CONCISE
DICTIONARY
OF
SCIENTIFIC
BIOGRAPHY

American Council of Learned Societies

The American Council of Learned Societies, organized in 1919 for the purpose of advancing the study of the humanities and of the humanistic aspects of the social sciences, is a nonprofit federation comprising forty-five national scholarly groups. The Council represents the humanities in the United States in the International Union of Academies, provides fellowships and grants-in-aid, supports research-and-planning conferences and symposia, and sponsors special projects and scholarly publications.

MEMBER ORGANIZATIONS
AMERICAN PHILOSOPHICAL SOCIETY, 1743
AMERICAN ACADEMY OF ARTS AND SCIENCES, 1780
AMERICAN ANTIQUARIAN SOCIETY, 1812
AMERICAN ORIENTAL SOCIETY, 1842
AMERICAN NUMISMATIC SOCIETY, 1858
AMERICAN PHILOLOGICAL ASSOCIATION, 1869
ARCHAEOLOGICAL INSTITUTE OF AMERICA, 1879
SOCIETY OF BIBLICAL LITERATURE, 1880
MODERN LANGUAGE ASSOCIATION OF AMERICA, 1883
AMERICAN HISTORICAL ASSOCIATION, 1884
AMERICAN ECONOMIC ASSOCIATION, 1885
AMERICAN FOLKLORE SOCIETY, 1888
AMERICAN DIALECT SOCIETY, 1889
AMERICAN PSYCHOLOGICAL ASSOCIATION, 1892
ASSOCIATION OF AMERICAN LAW SCHOOLS, 1900
AMERICAN PHILOSOPHICAL ASSOCIATION, 1901
AMERICAN ANTHROPOLOGICAL ASSOCIATION, 1902
AMERICAN POLITICAL SCIENCE ASSOCIATION, 1903
BIBLIOGRAPHICAL SOCIETY OF AMERICA, 1904
ASSOCIATION OF AMERICAN GEOGRAPHERS, 1904
HISPANIC SOCIETY OF AMERICA, 1904
AMERICAN SOCIOLOGICAL ASSOCIATION, 1905
AMERICAN SOCIETY OF INTERNATIONAL LAW, 1906
ORGANIZATION OF AMERICAN HISTORIANS, 1907
COLLEGE ART ASSOCIATION OF AMERICA, 1912
HISTORY OF SCIENCE SOCIETY, 1924
LINGUISTIC SOCIETY OF AMERICA, 1924
MEDIAEVAL ACADEMY OF AMERICA, 1925
AMERICAN MUSICOLOGICAL SOCIETY, 1934
SOCIETY OF ARCHITECTURAL HISTORIANS, 1940
ECONOMIC HISTORY ASSOCIATION, 1940
ASSOCIATION FOR ASIAN STUDIES, 1941
AMERICAN SOCIETY FOR AESTHETICS, 1942
AMERICAN ASSOCIATION FOR THE ADVANCEMENT OF SLAVIC STUDIES, 1948
METAPHYSICAL SOCIETY OF AMERICA, 1950
AMERICAN STUDIES ASSOCIATION, 1950
RENAISSANCE SOCIETY OF AMERICA, 1954
SOCIETY FOR ETHNOMUSICOLOGY, 1955
AMERICAN SOCIETY FOR LEGAL HISTORY, 1956
AMERICAN SOCIETY FOR THEATRE RESEARCH, 1956
SOCIETY FOR THE HISTORY OF TECHNOLOGY, 1958
AMERICAN COMPARATIVE LITERATURE ASSOCIATION, 1960
AMERICAN ACADEMY OF RELIGION, 1963
AMERICAN SOCIETY FOR EIGHTEENTH-CENTURY STUDIES, 1969
ASSOCIATION FOR JEWISH STUDIES, 1969

CONCISE
DICTIONARY
OF
SCIENTIFIC
BIOGRAPHY

CHARLES SCRIBNER'S SONS / *NEW YORK*

Copyright © 1981 Charles Scribner's Sons

Library of Congress Cataloging in Publication Data
Main entry under title:

Concise dictionary of scientific biography.

"Published under the auspices of the American
Council of Learned Societies"—Verso t.p.
  1. Scientists—Biography. I. American Council
of Learned Societies. II. Dictionary of
Scientific biography.
Q141.C55   509'.2'2[B]   81–5629
ISBN 0–684–16650–X   AACR2

Published simultaneously in Canada
by Collier Macmillan Canada, Inc.
Copyright under the Berne Convention.

5 7 9 11 13 15 17 19   V/C   20 18 16 14 12 10 8 6 4

Printed in the United States of America

CONTENTS

PREFACE

The *Dictionary of Scientific Biography*, the 16-volume parent set of the present book, was designed to bring together in one work the extant knowledge of the history of science, by means of articles on the lives and achievements of scientists. It was prepared under the auspices of the American Council of Learned Societies with the endorsement of the History of Science Society and the support of the National Science Foundation. The scientists chosen for inclusion represented all periods, from classical antiquity to modern times, and all branches of science. No living scientists were included.

The authors of the entries are distinguished scientists and historians of science from over 90 countries. Each biography is based on original sources and gives an analytical account of the subject's career. It interprets his or her scientific work and personality and shows the relation of the accomplishment to that of the scientist's predecessors, contemporaries, and successors.

The *Concise Dictionary of Scientific Biography* faithfully follows the design of the parent work, whose present coverage takes in scientists who died before 1972. What this one-volume abridgment offers is the essential facts from all the entries, set forth briefly and clearly and in significant proportion to the scope of the original articles.

As in the larger work, the entries are alphabetical by the scientist's last name. Entries from the first supplement have been inserted in their appropriate places and a list of scientists by fields has been included. Bibliographies have been omitted; for such information the parent set should be consulted.

The reader of this concise volume will find in each entry: the subject's places and dates of birth and death, areas of research, major phases and aspects of his or her career, and a brief statement of outstanding achievements. When pertinent, educational and social-cultural connections are mentioned, as well as family relationships to other scientists treated in the volume.

The length of each concise entry is about 10 percent of the original, but the scale of reduction has been varied liberally, both to ensure clarity and to reflect the comparative judgments embodied in the larger set. Thus, in the short entries where the subject's career is the main concern, the facts given are those on which the original biographer put the main emphasis. In some of the longer entries, the full account and interpretation has been retained intact.

The *Concise Dictionary of Scientific Biography* is accordingly a work of ready reference for anyone who wishes to inform himself quickly and adequately about the life, the scientific thought, and the contribution to knowledge of more than 5,000 scientists. For the history of science in fullest detail, and to appreciate the interconnections among the workers in one or more fields, the large DSB must be referred to, beginning with its extensive and minute indexing of the fifteen volumes.

CHARLES SCRIBNER'S SONS

CONCISE
DICTIONARY
OF
SCIENTIFIC
BIOGRAPHY

CONCISE DICTIONARY

OF

SCIENTIFIC BIOGRAPHY

ABAILARD, PIERRE (*b. Le Pallet, or Palais, Brittany, France, 1079; d. near Chalon-sur-Saône, France, 1142*), logic, theology, philosophy.

Studied metaphysics, first at school of Roscelin in Loches (*ca.* 1094–96), then with William of Champeaux in Paris. His primary interest was the philosophy of language. Founded a new school outside Paris. His interest turned to theology (*ca.* 1114); he studied at the school of Anselme and Ralph of Laon; taught at the Cathedral School of Paris; and became a monk at St. Denis (*ca.* 1118). His dialectical theology proved unpopular, and his doctrines were condemned at the Councils of Soissons (1121) and Sens (1140). His independence of thought led to a peripatetic career: he moved from St. Denis to a new convent, the Paraclete; to the abbey of St. Gildas in Brittany; to his school on the Montagne Ste. Geneviève (*ca.* 1136); to Cluny; and to the priory of St. Marcel, where he died.

His logical writings include commentaries on the standard texts, and *Dialectica*, the first attempt at a comprehensive system of logic in the Latin West. His systematic study of conditional propositions (*consequentiae*) is easily translatable into modern symbolism.

ABANO, PIETRO D' (*b. Abano, Italy, 1257; d. Padua, Italy, ca. 1315*), medicine, natural history, alchemy, philosophy.

Studied in Padua and Paris. Wrote *Conciliator differentiarum philosophorum et praecipue medicorum* on philosophy of medicine, including astrological influences and the concept of "physician." He was accused of heresy and condemned forty years *after* his death.

ᶜABBĀS IBN FIRNĀS (*b. Ronda, Spain; d. 274/A.D. 887*), humanities, technology.

Constructed astronomical instruments; may have discovered rock crystal. Disseminated oriental science in the West, including *Zīj al-Sindhind.*

AL-ᶜABBĀS IBN SAᶜĪD AL-JAWHARĪ. *See* **al-Jawharī.**

ABBE, CLEVELAND (*b. New York, N.Y., 1838; d. Washington, D.C., 1916*), meteorology.

Studied under Oliver Wolcott Gibbs at the City College of New York; with the German astronomer F. F. E. Brünnow; at the University of Michigan; with B. A. Gould at the Coast Survey in Cambridge, Mass.; and was in contact with William Ferrel at the *Nautical Almanac* office. Spent two years at the Pulkovo Observatory (1864–66) in Russia.

The first official weather forecaster of the U.S. government and a promoter of research in atmospheric physics. Under his aegis the Weather Service of the Signal Corps, the predecessor of the present Weather Bureau, established a laboratory and a center for basic research.

ABBE, ERNST (*b. Eisenach, Germany, 1840; d. Jena, Germany, 1905*), physics.

After attending the Eisenach Gymnasium, studied at Jena and Göttingen (Ph.D., 1861), where he was much influenced by Riemann and Weber.

In 1866, Carl Zeiss began a technical and scientific collaboration with Abbe. Abbe's fortunes grew with those of the Zeiss company; he had become a partner in 1876 and also held a professorship at Jena. He became sole owner of Zeiss in 1888. Within ten years, the Zeiss workshop developed into an internationally famous industrial enterprise. The company's apochromatic lens was the greatest advance in technical optics made to that date. Around the same time, Abbe created the Carl Zeiss Foundation, to which he bequeathed his personal fortune.

Early on Zeiss had begun experiments to convert the production of his microscope, which consisted of an objective and an ocular lens, into a scientific process but at that time he had relied on trial and error to find the best lenses. Unable to solve this problem because of his limited scientific training, Zeiss turned to Abbe. During the following decade they constructed the machinery required for industrial production and turned out many commercially marketed instruments (illuminating apparatus for the microscope, known in England as "the Abbe," the Abbe refractometer, and others).

Abbe's most important scientific achievements were in radiation optics and undulatory optics. Joining forces with Zeiss and Abbe, glass chemist Otto Schott perfected production methods in his Jena glassworks by refining a great number of new optical glasses to high perfection. In 1886 the Zeiss Works celebrated its greatest triumph to that date with the development of an apochromatic

1

system in which not only the primary but also the secondary color spectrum had been eliminated.

ᶜABD AL-, ᶜABDALLAH. *See* **last element of name.**

ABEL, JOHN JACOB (*b. near Cleveland, Ohio, 1857; d. Baltimore, Md., 1938*), pharmacology, biochemistry. Ph.B., University of Michigan (1883).

After a year with Henry Newell Martin at Johns Hopkins, he studied in various European universities from 1884 to 1890. During this period he worked with Carl Ludwig and M. von Nencki, among others. M.D., Strasbourg (1888). From 1891 to 1893 he taught at the University of Michigan. In 1893 he became Johns Hopkins' first professor of pharmacology, a position he held until his retirement in 1932. Abel's conviction of the importance of chemistry to medical and physiological studies shaped his work and affected the growth of his field. His biochemical studies included work on sulfur metabolism, hormone isolation (epinephrine, 1897; insulin, 1925), and protein constituents of the blood. For the latter research he developed an artificial kidney apparatus (1912–13) and plasmaphaeresis techniques. He also pursued pharmacological and physiological studies. He played a significant role in the institutional development of American science through the founding of scientific societies and periodicals.

ABEL, NIELS HENRIK (*b. Finnöy, an island near Stavanger, Norway, 1802; d. Froland, Norway, 1829*), mathematics.

Educated at Cathedral School in Christiania (Oslo). Interested in algebraic equation theory, Abel first attempted to solve the quintic equation while still in school but found no one in Norway capable of criticizing his methods. Working on his own he disproved his own proof and went on to develop a theory of elliptic functions. His independent study continued when he entered the university (1821) where Christopher Hansteen was one of his professors. In 1823 he published the first solution of an integral equation, and traveled to Copenhagen to meet Ferdinand Degen and other Danish mathematicians. He proved the impossibility of solving the quintic equation (1824); this work had been anticipated by Paolo Ruffini, and is now referred to as the Abel–Ruffini theorem. Went to Berlin (1825) and met August Leopold Crelle, who published much of Abel's work, including an expanded paper on the quintic equation, a generalization of the binomial formula, and a paper on the summation of series. Important paper on transcendental functions seems to have been misplaced by Cauchy before it could be published. The "Recherches sur les fonctions elliptiques" is a comprehensive and influential work. A rivalry in the field of elliptic functions erupted when Carl Gustav Jacob Jacobi published on the subject in September 1827; Legendre praised both men in his letters to them.

ABEL, OTHENIO (*b. Vienna, Austria, 1875; d. Pichl am Mondsee, Austria, 1946*), paleontology, founder of paleobiology.

Ph.D. in geology and paleontology from University of Vienna (1899); assistant to Eduard Suess. *Mitarbeiter* at Imperial-Royal Geological State Institute (Vienna) from 1900 to 1907. From 1900 on *collaborateur étranger* of Royal Museum of Natural History of Belgium; influenced by Louis Dollo. Taught at University of Vienna (1901–35) and University of Göttingen (1935–40). Published extensively and directed paleontological excavations.

ABELARD, PETER. *See* **Abailard, Pierre.**

ABENARE. *See* **Ibn Ezra.**

ABENGUEFITH. *See* **Ibn Wāfid.**

ABETTI, ANTONIO (*b. S. Pietro di Gorizia, Italy, 1846; d. Arcetri [Florence], Italy, 1928*), astronomy.

Although he received a degree in engineering from Padua (1867), he abandoned that field in 1868. Astronomer at University of Padua (1868–93). Appointed director of Arcetri observatory and professor of astronomy at University of Florence (1894–1921). Continued researches at university after retirement (1921–28). Worked primarily in positional astronomy, theory of observations, longitude differences. Participated in 1874 expedition to observe transit of Venus.

ABICH, OTTO HERMANN WILHELM (*b. Berlin, Germany, 1806; d. Vienna, Austria, 1886*), geology.

Ph.D. University of Berlin (1831), teachers included Humboldt and Buch. Appointed extraordinary professor of mineralogy at Dorpat and moved to Russia in 1843. Worked for Corps of Mining Engineers. Studied all aspects of geology of the Caucasus from 1843 to retirement in 1876. Did work of importance in mineralogy, petrography, paleontological stratigraphy, tectonics, and economic geology. Supported volcanistic theory. Developed anticlinal theory of oil prospecting.

ABNEY, WILLIAM DE WIVELESLIE (*b. Derby, England, 1843; d. Folkestone, England, 1920*), photography, astronomy.

Abney was one of the founders of modern photography. A graduate of the Royal Military Academy, he served for several years with the Royal Engineers in India. In later life his interest in color photography led him to investigate theories of color vision. His first book was *Chemistry for Engineers* (1870); his second, *Instruction in Photography* (1871), rapidly became a standard text.

Abney was a pioneer in the quantitative sensitometry of photographic images. Invented a dry photographic emulsion (1874), which remained in use for general as well as solar photography until superseded by commercial gelatin products. Studied the chemistry of latent image developing (1877) and introduced hydroquinone (1880), one of the best developing agents known.

Abney was the first to suggest (1877) that stars with rapid axial rotation could be detected by broadened lines in their spectra—an idea later to have wide application. He devised a red-sensitive emulsion and with it made the first spectroscopic analyses of the structure of organic molecules (1882) and the first photographs of the solar spectrum in the infrared (1887). Also did comparative studies on how sunlight is altered by the atmosphere.

ABOALY. *See* **Ibn Sīna.**

ABRAHAM. *See also* **Ibrāhīm.**

ABRAHAM BAR ḤIYYA HA-NASI, also known as **Savosorda** (*fl., Barcelona, before 1136*), mathematics, astronomy.

Savasorda's most influential work, the *Ḥibbūr ha-meshīḥah we-ha-tishboret,* is the earliest exposition of Arab algebra written in Europe, and it contains the first complete solution in Europe of the quadratic equation, $x^2 - ax + b = 0$.

The *Ḥibbūr* was among the earliest works to introduce Arab trigonometry into Europe, and it was also the earliest to treat of Euclid's *Book of Divisions.* Savasorda included the division of geometric figures in a practical treatise, thus effecting a synthesis of Greek theory with the pragmatic aspects of mathematics.

He did not accept the Pythagorean figurate numbers in his explanation of plane and square numbers.

ABRAHAM BEN JACOB. *See* **Ibrāhīm ibn Yaʿqūb.**

ABRAHAM BEN MEIR IBN EZRA. *See* **Ibn Ezra.**

ABRAHAM JUDAEUS. *See* **Ibn Ezra.**

ABRAHAM, MAX (*b. Danzig, Germany, 1875; d. Munich, Germany, 1922*), physics.

Abraham studied under Max Planck and completed his doctoral dissertation in 1897. He then assisted Planck at Berlin and in 1900 assumed the position of *Privatdozent* at Göttingen. His lifework amounted to the explication of Maxwell's theory.

Abraham is best remembered for his two-volume textbook, *Theorie der Elektrizität.* Volume II, subtitled "Der Elektromagnetische Theorie der Strahlung" ("The Electromagnetic Theory of Radiation"), contained Abraham's theory of electrons.

Abraham himself remained unalterably opposed to Einstein's theory of relativity throughout his life. His objections were not based on misunderstanding of the theory of relativity; he was simply unwilling to accept postulates he considered contrary to classical common sense.

ABREU, ALEIXO DE (*b. Alcáçovas, Alentejo, Portugal, 1568; d. Lisbon, Portugal, 1630*), tropical medicine.

Abreu studied at Évora University in 1577 and graduated as bachelor of arts about 1583. Afterward he studied medicine at Coimbra University on a royal scholarship and seven years later graduated as a licentiate of medicine. During a tropical sojourn in Brazil Abreu contracted amoebiasis and yellow fever. His *Tratado de las siete enfermedades* (1623) described his illness. In it Abreu discussed his own case of liver involvement in recurrent amoebiasis. His early description of scurvy, which he called *mal de loanda* emphasized gingivitis gum ulcers. He also described the *Tunga penetrans* or Brazilian *tungiasis,* the flea that penetrates the skin of the foot, and the Guinea worm, the macrofilaria *Dracunculus medinensis.*

ABŪ BAKR MUḤAMMAD IBN AL-ḤASAN AL-KARAJĪ, AL-ḤĀSIB. *See* **al-Karaji.**

ABU'L-BARAKĀT AL-BAGHDĀDĪ, HIBAT ALLAH (*b. Iraq, ca. 1080; d. Baghdad, Iraq, after 1164/1165*) physics, psychology, philosophy.

Abu'l-Barakāt's writings include *Kitāb al-Muʿtabar* ("The Book of What Has Been Established by Personal Reflection"); a philosophical commentary on the Ecclesiastes, written in Arabic in Hebrew characters; and the treatise "On the Reason Why the Stars Are Visible at Night and Hidden in Daytime."

In his psychology. as well as in his physics, Abu'l-Barakāt bases his views on what he regards as immediate certainties rather than on an assessment of empirical data. The use of this method clearly renders both the Aristotelian approach and many Aristotelian theories unacceptable to him. Abu'l-Barakāt considers that immediate self-awareness, the awareness of one's own existence and of one's own actions, constitutes an unchallengeable proof of the existence and activity of the soul (identified with the ego).

ABU'L-FIDĀʾ ISMĀʿĪL IBN ʿALĪ IBN MAḤMŪD IBN . . . AYYŪB, ʿIMĀD AL-DĪN (*b. Damascus, Syria, 1273; d. Ḥamā, Syria, 1331*), history, geography.

Among the most distinguished of Abu'l-Fidāʾ's historical-literary works is the *Mukhtaṣar taʾrīkh al-bashar,* a historical treatise that begins with pre-Islamic Arabia and becomes most interesting when it deals with happenings during the author's lifetime. This work became the basis for several historical syntheses by eighteenth-century Orientalists, which explains the strong influence it exerted on nineteenth-century Western historiography.

Abu'l-Fidāʾ's outstanding scientific work, the *Taqwīm al-buldān* ("A Sketch of the Countries"), is a general geography.

ABŪ ḤĀMID AL-GHARNĀṬĪ, also known as **Abū ʿAbdallāh Muḥammad ibn ʿAbd al-Raḥīm . . . al-Māzinī al-Andalusī** (*b. Granada, Spain, 1080; d. Damascus, Syria, 1169*), geography.

Abū Ḥāmid's two most important works, the *Muʿrib* and the *Tuḥfa,* influenced later Arabic cosmographers.

The work *Muʿrib ʿan baʿd ʿajāʾib al-Maghrib* ("Anthology of the Marvels of the Maghrib") contains a description of some of the marvels of Andalucía and some long dissertations on astronomical, astrological, and chronological matters.

The *Tuḥfat al-albāb wa-nukhbat al-ʿajāʾib* ("Gift from the Heart and Selection of Marvelous Things") contains descriptions of the world and the men and the spirits who inhabit it; strange countries; the seas and their animals; and a discussion of caves and tombs.

ABŪ JAʿFAR AL-KHĀZIN. *See* **al-Khāzin.**

ABŪ KĀMIL SHUJĀʿ IBN ASLAM IBN MUḤAMMAD IBN SHUJĀʿ (*b. ca. 850, d. ca. 930*), mathematics.

Abū Kāmil was one of Islam's greatest algebraists in the period following the earliest Muslim algebraist, al-Khwārizmī.

The *Kitāb . . . al-mukhammas wa-al-muʿashshar. . .* ("On the Pentagon and Decagon") is a work of both geometric and algebraic interest. The text is algebraic in treatment and contains solutions for a fourth-degree equation and for mixed quadratics with irrational coefficients.

Another manuscript is the most advanced work on indeterminate equations by Abū Kāmil. The solutions are not restricted to integers; in fact, most are in rational form.

Abū Kāmil put together a sophisticated algebra with an elaborated geometry. Thus Abū Kāmil effected the integration of ancient Mesopotamian practice and Greek theory to yield a wider approach to algebra.

ABŪ MAᶜSHAR AL-BALKHĪ, JAᶜFAR IBN MU-ḤAMMAD, also known as **Albumasar** *(b. in or near Balkh in Khurasan, 787; d. al-Wāsiṭ, Iraq, 886),* astrology.

Abū Maᶜshar was a leading exponent of the theory that all different national systems of thought are ultimately derived from a single revelation.

He began his career as an expert in *hadīth,* the sayings traditionally ascribed to Muḥammad and his companions, Proficienct in the pre-Islamic Arabic calendar and the chronology of the early caliphs.

His philosophical proof of the validity of astrology was probably most elaborately presented in his lost *Kitāb ithbāt ᶜilm al-nujūm* ("Book of the Establishment of Astrology"), where the argument is largely Aristotelian, with some Neoplatonic elements.

ABŪ NAṢR AL-FĀRĀBĪ. *See* **al-Fārābī.**

ABŪ'L-RAYḤĀN MUḤAMMAD IBN AḤMAD AL-BĪRŪNĪ. *See* **al-Bīrūni.**

IBN ABŪ'L-SHUKR. *See* **Muḥyi al-Dīn al-Maghribī.**

ABŪ ᶜUBAYD AL-BAKRĪ. *See* **al-Bakrī.**

ABŪ'L-WAFĀ᾿ AL-BŪZJĀNĪ, MUḤAMMAD IBN MUḤAMMAD IBN YAḤYĀ IBN ISMĀᶜĪL IBN AL-ᶜABBĀS *(b. Būzjān [now in Iran], 940: d. Baghdad [now in Iraq], 997 or 998),* mathematics, astronomy.

Abū'l-Wafā᾿ became the last great representative of the mathematics-astronomy school that arose around the beginning of the ninth century. Abū'l-Wafā᾿ conducted astronomical observations at the Baghdad observatory. He continued the tradition of his predecessors, combining original scientific work with commentary on the classics —the works of Euclid and Diophantus. He also wrote a commentary to the algebra of al-Khwārizmī.

Abū'l-Wafā᾿'s textbook on practical arithmetic, *Kitāb fī mā yaḥtaj ilayh al-kuttāb wa'l-ᶜummāl min ᶜilm al-ḥisāb* ("Book on What Is Necessary From the Science of Arithmetic for Scribes and Businessmen"), enjoyed widespread fame. This book indicates that the Indian decimal positional system of numeration with the use of numerals did not find application in business circles and among the population of the Eastern Caliphate for a long time. All numbers and computations he described only with words.

Another practical textbook by Abū'l-Wafā᾿ is *Kitāb fī mā yaḥtaj ilayh al-ṣāniᶜ min al-aᶜmāl al-handasiyya* ("Book on What is Necessary From Geometric Construction for the Artisan"). It includes simple planar constructions and construction of regular and semiregular polyhedrons inscribed in a given sphere. Abū᾿l-Wafā᾿ was the first to solve a large number of problems using a compass with an invariable opening.

His large astronomical work, *al-majisṭī,* or *Kitāb al-kāmil* ("Complete Book"), closely follows Ptolemy's *Almagest.*

He enriched the apparatus of spherical trigonometry, simplifying the solution of its problems, and he applied the theorem of tangents to the solution of spherical right triangles. One of the first proofs of the general theorem of sines applied to the solution of oblique triangles was also originated by Abū'l-Wafā᾿. To honor Abū'l-Wafā᾿, a crater on the moon was named after him.

ACCUM, FRIEDRICH CHRISTIAN *(b. Bückeburg, Germany, 1769; d. Berlin, Germany, 1838),* applied chemistry.

About 1800 Accum established his own laboratory; he was also "assistant chemical operator" to Humphrey Davy, resigning in September 1803. In 1802 he began public lecturing, and the steady stream of laboratory pupils included the Americans Benjamin Silliman and William Peck. The value of Accum's work lies in the way he saw and exploited the technological possibilities of the rapidly advancing science of chemistry. He wrote the 1815 treatise that became the classic text of gas technology. Equal fame surrounded his work on food adulteration. His deliberately sensational 1820 work (motto "There is death in the pot") did much to awaken that public concern that eventually resulted in the Adulteration Act of 1860.

ACHARD, FRANZ KARL *(b. Berlin, Germany, 1753; d. Kunern, Germany, 1821),* chemistry, experimental physics.

Of Achard's early education virtually nothing is known. At the age of twenty he began his career in association with the botanist J.G. Gleditsch and with the renowned chemist A.S. Marggraf. When Marggraf died in 1782, Achard succeeded him as director of the "Class of Physics" of the Berlin Academy. He is best known for his development of a method of extracting sugar from beets in large quantity. His process of obtaining sugar was simple but costly. In France the Institute made several valuable recommendations, the most important of which was that the beets be pressed without cooking them. Achard afterward adopted this technique in order to reduce the considerable expenditures for fuel.

ACHARIUS, ERIK *(b. Gavle, Sweden, 1757; d. Vadstena, Sweden, 1819),* botany.

Acharius was the last to defend his thesis under Linnaeus, and all his life pursued the Linnaean tradition of research in his botanical work. He studied medicine, first at the University of Uppsala and then at Lund, where he received the M.D. in 1782. He devoted himself almost exclusively to the study of lichens, and his description and classification of them laid the foundation for later scholarship.

ACHILLINI, ALESSANDRO *(b. Bologna, Italy, 1463; d Bologna, 1512),* anatomy.

Achillini was graduated doctor of philosophy and of medicine from the University of Bologna in 1484. During his lifetime, he was known mainly as a philosopher. Today he is remembered for his considerable activity in research on human anatomy. He gave a good description of the veins of the arm, and he described the seven bones of tarsus, the fornix of the brain, the cerebral ventricles, the infundibulum, and the trochlear nerve. He also described, exactly, the ducts of the submaxillary salivary glands and the ileocecal valve. Finally, to Achillini is attributed the first description of the two ossicles of the ear, the malleus and incus.

ACOSTA, CRISTÓBAL (*b. Bôa Ventura, Santo Antão, Cape Verde Islands, ca. 1525; d. La Peña de Tharsis* [?], *Huelva, Spain, ca. 1594*), natural history, medicine.

Acosta studied arts and medicine in Salamanca. His *Tratado de las drogas, y medicinas de las Indias orientales* offers systematic, firsthand observations of the Oriental drugs and is illustrated by woodcuts made from his own accurate drawings.

ACOSTA, JOSÉ DE (*b Medina del Campo, Spain, 1539; d. Salamanca, Spain, 1600*), geography.

Acosta was one of the first Europeans to provide a detailed image of the physical and human geography of Latin America.

Acosta's most important scientific work, *Historia natural y moral de las Indias,* provides first-hand observations on altitude sickness, the nature and uses of coca, and the crops, farm techniques, and domesticated animals of America. Equally important are his descriptions of Inca and Aztec history, religious observances, folk customs, and statecraft.

ACTEDIUS, PETRUS. *See* **Artedi, Peter.**

ACYUTA PIṢĀRAṬI (*b. Trkkantiyūr* [*Sanskrit, Kuṇḍapura*], *Kerala, India, ca. 1550; d. Kerala, 1621*), astronomy.

Acyuta studied astronomy under Jyeṣṭhandeva. and is the author of several works dealing largely with astronomy: *Pravesaka; Karaṇottama; Uparāgakriyākrama; Sphuṭanirnaya; Chāyāṣṭaka; Uparāgavimśati; Rāśigolasphuṭānīti; Venvārohavyākhyā;* and *Horāsāroccaya.*

ADAM OF BODENSTEIN (*b. 1528; d. Basel, Switzerland, 1577*), medicine, alchemy.

Adam was doctor of arts and medicine at Basel, where he studied and practiced medicine. He was a follower of the doctrines of Paracelsus and participated with other scholars of his time editing and publishing the works of Paracelsus still in manuscript. In close association with Paracelsus' special predilection for the use of metallic compounds, Adam developed an interest in minerals, particularly in the traditional alchemical process of transmuting baser metals into gold.

ADAMS, FRANK DAWSON (*b. Montreal, Canada, 1859; d. Montreal, 1942*), geology.

At nineteen Adams graduated with first rank honors in natural science from McGill University. He studied chemistry and mineralogy at Yale and later to attend several sessions at Heidelberg University. Through the use of the petrographic microscope, he was able to demonstrate conclusively not only the igneous origin of the anorthosites but also the sedimentary origin of some of the Grenville crystalline rocks in the Laurentian series (1893).

He established that the anorthosite in the upper division of the Laurentians was composed largely of plagioclase feldspar, and established its igneous nature both by his petrographic determinations in the laboratory and by its intrusive contacts with the Grenville rocks. He attributed the marked differences in grain size to crystal

fracturing. Adams also recognized that the Laurentian granites were intrusive into metamorphic rocks, which therefore must have preceded them in time and space. These conclusions were among the foundations upon which the modern classification of the Precambrian series rests.

Adams devoted the summers of 1902 to 1908 to the mapping and description of the Haliburton and Bancroft areas of southern Ontario. His discovery of nepheline syenite adjacent to granite and marble bodies was of great scientific importance.

To Adams must go the credit for establishing experimentation in geological investigation upon a sure engineering foundation.

Following his retirement he published the first complete geological report and map of Ceylon (1929). His scholarly work, *Birth and Development of the Geological Sciences* (1938), is a text that will long remain a standard treatment of the subject.

ADAMS, JOHN COUCH (*b. Laneast, Cornwall, England, 1819; d. Cambridge, England, 1892*), astronomy, mathematics.

Adams graduated from Cambridge in 1843. The same year he investigated the irregularities in the motion of the planet Uranus, a problem which required, among other procedures, the solution of ten simultaneous equations of condition for as many unknowns. Adams' first result convinced him that the disturbances of Uranus were due to an undiscovered planet.

In the meantime a French astronomer, Urbain Jean Joseph Leverrier, independently reached the same conclusions as Adams. In September 1846 the perturbing body—Neptune—was discovered as a result of his efforts. Adams' earlier prediction, which agreed closely with Leverrier's, was thus far unpublished.

In 1851 Adams began to work on lunar theory. He finished new tables of the moon's parallax which corrected several errors in lunar theory and gave more accurate positions. His paper on the secular acceleration of the moon's mean motion caused a sharp scientific controversy; a number of independent investigations confirmed Adams' result.

The brilliant Leonid meteor shower of November 1866 stimulated Adams to investigate the elements of the Leonid system.

He enjoyed the calculation of exact values for mathematical constants. In 1877 he published thirty-one Bernoullian numbers, thus doubling the known number.

ADAMS, ROGER (*b. Boston, Mass., 1889; d. Urbana, Ill., 1971*), organic chemistry.

Educated Harvard (B.A. 1909, Ph.D. 1912); studied in Germany with Diels and Willstätter. Taught at University of Illinois (from 1916); as head of chemistry department (from 1926), and through wide contacts, he fostered the rapid growth of American chemistry and its integration with industry and government; his department became a prolific source of industrial chemists and also developed valuable synthetic methods. Served on major national boards and committees; fostered private patronage of research. Worked on synthesis of aromatic compounds; developed "Adams catalyst," a colloidal platinum oxide now standard in hydrogenation; studied stereochemistry of substituted biphenyl and biaryl compounds; analyzed and synthesized marijuana alkaloids; synthesized local anesthetics.

ADAMS, WALTER SYDNEY (*b. Kessab, near Antioch, Syria, 1876; d. Pasadena, California, 1956*), astrophysics.

Adams graduated with the A.B. from Dartmouth College in 1898 and entered the University of Chicago. He gained his first practical observing experience under George Ellery Hale. After receiving his M.A. in 1900, he went to the University of Munich. The following year he returned to Yerkes as computer and general assistant.

At the Mount Wilson Observatory he contributed significantly to the design of instruments and helped to make the Mount Wilson and Palomar observatories preeminent.

His earliest work, on the polar compression of Jupiter, was followed by research on radial velocities in B–type, or helium, stars, which would prove important in discussions of stellar motions, especially in the recognition of the so-called K–term.

At Mount Wilson he joined George Hale in an intensive study of the sun, first with the horizontal Snow reflector, then with the sixty-foot and 150-foot tower solar telescopes. For the first time, it became possible to study spot spectra photographically with adequate apparatus. Adams became interested in the problem of solar rotation, and in 1909, with Hale, he succeeded in photographing the flash spectrum without eclipse.

His studies with the sixty-inch reflecting telescope on Mount Wilson included the first thorough investigation of the differences in the spectra of the large and massive stars of high luminosity called giants and the comparatively dense bodies of very low luminosity known as dwarfs.

In 1914, Adams compared pairs of stars of nearly the same spectral type, and the same temperature, but of very different luminosity. This ingenious method of obtaining "spectroscopic parallaxes," applied to thousands of stars, has become a fundamental astronomical tool of immense value in gaining knowledge of giant and dwarf stars and of galactic structure.

In 1917 the 100-inch telescope went into operation.

In the 1920's and 1930's Adams applied the spectrograph to studies of the atmospheres of Venus and Mars. Other investigations included Cepheids, spectroscopic binaries, and, from 1901 to 1936, the spectra of novae. His last extensive research was on the clouds of interstellar gas.

ADANSON, MICHEL (*b. Aix-en-Provence, France, 1727; d. Paris, France, 1806*), natural history, philosophy.

Adanson was educated at the Plessis Sorbon, the Collège Royal, and the Jardin du Roi. On a scientific expedition to Senegal, Adanson made a general survey of the living mollusks he found there. His classification of mollusks was an original one, based on the anatomical structure of the living animals inside the shells.

In 1763–64 he published *Familles des plantes,* in which he proclaimed his contempt for "systems" and proposed a natural classification based upon all characters rather than upon a few arbitrarily selected ones, an attempt that brought him into conflict with Linnaeus. He soon recognized that his *Familles des plantes* was only an outline of his

general conception, and in 1769 he prepared a new edition that was never published.

ADDISON, THOMAS (*b. Long Benton, England, ca. 1793; d. Brighton, England, 1860*), medicine.

Addison's father had wished him to become a lawyer, but in 1812 he entered the University of Edinburgh as a medical student. His numerous clinical studies include works on the clinical signs of a fatty liver (1836), appendicitis (1839), pneumonia (1843), phthisis (1845), and xanthoma (1851). In 1849 he described Addison's anemia before a meeting of the South London Medical Society. This excellent description of pernicious anemia was quite overshadowed by his spectacular discovery of the disturbance of the suprarenal capsules. In 1855, in a paper entitled "On the Constitutional and Local Effects of Disease of the Suprarenal Capsules," he described what is now known as Addison's disease.

ADELARD OF BATH (*b. Bath, England; fl. 1116–42*), mathematics, astronomy.

Adelard of Bath who traveled widely and studied at Tours was one of the foremost medieval English translators and natural philosophers who made the first wholesale conversion of Arabo-Greek learning from Arabic into Latin.

Adelard's modest contributions to medieval philosophy are found in two of his works: *De eodem et diverso* and *Quaestiones naturales.*

In astronomy Adelard's most significant achievement was his translation of the *Astronomical Tables* of al-Khwārizmī, *Ezich Elkauresmi per Athelardum bathoniensem ex arabico sumptus.* The *Tables* provided the Latin West with its initial introduction to the complex of Hellenistic-Indian-Arabic tabular material.

Adelard's earliest efforts in arithemetic appear in a work entitled *Regule abaci.* He was the first to present a full version, or versions, of the *Elements* of Euclid in Latin and thus to initiate the process that led to Euclid's domination of high and late medieval mathematics.

ADET, PIERRE-AUGUSTE (*b. Nevers, France, 1763; d. Paris, France, 1834*), chemistry.

Adet participated in the founding of the *Annales de chimie,* which was designed to permit easy publication of papers on antiphlogistic chemistry.

He proposed a new system of chemical symbols which was never generally adopted. He also published a work on stannic chloride (1789).

In 1798 Adet investigated "acetous" and acetic acids. He concluded that the acids differed only in the proportion of water they contained; this conclusion was confirmed by Proust in 1802. In 1804 Adet published his textbook, *Leçons élémentaires de chimie.*

ADRAIN, ROBERT (*b. Carrickfergus, Ireland, 1775; d. New Brunswick, New Jersey, 1843*), mathematics.

Adrain's first mathematical contributions were in George Baron's *Mathematical Correspondent* (1804). In *The Analyst* (1808) Adrain's most interesting mathematical paper appeared, a study of errors in observations with the first two published demonstrations of the normal (exponential) law of errors. This volume also contains Adrain's paper on what he calls isotomous curves. Another article deals with the *catenaria volvens.*

In 1818 he published in *Transactions* a paper on the figure of the earth, in which he found 1/319 as its ellipticity. In the same issue of the *Transactions* he published a paper on the mean diameter of the earth.

ADRIAANSON, ADRIAAN. *See* **Metius, Adriaan.**

AEGIDIUS. *See* **Giles of Rome.**

AEPINUS, FRANZ ULRICH THEODOSIUS (*b. Rostock, Germany, 1724; d. Dorpat, Russia [now Tartu, Estonian Soviet Socialist Republic], 1802*), mathematics, electricity, magnetism.

Aepinus studied medicine and mathematics at Jena, under the guidance of G.E. Hamberger, and at Rostock, where he took his M.A. (1747) with a dissertation on the paths of falling bodies. Aepinus was vitally interested in the study of the tourmaline. He was particularly struck by the formal similarity between the tourmaline and the magnet in regard to polarity; he reconsidered the possibility that electricity and magnetism were basically analogous. This thought became the theme for his masterwork, *Tentamen theoriae electricitatis et magnetismi* (1759).

In experimenting on the tourmaline Aepinus came to the anti-Franklinian idea of a Leyden jar without the glass.

The *Tentamen* is one of the most original and important books in the history of electricity. It is the first reasoned, fruitful exposition of electrical phenomena based on action-at-a-distance.

AËTIUS OF AMIDA (*b. Amida, Mesopotamia [now Diyarbakir, Turkey], fl. ca. A.D. 540*), medicine.

Aëtius wrote a large medical encyclopedia that is called either *Sixteen Medical Books* or *Tetrabibloi* (i.e., four volumes, each containing four parts or books). Aëtius' originality has often been questioned, but since there exists only an incomplete critical edition of his work, the question cannot be answered conclusively.

IBN AFLAḤ. *See* **Jābir ibn Aflaḥ.**

AGARDH, CARL ADOLPH (*b. Bastad, Sweden, 1785; d. Karlstad, Sweden, 1859*), botany.

Professor at the University of Lund (1812–35).

The introduction to Agardh's *Synopsis algarum Scandinaviae* (1817) presented an entirely new systematic survey of everything then considered algae. Agardh's *Species algarum* (1821–28), and *Systema algarum* (1824), presented nodal points in the development of algology.

At the mineral springs of Karlsbad, he met the Romantic philosopher Schelling. Together they studied algal forms in the hot springs, and Agardh demonstrated their life cycle. His interests shifted from taxonomy to the problems of plant life and his views on the subject were published in *Lärobok i botanik* (1830–32), which was translated into German and dedicated to Schelling.

AGARDH, JACOB GEORG (*b. Lund, Sweden, 1813; d. Lund, 1901*), botany.

Son of the prominent botanist Carl Adolph Agardh, Jacob Agardh soon gained international renown as an algologist, specializing in sea algae.

His important *Algae maris Mediterranei et Adriatici* (1842) contained his first work on the taxonomy of the *Florideae,*

which was to become his most important field of research. His *magnum opus* as an algae taxonomist was *Species, genera et ordines algarum*, in six volumes, published during the course of more than half a century (1848–1901). It contains all the then known species of *Florideae* and all the known species of *Fucaceae* (brown algae) as well as their description and a general morphological survey, all in accordance with the Swedish Linnaean tradition.

Agardh's interest in taxonomy encompassed the entire plant kingdom, and he developed his ideas in *Theoria systematis plantarum* (1858). He considered each species had evolved from a lower to a higher state and had developed through the ages into different and progressively more perfect forms.

His algae collection, which had been started by his father, is one of the most varied in the world.

AGASSIZ, ALEXANDER (*b. Neuchâtel, Switzerland, 1835; d. mid-Atlantic, 1910*), zoology, oceanography, engineering.

Agassiz graduated from Harvard College in 1855, from the Lawrence Scientific School with a degree in engineering in 1857, and again from the Lawrence Scientific School with a degree in zoology in 1862. Although his fortune, made from the Michigan copper mines, placed him first among those late nineteenth-century captains of industry who supported science in the United States, Agassiz was distinguished as both a zoologist and an oceanographer.

In 1860 his theories were closer to those of his father, Louis Agassiz, about the geographical distribution of animals than to the ideas of Charles Darwin. His work from 1860 to the late 1870's was largely concerned with the study of zoology, beginning with the animals of the New England shore, especially the echinoderms, and culminating in his *Revision of the Echini* (1872–74).

In 1891 he explored the deep water of the Pacific from the Galápagos Islands to the Gulf of California to make a comparative study of marine fauna on both sides of the Isthmus of Panama. His interest from 1892 onward shifted strongly to the problem of the formation of coral atolls. In 1893 and 1894 he explored the Bahama and Bermuda islands, in 1896 the Great Barrier Reef, in 1897 the Fijis, in 1898–1900 the central Pacific, and (1900–02) the Maldives.

AGASSIZ, JEAN LOUIS RODOLPHE (*b. Motieren-Vuly, Switzerland, 1807; d. Cambridge, Massachusetts, 1873*), ichthyology, geology, paleontology.

Attended the universities of Zurich, Heidelberg, and Munich. Ph.D. in philosophy (1829) at the universities of Munich and Erlangen. Published a monograph on the fishes of Brazil that brought him to the attention of Georges Cuvier. Ph.D. in medicine from the University of Munich (1830). Agassiz's career had two distinct geographic and intellectual aspects. As a European, he published monographs on ichthyology, paleontology, and geology whose promise earned him the admiration of many of his famous contemporaries. As an American, Agassiz made nature study popular and appealing, explored the American environment, and established lasting institutions of research and education. His *Poissons fossiles,* written directly in the tradition of his mentor Cuvier, contained precise descriptions of more than 1,700 ancient species, together with illustrated recon-

7

structions based on principles of comparative anatomy.

From 1835 to 1845 Agassiz studied the glacial formations of Switzerland and compared them with the geology of England and central Europe. Agassiz interpreted glaciation in metaphysical terms. To him, the Deity had been responsible for the Ice Age, a catastrophe that provided a permanent physical barrier separating the species of the past from those of the present era.

Agassiz found the natural environment of the United States fascinating. In 1855 he announced a grand plan for the publication of a monumental ten-volume study, *Contributions to the Natural History of the United States.* Only four volumes appeared, valuable only for their descriptions of North American turtles.

He made Harvard University into a center for natural history instruction and research. The capstone of such efforts was the establishment at Harvard College in 1859 of the Museum of Comparative Zoology.

He convinced fellow scientists to establish the National Academy of Sciences in 1863. This achievement, coupled with his earlier efforts to advise the federal government on the operations of the U.S. Coast Survey and the Smithsonian Institution, revealed Agassiz in the prime of his American influence and international prestige.

AGATHINUS, CLAUDIUS *(fl. ca.* A.D. *50),* medicine.

Agathinus, a Spartan who lived in Rome, was among the important and influential physicians of the intellectually rich first century A.D.

He founded his own school, which he called episynthetic (i.e., eclectic) and which championed the intellectual unity of medicine as interpreted by Galen. Agathinus had many medical disciples, of whom the best known was the celebrated Archigenes.

AGNESI, MARIA GAETANA *(b. Milan, Italy, 1718; d. Milan, 1799),* mathematics.

Maria Gaetana Agnesi was the first woman in the Western world who can accurately be called a mathematician.

Agnesi's father encouraged her interest in scientific matters by securing a series of tutors for her education. He also established a cultural salon in his home where she could present theses in various subjects. Some 190 of the theses she defended appear in the *Propositiones philosophicae* (1738).

In 1748 her *Istituzioni analitiche ad uso della gioventú italiana* won immediate acclaim in academic circles all over Europe and brought recognition as a mathematician. Her objective was to give a complete, integrated, comprehensible treatment of algebra and analysis, with emphasis on concepts that were new in the mid-eighteenth century. She covered the range from elementary algebra to the classical theory of equations, to coordinate geometry, and then on to differential calculus, integral calculus, infinite series and finally to the solution of elementary differential equations. She treated finite processes in the first volume and infinitesimal analysis in the second.

Of greatest significance to Agnesi were two letters from Pope Benedict XIV, who, in 1750, appointed her to the chair of mathematics and natural philosophy at Bologna. She never taught there, however.

AGRICOLA, GEORGIUS, also known as **Georg Bauer** *(b. Glauchau, Germany, 1494; d. Chemnitz, Germany [now*

Karl-Marx-Stadt, German Democratic Republic], *1555),* mining, metallurgy.

Agricola received the B.A. from Leipzig University in 1515 and remained there as lecturer in elementary Greek until he was chosen *ludi moderator* at Zwickau in 1517. He returned to Leipzig in 1523 to study medicine under Heinrich Stromer von Auerbach. In 1527 he was elected town physician and apothecary of St. Joachimsthal. Agricola studied not only the ailments of miners in St. Joachimsthal but also their life, labor, and equipment. He recorded his impressions in *Bermannus sive de re metallica dialogus* (1530).

His next books were political and economic: *Oratio de bello adversus Turcam suscipiendo* (1531) and *De mensuris et ponderibus* (1533).

Agricola decided to return to Chemnitz, to be town physician where after fifteen years of hard work, he succeeded in finishing a complete series of inquiries concerning the principles of geology and mineralogy. Later new books appeared: *De animantibus subterraneis* (1549) and an enlarged edition of *De mensuris et ponderibus* (1550). Agricola's studies during the plague led him to publish *De peste libri III* (1554).

In 1534 Georg the Whiskered had nominated Agricola as historiographer of the court of Saxony. For twenty years Agricola studied yellowed parchments and old chronicles. He recorded his findings very frankly—much to the disappointment of Augustus, third duke after Georg the Whiskered. It is no wonder, then, that the *Sippschaft des Hausses zu Sachssen,* an evaluation of all the rulers of Saxony, remained unpublished until 1963. Four months after his death, his chief work, *De re metallica libri XII,* illustrated with 292 woodcuts, appeared. A year later an Old German translation by Philippus Bech was published using the same woodcuts, which were used for 101 years in seven editions.

AGRIPPA, HEINRICH CORNELIUS, also known as **Agrippa von Nettesheim** *(b. near Cologne, Germany, 1486; d. Grenoble, France, ca. 1535),* magic, alchemy, philosophy, medicine.

Agrippa enrolled at the University of Cologne on 22 July 1499. He later studied in Paris and London before returning to Cologne where he held theological disputations. In 1530 he published his polemic *De incertitudine et vanitate scientiarum atque artium declamatio et de excellentia verbi Dei.* In 1531 he published the first of the three books of the *De occulta philosophia* (the fourth book is apocryphal), which had probably been written around 1510–15.

Agrippa's personality and *curriculum vitae* are still open to dispute, as is the authorship of his works. Today Agrippa's importance is considered to lie in the social criticism embodied in his works on magic as well as in his polemic against the vanity and uncertainty of science.

Considered the historical prototype of Goethe's Faust.

AGUILON, FRANÇOIS D' *(b. Brussels, Belgium, 1546; d. Antwerp, Belgium, 1617),* physics, mathematics.

The son of the secretary to Philip II, Aguilon became a Jesuit in 1586. His master treatise on optics synthesized the works of Euclid, Ibn al-Haytham (Alhazen), Vitellion, Roger Bacon, Pena, Ramus (Pierre de la Ramée), Risner, and Kepler. Only the first part exists, with six frontispieces drawn by Rubens: *Francisci Aguilonii e Societate Jesu Opticorum libri sex juxta ac mathematicis utiles* (1613).

Aguilon treated the eye, the object, and the nature of vision; the optic ray and horopter; the general ideas that make possible the knowledge of objects; errors in perception; luminous and opaque bodies; and projections.

AHMAD IBN IBRĀHĪM AL-UQLIDĪSĪ. *See* **al-Uqlidīsī.**

AHMAD IBN MUHAMMAD IBN ʿABD AL-JALĪL AL-SIZJĪ. *See* **al-Sizji.**

AHMAD IBN MUHAMMAD IBN AL-BANNĀʾ. *See* **Ibn al-Bannāʾ.**

AHMAD IBN MŪSĀ IBN SHĀKIR. *See* **Banū Mūsā.**

AHMAD IBN YŪSUF (*b. Baghdad, Iraq* [?] *; fl. ca 900–905; d. Cairo, Egypt, 912/913* [?]), mathematics.

Ahmad ibn Yūsuf wrote a work on similar arcs, a commentary on Ptolemy's *Centiloquium*, and a work on the astrolabe.

Ahmad's most significant work is the treatise on ratio and proportion. The work is largely an expansion of and commentary on Book V of Euclid's *Elements*. The latter part of the treatise on ratio and proportion is actually an extension of two lemmas from Book I of Ptolemy's *Almagest.*

AHMAD IBN YŪSUF AL-TĪFĀSHĪ. *See* **al-Tīfāshī.**

AIDA YASUAKI, also known as **Aida Ammei** (*b. Yamagata, Japan, 1747; d. Edo* [*now Tokyo*]*, Japan, 1817*), mathematics.

Aida studied mathematics under Yasuyuki Okazaki in Yamagata. Aida went to Edo, determined to become the best mathematician in Japan. The famous mathematician Sadasuke Fujita did not receive Aida as a pupil. Aida, in his *Kaisei sampo* (1781), criticized and revised Fujita's highly regarded *Seiyo sampo* of 1781.

In 1788 Aida published *Sampo tensei shinan*, a collection of conventional geometry problems. In the course of his research he developed a table of logarithms, transmitted from China, that differed substantially from that of Ajima, being calculated to the base of two.

Aida also worked in number theory and gave an explanation of approximate fractions by developing a continued fraction.

AILLY, PIERRE D', also known as **Petrus de Alliaco** (*b. Compiègne, France 1350; d. Avignon, France, 1420*), theology, cosmography.

Studied at the College of Navarre of the University of Paris, doctorate, 1381. D'Ailly wrote commentaries on Aristotle (the *De anima* and the *Meteorologica*), as well as a number of astronomical and astrological works, including a commentary on the *De sphaera* of Sacrobosco.

His most significant scientific work is a collection of cosmographical and astronomical treatises with the collective title *Imago mundi.*

In his philosophical and scientific outlook, d'Ailly is considered a nominalist; however, his scientific writing shows little originality and much unacknowledged borrowing. He has a more significant claim to historical prominence as a leader of the conciliar movement.

AIRY, GEORGE BIDDELL (*b. Alnwick, Northumberland, England, 1801; d. Greenwich, England, 1892*), astronomy.

Attended Cambridge and was elected fellow of Trinity College in 1824.

He transformed the Royal Greenwich Observatory into a highly efficient institution. The cost, however, was high. No independent thought could be tolerated, and as a result no scientists were trained there.

Airy supplied all the major participants in the discovery of the planet Neptune with the observational data they requested, and the only basis for the subsequent attacks upon him for withholding these observations was that he was not at home when John Adams, then a young Cambridge mathematician, called unannounced to present one of his early predictions that such a planet as Neptune had to exist in order to account for the motions of the other planets. Airy's great efficiency in the observatory was noted by other government services and he rapidly became the prototype of the modern government scientist.

AITKEN, ROBERT GRANT (*b. Jackson, California, 1864; d. Berkeley, California, 1951*), astronomy.

Aitken first intended to become a minister, but his studies in biology and astronomy at Williams College (1883–87) diverted his interest to science. During forty years at the Lick Observatory, Aitken was an outstanding observer of double stars, and his *New General Catalogue of Double Stars Within 120° of the North Pole* (1932) is still a standard work. In 1899 he embarked on a systematic survey of double stars. He was soon joined by W. J. Hussey. This survey resulted in the discovery of over 4,400 new pairs with separations mostly below 5″. He published statistical investigations of this material in 1918 in *The Binary Stars.*

AITON, WILLIAM (*b. Avondale, Lanarkshire, Scotland, 1731; d. Kew, Surrey, England, 1793*), horticulture.

Aiton was trained as a gardener and eventually became assistant to Philip Miller, curator of Chelsea Physic Garden. He was engaged in 1759 by Princess Augusta to plant a botanical garden at Kew House; this was the inauguration of the present-day Royal Botanic Gardens. Aiton assumed control of the garden in 1783.

He published his *Hortus Kewensis* in 1789. This three-volume work is of fundamental importance as a catalog of some 5,500 plants under cultivation at the time, and records their provenance and the date of their introduction. It also contains descriptions of new species.

Aiton is commemorated by the interesting monotypic South African genus *Aitonia*, which was described by Carl Peter Thunberg in 1780.

AITON, WILLIAM TOWNSEND (*b. Kew, Surrey, England, 1766; d. Kensington, London, England, 1849*), horticulture.

Aiton was greatly interested in landscaping and acquired a considerable reputation as a landscape gardener having started out an assistant to his father.

In 1793, upon the death of his father, William Aiton, he succeeded to the control of the gardens at Kew and Richmond, and of other royal gardens.

Aiton was one of the seven gentlemen who founded the Royal Horticultural Society in 1804.

AJIMA NAONOBU, also known as **Ajima Chokuyen** (common name, **Manzo;** pen name, **Nanzan**) *(b. Shiba, Edo [now Tokyo], Japan, ca. 1732; d. Shiba, 1798),* mathematics.

Ajima first studied mathematics under Masatada Irie of the Nakanishi school and later he studied both mathematics and astronomy under Nushizumi Yamaji who initiated him into the secret mathematical principles of the Seki school. In the traditional succession of the Seki school, Ajima is in the fourth generation of masters. Most of the essential points of his work are summarized in his *Fukyu sampo,* a book that Ajima intended as an emendation of Sadasuke Fujita's *Seiyo sampo,* which was then a popular textbook.

Influenced by Takakazu Seki, his works reflect an innovative trend toward geometry within a tradition that was basically algebraic and numerical in approach. This trend is exemplified in the development of *yenri,* a method for determining the area of a circle, of a sphere, or of plane figures composed of curved lines. In the same year Ajima discovered a way to obtain the volume common to two intersecting cylinders by using double integration, which he presented in *Enchu kokuen jutsu.*

For his work with logarithms, Ajima drew upon *Suri seiran,* a book published in China in 1723 that almost certainly incorporated some of the Western principles brought to China by the Jesuits. Ajima's table and its uses are described in *Fukyu sampo.*

Ajima drew upon Japanese mathematical tradition for *yo jutsu,* problems involving transcribing a number of circles in triangles and squares.

AL-. *See* **next element of name.**

ALAIN DE LILLE, also known as **Alanus de Insulis** *(b. Lille, France, first half of the twelfth century; d. Cîteaux, France, 1203),* theology, philosophy.

Alain's reputation rests largely on two literary works, the *De planctu naturae* and the very famous *Anticlaudianus.* The *De planctu* is an exposition of Neoplatonic Christian naturalism.

ALBATEGNI. *See* **al-Battānī.**

ALBERT I OF MONACO (HONORÉ CHARLES GRIMALDI) *(b. Paris, France, 1848; d. Paris, 1922),* oceanography.

Each year for nearly forty years Albert made voyages in the North Atlantic, taking soundings wherever he went.

In physical oceanography, Albert studied currents, especially the Gulf Stream (1885). One of his major achievements was a general atlas to the millionth, which had twenty-four plates and illustrated the bathymetry of all the oceans.

The results of Albert's research on the *Physalia* became a first step toward the discovery of anaphylaxis.

ALBERT OF BOLLSTÄDT. *See* **Albertus Magnus.**

ALBERT OF SAXONY *(b. Helmstedt, Lower Saxony, ca. 1316; d. Halberstadt, Saxony, 1390),* physics, logic, mathematics.

Albert studied at Prague and then at Paris where he obtained the degree of master of arts in 1351. His significance in the history of science is primarily that of a transmitter and an intelligent compiler of scientific ideas.

Despite his lack of originality Albert had the particular merit of seeing the importance of bringing together the mathematical treatments of motion in its kinematic aspect.

Albert's textbook of logic is one of the best organized of the late medieval works in the field.

Despite its excellence as a textbook, this work did not achieve the popularity or influence attained by Albert's *Tractatus proportionum* and by his questions on the physical treatises of Aristotle. These became the principal means by which the contributions of the northern Scholastics of the fourteenth century to the science of mechanics were made known to the physicists and mathematicians of Italy.

ALBERTI, FRIEDRICH AUGUST VON *(b. Stuttgart, Germany, 1795; d. Heilbronn, Germany, 1878),* geology, mining.

Alberti's most important technical improvement was the introduction of steam heating into salt processing. He was considered one of the foremost salt-mining engineers and a scientist of significant achievement.

His investigations of the Triassic period and its fossils were of fundamental significance.

ALBERTI, LEONE BATTISTA *(b. Genoa, Italy, 1404; d. Rome, Italy, 1472),* mathematics, physics, natural history, technology.

Alberti started his advanced education at Padua. After 1421 he continued it at Bologna, where he began the study of law. He received a doctorate in canon law. In Rome Alberti discovered antiquity and became the artist we know today—painter, sculptor, and then architect. At the court of Rimini, Alberti conceived and partially executed his most important architectural work, the Malatesta Temple, a chapel designed to shelter the tombs of the Malatesta family.

Unfortunately, a large part of Alberti's scientific work has been lost. Alberti's mathematics is exactly that of his times. Not much is known about his physics. In his writings on the natural sciences, Alberti speculated on nature rather than on scientific data.

His best-known work, containing many of his scientific ideas, is his *De re aedificatoria.*

ALBERTI, SALOMON *(b. Naumburg, Germany, 1540; d. Dresden, Germany, 1600),* medicine.

Alberti studied medicine at Wittenberg (M.D. 1574) and taught there for many years. His study of the venous valves was his most noteworthy achievement and he was the first to provide illustrations of venous valves in his *Tres orationes* (Nuremberg, 1585). Alberti also studied and described the lacrimal apparatus (*De lacrimis,* 1581). He provided an extended account of the ileocecal valve, the cochlea, and the renal papillae (*Orationes duae,* 1575). Alberti discussed the problem of deafness and muteness in

Oratio de surditate et mutitate (1591). His interest in the problem of scurvy led to the treatise *De schorbuto* (1591).

ALBERTUS MAGNUS, SAINT, also known as **Albert the Great** and **Universal Doctor** *(b. Lauingen, Bavaria, ca. 1200; d. Cologne, Prussia, 1280).* Proficient in all branches of science, he was one of the most famous precursors of modern science in the High Middle Ages.

Albertus Magnus studied liberal arts at Padua, where he was recruited into the Dominican Order. His principal importance for the history of modern science derives from the role he played in rediscovering Aristotle and introducing Greek and Arab science into the universities of the Middle Ages.

In the 1240's, he probably began his monumental paraphrase of all the known works of Aristotle and Pseudo-Aristotle.

He pointed out that science consists not in simply believing what one is told but in inquiring into the causes of natural things. Albert recognized the importance of mathematics for the physical sciences and composed treatises on its pure and applied branches. His mechanics was basically that of Aristotle.

He speculated on the cause of sound and also the cause of heat, studying in detail how light from the sun produces thermal effects.

Although he had no telescope, he postulated that the Milky Way is composed of stars and attributed the dark spots on the moon to configurations on its surface, not to the earth's shadow. His treatise on comets is notable for its use of simple observation to verify or falsify theories that had been proposed to explain them.

On the structure of matter, when discussing the presence of elements in compounds, Albert attempted to steer a middle course between the opposed positions of Avicenna and Averroës, thereby preparing for Aquinas' more acceptable theory of "virtual" presence. He benignly viewed Democritus' atoms as equivalent to the *minima naturalia* of the Aristotelians. He seems to have experimented with alchemy and is said to have been the first to isolate the element arsenic. He compiled a list of some hundred minerals, giving the properties of each. He was acquainted with fossils, and made accurate observations of "animal impressions."

In the biological sciences his powers of observation and his skill at classification earned for him an unparalleled reputation. His *De vegetabilibus et plantis,* in particular, is a masterpiece for its independence of treatment, its accuracy and range of detailed description, its freedom from myth, and its innovation in systematic classification. His general classification of the vegetable kingdom followed that proposed by Theophrastus.

On plant evolution, Albert proposed that existing types were sometimes mutable and described five ways of transforming one plant into another.

Albert's *De animalibus* includes descriptions of some fabulous creatures, but it also rejects many popular medieval myths and is especially noteworthy for its sections on reproduction and embryology. His system of classification for the animal kingdom was basically Aristotelian. His anthropology was more philosophical than empirical in intent. Albert made significant contributions also to veterinary and medical science, dentistry included.

ALBINUS, BERNARD *(b. Dessau, Anhalt, Germany, 1653; d. Leiden, Netherlands, 1721),* medicine.

First educated privately then at the University of Leiden, M.D. (1676). Traveled to the Netherlands and France to learn the latest developments in anatomy, surgery and medicine. Professor of medicine at the University of Frankfurt-an-der-Oder. Ph.D., University of Frankfurt-an-der-Oder (1681). Court physician to Friedrich Wilhelm, elector of Brandenburg, and Frederick I of Prussia. Taught theoretical and practical medicine at the University of Leiden (1702). Laid the foundation for the fame of Leiden as a world center for the study of medicine.

ALBINUS, BERNARD SIEGFRIED *(b. Frankfurt-an-der-Oder, Germany, 1697; d. Leiden, Netherlands, 1770),* anatomy, medicine.

Matriculated at Leiden (1709). From 1721 taught anatomy and surgery at Leiden. Reissued (with Boerhaave) the anatomical atlas of Vesalius and, later, the anatomical works of Fabrici (1737) and of Eustachi (1744). Edited the complete works of William Harvey (1736). Published his own plates, on the human bones (1726), on the human muscles (1734), and on the development of the human skeleton (1737). Devised a method for accurately rendering the proportions of a human skeleton much like the one devised by Albrecht Dürer. In 1747 his work on the human skeleton and muscles was published in thirty-five sheets; in 1748, his illustration of the gravid uterus in nine sheets; and in 1753, an atlas of the human bones, drawn separately, in thirty-four sheets. Between 1754 and 1768, his studies on human physiology were published in eight volumes.

ALBINUS, CHRISTIAAN BERNARD *(b. Berlin, Germany, 1698 / 1699; d. Utrecht, Netherlands, 1752),* anatomy.

Ph.D. University of Leiden, 1722. Professor of anatomy and surgery at the University of Utrecht. Known as the editor of the second English edition of William Cowper's anatomical atlas.

ALBINUS, FREDERIK BERNARD *(b. Leiden, Netherlands, 1715; d. Lieden, 1778),* anatomy, medicine.

Matriculated as a student of literature at Leiden (1731); doctor of philosophy and of medicine (1740). Lecturer in anatomy and surgery at the University of Leiden.

ALBRECHT, CARL THEODOR *(b. Dresden, Germany, 1843; d. Potsdam, Germany, 1915),* surveying, astronomy.

Graduated from the University of Leipzig (1869). From 1873 until his death, Albrecht was director of the astronomy department of the Geodetic Institute in Potsdam, which quickly became one of the leading research institutes in astronomy and geodesy.

ALBUMASAR. *See* **Abū Maꜥshar.**

ALCABITIUS. *See* **al-Qabīṣī.**

ALCMAEON OF CROTONA *(b. Crotona, Magna Graecia, ca. 535* B.C.*),* medicine, natural philosophy.

Alcmaeon, the son of Peirithoos and a pupil of Pythagoras, is often reported to have been a physician although there is no support for this in ancient sources. He also wrote about meteorological and astrological problems and about such philosophical questions as the immortality of the soul. It may, therefore, be best to call him a natural philosopher, deeply versed in medicine, who was in close contact with both the Pythagoreans and the physicians in Crotona.

May have written the very first Greek prose book, a *physikos logos;* and he furnished medicine with the first material for a fundamental intellectual mastery of the nontraumatic internal diseases.

ALCUIN OF YORK *(b. York, England, ca. 735; d. Tours, France, 804),* education.

As Charlemagne's educational advisor, Alcuin brought Anglo-Saxon learning and teaching methods to the Franks. He popularized the study of the seven liberal arts in France and wrote elementary textbooks on these subjects. His dialogue method of instruction brought needed vitality to teaching.

ALDER, KURT *(b. Königshütte, Germany [now Chorźow, Poland],* 1902; d. Cologne, Germany, 1958), organic chemistry.

Studied at the University of Berlin and University of Kiel (Ph.D. 1926). Alder's principal contributions to organic chemistry are associated with the diene synthesis, first reported in 1928. The synthetic method, frequently referred to as the Diels-Alder reaction, involves the addition of dienes to dienophiles. The Diels-Alder reaction became useful in structural studies because it provided an analytical means for the detection of conjugated double bonds. The diene synthesis also stimulated the understanding of terpene chemistry. With Otto Diels, Alder received the Nobel Prize for chemistry in 1950.

ALDEROTTI, TADDEO, also known as **Thaddaeus Florentinus** *(b. Florence, Italy, 1223; d. Bologna, Italy, ca. 1295),* medicine.

One of the founders of medical study at Bologna. Alderotti's commentaries on various classical and Islamic writers established the dialectical method of teaching in the medical school, a method that was used until the sixteenth century. He also developed a new form of medical literature, the *Consilia,* a collection of clinical cases with advice on how to treat them.

ALDINI, GIOVANNI *(b. Bologna, Italy, 1762; d. Milan, Italy, 1834),* physics.

In the controversy over Galvani's "animal electricity" and Volta's "galvanic current," Galvani's nephew, Giovanni Aldini, wrote, lectured, and published in Italian, French, and English on his own theories and those of his uncle. His best-known work was *Essai théorique et expérimentale sur le galvanisme* (1804). The *Dissertatione duae* resulted from Aldini's galvanic experiments, including those on warm-blooded animals.

ALDROVANDI, ULISSE *(b. Bologna, Italy, 1522; d. Bologna, 1605),* natural sciences.

As a professor at the University of Bologna, Aldrovandi carried out studies in botany, teratology, embryology, ichthyology, and ornithology.

His observations did not contribute greatly to the progress of embryology but they had the merit of recall-

ing to the attention of scholars the method of direct observation of natural phenomena.

Although he did not practice medicine, Aldrovandi's efforts to place botany and pharmacology on a scientific plane and the lucidness and modernity of the legislation he suggested for public health and the civic sanitation of Bologna suggest that he was a pioneer in hygiene and pharmacology.

ALEMBERT, JEAN LE ROND D' *(b. Paris, France, 1717; d. Paris, 1783),* physics, mathematics.

D'Alembert was the illegitimate child of a salon hostess and a cavalry officer. He is best known for his work in mathematics and rational mechanics and as scientific editor of the *Encyclopédie.*

In his most famous scientific work, the *Traité de dynamique* (1743), he developed his own three laws of motion. For the first and second laws, the law of inertia and of the parallelogram of motion, d'Alembert's reasoning was geometric. Only for the third law are physical assumptions involved. This law deals with equilibrium, and amounts to the principle of the conservation of momentum in impact situations. In the *Traité,* d'Alembert gives the first statement of what is now known as d'Alembert's principle which is actually not so much a principle as it is a rule for using the laws of motion stated in the *Traité.* It can be stated as follows: in any situation where an object is constrained from following its normal inertial motion, the resulting motion can be analyzed into two components: the motion the object actually takes, and the motion "destroyed" by the constraints.

In the *Traité de l'equilibre et du mouvement des fluides* (1744), d'Alembert used his principle to describe fluid motion, treating the major current problems of fluid mechanics and giving an alternative treatment to one already published by Daniel Bernoulli.

His *Réflexions sur la cause générale des vents* (1747) contained the first general use of partial differential equations in mathematical physics. In a 1747 article the wave equation made its first appearance in physics, but d'Alembert's solution, while correct, did not match well the observed phenomena.

In *Recherches sur la précession des équinoxes et sur la nutation de la terre* (1749) his method of attacking the problem of the precession of the equinoxes was similar to Clairaut's, but he arrived at a solution that was more in accord with the observed motion of the earth.

The *Essai d'une nouvelle théorie de la résistance des fluides* (1752), in which the differential hydrodynamic equations were first expressed in terms of a field and the hydrodynamic paradox was put forth, generated considerable dispute. The Prussian Academy awarded no prize in the competition for which it was written on the basis that nobody had submitted experimental proof of the theoretical work. It has been claimed that d'Alembert's work, although the best entered, was marred by errors. D'Alembert himself viewed his denial of the prize as the result of Euler's influence, and relations between the two scientists already strained, deteriorated further. Credit for the development of fluid mechanics has been variously assigned to both.

D'Alembert wrote the *Discours préliminaire* of the *Encyclopédie,* a cardinal document of the Enlightenment and a manifesto of the *philosophes.* D'Alembert's articles in the

Encyclopédie reached far beyond mathematics. His propagandistic article on Geneva was the immediate cause of the suspension of the license for the *Encyclopédie,* and he resigned, convinced that the enterprise must founder.

D'Alembert's chief scientific output after 1760 was his *Opuscules mathématiques* a mixed bag, including many new solutions to problems he had previously attacked. D'Alembert was almost alone in his day in regarding the differential as the limit of a function, a key concept around which the calculus was eventually rationalized.

The requirement of continuity probably led him to his idea of the limit, and to his test for convergence, now called d'Alembert's theorem. But in spite of such original contributions to mathematical manipulation, his chief concern was in making this language not merely descriptive of the world, but congruent to it.

ALEXANDER OF APHRODISIAS (*fl. second-third century* A.D.), philosophy.

A Peripatetic philosopher of the second-third century, among whose masters were Herminus, Sosigenes, and Aristocles. His fame rests mainly on his interpretation of Aristotle's doctrines, the scholarly qualities of which earned him the sobriquet of "the interpreter." Of his works other than commentaries, four have survived in Greek manuscripts: *On the Soul; On Fate;* a writing going under the title *On Mixture;* and another, in four books, going under the title *Natural Questions.* The assertion or the denial of the correctness of Alexander's interpretation of Aristotle and, even more, the correctness of the doctrine became one of the great controversies of the Middle Ages and early modern times.

ALEXANDER OF MYNDOS (*b. Myndos, Caria; fl. ca.* A.D. *25–50),* biology.

Alexander's principal work in natural history was entitled *On Animals.* The extant fragments from his zoological writings are a mixture of fact and fancy, in which the strange, unusual, or fabulous behavior of land animals and birds is emphasized.

ALEXANDER OF TRALLES (*b. Tralles, in Lydia, first half of the sixth century* A.D.; *fl. in the time of Justinian),* medicine.

Alexander's importance lies within the framework of Byzantine medicine. He did not simply edit a medical anthology composed of other people's texts but wrote a work of his own.

ALEXIS OF PIEDMONT. *See* **Ruscelli, Girolamo.**

ALFONSO EL SABIO (*b. Toledo, Spain, 1221; d. Seville, Spain, 1284),* astronomy, dissemination of science and learning.

Alfonso el Sabio, "the learned," became Alfonso X in 1252. Alfonso gave Spain a great legal code, *Las siete partidas,* and sponsored important scientific translations from Arabic into Latin and Castilian. He gained his most lasting scientific fame by supporting a new edition of the Toledan Tables of the Cordoban astronomer al-Zarqālī (Arzachel).

ALFRAGANUS. *See* **al-Farghānī.**

ALHAZEN. *See* **Ibn al-Haytham.**

ᶜ**ALI.** *See* **last element of name.**

ALKINDUS. *See* **al-Kindī.**

ALLEN, EDGAR (*b. Canyon City, Colorado, 1892; d. New Haven, Connecticut, 1943),* endocrinology.

Allen attended Brown University (Ph.B., 1915; M.A., 1916; Ph.D. 1921). He was professor of anatomy and chairman of the department at Yale School of Medicine from 1933.

ALLIACO, PETRUS DE. *See* **Ailly, Pierre d'.**

ALLONVILLE, J. E. D'. *See* **Louville, J. E. d'A., Chevalier de.**

ALPETRAGIUS. *See* **al-Biṭrūjī.**

ALPHARABIUS. *See* **al-Fārābī.**

ALPINI, PROSPERO (*b. Marostica, Italy, 1553; d. Padua, Italy, 1616),* botany.

Alpini studied medicine at the University of Padua (1578). He was among the first of the Italian physician-botanists of the sixteenth century to examine plants outside the context of their therapeutic uses.

From a scientific point of view, the *De plantis Aegypti* (1592) is his most important work. It introduced exotic Egyptian plants to the still parochial European botanical circles. Linnaeus regarded Alpini with sufficient esteem to name the genus *Alpinia (Zingiberaceae)* in his honor.

De balsamo dialogus (1591) discusses the source of balsam and its medical uses; *De rhapontico* (1612), the source and therapeutic properties of rhubarb and *De plantis exoticis,* the flora of Crete.

Alpini's interest in medicine was expressed in several books: *De medicina Aegyptiorum* (1591) was primarily an examination of contemporary Egyptian (i.e., Turkish) medicine, ranking as one of the earliest studies of non-European medicine; *De praesagienda vita* (1601) is a detailed study of prognostics in which attention is devoted to the patient's mental state and its bearing on health, as well as to the usual physical and diagnostic signs.

His *Rerum Aegyptiarum* was a pioneer contribution to Egyptology.

ALSTED, JOHANN HEINRICH (*b. Ballersbach, Germany, 1588; d. Weissenburg [after 1715 Karlsburg; now Alba Ivlia, Rumania] 1638),* natural philosophy.

Alsted studied at Frankfurt am Main, Heidelberg, Strasbourg and Basel. The majority of his writings were on theology. Throughout the areas of Calvinist influence, Alsted's systematic treatises on educational theory, theology, and philosophy exerted great influence in the universities during most of the seventeenth century.

His major monographs display a strikingly uniform organization, at the cost of oversimplification, an inherent danger of the Ramist approach. The *Systema physicae harmonicae* (1612) is typical of this.

The *Methodus admirandorum* discusses improved techniques of surveying and physical astronomy and the merits of the Copernican hypothesis.

Alsted's ultimate fame rests upon his conception of the encyclopedia as a universal system of knowledge.

ALZATE Y RAMÍREZ, JOSÉ ANTONIO (*b. Ozumba, Mexico, 1738; d. Mexico City, Mexico, 1799*), natural history, mathematics, geography, astronomy.

In 1756 Alzate received a bachelor of divinity degree from the University of Mexico, and was subsequently ordained a Catholic priest. He embraced the ideas of the Enlightenment and devoted his life to the study of all branches of natural science. His principal aim was to promote the development of technology in New Spain. Alzate founded several scientific periodicals: *Diario literario de México* (1768); *Asuntos varios sobre ciencias y artes* (1772); *Observaciones sobre la física, historia natural y artes utiles* (1787); and *Gazeta de literatura* (1788–95).

AMAGAT, ÉMILE (*b. Saint-Satur, Cher, France, 1841; d. Saint-Satur, 1915*), physics.

Amagat became *docteur-es-sciences* at Paris in February 1872 and was then successively, *agrégé,* professor of physics at the Faculté Libre des Sciences of Lyons, and examiner at the École Polytechnique.

His work dealt with fluid statics. He devoted the active phase of his career to the search for the laws of the coefficients of compressibility, the coefficients of expansion under constant pressure and constant volume, the coefficients of pressure when both pressure and temperature are varied, and the limits toward which these laws tend when matter is more and more condensed by pressure.

AMATUS LUSITANUS. *See* **Lusitanus, Amatus.**

AMEGHINO, FLORENTINO (*b. Moneglia, Liguria, Italy, ca. 1853; d. La Plata, Argentina, 1911*), paleontology, prehistory, anthropology, geology.

Ameghino's first important geological work was "El Tajamar y sus futuras consecuencias y el origen de la Tosca." His principal work, *Contribución al conocimiento de los mamíferos fósiles de la República Argentina* (1880), brought him gold medals at the Paris Exposition of 1889 and the Chicago Exposition of 1892. In 1880–81 he published *La antigüedad del hombre en el río de La Plata,* the first work on Argentine prehistory in both Spanish and French. In 1884 Ameghino published *Filogenia,* in which he proposed to find irrefutable proof of transformism. *Proceedings of the Zoological Society of London* published his account of the plexodontal molars of mammals in 1899. Ameghino's most controversial theory was that these fossils were older than those of other countries and that Argentina was the center from which those creatures had spread. This brought him into conflict with Europeans over the characteristics he attributed to Pampean man.

AMES, JOSEPH SWEETMAN (*b. Manchester, Vermont, 1864; d. Baltimore, Maryland, 1943*), physics.

Graduated Johns Hopkins (1886); Ph.D. (1890). Ames's research was limited in quantity and largely confined to the field of spectroscopy. In the 1890's, he struggled with the problem of finding relationships among the lines of particular spectra.

In World War I Ames served on the National Advisory Committee for Aeronautics, created by Congress in 1915 to promote the scientific study of flight. Ames got into trouble for writing publicly that the government's ambitious aircraft program was far behind schedule; Secretary of Commerce William C. Redfield considered the statement a treasonous act. But Ames was right, and he later became chairman of the NACA.

AMES, WILLIAM (*b. Ipswich, Suffolk, England, 1576; d. Rotterdam, Netherlands, 1633*), theology, natural philosophy.

Ames matriculated as a pensioner at Christ's College, Cambridge (1593/94), obtaining his B.A. (1597/98) and M.A. (1601). He achieved prominence at the Synod of Dordrecht (1618), where he advised the Calvinist faction. He occupied a prominent role in the Protestant theology of the first half of the seventeenth century, systematizing and developing certain aspects of the Calvinist theology of Perkins. Two particular points—practical divinity and Ramist philosophy—make Ames significant, not only for theology but also for the general intellectual history of the seventeenth century.

AMICI, GIOVAN BATTISTA (*b. Modena, Italy, 1786; d. Florence, Italy, 1868*), optics, microscopy, natural sciences.

Graduated as engineer architect from the University of Bologna (1807). Head of Royal Museum of Physics and Natural History until 1859. In 1818 Amici, after having built a type of catadioptric microscope that was free of chromatic aberrations, succeeded in appreciably improving the knowledge of the circulation of protoplasm in *Chara* cells.

In 1837 Amici arrived at a resolving power of 0.001 mm. with a new type of microscope that had a numerical aperture of 0.4 and was capable of magnifying up to 6,000 times.

Shortly thereafter values ranging around 1,000X were generally achieved.

Amici invented widely used prisms that still bear his name, and reconsidered the direct-vision prism, which had been forgotten. He also built concave mirrors and astronomical lenses. His masterpiece was a lens with a diameter of 285 mm. He also invented new micrometers to improve the accuracy of astronomical measurements, and new types of distance-measuring telescopes.

The discovery that made him famous was that of the fertilization of phanerogams, particularly the travel of the pollen tube through the pistil of the flower (1821).

AMMONIUS, SON OF HERMIAS (*d. Alexandria, Egypt, ca. A.D. 517–526*), philosophy.

Ammonius was head of the Platonic school in Alexandria from 485. A sober and scholarly interpreter of Plato and Aristotle.

AMONTONS, GUILLAUME (*b. Paris, France, 1663; d. Paris, 1705*), physics.

His first scientific production was a hygrometer in 1687. In 1688 he developed his shortened barometer. His optical telegraph consisted of a series of stations for the rapid transmission of signals.

In 1695 Amontons sought to renew the use of the clepsydra as a timing apparatus on ships in order to solve the problem of determining longitude at sea.

As early as 1699 he proposed a thermic motor: a machine using hot air and external combustion with direct rotation.

Amontons produced the first known study on the question of losses caused by friction in machines. He then established the laws of proportionality between the friction and the mutual pressure of the bodies in contact.

In 1702, having noted that water ceases to increase its temperature from the boiling point, he proposed that the latter be the fixed thermometric point. He also observed that for an equal elevation of temperature, the increase of pressure of a gas always exists in the same proportion, no matter what the initial pressure.

Amontons indicated practical ways of graduating ordinary alcohol thermometers. Among his last works was a barometer with a U-tube, without an open surface of mercury, to be used on shipboard. Also, using a barometer as an altimeter, he tried to verify the exactitude of Mariotte's (Boyle's) law at low pressures.

AMPÈRE, ANDRE-MARIE (b. *Lyons, France, 1775; d. Marseilles, France, 1836*), mathematics, chemistry, physics.

Ampère was educated along the lines laid down in Rousseau's *Émile.* He was exposed to a considerable library and left to educate himself as his own tastes dictated. Probably the most important influence was the *Encyclopédie,* but he was also thoroughly instructed in the Catholic faith. After a position as a mathematics teacher at Lyons, he became professor of physics and chemistry at the école centrale of Bourg-en-Bresse (1802). In that same year he began work on an original paper on probability theory, on the strength of which he was named *répétiteur* in mathematics at the École Polytechnique in Paris. In 1808 Ampère was named inspector general of the newly formed university system, a post he held, except for a few years in the 1820's, until his death. In 1814 he was named a member of the class of mathematics in the Institut Impérial. In 1819 he was authorized to offer a course in philosophy at the University of Paris, and in 1820 he was named assistant professor (*professeur suppléant*) of astronomy. In August 1824 Ampère was elected to the chair of experimental physics at the Collège de France.

There are, according to Ampère, two levels of knowledge of the external world. There are phenomena, presented to us directly through the senses, and there are noumena, the objective causes of phenomena. We can also know relations between phenomena and relations between noumena, and these relations are just as objectively real as noumena.

In 1814 Ampère published his "Lettre de M. Ampère à M. le comte Berthollet sur la détermination des proportions dan lesquelles les corps se combinent d'après le nombre et la disposition respective des molécules don leurs particules intégrantes sont composées." From the theory of universal attraction used to account for the cohesion of bodies and the fact that light easily passes through transparent bodies, Ampère concluded that the attractive and repulsive forces associated with each molecule hold the ultimate molecules of bodies at distances from one another that are, as Ampère put it, "infinitely great in comparison to the dimensions of these molecules."

Ampère's molecules were assumed to group themselves in various ways to form particles that had specific geometric forms. Thus there would be particles composed of four molecules that formed tetrahedrons, of eight molecules that formed an octahedron, etc. These geometrical forms were of the greatest importance in

Ampère's theory, for they allowed him to deal with the problem of elective affinity and also to deduce Avogadro's law.

The continuing intellectual passion of Ampère's life from 1800 to his death was his philosophical system but these years were also devoted to scientific research of considerable originality. From 1800 to about 1814, he devoted himself primarily to mathematics. As his mathematical interests declined, he became fascinated with chemistry and, from 1808 to 1815, he spent his spare time in chemical investigations. From 1820 to 1827, he founded and developed the science of electrodynamics, the scientific work for which he is best known and which earned him his place in the first rank of physicists.

Ampère's largest mathematical memoir, "Mémoire sur l'intégrations des équations aux différences partielles" (1814), concerns various means of integrating partial differential equations.

In 1816 Ampère turned to the phenomenal relations of chemistry in a long paper on the natural classification of elementary bodies ("Essai d'une classification naturelle pour les corps simples"). Here he drew attention to the similarities between Lavoisier's and his followers' classification of elements in terms of their reactions with oxygen and Linnaeus' classification of plants in terms of their sexual organs. By discovering a natural classification, i.e., one that tied the elements together by real rather than artificial relations, Ampère hoped to provide a new insight into chemical reactions. His classificatory scheme, therefore, was not merely an ordering of the elements but a true instrument of chemical research. Although he looked for more analogies among elements than Lavoisier had, the ones he selected offered little insight into the relations between the groups founded on them. The paper may be noted, however, as an early attempt to find relationships between the elements that would bring some order into the constantly growing number of elementary bodies.

It was the noumenal aspect of chemistry that fascinated Ampère. Although his derivation of Avogadro's law came three years after Avogadro had enunciated it, the law is known today in France as the Avogadro-Ampère law.

By 1820 Ampère had achieved a certain reputation as both a mathematician and a somewhat heterodox chemist. Hans Christian Oersted's discovery of electromagnetism in the spring of 1820 opened up a whole new world to Ampère. On 18 September he read his first paper on the subject to the Academy. On 25 September and 9 October he continued the account of his discoveries. In these feverish weeks the science of electrodynamics was born.

In the "Mémoire sur l'action naturelle de deux courants électriques . . ." (1820), Ampère stated that his mind leaped immediately from the existence of electromagnetism to the idea that currents traveling in circles through helices would act like magnets. He applied his theory to the magnetism of the earth, and the genesis of electrodynamics may, indeed, have been as Ampère stated it. It would appear that Oersted's discovery suggested to Ampère that two current-carrying wires might affect one another. Since the pattern of magnetic force around a current-carrying wire is circular, it was no great step for Ampère, the geometer, to visualize the resultant force if the wire were coiled into a helix. What Ampère had done was to present a new theory of magnetism as electricity in motion.

Having established a noumenal foundation for electro-dynamic phenomena, Ampère's next steps were to discover the relationships between the phenomena and to devise a theory from which these relationships could be mathematically deduced. This double task was undertaken in the years 1821–25, and his success was reported in his greatest work, the *Mémoire sur la théorie mathématique des phéonomènes électrodynamique, uniquement déduite de l'expérience* (1827). In this work, the *Principia* of electrodynamics, Ampère first described the laws of action of electric currents, which he had discovered from four extremely ingenious experiments.

From these cases Ampère was able to deduce consequences that permitted him to apply mathematics to the phenomena and attack the theory of magnetism quantitatively. In short, he was able to unify the fields of electricity and magnetism on a basic noumenal level.

AMSLER (later **AMSLER-LAFFON**), **JAKOB** (*b. Stalden bei Brugg, Switzerland, 1823; d. Schaffhausen, Switzerland, 1912*), mathematics, precision instruments.

Amsler studied theology at the universities of Jena and Königsberg. At Königsberg he came under the influence of Franz Neumann. Ph.D. 1848. Until 1854 his interests lay in the area of mathematical physics; he published articles on magnetic distribution, the theory of heat conduction, and the theory of attraction. One result of his work was a generalization of Ivory's theorem on the attraction of ellipsoids and of Poisson's extension of that theorem. Amsler's major contribution to mathematics was the polar planimeter, a device for measuring areas enclosed by plane curves (1854). The instrument, described in "Ueber das Polarplanimeter" (1856), proved especially useful to shipbuilders and railroad engineers.

To capitalize on his inspiration, Amsler established his own precision tools workshop in 1854.

ANARITIUS. *See* **al-Nayrīzī.**

ANATOLIUS OF ALEXANDRIA (*b. Alexandria; d. Laodicea; fl. ca. A.D. 269*), mathematics, philosophy.

Learned in arithmetic, geometry, astronomy, and other sciences both intellectual and natural, Anatolius was also outstanding in rhetoric. *The Canons of Anatolius on the Pascha* displays Anatolius' grasp of astronomy in the discussion of the position of the sun and moon in the zodiac at the time of Easter. Anatolius sometimes deals in Aristotelian terms with questions about mathematics, its name, its philosophical importance, and some of its methods. His *Introduction to Arithmetic* may have dealt with each of the first ten natural numbers.

ANAXAGORAS (*b. Clazomenae, Lydia, 500 B.C. [?]; d. Lampsacus, Mysia, 428 B.C. [?]*), natural philosophy.

Anaxagoras became a friend of Pericles in Athens and brought Ionian physical speculation to Athens at the height of its intellectual development.

Anaxagoras sought to reconcile Parmenides' logic with the phenomena of multiplicity and change. His concept of a separate, immaterial moving cause paved the way for a fully teleological view of nature.

ANAXILAUS OF LARISSA (*described by Eusebius as a Pythagorean magician who was banished from Italy by Augustus in Olympiad 188, 1 [28 B.C.]*).

Anaxilaus wrote about the "magical" or peculiar effects of some minerals, herbs, and animal substances and of the drugs made with them. He seems to have been famous for his magical tricks.

ANAXIMANDER (*b. 610 B.C.; d. ca. 546/545 B.C.*), astronomy, natural philosophy.

Anaximander tried to explain different phenomena as the result of one law that rules everything (here paraphrased): All things pass away into that from which they took their origin, the infinite, as it is necessary; for they make reparation to one another for their injustice in the fixed order of time.

ANAXIMENES OF MILETUS (*fl. 546/545 B.C.*), philosophy.

Anaximenes' cosmological and astronomical views are very close to those of Anaximander. Like Anaximander, Anaximenes thought that the source from which all things come into being is infinite. He further qualified this original substance by saying that it is air, for he had discovered a mechanism that could account for the transformation of one thing into another: the mechanism of condensation and rarefaction.

ANCEL, PAUL ALBERT (*b. Nancy, France, 1873; d. Paris, France, 1961*), biology.

Ancel became an intern in the Nancy hospitals in 1898 and received the M.D. in 1899 and the *docteur ès sciences* from the University of Nancy in 1903. Throughout his life he taught at the Universities of Lyons, Nancy, and Strassbourg. His work can be divided into three sections. His research in cytology furnished the material for an important thesis on the hermaphroditic genital glands of the snail. Secondly, he collaborated for twenty-five years with Pol Bouin in investigations on the physiology of reproduction in mammals. Finally, Ancel became one of the creators of present experimental embryology, and particularly of teratogenesis, by using physical and chemical means.

ANDERNACH, GUNTHER. *See* **Guenther, Johann.**

ANDERSON, ERNEST MASSON (*b. Falkirk, Scotland, 1877; d. Edinburgh, Scotland, 1960*), geology.

Anderson was educated at Edinburgh University, (B.Sc., 1897; M.A., 1898; D.Sc., 1933). His main scientific work concerned the dynamics of faulting and dyke formation and igneous intrusion, the lineation of schists, crustal heat and structure, and volcanism. After his retirement he expanded his studies by mathematical analysis.

Anderson gave the first fully satisfactory explanation of the "Becke line" effect seen in transparent mineral sections under the microscope (1910).

ANDERSON, OSKAR JOHANN VIKTOR (*b. Minsk, Russia, 1887; d. Munich, German Federal Republic, 1960*), mathematics.

After studying for one term at the mathematical faculty of Kazan University, Anderson entered the economics faculty of the Petersburg Polytechnic Institute in 1907. Graduated, 1912; dissertation published in *Biometrika*, 1914. From 1947 until his death he held the chair of statistics at the economics faculty of the University of Munich. Anderson considered himself a representative of the "Continental direction" of mathematical statistics. He was a pioneer in the field of sampling and was engaged mainly in the application of statistics to economics. He advocated the application of mathematical statistics to economics.

ANDERSON, THOMAS (*b. Leith, Scotland, 1819; d. Chiswick, England, 1874*), organic chemistry.

Graduated in medicine from Edinburgh University in 1841. Anderson carried out numerous analyses of soils, manures, and cattle foods. As chemist he examined the composition of wheat, beans, and turnips at various stages of growth.

In the distillation of bone oil (1848–68) Anderson found pyridine and its methyl derivatives.

ANDOYER, HENRI (*b. Paris, France, 1862; d. Paris, 1929*), astronomy, mathematics.

Graduated École Normale Supérieure (1884). Wrote doctoral thesis (1887) on the theory of intermediate orbits as applied to the moon. Taught astronomy at the Sorbonne for thirty-seven years. His research dealt with celestial mechanics: perturbation theory, special cases of the three-body and of the *n*-body problem, and the motions of the moon. He developed special methods for use in computing ephemerides.

ANDRÉ, CHARLES LOUIS FRANÇOIS (*b. Chauny, Aisne, France, 1842; d. St. Genis-Laval, Rhône, France, 1912*), astronomy, meteorology.

Graduated 1864 from the École Normale Supérieure in Paris with a degree in physics. Director of the Paris Observatory. André worked on observational techniques for determining the distance to the sun—the problem of the solar parallax. Difficulties encountered in timing the transit of Venus in 1874 led him to investigate effects of diffraction in optical instruments.

ANDREAE, JOHANN VALENTIN (*b. Herrenberg, Württemberg, 1586; d. Stuttgart, Württemberg, 1654*), theology, Christian learning.

Studied at Tübingen (B.A., 1603; M.A., 1605). Andreae wrote a large number of small works, most of them in Latin, whose general aim was the universal spiritual reformation of mankind.

These are the three so-called original Rosicrucian writings, the *Fama fraternitatis* (1614), the *Confessio* (1615), and the *Chymische Hochzeit Christiani Rosencreutz* (1616).

All three works were written in a satirical vein, but the fiction was mistaken for the truth and Andreae soon found himself compelled to reject them as a misunderstood joke in the *Turris Babel sive Judiciorum de fraternitate rosaceae crucis chaos* (1619).

ANDREWS, THOMAS (*b. Belfast, Ireland, 1813; d. Belfast, 1885*), chemistry.

Andrews studied medicine for four years at Dublin and for a year at Edinburgh (M.D. 1835). Professor of chemistry at Belfast. He published two pamphlets, *Studium generale* and *The Church in Ireland,* which he called "chapters of contemporary history."

Andrews' research on the problems of ozone led him to conclude that all the supposed varieties of ozone were identical and that it was, in fact, oxygen in an altered or allotropic condition.

Best known for his studies on the continuity of the gaseous and liquid states and for his discovery of critical temperature of carbon dioxide in 1861.

ANDRONOV, ALEKSANDR ALEKSANDROVICH (*b. Moscow, Russia, 1901; d. Gorky, U.S.S.R., 1952*), theoretical physics.

Graduated from the physical-mathematical faculty of Moscow University (1925). L. I. Mandelshtam played a major role in Andronov's development as a physicist even after Andronov had achieved recognition on his own. Almost all his research dealt with extremal Poincaré cycles and oscillatory theory. Working at the university in Gorky, Andronov wrote with S. E. Khaykin his book on the theory of oscillations (1937). He also wrote on the works of Maxwell, Vyshnegradsky, and A. Ştodola.

ANDRUSOV, NIKOLAI IVANOVICH (*b. Odessa, Russia, 1861; d. Prague, Czechoslovakia, 1924*), geology, paleontology.

Graduated (1884) Novorossiysk University in Odessa. I. I. Mechnikov and V. O. Kovalevski were his instructors. M.A., Petersburg University, 1890; Ph.D., 1897. Andrusov's chief attention was directed to recent bottom sediments and outcrops of bedrock. The major part of his work was devoted to the Neocene period in southern Russia. He studied these deposits and the fauna embedded in them. Andrusov's study of mollusks in marine basins and closed basins with abnormal salinity was especially important.

A significant place in Andrusov's paleontological-stratigraphical works was allotted to the elucidation of the paleogeographic conditions of the period under study. His works that deal with this elucidation contain models of analysis of facies relationships and ecological features in the habitat of fossil organisms.

Andrusov is recognized as the founder of the stratigraphy of the Neocene deposits in southern Russia and contiguous territories; and the schema he worked out for the subdivision of Upper Tertiary deposits has become the standard for all investigators of the Cenozoic era.

ANGELI, STEFANO DEGLI (*b. Venice, Italy, 1623; d. Venice, 1697*), mathematics, physics.

Studied at the University of Bologna under Bonaventura Cavalieri. His studies in mathematics include a development of the methods of indivisibles to solve problems dealing with infinitesimals and with the areas, volumes, and centers of gravity of given geometric figures.

Angeli's works on mathematics include: *De infinitorum spiralium spatiorum mensura* (1660) and *De infinitarum cochlearum mensuris ac centris gravitatis* (1661).

Angeli's *Della gravità dell'aria e fluidi,* largely experimental in character, examines the fluid statics, based on Archimedes' principle and on Torricelli's experiments. It also contains theories of capillary attraction.

ANGELUS (ENGEL), JOHANNES *(b. Aichach, Germany, 1453 [?]; d. Vienna, Austria, 1512),* astronomy.

Pupil of Regiomontanus at University of Vienna (B.A. 1471). Practiced medicine and astrology in Augsburg after further education; taught at Vienna (from 1494). Esteemed as astronomer by contemporaries; published astrological works, tables based on Regiomontanus, a translation of Abu Maʿshar's *De magnis conjunctionibus,* and a treatise on calendar reform; worked on revision of Peurbach's tables.

ÅNGSTRÖM, ANDERS JONAS *(b. Lögdö, Medelpad, Sweden, 1814; d. Uppsala, Sweden, 1874),* astronomy, physics.

Ph.D. University of Uppsala (1839) with a dissertation on the optics of conical refraction. Ångström's wrote on spectroscopy, terrestrial magnetism and the conduction of heat. His "Optiska undersökningar" ("Optical Researches") established him as one of several significant predecessors of Kirchhoff in formulating the foundations of modern spectroscopy.

After 1861 Ångström intensively studied the spectrum of the sun, noting the presence of hydrogen in the solar atmosphere. His monumental *Recherches sur le spectre solaire* (1868) expressed wavelength measurements in units of one ten-millionth of a millimeter—a unit of length that has been named the angstrom unit in his honor. Ångström's wavelength measurements provided a precise and convenient reference and became a competing authoritative unit until more precise tables were published by Henry Rowland (1887). In 1867 Ångström was the first to examine the spectrum of the aurora borealis. Ångström believed that each chemical element had a single characteristic spectrum that remained essentially unchanged.

ANGUILLARA, LUIGI (real name, **LUIGI SQUALERMO**) *(b. Anguillara, Sabazia, Italy, ca. 1512; d. Ferrara, Italy, 1570),* botany.

Anguillara's only known book, the *Semplici* (1549–60), is devoted principally to the identification of the plants known to Dioscorides and the other ancient writers on materia medica. Because of his travels, Anguillara was among the best-equipped of sixteenth-century botanists to make such a study. Approximately 1,540 plants are discussed by Anguillara. He is commemorated today by the genus *Anguillaria (Liliaceae).*

ANSCHÜTZ, RICHARD *(b. Darmstadt, Germany, 1852; d. Darmstadt, 1937),* chemistry.

Ph.D. University of Heidelberg, 1874. Anschütz successfully combined physical methods and chemical synthesis as a means of establishing chemical structure. He also pioneered in methods of vacuum distillation (1887).

His major publications dealt with organic chemistry. In his research on oxalic acid and its derivatives, he recognized the value of using oxalic acid as a dehydrating agent in the preparation of the anhydrides of dicarboxylic acids from the corresponding chlorides.

In 1883, he synthesized anthracene by the action of aluminum chloride on a mixture of benzene and acetylene tetrabromide. The result of one of his experiments was the discovery of a crystalline salicylide chloroform that is one-third chloroform by weight. From it chloro-

form of high purity can be extracted. This chloroform, named "Anschütz," is used for narcosis.

In his work on dioxytartaric acid and tartrazine, Anschütz was able to furnish proof that tartrazine is a derivative of pyrazoline, and not an osazone. Anschütz also wrote many papers on the tetronic and benzotetronic acids.

ANTHELME, VOITURET *(b. Chatenay-Vaudin, France, ca. 1618; d. Dijon, France, 1683),* astronomy.

Anthelme's work concentrated on the constellations Cygnus and Cassiopeia and, consequently, he discovered the nova Variable R Volpecula, which was observed between 1670 and 1672. He prepared one of the first ephemerides of a variable star, dealing with Mira Ceti.

The appearance of a comet in 1680 occasioned the treatise *Explication de la comète* (1681).

ANTHEMIUS OF TRALLES *(fl. sixth century* A.D., *during the reign of Justinian),* architecture, mathematics.

Anthemius' interest in conic sections as well as in reflectors is shown by the work *On Remarkable Mechanical Devices.* He describes the construction of an elliptical reflector.

ANTHONISZ. *See* **Metius**

ANTIGONE OF CARYSTUS. *See* **Diocles Carystius.**

ANTIPHON *(lived in Athens in the second half of the fifth century* B.C.), mathematics, cosmology, psychology.

Antiphon was the first native Athenian to be classed as a "Sophist" in the sense of "professional teacher of young men." Four works are clearly ascribed to Antiphon the Sophist *(On Truth, On Concord, The Statesman, On Interpretation of Dreams),* and a fifth *(The Art of Avoiding Pain)* may also be his.

His method of squaring the circle has been considered of interest as anticipating the method of exhaustion used by Euclid and the method of approximation of Archimedes. Antiphon's most famous doctrine is his opposition of nature and convention. But in *On Concord* he defends the authority of the community as a safeguard against anarchy. In *On Truth* he argues that there is a basic human nature common to Greeks and barbarians, and in *The Art of Avoiding Pain,* if it is his, he was also concerned with ways in which the individual could achieve the fulfillment of his nature without having to suffer.

ANTONIADI, EUGÈNE M. *(b. Constantinople [now Istanbul], Turkey, 1870; d. Meudon, France, 1944),* astronomy.

Antoniadi's long series of observations in Constantinople and on the island of Prinkipe were published in *L'astronomie,* the bulletin of the Astronomical Society of France.

In 1893 Antoniadi was able to employ a forty-two-centimeter equatorial to observe Mars. In 1909 he made important discoveries regarding the constitution of the surface details of Mars. His drawings show terrain covered with sparse vegetation, volcanic soil, and vast deserts. During the opposition of 1924 Antoniadi observed shining protuberances which seemed to oscillate above the surface of the planet and was thus able to confirm the period of rotation about its axis which had been determined by Giovanni Schiaparelli.

In later life Antoniadi became interested in the history of Greek and Egyptian astronomy; he also conducted important archeological studies on the basilica of Saint Sophia in Constantinople.

ANUCHIN, DMITRII NIKOLAEVICH (b. St. Petersburg, Russia, 1843; d. Moscow, Union of Soviet Socialist Republics, 1923), geography, anthropology, ethnography.

Anuchin studied at the Physics and Mathematics Faculty of Moscow University, where Darwin's concept of evolution and the mutual influence of natural phenomena were advocated and became the basis for his scientific research. He did a study of the geographical distribution of Russia's male population according to height (1889). Achieved wide fame as the founder and editor of the journal Zemlevedenie ("Geography").

Anuchin's basic works in general geography—including "Rel'ef poverkhnosti Evropejskoj Rossii" ("Surface Relief of European Russia," 1895), "Sushcha" ("Land," 1895), and Verkhnevolzhskie ozera i verkhov'ja Zapadnoj Dviny ("The Upper Volga Lakes and the Upper Reaches of the Western Dvina," 1897)—played an important role in the development of geomorphology and hydrology. His studies of man's racial types were also significant. He wrote several fundamental works on the physical types of various nationalities, among them a monograph on the Ainu people (1876).

ANVILLE, JEAN-BAPTISTE BOURGUIGNON D' (b. Paris, France, 1697; d. Paris, 1782), cartography.

Chief royal geographer and assistant geographer to the Académie Royale des Sciences, D'Anville contributed greatly to the renaissance of geography and cartography in France in the eighteenth century. His maps were solidly based on triangulation nets. The maps of China were the first to give an accurate indication of the Pacific coastline. D'Anville also drew maps of France for Longuerue's Description de la France (1719), and maps of Africa and Santo Domingo. In his Traité des mesures itinéraires anciennes et modernes (1769), he established remarkably accurate maps for Rollin's Histoire ancienne, Rollin and Crevier's Histoire romaine, and the Histoire des empereurs romains.

APÁTHY, STEPHAN (b. Budapest, Austria-Hungary, 1863; d. Szeged, Hungary, 1922), medical science, histology, zoology.

Apáthy attended the University of Budapest (Ph.D., 1885). His scientific achievements were in three fields: zoology, neurohistology, and microscopic technique. In zoology his most important contributions concerned the systematic and comparative anatomy of Hirudinea, especially of their nervous system. In neurohistology Apáthy defended the concept of a continuous network of neurofibrils, passing from one neuron to another. Apáthy's work in microscopic technique constituted a great contribution to the development of modern histological techniques. His Die Mikrotechnik der thierischen Morphologie was an indispensable handbook for two generations of histologists. His greatest achievement is that he made microscopic technique a scientific method, based not only on empirical knowledge but also on systematic comparisons and investigations.

APELT, ERNST FRIEDRICH (b. Reichenau bei Zittau, Germany, 1812; d. Oppelsdorf, Germany, 1859), philosophy, history of science.

Apelt's special contribution to the Kantian tradition was his insistence that scientific knowledge should be the epistemologist's touchstone and that a careful historical scrutiny of the sciences should be absolutely essential for epistemology. His most important work in the philosophy of science was his Theorie der Induction (1854).

APIAN, PETER, also known as **Petrus Apianus, Peter Bienewitz** (or **Bennewitz**) (b. Leisnig, Germany, 1495; d. Ingolstadt, Germany, 1552), astronomy, geography.

Apian studied mathematics and astronomy at Leipzig and Vienna. He was a pioneer in astronomical and geographical instrumentation. His first major work, Cosmographia seu descriptio totius orbis (1524), was based on Ptolemy and was one of the most popular texts of the time. His second major work, Astronomicon Caesareum (1540), is notable for his pioneer observations of comets. Of greater scientific significance, however, is Apian's Instrumentum sinuum sive primi mobilis (1534), where he calculates sines for every minute, with the radius divided decimally.

APOLLONIUS OF PERGA (b. second half of third century B.C., d. early second century B.C.), mathematical sciences.

Apollonius was born at Perga (Perge), a Greek city in southern Asia Minor. Lived for some time in Alexandria, and visited Pergamum and Ephesus. During this period he was in correspondence with several mathematicians, including Eudemus of Pergamum, Attalus (?of Rhodes), and notably the well-known Epicurean philosopher Philonides (the only reliable evidence for dating Apollonius' Conics). When he wrote the Conics he was already old enough to have a grown son (also called Apollonius). That is all that one can safely say about his life on the basis of the meager ancient sources (principally his own prefaces to the several books of his Conics).

The Conics, was originally in eight books. Books I–IV survive in the original Greek, Books V–VII in Arabic translation, while Book VIII is lost. As we learn from Apollonius' preface to Book I, he had originally composed the treatise hurriedly at the request of the geometer Naucrates; the Conics as we know it constitutes a revised version. It can be dated to (very roughly) 190 B.C.

In order to assess Apollonius' achievement in the Conics, we have to compare it with what preceded. But Apollonius' treatise was so successful that it led to the disappearance of its predecessors. To reconstruct them, we have to use the sometimes unreliable reports of ancient writers, and the works of Archimedes (of the generation before Apollonius), who makes extensive use of conics. The theory was invented by Menaechmus (ca. 350 B.C.), and by ca. 300 B.C. there were already textbooks on it, attributed to Aristaeus and Euclid. In these, the three principal conic sections were obtained by cutting a right circular cone by a plane at right angles to a generator. According to whether the cone has a right angle, an obtuse angle or an acute angle at its vertex, the resultant section is respectively a parabola, a hyperbola, or an ellipse. These sections were therefore named by the earlier Greek investigators "section of a right-angled cone", "section of an acute-angled cone" and "section of an obtuse-angled cone" respectively, names which are still used by Archimedes. The curves were, however, soon characterized by what was called a "symptom", a constant relationship between magnitudes which vary with the position of an arbitrary point on the curve, which may be represented by the modern equations $y^2 = px$ for the parabola, and $\frac{y^2}{x_1 x_2} = \frac{p}{a}$ for the hyperbola and ellipse. In this the ordinate, y, is always orthogonal to the abscissa, x, hence it is a system of "orthogonal conjugation".

Apollonius, in contrast, generates all three curves from the double oblique circular cone, by varying the position of the cutting plane. He is then able to derive "symptoms" which we may express by the modern equations $y^2 = px$ for the parabola, $y^2 = x \left(p + \frac{p}{a} x\right)$ for the hyperbola, and $y^2 = x \left(p - \frac{p}{a} x\right)$ for the ellipse. These symptoms are then expressed by the traditional Greek method of "application of areas", in which a rectangle of side x (equal to the abscissa) and of area y^2 (where y is the ordinate) is applied to (παραβάλλεται) the constant line-length p, which exactly fits it in the case of the parabola, but exceeds it (ὑπερβάλλει) or falls short of it (ἐλλείπει) by a rectangle similar to p/a in the case of hyperbola and ellipse respectively. Hence Apollonius gives the names παραβολή, ὑπερβολή and ἔλλειψις (from which the modern names are derived) to the three curves.

What is new in this, and indeed throughout Books I–IV of the *Conics,* is not so much the content as the greater generality of approach. For instance, in this method of generation, ordinate and abscissa are not necessarily at right angles to one another, i.e. this is a system of "oblique conjugation"; in modern terms, Apollonius refers the equation of the curve to a coordinate system in which one axis is an arbitrary diameter and the other the tangent at one end of that diameter. Another advantage is that it immediately produces both branches of the hyperbola. Now oblique conjugation was certainly known to Archimedes, and the method of defining the curves by the application of areas was probably even earlier. Even the names "parabola", "hyperbola" and ellipse" may not have been coined by Apollonius (as is generally supposed), but merely standardized by him. But his treatment of the elements of conics (in Books I–IV) gathered the scattered, unsystematic results of his predecessors in a consistent system characterized by powerful generality.

The *Conics* makes no claim to be exhaustive: Books V–VIII (which in content are much more original than I–IV) deal with certain special problems. Apollonius deliberately omitted certain topics (e.g. the focal properties of the parabola, treated by his contemporary Diocles). In a number of other short but remarkable works on higher geometry he dealt with some related problems. These are known to us mainly from the discussions of them in the *Synagoge* of Pappus (fourth century A.D.). They are: (1) *Cutting off of a Ratio* (which survives in Arabic translation: on the Arabic tradition of Apollonius see Fuat Sezgin, *Geschichte des Arabischen Schrifttums* V, 1974, 136–143), (2) *Cutting off of an Area.* (3) *Determinate Section.* (4) *Tangencies* (which included the famous problem of drawing a circle to touch three given circles). (5) *Inclinations.* (6) *Plane Loci.* Besides these, we hear from ancient sources of works on a method of expressing very large numbers by (in effect) a place-value system with base 10,000 (a refinement of Archimedes'

Sand-reckoner), on the foundations of geometry, on "unordered irrationals", and on the calculation of accurate limits for π.

Apollonius was also famous in antiquity for his astronomical studies. The only detail we know of these is an ingenious proof (given by Ptolemy in Almagest XII) of the method of finding the stationary point of a planet in a simple epicyclic system or the equivalent eccentric. Apollonius obviously made important contributions to the theoretical study of the application of geometry to astronomy, but not, it seems, to its practical application as a predictive science (which does not, in the Greek world, predate Hipparchus, ca. 140 B.C.).

The attribution of a work *On the Burning-Mirror* to Apollonius by a single source in late antiquity is probably a misattribution of Diocles' work.

Apollonius' *Conics* I–IV soon became the standard text book, and dominated the approach to the subject, not only in antiquity, but also in Islamic mathematics and (beginning in the 16th century) in western Europe, until the rise of analytic geometry. The later books of the *Conics* were also influential in Islamic countries, but knowledge of them did not reach Europe until the later 17th century, when they were already only a historical curiosity. Much more influential on the development of European mathematics was Pappus' account of Apollonius' lost works (which became generally known through Commandino's Latin translation of the *Synagoge* published in 1589).

APPELL, PAUL (-ÉMILE) (*b. Strasbourg, France, 1855; d. Paris, France, 1930*), mathematics, mathematical physics.

Appell attended the École Normale, from which he graduated first in his class (1876). He and Henri Poincaré formed a friendship there that lasted until the latter's death. After Appell's thesis (1876) in projective geometry, he turned to algebraic functions, differential equations, and complex analysis. He generalized many classical results to the case of two or more variables. His activity continued to shift toward mechanics, and in 1893 Volume I of the monumental *Traité de mécanique rationnelle* appeared. Volume V (1921) included the mathematics required for relativity, but the treatise is essentially an exposition of classical mechanics of the late nineteenth century.

APPLETON, EDWARD VICTOR (*b. Bradford, Yorkshire, England, 1892; d. Edinburgh, Scotland, 1965*), radio physics.

Appleton matriculated at the University of London at sixteen and won a scholarship to St. John's College, Cambridge, at eighteen. Graduated (1913) and started postgraduate work in crystallography under William Henry Bragg. Wrote *Thermionic Vacuum Tubes* (1932). In 1924 he and Miles Barnett performed a crucial experiment that led to a measurement of the height of the reflecting atmospheric layer of ionized gases.

Won the Nobel Prize in physics (1947) for his investigation of the physics of the upper atmosphere, especially for the discovery of the so-called "Appleton layers." His work is of prime technological significance, not only in regard to radio transmission but also as a milestone in the development of radar. Founded *Journal of Atmospheric Research* ("Appleton's Journal").

AQUINAS

AQUINAS, SAINT THOMAS (*b. Roccasecca, near Monte Cassino, Italy, ca. 1225; d. Fossanuova, near Maenza, Italy, 1274*), not a scientist in the modern sense, but a philosopher and theologian whose synthesis of Christian revelation with Artistotelian science has influenced all areas of knowledge—including modern science, especially in its early development.

Educated at abbey of Monte Cassino, at Naples and Cologne. From 1256 to 1259, Thomas composed his commentary on the *Sentences,* some smaller treatises—including the highly original *De ente et essentia* ("On Being and Essence")—and the disputed question *On Truth;* he also began work on the *Summa contra gentiles,* of special importance for its evaluation of Arab thought. At Rome (1265–67), he began his famous *Summa theologiae.* At the University of Paris (1269–72), he combated both the traditional Augustinian orthodoxy and the heterodox Aristotelianism of the Latin Averroists. The condemnation of certain Averroist theses drew a series of polemical treatises from Aquinas' pen, including *De aeternitate mundi contra murmurantes* ("On the Eternity of the Universe, Against the 'Murmurers' " i.e., the traditionalist Augustinians) and *De unitate intellectus contra Averroistas* ("On the Unity of the Intellect, Against the Averroists"). The intellectual ferment also stimulated him to further efforts at philosophical and theological synthesis. He subsequently was approved by the Roman Catholic Church as its most representative teacher. At the University of Paris, in an atmosphere dominated by faith, he turned the theologians to a study of the pagan Aristotle, to the use of what was then a rigorous scientific method, learned from investigating the world of nature, for probing the mysteries of revelation.

Aquinas was preoccupied with questions about God, the angels, and man; first and foremost he was a metaphysician and a theologian. For a man not usually recognized as a scientist, he made noteworthy contributions to medieval science. His more significant teachings related to the medieval counterparts of physics, astronomy, chemistry, and the life sciences.

In dynamics, he inaugurated some new directions in the study of causality affecting gravitational and projectile motions. He disagreed with those who defined gravitation as something absolute; it is a principle of motion, either actively or passively, depending on the particular motion that results.

On the subject of *impetus,* Thomas clearly defends the original Aristotelian teaching on the proximate cause of projectile motion. Aquinas took up the problems of the magnet, of tidal variations, and of other "occult" phenomena in a letter entitled *De occultis operationibus naturae* ("On the Occult Workings of Nature"). Commenting as he did on the *De caelo* and on the cosmogony detailed in Genesis, Thomas could not help but evaluate the astronomical theories of his contemporaries. His view of the structure of the universe was basically Aristotelian. The astronomical data reported by Aquinas were those of a well-informed thirteenth-century writer. His treatise on comets is one of the most balanced in the high Middle Ages, rejecting fanciful explanations and pointing out how little is actually known about these occurrences.

One topic that had important bearing on later views of the structure of matter was that of the presence of elements in compounds. His basic explanation continued to be taught through the sixteenth century and, coupled with Aristotelian teaching on *minima naturalia,* became the major alternative to a simplistic atomist view of the structure of matter before the advent of modern chemistry. In biology and psychology, his work is noteworthy more for its philosophical consistency than for its scientific detail.

He believed in spontaneous generation and countenanced a qualified type of evolution in the initial formation of creatures. Catholic thinkers, on the basis of his philosophy, have been more open to evolutionary theories than have fundamentalists, who follow a strict, literal interpretation of the text of Genesis.

Thomas offered proof where it could be adduced, appealing to experience, observation, analysis, and (last of all) authority. He sought a complete integration of all knowledge, divine as well as human, and provided a striking example for all who were to be similarly motivated in the ages to come.

ARAGO

ARAGO, DOMINIQUE FRANÇOIS JEAN (*b. Estagel, France, 1786; d. Paris, France, 1853*), physics, astronomy.

Arago graduated from École Polytechnique in 1803. He succeeded Monge as professor of descriptive geometry there and remained until his retirement in 1830. Arago's most important original work in science was carried out before 1830. His earliest investigations centered on the factors affecting the refraction of light passing through the atmosphere of the earth. Arago passed beams of polarized light through a variety of gaseous and crystalline substances to study the light's properties. His results, which suggested the usefulness of the undulatory theory, included the discovery of chromatic polarization by the use of thin mica plates (1811); the elaboration of the conditions necessary to produce Newton's rings (1811); and the observation of special cases of rotary polarization (1812), which were shortly thereafter made a general law of optics by Biot. In 1811 he invented the polariscope. With the addition of a series of properly graduated plates Arago transformed his polariscope into a polarimeter, which he used to verify one of the few mathematically expressed laws he discovered: the cosine-squared law for calculating the intensity of the ordinary ray in double refraction. In 1833 he derived from it the ratio of the amount of polarized light to neutral light.

In 1815 Arago built a primitive cyanometer to measure the degree of blueness of the atmosphere, which was later adapted for use in hydrographical determinations of the depth of the sea. In 1833 he proposed a photometer to measure comparative intensities of stellar light. He also perfected an ocular micrometer for measuring small angles. Offered an explanation of the scintillation of stars by the use of interference phenomena and the realization of the asymmetry of the layers of atmosphere with reference to the observer.

In 1820 Arago played a significant role in the elaboration of electrodynamic and electromagnetic theories. In Geneva he witnessed the verification of Oersted's experiments linking electricity to magnetism. Arago repeated the Geneva experiments at the Paris Academy, thereby inspiring Ampère to elaborate his electrodynamic theory of electricity and magnetism.

In 1820 Arago made the discovery of the temporary magnetization of soft iron by an electric current. He noticed the dampening effect that metallic substances had on the oscillations of the compass needle. He later announced that the rotation of nonmagnetic metallic substances (especially copper) created a magnetic effect on a magnetized needle—Arago's "disc" or "wheel."

ARANZIO, GIULIO CESARE (*b. Bologna, Italy, ca. 1529/1530; d. Bologna, 1589*), surgery, anatomy.

Nephew and pupil of Bartolomeo Maggi; studied at Universities of Padua and Bologna (M.D., 1556); taught at Bologna (from 1556), was first to hold professorship of anatomy (separated from surgery 1570—he held both). Accomplished anatomist, investigating function as well as form; discovered elevator muscle of upper eyelid, *pedes hippocamp*, cerebellum cistern, and arterial duct (erroneously attributed to Botallo). Performed rhinoplastic surgery several years before Tagliacozzi, but did not write about it.

ARATUS OF SOLI (*b. Soli, Cilicia, ca. 310* B.C.; *d. ca. 240/239* B.C.), astronomy.

Aratus' only extant work is *Phaenomena*, a poem dealing with various celestial phenomena. It possesses some literary value and is indebted mainly to Hesiod and Homer for vocabulary and syntax. Aratus' adherence to Stoicism is patent throughout the poem. From an astronomical standpoint the poem contains many errors.

ARBER, AGNES ROBERTSON (*b. London, England, 1879; d. Cambridge, England, 1960*), botany.

Studied at University College, London, and the Botany School, Cambridge. Arber engaged in the study of early printed herbals, and her book on them (1912) became a standard work. Her many papers on comparative anatomy were coordinated in three books: *Water Plants: A Study of Aquatic Angiosperms; Monocotyledons: A Morphological Study;* and *The Gramineae.*

ARBOGAST, LOUIS FRANÇOIS ANTOINE (*b. Mutzig, Alsace, 1759; d. Strasbourg, France, 1803*), mathematics.

Arbogast was responsible for the law introducing the decimal metric system in the whole of the French Republic. His interest in the history of mathematics led to his classification of papers left by Marin Mersenne. In 1787 Arbogast showed that arbitrary functions may tolerate not only discontinuities in the Eulerian sense of the term, but also "combinations of several portions of different curves or those drawn by the free movement of the hand." Two years later, Arbogast sent a report to the Académie des Sciences de Paris on the new principles of differential calculus. The principal aim of the calculus of derivatives, as Arbogast understood it, was to give simple and precise rules for finding series expansions.

Arbogast's work is dominated by operational calculus. He clearly saw the difference that should be made between function and operation.

ARBOS, PHILIPPE (*b. Mosset, France, 1882; d. Andancette, Drôme, France, 1956*), geography.

Graduated (1907) from the École Normale Supérieure. Arbos' doctoral thesis on pastoral life in the French Alps clarified the general principles of pastoral life, little known and poorly understood until then.

His study of the urban geography of Clermont-Ferrand (1930) has not become outdated, and his book on the Auvergne (1946) is a classic of regional geography.

ARBUTHNOT, JOHN (*b. Arbuthnot, Kinkardineshire, Scotland, 1667; d. London, 1735*), mathematical statistics.

Doctor's degree in medicine at St. Andrews (1696). Arbuthnot became especially famous for his political satire. He was a close friend of the wits and literary men of his day: with Swift, Pope, John Gay, and Thomas Parnell he was a member of the Scriblerus Club. Invented the character John Bull.

His scientific importance resides in a short paper in the *Philosophical Transactions of the Royal Society,* which has been taken as the very origin of mathematical statistics: "An Argument for Divine Providence, Taken From the Constant Regularity Observ'd in the Birth of Both Sexes." Arbuthnot's argument is the first known example of a mathematical statistical inference and, in fact, is the ancestor of modern statistical reasoning.

ARCHIAC, ÉTIENNE-JULES-ADOLPHE DESMIER (or DEXMIER) DE SAINT-SIMON, VICOMTE D' (*b. Rheims, France, 1802; d. Paris, France, 1868*), geology, paleontology.

In 1835 d'Archiac published a summary of his research on sedimentary formations. His "Essais sur la coordination des terrains tertiaires du nord de la France, de la Belgique et de l'Angleterre" appeared in 1839. In 1843 he published a geological map of Aisne on the scale of 1:160,000 in a serial monograph. In 1854 he published *Coupe géologique des environs des Bains de Rennes (Aude), suivie de la description de quelques fossiles de cette localité.* In 1857 he presented to the Geological Society his newly completed geological map of the regions adjacent to Aude and Pyrénées-Orientales. In 1842, he published a description of Devonian fossils of the Rhineland. In 1846 and 1850 he described and illustrated finds made by geologists at Bayonne and Dax. In 1853 he published, in collaboration with Jules Haime, *Description des animaux fossiles du groupe nummulitique de l'Inde, précédée d'un résumé géologique et d'une monographie des Nummulites.* This work has remained the basic work for every paleontological laboratory interested in the determination of Foraminifera.

In 1847 d'Archiac began publication of *Histoire des progrès de la géologie* with Volume I (*Cosmogénie et géogénie, physique du globe, géographie physique, terrain moderne*). D'Archiac's abstracts make up eight other volumes published between 1848 and 1860.

ARCHIGENES (*b. Apameia, Syria, ca.* A.D. *54; fl. Rome, 98–117*), medicine.

Archigenes' main contributions were in pathology, surgery, and therapeutics. His main work in general medicine was the semidiagnostic "On Places Affected", in which he sought to explain the causes of diseases by concentrating upon their localized manifestations. He devoted a special treatise to the pulse, his "On the Pulses." Archigenes was highly regarded for his writings on therapeutics and materia medica.

ARCHIMEDES (*b. Syracuse, ca. 287* B.C.; *d. Syracuse, 212* B.C.), mathematics, mechanics.

Few details remain of Archimedes' life: his father was the astronomer Phidias; he was perhaps a kinsman of

King Hieron II of Syracuse, to whose son Gelon he dedicated *The Sandreckoner;* he almost certainly visited Alexandria, where no doubt he studied with the successors of Euclid; and he composed most of his works in Syracuse where he died during its capture by the Romans. Archimedes' birth date is deduced from a remark by the twelfth-century Byzantine poet and historian John Tzetzes, who declared that Archimedes "worked at geometry until old age, surviving seventy-five years." Most accounts of Archimedes' death agree that he was killed by a Roman soldier and picture him engaged in mathematics at the time.

Archimedes reputation in antiquity was founded upon a series of mechanical contrivances as well as upon his mathematical works. He invented the water snail, a screw-like device to raise water for irrigation; an endless screw used to launch a ship; and the compound pulley. Of doubtful authenticity is the oft-quoted story told by Vitruvius that Hieron wished Archimedes to check whether a certain crown or wreath was of pure gold and Archimedes arrived at a solution while sitting in a bath tub.

The mathematical works of Archimedes can be loosely classified in three groups. The first group consists of those that have as their major objective the proof of theorems relative to the areas and volumes of figures bounded by curved lines and surfaces: *On the Sphere and the Cylinder; On the Measurement of the Circle; On Conoids and Spheroids; On Spirals;* and *On the Quadrature of the Parabola,* which, in respect to its Propositions 1–17 belongs also to the second category of works. The second group comprises works that lead to a geometrical analysis of statical and hydrostatical problems and the use of statics in geometry: *On the Equilibrium of Planes; On Floating Bodies; On the Method of Mechanical Theorems;* and the aforementioned propositions from *On the Quadrature of the Parabola.* Miscellaneous mathematical works constitute the third group: *The Sandreckoner; The Cattle Problem;* and the fragmentary *Stomachion.* Several other works not now extant are alluded to by Greek authors. Further works are attributed to Archimedes by Arabic authors, and, for the most part, are extant in Arabic manuscripts: *The Lemmata,* or *Liber assumptorum* (in its present form is certainly not by Archimedes since his name is cited in the proofs), *On Water Clocks, On Tangent Circles, On Parallel Lines, On Triangles, On the Properties of the Right Triangle, On Data,* and *On the Division of the Circle into Seven Equal Parts.*

In proving theorems relative to the area or volume of figures bounded by curved lines or surfaces, Archimedes employs the so-called Lemma of Archimedes or some similar lemma, together with a technique of proof that is generally called the "method of exhaustion," other special Greek devices such as *neusis,* and principles taken over from statics.

Archimedes demonstrated a host of theorems that have become a basic part of geometry. "The surface of any sphere is equal to four times the greatest circle in it," equivalent to the modern formulation $S = 4\pi r^2$. "Any sphere is equal to four times the cone which has its base equal to the greatest circle in the sphere and its height equal to the radius of the sphere." Its corollary, that "every cylinder whose base is the greatest circle in a sphere and whose height is equal to the diameter of the sphere is 3/2 of the sphere and its surface together with its base is 3/2 of the surface of the sphere," was illus-

trated on the tombstone of Archimedes, according to Cicero's account. The modern equivalent of Prop. 34 is $V = 4/3\pi r^3$. "Any right or oblique segment of a paraboloid of revolution is half again as large as the cone or segment of a cone which has the same base and the same axis." He was also able by his investigation of what are now known as Archimedean spirals not only to accomplish their quadrature but also to perform the crucial rectification of the circumference of a circle. This, then, would allow for the construction of the right triangle equal to a circle that is the object of *On the Measurement of a Circle.*

Archimedes employed statical procedures (in the solution of geometrical problems and the demonstration of theorems) which are evident in *On the Quadrature of the Parabola* and also in *On the Method.* In the latter work he also uses an entirely new assumption, that a plane figure can be considered as the summation of its line elements (presumably infinite in number) and that a volumetric figure can be considered as the summation of its plane elements. Archimedes also made important excursions into numerical calculation, although his methods are by no means clear. In *On the Measurement of the Circle,* he calculated the ratio of the circumference to diameter (not called π until early modern times) as being less than 3-1/7 and greater than 3-10/71. In the course of this proof Archimedes showed that he had an accurate method of approximating the roots of large numbers. It is also of interest that he there gave an approximation for the $\sqrt{3}$. In the tract known as *The Sandreckoner,* Archimedes presented a system to represent large numbers, a system that allows him to express a number P^{10^8}, where P itself is $(10^8)^{10^8}$. He invented this system to express numbers of the sort that, in his words, "exceed not only the number of the mass of sand equal in magnitude to the earth . . . , but also that of a mass equal in magnitude to the universe."

Archimedes is celebrated as the first to apply geometry successfully to statics and hydrostatics. In his *On the Equilibrium of Planes,* he proved the law of the lever in a purely geometrical manner. In demonstrating Proposition 6, "Commensurable magnitudes are in equilibrium at distances reciprocally proportional to their weights," his major objective was to reduce the general case of unequal weights at inversely proportional distances to the special case of equal weights at equal distances.

In his *On Floating Bodies,* the emphasis is again on geometrical analysis. In Book I, a somewhat obscure concept of hydrostatic pressure is presented as his basic postulate. By his procedures, Archimedes was able to formulate propositions concerning the relative immersion in a fluid of solids less dense than, as dense as, and more dense than the fluid in which they are placed. Prop. 7, relating to solids denser than the fluid, expresses the so-called principle of Archimedes. This is usually succinctly expressed by saying that such solids will be lighter in a fluid by the weight of the fluid displaced. In Book II Archimedes returns to the basic assumption found in *On the Equilibrium of Planes, On the Quadrature of the Parabola,* and *On the Method,* namely that weight verticals are to be conceived of as parallel rather than as convergent at the center of a fluid sphere.

The works of Archimedes were not widely known in antiquity. Our present knowledge of his works depends largely on the interest taken in them at Constantinople from the sixth through the tenth centuries. It is with the activity of Eutocius of Ascalon, who was born toward the end of the fifth century and studied at Alexandria, that the textual history of a collected edition of Archimedes properly begins. Eutocius composed commentaries on three of Archimedes works: *On the Sphere and the Cylinder, On the Measurement of the Circle,* and *On the Equilibrium of Planes.* The works of Archimedes and the commentaries of Eutocius were studied and taught by Isidore of Miletus and Anthemius of Tralles, Justinian's architects of Hagia Sophia in Constantinople. It was apparently Isidore who was responsible for the first collected edition of at least the three works commented on by Eutocius as well as the commentaries. Later Byzantine authors seem gradually to have added other works to this first collected edition until the ninth century when the educational reformer Leon of Thessalonica produced the compilation represented by Greek manuscript A (adopting the designation used by the editor, J.L. Heiberg). Manuscript A contained all of the Greek works now known excepting *On Floating Bodies, On the Method, Stomachion,* and *The Cattle Problem.* This was one of the two manuscripts available to William of Moerbeke when he made his Latin translations in 1269. It was the source, directly or indirectly, of all of the Renaissance copies of Archimedes. A second Byzantine manuscript, designated as B, included only the mechanical works: *On the Equilibrium of Planes, On the Quadrature of the Parabola,* and *On Floating Bodies.* It too was available to Moerbeke. But it disappears after an early fourteenth-century reference. Finally, we can mention a third Byzantine manuscript, C, a palimpsest whose Archimedean parts are in a hand of the tenth century. It contains large parts of *On the Sphere and the Cylinder,* almost all of *On Spirals,* some parts of *On the Measurement of the Circle* and *On the Equilibrium of Planes,* and a part of the *Stomachion.* More important, it contains most of the Greek text of *On Floating Bodies* (a text unavailable in Greek since the disappearance of manuscript B) and a great part of *On the Method of Mechanical Theorems,* hitherto known only by hearsay.

At about the same time that Archimedes was being studied in ninth-century Byzantium, he was also finding a place among the Arabs. The Arabic Archimedes consisted of the following works: (1) *On the Sphere and the Cylinder* and at least a part of Eutocius' commentary on it. This work seems to have existed in a poor, early ninth-century translation, revised in the late ninth century, first by Isḥāq ibn Ḥunayn and then by Thābit ibn Qurra. It was reedited by Naṣīr al-Dīn al-Ṭūsī in the thirteenth century and was on occasion paraphrased and commented on by other Arabic authors. (2) *On the Measurement of the Circle,* translated by Thābit ibn Qurra and reedited by al Ṭūsī. (3) A fragment of *On Floating Bodies,* consisting of a definition of specific gravity not present in the Greek text, a better version of the basic postulate than exists in the Greek text, and the enunciations without proofs of seven of the nine propositions of Book I and the first proposition of Book II. (4) Perhaps *On the Quadrature of the Parabola*—at least this problem received the attention of Thābit ibn Qurra. (5) Some material from *On the Equilibrium of Planes* found in other mechanical works translated into Arabic (such as Hero's *Mechanics,* the so-called Euclid tract *On the Balance,* the *Liber karastonis,* etc.). (6) In

addition, other works attributed to Archimedes by the Arabs and for which there is no extant Greek text.

The Latin West received its knowledge of Archimedes from both the sources just described: Byzantium and Islam. There is no trace of the earlier translations imputed by Cassidorus to Boethius. Such knowledge that was had in the West before the twelfth century consisted of some rather general hydrostatic information that may have indirectly had its source in Archimedes. It was in the twelfth century that translation of Archimedean texts from the Arabic first began. The small tract *On the Measurement of the Circle* was twice translated from the Arabic. The first translation was a rather defective one and was possibly executed by Plato of Tivoli. The second translation was almost certainly done by Gerard of Cremona.

Not only was Gerard's translation widely quoted by Gerard of Brussels, Roger Bacon, and Thomas Bradwardine, it also served as the point of departure for a whole series of emended versions and paraphrases of the tract during the thirteenth and fourteenth centuries.

In addition to his translation of *On the Measurement of the Circle,* Gerard of Cremona also translated the geometrical *Discourse of the Sons of Moses (Verba filiorum)* composed by the Banū Mūsā. This Latin translation was of particular importance for the introduction of Archimedes into the West. We can single out these contributions of the treatise: (1) A proof of Prop. I of *On the Measurement of the Circle* somewhat different from that of Archimedes but still fundamentally based on the exhaustion method. (2) A determination of the value of π drawn from Prop. 3 of the same treatise but with further calculations similiar to those found in the commentary of Eutocius. (3) Hero's theorem for the area of a triangle in terms of its sides, with the first demonstration of that theorem in Latin. (4) Theorems for the volume and surface area of a cone, again with demonstrations. (5) Theorems for the volume and surface area of a sphere with demonstrations of an Archimedean character. (6) A use of the formula for the area of a circle equivalent to $A = \pi r^2$ in addition to the more common Archimedean form, $A = \frac{1}{2} cr.$ Instead of the modern symbol π the authors used the expression "the quantity which when multiplied by the diameter produces the circumference." (7) The introduction into the West of the problem of finding two mean proportionals between two given lines. In this treatise we find two solutions: *(a)* one attributed by the Banū Mūsā to Menelaus and by Eutocius to Archytas, *(b)* the other presented by the Banū Mūsā as their own but similiar to the solution attributed by Eutocius to Plato. (8) The first solution in Latin of the problem of the trisection of an angle. (9) A method of approximating cube roots to any desired limit.

Some of the results and techniques of *On the Sphere and the Cylinder* also became known through a treatise entitled *De curvis superficiebus Archimenidis* and said to be by Johannes de Tinemue. This seems to have been translated from the Greek in the early thirteenth century or at least composed on the basis of a Greek tract. The *De curvis superficiebus* contained ten propositions with several corollaries and was concerned for the most part with the surfaces and volumes of cones, cylinders, and spheres. Like Gerard of Cremona's translation of *On the Measurement of the Circle,* the *De curvis superficiebus* was emended by Latin authors, with two original propositions being added to another (represented by manuscript M of the *De curvis*).

In 1269 the next important step was taken in the passage of Archimedes to the West when much of the Byzantine corpus was translated from the Greek by William of Moerbeke. Except for *The Sandreckoner* and Eutocius' *Commentary on the Measurement of the Circle,* all the works included in manuscripts A and B were rendered into Latin by William. *On the Method, The Cattle Problem* and the *Stomachion,* are not in manuscripts A and B. We possess the original holograph of Moerbeke's translations (MS Vat. Ottob. lat. 1850). This manuscript was not widely copied, but the Moerbeke translations were utilized more than one would expect from the paucity of manuscripts. Chief among those who used them was the astronomer and mathematician John of Meurs, who appears to have been the compositor of a hybrid tract in 1340 entitled *Circuli quadratura.* This tract consisted of fourteen propositions: the first thirteen were drawn from Moerbeke's translation of *On Spirals* and the fourteenth is Proposition 1 of Moerbeke's translation of *On the Measurement of the Circle.* Within the next decade or so after John of Meurs, Nicole Oresme, also at the University of Paris, in his *De configurationibus qualitatum et motuum* revealed knowledge of *On Spirals,* at least in the form of the hybrid *Circuli quadratura.* At the University of Paris, in the mid-fourteenth century, six of the nine Archimedean translations of William of Moerbeke were known and used: *On Spirals, On the Measurement of the Circle, On the Sphere and the Cylinder, On Conoids and Spheroids, On Floating Bodies,* and Eutocius' *Commentary on the Sphere and the Cylinder.*

In the fifteenth century, knowledge of Archimedes in Europe began to expand. A new Latin translation was made by James of Cremona in about 1450 by order of Pope Nicholas V. Since this translation was made exclusively from manuscript A, the translation failed to include *On Floating Bodies,* but it did include the two treatises in A omitted by Moerbeke, namely, *The Sandreckoner* and Eutocius' *Commentary on the Measurement of the Circle.* There are at least nine extant manuscripts of this translation, one of which was executed with corrections by Regiomontanus. The fate of Greek manuscript A and its various copies has been traced skillfully by J.L. Heiberg in his edition of Archimedes' *Opera.* The first printed Archimedean materials were Latin excerpts in George Valla's 1501 *De expetendis et fugiendis rebus opus.* The earliest actual printed texts of Archimedes were the Moerbeke translations of *On the Measurement of the Circle* and *On the Quadrature of the Parabola (Tetragonismus, id est circuli quadratura etc.),* published in 1503. In 1543, Tartaglia republished these same two translations and the Moerbeke translations of *On the Equilibrium of Planes* and Book I of *On Floating Bodies.* Curtius Trioianus published from the legacy of Tartaglia both books of *On Floating Bodies* in Moerbeke's translation (Venice, 1565).

The key event in the further spread of Archimedes was the *editio princeps* of the Greek text with the accompanying Latin translation of James of Cremona at Basel in 1544. Since the Greek text rested ultimately on manuscript A, *On Floating Bodies* was not included. A further Latin translation of the Archimedean texts was published by Federigo Commandino in Bologna in 1558. Already in the period 1534–49, a paraphrase of Archimedean texts had been made by Francesco Maurolico. This was published in Palermo in 1685. One other Latin translation of the sixteenth century by Antonius de Albertis remains in manuscript only. After 1544 the publication and use of Archimedes' works began to multiply markedly. His works presented quadrature problems and propositions that mathematicians sought to solve and demonstrate not only with his methods, but also with a developing geometry of infinitesimals that was to anticipate in some respect the infinitesimal calculus of Newton and Leibniz.

Of the many editions prior to the modern edition of Heiberg, the most important was that of Joseph Torelli (Oxford, 1792), by which time Archimedes' works had been almost completely absorbed into European mathematics and had exerted their substantial and enduring influence on early modern science.

ARCHYTAS OF TARENTUM (*fl. Tarentum now Taranto, Italy, ca. 375* B.C.), philosophy, mathematics, physics.

Archytas made important contributions to the theory of numbers, geometry, and the theory of music. He was deeply concerned with the foundations of the sciences and with their interconnection. Affirmed that the art of calculation is the most fundamental science and makes its results even clearer than those of geometry. Also discussed mathematics as the foundation of astronomy.

A central point in Archytas' manifold endeavors was the theory of means and proportions. His most famous mathematical achievement was the solution of the "Delian" problem of the duplication of the cube. Elaborated a physical theory of sound and is credited with the invention of a wooden dove that could fly.

ARDUINO (or **ARDUINI**), **GIOVANNI** (*b. Caprino Veronese, Italy, 1714; d. Venice, Italy, 1795*), geology.

Arduino received a good mathematical and literary education at Verona but did not take a degree. By applying Galilean methodology to investigations of the earth's structure and composition for the first time, he achieved results of lasting validity. The diversity of problems faced by Arduino in agriculture and industry is striking. His lifelong passion, however, was mining. He was receptive to the new discipline of geology. By observing the phenomena of nature without prejudice or consideration of the opinions of contemporary scientists, he was able to identify four very distinct geological units of successively later periods in the Atesine Alps, the foothills of the Alps, the subalpine hills, and the plains of the Po.

ARETAEUS OF CAPPADOCIA (*fl. ca.* A.D. *50*), medicine.

Aretaeus is known for his text on the causes, symptoms, and treatment of acute and chronic diseases. He belonged to the so-called Pneumatic school of physicians, which had been founded in the first century B.C.

ARFVEDSON, JOHANN AUGUST (*b. Skagerholms-Bruk, Skaraborgs-Län, Sweden, 1792; d. Hedensö, Sweden, 1841*), chemistry.

Arfvedson studied mining at Uppsala and then worked in Berzelius' laboratory. His research centered on oxides of manganese, determining the composition of manganous oxide (MnO) and manganosic oxide (Mn_3O_4). He isolated a new alkali from petalite, one of lower equivalent weight than any of the alkalies then known. He and Berzelius named it "lithia" (lithium oxide). Recognized as discoverer of lithium, although he never isolated the element. Also discovered beryllium hydroxide (mistaking it for silica) and uranous oxide.

ARGAND, ÉMILE (*b. Geneva, Switzerland, 1879; d. Neuchâtel, Switzerland, 1940*), geology.

Argand began his studies in Geneva but soon transferred to Lausanne, where he met Maurice Lugeon and became interested in the problems of Alpine structure. His classic map of the Dent Blanche massif and the memoir explaining his results (1908) revealed a new world of forms.

He attempted a synthetic picture of the structure of the arc of the western Alps. The results were condensed in his famous four plates of 1911. Argand next tried to synthesize Eduard Suess's five-volume *Das Antlitz der Erde* in a tectonic map of Eurasia.

In 1915 he announced a new branch of research which he called embryotectonics. It was the sequential analysis of the evolving structure back to the original sedimentary terrain.

In 1915 Alfred Wegener's hypothesis of continental drift became the frame within which Argand created a new concept of Eurasian structural development. *La tectonique de l'Asie* (1924) is not only a fundamental geology text but also a work of art.

ARGAND, JEAN ROBERT (*b. Geneva, Switzerland, 1768; d. Paris, France, 1822*). mathematics.

Argand's single original contribution to mathematics was the invention and elaboration of a geometric representation of complex numbers and the operations upon them. The purely geometric-intuitive interpretation and reasoning leading to his results seem to have been original with Argand, who defined his goals as clarifying thinking about imaginaries by setting up a new view of them and providing a new tool for research in geometry. He used complex numbers to derive several trigonometric identities, to prove Ptolemy's theorem, and to give a proof of the fundamental theorem of algebra.

ARGELANDER, FRIEDRICH WILHELM AUGUST (*b. Memel, Prussia, 1799; d. Bonn, Germany, 1875*), astronomy.

Argelander entered the University of Königsberg (1817) to study political economy and political science. He attended the astronomy lectures of Bessel, was won over to astronomy, and appointed an assistant in the observatory. Argelander devoted all his energies to the problem of spatial motions. His catalog of 560 stars, which was based on his observations (1835), is incontestably the most exact of the contemporary catalogs. His investigation, *Über die eigene Bewegung des Sonnensystems, hergeleitet aus den eigenen Bewegungen der Sterne* ("Concerning the Peculiar Movement of the Solar System as Deduced From the Proper Motions of the Stars," 1837) is one of the few theoretical works in which he found the basis of his observations conclusive enough to make deductions.

Argelander saw in his observations an opportunity to derive anew the motion of the sun. His result verified the accuracy of Herschel's pioneering work. Argelander's merit lies in the recognition of the significance of the dynamics of the stellar system and in his provisions that enabled later astronomers to solve the problem.

His *Uranometria nova* (1843), which recorded all stars visible to the naked eye, settled the nomenclature that had been used arbitrarily.

By qualitatively determining the changing brightness of stars, Argelander opened a completely new field of research. His goal was a uniform registration of all stars up to the ninth magnitude and the cataloging of their positions and magnitudes with an exactness sufficient for further identification. The *Bonner Durchmusterung,* a three-volume catalog of stars and a forty-plate atlas, has since provided the working basis for every observatory.

ARGENVILLE, ANTOINE-JOSEPH DEZALLIER D' (*b. Paris, France, 1680; d. Paris, 1765*), natural history, engraving, art history.

After studying at the Collège du Plessis, Argenville devoted himself to the fine arts under the direction of the engraver Bernard Picart, the painter Roger de Piles, and the architect Alexander Le Blond. In 1709 his first work, *Traité sur la théorie et la pratique du jardinage,* was published. Today d'Argenville is known through his *Abrégé de la vie des plus fameux peintres* (1745–52), a mediocre work. He also produced *L'histoire naturelle éclaircie dans deux de ses parties principales, la lithologie et la conchyliologie* (1742).

ARGOLI, ANDREA (*b. Tagliacozzo, Italy, 1570 [1568?]; d. Padua, Italy, 1657*), astrology, astronomy.

Argoli held the chair of mathematics at Sapienza in Rome (1622–27). Evidence suggests that he lost his post because of his enthusiasm for astrology. Argoli's extensive astronomical ephemerides gave a permanence to his reputation that his other writings would scarcely have achieved. In his *Astronomicorum* (1629), Argoli proposed his own geocentric system of the world.

ARISTAEUS (*fl. ca. 350–330 b.c.*), mathematics.

Aristaeus played a major part in the development of the conic section theory. According to Pappus, he introduced the terms "section of the acute-angled, right-angled and obtuse-angled cone."

ARISTARCHUS OF SAMOS (*ca. 310–230 b.c.*), mathematics, astronomy.

Aristarchus was a pupil of Strato of Lampsacos, third head of the Lyceum founded by Aristotle. He is celebrated as being the first man to have propounded a heliocentric theory, eighteen centuries before Copernicus.

The heliocentric theory never attracted much attention in antiquity since the main course of development of Greek astronomy was mathematical not physical.

Aristarchus' accomplishments as an astronomer have tended to detract attention from his attainments as a mathematician. *On Sizes and Distances* marks the first attempt to determine astronomical distances and dimensions by mathematical deductions based upon a set of assumptions.

Anticipating future trigonometric methods, he was the first to develop geometric procedures for approximating the sines of small angles.

ARISTOTLE (*b. Stagira, Chalcidice, 384 b.c.; d. Chalcis, 322 b.c.*), physics, astronomy, meteorology, biology, psychology.

Aristotle's father served as personal physician to Amyntas II of Macedon, grandfather of Alexander the

Great. Aristotle's interest in biology and disssection is sometimes ascribed to his father's influence, but both parents died when Aristotle was a boy and his knowledge of human anatomy and physiology remained a weak spot in his biology. In 367 he became a member of the Academy at Athens, where he remained until Plato died (347). In 342 he became tutor to the young prince Alexander. He returned to Athens in 335, but on the death of Alexander the Great (323) and faced with a charge of impiety and the revival of Macedon's enemies, he went into voluntary exile. He died on his maternal estate.

The starting point in Aristotle's scientific progress must be his years in the Academy. At the Academy, Aristotle reversed Plato's priorities, putting dialectic, the Socratic examination of assumptions made in reasoning, ancillary to mathematics. For him the pattern of a science is an axiomatic system in which theorems are validly derived from basic principles—"hypotheses," "definitions," and "axioms." The proof-theory characteristic of Greek mathematics is accepted as the chief aim of any science, which should not merely record but must explain and thus generalize.

Aristotle enlarges the mathematical model to provide for the physical sciences but a physical thing (any thing involved in regular natural change—a man, a tree, a flame) calls for more explanation than the abstractions with which mathematics deals. Again, physics, unlike mathematics, deals in generalizations that are true in most cases but not necessarily in all. He generally seems to hold that exceptions are not themselves inexplicable, but fails to maintain a sharp distinction between laws of necessary conditions and laws of sufficient conditions.

First the phenomena, then the theory to explain them. Aristotle recommends this Baconian formula not only for physics, astronomy, and biology, but for all arts and sciences. But "phenomena," like many of his key terms, is a word with different uses in different contexts. It means observations in biology, meteorology, and sometimes in astronomy, but the common convictions and linguistic usage of his contemporaries supplemented by the views of other thinkers when he expounds principles in the *Physics,* or again the nature and interaction of the elements in *De caelo* or *De generatione et corruptione.*

The point that he is not inventing a new vocabulary nor assigning new meanings to popular words must be borne in mind when *dunamis* ("power" or "ability") or *ischus* ("strength") is translated as "force." For example, Aristotle adduces the proportionalities in the *Physics* to show that the strength required for keeping the sky turning for all time would be immeasurable. He does not quote empirical evidence and he could not do so. He simply comments that the rules of proportion require this to be true. Aristotle's universe is finite, spherical, and geocentric, and natural motions are basic to his cosmology. Natural motions are the unimpeded rectilinear movements of the four sublunary elements: earth, water, fire and air, which terminate, unless blocked, in the part of the universe that is the element's natural place. The motion of the fifth element, ether, the substance of the spheres that carries the heavenly bodies, is circular and cannot be blocked.

When he comes to the birth of plants and animals, the apparent coming of something from nothing, he believes that even the emergence of a new individual must involve a substrate, "matter," which passes between two contrary conditions, the "privation" and the "form." But the

question "What are the essential attributes of matter?" must go unanswered for Aristotle rejects all theories that explain physical change by the rearrangement of some basic stuff or stuffs endowed with fixed characteristics. In particular he rebuts atomism. Physics studies the regularities of change, and matter determines what kinds of change are open to a given thing. The chief influence of Aristotle's concept of matter was on metaphysics, but his concept of *form,* the universal element in things that allows them to be known and classified and defined, remained a powerful influence in science. The formal element is inseparable from the things classified; the physical world is all.

When Aristotle contrasts mathematics and physics he says that the physicist must, as the mathematician does not, treat the geometric properties of physical bodies as attributes—he must be prepared to explain the application of his model. This readiness to import mathematics into physics is complemented by an insistence that any mathematics must be directly applicable to the world.

In the works on the exact sciences *(Posterior Analytics, Topics, Physics, De caelo,* and *De generatione),* his main concerns were the methodology of the sciences and a meticulous derivation of their technical equipment from common assumptions. His influence on science stemmed from an incomparable cleverness and sensitiveness to counterarguments, rather than from any breakthrough comparable to those of Eudoxus or Archimedes.

Aristotle probably began his zoölogical treatises in 344–342 B.C., when he was living on Lesbos, and after his philosophical framework was established. The zoölogical treatises are a fourth of the whole corpus and both data and discussion are concise. How much was his own work is unclear. The treatises form a course of instruction in which the *Historia animalium,* the chief collection of data, is referred to as the descriptive textbook.

In the Academy there were two issues: to identify the formal groups of animals and to explain their functioning as part of nature, and Aristotle followed this approach. His earliest zoology is in the *De partibus animalium,* the *De incessu animalium,* and the *Parva naturalia,* in which he sets out the "causes" of tissue and structures and of such significant functions as locomotion, respiration, aging, and death. Here the a priori element in his theory appears strongly: for example, right is superior to left.

But the teleological explanation is argued maturely with evidential support. In the next great treatise, *De generatione animalium,* he applies his concepts of form and matter, actuality and potentiality, to the problems of reproduction, inheritance, and growth of such inessential characters as color. Aristotle's teleology differs from others for he bases the teleology on the existence of forms. To explain an organ we must first grasp the complete animal's form and functions—what it means to be that animal. Our explanation will include both the "necessary" causes and the "end" toward which development tends—the perfect condition of the whole animal, "for the sake of which" each part develops.

In his biology as well as in the *Metaphysics* and *De anima,* the soul is not an independent substance but is the form of the body as well as the source of action. It causes growth, reproduction, sensation, and in man, has a third faculty, intellect, the only faculty that is not the form of body and could therefore be separable. According to the *Metaphysics,* the form toward which animals grow is their species: individual differences arise from matter and consequently are unknowable to science. In *De generatione animalium* he implies that individuals may differ in form. If the fetus develops regularly, the father's form will be actualized; failing that, the mother's; failing that again, more distant ancestors successively, until the form may merely be that of the species, or even just the genus *Animal* (that is, a monstrous birth).

Aristotle accepts Plato's four elements—fire, air, water, and earth—and systematizes them in a formula that survived through the Middle Ages. He treats the four elements as combinations of hot, cold, wet and dry. Whether he really intended a fifth element, *pneuma,* is debatable. He compares the *aither,* the fifth substance in the outer heaven, to the bodily *pneuma,* the material of the animal seed that conveys soul and generative warmth.

Classification of animals was a difficulty, and he suggested taking an animal's vital heat as an index of its superiority, but he does not produce an actual scheme. For practical purposes he discusses the animals by major groups, those with and those without blood (roughly vertebrates and invertebrates).

Historia animalium began as a comparative study of characters under the headings *parts, activities, lives, dispositions.* It approximates a descriptive zoology. The work is a theoretical study, not so much about animals as about *Animal.* His standard of judgment is function rather than morphology. He names about 500 "kinds" of animals; between 550 and 600 species can be distinguished, as many as 200 mentioned in connection with only one character. The great majority are native to Greece and its colonies in Asia Minor. Some of his data come from deliberate dissection, other information is gathered from casual observations in the kitchen or at augury. Many of the exterior observations presuppose prolonged study of the habits of birds, insects, and sea animals. His chief sources of information are fishermen, farmers, and hunters. He applies primarily observational checks, made either on the same type of animal or on "analogous" types. His favorite method is the counterinstance. Where observational checks are not available he tests by inherent probability—that is, by reference to theory. But he makes it clear that theory must always yield to reliable observation. Many of the mistakes stem from faulty observation that agreed with theory.

In his discussion of animals Aristotle gives great importance to the heart, the blood vessels, and the blood—departing from the physiological ideas of the Hippocratic writers. He gave one of the earliest accurate descriptions of the cardiovascular system, emphasizing the heart as its center. His success in dissection of blood vessels lay in his procedure of starving and strangling instead of stunning and then bleeding, thereby retaining all the blood within the vessels. Strangulation constricts the small arteries in the lungs, cutting off the supply of blood to the left side of the heart. Almost all the blood in the body accumulates in the venous system and in the right side of the heart, which is enormously swollen. Instead of four cavities, the heart will appear to have only three, the united right auricle and ventricle, appearing largest; the left ventricle; and the left auricle. This faulty observation had disastrous consequences for later anatomy. Aristotle did not distinguish between arteries and veins and applied the same term, *phleps,* to both. He traced the main branches

of both the venous and arterial systems and described the blood vessels as a system coextensive with the body. He described respiration as cooling and moderating the heat of the blood and the heart. He considered the brain to be cold and the heart hot. He did not know of the existence of the nervous system and did not conceive of the central role of the brain.

The Greek corpus of Aristotle's writings, typically represented by the Berlin Academy edition (1835), based mainly on lectures and elaborations of collected material, must have begun to be organized by Aristotle himself and his pupils. About 250 years after his death the quasi-final organization seems to have been accomplished by Andronicus of Rhodes. From this edition there derived the texts as we know them in Greek. By the second century A.D. the texts were already widely spread. The ban on pagan schools in 529 halted production until the revival of the late eight and ninth centuries. In the eleventh century uninterrupted transcription and transmission began. By the thirteenth and fourteenth centuries Aristotle was dominating the higher philosophical studies, side by side with Plato. A new impetus was given in the fifteenth century by the migration of scholars from the Greek world to Italy, where the first printed edition, the Aldine, appeared (1495–98). With the exception of the eighteenth century, when Aristotle was "out", the process of new editions has continued.

Although the Greek tradition was basic, the Latin was more important and permanent in the spread of Aristotle's works. Most important were direct translations from the Greek. Translations and expositions were made by both Neoplatonic Christians and the pagan revivalists of Themistius' school in Constantinople. The *Categories,* in its exposition by one of the latter, was later ascribed to St. Augustine and initiated the Latin Aristotelianism of the Middle Ages. Aristotle was a faded, but not a lost, memory when, in the sixth century, Boethius managed to obtain a copy of his logical texts and translated them into Latin. We still have his translations of *Categories, De interpretatione, Prior Analytics, Topics,* and *Sophistici elenchi.*

In the twelfth century Aristotle was again discovered and translated into Latin, not—as is commonly held—primarily from Arabic, but first and foremost from the Greek. The most important of the many translators of the Latin Middle Ages was James (Iacobus), a Venetian-Greek, who translated at least the *Posterior Analytics, Sophistici elenchi, De anima, Physics,* and *Metaphysics.* In the second half of the twelfth century, the Italian Gerard of Cremona translated from the Arabic what was accessible to him of the more scientific works of Aristotle, including *Meteorologics* I–III and *De caelo,* which did not exist in translation from the Greek. By the end of the twelfth century, therefore, most of his works had been translated into Latin. The works were not widely accessible until the mid-thirteenth century when Robert Grosseteste and William of Moerbeke took an interest in them. Michael Scot translated from the Arabic the first Latin version of the *Books on Animals,* and his translation of most of the Metaphysics with Averroës' *Great Commentary* was used by many students. By the end of the century almost all of the Aristotelian corpus as we know it was available in Latin.

The transmission of Aristotle in the Orient began in the Greek philosophical schools of the fifth and sixth centuries. The Syriac tradition formed the basis of a considerable proportion of Arabic texts and through them, of some Latin versions. Arabic translations were made in the ninth and tenth centuries.

ARISTOXENUS (*b. Tarentum, ca. 375–360* B.C.; *d. Athens [?]*), harmonic theory.

Aristoxenus was a pupil of Aristotle in Athens and hoped to succeed him as head of the Lyceum. Aristoxenus was the most famous and influential musical theorist of antiquity, but he turned his back upon the mathematical knowledge of his time to adopt and propagate a radically "unscientific" approach to the measurement of musical intervals. He stated that the ear was the sole criterion of musical phenomena. Writers on harmonics, from Aristoxenus on, fall into two schools: his followers, and the "Pythagoreans," who elaborated ratios for the intervals of the scale.

Aristoxenus drew a clear distinction between rhythm, which was an organized system of time units expressible in ratios, and the words, melodies, and bodily movements in which it was incorporated *(ta rhythmizomena)* and from which it could be abstracted.

ARISTYLLUS (*fl. ca. 270* B.C.), astronomy.

Aristyllus is mentioned by Plutarch as an astronomer who wrote in prose. According to Ptolemy, the observations of Aristyllus were not very accurate.

ARKADIEV, VLADIMIR KONSTANTINOVICH (*b. Moscow, Russia, 1884; d. Moscow, U.S.S.R., 1953*), physics.

Arkadiev attended the Physics and Mathematics Faculty of Moscow University where Umov and P.N. Lebedev lectured. In 1907, under Lebedev's direction, he began an experimental study of the magnetic properties of ferromagnetic substances in high-frequency fields of which the wavelength was on the order of one centimeter. In 1908 he obtained new results—ferromagnetic properties of iron and nickel disappeared when the wavelength was on the order of three centimeters.

Arkadiev was the first to determine experimentally the exact relationship between wavelength and the complex magnetic permeability of iron and nickel (1912).

In 1913, Arkadiev discovered ferromagnetic resonance. Between 1934 and 1936 he developed the concept of "magnetic viscosity," and the theory of the magnetization and demagnetization of bodies with various shapes.

ARKELL, WILLIAM JOSCELYN (*b. Highworth, Wiltshire, England, 1904; d. Cambridge, England, 1958*), geology, paleontology.

Graduated in geology from New College Oxford (1922). Arkell's first research culminated in the publication of two works: "The Corallian Rocks of Oxford, Berkshire, and North Wiltshire" (1927) and "A Monograph of British Corallian Lamellibranchia." He extended his studies to the Jurassic, in "The Stratigraphical Distribution of the Cornbrash" (1928, 1932), and to the Continent, in "A Comparison Between the Jurassic Rocks of the Calvados Coast and Those of Southern England" (1930).

Arkell wished to revise Albert Oppel's *Die Juraformation Englands, Frankreichs und des sudwestlichen Deutschlands* (1856–58) and extend its coverage throughout Europe and the rest of the world. Arkell's book *The Jurassic System*

in Great Britain (1933) was the first stage of a larger program. He made numerous contributions to the corpus of knowledge of Jurassic stratigraphy, and gradually stabilized many stratigraphically significant zonal assemblages. In 1946 his "Standard of the European Jurassic," advocated a commission to formulate a code of rules for stratigraphical nomenclature.

In 1956 Arkell's *Jurassic Geology of the World* reviewed critically the information dispersed throughout the enormous literature on the world's Jurassic stratigraphy. In 1957 Arkell contributed the section on Jurassic Ammonoidea to the *Treatise on Invertebrate Paleontology.*

ARMSTRONG, EDWARD FRANKLAND (*b. London, England, 1878; d. London, 1945*), chemistry

Studied with van't Hoff at the University of Berlin, Ph.D. (1901). During World War I, Armstrong solved a problem of great wartime importance—the large-scale catalytic production of acetic acid and acetone from ethyl alcohol. He was also instrumental in ensuring the inclusion of science in the programs of UNESCO.

ARMSTRONG, EDWIN HOWARD (*b. New York, N.Y., 1890; d. New York, 1954*), radio engineering.

Graduated from Columbia University (1913). The first of Armstrong's many inventions was the triode feedback (regenerative) circuit. His second important invention was the superheterodyne circuit.

In 1921 Armstrong made his third important discovery, superregeneration—a method of overcoming the regenerative receiver's principal limitation, the tendency to burst into oscillations just as the point of maximum amplification was reached.

Armstrong's greatest invention was frequency modulation (FM).

ARMSTRONG, HENRY EDWARD (*b. Lewisham, London, England, 1848; d. Lewisham, 1937*), chemistry, science education.

Armstrong entered the Royal College of Chemistry, London, in 1865. At the suggestion of Sir Edward Frankland he went to Leipzig to study under Hermann Kolbe. Ph.D., 1870. Armstrong did pioneer work on the structure of benzene, and his work with W. P. Wynne on the structure and reactions of naphthalene helped establish the dye industry.

He was among the first to base instruction and writing in chemistry upon Mendeleev's periodic table, and he early emphasized that molecules must have spatial configurations that determine crystal structures. His researches in crystallography were significant and antedated X-ray diffraction methods.

He was the first to devise curricula to relate chemistry and engineering, and he came to be regarded as the father of chemical engineering.

ARNALD OF VILLANOVA (*b. Aragon, Spain, ca. 1240; d. at sea off Genoa, Italy, 1311*), medical sciences.

Student at Montpellier (*ca.* 1260). His teaching and writings at Montpellier were of the first importance in establishing the content of scholastic medicine there.

Arnald was the principal figure in Montpellier's fusion of the Western empirical tradition with the systematic medical philosophy of the Greeks and Arabs. In the

1280's he translated, from Arabic into Latin, Avicenna's *De viribus cordis,* and Galen's *De rigore;* he also translated a work on drugs by Albuzale and one on regimen by Avenzoar. Arnald tried to develop a coherent, systematic science of medicine on the Galenic foundations. In the earlier works (e.g., the *De intentione medicorum*) his primary concern is to defend pragmatically the presence of a rational element in medicine.

Gradually Arnald became more preoccupied with problems of philosophy apart from any practical applications, and the later Montpellier treatises are highly technical discussions of sophisticated medical theory.

Arnald's attention to philosophical medicine coincided with the development of his theological position, and one concern may well have inspired the other.

ARNAULD, ANTOINE (*b. Paris, France, 1612; d. Brussels, Belgium, 1694*), mathematics, linguistics.

Arnauld was ordained a priest and received the doctorate in theology in 1641. Entered the Sorbonne in 1643 but was expelled for his Jansenist views in 1656. In *Logic* and *Port-Royal Grammar* he assumed that linguistic and mental processes are virtually identical, that language is thus to be studied in its "inner" and "outer" aspects. This view underlies the project for a universal grammar and the notion of the "transparency" of language.

His *Élémens* (1667) undertakes a reworking and reordering of the Euclidean theorems in the light of the contemporary literature and Pascal's influence.

ARNOLD, HAROLD DE FOREST (*b. Woodstock, Connecticut, 1883; d. Summit, New Jersey, 1933*), electronics.

B.A., M.A. Wesleyan University in Connecticut; Ph.D. University of Chicago (1911). Studied under Robert Millikan. Arnold was one of the founders of the Bell Telephone Laboratories. He was among the first to recognize the importance of high vacuum, and quickly developed designs that utilized reliable triodes and made long-distance telephony possible.

Arnold made a number of important contributions to the development of new magnetic alloys used in sound reproduction and to electroacoustics in general.

AROMATARI, GIUSEPPE DEGLI (*b. Assisi, Italy, 1587; d. Venice, Italy, 1660*), embryology.

Studied philosophy and medicine in Perugia, Montpellier, and Padua where he attended Fabricius' lectures. M.D. (1605). Aromatari was famous as a man of letters as well as a physician. He is remembered for his hypothesis of the preformation of the germ. He also investigated the so-called permeability of the interventricular septum of the heart.

In 1625 Aromatari published his famous *Epistola de generatione plantarum ex seminibus* ("Letter on the Generation of Plants from Seeds"). His hypothesis of germinal preformation became the new idea of the seventeenth century.

ARONHOLD, SIEGFRIED HEINRICH (*b. Angerburg, Germany [now Węgorzewo, Poland], 1819; d. Berlin Germany, 1884*), mathematics.

Aronhold attended the University of Königsberg (1841–45) and later continued his studies in Berlin. Ph.D. University of Königsberg (1851). Aronhold was particu-

larly attracted by the theory of invariants, then the center of mathematical interest, and was the first German to do research in this area. In 1863 he collected his ideas in a treatise entitled "Über eine fundamentale Begründung der Invariantentheorie."

AROUET, FRANÇOIS-MARIE. *See* **Voltaire.**

ARREST, HEINRICH LOUIS D' (*b. Berlin, Germany, 1822; d. Copenhagen, Denmark, 1875*), astronomy.

D'Arrest attended the Collège Français in Berlin before entering the University of Berlin. Ph.D. University of Leipzig (1850). A diligent investigator of comets, asteroids, and nebulae, d'Arrest is known today chiefly for his role in the discovery of the planet Neptune, and for the periodic comet that bears his name. This comet, which he discovered in 1851, was also seen in October 1963 and is significant because its orbit is gradually getting larger through the action of some nongravitational force.

ARRHENIUS, SVANTE AUGUST (*b. Vik, Sweden, 1859; d. Stockholm, Sweden, 1927*), chemistry, physics.

After attending the Cathedral School in Uppsala, Arrhenius studied mathematics, chemistry, and physics at the University of Uppsala, doctorate, 1884. He passed the candidate's examination in 1878 and in 1881 went to Stockholm to work under physicist Erik Edlund of the Swedish Academy of Sciences. His first independent research led to his paper "The Disappearance of Galvanic Polarization in a Polarization Vessel, the Plates of Which Are Connected by Means of a Metallic Conductor" (1883). His doctoral dissertation discussed the electrolytic theory of dissociation. He was appointed lecturer in physical chemistry at the University of Uppsala (1884). A travel grant from the Swedish Academy enabled him to work abroad with Ostwald, Kohlrausch, Boltzmann, and van't Hoff. In 1905 he became director of the physical chemistry department of the Nobel Institute.

Arrhenius' aim was to find a method for determining the molecular weight of dissolved nonvolatile compounds by measuring electric conductivity. He completed his experimental work in the spring of 1883 and submitted a long two-part memoir to the Swedish Academy "Recherches sur la conductibilité galvanique des electrolytes" (1884). The main importance of this memoir lies in the development of general ideas that contain the germ of the theory of electrolytic dissociation–although the term is not used.

In 1887 Arrhenius published a much revised, extended, and consolidated version of his theory of electrolytic dissociation in its quantitative formulation under the title "Ueber die Dissociation der im Wasser gelösten Stoffe."

Among Arrhenius' most important contributions to this theory are his publications on isohydric solutions, solutions of two acids that can be mixed without any change in the degree of dissociation (1888); the relation between osmotic pressure and lowering of vapor tension (1889); the condition of equilibrium between electrolytes (1889); the determination of electrolytic dissociation of salts through solubility experiments (1892); the hydrolysis of salts and weak acids and weak bases (1894); and the alteration of the strength of weak bases by the addition of salts (1899).

In his "Ueber die Reaktionsgeschwindigkeit bei der Inversion von Rohrzucker durch Säuren" (1889), Arrhenius studied the influence of an increase in temperature on the reaction velocity.

After 1900 Arrhenius devoted his attention to the physics and chemistry of cosmic and meteorological phenomena. In 1903 he published his *Lehrbuch der kosmischen Physik*, the first textbook on cosmic physics. He was also concerned with the theory of immunity, an interest that resulted in two textbooks: *Immunochemistry* (1907) and *Quantitative Laws in Biological Chemistry* (1915).

ARSONVAL, ARSÈNE D' (*b. Chateau de la Borie, St. Germain-les-Belles, La Porcherie, France, 1851; d. Chateau de la Borie, 1940*), biophysics.

D'Arsonval studied at the University of Poitiers (1869) and later at Limoges and Paris with Claude Bernard.

In 1882 d'Arsonval was awarded the Prix Montyon of the Académie des Sciences for his ingenious apparatus for studying the problems of animal heat and body temperature. His double-chambered calorimeter was remarkably accurate and based upon a new approach.

D'Arsonval became involved in famous experiments on endocrine extracts which revealed clues to the later controversial hormone theory of wound healing.

His most outstanding scientific contributions involved the biological and technological applications of electricity. His early studies dealt with the electrical properties of muscle contraction. This interest in muscle current led to a series of practical inventions in the early 1880's. They included nonpolarizable silver chloride electrodes for biological research, refinement of carbon-rod microphones, and the invention with Marey of myographic equipment. D'Arsonval, in cooperation with Deprez, invented the mobile circuit galvanometer in 1882.

Gradually d'Arsonval's interests shifted from pure biological research to technological problems. The d'Arsonval incubator was used well into the twentieth century. In later years d'Arsonval became involved in the application of electricity to industry.

His contribution to medicine, now overshadowed by the antibiotic era, created a minor revolution in clinical therapeutics. D'Arsonval literally founded the paramedical field of physiotherapy. The first high frequency heat therapy unit was established under d'Arsonval's direction at the Hôtel-Dieu Hospital in 1895. Indeed, electrotherapy was called *d'Arsonvalization* until the broader term *diathermy* came into use after 1920.

ARTEDI, PETER (*b. Anundsjö, Angermanland, Sweden, 1705; d. Amsterdam, the Netherlands, 1735*), biology.

Artedi matriculated at Uppsala University in 1724. *Petri Artedi sueci, medici, ichthyologia sive opera omnia de piscibus* (1738), Artedi's taxonomically most important work assured him the honor of being the father of the science of ichthyology. He was the first to settle the notion of genus in zoology; the distinction between species and variety; and the classification into classes, orders, and maniples (families).

ARTIN, EMIL (*b. Vienna, Austria, 1898; d. Hamburg, Germany, 1962*), mathematics.

Studied University of Vienna, then Leipzig (Ph.D., 1921). In 1923 Artin began the investigations that led him to the general law of reciprocity which he proved in 1927.

With the aid of the theorem, Artin traced Hilbert's assumption, according to which each ideal of a field becomes a principal ideal of its absolute class field, to a theory on groups that had been proven in 1930 by Philip Furtwaengler. In 1923 Artin derived a functional equation for his L-series that was completed by Richard Braver in 1947.

With the help of the theory of formal-real fields, Artin in 1927 solved the Hilbert problem of definite functions. In his work on hypercomplex numbers in 1927, Artin expanded the theory of algebras of associative rings; in 1944 he postulated rings with minimum conditions for right ideals (Artin rings). In 1927 he presented a new foundation for, and extension of, the arithmetic of semisimple algebras over the field of rational numbers.

ARTSIMOVICH, LEV ANDREEVICH (*b. Moscow, Russia, 1909; d. Moscow, U.S.S.R., 1973*), physics. Graduated from Belorussian State University, Minsk (1928); taught at Leningrad Physical-Technical Institute, Leningrad Polytechnical Institute, Leningrad University, Moscow Physical-Engineering Institute, and Moscow State University. Studied complete internal reflection of X rays from thin layers (1933); capture of neutrons by protons (1935); demonstrated strict correctness of laws of conservation during electron-positron annihilation; studied interaction of fast electrons with matter; electronic optics and radiation loss in betatron. Technological contributions included electromagnetic separation of isotopes; directed group working toward controlled thermonuclear reactions. Active member of Pugwash Movement.

ĀRYABHAṬA I (*b.* A.D. 476).

Āryabhata I wrote two works: the *Āryabhaṭīya* in 499, and another, lost treatise in which he expounded the *arddharātrika* system. The *Āryabhaṭīya* consists of three parts and a brief introduction: *Daśagītikā,* introduction; *Gaṇitapāda,* mathematics; *Kālakriyāpāda,* the reckoning of time and the planetary models; *Golapāda,* on the sphere, including eclipses. It was particularly studied in south India.

ĀRYABHAṬA II (*fl. between ca.* A.D. *950 and 1100*).

Author of *Mahāsiddhānta* (or *Āryasiddhānta*), which discusses the solar system and mathematics.

ARZACHEL *See* **al-Zarqālī.**

ASADA GŌRYŪ (*b. Kizuki, Bungo Province, Japan, 1734; d. Osaka, Japan, 1799*), astronomy.

Asada taught himself medicine and astronomy. He was instrumental in turning Japanese astronomy and calendrical science away from the traditional Chinese style and toward Western models. He placed great weight upon empirical verification and he determined the value of new theories by observation. The earliest record of an observation by him is that of a lunar eclipse in 1757.

Asada and his school introduced modern instruments and observational methods into Japan. He ground lenses and made a telescope, which he used to observe the movements of Jupiter's satellites.

Jikkenroku ("Records Based on Observations," 1786), gives the essentials of his calendar. The constants he employed for calculation were mostly new ones that Asada had worked out from his own data.

In 1793 he made a considerable correction in the constant for the distance between the sun and the earth, and corrected other constants affected by it.

When the shogunate proposed to revise the current Japanese calendar by use of the new theories of Western astronomy, Asada recomended two pupils from his own school, Takahashi Yoshitoki (1764–1804) and Hazama Shigetomi (1756–1816).

Asada formulated a modified conception in which the length of the ancient tropical year tended to decrease until it reached a minimum in the Middle Ages and to grow longer afterward, varying in a precession cycle of 25,400 years. He also presumed that the only perpetual constant was the length of the anomalistic (sidereal) year. Asada's pupils succeeded in applying his variation term to the *Kansei* calendar promulgated in 1798. In the 1830's it was realized that observations did not agree with the *Kansei* calendar.

His pupils claimed for Asada the honor of having independently discovered the relationship between the distances of planets from the sun and the periods of their revolution (in other words, Kepler's third law), although he did not publish it.

Asada's style in medicine was not Western, but that of the positivistic and clinical *koihō* (ancient medical learning) school that flourished during the mid-eighteenth century in Japan.

ASCLEPIADES (*b. Prusa, Bithynia, ca. 130* B.C.; *d. Rome, ca. 40* B.C.), medicine.

Trained originally as a philosopher and orator, Asclepiades achieved fame as a physician in Rome. He did much to overcome the Roman prejudice against Greek medicine. The most important ideas he derived from his predecessors were a theory of knowledge based upon sensory appearances alone and the rejection of teleology.

ASELLI, GASPARE (*b. Cremona, Italy, 1581; d. Milan, Italy, 1625*), anatomy.

Aselli revealed a marked propensity for the natural sciences early in his schooling. He studied medicine at the University of Pavia where one of his teachers was G. Carcano-Leone, a pupil of Falloppio. He discovered the chylous vessels, although both Hippocrates and Aristotle had already pointed to the existence of the so-called absorbent vessels. The results of his investigations were collected in *De lactibus sive Lacteis venis quarto vasorum mesaraicorum genere novo invento Gasparis Asellii Cremonensis anatomici Ticinensis dissertatio* (1627). They were the first anatomical illustrations to appear in color.

ASHMOLE, ELIAS (*b. Lichfield, England, 1617; d. London, England, 1692*).

Ashmole's was influenced by the mathematicians and astrologers with whom he associated during the English Civil War (1641–46). His first published writings were two short translations of astrological works in Lilly's *World's Catastrophe* (1647). Ashmole aspired to publish the "choicest flowers" of alchemical literature, and his first book, the *Fasciculus chemicus* (1650), was a modest translation of works by Arthur Dee and Jean d'Espagnet. He hoped to produce a comprehensive collection

of English verse and prose alchemical works, drawn from manuscript sources. The project had an auspicious beginning with the publication of the *Theatrum chemicum Britanicum* (1652) a collection of alchemical works. The *Prolegomena* indicate familiarity and agreement with the leading themes of Hermetic philosophy. The only other English alchemical work he published was *The Way to Bliss* (1658). Ashmole was zealous in his desire to replace ephemeral personal "cabinets" with permanent public museums. In 1675 he offered his collections to Oxford University, on the condition that suitable housing was provided for it. This was the first English public museum, and it became the focus of scientific activity at Oxford.

ASSALTI, PIETRO (*b. Acquaviva Picena, Italy, 1680; d. Rome, Italy, 1728*), medicine.

Assalti received his early education in Acquaviva Picena. At fifteen he went to Fermo to study. Four years later he went to Rome to study law, languages and natural history. He soon earned a reputation as a scholar and was chosen by Pope Clement XI to be one of the "writers" of the Vatican Library.

Assalti collected the works of Lancisi and published them in two volumes (1718), and was almost certainly the author of the annotations to Michele Mercati's *Metallotheca* (1717). His unpublished "Oratio de incrementis anatomicae in hoc saeculo XVIII" deals with the function of the spleen, among other topics.

ASTBURY, WILLIAM THOMAS (*b. Longton* [*now part of Stoke-on-Trent*], *England, 1898; d. Leeds, England, 1961*), X-ray crystallography, molecular biology.

Astbury read chemistry at Cambridge and began research under Sir William Bragg at University College, London, in 1921, moving with him to the Royal Institution in 1923. In 1928 he was appointed lecturer in textile physics at the University of Leeds, then reader, and finally professor of biomolecular structure. Worked on the structure of tartaric acids, measured diffraction intensities photometrically, and with Kathleen Lonsdale produced the first tables of space groups. In 1930 he discovered that two diffraction patterns can be produced from the same wool fiber by exposing it to the X-ray beam when relaxed and when under tension. He noted the similarity of the stretched, or beta form of keratin to silk and proposed for both a two-dimensional grid structure, the cross-links between the polypeptide chains being through salt linkages and sulfur bridges. Astbury's work was henceforth dominated by this theory of the reversible transformation of keratin. In 1951 Astbury's models were discarded.

Although his structures for proteins were all wrong in detail, they represent the first attempt at molecular models in which specific crosslinkages hold the polypeptide chains in a characteristic conformation. Nowhere did he utilize helical models, but his picture of DNA as a dense molecule with the bases stacked one above another 3.4 A apart was the first step toward the elucidation of its structure.

ASTON, FRANCIS WILLIAM (*b. Harbonne, Birmingham, England 1877; d. Cambridge, England, 1945*), experimental chemistry, physics.

After four years at Malvern College, in 1893 he entered Mason's College, Birmingham, where he studied for the London intermediate science examination with W.A. Tilden, P.F. Frankland and J.H. Poynting. Later he worked with Frankland on the stereochemistry of acid esters. From 1903 to 1908 he worked as physics research assistant with Poynting. From 1910 to 1919 Aston worked with J.J. Thomson at the Cavendish Laboratory, Cambridge, and the Royal Institution, London. During World War I, he returned to chemistry as a technical assistant at the Royal Aircraft Establishment, Farnborough. In 1919 he was elected a fellow of Trinity College, Cambridge.

The appearance of Thomson's *Conduction of Electricity Through Gases* in 1903 opened up the physicist's world for Aston. He began to work on the variable structure of phenomena observed during gaseous conduction at low pressures. In 1908 he detected a new "primary cathode dark space" about a millimeter thick and directly adjoining the cathode. The phenomenon now bears Aston's name.

He produced an improved spherical discharge tube, finely engineered cathode slits, an improved pump, a coil for detecting vacuum leaks, and an ingenious camera for photographing the parabolas. In 1912 he thought this apparatus for positive ray analysis gave a rigorous proof that all the individual molecules of any given substance had the same mass. This Daltonian belief was shattered in the same year when Thomson obtained two parabolas, of mass 20 and 22, for neon. Aston tried to separate the meta-neon of radioactive isotopes by fractional distillation, and later by diffusion. The partial separation of a new element, with the same properties as neon, was announced in 1913. In 1919 Aston built a positive ray spectrograph. But since the mass spectrograph was unsuitable for detecting minute amounts of isotopes, he missed finding those of oxygen and hydrogen. In 1930 Aston showed how his instrument could be used photometrically to determine and correct chemical atomic weights.

In December 1919 Aston announced the "whole-number rule" that atomic masses were integral on the scale of O^{16} (a notation introduced by Aston in 1920).

His achievements were kept continually before the scientific public by revised editions of his excellent book *Isotopes* (1922).

ASTRUC, JEAN (*b. Sauve, Gard, France, 1684; d. Paris, France, 1766*), medicine.

After receiving a doctorate in medicine at Montpellier in 1703, Astruc temporarily occupied Pierre Chirac's chair of medicine in 1706. Passed the competitive examination of the Faculty of Medicine of Toulouse (1711); held chair of medicine, Montpellier (1716–28). Physician to Augustus II of Poland. In 1751 he occupied E.F. Geoffroy's chair of pharmacy at the College Royal. His *Traité sur les maladies des femmes* (1761) describes septicemia caused by uterine infections and puerperal fever; ovarian cysts; tubal pregnancies; and lithopedions.

In 1743 Astruc compared the transformation of an impression or sensation into a motor discharge to a ray of light reflected on a surface; he called it *reflex*.

Astruc's best-known work is a treatise on venereology, *De morbis venereis* (1773–74). His Old Testament studies resulted in the *Conjectures sur la Genèse* (1753).

ATHENAEUS OF ATTALIA (*b. Attalia in Pamphylia now Antalya, Turkey*), medicine.

Athenaeus, a physician who practiced in Rome, founded the Pneumatic school of medicine. The name of Athenaeus' school came from a new term, *pneuma* ("breath" or "spirit"), that he introduced into medical theory from Stoic philosophy. He taught that the body was composed, ultimately, of the traditional four qualities —hot, cold, wet, dry—but that these were held together and governed by pneuma, which permeated the entire body.

ATWATER, WILBUR OLIN (*b. Johnsburg, New York, 1844; d. Middletown, Connecticut, 1907*), agricultural chemistry, physiology, scientific administration.

Atwater studied for two years at the University of Vermont and received his bachelor's degree at Wesleyan College in 1865. Ph.D. at Yale University Sheffield Scientific School (1869). Atwater became increasingly involved in fertilizer investigation and testing, using this work partly as a means of gaining agricultural support for scientific research.

Atwater and E. B. Rosa designed and constructed the Atwater-Rosa calorimeter. He was concerned not only with metabolism as a problem in physiology, but also with the use of his new techniques for the determination of improved dietary standards for the working class.

Vigorous though Atwater's scientific work was, his greatest contribution to the development of science in the United States was organizational and administrative —especially his efforts to establish scientific standards for experiment station research.

ATWOOD, GEORGE (*b. England, 1745; d. London, England, 1807*), mathematics, physics.

Atwood was awarded a scholarship to Trinity College, Cambridge where he received a B.A. (1769) and M.A. (1772). The work for which he is best known and which bears his name—Atwood's machine—is described in *A Treatise on the Rectilinear Motion . . .* (1784), which is essentially a textbook on Newtonian mechanics. Atwood's machine was designed to demonstrate the laws of uniformly accelerated motion due to gravity. Most of Atwood's other published work consisted of the mathematical analysis of practical problems.

AUBERT DUPETIT-THOUARS, L. M. *See* **Dupetit-Thouars, L. M. Aubert.**

AUBUISSON DE VOISINS, JEAN-FRANÇOIS D' (*b. Toulouse, France, 1769; d. Toulouse, 1841*), mining, geology, hydraulics.

Aubuisson de Voisins attended the Benedictine College of Sorèze and the Artillery School of Metz. Later he attended the Bergakademie (1800–01) and in 1802 published *Des mines de Freiberg en Saxe et de leur exploitation*.

In 1819 d'Aubuisson published *Traité de géognosie, ou Exposé des connaissances actuelles sur la constitution physique et minérale du globe terrestre*, the first competent treatment of general geology published in France.

In 1825 d'Aubuisson found that in an airshaft the resistance to passage of the air is directly proportional to the length of the pipe and the square of the speed of the air flow, and inversely proportional to the diameter.

D'Aubuisson also found that the volumes of two gases streaming from equal openings and under the same pressure are inversely proportional to the square roots of their densities. A further accomplishment was the establishment of a simple formula that made it possible to use cast-iron water pipes with walls half as thick as those previously used. He published *Traité d'hydraulique à l'usage des ingénieurs* (1834) and *Traité du mouvement de l'eau dans les tuyaux de conduite* (1827).

AUDOUIN, JEAN VICTOR (*b. Paris, France, 1797; d. Paris, 1841*), zoology.

Audouin began his studies at Rheims in 1807 and continued in Paris at Lycée Louis-le-Grand. He presented his doctoral thesis in 1826. He began to study law, but soon abandoned it for medicine, pharmacy, and the natural sciences. Audouin's work is both that of a scrupulously careful morphologist and anatomist of Cuvier's school and that of a biologist who has left behind important observations on the physiology of crustacea as well as on the ethology of various insects harmful to cultivated plants. This last phase of his research marks Audouin's work as the precursor of modern applied entomology.

AUDUBON, JOHN JAMES (*b. Les Cayes, Santo Domingo [now Haiti], 1785; d. New York, N.Y., 1851*), ornithology.

Audubon had no formal training in natural history, having had only a brief acquaintance with the obscure naturalist Charles d'Orbigny and a period in New York as a taxidermist under the many-faceted Samuel L. Mitchell. In 1821–24, Audubon came into his full powers as a gifted painter of birds and master of design. In England he brought out the 435 huge, aquatint copperplates of *The Birds of America* over a period of twelve years. The dramatic impact of his ambitious, complex pictures, and a romantic image as "the American woodsman" secured for Audubon entry into the scientific community. The text for Audubon's pictures emerged as the five-volume *Ornithological Biography.*

Audubon's remaining efforts were devoted to the hopeless task of including all the birds of North America in his work. Audubon's enduring fame rests on his much-debated, but obviously significant, efforts as an artist.

AUENBRUGGER, JOSEPH LEOPOLD (*b. Graz, Austria, 1722; d. Vienna, Austria, 1809*), medicine.

Auenbrugger received his medical education at the University of Vienna. He is considered the founder of chest percussion and was undoubtedly aided in developing this diagnostic technique by his musical knowledge which enabled him to perceive differences in tone when the chest was tapped. Auenbrugger's method permitted the determination of disease-caused changes in the lungs and heart of a live patient and thus gave a new, dependable foundation to the diagnosis of chest diseases. Even with the more recent development of X rays, this method still has diagnostic value.

AUGUSTINE OF HIPPO, SAINT, also known as **Aurelius Augustinus** (*b. Tagaste, North Africa, 354; d. Hippo, North Africa, 430*), theology, philosophy.

Augustine's was one of the most powerful minds the Christian church had known until the fourth century, perhaps the most creative it has ever known. He wrote such great creative works as *The City of God, On the Trinity,* and his incomparable *Confessions.* The success of his efforts to isolate and define the heretical elements in the work of Pelagius, Arius, and a legion of others gave to Roman Christianity a self-understanding, a methodology, and a philosophical power and scope it had never before possessed. The categories in which the medieval church thought of man, of the world, and of God, were largely those developed by Augustine. His metaphysics resembled those of Neoplatonism, but with *creation* replacing *emanation* as the focal concept. But what shaped his thought was not primarily the categorial systems of the Greek and Roman philosophers; rather, it was the overwhelming experience of sin and of conversion he had known in his own life. He built his philosophy around the certainties and realities of a profound inner experience. Augustine's theory of knowledge is built around the notion of a Divine illumination which is integral to any genuine human act of understanding, and his theory of will centers on the idea of grace—that is, the aid God freely gives man to strengthen his will in pursuit of the good.

Augustine's work can be seen as marking the second crucial stage in the development of the peculiar matrix of thought and value within which natural science, as we know it, emerged in the West. Augustine stands at a fateful parting of the ways between West and East. His influence on the growth of the approach to nature and the knowledge of nature that science would one day demand was considerable.

Augustine's theory of knowledge dominated all discussions of scientific method for almost a millennium, until challenged by Aristotelian doctrines in the schools of Paris and Oxford in the mid-thirteenth century.

Three Augustinian doctrines are worth noting because of the part they played in the early history of the natural sciences. The first of these is the doctrine of *rationes seminales,* which has often been said to prefigure the theory of an evolutionary origin of species. A second characteristically Augustinian emphasis is the preeminence of mathematics in the constructing of a science of nature. A final feature of Augustine's thought that laid its impress upon medieval science was his basic metaphor of illumination, the principal causal mode relating God and man.

AUSTEN, RALPH A.C. *See* **Godwin-Austen, Ralph A.C.**

AUSTIN, LOUIS WINSLOW (*b. Orwell, Vermont, 1867; d. Washington, D.C., 1932*), radio physics.

Austin graduated from Middlebury College in Vermont in 1889 and received the doctorate from the University of Strasbourg in 1893. His researches on radio transmission made him world famous. The scope of his research was considerably enhanced by the establishment of a naval radiotelegraphic laboratory at the Bureau of Standards in 1908. Austin and his collaborator Louis Cohen established the Austin-Cohen formula, a semiempirical method for predicting the strength of radio signals at remote locations. The formula played an important role in the design and manufacture of improved apparatus. He contributed significantly to the understanding of the sources of radio atmospheric disturbances ("static"), a field in which he was active until his death.

AUTOLYCUS OF PITANE (*fl. ca. 300* B.C.), astronomy, geometry.

Autolycus was a successor to Eudoxus in the study of spherical astronomy and attempted to defend the Eudoxian system of concentric rotating spheres. The two treatises of Autolycus, *On the Moving Sphere* and *On Risings and Settings,* are among the earliest works in Greek astronomy to survive in their entirety.

AUVERGNE, WILLIAM OF. *See* **William of Auvergne.**

AUWERS, ARTHUR JULIUS GEORG FRIEDRICH VON (*b. Göttingen, Germany, 1838; d. Lichterfelde bei Berlin, Germany, 1915*), astronomy.

Auwers attended the gymnasia in Göttingen and Schulpforta from 1847 to 1857. He wrote his dissertation, *Untersuchungen über veränderliche Eigenbewegungen,* in 1862. His lifework was the meticulous observation and calculation necessary to draw up star catalogs with highly accurate positions of stars. He made new reductions of previous observations such as Bradley's Greenwich observations, the oldest measurements of tolerable precision. His publication of Bradley's observations (1882–1903) was the basis of all modern star positions and proper motions. Auwers' *Neue Fundamentalcatalog der Astronomischen Gesellschaft* was the foundation of all present precise measurements. Auwers also initiated the *Geschichte des Fixsternhimmels,* a reduction and listing of all meridian observations of fixed stars from 1743 to 1900.

AUWERS, KARL FRIEDRICH VON (*b. Gotha, Germany, 1863; d. Marburg, Germany, 1939*), chemistry.

Auwers was a student of A.W. von Hofmann at Berlin, an assistant to Victor Meyer at Göttingen and Heidelberg, and then director of the chemical institute at the University of Marburg. He was a master organic chemist who investigated problems in structural theory for more than fifty years. His studies on isomerism led him into a lifelong investigation of stereochemical and spectrochemical problems.

AUZOUT, ADRIEN (*b. Rouen, France, 1622; d. Rome, Italy, 1691*), astronomy, physics, mathematics.

Auzout approached science with instruments rather than with mathematics. By 1660 his career centered on astronomical instruments. He made a significant contribution to the final development of the micrometer and to the replacement of open sights by telescopic sights.

AVEBURY, BARON. *See* **Lubbock, John.**

AVEMPACE. *See* **Ibn Bājja.**

AVENARE. *See* **Ibn Ezra.**

AVERROËS. *See* **Ibn Rushd.**

AVERY, OSWALD T. (*b. Halifax, Nova Scotia, Canada, 1877; d. Nashville, Tennessee, 1955*), biology.

Avery attended Colgate University (B.A., 1900), and received his medical degree from the Columbia University College of Physicians and Surgeons in 1904. In 1913

he became a member of the staff of the Rockefeller Institute Hospital, where he remained until 1948.

Avery showed that, in one instance at least, DNA was the active causative factor in an inherited variation in bacterial cells. It was to a great extent through his work that the stage was set for the rapidly ensuing elaboration of the structure, function, and importance of DNA.

AVICENNA. *See* **Ibn Sīnā.**

AVOGADRO, AMEDEO (*b. Turin, Italy, 1776; d. Turin, 1856*), physics, chemistry.

He received his first education at home and then attended grammar school in Turin. Avogadro was guided toward a legal career and in 1792 he became a bachelor of jurisprudence. In 1796 he gained his doctorate in ecclesiastical law and began legal practice. Also interested in natural philosophy, in 1800 he began to study physics and mathematics privately.

Appointed demonstrator at the college attached to the Academy of Turin (1806). Professor of natural philosophy at the College of Vercelli (1809). In 1820 he was appointed to the first chair of mathematical physics in Italy, at Turin.

Avogadro was elected a corresponding member of the Academy of Sciences of Turin in 1804, and in 1819 he became a full member. As president of a commission on weights and measures, he was largely responsible for the introduction of the metric system in Piedmont.

Avogadro is known principally for Avogadro's hypothesis, which he modestly presented as an extension of the work of Gay-Lussac. Avogadro's hypothesis provided a much-needed key to the problems of nineteenth-century chemistry by distinguishing between atoms and molecules: *"the number of integral molecules in any gas is always the same for equal volumes, or always proportional to the volumes."*

From Avogadro's hypothesis there immediately follows the inference that the relative weights of the molecules of any two gases are the same as the ratios of the densities of these gases under the same conditions of temperature and pressure. Molecular weights could thus be determined directly.

It should be noted that Avogadro's molecular weights are values based on the comparison with the weight of a molecule of hydrogen rather than an atom of hydrogen. The molecular weights given in Avogadro's paper of 1811 are therefore half the modern values.

Avogadro had a solution to the problem that arose when the hypothesis of equal volumes was applied to compound substances. He postulated compound molecules—the second and most important part of Avogadro's hypothesis. Unlike the first part, it seems completely original. Compound molecules of gases must therefore be composed of two or more atoms and Avogadro implied that there are always an even number of atoms in the molecule of a gas. He suggested that his hypothesis could be used to correct the theory of definite proportions, which he saw as "the basis of all modern chemistry and the source of its future progress." In 1811 Avogadro had been able to give the modern formulas (in words) for water vapor, nitric oxide, nitrous oxide, ammonia, carbon monoxide, and hydrogen chloride. In 1814 he was able to give the correct formulas for several compounds of carbon and sulfur. Falling back on analogy when experimental evidence was lacking, he reasoned correctly that silica was SiO_2 by comparison with CO_2. He extended his earlier treatment of metals in the hypothetical gaseous state and gave molecular weights for many elements based on analyses of their compounds. His mention of "gaz métalliques" may have done more harm than good to the reception of his hypothesis.

In 1821 Avogadro was able to state the correct formulas of several compounds including those of phosphorus and the oxides of nitrogen. After deducing the formulas of such inorganic compounds from combining volumes, densities, or merely by analogy, he turned to organic chemistry. He gave the correct empirical formulas for turpentine, alcohol, and ether.

Avogadro's claim to the hypothesis that is named after him rests on more than his mere statement of it because to him belongs the distinction of applying his hypothesis to the whole field of chemistry.

It is clear that Avogadro stated his new hypothesis in print repeatedly over the period 1811–21. Unfortunately these later memoirs were published in Italy, then at the periphery of the scientific world. Influential editors in France, England, and Germany generally ignored his work.

One of the most remarkable features of Avogadro's hypothesis was the way in which it was neglected by the vast majority of chemists for half a century after its initial publication. But despite the failure of chemists to appreciate the full significance of Avogadro's hypothesis, he could claim in 1845 that his statement that the mean distances between the molecules of all gases were the same under the same conditions of temperature and pressure and the consequence that the molecular weight was proportional to the density was generally accepted by physicists and chemists either explicitly or implicitly. What was ignored, however, was the use of the hypothesis to determine atomic weights.

Avogadro's first two published memoirs (1806, 1807) were on electricity. He considered the state of a nonconductor placed between two oppositely charged elementary layers. If there was air between two charged bodies, it would become charged. In a subsequent memoir (1842) Avogadro suggested that the capacity of a condenser was independent of the gas between the plates and that there would be the same process of induction even in a vacuum.

Avogadro's 1822 memoir "Sur la construction d'un voltimètre multiplicateur" was given publicity by Oersted. Avogadro's "multiplier" was one of the most sensitive instruments of the time, and by using it he found that when certain pairs of metals are plunged into concentrated nitric acid the direction of the electric current is momentarily reversed. This condition was sometimes referred to as "Avogadro's reversal."

Avogadro published his first article dealing only with chemistry in 1809. This memoir illustrates his abiding concern with chemical affinity and, incidentally, the great influence exerted on him by Berthollet. The opening paragraph, which criticizes the oxygen theory of acidity, illustrates his radical approach to post-Lavoisier chemistry. He postulated a relative scale of acidity, with oxygen and sulfur toward the acid end of the scale, neutral substances in the middle, and hydrogen at the alkali end. A

significant feature of the scale was that it was continuous.

Avogadro might claim to share with Berthollet the honor of having been a founder of physical chemistry. Certainly he saw no boundary between physics and chemistry and made constant use of a mathematical approach. He thus saw a means of relating chemical affinity to specific heat.

In 1822 Avogadro considered himself justified in making the generalization that the specific heats at constant volume of gases were proportional to the square root of the attractive power of their molecules for caloric. In 1824 he made further progress toward an evaluation of a true affinity for heat, to which he could assign a numerical value. Avogadro concluded with a table of twenty-nine substances, headed by acids and terminating with bases. By dividing each affinity for heat by that of oxygen, he obtained a series of what he called "affinity" numbers. He claimed that he had succeeded in deriving affinity numbers from atomic volumes and by a method independent of all chemical considerations—reminding us of his predominantly physical attitude.

Toward the end of his life Avogadro devoted four memoirs to atomic volumes. In the first (1843) he pointed out the connection with his classic memoir of 1811—the mean distance between the molecules of all gases is the same under the same conditions of temperature and pressure. In 1824 he had stated that the atomic volumes of all substances in the liquid or solid state would be the same if it were not for certain factors and in particular the different affinities of bodies for caloric. But the latter factor was directly related to the electronegativity of the element. Comparing the densities of the elements with their atomic weights, he now concluded that the distances between the molecules of solids and liquids, and consequently their volumes, were greater, and hence their densities compared with their atomic weights were less as the body became more electropositive. Alternatively expressed, the atomic volume (atomic weight/density) is greater for the more electropositive elements, and this is now accepted.

IBN AL-ʿAWWĀM ABŪ ZAKARIYYĀ YAḤYĀ IBN MUḤAMMAD (*fl. Spain, second half of the twelfth century*), agronomy.

The work of Ibn al-ʿAwwām, published in Spanish at the beginning of the nineteenth century, is devoted to agronomy and related matters. The *Kitāb al-filāḥa* was designed to increase the value of land through the education of the farmer.

AZARA, FÉLIX DE (*b. Barbuñales, Huesca, Spain, 1742; d. Huesca, 1821*), mathematics, geography, natural history.

Studied philosophy, arts, and law from 1757 to 1761 at the University of Huesca. He continued his mathematical training at Barcelona and by 1769 he was assisting in hydrographic surveys being carried out near Madrid.

Between 1784 and 1796 he prepared at least fifteen maps of the Brazilian frontier. He enlarged the study of natural history by discovering a large number of new species. Visualized great biological concepts expanded by Cuvier and Darwin, both of whom quoted and accepted his views; for instance, on the variation undergone by horses under domestication.

BAADE, WILHELM HEINRICH WALTER (*b. Schröttinghausen, Westphalia, Germany, 1893; d. Bad Salzuflen, Westphalia, Germany, 1960*), astronomy.

Baade attended the University of Münster, transferring to the University of Göttingen in 1913. He served for three years as assistant to the mathematician Felix Klein.

When Baade was invited to join the staff at Mt. Wilson Observatory near Pasadena, California (1931), he realized his dream of working with the best telescopes in the world. His concern with distance criteria soon had spectacular results. Baade reasoned correctly that the Andromeda galaxy was more distant than had previously been thought. Announced in 1952, this conclusion essentially doubled the size of the universe. His theory of stellar populations represented a major step toward today's understanding of the life cycles of stars.

Baade left his mark on another aspect of astronomy when he identified, in photographs he had taken with the 200-inch Palomar telescope, several objects first detected by radiotelescopes (1954). In a final contribution to the understanding of objects later called quasars, Baade showed that a jet issuing from the galaxy M87 emitted strongly polarized light (1956).

BABBAGE, CHARLES (*b. Teignmouth, England, 1792; d. London, England, 1871*), mathematics, computer logic, computer technology.

As a child Babbage was privately educated. Entering Cambridge University in 1810, he soon found that he knew more than his teachers. In a famous alliance with George Peacock and John Herschel, he began campaigning for revitalization of mathematics teaching. To this end the trio translated S.F. Lacroix's *Differential and Integral Calculus.*

Babbage wrote notable papers on the theory of functions and on various topics in applied mathematics. He was absorbed by problems of the mechanization of computation and is especially known for the devising of a notation that not only simplified the making and reading of engineering drawings but also helped a good designer simplify his "circuits." Babbage realized that existing mathematical tables were peppered with errors. He was enthusiastic about the application of the method of differences to tablemaking. (His finished table of eight-figure logarithms for the first 108,000 natural numbers is among the best ever made.) Babbage turned to the planning of a machine that would handle twenty-decimal numbers and sixth-order differences, plus a printout device. Two factors militated against the production of the difference engine. One was cost, and the other was the inventor's espousal of what he called an analytical engine. Babbage saw the possibility of using punched cards to code quantities and operations in an automatic computing system and he drew up plans for a machine of almost unbelievable versatility and mathematical power. Although the analytical engine foreshadowed modern equipment, an important difference obtains: it was decimal, not binary. Having to use wheels meant that his system was not "purely" digital, in the modern sense.

BABCOCK, STEPHEN MOULTON (*b. Bridgewater, New York, 1843; d. Madison, Wisconsin, 1931*), agricultural chemistry.

Received the B.A. from Tufts College in 1866. His engineering studies at Rensselaer Polytechnic Institute were cut short when he had to manage the family farm after his father's death. He soon took more chemistry courses at Cornell University and in 1875 was made an instructor. In 1877 he began graduate studies at the University of Göttingen under Hans Hübner (Ph.D., 1879).

Babcock is best known for his test for butterfat in milk, introduced in 1890. With the bacteriologist Harry L. Russell, he developed the process for cold curing of cheese in 1900. His most important contribution arose from his skepticism regarding the biological equivalency of chemically similar feeds from different crops.

BABINET, JACQUES (*b. Lusignan, France, 1794; d. Paris, France, 1872*), physics, meteorology.

Babinet entered the École Polytechnique in 1812. After graduation he held professorships at Fontenay-le-Comte and Poitiers. In 1820 he became professor of physics at the Collège Louis-le-Grande in Paris. He was elected a member of the physics section of the Academy of Sciences in 1840 and a year later was appointed Librarian at the Bureau of Longitudes.

He did important work in the theory of diffraction, meteorological optics, and optical instrumentation. He was an early proponent of the wave theory of light. He formulated the concept known today as Babinet's principle. Babinet constructed a portable goniometer and invented the Babinet compensator.

BABINGTON, CHARLES CARDALE (*b. Ludlow, England, 1808; d. Cambridge, England, 1895*), botany.

Graduated from St. John's College, Cambridge (B.A., 1830; M.A., 1833), where he was influenced by J. S. Henslow, whom he later succeeded in the chair of botany (1861).

Babington's *Manual of British Botany* (1843) was considered to be his *magnum opus.* With the exception of Hooker's *British Flora,* it was the first complete guide to British plants arranged according to a natural system. His *British Rubi* (1869) described in impressive detail some forty-five species.

BABINGTON, WILLIAM (*b. Port Glenone, Antrim, Northern Ireland, 1756; d. London, England, 1833*), mineralogy, geology.

Received M.D. from Aberdeen University (1795); practiced medicine in London. Interest in mineralogy arose through purchase of collection of minerals.

Babington's study of minerals, *New System of Mineralogy* (1799), classified minerals by the Linnaean system, the main subdivisions being based on chemical composition. This constituted an advance on the Wernerian system, which was based principally on external characters. A founder of the Geological Society of London (1807).

BACCELLI, GUIDO (*b. Rome, Italy, 1830; d. Rome, 1916*), clinical medicine.

Graduated from Roman School of Medicine (1853). Director of Medical Clinic of Rome (1863–1916). Greatest achievement was founding of Policlinico Umberto I, a medical center in Rome (1906). One of first supporters of oxygen therapy (1870). However, his major merit was "to have opened the way of the veins to the heroic drugs." In 1890, first injected quinine chlorhydrate into a vein of a woman, thereby saving her from death by pernicious malaria. In 1906 announced positive results from intravenous injection of strophantine in the treatment of heart failure.

BACH, ALEKSEI NIKOLAEVICH (*b. Zolotonosha [now in Ukrainian S.S.R.], Russia, 1857; d. Moscow, U.S.S.R., 1946*), biochemistry, physical chemistry.

Studied chemistry at Kiev University. Forced by his politics to leave Russia in 1885, performed chemical investigations in laboratories in Paris and Switzerland, returning to Russia in 1917. Under his directorship, the L. Y. Karpov Institute of Physics and Chemistry developed into a major scientific center.

Most important works are studies of carbon assimilation by plants and of slow oxidation and biological oxidation. Developed general theory of oxidation. His theory of slow oxidation was later named the Bach-Engler peroxide theory of oxidation. Subsequently extended the peroxide theory to processes of biological oxidation. His methods of industrial biochemistry are widely used.

BACHE, ALEXANDER DALLAS (*b. Philadelphia, Pa., 1806); d. Newport, R.I., 1867*), physics.

Graduated from West Point (1825); taught at University of Pennsylvania (1827–36, 1842–43); organized Girard College (1836) and was responsible for its observatory, first of its kind in the U.S. Director of Coast Survey (1843–67) and head of Office of Weights and Measures. His investigation of the explosion of steam boilers for the federal government (1836) was one of the first deliberate uses of science by government for solution of a practical problem. With Joseph Henry, established many of the patterns of interaction of science and the federal government. Formation of the National Academy of Sciences (1863), with Bache as its first president, was the concrete culmination of his influence.

BACHELARD, GASTON (*b. Bar-sur-Aube, France, 1884; d. Paris, France, 1962*), philosophy of science, epistemology.

Became philosopher late in life; previously taught physics and chemistry.

Knowledge of physics enabled him to determine the epistemological change brought about by modern science. His *Essai sur la connaissance approchée* (1928) penetrated to the heart of the new mathematical physics. *Étude sur l'évolution d'un problème de physique* (1928) was designed to show how thermodynamics was both established by and liberated from its early, very poor intuitions. *La formation de l'esprit scientifique* (1938) examines mental resistances and prejudices anthropologically and methodologically. From his thoughts on alchemy came his celebrated analyses of the classical four elements and of dreams, space, time, and imagination.

BACHELIER, LOUIS (*b. Le Havre, France, 1870; d. Saint-Servan-sur Mer, Ille-et-Villaine, France, 1946*), mathematics.

Under the name "théorie de la spéculation" introduced continuity into problems of probability. First to examine the stochastic methods of the Markovian type, on which A. N. Kolmogorov's theory is based. His papers and books on probability contributed to the diffusion of probabilistic thought. His studies were not of scientific importance, however.

BACHET DE MÉZIRIAC, CLAUDE-GASPAR (*b. Bourg-en-Bresse, France, 1581; d. Bourg-en-Bresse, 1638*), mathematics.

Early education with Jesuits, later at Padua. Author, poet, and mythologist. Most important for contributions to the theory of numbers and to the field of mathematical recreations, in which he was one of the earliest pioneers. The two mathematical works for which he is remembered are his first edition of the Greek text of Diophantus of Alexandria's *Arithmetica*, accompanied by prolix commentary in Latin (1621), and his *Problemes plaisans et delectables qui se font par les nombres* (1612).

BACHMANN, AUGUSTUS QUIRINUS, also known as **Augustus Quirinus Rivinus** (*b. Leipzig, Germany, 1652; d. Leipzig, 1723*), botany.

Studied at Leipzig; received degree from University of Helmstedt (1676). Practiced medicine in Leipzig; taught at University of Leipzig (1677–1723).

Main scientific interest was botanical taxonomy. Published atlases of tables of plants with irregular flowers of one, four, and five petals. He anticipated Tournefort and Linnaeus in devising an artificial system of plant classification. Attempt to base classification on a single part of a plant led to controversy with the famous English naturalist John Ray, who held the sound view that the whole plant must be considered. Since he emphasized the need for short plant names of no more than two words, Rivinus was a pioneer of modern binomial nomenclature.

BACHMANN, PAUL GUSTAV HEINRICH (*b. Berlin, Germany, 1837; d. Weimar, Germany, 1920*), mathematics.

Studied at Göttingen and Breslau; received doctorate at Berlin (1862). Taught at Breslau and Münster.

Main project was a complete survey of the state of number theory, *Zahlentheorie. Versuch einer Gesamtdarstellung dieser Wissenschaft in ihren Hauptteilen* (1892–1923). It includes not only a review of known results but also an evaluation of the various methods of proof and approach, labors for which his close association with Dirichlet, Kummer, Dedekind, and Hensel made him ideally suited.

BACK, ERNST E. A. (*b. Freiburg im Breisgau, Germany, 1881; d. Munich, Germany, 1959*), physics.

Received doctorate at Tübingen (1913); stayed to continue scientific research as assistant in Friedrich Paschen's institute.

Most important technical innovations were in the design and fabrication of the light source of spectrographs. Although Back was able to rule out a number of apparent exceptions to Preston's rule, it was Paschen who saw the solution to the difficulty: in sufficiently strong magnetic fields the several splitting patterns characteristic of the different types of series are transformed into the normal triplet (the Paschen-Back effect, 1912). During the following years this effect was regarded by leading theorists both as one of the most important problems in atomic physics and as one of the most promising sources of information on the subject of atomic structure.

BACKLUND, JÖNS OSKAR (*b. Långhem, Sweden, 1846; d. Pulkovo, Russia, 1916*), astronomy.

Received Ph.D. at Uppsala (1875); worked at Dorpat and Pulkovo observatories (director, 1895–1916).

The main object of his research was comet 1786 I, known as Encke's comet or (in the U.S.S.R.) comet Encke-Backlund. Despite its forty-eight observed returns to perihelion between 1786 and 1967, this comet still puzzles astronomers: Backlund was the first to show that the long-term acceleration in its motion is subject to irregular changes, attributable to nongravitational forces.

BACON, FRANCIS (*b. London, England, 1561; d. London, 1626*), philosophy of science.

Educated at Trinity College, Cambridge. Spent life in court circles, politics, and law.

Knighted in 1603; lord chancellor, 1618–21; viscount St. Albans, 1621. Bacon's place in the history of science rests chiefly upon his natural philosophy, his philosophy of scientific method, his projects for the practical organization of science, and the influence of all these upon the science of the later seventeenth century. During and immediately following his lifetime his principal publications in these areas were *The Advancement of Learning* (1605), expanded and latinized as *De augmentis scientiarum* (1623); *De sapientia veterum* (1609); *Novum organum* (1620); and *Sylva sylvarum* and *New Atlantis* (1627).

Bacon's closest associations with contemporary science were with atomism and with the Renaissance tradition of natural magic. In *De augmentis scientiarum,* which is concerned primarily with the classification of philosophy and the sciences, Bacon develops his influential view of the relation between science and theology. According to Bacon's method, the aim of scientific investigation is practical application of the understanding of nature to the improvement of man's condition. Thus with proper organization and financial support, it should be possible to complete the edifice of science in a few years and to gather all the practical fruit that it promised for the good of men. Throughout his life he used his status and influence in a succession of frustrated attempts to obtain the Crown's support for this enterprise. His unfinished account of the ideal scientific society was published posthumously in *New Atlantis,* which ranks among the best-known and most delightful Utopian writings.

BACON, ROGER (*b. England, ca. 1219; d. ca. 1292*), natural philosophy, optics, calendar reform.

Virtually all biographical information on Bacon comes from his own writings. He took his M.A. at either Oxford or Paris (probably about 1240) and lectured at Paris. Most of the content of his writings was derived from Latin translations of Greek and Arabic authors. When he learned Greek is not certain, but his Greek grammar may be placed after 1267. (He also wrote a Hebrew grammar to help in the understanding of Scripture.) At Oxford (about 1247) he underwent a radical intellectual change as a result of his new friendship with Robert Grosseteste, whose influence is evident. He entered the Franciscan order (*ca.* 1257), and after twenty years was condemned and imprisoned by the order for an undetermined period and obscure reasons. He probably composed his three famous works, *Opus maius* (including *De speciebus et virtutibus agentium* and *De scientia perspectiva* as supplements),

Opus minus, and *Opus tertium,* to comply with a mandate for a copy of his philosophical writings from Pope Clement IV (1266). These works (the second and third are résumés, corrections, and additions to the first) contain the essence of his conception of natural philosophy and consequential proposals for educational reform. He identified four chief obstacles to the grasping of truth: frail and unsuitable authority, long custom, uninstructed popular opinion, and the concealment of one's own ignorance in a display of apparent wisdom. The one wisdom of the Holy Scriptures had to be developed by reason as confirmed by experience. The two kinds of experience are obtained through interior mystical inspiration and through the exterior senses, aided by instruments and made precise by mathematics. The necessary sciences were languages, mathematics, optics, *scientia experimentalis,* and alchemy, followed by metaphysics and moral philosophy.

His writings are not as unusual as legend suggests; they have the virtues rather than the vices of Scholasticism. His mathematics included, on the one hand, astronomy and astrology, and on the other a geometrical theory of physical causation that came straight from Grosseteste and provided the efficient cause of every occurrence in the universe.

In thus trying to reduce different phenomena to the same terms, Bacon exhibited sound physical insight (his technical performance was weak). For him optics was the fundamental physical science and his most effective work was in that field. Apparently original is his classification of the properties of convex and concave spherical surfaces with the eye in various relationships to the refracting media. He made an important contribution to the history of physiological optics in the West by his exposition of Ibn al-Haytham's account of the eye as an image-forming device. There he introduced a new concept of laws of nature, referring to the "laws of reflection and refraction" as *leges communes nature;* elsewhere he discusses a *lex nature universalis.* Universal nature constituted from these common laws was superimposed on the system of particular natures making up the Aristotelian universe—not yet the seventeenth-century concept but perhaps a step toward it.

His *scientia experimentalis* embraces "natural magic" as well as "experience." It certifies the conclusions of deductive reasoning and provides knowledge that is undiscoverable by deduction. The *scientia* would also expose the frauds of magicians by revealing the natural causes of effects.

Bacon's mathematics and astronomy were almost wholly derivative, and he was not always a good judge of competence. His deep and novel insight into the role of mathematics in science is to the modern mind almost platitudinous; he argued for the usefulness of mathematics in almost every academic realm. Apart from mathematically trivial results in practical contexts, his works apparently contain not a single proof, not a single theorem; and we must take on trust the story of the difficult problems he devised for the young Paris masters. Almost everything he wrote under the title of mathematics is best regarded as being at a metaphysical level. His philosophy of science was inherently empiricist.

His geography was a compilation of works on descriptive geography. In one case he argued as cogently from available longitudes and latitudes as from classical authors, for example, his statement in the *Opus maius* of the possibility of voyaging from Spain to India. Although Columbus may not have read this passage until after his first voyage, he quoted it.

Bacon believed in astrology, holding that the stars did not necessarily subjugate the human will but that it was possible to predict human behavior statistically. His skepticism was useful in his writings on calendar reform, where he shows as much insight as anyone before Regiomontanus. The data were not his own. He first asserted that the length of the Julian year (365¼ days) was in excess by about one day in 130 years, and seems finally to have recommended the removal of one day in 125 years. (The correct figure for his time was one day in a little over 129 years.) He was five centuries ahead of English legislation.

Bacon continued to garner admirers after his death, largely for his calendar reform and his optics. His accounts of alchemy and natural magic brought him more dubious fame, varying with popular prejudices.

BADĪ AL-ZAMĀN AL-JAZARĪ. *See* **al-Jazarī.**

BAEKELAND, LEO HENDRIK (*b. Ghent, Belgium, 1863; d. Beacon, N.Y., 1944*), chemistry.
Graduated from University of Ghent (doctorate, 1884), staying on to teach until 1889, when he settled in the U.S. As head of his own company, manufactured photographic "gaslight paper."
Developed the manufacture of condensation products from phenol and formaldehyde. He distinguished three stages of reaction, with a soluble intermediate product. Manufacture of Bakelite resins started in 1907.

BAER, KARL ERNST VON (*b. Piep, near Jerwen, Estonia, 1792; d. Dorpat, Estonia [now Tartu, Estonian S.S.R.], 1876*), biology, anthropology, geography.
Received M.D. at Dorpat (1814) under Karl Friedrich Burdach. Continued studies in Berlin and Vienna; at Würzburg came under strong influence of Ignaz Döllinger. Taught at Königsberg (1817–34), making most of his contributions to embryology while there. Moved to Academy in St. Petersburg (1834–62).
Known for his discovery of the mammalian egg and for the treatise *Ueber die Entwickelungsgeschichte der Thiere, Beobachtung und Reflexion* (1828, 1837), which provided a basis for systematic study of animal development. Made a number of specific discoveries in vertebrate morphogenesis relating to the development of particular organs or organ systems. First to discover and describe the notochord. Among the first to recognize that the neural folds represent the rudiment of the central nervous system and that they form a tube. First to describe and name the five primary brain vesicles. Made considerable advances in the understanding of the development and function of the extraembryonic membranes in the chick and the mammal. Responsible for introduction of the term "spermatozoa." Baer's greatest contributions to embryology were of far wider general significance. In 1826 he discovered the egg of the mammal in the ovary, bringing to completion a search begun at least as early as the seventeenth century. He concluded that "every animal which springs from the coition of male and female is developed from an ovum, and none from a simple formative liquid,"

a unifying doctrine whose importance cannot be overemphasized. Equally important were Baer's careful descriptions and thoughtful interpretations of the whole course of vertebrate development. Described the development of vertebrates from conception to hatching or birth. Baer observed the formation of the germ layers and described the way in which they formed various organs by tubulation. He emphasized that development is epigenetic, that it proceeds from the apparently homogeneous to the strikingly heterogeneous, from the general to the special. Also made a number of important discoveries in natural history and geology. Classified man into six categories according to degree of primitiveness, and established a craniological collection at the Academy.

BAEYER, ADOLF JOHANN FRIEDRICH WILHELM VON (*b. Berlin, Germany, 1835; d. Starnberg, Oberbayern, Germany, 1917*), chemistry.
Educated at Heidelberg, Ghent, and Berlin (doctorate, 1858). Taught at Berlin, Strasbourg, and Munich.
Received Nobel Prize (1905) for work on dyes and hydroaromatic compounds. Best-known research, on indigo, was begun in 1865 and followed up earlier work on phthalein dyes. In 1870 produced indigo by treatment of isatin with phosphorous trichloride, followed by reduction. Finally in 1883 he showed the exact structural formula. Did extensive research on structure of benzene and on oxonium compounds. Much of his research extended Kekulé's work on tetravalency of carbon; other work grew from Liebig's work on uric acid derivatives. Stimulated the chemical dye industry through his work on indigo, and laid the foundation for subsequent work in biochemistry through his investigation of complex ring structures.

AL-BAGHDĀDĪ, ABŪ MANṢŪR ʿABD AL-QĀHIR IBN ṬĀHIR IBN MUḤAMMAD IBN ʿABDALLAH, AL-TAMĪMĪ, AL-SHAFIʿĪ (*b. Baghdad; d. 1037*), arithmetic.
Wrote two works on arithmetic, one being a small book on mensuration; the second, *al-Takmila fiʾl-ḥisāb*, presents seven systems of reckoning as then known: (1) Indian arithmetic of integers. (2) Indian arithmetic of fractions. (3) The sexagesimal scale, in the Indian fashion. (4) Finger reckoning, adding to the Indian system such Greek topics as summation of finite series. (5) Arithmetic of irrational numbers. (6) Properties of numbers. (7) Business arithmetic. Also known for theological works.

BAGLIVI, GEORGIUS (*b. Republic of Dubrovnik [now a part of Yugoslavia], 1668; d. Rome, Italy, 1707*), biology.
Educated at Jesuit College of Dubrovnik, at Naples, and probably received M.D. at Salerno (1688). Physician in many Italian hospitals before settling in Bologna to work with Malpighi (1691–94). Appointed pope's physician (1695); taught at the Sapienza in Rome (from 1696). His book, *De praxi medica* (1696), gave a lucid program of future medicine, attacked medico-philosophical systems, and defended Hippocratic principles of sound clinical observation.

BAIER, JOHANN JACOB (*b. Jena, Germany, 1677; d. Altdorf, Bavaria, 1735*), medicine, geology, paleontology.
Received M.A., Ph.D., and M.D. from University of Jena (1700). Practiced medicine in Nuremberg; taught at University of Altdorf in Nuremberg (1704–35).

Scientific fame rests on his studies of minerals and fossils. His *Oryctographia norica* (1708) laid the foundations for the investigation of Jurassic fauna and of scientific paleontology in general, preparing the ground for the next generation to determine historically the geological structure of mountains and to transform oryctography into geology.

BAILAK AL-QABAJAQĪ. *See* **Baylak al-Qibjāqī.**

BAILEY, EDWARD BATTERSBY (*b. Marden, England, 1881; d. London, England, 1965*), geology.

Graduated from Clare College, Cambridge (1902). Worked for Geological Survey of Great Britain (in Scotland), 1902–29 and 1937–45; taught at Glasgow University, 1929–37.

Made notable contributions to tectonics and metamorphism, to igneous and general geology, and to the history of the development of geological ideas. From 1910 introduced new or modified stratigraphical groupings and reinterpreted structure in terms of great recumbent folds and contemporaneous slides (fold faults). Main contributions to Scottish igneous geology stemmed from work with C. T. Clough and H. B. Maufe. Bailey's compilation of the memoir on the Tertiary volcanic complex of Mull (1924), and its accompanying intricate map, was recognized as a major scientific achievement. He also reassessed the intrusion tectonics of the Arran granite (1926) and of the volcanic complex of Rhum (1945), both of the Tertiary period.

BAILEY, LIBERTY HYDE, JR. (*b. South Haven Township, Mich., 1858; d. Ithaca, N.Y., 1954*), botany, horticulture, agriculture.

Received B.S. (1882) and M.S. (1886) from Michigan State (Agricultural) College. Occupied first chair of practical and experimental horticulture in America (Cornell, 1888–1903); in 1903 became director of College of Agriculture. In 1904 made first dean and director of experiment station of New York State College of Agriculture. Wrote over sixty books, hundreds of papers, and founded horticultural and botanical societies and journals.

A recognized authority on *Carex, Rubus, Cucurbita,* the palms, *Vitis,* and certain of the cultivated groups, notably *Brassica.* Most remembered, however, for his great encyclopedias and important manuals of horticulture and agriculture; his summaries of progress; his texts; his books on principles of cultivation, harvesting, plant breeding, and evolution; his *Hortus;* his beautiful and informative "garden" books; and his so-called background books.

BAILEY, LORING WOART (*b. West Point, N.Y., 1839; d. Fredericton, Canada, 1925*), geology.

Received B.A. (1859) and M.S. (1861) from Harvard. Taught at University of New Brunswick (1861–1907).

With George F. Matthew and Charles F. Hartt, Bailey was first to find fossils of Cambrian age in New Brunswick, thus establishing the base for deciphering chronostratigraphic interrelationships of a large area. Provided an extensive foundation for further work in New Brunswick and contributed to understanding of geology of neighboring New England, especially Maine. His *Report on the Mines and Minerals of New Brunswick* (1864) and *Observations on the Geology of Southern New Brunswick* (1865) are classics of regional geology.

BAILEY, SOLON IRVING (*b. Lisbon, N.H., 1854; d. Norwell, Mass., 1931*), astronomy, meteorology.

Received M.A. from Boston University (1884) and M.A. from Harvard (1888). Associated with Harvard Observatory for forty-four years; established Harvard's Boyden station near Arequipa, Peru; published data accumulated from meteorological stations in Peru and Chile in "Peruvian Meteorology" (1889–1930). Published *History and Work of the Harvard Observatory, 1839–1927* (1931).

Pioneered in studies in the southern hemisphere at a time when there were no large telescopes south of the equator. Main contributions to astronomy were studies of variable stars in globular clusters and his long-exposure photographs, which not only helped to elucidate the structure of our galaxy but also showed the value of photography in detecting extragalactic objects.

BAILLIE, MATTHEW (*b. Shots Manse, Lanarkshire, Scotland, 1761; d. Duntisbourne, Gloucestershire, England, 1823*), medicine.

Studied at Glasgow University and Oxford (M.D., 1789). Succeeded his uncle, William Hunter (1718–1783), as master of Windmill Street School of Anatomy. By 1800 had largest medical practice in London.

His *Morbid Anatomy of Some of the Most Important Parts of the Human Body* (1795) was the first English text on pathology, and the first systematic study in any language. Baillie was the first to take the organs of the body serially and set forth the diverse morbid conditions of each.

BAILLOU, GUILLAUME DE, also known as **Baillon** and **Ballonius** (*b. Paris, France, ca. 1538; d. Paris, 1616*), medicine.

Became physician in 1570 and dean of the Faculty of Medicine in 1580. During the many epidemics in Paris (1570–79), Baillou developed the idea of the ephemerides. He was thus the first Occidental epidemiologist since Hippocrates. Left excellent descriptions of the plague (and possibly of typhoid fever); of measles, which he distinguished from variola; and of diphtheria, whose choking false membranes he identified. Baillou is also credited with the first mention of adhesive pericarditis complicated by edema, and of whooping cough. Brought rheumatism into nosology.

BAILLY, JEAN-SYLVAIN (*b. Paris, France, 1736; d. Paris, 1793*), astronomy.

Studied mathematics with Montcarville of the Collège Royal. Bailly approached the problem of inequalities in the motions of the four known satellites of Jupiter with Clairaut's lunar theory in mind. He was the first to attempt to achieve better tables of the motions theoretically, by treating each satellite in turn as the third body in a three-body problem. His success was not complete, but he did demonstrate that the problem was amenable to solution by Newtonian principles. One of his best scientific papers, his 1771 memoir on the inequalities of the light of Jupiter's satellites, suggested a standard observing method to reduce instrument and observer errors. His four-volume history of astronomy (1775–82) represents his most lasting achievement. Established his own observatory in the Louvre, where he undertook astronomical research.

BAILY, FRANCIS (*b. Newbery, Berkshire, England, 1774; d. London, England, 1844*), astronomy, metrology.

After careers as explorer and stockbroker, during which he published in both areas, he devoted his full time to astronomy. A founder of the Astronomical Society of London.

Remembered today for "Baily's beads," a transient phenomenon often seen at the beginning and end of totality in a solar eclipse, when the edge of the moon is close to inner tangency and a thin crescent of sunlight shines between mountains on the moon's limb. Also did important work on methods of determining latitude and time by the stars and on redetermining the density of the earth.

BAIN, ALEXANDER (*b. Aberdeen, Scotland, 1818; d. Aberdeen, 1903*), philosophy, psychology.

Received M.A. (1840) at Marischal College, Aberdeen, staying for five years to teach mental and moral philosophy. In 1860 was elected to chair of logic at newly formed Aberdeen University. The influence of John Stuart Mill, Comte, and Whewell are apparent in his many writings.

Two powerful and complementary ideas of Bain's philosophy concerned the unity of the mind and the active power of the mind. Bain's study of the nervous system gave him a way of correlating every mental process with some physiological process. Founded the philosophical journal *Mind* (1876).

BAIRD, SPENCER FULLERTON (*b. Reading, Pa., 1823; d. Woods Hole, Mass., 1887*), zoology, scientific administration.

Graduated from (B.A., 1840; M.A., 1843) and later taught at (1846–50) Dickinson College. Received training in zoology through self-study and informal instruction from established naturalists—Dana, Audubon, and Lawrence. Assistant to and eventually succeeded Joseph Henry, secretary of Smithsonian Institution (1850–87). Directed establishment of U.S. Fish Commission (1871).

Most notable scientific papers were taxonomic studies of birds and mammals, but also wrote on reptiles, amphibians, and fishes, usually in collaboration with Charles Girard. His scientific writings earned Baird his reputation as the leading vertebrate zoologist of mid-nineteenth-century America. Four works were especially significant: *Mammals* (1857) and *Birds* (1858) were comprehensive monographs based on American collections taken north of Mexico by fifteen governmental surveys and by numerous individual naturalists. "The Distribution and Migrations of North American Birds" revealed Baird's support of organic evolution—one of the major commentaries on Darwinian evolution produced by American naturalists during this era. His final major work, a three-volume study of land birds, *A History of North American Birds* (1874), presented the first comprehensive information on behavior of birds in Arctic breeding grounds.

BAIRE, RENÉ LOUIS (*b. Paris, France, 1874; d. Chambéry, France, 1932*), mathematics.

Studied at the École Normale Supérieure, doctorate, 1889. Taught at Montpellier, the Collège de France, and Dijon.

Baire's doctoral thesis, on the theory of functions of real variables, solved the general problem of the characteristic property of limit functions of continuous functions. His success greatly influenced the orientation of the French school of mathematics. Baire put an end to the privileged status of continuity and gave the field to aggregate-oriented considerations for the definition and study of functions. Moreover, the class of Baire's functions, according to the definition adopted by Charles de la Vallée Poussin, remains unattainable as far as the evolution of modes of expression is concerned.

AL-BAIRŪNĪ. *See* **al-Bīrūnī.**

IBN AL-BAIṬĀR. *See* **Ibn al-Bayṭār.**

IBN BĀJJA, ABŪ BAKR MUḤAMMAD IBN YAḤYĀ IBN AL-ṢĀʾIGH, also known as **Avempace** or **Avenpace** (*b. Saragossa, Spain, end of the 11th century; d. Fez, Morocco, 1138/1139*), philosophy.

Often described as the earliest Arabic Aristotelian in Spain. His *Tadbīr al-mutawaḥḥid* ("The Regimen of the Solitary") deals with the various categories of men; with various regimens; and with the position that the philosopher should adopt in relation to the imperfect communities in which he has to live. Ibn Bājja's dynamics may be regarded as an attempt to unify the Aristotelian theory of movement by replacing the multiform concept of cause with the notion of force. The most influential of Ibn Bājja's physical theories was the one sometimes described as the doctrine concerning the original time of motion; this theory, which was known in Latin Europe through the exposition of Ibn Rushd, who refuted it, influenced Thomas Aquinas, Duns Scotus, and other Schoolmen.

BAKER, HENRY (*b. London, England, 1698; d. London, 1774*), microscopy.

Did valuable work on teaching of deaf and dumb, but especially noted for popularization of the use of the microscope and for his contribution to the study of crystals.

His work with the deaf attracted the interest of Daniel Defoe, one of whose early novels, *The Life and Adventures of Duncan Campbell* (1720), was about a deaf conjurer. Defoe and Baker established the *Universal Spectator and Weekly Journal* (1728). Microscopical examinations of water creatures and fossils were the subject of a majority of his papers and were included in his books on microscopy. *The Microscope Made Easy* appeared in 1742, and *Employment for the Microscope* in 1753. In 1743 he published *An Attempt Towards a Natural History of the Polype*. His most important scientific achievements were the observation under the microscope of crystal morphology and his account of an examination of twenty-six bead microscopes bequeathed to the Royal Society by Antony van Leeuwenhoek. Made bequest to Royal Society to establish Bakerian Lecture.

BAKER, JOHN GILBERT (*b. Guisborough, England, 1834; d. Kew, England, 1920*), botany.

Studied natural history at Friends' School at Bootham, York.

Helped create Botanical Exchange Club of the Thirsk Natural History Society, later moving the Club to London. Staff member of the herbarium at the Royal Botanic Gardens, Kew; his very able work completing Hooker's *Synopsis Filicum* earned Baker wide recognition as an expert on vascular cryptogams. Published monographic accounts of plant families and genera; made substantial contributions to *Flora of Tropical Africa, Flora Capensis,* and *Flora of British India.* Lectured on botany at London Hospital Medical School and at Chelsea Physic Garden. One of the great English taxonomists and a pioneer investigator in plant ecology.

BAKEWELL, ROBERT (*b. England, 1768; d. Hampstead, England, 1843*), geology.

Bakewell's *Introduction to Geology* (1813) was widely read and appreciated because it used examples and illustrations taken from the English countryside. Found evidence in rocks for geological revolutions of great magnitude with quiet intervals lasting tens of thousands of years.

BAKH, ALEKSEI NIKOLAEVICH. *See* **Bach, Aleksei Nikolaevich.**

AL-BAKRĪ, ABŪ ʿUBAYD ʿABDALLĀH IBN ʿABD AL-ʿAZĪZ IBN MUḤAMMAD (*b. ca. 1010; d. 1094*), geography.

Al-Bakrī was a Hispano-Arabic geographer who studied in Córdoba with historian Ibn Ḥayyān (*d.* 1075) and geographer al-ʿUdhrī (*d.* 1085). His main scientific works are (1) *Muʿjam mā istaʿjam,* a geographical collection of place names that are mainly Arabian; (2) *Kitāb al-masālik waʾl-mamālik,* a description of land and sea routes written to facilitate travel, also including historical and social data; (3) *Aʿyān al-nabāt* or *Kitāb al-nabāt,* about simple medicines.

BALANDIN, ALEKSEY ALEKSANDROVICH (*b. Yeniseysk, Siberia, Russia, 1898; d. Moscow, U.S.S.R., 1967*), chemistry.

Graduated from Moscow University (1923); professor of chemistry from 1934.

Founder of an important school of catalytic chemistry. His universal catalysis theory is known as the universal "multiplet" theory of catalysis. On the basis of the multiplet theory, Balandin proposed a classification of the organic catalytic reactions that reflected the positions of the atoms in the reacting molecule on the catalyst surface in relation to the active center. Introduced a number of basic concepts and equations into chemical kinetics.

BALARD, ANTOINE JÉROME (*b. Montpellier, France, 1802; d. Paris, France, 1876*), chemistry.

Studied at the École de Pharmacie under Jacques Étienne Bérard; degree in pharmacy (1826). He succeeded Anglada at Montpellier (1834), Thénard at the Sorbonne (1842), and Pelouze at the Collège de France (1851).

About 1825 he made his discovery of the element bromine. The discovery, a by-product of his more general chemical investigations of the sea and its life forms, made manifest the most striking "family" of elements—the halogens—in which bromine possessed an atomic weight that was approximately the arithmetic mean between those of chlorine and iodine. Also devoted research to the inexpensive extraction of salts from the sea, the discovery of oxamic acid from the decomposition by heat of ammonium hydrogen oxalate, and the study and naming of amyl alcohol. Taught Pasteur and Berthelot.

BALBIANI, EDOUARD-GÉRARD (*b. Port-au-Prince, Haiti, 1823; d. Meudon, France, 1899*), biology.

Studied in Paris, attracted to natural sciences by teaching of de Blainville at the Muséum National d'Histoire Naturelle. Received M.D. in 1854.

Early research on protozoa. Discovered sexual reproduction in the ciliata. While studying binary fission of infusoria, Balbiani set forth its laws (1861). Performed microsurgical experiments that enabled him to specify the role of the nucleus. Introduced the technique and the term "merotomy." Researched the formation of the sexual organs of the *Chironomus;* investigated the reproduction of aphids; worked on pebrine, a disease of the silkworm. Known eponymously through his research on cytoplasmic inclusions (the Balbiani vesicle). Founded *Archives d'anatomie microscopique,* and the Société de Micrographie.

BALBUS (BALBUS MENSOR [?]) (*fl. ca.* A.D. *100*), surveying, mathematics.

Very little is known of Balbus' life.

His only authenticated work, "Balbi ad Celsum expositio et ratio omnium formarum," is a geometric manual for surveyors, referring back to works of Hero of Alexandria. Other works of uncertain origin have been attributed to him, including a list of cities and works on fractions and geometry.

BALDI, BERNARDINO (*b. Urbino, Italy, 1553; d. Urbino, 1617*), mechanics.

Studied at Urbino and Padua. Made his scientific contributions while abbot of Guastalla (1585–1609) and historian and biographer to the duke of Urbino (1609–17).

Wrote biographies of some 200 mathematicians (1558–89). Principal contribution to physics was a commentary on the pseudo-Aristotelian *Questions of Mechanics* (1621), one of the most important works of its kind to appear up to that time. Especially significant for its development and application of the concept of centers of gravity, particularly with regard to stable and unstable equilibrium. Probably drew his chief ideas from manuscripts of Leonardo da Vinci. In 1589 published translation of Hero's *Automata,* prefaced by a history of mechanics. Final scientific contribution was a translation of Hero's *Belopoeica* into Latin, accompanied by the Greek text and by Baldi's Latin *Life of Hero* (1616).

BALFOUR, FRANCIS MAITLAND (*b. Edinburgh, Scotland, 1851; d. near Courmayeur, Switzerland, 1882*), embryology.

Educated at Harrow and Trinity College, Cambridge, teaching at the latter (1873–82). In 1882, Cambridge created a lifetime professorship of animal morphology for him; but before the year was out, Balfour died scaling an unconquered peak in the Alps.

In 1878 he completed his outstanding monograph on elasmobranch development. In it, Balfour included a detailed and superb description of the development of the excretory system. Within three years of this he finished his two-volume *Treatise on Comparative Embryology* (1880–81), the first successful attempt at a complete comparative embryology text; one finds important references to it for decades thereafter. Not only did Balfour survey developments peculiar to each phylum and give a comparative survey of the embryology of each organ system, but he also included introductory chapters on gamete formation, fertilization, and early cleavage, additions that demonstrated his keen interest in the most recent advances in cytology.

BALFOUR, ISAAC BAYLEY (*b. Edinburgh, Scotland, 1853; d. Haslemere, England, 1922*), botany.

Son of botanist John Hutton Balfour (1808–84). Graduated from Edinburgh (B.S., 1873; M.B., 1877). Studied further at Würzburg and Strasbourg. Taught at Glasgow (1879–84) and Oxford (1884–87).

From 1888 was professor of botany, queen's botanist in Scotland, and Regius keeper of the Royal Botanic Garden. Edinburgh became an exemplar of horticultural practice. Gained distinction in several fields of activity: taxonomy, teaching, horticulture, and administration. Concentrated on *Rhododendron* and *Primula;* taxonomic papers appeared in *Notes From the Royal Botanic Garden, Edinburgh,* which he founded in 1900. Authority on vegetation of Himalayas and western China. Modernized teaching methods of three universities, and for a generation Edinburgh was the main center for teaching taxonomy.

BALFOUR, JOHN HUTTON (*b. Edinburgh, Scotland, 1808; d. Edinburgh, 1884*), botany.

Educated at St. Andrews, Paris, and Edinburgh (M.D., 1832).

Succeeded Sir William J. Hooker as professor of botany at Glasgow University (1841); elected to the chair of botany at Edinburgh (1845). Effected marked improvements in the botanic gardens at Edinburgh. Made extensive use of the microscope in his demonstrations and placed great emphasis on the value of botanical excursions. Textbooks include *Manual of Botany* (1849) and *Class Book of Botany* (1852). Botanico-religious books include *Phyto-Theology* (1851), *Plants of the Bible* (1857), and *Lessons from Bible Plants* (1870). Father of botanist Isaac Bayley Balfour (1853–1922).

BALIANI, GIOVANNI BATTISTA (*b. Genoa, Italy, 1582; d. Genoa, 1666*), physics.

Trained in law; spent most of life in public service. Scientific interests began when, as prefect of fortress at Savona (1611), he noted the equal speed of fall of cannon balls differing greatly in weight. Also devised an apparatus for cooking by frictional heat—an iron pot rotating on a concave iron base. Corresponded with Galileo concerning experimental determination of the weight of air, falling bodies, and the failure of a siphon that had been expected to carry water over a rise of about sixty feet. Speculated that terrestrial motion was possible cause of tides. In 1638 he published a short treatise on motions of heavy bodies, and in 1647 a treatise on the plague, suggesting a chemical explanation of its nature and its contagious character. Also anticipated the Malthusian law. His most important contribution, a discussion of elastic shock, seems to have gone unnoticed until recently.

AL-BALKHĪ. *See* **Abū Maᶜshar.**

BALLONIUS. *See* **Baillou, Guillaume.**

BALLOT, CHRISTOPH BUYS. *See* **Buys Ballot, Christoph.**

BALMER, JOHANN JAKOB (*b. Lausen, Basel-Land, Switzerland, 1825; d. Basel, Switzerland, 1898*), mathematics, physics.

Studied at Karlsruhe and Berlin; received doctorate at Basel (1849). Taught secondary school in Basel and at the university.

His field of professional interest was geometry. Spectral series, the topic of his most noted contribution, was an area in which he became involved late in life. The earliest attempts to establish relationships between the observed lines of an elementary spectrum were organized primarily within the theoretical context of a mechanical acoustical analogy. The essentially successful mathematical organization of the data began in 1885 with Balmer's presentation of the formula for the hydrogen series. This formula could be used to generate, with considerable accuracy, the wavelengths of the known characteristic spectral lines for hydrogen. Later investigators demonstrated that the formula, with a slightly altered constant, represented the whole series, including additional lines, with unusual accuracy. Balmer's work served as a model for other series formulas, especially the more generalized formulas of Rydberg, Kayser, and Runge.

BAMBERGER, EUGEN (*b. Berlin, Prussia, 1857; d. Ponte Tresa, Switzerland, 1932*), chemistry.

Studied at Breslau, and at Heidelberg with Bunsen. Completed degree at Berlin under A. W. Hoffmann, also working with Carl Liebermann. Assistant to Karl Rammelsberg at the Technische Hochschule of Berlin-Charlottenburg. In 1883 went to Munich as Baeyer's assistant; in 1893 accepted professorship at the Eidgenössische Technische Hochschule in Zurich; after 1905 did private research.

Investigated aromatic hydrocarbons and elucidated the structures of retene, chrysene, pyrene, and the glycoside picein. Bamberger believed that a formula similar to that of nitrosamines could be used to represent those isodiazo compounds which on hydrolysis yielded normal diazo compounds. In 1894 this view was sharply criticized by Arthur Hantzsch. The controversy continued for years, and only with the rejection of pentavalent nitrogen could a new formula for diazo compounds be proposed. Bamberger later reduced nitrobenzene to nitrosobenzene and phenylhydrozylamine with zinc dust in a neutral solution, but refused to patent the process.

BANACH, STEFAN (*b. Krakow, Poland, 1892; d. Lvov, Ukrainian S.S.R., 1945*), mathematics.

Doctorate, Institute of Technology, Lvov (1919), where he also taught. Cofounder *Studia mathematica.* His thesis, "Sur les opérations dans les ensembles abstraits et leur application aux équations intégrales" (1922), sometimes said to have marked the birth of functional analysis. Significant contribution to theory of orthogonal series; his theorem on locally meager sets is of lasting importance in general topology. Contribution to theory of measure and integration stimulated discovery of the Radon-Nikodým theorem. Introduced concept of normed linear spaces, proving three fundamental theorems: the extension of continuous linear functionals (Hahn-Banach theorem); bounded families of mappings (Banach-Steinhaus theorem); and continuous linear mappings of Banach spaces, which is both an indispensable tool and the basis of contemporary theory of more general linear spaces. It also provided the stimulus and starting point for other branches of functional analysis.

BANACHIEWICZ, THADDEUS (*b. Warsaw, Poland, 1882; d. Cracow, Poland, 1954*), astronomy.

Graduated from Warsaw University (1904) and Moscow University (1910). Taught at Dorpat (1915–18) and at Cracow (from 1918), also serving as director of Cracow Observatory.

His work concerned many important problems of astronomy, geodesy, geophysics, mathematics, mechanics, and numerical calculus. His "Über die Anwendbarkeit der Gyldén-Brendelschen Störungstheorie auf die Jupiternahen Planetoiden" (1906) gave a brilliant analysis of Gyldén-Brendel's theory, pointing out its illusiveness when applied to small planets in the vicinity of Jupiter. Published several papers on Gauss's equation and gave useful tables to facilitate its numerical solution. One of his great achievements in theoretical astronomy was the simplification of Olbers' method of determining parabolic orbits. These new methods used a much improved technique of computing, for which Banachiewicz had invented the cracovian calculus. Investigations into the theory of linear equations produced interesting applications of the cracovian method. Cracovian formulas led to a general solution that comprised the formulas of Turner and those of the dependency method. He also simplified the classical method of least squares.

Banachiewicz was not only a prominent theorist but also a gifted and assiduous observer. He organized gravimetric observations and first-order leveling in Poland. He was interested in photometric problems and illumination of planetary disks and of our sky. First in Poland to appreciate the value of radio signals for the time service and of phototubes in photometry. Founder and editor of *Acta astronomica, Ephemerides of Eclipsing Binaries,* and *Circulaire de l'Observatoire de Cracovie.*

BANCROFT, WILDER DWIGHT (*b. Middletown, R.I., 1867; d. Ithaca, N.Y., 1953*), chemistry.

Educated at Harvard (B.A., 1888), Strasbourg, Berlin, Leipzig (Ph.D., 1892), and Amsterdam.

One of the first physical chemists in the United States. Taught at Harvard (1893–95) and Cornell (1895–1937), trained graduate students, wrote a text entitled *The Phase Rule* (1897), and founded the *Journal of Physical Chemistry* (1896). Early investigations in electrochemistry. Studied heterogeneous equilibria, applying the phase rule to a great variety of systems. Early work on emulsions and the chemistry of photography led him into theories of dyeing, of the color of colloids, and of the colloidal phenomena associated with anesthesia, asthma, insanity, and drug addiction.

BANISTER, JOHN (*b. Twigworth, Gloucestershire, England, 1650; d. on Roanoke River, Va., 1692*), botany, entomology, malacology, anthropology.

Educated at Magdalen College, Oxford (B.A., 1671; M.A., 1674), before coming to Virginia in 1678.

Contributed to English horticulture, to Linnaeus' understanding of the American flora, to Martin Lister's iconography of mollusks, and to James Petiver's catalog of insects. Approximately 340 plant descriptions, specimens, and at least eighty plant drawings by Banister are behind the citations in John Ray's *Historia,* Robert Morison's *Historia,* and Leonard Plukenet's *Phytographia* and texts cited in Linnaeus' *Species plantarum* (1753). One of the first to describe the internal anatomy of a snail, and the first to explain the function of balancers of *Diptera.* Wrote the significant "Natural History of Virginia." His citations are a comprehensive bibliography of the natural history of the New World. Appointed to the committee to establish the College of William and Mary.

BANKS, JOSEPH (*b. London, England, 1743; d. Isleworth, England, 1820*), botany.

Received only formal training in botany at Christ Church, Oxford, then settled in London.

His chief reputation was based on his ability to organize and administer scientific affairs. He became a patron of science. His botanical specimens from Labrador and Newfoundland marked the beginning of the famous Banks Herbarium. Participated in the famous first voyage of Captain James Cook on the *Endeavour;* observed the transit of Venus (1769); explored the South Seas for the southern continent that was thought to exist. During the voyage over 800 previously unknown specimens were collected. This expedition, one of the first to carry a professional naturalist, made a reputation for Banks that would greatly aid him in his later career. His herbarium and library went to the British Museum. Dominated the British scientific community. Persuaded King George III to turn Kew Gardens, already noted for their beauty, into a botanical research center. Recognized that various plants could be adapted for cultivation in the broad reaches of the British Empire. Suggested growing of Chinese tea in India. Instrumental in importing merino sheep to improve the quality of English wool.

Best remembered for his long tenure as president of the Royal Society (1778–1820).

IBN AL-BANNĀ᾽ AL-MARRĀKUSHĪ, also known as **ABŪ'L-ʿABBĀS AḤMAD IBN MUḤAMMAD IBN ʿUTHMĀN AL-AZDĪ** (*b. Marrakesh, Morocco, 1256; d. Marrakesh [?], 1321*), mathematics.

Studied in Fez and Marrakesh under various teachers; taught arithmetic, algebra, geometry, and astronomy in Fez.

His most important scientific works are an introduction to Euclid; a treatise on areas; an algebra text dedicated to Abū ʿAlī al-Ḥasan al-Milyānī; a book about acronical risings and settings; and an almanac. The *Talkhīṣ* is a summary of the lost works of the twelfth- or thirteenth-century mathematician al-Ḥaṣṣār. The *Kitāb minhāj al-ṭālib li taʿdīl al-kawākib* is a very practical book for calculating astronomical ephemerals.

BANTI, GUIDO (*b. Montebicchieri, Italy, 1852; d. Florence, Italy, 1925*), pathology.

Most eminent Italian pathologist of the early twentieth century. Studied at Pisa and the Medical School of Florence, working and teaching at the latter (1877–1924). Wrote that clinical observation, anatomical report, and laboratory examination are three links in the same chain.

Studied heart enlargement (1886), the surgical treatment of hyperplastic gastritis (1898), and acute appendicitis (1905). Studied cancer cells (1890–93). Published first Italian textbook of bacteriological technique (1885). Contributed decisively to the advancement of the study of human pathology. Integrated bacteriology with the pathogenesis of infectious diseases. Made first observations of typhoid without intestinal localizations. Did remarkable experimental work on the destruction of bacteria in organisms (1888), contributing to development of Metchnikoff's views on the phagocytic defense of the organism against bacterial invasion. Illustrated several forms of endocarditis and described arteriosclerosis of the kidney (1895). Anticipated the modern view of nephrosis. Contributed to the understanding of aphasia (1886); confuted Pierre Marie's views on the motor type of aphasia. Especially remembered for his contributions to knowledge of pathology of the spleen and of leukemia. In 1913, he gave his nosographic definition of the leukemias and demonstrated the relationship of the spleen to hemolysis *in vivo*. From 1882 to 1914 studied the so-called primitive splenomegalies. He was able by 1894 to describe a new morbid entity, later known as Banti's disease.

Concluded that the leukemias are systematic diseases arising from hemopoietic structures, lymph glands, and bone marrow, and that they are the consequence of the limitless proliferative power of staminal blood cells which have lost their maturative capacity.

BANTING, FREDERICK GRANT (*b. Alliston, Ontario, 1891; d. near Musgrave Harbour, Newfoundland, 1941*), endocrinology.

Studied at the University of Toronto. Discovered (with Charles H. Best) the hormone insulin (1922) used as specific remedy for diabetes. At Western University in London, Ontario, and later at the University of Toronto, Banting investigated the effects of tying off the pancreas ducts of dogs and eventually taking extracts of the glands. With Best and E. C. Noble he employed a technique, which he had developed, for complete pancreatectomy in one operation. Of the extract of the degenerated gland 5 cc. were administered intravenously to the depancreatized dog. The blood sugar fell from 0.200 to 0.11 percent in two hours, and at the same time the clinical condition of the dog was much improved. The next phase of experimentation led toward the production of insulin (a name introduced by J. J. R. Macleod but suggested as early as 1910 by Sharpey-Schafer). His almost instantaneous worldwide fame was first attested by the "insulin rush," the descent on Toronto of diabetic patients. The Nobel Prize in physiology or medicine was awarded to Banting and Macleod in 1923. In 1930 the Banting Institute at Toronto was opened, and he spent the rest of his life as director of the Banting-Best Department of Medical Research. His later research was devoted largely to cancer, coronary thrombosis, and silicosis.

BANŪ MŪSĀ. Three brothers—**Muḥammad, Aḥmad, and al-Ḥasan**— always known under the one name, which means "sons of Mūsā" (*b. Baghdad, Iraq, beginning of ninth century; d. Baghdad. Muhammad, the eldest, d.* A.D. *873*), mathematics, astronomy.

Enrolled in the House of Wisdom; excelled in mathematics, astronomy, and mechanics, especially in geometry. Led the astronomical observations in Baghdad and organized a school of translators who rendered many Greek scientific manuscripts into Arabic. Two of the most famous translators were Ḥunayn ibn Isḥāq and Thābit ibn Qurra. Among the first Arabic scientists to study the Greek mathematical works and to lay the foundation of the Arabic school of mathematics. It is difficult to distinguish the role played by each of the brothers in their common works. Of the many works ascribed to the Banū Mūsā, the most important was the geometrical treatise called *Book on the Measurement of Plane and Spherical Figures.* The main purpose of the treatise was to demonstrate the most important part of the Greek method of determining area and volume. In the treatise the method was applied to the measurement of the circle and the sphere. In addition, three classical Greek problems were solved in the treatise: (1) a proof of "Hero's theorem"; (2) the determination of two mean proportionals; and (3) the trisection of the angle.

BÁRÁNY, ROBERT (*b. Vienna, Austria, 1876; d. Uppsala, Sweden, 1936*), oto-rhino-laryngology.

Graduated University of Vienna (1900). His main contribution was the clinical application of experimental data to humans, which led to the development of methods of investigating the human equilibrium system. Discovered laws governing rotatory reactions; defined subjective sensations of dizziness by means of such objective indications as definite eye movements and reactions of the body's muscular system. Most important discovery was the caloric nystagmus. He proved the connection between the organ of equilibrium and centers in the brain. His work made possible systematic interpretation of many aspects of vertigo and equilibrium disturbances. Investigated the relationship between equilibrium apparatus and the nervous system, thus creating the basis for an entirely new field, otoneurology. Awarded Nobel Prize (1915) for work on the vestibular apparatus.

BARANZANO, GIOVANNI ANTONIO (*b. Serravalle in Sesia, Vercelli, Italy, 1590; d. Montargis, France, 1622*), philosophy of astronomy.

Studied in Crevalcuore, Vercelli, Novara, and Milan. Took vows as Barnabite (1609). Taught philosophy in Annecy and later in Montargis.

Most important work was *Uranoscopia seu De coelo* (1617), in which he defended the Copernican system. Obliged by the Church to withdraw his assertions, he wrote a small tract in which he presented his excuses for having departed from Scriptures. Entitled *Nova de motu terrae Copernicolo iuxta Summi Pontificis mentem disputatio* (1618), it was appended to the *Uranoscopia.*

BARBA, ALVARO ALONSO (*b. Lepe, Huelva, Spain, 1569; d. Potosí[?], Peru [now Bolivia], ca. 1640*), metallurgy.

Sent by the Church to Peru, where he combined priestly duties with studies of mineral deposits, mining, and especially the treatment of silver ores by amalgamation. In 1617, perfected his new procedures for treating silver ore. His *El arte de los metales* (1640) was the first significant Spanish treatise on metals and the only seventeenth-century treatise that was largely original. One of the first writers to advocate what amounts to a laboratory control of an entire plant process as well as the computation of all costs. Described pre-Columbian smelting practice, and the use of the reverberatory furnace for smelting considerably before its widespread adoption.

BARBIER, JOSEPH-ÉMILE (*b. St.-Hilaire-Cotter, Pas-de-Calais, France, 1839; d. St.-Genest, Loire, France, 1889*), mathematics, astronomy.

Attended the École Normale Supérieure (agrégation, 1860). Assistant astronomer at the Paris Observatory under Le Verrier. Career interrupted by period of mental instability. The numerous reports published thereafter were irreproachably sound and often most original. Several of his early studies (1860–66) bear on the mathematical aspects of astronomy, construction of new thermometers, and other aspects of instrumental techniques; infinitesimal calculus and elementary and infinitesimal geometry; and the calculus of probabilities. His last works (1882–87) dealt almost entirely with mathematics and made several interesting contributions to geometry (the theory of polyhedra, the indicatrix of Dupin), integral calculus, and the theory of numbers.

BARBOUR, HENRY GRAY (*b. Hartford, Conn., 1885; d. New Haven, Conn., 1943*), physiology, pharmacology.

Educated at Trinity College, Hartford (B.A., 1906), and Johns Hopkins University (M.D., 1910).

His single most important scientific contribution was his delineation of the reactions of the body temperature-regulating center in the brain. Taught pharmacology at Yale University, McGill University, and the University of Louisville. From 1912 until the 1940's amassed more precise information on phenomena of temperature regulation, and became a leading authority on the mechanism of body temperature regulation and the effect of pyretic and antipyretic drugs. Showed that there are two temperature control centers: a heat loss center in the anterior hypothalamus and a heating center in the posterior hypothalamus. Control of water-shifting mechanisms, and of the concentration of the bodily fluids, was found to be associated with the anterior hypothalamic region.

BARCHUSEN, JOHANN CONRAD (*b. Horn, Germany, 1666; d. Utrecht, Netherlands, 1723*), chemistry, medicine.

Studied pharmacy in Berlin, Mainz, and Vienna.

In Utrecht, he taught chemistry (from 1694). Works reflect a development from practicing pharmacist to professor of a new academic discipline, chemistry. His first book was a pharmaceutical text, *Pharmacopoeus synopticus* (1690). His chemical writings are contained in three works: the *Pyrosophia* (1698), later revised and republished as *Elementa chemiae* (1718); the *Acroamata* (1703), a collection of his public lectures on chemistry; and the *Compendium ratiocinii chemici* (1712), a brief work that attempts to set out the principles of chemistry in the form of a geometry textbook—definitions, postulates, theorems, etc. *Historia medicinae* (1710) discusses historical themes and systems in medicine (revised as *De medicinae origine et progressu dissertationes*, 1723). The *Collecta medicinae practicae generalis* (1715) contains important clinical observations.

BARCLAY, JOHN (*b. Perthshire, Scotland, 1758; d. Edinburgh, Scotland, 1826*), anatomy.

Received M.D. at Edinburgh (1796).

He was the leading teacher of anatomy in Edinburgh at the beginning of the nineteenth century. First to confine his attention to anatomy and not to engage in practice. Made a number of valuable contributions to human and comparative anatomy. The Barclay Collection of Comparative Anatomy was bequeathed by him to the Royal College of Surgeons.

BARCROFT, JOSEPH (*b. Newry, Ireland, 1872; d. Cambridge, England, 1947*), physiology.

Received B.Sc. from University of London; graduated from King's College, Cambridge (1896), where he taught for nearly fifty years and did research in the Physiological Laboratory.

Measured effects of stimulating the submaxillary gland upon its metabolism, to throw light on its innervation. He was able to show that stimulation of the chorda tympani substantially increased the oxygen uptake and carbonic acid output. Next he turned to the pancreas, kidney, and heart, finding in each case a correlation between increased or decreased activity and the rate of metabolism of the organ. Returned to the study of the submaxillary gland, to take up the problem of how oxygen is transferred from blood to secretory cells. He decided to check the oxygen dissociation curves for himself, discovering that a variation in the salts present in a solution of hemoglobin alters the hemoglobin's dissociation curve for oxygen. His main focus of research shifted to further elucidation of the oxygen dissociation curve. In 1913 Barcroft summarized his researches in *The Respiratory Function of the Blood*, a landmark in respiratory physiology. During World War I, he investigated the effects of gas poisoning and methods for treating patients. After the war Barcroft extended his study of high-altitude physiology. Between 1925 and 1928 he developed several methods for observing changes in the size of the spleen, so that he could tell whether it adds a significant amount of blood to the circulation when it contracts. He found not only that it does, but that its contractions are correlated with increased demands for circulating blood, so that the organ serves as a regulator of blood volume. In 1928 Barcroft became involved in a full investigation of fetal respiration, which broadened into a study of embryonic circulatory and nervous development. Also wrote broadly on the nature of physiological processes, the most notable work being *Features in the Architecture of Physiological Function* (1934).

BARGER, GEORGE (*b. Manchester, England, 1878; d. Aeschi, Switzerland, 1939*), organic chemistry.

Studied at University College, London, and King's College, Cambridge (graduated 1901). First professor of chemistry in relation to medicine at Edinburgh (1919); regius professor of chemistry, Glasgow (1937). Worked on isolation, structure determination, synthesis, and pharmacological importance of alkaloids and of naturally occurring amino acid degradation products; isolated first active ergot alkaloid (1906); isolated and identified amino acid derivatives from ergot extracts; worked with Henry Hallett Dale on sympathomimetic amines.

BARKHAUSEN, HEINRICH GEORG (*b. Bremen, Germany, 1881; d. Dresden, Germany, 1956*), electronic engineering.

Attended universities of Munich, Berlin, and Göttingen. In 1911 the Technische Hochschule in Dresden appointed him to the first professorship anywhere in the communications branch of electrical engineering. Contributed to the theories of nonlinear switching elements and of spontaneous oscillation, and formulated the electron-tube coefficients and the equations relating them. His four-volume text on electron tubes and their technological applications was a standard work. First proposed subjective measurement of loudness and the use of the *phon* as a unit of loudness. Discovered by acoustical methods the discontinuities that occur as a ferromagnetic material is magnetized (the Barkhausen effect), which played a part in the elucidation of the discrete nature of magnetism by the domain theory. Best known for the Barkhausen-Kurz oscillator (1920), an electron tube capable of continuous-wave oscillation at ultrahigh frequencies, the forerunner of a series of microwave tubes.

BARKHAUSEN, JOHANN CONRAD. See **Barchusen, Johann Conrad.**

BARKLA, CHARLES GLOVER (*b. Widnes, Lancashire, England, 1877; d. Edinburgh, Scotland, 1944*), physics.

Attended University College, Liverpool (B.Sc., 1898; M.Sc., 1899; D.Sc., 1904); and Trinity College, Cambridge (B.A.). Began researches at the Cavendish Laboratory in 1899. Taught at Liverpool (1905–09); King's College, London (1909–13); and Edinburgh (1913–44). Nobel Prize for physics (1917) for discovery that each element emits a characteristic spectrum of X rays. At Cambridge, began his lifelong investigations of the secondary X rays emitted by substances in the path of a beam of X radiation. In 1903 showed that the secondary radiation emitted by "all gases" was of the same absorbability (average wavelength) as that of the primary beam. Demonstration of the existence of such an unmodified scattered radiation was strong support for the "ether pulse" theory. Barkla found another property of the secondary radiation which argued strongly that X rays were indeed transverse electromagnetic radiations. By 1904 he could demonstrate polarization. By confining himself to the scattering by light elements, Barkla was able, at first, to deny that the secondary X radiation was softer than the primary, and thus to construe the emission of these secondary radiations as a classical scattering of the primary beam. In 1907 Barkla was joined by Charles A. Sadler. Their first results showed the homogeneity of secondary radiation (the criterion being exponential decrease of intensity in traversing a homogeneous absorber). By 1911 Barkla was the leading physicist in the field of secondary X rays.

BARLOW, PETER (*b. Norwich, England, 1776; d. 1862*), mathematics, physics.

Self-educated; taught at Royal Military Academy, Woolwich. Published *An Elementary Investigation of the Theory of Numbers* (1811), *A New Mathematical and Philosophical Dictionary* (1814), and *New Mathematical Tables* (1814), later known as *Barlow's Tables*. Reputation established with his *Essay on the Strength and Stress of Timber* (1817).

Essay on Magnetic Attractions (1820) described a method of correcting ships' compasses by use of a small iron plate. In 1827 developed an improved telescope lens, the "Barlow lens." Conducted experiments and made calculations on the best shape for railroad rails and the effect of gradients and curves.

BARLOW, WILLIAM (*b. Islington, London, England, 1845; d. Great Stanmore, Middlesex, England, 1934*), crystallography.

Barlow's view of the nature of crystalline matter united the mathematical system of symmetry with an anticipation of the new determinations of atomic structure that were to follow after 1910. His theories of the properties of crystals were based on the close packing of atoms. In his first paper (1883), he recognized that body-centered cubic and simple cubic structures admit packing of spheres of two kinds (but of equal size), and are therefore suited to be structures of the alkali halides. Explained the widest range of crystal phenomena with his structures: cleavage, such polar properties as pyroelectricity, varieties of crystal growth, solid solution, and chemical reactivity. Used his concept of pseudosymmetry as a structural explanation of twinning, polymorphism, oriented overgrowth, and anomalous birefringence in crystals. His 1897 paper on crystal structure incorporated his work with space groups. He could not go further in solving the puzzle without one very important piece of information, however: the size, or at least the relative size, of the atoms. For fifteen years worked with W. H. Pope in assembling data on solid-solution substitutions and the variation of the morphological axial ratios that should reflect variations in atomic size.

BARNARD, EDWARD EMERSON (*b. Nashville, Tenn., 1857; d. Williams Bay, Wis., 1923*), astronomy.

From 1883 to 1887 Barnard was associated with Vanderbilt University as both student and instructor. Career in four parts: before 1883, an enthusiastic amateur working with his own five-inch telescope; 1883–87, Vanderbilt University; 1888–95, Lick Observatory; 1895–1923, Yerkes Observatory. First published notes concern the transit of Mercury of 6 May 1878. Of considerable significance were his drawings of Jupiter in 1879 and 1880. An excellent summary of his early work, together with forty-five of his drawings, appeared in *Publications of the Astronomical Society of the Pacific* (1889). He made two comet discoveries in 1881 and 1882. Seven new comet discoveries during his time at Vanderbilt University are credited to him, in addition to discoveries of new nebulae. Independently discovered the *Gegenschein* in late 1883 and identified its true character and position (1918). Discovered the duplicity of the star β' Capricorni. At Lick discovered seven more comets and several new nebulae and took the first photographs of the Milky Way.

His most sensational discovery at Lick was that of Jupiter's fifth satellite. His micrometric measures of the diameters and dimensions of planets, satellites, and asteroids were reliable, and later verification of them has often taxed the most refined techniques. He joined the University of Chicago in 1895. His work at Yerkes included studies and discovery (often visually) of variable stars, novae, double stars, and faint satellites; observations of Eros to determine the basic astronomical distance, the astronomical unit; continuation of his monumental studies of the forms of comet tails; extension of his Milky Way photography with the Bruce telescope; planetary photography and drawing; aurorae; cometary positions; and solar and lunar eclipses. He discovered a star having (until 1968) the largest known proper motion, 10 seconds of arc per year; it is now known as Barnard's star.

BAROCIUS, FRANCISCUS, also known as **Francesco Barozzi** (*b. Candia, Crete, 1537; d. Venice, Italy, 1604*), mathematics, astronomy.

Studied and lectured at University of Padua.

Barocius' edition of Proclus' commentary on the first book of Euclid's *Elements* was the first important translation of this work (1560). In 1572, brought out a Latin translation of Hero's book on war machines; in 1588, completed his corrections of Commandino's translation of Pappus' *Collectio.* His translation of the Archimedean *De dimensionibus* is still in manuscript. Wrote in Italian on *rythmomachia* (1572). Composed a Latin treatise on thirteen ways to draw two parallel lines in a plane (1572) and an elementary *Cosmographia* (1585).

BARRANDE, JOACHIM (*b. Sangues, Haute-Loire, France, 1799; d. Frohsdorf, Austria, 1883*), paleontology, stratigraphy.

Educated in Paris at the École Polytechnique and the École des Ponts et Chaussées.

Tutor to the grandson of Charles X. Acquisition of fossils and examination of strata near Prague later became his chief occupation. From 1840 to his death Barrande collected, described, and drew fossils of the central Bohemian basin—the Barrandian. His *Système silurien du centre de la Bohême* (1852–1902) is still used as a reference book by paleontologists.

BARRÉ DE SAINT VENANT. *See* **Saint Venant, A. J. C. Barré de.**

BARRELL, JOSEPH (*b. New Providence, N. J., 1869; d. New Haven, Conn., 1919*), geology.

Studied engineering at Lehigh University (E.M., 1893; M.S., 1897; D.Sc., 1916); Ph.D. in geology from Yale (1900). Professor of structural geology at Yale (1908–19). Chief contributions were in isostasy, sedimentology, and metamorphism. In 1901 joined U.S. Geological Survey in Montana to study Marysville mining district and large Marysville and Boulder granite batholiths. His *Geology of the Marysville Mining District, Montana* (1907) is a geological classic. He was a pioneer dry-land geologist, greatly influencing the manner in which stratigraphic problems were subsequently approached and conceptualized. Early recognized causal relationships between climatic variation and sedimentation. Outlined numerous covarying factors of deposition in "Criteria for the Recognition of Ancient Delta Deposits" (1912). Read history of the earth in its strata and interpreted their irregularities as meaning that geological processes are halting and discontinuous. Antiuniformitarian arguments forcefully presented in "Rhythms and the Measurements of Geologic Time" (1917). Eight papers (1914–15) under the series title "Strength of the Earth's Crust" present his views on isostasy and terrestrial dynamics. He was concerned with the effects of physical agents on the evolution of the earth and its inhabitants.

BARRESWIL, CHARLES-LOUIS (*b. Versailles, France, 1817; d. Boulogne-sur-Mer, France, 1870*), chemistry.

Studied chemistry in Paris under Robiquet, Bussy, and Pelouze. Taught in Paris.

Published articles on chemical analysis, notably on a new process for separating cobalt from manganese (1846) and on the cupropotassic solution as a reagent facilitating the detection of sugar (1844). Rayer introduced the "blue liquid of Barreswil" into the systematic clinical detection of diabetes (the Fehling solution used today). Participated in many of Claude Bernard's researches; both signed the two basic communications on the presence of sugar in the liver (1848) and in egg whites (1849). Discovered a new chrome compound, blue chromic acid (1847), and prepared quinine tannate.

BARROIS, CHARLES (*b. Lille, France, 1851; d. Ste.-Geneviève-en-Caux, Seine Maritime, France, 1939*), geology, paleontology.

Studied with the Jesuits in Lille. Jules Gosselet's devoted disciple for half a century. In 1871 named to Faculté des Sciences of Lille. His doctoral thesis on the Cretaceous formations of England (1876) became the first volume of the *Mémoires de la Société géologique du Nord,* founded by Gosselet and Barrois. Studied Cretaceous formation of northern and eastern France and Primary formations of northern Spain; made field studies in Asturias, Galicia, and the Sierra Nevada. In 1878 toured the most important stratigraphic sequences in New York State with James Hall. His great work was mapping geological formations of Brittany. From 1880 to 1909 published twenty geological maps, representing more than 25,000 square kilometers. Founded the Musée Houiller in 1907. His design of a completely different tectonics for the Franco-Belgian coal basin led him to anticipate far smaller coal reserves. Studied the fossil corals, Spongiae, Bryozoa, brachiopods, and especially graptolites. Wrote extensive monograph on Devonian fauna of Erbray (1888). Translated into French the five volumes of Zittel's *Handbuch der Palaeontologie* (1883–94).

BARROW, ISAAC (*b. London, England, 1630; d. London, 1677*), geometry, optics.

Educated at Trinity College, Cambridge; M.A., 1652. In 1660 took holy orders. In 1663 became first Lucasian professor of mathematics at Cambridge. Prepared three series of *Lectiones* on which his scientific fame rests. The first, the *Lectiones mathematicae* (1664–66), discourse on the foundations of mathematics from an essentially Greek standpoint. The *Lectiones geometricae* were intended as the technical study of higher geometry for which the preceding course had paved the way. In his first five geometrical lectures he considered the properties of curves generated by combinations of moving points and lines, evolving a simple Robervallian construction for tangents. Later lectures (6–12) are a systematic generalization of tangent, quadrature, and rectification procedures. The final *Lectio,* 13, is an unconnected account of the geometrical construction of equations. Barrow's optical lectures were rendered obsolete by the Newtonian *Lectiones opticae.* The most original contributions of the work are his method for finding the point of refraction at a plane interface and his point construction of the diacaustic of a spherical interface.

BARRY, MARTIN (*b. Fratton, Hampshire, England, 1802; d. Beccles, Suffolk, England, 1855*), embryology, histology.

M.D., Edinburgh (1833). His three-part "Researches in Embryology" (1838–40) followed the mammalian ovum through its early stages of development. Barry made two notable embryological observations: the segmentation of the yolk in the fertilized mammalian ovum and the penetration of the spermatozoon into the mammalian ovum. In a note to the Royal Society (1842) he announced that he had recently seen spermatozoa within the ova of a rabbit. A second series, "On the Corpuscles of the Blood," was devoted to many types of tissues and his arguments that they had all arisen in the same manner from the same basic elements, thus developing further his ideas about the unity of all animal life. The greatest portion of Barry's later work was aimed at promoting his conclusions on the origin of blood corpuscles and the formation of animal tissues from them.

BARTELS, JULIUS (*b. Magdeburg, Germany, 1899; d. Göttingen, Germany, 1964*), geophysics.

Educated at University of Göttingen (Ph.D., 1923). Head of Meteorological Institute at the Fortliche Hochschule in Eberswalde (1927–41); taught at University of Berlin (1941–45); professor of geophysics and director, Geophysical Institute of the University of Göttingen from 1945 on; director of the Max Planck Institute of Aeronomy. His statistical analyses led him to make the first clear discrimination between geomagnetic variations caused by wave and particle radiation from the sun. Developed reliable measures, based on geomagnetic observations, of the two types of radiation. Elucidated features of tides in the earth's atmosphere that are caused by the moon's gravitational attraction. Postulated existence in the sun of certain magnetically active regions (*M* regions), which astronomers later connected with the development of sunspots.

BARTHEZ, PAUL-JOSEPH (*b. Montpellier, France, 1734; d. Paris, France, 1806*), physiology.

Received medical degree and later became professor of medicine at Montpellier. His vitalistic doctrines were expounded in three books: *De principio vitali hominis* (1773), *Nova doctrina de fonctionibus naturae humanae* (1774), and his most important work, *Nouveaux éléments de la science de l'homme* (1778). His vitalism is based on the distinction between three different types of phenomena—matter, life, and soul. His emphasis on the development of clinical teaching and research aroused a controversy that caused him to resign his position at Montpellier in 1781. In 1798 he published *Nouvelle méchanique des mouvements de l'homme et des animaux*. Also published several practical medical handbooks.

BARTHOLIN, CASPAR (*b. Malmö, Denmark [now Sweden], 1585; d. Sorø, Denmark, 1629*), theology, anatomy.

Studied at several universities and with many learned physicians and philosophers in Germany, Holland, France, and England. Taught at University of Copenhagen, first medicine, and later theology. In Naples, helped prepare engravings for Casserio's work on the sense organs, and his anatomical studies there formed basis for the manual *Anatomicae institutiones corporis humani* (1611),

which made him famous. First manual to describe the olfactory nerves, found by Casserio, as first pair of cerebral nerves. Also published several manuals of logic, physics, and ethics. In 1628 published the textbook *De studio medico*. Father of Erasmus (1625–98) and Thomas (1616–80).

BARTHOLIN, ERASMUS (*b. Roskilde, Denmark, 1625; d. Copenhagen, Denmark, 1698*), mathematics, physics.

Son of Caspar Bartholin (1585–1629) and brother of Thomas (1616–80). Studied at University of Leiden; received M.D. at Padua (1654). Taught at University of Copenhagen. Numerous publications in pure mathematics; main interest in theory of equations, directly influenced by Frans Van Schooten. In astronomy, studied comets with Ole Rømer. Major contribution to science was undoubtedly his study of Icelandic spar. In physics, as in mathematics, he was a fervent admirer of Descartes; he argued that double refraction could be explained in the Cartesian theory of light by assuming a double set of "pores" in the spar.

BARTHOLIN, THOMAS (*b. Copenhagen, Denmark, 1616; d. Copenhagen, 1680*), physiology, anatomy.

Son of Caspar Bartholin (1585–1629) and brother of Erasmus (1625–1698). Studied at the Universities of Copenhagen, Leiden, Padua, and Basel. In 1641 revised his father's *Institutiones anatomicae* (1611). Taught at Copenhagen, where he studied anatomy extensively. Known eponymously for Bartholin's gland and Bartholin's duct. After being informed by his brother of Pecquet's discovery in dogs of the thoracic duct and the cisterna chyli, Bartholin undertook a search for them in the cadavers of two criminals. He found the duct, which he reported in 1652. Bartholin's greatest contribution to physiology was his discovery that the lymphatic system is a separate system (1652). In 1654, confirmed the existence of the human lymphatic system. His *Dispensatorium hafniense* (1658) was the first Danish pharmacopeia. The *Historarium anatomicarum rariorum centuria I–VI* (1654–61) dealt with numerous limited problems of human and comparative anatomy, and *Cista medica hafniensis* (1662) was a medical miscellany. Responsible for the royal decree of 1672 that decided the organization of Danish medicine for the next hundred years. In 1673 established the first examination in midwifery at Copenhagen, and began publication of the first Danish scientific journal, *Acta medica et philosophica hafniensa*.

BARTOLI, DANIELLO (*b. Ferrara, Italy, 1608; d. Rome, Italy, 1685*), physics.

In 1650 became historian of the Jesuits. From 1671 to 1673 rector of the Collegio Romano, the principal Jesuit university. Published histories of the first century of Jesuit activity in England, Italy, China, and Japan. Also wrote extensively on Italian literary matters and on morals. Popularized the work of contemporary physicists, particularly barometric experiments and the concept of atmospheric pressure (1677). Wrote works on the physical analysis of sound, sound waves, and the sense of hearing (1679), and on the phenomena of freezing (1681).

BARTOLOTTI, GIAN GIACOMO (*b. Parma, Italy, ca. 1470; d. after 1530*), medicine, history of medicine.

Studied at Bologna and Ferrara. Made an Italian translation of the *Table (Pinax)*, a dialogue attributed to Cebes, the Theban philosopher. His *Opusculum de antiquitate medicinae* is a treatise on the history of ancient medicine.

BARTON, BENJAMIN SMITH (*b. Lancaster, Pa., 1766; d. Philadelphia, Pa., 1815*), botany, zoology, ethnography, medicine.

Studied at Edinburgh, Göttingen, and Lisbon.

Author of first botanical textbook published in the United States, *Elements of Botany* (1803); influential teacher at University of Pennsylvania; patron of Frederick Pursh and Thomas Nuttall, with whose specimens he hoped to produce a flora of North America; owner of largest private natural history library of his time. Between 1797 and 1807 assembled what was then the largest herbarium of native plants (1,674 specimens). Wrote numerous articles on medicine, natural history, physical geography, and lives of naturalists.

BARTRAM, JOHN (*b. Marple, Pa., 1699; d. Kingsessing, Pa., 1777*), botany.

Self-taught botanist; ranked with Franklin and Rittenhouse as one of America's authentic natural geniuses.

Bartram introduced more than a hundred American species into Europe. Peter Collinson ordered seeds, plants, and shrubs, got Bartram other customers, and advised him on what would sell in England. The yield to science from Bartram's botanical journeys to distant parts of the country was great. Copies of his journals circulated in manuscript in London. From his letters Collinson fashioned communications that were printed in the Royal Society's *Philosophical Transactions*. Bartram wrote almost nothing for publication. The close of the French and Indian War brought Great Britain a vast increase of territory in North America and Bartram set out to explore it. Father of William Bartram (1739–1823).

BARTRAM, WILLIAM (*b. Kingsessing, Pa., 1739; d. Kingsessing, 1823*), botany, ornithology.

Studied at the Academy of Philadelphia; accompanied his father, John (1699–1777), on botanizing expeditions.

After brief, unsuccessful careers as merchant and planter, he set out in 1773 on travels that were to make his reputation. For four years he traveled through South Carolina, Georgia, and Florida making notes on birds, animals, fishes, and plants and recording the life of the Indians. Returned to Kingsessing in 1778 and wrote up his notes. The *Travels* appeared in 1791 and was widely reprinted. It is for its style that the *Travels* is best known, and for its influence on romantic literature that it has its most lasting fame. He wrote down his observations of the Creek and Cherokee Indians for Benjamin Smith Barton, illustrated Barton's *Elements of Botany* (1803), and wrote papers for Barton's *Philadelphia Medical and Physical Journal*. The ornithologist Alexander Wilson owed much of his training to Bartram.

BARUS, CARL (*b. Cincinnati, Ohio, 1856; d. Providence, R.I., 1935*), physics.

Studied at Columbia University's School of Mines, and at Würzburg (Ph.D., 1879). Worked for U.S. Geological Survey (1880–92), U.S. Weather Bureau (1892–93),

Smithsonian Institution (1893–94), and taught at Brown University (1895–1926). Developed methods of measuring, with thermocouples, temperatures over a range of some 1,000° C. Internationally known as authority on pyrometry. Studied effects of X rays and radioactivity on condensation in a fog chamber. Assisted Samuel P. Langley in development of the flying machine. A founder of the American Physical Society (1899).

BARY, HEINRICH ANTON DE. *See* **DeBary, Heinrich Anton.**

BASIL, VALENTINE. *See* **Valentine, Basil.**

BASSANI, FRANCESCO (*b. Thiene, Vicenza, Italy, 1853; d. Capri, Italy, 1916*), paleontology.

Studied at Padua, Paris, Vienna, and Munich. Taught in secondary schools in Padua, Modena, and Milan, while actively investigating fossil fishes of northern Italy and adjacent regions (1879–87). Taught at Naples (1887–1916). Primarily a student of fossil fishes; also investigated other geological problems, particularly stratigraphic relations and geologic age, volcanic phenomena, contemporaneity of man and extinct animals, and marine mammals. Most significant work on faunal revisions; reviewed nearly all important fossil fishes of Mesozoic and Cenozoic in Italy. Developed concept of fish species evolving slowly through geologic time.

BASSI, AGOSTINO MARIA (*b. Mairago, Italy, 1773; d. Lodi, Italy, 1856*), law, agriculture, natural science.

Studied at Pavia under Scarpa, Volta, Rasori, and Spallanzani. Received law degree and worked as civil servant.

Experimented over many years to determine cause of the *mal del segno,* or muscardine, the silkworm disease then prevalent. He discovered the microscopic fungus parasite that caused this malady, commonly believed to be of spontaneous origin. He reported his experiments and conclusions in *Del mal del segno . . .* (1835–36). The minute fungus parasite was later named for Bassi, *Botrytis bassiana* (today *Beauvaria bassiana*). Later writings showed continuing interest in contagion, suggesting that parasites, animal or vegetable, were the cause of various diseases, including plague, smallpox, syphilis (1844), and cholera (1849). Since the minute germs spread, he advocated quarantine and various modes of prevention and disinfection, employing both asepsis and antisepsis.

BASSLER, RAYMOND SMITH (*b. Philadelphia, Pa., 1878; d. Washington, D.C., 1961*), paleontology.

Studied at University of Cincinnati and at George Washington University (M.S. and Ph.D.). Associated with the latter and the U.S. National Museum for nearly forty years. Strongly influenced by E. O. Ulrich throughout entire career. A world authority on Silurian and Ordovician Bryozoa, Bassler assembled an outstanding collection of these fossils, now at the Smithsonian Institution. Also published valuable bibliographic indexes relating to them. His study of other phyla resulted in the compilation of the *Bibliographic Index of Paleozoic Ostracoda* (1934) and *Bibliographic and Faunal Index of Paleozoic Echinoderms* (1943), as well as shorter papers on tetra corals, Cystoidea, and conodonts.

BASSO, SEBASTIAN (*fl. second half of sixteenth century*), natural philosophy.

Little known of his life except that he was a physician and had studied at the new Academia Mussipontana (Pont à Mousson).

Famous as a reviver of the atomic philosophy. Known only as the author of *Philosophiae naturalis adversus Aristotelem.* Basso's central doctrines are that all matter consists of very small atoms of different natures and that a very fine, corporeal ether extends throughout the universe and fills the pores between the atoms.

BASTIAN, HENRY CHARLTON (*b. Truro, England, 1837; d. Chesham Bois, England, 1915*), neurology, bacteriology.

Received M.B. (1863) and M.D. (1866) from University College, London. Practiced medicine and taught at St. Mary's Hospital, University College Hospital, and the National Hospital.

Spent most of hospital and academic life in clinical neurology. In 1869 began to publish series of papers on speech disorders. Described a visual and an auditory word center, and in 1869 gave the first account of word blindness (alexia) and of word deafness, which is known today as "Wernicke's aphasia." Important pioneer of neurology as a science; in addition, his anatomical skill is revealed by the discovery in 1867 of the anterior spinocerebellar tract of the spinal cord. First to show (1890) that complete section of the upper spinal cord abolishes reflexes and muscular tone below the level of the lesion; known occasionally as Bastian's law. Bastian himself claimed that his studies on abiogenesis were more significant. As Pasteur's main opponent, he was responsible for the development of some of the techniques that advanced bacteriology. Bastian denied that boiling destroyed all bacteria, as Pasteur claimed, and thereby opened the way for the discovery of heat-resistant spores. Devoted the last fifteen years of his life to the fundamental problem of the origin of life. He was one of the last scientific believers in spontaneous generation.

BATAILLON, JEAN EUGÈNE (*b. Annoire, Jura, France, 1864; d. Montpellier, France, 1953*), biology, zoology.

Assistant in zoology at the University of Lyons, 1887 (doctorate, 1891). Seconded by Pasteur, he was made lecturer at the Faculté des Sciences at Lyons and at Dijon in 1892; professor of general biology (1903), dean (1907). While at Dijon discovered the traumatic parthenogenesis of the batrachians. Held positions at Strasbourg and Clermont-Ferrand between 1919 and 1923. Appointed professor of zoology and comparative anatomy at Montpellier (1924), where he met his principal collaborator, Chou Su. His unchallenged discovery of traumatic parthenogenesis is important, but even more important is his remarkable analysis of the process, which clarified the complex phenomena of fertilization.

BATE, HENRY. *See* **Henry Bate of Malines.**

BATEMAN, HARRY (*b. Manchester, England, 1882; d. Pasadena, Calif., 1946*), mathematics, mathematical physics.

Attended Trinity College, Cambridge (B.A., 1903; M.A., 1906). Taught at Liverpool, Manchester, and Bryn

Mawr. Lectured at Johns Hopkins (1912–17); Ph.D., 1913. Professor of mathematics, theoretical physics, and aeronautics at Throop College (later California Institute of Technology), 1917–46. Much of his work consisted of finding special functions to solve partial differential equations, including Bateman's expansion and Bateman's function. Used definite integrals to extend E. T. Whittaker's solutions of the potential and wave equations. These and later results he applied to the theory of electricity and, with Ehrenfest, to electromagnetic fields (1924). His most significant single contribution to mathematical physics was a paper (1909) in which, following the work of Lorentz and Einstein on the invariance of the equations of electromagnetism under change of coordinates of constant velocity and constant acceleration, he showed that the most general group of transformations which preserve the electromagnetic equations and total charge of the system and which are independent of the electromagnetic field is the group of conformal maps of four-dimensional space.

One of the first to apply Laplace transform methods to integral equations (1906). Solved the system of ordinary differential equations arising from Rutherford's description of radioactive decay (1910). Worked on problems of electromagnetism and classical atomic models that were solved by the quantum theory (1926). In 1934, completed a monumental report on hydrodynamics.

BATES, HENRY WALTER (*b. Leicester, England, 1825; d. London, England, 1892*), natural history.

Began scientific investigations with Alfred Russel Wallace; in 1848 they arrived at Pará, Brazil, near the mouth of the Amazon River, to explore and collect. Bates remained eleven years. Collected 14,712 animal species (primarily insects)—more than 8,000 new to science. In 1859, began work on his enormous collections under influence of Darwin's *Origin of Species.* First naturalist to venture comprehensive scientific explanation for phenomenon he labeled "mimicry" (Batesian mimicry), which Darwin used to rebut critics of his theory. Discussion was unobtrusively buried in his classic article, "Contributions to an Insect Fauna of the Amazon Valley. *Lepidoptera: Heliconidae.*" On Darwin's urging, published his two-volume narrative, *The Naturalist on the River Amazon* (1863). Assistant secretary, Royal Geographical Society of London; edited *Journal* and *Proceedings,* carried on vast correspondence, and actually managed the Society. Greatest contribution to systematic entomology appeared in the *Biologia Centrali-Americana.* Preeminent authority on Coleoptera. His catalog of the Erycinidae (Riodinidae) butterflies laid a foundation upon which subsequent authors worked.

BATESON, WILLIAM (*b. Whitby, England, 1861; d. Merton, London, England, 1926*), morphology, genetics.

B.A. (1883), St. John's College, Cambridge; various positions he held culminated in first professorship of genetics (1908). First director of John Innes Horticultural Institution, Merton (1910).

During his early career (1883–1900) he turned from orthodox embryological Darwinizing to the rigorous study of heredity and variation. Bateson's Mendelian period lasted from 1900 until about 1915. His contributions toward the establishment of a Mendelian conception of heredity and variation were enormous. Proved that Mendelian behavior holds for animals as well as plants. In the third period (*ca.* 1915–26) he attacked the chromosome theory, and concentrated upon problems of somatic segregation. His science, genetics (so named by Bateson in 1905–06), turned largely toward chromosomes and genes. In place of the chromosome theory he devised an ostensibly nonmaterialistic vibratory theory of inheritance, founded on force and motion, but this theory was unacceptable to most geneticists. Bateson and R. C. Punnett began the *Journal of Genetics* in 1910.

BATHER, FRANCIS ARTHUR (*b. Richmond, Surrey, England, 1863; d. Wimbledon, England, 1934*), paleontology.

Attended Oxford (B.A., 1886; M.A., 1890; doctor of science, 1900). Geologist and curator at British Museum (1887–1928). Carried out research in paleontology and contributed many fundamental studies on echinoderm morphology: *Crinoidea of Gotland,* pt. 1 (1893), and *The Echinoderma* (1900), the leading exposition of echinoderm morphology for decades.

AL-BATTĀNĪ, ABŪ ʿABD ALLĀH MUḤAMMAD IBN JĀBIR IBN SINĀN AL-RAQQĪ AL-ḤARRĀNĪ AL-ṢĀBIʾ, also **Albatenius, Albategni,** or **Albategnius** (*b. probably at or near Ḥarrān, Mesopotamia, before* A.H. *244* [A.D. *858*]), astronomy, mathematics.

The widespread belief among Western historians that al-Battānī, one of the greatest Islamic astronomers, was a noble, a prince, or even a king of Syria is erroneous. His *Zīj* ("Astronomical Treatise") is one of the most important books written in the Middle Ages. A single copy in Arabic survives, and there is a Latin version by Plato of Tivoli. He also wrote three minor astrological works.

Al-Battānī wrote the *Zīj* to improve on Ptolemy's *Almagest,* on the basis of new observations; but he did not intend just a new *Almagest.* Unlike the *Almagest,* the *Zīj* is so predominantly practical that it is sometimes unclear and even evokes a totally wrong impression. Among his many important achievements are his improvement of the moon's mean motion in longitude; his measurements of the apparent diameters of the sun and of the moon and their variation in the course of a year, or of an anomalistic month, respectively, from which he concludes that annular solar eclipses (impossible according to Ptolemy) must be possible; and his new and elegant method of computing the magnitude of lunar eclipses.

For the precession of equinoxes, al-Battānī accepts and confirms Thābit ibn Qurra's value, far better than Ptolemy's—but about 10 percent too fast. His catalog of fixed stars is far less comprehensive than Ptolemy's. He has a good deal in common with the Banū Mūsā, Thābit, and al-Farghānī, but makes no reference whatever to his Islamic predecessors.

Although no Hebrew translation of the *Zīj* seems to have existed, its impact on Jewish scholarship was great. Maimonides follows it closely, without mentioning al-Battānī, in part of his *Mishne Tŏrā.* He also follows al-Battānī's method in his prescriptions for determining the limits of visibility of the new moon. Among Islamic astronomers and historians, al-Battānī holds a place of honor, and Albertus Magnus, Copernicus, Regiomontanus, Kepler, and Galileo also evidenced interest in his work.

IBN BAṬṬŪṬA (*b. Tangier, Morocco, 1304; d. Morocco, ca. 1368-69*), Muslim traveler.

All the details of Ibn Baṭṭūṭa's life and accomplishments come from his *Travels,* written to enlighten the reader about remarkable and often marvelous things and events in other countries and to deepen the understanding of human society and respect for the divine handiwork in all its richness and variety. This purpose was uniquely achieved and has given the *Travels* its lasting greatness. The work was not the product of scholarly or scientific research—the only systematic treatment of observed facts concerns the trees, fruits, and grains of South Arabia, India, and the Maldives—but it is a source of unmatched importance for fourteenth-century India (to which about one-fifth of it is devoted), and even more so for the Maldives, southern Russia, and especially Negro Africa. He is often the only medieval author to give us information on these areas.

BAUDRIMONT, ALEXANDRE ÉDOUARD (*b. Compiègne, France, 1806; d. Bordeaux, France, 1880*), chemistry, physiology.

M.D., Paris (1831), first-class degree in pharmacy (1834). Also obtained degrees in pure science: licentiate, 1839; doctorate, 1847. Taught at University of Bordeaux (1847-80). Published *Introduction à l'étude de la chimie par la théorie atomique* (1833), a mineralogy and geology textbook (1840), and the two-volume *Traité de chimie générale et expérimentale* (1844–46). Devoted attention to molecular structure, leading him to adumbrate a theory of chemical types. One of the few proponents of Avogadro's gas hypothesis in the 1830's and 40's. He made an important study of aqua regia. His greatest recognition came from work with Martin Saint-Ange on chemical changes in embryonic development in chickens and amphibia and the toxological effects of various gaseous substances on the embryo. Also performed experiments on testing of metals and published works on geometry, philosophy of science, music theory, and linguistics.

BAUER, EDMOND (*b. Paris, France, 1880; d. Paris, 1963*), physics, physical chemistry.

Graduated from University of Paris; taught at Strasbourg and Paris; worked in Langevin's laboratory at the Collège de France.

Bauer's main experimental and theoretical research dealt with radiation emitted by flames and metallic vapors, which he showed to be thermal; precise determination of the Stefan constant; diffusion of light by high-altitude atmosphere, at the Mont Blanc observatory; the ferromagnetic equation of state; group theory and quantum mechanics; hydrogen bonding and the structure of water and ice, determined from vibration spectra; differential infra-red detection of impurities in gas; dielectric dispersion and phase transformation, involving relaxation time and lifetime of hydrogen bonds; and chemical kinetics.

BAUER, FERDINAND LUCAS (*b. Feldsberg, Lower Austria, 1760; d. Hietzing, near Vienna, Austria, 1826*), scientific illustration.

Educated at a monastery in Feldsberg and worked under Jacquin in Vienna.

His fame rests chiefly on his illustrations for John Sibthorp's *Flora Graeca* (1806–40), the most beautiful flora of all time. The 2,750 plates of Boccius' fourteen-volume manuscript, *Hortus botanicus,* were chiefly the work of Ferdinand and his brothers. In Australia Bauer and the botanist Robert Brown made a rich collection of material that included over 2,000 sketches by Bauer, 1,541 being of plants. The overthrow of Linnaean taxonomy was partly due to this work.

BAUER, FRANZ ANDREAS (*b. Feldsberg, Lower Austria, 1758; d. Kew, England, 1840*), botanical illustration, microscopy.

Educated with his brother Ferdinand at a monastery in Feldsberg and worked under Jacquin in Vienna.

Sir Joseph Banks engaged Bauer as artist at Kew. He studied the intricacies of flower structure in strelitzias and orchids, the nature of red snow, and the structure of pollen grains. Illustrated the works of friends with microscopical and anatomical drawings. Achieved recognition as a microscopist but made no lasting contribution to that field.

BAUER, GEORG. See **Agricola.**

BAUER, LOUIS AGRICOLA (*b. Cincinnati, Ohio, 1865; d. Washington, D.C., 1932*), geophysics.

Originally trained as civil engineer, worked for U.S. Coast and Geodetic Survey (1887–92, 1899–1906). Ph.D, University of Berlin (1895). Taught at University of Chicago (1895–96) and University of Cincinnati (1897–99).

Founder of department of terrestrial magnetism of the Carnegie Institution of Washington (1904). Extensive mapping of the earth's magnetic field on a vast area of the seas. Promoted establishment of magnetic stations; active in mathematical analysis of observations and in development of a mathematical theory. Studied atmospheric electricity and extraterrestrial influences on the earth's magnetism. Founder (1896) and editor (until 1927) of *Terrestrial Magnetism* (now *Journal of Geophysical Research*).

BAUHIN, GASPARD (*b. Basel, Switzerland, 1560; d. Basel, 1624*), anatomy, botany.

Studied at Basel (doctorate, 1581), Bologna, Padua, Montpellier, Paris, and Tübingen. Held position at Basel on Faculty of Medicine (1581–1624). Believed that he was the first to describe the ileocecal valve, which was long known as the *valvula Bauhini.* His greatest contribution to anatomy was the reform he introduced into nomenclature, particularly into that of muscles, veins and arteries, and nerves. In 1605 his anatomical writings were published in Bauhin's most celebrated anatomical textbook, *Theatrum anatomicum,* accompanied by copper engravings; and, conflated with the textbook of Laurentius, published under title, *Microcosmographia, A Study of the Body of Man.* Medical works include treatises on the bezoar stone, Caesarean section, hermaphrodites and other monstrous births, and the pulse. His two pharmacological writings are designed as handbooks for young physicians. As in anatomy, his great contribution to botany was to nomenclature. His botanical fame rests chiefly on his *Prodromos* (1620) and *Pinax* (1623). He distinguished between genus and species and introduced a system of bi-

nomial nomenclature. In 1658 his son Jean Gaspard published the first volume, all that was ever published of the intended twelve, of his father's *Theatrum botanicum.* His botanical work was commemorated by L. P. C. Plumier, who gave the name *Bauhinia* to a family of tropical trees; and Linnaeus, in memory of both Gaspard and his brother Jean, called one species of this family *Bauhinia bijuga.*

BAUHIN, JEAN (*b. Basel, Switzerland, 1541; d. Montbéliard, principality of Württemberg-Montbéliard, 1613*), botany.

Studied at Basel, at Montpellier under Rondelet, and at Zurich under Gesner, who became his fellow traveler and correspondent.

In 1571, became physician to Duke Frederick of Württemberg. His first garden was established about 1564 at Lyons, where he collaborated with Jacques Daleschamps in studying local flora. Established botanical gardens at Montbéliard and Stuttgart. His *De plantis a divis sanctisve nomen* (1591) is an alphabetical list of plants named after saints, with full citations to the botanical literature. *De plantis Absynthii nomen* (1593) underlines the great confusion that existed over a single type. A specifically medical work described the remedies for diseases contracted as a result of animal bites (*Histoire notable de la rage,* 1591). His longest and most popular medical work, a description of European mineral waters and baths (*Historia novi et admirabilis fontis,* 1598), contains a series of illustrations, mostly of his fossil collections, in the appendix. His reputation as a botanist rests upon the encyclopedic *Historia plantarum universalis* (1650–51). Contains descriptions and synonyms of 5,226 plants, primarily from Europe. His work was paralleled by his brother Gaspard's *Pinax theatri botanici* (1623).

BAUMÉ, ANTOINE (*b. Senlis, France, 1728; d. Paris, France, 1804*), chemistry, pharmacy.

Trained as pharmacist; opened own dispensary in 1753.

Supplied drugs in bulk to pharmacies and hospitals and manufactured drugs and other chemicals. In 1767 began the first large-scale production of sal ammoniac in France. Also supplied industrial and laboratory apparatus. His areometer (1768) was an important step forward. In 1757, he and Macquer began a series of courses in chemistry and pharmacy: *Plan d'un cours de chymie expérimentale et raisonnée . . .* was published in 1757. Published a number of works on chemistry and pharmacy that ran into several editions, and contributed to the *Dictionnaire des arts et métiers* (1766).

BAUMHAUER, EDOUARD HENRI VON (*b. Brussels, Belgium, 1820; d. Haarlem, Netherlands, 1885*), chemistry.

Graduated from Utrecht (1844).

Professor of physics and chemistry at Royal Athenaeum in Maastricht (1845–47); professor of chemistry at Athenaeum Illustre in Amsterdam (1848–65). Although primarily a teacher, did much practical work in chemistry. Developed a method for quantitative determination of oxygen in organic substances. Effected passage of a municipal regulation calling for inspection of food. In 1859 he began work on accurate determination of the strength of alcohol. Published papers on such diverse subjects as diamonds, marine pileworms, and meteorology.

BAUMHAUER, HEINRICH ADOLF (*b. Bonn, Germany, 1848; d. Fribourg, Switzerland, 1926*), chemistry, mineralogy.

Studied at Bonn under Kekulé (graduated, 1869).

Taught at the agricultural school of Lüdinghausen, Westphalia (1873–96), and at Fribourg (from 1896). Crystallography and mineralogy were principal interests. In 1870, wrote a tract on the relation between atomic weights and properties of elements. Wrote textbooks on inorganic chemistry (1884), organic chemistry (1885), mineralogy (1884), and a popular work on crystallography (1889). Best known for study of etch figures produced on crystal faces by various solvents, a method of study that for a long time provided one of principal means for establishing symmetry of crystals. His *Die Resultate der Aetzmethode* (1894) was the standard and only work on the subject until 1927. Foremost authority on sulfosalts of Binnental occurrence; made extensive morphological studies of minerals.

BAYEN, PIERRE (*b. Châlons-sur-Marne, France, 1725; d. Paris, France, 1798*), chemistry, pharmacy.

Studied at the Collège de Troyes and in Paris. Worked as apothecary for army.

First publication was analysis of mineral waters of Bagnères-de-Luchon (1765). Most important contribution to chemistry was a series of four memoirs on precipitates of mercury (1774–75). His observations led him to doubt the phlogiston theory. Helped to make known the work of Jean Rey, whose theory of calcination was very similar to his own. In 1781, he produced a report concluding that commercial tin contained only a trace of arsenic at most, and was thus safe for cooking utensils.

BAYER, JOHANN (*b. Rain, Germany, 1572; d. Augsburg, Germany, 1625*), astronomy.

Established the modern nomenclature of stars visible to the naked eye. In his *Uranometria* (1603) he assigned to each star in a constellation one of the twenty-four letters of the Greek alphabet, also reproducing the traditional numeration of the stars and their many different names. The popularity of his work was enhanced by his forty-ninth plate, which displayed twelve new southern constellations.

BAYES, THOMAS (*b. London, England, 1702; d. Tunbridge Wells, England, 1761*), probability.

Privately educated; minister at Tunbridge Wells.

Bayes's *Divine Benevolence* (1731) and *Introduction to the Doctrine of Fluxions* (1736) are his only works known to have been published during his lifetime. The latter is a response to Bishop Berkeley's *Analyst*, a stinging attack on the logical foundations of Newton's calculus. Bayes is remembered for his brief "Essay Towards Solving a Problem in the Doctrine of Chances" (1763), the first attempt to establish foundations for statistical inference. A generalization on a deduction in his analysis is often called Bayes's theorem or Bayes's formula. Due to Laplace's influence, Bayes's ideas were almost unchallengeable until Boole's protest (1854). Since then, Bayes's technique has been a constant subject of controversy.

BAYLAK AL-QIBJĀQĪ (*fl. Cairo, Egypt, ca. 1250*), mineralogy.

Baylak's only known book is his mineralogical work, *Treasure of the Merchants on the Knowledge of Minerals.* First author writing in Arabic to treat the use of the magnetic needle as a ship's compass, which he observed while on a voyage to Alexandria.

BAYLISS, LEONARD ERNEST (*b. London, England, 1900; d. London, 1964*), physiology.

Graduated from Trinity College, Cambridge, in 1922; in 1925 received Ph.D. Spent short periods throughout his life working and teaching at University College, London; Marine Biological Station, Plymouth; and University of Edinburgh. In 1939 revised a version of his father's (William Maddock Bayliss) famous book, *Principles of General Physiology.* By 1960 he had completed his project, entirely rewriting the *Principles* and expanding it to two volumes. At University College worked on the metabolism of dog heart-lung preparations; devised pump-oxygenator perfusion techniques for kidneys; and studied serotonins in defibrinated blood, water diuresis, and glomerular permeability in both cold-blooded and warm-blooded animals. His interest in invertebrates was strengthened at the Plymouth Marine Biological Station. Rheology of blood was a major but intermittent interest during his later years.

BAYLISS, WILLIAM MADDOCK (*b. Wednesbury, Staffordshire, England, 1860; d. London, England, 1924*), general physiology.

Studied at University College, London (B.Sc., 1882) and Oxford. Strongly influenced by Burdon-Sanderson and Lankester. In 1888 returned to University College for rest of life. Father of Leonard Ernest Bayliss. Deeply interested in emergence of physical chemistry and biochemistry and their relations to problems of general physiology. Often collaborated with E. H. Starling. In electrophysiology, studied changes in electric potential involved in the act of secretion, and electromotive phenomena of mammalian heart. Study of vascular system resulted in a new form of optically registered blood pressure apparatus and a paper on innervation of mammalian heart. Studied movements and innervation of the intestines; elucidated peristaltic wave. Discovered the excitant substance, *secretin*, thus recognizing the existence of a new class of chemical messengers, hormones. In research on enzyme action, studied activation of trypsin in pancreatic juice. His work on colloids led to a study of osmotic pressure of Congo red and electrical equilibria. His work on wound shock resulted in replacing lost blood with gum saline solution. His *Principles of General Physiology* (1914) is a landmark in biological literature.

IBN AL-BAYṬĀR AL-MĀLAQĪ, ḌIYĀ᾽ AL-DĪN ABŪ MUḤAMMAD ᶜABDALLĀH IBN AḤMAD (*b. Málaga, Spain, ca. 1190; d. Damascus, Syria, 1248*), pharmacology, botany.

Studied in Seville, where he gathered herbs with his teachers. About 1220, migrated to the Orient. Settled in Cairo, named chief herbalist. His *Al-Mughnī fī 'l-adwiya al-mufrada* deals with simple medicines appropriate for various illnesses. *Al-Jāmiᶜ* enumerates alphabetically some 1,400 animal, vegetable, and mineral medicines. His main contribution was the systematization of discoveries made by Arabs during the Middle Ages, which added

300–400 medicines to the thousand known since antiquity.

BEALE, LIONEL SMITH (*b. London, England, 1828; d. London, 1906*), microscopy.

Attended King's College, University of London (M.B., 1851), later teaching there (1853–96). In his private laboratory, pioneered in teaching the use of the microscope in pathological anatomy. His practical books on the microscope are basic laboratory manuals. A lecture series, "On the Structure of the Simple Tissue of the Human Body" (1861), demonstrates his mastery of recently introduced techniques of vital staining, illustrated by his excellent plates. *Protoplasm,* a polemical work, asserted that a vital force was necessary for life. *On Disease Germs* (1870) proposed that disease germs are minute particles of degraded protoplasm derived by direct descent from normal protoplasm of the diseased organism. Two eponyms were awarded to Beale: "Beale's solution" (carmine in ammonia), an effective histological stain, and "Beale's cells," the pyriform nerve ganglion cells.

BEAUGRAND, JEAN (*b. Paris [?], France, ca. 1595 [?]; d. Paris [?], ca. 1640*), mathematics.

Studied with Viète, whose *In artem analyticam isagoge* he published (1631, with scholia). Served as *secrétaire du roi* (from 1635); met Castelli, Cavalieri, and Galileo in Italy and later corresponded with them. Initially friendly with Fermat, Desargues, Mersenne, and others; his *Géostatique* (1636), whose main thesis was that the weight of a body varies as its distance from the center of gravity, led to lengthy controversies: Beaugrand wrote anonymous pamphlets against Descartes accusing him of plagiarism, criticized Desargues's *Brouillon projet,* and lost the friendship of Fermat.

BEAUMONT, ÉLIE DE. *See* **Élie de Beaumont, Jean B.**

BEAUMONT, WILLIAM (*b. Lebanon, Conn., 1785; d. St. Louis, Mo., 1853*), physiology.

Learned medicine through apprenticeship; joined army as surgeon (1812), resigned for five years (1815–20), then became post surgeon at Fort Mackinac (Michigan) where an accidental gunshot wound suffered by Alexis St. Martin, a trapper (1822), led to important physiological studies. St. Martin gradually recovered from the extensive injury in his left side, but during the healing process a gastric fistula developed; Beaumont grasped the opportunity to study human digestion *in vivo,* and carried out four groups of experiments (1825–33). His studies included: confirmation that digestion is a chemical process; measurement of digestibility of various foods and of action of stimulants; description of gastric mobility; observations of gastritis and its causes; demonstration that gastric juice is not found in the stomach in the absence of food and that water and other fluids pass very rapidly and directly from the stomach through the pylorus; observation of a retrograde passage of the duodenal contents; demonstration that psychic influences have considerable effect on gastric secretion and digestion; and removal of samples of gastric juice, which were sent to Dunglison, Silliman, and Berzelius for analysis. These results, published in two articles (1825, 1826) and as *Experiments and Observations on the Gastric Juice and the*

Physiology of Digestion (1833), had a profound influence on many investigators, including Müller, Schwann, and Purkinje. Blondlot was led to establish artificial gastric fistulas in animals.

BECCARI, NELLO (*b. Bagno a Ripoli, near Florence, Italy, 1883; d. Florence, 1957*), anatomy.

M.D., Florence (1907); worked and taught at Institute of Human Anatomy, under Chiarugi (1907–15); directed Institute of Human Anatomy at Catania (1921–25); returned to Florence to direct Institute of Comparative Anatomy (1925–53). Principal work was in neurology: made precise observations on rhombencephalon, including function of Mauthner's fibers, importance of tegmental centers, and role of rhombencephalon in determination of static extrapyramidal motility; defended fundamental principle of neuron; stated that in vertebrates metamery begins only when the nerves appear. In cytology, studied genesis of the germ cells and early differentiation of sex cells in *Bufo:* found that primary germ cells are female, and that sexual determination results from later embryonic development; elucidated sebaceous secretion; demonstrated functional synergism between epithelial cells and melanophores.

BECCARIA, GIAMBATISTA (*b. Mondovì, Italy, 1716; d. Turin, Italy, 1781*), electricity.

Christened Francesco, became Giambatista on joining Piarists (1732); appointed to chair of physics at Turin (1748). In search of arguments against Cartesians, undertook study of electricity: publicized and extended Franklin's experiments, writing five books; sought to explain meteorological and geophysical phenomena as manifestations of "natural" electricity; asserted, against prevailing view, that air is a better conductor than pure water; designed useful apparatus, including electrical thermometer; constructed parallel plate condensers and attempted to estimate their relative powers; developed complicated theory of electrical atmospheres and "vindicating," or regenerating, electricity, which led Volta to invention of the electrophorus.

BÉCHAMP, PIERRE JACQUES ANTOINE (*b. Bassing, Moselle, France, 1816; d. Paris, France, 1908*), chemistry, biochemistry.

Trained and worked first as pharmacist; doctorates in science (1853) and medicine (1856); taught at Strasbourg (1853–56), Montpellier (1856–76), and Lille (1876–86). Did important work on albuminoid substances, using optical activity to distinguish large number of complex compounds; developed cheap industrial process to produce aniline (1852); identified parasitic nature of two silkworm diseases, anticipating Pasteur's results. Quarreled with Pasteur over theory of life: claimed that living organisms are composed of inert chemical substances and of *microzymas,* subcellular molecular granulations that are essentially eternal and polyvalent and that act as organizing principles.

BECHER, JOHANN JOACHIM (*b. Speyer, Germany, 1635; d. London, England, 1682*), chemistry, economics.

Largely self-educated, his far-flung interests included alchemy, medicine, theology, politics, economics, and formulation of a universal language. Publication of first book, *Naturkündigung der Metallen* (1661), established him as iatrochemist; M.D., University of Mainz (1661), appointed professor of medicine (1663). Subsequent royal and imperial appointments in Munich and Vienna involved him in economic policy, technical education reform, and alchemy; moved to Holland (1678), then England (1679), following experiments in extraction of gold from sea sand. His chemical theory held that air, water, and earth were the true elementary principles and were not interchangeable; the essential substance of metals and stones is earth, which occurs in three types: *terra vitrescible,* giving substance; *terra fluida,* giving form, odor, and weight; and *terra pinguis,* giving color and combustibility. Stahl developed the concept of oily, combustible *terra pinguis* into the phlogiston theory, praising Becher's work.

BECKE, FRIEDRICH JOHANN KARL (*b. Prague, Czechoslovakia, 1855; d. Vienna, Austria, 1931*), mineralogy, petrography.

Studied under Tschermak at University of Vienna; taught at universities of Czernowitz (1882), Prague (1890), and Vienna (1898); edited *Mineralogische und petrographische Mitteilungen* (from 1899). Did fundamental work in elucidation of metamorphism, combining exact observations with bold and sophisticated theoretical considerations; introduced terminology, developed graphic representation of rock components. Developed method for relative determination of light refraction by means of Becke line (1893). Stated (1896) Becke volume rule: assuming isothermal conditions, with increased pressure, the formation of minerals with the smallest molecular volume will be favored.

BECKER, GEORGE FERDINAND (*b. New York, N.Y., 1847; d. Washington, D.C., 1919*), geology.

Degrees from Harvard, University of Heidelberg, and Royal Academy of Mines, Berlin. Joined U.S. Geological Survey under Clarence King, contributing studies of mining districts and accounts of the Pacific Coast ranges and the Sierra Nevada. Supported theory of rigid earth. Helped found and was director of Carnegie Geophysical Laboratory.

BECKMANN, ERNEST OTTO (*b. Solingen, Germany, 1853; d. Berlin, Germany, 1923*), chemistry.

Studied at Leipzig (graduated 1878) under Kolbe, and later under Wislicenus and Ostwald; taught at Giessen (1891), Erlangen (1892–97), and Leipzig (1897–1912); director of Kaiser Wilhelm Institute of Applied and Pharmaceutical Chemistry (from 1912). Investigated isonitroso compounds; discovered (1886) Beckmann transformation, in which ketoximes are converted into amides by action of acids, acid chlorides, or phosphorus pentachloride. This reaction drew attention to isomerism in nitrogen bonding. Developed thermometer with variable range, useful in molecular weight determination.

BECKMANN, JOHANN (*b. Hoya, Germany, 1739; d. Göttingen, Germany, 1811*), economy, technology.

Studied at Göttingen (1759–62) and taught there (1766; professor of economics, 1770). Founded the independent science of agriculture with his textbook *Grundsätze der teutschen Landwirthschaft* (1769), stressing need of scientific foundation for practical agriculture. Interest in processing of raw materials by different trades led to *Anleitung zur Technologie* (1777), the first advanced textbook in this field, noteworthy for systematic approach; introduced technology into high school curriculum. Used primary literary material to write history of inventions; also wrote on natural sciences and philology.

BECQUEREL, ALEXANDRE-EDMOND (*b. Paris, France, 1820; d. Paris, 1891*), experimental physics.

Son of Antoine-César Becquerel (1788–1878), whom he assisted when young and eventually succeeded as director of the Muséum d'Histoire Naturelle (1878). Attended University of Paris (D.Sc., 1840); taught at Conservatoire des Arts et Métiers (1852–60), and Société Chimique de Paris (1860–63). Did important work in electricity, magnetism, and optics. In electricity, measured properties of currents and investigated conditions under which they arose. Studied diamagnetism (1845–55); conceived "Archimedean law" of magnetic action, that substances less magnetic than their surroundings are pushed away from a magnet whereas the more magnetic ones are attracted to it; measured magnetic properties of oxygen. Discovered (1840) electrical currents produced by photochemical reactions; constructed actinometer to measure intensity of light through photochemically-induced currents. Invented phosphoroscope; showed that fluorescence is a phosphorescence of extremely short duration. Studied spectra of luminescent bodies and the sun.

BECQUEREL, ANTOINE-CÉSAR (*b. Châtillon-sur-Loing, Loiret, France, 1788; d. Paris, France, 1878*), electrochemistry.

Graduated from École Polytechnique. First occupant of chair of physics at Muséum d'Histoire Naturelle (1838). His son Alexandre-Edmond succeeded him at the Museum, and his grandson Antoine-Henri (1852–1908) was the discoverer of radioactivity. Study of minerals with Brongniart led to electrical experiments on compression of crystals, electrical effects of heating minerals, and electrical measurement of temperature. Of perhaps greater interest was his work on the voltaic cell. In 1829 employed Davy's discovery that a battery could be made of two liquids separated by a solid barrier in the construction of the first battery that, not being polarized, could supply current at a reasonably constant EMF. Using these cells, he performed small-scale experiments on the synthesis of mineral substances. Of his joint papers, most were written in collaboration with his son, but co-workers also included Ampère and Biot. Corresponded with Faraday over diamagnetism. Invented an electromagnetic balance and a differential galvanometer.

BECQUEREL, [ANTOINE-] HENRI (*b. Paris, France, 1852; d. Le Croisic, Brittany, France, 1908*), physics.

Known mainly for discovery of radioactivity, for which he received the Nobel Prize for physics jointly with the Curies (1903). Held three chairs of physics in Paris—Museum of Natural History, École Polytechnique, and Conservatoire National des Arts et Métiers. His father, Alexandre-Edmond, and grandfather, Antoine-César, were also renowned physicists. His early research was almost exclusively optical. His first extensive investigations (1875–82) dealt with rotation of plane-polarized light by magnetic fields. Obtained doctorate from Faculty of Sciences of Paris (1888). By 1896, Becquerel's discovery of radioactivity was complete, although he continued with ionization studies of his penetrating radiation. He had established the occurrence and properties of that radiation and showed that the power of emitting penetrating rays was a particular property of uranium. Characterized his own achievement as the first observation of phosphorescence in a metal. This discovery opened the way to nuclear physics. Later, he identified electrons in the radiations of radium (1899–1900) and published the first evidence of a radioactive transformation (1901). He united two descriptive traditions, the magneto optics of his own experience and a line of qualitative studies of the discharge of electricity through gases. By 1900, Becquerel had duplicated J. J. Thomson's experiments for the radium radiation and had shown that it too consisted of negatively charged ions. His pioneer investigations opened the way to the Curies' discoveries, and their discoveries validated and showed the importance of his own.

BECQUEREL, PAUL (*b. Paris, France, 1879; d. Évian, France, 1955*), biology.

Grandson of Edmond Becquerel and nephew of Henri Becquerel. Licentiate in natural sciences from Faculty of Sciences at Paris (1903); doctorate, 1907; assistant at Faculty of Sciences. After World War I, member of Faculty of Sciences at Nancy; in 1927, appointed professor of general botany at Poitiers.

Becquerel did much to explain physiological nature of the plant seed and the reactions of protoplasm to freezing and dehydration. Concluded that a portion of the seed always lived, protected from hostile external environments by an impermeable protective layer. Showed that plant and animal tissue could attain a state of suspended or latent life. Studied effects of freezing on vegetable protoplasm; showed in 1939 that plant cells are not killed by plasmolysis upon freezing.

BEDDOE, JOHN (*b. Bewdley, Worcestershire, England, 1826; d. Bradford-on-Avon, England, 1911*), physical anthropology.

Studied medicine at University College, London, University of Edinburgh (M.D., 1853) and Vienna. Practiced medicine in Clifton (1857–91). Founding member of Ethnological Society (1857). Beddoe was a descriptive physical anthropologist, who wanted to explain the observed physical variation of man in terms of the spread of language and culture. His keen observations of physical variations in man resulted in his *Contributions to Scottish Ethnology* (1853). His essay on the origin of the English nation, *The Races of Britain: A Contribution to the Anthropology of Western Europe* (1885), was extended to cover all Europe in *The Anthropological History of Europe, Being the Rhind Lectures for 1912*.

BEDDOES, THOMAS (*b. Shifnal, Shropshire, England, 1760; d. Clifton, England, 1808*), medicine, chemistry.

Studied at Pembroke College, Oxford, and Edinburgh. Popular teacher of chemistry at Oxford (from 1788). Perhaps his most important contribution to science was his discovery of Humphry Davy. Well known in his own day for popular works on preventive medicine and investiga-

tions of use of gases in treating diseases. Among his publications are *Isaac Jenkins,* a moral tale (1792); *Essay on Consumption* (1799); and *Hygëia,* a series of essays describing the regimen necessary for avoiding disease (1802–03). In 1798, set up his Pneumatic Institution at Clifton for treating diseases by administration of gases, later a clinic of preventive medicine.

BEDE, THE VENERABLE (*b. Northumbria, England,* A.D. *672/673; d. Jarrow-on-Tyne, England,* A.D. *735*), philosophy.

Spent entire life at a monastery at Jarrow, which had unusual scientific resources.

Half of Bede's volumes are scriptural exegesis, an art in which he excelled. Five of the remaining six volumes contain homilies, hagiography, history, a guide to holy places, religious and occasional verses, and letters. They include his renowned work, *Historia ecclesiastica gentis Anglorum.* The remaining volume contains Bede's several *opera didascalica,* textbooks designed for courses in the emerging vocational curriculum of monastic schools. Bede reproduced or created tables of calculation, Easter tables, calendars, formularies, and mnemonic verses. First to have created, or at least to have recorded, on the basis of the Metonic nineteen-year lunar cycle, a perpetual (532-year) cycle of Easters and to have tabulated it. Built upon the work of Dionysius Exiguus and took his anchor date, the *annus Domini.* Became first historian to use the Christian era, and first stated the tidal principle of "establishment of port."

BEECKMAN, ISAAC (*b. Middelburg, Zeeland, Netherlands, 1588; d. Dordrecht, Netherlands, 1637*), physics, mechanics.

Studied at Leiden, Saumur, Amsterdam, and Caen (M.D., 1618). As apprentice received valuable experience in combustion, pumping, and hydrodynamics. Named rector of Latin school at Dordrecht (1627), where in 1628 he established the first meteorological station in Europe. Some of the greatest French philosophers went to see him—Descartes, Gassendi, and Mersenne. Early proponent of application of a mathematical method in physics. In 1613, rejecting any internal cause of motion, he put forward a principle of inertia for both circular and rectilinear movement. In 1618 he worked out a law of uniformly accelerated movement of bodies falling *in vacuo.* His experimental work was as concerned with purely scientific inquiry as with practical applications. He made both appreciative and devastating comments on the experiments contained in Francis Bacon's *Historia experimentalis.* He deemed much of Gilbert's work conformable to his own findings but rejected "internal magnetical force" as the motive power of the earth, holding that earth is subject to inertial motion in empty space. Considered Galileo's theory of tides a strong argument for the rotation of the earth, but suggested first making a mechanical model to test it.

BEER, WILHELM (*b. Berlin, Germany, 1797; d. Berlin, 1850*), astronomy.

A banker by profession; by avocation an amateur astronomer and owner of a private observatory. His place in the history of astronomy is due to contributions he and Johann Mädler made (1830–40) to selenography and solar-system studies in general. Their first joint work was *Physikalische Beobachtungen des Mars in der Erdnähe* (1830), and their chef d'oeuvre was *Mappa selenographica totam lunae hemisphaeram visibilem complectens* (1836), which constitutes a milestone in development of selenographical literature. His name remains inseparably connected with the best map of the moon produced in the first half of the nineteenth century. Half brother of the composer Meyerbeer.

BEEVOR, CHARLES EDWARD (*b. London, England, 1854; d. London, 1908*), neurology, neurophysiology.
Educated at University College, London (M.B., 1879; L.S.A., 1880; M.D., 1881). His main ambition was to make possible more accurate diagnosis of diseases of the nervous system. His *Diseases of the Nervous System: A Handbook for Students and Practitioners* (1898) revealed his clinical ability. In addition to being physician at hospitals in London, carried out neurophysiological investigations and practiced clinical neurology. Did landmark work in development of the concept of cerebral localization. Observed the function of muscles and muscle groups both in health and in disease. Carried out experiments on the human brain in order to discover the areas of distribution of the five main arteries.

BÉGHIN, HENRI (*b. Lille, France, 1876; d. Paris, France, 1969*), mechanics.
Studied at the École Normale Supérieure; taught in many schools, including Montpellier, Lille, and Paris.
Organized training of radio electricians during World War I. Associated with the most general treatment of systems of nonholonomic linkage, through which he demonstrated how to use Lagrange's equations in percussion problems. Provided an elegant extension of Carnot's theorem that leads to an exhaustive formulation. Extended the solution of Painlevé's paradox by increasing the examples of dynamic interference due to friction. The theory of the gyrostatic compass, which Béghin published in 1921 and later perfected, is significant for his fusion of the extensions of rational mechanics with technical and experimental data.

BEGUIN, JEAN (*b. Lorraine, France, ca. 1550; d. Paris, France, ca. 1620*), chemistry.
Little known of his early life. Best known for public lectures on chemical techniques, unveiling mysteries of iatrochemistry and teaching chemistry as the art of separating and recombining natural mixed bodies to produce agreeable and safe medicines. Published the lectures in the *Tyrocinium chymicum* (1610), which grew from 70 to nearly 500 pages in its later editions and translations.

BÉGUYER DE CHANCOURTOIS, ALEXANDRE-ÉMILE (*b. Paris, France, 1820; d. Paris, 1886*), geology.
Studied at the École Polytechnique and the École des Mines, teaching at the latter. He and Élie de Beaumont, whose geological theories greatly influenced him, explored the Haute-Marne regions for the French Geological Survey. This resulted in Béguyer's publication in 1860 of geological map (drawn by M. Duhamel) and collaboration with Élie de Beaumont on *Études stratigraphiques sur le départ de la Haute-Marne* (1862). He formulated a method for classifying chemical elements based upon the distri-

bution of these elements in the crust of the globe. His scheme, a precursor of Mendeleev's periodic table, was put forth in "Vis tellurique" (1862), the model for his theory being the "telluric screw," a heliacal graph wound about a cylinder. Participated in the voyage of the *Reine Hortense* to the polar regions (1856). Appointed director general of mines (1875).

BEHAIM, MARTIN, also known as **Martin of Bohemia** (*b. Nuremberg, Germany, 1459; d. Lisbon, Portugal, 1507*), geography.
Disciple of Regiomontanus; influenced by his *Ephemerides*. In Portugal, became a member of the Council of Mathematicians. Took part in the expedition of Diogo Cão (1485–86) that followed the coast of Africa to Cape Cross. Spent 1491 to 1493 in Nuremberg, where he built his famous globe which places him among the greatest geographers of the Renaissance. The globe, still extant, is covered with parchment adorned with many figures (111 miniatures, forty-eight banners, and fifteen coats of arms), with inscriptions explaining the geography. A nautical chart, since lost, that showed the strait discovered years later by Magellan was attributed to Behaim.

BEHREND, ANTON FRIEDRICH ROBERT (*b. Harburg [now part of Hamburg], Germany, 1856; d. Hannover, Germany, 1926*), chemistry.
Ph.D. Leipzig (1881); taught at Leipzig (until 1895) and at the Technische Hochschule, Hannover (1895–1925). Best known for synthetic organic chemistry: first synthesis of uric acid (1888), confirming Fischer's formulas for purine group. Also showed existence of two forms of d-glucose (1904) and proved its ring structure (1910).

BEHRING, EMIL VON (*b. Hansdorf, Germany, 1854; d. Marburg, Germany, 1917*), medicine, serology.
Attended Friedrich Wilhelms Institute in Berlin (M.D., 1878). Wrote early papers on sepsis and antisepsis in theory and practice. His iodoform experiments began his preoccupation with antitoxic blood-serum therapy. In 1889, joined Koch's Institute for Hygiene at the University of Berlin. Between 1889 and 1895, developed his pioneering ideas on serum therapy and his theory of antitoxins. In 1890 Behring and Kitasato published their first paper on blood-serum therapy, followed by another by Behring discussing the blood-serum therapy not only in the treatment of tetanus but also of diphtheria. Ehrlich's 1891 demonstration that even vegetable poisons led to the formation of antitoxins in the organism confirmed Behring's theory. From 1893 on, serum therapy experimentation was conducted on a more extensive scale. In 1894 appointed professor of hygiene in Halle and in 1895, in Marburg, where he carried on intensive research and organized what is now known as the Behring Institute. In 1901 his lifework was crowned with the first Nobel Prize in physiology and medicine. In 1889, Behring began to study tuberculosis. His vaccination attempts failed, but he ascribed the spread of tuberculosis mainly to the consumption by infants of milk containing tuberculosis bacilli. His suggestions for combating bovine tuberculosis brought about vital changes in public health policy. In 1913 he introduced active preventive vaccination against diphtheria.

BEIJERINCK, MARTINUS WILLEM (*b. Amsterdam, Netherlands, 1851; d. Gorssel, Netherlands, 1931*), microbiology, botany.

Studied at Delft Polytechnical School and University of Leiden (Ph.D., 1877); taught in agricultural schools, worked in Dutch Yeast and Spirit Factory (1884–95), taught at Polytechnical School in Delft (1895–1921). Wrote over 140 papers on botany, microbiology, chemistry, and genetics. Research on biology of gall wasps and gall formation (1882) led to theory of ontogeny in higher plants and animals as being controlled by a series of growth enzymes that become active in fixed succession (1917). Made major contributions to microbiology: developed technique of enrichment culture (simultaneously with Vinogradsky) permitting isolation of highly specialized microorganisms; cultivated and isolated *Rhizobium leguminosarum*, a bacillus that fixes free nitrogen and causes formation of nodules on roots of Leguminosae; characterized *Azotobacter* as nitrogen-fixing; isolated new genus, *Aerobacter*. In studying tobacco mosaic disease, concluded that filterable pathogen was a *contagium vivum fluidum*, a term coined to convey his concept of a living infectious agent in a fluid (noncellular) form—a revolutionary idea at a time when life and cellularity were thought to be inextricably connected.

BEILSTEIN, KONRAD FRIEDRICH (*b. St. Petersburg, Russia, 1838; d. St. Petersburg, 1906*), chemistry.

Studied with Bunsen and Kekulé at Heidelberg, Liebig at Munich, and Wöhler at Göttingen (Ph.D, 1858). Continued studies with Wurtz and Charles Friedel in Paris, and with Löwig in Breslau. In 1860 began to teach at Göttingen. Moved to Technical Institute of St. Petersburg in 1866 and remained there the rest of his life. At Göttingen, had attempted to bring order into organic chemistry by starting his *Handbuch der organischen Chemie.* The first edition (1880–82) described 15,000 compounds. After his death the Deutsche Chemische Gesellschaft continued the work.

BEKETOV, NIKOLAI NIKOLAEVICH (*b. Alferevka village, Penzensky district, Russia, 1827; d. St. Petersburg [now Leningrad], Russia, 1911*), chemistry.

Graduated from Kazan University (1849). In 1855, junior scientific assistant at Kharkov University; 1859–86, professor of chemistry. Began his scientific activity with work in organic chemistry, studying esterification reactions; later interests were physical and inorganic chemistry. As a result of his studies of liberation of certain metals by hydrogen and by other metals, he established an activity series of metals. The results were stated in his doctoral dissertation (1865). Later discovered and substantiated the theoretical possibility that metals could be reduced from their oxides by using aluminum, thus opening the way to the creation of the method of aluminothermal reduction.

BEKHTEREV, VLADIMIR MIKHAILOVICH (*b. Sorali, Vyatskaya oblast, Russia, 1857; d. Leningrad, U.S.S.R., 1927*), neurology, psychology.

Graduated from the Medical and Surgical Academy of St. Petersburg (1878). In 1881, defended dissertation for M.D., which dealt with the possible relation between body temperature and some forms of mental illness; then

began work with Flechsig and Meinert, Westfall and Charcot, Du Bois-Reymond, and Wundt. In 1885, became professor of psychiatry at Kazan University, where he organized the first laboratory for research on the anatomy and physiology of nervous system. Completed investigations of the role of the cortex in regulation of the functions of internal organs. From 1893 to 1913, headed the department of nervous and psychic diseases of the Military Medical Academy in St. Petersburg. Defined more precisely the path and separation of posterior rootlets of the spinal cord and described a group of cells on the surface of the shaft of the posterior horn (Bekhterev cells) and the internal bundle of the lateral column. Described the large bundles of the brain stem and the pia mater nodes of the base of the brain; studied in detail and described the reticular formation in 1885; and established the precise location of the taste center within the brain cortex in 1900. Isolated a number of reflexes and symptoms that have important diagnostic significance, and described new illnesses, notably numbness of the spine (Bekhterev's disease).

BELAIEW, NICHOLAS TIMOTHY, in Russian **Nikolai Timofeevich Beliaev** (*b. St. Petersburg, Russia, 1878; d. Paris, France, 1955*), metallurgy.

Studied at Mikhailovskoi Artilleriiskoi Akademii in St. Petersburg (1902–05); remained to teach metallurgical chemistry (1909–14). Strongly influenced by D. K. Chernoff. Wrote classic paper on the history and metallurgy of Damascus steel (1918). Studied, in engineering steels, the coalescence of iron carbide that the Oriental swordmakers had unknowingly achieved through their methods of forging. Showed that the geometric Widmanstätten structure could also be produced in steel under certain conditions of cooling. His emphasis on the crystallographic basis of the change and his detailed analysis of the geometry had great influence.

BÉLIDOR, BERNARD FOREST DE (*b. Catalonia, Spain, 1697/98; d. Paris, France, 1761*), mechanics, ballistics, military and civil architecture.

Bélidor's life mingled the scientific with the military. With Jacques Cassini and Philippe de La Hire, surveyed meridian from Paris to the English Channel. As professor of mathematics at artillery school at La Fère, he wrote textbooks and technical manuals in the 1720's and 1730's: *Nouveau cours de mathématique,* a text for artillery cadets and engineers; *Le bombardier françois,* for use in combat. With *La science des ingénieurs* (1729) and *Architecture hydraulique* (1737–39) Bélidor entered into the science of mechanics proper with a summons to builders to base design and practice on its principles. The first work concerned erection and reduction of fortifications. The second embraced civil constructions.

BELL, ALEXANDER GRAHAM (*b. Edinburgh, Scotland, 1847; d. Baddeck, Nova Scotia, 1922*), technology.

Bell achieved fame as inventor of the telephone and fortune under a broad interpretation given to the patent granted him in 1876. Did early telephone work in Boston, later moving to Washington. His interest in the deaf (his mother and wife were deaf) led Bell to publish several articles on hereditary deafness. This in turn led to studies on longevity and a series of experiments in which, after twenty years of selection, he had a flock of six-nippled sheep. As he had suspected, twin production increased with the number of nipples. Conceived the idea of the journal *Science* (1883). Donated funds for the establishment of the Smithsonian's astrophysical observatory and the National Geographic Society.

BELL, CHARLES (*b. Edinburgh, Scotland, 1774; d. Hallow, Worcestershire, England, 1842*), anatomy.

Studied medicine privately and at Edinburgh University. Co-owner of and principal lecturer at Great Windmill Street School of Anatomy (1812–25); a founder of Middlesex Hospital Medical School (1828). Returned to Edinburgh as professor of surgery (1836). Developed his experimental techniques involving the peripheral nerves to discover how the brain functions. In 1811 published *Idea of a New Anatomy of the Brain*. His techniques and observations led to Johannes Müller's generalizations on sensory functions of the nervous system. Bell did not deduce the Bell-Magendie law—that the anterior roots are motor, the posterior sensory—from his experiments. Magendie did his own experimental work, formulating and publishing the Bell-Magendie law (1822) after hearing of Bell's work. The law was a special case of the general principle of nervous function that Bell had worked out, but it was the special case that was noted and became the subject of a bitter priority dispute between Bell and Magendie.

BELL, ERIC TEMPLE (*b. Aberdeen, Scotland, 1883; d. Watsonville, Calif., 1960*), mathematics.

Migrated to the United States in 1902. Attended Stanford, University of Washington (M.A., 1908), Columbia (Ph.D., 1912). Bell had a lifelong interest in elliptic functions and number theory. Produced about 250 mathematical research papers, four learned books, eleven popularizations, and as "John Taine," seventeen science fiction novels, many short stories, and some poetry. At the University of Washington from 1912, he published significant contributions on numerical functions, analytic number theory, multiply periodic functions, and Diophantine analysis. Taught at California Institute of Technology (1926–53). Known for his *Men of Mathematics* (1937) and *The Development of Mathematics* (1940).

BELL, ROBERT (*b. Toronto, Ontario, 1841; d. Rathwell, Manitoba, 1917*), geology.

Graduated from McGill University (1861); taught at Edinburgh (1862) and Queen's University (1863–67). Worked for Canadian Geological Survey part-time from age fifteen, full-time from 1867 to 1906. Gained M.D.,C.M. degree in 1878. In 1870 commenced thirty continuous years of exploration of the territory from Lake Superior northward to the Arctic and from Saskatchewan to the east shore of Hudson Bay—work that today would be classified as reconnaissance mapping. Traveled mainly by canoe; his only instruments were the compass, sextant, boat log, and Rochon micrometer. His most important contribution was mapping both shores of Hudson Bay and parts of the Nottaway, Churchill, and Nelson rivers. Produced more than thirty reports on the geology of the areas surveyed, the balance of his more than 200 titles dealing with geography, zoology and botany, resources, and Indian lore.

BELLANI, ANGELO (*b. Monza, Italy, 1776; d. Milan, Italy, 1852*), physics, chemistry.

Educated in religious institutions; ordained a priest in Milan. Began scientific activity with construction and study of thermometers. Designed the "thermometergraph." Made instrument with a double scale, helpful in automatic registering of maximum and minimum temperatures. In 1808, demonstrated how "zero" on the scale is subject to variations caused by deformations of the glass over the years; established thermometer factory in Milan. After 1815 studied meteorology, agriculture, and natural history. Made a hygrometer from a fish bladder (1836) and perfected Landriani's *atmidomètre*. In 1834 defined his theory on formation of hail.

BELLARDI, LUIGI (*b. Genoa, Italy, 1818; d. Turin, Italy, 1889*), paleontology, entomology.

Self-taught in the natural sciences through collections and travels. Taught natural history for thirty years at the Liceo Gioberti; curator of paleontological collection of the Royal Geological Museum, Turin. His major scientific activity concentrated on the Cenozoic Mollusca of the Piedmont and of Liguria. Between 1854 and 1874 studied Piedmont diptera. First in Italy to discuss phylloxera and relationship to viticulture. Immediately understood the fundamental importance of the new evolutionary ideas; his last works show relationships between different forms of Mollusca and their probable filiation through geological time.

BELLARMINE, ROBERT (*b. Montepulciano, Italy, 1542; d. Rome, Italy, 1621*), theology, philosophy.

Joined Jesuit order (1560), took master's degree in philosophy at Roman College (1563). Ordained priest in 1570; completed theological studies in Louvain. Leading Catholic theologian on norms for proper interpretation of Scripture. His *Disputationes de controversiis* was the most effective piece of Catholic polemic scholarship of the century. Recognized as the leading defender of the papacy. Made rector of Roman College in 1592, cardinal in 1599, and archbishop of Capua in 1602. Lived at the Vatican as the pope's major theological adviser. Bellarmine's relevance to the history of science comes from his role in the Galileo story. In 1611 he was among the Roman dignitaries Galileo invited to see the new-found wonders in the sky. Disturbed at implications of what he saw, he asked astronomers of his old college to test the accuracy of Galileo's claims. Bellarmine emphasized that since the heliocentric theory of Copernicus could in no way be "strictly demonstrated," the troublesome scriptural phrases about the motion of the sun could not be regarded as metaphorical. In the *Dialogo*, Galileo attempted to meet Bellarmine's challenge to provide a dynamical proof of the earth's motion. In 1616, the pope asked Bellarmine to notify Galileo officially, in person, of the contents of the decree outlawing Copernicanism.

BELLAVITIS, GIUSTO (*b. Bassano, Vicenza, Italy, 1803; d. Tezze, near Bassano, 1880*), mathematics.

Self-taught in mathematics; appointed full professor, University of Padua (1845). In geometric calculus, developed method of equipollencies (two line segments are equipollent if they are equal, parallel, and pointing in same direction), a barycentric calculus that paved the way for W. R. Hamilton's quaternions and for vector theory. In algebraic geometry, worked on classification of curves; offered graphical solution of spherical triangles, based on transformation—through reciprocal vector radia—of a spherical surface into a plane. In algebra, continued Ruffini's research on numerical solution of an algebraic equation of any degree; studied theory of numbers and of congruences. Wrote also on infinitesimal analysis, physics, history of mathematics, and on problem of a universal scientific language.

BELLEVAL, PIERRE RICHER DE (*b. Châlons-sur-Marne, France, ca. 1564; d. Montpellier, France, 1632*), medicine.

Studied medicine at Avignon (physician's degree, 1587) and Montpellier (doctorate, 1595). Taught at medical college of Montpellier and devoted time and money to first botanical garden in France, at Montpellier (from 1593). Planning a general herbarium of Languedoc when he died; many of the plates that were to illustrate it are extant.

BELLINGSHAUSEN, FABIAN VON. *See* **Bellinsgauzen, Faddei.**

BELLINI, LORENZO (*b. Florence, Italy, 1643; d. Florence, 1704*), physiology, medical theory.

Attended University of Pisa. Appointed professor of theoretical medicine (1663) and anatomy (1668) at Pisa. First physician to Duke Cosimo III of Tuscany (*ca.* 1693). Considered a founder of Italian iatromechanism; pioneer in applying mechanical philosophy to explanation of functions of human body. The *Exercitatio anatomica de usu renum* (1662) was an important study of structure and function of the kidneys; discovered complicated structure composed of fibers, open spaces, and densely packed tubules opening into the pelvis of the kidney, which provided the key to true renal function. His 1665 essay on taste, *Gustus organum*, included sections on functional anatomy of the tongue. In 1683 published *De urinis et pulsibus et missione sanguinis*, the first important attempt by an Italian to apply mechanical philosophy to medical theory. The *Opuscula aliquot* (1695) treats problems ranging from hydraulics of intrauterine and extrauterine circulation to mechanics of the "contractile villi."

BELLINSGAUZEN, FADDEI F. (*b. Arensburg, on the island of Oesel, Russia* [*now Kingissepp, Sarema, Estonian Soviet Socialist Republic*], *1779; d. Kronstadt, Russia, 1852*), navigation, oceanography.

Began his naval career in 1789 in Kronstadt. Participated in the first round-the-world voyage by a Russian ship, the *Nadezhda* (1803–06). Military governor of Kronstadt (1839–52). One of the founders of the Russian Geographic Society (1845). Commander of the 1819–21 Russian Antarctic expedition. Came within twenty miles of the Antarctic mainland; this was the first view of the earth's sixth continent. He made the first attempt to describe and classify the Antarctic ice. Explained the origin of coral islands and determined the position of the South Magnetic Pole. His table of compass variations was published in Leipzig by Gauss (1840).

BELON, PIERRE (*b. Soultière, near Cerans, France, 1517; d. Paris, France, 1564*), zoology, botany.

Studied at University of Wittenberg under Valerius Cordus; obtained licentiate in medicine from Paris Faculty of Medicine (1560). In *Histoire naturelle des estranges poissons marins* (1551), he presented an orderly classification of fish (sturgeon, tuna, *malarmat*), dolphin, and hippopotamus. Considered the originator of comparative anatomy, he also set forth the first notions of embryology. One of the first explorer-naturalists, undertook long voyages through Greece, Asia, Judaea, Egypt, and Arabia. First to bring order into the world of feathered animals. More interested in practical uses of plants than scientific description. Advocated acclimatization of exotic plants in France. Clarified the therapeutic use of bitumen.

BELOPOLSKY, ARISTARKH APOLLONOVICH (*b. Moscow, Russia, 1854; d. Pulkovo, U.S.S.R., 1934*), astrophysics.

Graduated from Faculty of Physics and Mathematics of Moscow University (1877). Worked under Bredikhin at Moscow Observatory (1877–88) and at Pulkovo Observatory (from 1888). Worked on positional astronomy but did major work in photography: photographed the sun, studied law of its rotation; photographed eclipse of 1887; was first in Russia to attempt to photograph stars. At Pulkovo did astrometry; in 1895 began spectrographic studies: established latitudinal differences in Jupiter's axial rotation; confirmed that Saturn's rings are not solid. Determined radial velocities, discovered spectral duality of many stars. Discovered variability of spectrum of α_2 Canum Venaticorum, showing strong perturbations in its atmosphere. In studying spectra of Cepheid variables, discovered noncoincidence of the phases of changes in brightness and changes of radial velocities. Determined temperature of sunspots. Laboratory investigations included the rotation of liquid in glass flasks in analogy with the sun's surface, and verification of Doppler's principle in optics.

BELTRAMI, EUGENIO (*b. Cremona, Italy, 1835; d. Rome, Italy, 1900*), mathematics.

Studied mathematics at Pavia under Francesco Brioschi and in Milan. Taught at Bologna (1862–64 and 1866–73), Pisa (1864–66), Rome (1873–76 and 1891–99) and Pavia (1876–91). His works can be divided into two main groups: those before *ca.* 1872, which deal with differential geometry of curves and surfaces and were influenced by Gauss, Lamé, and Riemann; and the later ones, concerned with topics in applied mathematics that range from elasticity to electromagnetics. His most lasting work belongs to the first period. In "Saggio di interpretazione della geometria non-euclidea" (1868) Beltrami showed how possible contradictions in non-Euclidean geometry would reveal themselves in the Euclidean geometry of surfaces; this removed for most mathematicians the feeling that non-Euclidean geometry might be wrong. Later, extended representation of non-Euclidean geometry to manifolds of $n > 2$ dimensions in "Teoria fondamentale degli spazi di curvatura costante." Rescued from oblivion the Jesuit mathematician and logician, Giovanni Saccheri (1667–1733), whose work foreshadowed non-Euclidean geometry. Beltrami's "Ricerche di analisi applicata alla geometria" showed the power of using so-called differential parameters in surface theory, considered the beginning of the use of invariant methods in differential geometry. Also studied potential theory, wave theory, thermodynamics, optics, conduction of heat, and linear partial differential equations. Other papers deal with Maxwell's theory and its mechanistic interpretation.

BENEDEN, EDOUARD VAN (*b. Louvain, Belgium, 1846; d. Liège, Belgium, 1910*), zoology, embryology.

Son of P. J. Van Beneden. Appointed professor at University of Liège (1870). Collected many zoological specimens in Brazil and while at his father's laboratory on Belgian seacoast. Continued his father's studies of protozoa, hydraria, cestodes, nematodes, and tunicates. Extended these studies to dicyemida and vertebrates. Showed, in a contribution to ascidian embryology that represents one of the first and best works on segmentation of the egg, that the germ in formation shows a bilateral symmetry and a clear polarity. In 1884 Van Beneden and Charles Julin were first to follow, in a strictly bilateral egg, what is now called cell lineage. In 1887, they published an important paper on tunicate morphology. His most famous contributions to science are his papers on maturation and fertilization of the egg of *Ascaris megalocephala,* first published in 1883. In this paper he revealed the essential nature of fertilization: the union of two half-nuclei, one female and the other male. The individuality of the single chromosome was thus first demonstrated. With the photographer Neyt (1887), Van Beneden described the centrosome and showed that it was a permanent cell organ. Worked with the problem of the origin of vertebrates. His first interpretation of the didermic mammalian embryo was immediately accepted. His 1888 study of the gastrulation of mammals posthumously became a classic.

BENEDEN, PIERRE-JOSEPH VAN (*b. Mechelen [French, Malines], Belgium, 1809; d. Louvain, Belgium, 1894*), zoology.

Studied medicine at University of Louvain (M.D.) and zoology at Paris. Professor of zoology at Catholic University of Louvain (from 1835). His contributions to zoology are characterized by the importance given to embryology in the recognition of systematic affinities. His main contribution was the discovery of the life cycle of the cestodes (1849), concluding that a cysticercus is an incomplete taenioid. A paper on the mode of development and transmission of intestinal worms (1858) covers a wide range of data on parasites, ending with a masterly treatment of the systematics of worms that is based on embryology. After 1859 he studied Cetacea, both living and fossil.

BENEDETTI, ALESSANDRO (*b. province of Verona, Italy, ca. 1450; d. Venice, Italy, 1512*), anatomy, medicine.

Studied and taught at Padua. Practiced medicine in Venice. Improved the text of the thirty-seven books of Pliny's *Natural History.* His place in natural science rests upon his contributions to the study of anatomy: dissection before his students and his treatise, *Historia corporis humani sive anatomice* (1502). He followed the same firsthand methods in practicing medicine and in his encyclopedic *Omnium a vertice ad calcem morborum signa, causae, indicationes et remediorum compositiones utendique rationes* (1539).

BENEDETTI, GIOVANNI BATTISTA (*b. Venice, Italy, 1530; d. Turin, Italy, 1590*), mathematics, physics.

Studied privately with his father. Court mathematician to Duke Ottavio Farnese at Parma (1558–66). Lectured at Rome on Aristotle. Invited to Turin by the duke of Savoy (1567) and remained until his death, teaching mathematics and science at court. His *Resolutio* (1553) concerns the general solution of all the problems in Euclid's *Elements,* using only a compass of fixed opening. His first important contribution to birth of modern physics in the *Resolutio* treated the speeds of fall mathematically and was based on the principle of Archimedes. His "buoyancy theory of fall" is in many respects identical with that which Galileo set forth. His second book, *Demonstratio* (1554), restated the argument and cited the particular texts of Aristotle that it contradicted. He maintained that unequal bodies of the same material would fall at equal speed through a given medium. The second edition stated that resistance of the medium is proportional to the surface rather than the volume of the falling body. His ultimate expansion of the discussion of falling bodies includes an explanation of their acceleration in terms of increments of impetus successively impressed *ad infinitum.* Two letters on music entitle Benedetti to be considered the true pioneer in investigation of mechanics of production of musical consonances. His empirical approach to musical theory, as applied to tuning of instruments, anticipated the later method of equal temperament. His book on the theory and construction of sundials, *De gnomonum* (1573), dealt with construction of dials at various inclinations and with dials on cylindrical and conical surfaces. Followed by *De temporum emendatione,* on the correction of the calendar (1578). The 1579 *Consideratione* is a polemic work concerning a dispute over the relative volumes of the elements earth and water. His final work, containing the most important Italian contribution to physical thought prior to Galileo, was the *Diversarum speculationum* (1585). It includes a number of arithmetical propositions demonstrated geometrically, a treatise on perspective, a commentary on the fifth book of Euclid's *Elements,* many geometrical demonstrations, and a section on mechanics. Following that is an attack on many of Aristotle's basic physical conceptions. He described hydrostatic pressure and the idea of a hydraulic lift. His scientific originality and versatility afforded a basis for the overthrow of Aristotelian physics.

BENEDICKS, CARL AXEL FREDRIK (*b. Stockholm, Sweden, 1875; d. Stockholm, 1958*), metallography.

Studied at the University of Uppsala (Ph.D., 1904). Appointed professor of physics at University of Stockholm (1910). Regarded as the father of Swedish metallography. A founder and director of Swedish Institute of Metallography. Worked at Laboratorium Benedicks. Pioneered in metal microscopy. Some investigations were published as "Experimental Researches on the Cooling Power of Liquids on Queendring Velocities and on Constituents Troostite and Austenite."

BENEDICT, FRANCIS GANO (*b. Milwaukee, Wis., 1870; d. Machiasport, Me., 1957*), chemistry, physiology.

Studied chemistry at Massachusetts College of Pharmacy and Harvard (B.A., 1893; M.A., 1894). Ph.D., Heidelberg (1895). Taught at Wesleyan University. World's foremost expert on animal calorimetry and respiratory gas analysis. At Boston Nutrition Laboratory, 1907–37. W. O. Atwater and Benedict confirmed the validity of energy conservation in animal metabolism. His most important contribution was the invention of an apparatus to measure simultaneously, directly, and accurately oxygen consumption, expired air, and heat (1924). His respirator provided the foundation for the basal metabolic-rate test. His 1919 standards for basal metabolic rates of humans are still valuable. Insensible perspiration was found proportional to basal metabolism and body weight (1926), variations in temperature of anatomical structures were mapped out (1911), lipogenesis investigated, and caloric values of foods established. Benedict revised clinical treatment of diabetics by demonstrating that their metabolic rate was higher, not lower, than normal (1910).

BENIVIENI, ANTONIO (*b. Florence, Italy, 1443; d. Florence, 1502*), pathological anatomy.

Studied medicine at Pisa and practiced in Florence. Left a number of works in manuscript—*De pestilentia ad Laurentium Medicem; Consilium contra pestem Magistri Antonii Benivieni; De virtutibus*, an essay on Galenic physiology; notes on *De opinionibus antiquorum;* the title of a chapter of a *Liber de cometa ad Julianum Medicem;* separate notes on fossils and minerals; and a treatise, *De chirurgia*. Occupies a place in the history of science for his *De abditis nonnullis ac mirandis morborum et sanationum causis,* an early essay on pathological anatomy (1507).

BENOIT, JUSTIN-MIRANDE RENÉ (*b. Montpellier, France, 1844; d. Dijon, France, 1922*), physics.

Medical doctorate, Montpellier (1869). Then entered the laboratory of the École des Hautes Études (*doctorat ès sciences,* 1873). Director of the Bureau International des Poids et Mesures (1889–1915). Played a large role in standardizing units of length, temperature, and electrical resistance.

BENSLEY, ROBERT RUSSELL (*b. Hamilton, Ontario, 1867; d. Chicago, Ill. 1956*), anatomy.

Graduated from University College of the University of Toronto. Entered the medical department at Toronto (M.B., 1892) and became assistant demonstrator in biology. Joined anatomy department of the University of Chicago (1901), becoming acting head and then director (1907). Differentially stained the cells of the islands of Langerhans in 1906, which led to Banting's discovery of insulin. Confirmed presence of the Golgi apparatus of cells in 1910 and, with B. C. H. Harvey in 1912, demonstrated the mechanism of the gastric secretion of hydrochloric acid. Pioneered in study of cell organelles. Modified I. Altman's freezing-drying technique so that mitochondria could be isolated and subjected to microchemical analysis.

BENTHAM, GEORGE (*b. Stoke, near Plymouth, England, 1800; d. London, England, 1884*), botany.

Attended the faculty of theology at Montauban, where he made his first dried specimens and thus began a herbarium which through his own collecting, purchase, and gift amounted to over 100,000 specimens when he gave it to Kew in 1854. Published *Catalogue des plantes indigènes des Pyrénées et du bas Languedoc* (1826). Studied law at Lin-

coln's Inn, but gave up the legal profession for botany in 1833. Corresponded with most of the leading botanists of the day. His *Labiatarum genera et species* (1832–36) was a masterly treatment. In 1848, contributed a revision of the group for Candolle's *Prodromus*. At Kew, Bentham was given special facilities to continue his research. The *Genera plantarum* (1862–83), the fulfillment of complete collaboration with Joseph D. Hooker, was the culmination of his scientific career.

BENZENBERG, JOHANN FRIEDRICH (*b. Schöller, near Düsseldorf, Germany, 1777; d. Bilk, near Düsseldorf, 1846*), astronomy, geodesy, physics.

Studied theology in Herborn and Marburg, but later, in Göttingen, became interested in the natural sciences. Received his doctorate from the University of Duisburg (1800). Professor of mathematics at the Lyceum in Düsseldorf (1805). With H. W. Brandes, made first simultaneous observations of meteors that made use of terminal points on a basis of either ten or fifteen kilometers and determined height and velocity. Determined the displacement toward the east of falling lead spheres, thereby demonstrating the revolution of the earth some fifty years before Foucault. Also did ballistic experiments and published on geodetical, astronomical, and physical subjects.

BÉRARD, JACQUES ÉTIENNE (*b. Montpellier, France, 1789; d. Montpellier, 1869*), chemistry.

Studied at Paris and Montpellier (M.D. 1817). Became professor of chemistry. First published work (1809–10) was on the analysis of salts and a study of solubilities, at the behest of Berthollet. Collaborated with Malus in a study of infrared and ultraviolet radiation, finding that both can be polarized. His best-known research was carried out in collaboration with François Delaroche on specific heats of gases. Made first investigations of the effect of different atmospheres on ripening of fruit.

BÉRARD, JOSEPH FRÉDÉRIC (*b. Montpellier, France, 1789; d. Montpellier, 1828*), medicine.

M.D., Montpellier (1811). Contributed articles on cranioscopy, the elements, trance, and muscle strength to the *Dictionnaire des sciences médicales*. Appointed professor of public health, Faculté de Médecine of Montpellier (1823). Essentially an analyst of ideas and a philosopher as well as a historian.

BERENGARIO DA CARPI, GIACOMO (*b. Carpi, Italy, ca. 1460; d. Ferrara, Italy, 1530[?]*), medicine.

Received medical degree at University of Bologna (1489), where he practiced and taught surgery. Frequently called to Rome for medical consultation. In 1514 he produced an edition of Mondino da Luzzi's early fourteenth-century *Anothomia*. Placed in charge of postoperative care for Lorenzo de' Medici, who had received a gunshot wound and an occipital skull fracture in battle. His second book, *Tractatus de fractura calvae sive cranei* (1518), was the most original neurosurgical treatise until then. In the *Commentaria* (1521) he refers to a number of specific dissections he had performed on adult cadavers and on fetuses. The *Commentaria,* which contained twenty-one pages of illustrations, was the first work since the time of Galen to display any considerable amount of anatomical information based upon personal investigation and observation. He was the first anatomist to recognize the significance of anatomical illustrations properly related to the text. In 1522 he published an edition of Galen's work on medical prognostication. Despite his intermittent criticisms of Galenic anatomy, Berengario remained a supporter of the "prince of physicians." A much more important publication, in 1522, was the compendium of the *Commentaria*, entitled *Isagogae breves. . . .* a condensed version of *Commentaria* intended as a manual for his students and a replacement of his edition of Mondino's *Anothomia*. When Berengario retired to Ferrara, he edited a collection of Latin translations of Galen (1529).

BERG, LEV SIMONOVICH (*b. Bendery, Bessarabia, Russia, 1876; d. Leningrad, U.S.S.R., 1950*), geography, ichthyology.

Graduated Moscow University (1898). Studied lakes and rivers of central Asia and Kazakhstan until 1902. Studied oceanography in Bergen, Norway 1902–03. Zoologist and director of the ichthyology section of the Zoological Museum of the Academy of Sciences in St. Petersburg (1904–13). Received degrees of doctor of geography (1909) and zoology (1934). In 1913 the Moscow Agricultural Institute made Berg professor of ichthyology. In 1917 Petrograd University appointed him professor of geography; he spent the rest of his life there. Berg's works deal with a wide range of topics in geography and zoology. His early detailed investigations were the beginning of limnology in Russia. Also played an important role in the development of climatology as a science. His ichthyological works are valuable for information on anatomy, embryology, and paleontology, as well as on the systematics and geographical distribution, of all fishes in the U.S.S.R.

The most significant of his works are on geography, classifying the earth's surface according to climatic, soil, biological, and other natural factors. Coordinated his paleoclimatologic and paleogeographic reconstructions with the origin of various sedimentary rocks, the history of relief development, the formation of various soils, and the displacement of landscape zones. His investigations contributed to the intimate coordination of modern geography with historical geology.

Stressed the significance of living organisms in migration of chemical elements and in formation of sedimentary rocks. Determined with reasonable precision the time of the appearance of glacial epochs and the periods in which the climate grew warmer. Devoted serious attention also to history of geography.

BERGER, HANS (*b. Neuses bei Coburg, Germany, 1873; d. Jena, Germany, 1941*), psychiatry, electroencephalography.

Berger entered the University of Jena in 1892, first studying astronomy before switching to medicine. He remained at Jena until he retired in 1938. Berger's career was marked by continuing efforts to establish a correlation between the objective physical activities of the brain and its subjective psychic processes. After some unsuccessful experimentation, he discovered in 1924 the human electroencephalogram. Electroencephalography has proven to be of ever increasing importance in diagnosing and treating neurological diseases. After 1925

Berger specialized in registering the spontaneous fluctuations in electrical potential that could be recorded through the skull from the cortex.

BERGER, JOHANN GOTTFRIED (*b. Halle, Germany, 1659; d. Wittenberg, Germany, 1736*), physiology, medicine.

Berger, whose father was an important educator, graduated in medicine from Jena (1682). He taught at Wittenberg (1688–1736) and was physician to Friedrich August I, king of Poland and Saxony. His chief scientific work is *Physiologia medica* (1701), which deals with the physiological functions of the organs and organ systems and leans heavily toward iatromechanics. It is a general, critical presentation of contemporary physiology from the "modern" point of view; he fought against the weak points of the Galenists and Paracelsians as well as against Stahl.

BERGIUS, FRIEDRICH (*b. Goldschmieden, near Breslau, Germany, 1884; d. Buenos Aires, Argentina, 1949*), chemistry.

Bergius, whose father headed a chemical plant, received his Ph.D. at Leipzig (1907) and set up his own laboratory. He developed a coal similar to that produced in nature through his process of carbonization of peat and cellulose. His first patent was for the manufacture of liquid hydrocarbons from coal (1913). In the 1920's he obtained complete hydrolysis of wood cellulose, producing either dextrose, ethanol, or a nutrient yeast with a 50 percent albumin content. Nobel Prize for chemistry with Carl Bosch, 1931.

BERGMAN, TORBERN OLOF (*b. Katrineberg, Sweden, 1735; d. Medevi, Sweden, 1784*), chemistry, mineralogy, astronomy, physics, geography.

Bergman received the Ph.D. at Uppsala (1758) and taught physics (1758), mathematics (1761), and chemistry (1767) there. He studied insect larvae, notably describing the life cycle of the winter moths that damaged fruit trees. In physical science he discovered an atmosphere on Venus (1761). In *De tubo feruminatoria* (1779) he gave a full account of the blowpipe, which was excellent for qualitative analysis. In *De analysi aquarum* (1778) he gave the first comprehensive analysis of mineral waters. He successfully prepared artificial seltzer and Pyrmont waters (from 1773). In *De minerarum docimasia humida* (1780) he described his procedures for qualitative and quantitative analysis of minerals by wet methods.

Bergman demonstrated (1773) for the first time that all calcite crystals were composed of rhombohedra and that other shapes were built up from these. He accepted the Newtonian theory that crystals were formed by the mutual attraction of the molecules of matter. This belief, and his vast knowledge of chemical reactions, put him in a good position to study chemical affinity. His *Disquisitio de attractionibus electivis* (1775) included tables of affinities. He attempted a general reform of the system of nomenclature in *Sciagraphia regni mineralis* (1782) and in *Meditationes de systemate fossilium naturali* (1784), his last major work (which shows the influence of Guyton de Morveau). Following Linnaeus, he divided inorganic substances into classes, genera, and species defining each class and genus by one word and each species by two. His nomenclature was closely related to his classification of minerals by composition.

BERGMANN, MAX (*b. Fürth, Germany, 1886; d. New York, N.Y., 1944*), biochemistry, organic chemistry.

Graduated from University of Munich (1907); studied and worked at University of Berlin (Ph.D. 1911, *Privatdozent,* 1920); directed Leather Research Institute, Dresden (1921–33); moved to United States, worked at Rockefeller Institute until his death. Elucidated structure of glucal; developed new methods for preparation of α-monoglycerides. In protein chemistry, he devised the "carbobenzoxy" method for synthesis of peptides (1932), leading to discovery of first synthetic peptide substrates for proteolytic enzymes (1936–39, with Fruton); he developed new methods for quantitative analysis of amino acid composition of proteins and proposed a periodic arrangement in the protein chain (1938).

BERGSON, HENRI LOUIS (*b. Paris, France, 1859; d. Paris, 1941*). philosophy.

He was educated at the École Normale Supérieure in Paris and taught philosophy. After 1900 he taught at the Collège de France (to 1921) and achieved an international reputation. He received the Nobel Prize for Literature in 1928. His philosophy offers a new interpretation of four main ideas: time, freedom, memory, and evolution. His anti-materialist, anti-mechanist, and anti-determinist doctrine strongly emphasizes the phenomenon of change or process through unpredictable novelties and the importance of direct, conscious experience as the source of man's most reliable knowledge. His *Essai sur les données immédiates de la conscience* (*Time and Free Will,* 1889) drew a distinction between two kinds of time: measurable, divisible time and the time we experience directly, which he called *durée,* or duration, and which cannot be represented by the fictional units (days, hours, minutes) of mathematical time.

Matière et mémoire (1896) advocates a dualism of body and mind, which are not two entities connected spatially but related temporally through the memory. In *Introduction à la métaphysique* (1903) he contrasted "pure perception," or "intuition," detached from memory and action, with conceptual thought.

In his most famous book, *L'évolution créatrice* (1907) Bergson accepted the historical fact of evolution but rejected Darwin, Lamarck, and Spencer and all mechanistic or materialistic explanations. His theory of cosmic evolution goes beyond biology to metaphysics. In his later works, including *Les deux sources de la morale et de la religion* (1932), the religious element becomes more pronounced. Evolution is nothing less than God's "undertaking to create creators." Bergson's use of biological and psychological material to support his contentions, his capacity to invent striking metaphors, and above all his fluent, persuasive style gave his philosophy wide appeal.

BÉRIGARD, (in modern French, **Beauregard**), **CLAUDE GUILLERMET DE** (*b. Moulins, France, 1578 [according to Niceron; possibly as late as 1591]; d. Padua, Italy, 1663/1664*), medicine, physics, philosophy.

Bérigard studied medicine and philosophy at Aix-en-Provence. He taught philosophy at Pisa from 1628 until 1640, when he went to Padua. He became a well-known teacher there. He was abreast of the scientific movement of his time and well disposed to change, as his synopsis of his courses, *Circulus pisanus* (1643) shows. He always

praised Galileo, yet his *Dubitationes* (1632), on Galileo's *Dialogue* (condemned in 1633) declared firmly the earth's immobility. He probably follows Gassendi in reviving atomism, although Gassendi is usually said to have followed him. He was not aware of the implications of his own qualitative atomism or the importance of universal mechanism.

BERING, VITUS (*b. Horsens, Denmark, 1681; d. Bering Island, Russia, 1741*), geography.

Officer in the Russian navy. Undertook an expedition (starting 1725) for Peter the Great to determine whether Asia and America were joined by land: traveled overland to Kamchatka Peninsula (and was the first to map it); sailed north along coast to the Bering Strait (1728) but poor visibility prevented his sighting America. A second expedition left St. Petersburg (1733), investigated Kurile Islands and Japan, landed in Alaska, and returned along the hitherto unknown Aleutian Islands; forced to winter on uninhabited Bering Island, where Bering died.

BERINGER, JOHANN BARTHOLOMAEUS ADAM, also known as **Johann Barthel Adam Behringer** (*b. Würzburg, Germany, ca. 1667: d. Würzburg, 1738*), medicine, natural history.

Beringer's father was dean of the Faculty of Medicine at Würzburg where Johann studied and where he spent his entire career. After 1700 he held the post previously held by his father. A typically curious scholar, his interest in the petrifactions in the Würzburg Muschelkalk led to his involvement in the famous Würzburg *Lügensteine* hoax. Stones of shell lime carved in a great variety of forms were hidden about Mount Eibelstadt by two of Beringer's colleagues at the University. He found the stones. The hoaxers soon realized the enormity of their actions, but in spite of their best efforts to dissuade him, he published a report on the stones, *Lithographiae Wirceburgensis* (1726). The fraud was discovered, the culprits punished, and he remained on the university staff.

BERKELEY, GEORGE (*b. County Kilkenny, Ireland, 1685; d. Oxford, England, 1753*), philosophy of science.

Berkeley was a critic of seventeenth- and eighteenth-century philosophical, scientific, mathematical, moral, political, and theological ideas and an important link in the development of general philosophy between the period of Descartes and Locke and that of Hume and Kant. From his earliest days at Trinity College, Dublin (1700–13), he came under the influence of Bacon, Boyle, Newton, Locke and Malebranche. In London he formed intellectual associations with such prominent figures as Clarke, Swift, Addison, Steele and Pope. After a brief interlude in America, connected with his abortive attempt to found a college in Bermuda (1729–31), he retired to the bishopric of Cloyne (1734). He moved to Oxford in 1752.

Berkeley's interests ranged from those with a primarily scientific focus to the scientifico-philosophical. *A New Theory of Vision* (1709) is reckoned by *Brett's History of Psychology* to have been the most significant contribution to psychology produced in the eighteenth century. The close interweaving of science with epistemology, as well as of metaphysics with theology, is very prominent in Berkeley's last major work, *Siris* (1744). The body of the book consists, on the one hand, of a discussion of contemporary chemical theory and, on the other, of a critique of Newtonian principles of explanation, of space and time, and of the true interpretation of the concept of causation. The sections on chemistry display considerable acquaintance with most of the major chemical doctrines of Berkeley's period. *Siris* thus involves an attempt to assimilate Newtonian concepts to the more complex phenomena of chemistry and animal physiology. Apart from his more specifically scientific preoccupations, Berkeley's more general aim in these writings is to show that the goal of science can be no more than describing phenomena through the laws and theories of science that govern them.

BERKELEY, MILES JOSEPH (*b. Biggin Hall, Oundle, Northamptonshire, England, 1803; d. Sibbertoft, Market Harborough, Northamptonshire, 1889*), mycology.

Berkeley took the B.A. at Christ's College, Cambridge (1825) and was ordained (1826). He was an active clergyman all his life. His preeminence as a mycologist was established by his treatment of fungi in one volume of J. E. Smith's *The English Flora;* his meticulous descriptions, mostly from living material, remain unsurpassed. He established the constant presence of basidia with apically borne spores in a large group of fungi, thus laying the basis of the primary classification into Basidiomycetes and Ascomycetes. He was the first to appreciate the economic importance of the incidence of plant disease caused by fungi.

BERNAL, JOHN DESMOND (*b. Nenagh, County Tipperary, Ireland, 1901; d. London, England, 1971*), crystallography, molecular biology.

Studied at Emmanuel College, Cambridge, becoming interested in crystallography and deriving the 230 space groups by means of Hamiltonian quaternions. Worked with W. H. Bragg at the Royal Institution, and soon gained a reputation as an outstanding crystallographer; created the Bernal chart, a diagram for interpreting X-ray photographs. Returned to Cambridge (1927) to establish a department of crystallography; did major pioneer work, taking X-ray photographs of biologically important molecules and effectively initiating the field of molecular biology; strove to find explanations of the origin of life (biopoesis) in the geometry and physical structure of such molecules. During World War II he was active in scientific service to England and helped to plan the invasion of Europe by analyzing the condition of beaches. After the war, he worked at Birkbeck College, London University, on the structure of liquids. After the rise of Nazism, politics became his most imperative concern; he was a committed Marxist who was in demand to support Communist causes, and who was absorbed in trying to prevent another war.

BERNARD OF CHARTRES, also known as **Bernardus Carnotensis** (*d. Chartres, France, ca.1130*), philosophy.

An older brother of Thierry of Chartres, Bernard taught the masters responsible for the glory of the school of Chartres. His work survives only in fragments cited in John of Salisbury. He introduced the image "We (the moderns) are like dwarfs sitting on the shoulders of giants (the ancients)."

BERNARD OF LE TREILLE (TRILIA) (*b. near what is now Nîmes, France, ca. 1240; d. Avignon, France, 1292*), astronomy, philosophy.

Bernard was the earliest known French Dominican to be identified as a Thomist but cannot have actually studied under either Thomas Aquinas or Albertus Magnus. He defended Aquinas' teachings on the pure potentiality of primary matter and on the unicity of substantial form. His *Quaestiones* on the *Sphere* of John of Sacrobosco shows him to favor the Ptolemaic system.

BERNARD SILVESTRE (BERNARDUS SILVESTRIS), also known as **Bernard de Tours (Bernardus Turonensis)** (*fl. mid-twelfth century*), philosophy.

Bernard's most famous work (and only certain dating) is the *Cosmographia* (sometimes, improperly, *De mundi universitate*), written 1145–48. In prose and verse it describes the creation of the universe and of man and interprets philosophical thought from many sources. It shows that the heritage of Greek science had not been entirely lost in the first half of the twelfth century and that a man of letters could have mastered much of it simply by reading the available Latin texts.

BERNARD OF TREVISAN, also known as **Bernard of Treviso, Bernard of Treves** (*fl. ca. 1378 or 1400's–1500's [?] in France, Italy, or Germany*), alchemy.

The contents of all the tracts bearing the name of Bernard of Trevisan fit well with fourteenth-century alchemy where his name first appears. He maintained the dominant fourteenth-century theory that gold is made solely from mercury, which contains all four elements, rejecting the thirteenth-century theory that sulfur was also necessary. This doctrine of the composition of the philosophers' stone was reiterated in *Tractatus singularis. . . . De lapide philosophorum* (1647) and in *Traicté de la nature de l'oeuvf* (1659), both bearing his name. With other alchemists of the fourteenth century, he likened the production of the philosophers' stone to human generation, and the mercury of the philosophers to the philosophers' egg. His *Chymica miracula* (1567) has a long autobiographical account of his quest for the philosophers' stone.

BERNARD OF VERDUN, also known as **Bernardus de Virduno** (*France, fl. latter part of the thirteenth century*), astronomy.

Bernard is known only to have been a Franciscan teacher. His *Tractatus super totam astrologiam,* both a defense and a clear, although simplified, description of the Ptolemaic system, contains no astrological allusions. It combined solid spheres with epicycles and eccentrics; its tables of the relative sizes and distances of the sun, moon, and planets were undoubtedly canonical. Its description of the turquet may derive from that of a manuscript (dated 1284) of Francon de Pologne. As a technical treatise on astronomy, the *Tractatus* falls in the same medieval astronomical tradition as the "theory of the planets" literature.

BERNARD, CLAUDE (*b. St.-Julien, near Villefranche, Beaujolais, France, 1813; d. Paris, France, 1878*), physiology.

Bernard was apprenticed to an apothecary (1832), but planned a literary career, and to earn a living took the

M.D. at the Faculty of Medicine in Paris (1843). He discovered his real vocation, physiological experimentation, as *préparateur* to Magendie at the Collège de France (1841–44). He taught there from 1847 and when Magendie retired (1852) took over his chair and the laboratory. He took a doctorate in zoology at the Sorbonne (1853). Honor soon followed honor: a new chair of general physiology at the Faculty of Sciences in Paris and a chair at the Sorbonne (1854–68) and the Muséum d'Histoire Naturelle (from 1868); senator of the Empire (1869); president of the Académie Française (1869).

Bernard founded modern experimental physiology. His most impressive discoveries in digestion concern the functions of the pancreas, especially the importance of pancreatic juice in the digestion and absorption of fats.

His principal discoveries began with the chemistry and nerve control of gastric digestion (1843–45). Thereafter followed his first experiments with curare, the discovery of the role of bile in the digestion of proteins, and research on the innervation of the vocal cords and the functions of the cranial nerves (1844–45). He began work on the mechanism of carbon monoxide intoxication (1846), discovered the difference between the urine of herbivores and that of carnivores, began studies on absorption of fats and the functions of the pancreas, and observed the inhibitory action of the vagus nerve on the heart. He solved the problem of "recurrent sensitivity" in 1847. He made important discoveries concerning sugar in the blood, liver and urine. He demonstrated the role of the pancreas in the first phase of fat metabolism (1849), and discovered (1852) the so-called Horner-Bernard ocular syndrome (paralysis of the sympathetic nerve provokes miosis, narrowing of the palpebral fissure, and enophthalmos on the side of the lesion). He consolidated and completed his physiological discoveries: the experiment of the perfused liver and discovery of glycogen (1855); isolation of glycogen (1857). Brown-Séquard and others offered knowledge of the vasoconstrictor nerves; Bernard alone was responsible for the second stage in the explanation of vasomotor function: the discovery of the vasodilator nerves and the active vasodilator reflex, and the establishment of the concept of the physiological equilibrium of the two antagonistic innervations. He was deeply involved in the problems of animal heat production and regulation. He made two fundamental modifications of Lavoisier's theory: (1) Combustion was not direct but indirect, taking place with the aid of special ferments; and (2) Organic combustion occurred not only in the lungs but in all tissues. He experimented with lowered body temperature, the mechanism of death by exposure to high temperature, rigor mortis, and the acidity and alkalinity of muscles after death.

Bernard's principal theoretical work is *Introduction à l'étude de la médecine expérimentale* (1865). In his *Rapport sur les progrès et la marche de la physiologie générale en France* (1867) he passionately stated his unified synthetic physiology, founded on his notion of the "milieu intérieur" (a term he had coined in 1857) and on the regulatory functions that, under the control of the nervous system, maintain the stability of the fluids and the living tissues. His central notion of "milieu intérieur" arose from his view that life is a permanent conflict between the living particles and the outer world. The stability of the "milieu intérieur" is the precondition of a free, independent life.

The notion of homeostasis and even the beginnings of cybernetics relate to his ideas on the way in which the equilibrium between the "milieu intérieur," the tissues, and the outside world is maintained. Although he contributed to the spread of the cellular theory in France, for him life was protoplasmic and not really cellular, tied more closely to chemical compounds than to histological structures. His criticism of Pasteur's experiments on spontaneous generation today appears as an extraordinary anticipation of molecular biology.

BERNARD, NOËL (*b. Paris, France, 1874; d. Mauroc [near Poitiers], France, 1911*), botany.

Bernard's work on the endophytic fungi found in orchids was primarily done before he received a university professorship (1909, at Poitiers). He began by isolating for the first time three new species of the fungus, including *Rhizoctonia repens,* widespread in the Orchidaceae. He showed that the fungus was necessary for orchid germination (1900–01). On the physiological mechanism, he concluded that the fungus converted starch into sugar, and that the increased osmotic pressure stimulated growth and germination (later shown to be not entirely correct). His career was cut short by his untimely death.

BERNHEIM, HIPPOLYTE (*b. Mulhouse, France, 1840; d. Paris, France, 1919*), psychology.

Bernheim taught at the Faculté de Médecine in Nancy. He investigated a special form of the right asystole (the "Bernheim syndrome" in the South American school of cardiology). He is best known as a master of psychotherapy. He opposed Charcot's concepts of hypnosis and demonstrated (1904) that the four-phase hysteria described by Charcot was a psychoneurotic reaction brought about by suggestion and curable by the same process. He has been called a father of psychoanalysis and greatly impressed Freud, who translated into German two of his works on suggestion (*De la suggestion et de ses applications à la thérapeutique,* 1886; *Hypnotisme, suggestion, psychothérapie études nouvelles,* 1891); however, he always remained a classical psychologist.

BERNOULLI, DANIEL (*b. Groningen, Netherlands, 1700; d. Basel, Switzerland, 1782*), medicine, mathematics, physics.

Son of Johann I Bernoulli. Bachelor's degree (1715), master's degree (1716) in philosophy. Learned mathematics from his father and, especially his older brother Nikolaus II. Doctorate in medicine at Basel (1721). His Petersburg years with his brother (1725–27) and, after his brother's death, with Euler (1727–33) appear to have been his most creative period. About the same time he published his principal work, *Hydrodynamica* (completed 1734, publ.1738), his father published *Hydraulica,* predated to 1732 in an attempt to insure priority—one of many exhibitions of Johann Bernoulli's antagonism toward his second son. After several attempts (from 1721), Daniel finally obtained a chair at Basel, in anatomy and botany (1732–43), then in physiology (1743–50), and finally in physics (1750–76). In physiology he furnished a clear contribution to the determination of the shape and the location of the entrance of the optic nerve into the bulbus or blind spot (1726) and in a 1737 lecture on the computation of the mechanical work done by the heart *(vis cordis)* developed a correct method of lasting significance. He was the first to link Newton's ideas with Leibniz' calculus. He did not, however, solve problems by fundamental Newtonian equations; rather, he preferred to use the first integrals of these equations, especially Leibniz' principle of the conservation of living force, which his father had emphasized.

In rational mechanics the fields of oscillations of rigid bodies and the mechanics of flexible and elastic bodies were new areas that Bernoulli and Euler dominated for many years. Bernoulli's first publication in mechanics (1726) attempted to prove the principle of the parallelogram of forces, today considered an axiom. He also investigated friction of solid bodies and the movement of solid bodies in a resisting medium, based on Newton.

Traditionally, Bernoulli's fame rests on his *Hydrodynamica*. It gives formulas for velocity, duration, and quantity of fluid flowing out of the opening of a container. There is a theory of machinery, lifting devices, pumps, the screw of Archimedes, and windmill sails. His "kinetic gas theory" enabled him to explain the basic gas laws and to anticipate—in incomplete form—Van der Waals' equation of state. It also contains the first derivation of a formula for the flow velocity of air streaming from a small opening.

Bernoulli and Euler dominated the mechanics of flexible and elastic bodies from 1728, when they derived the equilibrium curves. Bernoulli in one stroke derived the entire series of such curves as the velaria, linteria, catenaria, etc. More original was his determination of the curvature of a horizontal elastic band fixed at one end. One of his finest works, "Theoremata de oscillationibus . . ." (completed 1733) for the first time defined the "simple modes" and the frequencies of oscillation of a system with more than one degree of freedom, the points of which pass their positions of equilibrium at the same time. For a uniform, free-hanging rope, he found the displacement of the oscillations at a given distance from the lower end by means of an equation which is the occasion of the first appearance of Bessel's function and which has an infinite number of real roots.

His notable work on vibrating strings (1753) is in reaction to d'Alembert and Euler. Bernoulli deduced that the most general motion could be represented by the superposition of the single vibrations of a string. His beautiful treatment of the oscillations inside organ pipes (1762) contains the first theory of conical pipes and an arrangement consisting of two coaxial pipes of different cross sections as well as a series of new experiments. Working on the vibrations of strings of uneven thickness (1765) he offers the first solutions for the determination of vibration curves from the distribution of density.

Bernoulli's most influential work on probability theory was *De mensura sortis* (1730), which contains an unusual evaluation of capital gains and thus the mathematical formulation of a new kind of value theory in political economy: the larger a person's fortune, the smaller the moral expectation (hope) of a given increment in the fortune. He later (1760) treated a similar problem, statistics on the rate of mortality from smallpox at various ages, defining the relationship between the number of survivors and the number of those who at age x have not yet had smallpox as a function of x. In dealing with the

theory of errors in observation as a branch of probability theory (1777), he challenges the assumption of Simpson and Lagrange that all observations are of equal importance, maintaining that small errors are more probable than large ones.

BERNOULLI, JAKOB (JACQUES) I (*b. Basel, Switzerland, 1654; d. Basel, 1705*), mathematics, mechanics, astronomy.

Bernoulli took degrees in philosophy (1671) and theology (1676) and studied mathematics and astronomy. He lectured at Basel in experimental mechanics (1683–87) and mathematics (1687). He showed his mastery of Leibnizian calculus with his analysis (1690) of Huygens' and Leibniz' solutions to the problem of the curve of constant descent in a gravitational field, using the term "integral" for the first time in its present mathematical sense. Typically careful and critical was his solution (1696) of the so-called Bernoullian differential equation (1696).

Jakob taught his younger brother, Johann, mathematics. Both were self-willed, obstinate, aggressive, vindictive, beset by feelings of inferiority, yet firmly convinced of their own abilities. Jakob's decisive scientific achievement lay not in the formulation of theories, but in the clever and preeminently analytical treatment of individual problems. His primary basic notion was the continuity of all processes of nature (*natura non facit saltum*). Although he assigned great significance to experimental research, he limited himself to a few basic facts on which he sought to base full theories (for example, on the center point of oscillation and on the resistance of elastic bodies). For this reason his final results were intellectually interesting and significant as points of departure. The five dissertations in his *Theory of Series* (1682–1704) contain sixty propositions. In these dissertations on series he apparently wished to reproduce everything he knew; he was primarily concerned with careful rendering of the results and not so much with originality. The *Ars conjectandi* (1713), which is incomplete, is his most original work. After a first-rate commentary on Huygens' *De ratiociniis in aleae ludo,* he takes up the theory of combinations. The chief result here is the rigid derivation of the experimental series through complete induction by means of the so-called Bernoullian numbers. He contributed decisively to the further development of the theory of probability, particularly through de Moivre. He greatly advanced algebra, the infinitesimal calculus, the calculus of variations, mechanics, and the theory of series.

BERNOULLI, JAKOB (JACQUES) II (*b. Basel, Switzerland, 1759; d. St. Petersburg, Russia, 1789*), mathematics.

Son of Johann II. Graduated in Jurisprudence (1778). The drawing of lots for the chair of his uncle Daniel went against him. He received a call to St. Petersburg, and published several treatises there.

BERNOULLI, JOHANN (JEAN) I (*b. Basel, Switzerland, 1667; d. Basel, 1748*), mathematics.

Younger brother of Jakob I Bernoulli and the tenth child in the family. He proved unsuited for a business career and studied mathematics with Jakob I at Basel. M.A. (1685), degree in medicine (1690), and doctorate (1694). He achieved equal rank with Jakob I on taking the chair of mathematics at Groningen (1695). Johann succeeded to Jakob's chair at Basel on Jakob's death. Both were engrossed in infinitesimal mathematics (from 1687) and were the first to fully understand Leibniz' differential calculus. By virtue of a "golden theorem" (stemming actually from Jakob)—the spectacular determination of the radius of curvature of a curve, he became known in Paris (1691) as a representative of the new Leibnizian calculus. He taught it to L'Hospital who has been credited with *Analyse des infiniments petits,* the first textbook in differential calculus, but Bernoulli's authorship is now substantiated. His two most important achievements were the investigations of the function $y = x^x$ and the discovery (1694) of a general development in series by means of repeated integration by parts. Johann's exponential calculus, developed in "Principia calculi exponentialium seu percurrentium" (1697) is the infinitesimal calculus of exponential functions. The distinct talents of the two brothers were publicly demonstrated in their solutions to the problem of the brachistochrone, the problem of determining the "curve of quickest descent," which Johann posed. Johann solved the problem by ingenious intuition, which enabled him to reduce the mechanical problem to the optical problem already resolved by means of Fermat's principle of least time. He deduced the differential equation of the cycloid from the law of refraction.

The brothers' differing solutions (1701) to a new variational problem, the isoperimetric problem (posed by Jakob 1697) was the beginning of their alienation and open discord—and also the birth of the calculus of variations.

After Newton's death Bernoulli was the unchallenged mathematical preceptor to Europe. His advocacy of the Cartesian vortex which Newton had severely criticized, delayed the acceptance of Newtonian physics on the Continent. His work on hydraulics (1732) was generally considered a piece of plagiarism from the hydrodynamics of his son Daniel. His pugnacity, which involved him in the Leibniz-Newton priority dispute on Leibniz' side as well as polemics with his brother, was matched by his energy as a correspondent, notably with Leibniz.

BERNOULLI, JOHANN (JEAN) II (*b. Basel, Switzerland, 1710; d. Basel, 1770*), mathematics.

Doctorate in jurisprudence (1727), won four prizes of the Paris Academy, and succeeded his father Johann I in the chair of mathematics at Basel. His mathematical production thereafter was meager, but he corresponded extensively with scientific colleagues and furthered publication of his father's *Opera omnia.*

BERNOULLI, JOHANN (JEAN) III (*b. Basel, Switzerland, 1744; d. Berlin, Germany, 1807*), mathematics, astronomy.

Son of Johann II. He reorganized the astronomical observatory at the Berlin Academy (1764). With Hindenburg he published the *Leipziger Magazin für reine und angewandte Mathematik* (1776–89).

BERNOULLI, NIKOLAUS I (*b. Basel, Switzerland, 1687; d. Basel, 1759*), mathematics.

Nikolaus' father was a Basel alderman and painter; he studied with his two uncles, Jakob I and Johann I. He

obtained his master's degree (1704) by defending Jakob I's last thesis on infinite series, and took a doctorate in jurisprudence (1709). He taught logic (1722–31) and law (from 1731) at Basel. He formulated for the first time the problem of probability theory, later known as the St. Petersburg problem. He solved the problem of the sum of reciprocal squares which had confounded Leibniz and Jakob I. He published his uncle Jakob I's *Ars conjectandi* and *Opera omnia.* In the priority quarrel with Newton, he defended Leibniz.

BERNOULLI, NIKOLAUS II (*b. Basel, Switzerland, 1695; d. St. Petersburg, Russia, 1726*), mathematics.

Nikolaus II, the favorite son of Johann I, was a licientiate in jurisprudence (1715). He assisted his father with his correspondence, particularly in the Leibniz-Newton priority quarrel. He died of a hectic fever shortly after he and his brother Daniel were appointed to the St. Petersburg Academy.

BERNSTEIN, FELIX (*b. Halle, Germany, 1878; d. Zurich, Switzerland, 1956*), mathematics.

As a student in Cantor's seminar at Halle, Bernstein gave the first proof (1897) of the equivalence theorem of sets, which establishes the notion of cardinality and is thus the central theorem in set theory. He made some of the earliest applications of set theory outside pure mathematics. He later studied at Göttingen (doctorate, 1907) and taught mathematical statistics there (from 1911) and founded and directed the Institute of Mathematical Statistics (1921–34). He left Germany in 1934, emigrated to the United States and taught at Columbia, New York, and Syracuse Universities. He contributed decisively to the development of population genetics: by analyses of racially variant blood-group frequencies he showed (1924) that the A, B, and O blood groups must be inherited by a set of triple alleles, not two pairs of genes. He also applied the techniques of population genetics to such problems as linkage and measures of individual and group inbreeding.

BERNSTEIN, JULIUS (*b. Berlin, Germany, 1839; d. Halle, Germany, 1917*), physiology.

Studied medicine at Breslau and Berlin (M.D. 1862) under Heidenhain and du Bois-Reymond; worked with Helmholtz at Heidelberg (1864–71); professor of physiology at University of Halle (from 1872). Published important work in many areas of physiology, most notably in the area of irritable structures. Improved apparatus, perfected techniques of stimulation and measurement; determined that synapse time for the neuromuscular junction is 0.3 milliseconds (1882); measured the velocity, form, and course of the excitation wave; recommended use of cathode rays to record bioelectric activity (1912). Applied the ideas and techniques of electrochemistry, molecular physics, and thermodynamics to elucidate the nature of the excitation process: developed a theory that the cell membrane includes an electrically charged double layer of ions, due to selective permeability; upon stimulation, the membrane's permeability increases as a result of a chemical change and the excited portion becomes negatively charged (that is, the membrane's potential decreases upon stimulation); this alteration propagates in the fiber in a wavelike manner—it is the origin of the electric excitation wave. Supported a mechanistic theory of life. Father of Felix Bernstein.

BERNSTEIN, SERGEY NATANOVICH (*b. Odessa, Russia, 1880; d. Moscow, U.S.S.R., 1968*), mathematics.

Studied at Paris and Göttingen (doctorate Paris, 1904) and at Kharkov (master's 1908; doctorate 1913); taught at Kharkov (1907–33), Leningrad (1933–43), and Moscow (from 1943), worked at Mathematical Institute of U.S.S.R. Academy of Sciences. Edited Chebyshev's collected works. United Russian mathematical tradition with European thought. In the field of partial differential equations, solved Hilbert's nineteenth and twentieth problems (in dissertations of 1904, 1908); developed theorems on differential geometry of surfaces, particularly on theory of minimal surfaces. Expanded Chebyshev's work on the theory of best approximation of functions, introduced an important new class of quasi-analytical functions. Also did influential work in probability theory, suggesting a system of axioms (1917) and conducting many fundamental studies, including applications to genetics.

BERNTHSEN, HEINRICH AUGUST (*b. Krefeld, Prussia, 1855; d. Heidelberg, Germany, 1931*), chemistry.

Bernthsen studied at Bonn and Heidelberg. He taught at Heidelberg (1879–87), then headed the laboratory of the Badische Analin- und Sodafabrik (from 1887). He dealt with dyes of the acridine and azine groups, giving the correct composition of sodium hyposulfite, and developed technically feasible processes for producing indigo, rhodamine, and tolyl red.

BERT, PAUL (*b. Auxerre, France, 1833; d. Hanoi, Indochina [now People's Republic of Vietnam], 1886*), physiology, comparative anatomy, natural history, education.

Bert, the son of a lawyer, took degrees in law, medicine (1863), and natural sciences (1866) at Paris. He held the chair of comparative physiology at the Muséum d'Histoire Naturelle (1868–70) and succeeded Claude Bernard in physiology at the Sorbonne (1869–70). He was a *revanchist* member of the Chamber of Deputies (from 1872) and a pro-secularist minister of public instruction (1881–82).

A staunch defender of French colonial expansion in Indochina, he was the first civil governor of the French colonies Annam and Tonkin (1886), where he died.

Bert's first important work was in the transplantation of animal tissue and organs as studies in general physiology. He studied the mechanism of death in marine fishes exposed to fresh water and did a classic study of the "sensitive plant" *(Mimosa pudica)*, showing that its spontaneous movements depend on differences of osmotic pressure, regulated by light and darkness. This first phase of his career ended with his monograph on the comparative physiology of respiration (1870). His definitive work, *La pression barométrique* (1878) was an environmental study on the largest scale. Bert showed the physiological importance of the partial pressures of the respiratory gases. He described the relationship between the external partial pressure and the behavior of the blood gases and recognized that mountain sickness and altitude sickness are a consequence of the low partial pressure of oxygen. He introduced oxygen apparatus to

avert the dangerous consequences of ascent. He discovered and described oxygen poisoning, differentiating it from suffocation from lack of oxygen, and explained the cause and mechanism of caisson disease. His hypothesis that people living at high altitudes might possess more red corpuscles was proved correct by François Viault (1890–92). His elementary and secondary textbooks on natural history, zoology, and the physical sciences were often reprinted and translated.

BERTHELOT, PIERRE EUGÈNE MARCELLIN (*b. Paris, France, 1827; d. Paris, 1907*), chemistry.

Graduated from the Paris Faculty of Science (1849). He worked at Pelouze's private laboratory; was demonstrator to Balard at the Collège de France (1851); took his doctorate (1854); and graduated from the École de Pharmacie in Paris (1858). Taught organic chemistry at the École de Pharmacie (from 1859) and the Collège de France (from 1865). During the siege of Paris (1870–71) he was president of the Comité Scientifique pour la Défense de Paris and was elected to the Senate although he had not run (1871). He served on several commissions on explosives. He was elected a permanent senator (1881) and sat on the left. He presided over a commission on laicization of primary education (1886) and was minister of education for five months (1886–87) and foreign minister for five months (1895). He was permanent secretary of the Académie des Sciences (from 1889).

Berthelot not only made outstanding contributions to chemistry but also extensively studied its history. He took the view that alchemy had developed as a misunderstanding of the earlier empirical knowledge of Egyptian metalworkers. His analysis of metallic objects from ancient Egypt and Mesopotamia laid the foundations of chemical archaeology. His last books concentrated on his concept of science as an all-embracing, ever-progressing philosophy. He foresaw a Utopia through science, particularly chemistry, by the year 2000. He favored a positivistic philosophy; accepting only the observable, he regarded atomic and molecular theories with great suspicion. His vast work over six decades led to some 1,600 titles, the most important being in organic chemistry.

Berthelot's initial achievements in organic chemistry were on alcohols and culminated in his definitive work on organic synthesis. He concluded (1851) that the synthesis of naphthalene, benzene, and possibly phenol was an established fact. This was one of the first examples of the use of the word synthesis to denote the production of organic compounds from their elements. In his research on the derivatives of glycerin (1853–54), he concluded that glycerin in organic chemistry corresponded to phosphoric acid in inorganic chemistry as alcohol corresponded to nitric acid—the beginning of the idea that, corresponding to polybasic acids in inorganic chemistry, there were polyatomic alcohols in organic chemistry. Hardly less important was his synthesis of stearin and palmitin, the chief constituents of ordinary hard fats. He showed that sugars behave partly as polyatomic alcohols and partly as aldehydes, and divided carbohydrates into three classes: ordinary sugars, carbohydrates, and polysaccharides. He gave cane sugar the systematic name *saccharose.* He defined alcohols as neutral compounds of carbon, hydrogen, and oxygen which with acids had water eliminated to form another neutral compound. He was the first to consider the phenols as a group, and similarly characterized them.

He obtained (1856) formic acid identical to that occurring naturally in the ant and achieved the first true synthesis of an aliphatic alcohol (methyl alcohol, 1857). His monumental *Chimie organique fondée sur la synthèse* (2 vols., 1860) reviewed his ten years of work in organic chemistry.

In the 1860's he achieved the synthesis of acetylene, benzene, and aromatic compounds occurring in coal tar; collaborated with Péan de Saint-Gilles on the formation and decomposition of esters, research that constituted a bridge between organic and physical chemistry; and used hydrogen iodide to reduce organic compounds. He opened a new field in his systematic investigation of hydrocarbons obtained by heating substances in the temperature range from red to white heat. His most famous experiment was the heating of acetylene in a glass tube; polymerization took place, forming benzene with some toluene—the first demonstration of a simple conversion of an aliphatic to an aromatic compound. He distinguished hydrocarbons according to their degree of saturation. He rejected Kekulé's formula for benzene (1865–66), and did not accept modern structural formulas until 1897. His last major research in organic chemistry was the application of hydrogen iodide as a reducing agent—he called it "une méthode universelle d'hydrogénation."

Berthelot's work in physical chemistry arose from his studies of the mechanical factors on which he believed chemical reactions depend. His interest in thermochemistry was really in the heat changes involved in the formation and decomposition of organic compounds so that these could be compared with the basic thermochemistry of inorganic chemistry. He introduced the terms *exothermic* and *endothermic* (1865). The accuracy of his thermochemical data has often been criticized. His major summary was *Essai de mécanique chimique fondée sur la thermochimie* (2 vols., 1879). He introduced the use of the bomb calorimeter determining heats of combustion with an accuracy hitherto unattainable. With Jungfleisch he arrived at the partition law (1869–72) and partition coefficient. In his *Sur la force des matières explosives d'après la thermochimie* (1871; 3rd. ed., 2 vols., 1883) he showed how the power of explosive materials could be quantitatively expressed and laid the foundations of a science of the mechanism of explosions.

He founded a research establishment for vegetable chemistry (1883) and his most original work in his last years was in this field, and in the history of science. With Guignard, he succeeded (1893) in isolating and forming a culture of bacteria capable of fixing nitrogen (*Chimie végétale et agricole,* 1899).

BERTHIER, PIERRE (*b. Nemours, France, 1782; d. Paris, France, 1861*), mineralogy, mining engineering, agricultural chemistry.

Berthier studied at the École Polytechnique and the École des Mines. He was professor of assaying and chief of laboratory there from 1816 to 1848. He pioneered in locating deposits of native phosphates and discovered several new mineral species, including bauxite and berthierite (named for him). His well-known *Traité des essais par la voie sèche* (1834) was widely used by mineralogists and mining engineers.

BERTHOLD, ARNOLD ADOLPHE (*b. Soest, Germany, 1803; d. Göttingen[?], Germany, 1861*), physiology.

Berthold took his doctorate in medicine at Göttingen (1823), taught there (from 1825), and practiced medicine. All historical accounts consider him a forerunner of modern endocrinology for his "Transplantation der Hoden" (1849), on the successful grafting of testicles from one cockerel to another, the first experimental demonstration of the correlation of a gland with the *milieu intérieur* of an organism. He had no immediate successors, however. He did other work in the physiology of reproduction, and with Bunsen (1834) he discovered hydrated iron oxide as an antidote for arsenic poisoning.

BERTHOLLET, CLAUDE LOUIS (*b. Talloire, near Annecy, Savoy, 1748; d. Arcueil, France, 1822*), chemistry.

Qualified as a physician at the University of Turin (1768); studied in Paris under Macquer and Bucquet (1772); took a doctorate of medicine at the University of Paris (1778). Inspector of dye works and director of Manufacture Nationale des Gobelins (from 1784). Taught at the École Normale (1794), and with his lifelong friends Monge and Guyton de Morveau organized the École Polytechnique, where for a time he taught animal chemistry. In 1804 Napoleon made him a count, senator for Montpellier, administrator of the mint, and *grand officier* of the Légion d'Honneur. After this, he led a semi-retired existence in Arcueil, where he and Laplace founded the Société d'Arcueil (1807).

Berthollet opposed Lavoisier and defended the phlogiston theory. He seized on the real weakness of Lavoisier's explanation of combustion: that it was not only a chemical phenomenon in which something (oxygen) was absorbed, but also a physical phenomenon in which something (energy or, rather, enthalpy, heat minus entropy) was released. He rejected the phlogiston theory in 1785, explicitly stating for the first time that phlogiston had at last become a useless hypothesis. One of Berthollet's most important contributions was his analysis of prussic acid (1787), which he correctly showed to be composed of hydrogen, carbon, and nitrogen; he was convinced it contained no oxygen. A valuable consequence of his adherence to Lavoisier was his determination of the composition of ammonia (1785).

During his two years in Egypt with Napoleon's expedition he sought an explanation for the apparently inexhaustible source of sodium carbonate constituted by Lake Natron in terms of a chemical theory of affinity, reasoning from the chemical properties of the layer of ordinary salt covering the ground surface of Egypt and the limestone of the mountains of Libya and the physical conditions in the area (1801). His complete new system of chemistry was fully developed in the comprehensive *Essai de statique chimique* (2 vols., 1803). His main contribution to the notion of affinity was the proof that it was not an absolute, but varied with the physical conditions accompanying an experiment. According to the *Essai,* there were two main natural forces: gravitation, which accounted for astronomical phenomena, and chemical affinity. He envisaged substances as composed of minute particles or molecules —roughly, atoms—all in a state of equilibrium. All chemical combinations were caused by an interplay of the several kinds of forces of the molecules composing the reactants. The different forces he distinguished as: (1) Chemical affinity; (2) Quantity; (3) Distance (cohesion and elasticity).

Thanks to his model and analysis of chemical reactions, especially combination, the idea of affinity had been replaced by a group of concepts. This had two important immediate influences: chemists dispensed with the use of tables of affinity as guiding hypotheses, and tried to provide theories accompanied by adequate models showing the internal workings and structure of chemical substances.

J. L. Proust asserted (1799) that all combinations occurred in definite proportions. From Berthollet's concept of chemical mass it followed that the proportion in which one substance combined with another increased directly with its chemical mass, and was not fixed, at least within limits. This was not borne out, however, by the facts in all cases. To reconcile this conflict he cited special conditions as sometimes abrogating the general law, and also the poverty or superficiality of experimental observations.

BERTHOLON, PIERRE (*b. Lyons, France, 1741; d. Lyons, 1800*), physics.

Bertholon, a priest of the Lazarist order, taught all aspects of science at Montpellier. He is best known for his work in physics, particularly through his studies of electricity in relation to all atmospheric manifestations and as applied to human ailments and electrotherapies and to the growth of plants for which he invented an electrovegetometer.

BERTI, GASPARO (*b. Mantua [?], Italy, ca. 1600; d. Rome, Italy, 1643*), physics, astronomy.

Inspired by Galileo's statement in *Discorsi* (1638) that water could not be raised more than eighteen cubits by a lift pump, Berti created experimental apparatus for a procedure he thought refuted the claim. His historical importance lies in this apparatus, which Torricelli adapted for mercury for his work in atmospheric pressure (1644).

BERTIN, LOUIS-ÉMILE (*b. Nancy, France, 1840; d. La Glacerie, France, 1924*), naval architecture, hydraulics.

Bertin graduated from the École Polytechnique in 1860 and joined the Naval Engineering Corps. He headed the Technical Department of Naval Construction (1895–1905). His enduring work was the design (1881) of the first French-built compartmentalized cruiser. When completed, it attained a speed of eighteen knots, a world record.

BERTINI, EUGENIO (*b. Forlì, Italy, 1846; d. Pisa, Italy, 1933*), mathematics.

Bertini took a degree at Pisa (1867) and taught there (1875–80, 1892–1921) and also at the University of Pavia (1880–92). His work in algebraic geometry followed the line take by Luigi Cremona. He succeeded (1877) in determining the types of plane involution that may be reduced by Cremona's transformations.

BERTRAND, CHARLES-EUGÈNE, or **Charles-Egmont** (*b. Paris, France, 1851; d. Lille, France, 1917*), plant anatomy.

Bertrand studied natural science at the Sorbonne and spent virtually his entire career at the University of Lille, where he established a famous laboratory. He collaborated with his son Paul, a paleobotanist. He himself was primarily a botanist, but much of his work furthered geologists' understanding of coals and the evolution of the extinct plants found in them.

BERTRAND, GABRIEL (*b. Paris, France, 1867; d. Paris, 1962*), biochemistry.

Bertrand, the son of a merchant, took a B.A. (1886) at Paris, was *préparateur* to Albert Arnaud (1890–1900), and taught biochemistry at the Institut Pasteur (from 1900) and the Faculté des Sciences, Paris (1904–37). He introduced both the term "oxidase" and the concept of trace elements. Investigating the darkening of the latex of lacquer trees, he recognized the cause as the oxidation of a phenol in the presence of laccase. He first used the term "oxidase" for these oxidizing enzymes in 1896. He further observed that laccase ash contained a large proportion of manganese (1897) and developed his concept of the trace element as essential and necessary to the functioning of the enzyme. He further explored the organic effects of various metals in hundreds of papers. His work was immediately applied to the elimination of previously undiagnosable deficiencies of trace elements.

BERTRAND, JOSEPH LOUIS FRANÇOIS (*b. Paris, France, 1822; d. Paris, 1900*), mathematics.

Bertrand entered the École Polytechnique at age eleven under the tutelage of his uncle and guardian, Jean Marie Constant Duhamel. In 1839 (at age seventeen) he became doctor of science in thermomechanics. At the École Polytechnique (from 1844) he was professor of Analyses (1856–95) and at the Collège de France (from 1847) he succeeded Biot (1862–1900). He was perpetual secretary of the Académie des Sciences (1874) and was elected to the Académie Française (1884). His many textbooks were widely used. In mathematics he covered many fields, but produced no fundamental works. Many of his studies on the theory of curves and surfaces, of differential equations and their application to analytical mechanics, of probability, and of the theory of errors were elegant and all were widely read. His name has been given to the so-called problem of Bertrand, to find the subgroups of the symmetric groups of lowest possible index (1845); to the curves of Bertrand, those with the property that a linear relation exists between first and second curvature (1850); and to Bertrand's paradox, the problem in continuous probabilities (in his *Calcul des probabilités*, 1889) for which the probability turns out to be undetermined unless specific assumptions are made about what constitute equally likely cases.

BERTRAND, MARCEL-ALEXANDRE (*b. Paris, France, 1847; d. Paris, 1907*), geotectonics, stratigraphy, general geology.

Bertrand, the son of Joseph Bertrand, studied at the École Polytechnique and the École des Mines in Paris, worked in the Geological Survey of France, and taught at the École des Mines (1886). He was the first to conceive of the overthrust structure of the Alps. He developed an orogenic wave concept and demonstrated that the European continent was built up gradually from north to south (1887). He formulated an original conception of the complete sedimentary cycle with recurring facies (1894).

BERWICK, WILLIAM EDWARD HODGSON (*b. Dudley Hill, England, 1888; d. Bangor, Wales, 1944*), mathematics.

Berwick's work is primarily concerned with the theory of numbers and related topics. His *Integral Bases* (1927) was the first to develop methods for constructing an integral basis for the algebraic integers in a rational field applicable to simple algebraic extensions in general.

BERZELIUS, JÖNS JACOB (*b. Väversunda, Östergötland, Sweden, 1779; d. Stockholm, Sweden, 1848*), chemistry.

Assisted Sven Hedin, chief physician at the Medevi mineral springs (1800). Doctorate in medicine (1802) at Uppsala. With Wilhelm Hisinger he discovered (1803) a new element, cerium (discovered at the same time by Klaproth). Professor of medicine and pharmacy at the College of Medicine (1807; later the Karolinska Institute). Friedrich Wöhler, a close personal friend, translated many of his important works into German. Berzelius was president (1810) and then secretary (1818) of the Swedish Academy of Science and the recognized authority on chemistry. He engaged in polemics, especially with Dumas and Liebig. An early friendship with Humphry Davy later cooled, after Berzelius' criticism of Davy. His earliest experiments (1803) convinced him of the significance of electricity in binding chemical elements together and also strengthened his conviction, gained from reading Lavoisier, that oxygen was an essential constituent of bases as well as acids. From these ideas he developed his dualistic theory of the nature of salts. His first book (1802) reviewed all prior work on the action of electricity on salts and minerals. His first Swedish textbook, on animal chemistry (1806) noted his finding that muscle tissues contain lactic acid, a substance previously found by Scheele in milk. His textbook, *Lärbok i kemien* (2 vols., 1808–12), became the most authoritative chemical text of its day.

Berzelius' new analytical methods showed his genius. In general he based his work on oxygen compounds. He reported his analyses in terms of the positive and negative components; for example, calcium sulfate as CaO and SO_3. All his analyses fitted into his original assumption of the validity of the law of constant proportions and his results permitted him to determine the atomic weights of the elements. He published revised tables of atomic weights in 1814, 1818 (this included forty-five of the forty-nine known elements and the chemical composition of nearly 2,000 compounds), and 1828.

His suggestion for a simple and logical system of symbols to represent compounds was that the first letter of the Latin name be used as the symbol for each element. Where more than one element began with the same letter, the next letter of the name was to be added for one of the two elements. The letter also stood for the atomic weight of the element as well, and so the chemical formulas of compounds represented the chemical proportions of the elements in the compound. To indicate these proportions he wrote the appropriate small numbers in the formulas, as superscripts resembling algebraic expo-

nents, a practice continued in France; elsewhere the numbers came to be written as subscripts.

In his laboratory, Berzelius himself discovered selenium and thorium; his students isolated lithium (Arfwedsen), vanadium (Sefström), and a number of rare earth elements (Mosander).

Berzelius had found that an electric current splits salts into positive and negative components, and he believed in the two-fluid theory of electricity and in unipolarity (and the intensity of polarity) as determining behavior in a substance.

Among his generalized definitions upon which much later chemistry developed were his terms isomerism (1831), catalytic force and catalysis (1835), and allotropy (1840). He proposed the word "protein" to Gerardus Mulder.

Berzelius remained a respected figure, but his opinions were generally disregarded. With the appearance of electron theories of chemical bonding, the Berzelius dualism was seen to contain much truth, at least for polar compounds.

BESSEL, FRIEDRICH WILHELM (*b. Minden, Germany, 1784; d. Königsberg, Germany [now Kaliningrad, U.S.S.R.], 1846*), astronomy, geodesy, mathematics.

Bessel was an unpaid apprentice to a mercantile firm (1799–1806) and self-taught in practical navigation and astronomy, when he used Harriot's 1607 observations of Halley's Comet to determine its orbit, and presented his determination to Olbers (1804), who had the work printed. It attracted much attention because of his circumstances. He became assistant (1806) at Schröter's private observatory and was appointed (1809) director and professor of astronomy of the observatory being built at the Prussian Emperor's command in Königsberg.

He has been called the founder of the German school of practical astronomy and was one of the most skillful and diligent observers of his century, as is evidenced in his *Beobachtungen der Königsberger Sternwarte* (21 vols.).

He presented the positions of Bradley's stars valid for 1755 as *Fundamenta astronomiae pro anno 1755* (1818), which also gives the proper motions of the stars, as derived from his own, Bradley's, and Piazzi's observations. It constitutes a milestone in the history of astronomical observations for its accuracy on the positions of stars. Auwers improved Bessel's reductions (star catalog, 1882–1903). Bessel improved the measurement of the positions and proper motions of stars by determining the position of the vernal equinox with an accuracy of .01 second through observations of both Maskelyne's stars and the sun (1820). His *Tabulae Regiomontanae* (1830) included the mean and the apparent positions of thirty-eight stars for the period 1750–1850. (He added the two polar stars α and δ Ursae Minoris to Maskelyne's thirty-six). It was the first modern reference system for the measurement of the positions of the sun, the moon, the planets, and the stars, and for many decades the Königsberg tables were used as ephemerides. With their aid, all observations of the sun, moon, and planets made since 1750 at the Royal Greenwich Observatory could be used for the theories of planetary orbits. He discovered the variation of the proper motions of the stars α Canis Major (Sirius) and α Canis Minor (Procyon) and concluded that they must have dimmer companions. The variation led to the discovery, in this century, of stars with extremely low luminosity (dark companions).

He pursued two aims: the determination of the motions of the stars so that their positions could be predicted for all time, and the definition of a reference system for the positions of the stars. He determined the positions of approximately 75,000 stars (brighter than ninth magnitude) in zones of declination between −15° and +45°. These observations were continued by Argelander, who measured the positions of stars in zones of declination from +45° to +80° and from −16° to −32°. The work of Bessel and Argelander encouraged the establishment of two large-scale programs: Argelander's *Bonner Durchmusterung* and the first catalog of the Astronomische Gesellschaft *(AGK 1)* with the positions of the stars of the entire northern sky.

One of Bessel's greatest achievements was the first accurate determination of the distance of a fixed star which he calculated using the change of position of the stars, as evidenced by the motion of the earth. In determining proper motions, Bessel found that individual stars are marked by especially great motions and that these stars are not among the brightest. He concluded that great proper motions are, in most cases, the result of small star distances.

To determine the parallax Bessel used the Fraunhofer heliometer with which he could measure greater angular distances than with the micrometer. After observing for eighteen months, by the fall of 1838 Bessel had enough measurements for the determination of a reliable parallax. This work was published in the *Astronomische Nachrichten* (1838), the first time the distance of a star became known.

Bessel was also an outstanding mathematician whose name became generally known through a special class of functions that have become an indispensable tool in applied mathematics, physics, and engineering. Bessel left few mathematical works that do not have some practical application.

Like nearly all great astronomers of his era, Bessel was obliged to spend part of his time surveying wherever the government wished. He describes the triangulation in East Prussia and its junction with the Prussian-Russian chain of triangulation in a book written with J. J. Baeyer (1838).

Among Bessel's works that contributed to geophysics were his investigations on the length of the simple seconds' pendulum (1826), the length of the seconds' pendulum for Berlin (1835), and the determination of the acceleration of gravity derived from observing the pendulum. Bessel achieved the standardization of the units of length then in use.

BESSEMER, HENRY (*b. Charlton, Hertfordshire, England, 1813; d. Denmark Hill, London, England, 1898*), technology.

A prolific inventor from youth, Bessemer learned metal processing in his father's type foundry and machine design and chemistry in London. An attempt to develop grooved artillery shot which would rotate when fired from smooth-bore cannons led to a need for stronger cannons: cast iron was too brittle and steel was too expensive; he developed the inexpensive Bessemer converter (1856), which blew air through molten pig iron to remove the carbon that made it brittle. But when ironmakers bought the process, their product was brittle; this turned out to be due to phosphorus contamination common in British ores (but not in the ore Bessemer had used). Subsequently he opened his own steel plant and learned how to add spiegeleisen (a mixture of carbon, iron, and manganese) to recarburize the refined iron and to remove oxygen bubbles; Bessemer steel proved ideal for rails, structural steel, and plate.

BESSEY, CHARLES EDWIN (*b. Milton Township, Ohio, 1845; d. Lincoln, Neb., 1915*), botany, education.

Studied at Michigan Agricultural College (graduated 1869); taught at Iowa Agricultural College, Ames (1869–84), where he inaugurated botany and horticulture, and University of Nebraska (from 1884). His textbook *Botany for High Schools and Colleges* (1880), an adaptation of Julius von Sachs's *Lehrbuch der Botanik* made at the suggestion of Asa Gray, reoriented botanical instruction in this country. Was associate editor of *American Naturalist* (1880–97) and *Science* (1897–1915). Devised a system of angiosperm classification that by its logic and attractive phyletic patterns—based on a refinement of Candolle's theory of differentiation—has proven effective in teaching systematic botany.

BETANCOURT Y MOLINA, AUGUSTIN DE (*b. Tenerife, Canary Islands, 1758; d. St. Petersburg, Russia, 1824*), physics, engineering.

Sent by Spanish government to France, England, Germany, and Holland to study methods of shipbuilding, navigation, mechanics, and using steam engines. Reported to Paris Academy on English double-action steam engine. Studied relation of temperature and steam pressure (1790). Constructed optical telegraphy line from Madrid to Cadiz. Worked in civil engineering in Spain, France, and Russia (from 1808).

BETTI, ENRICO (*b. near Pistoia, Italy, 1823; d. Pisa, Italy, 1892*), mathematics.

Studied at University of Pisa and taught there (from 1865; students included Dini, Bianchi, and Volterra). In algebra, sought to explicate Galois's ideas by relating them to previous research of Ruffini and Abel; obtained fundamental results on the solubility of algebraic equations by means of radicorational operations, restating the theory of substitutions. Wrote on theory of elliptic functions (1860–61) and on topology of hyperspace (1871; this work inspired Poincaré, who originated the term "Betti numbers" for numbers characterizing the connection of a variety). Inspired by Riemann to work on mathematical physics: demonstrated "Betti's theorem," a law of reciprocity in elasticity theory (1878); applied Green's methods to mathematics of elasticity and of heat.

BEUDANT, FRANÇOIS-SULPICE (*b. Paris, France, 1787; d. Paris, 1850*), mineralogy, geology.

Educated at École Polytechnique and École Normale Supérieure; taught in Paris, Avignon (1811), Marseilles (1813); early studies were in zoology and paleontology, particularly on interadaptability of saltwater and freshwater mollusks. Interest turned to geology when appointed to catalog mineralogical collection of Comte de Bournon

(1814); wrote on geology and mineralogy of Hungary (1822); professor of mineralogy at Sorbonne (1820–39). Experiments led to Beudant's law: some compounds dissolved in the same solution precipitate together, forming a crystal whose properties they determine in common; the interfacial angles of the new crystal have a value intermediate between angles of the original compounds, proportional to the quantity of each. Mitscherlich generalized this idea in his law of isomorphism (1819).

BEXON, GABRIEL-LÉOPOLD-CHARLES-AMÉ (*b. Remiremont, France, 1747; d. Paris, France, 1784*), biology.
Educated in theology (doctorate, Besançon, 1766 or 1767); ordained 1772. An avid student of natural history, who met Buffon in 1772 and volunteered to help with preparation of the *Histoire naturelle;* he made numerous contributions to six volumes of *Histoire des oiseaux* and to *Histoire des minéraux.*

BEYRICH, HEINRICH ERNST (*b. Berlin, Germany, 1815; d. Berlin, 1896*), geology, paleontology.
Studied at universities of Berlin and Bonn (Ph.D., Berlin, 1837), influenced by Leopold von Buch; taught at Berlin from 1841; one of founders of German Geological Society (1848); directed Königliche Geologische Landesanstalt und Bergakademie and Museum of Natural History (from 1873). Traveled extensively through Germany, Switzerland, and Italy, observing geology and meeting many eminent scientists. Made a geological survey of Silesia; publication of his findings (1844) established his reputation as a geologist and stratigrapher. Studied north German Tertiary formations, proposed (1854) concept of independent Oligocene (north German counterpart of the Belgian Tongrian and Rupelian) interpolated between Lyell's Eocene and Miocene. Also studied German Paleozoic stratigraphy: clarified tectonically complicated conditions of the Devonian in the Harz Mountains; defended division of the Carboniferous in Germany into an older and a younger system. Did far-ranging work in paleontology and biostratigraphy, including important elucidation of crinoidean skeleton; attempted to establish connections between Triassic and Jurassic ammonites; clarified conchological taxonomy; established phylogeny of *Mesopithecus pentelici;* studied Tertiary and Carboniferous plants. In geological cartography, mapped Harz Mountain region; became director of geological mapping in Prussia and Thuringia; introduced 1:25,000 topographic map scale.

BEZOLD, ALBERT VON (*b. Ansbach, Bavaria, 1836; d. Würzburg, Bavaria, 1868*), physiology.
Studied medicine at Munich, Würzburg, and Berlin (M.D., Würzburg, 1859); assisted Emil Du Bois-Reymond (1858); was appointed to newly created chairs of physiology at Jena (1859) and Würzburg (1865). Worked on neurophysiology of the heart: localized intracardial sources of stimulation in ganglia of *septum interatriale* (Bezold's ganglia); clarified relation of the vagus nerve to heartbeat; studied the function of the sympathetic nerve. Pharmacological experiments with veratrine led to the discovery of the "Bezold-Jarisch reflex" (reexamined by Adolf Jarisch, 1937), a regulatory heart-circulation reflex characterized by bradycardia and lowering of the blood pressure.

BEZOUT, ÉTIENNE (*b. Nemours, France, 1739; d. Basses-Loges, near Fontainebleau, France, 1783*), mathematics.
Taught practical mathematics and mechanics to naval and artillery officer candidates; published *Cours de mathématiques* (6 vols., 1764–69), which was widely used in France, translated into English, and considerably influenced the form and content of American mathematical education in the nineteenth century. Research papers focused on the theory of equations, often following a "method of simplifying assumptions," concentrating on those specific cases of general problems which could be solved. Bezout related the problem of solving nth-degree equations in one unknown to the problem of solving simultaneous equations by elimination: given n equations in n unknowns, the central problem was to find and study what he called the resultant equation in one of the unknowns and to find its degree; he constructed a determinant (the Bezoutiant) of the coefficients of the simultaneous equations and used it both in solving the equations and as a criterion for their solvability (1764). Bezout's theorem (1779) stated that "the degree of the final equation resulting from any number of complete equations in the same number of unknowns, and of any degrees, is equal to the product of the degrees of the equations"; he gave its geometric interpretation as "the surfaces of three bodies whose nature is expressible by algebraic equations cannot meet each other in more points than there are units in the product of the degrees of the equations." This theorem is crucial to the study of the intersection of manifolds in algebraic geometry.

BHABHA, HOMI JEHANGIR (*b. Bombay, India, 1909; d. Mont Blanc, France, 1966*), physics.
Graduated from Gonville and Caius College, Cambridge, in mechanical engineering (1930); research student at Cavendish Laboratory (1930–39); Ph.D., Cambridge (1935); visited Continental laboratories (1934–36), including Fermi's, Pauli's, and Bohr's. The outbreak of World War II caught him on holiday in India; a position was created for him at the Indian Institute of Science, Bangalore, where he stayed until the Tata Institute for Fundamental Research (founded at his suggestion and directed by him) was relocated in Bombay (1945). His vigorous advocacy of a nuclear-powered electrical system for India led to the creation of the Indian Atomic Energy Commission (1948) with him as chairman. He promoted international cooperation in science, particularly in peaceful uses of atomic energy; became a governor of the International Atomic Energy Agency. Bhabha's research in cosmic ray and nuclear physics included: expression (1935) of the probability of scattering of positrons by electrons (Bhabha scattering); theory of electron- and gamma-ray-induced cosmic ray showers (1937); nature of the penetrating component of cosmic ray showers; an exchange model for vector mesons in nuclear force theory. He was the first to point out (1938) that the lifetimes of fast, unstable cosmic ray particles would be increased because of the time-dilation effect that follows as a consequence of Einstein's special theory of relativity. He also wrote highly abstract papers on the classical theory of point particles moving in a general field, and on relativistic wave equations.

BHĀSKARA I (*fl. 629*), astronomy.

One of leading exponents of Āryabhaṭa I's two systems of astronomy. Author of three works: *Āryabhaṭīyabhāṣya*, *Laghubhāskarīya*, and *Mahābhāskarīya;* commentators on latter two works include Parameśvara.

BHĀSKARA II (*b. 1115*), astronomy, mathematics.

One of most impressive Indian astronomers and mathematicians, whose works inspired many commentaries and editions. Author of at least six works: *Līlāvatī*, on arithmetic, geometry, and algebra; *Bījaganita*, on algebra, including indeterminate quadratic equations; *Siddhānta-śiromaṇi*, comprising *Grahaganitādhyāya* (or *Ganitādhyāya*) on mathematical astronomy and *Golādhyāya* on the sphere (largely an expansion and explanation of the *Ganitādhyāya*); *Vāsanābhāṣya* or *Mitākṣarā*, Bhāskara II's own commentary on his *Siddhāntaśiromaṇi; Karaṇakutūhala* (or *Brahmatulya* or *Grahāgamakutūhala* or *Vidagdhabuddhivallabha*) on mathematical astronomy, with simpler rules than in *Siddhāntaśiromaṇi;* and *Vivaraṇa*, a commentary on Lalla's *Śisyadhīvṛddhidatantra*. The *Bījopanaya*, formerly attributed to Bhāskara II, is now thought to be a late forgery.

BIAGGIO PELICANI. See **Blasius of Parma.**

BIAŁOBRZESKI, CZESŁAW (*b. Pošechonje, near Jaroslavl, Russia, 1878; d. Warsaw, Poland, 1953*), physics, natural philosophy.

Studied physics at University of Kiev (1896–1901); worked in Langevin's laboratory, Collège de France (1908–10); taught at Kiev (1914–19) and Warsaw University (from 1921). Member of International Institute of Intellectual Cooperation of the League of Nations (from 1935). Did experimental and theoretical studies of electrical and optical phenomena in fluid and solid dielectrics (1900–12); wrote on stellar thermodynamics, radiation pressure, and mechanism of light absorption (1912–31); after 1931 was concerned with epistemology of physics, primarily of quantum theory.

BIANCHI, LUIGI (*b. Parma, Italy, 1856; d. Pisa, Italy, 1928*), mathematics.

Studied under Betti and Dini at the University of Pisa (graduated 1877), and later at Munich and Göttingen, chiefly under Klein. Taught in Pisa at Scuola Normale Superiore (from 1881) and at university. Principal research was in metric differential geometry. Among his major results was the discovery of all the Riemannian geometries that allow for a continuous group of movements; these results found application in Einstein's studies on relativity. He did an extensive study of non-Euclidean geometries. Other topics included functions of a variable complex, elliptic functions, and continuous groups of transformations.

BICHAT, MARIE-FRANÇOIS-XAVIER (*b. Thoirette, Jura, France, 1771; d. Paris, France, 1802*), surgery, anatomy, physiology.

Learned surgery and anatomy from Marc-Antoine Petit in Lyons and from Pierre Desault (whose posthumous works Bichat published) in Paris. One of founders of Société Médicale d'Émulation (1796). Gave private courses in anatomy, surgery, and physiology (using ani-

mal vivisection). His most important contribution to modern anatomy was a generalization of a theory of Pinel: pathology must be based upon the structure of the tissues making up the organs, regardless of the location of the latter in the organism. Tissues differ from each other in the composition and the arrangement of their fibers; Bichat distinguished twenty-one organized elements, characterized by their textures and their properties. Since it differs from others in its vital properties, each tissue also differs in its diseases. In his view, vital properties were irreducible to physical laws: "Life is the ensemble of functions that resist death." His ideas had a profound influence not only in medicine but also in philosophy.

BICKERTON, ALEXANDER WILLIAM (*b. Alton, England, 1842; d. London, England, 1929*), cosmology, natural philosophy.

An engineer whose interest turned to science. He wrote on the relation between electricity and heat, and on cosmogony: developed the controversial theory of the build-up of celestial bodies by collisions.

BIDDER, FRIEDRICH HEINRICH (*b. Kurland, Russia, 1810; d. Dorpat, Russia [now Tartu, Estonian S. S. R.], 1894*), anatomy, physiology.

Bidder took a medical degree at the University of Dorpat (1834) and taught there (from 1835), serving as dean of the medical faculty (1843–45) and rector (1858). His command of anatomy, physiology, histology, and embryology permitted him to single out important questions for him and his collaborators to study, but he did not make any major innovations. He discovered the auriculoventricular and interauricular ganglion cells in the hearts of frogs ("Bidder's ganglia") and demonstrated that the ganglia contained fibers of the vagus nerve. His classic *Verdauungssäfte und der Stoffwechsel* (1852; with Carl Schmidt) was the first major publication on intermediary metabolism. It showed that bile was not an excretion but a secretion serving a physiological function. This work and his contribution on the nervous system were too advanced for most of his contemporaries.

His best-known work on the nervous system (1842; with Alfred W. Volkmann) was an extensive histological study of the autonomic nervous system and the spinal cord which provided anatomical evidence for the theory of double innervation of the organs from the sympathetic chain and the ganglionic system.

BIDLOO, GOVARD (*b. Amsterdam, Netherlands, 1649; d. Leiden, Netherlands, 1713*), anatomy, biology.

Apprenticed to a surgeon; attended lectures of Ruysch and Blasius; M.D. from University of Franeker (1682). Taught at the Hague and in Rotterdam (from 1688); appointed superintendent of military medicine (1690) by William III of Orange, and later one of his personal physicians; professor at University of Leiden (from 1694); after death of William III (1702), became a very good teacher and developed a large practice. Chief work was his anatomical atlas (1685), with 105 plates by Gerard de Lairesse, including many microscopical drawings of human organs, and with brief descriptions; this atlas was criticized at length by Ruysch. All the same plates were used by William Cowper in his *Anatomy of Humane Bodies* (1698), perhaps the most flagrant case of plagiarism in the history of medicine. Other notable work included proof that nerves are not hollow, and thus that the animal spirits that nerves supposedly conducted did not exist; in biology, he described his painstaking work on the liver fluke *(Fasciola hepatica)* in a letter to Leeuwenhoek, who had it published.

BIELA, WILHELM VON (*b. Rossla, Stolberg am Harz, Germany, 1782; d. Venice, Italy, 1856*), astronomy.

The son of a Bohemian noble family, Biela had an army career (to 1844) during which he made many valuable astronomical observations. The most remarkable (1826) was of a comet, whose period he found to be six years and nine months, a discovery that made him famous. A crater on the moon was named for him, and the Andromedides are now called Bielides or Belides.

BIENAYMÉ, IRÉNÉE-JULES (*b. Paris, France, 1796; d. Paris, 1878*), probability, mathematical statistics, demography, social statistics.

After studying at the École Polytechnique, he entered civil service; became inspector in Administration of Finances; held a temporary appointment at the Sorbonne; was statistical expert in government of Napoleon III. One of the founders of Société Mathématique de France. He had a penchant for controversies: criticized Cauchy, Poisson, and others, while defending the views of Laplace. In demography and social statistics, he discussed the accuracy of life expectancy tables then in use, stability of insurance companies, and the mathematical theory of juries. Made major methodological contributions to probability and mathematical statistics. Was a founder of the "Continental direction" of statistics, concerned with the stability and dispersion theory of statistical trials: introduced the physical principle of *durée des causes;* showed (1840) an understanding of the statistical concept of sufficiency. Extended Laplace's asymptotic treatment of linear least squares; deduced (1852) an almost final form of the chi square criterion; obtained (1853) Bienaymé-Chebyshev inequality via method of moments; stated (1845) the criticality theorem for simple branching processes; developed a simple combinatorial test for randomness of observations on a continuously varying quantity, by counting the number of local maxima and minima in the series.

BIENEWITZ, PETER. *See* **Apian, Peter**

BIESTERFELD, J.H. *See* **Bisterfeld, Johann Heinrich**

BIGOURDAN, CAMILLE GUILLAUME (*b. Sistels, Tarn-et-Garonne, France, 1851; d. Paris, France, 1932*), astronomy, history of science.

Bigourdan, who came from a peasant family, was astronomer-in-chief at the Paris Observatory (1897–1925) and directed the Bureau International de l'Heure (1919–29). A remarkable observer, he was known for his visual surveys of position, especially of nebulae. His studies on time and the history of astronomy are still of value.

BILHARZ, THEODOR (*b. Sigmaringen, Germany, 1825; d. Cairo, Egypt, 1862*), anatomy, zoology.

Bilharz, the son of a counsellor of the exchequer, received the M.D. at the University of Tübingen in 1849. He was assistant to the director (1850–52) and chief physician (1852–56) of the Egyptian Department of Hygiene, and taught anatomy at the Cairo medical school (from 1856). He discovered (1851) the cause of the disease bilharziasis, calling the flatworm parasite *Distomum haematobium.* At the same time he also depicted *Schistosomum mansoni,* which was named for Patrick Manson in 1907. Neither he nor his contemporaries considered his discovery of the agent of tropical hematuria to be epochal, but it introduced a new era of tropical parasitology and initiated a successful fight against an illness that still infects millions.

BILLINGS, ELKANAH (*b. Billings Bridge, near Bytown [now Ottawa], Ontario, 1820; d. Montreal, Quebec, 1876*), paleontology.

Billings, a lawyer and editor of the Bytown *Citizen* was self-taught in paleontology and became paleontologist with the Geological Survey of Canada (from 1856). He published descriptions of sixty-one new genera and 1,065 new species of fossils. In addition to this remarkable achievement, he also determined the age of the rocks of the "Quebec Group" as Beekmantown and Chazy, from which Logan created "Logan's line." He concentrated on the descriptive taxonomy of fossils, mostly from Paleozoic formations of Eastern Canada.

BILLROTH, CHRISTIAN ALBERT THEODOR (*b. Bergen, on the island of Rügen, Germany, 1829; d. Abbazia, Istria, Italy [now Opatija, Yugoslavia], 1894*), pathological anatomy.

Billroth, the son of a clergyman, took a doctorate in medicine at Berlin (1852) and directed the surgical clinic at Zurich (1860–67) and the University of Vienna (to 1894). A devoted amateur musician, in Vienna he became friends with Johannes Brahms, who dedicated two string quartets to him. His *Die allgemeine chirurgische Pathologie und Chirurgie in fünfzig Vorlesungen* (1863) is a classic surgical textbook. He helped introduce antisepsis on the Continent, and was the first to resect the esophagus (1872), to perform total laryngectomy (1873), and to resect a cancerous pylorus (1881). His methods of resection, although modified, remained in use for many years. Plastic surgery, especially of the face, was another of his specialties. His pupils spread his teaching all over the Continent.

BILLY, JACQUES DE (*b. Compiègne, France, 1602; d. Dijon, France, 1679*), mathematics, astronomy.

A Jesuit, Billy taught theology and mathematics in Champagne. Parts of his *Doctrinae analyticae inventum novum* (1670), an elaborate study of Fermat's techniques of indeterminate analysis, originated in correspondence with Fermat. It is one of the few pertinent documents on this line of Fermat's activities.

BINET, ALFRED (*b. Nice, France, 1857; d. Paris, France, 1911*), psychology.

Binet, the founder of French experimental psychology, studied law and the sciences at the Sorbonne, for which he qualified in 1878. He became doctor of natural sciences in 1892. Was assistant director (1892) and director of the Laboratory of Physiological Psychology (1895–1911) at the Sorbonne. With Henri Beaunis he founded the first French journal of psychology, *Année psychologique* (1895) and with Ferdinand Buisson founded the Société Libre pour l'Étude Psychologique de l'Enfant (1898), later the Société Alfred Binet. He expanded the idea of experimentation in psychology, preferring questionnaires, investigations, and personal interviews to the apparatus of the laboratory.

His major contribution to psychology, the metric intelligence scale (1905), was based on the idea of classifying subjects by observed difference in individual performances. He drew up a series of tests for children, on problems related to daily situations, arranged by mental level; the measure of intelligence was established by comparison and classification of the results. He made an important innovation (1908): assuming that intelligence increases with age, he distinguished mental age from chronological age. This latter work, with Théodore Simon, began a new era in testing; its final form was in their *Le mesure du développement de l'intelligence chez les enfants* (1911).

BION, NICOLAS (*b. ca. 1652; d. 1733*), instrumentation.

Bion, who maintained his workshop in Paris, was king's engineer for mathematical instruments. He was less specialized than most of his colleagues, and remained accurate in a range of instruments. Few of his instruments are extant. His treatises on globes and cosmography (1699), astrolabes (1702), and on precision instruments in general (1709) contributed to his fame.

BIOT, JEAN-BAPTISTE (*b. Paris, France, 1774; d. Paris, 1862*), physics.

Graduated from the École Polytechnique (1791). He instructed his wife, a competent linguist, in science and mathematics, and she collaborated with him in translating E. G. Fischer's physics textbook into French. Professor of astronomy at the Paris Faculté des Sciences (1808–49), where he also taught physics (1816–26) and served as dean (1840–49). Vice-president of the Académie des Sciences (1835); elected to the Académie Française (1856). Wrote a biography of Newton for the *Biographie universelle.*

He initiated (1803) a general recognition in France of the reality of meteorites. With Thenard (1807) he made one of the earliest identifications of what was later called dimorphism. In his attempts to solve the discrepancy between Newton's formula for the velocity of sound and the value obtained in practice, he found a value for the velocity of sound in cast iron 10.5 times that in air, long considered authoritative. From a comparison of his many geodesic determinations he concluded that the weight of a given body is not the same on all points with the same latitude, nor is its variation uniform along a particular meridian. This work established the necessity of revising the generally accepted simple ellipsoid theory of the earth. He derived a formula (occasionally referred to as Biot's law) relating the intensity of solar radiation to the thickness of the atmosphere. He edited and presented (1801) the official report of the Institute on the voltaic pile. After Oersted's discovery of the connection between magnetism and electricity, he and Savart (1820) mea-

sured the rate of oscillation of a suspended magnet at various distances from a conductor and showed that the magnetic force acts at right angles to the perpendicular joining the point considered to the conductor, and that its intensity is inversely proportional to the distance (Biot and Savart's law).

Biot repeated Arago's experiments on the splitting of polarized white light into two different color beams and established the relationship between the thicknesses of the crystal plates and the colors produced. He interpreted his results in terms of a repulsive force that caused polarization by acting on the particles of light (1812). Biot clearly distinguished (1818) a uniaxial form of magnesia mica from the more common biaxial types (commemorated in the name biotite for a type of mica, J. F. L. Hausmann, 1847). He discovered (1815) that the property of rotating the plane of polarized light was shared by liquids. He appreciated the immense importance of his discovery—that since this was a property of liquids, it must be a property of the molecules. To confirm this, he demonstrated that the effect on polarized light applied equally to turpentine in the liquid and vapor states. He distinguished what he called right-handed and left-handed quartz (1815). He found that liquids also had opposite effects on polarized light. If liquids that rotated the plane of polarization in opposite directions were mixed in suitable proportions, the effect was cancelled out. For this effect, he introduced the term *compensé* ("compensated"). He introduced the practice of denoting the effect of polarized light on a liquid or solution by the value of the rotation produced by a column of standard length. He designed one of the first polariscopes.

Biot worked mainly in astronomy and electricity (1820–32), then resumed his optical research. He found (1836) that tartaric acid constituted an outstanding exception to his law of inverse squares (of wavelength). He accordingly divided optically active substances into two classes, those that obeyed his law and those that did not.

BIRD, JOHN (*b. Bishop Auckland, England, 1709; d. London, England, 1776*), mathematics, optics.

An eminent maker of mathematical instruments. His instruments were the most accurately divided prior to invention of the dividing engine, and made possible considerable advancement of practical astronomy; his methods were made available to others in two published works. Provided quadrants and other instruments to observatories at Greenwich, St. Petersburg, Paris, Cadiz, Göttingen, and Oxford. Made standard measures for governmental committees.

BIRGE, EDWARD ASAHEL (*b. Troy, N.Y., 1851; d. Madison, Wis., 1950*), limnology.

First great American limnologist. Attended Williams College (1869–73); studied briefly with Agassiz (1873), then transferred to Harvard Graduate School (Ph.D., 1878); taught at University of Wisconsin from 1876 and held state positions as well; studied under Ludwig and Gaule, University of Leipzig (1880–81). Studied plankton crustaceans in Lake Mendota in relation to depth, light, temperature, and currents; independently discovered thermocline. From 1900, collaborated with Chancey Juday; studied dissolved gases in lakes and their biological significance; investigated physical factors in lakes, especially heat distribution and light penetration; developed principle of heat budget of lakes; invented pyrlimnometer to measure light penetration at different depths.

BIRINGUCCIO, VANNOCCIO (*b. Siena, Italy, 1480; d. Rome [?], Italy, ca. 1539*), metallurgy.

Held varied governmental and private positions. Wrote first comprehensive account of the fire-using arts to be printed, *Pirotechnia* (1540), a prime source on many practical aspects of inorganic chemistry. Emphasized the adaptation of metals and minerals to use—alloying, working, and especially the art of casting. Criticized alchemical philosophy; advocated practical (but not theoretical) experimentation. Some sections of his work were appropriated by Agricola.

BIRKHOFF, GEORGE DAVID (*b. Overisel, Mich., 1884; d. Cambridge, Mass., 1944*), mathematics.

Regarded as leading American mathematician of his day. Studied at University of Chicago, Harvard (A.B., 1905), and again at Chicago (Ph.D., 1907); influenced especially by Maxime Bôcher and E. H. Moore. Taught at University of Wisconsin (1907–09), Princeton (1909–12), and Harvard (from 1912). Earliest paper was on number theory (1904); thesis was on asymptotic expansions, boundary-value problems, and the Sturm-Liouville theory. His interest then turned to linear differential equations, difference equations, and the generalized Riemann problem: he sought to construct a system of linear differential equations of the first order with prescribed singular points and a given monodromy group, then extended this to systems of difference equations. His major interest in analysis was in extending Poincaré's work in dynamical systems, particularly in celestial mechanics; he won fame for the proof (1913) of the "last geometric theorem" of Poincaré (on the three-body problem); introduced concepts of minimal or recurrent sets of motions, and of wandering, central, and transitive motions; his topological concepts of metric transitivity and the minimax principle have had great impact. Also influential is his pointwise ergodic theorem, stimulated by Von Neumann. Other concerns included the foundations of relativity and of quantum mechanics, function spaces, and quantitative aesthetics.

BIRMINGHAM, JOHN (*b. probably at Millbrook, near Tuam, Ireland, ca. 1816; d. Millbrook, 1884*), astronomy.

An amateur astronomer who became known by the discovery of nova T Coronae, the first nova to be identified with an existing star and the first to be examined spectroscopically (by Huggins). He subsequently revised Schjellerup's catalog of red stars (1872–76) and published observations of members of the solar system.

BIRT, WILLIAM RADCLIFF (*b. Southwark [London], England, 1804; d. Leytonstone, England, 1881*), astronomy.

Assisted Sir John Herschel in the analysis of barometric measurements (1839–43); studied atmospheric electricity; proposed the use of the barometer by ships' captains to steer away from the center of cyclones (1853). In astronomy, best known for selenography: he worked on a committee to revise a map by Beer and Mädler; devised a scale of lunar tints; detected the "secular variation of

tint" on the floor of the crater Plato. He also studied stellar fluctuations and made systematic observations of sunspots.

AL-BĪRŪNĪ (or **Bērūnī**), **ABŪ RAYḤĀN** (or **Abu'l-Rayḥān**) **MUḤAMMAD IBN AḤMAD** (*b. Khwārazm [now Kara-Kalpakskaya A.S.S.R.], 973; d. Ghazna [?] [now Ghazni, Afghanistan], after 1050*), astronomy, mathematics, geography, history.

Nothing is known about al-Bīrūnī's ancestry and childhood. He was taught by Abū Naṣr Manṣūr. At the age of seventeen he used a ring graduated in halves of a degree to observe the meridian solar altitude at Kāth, thus inferring its terrestrial latitude. Four years later he made plans to carry out a series of such determinations and prepared a ring fifteen cubits in diameter.

On 24 May 997, al-Bīrūnī observed a lunar eclipse at Kāth, having arranged previously with Abu'l Wafāʾ that the latter should simultaneously observe the same event from Baghdad. The time difference so obtained enabled them to calculate the difference in longitude between the two stations. He also engaged in an acrimonious correspondence with the brilliant Bukharan philosopher and physician Avicenna on the nature and transmission of heat and light. Al-Bīrūnī traveled and resided in various parts of India, determining the latitude of some eleven Indian towns. Al-Bīrūnī himself writes that while living at Nandana Fort, he used a nearby mountain to estimate the earth's diameter. It is also clear that he spent a great deal of time at Ghazna. The cluster of recorded observations made by him there commences with a series of meridian solar transits covering the summer solstice of 1019, and includes the lunar eclipse on 16 September of the same year. He continued to observe equinoxes and solstices at Ghazna, the last being the winter solstice of 1021.

When he was sixty-three years old, Al-Bīrūnī prepared a bibliography of the works of the physician Muhammad ibn Zakariyya al-Rāzī, to which he appended a list of his own books. This runs to 113 titles partially arranged by subject matter and occasionally with a brief indication of the contents. This list is incomplete, for al-Bīrūnī lived at least fourteen years after this, working until he died. Moreover, seven additional works by him are extant and many more are named. Roughly four-fifths of his work has vanished beyond hope of recovery. Of what has survived, about half has been published. Al-Bīrūnī's interests were very wide and deep, and he labored in almost all the branches of science known in his time. He was not ignorant of philosophy and the speculative disciplines, but his bent was strongly toward the study of observable phenomena, in nature and in man. Within the sciences themselves he was attracted by those fields then susceptible of mathematical analysis. He also did serious work in mineralogy, pharmacology, and philology, subjects where numbers played little part; but about half his total output is in astronomy, astrology and related subjects, the exact sciences par excellence of those days. Mathematics in its own right came next, but it was invariably applied mathematics.

Al-Bīrūnī's works still available are: *Chronology; Astrolabe; Sextant; Taḥdīd; Densities; Shadows; Chords; Patañjali; Tafhīm; India; Ghurra; Canon; Transits; Gems;* and *Pharmacology.* Speculation played a small role in his thinking; he was in full command of the best scientific theories of his time, but he was not profoundly original or a constructor of new theories.

BISCHOF, CARL GUSTAV CHRISTOPH (*b. Wörth, near Nuremberg, Germany, 1792; d. Bonn, Germany, 1870*), chemistry, geology.

Bischof took a Ph.D. at the University of Erlangen and taught chemistry at the University of Bonn (from 1819). He concentrated on chemical changes accompanying geological processes in the Rhineland, other German areas, and foreign regions. He was a gifted experimentalist, basically a laboratory chemist with a flair for the practical uses of science. The main source of his fame was his *Lehrbuch der chemischen und physikalischen Geologie* (3 vols., 1846–55). The second edition (1863–71) became the standard geochemical text. In the course of preparing the book he became as fervent a neo-neptunist as he had been a volcanist. He exaggerated the role of water in his experiments, extrapolating from laboratory results to natural phenomena without adequate observations. He promoted the use of analogies with experiments, introducing (1849) the so-called oxygen coefficient into chemical comparisons of rocks. His discussion of the reactions by which gypsum or anhydrite forms in one case and sulfur in another contributed to the suggestion decades later that massive stratiform sulfide deposits may be sedimentary or exhalative-sedimentary.

BISCHOFF, GOTTLIEB WILHELM (*b. Dürkheim an der Hardt, Germany, 1797; d. Heidelberg, Germany, 1854*), botany.

Bischoff, who came from a family of pharmacists, first trained as a graphic artist and then studied botany at Heidelberg, teaching there (from 1825) and directing the Botanical Garden (from 1839). His excellent observations and experiments on spores in his unfinished *Die kryptogamischen Gewaechse* (1828) prepared the way for Hofmeister's discovery of the alternation of generations. His *Lehrbuch der Botanik* (3 vols., 1834–40) contains one of the first histories of botany. His *Handbuch der botanischen Terminologie und Systemkunde* (3 vols., 1833–44) is still of value.

BISCHOFF, THEODOR LUDWIG WILHELM (*b. Hannover, Germany, 1807; d. Munich, Germany, 1882*), physiology, comparative anatomy.

Bischoff, the son of a physician who taught at the University of Bonn, took an M.D. at Heidelberg (1832) under Friedrich Tiedemann and taught at Heidelberg (1836–54) and Munich (1854–78). His most important work was on the embryology of mammals and of man. His work in physiology included an attempt to determine the amount of blood in a fresh corpse (1856) and (with P. G. von Jolly) the first experiments on blood-bound oxygen and carbon dioxide. His *Der Harn als Maass des Stoffwechsels* (1853) substantiated Liebig's theory of nitrogen-containing structural foodstuffs and respiratory nitrogen-free foods. With Carl Voit, he investigated nutrition in carnivores (1860). In embryology he achieved excellent results, doing important research on animal eggs. His discovery that the embryonic vesicle consists of cells enabled him to establish the connection between embryology and the then new science of cytology. He supported Darwinism with some reservation. He investi-

gated the cerebral convolutions (1868) and the weight of the human brain (1880), and found no relationship between intelligence and brain weight. Among his works is *Entwicklungsgeschichte der Säugetiere und des Menschen* (1843).

BISTERFELD, JOHANN HEINRICH (*b. Siegen, Germany, ca. 1605; d. Weissenburg [after 1715 Karlsburg, now Alba Iulia, Rumania], 1655*), philosophy, theology.

Bisterfeld studied under Comenius' teacher, Johann Heinrich Alsted at the University of Herborn and matriculated at the University of Leiden in 1626. He taught at the Transylvanian academy in Weissenberg (from 1629) and he performed a diplomatic mission for György Rákóczy I, prince of Transylvania. A Ramist, Bisterfeld had great insight into the philosophical requirements of the system that would reveal the universal harmony and thus put man in control of nature. He realized more fully than his contemporaries the value of an *ars combinatoria*, or a logic of relations, by which all things could be referred back to God. His works in this direction, *Philosophiae primae seminarium* (1657), *Phosphorus catholicus* (1649), and *Elementorum logicorum libri tres* (1657), had a strong effect on Leibniz and seem to have been the first in which Leibniz encountered the idea of universal harmony and the suggestion of a mathematical mode of logical calculation.

AL-BIṬRŪJĪ AL-ISHBĪLĪ, ABŪ ISḤĀQ, also known as **Alpetragius** (*his surname probably derives from Pedroche, Spain, near Cordoba; fl. Seville, ca. 1190*), astronomy, natural philosophy.

Outstanding astronomer among the Spanish Aristotelians. His only known work is *Kitāb fi 'l-hayᵓa* (translated by Michael Scot as *De motibus celorum circularibus*, 1217). A pupil of Ibn Ṭufayl, he valued the mathematical accuracy of Ptolemy's cosmology but denied its physical validity. His own system, whose sources are a matter for debate, comprised a Prime Mover, the ninth sphere, whose motion is transmitted to the successively slower lower spheres and to the sublunar elements; transmission of motion is explained by the impetus theory. The ninth sphere moves around the poles of the equator, from east to west, completing one revolution in twenty-four hours; next is the eighth sphere, that of the fixed stars, whose poles (those of the ecliptic) describe two small circles around the poles of the universe, since they participate in the diurnal movement of the ninth sphere (variable precession is thus explained); motion of the stars follows a curve called *lawlab ḥalazūnī* (interpreted as a spiral). Planetary motion is explained with the aid of a polar deferent and an epicycle; the order of the inferior planets is moon, Mercury, sun, Venus, Mars. Al-Biṭrūjī's cosmology was spread through much of Europe in the thirteenth century by William the Englishman, Grosseteste, Albertus Magnus, Vincent of Beauvais, Roger Bacon, and others; Regiomontanus wrote a brief work on his errors, and Copernicus cited his order of the planets.

BIZZOZERO, GIULIO CESARE (*b. Varese, near Milan, Italy, 1846; d. Turin, Italy, 1901*), histology.

Bizzozero, the son of a manufacturer, took an M.D. at Pavia (1866) and taught pathology at Turin (1872–1901), establishing one of the first Italian centers in pathology. He early understood the importance to medicine of the microscope (*Manuale di microscopia clinica,* 1879). He founded the *Archivio per le scienze mediche* (1876). An outstanding histologist of his time, he first called the staminal element of lymph nodes *cellula del reticolo* (1872). He also demonstrated the erythrocytopoietic function of bone marrow (1868) and discovered the megakaryocytes (1869). He was a pioneer in the modern study of inflammation. He affirmed before Metchnikoff, that reticular cells of lymph nodes act also against infection (1873). He demonstrated (1882) that platelets were normal elements of the blood and were linked to the phenomenon of thrombosis—hence the name "thrombocytes."

BJERKNES, CARL ANTON (*b. Christiania [now Oslo], Norway, 1825; d. Kristiania, 1903*), mathematics, physics.

The son of a veterinarian, Bjerknes took a degree in mining engineering (1848) and taught at the University of Christiania (from 1861). He collaborated closely with his son Vilhelm on his chief research interest, hydrodynamics, but was otherwise isolated. He arrived at the historic conclusion (1875) that two harmoniously pulsating balls moving through frictionless fluid react as though they were electrically charged, i.e., attract or repel one another with a force similar to that of Coulomb's law. His "hydrodynamic picture of the world" and his efforts to explain electromagnetic forces through hydrodynamics are today more a fascinating analogy than a basic physical theory, but he anticipated later developments in several fields, for example, recognizing the force known today as the hydrodynamic transverse force.

BJERKNES, VILHELM FRIMANN KOREN (*b. Christiania [now Oslo], Norway, 1862; d. Oslo, 1951*), physics, geophysics.

Bjerknes gave a clear, general and independent explanation of the theoretical thinking of his father, Carl Anton Bjerknes, in *Vorlesungen über hydrodynamische Fernkräfte nach C. A. Bjerknes's Theorie* (2 vols., 1900–02). He took an M.S. (1888) and a Ph.D. (1892) at the University of Christiania and taught at the universities of Stockholm, Christiania, Leipzig, and Bergen.

His collaboration with Heinrich Hertz (1890–92) on resonance in oscillatory circuits led to his discovery of theoretical and experimental resonance curves. His generalization of Kelvin's and Helmholtz's propositions on the so-called velocities of circulation and the conservation of the circular vortex, which he applied to the movements in the atmosphere and the ocean, led him to formulate the theory of physical hydrodynamics. His final goal was to calculate future conditions of the atmosphere and hydrosphere (*Dynamic Meteorology and Hydrography,* 2 vol., 1910–11, with J. W. Sandström, Th. Hesselberg, and O. Devik; *Physikalische Hydrodynamik mit Anwendung auf die dynamische Meteorologie,* 1933, with J. Bjerknes and H. Solberg). His now classic work *On the Dynamics of the Circular Vortex with Applications to the Atmosphere and to Atmospheric Vortex and Wave Motion* (1921) is a clear explanation of his most important basic ideas.

BJERRUM, NIELS JANNIKSEN (*b. Copenhagen, Denmark, 1879; d. Copenhagen, 1958*), chemistry, physics, history of science.

Bjerrum took a Ph.D. at the University of Copenhagen (1908) and taught chemistry at the Royal Veterinary and Agricultural College in Copenhagen (1914–49). In chemical physics (1911–14) he applied the kinetic and quantum theories to elucidate the constitution and the optical and thermal properties of matter. He succeeded in demonstrating the interdependence of specific heats and the spectrum as required by the quantum theory.

Physical chemistry, theoretical as well as analytical, was his lifelong interest. He developed (1905) a well-known extrapolation method for the elimination of the diffusion potential. He extended (1916) Arrhenius' theory to the view that some acids and hydroxyl compounds and most salts are almost completely dissociated into ions in the dissolved state. He developed a novel method of using the experimentally determined strength constants of different acidic and basic groups in a molecule to establish the constitution and dissociation constants of ampholytes, particularly of amino acids. His *Structure and Properties of Ice* (1951) treats the position of the hydrogen atoms and their zero-point entropy, changes in configuration, ionization and "molecular turns," and the proton-jump conductivity of ice and water.

BLACK, DAVIDSON (*b. Toronto, Canada, 1884; d. Peking, China, 1934*), anatomy, anthropology.

Black took an M.D. and an M.A. at the University of Toronto (1909). A year of study with Grafton Elliot Smith (1914) at Manchester turned his interest to anthropology. At the Peking Union Medical College (1920–34), he studied fossil-bearing material and searched for hominid fossils, concentrating on Chou K'ou-tien. When in 1927 at that site a well-preserved left molar was recovered Black pronounced it a new hominid genus, which he named *Sinanthropus pekinensis.* The site later yielded many bone fragments, notably an almost complete skull cap (1929) and a second skull (1930). He wrote reports on the discovery, morphology, and environment of *Sinanthropus pekinensis* (now classed as *Homo erectus*).

BLACK, JAMES (*b. Scotland, ca. 1787; d. Edinburgh, Scotland, 1867*), medicine, geology.

Black, a practicing physician, wrote *Capillary Circulation* (1825), which reported his only experimental work, mainly on ducks and frogs. His *The Nature of Fever* (1826) similarly reviewed alternative hypotheses and contemporary practice. He was a competent amateur geologist and paleontologist and helped found the Manchester Geological Society and the British Association.

BLACK, JOSEPH (*b. Bordeaux, France, 1728; d. Edinburgh, Scotland, 1799*), chemistry, physics, medicine.

He was William Cullen's assistant at the University of Glasgow (1744–52). At the University of Edinburgh, he took the M.D. (1754) with his now historic dissertation *De humore acido a cibis orto et magnesia alba.* The second half, the chemical experiments, considerably expanded, formed his classic paper "Experiments Upon Magnesia Alba, Quicklime, and Some Other Alkaline Substances" (1756)—the chief basis of his scientific renown as a founder of modern quantitative chemistry and his only major publication. In it he demonstrated that an aeriform fluid he called "fixed air" (carbon dioxide gas) was a quantitative constituent of certain alkaline substances. He replaced Cullen in Glasgow (1756–66) and carried on an active medical practice, then replaced Cullen at Edinburgh (from 1766). He founded the Oyster, a weekly dining club, with his two closest friends, Adam Smith and the geologist James Hutton; its members were the scientific luminaries of the remarkable Scotch Renaissance.

The "Experiments," in Part I recounts the experiments on *magnesia alba*, presenting his theory without equivocation: this substance he now describes as "a compound of a peculiar earth and fixed air." Part II describes experiments that enabled him to generalize the theory and to support his explanation of causticity as associated with a definite chemical entity of a definite solubility. Boiling quicklime with a mild alkali transfers fixed air from the mild alkali to the quicklime, uncovering the inherent causticity of the alkali. A conclusive test of his theory was his demonstration that both quicklime and *magnesia usta* could be produced without the use of fire.

Black's second major achievement, the discovery of latent and specific heats, was originally stimulated by Cullen's observation of the intense cold produced when highly volatile substances like ether evaporate and by Fahrenheit's observation that water can be cooled below the freezing point without congealing unless it is shaken. This showed that solidification (or liquefaction) required the transfer of substantial quantities of heat not directly detectable by the thermometer; in Black's term, *latent* heat. His earliest experiments on heat (1760) ascertained the reliability of the thermometer as a measuring tool. Crucial to his experiments was his recognition of the distinction between *quantity of heat* and *temperature*. Although not the first to notice this distinction, he was the earliest to sense its fundamental importance and to make systematic use of it. He measured the latent heat of fusion (1761). He also measured the latent heat of vaporization (1762), later obtaining more accurate figures.

His second, and closely related, discovery on heat was that different substances have different heat capacities. (It is commonly but falsely assumed that he discovered *specific heats* before his work on latent heat.)

Black never made or used the mythical ice calorimeter associated with his name and fully credited the French scientists for its independent invention and first use. The measurements made by Black, his student William Irvine, and Watt on the specific heats of various substances (1764) are the earliest known.

On the question of the "elements" or "principles" of bodies, Black was typically cautious, not crediting the venerable doctrine of the four elements. On combustion, fermentation, and the calcination of metals, he presented a version of the phlogiston theory.

His most interesting and pervasive doctrine is the theory of chemical affinity. Chemical reactions result from the differential or "elective" attraction of chemical individuals for one another. Simple elective attractions are those produced by heat; "double elective attractions," reactions of double decomposition, chiefly take place in solution. He saw no reason for avoiding the term "attraction," as did the French chemists who spoke instead of "affinities" or "rapports." As Newton had insisted, "attraction" was a descriptive term, not a causal explanation. His earliest use of this concept, and of Geoffroy's well-known table of affinities, appears in his "Experiments," to show the differential behavior of alkaline substances towards acids and "fixed air." It became a centrally important pedagogical device. He developed a diagram of

segmented circles without numbers to indicate the relative attractions. Unlike Cullen, he did not explicitly link his discussion of elective attractions with the corpuscular or atomic doctrine. He rejected all hypothetical explanations.

BLACKMAN, FREDERICK FROST (*b. Lambeth, England, 1866; d. Cambridge, England, 1947*), plant physiology.

Blackman, the son of a doctor, trained as a doctor (1885), then at St. John's College, Cambridge, read science (1887), was a fellow (1895–1947), served as steward (1908–14), taught botany (1891–1936), and developed a subdepartment of plant physiology (1931). Many papers by pupils in his laboratory bear his stamp if not his name, and much of his contribution was in his lectures. His and his pupils' papers were published in a series called the "Experimental Researches in Vegetable Assimilation and Respiration" (1895–1933). They included the demonstration by his pupil G. L. C. Matthaei that temperature had little effect on the rate of carbon assimilation at low illumination, while at high intensities the effect was comparable with that of many chemical reactions (1904); and Blackman's classic "Optima and Limiting Factors" (1905), which pioneered in the application of physicochemical ideas to biological problems. The process limiting the rate of carbon assimilation at high intensities of illumination was later named the Blackman reaction by Otto Warburg. In plant respiration, he studied the effect of the partial pressure of oxygen on the carbon dioxide production of apples (1928).

BLAEU, WILLEM JANSZOON (*b. Alkmaar [?], Holland, 1571; d. Amsterdam, Holland, 1638*), cartography.

Blaeu was a carpenter who worked at Tycho Brahe's observatory (1595–96) and established himself as a merchant of maps and globes created by himself or others and published at his own plant. Notable were his sea atlas, *Het Licht der Zeevaert* (1608) and his once-famous world atlas, *Novus atlas* (1634). He was the official cartographer of the Dutch East India Company (1633–38).

BLAGDEN, CHARLES (*b. Wooten-under-Edge, Gloucestershire, England, 1748; d. Arcueil, France, 1820*), physical chemistry.

Blagden, trained as an M.D. at Edinburgh (1768), was Cavendish's assistant (*ca.* 1782–89) and secretary of the Royal Society (from 1784) and was involved in the prolonged "water controversy"—the priority of Cavendish, James Watt, and Lavoisier in discovering the composition of water. There appears little ground for the charge by Watt's supporters that Blagden deliberately falsified evidence in favor of Cavendish—he was simply careless. In his own study of the effects of dissolved substances on the freezing point of water he concluded (1788) that salt lowers the freezing point in the simple inverse ratio of the proportion the water bears to it in the solution (now known as Blagden's law).

BLAINVILLE, HENRI MARIE DUCROTAY DE (*b. Arques, France, 1777; d. Paris, France, 1850*), anatomy, zoology.

Blainville took an M.D. at Paris (1808), was Cuvier's deputy (*ca.* 1810), and taught at the Muséum d'Histoire

Naturelle (from 1830). He was an outstanding comparative anatomist. His lifelong objective in natural history was order, derivable from principles of *la philosophie chrétienne.* A Roman Catholic, his religion was largely an elaboration of deism. God's plan for ordering animals and plants was the long-familiar scale of being, or *série,* which he defended against Cuvier's attacks. The defining characteristic of life, *sensibilité,* was to biology what gravitation was to the Newtonian world machine; it gave meaningful substance to the essential fact of relation. He became the friend, disciple, and mentor of Comte.

BLAIR, PATRICK (*d. Boston, England, 1728*), botany, biology, medicine.

Blair worked as a surgeon in Dundee, Scotland for some years. He gave the earliest known description of pyloric stenosis (1717) but is best known as a botanist, particularly for his work on plant sexuality, *Botanick Essays* (1720). He was an "ovulist" rather than a "pollenist."

BLAISE. *See* **Blasius of Parma.**

BLANC, ALBERTO-CARLO (*b. Chambéry, France, 1906; d. Rome, Italy, 1960*), prehistory, ethnology.

Blanc, whose father was a distinguished naturalist, studied at the universities of Pisa and Rome, and later taught geology at Pisa. In 1939 he discovered what was then the most complete Neanderthal skull while honeymooning at San Felice Circeo (Littoria). The Monte Circeo skull quickly became a classic. After 1939 he taught at Rome. He was the moving spirit behind the magazine *Quaternaria.* Blanc discovered six of the seven known Neanderthal fossils of Italy. He formulated a theory of the formation of ethnic groupings by a process he termed ethnolysis: differentiation by loss of characteristics. He extended this to the process of cosmolysis, which embraced the entire physical, biological, and human universe.

BLANCHARD, RAOUL (*b. Orléans, France, 1877; d. Paris, France, 1965*), geography.

Blanchard's thesis on Flanders (University of Lille, 1906) was one of the first important works of regional geography based on field research. As a teacher at the University of Grenoble (1905–48) he made it into an active center for geography. He was the creator of French Alpine geography, founding the *Revue de géographie alpine,* instituting field observation for the study of mountains, and completing *Les Alpes occidentales* (12 vols., 1941–58).

BLASCHKE, WILHELM JOHANN EUGEN (*b. Graz, Austria, 1885; d. Hamburg, Germany, 1962*), mathematics.

Blaschke, whose father taught descriptive geometry, took a Ph.D. at Vienna (1908) and taught at the University of Hamburg (1919–53), gaining worldwide recognition for the department of mathematics. He founded *Abhandlungen aus dem mathematischen Seminar der Universität Hamburg* and *Hamburger mathematische Einzelschriften.* His research concentrated on differential and integral geometry and kinematics, combining an unusual power of geometrical imagination with a consistent and suggestive use of analytical tools.

Blaschke made "kinematic mapping" (independently discovered by Josef Grünwald in 1911) a central tool in kinematics. His *Kreis und Kugel* (1916) investigated the isoperimetric properties of convex bodies, supplying existence proofs omitted by Jakob Steiner. His *Vorlesungen* (3 vols., 1921–29) covered classical geometry, affine differential geometry, and the differential geometry of circles and spheres. He originated topological differential geometry (*Geometrie der Gewebe,* 1938; *Einführung in die Geometrie der Waben,* 1955).

BLASIUS OF PARMA (*b. Parma, Italy, ca. 1345; d. Parma, 1416*), natural philosophy.

Blasius took his doctorate at the University of Pavia (*ca.* 1374) and taught there, and at Bologna, Padua, Venice, and Florence. During the 1390's at the summit of his career, he was at Pavia as professor of "mathematical arts and both philosophies" (moral and natural). Although he was not an original thinker, he did absorb sympathetically the new ideas of the Parisian Scholastics, which he disseminated and popularized in Italy. He seems to have been a materialist and determinist, and to have written the bulk of his extant work before 1396, when he was compelled to recant unspecified transgressions against the Church. Of his many treatises, only those on optics, statics, and intension and remission of forms are available in adequate modern editions. His *Quaestiones perspectivae* (*ca.* 1390) is empiricist in outlook and makes visual sensation the basis for human knowledge. One of his two treatises on intension and remission of forms, *Questiones de latitudinibus formarum,* included both the English (arithmetic) and French (geometric) fourteenth-century versions of the mean speed theorem. He may have introduced both versions into Italy. In *Questiones super octo libros physicorum* (1397), he denied that the impetus theory could explain acceleration in free fall or the rebound of bodies.

BLAUW, WILLEM. *See* **Blaeu, Willem.**

BLAZHKO, SERGEI NIKOLAEVICH (*b. Khotimsk-Mogilevskaya province, Russia, 1870; d. Moscow, U.S.S.R., 1956*), astronomy.

Blazhko took a Ph.D. (1911) and taught (1910–53) at Moscow University; he was director of the Moscow Observatory (1920–31) and of the university's Scientific Research Institute of Astronomy and Geodesy (1922–31). His primary sphere of scientific activity was the study of variable stars.

BLICHFELDT, HANS FREDERICK (*b. Illar, Denmark, 1873; d. Palo Alto, California, 1945*), mathematics.

Blichfeldt, the son of a farmer who emigrated to the United States about 1888, studied at Stanford University (B.A., 1896; M.A., 1897) and under Sophus Lie at the University of Leipzig (Ph.D., 1900). He taught at Stanford (1898–1938) and chaired the mathematics department (1927–38). His contributions in group theory and group characteristics, including *Finite Collineation Groups* (1917) and *Theory and Applications of Finite Groups* (1916, with G. A. Miller and L. E. Dickson) are now of considerable importance because of recent applications of Lie groups in the sciences.

BLISS, GILBERT AMES (*b. Chicago, Illinois 1876; d. Harvey, Illinois, 1961*), mathematics.

Bliss was educated at the University of Chicago (B.A., 1897; M.A., 1898; Ph.D., 1900) and taught mathematics and worked there (1908–41). His scientific interests ranged broadly in analysis, especially the basic existence theorems; but his focal point was the calculus of variations, and he was one of the chief architects of this edifice and exerted a strong influence on the American mathematical scene. His definitive *Lectures on the Calculus of Variations* (1946) firmly established its theoretical foundations.

BLISTERFELD, J. H. *See* **Bisterfeld, Johann Heinrich.**

BLOMSTRAND, CHRISTIAN WILHELM (*b. Växjö, Sweden, 1826; d. Lund, Sweden, 1897*), chemistry, mineralogy.

Blomstrand's doctorate at the University of Lund (1850) was in mineralogy; he then turned to chemistry and taught at Lund (1856–95). A scientific and political conservative in a period of transition in chemistry, he sought to reconcile Berzelius's dualistic theory with the unitary and type theories. His chain theory (even though displaced 1893 by Alfred Werner) was the most successful of many attempts to explain the constitution of metalamines.

BLONDEL, ANDRÉ EUGÈNE (*b. Chaumont, France, 1863; d. Paris, France, 1938*), physics, engineering.

Blondel was educated at the École Polytechnique and the École des Ponts et Chaussées and taught electrotechnology there and at the École des Mines (to 1900). Thereafter he devoted himself to research in his own laboratory. He invented the system of photometric units (lumens) of measurement (1894) now in use, introducing the fundamental concept of luminous flux and defining illumination according to the flux received by the unit surface (adopted by the International Electrical Congress, 1896). He also invented the oscillograph (1893; patented 1897).

BLONDEL, NICOLAS-FRANÇOIS (*b. Ribemont, France [baptized there 1618]; d. Paris, France, 1686*), military engineering, architecture.

Blondel held several naval engineering posts, lectured (1656) in mathematics at the Collège Royal (later the Collège de France), carried out several diplomatic missions, and was commissioner general of the navy. He was first director of the Royal Academy of Architecture (1671), in charge of public works for Paris (1672), and mathematics tutor to the dauphin (1673). His *Cours d'architecture* (1675–83) remained the definitive reference work for French architects for more than a century. In it he formulated "Blondel's rule," still in use, on the ratio between tread and risers on staircases. His *Résolution des quatre principaux problèmes d'architecture* (1673) dealt with the sketching of columns, rampant arches, and beams of equal resistance.

BLONDLOT, RENÉ-PROSPER (*b. Nancy, France, 1849; d. Nancy, 1930*), physics.

Blondlot taught physics at the University of Nancy. He did important work on Maxwell's theories of electromagnetism. Great notoriety attended his claim (1903) to have found a new kind of invisible radiation, which he called N rays. The claim was taken up by others, including Jean Becquerel, but his experiments proved unreproducible and the *Revue Scientifique* pronounced N rays chimerical (1904). He finally recanted and spent the rest of his life in relative obscurity.

BLUMENBACH, JOHANN FRIEDRICH (*b. Gotha, Germany, 1752; d. Göttingen, Germany, 1840*), natural history, anthropology, comparative anatomy.

Blumenbach received the M.D. at the University of Göttingen (1775). His dissertation, *De generis humani varietate nativa liber* (1776), which became world-famous, is a basic work in scientific anthropology. He was one of the first scientists to view man as an object of natural history, "the most perfect of all domesticated animals," yet distinct from animals. He formulated the first reliable survey of the characteristics and distribution of the various human races. His lectures and his textbook on comparative (physiological) anatomy were epoch-making; he was probably the first, at least in Germany, to lecture and publish on the subject. His *Handbuch der Naturgeschichte* (1779) and his *Beyträge zur Naturgeschichte* (2 vols., 1806–11) ushered in a new era in natural history.

BLYTH, EDWARD (*b. London, England, 1810; d. London, 1873*), natural history.

Blyth studied chemistry and opened a small druggist's shop in Surrey but his real efforts went into natural history, which gained him an excellent reputation. He was curator for the Royal Asiatic Society of Bengal (1841–62), and after resigning this post and returning to England contributed extensive notes and articles under the pseudonym "Zoophilus" or "Z."

Blyth's perceptive observations on variation in nature begin in two excellent articles published in 1835 to 1837. They discuss variation, the struggle for existence, sexual selection, and natural selection in Darwinian-sounding terms. While Blyth was in India he corresponded frequently and at length with Darwin. In 1855 he suggested that Darwin read these two articles and in the same year warmly recommended A. R. Wallace's first evolutionary paper to Darwin; this was perhaps Darwin's first clear warning of Wallace's work. Blyth undoubtedly supplied detailed information, comments, and recommendations, and probably did influence Darwin far more than most scholars have previously recognized. Blyth no doubt provided Darwin with many insights and possibly reconfirmed certain ideas, but it was Darwin's *On the Origin of Species* which seems to have revolutionized Blyth's ideas on species, and not vice versa.

BOAS, FRANZ (*b. Minden, Germany, 1858; d. New York, N.Y., 1942*), anthropology.

Boas exercised considerable influence in the "historical" and "scientific" reorientation of anthropology from about 1890 to 1925. He made significant contributions to formulation of problems and methods in human growth, linguistics, folklore, art, and the ethnology of the Indians of the Northwest Coast. He studied at Heidelberg, Bonn, and Kiel and took a doctorate in physics (1881), studied anthropometry with Rudolf Virchow (1882), and was geographer/anthropologist with an expedition to Baffin Island (1883–84). He was an assistant for the Museum für Völkerkunde (1884–87) and arranged the first of his thirteen field trips among the Indians of the Northwest Coast (the last was in 1931). He emigrated to the United States and became assistant editor of *Science* (1887) and taught anthropology at Clark University (to 1892). He was F. W. Putnam's assistant at the Field Museum (1892–94), then curator (1894), and became curator of ethnology and somatology (from 1896) and of anthropology (1901–05) at the American Museum of Natural History. He taught physical anthropology at Columbia University (1897–1937).

Boas took the empirical-inductive position, which was not novel in natural science; but only he seems to have understood its full implications for anthropology. The then-dominant "evolutionary" anthropology operated deductively with a number of unproved assumptions and an uncritical "comparative method." In the course of destroying this pseudo-anthropology, he contributed some basic principles: (1) The error of forcing the logic of one's own categories of thought on the "primitive" must be avoided. (2) Classification must be put aside until data has been collected on process—what actually happens, how forms change, recorded by showing variations in forms and their causes. (3) To be comparable, culture elements must show similarities not only in outward form but also in their histories. (4) Coincidence is not causal connection, as in the alleged relation linking race, language, and culture, which vary independently.

Boas rejected a uniform systematic history of the evolution of culture and advocated the historical method. By plotting culture "elements" in space, historical relations could be outlined and psychological processes recovered from the alterations of reinterpretations. Identical psychological processes could not be assumed unless the possibilities of contact, migration, and convergence could be discarded. At all times the investigator must stay within the limits of available data. He was a prime contributor to the emergence of the culture concept, stressing "social tradition" as a molding force in human behavior. Two of his students, Ruth Benedict and Margaret Mead, broke new ground in studying how cultures stimulate the development of unique personality types.

Boas concentrated on investigation of "mental phenomena" in art (*Primitive Art,* 1927), language, and mythology (*The Mind of Primitive Man,* 1911). He was thus diverted from the study of cultures in their organizational and functional operations, and was indifferent to the changes then taking place in Indian cultures. His method of reducing larger culture units to elemental parts to trace historical relations prevented full appreciation of the stylistic integration of culture patterns or literary style. He studied folklore and myth by compiling elements and extracting the psychological processes by which they had been altered. His publications covered a remarkable number of Pacific Coast and inland tribes, including the voluminous and quantitative *Tsimshian Mythology* (1916) and *Kwakiutl Ethnography* (1966). He became convinced that culture seldom diffused as a complex and unified whole and opposed the *Kulturkreislehre,* which assembled disparate elements into "culture complexes" which diffused *en bloc.* He held that no individual culture could become a thoroughly consistent and integrated whole. His methodical recording of myths and of languages became a platform for future investigations. His interest in physical anthropology arose from his be-

lief that although heredity predominates over environment, physical variability was not a matter of biology but the result of unknown influences on the more permanent characteristics. The plotting of human types of geographic distribution was thus his first concern.

BOBILLIER, ÉTIENNE (*b. Lons-le-Saulnier, France, 1798; d. Châlons-sur-Marne, France, 1840*), geometry, mechanics.

Bobillier studied at the École Polytechnique for a year; financial need caused him to leave for a teaching post at the École des Arts et Métiers at Châlons (1818–29, 1832–40). Isolated in the provinces, he never met J. D. Gergonne (whose disciple he was in some respects), Adolphe Quetelet, or Michel Chasles. Both he and Chasles rediscovered Poncelet's method for treating metric proportion (1824); Bobillier was first to publish it. He is best known for his studies of successive polars of curves or algebraic surfaces, and for his abridged notation, particularly in his essay on a new mode of research on the properties of space (1828), which he applied to some elementary geometric propositions with great efficacy (1828).

In statics, his "De l'équilibre de la chaînette sur une surface courbe" remains most elegant. In kinematics, he is remembered for the "Bobillier construction."

BOCHART DE SARON, JEAN-BAPTISTE-GASPARD (*b. Paris, France, 1730; d. Paris, 1794*), astronomy.

Bochart followed family tradition by choosing a legal career. An enlightened and generous amateur of science, he commissioned one of Europe's largest and finest collections of astronomical instruments. He aided Messier in finding comets after they had disappeared behind the sun. His correct supposition on the orbit of Herschel's comet was important in identifying it as the planet Uranus. He was First President of the Parliament of Paris and was beheaded during the reign of terror.

BÔCHER, MAXIME (*b. Boston, Mass., 1867; d. Cambridge, Mass., 1918*), mathematics.

Bôcher graduated from Harvard (1888) and took a Ph.D. at Göttingen (1891). He taught at Harvard (from 1891). He wrote many articles on the theory of differential equations and related questions.

BOCK, JEROME (*b. Heidesbach, or Heidelsheim, Germany, 1498; d. Hornbach, Germany, 1554*), botany.

Bock (also known as Hieronymus Tragus) was one of the three "German fathers of botany." With Otto Brunfels and Leonhard Fuchs, he represented the transition from late medieval botany, with its philological scholasticism, to early modern botany, with its demand that descriptions and illustrations be derived from nature. Little is known of his early life or education, but he is known to have been a Benedictine canon, to have become a follower of Luther, and to have served briefly as personal physician to the Landgraf Philipp II of Nassau. His *Neu Kreütterbuch* (1539) marked a new beginning in botany. As the first to describe the local flora, he has been credited with discovering many new species. By combining personal observation and precise description of details of structure with an attempt to establish a new taxonomy, he broke sharply with the past. He based descriptions on the morphological characteristics of the vegetative portions.

His ignorance of plant sexuality limits the taxonomic interest of his work, but by shifting attention from classical authority to the plants themselves and by leading the exodus from the library to the field he laid down methodological canons whose future importance transcended even his own accomplishments. Charles Plumier named the genus *Tragia (Euphorbiaceae)* in his honor.

BODE, JOHANN ELERT (*b. Hamburg, Germany, 1747; d. Berlin, Germany, 1826*), astronomy.

Bode was self-taught and privately tutored. He was only nineteen when his famous *Anleitung zur Kenntnis des gestirnten Himmels* (1768) appeared. He directed compilation for the *Astronomisches Jahrbuch* of the Berlin Academy for the years 1776–1829. He was royal astronomer, director of the astronomical observatory, and member of the Berlin Academy (1786–1825). His two sky atlases, *Vorstellung der Gestirne* (1782) and *Uranographia* (1801) were long standard works. He gave the name Uranus to Herschel's newly discovered planet.

BODENHEIMER, FRITZ SIMON (*b. Cologne, Germany, 1897; d. London, England, 1959*), entomology, zoology, history of science.

Bodenheimer took a Ph.D. at Bonn (1921), headed the department of entomology at the agricultural experiment station of the Jewish Agency in Palestine (1922–28), and taught at the Hebrew University (1928–53). His *Animal Life in Palestine* (1935) was the generally accepted survey, but his main interest was the ecological relations of animals, chiefly insect pests. He also wrote *Animal Life in Bible Lands* (2 vols., 1949–56) and *History of Biology* (1958).

BODENSTEIN, ADAM OF. *See* **Adam of Bodenstein.**

BODENSTEIN, MAX (*b. Magdeburg, Germany, 1871; d. Berlin, Germany, 1942*), chemistry.

Studied under Victor Meyer at University of Heidelberg (doctorate, 1893), Liebermann at Berlin, and Nernst at Göttingen. Early research was on chemical kinetics of gas reactions. Investigated kinetics of catalytic processes with Ostwald's researchers, Leipzig (1900–06); was the first to suggest the significance of concentration at the surface of a catalyst in heterogeneous catalysis. With Nernst in Berlin (1906–08), he studied catalysis in flowing systems: the dimensionless quotient obtained by multiplying the velocity of flow by pipe length and dividing by diffusion constant is known as the Bodenstein number. While teaching at the Technische Hochschule, Hannover, he initiated a significant study of the photochemical chlorine hydrogen reaction: explained anomalies (velocity was proportional to the square of chlorine concentration and inversely proportional to oxygen concentration, and the yield exceeded Einstein's law of equivalents by a factor of 10^4) by the concept of chain reaction, thus stimulating much important research.

BOË, FRANZ DE LA. *See* **Sylvius, Franciscus.**

BOEHME, JACOB (*b. Alt Seidenberg, near Görlitz, Germany, 1575; d. Görlitz, 1624*), theology, mysticism.

Boehme was a master cobbler. A profound mystical experience (1600) inspired his writing, which is in the Lutheran tradition and is indebted especially to Paracel-

sus and the sixteenth-century Protestant mystics. His vision and philosophy began with the revelation of the hidden God under and in the visible creation. God's self-knowledge finds expression in nature; man's path to regeneration is renewed revelation of the secrets of nature. In the seventeenth century, this view was more widely derived from Boehme than from Paracelsus. He claimed the gift of vision into the heart and being of all things in creation; he also claimed God-given insight into the language of nature. He recorded his experience in his first (unfinished) work, *Aurora oder Morgenröthe im Aufgang* (1612), which circulated in manuscript. Most of his works were first published in England between 1644 and 1663, where he had a wide and varied influence, most clearly among the Quakers. In Germany he did not gain prominence until he was taken up by the Pietists during the eighteenth century. He had a strong impact on German Romantic thought and on post-Kantian idealism, and a strong and enduring influence on Russian writers.

BOERHAAVE, HERMANN (*b. Voorhout, Netherlands, 1668; d. Leiden, Netherlands, 1738*), medicine, botany, chemistry.

Boerhaave took a degree at the University of Leiden in philosophy (1690) and a medical degree at the academy of Harderwijk (1693). He taught medicine at Leiden (from 1701 to 1729) and at one time he held simultaneously three of the five chairs that constituted the whole of Leiden's Faculty of Medicine. He was largely responsible for Leiden's pre-eminence as a medical center and he became the most famous man of science in Europe. The medical faculties at Vienna, Göttingen, and Edinburgh were begun or reformed on the system he instituted at Leiden. The modern medical curriculum—with its emphasis on natural science, anatomy, physiology, pathology, and, in particular, clinical training—owes much to him.

With Stahl and Hoffmann, he was a great systematist of the early eighteenth century. He accepted the corpuscular theory of the structure of matter, and his system was essentially mechanistic, although he acted eclectically. But his lasting influence on medicine lies in his teaching. He indoctrinated his pupils with the old Hippocratic method of bedside observation and taught them to examine their patients methodically.

His most important contributions to science were perhaps in chemistry. He introduced exact, quantitative methods into chemistry by measuring temperature and using the best available balances made by Fahrenheit; indeed, he may be considered the founder of physical chemistry as well as a contributor to pneumatic chemistry and biochemistry. He was the first to obtain urea and to discover its diuretic properties and its cooling effect when dissolved in water. He described a rapid method of making vinegar sometimes called Boerhaave's method. His textbook *Elementa chemiae* (1724) later translated into English and French, was the authoritative chemical manual for decades.

BOETHIUS, ANICIUS MANLIUS SEVERINUS (*b. Rome [?], ca. 480; d. near Pavia, Italy, 524/525*), logic, mathematics, music, theology, philosophy.

Very little is known of Boethius' life before his downfall, imprisonment, and execution (522–525). He belonged to an eminent aristocratic family. There is no reason to believe that he ever left Italy. Theodoric appointed him to high office as consul (510) but did not take into account his attachment to the Senate and to the idea of the Roman Empire and Roman "freedom." His appointment to one of the highest offices in the Roman Gothic kingdom, the *magisterium officiorum,* is hypothesized but not certain. When he defended Albinus against the charge of betraying the Gothic king for the Roman emperor, Theodoric ordered Boethius' imprisonment and death. Centuries later he became the broadcaster of Greek knowledge. He planned to leave behind, in Latin, the achievement of the Greek past, but did not outline any such plan. He did state two intentions: First, to translate and comment upon as many works by Aristotle and Plato as he could "get hold of," and to "try to show that their philosophies agree." This echoed Porphyry, who was often his source. Second, he intended to produce a handbook for each of the four mathematical disciplines already linked in the Greek tradition— arithmetic, music, geometry, astronomy—which he calls the *quadrivium,* probably the first use of the word. (This led, by analogy, to the term *trivium* for the disciplines dealing with words.)

He adapted from the Greek, but presented as original, several of his "original" works of logic and, perhaps, of theology. Of his works, the following translations are indisputably his: Porphyry's *Isagoge* (with commentary); Aristotle's *Categories* (with commentary), *De interpretatione* (with commentary), *Prior Analytics, Topics,* and *Sophistical Refutations.* The translations suggest that his knowledge of Greek was by no means excellent. *On Definitions,* ascribed to him from the twelfth to the nineteenth centuries, is the work of Marius Victorinus. None of the texts on astronomy tentatively connected with him can as yet be definitely ascribed to him. His theological works are obviously didactic or scholastic, a character shared, but veiled in a literary form, by his one personal, original, and attractive work, *The Consolation of Philosophy* (523–524), written in verse and prose while he was awaiting execution.

Originality is rare in Boethius' works especially in logic, mathematics, and theology. His texts contributed more than anything else to popularization of the Aristotelian divisions of philosophy and the general plan of logic. Especially important are his distinctions between "things as they are" and "things as they are conceived" and his mention of the theory of *indifferentia,* which became the doctrine of a main early twelfth century school of thought.

In *De divisione* (ca. 507) four kinds of "division" are listed: (1) of a genus by fundamental differences and by species, which are determined by at least some of these differences—indispensable for satisfactory definitions; (2) of a whole into its constituent parts, for precision in accounting for the nature and structure of the whole; (3) "division of words," classification of meanings or functions of individual words, to avoid confusion and sophistry; and (4) "division of accidents," classification of nonessentials. In *De syllogismis hypotheticis* (ca. 518) the one element useful for scientific method is the distinction between accidental connection or coincidence ("Fire being warm, the heavens are spherical") and natural connection ("If the Earth comes in between, there follows an eclipse of the moon"). The importance of his *De differentiis*

topicis (ca. 523) lies mainly in its critical evaluation of kinds of arguments.

Two Natures and One Person in Christ provides an analysis of the four meanings of *natura* and the definition of *persona* which became traditional in theology and is at the basis of most of our usages of "person."

His mathematical works reproduced Greek works that have not been clearly identified. The neo-Pythagorean theory of number as the divine essence of the world is the view around which the four sciences of the *quadrivium* are developed. His *Arithmetic* passes on to the Latin reader many of the basic terms and concepts of arithmetical theory. His understanding of arithmetic, and possibly of Greek, was limited. He does not, however, miss such elementary things as the multiplication table up to ten. His *Geometry* includes a description of the abacus, the elementary computer based on a decimal system, individual numbers are classified and there are rules for multiplication and division. One additional contribution to mathematics reached the Middle Ages through Boethius: the formula $n(n-1)/2$ for the number of possible combinations of two elements in a class of n elements.

The *De consolatione philosophiae* is on the whole a restatement of the eclectic Neoplatonic cosmology. It particularly impressed three doctrines into the minds of philosophers and scientists: (1) Independently of any revelation, the mind can achieve certainty about the existence of God, his goodness, and his power. (2) The universe is ordered according to unbroken chains of causes and effects; necessity is determined by God, and chance is nothing more than the coincidental intersection of distinct lines of causation. (3) The order of the universe includes a descent from the first cause to the lowest effects and a return from the lowest ends to the highest beginning. Causality, in the more restricted modern sense, and teleology have preserved a stronger hold on the minds of many generations because of its enormous popularity until the sixteenth century. But his insistence on the possibility of combining freedom of the will with God's eternally present knowledge of the order he willed engaged scholars in theological subtleties more than in any scientific approach.

BOETIUS DE BOODT, ANSELMUS. *See* **Boodt, Anselmus Boetius de.**

BOETTGER, RUDOLPH CHRISTIAN VON. *See* **Böttger, Rudolph Christian.**

BOGDANOV (MALINOVSKY), ALEKSANDR ALEK-SANDROVICH (*b. Tula, Russia, 1873; d. Moscow, U.S.S.R., 1928*), philosophy, medicine.

Educated at Moscow University and at Kharkov University (M.D. 1899); active in politics from student days. Wrote extensively on political economy, historical materialism, philosophy, science, and proletarian culture. Attempted to create a "universal organizational science," tectology, harmonizing Marxism and modern science: united subjective and objective realms of experience in a new philosophical system, empiriomonism; all existing objects could be distinguished in terms of the degree of their organization; living beings and automatic machines are dynamically structured complexes in which "bi-regulators" provide for the maintenance of order (some commentators consider this an anticipation of the concept of cybernetic feedback). His medical contribution consists chiefly in the organization of hematological research in Soviet Russia; he carried out transfusion experiments on himself.

BOGUSLAVSKY, PALM HEINRICH LUDWIG VON (*b. Magdeburg, Prussia, 1789; d. Breslau, Prussia, 1851*), astronomy.

Boguslavsky, an amateur astronomer, taught astronomy and was director of the astronomical observatory at the University of Breslau (from 1843). He was concerned primarily with observations and orbit computation of comets, meteor groups, planets, and solar eclipses.

BÖHEIM, MARTIN. *See* **Behaim, Martin.**

BOHL, PIERS (*b. Walka, Livonia [now Latvian S.S.R.], 1865; d. Riga, Latvia, 1921*), mathematics.

Bohl took degrees at the University of Dorpat (1887, 1893, 1900) and taught at Riga Polytechnic Institute (1895–1919) and the University of Latvia (1919–21). He introduced (1893) and studied the functions named quasi-periodic in 1903 by E. Esclangon, who had discovered them independently. Bohl presented (1900) a new development of topological methods of systems of differential equations of the first order.

BOHN, JOHANNES (*b. Leipzig, Germany, 1640; d. Leipzig, 1718*), medicine, physiology.

Bohn took a doctorate in medicine at Leipzig (1665) and taught there (from 1668). An innovator in physiology, he completely forsook the Galenic tradition. His *Exercitationes physiologicarum* (1668–77) and his *Circulus anatomicus-physiologicus seu Oeconomia corporis animalis* (1680) dedicated to Malpighi, cite contemporary authors almost exclusively, describe and discuss all major body functions, and rely much on firsthand experiments. His basic attitude was mechanistic. He was a founder of forensic medicine and of forensic autopsy.

BOHR, HARALD (*b. Copenhagen, Denmark, 1887; d. Copenhagen, 1951*), mathematics.

Bohr, a younger brother of Niels Bohr, was educated at the University of Copenhagen (1910), and taught there (1910–15) and at the College of Technology (1915–30). He headed the new Institute of Mathematics at Copenhagen (from 1930). He was a leading analyst of his time, with international influence. All his work was on Dirichlet series. His collaboration with Landau, mainly on the theory of the Riemann zeta-function, culminated in the so-called Bohr-Landau theorem (1914) on the distribution of its zeros. His main achievement was the theory of almost-periodic functions (1924–26). Von Neumann extended it to functions on arbitrary groups (1930's) and it became central in contemporary mathematics.

BOHR, NIELS HENRIK DAVID (*b. Copenhagen, Denmark, 1885; d. Copenhagen, 1962*), atomic and nuclear physics, epistemology.

Upon completing his graduate research in electron theory at the University of Copenhagen in 1911, Bohr went to England where, after a brief association with J. J. Thomson in Cambridge, he moved to Rutherford's labo-

ratory in Manchester. There, during the short period from March to July, 1912, Bohr laid the foundations of his greatest achievement in physics, the theory of atomic constitution.

Quick to perceive the profound theoretical significance and heuristic value of the "nuclear" model of the atom, proposed by Rutherford in 1910, Bohr used it to show the following: 1) that the chemical properties of an atom, including its place in the periodic table, depended on the configuration of its electrons, 2) that the radioactive properties were associated with the nucleus, 3) that isotopes corresponded to atoms with identical electrons but different mass nuclei, and 4) that radioactive decay changed the charge on the nucleus, and hence the number of electrons and the chemical identity of an atom.

Bohr next undertook to determine the exact nature of the relation between the atomic number of an element, which summarized its chemical behavior, and the number of electrons in the atom—a problem that amounted to a dynamic analysis of the nuclear model. Following J. J. Thomson's example, he assumed that the electrons would be symmetrically distributed around the nucleus in concentric rings, but he had to account for the stability of such a structure, which in this model could not be maintained by electrostatic forces alone. The theoretical inconsistencies that Bohr had met with earlier in his doctoral study of electrons in metals had convinced him of the need to depart from classical mechanics in describing atomic phenomena. In fact, he had no doubt that Planck's quantum of action would figure in his analysis of atomic structure. He proceeded to "quantize" the motions of the peripheral electrons by defining a series of allowable states of motion, with binding energies differing by integral multiples of the expression $Kh\nu$ (K = a numerical factor to be determined by experiment, h = Planck's constant, ν = the frequency of the motion), determinable optically by the scattering of light by the atom. While a rough check of this formula was encouraging within the appropriate orders of magnitude, it did not suffice to determine the precise quantum condition, and Bohr dropped the problem temporarily.

He then used the nuclear model to calculate the energy lost by a particle traversing matter because of the electrical interaction between the particle and atomic electrons. The success of this analysis suggested to him that one must expect 1) a gradual merging of the quantum theory into the classical one for motions of progressively lower frequencies, and 2) that the classical theory could be used for estimating the effect of a very slow modification of the forces acting on or within an atomic system. Bohr developed those two insights into powerful heuristic principles. He used the second principle to analyze simple atomic and molecular structures, and to show that the Rutherford model yielded a clear-cut distinction between atom and molecule, the latter being defined as a system with more than one nucleus. That definition led to the understanding that the chemical bond is produced by the formation of a configuration of electrons shared by the combining atoms.

Relative to the theory of atomic constitution, Bohr went on to show that the classical theory provides a non-quantal relation between the frequency of the peripheral electrons and their binding energy, thus making it possible to eliminate the frequency from the quantum condition. He was then able to obtain an extremely simple expression for the quantized binding energies W_n depending only on the integer n: $W_n = A/n^2$ (where $A = \pi^2 e^4 m/2K^2 h^2$; all being known constants except for the factor K).

Bohr left Manchester in July 1912 and returned to Copenhagen to take up the duties of assistant at the university. Early in 1913, he turned to the phenomenon of atomic radiation, which gave him the missing clue to the structure of the nuclear atom. Once he had been introduced to the empirical formula $\nu_{nm} = R \left(\frac{1}{n^2} - \frac{1}{m^2} \right)$, discovered by J. R. Rydberg as representing the apparently indecipherable spectral lines of elements as functions of a pair of integral variables, Bohr recognized at once the formal similarity between the Rydberg terms R/n^2 and his own terms for the possible energy states (A/n^2) of the quantized atom. Assuming that when an atom emits light of frequency ν it does so in quanta of energy $h\nu$, Bohr was able to interpret Rydberg's formula as indicating that for each such emission the atom would pass from one stationary state W_n to another W_m, of correspondingly lower energy. He was now in a position to calculate Rydberg's empirical constant R in terms of his own theoretical constant A by the simple relation $Rh = A$. The accuracy of that calculation was strong evidence for the validity of his interpretation.

A peculiar feature of this new theory of atomic constitution and radiation was the fact that the frequencies of the emitted light did not coincide with any of the allowed frequencies of the electrons or their harmonics, but Bohr accepted that anomaly as a necessary consequence of the acute conflict between the classical description of atomic phenomena and their quantal features. Although the stationary states of an atomic system can be described by classical mechanics, the transition from one state to another is a nonclassical process, the result of which can be accounted for by Planck's relation between the energy and frequency of the quantum of light emitted or absorbed.

Bohr recognized the need to extend his atomic theory beyond the simple structures he had used at first: to generalize it, explore its consequences, and analyze more deeply the relation between its classical and quantal aspects. To achieve all that was a challenging research program for a whole generation of physicists during the next two decades. After the Danish authorities had established the Institute for Theoretical Physics in Copenhagen in 1920, Bohr and the collaborators who joined him there — including György Hevesy, Hendrik A. Kramers, Oskar Klein, Wolfgang Pauli, and Werner Heisenberg—devoted their talents to the theory of atomic phenomena. The long series of their experimental results and theoretical interpretations were of primary importance to the creation of the theory of quantum mechanics.

In the development of his theory of atomic structure, dynamics, and radiation, Bohr continued to make major scientific contributions. He used the concept of adiabatic invariants (suggested by Paul Ehrenfest in 1911) to account for the complex motion of the electrons in large atoms.

That was followed by the introduction of the modern concept of groupings of electron orbits in "shells" specified by definite sets of "quantum numbers" according to rules inferred from spectroscopic data. This new model not only accounted for the main classification of stationary states but also led to an understanding of the intensities of the quantal transitions between such states—phenomena describable hitherto only by empirical spectroscopic rules.

Bohr was now able to set forth a description of the atom as a multiply periodic system whose states of motion could be represented by superpositions of harmonic oscillations of specified frequencies and their integral multiples, each occurring with a definite amplitude. He demonstrated that the classical description of the radiation would tend towards the frequencies of the quantal transitions in the limiting cases of large quantum numbers. He further postulated that the amplitudes of the harmonics of the classical motion should in all cases give an *estimate* of the corresponding quantal amplitudes. This so-called "correspondence argument" of Bohr's was immediately applied by Kramers to the splitting of the hydrogen lines in an electric field, as well as to the interpretation of other spectroscopic data. (Eventually it gave Heisenberg the decisive clue to the mathematical structure of a consistent quantum mechanics.)

Bohr's theory of atomic structure provided chemists with powerful and refined spectroscopic methods, and led to the discovery by Dirk Koster and Hevesy of the element with atomic number 72, hafnium, in 1922 (the year Bohr won the Nobel prize in physics).

In spite of the triumphs of his theory, Bohr remained unconvinced that the model he was using to describe atomic phenomena—simple point charges interacting by electrostatic forces according to the laws of classical mechanics—bore a close resemblance to reality. He was aware of the deficiencies of his model that showed up in the fine structure of spectroscopic analysis; and the limited correspondence between the quantal radiation processes and their classical counterparts suggested to him that the classical model was only a useful guide.

In 1924, in a paper entitled the "Quantum Theory of Radiation," he expressed his doubts and emphasized the "virtual" character of the classical model. He even went so far as to question the absolute validity of the classical conservation laws of mass and energy, suggesting that they might hold true only on the average.

While the latter suggestion was refuted experimentally by A. H. Compton and A. W. Simon, Bohr's skepticism was influential in establishing the conviction that the classical mode of describing atomic processes would eventually have to be relinquished. The additional quantum numbers hypothesized by Pauli in 1925, and later interpreted as electron "spin," taken together with Pauli's "exclusion principle," added to the already considerable difficulty of treating the atom as a classical dynamic system.

In the same year, Heisenberg abandoned the search for a classical interpretation of quantal processes and constructed instead a formal algebraic system that described atomic phenomena only in terms of the relations between observable quantities. Heisenberg's approach was essentially a statistical one: he interpreted quantum amplitudes as providing the probabilities of the transitions between stationary states, and he introduced the correspondence between classical and quantal amplitudes only as part of the set of mathematical rules the quantal amplitudes had to obey.

In the course of the next two years, Heisenberg's ideas were developed by Max Born, P. A. M. Dirac, and others into a general theory of quantum mechanics. This new conceptual scheme had peculiar features. The classical concept of a particle appeared in it only in conjunction with a wave field, and the classical concept of a trajectory became the limiting case of a more general statistical description of the motion of the particle. Another peculiar feature was the limitation the theory imposed on the exactness with which certain pairs of classical magnitudes (e.g., position and momentum) could be determined jointly in a particular case. According to Heisenberg's "uncertainty principle" the product of the degree of uncertainty of the two magnitudes could not be less than Planck's constant. Thus the precision of one measurement was achieved *in principle* at the expense of the precision of the other. This represented the extention of quantum rules to classical concepts.

Bohr accepted the new theory wholeheartedly. Although he had predicted the fundamental break with classical theory, he was gratified that the abstract character of the new theory made it possible to retain every element of the classical description, within the limits suggested by experience.

He contributed to explaining the strange features of quantum mechanics and resolving many of its apparent contradictions by operational analysis of the concepts in question. In these endeavors he was spurred on by the subtle objections of Albert Einstein, who was out of sympathy with the statistical foundations of the theory.

Bohr's investigations of quantum mechanics convinced him that the decisive element introduced by the quantum of action was what he called the "individual character" of quantal processes. Every such process (for example, the emission of radiation by an atom) occurs *as a whole*. It is well defined only when completed and cannot be subdivided like the processes of classical mechanics, which involve an immense number of quanta. He also perceived in the wave-particle duality and the uncertainty principle, profound epistemological implications that affect our view of the role and meaning of science. Bohr called that aspect of knowledge "complementarity." Two "complementary" descriptions of a phenomenon, although mutually exclusive in a given case, are both indispensable for the full description of our experience.

By the mid 1930's, the main interest in Copenhagen as elsewhere had shifted to nuclear physics, and Bohr helped to resolve some of the early theoretical difficulties encountered by physicists in dealing with nuclear reactions. His "droplet model" for the nucleus (1936) explained the nuclear "capture" of a neutron as well as the "escape" of a nucleon from a compound nucleus.

This theory was to have an important application in explaining nuclear fission—in which a heavy nucleus, after the impact of a neutron, splits into two fragments of about the same mass and charge. When Otto Hahn identified two such fragments as decay products of uranium under neutron bombardment, O. R. Frisch and Lise Meitner were led to the conclusion that this could be only the result of nuclear fission. The first experiments actually showing the emission of these fragments were performed in Copenhagen by Frisch in January 1939. In the same month, Bohr outlined a theory of the process, later elaborating his ideas with the help of J. A. Wheeler.

Bohr was later able to explain the differential efficacy of fast and slow neutrons in producing nuclear fission in uranium, by showing that only the rare isotope U-235 is fissile by slow neutrons, while the abundant U-238 was not; and he demonstrated by an ingenious argument that the difference was the result of the first isotope having an even number of neutrons and the second an odd one.

The discovery that the unstable fission fragments emitted neutrons suggested the possibility of a chain reaction with the release of huge amounts of nuclear energy. This was confirmed in Chicago, in 1942, by the experimental production of the first self-sustained nuclear reaction, and later by the explosion of the atomic bomb.

After World War II, Bohr, who had attempted earlier and without success to persuade the allied leaders to accept his views as to the international initiatives that should be taken to limit the dangers of nuclear warfare, published an open letter to the United Nations in 1950, repeating his plea for an "open world" as a precondition of peace.

Among his later scientific activities was the leading role he played in 1955 in the organization of a Danish establishment for the constructive use of nuclear energy.

BOISBAUDRAN, PAUL ÉMILE LECOQ DE (called **François**) (*b. Cognac, France, 1838; d. Paris, France, 1912*), chemistry.

Boisbaudran had no formal schooling. He worked in the family wine business, and studied chemistry and physics in a home laboratory. He is best known for his spectroscopic methods of elementary analysis. His *Spectres lumineux* (2 vols., 1874) reported the results of extensive and refined spectral examinations of thirty-five elements. He spectroscopically discovered (1875) a new element, gallium. He also discovered samarium; dysprosium, terbium, europium (1885); gadolinium (1886).

BOISLAURENT, FRANÇOIS BUDAN DE. *See* **Budan de Boislaurent, François.**

BOLK, LODEWIJK, usually called **Louis** (*b. Overschie, Netherlands, 1866; d. Amsterdam, Netherlands, 1930*), anatomy.

Bolk took a medical degree at Amsterdam University (1896), taught there (from 1898), and served as rector (1918). He was knighted in 1918. With Winkler he started (1900) the anatomical periodical *Petrus Camper*, publishing in it his work on the comparative anatomy of the cerebellum and its nerves. His research dealt with the ontogeny of the teeth, left and right handedness, the length of the body in the Nordic and Alpine races, endocrinology, and general ontogeny.

BOLOS OF MENDES, also known as **Bolos the Democritean** (*b. Mendes, Egypt; fl. ca. 200* B.C.), biology.

Bolos' reputation in antiquity rivaled that of Aristotle in natural history. No detailed reconstruction of any of his works or of his influence is possible because only a few identifiable fragments remain; because he deliberately passed off his writings under Democritus' name; and because later pseudo-Democritean works were attributed to him. The evidence suggests that he made no original contribution and that he collected unsystematically a large and diverse body of information, largely supernatural, suitable to the exploitation of the irrational in Hellenistic times.

BOLOTOV, ANDREI TIMOFEEVICH (*b. Dvoryaninovo, Tula oblast, Russia, 1738; d. Dvoryaninovo, 1833*), agronomy, biology.

Bolotov devoted himself to agronomy after retiring (1762) from military service. His most noteworthy achievement was the defense against the reigning humus theory and further development of the theory that plants need mineral nourishment. His precise description (1778) of dichogamy antedated Sprengel's work. He was the author of more than 300 works.

BOLTWOOD, BERTRAM BORDEN (*b. Amherst, Mass., 1870; d. Hancock Point, Me., 1927*), radiochemistry.

Boltwood graduated in chemistry from Yale's Sheffield Scientific School (1892); studied under Alexander Krüss in Munich (1892–94), and took a Ph.D. at Yale (1897). He taught physics (1906–09) and radiochemistry (1910–27) at Yale College and directed the college chemical laboratory (1918–27).

In 1904, to support Rutherford's theory that radioactive atoms decay and transmute into other elements, Boltwood determined to measure radium's first daughter product, emanation, as an indication of the amount of radium present. He thus overcame the difficulty of testing minute traces of radium quantitatively. He showed that the activity of radium emanation was directly proportional to the amount of uranium in each of his samples. Seeking direct proof that uranium decays into radium, he established, in collaboration with Rutherford, the equilibrium amount of radium (1906). He hypothesized a long-lived decay product between uranium X and radium, for a time identifying it as actinium (wrongly, as Rutherford and Soddy insisted). He named "ionium," one of the constituents in actinium, as the immediate parent of radium (1907; proved by Soddy 1919). From this work grew a superior method for the determination of the half-life of radium; recognition of chemically-identical isotopes; and Boltwood's own method of radioactive dating of rocks by lead content. His claim for a billion-year span in the age of the earth initially met some skepticism, but the work of Arthur Holmes, an understanding of isotopes, and increasing accuracy of decay constants and analyses brought widespread acceptance in the 1930's.

BOLTZMANN, LUDWIG (*b. Vienna, Austria, 1844; d. Duino, near Trieste, 1906*), physics.

Boltzmann, the son of a civil servant, took a doctorate at the University of Vienna (1867) and taught at Graz, Vienna, Munich, and Leipzig.

He began his lifelong study of the atomic theory of matter by seeking to establish a direct connection between the second law of thermodynamics and the mechanical principle of least action (1866), but the analogy was insufficient. The missing element was the statistical approach to atomic motion introduced by James Clerk Maxwell (1859, 1866). Assuming as Maxwell had, that the gas was in an equilibrium state, Boltzmann extended Maxwell's theory of the distribution of energy among colliding gas molecules, treating the case when external forces are present (1868). The result was a new exponential formula for molecular distribution, now known as the

"Boltzmann factor" and basic to all modern calculations in statistical mechanics.

Maxwell and Boltzmann thought that the kinetic theory should also be able to show that a gas will actually tend to equilibrium if it is not there already. It was Boltzmann's achievement to show in detail how thermodynamic entropy is related to the statistical distribution of molecular configurations, and how increasing entropy corresponds to increasing randomness on the molecular level (1872). Taking Maxwell's theory as the starting point, he arrived at a special case of the general Boltzmann transport equation. Once the Maxwellian state has been reached, no further change in the velocity distribution function can occur. He then showed how the diffusion, viscosity, and heat conduction coefficients of a gas could be calculated by solving the general Boltzmann transport equation. It is difficult to obtain exact solutions of this equation except when the molecules interact with inverse fifth-power forces, a case for which Maxwell had found an important simplification. The equation is now used in research on fluids, plasmas, and neutron transport.

It would be possible (as many modern texts do) to take the Maxwell-Boltzmann distribution function as the basic postulate for calculating all the equilibrium properties of a system. Boltzmann, however, preferred another approach. He developed and applied (1877) the famous relation between entropy and probability which assumes equal a priori probability of all microstates of the system. Boltzmann and Maxwell also introduced what is now called the "ergodic hypothesis": a single system will eventually pass through all possible microstates.

Half of Boltzmann's publications were not in kinetic theory but range in physics, chemistry, mathematics, and philosophy. He worked out a theoretic derivation (1883) of the fourth-power law found experimentally by Stefan. The Stefan-Boltzmann law for radiation was later exploited in the quantum theory.

Throughout his career, Boltzmann was concerned with the mathematical problems arising from the atomic nature of matter. His concern about the consistency of atomic theories may have seemed excessive until, toward the end of the century, the various paradoxes—specific heats, reversibility, and recurrence—were taken more seriously as defects of atomism, and he was cast in the role of principal defender of the kinetic theory and of the atomistic-mechanical view in general. He engaged in bitter debates with those who were in reaction against "materialist" science and preferred empirical or phenomenological theories to atomic models (Ernst Mach, Wilhelm Ostwald, Pierre Duhem, George Helm).

BOLYAI, FARKAS (WOLFGANG) (*b. Bolya [German, Bell], near Nagyszeven [German, Hermannstadt], Transylvania, Hungary [now Sibiu, Rumania], 1775; d. Marosvásárhely, Transylvania, Hungary [now Târgu-Mures, Rumania], 1856*), mathematics.

Bolyai studied at the University of Göttingen (1796–99), meeting there his lifelong friend Carl Friedrich Gauss. He taught at the Evangelical-Reformed College at Marosvásárhely (1804–53). Working in almost total scientific isolation, he concentrated on the theory of parallels. His principal work, *Tentamen* (2 vols., 1832), was an attempt at a rigorous and systematic foundation of geometry, arithmetic, algebra, and analysis. It contained, as an appendix, an essay by his son János, who had developed an entirely unorthodox system of geometry based on the rejection of the parallel axiom, something with which his father could not agree. Unwittingly, the son's paper gave the father's book immortality. Bolyai published a German summary of his *Tentamen, Kurzer Grundriss eines Versuches* (1851).

BOLYAI, JÁNOS (JOHANN) (*b. Koloszvár [German, Klausenburg], Transylvania, Hungary [now Cluj, Rumania], 1802; d. Marosvásárhely, Hungary [now Tárgu-Mureș, Rumania], 1860*), mathematics.

Bolyai, the son of Farkas Bolyai, was educated at the imperial engineering academy in Vienna (1818–22). After a military career (1822–33) he was pensioned off as a semi-invalid and returned home. By 1823 he had begun constructing a geometry without the parallel axiom. He showed his father (1825) a manuscript that contained his theory of absolute space. His father rejected it but sent the manuscript to his lifelong friend, Carl Friedrich Gauss. Gauss's famous reply (1832) expressed his astonishment and delight at the almost complete agreement with his own thoughts. The letter was a terrible blow to János, robbing him of priority. His classic essay of twenty-four pages, published in the elder Bolyai's *Tentamen* (1832) an "Appendix Explaining the Absolutely True Science of Space," was the only one of his works published in his lifetime. It evoked no response from other mathematicians, and he avoided mathematics for long periods. The "Appendix" was practically forgotten until Richard Baltzer discussed it in his *Elemente der Mathematik* (2nd ed., 1867). Jules Houel translated it into French (1868), and full recognition came with the work of Eugenio Beltrami (1868) and Felix Klein (1871).

BOLZA, OSKAR (*b. Bergzabern, Germany, 1857; d. Freiberg im Breisgau, Germany, 1942*), mathematics.

Bolza took a Ph.D. at the University of Göttingen (1886) under Felix Klein. He taught at the University of Chicago (1893–1910) and at Freiberg (1910–26, 1929–33). His principal mathematical investigations were in the reduction of hyperelliptic integrals to elliptic integrals, elliptic and hyperelliptic functions, and the calculus of variations. His most significant single contribution was the unification of the problems of Lagrange and Mayer into his more general problem of Bolza.

BOLZANO, BERNARD (*b. Prague, Czechoslovakia, 1781; d. Prague, 1848*), philosophy, mathematics, logic, religion, ethics.

Bolzano took a degree (1800) in philosophy and in theology, took orders (1804), and was called to the new chair in the philosophy of religion at the University of Prague (1805). In the struggle between the Catholic restoration and the Enlightenment, he was charged (1816) at the court in Vienna and dismissed (1819) from the chair and from his post as dean of the philosophy faculty, which he had held for a year. He was forbidden to publish and was kept under police supervision until intervention by the influential nationalist leader J. Dobrovsky ended the action (1825).

Bolzano's *Rein analytischer Beweis* (1817) gives the first definition of a continuous function that did not involve infinitesimals. The book also used a lemma which proved to be the cornerstone of the theory of real numbers.

Bolzano's *Functionenlehre* contained a fairly complete theory of real functions, including many of the fundamental results rediscovered after his death. It uses the so-called Bolzano-Weierstrass theorem that a bounded infinite point set has an accumulation point. Most remarkable, however, is the so-called Bolzano function: a function constructed as the limit of a sequence of continuous functions which is continuous on the closed interval (0, 1) such that it is in no subinterval monotone. The importance of this function derives from its non-differentiability, preceding Weierstrass's different example (1875), which roused wide interest and even indignation. Bolzano completed the firm base for the theory of functions, the theory of quantities (real numbers), in 1832–35 (published 1962). This, like much of his bold enterprise, long remained in manuscript and failed to exercise any influence. Real numbers he named measurable infinite number-expressions. The essential difference between his incomplete theory of real numbers and those of, for instance, Weierstrass and Cantor is the possibility of creating new mathematical objects by means of definition by abstraction, based on equivalence relations, of which he was unaware. This is also clear in his *Paradoxien des Unendlichen* (1851), in which he is at the border of cardinal arithmetic, a border he is unable to cross.

Bolzano's *Wissenschaftslehre* (4 vols., 1837) did not induce a complete revision of science, as he had hoped, but remained unnoticed. The rise of logical semantics (1930's) revived study of his logic and his theory of an ideal language, and he is regarded as a precursor of modern logic in his development of the concepts of abstract proposition, abstract idea, and truth, and of notions of derivability, consistency, and entailment as relations of propositions.

BOMBELLI, RAFAEL (*b. Bologna, Italy, 1526; d. 1572*), algebra.

Bombelli was an engineer-architect serving Alessandro Rufini, a favorite of Pope Paul III. His major project was the reclamation of the marshes of the Val di Chiana (by 1551–60). He wrote (1557–60) a systematic and logical exposition of algebra that, he hoped, would enable anyone to master the subject without the aid of any other text and would improve the clarity of Cardano's exposition. He gave a comprehensive account of existing knowledge of algebra, enriched with his own contributions. These included the cube root of a complex number occurring in the solution of the irreducible case of the cubic equation. His rules for operating with complex numbers show him to be far ahead of his time. He helped to raise algebra to the status of an independent discipline and was the first to popularize Diophantus in the West; he used 143 of Diophantus' problems. Also significant was his notation. The last of the algebraists of Renaissance Italy, he had a strong influence on Simon Stevin and later on Leibniz.

BONANNI, FILIPPO. *See* **Buonanni, Filippo.**

BONAPARTE, LUCIEN JULES LAURENT, called **Charles Lucien** (*b. Paris, France, 1803; d. Paris, 1857*), zoology.

A son of Napoleon's younger brother Lucien, Bonaparte went to the United States (1822), where he started a promising career as a naturalist. He returned to Italy (1828) and began his great political activity. He left politics in 1850 and turned exclusively to science. In the United States he had applied himself to the continuation of Wilson's work on birds, then (1831) became interested in the great principles of classification and was critical of Cuvier's concepts. He published many synopses, conspectuses, and catalogs. He conceived, with Victor Meunier, a general work on the fauna of France in the year he died.

BONAVENTURA, FEDERIGO (*b. Ancona, Italy, 1555; d. Urbino [?], Italy, 1602*), meteorology.

Bonaventura was educated under the duke's favor and several times served as Urbino's ambassador to European courts. His meteorological works examine the philological meanings of ancient authors, Theophrastus particularly, without resort to experiment or observation for verification. He also translated into Latin works of Theophrastus, Themistius, and Ptolemy.

BONCOMPAGNI, BALDASSARRE (*b. Rome, Italy, 1821; d. Rome, 1894*), history of mathematics, history of physics.

Boncompagni, whose father was prince of Piombino, studied with Barnaba Tortolini. His most important historical works were on Leonardo Fibonacci, then little known, and he made his importance clear. His edition of the *Scritti di Leonardo Pisano* (1857–62) was an accurate one. He established his own printing plant, which published such important documents on the history of science as letters of Lagrange and Gauss, the journal *Bullettino Boncompagni* (1868–87), and the transactions of the Pontifical Academy of the New Lincei.

BOND, GEORGE PHILLIPS (*b. Dorchester, Mass., 1825; d. Cambridge, Mass., 1865*), astronomy.

A son of William Cranch Bond, the first director of Harvard Observatory, Bond collaborated intimately with his father. He has been called "the father of celestial photography." His pioneering daguerreotype work (1847–51) with his father resulted in the first photograph of a star, Vega. His 1857 experiments with wet collodion photography achieved still greater success. He discovered Saturn's satellite Hyperion (1848) and its crepe ring (1850). He directed the Harvard Observatory (1859–65). His report on the comparative brightness of the sun, moon, and Jupiter (1860) established "Bond albedo" in the vocabulary.

BOND, WILLIAM CRANCH (*b. Falmouth [now Portland], Me., 1789; d. Cambridge, Mass., 1859*), astronomy.

Bond left school early to help in his father's clockmaking shop, where his rare mechanical ability was invaluable. He independently found the Comet of 1811. As an expert clockmaker, he rated the chronometers for many longitude determinations in the eastern states. He was the unpaid astronomical observer to Harvard University (1839), where he transferred his own equipment, until the great sun-grazing comet of 1843 led to the building of a large 15-inch telescope at Harvard (1847). He and his son, George Phillips Bond, first used (1847–51) the daguerreotype process to photograph stars.

BONNET, CHARLES (*b. Geneva, Switzerland, 1720; d. Geneva, 1793*), natural history, biology, philosophy.

Bonnet took a doctorate in law (1744) to please his father but was already deeply interested in natural science. While still young, he became increasingly deaf, almost completely blind, and subject to severe asthma. He nevertheless became one of the fathers of modern biology, distinguished for his experimental research on insects and plants. His first and greatest discovery was the parthenogenesis of the aphid (1746). He also demonstrated that each piece of a rainwater worm of the species *lumbriculus* regenerates a perfectly constituted new worm (1745). He was one of the first to investigate photosynthesis experimentally. He discovered the epinastic phenomena. After 1750 he could no longer observe with his own eyes, but through his collaborators and voluminous correspondence he continued to be a fertile instigator of many fundamental experiments. His *Recherches sur l'usage des feuilles dans les plantes* (1754) was of prime importance.

BONNET, PIERRE-OSSIAN (*b. Montpellier, France, 1819; d. Paris, France, 1892*), mathematics.

Bonnet took a degree at the École des Ponts et des Chaussées (1841), taught at the École Polytechnique (from 1844), was director of studies there (from 1868), taught at the Sorbonne (from 1878), and was a member of the Bureau des Longitudes (from 1883). His fame is based on his work in the differential geometry of curves and surfaces. He introduced the concepts of geodesic curvature and torsion, and proved a series of theorems, including the one known as the Gauss-Bonnet theorem. He gave a definition of the limit for functions of a real variable (1871).

BONNEY, THOMAS GEORGE (*b. Rugeley, England, 1833; d. Cambridge, England, 1923*), geology.

Bonney, the son of a grammar school headmaster, graduated (1856) from St. John's College, Cambridge, in mathematics and classics. He was ordained and elected a fellow of the college, where he taught (from 1861), molding the Cambridge school of geology. He also taught at University College, London (1877–1901). A leading figure in early British petrography, he demonstrated the true character of British serpentines. His paper on the use of microscopic analysis in the physical geography of the past (1886) was a remarkable pioneering achievement in sedimentology.

BONNIER, GASTON (*b. Paris, France, 1853; d. Paris, 1922*), botany.

Bonnier studied and taught at the École Normale in Paris, then held the chair of botany at the Sorbonne (1887–1922). He founded and directed the Laboratoire de Biologie Végétale at Fontainebleau (1889–1922). He helped transfer botany from a descriptive to an experimental science by several important though not revolutionary discoveries. He discovered that seeds, grains, and bulbs are not physiologically "dead" (1880–82). On plant respiration, his most crucial discovery (with Louis Mangin) was that respiration proceeds most rapidly in the absence of light (1883–85). His masterpiece was *Flore complète . . . de France, Suisse et Belgique* (12 vols., 1912–34).

BONOMO, GIOVAN COSIMO (*b. Leghorn, Italy, 1666; d. Florence, Italy, 1696*), medicine.

Bonomo took a degree in medicine at the University of Pisa (1682) and was physician in the navy of Grand Duke Cosimo III and physician to the duke's daughter (1691–94). He offered the first clinical and experimental proof that scabies is transmitted by mites (1687).

BONVICINO (also known as **Bonvoisin** or **Buonvicino**), **COSTANZO BENEDETTO** (*b. Centallo, near Cuneo, Piedmont, 1739; d. Turin, Italy, 1812*), chemistry.

Bonvicino took a degree in medicine (1764) and taught pharmaceutical chemistry at the University of Turin (from 1800). He was president of the Academy of Sciences of Turin (1801–02), directed its laboratory, and worked in industrial chemistry and applied mineralogy. His best work was on the analysis of water and salts, particularly his tackling of the problems of quantitative analysis. His *Elementi di chimica* (2 vols., 1804–10) was a rich compendium of his university courses.

BOODT, ANSELMUS BOETIUS DE (*b. Bruges, Belgium, ca. 1550; d. Bruges, 1632*), mineralogy.

Boodt took an M.D. in Padua. He was physician to the burgrave of Prague (1583–1604) and physician to Rudolf II (1604–12), then a town councillor in Bruges (1612–32). His chief work, *Gemmarum et lapidum historia* (1609), made the first attempt at a systematic and lengthy description of minerals. He criticized Paracelsus but accepted the existence of the four elements and three principles; he also mentioned atoms.

BOOLE, GEORGE (*b. Lincoln, England, 1815; d. Cork, Ireland, 1864*), mathematics.

Boole was largely self-educated, yet at the age of fifteen he began teaching, soon setting up a school of his own in Lincoln. He continued his independent study of mathematics, reading Newton's *Principia* and Lagrange's *Mécanique analytique* and gaining a considerable local reputation. In 1835 he published his first scientific work (on Newton). Although he did not hold any university degree, he was appointed professor of mathematics at Queen's College, Cork; he remained in this position until his death.

Boole's scientific writings include some fifty papers, two textbooks, and two volumes on mathematical logic. In papers of 1841 and 1843 he dealt with linear transformations of binary quadratic forms and drew attention to the absolute invariants of the transformation; this was the starting point of the theory of invariants, which was rapidly developed by others. His textbooks, on differential equations (1859) and on finite differences (1860), incorporated and extended much of the material published in his research papers. In them he greatly increased the power of the operational calculus: he made extensive use of the differential operator D and introduced new operators, π and ρ, whose use he demonstrated in solving certain types of linear difference equations.

Throughout this work Boole was striving to make his foundations secure; there is also the beginning of the recognition of the nonnumerical variable as a genuine part of mathematics. The development of this notion in his later and most important work appears to have been stimulated by the quarrel between Sir William Hamilton and Boole's friend Augustus de Morgan over the applicability of mathematics to logic. Boole's *Mathematical Analy-*

sis of Logic (1847) was offered as a construction, in symbolic terms, of logic as a doctrine, like geometry, resting upon a groundwork of acceptable axioms. Attempts at the reduction of Aristotelian logic to an algebraic calculus had already been made; Boole succeeded where others had failed by recognizing the need for a new set of rules, in effect, a new algebra.

In the symbolism of the Boolean algebra of logic (an algebra of sets) U, the universal set, is denoted by 1. Subsets are specified by elective operators $x, y, \ldots$; these operators may be applied successively. Many of the rules of the algebra of real numbers are thus valid: $yx = xy, x(yz) = (xy)z, x + y = y + x$, etc.; but, by definition, $x^2 = x$. This is the idempotent law, also expressed as $x(1 - x) = 0$. Boole used the sign $+$ in the exclusive sense, with the sign $-$ as its inverse; he did not write $x + y$ unless the sets x,y were mutually exclusive. Much of the 1847 book is devoted to symbolic expressions for the forms of the classical Aristotelian propositions and the moods of the syllogism. For particular propositions he introduced the elective symbol v for a subset of indefinite membership.

The concept of the "development" of a function of the elective symbols is fundamental to Boole's logical operations and occupies a prominent place in *Investigation of the Laws of Thought* (1854). If $f(x)$ involves x and the algebraic signs, then it must denote a subset of the universe of discourse and must therefore be made up of elements from x and $\bar{x}$ ("not x"); thus $f(x) = Ax + B\bar{x}$, where the coefficients A and B are determined by giving x the values of 0 and 1. Logical problems which can be expressed in terms of elective symbols may then be reduced to standard forms expediting their solution. In this book Boole also analyzes the theory of probability.

Subsequent development of Boolean algebra by Jevons, Venn, and C. S. Peirce modified the use of the plus sign to an inclusive sense, permitting both a duality between sum and product and the elimination of subtraction and division. Numerical interpretation of the idempotent law as an equation whose only roots are $x = 0$, $x = 1$ leads to a two-valued algebra (as Boole himself established); this has found modern application in electrical circuit design, particularly in computer technology.

BORCH, OLUF. *See* **Borrichius, Olaus.**

BORCHARDT, CARL WILHELM (*b. Berlin, Germany, 1817; d. Rudersdorf, near Berlin, 1880*), mathematics.

Borchardt took a Ph.D at the University of Königsberg (1843) under Jacobi and taught at the University of Berlin (from 1848). He edited (1856–80) the celebrated *Crelle's Journal.* He wrote 25 papers applying the theory of determinants to algebraic questions and studying the arithmetic-geometric mean.

BORDA, JEAN-CHARLES (*b. Dax, France, 1733; d. Paris, France, 1799*), physics, mathematics.

Borda was educated at the Jesuit Collège de la Flèche and the École du Génie de Mézières before entering the navy. His naval career was distinguished. In addition, he was a key figure in the renaissance of exact physics in the eighteenth century and skillfully unified the use of calculus and experiment. He developed instruments for navigation and geodesy, designed the platinum standard meter and the standard seconds pendulum, demonstrated that Newton's theory of fluid resistance was untenable and that the resistance is proportional to the square of the fluid velocity and to the sine of the angle of incidence.

BORDET, JULES (*b. Soignies, Belgium, 1870; d. Brussels, Belgium, 1961*), bacteriology, immunology.

Bordet took an M.D at the University of Brussels (1892); worked on humoral immunity at the Institut Pasteur (1894–1901), directed the Institut Pasteur de Brabant (1901–40), and taught at the Free University of Brussels (1907–35). His work was important to Wassermann in the diagnosis of syphilis and more recently in the diagnosis of virus infections. With Gengou he discovered the whooping cough bacillus and prepared a vaccine (1906). He isolated the germ of bovine peripneumonia and that of avian diphtheria (1909). He was awarded the 1919 Nobel Prize in medicine for his work in immunology.

BORDEU, THÉOPHILE DE (*b. Izeste, France, 1722; d. Paris, France, 1776*), medicine.

Bordeau took an M.D. at Montpellier (1743), superintended the mineral waters of Aquitaine (1749–52), took another M.D. at Paris (1754). He founded modern hydrotherapy, publicizing the therapeutic value of mineral waters, and he was a fine clinician, as his two contributions to the *Encyclopédie* on crises demonstrate. Since Bordeu, physicians take the pulse by applying the tips of the four fingers to the hollow of the radius. Among his works are *Recherches anatomiques sur les différentes positions des glands et sur leur action* (1752), *Recherches sur le tissu muqueux* (1767).

BORDONE DELLA SCALA, GIULIO. *See* **Scaliger, Julius Caesar.**

BOREL, ÉMILE (FÉLIX-ÉDOUARD-JUSTIN) (*b. Saint-Affrique, Aveyron, France, 1871; d. Paris, France, 1956*), mathematics.

Borel graduated first in his class at the École Normale Supérieure (1893), where he wrote his thesis (1894) and taught (1897–1920). At the Sorbonne he held the chair of theory of functions created for him (1909–20) and of probability and mathematical physics (1920–40). After 1921 he moved into politics, as a Radical-Socialist deputy (1924–36) and minister of the navy (1925).

Borel's ideas initiated the modern theories of functions of a real variable, measure, divergent series, nonanalytic continuation, denumerable probability, Diophantine approximation, and the metrical distribution theory of values of analytical functions. They are related to Cantorian ideas, especially to the notion of a denumerable set. This is obvious for the two most famous results of his thesis, the Heine-Borel covering theorem and the proof that a denumerable set is of measure zero. His *Leçons* (1898) and other works laid the basis of measure theory so solidly that in that field the letter B means Borel. Many of his solutions opened whole fields: his "elementary" proof of Picard's theorem (1896) set the theme of complex function theory for a generation. He was the inventor, if not the founder, of game theory (1921–27). He was the most successful of his generation in using specific

problems and results as scientific parables pointing the way to broad theories.

BOREL, PIERRE (*b. Castres, Languedoc, France, ca. 1620; d. Paris, France, 1671*), history, medicine, chemistry.

Borel took an M.D. at Montpellier (1641) and practiced in Castres (1641–ca. 1653) and Paris. Among his original contributions to medicine are the statement that a cataract is a darkening of the crystalline lens, and his use of concave mirrors in diagnosis of the nose and throat. He is credited with the first description of brain concussions.

BORELLI, GIOVANNI ALFONSO (*b. Naples, Italy, 1608; d. Rome, Italy, 1679*), astronomy, epidemiology, mathematics, physiology, iatromechanics, physics, volcanology.

Because Borelli's mechanics was completely overshadowed by Newton and his iatromechanics bore little immediate fruit, his work has sometimes been undervalued. But his contributions were significant and were important in establishing and extending the new experimental-mathematical philosophy. He was very much ahead of his time, even if he did not produce successful general synthetic solutions. His career is an illuminating record of an original scientist politically active in Counter-Reformation Italy. When Borelli obtained the public lectureship in mathematics in Messina (*ca.* 1635–56), he quickly became known as the best mathematician after Cavalieri in Italy. He taught at the University of Pisa (1656–66) and, at the flourishing anatomical laboratory in his own house, taught among others Marcello Malpighi. He seems to have been the principal but not the sole mover in the Accademia del Cimento, which was established a year after he arrived and largely ceased to function the year he returned to Messina. There he was active in local agitation against the Spanish: he was declared a rebel in 1672 and a price was placed on his head. He ended his life in political exile in Rome, poverty-stricken, teaching elementary mathematics at a convent school.

Borelli's work on a fever epidemic in Sicily (1649) concluded that the cause was not meteorological or astrological, but rather something chemical getting into the body from the outside, and he prescribed a chemical remedy, sulfur. A section on digestion characterized the process as the action of a *succo acido corrosivo* turning food into a liquid form. He edited an edition (1661) of the then unknown Books V, VI, and VII of the *Conics* of Apollonius, from an Arabic version. His *Euclides restitutus* (1658) aimed at a clear and concise restatement; he also proposed his own version of the parallel postulate and tried to establish the theory of proportions on firmer ground. A small paper on his observations of a comet in 1664–65 showing that the comet changed in its absolute distance from the earth, raised obvious difficulties for the Ptolemaic and Tychonic systems, and presented difficulties for the Keplerian system as well. This material he published under a pseudonym Pier Maria Mutoli. His *Theoricae mediceorum planetarum ex causis physicis deductae* (1666) masks clear Copernican implications by seeming to focus on the motions of the moons of Jupiter; it explains among other things, how the elliptical orbits of planetary bodies could be understood in terms of three types of action. Two major studies were not only exercises in pure mechanics but also, in his opinion, necessary introductions to his most important work, *De motu animalium.* Both *De vi percussionis* (1667) and *De motionibus naturalibus a gravitate pendentibus* (1670) cover wide ground. The first touches on some general problems of motion, gravity, magnetism, the motion of fluids, the vibrations of bodies, and pendular motion. The second argues against positive levity, discusses the Torricellian experiment, takes up siphons, pumps, and the nature of fluidity, and deals with fermentation and other chemical processes. All this was the product of years of experimental and theoretical investigation, and he did not allow the works to be brought out by the Cimento, which required collective anonymity. His *De motu animalium* (2 vols., 1680–81) treated external motions, or the motions produced by the muscles, as well as internal motions, such as movements of the muscles themselves, circulation, respiration, the secretion of fluids, and nervous activity.

BORGOGNONI OF LUCCA, THEODORIC (*b. Parma or Lucca, Italy, ca. 1205; d. Bologna, Italy, 1298*), medicine, surgery.

Theodoric, a Dominican friar and bishop, practiced surgery in Bologna. His most famous work is his *Surgery* (*Chirurgia,* sometimes entitled *Filia principis;* released 1266, pub. 1498), which confirmed and supplemented the surgical practices of his father, Hugh of Lucca, a pioneer of Italian surgery. Theodoric's methods were revolutionary, particularly his advocacy of antiseptic surgery and his condemnation of the generation of pus in a wound, at a time when everyone held the theory of "laudable pus." He detailed his own revolutionary methods for cleaning the wound, eliminating dead tissue and foreign matter, accurately reapproximating the wound walls, using stitches where necessary, and adequately protecting the area.

BORN, IGNAZ EDLER VON (*b. Karlsburg, Transylvania* [*now Alba Iulia, Rumania*], *1742; d. Vienna, Austria, 1791*), mineralogy.

Born studied with the Jesuits in Vienna and settled in Prague, where he was with the department of mines and the mint (from 1770), counselor of mines (from 1770) and counselor of the court chamber (from 1779). His works include *Lithophylacium Bornianum* (1772), on his own collection; catalogs of fossil and mineral collections; and descriptions of mines and mining equipment. He invented an amalgamation process for removing gold and silver from various ores which was adopted in copper mines throughout Hungary.

BORN, MAX (*b. Breslau, Germany* [*now Wrocław, Poland*], *1882; d. Göttingen, Germany, 1970*), theoretical physics.

Studied at the universities of Breslau, Heidelberg, Zurich, and at Göttingen (doctorate, 1907), where he assisted Hilbert and took courses from Minkowski, Klein, and others. Collaborated with Minkowski (1908–09) and edited his papers; developed a theory of self-energy of the relativistic electron. With Kármán, published (1912) a theoretical foundation for the deviations from Einstein's quantum formula for specific heat that had been experimentally ascertained by Nernst and his collaborators; this theory was less popular than Debye's, but more reliable at very low temperatures. He undertook to erect a unified crystal physics on atomic foundations: in *Dyna-*

mik der Kristallgitter (1915) he assumed very small deviations of the "crystal particle" from the position of rest and was able to derive the essential physical properties of the crystals; *Dynamical Theory of Crystal Lattices* (1954) was a reworking based on quantum theory. At Frankfurt (1919) he undertook direct molecular-ray measurement of the parameters of gas theory, particularly of the free path length of molecules. At Göttingen (1921–33) he established an influential training-ground for theoretical physicists and engaged in productive collaborative work; inspired by Bohr's correspondence principle, he sought to elucidate atomic structure by constructing a "quantum mechanics" (1924); with Pascual Jordan he replaced the differential operators of classical mechanics by difference operators and calculated the absorption and emission of a resonator in the radiation field; they found that quantum physics pertained not to individual states but to pairs of states, to which a "transition amplitude" must be assigned. Born, Jordan, and Heisenberg went on to develop matrix mechanics, a useful new method for computing the atom's stationary states (1925) which was further elaborated in collaboration with Wiener (1926). Using Schrödinger's method of treating atomic scattering processes, he developed the "Born approximation method" of statistical quantum mechanics (1926): this method yields the statistics of scattering processes directly; with it he derived the existence of energy thresholds, a typically quantum mechanical effect in inelastic scattering processes, and thereby established a connection between the theory and the experiments of Franck and Hertz; for this work he received the Nobel Prize in physics (1954). The anti-Semitism of 1933 led him to leave Germany; he settled first in Cambridge (1933–36), where with Leopold Infeld he worked out the Born-Infeld theory of nonlinear electrodynamics; at Edinburgh (1936–53) he gathered a new group of researchers, including a number of Chinese; in 1954 he returned to Germany. His later writings were on optics, statistical mechanics of condensed systems (with Herbert S. Green), and history of science. He joined with other Nobel laureates in condemning the development of atomic weapons.

BORODIN, ALEKSANDR PORFIREVICH (*b. St. Petersburg, Russia, 1833; d. St. Petersburg, 1887*), chemistry.

Borodin, a professor at the Academy of Medicine and Surgery (from 1864), was also well-known as the composer of *Prince Igor,* the first heroic opera on a Russian theme, and other musical works. In the field of chemistry, he was among the first to obtain fluorine benzol and developed a method for the fluorination of organic compounds (1861). He investigated the polymerization and condensation of aldehydes (1863–74). His azotometric method and apparatus for the quantitative determination of urea (1876) was widely adopted in biochemical and clinical laboratories and was known by his name.

BORREL, JEAN. *See* **Buteo, Johannes.**

BORRICHIUS (or **Borch**), **OLAUS** (*b. Nørre Bork, in Ribe, Denmark, 1626; d. Copenhagen, Denmark, 1690*), chemistry.

Borrichius was greatly influenced by the alchemist G. F. Borri. He himself became famous in his own time as a physician, a polemicist, a defender of Hermeticism (particularly against Hermann Conring), and a prolific writer on chemistry, botany, and philology, the three fields he taught at the University of Copenhagen (from 1664). His histories of chemistry are among his best-known works.

BORRIES, BODO VON (*b. Herford, Westphalia, Germany, 1905; d. Cologne, Germany, 1956*), electron microscopy.

Borries studied electrical engineering at Karlsruhe, Danzig, and Munich. As an assistant-at the High-Voltage Institute of the Technische Hochschule in Berlin (1930–37), he was involved in electron microscopy from its conception and later helped to introduce its techniques into many fields, notably the life sciences. He helped organize German and international societies for electron microscopy and was president of the International Federation (1954–56).

BORRO, GIROLAMO, also known as **Borri** and **Hieronymus Borrius** (*b. Arezzo, Italy, 1512; d. Perugia, Italy, 1592*), natural philosophy, methodology of science.

Served Cardinal Giovanni Salviati as theologian (1537–53); taught natural philosophy at University of Pisa (1553–59, 1575–86); after dismissal from Pisa, may have taught at Perugia. A rather backward-looking Aristotelian; he emphasized an experiential approach to the study of natural philosophy (as opposed to a mathematical one). Published a theory of the tides (1561) and an exposition of scientific method according to Aristotelian principles (1584). In *De motu gravium et levium* (1575), he described an experimental study of falling lead vs. wood balls in which the wood fell faster. Galileo knew his writings and may have been his student.

BORTKIEWICZ (or **Bortkewitsch**), **LADISLAUS** (or **Vladislav**) **JOSEPHOWITSCH** (*b. St. Petersburg, Russia, 1868; d. Berlin, Germany, 1931*), mathematics, statistics.

Bortkiewicz, a representative of the "Continental direction" in mathematical statistics, was educated in political economy and statistics at St. Petersburg and in philosophy at Göttingen. He taught statistics and political economy at the University of Berlin (1901–31). He worked on probabilities in statistics, actuarial science, and political economy. He was a pioneer in order statistics.

BORTOLOTTI, ETTORE (*b. Bologna, Italy, 1866; d. Bologna, 1947*), mathematics, history of mathematics.

Bortolotti graduated from the University of Bologna in 1889 and later taught there and at the University of Modena. In mathematics his work was in topology and analysis. He edited Ruffini's *Opere matematiche* (1953–54), studied the development of infinitesimal analysis in the seventeenth century, found and published (1929) the manuscript of books IV and V of Bombelli's *L'algebra*, and reconstructed the argument of the Sumerian, Assyrian, Babylonian, and Egyptian mathematicians.

BORY DE SAINT-VINCENT, JEAN BAPTISTE GEORGES MARIE (*b. Agen, France, 1778; d. Paris, France, 1846*), biology.

An amateur naturalist since childhood, Bory de Saint-Vincent was conscripted into the army in 1799 and remained an officer until retirement in 1840. He is remembered as the leader of successful botanical expeditions and for contributions to the theory, principles, and knowledge of island faunas; the zoogeography of the seas; and the classification of man by physical type.

BOSC, LOUIS AUGUSTIN GUILLAUME, known in his youth as **Dantic** (*b. Paris, France, 1759; d. Paris, 1828*), natural history, agronomy.

A remarkable artisan of natural history and a pioneer in practical natural history, Bosc was educated at the Collège de Dijon. He served in the Girondist government in 1792. Later he fled to Montmorency and visited South Carolina. As a naturalist, he discovered, described, drew, and named many species. His first published article (1784) was a masterful description of an unusual cochineal, a new genus, which he named (1792) *Ripiphorus,* a coleopteron later elevated to the rank of family by Thomson (1864). He wrote on agriculture and edited the three last volumes of the *Encyclopédie de Panckoucke* (1813–21) and was one of the leading editors of the *Annales de l'agriculture française* (1811–28).

BOSCH, CARL (*b. Cologne, Germany, 1874; d. Heidelberg, Germany, 1940*), chemistry.

Bosch took a doctorate at Leipzig and while working at a technical firm tested Wilhelm Ostwald's claimed process for obtaining ammonia from nitrogen and hydrogen and found Ostwald's error. He undertook (1909) to transform Fritz Haber's laboratory experiments on the synthesis of ammonia into large-scale technological experiments; within five years a huge industry developed. He became president of I. G. Farben (1925) and shared the Nobel Prize with Bergius in 1931 "for the discovery and development of chemical high-pressure methods."

BOSE, GEORG MATTHIAS (*b. Leipzig, Germany, 1710; d. Magdeburg, Germany, 1761*), electricity.

Bose was educated at the University of Leipzig and taught natural philosophy at the University of Wittenberg (1738–60). He came to the study of electricity late, but then vigorously and successfully promoted it in Germany, producing wonderful displays with his electrical machine, a revival of Hauksbee's with greatly enhanced power. Musschenbroek's experiments—culminating in the Leyden jar—began with a repetition of a Bosean demonstration.

BOSE, JAGADISCHANDRA (*b. Mymensingh, India [now Nasirabad, Bangladesh], 1858; d. Giridih, India, 1937*), physics, plant physiology.

First modern Indian scientist to establish an international reputation. Studied at St. Xavier's College, Calcutta (B.A., 1879), Christ's College, Cambridge (B.A., 1884), and London University (B.Sc., 1884; D.Sc., 1896); his teachers at Cambridge included Sydney Vines, Francis Darwin, and Lord Rayleigh. Professor of physics at Presidency College, Calcutta (from 1884); director of Bose Research Institute (from 1917). Early research was on generation, reception, and properties of radio waves with wavelengths of about one centimeter; conducted wireless telegraphy demonstrations (1895); observed fatigue in inorganic materials exposed to radiation and undertook comparative studies of responses of plants to electrical and mechanical stress. His precise measurements of plant response were generally considered valid, but his conclusions were not. Knighted in 1916.

BOSE, SATYENDRANATH (*b. Calcutta, India, 1894; d. Calcutta, 1974*), physics.

Studied at Presidency College, Calcutta (M.Sc. 1915); taught at University College of Science, Calcutta (1917–21), University of Dacca (1921–45), and Calcutta University (1945–56); subsequently served Indian government. Publications include work on statistical mechanics, electromagnetic properties of the ionosphere, the theories of X-ray crystallography and thermoluminescence, and unified field theory. Known outside India primarily for deriving the Planck blackbody radiation law without reference to classical electrodynamics (1924); Einstein himself translated the paper into German and had it published, and his generalization of Bose's method led to the first of two systems of quantum statistical mechanics, known as the Bose-Einstein statistics (Paul Dirac later coined the term "boson" for particles that obey these statistics). Bose's paper showed that the Planck law was completely consistent with Einstein's quantum gas model; his derivation followed a general procedure introduced by Boltzmann for determining the equilibrium energy distribution of the microscopic entities that constitute a macrosystem, Bose's innovation being to assume the identity of two or more photons that differed only in the permutation of their phase points within a subregion of phase space of volume h^3 (where h is Planck's constant). This method of counting has the effect of enhancing the population of lower-energy photon states at the expense of those of higher energy, and leads to the correct Planck distribution law.

BOŠKOVIĆ, RUDJER J. (*b. Dubrovnik, Yugoslavia, 1711; d. Milan, Italy, 1787*), natural philosophy, mathematics, astronomy, physics, geodesy.

Bošković became a Jesuit and studied at the Collegium Romanum (from 1725), learning the exact sciences independently. A polymath, his first interest was mathematics, which he taught at the Collegium Romanum (1740–59). His textbook, *Elementa universae matheseos* (1754), contains an original theory of conic sections. He traveled widely (1759–63), then was professor of mathematics at the University of Pavia (1763–72). He helped organize and directed the Jesuit observatory at Brera near Milan (1764–72) until the opposition he provoked there led the court in Vienna to relieve him of the post. In despair he resigned his professorship as well. In 1773 the pope suppressed the Jesuit order. Bošković went to Paris as director of optics for the navy and became a French subject. He returned to Italy (1782) to prepare for publication his *Opera* (5 vols., 1785), then settled down at the Brera observatory.

In astronomy, optics, and geodesy Bošković was consistently interested in instrumentation and in eliminating procedural errors. His widely-read work on comets (1746) included his first method for the determination of parabolic orbits, which later occasioned a polemic with Laplace. In a broadly critical work on light (1748), he challenged the central Newtonian positions in optics; perhaps most interesting is his view of rectilinear propagation as an unproved hypothesis. He was the first to formulate a general photometric law of illumination and

enunciated the law of emission of light known by Lambert's name. Among the many astronomical instruments he invented, perhaps the most ingenious were a leveler that determined the plane of the edge of a quadrant, and a micrometric wedge to measure the distances between two planes. He conceived of the idea of a kind of gravimeter for measuring gravitation even in the ocean. Drawn to the problem of the shape and size of the earth, he initiated a critical investigation (1739) of existing measurements of the length of a degree along the meridian, and with Christopher Maire surveyed the length of two degrees of the meridian between Rome and Rimini, confirming among other things the geodetic consequences of unevenness in the earth's strata, the possibility of determining surface irregularities by such measures, and the deviation of meridians and parallels from a spherical shape (1755). He originated the earliest device for verifying the points of division on the edge of an instrument. His method of compensating errors was applicable to astronomical as well as geodetic observations, an important step toward the newer practical astronomy before Bessel. The French edition of his report (1770) included the first theory of the combination of observations based on a minimum principle for determining their most suitable values, making use of absolute values instead of their squares, as Gauss later did.

Idiosyncratic for his age, he took his lead in physics from Leibniz and in mathematical analysis from Newton. In mechanics his heterodoxy is notable in his "universal law of forces," which modified the Newtonian corpuscles into immaterial centers of force, distinguished from geometric points only by their inertia and their mutual interaction. Bošković held it impossible to prove the principle of inertia, or indeed any metaphysical principle, either a priori or a posteriori. He introduced the notion that inertia as it is observed is relative to a space chosen to include all bodies in the universe that are within range of our senses, i.e., all the subjects of all our experiments and observations, and concluded that experiment and observation could never decide whether inertia is relative or absolute. He had a clear understanding of the hypothetical-deductive nature of geometry. In his view our universe is no more than a grain of sand in a horde of other universes; there might well be other spaces quite unconnected to our own and other times that run some different course.

BOSS, LEWIS (*b. Providence, R.I., 1846; d. Albany, N.Y., 1912*), positional astronomy.

Boss studied classics at Dartmouth College and took up astronomy as an avocation. Appointed assistant astronomer for the Survey of the 49th parallel, he developed a homogeneous system of declinations. He was director of the Dudley Observatory (1876–1912), and of the Carnegie Institution's new department of meridian astrometry (from 1906). He and his son Benjamin, who directed the meridian astrometry after his death, prepared four great star catalogs.

BOSSE, ABRAHAM (*b. Tours, France, 1602; d. Paris, France, 1676*), geometry, graphic techniques.

Bosse was a draftsman and engraver. His drafting technique derived from Girard Desargues's method of perspective, and, through his ardent propagandizing, Desargues's methods achieved some success among artists. He published two complex expositions (1643) of essays by Desargues on the cutting of stone and on gnomonics. His *Manière universelle de Mr. Desargues pour pratiquer la perspective* (1648) included Desargues's previously unpublished famous theorem on perspective triangles.

BOSSUT, CHARLES (*b. Tartaras, Rhône-et-Loire, France, 1730; d. Paris, France, 1814*), mathematics, mechanics.

Bossut studied mathematics at the Jesuit Collège de Lyon; he took minor ecclesiastical orders and was an *abbé* (to 1792). He was an important figure in education in physics and engineering. His own and Étienne Bézout's texts best represent the emergence in the eighteenth century of standardized, widely-used, rigorous textbooks in engineering physics. He taught mathematics (1752–68) and was examiner (1768–94) at the École du Génie at Mézières and held the chair of hydrodynamics at the Louvre (1775–80). His history of mathematics was highly successful.

BOSTOCK, JOHN (*b. Liverpool, England, 1773; d. London, England, 1846*), medical chemistry.

Bostock took an M.D. at Edinburgh (1798) and was physician to the General Dispensary at Liverpool (to 1817), then chemical lecturer at Guy's Hospital in London (from 1817). His research was largely in medical chemistry and he made valuable contributions to the study of body fluids and urinary components. He also gave the first complete description of hay fever. He wrote prolifically; most successful work was his *Elementary System of Physiology* (3 vols., 1824–27).

BOTALLO, LEONARDO (*b. Asti, Italy, ca. 1519; d. Chenonceaux or Blois, 1587/88*), medicine.

Botallo took a medical degree at Pavia, studied with Gabriele Falloppio, became a noted military surgeon with the French forces (by 1544) and was a physician to Charles IX (by 1560), the queen mother, Catherine de' Medici, whose favor he always enjoyed, and her favorite son, the duke of Anjou (later Henry III). His *De curandis vulneribus sclopettorum* (1560) is notable chiefly as supporting the opinion that gunshot wounds were not envenomed and ought to receive mild rather than harsh treatment. The eponymous Botallo's duct *(ductus arteriosus)* and Botallo's foramen *(foramen ovale cordis)* are actually incorrectly attributed to him.

BOTHE, WALTHER WILHELM GEORG (*b. Oranienburg, Germany, 1891; d. Heidelberg, Germany, 1957*), physics.

Bothe took his doctorate at the University of Berlin under Max Planck (1914). He worked with Hans Geiger at the radioactivity laboratory of the Physikalische-Technische Reichsanstalt (from 1920), taught at the universities of Berlin and Giessen, and directed the Max Planck Institute (1934–57). He shared the Nobel Prize with Max Born in 1954. He and Geiger performed an important experimental test of the Bohr-Kramers-Slater quantum theory of radiation by examining individual Compton collisions, and he made important modifications on the Geiger counter.

BOTTAZZI, FILIPPO (*b. Diso, Apulia, Italy, 1867; d. Diso, 1941*), physiology.

Bottazzi took an M.D. at Rome (1893). He was at Naples University from 1905 to 1923. His *Elementi di chimica fisica* (1906) and *Trattato di chimica fisiologica* (2 vols., 1898–99) were for decades standard in Italy. In his research on the osmotic pressure of the organic liquids, he concluded that homeo-osmosis is a relatively late philogenetic acquisition, and he distinguished homeo-osmotic and poikilosmotic animals (similar to the distinction between homeo-thermic and poikilothermic animals).

BÖTTGER, RUDOLPH CHRISTIAN (*b. Aschersleben, Germany, 1806; d. Frankfurt am Main, Germany, 1881*), chemistry.

Böttger took a doctorate in chemistry at Halle (1837) and taught physics and chemistry at the Physikalischer Verein at Frankfurt (1835–81). His qualitative laboratory work concentrated on practical applications. He demonstrated electrodeposition of nickel on other metals (1843) before technological advances allowed commercial use. He discovered guncotton independently of Schönbein (1846), and he developed a striking match head (1847). His tests for nitrites and chlorates are still used.

BOUCHER DE CRÈVECOEUR DE PERTHES, JACQUES (*b. Rethel, Ardennes, France, 1788; d. Abbeville, France, 1868*), prehistory, human paleontology.

Officer in Customs Administration, appointed to Abbeville (1825). Wrote on literary, philosophical, economic, and social questions, including a theory of the universal evolution of nature (*De la création*, 1838–41). Membership in Abbeville Société d'Émulation led to an interest in archaeology and paleontology. Skillful excavation and rigorous stratigraphic method brought him to the conclusion that the stone axes and tools mixed with mammalian fossil bones of extinct species in "diluvial" beds were the artifacts of "homme antédiluvien," contemporary with the extinct species and therefore much older than any known human population. These results, first published in 1846, were slow to find acceptance; support finally came from Prestwich, Falconer, and Lyell, after examining the Abbeville evidence (1858–59), and subsequent finds of human fossils confirmed the validity of the idea of a human paleontology.

BOUÉ, AMI (diminutive of **Amédée**) (*b. Hamburg, Germany, 1794; d. Vöslau, Austria, 1881*), geology.

Boué took an M.D. at Edinburgh (1817) but turned his interest exclusively to geology. In addition to field work and published studies on Scotland (1820) and Germany (1822, 1829), he summarized annual geological progress in foreign countries (1830–34), wrote *Guide du géologue-voyageur, sur le modèle . . . de Leonhard* (2 vols., 1835–36), and attempted to synthesize geological knowledge in *Essai de carte géologique du globe terrestre* (1845).

BOUELLES, CHARLES DE. *See* **Bouvelles, Charles.**

BOUGAINVILLE, LOUIS ANTOINE DE (*b. Paris, France, 1729; d. Paris, 1811*), geography, mathematics.

Bougainville's contributions to mathematics and great fame as the first Frenchman to sail around the world (1766–69) were achieved during his army services. The clarity of his *Traité du calcul-intégral* (2 vols., 1754–56) gained him recognition. During the famous voyage its botanist, Commerson, named the bougainvillea after him, and Bougainville discovered several islands. His *Voyage autour du monde* (1771) was immediately popular. He made the first charts of longitude in the Pacific.

BOUGUER, PIERRE (*b. Croisic, France, 1698; d. Paris, France, 1758*), geodesy, hydrography, physics.

Bouguer, son of Jean Bouguer, the royal professor of hydrography, was a prodigy who at fifteen succeeded to the professorship and became the French theoretical authority on all things nautical. He was on the celebrated expedition to Peru (1735–44) to measure an arc of the meridian near the equator. He invented the heliometer (1748). Bouguer is now best known as the father of photometry. His *Essai d'optique sur la gradation de la lumière* (1729) discussed his two great optical discoveries: that the eye could be used not as a meter but to establish the equality of brightness of two adjacent surfaces and Bouguer's law. *Traité d'optique sur la gradation de la lumière* (1760) included a method of goniophotometry and a valid theory of the horizontal visual range.

BOUILLES, CHARLES DE. *See* **Bouvelles, Charles.**

BOUIN, POL ANDRÉ (*b. Vendresse, Ardennes, France, 1870; d. Vendresse, 1962*), biology.

The son and grandson of veterinary surgeons, Bouin fixed his attention on testicular physiology and pathology. He was educated at Nancy and taught there and at Strasbourg (1919–39) and directed the Institute of Histology. With Paul Ancel (1903–36) he laid the groundwork for the rapid development of reproductive endocrinology and pioneered in the physiology of reproduction long before the isolation (around 1930) of sex hormones.

Bouin's work included classic drawings of spermatogenesis in myriapods. *Traité d'histologie* (2 vols., 1904–11, with A. Prenant) is valuable as a source of iconography. *Éléments d'histologie* (2 vols., 1929–32) contained illustrations that have been reproduced in later standard works.

BOULE, MARCELLIN (*b. Montsalvy, Cantal, France, 1861; d. Montsalvy, 1942*), human paleontology, geology.

Boule was educated at Toulouse and at the Museum of Natural History in Paris, where he taught (to 1936). He was the first director of the Institute for Human Paleontology (1920–42) and edited its *Archives* and *L'anthropologie* (1893–1920), and was thus the commanding figure in French prehistory for decades. His classical anatomical account of Neanderthal man as a distinct species not ancestrally related to modern man was for a long time the cornerstone of French theory. His central accomplishment was *Les hommes fossiles: Éléments de paléontologie humaine* (1921).

BOULLANGER, NICOLAS-ANTOINE (*b. Paris, France, 1722; d. Paris, 1759*), geology, philosophy.

Boullanger was educated at Beauvais College, Paris. He was with the Département des Ponts et Chaussées (1745–58), where he deduced—from rather cursory observations of the strata of the Loire and the Marne—a theory that formation of the earth involved a universal deluge ("Déluge," *Encyclopédie*, IV, 1754). The modern

distribution of the oceans suggested to him a complementary hypothesis: elasticity of the earth's strata, half of which had, by bending, elevated the other half (*Nouvelle mappemonde dédiée au progrès de nos connoissances*, 1753).

BOULLIAU, ISMAEL (*b. Loudun, France, 1605; d. Paris, France, 1694*), mathematics, astronomy.

Boulliau was an early Galilean convert. His *Astronomia philolaica* (1645) was one of the most important treatises between Kepler and Newton. In it he accepted the ellipticity of orbits—he was one of the very few who did—but rejected all of Kepler's revolutionary suggestions of variation in celestial forces. In astronomy, he first established the periodicity of a variable star, Mira Ceti (1667). Perhaps his most important role was as a correspondent, in which he rivaled Mersenne; a confidant, particularly of Huygens; and a distributor of news and scientific publications. His post as librarian to the Bibliothèque Royale in Paris aided in this.

BOUQUET, JEAN-CLAUDE (*b. Morteau, Doubs, France, 1819; d. Paris, France, 1885*), mathematics.

Bouquet took a doctorate (1842) at the Faculty of Sciences, Paris, and taught at the Sorbonne (1874–84). His long collaboration with Charles Briot (from 1853) resulted in a profound study and clarification of the analytic work of Augustin Cauchy.

BOUR, EDMOND (*b. Gray, Haute-Saône, France, 1832; d. Paris, France, 1866*), mathematics, analytical mechanics, celestial mechanics.

Bour graduated from the École Polytechnique in 1852 and then studied at the École des Mines. He was professor of mechanics at the École Polytechnique (1861–66). He wrote valuable works in mathematical analysis, algebra, mechanics, and infinitesimal geometry. His "Théorie de la déformation des surfaces" (1861) contained several theorems on ruled and minimal surfaces.

BOURBAKI, NICOLAS.

Bourbaki is the collective pseudonym of an influential group of mathematicians preparing its own definitive survey of mathematics as *Elements of Mathematics* (in installments: 1st, 1939; 33rd, 1967; many revised and reissued). The original group included H. Cartan, C. Chevalley, J. Dieudonné, A. Weil; the number is understood to be from ten to twenty, including many younger French mathematicians and two or three Americans. The founding members are said to have agreed to retire at age fifty. The exact composition varies from year to year and is now deliberately secret.

Mathematics for Bourbaki begins with set theory, followed in order by (abstract) algebra, general topology, functions of a real variable (including ordinary calculus), topological vector spaces, and the general theory of integration. Bourbaki has been influential for a number of reasons. He gave the first systematic account of some topics previously available only in scattered articles. His orderly and very general approach, his insistence on precision of terminology and argument, and above all his strict adherence to axiomatization applied to parts of mathematics with the widest possible scope. Much of the originally unconventional terminology has been widely accepted and has changed the vocabulary of research.

BOURDELIN, CLAUDE (*b. at or near Villefranche-sur-Saône, France, ca.1621; d. Paris, France, 1699*), chemistry.

Bourdelin, apothecary to Gaston of Orléans, the king's brother, installed the new Academy of Science's laboratory (1666) and worked there himself (1667–86). His importance lies in his clear advocacy of less antiquated experimental methods and the need for hypotheses in research.

BOURDELOT, PIERRE MICHON (*b. Sens, France, 1610; d. Paris, France, 1685*), medicine, dissemination of science.

Pierre Michon was adopted by an uncle who was a royal physician and gave him the name Bourdelot (1634). He became physician to Prince Henri II de Condé (1638–46), to his son Louis II (1646–51, from 1659), and to Queen Christina of Sweden (1651–53) during the Great Condé's arrest and exile. Eager for fame, he founded the Académie Bourdelot, which played an important role in creating a favorable climate for the spreading of scientific ideas in Paris.

BOURDON, EUGÈNE (*b. Paris, France, 1808; d. Paris, 1884*), instrumentation.

Bourdon had an instrument and machine shop (1832–72) in Paris. His most important single design was his "metallic manometer" (patent 1849), a "pressure gauge without mercury," still the most widely used for pressures of 15 to 100,000 pounds per square inch. The sensing element, or transducer, is the Bourdon tube.

BOURGUET, LOUIS (*b. Nîmes, France, 1678; d. Neuchâtel, Switzerland, 1742*), archaeology, philology, philosophy, biology, geology, crystallography, physics.

Traveled frequently between Switzerland and Italy on business until settling in Neuchâtel in 1716; appointed professor of philosophy and mathematics (1731). Corresponded with more than seventy persons, including Scheuchzer and Leibniz, and played an important role in the diffusion of ideas. Founded two periodicals, *Bibliothèque italique* (1728) and *Mercure suisse* (1732; later named *Journal helvétique*). Of vast erudition (he read or spoke a great many languages, and his projects included a philological investigation of the Etruscan alphabet), he published numerous articles (many pseudonymously or anonymously) and two books. *Lettres philosophiques* (1729) demonstrates the animal origin of belemnites and *pierres lenticulaires* and compares elementary processes of the mineral world (crystallization) and of the living world (generation, assimilation, growth); it presents a theory of crystallization derived from the idea of a chain of immaterial beings that he adapted from Cudworth and Grew and modified to fit a Leibnizian context: even if the actual microscopic order escapes our senses, everything is organized in matter; all organization in the universe was originally and simultaneously created by God. Bourguet was thus a preformationist, and also held that there are neither special organic molecules nor occult vital forces: the elementary corpuscles circulate ceaselessly and by their combinations constitute the infinitely complex tissues of organisms. In *Traité des pétrifications* (1742), which contained a paleontological atlas, Bourguet sought to arrange all mineral and organic species in a single chain. In *Mémoire sur la théorie de la terre*, appended to

Lettres philosophiques, he stated that all parts of the earth as presently constituted are more or less coeval, dating from the Flood which was an amplification of normal processes and an exceptional convergence, ordained by God, of ordinary causes. Orogeny is linked to the dynamics of terrestrial rotation: mountains were formed near the end of the renovation of the earth by the Flood when the hardening new strata were given an upward thrust by the earth's spin; mountains and all their topographic features were carved by the retreating sea (hence their zigzag patterns and ripplelike marks). Bourguet rejected the theory of Henri Gautier (1721) that rain and rivers had leveled the mountains over long periods of time, and that the material was thus removed and deposited in the seas and later formed the strata of new mountains erected by lateral upheaval; but his discussion of the theory may have introduced it to Hutton.

BOURNON, JACQUES-LOUIS, COMTE DE (*b. Metz, France, 1751; d. Versailles, France, 1825*), mineralogy.

Bournon had a military career. In exile in England (1792–1814) he gave the first description of the mineral bournonite (1804) and wrote his major work, *Traité complet de la chaux carbonatée et de l'arragonite* (1808).

BOUSSINESQ, JOSEPH VALENTIN (*b. St.-André-de-Sangonis, Hérault, France, 1842; d. Paris, France, 1929*), mechanics, theoretical physics.

Boussinesq took a doctorate in science (1867) and taught mechanics, physics, and probabilities calculus at Paris. He was dean of the Académie des Sciences and at his death the oldest member. One of the last scientists loyal to classical mechanics and sure of the reality of the ether, he was hostile to relativist innovation. He made important contributions to all branches of mathematical physics except electromagnetism.

BOUSSINGAULT, JEAN BAPTISTE JOSEPH DIEUDONNÉ (*b. Paris, France, 1802; d. Paris, 1887*), agricultural chemistry.

Boussingault brought the problem of plant nitrogen to the threshold of its modern microbiological formulation through organic analysis in field and laboratory research on his Alsatian farm. He did important work on legumes, *Helianthus,* and nitrates.

BOUTROUX, PIERRE LÉON (*b. Paris, France, 1880; d. France, 1922*), mathematics, history, philosophy of science.

Boutroux's father was the celebrated philosopher Émile Boutroux; his uncles were the Poincarés. He took a *licence* at the University of Paris (1900). He was professor of integral calculus at Poitiers (1908–20). He was the first and only historian of science to hold the chair of history of science at the Collège de France (1920–22). His chief contribution in pure mathematics was his study of multiform functions (1908), which extended work by Painlevé, Poincaré, and Picard. His *Les principes de l'analyse mathématique* (2 vols., 1914–19) presents the view that mathematical analysis is a reconciliation of empiricism and rationalism. His foremost work is *L'idéal scientifique des mathématiciens dans l'antiquité et dans les temps modernes* (1920). In it he identifies three stages in the evolution of mathematics: the aesthetic, contemplative Greek; the synthetic conception of Cartesian algebra; and the apparently groping and incoherent contemporary mathematics.

BOUVARD, ALEXIS (*b. Contamines, Haut Faucigny, France, 1767; d. Paris, France, 1843*), astronomy.

Bouvard, a self-educated Alpine peasant, became a brilliant and indefatigable calculator. He assisted Laplace, through whom he became a member of the Bureau des Longitudes (1804). He is known chiefly for his *Tables astronomiques* of Jupiter, Saturn, and Uranus (1821), which were to predict future locations. When the Uranus tables failed to predict the planet's position, he became convinced that the cause was an unknown perturbing body; the failure hastened discovery of Neptune by Adams and Leverrier, probably by several decades.

BOUVELLES, CHARLES (*b. Saucourt, Picardy, France, ca. 1470; d. Noyon, France, ca.1553*), philosophy, theology, philology, mathematics.

Bouvelles was also known as Charles de Bouelles. His most important mathematical work was *Geometricae introductionis* (1503), which includes chapters on stellated polygons and on the old problem of the quadrature of the circle, to which he returned several times. His *Liber de XII numeris* (1510) is on perfect numbers. His *Géométrie en françoys* (1511) is probably the first geometrical treatise printed in French.

BOVERI, THEODOR (*b. Bamberg, Germany, 1862; d. Würzburg, Germany, 1915*), biology.

Boveri took a doctorate at the Anatomical Institute in Munich (1885), worked under Richard Hertwig at the Zoological Institute in Munich (1885–93), and directed the Zoological-Zootomical Institute at Würzburg from 1893. His biologist wife, Marcella O'Grady, participated in many of his investigations. His demonstrations of chromosome individuality and his experimental proof of the differential value of the chromosomes were primary in leading to the cytological explanation of Mendel's law of heredity via the chromosomal theory. In three exhaustive and brilliant observational studies of *Ascaris* morphology, he first described some aspects of maturation of the egg and formation of its polar bodies (1887). He then demonstrated the individuality of the chromosomes, a discovery fundamental to the subsequent development of theories on the role of chromosomes in inheritance (1888). His third study confirmed that at fertilization the egg and spermatozoon contribute equivalent sets of chromosomes to the new individual (1890). In his *Ascaris* studies he also showed that the centrosome introduced into the egg at fertilization by the midpiece of the spermatozoon provides the division centers for the dividing egg cell and all its progeny. In further observations of *Ascaris* he gave the first description of chromatin diminution. He wrote forcefully on the significance of reciprocal interaction between nucleus and cytoplasm at a time when it was otherwise ignored.

BOVILLUS. *See* **Bouvelles, Charles.**

BOWDITCH, HENRY PICKERING (*b. Boston, Mass., 1840; d. Boston, 1911*), physiology.

Bowditch, a grandson of Nathaniel Bowditch, was educated at Harvard College (1861), Lawrence Scientific

School, Harvard Medical School (M.A., 1866; M.D., 1868), and by French and German physiologists, especially Carl Ludwig. He improved Ludwig's kymograph (1869) and invented the "Bowditch clock" for marking elapsed time. He taught physiology (1871–1906) and served as dean (1883–93) at Harvard Medical School. He established the first teaching laboratory for physiology in the United States (1871). One of his most important experiments brought a controversy to a close: he gave final demonstration of the indefatigability of the nerve trunk, of fundamental importance in the physiology of the nervous system (1885). His series of studies in anthropometry, examining the rate of growth in Boston school children, indicated that modes of life—nutrition and environment—were probably more important than race in determining size (1872–81).

BOWDITCH, NATHANIEL (*b. Salem, Mass., 1773; d. Boston, Mass., 1838*), astronomy.

An apprentice to a ship's chandler and later a ship's master and an insurance actuary, Bowditch was self-educated in astronomy and mathematical physics. He delighted in mathematical computations and his early work often consisted of corrections of others' errors. He revised John Hamilton Moore's *New American Practical Navigator* and after 1802 the work bore Bowditch's name as author, as it still does today. His article (1811) on the 1807 meteor explosion over Weston, Connecticut, was his most spectacular; his report on the motion of a pendulum suspended from two points was probably his most significant (1815). His translation of the first four volumes of the *Mécanique céleste* (1829–39) was, in English-speaking countries, often the means of learning about the mechanics of the heavens.

BOWEN, NORMAN LEVI (*b. Kingston, Ontario, 1887; d. Washington, D.C., 1956*), geology.

Bowen, who led the magmatist school of geology, was educated at Queen's University at Kingston and Massachusetts Institute of Technology; was at the Geophysical Laboratory, Carnegie Institution (1920–37; 1947–56); and taught at the University of Chicago (1937–45). His critical phase diagrams for the study of the major igneous rocks included a plagioclase diagram (1913) on which he based his theory of the evolution of igneous rocks (1915). His principle of the continual reaction of early-formed crystals with liquid is now a fundamental concept of geology. His conclusions on the physical-chemical bases for geological processes were brought together in *The Evolution of Igneous Rocks* (1928).

BOWER, FREDERICK ORPEN (*b. Ripon, England, 1855; d. Ripon, 1948*), botany.

Bower studied at Trinity College, Cambridge (1877), and at Würzburg and Strasbourg. He held the Regius chair of botany at the University of Glasgow (1885–1925). His deep interest in teaching is apparent in *Sixty Years of Botany in Britain (1875–1935)* (1938). His extensive work on vascular cryptogams resulted in his monumental work on classification, *The Ferns* (3 vols., 1923–28). His *The Origin of a Land Flora* (1908) developed Celakovsky's theory of the origin of alternation of generations by the interpolation of the sporophyte by division and progressive sterilization of the zygote of a primitive sexually reproducing plant. His was the accepted exposition of the "antithetic" as opposed to the "homologous" theory of alternation. He later reconsidered these views in *Primitive Land Plants* (1935). His *Size and Form* (1930) pointed to the need in plant tissues to maintain a certain relationship between surface and bulk.

BOWIE, WILLIAM (*b. Grassland, Anne Arundel County, Md., 1872; d. Washington, D.C., 1940*), geology.

Bowie took a C.E. degree at Lehigh University (1895) and a B.S. degree at Trinity College, Connecticut (1907). He had a lifelong association with the U.S. Coast and Geodetic Survey (1895–1940). As chief of the Division of Geodesy, he established many controls over triangulation, leveling, and gravity effect surveys. He achieved acceptance of the North American Datum by the United States, Canada, and Mexico. His major work is *Isostasy* (1927). His reduction tables for the depths of compensation brought the study of isostasy into the realm of mathematical computation.

BOWMAN, ISAIAH (*b. Waterloo, Ontario, 1878; d. Baltimore, Maryland, 1950*), geography.

Bowman took a B.S. at Harvard (1905) and a Ph.D. at Yale (1909), then taught there. He initiated the mapping of Hispanic America for the International Millionth Map. He was president of Johns Hopkins University (1935–48) and its department of geography was renamed for him (1948). His *Forest Physiography* (1911) was the first comprehensive account for the United States. His principal geographic works were on the Andes (1916) and modern frontiers.

BOWMAN, WILLIAM (*b. Nantwich, England, 1816; d. Dorking, England, 1892*), medicine.

Bowman studied surgery under Joseph Hodgson (from 1832) and was at King's College, London (1838) where he was surgeon (1840–56). He was the father of histological anatomy and ophthalmic surgery in England. For his and R. B. Todd's *Cyclopaedia of Anatomy and Physiology* (5 vols., 1836–52) and *Physiological Anatomy and Physiology of Man* (2 vols., 1843–56) he made unprecedented microscopic investigations for new and detailed descriptions of skin, muscle, nerves, sense organs, kidney, bone, and cartilage.

In histology, Bowman described the cornea, including its anterior elastic membrane, Bowman's membrane, and the radial fibers of the ciliary muscle, Bowman's muscle. "Bowman's tubes" is the name for certain tubular appearances between the corneal lamellae, which he produced artificially by injection of mercury. "Bowman's operation" is for artificial pupil in cases of corneal opacity or closure of the pupil. "Bowman's probes" for the obstructed lacrymal ducts are still in daily use; most of his anatomical observations have been confirmed, but many of his surgical procedures have been superseded. More important was the impetus he gave to the study and understanding of eye disease. He was created a baronet in 1884.

BOYLE, ROBERT (*b. Lismore, Ireland, 1627; d. London, England, 1691*), natural philosophy, physics, chemistry.

The son of Richard Boyle, a great and affluent Elizabethan adventurer, Boyle was related to all the great Anglo-

Irish families of his day. His laboratory in London (from 1668) became a center for research. He was honored in his lifetime as an original chemist and physicist, a great exponent of English experimental philosophy, a founder, and throughout his life the most notable fellow, of the Royal Society. His first published scientific book, *New Experiments Physico-Mechanicall, Touching the Spring of the Air and its Effects* (1660), established his fame. It included a brilliant series of experiments, using an air pump, which proved that the phenomena of Torricelli's experiment were indeed caused by the air, that sound was impossible in a vacuum, that air was truly necessary for life and flame, and that air was permanently elastic. In an appendix to the second edition (1662), he developed this last discovery into a quantitative relationship, that volume varies inversely with pressure, rightly called Boyle's law. Perhaps the most influential of his many experiments *in vacuo* were those showing that many fruits and vegetables contain air (actually carbon dioxide), which they give off during fermentation—the eighteenth-century chemist's "fixed air."

An eclectic, what mattered most to him was destroying all Aristotelian forms and qualities and substituting for them rational, empirically based, mechanical explanations in terms of matter and motion. His second aim was to show that this was best done by experiment, and he devised, conducted, and faithfully described experiments that should demonstrate the nonexistence of the Aristotelian forms and the positive existence of particles whose size, shape, and motion could easily and rationally account for the observed behavior and properties of matter. Since he rejected both the atoms of the Epicureans and the complex hierarchy of particles of Descartes, preferring the neutral word "corpuscle," his discussions were acceptable and convincing to all except dedicated Aristotelians. Rationalists (Huygens, Leibniz, Spinoza) rejected experiment as a means of proof; experiment could only confirm or (possibly) refute. To Boyle, experiment was an essential ingredient of proof, and logical argument merely the employment of *a priori* hypotheses. This was an important difference in scientific method in the seventeenth century; although he at first had few disciples, he eventually helped establish the experimental method in many branches of physics and chemistry.

His first approaches to the nature and structure of matter were chemical; *Certain Physiological Essays* (1661), his first work on the corpuscular theory, contains his first published chemical experiment, an attempt, using niter, to demonstrate the strong probability of the existence of particles that could persist through physical and chemical changes. He recognized this as a novel approach. Before chemists thought in corpuscular terms, the only possibility of breaking down such a substance as niter was to resolve it into its component "elements," which were like the Greek elements—not only the simplest bodies of a substance, but also the necessary ingredients of all bodies. He, on the other hand, thought that corpuscles were the only things universally present in all bodies. In the *Sceptical Chymist* (1661) he did not, as is commonly said, give a modern definition of an element, but (intentionally) a clear definition of an element as then understood. Its chief value in its day, aside from its main message, was the wealth of chemical experiment that showed how to employ corpuscular terms in chemical explanation and also presented new chemical facts. A prolific experimenter, he almost always found new chemical combinations and reactions, as well as a few new chemical substances; the best-known is hydrogen. He discovered, for example, the chief chemical and physical properties of phosphoric acid, in 1680 and 1682. He never stressed such novelties, only the reactions and their interpretation. He never approached the modern definition of element, which emerged during the eighteenth century under the influence of his teaching. Far more useful to chemistry than the old notion of element was his identification of substances empirically, via the color changes he observed in the course of chemical reactions. In *Experiments and Considerations Touching Colours* (1664) he claimed to be the first to realize that not only some, but all acids turned the blue syrup of violets red, and that those substances that did not were not acids. Similarly, he claimed to be the first to note that alkalies—all alkalies—turned syrup of violets green. This left him with three classes of salts: acid, alkali, and those that were neither. He also used color reactions to determine the relative strength of acidic and alkaline solutions. He demonstrated (what he claimed to have deduced) that different alkalies give differently colored precipitates, and he could distinguish among all the common alkalies. He used a host of other specific tests: for copper, silver, sulfur, and various mineral acids—some new, others known for centuries. The importance of these tests, upon which he relied absolutely, was very great, for in the late seventeenth century there was still great confusion over the identity, not to mention the composition, of various simple substances. He was unique also in testing for purity as well as for composition and chemical differences and similarities. His tests enabled him to discuss the composition of substances in positivistic terms of empirically determined components. This was perhaps his greatest contribution to chemistry.

Truly devout in his Catholicism, he was not dogmatic. Many of his religious books were an offshoot of his scientific work, and it was these among his religious books that were influential. His endowment of the Boyle lectures (really sermons) for the confutation of atheism was interpreted by his contemporaries as meaning arguments against atheism to be drawn from the scientific advances of his day; hence the first and most famous, by Robert Bentley, initiated a characteristically eighteenth-century form of "natural" religion, much less formal and theological than anything usual in his day. In this, as in so much else, he set the tone and inspired the methods of thought widely accepted by the next two generations, not least by Newton.

BOYS, CHARLES VERNON (*b. Wing, Rutlandshire, England, 1855; d. St. Mary Bourne, Andover, Hampshire, England, 1944*), physics.

Studied at Royal School of Mines, London; taught at Normal School of Science (1881–97), then became a metropolitan gas referee. Notable as great experimenter and creator of precise instruments. Designed radiomicrometer (1887) to detect infrared radiation, incorporating a blackened thermojunction into the suspension of a moving-coil galvanometer, with which he detected radiant

heat from the lunar surface. Produced fused quartz fibers, found them to have a low expansion coefficient and remarkably low hysteresis. Measured the constant of gravitation with precision (6.6576×10^{-8} in cgs units, within 0.5% of the modern estimate) and discussed the optimum size of apparatus. His later work was primarily in applied physics. Invented a rotating lens camera for photographing lightning flashes (1900); developed a system for spark photography of flying bullets, obtaining widely reproduced pictures of shock waves. Knighted in 1935.

BRACE, DE WITT BRISTOL (*b. Wilson, N.Y., 1859; d. Lincoln, Neb., 1905*), optics.

Brace, professor of physics and specialist in optics at the University of Nebraska (1888–1905) invented the Brace spectropolariscope and the Brace spectrophotometer. He is best remembered for his experimental test of the Lorentz-Fitzgerald contraction hypothesis (1904), establishing the absence of double refraction in a moving transparent medium.

BRACHET, ALBERT (*b. Liège, Belgium, 1869; d. Brussels, Belgium, 1930*), embryology.

Brachet took an M.D. (1894) at the University of Liège, studying with Edouard van Beneden. He directed the anatomy laboratory at Liège (1900–04) and directed the Institute of Anatomy of the University of Brussels (1904–14, from 1918). He concentrated on comparative studies of the organization of the ovum, the nature of fertilization, and the patterns of segmentation and early embryonic differentiation. He analyzed the inherent capacities of the egg cell. Perhaps more than any other biologist of his time, he bequeathed the understanding that the fertilized egg cell develops into an adult not by preformation or epigenesis, but as a packet of living materials endowed with potentialities of growth and differentiation under inherent physical and chemical influences (*L'oeuf et les facteurs de l'ontogénèse* [1917]; *Traité d'embryologie des vertèbres* [1921]).

BRACONNOT, HENRI (*b. Commercy, France, 1780; d. Nancy, France, 1855*), chemistry.

Braconnot pioneered in plant and animal chemistry. He was a pharmacist who studied with Fourcroy and became director of the Jardin Botanique de Nancy (1807–55). He attempted to elucidate the steps by which the complex organic constituents of plants were synthesized from simple inorganic substances. His discoveries included a cellulose substance in mushrooms which he named fungine; ellagic acid in nutgalls (1818); a sugarlike substance he called *sucre de gélatine* (later glycine); pectic acid; legumin, a substance in beans he thought analogous to albumin; populin (benzoylsalicin); pyrogallic acid; and xyloïdine (nitrocellulose).

BRADFORD, JOSHUA TAYLOR (*b. Bracken County, Ky., 1818; d. Augusta, Ky., 1871*), medicine, surgery.

Bradford took an M.D. at the University of Transylvania, Kentucky (1839). He became the most successful early ovariotomist, keeping deaths at less than 10 percent. He believed boiled water was the best surgical dressing. He devised an ointment effective against skin cancer.

BRADLEY, JAMES (*b. Sherbourne, Gloucestershire, England, 1693; d. Chalford, Gloucestershire, England, 1762*), astronomy.

Bradley took a B.A. (1714) and an M.A. (1717) at Balliol College, Oxford, and was ordained (1719). He taught astronomy at Oxford (1721–41). His celebrated discovery of the aberration of light occurred as he attempted to measure the parallax of the star Gamma Draconis (with Samuel Molyneux, 1725). He detected a displacement too large and in the wrong direction to be due to its parallax. He finally concluded that the phenomenon was due to the combined effect of the velocity of light and the orbital motion of the earth, and that the parallaxes of the stars were much smaller than hitherto supposed. The discovery (1729) not only provided an essential correction for star positions but was also the first direct observational proof of the Copernican theory that the earth moves round the sun. Noticing a small "annual change of declination in some of the fixed stars" for which neither precession nor aberration could completely account (1727), he continued observation, guessing (1732) the real cause, the moon's action "on the equatorial parts of the earth." He called the effect on star positions "nutation." As astronomer royal (from 1742), his intensive program of star observations (at least 60,000, 1750–62) was high in accuracy and is still useful. The value of his observations increases with time, for they provide a firm starting point for long-term investigations of stellar motions.

BRADLEY, RICHARD (*d. Cambridge, England, 1732*), botany.

A prolific science writer, whose publications did much to encourage a scientific approach to gardening and husbandry; held chair of botany at Cambridge (1724–32). Performed experiments on movement of sap and on sexual reproduction of plants. Also wrote on plague, with prophylactic suggestions (1721, 1722). Claimed to have invented the kaleidoscope, which he used for preparing symmetrical designs for formal gardens. Advocated steam-powered irrigation.

BRADWARDINE, THOMAS (*b. England, ca. 1290–1300; d. Lambeth, England, 1349*), mathematics, natural philosophy, theology.

Received four degrees from Oxford University (B.A., M.A., B.Th., and D.Th.—dates uncertain). Held academic positions, including fellow of Balliol College (1321) and of Merton College (1323). His ecclesiastical career began in Lincoln in 1333; he was subsequently chancellor of St. Paul's, London (1337), chaplain to Edward III (*ca.* 1338/39), and archbishop of Canterbury (1349).

Bradwardine wrote at least two early works on logic: *De insolubilibus* and *De incipit et desinit*, the latter addressed to the problem of ascribing what we would call intrinsic or extrinsic boundaries to physical changes or processes occurring within the continuum of time.

His *Tractatus de proportionibus velocitatum in motibus* (1328) deals with the question of how correctly to relate a variation in the speeds of a mobile (expressed, as in the work's title, as a "ratio of speeds") to a variation in the causes, which is to say the forces and resistances, determining these speeds; his solution (Bradwardine's function, or law), in modern terms, is that speeds vary arithmetically while the ratios of forces to resistances determining these speeds vary geometrically. Thus Bradwardine succeeded in discovering a mathematical relation governing speeds, forces, and resistances that fit more adequately than others the Scholastic-Aristotelian postulates of motion; his function may have originated in medieval pharmacology, from al-Kindī's discussion of the relation between the strengths of the ingredients of a compound medicine and the effect of that medicine on the body, but he went further than the pharmacologists and developed the mathematics behind his function by axiomatically connecting it with the whole medieval mathematics of ratios as he knew it. Significant generalization and development of Bradwardine's function were achieved by John of Dumbleton, Richard Swineshead, and Nicole Oresme.

Bradwardine wrote *Tractatus de continuo* to combat the rising tide of anti-Aristotelian indivisibilism, or atomism. It is mathematical in form as well as in content, having been modeled on the axiomatic pattern of Euclid's *Elements;* its "Conclusions" purport to reveal the absurdity of atomism in all branches of knowledge, but its emphasis is on geometrical arguments, such as the sequence of propositions in which he proves that the superposition of any two geometrical entities systematically excludes their forming a single continuum and consequently that the urgently needed contact of atoms is geometrically inadmissible.

Other writings include two elementary mathematical texts, and a major theological work, *De causa Dei contra Pelagium et de virtute causarum ad suos Mertonenses,* that contains discussions of questions relevant to natural philosophy.

BRAGG, WILLIAM HENRY (*b. Westward, Cumberland, England, 1862; d. London, England, 1942*), physics.

Studied at Trinity College, Cambridge (1881–85), receiving first-class honors in mathematics. Professor of mathematics and physics at University of Adelaide (1886–1908); professor of physics at Leeds (1909–15); Quain professor of physics at University College, London (1915); head of Royal Institution (1923); president of Royal Society (1935–40).

In 1904 Bragg began experiments on the absorption of α particles emitted by a radium bromide source. He found that they fell into a few groups, each of which had a definite range, and thus a definite initial velocity. Each group corresponded to a different radioactive species in the source, so that the measurement of α particle ranges soon became an invaluable tool in identifying radioactive substances. In 1907 he hypothesized that γ and X rays might be "of a material nature," specifically neutral pairs consisting of an electron and an α particle, and drew the inference that the ionization accompanying the passage of X rays and γ rays through matter is not produced by the direct action of these rays, but is entirely a secondary effect occurring only after the ray has been converted into a high-speed electron (through removal of the neutralizing positive charge). This inference was disputed, most actively by Barkla, until supported by cloud-chamber evidence (1911).

Bragg and his son, William Lawrence, were awarded the Nobel Prize in physics (1915) for their development of X-ray crystallography. Having convinced himself that a wave-interpretation of X rays was unavoidable in order to explain their diffraction (1912), Bragg constructed the first X-ray spectrometer (1913); he initially studied the properties of the rays, but soon father and son were inverting the latter's relation of X-ray wavelength to crystal angle ($n\lambda = 2d \sin \theta$) and using a known wavelength in order to determine d, the distances between the atomic planes, and thus the structure of the crystal mounted in the spectrometer. By the end of 1913 they had reduced the problem of crystal structure analysis to a standard procedure.

During World War I Bragg assisted the navy in research on submarine detection. He was knighted in 1920. At the Royal Institution (from 1923) his research group excelled in the analysis of organic crystals.

BRAGG, SIR WILLIAM LAWRENCE (*b. Adelaide, Australia, 1890; d. Ipswich, England, 1971*), X-ray crystallography, physics.

Educated at University of Adelaide and Trinity College, Cambridge (graduated 1912); professor of physics at University of Manchester (1919) and Cambridge (1938); professor of chemistry, Royal Institution, London (1954–66). First important work was with his father, William Henry Bragg, investigating Laue's discovery of diffraction of X rays by a crystal: Bragg conceptualized the effect as that of the reflection of X rays off crystal planes, and formulated this (1912) in the expression $\lambda = 2d \cos \theta$, which showed the relationship between angle of incidence θ, wavelength λ, and distance between parallel atomic planes d (in the form $n\lambda = 2d \sin \theta$, this became known as Bragg's law). The process of diffraction was thus rendered easier to visualize and to calculate. Bragg and his father went on (1913–14) to develop diffractometer and ionization spectrometer techniques, to elucidate the atomic structure of simple crystals, and to calculate X-ray wavelengths in a brilliant collaboration that won them the Nobel Prize for physics (1915). Bragg continued this work after World War I and is associated with the entire history and development of X-ray crystallography. He and his collaborators laid a sound methodological basis for the development of quantitative studies through work on absolute intensities; they established that silicate structures depend on the ratio of silicon to oxygen atoms, and thus revolutionized the basis of mineralogy. In his later years he also devoted himself to the popularization and teaching of science, including the history of science.

BRAHE, TYCHO (*b. Skåne, Denmark [now in Sweden], 1546; d. Prague, Czechoslovakia, 1601*), astronomy.

Son of a noble family, Tycho did not need a university degree to establish himself in a profession. He attended the Lutheran University of Copenhagen from April 1559 to February 1562. On 21 August 1560 the occurrence at the predicted time of a solar eclipse, although only partial in Copenhagen, turned Tycho toward observational astronomy, which was not part of the university curriculum. He immediately obtained a copy of Stadius' *Ephemerides,* based on the *Prutenic Tables* and, consequently, on the Copernican system. To encourage him to study law rather than science, his family sent him to Leipzig with a tutor (1562–65); but he pursued astronomy secretly, while his tutor slept. A conjunction of Saturn and Jupiter in August 1563 was later regarded by Tycho as the turning point in his career. Although equipped with only a pair of compasses, he recorded his observations relative to it. The discrepancy between the time of the observed closest approach of the two planets and that computed from the tables, about a month using the *Alphonsine Tables* and a few days by the *Prutenic Tables,* greatly impressed him; in May 1564 he began observing with a radius, or cross staff.

From 1565 to 1570 Tycho combined travels with studies and observational work, and began to acquire accurate instruments. He spent time successively at Wittenberg, the University of Rostock (1566–68), the University of Basel (1568–69), and Augsburg, before returning to Copenhagen. He devoted himself to chemical experiments until 11 November 1572 when, almost directly overhead, in the constellation Cassiopeia he noticed a star shining more brightly than all the others and immediately realized it had not been there before. Using a sextant he measured the angular distance of the new star, at both upper and lower culmination, from the star Schedar (α Cassiopeia), which crossed the meridian at nearly the same time, and found no parallax. He measured the distance of the nova from nine stars in Cassiopeia and found no variation between observations. Had the new star been as close to the earth as the moon, a parallax of 58'30" would have been found. Tycho concluded that it was a star, not a comet, situated in the region of the fixed stars—thus undermining the traditional Aristotelian cosmology. He described his discovery in a brief tract, *De nova et nullius aevi memoria prius visa stella . . .* (1573), and further in the *Progymnasmata* (1602). His records of its variations in color and magnitude identify it as a supernova. He estimated its real diameter at its first appearance as $7\frac{1}{8}$ times that of the earth; he assigned the diminution in light to actual decrease in size, and thought it not impossible that it would cease to be visible.

After teaching a course at Copenhagen, Tycho spent 1575 in travels, meeting astronomers and inspecting astronomical instruments. He went first to Kassel, where he made observations with Landgrave William IV for more than a week and impressed him greatly; he then went to Frankfurt am Main, Basel, Venice, Augsburg, Regensburg, Saalfeld, and Wittenberg, before returning home.

In February 1576 King Frederick II offered Tycho the island of Hven in the Danish Sound and asked him to erect suitable buildings and construct instruments there; he accepted gladly, and by 1584 had built two fantastically ornate but exceedingly useful observatories: Uraniborg (heavenly castle) and Stjerneborg (castle of the stars). The island's facilities eventually included workshops for the construction of instruments, a printing office, a windmill, a paper mill, nearly sixty fishponds, and indoor running water. In these luxurious surroundings Tycho and his assistants (Longomontanus, Willem Blaeu, Paul Wittich, and Peter Jacobsøn Flemløs, among others) studied the skies. The accuracy of the observations depended on the instruments and the care with which they were used; although the instruments were without magnification, error was minimized by their huge size and by the graduations carefully marked on them to facilitate angular measurements on the celestial sphere, altitudes, and azimuths. Tycho checked instruments against each other and corrected for instrumental errors.

He observed regularly and achieved an accuracy within a fraction of a minute of arc, an accuracy unsurpassed from the time of Hipparchus to the invention of the telescope. Tycho drew up, without proof, a set of rules for solving plane and spherical triangles based on the prosthaphaeretic method of replacing multiplications and divisions with additions and subtractions, and supplied his assistants with manuscript copies.

In the southwest room on the ground floor at Uraniborg, affixed to a wall in the plane of the meridian, was Tycho's most famous instrument, the mural quadrant with a radius of about six feet. Each minute of a degree was divided by transversal points into six subdivisions of ten seconds each, making it possible to read off measurements of five seconds; the observer's reading was recorded by an assistant, while a third person read the time from two clocks.

On 13 November 1577 Tycho noticed, for the first time, a large comet with a very long tail; he observed it until 26 January, by which time it was barely distinguishable. He traced the comet's path from west to east, and found that its rate of motion gradually decreased. Its tail, 22° long in the beginning, gradually became smaller and shorter; Tycho argued from the direction of comets' tails that they were merely solar rays transmitted through the head of the comet. Shortly after the comet ceased to be visible he described it in a short German tract (first published in 1922), emphasizing the comet's lack of parallax and the resultant untenability of the so-called Aristotelian doctrine of solid spheres in an unchanging heaven. The tract hints at Tycho's own system of the universe, on which he was already working; it also deals at length with the astrological implications of the comet's appearance (Tycho considered astrology to be a science for which both accurate knowledge of the course of the stars and experience gained from signs seen in the elementary world were needed; he himself made accurate predictions of weather and of human events, and cast annual horoscopes for Frederick II). *De mundi aetherei recentioribus phaenomenis* (1588), intended for a more scholarly audience, contains detailed records of Tycho's observations and computations on the comet and is profusely illustrated with useful diagrams; in discussing the comet's supralunar position he included a description of his own geoheliocentric system of the universe. The comet, whose greatest elongation from the sun was 60°, moved about that body in a circle outside that of Venus.

The Tychonic system was never presented in detail. In it the earth is at rest in the center of the universe, and there is still need for a sphere of fixed stars revolving in twenty-four hours. The planets circle the sun while the sun circles the earth. The orbits of Mercury and Venus intersect the orbit of the sun in two places but do not encompass the earth. The orbit of Mars also twice intersects that of the sun, but encloses the earth and its orbiting moon. The orbits of Jupiter and Saturn enclose the entire path of the sun. Tycho prized parts of the Copernican doctrine but could not bring himself to accept a sun-centered universe, largely due to his inability to conceive of a universe so immense that an observer as accurate as he knew himself to be could not detect any stellar parallax, the necessary consequence of the earth's motion around the sun. The Tychonic system was timely and gained acceptance in many quarters. It did not contradict

Scripture, yet it cared for observed phenomena, including the motion of comets through space (which had necessitated Tycho's rejection of the Aristotelian spheres). It could also account for the phases of Venus, first observed by Galileo.

Tycho's main occupation on Hven was redetermination of the positions of the fixed stars and observation of the planets, the sun, and the moon for the purpose of improving the theory of their motions. Starting with observations of Venus and the sun (1582–88), the right ascensions of eight standard stars were eventually determined; to find the position of another star, two or three standard stars were used as reference. Included in the *Progymnasmata* (1602) are a catalog giving the positions of 777 fixed stars (to which 223 were later added) and revisions of the solar and lunar theories. Tycho determined the equinoxes for the years 1584–88. He believed that the sun moved uniformly in an eccentric circle, and considered his tables of the sun's motion to be accurate within $10''$ or at most $20''$. His values were $95°30'$ for the longitude of the apogee with an annual motion of $45''$ and .03584 for the eccentricity of the orbit, the greatest equation of the center being $2°3'15''$. The difference in the colatitude as determined from his solar observations and his observations of the polestar led him to investigate the effects of refraction and to compose a refraction table; he erred in believing refraction negligible at 45° and over, but made a step forward in determining the refraction for an observation and in correcting the instruments.

Tycho's handling of the lunar theory illustrates not only the accuracy of his observations and his awareness of the need to observe over long periods of time and over the whole course of the moon's orbit, but also his computational prowess and talent for theory construction. His discoveries of new inequalities in both longitude and latitude stem from his efforts at accurate determination of eclipses and his interest in parallax. At his death all the important lunar perturbations, with the exception of the secular variation of the mean motion, were known; his theory was put into its finished form by Longomontanus in 1601.

Other concerns at Hven included the keeping of a daily weather record (1582–97); carrying on a vast correspondence that kept alive the personal contacts made in Tycho's student days, apprised the scholarly world of his work, and provided him with the observations of others for comparison with his own; and entertaining such noble visitors as James VI of Scotland (1590).

After the death of Frederick II (1588) Tycho gradually lost the favor he had enjoyed at court. In 1597 he left Hven, and after short stays in Copenhagen and Rostock he took up residence in the castle at Wandsbeck, near Hamburg, where he continued his observations. Here he also completed the *Mechanica* (1598), which contained descriptions of his instruments, of Hven and its buildings, and a brief autobiography. In June 1599 Tycho and his entourage moved to Prague, where he received financial support from the emperor; in February 1600 Johannes Kepler became one of Tycho's assistants. Kepler worked on the theories of Mercury, Venus, and Mars; the relations between them were frequently strained, but on his deathbed Tycho begged Kepler to complete the *Rudolphine Tables* as quickly as possible and expressed the wish that their theory be demonstrated in accordance with the Tychonic system (the *Tables* were published in 1627, in conformity with a heliocentric system). Giving him due credit, Kepler used the records of Tycho's observations, especially of Mars, to derive the laws of planetary motion; he did not obtain Tycho's instruments, the ultimate fate of which is uncertain.

BRAHMADEVA (*fl. ca. 1092*), astronomy.

Brahmadeva's only work, *Karaṇaprakāśa* (1092), is based on the *Āryabhaṭīya* of Āryabhaṭa I. It was particularly popular in Madras, Mysore, and Mahārāṣṭra.

BRAHMAGUPTA (*b. 598; d. after 665*), astronomy.

Brahmagupta composed the *Brāhmasphuṭasiddhānta* (ca. 628) and the *Khaṇḍakhādyaka* (665), the best-known treatise on the *ārddharātrika* system. The extent and authorship of an appendix to the latter is in doubt. Virtually every paper on every aspect of Indian astronomy discusses him.

BRAIKENRIDGE (BRAKENRIDGE), WILLIAM (*b. ca. 1700; d. 1762*), mathematics.

Braikenridge was a noted theologian whose scientific reputation rests mainly on his *Exercitatio geometrica de descriptione linearum curvarum* (1733), which contributed to the revived interest in geometry in his time. He independently discovered many of Colin Maclaurin's theorems, notably the Braikenridge-Maclaurin theorem: If the sides of a polygon are restricted so that they pass through fixed points while all the vertices except one lie on fixed straight lines, the free vertex will describe a conic or a straight line.

BRAMER, BENJAMIN (*b. Felsberg, Germany, ca. 1588; d. Ziegenhain, Germany, 1652*), mathematics.

Bramer was master builder to the court in Marburg (1612–30) and in Ziegenhain, where he was also treasurer (1635). His mathematical interests were wide but unconcentrated; he wrote on the vacuum (1617) and on empty space. By a method described in his *Trigonometria planorum* (1617), he developed (1630) a device to draw accurate geometrical perspectives true to nature.

BRANDE, WILLIAM THOMAS (*b. London, England, 1788; d. London, 1866*), chemistry.

The Brandes were apothecaries to George III in both London and Hannover. Brande also lectured on chemistry and pharmacy at London medical schools (from 1808) and succeeded Davy at the Royal Institution (1813–52). Faraday assisted him in the laboratory, in teaching, and in editing the Institution's *Quarterly Journal* (from 1815). Brande showed that the alcohol in fermented liquors was not a result of distillation (1813); he also ascertained the alcohol content of many wines.

BRANDES, HEINRICH WILHELM (*b. Groden, near Cuxhafen, Germany, 1777; d. Leipzig, Germany, 1834*), astronomy, physics.

Brandes taught at Breslau (1811–26) and Leipzig (from 1826). His popular works on astronomy were widely read.

BRANDT, GEORG (*b. Riddarhyttan, Sweden, 1694; d. Stockholm, Sweden, 1768*), chemistry, mineralogy.

Brandt studied at Uppsala, with Boerhaave at Leiden, and took an M.D. at Rheims (1726). He was director of the chemical laboratory of the Swedish Council of Mines and warden of the Royal Mint (1730). He did the first detailed research on arsenic, establishing it as a metal (1733). In a work on semimetals (1735) he showed that cobalt is a distinct metal; he is chiefly known for his discovery of this element. He proved that thermal brittleness in iron was due to the sulfur content (1751).

BRANDT, JOHANN FRIEDRICH (*b. Jüterbog, Germany, 1802; d. Baths of Merreküll, Finland, 1879*), zoology, paleontology, botany.

Brandt took an M.D. at the University of Berlin (1826) and lectured there. He went to Russia (1831), where he directed the zoological museum of the Academy of Sciences, St. Petersburg, and taught at the Military-Medical Academy (1851–69). Of his 318 scientific works, 176 are in zoology, 24 in comparative anatomy, and 35 in paleontology. His fame is based essentially on his paleontological studies of the fossil Mammalia, particularly *Untersuchungen über die fossilen und subfossilen Cetaceen Europa's* (1873) on all known European Cetacea. He did exhaustive paleontological monographs on *Elasmotherium; Dinotherium; Rhytina;* the elk; the mammoth; and on the Sirenia and their relations to different orders.

BRASHEAR, JOHN ALFRED (*b. Brownsville, Pa., 1840; d. Pittsburgh, Pa., 1920*), astrophysical instruments.

Brashear was a mechanic in a steel mill. An amateur telescope maker, he established a workshop, the John A. Brashear Company, for making astrophysical instruments (1881). With the help of Samuel Pierpont Langley and William Thaw, he produced many major instruments: a widely used process for silvering glass mirrors (1880); spectroscopes for the Allegheny, Lick, Princeton, and Yerkes observatories; and many telescope objectives, culminating in the 72-inch-aperture primary mirror for the Dominion Observatory in Canada.

BRASHMAN, NIKOLAI DMITRIEVICH (*b. Rassnova, near Brno, Czechoslovakia, 1796; d. Moscow, Russia, 1866*), mathematics, mechanics.

Brashman was educated in Vienna and taught at the University of Moscow (from 1834) laying the foundations of instruction in mechanics. His textbooks included one of the best in analytical geometry in his time (1836); *Teoria ravnovesia tel tverdykh i zhidkikh* (1837), an original presentation of problems of statics and hydrostatics; *Teoreticheskaya mekhanika* (1859), on the theories of equilibrium and the motion of a point and of a system of points.

BRAUN, ALEXANDER CARL HEINRICH (*b. Regensburg, Germany, 1805; d. Berlin, Germany, 1877*), botany, philosophy.

Braun took a doctorate at Tübingen (1829) and was professor of botany and director of the botanical gardens at the University of Berlin (1851–77). He was the most highly regarded botanist of the *Naturphilosoph* school. Several species of cryptogams he discovered bear his name: *Chara braunii, Orthotrichum braunii,* and *Aspidium braunii.* With Carl Schimper, he established the Schimper-Braun theory of spiral phyllotaxis (1830–1835).

Braun's most important single work was *Betrachtungen über die Erscheinung der Verjüngung in der Natur* (1851). It contained significant contributions to the morphology of plants, to the biology of freshwater algae, and especially to cell theory. He opposed Darwinian selection and remained a genuine *Naturphilosoph* when that mode of thought was becoming unfashionable.

BRAUN, FERDINAND (*b. Fulda, Germany, 1850; d. Brooklyn, N.Y., 1918*), physics.

Braun took a Ph.D. at the University of Berlin (1872). He shared the Nobel Prize in physics with Marconi (1909) for his fundamental modification of Marconi's transmitting system, increasing its range over 15 kilometers by producing a sparkless antenna circuit (patented 1899), a principle applied to radio, radar, and television. His discovery that mineral metal sulfide crystals conducted electric currents in only one direction (1874) was used in crystal radio receivers. His oscilloscope, or Braun tube (1897), based on moving an electron beam by alternating voltage, has in its modifications become essential to electronics.

BRAUNER, BOHUSLAV (*b. Prague, Czechoslovakia, 1855; d. Prague, 1935*), chemistry.

Brauner studied under Bunsen, took a Ph.D. at Prague (1880), and taught at the Czech branch of Charles University, Prague (1882–1925). In the laboratory he perfected Mendeleev's periodic law and classification of the elements. After 1882 he concentrated on the rare earth elements. He isolated and computed atomic weights of cerium, lanthanum, praseodymium, neodymium, samarium, and placed the rare earths between lanthanum (57) and hafnium (72). His value for tellurium 127.61, although still an inversion, remains accepted. He advocated (1888) oxygen instead of hydrogen as the standard for calculating atomic weights (adopted internationally 1904). He contributed sections on atomic weights for Abegg's *Handbuch der anorganischen Chemie* and a section on rare earth elements for a revision of Mendeleev's *Principles of Chemistry* (1906).

BRAUNMÜHL, ANTON VON (*b. Tiflis, Russia, 1853; d. Munich, Germany, 1908*), history of mathematics.

Braunmühl studied and taught the history of mathematics at the Munich Technical University (from 1888). His work in the history of trigonometry was notably thorough and precise, and he was regarded as one of the leading German authorities on the history of mathematics.

BRAVAIS, AUGUSTE (*b. Annonay, France, 1811; d. Le Chesnay, France, 1863*), botany, physics, astronomy, crystallography.

Bravais was educated at the École Polytechnique (1831), took a Ph.D. at Lyons (1837), and entered into a naval career (from 1831). He taught astronomy at Faculté des Sciences (1841–45) and physics at the École Polytechnique (1845–56). His most important work was on crystals. In an exhaustive study of the properties of lattices (1848), he derived the fourteen possible arrangements of points in space. His *Études cristallographiques* (1866) concentrated on the relationships between the ideal lattice and the material crystal. The Bravais rule

afforded a method by which mineralogists could determine lattice types and, in the simplest cases, structures. He provided the mathematical and conceptual basis for the determination of crystal structures after Laue's discovery of X-ray diffraction in 1911. Solid-state physics has publicized Bravais's originating role in applying the mathematics of symmetry and groups to the theory of solids.

BREDIKHIN, FEDOR ALEKSANDROVICH (*b. Nikolaev, Russia, 1831; d. St. Petersburg, Russia, 1904*), astronomy.

Bredikhin graduated from Moscow University (1855; M.A., 1862; Ph.D., 1865) and taught there (from 1858). He directed the Moscow observatory (1873–90) and the Pulkovo observatory (1890–95). Comets were his major work. He was a theoretician and a tireless observer of all major aspects of contemporary astronomy, including gravimetry. He developed the so-called mechanical theory of a comet's form: Assuming that particles of matter, which fly off from the core, are repelled by the sun in hyperbolic trajectories, he developed a method for determining the value of the repulsive accelerations in the tails of comets and thus classified tails. The theory has largely been retained, as has his classification of comet tails. He developed a theory of the movement of matter in sunspots and in the rays of the solar corona. He correctly noted the intimate connection between coronal eruptions and chromospheric protuberances and the absence of a direct connection between coronal eruptions and sunspots.

BREDON, SIMON (*b. Winchcomb, England, ca. 1300; d. ca. 1372*), mathematics, astronomy, medicine.

Bredon was a fellow and junior proctor of Oxford and keeper of the Langton chest (1339). After 1348 he held various church appointments. Among his works in mathematics is an explanation of Boethius' *Arithmetic*. In astronomy he wrote on the use of the astrolabe and *Theorica planetarum*, sometimes attributed to Walter Brytte or Gerardo da Sabbionetta. *De equationibus planetarum*, once ascribed to him, is now credited to Chaucer. His commentary on the first three books of Ptolemy's *Almagest* survives incompletely. Of his most ambitious work, *Trifolium*, a medical compilation modeled on Avicenna's *Canon*, only a twelfth survives.

BREFELD, JULIUS OSCAR (*b. Telgte, Germany, 1839; d. Schlachtensee, near Berlin, Germany, 1925*), mycology.

Brefeld, a founder of modern mycology, qualified in pharmacy (1863) and took a Ph.D. at Heidelberg (1864) in chemistry. He taught at the Royal Botanical Institute and directed the botanical garden at Münster (1884–98) and directed the Institute of Plant Physiology at Breslau (1898–1907); glaucoma forced his resignation. His monumental work *Botanische Untersuchungen über Schimmelpilze* (pts. 1–5, 1872–83), continued under the title *Untersuchungen aus dem Gesammtgebiete der Mykologie* (pts. 6–15, 1884–1912), often termed the bible of mycology, summarized his contributions. He originated (by 1874) the gelatinized nutrient medium wrongly credited to Koch. His pioneer work on cereal smuts, especially of wheat, yielded vast indirect practical benefits. He investigated the mechanisms of infection, and host susceptibility in several smut diseases (1895, 1905). He made thousands of cultures and studied the developmental history and systematic relations of vast numbers of fungi, including Zygomycetes (a subclass of which he characterized *penicillium*), Basidiomycetes, Myxomycetes, Entomophthorales (1884), and Ascomycetes.

BREGUET, LOUIS FRANÇOIS CLÉMENT (*b. Paris, France, 1804; d. Paris, 1883*), instrumentation.

Breguet took over his family's famous clockworks (1830) and began to make precision electrical apparatus: electric clocks (from 1839); an electrical thermometer (1840); and a genuine induction coil (1842). He constructed the Foy-Breguet instrument used in the French telegraphic system. After his son, Antoine, became his partner (1873), the company produced Daniell and Leclanché batteries; arc lamps; Gramme dynamos; metal thermometers, barometers, and manometers; and set up the French telephone system (1876).

BREISLAK, SCIPIONE (*b. Rome, Italy, 1750; d. Milan, Italy, 1826*), geology, natural history.

Breislak, a priest who taught the natural sciences, was a founder of volcanology in Italy (*Topografia fisica della Campania*, 1798). He was the first to determine that basaltic rocks were of extrusive origin and emphasized the underwater origin of tufaceous deposits.

BREITHAUPT, JOHANN FRIEDRICH AUGUST (*b. Probstzella, Germany, 1791; d. Freiberg, Germany, 1873*), mineralogy.

Breithaupt studied at the Bergakademie at Freiberg under Abraham Werner (1811), taught at the Mining Academy (1813), was the last gem inspector (1813), and became professor of mineralogy (1826–66). A great observer, he named more than eighty minerals; about half —including monazite, phlogopite, and orthoclase—are still regarded as valid. More fundamental was his *Über die Echtheit der Krystalle* (1815), on pseudomorphs. He was the first to distinguish amorphous minerals ("porodine," now an obsolete term). His greatest contribution was *Die Paragenesis der Mineralien* (1849), the first comprehensive study of regularities and the importance of age relations in mineral associations. His term "paragenesis" was quickly and generally adopted and remains important in mineralogy, geochemistry, petrology, and ore geology.

BREMIKER, CARL (*b. Hagen, Germany, 1804; d. Berlin, Germany, 1877*), astronomy, geodesy.

Connected with the royal observatory at Berlin.

Bremiker was an editor of widely used mathematical and astronomical tables. By the advent of the calculating machine his *Logarithmisch-trigonometrische Handbuch* (1856) had gone through forty editions.

BRENDEL, OTTO RUDOLF MARTIN (*b. Niederschönhausen, near Berlin, Germany, 1862; d. Freiburg, Germany, 1939*), astronomy.

Brendel was a disciple of Gyldén in the development of mathematical estimates for the influence of perturbations on orbits (*Theorie der kleinen Planeten*, 4 vols., 1897–1911). He helped establish the Internationales Planeteninstitut, and directed the University of Frankfurt observatory (1914–27).

BRESCHET, GILBERT (*b. Clermont-Ferrand, France, 1783; d. Paris, France, 1845*), anatomy.

Breschet took an M.D. (1812), headed anatomical studies at the Hôtel Dieu (1819), was *agrégé* (1825). He became professor of anatomy at the Faculty of Medicine (1836), Paris, the only doctor-naturalist there. He studied anatomy with great industry, particularly the veins of the spine and the human skull, the auditory system in vertebrates, and the arterial plexuses of the Cetacea, showing their adaptation for diving. With Roussel de Vauzème he discovered the sweat glands, and he coined the word "phlebitis" (1818).

BRET, JEAN JACQUES (*b. Mercuriol, Drôme, France, 1781; d. Grenoble, France, 1819*), mathematics.

Bret studied civil engineering at the École Polytechnique and eventually (1812) received the D.S. from the Faculté des Sciences. He taught at the lycée (1804–11) and at the Faculté des Sciences (1811–19) in Grenoble. Most of his twenty or so articles deal with analytical geometry on plane surfaces and in space, notably with the theory of conics and quadrics.

BRETHREN OF PURITY. *See* **Ikhwān al-Ṣafāʾ**.

BRETONNEAU, PIERRE (*b. St.-Georges-sur-Cher, France, 1778; d. Passy, France, 1862*), medicine.

Bretonneau studied at the École de Santé in Paris (1795–1801), became a public health officer, took a doctorate (1815), was chief physician at the Tours hospital (1815–38), then practiced medicine among the poor. He developed G. L. Bayle's and Laennec's concept of physical lesions as classificatory in his identification of two diseases of the mucous membranes. He individualized typhoid fever (called *dothinentérie;* 1819). He also distinguished exanthematic typhus from typhoid. He invented the double cannula and with it performed the first tracheotomy (1825), preventing fatal asphyxia in a croup patient.

BREUER, JOSEF (*b. Vienna, Austria, 1842; d. Vienna, 1925*), medicine, physiology, psychoanalysis.

Studied at University of Vienna (M.D. 1867); entered private practice in 1871; qualified as *Privatdozent* in internal medicine (1875) but resigned in 1885. His formal relationship to the medical faculty was thus tenuous and strained, yet he was considered one of the best physicians and scientists in Vienna. Although he published relatively few major scientific articles at relatively long intervals, he was one of the great physiologists of the nineteenth century. His first major study, in collaboration with Ewald Hering, led to the discovery of the reflex regulation of respiration (1868)—one of the first "feedback" mechanisms to be demonstrated in the mammal. The underlying reflex is still known as the Hering-Breuer reflex.

Breuer next began a long series of investigations of the labyrinth, remarkable for their importance and even more remarkable because he conducted them privately, in his own home and at his own expense. He developed the theory (1873, simultaneously with Mach and with Crum Brown) that the semicircular canals detect motion via the angular acceleration of the endolymph within them, and supported his theory with the evidence of many experiments. In addition he called attention to the importance of the otoliths and hair cells of the utricle as static position receptors, and gave a clear-cut depiction of the relationship of the labyrinthine reflexes to optical nystagmus. His work was by no means immediately accepted, but today is recognized as the foundation of our knowledge of the sensory receptors for sensations of posture and movement.

In the summer of 1880 one of Breuer's patients, "Anna O.," began to suffer severe psychological and physical disturbances. He noted that she showed two markedly different states of consciousness each day: during one she seemed relatively normal, during the other she was "clouded." He also found that if, during her normal state, she could be induced to tell him the fantasies that occupied her during her clouded state her restlessness was greatly reduced. To facilitate this "catharsis," he began to hypnotize her. He eventually noted that under special circumstances of recall she would trace a series of memories back over time until she reached the memory of a "traumatic" episode that had been transformed into a symptom; he gradually succeeded in relieving all of her symptoms by this process of catharsis over a period of two years. From this case Breuer drew two important conclusions: (1) that the symptoms of his patient were the result of "affective ideas, deprived of the normal reaction" which remained embedded in the unconscious, and (2) that the symptoms vanished when the unconscious causes of them became conscious through being verbalized. These two observations form the cornerstone upon which psychoanalysis was later built.

Breuer did not publish or publicize this case, but did discuss it with Freud. Freud first used the cathartic method in either 1888 or 1889, under Breuer's guidance, and for several years they jointly explored this form of psychotherapy—Freud treating the patients, and Breuer discussing the techniques and results with him. The practical and theoretical conclusions they reached through their collaboration were published in an article in 1893 and as a book (*Studien über Hysterie*) in 1895. Although they had been very close for many years, Freud and Breuer separated in 1896 and never spoke again—due at least partly to quarrels over their groundbreaking work on psychotherapy.

BREUIL, HENRI ÉDOUARD PROSPER (*b. Mortain, Manche, France, 1877; d. L'Isle-Adam, Seine-et-Oise, France, 1961*), prehistory.

Breuil was an ordained priest (1900) who taught at Fribourg (1905–10), the Institut de Paléontologie Humaine (1910–29), and the Collège de France (1929–47). He was for years the doyen of Paleolithic studies, painstakingly recording and analyzing Paleolithic cave art at Altamira (1906), Les Eyzies (1910, 1924), Tuc d'Audoubert (1912), Les Trois-Frères (1916), and other important sites. He was the first archaeologist to visit and describe Lascaux (1940). His other main contribution was his reclassification of Paleolithic industries (1912).

BREWSTER, DAVID (*b. Jedburgh, Scotland, 1781; d. Allerly, Melrose, Scotland, 1868*), optics.

Brewster studied at the University of Edinburgh (from 1794) and was licensed to preach in the Church of Scotland (1804). A leading evangelical, he became a member of the Free Church of Scotland (1843) and made his living from writing and editing scientific articles. Brewster attempted to determine the law of polarization of light. He searched for the law of polarization by reflection, concluding that "the index of refraction is the tangent of the angle of polarization" (Brewster's law). His popular reputation was established in 1816 by his invention of the kaleidoscope. From his study of metallic reflection he deduced laws that accurately predicted the quantities and angles of polarization of light, and he also created the new fields of optical mineralogy and photoelasticity. He was able (1819) to group all but a few of hundreds of minerals and crystals into mutually consistent optical and mineralogical categories. He deduced equations that permitted him to predict the shapes, numbers, and colors of patterns that would be produced by changes in configuration, temperature, pressure, and method of observation. In an attempt to improve colored eyeglasses and microscopy, he studied absorption spectroscopy (from 1821), a line that led to his dissent from Newton's doctrine of colors and to his most effective defense of a "Newtonian" emission theory of light. To establish techniques for optical chemical analysis, he examined the spectrum of plant juices, gases, and the earth's atmosphere. Not only did he succeed in identifying bodies by their characteristic dark lines, but he also added some 1,600 dark lines to Fraunhofer's 354. After the 1830's optics was increasingly dominated by the undulatory theory of light, based on a hypothetical ether; he never wholeheartedly accepted the theory, finding the hypothesis to be unbridled speculation. Brewster was knighted in 1832 and in 1838 became principal of the United Colleges of St. Salvator St. Leonard, and St. Andrews. In 1859 he was elected principal of the University of Edinburgh and later became vice-chancellor.

BRIANCHON, CHARLES-JULIEN (*b. Sèvres, France, 1783; d. Versailles, France, 1864*), mathematics.

Brianchon was a student at the École Polytechnique (1804–08) when he published "Sur les surfaces courbes du second degré" (1806), which contained the famous theorem named after him: If all the sides of a hexagon are tangent to a conic, then the diagonals joining opposite vertices are concurrent. He published several works in geometry and taught at the Artillery School of the Royal Guards (from 1818). His last work in mathematics contains the first use of the term "nine-point circle" and the first complete proof of this rediscovered theorem (1820).

BRIDGES, CALVIN BLACKMAN (*b. Schuyler Falls, N.Y., 1889; d. Los Angeles, Calif., 1938*), genetics.

Bridges' work on the genetics of *Drosophila* (1910–27), on which he became the outstanding authority, began when he was a scholarship student at Columbia (1909–12) assisting in T. H. Morgan's laboratory. He continued at Columbia after graduation and from 1915 was also research associate of the Carnegie Institution. In 1928 he moved to the California Institute of Technology. He greatly advanced research techniques, particularly in standardization of culturing. The information and stocks of *Drosophila* he accumulated are still in constant use. In his account of the exceptions to the usual rules for the inheritance of sex-linked genes he named the phenomenon "nondisjunction" (1913), and in microscopic study of the chromosomes (1914) and in his doctoral thesis (1916) he produced a convincing proof of the chromosome theory of heredity. His study of nondisjunction of the small fourth chromosome led to his development of the idea of genic balance.

BRIDGMAN, PERCY WILLIAMS (*b. Cambridge, Mass., 1882; d. Randolph, N.H., 1961*), physics, philosophy of science.

Bridgman was educated at Harvard (B.A., 1904; M.A., 1905; Ph.D., 1908) and taught there (1908–61). He received the Nobel Prize in physics (1946) for his apparatus that produced high pressures. The ultimate limitation of his pressure apparatus was the strength of the metal parts. He reached pressures of 20,000 atmospheres (1910) and still higher pressures (1930's) only by the development of the cobalt-bonded tungsten carbides. He settled on an electric-furnace chrome-vanadium steel for most of his vessels and tubes, and was able to contain pressures far in excess of predictions based on simple elastic criteria. He obtained a maximum fluid pressure for routine measurements of the mechanical, electrical, and thermal properties of matter of 30,000 atmospheres; in quasi-fluid systems, he obtained 400,000 atmospheres. The realm above 3,000 atmospheres was entirely new to physics; in a span of fifty years he provided a large part of all high-pressure measurements now used. His *The Physics of High Pressure* (1931) is still basic. His massive treasure of data has proved invaluable for the development of solid state physics. He lived to see the artificial production of many natural high-pressure mineral forms (diamond, coesite, jadeite) based on his discoveries. For the Manhattan Project he measured the compressibility of uranium and plutonium.

In the area of the philosophy of science, Bridgman examined Einstein's demonstration of the meaninglessness of the concept of absolute simultaneity. He proposed physical and mental "operations" as the measure of meaning. Initially the term must have been closely related to his own manifold physical activities in shop and laboratory. He brilliantly argued in *The Logic of Modern Physics* (1927) that a concept is nothing more than, and synonymous with, a set of operations, and that a question has meaning only if operations exist by which answers may be given to it. He proposed operational analysis as an aid to clear thinking, not as a solution to all the problems of philosophy. His other works include *The Nature of Physical Theory* (1936), *The Nature of Thermodynamics* (1941), and *A Sophisticate's Primer of Relativity* (1962).

BRIGGS, HENRY (*b. Warleywood, Yorkshire, England, 1561; d. Oxford, England, 1630*), mathematics.

Briggs took a B.A. (1581) and an M.A. (1585) at St. John's College, Cambridge, where he held a fellowship (1589) and lectured. He was the first professor of geometry at the new Gresham College in London (1596–1620) and taught at Merton College, Oxford (1620–30). He was renowned for his work in logarithms. He added his own table to E. Wright's translation (1616) of Napier's *Canon mirificus* after discussions with Napier, and in his own *Logarithmorum chilias prima* (1617) justified the change. His *Arithmetica logarithmica* (1624) included thirty thousand logarithms and dissertations on the principles of construction and use. Briggs's tables of logarithmic sines and tangents were in *Trigonometria Britannica* (1633), edited by Henry Gellibrand.

BRIGHT, RICHARD (*b. Bristol, England, 1789; d. London, England, 1858*), medicine.

Bright took a medical degree at Edinburgh (1813) and became (1820) a physician at Guy's Hospital. He gave the first accurate account of appendicitis in *Elements of the Practice of Medicine* (1839, with Thomas Addison). He exercised his powers of observation at the bedside, the autopsy table, and the rudimentary clinical laboratory, thereby exemplifying the transition between the medical tradition of observation by the unaided senses and the just-burgeoning tradition of the laboratory. His great contribution was to perceive and prove a relationship between pathological changes in the kidney, chemical alteration (albumin in urine), and the clinical sign of edema. Bright's disease was later seen to be of enormous complexity, but his correlation of three known but hitherto unconnected features was brilliant.

BRILL, ALEXANDER WILHELM VON (*b. Darmstadt, Germany, 1842; d. Tübingen, Germany, 1935*), mathematics.

Brill, the nephew of Christian Wiener, studied with Alfred Clebsch at Giessen (1864; Ph.D., 1867) and taught at Tübingen (1884–1918). The first of his two noteworthy studies—both with Max Noether—was on properties of algebraic functions invariant under birational transformations (1874) and substantiates by algebraic-geometric methods many results obtained by Riemann, Clebsch, and Gordan by transcendental methods. The second was a survey of the development of algebraic functions (1894).

BRILLOUIN, MARCEL LOUIS (*b. Melle, Deux-Sèvres, France, 1854; d. Paris, France, 1948*), mathematics, physics.

Brillouin attended the École Normale Supérieure (1874–78), took doctorates in mathematics and physics (1881), and taught at the Collège de France (1900–31). His wide-ranging, open-minded interests included Kelvin (1893); meteorology (1900); Boltzmann (1902); viscosity (1906–07); the thermodynamics of liquids and solids, plasticity, and melting conditions; the propagation of electricity (1904); Helmholtz; the stability of airplanes; the problem of an electromagnetic source in uniaxial or biaxial crystals; and the physics of the earth, especially tides (from 1925). His new model of the Eötvös balance (built 1900, described 1908), named for him, was later used in oil prospecting. His attempted explanation (1918–22) of Bohr's condition of stable atom trajectories and their n, l, m quantum numbers was similar to conditions used by de Broglie and Schrödinger.

BRINELL, JOHAN AUGUST (*b. Bringetofta, Sweden, 1849; d. Stockholm, Sweden, 1925*), metallurgy, materials testing.

Brinell, who worked in the Swedish iron industry, is best known as the originator of a standard procedure (1900) for determining the hardness of a metal. The Brinell hardness number (Bhn) in kg/mm^2 is still one of the most widely used tests of hardness. He also did significant work on the metallurgy of steel (1885).

BRING, ERLAND SAMUEL (*b. Ausås, Kristianstad, Sweden, 1736; d. Lund, Sweden, 1798*), mathematics.

Bring studied law (1750–57) and taught history (from 1762) at Lund University. His main interest was mathematics, however, and in his *Meletemata* (1786) he succeeded in reducing a general fifth-degree equation to the trinomial form. Bring's achievement was not recognized until 1861, mainly through the efforts of Carl J. D. Hill.

BRINKLEY, JOHN (*b. Woodbridge, England, 1763; d. Dublin, Ireland, 1835*), astronomy, mathematics.

Brinkley was educated at Cambridge (B.A., 1788; M.A., 1791), was ordained (1791), and was elected first astronomer royal for Ireland (1792). He was named Bishop of Cloyne (1826). His great contribution was his approximation of the long-sought parallaxes of the fixed stars. His parallaxes for α Lyrae and other stars were disputed by Pond; the long controversy led to repeated tests of the observations and to study of differences between measurements at Dublin and Greenwich, and thus to the eventual detection of stellar parallaxes.

BRIOSCHI, FRANCESCO (*b. Milan, Italy, 1824; d. Milan, 1897*), mathematics, hydraulics.

Brioschi graduated from the University of Pavia (1845), taught there (1852–61), was secretary (1861–62) and member of Executive Council (1870–82) of the Ministry of Education, senator (from 1865), director of the Istituto Tecnico Superiore in Milan (1863–97), and president of the Accademia Nazionale dei Lincei (1884–97). His *Teoria dei determinanti* (1854) was the first nonelementary statement of the theory of determinants and its basic applications. His greatest achievement was to apply elliptical modular functions to the solution of fifth-degree equations (simultaneously with Kronecker). His second great achievement was the solution of sixth-degree equations using hyperelliptic functions.

BRIOT, CHARLES AUGUSTE (*b. St.-Hippolyte, France, 1817; d. Bourg-d'Ault, France, 1882*), mathematics, physics.

Briot taught at the Sorbonne and at the École Normale Supérieure (from 1864). He stressed the relation between thermodynamics and rational mechanics, and his many textbooks helped raise the level of mathematics teaching in France. He published, with Bouquet, an important work on elliptic functions (1875) and, alone, a treatise on Abelian functions (1879).

BRISBANE, THOMAS (*b. Brisbane House, Ayrshire, Scotland, 1773; d. Brisbane House, 1860*), astronomy.

Brisbane, who had a distinguished military career and was an able practical astronomer, is remembered as a munificent patron of science through his founding, equipping, and staffing of two observatories. When he was governor of New South Wales, he established an observatory at Paramatta (1822). On his return to Scotland, he built and equipped an astronomical observatory at Makerstoun (1826), and later a magnetic observatory there (1841). The results obtained at this magnetic station now constitute the most valuable fruits of his patronage.

BRISSON, BARNABÉ (*b. Lyons, France, 1777; d. Nevers, France, 1828*), hydraulic engineering, mathematics.

Brisson was trained at the École des Ponts et Chaussées (1798) and rose in the Corps des Ponts et Chaussées to the post of secretary of the Conseil Royal (from 1824), specializing in ship canals. He edited the fourth edition of Monge's *Géométrie descriptive* (1820). His application of functional calculus to the solution of linear equations with finite differences (1808, 1823) particularly impressed Cauchy.

BRISSON, MATHURIN-JACQUES (*b. Fontenay-le-Comte, Vendée, France, 1723; d. Brouessy, Commune of Magny-les-Hameaux, near Versailles, France, 1806*), physics, natural history.

Brisson was caretaker (1749–57) of the collection of the naturalist Réaumur, to whom he was related, and became personally involved in the great rivalry between Réaumur and Buffon. Brisson's *Règne animal* (1756) announced Réaumur's intent of giving a general description of the animal world to rival Buffon's *Histoire naturelle.* After Réaumur's death his collection went to the Cabinet du Roi, under Buffon and Daubenton, and Brisson was denied access to his direct documentation. He managed to complete his *Ornithologie* (6 vols., 1760), the speciality of Réaumur's collection; in spite of insufficient classification, it was one of the most complete in ornithology before Buffon's *Histoire des oiseaux.* Unable to continue as a naturalist, he turned to experimental physics. He taught at the Collège de Navarre, was royal tutor (from 1770), and taught at the Collège des Quatre Nations (1796–1806). He translated Priestley's *History of Electricity* (1771) and wrote *Pesanteur spécifique des corps* (1787) and *Traité élémentaire ou Principes de physique* (1789).

BRITTEN, JAMES (*b. London, England, 1846; d. Brentford, Middlesex, England, 1924*), botany.

Britten abandoned medical studies to work (1869–71) at the Royal Botanical Gardens, Kew, and in botany at the British Museum (from 1871). He produced the invaluable *Biographical Index of British and Irish Botanists* (with G. S. Boulger, 1893, 3 supp.); *Dictionary of English Plant Names* (1878–86); the mass of data from which was compiled *The Sloane Herbarium*, an annotated list (1958). He edited the *Journal of Botany* for almost forty-five years.

BRITTON, NATHANIEL LORD (*b. Staten Island, N.Y., 1859; d. New York, N.Y., 1934*), botany.

Britton trained as a mining engineer at Columbia College (1879), taught botany there (from 1887), and is best known as founder and director (1896–1929) of the New York Botanical Garden, which he made a great institution. His most important work was *Illustrated Flora of the Northern United States, Canada and the British Possessions* (3 vols., 1896–98). The periodical *Brittonia* (from 1931) is named for him, as are several genera.

BROCA, PIERRE PAUL (*b. Sainte Foy-la-Grande, near Bordeaux, France, 1824; d. Paris, France, 1880*), medicine, anthropology.

Broca took an M.D. at the University of Paris (1849), taught at the Faculty of Medicine (from 1853), and was an outstanding hospital surgeon. He is best known in medicine for providing the essential link in the argument (1861) favoring the localization of speech function in the left inferior frontal gyrus (Broca's convolution). He served on a commission to report on excavations in the cemetery of the Célestins (1847), and this led him to craniology and ethnology. He was mainly responsible for the formation of the Société d'anthropologie de Paris (1859), the *Revue d'anthropologie* (1872), and the École d'Anthropologie (1876).

BROCARD, PIERRE RENÉ JEAN-BAPTISTE HENRI (*b. Vignot, France, 1845; d. Bar-le-Duc, France, 1922*), mathematics, meteorology.

Brocard was a French army engineering teacher and researcher (1867–1910), and an indefatigable correspondent to mathematical and scientific journals. His renown rests on his "Étude d'un nouveau cercle du plan du triangle" (1881), which announced the discovery of the circle now known as the Brocard circle of a triangle.

BROCCHI, GIOVANNI BATTISTA (*b. Bassano, Italy, 1772; d. Khartoum, Sudan, 1826*), geology.

Brocchi taught natural history at the gymnasium at Brescia (1802–08), was inspector of mines at Milan (1808–14), and organized the mining industry in Egypt (1822–26). His masterpiece is the *Conchiologia fossile subappennina* (1814), which includes a survey of paleontological studies in Italy, a detailed description of fossiliferous deposits, and a suggestive but incomplete analysis of the contrast between the Subapennine fossils, most of which were identifiable with living fauna, and those described by Lamarck from the Paris Basin, most of which were extinct.

BROCHANT DE VILLIERS, ANDRÉ-JEAN-FRANÇOIS-MARIE (*b. Villiers, near Mantes, France, 1772; d. Paris, France, 1840*), geology, mineralogy.

Brochant taught at the École des Mines (from 1804) and became inspector general of mines. He warmly supported Haüy's theories of crystal structure and A. G. Werner's principles in geology. With Armand Dufrénoy and Élie de Beaumont he executed a geological map of France (1841).

BRÖDEL, MAX (*b. Leipzig, Germany, 1870; d. Baltimore, Maryland, 1941*), medical illustration, anatomy.

Studied at Leipzig Academy of Fine Arts (1885–90); free-lance illustrator in Leipzig; worked at Johns Hopkins from 1894 (department established for him in 1910). He was an influential illustrator who insisted on close attention to anatomic detail and became an expert anatomist. His dissections led to the discovery of Brödel's line (for opening the kidney along a relatively avascular plane); developed Brödel's suture for attaching a prolapsed kidney.

BRODIE, BENJAMIN COLLINS (*b. Winterslow, Wiltshire, England, 1783; d. Broome Park, Betchworth, Surrey, England, 1862*), physiology, surgery.

Brodie was surgeon (from 1805) at St. George's Hospital, London, and lectured at the Windmill Street School (1808–30). His influential *Diseases of the Joints* (1818) was based on analysis of case histories. His six experimental reports to the Royal Society (1809–14) made a sensational impact. These reports of experiments in destroying an animal's brain, yet maintaining artificial respiration and heartbeat, indisputably challenged with empirical evidence the contemporary chemical theory of animal heat and showed that respiration was not the sole source of heat production, since destruction of the brain totally impaired heat production. He was knighted in 1834.

BRODIE, BENJAMIN COLLINS, JR. (*b. London, England, 1817; d. Torquay, England, 1880*), chemistry.

Brodie, the son of Benjamin Collins Brodie, graduated from Balliol College, Oxford (1845), worked under Liebig at Giessen (1845–47), and was Waynflete professor of chemistry at Oxford (1855–73). He early discovered and named cerotic acid, cerotin, and melissic acid (1848–49) and discovered graphitic acid, representing the new substances by conventional formulas. But he is interesting for his "The Calculus of Chemical Operations" (1866) and *Ideal Chemistry* (1880), containing his drastic proposals for an exact language for chemistry free from any association with Dalton's atomic theory and any hypothesis on the nature of matter. Brodie's calculus, never adopted, is a curious relic of the positivistic tendencies of nineteenth-century chemistry.

BRØGGER, WALDEMAR CHRISTOPHER (*b. Christiania [now Oslo], Norway, 1851; d. Oslo, 1940*), geology.

Brøgger took a B.A. at the University of Oslo (1869), founded the mineralogical institute at the new University of Stockholm (1881–90), taught at Oslo (1890–1917), was rector there, and was president of the Norwegian Academy of Science for many years. He was a member of the Storting (1900–06). His main research contribution was in the study of the Permian eruptive rocks of the Oslo district. He also pioneered in the theory of magmatic differentiation and published many geological maps.

BROGLIE, LOUIS-CÉSAR-VICTOR-MAURICE DE (*b. Paris, France, 1875; d. Neuilly-sur-Seine, France, 1960*), physics.

De Broglie was in the navy (1895–1908); and, after distinguishing himself by installing the first French shipboard wireless, he was allowed to follow his own bent. He took his *licence* at Marseilles (1900), and a Ph.D. at the Collège de France in ionic mobilities (1908). X-ray spectra became his chief interest (from 1912); using his "method of the rotating crystal," an application of Bragg's "focusing effect" to eliminate spurious spectral lines, he cautiously investigated a wide spectrum of X-ray emissions. He discovered the third L absorption edge (1916), which led to the exploration of "corpuscular spectra." His work with his brother Louis (1921–22) refined Bohr's specification of the substructure of the various atomic shells. He did pioneer work in nuclear physics and cosmic radiation.

BROILI, FERDINAND (*b. Mühlbach, Germany, 1874; d. Mühlbach, 1946*), paleontology, geology.

Broili took a Ph.D. at Munich (1898) under Karl von Zittel, whom he assisted (1899–1904) and succeeded (1904–39) at the State Paleontological Collection. His work in Texas with Charles Sternberg (1901) on fossils of the Permian era led to several works, especially on saurians (1904–13). He directed the Institute for Paleontology and Historical Geology of the University of Munich (1919–39). He was especially successful in his investigations of winged reptiles of the upper Malm, showing them to be warm-blooded (1919–26), and his many-faceted investigations of the Paleozoic and Mesozoic eras encompassed description, systematic explanation, and depiction of main life habits.

BROMELL, MAGNUS VON, known as **Bromelius** before ennoblement in 1726 (*b. Stockholm, Sweden, 1679; d. Stockholm, 1731*), geology.

Browell practiced medicine in Stockholm and headed the Collegium Medicum (1724) there; he directed the chemical laboratory of the Board of Mines (1724). He had a renowned cabinet of ores, minerals, and fossils. His *Mineralogia* (1730) essayed mineral classification by chemical characteristics.

BROMWICH, THOMAS JOHN I'ANSON (*b. Wolverhampton, England, 1875; d. Northhampton, England, 1929*), mathematics.

Bromwich was educated at Saint John's, Cambridge (1895; Sc.D, 1909), and taught there (from 1907). His two best works are his encyclopedic *Introduction to the Theory of Infinite Series* (1908) and *Quadratic Forms and Their Classification by Means of Invariant Factors* (1906); these introduced Kronecker's work to English readers and advanced knowledge of quadratic and bilinear forms.

BRONGNIART, ADOLPHE-THÉODORE (*b. Paris, France, 1801; d. Paris, 1876*), paleobotany, plant anatomy, plant taxonomy.

Brongniart was trained by his father, Alexandre Brongniart, and from 1822 began developing a new science of which he was the architect: the comparative morphology of living and fossil plants. He helped found the *Annales des sciences naturelles* (1824), took his *agrégation* in medicine (1827), and taught botany at the Muséum d'Histoire Naturelle (from 1833). He discovered the tetrads and the distinction between the fertilized egg and the seed (1827). His masterworks *Prodrome* (1828) and *Histoire des végétaux fossiles* (2 vols., 1837) clearly showed his two concerns: nomenclature and illustration. He identified four periods of vegetation, characterized geologically, and six classes in the vegetable kingdom. One of the first to use thin sections in paleobotany, his most notable use was in his famous anatomical observations on the *Sigillaria* (1839). His "Végétaux fossiles" (1849) was the first attempt at a synthesis of paleobotany: the inventory of fossil genera as a whole and the place of these genera in natural classification. His last great paleobotanical discovery was the pollen chamber in fossil cycads (1875).

BRONGNIART, ALEXANDRE (*b. Paris, France, 1770; d. Paris, 1847*), geology.

Brongniart studied at the École des Mines and the École de Médecine, taught at the Muséum d'Histoire Naturelle (from 1822), and was chief engineer of mines (from 1818). He directed the Sèvres porcelain factory (1800–47) and retained an interest in ceramics technology. His "Essai d'une classification naturelle des reptiles" (1800) offered a grouping essentially retained in modern systematics. His textbook *Traité élémentaire de minéralogie* (2 vols., 1807) adopted a simple classification based on physical properties, but made extensive use of Haüy's crystallographic work. These early studies coalesced in the geological work that made him famous: with Cuvier, who had already begun his spectacular reconstructions of extinct mammals from the Paris region, he determined the order of the strata in which the fossils had been found. Their "Essai sur la géographie minéralogique des environs de Paris" (1808) was quickly recognized as significant. (The geology seems to have been largely Brongniart's.) Brongniart's discovery of the value of fossils as a tool for stratigraphy was the first to be published, and had great influence. In a later edition (1822) of the work, he described strata equivalent to those of the Paris region from many different parts of Europe. He empirically demonstrated the primacy of fossil evidence over that of lithology and physical position as a criterion for age, wherever the evidence is conflicting. His *Histoire naturelle des crustacés fossiles* (1822) was important in the later unraveling of Paleozoic stratigraphy. He described the sinuous ridges of Sweden but did not recognize ice sheets as the cause. His last major geological work, *Tableau des terrains qui composent l'écorce du globe* (1829), was the culmination of his attempt to distinguish time units from rock units. In this he had little influence; but the valuable lists of characteristic fossils for each *terrain* (rock unit) back to the pre-Carboniferous were widely used in the following decade. The influence of his early work on the Paris region, and its later extension to the whole of western Europe, was the principal model for much of the research of 1810–40 and thus lay at the root of the greatest achievement of early nineteenth-century geology, the elucidation of the main outlines of the history of the earth and of life on earth.

BRONN, HEINRICH GEORG (*b. Ziegelhausen bei Heidelberg, Germany, 1800; d. Heidelberg, 1862*), paleontology, zoology.

Bronn studied and taught at (from 1833) Heidelberg. *Lethaea geognostica* (2 vols., 1835–38) and *Index paleontologicus* (2 vols., 1841–43) summarized all that was then known in stratigraphy and paleontology and were for decades the chief reference works in paleontology. He left unfinished *Die Klassen und Ordnungen des Thier-reichs* (from 1859). He attempted a synthesis of the developmental laws of nature from his paleontological studies (1857).

BRØNSTED, JOHANNES NICOLAUS (*b. Varde, Denmark, 1879; d. Copenhagen, Denmark, 1947*), chemistry.

Brønsted took the M.S. (1902) and Ph.D. (1908) at the University of Copenhagen and taught there after 1908; directed the Institute of Physical Chemistry (from 1930). He took over Julius Thomsen's idea of determining chemical affinity by measuring the maximum work of a chemical process, but used electromotive force measurements for galvanic cells (13 papers, 1906–21). Other achievements include his definition of acids and bases.

BROOKS, ALFRED HULSE (*b. Ann Arbor, Mich., 1871; d. Washington, D.C., 1924*), geology.

Brooks was dominant in the early geological exploration of Alaska. He was educated at Stuttgart, Munich, and Harvard (B.S., 1894) and at the École des Mines, Paris. He joined the U.S. Geological Survey (1894), becoming in time chief of the Alaska Branch. In his geological explorations there (1898–1917) he discovered and named

Rainy Pass, predicted and guided the discovery of the gold bonanzas at Nome, and discovered the tin placers of western Alaska. He laid a general conceptual framework for future studies of Alaska's geological history and topographical development in "The Geography and Geology of Alaska" (1906) and *Blazing Alaska's Trails* (1953). His work led to the mapping of Alaska and to major works on its coal and metal resources. He played a major role in creating the Alaska Railroad (completed 1923). The Brooks Range, Brooks Peak, and the Brooks River all bear his name.

BROOKS, WILLIAM KEITH (*b. Cleveland, Ohio, 1848; d. Baltimore, Md., 1908*), zoology, embryology.

Brooks was educated at Williams College (1870) and Harvard (Ph.D., 1875) and taught biology at Johns Hopkins University from 1875 until his death. A descriptive evolutionary morphologist for whom the adaptive response of the organism was paramount, he could not participate in the transformation of morphology from a comparative to a causal science. Yet four of his students (E. B. Wilson, T. H. Morgan, E. G. Conklin, R. G. Harrison) laid the groundwork for much of modern cytology, embryology, and genetics. His descriptions of the embryology, morphology, and life habits of marine invertebrates are classic. His major work was *The Foundations of Zoology* (1899).

BROOKS, WILLIAM ROBERT (*b. Maidstone, England, 1844; d. Geneva, N.Y., 1921*), astronomy.

Self-educated in astronomy, Brooks was a successful observer who discovered twenty-seven comets with portable apparatus of his own design and construction. In 1888 he became chief of the Smith Observatory, Geneva, New York, and he taught astronomy at Hobart College (from 1900) and at William Smith College (from 1908).

BROOM, ROBERT (*b. Paisley, Scotland, 1866; d. Pretoria, South Africa, 1951*), paleontology.

Broom took an M.D. at the University of Glasgow (1889) and practiced medicine in Australia (1892–96) and South Africa (1897–1928). He taught zoology and geology (1903–10) at Victoria College (now Stellenbosch University), and was curator of paleontology at the Transvaal Museum in Pretoria (1934–51). His major contributions were on the origin and skull structure of mammals, the history and classification of Permian and Triassic reptiles, and the discovery and interpretation of the earliest human fossils. His unusual talent for combining paleontology and embryology enabled him to contribute more to the story of mammalian origins than all his contemporaries together.

Studying the embryonic development of the skull in the Australian phalanger *Trichosurus* (from 1898), Broom discovered that the mammalian alisphenoid bone does not form in the wall of the braincase but arises from the palate, like the slender epipterygoid bone of lizards and other reptiles (1907). He later showed this transition from reptilian to mammalian condition in the skulls of various mammal-like reptiles, perhaps his most important contribution to vertebrate morphology. In a series of reconstructions (1911) he also suggested the mode of transition from the reptilian to the mammalian ear condition. In his famous studies of the fossil reptiles of the

Karroo, following descriptive work by Owen and Seeley, he revealed the details of the skull structure of mammal-like reptiles and thus placed their classification on a firm morphological basis. He proposed the suborder *Therocephalia* (1902). His basic groupings of the African forms (1905), modified in the light of later discoveries, are still used. He established the standard sequence of faunal zones and also described an unbelievably large number of fossils. He summarized this work in *The Origin of the Human Skeleton* (1930) and *The Mammal-like Reptiles of South Africa* (1932). He described his important Australopithecine discoveries in *The South African Fossil Ape-Men. The Australopithecinae* (1946, with G. W. H. Schepers); *Finding the Missing Link* (1950); and *Swartkrans Ape-Man, Paranthropus crassidens* (1952, with J. T. Robinson).

BROSCIUS, JOANNES. *See* **Brożek, Jan.**

BROUNCKER, WILLIAM (*b. 1620; d. Westminster, London, England, 1684*), mathematics.

Brouncker succeeded to the title viscount of Castle Lyons, Ireland, in 1645. He took the Doctor of Physick degree at Oxford (1647) and held several prominent administrative offices (at Gresham College, the navy, the treasury). His fame as a mathematician rests largely on his solutions of problems set by others, primarily John Wallis: an alternate expression for π in the form of an infinite product in terms of continued fractions; several solutions for the Diophantine equation $ax^2 + 1 = y^2$; and a solution of the quadrature of a rectangular hyperbola.

BROUSSAIS, FRANÇOIS JOSEPH VICTOR (*b. near St. Malo, France, 1772; d. Paris, France, 1838*), medicine.

Broussais took a medical degree at Paris (1802). His success as a physician and a teacher of practical medicine at the Val de Grâce hospital, Paris (1814–36), lasted until his physiological doctrine was proved wrong in the 1832 outbreak of cholera, which he treated (disastrously) as acute gastroenteritis. In 1834, in a final effort to regain popularity, he exploited the fashion for phrenology. In 1836 he began in his lectures to question the immortality of the soul and the existence of God. This led to such violent scenes that the police were called in to restore order and Broussais was forced to cease teaching.

BROUSSONET (or **Broussonnet** or **Broussounet**), **PIERRE-AUGUSTE-MARIE** (*b. Montpellier, France, 1761; d. Montpellier, 1807*), zoology, botany.

Broussonet, whose father taught medicine at Montpellier and whose brother Victor became dean in medicine, took a doctorate there (1779). By that time a convinced Linnaean, he went to London (1780). Sir Joseph Banks turned over to him his collection of fish from Cook's first expedition. The result was Broussonet's *Ichthyologia* (1782), which noted the important discovery of the *pseudobranchia*. He returned to France and completed his last work in ichthyology, a memoir on the *voilier* (1786). He taught (1783–89) rural economy at the Alfort Veterinary School. He was in sympathy with the Revolution but fled after witnessing the killing of Berthier. On his return (1795), the post of vice-consul at Morocco, where he could pursue his observations, was created for him (1797–99). He became professor at the medical school of

Montpellier (1803–06) in charge of the botanical garden there.

BROUWER, DIRK (*b. Rotterdam, Netherlands, 1902; d. New Haven, Conn., 1966*), astronomy.

Brouwer made elegant theoretical contributions to celestial mechanics. He took a Ph.D. at the University of Leiden (1927) and taught at Yale (from 1928), becoming director of the Yale Observatory (1941–66) and editor of the *Astronomical Journal* (1941–66). He searched for differences between predicted and observed positions of the moon that would reveal changes in the earth's rotation. His direct determination of planetary positions by numerical integration was in *Coordinates of the Five Outer Planets, 1653–2060* (1951). He influenced the International Astronomical Union to adopt new fundamental astronomical constants (1964) and suggested the name for Ephemeris Time (1950).

BROUWER, LUITZEN EGBERTUS JAN (*b. Overschie, Netherlands, 1881; d. Blaricum, Netherlands, 1966*), mathematics.

Brouwer took a Ph.D. at the University of Amsterdam (1907) and taught there (from 1912). His most important work was on the foundations of mathematics; his thesis took the view that mathematical existence did not mean freedom from contradiction but rather intuitive constructibility. In his constructivist conception (later called intuitionistic), mathematics was a free activity of the mind constructing mathematical objects from self-evident primitive notions. Formal logic only describes irregularities in the systems thus constructed. His *Over de Onbetrouwbaarheid der logische Principes* (1908) rejected the principle of the excluded third (*A* or not *A*). He first arrived at a satisfactory notion of the constructive continuum, the stumbling block to a reconstruction of mathematics, in his review (1914) of the Schoenflies-Hahn report on the development of set theory. He published a set theory independent of the principle of the excluded third (1918), a constructive theory of measure (1919), and a theory of functions (1923). To explain the notion of set in his constructivist theory, he introduced the notion of free-choice sequence and derived his fundamental fan theorem. With this theorem he showed that the principle of the excluded third is contradictory. His proof of the theorem is still not quite accepted, but it enabled him to derive results that diverge strongly from what is known from ordinary mathematics. Interest in intuitionist mathematics was revived in the late 1920's and, after World War II, by S. C. Kleene.

BROWN, ALEXANDER CRUM (*b. Edinburgh, Scotland, 1838; d. Edinburgh, 1922*), chemistry, physiology.

Crum Brown took an M.D. (1861) and a D.Sc. at London University (1862). Under Kolbe, he carried out what was probably the first synthesis of adipic acid (1862). He taught chemistry at Edinburgh (1863–1908). His thesis (1861) proposed a scheme to represent the structure of compounds by letter and lines similar to but independent of Archibald Couper's; the formulas used today most resemble Crum Brown's. He invented the symbol, still in use, of two parallel lines for a double bond (1865). He worked out an operational calculus (1867) more pragmatic in approach to the atomic theory than Brodie's, but

equally uninfluential. In physiology he correctly related vertigo to the motion of liquid in the semicircular canals of the inner ear.

BROWN, ERNEST WILLIAM (*b. Hull, England, 1866; d. New Haven, Conn., 1938*), celestial mechanics.

Brown was educated at Christ's College, Cambridge (B.A., 1887; M.A., 1891; D.Sc., 1897), and taught at Yale University (1907–32). His aim was to reconcile lunar theory and observations by finding the complete effect of the law of gravitation on the moon. He used his theory of lunar motion (1908) to construct (with H. B. Hedrick) new tables of the moon's motion, adopted by most national ephemerides (1923).

BROWN, ROBERT (*b. Montrose, Scotland, 1773; d. London, England, 1858*), botany.

Brown's work, like that of both William Sherard and Linnaeus, deals primarily with taxonomy and hence nomenclature. But Brown's works embody as well many profound observations, and his discovery of Brownian motion. The son of a Scottish Episcopalian clergyman, he took an M.D. (1795) at the University of Edinburgh. He sailed (1801) as naturalist in Matthew Flinders' voyage to survey the coast of Australia. On his return (1805) he brought samples of nearly 4,000 plant species; on government salary (to 1810) he described nearly 2,200 species, over 1,700 new (including 140 new genera), and selected about 2,800 representative specimens for a public collection. He was clerk to the Linnean Society of London (1806–22) and librarian to Joseph Banks (1810–20), who willed him an annuity and his Soho Square house. After Banks's death he transferred the Soho Square collection to the British Museum as the first nationally owned botanical collection available to the public. He headed the museum's independent botanical department (1827–58).

Through his wandering curiosity and his mastery of a subject detail by detail, Brown's early work on the flora of Australia led to many other matters. His classic "On the Proteaceae of Jussieu" (read 1809, pub. 1810) defined a new classification of genera. "On the Asclepiadeae" (1810) separated the family Asclepiadaceae from the Apocynaceae by the character of its pollen. His *Prodromus florae Novae Hollandiae* (1810), which introduced a new classification system, is still fundamental for Australian botany. His almost haphazard presentation of isolated parts of his vast studies makes almost all his publications liable to yield unexpected lines of inquiry in digressions or footnotes. He gave the first demonstration of the general occurrence of the nucleus in living cells and coined the term "nucleus." His important discovery of the fundamental difference between what were later named gymnosperms and angiosperms was also communicated as a digression (paper on Kingia, 1827).

Examining pollen grains of *Clarkia pulchella* in 1827, he observed particles suspended in a fluid within the grain which were evidently moving, and he concluded that their motion "arose neither from currents in the fluid nor from its gradual evaporation but belong to the particle itself." He characteristically extended his observations to all fresh pollen, preserved specimens, and every mineral he could reduce to a powder sufficiently fine to be suspended in water. His account, published in 1828, was a landmark of nineteenth-century science. It remained for others to demonstrate relevance of Brownian movement to the kinetic theory of gases.

BROWNE, THOMAS (*b. London, England, 1605; d. Norwich, England, 1682*), general science, natural history.

Browne was educated at Pembroke College, Oxford (M.A., 1629) and received the M.D. from both Leiden (1633) and Oxford (1637). He practiced medicine in Norwich. His pursuit of his hobbies, science and natural history, was conducted on the fringe of the scientific world. He was knighted by Charles II in 1671. His best-known book was *Religio medici* (1642). His *Pseudodoxia epidemica: or, Enquiries Into Very Many Received Tenents, and Commonly Presumed Truths* (1646) ranged over all knowledge, and mentions many of his experiments in physics, electricity (a word he coined), biology, and comparative anatomy.

BROWNRIGG, WILLIAM (*b. High Close Hall, Cumberland, England, 1711; d. Ormathwaite, Cumberland, England, 1800*), chemistry.

Brownrigg took an M.D. at Leiden (1737) and practiced in Whitehaven. He investigated (from 1741) the damps arising in the local mines. His views on gases and his techniques were an advance on Hales's, and he deserves a place in the direct line of British pneumatic chemistry. He also made the first investigation in Europe of platinum (1741–49).

BROWN-SÉQUARD, CHARLES-ÉDOUARD (*b. Port Louis, Mauritius, 1817; d. Paris, France, 1894*), physiology.

The son of C. E. Brown, an American naval officer, and Charlotte Séquard, a Frenchwoman, Brown-Séquard became a French citizen (1878). He took an M.D. at Paris (1846). He was restless, practicing medicine, teaching, and experimenting in New York, Paris, Port Louis, and London at various times. The high point of his scientific career was as professor of medicine at the Collège de France (1878–94). He showed (1849) that transverse hemisection of the spinal cord produces motor paralysis and hyperesthesia on the corresponding side and anesthesia on the opposite side of the body below the lesion (the Brown-Séquard syndrome). He demonstrated that section of the vagus nerve brought on dilation of the coronary arteries (1862). A pioneer of endocrinology, he proved that removal of the adrenal glands always caused death in animals (1856). His great achievement was understanding that through "internal secretion," the cells become dependent on one another by a mechanism other than the nervous system (1891).

BROŻEK (or **Broscius**), **JAN** (*b. Kurzelow, near Sieradz, Poland, 1585; d. Krakow, Poland, 1652*), mathematics.

Brożek took a degree at Krakow (1605), was ordained a priest, and received the M.D. from Padua in 1624. During most of his life he taught at the University of Krakow. His works on Copernicus and on mathematics won him the reputation of being the greatest Polish mathematician of his time. His most important works are *Arithmetica integrorum* (1620), *Aristoteles et Euclides defensus contra Petrum Ramum* (1638), and *De numeris perfectis* (1637, 1638). He is sometimes confused with Nicolas Brożek, another Polish mathematician to whom he was related.

BRUCE, DAVID (*b. Melbourne, Australia, 1855; d. London, England, 1931*), microbiology.

Bruce, who discovered the bacterial cause of Malta fever and did important research on trypanosomiasis, took an M.B. at Edinburgh (1881) and served in the Army Medical Service (from 1883) and the Royal Army Medical Corps, in which he became surgeon general. He was knighted (1908).

While stationed in Malta, Bruce found "micrococci" in the spleen of a patient who died of Malta fever (1886), and from splenic pulp of other patients he grew cultures of this micrococcus (1887). He then described the organism, which he named *Micrococcus melitensis*. The generic term *Brucella*, in Bruce's honor, was later adopted (1920) for these microorganisms. The term "brucellosis" has now replaced such names as Malta, Mediterranean, and undulant fever.

When he was stationed in Natal (1894), Bruce investigated an epizootic, nagana, that was affecting cattle in northern Zululand. Intensive microscopic study of blood specimens of affected oxen revealed a motile vibrating hematozoon, which he later concluded was a trypanosome. He showed that it infected healthy horses and dogs. His reports (1895, 1897) described the hematozoa of nagana, established the tsetse fly *Glossina morsitans* as the vector, and implicated regional wild game as the trypanosomal reservoir. The parasite was named *Trypanosoma brucei* by Plimmer and Bradford (1899). He headed the Royal Society's Sleeping Sickness Commission to Uganda (1903), which made use of the prior contributions of Aldo Castellani. Their "Progress Report" acknowledged Castellani's discovery; the "Further Report" minimized it. Bruce directed further research into the transmissibility of the disease in Uganda (1908–10) and Nyasaland (1911–13). The commission concluded that *T. rhodesiense* and *T. brucei* were identical, but this view now has no adherents.

BRUCE, JAMES (*b. Stirlingshire, Scotland, 1730; d. Stirlingshire, 1794*), exploration.

Bruce during his most notable journey found the source of the Blue Nile (1770). His *Travels* (5 vols., 1790) contains considerable meteorological and astronomical records, as well as descriptions of flora and fauna.

BRÜCKE, ERNST WILHELM VON (*b. Berlin, Germany, 1819; d. Vienna, Austria, 1892*), physiology.

Brücke took an M.D. at Berlin (1842) under Johannes Müller. He taught at Vienna (1849–90) where his school for physiologists gained an international reputation. The range of his physiological interests was vast, as his *Lectures on Physiology* (1873–74) show. He discovered the ciliary muscle named for him, and his *Anatomical Description of the Human Eye* (1847) has become the standard anatomical-histological work for contemporary oculists. He also did work on luminescence, blood coagulation, microscopy, and cells.

BRUHNS, KARL CHRISTIAN (*b. Plön, Germany, 1830; d. Leipzig, Germany, 1881*), astronomy.

Bruhns, a locksmith, took a degree at the University of Berlin (1856) in astronomy, taught at Leipzig (1861–81), and directed the observatory (1860–81). Much of his work was on determinations of longitude between his observatory and Berlin, Vienna, Paris, and Munich. More importantly, he helped to organize uniform world-wide weather observations, supervised the local observations, and promoted regular forecasts. His was the first comprehensive biography of Alexander von Humboldt (1871).

BRUMPT, ÉMILE (*b. Paris, France, 1877; d. Paris, 1951*), parasitology.

Brumpt was trained in Paris as a zoologist (1901) and a physician (1906) and originated medical parasitology in France. He taught at the Faculté de Médecine (from 1919). He demonstrated a development phase in leeches of the trypanosomes of batrachians and fish (1904). He described the life history of *Trypanosoma cruzi,* the agent of Chagas' disease (1912). He discovered a strain of *Plasmodium gallinaceum* invaluable in the chemotherapy of human malaria. He proved a genetic difference between the dysenteric amoeba and a nonpathogenic species (1923).

BRUNELLESCHI, FILIPPO (*b. Florence, Italy, 1377; d. Florence, 1446*), architecture, engineering, geometry.

Brunelleschi, the first great Renaissance architect, is sometimes credited with inventing monocular perspective, although modern research assigns him a more modest part. His ingenious painting of the baptistery of Sta. Maria del Fiore is in effect an optic box affording the viewer, by optical illusion, a three-dimensional representation. The idea for this optic box may well have been part of the common scientific fund of his time, but the painting demonstrates the artist's knowledge of conical projection and vanishing points.

BRUNFELS, OTTO (*b. Mainz, Germany, ca. 1489; d. Bern, Switzerland, 1534*), botany.

The earliest of the three "German fathers of botany" (with Jerome Bock and Leonhard Fuchs), Brunfels emancipated botany from medieval herbalism. He took an M.A. at Mainz (1508), entered a Carthusian monastery (1510–21), left the Catholic faith, became a Lutheran pastor, opened his own school in Strasbourg (1524), took an M.D. at Basel (1532), and was town physician in Bern. He wrote one of the earliest medical bibliographies, *Catalogus* (1530). His *Herbarum vivae eicones* (3 vols., 1530–36) changed the direction of botany. The text is unoriginal but the realism of the 238 woodcuts (executed by Hans Weiditz) taken from nature revolutionized botanical iconography. All portions of the plant were depicted with equal detail, in the typical habitat. These are the first printed botanical illustrations that have scientific value. Brunfels' German adaptation of the *Herbarum,* the *Contrafayt Kreüterbuoch* (2 vols., 1532–37), includes additional figures. His most important other work was *Reformation der Apotecken* (1536), which contains an early Swiss dispensatory.

BRUNHES, JEAN (*b. Toulouse, France, 1869; d. Boulogne-sur-Seine, France, 1930*), geography.

Educated at École Normale Supérieure (1889–96; doctorate, 1902). Taught at universities of Fribourg (1896) and Lausanne (1908); in 1912 the Collège de France created a chair of human geography for him. In his great work, *Géographie humaine* (1910), Brunhes presented the first attempt to coordinate the geographical phenomena resulting from the activities of man; although criticized by some, he gave a decisive impetus to human geography.

BRUNO, GIORDANO (*b. Nola, Italy, 1548; d. Rome, Italy, 1600*), philosophy.

Bruno entered the Dominican order in 1563, where he acquired a grounding in Scholastic philosophy. He fell under suspicion of heresy in 1576, fled Naples for Rome, abandoned the Dominican habit, and began a long odyssey through Switzerland, France, England, and Germany. While in England (1583–85), he published five dialogues, and it was on these works that his reputation as the instigator of a new philosophy rests.

In 1585 Bruno returned to Paris and the next year began his travels through Germany. In 1591 he returned to Italy, where he was promptly arrested and tried by a court of the Inquisition. He was convicted of heresy, which he recanted to no avail. He was imprisoned for eight years and finally burned alive in Rome.

Bruno's works were based on the beliefs of a mythical Egyptian sage, Hermes Trismegistus, who enjoyed great prestige in the Renaissance. He accepted the pseudo-Egyptian religion described in these Hermetic texts as the true religion. His belief in the magical animation of all nature, which the magus could learn to tap and use, his vision of the living earth moving around the sun, of an infinite universe of innumerable worlds moving like great animals in space, are all inseparably connected with his pseudo-Egyptian religion. Extraordinarily he seems to have believed that his religion could somehow be incorporated within a Catholic framework in the coming new dispensation.

In England he enjoyed the protection of the French ambassador, which allowed him to publish clandestinely his extremely provocative works criticizing Reformation Oxford and attacking the whole social order of Elizabethan England for having destroyed, without adequately replacing, the institutions of Catholic times. These published works (all in Italian) are *Cena de le ceneri* (1584), a defense of Copernican heliocentricity; *De la causa, principio e uno* (1584), an answer to the protests that arose over his previous work; *De l'infinito, universo e mondi* (1584) on his remarkable vision of an infinite universe and innumerable worlds infused with divine life; *Spaccio della bestia trionfante* (1584), on universal moral and religious reform; *De gli eroici furori* (1585), a beautiful poem sequence with commentaries.

The grounds on which Bruno was condemned as a dangerous heretic are known only second hand. To his major theological heresy, the denial of the divinity of the Second Person of the Trinity, was added suspicion of diabolical magical practices. He described Christ as a magus. It was probably mainly as a magician that he was burned, and as the propagator throughout Europe of some mysterious magico-religious movement. The legend that he was a martyr for modern science (for his defense of Copernicus) was born in the nineteenth century. Recent scholarship places him firmly in the Hermetic tradition. His influence is recognized most forcefully in the works of Leibniz and Spinoza.

BRUNSCHVICG, LÉON (*b. Paris, France, 1869; d. Aix-les-Bains, France, 1944*), philosophy.

Brunschvicg took his doctorate at the Sorbonne (1897) and taught there (from 1909) and at the École Normale Supérieure. A critical idealist opposed to *Naturphilosophie*, he believed that judgment is an action that defines the mind, that intelligence is always the victor over empiricism. Science, especially mathematics, he saw as the best expression of rationality. His *Les étapes de la philosophie mathématique* (1912) examined the history of innovations in mathematical thought and foresaw the unification of mathematics through the study of algebraic-topological structures. His *L'expérience humaine et la causalité physique* (1922) reviewed the historical stages of thought on concepts of nature, similarly confirming unity, as did his various studies on Pascal, Spinoza, and Descartes.

BRUNSCHWIG (also **Brunswyck** or **Braunschweig**), **HIERONYMUS** (*b. Strasbourg, France, ca. 1450; d. Strasbourg, ca. 1512*), surgery.

Brunschwig was educated in surgery and his works on anatomy, wounds, and the preparation of medicines are directed primarily to barbers and surgeons. His surgical texts are directed to laymen. His *Cirurgia* (1497) is an important cultural-historical source for medicine and pharmacy. His *Liber de arte distillandi, de simplicibus* (1500) was a pharmaceutical-technical authority far into the sixteenth century. His *Liber de arte distillandi, de compositis* (1507) contains a model pharmacopeia for poor people.

BRUNTON, THOMAS LAUDER (*b. Roxburgh, Scotland, 1844; d. London, England, 1916*), physiology, pharmacology.

Brunton took an M.D. (1868) and D.Sc. (1870) at Edinburgh and practiced at St. Bartholomew's Hospital (from 1871). He discovered that amyl nitrate was useful in the relief of angina pectoris (1867) through his physiological approach to therapeutics. He helped develop pharmacology into an independent and rigorous science. His *A Textbook of Pharmacology, Therapeutics and Materia Medica* (1885) was the first comprehensive physiological treatise on pharmacology. He was knighted (1900) and made a baronet (1909).

BRYAN, KIRK (*b. Albuquerque, N.M., 1888; d. Cody, Wyo., 1950*), geology, geomorphology.

Bryan took a B.A. (1910) and a Ph.D. (1920) at Yale, worked with the U.S. Geological Survey (1912–26), and taught at Harvard (1926–50). His "Erosion and Sedimentation in the Papago Country, Arizona" (1922) firmly established the term "pediment" in the literature of landscape evolution and outlined what came to be known as the "alluvial chronology" of late Pleistocene and recent time in the southwest. He was instrumental in introducing in America the use of pollen in the reconstruction of North American Pleistocene climate (from 1932) and the use of frost forms as stratigraphic and environmental indicators, coining the term "cryopedology" (1946). His work initiated the general interest of geologists in paleosoils.

BRYSON OF HERACLEA, mathematics.

The name Bryson occurs several times in Aristotle and in Plato, probably referring to the same person, who developed a method of squaring the circle and wrote *Diatribes*. Aristotle criticized his method.

BRYTTE (also **Britte, Brit,** or **Brute**), **WALTER** (*fl. Oxford, England, second half of fourteenth century*), astronomy.

Brytte may have been a fellow of Merton College; an old tradition is that he was a follower of John Wycliffe. The only work known to be his is *Theorica planetarum secundum dominum Walterum Brytte*. Its most interesting characteristic is its insight into kinematics, clearly stemming from the great Merton school of mechanics. His kinematic concepts are applied to planetary theory; he states the correct condition for a planet being stationary, yet is unable to deduce a correct geometrical construction from this principle.

BUACHE, PHILIPPE (*b. Paris, France, 1700; d. Paris, 1773*), cartography.

Buache was assistant geographer for the Royal Academy of Sciences (1730–73). His *Essai de géographie physique* (1752) contained influential studies of global structure. Was one of first to use hydrographic contour lines. In a later work, he posited the existence of Alaska and a connection between America and Asia (1753).

BUCH, [CHRISTIAN] LEOPOLD VON (*b. Stolpe, Germany, 1774; d. Berlin, Germany, 1853*), geology.

Buch was educated at the Bergakademie under A. G. Werner, and at Halle and Göttingen. His wealth allowed him to travel extensively. A true Wernerian and hence a *Naturphilosoph*, he disdained chemistry and chronology. Werner's Neptunist rule about the necessary order of succession of rock deposits, which needed no verification outside Saxony, led Buch to measure the heights of many formations, and he showed great versatility in inventing odd and drastic devices to explain disagreements between his observations and Werner's rigid theory. The solid core of his life's work was the first geological map of Germany (1826).

Buch's fundamental error in speculation sprang perhaps from the prejudice that the earth was specially created as a place for man to dwell. In 1798 he explored the Tyrol, often with his friend Alexander von Humboldt, and crossed the Brenner Pass. He expected a symmetrical arrangement on the south side of the Alps; to his distress, he found quite different formations and the whole of Werner's beautiful system collapsed in confusion. The device Buch used to impose order was one he returned to several times: the formation flood on the northern side of the pass had been stopped by the granite mountains (by Werner's theory, already there at full height). The floods from the south had arrived independently, at other stages, and hence had brought other rocks. His excursion to the Auvergne (1802) has often been referred to as momentous in allegedly converting him to Volcanism and even Plutonism. In his *Geognostische Beobachtungen auf Reisen durch Deutschland und Italien* (2 vols., 1802, 1809) and in some other works supposing that the towering heights of the Dolomites might be the result of upheaval occasioned by porphyry, including monazite, he concluded that the magnesia in this rock would also transform the original limestone into dolomite. He thus came to visualize great subterranean activities, ingeniously demonstrating (1815) the interdependence of the Canary Islands volcanoes. His view of effective subterranean masses soon encompassed the whole world.

"Ueber Granit und Gneiss" (1842) illustrates his later Wernerism and the remarkable consequences to which his refusal to consider erosion led him. To explain Silurian strata in Sweden and the Baltic he had recourse to the non-Wernerian principle of metamorphism. Stratigraphy and paleontology became his chief concern after 1824.

BUCHANAN, JOHN YOUNG (*b. Glasgow, Scotland, 1844; d. London, England, 1925*), oceanography, chemistry.

Buchanan graduated from the University of Glasgow (1863), was with the pioneering oceanographic expedition of Charles Wyville Thomson (1872–76), designed and improved oceanographic instruments and observational methods, and prepared the first reliable surface salinity map of the oceans in his own laboratory. He demonstrated as inorganic the gelatinous deep-sea deposit then thought to be protoplasmic, and pioneered in quantifying seasonal variations in heat content of lakes.

BUCHER, WALTER HERMAN (*b. Akron, Ohio, 1889; d. Houston, Tex., 1965*), geology.

Bucher took a Ph.D. at Heidelberg (1911) and taught at the University of Cincinnati (1913–40) and Columbia (1940–56). His major work, *The Deformation of the Earth's Crust* (1933), offers a thesis on the origin of orogenic belts, combining the contraction of the earth by cooling with gravitational forces. His reliance on radical forces is now less popular than theories of primarily tangential movement, such as continental drift.

BUCHERER, ALFRED HEINRICH (*b. Cologne, Germany, 1863; d. Bonn, Germany, 1927*), physics.

Bucherer studied at Johns Hopkins under Ira Remsen (1885), at Cornell (1893), at Strasbourg (1895), and at Leipzig with Ostwald. He taught at Bonn (1899–1923). In *Mathematische Einführung in die Elektronentheorie* (1904) he produced his own theory of the moving electron, falling midway between Abraham's prediction and the Lorentz-Einstein prediction. Bucherer's own measurements (1908) brought him to the conclusion that his data supported not his own theory but Einstein's. Despite this remarkable and abrupt turn, he was never completely happy with the relativistic formulation.

BUCHNER, EDUARD (*b. Munich, Germany, 1860; d. Focsani, Rumania, 1917*), chemistry.

Buchner took his doctorate at the Bavarian Academy of Sciences in Munich (1888) under Adolf von Baeyer. He taught at a number of schools, in Tübingen producing his pioneering work, *Alkoholische Gärung ohne Hefezellen* (1897). His most productive period, especially in the biochemistry of the fermentation process, was as professor of general chemistry at the College of Agriculture in Berlin and director of the Institute for the Fermentation Industry (1898–1909). Buchner's sensational discovery of cell-free fermentation (for which he received the Nobel Prize in chemistry in 1907) was the turning point in the study of enzymes. In three papers (1897) he gave the results of his first experiments with cell-free alcoholic fermentation. His comprehensive presentation, with his brother and Martin Hahn, was in *Die Zymase-Gärung* (1903). They subjected a paste of yeast and quartz sand to pressure, which yielded a fluid. The active, fermentation-producing agent of the expressed fluid was called "zymase," eliminating Pasteur's distinction between enzymes and ferments and establishing fermentation as a chemical, enzymatically catalyzed process.

He explored the chemical properties of the expressed fluid, identifying other enzymes it contained. The reaction chain of alcoholic fermentation was widely explored by Buchner and his associates (1904–17). His investigations of the fermentation phenomena of various microorganisms confirmed that characteristic life phenomena can be attributed to the regularities of enzyme-catalyzed chemical reactions.

BÜCHNER, FRIEDRICH KARL CHRISTIAN LUDWIG (*b. Darmstadt, Germany, 1824; d. Darmstadt, 1899*), medicine, philosophy, history of science.

Büchner, the most influential nineteenth-century German representative of materialism, took an M.D. at the University of Giessen (1848). He taught at Tübingen (1854) until furor over his most famous work, *Kraft und Stoff* (1855), forced his resignation. He then practiced medicine in Darmstadt. His many works to disseminate knowledge of the natural sciences were based on his definition of force as "expression for the cause of a possible or an actual movement" and on the unity of matter and force. No insight was conceivable without exact knowledge of matter and its laws, which are unchangeable and generally valid. He did much to disseminate Darwin's work in particular.

BUCHOLZ, CHRISTIAN FRIEDRICH (*b. Eisleben, Germany, 1770; d. Erfurt, Germany, 1818*), chemistry, pharmacy.

Bucholz took a Ph.D. at Rinteln (1808) and at Erfurt (1809), where he taught. His reputation was founded on a large number of analytical studies and did not long survive his death; he made a few important but no primary contributions to chemistry.

BUCKINGHAM, EDGAR (*b. Philadelphia, Pa., 1867; d. Washington, D.C., 1940*), physics.

Buckingham graduated from Harvard (1887) and Leipzig (Ph.D., 1893) and worked at the Bureau of Standards (1905–37). He is best known for his early book on thermodynamics (1900) and for showing more clearly than anyone before him how the method of dimensions, later called dimensional analysis, facilitates experimentation.

BUCKLAND, WILLIAM (*b. Axminster, England, 1784; d. Islip, England, 1856*), geology, paleontology.

Buckland was educated at Corpus Christi College, Oxford (1804), where he taught (1809–45). He took holy orders (1809), and was dean of Westminster (1845–49). His geological tours of the British Isles (1808–15) and Europe (from 1816) brought him international contacts, and he gave Oxford an international name in science.

His importance lay not in theorizing but in helping to redefine the nature and method of a geological explanation. He helped build a typically "British" geology based on local stratigraphy and local dynamic explanations but revivified by the addition of fossil evidence. He agreed with Saussure's idea of a massive "debacle" of water to explain valley excavation, distribution of alluvial gravel, and erratic transport, challenging the interpretation that the Mosaic flood occurred miraculously but left no traces. His major work on the geological evidence for a recent deluge was on the worldwide distribution of pebbles similar to the quartz pebbles of Lickey Hill in Worcestershire (read 1819). He continued to be skeptical of evidence of fossil human bones in strata earlier than the debacle. In paleontology his most interesting work was on still-existing forms, such as hyenas and bears, and on marine shells. Although his *Vindiciae geologicae* (1820) was ostensibly an orthodox defense of geology as useful to religion, it in fact shows him hewing out an independent position. He also showed that formations on Alpine mountain flanks were the equivalent of certain secondary formations in England, and that the regular order of succession in Alpine districts is identical with that of England. His *Reliquiae diluvianae* (1823) concluded that species of animals now existing together only in the tropics had coexisted in northern Europe with species still in existence, and that this demonstrated a tropical climate in antediluvial times. It was criticized for asserting the geological reality of the Mosaic flood, and this he finally abandoned, but his geological evidence for some large-scale unknown force acting in geologically recent times remained intact. His celebrated explanations of the habits of the fossil *Megatherium* and the present-day sloth—showing how perfect their organization is for their mode of life—appeared in his Bridgewater treatise, *Geology and Mineralogy Considered With Reference to Natural Theology*. In it he emphasized Paley's position that the world was made for all the species in it, not for man alone.

BUCQUET, JEAN-BAPTISTE MICHEL (*b. Paris, France, 1746; d. Paris, 1780*), chemistry.

Bucquet taught chemistry at the Faculty of Medicine in Paris (from 1770). He was convinced that chemistry held the key to natural history and medicine, and aimed to integrate it with all related subjects by verifying prior experimental work. His work on gases was probably of great use to Lavoisier, with whom he worked (from 1777). He seems to have been the first to teach Lavoisier's theory, as early as 1778. He produced and investigated "fixed air" (carbon dioxide). His book on plant chemistry (2 vols., 1773) seems to be the first detailed account of the subject.

BUDAN DE BOISLAURENT, FERDINAND FRANÇOIS DÉSIRÉ (*worked Paris, France, ca. 1800–at least 1853*), mathematics.

Budan's life is known only through the title pages of his published works. He was a doctor of medicine and an amateur mathematician. He independently discovered (1807) what became known as the rule of Budan and Fourier; it gives necessary conditions for a polynomial equation to have n real roots between two given real numbers. Lagrange greatly influenced him; he appears to have been led to the rule by Descartes's rule of signs. Budan's rule remains the most convenient for computation.

BUDD, WILLIAM (*b. North Tawton, Devon, England, 1811; d. Clevedon, Somerset, England, 1880*), medicine, epidemiology.

Budd was a pioneer epidemiologist and a precursor of the Pasteurian germ theory of disease. He took an M.D. at Edinburgh University (1838) and worked in Bristol at St. Peter's Hospital, Bristol Medical College, and the Bristol Royal Infirmary. His belief in specific infective agents in communicable diseases stemmed from his investigations of over eighty cases of typhoid at North Tawton (1839–40; *Typhoid Fever*, 1873). He concluded that the "poisons" of typhoid and cholera multiply in the victim's intestines and are "cast off." His *Malignant Cholera* (1849) declared this disease to be waterborne and his preventive regimen successfully curbed the 1866 outbreak in Bristol. He applied himself to such other communicable diseases as diphtheria, scarlet fever, and tuberculosis, a sheep-pox epizootic, rinderpest, and hog cholera.

BUERG, JOHANN TOBIAS. *See* **Bürg, Johann Tobias.**

BUFFON, GEORGES-LOUIS LECLERC, COMTE DE (*b. Montbard, France, 1707; d. Paris, France, 1788*), natural history.

Buffon studied in Dijon (Collège des Jésuites, 1717–23; law, 1723–26) and Angers (1728–30), where his interest turned to mathematics. He was *intendant* of the Jardin du Roi (1739–88). His works include *Mémoires* to the Académie des Sciences (1737–52) and the *Histoire naturelle* (36 vols.). Most of the memoirs he reconsidered in the *Supplément à l'Histoire Naturelle* (1774–77).

Buffon's most important writing on the nature and value of science is *Discours sur la manière d'étudier et de traiter l'histoire naturelle* (1749). Breaking with the spirit of his time, he attempted to separate science from metaphysical and religious ideas. He found fault with classifiers, especially Linnaeus, for trying to imprison nature within an artificial system. His ideas evolved considerably; later (1764 and 1765) he seemed to admit that man is actually capable of ascertaining fundamental laws of nature, and still later (1779) showed how the history of the earth obeys these laws. His *Histoire et théorie de la terre* (1749) states neptunian views, refuses to accept the notion of catastrophes, and advocates "real causes" and natural causes for change. He juxtaposed a plutonian cosmogony and a neptunian theory of the earth.

In biology, Buffon was most interested in reproduction as the essential property of living matter. He rejected the widely accepted theory of the preexistence and preformation of embryos, accepting epigenesis because it exists in nature and allows heredity to be understood. His thinking was formed by a mechanistic tradition, complicated by Newton's influence, and balanced by a diminishing tendency toward vitalism. In 1749 he saw only disorder in nature. The only notion that corresponded to reality was the idea of species. In *De la dégénération des animaux* (written 1766) he shows himself as a forerunner of Lamarck. His final point of view on the history of living beings affirms unity in the plan of animals' composition and, in variations on that plan, the principle of the subordination of organs. He studied at length the giant fossils discovered in Europe and North America, becoming one of the founders of paleontology. His work is above all a detailed description of quadrupeds, birds, and minerals. He aimed at an "exact history" of each animal which would include reproduction, care, education, instincts, habitats, diet, habits, "wiles," hunting methods, and psychology. His method became more and more comparative. He studied the human species by the same methods, including psychological, moral, and intellectual life.

Buffon's work is of exceptional importance because of its diversity, richness, originality, and influence. Although his cosmogony was inadequate and his theory of animal reproduction weak, and although he did not understand the problem of classification, he did establish the intellectual framework within which most naturalists up to Darwin worked.

BUGAEV, NICOLAY VASILIEVICH (b. Dusheti, near Tiflis [now Tbilisi], Russia, 1837; d. Moscow, Russia, 1903), mathematics.

Studied at Moscow University (graduated 1859; master's, 1863; doctorate, 1866), with Kummer and Weierstrass in Berlin, and with Liouville in Paris. Taught at Moscow University (from 1867); his own pupils included Sonin and Egorov. He promoted development of Russian mathematical terminology and dissemination of mathematical and technological knowledge. Wrote on mathematical analysis, number theory (used elliptic functions to prove Loiuville's formulas), and algebra.

BULLER, ARTHUR HENRY RÉGINALD (b. Birmingham, England, 1874; d. Winnipeg, Canada, 1944), mycology.

Buller took the B.Sc. at the University of London (1896) and the Ph.D. at the University of Leipzig (1899). At the University of Manitoba (1904–36) he founded the department of botany, which became outstanding in Canada. His Researches on Fungi (7 vols., 1909–50), his magnum opus, will long remain a primary reference source on the problems of spore production and liberation, social organization, and epidemiology in general.

An ardent Darwinian, Buller was looking for adaptations in form and function that made certain species successful and certain groups dominant. This and his insistence on dealing only with living materials exerted a profound influence in biology. Volume VII, on sexuality in rust fungi, contained basic contributions in epidemiology, genetics, and plant breeding as well as mycology and plant pathology. His most important single discovery was that, in the Hymenomycetes, a haploid mycelium could be diploidized by a dikaryotic diploid mycelium—designated by Quintanilha (1939) the Buller phenomenon. In his classic "The Diploid Cell and the Diploidisation Process in Plants and Animals" (1941) he redefined the phenomenon. He virtually revolutionized fungal taxonomy and made a science of the epidemiology of fungus spores.

BULLIALDUS, ISMAËL. See **Boulliau, Ismaël.**

BULLOCH, WILLIAM (b. Aberdeen, Scotland, 1868; d. London, England, 1941), bacteriology.

Bulloch took an M.D. at Aberdeen (1894). He took charge of the serum laboratories at the British (later Lister) Institute of Preventive Medicine (1895). He was bacteriologist to the London Hospital (1897–34) and Goldsmith professor of bacteriology at the University of London (1919–34). He published meticulous reports (1892–1910) on such matters as Ehrlich's diphtheria toxin "spectra" and antitoxin assay, Almroth Wright's opsonins and vaccine therapy, and the Wassermann test for syphilis. His painstaking review of hemophilia (1912) and diphtheria (1923) culminated in his scholarly masterpiece, The History of Bacteriology (1938).

BUNGE, GUSTAV VON (b. Dorpat [now Tartu], Estonia, 1844; d. Basel, Switzerland, 1920), physiology.

Bunge took a Ph.D. at Dorpat (1874), taught there (to 1884), took an M.D. at Leipzig (1882), and taught at Basel (from 1885), where his most famous student was Emil Abderhalden. He was a first-rate nutritional scientist, concentrating on mineral salts. His best-known work, Vegetarianismus (1885), was on the role of sodium chloride. The methods he applied to metabolic problems are still widely used.

BUNSEN, ROBERT WILHELM EBERHARD (b. Göttingen, Germany, 1811; d. Heidelberg, Germany, 1899), chemistry.

Bunsen took a Ph.D. at the University of Göttingen (1830). He taught at various German universities (Heidelberg from 1855), later he worked at a laboratory built for him by the government of Baden. He was an expert crystallographer and developed and improved several instruments, including the Bunsen burner (1850's). His most important work was the development of analytical techniques for identification, separation, and measurement of inorganic substances. In his only venture in physiological chemistry he discovered (1834) that hydrated ferric oxide could be used as an antidote for arsenic poisoning (still used today). He set forth the compositions and crystal measurements of a new series of double cyanides (1835–36) and discovered the double salt of ammonium ferrocyanide and ammonium chloride. His methods for the study of gases (1838–46) were included in his only book, Gasometrische Methoden (1857), which brought gas analysis to a new level of accuracy and simplicity. Using electrochemical techniques (from 1852) to isolate pure metals in quantities sufficient for determining their physical and chemical properties, he prepared chromium and magnesium. He therefore opened the door to the commercial use of magnesium as a brilliant light source. He prepared sodium and aluminum from their molten chlorides and isolated lithium and several alkaline earth metals from their fused chlorides. To obtain the specific heats of the rare elements of the cerium group he devised a sensitive ice calorimeter (mid-1850's). The Bunsen battery (1841) made possible the electrolysis of a variety of organic compounds and the isolation of organic radicals by Kolbe and Frankland. The Bunsen burner, with its nonluminous flame, quickly supplanted the blowpipe flame in the dry tests of analytical chemistry.

BUNYAKOVSKY, VIKTOR YAKOVLEVICH (b. Bar, Podolskaya gubernia [now Vinnitsa oblast], Russia, 1804; d. St. Petersburg, Russia, 1889), mathematics, mechanics.

Doctorate in mathematics, Paris (1825); taught in St. Petersburg from 1826 (at University from 1846); did scientific work at the Academy of Sciences. Best known for his monograph on inequalities relating to integrals in finite intervals (1859) in which he first stated the important integral inequality named for him (rediscovered and published by Hermann Schwarz in 1884 and sometimes given his name). He also worked in number theory (gave a new proof for the law of quadratic reciprocity), geometry (attempted a proof of Euclid's fifth postulate), applied mechanics, hydrostatics, and probability.

BUONAMICI, FRANCESCO (*b. Florence, Italy, first half of sixteenth century; d. 1603*), medicine, natural philosophy.

Buonamici, a Florentine physician, taught physics at Pisa while Galileo was a student there, giving credence to the theory that Galileo's *Juvenilia* were based on Buonamici's lectures. Galileo's early writings contain resemblances to *De Motu* (1591), Buonamici's principal work, although Galileo attacked Buonamici's teachings (1612). *De motu* is a complete course in natural philosophy, a masterpiece of Renaissance eclecticism, organized about the causes and types of motion, or change, and the relation of motion to the heavenly bodies. It shows him as an orthodox and traditional Aristotelian.

BUONANNI, FILIPPO (*b. Rome, Italy, 1638; d. Rome, 1725*), natural sciences.

Buonanni, a Jesuit, was curator of the Kircherian Museum (from 1698). He made extensive studies in the natural sciences, and constructed his own microscope with three lenses. He affirmed his belief in the spontaneous generation of mollusks and rekindled the controversy over generation, even though Redi and Malpighi had settled it.

BUONO, PAOLO DEL (*b. Florence, Italy, 1625; d. Poland, 1659*), mechanics, physics.

Del Buono was an eccentric cleric who aroused Leopoldo de' Medici's interest in science. He invented an instrument to demonstrate the incompressibility of water and stated that water enclosed in glass vials with very thin necks generates air in amounts dependent on the temperature of the environment.

BUONVICINO, COSTANZO BENEDETTO. *See* **Bonvicino, Costanzo Benedetto.**

BUOT, JACQUES (*d. ca. 1675*), astronomy, physics, geometry.

Buot, an original member of the Académie des Sciences, calculated the inclination of the ring of Saturn to the equator and to the ecliptic independently and with Huygens (1667). He invented the *équerre azimutale,* an instrument for finding the intersection of the meridian with a horizontal plane.

BURALI-FORTI, CESARE (*b. Arezzo, Italy, 1861; d. Turin, Italy, 1931*), mathematics.

Burali-Forti took a degree at Pisa (1884) and taught at the technical school in Turin (1887–1914) and at the Accademia Militare (1887–1931). He is famous for the antinomy he discovered (1897): To every class of ordinal numbers there corresponds an ordinal number which is greater than any element of the class. An early popularizer of Peano, he contributed a study of the foundations of mathematics to Peano's famous *Formulaire de mathématiques* project (1893) and as editor of the 1919 edition of *Logica mathematica* contributed much original material. His most valuable mathematical contributions were on

the foundations of vector analysis and linear transformations and their various applications, especially in differential geometry (with R. Marcolongo).

BURDACH, KARL FRIEDRICH (*b. Leipzig, Germany, 1776; d. Königsberg, Germany, 1847*), physiology.

Burdach was representative of the *Naturphilosophie* of the German Romantic period of the early nineteenth century. He took a Ph.D. (1798) and an M.D. (1799) at Leipzig and taught at Königsberg (from 1813), where he created and headed the Königliche Anatomische Anstalt (from 1817). He began extensive studies of the brain and of embryology, convinced that nature is a unity and that knowledge of it is obtained only through a combination of observation and analysis. His *Vom Baue und Leben des Gehirns* (3 vols., 1819–26) was one of the best examples of this Romantic approach to physiology. The first volume described the column of fibers in the spinal cord now called the fasciculus cuneatus but originally known as the "column of Burdach." He enlisted many collaborators for *Die Physiologie als Erfahrungswissenschaft* (6 vols., 1826–40), which was for a time widely read. The first three volumes dealt with the history of *Leben an sich:* generation, embryonic life, and independent life. The incomplete second part treated some of the systems involved in the vegetative aspects of life: the blood, the blood circulation, nutrition, secretion. Baer's original work on the formation of the embryo for Volume II was rearranged and split up by Burdach, to conform to his larger system; as a result, Baer published his work separately, as the first part of his *Ueber Entwicklungsgeschichte der Thiere* (1828), the first great work of modern embryology. Burdach's last major work was *Blicke ins Leben* (4 vols., 1842–48).

BURDENKO, NICOLAI NILOVICH (*b. Kamenka [near Penza], Russia, 1876; d. Moscow, U.S.S.R., 1964*), neurology.

Burdenko took two degrees at Yuriev University (Tartu) Medical School (1906, 1909), where he taught (from 1910). He headed the Voronezh Medical Institute surgical clinic (1918–23), taught at Moscow State University Institute (1923), and directed the neurological clinic of the Health Ministry's roentgenology institute (from 1929), now the Burdenko Neurosurgical Institute. He was a pioneer of Soviet experimental neurosurgery and the teacher of the first generation of Soviet neurosurgeons.

BURDON-SANDERSON, JOHN SCOTT (*b. Jesmond, near Newcastle-on-Tyne, England, 1828; d. Oxford, England, 1905*), pathology, physiology.

Burdon-Sanderson studied at Edinburgh (M.D., 1851), served on the staffs of several hospitals (1853–ca. 1870), taught at University College, London (1870–82), and was the first Waynflete professor of physiology at Oxford (1882–95) and Regius professor of medicine there (from 1895). He was important in establishing physiology as an independent discipline in England and urged an experimental approach to pathology as well as physiology. He superintended the Brown Institution, the first laboratory for pathology in England (1871–78). His reputation in pathology was primarily for his pioneer experimental investigations of contagious diseases and the infective processes. He was generally considered a leading exponent in England of the germ theory of disease, but his views were ambiguous. In electrophysiology his most notable work showed a pronounced electrical current on closing of the leaf of the Venus's-flytrap, in experiments for Charles Darwin (1873). He was created a baronet in 1899.

BÜRG, JOHANN TOBIAS (*b. Vienna, Austria, 1766; d. Wiesenau, Austria, 1834*), astronomy.

Bürg studied at Vienna University and taught there (1806–13). His most important work was the recalculation of lunar ephemerides from 1813 to 1820, used in the *Nautical Almanac* of the British Admiralty.

BURGER, HERMAN CAREL (*b. Utrecht, Netherlands, 1893; d. Utrecht, 1965*), physics, medical physics.

Burger took a Ph.D. at the University of Utrecht (1918) and taught there (1922–63). Before World War II his work was on intensity measurements and spectral analysis. He and Moll refined the apparatus for detecting radiation—vacuum thermoelements, the bolometer, and the galvanometer. With Van Cittert he experimented with high-resolution apparatus and studied the influence of the apparatus on the shape of the spectral line. With Ornstein he worked with intensity measurements themselves. His second interest (from 1938) was medical physics, primarily vectorcardiography, pursued with his physician brother, Eduard Burger.

BURGERSDIJK (or **Burgersdicius**), **FRANK** (*b. Lier, near Delft, Netherlands, 1590; d. Leiden, Netherlands, 1635*), natural philosophy.

Burgersdijk took a doctorate at the University of Leiden (1614) and became a leading teacher there (1620–35). His highly successful textbooks made him the dominant figure in the final stage of Dutch Scholasticism, and his authority extended to England and Germany. His textbooks were used long after his ideas had been eclipsed by Cartesianism.

BÜRGI, JOOST (*b. Liechtenstein, 1552; d. Kassel, Germany, 1632*), mathematics, astronomy.

Bürgi was court watchmaker at Kassel (1579–ca. 1603) and at Prague to Emperor Rudolf II and his successors Matthias and Ferdinand II. His proportional compasses competed with Galileo's. He was Kepler's assistant and computer. In his manuscript "Arithmetics" he uses (probably independently of Stevin) the decimal point and sometimes substitutes a small arc for it. The logarithmic system he discovered corresponds to our so-called natural logarithms with the base e (tables computed before 1603; publ. 1620). It had no apparent influence, however.

BURIDAN, JEAN (*b. Béthune, France, ca. 1295; d. Paris, France, ca. 1358*), philosophy, logic, physics.

Buridan, a secular cleric, was the most influential teacher of natural philosophy at the University of Paris in the fourteenth century. His extant writings consist of his lectures in the faculty of arts at Paris. His own textbook of logic, *Summula de dialectica*, was a "modern" revision and amplification of the text of Peter of Spain; his *Consequentiae* and *Sophismata* are among the most interesting works of late medieval logic. All of his other works are

commentaries (mss. only) and *Questions* on the Aristotelian corpus (*Physics, Metaphysics, De anima, Parva naturalia, Nicomachean ethics,* and *Politics*) published, as were the writings in logic, after the invention of the printing press. As a philosopher of science he was historically important in two respects. First, he vindicated natural philosophy as a respectable study in its own right. Second, he defined the objectives and methodology of scientific enterprise as autonomous with respect to dogmatic theology and metaphysics. Both of these achievements were the result of his thoroughgoing nominalist stance; he employed the logical and epistemological doctrines of nominalism in a methodological rather than a metaphysical way in formulating the character and evidential foundations of natural philosophy. His philosophy of science is formulated in his *Questions* on the *Metaphysics.* The Aristotelian definition of science is accepted. The significance of his theory of scientific evidence lies in its rejection of the thesis, held by most of the scholastic Aristotelians, that the principles of physics are established by metaphysics and that they are necessary in the sense that their contradictories are logically or metaphysically impossible. He was thus able to concede the absolute possibility of supernatural interference with the natural causal order, and yet to exclude such supernatural causes as irrelevant to the scientific enterprise. It is within his conception that science has operated since the late seventeenth century. In his *Questions* on the *Physics* and *De caelo et mundo* he accepts the Aristotelian conceptual framework as the working hypothesis of natural philosophy, but entertains alternative assumptions as being not only logically possible but also possibly preferable in accounting for the observed phenomena.

His major significance in the historical development of physics arises from his challenge to Aristotle's dynamic theory of local motion and from his proposal of an alternative dynamics which came to be known as the impetus theory. Accounting for projectile motion, he calls the tendency of the projectile to continue moving in the direction in which it is propelled *impetus,* a permanent power which would continue unchanged if it were not opposed by the gravity of the projectile and the resistance of the air. Buridan's significance in the history of science lies more in the questions he raised than in the answers he gave. He eliminated explanations in terms of final causes from the domain of physics. The mechanistic conception of nature, construed as a methodological assumption more than as a metaphysical thesis, emerged in the fourteenth century as a natural development from his philosophy of science.

BURLEY, WALTER (*b. England, ca. 1275; d. ca. 1345?*), logic, natural philosophy.

Burley took an M.A. degree at Oxford, and studied theology in Paris (?1310–27). He was an envoy of Edward III to the papal court (1327) and intermittently served other English public figures. Most of his writings deal with logic and philosophy, many being commentaries on Aristotle. His magnum opus in logic is *De puritate artis logicae.* In natural philosophy, his final redaction of his comments on the *Physica* (1334–37) contains his most significant contributions (more elaborately treated in other works). Two of his contentions are of more than ephemeral importance in natural philosophy: his view of the proper limits to be assigned temporal processes through the ascription of first or last instants, and his view of the nature of motion. He formulated what was to become a standard distinction between instants within and instants outside a given temporal process or change. In *Tractatus primus* (1320–27) he detailed his theory of intension and remission of forms: to Ockham's theory that motion is only a *forma fluens,* Burley added that it is also a flux *(fluxus formae).* By this he gained the ability to insist that a body at a given time had only one place, one quality of a given type (as hot or cold), and one quantity of a given type. The forms, analogous to points, could not be continuous. The motivation for Burley's conclusions was not simply a willingness to multiply entities beyond necessity, but also his view of forms as empirical, simple, and separate, and his refusal to assume hypothetical connections between them.

BURNET, THOMAS (*b. Croft, Yorkshire, England, ca. 1635; d. London, England, 1715*), cosmogony, geology.

Burnet took a B.A. (1655) and an M.A. (1658) at Cambridge. Ordained in the Anglican Church, he was Master of the Charterhouse (from 1685) and chaplain to William III and clerk of the closet. His *Telluris theoria sacra* (1681) was an attempt to combine the idealism of the Cambridge Platonists (with whom he was associated), Scripture, and an explanation of the features of the earth's surface in order to account for the past and present states of the earth and to offer a prophecy about its future. His *Archaelogiae philosophicae* (1692) aroused such opposition for its allegorical treatment of Scripture that he was forced to resign his position at court. Burnet's books were widely read, and for more than a hundred years any theorizing on the origin of and changes in the surface of the earth had to be reconciled with the account of creation in Genesis. Moreover, the importance of the Deluge as marking the end of "antedeluvian" times, creating mountains, and initiating a period of geological change was taken as given. This last aspect of the theory also helped popularize the idea that the features of the earth's surface were constantly changing.

BURNHAM, SHERBURNE WESLEY (*b. Thetford, Vermont, 1838; d. Chicago, Illinois, 1921*), astronomy.

Burnham was a self-trained amateur astronomer. He was professor of practical astronomy at the Yerkes Observatory (1897–1914). He discovered a host of visual binary systems, many of them new companions.

BURNSIDE, WILLIAM (*b. London, England, 1852; d. West Wickham, England, 1927*), mathematics.

A number of Burnside's results in the theory of groups of finite order have become an integral part of the modern theory of groups and their representations. His *Theory of Groups* (1897) was the first work on the subject in English.

BURRAU, CARL JENSEN (*b. Elsinore, Denmark, 1867; d. Gentofte, Denmark, 1944*), astronomy, actuarial mathematics.

Burrau lectured at Copenhagen University (1906–12). He pioneered in the systematic search for periodic orbits in the three-body problem, pointing out that a series of periodic orbits into which the third (massless) body

moves develops into a limiting orbit of ejection from (or collision with) one of the masses (1892).

BUSCH, AUGUST LUDWIG (*b. Danzig, Prussia, 1804; d. Königsberg, Prussia, 1855*), astronomy.

Busch assisted (from 1831) and succeeded (1846) Friedrich Bessel as director of the astronomical observatory at Königsberg. He took a daguerreotype of the eclipsed sun (1851).

BUSK, GEORGE (*b. St. Petersburg, Russia, 1807; d. London, England, 1886*), medicine, natural history, anthropology.

Busk was surgeon to the Seaman's Hospital Society (1832–54) and Hunterian professor (1856–59) and president of the Royal College of Surgeons (1871). He is credited with important observations on scurvy and with working out the pathology of cholera, for which there is no direct evidence. He described the pathology of fasciolopsiasis, which resembles cholera, describing the fluke now styled *Fasciolopsis buski.* He formulated (1856) the first scientific arrangement of the Bryozoa (Polyzoa); the name *Buskia* was given to one genus (1856). His opinions were much sought on fossil identification, and he provided corroborative evidence for the ideas of Darwin, Lyell, and Richard Owen.

BUTEO, JOHANNES (*b. Charpey, Dauphiné, France, ca. 1492; d. Romans-sur-Isère, Dauphiné, ca. 1564–72*), mathematics.

Buteo's original French name was Jean Borrel. He lived in the Abbaye de St.-Antoine (about 1508), serving as the abbot for two years. His most original work was *Ad problema cubi duplicandi,* in which he refutes Michael Stifel's claim of an exact solution and gives an approximate one. He gave an interesting proof that the author of the proofs of Euclid's *Elements* was Euclid himself, and initiated the famous dispute on the angle of contact by refuting Peletier (1559). His most important work was *Logistica* (1559), on arithmetic and algebra.

IBN BUṬLĀN, ABU'L-ḤASAN AL-MUKHTĀR IBN ᶜABDŪN IBN SAᶜDŪN (*b. Baghdad, ca. beginning eleventh century; d. Antioch, 460/1068*), medicine.

Ibn Buṭlān was a Christian physician who practiced in Baghdad and elsewhere (from 440/1049), then retired to a monastery in Antioch. In his cunning and tough attacks, on Ibn Riḍwān particularly, he displays wide scientific and philosophic knowledge, grappling with questions of physics, geometry, and Aristotelian definitions in his discussions of medical problems. He was part of the movement of science away from traditional translations toward clinical experimentation and observation by which to verify, extend, and correct the heritage of the Ancients.

BUTLEROV, ALEKSANDR MIKHAILOVICH (*b. Chistopol, Kazanskaya [now Tatarskaya, A.S.S.R.], Russia, 1828; d. Butlerovka, Kazanskaya, Russia, 1886*), chemistry.

Butlerov studied under N. N. Zinin at Kazan University (1844–49), taught there (1852–68), and was twice rector (1860–63). He took a doctorate at Moscow University (1854) and taught at St. Petersburg University (1868–85).

Theory in chemistry in the 1850's did not correspond to the sum of empirical data. Most chemists adhered to the Gerhardtian theory of polyatomic radicals, but several turned in despair to empirical formulas. At this juncture Butlerov created and gave impetus to the initial development of the classic theory of chemical structure. In 1861 he read his paper on the chemical structure of substances to the Congress of German Naturalists and Physicians in Speyer. In it, he defined "chemical structure" as the "chemical bond or capacity for the mutual union of atoms into a complex substance." He also advanced the basic proposition that "the chemical nature of a compound molecule is determined by the nature of its component parts, by their quantity, and by their chemical structure." The proposition broke with the traditional view that the properties of molecules are determined principally by the space grouping, relative position, and distances between their atoms but retained all the other propositions of the classical theory. He formulated rules for determining the chemical structure of molecules, giving primacy to those synthetic reactions in which the radicals retain their chemical structure. He wrongly defined isomers as compounds of the same elementary composition but different chemical structure and never wholly accepted stereochemistry. His explanation of the relationships of the properties and chemical structure of organic compounds by the existence of "the mutual influence of atoms," which gives different "chemical values," has in this century been given an electron interpretation.

Butlerov predicted and proved positional and skeletal isomerism (1864, 1866) and in investigations of unsaturated compounds supported the hypothesis that they contain multiple bonds (1870). His textbook on organic chemistry in Russian (1864–66) and German (1867–68) helped popularize the structural theory. He created the first Russian school of chemists, which included V. V. Markovnikov, A. M. Zaytsev, A. P. Popov at Kazan and A. E. Favorski and I. L. Kondakov at St. Petersburg.

BÜTSCHLI, OTTO (*b. Frankfurt am Main, Germany, 1848; d. Heidelberg, Germany, 1920*), zoology, mineralogy.

Bütschli was assistant to the paleontologist Karl von Zittel (1865–66), took a doctorate in mineralogy at Heidelberg (1868), and taught zoology and paleontology there (1878–1918). He pioneered in cytology and cell theory. He was the first to identify and order sequentially the stages of nuclear division in several types of animal cells, demonstrated that the polar bodies of eggs arise through atypical cell division, and was the first to describe the fertilization cone and to prove that normally only one sperm enters the egg. His deepest interest was in the cytoplasm as a physical-chemical system. He felt that life processes and the nature of protoplasm could be studied in unicellular organisms better than in Metazoa, and his *Protozoa* (3 vols., 1880–89) was a critical review of the whole field that included much original work.

His work on the structural problems of protoplasm led to his "alveolar theory" of protoplasm as a two-phase system similar to an emulsion (1889), summarized in *Untersuchungen über microskopische Schäume und die Struktur des Protoplasmas* (1892). This, with his *Untersuchungen über Strukturen* (1898), which included 300 pioneering photomicrographs, was a starting point for the subsequent development of colloid chemistry.

BUYS BALLOT, CHRISTOPH HENDRIK DIEDERIK (*b. Kloetinge, Netherlands, 1817; d. Utrecht, Netherlands, 1890*), meteorology, physical chemistry.

Buys Ballot took a doctorate at Utrecht (1844) and taught there (1845–88). He is best known for the law (1857) named for him (anticipated by William Ferrel): "When you place yourself in the direction of the wind, . . . you will have at your left the least atmospheric pressure." But his chief accomplishment was to help shape the new field of meteorology by emphasizing and himself collecting data from the widest possible network of simultaneous observations.

CABANIS, PIERRE-JEAN-GEORGES (*b. Cosnac, Corrèze, France, 1757; d. Rueil, near Paris, France, 1808*), philosophy, medicine, history and sociology of medicine.

Became doctor of medicine at Rheims (1784). Close friend of Condorcet. Taught hygiene at the Écoles Centrales (from 1794), was assistant to Corvisart, and taught history of medicine in the Écoles de Santé in Paris. His fundamental philosophical work, *Rapports du physique et du moral de l'homme* (1802), sets forth a psychology and an ethical system based on the necessary effects of an animal's organization on its relations with its environment. His principal work in medicine, *Coup d'oeil sur les révolutions et sur la réforme de la médecine* (1804), advocates methodically gathered tables of observations and experiments as the basis for reforms in treatment and medical instruction. In his *Observations sur les hôpitaux* (1790) he recognized that the hospital was the place where the reform of medicine must occur. His *Du degré de certitude de la médecine* (1798) is a defense of medical empiricism enriched by a history of medical practice.

CABEO, NICCOLO (*b. Ferrara, Italy, 1586; d. Genoa, Italy, 1650*), meteorology, magnetism, mathematics.

A Jesuit, Cabeo taught in Parma and in Genoa, where he met G. B. Baliani. Interpreted Baliani's experiments with falling weights as two different weights falling in the same length of time, a result reported by Vincenzo Renieri to Galileo in 1641. Published *Philosophia magnetica* (1629) and *In quatuor libros meteorologicorum Aristotelis commentaria* (1646).

CABRERA, BLAS (*b. Lanzarote, Canary Islands, Spain, 1878; d. Mexico City, Mexico, 1945*), physics.

Received Ph.D. (1901) at University of Madrid. He taught there (to 1910), directed Spanish Physical Research Institute (from 1910), worked with Pierre Weiss (1910–12), directed the National Institute of Physics and Chemistry (from 1932). Published over 150 papers. Contributed to establishment of Hund and Van Vleck's molecular field, established the variation of the atomic moment versus atomic number, modified the Curie-Weiss law for rare earths, and derived an equation for the atomic magnetic moment including temperature effect. Some of his magnetic susceptibility measurements have not been improved upon. In 1936 established laboratory for magnetic research in Paris. Taught at University of Mexico (1941–45).

CADET (or **Cadet de Gassicourt** or **Cadet-Gassicourt**), **LOUIS-CLAUDE** (*b. Paris, France, 1731; d. Paris, 1799*), chemistry.

Studied at the Collège des Quatre-Nations, worked with the Geoffroys, was *apothicaire-major* at the Hôtel Royal des Invalides (1753–59), and established his own highly reputed apothecary shop (1759). Earliest research was on analysis of mineral water, carried on initially with his teacher, Rouelle. Collaborated with Berthollet and Lavoisier at the Paris mint and served as royal commissioner at the Sèvres porcelain works. He discovered (1757) a "fuming liquor" later used by Bunsen in his isolation of the cacodyl radical. Improved methods for producing potassium acetate and ether. With Macquer and Lavoisier, tested the effect of heat on diamonds (1772).

CADET DE GASSICOURT (or **Cadet**), **CHARLES-LOUIS** (*b. Paris, France, 1769; d. Paris, 1821*), chemistry, public health.

Studied at the Collège Mazarin. Influenced later by lectures of Fourcroy, he abandoned law practice for pharmacy, becoming an enthusiastic partisan of the New Chemistry.

Helped found the influential *Bulletin de pharmacie* (1809), served as pharmacist to Napoleon and helped diffuse and popularize the New Chemistry, particularly in his *Dictionnaire de chimie* (4 vols., 1803). Responsible for establishment of influential health council in Paris (1802).

CADET DE VAUX (or **Cadet-Devaux** or **Cadet le jeune**), **ANTOINE-ALEXIS-FRANÇOIS** (*b. Paris, France, 1743; d. Nogent-les-Vierges, France, 1828*), chemistry, agriculture, nutrition, public health.

Succeeded his brother, Louis-Claude as *apothicaire-major* at the Hôtel Royal des Invalides (1759–66) and had his own pharmacy (1769–81). Co-founded first daily newspaper in Paris, *Le journal de Paris* (1777). His manifold projects included agriculture, nutrition, public health (particularly in prisons and industry), and the École de Boulangerie, which he founded (1780) with his close friend and collaborator, Parmentier. There they both lectured on chemistry and technology. He recommended to the government safe methods for large-scale disinterments (1783) and for cleaning out cesspools (1788), including the use of quicklime, a ventilator, and furnaces for both these hazardous operations. With Fourcroy he issued (1789) an enthusiastic report on Lavoisier's *Traité élémentaire de chimie.*

CAGNIARD DE LA TOUR, CHARLES (*b. Paris, France, 1777; d. Paris, 1859*), physics.

Studied at the École Polytechnique and the École du Génie Géographe. He was *auditeur* to the Council of State and director of special projects for Paris, notably the Crouzoles aqueduct. His wide interests in mechanics and physics led to several original results. The principle of the heat engine he proposed (1809) used his "cagniardelle" (a form of Archimedean screw). He discovered the existence of a critical state in the vaporization of liquids (1822). Invented an acoustical siren (1819) which both demonstrated the nature of sound and determined the frequency of vibration of any sonorous body. Helmholtz perfected the device. His most valuable work, on alcoholic fermentation, led him to the conviction that brewer's yeast contained a

living substance which releases carbon dioxide (1836). Schwann came to the same conclusion, but Liebig's violent opposition postponed exploration until Pasteur's 1857 work.

CAHOURS, AUGUSTE ANDRÉ THOMAS (*b. Paris, France, 1813; d. Paris, 1891*), chemistry.

Graduated from the École Polytechnique (1835), took a doctorate at the Faculty of Sciences (1845). Taught chemistry at the École Polytechnique, the École Centrale, and the Sorbonne. Did important research on derivatives of potato oil, and on abnormal vapor densities. He discovered toluene (1834), anisic acid, anisole, and polysulfides of alcohol, and achieved the etherification of the phenols. He paved the way for Gerhardt's discovery of the acid anhydrides.

CAILLETET, LOUIS PAUL (*b. Châtillon-sur-Seine, Côte-d'Or, France, 1832; d. Paris, France, 1913*), physics, technology.

Studied at the École des Mines, then managed the forges and rolling mills of his father's business, analyzing gases from the blast furnaces. Most famous for his liquefaction of the six gases that were considered permanent: oxygen, nitrogen, hydrogen, nitrogen dioxide, carbon monoxide, and acetylene (1877–78).

CAIUS (pronounced and sometimes written **Keys**), **JOHN** (*b. Norwich, England, 1510; d. London, England, 1573*), medicine.

Caius took a B.A. (1533) and an M.A. (1535) at Gonville Hall, Cambridge, and an M.D. at the University of Padua (1541), under Vesalius. Published a number of emendated Greek texts and Latin translations of Galenic and Hippocratic writings. Member of the College of Physicians of London and its president for nine terms (1555–73); successfully raised the level of medical education in England. Anatomical demonstrator to the Company of Barber-Surgeons (1546–63), practiced medicine in London, and was physician to Edward VI, Mary, and Elizabeth. His *Boke or counseill against the disease called the sweate* (1552) is a minor classic and the first original description of the disease (possibly influenza) to be written in English. He was empowered (1557) to refound his old college at Cambridge as Gonville and Caius College and became master there (1559–73).

CALANDRELLI, GIUSEPPE (*b. Zagarolo, near Rome, Italy, 1749; d. Rome, 1827*), astronomy.

Calandrelli taught mathematics at the Gregorian University of the Jesuit-run Collegio Romano in Rome, and codirected its observatory with A. Conti and G. Ricchebach, and with them published the series, Opuscoli Astronomica (1803–24).

CALANDRELLI, IGNAZIO (*b. Rome, Italy, 1792; d. Rome, 1866*), astronomy, mathematics.

Taught astronomy and directed observatory at University of Bologna, Pontifical University, and Observatory of the Campidoglio in Rome. Scientific work confined almost exclusively to positional astronomy.

CALCIDIUS (*fourth, possibly fifth century* A.D.), Platonist commentary.

Calcidius' Latin translation of the first two-thirds of Plato's *Timaeus* was the only extensive text of Plato known to western Europe for 800 years and thus transmitted classical cosmology to the Latin West. His commentary, six times as long as his translation, is eclectic and conflates Platonic, Aristotelian, and Christian concepts.

CALDANI, LEOPOLDO MARCANTONIO (*b. Bologna, Italy, 1725; d. Padua, Italy, 1813*), anatomy, physiology.

Caldani took the Ph.D. and M.D. at Bologna (1750) and taught there (to 1760) and at Padua (from 1764) where he succeeded Morgagni in the chair of anatomy (1773–1805). His early and continued advocacy of Haller's doctrine of differential sensibility and irritability of animal tissues and organs overcame the initial powerful resistance in Italy. His *Institutiones physiologiae* (1773), written in the style of Haller, was used by several universities as a text book.

CALDAS, FRANCISCO JOSÉ DE (*b. Popayán, New Granada* [*now Colombia*], *1768; d. Santa Fe* [*now Bogotá*], *New Granada, 1816*), botany, astronomy, geography.

Taught himself mathematics and astronomy. Received rest of education during travels with Humboldt and Bonpland. Director of first astronomical observatory in South America (from 1805, in Bogotá). Discovered method for measuring altitude by the boiling point of pure water; discovered many species and varieties of cinchona; and collaborated with Humboldt on study of distribution of plants according to altitude.

CALKINS, GARY NATHAN (*b. Valparaiso, Ind., 1869; d. Scarsdale, N.Y., 1943*), zoology.

Received B.A. in biology at the Massachusetts Institute of Technology (1890) and a Ph.D. at Columbia (1897); taught at Columbia (1894–1939). Worked at the Marine Biological Laboratory at Woods Hole for many years, held office in the American Statistical Association, and worked in cancer research. He is best known for *The Protozoa* (1901) and *The Biology of the Protozoa* (1926).

CALLAN, NICHOLAS (*b. near Dundalk, Ireland, 1799; d. Maynooth, Ireland, 1864*), electromagnetics.

Ordained a priest (1823) at St. Patrick's College, Maynooth, and taught natural philosophy there (from 1826). Financed his research by private means. A pioneer in the development of electromagnetism as a source of power, he built large batteries and electromagnets. Invented the induction coil (1836), for which Ruhmkorff has been credited; discovered the principle of the self-induced dynamo (1838), usually credited to Werner Siemens.

CALLANDREAU, PIERRE JEAN OCTAVE (*b. Angoulême, France, 1852; d. Paris, France 1904*), astronomy.

Graduated from the École Polytechnique (1874). Influenced by lectures of Puiseux at the Sorbonne to work on perfecting theories of celestial mechanics. Strongly influenced by Tisserand and Gyldén, further developing the work of both in mathematical astronomy. Initiated first systematic observation of shooting stars in France.

CALLENDAR, HUGH LONGBOURNE (*b. Hatherop, Gloucestershire, England, 1863; d. Ealing, England, 1930*), physics, engineering.

Graduated from Trinity College, Cambridge in classics (1884) and mathematics (1885). Taught physics in England and Canada, ultimately at the Royal College of Science (1902–30). An experimental scientist, particularly in heat thermodynamics. Introduced an improved platinum resistance thermometer which was adopted as the basis for a standard scale of temperature (1899). His method of continuous electrical calorimetry allowed the specific heats of liquids to be measured.

His study of the thermodynamic properties of gases and vapors led to his equation for an imperfect gas and to formulation of his steam equation. The *Callendar Steam Tables* (1915 ff.) give properties of steam up to and beyond the critical pressure.

CALLINICOS OF HELIOPOLIS (*fl. ca.* A.D. *673*), chemistry.

Credited with having invented or perfected "Greek fire." This liquid was propelled from flame projectors of Greek ships. The actual ingredients probably consisted of sulfur, pitch, petroleum, and some unknown substances added to known incendiary materials.

CALLIPPUS (*b. Cyzicus, Turkey, ca. 370* B.C.), mathematics, astronomy.

A great Greek astronomer of the line of Eudoxus and associated with the Academy and the Lyceum, Callippus corrected and completed Eudoxus' work on the motion of the planets, made accurate determinations of the lengths of the seasons, and constructed a seventy-six-year cycle to harmonize the solar and lunar years. This "Callippic period" was used by all later astronomers to record and date observations.

CALMETTE, ALBERT (*b. Nice, France, 1863; d. Paris, France, 1933*), bacteriology.

Studied microbiology under Roux at the Pasteur Institute in Paris (1889); directed the new Pasteur Institute in Lille (1895–1919); and was assistant director of the Pasteur Institute in Paris (1917–33), where he founded the tuberculosis department. One of first to prepare antivenin serums. He prepared tuberculosis vaccine BCG (Bacillus Calmette-Guérin) with Camille Guérin while at Lille.

CAMERARIUS (Camerer), RUDOLPH JAKOB (*b. Tübingen, Germany, 1665; d. Tübingen, 1721*), medicine, botany.

Studied (bachelor's degree, 1679; master's, 1682; doctorate, 1687) and taught (from 1688) at Tübingen. Most important scientific achievement was experimental demonstration of the sexuality of plants, published as *Epistola . . . de sexu plantarum* (1694): he concluded that anthers are the male organs of the plant, and ovary, with style and stigma, the female organs; he considered dioecious plants hermaphroditic. His experiments were confirmed by Johann Gottlieb Gleditsch in 1749, but doubts persisted until the work of K. F. von Gaertner (1844, 1849). In *De convenientia plantarum in fructificatione et viribus* (1699) Camerarius established similar healing properties, and hence similar composition, of plants with similar flower structures (confirmed by modern chemotaxonomical methods).

CAMPANELLA, TOMMASO (*b. Stilo, Calabria, Italy, 1568; d. Paris, France, 1639*), natural philosophy.

Entered Dominican order (1582). Influenced by Telesio's *De rerum natura* and by Giambattista della Porta; denounced to Inquisition for heresy (1592), imprisoned for long periods in Naples and Rome. Fled to Aix-en-Provence (1634) and then moved to Paris (1635) where Richelieu befriended him. Voluminous writings on wide range of subjects were strongly anti-Aristotelian. Best known for *Civitas solis*, on political philosophy, but also wrote on most other branches of philosophy. His natural philosophy, derived partly from Telesio, included heat and cold as the active forces of the universe, the concept of the void, and man as composed of the triad body-*spiritus*-soul. His world view allowed a key position to astrology and pseudoscience. In *Apologia pro Galilaeo* (1622) he supported Galileo's defense of the Copernican system, and the distinction of science from theology. Attempted to provide a new system of natural knowledge based on the empirical, Neoplatonic, and astrological traditions at his disposal.

CAMPANI, GIUSEPPE (*b. Castel San Felice, near Spoleto, Italy, 1635; d. Rome, Italy, 1715*), astronomy, microscopy, horology.

Educated in Rome. Active in production of lenses and optical instruments for more than fifty years. Among his inventions are a silent night clock, the composite lens eyepiece, a telescope with four lenses, a lens-grinding machine lathe, and a screw-barrel type of microscope.

CAMPANUS OF NOVARA (*b. [probably] Novara, Italy, first quarter of thirteenth century; d. Viterbo, Italy, 1296*), mathematics, astronomy.

The scant biographical data suggest a life spent tranquilly cultivating the mathematical sciences under the patronage of four popes, assisted by the income from a plurality of benefices. Best known for his Latin edition of Euclid's *Elements* (1255–59). Neither a translation nor a commentary, it was a free reworking of earlier translations, a textbook of elementary geometry and arithmetic readily comprehensible in form and language. Most of his other writings are on astronomy. The most influential, the *Theorica planetarum* (1261–64), describes the structure and dimensions of the universe according to the Ptolemaic theory, and gives instructions for the construction of the instrument later called an equatorium, the major influence toward the subsequent development of much more sophisticated equatoria. His *Computus maior* (1268), on the computation of Easter by various methods, including the use of tables, is one of the most successful examples of the genre. In later times he had a considerable reputation as an astrologer.

CAMPBELL, DOUGLAS HOUGHTON (*b. Detroit, Mich., 1859; d. Palo Alto, Calif., 1953*), botany.

Received M.A. (1882) and Ph.D. (1886) at the University of Michigan, Ann Arbor; taught at Indiana University (1888–91) and held the chair of botany (1891–1925) at Stanford University.

Wrote two important textbooks: *The Structure and Development of Mosses and Ferns* (1895), and *Lectures on the Evolution of Plants* (1899). Did extensive research on the Cryptogamia, especially Anthocerotaceae. Most important contribution was to link the ferns with the liverworts by way of *Anthoceros*. His important discoveries on *Anthoceros* led him to support the antithetic theory of the origin of the sporophyte generation. Especially remembered for his suggestion of the anthocerotean origin of the eusporangiate pteridophytes and his associated belief in the primitive character of the Eusporangiatae.

CAMPBELL, NORMAN ROBERT (*b. Colgrain, Dumbarton, Scotland, 1880; d. Nottingham, England, 1949*), physics, philosophy of science.

Educated at Eton and Trinity College, Cambridge. As a fellow of the college (1904), he established, with A. Wood, the radioactivity of potassium. He was Cavendish research fellow at Leeds (to 1913), on the staff of the National Physical Laboratories during the war, and at the General Electric Company, Ltd. (1919–34). Although he distinguished himself as an experimental physicist, largely in electricity, it is as a philosopher of science that he is best known. He was profoundly influenced by J. J. Thomson and by the ideas of Faraday and Maxwell, and took a mechanical view of physics. He considered at length the nature of physical measurement and its relation to purer mathematics. His continuing examination of the radical changes in physics taking place in his working lifetime can be seen in progressive editions of his *Modern Electrical Theory* (1907, 1913, 1923). His most notable thesis for the theory of science was the distinction between laws and theories as pivotal in understanding the nature and status of scientific proposition. With the basis of his account of the nature of scientific laws, he elaborated his major thesis of the structure of theories and their distinction from laws.

CAMPBELL, WILLIAM WALLACE (*b. Hancock County, Ohio, 1862; d. San Francisco, Calif., 1938*), astronomy, education.

Received B.S. at University of Michigan (1886); taught at Colorado (1886–88) and Michigan (1888–1901); joined Lick Observatory of University of California as staff astronomer (1891–1901) and director (1900–30). Served as president of the university (1923–30) and as president of the National Academy of Sciences (1931–35). Strong and successful exponent of use of scientific advice by government. In his major field, spectroscopic observation, he designed the classic Mills spectrograph (1893). Participated in seven eclipse expeditions. Published a handbook of practical astronomy. From observations, concluded (1894) that the atmosphere of Mars was deficient in oxygen and water vapor and unable to support life. Established a southern station of the Lick Observatory in Chile (1910), where he continued the program for which he is probably best known today: systematic radial velocity observation for the determination of the sun's path among the stars (begun 1896).

CAMPER, PETER (PETRUS) (*b. Leiden, Netherlands, 1722; d. The Hague, Netherlands, 1789*), anatomy, surgery, obstetrics, anthropology, ophthalmology.

Took degrees in science and in medicine from Leiden University (1746). Taught philosophy, medicine, and surgery at Franeker University, in Friesland (1749–55); anatomy, surgery and medicine at the Athenaeum Illustre in Amsterdam (1755–61); and theoretical medicine, anatomy, surgery, and botany at Groningen University (1763–73). In his lifetime he was one of the most famous scientists of western Europe. He practiced medicine and midwifery. In anatomy he described structures that are still associated with him: the *processus vaginalis (peritonei* and *testis),* Camper's fascia, and Camper's *chiasma tendinum digitorum manus.* Goethe sent his treatise on the *os inter maxillare* to Camper, whose measurements of the facial angle and the introduction of Camper's line contributed to the foundation of anthropology.

CAMUS, CHARLES-ÉTIENNE-LOUIS (*b. Crécy-en-Brie, France, 1699; d. Paris, France, 1768*), mathematics, mechanics, astronomy.

Studied at the Collège de Navarre. Served the Academy of Sciences as administrator, commissioner, and active scientist for forty years. Published memoirs on mathematics and mechanics. Secretary to the Academy of Architecture (after 1730), examiner of engineering students of the École du Génie at Mézières (from 1748) and examiner of artillery students (from 1755). These roles resulted in his *Cours de mathématiques.* Much of his most important work was with Maupertuis, Clairaut, and Lemonnier on the Academy's expedition to Lapland to determine the shape of the earth (1736).

CANANO, GIOVAN BATTISTA (*b. Ferrara, Italy, 1515; d. Ferrara, 1579*), anatomy.

Graduated in the arts and medicine at Ferrara (1543) and taught there (1544–52). Physician to Pope Julius III (1552–55) and chief physician of the Este principality (from 1555). His *Musculorum humani corporis picturata dissectio* (1541 or 1543) is outstandingly original, based exclusively on direct observation of the structures of the human body and of living animals. It constitutes the first use of copperplates, the first anatomical drawings of lumbricales and of the interossei of the hand, and the first description and drawing of the short palmar muscle and the oblique head of the adductor pollicis. Canano's discovery of the valves of the deep veins and the assertion that they prevent the reflux of the blood, although ignored until Fabrizio credited himself with the discovery, finally opened the way to greater knowledge of blood circulation.

CANCRIN (CANCRINUS), FRANZ LUDWIG VON (*b. Breitenbach, Hesse, Germany, 1738; d. St. Petersburg, Russia, 1812 or 1816*), mining, metallurgy.

Educated by his father and at the University of Jena (1759–62). Held a number of civil offices, including director of the mint (1774). His encyclopedic work, *Erste Gründe der Berg- und Salzwerkskunde* (21 vols., 1773–91), on the mining of metals and salt—including mineralogy, assaying, mathematics, and mechanics—brought him a European reputation. Served the Russian Empress Catherine II (from 1783), managing the Staraya Russa saltworks.

CANDOLLE, ALPHONSE DE (*b. Paris, France, 1806; d. Geneva, Switzerland, 1893*), botany, phytogeography.

Took a B.S. (1825) and a doctorate in law (1829) at Geneva, where he succeeded his father, Augustin-Pyramus de Candolle, in the chair of botany and the

directorship of the botanical gardens (1835–50). He made no important discoveries but wrote classic articles and books, particularly *Géographie botanique raisonnée* (1855), still the key work of phytogeography, which ushered in new methods of investigation and analyzed the causes of distribution of plant life.

CANDOLLE, AUGUSTIN-PYRAMUS DE (*b. Republic of Geneva, 1778; d. Geneva, 1841*), botany, agronomy.

Studied medicine at the Academy of Geneva and natural sciences in Paris. Strongly influenced by Vaucher, Sénebier, and Saussure. Held the chair of botany at the École de Médicine and the Faculté des Sciences in Montpellier (1808–16), and the chair in natural history (1816–35) at Geneva, where he completely reorganized the botanical gardens, helped create a museum of natural history, and founded the Conservatoire Botanique. Became a distinguished taxonomist and accomplished botanist. More than 300 plants, one family (Candolleaceae), and two genera *(Candollea* and *Candollina)* named for him. Published nearly 180 memoirs and other works. His most significant work, the *Prodromus systematis naturalis regni vegetabilis* (1824–39), is a huge botanical treatise on all aspects of science, containing allusions to the problems of evolution as well as forward-looking discussions of ecology, phytogeography, biometry, and agronomy. His most original contribution was as a forerunner in phytogeography. A worthy pupil of Lamarck, he accurately describes the relationships between plants and soil, which affect the distribution of vegetation. Father of Alphonse de Candolle (1806–93).

CANNIZZARO, STANISLAO (*b. Palermo, Sicily, 1826; d. Rome, Italy, 1910*), chemistry.

Studied medicine at the University of Palermo (1841–45) and chemistry at Pisa (1845–47). Taught chemistry at the Collegio Nazionale in Alessandria (1851–55), and the University of Genoa (1855–61), and returned to Palermo (1861–71), which he soon turned into the center of chemical education in Italy. At the University of Rome (1871–1909), he founded the Italian Institute of Chemistry to establish a functioning laboratory. Experimental work was in organic chemistry. Discovered (1853) the reaction of benzaldehyde with potassium hydroxide ("Cannizzaro reaction"). Lasting fame stems from his letter of 1858, "Sunto di un corso di filosofia chimica fatto nella Reale Università di Genova," later presented at the first international chemical congress (1860). At that time, there was no agreement on values for atomic, molecular, or equivalent weights; no possibility of systematizing the relationship of the elements; and no unanimity on the formulas for organic compounds. Cannizzaro restated Avogadro's hypothesis, supplied new evidence for it, and clearly distinguished between atoms and molecules. He chose hydrogen as the standard of atomic weight, unity being "half a molecule of hydrogen." It was the recognition of true atomic weights that permitted Lothar Meyer and Mendeleev to formulate the periodic law at the end of the 1860's. Cannizzaro's logic also opened the way for full development of the structural theory by Butlerov and others.

CANNON, ANNIE JUMP (*b. Dover, Delaware, 1863; d. Cambridge, Mass., 1941*), astronomy.

Cannon, the daughter of a Delaware state senator, took a degree at Wellesley College (1884), did graduate study there in mathematics, physics, and astronomy, and worked at the Harvard College Observatory (1896–1941), becoming curator of astronomical photographs (from 1911) and William Cranch Bond Astronomer (from 1938). Her greatest contributions were in stellar spectral classification. On photographic plates she discovered more than 300 variable stars and developed the definitive Harvard system of spectral classification. She proved that only a small number of spectral types exist and demonstrated that these could be arranged in a continuous series. The *Henry Draper Catalogue* (to 1924) classified virtually all stars brighter than ninth or tenth magnitude—a colossal enterprise embracing 225,300 stars; her *Henry Draper Extension* (1925–1936), about 47,000 more; her *Yale Zone Catalogue* and *Cape Zone Catalogue*, several thousand more; the *Annals* (1949), another 86,000.

CANNON, WALTER BRADFORD (*b. Prairie du Chien, Wis., 1871; d. Franklin, N.H., 1945*), physiology.

Graduated Harvard (1896; M.A., 1897). At Harvard Medical School (M.D., 1900) under Henry Bowditch, developed method of feeding gelatin capsules filled with bismuth subnitrate to animals to observe movements of alimentary tract by fluoroscopy (first public demonstration, 1896; summarized in *The Mechanical Factors of Digestion*, 1911). Adapted the case system of law study to medical education (1900). Taught at Harvard Medical School (1900–42). Observation of the effect of strong emotions on gastrointestinal motility led to examination of the sympathetic nervous system and its emergency function (*Bodily Changes in Pain, Hunger, Fear and Rage*, 1915). During World War I, served on American and British shock committees (*Traumatic Shock*, 1923). Returned to investigations on sympathetic nervous system and developed the denervated heart as an indicator of sympathetic activity. His extraordinary dexterity and surgical skill enabled him to remove the entire sympathetic nervous system, and the ensuing studies showed that the function of the autonomic nervous system is the maintenance of a uniform condition in the body fluids; this concept of self-regulation of physiological processes, or "homeostasis," was popularized in *Wisdom of the Body* (1932). Later work was on chemical transmission of nerve impulses: with Arturo Rosenblueth, hypothesized (in *Autonomic Neuro-Effector Systems*, 1937) existence of two sympathins, one excitatory and the other inhibitory (now known to be epinephrine and norepinephrine). From 1908, was in forefront of the struggle against antivivisection. His belief in the brotherhood of man and the universality of science involved him in formation of several national and international medical bodies.

CANTON, JOHN (*b. Stroud, England, 1718; d. London, England, 1772*), physics.

Earned living as a schoolmaster. One of the most distinguished self-made men who best represented English physics. Invented new method of making strong artificial magnets (*ca.* 1747); first in England to repeat successfully the French experiments confirming conjectures on lightning, and discovered independently that clouds came electrified both positively and negatively. Apparently to determine the sign of a cloud's charge, he designed experiments on electrostatic induction. Discovered that glass does not always charge positively by friction. Invented a strongly phosphorescent compound, "Canton's phosphor"—sulfur and calcined oyster shells (CaS)—and demonstrated the compressibility of water.

CANTOR, GEORG (*b. St. Petersburg, Russia, 1845; d. Halle, Germany, 1918*), mathematics, set theory.

Took a doctoral degree at the University of Berlin (1867) under Karl Weierstrass who influenced his early research on series and real numbers. He taught at the University of Halle (1869–1918). All his hopes of a better-endowed professorship in Berlin were blocked by Kronecker, who completely disagreed with his views on "transfinite numbers." He was president (1864–65) of the Berlin Mathematical Society; established and was the first president of the Association of German mathematicians (1890–93); and was responsible for the first international congress of mathematicians in Zurich (1897). From 1884 he suffered sporadically from deep depression and was often in a sanatorium. He died in Halle University's psychiatric clinic.

Cantor, the founder of set theory, made equally important contributions in classical analysis. In his treatise on trigonometric series (1872) he introduced real numbers defined in modern terms as an equivalence class of fundamental sequences. He further showed that any positive real number can be represented through a series, known today as Cantor series.

Knowing that it was possible to "count" the set of rational numbers, i. e., to put them into a one-to-one correspondence with the set of natural numbers, he succeeded in proving that the "aggregate" of real numbers was uncountable (letter to Dedekind, 1873); thus set theory was born. The significance of the proof shortly became clear; he succeeded in proving that the set of real algebraic numbers is countable—a new proof of Liouville's theorem. His first publication on set theory, "Über eine Eigenschaft des Inbegriffes aller reellen algebraischen Zahlen" (1874), included not only the theorem on algebraic numbers, but also the one on real numbers. He then generalized the problem: can the set of points of a square be mapped in a one-to-one correspondence onto the points of a line segment, and proved the affirmative (letter to Dedekind, 1877). His mapping seemed to have rendered the concept of dimension meaningless. But Dedekind recognized immediately that the map was discontinuous, suspecting that a continuous one-to-one correspondence between sets of points of different dimensions was not possible. Cantor attempted to prove this, but his deduction did not stand up. Brouwer (1910) furnished a complete proof. Cantor's next works dealt with the theory of point sets, and many of the now generally standard basic concepts in topology can be traced to him; for example, the "derivation of a point set," the idea of "closure," and the concepts "dense" and "dense in itself." He gave a remarkable example of a perfect discontinuous set (a "Cantor set"). He provided the first mathematically useful definition of the term "continuum," as a continuous perfect set (today usually altered to a compact continuous set). In his first published article on set theory he showed that, with the aid of the one-to-one correspondence, it becomes possible to distinguish differences in the infinite: There are *countable* sets and there are sets having the power of a *continuum*. Of root importance was his realization that for every set there is a set of higher power. He substantiated this through his subset theorem that for each set there is a set of a higher power: the set of subsets or the power set *P(M)*. The question of a general "set theory" thus became acute. He introduced "transfinite" numbers (cardinal numbers, ordinal numbers) and developed an arithmetic for them. With these numbers, explained in terms of transfinite sets, he opened up a new realm for mathematics. His attempts (1884, 1895, 1899) at the definition of the basic concept "a power or cardinal number" and of "ordinal number" have been much modified by John von Neumann and others. But he proved the most important theorems of the new theory himself and laid the groundwork for present-day definitions.

By his bold advance into the realm of the infinite, Cantor ignited twentieth-century research on the fundamentals. But Cantor himself was not an axiomaticist; he acknowledged (1883) his adherence to "the Platonic system." He was convinced that the actually infinite really existed "both concretely and abstractly." He believed the atoms of the "universal ether" to be an example of a set having the power of a continuum. His views in physics and philosophy appear quaint and antiquated unlike his pure mathematics.

CANTOR, MORITZ BENEDIKT (*b. Mannheim, Germany, 1829; d. Heidelberg, Germany, 1920*), mathematics.

Studied at Göttingen and Berlin. Took his degree at Heidelberg (1851) and taught there (1860–1913). A leading historian of mathematics in Germany at the turn of the century, he is best known for *Vorlesungen über Geschichte der Mathematik* (4 vols, 1880–1908), which gave impetus to the development of the history of mathematics as a scholarly discipline. Wrote most of the biographies of mathematicians in *Allgemeine Deutsche Biographie* (from 1875) and edited *Abhandlungen zur Geschichte der Mathematik* (1877–99).

CAPRA, BALDASSAR or **BALDESAR** (*b. Milan, Italy, ca. 1580; d. Milan, 1626*), astronomy.

Studied in Padua under Simon Mayr. Known as one of the first opponents of Galileo. Published his first attack on Galileo in 1605, on Galileo's observations of the new star of 1604. He then published as his own (1607) a brief Latin treatise on the proportional compass, which was scarcely more than a translation of Galileo's *Le operazioni del compasso* and was sprinkled with malevolent insinuations about Galileo. Had Capra only cited his source and renounced the absurd pretext of priority, he might have gained fame and some fortune from the work.

CARAMUEL Y LOBKOWITZ, JUAN (*b. Madrid, Spain, 1606; d. Milan, Italy, 1682*), mathematics.

Studied at Alcalá, Salamanca, and Louvain. Held various posts in Cistercian Order. Wrote some seventy works on many subjects. One of most important is *Mathesis biceps: Vetus et nova* (1670), which expounds the general principle of the numbering systems of base *n*, proposes a new method of approximation for trisecting an angle, and develops a system of logarithms which prefigures cologarithms.

CARANGEOT, ARNOULD (*b. Rheims, France, 1742; d. Meaux, France, 1806*), crystallography, entomology.

Studied in Paris under Romé de L'Isle; constructed a goniometer—a device combining the proportional compass and the protractor—and used it to make the first observation of the invariability of dihedral angles in mineral species. As an entomologist, he wrote the text of volumes IV–VIII (1785–93) of d'Orcy's *Papillons d'Europe peints d'après nature.*

CARATHÉODORY, CONSTANTIN (*b. Berlin, Germany, 1873; d. Munich, Germany, 1950*), mathematics.

Studied in Berlin, took a doctorate at Göttingen (1904), and taught in Bonn, Hannover, Breslau, Göttingen, and Berlin. Directed completion of the university in Smyrna (1920–22), taught at Athens (1922–24) and Munich (1924–50). Most notable Greek mathematician of recent times. In the calculus of variations, the theory of maxima and minima in curves, he showed that all of the theory for smooth curves can be applied to curves with corners. Published *Variationsrechnung und partielle Differentialgleichungen erster Ordnung* (1935). In the theory of functions, most important contributions were on conformal representation, particularly his theory of boundary correspondence. In the so-called theory of real functions and the theory of the measure of point sets and of the integral, his *Vorlesungen über reele Funktionen* (1918) began the modern axiomatization of this field.

CARCAVI, PIERRE DE (*b. Lyons, France, ca. 1600; d. Paris, France, 1684*), mathematics.

Custodian of the Royal Library (1663–83). Rendered great services to science through extensive correspondence with Huygens, Fermat, Pascal, Mersenne, Descartes, Galileo, and Torricelli, thus serving as a medium for the communication of scientific intelligence. Probably the first to recognize Fermat's extraordinary abilities, and Fermat entrusted him with publication of his treatises, in which Carcavi was not successful.

CARDANO, GIROLAMO (*b. Pavia, Italy, 1501; d. Rome, Italy, 1576*), medicine, mathematics, physics, philosophy.

Took a doctorate in medicine at Padua (1526) and became the most famous physician in Milan (from 1534). Held the chair of medicine at Pavia (1543–60) and Bologna (1562–70). Wrote more than 200 works on medicine, mathematics, physics, philosophy, religion, and music. His fame rests on his mathematics. He solved equations above the second degree, which contemporary algebra was unable to do. His major work, the *Ars magna* (1545), presented many new ideas in algebra. One was the rule ("Cardano's rule") for solving reduced third-degree equations. He is considered originator of the theory of algebraic equations. His *Liber de ludo aleae* was the first attempt to formulate the laws of probability, but was published after the work of Fermat and Pascal (1654). His two encyclopedias of natural science (1550, 1557) contained a little of everything, introduced new ideas, and inspired new investigations. In mechanics, he described many mechanical devices, among them "Cardano's suspension." In hydrodynamics he made many important observations. In physics, he made the first attempt to determine experimentally the relation between the densities of air and water. Responsible for several important geological theories.

CARLISLE, ANTHONY (*b. Stillington, Durham, England, 1768; d. London, England, 1840*), medicine, galvanism.

Resident surgeon at Westminster Hospital (from 1792), professor of anatomy at the Royal Academy of Surgeons (from 1808) and surgeon to the Prince Regent, on whose accession he was knighted. As a skilled surgeon, he devised effective modifications to several surgical instruments. His enduring reputation stems from a famous experiment in galvanism: with William Nicholson he electrolyzed water into its constituents (1800). The experiment was improved by Humphry Davy.

CARLSON, ANTON JULIUS (*b. Bohuslan, Sweden, 1875; d. Chicago, Ill., 1956*), physiology.

Received Ph.D. in neurophysiology at Stanford University (1902) and taught at the University of Chicago (to 1940). His studies on the heart of the horseshoe crab *Limulus* (1904) established the neurogenic mechanism of automaticity and of conduction of excitation. Long before the discovery of insulin his observations contributed to the proof that the antidiabetic substance of the pancreas is carried by the bloodstream and is capable of passing the placental barrier. He carried on extensive studies on physiology of the stomach. Among his many public services was leadership in the fight against antivivisectionists, and organization of the National Society for Medical Research.

CARNALL, RUDOLF VON (*b. Glatz, Germany [now Klodzko, Poland], 1804; d. Breslau, Germany [now Wrocław, Poland], 1874*), geology.

Trained as Prussian civil mining engineer; received Ph.D. at Berlin (1855). Served in various government positions. With von Buch and Rose, initiated the Deutsche Geologische Gesellschaft. Founded the official German mining journal. Published important papers on administrative, technical, mining, and geological problems. Heinrich Rose named the mineral carnallite after him.

CARNOT, LAZARE-NICOLAS-MARGUERITE (*b. Nolay, Côte-d'Or, France, 1753; d. Magdeburg, Germany, 1823*), mechanics, mathematics, engineering.

Known in France as the "Organizer of Victory" in the Revolution and in engineering for the principle of continuity in the transmission of power, Carnot is one of the few scientist-politicians who had a serious career in each domain. His father was one of the higher bourgeois; his elder son Sadi was famous in thermodynamics, and a grandson was president of the French republic (1887–94). Carnot graduated from the service school for the Royal Corps of Engineers. He became a republican (1791–92) out of a civic commitment natural to his class and family. After the overthrow of the monarchy his main responsibility on the Committee of Public Safety was military defense and attack; he was the leading member of the Directory.

The range and originality of Carnot's published works in mechanics, geometry, and the foundation of the calculus (1797–1807) must be unique in the annals of statesmen in political eclipse. His *Essai sur les machines en général*

(1783) contains all the elements of his engineering mechanics, in which it was the first truly theoretical work. It attracted no attention prior to his revision, *Principes fondamentaux de l'équilibre et du mouvement* (1803), which began to affect the actual treatment of problems only in the 1820's. The lag derived not from his content but from his purpose, which was to specify the optimal conditions for the operation of all machines. In his reasoning he gave impetus to what was to become the physics of energy, by starting with the elementary principle, the conservation of live force. The principle finding of the *Essai* was that a condition of maximum efficiency is that power be transmitted without percussion or turbulence (in hydraulic machines)—known as Carnot's principle until the late nineteenth century when it merged in the generality of conservation of energy, of which it was one of the many early partial instances.

He recognized that the product of the dimensions of force multiplied by distance was the quantity that might most conveniently estimate efficacy. In effect he transformed the discussion of force and motion into an analysis of the transmission of power. Dimensionally, this was nothing new, but the engineer in Carnot saw the advantage of applying the science of mechanics to analysis of the operation of machines. In the ideal case, live force reappears as moment of activity; or input equals output. He carried over the use of live-force conservation from hydrodynamics into engineering mechanics. The hydraulic application of principles and findings had a major place in his thinking. His reasoning also pointed to dimensional and vector analysis and the concept of reversible processes. To convert his equation expressing the principle of live force conservation into an expression applicable to all interactions in which motion was communicated, he introduced the notion he regarded as his most significant: geometric motions, which he defined as displacements depending for their possibility only on the geometry of a system quite independently of the rules of dynamics (later called virtual displacement). In the *Principes fondamentaux* he simplified his definition, but historically the first is more interesting; almost certainly it suggested to Sadi the idea of a reversible process.

In the *Essai* he derived a further fundamental equation, which differs from the first in that the actual physical velocity has been replaced by an idealized geometric velocity. He had derived conservation of moment of momentum or torque from conservation of energy or work by considering the ideal system within which no energy or work is lost. His conception of the science of machines, however, rather than his solution to its generalized problem, was what made him an important influence in mechanics, which became the basis of mechanical engineering. In the physics of work and energy, his analysis has been useful ever since those topics became explicit (1820–40's). Its most recognizable offspring was the heat cycle of Sadi Carnot. Carnot's operationalism distinguishes his mathematics as well as his mechanics.

His *Réflexions sur la métaphysique du calcul infinitésimal* (1797; Port., Ger., Eng., It., Russ. trs.) answered for well over a century to the needs of a public that wished to understand its use of calculus. In his account, the genius of the calculus was its procedural capacity to "compensate for" (eliminate) errors that it admitted into computation to facilitate a solution. His main geometric works were also motivated largely by the attempt to make reasonable the use of unreasonable quantity in analysis, with the focus on negative rather than infinitesimal quantity (*De la corrélation des figures de géométrie*, 1801; *Géométrie de position*, 1803). Errors in the calculus are eliminated through the process of computation, whereas in algebra they remain in the solution, where we recognize them by comparison with a rational or metrical reality, and that is where geometry comes in.

Géométrie de position was a vast exploration of the problem-solving reaches of geometry. He proposed to associate in a single treatment relations of magnitude as studied by the ancients with relations of position as studied more characteristically by the moderns, and thus to compare and unify the two main types of relation. It was a sort of engineering handbook of geometric systems that, were it ever completed, would permit resolving problems by considering unknown systems as correlatives of the set of primitive systems of which the properties were known. The formulas were to contain only real and intelligible expressions—no imaginary and no inverse quantities. This was preliminary to what was closest to his heart: the science of geometric motion.

CARNOT, NICOLAS LÉONARD SADI (*b. Paris, France, 1796; d. Paris, 1832*), thermodynamics.

Carnot, eldest son of Lazare Carnot, graduated from École Polytechnique (1814) and the École du Génie at Metz (1816). An appointment to the army general staff in Paris, through competitive examination, allowed him to pursue his own researches. He resigned from the army (1827); he died after contracting scarlet fever and then cholera. Nearly all his papers were burned after his death. Three major scientific works survive.

The earliest, "Recherche d'une formule propre à représenter la puissance motrice de la vapeur d'eau" (written probably 1823; unknown to 1966), is distinguished for the use of both an adiabatic working stage and an isothermal stage in which work is consumed.

Réflexions sur la puissance motrice du feu et sur les machines propres à développer cette puissance (1824) was regarded by contemporaries as primarily an essay on steam engines and had almost no influence on contemporary science. In the *Réflexions* Carnot set out three premises: the impossibility of perpetual motion; the caloric theory of heat which asserted that the quantity of heat absorbed or released by a body in any process depends only on the initial and final state of the body; and that motive power (work) is produced by the transfer of caloric from a warm to a cold body. In his concept of reversibility he implicitly assumed the converse as well: that the expenditure of motive power will return caloric from the cold to the warm body. In his analysis of heat engines he produced the ideal heat engine and the cycle that now bear his name. The "Carnot engine" consisted simply of a cylinder and a piston, a working substance he assumed to be a perfect gas, and two heat reservoirs maintained at different temperatures. The cycle incorporated the isothermal and adiabatic expansions and the isothermal compression of the steam engine, with a final adiabatic compression in which motive power was consumed to heat the gas to its original, boiler temperature. To describe the engine's properties, he introduced two fundamental thermodynamic concepts, completeness and reversibility. Joined together but operating in opposite directions, two such engines would produce no net effect. He postulated an engine that would produce more motive power than a "Carnot engine," and concluded that no engine whatsoever could do so. Formulating the result now known as "Carnot's theorem," he stated that "the motive power of heat is independent of the agents employed to realize it; its quantity is fixed solely by the temperatures of the bodies between which is effected, finally, the transfer of caloric." He then derived seven theorems, all now regarded as valid in their original form. A least three were major advances. These three state that the quantity of heat absorbed or released in isothermal changes is the same for all gases; that "the difference between specific heat under constant pressure and specific heat under constant volume is the same for all gases"; and that the fall of caloric produces more motive power when the temperature is lower than when it is higher. With Clausius' work showing that Carnot's theorem was correct as stated, Carnot's theorem became the second law of thermodynamics. A bundle of twenty-three loose sheets of rough manuscript notes (probably written 1824–26) shows that he had begun to work out the details of a kinetic theory of heat and anticipated nearly all of the groundwork for the first law of thermodynamics. They were not discovered until 1878.

CARO, HEINRICH (*b. Poznan, Poland, 1834; d. Dresden, Germany, 1910*), dye chemistry.

Career mirrors the dynamic expansion of the synthetic dye industry in cooperation with science. Trained as a dyer at the Gewerbeinstitut, simultaneously studying chemistry at Berlin (1852–55). As chemist in Manchester, discovered a more efficient synthesis of Perkin's mauve. Discovered induline, a useful aniline dye, and with Martius found and developed a commercial synthesis for Bismarck brown and Martius yellow. Worked in Bunsen's laboratory in Heidelberg (1866–68), then became director (1868–89) of perhaps the first industrial research organization, the Badische Anilin- & Soda-Fabrik in Ludwigshafen. Found a cheaper process to make alizarin commercially, and with Baeyer produced eosin, a fluorescent red dyestuff, and methylene blue, and commercially synthesized indigo. Discovered and produced chrysoidine, azo orange, and fast red. His last major finds were naphthol yellow and persulfuric acid (H_2SO_5), also known as Caro's acid. Helped formulate effective patent laws and practices for chemical inventions.

CAROTHERS, WALLACE HUME (*b. Burlington, Iowa, 1896; d. Philadelphia, Pa., 1937*), chemistry.

Received master's degree (1921) and Ph.D. (1924) at the University of Illinois in Urbana. He taught there (to 1926) and at Harvard (1926–28), then directed organic research at E. I. du Pont de Nemours and Company (1928–37). First industrial organic chemist elected to the National Academy of Sciences (1936). Helped found the synthetic rubber and synthetic fiber industries. His laboratory produced a number of fiber-forming polymers, one of which led to the first nylon, manufactured from 1939. Studies of the chemistry of vinylacetylene and divinylacetylene led to a wide range of derivatives: the most important was chloroprene, which converted to a polymer manufactured as neoprene from 1931.

CARPENTER, HENRY CORT HAROLD (*b. Bristol, England, 1875; d. Swansea, South Wales, 1940*), metallurgy.

Received degree at Merton College, Oxford (1896), and Ph.D. at Leipzig in organic chemistry. Headed the chemistry and metallurgy departments of the National Physical Laboratory (1901–06) and taught at Victoria University of Manchester (1906–13) and the Royal School of Mines (1913–40). A founder of the Institute of Metals; knighted in 1929. Made original contributions to the application of physicochemical principles to the metallurgy of iron and steel and of nonferrous metal alloys. Studied changes taking place in metals under repeated or cyclic temperature changes. Worked on production of aluminum and studied its remarkable properties.

CARPENTER, WILLIAM BENJAMIN (*b. Exeter, England, 1813; d. London, England, 1885*), medicine, natural history.

Studied at University College, London; became member of Royal College of Surgeons (1835), and received M.D. at Edinburgh (1839). Taught at the Royal Institution, University College, and London Hospital (from 1845). Registrar (1856–79) and Senator (from 1879) of London University. His output of writing on physiology and zoology was prodigious. From his *Principles of General and Comparative Physiology* (1839) developed his *Principles of Mental Physiology* (1874), which introduced new ideas on the working of nervous mechanisms and launched the controversy over his concept of "brain-change," a reflex action of the brain which found expression in thought and feeling. His essay review on the *Origin of Species* showed his acceptance and criticism of Darwinism, and carried much weight and influence. Propounded and executed important developments in the teaching of science. In microscopy, published *The Microscope and Its Revelations* (1856). In zoology, did pioneering work on descriptions and classification of the Foraminifera. Made several marine expeditions with Charles Wyville Thomson, leading to publications on the Crinoidea and throwing new light on many aspects of oceanography. Founding member of the Marine Biological Association.

CARPI, BERENGARIO DA. *See* **Berengario da Carpi, Giacomo.**

CARR, HERBERT WILDON (*b. London [?], England, 1857; d. Los Angeles, Calif., 1931*), philosophy.

Educated at King's College, University of London, and taught philosophy there (1918–25). Developed his philosophical ideas at the Aristotelian Society. A philosophical idealist, inspired by Leibniz, he held that the ultimate realities are active perceiving persons. He welcomed the general theory of relativity as providing scientific support for monadism and a relative theory of space and time (*The General Principle of Relativity*, 1920). Influenced by Bergson, he criticized mechanistic theories in biology.

CARREL, ALEXIS (*b. Lyons, France, 1873; d. Paris, France, 1944*), surgery, experimental biology.

Received M.D. at the University of Lyons (1900). Reputation for surgical skill, bold experiment, and technical originality, at the University of Chicago, led to appointment as member of the Rockefeller Institute for Medical Research (now Rockefeller University) in New York (1906–38). Developed first successful surgical techniques for suturing arteries and veins (1902), achieved pioneer successes with organ transplants (1904–08), and succeeded in cultivating the cells of warm-blooded animals outside the body (1908). Received Nobel Prize in 1912 for his surgical and cell-culture experiments. Aided by Charles A. Lindbergh, who devised a glass pump for circulating culture fluid through an excised organ, he kept organs alive and partially functioning for days or weeks, a pioneer step in the development of apparatus now used in surgery of the heart and great vessels. His widely read *Man the Unknown* (1935) expressed the hope that scientific enlightenment might confer upon mankind freedom from disease, long life, and spiritual advancement. In Paris during the German occupation in World War II he headed a self-created Institute for the Study of Human Problems.

CARRINGTON, RICHARD CHRISTOPHER (*b. London, England, 1826; d. Churt, Surrey, England, 1875*), astronomy.

Received B.A. at Trinity College, Cambridge (1848) and was observer at the University of Durham (1849–52). Set up his own observatory (1853) at Redhill, near Reigate, Surrey, so that he could complete the work of Bessel and Argelander by preparing a catalog of circumpolar stars brighter than the eleventh magnitude (*Catalogue of 3735 Circumpolar Stars*, 1857). Its reliability is unquestioned, but he is better remembered for his pioneering investigations (1853–61) of sunspots. In his *Observations of the Spots on the Sun* (1863) he determined the position of the sun's axis with unprecedented accuracy and established the important empirical laws of sunspot distribution and the variation in solar rotation as functions of the heliocentric latitude.

CARROLL, JAMES (*b. Woolwich, England, 1854; d. Washington, D.C., 1907*), bacteriology.

Received M.D. at the University of Maryland (1891), studied at Johns Hopkins University (1891–93), and became assistant to Walter Reed (1895–1902), succeeding him as curator of the Army Medical Museum and as professor at George Washington University (1902–07). He was Reed's second in command in the famous commission to Cuba to study yellow fever (1900). He took the bite of an infected mosquito and came down with the first experimental case of yellow fever, and acquired a heart disease from which he died a few years later, one of the genuine martyrs of science. He demonstrated, at Reed's suggestion, that the bacteriological agent of yellow fever is a filterable virus, one of the first established virus etiologies of a human disease.

CARTAN, ÉLIE (*b. Dolomieu, France, 1869; d. Paris, France, 1951*), mathematics.

Graduated from the École Normale Supérieure and taught at Montpellier, Lyons, Nancy, and finally Paris (1912–40). Shaped and developed analysis on differentiable manifolds, centering on Lie groups, partial differential systems, and differential geometry. Had a decisive influence on development of modern mathematics. His famous thesis on Lie groups extended Wilhelm Killing's "local" theory by classifying simple real Lie algebras and determining all irreducible linear representations. Discovered (1913) the spinors, later important in quantum mechanics. His methods in the theory of differential systems are perhaps his most profound achievement. His chief tool was the calculus of exterior differential forms, which he helped create and applied, revitalizing differential geometry. His was the first general idea of a fiber bundle, and his definition of a connection is now universal. His chief contribution to Riemannian geometry was the discovery and study of the symmetric Riemann spaces.

CARTESIUS, RENATUS. *See* **Descartes, René.**

CARUS, JULIUS VICTOR (*b. Leipzig, Germany, 1823; d. Leipzig, 1903*), zoology.

Doctorate in medicine and surgery from Leipzig (1849); studied also at Dorpat, Würzburg, and Freiburg im Breisgau. Conservator of Museum of Comparative Anatomy, Oxford (1849–51); taught comparative anatomy at Leipzig (from 1851). In *System der thierischen Morphologie* (1853) he stated that the aim of zoology is the explanation of animal forms, and he maintained the direct connection of presently living organisms with the earliest created forms. Corresponded with Darwin, translated and promulgated his works; also translated works by Thomas Huxley, Lionel Beale, and G. H. Lewes. Wrote a history of zoology (1872); with Wilhelm Engelmann edited *Bibliotheca zoologica;* founded and edited *Zoologischer Anzeiger.*

CARUS, PAUL (*b. Ilsenburg, Germany, 1852; d. La Salle, Ill., 1919*), philosophy of science.

Ph.D. from Tübingen (1876); moved to Dresden, England, New York, and then (*ca.* 1886) to La Salle, where he edited *The Open Court* and *Monist* and published philosophical and scientific classics. Wrote hundreds of articles and scores of books. His mission in all his writing was to conciliate science and religion; between 1890 and 1900 he elaborated a philosophy that he sometimes called "monism" and at other times "religion of science," by generalizing Grassmann's vector geometry: form is the quality not only of mind but of all reality; knowledge is the grasping of forms that are in the world; there is a one-to-one correspondence between knowledge and the external world. Carus rejected idealism and materialism, and questioned the subjectivism of Einstein's relativity.

CASAL JULIAN, GASPAR ROQUE FRANCISCO NARCISO (*b. Gerona, Spain, 1680; d. Madrid, Spain, 1759*), medicine, natural history.

Received bachelor of arts degree at University of Sigüenza (1713). Practiced medicine in Madrid (to 1717) and in Oviedo, Asturias (to 1751). His natural and medical history of Asturias (1762) describes the geography, climate, plants, animals, and diseases most frequently observed in the province, and discusses Hippocratic doctrines.

CASSEGRAIN (*fl. Chartres, France, 1672*), physics.

Cassegrain is known only for the arrangement of telescope mirrors he conceived, the "Cassegrain focus": a convex secondary mirror placed to intercept rays from the objective before they arrive at the focus and to reflect them straight back to the eyepiece through a hole in the objective (1672). Its real virtue—partial cancellation of spherical aberrations—was established by Ramsden a century later, and it has been popular in the construction of large reflectors.

CASSERI (or **Casserio**), **GIULIO** (*b. Piacenza, Italy, ca. 1552; d. Padua, Italy, 1616*), anatomy, surgery.

Received doctorate in medicine and philosophy at Padua (around 1580) under influence of Girolamo Fabrizio, and practiced as a surgeon (by 1585), giving private lessons in anatomy and occasionally substituting for the ailing Fabrizio. He was made public lecturer in surgery (1609) and replaced Fabrizio as anatomy lecturer (1614–16), achieving great fame as an anatomist. His *De vocis auditusque organis historia anatomica* (1600–01), on the comparative and descriptive anatomy of the larynx and of the ear, also deals with phonation, auditory function and acoustics, and the physiology of hearing. The *Pentaesthese-ion* (1609) contains five books on the organs of touch, taste, smell, hearing, and vision. His *Tabulae anatomicae* (1627) was to have formed a complete atlas of human anatomy. His illustrations were vigorous, concrete, and unusually accurate

CASSINI, GIAN DOMENICO (JEAN-DOMINIQUE) (CASSINI I) (*b. Perinaldo, Imperia, Italy, 1625; d. Paris, France, 1712*), astronomy, geodesy.

The first of a family of astronomers, Cassini I studied at the Jesuit college in Genoa, the abbey of San Fructuoso, and worked at the observatory at Panzano, near Bologna (1648–69). Studied with Riccioli and Grimaldi, Jesuits who probably reinforced his conservatism, especially toward Copernicus, and taught him the value of systematic observation and precision in methods and instruments. Held the chair of astronomy at the University of Bologna (1650–69). A large meridian constructed to his design (1653) and his observations of solar movements with it (*Specimen observationum Bononiensium . . .*, 1656), made him a brilliant reputation. In a period of public technical service, he worked on applied hydraulics and fortifications. Astronomy remained his preoccupation. His solar tables (1662) were used to construct the ephemerides, and he elaborated the first major theory of atmospheric refraction founded on the sine law. Proposed a Tychonian theory on the orbit of a comet (1664–65). Using Campani's and Divini's telescopes of great focal length, he made a remarkable series of observations of planetary surfaces. He detected the shadow of certain satellites, established a period for Jupiter close to the modern value, and established tables of movements of its satellites (*Ephemerides Bononienses mediceorem siderum,* 1668). Römer used the tables to demonstrate that light had a finite speed (1675), and they were used to determine longitude by navigators and astronomers. Became member of the new Académie Royale des Sciences in Paris (1667) and participated in setting up the observatory (1669). Assumed effective direction of the observatory (1671) and became a French citizen (1673). Discovered four satellites of Saturn. Discerned a band on the surface of the planet and discovered (1675) that its ring is subdivided into two parts, separated by a narrow band (Cassini's division). From observation he drew a large map of the moon (1679), and hypothesized correctly that the zodiacal light is cosmic, not meteorological. Obtained more accurate measure of arcs of meridian measuring (1683–1700) with several collaborators the arc of meridian from Paris to Perpignan. He then adopted the hypothesis of the lengthening of the terrestrial spheroid. His son, Jacques (1677–1756), gradually replaced him in his various functions.

CASSINI, JACQUES (CASSINI II) (*b. Paris, France, 1677; d. Thury, near Clermont, Oise, France, 1756*), astronomy, geodesy.

The son of Cassini I, he studied at the Collège Mazarin and at the Paris observatory, where he succeeded his father as *pensionnaire* (1712) and acting manager of the observatory (before 1710). Participated in his father's measurement of the meridian of Paris (1700–01) and supported the hypothesis of the elongation of the terrestrial ellipsoid until his retirement, like his father supporting the last Cartesians in the battle against the Newtonian hypothesis of flattening. Extended determination of the meridian of Paris to Dunkirk (1718) and used the results in his *De la grandeur et de la figure de la terre* (1722) to confirm his Cartesian position. To re-affirm the theory of elongation he determined the perpendicular to the meridian of Paris from Saint-Malo to Strasbourg (1733–34). In astronomy proper, his principal interests were the study of planets and their satellites, the observation and theory of comets, and the tides. Made valuable observations, particularly, in 1738, the revelation of the proper motions of the stars. Under continued challenge from Newtonians, he began to leave the polemic to his son, César-François (1714–84), and (from 1740) progressively abandoned scientific work.

CASSINI, JEAN-DOMINIQUE (CASSINI IV) (*b. Paris, France, 1748; d. Thury, near Clermont, Oise, France, 1845*), astronomy, geodesy.

Son of Cassini III; gradually took on the duties of directorship of the Paris observatory (from 1771), succeeding his father in 1784. Began to restore and reorganize the observatory and completed his father's great map of France. With Legendre and Méchain, participated in geodesic operations joining the Paris and Greenwich meridians (1787). Directed work on a portion of the new administrative maps and helped the Academy on a new metrological system (1791). He opposed the Revolution's reforms at the observatory in 1793 and gave up his duties there later that year.

CASSINI DE THURY, CÉSAR-FRANÇOIS (CASSINI III) (*b. Thury, near Clermont, Oise, France, 1714; d. Paris, France, 1784*), geodesy, astronomy.

Studied at the family home in the Paris observatory under Maraldi. Son of Cassini II; began his career at the height of the debate which centered on the form of the terrestrial sphere. Collaborated with his father in the geodesic work of 1733–34 and directed geodesic operations (1735–36) to reinforce his father's position, determining the two demiperpendiculars to the meridian of Paris. By 1737 he began to renounce the theory of elongation held by his father and took responsibility for conclusions resulting from this position (*La méridienne de l'Observatoire royal de Paris vérifiée dans toute l'étendue du royaume*, 1744). He gave up the polemic and devoted himself to

unremarkable astronomical observation and to his primary achievement, the first modern map of France. His official post of director of the observatory was created by the king in 1771, although the Cassinis had held that post in fact from 1671. Geodesic operations (1733–40) provided the essential elements for a new map of France. He supervised 400 principal triangles, and produced a preliminary map in eighteen sheets on the scale of 1:870,000 (1746 or 1747). The king delegated him the responsibility of establishing a map of France on a new model. He planned a map in 182 sheets; surveying began in 1750. At his death, only the map of Brittany remained to be done. His son, Cassini IV, completed it.

CASSIODORUS SENATOR, FLAVIUS MAGNUS AURELIUS (*b. Scylacium [now Squillace], Italy, ca. 480; d. Vivarium, Italy, ca. 575*), preservation and dissemination of knowledge.

Cassiodorus, who served the Ostrogoth kings (503–537), established a monastery, Vivarium (after 537). He established the scriptorium as a regular part of monastic life, equal in dignity to manual work. He also insisted that secular subjects were to be studied and copied by clerics along with the scriptures and the works of the Church Fathers. His greatest work, *Institutiones divinarum et humanarum litterarum*, a manual of instruction, maintains the Roman encyclopedic tradition and the importance of the seven liberal arts.

CASSIRER, ERNST ALFRED (*b. Breslau, Germany, 1874; d. New York, N.Y., 1945*), philosophy.

Studied at Berlin, Leipzig, Heidelberg, and Munich. Received doctorate at Marburg (1899) in philosophy. Taught at Berlin (1906–19), Hamburg (1919–33), Oxford (1933–35), Göteborg (1935–41), Yale University (1941–44), and Columbia University (1944–45). Most important of the younger circle of the neo-Kantian Marburg school. His major systematic work, *Das Erkenntnisproblem in der Philosophie und Wissenschaft der neueren Zeit* (4 vols., 1906–50), presents an analysis of the formation of philosophic concepts and shows the connection between the theory of knowledge and the general intellectual culture. His book, *Determinismus und Indeterminismus in der modernen Physik* (1937), provided logical clarification of the newly emerging problems of modern physics. He thought he could show that Einstein's theories did not conflict with those of Kant. *Philosophie der symbolischen Formen* (1923–31) developed the theory that human reason alone does not provide access to reality.

CASTALDI, LUIGI (*b. Pistoia, Italy, 1890; d. Florence, Italy, 1945*), anatomy.

Received M.D. at Florence (1914). Worked at the Institute of Human Anatomy of Florence (1919–22) and taught at the University of Perugia (1923–26) and the University of Cagliari (1926–43). Wrote important textbook on histology of the liver (1920). His precise work on the mesencephalon (1922–28) culminated in an exhaustive report (1937) on the extrapyramidal pathways of the central nervous system. In experimental work on the influence of the endocrine gland on morphogenesis (1920–28), he confirmed the relationship between iodine content and activity of the thyroid and established its influence on human height and development. He confirmed (1924–26) that the adrenal cortex can stimulate growth of the muscular and skeletal systems. In biometrics, he derived tables of average weights of thymus glands (1923), ovaries (1924), and the principal organs of the body (1927) by age, sex, body weight, and height.

CASTEL, LOUIS-BERTRAND (*b. Montpellier, France, 1688; d. Paris, France, 1757*), physics, mathematics.

Received early education at Jesuit school of Toulouse. Influenced by Fontenelle to move to Paris, where he taught at the Jesuit school in the rue Saint-Jacques, the present Lycée Louis-le-Grand. Published a creditable anti-Newtonian scientific theory that succeeded in delaying the acceptance of Newton's ideas in France; was spokesman of French scientists who saw Newton as a threat to the prestige of their hero, Descartes. They preferred an attractively reasoned system with daring ideas based on the logical process, rather than seeking scientific truth painfully and laboriously. Castel's ocular harpsichord, a scheme for making colors and musical tones correspond, spread his fame more than his scientific reputation.

CASTELLI, BENEDETTO (*b. Brescia, Italy, 1578; d. Rome, Italy, 1643*), hydraulics, astronomy, optics.

Entered the Benedictine order in Brescia (1595). Studied under Galileo in Padua. His scientific importance lay in his extension and dissemination of Galileo's work and methods and in his long and faithful service to Galileo in the two crises with the Inquisition. Galileo's first public discussion of the relation between science and religion was an expanded version of a letter to Castelli (1613). On Castelli's advice (1630) Galileo transferred the printing of the *Dialogue* from Rome to France, a maneuver vital to publication. Castelli taught at Pisa (1613–26) and Rome (from 1626) and was consultant to Pope Urban VIII on hydraulics. His *Della misura dell'acque correnti* (1628) began modern hydraulics. His pioneer work was carried much further by his pupil Torricelli. In other areas of research, he arrived independently at the photometric law that illumination is directly proportional to intensity and surface area of the source and inversely proportional to the squares of the distances of the lights from the illuminated body (1634); made many observations and conclusions with respect to the persistence of optical images; and carried on experiments with the absorption of radiant and transmitted heat by black and white objects.

CASTELNUOVO, GUIDO (*b. Venice, Italy, 1865; d. Rome, Italy, 1952*), mathematics.

Graduated from the University of Padua (1886) and taught at the University of Rome (1891–1935). Served as special commissioner of the Consiglio Nazionale delle Ricerche and president of the Accademia Nazionale dei Lincei. Principal field was algebraic geometry; his mathematical results particularly concerned algebraic surfaces and the theories constituting their background. In connection with these results is the theorem of Kronecker-Castelnuovo: "If the sections of an irreducible algebraic surface with a doubly infinite system of planes turn out to be reducible curves, then the above surface is either ruled or the Roman surface of Steiner" (1937).

CASTIGLIANO, (CARLO) ALBERTO (*b. Asti, Italy, 1847; d. Milan, Italy, 1884*), structural engineering.

Received degree at the Polytechnic of Turin (1873) and was chief of artwork, maintenance, and service for the Northern Italian Railroads (1873–84). His dissertation, *Intorno ai sistemi elastici* (1873), states the first of two theorems named for him: that the partial derivative of the strain energy, considered as a function of the applied forces (or moments) acting on a linearly elastic structure, with respect to one of these forces (or moments), is equal to the displacement (or rotation) in the direction of the force (or moment) of its point of application. In his second theorem (1875) the strain energy is considered a function of the unprescribed displacements of discrete boundary points; its derivative with respect to one of these displacements gives the corresponding force acting there. Menabrea's principle of least work is included in both theorems, and Castigliano claimed Menabrea's later demonstration did not credit him sufficiently, leading to a priority dispute. Principal continuations of his work were by Crotti and Donati.

CASTILLON, JOHANN (**Giovanni Francesco Melchiore Salvemini**) (*b. Castiglione, Tuscany, Italy, 1704; d. Berlin, Germany, 1791*), mathematics.

Received doctorate in jurisprudence at the University of Pisa (1729). Taught in Lausanne and Bern, then Utrecht (from 1751), where he received a doctorate in philosophy (1754). He was royal astronomer at the Berlin Observatory (from 1765) and directed the Mathematics Section of the Berlin Academy (1787–91). Known as an able geometer and general philosopher. Did elementary work in mathematics; named the cardioid curve. Wrote a useful commentary on Newton's *Arithmetica universalis* (1761).

CASTLE, WILLIAM ERNEST (*b. Alexandria, Ohio, 1867; d. Berkeley, Calif., 1962*), biology.

Received B.A. from Denison University (1889); and B.A. (1893), M.A. (1894), and Ph.D. (1895) at Harvard University, where he taught biology (1897–1936). Had a significant influence on American genetics through his training of graduate students at the Bussey Institution. Research associate in mammalian genetics at the University of California, Berkeley (1936–62). When Mendel's work was rediscovered in 1900, Castle helped carry the young science of genetics through the early days of skepticism and doubt. First to use *Drosophila* for extensive laboratory breeding (1901–06). Showed that inheritance of coat color in guinea pigs follows strictly Mendelian lines (1903–07). Was convinced that Mendel's laws could be generalized throughout the animal and plant worlds. With J. C. Phillips, he demonstrated dramatically the validity of Weismann's distinction between germ and somatic tissues (1909). His "Piebald Rats and Selection" (1914), the culmination of a series of experiments (1907–14), concluded that selection permanently modified genes by contamination. This attack on a fundamental assumption of Mendelian genetics, purity of the gametes, drew sharp criticism from T. H. Morgan's group at Columbia; Castle repeated his experiments (1914–19) and in "Piebald Rats and Selection: A Correction" (1919) conceded gracefully that the Morgan school multiple-factor hypothesis accounted for the results of selection. This put to final rest the assertion that selection itself created new and specific variability in the germ plasm by confirming for animals the results of Wilhelm Johannsen's experiments with plants. His later work was on the inheritance of quantitative characters, such as size, in mammals; the construction of genetic maps for small mammals, such as the rat and the rabbit; and the inheritance of coat colors in large mammals, particularly horses. Played an important role in organization and founding of genetics associations and journals.

CATALÁN, MIGUEL ANTONIO (*b. Zaragoza, Spain, 1894; d. Madrid, Spain, 1957*), experimental spectroscopy.

Studied at University of Zaragoza, and received D.Sc. at University of Madrid. Worked at the Laboratorio de Investigaciones Físicas in Madrid; was made chief of atomic spectroscopy of the Rockefeller Institute in Madrid (1930). In 1950 became head of spectroscopy at the Institute of Optics in Madrid. His extensive studies (1920–21) of the manganese spectrum revealed systems of multiplets; his further studies of chromium, selenium, molybdenum, and other elements showed the phenomenon was a general regularity. His "Series and Other Regularities in the Spectrum of Manganese" (1923) gave theoreticians and experimentalists the key to unraveling the spectra of the elements in the center of the periodic table, and contributed to establishing the structure of the atom.

CATALDI, PIETRO ANTONIO (*b. Bologna, Italy, 1552; d. Bologna, 1626*), mathematics.

Little known of his life. Taught at the Florentine Academy of Design, the University of Perugia, the Academy of Design in Perugia, and the Studio di Bologna (1584–1626). His *Trattato del modo brevissimo di trovar la radice quadra delli numeri* (1613), in which the square root of a number is found through the use of infinite series and unlimited continued fractions, made a notable contribution to the development of infinite algorithms. He also has a place in the history of the criticism of Euclid's fifth postulate, which he attempted to demonstrate on the basis of remainders. Wrote other didactic mathematical works.

CATESBY, MARK (*b. Castle Hedingham, Essex, England, 1683; d. London, England, 1749*), natural history.

Catesby's career as a naturalist began during a visit to the New World. The plants he sent back from America, Bermuda, and Jamaica brought him to the attention of English natural historians, and a subscribed journey to the New World (1722–26) resulted in his *Natural History of Carolina, Florida, and the Bahama Islands* (1729–47). He produced all save two of the 220 illustrations. His major contribution was in ornithology and bird illustration; Linnaeus used the work as the source for many designations of American birds.

CATTELL, JAMES McKEEN (*b. Easton, Pa., 1860; d. Lancaster, Pa., 1944*), psychology, scientific publishing.

Received Ph.D. at Leipzig (1886), where he was Wilhelm Wundt's first laboratory assistant. First person in the world to hold title of "professor of psychology," at the University of Pennsylvania (1888–91). Taught at Columbia University (1891–1917). His psychological work shows the influence of Wundt and Galton. He and his students greatly influenced American psychology in its bias toward experimentation and quantification. Principal importance is as a great scientific publisher and editor and as a powerful force in the development of the scientific and intellectual community. Owned and edited *Science* (1895–1944), willing it to the American Association for the Advancement of Science. Founded the Science Press of Lancaster, Pennsylvania (1923), to handle all the journals he owned or edited, including *Psychological Review, Popular Science Monthly,* and *American Men of Science.*

CAUCHY, AUGUSTIN-LOUIS (*b. Paris, France, 1789; d. Sceaux [near Paris], 1857*), mathematics, mathematical physics, celestial mechanics.

Cauchy was educated by his father, who held high administrative posts, including first secretary to the Senate. During the Terror his family escaped to Arcueil; Laplace and Berthollet were neighbors. Cauchy studied at the École Polytechnique (1805–07) and the École des Ponts et Chaussées, which he left (1809?) to become an engineer. He returned to Paris in 1813, and in 1816 agreed to succeed (by appointment) the republican and Bonapartist Gaspard Monge, who had been expelled. He taught (from 1815) at the École Polytechnique and held other chairs at the Faculté des Sciences and the Collège de France. He married (1818) Aloïse de Bure, daughter (or granddaughter) of the publisher of most of his works. After the July Revolution of 1830, he not only refused to take the oath of allegiance, which meant that he would lose his chairs, but exiled himself. It is not clear why. He taught at the University of Turin (to 1833); then in Prague, tutored Charles X's son, the crown prince. He returned to Paris in 1838, resuming work at the Academy; academicians were exempted from the oath of allegiance. Efforts to procure him a chair foundered on his intransigent refusals even to appear to have taken the oath of allegiance. When the Second Republic repealed the act requiring the oath, he resumed his chair at the Sorbonne (the only one vacant), and retained it under Napoleon III, who exempted the republican Arago and the royalist Cauchy from the reestablished oath. A devout Catholic, he took a leading part in church charities. His reputation has been that of a bigoted, selfish, narrow-minded fanatic; N. H. Abel called him mad, infinitely Catholic, and bigoted.

Cauchy did not master mathematics; he was mastered by it. If he hit on an idea he could not wait a moment to publish it. Before the weekly *Comptes rendus* came into being, he founded a private journal, *Exercices de mathématiques* (10 vols., 1826–40), filling its twelve issues a year himself with the most improbable subjects in the most improbable order. In less than twenty years the *Comptes rendus* published 589 notes by him; many more were not printed. He published in all at least seven books and more than 800 papers. Of all the mathematicians of his period he was the most careful in quoting others. His reports on his own discoveries have a remarkably naive freshness because he never forgot to sum up what he owed to others. Most of his work is hastily, but not sloppily written. More concepts and theorems have been named for him than for any other mathematician (in elasticity alone, sixteen concepts and theorems). All of them are absolutely simple and fundamental in their final form but not in his presentation. His classic *Cours d'analyse*

(1821) forcefully impressed his contemporaries. In method he aimed for "rigor" of geometry, and eschewed the "generality" of algebra. He discovered and formulated convergence criteria and used the limit sign. He proved Lagrange's and his own remainder theorem, first by integral calculus and later by his own generalized mean-value theorem, which sidestepped integral calculus. His celebrated *Calcul des limites* (1831–32) reduces convergence questions to those of geometric series. He invented our notion of continuity. He gave the first adequate definition of the definite integral as a limit of sums and defined improper integrals, the well-known Cauchy principal value of an integral with a singular integrand, and integrals of infinitely large functions over infinitely small paths. He also gave the proof of the fundamental theorem of algebra that uses the device of lowering the absolute value of an analytic function as long as it does not vanish. He calculated and transformed integrals and series developments. He was the first to state the meaning and use of semiconvergent series clearly. He was also the first to define continuity, but never proved the continuity of any particular function. The weakest point in his reform of calculus is that he never grasped the importance of uniform continuity.

Cauchy is most firmly associated with his fundamental theorems on complex functions. He moved slowly from initial hostility toward complex integration to the theorems that now bear his name, which depend first on some geometric idea on complex numbers and second on some more sophisticated ideas on definite integrals. The first comprehensive theory of complex numbers, in his *Cours d'analyse*, justified the algebraic and limit operations on complex numbers, considered absolute values, and defined continuity for complex functions. His integral theorem proved powerful; a host of old and new definite integrals could be verified. His *Mémoire sur les intégrales définies prises entre des limites imaginaires* (1825) took a long step toward what is now called Cauchy's integral theorem. He defined integrals over arbitrary paths in the complex domain; and through the Cauchy-Riemann differential equations he derived, by variation calculus, that fact that in a domain of regularity of $f(z)$ such an integral depended on the end points of the path only. His yield was the residue theorem with respect to poles, extended by P.A. Laurent (1843). He never used or quoted this memoir until 1851. But his indirect applications were manifold. He devised a method (1827) to check the convergence of a special power series for implicit functions, the so-called Lagrange series of celestial mechanics. It is a method that in the general case leads to the power series development. From this work he derived his integral formula from his integral theorem. Despite tremendous production in this one area, he had no clear overall view. He introduced arbitrary closed integration paths in 1846, proving his integral theorem anew by what is now called Green's formula. Still more important was his understanding of multivalued analytic functions, which could now be freely followed along rather arbitrary integration paths. This progress was just fine enough for elliptic and hyperelliptic integrals. The third of Cauchy's three studies (1824, 1837, 1853) of error theory produced the celebrated Cauchy stochastics in the course of his counterattack on Bienaymé, a supporter of fitting by least squares, who attacked the first two studies.

Two ideas are fundamentally new in Cauchy's approach to differential equations: (1) that the existence of solutions is not self-evident but has to be proved, and (2) that uniqueness has to be enforced by specifying initial (or boundary) data rather than by unimportant integration constants—famous as the Cauchy problem in partial differential equations. His work with linear partial equations led up to the outstanding device of the Fourier transform (Fourier's discovery, 1807, 1811; publ. 1824–26). Cauchy used it as early as 1815, and claimed independent discovery, but called the inversion formula after Fourier. He put it to greater use with greater skill than anybody at that time and for long after—Fourier and Poisson included; and he was the first to formulate the inversion theorem correctly.

Cauchy created (1822) the fundamental mathematical apparatus of elasticity theory, what some consider his greatest achievement. He based his equation of equilibrium of the elastic plane on a single force, "tension or pressure, of the same nature as hydrodynamic pressure . . . by a fluid against the surface of a solid . . . , derived as to magnitude and direction from the pressures or tensions exerted against three rectangular planes." Nearly all fundamental notions of the mechanics of continuous media were clear in his 1822 note: the concepts of tensors, the principle of obtaining equilibrium and motion equations by accepted elasticity theory of isotropic media. For anisotropic media he admitted a general linear dependence between stress and strain. He applied the general theory to several problems, particularly elastic light theory—one of the great pre-Maxwellian efforts necessary before physicists became convinced of the impossibility of any elastic light theory.

Cauchy's many contributions to celestial mechanics included proof that the infinite series astronomers used converged, and much detailed work on series, particularly for the solution of the Kepler equation and developments of the perturbative function. His best-known contribution to astronomy (1845) is his checking of Leverrier's cumbersome computation of the large inequality in the mean motion of Pallas by a much simpler method.

CAULLERY, MAURICE (*b. Bergues, France, 1868; d. Paris, France, 1958*), zoology, biology.

Received doctorate at the École Normale Supérieure (1895); taught at the École Normale, Lyons, Marseilles, and Paris. In 1909 succeeded Alfred Giard, who had greatly influenced him, in the chair of evolution at the Laboratoire d'Évolution des Êtres Organisés of the Faculté des Sciences, Paris, retiring in 1939. Also directed the Wimereux marine laboratory. Wrote numerous zoological works, many in collaboration with Félix Mesnil. He described new marine species, but gave the closest study to animals whose morphology, mode of reproduction, and ecology were of special interest or posed problems from the evolutionary point of view—Tunicata, Annelida, and Orthonectida. His important works on parasitic Protozoa precisely defined their sexual cycles.

CAVALIERI, BONAVENTURA (*b. Milan, Italy, probably 1598; d. Bologna, Italy, 1647*), mathematics.

Studied with Benedetto Castelli at Pisa (1616–20), and became a disciple of Galileo. Held the first chair in mathematics at Bologna (1629–47) largely through the recommendation of Galileo. Also held various religious appointments in the Jesuati order throughout his career. His work relates to an inquiry in infinitesimals and stems from revived interest in Archimedes' work. His major contribution to mathematics, the principle of indivisibles for finding areas and volumes, was first developed in his *Geometria indivisibilibus continuorum nova quadam ratione promota* (1635). The Cavalieri principle affirms that two integrals are equal if the integrands are equal and the integration limits are also equal. Furthermore, a constant that appears as a multiplier in the integrand may be carried out of the sign of integration without changing the value of the integral. Torricelli, who made the most significant progress along Cavalieri's path, rightly noted the "marvelous economy" over the method of exhaustion, yet it occasioned polemics with Guldin and others who were unaware of its Archimedean lineage. It later exerted a profound influence. Cavalieri's other contributions include the theorem of mean value, also known as the Cavalieri theorem, stated in geometric form in *Geometria;* the introduction of logarithms in Italy; noteworthy developments in trigonometry and applications to astronomy. In his theory of conics as applied to optics (*Lo specchio ustorio,* "The Burning Glass") he offered the idea of the reflecting telescope, preceding Gregory and Newton.

CAVALLO, TIBERIUS (*b. Naples, Italy, 1749; d. London, England, 1809*), physics.

Settled in England (1771) and became a member of the Royal Society (1779). His most important work was *A Complete Treatise on Electricity in Theory and Practice* (1777), which contained valuable details on medical electricity, Beccaria's obscure theories, and the design and operation of electrostatic instruments. *A Treatise on the Nature and Properties of Air and Other Permanently Elastic Fluids* (1781) was a judicious examination of contemporary work, particularly Priestley's. His last, most ambitious, most elementary, but least successful exposition was the *Elements of Natural Philosophy* (1803).

CAVANILLES, ANTONIO JOSÉ (*b. Valencia, Spain, 1745; d. Madrid, Spain, 1804*), botany.

Cavanilles took a doctorate in theology; he studied botany with A. Laurent de Jussieu and Lamarck (Paris, 1780). His most important work was *Monadelphiae* (10 monographs, 1785). He was professor and director of the Madrid Botanical Gardens (from 1801).

CAVENDISH, HENRY (*b. Nice, France, 1731; d. London, England, 1810*), natural philosophy.

Studied at St. Peter's College, Cambridge (1749–53), leaving without a degree. He fitted out his own laboratory and workshop in London and with his father, Lord Charles, was active in the organized scientific and intellectual life of London. He published no books and fewer than twenty papers (predominantly experimental and chemical) in a career of fifty years, but the many manuscripts uncovered gradually after his death show that he carried on profound experimental, observational and mathematical researches in literally all the physical sciences of his day. The vast bulk remains unpublished, except for the manuscripts on electricity collected by James Clerk Maxwell (1879) and some on chemistry and

dynamics collected by specialists (1921). A thoroughly Newtonian conception of natural philosophy as the search for the forces of particles animates and unifies all his work. Newton's *Principia* was his model of exact science. An early manuscript states his theory of heat and describes heat experiments in which he rediscovered the basic facts of specific and latent heats. His first published paper was on "factitious" airs, airs that are contained inelastically in other bodies but are capable of being freed and made elastic (1766). It helped discredit the notion that there is only one, true, permanent air. His most sustained and organized effort, on electrical theory (1771–81), led to his mathematical, single-fluid theory of electricity. His greatest predictive achievement lay buried in manuscript: the calculation and experimental confirmation of the precise quantities of electric fluid that bodies of different geometrical form and size can contain at any electrical tension. In his renewed work on elastic airs (1783–88), the most important fruit was his celebrated publication (1784) on the synthesis of water from inflammable and common air, concluding that inflammable air is phlogiston united to water. The basic themes of this research were the agency of electricity, the transition between elastic and inelastic states of matter, and the generation of heat. In work on freezing points (1783–88), his most important conclusion was that the extraordinarily low readings recorded on mercury thermometers were due merely to the shrinkage of solidifying mercury. Between 1784 and 1809 he published five papers on astronomy, the only notable one being on his determination of the density of the earth (1798) by means of John Michell's torsion balance.

CAVENTOU, JOSEPH-BIENAIMÉ (*b. Saint-Omer, France, 1795; d. Paris, France, 1877*), chemistry.

Studied at the School of Pharmacy and the Faculty of Sciences (Paris), was an intern in pharmacy at the Saint-Antoine Hospital (1816–26), and taught at the École Supérieure de Pharmacie (1826–59). Published a handbook of chemistry, *Nouvelle nomenclature chimique* (1816). His collaboration with Pierre-Joseph Pelletier (1817–42) led to their extraction of a number of important alkaloids from plants. They isolated strychnine (1818), brucine and veratrine (1819), and cinchonine and quinine (1820). They also discovered caffeine (1821). The discovery of quinine soon led to a worldwide demand for it as a therapeutic agent. In phytochemistry, they studied and named chlorophyll (1817), and with François isolated cahinca acid (1830).

CAYEUX, LUCIEN (*b. Semousies, Nord, France, 1864; d. Mauves-sur-Loire, Loire-Inférieure, France, 1944*), sedimentary petrography, stratigraphy.

Received master's degree and doctorate (1897) at Lille under Gosselet and Barrois, was *préparateur* at the National School of Mines in Paris (1891–98) and taught there (1904–12), then held the chair of geology of the Collège de France (1912–36). Worked and taught at the National Agronomical Institute (1898–1904). Spent his years at the Collège de France developing the teaching of the petrography of sedimentary rocks. He relied heavily on the data collected by the *Challenger* expedition to understand the genesis of ancient sediments on the basis of recent ones. Hence he created a new approach: paleooceanography. He investigated the chalk of the Paris basin (1897) and the sedimentary rocks of France and its colonies. In his studies of carbonate rocks particularly (1935), he anticipated many modern trends on early diagenetic changes. His *Introduction à l'étude pétrographique des roches sédimentaires* (1916) exhaustively surveyed methods of analysis and the mineral species and organisms contributing to sedimentary deposits. Between 1900 and 1904 he served as geological adviser to archaeologists working in Greece and in the archipelago.

CAYLEY, ARTHUR (*b. Richmond, Surrey, England, 1821; d. Cambridge, England, 1895*), mathematics, astronomy.

Cayley, the son of a merchant, graduated (1842) from Trinity College, Cambridge, and was elected a fellow (1842) at the earliest age of any man of the century. He studied at Lincoln's Inn, was called to the bar (1849), and practiced law (to 1863). With J. J. Sylvester, who also divided his time between law and mathematics, he founded the algebraic theory of invariants. They drifted apart professionally when Cayley was elected to the new Sadlerian chair of pure mathematics at Cambridge (1863–95). He was active in such matters as the drafting of college and university statutes. He published only one book, *Treatise on Elliptic Functions* (1876), but nearly a thousand papers on mathematics, theoretical dynamics, and mathematical astronomy (repub. in *Collected Mathematical Papers of Arthur Cayley,* 13 vols., 1889–98) notable for clarity, elegance, and analytical power. Characteristically courteous and unassuming, he gave abundant assistance to others (F. Galton, C. Taylor, R. G. Tait, G. Salmon), even writing whole chapters of their texts. He was a pure mathematician, taking little inspiration from the physical sciences at his most original.

He is remembered above all for his contributions to invariant theory. Moved by Boole's 1841 paper, he calculated the invariants of the nth-order forms (1843). He then (1846) introduced the idea of covariance; he was the first to state the problem of algebraic invariance in general terms. Salmon diffused his results, and Sylvester was largely responsible for the theory's luxuriant vocabulary. His ten brilliant and influential "Memoirs on Quantics" (1854–78) included the renowned theorem on the number of linearly independent semivariants of degree i and weight w of a binary p-ic. He found an expression giving a number which he proved could not be less than that required. In perhaps the best-known memoir, the sixth (1859), he gave a new meaning to the metrical properties of figures. Hitherto, affine and projective geometry had been regarded as special cases of metric geometry. He showed how it was possible to interpret all as special cases of projective geometry.

Cayley is also responsible for creating a theory of matrices that did not require repeated reference to the equations from which their elements were taken. He established (1858) the associative and distributive laws, the special conditions under which a commutative law holds, and the principles for forming general algebraic functions of matrices. He later derived many important theorems of matrix theory and contributed original work in both the abstract algebraic structure tradition and the geometrical tradition as did Benjamin Peirce, often regarded as the cofounder of the theory of matrices. He

grasped the merits of matrices and quaternions more clearly than most of his contemporaries, but like them he chose a side (coordinates rather than quaternions) in this heated controversy.

His characteristic use of geometrical analogy in algebra and analysis and his studied avoidance of the highly physical interpretation of geometry typical of his day helped lead him to a geometry of n dimensions. He considered the properties of determinants formed around coordinates in n-space (1843), used four dimensions in the enunciation of specifically synthetic geometrical theorems (1846), and laid down in general terms, without symbolism, the elements of "hyperspace" in his "Memoir on Abstract Geometry" (1870), showing that he was conscious of the metaphysical issues.

ČECH, EDUARD (*b. Stračov, Bohemia, 1893; d. Prague, Czechoslovakia, 1960*), mathematics.

Studied at Charles University of Prague (1912–14) and University of Prague (mathematics degree, 1920). Studied with Fubini in Turin (1921–22), later collaborating on two papers on projective geometry. Taught at Prague (1922–23), University of Brno (1923–39), and Charles University (from 1945). Worked on improvement of mathematics teaching in secondary schools; was instrumental in founding two mathematics research centers in Czechoslovakia. His work on the general theory of homology in arbitrary spaces, the general theory of varieties, and theorems of duality showed him to be one of the foremost experts in combinatorial topology. In his paper, "On Bicompact Spaces" (1937), he stated precisely the possibilities of utilizing a new type of topological space, which later came to be known as Čech's bicompact envelope. He was one of the founders of systematic projective differential geometry.

CELAYA, JUAN DE (*b. Valencia, Spain, ca. 1490; d. Turia, Spain, 1558*), logic, natural philosophy.

Received master of arts (1509) and doctorate in theology (1522) at the Collège de Montaigu, Paris, where he was influenced by Gaspar Lax and John Dullaert of Ghent. Taught in Paris at the Collège de Coqueret (1510–15) and the College of Santa Barbara (1515–24), and at the University of Valencia (from 1525). The most important of his many works on logic and expositions, with questions, of Aristotle's works, was his commentary on *Physics,* which had a great influence on the development of modern science.

CELS, JACQUES-PHILIPPE-MARTIN (*b. Versailles, France, 1740; d. Montrouge, Hauts-de-Seine, France, 1806*), botany, horticulture.

Studied in Paris under Bernard de Jussieu and Louis-Guillaume Le Monnier. After the Revolution abolished his civil service office, he retired to Montrouge and devoted himself to the cultivation and sale of plants; his garden became one of the most beautiful in Europe. He propagated the rare plants introduced into France by naturalist voyagers, corresponded with the principal botanists of Europe, sent plants to the botanical garden at Kew, prevented the destruction of parks and châteaus during the Revolution, and contributed to the formation of the agricultural institutions at Le Raincy, Sceaux, and Versailles. Most of his writings appeared anonymously.

CELSIUS, ANDERS (*b. Uppsala, Sweden, 1701; d. Uppsala, 1744*), astronomy.

Studied at the University of Uppsala, and taught mathematics there for several years before traveling extensively to broaden his knowledge. He visited astronomers and observatories in Bérlin and Nuremburg, Italy and Paris. He joined Maupertuis's expedition (1735–37) to measure a meridian in the north and thus helped verify the Newtonian theory that the earth is flattened at the poles. In the subsequent controversy with the Cartesians he fired a literary broadside (1738) against Jacques Cassini. He returned to Uppsala, teaching astronomy and moving into the newly completed astronomical observatory. His famous observations on the 100-degree thermometer scale based on the freezing and boiling points of water (1742) led to general acceptance of the scale, known by his name from about 1800.

CELSUS, AULUS CORNELIUS (*fl. Rome, ca. A.D. 25*), collection of knowledge.

Little is known of Celsus, except that he compiled an encyclopedia entitled *Artes* and was, with his predecessor Varro, Rome's most important master of this literary form. It contained eight extant books on medicine, plus five books on agriculture, and sections on military science, rhetoric and possibly philosophy. His authorship is open to serious criticism on many points. He may have translated a single Greek text, or several, into Latin; or, more likely, may have "compiled" the contents. He was probably an aristocratic, Greek-educated Roman strongly interested in medicine who held an individual but not atypical point of view.

CENSORINUS (*fl. Rome [?], first half of the third century A.D.*), grammar, collection of knowledge.

Censorinus' two extant works enrich our view of Greek and Roman science and increase our knowledge of Varro, on whom the works are based. *De die natali* (A.D. 238) has sections on the life of man and on time and its divisions. *Fragmentum Censorini* is more important for the history of science, containing a series of short tractates from an encyclopedic work on astronomy, geometry, music, and metrics.

CENTNERSZWER, MIECZYSŁAW (*b. Warsaw, Poland, 1871; d. Warsaw, 1944*), chemistry.

Received Ph.D. (1898) at the University of Leipzig and an M.S. at the University of St. Petersburg (1904); taught at the Polytechnic of Riga (1905–29) and the University of Warsaw (from 1929). He was founder of the Baltic school of chemists, and his books on inorganic and physical chemistry were widely translated. He was concerned mainly with chemical kinetics.

CERVANTES, VICENTE (*b. Zafra, Badajoz, Spain, 1755; d. Mexico City, Mexico, 1829*), pharmacy, botany.

Member of royal botanical expedition to New Spain led by Martín Sessé (1786). Founded botanical garden in Mexico City (1788), and taught at University in Mexico City (1788–1829). Considerably expanded the knowledge of Mexican botany, and in his *Hortus mexicanus* described 1,400 botanical species. Started the training of Mexican botanists in the Linnaean system.

CESALPINO, ANDREA (or **Andreas Caesalpinus**) (*b. Arezzo, Italy, 1519; d. Rome, Italy, 1603*), medicine, botany, philosophy.

Studied philosophy and medicine at Pisa (doctorate, 1551) under Luca Ghini; taught there (1555–92) and at the Sapienza in Rome; physician to Pope Clement VIII. Philosophical views were largely Aristotelian. In medicine, studied anatomy and physiology of movement of blood: gave good descriptions, recognized heart as center of circulation, but did not discover the major blood circulation. Wrote first true textbook of botany, *De plantis libri XVI* (1583), containing first system of the plants based on a unified and coherent group of notions; this exerted little influence on his contemporaries, but was valued by later botanists, especially Joachim Jungius and Linnaeus.

CESÀRO, ERNESTO (*b. Naples, Italy, 1859; d. Torre Annunziata, Italy, 1906*), mathematics.

Studied at the École des Mines of Liège and at the University of Rome (doctorate, 1887). Taught at the University of Palermo (1886–91) and at Naples (1891–1906). He had remarkably wide-ranging interests, but his most important contribution was his intrinsic geometry (from 1883). His *Lezione di geometria intrinseca* (1896) used Darboux's method of a mobile coordinate trihedral to simplify the analytic expression and make it independent of extrinsic coordinate systems. The *Lezione* also describes the curves that bear his name, and deals with the theory of surfaces and multidimensional spaces in general. He emphasized the independence of his geometry from the axiom of parallels. He extended the results to multidimensional spaces with constant curvature and established other bases for non-Euclidean geometry in "Sui fondamenti della interseca non-euclidea" and "Fondamento intrinseco della pangeometria" (1904).

CESI, FEDERICO (*b. Rome, Italy, 1585; d. Acquasparta, Italy, 1630*), botany, scientific organization.

Educated at Rome by private tutors, he founded, administered and financed there the first truly modern scientific academy, the Accademia dei Lincei (1603). After the election of Galileo (1611) the Academy grew rapidly. Its aims were the study of science and mathematics, the pursuit of new knowledge, and the publication of scientific discoveries. Its first important publication was Galileo's book on sunspots (1613). Cesi supported freedom of opinion within the Academy when the Holy Office condemned the Copernican doctrine (1616), published Galileo's *Saggiatore* (1623), and would have published the later *Dialogue* if he had not died before the imprimatur was obtained. His pioneer work in systematic botanical classification and the microscopic study of plant structure is overshadowed by his work with the Academy. His phytosophic tables anticipated by more than a century the work of Linnaeus in formulating a rational system for the classification and nomenclature of plants.

CESTONI, GIACINTO (*b. Montegiorgio, Italy, 1637; d. Leghorn, Italy, 1718*), natural history.

Cestoni practiced pharmacy in Leghorn. His letters recounting his findings on the generation of insects were valuable to F. Redi and A. Vallisnieri in disproving the theory of spontaneous generation. He discovered the acarid etiology of mange with G. C. Bonomo (1687). His correspondence with Vallisnieri included relevant observations on the parthenogenesis and the viviparity of the aphides.

CEULEN, LUDOLPH VAN (*b. Hildesheim, Germany, 1540; d. Leiden, Netherlands, 1610*), mathematics.

Taught arithmetic, surveying and fortification at the engineering school in Leiden (1600–10). His computation of π (sometimes called Ludolph's number) in his principal work, *Van den Circkel* (1596), the best approximation then rendered, went to twenty decimal places. His *Arithmetische en geometrische fondamenten* (1615) took π to thirty-three places, always enclosing it between an upper and a lower limit. His final triumph, π to thirty-five places, was published in his disciple Willebrord Snell's *Cyclometricus* (1621).

CEVA, GIOVANNI (*b. Milan, Italy, 1647 or 1648; d. Mantua, Italy, 1734*), mathematics.

Ceva, a brother of Tomasso Ceva (1648–1737), studied at Pisa. When he died he was a salaried employee of the royal court. His most important work, *De lineis rectis* (1678), used the properties of the center of gravity of a system of points to obtain the relation of the segments produced by straight lines drawn through their intersections. This method, combining geometry and mechanics, he applied to prove, among others, the transversal theorem named for him on the concurrency of transverse lines through the vertices of a triangle. His *Opuscula mathematica* (1682) showed how geometric proofs can verify results determined mechanically, and sketched clearly his infinitesimal method. In his *Geometria motus* (1692), he attempted to determine the nature of motions geometrically, treated composite motions, and discussed the laws of pendulums. Although he used archaic and complicated formulations, the *Geometria* anticipates or at least suggests elements of infinitesimal calculus.

CEVA, TOMASSO (*b. Milan, Italy, 1648; d. Milan, 1737*), mathematics.

Ceva, a brother of Giovanni Ceva (*ca.* 1647–1734), entered the Society of Jesus (1663) and taught mathematics at Brera College in Milan. His contribution to mathematics (*Opuscula mathematica*, 1699) is the summation of all his work and is concerned with gravity, arithmetic, geometric-harmonic means, the cycloid, division of angles, and higher-order conic sections and curves. Carried on extensive correspondence with Guido Grandi. Also known as a great poet.

CHABRY, LAURENT (*b. Roanne, France, 1855; d. Paris, France, 1893*), physiology, embryology.

Received M.D. at the Collège de France (1881) and a doctorate in science at the Sorbonne (1887), taught at Lyon (1888–90), practiced medicine, and studied bacteriology at the Pasteur Institute. In his pioneering work on ascidians (1887), which showed that each of the primary cells of the embryo has a predetermined fate independent of later circumstances, he experimentally produced half-embryos by destroying, through *piqûre*, one of the two primary cells. He was the first to perform experimental operations on such a small egg. Collaborated with G. Pouchet and Charles Robin on other works on embryology.

CHAGAS, CARLOS RIBEIRO JUSTINIANO (*b. Oliveira, Minas Gerais, Brazil, 1879; d. Rio de Janeiro, Brazil, 1934*), medicine.

Chagas' uncle was a surgeon who established a hospital using the methods of Lister for the first time in Brazil, and exerted a great influence on his nephew. Chagas took an M.D. at the Instituto Oswaldo Cruz (1903), where he worked (from 1907), and where Cruz was a major influence in Chagas' career. His successful innovative technique for malaria control, using pyrethrum for disinfection, was described in *Prophylaxia do impaludismo* (1905), later used as a guide for the use of synthetic insecticides. During a new antimalaria campaign in the village of Lassance (1909–10) he discovered and described the disease that bears his name: he identified the pathogenic trypanosome as a new genus and species and proposed to name it *Schizotrypanum cruzi* (known generally as *Trypanosoma cruzi*). His was a unique feat in the history of medicine—the only instance in which a single investigator has described the infection, its agent, its vector, its manifestations, its epidemiology, and some of the hosts of the pathogenic genus. He later reorganized the Department of Health in Brazil, helped establish international centers for preventive medicine, and helped reformulate Brazilian medical education.

CHALCIDIUS. *See* **Calcidius.**

CHALLIS, JAMES (*b. Braintree, Essex, England, 1803; d. Cambridge, England, 1882*), astronomy.

Challis took a degree at Trinity College, Cambridge (1821), was elected a fellow (1826) and was ordained (1830). He was Plumian professor (1835–82) and director of the observatory (1835–61) at Cambridge. The peculiarity of his scientific views was evident in his *Notes on the Principles of Pure and Applied Calculation; and Application of Mathematical Principles to Theories of the Physical Forces* (1869), which attempted to show that all physical phenomena are mathematically deducible from a few simple laws. But it was his spectacular failure to discover Neptune in 1845–46 which ironically immortalized him. Under pressure from John Couch Adams and George Biddell Airy, Challis made the observations (August 1846), by which he could have discovered the new planet, but he did not examine or map his observations because, he later explained, he was busy reducing his comet observations.

CHAMBERLAIN, CHARLES JOSEPH (*b. Sullivan, Ohio, 1863; d. Chicago, Ill., 1943*), botany.

Received M.A. (1894) at Oberlin, and doctorate at Chicago (1897), teaching at the latter for over forty-five years. His lifelong interest was the morphology and phylogeny of the cycads. *The Living Cycad* (1919) is an account of his worldwide field expeditions. The collection of living cycads in the botanical garden at the University of Chicago, the foremost in the world, at his death contained all of the surviving nine genera and half the known species.

CHAMBERLAND, CHARLES EDOUARD (*b. Chilly le Vignoble, Jura, France, 1851; d. Paris, France, 1908*), bacteriology.

Studied at the École Normale Supérieure and became one of Pasteur's most famous associates there (1875–88), as director of the Pasteur Institute department which prepared vaccines (from 1888) and as assistant director of the Institute (from 1904). In the Pasteur-Bastian controversy on spontaneous generation, he investigated the causes of error in Bastian's experiments. His observations led him to new methods for sterilization of culture media, and resulted in the autoclave, which soon became indispensable. His studies with Jouan on microbes of the *Pasteurella* type have remained classic.

CHAMBERLIN, THOMAS CHROWDER   (*b. Mattoon, Ill., 1843; d. Chicago, Ill., 1928*), geology, cosmology.

Took an A.B. at Beloit College (1866) and did graduate work in geology at the University of Michigan. Geologist for the Wisconsin Geological Survey (1873–82); in the report, *Geology of Wisconsin* (1877–83), he dealt especially with glacial deposits, lead and zinc ores, and the Silurian coral reefs. Directed the glacial division of the U.S. Geological Survey (1881–1904), was president of the University of Wisconsin (1887–91), and chairman of geology at the new University of Chicago (1892–1918), where he established the *Journal of Geology* and developed a most distinguished geology department. He was one of the first to see the Ice Age as a time of multiple glaciation, and focused on the causes of glacial climates and the problem of the changing climates of the geological past. With F. R. Moulton he tested the Laplacian hypothesis concerning the origin and early history of the earth, abandoned it (1900), and developed (1905) the concept of planetary growth by accretion of planetoidal particles and bodies (planetesimals). He followed its far-reaching implications in fifteen papers in the *Journal of Geology* (1913–20) and a series of papers in the Yearbooks of the Carnegie Institution in Washington (1904–28).

CHAMBERS, ROBERT   (*b. Peebles, Scotland, 1802; d. St. Andrews, Scotland, 1871*), biology.

With his brother William, he formed the well-known Chambers publishing firm. He is best known for his *Vestiges of the Natural History of Creation* (1844), published anonymously. Its main thesis is that the organic world is controlled by the law of development, just as the inorganic is controlled by gravitation. Probably the strongest section is the quarter on geology and paleontology; it demonstrates that the fossils show a general progression from lower to higher types, extinctions and new appearances taking place until the appearance of the present species, man being very recent. Within the human species, development has finally produced the highest race, the Caucasian. The book brought together a large variety of data from geology and the life sciences bearing on the origin of species. It contravened contemporary theology, envisaging the Creator as working through natural laws. Its evolutionary view of nature eased the way for Darwin's *On the Origin of Species.*

CHAMISSO, ADELBERT VON   (*b. Ante parish, Marne, France, 1781; d. Berlin, Germany, 1838*), natural history, botany.

Served in Prussian army (1801–06); studied at University of Berlin (1812–15). Naturalist on the brig *Rurik*, under Kotzebue, for Pacific exploration (1815–18);

brought back rich botanical collections, notably from Marshall and Hawaiian islands, Kamchatka, the Aleutians, and California. On return to Berlin, appointed to Royal Botanical Gardens (curator from 1833). Wrote on botanical taxonomy, zoology, and geology; discovered alternation of generations in salps (1819); first to propose floating fruits as agents for populating islands, and to ascribe coloration of seawater to pigmented microorganisms. Noted also as poet and as author of *Peter Schlemihl's wundersame Geschichte* (1814).

CHANCEL, GUSTAV CHARLES BONAVENTURE (*b. Loriol, France, 1822; d. Montpellier, France, 1890*), chemistry.

Studied at the École Centrale in Paris; taught at Montpellier (from 1851); was dean of the faculty of sciences (from 1865) and rector of the Montpellier Academy (from 1879). His researches were primarily in analytical and organic chemistry. His analytical studies dealt with the separation and analysis of metals in solution. In 1858 he introduced a new method of precipitation. He investigated ketones in his first organic chemical researches. He helped to confirm Charles Gerhardt's homologous series for alcohols, successfully preparing propyl alcohol (1853). With Auguste Laurent he discovered butyronitrile (1847) and phenylurea and diphenylurea (1849). He confirmed Laurent's proposal of alcohol and ether as members of the water type (1850).

CHANCOURTOIS, A. E. BÉGUYER DE. *See* **Béguyer de Chancourtois, A. E.**

CHANDLER, SETH CARLO   (*b. Boston, Mass., 1846; d. Wellesley Hills, Mass., 1913*), astronomy.

Worked with Benjamin Apthorp Gould on the U.S. Coast Survey (1861–64). After many years as an actuary, became associated with Harvard College observatory, evolving with J. Ritchie the Science Observer Code (1881), a system for transmitting by telegraph information about newly discovered comets. Most important contribution was the discovery of the variation of latitude, after he devised the almucantar to relate positions of stars not to the meridian but to a small circle centered at the zenith.

CHAPLYGIN, SERGEI ALEKSEEVICH   (*b. Ranenburg [now Chaplygin], Russia, 1869; d. Moscow, U.S.S.R., 1942*), mechanics, engineering, mathematics.

Graduated from Moscow University (1890), later received master's degree (1897) and doctorate. Taught at Moscow University (1894–96), Moscow Technical College (1896–1906), and Moscow Women's College (1901–18). With his teacher and collaborator, N. E. Zhukovsky, helped organize the Central Aerohydrodynamic Institute (1918), becoming director on Zhukovsky's death (1921). Early work was devoted to hydromechanics and to the development of the general methods of classical mechanics. He first obtained general equations for the motion of nonholonomic systems. In his investigation of the mechanics of liquids and gases, he developed a method (1902) to solve the problem of the noncontinuous flow of a compressible gas. He stated the results of his work on the aerodynamic forces acting on an airplane wing in a paper on the so-called Chaplygin-Zhukovsky postulate, which gives a complete solution to the problem of the forces exerted by a stream on a body passing through it.

CHAPMAN, ALVAN WENTWORTH (*b. Southampton, Mass., 1809; d. Apalachicola, Fla., 1899*), botany.

Graduated from Amherst College (B.A., 1830); place and date of his M.D. are obscure. Botanized on the Apalachicola River in 1837 with Hardy Bryan Croom. Chapman's *Flora of the Southern United States* (1860) faithfully carried forward Torrey and Gray's plan for a comprehensive flora of the nation. Revisions served until Small's *Flora* (1903).

CHAPMAN, DAVID LEONARD (*b. Wells, Norfolk, England, 1869; d. Oxford, England, 1958*), chemistry.

Graduated from Christ Church, Oxford (1893), spent ten years on the staff at Owens College, Manchester, and taught at Jesus College, Oxford (1907–44), where he also superintended the laboratory. While at Owens College, he worked out the "Chapman equation," interpreting theoretically the gaseous explosion rates being measured there by H. B. Dixon. At Jesus College he opened a new field by being the first to carry out rate measurements on a homogeneous gas reaction, the thermal decomposition of ozone. He later worked on the kinetics and the inhibiting effect of oxygen, and catalysis of gas reactions by metals.

CHAPPE D'AUTEROCHE, JEAN-BAPTISTE (*b. Mauriac, Cantal, France, 1728; d. San José del Cabo, Cape Lucas, Baja California, 1769*), astronomy.

Studied at the Collège Louis-le-Grand. He was elected to the Academy of Sciences (1759) and then joined the Paris observatory staff. The high point of his career was his part in the two great voyages (Siberia, 1761; southern California, 1769) to observe the transits of Venus, the capstone of eighteenth-century observational activity. His astronomical observations were used by J. D. Cassini (1772) to arrive at a solar parallax of 8.5″. Between the years of the two transits, he made other important astronomical observations and was involved in sea tests of Ferdinand Berthoud's chronometer, on which he made an important report.

CHAPTAL, JEAN ANTOINE (*b. Nojaret, Lozère, France, 1756; d. Paris, France, 1832*), applied chemistry.

Received M.D. at Montpellier (1777). He held a new chair of chemistry there (1780–95) and then taught chemistry in the medical school. After his marriage (1781) he used the dowry and a large sum from his uncle to found one of the greatest chemical industries of his age. He was Bonaparte's minister of the interior (1801–04), the key post in the post-revolutionary period, and during his administration notably expanded technical education and reformed the Institute (later the Académie des Sciences). He was president from its founding (1801) of the Société d'Encouragement pour l'Industrie Nationale. He made few original contributions to pure chemistry, but was one of the greatest chemical manufacturers of his day. After 1804 he again took a close interest in his chemical factories. The one at Ternes, near Paris, produced oxalic acid, tartaric acid, corrosive sublimate, potassium and sodium arsenates, copper sulfate, tin and lead salts, alcohol, ether, and ammonia. Soda was refined there and sulfuric acid was concentrated in platinum vessels. The factory at La Folie, near Nanterre, produced hydrochloric acid, sulfuric acid, nitric acid, crude soda, potassium carbonate, potassium sulfate, and alum. The third factory, near Martigues, on the Mediterranean, mainly produced soda. He was always ready to apply the lessons of the laboratory to the factory, and was influential in advocating the introduction of science into the old craft procedures. In the production of wine he proposed the addition of sugar to improve fermentation, an effective method of improving yield which became known as "chaptalization." Among his many articles and books, his book, *Chimie appliquée aux arts* (1807), warned the industrialist of the danger of ignoring science.

CHARCOT, JEAN-BAPTISTE (*b. Neuilly-sur-Seine, France, 1867; d. at sea, 1936*), medicine, navigation, geography, oceanography, exploration.

Charcot, the son of the renowned J.-M. Charcot (1825–93) took an M. D. at the Faculté de Médecine (1895), was chief of its neurological clinic, and was associated with the Institut Pasteur. He abandoned medicine in 1903 for maritime expeditions, which he organized and led. He designed the first polar vessels built in France: the *Français*, which was used in the first French Antarctic expedition (1903–05), and the *Pourquoi Pas?*, which became the floating marine research laboratory of the École Pratique des Hautes Études (from 1911) and was often used by the Muséum National d'Histoire Naturelle. During the annual expeditions he commanded, work was done in hydrography, meteorology, atmospheric electricity, and gravitation, among many other fields; new lands were discovered; the problem of the South American Antarctic was resolved; and two new sciences (submarine geology, with the establishment of marine geological maps; and geological oceanography) were created. His last voyage, during which the ship foundered on reefs off Iceland and only the master helmsman survived, was to Greenland to locate the Victor mission.

CHARCOT, JEAN-MARTIN (*b. Paris, France, 1825; d. Lake Settons, Nièvre, France, 1893*), medicine, neurology.

Received M.D. at the Faculty of Medicine in Paris (1853), taught there (1872–82), created a major neurology department at the Salpêtrière clinic (1862–72) and taught there (from 1882). He described the neurogenic arthropathies popularly known as Charcot's disease, recorded the history of lateral amyotrophic sclerosis (also known as Charcot's disease), and discovered a progressive neuropathic muscular atrophy, later named Charcot-Marie (after Pierre Marie) amyotrophy. He initiated (1872) work on hysteria and hysterical hemianesthesia and before his death was exploring convulsive attacks in hysterical patients, and hypnotic theory. He was one of the first to demonstrate the clear and fruitful relationship between psychology and physiology. His work on hysteria stimulated Freud's investigations, and he was, with Duchenne, one of the founders of modern neurology.

CHARDENON, JEAN PIERRE (*b. Dijon, France, 1714; d. Dijon, 1769*), chemistry, medicine.

Practiced medicine in Dijon and was scientific secretary to the Académie des Sciences, Arts et Belles-Lettres de Dijon (1752–62). His interests in the chemical aspects of medicine included an inquiry into the nature of oil, which he showed could not be an element or principle because it could be decomposed on heating; and a naïve Newtonian theory on the cause of the weight increase of metals on calcination (1762), in which he criticized two earlier theories—one by Boyle and one by Béraut.

CHARDONNET, LOUIS-MARIE-HILAIRE BERNIGAUD, COMTE DE (*b. Besançon, France, 1839; d. Paris, France, 1924*), cellulose technology.

Trained as an engineer at the École Polytechnique; influenced by Pasteur's work on the silkworm to imitate as closely as possible the work of the silkworm. Devised a process in which a solution of cellulose nitrate was extruded through very fine glass capillaries to form continuous filaments. Established factories to produce the "artificial silk" (later known as rayon).

CHARLES, JACQUES-ALEXANDRE-CÉSAR (*b. Beaugency, France, 1746; d. Paris, France, 1823*), experimental physics.

After a non-scientific education, he was influenced by Franklin and studied the elements of nonmathematical, experimental physics. Gave public lectures (from 1781), became member of the Academy of Sciences (1795), taught experimental physics at the Conservatoire des Arts et Métiers, was librarian of the Institute, and (from 1816) president of the Class of Experimental Physics at the Academy. He conceived the idea of using hydrogen instead of hot air in the balloon and developed nearly all the essentials of modern balloon design. He made a successful balloon voyage from Paris of twenty-seven miles (1783). He discovered the law on gas expansion named for him in 1787; it was first made public by Gay-Lussac. Often confused with Charles le Géomètre (*d.* 1791).

CHARLETON, WALTER (*b. Shepton Mallet, Somerset, England, 1620; d. London, England, 1707*), natural philosophy, medicine.

Received doctor of physick degree at Magdalen Hall, Oxford (1643), where he was strongly influenced by John Wilkins. Served as physician-in-ordinary to the king. Published prolifically, mostly on medicine and natural philosophy. His most famous work, *Chorea gigantum* (1663), argued that Stonehenge was not a Roman temple, but rather the ruined meeting place of Danish chieftains. His most important scientific work was *Physiologia Epicuro-Gassendo-Charltoniana* (1654). It was widely read, by Boyle and Newton among others, as a convenient substitute for Gassendi's scarce works. He served as an expositor of the atomic philosophy at a time when its reception was in doubt. He was an original member of the Royal Society, and president of the Royal College of Physicians (1689–91).

CHARPENTIER, JOHANN (JEAN) DE (*b. Freiberg, Germany, 1786; d. Bex, Switzerland, 1855*), mining engineering, glaciology.

Graduated from the Mining Academy in Freiberg and worked at the Waldenburg coal mines. Became director of the salt mines of Bex (1813–55). He turned (1818) to a study of glaciers and the origins of the blocks of rock scattered in the Rhone valley from the Alps to the Jura. James Hutton's views on glaciation (1795) were not then known on the Continent. Charpentier analyzed all the hypotheses which had been advanced (meteorites, collapsed caverns in the earth, floodwaters, icebergs on rivers or lakes) and refuted them with evidence of his own finding (1834). Louis Agassiz, among others, visited Charpentier and, carried away with enthusiasm, rushed into print (1840). The origin of the theory of the Ice Age is still commonly attributed to Agassiz rather than to Charpentier. Charpentier received Agassiz's book three days before he finished his own *Essai sur les glaciers* (1841), a classic of scrupulous care in weighing evidence, describing the erratic blocks, and explaining the function of glaciers in transporting them.

CHARPY, AUGUSTIN GEORGES ALBERT (*b. Oullins, Rhône, France, 1865; d. Paris, France, 1945*), metallurgy, chemistry.

Received doctoral degree at the École Polytechnique, became engineer at the Laboratoire d'Artillerie de la Marine (1892), was technical director of the Compagnie de Châtillon Commentry (after 1898), and director general of the Compagnie des Aciéries de la Marine et Homécourt (from 1920). Taught at the École Polytechnique and the École Supérieure des Mines. He was, with Osmond and Henry Le Châtelier, a founder of the science of alloys in France. He devised the Charpy pendulum drop hammer to measure the brittleness of steel, and proposed the alloy of iron with 2 or 3 percent silicon, universally adopted for low-leakage magnetic circuits.

CHASLES, MICHEL (*b. Épernon, France, 1793; d. Paris, France, 1880*), synthetic geometry, history of mathematics.

Studied at the École Polytechnique, then devoted himself to research. Taught at the École Polytechnique (1841–51), and at the Sorbonne (1846–80). His overriding purpose was to show that the methods of synthetic geometry introduced by Carnot, Monge, and Poncelet, which included a systematic use of sensed magnitudes, imaginary elements, the principle of duality, and the transformations of figures, give to geometry the freedom and power of analysis. All his books elaborate points raised in his first major work, *Aperçu historique* (1837), a philosophical examination of these methods, which remains a classic of mathematical history written by a mathematician. He knew no German, and hence claimed many results which had been wholly or partly anticipated by German mathematicians. He saw clearly the basic concepts and their ramifications in what is now known as projective geometry, and his textbooks were influential in Germany and Great Britain as well as France. He did noteworthy work in what came to be called enumerative geometry and in analysis, particularly the attraction of ellipsoids.

CHÂTELET, GABRIELLE-ÉMILIE LE TONNELIER DE BRETEUIL, MARQUISE DU (*b. Paris, France, 1706; d. Lunéville, Meurthe-et-Moselle, France, 1749*), scientific commentary.

Received a literary, musical, and scientific education. After her marriage (1725) to the marquis du Châtelet she lived with her husband for several years; he then pursued a military career and visited her only briefly. After she returned to Paris (1730) she became intimate with Voltaire (1733); when he was threatened with arrest (1734) he withdrew to her château at Cirey, which they made into one of the most brilliant centers of French literary and philosophical life. Beyond her great influence on his work and public activity, Mme. du Châtelet contributed to the vitality of French scientific life and to parallel diffusion of Newtonianism and Leibnizian epistemology in her commentaries and syntheses. Her systematic study of Newton led her to write *Essai sur l'optique* and "Lettre sur les élémens de la philosophie de Newton" (1738), a defense of Newtonian attraction. In 1739 she published an important memoir on fire. Her *Institutions de physique* (1740) vigorously defended Leibniz's view on *forces vives*. Her translation of Newton's *Principia*, in collaboration with Clairaut (1759), remains the sole French translation.

CHAUCER, GEOFFREY (*b. London, England, ca. 1343; d. London, England, 1400*), literature, astronomy.

Chaucer's *Canterbury Tales* has tended to eclipse his other works, in particular *A Treatise on the Astrolabe* (1391) and *Equatorie of the Planetis* (1392), on the construction and use of these instruments. Both are written in the vernacular rather than the usual Latin, are clearly pedagogic, and display clear technical mastery of the line of instrumentation associated with Merton College, Oxford. Details of his scientific education are unknown: he is not recorded at Oxford.

CHAULIAC, GUY DE (*b. Chauliac, Auvergne, France, ca. 1290; d. in or near Lyons, France, ca. 1367*), medicine.

Studied at Toulouse, at Bologna under Bertrucius, and took a medical degree at Montpellier. He was private physician to Clement VI (1342–52), Innocent VI (1352–62), and Urban V (1362–70). He was one of the most influential surgeons of the fourteenth century. His *Inventorium sive collectorium in parte chirurgiciali medicine* (1363), usually called *Chirurgia* or *Chirurgia magna*, was the standard work throughout Europe until at least the seventeenth century, and probably accurately reflects the state of medical knowledge of the time; it is a mine of information.

CHAUVEAU, JEAN-BAPTISTE AUGUSTE (*b. Yonne, France, 1827; d. Paris, France, 1917*), physiology, veterinary medicine.

Received veterinary degree at Alford (1844), was head in anatomy and physiology at the Lyons veterinary school, and inspector general of veterinary schools (from 1886). He taught at the Museum of Natural History and was president of the Academy of Sciences (1907) and the Academy of Medicine (1913). Wrote a highly regarded text on the anatomy of domestic animals. He performed some of the earliest cardiac catheterizations on horses, showed that cattle could be infected with human tuberculosis, refuted Claude Bernard's view that glucose was metabolized in the lung but not in the muscle, and showed that the metabolism of protein requires energy.

CHAZY, JEAN FRANÇOIS (*b. Villefranche-sur-Saône, France, 1882; d. Paris, France, 1955*), celestial mechanics.

Studied at the École Normale Supérieure and the Sorbonne (doctorate, 1910) and taught at Grenoble, Lille, and the Sorbonne (1925–53). A classically trained mathematician, he did great work in celestial mechanics by pushing to its extreme limits the Newtonian model of mathematical astronomy. Attacking the three-body problem of Newtonian mechanics (from 1919), he was able to determine the region of the twelve-dimensional space defined by the positions and velocities of two of the bodies relative to the third within which the bounded trajectories can only exist—and thus to achieve a representation of planetary motions (1922). In his famous Newtonian critique of Newcomb's calculations for the advance of the perihelion of Mercury he furnished a very nearly exact value (1921).

CHEBOTARYOV, NIKOLAI GRIGORIEVICH (*b. Kamenets-Podolsk [now Ukrainian S.S.R.], 1894; d. Moscow, U.S.S.R., 1947*), mathematics.

Received degrees at Kiev (1916; doctorate, 1927), and taught at Odessa (1921–27) and at Kazan University (1928–47), where he founded his own school of algebra. His works deal with the algebra of polynomials and fields, the problem of resolvents, the distribution of the roots of an equation on the plane, the theory of algebraic numbers, the theory of Lie groups, geometry, and the history of mathematics.

CHEBYSHEV, PAFNUTY LVOVICH (*b. Okatovo, Kaluga region, Russia, 1821; d. St. Petersburg, Russia, 1894*), mathematics.

Received a bachelor's degree (1841) and a master's degree (1843) at Moscow University under N. D. Brashman and a doctorate at Petersburg (1849). He taught at Petersburg (1847–82). He was one of the first members of the Moscow Mathematical Society (of which Brashman was the principal founder and the first president). He was a member in applied mathematics of the Petersburg Academy of Sciences (from 1853); a member of its Artillery Committee (from 1856), to which he contributed particularly in ballistics; and, on the Scientific Committee of the Ministry of Education (1856–73), contributed to syllabi for secondary schools. He was the first Russian scientist to be a foreign member (1874) of the French Academy.

His and his disciples' studies of the theory of numbers advanced the theory in Russia to a level reached a century before by Euler. With Bunyakovski, he prepared an edition with commentary of Euler's works on the theory (1849). A systematic analysis with his own discoveries was long used as a textbook in Russian universities. His two classic memoirs on the distribution of prime numbers (1849, 1852) became widely known. He used the properties of Euler's zeta function in the real domain to prove the principal inaccuracy of Legendre's formula for the number of prime numbers not exceeding a given number.

His work on the integration of algebraic functions (1853–67) was directed toward determining conditions for integration in the final form of different classes of irrational functions, closely connected with the work of Abel, Liouville, and, in part, Ostrogradski. He gave (1853) the final solution of the problem of the integration of the binomial differential $x^m(a + bx^n)^p dx$. In the theory of elliptic integrals he substantially supplemented Abel.

His studies of the theory of hinge mechanisms aimed at the smallest deviation of the trajectory of any points from the straight line for the whole interval studied. A corresponding mathematical problem was to choose the function for which the greatest modulo error is the smallest under all considered values. His general theory proceeded from the approximation of functions by means of polynomials, seeking the uniform best approximation throughout the interval; this work proved to be his outstanding contribution, on which he was engaged for forty years (from 1854) and synthesized his technological and mathematical inclinations. He first formulated the "theory of polynomials deviating least from zero" in 1854. He extended the problem to all kinds of functions depending on n parameters, generalized on the method of solution, and analyzed two cases when the function is rational (1859). He extended his work to the theory of interpolation on the method of least squares (1855–75); the theory of orthogonal polynomials such as Hermite and Laguerre systems, in which he introduced polynomials by means of an expansion in continued fractions of certain integrals; the theory of moments, in which he similarly introduced expansion in continued fractions and solved a special case in mathematical terms; and the approximate calculus of definite integrals (1874).

On the theory of probability he demonstrated precisely and simply the generalized law of large numbers (1866). The theorems of Poisson and Jakob Bernoulli are special cases for sequences of random quantities. By developing his method of moments and of estimation of the limit values of integrals, he also extended to sequences of independent random quantities the central limit theorem of Moivre and Laplace (1887), thus facilitating application of the theory of probability to mathematical statistics and natural sciences. He was the first to estimate clearly and to use the concepts of "random quantity" and its "expectation (mean) value." He aimed to estimate exactly, as valid inequalities, the possible deviations from limit regularities.

Chebyshev initiated a new branch of the theory of surfaces in his "Sur la coupe des vêtements" (1878) in his investigation of a surface so that a net is formed whose two systems of lines form curvilinear quadrangles with equal opposite sides—the "Chebyshev net."

The influential Petersburg school he founded, which partly derived from Bunyakovsky and Ostrogradski, included Lyapunov and Markov, his prominent disciples. He especially valued solutions that achieved a "maximum possible advantage," that contributed to a "theory of the greatest and least values." He tended to set a concrete problem as a source of theoretical conclusions later generalized, and to seek the most effective solutions that approached computing algorithms. He saw the unity of theory and practice as the moving force of mathematical progress. He was a notable representative of the "mathematics of inequalities" of the late nineteenth century. He preferred elementary mathematical apparatus, particularly his almost exclusive use of functions in the real domain, and was especially adept at using continued fractions.

CHENEVIX, RICHARD (*b. Ballycommon, near Dublin, Ireland, 1774; d. Paris, France, 1830*), chemistry, mineralogy.

After education at University of Glasgow, he soon revealed his abilities as an analytical chemist in his analyses of a new variety of lead ore; of arsenates of copper; and

of sapphire, ruby, and corundum. His scientific reputation was badly damaged when he attacked Wollaston's discovery of palladium, and he left England for France (1804). There he published a significant paper in which he disputed Werner's classification of minerals by their chemical composition and adopted Haüy's criterion of classification by their physical characteristics.

CHERNOV, DMITRI KONSTANTINOVICH (*b. St. Petersburg, Russia, 1839; d. Yalta, U.S.S.R., 1921*), metallurgy.

Graduated from the St. Petersburg Practical Technological Institute (1858), taught there (to 1866), worked in a steel casting plant (1866–80), and taught at the Mikhailovsky Artillery Academy in St. Petersburg (from 1889). Founded an important school of metallurgists. He discovered (1866–68) the critical temperatures for phase transformations in steel and plotted a series of thermometric "Chernov points," particularly the temperature below which steel does not harden independently of the cooling and the temperature at which the dissolution of ferrite in austenite ceases during the heating of steel. He recognized the influence of carbon content on steel and made the first rough sketch of the "iron-carbon state" diagram later constructed by Roberts-Austin. His work gave scientific basis to contemporary metallurgy and the process for heat treatment of metals. He also presented a coherent theory of the crystallization of steel ingots (1879), confirmed the importance of the complete deoxidation of steel during smelting and the advisability of using complex deoxidizers, and improved the converter method of producing cast steel (1872).

CHERNYAEV, ILYA ILYICH (*b. Spasskoye, Vologda district, Russia, 1893; d. Moscow, U.S.S.R., 1966*), chemistry.

Graduated from St. Petersburg University (1915). Took an active part in organization and development of science from the beginning of the existence of the Soviet state. Worked in the platinum department of the Commission for the Study of the Productive Capacity of Russia (from 1917), at the Institute for Platinum and Other Precious Metals (1918–33), and headed the department of complex compounds of the Institute of General and Inorganic Chemistry of the Academy of Sciences of the U.S.S.R., directing the Institute from 1941 to 1964. He taught at Leningrad (1925–35) and at Moscow. His crowning achievement was the development of methods to obtain platinum, palladium, and rhodium in a spectroscopically pure state. His studies of thorium and uranium contributed greatly to the establishment of the nuclear fuel industry in the U.S.S.R.

CHERNYSHEV, FEODOSII NIKOLAEVICH (*b. Kiev, Russia, 1856; d. St. Petersburg, Russia, 1914*), geology, stratigraphy, paleontology.

Graduated from St. Petersburg Mining Institute (1880). From 1882 worked with the Geological Committee of Russia, becoming director in 1903, as well as director of the Mineralogical Museum of the Academy of Sciences. His geological surveys of the Devonian strata of the Urals had great significance in the clarification of the physical and geographical conditions of the Devonian period over a large part of the earth's surface, from Western Europe to America. Published an important monograph resulting from the large amount of geological and paleontological material collected on a difficult expedition to the Timan ridge. Studied the geological structure of the Donets coal basin and compiled a geological map of European Russia.

CHERWELL, LORD. *See* **Lindemann, F. A.**

CHEVALLIER, JEAN-BAPTISTE-ALPHONSE (*b. Langres, France, 1793; d. Paris, France, 1879*), chemistry, public health.

Taught at the École de Pharmacie in Paris and had a private analytical laboratory (from 1835). He successfully applied chemical expertise to a variety of public health problems, such as food and drug adulteration, industrial hygiene, toxicology, and disinfection, in a multitude of books, memoirs and reports. His *Dictionnaire des altérations et falsifications des substances alimentaires, médicamenteuses et commerciales* (1850–52) was the most important work of its kind in France.

CHEVALLIER, TEMPLE (*b. Bury St. Edmonds* [?], *England, 1794; d. Durham, England, 1873*), astronomy, education.

Studied at Pembroke College, Cambridge, was ordained (1818), and taught at Durham University (from 1835), where he largely planned the observatory, making use of its facilities in his work on the sun's diameter, solar eclipses, the planets, and meteorological phenomena. He founded an engineering class (1838) and a department of physics at Durham and helped found (1871) the College of Science at Newcastle (Armstrong College).

CHEVENARD, PIERRE ANTOINE JEAN SYLVES-TRE (*b. Thizy, Rhône, France, 1888; d. Fontenay-aux-Roses, France, 1960*), metallurgy.

Graduated from the École des Mines at Saint-Étienne (1910) and worked at the Société de Commenty Fourchambault et Decazeville (from 1910), becoming its scientific director (1935). In pursuing the investigations begun by Guillaume, he explored the physical properties of nickel, providing the clockmaking industry with a remarkable series of alloys. He brought out several alloys that showed good resistance to creep at high temperatures and especially high resistance to corrosion. He created a series of self-recording micromachines, almost all based on the optical tripod, which permitted the examination of heterogeneous pieces with a new exactness, and facilitated the use of certain physical methods to such a degree that his name has been passed from the device to the methods themselves. This is the case with the dilatometric and thermoponderal methods, through his differential dilatometer and his thermobalance.

CHEVREUL, MICHEL EUGÈNE (*b. Angers, France, 1786; d. Paris, France, 1889*), chemistry.

Chevreul was associated with the Muséum d'Histoire Naturelle for nearly ninety years as student, teacher, and director (1864–79). He was also director of dyeing at the Manufactures Royales des Gobelins (from 1824), and was president of the Academy of Sciences (1839, 1871). During his long and distinguished career he published many books and papers on a great variety of scientific subjects. His work on dyes, color theory and the chemistry of natu-

ral fats all stemmed from his association with Vauquelin at the Museum. His monumental *De la loi du contraste simultané des couleurs* (1839) was his most influential book. It stemmed from his discovery that the apparent intensity and vigor of colors depended less on pigmentation than on the hue of the adjacent color. To provide precise standards in the definition and use of colors, he defined almost 15,000 tones in a chromatic circle of seventy-two colors representing the entire visible spectrum. When science turned to measurement with optical instruments, his book continued to be influential among painters, designers, and decorators, particularly among the neo-impressionist painters who derived their methods from him.

Chevreul's studies of natural fats (from 1811) resulted in his *Recherches chimiques sur les corps gras* (1823), a major contribution to the early development of organic chemistry, the first full account of the nature of a natural organic substance, and the first model for exact analytical research. He showed that fats were composed of a few chemical species which were amenable to analysis and obeyed the same laws of chemical combination as inorganic substances. He obtained a whole series of new organic acids and isolated, studied, and named many of the fatty acid series from butyric to stearic acid. He concluded that saponification was essentially the chemical fixation of water, and that soaps were combinations of a fatty acid with an inorganic base and were therefore true salts. He developed methods of fractional solution to separate the immediate principles in fats and was chiefly responsible for introducing the melting point to establish the identity and purity of organic substances.

CHEYNE, GEORGE (*b. Aberdeenshire, Scotland, 1671; d. Bath, England, 1743*), medicine, mathematics, theology.

Cheyne studied medicine under Pitcairn in Edinburgh and practiced in London (1702–20) and in Bath (from 1720). He began as a principal representative of British "Newtonianism." His *A New Theory of Fevers* (1702) was based on Pitcairn's supposedly "mathematical" and "Newtonian" variety of iatromechanism. His *Fluxionum methodus inversa* (1703) was attacked by Moivre and may have provoked Newton to refutation (on "quadratures," *Opticks*, 1704 ed.). Cheyne's *Philosophical Principles of Natural Religion* (1705) claimed that the observed phenomena of attraction in the universe argued for a Supreme Being. This argument proved popular and may have impressed Newton (in *Opticks*, 1706 ed.). Cheyne's later series of practical guides emphasized moderation in diet and drink. In these works his emphasis on the bodily fibers, particularly in *De natura fibrae* (1725) and *The English Malady* (1733), aroused much interest in Britain in the fibers and mind-body metaphysics.

CHIARUGI, GIULIO (*b. Siena, Italy, 1859; d. Florence, Italy, 1944*), anatomy.

Studied at University of Siena, and graduated from the University of Turin (1882). Taught at Siena (1886–90) and at the Medical School of Florence (1890–1934), also directing the Institute of Human Anatomy in Florence (from 1890). One of the most eminent embryologists of last hundred years, he helped shape present-day anatomy and influenced thousands of medical students as a great teacher. In his studies of the human encephalon (1885,

1886), he confirmed that formation of the cerebral convolutions is passed on by heredity. In embryology, he was the first to demonstrate (1887) that activity of the heart begins in the very first stages of ontogeny, thus proving the theory of cardiac automatism. He later showed the dual origin of the vagus nerve.

CHICHIBABIN, ALEXEI YEVGENIEVICH (*b. Kuzemino, Poltava gubernia* [*now Ukrainian SSR*], *Russia, 1871; d. Paris, France, 1945*), chemistry.

Graduated from Moscow University (1892), taught there (1918–23) and at Moscow Higher Technical School (1909–30), and worked in the organic chemistry laboratory at the Collège de France (from 1930). Wrote an important chemistry textbook (1924). Organized production of pharmaceuticals in Russia; responsible for construction of first Russian alkaloid plant. He discovered new methods of synthesizing pyridine or alkylpyridine with the alkyl group in any position. With Seide, he discovered (1913) direct amination, now known as the Chichibabin reaction, which is applied to industrial preparation of 2-aminopyridine from pyridine. Study of the Chichibabin amination was extended to different pyridines, natural nicotine, and compounds of the quinoline and isoquinoline series.

CHILD, CHARLES MANNING (*b. Ypsilanti, Mich., 1869; d. Palo Alto, Calif., 1954*), zoology.

Received Ph.B. (1890) and M.S. (1892) at Wesleyan University, and a Ph.D. at Leipzig (1894). He taught at the University of Chicago (1895–1937), where he headed the department of zoology. His two main areas of research were sensitivity and reactivity of animal organisms, and the problems of reproduction and development. His main contribution, the gradient theory, took its name from Child's observation that regeneration of the organism occurs in graded physiological stages along the axis, with each gradient physiological process seemingly connected to those immediately adjacent to it.

CHILDREY, JOSHUA (*b. Rochester, England, 1623; d. Upwey, Dorsetshire, England, 1670*), meteorology, natural history.

Received B.A. from Magdalen College, Oxford (1646). Became doctor of divinity (1661); was made rector of Upwey (1664–70). In his astrological works, he sought to extend the Baconian method to astrology. His best-known work was his *Britannia Baconia: or, The Natural Rarities of England, Scotland and Wales, According as They Are to be Found in Every Shire. Historically Related, According to the Precepts of Lord Bacon* (1660). He made numerous observations on the weather and tides.

CH'IN CHIU-SHAO (*b. Szechuan, China, ca. 1202; d. Kwangtung, China, ca. 1261*), mathematics.

Ch'in, a genius in mathematics, has often been judged an intriguing and unprincipled character, notorious for poisoning those he found disagreeable. The son of a civil servant, he is known to have studied astronomy at the astronomical bureau in the Sung capital, Chung-tu (now Hangchow), in 1224–25. He himself mentions that he learned mathematics from an unidentified recluse scholar. He held a number of administrative posts, including a governorship in modern Hainan for a few

months (1258), but was dismissed on charges of bribery and corruption, returning home, we are told, with immense wealth. He was then a civil aid to an intimate friend, Wu Ch'ien, who became a minister, then lost favor (1260) and was given a lesser assignment in Kwangtung province. Ch'in received an appointment there shortly before he died. His celebrated *Shu-shu chiu-chang* ("Mathematical Treatise in Nine Sections") has been variously titled through the centuries; Sarton concluded that it and the *Shu-hsüeh* ("Outline of Mathematics") were separate works. *Shu-shu chiu-chang* apparently existed only in manuscript until the first known publication in 1842. Each of its nine sections includes two chapters of nine problems. The first section, on indeterminate analysis, brought the study of that topic in China to its highest point. Other sections on astronomical and calendrical calculations, land measurement, and surveying by triangulation, for example, contain much sociological information, from finance and commerce to the levy of taxes. The complete text has not been translated or investigated in full, although some individual problems have been studied.

From the third century, Chinese calendar experts had taken as their starting point the Grand Cycle (*Shang yuan*), the last time the winter solstice fell exactly at midnight on the fourth day of the eleventh month, which also happened to be the first day (*chia-tzu,* cyclic day) of a sixty-day cycle. For several hundred years, calendar experts had been working out the Grand Cycle from new astronomical data. The earliest elucidation of the method available to us comes from Ch'in. His method of solving indeterminate analysis is given in a German manuscript from Göttingen (*ca.* 1550), but it was not rediscovered in Europe before Lebesque (1859) and Stieltjes (1890). The identity of the Chinese rule with Gauss's formula was pointed out by Matthiessen in the last century, after Ch'in's study was first brought to the attention of the West by Alexander Wylie. Ch'in also deals with numbers which have common factors: he would go about searching for the least integral value of a multiple, an important intermediate stage in indeterminate analysis which became known as the *ta yen ch'iu i shu* ("the Great Extension method of searching for unity"). The term *ta yen* ("Great Extension") came from a method of divination in the *Book of Changes:* fifty yarrow stalks were taken, and one was set aside before the remaining forty-nine were divided into two random groups. Ch'in sought to explain the term *ta yen ch'iu i shu* in the first problem of his book by introducing the so-called "Great Extension number" 50 and the number 49 and showing how they could be arrived at from the numbers 1, 2, 3, 4. He also introduced many technical terms used in indeterminate analysis. He used the celestial monad (*t'ien-yuan*) to denote a known number, differing from the method employed by his contemporary Li Chih (*t'ien-yuan-shu*) and later known in Japan as the *tengen jutsu,* where it represents an unknown algebraic quantity.

He represented algebraic equations by placing calculating rods on the counting board so that the absolute term appeared on the top of the vertical column; immediately below it was the unknown quantity, followed by the increasing powers of the unknown. Negative quantities are denoted by an extra rod placed obliquely over the first figure of the number. The text is also the oldest extant in China to contain the zero symbol. He always arranged his equations so that the absolute term was negative, equivalent to Thomas Harriot's practice (1631). He used a method, probably not original, to solve numerical equations of any degree identical to that rediscovered by Paolo Ruffini (*ca.* 1805) and W. G. Horner (1819).

CHITTENDEN, RUSSELL HENRY (*b. New Haven, Conn., 1856; d. New Haven, 1943*), physiological chemistry.

Received Ph.D. (1880) at the Sheffield Scientific School of Yale University, taught there (1882–1922), and was permanent secretary, director (1898–1922), and treasurer (1898–1930). He attained wide recognition both as an administrator and as a teacher. His students carried his principles and methods of physiological chemistry to almost every other medical school in the country. He was first to observe the occurrence of free glycine in nature (1875). His work with W. Kühne of Heidelberg on the nature of proteins contributed the sound basic premise that digestion is a gradual process and laid a firm technical foundation for the study of enzymes. His most important contribution was his study of the protein requirement of man; his experiments on himself and others established that about fifty grams a day, rather than the current standard of 118, was sufficient to maintain good health (1904). He also did outstanding work on the effects of alcohol on man and the effects of sodium benzoate and other commercial additives to human food (1908–15).

CHLADNI, ERNST FLORENZ FRIEDRICH (*b. Wittenberg, Germany, 1756; d. Breslau, Germany, 1827*), physics.

Received degree in jurisprudence at Leipzig (1782) but devoted himself to the study of acoustics and vibration. He designed and constructed two keyboard instruments, the euphonium and the clavicylinder. He alternated between his experimental studies at his home in Wittenberg and travels in Europe. His most important work was his demonstration of the vibrations of plates, using his sand pattern technique, running a violin bow over sand covered plates (1787). He classified the structure of the vibrations by geometrical shape, noting for each the corresponding pitch. He showed that the patterns and sounds of a vibrating plate are analogous to the shapes and tones of the modes in the harmonic series of a string. His demonstrations evoked great interest throughout Europe, particularly in France, and led to much work on the mathematical theory of vibration. Using the same sand figure method, he also studied the vibrations of cylindrical and prismatic rods.

CHODAT, ROBERT (*b. Moutier-Grandval, Switzerland, 1865; d. Geneva, Switzerland, 1934*), botany, algology, plant physiology.

Received doctorate at Geneva (1887), taught there (from 1888), and was director of the Institut de Botanique (from 1900). His voluminous *Monographia Polygalacearum* (1893) attracted worldwide attention. He was one of the first to obtain a pure culture of isolated algae (1893) and discovered the cause of the vine disease now known as acariasis. Besides algology, his work covered floristics, ecology, plant anatomy, cytology, teratology, and pathology. He collaborated on the monu-

mental *Handbuch der biologischen Arbeitsmethoden* from its very inception.

CHRISTIANSEN, CHRISTIAN (*b. Lónborg Jutland, Denmark, 1843; d. Copenhagen, Denmark, 1917*), physics.

Received M.S. at University of Copenhagen (1866). Taught at the University of Copenhagen and at the Polytechnical Institute and the Agricultural College of Copenhagen (from 1886). Under influence of Ludvig Lorenz, laid foundation for the study of theoretical physics at Copenhagen; students on whom he exerted great influence included Martin Knudsen and Niels Bohr. Discovered anomalous dispersion of light in fuchsine solutions (1870); constructed water-jet pump to produce low pressures (1872).

CHRISTIE, SAMUEL HUNTER (*b. London, England, 1784; d. Twickenham, London, 1865*), magnetism.

Graduated from Trinity College, Cambridge (1805) and taught at Woolwich Military Academy (1806–1854). Almost all his investigations were related to terrestrial magnetism. He discovered that the simple rotation of an unmagnetized iron plate had a considerable influence on its magnetic properties (1821; prior to Arago). He concluded that the magnetism is communicated from the earth and speculated that the earth receives its magnetism from the sun, later also speculating that diurnal variation of the earth's magnetic field is caused by thermoelectric currents in the earth produced by the sun's heating (1823). From experimental evidence he supported the theory that voltaelectricity, thermoelectricity, and magnetoelectricity are identical (1833). Father of Sir William H. M. Christie (1845–1922).

CHRISTIE, WILLIAM HENRY MAHONEY (*b. Woolwich, England, 1845; d. at sea, 1922*), astronomy.

Christie, the son of S. H. Christie (1784–1865), was educated at King's College, London, and Trinity College, Cambridge, became chief assistant at the Royal Observatory (1870) and astronomer royal (1881–1910). He engaged primarily in positional astronomy, later encouraging more physical observations at the observatory. His contribution was greater in administration than in theory; under him the scope of observations went far beyond utilitarian needs, and the observatory prospered materially with the acquisition of many new instruments and the addition of several new buildings.

CHRISTMANN, JACOB (*b. Johannesberg, Rheingau, Germany, 1554; d. Heidelberg, Germany, 1613*), oriental studies, mathematics, chronology, astronomy.

Studied oriental subjects and taught at Heidelberg (from 1584), becoming rector in 1602 and professor of Arabic in 1608. The latter position he had advocated to open possibilities for teaching philosophy and medicine from the original sources. After inheriting some astronomical instruments, he was the first to use the telescope in conjunction with such instruments as the sextant or Jacob's staff (1611). In his books on chronology, he disputed the work of Scaliger and Lipsius.

CHRISTOFFEL, ELWIN BRUNO (*b. Montjoie [now Monschau], near Aachen, Germany, 1829; d. Strasbourg, France [then Germany], 1900*), mathematics.

Received doctorate at the University of Berlin (1856) and taught at Berlin, the Polytechnicum in Zurich, the Gewerbsakademie in Berlin, and at the University of Strasbourg (1872–92). He was a very conscientious mathematician and teacher. He extended Riemann's theta function studies (1901) and made an early contribution to the theory of shock waves (1877). His best-known work, "Über die Transformation der homogenen Differentialausdrücke zweiten Grades" (1869), introduced the three index symbols now called Christoffel symbols of the first and second order, and a series of symbols of more than three indices, of which the four index symbols are now known as the Riemann-Christoffel symbols, or coordinates of the Riemann-Christoffel curvature tensor.

CHRISTOL (CRISTOL), JULES DE (*b. Montpellier, France, 1802; d. Montpellier, 1861*), paleontology.

Received doctorate at Montpellier (1834) and taught at Dijon (from 1837), where he became dean of the Faculty of Sciences (1853). A mediocre geologist but a competent osteologist, he specialized in the study of the Tertiary and Quaternary mammals of the south of France, particularly those from caves and osseous breccia. He is often cited as the founder of prehistory for his daring statement (1829) identifying certain human bones as fossil man and thus challenging Cuvier.

CHRYSTAL, GEORGE (*b. Mill of Kingoodie, near Old Meldrum, Aberdeenshire, Scotland, 1851; d. Edinburgh, Scotland, 1911*), education, mathematics, physics.

Graduated from Aberdeen University (1871) and Peterhouse, Cambridge (1875). He held the chair of mathematics at Edinburgh University (1879–1911) and was dean of the Faculty of Arts (1890–1911). He brought a progressive and substantial rise in the standard of the mathematical syllabus and teaching, and contributed much to preuniversity teaching throughout Scotland. His *Algebra* (1886) profoundly influenced teaching throughout Great Britain and beyond. Many of his biographies for the *Encyclopaedia Britannica* are still of value. He also wrote the surveys, "Electricity" and "Magnetism," for the ninth edition.

CHU SHIH-CHIEH (*fl. China, 1280–1303*), mathematics.

Little is known of the life of Chu except that he flourished as a mathematician and teacher in the two decades after the Mongol conquest of the Sung dynasty (1279) had reunified China. He wrote a textbook for beginners in mathematics in 1299 and, in 1303, his *Ssu-yüan yü-chien*, which contained the "method of the four elements" he invented and which took Chinese algebra to its peak. It also marked the end of the Golden Age of Chinese mathematics. After disappearing from China, probably toward the end of the eighteenth century, the manuscript was rediscovered and appeared in the vast imperial library collection prepared by Juan Yuan early in the nineteenth century. Lo Shih-lin's adaptation (1834) brought the "method of the four elements" much attention from Chinese mathematicians, including I Chih-han, Li Shan-lan, Wu Chia-shan, and Hua Heng-fang. There is a French translation by L. van Hée and an English translation by Ch'en Tsai-hsin. The "method of celestial elements" was probably known in China before the thirteenth century;

Chu extended it for the first time to express four unknown quantities in the same algebraic equation. Thus used, it became known as the "method of four elements" (*ssu-yüan shu*). Each "element" represents an unknown quantity. Chu was limited by the two-dimensional space of the counting-board; the method cannot be used to represent more than four unknowns or the cross product of more than two unknowns. He also dealt with numerical equations of higher degree, even up to the power fourteen. He sometimes used a transformation method (*fan fa*); he gives no description, but it could only be similar to the Horner-Ruffini method for the solution of cubic equations. Where the root of an equation was not a whole number, he sometimes found the next approximation by using the coefficients obtained from Horner's method. Where exact roots were not found, he would sometimes find the next decimal place for the root by continuing the process of root extraction. Like Ch'in, he also employed a method of substitution to give the approximate number. Sometimes he combined two methods. He advanced the study of higher series by dealing with bundles of arrows of various cross-sections, such as circular or square, and with piles of balls arranged so that they formed a triangle, a pyramid, a cone, and so on. No theoretical proofs are given. After Chu, the study of higher series in China was only revived by the Jesuits. Wang Lai, for example, generalized the first five of Chu's series. In the nineteenth century Chinese mathematicians further generalized and modernized his forms; in fact, certain relationships erroneously attributed to him can be traced only as far as Li Shan-lan. Also significant was Chu's application of the method of *chao-ch'a* ("finite differences")—originally used by Chinese astronomers to find arbitrary constants in formulas for celestial motions—to other problems.

CHUGAEV, LEV ALEKSANDROVICH (*b. Moscow, Russia, 1873; d. Gryazovets, Vologoskaya oblast, U.S.S.R., 1922*), chemistry.

Graduated from Moscow University (master's, 1903). Taught at the Bacteriology Institute in Moscow (1896–1904), Moscow Technical College (1904–08), and St. Petersburg University and St. Petersburg Institute of Technology (1908–22). Responsible for creation of the Institute for the Study of Platinum and Precious Metals (1918), and a founder of the Russian Scientific and Technical Institute of Nutrition (1918) and the Institute of Applied Chemistry (1919). His research covered problems in biochemistry and in organic, inorganic, and physical chemistry. Using his xanthogen method, he first synthesized a number of terpene hydrocarbons. His method was a classic of organic chemistry and has been applied for decades. Study of the optical properties of organic compounds allowed him to formulate the "rule of distance" (1908). He made important contributions in the synthesis and stereochemistry of the inner complex salts of copper, nickel, silver, cobalt, and the platinum metals, and studied the specific reactions of the platinum metals that can be used for their separation and purification.

CHUQUET, NICOLAS (*b. Paris [?], France; fl. second half of fifteenth century*), algebra.

Chuquet is known only through one work written before May 1484, of which only two parts have been published: the "Triparty," on the science of numbers (1880), and a set of 156 problems (1881). The analysis of these problems, a section on practical geometry, and another on commercial arithmetic remain unpublished. The "Triparty" states that he was a Parisian with a baccalaureate in medicine from Lyons. Several passages from the book were copied slavishly by "Master Étienne de la Roche" in his arithmetic text (1520), who cites Chuquet and his "Triparty," without adding that he is plagiarizing outrageously. Étienne thus confirms the existence and importance of Chuquet. If he had plagiarized the algebraic "règle des premiers" and its applications, mathematics would perhaps be grateful to him for his larcenies. But the most original part of Chuquet's work remained unknown until very recently.

The only claim Chuquet makes for priority is for his "règle des nombres moyens"; he does not stress his claim to the "règle des premiers," where his originality is obvious, as in his rules for decimal numeration. On fractions he is clear but, like all his contemporaries, always used a numerator smaller than the denominator, which led to unnecessary complications in calculation. Of his methods for his collection of remarkable linear problems, he said that after having solved a problem by the usual methods —double position or algebra (his "règle des premiers") —one must vary the known numerical quantities and analyze the sequence of computations in order to extract a canon (formula). His own analysis on these lines generally led him to a correct formula. Another of his original concepts is that adding or subtracting zero does not change the number. He reviewed the rules for addition and subtraction of negative numbers, carrying this farther than Fibonacci. His "règle des nombres moyens" allows solution of many otherwise unapproachable problems. It established that between any two given fractions a third can always be interpolated that has for numerator the sum of the numerator of the other two fractions, and for denominator the sum of their denominators (recently shown to permit solving any problem allowing for rational solution).

His most original concept was the "règle des premiers," which "does everything that other rules do and, in addition, solves a great many more difficult problems"— thus he announced the algebraic method. Like most algebraists of his time, he would have liked to go beyond the second degree but was not sure how to go about it.

The "Triparty" was an abstract treatise on algebra, without concrete applications, which greatly extended the concept of number—zero, negative numbers, and roots and combinations of roots all being included. Excellent notations prefigured, in particular, Bombelli. Its weak points were poor treatment of cases of indetermination and insolubility in linear algebra, lack of recognition of the importance of degree in the theory of equations, and traditional errors in equations of the second degree. His taste for needlessly complicated computation and the shortcomings of numerical algebra are painfully evident.

The 156 problems that follow the "Triparty" are only apparently concrete. One detects here not a number theorist but a pure algebraist. Many of the problems he chose are found in Bachet de Méziriac and Pacioli, and are part of an old tradition; his originality lay in his algebraic treatment. He used, at least five times, not one

unknown but two. He thus preceded Luca Pacioli's similar procedure in the Summa (1494) by ten years.

CHWISTEK, LEON (b. Zakopane, Poland, 1884; d. Berwisza, near Moscow, U.S.S.R., 1944), philosophy, logic, aesthetics.

Taught logic at the University of Lvov (1930–40), then sought refuge in the Soviet Union. In 1921 he published his theory of the plurality of realities: natural reality, physical reality, reality of sensation, and reality of images. Under the influence of Poincaré, he developed a strictly nominalistic attitude toward logic and mathematics. Dissatisfied with Russell's foundation of mathematics, Chwistek proposed his theory of constructive types in 1924. His main contribution was the foundation of logic and mathematics on his system of rational semantics.

CIAMICIAN, GIACOMO LUIGI (b. Trieste, Italy, 1857; d. Bologna, Italy, 1922), chemistry.

Studied at Vienna and at Giessen (Ph.D., 1880). Worked as Cannizzaro's assistant at Rome (1880); taught at Padua (1887) and Bologna (1889). His studies of pyrrole (1880–1905) established it as a secondary amine; among the many derivatives he prepared was iodol (tetraiodopyrrole), which has therapeutic use as a substitute for iodoform. He helped found photochemistry (1900–15) and discovered many photochemical reactions. With Ciro Ravenna he worked on the origin and function of organic substances in plants (1908–22), synthesizing glycosides in plants, and concluding that alkaloids had a function similar to that of hormones in animals.

CIRUELO, PEDRO, also known as **Pedro Sánchez Ciruelo** (b. Daroca, Spain, 1470; d. Salamanca [?], Spain, 1554), mathematics, logic, natural philosophy.

Studied at Salamanca and at Paris (1492–1502), taught mathematics at Paris (1502–ca. 1515) and theology at Alcalá and Salamanca thereafter. His Tractatus arithmeticae practicae (1495) and Cursus quatuor mathematicarum artium liberalium (1516) went through many printings. Among his other works were editions of Bradwardine, Sacrobosco, Boethius, and Peckham.

CLAIRAUT, ALEXIS-CLAUDE (b. Paris, France, 1713; d. Paris, 1765), mathematics, mechanics, celestial mechanics, geodesy, optics.

Educated by his father in the pioneering mathematics of the era, analytical geometry and infinitesimal calculus. Elected to the Academy of Sciences at sixteen, and there allied himself with Maupertuis and the group supporting Newton. Led an expedition to Lapland in 1736, returning to Paris in 1737. Guided the marquise du Châtelet's studies, particularly her translation of Newton's Principia; many of his works are used in it, including his Théorie de la figure de la terre (1743). In this classic is found the formula named for him expressing the earth's gravity as a function of latitude. This work helped gain acceptance for Newton's theory of gravitation in France. From his controversy with Buffon (1745) on Clairaut's suggested correction of Newton's law of attraction, he arrived at the first approximate resolution of the three-body problem in celestial mechanics (Théorie de la lune, 1752; Tables de la lune, 1754). He attacked the three-body problem in the case of comets by attempting to calculate precisely the passage of Halley's comet by calculating the perturbations due to Jupiter and Saturn. He was attacked by d'Alembert and Le Monnier, and the polemical flurry lasted a year. From this work came his *Théorie du mouvement des comètes* (1760?) and *Recherches sur la comète* (1762). He offered a theoretical proof (1737) of Bradley's discovery of the aberration of light and indicated corrections for the aberration of planets, comets and satellites (1746). He worked on the theoretical problem of refraction in Newton's corpuscular theory of light (from 1739) and on its applications to astronomical instruments (1761–62). In mathematics he made the first serious analytical study of the gauche curve (1731) and originated the differential equations named for him (1734). His ideas on pedagogy were influenced by his own mathematical education, which conformed little to university tradition, as his *Élémens de géométrie* (1741) and *Élémens d'algèbre* (1746) show.

CLAISEN, LUDWIG (*b. Cologne, Germany, 1851; d. Godesberg-am-Rhein, Germany, 1930*), chemistry.

Studied at Göttingen and at Bonn (doctorate, 1874). Taught at Bonn (1875–82); Owens College, Manchester, England (1882–85); Aachen Technische Hochschule (1890–97); and University of Kiel (1897–1904). Worked in Baeyer's laboratory at Munich (1886–90), Emil Fischer's laboratory in Berlin (1904–07), and established his own laboratory at Godesberg (1907–26). His discoveries placed him among the most renowned researchers in organic chemistry. He developed the so-called Claisen condensation for synthesizing keto esters and 1,3-diketones.

CLAPEYRON, BENOIT-PIERRE-ÉMILE (*b. Paris, France, 1799; d. Paris, 1864*), civil engineering.

Graduated from the École Polytechnique (1818), studied at the École des Mines, and worked in the mining corps, specializing in steam engine design and construction. Collaborated with Lamé on several papers. Taught at the École des Ponts et Chaussées (from 1844). He is best known for the relationship, which bears his name, between the temperature coefficient of the equilibrium vapor pressure over a liquid or solid and the heat of vaporization (1834), an application of Sadi Carnot's principle. The Clapeyron relationship was ignored until Kelvin and Clausius revealed its true significance as the basis for the second law of thermodynamics.

CLARK, ALVAN (*b. Ashfield, Mass., 1804; d. Cambridgeport, Mass., 1887*); **CLARK, ALVAN GRAHAM** (*b. Fall River, Mass., 1832; d. Cambridgeport, Mass., 1897*); **CLARK, GEORGE BASSETT** (*b. Lowell, Mass., 1827; d. Cambridgeport, Mass., 1891*), astronomical instrumentation.

In their factory at Cambridgeport, the Clarks made the first significant American contribution to astronomical instrument making. Almost every American observatory built during this period, and some observatories abroad, housed an equatorial refracting telescope, and often auxiliary apparatus as well, made by the Clarks. While testing the 18½-inch objective later installed in the Dearborn Observatory in Chicago, Alvan Graham discovered the predicted but hitherto unseen companion of Sirius.

CLARK, JOSIAH LATIMER (*b. Great Marlow, Buckinghamshire, England, 1822; d. London, England, 1898*), technology.

As an engineer in a telegraph company, Clark's interest in practical telegraphic matters led him into important scientific investigations. In 1863 he demonstrated the speed of a current pulse was independent of the voltage applied. He developed a zinc-mercury standard cell, suggested the establishment of standard electrical units, and helped Airy develop a telegraphic system for reporting Greenwich mean time.

CLARK, THOMAS (*b. Ayr, Scotland, 1801; d. Glasgow, Scotland, 1867*), chemistry.

Clark was an accountant and then a chemist with two leading Glasgow industrial companies (1816–26), taught chemistry at the Glasgow Mechanics' Institution (1826–29), took a medical degree at Glasgow University (1831), and taught chemistry at Marischal College in Aberdeen (from 1833). At the Mechanics' Institution he prepared (1827) tables of elements, compounds, and atomic and molecular weights, notable for the use and modernity of symbols. His discovery of sodium pyrophosphate (1827) paved the way for Thomas Graham's study of phosphoric acids and the concept of polybasic acids. He is, however, best known for "Clark's process" of softening water, by the addition of milk of lime (1841).

CLARK, WILLIAM MANSFIELD (*b. Meyersville, N.Y., 1884; d. Baltimore, Md., 1964*), chemistry.

Received master's degree at Williams College, and Ph.D. at Johns Hopkins (1910). His work on the bacteriology of milk products for the U.S. Department of Agriculture (1910–20) led to *The Determination of Hydrogen Ions* (1920), a classic in its field. As chief of the Division of Chemistry of the Hygiene Laboratory, Public Health Service, he began life-long studies on oxidation-reduction potentials of dyes, and the study of metalloporphyrins. Taught at Johns Hopkins Medical School (1927–52).

CLARKE, EDWARD DANIEL (*b. Willingdon, Sussex, England, 1769; d. London, England, 1822*), mineralogy, geology.

Received B.A. at Jesus College, Cambridge (1790), became a fellow there (1797); did extensive fieldwork (1790–1802) in Europe, Russia, and the Middle East; taught mineralogy at Cambridge (from 1807) and was university librarian (from 1817). He had a significant contemporary impact through his teaching of mineralogy in terms of crystallography and the new chemistry, through the topographical geology and volcanological observations in his widely read *Travels* (6 vols., 1810–23), and through his enthusiasm for minerals and scientific fieldwork. He maintained correspondence with many scientists in Europe and England, and was a leader in founding the Cambridge Philosophical Society (1819).

CLARKE, FRANK WIGGLESWORTH (*b. Boston, Mass., 1847; d. Chevy Chase, Md., 1931*), geochemistry.

Received B.S. at Lawrence Scientific School of Harvard University (1867); taught at Boston Dental College (1870–73), Howard University (1873–74), and the University of Cincinnati (1874–83); and was chief chemist to the U.S. Geological Survey (1883–1924). Under his direction the laboratories became internationally known. He used his compilations of rock, mineral, and natural water analyses (*The Data of Geochemistry,* 1908) to explain the chemical processes occurring at the earth's surface. He emphasized the importance of equilibrium in predicting and describing chemical reactions in nature, and subsequent generations of geochemists successfully applied equilibrium thermodynamics to the formation and alteration of igneous, sedimentary, and metamorphic rocks. With H. S. Washington he calculated the average composition of the earth's crust to a depth of ten miles. His work on silicates (1895) essentially closed the chemical era of silicate mineralogy based upon chemical composition and reactions; X-ray diffraction and electron microscopy later opened a new era. He calculated the average composition of igneous and sedimentary rocks, and computed the total amount of sedimentation occurring during geological time. He provided some of the first estimates of the relative contributions to the geological column of inorganic sediments and those precipitated biologically. He was instrumental in the formation of the American Chemical Society (1889).

CLARKE, SAMUEL (*b. Norwich, England, 1675; d. London, England, 1729*), metaphysics, mathematics.

Received B.A. (1695), M.A. (1698), and D.D. (1709) from Cambridge. Held various ecclesiastical positions throughout his life, including chaplain to bishop of Norwich and to Queen Anne. His contemporaries ranked him almost with Newton in the force of his intellect. His notes to his Latin translation of Rohault's *Physics* turned a Cartesian treatise into a vehicle for disseminating the ideas of Newton; it was the major text at Cambridge for over forty years. His Latin translation (1706) of Newton's *Opticks* was commissioned by Newton himself. The sixteen sermons he delivered at the Boyle lectures for 1704 were published as *The Being and Attributes of God.* His Arianism became obvious with publication of his *Scripture Doctrine of the Trinity* (1712), and led to a long pamphlet war with Daniel Waterland. In a long controversy with Leibniz over the interpretation of the physical universe and its phenomena, Clarke maintained that time and space were real entities. His most direct contribution to physics came in correspondence with Leibniz, in which he considered the problem of computing the force of a moving body, strongly advocating the Newtonian position that such force could be expressed as the product of mass and velocity.

CLARKE, WILLIAM BRANWHITE (*b. East Bergholt, England, 1798; d. Sydney, Australia, 1878*), geology.

Received B.A. (1821) and M.A. (1824) at Jesus College, Cambridge. He emigrated to New South Wales (1839) and there laid the foundation for Australian geology. His contention that the carboniferous basins of New South Wales were lower in Paleozoic sequence than those of Europe and India generated a thirty-year controversy with Frederick McCoy until he was upheld by Koninck and Feistmantel (1876–79). Much of his impact on science stemmed from his continuing contact with scientists abroad. He was one of the first Australians to accord *The Origin of Species* an open-minded reception. He was a founder of the Royal Society of New South Wales (1867).

In addition to his works on Australian stratigraphy, he published some eighty monographs and papers on geology and mineralogy of Australia.

CLASSEN, ALEXANDER (*b. Aachen, Germany, 1843; d. Aachen, 1934*), analytical chemistry.

Studied at Giessen and Berlin. Taught at Technische Hochschule, Aachen (professor from 1883); directed Electrochemical Institute (1894–1914). First to make thorough study of electrogravimetric analysis (*Quantitative Analyse auf elektrolytischem Weg,* 1881); his innovative methods, which became standard practice, included use of warm solutions, introduction of measuring devices into the circuit, and substitution of storage cells for galvanic cells.

CLAUDE, FRANÇOIS AUGUSTE (*b. Strasbourg, France, 1858; d. Paris, France, 1938*), astronomy.

Spent his entire scientific career at the observatory of the Bureau des Longitudes in Paris (from 1884), becoming its director (1929–38). Improved techniques for telephonic and radiotelegraphic transmission of signals and observations of the passage and altitude of stars. He invented the prismatic astrolabe (1899) for the determination of geographic coordinates. With L. Driencourt he adapted it to the needs of geodesy (1905). A. Danjon adapted the principle in his "impersonal astrolabe" (1938), now a fundamental astronomical instrument.

CLAUDE, GEORGES (*b. Paris, France, 1870; d. St. Cloud, France, 1960*), technology.

Graduated from the municipal school of physics and chemistry in 1889 and worked at the Usines Municipales d'Électricité des Halles. At the Compagnie Française Houston-Thomson (1896–1902) he developed the method of handling acetylene by dissolving it in acetone and began his work on the manufacture of liquid air. He used thermodynamic principles to improve methods that used the energy of the expanding gas for producing electricity.

CLAUS, ADOLF CARL LUDWIG (*b. Kassel, Germany, 1838; d. Gut Horheim, near Freiburg im Breisgau, Germany, 1900*), chemistry.

Studied at Marburg and Göttingen and taught at the University of Freiburg im Breisgau (1862–1900), where he directed the chemical institute (from 1883). Published almost 400 papers in organic chemistry. His best-known experimental discovery was the synthesis of phenazine (1872). He was one of the first organic chemists to understand the importance of structural relationships in organic compounds, and helped to make the Kekulé-Couper structural ideas known to all chemists.

CLAUS, CARL ERNST (*b. Dorpat, Russia [now Tartu, Estonian S.S.R.], 1796; d. Dorpat, 1864*), chemistry, pharmacy.

Received bachelor's and master's degrees in chemistry and a doctorate in pharmacy (1839) at Dorpat. He taught and directed the chemistry laboratory (1838–52) at the University of Kazan and taught at Dorpat (1852–64). He discovered ruthenium (1844), achieved a worldwide reputation for his research on the platinum metals, and made important contributions to the study of the formation of platinum ammines and the analogy between metal ammines and salt hydrates.

CLAUSEN, THOMAS (*b. Snogbaek, Denmark, 1801; d. Dorpat, Estonia [now Tartu, Estonian S.S.R.], 1885*), mathematics, astronomy.

Clausen was a self-made man, tutored by a local pastor. He assisted H. C. Schumacher at his Altona observatory (1824–28), worked at the Joseph von Utzschneider Optical Institute, Munich (1828–40), and worked at the Dorpat observatory (from 1842), becoming director (1866–72) and teaching at the university. His approximately 150 published works are devoted to a multitude of subjects, from pure and applied mathematics to astronomy, physics, and geophysics. He calculated fourteen paths of comets and constructed (1840) the Staudt-Clausen theorem dealing with Bernoullian numbers, using as a basis his own new method of factoring numbers into their prime factors.

CLAUSIUS, RUDOLF (*b. Köslin, Prussia [now Koszalin, Poland], 1822; d. Bonn, Germany, 1888*), physics.

Clausius was educated at Berlin and at Halle (Ph.D., 1847). He taught at the new Polytechnicum in Zurich (1855–67), the University of Würzburg (1867–69), and Bonn (from 1869), where he was rector during his final years.

He established the foundations for modern thermodynamics in his first great paper "Über die bewegende Kraft der Wärme" (1850). It showed his distinctive approach: grasp of fundamental facts and equations, a microscopic model to account for them, and an attempt to correlate the two with mathematics. He denied the fundamental assumptions of the caloric theory, basing the denial on what has become the first law of thermodynamics—that whenever work is produced by heat, a quantity of the heat equivalent to the work is consumed. He also provided a new mechanical explanation for the traditional concepts of free and latent heat: real existence belonged only to free heat, understood as the *vis viva* (kinetic energy) of the fundamental particles of matter and the determiner of temperature. Latent heat was the heat destroyed by conversion into work. He made an important distinction between internal work, which is a state of function, subject solely to the initial and final conditions of change, and external work, which depends on the conditions under which the change occurs. Even in the final (1887) edition of *Die mechanische Wärmetheorie* (1865–67), in which he introduced the function U into thermodynamics in the classic thermodynamic expression $dQ = dU + dW$, the function U was simply the energy in the body, undifferentiated in molecular form. Later in his developed theory U was simply the sum of H (heat) and J (external work), but initially he assured complete generality by employing an extremely tedious analysis of an infinitesimal Carnot cycle. The approach, independent of molecular assumptions, became normative in thermodynamic thought. His brilliant vision of the traditional Carnot argument allowed him to incorporate the most significant results of the caloric theory in the new structure. He derived Clapeyron's equation for the universal temperature function C and continued Clapeyron's fruitful handling of the vapor-liquid equilibrium. He established that $C = A(a + t)$, where A is the mechanical equivalent of heat and a the coefficient of expansion for gases. He introduced the symbol T for this universal function of temperature $(a + t)$ in his second important paper, "Ueber eine veränderte Form des zweiten Hauptsatzes der mechanischen Wärmetheorie" (1854), in which he developed the concept of entropy, there calling it simply the principle of equivalence of transformations. In a unique engine cycle he portrayed two transformations: a conversion of heat into work at one temperature and a transfer of heat from a higher to a lower temperature. These were "equivalent" because they could replace one another. By assigning positive transformation values to these processes and equal negative values to their opposites, he established that the transformation values could only be universal functions of heat and temperature. He derived a new function of state similar to Rankine's and Kelvin's but made distinctive by his consideration of the case of irreversible processes. He later capsuled his theorem of transformation values, that the sum of transformation values in any cycle could only be zero (reversible) or positive (irreversible), in his couplet for the two laws of thermodynamics: "Die Energie der Welt ist constant; die Entropie strebt einen Maximum zu" (1865). He chose the term "entropy" from the Greek for transformation (1865).

In his "Über die Art der Bewegung, welche wir Wärme nennen" (1857) he ascribed rotatory and vibratory, as well as translational, motion to molecules. He demonstrated that non-translational motions must exist by showing that translational motions alone could not account for all the heat in a gas. Thus he established the first significant tie between thermodynamics and the kinetic theory of gases. He also presented the first physical, non-chemical argument for Avogadro's hypothesis. He wrongly claimed priority for Avogadro's hypothesis of diatomic molecules (1857) and for the diatomic nature of the oxygen molecule (1866). He developed (1858) the idea of the mean length of path of a moving molecule: the true mean length of path would be reduced by 3/4 because the relative velocity is 4/3 the actual average velocity. From this a neat relationship seemed to exist—the ratio between the mean length of path and the radius of the collision sphere being equal to the ratio of the average space between molecules and the volume of the collision sphere for each molecule. He completely failed to grasp the significance of Maxwell's famous law and never did adopt Maxwell's distribution function.

In his work on the second law of thermodynamics he introduced the concept of disgregation (1862): the work which can be done by heat in any change of the arrangement of a body is proportional to the absolute temperature multiplied by a function of molecular arrangement, the disgregation Z. He thus proved his theorem of the equivalence of transformations and separated the equivalence function (entropy) into a temperature-dependent and a configurational-dependent term. In his attempts to derive an equation in pure mechanics to correspond to his idea, he was led (1871) to what turned out to be essentially the same reduction of the second law as Boltzmann's claim to priority and (to 1875) elaborated what he thought represented a new and unique idea, a variation in the force function itself. He ignored the new directions in Boltzmann's thought and never once sought a mechanical explanation or a molecular understanding for the irreversible increase of entropy, which was his great legacy to physics.

CLAVASIO, DOMINICUS DE. *See* **Dominicus de Clavasio.**

CLAVIUS, CHRISTOPH (*b. Bamberg, Germany, 1537; d. Rome, Italy, 1612*), mathematics, astronomy.

Taught at the Collegio Romano in Rome (1565–1612). His major work, *The Elements of Euclid* (1574), contains notes from previous commentators as well as some criticisms and elucidations of his own. In his *In Sphaeram Ioannis de Sacro Bosco commentarius* (1581) he was the first to accuse Copernicus of presenting a physically absurd doctrine and contradicting Scripture. In a report to the Holy Office (1611), he confirmed Galileo's discoveries, but not his theory. In mathematical works, he offered an explanation for finding the lowest common multiple, introduced into Italy the German plus (+) and minus (−) signs, algebraic symbols used by Stifel, and related nearly all the contemporary knowledge of trigonometry. His improvement of the Julian calendar was adopted by Pope Gregory XIII.

CLAY (CLAIJ), JACOB (*b. Berkhout, Netherlands, 1882; d. Bilthoven, Netherlands, 1955*), physics.

Received Ph.D. at Leiden University (1908) and taught at Delft (1913–20) and Bandung (1920–29) technological universities and the University of Amsterdam (from 1929). On voyages from Indonesia to the Netherlands he discovered the latitude effect, a diminution in the intensity of cosmic radiation in the equatorial regions that is caused by the earth's magnetic field, thus establishing the presence of charged particles in primary cosmic radiation. He wrote books on cosmic rays, philosophy, and measurement of radioactivity.

CLEAVELAND, PARKER (*b. Rowley [Byfield Parish], Mass., 1780; d. Brunswick, Me., 1858*), mineralogy.

Graduated from Harvard College (1799) and taught at Bowdoin College (from 1805). His *An Elementary Treatise on Mineralogy and Geology* (1816) was the first important American mineralogical text, the theoretical part compiled from writings of European scientists, and much valuable data on American minerals collected from almost every contemporary naturalist. Cleavelandite, in the feldspar family, was named for him (1936).

CLEBSCH, RUDOLF FRIEDRICH ALFRED (*b. Königsberg, Germany [now Kaliningrad, U.S.S.R.], 1833; d. Göttingen, Germany, 1872*), mathematics.

Received doctorate at the University of Königsberg and taught at Karlsruhe (1858–63), Giessen (1863–68), and Göttingen (1868–72). With Carl Neumann he founded *Mathematische Annalen* (1868). He came to the fore in German mathematics with his contributions to the theory of projective invariants and algebraic geometry, which included the Plücker-Clebsch principle of the resolubility of several algebraic equations. He completed the symbolic calculus for forms and invariants created by Aronhold with the Clebsch-Aronhold symbolic notation. He helped initiate the theory of algebraic surfaces in his descriptions of the plane representations of the various rational surfaces, especially the general cubic surface. He also intro-

duced the first birational invariant of an algebraic surface. With Paul Gordan (*Theorie der Abelschen Funktionen*, 1866), he contributed essential steps in establishing the Riemann theory on pure algebraic geometry. Clebsch's successors were his pupils Brill and M. Noether.

CLÉMENT, NICHOLAS (*b. Dijon, France, ca. 1778; d. Paris, France, 1841*), chemistry.

Studied in Dijon and at the Jardin des Plantes in Paris. Through connections at the École Polytechnique, he established a collaboration with Charles-Bernard Desormes (from 1801), whose daughter he married. He often used the name Clément-Desormes, which has led to confusion of the two men. Clément taught at the Conservatoire des Arts et Métiers (from 1819), and was consulting engineer to several large companies. The scientific work of Clément and Desormes began with the exact determination of the composition of carbon monoxide and carbon disulfide (1801–02). They analyzed ultramarine (1806); established that the commercially preferred coloring of Italian alum was the result of impurities, thus opening the way for the French alum industry; and analyzed the chemical reactions in the manufacture of sulfuric acid. Their study of the mechanical power of heat (*ca.* 1812–19) yielded a number of a satisfactory order of magnitude for absolute zero, as well as an 1819 memoir on steam engines which Clément lent to Sadi Carnot.

CLEMENTS, FREDERIC EDWARD (*b. Lincoln, Neb., 1874; d. Santa Barbara, Calif., 1945*), botany.

Received B.S. (1894) and Ph.D. (1898) at University of Nebraska, taught there (1897–1906), headed the botany department at the University of Minnesota (1907–17), and was research associate of the Carnegie Institution of Washington (from 1917). The most influential ecologist of his time; protagonist of "plant succession" and its component concepts of formation and climax; glossarist (introduced "sere," "ecad," etc.); and adviser to the U.S. government on policies of range management, forestry, and Dust Bowl rehabilitation. Gave direction in the U.S. to emergent plant ecology. Established Alpine Laboratory on Pikes Peak, where he spent summers and where scientists came to observe "dynamic ecology." His *Plant Succession* (1916) espoused a conservative, inclusive interpretation of plant species, seeking to demonstrate experimentally that some species might be transformed under the impact of environment. His wife, Edith Schwartz, was inseparably associated with his work.

CLEOMEDES, astronomy.

Cleomedes probably lived not earlier than the first century B.C. and not later than the early second century A.D. He wrote an elementary handbook of astronomy entitled "Circular Theory of the Heavens." Such handbooks exerted considerable influence on Roman and medieval writers. His chief authority is Posidonius, and it is unlikely that he himself added anything original, but he also used other sources that sometimes disagreed with Posidonius' views. He was the only Greek writer whose extant work gives details of methods of Eratosthenes and Posidonius for estimating the circumference of the earth.

CLERCK, CARL ALEXANDER (*b. Stockholm, Sweden, 1709; d. Stockholm, 1765*), entomology.

Clerck studied at Uppsala University (1726), became a tax agent, and pursued entomology as a sideline. He invented "butterfly tongs" and an ingenious box for collecting spiders. His *Aranei Suecici* (1757) became a standard work for spider nomenclature and the only pre-Linnaean work on nomenclature incorporated in modern science. *Icones insectorum rariorum* (1759–64) deals with Swedish and tropical butterflies and moths.

CLERSELIER, CLAUDE (*b. Paris, France, 1614; d. Paris, 1684*), publication of scientific works.

Clerselier, a counsel to the Parlement of Paris, used his considerable fortune in his role as translator, apologist, mediator (particularly with Gassendi), and publisher of Descartes. He published the first French translation of the *Méditations* (1647); *Lettres* (1657–67); *L'homme* and *Traité de la formation du foetus* (1659); and *Le monde ou Traité de la lumière* (1677).

CLEVE, PER TEODOR (*b. Stockholm, Sweden, 1840; d. Uppsala, Sweden, 1905*), mineralogy, chemistry, oceanography.

Studied in Stockholm under Mosander, received Ph.D. at Uppsala (1863), and taught at the Technological Institute in Stockholm and at Uppsala. He led Swedish natural science research in the last decades of the century. His analyses of the rare earth metals confirmed Mendeleev's prediction that they were trivalent and that ekabor existed; he identified it as the new element scandium. He discovered the elements holmium and thulium (1879). In organic chemistry he discovered the aminosulfon acids known for a time as "Cleve's acids." He originated the idea that diatoms make good index fossils. His *The Seasonal Distribution of Atlantic Plankton Organisms* (1900) is a basic oceanography text.

CLIFFORD, WILLIAM KINGDON (*b. Exeter, England, 1845; d. Madeira, 1879*), mathematics.

Studied at King's College, London, graduated from Trinity College, Cambridge (1867), and taught at University College, London (from 1868). He is most widely remembered for his popular pieces, especially on the relations between metaphysics, epistemology, and science, but he was one of the best mathematicians of his generation. He helped introduce the ideas of Riemann and non-Euclidean geometry into England and did his best work in this field. He showed how a certain three parallels define a ruled second-order surface (later known as a "Clifford's surface"); Bianchi and Klein later investigated its properties. His papers on biquaternions and the classification of loci and his establishment of some important topological equivalences for Riemann surfaces (1877) were among his memorable works.

CLIFT, WILLIAM (*b. Burcombe, Cornwall, England, 1775; d. London, England, 1849*), comparative anatomy, paleontology.

Clift was apprenticed to John Hunter, the great London surgeon and biologist, and on Hunter's death (1793) became curator of his collections, which became the Hunterian Museum. He organized and extended Hunter's collections, to display the processes of life in extant and fossil animals, arranged by functional body systems. The museum attracted worldwide interest and redirected the method and purpose of museum display. He became an acknowledged authority in comparative anatomy, especially in the identification of fossil bones, and helped to formulate scientific paleontology. He also used his notable artistic skills in scientific illustrations for a number of works. His assistant and successor, Richard Owen, became the greatest British comparative anatomist of the century.

CLOOS, HANS (*b. Magdeburg, Germany, 1885; d. Bonn, Germany, 1951*), geology.

Received doctorate at Freiburg im Breisgau and taught at Marburg (1914–19), Breslau (1919–26), and Bonn (from 1926). He developed the field later known as granite tectonics, the reconstruction of the dynamics of emplacement of a mobilized pluton from its internal structure (1921, 1922, 1925). He first worked on massifs of Silesia, then applied granite tectonics to the Bavarian forest and in Norway and North America (1928). For a time he engaged in polemics with Bruno Sander, who was using structural petrology for the same problems. He reproduced tectonic phenomena in his laboratory (from 1926), making what may have been the first extensive use of wet clay, notably in experiments on rift valley formation (1931). He wrote an outstanding textbook on internal dynamics (1936).

CLOUET, JEAN-FRANÇOIS (*b. Singly, Ardennes, France, 1751; d. Cayenne, French Guiana, 1801*), chemistry, metallurgy.

Studied at the École du Génie at Mézières, where he assisted Gaspard Monge and succeeded him (1784). His work in metallurgy helped orient French chemical research toward the modernization of the metallurgical industry. During the Revolution he reorganized several metallurgical establishments. In 1799, left civilized life behind for Guiana.

CLUSIUS, CAROLUS. *See* **L'Écluse, Charles de.**

COBLENTZ, WILLIAM WEBER (*b. North Lima, Ohio, 1873; d. Washington, D. C., 1962*), infrared spectroscopy.

Graduated from Case School of Applied Science (1900) and Cornell University (M.S., 1901; Ph.D., 1903). At the National Bureau of Standards (from 1904) he was chief of the radiometry section (1905–45). He was the first to determine accurately the radiation constants of a blackbody and thus to verify Planck's law. The exceptionally sensitive thermopiles he constructed were widely used. His thoroughness and accuracy led to the adoption of radiometric standards.

COCCHI, IGINO (*b. Terrarossa, Massa e Carrara, Italy, 1827; d. Leghorn, Italy, 1913*), geology.

Cocchi took a degree at Pisa (1848) and taught at the Institute of Higher Studies (now the University) of Florence (1859–73). He organized the geological study and mapping of Italy, as first president of the Italian Geological Committee and founder and president of the Italian Geological Society. He was responsible for the compilation of a geological map, on a scale of 1:600,000, of almost all of Italy. His most original contribution was his geological-paleoethnological study of a fossil human cranium found at Olmo (1862).

COCHON DE LAPPARENT. *See* **Lapparent, Albert.**

COCHRANE, ARCHIBALD. *See* **Dundonald, Archibald Cochrane, Earl of.**

COCKCROFT, JOHN DOUGLAS (*b. Todmorden, Yorkshire, England, 1897; d. Cambridge, England, 1967*), physics.

Studied at the University of Manchester (M.Sc.Tech., 1922) and St. John's College, Cambridge (B.A., 1924). He joined Rutherford's team at Cavendish Laboratory (1924–39) and was responsible for a major reconstruction of the laboratory, including the building of a cyclotron (1935–39). His early work on radar, building stations to detect submarines and low-flying aircraft, led to his appointment as chief superintendent of the Air Defense Research Development Establishment at Christchurch, Hampshire (1941–44). He directed the Anglo-Canadian atomic energy research laboratory in Montreal (1944–46) and then directed the new British Atomic Energy Research Establishment (1946–59), guiding nuclear developments from basic research to power stations. He was master of Churchill College, Cambridge (from 1959), and received a knighthood. He shared the 1951 Nobel Prize for physics with E.T.S. Walton. They designed an accelerator for protons which yielded a steady potential of 710,000 volts and overcame the difficulty of maintaining the necessary degree of vacuum. Using a lithium target, they performed the first nuclear transformation by artificial means (1930). They achieved similar effects with boron and fluorine targets. After discovery of the neutron they bombarded lithium, boron, and carbon with deuterons from their accelerating apparatus (1933).

CODAZZI, DELFINO (*b. Lodi, Italy, 1824; d. Pavia, Italy, 1873*), mathematics.

Codazzi, who taught at the University of Pavia (1865–73), wrote a paper on the applicability of surfaces (1859) containing his formulas, based on Mainardi's but of wider application. Bonnet used Codazzi's formulas to prove the existence theorem in the theory of surfaces.

COGHILL, GEORGE ELLETT (*b. Beaucoup, Ill., 1872; d. Gainesville, Fla., 1941*), embryology, anatomy, psychobiology.

Coghill took an A.B. (1896) and a Ph.D. (1902) at Brown University, and taught at the University of Kansas Medical School (1913–25), and at the Wistar Institute of Anatomy and Biology, Philadelphia (1925–35). His analysis of the developing nervous system of *Ambystoma* permitted him to formulate a universal law which states that the total pattern of development of the central nervous system and behavior dominates the partial patterns. He was a founder of the American school of psychobiology.

COGROSSI, CARLO FRANCESCO (*b. Caravaggio, Italy, 1682; d. Crema, Italy, 1769*), medicine.

Cogrossi took a medical degree at Padua (1701), practiced medicine, and taught at Padua (1721–33). His major work, *Nuova idea del male contagioso de'buoi* (1714), clearly formulated the "contagium vivum seu animatum." His work was stimulated by an outbreak of cattle plague in Italy. He conjectured that parasitism might occur at the microscopic level, accounting for the ease with which diseases are transmitted. To rid a nation of a contagious disease, he advocated isolating and curing those infected, isolating the suspect ones, and disinfecting the personal belongings of both, in order to exterminate the causative agent and its eggs. He also speculated on the entrance routes of the infection and its transmission through secretions and excretions of the infected animal.

COHEN, ERNST JULIUS (*b. Amsterdam, Netherlands, 1869; d. Auschwitz [Oświęcim], Poland, 1944*), physical chemistry, history of chemistry.

Received doctorate at Amsterdam (1893) under van't Hoff and taught there (1896–1902) and at Utrecht (1902–39). He is known primarily for his famous series of investigations on physical isomerism, particularly his lifelong study (from 1899) of the allotropy of tin, much of it with C. van Eyk, and what he called cases of physical isomerism: enantiotropy, with a transition point as in tin, and monotropy, in which one modification is always stable and the other always metastable. He concluded that enantiotropy and monotropy were exceedingly common in elements and compounds and that most metals in common use were metastable or at least mixtures of stable and metastable phases. He also studied the electrochemistry of the galvanic cells and piezochemistry.

COHEN, MORRIS RAPHAEL (*b. Minsk, Russia, 1880; d. Washington, D.C., 1947*), philosophy of science.

Cohen emigrated from Russia to New York City (1892), graduated from the College of the City of New York (1900), received Ph.D. at Harvard (1906), and taught at City College (1906–38) and the University of Chicago (1938–41). Unlike other philosophic naturalists of his time, he turned from an empiricist interpretation of scientific method to an older conception of rationalism as the ally of science in combating the forces of superstition, supernaturalism, and authoritarianism. Further, he believed that man does not merely impose the universal laws of science upon the external world of nature, but discovers them there. He pointed out that it is only the intelligibility of things, not their existence, that is dependent upon invariant scientific laws.

COHN, EDWIN JOSEPH (*b. New York, N.Y., 1892; d. Boston, Mass., 1953*), biochemistry.

Cohn took a Ph.D. at Harvard (1917) and taught in the medical school there (from 1920), directing the department of physical chemistry. He initiated active research on the physical chemistry of proteins, especially on their solubilities in different media and their acidic and basic properties. His work on the polar molecules of amino acids and peptides laid a foundation for further study of proteins. During World War II he initiated and directed a major program for the large-scale fractionation of human blood plasma.

COHN, FERDINAND JULIUS (*b. Breslau, Lower Silesia [now Wrocław, Poland], 1828; d. Breslau, 1898*), botany, bacteriology.

Studied at the University of Breslau (1842–46) but was barred as a Jew from the degree examinations; received doctorate in botany at Berlin (1847). Taught at Breslau (from 1850), where he founded the first institute for plant physiology (1866) and the journal intended to publish its work, *Beiträge zur Biologie der Pflanzen* (1870), in which appeared the founding papers of modern bacteriology. He was chairman for botany of the Schlesische Gesellschaft für Vaterländische Kultur (1856–86). He summed up his early work in a treatise on the developmental history of microscopic algae and fungi (1854), notable for the section on bacteria, then called Vibrionia. He was the first to argue that they were not animals but plants, developmentally akin to algae. He then demonstrated two cases of sexuality in algae (1855–56) and showed that contractility was not confined to animal tissue but was present in plants as well (1860). All this work led to his first major contribution to the development of bacteriology: "Untersuchungen über Bacterien" (1872). His second "Researches on Bacteria" (1875) defended his classification by external form on the ground that physiological phenomena, especially specific fermentative activities, were associated with specific forms. It also reported his second great contribution to bacteriology, his discovery of spores. He also showed that growth, development, and spore formation were dependent on the presence of air. Forearmed with these results, John Tyndall carried the argument against spontaneous generation to a new level of completeness with his work on sterilization by discontinuous heating.

COHN, LASSAR (*b. Hamburg, Germany, 1858; d. Königsberg, Germany [now Kaliningrad, U.S.S.R.], 1922*), chemistry.

Published under the name of Lassar-Cohn. Studied at Heidelberg, Bonn, and Königsberg; taught at Munich (1897–98) and Königsberg (1894–97, 1902–09). He was associated with various industrial firms; he conducted researches in organic and physiological chemistry and chemical technology. Most elaborate investigation was isolation of acids in ox and human bile by means of saponification, acidification, and solvent extraction. Developed an improved nitrometer and invented a new saccharimeter. His *Arbeitsmethoden für organisch-chemische Laboratorien* (1891) was a valuable compilation of all the methods for particular laboratory operations in organic chemistry.

COITER, VOLCHER (*b. Groningen, Netherlands, 1534; d. Champagne, France, 1576*), anatomy, physiology, ornithology, embryology, medicine.

Studied under Falloppio and Eustachi, and took a doctorate in medicine at Bologna (1562), where he taught briefly. He was physician to the city of Nuremberg (from 1569). By 1569 dissection had become the most important part of anatomy for him. His treatise on the skeleton of the fetus and of a child six months old pointed up the differences between these and adult skeletons and showed where ossification begins. In comparative anatomy, he covered almost all vertebrates and was the first to raise this field to independent status. His epochal studies of the chick, based on observations on twenty consecutive days, were the first systematic statement after Aristotle's.

COLDEN, CADWALLADER (*b. Ireland, 1688; d. Flushing, N.Y., 1776*), botany, medicine, physics.

Graduated from the University of Edinburgh (1705), studied medicine in London, and emigrated to America (1710). In botany he carefully cataloged and described a collection of American plants which he sent to his regular

correspondent Linnaeus, who published it as "Plantae Coldenghamiae" (1743), and who named the Coldenia for Colden (1747). His major scientific effort was devising an explanation of gravity, which Newton had admitted he did not understand. Colden's *An Explication of the First Causes of Action in Matter* (1746) was, although he did not realize it, in direct conflict with the laws of motion of the *Principia*, and he resented being called an opponent of Newton. It was ultimately rejected. Nevertheless his constructive achievements in botany and other fields made him important in the American scientific community.

COLDING, LUDVIG AUGUST (*b. Holbaek, Denmark, 1815; d. Copenhagen, Denmark, 1888*), engineering, physics.

Studied and taught at Copenhagen Polytechnic Institute (graduated 1841; professor from 1869). Greatly influenced by Oersted, director of the Polytechnic and a family friend. Gained a reputation for career as civil engineer, overseeing an extraordinary number of municipal projects. He made major contributions in hydrodynamics, meteorology, and thermodynamics. Through the conviction that "the forces of nature must be related to the spiritual in nature," and thus must be imperishable, he was led to an independent statement of the conservation of energy (1843; papers published 1850, 1852, and 1856): he summarized data indicating that the heat evolved during compression or friction is "proportional to the lost moving forces" and concluded that "when a force seems to disappear it merely undergoes a transformation, whereupon it becomes effective in other forms."

COLE, FRANK NELSON (*b. Ashland, Mass., 1861; d. New York, N. Y., 1926*), mathematics.

Cole took an A.B. (1882) and a Ph.D. (1886) at Harvard and taught at Michigan (1888–95) and Columbia (1895–1926). His research dealt mainly with prime numbers, number theory, and group theory. He helped found the American Mathematical Society and was its secretary (1896–1920) and an influential editor of its *Bulletin* (1897–1920).

COLLET - DESCOTILS,   HIPPOLYTE - VICTOR (*b. Caen, France, 1773; d. Paris, France, 1815*), chemistry.

Studied at the Collège du Bois of the University of Caen, in Paris under Charles and Vauquelin, and at the École des Mines in Paris. Member of Napoleon's expedition to Egypt (1798), remaining a member of the Institut d'Égypte until 1801. Returned to Paris as professor and later director at the École des Mines. Developed a procedure for precipitating iridium from a platinum solution.

COLLIE, JOHN NORMAN (*b. Alderley Edge, Cheshire, England, 1859; d. Sligachan, Isle of Skye, Scotland, 1942*), chemistry.

Collie took a Ph.D. at Würzburg (1885) and taught at University College, London (1887–96), where he later became the first professor of organic chemistry (1902–28). His study of β-aminocrotonic ester led him to major works on polyketides and pyrones. His work on dehydracetic acid culminated in his generalization of the multiple ketene group. He speculated on the formation of sugars and fats, with the multiple ketene group as the fundamental building block.

COLLINS, JOHN (*b. Wood Eaton, near Oxford, England, 1625; d. London, England, 1683*), algebra.

Although he had no university education, Collins taught mathematics in London and did much to revive the London book trade after the disastrous 1666 fire. His published works are essentially derivative, but reveal his competence in mathematics. His scientific importance lies in his untiring effort, by correspondence and word of mouth, to be an efficient "intelligencer" of current mathematical news and promote scientific learning. His still-intact collection of some 2,000 books and uncounted original manuscripts of such men as Newton, Barrow, and Halley, is a major primary source for the modern historian of science.

COLLINSON, PETER (*b. London, England, 1693/94; d. Mill Hill, Middlesex, England, 1768*), natural history, dissemination of science.

Collinson was largely self-taught and took over his father's shop as mercer and haberdasher. A gardener who had considerable success domesticating foreign plants, he is credited with introducing or reintroducing 180 new species into England, over fifty being American. Through his American business connections he became unpaid London agent for the Library Company of Philadelphia (from 1732), the first scientific institution of that city, and the books, instruments, and reports he sent were central in American cultural development. He secured most of the planting lords and gentlemen of England as customers for John Bartram's seeds and plants. He played a lesser but important role in sending Benjamin Franklin and his associates accounts of German electrical experiments, which launched Franklin's researches, and saw to the publication of Franklin's *Experiments and Observations on Electricity* (1751–54) in London. From the 1730's he was the center of a network of intelligence reaching from Peking to Philadelphia. He was the European literary agent and source of influence for virtually every American naturalist of significance.

COLLIP, JAMES BERTRAM (*b. Thurold Township, near Belleville, Ontario, 1892; d. London, Ontario, 1965*), endocrinology.

Collip took a B. A. (1912), M.A. (1913), and Ph.D. (1916) at Trinity College, University of Toronto, and a D.Sc. (1924) and M.D. (1926) at the University of Alberta. He taught at the University of Alberta (1915–21, 1922–27); was chairman of the biochemistry department (1927–41) and professor and director of the Institute of Endocrinology (1941–47) at McGill University; and dean of medicine (1947–61) and director of medical research at the new Collip Medical Research Laboratory (1947–65) at the University of Western Ontario. His chief work in endocrinology began in 1921 when he worked with Banting and Best at Toronto to develop a pancreatic extract to combat diabetes. He developed the method for preparing insulin from cattle or hog pancreas, using alcohol to obtain a differential precipitation of the impurities, which allowed its first clinical use, as reported in his "Pancreatic Extracts in the Treatment of Diabetes Mellitus" (1922; with Banting, Best, Campbell, and Fletcher). He made extensive discoveries by relating the hormonal control of calcium and phosphorus metabolism to an active principle in the parathyroid gland. His

further research, always in areas where it seemed directly possible to discover new treatments for human diseases, included the separation (1933) of pituitary growth hormone free from both adrenocorticotrophic hormone (ACTH) and thyrotrophic hormone (TSH), and the preparation of ACTH pure enough for administration to humans. After 1938 he devoted himself to organization of medical research in Canada for the National Research Council.

COLOMBO, REALDO (*b. Cremona, Italy, ca. 1510; d. Rome, Italy, 1559*), anatomy, physiology.

Received medical degree at Padua (prob. 1541). He replaced Vesalius in anatomy at Padua (1543–45), taught anatomy at Pisa (1545–48) and at the Sapienza in Rome (1548–59). Vesalius' enmity was roused when Colombo criticized him publicly for anatomical errors. Many of Colombo's discoveries and his numerous corrections of Vesalius were in *Historia de la composición del cuerpo humano* (1556) by his student Juan de Valverde, and in his own *De re anatomica* (1559), which displayed his rich experience in dissection, vivisection, autopsy, and surgery and gave a clear, brief account of human anatomy. His bad relations with Vesalius and with Falloppio, who insinuated plagiarism in the discovery of the *levator palpebrae superioris* muscle and the stapes, as well as Colombo's lack of classical learning, diminished the esteem of Italian anatomists for the work. He is best known for the discovery of the pulmonary circuit (the passage of blood from the right cardiac ventricle to the left through the lungs). There is good evidence that he discovered it on his own through vivisections, and that he did not know the relevant passages of Galen. His work represents a significant advance in the understanding of the operations of the heart, lungs, and arteries. He quite consciously diminished the status of the heart to that of distributing, not generating, the arterial blood. He also observed that contraction is more strenuous than dilation and that the arteries dilate when the heart contracts.

COLONNA, EGIDIO. *See* **Giles of Rome.**

COLUMBUS, CHRISTOPHER (*b. Genoa, Italy, 1451; d. Valladolid, Spain, 1506*), exploration.

Nothing certain is known about Columbus' early years; he first went to sea at eighteen; went to Madeira (*ca.* 1479) and then to Porto Santo; moved to Spain (*ca.* 1485), and back to Portugal (1488) where he was present at Bartolomeo Dias's return from his southern exploration of 1487–88; returned to Spain by 1492. His observations on magnetic declination, its variation, and the daily movement of the lodestar around the pole reveal that he was a very competent navigator. Nevertheless, his discovery of the New World was made possible by two major errors of calculation: in correlating the data of Paolo dal Pozzo Toscanelli with ancient and medieval sources, Columbus seems to have reduced the length of a degree of longitude by one-quarter, and to have grossly overestimated the length of the Eurasian continent; he concluded that after sailing only 2,400 miles westward he would reach Japan, whereas in reality that is the distance to the West Indies.

On 3 August 1492, accompanied by his brothers Bartolomeo and Diego, he sailed from Palos with the *Santa*

Maria, the *Pinta,* and the *Niña,* having received the title of admiral and the viceroyalty and governorship of any lands he might discover; on 12 October they landed on Guanahaní in the Bahamas and named it San Salvador (now Watling Island). He went on to Cuba, Great Inagua, and Haiti (where he established a séttlement), and arrived back in Palos on 13 March 1493. His second expedition (25 September 1493 to 11 June 1495) took him to the Leeward Islands, Puerto Rico, Haiti, and Jamaica; the third (30 May 1498 to November 1500), to Trinidad, the mouth of the Orinoco (thus discovering the American continent), and Santo Domingo. His inadequacies as governor of the Hispaniola colony diminished his standing in Spain, and he was returned from his third voyage in chains after an investigation of his harsh disciplinary methods; despite his disgrace he was permitted to make a fourth voyage, but was stripped of his governorship. He left Seville on 3 April 1502 and sailed to Santo Domingo, Honduras, Nicaragua, Costa Rica, Panama, and Colombia; he arrived at Jamaica with damaged vessels, and was rescued nearly a year later (28 June 1504). Broken and ill, he died ignorant of the extent of his discoveries.

COMAS SOLÁ, JOSÉ (*b. Barcelona, Spain, 1868; d. Barcelona, 1937*), astronomy.

Graduated from University of Barcelona (1890) and founded and directed the Observatorio Fabra. He made the first Spanish relief map of Mars (1894), made an early attempt to harmonize the wave and corpuscular theories of radiation (1915), invented the stereogoniometer, discovered two comets, and was the first in Spain to discover asteroids. Wrote several popular science books.

COMBES, CHARLES-PIERRE-MATHIEU (*b. Cahors, France, 1801; d. Paris, France, 1872*), technology, mechanics.

Studied at the École Polytechnique and the École des Mines and made his career in mining both as a teacher and administrator. Studied the development of mines, ventilation in underground work areas, and directed the regulation and certification of all steam machines.

COMBES, RAOUL (*b. Castelfranc, France, 1883; d. Paris, France, 1964*), plant physiology, history of science.

Received doctorate in science (1910) and taught at the Sorbonne (from 1921). Taught at the Institut National Agronomique and the École Nationale d'Horticulture (1912–21). Guided development of the Fontainebleau laboratory (1933) and founded the laboratory of applied biology of the "Station du Froid" at Bellevue (1943). Directed establishment of the Adiopodoumé and Bondy research institutes. Among other works, he studied the effects of environment on the form and physiology of plants. The original conclusions of his experiments remain classic: in weak lighting or under water, plant cells accumulate nitrates, and at high altitudes carbohydrates are stored.

COMENIUS, JOHN AMOS (*b. Nivnice [near Uherský Brod], Moravia, 1592; d. Amsterdam, Netherlands, 1670*), theology, pansophy, pedagogy.

Studied at the Reformed University of Herborn under the strong influence of Alsted, and at Heidelberg; was ordained in the Bohemian Brethren (1616). Thereafter he shepherded his flock and worked and wrote on pansophy and educational reform in Moravia and, after the expulsion of the Brethren from the empire (1628), in Poland, Sweden, Transylvania, and Amsterdam. He gained European fame with his *Janua linguarum reserata* (1633), a new method of teaching Latin. His work on Christian pansophy was first published in 1637. His *Orbis sensualium pictus* (1658) was the first school book consistently to use pictures of things in the learning of languages. His great work, *De rerum humanarum emendatione consultatio catholica* summed up his lifelong deliberations on improvement through universal education and overcoming confusion of languages.

COMMANDINO, FEDERICO (*b. Urbino, Italy, 1509; d. Urbino, 1575*), mathematics.

Studied at Padua for ten years and took a medical degree at Ferrara. In the sixteenth century, Western mathematics emerged from a millennial decline partly due to the works edited, translated into Latin, and commented on by Commandino.

COMMERSON, PHILIBERT (*b. Châtillon-les-Dombes, Ain, France, 1727; d. St.-Julien-de-Flacq, Île de France [now Mauritius], 1773*), natural history.

Took a doctorate in medicine at Montpellier (1754), then turned to botany. He was appointed botanist and naturalist to the king for Bougainville's expedition (1767–68), then botanized in Mauritius, Madagascar, and Réunion. His manuscripts and herbarium of 3,000 new species and genera were turned over to the Jardin du Roi on his death.

COMMON, ANDREW AINSLIE (*b. Newcastle-upon-Tyne, England, 1841; d. Ealing, London, England, 1903*), astronomy.

Common, by profession a sanitary engineer, was noted for his pioneer work in celestial photography and the design and construction of large telescopes. By devising a photographic plate holder that could be moved during exposure to counteract errors in the clock drive of the telescope, he was the first to make really long exposures successfully. He constructed many large parabolic mirrors and high-quality flat mirrors, aided by a very sensitive spherometer of his own design. Designed gunsights for the Royal Navy.

COMPTON, ARTHUR HOLLY (*b. Wooster, Ohio, 1892; d. Berkeley, Calif., 1962*), physics.

Compton shared the 1927 Nobel Prize in physics for his discovery of the Compton effect. His oldest brother, Karl (1887–1954), was his closest adviser. He graduated from Wooster (1913), and at Princeton took an M.A. (1914) and a Ph.D. (1916). At Cavendish Laboratory at Cambridge (1919–20) he developed a close relationship with J. J. Thomson. He was head of the physics department at Washington University, in St. Louis, Missouri (1920–23) when he made his greatest single discovery.

Compton used a Bragg crystal spectrometer to measure accurately the change in wavelength of the X rays scattered from a target at various angles and showed the change to depend on the scattering angle—universally known as the Compton effect. After struggling to keep within the classical concept of the momentum of radiation despite his experimental results. He arrived at his revolutionary quantum theory rather suddenly (1922), by treating the interaction as a simple collision between a free electron and an X-ray quantum having energy $h\nu$ and momentum $h\nu/c$ and obeying the usual conservation laws. The concept of an X-ray photon with linear momentum as well as energy gave perfect agreement with his data and led him to a quantum Compton wavelength h/mc for the electron.

The Compton effect provided conclusive proof of Einstein's concept of a photon with both energy and directed momentum. But Compton's use of a Bragg crystal spectrometer, which depended directly on the wave nature of X rays, clearly necessitated a more general synthesis incorporating both the corpuscular photon and the electromagnetic wave as they behaved in experiment. Later experiments on the effect proved conclusively that the basic interaction between quantum and electron obeys the conservation laws in individual events and not just statistically. The final great synthesis of quantum mechanics and quantum electrodynamics was forced upon physics by the crucial experiments of the Compton effect, electron diffraction, space quantization, and the existence of sharp spectral lines, which could not be brought into line with classical theory. Another development, basic to both astrophysics and high-energy accelerator physics, is the inverse Compton effect, in which a high-speed electron imparts great energy to a photon.

Compton's further research was done at the University of Chicago (1923–45). He made the first successful application of a ruled diffraction grating to the production of X-ray spectra, thus extending X rays as a branch of optics. One of its more important consequences was values for the Avogadro number and for the electronic charge; it definitively clarified discrepancies in the values of fundamental atomic constants. His worldwide study of cosmic rays supported Jacob Clay's observations that their intensity depends on geomagnetic latitude and on altitude, proved that a significant fraction of primary rays are charged particles and thus subject to the earth's magnetic field, and gave the first indication of the radioactivity of mesons. As chairman of the National Academy of Sciences on Uranium, Compton masterfully set forth the possibilities opened up by the discovery of plutonium (1941). He helped initiate the Manhattan Project and organized and directed the Metallurgical Laboratory of the Manhattan District of the Corps of Engineers at the University of Chicago, which was responsible for the production of plutonium. He was in charge when Enrico Fermi obtained the first successful nuclear reaction (1942). After the war he served as chancellor of Washington University (1945–54).

COMPTON, KARL TAYLOR (*b. Wooster, Ohio, 1887; d. New York, N.Y., 1954*), physics.

Compton, the brother of Arthur Holly Compton (1892–1962), received his M.A. at Wooster College (1909) and Ph.D. at Princeton (1912) under O. W. Richardson, whom he assisted in providing experimental evidence for the validity of Einstein's quantum theory of the photoelectric effect. He taught at Reed College in Portland, Oregon, and at Princeton. His experience in World War I stimulated his interest in scientific research applied to modern warfare. From 1918 to 1930 he published

nearly 100 scientific papers on various aspects of electron physics, in fields which were a part of the rapid evolution of atomic physics. As president of M.I.T., he built one of the world's leading centers of graduate education in the physical sciences. As member of the National Defense Research Committee, he directed the development of many electronic devices, especially radar, that revolutionized military technology.

COMRIE, LESLIE JOHN (*b. Pukekohe, New Zealand, 1893; d. London, England, 1950*), astronomy, computation.

Studied astronomy at St. John's College, Cambridge. He successfully applied new computing techniques to the problems of spherical and positional astronomy. As deputy (1925–30) and superintendent (1930–36) of the *Nautical Almanac*, he revised it and introduced into astronomy the concept of the standard equinox. He founded the Scientific Computing Service, where he showed how to program commercial machines for scientific computation, developed interpolation techniques and, produced mathematical tables of the highest accuracy.

COMSTOCK, GEORGE CARY (*b. Madison, Wis., 1855; d. Madison, 1934*), astronomy.

Studied at the University of Michigan (1873–77) under James Watson and assisted him at the Washburn Observatory at Wisconsin (from 1879). He produced a useful general formula for atmospheric refraction, and demonstrated the existence of relatively large proper motions for twelfth-magnitude stars.

COMTE, ISIDORE AUGUSTE MARIE FRANÇOIS XAVIER (*b. Montpellier, France, 1798; d. Paris, France, 1857*), philosophy, sociology, mathematics.

Comte, the son of a civil servant, was expelled from the École Polytechnique (1816) in the royalist reorganization there, was private secretary to Saint-Simon (1817–23), and thereafter subsisted on money from public lectures in mathematics at the École Polytechnique in the 1830's and the benevolence of such admirers as Mill and Grote. His association with Mme. Clothilde de Vaux (from 1840's) changed his intellectual orientation. He founded (1848) the Société Positiviste, to promote the "Cult of Humanity," a godless religion, and established more than a hundred congregations in Europe and North America.

Comte's methodological and epistemological doctrine of positivism was distinctive in its firm commitment to scientific knowledge as prototypical of the history of knowledge. The most famous result of his approach is the law (formulated 1822) of three historical phases of human thought: the theological (or fictional), the metaphysical (or abstract), and the positive (or scientific), which repudiates both gods and causal forces and restricts itself to expressing precise, verifiable correlations between observable phenomena. Most of his *Cours de philosophie positive* (6 vols., 1830–42) assesses the degree of progress toward the positive stage of each science. Its major impact on contemporaries was methodological. His conception of sociology required a unique method, the "historical," which none of the other sciences exemplified; hence he had to establish that different sciences use different methods, and was manifestly not a reductionist. His strictures on mysticism and naïve empiricism and his stress on verification are largely responsible for the wide currency the doctrine of verifiability enjoys in recent philosophy and science.

Astronomy came closest to his positive ideal. To the physical theories of his day he was generally antagonistic, seeing in them vestiges of the metaphysical. His most original and most influential treatment was of "social physics" (after 1840, "sociology"). Social statistics began with Aristotle, but Comte made the unexplored realm of social dynamics—the birth, growth, and life cycle of a social ensemble—the subject of sociology.

CONDILLAC, ÉTIENNE BONNOT, ABBÉ DE (*b. Grenoble, France, 1714; d. Beaugency, France, 1780*), philosophy, psychology.

After taking holy orders and studying at the seminary at Saint-Sulpice and at the Sorbonne, Condillac entered the inner circle of the philosophes. His philosophy of science as language stood midway in the evolution of scientific epistemology between the empiricism of Locke and the positivism of Comte. He contributed more decisively to the synthesis of epistemology and psychology characteristic of the French Enlightenment than any other writer. Condillac stressed that the operations of language are the cause of intellectual functions. The generation of scientists that followed him was most influenced by his *La logique* (1780) and *La langue des calculs* (pub. posthumously), which eschewed geometry for algebra as the model of a "well-made language" and a method of analysis, to be applied in science and in social life. His lasting influence is evident in the terminology and symbolism of modern chemistry; in the reform of chemical nomenclature to identify a compound in its name; and in taxonomy and its identification with analysis in botany, in zoology, and even in the classification of geometric surfaces by mode of generation.

CONDORCET, MARIE-JEAN-ANTOINE-NICOLAS CARITAT, MARQUIS DE (*b. Ribemont, France, 1743; d. Bourg-la-Reine, France, 1794*), mathematics, applied mathematics.

Condorcet's family were provincial nobility; he graduated from the Collège de Navarre in Paris (1759) and established himself as a mathematician in Paris, becoming friendly with d'Alembert and Turgot and marrying Sophie de Grouchy (1786), who held a leading salon. He was elected to the Académie des Sciences (1769) and was its assistant secretary (1773) and permanent secretary (from 1776). On the eve of the Revolution he was also inspector of the mint (from 1776). After 1787 he was wholly absorbed in reforming the regime on liberal bourgeoise lines. He was a delegate to the Legislative Assembly and later to the Convention of 1792. Closely linked to the Girondists, he came under suspicion after their expulsion, and after his arrest was ordered he went into hiding (July 1793), composing his philosophical masterpiece, *Esquisse d'un tableau des progrès de l'esprit humain.* The morning after his arrest and imprisonment he was found dead in his cell. The rumor, originating in 1795, that he committed suicide by poison has never been verified.

The typical and perhaps last Encyclopedist, he was fascinated by all knowledge—applications of science, the organization of scientific education, a universal scientific

language. His entire concept of scientific knowledge was essentially probabilistic. One suspects that friendship and the respect due the secretary of the Academy dulled the critical sense of his contemporaries and exaggerated his mathematical abilities. His interpretation of probability had far-reaching consequences.

His most significant work was in an entirely new field, a scientific comprehension of human phenomena using the empirical approach of natural sciences with mathematics as its tool. "Social mathematics" was to comprise a statistical description of society, a Physiocratic theory of political economy, and a combinatorial theory of intellectual processes. His greatest work was *Essai sur l'application de l'analyse à la probabilité des décisions rendues à la pluralité des voix* (1785).

CONGREVE, WILLIAM (*b. Middlesex, England, 1772; d. Toulouse, France, 1828*), rocketry.

Studied at Trinity College, Cambridge (B.A., 1793; M.A., 1795). In 1814 succeeded his father as comptroller of the royal arsenal. Perfected the rocket as a military weapon; England used "Congreve rockets" against the French, and they were copied by most European armies by 1830. Among his other inventions were new methods of mounting naval ordnance, gunpowder manufacture, printing unforgeable currency, and gas lighting.

CONKLIN, EDWIN GRANT (*b. Waldo, Ohio, 1863; d. Princeton, N.J., 1952*), biology.

Conklin took a B.A. at Ohio Wesleyan (1886) and a Ph.D. at Johns Hopkins (1891). He taught at Rust University, Mississippi; Ohio Wesleyan; Northwestern University; Pennsylvania; and Princeton (1908–33). He was a member and officer of numerous professional and biological organizations, and edited a number of journals. He was a founder of the *Journal of Experimental Zoology* (1904). His study of the cell lineage of the *Crepidula,* following the fate of daughter cells during embryonic cleavage, showed a homology in cleavage with *Nereis* and thus furthered understanding of evolutionary relationships. His similar study of the naturally pigmented egg of *Cynthia* showed that specific regions of the egg always give rise to specific parts of the later embryo, thus providing evidence for the mosaic theory of development of eggs against the regulative theory of nonspecificity. He also wrote and lectured widely on the relations between science and social questions, and defended Darwinism.

CONON OF SAMOS (*b. Samos; fl. Alexandria, 245* B.C.), mathematics, astronomy, meteorology.

Conon, court astronomer to Ptolemy III, was a close friend and important correspondent of Archimedes. He played a notable part in the development of the *parapegma,* the Greek astronomical and meteorological calendar, and became a symbolic figure for the astronomer. He is famous chiefly for his identification of the constellation *Coma Berenices* (*ca.* 245 B.C.).

CONRAD, TIMOTHY ABBOTT (*b. near Trenton, N.J., 1803; d. Trenton, 1877*), paleontology, malacology.

Attended Quaker schools and taught himself languages and natural history. He was one of the first American paleontologists to try to determine the geologic significance of fossils, to correlate regional Tertiary strata by their contained fauna, to compare American with foreign fossils, and to attempt intercontinental correlation. He was paleontologist of the New York State Geological Survey (from 1837) and helped organize the Association of American Geologists (1840). He published the first geologic map of Alabama (1835).

CONSTANTINE THE AFRICAN (*b. Carthage, North Africa; d. Monte Cassino, Italy; fl. 1065–85*), medicine.

The details of Constantine's life and works are not clear. A Muslim who may have become a Christian and joined the Benedictine community at Monte Cassino, he was in any case the first important figure to transmit Greco-Arabic science to the West, and most of the Latin medical texts bearing his name show signs of having been written at the monastery. In all his works, whether translations or originals, he saw himself responsible for summarizing, explaining, and expanding the substance primarily to satisfy requests or fill a practical or pedagogical need. Many of what are identifiably translations are from Isaac Judaeus; others are from Ibn al-Jazzār (*Viaticum*) or Haly Abbas, whose *Kitāb al-malikī* became Constantine's most ambitious and most influential production, *Pantechne*, covering medical theory and practice. It was completed by his disciple Johannes Afflacius. The charge of plagiarism leveled first by Stephen of Antioch in his translation of the *Kitāb* (1127), and often repeated, rested on Constantine's suppression of Haly Abbas' name. But the charge disregards Constantine's approach and aims in translation, and no clear line can be drawn between his translations and his original collections on single topics. His work formed the core of the *Ars medicine*, the foundation of much European medical instruction well into the Renaissance, and was the first impetus in Salerno toward the treatment of medicine as a fundamental constituent of natural philosophy, which triumphed in the twelfth century.

CONYBEARE, WILLIAM DANIEL (*b. London, England, 1787; d. Llandaff, Wales, 1857*), geology.

Conybeare was educated at Christ Church, Oxford, and was a cleric by profession. He was one of the most active of the "Oxford school" of geology, a close associate of William Buckland, and an abler and more moderate exponent than Buckland of the catastrophist-progressionist synthesis which dominated geology in the 1820's and 1830's. One of the most important defenses of progressionism was his "On Mr. Lyell's 'Principles of Geology'" (1830). His theoretical viewpoint combined an actualist method with acceptance of occasional paroxysms, earth history tending to progressively less intense geologic processes and progressively greater complexity in the organic world. His *Outlines of the Geology of England and Wales* (1822), an improvement of William Phillips' compilation, was then unrivaled in detail and accuracy.

COOK, JAMES (*b. Marton-in-Cleveland, Yorkshire, England, 1728; d. Kealakekua Bay, Hawaii, 1779*), maritime discovery.

Received only an elementary education; as an apprentice to a shipowner, he became a first-rate seaman and practical navigator. He joined the navy (1755) and became a planner of voyages, practical seaman, observer,

marine surveyor, and hydrographer. He commanded the *Endeavour* expedition to Tahiti to observe the transit of Venus (1768–71) and (under secret orders) to search for a continent down to latitude 40° south. The harvest of this voyage in geographical, ethnological, and botanical knowledge led to his next remarkable voyage, on the ships *Resolution* and *Adventure*, to discover whether there was a continent in the Southern Hemisphere. This circumnavigation of the world (1772–75) destroyed the ancient hypothesis of a great southern continent, made new and coordinated old discoveries (Easter Island, the Marquesas, New Hebrides), proved the utility of the chronometer, and avoided any death from scurvy. He died during his third voyage (1776–79), attempting to find a northwest passage through America from the Pacific coast, discovering Hawaii on the way. His conquest of scurvy at sea would alone have made him famous.

COOKE, JOSIAH PARSONS, JR. (*b. Boston, Mass., 1827; d. Newport, R.I., 1894*), chemistry.

Graduated from Harvard College (1848) and was professor of chemistry and mineralogy there (1850–94). He adopted Liebig's method of laboratory instruction and demonstration experiments during lectures, and in effect founded Harvard's chemistry department. His influence, particularly through his *Principles of Chemical Philosophy* (1868), spread to other American colleges. He made several important determinations of atomic weights.

COOLIDGE, JULIAN LOWELL (*b. Brookline, Mass., 1873; d. Cambridge, Mass., 1954*), mathematics.

Coolidge took a B.A. at Harvard (1895), a B.Sc. at Oxford (1897), and a Ph.D. at Bonn (1904). He taught at Harvard (1899–1902; 1904–40). His *Introduction to Mathematical Probability* (1925) was one of the first modern English texts on the subject. He wrote four other mathematical books in the tradition of the Study-Segre school, as well as three on the history of mathematics.

COOPER, THOMAS (*b. London, England, 1759; d. Columbia, S.C., 1839*), chemistry.

Cooper studied at Oxford, became a barrister (1787), and pioneered in commercial bleaching by chlorine (*ca. 1790*). He emigrated to America (1794) and taught chemistry at Dickinson College (1811–15), University of Pennsylvania (1815–19) and South Carolina College (1819–34). Much of his time was spent on political causes. His greatest service to science was in the dissemination of information; he brought out American editions of a number of English chemistry textbooks, adding comprehensive notes on recent advances. As a practicing scientist he was largely a dilettante; his most notable achievement was the preparation of potassium, almost certainly for the first time in America, by strongly heating potash with iron in a gun barrel.

COPAUX, HIPPOLYTE EUGÈNE (*b. Paris, France, 1872; d. Étampes, France, 1934*), chemistry.

Studied at the École de Physique et de Chimie Industrielles de Paris, took the *licence* (1896) and his doctorate (1905) and taught there (from 1900). His first studies dealt with chemistry and crystallography of mineral substances. During World War I, assigned to the Patent Office, he developed a process for the rapid preparation of phosphoric acid. In 1919 he perfected a method for obtaining beryllium oxide from beryl.

COPE, EDWARD DRINKER (*b. Philadelphia, Pa., 1840; d. Philadelphia, 1897*), vertebrate paleontology, zoology.

Privately educated and independently wealthy, he was a pioneer in the development of American vertebrate paleontology who gained notoriety for his disputes with O. C. Marsh and fame as the leading theorist of the neo-Lamarckian movement in American biology. Only academic positions were at Haverford College (1866–67) and University of Pennsylvania (1889–97). Studied natural history at prominent museums; by 1866 had begun to study fossils. From 1871 to 1879 Cope spent eight months of each year with one of the U.S. geological surveys, collecting fossils and gaining knowledge; his writings of 1875 and 1884 represent first comprehensive descriptions of vertebrates from the early Eocene, and pushed the origin of the "age of the mammals" further back into time. His evolution theory, first articulated in 1866 and expressed in more than fifty articles and books, stressed importance of the environment and inheritance of acquired characteristics; in "On the Origins of Genera" (1868) he attacked Darwin's theory of natural selection. When Marsh, a bitter rival since 1872, was appointed to the newly consolidated U.S. Geological Survey (1879), Cope's affiliation with it ceased.

COPERNICUS, NICHOLAS (*b. Torun, Poland, 1473; d. Frauenburg [Frombork], Poland, 1543*), astronomy.

Copernicus, the founder of modern astronomy, studied at the University of Cracow (from 1491). Through his uncle, the bishop of Varmia (Ermland), he was elected a canon of the cathedral chapter of Frombork (Frauenburg), whose members enjoyed an ample lifetime income. He served the chapter to his death, except for periods of studying canon law at the University of Bologna (1496–1500), medicine at Padua (1501), and canon law at Ferrara, where he took a doctoral degree (1503). At Varmia he constructed a roofless little tower (1513) in which he used a parallactic instrument, mainly for observing the moon; a quadrant, for the stars; and an astrolabe, or armillary sphere, for the stars. He wrote the first draft of his new astronomical system, the compact *De hypothesibus motuum coelestium a se constitutis commentariolus*, between 15 July 1502 and 1 May 1514 and discreetly circulated a few manuscript copies among trusted friends. With his customary prudence he deliberately withheld his name from it. It challenged the astronomical system which had dominated Western thought since Aristotle and Ptolemy, proclaiming the center of the universe to be the sun, not the earth, and ascribing motion to the earth. His disciple Rheticus drafted (1539) *Narratio prima* to present the Copernican system in printed form. In Copernicus' stirring plea for freedom of thought which serves as the dedication of his *De revolutionibus orbium coelestium* (*Revolutions of the Heavenly Spheres;* written June 1542) he named Philolaus and Ecphantus as Pythagorean forerunners, but carefully deleted a reference associating Aristarchus, to whom charges of impiety might attach, with ideas of the earth's motion. The enormous remoteness of the stars, a fundamental consequence of heliocentrism, was expressed in *Commentariolus*. To gain acceptance for his revival of the concept of a moving earth, he had to

overcome the ancient objections. Earth was traditionally one of the four terrestrial elements, capable of rectilinear motion; the heavenly bodies consisted of a fifth element, capable of circular motion. He transferred the earth to the category of the heavenly bodies, and as a whole it had only circular motion. Both "the watery element" joined with the earth and the lower layers of air are firmly attached to the earth and rotate daily with it. This answers the argument that "objects falling in a straight line would not descend perpendicularly to their appointed place, which would meantime have been withdrawn by so rapid a movement" as the earth's rotation. In addition to the diurnal rotation and annual revolution, he also ascribed to the earth what he called its "motion in declination." In performing the annual revolution around the sun, the earth describes what he termed the "grand circle," the plane of which cuts the celestial sphere in the ecliptic. If the earth were subject only to the diurnal rotation and annual revolution, "no inequality of days and nights would be observed." The function of this motion in declination was to keep the earth presenting a virtually unchanging aspect to the observer viewing it from a distant star (instead of describing a huge conical surface in space), whereas to a spectator on the sun it would constantly pass through its cyclical seasonal changes. The rotational axis, however, is not directed toward precisely the same distant star.

That Copernicus had any direct acquaintance with the thinking of Ibn al-Shāṭir, Nicole Oresme, or Jean Buridan seems out of the question. The absence of the earth's orbital revolution from the thinking of these predecessors, as well as his use of Arabic observational results, indicate that he did not conceal any intellectual indebtedness.

The astronomer in Copernicus' cosmos watches the stately celestial ballet from an observatory that is itself both spinning and advancing. The three outer planets, Mars, Jupiter, and Saturn, revolve around the sun in orbits larger in size and longer in period than the earth's. He correctly located Venus and Mercury as the inferior, inner planets, revolving around the central sun inside the earth's orbit and at greater speed. The kinks or loops in the planetary orbits which are observed from the earth he showed to be not real itineraries but optical illusions, side effects of the observation of a planet from the moving earth. He called this "the motion in parallax."

Ptolemaists and Copernicans alike separated the moon from the outer planets. Not so the sun; in the Ptolemaic system nominally a planet, it actually had a privileged status, never explained, so that its orbital motion was integral to the theory of the five other planets. Among Copernicus' most influential contributions was making the earth a planet and deplanetizing the sun. The behavior of the other planets was thus explicable by physical facts related to their positions vis-à-vis the earth.

From his determination of the maximum elongation of Venus, he also obtained the first approximately correct planetary distances, which he expressed in terms of the distance earth–sun, subsequently the fundamental astronomical unit (he grossly underestimated it).

He neither accepted nor explicitly rejected the widespread belief that every planet was moved by a resident angel or spirit. He held instead that "the motion appropriate to a sphere is rotation in a circle." He always assumed the physical existence of the unseen celestial spheres. Thus *orbium* in the title of his *De revolutionibus orbium coelestium* referred not to the planetary bodies themselves but to the spheres which carried them. It was left to Tycho Brahe to banish these spheres from astronomy.

The center of Copernicus' universe was not the body of the sun, but a nearby unoccupied point, a purely mathematical entity. Whereas the pre-Copernican cosmos had known only a single center of gravity, he endowed the physical universe with multiple centers, thus opening the road to universal gravitation, one of the basic concepts of modern physics and cosmology.

He was firmly convinced that he was talking about the actual physical world when he transformed the earth into a satellite spinning about its axis as it whirled around the sun. By a quirk of fate, the printing of the first edition of *De revolutionibus* was in the hands of an editor who shared Buridan's fictionalist conception. Andreas Osiander inserted in the most prominent place available—the verso of the title page—an unsigned note to the reader concerning the "hypotheses of this work." The reader was not informed that Copernicus used the word "hypothesis" to mean "fundamental categorical proposition" rather than "tentative conjecture," although in private correspondence with the editor, Copernicus had steadfastly repudiated this interpretation. Thus *De revolutionibus*, now universally recognized as a classic of science, was first presented in a guise which falsified its essential nature and fooled many readers, including J. B. J. Delambre.

CORDIER, PIERRE-LOUIS-ANTOINE (*b. Abbeville, France, 1777; d. Paris, France, 1861*), geology, mineralogy.

Cordier entered the École des Mines (1795) and made his career there, pioneering in the geological, technical, and economical analysis of French mining. He played an important role in the organization of French railroads, steamboat navigation, and road construction, and had a powerful voice in French mining affairs as president of the Conseil des Mines (1831–61). He began the use of the polarizing microscope in geology. The metamorphic aluminum silicate Cordierite was named for him by Haüy.

CORDUS, EURICIUS (*b. Simtshausen bei Marburg, Germany, 1486; d. Bremen, Germany, 1535*), medicine, poetry, botany.

Received master of arts degree at Erfurt (1516) and doctor's degree at Ferrara (1521). Taught at Marburg (1527–33), and was municipal physician and professor at the Gymnasium in Bremen (1533–35). His works included poetry and medical and botanical writings. His *Botanologicon* (1534) is generally considered to be the first attempt at a scientific systematization of plants.

CORDUS, VALERIUS (*b. Erfurt, Germany, 1515; d. Rome, Italy, 1544*), botany, pharmacy.

Received bachelor's degree at Marburg (1531), under the important influence of his father, Euricius (1486–1535). Completed training in apothecary shops and at the universities in Leipzig and Wittenberg. Authored the first official pharmacopoeia in Germany (*Dispensatorium*, 1546). Enriched the fields of botany, pharmacognosy and pharmacy by his critical plant characterizations (*Annotationes*, 1549; *Historiae*, 1561) and by new teaching methods. He is generally called the discoverer of ether (probably based on work by his predecessors), and is quite justifiably regarded as one of the fathers of pharmacognostics.

CORI, GERTY THERESA RADNITZ (*b. Prague, Austria-Hungary [now Czechoslovakia], 1896; d. St. Louis, Mo., 1957*), biochemistry.

Received M.D. at the German University of Prague (1920). At the New York State Institute for the Study of Malignant Diseases, in Buffalo (1922–31), she and her husband, Carl, initiated a close collaboration in research on the metabolism of carbohydrates in animals. She held a research appointment at Washington University School of Medicine in St. Louis, Missouri (from 1931), where she also taught biochemistry (1947–57). Continuing their research, the Coris identified and isolated several enzymes which form and break down the glycogen molecule, and made the first synthesis of glycogen in the test tube. For this they were awarded the 1947 Nobel Prize in physiology or medicine. She defined the molecular structure of glycogen chemically (1952), and by isolating and characterizing individual enzymes, illuminated the nature of the glycogen storage diseases (1953).

CORIOLIS, GASPARD GUSTAVE DE (*b. Paris, France, 1792; d. Paris, 1843*), theoretical and applied mechanics.

Graduated from the École Polytechnique, where he taught (1816–38) and was director of studies (1838–43). He contributed fundamental elements in the theory of classical mechanics. From his belief that rational mechanics should enunciate general principles on the operation of motors, which inspired his *Du calcul de l'effet des machines* (1829), came a method and new terminology more important than he knew. He discovered the remarkable characteristic that the value of the work of a system of forces of which the resultant equals zero is independent of the frame of reference for changes of position. He compared (1831) two systems of reference in rectilinear translation moving uniformly, for which the work done by inertial forces is identical. From this he generalized to a major advance: the expression for complementary acceleration, derived from the momentum of relative velocity and the instantaneous rotation of the frame of reference. History remembers him only for the Coriolis force present in a rotating frame of reference. One application of that force is to fluid masses on the earth's surface.

CORNETS DE GROOT, JAN. See **De Groot, Jan Cornets.**

CORNETTE, CLAUDE-MELCHIOR (*b. Besançon, France, 1744; d. Rome, Italy, 1794*), chemistry, medicine.

Studied chemistry and pharmacy in Paris, and medicine at Montpellier. Carried on research in Lassone's laboratory at Marly-le-Roi, and served as physician to the royal family. His works on chemistry followed Rouelle's theories. He wrote several memoirs on salts and their decomposition by mineral acids, and on the reaction of acids with oils. He later turned to chemical drugs (soap, mercury, etc.) at the expense of pure chemistry.

CORNU, MARIE ALFRED (*b. Orléans, France, 1841; d. La Chansonnerie, near Romartin, France, 1902*), optics.

Studied at the École Polytechnique (doctorate, 1867) and at the École des Mines, and taught at the Polytechnique (from 1864). His attraction to experimental optics led to a redetermination of the velocity of light by Fizeau's method. He made a number of important contributions to spectrum analysis, including very precise measurements of the wavelengths of certain lines in the hydrogen spectrum. He is remembered for the elegant method of the so-called Cornu spiral for the determination of intensities in interference phenomena.

CORONEL, LUIS NUÑEZ (*b. Segovia, Spain, second half of fifteenth century; d. Spain or Canary Islands, 1531*), logic, natural philosophy.

Coronel was educated at Salamanca and Paris, was ordained (1512), and took a doctorate in theology (1514). While with the Inquisition at Brussels (1521 or 1522) he met Erasmus, who saw him as an ally and with whom he later corresponded. He became bishop of Las Palmas, Canary Islands (1527). His *Physicae perscrutationes* (1511) contains work in the framework of Aristotle's *Physics,* with long digressions on motion and on infinity.

CORONELLI, VINCENZO MARIA (*b. Venice, Italy, 1650; d. Venice, 1718*), geography.

Became a Minorite friar (1655) and received doctorate in theology at Rome (1674). Interested in maps and globes from early youth, he built a terrestrial globe and a celestial globe for Louis XIV, the largest made until the 1920's. Founded the Accademia Cosmografica degli Argonauti, the first geographical society (1684, Venice). Traveled extensively through Europe, designed two major atlases, and became known as a civil engineer and geographer.

CORRENS, CARL FRANZ JOSEPH ERICH (*b. Munich, Germany, 1864; d. Berlin, Germany, 1933*), botany, plant genetics.

Graduated from Munich (1889), studied at Berlin and Tübingen, and taught at Münster (1909–13). He was the first director of the Kaiser Wilhelm Institut für Biologie (1913–33). Of the three rediscoverers of Mendel's laws, he showed the deepest understanding and the most subtlety. Unlike de Vries, he concentrated on complexities and exceptions, beginning with the xenia question. He was the first to correlate Mendelian segregation with reduction division and to show that segregation does not require the dominant-recessive relationship, and that characters can be "coupled" or "conjugated" in heredity and are therefore unable to show independent assortment (Mendel's second law). He proved that sex is inherited in a Mendelian fashion in classic experiments with *Bryonia* (1907). He also obtained the first proof of cytoplasmic inheritance in plants, independently of Erwin Baur (1909).

CORTÉS DE ALBACAR, MARTÍN (*b. Bujaraloz, Spain; d. Cádiz, Spain, 1582*), cosmography, navigation.

Cortés is known only through his *Breve compendio de la esfera* (1551), with sections on the composition of the world and the universal principles of navigation; movements and effects of the sun and moon; the construction and use of cross-staffs, astrolabes, and compasses; and particularly on practical navigation. His rejection of maps with rectangular projections led to the cylindrical projection of Alonso de Santa Cruz. He accepted and affirmed Columbus' discovery of the variation of magnetic declination when it was still doubted.

CORTI, ALFONSO GIACOMO GASPARE (*b. Gambarana, near Pavia, Italy, 1822; d. Corvino San Quirico, near Casteggio, Italy, 1876*), microscopic anatomy.

Studied medicine in Pavia (1841–45) and took his M.D. in Vienna (1847). One of the biologists who sought to explain the fine structure of organs, he introduced carmine staining into microscopic technology and described the most important components of the membranous cochlea. He later proved that the cells of the various tissues of the elephant are the same relative size as corresponding cells of other mammals. He is now generally known for the organ in the cochlea described by him, the organ of Corti.

CORTI, BONAVENTURA (*b. Scandiano, Modena, Italy, 1729; d. Reggio nell' Emilia, Italy, 1813*), physics, botany.

Corti studied and taught at Reggio nell' Emilia. He directed the Collegio dei Nobili in Modena (1783–1804), and taught at the University of Modena (1804–09). His two-volume treatise on physics, *Institutiones physicae* (1769), predates the discoveries of Galvani and Volta. His *Osservazioni microscopiche sulla Tremella . . .* (1774) clearly anticipated later descriptions of the movements of the protoplasm in the cell.

CORVISART, JEAN-NICOLAS (*b. Dricourt, France, 1755; d. Paris, France, 1821*), medicine.

Received medical degree at Paris (1782) and worked at the Hôpital de la Charité, holding a professorship of internal clinical medicine created for him (1794–1801). He also taught at the École de Médecine and the Collège de France, and became Napoleon's chief physician (1801) and surgeon general. He wrote the first treatise on cardiology (1806). A meticulous observer, he instituted systematic examination and the analytical interpretation of physical symptoms for diagnosis, which established him as the true promoter of clinical medicine in France.

COSSERAT, EUGÈNE MAURICE PIERRE (*b. Amiens, France, 1866; d. Toulouse, France, 1931*), geometry, mechanics, astronomy.

Studied at the École Normale Supérieure and at the University of Toulouse (1886–1931), where he took a doctorate (1888) and directed the observatory (from 1908). He divided his time between his duties at the observatory and research in geometry. In studying deformation of surfaces, he worked on the theory of elasticity. Although his concepts had originality, they were already being called into question by the theory of relativity and progress in physical theory. At the observatory he organized meridian observations, photography, and computations of positions for the international project of the Carte du Ciel.

COSTA, CHRISTOVÃO DA. *See* **Acosta, Cristóbal.**

COSTA IBN LUCA. *See* **Qusṭā ibn Lūqā.**

COSTANTIN, JULIEN NOËL (*b. Paris, France, 1857; d. Paris, 1936*), botany.

Costantin studied at the École Normale Supérieure, took a doctorate (1883), and taught at the Muséum d'Histoire Naturelle (1901–36). A convinced Lamarckian, he sought to establish the influence exerted by environment on the structure of higher plants and to provide a solid foundation for the theory of inheritance of acquired characters. For many years mushrooms and their cultivation were his principal interest; after 1914 he devoted his research to the action of symbiosis in the development and maintenance of life.

COSTER, DIRK (*b. Amsterdam, Netherlands, 1889; d. Groningen, Netherlands, 1950*), physics.

Studied physics under Ehrenfest at Leiden (doctorate, 1922), and received degree in electrical engineering at Delft Technological University. At Bohr's laboratory in Copenhagen, he completely worked out the linking up of X-ray experimental data with Bohr's theory of atomic structure and the periodic table of the elements. With von Hevesy he discovered the element hafnium (1923). Taught at Groningen University (1924–49), where he introduced X-ray work and mounted a Rowland grating for studying band spectra, mostly of diatomic molecules.

COTES, ROGER (*b. Burbage, Leicestershire, England, 1682; d. Cambridge, England, 1716*), mathematics, astronomy.

Received B.A. (1702) and M.A. (1706) at Trinity College, Cambridge, and taught astronomy and natural philosophy at Cambridge (1706–16). Worked with Newton on the second edition of Newton's *Principia*, and his preface defended the Newtonian hypothesis against the Cartesian theory of vortices. His mathematical papers are collected as *Harmonia mensurarum* (1722). In the section on systematic integration is a geometrical result now known as Cotes's theorem, which, expressed in analytical terms, is equivalent to finding all the factors of $x^n - a^n$ where n is a positive integer. His essay on Newton's differential method describes how, given n points at equidistant abscissae, the area under the curve of the nth degree joining these points may be evaluated. A modernized form of his result is known as the Newton-Cotes formula. His method for evaluating the most probable result of a set of observations comes very near to the method of least squares, anticipating Gauss (1795) and Legendre (1806).

COTTA, CARL BERNHARD VON (*b. Zillbach, Saxe-Weimar-Eisenach [now German Democratic Republic], 1808; d. Freiberg, Saxony [now German Democratic Republic], 1879*), geology.

Graduated from the Freiberg Bergakademie (1831) and received doctorate at Heidelberg (1832). For the next ten years he worked at his father's Tharandt Forestry Academy near Dresden, and participated in a geological survey of Saxony. He taught at the Bergakademie (1842–74). He traveled extensively and did a special mapping of Thuringia, and was Royal Saxon mining adviser (from 1862). A philosopher of geology in a time of increasingly detailed research, he marked the culmination and end of Werner's macroscopic descriptive petrography. The principal groupings of his genetic system of petrography (1866) are still in use. He instituted at Freiberg what was probably the first course on ore deposits and helped originate that science. The "Freiberg school," based on his textbooks, gained world fame. He ardently defended the concept of evolution even in the inorganic realm. A forerunner of Darwin in Germany, as early as 1848 he expressed the basic biogenetic law.

COTTE, LOUIS (*b. Laon, France, 1740; d. Montmorency, France, 1815*), meteorology.

Cotte was educated in Oratorian *collèges,* entered the order (1758), but renounced the priesthood to marry (1795). He was assistant librarian at the Bibliothèque Sainte-Geneviève in Paris (1798–1802) and a member of the Institut de France (1803). He carried on a vast correspondence and routinely recorded meteorological observations. Widely known as a compiler, he made no startling contributions to meteorology, but was self-appointed clearing house for meteorological information and a chronicler and propagandizer of the science. He saw meteorology as primarily useful in agriculture and secondarily in medicine. He saw it as embracing earthquakes, aurora borealis, terrestrial magnetism, atmospheric electricity, and lunar periodicity as well as temperature, atmospheric pressure, winds and precipitation, and assumed relationships merely awaiting discovery among all these.

COTTRELL, FREDERICK GARDNER (*b. Oakland, Calif., 1877; d. Berkeley, Calif., 1948*), engineering, chemistry.

Cottrell took a B.S. at the University of California at Berkeley (1896) and a Ph.D. at Leipzig (1902). He invented electrostatic precipitators to remove suspended particles from gases; these devices are widely used to abate pollution by smoke from power plants and dust from cement kilns and other industrial sources. He founded the non-profit Research Corporation (1912) and arranged for it to secure and develop patents for inventors. He taught at California (1902–11), worked at the U.S. Bureau of Mines (1911–20), the National Research Council (1921–22), and directed the Fixed Nitrogen Research Laboratory (1922–30).

COTUGNO, DOMENICO FELICE ANTONIO (*b. Ruvo di Puglia, Italy, 1736; d. Naples, Italy, 1822*), anatomy, physiology, medicine.

Studied medicine at the University of Naples and the Ospedale degli Incurabili and devoted his career to these institutions. His medical career exemplified the true investigative and selfless spirit in anatomy and medicine. His research fused anatomy and physiology: he traced the course of the nasopalatine nerve (1761) prior to Antonio Scarpa, described parts of the internal ear, demonstrated the existence of the labyrinthine fluid, and formulated a theory of resonance and hearing. In differentiating between arthritic and nervous sciatica, he described extensively for the first time the cerebrospinal fluid (1764).

COUES, ELLIOTT (*b. Portsmouth, N.H., 1842; d. Baltimore, Md., 1899*), ornithology.

Received an A.B. (1861) and an M.D. (1863) at Columbian College (now George Washington University), and taught anatomy there (1877–86) after a stint as army surgeon and naturalist. He was editor in natural history for the *Century Dictionary*. His extensive travels enabled him to write the popular *Key to North American Birds* (1872), *Check-List of North American Birds* (1873), and *Field Ornithology* (1874). In the 1890's he checked and annotated manuscripts of several American western explorations.

COULOMB, CHARLES AUGUSTIN (*b. Angoulême, France, 1736; d. Paris, France, 1806*), physics, applied mechanics.

A major figure in the history of physics and engineering, Coulomb's main contributions were in the fields of electricity, magnetism, applied mechanics, friction and torsion. Following education at the Military Engineering School at Mézières, France, Coulomb entered a military engineering career in 1761 where he then served with great distinction for thirty years at numerous posts including Martinique and near Rochefort, where he initiated his most important studies in mechanics. He won two memoir competitions at the Paris Academy of Sciences which led to his election to the Academy in 1781 and allowed him to reside thereafter in Paris. It was only then that he was able to devote the major portion of his time to research in the physics of torsion, electricity, and magnetism. His mechanics studies included fundamental memoirs on structural mechanics, rupture of beams and masonry piers, soil mechanics, friction theory, and ergonomics. With the exception of his friction studies, most of Coulomb's mechanics memoirs were little utilized by engineers until the nineteenth century.

Coulomb's later work in physics is tied closely to his work in mechanics. His concern with friction and cohesion and his emphasis upon the importance of shear in structural mechanics appear again in his studies of torsion, in his ideas of "coercive force" in electrostatics and magnetism, and in his final studies in magnetism and the properties of matter. Coulomb invented the torsion balance and employed it subsequently to measure the force relationships in various physical disciplines. He developed both theoretically and experimentally the fundamental equation for torque in thin cylinders.

The period of Coulomb's memoirs in electricity and in magnetism began in 1777 with a paper on magnetic compasses and continued for about two decades. In the broadest sense Coulomb participated in the articulation and extension of the Newtonian theory of forces to the disciplines of electricity and magnetism. At the same time Coulomb's researches illustrate the emergence of the "empirical" areas of physics (areas such as heat, electricity, magnetism, crystallography) from within traditional natural philosophy to positions of sophisticated disciplines in physics. Coulomb worked particularly to obtain exact quantifications of the electric and magnetic laws, supporting the Newtonian theory of central forces against the Cartesian idea of vortices. With regard to electricity and magnetism he said "One must necessarily resort to attractive and repulsive forces of the nature of those which one is obliged to use in order to explain the weight of bodies and celestial physics." In his electrical studies Coulomb determined the quantitative force law, gave the notion of electrical mass, and studied charge leakage and the surface distribution of charge on conducting bodies. In magnetism he determined the quan-

titative force law, created a theory of magnetism based on molecular polarization, and introduced the idea of demagnetization.

Coulomb performed significant public service as intendant of the royal waters and fountains, and as consultant for hospital reform and, under Napoleon, in school reform. Those academicians with whom Coulomb worked most closely were mathematicians and others interested in physics, including those we would today call engineering physicists.

COUNCILMAN, WILLIAM THOMAS (*b. Pikesville, Md., 1854; d. York Village, Me., 1933*), pathology.

Received M.D. at the University of Maryland (1878), studied pathology abroad, and taught at Johns Hopkins Medical School (1883–92) and at Harvard Medical School (from 1892). His paper on the pathology of malaria was his first significant research. His monograph on amoebic dysentery (1891) established it as an independent disease entity. He also did research on cerebrospinal meningitis, chronic nephritis, smallpox, and diphtheria. He was the principal founder of the American Association of Pathologists and Bacteriologists, greatly stimulating the development of pathology in the United States.

COUPER, ARCHIBALD SCOTT (*b. Kirkintilloch, Dumbartonshire, Scotland, 1831; d. Kirkintilloch, 1892*), chemistry.

Couper studied at Glasgow, Edinburgh, and Berlin, and worked in Wurtz's Paris laboratory (1856–58). At the same time as Kekulé and independently, he introduced principles that underlie the modern structural theory of organic chemistry and brought into practice the use of lines to represent valence bonds in chemical formulas. In experiments on the bromination of benzene, he isolated two new compounds, bromobenzene, and *p*-dibromobenzene. His results from studying the constitution of the benzene derivative salicylic acid represented the first time that the relations between the individual carbon atoms of benzene had been depicted in a formula. He introduced the first ring formula into organic chemistry, to represent the structure of cyanuric acid.

COURNOT, ANTOINE-AUGUSTIN (*b. Gray, France, 1801; d. Paris, France, 1877*), applied mathematics, philosophy of science.

Studied at the École Normale Supérieure and the Sorbonne, took a doctorate in science (1829), and became a high official of the French university system (from 1834), as inspector general of public education (1838–54), chairman of the Jury d'Agrégation in mathematics (1839–53), and rector at Dijon (1854–62). Mediocre in pure mathematics, his work on the philosophy of science forcefully and originally opened up unexplored fields in applied mathematics. With his *Recherches sur les principes mathématiques de la théorie des richesses* (1838), he was the true founder of mathematical economics. He was the first to formulate the data of the diagram of monopolistic competition, thus defining a type of solution famous as "Cournot's point." His original examination of the calculus of probability was the first which radically dissociated various still obscure ideas, allowing deeper and more systematic research. He also showed clearly the importance of the applications of the calculus of probability to the scientific description and explanation of human acts. More than for his mathematical originality, he is known for his views on scientific knowledge. He defined science as logically organized knowledge, comprising both a classification of the objects with which it deals and ordered concatenation of the propositions it sets forth. He was a forerunner of a completely modern structural concept of the scientific object. For Cournot, the scientific explanation of the phenomena of life requires a specific principle that, in the organism, must control the laws of physics and chemistry. This separation from the state of nature is accomplished by man in the course of a development that causes him to cultivate religion, art, history, philosophy, and science.

COURTIVRON, GASPARD LE COMPASSEUR DE CRÉQUY-MONTFORT, MARQUIS DE (*b. Château de Courtivron, Côte-d'Or, France, 1715; d. Château de Courtivron, 1785*), mechanics, optics, technology.

Courtivron gave up a military career for a scientific one. In mechanics, he brought together the principles of Leibniz, Johann I Bernoulli, and d'Alembert, moving toward a formulation of the concept of the conservation of work. In optics, he assailed the Cartesian concept of light and championed the Newtonian. His career covers a broad spectrum of scientific endeavor, and reflects the style of Enlightenment science.

COURTOIS, BERNARD (*b. Dijon, France, 1777; d. Paris, France, 1838*), chemistry.

Studied under Fourcroy at the École Polytechnique, worked as a military pharmacist and as assistant to Thenard and to Armand Séguin. Took over his father's saltpeter business in Dijon. He discovered a new substance which was later established by Gay-Lussac and Humphry Davy as a new element, "iode" (iodine).

COUTURAT, LOUIS (*b. Paris, France, 1868; d. between Ris-Orangis and Melun, France, 1914*), logic, mathematical philosophy, linguistics.

Graduated from the École Normale Supérieure (1892) and took a doctorate at the Sorbonne with a thesis, *De l'infini mathématique* (1896), which brought to metaphysicians and logicians the theories of the new mathematics. He examined Leibniz' metaphysics in *La logique de Leibniz* (1901), and prepared an influential edition (1905) of Bertrand Russell's *Principia mathematica*. He became a prime mover in developing an auxiliary international language, constructing the complete vocabulary of Ido, a language derived from Esperanto (1908).

COWELL, PHILIP HERBERT (*b. Calcutta, India, 1870; d. Aldeburgh, Suffolk, England, 1949*), dynamical astronomy.

Graduated from Trinity College, Cambridge (1892), was chief assistant at the Royal Observatory (from 1896) and superintendent of the *Nautical Almanac* (from 1910). Made contributions to development of a theory of the motion of the moon. His name is perpetuated in "Cowell's method" of step-by-step numerical integration for the solution of the relatively simple differential equations in rectangular coordinates defining the motions of bodies under their mutual gravitational attraction.

CRABTREE, WILLIAM (*b. Broughton, England, 1610; d. Broughton, 1644[?]*), astronomy.

Crabtree is remembered chiefly for his influence on and relationship to Jeremiah Horrocks. He convinced Horrocks of the superiority of Kepler's new astronomy, accepting the latter's elliptical orbits and concurring in his call for the creation of a celestial physics. Both made many corrections to Kepler's *Rudolphine Tables*, and Crabtree converted them to decimal form.

CRAIG, JOHN (*b. Scotland, second half of seventeenth century; d. London, England, 1731*), mathematics.

Little known of his early life. Studied at Edinburgh, took holy orders, and spent most of life in Cambridge. One of the few Englishmen who realized the vast possibilities of the newly invented calculus, he compiled three major works: "Method of Determining the Quadratures of Figures Bounded by Curves and Straight Lines" (1685), "Mathematical Treatise on the Quadratures of Curvilinear Figures" (1693), and "On the Calculus of Fluents" (1718).

CRAMER, GABRIEL (*b. Geneva, Switzerland, 1704; d. Bagnols-sur-Cèze, France, 1752*), geometry, probability theory.

Cramer was educated in Geneva and taught at the Académie de Calvin there (from 1924). His extensive correspondence on mathematical and philosophical topics and the acquaintanceships formed in his travels show his function as a stimulator and intermediary in the spread of problems and ideas. He proposed the Castillon (Castillon-Cramer) problem. He is best known for Cramer's rule and Cramer's paradox, although neither was original with him. The rule is a general and convenient one for the solution of a set of v linear equations in v unknowns. The paradox grew out of combining the formula $v^2/2 + 3v/2$ with the theorem that mth- and nth-order curves intersect in mn points. The formula says, for example, that a cubic curve is uniquely determined by nine points; the theorem, that two *different* cubic curves would intersect in nine points.

His most original contributions are less well known: the general content and organization of his *Introduction à l'analyse des lignes courbes algébriques* (1750), and his concept of mathematical utility (related to mathematical expectation and a link between mathematical economics and probability theory).

CRAMER, JOHANN ANDREAS (*b. Quedlinburg, Germany, 1710; d. Berggiesshübel, near Dresden, Germany, 1777*), chemistry.

After brief legal career, entered University of Helmstedt to study chemistry and metallurgy (1734); lectured at Leiden, traveled to England, appointed director of Brunswick Mining and Metallurgy Administration in Harz mountains (1743), worked also in Saxony and Prussia. *Elementa artis docimasticae* (1737) was the first textbook of its kind, covering the entire art of assaying in two parts, one theoretical and one practical; all instruments and apparatus were illustrated and described exactly, including the first description of the use of the blowpipe in analysis.

CRAWFORD, ADAIR (*b. Ireland, 1748; d. Lymington, England, 1795*), physiology, physics, chemistry.

Studied at University of Glasgow (1764–76) and at University of Edinburgh medical school. Became champion of heat theory of William Irvine: heat is physically contained in substances having varying capacities for it. Performed first experiments (1777) designed to determine specific heats of gases; published theory of respiration and combustion based on three propositions: atmospheric air inhaled into lungs contains more absolute heat than air exhaled, arterial blood leaving lungs contains more absolute heat than venous blood pumped into lungs, and a body's capacity for heat is reduced by chemical fixation of phlogiston and increased by separation of phlogiston. The challenge posed by his theory was soon taken up by Lavoisier and Laplace, whose experiments failed to support it; John Dalton continued to advocate it until it was disproved by Delaroche and Bérard (1812).

CREDNER, (KARL) HERMANN GEORG (*b. Gotha, Germany, 1841; d. Leipzig, Germany, 1913*), geology.

Credner took a Ph.D. at Göttingen (1864), worked in North America as an expert on gold mining, taught at Leipzig, and directed the Geologische Landesanstalt. His *Elemente der Geologie* (1871) was the leading German text for thirty-five years. He was one of the first scientists to recognize the consequences of the European ice ages; did intensive work on Saxon Stegocephalia; and made a complete cumulative survey map of Saxony on the scale of 1:250,000.

CREIGHTON, CHARLES (*b. Peterhead, Aberdeenshire, Scotland, 1847; d. Upper Boddington, Northamptonshire, England, 1927*), medical history.

Creighton took an M.A. (1867), M.B. and M.S. (1871), and M.D. (1878) at Aberdeen. His chief work was *A History of Epidemics in Britain* (1891–94), a unique source book on the interrelations of epidemic diseases and social history. Despite his industry, rare scholarly insights, and splendid style, he incurred contemporary disdain for a comprehensive article on pathology (1885) which cast doubt on the existence of pathogenic bacteria and the germ theory of infectious diseases. He denounced Jennerian vaccination in *The Natural History of Cowpox and Vaccinal Syphilis* (1887) and in *Jenner and Vaccination* (1889). He clung perversely to the last defensible aspects of Rokitansky's humoral theory of pathology and Virchow's early skepticism about bacteriology.

CRELL, LORENZ FLORENZ FRIEDRICH VON (*b. Helmstedt, Germany, 1745; d. Göttingen, Germany, 1816*), chemistry.

Crell took an M.D. (1768) at Helmstedt and taught there (1774–1810) and at Göttingen (1810–16). On a study tour to Strasbourg, Paris, Edinburgh, and London, he came under the strong influence of William Cullen and Joseph Black. He founded and edited a journal for chemistry which became the first successful discipline-oriented journal in science and the model for others, and which forged a German chemical community. He first titled it *Chemisches Journal für die Freunde der Naturlehre, Arzneygelahrtheit, Haushaltungskunst und Manufacturen* (1778–80), then *Die neuesten Entdeckungen in der Chemie* (quarterly, 1781–83), then *Chemische Annalen für die Freunde...* (monthly, 1784–1804). His influential backing of R. Kirwan's notion that inflammable air (hydrogen) was phlogiston and his opposition to Lavoisier finally only discredited him and led to the founding of an antiphlogistonist rival journal by A. N. Scherer.

CRELLE, AUGUST LEOPOLD (*b. Eichwerder, near Wriezen, Germany, 1780; d. Berlin, Germany, 1855*), mathematics, civil engineering.

Crelle trained as a civil engineer and was a Prussian civil servant engaged in construction of new roads and a railway line when he took a doctorate in mathematics at Heidelberg (1816). Later he transferred to the Ministry of Education as advisor on mathematics (1828). He is best remembered as the founder of the *Journal für die reine und angewandte Mathematik*, still universally known as *Crelle's Journal* (1826). He edited fifty-two volumes, and through the journal exercised his unique sensitivity to mathematical genius. For his lifelong, unselfish intercession, he deserves a place in the history of science. He also wrote many mathematical and technical papers, textbooks, and mathematical tables.

CREMONA, ANTONIO LUIGI GAUDENZIO GIUSEPPE (*b. Pavia, Italy, 1830; d. Rome, Italy, 1903*), mathematics.

Cremona took a doctorate in civil engineering and architecture at Pavia (1853). He taught at Bologna (1860–67) and at the Technical Institute in Milan (1867–73), directed the new Polytechnic School of Engineering in Rome (1873–77), and taught at the University of Rome (from 1877). A main contribution to mathematics was his theory of birational transformations (Cremona transformations). These have been used to study rational surfaces, elliptic integrals, and Riemann surfaces and to resolve singularities of plane and space curves. Another contribution was his skillful use of the funicular diagram, or reciprocal figure, in graphic statics, which helped popularize Maxwell's theorem on reciprocal figures. Although he made no startling discoveries in projective geometry, this discipline pervades all his work, and he derived many properties of projectively related figures.

CRESCAS, HASDAI (*b. Barcelona[?], Spain, ca. 1340; d. Zaragoza, Spain, 1412*), philosophy, theology.

Crescas, a leader of the Spanish Jewish community, attacked much of the foundation of Aristotelian physics in the natural science section of his *Or Adonai* ("Light of the Lord"), examining twenty-five propositions of Maimonides that summarize medieval Aristotelian physics and metaphysics. The drift of his critique is toward a conception of infinite space, with the possibility of infinite worlds, and the uniformity of nature. His position is similar to that of Giordano Bruno.

CROLL, JAMES (*b. Cargill, Perthshire, Scotland, 1821; d. Perth, Scotland, 1890*), geology.

Croll studied theology and metaphysics during an unsuccessful business career. He began to publish papers in chemistry and physics, and became resident geologist in the new Edinburgh office of the Geological Survey (1867–80). His chief importance was as a controversialist, propounding the broadest climatological and cosmological theories and defending them against the mathematically adept, thus stimulating others to develop better evidence and more quantitative theories.

CROLLIUS, OSWALD (*b. Wetter, near Marburg, Germany, ca. 1560; d. Prague, Czechoslovakia, 1609*), medicine, iatrochemistry.

Crollius was educated at Marburg, Heidelberg, Strasbourg, and Geneva, taking a doctorate in medicine about 1582. As a physician in Prague, he performed practical chemical experiments to determine the properties of various chemical remedies. His vastly successful *Basilica chymica* (1609) became the standard scientific work of iatrochemistry. Healing by purely spiritual means was his ultimate goal, but in practice he insisted on real, often drastic, remedies, usefully describing in detail their composition and application. He gained academic recognition of many chemicals previously rejected as remedies.

CROMMELIN, ANDREW CLAUDE DE LA CHEROIS (*b. Cushendun, Northern Ireland, 1865; d. London, England, 1939*), astronomy.

Crommelin took a degree at Trinity College, Cambridge (1886), and was observer and computer at the Royal Observatory, Greenwich (1891–1927). He calculated preliminary orbits for many comets. With Cowell, he developed a direct method for studying the orbit of Jupiter's eighth satellite and applied it to Halley's comet, correctly predicting its return in 1910 within three days. He demonstrated (1929) the identity and the orbit of the comet variously named Pons, Coggia-Winnecke, and Forbes, and the International Astronomical Union renamed it for him. From 1891 to 1937 he wrote the annual reports on minor planets in the *Monthly Notices of the Royal Astronomical Society* and from 1916 reports on comets.

CRONSTEDT, AXEL FREDRIK (*b. Turinge, Sweden, 1722; d. Säter, Sweden, 1765*), chemistry, mineralogy.

Cronstedt became a first-rate mining expert through field study and work with Georg Brandt. He was a director of the East and West Bergslagen, a large area in the richest ore-bearing region of central Sweden (from 1748). He discovered that nickel (1751), which he so named for the material from which he obtained it, "copparnickel" in Swedish, was not a mixture of several substances but a new metal. His experiments, oriented toward the chemistry of metals, gave him unprecedented insight into the inner structure of minerals, and he attempted a new mineralogical classification in his *Försök til mineralogie, eller mineralrikets upställning* (1758). He established the first correct distinction between simple minerals and rock minerals consisting of a mixture of several minerals. He methodically applied the blowpipe to examination of minerals, and Berzelius declared him the founder of chemical mineralogy.

CROOKES, WILLIAM (*b. London, England, 1832; d. London, 1919*), chemistry, physics.

Crookes was personal assistant to A. W. Hoffman at the Royal College of C .:mistry in London (1850–54). He became a free-lance chemical consultant (using a home laboratory) and editor of photographic and scientific journals. He was nominal editor, and proprietor of the most successful and important of these, *Chemical News* (1859–1919). He was knighted in 1897, and was presi-

dent of the British Association (1898) and the Royal Society (1913–15).

Brilliance in experimentation was the dominant feature of his career; his success in producing a vacuum of the order of one millionth of an atmosphere made possible the discovery of X rays and the electron. Much of his experimental work was done by assistants after 1870, notably (1882–1919) by James H. Gardiner (scandium, "Crookes lenses").

After the death of a brother, Crookes began attending Spiritualist séances (1867) and was persuaded, after experimenting, that despite the frauds he detected, a few mediums, notably D. D. Home and Florence Cook (1874) genuinely possessed a "psychic force" that could modify gravity and produce other strange effects and he staked his scientific repute on the validity of the phenomena he described. He was the most experienced, if not always the most critical, of all nineteenth-century psychic investigators. He was president of the Society for Psychical Research (1897) and joined the Theosophy movement (1883). Until his wife's death (1916) he never believed that the "spirits" appearing in séances were unequivocally those of human dead. He is best described, therefore, as an occultist, a man for whom traditional science left huge areas of creation unexplored.

In his early attempts to apply photography to the scientific recording of polarization, astronomical objects, and spectra, he devised the first dry collodion process, with John Spiller (1854). After Bunsen and Kirchhoff announced (1860) the discovery of two new elements detected by spectrum analysis, he immersed himself in spectroscopy, and found an anomalous bright green line in selenium wastes in his laboratory. This he identified as a new element, thallium (announced 1861; isolated simultaneously on a larger, more obviously metallic scale by C. A. Lamy). It brought him fame and election to the Royal Society (1863).

Working with his Oertling balance in a vacuum, he noticed that warmer bodies appeared to be lighter than colder ones. He found that if a large mass was brought close to a lighter one suspended in an evacuated space, it would move, increasingly with decreased pressure. He supposed (1873) this was due to a repulsive action of light or heat radiation, and concluded—erroneously—that he had found the "pressure of light" postulated by Maxwell's as yet unaccepted electromagnetic theory. This belief led him to devise (1875) the "light mill," or radiometer. The explanation of its action provoked controversy, exacerbated by his psychic activities. Eventually he accepted (1876) Johnstone Stoney's explanation that the motion was due to the internal movements of the molecules in the residual gas. This gave a good qualitative explanation of all Crookes's subsequent radiometer work. He showed how the radiometer confirmed Maxwell's prediction that the viscosity of a gas was independent of its pressure except at the highest exhaustions (1877–81).

By attempting to determine the actual paths of "lines of molecular pressure" causing movement in the radiometer, on the analogy of Faraday's lines of magnetic force, he came to the cathode rays. An electric radiometer whose vanes acted as a cathode showed that the dark space between cathode and cathode glow extended farther from the blackened side of the vane, and that only when pressure was reduced to a point at which the dark space touched the sides of the radiometer tube did rotation occur. This suggested that the electric discharge in an evacuated tube (a "Crookes tube") was an actual illumination of the lines of molecular pressure. The dark space was soon called the "Crookes dark space." Adapting (1876) Faraday's concept of "radiant matter" to the lines of molecular pressure, Crookes showed that this matter traveled in straight lines and was corpuscular. For him, cathode rays were negatively charged molecules, but for J. J. Thomson "radiant matter" became the electron.

Crookes's examination of the phosphorescent spectra produced by bombarding minerals with radiant matter led him to speculate about the origin of the elements. His elegant fractionations (to 1906), which turned out to be useless for characterizing elements, confused the relationships between the rare earth elements for years. Had he pursued the fractionation of calcium salts, which he began, he undoubtedly would have separated calcium isotopes. But the similarity between the rare earth elements was also for him certain evidence of origin in a common matter (1886, 1888), "protyle." With remarkable vision he showed how elements, with their periodic properties, could be conceived of as arising under the action of an imaginary cosmic pendulum swung by electricity and heat and dampened by two lawful oscillatory motions thus producing J. Emerson Reynolds' curve of the periodic system. But genesis occurred in space, and he conceived a third oscillatory motion, and constructed an actual three-dimensional figure-eight model of the genesis of the elements, such that similar elements were located in a vertical plane on identical parts of the helix. The universe was in continual creation, radiant heat transforming into protyle. Definite quantities of electricity were given to each element at its genesis, determining the element's valence and, hence, its chemical properties. Atomic weight was only a measure of the cooling conditions at the moment of the element's birth and not, as in Mendeleev, a measure of its properties; it was conceivable that atomic weights really represented an average weight. He called the closely related atoms "meta-elements" or "elementoids," and in 1915 tried to liken these to isotopes, as in 1902 he identified protyle with the electron. The theory of genesis was indeed the high-water mark of his speculative genius, hardly equaled in science. Even the idea of the noble gases was implicit in his double helix model.

Crookes supplied a fundamental datum for Rutherford's theory of radioactivity. Using photographic plates as indicators of activity, he showed that purified uranium could be separated chemically into a non-active and a radioactive ("uranium X") portion (1900). (Soddy later showed that uranium emitted α rays and uranium X penetrating β rays.) Crookes also developed (1903) the spinthariscope; even after the invention of more sophisticated electric counting devices, Rutherford used this scintillation-counting method to estimate α activity.

CROONE, WILLIAM (*b. London, England, 1633; d. London, 1684*), physiology.

Croone graduated from Emmanuel College, Cambridge (1650), and taught rhetoric at Gresham College, London (1659–70), and anatomy at Surgeons' Hall (1670–84). He was the "register" of the circle which be-

came the Royal Society and was one of its first fellows. He was created M.D. by royal mandate (1662). His most significant discovery in experimental physics was that water has its maximum density above its freezing point. He was one of the earliest to use alcohol as a preservative of animal tissue (1662). His long-standing interest in muscle physiology led to two important contributions: he showed in experiments that the "spirit" which passes along the nerve from the brain during contraction is a definite physical "juice" and introduced the idea that a chemical reaction may be involved in contraction. He also suggested that the nerve impulse might be a disturbance or vibration along the nerves rather than a flow of substance. He was closely associated with Boyle in the latter's classic studies of aerial physics.

CROSS, CHARLES WHITMAN (*b. Amherst, Mass., 1854; d. Chevy Chase, Md., 1949*), petrology.

Cross took a B.S. at Amherst (1875) and a Ph.D. at Leipzig (1880) and was with the U. S. Geological Survey (1880–1925). His accurate field investigations in Colorado and elsewhere constitute his greatest contribution to geology. He and his assistants mapped the rock formations of seven quadrangles in the rugged terrain of the San Juan Mountains. With Iddings, Pirsson, and Washington, he devised a quantitative chemico-mineralogical classification and nomenclature of igneous rocks, the C.I.P.W. system. He was instrumental in the establishment of the Geophysical Laboratory, and a charter member of the Petrologists' Club.

CROUSAZ, JEAN-PIERRE DE (*b. Lausanne, Switzerland, 1663; d. Lausanne, 1750*), theology, philosophy, mathematics.

Crousaz was educated at the Academy of Lausanne and taught there (1700–24, 1733–49). He tutored Prince Frederick of the house of Hesse-Kassel (1726–33), having acquired a solid pedagogical reputation through his *Nouvelles maximes sur l'éducation des enfants* (1718) and *Traité de l'éducation des enfants* (1722). In analysis the work that made him famous is the *Commentaire sur l'analyse des infiniment petits* (1721). Among his other works are memoirs on the theory of movement, the causes of elasticity, the nature and propagation of fire, the different states of matter, and a harsh critique of Leibniz's preestablished harmony. He maintained a large correspondence with many eminent scientists.

CRUIKSHANK, WILLIAM CUMBERLAND (*b. Edinburgh, Scotland, 1745; d. London, England, 1800*), anatomy.

Cruikshank took an M.A. at Glasgow (1767) and an M.D. in 1783. He became William Hunter's partner at the Windmill Street School of Anatomy, running it jointly with Matthew Baillie after Hunter's death. His best-known piece of research was *The Anatomy of the Absorbing Vessels of the Human Body* (1786). In a series of experiments he confirmed Regnier de Graaf's theories on generation in the rabbit (1778). He had a large but not very lucrative medical practice.

CRUM, WALTER (*b. Glasgow, Scotland, 1796; d. Rouken, Scotland, 1867*), chemistry.

Crum studied at Glasgow under Thomas Thomson. For forty years he devoted himself to the improvement of calico printing by the application of chemical knowledge. He undertook an analysis of indigo, preparing pure indigo by sublimation and determining its composition in a remarkably accurate piece of organic research. In analytical chemistry he discovered the lead dioxide test for manganese, developed an ingenious method for the analysis of nitrates, and was the first to prepare copper peroxide and colloidal alumina. He proposed a theory of dyeing that involved both a mechanical and a chemical aspect.

CRUM BROWN, ALEXANDER. *See* **Brown, Alexander Crum.**

CRUVEILHIER, JEAN (*b. Limoges, France, 1791; d. Sussac, Haute-Vienne, France, 1874*), anatomy, pathology.

Cruveilhier took a doctoral degree at Paris (1816), and taught at Montpellier and at Paris (from 1825), holding the first chair of pathological anatomy there (1836). He had an enormous practice, following a very strict ethic he condensed in his *Des devoirs et de la moralité du médecin* (1837). He was essentially a researcher and experimenter. His injections of mercury into blood vessels and bronchial systems made possible the concepts of embolism and infarction developed by Virchow. A valvula at the distal end of the lacrimonasal canal and a vertebral nerve in the posterior cervical plexus are named for him. His anatomical texts (1830, 1834–36) played a major role in the progress of anatomical studies at Paris. He is best known for his *Anatomie pathologique du corps humain* (1828–42) and *Traité d'anatomie pathologique générale* (1849–64).

CRUZ, OSWALDO GONÇALVES (*b. São Luís de Paraitinga, São Paulo, Brazil, 1872; d. Petrópolis, Rio de Janeiro, Brazil, 1917*), public health, medicine.

M.D., Rio de Janeiro (1892); also studied in Paris (1896–99), especially at Pasteur Institute. Appointed to Serum Therapy Institute of Manguinhos (director from 1902); took charge of Brazil's first large-scale and systematic sanitation campaign (1903–09) and rid Rio de Janeiro of yellow fever and bubonic plague. At his request, institute became Institute of Experimental Pathology (1907; renamed Cruz Institute, 1908) and combined preparation of vaccines and serums, teaching, and research, thus becoming first important center for medical research in Brazil.

CTESIBIUS (KTESIBIOS) (*fl. Alexandria, 270* B.C.), invention.

Ctesibius developed the science of pneumatics, now called hydraulics, probably in collaboration with Strato of Lampsacus. He wrote a book about his inventions, which were of the first order. We owe to him force pumps for air and water; the hydraulic organ with its keyboard and rows of pipes; and the water clock. His *parerga* for water clocks survive in the cuckoo clock.

CUDWORTH, RALPH (*b. Aller, England, 1617; d. Cambridge, England, 1688*), philosophy.

Cudworth, a Cambridge Platonist, was successively fellow and tutor of Emmanuel College (1639), master of Clare Hall (1644), Regius professor of Hebrew (1645), and master of Christ's College (1654). His attempt to combine Neoplatonism and the mechanical philosophy in *The True Intellectual System of the Universe* (1678) is important in understanding the background to Newton and the early Newtonians.

CUÉNOT, LUCIEN (*b. Paris, France, 1866; d. Nancy, France, 1951*), zoology, general biology.

Cuénot took a doctorate at the Sorbonne (1887) and taught zoology at Nancy (1890–1937). His comparative studies of living and fossil fauna led to a description of many new species and detailing their ecology and ethology. In his cross-breeding of mice he showed (simultaneously with Bateson) that Mendelism extended to the animal kingdom. He discovered the impossibility of cross-breeding pure yellow mice, and thus the first example of lethal genes (1905). He also studied heredity of variegation, experimental production of atavism, the intransmissibility of cataract caused by naphthalene, and the heredity of predisposition to cancer. He early compared the activity of genes to that of enzymes. After 1918 he worked largely on adaptation and speciation, attributing importance to mutation but disputing natural selection.

CULLEN, WILLIAM (*b. Hamilton, Scotland, 1710; d. Kirknewton, near Edinburgh, Scotland, 1790*), medicine, chemistry.

Cullen studied at Edinburgh, received M.D. at Glasgow (1740), practiced medicine (1736–44), taught the first independent course in chemistry in the British Isles (in Glasgow, 1747–55), and taught medicine at Glasgow (1751–55). At Edinburgh he taught chemistry (from 1755) and the theory of medicine (from 1766). In his teaching of chemistry he was strongly influenced by Boyle rather than the fashionable narrow Newtonianism, largely ignored atoms, but was probably the first to give symbolic precision to "affinity" tables, using reversed arrows for "double decompositions." His only scientific paper was "Of the Cold Produced by Evaporating Fluids and of Some Other Means of Producing Cold" (1756), but he also made contributions to nosology and to the understanding of contemporary empirical philosophy.

CULMANN, KARL (*b. Bergzabern, Lower Palatinate, Germany, 1821; d. Zurich, Switzerland, 1881*), graphic statics.

Culmann graduated from the Polytechnikum in Karlsruhe, served as engineer in the Bavarian civil service (1841–55), and taught at the new polytechnic institute (now ETH) in Zurich (1855–81). After a study trip abroad, he wrote important reports on wooden bridges of the U.S. and iron bridges of England and America. His principal work, *Die graphische Statik* (1866), presents the graphical calculus as a symmetrical whole, a systematic introduction of graphical methods into the analysis of all kinds of structures—beams, bridges, roof trusses, arches, and retaining walls. He did not use the customary equations to analyze particular designs, but fundamental and widely applicable geometric constructions. He introduced the use of force and funicular polygons, the method of sections, and the diagram of internal forces based on the equilibrium conditions of successive joints. His book was eagerly and widely applied, and his work, which was carried forward after his death by W. Ritter, was fundamental to present analytical procedures.

CUMMING, JAMES (*b. London, England, 1777; d. North Runcton, Norfolk, 1861*), physics.

Cumming graduated from Trinity College, Cambridge (1801), and taught chemistry there (1815–60). His research (1822–33) in electromagnetism led him to independent invention of the galvanometer (1821) and independent discovery of thermoelectricity (1823). He was active in the founding of the Cambridge Philosophical Society.

CUNHA, JOSÉ ANASTÁCIO DA (*b. Lisbon, Portugal, 1744; d. Lisbon, 1787*), mathematics.

Studied mathematics and physics on his own; served as artillery officer; became known as progressive thinker; taught at Coimbra University (1773–77); imprisoned by Inquisition (1777–81); taught at College of São Lucas. Wrote *Principios mathemáticos*, a concise encyclopedia of mathematics in twenty-one parts (published serially from 1782, and as book in 1790). He was one of the main precursors of the reform of the foundations of infinitesimal calculus, presented a new theory of the exponential function based on use of solely convergent series, and gave a new definition of "differential."

CURIE, MARIE (MARIA SKLODOWSKA) (*b. Warsaw, Poland, 1867; d. Sancellemoz, France, 1934*), physics.

Marie took part in a Polish anticlerical, proscience underground university whose journal preached the cult of science. She read everything in the original. She joined her sister in Paris (1891), took a *licence* in physics (1893) and mathematics (1894), and placed first on the women's *agrégation* in physics (1896). She married Pierre Curie in 1895. For her thesis topic she chose to determine whether rays resembling those Roentgen had just discovered were emitted by elements other than uranium, which Becquerel had already shown to emit such rays. Her thesis, *Recherches sur les substances radioactives* (1904), embodied her discovery of polonium and her discovery, isolation, and measurement of the atomic weight of radium. She received jointly with her husband and Henri Becquerel the Nobel Prize for physics in 1903 for the discovery of radioactivity. She was named Pierre's assistant (1904), and after his death, after refusing a pension, held the chair of physics created for him at the Sorbonne (from 1906). She was the first woman to teach there. She received the Nobel Prize for chemistry in 1911 for the discovery of radium and polonium, the first time a scientist had received it twice.

Her method of pursuing her thesis problem was to calculate by electrical measurement the effects of each element on the conductivity of air, one of the effects of Roentgen rays (X rays) identified by Roentgen. Her first result was that thorium was "radioactive" (her term). She also identified two uranium ores as more active than uranium itself, suggesting the presence of elements more active than uranium. To prove that an imponderable mass of an unknown element, too minute to yield an optical spectrum, could be the source of measurable and characteristic effects, she undertook the immense labor needed to concentrate the active substances and measure the products (her husband joining her from this time). She showed that natural pitchblende after chemical treatment was 400 times as active as uranium and contained an unidentified metal resembling bismuth, which they

named "polonium." She also discovered a second element resembling barium—radium (1898). While her husband studied the radiations, she concentrated on isolating the two new elements and determining the atomic weight of radium. She finally isolated a decigram of pure radium (1902) and determined its atomic weight as 225 (currently 226). Until 1906, she pursued experimental proof that radium did not act on its "surroundings," material atoms or the ether in a vacuum, to produce the atomic transformations, then finally applied the Rutherford-Soddy exponential law of decay for the first time. Many difficulties remained in interpreting the experimental results: the emanation (radon), induced radioactivity, and short-lived radioactivity. The phenomenon of radioactivity substantiated the connection between matter and electricity; the causes of the atomic explosion of energy remained to be discovered. Among her contributions to the growing vocabulary were the terms "disintegration" and "transmutation."

She set the official standards for radium for the Radiology Congress (1910); the congress also defined the curie (named for her husband), a new unit based on the quantity of emanation (radon) from one gram of radium. She was a member of the Council of the Radium Institute (formed 1914), and through the institute pursued basic research and medical applications. During World War I she equipped ambulances with portable X-ray apparatus, accompanied them to the front lines, and organized courses in radiology for military medical personnel. Through the Curie Foundation (1920) and her election to the Académie de Médecine (1922) she pursued the development of "curietherapy" and the establishment of safety standards for workers. Among her collaborators at the Radium Institute was her daughter Irène, her first experimental assistant and *préparateur*, who discovered artificial radioactivity with her husband, Frédéric Joliot (1933). Marie Curie's last work included the preparation of derivatives of actinium that had not yet been isolated.

CURIE, PIERRE (*b. Paris, France, 1859; d. Paris, 1906*), physics.

Curie received a B.S. (1875) and a *licence* in physical sciences at the Faculty of Sciences in Paris (1877). He was laboratory assistant at the Sorbonne physics laboratory (1878–82) and director of the laboratory at the École Municipale de Physique et Chimie (1882–1904), where his wife, Marie Curie, worked until 1905. He died before he could take his chair of physics at the Sorbonne. He shared the Nobel Prize in physics in 1903 with his wife and Henri Becquerel for the discovery of radioactivity.

With his brother Jacques, a mineralogist, he discovered piezoelectricity, a property of non-conducting crystals that have no center of symmetry (1880). They also built the remarkable piezoelectric quartz balance, which supplied electricity proportional to weights suspended from it, later used by the Curies in work on radioactivity.

After his brother left Paris, Pierre developed in crystallography what are today called Curie's laws of symmetry (1894): When certain causes produce certain effects, the symmetry of the causes reappears, in its entirety, in the effects; if the effect includes an asymmetry, it appears in the effective cause.

From his thesis (1895) stem all modern theories of magnetism. He showed that diamagnetism is a property

179

of atoms, a property of all matter, whereas ferromagnetism and paramagnetism are properties of aggregates of atoms and not of all matter. Ferromagnetism decreases with temperature rise and gives way to weak paramagnetism at a characteristic temperature known as a substance's "Curie point." Paramagnetism is inversely proportional to the absolute temperature (Curie's law). His experimental laws and a quantum mechanical version of his student Paul Langevin's theory of thermal excitation of atoms are the basis of modern theories of magnetism. He also invented and perfected many measuring devices important in the work on radioactivity.

Whereas his wife was trained mainly as a chemist and had a vast persevering firmness in pursuing a problem, he was a complete physicist—theoretician and experimenter. The reason for their success was the new method of chemical analysis based on the precise measurement of radiation emitted. After her first note (April, 1898) to the Academy, he joined in her research. They sought to isolate, from the ores from which uranium and thorium were extracted, new elements more active than either, by using the classical methods of analysis and chemical separations. They discovered polonium and, with G. Bémont, radium (1898). For a few centigrams of pure radium chloride they had to process two tons of uranium ore residue. Pierre Curie took up his wife's discovery of induced radioactivity (1899), and showed that the activity diminishes exponentially by a time constant equal for the emanation to 5,752 days, regardless of the experimental conditions (1902, 1903). This discovery was the point of departure for all modern measurements of archaeological and geological dating; he himself defined a standard for the absolute measurement of time on the basis of radioactivity (1902). His basic discovery of the vast heat released spontaneously by radium (1903) was the first appearance of atomic energy in the form of heat.

CURTIS, HEBER DOUST (*b. Muskegon, Mich., 1872; d. Ann Arbor, Mich., 1942*), astronomy.

Curtis took an A.B. (1892) and A.M. (1893) at the University of Michigan, taught Latin and Greek (1894–96) and mathematics and astronomy (1896–1900) at Napa College, took a Ph.D. in astronomy at the University of Virginia (1902), and joined the Lick Observatory (1902–20). He was the director of the Allegheny Observatory of the University of Pittsburgh (1920–30) and of the observatory of the University of Michigan (1930–42). He worked on nebular photography at the Lick Observatory in conjunction with his growing conviction of the truth of the "island universe" theory, presenting his case in opposition to Harlow Shapley at the National Academy of Sciences (1920). His later work was in teaching, administration, and construction of new instruments.

CURTISS, RALPH HAMILTON (*b. Derby, Conn., 1880; d. Ann Arbor, Mich., 1929*), astronomy.

Curtiss took a B.S. (1901) and a Ph.D. (1905) at the University of California. While at Allegheny Observatory of the University of Pittsburgh (1905–07), he designed his first stellar spectrograph and discovered with it a third component of the star Algol. At the University of Michigan (from 1907), he initiated a program of observing close binary stars, Cepheid variables, and stars of high

surface temperature with bright line spectra. Director of the university's Detroit observatory (1927–29).

CURTIUS, THEODOR (*b. Duisburg, Germany, 1857; d. Heidelberg, Germany, 1928*), chemistry.

Curtius studied under Bunsen in Heidelberg and took a doctorate under Kolbe at Leipzig (1882). He worked in Baeyer's laboratories in Munich (1882–86), in the analytical section of the chemical laboratories at Erlangen (1886–97), and directed the chemical institute at Heidelberg (1898–1926). He discovered the first known aliphatic diazo compound, diazoacetic ester (1886); hydrazine (1887); and hydrazoic acid (1890). In work on polypeptides (from 1882) he synthesized a hexapeptide, benzoyl pentaglycine-aminoacetic acid, by fusing ethyl hippurate with glycine. He discovered two reactions named for him: the conversion of an acid into an amine or an aldehyde (1894) and the conversion of an azide into an isocyanate (1913).

CURTZE, E. L. W. MAXIMILIAN (*b. Ballenstedt, Harz, Germany, 1837; d. Thorn, Germany [now Toruń, Poland], 1903*), mathematics.

Curtze studied in Greifswald and taught at the Gymnasium in Thorn. He translated mathematical works from Italian into German. The expert of his time on medieval mathematical texts, his editions pointed out new paths in a field that was then little investigated.

CUSA, NICHOLAS, also known as **Nikolaus von Cusa, Nicolaus Cusanus** (*b. Kues, Moselle, Germany, ca. 1401; d. Todi, Umbria, Italy, 1464*), philosophy, mathematics.

Nicholas studied at Heidelberg and took the degree *doctor decretalium* at the University of Padua (1423). He proved that the Donation of Constantine was an eighth-century forgery and discovered long-lost Latin works, including the *Natural History* of Pliny the Elder. He was ordained (*ca.* 1430), became a partisan of the papal faction (*ca.* 1436), and was an imaginative, skillful diplomat for the Curia. He was named a cardinal (1446) and legate for Germany (1450), but in later life was embroiled in ineffectual attempts to reform clergy, orders, and the Curia. In his major philosophical work, *De docta ignorantia* (completed 1440), he made new interpretations of those philosophically oriented introductory books of mathematics with which he was acquainted, notably Boethius and Bradwardine. Throughout his works he expounded his doctrine of *coincidentia oppositorum;* he made extensive use of geometric figures, because rational language was not suited to explaining the power of knowing that is superior to human reason. His cosmological reasoning, although garbled in theological language, anticipates scientific discovery. *De docta ignorantia* was respected and influential, but was attacked for pantheism and other heresies; after his *Apologia doctae ignorantiae* (1449) he wrote a number of short treatises, some on mathematics, and some 300 sermons, applying his philosophy. He shows considerable knowledge of the available practical geometries and the simpler Euclidean theorems and relies heavily on Thomas Bradwardine. He attempted to transform a circle into a straight line (1445), and offered numerous methods for determining physical parameters through such apparatus as scales and a water clock. In *Perfectio mathematica* (1458), he anticipated an infinitesimal concept of great significance by suggesting his method could yield an infinitely small arc of a circle and its corresponding chord. His later works include a number of relatively short treatises in which simple physical or mathematical examples are expanded into philosophical symbols.

CUSHING, HARVEY WILLIAMS (*b. Cleveland, Ohio, 1869; d. New Haven, Conn., 1939*), neurosurgery, neurophysiology.

Cushing took a degree at Yale and an M.D. at Harvard Medical School (1895), taught at Johns Hopkins Hospital (to 1911), at Harvard (1912–32), and at Yale (1933–37). The first American surgeon to specialize in neurological surgery, he inspired the Harvey Cushing Society (1932), now the American Association of Neurological Surgeons. His greatest contribution was in the field of intracranial tumors; he reduced mortality from almost 100 percent to less than 10 percent in a series of over 2,000 cases. He established the Hunterian Laboratory at Johns Hopkins (1905) and the Laboratory of Surgical Research at Harvard. His physiologically balanced substitute for pure sodium chloride, "Cushing's solution," is still in use. He anticipated the now routine use of positive-pressure endotracheal anesthesia. His classic demonstration that increased spinal fluid pressure initially produces a vagal effect with bradycardia, followed by high rise in arterial blood pressure, allowed safer craniotomies and stimulated further research. He introduced the first blood pressure apparatus in America and devised silver clips still used to control bleeding. He introduced electrocautery in brain surgery (1925). His early work on tumors of the pituitary gland (1912) is one of his most enduring; it elucidated the overriding influence of the pituitary and the other ductless glands. He identified pituitary basophilism, or Cushing's disease (1930).

CUSHMAN, JOSEPH AUGUSTINE (*b. Bridgewater, Mass., 1881; d. Sharon, Mass., 1949*), micropaleontology.

Cushman took a degree at Harvard College (1903), was curator at the Museum of the Boston Society of Natural History (1903–12), Foraminifera expert with the U.S. Geological Survey (1912–23), and established the Cushman Laboratory for Foraminiferal Research (1923). He established Foraminifera as a tool in biostratigraphy and paleoecology and as a major factor in the search for petroleum. His radical reclassification (*Foraminifera, Their Classification and Economic Use*, 1928) has been retained as a basic structure. By the 1940's he saw the potential of planktonic Foraminifera for worldwide stratigraphic zonation; this was widely accepted shortly after his death.

CUSHNY, ARTHUR ROBERTSON (*b. Fochabers, Morayshire, Scotland, 1866; d. Edinburgh, Scotland, 1926*), pharmacology, physiology.

Educated at University of Aberdeen (M.A., 1886; Bachelor of Medicine and Master of Surgery, 1889), at Bern (under Kronecker), and at Würzburg (under Schmiedeberg). Occupied chairs in pharmacology at University of Michigan (1893–1905) and at University College, London (1905–18), then chair of materia medica at University of Edinburgh. Made important contributions to three separate problems: the action and therapeutic application of digitalis, the secretion of urine by the kid-

ney, and the action and general biological relationships of optical isomers. Used myocardiograph and cardiometer to reveal two-stage effects of digitalis on mammalian heart, suggesting hypothesis of dynamic interplay between two antagonistic powers of digitalis series: direct stimulation of vagus nerve and of central inhibitory apparatus vs. direct tonic effect on cardiac muscles, the latter being main cause of therapeutic effects (*The Action and Uses in Medicine of Digitalis and Its Allies*, 1925). Discovered auricular fibrillation to be a factor in many cases of cardiac irregularity. In *The Secretion of Urine* (1917), advocated filtration-reabsorption theory, following extensive experimentation. In studying pharmacological action of optical isomers (*Biological Relations of Optically Isomeric Substances*, 1926) he provided decisive evidence that a pair of optical isomers could differ in their action on the cells of higher organisms; his later work demonstrated the full complexity of the subject. Also wrote *A Textbook of Pharmacology and Therapeutics* (1899).

CUVIER, FRÉDÉRIC (*b. Montbéliard, Württemberg, 1773; d. Strasbourg, France, 1838*), zoology.

Frédéric worked under his famous brother, Georges at the Muséum d'Histoire Naturelle in Paris (1797–1838). From 1818 to 1837, he published seventy installments of his *Histoire des mammifères*, in which approximately 500 species were described, naming important new species and genera. His most original work was on the behavior of mammals in captivity; he was ahead of his time in studying mammalian social life, hoping that his study would make possible the better understanding of human societies.

CUVIER, GEORGES (*b. Montbéliard, Württemberg, 1769; d. Paris, France, 1832*), zoology, paleontology, history of science.

Cuvier's precocity brought him to the attention of the duke of Württemberg, who seconded him to the Caroline University (1784–88) where he studied under K.F. Kielmeyer. Étienne Geoffroy Saint-Hilaire summoned him to Paris where they lived and worked together for a year (1795). Cuvier presented the first new divisions of invertebrates into mollusks, crustaceans, insects, worms, echinoderms, and zoophytes. Cuvier and Geoffroy in one paper, on orangutans, audaciously proposed the idea of the origin of species from a single type. Because of his brilliance and a shortage of zoologists in Paris, he rapidly became assistant professor of animal anatomy at the Muséum (from 1795); a member of the Institut de France (1796) and permanent secretary for physical sciences (1803); professor at the Collège de France (from 1800); university counselor (from 1808); *chevalier* (1811); councillor of state (from 1814; presided over the Interior Department of the council 1819–32); member of the Académie Française (1818); *grand officier* of the Legion of Honor (1824); peer of France (1831).

At the Muséum, then the world's largest scientific research establishment, he greatly expanded the comparative anatomy collections. His three published works of general zoology contain classifications that are often a bit hasty and conservative and, except for fish, without the solidity of Lamarck's, Latreille's, or Geoffroy's. His great work, *Histoire des poissons* (with Achille Valenciennes; 22 vols., 1828–49), is the basis for modern ichthyology; most of the fish families he created were so soundly based that they have become orders or suborders in present classification. He was the first to deal systematically with mollusk anatomy.

Notes taken at his last courses at the Collège de France, published as *Histoire des sciences naturelles depuis leur origine*, made the first great work on this vast subject.

He made great strides in studying extinct animals with new accuracy. His famous paleontological reconstructions were based on the living being, assuming that any well-preserved piece of bone can reveal infallibly the class, order, genus, and even the species. He reconstructed the musculature of extinct animals from imprints left by the muscles on the bones. He conceived the notion of the balance of nature as an interdependent network, and believed that the network, like the species, was fixed at the time of creation, until his own paleontological discoveries forced him to admit creation in several stages (1812). With Alexandre Brongniart, he researched (from 1804) and wrote *Description géologique des environs de Paris* (1822, 1835), a landmark in geology. Cuvier played the lesser role in this work. Respecting the short chronology of the Bible, he was forced to assume the operation not only of Lamarck's "current causes," which act very slowly, but also the operation of rapid catastrophes and global upheavals which had no basis in fact.

For political, scientific, and religious reasons, he undertook a famous battle (1830) against his former friends Lamarck and Geoffroy—a battle often fought in secret and in which he tested his own political power. He first disputed and then accepted (1792) the theory of the chain of being. His collaboration with Geoffroy, whom he probably influenced in favor of the theory, occurred in 1795. He then rejected the theory again (1802–04). Geoffroy demonstrated that all vertebrates had the same type of body structure, which supported common origin. Two of Geoffroy's disciples, Laurencet and Meyranx, in an audacious and still worthy hypothesis, attempted (1829) to establish a structural analogy between fish and cephalopods, a possible transition between invertebrates and vertebrates. Cuvier sought to prevent the Academy from examining this work (1830) and accused Geoffroy and his disciples of being pantheists.

CYRIAQUE DE MANGIN, CLÉMENT. *See* **Henrion, Denis.**

CYSAT, JOHANN BAPTIST (*b. Lucerne, Switzerland, ca. 1586; d. Lucerne, 1657*), astronomy.

Cysat entered the Jesuit order (1604), taught at Ingolstadt (from 1618), and later held many administrative posts. He is mainly known for his observations of the comet of 1618–19, the most nearly continuous series on this much argued-over comet. His aim was to show that it was supralunary. He proposed two different theories: a Tychonic-style circular orbit about the sun and a straight-line trajectory (*Mathemata astronomica . . .*, 1619).

CZEKANOWSKI, ALEKSANDER PIOTR (*b. Krzemieniec, Poland [now Kremenets, Ukrainian S.S.R.], 1833; d. St. Petersburg, Russia, 1876*), geology, exploration.

Czekanowski studied medicine at Kiev and mineralogy at Dorpat; he and many colleagues in a Polish freedom organization were arrested and deported to Siberia in 1863. He continued his intensive studies in the natural sciences. He made the first geological study of the Eastern Siberian Upland. He organized three scientific expeditions (1873–75) which gathered paleontological, zoological, and botanical data on the vast region between Mongolia and the Arctic Ocean. Several genera and many species of plant and animal fossils, four plants, a mountain range near the lower Glensk, and a peak of the Chamar-Daban range are named for him.

CZERMAK (ČERMAK), JOHANN NEPOMUK (*b. Prague, Czechoslovakia, 1828; d. Leipzig, Germany, 1873*), physiology, histology, phonetics, laryngology.

Czermak studied in Prague, Vienna, Würzburg, and in Breslau under the strong influence of Purkinje. He worked in Prague, Graz, Krakow, Vienna, Budapest, Jena, and Leipzig. He is best known for improving the laryngeal mirror and introducing it as a clinical tool. He was the first to use it for dorsal rhinoscopy. He also contributed to physiological experimental techniques and made contributions in phonetics and the physiology of sensations. The phenomenon of slow heartbeat and loss of consciousness from pressure on the neck is named for him, as are "Czermak spaces" (irregular gaps in dentin in teeth) and "Czermak lines," formed by Czermak spaces.

CZERSKI, JAN (*b. Svolna, Vitebsk, Russia [now Byelorussia, U.S.S.R.], 1845; d. confluence of Prorva and Kolyma Rivers, Siberia, Russia, 1892*), geology, zoology, Siberian exploration.

Czerski was exiled for taking part in the Polish insurrection of 1863, educated himself with the help of other exiled scientists, was natural science custodian of the Siberian branch of the Russian Geographical Society (1871–85) and worked in the geological museum of the St. Petersburg Academy (1885–92). He died on an expedition continuing the work of Czekanowski. He was responsible for the elucidation of the geology of Lake Baykal; the discovery of Quaternary mammals and Paleolithic occurrences of man in Siberia; the first synthetic geological cross section of Siberia from Baykal to the Urals; and for the assemblage of valuable zoological, geological, and ethnographical collections.

D', DA, DE, DEL', DELLA. Many names with these prefixes are listed under the next word of the name.

DAINELLI, GIOTTO (*b. Florence, Italy, 1878; d. Florence, 1968*), geology, geography.

Dainelli taught geography at Pisa and geology at Naples and Florence. As well as geographic studies of Italy, he made paleontologic and tectonic studies of the Friulian Prealps and a paleogeographic study of Italy during the Pliocene. On his expedition to the eastern Karakoram Range, he made contributions to anthropogeographic research and geology, encompassing terrain series and formations, problems of tectonics, and vast paleogeographic reconstructions. In eastern Africa, he constructed a vast synthesis of its geology, ranging from stratigraphic and paleontologic observations to paleogeographic reconstructions.

DALE, HENRY HALLETT (*b. London, England, 1875; d. Cambridge, England, 1968*), physiology, pharmacology.

Studied at Trinity College, Cambridge (graduated 1898), St. Bartholomew's Hospital (B. Chir., 1903; M.D., 1909), University College, London (under Starling and Bayliss), and Frankfurt (under Paul Ehrlich). Worked at Wellcome Physiological Research Laboratories (1904–14); on Medical Research Committee (1914–28); director of National Institute for Medical Research (1928–42); resident director of Royal Institution of Great Britain (1942–46). Shared Nobel Prize for medicine or physiology with Loewi (1936); knighted (Grand Cross Order of the British Empire, 1943). Research on physiological actions of ergot led to the discovery of the phenomenon of adrenalin reversal (1907); observation of oxytocic effects of posterior pituitary extracts (1909); identification of histamine poisoning with anaphylactic shock (1911); and demonstration of importance of chemical and humoral factors in control of the circulation. Pursuing studies of vasoactive substances, Dale published a comprehensive review of the physiological properties of acetylcholine, noting its muscarinic action and nicotinic action and calling attention to similarities with effects of stimulation of parasympathetic nervous system (1914). Subsequent work proved the natural occurrence of acetylcholine (1929) and extended the concept of chemical transmission of nerve impulses. Dale, with Thorvald Madsen, was largely responsible for adoption of an international scheme of standardizing drugs and antitoxins (1925).

DALÉCHAMPS, JACQUES (or **Jacobus Dalechampius**) (*b. Caen, France, 1513; d. Lyons, France, 1588*), botany, medicine.

Daléchamps took a doctorate in medicine at Montpellier (1547) and worked in Lyons (from 1552). A "medical humanist," he wrote the most complete botanical compilation of its time (*Historia generalis plantarum*, 1586–87), the first to describe the flora peculiar to the Lyons area. His *Chirurgie françoise* (1570) was based largely on Paul of Aegina. He made the first complete Latin translation of Theophrastus' known works as well as many other editions and translations into Latin and French.

DALENCÉ, JOACHIM (*b. Paris, France, ca. 1640; d. Lille, France, 1707*[?]), astronomy, physics.

Served as royal secretary and counsellor. Served as intermediary between Oldenburg and Huygens, was in communication with Leibniz, and served as liaison between the French Academy and Huygens. Published anonymously the first six collections of the *Connaisance des temps* (beginning 1679). His works on scientific instruments included a detailed description of the principal meteorological instruments of the period.

DALIBARD, THOMAS FRANÇOIS (*b. Crannes, France, 1703; d. Paris, France, 1779*), natural history.

Dalibard was the first naturalist in France to adopt Linnaeus' system (*Florae Parisiensis prodomus . . . ,* 1749). Linnaeus named a Canadian bramble for him. While translating Franklin's *Experiments and Observations on Electricity,* he reenacted Franklin's experiments and proved the accuracy of Franklin's theory that the materials of thunder and lightning were similar.

DALL, WILLIAM HEALEY (*b. Boston, Mass., 1845; d. Washington, D.C., 1927*), malacology, paleontology.

Dall studied under Louis Agassiz and A. A. Gould, but received no college degree. He was a naturalist with the Western Union International Telegraph Expedition to Alaska (1865), then its scientific director (1866), and thereafter devoted himself to exploring Alaska, the Aleutian chain, and the Pacific coast. He became acting assistant with the Coast Survey (1871–81), assistant with the Coast and Geodetic Survey (1881–84), and paleontologist for the U.S. Geological Survey (1884). His wide-ranging work—*Alaska and Its Resources* (1870), studies of mollusks, brachiopods, birds, land and marine mammals, fishes, climatology, anthropology, currents, and geology of Alaska and the Aleutians, and his immense collections of specimens—constitutes a primary source for the area. He named 5,427 genera, subgenera, and species of mollusks and brachiopods, recent and fossil. His reclassification of the pelecypods, largely by shell features, particularly the hinge, is still a standard reference.

DALTON, JOHN (*b. Eaglesfield, Cumberland, England, 1766; d. Manchester, England, 1844*), physics, chemistry, meteorology.

Dalton is a classic figure of the eighteenth-century English natural philosophy: of Quaker background, obscure education, and self-made opportunity. Put to work as a laborer, he was rescued (1781) by a place as assistant in a new Quaker boarding school in Kendal which had a good science library, apparatus, and a steady flow of itinerant natural philosophy lecturers, including John Banks. With his brother Jonathan he became joint principal (1785–92). A local Quaker, John Gough, taught him mathematics, meteorology, and botany. He taught at the "New College" established by Dissenters in Manchester (1792–1800), resigned, and opened (1800) his own private academy; success came quickly, and private teaching supported him from then on.

Elected to the Manchester Literary and Philosophical Society (1794), within a month he read his first major paper, characteristic in its careful observations and bold (in this case, mistaken) theorizing. It gave the first systematic account of color blindness, a defect he shared with his brother.

Not an orthodox Newtonian, Dalton was deeply indebted to the empirical and speculative British tradition of textbook and popular Newtonianism. His *Meteorological Observations and Essays* (1793) provided diligent tables, but far more interesting were the essays, particularly one on evaporation that includes the germs of his chemical atomic theory. His experiments seemed to show that, in modern terminology, the vapor pressure of water is constant at constant temperature, a conclusion at odds with belief in evaporation as a chemical process. Hence he, the mathematically inclined meteorologist, simply abandoned the chemistry. This first statement that in a mixture of gases, every gas acts as an independent entity (his law of partial pressures) and that the air is not a vast chemical solvent brought no immediate reaction. A paper on water vapor provided the earliest definition of the dew point (1800). Then came the really dramatic development, four papers (1801) which included his first clear statement that "When two elastic fluids, . . . *A* and *B*, are mixed together, the particles of *A* do not repel those of *B*, as they do one another. . . . The pressure or whole weight upon any one particle arises solely from those of its own kind"; the notion of the static, particulate gas was Newtonian. He also independently stated Charles's law: "all elastic fluids expand the same quantity by heat." Controversy was rapid and widespread. Convincing experimental proof was thenceforth his major aim, and hence the efficient cause of the chemical atomic theory. Led to the question of the solubility of gases in water, he extended the mechanical idea (1802) that a gas "is held in water, not by chemical affinity, but merely by the pressure." His close friend William Henry, in rival and chemically orthodox experiments to ascertain the order of affinities of gases for water, found what Dalton had failed to see—that at a given temperature the mass of the gas absorbed by a given volume of water is directly proportional to the pressure of the gas (Henry's law). Henry publicly admitted Dalton's mechanical explanation. In "The Absorption of Gases by Water and other Liquids" (read 1803), Dalton made it clear that different gases observe different laws; proposed that "the circumstance depends upon the weight and number of the ultimate particles of the several gases; those whose particles are lightest and single being least absorbable"; and closed with the first list of what we would now call atomic weights. His mechanist, visual, and realist view of atoms was joined with the prevailing vogue for numerical calculation and with the common assumption of one-to-one combination in such a way as to yield wholly new insights. He had a rationale for deciding both the formulas of compounds and their three-dimensional molecular structures. With his mechanical view, it was a simple matter for him to argue from the knowledge that eight ounces of oxygen combined with one of hydrogen, to the statement that the relative weights of their ultimate particles were as eight to one. There was no public reaction to his tables, which appeared to be just further unexplained variations on the widely known tables of affinity numbers. He himself only fully grasped the wider implications of his work in his *New System of Chemical Philosophy* (2 vols., 1808–1827). With this and more especially with T. Thomson's and W. H. Wollaston's 1808 papers on the practical power of his approach, the chemical atomic theory was finally launched. His later work mainly provided experimental measurements of atomic weights of known chemical compounds.

The equation of the concepts "atom" and "chemical element" is usually held to be one of his most important achievements, providing a new, fundamental, and enormously fruitful model of reality for the chemist. But the use and the extension of his ideas on atomic weights was plagued by methodological problems only slowly resolved by Gay-Lussac, Avogadro, and Cannizzaro. His ideas on the real physical existence and actual nature of chemical atoms were even more troublesome, initiating a continuing debate terminated only by Rutherford and Soddy. He used "atom" not as a complex result of an ordered and intricate internal structure, but as the given solid, the planet (1808); he also publicly abandoned the unity of matter (1810), quoting Newton's thirty-first query in the *Opticks* polemically. The eventual successes of the theory were so great as to hide from many these ambiguities and uncertainties.

The Manchester "Lit and Phil" offered Dalton an extensive library, a vehicle for publication, a home for his apparatus and experiments (from 1800), critical encour-

agement, and personal reward: he rose to president (1817–44). One of the first two recipients of the Royal Medal (1826) for his chemical atomic theory, he was a reluctant candidate for election to the Royal Society. He was a willing corresponding member (1816) and one of eight foreign associates (1830) of the French Academy, helped found the British Association for the Advancement of Science, chaired chemistry committees, and was vice-president-elect (1836) when severe paralytic attacks (1837) left him a semi-invalid.

DALTON, JOHN CALL (*b. Chelmsford, Mass., 1825; d. New York, N.Y., 1889*), medicine, physiology.

Studied at Harvard (A.B., 1844; M.D., 1847), attended lectures of Claude Bernard at Paris (1850); gave up medical practice to devote all of his time to physiology, the first American to do so. Taught at University of Buffalo, University of Vermont, Long Island College Hospital, and the College of Physicians and Surgeons (New York); served as surgeon in Civil War. Introduced vivisection demonstrations into American physiological education; wrote widely-used textbook (*A Treatise on Human Physiology,* 1859). Investigated action and secretion of gastric juice, chemical and physiological properties of bile, and effects of removal of cerebral hemispheres of birds. Defended Bernard's belief that the liver normally produces sugar (1871). Wrote works on history of physiology.

DALY, REGINALD ALDWORTH (*b. Napanee, Ontario, Canada, 1871; d. Cambridge, Mass., 1957*), geology, geophysics.

Daly took an A.B. at Victoria College, University of Toronto (1891), an M.A. (1893) and a Ph.D. (1896) at Harvard. He was geologist with the Canadian International Boundary Commission (1901–07) and taught geology at M.I.T. (1907–12) and Harvard (1898–1901, 1912–42). His extensive field work stimulated him to correlate countless observations into coherent genetic syntheses, in such theories as magmatic stoping, and glacial control in the development of coral atolls.

AL-DAMĪRĪ, MUḤAMMAD IBN MUSA (*b. Cairo, Egypt, 1341; d. Cairo, 1405*), natural history.

Al-Damīrī, who taught in the leading universities of Egypt, is best known as the author of *Ḥayāt al-ḥayawān* ("Life of the Animals"), an alphabetical collection of articles on animals mentioned in the Koran and Arabic literature. Although he contributed no observations of his own, he included information on grammatical and lexicographical peculiarities of the animals' names, descriptions of the animals, juridico-theological considerations, proverbs about the animals, and medicinal properties.

DANA, JAMES DWIGHT (*b. Utica, N.Y., 1813; d. New Haven, Conn., 1895*), geology.

Dana studied at Yale College under the strong influence of Silliman, and served as geologist and marine zoologist with the great American expedition led by Wilkes which circled the globe (1838–42). It gave him a competence in natural history then matched only by Darwin's, inspired his interest in volcanic and coral phenomena, and, with his religiosity, disposed him to sweepingly unitary conceptions. He wrote the expedition reports *Zoophytes* (1846), *Geology* (1849), and *Crus-*

tacea (1852). Taught natural history at Yale (1856–90).

The plant-like animals now called coelenterates, the corals in particular, were then little known. He not only classified the "animalcules," but also elucidated their individual and communal physiology and their ecology. His large divisions and a majority of his species are still accepted. His observations on atolls and barrier reefs independently confirmed Darwin's theory of subsidence as the evolutionary agent. His observations on coral phenomena appeared in his popular *Corals and Coral Islands* (1872).

He sided with Lyell and against Christian von Buch on the origin of craters. His study of the erosion of a volcanic cone, one of the earliest, emphasized the importance of stream erosion in shaping any land mass. In this and in his influential concept of the permanency of the continents and the ocean basins, first presented in his *Geology*, he outdid even Lyell in uniformitarianism. The principal exponent, if not the originator, of the geosynclinal-contraction hypothesis of mountain building, he relied for much of his physical information on G. H. Darwin. He mustered the extensive, regional geologic surveys in the western United States and the Alps into a coherent geological system which was the guiding theoretical framework of geodynamics through the first quarter of the twentieth century.

Like most other uniformitarians, he was a catastrophist in biology—man most emphatically excepted. He was driven by his observations of change and progress to devise a theory of "cephalization," the release, from lower species to higher, of the organs of locomotion to the service of the brain, which provided a measure of the intelligence of the species. He remained remarkably open-minded and progressively surrendered to Darwinism, continuing to insist on occasional events of supernatural intervention, particularly in the evolution of man.

DANDELIN, GERMINAL PIERRE (*b. Le Bourget, France, 1794; d. Brussels, Belgium, 1847*), mathematics, military engineering.

Dandelin studied at the École Polytechnique in Paris and taught engineering at Liège, Namur, and Brussels. He described a useful theorem named for him in descriptive geometry and a method of approximating the roots of algebraic equations (the Dandelin-Gräffe method).

DANFORTH, CHARLES HASKELL (*b. Oxford, Me., 1883; d. Palo Alto, Calif., 1969*), anatomy, genetics.

Danforth took a B.A. (1908) and an M.A. (1910) at Tufts College and a Ph.D. (1912) at Washington University, St. Louis. He taught at the latter (1908–22) and at Stanford (1922–49). He wrote some 125 papers in several different fields of anatomy and genetics, particularly dealing with problems of inheritance. He made a major contribution to physical anthropology in helping to measure young male Americans being discharged from the army. Throughout his career he was concerned with the problems of race and evolution.

DANIELL, JOHN FREDERIC (*b. London, England, 1790; d. London, 1845*), meteorology, chemistry, electricity.

Daniell received an extensive private education. He showed his gift for scientific manufacturing enterprises in

his new process for generating gas, as managing director of the Continental Gas Company (from 1817). His real métier was in useful observation, elegant classification, and improvement in instruments in the still imperfectly differentiated physical sciences of his day. His new dew-point hygrometer (1820) quickly became a standard instrument; his pyrometer to measure furnace heat (1830) was also successful. He is best known for his work in current electricity (from 1835). He devised the improved zinc-copper battery known familiarly as the Daniell cell, which maintained a continuous, even current (1836). As first professor of chemistry at the new King's College, London (1831–45), he was largely responsible for the establishment of the department of applied science. His *Meteorological Essays* (1823) was widely successful, as was his elegant *Introduction to the Study of Chemical Philosophy* (1839). He was a founding member and vice president of the Chemical Society of London (1841).

DANTI, EGNATIO (PELLEGRINO RAINALDI) (*b. Perugia, Italy, 1536; d. Alatri, Italy, 1586*), cosmography, mathematics.

Danti entered the Dominican order and established his reputation as a scholar in science and the arts, becoming cosmographer for Cosimo I de' Medici. His establishment of the vernal equinox confirmed the need for reform of the Julian calendar. In 1580, Pope Gregory XIII called Danti to Rome to reform the calendar. He published the earliest astronomical treatises in Italian and prepared topological maps of Italy.

DARBOUX, JEAN-GASTON (*b. Nîmes, France, 1842; d. Paris, France, 1917*), mathematics.

Darboux studied at the École Normale Supérieure (doctorate, 1866); he taught in secondary schools (1867–72), at the École Normale (1872–81), and at the Sorbonne (1873–1917). He was primarily a geometer, using both analytic and synthetic methods, notably in the theory of differential equations, and made discoveries in analysis and rational mechanics as well (*Leçons sur la théorie générale des surfaces*, 1887–96; *Leçons sur les systèmes orthogonaux*, 1898). The latter contained new results stemming from his earlier investigation of the cyclids.

D'ARCET, JEAN (*b. Doazit, near St. Sever, Landes, France, 1725; d. Paris, France, 1801*), chemistry.

D'Arcet took a degree at the Faculty of Medicine in Paris (1762), studied chemistry with G. F. Rouelle, and taught at the Collège de France (from 1774). His experiments on the effects of heat on minerals led to the manufacture of true porcelain in France. In working with fusible alloys, he discovered an alloy useful in the production of stereotype plates and a method of separating the copper from church bells to cast cannon. He published works on geology of the Pyrenees and on the action of strong heat on calcareous earth. He was inspector at the Gobelins dye works, director of the porcelain works at Sèvres, and inspector general of the mint.

D'ARCY (or D'ARCI), PATRICK (*b. Galway, Ireland, 1725; d. Paris, France, 1779*), mathematics, astronomy.

D'Arcy received a private education. His active military career furthered his tendency toward being something of a scientific gadfly. He did work in rational mechanics, military technology, and physics. In 1747, he presented his principle of conservation of areas, extending it to what he called the principle of conservation of action. He worked on the physics and chemistry of gunpowder mixtures, the dimensions and design of cannon, and the placement of the charge in cannon. With J. B. Le Roy he developed a floating electrometer (1749).

DARLINGTON, WILLIAM (*b. Dilworthtown, Chester County, Pa., 1782; d. West Chester, Pa., 1863*), botany.

Darlington took an M.D. at the University of Pennsylvania (1804) and practiced medicine. Botany, however, dominated his life. He was long a confidant of Asa Gray, and documented the growth of American botany in his extensive correspondence, his *Memorials of John Bartram and Humphry Marshall* (1849), his *Florula Cestrica* (1826; *Flora Cestrica*, 1837), *Agricultural Botany* (1847), and *American Weeds and Useful Plants* (1859).

DARWIN, CHARLES GALTON (*b. Cambridge, England, 1887; d. Cambridge, 1962*), applied mathematics, theoretical and general physics.

The grandson of Charles Darwin and the son of George Darwin, Charles Galton took a degree from Trinity College, Cambridge (1910), worked under Rutherford at Manchester, taught at Christ's College, Cambridge (1918–22) and the University of Edinburgh (1924–36), and was master of Christ's College from 1936 until the war, when he became director of the National Physical Laboratory (until 1949). Knighted, 1942. His most important contribution to theoretical physics was to lay the foundation for all subsequent interpretation of X-ray diffraction by crystals, anticipating P. P. Ewald's work. With Fowler, he developed the Darwin-Fowler method (1923), an effective foundation for quantum statistics which differs from the Maxwell-Boltzmann and Gibbs approaches by calculating directly the averages of physical quantities by the method of the steepest descents. He also developed a quantum mechanical theory of the electron which approximated Dirac's later relativist theory. In later years he devoted his attention to genetics and eugenics. His neo-Malthusian, pessimistic view of man as the last "wild" animal became well known through his *The Next Million Years* (1952).

DARWIN, CHARLES ROBERT (*b. The Mount, Shrewsbury, England, 1809; d. Down House, Downe, Kent, England, 1882*), natural history, geology, evolution.

Darwin was the grandson of Erasmus Darwin and the son of Robert Darwin. He studied medicine at Edinburgh University (1825–27), but attending operations (performed without anesthetics) turned him away from that career. Sent to Cambridge to prepare for the Church (1827–31), he accepted the Articles of Faith but thought his time wasted academically. He took a poor degree, but did meet John Stevens Henslow, who fired his interest in natural history, gave him confidence, and instigated his invitation to join the admiralty survey ship H.M.S. *Beagle* as unpaid naturalist on a voyage around the world. He sailed with no formal scientific training; he returned a hard-headed man of science.

When Darwin sailed on the *Beagle*, the most commonly accepted theory in geology was catastrophism. Charles Lyell in his *Principles of Geology* (1830) had challenged this view. In the *Beagle*, Darwin had with him Lyell's volume, which he had been advised to read but on no account to believe. Nevertheless he satisfied himself that Lyell's views accorded with the facts. His first geological study was in Santiago in the Cape Verde Islands. By applying Lyell's principles, he quickly unraveled the history of the island: subsidence and then elevation. But South America was the model for his observational and interpretive skill. Directly contrary to the accepted views of Sedgwick and Lyell, he proved that foliation and cleavage are not original phenomena dependent on the deposition of the strata, but had been superimposed by pressure. His demonstration of the origin of metamorphic rocks by deformation and of the distinction between cleavage and sedimentary bedding was a major contribution to geology. He witnessed an earthquake that elevated the land by several feet, observed a connection between elevation of the land and volcanic activity, examined a raised fossil forest which gave him proof of extensive subsidence followed by elevation. Making connections between geological phenomena and life in his observations of low-lying and raised beds of shells belonging to species still living, he concluded that the age of the earth must be vastly greater than was imagined, and that the fossil record must be expected to be erratic and incomplete. He challenged Lyell's theory that coral atolls were formed on the rims of submarine volcanic craters and offered his own deductive theory of subsidence to the required depth of 120 feet, a theory since confirmed. He mapped the coral reefs, finding atolls and a second type, barrier reefs, in zones of the Pacific which had undergone subsidence, and fringing reefs, a third type he identified, in parallel zones that had undergone elevation. Moreover, all the active Pacific volcanoes were in the zone of fringing reefs —a further confirmation of Lyell. His *Coral Reefs* (1842) remains the accepted explanation (with the slight addition of R. A. Daly's glacial control theory). Geology was his supreme interest when his *Journal of Researches into the Geology and Natural History of the Various Countries Visited by H.M.S. Beagle* was first published (1839); in the second edition (1845) geology took second place in the title.

In the *Beagle*, he gradually questioned the accepted view that living species were fixed at the creation. A few months after he returned to England, he posited that a common ancestor would explain a number of facts: fossil species resemble living species in the same area; why regional and continental differences were present in very similar species; why oceanic island fauna resembled species on the neighboring continent; and why individual islands in certain island groups (Cape Verde, Galapagos), although identical in climate and physical features, supported species differing in food habits and structure. An early entry in his *Notebook on Transmutation of Species* (begun 1837) further notes that descent from a common ancestor would also explain similarity of certain bones across species; similarity of embryos; useless rudimentary organs; the apparent relationship of species, rather than random distribution of forms across the whole field of possibilities. The form of his argument is important: he never claimed to demonstrate the change of one species into another, only that if evolution has occurred, it explains a host of otherwise inexplicable facts. But after he satisfied himself that evolution had occurred, he kept his views to himself.

He had clearly grasped the principle of natural selection by February 1838, before he saw how it was enforced in nature. This came to him in September, in a very simple flash of genius when he read Malthus' *Essay on the Principle of Population.* The remarkable note he scribbled down immediately pinpoints two notions: that evolution takes place in the economy of nature, each individual having an ecological niche; and that evolution goes on not in individuals, but in populations.

The formal theory of evolution by natural selection can be stated as follows: (1) The numbers of individuals in species remain more or less constant. (2) There is an enormous overproduction of pollen, seeds, eggs, larvae. (3) Therefore, there must be high mortality. (4) Individuals in species differ in innumerable anatomical, physiological, and behavioristic respects. (5) Some are better adapted to their available ecological niches, will survive more frequently, and will leave more offspring. (6) Hereditary resemblances between parents and offspring is a fact. (7) Therefore, successive generations will not only maintain but improve their degree of adaption, and as the environment varies, successive generations will not only differ from their parent but also from each other, giving rise to divergent stocks from common ancestors. Recent observations and controlled experiment have proved the theory correct.

Darwin wrote a rough sketch of this theory (1842) and expanded it into an essay (1844) but disclosed the theory only in 1856, to his friends Lyell and J. D. Hooker; neither accepted evolution, which they knew only through Lamarck. On their urging, he began a book on the theory (1856); in 1858 Alfred Russel Wallace sent him a letter summarizing identical views. Darwin's and Wallace's papers were read at the Linnean Society of London and published (1858). Darwin then wrote *On the Origin of Species by Means of Natural Selection, or the Preservation of Favoured Races in the Struggle for Life* (1859). Old-fashioned biologists protested that he indulged in hypotheses he could not prove (he did not pretend to prove them). Theologians were aghast: if man and the apes had a common ancestor, man no longer had a privileged position as created by God in his own image; moreover, if all plants and animals originated by natural selection, the argument for the existence of God based on design in nature was destroyed. Matters came to a head at the Oxford meeting of the British Association for the Advancement of Science in 1860, when the Reverend Samuel Wilberforce, bishop of Oxford, was annihilated by T. H. Huxley and Hooker, and Darwin's views started their conquest of the world. In the United States, Darwin's friend Asa Gray had already won a victory over Louis Agassiz.

In *The Descent of Man, and Selection in Relation to Sex* (1871), Darwin amplified *Origin.* He never claimed man was descended from apes, but that man's ancestor, if alive today, would be classed among the Primates, and would be even lower on the scale than the apes. On sexual selection, or the preferential chances of mating, Darwin's greatest contribution was to show that secondary sexual characteristics had evolved in relation to a complex pattern of behavior, itself the product of natural selection. His *The Expression of the Emotions in Man and Animals* (1872) founded the study of ethology and of communication theory and made a major contribution to psychology.

In the twelve years of experiments on fifty-seven species, Darwin discovered and demonstrated the fact of hybrid vigor (*Effects of Cross and Self Fertilization,* 1876). His demonstration of the advantages of cross-fertilization explains why sexual reproduction (as distinct from asexual budding) increases heritable variation and what the survival value of different sexes in a species is. Among his other work in botany, in *Climbing Plants* (1875) and *Power of Movement in Plants* (1880) his researches and experiments were the springboard for the science of growth hormones in plants.

DARWIN, ERASMUS (*b. Elston Hall, near Nottingham, England, 1731; d. Breadsall Priory, near Derby, England, 1802*), medicine, scientific poetry, botany, technology.

Darwin, the grandfather of Charles Darwin and Francis Galton, took an M.B. at St. John's College, Cambridge (1755), and studied with William Hunter and at Edinburgh Medical School (1754–55). He practiced medicine in Lichfield with spreading fame, individualizing treatment according to the symptoms. He was a founder of the Lunar Society in Birmingham (1766) and the Lichfield Botanical Society (early 1770's), through which he pursued a bitter quarrel with William Withering over Linnaean classification and over priority in the treatment of dropsy by digitalis. In 1781, he moved to Derby, there founding the Derby Philosophical Society (1783) for the discussion of science and applied technology. His Commonplace Book for the time includes his plans for a dispensary and for many ingenious devices which illustrate his protean imagination.

Darwin's first major work, *The Botanic Garden* (part 1, *The Economy of Vegetation,* 1791; part 2, *The Loves of the Plants,* 1789), was an annotated scientific poem in Augustan couplets covering all natural philosophy, embodying many contemporary researches and inventions, and personifying all scientific, technological, and natural phenomena. His repute as a poet was ruined by a devastating parody of his work, possibly aimed at the Lunar Society.

In his major work in medicine and natural science, *Zoonomia* (2 vols., 1794–96), he discusses the bases for laws of animal causation and his classification of diseases, defends spontaneous generation, and develops his theory of biological evolution. He gives the first consistent, all-embracing hypothesis of evolution, although his grandson said it had no effect on his *Origin of Species.*

His third major work, *Phytologia, or the Philosophy of Agriculture and Gardening* (1800), continues and applies to plants, considered inferior to animals, the discussion of biological evolution.

His last book, *The Temple of Nature; or the Origin of Society* (1803), another poem, tries to unite the ancient myths, as embracing basic natural truths, with the world of science; his extravagant theorizing does not mask his enthusiasm for progress and evolution.

DARWIN, FRANCIS (*b. Down, Kent, England, 1848; d. Cambridge, England, 1925*), botany.

The son of Charles Robert Darwin, Francis took degrees in mathematics (1869) and natural science (1870) at Trinity College, Cambridge, and an M.B. degree at the Brown Institute (1875). He was his father's secretary and botanical assistant (1874–82), and taught botany at Cambridge (1882–1903). He was knighted (1913). In studying the causes of plant curvature in response to light (*The Power of Movement in Plants*, 1880, with Charles Darwin), they showed that something in the apex of the root and shoot is acted on by light and gravity and transmits its effects to other plant parts. This and his further findings led to F. W. Went's isolation of a growth-promoting substance (1928).

In his study of water movement in plants he introduced the horn hygroscope for the study of stomatal function (1897), and the porometer for studying transpiration rate. His *Practical Physiology of Plants* (1894; with E. H. Acton) was the first of its kind in English. His informative and well-annotated *The Life and Letters of Charles Darwin* (3 vols., 1887) and *More Letters of Charles Darwin* (2 vols., 1903) are the basis for all subsequent work on Charles Darwin.

DARWIN, GEORGE HOWARD (*b. Down House, Kent, England, 1845; d. Cambridge, England, 1912*), mathematics, astronomy.

The son of Charles Darwin, George Howard took a degree at Trinity College, Cambridge (1868) and taught astronomy and experimental philosophy at Cambridge (1883–1912). His paper, "On the Influence of Geological Changes on the Earth's Axis of Rotation" (1876), marked the beginning of his investigations of geophysical problems, in which he was directly inspired by Lord Kelvin. His most significant contribution lies in his pioneering work in the application of detailed dynamical analysis to cosmological and geological problems. He devoted himself to the problems of mathematical cosmogony and the explanation of the various aspects of the history of the double stars, planetary system, and satellite systems.

DAŚABALA, astronomy.

Daśabala, a Buddhist, is known in astronomy for his two works *Cintāmaṇisāraṇikā* (A.D. 1055) and *Karaṇakamalamārtaṇḍa* (A.D. 1058).

DASYPODIUS, CUNRADUS (*b. Frauenfeld, Thurgau, Switzerland, ca. 1530; d. Strasbourg, France, 1600*), mathematics, astronomy.

Dasypodius studied in Strasbourg at Johannes Sturm's academy and taught there (from 1558). The textbooks Dasypodius wrote show that under Sturm, mathematics was more extensively studied than in many universities. Desiring the publication of all Greek mathematical works, Dasypodius made a beginning by editing and translating works of Euclid and others. His fame is based especially on his construction of an ingenious and accurate astronomical clock, which showed the influence of Hero.

DAUBENTON, LOUIS-JEAN-MARIE (*b. Montbard, France, 1716; d. Paris, France, 1800*), medicine, anatomy, mineralogy, zootechny.

M.D., Rheims (1741); assistant to Buffon at Jardin du Roi (from 1742); taught at Collège Royal (1778), veterinary school at Alfort (1783), and École Normale Supérieure; first director of Muséum National d'Histoire Naturelle (1793). Contributed some 200 descriptions of quadrupeds to Buffon's *Histoire naturelle* (vols. III–XV, 1749–67); his descriptions concentrated on skeleton, principal internal organs, brain, sexual organs, and em-

bryo and its enveloping membranes, with measurements, and were set out in a uniform manner to facilitate comparisons. Appears to have been first to apply comparative methods to fossil forms (1762). Also achieved fame for *Instruction pour les bergers et les propriétaires de troupeaux* (1782), which dealt with the physiology, therapeutics, and surgery of wool-bearing animals, as well as with pastures, races, and breeding methods, following his fifteen years of research into the improvement of wool.

DAUBENY, CHARLES GILES BRIDLE (*b. Stratton, Gloucestershire, England, 1795; d. Oxford, England, 1867*), chemistry, geology.

Daubeny took a B.A. at Oxford (1814) and an M.D. at Magdalen (1821), practiced medicine (to 1829), and taught chemistry (from 1822) and botany (from 1834) at Oxford. He carried out important research in chemistry, geology, and botany. In his *Description of Active and Extinct Volcanoes* (1826) he developed a chemical theory of volcanic action which stated that such action results from penetration of water to the free alkali and alkaline earth metals supposed to exist beneath the earth's crust. He was active in the reform of Oxford science teaching.

DAUBRÉE, GABRIEL-AUGUSTE (*b. Metz, France, 1814; d. Paris, France, 1896*), geology.

Daubrée took a doctorate in science at Paris (1849), taught at Strasbourg and the Museum of Natural History in Paris (from 1861), and directed the School of Mines (1872–84). He contributed to geochemistry, the application of engineering principles to geology and mineralogy, and economic exploitation of ores. His most important work was *Études synthétiques de géologie expérimentale* (1879), largely through its mechanical rather than its chemical experiments. During his later years he made important studies of meteorites and of the chemical action of underground water on limestone.

DAVAINE, CASIMIR JOSEPH (*b. St.-Amand-les-Eaux, France, 1812; d. Garches, France, 1882*), medicine, biology.

Davaine studied at Lille, took a doctorate in medicine in Paris (1837), and practiced medicine thereafter (from 1838). His most important contribution was in medical microbiology. He was the first to recognize the pathogenic role of bacteria, and one of the first to demonstrate that the *bactéridie (Bacillus anthracis)* is the sole cause of anthrax, and to differentiate it from bovine septicemia. He demonstrated the infective power of blood containing the bacilli. His conflicts with enemies of the germ theory of disease foreshadowed Pasteur's later disputes.

In his *Traité des entozoaires* (1860), he described tracking down intestinal worms by seeking the eggs in the stools, a procedure still followed. He also pioneered in plant pathology, studying the cycle of the wheat worm. He demonstrated that leukocytes can absorb foreign bodies, thus observing phagocytosis fourteen years before Metchnikoff (1883). He was also the first to recognize (1852) the protandrous hermaphroditism of oysters. He made numerous contributions on anatomic-pathological lesions observed in various animals.

DAVENPORT, CHARLES BENEDICT (*b. Stamford, Conn., 1866; d. Cold Spring Harbor, N.Y., 1944*), zoology, eugenics.

Davenport took a B.S. at the Polytechnic Institute of Brooklyn (1886) and an A.B. (1889) and Ph.D. (1892) at Harvard. He taught at Harvard (1892–99) and the University of Chicago (1899–1904). At Cold Spring Harbor, he directed the Station for Experimental Evolution (1904–34), the Eugenics Record Office (1910–34) which he established, and the Biological Laboratory Summer School of the Brooklyn Institute of Arts and Sciences (1898–1923). His main contribution, aside from the work of the three laboratories, was to introduce statistical methods (including those of Karl Pearson) into American evolutionary studies, especially through his *Statistical Methods With Special Reference to Biological Variation* (1899) and *Heredity in Relation to Eugenics* (1911).

DAVID, TANNATT WILLIAM EDGEWORTH (*b. near Cardiff, Wales, 1858; d. Sydney, Australia, 1934*), polar exploration, geology.

David took a B.A. in classics at Oxford (1880), studied at the Royal School of Mines, and taught geology at Sydney (1891–1924). He became the leading expert on Australian geology. As leading geologist on the Shackleton Expedition (1907–09), he carried out pioneering fieldwork in Antarctica. He made important contributions to the early delineation of strata in coalfields of New South Wales, foundational rocks under the coral atoll of Funafuti, past glaciation in Australia and India, and fossil evidences of life in Precambrian rocks near Adelaide. His comprehensive geological map of Australia with a summary of field data (1932) was later expanded into *Geological Map of the Commonwealth of Australia* (1950).

DAVIDOV, AUGUST YULEVICH (*b. Libav, Russia, 1823; d. Moscow, Russia, 1885*), mechanics, mathematics.

Davidov graduated from Moscow University (doctorate, 1851) and taught there (1850–85). He was the first to give a general analytic method for determining the position of equilibrium of a floating body. He made other valuable mathematics studies on equations with partial derivatives, elliptical functions, and the application of the theory of probability to statistics. He wrote a number of excellent geometry and algebra textbooks for secondary schools.

DAVIDSON, WILLIAM. *See* **Davison, William.**

DAVIS, WILLIAM MORRIS, (*b. Philadelphia, Pa., 1850; d. Pasadena, Calif., 1934*), geography, geomorphology, geology, meteorology.

Davis took a B.S. degree (1869) and a master's degree in engineering (1870) at Harvard, where he taught (1877–1912). He worked as meteorologist at the national observatory at Córdoba, Argentina, and assisted Pumpelly on the Northern Pacific survey. He was a founder of the Geological Society of America and the Association of American Geographers. Among his 501 titles in meteorology, geology, and geomorphology (1880–1938), his *Elementary Meteorology* (1894) was an admirable, up-to-date synthesis used for more than thirty years as a college text. His greatest contribution was in what he called physical geography—geomorphology: his concept of the cycle of erosion and the demonstration of its use to describe the earth's surface features and to decipher

earth history. He laid the cornerstone of the "Davisian system" of analysis in his "The Rivers and Valleys of Pennsylvania" (1889). He explained the origin of the landscape through the developmental, evolutionary concept of the cycle of erosion in a valley through youth, maturity, and old age; the end product was a nearly featureless plain, a "peneplain." For geologists, the form of the land thus provided a history even when no rock record was available. For physical geography, he sought to provide a store of ideal landscape types correlated with "structure, process, and time" (1902). He also summarized the facts and hypotheses advanced to explain coral reefs (1928) and developed the still-accepted interpretation of caves as the product of two stages of development (1930).

DAVISON, WILLIAM (*b. Aberdeenshire, Scotland, 1593; d. Paris, France, ca. 1669*), medicine, chemistry.

Davison took an M.A. at Marischal College, Aberdeen (1617) and an M.D. in France, and became the first teacher of chemistry at the Jardin Royal des Plantes (1648–51). He was director of the Royal Botanical Garden in Warsaw and physician to the wife of King John II Casimir of Poland (1651–67). His principal chemical work, the *Philosophia pyrotechnica* (1633–35) is characterized by long disquisitions on the metaphysical basis of his chemical theory. He elaborates on the Neoplatonic aspects of Paracelsian theory. His most ambitious work is his commentary (1660) on the *Idea medicinae philosophicae* of Peter Severinus.

DAVISSON, CLINTON JOSEPH (*b. Bloomington, Ill., 1881; d. Charlottesville, Va., 1958*), physics.

Davisson took a B.S. at Chicago (1908) and a Ph.D. at Princeton (1911), taught at the Carnegie Institute of Technology (1911–17), and did basic research at the Western Electric Company Laboratories (now Bell Telephone Laboratories). He shared the Nobel Prize in physics in 1937 with G. P. Thomson for their independent confirmations of electron waves. Through a series of laboratory experiments, with C. H. Kunsman and later L. H. Germer, he proved the wave nature of electrons, confirming de Broglie's theory. In the 1930's Davisson worked on applying electron waves to crystal physics and electron microscopy, developing a technique for electron focusing. From 1946 to 1954 he taught physics at the University of Virginia.

DAVY, HUMPHRY (*b. Penzance, England, 1778; d. Geneva, Switzerland, 1829*), chemistry.

While apprenticed to an apothecary-surgeon, Davy drew up for himself a formidable program of self-education, including theology and geography, seven languages, and a number of science subjects. He read philosophy and studied chemistry through Nicholson and Lavoisier. He became superintendent of Thomas Beddoes' Pneumatic Institution at Clifton (1798–1801). Within five years of reading his first chemistry book he was lecturing on chemistry at the Royal Institution (1801), which he made a center for advanced research and where he spent most of his working life. He was knighted in 1812 and made a baronet in 1818.

In an early essay (1799), Davy attacked Lavoisier's caloric theory for introducing imaginary substances and the theory-laden term, "caloric," and appealed to a theory of heat as motion and light as matter. In place of "caloric," he proposed "repulsive motion."

In his investigations of the therapeutic uses of gases at the Pneumatic Institution, Davy tried breathing nitrous oxide and discovered its anesthetic properties, giving classic subjective accounts in his book on it (1800) and showing his great facility for qualitative experiment and for volumetric analyses, which he preferred to more accurate gravimetric methods. The book, which made his reputation, is among his best.

Of all those who worked on Volta's pile, Davy was consistently the clearest-headed. From the first he held to the chemical reaction theory of electricity production, and ultimately proved that the current in the electrolytic cells separated compounds into components and did not synthesize new substances. He invented the carbon arc. His pioneering book on applying chemistry to agriculture remained a standard work for a generation.

Davy disproved Lavoisier's theory that oxygen was the principle of acidity. In the course of experiments, he isolated and described many of the properties of potassium and sodium (1807). He then analyzed the alkaline earths, isolating magnesium, calcium, strontium, and barium, and obtained boron and silicon. He established that chemical elements do not behave as "principles" of acidity or alkalinity and concluded that chemical properties were a function of the relative arrangements as well as of the components of a substance. Davy showed that oxygen was never produced in reactions with oxymuriatic acid unless water was present, placed oxymuriatic acid among the elements, and named it "chlorine."

He elucidated the nature and essential properties of iodine. In only three month's work (1815) on the explosive gas firedamp, he confirmed that methane was its main constituent and would ignite only at high temperatures, and created the Davy lamp, in which the open flame is surrounded by a cylinder of metallic gauze.

DAVY, JOHN (b. Penzance, England, 1790; d. Ambleside, England, 1868), physiology, chemistry, natural history.

Davy assisted his brother Humphry in the laboratory of the Royal Institution, took an M.D. at Edinburgh (1814), and joined the army medical service, rising to inspector general of hospitals. As a result of his work successfully defending his brother's views on chlorine, he first prepared, named, and characterized phosgene gas. He served many years abroad, and observed life habits and cultural practices of the native population, deriving his major scientific works from his medical service.

DAWES, WILLIAM RUTTER (b. London, England, 1799; d. Haddenham, near Thame, Oxfordshire, England, 1868), astronomy.

Dawes studied medicine at St. Bartholomew's Hospital and spent brief periods practicing medicine and as a pastor. At an observatory he constructed in Ormskirk and at George Bishop's observatory in Regent's Park, he devoted himself to measurement of hundreds of double stars. He continued to make observations wherever he lived, and established himself as a leading observer of

Saturn through numerous meticulous observations of the planet and especially of the various rings.

DAWSON, CHARLES (b. Fulkeith Hall, Lancashire, England, 1864; d. Uckfield, Sussex, England, 1916), paleontology.

Dawson, a solicitor, was by avocation a highly respected geologist, paleontologist, and archaeologist, and honorary collector for the British Museum. He discovered a new species of dinosaur, Iguanodon dawsoni, and a new Weald mammal, Plaugiaulax dawsoni. He is best known, however, as the discoverer of the fragments of Eoanthropus (1909–12) from which "Piltdown man," who had a more recent human cranium coupled with a simian mandible, was constructed. It was most likely he who had planted them, the associated bone and flint tools and Villefranchian fauna, and the second Piltdown specimen (1915), which he also discovered. In the following decades new discoveries rendered Piltdown man incredible, the sole example of a completely divergent evolutionary line. In the early 1950's new techniques for determining a fossil's age showed that the cranium was an Upper Pleistocene human, with the mandible from a modern orangutan, both stained with iron sulfate for uniform color; the teeth had been artificially abraded. If Dawson did not mastermind the hoax, he was in complicity with it, but his motives remain unknown.

DAWSON, JOHN WILLIAM (b. Pictou, Nova Scotia, 1820; d. Montreal, Quebec, 1899), geology.

Dawson took an M.A. at Edinburgh (1841), worked as a geologist, became superintendent of education for Nova Scotia (1850–55), and was principal of McGill University (1855–93); under him it acquired an international reputation. He founded the library and was its first librarian and taught geology and paleontology for many years. He was knighted (1884). His reputation was greatest and most enduring in paleobotany. His Acadian Geology (1855) had lasting influence. He gave a classic description of Psilophyton (1859), then the earliest land plant known. His Geological History of Plants (1888) was a textbook without competitor for several decades. His work in paleozoology was less uniform. His discovery and classic description of Cambrian(?) sponges is notable. His The Canadian Ice Age (1893) was, for its time, a remarkable treatment of events succeeding the Pleistocene glaciation. His theories and conclusions on prehistoric human remains are contained in his Fossil Men (1880).

DAY, DAVID TALBOT (b. Rockport [now Lakewood], Ohio, 1859; d. Washington, D.C., 1925), chemical geology.

Day took an A.B. (1881) and a Ph.D. (1884) at Johns Hopkins University, and was with the U.S. Geological Survey (1885–1914). As head of the statistical division, he presented the first statistics on minerals (1890 census); he also surveyed oil shales and became consulting chemist, transferring to the Bureau of Mines (1914–20). He wrote the invaluable Handbook of the Petroleum Industry (2 vols., 1922).

IBN AL-DĀYA. See **Ahmad ibn Yūsuf.**

DEAN, BASHFORD (b. New York, N. Y., 1867; d. Battle Creek, Mich., 1928), ichthyology.

Dean graduated from the College of the City of New York (1886) and received a Ph.D. at Columbia (1890). He was the first director of the summer school of biology at Cold Spring Harbor, N.Y. (1890), taught at Columbia (from 1891), and was curator of reptiles and fishes at the American Museum of Natural History (1903–10). His *Bibliography of Fishes* (1916–23) was exhaustive, and he solved several problems in fish evolution, including derivation of pectoral and pelvic fins from continuous fin folds.

DE BARY, (HEINRICH) ANTON (*b. Frankfurt-am-Main, Germany, 1831; d. Strassburg, Germany [now Strasbourg, France], 1888*), botany.

De Bary founded mycology and was its foremost practitioner in his day. He took a medical degree at Berlin (1853), studying botany under Alexander Braun. He taught botany at Freiburg im Breisgau (1855–67), where he established the first botany laboratory; at Halle; and at Strassburg, where he established a botanical institute. He clarified the life histories of various fungi at a time when they were still considered by some to arise through spontaneous generation, starting with the fungi that produced rusts and smuts in cereals (1853). From his developmental studies of the Myxomycetes, he showed that in one stage they were formless, motile masses of *sarcode*, the substance of the plasmodium, and thus evidence of the protoplasmic substratum of life. His direct observations of several fungi (1863) led him to deny spontaneous generation and to hold the contagion to be due to the germs of parasites and exterior conditions that favored invasion. He named the potato blight fungus *Phytophthora infestans*, produced the disease in healthy plants by inoculation, and reconstructed the fungus' life cycle by experiment and analogy. In his investigations of the rust of wheat and other grains he demonstrated that *Puccinia graminis* required different hosts during the different stages of its development and termed such species heteroecious, as opposed to autoecious species, which require only one host for development. He coined the word "symbiosis" (*Die Erscheinung der Symbiose,* 1879) to mean "the living together of unlike organisms" and describing a broad range of relationships. In his major works on morphology (1866–84) he established mycology as a science. He always attempted to observe life cycles in the living plant and introduced methods for sowing spores and observing development. As an opponent of spontaneous generation he was critical of culture procedures that allowed the easy intrusion of unknown organisms into apparatus.

DEBEAUNE (also known as **Beaune**), **FLORIMOND** (*b. Blois, France, 1601; d. Blois, 1652*), mathematics.

Debeaune studied law and bought the office of counselor to the court of justice in Blois (to 1648). He gained great renown for his *Notes brèves* on Descartes's *Géométrie* (pub. with 1st Latin ed., 1649); Descartes was right in believing that none understood it better. The notes clarify and illustrate some of the difficult passages and played a role in the belated spread of Cartesian mathematics. The second Latin edition (1659–61) also contained two short papers on algebra. One problem particularly identified with him (formulated 1638) ushered in what was called at the end of his century the "inverse of tangents" —the determination of a curve from a property of its

tangent. His discussion of it reveals his singular ability to translate physical questions into abstract language of mathematical analysis, fifty years before the language of Leibnizian calculus was available.

DEBENHAM, FRANK (*b. Bowral, New South Wales, Australia, 1883; d. Cambridge, England, 1965*), polar exploration, cartography, geography.

Debenham took a B.A. (1904) and a B.Sc. (1910) in geology at the University of Sydney, was with the second Scott Antarctic Expedition (1910–13), and taught at Cambridge (from 1913), becoming the first director of the Scott Polar Research Institute (from 1925) and the first professor of geography (1931–49). His many works include accounts of his various polar expeditions.

DEBRAY, HENRI JULES (*b. Amiens, France, 1827; d. Paris, France, 1888*), chemistry.

Debray took a doctorate at the École Normale Supérieure (1855), taught there (1855–68) and at the École Polytechnique (1868–88), and was assayer at the mint (1868–88). His *Cours élémentaire de chimie* appeared in eight editions between 1863 and 1871. He established a new standard meter in Paris from a platinum-iridium alloy. He also worked on dissociation phenomena and determined the density of mercurous chloride vapor.

DEBYE, PETER JOSEPH WILLIAM (*b. Maastricht, Netherlands, 1884; d. Ithaca, N.Y., 1966*), chemical physics.

Debye took an electrical engineering degree at the Technische Hochschule in Aachen (1905) and a Ph.D. in physics at Munich under Arnold Sommerfeld (1908). He taught at Göttingen (1913–20); directed the Physical Institute of the Eidgenössische Technische Hochschule in Zurich (1920–27), the experimental physics institute at Leipzig (1927–34), and the Berlin Institute of Physics, which he named the Max Planck Institute. After the outbreak of World War II he emigrated to the United States, heading the chemistry department at Cornell University (1940–50).

Each of his major achievements revised and developed a previously incomplete or inadequate treatment into an important generalization or a new method of investigation. He received the Nobel Prize in chemistry in 1936. He revised the Clausius-Mosotti equation for the dielectric constant so that the new equation not only represented the behavior of the dielectric constant satisfactorily, but also established the existence of a permanent electric doublet, or dipole, in many molecules and provided a means of determining the moment of the dipole and the geometry of the molecule; the unit of dipole moment later became the "Debye." By treating a solid as a system of vibrating atoms he modified Einstein's theory of specific heats in the "Debye equation," which employed the "Debye temperature," a characteristic of the particular solid, and which gave quantitative agreement with observed specific heat factors. His classical representation of dielectric behavior (often called "Debye behavior") was of much use in investigating molecular size and structure and intermolecular forces. His best-known work on X-ray scattering (1916; with Paul Scherrer) presented the Debye-Scherrer method, possibly the most powerful tool for the determination of the structure of crystals of high symmetry. His extension of his work on atomic structure and X-ray scattering to molecules and liquids developed tools which, because of the dualism of the wave and particle theories, provided a foundation for the electron diffraction method important in molecular structure determination. With E. Hückel he developed (1923), by mathematical analysis, the fundamental thermodynamics of electrolytic solutions and solved the problem of electrolytic conductance. Like much of his other work, this provided the theoretical basis for subsequent work in the field. He also developed light scattering as a tool for the absolute determination of molecular weights of polymers and the spatial extension of macromolecules in dilute solutions (1944).

DECHALES, CLAUDE FRANÇOIS MILLIET (*b. Chambéry, France, 1621; d. Turin, Italy, 1678*), mathematics.

Dechales, a Jesuit, taught at the Collège de Clermont in Paris, at Lyons, Chambéry, Marseilles, and the University of Turin. He is known for his *Cursus seu mundus mathematicus* (1674), a complete course of mathematics, including many related subjects that in his day were held to belong to the exact sciences.

DÉCHELETTE, JOSEPH (*b. Roanne, Loire, France, 1862; d. Nouron-Vingré, Aisne, France, 1914*), archaeology.

Déchelette studied with the Jesuits. His interest in archaeology was stimulated by travels for his family's fabric business. In 1899 he abandoned industry for archaeology. Among his works is his famous *Manuel d'archéologie préhistorique, celtique et gallo-romaine* (1908–14).

DECHEN, HEINRICH VON (*b. Berlin, Germany, 1800; d. Bonn, Germany, 1889*), mining.

Dechen was educated at the University of Berlin and the Haupt-Bergwerks-Eleven-Institut and rose in the mining administration to become superintendent of mines in Bonn (1841–59), director of Prussian mining, metallurgy, and salt mining (1859–60), and inspector general of mines in Bonn (1860–64). He prepared many classic geological maps, and after working on a systematic geological survey of Prussia was made curator of the new Geological Institute in Berlin (1875).

DEDEKIND, (JULIUS WILHELM) RICHARD (*b. Brunswick, Germany, 1831; d. Brunswick, 1916*), mathematics.

Studied at Collegium Carolinum (1848–50). Received doctorate from University of Göttingen (1852), where he was most influenced by Moritz Abraham Stern, Wilhelm Weber, and Carl Friedrich Gauss, and where he first met Georg Friedrich Bernhard Riemann. Became university lecturer (1854) after two years of further study. While teaching, Dedekind was still studying: he attended the lectures of Dirichlet (1855) and became his friend; he also heard Riemann's lectures (1855–56). His own lectures on Galois theory during this period may have been the first in any university. Dedekind's next appointment (1858–62) was at the Zurich Polytechnikum; in 1859 he and Riemann traveled to Berlin and met the leading mathematicians there. In 1862 he returned to the Brunswick Polytechnikum (created from the Collegium Carolinum) as professor and was content to remain there, near his family, until his death. He did not feel pressed to have a

more marked effect in the outside world; such confirmation of himself was unnecessary. He served as director of the Polytechnikum (1872–75) and chairman of its building commission; he continued lecturing after being made professor emeritus (1894).

In number theory (to which he was first introduced as a student at Göttingen) Dedekind is best known for the "Dedekind cut," to which he was led through consideration of the foundations of arithmetic. In 1858 he produced a purely arithmetical definition of continuity and an exact formulation of the concept of irrational numbers (published finally in 1872 as *Stetigkeit und irrationale Zahlen*) in which irrational numbers were explained as "cuts" in the realm of rational numbers. The continuum of real numbers thus comprises the system of rational numbers and an infinite number of cuts that are produced by irrational numbers. Further work in number theory and the foundations of mathematics was published in *Was sind und was sollen die Zahlen?* (1888); this work was criticized by such notables as Kronecker, Weierstrass, Hilbert, Frege, and Bertrand Russell, but was nevertheless recognized by them, as by others, as profoundly influential.

It fell to Dedekind to edit the posthumous works of Gauss on the theory of numbers; he was able not only to make the papers of his former teacher available to wider circles, but also to comment on them with deep understanding. He performed this service also for Dirichlet (*Vorlesungen über Zahlentheorie*, 1863) and Riemann (*Werke Bernhard Riemanns*, 1876, with Heinrich Weber). The editing of Dirichlet's lectures led him to examine the theory of generalized complex numbers; from 1871 he published important work on the theory of algebraic number fields and the theory of ideals, introducing such concepts as *ring* and *unit*. This work stimulated Emmy Noether, Hilbert, Paul Bachmann, Adolf Hurwitz, and Heinrich Weber to disseminate and expand his thoughts.

DEE, JOHN (*b. London, England, 1527; d. Mortlake, Surrey, England, 1608*), mathematics.

Educated St. John's College, Cambridge (B.A., 1545; M.A., 1548). Fellow of St. John's, foundation fellow of Trinity College (1546). In Louvain and Paris (1548–51) studied with Gemma Frisius and Gerhardus Mercator. Navigational adviser to various English voyages of discovery. Edited translation of Euclid (1570); wrote on determination of stellar parallax; may have encouraged revival of interest in work of Vitruvius. Interested in occult studies: alchemy, judicial astrology, psychic research. Defended calendar reform (1583).

DE FOREST, LEE (*b. Council Bluffs, Iowa, 1873; d. Hollywood, Calif., 1961*), electronics.

Graduated Yale University (1896; Ph.D., 1899); taught by J. W. Gibbs. Primary interest was radiotelegraphy; his improved systems were used in an attempt to report America's Cup races of 1903, and by European reporters in early part of Russo-Japanese War (1904–05). Invented the triode (1906) as an improved detector; this important prototype of all electronic amplifiers made transcontinental telephony possible for the first time and underlies all technological applications in which weak electrical signals are amplified—including the transistor, which is a type of triode. Active in development of radio industry (but thought its use should be cultural rather than commercial) and of sound motion pictures. A prolific inventor, he was granted more than 300 patents (litigation over his patent rights was frequent and expensive).

DeGOLYER, EVERETTE LEE (*b. Greensburg, Kan., 1886; d. Dallas, Tex., 1956*), geophysics.

Studied mining engineering at University of Oklahoma; received B.A. (1911) after interval of field work for U.S. Geological Survey and in Mexico. Specialized in oil exploration; formed a series of oil companies; advised governments on development of oil fields. DeGolyer developed a theory of the volcanic origin of salt domes, and then set out to locate salt domes by geophysical methods (torsion balance, refraction and reflection seismography). The discovery by his company of the Edwards oil field in Oklahoma (1930) by reflection survey ushered in the modern era of oil exploration.

DE GROOT, JAN CORNETS, also known as **Johan Hugo De Groot** or **Janus Grotius** (*b. near Delft, Netherlands, 1554; d. Delft, 1640*), mechanics.

Studied at University of Leiden; appointed curator (1594–1617); received doctorate of law (1596). Distinguished amateur scientist, best known through anti-Aristotelian experiment performed with Simon Stevin in which they proved that lead bodies of different weights falling on a board traverse the same distance in the same time. Translated Archimedes' *Measurement of the Circle* from Greek into Dutch for Ludolph van Ceulen.

DE HAAS, WANDER J. *See* **Haas, Wander J. de.**

DEHN, MAX (*b. Hamburg, Germany, 1878; d. Black Mountain, N.C., 1952*), mathematics.

Studied at Göttingen (Ph.D., 1900) under David Hilbert. Professor at Frankfurt University (1921–35) until ousted by Nazis; emigrated to U.S. (1940), where he held several academic positions. Influenced by Hilbert's work on axiomatization of geometry, Dehn discussed Legendre's theorem on the sum of the angles of a triangle. Did early report on topology (1907); proved an important theorem on topological manifolds (Dehn's lemma, 1910); elucidated problems of fundamental groups (following Poincaré).

DEINOSTRATUS. *See* **Dinostratus.**

DE LA BECHE, HENRY THOMAS (*b. London [?], England, 1796; d. London, 1855*), geology.

Of independent means, he was interested in geology from youth (elected to Geological Society of London, 1817; fellow of Royal Society, 1819). Toured Europe at length (from 1819), making many geological observations that he later published; his first paper was on the depth and temperature of Lake Geneva. Visited the family estate in Jamaica (1824) and published the first systematic account of the geology of the island, with a colored geological map (1827). His primary interest was in field geology, and he published many informative papers enhanced by clear and simple illustrations. He valued facts above theory, but did publish *Researches in Theoretical Geology* (1834) in which he suggested theories based on his knowledge of mineralogy, chemistry, and physics, as well as on his geological observations; some of his ideas

were well ahead of their time. De la Beche was closely involved in the formation and development of the official Geological Survey of Great Britain (established 1835): he had surveyed Devonshire (1832–35) for the government at his own suggestion, and was made director of the new survey; he directed it until his death, while continuing to do field work and to publish. The culmination of his official career was reached with the opening of the Museum of Practical Geology (1851); he was in charge of the School of Mines and the Mining Records Office.

DELAFOSSE, GABRIEL (*b. Saint-Quentin, France, 1796; d. Paris, France, 1878*), mineralogy, crystallography.

Studied under Haüy, assisted with editing and publication of his books. Worked at Muséum d'Histoire Naturelle (from 1817); also associated with Paris Faculté des Sciences (from 1822) and École Normale Supérieure (1826–57). Taught Pasteur. Founding member of Société Géologique de France. Considered symmetry a basic principle of crystallography. Sought the relation between structure and chemical composition. Suggested that Haüy's subtractive molecule comprised groups of chemical molecules, cleavage then could cut through subtractive molecules; and thus explained hemihedrism. Also studied relation between crystal form and physical properties; devised chemical/structural mineral classification system.

DELAGE, YVES (*b. Avignon, France, 1854; d. Sceaux, France, 1920*), zoology, anatomy, physiology, embryogeny, general biology.

Received doctorates in medicine (1880) and in science (1881) at Paris. Taught at Sorbonne and at Caen; directed marine laboratory at Roscoff (from 1902). Disciple of and assistant to Henri de Lacaze Duthiers. Applied experimental ingenuity and technical ability to many areas of zoological research, including crustacean circulation, embryogeny of the sponges, metamorphoses of the Anguillidae, physiology of the inner ear, and artificial (chemical) fertilization of sea urchins. Founded *Année biologique*. Was a Lamarckian and a believer in zoological types. After he became blind Delage studied the nature of dreaming.

DELAMAIN, RICHARD (*fl. London, England, first half of the seventeenth century*), mathematics.

Studied at Gresham College, London; became mathematical tutor to King Charles I. Constructed numerous mathematical instruments, including the circular slide rule; he and William Oughtred, his former teacher, quarreled violently over priority in the invention of the latter instrument. Is thought to have made King Charles's silver sundial.

DELAMBRE, JEAN-BAPTISTE JOSEPH (*b. Amiens, France, 1749; d. Paris, France, 1822*), astronomy, geodesy, history of astronomy.

From a poor background, supporting himself by working as a tutor, Delambre did not begin the study of astronomy until 1780 when he attended Lalande's lectures at the Collège de France; he quickly impressed Lalande by his literary and linguistic knowledge and scientific aptitude and became his assistant and then his collaborator. His employer (Geoffroy d'Assy) built him a private observatory on Lalande's recommendation. His first major observation (1786) was of the transit of Mercury; discrepancies in the astronomical tables of that time had led other Parisian astronomers to cease their observations before the transit had actually occurred, and only Delambre and Messier remained to see it. Delambre was eventually to publish his own greatly improved astronomical tables, which earned the recognition of the Académie des Sciences. He won the Academy's competition (1790) for the theory of Uranus, an especially challenging problem as the eight years of observation since the discovery of the planet represented only one-tenth of its sidereal period.

Delambre's skill in using and perfecting the methods of astronomical calculation led to his being chosen (1792), with Méchain, to do the geodetic survey that would establish the base of the Academy's proposed metric system. The new unit of measure was to be based on the length of one-quarter of a terrestrial meridian; Delambre and Méchain were to survey along the meridian between Dunkerque and Barcelona (9°.5 of arc), Delambre being responsible for the portion from Dunkerque to Rodez. This work took until 1799 to complete, due partly to the governmental upheavals of the French Revolution. The geodetic calculations were a worthy challenge to Delambre's skill: his instruments were calibrated in the proposed new centesimal units of angle-measure, which he found very convenient to use, while the logarithmic and trigonometric tables then available were based on degrees; until new tables could be prepared all observations had to be converted to degrees. Prony and Borda both produced new tables, to fourteen and to seven decimal places, respectively, and Delambre helped to see these to publication (1801). The final report of the geodetic expedition, *Base du système métrique décimal* (3 vols., 1806–10), was written by Delambre after the death of Méchain (1804). The recognized accuracy and importance of this work earned him positions in the Bureau des Longitudes (1795), the Instutut National (1803), and the Collège de France (1807).

Delambre continued to do work in positional astronomy and celestial mechanics, occasionally in collaboration with Laplace, and published new tables and fundamental astronomical texts. He also wrote major historical works, on mathematics (1810) and on astronomy (6 vols., 1817–27); the latter (*Histoire de l'astronomie*) was a comprehensive, technical work, offering no historical synthesis but rather a series of discrete analyses of one treatise (or other work) after another. He combined his historical and linguistic interests in assisting with the Abbé Halma's translation of Ptolemy's *Almagest* (1813–16).

From 1802 Delambre held various posts in the administration of public education. He retired from public life in 1815 and was made a *chevalier* of Saint Michel by the royal government. In 1821 he became an *officier* of the Legion of Honor.

DE LA RUE, WARREN (*b. Guernsey, 1815; d. London, England, 1889*), chemistry, invention, astronomy.

Began as a printer, improved its technology. In chemistry, made a small improvement to the Daniell battery; with August Wilhelm Hofmann, edited English version of first two volumes of Liebig and Kopp's *Jahresbericht*. His major contribution was in astronomy: James Nasmyth's

drawings of the moon inspired him to produce more accurate and detailed pictures of the sun, moon, and planets. To this end he set up his own observatory and made first drawings and then photographs; he made stereoscopic plates to reveal the topography of moon and sun; showed that sunspots are depressions in the sun's atmosphere; and invented the photoheliographic telescope to map the sun's surface photographically.

DELAUNAY, CHARLES-EUGÈNE (*b. Lusigny, France, 1816; d. at sea, near Cherbourg, France, 1872*), celestial mechanics.

Educated at École Polytechnique (graduated 1836) and University of Paris (Ph.D., 1841). Taught in various engineering schools and at University of Paris; director of Paris observatory (1870). Rival of Le Verrier. His work on lunar theory resulted in the Delaunay method (1846) of treating systems of canonical equations in analytical mechanics. Delaunay proposed the theory (1865) that a slowing of the earth's rotation due to tidal friction could account for the secular acceleration of the moon.

DELÉPINE, STÉPHANE-MARCEL (*b. St.-Martin-le-Gaillard [Seine Maritime], France, 1871; d. Paris, France, 1965*), chemistry.

Studied pharmacy and science in Paris (*docteur ès sciences physiques*, 1898). Worked at Collège de France (1895–1907) with Marcellin Berthelot as his *préparateur* until 1902; at École de Pharmacie (1904–30); and again at Collège de France as professor (1930–41). He continued to work in his laboratory until the year of his death. Influenced by the work of Alfred Werner. In organic chemistry he studied the thermodynamics of amines and amides derived from aldehydes; organic sulfur compounds (discovered monomeric sulfides of ethylene, and oxyluminescence of certain compounds of doubly-bound sulfur); and catalytic hydrogenation. In inorganic chemistry he studied coordination compounds, verifying Werner's theory; chemistry of iridium; and stereochemistry. Perfected preparation of tungsten.

DELILE (or **RAFFENEAU-DELILE**), **ALIRE** (*b. Versailles, France, 1778; d. Montpellier, France, 1850*), botany.

In Egypt with Napoleonic expedition (1798–1801); published extensively on botany of Egypt. Studied medicine intermittently: Paris (1795–98); Philadelphia (with Benjamin Smith Barton, 1806); New York (with David Hosack, 1807); Paris (M.D., 1809). Professor of botany at Faculty of Medicine, Montpellier (1819).

DELISLE, GUILLAUME (*b. Paris, France, 1675; d. Paris, 1726*), geography.

First modern scientific cartographer; published some ninety maps, distinguished for their accuracy and clarity; *premier géographe du roi* (1718). Studied under Gian Domenico Cassini. Brother of Joseph-Nicolas Delisle, who published some of his maps.

DELISLE, JOSEPH-NICOLAS (*b. Paris, France, 1688; d. Paris, 1768*), astronomy, geography.

Made astronomical observations in various private observatories and at Royal Observatory; produced astronomical tables for Jacques Cassini. Studied with Maraldi. Appointed to chair of mathematics at Collège Royal

(1718); taught Godin and Grandjean de Fouchy. Worked in optics. Invited by Peter the Great to establish an observatory and school at St. Petersburg (1725–47); directed geodetic and cartographic studies for a proposed large-scale map of Russia; published observations of eclipses of Jupiter's satellites, for longitude determinations. Made and collected meteorological observations; invented the "universal thermometer" (1738); attempted to use the transits of Mercury to determine the parallax of the sun. Returned to Collège Royal (1747–61); his students included Lalande and Messier. Corrected Halley's planetary tables; wrote on predicted return of Halley's comet; worked on longitude determinations for use in transit studies; and stimulated and coordinated worldwide observation of transit of Venus (1761).

DELLA PORTA, GIAMBATTISTA. *See* **Porta, Giambattista della.**

DELLA TORRE, GIOVANNI MARIA (*b. Rome, Italy, 1713; d. Naples, Italy, 1782*), natural sciences.

Widely interested in science; influenced by *De rerum naturae* of Lucretius. Studied optics, histology, volcanology, history. Most important work was scientific encyclopedia, *Scienza della natura* (2 vols., 1748–49), which anticipated the *Encyclopédie.*

DELLA TORRE, MARCANTONIO. *See* **Torre, Marcantonio Della.**

DELPORTE, EUGÈNE JOSEPH (*b. Genappe, Belgium, 1882; d. Uccle, Belgium, 1955*), astronomy.

Studied at Brussels University (Ph.D., 1903). Worked at Royal Observatory of Belgium, Uccle (1903–47; director from 1936). In the field of meridian astronomy he made thousands of transit observations of reference stars, including 3,533 stars for *Carte du ciel;* investigated errors of divisions of the meridian circle; determined longitude difference between Paris and Uccle. Transferred to department of equatorials (1919), concentrated on systematic observations of comets and asteroids; discovered many new asteroids and a comet. Edited two volumes of *Scientific Delimitation of Constellations* (1930) for International Astronomical Union.

DELUC, JEAN ANDRÉ (*b. Geneva, Switzerland, 1727; d. Windsor, England, 1817*), geology, meteorology, physics, natural philosophy, theology.

Traveled extensively both before and after moving to England (1773), and made geological observations; lived six years in Germany (1798–1804). Interested in earth sciences and theology. His great aim was to reconcile Genesis and geology: he considered the six days of the Creation as six epochs preceding the present state of the globe, which began when cavities in the interior of the earth collapsed and lowered the sea level, exposing the continents. There was thus a distinction between an older creative, or antediluvian, period and a newer, or diluvian, period. Of the former only a few primordial islands survived, accounting for the fossils of large animals and the antiquity of organic life. In the latter period (starting about 2200 B.C.) new geological processes were operative but were so ineffectual or incidental that the landscape remained unchanged. Mountains were remnants

left upstanding when adjacent areas collapsed catastrophically; erratic boulders were blown out when great interior caverns filled with some expansible fluid collapsed. Deluc opposed Hutton's ideas on present erosion.

In meteorology, he noticed the disappearance of some heat during the thawing of ice; probably originated the theory that the amount of water vapor contained in any space is independent of the density of the air or any other gaseous substance in which it is diffused; published improved rules for measuring heights by barometer; devised a hygrometer with an ivory bulb, which Humboldt found better than Saussure's hair hygrometer for use at sea level; influenced Daniell's account of atmospheric evaporation and condensation; disagreed with H. B. de Saussure on theory of the barometer (Deluc's view, now known to be correct, was that pure air is heavier than air mixed with water vapor). In physics and chemistry he discussed the mode of action of the galvanic pile and developed an "electric column"; he strenuously opposed Lavoisier's new chemical theory.

DEMBOWSKI, ERCOLE (*b. Milan, Italy, 1812; d. Monte de Albizzate [near Gallarate], Italy, 1881*), astronomy.

Measured distances and positions of double and multiple stars over a period of twenty-five years. Worked on revision of F. G. W. Struve's *Dorpat Catalogue;* these measurements were used by Argelander in work on proper motions. His collected observations were edited posthumously by G. V. Schiaparelli and Otto Wilhelm Struve.

DEMOCRITUS (*b. Abdera, Thrace; fl. late fifth century* B.C.), physics, mathematics.

Although Democritus had a great influence on Greek and later natural philosophy, his chronology is uncertain and only some three hundred alleged quotations survive of his more than sixty works. We know that Leucippus was one of his teachers, and that his own pupils included Nausiphanes who was in turn the teacher of Epicurus. What we know of his thought has been transmitted by Aristotle, Theophrastus, Epicurus, and others. Epicureanism represents a further elaboration of the physical theories of Democritus, and surviving writings of Epicurus and others provide further interpretations and sometimes specific information about earlier atomist doctrines. While some writers attempted to trace the origin of atomism to the Orient, there is no early evidence of external sources for Democritus' thought; Aristotle is probably right in explaining his views as developed in reply to the doctrines of the Eleatics. The possibility remains that the atomists were also influenced by what is sometimes called Pythagorean number-atomism, either before or after the time of Leucippus, and it is clear that Democritus did not invent atomism but received the essentials of the doctrine from Leucippus.

Atoms and void are the bases of Democritus' system for explaining the universe: solid corporeal atoms, infinite in number and shape, differing in size but generally invisibly small, lacking in other sensible qualities, physically indivisible (this is the meaning of the name *atomos*), homogeneous, containing no void nor interstices, and in perpetual motion in the infinitely extended void, probably moving equally in all directions. All movement and all change are the necessary result of the natural movement of the atoms. A cosmos is formed when a group of like atoms are whirled together into a spherical structure, and can be destroyed by collision with another cosmos. Apart from differences in shape, atoms differ in arrangement and position; the perceived qualitative differences between objects depend on the nature and arrangement of the relevant atoms and void, and on the state of the percipient. Fire and soul are composed of spherical atoms. Soul atoms are distributed throughout the living body in alternation with body atoms and are the immediate source of life; when depleted, the soul can be nourished by breathing in suitable atoms from the air (a possible explanation for resuscitation). In addition to the dispersed soul atoms there is another part of the soul, the mind, located in the head. There is no survival of the individual soul, although the soul atoms themselves survive because, like all atoms, they are indestructible. Sensation is based on touch, either directly or through imprinted air. Thought, like sensation, is the result of a disturbance of the soul atoms by configurations of atoms from outside; it is what occurs when the soul achieves a fresh balance after the movement which is sensation. But there are two kinds of knowledge: genuine knowledge operates on objects too fine for any sense to grasp, while bastard knowledge comes from the senses.

Democritus' cosmology had at its center a flat, elongated, stationary earth, with other bodies in the normal order of moon, Venus, sun, planets, and fixed stars. His meteorology was generally traditional also, although some explanations were atomistic (for example, magnetism is caused by the attraction of like atoms to like). Among his mathematical discussions are the nature of the sphere as "all angle"; the question of the equality or inequality of the two contiguous surfaces of a horizontally sliced cone; and the ratios of size between cylinders, pyramids, and prisms. Other attributions to Democritus include a theory of the development of civilization from lower levels to higher; a theory of *euthymia* ("contentment") as the end of ethics; and a respect for the importance of law.

DE MOIVRE, ABRAHAM. *See* **Moivre, Abraham de.**

DE MORGAN, AUGUSTUS (*b. Madura, Madras presidency, India, 1806; d. London, England, 1871*), mathematics.

Graduated Trinity College, Cambridge (1827). Chair of mathematics at University College, London (1828–31, 1836–66). Very influential: taught Todhunter, Routh, and Sylvester; helped found London Mathematical Society (1865); wrote prolifically. His main contributions were in analysis, where he gave a precise analytical definition of the limit and an original rule to determine the convergence of infinite series; algebra, where his "double algebra" helped to interpret complex numbers and suggested the idea of quaternions; and logic, where he developed a notation suitable for reasoning involving quantity and also presented a logic of relations. Also promoted history of mathematics and arithmetical bibliography; advocated decimal coinage; prepared an almanac; wrote on theory of probability applied to life contingencies.

DENIS, JEAN-BAPTISTE (*b. Paris, France, 1640*[?]; *d. Paris, 1704*), medicine.

Performed experiments on transfusion of blood between animals (1667) under aegis of Henri Habert de Montmor's Academy. Achieved celebrity and started medical controversy when the experiments were extended to transfusion from animals to man with some success.

DEPARCIEUX, ANTOINE (*b. Clotet-de-Cessous, France, 1703; d. Paris, France, 1768*), mathematics.

Published works on trigonometry (1741) with extensive tables, and on mortality statistics (1746); discussed concept of mean life expectancy; manufactured sundials; studied hydraulics.

DEPÉRET, CHARLES (*b. Perpignan, France, 1854; d. Lyons, France, 1929*), paleontology, stratigraphy.

Studied Tertiary geology and paleontology of France and Spain, made extensive fossil collections. Turned to Quaternary studies (1906) and supported theory of eustacy and alluvial Quaternary terraces.

DEPREZ, MARCEL (*b. Aillant-sur-Milleron, France, 1843; d. Vincennes, France, 1918*), engineering.

Major innovator in many fields of technology, including steam engine valves and indicators, ballistics, railroad engineering, and electrotechnology. Promoted and facilitated industrial use of electricity. Conducted public demonstrations of d.c. electric power transmission (1881–86); suggested and patented a.c. transmission with transformers (1881).

DERHAM, WILLIAM (*b. Stoughton, Worcestershire, England, 1657; d. Upminster, Essex, England, 1735*), natural history, natural theology.

B.A., Trinity College, Oxford (1679); ordained priest in Church of England (1682); vicar of Upminster (1689); royal chaplain (1714). Known primarily for natural theological writings, well grounded in natural history; wrote on meteorology, astronomy, and natural history. Edited important works of John Ray and Robert Hooke.

DEROSNE, (LOUIS-) CHARLES (*b. Paris, France, 1780; d. Paris, 1846*), chemistry, industrial technology, invention.

Associated with his brother, Jean-François, and Louis-Claude Cadet in pharmacy; investigated properties of acetone (1807). In sugar technology, improved beet sugar methods of Achard and Hermbstaedt; invented continuous distillation apparatus. Founded successful firm to manufacture industrial and railway machinery.

DERYUGIN, KONSTANTIN MIKHAILOVICH (*b. St. Petersburg, Russia, 1878; d. Moscow, U.S.S.R., 1938*), earth science, oceanography, zoology.

Associated with St. Petersburg University as student (graduated 1900; master's, 1909; doctorate, 1915) and as teacher (lecturer, 1917; professor, 1919); also on staff of State Hydrological Institute (Leningrad); organized and directed oceanographic stations at Murmansk and Vladivostok. Won fame chiefly as a marine zoologist, studying taxonomy and environmental effects on biogeography. Worked extensively on hydrology, biogeography, and geological history of the seas bordering the Soviet Union. Made many improvements in oceanographic methodology and equipment.

DESAGULIERS, JOHN THEOPHILUS (*b. La Rochelle, France, 1683; d. London, England, 1744*), experimental natural philosophy.

Of Huguenot parents. B.A., Christ Church, Oxford (1709), M.A., Hart Hall, Oxford (1712); ordained Church of England; Freemason; fellow of Royal Society (1714). Noted Newtonian popularizer and public demonstrator of natural philosophy in the Royal Society, at court, and in his own home. Translated works by Ozanam, Mariotte, 'sGravesande, Pitcairn, and others. Published extensively on optics, mechanics, and electricity. In theoretical mechanics and optics his work was largely unoriginal, relying on Newton and Hales. He emphasized the Newtonian duality of forces: attributed elasticity of air to repulsion between its particles; taught that light is a body, and optical phenomena result from varying attractions between light and the media through which it moves. Performed many electrical experiments; distinguished "electrics per se," which could be charged by friction, from "non-electric bodies," which were incapable of receiving charge directly although they were capable of being electrified indirectly when suitably suspended. Skilled in practical mechanics: analyzed machines, improved devices of others.

DESARGUES, GIRARD (*b. Lyons, France, 1591; d. France, 1661*), geometry, perspective.

Worked as an engineer, perhaps at the siege of La Rochelle (1628); his presence in Paris first recorded in 1626. Acquainted with the leading mathematicians of Paris through Mersenne's Académie Parisienne; conducted an indirect correspondence with Descartes. In 1626 published works on music (in Mersenne's *Harmonie universelle*) and on perspective. In his subsequent writings, many of which have been lost, he had two goals: to rationalize, coordinate, and unify the diverse graphical techniques by his "universal methods" of perspective; and to integrate projective methods into the body of mathematics by means of a purely geometric study of perspective. His profound intuition of spatial geometry led him to prefer a thorough renewal of the methods of geometry rather than the Cartesian algebraization. The *Brouillon project* on conics (1639) is a daring projective presentation of the theory of conic sections; the curves are studied as plane perspective figures by means of involution. Desargues introduced the principal concepts of projective geometry: consideration of points and straight lines to infinity, studies of poles and polars, the introduction of projective transformations, the general definition of focuses, the unitary study of conics, and so on. But the use of an original vocabulary and the refusal to resort to Cartesian symbolism made his work difficult to read and partially explain its meager success. The only geometer who really comprehended the originality and breadth of Desargues's views was the young Blaise Pascal, whose works have largely been lost; Desargues's example survived only in some of the youthful works of Philippe de la Hire and perhaps in a few essays of the young Newton. The rapid success of the Cartesian method of applying algebra to geometry was certainly an important reason for the poor diffusion of Desargues's ideas.

In his work on stonecutting and gnomonics Desargues encountered similar hostility. Although his private pupils valued his methods, his published work (1640) was both plagiarized and criticized in print and resisted by artisans in practice. One of his disciples, Abraham Bosse, promoted his work in two treatises (1643) that were distributed widely; but criticisms persisted. Bosse continued to publish works on his master's method (1648, 1653) which Desargues may have written partially. After 1644 Desargues seems to have largely withdrawn from active scientific debate and commenced another aspect of his work, that of architect and practitioner, first in Paris, then in Lyons (*ca.* 1649–57), then again in Paris. He was responsible for numerous individual rooms, spectacular staircases, and public as well as private buildings, and amply vindicated his much-criticized graphical methods. He was also active as an engineer, most notably in the use of epicycloidal wheels in a system for raising water at the château of Beaulieu.

Desargues's work was rediscovered and fully appreciated by the geometers of the nineteenth century.

DESCARTES, RENÉ DU PERRON (*b. La Haye, Touraine, France, 1596; d. Stockholm Sweden, 1650*), natural philosophy, scientific method, mathematics, optics, mechanics, physiology.

Descartes received from the Jesuits of La Flèche a modern education in mathematics and physics, philosophy, and the classics. After graduating in law from the University of Poitiers he met Isaac Beeckman, who aroused him to self-discovery as a scientific thinker and mathematician and introduced him to a range of problems, especially in mechanics and acoustics, the subject of his first work (the *Compendium musicae* of 1618; published posthumously, 1650). On 26 March 1619 he reported to Beeckman his first glimpse of "an entirely new science," which was to become his analytical geometry.

The primarily centrifugal direction of Descartes's thought—moving out into detailed phenomena from a firm central theory—is shown by the sequence of composition of his major writings. He set out his method in the *Rules for the Direction of the Mind*, left unfinished in 1628 and published posthumously, and in the *Discours de la méthode*, written in the Netherlands along with the *Météores, La dioptrique*, and *La géométrie*, which he presented as examples of the method. All were published in one volume in 1637. At the same time his investigation into the true ontology led him to the radical division of created existence into matter as simply extended substance, given motion at the creation, and mind as unextended thinking substance. This conclusion he held to be guaranteed by the perfection of God, who would not deceive true reason.

It was from these first principles that Descartes had given an account in *Le monde, ou Traité de la lumière* of cosmogony and cosmology as products simply of matter in motion, making the laws of motion the ultimate "laws of nature" and all scientific explanation ultimately mechanistic. This treatise remained unpublished in Descartes's lifetime; so too did the associated treatise *L'homme,* in which he represented animals and the human body as sheer mechanisms, an idea already found in the *Rules*. He withheld these essays, on the brink of publication, at the news of Galileo's condemnation in 1633, and instead published his general system of physics, with its Copernicanism mitigated by the idea that all motion is relative, in the *Principles of Philosophy* in 1644. Finally, he brought physiological psychology within the compass of his system in *Les passions de l'âme* in 1649.

No other great philosopher, except perhaps Aristotle, can have spent so much time in experimental observation. According to Baillet, over several years Descartes studied anatomy, dissected and vivisected embryos of birds and cattle, and went on to study chemistry. He did experiments on the weight of the air and on vibrating strings and made observations on optical phenomena.

In Descartes's letter prefaced to the French translation of the *Principles* (1647) he wrote that two, and only two, conditions determined whether the first principles proposed could be accepted as true: "First they must be so clear and evident that the mind of man cannot doubt their truth when it attentively applies itself to consider them"; and secondly, everything else must be deducible from them. But he went on to admit, "It is really only God alone who has perfect wisdom, that is to say, who has a complete knowledge of the truth of all things." To find the truth about complex material phenomena man must experiment, but as the sixth part of the *Discours* shows, the need to experiment was an expression of the failure of the ideal. The main issue in any historical judgment of Descartes here is not whether his own answers were correct but whether his questions were fruitful. In insisting that experiment and observation alone could show whether the model corresponded with actuality, he introduced further precision into his theory of demonstration.

The mathematics that served as model and touchstone for Descartes's philosophy was in large part his own creation and reflected in turn many of his philosophical tenets. Its historical foundations lie in the classical analytical texts of Pappus *(Mathematical Collection)* and Diophantus *(Arithmetica)* and in the cossist algebra exemplified by the works of Peter Rothe and Christoph Clavius. He apparently received the stimulus to study these works from Isaac Beeckman. His command of cossist algebra (evident throughout his papers of the early 1620's) was perhaps strengthened by his acquaintance during the winter of 1619–20 with Johann Faulhaber, a leading German cossist in Ulm; Descartes's treatise *De solidorum elementis* was quite likely also the result of their discussions.

Whatever the early influences on Descartes's mathematics, it nonetheless followed a relatively independent line of development during the decade preceding the publication of his magnum opus, the *Géométrie* of 1637. During this decade he sought to realize two programmatic goals. The first stemmed from a belief, first expressed by Petrus Ramus, that cossist algebra represented a "vulgar" form of the analytical method employed by the great Greek mathematicians. Descartes expressed his second programmatic goal in a letter to Beeckman in 1619. He envisaged "an entirely new science," a symbolic algebra of pure quantity by which problems of any sort could be analyzed and classified in terms of the constructive techniques required for their most efficient solution. He conceived of his "true mathematics" as the science of magnitude, or quantity, per se. He replaced the old cossist symbols with letters of the alphabet, using at first (in the *Rules*) capital letters to denote known quantities and lowercase letters to denote unknowns, and later (in the *Géométrie*) shifting to the a,b,c; x,y,z notation still in use today. In a more radical step, he

then removed the last vestiges of verbal expression (and the conceptualization that accompanied it) by replacing the words "square," "cube," etc., by numerical superscripts.

While all numbers are homogeneous, the application of algebra to geometry (Descartes's main goal in the *Géométrie*) required the definition of the six basic algebraic operations (addition, subtraction, multiplication, division, raising to a power, and extracting a root) for the realm of geometry in such a way as to preserve the homogeneity of the products. The famous "Problem of Pappus," called to Descartes's attention by Jacob Golius in 1631, provides the focus for Descartes's exposition of his new method. His classification of the various cases of Pappus' problem follows the order of difficulty of solving determinate equations of increasing degree. Solution of such equations carries with it the possibility of constructing any point (and hence all points) of the locus sought. The direct solvability of algebraic equations becomes in book II Descartes's criterion for distinguishing between "geometrical" and "nongeometrical" curves; for the latter (today termed "transcendental curves") by their nature allow the direct construction of only certain of their points. Descartes goes on to show that the equation of a curve also suffices to determine its geometrical properties, of which the most important is the normal to any point on the curve. His method of normals—from which a method of tangents follows directly—takes as unknown the point of intersection of the desired normal and the axis. Descartes's method is formally equivalent to Fermat's method of maxima and minima and, along with the latter, constituted one of the early foundations of the later differential calculus.

The central importance of determinate equations and their solution leads directly to book III of the *Géométrie* with its purely algebraic theory of equations. Entirely novel and original, Descartes's theory begins by writing every equation in the form $P(x)=0$, where $P(x)$ is an algebraic polynomial with real coefficients. From the assertion, derived inductively, that every such equation may also be expressed in the form $(x-a)(x-b)\ldots(x-s)=0$, where $a,b,\ldots,s$ are the roots of the equation, he states and offers an intuitive proof of the fundamental theorem of algebra (first stated by Albert Girard in 1629) that an nth-degree equation has exactly n roots.

In addition to presenting his new method of algebraic geometry, Descartes's *Géométrie* also served in book II to provide rigorous mathematical demonstrations for sections of his *Dioptrique* published at the same time. The mathematical derivations pertain to his theory of lenses and offer, through four "ovals," solutions to a generalized form of the anaclastic problem. The theory of lenses, a topic that had engaged him since reading Kepler's *Dioptrica* in 1619, took its form and direction in turn from Descartes's solution to the more basic problem of a mathematical derivation of the laws of reflection and refraction, with which the *Dioptrique* opens. Background to these derivations was Descartes's theory of light, an integral part of his overall system of cosmology. For him light was not motion (which takes time) but rather a "tendency to motion," an impulsive force transmitted rectilinearly and instantaneously by the fine particles that fill the interstices between the visible macrobodies of the universe. His model for light itself was the blind man's cane, which instantaneously transmits impulses from the objects it meets and enables the man to "see." To derive the laws of reflection and refraction, however, Descartes required another model more amenable to mathematical description; he chose the model of a tennis ball striking a flat surface and applied this motion to his description of the optical phenomena of refraction. He then applied two fundamental principles of his theory of collision: first, that a body in motion will continue to move in the same direction at the same speed unless acted upon by contact with another body; second, that a body can lose some or all of its motion only by transmitting it directly to another.

Following those derivations, Descartes devotes the remainder of the *Dioptrique* to an optical analysis of the human eye, moving from the explanation of various distortions of vision to the lenses designed to correct them or, in the case of the telescope, to increase the power of the normal eye. The laws of reflection and refraction reappear, however, in the third of the *Essais* of 1637, the *Météores*. There Descartes presents a mathematical explanation of both the primary and the secondary rainbow in terms of the refraction and internal reflection of the sun's rays in a spherical raindrop.

His contribution to mechanics lay less in solutions to particular problems than in the stimulus that the detailed articulation of his mechanistic cosmology provided for others.

Descartes' physiology grew and developed as an integral part of his philosophy. Important ideas on animal function occur briefly in the *Regulae* (1628), form a significant part of the argument in the *Discours de la méthode* (1637), and lie behind certain parts of the *Principia philosophiae* (1644) and all of the *Passions de l'âme* (1649). Descartes hinted at the most fundamental conceptions of his physiology relatively early in his philosophical development. Already in the twelfth *regula*, he suggested that all animal and subrational human movements are controlled solely by unconscious mechanisms. Closely associated with this notion of animal automatism was his belief that human sensation is a two-step process consisting, first, of the mechanical conveyance of physical stimuli from the external organs of sense to a common sensorium located somewhere in the body and, second, of the internal perception of these mechanically conveyed stimuli by a higher "spiritual" principle. Implicit in these two notions and seeming to tie them together is the assumption that all phenomena of the animate and inanimate world, with the sole exception of those directly connected with human will and consciousness, are to be explained in terms of mathematics, matter, configuration, and motion.

In June 1632 he informed Mersenne that he had already completed his work on inanimate bodies but still had to finish off "certain things touching on the nature of man." The allusion here was to the *Traité de l'homme*, which with the *Traité de lumière* was meant to form *Le monde;* both works were suppressed by Descartes, however, after the condemnation of Galileo in 1633. Although it thus had to await posthumous publication in the 1660's, the *Traité de l'homme* was obviously written as a full working out of the physiological hints included in the *Regulae* and elaborated in the light of his own philosophical development. A clearly stated dualist ontology runs through the *Traité*, while mechanistic details analo-

gous to those of the *Traité de lumière* are evident at almost every turn.

But the *Traité de l'homme* served not only to clarify and develop Descartes's physiological views; it also quickly became a rich fund of ideas upon which he drew throughout the rest of his intellectual life. In 1637, for example, he published two important works: *Discours de la méthode* and *Dioptrique*. In both he uses physiological ideas from the unpublished *Traité* at important points in his argument. The complicated arguments of the *Passions de l'âme*, published near the end of that decade, rest firmly on the extensive survey of basic Cartesian physiology incorporated in part I of the *Traité*, while Descartes's assertiveness in his correspondence and later philosophical writings on the "beast-machine" makes full sense only against a background provided by the *Traité*'s automaton.

Descartes, however, had left one major physiological problem untreated in the *Traité:* the reproductive generation of animals and men. His ideas on the subject really seem to have crystallized in the late 1640's, when he triumphantly announced his "solution" to the long-plaguing problem in a series of enthusiastic letters to Princess Elizabeth. The ideas alluded to in these letters appear to be those published as the *De la formation du foetus*, which Descartes completed not long before his death. First published by Clerselier in 1664, the *Formation* is a curious essay. Unlike the *Traité de l'homme*, which must precede it in date of composition, the *Formation* consists mainly of bald assertions and only the vaguest mechanisms. Everything in the animal's life now had an automatic, mechanical explanation.

DES CLOIZEAUX, ALFRED-LOUIS-OLIVIER LEGRAND (*b. Beauvais, France, 1817; d. Paris, France, 1897*), mineralogy, crystallography.

Studied in Paris with Armand Lévy, Alexandre Brongniart, and Armand Dufrénoy; doctorate from Faculté des Sciences (1857). Professor at Muséum d'Histoire Naturelle (1876–92); president of Académie des Sciences (1889). Studied form and optical properties of crystals, and interior structure of minerals; promoted crystallographic notation of Haüy and Lévy. Improved on polarizing microscope, determined optical characteristics of nearly 500 substances; established effects of high temperatures on positions of optic axes of certain crystals.

DESCOTILS, HIPPOLYTE VICTOR. *See* **Collet-Descotils, Hippolyte Victor.**

DESCOURTILZ, MICHEL ÉTIENNE (*b. Boiste, near Pithiviers, France, 1775; d. Paris, France, 1836*), medicine, natural history.

First trained as a surgeon. Lived in Santo Domingo (Haiti) 1798–1803, during the Negro revolution; wrote extensively on natural history of the area, particularly botany. Became doctor of medicine (Paris, 1814).

DESHAYES, GERARD PAUL (*b. Nancy, France, 1797; d. Boran-sur-Oise, France, 1875*), paleontology, malacology.

Independently educated in Paris; gave private geological lectures and led field trips (students included d'Archiac, Élie de Beaumont, Louis-Constant Prévost, Philippe de Verneuil). Professor at Muséum d'Histoire

Naturelle (1869). One of founders of Société Géologique de France. Amassed a significant collection of mollusks and a large library, which were sold to the French government (1868) for École des Mines, Paris. Major contributions were on paleontology and stratigraphy of Paris Basin. Described 1,074 species of mollusks, divided Tertiary into three periods based on proportion of living species among fossil forms, and provided statistical tables of Tertiary mollusk species for Lyell's *Principles of Geology*. Also published on mollusks of Algeria (1844–48), and many other works on conchology. Collaborated with Milne-Edwards on new edition (1833–58) of Lamarck's *Histoire des animaux sans vertèbres*.

DESLANDRES, HENRI (*b. Paris, France, 1853; d. Paris, 1948*), astronomy, physics.

Graduated from École Polytechnique (1874); served in army (1874–81); studied spectroscopy with M. A. Cornu. Worked at Paris observatory (1889); Meudon observatory (1897; director, 1908); director of both after merger (1926–29). President Académie des Sciences (1920). Formulated two useful laws (1886) of bands in molecular spectra that later proved to be consistent with quantum theory. Turned to astrophysics and measurement of line-of-sight velocities through Doppler-Fizeau effect: developed law of rotation of Saturn's ring (1895) and proved opposite direction of rotation of Uranus. Invented spectroheliograph (1894), independently of G. E. Hale; studied solar activity and structure of chromosphere; predicted solar Hertzian radiation.

DESMAREST, NICOLAS (*b. Soulaines-Dhuys, France, 1725; d. Paris, France, 1815*), geology, technology.

Educated at Oratorian college of Troyes. Moved to Paris (*ca.* 1746); worked as private tutor; assisted in editing *Journal de Verdun* (1749). Subsequently edited various works, including French edition of Hauksbee's *Physico-Mechanical Experiments* (1754). His first scientific work (1751) argued that England had once been joined to France by an isthmus whose destruction was recent, natural, and noncatastrophic. He published a theory of earthquakes (1756) and an article in the *Encyclopédie* (1757) on the origin of springs. His general outlook was neptunist, due to G. F. Rouelle's influence. In 1757 he began a career in study and regulation of French industry, developing special proficiency in papermaking technology; his travels as inspector took him to Auvergne (1763) where he saw prismatic basalt columns. He concluded (1765) that the columns were of volcanic origin, and that the presence of prismatic basalts infallibly indicates the former presence of volcanoes; a full report, with a geological map of the main volcanic district of Auvergne, was presented to the Académie des Sciences (1771). In this and later reports he dealt with such problems as the origin of the matter constituting the basalts, the volcanic history of the Auvergne region, and the alterations that the volcanic flows had undergone. By analogy, he was led to a consideration of the destructive effects of flowing water upon the Auvergne terrain; he applied the idea of aqueous degradation in such a way as virtually to enunciate a principle of uniformity in destructive geological processes. He considered volcanoes as feeding on some combustible or fermenting agent, and lavas as material heated accidentally; basalt was granite heated to a moderate de-

gree; volcanic action had a relatively recent appearance in geological history.

DESMIER DE SAINT-SIMON, ÉTIENNE J. A. *See Archiac, Vicomte d'.*

DESOR, PIERRE JEAN ÉDOUARD (*b. Friedrichsdorf, near Frankfurt am Main, Germany, 1811; d. Nice, France, 1882*), glacial geology, paleontology, stratigraphy.

Close friend and collaborator of Louis Agassiz. In America (1846–52), he was geologist for governmental agencies. Professor at Academy of Neuchâtel (1852–58) and president of Swiss Federal Assembly (1874). Wrote on glacial theory, Alpine studies, fossil echinoderms, geology of the Jura, and Bronze Age archaeology. Collaborated on a geological map of Switzerland.

DESORMES, CHARLES-BERNARD (*b. Dijon, Côte-d'Or, France, 1777; d. Verberie, Oise, France, 1862*), chemistry.

At École Polytechnique (1794–1804), as student and as *répétiteur* under Guyton de Morveau. Did important joint work in chemistry with Nicolas Clément (*q.v.*); also devised dry electric piles composed of metallic disks separated by a layer of salt paste (1801–04).

DESPAGNET, JEAN (*fl. ca. 1625*), alchemy.

Published two classic alchemical works (1623); regarded nature as a constant expression of divine will, thus illustrating the deepening sense of the spiritual on the part of post-Reformation physical alchemists.

DESSAIGNES, VICTOR (*b. Vendôme, France, 1800; d. Paris, France, 1885*), chemistry.

Degrees in law (1822) and medicine (1836); established a private chemical laboratory, achieved the recognition of other chemists although an amateur. Studied metabolism, structure of organic acids, transformations between malic, succinic, and tartaric acids. Synthesized hippuric acid and other organic substances.

DEVAUX, HENRI (*b. Étaules, Charente-Maritime, France, 1862; d. Bordeaux, France, 1956*), plant physiology, molecular physics.

Graduated from University of Bordeaux; doctorate in botany, University of Paris (1889); worked at Bordeaux (chair of plant physiology, 1906–32). Studied accumulation of polyvalent metallic ions in membranes of aquatic plants, and reversal of the process (now known as ion exchange); from 1903 worked on physics of surfaces, particularly monomolecular films of proteins which he used to calculate molecular weights.

DEVILLE, HENRI ÉTIENNE SAINTE-CLAIRE (*b. St. Thomas, Virgin Islands, 1818; d. Boulogne-sur-Seine, France, 1881*), chemistry.

Doctorates in medicine (1843) and science, Paris; taught by Thenard. Worked first in his own laboratory; professorships at University of Besançon (1845–51), École Normale Supérieure (Paris, 1851–80); lectured at Sorbonne (1853–66). Early studies in organic chemistry (e.g., turpentine); synthesized nitrogen pentoxide (1849) and turned to inorganic chemistry. Developed industrially useful methods for production of aluminum and sodium. Prepared silicon, boron, titanium. Studied metallurgy of platinum. Expert in high-temperature techniques. His measurements of vapor densities of compounds at various temperatures helped to confirm Avogadro's hypothesis. Discovered dissociation of heated chemical compounds and their recombination at lower temperatures.

DEWAR, JAMES (*b. Kincardine-on-Forth, Scotland, 1842; d. London, England, 1923*), chemistry, physics.

Studied at Edinburgh under J. D. Forbes and Lyon Playfair, became assistant to Playfair (1867–68) and then to Alexander Crum Brown (1868–73). Elected to professorships at Cambridge (1875–1923) and Royal Institution (1877–1923); knighted (1904). Best known for work in cryogenics at Royal Institution: when Cailletet and Pictet announced the liquefaction of oxygen and nitrogen in small amounts (1877) Dewar attacked the technical problems in order to study properties of matter near absolute zero temperature. He improved the techniques of Wróblewski and Olszewski and prepared large quantities of liquid air and oxygen (1885); discovered that liquid oxygen and ozone were magnetic (1891). By 1898 he produced liquid and solid hydrogen, utilizing the Joule-Thomson effect of the cooling of a compressed gas by expansion into a vacuum: hydrogen was cooled first by liquid air, then forced through a nozzle into a vacuum vessel where it liquefied; when the pressure was reduced the liquid solidified and was cooled to −260°C. With liquid hydrogen, every gas but helium could in turn be both liquefied and solidified. In 1908 Kamerlingh Onnes used Dewar's methods to liquefy helium; by boiling helium at reduced pressure Dewar could reach a temperature less than 1° from absolute zero. To pursue his low-temperature studies Dewar invented the vacuum-jacketed flask (1892), which he later improved (1905) by adding charcoal to the evacuated space to absorb the traces of gas remaining in the vacuum. His studies of the properties of matter at very low temperatures included chemical reactivity; properties of liquefied gases; emanations of radium (with Crookes); gases occluded by radium (with Pierre Curie); strength of materials; phosphorescence; electrical and magnetic properties of metals and alloys (with J. A. Fleming, 1892–95) for the range 200°C. to −200°C.; and calorimetry (1904–13). Determining atomic and molecular heats, he discovered that atomic heats of solid elements at a mean temperature of 50°K. were a periodic function of atomic weights.

Dewar did work of note in many other areas as well, including structural organic chemistry, where he proposed ring formulas for benzene (1867) and pyridine (1870); physiological chemistry; physiological optics; chemical reactions in the electric arc; monatomicity of sodium and potassium vapor (1883). Other investigations included extensive spectroscopic studies with G. D. Liveing (1877–1904); the invention of cordite (with Sir Frederick Abel, 1889); measurement of the rate of production of helium from radium (1908); thin films and bubbles; and measurement of infrared radiation. Dewar was a superb experimentalist; he published no theoretical papers.

DEZALLIER D'ARGENVILLE, ANTOINE-JOSEPH. *See* **Argenville, Antoine-Joseph d'.**

DICAEARCHUS OF MESSINA (*fl. 310 B.C.*).

Disciple of Aristotle. Author of many books (none of which is preserved) in different fields, including political theory, advocating a composite constitution, and a history of Greece, which inspired Varro's history of Rome. Following Eudoxus, Dicaearchus wrote a geography combining the actual knowledge of lands and seas with the theory of the earth as a sphere. The circumference was calculated at 400,000 or 300,000 stades (stades varied from 148 to 198 meters), and the highest mountains were "measured" at ten or fifteen stades high.

DICKINSON, ROSCOE GILKEY (*b. Brewer, Me., 1894; d. Pasadena, Calif., 1945*), physical chemistry, X rays, crystal structure.

Studied at Massachusetts Institute of Technology (B.S., 1915) and California Institute of Technology (Ph.D., 1920, the first awarded); taught at latter school all his life. Determined structure of many crystals, including those containing inorganic complexes, with X-ray diffraction methods; made first structure determination of a molecule of an organic compound (hexamethylenetetramine, with A. L. Raymond). Also studied photochemistry, chemical kinetics, Raman spectroscopy, properties of neutrons, and use of radioactive indicators in studying chemical reactions.

DICKSON, LEONARD EUGENE (*b. Independence, Iowa, 1874; d. Harlingen, Tex., 1954*), mathematics.

Educated at University of Texas (B.S., 1893; M.S., 1894) and University of Chicago (Ph.D., 1896, Chicago's first in mathematics); post-graduate study in Leipzig and Paris. Taught at universities of California (1898), Texas (1899), and Chicago (1900–39). Prolific and well-recognized writer in many areas, primarily in algebra and number theory; studies included finite linear groups, theory of finite fields, linear algebra, relationships between theory of invariants and number theory, and additive number theory (proved the ideal Waring theorem). Wrote a monumental work on history of number theory.

DICKSTEIN, SAMUEL (*b. Warsaw, Poland, 1851; d. Warsaw, 1939*), mathematics, history of mathematics, science education, scientific organization.

In mathematics, he was concerned mainly with algebra and history of mathematics; edited Leibniz-Kochański correspondence. His life was devoted to building up the organizational structure for Polish science: he founded several periodicals, a series of scientific textbooks in Polish, and scientific societies.

DIDEROT, DENIS (*b. Langres, France, 1713; d. Paris, France, 1784*), letters, technology.

From a family with close ties to the church, Diderot was educated by Jesuits; he moved to Paris 1728, received his master's degree from the University of Paris (1732). Had no fixed employment; educated himself in science while doing translations and small writing jobs for money. Became acquainted with the notable thinkers of Paris. Diderot is best remembered as editor of the *Encyclopédie*, but he was besides a prolific writer, few of whose works of philosophy, science, and literature were published in his lifetime. His philosophical position combined elements of skepticism, pantheism, and humanism. His radical views on personal freedom and antideistic naturalism, expressed in *Pensées philosophiques* (1746), *Les bijoux indiscrets* (1747), and *Lettre sur les aveugles* (1749), led to his detention by the authorities for three months in 1749, but his imprisonment did not interfere with his intellectual activities. Diderot's writings in science and philosophy, including *Le neveu de Rameau, De l'interprétation de la nature* (1753), and *Le rêve de d'Alembert*, reveal an anticipation of biological romanticism—an attempt to construct an account of the operations of nature in categories of organism and consciousness rather than impersonal matter in inanimate motion. The Experimental Art is the true road to a science of nature; that road lies through craftsmanship. Not some mathematical abstraction from nature but manual intimacy with nature is the arm of science. Nature is the combination of its elements and not just an aggregate. It is continuity that science is to seek in nature, not divisibility; there are no fixed limits in nature. The universe is a cosmic polyp, time its life unfolding, space its habitation, gradience its structure. The two ideas that mattered most to Diderot were those of social naturalism and universal sensibility.

The *Encyclopédie, ou Dictionnaire raisonné des sciences, des arts, et des métiers*, signet of the French Enlightenment, was published between 1751 and 1766 (with d'Alembert's assistance until 1758); publication was suspended by the authorities from 1759 to 1766, but work on the technical plates was continued. It had been instigated by a publisher who wanted a straightforward translation of two English encyclopedias; in Diderot's hands the project grew in size and adopted a philosophical purpose. He felt it should have "the character of changing the general way of thinking" in two areas: on the one hand he endeavored to unsettle the authorities by purveying tongue-in-cheek reflections on superstition and injustice in the guise of information, and on the other he aimed at the dignification of common pursuits and the rationalization and perfection of those pursuits in the light of modern knowledge. The second purpose was abetted by the eleven volumes of splendid plates, not all of which were original (some may have been lifted from engravings prepared by Réaumur for the Academy of Sciences); the plates presented something like an anatomy of machines, a physiology of processes, analogous to the technique of Vesalius (some of whose plates are included). In effect the *Encyclopédie* turned craftsmanship from lore to science and promoted the concept of uniform industrial method to be adopted by all producers. Although misunderstood and resented by many practitioners, its aim was the easing of labor, its liberation from routine, and the summons to pride in its enlightenment.

DIELS, OTTO PAUL HERMANN (*b. Hamburg, Germany, 1876; d. Kiel, Germany, 1954*), organic chemistry.

Studied at University of Berlin (Ph.D., 1899) and taught first there and then at Christian Albrecht University, Kiel (1916–48). Wrote a very popular textbook, *Einführung in die organische Chemie* (1907). Outstanding experimenter. Determined the structure of cholesterol by dehydrating with selenium to "Diels hydrocarbon," which proved to be the basic substance and structure of many natural products. Won Nobel Prize in chemistry (1950) with Kurt Alder for development of diene synthesis, combining a diene with a philodiene to form a ring-

shaped structure: the diene system opens at positions 1 and 4, and the terminal carbons are located at the double bond of the philodiene.

DIETRICH, BARON DE. *See* **Holbach, Paul-Henri d'.**

DIETRICH VON FREIBERG (*b. Freiberg, Germany, ca. 1250; d. ca. 1310*), optics, natural philosophy.

Studied at University of Paris (ca. 1275–77); may have been taught by Albertus Magnus. A Dominican who wrote extensively on philosophy (generally Aristotelian) and theology (Augustinian-Neoplatonic); opposed Thomas Aquinas; influenced development of speculative mysticism. In an important work on geometrical optics, *De iride et radialibus impressionibus*, he presented a theory of the rainbow arrived at by a combination of experimentation and Aristotelian reasoning. He attempted to duplicate nature's operation by isolating the component factors of that operation in a way that permitted their study at close range. He studied the paths of light rays through crystalline spheres and flasks filled with water, having recognized that a globe of water could be thought of as a magnified raindrop and that the bow is simply the aggregate of effects produced by many individual drops. He was the first to trace correctly the path of the light ray through the raindrop and to see that this involved two refractions at the surface of the drop nearer the observer and one internal reflection at the farther surface. He was also the first to see that each color is projected to the observer from a different drop or series of drops. He went on to detail the mechanism for production of the secondary, or upper, rainbow: this involves two refractions at the nearer surface of the drop and *two* internal reflections at the farther surface, and thus explains the inversion of colors in the secondary bow. His attempt at a theory of colors, involving an analogy with the theory of the elements, was less successful. He wrote also on the theory of matter, gravitational motion, and astronomy.

DIGBY, KENELM (*b. Gayhurst, Buckinghamshire, England, 1603; d. London, England, 1665*), natural philosophy, occult science.

Studied at Oxford (1618–20); knighted (1623). Catholic, royalist; traveled extensively; widely admired; early member of Royal Society. Collected books, manuscripts, and medical, chemical, and household recipes. Corresponded with Descartes, Fermat, Wallis, and Brouncker. Wrote on literature, religion, alchemy (gave a famous account of the "powder of sympathy" for curing wounds, 1658), botany (*Discourse Concerning the Vegetation of Plants*, 1661). Most important work in natural philosophy was "Of Bodies" (the first of his *Two Treatises*, 1644), dealing with both animate and inanimate bodies and referring frequently to Galileo's *Two New Sciences* (1638): the fundamental properties of bodies are quantity, density, and rarity, and from them motion arises; light is material and in motion and can exert pressure; motion is discussed extensively but qualitatively.

DIGGES, LEONARD (*b. England, ca. 1520; d. England, 1559[?]*), mathematics.

Interested in elementary practical mathematics, especially surveying, navigation, and gunnery. Wrote *Tectoni-*

con (1556) and *Pantometria* (1571), based largely on Peter Apian and Gemma Frisius, and *Stratioticos* (1579), and based partly on his gunnery experiments. Digges's son Thomas completed and published his father's works.

DIGGES, THOMAS (*b. Kent, England, 1546[?]; d. London, England, 1595*), mathematics.

Studied under his father (Leonard Digges) and John Dee; published his father's works on geometry, ballistics, and prognostication with his own additions. Leader of English Copernicans: made careful observations of 1572 nova in hope of proving Copernican theory; translated part of *De revolutionibus*, added concept of physical universe in which fixed stars were at varying distances in infinite space ("A Perfit Description of the Caelestiall Orbes," 1576, added to *Prognostication*).

DILLENIUS, JOHANN JACOB (*b. Darmstadt, Germany, 1687; d. Oxford, England, 1747*), botany.

Trained as a doctor (M.D., Giessen, 1713) but became interested in plants, primarily cryptogams. He was offered a job as a botanist by William Sherard (working on *Pinax*), moved to England (1721), eventually occupied chair of botany at Oxford (1734). Studied sexual organs and classification of cryptogams. Published *Catalogus plantarum circa Gissam sponte nascentium* (1719) comparing taxonomic systems: criticized Bachmann (Rivinus) in favor of Ray; made third edition of Ray's *Synopsis plantarum* (1724) incorporating many new species. Described and illustrated plants in garden of James Sherard (1732); introduced a new classification of lower plants, still partially in use today, in *Historia muscorum* (1741). Corresponded with Linnaeus.

DINAKARA (*b. Gujarat, India, ca. 1550*), astronomy.

Composed three sets of astronomical tables based on the work of Bhāskara II and Mahādeva; influenced Haridatta II.

DINGLER, HUGO ALBERT EMIL HERMANN (*b. Munich, Germany, 1881; d. Munich, 1954*), philosophy.

Grandson of Emil Erlenmeyer. Studied mathematics, physics, and philosophy at Erlangen, Göttingen, and Munich; teachers included Hilbert, Klein, Husserl, Minkowski, Roentgen, and Woldemar Voigt. Doctorate in mathematics (1907); taught at Technische Hochschule in Munich (1912) and University of Munich (1920–32), then Technische Hochschule in Darmstadt (1932–34). An antiempiricist, concerned with the validity of axioms, he treated the Kantian problem: How is pure science possible? His fundamental investigations were concerned exclusively with the logical and methodological aspect of exact research. He called for a reconstruction of the foundations and the elimination of every presupposition in order to be able to give an ultimate foundation even to the axioms themselves. Starting from the "untouched" situation, the will perceives the way to the goal of knowledge, constructing a system of pure synthesis according to the principle of simplicity. He conceived of experiment as a willed, intentional action. Only Euclidean geometry was demonstrable as a fully defined fundamental science; nevertheless non-Euclidean geometries were methodologically important. Dingler constructed a logical demonstration of biological evolution, completely within his sys-

tem of pure synthesis, that has since been confirmed experimentally.

DINI, ULISSE (*b. Pisa, Italy, 1845; d. Pisa, 1918*), mathematics.

Studied under Betti, Hermite, and Joseph Bertrand. Taught at University of Pisa (from 1866). Worked in infinitesimal geometry, primarily helicoid surfaces, ruled surfaces, and conformable representation of one surface on another; and (from 1871) in analysis, chiefly uniform functions, functions of a real variable, Fourier series, and integral equations.

DINOSTRATUS (*fl. Athens, fourth century* B.C.), mathematics.

Said by Pappus to have squared the circle (i.e., found a square equal in area to a circle) by means of the quadratrix (a curve discovered by Hippias) and to have demonstrated the proof *per impossibile*.

DIOCLES (*fl. ca. 190* B.C.), mathematics.

Only surviving work (recently discovered in Arabic translation, previously known only through excerpts in Eutocius' commentary on Aristotle's *Sphere and Cylinder*) is *On Burning Mirrors*, dealing largely with three problems in the theory of conic sections: 1) The focal property of the parabola is proved, and a parabolic mirror of given focal length is constructed using the focus-directrix property (which Diocles may have discovered). 2) Division of a sphere in a given ratio is solved using the intersection of a hyperbola and an ellipse. 3) The Delian problem of doubling the cube, in its equivalent form of finding two mean proportionals between two given magnitudes, is solved in two ways: by the intersection of two parabolas, and by a curve later named "cissoid."

DIOCLES OF CARYSTUS (*b. Carystus, Euboea; fl. Athens, late fourth century* B.C.), medicine.

Prominent and influential physician, known to rulers of his time; pupil of Aristotle, author of numerous and diverse works of which fragments remain. His medical writings show the influence of the Aristotelian teleological view of nature, and indicate he was the first physician to use a collection of Hippocratic writings. According to Galen, he was the first to write a book on anatomy and to use that term in the title. His embryological views followed Empedocles: he thought the embryo, to which both man and woman furnish seed, developed in forty days. Studied sterility. Physiology based on four elements, fire, water, air, earth: health depended on proper balance of elements and proper movement of pneuma. Wrote on hygiene; studied fevers; described ideal diet; stressed practical experience, observation, and the importance of diagnosis and prognosis. Was the first to write a herbal on the origin, recognition, nutritional value, and medical use of plants; thus he can be considered the founder of pharmacy.

DIONIS DU SÉJOUR, ACHILLE-PIERRE (*b. Paris, France, 1734; d. Vernou, near Fontainebleau, France, 1794*), astronomy, mathematics, demography.

Studied in Paris (Collège Louis-le-Grand and Faculté de Droit). With Mathieu-Bernard Goudin, he wrote on analytical geometry of plane curves and on theoretical astronomy. Applied the most recent analytic methods to the study of astronomical phenomena; proved near impossibility of collision of comet with earth; discussed varying appearance of rings of Saturn. Studied theory of equations. With Condorcet and Laplace, he undertook systematic inquiry to determine the population of France.

DIONYSODORUS (*fl. Caunus* [?], *Asia Minor, third–second centuries* B.C.), *mathematics.*

Many references to this name exist in Greek literature, and the exact identification of the individuals is uncertain. The Dionysodorus discussed here is recorded by Eutocius as having solved, by means of the intersection of a parabola and a hyperbola, the cubic equation to which (in effect) Archimedes had reduced the problem of so cutting a sphere by a plane that the volumes of the segments are in a given ratio. This may be the same Dionysodorus who gave a formula for the volume of a torus that is the earliest example of Guldin's (or Pappus') theorem, and who invented a conical sundial.

DIOPHANTUS OF ALEXANDRIA (*fl.* A.D. *250*), *mathematics.*

Little has been recorded of Diophantus' life, and few of his writings are known. Of his major work, *Arithmetica*, six (of thirteen) books survived in a Greek manuscript discovered by Regiomontanus in Venice (1464); four more books have recently been discovered in an Arabic translation and commentary (1198) by Qusṭā ibn Lūqā. The Arabic books are labeled IV to VII, and there is evidence suggesting that they were intended to follow the Greek books I–III: in the Arabic books all the methods or results needed, whether explicitly cited or not, are found in the first three (Greek) books, while methods used in the last three Greek books (among them the use of the second-degree equation) are totally absent from the Arabic books. In early Islamic time, the order of the books is confirmed by the order of the problems considered in al-Karajī's *Fakhrī*. This would indicate that (Greek) books IV–VI, although their content must be drawn from the original work of Diophantus, are the result of a later recension that changed the numbering, and perhaps the order of contents, of his work. Throughout the Greek books a great deal has fallen into disorder through the commentators or transcription.

The *Arithmetica* is not a work of theoretical arithmetic in the sense understood by the Pythagoreans or Nicomachus. It deals, rather, with logistic, the computational arithmetic used in the solution of practical problems. Although Diophantus knew elementary number theory and contributed new theorems to it, his *Arithmetica* is a collection of problems, both determinate and indeterminate (which, with one exception, are purely numerical). In the algebraic treatment of the basic equations Diophantus, by a sagacious choice of suitable auxiliary unknowns and frequently brilliant artifices, succeeded in reducing the degree of the equation (the unknowns reaching as high as the ninth power) and the number of unknowns (as many as ten) and thus arrived at a solution. He showed himself a master in the field of indeterminate analysis, and apart from Pappus he was the only great mathematician during the decline of Hellenism.

The symbolism, undoubtedly of his own devising, that Diophantus introduced, provided a short and readily comprehensible means of expressing an equation. Numbers which are not coefficients of unknowns are termed "units." The symbols for the powers of the unknowns are also employed for the reciprocal values $1/x$, $1/x^2$, etc., in which case an additional index, ^{x}, marks them as fractions. All these symbols—among which is one for the "square number," —were read as the full words for which they stand, as is indicated by their added grammatical endings. The sign for subtraction is interpreted as the paleographic abbreviation of the verb "to want." Addends are simply juxtaposed without any plus sign between them; since brackets had not been invented, negative members had to be brought together behind the minus symbol. To designate a fraction whose denominator is a long number or a polynomial, the numerator and denominator are separated by the Greek word for "divided by." The Greek system of numerals is used.

Since Diophantus did not wish to write a textbook, he gives only general indications for computation. Only two rules are stated explicitly: a negative term multiplied by a negative yields a positive, and a positive multiplied by a negative yields a negative. Only in the treatment of linear equations does he go into more detail: one should "add the negative terms on both sides, until the terms on both sides are positive, and then again . . . subtract like from like until one term only is left on each side."

The problems presented in the *Arithmetica* are heterogeneous and difficult to classify definitively. Some of the categories of indeterminate problems are: 1) polynomials (or other algebraic expressions) to be represented as squares; 2) polynomials to be represented as cube numbers; 3) to form two polynomials such that one is a square and the other a cube; 4) given numbers to be decomposed into parts; 5) a number is to be decomposed into squares. These are not grouped in the text by type but are scattered throughout the work, interspersed with many other types. Diophantus generally proceeds from the simple to the more difficult, both in the degree of the equation and in the number of unknowns; however, the books always contain exercises belonging to various groups of problems.

In only a few cases can one recognize generally applicable methods of solution in the computations that Diophantus presents, for he considers each case separately, often obtaining an individual solution by means of brilliant strategems. A solution must not be negative, but need not be a whole number; it must be rational. Although aware that many solutions are possible, he does not present a general solution. Achievement of a general solution would have been hampered by two circumstances: Diophantus can symbolically represent only one unknown—most often, definite numbers immediately take the place of the unknowns and particularize the problem; and he lacks a symbol for the general number n. Among the methods he uses are balancing and completion of equations; solving for one unknown in terms of another; reduction of the number of unknowns through the substitution of definite numbers at the beginning; reduction of the degree of the equation by substitution of a definite number, or a function of the first unknown, for one or more unknowns; reckoning backward; approximation to limits; and application of number-theory relations.

Many of the procedures used by Diophantus can be found in preexisting Greek, Babylonian, and Chinese texts. Consequently, he certainly was not, as he has often been called, the father of algebra. Nevertheless, his remarkable, if unsystematic, collection of indeterminate problems, with its new symbolism, is a singular achievement that was not fully appreciated and further developed until much later. His number-theory propositions were taken up by mathematicians of the seventeenth century, generalized, and proved, thereby creating modern number theory.

DIOSCORIDES, also known as **Pedanius Dioscorides of Anazarbus** (*b. Anazarbus, near Tarsus in Cilicia; fl.* A.D. *50–70*), pharmacy, medicine, chemistry, botany.

Although numerous treatises in Greek and Latin have been attributed to Dioscorides, only *De materia medica* is now considered to be his. Written in five books, the treatise discusses over 600 plants, thirty-five animal products, and ninety minerals in simple, concise Greek. It was by far the largest pharmaceutical guide in antiquity, and determined the general form of later pharmacopoeias, both Eastern and Western. Galen, always a severe critic, acknowledged Dioscorides' work to be the best of its kind and showed his respect by numerous citations. Dioscorides was an empiricist, who cautioned his readers that knowledge of plants was gained by experience. He cited the need to study each plant in relation to its habitat, to observe rigorously the plants at all seasons, to note all parts from the first shoots to the seeds, to prepare each medicine with precision, and to judge each medicine by its merits. For each item generally he gave a Greek synonym; a deposition on the substance's origin and physical characteristics; a discourse on the mode of preparation of the medicine; and, finally, a list of its medicinal uses with occasional notations of harmful side effects. Often he relates information about how the simple is compounded in a prescription; further, he gives dietetic hints and even tests for detecting a fraudulent preparation. Dioscorides also gives directions for the proper gathering and storage of medicines. He says that whenever possible he saw plants with his own eyes but that he also relied on questioning people in the course of his travels and on consulting previously written works. He was the first to recognize the extensive use of medicines from all three of the natural kingdoms—animal, vegetable, and mineral.

Dioscorides was largely responsible for determining modern plant nomenclature, both popular and scientific, because of the reliance of later authorities on his work. Numerous and extensive textual modifications obscure our knowledge of Dioscorides' own Greek text; also, it is not known whether the original illustrations were done by Dioscorides himself or by Crateuas the rhizotomist. The most illustrious edition of *De materia medica* was by Mattioli (Venice, 1554): so many editions and translations were made from this critical edition that it is said that this printing is the basic work for modern botany. A pseudo-Dioscoridean text known as *De herbis femininis*, based on Dioscorides but severely edited, with additions from other writers, was very popular during the early Middle Ages.

DIRICHLET, GUSTAV PETER LEJEUNE (*b. Düren, Germany, 1805; d. Göttingen, Germany, 1859*), mathematics.

Precociously interested in mathematics. Studied at Jesuit college in Bonn; teachers included Ohm. Went to Paris (1822) to pursue mathematical studies at Collège de France and Faculté des Sciences; work as a tutor led to acquaintance with leading intellectuals, including Fourier, whose work was to influence his. Encouraged by Humboldt to return to Germany (1826); taught at University of Breslau; moved to Berlin (1828) to teach at the military academy and the university. Visited Italy (1843–44) with his close friend Karl Gustav Jacobi. Replaced Gauss at University of Göttingen (1855).

Dirichlet worked extensively in algebraic number theory, inspired by Gauss's *Disquisitiones arithmeticae*. He addressed such topics as Fermat's equation, quadratic forms, prime divisors of polynomials, Gaussian integers, and the quadratic and biquadratic laws of reciprocity. In his first work on analytic number theory he proved the prime number theorem (1837): Any arithmetical series of integers $an + b$, $n = 0, 1, 2, \ldots$, where a and b are relatively prime, must include an infinite number of primes. He went on to study quadratic forms with rational coefficients, convergence of series, Gaussian sums, and to search for a general theory of algebraic numbers. The first application of Dirichlet's important "box principle" (if one distributes more than n objects in n boxes, then at least one box must contain more than one object) appears in a paper of 1842 on quadratic forms with Gaussian coefficients. One part of algebraic number theory, the theory of units, had its beginning in Dirichlet's work on an equation of John Pell, $x^2 - Dy = N$, when he succeeded (1846) in establishing the complete result for the Abelian group of units in an algebraic number field. Dirichlet's *Vorlesungen über Zahlentheorie* (1863) was published by his pupil and friend Richard Dedekind, who added several supplements of his own to later editions.

Another area of interest to Dirichlet was analysis and mathematical physics. In 1829 he published a method of determining convergence of Fourier series which became classic. He introduced (1837) the modern concept of a function $y = f(x)$ as a correspondence that associates with each real x in an interval some unique value denoted by $f(x)$. He applied his methods to problems in heat theory, hydrodynamics, and general mechanics. In the course of this work he dealt with the boundary value problem, now known as Dirichlet's problem, in which it is attempted determine a potential function satisfying Laplace's equation and having prescribed values on a given surface. This type of problem plays an important role in numerous physical and mathematical theories, such as those of potentials, heat, magnetism, and electricity. Mathematically it can be extended to an arbitrary number of dimensions.

DITTMAR, WILLIAM (*b. Umstadt, [near Darmstadt], Germany, 1833; d. Glasgow, Scotland, 1892*), chemistry.

While working in Bunsen's laboratory in Heidelberg was befriended by Henry Roscoe, who invited him to England; worked at Owens College, Manchester, Edinburgh University, and Anderson's College, Glasgow. Analyzed samples of seawater collected during the voyage of H.M.S. *Challenger* (1872–76); confirmed Forchhammer's discovery that although the salinity of seawater varies from place to place, the ratios of the principal constituents to each other remain almost constant. Also studied atomic weight of platinum and gravimetric composition of water.

DIVINI, EUSTACHIO (*b. San Severino delle Marche [near Ancona], Italy, 1610; d. Rome, Italy, 1685*), optical instrumentation.

Among the first to develop technology for production of scientifically designed optical instruments. Studied with Benedetto Castelli; was rival of Guiseppe Campani. Constructed an innovative compound microscope (1648); developed a doublet lens for microscopes; constructed telescopes of long focus. Using his instruments he made a map of the moon (1649) and observed the rings of Saturn and spots and satellites of Jupiter (leading to a controversy with Huygens).

DIVIŠ, PROKOP (also **Procopius Divisch** or **Diwisch**) (*b. Žamberk, Bohemia, 1698; d. Přímětice, near Znojmo, Moravia, 1765*), electricity.

One of most eminent Czech scholars of mid-eighteenth century, although largely self-educated. Most important studies were on atmospheric electricity: performed experiments demonstrating effects of the conductive point; applied point-effect analogy to prevention of lightning. Constructed (1754) a large metal conductor on a wooden frame, 108 feet high, connected to the ground by four iron chains. The grounding made his conductor the first to afford actual protection from lightning. Also interested in therapeutic applications of electricity.

DIXON, HAROLD BAILY (*b. London, England, 1852; d. Lytham, England, 1930*), chemistry.

Studied at Oxford with A. V. Harcourt; held chair of chemistry, Owens College, Manchester (from 1886). Leading authority on gaseous explosions, created international interest in combustion research. Discovered incombustibility of purified and dried gases; studied rate and propagation of explosions, finding very great flame speeds by photographic methods; measured ignition temperatures of gases and gas mixtures.

DIXON, HENRY HORATIO (*b. Dublin, Ireland, 1869; d. Dublin, 1953*), botany.

Graduated Trinity College, Dublin (1891); studied with Eduard Strasburger (Bonn, 1891–93); taught at Dublin. Did early work in cytology; developed sterile culture methods for seedlings (1892); studied resistance of seeds to heat, cold, and poisons. With John Joly published (1894) tension theory of ascent of sap in trees, building on work of Strasburger, François Donny, and Berthelot and on transpiration experiments. Continued to perfect the theory, published two further accounts (1909, 1914).

DIXON, JEREMIAH (*b. Bishop Auckland, Durham, England, 1733; d. Cockfield, Durham, England, 1779*), astronomy.

Through acquaintance with John Bird was appointed assistant to Charles Mason on Royal Society expedition to observe transit of Venus (1761, Cape of Good Hope). With Mason, surveyed long-disputed boundary between Pennsylvania and Maryland (1763–68), putting a stop to quarrels between the two colonies; also calculated length of a degree of latitude (363,763 feet, 470 less than mod-

ern figure). Observed 1769 transit of Venus at Hammerfest.

DOBELL, CECIL CLIFFORD (*b. Birkenhead, England, 1886; d. London, England, 1949*), protozoology.

Studied at Trinity College, Cambridge (B.A., 1906; M.A., 1910; Sc.D., 1942), under Adam Sedgwick; also in Munich, under Richard Hertwig (1907). Taught at Imperial College of Science and Technology, London; worked at Wellcome Bureau of Scientific Research, and National Institute for Medical Research, Hampstead. Best known for meticulous researches on human intestinal protozoa, including careful self-infection, which elucidated the *in vitro* life histories and the cross-infectivity of most species of human and simian intestinal amoebae. Also wrote on history of science, including a remarkable biography of Leeuwenhoek.

DÖBEREINER, JOHANN WOLFGANG (*b. Hof an der Saale, Germany, 1780; d. Jena, Germany, 1849*), chemistry.

Self-educated; served as apothecary's apprentice, then manufactured pigments and drugs and published on them. Through recommendation of A. F. Gehlen and support of Goethe, was invited to teach in technical college of University of Jena (1810). Taught and worked on practical chemistry (illuminating gas, conversion of starch into sugar, fermentation of alcohol). Studied platinum: investigated oxides, complex salts, and platinum black; constructed pneumatic gas lighter utilizing hydrogenation of spongy platinum. Wrote on stoichiometry. Studied catalytic action of pyrolusite. Developed method to separate calcium and magnesium. Chief contribution resulted from study of weights of chemical elements: elucidated relations of specific gravity and chemical affinity to atomic weight within triads of similar elements.

DODART, DENIS (*b. Paris, France, 1634; d. Paris, 1707*), botany, physiology.

Graduated from Faculty of Medicine, Paris (1660); practiced medicine, was active in Academy of Sciences. In botany, published preliminary study for Academy containing recommendations for methodology of botanical research, advocating phytochemical analysis. Studied influence of gravitation on development of roots and stems and on fertilization and reproduction of plants; applied preformationist ideas to plant embryology. In physiology, pointed out the role of vocal cords in phonation; performed iatromechanical "static" experiments on changes in weight of body with nutrition and perspiration.

DODGSON, CHARLES LUTWIDGE (*b. Daresbury, Cheshire, England, 1832; d. Guildford, Surrey, England, 1898*), mathematics, logic.

Of a complex and retiring personality, a stutterer and uninspiring lecturer in mathematics (at Christ Church, Oxford, his alma mater), was ordained in the Church of England but without ecclesiastic appointment. Dodgson published extensively: thirteen books (six for children, including the *Alice* books) and hundreds of pamphlets and papers. His scholarly output, which often reveals a lack of awareness of contemporary research, falls into four main groups: determinants, geometry, mathematics of tournaments and elections, and recreational logic. His most interesting publication in geometry was a five-act comedy, engagingly written, entitled *Euclid and His Modern Rivals*, which is an attack on the changing method of teaching classical geometry and not, as is sometimes assumed, on non-Euclidean geometry. In writing on tournaments and voting theory he advocated the use of degrees of preference in voting schedules, and was the first to use matrix notation in the handling of multiple decisions. His work on logic was written entirely under his pseudonym, Lewis Carroll; he was interested in diagrammatization of the logic of classes and modified Venn's diagrams by making their boundaries linear and by introducing colored counters.

DODOENS (DODONAEUS), REMBERT (*b. Mechelen, Netherlands [now Malines, Belgium], 1516; d. Leiden, Netherlands, 1585*), medicine, botany.

Licentiate in medicine, University of Louvain (1535); traveled extensively; municipal physician, Mechelen (1548–74); imperial physician, Vienna (1574–80); taught at Leiden University (from 1582). Published on cosmography, physiological tables, and, most importantly, on botany. Building on the work of Brunfels, Bock, and Leonhart Fuchs, he wrote extensively on medical botany, with illustrations and synonymy, and on the botany of the Flemish provinces. In *Stirpium historiae . . .* (1583), his major work, he divided plants into twenty-six groups and introduced many new families, adding a wealth of illustration either original or borrowed from Dioscorides, de l'Écluse, or de L'Obel.

DOELTER (CISTERICH Y DE LA TORRE), CORNELIO AUGUST SEVERINUS (*b. Arroyo, Guayama, Puerto Rico, 1850; d. Kolbnitz, Carinthia, Austria, 1930*), chemical mineralogy.

Studied at Paris, Freiburg, Heidelberg (Ph.D., 1872), and Vienna. Worked for Imperial Geological Survey (1873), University of Graz (1876–1907), and University of Vienna (1875–76, 1907–21). Did extensive and important work in petrology: investigated origin of dolomite, surveyed volcanic regions, explained laterite formation. Felt microscopic and chemical investigation of igneous rock and the exact observation of geological occurrence to be the foundation of all petrology, and insisted on confirmation of all suppositions through experiment. Using methods of physical chemistry, studied remelting and recrystallization, influence of mineralizers, behavior of fused silicates, melting points of minerals and mixtures, and magmatic differentiation. Experimentally verified Rosenbusch's order of crystallization series and related it to solubility, force and velocity of crystal growth, stability, cooling rates, and percentage of mineralizers; distinguished different types of differentiation. Measured viscosity. Also investigated mineral coloration, studying effects of radiation and of heating in gases.

DOGEL, VALENTIN ALEXANDROVICH (*b. Kazan, Russia, 1882; d. Leningrad, U.S.S.R., 1955*), zoology.

Graduated St. Petersburg University (1904) and taught there (1914–55). Established evolutionary regularity of development of protozoa—the phenomenon of polymerization. In ecological parasitology, studied relation of parasitofauna to type of diet, migrations, and hibernation of host. Formulated evolutionary regularities of invertebrates.

DOHRN, FELIX ANTON (*b. Stettin, Germany [now Szczecin, Poland], 1840; d. Munich, Germany, 1909*), zoology.

Intermittent university studies; habilitated at Jena (1868) after study with Gegenbaur and Haeckel. Early interest in entomology, then in crustaceans. Carried out combined morphological and embryological investigations in an attempt to elucidate the phylogeny of arthropods. Studied homologies between arthropods and vertebrates; speculated that vertebrates had been derived from annelids. Primary contribution was the establishment of the Zoological Station in Naples: not only the first laboratory set up specifically for marine studies, but also the first institute formally organized for the sole pursuit of research. The station was conceived by Dohrn in 1870, and the doors opened in February 1874. The initial funds came from Dohrn's father, Carl August (an entomologist), and from the Prussian Academy of Sciences. A public aquarium in the building brought in some revenue, but continuing funds were provided mainly through the support of individual work tables by governments and institutions, to be used by investigators of their choosing. This brilliant notion made the laboratory a truly international venture. When the station opened, there were ten tables; by 1910 there were eighty in use at a single time. Laboratory facilities were excellent, as was the library, and many important pioneering experimental investigations were carried out. Especially significant were studies in comparative physiology and experimental embryology, which became the foundations of whole new sciences.

DOKUCHAEV, VASILII VASILEVICH (*b. Milyukovo, Smolensk province, Russia, 1846; d. St. Petersburg, Russia, 1903*), natural science, soil science, geography.

Initially studied for priesthood, then at St. Petersburg University in natural sciences (master's, 1871; doctorate, 1878). Taught at St. Petersburg University and worked with numerous scientific and governmental groups. First major work was on formation of river valleys: made profound study of the geological, orographical, and hydrographical peculiarities of the Russian plain. Gave a coherent explanation of the genesis of landforms and their relation to specific physical and geographical conditions of the past; on this basis he may be considered one of the founders of geomorphology. Was a pioneer in soil science: studied chernozem, worked on soil map of European Russia, made agricultural appraisals based on full description of the natural history of a province (geology, soil, water, plant and animal life). Considered soil as a special body that has developed as a result of climate, bedrock, plant and animal life, age of the land, and topography. His approach to the evolution of soils allowed him to discover all the complex connections between the soil-forming factors, including the factors of time and human activity. Created new classification of soils according to natural history; established zonality of soil and its coincidence with the zonality of climate, vegetation, and animal life. Promoted establishment of museums of natural history, and soil institutes and departments of soil science in universities. During drought of 1891 made extensive study of climate, agriculture, and water management in steppe belt.

DÖLLINGER, IGNAZ (*b. Bamberg, Germany, 1770; d. Munich, Germany, 1841*), physiology, embryology.

Studied at Bamberg, Würzburg, Vienna, Pavia (M.D., Bamberg, 1794); taught at Bamberg, Würzburg, and Munich (from 1823). Applied *Naturphilosophie* to physiology and embryology, but major emphasis was on observation and experiment. Improved the microscope; made observations of blood circulation, paid special attention to red and white blood cells and their intravascular and extravascular fates in different tissues. Stimulated research on morphology of developing chick; recognized early stages of embryonic differentiation.

DOLLO, LOUIS ANTOINE MARIE JOSEPH (*b. Lille, France, 1857; d. Brussels, Belgium, 1931*), paleontology.

Graduated from University of Lille (1877), where taught by Gosselet and Giard. Worked at Royal Museum of Natural History, Brussels (from 1882); taught at Brussels University (from 1909). Studied adaptation among fossil reptiles and other vertebrates, laying foundations of ethological methodology; studied transitions between sea life and land life; elucidated evolution of lungfish. Applied ethological methods to invertebrates and to living forms, particularly to evolution of marsupials. Enriched Darwinism by laws on irreversibility of evolution.

DOLLOND, JOHN (*b. London, England, 1706; d. London, 1761*), optics.

Initially a silk weaver; joined eldest son, Peter, in optical instrument business (1752). Made improvements to telescope. Achieved fame for developing achromatic telescope objective lens, composed of two different kinds of glass (1758); this had been previously discovered (1729–33) by Chester More Hall, but not publicized or exploited by him, and Dollond was awarded the patent.

DOLOMIEU, DIEUDONNÉ (called **DÉODAT**) **DE GRATET DE** (*b. Dolomieu, Dauphiné, France, 1750; d. Châteauneuf, Saône-et-Loire, France, 1801*), geology.

Member of the Sovereign and Military Order of the Knights of Malta from youth. Made geological observations and collected minerals during frequent travels while in service of the Order: Anjou and Brittany (1775), Alps and Italy (1776), Portugal (1778). Retired from active service (1779 or 1780), maintaining residence in Malta, and continued travels: Sicily (1781), Pyrenees (1782), Italy and Elba (1784), Italy and Corsica (1786), and in the Alps in 1789 and frequently thereafter. Developed political differences with superiors and left Malta (1791) for Paris; initially sympathetic to Revolution, but dismayed by its excesses. Taught at École des Mines (from 1796). Member of Napoleon's expedition to Egypt (1798), maneuvered into taking part in negotiations for capitulation of Malta; a storm on the return voyage led to capture and imprisonment in Messina for twenty-one months. After release, began teaching at Muséum d'Histoire Naturelle, but died soon after.

Known primarily for studies of volcanic substances and regions, inspired by correspondence with Barthélemy Faujas de Saint-Fond. Considered basalt to be of volcanic origin. Studied nature and source of volcanic ejecta: mineralogical nature of lava depended on the conception of lavas as being warm and viscous, but never especially hot, with an intrinsic source of heat which might be or contain sulfur; lavas are not vitrifications, and their components do not decompose. Volcanic products constitute a significant proportion of the earth's features, but historically volcanic activity was an occasional event of inferior significance; volcanic effects were limited both spatially and temporally. Aqueous agents were the outstanding causes of geological change. The oldest rocks were precipitated out of a universal fluid which was not water alone, but contained another agent, perhaps of the nature of phlogiston; precipitation took place in reverse order of solubility, in a slow and orderly fashion. A series of violent upheavals (whose cause was uncertain) then determined once and for all the major irregularities of the earth's surface. Subsequent alterations were brought about by "transport," or mechanical deposits deriving from degradation of the mountainous uplands, and by catastrophic currents. Dolomieu steadfastly believed in recurrent catastrophic alteration of the fundamentally established order of things, and in the great variable intensity of geological forces; violent means were the principal causes of change in the earth's surface, and the geological time scale was accordingly short.

In mineralogy, worked toward a mineral classification based on Haüy's integrant molecule. Described a mineral later named for him, dolomite.

DOMAGK, GERHARD (*b. Lagow, Brandenburg, Germany, 1895; d. Burgberg, Germany, 1964*), medicine, chemistry, pharmacology.

M.D. from University of Kiel (1921). Taught at University of Greifswald, then at University of Münster (from 1925); director of research in experimental pathology and bacteriology at I. G. Farbenindustrie (from 1927). Did influential work in chemotherapy: in testing azo dyes as antibacterial agents, discovered antistreptococcal action of prontosil rubrum (4′-sulfonamide-2,4-diaminoazobenzol); published masterful evaluation of the new drug (1935). Other investigators established that the azo component dissociated *in vivo* and that the liberated sulfonamide radical was responsible for the antibacterial effect, an important discovery since sulfonamide could be produced far more cheaply than prontosil; the development of sulfa drugs followed rapidly. Domagk was awarded the 1939 Nobel Prize in physiology or medicine, but prevented from accepting it by the Nazis. Later work was on chemotherapy of tuberculosis with thiosemicarbazones, and on chemotherapy of cancer.

DOMBEY, JOSEPH (*b. Mâcon, France, 1742; d. Montserrat, West Indies, 1794*), medicine, botany.

Doctor (M.D., Montpellier, 1767) and naturalist (studied with Antoine-Laurent Jussieu and Lemonnier, from 1772, Paris). Explored Peru and Chile with Ruiz and Pavón (1777–85), studying botany, natural resources, archaeology; collected many plants; introduced Araucanian pine into naval construction.

DOMINGO DE SOTO. *See* **Soto, Domingo de.**

DOMINIC GUNDISSALINUS. *See* **Gundissalinus, Dominicus.**

DOMINICUS DE CLAVASIO, also known as **Dominicus de Clavagio, Dominicus Parisiensis,** or **Dominic de Chivasso** (*fl. mid-fourteenth century*), mathematics, medicine, astrology.

Wrote popular *Practica geometriae.* Also wrote *questiones* on *De caelo* of Aristotle. His theory of impetus influenced by Oresme and Buridan: impetus is a quality; a body in violent motion possesses both impetus and an "actual force." Dominicus may have connected impetus with acceleration rather than velocity.

DOMINIS, MARKO ANTONIJE (*b. Rab, Yugoslavia, 1560; d. Rome, Italy, 1626*), physics.

Studied at Padua; taught at Verona, Padua, and Brescia. Catholic archbishop whose *De republica ecclesiastica,* urging unity of all Christian churches, caused his flight to England and subsequent imprisonment in Rome by the Inquisition. Wrote work on geometrical optics and theory of the rainbow; knowledge of refraction incomplete. Also wrote work on tides, advocating sphericity of earth and theorizing that moon and sun influence the sea in a manner analogous to a magnet; summed up influences of both bodies in any position, thus accounting for all the different elevations of the sea; recognized vertical motion in tide wave.

DOMNINUS OF LARISSA (*b. Larissa, fl. fifth century* A.D.), mathematics, philosophy.

Fellow pupil with (and rival of) Proclus at Neoplatonic school of Athens. Nothing survives of his philosophy; held theory that comets were composed of dry vapor. Wrote manual of arithmetic, drawing on Euclid and Theon of Smyrna and turning away from ideas of Nicomachus of Gerasa; treated numbers and theory of means and proportions.

DONALDSON, HENRY HERBERT (*b. Yonkers, N.Y., 1857; d. Philadelphia, Pa., 1938*), neurology.

Studied at Yale, College of Physicians and Surgeons, Johns Hopkins (Ph.D., 1895, under G. Stanley Hall), and in Europe under Forel, Gudden, Golgi, and others. Taught at Johns Hopkins, Clark University (Worcester, 1889–92), University of Chicago (1892–98); head of Wistar Institute of Anatomy and Biology, Philadelphia, from 1905. Studied growth and development of human brain from birth to maturity; relationship of weight and length of brain and spinal cord to that of entire body; age equivalence between man and experimental rat. Helped to found Marine Biological Laboratory, Woods Hole.

DONATI, GIOVAN BATTISTA (*b. Pisa, Italy, 1826; d. Florence, Italy, 1873*), astronomy.

Studied under Mossotti at University of Pisa; worked at Florence observatory (director from 1864); supervised construction of Arcetri observatory (1864–72). Made many observations of comets (discovered comet named for him on 2 June 1858). Applied spectroscopy to astronomy, developed new spectroscopes, obtained first spectrum of a comet and deduced comet's composition, studied sun and atmosphere; wrote on physical structure of sun and its distance from earth.

DONDERS, FRANCISCUS CORNELIS (*b. Tilburg, Netherlands, 1818; d. Utrecht, Netherlands, 1889*), physiology, ophthalmology.

Trained in military medicine and at Utrecht University; M.D. from Leiden University (1840). Taught at University of Utrecht (from 1842), professor of physiology (from 1862), dean of medical faculty; influential in education, concerned to make science serve the needs of humanity. Research and teaching in histochemistry and physiology led to specialization in ophthalmology: visited eye clinics in England and France, used own money to establish polyclinic in Utrecht which became a center for both research and teaching.

DONDI, GIOVANNI (*b. Chioggia, Italy, 1318; d. Milan, Italy, 1389*), horology, astronomy, medicine.

Son of Jacopo de'Dondi dall'Orologio, with whom he is often confused. Physician to Emperor Charles IV. Taught at universities of Padua, Florence, and Pavia. Wrote on diet during times of plague, and on hot springs near Padua. Most known for elaborate astronomical clock, constructed from 1348 to 1364 and given a detailed, illustrated description in *Tractatus astrarii* or *Tractatus planetarii;* the astrarium, inspired by Campanus of Novara, is one of the earliest geared equatoria, driven by clockwork. A modern replica is in the Museum of History and Technology, Washington, D.C.

DONNAN, FREDERICK GEORGE (*b. Colombo, Ceylon, 1870; d. Canterbury, England, 1956*), physical chemistry.

Studied at Leipzig with Wislicenus and Ostwald, at Berlin with van't Hoff, and at University College, London, with Ramsay; taught at Liverpool and University College. Helped introduce physical chemistry into Britain; most influential work was on membrane equilibrium in the presence of a non-dialyzable electrolyte. Later interested in philosophy of biology.

DOPPELMAYR, JOHANN GABRIEL (*b. Nuremberg, Germany, 1671* [?]; *d. Nuremberg, 1750*), astronomy, mathematics, physics, history of mathematics.

Studied and later taught (from 1704) at Aegidien Gymnasium, Nuremberg. Wrote extensively, primarily expounding ideas of others. Made astronomical and meteorological observations, performed physical experiments. Translated works by Thomas Streete, John Wilkins, Nicolas Bion. Published important collection of biographies of mathematicians, artists, and instrument makers of Nuremberg. Popularized electrical experimentation.

DOPPLER, JOHANN CHRISTIAN (*b. Salzburg, Austria, 1803; d. Venice, Italy, 1853*), mathematics, physics, astronomy.

Taught at State Technical Academy, Prague (1841–47), Mining Academy at Schemnitz, and Physical Institute and Royal Imperial University of Vienna (1850–52). Famed for enunciation of Doppler principle (1842), which relates the observed frequency of a wave to the motion of the source or the observer relative to the medium in which the wave is propagated. Doppler mentioned application of the principle to acoustics and to optics, particularly to colored appearance of double stars, but his optical reasoning was not always cogent. First experimental verification of acoustical Doppler effect was performed by Buys Ballot (1845), using trumpeters on a moving train. Fizeau suggested application to spectral line shifts in astronomy (1848). Optical effect first confirmed terrestrially by Belopolsky (1901). Modified by relativity, the Doppler principle is a major astronomical tool.

DÖRFFEL, GEORG SAMUEL (*b. Plauen, Vogtland, Germany, 1643; d. Weida, Germany, 1688*), astronomy, theology.

Educated at Leipzig and Jena. An amateur observer who described path of comet of 1680, and possibly other comets, as a parabola with the sun at the focus. Published reports of measurements on comets of 1672, 1677, and 1682 (Halley's). Corresponded with Gottfried Kirch. Discovered new method for determining distance of a body from earth with observations from only one site.

DORN, GERARD (*b. Belgium [?]; fl. Basel, Switzerland, and Frankfurt, Germany, 1566–84*), medicine, alchemy, chemistry.

Contributed significantly, through translations, commentaries, and his own writings, to the rapid dissemination of Paracelsian doctrines. Published a dictionary of Paracelsian terms. His views on the philosophical aspects of alchemy were important to C. G. Jung.

DORNO, CARL W. M. (*b. Königsberg, Prussia [now Kaliningrad, U.S.S.R.], 1865; d. Davos, Switzerland, 1942*), biometeorology.

Studied at Königsberg University (doctorate, 1904). Established private physical-meteorological observatory in Davos to measure and record solar and celestial radiation; improved instrumentation. Determined energies of single spectral regions; investigated annual and diurnal variation of radiation; did studies of ultraviolet radiation; deduced concept of biological cooling.

DOROTHEUS OF SIDON (*fl. Egypt [?], first century* A.D.), astrology.

One of most influential astrologers of antiquity: his theories form the basis of the astrological treatises of Firmicus Maternus, Hephaestio of Thebes, and Rhetorius of Egypt, and he became one of the chief authorities for Arabic astrologers. His work was originally published as five books in hexameters.

DOSITHEUS (*fl. Alexandria, second half of the third century* B.C.), mathematics, astronomy.

Colleague of Conon of Samos; corresponded with Archimedes and transmitted his geometrical works to scholars of Alexandria. Cited by Geminus and Ptolemy for work on calendar and weather prognostications for *parapegma*.

DOUGLAS, JAMES (*b. Baads, Scotland, 1675; d. London, England, 1742*), medicine, natural history, letters.

M.D., Rheims (1699). Specialized in anatomy and obstetrics; writings include books on comparative myology (1707), the peritoneum (1730), natural history, and bibliography. Left an interesting series of case notes. Realized the importance of anatomical teaching to the advancement of medicine, and was among the first to advertise classes; provided strong encouragement to William Hunter, who came to him as a resident pupil in 1741.

DOUGLAS, JESSE (*b. New York, N.Y., 1897; d. New York, 1965*), mathematics.

Educated at City College of New York (B.S., 1916) and Columbia University (Ph.D., 1920); taught at Columbia (1920–26), Massachusetts Institute of Technology (1930–36), Brooklyn College and Columbia (1942–54), and City College (from 1955). Wrote on geometry, analysis, and group theory. Published complete solution to problem of Plateau (proving the existence of a surface of least area bounded by a given contour); Douglas' solution is highly generalized, applying even to a contour in space of any number of dimensions. Also published first complete solution of the inverse problem of the calculus of variations for three-dimensional space.

DOVE, HEINRICH WILHELM (*b. Liegnitz, Prussia [now Legnica, Poland], 1803; d. Berlin, Germany, 1879*), meteorology, physics.

Studied at University of Breslau with H. W. Brandes; taught at University of Königsberg (doctorate, 1826) and at University of Berlin (from 1829). In physics, studied terrestrial magnetism, polarization phenomena, especially the optical properties of crystals, and induced electricity; gave popular experiment-illustrated lectures. Main interest was meteorology: drew climatological maps of heat distribution; formulated "law of rotation" of meteorological phenomena, founded on assumption of wind as primary factor, and was thus first to find a system in weather changes.

DOWNING, ARTHUR MATTHEW WELD (*b. Carlow, Ireland, 1850; d. London, England, 1917*), astronomy.

Studied at Trinity College, Dublin (B.A., 1871; M.A., 1881); worked at Royal Observatory, Greenwich (1873–91), and Nautical Almanac Office (1892–1910); a founder of the British Astronomical Association (1890). Chief contribution was computation of precise positions and movements of astronomical bodies: corrected systematic errors of star tables, calculated (with G. Johnstone Stoney) perturbations of Leonid meteors. Greatly improved *Nautical Almanac* (1896–1912). Contributed significantly to amateur astronomy by advance publication of particulars of astronomical occurrences.

DRACH, JULES JOSEPH (*b. Sainte-Marie-aux-Mines, near Colmar, France, 1871; d. Cavalaire, Var, France, 1941*), mathematics.

Taught at universities of Clermont-Ferrand, Lille, Poitiers, Toulouse, and Paris (1913). Approached theory of integration of differential equations by "logical" classification of transcendental quantities satisfying the rational system verified by the solutions; introduced concept of "rationality group"; drew on results of Lie, Émile Picard, and Vessiot and extended studies of ballistic equations and equations of families of curves. With Émile Borel prepared lectures of Poincaré and Jules Tannery for publication; worked on publication of collected works of Poincaré.

DRAPARNAUD, JACQUES-PHILIPPE-RAYMOND (*b. Montpellier, France, 1772; d. Montpellier, 1804*), zoology, botany.

Published works on politics, philosophy, grammar, physics, mineralogy, zoology, and botany. In comparative physiology, introduced idea of vital phenomena common to animal and plant life and attempted to reduce these phenomena to physical and chemical laws. Studied history of confervae, and compiled herbal of algae.

DRAPER, HENRY (*b. Prince Edward County, Va., 1837; d. New York, N.Y., 1882*), astronomy.

Son of John William Draper. Educated (M.D., 1858) and employed (from 1860) in medicine at the University of the City of New York. Draper achieved fame primarily for his astronomical avocation, pursued at his own expense; he was a gifted inventor and deft technician who made most of his own equipment. A visit to Parsons' observatory in Ireland (1857) led to the idea of combining photography and astronomy; by 1861 he had ground his first mirror and installed it in his new observatory at Hastings-on-Hudson, and began making daguerreotypes of the sun and moon. He continually improved the techniques of telescope construction and photography (he was a founding member of the American Photographic Society). In 1865 he became interested in spectrum analysis, and from 1867 to 1872 made preliminary studies of elemental spectra, photographing the solar spectrum as a reference scale for wavelength determination. In 1872 he made the first photograph of stellar spectrum lines (of Vega), and devised the spectrograph. Directed photographic department of U.S. commission to observe 1874 transit of Venus. Organized expedition (Edison was a member) to Rockies to observe solar eclipse of 1878; spectroscopy revealed that the corona shines largely by reflected light from solar disk. Visit to Huggins and Lockyer (1879) and improvement of dry photographic plates stimulated him to return to stellar spectroscopy; confirmed Huggins' discovery of hydrogen in Vega. Obtained many high-quality spectra of bright stars, moon, Mars and Jupiter, comet 1881 III, and Orion nebula. Also perfected clockwork drive mechanism to permit long-exposure direct photography of the moon and of the Orion nebula. By 1881 he had succeeded in making photography the best means of studying the sky.

DRAPER, JOHN WILLIAM (*b. St. Helens, Lancashire, England, 1811; d. Hastings-on-Hudson, N.Y., 1882*), chemistry, history.

Studied at London University under Edward Turner, who interested him in photochemistry; immigrated to Virginia (1832); M.D., University of Pennsylvania (1836). Taught chemistry at New York University (from 1839): was a founder of the School of Medicine, and encouraged establishment of the Ph.D. degree. Did pioneer work in photography: made temporary images (1837), one of earliest daguerreotype portraits (1839), first photograph of moon (1840), photographs of slides through a microscope (1850–56, to illustrate a physiology textbook), and probably the first photograph of the diffraction spectrum (1844). Deep concern was with photochemistry: enunciated principle (Grotthuss-Draper law) that only absorbed rays produce chemical change (1841); constructed tithonometer (1843) to measure light intensity by its effect on the combination of hydrogen with chlorine. Proved (1847) that all solid substances become incandescent at the same temperature, that with rising temperature they emit rays of increasing refrangibility, and that incandescent solids produce a continuous spectrum.

Found that maxima of luminosity and of heat in the spectrum coincide. Developed cyclical theory of history, influenced by Comte's law of historical development and profiting from popularity of Darwinism. Defended science against religionists.

DREBBEL, CORNELIUS (*b. Alkmaar, Netherlands, 1572; d. London, England, 1633*), mechanics, optics, technology.

Trained as engraver, but became famous for mechanical inventions. Best-known inventions included: 1) a *perpetuum mobile* operating by changes in atmospheric temperature and pressure, and employed in a clock; 2) thermostatic regulators for ovens, furnaces, and incubators; 3) optical instruments, including compound microscopes as early as 1619; 4) a submarine, based on principle of diving bell and perhaps with air-purification device; 5) tin mordant process for dyeing scarlet with cochineal. Published works on alchemical theory and its application to medicine.

DREYER, JOHANN LOUIS EMIL (*b. Copenhagen, Denmark, 1852; d. Oxford, England, 1926*), astronomy.

Studied at Copenhagen University (M.A., 1874; Ph.D., 1882); worked in Ireland, at Parsonstown, Dublin, and Armagh observatories. Published star catalog (1886), revised Herschel catalog of nebulae and clusters (1888) and supplemented it with two index catalogs. Edited scientific papers of Sir William Herschel, wrote biographies of Herschel and Brahe, collected and edited all the works and correspondence of Brahe.

DRIESCH, HANS ADOLF EDUARD (*b. Bad Kreuznach, Germany, 1867; d. Leipzig, Germany, 1941*), biology, philosophy.

Studied with August Weismann (Freiburg, 1886) and Haeckel (Jena, doctorate, 1889). Influential work in experimental embryology was done independently, principally at Zoological Station in Naples. Professional appointments were in natural philosophy at Heidelberg (1909), systematic philosophy at Cologne (1919), and philosophy at Leipzig (1921). Initially a mechanist, but results of his own experiments led him to vitalist outlook by 1895. Working with sea urchin eggs, used shaking method of Richard and Oskar Hertwig and Theodor Boveri to separate blastomeres at two-cell stage (1891); found that in this egg, in contrast with that of the frog, each blastomere could form a whole rather than a half larva. He concluded that the fate of a cell is a function of its position in the whole; its prospective potency is greater than its prospective significance; it is a harmonious equipotential system. This work confirmed experimentally that development is epigenetic, and provided the conceptual framework for the organizer concept later developed by Hans Spemann. In further experiments Driesch separated cells at later developmental stages, fused two embryos, and compressed eggs to alter cleavage pattern and affect distribution of nuclei (formation of normal larvae showed that all nuclei were equivalent). He disturbed the organization of mesenchyme cells (which subsequently returned to normal positions), and studied regeneration in adult hydroids and ascidians. He postulated (1894) that factors external to a cell influence its cytoplasm, which in turn influences the nucleus to produce substances that affect the cytoplasm, and that the influence of the nucleus on the cell body is mediated through enzymes. He also discussed the possibilities of embryonic induction.

DRUDE, PAUL KARL LUDWIG (*b. Brunswick, Germany, 1863; d. Berlin, Germany, 1906*), physics.

Introduced to physical optics by W. Voigt at Göttingen, where he studied and worked until 1894; subsequently worked at Leipzig (1894–1901), then directed institutes of physics at Giessen (1901–05) and Berlin (1905–06). From 1889, edited *Annalen der Physik*. His early work concentrated on the relationship between the physical properties and the optical characteristics of crystals; he discovered that the optical constants of some crystals were not independent of the state of the crystal's surface, and undertook the determination of the optical constants of a wide variety of substances with remarkable accuracy. Although initially an adherent of Neumann's mechanical theory of light propagation, his intensive comparison of that theory with Maxwell's electromagnetic view led him first to declare that in terms of the differential equations and necessary boundary conditions the two theories were equivalent (1892), and eventually to advocate Maxwell's theory. He thought it should be possible to explain electrical and optical properties of matter as the interaction of electromagnetic fields with electrical charges contained within the body. In investigating the relationship between optical and electrical constants and the constitution of substances, he measured coefficients of absorption in a wide variety of solutions and compared these to coefficients of conductivity for the same solutions; rather than the universal correlation predicted by Maxwellian theory, he found that a whole class of substances absorbed seventy-five centimeters radiation quite independent of their coefficient of conductivity. He was able to show that this selective absorption was directly related to chemical structure and that it was the hydroxyl radical that was responsible, thus establishing a practical analytical tool. Drude also developed an electron theory of metals: every metal contains a large number of free electrons (which he treated as a gas), nonconductors containing relatively few; only negative electrons are mobile; although average kinetic energy is high, velocity is limited by their very small mean free path (due mainly to collisions with atomic centers). He used this theory to explain the optical, thermal, and electrical properties of metals.

DRYGALSKI, ERICH VON (*b. Königsberg, Eastern Prussia [now Kaliningrad, U.S.S.R.], 1865; d. Munich, Germany, 1949*), geography.

Studied under von Richthofen at Bonn, Leipzig, and Berlin; taught at Berlin (1898–1906) and Munich (1906–35). An authority on polar and oceanic exploration; led important expeditions to western Greenland (1891, 1892–93) and polar ship *Gauss* expedition to South Pole (1901–03); developed conclusions from latter voyage over many years.

DUANE, WILLIAM (*b. Philadelphia, Pa., 1872; d. Devon, Pa., 1935*), physics, radiology.

A.B. from University of Pennsylvania (1892) and Harvard (1893; A.M., 1895). Studied in Germany with Emil Warburg, Landolt, Wallach, Nernst, and Planck (doctorate, 1897, Berlin). Taught at University of Colorado

(1898–1906); did research at Curie laboratory, Paris, 1904–05 and 1907–13; from 1913 held joint appointments at Harvard and at Huntington Hospital, Boston. Early studies were on electromagnetism and on physical chemistry. Learned radioactivity techniques from Curies; determined the total ionization produced by a radioactive source of given intensity, and then the total charge carried by the α and β rays; measured rate of evolution of heat from minute samples of radioactive substances. In Boston, worked on treatment of cancer by implantation of sources of intense radiation. Investigated X-ray therapy, turned to frequency-potential relations; with Franklin L. Hunt, announced Duane-Hunt law (1915), stating that there was a maximum frequency in the radiation produced by electrons of a given energy, and for this frequency the equation $E = hv$ held very closely. In the next two years Duane developed his law into a precision method for determining h. Made accurate measurements (1918–21) of X-ray excitation for a variety of elements, which were valuable to theoretical physicists working on atomic structure. In cancer therapy, developed technique of measuring X-ray dosage in terms of ionization of air, and secured official international adoption of this standard in 1928. Attempted theoretical explanation of X-ray diffraction.

DUBINI, ANGELO (*b. Milan, Italy, 1813; d. Milan, 1902*), medicine, helminthology.

M.D., University of Pavia (1837); worked at Ospedale Maggiore, Milan (from 1842). Promoted the new clinical medicine emphasizing anatomical diagnosis; anatomical-pathological work led to his discovery of a new human intestinal worm, *Anchylostoma duodenale* (1842), a hookworm with a high frequency of occurrence. Diagnosed and described electric chorea (Dubini's disease).

DUBOIS, FRANÇOIS. *See* **Sylvius, Franciscus.**

DUBOIS, JACQUES (Latin, **JACOBUS SYLVIUS**) (*b. Amiens, France, 1478; d. Paris, France, 1555*), medicine.

Generally known as Sylvius. Studied informally at Paris, formally at Montpellier (M.B., 1529; M.D., 1530); taught anatomy in Paris. A convinced Galenist, who attacked Vesalius, his former student, upon publication of the *Fabrica*. His own most important anatomical book was *In Hippocratis et Galeni physiologiae partem anatomicam isagoge* (1555, posthumous), based on the writings of Galen and of Niccolo Massa and on a certain amount of human anatomical dissection. When his observations differed from Galen's descriptions, he criticized the human structure, which he declared to have degenerated and thus to have betrayed Galen's earlier, correct descriptions. The *Isagoge* is noteworthy for its systematic presentation, the clear scheme for muscle identification based on attachments, and the introduction of anatomical terminology that is still in use.

DUBOIS-REYMOND, EMIL HEINRICH (*b. Berlin, Germany, 1818; d. Berlin, 1896*), electrophysiology.

Studied at universities of Berlin (doctorate, 1843) and Bonn, becoming acquainted with many teachers and researchers. A founder of Physikalische Gesellschaft (Berlin, 1845). Taught at Berlin Academy of Art (1848–53) and at University of Berlin (from 1854; professor of physiology, 1858; rector, 1869–70 and 1882–83). Editor of *Archiv für Anatomie, Physiologie und wissenschaftliche Medizin;* permanent secretary of Prussian Academy of Sciences (from 1876). Early interest in the history of animal electricity led to his lifelong concentration on the experimental analysis of animal electricity using the techniques of physics; with his friends Brücke, Ludwig, and Helmholtz he became a pioneer in the new physical orientation of physiology, which sought to explain all processes in an organism by means of physical, molecular, and atomic mechanisms, without drawing upon hypothetical vital forces. By creating new electrophysiological methods and apparatus he was the first to succeed in clarifying, eliminating, or avoiding the many sources of error; most of his experimental findings and technical procedures have remained valid, although some of his theories have not. Among his theories was that of the muscle fiber being made up of numerous peripolar electromotive molecules, each consisting of a positive equatorial zone and two negative polar zones; he interpreted the currents from intact, injured, and contracting muscles as having a single cause; he considered it possible for a chemical mechanism for transmitting stimulation from nerves to muscle fibers to coexist with the electrical mechanism. Much of his study was on electric fishes. He was deeply interested also in the molecular physics of organic metabolism, and lectured on such topics as diffusion, adsorption, and secretion. He retained an interest in history, and in later years became increasingly active in the public discussion of the relation between the natural sciences and the humanities; he considered the history of science the most important, but most neglected, part of cultural history. His arguments on problems of scientific boundaries and principles still arouse great interest.

DU BOIS-REYMOND, PAUL DAVID GUSTAV (*b. Berlin, Germany, 1831; d. Freiburg, Germany, 1889*), mathematics.

Brother of Emil du Bois-Reymond. Initially studied medicine at University of Zurich, turned to mathematical physics at University of Königsberg, specializing in study of liquids; doctorate from University of Berlin (1859). Taught at universities of Heidelberg (1865), Freiburg (1870), and Tübingen (1874–84). Worked on problems of infinitesimal calculus: in theory of differential equations was one of first to follow up Monge's idea of the "characteristic" of a partial differential equation, which he generalized for equations of the *n*th order. Demonstrated the mean-value theorem for definite integrals, a valuable aid in the study of Fourier series; attempted general exposition of fundamental concepts of the theory of functions in *Die allgemeine Functionentheorie* (1882).

DUBOSCQ, OCTAVE (*b. Rouen, France, 1868; d. Nice, France, 1943*), protistology, cytology.

Doctorates in medicine (Paris, 1894) and in science (1899). Teacher (Caen, 1900; Montpellier, 1904; Paris, 1923); director of Arago Laboratory at Banyuls-sur-Mer. Early research was on microanatomy of arthropods; later studies, many in collaboration with Urbain-Louis-Eugène Léger, contributed to knowledge of Protista: structure and cycle of schizophytes, spirochetes, and eccrinids; phylogeny and classification of sporozoans; reproduction of flagellates; fertilization of sponges.

DU BUAT, PIERRE-LOUIS-GEORGES (*b. Tortizambert, Normandy, France, 1734; d. Vieux-Condé, Flanders [now part of Nord, France], 1809*), hydraulics.

Became military engineer at age of seventeen. Forced to flee France during Revolution. Wrote *Principes d'hydraulique* (1779) containing analytical section and results of 200 tests on flow in pipes, artificial channels, and natural streams which were to be used for generations. First to demonstrate that the shape of the rear of a body is as important as the front in controlling its resistance. Du Buat's paradox states that the force exerted upon a stationary body by running water is greater than that required to move the same body at the same relative speed through still water.

DUCHESNE, JOSEPH, also known as Josephus Quercetanus (*b. L'Esture, Armagnac, Gascony, France, ca. 1544; d. Paris, France, 1609*), chemistry, medicine.

Also known as Sieur de la Violette. Studied at Montpellier and Basel (M.D., 1573); lived in Kassel and Geneva (1584–93) before becoming physician in ordinary to King Henry IV in Paris. Important in literature as well as in science and medicine. Wrote many works in defense of iatrochemistry and gave new recipes for pharmaceuticals. His five-element principle system comprised the three Paracelsian principles plus the Aristotelian water and earth; he rejected the four humors; he believed in the doctrine of signatures. His *De priscorum philosophorum verae medicinae materia . . .* (1603) initiated the debate over the chemical medicine at Paris, and its influence extended for more than half a century.

DUCLAUX, ÉMILE (*b. Aurillac, Cantal, France, 1840; d. Paris, France, 1904*), biochemistry.

After studies at École Normale Supérieure (1859–62) became assistant to Pasteur, with whom he remained closely associated while working in various cities. Returned to Paris (1878) to teach at the Institut Agronomique and at the Sorbonne (gave a course in microbiology, the first of its kind); taught at the Institut Pasteur (from 1888), succeeded Pasteur as director (1895). Supporter of Pasteur's work and theories; excellent teacher (pupils included Émile Roux); founder of *Annales de l'Institut Pasteur*. Research included physics (osmosis, molecular adhesion, surface tension) and chemistry (fermentation, role of enzymes in digestion, analysis of milk, cheese formation).

DUCROTAY DE BLAINVILLE, HENRI MARIE. *See* Blainville, Henri Marie Ducrotay de.

DUDITH (DUDITIUS), ANDREAS (*b. Buda [now Budapest], Hungary, 1533; d. Breslau, Germany [now Wrocław, Poland], 1589*), astronomy, astrology, mathematics.

Combined political and religious activity with humanist and scientific interests; amassed large library, including collection of Greek mathematical manuscripts. Known mainly for *De cometarum significatione* (1579) in which, influenced by Erastus, he rejected astrology and the terrestrial effects of comets. Initially supported Aristotelian theory of comets as sublunar exhalations, but Hagecius' measurement of cometary parallax convinced him that comets originated beyond the moon.

DUDLEY, ROBERT (*b. Sheen House, Surrey, England, 1573; d. Villa di Castello, Florence, Italy, 1649*), navigation.

Student at Christ Church, Oxford; knighted (1596); moved to Italy in 1605. Published *Dell'arcano del mare* (3 vols., 1646–47), one of great sea atlases of all time and the first with all maps drawn on Mercator's projections, as modified by Edward Wright; besides maps of the entire world, it contained information on navigation, naval strategy, shipbuilding, and coastal fortification.

DUFAY (DU FAY), CHARLES-FRANÇOIS DE CISTERNAI (*b. Paris, France, 1698; d. Paris, 1739*), physics.

After early military service (1712–21), became chemist in Académie des Sciences (1723; director, 1733 and 1738); eventually published at least one paper in each branch of science recognized by the Academy, perhaps the only man ever to do so. First work (1723) was on mercurial phosphor (light sometimes produced in the tube of a barometer by jostling); later (1730) returned to phosphorescence, making lengthy and systematic studies and giving recipes for producing phosphors from a wide variety of substances. Studied magnetism (1728–31) with equal thoroughness. Most notable work was on electricity; through his conviction of the universal character of electricity, and through systematic study of previous experiments and organization of new ones, Dufay was able to make substantial discoveries (1733): the relation between electrostatic attraction and repulsion, the existence of two distinct "electricities" (resinous and vitreous), the shocking effect of electricity when his body was insulated and an assistant tried to touch him, and (with Nollet, his protégé) the visible spark just before contact when the experiment was repeated at night. As director of Jardin Royal des Plantes (1732–39) he restored its plantings and extended its relations with similar institutions.

DUFOUR, GUILLAUME-HENRI (*b. Constance, Switzerland, 1787; d. Les Contamines [near Geneva], Switzerland, 1875*), technology.

Military engineer in French and Swiss armies; civil engineer in Switzerland; one of founders of military school at Thun. From 1833 did pioneering work in triangulation for topographical mapping of Swiss Confederation. Presided over Geneva international congress, 1864.

DUFRÉNOY, OURS-PIERRE-ARMAND (*b. Sevran, Seine-et-Oise, France, 1792; d. Paris, France, 1857*), geology, mineralogy.

Studied at École Polytechnique and École des Mines; taught at École des Mines (director from 1846) and modernized its curriculum; professor of mineralogy, Muséum d'Histoire Naturelle (1847). With Élie de Beaumont and under direction of Brochant de Villiers, prepared first modern geological map of France; also published memoirs on geology and crystallographic and chemical mineralogy, *Traité de minéralogie* (1844–47), and (with Élie de Beaumont) *Voyage métallurgique en Angleterre* (1827).

DUGAN, RAYMOND SMITH (*b. Montague, Mass., 1878; d. Philadelphia, Pa., 1940*), astronomy.

Graduated from Amherst College (B.A., 1899; M.A., 1902); Ph.D. from University of Heidelberg (1905, under Max Wolf). Working at Princeton (from 1905), made

long series of observations on a selected few eclipsing variables, producing data on size, brightness, distance apart, tidal distortion, and density variation. He was the first to detect reflection of light from a brighter star to its weaker partner. With H. N. Russell, wrote excellent elementary astronomy text.

DUGGAR, BENJAMIN MINGE (*b. Gallion, Ala., 1872; d. New Haven, Conn., 1956*), plant pathology.

Graduate student at Alabama Polytechnic Institute (M.Sc., 1892), Harvard (M.A., 1895), and Cornell (Ph.D.); also studied in Europe. Held appointments at University of Missouri, Cornell, Washington University, Missouri Botanical Garden, and University of Wisconsin. A founder of American Society of Agronomy and American Phytopathological Society; editor of *Botanical Abstracts for Physiology*. Wrote *Fungus Diseases of Plants* (1909), first monograph in any language devoted exclusively to plant pathology. Leading investigator of tobacco mosaic virus. As consultant to Lederle Division of American Cyanamid Company, discovered Aureomycin (1948).

DU HAMEL, JEAN-BAPTISTE (*b. Vire, Normandy, France, 1623; d. Paris, France, 1706*), institutional history.

Distinguished priest and humanist; known as anatomist, but also author of works on astronomy and natural philosophy. Held various ecclesiastic and academic appointments. First secretary of Académie Royale des Sciences (1666–97) and author of its first history (1698).

DUHAMEL, JEAN-MARIE-CONSTANT (*b. St.-Malo, France, 1797; d. Paris, France, 1872*), mathematics, physics.

Taught at École Polytechnique (1830–69), at École Normale Supérieure, and at the Sorbonne; students included J. L. F. Bertrand. Earliest research was on mathematical theory of heat, based on work of Fourier and Poisson. In analyzing temperature distribution in a solid with variable boundary temperature, he generalized a solution by Fourier and arrived at Duhamel's principle in partial differential equations. In acoustics, studied vibrating strings, vibrations of air in cylindrical and conical pipes, and harmonic overtones.

DUHAMEL DU MONCEAU, HENRI-LOUIS (*b. Paris, France, 1700; d. Paris, 1782*), agronomy, chemistry, botany, naval technology.

Attended science lectures at Jardin du Roi; elected to Académie Royale des Sciences (1728) after his demonstration that blight of the saffron plant was caused by a parasite. In chemistry, studied Frobenius' ether (with Jean Grosse); argued that salts had different fixed alkaline components, which were essentially soda and potash. Interest in botany and agronomy led to study of cultivation and use of timber; became naval inspector, and wrote on structural properties of wood and rigging of ships. Contributed to improvement of French agriculture by exposition (and occasional criticism) of theories of Jethro Tull.

DUHEM, PIERRE-MAURICE-MARIE (*b. Paris, France, 1861; d. Cabrespine, France, 1916*), physics, rational mechanics, physical chemistry, history of science, philosophy of science.

Duhem attended the Collège Stanislas from his eleventh year and later chose the École Normale. He published his first paper, on the application of the thermodynamic potential to electrochemical cells, in 1884, while still a student. He proceeded with distinction through the *licence* and *agrégation*, after meeting a setback with a thesis for the doctorate on the concept of thermodynamic potential in chemistry and physics that included an attack on Marcellin Berthelot's twenty-year-old principle of maximum work. Duhem later published the thesis as a book, *Le potentiel thermodynamique* (1886). He was placed under the necessity of preparing another subject for the doctorate; he received the degree in 1888 for a thesis on the theory of magnetism, this one falling within the area of mathematics. Unfortunately the enmity between Berthelot and Duhem was not dissipated until after 1900. Duhem blamed Berthelot, who was minister of education in 1886–87, together with the circle of liberal and free-thinking scientists who advised successive ministers, for preventing him from ever receiving the expected call to a professorship in Paris; he taught at Lille (1887–93), Rennes (1893–94), and Bordeaux (1894–1916). In 1900 he was elected to corresponding membership in the Academy of Sciences. In 1913 he was elected one of the first six nonresident members of the Academy.

Duhem's interests fell roughly into periods. Thermodynamics and electromagnetism predominated between 1884 and 1900, although he returned to them in 1913–16. He concentrated on hydrodynamics from 1900 to 1906. His interest in the philosophy of science was mostly in the period 1892–1906, and in the history of science from 1904, although his earliest historical papers date from 1895. The extraordinary volume of Duhem's production is impressive—nearly 400 papers and some twenty-two books.

Duhem published his major philosophical work, *La théorie physique, son objet et sa structure,* in 1906 after having largely completed his researches in physical science. What his philosophy purported to establish was that an energeticist approach was no less legitimate than a mechanistic one. The discussion explains how theories are to be judged and looked at merely in point of preference or policy; and in the absence of concrete facts, either type of theory would in principle be acceptable, so long as no metaphysical import be loaded into the choice. The issue was one that Duhem discussed in *L'évolution de la mécanique* (1902) and also in the essay "Physique de croyant," included in later editions of *La théorie physique.*

The most impressive monument to the scholarly fertility of that claim remains his massive contribution to the knowledge of medieval science in his three-volume *Études sur Léonard de Vinci* (1906–13) and the ten-volume *Système du monde* (1913–59) contain a detailed exposition of two theses: (1) a creative and unbroken tradition of physics, cosmology, and natural philosophy was carried on in the Latin West from about 1200 to the Renaissance, and (2) the results of this medieval activity were known to Leonardo da Vinci and Galileo, and played a seminal role in the latter's transformation of physics.

He early became convinced that the underlying descriptive theory for all of physics and chemistry would emerge from a generalized thermodynamics. The central commitment of his scientific life was the building up of such a science, one that would include electricity and magnetism as well as mechanics. His attempts culminated in the *Traité d'énergétique* (1911).

Duhem's *Traité de mécanique chimique* (1897–99) and *Thermodynamique et chimie* (1902) provided a whole generation of French physicists and chemists with their knowledge of chemical thermodynamics. He was the first (1887) to publish a critical analysis of Gibbs's "Equilibrium of Heterogeneous Substances"; in Duhem's paper is the first precise definition of a reversible process. He later pointed out in the "Commentaire aux principes de la thermodynamique" that there exist situations such as hysteresis where the limiting set of equilibrium states for the direction AB is not the same as that for the direction BA. Therefore, it is possible to go from A to B and back by quasi-static processes, but not reversibly. Duhem believed that the "Commentaire" (1892–94) was one of his more significant contributions. It contains a very detailed analysis of the steps leading from the statement of the second law of thermodynamics to the definitions of entropy and thermodynamic potential. It also contains an axiomatic treatment of the first law of thermodynamics which is surprisingly good by present-day standards.

In "Sur les déformations permanentes et l'hystérésis" (1896–1902) Duhem considered in some detail the thermodynamics of nonreversible but quasi-static processes and some irreversible processes, including hysteresis and creep. He provided the first explicit unrestricted proof of the Gibbs phase rule, based on Gibbs's suggestions, in "On the General Problem of Chemical Statics" (1898). At the same time he extended it beyond the consideration of just the intensive variables, giving the conditions necessary to specify the masses of the phases as well.

He attached great importance to his thermodynamics of false equilibrium and friction. According to Duhem, false equilibria can be divided into two classes: *apparent,* as for example a supersaturated solution, which, as a result of a small perturbation, returns instantly to thermodynamic equilibrium; and *real,* as for example organic compounds, such as diamond or petroleum constituents. Such compounds are unstable thermodynamically with respect to other substances but have remained unchanged for large perturbations throughout geological periods of time. Yet they will transform into the stable products if the perturbations are large enough (diamond to graphite by heating).

A major portion of Duhem's interest was focused on hydrodynamics and elasticity. His second book, *Hydrodynamique, élasticité, acoustique* (1891), had an important influence on mathematicians and physicists because it called attention to Hugoniot's work on waves. Duhem was a pioneer in trying to prove rigorous general theorems for Navier-Stokes fluids and for finite elasticity in Kelvin-Kirchhoff-Neumann bodies. His results are important and of sufficient interest later that his *Recherches sur l'hydrodynamique* (1903–04) was reprinted in 1961. He was the first to study wave propagation in viscous, compressible, heat-conducting fluids using stability conditions and the full resources of thermodynamics (*Recherches sur l'hydrodynamique*). He showed the then startling result that no true shock waves or higher order discontinuities can be propagated through a viscous fluid. This is contrary to the result for rigorously nonviscous fluids.

In elasticity Duhem was again interested in rigorous general theorems (*Recherches sur l'élasticité*). He was the first to study waves in elastic, heat-conducting, viscous, finitely deformed systems. The results are similar to that for fluids; namely, in any finitely deformed viscous elastic system, whether crystalline or vitreous, no true waves can be propagated and the only possible discontinuities always separate the same particles. He was also the first to study the relationships between waves in isothermal and adiabatic finitely deformed systems without viscosity.

Duhem was a critic of Maxwell's electromagnetic theory, claiming that it not only lacked rigorous foundation but was not sufficiently general to explain the existence of permanent magnets (*Les théories électriques de J. Clerk Maxwell* [1902]).

DUJARDIN, FÉLIX (*b. Tours, France, 1801; d. Rennes, France, 1860*), protozoology.

Largely self-educated; trained in art, performed chemical experiments, published on paleontology and botany. Appointed to chair in geology and mineralogy at Toulouse (1839); professor of zoology and botany at Rennes (from 1840). His careful microscopic study of Foraminifera (classified as microscopic cephalopods by d'Orbigny) failed to reveal the expected internal structure: within the shells he found a semifluid internal substance having no apparent structure. He proposed (1835) a new family, Rhizopoda, for these plus similar organisms with less distinct casings, all having the amoeboid character of exuding and retracting pseudopodic rootlets. He named the internal substance "sarcode," and found that its property of spontaneously producing vacuoles by separating out a part of its water contradicted Ehrenberg's polygastric hypothesis (that the many cavities within infusoria were tiny stomachs connected by an intestine). Dujardin described the behavior of sarcode when subjected to various chemicals; he suggested that it was present in some higher animals, such as worms and insects, and later found it in white blood cells. His work was thus a major step toward the protoplasmic theory of life. Other important work included an influential treatise on intestinal worms (1844) and an improved method of microscopic illumination.

DULLAERT OF GHENT, JEAN (*b. Ghent, Belgium, ca. 1470; d. Paris, France, 1513*), logic, natural philosophy.

An Augustinian friar, pupil and colleague of John Maior at Collège de Montaigu (students included Celaya and Vives). Also taught at Collège de Beauvais (from 1510). Published questions and commentaries on Aristotle; edited works of Albertus Magnus, Buridan, and Paul of Venice. Held both realist and nominalist views; his teachings were criticized by humanists, but were appreciated and frequently cited during the early sixteenth century.

DULONG, PIERRE LOUIS (*b. Rouen, France, 1785; d. Paris, France, 1838*), chemistry, physics.

Studied briefly at École Polytechnique before trying a medical career; subsequently turned to botany and then chemistry. Became assistant to Thenard and then to Berthollet; held numerous teaching, examining, and administrative positions, including professorships at Faculté des Sciences and École Polytechnique, despite persistent poor health. Early studies were on decomposition of supposedly insoluble salts of barium (1811); went on to study of oxalates, concluding that a metal oxalate was a simple compound of the metal and carbonic acid. Discovered (1811) nitrogen trichloride, losing a finger

and the sight of one eye when it exploded spontaneously. Prepared and analyzed (1816) acids of phosphorus and oxides of nitrogen. With Berzelius (1819) determined gravimetric composition of water (H:O = 11.1:88.9). With Petit (1815–20) did important work on heat: compared mercury and air thermometers; determined absolute coefficient of expansion of mercury; determined laws of cooling in a vacuum. They measured specific heats of elements, related them to atomic weights, and concluded that "the atoms of all simple bodies have exactly the same capacity for heat" (law of Dulong and Petit). Their new law was used to settle disputed values of atomic weights. Dulong subsequently studied specific heats of gases (1829), animal heat, and heats of combustion; with Thenard (1823), studied catalytic phenomena; with Arago (1830), pressure of steam at high temperatures.

DUMAS, JEAN-BAPTISTE-ANDRÉ (*b. Alès [formerly Alais], Gard, France, 1800; d. Cannes, France, 1884*), chemistry.

Apprenticed to apothecary; emigrated to Geneva (1816) and studied under Gaspard de La Rive, Marc Pictet, and Augustin de Candolle; returned to France (1823) and taught at École Polytechnique, the Athenaeum, École Centrale des Arts et Manufactures (cofounder, 1829), Sorbonne, École de Médecine, and Collège de France, as well as private classes. Cofounder of *Annales des sciences naturelles* (1824); editor of *Annales de chimie et de physique* (from 1840). Active in politics (from 1848); with Haussmann, undertook transformation and modernization of Paris; permanent secretary of Academy of Sciences (1868). Earliest researches were in medicine and physiology (muscle contraction, fat metabolism) and in applied chemistry, including metallurgy, properties of glass, and dye chemistry (analysis of indigo and picric acid). Developed method of determining molecular weight by measuring vapor density (1826), but lack of clear distinction between atoms and molecules led to confusing results. Most important concern was classification of chemical substances: tried to classify organic compounds using theories of atomism and electrochemical dualism. Analyzed alcohol and ether, concluded that both were hydrates of ethylene, alcohol containing twice as much water as ether did (1827–28); explained the constitution of oxamide by postulating the existence of the amide radical (N_2H_4), described urea as made up of carbon [mon]oxide combined with two amide radicals (1830). Investigated methyl alcohol (1835) and showed how presence of a radical gave rise to a whole series of compounds, thereby adding the concept of isomerism to earlier dualistic theories, and predicting and discovering the whole methyl series. Was first to explain the mechanism of substitution reactions in organic chemistry with his theory of substitutions (1834): stated that the hydrogen in any compound could be replaced by an equivalent amount of a halogen, oxygen, or other element, and that "if the hydrogenized compound contains water (i.e., hydrogen linked to oxygen), the hydrogen is eliminated without replacement; but if a further quantity of hydrogen is subsequently removed, then it is replaced by an equivalent amount of chlorine, etc." From 1837 was dissatisfied with electrochemical dualistic theory, and favored a unitary view of the molecule as a single structure without polarization into negative and positive parts;

similarity between properties of substituted and of parent compounds led to theory (1840) that the properties were dependent upon the position and arrangement of the component elements, an early version of the theory of types (including an untenable division into chemical vs. mechanical types). From 1840, carried out an important revision of atomic weights of thirty elements; with Stas, made very precise determination of atomic weight of carbon ($12 \pm .002$); attempted to classify elements and to find "generating" relations similar to those defining series of organic compounds. His historically oriented *Leçons sur la philosophie chimique* (1837) was very influential upon subsequent studies in history of chemistry.

DUMBLETON. *See* **John of Dumbleton.**

DUMÉRIL, ANDRÉ-MARIE-CONSTANT (*b. Amiens, France, 1774; d. Paris, France, 1860*), zoology, herpetology, entomology.

Studied and taught medicine in Paris; taught zoology at Muséum d'Histoire Naturelle (from 1803). Encouraged in pursuit of natural history by Cuvier, edited first two volumes of latter's *Leçons d'anatomie comparée* (1800). Did important work in entomology. Published *Erpétologie générale* (9 vols., 1835–54)—a necessary sequel to the major works of Lamarck and Latreille on the invertebrates and of Cuvier on the fishes—which constitutes a crucial stage in the development of descriptive and systematic zoology. Early volumes were in collaboration with Gabriel Bibron. Duméril's son, Auguste (1812–70), assisted him from 1848, and continued working in the field after his father's death.

DU MONCEL, THÉODOSE ACHILLE LOUIS (*b. Paris, France, 1821; d. Paris, 1884*), electricity, magnetism.

Studied at the *collège* of Caen. Published some sixty-five books and papers on electricity and magnetism, concerned less with theory than with practical applications. His assiduous experiments and interpretations of the work of his colleagues helped organize the electrical innovations from the 1850's to the 1880's; his writings analyzed each discovery and invention in the framework of the entire science.

DUNCAN, JOHN CHARLES (*b. Duncan's Mill, near Knightstown, Ind., 1882; d. Chula Vista, Calif., 1967*), astronomy.

Educated at Indiana University (B.A., 1905; M.A., 1906) and University of California (Ph.D., 1909, under W. W. Campbell). Taught at Harvard (1909–16), Wellesley (1916–50), and University of Arizona (visiting professor, 1950–62). Author of *Astronomy* (1926), standard college textbook for over thirty years, illustrated with many of his own excellent photographs of nebulae and galaxies. Chief contribution to astronomy was photographic demonstration of expansion in the Crab nebula. Also studied comets, spectroscopic binary stars, and novae.

DUNDONALD, ARCHIBALD COCHRANE, EARL OF (*b. Culross Abbey [?], Scotland, 1749; d. Paris, France, 1831*), chemistry.

Spent most of life attempting to apply science to the art of manufactures; achieved considerable technical but little commercial success. Granted patent (1781) for manu-

facture of coal tar, founded British Tar Company (1782), but found no market. Chief contribution to industrial chemistry was production of soda from common salt (1795). Treatise on connection between agriculture and chemistry foreshadowed much of Humphry Davy's *Elements of Agricultural Chemistry*, including recognition of phosphorus as essential plant nutrient.

DUNÉR, NILS CHRISTOFER (*b. Billeberga, Sweden, 1839; d. Stockholm, Sweden, 1914*), astronomy.

Doctorate from University of Lund (1862); worked at Lund Observatory (1864–88) and at Uppsala University (1888–1909). Introduced methods of observational astronomy to Sweden with establishment of new observatory at Lund. Work included measurement of visual double stars; spectra of red stars (discovered more than 100); spectroscopic determination of solar rotation; observation and reduction of star positions; elucidation of the nature of the eclipsing binary Y Cygni; and geodesy of Spitsbergen Islands. Member of planning commission for *Carte photographique du ciel*.

DUNGLISON, ROBLEY (*b. Keswick, England, 1788; d. Philadelphia, Pa., 1869*), medical education, lexicography, physiology.

Studied medicine at Edinburgh, Paris, and London; obtained degree by examination, Erlangen; commenced practice in London (1819). Moved to America (1825), taught at University of Virginia as first full-time professor of medicine in United States; subsequently taught at University of Maryland (1833–36) and Jefferson Medical College, Philadelphia (1836–68). First American author of a textbook on physiology, a medical dictionary, and a history of medicine; pioneer in publication of works on public health, materia medica and therapeutics, medical jurisprudence and toxicology, medical education, and internal medicine; contributed to W. Beaumont's work on physiology of digestion; instrumental in establishing Jefferson Medical College as a leading medical center.

DUNOYER DE SEGONZAC, LOUIS DOMINIQUE JOSEPH ARMAND (*b. Versailles, France, 1880; d. Versailles, 1963*), physics.

Studied at École Normale Supérieure (1902–05); worked under Langevin and Marie Curie; professional positions, included professor at Institut d'Optique (1921–41) and director of Institut de Chimie Physique (1941–45). One of founders of Société de Recherches et de Perfectionnements Industriels. Conducted fundamental experiment on molecular beams, which verified kinetic theory of gases and was origin of preparation of thin films by thermal vaporization. Remarkable technician, dubbed "Grandfather of the Vacuum." Won prizes for work on magnetism (1908), fluorescence (1912), electrical and optical properties of metallic vapors (1913), cryogenics (1925), and photoelectricity (1930). Constructed first aluminized mirrors (1935).

DUNS SCOTUS, JOHN (*b. Roxburghshire, Scotland, ca. 1266; d. Cologne, Germany, 1308*), philosophy.

Franciscan, ordained 1291; studied at Oxford and Paris (D.Th., Paris, 1305). Wrote two commentaries on *Sentences* of Peter Lombard, *Opus Oxoniense* and *Reportata Parisiensis*, both unfinished. Sought to provide a new, metaphysical basis for a natural theology, freeing it from dependence upon natural phenomena. His key was the notion of being, which transcended the physical properties of specific beings known through the senses; it could be applied to God by considering it in its two main modes, infinite and finite: infinite being was by definition necessary and uncaused, while finite being was dependent upon another for its existence and, so, contingent. He thus took an important step in separating natural experience and reason from revealed theological truth and from the preordained determinism against which the condemnations of 1277 had been directed.

DUPERREY, LOUIS-ISIDORE (*b. Paris, France, 1786; d. Paris, 1865*), navigation, hydrography, terrestrial magnetism.

Naval officer. Made two circumnavigating expeditions (1817–20 and 1822–25); on second, commanded *Coquille* with Lesson and Garnot as naturalists. Produced new knowledge of behavior of ocean currents in Atlantic and Pacific, and of variations in intensity and direction of terrestrial magnetism; made observations of earth's magnetic equator.

DUPIN, PIERRE-CHARLES-FRANÇOIS (*b. Varzy, France, 1784; d. Paris, France, 1873*), mathematics, economics, education.

Studied naval engineering at École Polytechnique (graduated 1803); teachers included Monge. Worked as engineer while studying resistance of materials and differential geometry of surfaces; later taught at Paris Conservatoire des Arts et Métiers, gave popular lectures on mathematics and mechanics and their industrial applications. Made a baron (1824) and a peer (1838); active in politics (1828–70). Made many contributions to differential geometry, notably the introduction of conjugate and asymptotic lines on a surface, the so-called indicatrix of Dupin, and "Dupin's theorem," that three families of orthogonal surfaces intersect in the lines of curvature. Discovered the cyclid (1801).

DUPRÉ, ATHANASE LOUIS VICTOIRE (*b. Cerisiers, France, 1808; d. Rennes, France, 1869*), physics, mathematics.

Studied at École Normale Supérieure (1826–29); taught at Rennes (Collège Royale, 1829–47; Faculty of Science, from 1847). Contributed to several branches of mathematics and physics, most notably number theory; from 1859, concentrated on mechanical theory of heat and its implications for matter on the molecular scale. Made important contribution to dissemination in France of newly discovered principles of thermodynamics.

DÜRER, ALBRECHT (*b. Nuremberg, Germany, 1471; d. Nuremberg, 1528*), mathematics, painting, theory of art.

Studied goldsmithing with his father, and then painting and engraving with Michael Wolgemut. Traveled to Italy (1494–95) to learn more about the rediscoveries of Renaissance scholars and artists; became convinced that the new art must be based upon science—in particular, upon mathematics. Studied Euclid's *Elements* and Vitruvius' *De architectura;* experimented with scientific perspective and mathematical proportion, while achieving recognition as an artist (the figures in *Adam and Eve*

[1504] were constructed with compass and ruler). Probably met with Luca Pacioli on second trip to Italy (1505–07). Wrote three major theoretical books: *Underweysung der Messung . . .* (1525) on geometry and its applications, the second known mathematics book in German; *Befestigungslehre* (1527) on fortifications and architecture, the ideas of which were put to use in the strengthening of Nuremberg, Strasbourg, and Schaffhausen; and *Vier Bucher von menschlicher Proportion* (1528), in which Dürer set forth his formal aesthetic, based in the laws of optics: true form is the primary mathematical figure, constructed geometrically or arithmetically, and made beautiful by the application of some canon of proportion. The resulting beautiful form may be varied within limits of similarity. Dürer used the height of the human body as the basic unit of measurement and subdivided it linearly to reach a common denominator for construction of a unified artistic plan. In treating of the movement of bodies in space he was forced to present new, difficult, and intricate considerations of descriptive spatial geometry. He illustrated his influential theories at the end of this last book in the construction of his famous "cube man."

DU TOIT, ALEXANDER LOGIE (*b. Rondebosch, near Cape Town, South Africa, 1878; d. Cape Town, 1948*), geology.

Graduated from South Africa College; studied mining engineering at Royal Technical College, Glasgow, and geology at Royal College of Science, London. Taught at Royal Technical College, Glasgow, and University of Glasgow (1901–03). Worked with Geological Commission of the Cape of Good Hope (from 1903); consulting geologist to De Beers Consolidated Mines (1927–41). Most honored of South African geologists, did important work in stratigraphy, paleobotany, petrology, hydrogeology, geomorphology, and economic geology; mapped more than 100,000 square miles, much of it in detail. Visited South America (1923) and subsequently published *A Geological Comparison of South America with South Africa* (1927); became champion of theory of continental drift; first to realize that the southern continents had once formed the supercontinent of Gondwanaland.

DUTROCHET, RENÉ-JOACHIM-HENRI (*b. Néon, France, 1776; d. Paris, France, 1847*), animal and plant physiology, embryology, physics, phonetics.

Of a noble family, displaced by the Revolution. Studied medicine in Paris (1802–06), served as military doctor in Spain; long convalescence from typhoid led him to study of natural science. Earliest research (1806) was repetition of Ferrein's experiments on the larynx. In embryology (1814) studied thitherto neglected early stages of development of the egg within the ovary, its detachment, and the fetal membranes ("Dutrochet's membrane" is the external yolk membrane of the bird's egg). In physiology, stressed anatomical and mechanical arguments and similarity of plant and animal phenomena such as respiration, excitability, motility, osmosis, and diffusion. His ideas influenced younger colleagues, including Carl Ludwig and Emil du Bois-Reymond; he anticipated, but did not actually formulate, the cell theory.

DUTTON, CLARENCE EDWARD (*b. Wallingford, Conn., 1841; d. Englewood, N.J., 1912*), geology.

Graduate of Yale (1860). Entered army during Civil War, made it his career; served with U.S. Geological Survey, 1875–90. With J. W. Powell and G. K. Gilbert, his close collaborators, established some basic principles of structural geology (including theory of isostasy). From 1882, studied volcanism and earthquakes.

DUVAL, MATHIAS MARIE (*b. Grasse, France, 1844; d. Paris, France, 1907*), histology, physiology, comparative anatomy, embryology.

M.D., Strasbourg (1869). Taught in Paris at École Nationale Supérieure des Beaux-Arts (from 1873), École Pratique des Hautes Études (professor, 1880), and Faculty of Medicine (professor, 1885). Strongly influenced by Charles Robin and by Charles Darwin; promoted Darwin's theory of evolution. Did important original work in neurohistology.

DUVERNEY, JOSEPH-GUICHARD (*b. Feurs, France, 1648; d. Paris, France, 1730*), anatomy.

Studied at Avignon (M.D., 1667). Joined group of Parisian anatomists led by Claude Perrault, contributed to their anonymous publications on comparative anatomy. Assisted in publication of *Mémoires* of Académie des Sciences (1674). Held chair of anatomy at Jardin du Roi (1679). Published first thorough, scientific treatise on the human ear (1683), illustrating its sensory innervation and giving a mechanical interpretation of its function. Wrote on circulatory and respiratory systems in cold-blooded vertebrates (1699), including a highly accurate description of the tortoise heart; he recognized the respiratory function of the gills.

DYADKOVSKY, IUSTIN EVDOKIMOVICH (*b. Dyadkovo, Ryazan gubernia, Russia, 1784; d. Pyatigorsk, Russia, 1841*), medicine, philosophy.

Studied and taught at Moscow Medical-Surgical Academy (graduated 1812; M.D., 1816; professor from 1824); simultaneously professor at Moscow University (from 1831). Dismissed for atheism (1835). Opponent of *Naturphilosophie* and vitalism: believed that movement of matter underlies natural phenomena and that life is a continuous physicochemical process influenced by the interaction of the organism and its environment; thought that organic world evolved from the inorganic, and supported (1816) idea of transformation of species.

DYCK, WALTHER FRANZ ANTON VON (*b. Munich, Germany, 1856; d. Munich, 1934*), mathematics.

Studied in Munich, Berlin, and Leipzig. Assisted F. Klein at Leipzig (1882); professor at Munich Polytechnikum (from 1884), and as its director (from 1900) brought about its rise to university standing. Made noteworthy contributions to function theory, group theory, topology, potential theory, and the formative discussion on integral curves of differential equations. One of founders of *Encyclopädie der mathematischen Wissenschaften*. Organized edition of complete works of Kepler.

DYSON, FRANK WATSON (*b. Measham, near Ashby-de-la-Zouch, Leicestershire, England, 1868; d. on board ship near Cape Town, South Africa, 1939*), astronomy.

Graduated from Cambridge (1889). Chief assistant at Greenwich (1894), astronomer royal for Scotland (1905),

astronomer royal at Greenwich (1910); knighted 1915. Cooperated in, and directed, preparation of many fundamental measurements, including reobservation of stars of Groombridge's catalog to determine proper motions, measurement of wavelengths of solar chromosphere, and determination of gravitational deflection of starlight during 1919 eclipse. Developed geophysical and chronometric work at Greenwich.

EAST, EDWARD MURRAY (*b. Du Quoin, Ill., 1879; d. Boston, Mass., 1938*), genetics.

Studied chemistry at University of Illinois (bachelor's, 1900; master's, 1904; doctorate, 1907); interest turned to genetics when doing chemical analyses for selection experiments on corn, and he began experiments on inbreeding in corn; continued study of inbreeding and outbreeding at Connecticut Agricultural Experiment Station (1905–09). Taught at Harvard from 1909. In studying inheritance of continuously varying characters was able to show that some cases could be explained in terms of Mendelian inheritance. Popularized view that sexual reproduction leads to recombination in the germ plasm and thus to vastly increased numbers of heritable variations. Developed theory that inbreeding leads to increased homozygosity and thus to manifestation of deleterious recessive mutations. Concern with world food supply led to his support of eugenics and population control.

EASTON, CORNELIS (*b. Dordrecht, Netherlands, 1864; d. The Hague, Netherlands, 1929*), astronomy, climatology.

A journalist by vocation, but active as a respected amateur in many fields of science. Made drawings of Milky Way showing distribution of its brightness; proposed spiral galactic structure with center in direction of constellation Cygnus. Published statistical-historical study of climatology of western Europe.

EATON, AMOS (*b. Chatham, N.Y., 1776; d. Troy, N.Y., 1842*), geology, botany, scientific and applied education.

After his career as a lawyer was terminated by imprisonment for an alleged forgery (1810–15), Eaton turned in earnest to science, in which he had always been interested. Largely self-taught, he was a kind of "jack-of-all-sciences," opening new vistas and stressing simplicity and practicality. He wrote texts and articles on many subjects, most notably a *Manual of Botany for the Northern States* (1817), gave popular lectures, and executed geological and agricultural surveys across New York State. He attempted to develop an American nomenclature for New York stratigraphy, following Werner's fivefold classification and basing his distinctions on lithology and the structural attitude of beds. His final and most noteworthy contribution was to scientific education, through persuading Stephen Van Rensselaer to establish the Rensselaer School (now Rensselaer Polytechnic Institute), where Eaton implemented his theory of teaching science. His disciples included James Hall, Ebenezer Emmons, and E. N. Horsford.

EBEL, JOHANN GOTTFRIED (*b. Züllichau, Germany, 1764; d. Zurich, Switzerland, 1830*), medicine, geography.

Studied medicine at Frankfurt-an-der-Oder and at Vienna (M.D., 1788). Worked extensively in ethnology, statistics, and comparative anatomy, but best remembered for writing *Anleitung* (1793), a geological and historical guide to Switzerland, and for promoting the Swiss tourist industry.

EBERTH, CARL JOSEPH (*b. Würzburg, Germany, 1835; d. Berlin, Germany, 1926*), comparative anatomy, pathology, bacteriology.

Studied at University of Würzburg (M.D., 1859) under Kölliker, Heinrich Müller, Leydig, and Virchow. Taught at Würzburg, Zurich (1865–81), and Halle (1881–1911). Early papers were on histology, particularly of ciliated epithelium and of liver. Became interested in process of inflammation, and then in inflammations caused by microorganisms; was subsequently instrumental in bringing the study of bacteria and their actions to the attention of German scientists. In *Zur Kentniss der bacteritischen Mycose* (1872) Eberth reported his observations of the causative organisms of diphtheria and of anthrax; he discovered (1879) rod-shaped organisms in twelve cases of typhoid fever (but Gaffky was first to isolate and cultivate the bacillus, in 1884). Described process of amyloid deposition in tissues. With Schimmelbusch, demonstrated role of platelets in thrombosis. Published new edition (1889), with many additions and improvements, of Friedländer's *Microscopische Technik.*

ECKERT, WALLACE JOHN (*b. Pittsburgh, Pa., 1902; d. Englewood, N.J., 1971*), celestial mechanics, computation.

Educated at Oberlin (A.B., 1925), Amherst (M.A., 1926), and Yale (Ph.D., 1931). Applied mechanical computation to needs of astronomy at Columbia University (from 1929) and as director of U.S. Nautical Almanac Office (1940–45). Designed and developed the *American Air Almanac* (1940). Joined IBM (1945) as director of Watson Scientific Computing Laboratory (located at Columbia); worked on design of large-scale computers (SSEC, 1948; NORC, 1954). Computed planetary positions; worked on lunar theory, confirming predictions of E. W. Brown and providing improved lunar data.

EDDINGTON, ARTHUR STANLEY (*b. Kendal, England, 1882; d. Cambridge, England, 1944*), astronomy, relativity.

Studied at Owen's College, Manchester, under Arthur Schuster and Horace Lamb, and at Trinity College, Cambridge (1902–05). Appointed chief assistant at Royal Observatory, Greenwich (1906); returned to Cambridge (1913) as Plumian professor of astronomy and director of the observatory. Eddington's intuitive insight into the profound problems of nature, coupled with his mastery of the mathematical tools, led him to illuminating results in a wide range of problems. In astrophysics, he studied the motions and distributions of stars, using proper-motion data to confirm the existence of two star streams; analyzing stellar structure, he developed an equation for radiative equilibrium assuming perfect gas conditions, even for dwarf stars, and derived an important mass-luminosity relation (1924). He calculated the density of Sirius B, a white dwarf, to be 50,-000 gm./cc., and deduced a relativistic red shift in its spectrum which was confirmed by W. S. Adams's measurements (1924). Investigating the sources of stellar energy, he suggested the hypothesis of conversion of matter into radiation by annihilation of electrons and

protons (1917), and estimated the age of stars to be several trillion (10^{12}) years; he developed a theory of the absorption lines in stellar atmospheres that made possible the interpretation of many observed line intensities. He calculated the density and temperature of interstellar matter, and proposed the estimation of a star's distance by measurement of the intensity of its interstellar absorption lines. In addition, Eddington was the first interpreter of Einstein's relativity theory in English (1918), and made his own contributions to its development; Einstein considered Eddington's *Mathematical Theory of Relativity* (1923) the finest presentation of the subject in any language. Eddington was fascinated with the fundamental constants of nature; he formulated relationships between all the principal constants, attempting a vast synthesis in his provocative but uncompleted *Fundamental Theory.*

EDER, JOSEF MARIA (*b. Krems, Austria, 1855; d. Kitzbühel, Austria, 1944*), chemistry, photography.

Studied and taught in Vienna; founded graphic arts institute at state vocational high school (1882). Improved the use of photographic emulsions and made sensitometric studies. Photographed spectra of many elements, including rare earths. Published extensive handbook of photography; started photographic yearbook (1887); wrote history of photography.

EDISON, THOMAS ALVA (*b. Milan, Ohio, 1847; d. West Orange, N.J., 1931*), technology.

Entirely self-educated in science; had an early and avid interest in chemistry and electricity, and performed experiments at home and on the trains on which he worked as a peddler. Employed as a telegraph operator (1863–69), but determined to become an inventor. In 1870 he received $40,000 for improving the stock-ticker system and used the money to set up a private fifty-man laboratory; he became the epitome of the technologist-inventor, using an exhaustive "cut-and-try" procedure to develop inventions for which he perceived a practical need (exemplified by his work on multiplex telegraphy, incandescent lighting, magnetic iron-ore separation, and the storage battery). His only scientific discovery was the "Edison effect," the emission of electrons from a hot cathode (later exploited by J. A. Fleming), found when investigating the dark shadow within a light bulb.

EDWARDES (or **EDGUARDUS**), **DAVID** (*b. Northamptonshire, England, 1502; d. Cambridge [?], England, ca. 1542*), medicine.

Studied Greek at Oxford (B.A., 1521; M.A., 1525), and medicine at Oxford and Cambridge; taught medicine at Cambridge. Published first work in England to be devoted solely to anatomy, reflecting the new, humanistic Greek anatomical nomenclature and containing the first recorded (although legally unsanctioned) human dissection in England.

EDWARDS, WILLIAM FRÉDÉRIC (*b. Jamaica, West Indies, 1776; d. Versailles, France, 1842*), physiology, ecology, anthropology, ethnology, linguistics.

Studied medicine in Bruges and Paris (M.D., 1814); assisted Magendie in preparation of *Précis élémentaire de physiologie.* Studied influence of environmental factors on "animal economy," especially heat production and respiration; discovered need of some newborn animals for external heat supply. In ethnology, held that human races have fixed, persistent features; founded Société Ethnologique de Paris (1839); introduced word "ethnologie." Brother of Henri Milne-Edwards.

EGAS MONIZ, ANTONIO CAETANO DE ABREU FREIRE (*b. Avança, Portugal, 1874; d. Lisbon, Portugal, 1955*), neurology.

Studied medicine at University of Coimbra (M.D., 1899), then neurology and psychiatry at Paris and Bordeaux. Professor at Coimbra (1902) and at University of Lisbon (1911–45). Active in Portuguese politics. Developed diagnostic technique of cerebral angiography (1927). Received Nobel Prize in physiology or medicine (1949) for discovery of therapeutic value of frontal leucotomy (or lobotomy) in certain psychoses.

EGOROV, DIMITRII FEDOROVICH (*b. Moscow, Russia, 1869; d. Kazan, U.S.S.R., 1931*), mathematics.

Educated (diploma, 1891; doctorate, 1901) and taught at Moscow University; editor-in-chief of *Matematicheskii sbornik* (from 1922). Contributed greatly to differential geometry by studies on triply orthogonal systems and potential surfaces. Also studied theory of integral equations, and theory of functions of a real variable; Egorov's theorem states that any almost-everywhere converging sequence of measurable functions converges uniformly on a closed set, the complement of which has an infinitely small measure.

EHRENBERG, CHRISTIAN GOTTFRIED (*b. Delitzsch, near Leipzig, Germany, 1795; d. Berlin, Germany, 1876*), biology, micropaleontology.

Trained in medicine at Leipzig and Berlin (M.D., 1818); influenced by Karl Rudolphi and Heinrich Link to pursue botanical and zoological studies. Early work elucidated sexual generation of fungi (1818) and led him to deny spontaneous generation. Participated in expedition to Egypt (1820–25), collecting thousands of species of animals and plants (many of which were lost); his work on the coral polyps of the Red Sea included the first exact investigations on the anatomy, nourishment, and growth of corals. Persuaded by Humboldt to go on scientific expedition to Siberia (1827–31), where he collected plants and animals, undertook geological and paleontological studies, and made microscopical observations of Infusoria. Although appointed to the University of Berlin he did little teaching, but carried out research at the Berlin Academy; he published studies on material and observations from his expeditions, and on the organization and systematics of Infusoria. Believing that all animals possess with an equal degree of completeness the important organs of life, he endeavored to demonstrate the presence of complete organ systems in single-celled animals; while his research method was good, his microscope was inadequate. He did work of lasting importance in his study of single-celled fossils, giving exact descriptions of freshwater vs. marine shells and skeletons and becoming the founder of microgeology and micropaleontology in Germany. His marine studies led to his participation in international oceanographic projects.

EHRENFEST, PAUL (*b. Vienna, Austria, 1880; d. Amsterdam, Netherlands, 1933*), theoretical physics.

Received doctorate in physics at Vienna (1904) with dissertation on statistical mechanics under Boltzmann. First academic appointment was at Leiden (1912), where he revitalized the scientific community and excelled as a teacher. Critical ability evident in writings on statistical mechanics: proposed urn model (1907) that showed how the laws of probability could produce an average trend toward equilibrium, even though the behavior of the model was reversible in time and every one of its states would eventually recur. In analyzing quantum theory, he showed that the ratio of energy to frequency was the only variable that could be quantized for a harmonic oscillator; he went on to show (1913–16) that this ratio is invariant in every periodic system under slow (adiabatic) changes in its parameters, and proposed that only such adiabatic invariants could properly be quantized. Continuing to elucidate quantum mechanics and to stress its relationships with classical physics, he proved "Ehrenfest's theorem" that quantum mechanical expectation values of coordinates and momentum obey the classical equations of motion.

EHRET, GEORG DIONYSIUS (*b. Heidelberg, Germany, 1708; d. London, England, 1770*), botany.

A journeyman gardener who became known for his botanical drawings; illustrated Linneaus' *Hortus Cliffortianus* (1737); moved to England (1740) and worked as artist and teacher.

EHRLICH, PAUL (*b. Strehlen, Germany [now Strzelin, Poland], 1854; d. Bad Homburg, Germany, 1915*), hematology, immunology, chemotherapy.

Studied at Breslau University and at Strasbourg, where he was impressed by the anatomist Wilhelm von Waldeyer's broad comprehension of medicine; and the professor in turn noted his student's excellent histological preparations with his own modifications of new aniline dyes.

Although lacking formal courses in chemistry, Ehrlich became fascinated with the subject while studying for his *Physikum* at Strasbourg. Having passed this examination, he returned in 1874 to Breslau, where he completed studies for his medical degree and was influenced by the pathologists Julius Cohnheim and Carl Weigert, the physiologist Rudolf Heidenhain, and the botanist Ferdinand Cohn, sponsor of Robert Koch's researches on anthrax bacilli. His doctoral dissertation, "Beiträge zur Theorie und Praxis der histologischen Färbung," was approved at Leipzig in 1878, and included descriptions of large, distinctively stained cells containing basophilic granules, for which Ehrlich coined the term "mast cells," observed in connective tissue by Waldeyer. In 1879 he defined and named the eosinophil cells of the blood.

Upon graduation Ehrlich was appointed head physician in Friedrich von Frerichs' renowned medical clinic at the Charité Hospital in Berlin. Frerichs encouraged Ehrlich's histological and biochemical researches, and the latter thereby gained lasting insights into diagnostic and therapeutic problems. His observation that basic, acidic, and neutral dyes reacted specifically with such cellular components as leukocyte granules and nuclei implanted in Ehrlich's mind the fundamental concept underlying his future work: that chemical affinities govern all biological processes.

Ehrlich was determined to explore the avidity of living tissues for certain dyes. In 1885 a monograph, *Das Sauerstoffbedürfnis des Organismus,* reporting his investigations into the distribution of oxygen in animal tissues and organs, gained widespread attention from medical scientists. The monograph won the Tiedemann Prize and served as Ehrlich's *Habilitation* thesis before he became *Privatdozent* in internal medicine at Berlin University. In 1886 he described methylene blue as a selective vital stain for ganglionic cells, axis cylinders, and nerve endings. Later, with A. Leppmann, he used this dye therapeutically to kill pain in neuralgias; and in 1891, with P. Guttmann, he pursued to its logical conclusion the finding that malaria parasites stain well with methylene blue, administering the dye to two malarial patients with apparent success.

In 1889 Ehrlich set up a small private laboratory in a rented flat and launched a series of fundamental studies in immunity. He first described these observations in two papers entitled "Experimentelle Untersuchungen über Immunität" (1891). Ehrlich also reported his findings at the Seventh International Congress for Hygiene and Demography at London in 1891. Thereafter he performed his immunological studies in a small laboratory at the newly founded Institute for Infectious Diseases in Berlin, of which Koch had become director.

Ehrlich investigated bacterial toxins and antitoxins by methods comparable with those employed in his plant protein studies. With L. Brieger he produced potent antitoxic serums in actively immunized large animals and demonstrated that these substances could be concentrated and partially purified. In 1894 he reported, with H. Kossel and A. von Wassermann, on 220 unselected diphtheric children treated with antitoxin, stressing the importance of early, liberal dosages.

Early in 1895 an antitoxin control station was established at Koch's institute under the supervision of Ehrlich, assisted by Kossel and Wassermann. This function was transferred in 1896 to a center for serum research and testing at Steglitz, a Berlin suburb. Ehrlich was appointed director, with Wilhelm Dönitz, and later Julius Morgenroth and Max Neisser, as his associates.

Ehrlich took pride in his unpretentious establishment, and excellent work was done in it. His recommendations were widely adopted, and the Lt, or *Limes-Tod,* designation for the test dose survives among his striking legacy of biomedical terms.

Although certain of Ehrlich's proposals set forth in the papers, "Die Wertbemessung des Diphtherieheilserums und deren theoretische Grundlagen" (1897) and "Ueber die Constitution des Diphtheriegiftes" (1898), mystified some readers and aroused opposition from others, in the main they won acceptance and brought the author international recognition. People realized that Ehrlich's genius deserved better facilities, and construction of a suitable building near the Frankfurt city hospital was arranged. Opened in 1899, the Royal Prussian Institute for Experimental Therapy was directed by Ehrlich until his death sixteen years later.

The new "Serum Institute" was not only responsible for routine state control of immunotherapeutic agents such as tuberculin and diphtheria antitoxin, but also for research and training in experimental therapy.

Ehrlich's activities in Frankfurt fall into three periods. The first, 1899–1906, was marked by the emergence and elaboration of his side-chain theory, the conclusion of his work on diphtheria, extensive researches into the mechanisms of hemolytic reactions and his cancer investigations. The second period dates from an address at the ceremonial opening of the Georg-Speyer-Haus in 1906, in which Ehrlich prophesied the creation of substances "as the chemist's retort" that would "be able to exert their full action exclusively on the parasite harbored within the organism and would represent, so to speak, magic bullets which seek their target of their own accord." It culminated in his momentous announcement before the Congress for Internal Medicine at Wiesbaden, in 1910, that a synthetic arsenical compound (Salvarsan, later arsphenamine) had shown curative properties in relapsing fever and early syphilis. The third period, 1910–15, covered Ehrlich's gallant struggle to handle the multiple problems that followed the discovery of Salvarsan. Shared 1908 Nobel Prize with Metchnikoff for their work on immunity.

EICHENWALD, ALEKSANDR ALEKSANDROVICH (*b. St. Petersburg, Russia, 1864; d. Milan [?], Italy, 1944*), physics, engineering.

Graduated from St. Petersburg Railway Institute (1888); worked as engineer, then studied physics at Strasbourg (Ph.D., 1897). Worked at Moscow Engineering College (1897–1921; received doctorate 1904) and at Moscow University (1906–11). Won world fame for unquestionable proof that motion of an electrically charged body produces an electric field, by exact proof of equivalence of convection and conduction currents, and by first proof, based on direct measurements, of existence of a magnetic field when the polarization of a dielectric changes, i.e., a magnetic field of a displacement current (1901–04, using the Eichenwald experiment). Wrote also on motion of light energy in reflection, and on sound waves of large amplitude.

EICHLER, AUGUST WILHELM (*b. Neukirchen, Germany, 1839; d. Berlin, Germany, 1887*), botany.

Studied at University of Marburg (1857–61); influenced by Albert Wigand. Assisted Karl Friedrich von Martius in editing *Flora Brasiliensis.* Taught at Munich, Graz, Kiel, and Berlin (from 1877). One of most prominent systematic and morphological botanists of his time; his main contributions concerned symmetry of flowers and taxonomy of higher plants.

EICHWALD, KARL EDUARD IVANOVICH (*b. Mitau, Latvia [now Jelgava, Latvian S.S.R.], 1795; d. St. Petersburg, Russia, 1876*), geology, paleontology.

Studied at Dorpat, Berlin, Vienna, Paris, and Vilna (M.D., 1819); a naturalist of wide interests who held varied teaching positions and successfully devoted himself, at different periods, to medicine and zoology, as well as to botany, geology, paleontology, anthropology, ethnography, and archaeology. Became leading Russian paleontologist, studying flora and fauna of all orders and classes throughout the entire geologic sequence; discovered many new species; drew stratigraphic, paleogeographic, and paleoecological conclusions; published extensive summary, *Lethaea Rossica* (1853–68, 3 vols.). His geological theories were progressive for his time: in 1827, for example, he wrote that folding results from the combined effect of gravity and lateral compression.

EIGENMANN, CARL H. (*b. Flehingen, Germany, 1863; d. Chula Vista, Calif., 1927*), ichthyology.

Studied under David Starr Jordan at Indiana University (bachelor's, 1886; Ph.D., 1889), and followed him as professor of zoology (1891); director of Biological Survey of Indiana (from 1892). Primary interest was in painstaking analysis of classification, distribution, and evolution of freshwater fishes of South America, based on studies of museum collections and on results of his own expeditions; major publication was on American Characidae; comparing South American and African species, deduced pre-Tertiary land connection between the continents. Also studied degenerative evolution of cave fauna.

EIJKMAN, CHRISTIAAN (*b. Nijkerk, Netherlands, 1858; d. Utrecht, Netherlands, 1930*), medicine, physiology, nutrition.

M.D., Zaandam (1883); worked as medical officer in Dutch East Indies (1883–85); studied bacteriology with Robert Koch (1886). With C. A. Pekelharing and C. Winkler went on government mission to Dutch East Indies (1886) to study beriberi, then thought to have a bacteriological origin; found similar disease in fowl, and a chance variation in their diet, followed by extensive food experiments, led to discovery that unpolished rice had both a preventive and a curative effect. He did not perceive the correct explanation, but his work led eventually to the discovery of thiamine (vitamin B_1) as the substance protecting against beriberi. He shared the Nobel Prize in physiology or medicine (1929) with F. G. Hopkins. From 1898 to 1928 he taught at the University of Utrecht.

EINSTEIN, ALBERT (*b. Ulm, Germany, 1879; d. Princeton, N.J., 1955*), physics.

Einstein, who was a slow child and disliked the regimentation of school, had his scientific interests awakened early by his family and by his reading at home. He left school for a year when his family moved to Milan (1894); he then went to Switzerland, finished the Gymnasium, and graduated in physics and mathematics from the Zurich Polytechnikum with the hope of teaching. He found no regular employment for two years, and then accepted the position of examiner in the Swiss Patent Office at Berne; during the seven years he spent in this job he devoted his nonworking hours to the serious pursuit of theoretical physics that brought him academic recognition. His first teaching appointment (1909) was as associate professor of physics at the University of Zurich. From there he moved to the German University in Prague (1911), the Zurich Polytechnikum (1912), and then to Berlin (1914) as director of the Kaiser Wilhelm Institute for Physics. He remained in Berlin until the menace of the Nazi regime led him to accept an offer from the Institute for Advanced Study in Princeton (1933); he became an American citizen in 1940.

Throughout his life Einstein was an outspoken pacifist; in the 1930s, however, he became convinced that Hitler must be put down by force. In 1939 he agreed to write to President Roosevelt to warn him that Germany might be developing dangerous nuclear weapons; this letter helped to initiate the American efforts that eventually produced the nuclear reactor and the fission bomb, but Einstein neither participated in nor knew anything about these efforts. After the war he worked toward a world government, the renunciation of nuclear weapons, and the abolition of war. He had long been a Zionist; in 1952 he was offered, but did not accept, the presidency of Israel. Despite his concern with world problems his ultimate loyalty was to his science. His honors included the Nobel Prize in physics (1921).

Einstein's earliest work was mainly in statistical mechanics. He rederived the basic results, emphasizing that the probabilities are to be understood as having a physical meaning: the probability of a macroscopically identifiable state of a system is the fraction of time that the system spends in this state. Equilibrium is therefore dynamic. The physical significance of Boltzmann's constant, k, is that it defines the scale of fluctuation phenomena; by measuring fluctuations one could determine k, and hence Avogadro's number and the mass of an atom. He went on to discuss Brownian motion (1905), which was predicted by the molecular theory of heat; the equation he suggested to describe the motion was confirmed by Jean Perrin, who used it to determine Avogadro's number. These results helped to convince the remaining skeptics, such as Ostwald, that molecules were real and not just a convenient hypothesis. Einstein subsequently generalized fluctuation theory (1910).

This early work, significant as it was, does not represent the predominant concern of Albert Einstein throughout his career: the search for a unified foundation for all of physics, which led to his most important early work—the special theory of relativity and the theory of quanta. Neither the attempts at a mechanical theory of the electromagnetic field nor the recent efforts to base mechanics on electromagnetism had been successful. The disparity between the discrete particles of matter and the continuously distributed electromagnetic field came out most clearly in Lorentz' electron theory, where matter and field were sharply separated for the first time (this theory strongly influenced Einstein, who often referred to the basic electromagnetic equations as the Maxwell-Lorentz equations). In considering black-body radiation, whose predicted frequency distribution was incompatible with experimental results, Einstein made the bold suggestion (1905) that light be considered a collection of independent particles of energy, which he called light quanta. He used the methods of thermodynamics and statistical mechanics to show that the entropy of black-body radiation in a given frequency interval depends on the volume of the enclosure in the same way that the entropy of a gas depends on its volume, and leaped to the conclusion that the radiation, like a gas, must consist of independent particles of energy. The energy E of the particles would then be proportional to the frequency ν of the radiation, $E = h\nu$, where the universal proportionality constant h was the product of k and one of the constants in Wien's distribution law. Einstein used this expansion of Planck's (1900) quantum theory to predict the quantitative relationships of the photoelectric effect; to account for departures from the specific heat rule of Dulong and Petit; and to predict a new law of specific heats at low temperatures (1907). These achievements awakened the interest of physicists in the quantum theory. Subsequent developments included Einstein's proposal (1909) of a field theory based on partial differential equations from which quanta would emerge as singular solutions, in an attempt to overcome the wave-particle duality in radiation; Bohr's theory of the hydrogen atom (1913); Einstein's suggestion of the identity of physical and chemical changes at the molecular level (1914); Einstein's argument for the directionality of light quanta (confirmed by the Compton effect, 1923); the Bose-Einstein statistics of an ideal gas (1924); de Broglie's theory of a wave-particle duality for matter (1924); Schrödinger's wave mechanics, inspired by Einstein's support for de Broglie's theory; and the new quantum mechanics (1927). Despite the enormous success of quantum mechanics Einstein never accepted the finality of its renunciation of causality or its limitation of physical theory to the unambiguous description of the outcome of fully defined experiments. He was convinced that a fundamental theory could not be statistical, "that *He* doesn't play dice"; he would not give up the idea that there was such a thing as "the real state of a physical system, something that objectively exists independently of observation or measurement, and which can, in principle, be described in physical terms." The search for a theory that could provide such a description of reality was Einstein's program. He never lost his hope that a field theory of the right kind might eventually reach this goal.

Just as Einstein had introduced the particle concept from mechanics into the theory of light in his light-quantum study, so he introduced the mechanical concept of relativity into field theory in his relativity study. The principle of relativity did not originate with Einstein: both Maxwell and Poincaré had discussed the necessity of such a principle to unify the current physical theories. Einstein went beyond them in rejecting the concept of the ether. In his first paper on relativity (1905) his purpose was to present "a simple and consistent theory of the electrodynamics of moving bodies based on Maxwell's theory for stationary bodies." Using the model of thermodynamics, which he characterized as a theory of principle, he refounded the Maxwell-Lorentz theory on a new kinematics based on two universal postulates: the first, the "principle of relativity," stipulated that "the same laws of electrodynamics and optics will be valid for all frames of reference for which the equations of mechanics hold good"; the second stipulated that light always moves with the same velocity in free space, regardless of the motion of the source. To reconcile these two postulates it was necessary to modify the classical transformation equations for relating the space and time coordinates of different inertial systems; this led Einstein to propose a new concept of simultaneity and then to deduce a new set of equations relating the four coordinates x', y', z', t' in the system K' to the coordinates x, y, z, t in the inertial system K, with respect to which K' was in uniform translatory velocity v along the x-axis:

$$x' = \frac{x - vt}{(1 - v^2/c^2)^{1/2}},$$
$$y' = y,$$
$$z' = z,$$
$$t' = \frac{t - vx/c^2}{(1 - v^2/c^2)^{1/2}}.$$

(Unknown to Einstein, these transformation equations had already appeared in a paper published in 1904 by Lorentz; they are therefore called the Lorentz transformation.) As Einstein perceived, the new transformation presented a revolutionary theory of space and time. Lengths and time intervals are shown to be magnitudes relative to the inertial systems in which they are measured. The reciprocity of length contraction and time dilation between any two inertial systems renders physically meaningless questions as to whether such effects are "apparent" in one system and "real" in the other, or vice versa. Because of the complete generality of Einstein's first postulate, it follows that the fundamental principle of the special theory of relativity can be expressed by stating that the laws of physics are invariant with respect to the Lorentz transformation. By applying the transformation equations Einstein derived several other theorems in the optics and electrodynamics of moving bodies on the basis of the theory for stationary bodies. He also revised some of the laws of classical mechanics. In a second paper of 1905 he calculated the loss of kinetic energy for a body emitting radiation energy and was able to deduce that the mass of the body had been diminished; he concluded that the mass of a body is a measurement of its energy content, thus bridging the concepts of mechanics and electromagnetism. He developed his famous equation, $E = mc^2$, in 1907. The universal geometrical implications of Einstein's theory were first clearly revealed by Minkowski (1908), who developed the formalism of the world as a four-dimensional flat space-time in which events are points, the history of a particle is a curve, and inertial frames correspond to Cartesian coordinates spanning this space-time; this ultimately led to Einstein's belief that all laws of nature should be geometrical propositions concerning space-time.

Einstein arrived at the general theory of relativity, which extended the earlier theory to include accelerated coordinate systems, through work on the theory of gravitation. In 1907 he stated his equivalence principle, that inertial mass and gravitational mass are equal (so that all bodies in free fall have the same acceleration). In 1912 he suggested that the mass of a body arises from gravitational interaction with all other bodies in the universe (in 1918 he called this Mach's principle). In 1913 he insisted that the conservation laws must be retained; he used more general frames of reference and deduced that the gravitational field must be characterized by ten functions, and thence that gravitation is explicitly related to the geometrical structure of space-time; and he gave the equation of motion of a particle in a gravitational field, one of the three steps necessary for any theory of gravitation. The theory was completed by field equations for motion of the electromagnetic field in the presence of a gravitational field (1914) and the field equations of gravitation (1915). The final theory (definitively presented in 1916) was of immense sweep and great conceptual simplicity. All frames of reference are equally good; the classical conservation laws fade away—they are no longer laws but mere identities and lose their former significance. There are no gravitational forces in the sense in which the theory contains electromagnetic ones, or elastic ones; gravitation appears in a different way: it is the name given to those phenomena that appear because space-time is not flat. The fixed, given space-time of the special theory has gone; what before had erroneously been labeled as the influence of a body by gravitation on the motion of another is now given as the influence of one body on the geometry of space-time in which the free motion of the other body occurs. This free motion in the altered space-time is what was mistaken as forced motion (forced by a gravitational field) in an unaltered space-time. The curvature of space-time is due to its energy and mass content. The laws of nature are now geometrical propositions concerning space-time.

Among the experimental predictions of the new theory were two whose confirmation led to wide and rapid recognition of Einstein's achievement. The first was a new calculation of the motion of the planet Mercury: general relativity added a precession factor sufficient to bring the precession value calculated from Newtonian theory up to the observed value. The second prediction was that light rays will be bent in the vicinity of a gravitating body, and this was confirmed by observations during a solar eclipse (1919). (A third prediction, that spectral lines will be shifted in wave length by a gravitational field, was confirmed by astrophysicists in 1960.) Einstein was not satisfied with his theory, however. He felt that, among other difficulties, the equations of motion of the electromagnetic field were not geometrical propositions; he therefore continued to work on the mathematical structure of relativity theory and, for the rest of his life, to search for a unified field theory where all the laws would have geometrical significance.

EINTHOVEN, WILLEM (*b. Semarang, Java, 1860; d. Leiden, Netherlands, 1927*), physiology.

Studied medicine at Leiden (Ph.D., 1885) and held professorship of physiology (from 1885). Received Nobel Prize for physiology or medicine (1924) for his development of electrocardiography. Working with Lippmann's capillary electrometer, he calculated the curve for the action current of the heart; to record the curve directly, he invented the string galvanometer (1896); in 1903 he defined the standard measures for general use. He developed telecardiography to study hospital patients (1906), and constructed a string recorder and a string myograph to prove that the electrocardiogram and muscle contraction are inseparably connected.

EISENHART, LUTHER PFAHLER (*b. York, Pa., 1876; d. Princeton, N.J., 1965*), mathematics.

Studied at Gettysburg College (1892–96) and at Johns Hopkins University (Ph.D., 1900); taught at Princeton. Did noteworthy work in differential geometry. Until about 1920, concentrated on theory of deformations of surfaces and systems of surfaces, contributing a unifying principle: The deformation of a surface defines the congruence of lines connecting a point and its image; in general a congruence contains two families of developable surfaces. Eisenhart recognized that in all known cases, the intersections of these surfaces with the given surface and its image form a net of curves with special properties. Later work was on Riemannian geometry and its generalization; he started the topic of recurrent fields and harmonic spaces; and he produced Eisenhart's theorem (1923): If a Riemannian geometry admits a second-order, symmetric, covariant constant tensor other than

the metric, the space behaves locally like the product of two lower-dimensional spaces.

EISENSTEIN, FERDINAND GOTTHOLD MAX (*b. Berlin, Germany, 1823; d. Berlin, 1852*), mathematics.

Interested in mathematics from early youth; teachers included Schellbach and Dove, but much study was independent. Entered University of Berlin (1843), earned esteem of Crelle, in whose journal he published twenty-five papers in one year (1844); Humboldt became his patron and promoter. Corresponded with Gauss (1844). Taught at Berlin as *Privatdozent*. Published numerous papers on theory of elliptic functions, quadratic and cubic forms, fundamental theorems for quadratic and biquadratic residues, the reciprocity theorem for cubic residues, cyclotomy, and quadratic partition of prime numbers.

EKEBERG, ANDERS GUSTAF (*b. Stockholm, Sweden, 1767; d. Uppsala, Sweden, 1813*), chemistry, mineralogy.

Studied at Uppsala, Greifswald, and Berlin; taught at Uppsala (from 1794). A pupil of C. E. Weigel, the German translator of Lavoisier; became first to publish the antiphlogiston theory in Sweden (1795, anonymously). In analyzing minerals from Ytterby, Ekeberg discovered tantalum, a new heavy metal.

EKMAN, VAGN WALFRID (*b. Stockholm, Sweden, 1874; d. Gostad, Stockaryd, Sweden, 1954*), oceanography.

Studied at University of Uppsala with Vilhelm Bjerknes and Fridtjof Nansen; worked at International Oceanographic Laboratory, Oslo (1902–08), then taught at Lund. Published mathematical theory of influence of earth's rotation on oceanic circulation (1902); complete mathematical theory for wind-driven circulation in an oceanic basin (1923); studies of the dead water effect in Norwegian fjords (1904). Constructed oceanographic instruments, including a current meter that is still a standard tool.

ELHUYAR (or **ELHUYART**), **FAUSTO D'** (*b. Logroño, Spain, 1755; d. Madrid, Spain, 1833*), chemistry, mineralogy, assaying.

Younger brother of Juan José D'Elhuyar. Studied in Paris (1772–77) and at the Mining Academy in Freiberg; taught in Vergara, founded Real Escuela Metalúrgica. Assisted his brother in experiments leading to discovery of metallic tungsten; worked on separation of platinum; improved Ignaz von Born's method of amalgamation for gold and silver ores; discovered chloroargentic acid.

ELHUYAR (or **ELHUYART**), **JUAN JOSÉ D'** (*b. Logroño, Spain, 1754; d. Bogotá, Nueva Granada [now Colombia], 1796*), chemistry, mineralogy, metallurgy.

Older brother of Fausto D'Elhuyar. Studied in Paris (1772–77), at the Mining Academy in Freiberg, and at University of Uppsala. His teachers included Hilaire-Marin Rouelle, Werner, and Bergman. Appointed (1783) director of mines of Nueva Granada. Discovered metallic tungsten (1783) after working with Bergman and Scheele; perfected Born's method for amalgamating silver and mercury; recommended new process for isolation of platinum.

ÉLIE DE BEAUMONT, JEAN-BAPTISTE-ARMAND-LOUIS-LÉONCE (*b. Canon, Calvados, France, 1798; d. Canon, 1874*), geology.

Studied at École Polytechnique (1817–19) and at École Royale des Mines (1819–23); went on study trips to the Vosges with Philippe Voltz (1821) and to Switzerland with Johann de Charpentier (1822). In 1823, went with Brochant de Villiers and Dufrénoy on a mission to confer with English geologists; visited mines and ironworks. From 1825, was in charge of the eastern division of the geological mapping of France: with Dufrénoy, published *Carte géologique générale de la France* (1841). At the same time he was teaching geology at the École des Mines (from 1827) and at the Collège de France (from 1832). One of the founders of the Société Géologique de France (1830). Chairman of Conseil Général des Mines (1861–68); director of Service de la Carte Géologique (1865–68). Aside from the first complete theory of metalliferous veins (1847), his theories, including a development of Leopold von Buch's theory of elevation craters (1833) and the hypothesis of a pentagonal grid structure for the earth's crust, were less successful than his practical work.

ELKIN, WILLIAM LEWIS (*b. New Orleans, La., 1855; d. New Haven, Conn., 1933*), positional astronomy, meteoritics.

Graduated from Royal Polytechnic School, Stuttgart (1876), then studied astronomy at Strasbourg (Ph.D., 1880). Worked with David Gill at Cape of Good Hope, determining stellar parallaxes; was called to Yale University Observatory (1884; director, 1896–1910). Did numerous heliometric determinations of stellar parallaxes; cooperated in measurement of solar parallax; determined positions of stars near the north celestial pole. Made photographic study of meteors, including first successful interrupted photographs of meteor trails.

ELLER VON BROCKHAUSEN, JOHANN THEODOR (*b. Plötzkau, Germany, 1689; d. Berlin, Germany, 1760*), medicine, chemistry.

Studied medicine at Jena, Halle, Leiden, and Amsterdam, and mineralogy and chemistry at Paris (with Lemery and Homberg) and London (with Hauksbee and Desaguliers). Held the highest medical positions in Prussia. His medical writings consist largely of compilations of case histories; his theoretical chemistry gave a central role to heat, which was material in nature and (as fire) was the sole cause of fluidity.

ELLIOT SMITH, GRAFTON (*b. Grafton, Australia, 1871; d. Broadstairs, England, 1937*), anatomy.

Studied at University of Sydney (M.D., 1895) and at Cambridge. Taught at Government School of Medicine, Cairo (1900), Manchester (1909), and University College, London (1919); knighted in 1934. Noted for detailed comparative anatomical descriptions of the brains of reptiles and nonplacental and placental mammals, which contributed to the study of evolution as well as to neurology. His descriptions of Egyptian mummies were the first to be so comprehensive and so detailed. His theory of the diffusion of culture has never been generally accepted.

ELLIS, WILLIAM (*b. Greenwich, England, 1828; d. Greenwich, 1916*), geomagnetism, meteorology, astronomy.

Employed at Royal Observatory from age of thirteen (except for one year at Durham University, 1852–53) in various capacities; from 1875 to 1893 was superintendent in the magnetic and meteorological department. He carried out work which was accepted as proof of the relationship between terrestrial magnetism and sunspots suggested in 1852 by Sabine and others.

ELSTER, JOHANN PHILIPP LUDWIG JULIUS (*b. Bad Blankenburg, Germany, 1854; d. Bad Harzburg, Germany, 1920*), experimental physics.

Studied in Heidelberg (1875–77), Berlin (1877–78), and again in Heidelberg under Quincke (doctorate, 1879). Taught mathematics and physics at Herzoglich Gymnasium in Wolfenbüttel, near Brunswick. From 1884, collaborated with Hans Geitel in pioneering researches into atmospheric electricity, including measurement of the electric field of the earth. With Geitel, studied the photoelectric effect and thermal electron emission, and the use of photocells in photometry; electrical phenomena in gases, including discovery (1887) of the "electrification of gases by means of incandescent bodies"; and radioactivity, which they interpreted as resulting from the spontaneous release of energy by the atom. They devised a method of measuring the concentration of radium emanation (radon) in the atmosphere (the Elster-Geitel activation number) and made extensive studies of its distribution and the factors affecting it.

ELVEHJEM, CONRAD ARNOLD (*b. McFarland, Wis., 1901; d. Madison, Wis., 1962*), biochemistry.

Entire career spent at University of Wisconsin (president from 1958), where he started teaching immediately following his studies (B.S., 1923; M.S., 1924; Ph.D., 1927). Published more than 800 papers on animal nutrition, particularly the role of trace elements and vitamins. Contributed to the growth of understanding of members of vitamin B complex: showed that nicotinic acid cured blacktongue, the canine equivalent of human pellagra (1937); showed that tryptophan can serve as a substitute for nicotinic acid; pioneered in testing role of vitamins in nutrition of higher animals. Also helped clarify role of intestinal bacteria in the synthesis of various trace nutrients.

EMANUELLI, PIO (*b. Rome, Italy, 1888; d. Rome, 1946*), astronomy.

Made first observation at age of eleven; became astronomer at Vatican Observatory when twenty-two. Worked on international *Astrographic Catalogue*; computed orbits of asteroids, elements of solar eclipses, and relativistic deflections of stars near the eclipsed sun; composed tables for conversion of the equatorial in galactic coordinates.

EMBDEN, GUSTAV (*b. Hamburg, Germany, 1874; d. Frankfurt, Germany, 1933*), physiological chemistry.

Studied medicine at universities of Freiburg im Breisgau, Munich, Berlin, and Strasbourg (M.D., 1899). Worked at Physiological Institute of Frankfurt-Sachsenhausen (from 1904) and at University of Bonn (from 1907). Studied intermediate metabolism of liver, using a special perfusion technique: revealed oxidative deamination, synthesis of sugar from lactic acid, and acetoacetic acid and acetone as products of pathological sugar metabolism. Then turned to the chemical processes in muscle: discovered hexose monophosphate ("Embden ester," 1927) and adenyl phosphoric acid in muscle; first to recognize the rapid reversibility of chemical processes in muscle contraction.

EMDEN, ROBERT (*b. St. Gallen, Switzerland, 1862; d. Zurich, Switzerland, 1940*), astrophysics.

Studied physics at Strasbourg (doctorate, 1887). Taught at Technische Hochschule, Munich (1907–28) and at University of Munich (from 1928). Wrote influential astrophysics textbook (1907); introduced concept of polytropic change of state; first to give a derivation for radiative equilibrium for nondiscernible particles; studied atmospheric physics.

EMERSON, BENJAMIN KENDALL (*b. Nashua, N.H., 1843; d. Amherst, Mass., 1932*), geology.

Graduated from Amherst; studied geology at Berlin and Göttingen (Ph.D., 1870); taught at Amherst (professor from 1872). On staff of U.S. Geological Survey; member of Harriman expedition to Alaska (1899); a founder of Geological Society of America. Made important contributions to geology of the Connecticut Valley and bordering plateaus; his interpretations served as a progressive link between nineteenth-century and early twentieth-century geology. Cataloged mineral occurrences in south-central New England.

EMERSON, ROBERT (*b. New York, N.Y., 1903; d. New York, 1959*), plant physiology.

Studied at Harvard, then under Otto Warburg at Berlin (doctorate, 1927). Worked at Carnegie Laboratory of Plant Biology, Stanford (1937–40); California Institute of Technology (1930–37, 1940–47); and University of Illinois, Urbana (from 1947). Concentrated on precise, quantitative study of photosynthesis: determined quantum requirement in algae of various colors, establishing that the minimum quantum requirement for all plants is eight. Discovered "Emerson effect," the restoration of photosynthetic yield under longwave light ("red drop") to normal level by additional illumination with shortwave light; studied photosynthesis in flashing light, to analyze its component reactions.

EMMONS, EBENEZER (*b. Middlefield, Mass., 1799; d. Brunswick County, N.C., 1863*), geology.

Studied at Williams College and at Berkshire Medical School (and practiced medicine, chiefly obstetrics, throughout his life). Taught at Williams, at Rensselaer School, and at Albany Medical College. A principal figure in the first geological survey of New York (1837–43), he played a leading role in the establishment of a geological column for America and a stratigraphy independent of the Anglo-Continental model; the strata were characterized both paleontologically and lithologically. The system of nomenclature by geographic reference, adopted for the first time in North America, was specifically his work. These contributions were overshadowed, however, by the controversy provoked among leading geologists by his delineation of the Taconic System as a vast new sedimentary series between the Potsdam and the primary, the true primordial system and the base of the sedimentary column.

EMMONS, SAMUEL FRANKLIN (*b. Boston, Mass., 1841; d. Washington, D.C., 1911*), geology, mining.

Studied at Harvard (A.B., 1861; A.M., 1866), at École Impériale des Mines, Paris (1862–64), and at Bergakademie, Freiberg (1864–65). Worked on geological exploration of fortieth parallel (1867–77); headed Rocky Mountain Division (from 1879) and then Division of Economic Geology of the U.S. Geological Survey. A founder of the Geological Society of America (1888) and of the Colorado Scientific Society (1882). Major interest was origin of ore deposits: concluded they had been derived mainly from intruded igneous rocks and deposited in adjacent sedimentary rocks by hot aqueous solutions. With G. F. Becker, worked on statistics of precious metals for the *Tenth Census Reports* (1880).

EMPEDOCLES OF ACRAGAS (*b. Acragas [now Agrigento, Sicily]*, *ca. 492* B.C.; *d. ca. 432* B.C.), natural philosophy.

Author of two hexameter poems, a physical-cosmological one traditionally entitled "On Nature" and a religious-mystical one, "Purifications," from both of which a total of 450 lines has been preserved in the form of quotations by later authors. Was referred to as a physician, dramatist, and logician, but no texts survive. In developing and moderating the metaphysics of Parmenides, he originated the four-element theory of matter: he postulated four eternal and unchanging elements, earth, water, air, and fire, and two forces, Love and Hate. Various combinations of the elements produce the familiar entities of the manifest world, and change is wrought through aggregation and dispersal of the elements by the two cosmic forces. This theory was adopted by Plato and Aristotle and inspired or influenced Hippocratic medicine, and thus persisted until the seventeenth-century revival of atomism. Empedocles explained the origin of animals by chance and natural selection: stray limbs and organs combined randomly, producing monsters which perished and viable organisms which persisted. He was the first to explain respiration and movement of the blood in terms of ebbing and flowing. He postulated a four-phase cosmic cycle: complete mixture of the elements in a homogeneous sphere, increasing separation by Hate, total separation, and increasing integration by Love. His universe was a spherical plenum, with an encompassing crystalline firmament.

ENCKE, JOHANN FRANZ (*b. Hamburg, Germany, 1791; d. Spandau [near Berlin], Germany, 1865*), astronomy.

Studied under Gauss at University of Göttingen. Worked at Seeberg observatory (from 1816); appointed professor at Academy of Sciences and director of Berlin observatory (1825); taught at University of Berlin (professor, 1844). Noted for calculations of cometary orbits and of perturbations of asteroids; computed orbit of Pons's comet (now called Encke's comet) and found its period to be less than four years, far shorter than other known periods. Edited *Berliner astronomisches Jahrbuch* (1830–66).

ENGEL, FRIEDRICH (*b. Lugau, near Chemnitz [now Karl-Marx-Stadt], Germany, 1861; d. Giessen, Germany, 1941*), mathematics.

Studied mathematics in Leipzig and Berlin (doctorate, Leipzig, 1883); taught at Leipzig (1885–1904), Greifswald (1904–13), and Giessen (1913–31). Became closest student and indispensable assistant of Sophus Lie, first in Christiania (1884–85) and then at Leipzig: collaborated on *Theorie der Transformationsgruppen*, completed Lie's theory of differential equations, edited his collected papers. Also edited works of Hermann Grassmann; studied history of non-Euclidean geometry (with Stäckel), and translated essential works of Lobachevsky.

ENGEL, JOHANN. *See* **Angelus, Johannes.**

ENGELMANN, GEORGE (*b. Frankfurt am Main, Germany, 1809; d. St. Louis, Mo., 1884*), botany.

Studied at universities of Heidelberg, Berlin, and Würzburg (M.D., 1831). Moved to St. Louis in 1833, practiced medicine there from 1835 while studying many taxonomically difficult plant groups and publishing fundamental revisions. Initiated study of oligotropic pollination with work on *Yucca;* analyzed diseases of grapes (1873). Operated a clearinghouse in St. Louis for botanical explorers of the West, transmitting their discoveries to study centers in the East. Influential in the founding of the Missouri Botanical Garden (1859).

ENGELMANN, THEODOR WILHELM (*b. Leipzig, Germany, 1843; d. Berlin, Germany, 1909*), physiology.

Studied natural sciences and medicine at Jena, Heidelberg, Göttingen, and Leipzig (doctorate, 1867). Went to Utrecht (1867) as assistant to Donders (succeeded to his chair, 1888); subsequently professor at Berlin (1897). Early interest was in microscopy and cellular physiology, including flagellating movements of protozoa and connection between nerves and muscle fibers. Advocated myogenic formation and conduction of stimuli (1869), and proved it for the heart with famous "zig-zag experiment" (1875) in which a frog heart was dissected spirally. First to distinguish four types of activity of cardiac nerves. Made extensive studies of physiology of muscle contraction and developed controversial theories. Proved that retinal cones of frog shift in course of change from light to darkness. Editor of *Archiv für Anatomie und Physiologie* (1900–09).

ENGELS, FRIEDRICH (*b. Barmen [now part of Wuppertal], Prussian Rhineland, 1820; d. London, England, 1895*), history, sociology, political science, economics, philosophy, history and philosophy of science and technology, military science.

Strongly encouraged by his father to enter the business world rather than attend a university to study law, as he had wished, Engels left the gymnasium a year before his graduation. He worked for a year at his father's firm, then for about two years as a clerk at Bremen. He volunteered for an artillery guards' regiment at Berlin before going to England in November 1842 to work in his father's textile mill at Manchester.

At school and in Bremen, Engels published several dozen writings under pseudonyms. While still a clerk, he was deeply affected by David Friedrich Strauss's just-published *Life of Jesus.* Strauss led him to Hegel; first the *Philosophy of History,* and then the logical treatises and the

Phenomenology of Mind, and soon back into the writings of Kant and other predecessors.

During his military year (1841), Engels lived privately and plunged into life among university students and an informal club of young Left Hegelians called "The Free"; he attended Schelling's inaugural lecture, was outraged by Schelling's rejection of reason, science and progress, and proceeded to publish three anonymous pamphlets in defense of progressive Hegelianism and against Schelling. That year he was influenced by Ludwig Feuerbach's works, which confirmed both his total breakaway from his Christian upbringing, and his abiding belief in the humanist basis and purpose of any reasonable ethical principles. And then came a decisive turn: he was impressed by Moses Hess, who brought the French socialism of Saint-Simon into the Left Hegelians' discussions.

In 1842 he wrote for Marx's newspaper, the *Rheinische Zeitung,* and the two met briefly at Cologne. While in England for the next two years, Engels continued his commercial training at the family firm and investigated English social and economic conditions. During this period Engels published his first economic work—the anticipation of Marx's later critique of economic categories, *Outlines of a Critique of Political Economy.*

During his return journey to Barmen in August 1844, Engels stopped for ten days in Paris, to see Marx. The visit was decisive for both; their friendship and collaboration began then. Engels returned to Barmen to visit his family, to plan his business career, to undertake political activity with Hess and other socialists in the Rhineland, and to write *The Condition of the Working Class in England.*

Thereafter he continued his work on concrete social matters, both contemporary and historical: *The Peasant War in Germany* (1850); twenty articles on the 1848 revolution in Germany for the *New York Tribune* (1851–52)—signed by Marx; and six articles on housing (1872). He also produced philological studies on the history of German dialects; several dozen significant articles and pamphlets on tactical and political-military subjects; and an essay and notes on the history of science and technology (which were used in his longer theoretical works and in *Dialectics of Nature*).

In 1844–45, Engels had joined Marx in a number of projects, the first being their sarcastic critique of "speculative" Left Hegelians, *The Holy Family* (1845). It was followed by *The German Ideology* (unpublished until 1932).

In 1848 came the famous *Manifesto of the Communist Party,* written by Marx but influenced by Engels, and anticipated in many aspects by Engels' *Principles of Communism* (1847). Engels aided Marx with more than 170 articles as European correspondent for the *New York Tribune* and nine, chiefly on military subjects, for the *New American Cyclopedia* (1857–62). After Marx's death in 1883, Engels put the incomplete manuscripts in order and prepared the second and third volumes of Marx's *Capital* for publication (1885, 1894), as well as some eighteen new editions of Marx's other works.

After his retirement in 1869, Engels settled in London to continue scientific work, writing, political activity, and work with Marx. He wrote *Anti-Dühring* (1876–78), the most popularly effective of all his and Marx's expositions of their world view; *The Origin of the Family, Private Property and the State* (1884), based in part on Marx's anthropological notes; and *Ludwig Feuerbach and the Outcome of Classical*

German Philosophy (1886); he also drafted parts of his proposed work on the philosophy of science, a "dialectic of nature."

Scientific ideas were both classless and class-situated for Engels. With Marx, he had written decisively about the role of ruling-class interests in the thought of an epoch. Science and all scientific theories of nature were irrevocably social and must be examined as such. Neither Marx nor Engels wrote about the nature of science in a future classless society, in a society with a minimum of necessary labor and without the exquisite specialized division of labor that thus far had characterized industry and science alike.

To Engels, it was inevitable that scientific truths would have ideological impacts and exploitation. Science existed in society, subject to social uses and understandings. He saw that science, like all social activities, would have its struggles—those about its findings, those about its direction, and those within its thought.

ENGLER, HEINRICH GUSTAV ADOLF (*b. Sagan, Silesia, Germany [now Zagán, Poland], 1844; d. Berlin-Dahlem, Germany, 1930*), botany.

As scientist and organizer, Engler dominated an entire era in systematic botany. After obtaining a doctorate under Goeppert at Breslau, he taught there; he then worked at the Botanische Staatsansalt, Munich, under Naegeli, where he contributed to the *Flora Brasiliensis* and developed his comparative morphological method supplemented with elements from phytogeography, anatomy, embryology, and phytochemistry; he next taught at Kiel (1878), then Breslau (1884), and finally at Berlin (1889). His achievements included the founding of *Botanische Jahrbücher für Systematik, Pflanzengeschichte und Pflanzengeographie* (1880), a leading journal in its field; *Versuch einer Entwicklungsgeschichte der Pflanzenwelt . . .* (1879–82), the first attempt at a genetic and historical theory of the origin of the floristic diversity of the Northern Hemisphere; and a collaborative encyclopedia, *Die natürlichen Pflanzenfamilien* (1887–1915), in which he expounded his influential taxonomic system.

ENRIQUES, FEDERIGO (*b. Leghorn, Italy, 1871; d. Rome, Italy, 1946*), mathematics, philosophy and history of mathematics and science.

Graduated from University of Pisa (1891); taught at universities of Bologna (professor, 1896) and Rome (from 1923); founded Italian National Institute for the History of Science. Specialized in theory of algebraic surfaces, in collaboration with Castelnuovo; also contributed to differential geometry of hyperspace. Applied interest in foundations of mathematics to the writing of textbooks, and greatly influenced Italian education.

ENSKOG, DAVID (*b. Västra Ämtervik, Värmland, Sweden, 1884; d. Stockholm, Sweden, 1947*), physics.

Ph.D., Uppsala University (1917); professor of mathematics and mechanics, Royal Institute of Technology, Stockholm (from 1930). Best known for developing a method for solving the Maxwell-Boltzmann transport equations in the kinetic theory of gases (1911–12, simultaneously with Sydney Chapman in England, and F.W. Dootson in 1917); this work provided the basis for a revival of activity in kinetic theory after 1945.

ENT, GEORGE (*b. Sandwich, Kent, England, 1604; d. London, England, 1689*), medicine.

Educated at Sidney Sussex College, Cambridge (M.A., 1631) and at Padua (M.D., 1636). Prominent at College of Physicians; a founder of the Royal Society; knighted in 1665. A friend of William Harvey and one of first to write in his defense (*Apologia pro circulatione sanguinis*, 1641); edited Harvey's *De generatione* (1651); in charge of dispersing Harvey's library.

EÖTVÖS, ROLAND, BARON VON (*b. Budapest, Hungary, 1848; d. Budapest, 1919*), physics.

Studied at universities of Budapest, Heidelberg, Königsberg; received doctorate from Heidelberg (1870); influenced by such professors as Kirchhoff, Helmholtz, and Franz Neumann. Taught at University of Budapest from 1871. Early research was on capillarity; discovered that the temperature coefficient of the molecular surface energy of a liquid is independent of the nature of simple unassociated liquids. Later work concentrated on gravitation and the development and perfection of the Eötvös torsion balance; the balance was applied to geophysical exploration and to proving the equivalence of gravitational and inertial mass. He also investigated the magnetic anomalies accompanying the gravitational effects, and became interested in paleomagnetic study of bricks and other ceramic objects. One of founders of the (Hungarian) Society for Mathematics (1885).

EPICURUS (*b. Samos, 341 B.C.; d. Athens, 270 B.C.*), moral and natural philosophy.

After establishing schools in Mytilene and Lampsacus, Epicurus moved to Athens (ca. 307/306 B.C.). He became known for his moral philosophy, a moderate hedonism wherein the pain of unsatisfied desire is to be avoided by limiting one's desires, and for his cosmology, a modification of the atomism of Leucippus and Democritus aimed at reducing man's anxiety over his ignorance of the forces of Nature. Epicurus' atom has "minimal parts" that can be distinguished theoretically but not split off physically; its weight gives it a natural downward motion, but it swerves unpredictably from time to time. Epicurean atomism was preserved in the works of Diogenes Laertius, Cicero, and Lucretius, and was thus transmitted to post-Renaissance philosophers.

ERASISTRATUS (*b. Iulis, Chios, ca. 304 B.C.; d. Mycale*), anatomy, physiology.

Studied medicine in Athens, Cos, and Alexandria; spent last years in research at Museum of Alexandria. Wrote many works on anatomy and medicine, none of which has survived. With Herophilus, his teacher, Erasistratus laid the foundations for the scientific study of anatomy and physiology, and their careful dissections provided a basis and stimulus for the anatomical investigations undertaken by Galen. Erasistratus compared the findings of human dissection and animal vivisection, and developed a broad knowledge of anatomy and a physiology that combined a corpuscular theory with the doctrine of the pneuma. He conceived of the particles as very small, imperceptible, corporeal entities surrounded by a vacuum in a finely divided or discontinuous condition; physiological processes were explained by the *horror vacui,* derived from Strato, whereby those

229

empty spaces which suddenly form in the living body are continually filled. He found that all organic parts of the living creature were a tissue composed of vein, artery, and nerve, bodies so fine that they were knowable only by reason; the vein carried the food, the artery the pneuma, and the nerve the psychic pneuma. Blood, which nourishes the body, is formed in the liver and conveyed via the vena cava to the heart, which pumps it into the veins. Pneuma is inhaled into the lungs and transmitted through the pulmonary vein to the heart, to be pumped into the arteries; the brain transforms its vital pneuma into psychic pneuma and transmits it to the body via the nerves; both types of pneuma help to transmit the natural activity of the bodily processes. Erasistratus made a study of the brain, which he held to be the seat of the central intelligence; he distinguished the cerebrum from the cerebellum, described the ventricles and meninges, and traced the nerves to their origin. In pathology, he rejected the humoral theory and held the main cause of disease to be plethora (the flooding of the veins with a superfluity of blood engendered by an excessive intake of nourishment); his preferred treatment was starvation rather than phlebotomy. He also stressed the importance of hygiene, and pioneered in the study of pathological anatomy.

ERASTUS (LIEBER), THOMAS (*b. Baden, Switzerland, 1523; d. Basel, Switzerland, 1583*), medicine, natural philosophy, theology.

Studied theology and philosophy at Basel (1540–44), medicine at Bologna and Padua (1544–55; M.D., 1552). Taught medicine at Heidelberg (from 1558) until his anti-Calvinist views led to his fall from favor; taught theology and moral philosophy at Basel (from 1580). Remembered chiefly as a critic of astrology, natural magic, and particularly of Paracelsus and iatrochemistry. In his medical practice he adhered to traditional humoralism and ancient practice, but criticized Galen.

ERATOSTHENES (*b. Cyrene [now Shahhat, Libya], ca. 276 B.C.; d. Alexandria, ca. 195 B.C.*), geography, mathematics.

Educated in Athens; spent most of working life as librarian at Museum in Alexandria. One of the foremost scholars of his time, producing works (of which only fragments remain) on geography, mathematics, philosophy, chronology, literary criticism, and grammar; he also wrote poetry. His *Geography* (in three books) was the first scientific attempt to put geographical studies on a sound mathematical basis: it contained a discussion of the terrestrial globe, which he divided into five zones; a remapping of the *oikoumene* (inhabited world), with numerous estimates of distances along a few roughly defined parallels and meridians; and some material descriptive of peoples and places. Eratosthenes is noted for his measurement of the earth's circumference which he determined to be 250,000 stades (adjusted to 252,000 in order to make it divisible by 60), approximately equivalent to 29,000 English miles. He also measured the obliquity of the ecliptic, estimating it to be 11/83 of a circle (or 23°51′). His *Geography* long remained a prime authority.

Eratosthenes' chief mathematical work seems to have been the *Platonicus*, in which he discussed such topics as proportion and progression, and the theory of musical

scales; he also gave the solution of the famous Delian problem of doubling the cube and described an apparatus for obtaining the solution by mechanical means (this solution was his proudest achievement). In arithmetic, he invented the "sieve" method for finding prime numbers. He was the first Greek writer to make a serious study of chronological questions, and established the system of dating by olympiads; his datings remained authoritative throughout antiquity.

ERCKER (also **ERCKNER** or **ERCKEL**), **LAZARUS** (*b. Annaberg, Saxony, ca. 1530; d. Prague, Bohemia, 1594*), chemistry, metallurgy.

Studied at University of Wittenberg (1547–48). Held various mining and minting positions in Saxony and Bohemia; chief inspector of mines under Rudolf II, knighted 1586. His *Beschreibung allerfürnemisten mineralischen Ertzt* (1574) is considered the first manual of analytical and metallurgical chemistry: it presents a systematic review of methods of testing, refining, and compounding, describes laboratory procedures and equipment, and contains interesting observations of the behavior of copper and iron in solution.

ERDMANN, OTTO LINNÉ (*b. Dresden, Germany, 1804; d. Leipzig, Germany, 1869*), chemistry.

Graduated in medicine from University of Leipzig (1824), where he became a researcher and teacher of chemistry. His textbooks and his encyclopedia of industrial chemistry were influential. Created (1834) *Journal für praktische Chemie.* Did descriptive and analytical research in mineralogical, industrial, inorganic, and organic chemistry. With R. F. Marchand, redetermined atomic weights and found them to be close to whole numbers (1841–50).

ERIUGENA, JOHANNES SCOTTUS (*b. Ireland, first quarter ninth century; d. England [?], last quarter ninth century*), philosophy.

A noted scholar with an exceptional command of Greek. Believed a knowledge of the seven liberal arts to be essential to the study of philosophy and theology; taught at the palace school in Laon, established a curriculum influential throughout Europe from the ninth to the twelfth centuries. In *Periphyseon* or *De divisione naturae* (866), synthesized the Western and Eastern forms of Neoplatonism within a Christian context.

ERLANGER, JOSEPH (*b. San Francisco, Calif., 1874; d. St. Louis, Mo., 1965*), physiology.

Studied chemistry at University of California and medicine at Johns Hopkins. Taught at Johns Hopkins, the University of Wisconsin (from 1906), and Washington University, St. Louis (from 1910). In neurophysiology, succeeded in localizing the exact position in the spinal cord of the motor nerve cells that innervate a given muscle (1900). Majority of work was in cardiac physiology: designed sphygmomanometer (1904) to study pulse wave and distinguish between effects of pulse pressure and arterial pressure; did pioneering experiments on auriculoventricular block, to elucidate conduction of excitation in the heart; analyzed source of sounds of Korotkoff as breaking of crest of pulse wave. From 1921, worked with Herbert Gasser to apply cathode-ray oscillography to neurophysiological studies, which led to their law that nervous impulse velocity is directly proportional to fiber diameter; they shared the Nobel Prize (1944) for this work.

ERLENMEYER, RICHARD AUGUST CARL EMIL (*b. Wehen, Germany, 1825; d. Aschaffenburg, Germany, 1909*), chemistry.

Studied at Giessen under Liebig, and then at Heidelberg, as one of Kekulé's first private students. Taught at Munich Polytechnic School (1868–83); an editor of *Zeitschrift für Chemie und Pharmazie* and of Liebig's *Annalen der Chemie;* one of authors of *Lehrbuch der organischen Chemie* (1867–94). Experimental work was primarily on synthesis and constitution of aliphatic compounds. In theoretical organic chemistry his remarks on valence and structure fostered the new ideas; he introduced the terms "Strukturchemie," "monovalent," "divalent," and so on; he modified Crum Brown's graphic formulas (1864) to introduce modern structural notation (1866); he proposed the triple bond to represent acetylene, and the modern naphthalene formula. The Erlenmeyer rule (1880) states that all alcohols in which the hydroxyl group is attached directly to a double-bonded carbon atom become aldehydes or ketones.

ERMAN, GEORG ADOLPH (*b. Berlin, Germany, 1806; d. Berlin, 1877*), physics, meteorology, geophysics, geography, geology, paleontology.

Doctorate in physics from University of Berlin (1826), where he later taught. Made geographic and geodesic surveying voyage around the world on a Russian ship (1828–30), reported in his *Reise um die Erde* (7 vols., 1833–48). Edited *Archiv für wissenschaftliche Kunde von Russland* (1841–67).

ERRERA, LÉO-ABRAM (*b. Laeken, Belgium, 1858; d. Uccle, Belgium, 1905*), botany, biology, philosophy.

Educated at University of Brussels (baccalaureate; doctorate, 1879), where he later taught (from 1884). A remarkable teacher, responsible for countless academic and pedagogic reforms. Made contributions to plant physiology, which he approached from a strictly physicochemical perspective. First to reveal presence of glycogen in Ascomycetes, as well as in a series of microorganisms.

ESCHER VON DER LINTH, HANS CONRAD (*b. Zurich, Switzerland, 1767; d. Zurich, 1823*), geology, hydraulics.

Ran the family textile factory, held political positions. Devised plan to control flooding of Linth River by diverting it into Lake of Walen. Made numerous studies of Alpine geology, of which only a few were published: observed inverse stratification, theorized its connection with tectonic nappe structure; considered water erosion to be major cause of valley formation, in opposition to ideas of Buch; recognized that distribution of erratic boulders corresponds to watersheds of the great Alpine rivers.

ESCHERICH, THEODOR (*b. Ansbach, Germany, 1857; d. Vienna, Austria, 1911*), pediatrics.

Studied at Strasbourg, Kiel, Berlin, Würzburg, and Munich (M.D., 1881); took further training in Paris and Vienna. Taught at University of Munich (1886), Graz (1890), and Vienna (from 1902). A pioneer pediatrician whose clinical insights and organizational abilities—linked to profound interests in bacteriology, immunology, and biochemistry—were devoted to improving child care, particularly infant hygiene and nutrition. Publication of his monograph on the relationship of intestinal bacteria to the physiology of digestion in the infant (1886), which included a classic description of *Bacterium coli commune* (later designated *Escherichia coli*), established him as the leading bacteriologist in the field of pediatrics; he went on to study artificial nutrition, to devise new formulas, and to advocate breast-feeding. In 1889 he confirmed the causal role of the Klebs-Löffler bacillus in a diphtheria epidemic; he instituted antitoxin theraphy in 1894. Escherich was intensely interested in the diagnosis, pathogenesis, and control of tuberculosis, and pioneered in X-ray detection of the disease in children. In 1890 he began to study infant tetany; he became the leading authority on the disease, and correctly ascribed it to parathyroid insufficiency (1909). In Vienna he renovated the St. Anna Children's Hospital and started an exemplary school for infant nursing.

ESCHOLT, MIKKEL PEDERSÖN (*b. ca. 1610; d. Christiania [now Oslo], Norway, 1669*), geology.

Primarily a theologian, but also author of *Geologia norvegica* (1657), the first scientific treatise printed in Norway. The book contains surprisingly modern views; Escholt was aware of the relation of earthquakes to volcanism, demonstrated the regularity of earthquakes in the Oslo region (two each century), and was first to use the word "geology" in the modern sense.

ESCHSCHOLTZ, JOHANN FRIEDRICH (*b. Dorpat, Russia [now Tartu, Estonian S.S.R.], 1793; d. Dorpat, 1831*), medicine, zoology.

Studied medicine at Dorpat University, where he taught from 1819. Physician and naturalist to round-the-world expeditions of Kotzebue (1815–18).

ESCLANGON, ERNEST BENJAMIN (*b. Mison, France, 1876; d. Eyrenville, France, 1954*), astronomy, mathematics, physics.

Trained as mathematician at École Normale Supérieure (doctorate, 1904); developed theory of quasi-periodic functions. Worked as astronomer at Bordeaux (1899), then director of observatories of Strasbourg (1918) and Paris (1929–44). Explored all branches of fundamental astronomy, devoting special attention to perfecting instruments. Developed techniques of sound-ranging during World War I. Directed Bureau International de l'Heure (1929–44), devised the "talking clock" (1933).

ESKOLA, PENTTI ELIAS (*b. Lellainen, Honkilahti, Finland, 1883; d. Helsinki, Finland, 1964*), petrology, mineralogy, geology.

Studied at University of Helsinki (enrolled 1901; Ph.D., 1914) and taught there after working on Finnish Survey (1922–24). Strove constantly to combine laboratory results with field data. Major contribution to earth sciences was his concept of mineral facies: originally he differentiated between five separate facies, stressing their independence of mode of formation and naming them the sanidine, hornfels, greenschist, amphibolite, and eclogite facies. By 1939 this nomenclature had evolved into a two-dimensional temperature-pressure classification further differentiated into metamorphic and magmatic facies. Eskola was active also in the interpretation of pre-Cambrian stratigraphy.

ESPY, JAMES POLLARD (*b. Washington County, Pa., 1785; d. Cincinnati, Ohio, 1860*), meteorology.

Turned from teaching to full-time meteorological work in mid-1830's; founded a system of observations in Pennsylvania (1836) and strove to establish a national system of volunteer weather observers (*ca.* 1840–52). Performed experiments in search of physical concepts, most notably centering on heat effects: constructed a nepheloscope to measure the dry and moist adiabatic cooling rates in clouds, and deduced the role of latent heat in cloud formation and rainfall. His ideas were transmitted to the British Association (1840) and the French Academy (1841).

ESSON, WILLIAM (*b. Carnoustie, Scotland, 1839* [*perhaps 1838*]; *d. Oxford, England, 1916*), chemistry.

Studied mathematics at St. John's College, Oxford; taught mathematics at Merton College; professor of geometry from 1897. Contributed greatly to the employment of higher mathematics in chemistry. With Vernon Harcourt, studied many problems of chemical kinetics and nearly succeeded in formulating the law of mass action (1864): they studied the reaction of potassium permanganate with oxalic acid, and concluded that "in unit volume of a dilute solution at constant temperature the rate of chemical change varies directly with the mass of each of the interacting substances."

ESTIENNE (STEPHANUS), CHARLES (*b. Paris, France, ca. 1505; d. Paris, 1564*), anatomy, natural history, scientific publication.

Member of famous dynasty of Parisian printers and publishers. Studied classical philology in Padua, then medicine under Jacques Dubois (Sylvius) in Paris; awarded bachelor's degree by Faculté de Médecine (1540), where he taught anatomy (1544–47). Wrote works on gardening, the names of plants and birds, diet, and a rural encyclopedia; major scientific work was *De dissectione partium corporis humani* (1545) with many original observations, antedating Vesalius' *Fabrica* in actual composition but delayed in its publication by a lawsuit.

EUCKEN, ARNOLD THOMAS (*b. Jena, Germany, 1884; d. Chiemsee, Germany, 1950*), physical chemistry.

Studied at universities of Kiel, Jena, and Berlin (doctorate, 1906); assistant in Nernst's laboratory (from 1908); director of physical chemistry at Technische Hochschule, Breslau (1919), and at University of Göttingen (from 1930). Worked on heat theory, determining specific heats and testing many heat laws experimentally. Later research was on reaction kinetics.

EUCLID (*fl. Alexandria* [*and Athens?*], *ca. 295* B.C.), mathematics.

Although Euclid is the most celebrated mathematician of all time only two facts of his life are known, and even these are not beyond dispute. One is that he was interme-

diate in date between the pupils of Plato (*d.* 347 B.C.) and Archimedes (*b. ca.* 287 B.C.); the other is that he taught in Alexandria. His birthplace is unknown, and the date of his birth can only be guessed. It is highly probable, however, that he attended the Academy, for Athens was the great center of mathematical studies at the time. Euclid is regarded as the founder of the great school of mathematics at Alexandria.

Euclid's fame rests preeminently upon the *Elements*, which he wrote in thirteen books. There had been *Elements* written before Euclid, but Euclid's work superseded them so completely that they are now known only from Eudemus' references as preserved by Proclus. Euclid's *Elements* was the subject of commentaries in antiquity by Hero, Pappus, Porphyry, Proclus, and Simplicius; and Geminus had many observations about it in a work now lost. In the fourth century Theon of Alexandria reedited it, altering the language in some places with a view to greater clarity, interpolating intermediate steps, and supplying alternative proofs, separate cases, and corollaries. All the manuscripts of the *Elements* known until the nineteenth century were derived from Theon's recension. Then Peyrard discovered in the Vatican a manuscript, known as *P*, which obviously gives an earlier text and is the basis of Heiberg's definitive edition.

The subject matter of the first six books of the *Elements* is plane geometry. It is, on the whole, a compilation of things already known, and its most remarkable feature is the arrangement of the matter so that one proposition follows on another in a strictly logical order, with the minimum of assumption and very little that is superfluous. It would appear that the fundamental discoveries were made before Euclid but that the orderly arrangement of propositions is his work.

The significance of Euclid's *Elements* in the history of thought is twofold. In the first place, it introduced into mathematical reasoning new standards of rigor which remained throughout the subsequent history of Greek mathematics and, after a period of logical slackness following the revival of mathematics, have been equaled again only in the past two centuries. In the second place, it marked a decisive step in the geometrization of mathematics. It was Euclid who ensured that the geometrical form of proof should dominate mathematics. This decisive influence of Euclid's geometrical conception of mathematics is reflected in two of the supreme works in the history of thought, Newton's *Principia* and Kant's *Kritik der reinen Vernunft*. Newton's work is cast in the form of geometrical proofs that Euclid had made the rule, even though Newton had discovered the calculus, which would have served him better and made him more easily understood by subsequent generations; and Kant's belief in the universal validity of Euclidean geometry led him to a transcendental aesthetic which governs all his speculations on knowledge and perception.

It was only toward the end of the nineteenth century that the spell of Euclidean geometry began to weaken and that a desire for the "arithmetization of mathematics" began to manifest itself; and only in the second quarter of the twentieth century, with the development of quantum mechanics, have we seen a return in the physical sciences to a neo-Pythagorean view of number as the secret of all things.

Any attempt to plot the course of Euclid's *Elements* from the third century B.C. through the subsequent history of mathematics and science is an extraordinarily difficult task. No other work has, in making its way from antiquity to the present, fallen under an editor's pen with anything approaching an equal frequency. And with good reason: it served, for almost 2,000 years, as the standard text of the core of basic mathematics.

The *Data,* the only other work by Euclid in pure geometry to have survived in Greek, is closely connected with books I–VI of the *Elements.* It is concerned with the different senses in which things are said to be given. Thus areas, straight lines, angles, and ratios are said to be "given in magnitude" when we can make others equal to them. Rectilineal figures are "given in species" or "given in form" when their angles and the ratio of their sides are given. Points, lines, and angles are "given in position" when they always occupy the same place, and so on. After the definitions there follow ninety-four propositions, in which the object is to prove that if certain elements of a figure are given, other elements are also given in one of the defined senses.

The concept behind the *Data* is that if certain things are given, other things are necessarily implied, until we are brought to something that is agreed. The *Data* then is a collection of hints on analysis.

Marinus of Naples, the pupil and biographer of Proclus, wrote a commentary on, or rather an introduction to, the *Data.* It is concerned mainly with the different senses in which the term "given" was understood by Greek geometers.

Proclus preserved *On Divisions of Figures* along with the titles of other works of Euclid and gives an indication of its contents. The book has not survived in Greek, but all the thirty-six enunciations and four of the propositions have been preserved in an Arabic translation discovered by Woepcke and published in 1851; the remaining proofs can be supplied from the *Practica geometriae* written by Leonardo Fibonacci in 1220, one section of which, it is now evident, was based upon a manuscript or translation of Euclid's work no longer in existence. The work was reconstructed by R. C. Archibald in 1915. The figures which are divided in Euclid's work are the triangle, the parallelogram, the trapezium, the quadrilateral, a figure bounded by an arc of a circle and two lines, and a circle.

Euclid also wrote a three-book work called *Porisms.* Pappus, who includes the work in the *Treasury of Analysis,* adds the information that it contained 171 theorems and thirty-eight lemmas. It has not survived—most unfortunately, for it appears to have been an exercise in advanced mathematics; but the account given by Pappus encouraged such great mathematicians as Robert Simson and Michel Chasles to attempt reconstructions, and Chasles was led to the discovery of anharmonic ratios.

Pappus explains that according to the older writers a porism is something intermediate between a theorem and a problem. The term, he says, is used both for "such theorems as are established in the proofs of other theorems, being windfalls and bonuses of the things sought, and also for such things as are sought, but need discovery, and are neither pure bringing into being nor pure investigation." As examples of a porism in this sense, Proclus gives two: first, the finding of the center of a circle, and second, the finding of the greatest common

measure of two given commensurable magnitudes. Euclid's *Porisms* would appear to have been the earliest known treatise on projective geometry and transversals.

We know from Pappus that Euclid wrote a four-book work on conic sections, but it has not survived even in quotation.

He doubtless shared the early Greek view that conic sections were generated by the section of a cone by a plane at right angles to a generator. He was also aware that a conic may be regarded as the locus of a point having a certain relationship to three or four straight lines. Pappus says that Euclid "wrote so much about the locus as was possible by means of the *Conics* of Aristaeus but did not claim finality for his proofs" and that "neither Apollonius himself nor anyone else could have added anything to what Euclid wrote, using properties of conics which had been proved up to Euclid's time."

It would appear that Euclid's work was no advance on that of Aristaeus, which would account for the fact that the latter's *Conics* was still extant, although that of Euclid had been lost, by the time of Pappus.

Surface Loci, a work in two books, is attributed to Euclid by Pappus and included in the *Treasury of Analysis.* It has not survived, and its contents can be conjectured only from remarks made by Proclus and Pappus about loci in general and two lemmas given by Pappus to Euclid's work.

It seems probable that Euclid's *Surface Loci* was concerned not merely with cones and cylinders (and perhaps spheres), but to some extent with three other second-degree surfaces of revolution: the paraboloid, the hyperboloid, and the prolate (but not the oblate) spheroid. If so, he anticipated to some extent the work that Archimedes developed fully in his *On Conoids and Spheroids.*

Proclus mentions Euclid's *Book of Fallacies* which has not survived but is identical with the work referred to as *Pseudographemata* by Michael Ephesius in his commentary on the *Sophistici elenchi* of Aristotle.

The textbook, *Phaenomena,* which the Greeks called *sphaeric,* intended for use by students of astronomy, survives in two recensions, of which the older must be the nearer to Euclid's own words. It was included in the collection of astronomical works which Pappus calls *The Treasury of Astronomy,* alternatively known as *The Little Astronomy,* in contrast with Ptolemy's *Syntaxis,* or *Great Astronomy.* In the older, more authentic recension it consists of a preface and sixteen propositions.

The *Optica,* attributed to Euclid by Proclus and also attested by Pappus, survives in two recensions; there is no reason to doubt that the earlier one is Euclid's own work. An elementary treatise in perspective, it was the first Greek work on the subject and remained the only one until Ptolemy wrote in the middle of the second century.

Proclus also attributes to Euclid a book entitled *Catoptrica,* that is, on mirrors. The work which bears that name in the editions of Euclid is certainly not by him but is a later compilation, and Proclus is generally regarded as having made a mistake.

Proclus attributes to Euclid a work with the title *Elements of Music.* Two musical treatises are included in the editions of Euclid's works, but they can hardly both be by the same author, since the *Sectio canonis,* or *Division of the Scale* expounds the Pythagorean doctrine that the musical intervals are to be distinguished by the mathematical ratio of the notes terminating the interval, while the *Introduction to Harmony* is based on the contrary theory of Aristoxenus, according to which the scale is formed of notes separated by a tone identified by the ear. It is now universally accepted that the *Introduction to Harmony* is the work of Cleonides, the pupil of Aristoxenus, to whom it is attributed in some manuscripts. The strongest argument for *Sectio cahonis* authenticity is that Porphyry in his commentary on Ptolemy's *Harmonica* quotes almost the whole of it except the preface, although the passages cited by Prophyry differ greatly from the text in dispute. All that it seems possible to say with certainty is that Euclid wrote a book entitled *Elements of Music* and that the *Sectio canonis* has some connection with it.

No work by Euclid on mechanics is extant in Greek. According to Arabic sources, however, he wrote a *Book on the Heavy and the Light;* when Hervagius was about to publish his 1537 edition there was brought to him a mutilated fragment, *De levi et ponderoso,* which he included as one of Euclid's works. As it stands, such a work could derive from a work by Euclid, but it is unlikely to be a direct translation of a Euclidean original.

EUCTEMON (*fl. Athens, fifth century* B.C.), astronomy.

Collaborated with Meton in observations of the summer solstice, in suggesting an intercalation cycle of nineteen years (the Metonic cycle) to correlate the lunar month with the solar year. Together they composed an influential parapegma (a type of almanac) whose weather prognostications were frequently cited in Greek calendars.

EUDEMUS OF RHODES (*b. Rhodes; fl. second half of fourth century* B.C.), philosophy, history of science.

A favored pupil of Aristotle, and one of those who made the works of Aristotle available to the world. Whether Eudemus was the author, or perhaps the editor, of the *Eudemian Ethics* has been matter for debate; he did write a *Physics* based on Aristotle's work, and this was used by Simplicius in his elucidation of Aristotle. Eudemus and Theophrastus together developed Aristotelian logic: they added five moods to the four in the first syllogistic figure, developing a distinction between necessary and merely factual premises and conclusions and saying that the conclusion must be like the "inferior premise." Eudemus is also important for his studies in the history of science, among the earliest in that field; although none of his works survive, they were used extensively by later writers and have thus given us what knowledge we have of early Greek science. Besides *History of Arithmetic, History of Geometry,* and *History of Astronomy,* he may have written a history of theology, a work *On the Angle,* a work on animals, and a history of Lindos.

EUDOXUS OF CNIDUS (*b. Cnidus, ca. 400* B.C.; *d. Cnidus, ca. 347* B.C.), astronomy, mathematics.

An eminent scholar and scientist who contributed to the development of astronomy, mathematics, geography, and philosophy. His teachers included Archytas and Plato; he founded a school at Cyzicus, and also taught in Cnidus. In mathematics his thinking lies behind much of Euclid's *Elements,* especially books V, VI, and XII. His theory of proportion embraced incommensurable quantities, and amounts to a rigorous definition of real number which

gave new impetus to number theory; he also attempted a strictly geometrical solution to the duplication of the cube. His method of exhaustion, used in calculation of the volume of solids, was an important step toward the development of integral calculus. He studied the axiomatic method, and the "Euclidean" presentation of axioms and propositions may well have been first systematized by him. His most influential achievement was the application of spherical geometry to astronomy: in *On Speeds* he expounded a system of geocentric, homocentric rotating spheres designed to explain the irregularities in the motion of planets as seen from the earth; he used the hippopede, an eight-shaped curve, to represent a planet's apparent motion in latitude as well as its retrogradation; in explaining his system he gave close estimates of the planetary synodic periods. Other works included two catalogs of stellar observations, a geography, and a calendar.

EULER, LEONHARD (*b. Basel, Switzerland, 1707; d. St. Petersburg, Russia, 1783*), mathematics, mechanics, astronomy, physics.

Euler's father gave his son his elementary education, including mathematics. Euler later spent several years in Basel, studying at a rather poor local Gymnasium; mathematics was not taught at all, so he studied privately with Johann Burckhardt, an amateur mathematician. In the autumn of 1720, being not yet fourteen, Euler entered the University of Basel in the department of arts to get a general education before specializing. Among his professors there was Johann I Bernoulli, who had followed his brother Jakob in the chair of mathematics. In 1722 Euler received the equivalent of the bachelor of arts degree, and in 1723 a master's degree in philosophy.

At the age of eighteen, he began his independent investigations. His first work, a small note on the construction of isochronous curves in a resistant medium, appeared in *Acta eruditorum* (1726); this was followed by an article in the same periodical on algebraic reciprocal trajectories (1727).

Euler received an invitation to serve as adjunct of physiology in St. Petersburg in the autumn of 1726. In 1727 he left Basel for St. Petersburg. He was at once given the chance to work in his real field and was appointed an adjunct member of the Academy in the mathematics section. He became professor of physics in 1731 and succeeded Daniel Bernoulli, who returned to Basel in 1733 as professor of mathematics. Already in August 1727 he had started making reports on his investigations at sessions of the Academy; he began publishing them in the second volume of the academic proceedings, *Commentarii Academiae scientiarum imperialis Petropolitanae (1727)* (St. Petersburg, 1729).

During his fourteen years in St. Petersburg Euler made brilliant discoveries in such areas as analysis, the theory of numbers, and mechanics. By 1741 he had prepared between eighty and ninety works for publication. He published fifty-five, including the two-volume *Mechanica.*

He was a member of both the St. Petersburg and Berlin academies, and was later elected a member of the Royal Society of London (1749) and the Académie des Sciences of Paris (1755). He was elected a member of the Society of Physics and Mathematics in Basel in 1753.

After fourteen years of living in Russia, Euler moved to Berlin in 1741 where he remained for the next twenty-five years. His work was still in both the Berlin and St. Petersburg academies. He was very active in transforming the old Society of Sciences into a large academy—officially founded in 1744 as the Académie Royale des Sciences et des Belles Lettres de Berlin.

During this period Euler greatly increased the variety of his investigation. Competing with d'Alembert and Daniel Bernoulli, he laid the foundations of mathematical physics; and he was a rival of both A. Clairaut and d'Alembert in advancing the theory of lunar and planetary motion. At the same time, Euler elaborated the theory of motion of solids, created the mathematical apparatus of hydrodynamics, successfully developed the differential geometry of surfaces, and intensively studied optics, electricity, and magnetism. He also pondered such problems of technology as the construction of achromatic refractors, the perfection of J. A. Segner's hydraulic turbine, and the theory of toothed gearings.

During the Berlin period Euler prepared no fewer than 380 works, of which about 275 were published, including several lengthy books: a monograph on the calculus of variations (1744); a fundamental work on calculation of orbits (1745); a work on artillery and ballistics (1745); *Introductio in analysin infinitorum* (1748); a treatise on shipbuilding and navigation, prepared in an early version in St. Petersburg (1749); his first theory of lunar motion (1753); and *Institutiones calculi differentialis* (1755). The last three books were published at the expense of the St. Petersburg Academy. Finally there was the treatise on the mechanics of solids, *Theoria motus corporum solidorum seu rigidorum* (1765). The famous *Lettres à une princesse d'Allemagne sur divers sujets de physique et de philosophie,* which originated in lessons given by Euler to a relative of the Prussian king, was not published until Euler's return to St. Petersburg. The book was an unusual success and ran to twelve editions in the original and was translated into many other languages.

In the 1740's and 1750's Euler took part in several philosophical and scientific arguments—such as the dispute over the monadology of Leibniz and of Christian Wolff.

In 1751 an argument began when S. König published some critical remarks on Maupertuis's principle of least action (1744) and cited a letter of Leibniz in which the principle was, in König's opinion, formulated more precisely. Submitting to Maupertuis, the Berlin Academy rose to defend him and demanded that the original of Leibniz' letter be presented. When it became clear that the original could not be found, Euler published, with the approval of the Academy, "Exposé concernant l'examen de la lettre de M. de Leibnitz" (1752), where, among other things, he declared the letter a fake. The conflict grew critical when later in the same year Voltaire published his *Diatribe du docteur Akakia, medécin du pape,* defending König and making laughingstocks of both Maupertuis and Euler. Frederick rushed to the defense of Maupertuis, quarreling with his friend Voltaire and ordering the burning of the offensive pamphlet.

Three other disputes in which Euler took part were much more important for the development of mathematical sciences: his argument with d'Alembert on the problem of logarithms of negative numbers, the argument with d'Alembert and Daniel Bernoulli on the solution of the equation of a vibrating string, and Euler's polemics with Dollond on optical problems.

After Maupertuis died in 1759 Euler managed the Berlin Academy, but under the direct supervision of the king. But relations between Frederick and Euler had long since spoiled. In 1763 it became known that Frederick wanted to appoint d'Alembert to the post of president of the Academy and Euler thus began to think of leaving Berlin. During 1765 and 1766 grave conflicts over financial matters arose between Euler and Frederick. On 9 June 1766, Euler left Berlin for St. Petersburg.

Soon after his return to St. Petersburg he suffered a brief illness, which left him almost completely blind. But his blindness did not lessen his scientific activity. Only in the last years of his life did he cease attending academic meetings and his literary output even increased—almost half of his works were produced after 1765.

Euler was a geometer in the wide sense in which the word was used during the eighteenth century. In his work, mathematics was closely connected with applications to other sciences, to problems of technology, and to public life.

In Euler's mathematical work, first place belongs to analysis; seventeen volumes of the *Opera omnia* are in this area. He contributed numerous particular discoveries to analysis, systematized its exposition in his classical manuals and contributed immeasurably to the founding of several large mathematical disciplines: the calculus of variations, the theory of differential equations, the elementary theory of functions of complex variables, and the theory of special functions.

Euler introduced many of the present conventions of mathematical notation: the symbol e to represent the base of the natural system of logarithms (1727, published 1736); the use of letter f and of parentheses for a function $f([x/a] + c)$ (1734, published 1740); the modern signs for trigonometric functions (1748); the notation $\int n$ for the sum of divisors of the number n (1750); notations for finite differences, Δy, $\Delta^2 y$, etc., and for the sum Σ (1755); and the letter i for $\sqrt{-1}$ (1777, published 1794).

A large series of Euler's works is connected with the theory of divisibility. He proved by three methods Fermat's lesser theorem, the principal one in the field (1741, 1761, 1763); he suggested with the third proof an important generalization of the theorem by introducing Euler's function $\phi(n)$, denoting the number of positive integers less than n which are relatively prime to n: the difference $a^{\phi(n)} - 1$ is divisible by n if a is relatively prime to n.

In the field of algebra Euler stated for the first time the theorem that every algebraic polynomial of degree n with real coefficients may be resolved into real linear or quadratic factors, that is, possesses n roots of the form $a + bi$. He also gave the first proof of the theorem that two algebraic curves of degrees m and n respectively intersect in mn points.

In Euler's works, infinite series, which previously served mainly as an auxiliary means for solving problems, became a subject of study. Euler demonstrated that for any even integer number $2k > 0$,

$$\zeta(2k) = a_{2k}\pi^{2k},$$

where a_{2k} are rational numbers (1740), expressed through coefficients of the Euler-Maclaurin summation formula (1750) and, consequently, through Bernoulli numbers (1755).

The summation formula was discovered by Euler no later than 1732 (1738) and demonstrated in 1735 (1741). The formula, one of the most important in the calculus of finite differences, represents the partial sum of a series, $\sum_{n=1}^{m} u(n)$, by another infinite series involving the integral and the derivatives of the general term $u(n)$.

The functions studied in the eighteenth century were, with rare exceptions, analytic, and therefore Euler made great use of power series. His special merit was the introduction of a new and extremely important class of trigonometric Fourier series. In a letter to Goldbach (1744), he expressed for the first time an algebraic function by such a series (1755),

$$\frac{\pi}{2} - \frac{x}{2} = \sin x + \frac{\sin 2x}{2} + \frac{\sin 3x}{3} + \cdots .$$

Discoveries in the field of analysis made in the middle of the eighteenth century were systematically summarized by Euler in the trilogy *Introductio in analysin infinitorum* (1748), *Institutiones calculi differentialis* (1755), and *Institutiones calculi integralis* (1768–70).

Starting with several problems solved by Johann and Jakob Bernoulli, Euler was the first to formulate the principal problems of the calculus of variations and to create general methods for their solution. In *Methodus inveniendi lineas curvas . . .* he systematically developed his discoveries of the 1730's (1739, 1741). The very title of the work shows that Euler widely employed geometric representations of functions as flat curves. Here he introduced, using different terminology, the concepts of function and variation and distinguished between problems of absolute extrema and relative extrema, showing how the latter are reduced to the former. The problem of the absolute extremum of the function of several independent variables,

$$\int_a^b F\,(x,\ y,\ y')\ dx,$$

where F is the given and $y(x)$ the desired minimizing or maximizing function, is treated as the limiting problem for the ordinary extremum of the function

$$W_n\,(y_0,\ y_1,\ \ldots,\ y_n) = \sum_{k=0}^{n-1} F\left(x_k,\ y_k,\ \frac{y_{k+1}-y_k}{\Delta x}\right)\Delta\ x,$$

where $x_k = a + k\ \Delta\ x$, $\Delta\ x = (b - a)/n$, $k = 0, 1, \ldots, n$ (and $n \to \infty$). Thus Euler deduced the differential equation named after him to which the function $y(x)$ should correspond; this necessary condition was generalized for the case where F involves the derivatives y', y'', $\ldots$, $y^{(n)}$. In this way the solution of a problem in the calculus of variations might always be reduced to integration of a differential equation. A century and a half later the situation had changed. The direct method imagined by Euler, which he had employed only to obtain his differential equation, had (together with similar methods) acquired independent value for rigorous or approximate solution of variational problems and the corresponding differential equations.

Most of Euler's geometrical discoveries were made by application of the methods of algebra and analysis. He gave two different methods for an analytical exposition of the system of spherical trigonometry (1755, 1782). He showed how the trigonometry of spheroidal surfaces might be applied to higher geodesy (1755). In volume II of the *Introductio* he surpassed his contemporaries in giving a consistent algebraic development of the theory of second-order curves, proceeding from their general equation (1748). He constituted the theory of third-order curves by analogy. But Euler's main achievement was that for the first time he studied thoroughly the general equation of second-order surfaces, applying Euler angles in corresponding transformations.

Euler's studies of the geodesic lines on a surface are prominent in differential geometry. Still more important were his pioneer investigations in the theory of surfaces, from which Monge and other geometers later proceeded. In 1763 Euler made the first substantial advance in the study of the curvature of surfaces; in particular, he expressed the curvature of an arbitrary normal section by principal curvatures (1767). He went on to study developable surfaces, introducing Gaussian coordinates (1772), which became widely used in the nineteenth century. In a note written about 1770 but not published until 1862 Euler discovered the necessary condition for applicability of surfaces that was independently established by Gauss (1828). In 1775 Euler successfully renewed elaboration of the general theory of space curves (1786), beginning where Clairaut had left off in 1731.

Euler was also the author of the first studies on topology. In 1735 he gave a solution to the problem of the seven bridges of Königsberg: the bridges, spanning several arms of a river, must all be crossed without recrossing any (1741). In a letter to Goldbach (1750), he cited (1758) a number of properties of polyhedra, among them the following: the number of vertices, S, edges, A, and sides, H, of a polyhedron are connected by an equality $S - A + H = 2$. A hundred years later it was discovered that the theorem had been known to Descartes. The Euler characteristic $S - A + H$ and its generalization for multidimensional complexes as given by H. Poincaré is one of the principal invariants of modern topology.

In an introduction to the *Mechanica* (1736) Euler outlined a large program of studies embracing every branch of the science. The distinguishing feature of Euler's investigations in mechanics as compared to those of his predecessors is the systematic and successful application of analysis. Previously the methods of mechanics had been mostly synthetic and geometrical; they demanded too individual an approach to separate problems. Euler was the first to appreciate the importance of introducing uniform analytic methods into mechanics, thus enabling its problems to be solved in a clear and direct way. Euler's concept is manifest in both the introduction and the very title of the book, *Mechanica sive motus scientia analytice exposita*.

The *Theoria motus corporum solidorum*, published almost thirty years later (1765), is related to the *Mechanica*. In the introduction to this work, Euler gave a new exposition of punctual mechanics and followed Maclaurin's example (1742) in projecting the forces onto the axes of a fixed orthogonal rectilinear system. Establishing that the instantaneous motion of a solid body might be regarded as composed of rectilinear translation and instant rotation, Euler devoted special attention to the study of rotatory motion. Thus, he gave formulas for projections of instantaneous angular velocity on the axes of coordinates (with application of Euler angles), and framed dynamical differential equations referred to the principal axes of inertia, which determine this motion.

In one of the two appendixes to the *Methodus* . . . Euler suggested a formulation of the principle of least action for the case of the motion of a point under a central force. In the other appendix to the *Methodus* Euler studied bending and vibrations of elastic bands (either homogeneous or nonhomogeneous) and of a plate under different conditions; considered nine types of elastic curves; and deduced the famous Euler buckling formula, or Euler critical load, used to determine the strength of columns.

His first large work on fluid mechanics was *Scientia navalis*. Volume I contains a general theory of equilibrium of floating bodies including an original elaboration of problems of stability and of small oscillations in the neighborhood of an equilibrium position. The second volume applies general theorems to the case of a ship.

From 1753 to 1755 Euler elaborated in detail an analytical theory of fluid mechanics in three classic memoirs —"Principes généraux de l'état d'équilibre des fluides"; "Principes généraux du mouvement des fluides"; and "Continuation des recherches sur la théorie du mouvement des fluides"—all published simultaneously (1757). Somewhat earlier (1752) the "Principia motus fluidorum" was written; it was not published, however, until 1761. Here a system of principal formulas of hydrostatics and hydrodynamics was for the first time created; it comprised the continuity equation for liquids with constant density; the velocity-potential equation (usually called after Laplace); and the general Euler equations for the motion of an incompressible liquid, gas, etc. The main innovations were in the application of partial differential equations to the problems.

Euler's studies in astronomy embraced a great variety of problems: determination of the orbits of comets and planets by a few observations, methods of calculation of the parallax of the sun, the theory of refraction, considerations on the physical nature of comets, and the problem of retardation of planetary motions under the action of cosmic ether. His most outstanding works, for which he won many prizes from the Paris Académie des Sciences, are concerned with celestial mechanics.

In 1751 he had written his own *Theoria motus lunae exhibens omnes ejus inaequalitates* (published in 1753), in which he elaborated an original method of approximate solution to the three-body problem, the so-called first Euler lunar theory. The theory had an important practical consequence: T. Mayer, an astronomer from Göttingen, compiled, according to its formulas, lunar tables (1755) that enabled the calculation of the position of the moon and thus the longitude of a ship with an exactness previously unknown in navigation.

From 1770 to 1772 Euler elaborated his second theory of lunar motion, which he published in the *Theoria motuum lunae, nova methodo pertractata* (1772).

Euler's works on optics were widely known and important in the physics of the eighteenth century. Rejecting the dominant corpuscular theory of light, he constructed his own theory in which he attributed the cause of light to peculiar oscillations of ether. His *Nova theoria lucis et colorum* (1746) explained some, but not all, phenomena.

EULER-CHELPIN, HANS KARL AUGUST SIMON VON (*b. Augsburg, Germany, 1873; d. Stockholm, Sweden, 1964*), biochemistry.

Turned to science from painting; studied under leading chemists and physicists at Berlin, Göttingen, Stockholm; qualified as *Privatdozent* in physical chemistry at Stockholm, 1898 (professor of general and organic chemistry from 1906). Shared Nobel Prize in chemistry (1929) with Arthur Harden for studies on fermentation: Euler-Chelpin and his associates clarified the role of cozymase by use of inhibitors. He also studied the chemical nature of cozymase, showing its structure to be that of diphosphopyridine nucleotide (DPN); investigated the role of nucleic acids in tumor growth; and contributed to our understanding of vitamin activity.

EUSTACHI, BARTOLOMEO (*b. San Severino, Ancona, Italy, ca. 1500–10; d. on the Via Flaminia en route to Fossombrone, Italy, 1574*), medicine.

Appears to have studied medicine at the Sapienza in Rome; began to practice medicine about 1540; moved to Rome (1549) and subsequently taught anatomy at Sapienza. Wrote two early works directed against the anti-Galenism of Vesalius (1561), and remarkable treatises on the kidney, the auditory organ, the venous system, and the teeth (written 1562–63, published together in 1564). Is remembered eponymously for the Eustachian tube (*tuba auditiva*) and the Eustachian vavle (*valvula venae cavae* in the right auricle). His work on the kidney was the first specifically dedicated to that organ and displays detailed, accurate knowledge; his pioneering study of the teeth was based on the dissection of fetuses and newborn children. In 1552 Eustachi prepared forty-seven strikingly modern anatomical illustrations (copperplate) of which eight were published in his work of 1554 (the rest were published by Lancisi in 1714).

EUTOCIUS OF ASCALON (*b. Palestine, ca. A.D. 480*), mathematics.

Eutocius is not known to have done any original mathematical work, but was the author of commentaries on three works by Archimedes (*On the Sphere and Cylinder, Measurement of a Circle,* and *On Plane Equilibria*) and edited and commented on the first four books of the *Conics* of Apollonius. In his commentaries he preserves solutions of mathematical problems by the earlier Greek geometers that are sometimes the sole evidence for their existence, including a valuable collection of solutions to the problem of finding two mean proportionals to two given straight lines, and Archimedes' solution of a cubic equation by the intersection of conics. His commentaries on Archimedes were translated into Latin, along with the parent works, by William of Moerbeke in 1269.

EVANS, ALEXANDER WILLIAM (*b. Buffalo, N.Y., 1868; d. New Haven, Conn., 1959*), botany.

Educated at Yale University (Ph.B., 1890; M.D., 1892; Ph.D., 1899; D.Sc., 1947), where he taught from 1895 until his death. Evans' interest turned from medicine to botany while he was an undergraduate; after his internship he studied botany at Berlin and Munich, and he never practiced medicine. He became the undisputed leader in two unrelated areas of botanical research, hepaticology and lichenology. In hepaticology he made effective use of morphological detail in interpreting relationships; his account of reduction as a prevailing trend in liverwort evolution and his scheme of classification based on that trend reflect a thoroughly modern point of view. Evans began to collect lichens in 1924, and from 1930 he specialized in the study of *Cladonia*; his major achievement was the successful use of chemistry to define species (chemotaxonomy), identifying distinctive substances microscopically by their crystalline structure. He also wrote on antibiotic properties of lichens. He served as editor of *Bulletin of the Torrey Botanical Club* (1914–24) and as associate editor of *Bryologist.*

EVANS, FREDERICK JOHN OWEN (*b. London* [*?*], *England, 1815; d. London, 1885*), hydrography, geomagnetism.

Volunteered for the navy at thirteen; began survey work in 1833. In 1841, as master and senior surveying officer of H.M.S. *Fly,* he charted a safe and easy passage through the Torres Strait and thus contributed to the development of New South Wales. Appointed superintendent of the Compass Department (1855), hydrographer to the navy (1874); knighted in 1881. Scientific recognition comes from his solution of the problems associated with compass navigation in iron and armor-plated ships and from his observations leading to the publication of a chart of curves of equal magnetic declination for the navigable world (with mathematical help from Archibald Smith). An important indirect contribution to oceanography was the compilation of magnetic instructions by Evans and Smith for the *Challenger* voyage.

EVANS, LEWIS (*b. Llangwnadl, Carnarvonshire, Wales, 1700; d. New York, N.Y., 1756*), cartography, geography, geomorphology, geology.

Evans came to Philadelphia sometime before 1736 and became known as a surveyor, draftsman, and mapmaker; he also gave lectures on electricity and wrote on climatology. The notes to his two great maps of the middle colonies (1749, 1755) reveal him as an early student not only of landscape but also of fossils and the relation of bedrock to surface morphology. He was the first in America to recognize the principles of isostasy (recorded in the journal of his expedition with John Bartram to Lake Ontario, 1743).

EVANS, WILLIAM HARRY (*b. Shillong, Assam, India, 1876; d. Church Whitfield, Dover, England, 1956*), entomology.

Career officer with Royal Engineers in India (1896–1931); collected and studied butterflies in his spare time and published *Identification of Indian Butterflies* (1927), the only work dealing fully with the subject of identification. After his retirement he published a series of catalogues of the Hesperiidae in the British Museum, establishing a complete classification of the Hesperiidae.

EVELYN, JOHN (*b. Wotton, Surrey, England, 1620; d. London, England, 1706*), arboriculture, horticulture.

Studied at Balliol College, Oxford (1637–40); traveled through France and Italy, studying anatomy in Padua (1645–46) and chemistry in Paris (under Niçaise Le Febvre, 1646), and visiting hospitals. In 1652 Evelyn set-tled at Sayes Court, his father-in-law's estate at Deptford in Kent, where he spent the next forty years and where he laid out gardens that became famous. He was instrumental in obtaining royal patronage and the name of "Royal Society" for the Gresham College group in 1662, and he wrote the first book published by order of the Society: *Sylva* (1664), an influential report on the propagation of timber trees drawn up at the request of the navy commissioners, with other horticultural tracts appended. Other scientific writings included *Fumifugium* (1661), on the pollution of the air in London; a translation of the first book of Lucretius' *De rerum natura* (1656) with a commentary on the works of Gassendi and atomism; translations of important French horticultural works; and a book on architecture (1664). Evelyn held many public appointments; his activities were guided by religious and patriotic motives. His *Diary,* which he kept throughout his life, is his greatest contribution, albeit to letters rather than to science.

EVERSHED, JOHN (*b. Gomshall, Surrey, England, 1864; d. Ewhurst, Surrey, England, 1956*), solar physics.

An ingenious designer of optical instruments and an indefatigable and meticulous observer. As a young man, studied solar and experimental spectroscopy in his private observatory; inherited A. C. Ranyard's astronomical instruments. Went on solar eclipse expeditions, first photographed (1898) continuous spectrum to the ultraviolet of the Balmer series limit at λ 3646. Through Huggins he was appointed to Kodaikanal and Madras observatories, India, where he began a long series of spectroheliograms. Discovered (1909) radial motion of gases in sunspots (Evershed effect). Confirmed Einstein's prediction of red shift of spectrum lines (Kashmir, 1915). Retired to England (1923), did high-dispersion work to determine exact wavelengths of the solar spectrum, sunspots, prominences, and minute line-shifts, and to study the Zeeman effect in assessing the strength of magnetic fields of sunspots.

EWING, JAMES (*b. Pittsburgh, Pa., 1866; d. New York, N.Y., 1943*), pathology.

Studied at Amherst College (A.B., 1888; M.A., 1891) and at College of Physicians and Surgeons, Columbia (M.D., 1891); taught at Columbia (1893–98) and then at Cornell University Medical College (1899–1939). After early work on pathology of the blood, pathogenesis of infectious diseases, immunity and blood serum reactions, and medicolegal questions, Ewing began experimental cancer studies (1902) and soon became one of the foremost American spokesmen in experimental oncology. His awareness of the need for a comprehensive organization of anticancer activities and his influence as president of the Medical Board of General Memorial Hospital (1913; director, 1931–39) led to the creation of a primary cancer facility—the present Memorial Sloan-Kettering Cancer Center in New York City. Ewing recorded a number of significant discoveries in tumor morphology in *Neoplastic Diseases* (1919), the cornerstone of modern oncology. He was a founder of the American Association for Cancer Research (1907) and of the American Cancer Society (1913), and was appointed to the first National Advisory Cancer Council (1937).

EWING, JAMES ALFRED (*b. Dundee, Scotland, 1855; d. Cambridge, England, 1935*), physics.

Engineering student at University of Edinburgh, influenced by Peter Tait and Fleeming Jenkin; with Jenkin, did early research on the harmonic analysis of vowel sounds. Taught at University of Tokyo (1878–83), where he established a seismological observatory, devised a new seismograph to record motion continuously during an earthquake, and began experimental study of magnetism. Held subsequent positions at University of Dundee (1883–90), Cambridge University (1890–1903), and University of Edinburgh (1916–29). Was director of naval education 1903–16, and during World War I he was in charge of "Room 40," a group that intercepted and deciphered German messages. Ewing was influential in establishing engineering education; he was knighted in 1911. In physics, he was one of the first to observe the phenomenon of hysteresis (1881), which he named.

EYTELWEIN, JOHANN ALBERT C. (*b. Frankfurt am Main, Germany, 1764; d. Berlin, Germany, 1848*), hydraulic engineering, mechanics.

Joined Prussian artillery at fifteen; studied civil engineering privately, entered the civil service where he made his career as hydraulic engineer (1790–1830). He was a strong influence in elevating the standards of engineering education. Concerned over the lack of a training program for civil engineers, he published a collection of problems in applied mathematics for surveyors and engineers (1793). He was one of the first to write on the application of mechanics and mathematics to the design of structures and machines. In 1797 he was a co-founder of the first civil engineering journal in Germany. His continued efforts on behalf of an engineering institution led to the founding of the Berlin Bauakademie (1799), of which he was director (1799–1806) and where he lectured. He also lectured at the University of Berlin (1810–15). His *Handbuch der Mechanik . . .* (1801) was the most important book of this era, for it was the first to combine practice and theory.

IBN EZRA, ABRAHAM BEN MEIR, also known as **Abū Isḥāq Ibrāhim al-Mājid ibn Ezra,** or **Avenare** (*b. Toledo, Spain, ca. 1090; d. Calahorra, Spain, ca. 1164–67 [?]*), mathematics, astronomy.

A Hebrew grammarian, exegete, astrologer, translator from Arabic into Hebrew, and poet, as well as a scientist, Ibn Ezra disseminated rationalistic and scientific Arabic learning in France, England, and Italy. Three of his treatises were devoted to numbers; others dealt with permutations and combinations, chronology and calendric science, and the astrolabe.

FABBRONI (or erroneously **FABRONI**), **GIOVANNI VALENTINO MATTIA** (*b. Florence, Italy, 1752; d. Florence, 1822*), economics, physics.

Worked at Museum of Physics and Natural Sciences in Florence (from 1768), except for years spent in Paris and London (1776–78); member of many learned academies. Wrote on economics, defending free trade, and on agriculture, botany, chemistry, physics, archaeology, and philology. In memoirs of 1792 and 1799 Fabbroni maintained that galvanic phenomena were not due to the action of an electric fluid, but to the reciprocal action of dissimilar metals upon contact, in the presence of moisture—an idea that influenced the emergence in the first years of the nineteenth century of the chemical theory of the battery.

FABRE, JEAN HENRI (*b. Saint-Léons, Aveyron, France, 1823; d. Sérignan, Vaucluse, France, 1915*), entomology, natural history.

Trained as a teacher, taught at various lycées (from 1842) while studying science (received *doctorat ès sciences naturelles,* Paris, 1854); remainder of life was devoted to research on the biology and behavior of insects. His principal discoveries were the hypermetamorphosis of *Meloidae;* the relationship between sex of the egg and dimensions of the cell among the solitary bees; the habits of dung beetles; and the paralyzing instinct of solitary wasps. His work demonstrated the importance of instinct among the insects and provoked much discussion (and some criticism); Fabre was opposed to evolution, and felt that each species was created with the same instinctual equipment it displays today. His *Souvenirs entomologiques* (10 vols., 1879–1907) contained many original observations on insect behavior, and led more than one person to become a naturalist. Fabre also wrote some forty works of scientific popularization, and was awarded the Legion of Honor for isolating alizarin from madder (1866).

FABRI, HONORÉ, (or **HONORATUS FABRIUS**) (*b. Virieu-le-Grand, Dauphiné, France, 1607; d. Rome, Italy, 1688*), mathematics, natural philosophy.

Educated as a Jesuit and ordained in 1636, Fabri combined important work in church politics and theology with wide-ranging scientific research. He taught at Collège de la Trinité in Lyons (1640–46) until his Cartesianism caused his transfer to Rome, where he served on the Penitentiary College (the Inquisition) until 1680. In astronomy, he opened a controversy with Huygens over Saturn's rings (1660), defended heliocentrism (leading to his imprisonment for fifty days), and discovered the Andromeda nebula (1665). In biology, he discovered—independently of Harvey—the circulation of the blood, which he taught publicly (1636). In his principal mathematical work, *Opusculum geometricum* (1659), he reinterpreted Cavalieri's concept of indivisibles by means of a dynamically formulated concept of *fluxus,* and presented various quadratures and cubatures as well as centroid determinations of sinusoidal and cycloidal segments together with their elements of rotation about both axes. His natural philosophy was less successful, but he did attempt to introduce a priori methods; he used the concept of the static moment, attempted a lunar explanation of the tides, studied capillarity, and used the principle of dispersion to explain the blue color of the sky.

FABRI, NICOLAS DE PEIRESC. *See* **Peiresc, Nicolas Fabri de.**

FABRICI, GIROLAMO (or **FABRICIUS AB AQUAPENDENTE, GERONIMO FABRIZIO**) (*b. Aquapendente, near Orvieto, Italy, ca. 1533; d. Padua, Italy, 1619*), anatomy, physiology, embryology, surgery.

Pupil of Falloppio at Padua (degree in medicine and philosophy *ca.* 1559); taught anatomy privately (1563–65) and then at the university (1565–1613), and taught surgery until 1609. Among his students were William Harvey, Salomon Alberti, Olaus Worm, and Caspar Bartholin. As a surgeon and physician Fabrici enjoyed high professional acclaim and the patronage of many eminent people; his patients included Galileo and Paolo Sarpi, as well as members of the nobility. As a scientist he was an indefatigable and scrupulous observer, but his interpretations were often shaped by tradition; he was more concerned with finding philosophically based principles than with morphological detail and tended to modify observations that did not verify such principles. His interpretation of nature was teleological, and his methods of observation derived largely from Galen.

Fabrici published several scientific volumes, of which the most famous is *De venarum ostiolis* (1603) on his observation of the venous valves (he first saw them in 1574). His Galenic approach caused him to miss the real significance of the valves, however; he thought their function to be the slowing down of the influx of the blood to provide for its even distribution to various parts of the body. He described them as corresponding to the openings of collateral branches, and thought they also served to prevent excessive stretching of the blood vessels. Perhaps the most notable contribution of *De venarum ostiolis* is that Harvey drew upon it in beginning his studies.

Two embryological treatises assure Fabrici's place among the most important biologists of his time. *De formatione ovi et pulli* (published posthumously in 1621) deals with the formation of the egg and with the generation of the chick within the egg; Fabrici excludes from his list of oviparous creatures only mammals and those insects that he believes to be the products of spontaneous generation. The work is illustrated with the first printed figures of the development of the chick, beginning with the third or fourth day of incubation.

Fabrici's other major embryological work, *De formato foetu* (1604), reveals the way in which nature provides for the necessities of the fetus during its intrauterine life. It treats specifically of the umbilical vessels, the urachus, the fetal membranes, fetal waste products, the placenta, and the uterus, and includes comparative studies; the value of the observations is lessened, however, by the Galenic interpretation imposed upon them. Fabrici was the first to give a reasoned classification of the various forms of placentas, and the first to study human decidua and the subplacenta of the guinea pig; he also was first to provide illustrations of many aspects of the anatomy of the uterus and the fetus.

FABRICIUS AB AQUAPENDENTE. *See* **Fabrici, Girolamo.**

FABRICIUS, JOHANN CHRISTIAN (*b. Tønder, South Jutland, Denmark, 1745; d. Kiel, Germany, 1808*), entomology.

Studied for two years under Linnaeus in Uppsala (1762–64) and traveled extensively thereafter. Professor of natural science and economics, first at University of Copenhagen and then at Kiel. Fabricius' work in entomology was admired by Linnaeus and by other colleagues throughout the world. His extensive writings on taxonomy were guided by two basic principles: the distinction between artificial and natural characteristics, and the importance of the various structures of the mouth. He named and described some 10,000 insects, and at-

tempted to build a system based on the naturally defined genera. He was a convinced evolutionist who considered it possible that a species could be formed through mixing existing species and through morphological adaptation and modification. He also discussed the influence of environment on the development of the species, as well as some selective phenomena.

FABRY, CHARLES (*b. Marseilles, France, 1867; d. Paris, France, 1945*), physics.

Graduated from École Polytechnique, Paris; received doctorate in physics from University of Paris (1892). Taught at Marseilles (1894–1920) and then at the Sorbonne and École Polytechnique. Fabry's research was primarily on the precise measurement of optical interference effects. With Alfred Pérot he invented an interferometer (1896) based upon multiple reflection of light between two plane parallel half-silvered mirrors; for about a decade they applied the instrument to spectroscopy and metrology. From 1906 Fabry worked with Henri Buisson; in 1912 they verified for helium, neon, and krypton the Doppler-broadening of emission lines predicted by the kinetic theory of gases. In 1914 they devised a simple method to confirm experimentally in the laboratory the Doppler effect for light. Fabry also used his interferometer to study solar and stellar spectra, and improved the techniques of photometry of the nocturnal sky; as part of this work he showed that the ultraviolet absorption in the upper atmosphere is due to ozone.

FABRY, LOUIS (*b. Marseilles, France, 1862; d. Les Lecques, near Toulon, France, 1939*), astronomy, applied celestial mechanics.

Older brother of Charles Fabry. Studied at École Polytechnique, at Marseilles, and at the Paris Observatory; held positions at the observatories of Nice (1886–90) and Marseilles (1890–1925). Fabry discovered a comet while still a student; his dissertation (1893) proved by statistical methods that the distribution of the elements of hyperbolic cometary orbits was incompatible with the hypothesis that such comets originated outside the solar system. He later showed that hyperbolic orbits had become so by the action of planetary perturbations and were originally elliptical. Fabry also developed rapid methods for identifying asteroids and for calculating and improving their ephemerides.

AL-FAḌL IBN ḤĀTIM AL-NAYRĪZĪ. *See* **al-Nayrizi.**

FAGNANO DEI TOSCHI, GIOVANNI FRANCESCO (*b. Sinigaglia, Italy, 1715; d. Sinigaglia, 1797*), mathematics.

An archpriest (from 1755); son of Giulio Carlo Fagnano. Made important contributions to geometry of the triangle, such as the theorem that the triangle which has as its vertices the bases of the altitudes of any triangle has these altitudes as its bisectors.

FAGNANO DEI TOSCHI, GIULIO CARLO (*b. Sinigaglia, Italy, 1682; d. Sinigaglia, 1766*), mathematics.

Son of a noble family; self-taught in mathematics, but rose rapidly to international prominence and corresponded with many contemporary mathematicians. In algebra he suggested new methods for solution of equations of the second, third, and fourth degrees; he also clarified the field of imaginary numbers and established the well-known formula

$$\frac{\pi}{4} = \log \left(\frac{1-i}{1+i} \right)^{1/2}.$$

In geometry Fagnano formulated a general theory of geometric proportions, but of even more importance is his fundamental work on the geometry of the triangle. Two major findings are (1) that the sum of the squares of the distances of the center of gravity of a triangle from the vertices equals one-third the sum of the squares of the sides and (2) that given a triangle, *ABC*, for every point *P* of *BC* we may construct an inscribed triangle, with its vertex at *P*, of minimum perimeter. Eminent in analytical geometry and integral calculus, Fagnano rectified the lemniscate of Jakob I Bernoulli and found its area; he gave their name to "elliptic integrals," and his work is considered by some to be the forerunner of the theory of elliptic functions.

FAHRENHEIT, DANIEL GABRIEL (*b. Danzig* [*Gdansk*], *Poland, 1686; d. The Hague, Netherlands, 1736*), experimental physics.

Sent to Amsterdam at fifteen to learn business, but became fascinated by the manufacture of scientific instruments. Spent ten years in travel, visiting scientists and instrument makers (met Olaus Roemer in Copenhagen, 1708); returned to Amsterdam in 1717 and established his own business. Fahrenheit's most significant achievement was his development of the standard thermometric scale that bears his name. He started graduating his thermometers by what he believed to be Roemer's methods: the upper fixed point, labeled 60°, was at body temperature, and the lower, labeled 30°, was determined by an ice and water mixture; he later (1717) moved the upper point to 96° and the lower one to 32° for more convenient calculation, and after his death it became standard practice to set the upper point at 212°, the boiling point of water (thus moving body temperature to 98.6°). In perfecting his thermometers Fahrenheit studied such problems as the expansion of glass, the thermometric behavior of mercury and alcohol, and density determination. He constructed a hypsometric thermometer to determine the atmospheric pressure directly from a reading of the boiling point of water, and invented a hydrometer.

FALCONER, HUGH (*b. Forres, Scotland, 1808; d. London, England, 1865*), paleontology, botany.

Studied at universities of Aberdeen (M.A.) and Edinburgh (M.D.). Held botanical posts in India (1832–42, 1848–55), where he explored mountainous country and made immense collections of plants, and was largely responsible for starting the cultivation of Indian tea and for the introduction into India of the quinine-bearing plant. Most known for study (with Proby Cautley) of Tertiary vertebrate fossils, particularly mammals, that they discovered in the Siwalik Hills. His later studies were on Pleistocene mammals and the evidences of prehistoric man in Britain and Europe.

FALLOPPIO, GABRIELE (*b. Modena, Italy, 1523* [*?*]; *d. Padua, Italy, 1562*), medicine.

Studied medicine in Modena, perhaps in Padua, and in Ferrara; held chair of pharmacy at Ferrara, chair of anat-

omy at Pisa (1549), and chair of anatomy at Padua (from 1551). Of the various works attributed to him only the *Observationes anatomicae* (1561) was published during his lifetime and can be said with certainty to be fully authentic; rather than a systematic text it is an unillustrated commentary on the *De humani corporis fabrica* of Vesalius, seeking to correct its errors and to present new material. Falloppio's criticism is temperate and friendly, for he recognized the influence of Vesalius' work on his own studies. He based his comments on many dissections, not only of human bodies but also of fetuses, newborn infants, and young children, and presented many important contributions to the knowledge of primary and secondary centers of ossification, the stages of dentition, the anatomy of the auditory apparatus, the arrangement and action of the muscles of the head, the anatomy of the kidneys and bladder, and female reproductive anatomy. His name is most closely associated with his description of the uterine or Fallopian "tubes" (his word for them was *tuba*, because of their resemblance to small trumpets).

FANKUCHEN, ISIDOR (*b. Brooklyn, N.Y., 1905; d. Brooklyn, 1964*), crystallography.

Received degrees from Cooper Union (B.S., 1926), Cornell University (Ph.D., 1933), and Cambridge University (Ph.D., 1942); worked under W. L. Bragg in Manchester (1934–36), then under J. D. Bernal in Cambridge (1936–38) and in London (1938–39). As an active member of the Bernal group he studied molecular weight and crystal structure of macromolecular compounds. From 1942 he taught at the Polytechnic Institute of Brooklyn, where he exerted a great influence on the teaching of crystallography and X-ray diffraction. He applied X-ray diffraction to new problems and refined or developed the necessary techniques and apparatus. His later studies were on fibers, metal films, and bones and teeth. First American editor of *Acta crystallographica* (1948–64); first president of American Crystallographic Association (1950); founder of Polycrystal Book Service.

FANO, GINO (*b. Mantua, Italy, 1871; d. Verona, Italy, 1952*), geometry.

While a student under Segre at Turin (1888–92) Fano translated Felix Klein's Erlanger Programm; he later met Klein in Göttingen (1893–94). Assisted Castelnuovo in Rome (1894–99), taught at Messina (1899–1901) and then at Turin (1901–38) until ousted by the Fascists. Worked mainly in projective and algebraic geometry of n-space S_n. Early studies deal with line geometry and linear differential equations with algebraic coefficients; he also pioneered in finite geometry. Later work is on algebraic and especially cubic surfaces, manifolds, birational contact transformations, and non-Euclidean and non-Archimedean geometries.

AL-FĀRĀBĪ, ABŪ NAṢR MUḤAMMAD IBN MUḤAMMAD IBN ṬARKHĀN IBN AWZALAGH (Latin Alf[h]arabius, Abunazar, among other forms) (*b. Wasīj, district of Fārāb, ca. 870; d. Damascus, 950*), philosophy, music.

Traveled widely, but most productive years were spent in Baghdad, where he perfected his knowledge of Arabic and established a reputation as the foremost Muslim philosopher and the greatest philosophic authority after Aristotle; his influence persisted in the learned tradition of the study of and commentary on Aristotle and Plato in Arabic, Hebrew, and Latin. Al-Fārābī believed that science (that is, philosophy) had reached its highest development in the Socratic tradition; his effort to recover, explain, defend, and reestablish this view of science as the highest stage of human wisdom took into account the gulf that separated the cultural environment of Greek science from the new Islamic environment. His teaching activity followed an elaborate philosophic syllabus developed on a number of levels and based on the writings of Aristotle, a number of Platonic dialogues, and the works of Hippocrates and Galen, Euclid and Ptolemy, Plotinus and Porphyry, and the Greek commentators of the schools of Athens and Alexandria.

Al-Fārābī's specialized writings on natural science are for the most part polemical, although it seems that his intention was not primarily to defend the doctrines of Aristotle against his critics, but rather to clarify the questions at issue. In mathematics, he wrote a major work on music: *Kitāb al-mūsīqā al-kabīr,* on musical history, theory, and practice; included are the physics of sound, definitions of the basic elements of note, pitch, and interval, a detailed exposition of various tetrachord species, an analysis of rhythm, a presentation of the differing scales obtainable on the main melody instruments, and an account of various types of voice production and ornamentation and the way these should be utilized in the course of a composition.

FARADAY, MICHAEL (*b. Newington, Surrey [now part of Southwark, London], England, 1791; d. Hampton Court, Middlesex, England, 1867*), chemistry, physics.

Faraday's formal education was almost nil, consisting of the rudiments of reading, writing, and ciphering. When fourteen, he was apprenticed to learn the art of bookbinding. The proximity of books stimulated his mind and he became an omnivorous reader. His passion for science was first aroused by a chance reading of the article "Electricity" in a copy of the *Encyclopaedia Britannica* which he was rebinding. In February 1810, Faraday attended his first lecture at the City Philosophical Society, a group of young men with a common passion for science led by John Tatum. There he received a basic education in the sciences.

Faraday's interest in science led him to a work which he lauded throughout his life, Jane Marcet's *Conversations on Chemistry.* His thoughts were directed specifically to chemistry, and, most important of all, he was introduced to the thoughts of Humphry Davy.

In late October 1812 Davy was temporarily blinded by an explosion in his laboratory at the Royal Institution. Faraday was recommended to Davy as an amanuensis, and Davy was pleased to have him. In March 1813, Faraday took up his new position as laboratory assistant.

Soon after Faraday's employment at the Royal Institution, Davy decided to visit the Continent, and he asked Faraday to accompany him. During this tour, Davy discoursed on every scientific subject under the sun, and Faraday eagerly drank it all in.

Upon his return to London in 1815, Faraday threw himself into chemistry. In 1816 he published his first

paper, "Analysis of Caustic Lime of Tuscany." By 1820 Faraday had established a modest but solid reputation as an analytical chemist. In 1820 he produced the first known compounds of chlorine and carbon, C_2Cl_6 and C_2Cl_4, by the substitution of chlorine for hydrogen in "olefiant gas," our modern ethylene. This was the first substitution reaction.

Beyond his work in analytical and pure chemistry, Faraday showed himself to be a pioneer in the application of chemistry to problems of technology. In 1818, together with James Stodart, a cutler, he began a series of experiments on the alloys of steel. In 1824 Faraday was asked by the Royal Society to conduct experiments on optical glass.

By 1821 Faraday was aware of and even toying with the concept of Boscovichean point-atoms. This is not to say that Faraday was a disciple of Boškovic, for he certainly did not follow the Boscovichean system in his work; but the notion of atoms as centers of force; Had a strong appeal for him, and it is this notion that provided the conceptual framework for his work on electricity.

After Oersted's announcement of the discovery of electromagnetism in 1820, editors of scientific journals had been inundated with articles on the phenomenon. It was to answer questions about this phenomenon that the editor of *Philosophical Magazine* turned to Faraday to undertake a short historical survey.

His enthusiasm was aroused in September 1821, when he turned to the investigation of the peculiar nature of the magnetic force created by an electrical current. His paper "On Some New Electro-Magnetical Motions, and on the Theory of Magnetism" (1821) records the first conversion of electrical into mechanical energy. It also contains the first notion of the line of force.

In the years between 1821 and 1831, Faraday returned sporadically to the question of electromagnetism. He demonstrated the reverse of Oersted's effect, namely, the conversion of magnetic force into electrical force. Further investigation led him to the invention of the first dynamo, whereby the reverse of his 1821 discovery of electromagnetic rotations could be accomplished. Mechanical force could be converted into electrical force by a simple machine.

The first and second series of Faraday's *Experimental Researches* had been concerned with the relations between electricity and magnetism. In the summer of 1832 Faraday appeared to go off on a tangent, with an investigation into the identity of the electricities produced by the various means then known. Insofar as electricity affected a galvanometer needle, Faraday gave conclusive proof of the identity of static and voltaic electricity. He had furthermore devised an instrument for the measurement of relative quantities of electricity.

But one more question needed to be solved. Could not the quantity of electricity be correlated with the products of electrochemical decomposition? In answering this question, Faraday enunciated his two laws of electrochemistry: (1) Chemical action or decomposing power is exactly proportional to the quantity of electricity which passes in solution; (2) The amounts of different substances deposited or dissolved by the same quantity of electricity are proportional to their chemical equivalent weights.

By 1838 Faraday was in a position to put all the pieces together into a coherent theory of electricity. The particles of matter were composed of forces arranged in complex patterns which gave them their individuality. These patterns could be distorted by placing the particles under strain. Electrical force set up such a strain. In electrostatics, the strain was imposed on molecules capable of sustaining large forces; when the line of particulate strain gave way, it did so with the snap of the electric spark. Lightning was the result of the same process on a larger scale. In electrochemistry, the force of the breaking strain was that of the chemical affinities of the elements of the chemical compound undergoing electrochemical decomposition. The shift of the particles of the elements toward the two electrodes momentarily relaxed the strain, but it was immediately re-created by the constant application of electric force at the electrodes upon the nearest particles of the electrolyte. This buildup and breakdown of interparticulate strain, passing through the electrolyte, constituted the electrical "current." It was a transfer of energy which did not entail a transfer of matter.

In 1845 Faraday performed an experiment showing the angle of rotation of a ray of plane polarized light to be directly proportional to the strength of magnetic force applied to it. This indicated for him the direct effect of magnetism upon light. Yet, not all bodies reacted in the same way to the magnetic force. Some, like iron, aligned themselves along the lines of magnetic force and were drawn into the more intense parts of the magnetic field. Others, like bismuth, set themselves across the lines of force and moved toward the less intense areas of magnetic force. The first group Faraday christened "paramagnetics"; the second, "diamagnetics."

Faraday went on to show that the lines of magnetic force, unlike their electrostatic cousins, are continuous curves having no termini. They cannot be accounted for in terms of force-atoms under strain, and Faraday ignored his earlier model of interparticulate strain for the transmission of magnetic force.

But his explanations remained unsatisfactory. Only one point emerged clearly, and this point was of fundamental importance. Whatever the cause of magnetism, the manifestation of magnetic force took place in the medium surrounding the magnet. This manifestation was the magnetic field, and the energy of the magnetic system was in the field, not in the magnet. By extension, the same could be said of electrical and gravitational systems. This is the fundamental axiom of classic field theory.

FAREY, JOHN (*b. Woburn, Bedfordshire, England, 1766; d. London, England, 1826*), geology.

Employed first as a land steward (1792–1802) and eventually as a mineral surveyor, Farey contributed to geology both indirectly—through promotion of the pioneering work of William Smith, who had taught him—and directly. He drew geological sections of the area between London and Brighton and between Ashover (Derbyshire) and the Lincolnshire coast in which he recognized anticlinal structure and denudation. The first volume of his survey of Derbyshire (1811) for the Board of Agriculture includes the first published geological map of an English county and two colored plates of block diagrams.

AL-FARGHĀNĪ, ABU'L-ʿABBĀS AḤMAD IBN MU-HAMMAD IBN KATHĪR (*b. Farghāna, Transoxania; d. Egypt, after 861*), astronomy.

As an engineer, supervised construction of the Great Nilometer for al-Mutawakkil. Employed as an astronomer-astrologer by al-Maʾmūn. Wrote *Jawāmiʿ*, or *Elements* (also known under various other titles), a comprehensive, nonmathematical account of the elements of Ptolemaic astronomy that was commented on by al-Qabīsī, translated by John of Seville and by Gerard of Cremona, and was widely influential in medieval Europe. In it the Maʾmūnic value of the obliquity of the ecliptic is given as 23° 35', and of the circumference and the diameter of the earth as 20,400 and approximately 6,500 miles, respectively. Al-Farghānī also wrote works on sundials, on the mathematical theory of the astrolabe, and on the astronomical tables of al-Khwārizmī (his commentary has been lost, but was available to and made use of by al-Bīrūnī).

FARKAS, LASZLO (LADISLAUS) (*b. Dunaszerdahely, Hungary [now Dunajska Streda, Czechoslovakia], 1904; d. near Rome, Italy, 1948*), physical chemistry.

Studied chemistry at Technische Hochschule in Berlin (doctorate, 1927); worked at Kaiser Wilhelm Institute, at Cambridge University, and finally at Faculty of Sciences of Hebrew University, Jerusalem (1936–48). Did research on photochemical sensitizing in the region of the ultraviolet and then on equilibrium distribution of ortho-hydrogen and para-hydrogen, before turning to pioneering work on deuterium and heavy water. With his brother he developed an electrolytic method that resulted in the simplest known procedure for producing heavy water.

FARMER, JOHN BRETLAND (*b. Atherstone, Warwickshire, England, 1865; d. Exmouth, Devon, England, 1944*), botany.

Graduated from Oxford in natural sciences (1887) and taught there (1887–92); from 1892 taught at Royal College of Science and promoted training of applied biologists to work in underdeveloped countries. Did research in pure botany and in cytology; made extensive studies of reduction division, demonstrating it in spore formation and showing similarities between division in plant and animal cells. With J. E. S. Moore (1904) introduced term "maiotic phase" (later changed to "meiotic phase"). Edited *Annals of Botany, Science Progress,* and *Gardeners' Chronicle.* Knighted, 1926.

FARRAR, JOHN (*b. Lincoln, Mass., 1779; d. Cambridge, Mass., 1853*), mathematics, physics, education.

Responsible for sweeping modernization of the science and mathematics curriculum at Harvard College, his alma mater. Translated and published the best French and other European writings; much of the responsibility for shifting from the Newtonian fluxional notations to Leibniz's algorithm for the calculus was his.

IBN AL-FARRUKHĀN. *See* ʿUmar ibn al-Farrukhān.

FATOU, PIERRE JOSEPH LOUIS (*b. Lorient, France, 1878; d. Pornichet, France, 1929*), mathematics.

Attended École Normale Supérieure (1898–1901; doctorate, 1907); worked at Paris Observatory in practical astronomy: on absolute positions of stars and planets, on instrumental constants, and on measurements of twin stars. Also did mathematical research, contributing important results on Taylor series, the theory of the Lebesgue integral, and iteration of rational functions of a complex variable.

FAUJAS DE SAINT-FOND, BARTHÉLEMY (*b. Montélimar, Dauphiné, France, 1741; d. Saint-Fond, Dauphiné, 1819*), geology.

Turned from legal career to natural history, worked at Muséum d'Histoire Naturelle (Paris) from 1778 (professor of geology from 1793). Studied basalt of Vivarais and Velay districts, showed it to be volcanic (1778). Continued to study basalt in journey through England to Scotland (1784, full account published in 1797). In the chalk of Maastricht Faujas found a huge reptilian skull, later discussed by Cuvier (1824) and named mosasaur by Conybeare. Wide-ranging interests included physics and chemistry as well as geology, and their practical applications; he found, analyzed, and opened up a deposit of volcanic tuff for the cement industry, and wrote on balloon construction and navigation.

FAULHABER, JOHANN (*b. Ulm, Germany, 1580; d. Ulm, 1635*), mathematics.

A weaver whose natural abilities led him to mathematics, and who became one of the most significant Cossists and the first to take algebra into equations higher than the third degree. He laboriously translated the Latin texts he needed into simple German. In 1600 he founded a school in Ulm; his school became an educational institute for higher mathematical sciences, and an artillery and engineering school was later added. He excelled in the dissemination of mathematical knowledge for general use; his lasting accomplishment was the publication and explanation of the logarithmic method of calculation in *Ingenieurs-Schul . . .* (1630–33), *Appendix oder Anhang . . . Ingenieurs-Schul* (1631), and *Zehntausend Logarithmi . . .* (1631).

Particular mathematical problems addressed by Faulhaber include formulas for the sum of the powers for natural numbers up to the thirteenth power, the stereometric analog to the Pythagorean theorem (1620), and the radius and angle measurements of an irregular circle-heptagon (in *Ingenieurs-Schul*). His interests also extended to alchemy, which he practiced as a believer in Andreae's Rosicrucianism; military engineering in many localities; and physical and technical inventions. He published several works on Biblical numerology, thereby incurring the enmity of the clergy and the displeasure of the civil authorities. With Kepler, he designed a gauging kettle for the measurement of length, volume, and weight (1622). He was esteemed by Descartes, who studied with him in 1620.

FAVORSKY, ALEXEI YEVGRAFOVICH (*b. Pavlovo, Russia, 1860; d. Leningrad, U.S.S.R., 1945*), chemistry.

Studied under Butlerov at St. Petersburg (graduated 1882); professor from 1896, and responsible for a large school of chemists (including Ipatiev and Lebedev). Studied reactions of organic unsaturates, primarily the acetylenic hydrocarbons; the results of his work form the basis of many general methods of synthesis, including a number that are of industrial significance. Discovered the iso-

merization phenomena of acetylenic hydrocarbons (1884); predicted existence of polyene compounds (1891); explained phenomena of tautomerism and reversible isomerization in one set of reactions; studied condensation of ketones with acetylenic hydrocarbons (1905–07) and used this reaction in developing a simple method for synthesizing isoprene (1932). Edited *Zhurnal Russkago fizikokhimicheskago obshchestva* (1900–30).

FAVRE, PIERRE ANTOINE (*b. Lyons, France, 1813; d. Marseilles, France, 1880*), chemistry.

Studied medicine in Paris before turning to chemistry; held positions in Paris, Besançon, and Marseilles. Did notable work in thermochemistry, and is perhaps best known for using the term "calorie" (1853). Studied heats of combustion with J. T. Silbermann (1845–53), using a newly-devised mercury calorimeter; their results were somewhat inaccurate, but were widely used, and their work was influential in replacing the vague notion of chemical affinity with more precise thermodynamic expressions. In 1857 Favre substantiated Joule's ideas on the conservation of energy by means of a voltaic battery operating an electric motor that raised a weight, showing that the total heat evolved in battery and circuit, added to the equivalent in heat required to raise the weight, equaled that evolved by the battery alone when it was short-circuited.

FAYE, HERVÉ (*b. St. Benoît-du-Sault, France, 1814; d. Paris, France, 1902*), astronomy, geodesy.

Studied at École Polytechnique and later taught there (from 1848); entered Paris Observatory in 1836, where he discovered the periodic comet of 1843 and computed its orbit. Later professor of astronomy at Nancy and president of the Bureau des Longitudes. Improved observational techniques in astronomy; developed theories of the tails of comets, of meteorites as related to comets, of the gaseous nature of the sun; developed and improved Laplace's cosmogony. Spent much effort on geodetic projects; introduced an idea close to isostasy.

AL-FAZĀRĪ, MUHAMMAD IBN IBRĀHĪM (*fl. second half of the eighth century*), astronomy.

Al-Fazārī's work was almost entirely derivative, and he did not produce a unified system of astronomy, but he did help to introduce a large body of Indian astronomical parameters and computational techniques to Islamic scientists through his *Zīj al-Sindhind al-kabīr* (combining elements of the *Zīj al-Sindhind*, the *Zīj al-Shāh*, and the *Āryabhaṭīya*). He also wrote another set of astronomical tables, with calendric conversion tables and a list of the countries of the world and their dimensions.

FEATHERSTONHAUGH, GEORGE WILLIAM (*b. London, England, 1780; d. Le Havre, France, 1866*), geology.

Did not enter a university; after travels, moved to U.S. (1806) and became interested in agriculture. Returned briefly to England (1826–27), where he met the leading geologists and acquired both knowledge and large collections of minerals, fossils, and shells. Advanced American geology through distribution of collections to museums and societies; through public lectures; through correspondence with English geologists; and through his short-lived *Monthly American Journal of Geology and Natural Science* (1831). Began field work in 1832, and in 1834 became first U.S. government geologist; published reports on the Ozark Mountains and on Wisconsin and Minnesota (the latter report included observations between Washington and Green Bay). Served as commissioner in boundary dispute between Maine and New Brunswick (1839); delivered his report to England and never returned to America. His later years were spent in diplomatic work.

FECHNER, GUSTAV THEODOR (*b. Gross-Särchen, near Halle, Germany, 1801; d. Leipzig, Germany, 1887*), psychology.

In 1817 Fechner matriculated at the University of Leipzig, where he spent the rest of his life (M.D., 1822; professor of physics, 1834–39). Early work in physics was on electricity, particularly on Ohm's law; published *Massbestimmungen über die galvanische Kette* (1831), a paper of great importance on quantitative measurements of the galvanic battery. A long, serious neurotic illness caused his resignation from his chair of physics; on recovering from this illness he developed what has been called his panpsychism: since mind and matter were two aspects of the same thing (his earlier *Tagesansicht*), the entire universe could be looked at from the point of view of its mind. In 1850 he decided to make the relative increase of stimulation the measure of the increase of the corresponding sensation, with the anticipation that the arithmetical series of perceived intensities might correspond to a geometrical series of external energies; after a decade of thought and experiment he published *Elemente der Psychophysik* (1860), the foundation of the new science of psychophysics, containing basic methodology and, more importantly, Fechner's development of the Weber fraction into what has come to be known as the Weber-Fechner law. E. H. Weber had stated that the just noticeable difference in stimulus intensity is a constant fraction of the total intensity at which it is measured, expressible as $\frac{\Delta R}{R}$ = constant, where R is *Reiz*, or stimulus; Fechner assumed that on the mental side there is a corresponding increase in sensation, ΔS, and that all such ΔS's are equal and can be treated as units, and arrived at $S = C \log R$, where R is measured in units of its threshold value. This is the fundamental relation between mind on the left-hand side of the equation, and matter on the right. The *Elemente* kindled immediate controversy, which persists. In Fechner's next work, *Vorschule der Ästhetik* (1876), he founded experimental aesthetics.

FEDDERSEN, BEREND WILHELM (*b. Schleswig, Germany, 1832; d. Leipzig, Germany, 1918*), physics.

Studied in Göttingen, Berlin, Leipzig, and Kiel (doctorate, 1858). Investigated electric-spark discharges; showed that the discharge of a Leiden flask produces a train of damped oscillations, which he photographed. His finding that a circuit made up of a capacitance, a resistance, and an inductance produces oscillations whose frequency and amplitude depend on these components proved to be of considerable technological importance, and his photographs served to confirm William Thomson's theory (1853) of long-distance signaling. Feddersen is also remembered for his contributions to scientific bibliography through participation in (and financial

support of) Poggendorff's *Biographisch-literarisches Handwörterbuch*.

FÉE, ANTOINE-LAURENT-APOLLINAIRE (*b. Ardentes, France, 1789; d. Paris, France, 1874*), botany.

Served as military pharmacist and operated own pharmacy in Paris before earning M.D. from Strasbourg (1833) and becoming professor of botany there. Contributed to cryptogamic botany through extensive descriptive study of ferns (1844–66) and work on lichens and cryptogams occurring on medicinal barks. In plant physiology, studied movement in plants, especially as affected by light. Also wrote on plants mentioned in classical literature, and published biographies of prominent botanists.

FEIGL, GEORG (*b. Hamburg, Germany, 1890; d. Wechselburg, Germany, 1945*), mathematics.

Received doctorate from University of Jena (1918); taught at universities of Berlin (1919–35) and Breslau (from 1935). Worked on foundations of geometry and topology, but more important was his reform of mathematical education through introduction of the modern mathematics based on axioms and structures into universities and even high schools. Managing editor of *Jahrbuch über die Fortschritte der Mathematik* (1928–35).

FEJÉR, LIPÓT (*b. Pécs, Hungary, 1880; d. Budapest, Hungary, 1959*), mathematics.

Studied at universities of Berlin and Budapest (doctorate, 1902); taught at Budapest (1902–05, 1911–59) and at Kolozsvár (now Cluj, Rumania—1905–11), and became head of the most successful Hungarian school of analysis. His main works deal with harmonic analysis; his classic theorem on (C,1) summability of trigonometric Fourier series (1900) not only gave a new direction to the theory of orthogonal expansions, but also, through significant applications, became a starting point for the modern general theory of divergent series and singular integrals. In 1910 Fejér found a new method of investigating the singularities of Fourier series that was suitable for a unified discussion of various types of divergence phenomena. Contributed also to approximation theory and the constructive theory of functions, to mechanical quadrature, and to complex analysis.

FENNEMAN, NEVIN MELANCTHON (*b. Lima, Ohio, 1865; d. Cincinnati, Ohio, 1945*), geology.

Studied at Heidelberg College and University of Chicago (Ph.D., 1901). Taught at universities of Colorado and Wisconsin before going to University of Cincinnati, where he started a department of geology and geography (1907); served state surveys of Wisconsin (1900–02), Illinois (1906–08), and Ohio (1914–16), as well as with U.S. Geological Survey (from 1901). Pioneered in applying regionally the scientific principles of landform study. His map "Physiographic Divisions of the United States" (1916) was the original for all such maps and was adopted by the U.S. Geological Survey and all other government agencies; it served as the basis of regional work in the U.S. and of university courses on the subject. Two later publications gave the definitive genetic description and analysis of the physiography of the U.S., subdivision by subdivision.

FENNER, CLARENCE NORMAN (*b. near Clifton, N.J., 1870; d. near Clifton, 1949*), petrology, volcanology.

Studied at Columbia University (Engineer of Mines, 1892; M.A., 1909; Ph.D., 1910); employed at Geophysical Laboratory, Carnegie Institution of Washington (1910–38). Published widely, on a variety of subjects. His principal contributions to petrology are his experimental determination of the thermal stability of the various polymorphs of silica; field description, chemical analysis, and structural and theoretical study of the great eruption of Mt. Katmai, in Alaska (1912); recognition of a type of basalt crystallization leading to iron enrichment; and a physico-chemical theory of rock solution and of ore deposition by gaseous emanations. In addition he investigated uranium and thorium minerals bearing on the age of the earth and devised chemical methods for their separation and analysis. During World War I he helped to establish the optical glass industry.

FERCHAULT, RENÉ ANTOINE. *See* **Réaumur, René Antoine Ferchault de.**

FERGUSON, JAMES (*b. near Rothiemay, Banffshire, Scotland, 1710; d. London, England, 1776*), astronomy, instrument making.

Son of a farmer and entirely self-educated, Ferguson became a skilled designer of clocks and planispheres and an accomplished public lecturer and expounder of Newtonian ideas. His models of the planetary system were classics of engineering design whose accuracy far surpassed anything previously available; his scientific work was neither original nor distinguished, but he excelled in popularization. His *Astronomy Explained Upon Sir Isaac Newton's Principles* (1756) went through seventeen editions.

FERMAT, PIERRE DE (*b. Beaumont-de-Lomagne, France, 1601; d. Castres, France, 1665*), mathematics.

Having received a solid classical secondary education locally, Fermat may have attended the University of Toulouse, although one can say with certainty only that he spent some time in Bordeaux toward the end of the 1620's before finally receiving the degree of Bachelor of Civil Laws from the University of Orleans in 1631.

As a lawyer and *parlementaire* in Toulouse, Fermat seems to have benefited more from the high rate of mortality among his colleagues than from any outstanding talents of his own. Fermat's letters suggest that his performance in office was often less than satisfactory. His letters and papers, most of them written after 1636 for friends in Paris, also provide the few available hints regarding his development as a mathematician. One can infer that his stay in Bordeaux most decisively shaped his approach to mathematics; almost all of his later achievements derived from research begun there. It was apparently in Bordeaux that Fermat studied in depth the works of François Viète. From Viète he took the new symbolic algebra and theory of equations that served as his basic research tools. More important, however, Viète's concept of algebra as the "analytic art" and the program of research implicit in that concept largely guided Fermat's choice of problems and the manner in which he treated them.

Believing that the so-called "analytical" works cited by Pappus contained the desired clues, Fermat followed Viète and others in seeking to restore those lost texts, such as Apollonius' *Plane Loci* and Euclid's *Porisms*. Another supposed source of insight was Diophantus' *Arithmetica*, to which Fermat devoted a lifetime of study. These ancient sources, together with the works of Archimedes, formed the initial elements in a clear pattern of development that Fermat's research followed. Taking his original problem from the classical sources, Fermat attacked it with the new algebraic techniques at his disposal. His solution, however, usually proved more general than the problem that had inspired it. By skillful application of the theory of equations in the form of a "reduction analysis," Fermat would reformulate the problem in its most general terms, often defining thereby a class of problems; in many cases the new problem structure lost all contact with its Greek forebear. In Fermat's papers algebra as the "analytic art" achieved equal status with the traditional geometrical mode of ancient mathematics. With few exceptions he presented only the algebraic derivation of his results, dispensing with their classical synthetic proofs.

Fermat never wrote for publication and adamantly refused to edit his work or to publish it under his own name. He freely sent papers to friends without keeping copies for himself. His "Observations on Diophantus," a major part of his work on number theory, was published by his son on the basis of the marginalia in Fermat's copy of the Bachet edition of the *Arithmetica*.

By the time Fermat began corresponding with Mersenne and Roberval in 1636, he had already composed his "Ad locos planos et solidos isagoge," in which he set forth a system of analytic geometry almost identical with that developed by Descartes in the *Géométrie* of 1637. Despite their simultaneous appearance, the two systems stemmed from entirely independent research. Fermat received the first impetus toward his system from an attempt to reconstruct Apollonius' lost treatise *Plane Loci* (loci that are either straight lines or circles). His completed restoration, although composed in the traditional style of Greek geometry, nevertheless gives clear evidence that Fermat employed algebraic analysis in seeking demonstrations of the theorems listed by Pappus. This application of algebra, combined with the peculiar nature of a geometrical locus and locus demonstrations, appears to have revealed to Fermat that all of the loci discussed by Apollonius could be expressed in the form of indeterminate algebraic equations in two unknowns, and that the analysis of these equations by means of Viète's theory of equations led to crucial insights into the nature and construction of the loci.

Like Descartes, Fermat did not employ a coordinate system, but a single axis with a moving ordinate; curves were not plotted, they were generated. Although the analytic geometries of Descartes and Fermat are essentially the same, their presentations differed significantly. Fermat concentrated on the geometrical construction of the curves on the basis of their equations, relying heavily on the reader's knowledge of Viète's algebra to supply the necessary theory of equations. By contrast, Descartes slighted the matter of construction and devoted a major portion of his *Géométrie* to a new and more advanced theory of equations.

In the years following 1636, Fermat made some effort to pursue the implications of his system. In an appendix to the "Isagoge," he applied the system to the graphic solution of determinate algebraic equations, showing, for example, that any cubic or quartic equation could be solved graphically by means of a parabola and a circle. In his "De solutione problematum geometricorum per curvas simplicissimas et unicuique problematum generi proprie convenientes dissertatio tripartita" he took issue with Descartes's classification of curves in the *Géométrie* and undertook to show that any determinate algebraic equation of degree $2n$ or $2n - 1$ could be solved graphically by means of curves determined by indeterminate equations of degree n.

In 1643, in a memoir entitled "Isagoge ad locos ad superficiem" Fermat attempted to extend his plane analytic geometry to solids of revolution in space and perhaps thereby to restore the content of Euclid's *Surface Loci*, another text cited by Pappus.

Although Fermat never found the geometrical framework for a solid analytic geometry, he nonetheless correctly established the algebraic foundation of such a system. In 1650, in his "Novus secundarum et ulterioris ordinis radicum in analyticis usus" he noted that equations in one unknown determine point constructions; equations in two unknowns, locus constructions of plane curves; and equations in three unknowns, locus constructions of surfaces in space. The change in the criterion of the dimension of an equation—from its degree, where the Greeks had placed it, to the number of unknowns in it—was one of the most important conceptual developments of seventeenth-century mathematics.

The method of maxima and minima, in which Fermat first established what later became the algorithm for obtaining the first derivative of an algebraic polynomial, also stemmed from the application of Viète's algebra to a problem in Pappus' *Mathematical Collection.* In a lemma to Apollonius' *Determinate Section,* Pappus sought to divide a given line in such a way that certain rectangles constructed on the segments bore a minimum ratio to one another, noting that the ratio would be "singular." In carrying out the algebraic analysis of the problem, Fermat recognized that the division of the line for rectangles in a ratio greater than the minimum corresponded to a quadratic equation that would normally yield two equally satisfactory section points. A "singular" section point for the minimum ratio, he argued, must mean that the particular values of the constant quantities of the equation allow only a single repeated root as a solution.

Fermat's method of maxima and minima, which is clearly applicable to any polynomial $P(x)$, originally rested on purely finitistic algebraic foundations. It assumed, counterfactually, the inequality of two equal roots in order to determine, by Viète's theory of equations, a relation between those roots and one of the coefficients of the polynomial, a relation that was fully general. This relation then led to an extreme-value solution when Fermat removed his counterfactual assumption and set the roots equal. Borrowing a term from Diophantus, Fermat called this counterfactual equality "adequality."

The original method of maxima and minima had two important corollaries. The first was the method of tangents by which, given the equation of a curve, Fermat could construct the tangent at any given point on that curve by determining the length of the subtangent. The second was a method for determining centers of gravity of geometrical figures.

Fermat's method of maxima and minima and its corollary method of tangents formed the central issue in an acrid debate between Fermat and Descartes in 1638.

Fermat's research also delved into methods of quadrature, but like his method of tangents, his method of quadrature lacked even the germ of several concepts crucial to the development of the calculus.

As a result of limited circulation in unpublished manuscripts, Fermat's work on analytic geometry, maxima and minima and tangents, and quadrature had only moderate influence on contemporary developments in mathematics. His work in the realm of number theory had almost none at all. It was neither understood nor appreciated until Euler revived it and initiated the line of continuous research that culminated in the work of Gauss and Kummer in the early nineteenth century. Indeed, many of Fermat's results are basic elements of number theory today. Although the results retain fundamental importance, his methods remain largely a secret known only to him. In an important sense Fermat invented number theory as an independent branch of mathematics. He was the first to restrict his study in principle to the domain of integers. His refusal to accept fractional solutions to problems he set in 1657 as challenges to the European mathematics community initiated his dispute with Wallis, Frénicle, and others, for it represented a break with the classical tradition of Diophantus' *Arithmetica,* which served as his opponents' model. The restriction to integers explains one dominant theme of Fermat's work in number theory, his concern with prime numbers and divisibility. A second guiding theme of his research, the determination of patterns for generating families of solutions from a single basic solution, carried over from his work in analysis.

To prove his decomposition theorems and to solve the equation $x^2 - 1 = my^2$, Fermat employed a method he had devised called "infinite descent." The method, an inverse form of the modern method of induction, rests on the principle (peculiar to the domain of integers) that there cannot exist an infinitely decreasing sequence of integers.

FERMI, ENRICO (*b. Rome, Italy, 1901; d. Chicago, Ill., 1954*), physics.

Fermi was primarily self-taught. By his seventeenth year, while still in high school, he had acquired a thorough knowledge of classical physics, comparable to that of an advanced graduate student in a university. Furthermore, Fermi and his schoolmate and lifelong friend, Enrico Persico, performed many experiments with apparatus they had built themselves, and thus had acquired an excellent grasp of contemporary experimental physics. Fermi received his doctorate from the University of Pisa in 1922 and then returned to Rome.

In Rome he met Orso Mario Corbino, director of the physics laboratory at the University of Rome. Corbino immediately recognized Fermi's talent and became his lifelong friend and patron. Fermi spent some time at Max Born's institute at Göttingen and then with Paul Ehrenfest at Leiden. Fermi returned to Florence with the post of lecturer.

Up to this time Fermi's work had been primarily in general relativity (tensor analysis), where he had developed a theorem of permanent value: that in the vicinity of a world line, space can always be approximated by a pseudo-Euclidean metric. In statistical mechanics he had written subtle papers on the ergodic hypothesis and on quantum theory. Here he had developed an original form of analyzing collisions of charged particles. He developed the field produced by the charged particle by the Fourier integral and used the information from optical processes to determine the result of the collision. Other studies on the entropy constant of a perfect gas are historically important as preparation for things to come. An experiment done with Rasetti, who was also in Florence, on the depolarization of resonance light in an alternating magnetic field was the subject of Fermi's first important experimental paper.

Early in 1926, Fermi, realizing that Bose-Einstein statistics were not applicable to particles obeying Pauli's recently discovered exclusion principle, began developing a new type of statistics. Fermi statistics, which are applicable to electrons, protons, neutrons, and all particles of half integral spin, have a pervading importance in atomic and nuclear physics and in solid-state theory.

In 1927 a chair in theoretical physics was established at the University of Rome. In the competition for the position Fermi placed first.

Fermi's next important study was the application of his statistics to an atomic model. This had been anticipated, however, by L. H. Thomas, who was working independently. The Thomas-Fermi atom gives very good approximations in a great number of problems. The fundamental idea was to compute the density of the electronic cloud around the nucleus as an atmosphere of a totally degenerate gas of electrons attracted by the nucleus. Fermi made numerous applications of his method to X-ray spectroscopy, to the periodic system of the elements, to optical spectroscopy, and later to ions.

In another important group of papers devoted to the reformulation of quantum electrodynamics he developed by Fourier analysis the electromagnetic field which obeys Maxwell's equations and quantized the single harmonic components as oscillators. He thus wrote the Hamiltonian of the free field, giving a Hamiltonian form to Maxwell's theory. To this Hamiltonian, he added the Hamiltonian of an atom and a term representing the interaction between atom and radiation. The complete system was then treated by perturbation theory.

Fermi decided to switch to nuclear physics. He initially investigated the theory of the hyperfine structure of the spectral lines and the nuclear magnetic moment, a suitable subject for making the transition from atomic to nuclear physics.

In Rome, about 1929, Rasetti and Fermi began experiments on nuclear subjects. The Solvay Conference of 1933 was devoted to the nucleus, and shortly thereafter Fermi developed the theory of beta decay, based on the hypothesis of the neutrino formulated for the first time in 1930 by Wolfgang Pauli. Beta decay—the spontaneous emission of electrons by nuclei—presented major theoretical difficulties. Apparently, energy and momentum were not conserved. There were also other difficulties with angular momentum and the statistics of the nuclei. Pauli sought a way out of the apparent paradoxes by postulating the simultaneous emission of the electron and of a practically undetectable particle, later named "neutrino" by Fermi.

An entirely new type of force had to be postulated, the so-called weak interaction, occurring between all particles and thus unlike electromagnetic or strong interactions, which are restricted to certain particles. The first manifestation of the weak interaction to be treated in detail was the beta decay. The treatment was accomplished by applying second quantization and destruction and creation operators for fermions and by adopting (or better, guessing) a Hamiltonian for weak interactions on the basis of formal criteria, such as relativistic invariance, linearity, and absence of derivatives. Of the five possible choices which satisfied the formal requirements, Fermi treated the vector interaction in detail, mainly because of its analogy with electromagnetism.

In his paper on beta decay, Fermi also introduced a new fundamental constant of nature, the Fermi constant, G, which plays a role analogous to that of the charge of the electron in electromagnetism. This constant has been experimentally determined from the energy available in beta decay and the mean life of the decaying substance. Its value is 1.415×10^{-49} erg cm^3. The famous paper in which Fermi developed this theory had far-reaching consequences for the future development of nuclear and particle physics.

The Joliots' discovery of artificial radioactivity provided the occasion for experimental activity which Fermi continued for the rest of his life. Fermi reasoned that neutrons should be more effective than alpha particles in producing radioactive elements because they are not repelled by the nuclear charge and thus have a much greater probability of entering the target nuclei.

Acting on this idea, Fermi bombarded several elements of increasing atomic numbers with neutrons. He hoped to find an artificial radioactivity produced by the neutrons. His first success was with fluorine. Immediately thereafter Fermi carried out a systematic investigation of the behavior of elements throughout the periodic table. In most cases he performed chemical analysis to identify the chemical element that was the carrier of the activity. In the first survey, out of sixty-three elements investigated, thirty-seven showed an easily detectable activity. The nuclear reactions of (n, α), (n, p), and (n, γ) were then identified, and all available elements, including uranium and thorium, were irradiated. In uranium and thorium the investigators found several forms of activity after bombardment but did not recognize fission. Fermi and his collaborators, having proved that no radioactive isotopes were formed between lead and uranium, put forward the natural hypothesis that the activity was due to transuranic elements.

In October 1935 Fermi and his collaborators observed that neutrons passed through substances containing hydrogen have increased efficiency for producing artificial radioactivity. Fermi interpreted this effect as due to the slowing down of the neutrons by elastic collisions with hydrogen atoms. Thus slow neutrons were discovered.

By 1938 the deteriorating political situation in Italy was materially hampering his work. In December 1938 Fermi received the Nobel Prize and proceeded directly from Stockholm to New York and settled at Columbia University. Shortly thereafter Bohr brought to the United States the news of the discovery of fission. Fermi and others immediately saw the possibility of the emission of secondary neutrons and perhaps of a chain reaction; he started at once to experiment in this direction.

The first problem was to investigate whether on the fission of uranium secondary neutrons were in fact emitted. If such did occur, it might be possible to use these neutrons to produce further fission, and under favorable circumstances one could obtain a chain reaction.

In order to analyze the problems facing him, Fermi needed a great amount of quantitative information on cross sections, delayed neutrons, branching ratios of the fission reactions, and nuclear properties of several nuclei to be used in a future reactor. This information was not available. He then proceeded to collect it with the help of many collaborators.

The potential overwhelming practical importance of this work was clear to physicists, and Fermi, together with George B. Pegram, chairman of the physics department at Columbia and a close personal friend, tried to alert the U.S. government to the implications of the recent discoveries. A small subsidy for further research was obtained from the U.S. Navy; and the studies that were to culminate in the atomic bomb were initiated.

Fermi concentrated his efforts on obtaining a chain reaction using ordinary uranium of normal isotopic composition. As soon as it was established that of the two isotopes present in natural uranium, only U^{235} is fissionable by slow neutrons, it became apparent that if one could obtain pure U^{235} or even enrich the mixture in U^{235}, the making of a reactor or possibly even of an atom bomb would be comparatively easy. Still, the isotope separation was such a staggering task that it discouraged most physicists.

In 1939 and 1940, however, isotope separation was very uncertain and other avenues had to be explored. In December 1940, Fermi and Segrè discussed another possibility: the use of the still undiscovered element 94 (plutonium) of mass 239 (Pu^{239}). This substance promised to undergo slow neutron fission and thus to be a replacement for U^{235}. If it could be produced by neutron capture of U^{238} in a natural-uranium reactor, followed by two beta emissions, one could separate it chemically and obtain a pure isotope with, it was hoped, a large slow-neutron cross section. Arthur Wahl undertook the preparation and measurement of the nuclear properties of Pu^{239}, using the Berkeley cyclotron. The favorable results of these experiments (January–April 1941) added impetus to the chain-reaction project. By December 1941, the whole world was engulfed in war, and military applications were paramount. The United States developed, under government supervision, an immense organization, which evolved according to the technical necessities and led to the establishment of the Manhattan Engineer District (MED). The purpose of the MED was to make an atomic bomb in time to influence the course of the war. Fermi had a technically prominent part in the whole project. His work at Columbia was still on a small scale, but in 1942 he transferred to Chicago, where it was expanded. It culminated on 2 December 1942 with the first controlled nuclear chain reaction at Stagg Field at the University of Chicago.

When his work at Chicago was finished, Fermi went to Los Alamos, New Mexico, where the Los Alamos Laboratory of the Manhattan Engineer District, under the direc-

tion of J. R. Oppenheimer, had the assignment of assembling an atomic bomb. Fermi spent most of the period from September 1944 to early 1946 at Los Alamos, where he served as a general consultant. He also collaborated in the building of a small chain reactor using enriched uranium in U^{235} and heavy water. Fermi actively participated in the first test of the atomic bomb in the desert near Alamogordo, New Mexico, on 16 July 1945.

Following the successful test of the bomb, he was appointed by President Truman to the interim committee charged with advising the president on the use of the bomb and on many fundamental policies concerning atomic energy.

In 1946 the University of Chicago created the Institute for Nuclear Studies and offered a professorship to Fermi. He and his family left Los Alamos for Chicago, where he remained at the University of Chicago for the rest of his life.

As soon as the Chicago cyclotron was ready for operation, Fermi again started experimental work on pion-nucleon scattering. (He had coined the word "pion" to indicate pi-mesons.) He found experimentally the resonance in the isotopic spin 3/2, ordinary spin 3/2 state, which had been predicted by Keith Bruckner. The investigation became a major one. With H. L. Anderson and others, Fermi worked out the details up to an energy of about 400 MeV lab of the nucleon-pion interaction.

In addition to this experimental activity, Fermi did theoretical work on the origin of cosmic rays, devising a mechanism of acceleration by which each proton tends to equipartition of energy with a whole galaxy. He also developed a statistical method for treating high-energy collision phenomena and multiple production of particles. This method has also received wide and useful applications.

FERNALD, MERRITT LYNDON (*b. Orono, Me., 1873; d. Cambridge, Mass., 1950*), botany.

Graduated from Harvard's Lawrence Scientific School (B.S., 1897) and spent rest of career at Harvard. Wrote over eight hundred papers, chiefly on the flora of the northeastern United States; achieved a complete revision in 1950 of Asa Gray's *Manual of the Botany of the Northern United States* (1908). Made an outstanding contribution to phytogeography with his theory of the persistence of plants on nunataks.

FERNEL, JEAN FRANÇOIS (*b. Montdidier, France, 1497 [?]; d. Fontainebleau, France, 1558*), medicine.

M.A., Collège de Ste. Barbe, Paris (1519). Fernel turned from philosophy, mathematics, and astronomy, in which he published two books (*Cosmotheoria*, 1528, contains an accurate estimate of a degree of meridian), to the study of medicine, and obtained his *venia practicandi* in 1530. He soon became one of the most famous physicians in France, with royal patients and a large following of students. Fernel brought a new approach to medicine, emphasizing the value of practice and experience and, eventually, condemning astrology. His observations included peristalsis, the systole and diastole of the heart, early descriptions of appendicitis and endocarditis, and the first description of the spinal canal. He introduced the term "physiology" for the science of the functions of the body, but his own physiology was still the humoral medicine of his time. He wrote general medical texts and works on the cure of syphilis and of fevers.

FERRARI, LUDOVICO (*b. Bologna, Italy, 1522; d. Bologna, 1565*), algebra.

A public lecturer in mathematics in Milan (from 1540), then employed by Ercole Gonzaga, cardinal of Mantua, and finally a lecturer at the University of Bologna (1564–65), Ferrari learned mathematics from Cardano while a member of his household (from 1536) and collaborated with him on the study of cubic and quartic equations. Cardano had learned of a method of solving $x^3 + ax = b$, where a and b are positive, from Tartaglia (under a promise of secrecy) and from Scipione Ferro's notes; Cardano and Ferrari then extended their researches to other types of cubics and to the quartic. Ferrari found geometrical demonstrations for Cardano's formulas for solving $x^3 + ax = bx^2 + c$ and $x^3 + ax^2 = b$; he also solved the quartic of the form $x^4 + ax^2 + b = cx$, where a, b, c are positive, by reducing the equation to a cubic. The results were embodied in Cardano's *Ars magna* (1545) and led to the celebrated feud between Ferrari and Tartaglia that involved twelve published letters, sets of problems sent by each to the other, and a public disputation (1548).

FERRARIS, GALILEO (*b. Livorno Vercellese, Italy, 1847; d. Turin, Italy, 1897*), electrical engineering, physics.

Graduated from Scuola d'Applicazione di Torino (1869); received doctorate from University of Turin (1872); taught technical physics at Regio Museo Industriale, Turin. His studies of light waves and the optical characteristics of telescopes, especially the phase difference of two waves in sinusoidal motion, led to the concept of phase-displaced electrical waves and a rotating electromagnetic field. Ferraris visualized the placing of two electromagnets, each fed by a current displaced 90° out of phase, at right angles to each other, thereby producing the equivalent of a revolving magnetic field; this could induce currents in an included copper drum (or rotor), and the resulting torque would be equivalent to the power of an alternating current electric motor—then still the missing unit in the production of an alternating current system. He constructed such a device in 1885, leading to the type of motor that today is responsible for the bulk of conversion of electrical power to mechanical power.

FERREIN, ANTOINE (*b. Frespech, near Agen, Lot-et-Garonne, France, 1693; d. Paris, France, 1769*), anatomy.

Studied medicine at Montpellier (M.B., 1716 M.D., 1728), taught there and then in Paris (from 1732; M.B., 1736 M.D., 1738), where his courses became famous. Influenced by iatromechanics, he followed the idea of an *anatomie subtile* which would seek out in the *petites machines* of the body the explanation of most physiological and pathological phenomena. Propounded (1731) a new and accurate explanation of the heart's beating against the thoracic wall, maintaining that the heart shrank during systole and that its tip curled over and forward. Published (1733) microscopic research on the parenchymatous and vascular structure of the liver. Studied phonation experimentally by forcing air through the detached larynxes of various animals, the first since Leonardo to do so. De-

scribed the pyramids and the tubular structure of the kidneys, but misconstrued their function. Formulated the rules for examination of the abdominal organs by palpation.

FERREL, WILLIAM (*b. Bedford [now Fulton] County, Pa., 1817; d. Maywood, Kan., 1891*), mathematical geophysics.

Largely self-educated in science, Ferrel taught school for a living and attended college when he could (graduated 1844, Bethany College). His career as a scientist began about 1850 with his study of Newton's *Principia;* concentrating on tidal theory, he conjectured "that the action of the moon and sun upon the tides must have a tendency to retard the earth's rotation on its axis." Laplace had discounted any such effect, but in his first published paper (1853) Ferrel showed that Laplace had neglected the second-order terms that should cause tidal retardation. Ferrel's was the first quantitative treatment of tidal friction; he later made important contributions to the techniques of tidal prediction (1874) and designed a tide-predicting machine (1880).

His early publications led to his first scientific post, on the *American Nautical Almanac* staff (1858–67); subsequently he worked with the U.S. Coast Survey (1867–82) and the U.S. Army's Signal Service (predecessor of the weather bureau) until 1886. He pioneered in the development of meteorology from a descriptive science to a branch of mathematical physics. He was the first to understand in mathematical detail the significance of the earth's rotation for the motion of bodies at its surface, having deduced that both winds and currents must be deflected. Ferrel's law (1858) states that "if a body is moving in any direction, there is a force, arising from the earth's rotation, which always deflects it to the right in the northern hemisphere, and to the left in the southern." His application of this principle to explain both the general circulation and the rotary action of cyclonic storms began to be generally accepted in the 1870's.

FERRIER, DAVID (*b. Aberdeen, Scotland, 1843; d. London, England, 1928*), neurophysiology, neurology.

M.A., Aberdeen University (1863); M.B. (1868) and M.D. (1870), University of Edinburgh. Worked at King's College Hospital and Medical School (1871–1908) and also held appointments at West London Hospital and at National Hospital, Queen Square. Founding member, Physiological Society (1876); founding editor of *Brain* (1878); knighted, 1911. In 1873 he began detailed, systematic exploration of the cerebral cortex in different vertebrates, ranging from the lowest to the highest and including the ape, with the express purpose of confirming or refuting the theoretical suggestions made by Hughlings Jackson with regard to the localized cortical areas of function. Using faradic stimulation to the cortex (an important technical advance), and studying mainly primates, he mapped much of the cerebral cortex and carefully delineated the "motor-region"; the scheme of localized function that he put forward was based on the concept of "motor" and "sensory" regions. Although he was occasionally in error, and was guilty of unwarranted extrapolation from his findings in animals to the human brain, his *The Function of the Brain* (1876) is one of the most significant publications in the field of cortical localization. In addition he had an important influence on the embryonic field of brain surgery, for he urged his surgical colleagues to attack cerebral lesions operatively.

FERRO (or FERREO, DAL FERRO, DEL FERRO), SCIPIONE (*b. Bologna, Italy, 1465; d. Bologna, 1526*), mathematics.

Lecturer in arithmetic and geometry at University of Bologna (1496–1526). No work of his survives, but he was reported by his disciples Annibale della Nave and Antonio Maria Fiore, and subsequently by Cardano and Ferrari, to have discovered the solution to the cubic equation $x^3 + px = q$, where p and q are positive numbers. He also contributed to the study of fractions with irrational denominators, and studied the geometry of the compass with a fixed opening.

FERSMAN, ALEKSANDR EVGENIEVICH (*b. St. Petersburg, Russia, 1883; d. Sochi, U.S.S.R., 1945*), mineralogy, geochemistry.

Began collecting minerals as a youth. Studied at universities of Novorossisk (1901–03) and Moscow (1903–07). Worked under Vernadsky in Moscow, then under Victor Goldschmidt in Heidelberg (they collaborated on *Der Diamant*, 1911). Curator of mineralogy, Russian Academy of Sciences (1912); lectured on geochemistry at Shanyavsky University (1912); an organizer of journal *Priroda*. From 1915, studied natural resources for Academy of Sciences. During both World Wars, was active in military geology. Taught at Petrograd University (1919–20). Active in Academy of Sciences as teacher, researcher, and leader. Fersman made major contributions to geochemistry, which he defined as concerning the history of atoms of chemical elements in the earth's crust and their behavior under various thermodynamic, physical, and chemical conditions of nature; it appeared to him that at the foundation of all life lay the laws of the dispersion and combination of ninety chemical elements, from which the earth and all of space are constructed. He established the frequency of distribution of most of the elements (proposing the term "clarke" for the concentration of an element in the earth's crust); discovered the independence of geochemical abundances from the positions of the elements in the periodic system; showed that abundances within the earth's crust were determined by the effects of the migration of the elements, while abundances in space were related to the stability of the atomic nucleus; and showed that man concentrates certain elements (gold, platinum, silver, etc.) and disperses others (such as carbon, tin, magnesium, and silicon). Fersman wrote an important work on pegmatites (1932) through which scientists have come to a deeper understanding of the world's structure and of the role of atoms in that structure. He discovered valuable deposits of apatite in the Khibiny Mountains and of virgin sulfur in the Karakum Desert; and he wrote popular articles and books helping to explain the practical significance of theoretical research in geology.

FESSENDEN, REGINALD AUBREY (*b. Milton, Quebec, Canada, 1866; d. Hamilton, Bermuda, 1932*), radio engineering.

Educated in Canada. Worked for Thomas Edison and for Westinghouse Electric and Manufacturing Co. (1890–92); taught at Purdue University and at Western University of Pennsylvania (1893–1900). Worked with U.S. Weather Bureau on adapting radiotelegraphy to weather forecasting (1900–02); and was general manager of National Electric Signalling Company (1902–10), a company formed to exploit his ideas. First contribution was development of the electrolytic detector (1900), making radiotelephony feasible for the first time; invented the heterodyne receiver; transmitted the first voice signals over long distances (1906); obtained some 300 patents.

FEUERBACH, KARL WILHELM (*b. Jena, Germany, 1800; d. Erlangen, Germany, 1834*), mathematics.

By the age of twenty-two, Feuerbach had been awarded the Ph.D., had made a significant contribution to the geometry of the triangle, and had been named professor of mathematics at the Erlangen Gymnasium. His theorem, in which one recognizes the nine-point circle of a triangle, states that "the circle which passes through the feet of the altitudes of a triangle touches all four of the circles which are tangent to the three sides of the triangle; it is internally tangent to the inscribed circle and externally tangent to each of the circles which touch the sides of the triangle externally" (1822). In 1827 he independently discovered the theory of the homogeneous coordinates of a point in space.

FEUILLÉE, LOUIS (*b. Mane, Basses-Alpes, France, 1660; d. Marseilles, France, 1732*), astronomy, botany.

Royal mathematician, astronomer for Académie des Sciences. Best-known work is *Journal des observations physiques, mathématiques, et botaniques . . .* (1714) on his exploration of the South American coast. His description of the flora of the coasts of Peru and Chile is still much appreciated.

FEULGEN, ROBERT JOACHIM (*b. Werden, Germany, 1884; d. Giessen, Germany, 1955*), biochemistry, histochemistry.

Studied medicine at University of Freiburg im Breisgau (from 1905), completed training at Kiel; worked at physiological institutes of Berlin (1912–18) and Giessen (from 1920). Discovered (1914) the nucleal reaction: thymonucleic acid (DNA), treated with $1N$ HCl and then with Schiff's reagent, showed the magenta color indicative of furan. In 1923 he applied his reaction as a histochemical stain, and was able to show that thymonucleic acid is found only in the nucleus and that both plant and animal cells give a positive nucleal reaction, thus banishing the old division of nucleic acids.

FIBONACCI, LEONARDO (or **LEONARDO OF PISA**) (*b. Pisa, Italy, ca. 1170; d. Pisa, after 1240*), mathematics.

Leonardo's father, as secretary of the Republic of Pisa, was entrusted around 1192 with the direction of the Pisan trading colony in Bugia (now Bougie), Algeria. He soon brought his son there to have him learn the art of calculating, since he expected Leonardo to become a merchant. It was there that Leonardo learned methods "with the new Indian numerals," and he received excellent instruction. On the business trips on which his father evidently soon sent him and which took him to Egypt, Syria, Greece (Byzantium), Sicily, and Provence, he acquainted himself with the methods in use there through zealous study and in disputations with native scholars. All these methods, however, as well as "algorismus" and the "arcs of Pythagoras" (apparently the abacus of Gerbert) appeared to him in "error" in comparison with the Indian methods.

Around the turn of the century Leonardo returned to Pisa. For the next twenty-five years he composed works in which he presented not only calculations with Indian numerals and methods and their application in all areas of commercial activity, but also much of what he had learned of algebraic and geometrical problems. His most important original accomplishments were in indeterminate analysis and number theory.

As the first great mathematician of the Christian West, he did pioneering work in many areas: use of the chain rule in the "Rule of Three"; rules for factoring numbers and formation of perfect numbers; and the famous Fibonacci series, the first recurrent series, seeking a solution to the rabbit problem (if one starts with a single pair of rabbits, how many pairs will one have after n months?). He treated indeterminate equations of the first and second degrees in a new manner; applied new methods of algebra to geometric problems; developed a new concept of number which recognized negative quantities and even zero as numbers; and arithmetized the Euclidean propositions.

Five works by Leonardo are preserved: *Liber abbaci* (1202; 1228); *Practica geometriae* (1220/1221); a writing entitled *Flos* (1225); an undated letter to Theodorus, the imperial philosopher; and *Liber quadratorum* (1225). We know of further works, such as a book on commercial arithmetic, *Di minor guisa;* especially unfortunate is the loss of a tract on book X of the *Elements,* for which Leonardo promised a numerical treatment of irrationals instead of Euclid's geometrical presentation.

With Leonardo a new epoch in Western mathematics began; however, not all of his ideas were immediately taken up. Direct influence was exerted only by those portions of the *Liber abbaci* and of the *Practica* that served to introduce Indian-Arabic numerals and methods and contributed to the mastering of the problems of daily life.

Leonardo was also the teacher of the "Cossists," who took their name from the word *causa,* which was used for the first time in the West by Leonardo in place of *res* or *radix.* His alphabetical designation for the general number or coefficient was first improved by Viète (1591), who used consonants for the known quantities and vowels for the unknowns.

FICHOT, LAZARE-EUGÈNE (*b. Le Creusot, Saône-et-Loire, France, 1867; d. Tabanac, Gironde, France, 1939*), marine hydrography.

Graduated from École Polytechnique (1886) and joined Marine Corps of Hydrographic Engineers. Made numerous hydrographic, geologic, and meteorologic observations along the coasts of France and the French colonies in Asia and Africa. Discovered (1908) a new navigational route along the coast of Indochina. Wrote on tidal theory (with Poincaré, 1938–41) and on industrial utilization of the tides (1923).

FICK, ADOLF EUGEN (*b. Kassel, Germany, 1829; d. Blankenberge, Belgium, 1901*), physiology, physical medicine.

Studied with Carl Ludwig at Marburg (doctorate, 1851) and with Helmholtz and du Bois-Reymond at Berlin (1849–50). Worked as anatomist at Marburg (1851) and Zurich (1852–61), and as professor of physiology at Zurich (1861–68) and Würzburg (1868–99). Became one of the main proponents of the new orientation of physiology toward physics, whose objective was to determine quantitatively, whenever possible, the fundamental capabilities of the organism's components and to explain them on the basis of general physicochemical laws of nature. Worked with great success on problems of molecular biophysics (especially diffusion), mechanics of solids (including the geometry of articulations, and statics and dynamics of muscles), optics, and bioelectricity. Fick was gifted in constructing physiological measuring devices and in arriving at the precise mathematical expression of physiological processes; his gift for mathematical-physical thinking is most clearly exhibited in his numerous studies on the nature of heat, on the causes of thermal expansion of bodies, and on the nature, magnitude, and origin of body heat (he ascribed all processes of heat generation to the expenditure of chemical energy). In hemodynamics he developed a principle, which came to be called Fick's law (1870), that permits calculation of the cardiac output from the measurement of the minute volume of oxygen consumption and arteriovenous oxygen difference in the living organism.

FIELDS, JOHN CHARLES (*b. Hamilton, Ontario, Canada, 1863; d. Toronto, Ontario, Canada, 1932*), mathematics, education.

Studied at University of Toronto (B.A., 1884), Johns Hopkins (Ph.D., 1887), and in Europe (primarily Berlin and Paris, 1892–1902). Taught at Allegheny College (1889–92) and at Toronto (1902–32). Wrote on algebraic functions; established a general plan for proving the Riemann-Roch theorem (1906). Conceived and funded the Fields Medal, an international medal for mathematical distinction first awarded in 1936.

FIESSINGER, NOËL (*b. Thaon-les-Vosges, France, 1881; d. Paris, France, 1946*), medicine, biology.

Held high positions in Paris hospitals, including chair of clinical medicine at Hôtel-Dieu; promoted the idea that clinical medicine must be closely associated with biological research. Elucidated the histogenesis of cirrhosis (1908); demonstrated that white cells contain either protease or lipase; among the first to define the principles of functional exploration of an organ, and developed liver function tests; discovered Fiessinger-Leroy-Retter disease. During World War I, made major observations in biology of war wounds.

FINE, HENRY BURCHARD (*b. Chambersburg, Pa., 1858; d. Princeton, N.J., 1928*), mathematics.

Studied under George Halsted at Princeton (graduated 1880) and taught there before going to Germany to study (Ph.D., Leipzig, 1885); returned to Princeton and taught there until his death (dean of faculty from 1903, dean of departments of science from 1912). His impact on science lies mainly in his support of science and mathematics at Princeton; as dean of the faculty he promoted Luther Eisenhart and brought in Oswald Veblen, G. A. Bliss, George Birkhoff, and J. H. M. Wedderburn. His most important papers were on Newton's method of approximation (1916) and an exposition of a theorem of Kronecker's on numerical equations (1914).

FINE, ORONCE (*b. Briançon, France, 1494; d. Paris, France, 1555*), astronomy, mathematics, cosmography.

Fine earned a medical degree in Paris (M.B., 1522), but his career developed outside the university; from 1515 he edited astronomical and mathematical writings for printers in Paris andabroad (his editions included Peuerbach's *Theoricae planetarum*, Sacrobosco's *De sphaera* [1516], and Euclid's *Elements*). In 1531 he was appointed to the chair of mathematics at the Collège Royal, where he taught until his death. His scientific work may be briefly characterized as encyclopedic, elementary, and unoriginal; the goal of his publications, which ranged from astronomy to instrumental music, appears to have been to popularize the university science that he himself had been taught. Fine wrote several works on astronomical instruments; in his discussion of the equatorium (1526) he ingeniously exploited the possibilities of curves traced by points (the diagrams of the equations of center), used to facilitate the placement, with respect to the equant, of the mean apsidal line on the epicycle. His *Théorique des cieux* (published anonymously in 1528) gave the first detailed exposition of the Alphonsine epicyclic theory in French. *De arithmetica practica* (1532) contains a multiplication table facilitating the use of sexagesimal fractions; in a minor work on astrology Fine gave an original definition of the unequal hours (as the equal divisions of the ecliptic computed, at each moment, from its intersection with the horizon) that found an application in the astrolabic dial of the planetary clock at the Bibliothèque Ste. Geneviève (his replacement of this dial is most likely his only contribution to the clock). His efforts at quadrature of the circle were vehemently attacked by some of his contemporaries.

FINK (FINCKE), THOMAS (*b. Flensburg, Denmark [now Germany], 1561; d. Copenhagen, Denmark, 1656*), mathematics, astronomy, medicine.

Received M.D. (Basel, 1587) after study at several universities; worked as a physician until appointed professor of mathematics at Copenhagen (1591; rhetoric, 1602; medicine, 1603). Self-taught in mathematics, but wrote influential textbook (*Geometriae rotundi*, 1583) that was used by such mathematicians as Lansbergen, Clavius, Napier, and Pitiscus; Fink based his work mainly on that of Ramus, but introduced such terms as "tangent" and "secans" and devised new formulas, such as the law of tangents.

FINLAY, CARLOS JUAN (*b. Puerto Príncipe [now Camagüey], Cuba, 1833; d. Havana, Cuba, 1915*), medicine.

Studied at Jefferson Medical College (M.D., 1855) under Robley Dunglison and S. Weir Mitchell; practiced general medicine and ophthalmology in Havana. Working closely with U.S. Yellow Fever Commission, he reached the conclusion that the disease was transmitted by the household mosquito, *Culex fasciatus,* now called *Aedes aegypti;* he conducted 103 experiments (1881–98) wherein he induced mosquitoes to bite yellow fever patients and then bite healthy recent immigrants (volunteers). Finlay's experiments were inconclusive and his

theories were ridiculed, but he was vindicated by the work of the Yellow Fever Board (1900–01), whom he provided with mosquitoes and eggs and whom he assisted with diagnosis.

FINSEN, NIELS RYBERG (*b. Thorshavn, Faeroe Islands, 1860; d. Copenhagen, Denmark, 1904*), therapeutic medicine.

Studied medicine at University of Copenhagen (M.D., 1891) and taught there briefly before turning to pioneering studies in phototherapy. He first investigated the injurious influences of light on smallpox lesions, and found that blue and ultraviolet rays were harmful, while red and infrared rays were beneficial (1893–94). In 1895 he began successful treatment of lupus vulgaris with high concentrations of ultraviolet light; in 1896 he was put in charge of a new institute for phototherapy. Severely incapacitated by constrictive pericarditis, he performed a self-study on water and salt metabolism, the results of which laid the scientific foundations for the low-fluid and low-salt-intake therapy. He was awarded the Nobel Prize for Medicine or Physiology in 1903.

FIRMICUS MATERNUS (*b. Sicily, fl.* A.D. *330–354*), astrology.

Author of *De errore profanarum religionum*, an attack upon pagan cults, and of *Mathesis*, a comprehensive handbook of astrology representing popular traditions of the previous four centuries and containing many errors of astronomy. *Mathesis* appears to have become popular in the eleventh century.

FISCHER, EMIL HERMANN (*b. Euskirchen, near Bonn, Germany, 1852; d. Berlin, Germany, 1919*), chemistry.

Studied at Bonn and Strasbourg under Kekulé and Baeyer; doctorate in 1874. Taught at Munich, Erlangen, Würzburg, and Berlin. Father of Herman Fischer. First published on organic derivatives of hydrazine. By 1888 established structures of hydrazones and osazones. Worked with Otto Fischer on constitution of analine dyestuffs. Explored the whole series of purines, established structures, and synthesized about 130 derivatives. His research became the basis of the German drug industry, including production of caffeine, theophylline, theobromine, and phenobarbital. Elaborated complex structures and chemistry of carbohydrates, synthesized many, and established configurations of the sixteen possible stereoisomers of glucose. (Nobel Prize for chemistry for syntheses in sugar and purine groups, 1902.) Laid foundations of enzyme chemistry; turned to study of proteins; modified Curtius' method for separation of amino acids. Synthesized about 100 polypeptides.

FISCHER, HANS (*b. Höchst am Main, Germany, 1881; d. Munich, Germany, 1945*), chemistry.

Son of a dye chemist; had an early acquaintance with chemistry of pigments. Studied medicine and chemistry at Marburg, Munich, and Berlin. Taught at Innsbruck and Vienna. Head, Institute of Organic Chemistry, Technische Hochschule of Munich (1921). Worked on bile pigments and related substances. Did systematic study of synthetic pyrrole derivatives; more than 60,000 microanalyses carried out in his laboratory. First synthesized porphyrin (1926) and hemin (1929). For the latter he received the 1930 Nobel Prize in chemistry. Later determined the structure of bilirubin.

FISCHER, HERMANN OTTO LAURENZ (*b. Würzburg, Germany, 1888; d. Berkeley, Calif., 1960*), biochemistry.

Son of Emil Fischer. Studied at Cambridge, Berlin, and Jena (Ph.D., 1912). Began research under his father at Berlin (1912) on carbomethoxy derivatives of acids (1913). Taught at Chemical Institute of Berlin University (1922–31), Basel (1932–36), Banting Institute of the University of Toronto (1937–47), and the new department of biochemistry at University of California (1948–1956). Elucidated the structures of quinic acid, shikimic acid, and their derivatives. Worked on the trioses, dihydroxyacetone and glyceraldehyde. Investigated chemical and biological relationships between hexoses and inositols, and chemical synthesis of intermediate products of sugar metabolism.

FISCHER, NICOLAUS WOLFGANG (*b. Gross-Meseritz, Bohemia [now Mezirici Velké, Czechoslovakia], 1782; d. Breslau, Germany [now Wrocław, Poland], 1850*), chemistry.

Studied medicine in Erfurt; practiced in Breslau. Taught chemistry at Breslau (1811–50). Employed triple salt $K_3Co(NO_2)_6$ ("Fischer's salt") in analytical separation of nickel from cobalt. Studied osmosis in animal bladders; the relationship between chemical affinity and galvanism; and the construction of voltaic cells.

FISHER, RONALD AYLMER (*b. London, England, 1890; d. Adelaide, Australia, 1962*), statistics, biometry, genetics.

Studied mathematics and theoretical physics at Cambridge (1909–12). Statistician at Rothamsted Experimental Station (1919–33). Taught eugenics at University College, London (1933–43), and genetics at Cambridge (1943–59). Spent his last three years in Australia in Division of Mathematical Statistics of the Commonwealth Scientific and Industrial Research Organization. Knighted in 1952. In mathematical statistics, he erected a comprehensive theory of hypothesis testing; introduced the analysis of variance and covariance; and made numerous contributions to such topics as multivariate analysis, bioassay, time series, contingency tables, and the logarithmic distribution. His doctrine of "fiducialism" was opposed by Jerzy Neyman's theory of confidence limits (*ca.* 1930). In genetics, he laid the foundations for biometric genetics; worked on the phenomenon of dominance; carried out breeding experiments with various animals; and enunciated a fundamental theorem of natural selection.

FITCH, ASA (*b. Salem, N.Y., 1809; d. Salem, 1879*), economic entomology, medicine.

Studied science under Amos Eaton at Rensselaer; and medicine at various medical schools in New York and Vermont. Began a life-long diary on geological expedition with Eaton. Taught natural history briefly at Rensselaer. State entomologist for New York (1854–70). Collected, studied, and reported on insects, especially with respect to injurious or beneficial effects upon crops.

FITTIG, RUDOLPH (*b. Hamburg, Germany, 1835; d. Strasbourg, Alsace [France], 1910*), chemistry.

Received doctorate from Göttingen (1858). Taught at Göttingen, Tübingen, and Strasbourg. Editor of *Zeitschrift für Chemie*. Published extensively; wrote massive textbook of chemistry; trained many chemists, notably William Ramsay and Ira Remsen. His work in experimental chemistry extended Wurtz's work in developing the Wurtz-Fittig reaction: sodium acted on benzene halides to produce new aromatic compounds, including biphenyl.

FITTON, WILLIAM HENRY (*b. Dublin, Ireland, 1780; d. London, England, 1861*), geology.

Studied medicine, but gave up practice in 1820. Interest in geology stimulated by lectures of Robert Jameson and T. C. Hope at Edinburgh. Wrote many reviews for geological and medical books. Best known for contributions to stratigraphy and elucidation of the succession of Upper Jurassic and Lower Cretaceous strata of southern England.

FITZGERALD, GEORGE FRANCIS (*b. Dublin, Ireland, 1851; d. Dublin, 1901*), physics.

Studied and taught at Trinity College, Dublin. One of the initial group, which included Heaviside, Hertz, and Lorentz, that took Maxwell's electromagnetic theory seriously and began to explore its consequences. Together with Lorentz, he first explained the null results of the Michelson-Morley experiment as due to the contraction of an arm of the interferometer, which resulted from its motion through the ether (the FitzGerald-Lorentz contraction).

FITZROY, ROBERT (*b. Ampton Hall, Suffolk, England, 1805; d. Upper Norwood, London, England, 1865*), hydrography, meteorology.

Attended Royal Naval College at Portsmouth. Commander of *Beagle* expeditions to survey the southern coasts of South America (1828–36). Chose the young Charles Darwin to accompany him on the second voyage. Published a narrative of the two expeditions. Brief political career; retired from the navy in 1850. As head of the Meteorologic Office (from 1855) he inaugurated weather forecasting.

FIZEAU, ARMAND-HIPPOLYTE-LOUIS (*b. Paris, France, 1819; d. Venteuil, near Jouarre, France, 1896*), experimental physics.

Studied optics at Collège de France with H.-V. Regnault; influenced by François Arago while studying at Paris observatory. Collaborated with Léon Foucault on experiments involving heliography, interference fringes, and the relative speeds of light in water and in air. In 1848, Fizeau published a paper on exactly the same subject as Christian Doppler had in 1842, unknown to Fizeau. The Doppler-Fizeau effect relates the observed frequency of a wave to the motion of the source or the observer relative to the medium in which the wave is propagated. Invented ingenious experimental techniques which he left for his followers and collaborators to develop and perfect. Much of the career of A. A. Michelson was built on Fizeau's unfinished business.

FLAMMARION, CAMILLE (*b. Montigny-le-Roi, France, 1842; d. Juvisy, France, 1925*), astronomy.

Began work in astronomy under Le Verrier at Paris Observatory, in Bureau de Calcul, later in Bureau des Longitudes. Important popularizer of science, notably through publications, including the best seller *Astronomie populaire* (1880). Founded Juvisy Observatory (1883). Did research on hypothetical habitability of Mars. Founded French Astronomical Society (1887). Scientific output concerned many subjects, including philosophy, psychic phenomena, and volcanology.

FLAMSTEED, JOHN (*b. Denby, England, 1646; d. Greenwich, England, 1719*), astronomy.

Mostly self-taught in astronomy due to ill health, which plagued him throughout his life. Took M.A. at Cambridge by letters-patent (1674). Career launched through influence of Sir Jonas Moore. Appointed first astronomer royal at Royal Observatory at Greenwich (1675). Mandate was to apply himself ". . . to the rectifying the tables of the motions of the heavens, and the places of the fixed stars," to bring positional astronomy abreast of the new descriptive astronomy. Re-worked, tabulated, and elucidated Horrox' lunar theory. Published 3,000-star "British Catalogue," vol. III of his *Historia coelestis Britannica* (1725). His accuracy in fundamental astronomical observations was unsurpassed before Bradley. Achieved precise determinations of the latitude of Greenwich, the obliquity of the ecliptic, and position of the equinox. Also worked on motion of the sun, satellites of Jupiter, and tables of atmospheric refraction and tides. Controversy with Newton and Halley, primarily over his slowness in publishing his observations.

FLECHSIG, PAUL EMIL (*b. Zwickau, Germany, 1847; d. Leipzig, Germany, 1929*), neuroanatomy, psychiatry, neurology.

Educated at Leipzig; influenced by Karl Ludwig. Worked in Institute of Pathology and appointed head of histology in Institute of Physiology (1873) at Leipzig. Became professor of psychiatry, studied psychiatry in European centers, and returned to open a clinic (1882). Rector at Leipzig 1894–95. With Wilhelm His, helped found the International Brain Commission (1901), to unify nomenclature, standardize methods, collect material, and encourage research in neuroanatomy. Contributed to clinical and pathological study of hysteria, epilepsy, neurosyphilis, and chorea. Fame due mainly to his technique of myelogenesis for examination of the brain and spinal cord. Described the dorsal spinocerebellar, now called Flechsig's tract. Monumental work on pyramidal tract.

FLEISCHER, JOHANNES (*b. Breslau, Germany [now Wrocław, Poland], 1539; d. Breslau, 1593*), optics.

Educated at Wittenberg. Published treatise on the rainbow, considerably clarifying the mechanism of reflection and refraction described by Witelo.

FLEMING, ALEXANDER (*b. Lochfield, Ayrshire, Scotland, 1881; d. London, England, 1955*), bacteriology.

Educated and worked at St. Mary's Hospital Medical School, Paddington; and University of London. Disciple of Sir Almroth Wright at St. Mary's. Devoted to investi-gating human body's defenses against bacterial infections. Upheld and practiced Wright's doctrine of specific immunization against bacterial infection through vaccine therapy. Among the first to treat syphilis with Salvarsan. Served in wound-research laboratory at Boulogne during World War I. Detected and named lysozyme (1921). Discovered penicillin (1928), but the antibiotic's powers were not established until it was stabilized and purified by Ernst Chain, Howard Florey, and their co-workers at Oxford (1940). Knighted in 1944; received Nobel Prize in medicine, jointly with Florey and Chain, in 1945.

FLEMING, JOHN (*b. Kirkroads, near Bathgate, Linlithgowshire, Scotland, 1785; d. Edinburgh, Scotland, 1857*), zoology, geology.

Studied at Edinburgh; taught at King's College, Aberdeen, and New College (Free Church), Edinburgh. Scotland's foremost zoologist as early as 1815; concerned largely with description and classification of freshwater and marine invertebrates, advocating the binary or dichotomous system of classification. Wrote detailed description and classification of British fauna. Controversy with William Buckland over nature of the deluge, and with William Conybeare over fossil evidence for a warmer climate in the past. Rejected Lyell's uniformitarian views for earth history as a whole.

FLEMING, JOHN AMBROSE (*b. Lancaster, England, 1849; d. Sidmouth, Devon, England, 1945*), electrical engineering.

Attended University College, London. Worked at Cambridge under James C. Maxwell in the new Cavendish Laboratory; taught at University College at Nottingham. In London, served briefly as consultant to Edison Electric Light Co. and taught at University College (1885–1926). Made many contributions to design of transformers, understanding properties of materials at liquid-air temperatures, photometry, and electrical measurements. Right-hand rule (a mnemonic aid relating direction of magnetic field, conductor motion, and induced electromotive force) is attributed to him. Experimented widely with wireless telegraphy; repeated Edison's experiments on the "Edison effect" (1889), resulting in a patent for the first electron tube, the diode (1904). Helped Marconi design a transmitter for spanning the Atlantic (1901). Wrote monumental *Principles of Electric Wave Telegraphy* (1906). Knighted in 1929.

FLEMING, WILLIAMINA PATON (*b. Dundee, Scotland, 1857; d. Boston, Mass., 1911*), astronomy.

Worked with Edward C. Pickering at Harvard College Observatory and became the leading woman astronomer of her day. Discovered more than 200 variable stars and ten novae. Classification of 10,351 stars published in *Draper Catalogue of Stellar Spectra*, Vol. XXVII of *Annals of Harvard College Observatory* (1890). Fifth woman member (honorary) of Royal Astronomical Society (1906).

FLEMMING, WALTHER (*b. Sachsenberg, Mecklenburg, Germany, 1843; d. Kiel, Germany, 1905*), anatomy, cytology.

Studied at Göttingen, Tübingen, Berlin, and Rostock. Worked and studied at several places in Europe from

1869 to 1876. Settled at University of Kiel (1876–1901). Published great work on cell division, *Zellsubstanz, Kern und Zelltheilung* (1882). Coined several terms used in study of cell division: mitosis, chromatin, achromatin, monocentric and dicentric phases. Improved Flesch's fixative in 1882 by addition of acetic acid to give Flemming's fluid; introduced Flemming's stain (safranine–gentian violet–Orange G) in 1891.

FLETCHER, WALTER MORLEY (*b. Liverpool, England, 1873; d. London, England, 1933*), physiology.
   Studied at Trinity College, Cambridge, receiving B.A. (1894), M.A. (1898), M.B. (1900), M.D. (1908), and Sc.D. (1914). Taught at Cambridge; strongly influenced students, one of whom, A. V. Hill, won a Nobel Prize in 1922. Left Cambridge when appointed by Ministry of Health as first secretary of Medical Research Committee (1914), later the independent Medical Research Council (1920). Served on several other important government bodies, helping to secure money for medical research. Most of his work was devoted to the problem of muscular metabolism and fatigue. With Frederick Gowland Hopkins, challenged the "inogen" theory of muscular metabolism.

FLETT, JOHN SMITH (*b. Kirkwall, Orkney, Scotland, 1869; d. Ashdon, Essex, England, 1947*), geology, petrology.
   Entered University of Edinburgh at seventeen, received M.A., B.Sc., M.B. and C.M. (1894), and D.Sc. (1899). Taught petrology at Edinburgh; did early research on stratigraphy and petrology of Orkney. Worked for Geological Survey of Great Britain as petrographer (1901–11) and director (1921–35); Geological Survey in Scotland (1911–21). Knighted 1925. Made important contributions to geology of Cornwall, especially sediments, metamorphic rocks, and igneous masses of the Lizard and adjacent areas. Formulated spilite suite, a worldwide type characteristic of early geosynclinal history.

FLEXNER, SIMON (*b. Louisville, Ky., 1863; d. New York, N.Y., 1946*), pathology, bacteriology.
   Received M.D. from University of Louisville (1889). Studied and worked at Johns Hopkins Hospital with William H. Welch. Taught at University of Pennsylvania (great influence on Hideyo Noguchi). Director of Rockefeller Institute for Medical Research in New York City. During a stay in Manila, isolated the "Flexner bacillus," which causes a form of dysentery. Led battle against bubonic plague in California (1901), cerebrospinal meningitis (1906), and poliomyelitis in New York City (1910).

FLOREY, HOWARD WALTER (*b. Adelaide, Australia, 1898; d. Oxford, England, 1968*), pathology.
   Studied at Adelaide, Oxford, and Cambridge. Influenced by Sir Charles Sherrington at Oxford, and by Sir Frederic Gowland Hopkins at Cambridge. Taught at University of Sheffield and at Oxford's Sir William Dunn School of Pathology. Later provost of Queen's College, Oxford. Career devoted to experimental study of disease processes. With E. B. Chain, developed penicillin as a systemic antibacterial antibiotic suitable for use in man; shared the Nobel Prize for physiology or medicine (1945) with Fleming and Chain. Knighted in 1944.

FLOURENS, MARIE-JEAN-PIERRE (*b. Maureilhan, near Béziers, France, 1794; d. Montgeron, near Paris, France, 1867*), physiology, history of science.
   Studied medicine at Montpellier. Lectured before Cercle Athénée. Under Cuvier's influence, taught at Collège de France. With Arago, founded *Comptes rendus,* reports of meetings of Academy of Sciences. Did landmark research on the physiology of the nervous system; localization of respiratory center in medulla oblongata; reunion of nerves; role of periosteum in formation and growth of bone; discovery of anesthetic properties of chloroform on animals.

FLOWER, WILLIAM HENRY (*b. Stratford-on-Avon, England, 1831; d. London, England, 1899*), zoology.
   Studied at University College, London; Middlesex Hospital; and London University. Appointed surgeon, lecturer in anatomy, and curator at museum of Middlesex Hospital. Conservator of Hunterian Museum at Royal College of Surgeons (1861–84); superintendent (later director) of Natural History Departments of British Museum (1884–98). Lectured extensively, particularly as Hunterian professor of comparative anatomy and physiology (1870–84). In addition to curatorial duties, made significant contributions to clarification of the classification of carnivores (1869), rhinoceroses (1875), and edentates (1882). Prime research interest was the Mammalia, especially Cetacea.

FLUDD, ROBERT (*b. Milgate House, Bearsted, Kent, England, 1574; d. London, England, 1637*), alchemy, medicine.
   Received B.A. (1596) and M.A. (1598) from St. John's College, Oxford. Spent six years as student of medicine, chemistry, and the occult sciences on the Continent. Received M.B. and M.D. at Christ Church, Oxford (1605). Medical practice in London. Published massive description of the macrocosm and the microcosm, the *Utriusque cosmi maioris scilicet et minoris, metaphysica, physica atque technica historia,* attacking Aristotle, Galen, and the universities, which to him seemed dedicated to preserving the authority of the ancients. He sought instead a new understanding of nature based on Christian principles. Attracted much controversy, particularly from Kepler, Mersenne, and Gassendi.

FOERSTE, AUGUST FREDERICK (*b. Dayton, Ohio, 1862; d. Dayton, 1936*), invertebrate paleontology, stratigraphy.
   Received B.A. from Denison University, M.A. (1888) and Ph.D. (1890) from Harvard, and did advanced study at Heidelberg and the Collège de France. Also worked part-time for the U.S. Geological Survey. Chose to teach science in a high school rather than accept a more prestigious position, in order to spend more time on research. Worked in state geological surveys of Indiana, Ohio, and Kentucky, and the Geological Survey of Canada. One of the founders of the Paleontological Society of America. Influenced by C. L. Herrick at Denison, and E. O. Ulrich. Herrick and Foerste founded *Bulletin* (now *Journal*) *of the Scientific Laboratories of Denison University* (1885). Re-studied, re-described, and illustrated hundreds of species of invertebrate fossils inadequately de-

scribed by earlier writers. Did systematic study of Ordovician and Silurian cephalopods.

FOL, HERMANN (*b. St. Mandé, France, 1845; d. at sea, 1892*), biology.

Studied medicine and zoology at Jena, Heidelberg, Zurich, and Berlin. Strongly influenced by Gegenbauer and Haeckel. Chose zoological research over medical research; accepted titular professorship (without pay) at Geneva. Wintered and eventually retired in Villefranche, near Nice, where in 1880 he established a marine laboratory. Did research on the anatomy and development of Ctenophora, and the embryology of Mollusca; made microscopic studies of fertilization, cell division, and early embryonic growth. His investigations enabled later workers (Boveri, Weismann, and Strasburger) to clarify the hereditary function of the nucleus. Founder of Geneva Photographical Society and *Recueil zoologique suisse*.

FOLIN, OTTO (*b. Asheda, Sweden, 1867; d. Boston, Mass., 1934*), biochemistry.

Educated at Minnesota and Chicago (Ph.D., 1898). Studied biochemistry with Kossel at Marburg, Hammarsten at Uppsala, and Salkowski in Berlin. Taught at University of West Virginia; in charge of the first laboratory for biochemical research in a hospital, McLean Hospital for the Insane at Waverley, Massachusetts. Appointed to the first chair of biochemistry in Harvard Medical School (1907). With Hsien Wu (1919), developed analytical methods for biochemical research; published classic paper on microchemical methods of blood analysis.

FOLKES, MARTIN (*b. London, England, 1690; d. London, 1754*), antiquarianism.

Educated at Saumur, France, and Clare Hall (Clare College), Cambridge. Publications on coins. Controversial president of Royal Society (1741–52).

FONTAINE (FONTAINE DES BERTINS), ALEXIS (*b. Claveyson, Drôme, France, 1704; d. Cuiseaux, Saône-et-Loire, France, 1771*), mathematics.

Studied at Collège de Tournon, and at Paris under Père Castel. Presented several memoirs to the Académie des Sciences; admitted in 1733. Work mainly in the fields of calculus of variations, differential equations, and theory of equations. Independently of Euler and Clairaut, discovered the relation termed homogeneity.

FONTANA, FELICE (*b. Pomarolo, Italy, 1730; d. Florence, Italy, 1805*), neurology, biology.

Educated at Rovereto, Verona, Parma, and Padua. In Bologna in 1755, collaborated with L. M. A. Caldani in research on irritability and sensitivity of parts of the animal body. Taught at University of Pisa. Summoned by Leopold I, grand duke of Tuscany, to Florence to organize and develop the court's physics laboratory; opened Museum of Physics and Natural History (1775). Research on movements of the iris and on viper venom was tied to research on irritability. One of the major microscopists of the eighteenth century. Discovered Fontana's canal in the ciliary body of the eye. Also noteworthy are his model of the eudiometer, an apparatus for oxygen therapy, and studies on absorbent powers of coal.

FONTENELLE, BERNARD LE BOUYER (or **BOVIER) DE** (*b. Rouen, France, 1657; d. Paris, France, 1757*), dissemination of knowledge, mathematics, astronomy.

Studied at the Jesuit *collège* in Rouen. *Secrétaire perpétuel* of Académie des Sciences (later *sous-directeur* and *directeur*). Published forty-two volumes of the *Histoire de l'Académie*, containing sixty-nine *éloges*. Published additional *éloges* separately. Most famous work, *Entretiens sur la pluralité des mondes* (1686, 1687), set forth the different astronomical systems of Ptolemy, Copernicus, and Tyco Brahe; first example in French of a learned work placed within reach of an educated but nonspecialized public.

FÖPPL, AUGUST (*b. Grossumstadt, Germany, 1854; d. Ammerland, Germany, 1924*), engineering, physics.

Studied at Darmstadt, Stuttgart, and the Polytechnic in Karlsruhe. Received doctorate from Leipzig in 1886. Taught at the Trades School in Leipzig (1877–92) and then at the university (1892–94). Wrote immensely successful *Einführung in die Maxwellsche Theorie der Elektrizität* (1894). Professor of theoretical mechanics and director of strength-of-materials laboratory at Technische Hochschule in Munich (from 1894). Published *Vorlesungen über technische Mechanik*.

FORBES, ALEXANDER (*b. Milton, Mass., 1882; d. Milton, 1965*), physiology.

Attended Harvard (B.A., 1904; M.A., 1905; M.D., 1910). Studied with Sherrington at Liverpool (1911–12) and Lucas at Cambridge (1912). Taught at Harvard Medical School; after 1948 continued research in Harvard biological laboratories. Greatest contributions were to neurophysiology. His paper on the flexion reflex of the decerebrate cat, timed by means of a string galvanometer, was a landmark in neurophysiology. His influence on Wiener and Rosenblueth contributed significantly to the development of cybernetics. Contributed to the final establishment of the all-or-none law of nerve conduction.

FORBES, EDWARD, JR. (*b. Douglas, Isle of Man, England, 1815; d. Edinburgh, Scotland, 1854*), biogeography, invertebrate zoology, invertebrate paleontology.

Studied medicine at Edinburgh; strongly influenced by Robert Graham in botany and Robert Jameson in geology. Attended biological lectures of Blainville and Geoffroy Saint-Hilaire in Paris. Interests focused strongly upon marine animals and distribution of species. Taught botany at Kings College, London; curator of Geological Society of London; and paleontologist for Geological Survey. Appointed to Regius chair of natural history at Edinburgh, but his death soon followed. Important work in biogeography and paleontology carried him close to the concept of biotic communities. Believed in the continuity of forms of species as the result of a creation plan rather than of evolution.

FORBES, JAMES DAVID (*b. Edinburgh, Scotland, 1809; d. Clifton, Scotland, 1868*), physics, geology.

Studied at Edinburgh; influenced by Leslie and Brewster. Appointed to chair of natural philosophy at Edinburgh (1833). His discovery of the polarization of radiant heat strengthened belief in the identity of thermal and luminous radiation and contributed to development of the concept of a continuous radiation spectrum. His detailed studies of glaciers aided in the establishment of modern theories of their formation and movement. Controversy with Agassiz on movement of glaciers. Principal of United College of St. Andrews (1860–68).

FORBES, STEPHEN ALFRED (b. *Silver Creek, Stephenson County, Ill., 1844; d. Urbana, Ill., 1930*), biology.

Studied medicine; taught school while studying natural history on his own. Curator of Museum of the State Natural History Society, Normal, Illinois (1872); transformed it into Illinois State Laboratory of Natural History in 1877. Moved it to Urbana when he became professor at University of Illinois. Received Ph.D. from Indiana (1884). State entomologist, Illinois; this office and State Laboratory combined into State Natural History Survey; Forbes was chief of the Survey until his death. First professional concern was how to teach natural history in public schools. Work dominated by interest in ecology. Studied food of fish and birds because he saw predator-prey relation as the most direct ecological link between species. "The Lake as a Microcosm" was hailed as minor classic by ecologists for its early statement of the concept of community.

FORCHHAMMER, JOHAN GEORG (b. *Husum, Denmark, 1794; d. Copenhagen, Denmark, 1865*), geology, oceanography, chemistry.

Studied physics, chemistry, pharmacy, mathematics, and mineralogy at Kiel; doctorate from Copenhagen (1820). Taught at Copenhagen; professor and later director at Polytechnic Institute. His fundamental researches on the composition of seawater brought him international acclaim. Called "father of Danish geology." *Danmarks geognostiske Forhold* (1835) was the first work on the structural geology of Denmark.

FORDOS, MATHURIN-JOSEPH (b. *Sérent, France, 1816; d. Paris, France, 1878*), chemistry.

Directed pharmacy services at three Paris municipal hospitals: Midi (1841–42), Saint-Antoine (1842–59), and Charité (1859–78). With others, founded the Société d'Émulation pour les Sciences Pharmaceutiques. With Amédée Gélis he investigated inorganic sulfur compounds, discovered sodium tetrathionate, and elucidated the composition of sulfur nitride. Isolated pyocyanine; worked on public health aspects of lead toxicity.

FOREL, AUGUSTE-HENRI (b. *near Morges, Switzerland, 1848; d. Yvorne, Switzerland, 1931*), medicine, neurology, entomology.

Studied at Zurich; doctorate from Vienna (1872). Taught psychiatry at Zurich Medical School; director of Burghölzli Clinic; established Asile d'Ellikon. In addition to psychiatry, did important research in Hymenopteran taxonomy and made remarkable studies of the brain. A region of the hypothalamus was named campus Foreli in his honor.

FOREL, FRANÇOIS ALPHONSE (b. *Morges, Switzerland, 1841; d. Morges, 1912*), limnology, earth sciences.

Studied at Académie de Genève, Montpellier, and Würzburg. Taught briefly at Würzburg, and for twenty-five years at Académie de Lausanne. Founder of limnology, most research done at Lake Geneva. Wrote

three-volume monograph on Lake Geneva (1892–94) and first limnology text (1901).

FORSSKÅL (also **FORSSKÅHL** or **FORSKÅL), PETER** (b. *Helsinki, Finland [then Sweden], 1732; d. Yarīm, Yemen, 1763*), botany.

Studied in Uppsala (1751–53, 1756–60) and Göttingen (1753–56). Gifted pupil of Linnaeus. Member of research voyage to Arabia sponsored by King Frederick V of Denmark. Although he died on the expedition his work, *Flora aegyptiaco-arabica*, was published posthumously. Its introduction surveys the phytogeography of Egypt.

FORSTER, (JOHANN) GEORG ADAM (b. *Nassenhuben [or Nassenhof], near Danzig, Germany [now Gdansk, Poland], 1754; d. Paris, France, 1794*), natural philosophy, geography.

Well schooled by his father, Johann Reinhold Forster. Studied at Dissenters' Academy; received M.D. from Halle. Accompanied his father on Cook's second voyage (1772–75); published *A Voyage Round the World* (1777). Taught at Collegium Carolinium in Kassel, and Vilna, Poland. Had prolific correspondence with men of science and letters throughout Europe. Librarian at University of Mainz (1788). Wrote *Ansichten vom Niederrhein* (1791–94), an account of his journey with Humboldt to England via Rhineland and the Low Countries.

FORSTER, JOHANN REINHOLD (b. *Dirschau [now Tczew], Poland, 1729; d. Halle, Germany, 1798*), natural philosophy, geography.

Educated as a clergyman at Berlin and Halle. Began wide scientific correspondence. Taught at Dissenters' Academy in Warrington, Lancashire; and at Halle. Published on zoology, ornithology, and ichthyology. With his son, Georg, accompanied Cook on *Resolution* voyage (1772–75); published *Observations Made During a Voyage Round the World* (1778). Influenced Humboldt and Blumenbach.

FORSYTH, ANDREW RUSSELL (b. *Glasgow, Scotland, 1858; d. London, England, 1942*), mathematics.

Educated at Trinity College, Cambridge, under Cayley. Taught at University College, Liverpool; Cambridge; and Imperial College, London. First to realize deficiencies of Cambridge mathematical school, to which he brought the modern style of mathematics, first through his *Theory of Functions* (1893).

FORTIN, JEAN NICOLAS (b. *Mouchy-la-Ville, Île-de-France, France, 1750; d. Paris, France, 1831*), scientific instruments.

Devised many instruments used in famous experiments by scientists and engineers such as Lavoisier, Gay-Lussac, Arago and Dulong, Biot and Arago. Of special note are a precision balance and the Fortin barometer.

FOSTER, HENRY (b. *Wood Plumpton, England, 1797; d. Chagres River, Isthmus of Panama, 1831*), geophysics.

Involved with geophysical observations during his naval career. Performed most investigations on expeditions to the Arctic (1824–25) and to the South Seas (1828–31). Studied geomagnetism, velocity of sound, atmospheric refraction, acceleration of gravity, meteorology, and oceanography.

FOSTER, MICHAEL (*b. Huntingdon, England, 1836; d. London, England, 1907*), physiology.

Received M.B. (1858) and M.D. (1859) from University College, London. Studied clinical medicine in Paris; briefly practiced medicine in Huntingdon. Taught at University College, where he came under the influence of William Sharpey (1867–69). Taught at Trinity College, Cambridge (1870–1903). Greatly influenced by Thomas Henry Huxley. In 1870 biological sciences and the medical school at Cambridge were largely moribund; Foster determined to build a great school of biology and physiology. Founder of the Cambridge School of Physiology; the eminent physiologists trained while he was there are his chief contributions to science. Did original research on the heartbeat; published several important textbooks on physiology. A founder of the British Physiological Society (1876); founded the *Journal of Physiology* (1878).

FOUCAULT, JEAN BERNARD LÉON (*b. Paris, France, 1819; d. Paris, 1868*), experimental physics.

Educated at home due to delicate health. Abandoned medical studies; wrote a newspaper column giving the latest from the world of science. Did research in home laboratory until given a position as physicist at the Paris observatory (1853). Determined velocity of light (1850, 1862) independently of Fizeau. With Fizeau, made first daguerreotype of sun (1845), and performed other experiments strengthening the wave theory of light. Best known for the Foucault pendulum, which mechanically demonstrated the earth's rotation (1851, 1852). He mounted a pendulum with a five-kilogram bob suspended from a steel thread two meters long, free to swing in any direction and tied at the extremity of its swing with a thread. When the thread was set afire, the pendulum began swinging, gradually turning "in the direction of the diurnal movement of the celestial sphere." In 1852 he invented the gyroscope. Among his many other technical inventions, the most significant were a modern technique for silvering glass to make mirrors for reflecting telescopes (1857) and his simple but accurate methods for testing and correcting the figure of both mirrors and lenses (1858).

FOUCHY, JEAN-PAUL GRANDJEAN DE (*b. Paris, France, 1707; d. Paris, 1788*), astronomy.

Studied astronomy under Joseph Nicolas Delisle. Presented an early important paper on the meridian of mean time. Produced many observational reports on specific astronomical phenomena. Judged by Delambre to be more an amateur than a true astronomer. Perpetual secretary of Academy of Sciences (1743–76); wrote over sixty *éloges.*

FOUQUÉ, FERDINAND ANDRÉ (*b. Mortain, Manche, France, 1828; d. Paris, France, 1904*), geology, mineralogy.

Worked briefly in chemical industry; received doctorate in medicine in 1858. Traveled extensively to study volcanoes, both active and extinct. Taught at Collège de France; served on French geological survey commission. Added significantly to knowledge of volcanic phenomena and products: generalized Henri Sainte-Claire Deville's explanation of the chemical composition of emanations of fumaroles. With Auguste Michel-Lévy, introduced into France the study of rocks by microscopical petrography and synthesized a large number of igneous rocks.

FOURCROY, ANTOINE FRANÇOIS DE (*b. Paris, France, 1755; d. Paris, 1809*), chemistry, medicine.

Studied at Paris Faculty of Medicine. Lectured on relations between chemistry and natural history and their application to medicine. Taught at École Royale Vétérinaire at Alfort, near Paris, and at Jardin du Roi. Lectured at the Lycée founded by J. F. Pilatre de Rozier; later also taught at École Polytechnique and École de Médecine at Paris. In 1787 he collaborated with Lavoisier, Guyton de Morveau, and Berthollet in the revision of chemical nomenclature; completed the chemical section of *Encyclopédie méthodique* (1789). Interest in application of chemistry to medicine led to study of various solids and fluids of human and animal body in health and sickness. Entered politics during French Revolution; served on Committee of Public Instruction and Committee of Public Safety. Collaborated with Vauquelin in important research in inorganic chemistry; isolated urea (1799).

FOURIER, JEAN BAPTISTE JOSEPH (*b. Auxerre, France, 1768; d. Paris, France, 1830*), mathematics, mathematical physics.

Fourier lost both his father and his mother by his ninth year and was placed by the archbishop in the town's military school. Later he was sent on to a Benedictine school at St. Benoît-sur-Loire. In 1789 he returned to Auxerre to accept a teaching position at his old school.

During the Revolution, Fourier was prominent in local affairs, and his courageous defense of the victims of the Terror led to his arrest in 1794. He was released after Robespierre's execution. When the École Polytechnique started in 1795 he was appointed assistant lecturer, to support the teaching of Lagrange and Monge. In 1798 Monge selected him to join Napoleon's Egyptian campaign. He became secretary of the newly formed Institut d'Égypte, and held other diplomatic posts as well as pursuing research.

After his return to France in 1801, Fourier wished to resume his work at the École Polytechnique; but Napoleon appointed him prefect of the Department of Isère, centered at Grenoble and extending to what was then the Italian border. Fourier was still at Grenoble in 1814 when Napoleon fell. Later Napoleon made him a count and appointed him prefect of the neighboring department of the Rhône, centered at Lyons. But before the end of Napoleon's Hundred Days, Fourier had resigned his new title and prefecture in protest against the severity of the regime and had come to Paris to try to take up research full time.

A former student at the École Polytechnique and companion in Egypt, Chabrol de Volvic, now was prefect of the department of the Seine and appointed him director of its Bureau of Statistics. In 1816 Fourier was elected to the reconstituted Académie des Sciences, but Louis XVIII could not forgive his having accepted the prefecture of the Rhône from Napoleon, and the nomination was refused. His renomination in 1817 was not opposed.

Fourier was left in a position of strength after the decline of the Société d'Arcueil, led by Laplace in the physical sciences, and gained the favor and support of the aging Laplace himself in spite of the continued enmity of Poisson. In 1822 he was elected to the powerful position of *secrétaire perpétuel* of the Académie des Sciences, and in 1827—after further protests—to the Académie Française. He was also elected a foreign member of the Royal Society.

Fourier's achievements lie in the study of the diffusion of heat and in the mathematical techniques he introduced to further that study. In 1807 he presented a long paper to the Academy on heat diffusion between disjoint masses and in special continuous bodies based on the diffusion equation. Lagrange opposed it—due, to some extent, to the Fourier series required to express the initial temperature distribution in certain of these bodies, which contradicted Lagrange's own denigration of trigonometric series. The paper was never published.

A prize problem on heat diffusion was proposed in 1810, however, and Fourier sent in the revised version of his 1807 paper, together with a new analysis on heat diffusion in infinite bodies. In these cases the periodicity of the Fourier series made it incapable of expressing the initial conditions, and Fourier substituted the Fourier integral theorem. He expanded the mathematical parts of the paper into his book *Théorie analytique de la chaleur* (1822).

The history of Fourier's main work in mathematics and mathematical physics has long been confused by an exclusive concentration on only two results, Fourier series and Fourier integrals, and by the application of anachronistic standards of rigor in judgments on their derivation. Fourier's achievement is twofold: first, the formulation of the physical problem as boundary-value problems in linear partial differential equations, which achieved the extension of rational mechanics to fields outside those defined in Newton's *Principia;* and second, the powerful mathematical tools he invented for the solution of the equations, which yielded a long series of descendants and raised problems in mathematical analysis that motivated much of the leading work in that field for the rest of the century and beyond.

Although Fourier studied the physical theory of heat for many years, his contributions, based primarily on the phenomena of radiation, did not long survive. His concern for applying his theory produced an analysis of the action of the thermometer, of the heating of rooms, and, most important, the first scientific estimate of a lower bound for the age of the earth.

FOURNEAU, ERNEST (*b. Biarritz, France, 1872; d. Ascain, France, 1949*), chemistry.

Studied chemistry in Germany under Theodor Curtius, Ludwig Gatterman, Emil Fischer, and Richard Willstätter. Returned to France and became director of pharmaceutical chemistry laboratory in factory at Ivry-sur-Seine. Named chief of new therapeutic chemistry service at Institut Pasteur (1911-46); after retirement worked at Rhône-Poulenc chemical company. Published more than two hundred books, articles, and lectures in collaboration with other researchers on amino alcohols and ethylene oxides (stovaine). Helped establish fundamental laws of chemotherapy.

FOURNEYRON, BENOÎT (*b. Saint-Étienne, Loire, France, 1802; d. Paris, France, 1867*), hydraulic machinery.

Constructed hydraulic turbines, determining their power and efficiency through first practical application of the Prony brake. Also wrote on water pressure, pipe design, and lock gates.

FOWLER, ALFRED (*b. Wilsden, Yorkshire, England, 1868; d. Ealing, London, England, 1940*), astrophysics.

Attended and taught at Normal School of Science (later the Royal College of Science) at South Kensington. Close association and participation with Norman Lockyer in the new field of application of the spectroscope to astronomy. Appointed Yarrow research professor of Royal Society (1923); a founder of the International Astronomical Union (1919). His contributions to astrophysics were based on exceptionally intimate knowledge of the characteristic spectra of the elements; he elucidated the structure of atoms.

FOWLER, RALPH HOWARD (*b. Roydon, Essex, England, 1889; d. Cambridge, England, 1944*), physics.

Educated at Winchester and at Trinity College, Cambridge (B.A., 1911). Taught at Cambridge (1919-38). One of the founders of modern theoretical astrophysics. Provided one of the earliest applications of the new "quantum statistics" of E. Fermi and P. A. M. Dirac. Introduced problems from the quantum theory into discussions of the more experimentally inclined physicists. His *Statistical Mechanics* became a standard reference work on the subject. Knighted in 1942.

FOWNES, GEORGE (*b. London, England, 1815; d. Brompton, England, 1849*), chemistry.

Earned doctorate under Liebig at Giessen (1839). Assistant to Thomas Graham at University College, London. Lectured in chemistry at Charing Cross and Middlesex hospitals and at the Royal Institution. First director of Birkbeck Laboratory at University College (1845). Most notable achievement was the isolation of two new organic bases, furfural and benzoline.

FRACASTORO, GIROLAMO (*b. Verona, Italy, ca. 1478; d. Incaffi [now hamlet of Affi, Verona], 1553*), medicine, philosophy.

Studied literature, mathematics, astronomy, philosophy, and medicine at Academy in Padua. Taught logic at University of Padua for several years; practiced medicine in Verona. Narrative poem, *Syphilis sive morbus Gallicus* (1530), brought him universal fame; in it the nature and cure of syphilis are illustrated. *De morbo Gallico* laid the first foundations of his doctrine of infections. *Homocentrica sive de stellis* (1538) attempts to solve certain problems in astronomical and terrestrial physics. His scientific thought culminates in *De contagione et contagiosis morbis et curatione* (1546), in which he describes numerous contagious diseases and illustrates three means by which contagion can be spread.

FRAENKEL, ADOLF ABRAHAM (*b. Munich, Germany, 1891; d. Jerusalem, Israel, 1965*), mathematics.

Studied at Munich, Marburg, Berlin, and Breslau. Taught at Marburg (1916-28), Kiel (1928), and Hebrew University of Jerusalem (1929-59). As mathematician, was interested in axiomatic foundation of mathematical theories. Encyclopedic knowledge of set theory. Developed ZF (Zermelo-Fraenkel) set theory to include theories of order and well-order.

FRAIPONT, JULIEN (*b. Liège, Belgium, 1857; d. Liège, 1910*), zoology, paleontology, anthropology.

Studied and taught at University of Liège; inspired by example and teaching of his mentor, Edouard Van Beneden. Zoological works dealt with systematics, and with the morphology of Protozoa, Hydrozoa, Trematoda, Cestoda, and, most importantly, Archiannelida. In his paleontological research, he studied various fossils of the Upper Devonian and Lower Carboniferous. Involved in study of human fossils discovered at Spy, near Namur (Belgium); this was the first discovery of relatively complete documents of Neanderthal man, exhumed in perfectly established stratigraphic conditions that fixed their age and guaranteed their authenticity.

FRANÇAIS, FRANÇOIS (JOSEPH) (*b. Saverne, Bas-Rhin, France, 1768; d. Mainz, Germany, 1810*), mathematics.

Taught at the *collège* in Colmar (1791), the *collège* in Strasbourg (1792), the École Centrale du Haut-Rhin in Colmar (1797–1803), the lycée at Mainz (1803), the École d'Artillerie at La Fère (1804), and the École d'Artillerie in Mainz. Highly esteemed by mathematicians of the Paris Academy. Worked on development of the calculus of derivations and its applications, and on integration of partial differential equations. Works often confused with those of his brother, Jacques Frédéric (*q.v.*).

FRANÇAIS, JACQUES FRÉDÉRIC (*b. Saverne, Bas-Rhin, France, 1775; d. Metz, France, 1833*), mathematics.

Studied at the *collège* of Strasbourg, the École Polytechnique, and the École du Génie. Served in French army; professor of military art at the École d'Application du Génie et de l'Artillerie in Metz (1811–33). Published papers of his brother (François) posthumously; source of inspiration to him. Works often confused with those of François (*q.v.*).

FRANCESCA, PIERO DELLA (or **Piero dei Franceschi**), also known as **Petrus Borgensis** (*b. Borgo San Sepolcro [now Sansepolcro], Italy, between 1410 and 1420; d. Sansepolcro, 1492*), mathematics.

Nothing is known of his life until 1439, when he was the associate of Domenico Veneziano at Florence. After a career as an artist, wrote major work on mathematics of painting, *De prospettiva pingendi*.

FRANCIS OF MARCHIA (*b. Appignano, Italy; fl. first half of the fourteenth century*), theology, natural philosophy.

A Friar Minor (Franciscan); received degree as teacher of theology at University of Paris. Lectured at Studio Generale of Franciscans at Avignon. Rebelled against Pope John XXII; excommunicated (1328) and expelled from the order (1329). In 1344 made formal recantation; reconciled with church and order. Wrote commentaries on Aristotle's *Physics;* first medieval philosopher to employ theory of impetus to explain movement of projectiles. Also used theory to explain movement of celestial spheres. Proponent of the then new theory of actual infinity.

FRANCIS OF MEYRONNES (*b. Meyronnes, Provence, France, ca. 1285; d. Piacenza, Italy, ca. 1330*), theology, natural philosophy.

Member of Franciscan order of Provence; pupil and follower of doctrines of Duns Scotus. Taught in England.

Bachelor of faculty of theology at Paris. Lectured on Peter Lombard's *Sentences;* doctor of theology (1323). As theologian, commented on Aristotle's cosmology, correcting it in light of physics presented in Scriptures.

FRANCK, JAMES (*b. Hamburg, Germany, 1882; d. Göttingen, Germany, 1964*), physics.

Studied at Heidelberg, and at Berlin under Rubens, Emil Warburg, and Planck. In Warburg's laboratory Franck and Gustav Hertz performed famous experiments on elastic collisions, leading to discovery of the quantized transfer of energy in inelastic collisions between electrons and atoms; shared Nobel Prize, 1926. From 1917 to 1921 at Kaiser Wilhelm Institut für Physikalische Chemie Franck extended his previous work. In 1921 he moved to Zweite Physikalische Institut in Göttingen; he worked with Max Born on study of atoms in collision, and the formation and dissociation of molecules and their vibration and rotation. Franck was led to his method of determining the energy of dissociation of molecules by extrapolation of vibrational levels and to the principle which, after its wave-mechanical formulation by Condon, became known as the Franck-Condon principle. After Hitler came to power, Franck spent a year in Copenhagen, then accepted a professorship at Johns Hopkins University in Baltimore. In 1938 he moved to University of Chicago, where he did important research in the laboratory for photosynthesis. Worked on atomic bomb project; afterwards he and many other scientists released the Franck Report, urging the government to consider use of the bomb a fateful political decision.

FRANCK, SEBASTIAN (*b. Donauwörth, Bavaria, Germany, 1499; d. Basel, Switzerland, 1542*), theology.

Studied at Arts Faculty of University of Ingolstadt and at Dominican college at Heidelberg. Entered Catholic priesthood, later Protestant pastor for short time. Earned living as popular writer, printer, and soapmaker, wandering from place to place as he was banned from one town after another for his unorthodox writings. His great work, *Chronica, Zeitbuch und Geschichtbibel* (1531), which brought complaints from many sides, was confiscated and he was arrested and expelled from Strasbourg. Later expelled from Ulm, allowed to remain in Basel. In addition to theological works, he published a book on geography, folklore, and anthropology, and a history and description of Germany. His theological thought was guided by individualism, spiritualism, rationalism, and radical universalism. Scriptures have no part in his theology, hence his profound doubts about the Trinity and the divinity of Christ. Strongly influenced by Renaissance humanism and the Neoplatonic tradition.

FRANK, PHILIPP (*b. Vienna, Austria, 1884; d. Cambridge, Mass., 1966*), physics, mathematics, philosophy of science, education.

Received doctorate in physics from Vienna under Ludwig Boltzmann (1907). Worked on fundamental problems of theoretical physics. His greatest interest, the philosophy of science, led to a paper analyzing the law of causality, later expanded into his widely influential work, *Das Kausalgesetz und seine Grenzen* (1932). Sought to bring philosophy and science closer together. Succeeded Einstein as professor of theoretical physics at German University of Prague (1912). Came to U.S. as lecturer on physics and mathematics at Harvard (1938–54).

FRANKENHEIM, MORITZ LUDWIG (*b. Brunswick, Germany, 1801; d. Dresden, Germany, 1869*), crystallography.

Received doctorate at Berlin (1820). Taught at Berlin (1826) and Breslau (1827–66). His importance lies especially in field of crystallography.

FRANKLAND, EDWARD (*b. Catterall, near Churchtown, Lancashire, England, 1825; d. Golaa, Gudbrandsdalen, Norway, 1899*), chemistry.

Studied with A. W. H. Kolbe while employed in Lyon Playfair's laboratory at Museum of Economic Geology, London. Received doctorate at Marburg under Bunsen; briefly studied with Liebig at Giessen. Taught at Putney (1850–51); Owens College, Manchester (1851–57); St. Bartholomew's Hospital; Addiscombe Military College; and the Royal Institution. Professor of chemistry at Royal College of Chemistry (1865–85). Member of the X Club. Founder of Institute of Chemistry (1877). Knighted in 1897. Deeply conscious of importance of applied science; worked on improving water and gas supplies. Did research in organic, physical, and applied chemistry. Work on radicals led to isolation of zinc methyl; developed concept of valence. In biology, designed an experiment to test Liebig's theory of the source of muscular energy. His calorimetric experiments laid the foundation for quantitative dietetics. Humanitarian and scientific interest in water analysis was continued by his son Percy.

FRANKLAND, PERCY FARADAY (*b. London, England, 1858; d. House of Letterawe, on Loch Awe, Argyllshire, Scotland, 1946*), chemistry, bacteriology.

Son of Edward Frankland (*q.v.*), who greatly influenced his work. Studied at Royal School of Mines under his father and Thomas Henry Huxley; Ph.D. from Würzburg (1880); B.Sc. from University of London (1881). Taught at University College, Dundee (1888–94); and Mason Science College (later University of Birmingham) (1894–1919). Worked with Chemical Warfare Committee on synthetic drugs, explosives, and mustard gas during World War I. Undertook systematic study of coal gas and water supplies, particularly developed methods for analyzing and preventing contamination of water supplies. Other research concerned stereochemistry of optically active substances.

FRANKLIN, BENJAMIN (*b. Boston, Mass., 1706; d. Philadelphia, Pa., 1790*), electricity, general physics, oceanography, meteorology, promotion and support of science and international scientific cooperation.

Benjamin Franklin was the first American to win an international reputation in pure science and the first man of science to gain fame for work done wholly in electricity. His principal achievement was the formulation of a widely used theory of general electrical "action" (explaining or predicting the outcome of manipulations in electrostatics: charge production, charge transfer, charging by electrostatic induction). He advanced the concept of a single "fluid" of electricity, was responsible for the principle of conservation of charge, and analyzed the distribution of charges in the Leyden jar, a capacitor. He

introduced into the language of scientific discourse relating to electricity such technical words as "plus" and "minus," "positive" and "negative," "charge" and "battery." By experiment he showed that the lightning discharge is an electrical phenomenon, and upon this demonstration (together with his experimental findings concerning the action of grounded and of pointed conductors) he based his invention of the lightning rod.

Franklin made contributions to knowledge of the Gulf Stream, of atmospheric convection currents, and of the direction of motion of storms. His observations on population were of service to Malthus. He was the principal founder of the American Philosophical Society, the New World's first permanent scientific organization.

In spite of his extraordinary scientific accomplishments, the public at large knows of Franklin primarily as a statesman and public figure, and as an inventor rather than as a scientist—possibly because he devoted only a small portion of his creative life to scientific research. One of the three authors of the Declaration of Independence, he was a member of the Second Continental Congress and drew up a plan of union for the colonies. Sent to Paris in 1776 as one of three commissioners to negotiate a treaty, in 1778 he was appointed sole plenipotentiary, and in 1781 he was one of three commissioners to negotiate the final peace with Great Britain.

In France, Franklin enjoyed contact with many scientists and made the acquaintance of Volta, a strong supporter of Franklin's one-fluid theory; Volta began the next stage of electrical science with his invention of the battery, which made possible the production of a continuous electric current. Franklin appears to have been the first international statesman of note whose international reputation was gained in scientific activity.

FRANKLIN, ROSALIND ELSIE (*b. London, England, 1920; d. London, 1958*), physical chemistry, molecular biology.

After graduating from Newnham College, Cambridge (1941), stayed on to investigate gas-phase chromatography. In 1942 joined British Coal Utilisation Research Association; applied expertise in physical chemistry to the problem of the physical structure of coals and carbonized coals. From 1947 to 1950 worked at Laboratoire Central des Services Chimiques de l'État, Paris, developing her skill in X-ray diffraction techniques and applying them to a detailed and illuminating study of carbons and structural changes accompanying graphitization. In 1951 joined King's College Medical Research Council Biophysics Unit (London), where she and Raymond Gosling applied these techniques to problems of the structure of DNA. In 1953 moved to Crystallography Laboratory of Birkbeck College, London, to work similarly on even more exacting problems of virus structure.

FRAUNHOFER, JOSEPH (*b. Straubing, Germany, 1787; d. Munich, Germany, 1826*), optics, optical instrumentation.

Little formal education; after several years as apprentice and journeyman to a mirror-maker and glass cutter, entered optical shop of Munich philosophical (scientific) instrument company. Developed expertise in practical optics and knowledge of mathematics and optical science. Working with Pierre Louis Guinand, he improved homogeneity of optical glass and increased size of striae-free blanks, so that large-diameter lenses could be made. During research to determine optical constants of glass, found solar spectrum crossed with many fine dark lines (Fraunhofer lines); designated the more distinct lines with capital letters, mapping many of the 574 observed. Through his observations of the spectral lines and his interpretation of diffraction spectra, he designed and produced many optical and mechanical instruments, notably the nine-and-a-half-inch Dorpat refracting telescope and equatorial mounting, and the six-and-a-quarter-inch Königsberg heliometer.

FRAZER, JAMES GEORGE (*b. Glasgow, Scotland, 1854; d. Cambridge, England, 1941*), anthropology.

Attended University of Glasgow and Trinity College, Cambridge; elected to fellowship at latter which was renewed for rest of his life. Spent one year (1907–08) teaching social anthropology at Liverpool. Knighted in 1914. Popularizer of comparative anthropology. Wrote *The Golden Bough* (12 vols., 1911–15) about rites and practices of European countries similiar to those of more primitive societies. Although he made no original observations in anthropology, his inductive method of reading published literature, making notes which he later classified, assembled, and discussed, brought together volumes of data on customs and beliefs, classified and documented to stimulate other workers.

FREDERICK II OF HOHENSTAUFEN (*b. Iesi, Italy, 1194; d. Castelfiorentino, Italy, 1250*), natural sciences.

King of Sicily, 1198–1212. Holy Roman emperor (1220–50). Patron of literature and science; drew scholars of widely different backgrounds and interests to his court. Wrote six-book composition, *De arte venandi cum avibus* (*ca.* 1244–48): the first book is a remarkable survey of general ornithology; later books are more technical and specialized, treating falconry, use of the lure, and hawking with various birds.

FREDERICQ, LÉON (*b. Ghent, Belgium, 1851; d. Liège, Belgium, 1935*), physiology.

Received doctor's degree in natural sciences (1871) and M.D. (1875) at University of Ghent. From 1875 to 1879, studied and worked at Ghent, Paris, Strasbourg (under Hoppe-Seyler), Roscoff (under Lacaze-Duthiers), and Berlin (under Emil du Bois-Reymond). Did classic work on blood coagulation. In 1879 appointed professor of physiology at University of Liège. Did research on blood salinity of marine invertebrates, osmoregulation, regulation of temperature in mammals, and circulation physiology. Discovered phenomenon of autotomy. Built a better aerotonometer for demonstrating laws of gas diffusion in lungs and gills.

FREDHOLM, (ERIK) IVAR (*b. Stockholm, Sweden, 1866; d. Stockholm, 1927*), applied mathematics.

Educated at Polytechnic Institute in Stockholm; Uppsala (B.S., 1888; D.Sc., 1898); and University of Stockholm, under Mittag-Leffler. Taught at University of Stockholm (1898–1927). Concentrated in area of equations of mathematical physics. Most significantly, he solved, under quite broad hypotheses, a very general class of integral equations that had been the subject of extensive research

for almost a century (Fredholm's equation). His work led indirectly to the development of Hilbert spaces and so to other more general function spaces.

FREGE, FRIEDRICH LUDWIG GOTTLOB (*b. Wismar, Germany, 1848; d. Bad Kleinen, Germany, 1925*), logic, foundations of mathematics.

Studied at Jena and Göttingen (Ph.D., 1873). Taught at Jena (1879–1917). Found ordinary language insufficient to give a satisfactory definition of number and a rigorous foundation to arithmetic; wrote his *Begriffschrift* (1879), intended to be a formula language for pure thought, written with specific symbols and modeled upon that of arithmetic. This tool gradually developed into modern mathematical logic, of which Frege may justly be considered the creator.

FREIESLEBEN, JOHANN KARL (*b. Freiberg, Saxony, Germany, 1774; d. Nieder-Auerbach, Saxony, Germany, 1846*), geology, mineralogy, mining.

Studied at Mining Academy in Freiberg under Abraham Gottlob Werner, whose theories Freiesleben later applied and extended. Made scientific journeys through Saxony and Thuringia with Leopold von Buch, explored Thuringian Forest with E. F. von Schlotheim, and traveled to Bohemia, the Swiss Jura, the Alps, and Savoy with Alexander von Humboldt. Visited Harz Mountains often while studying in Leipzig. Director of copper and silver mines in Eisleben (1800–08); joined Bureau of Mines in Freiberg (1808); in charge of all Saxon mining operations (1838–42). Received doctorate from Marburg (1817). Wrote important works on mineralogy, mining, and stratigraphy of Harz Mountains, Saxony, and Thuringia. Devised technical improvements in mining and metallurgy.

FREIND, JOHN (*b. Croughton, Northamptonshire, England, 1675; d. London, England, 1728*), chemistry, medicine.

Studied at Christ Church, Oxford (B.A., 1698; M.A., 1701; M.B., 1703; M.D., 1707). Lectures on chemistry at Ashmolean Museum notable for his adoption of Newtonian attraction. Successful medical career, ultimately royal physician. Medical works concerned with therapeutics and English medieval and Renaissance medicine.

FRÉMY, EDMOND (*b. Versailles, France, 1814; d. Paris, France, 1894*), chemistry.

Taught at the École Polytechnique and Muséum d'Histoire Naturelle. Continued and expanded Pelouze's studies of iron oxides. Among other scientific investigations, synthesized rubies. At the museum he sought to prove the transformation of plant materials into coal. Organized collaboration of professors and industrialists on a chemical encyclopedia.

FRENET, JEAN-FRÉDÉRIC (*b. Périgueux, France, 1816; d. Périgueux, 1900*), mathematics.

Studied at the École Normale Supérieure; doctorate from University of Toulouse (1847). His thesis contains what are known in the theory of space curves as the Frenet-Serret formulas. Taught at Toulouse and Lyons. His *Recueil d'exercises sur le calcul infinitésimal* (1856) was popular for more than half a century.

263

FRENICLE DE BESSY, BERNARD (*b. Paris, France, ca. 1605; d. Paris, 1675*), mathematics, physics, astronomy.

An accomplished amateur mathematician; held an official position as counselor at Cour des Monnaies in Paris. Maintained correspondence with the most important mathematicians of his time—Descartes, Fermat, Huygens, and Mersenne. Solved many mathematical problems proposed by Fermat. First to use the so-called secant transformation.

FRENKEL, YAKOV ILYICH (*b. Rostov, Russia, 1894; d. Leningrad, U.S.S.R., 1954*), physics.

Graduated from St. Petersburg University in 1916. Taught at Tavrida University in Simferopol (1918). Worked at Physico-Technical Institute in Petrograd (Leningrad) (1921–54). Also taught at Leningrad Polytechnic Institute. Spent one year lecturing at University of Minnesota. Published many scientific books and articles, encompassing extremely varied fields of theoretical physics. One of the founders of modern atomic theory of solids (metals, dielectrics, and semiconductors). In his study of the absorption of light in solid dielectrics and semiconductors, he pointed out a second type of excitation associated with ionization, with the formation of a free electron and a free hole; when bound together the electron and hole form a unique neutral system called "Frenkel's exciton." The "Frenkel defect" in a crystal lattice is caused by an atom or ion being removed from its normal position in the lattice (thus causing a vacancy) and taking up an interstitial position. His research had an essential influence on the development of electrodynamics and the theory of electrons, as well as the theory of atomic nuclei.

FRENZEL, FRIEDRICH AUGUST (*b. Freiberg, Germany, 1842; d. Freiberg, 1902*), mineralogy.

Studied at the Mining Academy in Freiberg. Mine chemist for the state mines for over 25 years. Lectured at Royal Mining School. Discovered eight new minerals. His *Mineralogisches Lexikon für das Königreich Sachsen* (1874) contained descriptions of 723 minerals. Assembled two large mineral collections. Also wrote numerous articles on ornithology.

FRERE, JOHN (*b. Westhorpe, Suffolk, England, 1740; d. East Dereham, Norfolk, England, 1807*), archaeology.

Educated at Cambridge (B.A., 1763; M.A., 1766). Professional career was in law and politics; scientific work mainly a hobby. His discovery of flint weapons at a brickyard near Hoxne aroused little or no interest until 1840, when Boucher de Perthes found similar implements in the Somme. These flints probably exhibited the best known workmanship of the lower Paleolithic period, and further excavations were made later in late Acheulean deposits at Hoxne.

FRESENIUS, CARL REMIGIUS (*b. Frankfurt am Main, Germany, 1818; d. Wiesbaden, Germany, 1897*), analytical chemistry.

Studied at University of Bonn; received doctorate from Giessen (1842) under Liebig. Faced with lack of guidelines for systematic qualitative analysis, he devised a method of his own for systematic identification and separation of the individual metals (cations) and nonmetals (anions), selecting from the great multitude of reactions those which struck him as most suitable. In 1841 he expanded his system into a book, *Anleitung zur qualitativen chemischen Analyse;* its enormous success clearly shows the magnitude of the gap in scientific knowledge which the Fresenius system of qualitative analysis filled. In 1845 he moved to Wiesbaden Agricultural College, where he taught and established a laboratory which eventually became the Fresenius Training and Research Institute. Founded the journal *Zeitschrift für analytische Chemie* (1862). Also published a book on quantitative chemical analysis and played a large role in shaping the science of chemical analysis to meet the requirements of an industrial age.

FRESNEL, AUGUSTIN JEAN (*b. Broglie, France, 1788; d. Ville-d'Avray, France, 1827*), optics.

Studied at the École Polytechnique in Paris and the École des Ponts et Chaussées. Entered government service as civil engineer. Began his investigations of the wave nature of light during periods of leave from the Corps des Ponts et Chaussées. Whenever possible, he returned to Paris to pick up the thread of his research. His later work with the Lighthouse Commission put severe demands on his time. Worked with François Arago. His scientific work shows an essential unity. Above all, his research found its motivation and direction in an attempt to demonstrate that light is undulatory and not corpuscular. With only the most general knowledge of the work of his predecessors, he challenged the prevailing Newtonian view and undertook a series of brilliant investigations which systematically elaborated the wave concept and established its conformity with experience.

FREUD, SIGMUND (*b. Freiberg, Moravia [now Příbor, Czechoslavakia], 1856; d. London, England, 1939*), psychology.

In 1873 Freud entered the University of Vienna to study medicine. He spent three more years than was necessary in qualifying for his medical degree, which he finally received in 1881. This delay resulted from starting what he intended to be a career in biological research. He later decided to obtain the clinical experience that would gain him respectable status as a practitioner. He joined the resident staff of the Vienna General Hospital in 1882 and remained there until 1885, working in the various clinical departments of the hospital for short periods of time. He stayed fourteen months in the department of nervous diseases because he wished to specialize in neuropathology; he also found time to continue his anatomical research on the human brain, tracing the course of nerve tracts in the medulla oblongata.

In the early years of his practice he went several times a week to Kassowitz's Children's Clinic, where he headed the department of neurology. Throughout his career he was on the faculty of the University of Vienna, where he lectured, first on neuropathology and then on psychoanalysis. Freud made a solid contribution to conventional neuropathology. His first book was *Aphasia* (1891). Part of his motivation to write it must have been the desire to get at the neurological events underlying complex psychological processes. In this it foreshadowed his *Psychology for Neurologists* (1895). His three works on cerebral paralysis in children, published in 1891, 1893, and 1897, were immediately recognized as definitive works on the subject and have remained so valued.

The development of Freud's psychoanalytic thought can be described as occurring in three phases. In the first phase he gradually developed his ideas during his experience in the therapy of hysteria. In the second phase, in the middle of the 1890's, he developed his ideas more rapidly and with less reference to clinical experience than he had before and would later. He wrote the crucial document of this second phase of development in 1895: the "Project for a Scientific Psychology" was a comprehensive theory of the neurological events underlying human thought and behavior. In the third phase, which lasted from the late 1890's until the end of his career, Freud elaborated greatly on the ideas developed during the first two phases. There was again much reference to his clinical experience, but it was often interpreted so that it fit his previous ideas.

The *Interpretation of Dreams* (1901) has usually been considered Freud's most important work. In the famous seventh chapter he published for the first time much of the general theory he had formulated in the "Project" in 1895; in this chapter the brain becomes the "psychic apparatus" and most other neurological terms are replaced by psychological and psychoanalytic terms. The volume contains many detailed accounts of dreams and many interpretations, primarily of his own dreams, following his formulation of the wish-fulfillment theory. In carrying out these interpretations, Freud refined his understanding of the mode of operation of the unconscious.

In 1905 Freud published *Three Essays on the Theory of Sexuality* the second in importance of his books. His last major contribution to psychoanalytic theory was *The Ego and the Id* (1923), in which he elaborated on the concept of the superego. The superego was a part of the ego that did not involve consciousness. *Totem and Taboo*, published in 1913, was Freud's first and most important volume on social theory.

The dispersion of Freud's thought in Europe centered in the psychoanalytic movement. The weekly meetings that began at his house in 1902 developed into the International Psychoanalytic Association, established at Nuremberg in 1910.

FREUNDLICH, ERWIN FINLAY (*b. Biebrich, Germany, 1885; d. Wiesbaden, Germany, 1964*), astronomy.

Studied briefly at Leipzig; received Ph.D. from Göttingen (1910). Worked as astronomer at the Royal Observatory in Berlin and at its new site in Neubabelsberg (1910–18). Influenced by Felix Klein, Emil Fischer, and Einstein. Resigned his post to work full-time with Einstein on his still incomplete theory of general relativity, financed by the Kaiser Wilhelm Gesellschaft (1918–20). Appointed observer and later professor at the Einstein Institute at the Astrophysical Observatory, Potsdam (1921–33). Worked on solution of solar red-shift problem. Emigrated to Turkey; helped reorganize the University of Istanbul and create a modern observatory (1933–37). Wrote first astronomical textbook published in Turkish (1937). Taught briefly at Charles University in Prague. Accepted offer from St. Andrews University, Scotland, to build an observatory and create a new department of astronomy (1939–59); improved astronomical instruments at the observatory. Continued research on redshift theory.

FREUNDLICH, HERBERT MAX FINLAY (*b. Berlin-Charlottenburg, Germany, 1880; d. Minneapolis, Minn., 1941*), colloid and interface science.

Older brother of astronomer Erwin Freundlich (1885–1964). Studied at Munich and Leipzig. Remained at Leipzig as Wilhelm Ostwald's chief assistant (1903–11). Taught at Technische Hochschule in Brunswick (1911–19). Worked at Kaiser Wilhelm Institute for Physical Chemistry and Electrochemistry in Berlin-Dahlem (1919–33), where his laboratory was one of the world's chief centers of research in colloid and interface science; followed Fritz Haber's example of linking fundamental research to industrial processes. Taught at University College, London (1933–37), and at University of Minnesota until his death.

FREY, MAXIMILIAN RUPPERT FRANZ VON (*b. Salzburg, Austria, 1852; d. Würzburg, Germany, 1932*), physiology.

Studied at Vienna and Freiburg; graduated from Leipzig in 1877. Worked in Carl Ludwig's physiology laboratory at Leipzig (1880–97); taught at Leipzig (1882–1897). Taught at Zurich (1897–99) and Würzburg (1899–1932). His three fields of research were muscle physiology; mechanics of circulation; and investigation of the "lower senses," i.e., sensory organs of the skin and "deep sensibility."

FRIBERGIUS, KALBIUS. *See* **Rülein von Calw, Ulrich.**

FRIEDEL, GEORGES (*b. Mulhouse, France, 1865; d. Strasbourg, France, 1933*), crystallography.

Studied at École Polytechnique and School of Mines, Paris. Taught and later became director at School of Mines at Saint-Étienne. After World War I was chairman of the Institute of Geological Sciences at French University of Strasbourg; one of the founders of the Petroleum Institute. His work is remarkable for its diversity; essentially crystallographic and mineralogical, it also deals with petrology, geology, and even engineering and pedagogy. Established validity of the law of Bravais as a law of observation, regardless of theory (1904). Enunciated the empirical law of mean indices (1908). In 1905 he proved the physical reality of the Bravais lattice by noting that irrational threefold axes had never been found in crystals (Friedel's law of rational symmetric intercepts). In 1904 he completed Bravais's and Mallard's theory of twinning and stated the general law that governs all twins. His work on the mesomorphous stases is perhaps the most important of all his contributions. He enumerated the eleven centrosymmetries that can be determined by X rays (Friedel's law). His theory of crystal growth explains negative crystals.

FRIEDMANN, ALEKSANDR ALEKSANDROVICH (*b. St. Petersburg, Russia, 1888; d. Leningrad, U.S.S.R., 1925*), mathematics, physics, mechanics.

Graduated from St. Petersburg University (1910). Worked at aerological observatory in Pavlovsk; studied means of observing the atmosphere. Director of Russia's first factory for manufacture of measuring instruments used in aviation. Taught at Perm University (1918–20); worked at main physics observatory of Academy of Sciences, Petrograd (1920–25); taught courses in higher mathematics and theoretical mechanics at various colleges in Petrograd. Scientific activity concentrated in theoretical meteorology and hydromechanics; one of the founders of dynamic meteorology. His important work in hydromechanics gave the fullest theory of vortical motion. His work on the theory of relativity dealt with its cosmological problem.

FRIEND, JOHN ALBERT NEWTON (*b. Newton Abbot, Devonshire, England, 1881; d. Birmingham, England, 1966*), chemistry.

Attended Birmingham University (B.Sc., 1902; M.Sc., 1903; D.Sc., 1910) and Würzburg (Ph.D., 1908). Taught at Darlington Technical College (1908–12); Victoria Institute Science and Technical Schools, Worcester (1912–15, 1918–20); and Birmingham College of Advanced Technology (1920–46). Served in scientific capacities during both world wars. Best known as a teacher and an author; vigorously pursued research on valence theory, persulfates, metallic corrosion, paints, linseed oil, rare earths, solubilities of salts, viscosities of organic liquids, analysis of ancient artifacts, and the history of science. Wrote *Textbook of Inorganic Chemistry* (22 vols., 1914–30).

FRIES, ELIAS MAGNUS (*b. Femsjö, Sweden, 1794; d. Uppsala, Sweden, 1878*), botany.

Received degree in philosophy from University of Lund (1814), studying botany under C. A. Agardh, and stayed there to teach until 1835; taught at Uppsala from 1835. His foremost accomplishment in botany was in systematics; under the influence of Lorenz Oken and C. G. Nees von Esenbeck, he wrote *Systema mycologicum* (1821–32). Three important characteristics of his systematics are the idealistic conception of natural relationships, the distinction between affinity and analogy, and his ideas on evolution.

FRIES, JAKOB FRIEDRICH (*b. Barby, Germany, 1773; d. Jena, Germany, 1843*), philosophy, physics, mathematics.

Educated at Leipzig and Jena. Taught at Heidelberg (1805–16) and Jena (1816–17, 1824–43). Considered himself Kant's most loyal disciple; believed that Kant had finished the philosopher's task for all time and that only individual elements of his doctrine were susceptible to correction. Despite this belief Fries himself decisively altered the Kantian formulation by psychologizing Kant's transcendental idealism. He also spoke for contemporary positive scientific research, writing on physiological optics, theory of probabilities, and experimental physics. His influence led his student J. M. Schleiden to become the founder of modern cytology.

FRISI, PAOLO (*b. Milan, Italy, 1728; d. Milan, 1784*), mathematics, physics, astronomy.

A member of Barnabite order. In physics research he interpreted certain phenomena of light and aspects of electricity. As an astronomer, he was concerned with daily movement of the earth, obliquity of the ecliptic, motion of the moon, determination of the meridian cir-

cle, and matters concerning gravity in relation to Newton's general theories. His mathematical activity included studies on kinematics and isoperimetry. Also did work in hydraulics.

FRISIUS, GEMMA. *See* **Gemma Frisius, Reiner.**

FRITSCH, GUSTAV THEODOR (*b. Cottbus, Germany, 1838; d. Berlin, Germany, 1927*), anatomy, physiology, zoology, anthropology, photography.

Studied at Berlin, Breslau, and Heidelberg. Made several anthropological, geographical, and astronomical expeditions to South Africa, Aden, Egypt, Persia, and Smyrna. His photographic skill was valuable on expeditions and he later applied it to photomicrography and stereoscopy in microscopic anatomy. Worked under Berlin anatomist Karl B. Reichert; at the Institute of Pathology under Emil du Bois-Reymond and Theodor Wilhelm Engelmann; and in the Anatomy Institute with Wilhelm Waldeyer and Adolf Fick. With Eduard Hitzig he made an important contribution to the electrophysiology of the brain, establishing the existence of functional localization in the cerebral cortex of the dog. His work in anthropology and ethnology revolved about the concept of racial dominance.

FRITZSCHE, CARL JULIUS (*b. Neustadt, Saxony, Germany, 1808; d. Dresden, Germany, 1871*), chemistry.

Obtained doctorate in botany at Berlin (1833). Emigrated to Russia (1834); became manager of H. W. Struve's mineral-water works in St. Petersburg. Did long series of researches on indigo; discovered aniline; isolated and named crysanilic and anthranilic acids. Worked with N. N. Zinin of University of Kazan.

FROBENIUS, GEORG FERDINAND (*b. Berlin, Germany, 1849; d. Charlottenburg, Berlin, Germany, 1917*), mathematics.

Began his studies at Göttingen; received a doctorate from Berlin (1870). Taught at Berlin and at Eidgenössische Polytechnikum in Zurich. His major achievements were in group theory, which produced the concept of the abstract group. Worked with Issai Schur on the theory of finite groups of linear substitutions of *n* variables.

FROST, EDWIN BRANT (*b. Brattleboro, Vt., 1866; d. Chicago, Ill., 1935*), astronomy.

Graduated from Dartmouth (1886); greatly influenced by C. A. Young while studying astronomy at Princeton. Studied at Strasbourg and with H. C. Vogel at Potsdam Observatory. Taught at Dartmouth (1892–1902); professor of astrophysics at the new Yerkes Observatory (1898–1905; director, 1905–32). Principal research was in stellar spectroscopy, specifically determination of the radial velocities of stars, especially stars of early spectral type. Published *A Treatise on Astronomical Spectroscopy* (1894), a translation and revision of Scheiner's *Die Spectralanalyse der Gestirne.*

FROUDE, WILLIAM (*b. Dartington, Devonshire, England, 1810; d. Simonstown, Cape of Good Hope [now Union of South Africa], 1879*), ship hydrodynamics.

Studied at Oriel College, Oxford; worked as a civil engineer and became interested in naval architecture.

Did analytical and experimental study of the resistance and rolling of ships; controlled rolling by the use of bilge keels. Secured support of the Admiralty for construction of a model towing tank for studying resistance on scale models, based upon his hypothesis that the total resistance could be considered the sum of wave formation and skin friction and that each could be scaled independently. Showed that wave effects would be similar in model and prototype if velocity were reduced in proportion to the square root of the length (Froude's law of similarity).

FUBINI, GUIDO (*b. Venice, Italy, 1879; d. New York, N.Y., 1943*), mathematics.

Graduated from the Scuola Normale Superiore di Pisa; greatly influenced by Luigi Bianchi. Taught at Catania, Genoa, Politecnico in Turin, University of Turin (1908–38), and New York University; worked at Institute for Advanced Study at Princeton. Was one of Italy's most fecund and eclectic mathematicians. In analysis, he worked on linear differential equations, partial differential equations, analytic functions of several complex variables, and monotonic functions. In the field of discontinuous groups, he studied linear groups and groups of movement on a Riemannian variety. In the field of non-Euclidean spaces, he introduced sliding parameters. In differential projective geometry, he elaborated general procedures of systematic study that still bear his name.

FUCHS, IMMANUEL LAZARUS (*b. Moschin, near Posen, Germany [now Poznan, Poland], 1833; d. Berlin, Germany, 1902*), mathematics.

Received doctorate from Berlin (1858), studying with Kummer and Weierstrass. Taught at Berlin (1865–66; 1882–1902), the Artillery and Engineering School, Greifswald, Göttingen, and Heidelberg. A gifted analyst whose works form a bridge between the fundamental researches of Cauchy, Riemann, Abel, and Gauss and the modern theory of differential equations discovered by Poincaré, Painlevé, and Picard. Except for early papers in higher geometry and number theory, all his efforts were devoted to differential equations. The "Fuchsian theory" was named for him.

FUCHS, JOHANN NEPOMUK VON (*b. Mattenzell, Bavaria, Germany, 1774; d. Munich, Germany, 1856*), chemistry, mineralogy.

Studied at Vienna, Heidelberg, and Munich. Under Jacquin's influence he became interested in chemistry and mineralogy. Taught at University of Landshut and Ludwig-Maximilian University, Munich. Served as chemist on Obermedizinalausschuss and Supreme School Board. One of the first in Germany to introduce practical laboratory instruction in chemistry at the university level. His scientific work was mainly practical and empirical. Stressed importance of chemistry in study of mineralogy; determined composition of many minerals and mineral waters used for medicinal purposes.

FUCHS, LEONHART (*b. Wemding, Germany, 1501; d. Tübingen, Germany, 1566*), medicine, botany.

Educated at Erfurt and Ingolstadt (master's, 1521; doctorate, 1524). Practiced medicine in Munich, taught at Ingolstadt (1526–28) and Tübingen (1535–66). While at Tübingen he continued to practice medicine. In attempt-

ing to reform medicine, he emphasized the importance of relying upon ancient Greek authorities rather than later authors. Wrote medical textbooks and a pharmaceutical herbal, *De historia stirpium* (1542), the latter with impressive illustrations.

FÜCHSEL, GEORG CHRISTIAN (*b. Ilmenau, Germany, 1722; d. Rudolstadt, Germany, 1773*), geology.

Studied medicine at Jena and medicine, natural sciences, and theology at Leipzig. Settling in Rudolstadt, he engaged in the "salon" science of natural history cabinets and mineral collections and practiced medicine. His major work, "Historia terrae et maris, ex historia Thuringiae, per montium descriptionem, eruta" (1761), is unusual for its purely geological orientation. It contains an enunciation and substantiation of general principles of historical geology, the extensive description of all stratified rocks of Thüringer Wald, and explanations of the causes of dynamic changes in the earth's crust and the origin of veins and their minerals. Produced the first published geological map.

FUETER, KARL RUDOLF (*b. Basel, Switzerland, 1880; d. Brunnen, Switzerland, 1950*), mathematics.

Graduated from Göttingen (1903). After further study in Paris, Vienna, and London and teaching in Marburg and Clausthal, he taught at Basel (1908–13), the Technische Hochschule in Karlsruhe (1913–16), and finally at the University of Zurich (1916). Field of interest was theory of numbers as presented in David Hilbert's work. Derived the class formula for an entire group of Abelian number fields over an imaginary quadratic base field. Later founded his own school of thought on the theory of functions of a quaternion variable.

FUHLROTT, JOHANN KARL (*b. Leinefelde, Germany, 1804; d. Elberfeld [now Wuppertal], Germany, 1877*), natural history, human paleontology.

Obtained a doctorate from Bonn (1830); became a science teacher at Elberfeld, subsequently vice-director of the Realschule. Won modest recognition as a naturalist. In 1856, he received fossilized bones found by quarry workers in Feldhofer cave of the Neander Valley; Fuhlrott identified them as *Homo neanderthalensis*, but reaction to his discovery was hostile, and extensive controversy ensued. It was not until after his death and the discovery of fossil men at Spy, Belgium, and Gibraltar that opposition to the notion of Neanderthal man was finally silenced.

FULTON, JOHN FARQUHAR (*b. St. Paul, Minn., 1899; d. New Haven, Conn., 1960*), physiology, history of medicine.

Studied at University of Minnesota and Harvard (B.Sc., 1921). Spent a year at Magdalen College, Oxford, under the influence of C. S. Sherrington. Strongly influenced at Harvard by Harvey Cushing. Taught at Yale Medical School (1929–60); organized first primate laboratory for experimental physiology in America. Studied the function of brains most closely resembling that of man. Wrote textbook, *The Physiology of the Nervous System*, and was a founder of the *Journal of Neurophysiology*. His deep interest in history of medicine is evidenced in the many biographical and bibliographical sketches he wrote.

FUNK, CASIMIR (*b. Warsaw, Poland [then Russia], 1884; d. New York, N.Y., 1967*), biochemistry.

Received Ph.D. at Bern. Following work at Pasteur Institute, Wiesbaden Municipal Hospital, and University of Berlin, took a post at the Lister Institute in London. Immigrated to New York (1915); held several industrial and university positions there. Worked at State Institute of Hygiene in Warsaw; consultant to a pharmaceutical firm in Paris; returned to New York as consultant to U.S. Vitamin Corporation; president of Funk Foundation for Medical Research. Did extensive work on vitamins—proposed the term "vitamine" (for vital amine)—animal hormones, and the biochemistry of cancer, ulcers, and diabetes.

FUSORIS, JEAN (*b. Giraumont, Ardennes, France, ca. 1365; d. 1436*), astronomy.

Studied at University of Paris (masters in arts and medicine). Successively named canon of Rheims (1404), Paris (1411), Nancy, and curate of Jouarre-en-Brie; resided in Paris until 1416. Directed a large workshop for manufacture of astronomical instruments. Exiled in 1416 to Mézières-sur-Meuse. Among instruments made in his laboratory were astrolabes, dials, armillary spheres, clocks, and at least one equatorium; many have survived. Written works include texts on the construction and use of the astrolabe and equatorium, cosmography, and astronomical tables.

FUSS, NICOLAUS (or **Nikolai Ivanovich Fus**) (*b. Basel, Switzerland, 1755; d. St. Petersburg, Russia, 1826*), mathematics, astronomy.

Fuss's mathematical abilities led Daniel Bernoulli to recommend him to Euler, then in Russia, as a secretary. Junior scientific assistant of St. Petersburg Academy of Sciences (1776–83), academician in higher mathematics (1783–1800), and permanent secretary (1800–26). Also taught at military and naval cadet academies; active in reform of Russian national education system. Most of his writings contain solutions to problems raised in Euler's work: spherical geometry, trigonometry, theory of series, geometry of curves, integration of differential equations, mechanics, astronomy, and geodesy. His textbooks also show Euler's influence.

FYODOROV (or **Fedorov**), **EVGRAF STEPANOVICH** (*b. Orenburg, Russia [now Chkalov, U.S.S.R.], 1853; d. Petrograd [now Leningrad], U.S.S.R., 1919*), crystallography, geometry, petrography, mineralogy, geology.

Studied mathematics independently while attending the Petersburg Military Engineering School, the Military Medical and Surgical Academy, and the Technological Institute. Graduated from the Mining Institute in 1883. Joined Mining Department expedition to investigate northern Urals (1883). Published more than 500 scientific works; the foundation of all his work was geometry. Exerted a very strong influence on the development of mineralogy; his classification of symmetry groups governing the periodic distribution within crystalline matter led to the working out of a new nomenclature of systems and point group symmetries (Fyodorov-Groth nomenclature). His two-circle optical goniometer produced a revolution in the method of investigating minerals. Constructed a universal stage (Fyodorov table) for the petrographic microscope that would locate the specimen at the center of two glass hemispheres (Fyodorov method). Conducted important research on northern Urals, Bogoslovsky district, coast of the White Sea, the Caucasus, and Kazakhstan.

GABB, WILLIAM MORE (*b. Philadelphia, Pa., 1839; d. Philadelphia, 1878*), geology.

Pupil and assistant of James Hall; spent some time at Academy of Natural Sciences of Philadelphia; joined group around Spencer F. Baird at the Smithsonian Institution. A foremost authority on Cretaceous fossils, he joined California State Geological Survey under Josiah Dwight Whitney (1862–68). Conducted topographical and geologic surveys of Santo Domingo (1869–72) and Costa Rica (1873–76).

GABRIEL, SIEGMUND (*b. Berlin, Germany, 1851; d. Berlin, 1924*), chemistry.

Studied at Berlin under August Wilhelm von Hofmann and E. A. Schneider; received doctorate from Heidelberg (1874) under Bunsen. Taught at Berlin, working with Hofmann and Emil Fischer. His most significant contributions were his method of preparing primary amines (Gabriel synthesis) and his studies of heterocyclic compounds of nitrogen.

GADOLIN, JOHAN (*b. Åbo [now Turku], Finland, 1760; d. Wirmo, Finland, 1852*), chemistry, mineralogy.

Studied at Åbo and Uppsala. Taught at Åbo (1785–1822). As an educator, was significant for opening his chemical laboratory to students. His *Inleding till chemien* (1798) the was first Swedish-language textbook written in the spirit of the new combustion theory; spokesman in Scandinavia for Lavoisier's nomenclature and combustion theory. Best remembered for studies in mineralogy; gadolinite and gadolinium are named for him.

GAERTNER, JOSEPH (*b. Calw, Germany, 1732; d. Calw, 1791*), botany.

Received M.D. from Tübingen (1753); traveled in Europe pursuing mathematics, optics, mechanics, and eventually botany. Taught at Tübingen and St. Petersburg. Best known for *De Fructibus et seminibus plantarum* (1788–92), which describes fruits and seeds of 1,050 genera. His valuable reflections on sexuality in plants were of great theoretical significance. Father of botanist Karl Friedrich von Gaertner (1772–1850).

GAERTNER, KARL FRIEDRICH VON (*b. Göppingen, Germany, 1772; d. Calw, Württemberg, Germany, 1850*), botany.

Son of botanist Joseph Gaertner (1732–91). Studied at the Hohe Karlsschule, Jena, and Göttingen; received medical degree from Tübingen (1796); set up practice in Calw. Traveled in Europe, meeting leading natural scientists. Forced by an eye ailment to give up medical practice and microscopical investigations, he devoted his energies to research on plant hybridization as an independent scholar. His writings constituted the first comprehensive treatment of the problem of hybridization; in them the sexuality of plants was definitively established, having great influence on later work of Charles Darwin and Gregor Mendel.

GAFFKY, GEORG THEODOR AUGUST (*b. Hannover, Germany, 1850; d. Hannover, 1918*), bacteriology, public health.

Received M.D. from Berlin (1873); was a military surgeon for several years. In 1880 he and Friedrich Löffler joined Robert Koch at the imperial health office in Berlin. Under Koch's tutelage, Gaffky participated in developing new bacteriological methods and demonstrating causes of infectious disease. His most important contribution was isolation and culture of the bacillus that is the causative agent of typhoid fever. Succeeded Koch as director of the imperial health office (1885). Taught at Giessen and directed the Hygienic Institute there (1888–1904). Succeeded Koch as director of Institut für Infektionskrankheiten (1904–13).

GAGLIARDI, DOMENICO (*b. Rome [?], Italy, 1660; d. Rome [?], ca. 1725*), anatomy.

There is little or no information on his life. Acquired great fame as doctor and anatomist. Did morphological and microscopic work accompanied by anatomicopathologic research. His *Anatome ossium novis inventis illustrata* (1689) contains the first description of what is presumably tuberculosis of the bone. Also wrote on medical deontology and scientific popularization.

GAGNEBIN, ÉLIE (*b. Liège, Belgium, 1891; d. Lausanne, Switzerland, 1949*), geology.

Received doctorate at Lausanne (1920), where he worked with and eventually succeeded Maurice Lugeon as professor. As a field geologist, worked for Swiss Geological Commission and Service de la Carte Géologique de France. Published on stratigraphy and tectonics of Préalpes Bordières, formation of the Alps by continental drift, and paleontology.

GAHN, JOHAN GOTTLIEB (*b. Ovanåker, Sweden, 1745; d. Falun, Sweden, 1818*), mineralogy, chemistry.

Studied physics and chemistry at Uppsala (1762–70); laboratory assistant to Torbern Bergman. Worked for the College of Mining at the Falun mine in the Kopparberg district, exclusively with copper smelting, introducing important improvements and solving many technical problems. He modernized methods for using byproducts of the smelting process. Performed chemical research in the well-equipped laboratory he installed himself at Falun, which became mecca for scholars, factory owners, and industrialists seeking advice and guidance in technical problems. Collaborated with Bergman, Scheele, and Berzelius. Discovered the metal later named manganese.

GAILLOT, AIMABLE JEAN-BAPTISTE (*b. Saint-Jean-sur-Tourbe, Marne, France, 1834; d. Chartres, France, 1921*), astronomy, celestial mechanics.

Spent his entire career at the Bureau of Computation of the Paris observatory. Collaborated with Urbain Le Verrier. Directed publication of the *Catalogue de l'Observatoire de Paris*, which classified the 387,474 meridian observations made between 1837 and 1881.

GAIMARD, JOSEPH PAUL (*b. St. Zacherie, France, 1796; d. Paris [?], France, 1858*), natural history, scientific exploration, naval medicine.

Studied at naval medical school at Toulon; named surgeon in royal navy. Made exploratory voyages to South Pacific, Iceland, Greenland, Lapland, Spitsbergen, and the Faeroes. Wrote numerous reports on zoology and ethnography of the Pacific area, as well as a classic account of a cholera epidemic. Collaborated with Jean René Constant Quoy on zoological collections and discoveries.

GAINES, WALTER LEE (*b. Crete, Ill., 1881; d. Urbana, Ill., 1950*), dairy science.

Educated at Illinois (B.S., 1908; M.S., 1910) and Chicago (Ph.D., 1915). Professor of milk production at University of Illinois (1919–49). Leader in the United States of the scientific approach to problems of milk secretion.

GALEAZZI, DOMENICO GUSMANO (*b. Bologna, Italy, 1686; d. Bologna, 1775*), anatomy, biochemistry.

Graduated Doctor of Philosophy and Medicine in 1709 from Jesuit College in Bologna. Taught at Bologna (1716–56). Most important anatomical discoveries were in the gastro-intestinal system: described layers of muscle fibers in the stomach and intestines, described glands in the intestines, and clarified structure of villi.

GALEN (*b. Pergamum, A.D. 129/130; d. 199/200*), medicine.

A dream allegedly caused Galen and his father to decide definitely that he should undertake medical studies. His first medical teacher in Pergamum was Satyrus and Galen composed several works while still a student there. He himself names three of them: *On the Anatomy of the Uterus,* the *Diagnosis of Diseases of the Eye,* and *On Medical Experience.* The work on medical experience was written at the end of his first period in Pergamum (*ca.* 150) and reflects a two-day debate between the physicians Pelops and Philippus in Smyrna. This contact with Pelops induced Galen to go to Smyrna as his student.

In philosophy Galen was most influenced by Platonism, just as Hippocratism exercised the greatest influence on him in medicine; indeed, he set forth a connection between the two in his great work *On The Doctrines of Hippocrates and Plato.*

From Smyrna, Galen went to Corinth to continue his medical education with Numisianus, and finally to Alexandria, then the most famous center of research and training in medicine. At the age of twenty-eight he returned to his native Pergamum as physician to the gladiators, having studied medicine for about twelve years, much longer than was then customary. In the year 161 he arrived at Rome where he quickly established a medical practice. Galen himself vigorously insisted that it was not primarily *logoi sophistikoi* but rather medical successes that established his fame in Rome. On the other hand, the Second Sophistic exercised a great influence on him, and he cannot be seen apart from this intellectual movement.

When the great plague broke out, Galen left the city and hastened home. It is not known whether he spent the last years of his life in Rome or in his native city.

As a physician Galen accepted the "fourfold scheme" which brought the humors, the elementary qualities, the elements, the seasons, age and other factors into common accord. He attempted to restore medicine to its Hippocratic basis. He constructed his own Hippocratism, however; Hippocrates himself was not acquainted with any fourfold system in Galen's sense.

Galen's anatomy suffers from a similar conflict. On the one hand, he was an energetic advocate of anatomy as the foundation of medicine. On the other, his anatomy necessarily suffered from the lack of opportunity to examine human cadavers and he necessarily introduced a speculative element.

The same is true of his physiology. He had a clear conception of the importance of physiological experiment, and his knowledge of the physiology of the nerves was considerable. Yet again there is speculation, in substantial part teleological, as in the great physiologico-anatomical treatise *On the Usefulness of the Parts of the Body.*

As a dietitian, he continued an illustrious and ancient tradition. In this field he composed his most interesting and exciting works, especially the *Hygieina.*

In the area of prognosis, Galen remained a Hippocratic: first, he developed, as a general principle, a self-reliance in prognosis that was unjustified. As a clinician, he cherished the same speculative conception as Hippocrates, who had employed the consistency, the sediments, and the color of the urine not only in diagnosis but also in prognosis. The crucial thing is that Galen, like Hippocrates, did not apply the three criteria of consistency, sediments, and color in an exact fashion, but rather in a vague, subjective way.

The impression that Galen possessed all clinical skills is only apparent. On closer examination he seems to have had no experience in operative gynecology and obstetrics or in surgery in general, and it is obviously for this reason that he devoted none of his own writings to these fields. As a physician, Galen was a Hippocratic and, as a scientist (anatomist and physiologist), an Aristotelian, and he adhered to these basic commitments even when he was ostensibly an eclectic.

Aside from his medico-philosophical efforts, Galen not only interpreted the work of other philosophers, but also became known as a philosopher in his own right, above all in the field of logic, in such works as *On Scientific Proof* and *Introduction to Logic.*

He exhibits his ability as a philologist and grammarian in his commentaries on Hippocrates. He also wrote a series of works dealing with lexicographical and stylistic problems.

The influence of Galen, transmitted equally by his own writings, in both the original Greek texts and translations, and by summaries, compendia, commentaries by other physicians, and even forgeries, created Galenism, which dominated the medicine of the Middle Ages.

Galen's physiological system was, from the second century A.D. until the time of William Harvey, the basis for the explanation of the physiology of the body. His physiological theories are of particular interest because they included concepts which together formed a comprehensive and connected account of the functioning of the living animal body. The fundamental change which Galen made in the physiology of the heart, lungs, and vessels showed that both the left ventricle of the heart and the arteries invariably contain blood and that this is their normal condition. By his demonstration of the normal presence of blood in the arteries, Galen destroyed Erasistratus' theory of how the pneuma was conveyed to the whole body. Galen's proof of the normal presence of

blood in the arteries is contained in his short work *Whether Blood Is Contained in the Arteries in Nature.* However, in his work *On the Usefulness of the Parts of the Body,* Galen considered that both ventricles contained both blood and pneuma, but that the left ventricle contained pneuma in larger proportion. He showed in his physiological system that the liver and the veins supplied the body with nutrition; the lungs, the left ventricle of the heart, and the arteries maintained the pneuma and the innate heat throughout the body; while the brain and nerves controlled sensation and muscular movement through the medium of a special psychic pneuma.

GALERKIN, BORIS GRIGORIEVICH (*b.* *Polotsk, Russia, 1871; d. Moscow, U.S.S.R., 1945*), mechanics, mathematics.

Graduated from Petersburg Technological Institute (1899). Worked at Kharkov Locomotive Building Mechanical Plant and Northern Mechanical and Boiler Plant, St. Petersburg. Traveled in Russia and Europe to study factories and engineering installations. Taught at Petersburg Polytechnical Institute, Leningrad Institute of Communications Engineers, and Leningrad University. Scientific work was devoted to difficult problems in the theory of elasticity and structural mechanics, particularly longitudinal curvature, curvature of thin plates, and theory of casing. Proposed a method for approximate integration of differential equations, used widely for the solution of problems in mathematics, physics and technology (Galerkin's method).

GALILEI, GALILEO (*b. Pisa, Italy, 1564; d. Arcetri, Italy, 1642*), physics, astronomy.

Galileo is linked with the advent, early in the seventeenth century, of a marked change in the balance between speculative philosophy, mathematics, and experimental evidence in the study of natural phenomena. The period covered by his scientific publications began with the announcement of the first telescopic astronomical discoveries in 1610 and closed with the first systematic attempt to extend the mathematical treatment of physics from statics to kinematics and the strength of materials in 1638.

Galileo was first tutored at Pisa by one Jacopo Borghini. Early in the 1570's, the family returned to Florence. Galileo was then sent to school at the celebrated monastery of Santa Maria at Vallombrosa. In 1578 he entered the order as a novice, against the wishes of his father, who removed him again to Florence. In 1581 he was enrolled at the University of Pisa as a medical student.

The chair of mathematics appears to have been vacant during most of Galileo's years as a student at Pisa. His formal education in astronomy was thus probably confined to lectures on the Aristotelian *De caelo* by the philosopher Francesco Buonamici. Physics was likewise taught by Aristotelian lectures, given by Buonamici and Girolamo Borro. His interest in medicine was not great; he was instead attracted to mathematics in 1583, receiving instruction from Ostilio Ricci outside the university. Galileo's studies of mathematics, opposed at first by his father, progressed rapidly; in 1585 he left the university without a degree and returned to Florence, where he pursued the study of Euclid and Archimedes privately.

From 1585 to 1589 Galileo gave private lessons in mathematics at Florence and private and public instruction at Siena. During a visit to Rome in 1587, he made the acquaintance of the Jesuit mathematician Christoph Klau (Clavius). In 1589 Galileo gained the mathematics chair at Pisa, where he was not on cordial terms with many of the professors, chiefly because of his campaign to discredit the prevailing Aristotelian physics. His alleged demonstration at the Leaning Tower of Pisa that bodies of the same material but different weight fall with equal speed was clearly not an experiment but a public challenge to the philosophers.

In the treatise *De motu* Galileo derived the law governing equilibrium of weights on inclined planes and attempted to relate this law to speeds of descent. After his father's death in 1591, Galileo moved to the chair of mathematics at Padua. He lectured publicly on the prescribed topics and composed several treatises for the use of his students. One, usually known as *Le meccaniche,* survives in three successive forms (1593, 1594, 1600). In this treatise, besides developing further his treatment of inclined planes, he utilized as a bridge between statics and dynamics the remark that an infinitesimal force would serve to disturb equilibrium.

Late in August 1609 Galileo arrived at Venice with a nine-power telescope, three times as effective as any other. Galileo's swift improvement of the telescope continued until, at the end of 1609, he had one of about thirty power. This was the practicable limit for a telescope of the Galilean type, with plano-convex objective and plano-concave eyepiece. He turned this new instrument to the skies early in January 1610, with startling results. Not only was the moon revealed to be mountainous and the Milky Way to be a congeries of separate stars, contrary to Aristotelian principles, but a host of new fixed stars and four satellites of Jupiter were promptly discovered. Working with great haste but impressive accuracy, Galileo recited these discoveries in the *Sidereus nuncius,* published at Venice early in March 1610. In the summer of 1610, he resigned the chair at Padua and returned to Florence as mathematician and philosopher to the grand duke of Tuscany, and chief mathematician of the University of Pisa, without obligation to teach.

Galileo's *Letters on Sunspots* was published at Rome in 1613 under the auspices of the Lincean Academy. In this book Galileo spoke out decisively for the Copernican system for the first time in print. But attacks against Galileo and his followers soon appeared in ecclesiastical quarters. These came to a head with a denunciation from the pulpit in Florence late in 1614.

In December 1613 it had happened that theological objections to Copernicanism were raised, in Galileo's absence, at a court dinner, where Galileo's part was upheld by Benedetto Castelli. Learning of this, Galileo wrote a long letter to Castelli concerning the inadmissibility of theological interference in purely scientific questions. After the public denunciation in 1614, Castelli showed this letter to an influential Dominican priest, who made a copy of it and sent it to the Roman Inquisition for investigation. Galileo then promptly sent an authoritative text of the letter to Rome and began its expansion into the *Letter to Christina,* composed in 1615 and eventually published in 1636. Galileo argued that neither the Bible nor nature could speak falsely and that the investigation

of nature was the province of the scientist, while the reconciliation of scientific facts with the language of the Bible was that of the theologian.

Late in 1615 Galileo went to Rome to clear his own name and to prevent, if possible, the official suppression of the teaching of Copernicanism. In the first, he succeeded; no disciplinary action against him was taken on the basis of his letter to Castelli or his Copernican declaration in the book on sunspots. In the second objective, however, he failed. Galileo was instructed on 26 February 1616 to abandon the holding or defending of that view. Returning to Florence, Galileo took up a practical and noncontroversial problem, the determination of longitudes at sea.

It is probable that Galileo also returned during this period to his mechanical investigations, interrupted in 1609 by the advent of the telescope. A Latin treatise by Galileo, *De motu accelerato,* correctly defines uniform acceleration and much resembles the definitive text reproduced in his final book.

In 1618 three comets attracted the attention of Europe and became the subject of many pamphlets and books. One such book, written anonymously by Orazio Grassi, was criticized in the Florentine Academy by Guiducci, coached by the bedridden Galileo. The outcome of the quarrel was one of the most celebrated polemics in science, Galileo's *Il saggiatore (The Assayer).* It was addressed to Virginio Cesarini, a young man who had heard Galileo debate at Rome in 1615–16 and had written to him in 1619 to extol the method by which Galileo had opened to him a new road to truth. Since he could no longer defend Copernicus, Galileo avoided the question of the earth's motion; instead, he set forth a general scientific approach to the investigation of celestial phenomena. He gave no positive theory of comets, but in the course of his arguments, Galileo distinguished physical properties of objects from their sensory effects, repudiated authority in any matter that was subject to direct investigation, and remarked that the book of nature, being written in mathematical characters, could be deciphered only by those who knew mathematics.

The *Saggiatore,* printed in 1623 under the auspices of the Lincean Academy, was dedicated to Pope Urban VII. Galileo journeyed to Rome in 1624 to pay his respects to Urban, and although the pope refused to rescind the edict of 1616, he gave him permission to discuss the Copernican system in a book, provided that the arguments for the Ptolemaic view were given an equal and impartial discussion.

The *Dialogue Concerning the Two Chief World Systems* occupied Galileo for the next six years. It has the literary form of a discussion between a spokesman for Copernicus, one for Ptolemy and Aristotle, and an educated layman for whose support the other two strive. Galileo thus remains technically uncommitted except in a preface which ostensibly supports the anti-Copernican edict of 1616.

Important in the *Dialogue* are the concepts of relativity of motion and conservation of motion, both angular and inertial, introduced to reconcile terrestrial physics with large motions of the earth, in answer to the standard arguments of Ptolemy and those added by Tycho Brahe. The law of falling bodies and the composition of motions are likewise utilized. Corrections concerning the visual sizes and the probable distances and positions of fixed stars are discussed. A program for the detection of parallactic displacements among fixed stars is outlined, and the phases of Venus are adduced to account for the failure of that planet to exhibit great differences in size to the naked eye at perigee and apogee. Kepler's modification of the circular Copernican orbits is not mentioned; indeed, the Copernican system is presented as more regular and simpler than Copernicus himself had made it. Technical astronomy is discussed with respect only to observational problems, not to planetary theory.

To the refutation of conventional physical objections against terrestrial motion, Galileo added two arguments in its favor. One concerned the annual variations in the paths of sunspots, which could not be dynamically reconciled with an absolutely stationary earth. The second new argument concerned the existence of ocean tides, which Galileo declared, quite correctly, to be incapable of any physical explanation without a motion of the earth.

The *Dialogue* appeared at Florence in March 1632. A few copies were sent to Rome, and for a time no disturbance ensued. Then, quite suddenly, the printer was ordered to halt further sales, and Galileo was instructed to come to Rome and present himself to the Inquisition during the month of October.

Confined to bed by serious illness, he at first refused to go to Rome. The grand duke and his Roman ambassador intervened stoutly in his behalf, but the pope was adamant.

The outcome of the trial, which began in April, was inevitable. Galileo was persuaded in an extrajudicial procedure to acknowledge that in the *Dialogue* he had gone too far in his arguments for Copernicus. On the basis of that admission, his *Dialogue* was put on the Index, and Galileo was sentenced to life imprisonment after abjuring the Copernican "heresy." The terms of imprisonment were immediately commuted to permanent house arrest under surveillance. He was at first sent to Siena where he began the task of putting his lifelong achievements in physics into dialogue form, using the same interlocutors as in the *Dialogue.*

In 1634 Galileo was transferred to his villa at Arcetri, in the hills above Florence. It was probably on the occasion of his departure from Siena that he uttered the celebrated phrase "Eppur si muove," apocryphally said to have been muttered as he rose to his feet after abjuring on his knees before the Cardinals Inquisitors in Rome. Galileo was particularly anxious to return to Florence to be near his elder daughter. But she died shortly after his return. For a time, Galileo lost all interest in his work and in life itself. But the unfinished work on motion again absorbed his attention, and within a year it was virtually finished. Now another problem faced him: the printing of any of his books, old or new, had been forbidden by the Congregation of the Index. A manuscript copy was nevertheless smuggled out to France, and the Elzevirs at Leiden undertook to print it. By the time it was issued, in 1638, Galileo had become completely blind.

His final work, *Discourses and Mathematical Demonstrations Concerning Two New Sciences,* deals with the engineering science of strength of materials and the mathematical science of kinematics. Of the four dialogues contained in the book, the last two are devoted to the treatment of uniform and accelerated motion and the discussion of parabolic trajectories. The first two deal with problems related to the constitution of matter; the nature of mathematics; the place of experiment and reason in science; the weight of air; the nature of sound; the speed of light; and other fragmentary comments on physics as a whole.

Galileo lived four years, totally blind, beyond the publication of his final book. During this time, he had the companionship of Vincenzio Viviani, who succeeded him (after Evangelista Torricelli) as mathematician to the grand duke and who inherited his papers.

GALILEI, VINCENZIO (*b. Santa Maria a Monte, Italy, ca. 1520; d. Florence, Italy, 1591*), music theory, acoustics.

Father of Galileo Galilei. Studied music at Florence and at Venice under Gioseffo Zarlino, foremost music theorist of the time. Attacked the prevailing basis of musical theory in his *Dialogo della musica antica e della moderna* (1581), which resulted in a bitter polemic with Zarlino. Put to direct experimental test teachings of Zarlino concerning intonation and tuning.

GALITZIN, B. B. *See* **Golitsyn, B. B.**

GALL, FRANZ JOSEPH (*b. Tiefenbronn, near Pforzheim, Germany, 1758; d. Paris, France, 1828*), neuroanatomy, psychology.

Studied medicine at Strasbourg; received M.D. from Vienna (1785). Had a successful medical practice in Vienna and Paris; lectured in Vienna, Paris, and other European cities; visited schools, hospitals, prisons, and insane asylums with Johann C. Spurzheim to gather evidence and demonstrate their doctrines. Took up residence in Paris (1807). Founder of phrenology; studied brains and skulls of men and animals to establish the relationship between mental faculties and shape of brain and skull. Pointed out that gray matter in the brain was a matrix of the nerves, while fibrous white matter served a conducting function. Popular application of his theories in the form of phrenology came to be seen as pseudoscience and quackery; but his work was recognized as seminal in three spheres: (1) origination of the modern doctrine of cerebral localization of functions, (2) establishment of psychology as a biological science, and (3) use of his work as a vehicle for a naturalistic approach to the study of man which was very influential in development of evolutionary theory, physical anthropology, and sociology.

GALLE, JOHANN GOTTFRIED (*b. Pabsthaus, near Gräfenhainichen, Germany, 1812; d. Potsdam, Germany, 1910*), astronomy.

Received doctorate from Berlin (1845). In 1835 began working at Berlin Observatory with Encke, whose influence can be seen throughout Galle's lifework. Collaborated on computation of astronomical material collected by Alexander von Humboldt. First to observe "Le Verrier's planet," Neptune, after being informed by Le Verrier of its presumed position. In 1851 became director of observatory and professor at Breslau. Taught astronometry and meteorology; devoted research to comets and planetoids. Proposed in 1872 that corresponding data on minor planets, observed at close approach to earth, be used to determine solar parallax. Exerted great influence on several generations of German astronomers.

GALLOIS, JEAN (*b. Paris, France, 1632; d. Paris, 1707*), history of science.

Best known as a publicist, particularly for making the *Journal des sçavans* a success after the violent polemics which led to its suspension.

GALOIS, EVARISTE (*b. Bourg-la-Reine, near Paris, France, 1811; d. Paris, 1832*), mathematics.

Studied at the Collège Louis-le-Grand and École Normale Supérieure. A militant republican; died before age twenty-one in a duel; left a body of work—most published posthumously—of less than 100 pages but of astonishing richness. Continuing the work of Abel, he produced with the aid of group theory a definitive answer to the problem of solvability of algebraic equations, thereby laying one of the foundations of modern algebra. Two days before his death he wrote a testamentary letter attempting to sketch the results he had achieved; it contained, notably, a daring generalization of the theory of congruences by means of new numbers that are today called Galois imaginaries and its application to research in those cases where a primitive equation is solvable by radicals. Beyond the precise definition of decomposition of a group, it included applications of Galois's theory to elliptic functions.

GALTON, FRANCIS (*b. Birmingham, England, 1822; d. Haslemere, Surrey, England, 1911*), statistics, anthropometry, experimental psychology, heredity.

Formal education consisted of a few mathematics courses at Cambridge and unfinished medical studies in London. Journeying through unknown parts of southwestern Africa, he acquired fame as an intrepid explorer. Earliest notable research was on meteorology; he first recognized and named the anticyclone. Most experiments were done at home, while traveling, or farmed out to friends. He believed virtually anything is quantifiable. In psychology, he sowed the seeds of mental testing, measuring sensory acuity, and scaling and typing. In statistics he originated the concepts of regression and correlation. Best-known work was on the inheritance of talent —found strong evidence of inheritance; coined the word "eugenics." Galton's law of ancestral heredity set the average contribution of each parent at 1/4, of each grandparent at 1/16, etc., the sum, over all ancestors of both parents, being asymptotic to unity. Established fingerprinting as a means of human identification and set up taxonomy of prints. Knighted in 1909.

GALVANI, LUIGI (*b. Bologna, Italy, 1737; d. Bologna, 1798*), anatomy, physiology, physics.

Received degree in medicine and philosophy from Bologna (1759). Practiced medicine. Taught at Bologna; curator and demonstrator of anatomical museum in Bologna; professor of obstetric arts at Istituto delle Scienze. Best remembered for investigations on problems of animal electricity. Performed an extensive and meticulous series of experiments on irritable responses elicited by static electricity in properly prepared frogs. Hit upon central phenomenon of galvanism: the production of electric current from contact of two different metals in a moist environment; however he interpreted this as clear and unmistakable proof of a special animal electricity.

GAMALEYA, NIKOLAY FYODOROVICH (*b. Odessa, Russia, 1859; d. Moscow, U.S.S.R., 1949*), microbiology.

Studied in Strasbourg; graduated from Novorossysky University (1881) and Military Medical Academy at St. Petersburg (1883). Commissioned by Odessa Society of Physicians to familiarize himself at Pasteur's laboratory with technique of performing antirabies inoculations; worked in France 1886–92; first to inoculate himself with antirabies vaccine, thereby proving its harmlessness to healthy organisms. Founded and worked at Bacteriological-Physiological Institute in Odessa. His textbook, *Foundations of General Bacteriology*, had great significance for development of the new science. Outstanding researcher and fighter against bubonic plague, typhus, smallpox, cholera, anthrax, and tuberculosis. Director of several Russian microbiological institutes.

GAMBEY, HENRI-PRUDENCE (*b. Troyes, France, 1787; d. Paris, France, 1847*), precision instrumentation.

Worked at the École des Arts et Métiers in Compiègne, and in Châlons-sur-Marne. Returned to Paris, set up shop in St. Denis, where he manufactured high-quality precision instruments for physicists and astronomers, notably the first cathetometer, and a mural circle for the Paris observatory.

GAMOW, GEORGE (*b. Odessa, Russia, 1904; d. Boulder, Colorado, 1968*), physics.

Studied at Novorossysky University; graduated from University of Petrograd (Leningrad) (1928). Worked at Copenhagen Institute of Theoretical Physics with Niels Bohr, Cavendish Laboratory at Cambridge; and taught at Leningrad, George Washington University, and University of Colorado. Contributions in theoretical nuclear physics included the theory of nuclear α decay and the Gamow-Teller selection rule for β decay. Applied nuclear physics to astronomical phenomena; strong advocate of the expanding-universe theory.

GAṆEŚA (*b. Nandod, Gujarat, India, 1507*), astronomy.

Son of the astronomer Keśava, under whom he studied. Wrote a number of works on astronomy, astrology, and Hindu law, including many commentaries. His main work on astronomy was *Grahalâghava*.

GARNETT, THOMAS (*b. Casterton, Westmorland, England, 1766; d. London, England, 1802*), medicine, natural philosophy.

Received M.D. from Edinburgh (1788), where he was profoundly influenced by Joseph Black. Supplemented medical practice with chemical analyses and lectures. Taught natural philosophy at Anderson's Institution in Glasgow. In 1799 joined the Royal Institution in London as first professor of natural philosophy and chemistry; had great influence on its aims, style, and method of operation.

GARNOT, PROSPER (*b. Brest, France, 1794; d. Paris, France, 1838*), medicine, zoology, anthropology, ethnology.

Assistant surgeon in the French navy. Made several voyages as a naturalist to Cayenne, Martinique, the Antilles, Falkland Islands, and the South Pacific, including Duperrey's on the *Coquille*. Made contributions to geography, zoology, and anthropology. Found a plant, named garnotia. Later practiced medicine in France and Martinique.

GARREAU, LAZARE (*b. Autun, France, 1812; d. Lille, France, 1892*), botany.

After serving as military surgeon, taught at University of Lille. Did research on transpiration, osmosis, respiration, nutrition, and heat production in plants.

GASCOIGNE, WILLIAM (*b. Middleton, Yorkshire, England, ca. 1612; d. Marston Moor, Yorkshire, 1644*), optics, astronomy.

Formal education slight and unclear. Preceded Auzout and Picard in improving the telescope by introduction of cross hairs into the image plane and invention of a micrometer to measure small angular distances, but his work essentially died with him. Some scholarly correspondence survived him.

GASKELL, WALTER HOLBROOK (*b. Naples, Italy, 1847; d. Great Shelford, near Cambridge, England, 1914*), physiology, morphology.

Received B.A. (1869) and M.D. (1878) from Cambridge. Under the powerful influence of Michael Foster, devoted himself to physiological research rather than medicine. Worked under Carl Ludwig in Leipzig. Taught at Cambridge (1883–1914). His research was divided into four periods: (1) 1874–79, vasomotor action, investigating effects of nerve action on circulation in muscle arteries of the frog and dog; (2) 1879–83, heartbeat, resulting in physiological and histologico-evolutionary evidence of the myogenic theory; (3) 1883–87, involuntary nervous system, discovery that cold-blooded animals possess augmentor as well as inhibitory cardiac nerves, and that the connection between the central nervous system and the chain of sympathetic ganglia is unidirectional; and (4) 1888–1914, origin of vertebrates, culminating in *The Origin of Vertebrates* (1908), which attempted to trace vertebrates to an arthropod ancestor.

GASSENDI (GASSEND), PIERRE (*b. Champtercier, France, 1592; d. Paris, France, 1655*), philosophy, astronomy, scholarship.

Obtained doctorate at Avignon (1614); took holy orders at Aix, where he taught (1617–23); canonry at Digne; taught at Collège Royal in Paris (1645–48). Greatly influenced by Peiresc; maintained correspondence with Peiresc, Galileo, Mersenne, Luillier. Published works on philosophy, astronomy, and lives of astronomers. Opposed Descartes. Emphasized nominalism, finality, and vitalistic or chemical analogies, to achieve synthesis between Epicureanism and Christianity. His observation of the transit of Mercury in 1631 confirmed Kepler and, indirectly, Copernicus. Had great influence on Boyle. A convinced atomist, belated humanist, precursor of Locke, Condillac, and positivists and empiricists of the eighteenth and nineteenth centuries.

GASSER, HERBERT SPENCER (*b. Platteville, Wis., 1888; d. New York, N.Y., 1963*), physiology.

Educated at University of Wisconsin and Johns Hopkins. Involved in teaching or research at Wisconsin (1911–16); Washington University, St. Louis (1916–31); Chemical Warfare Service (1918); Cornell University

Medical College (1931–35); Rockefeller Institute for Medical Research (1935–53). His pioneering work on the study of nerves culminated in sharing the Nobel Prize with Erlanger in 1944 for discoveries relating to nerve fibers.

GASSICOURT. *See* **Cadet de Gassicourt.**

GASSIOT, JOHN PETER (*b. London, England, 1797; d. Isle of Wight, 1877*), electricity.

One of founders of Chemical Society (1841). Investigated voltaic electricity and the discharge of electricity through gases at low pressure. Perfected rotating and vibrating mirror technique. Designed and had constructed a spectroscope for Kew observatory.

GATES, REGINALD RUGGLES (*b. Middleton, Nova Scotia, 1882; d. London, England, 1962*), genetics.

Educated at Mount Allison University, Sackville, New Brunswick, Canada (B.A., 1903; M.A., 1904); McGill (B.Sc., 1906); and Chicago (doctorate, 1908). Worked at Woods Hole Biological Laboratory and Missouri Botanical Garden; taught at St. Thomas's Hospital, London, and King's College, University of London. One of several early geneticists who tried, unsuccessfully, to unravel the genetics of *Oenothera* (evening primrose), a particularly important botanical genus. Traveled widely, often combining travels with eugenic investigations; discovered gene for hairy ear rims on the Y chromosome. Founded *Mankind Quarterly*.

GAUDIN, MARC ANTOINE AUGUSTIN (*b. Saintes, France, 1804; d. Paris, France, 1880*), chemistry.

Gained inspiration for his work from Ampère's lectures at the Collège de France. Calculator at Bureau des Longitudes in Paris (1835–64). Most important work was concerned with arrangement of atoms within molecules and of molecules within crystals; supported gas hypothesis of Avogadro twenty-five years before the work of Cannizzaro and the Karlsruhe Congress made the hypothesis acceptable; studied the relationship between physical and chemical properties of substances and the spatial arrangement of the atoms that composed them.

GAUDRY, ALBERT JEAN (*b. St.-Germain-en-Laye, France, 1827; d. Paris, France, 1908*), paleontology.

Worked at Muséum d'Histoire Naturelle in Paris with P. L. A. Cordier and Alcide d'Orbigny. Excavated in Attica, in Tertiary mammal deposit at Pikermi; and at St.-Acheul, near Amiens. Established remarkable genealogical trees of five large groups of mammals; removed last doubts concerning contemporaneity of man and large extinct mammals. Worked to make paleontology an independent science. Taught paleontology at the Sorbonne (1868–71) and at Muséum d'Histoire Naturelle from 1872.

GAULTIER DE CLAUBRY, HENRI-FRANÇOIS (*b. Paris, France, 1792; d. Paris, 1878*), chemistry, toxicology, public health.

Taught chemistry and toxicology at the École de Pharmacie. Work in chemistry included the discovery with J.-J. Colin of the blue color imparted to starch by free iodine (1814) and research on coloring matter in madder. Significant in toxicology was his treatise on legal chemistry.

Writings on public health dealt with food adulteration, environmental health, disinfection, industrial hygiene.

GAUSS, CARL FRIEDRICH (*b. Brunswick, Germany, 1777; d. Göttingen, Germany, 1855*), mathematical sciences.

Gauss's father was persuaded to allow him to enter the Gymnasium in 1788 and to study after school instead of spinning to help support the family. When he entered the Brunswick Collegium Carolinum in 1792, he possessed a scientific and classical education far beyond that usual for his age at the time. During his three years at the Collegium, Gauss continued his empirical arithmetic. Before entering the University of Göttingen in 1795 he had rediscovered the law of quadratic reciprocity, related the arithmetic-geometric mean to infinite series expansion, conjectured the prime number theorem and found some results that would hold if "Euclidean geometry were not the true one."

In 1796, as a by-product of a systematic investigation of the cyclotomic equation, Gauss obtained conditions for the constructibility by ruler and compass of regular polygons and was able to announce that the regular 17-gon was constructible by ruler and compasses, the first advance in this matter in two millennia.

During the five years from 1796 to 1800, mathematical ideas came so fast that Gauss could hardly write them down. In 1798 he returned to Brunswick, where he lived alone and continued his intensive work. The next year, with the first of his four proofs of the fundamental theorem of algebra, he earned the doctorate from the University of Helmstedt under the rather nominal supervision of J. F. Pfaff. In 1801 the creativity of the previous years was reflected in two extraordinary achievements, the *Disquisitiones arithmeticae* and the calculation of the orbit of the newly discovered planet Ceres.

In his *Disquisitiones* Gauss summarized previous work on number theory in a systematic way, solved some of the most difficult outstanding questions, and formulated concepts and questions that set the pattern of research for a century and still have significance today. He introduced congruence of integers with respect to a modulus, the first significant algebraic equivalence relation. He proved the law of quadratic reciprocity, developed the theory of composition of quadratic forms, and completely analyzed the cyclotomic equation.

In January 1801 G. Piazzi had briefly observed and lost a new planet. During the rest of that year the astronomers vainly tried to relocate it. By December the task was done, and Gauss found Ceres in the predicted position.

The decade that began so auspiciously with the *Disquisitiones* and Ceres ended with *Theoria motus corporum coelestium in sectionibus conicis solem ambientium* (1809), in which Gauss systematically developed his methods of orbit calculation, including the theory and use of least squares. Professionally this was a decade of transition from mathematician to astronomer and physical scientist. Gauss decided on a career in astronomy and began to groom himself for the directorship of the Göttingen observatory. When he accepted the position in 1807, he was already well established professionally.

In his first years at Göttingen, Gauss experienced a second upsurge of ideas and publications in various fields of mathematics. Among the latter were several notable papers inspired by his work on the tiny planet Pallas, perturbed by Jupiter: *Disquisitiones generales circa seriem infi-*

nitam (1813), an early rigorous treatment of series and the introduction of the hypergeometric functions, ancestors of the "special functions" of physics; *Methodus nova integralium valores per approximationem inveniendi* (1816), an important contribution to approximate integration; *Bestimmung der Genauigkeit der Beobachtungen* (1816), an early analysis of the efficiency of statistical estimators; and *Determinatio attractionis quam in punctum quodvis positionis datae exerceret planeta si eius massa per totam orbitam ratione temporis quo singulae partes describuntur uniformiter esset dispertita* (1818), which showed that the perturbation caused by a planet is the same as that of an equal mass distributed along its orbit in proportion to the time spent on an arc.

Astronomical chores soon dominated Gauss's life. He began with the makeshift observatory in an abandoned tower of the old city walls. A vast amount of time and energy went into equipping the new observatory, which was completed in 1816 and not properly furnished until 1821. He ended his theoretical astronomical work in 1817 but continued positional observing, calculating, and reporting his results until his final illness.

It was during these early Göttingen years that Gauss matured his conception of non-Euclidean geometry. He had experimented with the consequences of denying the parallel postulate more than twenty years before, and during his student days he saw the fallaciousness of the proofs of the parallel postulate that were the rage at Göttingen; but he came only very slowly and reluctantly to the idea of a different geometric theory that might be "true."

But Gauss continued to find results in the new geometry and was again considering writing them up, possibly to be published after his death, when in 1831 came news of the work of János Bolyai.

By 1817 Gauss was ready to move toward geodesy. He began discussing the possibility of extending into Hannover a survey of Denmark. The triangulation of Hannover was not officially approved until 1820, but already in 1818 Gauss began an arduous program of summer surveying in the field followed by data reduction during the winter. After 1825 he confined himself to supervision and calculation, which continued to completion of the triangulation of Hannover in 1847. An early by-product of fieldwork was the invention of the heliotrope, an instrument for reflecting the sun's rays in a measured direction. He designed the instrument and had the first model built in 1821.

The period of preoccupation with geodesy was in fact one of the most scientifically creative of Gauss's long career. Already in 1813 geodesic problems had inspired his *Theoria attractionis corporum sphaeroidicorum ellipticorum homogeneorum methodus nova tractata*, a significant early work on potential theory. The difficulties of mapping the terrestrial ellipsoid on a sphere and plane led him in 1816 to formulate and solve in outline the general problem of mapping one surface on another so that the two are "similar in their smallest parts," published in 1825 as the *Allgemeine Auflösung der Aufgabe die Theile einer gegebenen Fläche auf einer anderen gegebenen Fläche so auszubilden dass die Abbildung dem Abgebildeten in den kleinsten Theilen ähnlich wird.* This paper, his more detailed *Untersuchungen über Gegenstände der höhern Geodäsie* (1844–47), and geodesic manuscripts later published in the *Werke* were further developed by German geodesists and led to the Gauss-Krueger projection (1912), a generalization of the transverse Mercator projection, which attained a secure position as a basis for topographic grids taking into account the spheroidal shape of the earth.

Surveying problems also motivated Gauss to develop his ideas on least squares and more general problems of what is now called mathematical statistics. The result was the definitive exposition of his mature ideas in the *Theoria combinationis observationum erroribus minimis obnoxiae* (1823, with supplement in 1828). In the *Bestimmung des Breitenunterschiedes zwischen den Sternwarten von Göttingen und Altona durch Beobachtungen am Ramsdenschen Zenithsector* of 1828 he summed up his ideas on the figure of the earth, instrumental errors, and the calculus of observations. However, the crowning contribution of the period, and his last breakthrough in a major new direction of mathematical research, was *Disquisitiones generales circa superficies curvas* (1828), which grew out of his geodesic meditations of three decades and was the seed of more than a century of work on differential geometry.

In September 1829 Quetelet visited Göttingen and found Gauss very interested in terrestrial magnetism but with little experience in measuring it. The new field had evidently been selected, but systematic work awaited Weber's arrival in 1831. Meanwhile, Gauss extended his long-standing knowledge of the physical literature and began to work on problems in theoretical physics, and especially in mechanics, capillarity, acoustics, optics, and crystallography. The first fruit of this research was *Über ein neues allgemeines Grundgesetz der Mechanik* (1829). In it Gauss stated the law of least constraint: the motion of a system departs as little as possible from free motion, where departure, or constraint, is measured by the sum of products of the masses times the squares of their deviations from the path of free motion. He presented it merely as a new formulation equivalent to the well-known principle of d'Alembert. This work seems obviously related to the old meditations on least squares, but Gauss wrote to Olbers on 31 January 1829 that it was inspired by studies of capillarity and other physical problems. In 1830 appeared *Principia generalia theoriae figurae fluidorum in statu aequilibrii,* his one contribution to capillarity and an important paper in the calculus of variations, since it was the first solution of a variational problem involving double integrals, boundary conditions, and variable limits. In 1831 Gauss and Weber began their close collaboration and intimate friendship. Their joint efforts soon produced results. In 1832 Gauss presented to the Academy the *Intensitas vis magneticae terrestris ad mensuram absolutam revocata* (1833), in which appeared the first systematic use of absolute units (distance, mass, time) to measure a nonmechanical quantity. Stimulated by Faraday's discovery of induced current in 1831, the pair energetically investigated electrical phenomena. They arrived at Kirchhoff's laws in 1833 and anticipated various discoveries in static, thermal, and frictional electricity but did not publish, presumably because their interest centered on terrestrial magnetism.

The thought that a magnetometer might also serve as a galvanometer almost immediately suggested its use to induce a current that might send a message. Working alone, Weber connected the astronomical observatory and the physics laboratory with a mile-long double wire that broke "uncountable" times as he strung it over houses and two towers. Early in 1833 the first words were

sent, then whole sentences. This first operating electric telegraph was mentioned briefly by Gauss in a notice in the *Göttingische gelehrte Anzeigen* but it seems to have been unknown to other inventors. Other inventors (Steinheil in Munich in 1837, Morse in the United States in 1838) had independently developed more efficient and exploitable methods, and the Gauss-Weber priority was forgotten.

In 1834 there were already twenty-three magnetic observatories in Europe, and the comparison of data from them showed the existence of magnetic storms. Gauss and Weber organized the Magnetische Verein, which united a worldwide network of observatories. Its *Resultate aus den Beobachtungen des magnetischen Vereins* appeared in six volumes (1836–41) and included fifteen papers by Gauss, twenty-three by Weber, and the joint *Atlas des Erdmagnetismus* (1840). These and other publications elsewhere dealt with problems of instrumentation (including one of several inventions of the bifilar magnetometer), reported observations of the horizontal and vertical components of magnetic force, and attempted to explain the observations in mathematical terms.

The most important publication in the last category was the *Allgemeine Theorie des Erdmagnetismus* (1839). Here Gauss broke the tradition of armchair theorizing about the earth as a fairly neutral carrier of one or more magnets and based his mathematics on data. Using ideas first considered by him in 1806, well formulated by 1822, but lacking empirical foundation until 1838, Gauss expressed the magnetic potential at any point on the earth's surface by an infinite series of spherical functions and used the data collected by the world network to evaluate the first twenty-four coefficients.

As Gauss was ending his physical research, he published *Allgemeine Lehrsätze in Beziehung auf die im verkehrten Verhältnisse des Quadrats der Entfernung wirkenden Anziehungs- und Abstossungskräfte* (1840). Growing directly out of his magnetic work but linked also to his *Theoria attractionis* of 1813, it was the first systematic treatment of potential theory as a mathematical topic, recognized the necessity of existence theorems in that field, and reached a standard of rigor that remained unsurpassed for more than a century. In the same year he finished *Dioptrische Untersuchungen* (1841), in which he analyzed the path of light through a system of lenses and showed, among other things, that any system is equivalent to a properly chosen single lens. Although Gauss said that he had possessed the theory forty years before and considered it too elementary to publish, it has been labeled his greatest work by one of his scientific biographers. In any case, it was his last significant scientific contribution.

GAUTIER, ARMAND E.-J. (*b. Narbonne, France, 1837; d. Cannes, France, 1920*), chemistry.

Received medical degree from Montpellier (1862); worked in Paris laboratory of Adolphe Wurtz. Isolated in 1866 isonitriles (isomers of the nitriles), or carbylamines, as he called them. Worked in the chemical laboratory of École Pratique des Hautes-Études (1869–74) and Faculté de Médecine (1874–1912). Published numerous textbooks.

GAUTIER, PAUL FERDINAND (*b. Paris, France, 1842; d. Paris, 1909*), astronomical instrumentation.

From age eighteen occupied with construction of astronomical instruments. Most important include equatorial visual telescopes, double astrographs, reflectors, and *coudé* telescopes at leading observatories in France, Austria, Greece, the Netherlands, Vatican City, Spain, Algeria, Argentina, and Brazil.

GAY, FREDERICK PARKER (*b. Boston, Mass., 1874; d. New Hartford, Conn., 1939*), bacteriology, pathology.

Studied at Harvard (B.A., 1897) and Johns Hopkins Medical School (1897–1901). Taught or did research at Pennsylvania (1901–03), under Simon Flexner; Pasteur Institute in Brussels (1903–06), with Jules Bordet; Harvard Medical School (1907–09); University of California at Berkeley (1910–23); and Columbia University College of Physicians and Surgeons (from 1923). Made studies on serum reactions, anaphylaxis, typhoid, hemolytic streptococcic infections, viral diseases, and a multitude of related subjects. Wrote *Agents of Disease and Host Resistance* (1935). Besides scientific interests he was concerned with social philosophy and humanism.

GAYANT, LOUIS (*b. Beauvais, France; d. Maastricht, Netherlands, 1673*), comparative anatomy.

Trained in medicine, served as military physician. Collaborated with Jean Pecquet, and Claude Perrault, among others, in anatomical work published in the *Mémoires*. In particular, he dissected a female cadaver to demonstrate the venous system; did transfusions of blood in dogs; and wrote on comparative anatomy.

GAY-LUSSAC, JOSEPH LOUIS (*b. St.-Léonard, France, 1778; d. Paris, France, 1850*), chemistry, physics.

Graduated from the École Polytechnique in 1800 and entered the civil engineering school, the École Nationale des Ponts et Chaussées. In the winter of 1800–01, the chemist Berthollet, impressed by the ability of the young man, took him to his country house at Arcueil as an assistant. Having already had an excellent mathematical education, Gay-Lussac received training in chemical research from Berthollet, who also played a key role in the professional advancement of his protégé.

Gay-Lussac was successively *adjoint* and *répétiteur* at the École Polytechnique. He was given the honorary title of professor of practical chemistry, but upon the death of Fourcroy he was appointed to succeed him as professor of chemistry. On the creation of the Paris Faculty of Science, he was appointed professor of physics; in 1832 he gave up this chair in favor of that of general chemistry at the Muséum National d'Histoire Naturelle.

Gay-Lussac's first major research was on the thermal expansion of gases. There was conflicting evidence about the expansive properties of different gases when heated. He concluded that equal volumes of all gases expand equally with the same increase of temperature. Over the range of temperature from 0° C. to 100° C. the expansion of gases was 1/266.66 of the volume at 0°C. for each degree rise in temperature.

Gay-Lussac made an ascent in a hydrogen balloon first with Biot and later alone in 1804. The primary objective of the ascents was to see whether the magnetic intensity at the earth's surface decreased with an increase in altitude. They concluded that it was constant up to 4,000 meters. They also carried long wires to test the electricity of different parts of the atmosphere. Another objective was to collect a sample of air from a high altitude to compare its composition with that of air at ground level.

One of Gay-Lussac's early collaborators was Alexander von Humboldt. They collaborated in an examination of various methods of estimating the proportion of oxygen in the air, particularly the use of Volta's eudiometer. In 1805 Gay-Lussac embarked on a year of European travel with Humboldt. Their principal object, however, was to record the magnetic elements at different points along their route. Their general conclusion was that the horizontal component of the earth's magnetic intensity increased from north (Berlin) to south (Naples) but that the total intensity decreased on approaching the equator.

In 1807 Gay-Lussac carried out a series of experiments designed principally to see whether there was a general relationship between the specific heats of gases and their densities. From a modern viewpoint the importance of his work was his establishment of basic principles of physics, since it follows from his experiments that the internal energy of an ideal gas depends on the temperature only. He wished to find the relationship between heat absorbed and heat evolved and from his experiments he drew the valuable conclusion that these were equal within the limits of experimental error. The change of temperature was directly proportional to the change of pressure.

Probably Gay-Lussac's greatest single achievement is based on the law of combining volumes of gases, which he announced in 1808. His own statement was that "gases combine in very simple proportions . . . and . . . the apparent contraction in volume which they experience on combination has also a simple relation to the volume of the gases, or at least to one of them."

The work of Volta inspired many chemists to investigate the chemical effects of the voltaic pile. Gay-Lussac and Thenard were among this number. They were influenced particularly by the news in the winter of 1807–08 of Davy's isolation of potassium and sodium by the use of the giant voltaic pile at the Royal Institution. Napoleon ordered the construction of an even larger pile at the École Polytechnique and Gay-Lussac and Thenard were placed in charge of it. Their research, reported in part 1 of their *Recherches physico-chimiques* was basically a repetition of Davy's experiments. Although Davy seems to have exhausted the most obvious possibilities, Gay-Lussac and Thenard's report does contain the suggestion that the rate of decomposition of an electrolyte depends only on the strength of the current, and they used chemical decomposition as a measure of electric current thirty years before Faraday.

Gay-Lussac and Thenard's really important contribution stemming from Davy's work was their preparation of potassium and sodium in reasonable quantities and by purely chemical means.

In a further memoir, Gay-Lussac and Thenard described an experiment in which potassium was heated in dry ammonia, forming a solid (KNH_2) and liberating hydrogen. Other related experiments seemed to indicate to them that potassium was not an element at all but a hydride, and they argued this at length with Davy. Despite their mistaken conclusions on this point, the French chemists deserve credit for their discovery of a new class of compounds, the amides of metals.

Their discovery of boron was first announced in November 1808. On 20 June 1808 they had mentioned an olive-gray substance obtained by the action of potassium on fused boric acid, but it was not until 14 November that they claimed to have isolated a new element and discovered its properties. This is one case where the work of Gay-Lussac and Thenard is indubitably prior to that of Davy. Davy had described in a footnote on 30 June 1808 how he had ignited boric acid and heated the product with potassium in a gold tube; this process yielded a black substance, which he did not identify but which was later recognized to be boron. Gay-Lussac and Thenard gave it the name *bore* (boron) and noted the similarity of its properties to those of carbon, phosphorus and sulfur. Their success in decomposing boric acid and isolating its "radical" led Gay-Lussac and Thenard to apply their new reagent, potassium, to the isolation of other radicals.

Apart from their early contribution to photochemistry, Gay-Lussac and Thenard made a fundamental contribution to the realization that so-called oxymuriatic acid contained no oxygen and was an element. At first they had suggested unequivocally that oxymuriatic gas was an element. Their patron, Berthollet, unfortunately persuaded them to alter their remarks to make this no more than a possibility. Because of the pressure he exerted on Gay-Lussac and Thenard, Davy is usually credited with the discovery of the elementary nature of chlorine, which he announced in 1810. Another area in which the contributions of Gay-Lussac were eclipsed by Davy was in the understanding of the properties of iodine.

In 1809 Gay-Lussac established by purely empirical means the general principle that the weight of acid in salts is proportional to the oxygen in the corresponding oxide. He used this principle (occasionally referred to as a law) to determine the composition of some soluble salts.

Among his other work in inorganic chemistry, he investigated the thermal decomposition of sulfates. He also carried out research on sulfides. The most important part of this work for the subsequent history of qualitative analysis was his investigation of the precipitation of metal sulfides. He successfully demonstrated that the sulfides of certain metals could be precipitated if they were present as salts of acetic, tartaric, or oxalic acids (that is, weak acids) or, better, in the presence of an alkali, such as ammonia.

In 1809 Gay-Lussac carried out a study of the combining volumes of nitric oxide and oxygen and recognized the five oxides of nitrogen. He demonstrated conclusively that there was a definite class of acids that, instead of containing oxygen, contained hydrogen. He introduced the term "hydracid" to denote this class, which included hydrochloric acid, hydriodic acid, and hydrogen sulfide. Gay-Lussac thus introduced the name hydrochloric acid *(acide hydrochlorique)* for what had been called muriatic acid.

His important research on prussic acid began with his successful preparation in 1811 of the anhydrous acid by the action of hydrochloric acid on mercuric cyanide. In 1815 he determined the physical constants of the acid, including its vapor density.

Gay-Lussac's study of the solubility of salts is of considerable importance, since he was the first to construct a solubility curve showing the variation of solubility of vari-

ous salts in water at different temperatures. He recognized that the amount of solid has no influence on the ultimate solubility and understood that the solubility of a salt in water at a given temperature is a constant in the presence of excess solute. He noticed the break in the solubility curve of hydrated sodium sulfate and that this occurs at the point of maximum solubility.

Gay-Lussac studied the effect of the material and form of different vessels on the constancy of boiling points of liquids and found that the vapor pressure of a solution is lower than that of the pure solvent.

In considering the action of chlorine on alkalies, he stated, "There is a general rule that in every case where the same elements can form compounds of different stability (but are capable of existing simultaneously under the same given conditions), the first to be formed is the least stable."

He made several contributions to an understanding of chemical equilibrium and the realization of the relevance to a reaction of the mass of the reactants. Toward the end of his career, Gay-Lussac wrote a long historical article on affinity.

Although he is probably best known for his work in physical and inorganic chemistry, he also made a number of important contributions to organic chemistry. He and Thenard divided vegetable substances into three classes according to the proportion of oxygen and hydrogen contained in them. This classification was accepted by William Prout, who referred to this group as the saccharine class, later called carbohydrates.

Gay-Lussac also contributed to the early history of isomerism. His vital work on volumetric analysis occupied much of the later part of his life. The concept of titration passed into general chemical practice from the method proposed by Gay-Lussac for estimating the purity of silver. His 1824 paper contains the first use of the terms *pipette* and *burette* for the respective pieces of apparatus that have since become standard.

He made a major contribution to chemical analysis in 1832 when he introduced a volumetric method of estimating silver, which he justly claimed was much more accurate than the centuries-old method of cupellation.

GEER, CHARLES DE (*b. Finspång, Sweden, 1720; d. Leufsta, Sweden, 1778*), entomology.

Using Leeuwenhoek's and Swammerdam's techniques of microscopy, and Réaumur's method of biological observation, he studied the life and metamorphosis of insects, making morphological observations and drawings of their structures, and produced *Mémoires pour servir à l'histoire des insectes* (1752–78).

GEER, GERHARD JAKOB DE (*b. Stockholm, Sweden, 1858; d. Saltsjöbaden, Sweden, 1943*), geology, geochronology.

Received master's degree from Uppsala (1879); appointed to Swedish Geological Survey (1878). His lifetime interest was the study of Quaternary (Pleistocene) geology. Made expeditions in 1882, 1896, 1899, 1901, and 1908, including the Swedish-Russian meridian expedition. Introduced terrestrial photogrammetry. Coined the term "marine limit" (the highest shoreline of the sea at any particular locality). Taught at Stockholm (1897–1924); established the varve chronology. Retired (1924)

278

and became head of Institute of Geochronology at University of Stockholm.

GEGENBAUR, CARL (*b. Würzburg, Germany, 1826; d. Heidelberg, Germany, 1903*), comparative anatomy and morphology, zoology.

Received medical diploma from Würzburg (1851), while studying natural history independently. Taught at Würzburg, Jena, and Heidelberg. His anatomical investigations were distributed into three periods: At Würzburg and during the early years at Jena, his attention was devoted to life cycles and morphology of different stages of various marine animals. At Jena, he discovered Darwin and the descent theory, which over the next several years achieved full hegemony over Gegenbaur's zoological and anatomical outlook. He began intensive comparative examination of vertebrate musculature, osteology, and neural structures. This work continued into a third period, at Heidelberg, and included much effort directed toward specifying in detail the anatomical bases for regarding man as an animal. Worked closely with Ernst Haeckel on descent theory.

GEHLEN, ADOLF FERDINAND (*b. Bütow, Pomerania [now Bytów, Poland], 1775; d. Munich, Germany, 1815*), pharmacy, chemistry.

Received M.D. from University of Königsberg. Worked in Berlin with Klaproth and Valentin Rose. Edited several chemical journals, enlisting a large circle of distinguished collaborators. Taught at Halle (1806). Appointed *akademischer Chemiker* at the Bavarian Academy of Sciences. Favorite field of study remained pharmacy; with J. A. Buchner founded the Pharmazeutischer Verein in Baiern and began publication of *Reportorium für die Pharmacie.* Gehlenite, a silicon compound, named in his honor by Georg F. C. Fuchs.

GEIGER, HANS (JOHANNES) WILHELM (*b. Neustadt an der Haardt [now Neustadt an der Weinstrasse], Rheinland-Pfalz, Germany, 1882; d. Potsdam, Germany, 1945*), physics.

Studied at Munich; doctorate from Erlangen (1906). Worked with Arthur Schuster and Ernest Rutherford at Manchester, England (1906–12); with the latter investigated charge and nature of the α particle, resulting in a proto-"Geiger counter" (1908). Studied scattering of α particles with Ernest Marsden. At Rutherford's suggestion, Geiger and John Michael Nuttall established the Geiger-Nuttall rule connecting the range of an α particle with the average lifetime of the parent atom (1911–12), later revised by Geiger (1921). Director of laboratory for radium research at Physikalisch-Technische Reichsanstalt, Berlin (1912–24); continued experiments on counting α and β particles. Taught at University of Kiel (1925–29); Tübingen (1929–36); and Technische Hochschule, Berlin (1936–44). At Kiel developed with Walther Müller the Geiger-Müller counter based on the 1908 prototype, for detecting and counting individual charged particles, and eventually cosmic radiation. Production of the counters from 1928 marked the introduction of modern electrical devices into radiation research.

GEIKIE, ARCHIBALD (*b. Edinburgh, Scotland, 1835; d. Haslemere, Surrey, England, 1924*), geology.

Studied geology independently in Edinburgh before studying at Edinburgh University. In 1855 began working for the Geological Survey of Great Britain under Sir Roderick Murchison and Andrew Ramsay, whom he succeeded as head (1881–1901). Simultaneously taught at Edinburgh University (1871–81); succeeded by his brother, James (1839–1915). Knighted, 1891. His main publications fall under the following classifications: (1) geological treatises on ancient volcanism, Old Red Sandstone, and glaciation; (2) official Geological Survey memoirs, particularly on the Edinburgh neighborhood, Fife, and a series of stratigraphical monographs; (3) incomparable textbooks, including *Text-book of Geology* (1882); (4) biographies of geologists, and belles-lettres.

GEIKIE, JAMES (*b. Edinburgh, Scotland, 1839; d. Edinburgh, 1915*), geology.

Attended University of Edinburgh; worked for Geological Survey (1861–82); succeeded his brother, Archibald (1835–1924) as Murchison professor of geology at University of Edinburgh (1882). One of the founders of the Royal Scottish Geographical Society (1884). Reputation rests on the study of Pleistocene geology in general and glacial deposits in particular, in addition to his unofficial papers and books, particularly *The Great Ice Age* (1874).

GEISER, KARL FRIEDRICH (*b. Langenthal, Bern, Switzerland, 1843; d. Küsnacht, Zurich, Switzerland, 1934*), mathematics.

Graduated from the Polytechnikum in Zurich and University of Berlin. Taught at Zurich Polytechnikum (later renamed Eidgenössische Technische Hochschule) from 1873. Scientific works concerned especially with algebraic geometry; an involution he discovered bears his name.

GEISSLER, JOHANN HEINRICH WILHELM (*b. Igelshieb, Thuringia, Germany, 1815; d. Bonn, Germany, 1879*), glassmaking, technology.

Little known of his life. Practiced glassblowing at several universities, including Munich. Around 1852 settled as a mechanic at the University of Bonn and established a workshop for producing chemical and physical instruments for such scientists as W. H. Theodor Meyer, Julius Plücker, H. P. J. Vogelsang, Eduard Pflüger, and Franz Müller, who succeeded him as owner of the workshop. With Plücker he constructed his famous standard thermometers, whose difference was due to their thin glass, application of capillarity, and high precision (1852); in 1855 constructed an improved mercury air pump. Through the use of these inventions he was able to make rather small glass tubes with electrodes melted into the ends and filled with rarefied gases (Geissler's tubes). By using these tubes Plücker studied discharges in very rarefied gases. The technology of Geissler's tubes helped introduce a new branch of physics which led directly to discovery of cathode rays.

GEITEL, F. K. HANS (*b. Brunswick, Germany, 1855; d. Wolfenbüttel, Germany, 1923*), experimental physics.

Studied at Heidelberg (1875–77) and Berlin (1877–79); taught in Wolfenbüttel (1880–1920). In collaboration with Elster, published works on atmospheric electricity, radioactivity, and photoelectric methods of measurement.

GELFOND, ALEXANDR OSIPOVICH (*b. St. Petersburg [now Leningrad], Russia, 1906; d. Moscow, U.S.S.R., 1968*), mathematics.

Studied at Moscow University (1924–30); taught at Moscow Technological College (1929–30) and Moscow University (1931–68). From 1933 also worked in Soviet Academy of Sciences Mathematical Institute. Most important work was in analytical theory of numbers and theory of interpolation and approximation of functions of a complex variable; used and improved methods of theory of functions.

GELLIBRAND, HENRY (*b. London, England, 1597; d. London, 1636*), navigation, mathematics.

Received B.A. (1619) and M.A. (1623) from Trinity College, Oxford. Professor of astronomy at Gresham College, London, from 1627. Completed second volume of Henry Briggs's *Trigonometria Britannica* (1633). His most widely appreciated scientific discovery, shared with John Marr, was that of the secular change in magnetic variation (declination) of the earth. His textbooks on navigation helped raise English standards of navigation to new heights.

GELMO, PAUL JOSEF JAKOB (*b. Vienna, Austria, 1879; d. Vienna, 1961*), chemistry.

Received doctorate from the Technische Hochschule in Vienna (1906). Chief chemist for Austrian State Printing Office (1910–38); taught at Technische Hochschule from 1929. Synthesized sulfonanilamide, later discovered to be capable of controlling streptococcal infections. It became the most widely used of the sulfa drugs, and its commercial manufacture was accomplished essentially by his method.

GEMINUS (*fl. Rhodes [?], ca. 70 B.C.*), astronomy, mathematics.

Nothing is known of the circumstances of his life, but the date and place of his work may be inferred from internal evidence in his *Isagoge,* an early example of an elementary astronomical handbook written to popularize the main ideas in the technical treatises of the scientists. A work on mathematics (known only from extracts quoted by later writers) is also attributed to Geminus; its title was probably *Theory of Mathematics,* and apparently dealt with logical subdivision of the mathematical sciences, discussing the philosophical principles of their classification.

GEMINUS (also known as **Lambrit** or **Lambert**), **THOMAS** (*b. Lixhe, Belgium, ca. 1510; d. London, England, 1562*), medicine.

Little known of his life. Migrating to England about 1540, he practiced the arts of engraving, printing, and instrument making. Was penalized for practicing medicine without a license. His most important work was a series of handsome, copper-engraved anatomical figures, most of them plagiarized from Vesalius' *Fabrica* and a few from his *Epitome;* its translations and editions were of considerable influence and were in turn plagiarized by later authors.

GEMMA FRISIUS, REINER (*b. Dokkum, Netherlands, 1508; d. Louvain, Belgium, 1555*), geography, mathematics.

Studied, practiced medicine, and taught at Louvain, but is remembered for his contributions to geography and mathematics, his avocations. Designed globes and astronomical instruments that were well known and much sought after. Was the first to propose and illustrate the principle of triangulation as a means of carefully locating places and accurately mapping areas, and first to suggest in explicit terms the use of portable timepieces to measure longitude by lapsed time.

GENTH, FREDERICK AUGUSTUS (*b. Wächtersbach, Hesse, Germany, 1820; d. Philadelphia, Pa., 1893*), chemistry, mineralogy.

Studied at Heidelberg (1839–40) under Gmelin, Blum, and Leonhard; at Giessen (1841–43) under Fresenius, Kopp, and Liebig; and Marburg (doctorate, 1845) under Bunsen. Was Bunsen's assistant for three years before immigrating to the United States. Taught at University of Pennsylvania (1872–88). Best-known research involved ammonia-cobalt bases (cobalt ammines), developed jointly with Gibbs. His chief chemical contributions to mineralogy are contained in fifty-four papers describing 215 mineral species; he himself discovered twenty-four new minerals.

GENTZEN, GERHARD (*b. Greifswald, Germany, 1909; d. Prague, Czechoslovakia, 1945*), logic, foundations of mathematics.

Studied mathematics under such renowned scholars as Carathéodory, Hilbert, Kneser, Landau, and Weyl, receiving doctorate at Göttingen in 1933. Hilbert's assistant from 1934 to 1943 except for a two-year period teaching at Prague. Combined an exceptional inventiveness and talent for coordinating diverse existing knowledge into a systematic conceptual framework. Succeeded in making classical logic appear as a simple extension of intuitionist logic and in enunciating his *Hauptsatz* (chief theory), which says that in both intuitionist and classical predicate logic, a purely logical sequent can be proved without "cut." Sharpened the *Hauptsatz* for classical logic to the midsequent theorem (Herbrand-Gentzen theorem).

GEOFFROY, CLAUDE JOSEPH (*b. Paris, France, 1685; d. Paris, 1752*), chemistry, botany.

Geoffroy the Younger (le Cadet) was the brother of Étienne François Geoffroy (the Elder) (1672–1731). Qualified as apothecary (1703), took over family pharmacy (1708). Appointed inspector of the pharmacy at Hôtel-Dieu (the Paris hospital). Elected to Académie des Sciences as botanist (1707), transferred to chemical section (1715). Did research on chemical explanation of colors of plants and on pharmaceutical chemistry.

GEOFFROY, ÉTIENNE FRANÇOIS (*b. Paris, France, 1672; d. Paris, 1731*), chemistry, medicine.

Geoffroy the Elder (l'Aîné) was the brother of Claude Joseph (Geoffroy the Younger) (1685–1752), and father of Étienne Louis Geoffroy (1725–1810). Studied at Montpellier; qualified as pharmacist (1694); M.D. from Paris (1704). Taught at Collège Royal (now Collège de France)

(1709–31) and Jardin du Roi (1707–30). A Paris pharmacopoeia, *Codex medicamentarius seu pharmacopoeia parisiensis,* largely his work, contained many chemical remedies in addition to traditional galenicals, as did his unfinished book on materia medica. In experimental chemistry, he theorized a "sulfurous principle" being common to vegetable matter and metals and giving metals their properties of fusibility and ductility (1705). In 1720 he identified his "sulfurous principle" with Georg Stahl's phlogiston. To advance the theory that certain substances could displace others from compounds, he prepared a sixteen-column table showing the order of displacement of some common substances.

GEOFFROY, ÉTIENNE LOUIS (*b. Paris, France, 1725; d. Chartreuve, near Soissons, France, 1810*), zoology, medicine.

Son of Étienne François Geoffroy (1672–1731). Studied medicine at Paris under Ferrein, Rouelle, Bernard de Jussieu, and Astruc. Practiced medicine while pursuing research in zoology. Wrote important works on taxonomy of insects and comparative anatomy.

GEOFFROY SAINT-HILAIRE, ÉTIENNE (*b. Étampes, France, 1772; d. Paris, France, 1844*), zoology.

Studied at Collège de Navarre, Paris; Collège du Cardinal Lemoine, Paris; and the Collège de France. Taught for forty-seven years at the Muséum d'Histoire Naturelle and for thirty-two at the Sorbonne. Part of Bonaparte's famous Egyptian campaign (1798–1801); studied and published the rich material gathered in *Description de l'Égypte par la Commission des sciences* (1808–24). Believed in non-fixity of species; by comparative anatomy, teratology, and paleontology he strove to prove that species are transformed in the course of time, the simpler ones engendering the more complex. Established two fundamental principles of comparative anatomy: the principle of anatomical connections, which allows one to trace an organ from species to species despite its transformations; and the principle of balance (equilibration of the organs), which manifests itself in reduction in size of organs when a neighboring organ hypertrophies. His belief in the theory of the chain of being led to his famous controversy of 1830 with Cuvier (*q.v.*). His varied researches led to the beginning of scientific teratology, experimental embryology, and evolutionary paleontology. Father of Isidore Geoffroy Saint-Hilaire (1805–61).

GEOFFROY SAINT-HILAIRE, ISIDORE (*b. Paris, France, 1805; d. Paris, 1861*), zoology.

Son of Étienne Geoffroy Saint-Hilaire (1772–1844). Replaced his father at the Faculté des Sciences (1837) and at the Muséum d'Histoire Naturelle (1841). Taught at the Sorbonne from 1850. Continued much of his father's work. In 1832 he coined the word *teratology* to designate the science of monsters. His description and classification of mammals, especially of the apes, was original and successful. Long before L. Bolk enunciated his theory of neoteny (1921), Geoffroy Saint-Hilaire suggested that the adult human's large brain and potential for adaptation might likewise represent the persistence of an infantile form. Founded the Société d'Acclimatation and the Jardin d'Acclimatation in the Bois de Boulogne, Paris.

GERARD OF BRUSSELS (*fl. first half of the thirteenth century*), geometry.

Played a minor but not unimportant role in the development of kinematics and the measure of geometrical figures. His *Liber de motu* was written between 1187 and 1260.

GERARD OF CREMONA (*b. Cremona, Italy, ca. 1114; d. Toledo, Spain, 1187*), translation of scientific and philosophical works from Arabic into Latin.

Few details of Gerard's life are known with certainty. A biography found inserted at the end of some copies of his translation of Galen's *Tegni,* along with a list of his translations drawn up by his associates *(socii),* states that he completed his education in the schools of the Latins before going to Toledo, and it seems likely that he reached Toledo by 1144 at the latest. The biography recalls that it was the love of the *Almagest,* which he knew was not available in Latin, that led Gerard to Toledo and to the study of Arabic; he became the most prolific translator of scientific and philosophical works from Arabic in the Middle Ages. Through their abundance, subject matter, and quality, Gerard's translations made a decisive contribution to the growth of medieval Latin science. The impact of his work was felt well into the early modern period.

Gerard's approach to translation was strongly influenced by that of John of Seville, whom he may have known. He appears to have weighed earlier Latin translations against the Arabic original, retaining what seemed to him passable and simultaneously reducing the lexical usage to a standard one, and restoring all passages and constructions omitted in earlier versions. The mutual characteristics of the two translators are closeness to the Arabic original, preservation as far as possible of the construction of the Arabic sentences, and scrupulous rendering of nearly every word contained in the Arabic.

The listing by the *socii,* which is not complete, names seventy-one translations by Gerard. It would seem that he sought out pedagogical collections of required works, particularly in mathematics, astronomy, and medicine, in order to translate them as a corpus in each branch of the *quadrivium.* Although medicine was not part of the *quadrivium,* it was in this field that Gerard produced the greatest number—at least twenty-one—and the highest quality of translations, including Ibn Sīnā's *Canon,* al-Rāzī's *Almansorius,* and ten writings of Galen; consequently his translations had an immeasurable impact upon Latin medicine of the Middle Ages, which profited greatly from the advanced state of medicine in medieval Islam. Second in importance in both number and quality were his translations in geometry, mathematics, and astronomy, totaling some thirty works and including Euclid's *Elements* and Ptolemy's *Almagest;* here again, his translations influenced the strivings of Latin scholars toward a scientific approach to knowledge of nature that subordinated philosophical and theological inclinations. Six additional works on geomancy and alchemy also contributed largely to the scientific orientation of the medieval West. Gerard's eleven translations of works in philosophy and three on dialectics appear to have had a rather minimal influence; they seem to have been selected for their relevance to the epistemology of natural science and to a scientific interpretation of the cosmos. The evolution of the University of Paris curriculum during the thirteenth and fourteenth centuries reveals the slow but sure penetration of many of Gerard's translations, which nourished the awakened interest in natural science until the end of the Middle Ages. His influence waned, but did not disappear, in the Renaissance (when scholarship focused on Greek texts at the expense of their Arabic counterparts); the first Latin *Almagest* to be printed (Venice, 1515) was Gerard's, of which it seems that Copernicus soon procured a copy.

There is still much uncertainty about the number, value, and even the existence of Gerard's original works. *Theorica planetarum,* attributed by some to him and by others to Gerard of Sabbioneta, may actually have originated with John of Seville, whose style it matches perfectly. It may have been reworked in some fashion by Gerard of Cremona.

GERARD OF SILTEO (SILETO) (*fl. thirteenth century*), astronomy.

A Dominican friar about whom little is known except that he composed a *Summa de astris.* It is divided into three parts: astronomy, astrology, and a critical refutation of astrological excesses.

GERARD, JOHN (*b. at or near Nantwich, Cheshire, England, 1545; d. Holborn, London, England, 1612*), botany, pharmacy, horticulture.

A barber-surgeon best known for his horticultural interests. In addition to overseeing his own well-stocked garden, he was superintendent of gardens belonging to William Cecil, Lord Burleigh, at the Strand, London, and at Theobalds, Hertfordshire (1577–98), and curator of a physic garden belonging to the College of Physicians of London (1586–ca. 1604). His main work, *The Herball or Generall Historie of Plantes* (1597), is the best-known and most often quoted herbal in the English language.

GERASIMOVICH, BORIS PETROVICH (*b. Kremenchug, Russia, 1889; d. Moscow, U.S.S.R., 1937*), astrophysics.

Educated at Kharkov University, later teaching there and at other higher educational institutions in Kharkov. Studied at Pulkovo Observatory under Belopolsky and Kostinsky, eventually becoming senior astronomer, professor of astronomy, head of astrophysics section (1920–33), and director (1933). Visiting professor at Harvard Observatory (1926–29), working with Shapley, Otto Struve, Luyten, and Menzel. His range of astronomical interests was very broad, with about 170 publications. Pioneer in study of planetary nebulas. First to emphasize the important role of computation of interstellar light absorption in study of structure of the Galaxy. Responsible for important investigation of dynamics of the stellar system as a site of simultaneous action of regular and irregular forces. The study of the sun and organization of and participation in expeditions to observe total solar eclipses occupied a special place in his work.

GERBERT, also known as **Gerbert d'Aurillac,** later **Pope Sylvester II** (*b. Aquitaine, France, ca. 945; d. Rome, 1003*), mathematics.

Received an ecclesiastical education, later concentrating on mathematics. Assigned to Adalbero, archibishop of Rheims; reorganized cathedral school with such success that pupils flocked there from many parts of the empire. His influence probably extended to other cathedral or monastic schools; this school of training in the quadrivium (music, geometry, arithmetic, astronomy) indicated the vivid interest in mathematics beginning to appear in western Europe. Constructed armillary spheres and an *oralogium* and taught with a special twenty-seven column abacus. Archbishop of Rheims (991), archbishop of Ravenna (998), and pope (999), through the influence of Otto III. A lover of arts and sciences, Otto hoped that the emperor and pope would revive the Carolingian Renaissance; significantly, Gerbert assumed the name Sylvester II, Sylvester I having been pope at the time of Constantine and participant in the first holy alliance of pope and emperor. However, the great scheme came to naught with the death of Otto in 1002 and of Gerbert in 1003.

GERBEZIUS, MARCUS, also known as **Marko Gerbec** (*b. St. Vid, near Stična, Slovenia, 1658; d. Ljubljana, Slovenia, 1718*), medicine.

Studied philosophy in Ljubljana, then medicine in Vienna, Padua, and Bologna, where he obtained a doctorate in philosophy and medicine in 1684. Returning to his native country, he became the most sought-after physician in Ljubljana. Admitted to Academia Leopoldina Naturae Curiosorum (1688), to which he sent a great many medical, meteorological, and zoological observations. Founding member of Academia Operosorum in Ljubljana (1701). His views are a mixture of Dutch and German iatrochemical ideas with English neo-Hippocratic ideas. Published first detailed observation of an auriculoventricular block (1692).

GERGONNE, JOSEPH DIAZ (*b. Nancy, France, 1771; d. Montpellier, France, 1859*), geometry.

Gergonne began his mathematical career at the École Centrale in Nîmes, and at the École Polytechnique in Paris under the influence of Gaspard Monge. Taught at University of Montpellier (1816–44). In 1810 founded the *Annales de mathématiques pures et appliquées,* the first purely mathematical journal, known as the *Annales de Gergonne.* Almost all his papers appear in the *Annales,* which played an essential role in the creation of modern projective and algebraic geometry. His geometry papers stressed polarity and duality, first mainly in connection with conics, then also with structures of higher order. A priority struggle developed with Poncelet after his publication of this new geometry in book form.

GERHARDT, CHARLES FRÉDÉRIC (*b. Strasbourg, France, 1816; d. Paris, France, 1856*), chemistry.

Studied at Giessen under Liebig and at the Faculty of Sciences in Paris under Dumas; won degrees of licentiate and doctor (1841). Worked and taught at the Faculty of Sciences in Montpellier (1841–51) with frequent leaves to Paris. In 1854 accepted positions at Strasbourg, in the Faculty of Sciences and the School of Pharmacy. In 1844 began a close friendship and collaboration with Laurent, at Bordeaux. Many of Gerhardt's most revealing articles appear in the journal they founded, *Comptes rendus mensuels des travaux chimiques* (1845–51). Involved in many disputes, notably with Dumas and Liebig. Became one of the seminal figures in the history of nineteenth-century chemistry. His most conspicuous contribution to the development of organic chemistry was his homologous series. His most notorious was a reform of the presuppositions then underlying the determination of chemical equivalents. Also notable were his redefinition of acids and his preparation of acid anhydrides. One of his principal claims to fame was his "type" theory (1853–56), which illustrated how one could envisage organic compounds as substitutionary derivatives of a minimal number of inorganic compounds: water, ammonia, hydrogen, and hydrogen chloride.

GERMAIN, SOPHIE (*b. Paris, France, 1776; d. Paris, 1831*), mathematics.

France's greatest female mathematician prior to the present era. Her father's extensive library enabled her to educate herself at home. She obtained lecture notes of Lagrange's courses at the École Polytechnique; under the pseudonym, Le Blanc, wrote a paper on analysis for him; he was astounded and sought out its author, becoming her sponsor and mathematical counselor. Correspondence with great scholars became the means by which she obtained higher education in mathematics, literature, biology, and philosophy. The Legendre-Germain correspondence was so voluminous that it was virtually a collaboration. She also corresponded with Gauss, initially under her pseudonym. One of her theorems related to the still unsolved problem of obtaining a general proof for "Fermat's last theorem." She also made contributions to the applied mathematics of acoustics and elasticity; awarded a prize by the Académie des Sciences for her treatise on vibration of elastic plates (1816). Created the concept of mean curvature.

GERMANUS, HENRICUS MARTELLUS (*fl. Florence, Italy, 1480–1496 [?]*), geography.

Drew maps remarkable for high artistic quality and new geographical concepts, including two sets to illustrate Ptolemy's *Geography*, five codices of an *Insularium*, or Book of Islands, and a large world map (43″ by 75″). His world maps served as the model for Martin Behaim's celebrated 1492 globe, the oldest surviving globe in the Western world, and probably inspired the geographic ideas of Columbus.

GESELL, ARNOLD LUCIUS (*b. Alma, Wis., 1880; d. New Haven, Conn., 1961*), psychology.

Educated at University of Wisconsin (B.Ph., 1903), Clark University (Ph.D., 1906), and Yale (M.D., 1915). Interest in the study of retarded children led to the founding of the Clinic of Child Development at Yale (1911), later to become Gesell Institute of Child Development (1950). Taught in Yale Graduate School of Medicine (1915–48); attending pediatrician at New Haven Hospital (1928–48). Study of retarded children led to work on mental development of children generally. Introduced the use of cinematography and the one-way observation dome into psychological research. Published many writings, some in cooperation with Louise Ames and Frances L. Ilg. His significance lies in the development of new methods in the study of children, placing particular emphasis on preschool years. His conclusions about the psychological care of infants and the guidance of children exerted important influence on attitudes and

practices of nursery schools, kindergartens, elementary schools, as well as parents. His institute inspired active disciples who are continuing his work.

GESNER, KONRAD (*b. Zurich, Switzerland, 1516; d. Zurich, 1565*), natural sciences, medicine, philology.

Studied at Bourges, Paris, and Basel (doctorate, 1541). Taught Greek at Lausanne Academy (1537–40); studied botany at Montpellier; settled in Zurich as chief physician. Made many botanical and zoological expeditions. His four-volume *Bibliotheca universalis* (1545–55), an index to Greek, Latin, and Hebrew writers, earned him fame as the founder of bibliography. His monumental treatise, *Opera botanica*, for which he drew nearly 1,500 plates, was published through the efforts of C. Schmiedel (1551–71), and had an influence on Linnaeus. Also wrote *Historia animalium*, a 4,500-page work which influenced Cuvier. Did pioneering work in paleontology, veterinary science, and crystallography.

GESSNER (GESNER), JOHANNES (*b. Zurich, Switzerland, 1709; d. Zurich, 1790*), botany, geology.

Studied at Leiden, where his interest in botany was stimulated by Boerhaave and Haller; and at Paris and Basel (medical degree, 1729). Taught mathematics at Basel. Practiced medicine in Zurich. Founded the Société de Physique in 1757 in Zurich, where he remained for the rest of his life. Accomplished in medicine, physics, botany, and mathematics; maintained imposing correspondence with most scientists of his time, particularly with Linnaeus, whose system of classification he did much to popularize in his writings in systematic botany. One of the founders of paleobotany; specialized in study of Alpine flora; found many new species which now bear his name.

GEUTHER, ANTON (*b. Neustadt, near Coburg, Germany, 1833; d. Jena, Germany, 1889*), chemistry.

Studied at Jena under Wackenroder and Schleiden, then at Berlin, and at Göttingen (doctorate, 1855), where he worked at Wöhler's institute. At Göttingen, devoted himself to inorganic chemistry. At Jena (from 1863) organic chemistry took precedence in his work. His most important discovery was the synthesis of acetoacetic ester; as the first example of a keto-enol tautomerism, it was of great significance in the development of theoretical organic chemistry.

GHETALDI (GHETTALDI), MARINO (*b. Ragusa, Dalmatia [now Dubrovnik, Yugoslavia], 1566 [1568?]; d. Ragusa, 1626*), mathematics.

Lived a peripatetic life, traveling extensively through Europe, studying in Rome under Clavius, Antwerp with Coignet, and in Paris with Viète. His first publications were a part of beginning research on Archimedes; also worked on reconstructing content of lost works of Apollonius. Considered by some the precursor of analytic geometry.

GHINI, LUCA (*b. Croara d'Imola, Italy, ca. 1490; d. Bologna, Italy, 1556*), botany.

Studied and taught medicine and botany at Bologna; taught at Pisa (1544–54), but maintained a private garden in Bologna. Prominent pioneer in creation of the first botanical gardens in sixteenth-century Italy (Pisa, Florence), and in collection of the earliest herbaria. Probably introduced the technique for pressing and drying plants for future reference.

GHISI, MARTINO (*b. Soresina, Italy, 1715; d. Cremona, Italy, 1794*), medicine.

Practiced medicine in Cremona after studying in Cremona and graduating from Florence. Made one of the first—if not the first—descriptions of diphtheria to be complete and valid both clinically and anatomicopathologically.

GIARD, ALFRED (*b. Valenciennes, France, 1846; d. Paris, France, 1908*), botany, zoology, embryogeny, general biology.

Received doctorate from the École Normale Supérieure (1872); taught at the Faculté des Sciences of Lille (1875–86), École Normale Supérieure (1887), and the Faculté des Sciences of Paris (1888–1908). Morphologist, phylogenist, ethologist—a complete naturalist who studied many different animals, investigating several problems of biology. Considered examination of living creatures in their environment to be superior to laboratory studies. Founded the biological station at Wimereux (1874) to introduce students to marine and terrestrial flora and fauna. Influenced by Haeckel; thought Lamarckism and Darwinism complemented each other. Created new biological terms, some of which became classic.

GIBBS, JOSIAH WILLARD (*b. New Haven, Conn., 1839; d. New Haven, 1903*), theoretical physics.

Gibbs grew up in New Haven and graduated from Yale College in 1858. He continued at Yale as a student of engineering in the new graduate school, and in 1863 he received one of the first Ph.D. degrees granted in the United States. After serving as a tutor in Yale College for three years, giving elementary instruction in Latin and natural philosophy, he left New Haven for further study at Paris, Berlin, and Heidelberg. He returned to New Haven in 1869 and taught at Yale (1871–1903).

Gibbs first turned his attention to thermodynamics in the early 1870's. His first scientific paper, "Graphical Methods in the Thermodynamics of Fluids," appeared in 1873. He assumed from the outset that entropy is one of the essential concepts to be used in treating a thermodynamic system, along with energy, temperature, pressure, and volume. In his first paper he limited himself to a discussion of what could be done with geometrical representations of thermodynamic relationships in two dimensions, and showed how some of the interrelations among the curves describing, respectively, states of equal pressure, equal temperature, equal energy, and equal entropy were independent of how the thermodynamic diagram was constructed and followed directly from the stability of equilibrium states.

In his second paper, which appeared later in 1873, Gibbs extended his geometrical discussion to three dimensions by analyzing the properties of the surface representing the fundamental thermodynamic equation of a pure substance. The thermodynamic relationships could be brought out most clearly by constructing the surface using entropy, energy, and volume as the three orthogonal coordinates.

Gibbs showed how one could use the thermodynamic surface to discuss the coexistence of the various phases of a pure substance and the stability of these states under given conditions of temperature and pressure.

"On the Equilibrium of Heterogeneous Substances" contains Gibbs's major contributions to thermodynamics. In this single memoir of some 300 pages he vastly extended the domain covered by thermodynamics, including chemical, elastic, surface, electromagnetic, and electrochemical phenomena in a single system. The basic idea had been foreshadowed in his two earlier papers, in which Gibbs had directed his attention to the properties characterizing the equilibrium states of simple systems rather than to the heat and work exchanged in particular kinds of processes. In the abstract of his memoir he formulated the criterion for thermodynamic equilibrium in two alternative and equivalent ways. He indicates that thermodynamic equilibrium is a natural generalization of mechanical equilibrium, both being characterized by minimum energy under appropriate conditions. The consequences of this criterion could then be worked out as soon as the energy of the system was expressed in terms of the proper variables. Gibbs's first and probably most significant application of this approach was to the problem of chemical equilibrium.

Gibbs's memoir showed how the general theory of thermodynamic equilibrium could be applied to phenomena as varied as the dissolving of a crystal in a liquid, the temperature dependence of the electromotive force of an electrochemical cell, and the heat absorbed when the surface of discontinuity between two fluids is increased. But even more important than the particular results he obtained was his introduction of the general method and concepts with which all applications of thermodynamics could be handled.

During the 1880's Gibbs seems to have concentrated on optics and particularly on Maxwell's electromagnetic theory of light. He emphasized that a theory of dispersion requires one to treat the local irregularities of the electric displacement due to the atomic constitution of the medium. In the last two papers of this series, published in 1888 and 1889, Gibbs appeared as a defender of the electromagnetic theory of light against the latest versions of purely mechanical theories. These were based on special elastic ethers still being proposed by William Thomson. Gibbs showed that although such theories might account for the phenomena, they required rather artificial assumptions as to internal forces, while Maxwell's theory was "not obliged to invent hypotheses."

Gibbs's reading of Maxwell's *Treatise on Electricity and Magnetism* led him to a study of quaternions, since Maxwell had used the quaternion notation to a limited extent. Gibbs decided, however, that quaternions did not really provide the mathematical language appropriate for theoretical physics, and he worked out a simpler and more straightforward vector analysis. He wrote a pamphlet on this subject which he had printed in 1881 and 1884 for private distribution to his classes and to selected correspondents.

During the academic year 1889–90 Gibbs announced "A short course on the a priori Deduction of Thermodynamic Principles from the Theory of Probabilities," a subject on which he lectured repeatedly during the 1890's. Gibbs did not publish anything more than a very brief abstract on this subject (1884) until 1902, when his book *Elementary Principles in Statistical Mechanics Developed With Special Reference to the Rational Foundation of Thermodynamics* appeared. The principal theme of Gibb's book is the analogy, as he describes it, between the average behavior of a canonical ensemble of systems and the behavior of a physical system obeying the laws of thermodynamics.

Gibbs was very much aware of the gaps in his statistical mechanics. He had supplied a "rational foundation" for thermodynamics in statistical mechanics to the extent that thermodynamic systems could be treated as if they were conservative mechanical systems with a finite number of degrees of freedom. He could not incorporate the phenomena of radiation that were of so much interest at the turn of the century, nor could he surmount the long-standing difficulties associated with the theorem of the equipartition of energy. For these reasons he disclaimed any attempts "to explain the mysteries of nature" and put his work forward as the statistical "branch of rational mechanics." Despite these difficulties Gibbs's work in statistical mechanics constituted a major advance. His methods were more general and more readily applicable than Boltzmann's and eventually came to dominate the whole field.

GIBBS, (OLIVER) WOLCOTT (*b. New York, N.Y., 1822; d. Newport, R.I., 1908*), chemistry.

Received M.D. from College of Physicians and Surgeons (1845); also studied in France, influenced in Berlin by Heinrich Rose. Taught at what is now City College of the City University of New York (1849–63) and at Harvard (1863–87). Specialized in analytic and inorganic chemistry. Worked on platinum metals (1861–64) and developed an electrolytic method for determination of copper. Member of the "Lazzaroni" around Alexander Dallas Bache.

GIESEL, FRIEDRICH OSKAR (*b. Winzig, Silesia, Germany, 1852; d. Brunswick, Germany, 1927*), commercial chemistry.

Studied at the Königliche Gewerbeakademie in Berlin (1872–74); received doctorate from Göttingen (1876). Collaborated at Gewerbeakademie until 1878 with Carl Liebermann, with whom he continued to publish until 1897. Concentrating upon alkaloid research, they achieved a partial synthesis of cocaine and patented the technique in 1888. Working at Buchler & Co., a *Chininfabrik* in Brunswick, Giesel developed the use of radioactive luminous compounds and published over thirty papers on radioactivity between 1899 and 1909. Through his research, pure radium bromide became commercially available for research. When Elster and Geitel obtained inconclusive results regarding magnetic influence upon Becquerel rays, Giesel provided a key to these rays' non-X-ray character by his decisive proof of their magnetic deflectability (1899). Discovered "emanium X" (actinium X) simultaneously with Godlewski (1905).

GILBERT, GROVE KARL (*b. Rochester, N.Y., 1843; d. Jackson, Mich., 1918*), geology, geomorphology.

Received A.B. at University of Rochester (1862). After work on other surveys, joined John Wesley Powell's Rocky Mountain geographical and geological survey (1874), which five years later was combined with other federal surveys to form the U. S. Geological Survey. Thus began the long and fruitful association of Powell, Gilbert, and Clarence Edward Dutton. On their work were founded the fundamental principles of a new subscience, geomorphology. Gilbert served as chief geologist of the Survey (1889–92).

GILBERT, J. H. *See* **Lawes, J. B.**

GILBERT, WILLIAM (*b. Colchester, Essex, England, 1544; d. London, England, 1603*), magnetism, electricity.

Educated at St. John's College, Cambridge (A.B., 1561; M.A., 1564; M.D., 1569). Practiced medicine in London; royal physician to Elizabeth I and James I. His most famous and influential work, *De magnete, magneticisque corporibus, et de magno magnete tellure; physiologia nova, plurimis & argumentis, & experimentis demonstrata,* provided the only fully developed theory dealing with all five of the then known magnetic movements (coition, direction, variation, declination, revolution) and the first comprehensive discussion of magnetism since the thirteenth-century *Letter on the Magnet* of Peter Peregrinus. The first of its six books deals with the history of magnetism and introduces his new basic idea which was to explain all terrestrial magnetic phenomena: his postulate that the earth is a giant lodestone and thus has magnetic properties. The remaining five books deal with the five magnetic movements. He distinguished between magnetic phenomena and the amber effect, introducing the vocabulary of electrics, and devised a testing instrument, the versorium, to determine electrics. Used a small spherical magnet called a terrella to represent the earth in his demonstrations of magnetism. Other writings published after his death by his younger half brother, William Gilbert of Melford, under the title *De mundo nostro sublunari philosophia nova* (1651). The first section, "Physiologiae nova contra Aristotelem," is an expansion of the cosmology of *De magnete* and discusses his ideas on structure of the earth, other globes, and the universe. The second section, "Nova meteorologia contra Aristotelem," follows the general pattern of Aristotle's *Meteorology;* it contains Gilbert's theories, with summaries of others mixed in, on comets, the Milky Way, clouds, winds, the rainbow, origin of springs and rivers, and nature of the sea and tides. The *De mundo* did not have the influence of the *De magnete,* since his cosmology was less acceptable than either his magnetic theory or his electric theory.

GILES (AEGIDIUS) OF LESSINES (*b. Lessines [now Hainaut, Belgium], ca. 1235; d. 1304 or later*), astronomy, natural philosophy.

Dominican who probably studied under Albertus Magnus at Cologne and Thomas Aquinas at Paris. First to develop Thomistic doctrine; wrote most complete study of usury in the Middle Ages. Among his works is the classic *De essentia, motu et significatione cometarum,* divided into ten chapters: seven on astronomical and meteorological discussion of comets, three on their astrological significance, and one on the history of comets and their sequels.

GILES (AEGIDIUS) OF ROME (*b. Rome, Italy, before 1247; d. Avignon, France, 1316*), physics, astronomy, medicine.

Studied in Paris with Thomas Aquinas; taught theology. Chosen general of the Hermits of St. Augustine (1292) and archbishop of Bourges (1295). Mainly philosopher and theologian, but frequently dealt with problems relating to natural philosophy, notably in his commentaries on Aristotle which were often utilized by such fourteenth-century physicists as Buridan and Marsilius of Inghen. Wrote numerous works, including treatises on embryology and cosmology.

GILL, DAVID (*b. Aberdeen, Scotland, 1843; d. London, England, 1914*), astronomy.

Education and early experience mostly in clockmaking, gave him experience and knowledge of fine mechanisms. Gained invaluable knowledge and firsthand experience in planning and supervising building of an observatory for Lord Lindsay at Dun Echt, near Aberdeen (1872–76). Made expeditions to Mauritius (1874) and Ascension Island (1877), using the Dun Echt heliometer to determine the distance of the sun and associated constants, by observing the transit of Venus and near approach of Mars, respectively. Appointed royal astronomer at Royal Observatory at Cape Town (1879–1906). Knighted, 1900. Transformed the observatory from a small, run-down institution into one of the best equipped in the world, with a large, young, keen staff, and a constant stream of visiting astronomers. His most notable contributions were the determination of solar parallax by systematic observations of three minor planets, his value being used until 1968; and the *Cape Photographic Durchmusterung*, which gives the approximate positions and brightness of nearly half a million southern stars, and which was the first major astronomical work to be carried out photographically.

GILL, THEODORE NICHOLAS (*b. New York, N.Y., 1837; d. Washington, D.C., 1914*), ichthyology.

Educated at Wagner Free Institute of Science in Philadelphia, and Columbian College (now George Washington University) (M.A., 1865; M.D., 1866; Ph.D., 1870; LL.D., 1895). From 1860 held various appointments at Columbian College, including professor of zoology (1884–1910). Librarian of Smithsonian Institution (1862–66) and assistant librarian at Library of Congress (1866–74). One of Spencer F. Baird's close-knit coterie in the U.S. Fish Commission, he was an outstanding taxonomist and synthesizer of scientific literature. His very large number of relatively short papers constituted a major contribution to ichthyology.

GIORGI, GIOVANNI (*b. Lucca, Italy, 1871; d. Castiglioncello, Italy, 1950*), electrical theory, electrical engineering, mathematics.

Received degree in civil engineering from the Institute of Technology in Rome. Director of Technology Office of the city of Rome (1906–23). Taught at Universities of Rome, Cagliari, and Palermo, and at the Royal Institute of Higher Mathematics. Chief fame arises from his concept of a new absolute system of measurement to be simultaneously applicable to all electrical, magnetic, and mechanical units, which he first proposed in a letter to the English periodical *Electrician* (1895). In a subsequent paper (1901) he presented a consistent measurement system based on the meter, kilogram, and mean solar second (hence called the M.K.S. system, as well as the Giorgi International System). It was half a century before the final adoption of his system.

GIRARD, ALBERT (*b. St.-Mihiel, France, 1595; d. Leiden, Netherlands, 1632*), mathematics.

Not much known of his education or life. Works include many translations and editions of mathematical works. Made contributions in areas of spherical trigonometry, arithmetic, theory of numbers, algebra, and cubic and biquadratic equations.

GIRARD, PIERRE-SIMON (*b. Caen, France, 1765; d. Paris, France, 1836*), hydraulic engineering.

Educated at Caen, admitted to École des Ponts et Chaussées, and in 1789 appointed engineer in the Corps des Ponts et Chaussées. Part of Napoleon's expedition to Egypt (1798–1803); one of eight authors of a comprehensive report of the expedition—his study covering agriculture, commerce, and industry. Appointed director of the Paris water supply, with the special task of connecting the Seine and Ourcq rivers with a ship canal to serve the capital. First barges reached Paris in 1813; his account of the project is found in his major treatise, *Mémoire sur le canal de l'Ourcq . . .* , a two-volume work plus atlas (1831–43).

GIRAUD-SOULAVIE, J. L. *See* **Soulavie, J. L. Giraud.**

GIRTANNER, CHRISTOPH (*b. St. Gall, Switzerland, 1760; d. Göttingen, Germany, 1800*), medicine, chemistry.

Studied at Lausanne and at Göttingen (doctorate, 1782). Settled in Göttingen after traveling; in 1793 became privy councillor to the duke of Saxe-Coburg. Books on medicine and chemistry included *Anfangsgründe der antiphlogistischen Chemie.*

GLADSTONE, JOHN HALL (*b. London, England, 1827; d. London, 1902*), chemistry.

Studied at University College, London, with Thomas Graham; received Ph.D. from Giessen under Liebig. Lectured at St. Thomas' Hospital, London (1850–52). Elected fellow of Royal Society (1853); Fullerian professor of chemistry at Royal Institution (1874–77). A founder of the Physical Society (1874). Best known for the application of optical phenomena to chemical problems.

GLAISHER, JAMES (*b. Rotherhithe, England, 1809; d. Croydon, England, 1903*), meteorology.

Largely self-educated; acquired interest in science on visits to Greenwich observatory. Appointed by George Airy as assistant at Cambridge observatory (1833); followed Airy to Greenwich (1835), where he became superintendent of the magnetic and meteorological department (1838–74). Effectively organized meteorological observations and climatological statistics in United Kingdom. His *Hygrometrical Tables Adapted to the Use of the Dry and Wet Bulb Thermometer* (1847) remained in use for almost a century. Made scientific balloon ascents with aeronaut Henry Coxwell (1862).

GLAISHER, JAMES WHITBREAD LEE (*b. Lewisham, Kent, England, 1848; d. Cambridge, England, 1928*), mathematics, astronomy.

Son of astronomer James Glaisher (1809–1903). Educated at St. Paul's School, London, and Trinity College, Cambridge, remaining at the latter the rest of his life. Awarded new D.Sc. degree in 1887 by Cambridge. Published nearly 400 articles and notes in mathematics and astronomy, notably in areas of special functions, tables, and history of mathematics. Characterized as a mathematical stimulus to others rather than a pioneer, his influence on Thomas S. Fiske led to the latter's organization of the New York Mathematical Society (1888) and its *Bulletin*.

GLANVILL, JOSEPH (*b. Plymouth, England, 1636; d. Bath, England, 1680*), theology, apologetics, history and philosophy of science.

Educated at Exeter College, Oxford (B.A., 1655), and Lincoln College (M.A., 1658); ordained in 1660, rector at abbey church at Bath (1666–80). Elected fellow of Royal Society (1664). Made a few minor contributions to natural history in the form of reports on mines and medicinal springs. Principal contribution to the work of the Royal Society was to defend it against its critics. In *The Vanity of Dogmatizing* (1661) and its revision, *Scepsis scientifica* (1664), he argued that the new experimental philosophy was beneficial in practical terms, had already advanced knowledge beyond what antiquity could claim and would rapidly advance it still further, and was harmless—indeed, it was helpful—to the cause of religion. Throughout his career he was a prominent apologist for latitudinarian Anglicanism as well as for the new philosophy, and his two lines of apologetic endeavor were frequently intertwined. In later years he wrote primarily on specifically religious and religiopolitical questions, and above all to combat disbelief in witches.

GLASER, CHRISTOPHER (*b. Basel, Switzerland, ca. 1615; d. Paris, France, 1672 [?]*), pharmacy, chemistry.

Little is known of his early and later life. Trained as a pharmacist, practiced as an apothecary. Appointed demonstrator in chemistry at the Jardin du Roi in Paris (1662). In 1663 published chemistry textbook, *Traité de la chymie*, which appeared in fourteen editions, including one English and five German versions. Glaser's recipe for a *sel antifebrile* became known as *sel polychrestum Glaseri;* the naturally occurring mixed sulfate of sodium and potassium was named glaserite in his honor. Disappeared from public life after his implication as the source of a poison recipe in the famous Brinvilliers poison case (1672).

GLASER, JOHANN HEINRICH (*b. Basel, Switzerland, 1629; d. Basel, 1679*), anatomy, botany, surgery.

Studied in Geneva, Paris, and Basel (doctorate, 1661). Medical practice in Basel soon brought him international fame. Taught at Faculté de Médecine at Basel. Glaser owes lasting fame to his work on the brain, nerves, and bones of the head, *Tractatus de cerebro* (1680). Fissure of the temporal bone through which the tympanic cords pass is known as the Glaserian petrotympanic fissure.

GLAUBER, JOHANN RUDOLPH (*b. Karlstadt, Germany, 1604; d. Amsterdam, Netherlands, 1670*), chemistry, medicine, metallurgy.

Unlike most iatrochemists, he did not attend a university, but set out in quest of alchemical wisdom, visiting laboratories in Paris, Basel, Salzburg, and Vienna. Eventually settled in Amsterdam and outfitted the most impressive laboratory in Europe. Best practical chemist of his day and the first industrial chemist. His instructions for improvement of laboratory technique were instrumental in preparing the way for the chemical revolution of the next century. In his *Furni novi philosophici* (1646–49) he carefully described the materials and dimensions for construction of his famous distillatory furnaces, which made it possible to obtain high temperatures and to heat substances under a variety of conditions. The *Pharmocopoea spagyrica* (1654–68) is a collection of medical preparations he found most reliable. *Dess Teutschlands-Wohlfahrt* (1656–61) encourages Germans to make better use of their natural resources and become economically self-sufficient, and contains considerable discussion of transmutation. In *Miraculum mundi* (1653–60) he specified that the universal salt is niter. In 1658 the *Tractatus de natura salium* appeared, and in 1660 a second part of the *Miraculum mundi*. Only then did he recognize the significance of his "sal mirabile" (Glauber's salt) and begin to utilize it, not very successfully, in the central position that niter formerly held. It was produced in its most interesting form as a by-product of his secret process for hydrochloric acid: from common salt and sulfuric acid. Today hydrated sodium sulfate is familiarly known as Glauber's salt.

GLAZEBROOK, RICHARD TETLEY (*b. West Derby, Liverpool, England, 1854; d. Limpsfield Common, England, 1935*), physics.

Received B.A. (1876) and M.A. (1879) from Trinity College, Cambridge. Worked at Cavendish Laboratory under Maxwell and Rayleigh. Lectured in mathematics and physics (1881–97). Assistant director of Cavendish Laboratory (1891–98). Resigned to become principal of University College, Liverpool (1898). Became first director of the National Physical Laboratory (1900–1919). Pressed for determination of fundamental electrical standards for both scientific and industrial purposes.

GLEICHEN-RUSSWORM, WILHELM FRIEDRICH VON (*b. Bayreuth, Germany, 1717; d. Schloss Greifenstein, Bonnland, Hammelburg, Germany, 1783*), microscopy.

Received little formal education; did independent research. Interest in microscopy stimulated by Martin Ledermüller. Particularly interested in processes of fertilization in plants and animals: his *Das neueste aus dem Reiche der Pflanzen* (1763–66[?]) contains fifty-one colored plates illustrating numerous details of floral structure and various pollens, plus six plates devoted to modifications and accessories he designed for the microscope. His most important contribution was his description of the technique of phagocytic staining (1778).

GLISSON, FRANCIS (*b. England, 1597[?]; d. London, England, 1677*), medicine, philosophy.

Received B.A. (1620–21), M.A. (1624), and M.D. (1634) from Cambridge, where he held the position of regius professor (1636–77). London was the seat of his professional and scientific life. Collaborated on a book on rickets, *De rachitide* (1650), which contained classic anatomical and clinical descriptions of the disease. This and other publications incorporated empirical findings into a scholastic framework of reasoning. *Anatomia hepatis* (1654) and *Tractatus de ventriculo et intestinis* (1677) constitute a monumental work on general anatomy and on anatomy and physiology of the digestive organs. In the former work, he used the word "irritability" to connote the ability of a part to become irritated, that is, to perceive an irritant and to try to rid itself of it. This doctrine of irritability acquired fame because in later years Haller traced the origin of the term back to Glisson.

GMELIN, JOHANN GEORG (*b. Tübingen, Germany, 1709; d. Tübingen, 1755*), botany, natural history, geography.

Received medical degree from Tübingen (1727). In St. Petersburg, studied and then lectured at Academy of Sciences (1728–33). From 1733 to 1743 took part in the imperial scientific expedition to eastern Siberia with Gerhard Friedrich Müller. Gmelin to studied the natural history of territories visited. Upon his return, resumed academic functions at the Academy and worked on *Flora sibirica sive historia plantarum Sibiriae* (1747–69), which contains descriptions of 1,178 species and illustrations of 294 of these. Also contributed to knowledge of the zoology, geography, geology, ethnography, and natural resources of explored regions. In 1747 returned to Tübingen, becoming professor at the University in 1749.

GMELIN, LEOPOLD (*b. Göttingen, Germany, 1788; d. Heidelberg, Germany, 1853*), chemistry.

Studied at Tübingen and Göttingen (medical doctorate, 1812); also qualified as chemist. Taught at Heidelberg (1813–51); director of the Chemical Institute, which became independent in 1818. Improved teaching of chemistry; made extensive laboratory studies that embraced physiology, organic chemistry, inorganic chemistry, and mineralogy, in addition to purely theoretical studies. The *Handbuch der theoretischen Chemie* (1817) was his masterwork. In 1922 the Deutsche Chemische Gesellschaft assumed the obligation to continue the monumental work; the eighth edition, now entitled *Gmelins Handbuch der anorganische Chemie*, began publication in 1924 and is still being published. In it, Gmelin sought the complete presentation of the prevailing state of chemistry; planned to adduce all pertinent facts, arrange them by element and compound, and give appropriate references. Maintained that inorganic and organic substances must be distinguished from each other. Also did pioneering work with Tiedemann in the chemistry of digestion, designed and described some chemical apparatus, and introduced the terms "racemic acid," "ester," and "ketone."

GOBLEY, NICOLAS-THÉODORE (*b. Paris, France, 1811; d. Bagnères-de-Luchon, France, 1876*), chemistry.

Apprenticed to the eminent pharmacist and chemist Pierre Robiquet. Studied pharmacy in Paris; directed his own pharmacy (1837–61). Taught at School of Pharmacy (1842–47). Most significant work on chemistry of phosphatides. In 1845 discovered a fatty substance containing phosphorus which in 1850 he named lecithin. Collaborated with J. L. M. Poiseuille in a study of blood levels of urea and its secretion from the kidneys.

GODDARD, ROBERT HUTCHINGS (*b. Worcester, Mass., 1882; d. Baltimore, Md., 1945*), physics, rocket engineering.

Graduated from Clark University (M.A., 1910; Ph.D., 1911), where he also taught from 1913. After the advent of ballistic missiles and space exploration, Goddard became posthumously world-famous as one of three scientific pioneers of rocketry. He worked out the theory of rocket propulsion independently; and then almost alone he designed, built, tested, and flew the first liquid-fuel rocket on 16 March 1926. During the 1930's he worked near Roswell, New Mexico, demonstrating progressively more sophisticated experimental boosters and payloads. Laid the foundation from which team workers could launch men to the moon. Over 200 patents.

GODFREY, THOMAS (*b. Bristol Township, Pa., 1704; d. Philadelphia, Pa., 1749*), technology.

Major contribution to science was the invention of the double reflecting quadrant which became generally known as Hadley's quadrant and is, essentially, the navigational sextant used today. Hadley had priority of publication of the two identical independent inventions. Godfrey also published almanacs (1729–36) and gave instruction in navigation, astronomy, and mathematics.

GODIN, LOUIS (*b. Paris, France, 1704; d. Cádiz, Spain, 1760*), astronomy.

Studied under Joseph Delisle at the Collège Royal. Entered Academy of Sciences in 1725; edited Academy's *Mémoires* for the years 1666–99, wrote its *Histoire* for nineteen of those years, prepared an index of these materials (*Histoire et les Mémoires de l'Académie Royale des Sciences*) for 1666–1730; prepared Academy's annual ephemeris, *Connaissance des temps*, 1730–35. Many publications on astronomical topics: meteor and eclipse observation; lunar and solar parallax determination; pendulum observation. Made expedition to Ecuador which verified oblateness of earth. Taught at University of San Marcos (1743–51); director of Academy of Naval Guards at Cádiz, Spain (1752–60).

GODWIN-AUSTEN, ROBERT ALFRED CLOYNE (*b. Guildford, England, 1808; d. Guildford, 1884*), geology.

Educated in France and at Oriel College, Oxford (B.A., 1830). Interest in geology kindled by William Buckland at Oxford. Remembered for contributions on stratigraphy of southern England, as one of the first European paleogeographers, and for his prediction that a coalfield would be discovered beneath the younger rocks of Kent. Also pioneer in elucidation of the history of the English Channel.

GOEBEL, KARL (*b. Billigheim, Baden, Germany, 1855; d. Munich, Germany, 1932*), botany.

Received inspiration in botany from Wilhelm Hofmeister (Tübingen), Heinrich Anton de Bary (Strasbourg, doctorate), and Julius von Sachs (Würzburg). Sachs's assistant for four years. Taught at Rostock and Marburg. In Munich taught botany and later became general director of State Scientific Collections; he moved the botanical laboratories and gardens from the center of town to the edge of the Bavarian royal park at Nymphenburg. Enriched gardens and greenhouses with specimens collected on his many botanical journeys. Published more than 200 works, his principal one being *Organographie der Pflanzen*, not fully published until the year after his death. The significance of his organography for botanical science lay in the fact that it provided one of the main bridges from the achievements of observation in the late nineteenth century to the fully fledged experimental science of the twentieth century.

GOEDAERT, JOHANNES (*b. Middelburg, Netherlands, ca. 1617; d. Middelburg, 1668*), entomology.

Little known of his life. One of the earliest authors on entomology, first to write on insects of the Netherlands. First to base discussions entirely on firsthand observation. His only work, *Metamorphosis naturalis,* describes his observations of and experiments with insects made between 1635 and 1658. His technique was to catch "worms" (larvae) in the field and rear them, feeding them with their natural nutrients and observing and recording their metamorphosis, until finally the mature animal could be observed and drawn. In this way, studied life cycles of a variegated collection of butterflies, bees, wasps, flies, and beetles. He is remembered as a painter, more particularly as a watercolorist, whose subjects were mainly birds and insects.

GOEPPERT, HEINRICH ROBERT (*b. Sprottau, Lower Silesia, Germany [now Szprotawa, Poland], 1800; d. Breslau, Germany [now Wrocław, Poland], 1884*), paleobotany, botany.

Studied medicine at Breslau and Berlin. In 1827 became *Privatdozent* at Faculty of Medicine at Breslau, and eventually full professor in 1839. In 1852 assumed chair of botany and was appointed director of botanical garden and museum. Lectured in many fields: pharmacology, toxicology, forensic chemistry, systematic botany, plant physiology, plant geography, and paleobotany. His most distinguished work was done in the field of paleobotany, particularly the study of Carboniferous flora. Published works on fossil flora of almost all geological periods.

GOETHE, JOHANN WOLFGANG VON (*b. Frankfurt am Main, Germany, 1749; d. Weimar, Germany, 1832*), zoology, botany, geology, optics.

Law degree from Strasbourg (1771). Summoned in 1775 to the court of Weimar, where his duties included supervision of mining. Established a lasting reputation as Germany's greatest poet. His first scientific paper (1784) claimed to demonstrate the presence of the intermaxillary bone in man: to deny man the bone would be to impugn the unity of nature. Goethe thought that the biologist, by comparing a large number of plant and animal forms, can obtain a clear idea of underlying archetypes. He also constructed his idea of the archetype from a study of function, in accordance with the principle of compensation derived from Aristotle and extended his unity of type to cover not only vertebrates but all animals. He argued that the vertebral column preserves some indication of an underlying identity of the units forming the vertebrate archetype, and that the skull is really a series of bones seen to be variations of vertebrae. Lorenz Oken shared these views. Goethe sought in botany and zoology a theory that would explain all living forms. His concern with geology sprang from his superintending the reopening of copper slate mines at Ilmenau in 1784. At that time most rocks were regarded as chemical precipitates from saline seas. It is an important part of his theory of rock origin that the joint planes which divide granite masses into blocks were original, not shrinkage cracks due to

cooling or drying. His repugnance for theories involving terrestrial violence sometimes led him to pioneer a correct path, most notably his glacial interpretation of erratic blocks at a time when violent and catastrophic movement was being invoked to explain their remoteness from their parent rocks. His whole approach to rocks reflects the insistence on types which distinguishes his biological thinking. His first publications on optics (1791) culminated in *Zur Farbenlehre* (1810), his longest and, in his own view, best work, today known principally as a fierce and unsuccessful attack on Newton's demonstration that white light is composite. Goethe supposed that the pure sensation of white can be caused only by a simple, uncompounded substance. His chapter on physiological colors (those which depend more on the condition of the eye than on the illumination) is most successful and also typifies his psychological approach to color.

GOETTE, ALEXANDER WILHELM (*b. St. Petersburg, Russia, 1840; d. Heidelberg, Germany, 1922*), zoology.

Studied at Dorpat (1860–65) and Tübingen (M.D. under Leydig). Taught and was an assistant in the Zoological Institute at Strasbourg (1872–81); director of zoological collection of Municipal Museum of Strasbourg (1880–81). Professor of zoology at Rostock (1882–86); returned to Strasbourg (1886–1918); spent his last years in Heidelberg (1918–22). In his principal work, he gave a detailed description of development of the organs of *Bombinator igneus,* plus a detailed presentation of methods and problems of ontogenetic research, emphasizing the necessity of investigating purely ontological and physiological regularities as a basis for understanding morphological phenomena, which led to controversy with Haeckel and his gastraea theory and the "biogenetic law."

GOHORY, JACQUES (*b. Paris, France, 1520; d. Paris, 1576*), natural history, alchemy, medicine.

From 1572 maintained a private academy called the Lycium Philosophal San Marcellin at his home in the Faubourg Saint-Marcel, devoted to encyclopedic cultivation of the arts in the Italian Neoplatonic tradition, with stress on alchemy, botany, and magical arts. Gohory was important as an early disseminator of Paracelsian ideas in France. The Lycium became a center for preparation of chemical medicines.

GOLDBACH, CHRISTIAN (*b. Königsberg, Prussia [now Kaliningrad, R.S.F.S.R.], 1690; d. Moscow, Russia, 1764*), mathematics.

Studied medicine and mathematics at Königsberg before embarking on a series of travels around Europe, where he formed acquaintances with leading scientists of his day. Held several positions at the Imperial Academy of Sciences in St. Petersburg. Ended ties with the Academy when promoted to *Staatsrat* in Ministry of Foreign Afrairs (1742). Political success prevented his talent in mathematics from attaining full promise; however he maintained important correspondence with Nikolaus II Bernoulli, Daniel Bernoulli, and Leonhard Euler; that with Euler on number theory marking him as one of the few men of his day who understood the implications of Fermat's new approach to the subject.

GOLDBERGER, JOSEPH (*b. Girált, Hungary, 1874; d. Washington, D.C., 1929*), epidemiology.

Graduated from Bellevue Hospital Medical School (1895). Worked for U.S. Public Health Service (1899–1929). Played an increasingly responsible role in field investigations of yellow fever, typhus, dengue, and measles, making several important epidemiological contributions. In 1914 he undertook direction of an expanded antipellagra program. Almost immediately decided pellagra was a consequence of improper diet. In three major steps he succeeded by 1916 in marshaling extremely strong evidence for his position: 1) by supplementing diets in particular institutional populations, he almost completely eliminated the disease; 2) he induced symptoms of pellagra in prison-farm volunteers by providing an abundant but protein-deficient diet; 3) he and co-workers were unable to produce symptoms in themselves through ingestion and injection of the excreta and secretions of patients. He then turned his efforts toward identification of constituent(s) lacking in a pellagra-producing diet, suspecting some amino acid component of such protective foods as meat and yeast.

GOLDSCHMIDT, RICHARD BENEDICT (*b. Frankfurt am Main, Germany, 1878; d. Berkeley, Calif., 1958*), zoology, general biology.

Studied at Heidelberg under Bütschli and Gegenbaur and at Munich under Hertwig; Hertwig's assistant and later *Privatdozent* (1903–13). In 1913 appointed director of genetics department at Kaiser Wilhelm Institute for Biology in Berlin. Taught at University of California at Berkeley (1936–58). Produced more than 250 memoirs and articles and about twenty books in which three orientations emerge: 1) morphological problems and cytology, fertilization, meiosis, histology, comparative anatomy, and embryology of trematodes, nematodes, and the Acrania; 2) researches on moths of genus *Lymantria* which lasted twenty-five years—population genetics, genetics of geographic variation, and theory of genes; 3) physiological genetics of the *Drosophila*. Founded *Archiv für Zellforschung* (1906).

GOLDSCHMIDT, VICTOR (*b. Mainz, Germany, 1853; d. Salzburg, Austria, 1933*), crystallography, harmonics.

Educated at Freiberg Bergakademie, Munich, Prague, and Heidelberg (Ph.D., 1880). At Vienna from 1882 to 1887. From 1888 spent most of his time teaching and doing research in Heidelberg. In 1916 he and his wife established the Eduard und Josefine von Portheim Stiftung, of which the Victor-Goldschmidt-Institut für Kristallforschung was a part. One of the founders of modern crystallography, his contribution centered mainly on complete indexing and recording of mineral crystal forms, to link these external variations of form to the physicochemical variations of composition and of physicochemical factors present during formation. Part of his contribution consisted of improving existing instruments and inventing new ones.

GOLDSCHMIDT, VICTOR MORITZ (*b. Zurich, Switzerland, 1888; d. Oslo, Norway, 1947*), geochemistry, chemistry, mineralogy.

Doctorate from University of Christiania (now Oslo) under strong influence of W. C. Brøgger (1911); also influenced by von Groth at Munich and Becke at Vienna.

Taught at Christiania, directed mineralogical institute. A pioneer in geochemistry. Petrological studies on regional metamorphism led to mineralogical phase rule. In 1917 became chairman of Government Commission for Raw Materials and director of Raw Materials Laboratory, investigating factors governing distribution of chemical species in nature: he and associates worked out crystal structures of 200 compounds of seventy-five elements to form a background for elucidation of laws of geochemical distribution. In 1929 became full professor in Faculty of Natural Sciences at Göttingen and head of the mineralogical institute. In 1935 returned to Oslo to a similar position. Suffered much adversity at the hands of Nazis: imprisoned several times, went into hiding, made his way to Sweden and then Great Britain, applying his geochemical concepts to soil science at the Macaulay Institute for Soil Research and at Rothamsted.

GOLDSTEIN, EUGEN (*b. Gleiwitz, Upper Silesia [now Gliwice, Poland], 1850; d. Berlin, Germany, 1930*), physics.

Studied at Breslau; received doctorate from Berlin under Helmholtz (1881). Spent most of his long professional career as physicist at Potsdam observatory: lifelong interest in electrical discharges in moderate to high vacuums. Discoverer (1886) of canal rays, which emerged from channels or holes in anodes in low-pressure discharge tubes. Many of his students carried on his work, notably Wilhelm Wien and Johannes Stark.

GOLGI, CAMILLO (*b. Corteno [now Corteno Golgi], Brescia, Italy, 1843; d. Pavia, Italy, 1926*), histology, pathology.

Medical degree at University of Pavia (1865). Conducted histological research in Bizzozero's laboratory of experimental pathology; practiced medicine at Abbiategrasso. Taught at Universities of Siena (1879) and Pavia (1875–78, 1880–1918). Shared 1906 Nobel Prize for medicine or physiology with Santiago Ramón y Cajal, for his work on neuroanatomy. Invented original method for studying the nervous system based on the coloration of cells and nerve fibers by means of prolonged immersion of samples, previously hardened with potassium bichromate or ammonium bichromate, in a 0.5 to 1 per cent solution of silver nitrate. This technique brings out clearly features of nerve elements. In cytology, was the first to describe (1898) the existence in cytoplasm of the nerve cell of a special small organ, in the shape of a fine and elegant network of anastomosed and interlaced threads (Golgi's internal reticular apparatus), now considered of fundamental importance in cytometabolic processes. Also did important research on malaria, making it possible to diagnose different forms of the disease, to establish a sequence in the appearance of fever fits, and to treat it efficiently with quinine.

GOLITSYN, BORIS BORISOVICH (*b. St. Petersburg [now Leningrad], Russia, 1862; d. Petrograd [now Leningrad], 1916*), physics, seismology.

Graduated from the hydrographic section of the Maritime Academy (1887) and from the Physics and Mathematics Faculty of University of Strasbourg (1890). Began teaching at Moscow University in 1891. His master's thesis (1893), "Investigations in Mathematical Physics," in which he departed from the electrodynamics of Faraday and Maxwell by first considering the space occupied by radiation as a kind of medium to which the concept of temperature is applicable, created a great controversy with Stoletov and Sokolov. After 1898 occupied himself mainly with seismology and seismometry. Laid foundations of scientific seismometry and developed an improved type of seismograph.

GOLTZ, FRIEDRICH LEOPOLD (*b. Posen, Germany* [*now Poznan, Poland*], *1834; d. Strasbourg, France, 1902*), physiology, encephalology.

Medical degree from Königsberg (1858). Taught at Königsberg (1860–69), Halle (1870–72), and Strasbourg (from 1872). Principal research on reflex phenomena, particularly the spinal cord of the frog. The Goltz *Kochversuch* ("cooking test," 1860) called for slow heating of a spinal (decerebrated) frog in a water bath. His *Klopfversuch* ("tapping test," 1862) also became famous: when the abdominal wall of a frog is tapped, the heart stops momentarily because of the reflex vagus effect. He also demonstrated the "embracing reflex" and the "croaking reflex." Analyzed functions of the labyrinth of the inner ear in frogs and pigeons; first to recognize importance of semicircular canals in maintaining equilibrium. Did important research on functions of the cerebrum (1876). A dog whose cerebrum had been removed was without intellect, memory, and intelligence.

GOMBERG, MOSES (*b. Elisavetgrad, Russia* [*now Kirovograd, U.S.S.R.*], *1866; d. Ann Arbor, Mich., 1947*), organic chemistry.

Educated at University of Michigan (B.S., 1890; M.S., 1892; Ph.D., 1894). Taught at Michigan (1893–1936) except for leave to work in von Baeyer's laboratory in Munich and with Victor Meyer in Heidelberg. Prepared the first stable free radical, triphenylmethyl, $(C_6H_5)_3C$, developing understanding of experimental conditions necessary for successful synthesis of related compounds.

GOMPERTZ, BENJAMIN (*b. London, England, 1779; d. London, 1865*), mathematics.

Denied matriculation at the universities because he was Jewish, he joined the Society of Mathematicians of Spitalfields in 1797 and educated himself by reading the masters, especially Newton, Colin Maclaurin, and William Emerson. In various learned societies he found intellectual stimulation that led to many publications and a wide spectrum of accomplishments. Pioneer in actuarial science. Applied method of fluxions to investigation of various life contingencies. In 1824 was appointed actuary and head clerk of the newly founded Alliance Assurance Company. In 1825 published Gompertz's law of mortality, ". . . the average exhaustion of man's power to avoid death to be such that at the end of equal infinitely small intervals of time he lost equal portions of his remaining power to oppose destruction which he had at the commencement of these intervals."

GONSÁLEZ, DOMINGO. *See* **Gundissalinus, Dominicus.**

GOODRICH, EDWIN STEPHEN (*b. Weston-super-Mare, England, 1868; d. Oxford, England, 1946*), comparative anatomy, embryology, paleontology, evolution.

In 1888 entered Slade School at University College, London, as an art student; E. Ray Lankester interested him in zoology and in 1892 made him his assistant at Oxford, where he stayed until 1945. Became the greatest comparative anatomist of his day. Traveled extensively, studying marine fauna. Most important area of his work involved unraveling the significance of sets of tubes connecting the centers of bodies of animals with the outside: nephridia serve the function of excretion, and coelomoducts serve to release the germ cells. In his various researches his attention was always focused on evolution, to which he made notable contributions, firmly adhering to Darwin's theory of natural selection.

GOODRICKE, JOHN (*b. Groningen, Netherlands, 1764; d. York, England, 1786*), astronomy.

Despite the handicap of deafness and dumbness and a lamentably brief life, his discoveries laid the foundations of an important branch of stellar astronomy. Educated at Warrington Academy. Discovered the first known short-period variable star (β Persei, or Algol) and established a remarkably accurate estimate of its period. Also discovered the variability of β Lyrae and δ Cephei, both of which became prototypes of other classes of variable stars. His bold suggestion that Algol (and β Lyrae) was an eclipsing variable, as they are now called, was made too early to gain speedy acceptance among contemporary astronomers.

GOODSIR, JOHN (*b. Anstruther, Fife, Scotland, 1814; d. Edinburgh, Scotland, 1867*), anatomy, marine zoology.

Studied at St. Andrews University and Edinburgh University. During his early medical practice, he did important investigation into the development of teeth—demonstrated the independent origin of deciduous and permanent dentitions. He and Edward Forbes published jointly on marine biology. At the University of Edinburgh Museum he was successively conservator of human and comparative anatomy (1840–42), curator of anatomy and pathology (1843), demonstrator in anatomy (1844), and curator of entire museum (1846). His ambition was to create a teaching museum second to none in Britain. Elected to the chair of anatomy at Edinburgh (1846). Also served as conservator of the museum of the Royal College of Surgeons (1841–43), where his research included fundamental observations on cell structure. His later work in the mathematics of form, trying to perceive an underlying "crystal" arrangement of the fine structure of muscle, bone, and other tissues and organs, led him to formulate a theory of the triangle as the universal image of nature.

GÖPEL, ADOLPH (*b. Rostock, Germany, 1812; d. Berlin, Germany, 1847*), mathematics.

Earned doctorate at Berlin (1835). Taught at Werder Gymnasium and at Royal Realschule before becoming an official at the royal library in Berlin. Little known of his life; he owes his fame to "Theoriae transcendentium Abelianarum primi ordinis adumbratio levis," published after his death. Continuing the work of C. G. J. Jacobi, he obtained the result that the quotients of two theta functions are solutions of the Jacobian inverse problem for $p = 2$. In his calculations he linked four quadratics through a homogeneous fourth-degree relation, later named the "Göpel relation," which coincides with the equation of the Kummer surface.

GORDAN, PAUL ALBERT (*b. Breslau, Germany, 1837; d. Erlangen, Germany, 1912*), mathematics.

Studied at Berlin under Ernst Kummer, at Breslau, and at Königsberg under Karl Jacobi. Taught at Erlangen (1874–1910). Expert in invariant theory, developing many techniques for representing and generating forms and their invariants. In 1868 proved by constructive methods that the invariants of systems of binary forms possess a finite base (Gordan finite basis theorem). Second major area of contributions was in solutions of algebraic equations and their associated groups of substitutions. His only doctoral student, Emmy Noether (1882–1935), carried on his work in invariant theory.

GORDON, WALTER (*b. Apolda, Germany, 1893; d. Stockholm, Sweden, 1940*), theoretical physics.

Obtained Ph.D. at Berlin (1921); remained until 1929, when he began teaching at Hamburg. Lost position in 1933 like other professors of Jewish origin; became member of Institute of Mathematical Physics at University of Stockholm. Made several important contributions to relativistic generalization of nonrelativistic quantum mechanics. Published papers containing important contributions to Dirac's theory of the electron.

GORE, GEORGE (*b. Bristol, England, 1826; d. Birmingham, England, 1908*), electrochemistry.

Chemist for firm in Birmingham that manufactured phosphorus. Published many articles on electrodeposition of metals. Studied properties of electrodeposited antimony. Published study of preparation and properties of anhydrous hydrofluoric acid. Lectured at King Edward's School in Birmingham (1870–80); formed Institute of Scientific Research (1880), serving as director till his death.

GÖRGEY, ARTHUR (*b. Toporc, Hungary [now Toporec, Czechoslovakia], 1818; d. Visegrád, Hungary, 1916*), chemistry.

Studied chemistry at Prague, remaining as assistant to Joseph Redtenbacher. Returned to Hungary after Revolution of 1848, joined national army, and by 1849 was commander-in-chief. His military and political activity are the subject of many books and plays. It is almost forgotten that he is the same Görgey who is cited in organic chemistry textbooks as the discoverer of lauric acid. The discovery was made while carrying out an analysis of coconut oil during his stay in Prague.

GOSSELET, JULES-AUGUSTE (*b. Cambrai, France, 1832; d. Lille, France, 1916*), geology, paleontology.

Greatly influenced by Constant Prévost and Edmond Hébert at the Sorbonne, he worked with the former as *préparateur* in geology for seven years. His studies of Devonian and Carboniferous strata in nearby quarries led to his important researches on primary formations, which he submitted for the doctorate in natural sciences. Taught physics and chemistry at the *lycée* in Bordeaux, natural history in the Faculty of Science at Poitiers, and geology at Lille. Worked for the Service de la Carte Géologique de France and the Service de la Carte Géolo-

gique de Belgique. Among his several famous discoveries were establishing that the basins of Dinant and Namur had existed since the Devonian; recognizing the continuity of folding in the two distinct geographic massifs of the Boulonnais and the Ardennes; and "revealing the evolution of a great tectonic line along which the earth's crust had contracted in a persistent and periodic manner since the beginning of time."

GOSSET, WILLIAM SEALY (also known as **"Student"**) (*b. Canterbury, England, 1876; d. Beaconsfield, England, 1937*), statistical theory.

Studied at Winchester College and New College, Oxford. Worked for Arthur Guinness and Sons, brewers, in Dublin from 1899 until 1935, when he moved to London to take charge of a new brewery. Guinness sent him to work under Karl Pearson at University College, London, when the firm needed more accurate statistical analysis of a variety of processes (1906). His most notable contribution to statistical theory was published under the pseudonym "Student." What came to be called Student's t-test of statistical hypotheses consists in rejecting a hypothesis if and only if the probability, derived from t, of erroneous rejection is small. The statistic proved basic for statistical analysis of the normal distribution and paved the way for the analysis of variance.

GOULD, AUGUSTUS ADDISON (*b. New Ipswich, N.H., 1805; d. Boston, Mass., 1866*), conchology, medicine.

Received B.A. from Harvard College (1825) and M.D. from Harvard Medical School (1830). Greatest contribution to science in conchology: his "Results of an Examination of the Species of Shells of Massachusetts and Their Geographical Distribution" (1840) and *Report on the Invertebrata of Massachusetts* (1841) gave him an international reputation. Collaborated with Louis Agassiz on *Principles of Zoology* (1848). Wrote major works on shells collected by Couthouy during U.S. Exploring Expedition (1838–42) and by William Stimpson for the North Pacific Exploring Expedition (1853–55). His profession remained medicine, and he encouraged and advised W. T. G. Morton, discoverer of ether, mediating a priority dispute with Charles T. Jackson.

GOULD, BENJAMIN APTHORP (*b. Boston, Mass., 1824; d. Cambridge, Mass., 1896*), astronomy.

Studied at Harvard College under Benjamin Peirce, at Berlin, and at Göttingen under Gauss (doctorate, 1848). Upon return to U.S., vowed to raise the reputation of American astronomy; began by founding the *Astronomical Journal* (1849). As executive officer and later director of Dudley Observatory in Albany (1855–59) devoted much effort to converting the observatory into a worthy scientific institution and traveled to Europe to order equipment. Head of longitude department of U.S. Coast Survey (1852–67); measured longitude difference between Greenwich and Washington over first transatlantic cable. After leaving Albany, set up an observatory near Cambridge, collaborating with Lewis Rutherfurd in application of photography to astrometry (1866). In 1870 founded Argentine National Observatory in Córdoba. Before instruments arrived, he and four assistants, using only binoculars, determined magnitudes and positions of all the naked-eye stars in the southern heavens, establishing "Gould's belt" of bright stars, spread in a broad band inclined at some 20 degrees to the galactic equator. Returned to Cambridge in 1885.

GOULD, JOHN (*b. Lyme Regis, England, 1804; d. London, England, 1881*), ornithology.

As a gardener he had opportunity to observe birds and teach himself taxidermy. Taxidermist for Zoological Society of London (1826–81). In 1830 received a collection of bird skins from the Himalayas, and from them produced a volume of colored illustrations with text by Nicholas Vigors. Issued in all forty-one volumes in elephant folio containing some 3,000 plates, mostly of birds from all over the world. The plates, all lithographed and hand-painted, are among the finest bird pictures ever produced. Most significant work was *The Birds of Australia* (1840–69), plates with a page of description of the species, notes on distribution and adaptation to environment, index of species, and a systematic table. Also made plates for reports on birds collected by expeditions of the *Beagle* and the *Sulphur.*

GOURSAT, ÉDOUARD JEAN-BAPTISTE (*b. Lanzac, Lot, France, 1858; d. Paris, France, 1936*), mathematics.

Greatly influenced by Émile Picard, Claude Bouquet, Charles Briot, Jean Darboux, and Charles Hermite while studying at the École Normale Supérieure (D.Sc., 1881). Taught at the Faculty of Sciences, Toulouse (1881–85); École Normale Supérieure (1885–97); and Paris (1879–81 and 1897–retirement). Also tutored in analysis at the École Polytechnique (1896–1930) and the École Normale Supérieure, St.-Cloud (1900–29). Leading analyst of his day—made original contributions to almost every important area of analysis, notably in *Cours d'analyse mathématique* (1902–05). One of his earliest works removed the redundant requirement of the continuity of the derivative in Augustin Cauchy's integral theorem. The theorem is now known as the Cauchy-Goursat theorem.

GOUY, LOUIS-GEORGES (*b. Vals-les-Bains, Ardèche, France, 1854; d. Vals-les-Bains, 1926*), general physics, optics.

Almost nothing known of his early life and education; spent most of his productive life as professor at the Faculty of Sciences at University of Lyons. A prolific researcher, published dozens of articles on some of the more obscure problems of optics. Important research on velocity of light in dispersive media, propagation of light waves, and diffraction produced by passage of light across the edge of an opaque screen. In other areas of experimental and mathematical physics, he made important studies on inductive powers of dielectrics, on electrocapillarity, on the effects of a magnetic field on electrical discharge in rarefied gases, and spectroscopy.

GRAAF, REGNIER DE (*b. Schoonhoven, Netherlands, 1641; d. Delft, Netherlands, 1673*), medicine, anatomy, physiology.

Studied at Utrecht, Leiden, and Angers (M.D., 1665). Well-known practicing physician in Delft; privately did scientific research. One of the creators of experimental physiology; many editions and translations of his works followed each other in rapid succession. Published on very diverse subjects; devised the method of pancreatic fistula; best known through the term "Graafian follicle," which commemorates his crucial role in the accurate and concrete description of anatomy and physiology of female mammalian reproductive organs. Adopted the name "ovary" for the female mammalian gonad. Bitter quarrel with Jan Swammerdam over priority dispute concerning a new technique of injecting vessels with colored substances. Even today the physiology of the ovary can be illustrated by utilizing his plates without modification.

GRABAU, AMADEUS WILLIAM (*b. Cedarburg, Wis., 1870; d. Peking, China, 1946*), geology, paleontology.

Received B.S. from M.I.T. (1896), and M.S. (1898) and D.Sc. (1900) from Harvard. After a short stay at Rensselaer (1899–1901), taught paleontology at Columbia until 1920, when he moved to China, becoming professor of paleontology at the National University and chief paleontologist of the Geological Survey of China. Principal distinction is his anticipation of several principles of stratigraphy and paleontology that became more generally recognized by later geologists. A pioneer in sedimentary petrology, he proposed a genetic classification of sedimentary rocks that strongly influenced advances in the field. He early emphasized importance of the environment of deposition in determining rock characters and organic assemblages: the field of paleoecology. His polar control theory of the distribution of climatic zones through the geologic record stated that the poles remained stable with respect to the earth's interior, retaining latitudinal climatic zones, but that the outer crust wandered from these poles. He believed that the continents once formed a single continental mass, Pangaea, that had been disrupted through relative movements among its dismembered parts. His pulsation theory attributed the distribution of the principal stratigraphic units to great rhythmic advances and regressions of the seas, which were in turn dependent on restriction and expansion of capacities of ocean basins. He gave scientific life in China a great stimulus, and had an important influence on his many students.

GRAEBE, KARL JAMES PETER (*b. Frankfurt am Main, Germany, 1841; d. Frankfurt, 1927*), chemistry.

Studied at the Technische Hochschule at Karlsruhe, at Marburg with Kolbe, at Heidelberg with Bunsen and Erlenmeyer, and at Berlin with Adolf von Baeyer. Taught at Königsberg, Zurich, and Geneva (the latter, 1878–1906). With the work of F. A. Kekulé as a starting point, he studied compounds related to benzene, particularly the quinones. With Carl Liebermann, discovered and synthesized alizarin, spurring development of the synthetic dye industry. Collaborated with several other chemists in work on other organic dyes and quinone derivatives. Introduced the terms "ortho," "meta," and "para" for disubstituted benzene compounds.

GRAFF, KASIMIR ROMUALD (*b. Prochnowo, Germany [now Próchnowo, Poland], 1878; d. Breitenfurt, near Vienna, Austria, 1950*), astronomy.

Received Ph.D. from Berlin (1901). Employed as astronomer at Urania Observatory in Berlin, and at the observatory in Hamburg and later Bergedorf. Taught at Vienna (1928–38, 1945–48), modernizing the great university observatory. One of the last pioneers in astrophysics who by visual observations promoted photometry and colorimetry, as well as planetary and lunar research.

GRÄFFE, KARL HEINRICH (*b. Brunswick, Germany, 1799; d. Zurich, Switzerland, 1873*), mathematics.

Graduated from Göttingen (1825). Taught at the Technische Institut and Oberen Industrieschule in Zurich; appointed to University of Zurich in 1860. His name remains attached to a method for the numerical solution of algebraic equations; it may be extended to equations with equal roots and with complex roots.

GRAHAM, GEORGE (*b. near Rigg, Cumberland, England, ca. 1674; d. London, England, 1751*), scientific instrumentation.

Trained as clockmaker; employed by a leading clock, watch, and instrument maker, Thomas Tompion, later taking over the business (1713). With Tompion he made the original machine (later named an orrery) to demonstrate the motions of heavenly bodies by means of geared models. Devised a mercury-compensated pendulum and invented the deadbeat escapement. Among the many precision instruments he made were an improved eight-foot quadrant for Halley at Greenwich, an improved twenty-four-and-one-quarter-foot zenith sector for Molyneux at Kew, and a twelve-and-a-half-foot zenith sector for James Bradley. Most important contributions were kinematic designs, among them more accurate graduations and micrometer screws for precise subdivisions, including a micrometer eyepiece.

GRAHAM, THOMAS (*b. Glasgow, Scotland, 1805; d. London, England, 1869*), chemistry, physics.

Received M.A. from Glasgow (1826), interest in chemistry stimulated by Thomas Thomson. Taught at Anderson's College (later Royal College of Science and Technology) (1830–36) and at University College, London (later University of London) (1837–54), then succeeding Sir John Herschel as master of the mint. Founder of colloid chemistry. Graham's law, first published in 1829, states that the rate of diffusion of a gas is inversely proportional to the square root of the density of that gas. Major contribution to inorganic chemistry, "Researches on the Arseniates, Phosphates, and Modifications of Phosphoric Acid" elucidates the differences between the three phosphoric acids. Discovery of polybasicity of these acids provided Justus Liebig with a clue to the modern concept of polybasic acids. In laying the foundations for colloid chemistry, "On the Diffusion of Liquids" showed that the rate of diffusion of liquids was approximately proportional to the concentration of the original solution. Developed a "dialyzer," which he used to separate colloids, which dialyzed slowly, from crystalloids, which dialyzed rapidly.

GRAM, HANS CHRISTIAN JOACHIM (*b. Copenhagen, Denmark, 1853; d. Copenhagen, 1938*), biology, medicine.

Received B.A. from Copenhagen Metropolitan School (1871) and M.D. from University of Copenhagen (1878), defended a doctoral thesis on the size of human erythrocytes at Copenhagen in 1883. From 1883 to 1885 traveled in Europe, studying pharmacology and bacteri-

ology; in 1884, while working with Friedländer in Berlin, published his famous microbiological staining method. Experimented with staining pneumococcal bacteria by modifying Ehrlich's alkaline aniline solutions. Gram stained his preparations with aniline gentian violet, adding Lugol's solution for from one to three minutes. When he removed the nonspecific attributed stain with absolute alcohol, certain bacteria retained the color (gram-positive), while other species bleached (gram-negative). Taught at University of Copenhagen (1891–1923), in addition to a large medical practice.

GRAMME, ZÉNOBE-THÉOPHILE (*b. Jehay-Bodegnée, Belgium, 1826; d. Bois-Colombes, near Paris, France, 1901*), technology.

Worked as a model maker in a Paris firm manufacturing electrical apparatus. In 1869 built a successful direct-current dynamo, drawing on the work of Pacinotti and other earlier physicists who had theorized autoexcitation in revolving machines. Used in metallurgy as well as production of electric light, the dynamo depended upon a ring winding to hold the conductors in place on the surface of the revolving armature. Accomplished long-distance transmission of direct-current electricity. With Hippolyte Fontaine opened a factory (1871)—the Société des Machines Magnéto-Électriques Gramme—which manufactured the Gramme ring, Gramme armature, and Gramme dynamo, among other things.

GRAMONT, ANTOINE ALFRED ARNAUD XAVIER LOUIS DE (*b. Paris, France, 1861; d. Savennières, Maine-et-Loire, France, 1923*), physics, mineralogy.

First studies in organic synthesis were followed by artificial production of several minerals, including boracite and datholite. Investigated, with Georges Friedel, the pyroelectricity of scolecite. Contributed new methods to spectroscopy. Wrote a major work on spectroscopy with P. E. L. de Boisbaudran.

GRAND'EURY, CYRILLE (*b. Houdreville, Meurthe-et-Moselle, France, 1839; d. Malzéville, near Nancy, France, 1917*), paleobotany.

Studied at the École Loritz in Nancy and the École des Mines at St.-Étienne. Worked for several years as an engineer at Roche-la-Molière mines, then accepted a post as *répétiteur* and later professor of trigonometry at the École des Mines at St.-Étienne (1863–99). Traveled for ten years in northern Europe, Upper Silesia, and the Urals; resulting in works on paleobotanical stratigraphy, reconstruction of Paleozoic plants, their ecology, and deposition and formation of coal beds, particularly of the Loire and Gard basins.

GRANDI, GUIDO (*b. Cremona, Italy, 1671; d. Pisa, Italy, 1742*), mathematics.

While teaching mathematics at a monastery in Florence, his study of Newton's *Principia* led to discovery of new properties of the cissoid and the conchoid. Taught at University of Pisa from 1700, leaving voluminous scientific correspondence. As collaborator in the first Florentine edition of the works of Galileo, Grandi gave the first definition of a curve he called the *versiera*. His reputation rests especially on the curves he named "rodonea" and "clelia," arrived at while attempting to define geometrically the curves that have the shape of flowers, in particular the multi-leaved roses. Introduced Leibnizian calculus into Italy.

GRANGER, WALTER WILLIS (*b. Middletown Springs, Vt., 1872; d. Lusk, Wyo., 1941*), paleontology.

Began a lifelong career at American Museum of Natural History in 1890, after only two years of high school, eventually advancing to curator of fossil mammals. Spent summers in the field—western U.S., Egypt, China, central Asia, Gobi Desert of Mongolia—leading to many published works on vertebrate paleontology. Important studies of primitive fossil horses, the early Tertiary geology of the Rocky Mountains, systematics of Eocene mammals, and vertebrate fossils from Mongolia and China. Wrote popular accounts of the Gobi exploration.

GRASHOF, FRANZ (*b. Düsseldorf, Germany, 1826; d. Karlsruhe, Germany, 1893*), applied mechanics, thermodynamics, machine design.

Studied and taught at the Gewerbe-Institut in Berlin; director of Office of Weights and Measures. Founding member (1856), editor, and long-time director of the Verein Deutscher Ingenieure (VDI). Later taught at the Polytechnikum in Karlsruhe. Authority on mechanical engineering in its broadest sense. Influenced a generation of engineers by bringing mathematical and scientific considerations to the burgeoning problems of the steam-engine age. Was first to present fundamental equations of theory of elasticity, in a text on strength of materials. Name perpetuated in the dimensionless Grashof number of heat transfer in free-convection flow systems for the transition from laminar to turbulent flow, and the Grashof criterion used in kinematics for establishing whether one link of a four-bar chain can rotate completely.

GRASSI, GIOVANNI BATTISTA (*b. Rovellasca, Italy, 1854; d. Rome, Italy, 1925*), entomology, parasitology.

Graduated from Pavia (1878); in Heidelberg, worked with Bütschli and Gegenbaur. Taught at Catania (1883–95) and Rome University (1895–1925). His scientific production was enormous; remembered essentially for studies in parasitology and practical and applied entomology. In study of malarial parasites, he discovered that the agent transmitting malaria to man is the female *Anopheles* mosquito; Ronald Ross claimed priority and received the 1902 Nobel Prize. Launched a great antimalaria campaign, emphasizing human protection through window screens, prophylaxis with quinine, and destruction of *Anopheles* with *Gambusia*, which devours its larvae. In another field of research, he studied phylloxera of grapes, leading to a precise and monumental analysis of morphology and biology of Italian and other European genera and making it possible to begin the fight against this agricultural pest.

GRASSMANN, HERMANN GÜNTHER (*b. Stettin, Pomerania [now Szczecin, Poland], 1809; d. Stettin, 1877*), mathematics.

Grassmann came from a family of scholars. He received his earliest instruction from his mother and at a private school before attending the Stettin Gymnasium. In 1831, at Berlin, he took the examination for teaching at the Gymnasium level. In 1839 he passed the examination in Stettin and the following year at Berlin that fully qualified him to teach all grades of secondary school. By 1840 he had decided to concentrate entirely on mathematical research.

At first, however, Grassmann devoted considerable effort to teaching in Stettin. He wrote several brief textbooks for use in secondary school. They included *Grundriss der deutschen Sprachlehre* (1842) and *Leitfaden für den ersten Unterricht in der lateinischen Sprache* (1842).

In the fall of 1843, Grassmann had completed the manuscript of the first volume of his chief work, *Die lineale Ausdehnungslehre*, which appeared the following year as *Die Wissenschaft der extensiven Grösse oder die Ausdehnungslehre*. The *Ausdehnungslehre* concerns geometric analysis, a border region between analytic geometry, which uses only the algebra of coordinates and equations, and synthetic geometry, which dispenses with all algebraic aids. The book was totally disregarded by the experts.

As an application of the *Ausdehnungslehre*, which is based on the general concept of connectivity, Grassmann published *Neue Theorie der Elektrodynamik* (1845), in which he replaced Ampere's fundamental law for the reciprocal effect of two infinitely small current elements with a law requiring less arbitrary assumptions.

In 1847 the Fürstlich Jablonowsky'sche Gesellschaft der Wissenschaften in Leipzig published his *Geometrische Analyse*.

Soon after the political unrest of 1848–49 had subsided, Grassmann began to study comparative linguistics and developed a theory of the physical nature of speech sounds (1854).

In "Zur Theorie der Farbenmischung" (1853) he opposed certain conclusions that Helmholtz had drawn from experiments on the mixing of colors.

Around the middle of 1854 Grassmann resumed work on the *Ausdehnungslehre*. Rather than writing a second volume of the work, as he had originally intended, Grassmann decided to rework the text. *Die Ausdehnungslehre. Vollständig und in strenger Form bearbeitet* was published at Berlin in 1862. The new version fared no better than the first.

Disappointed by his continued lack of success, Grassmann gradually turned away from mathematics and concentrated on linguistic research. Works on phonetics that were based on the historical study of language (1860, 1862) were followed by the important "Über die Aspiranten und ihr gleichzeitiges Vorhandensein im An- und Auslaute der Wurzeln" (1863), in which he formulated the law of aspirates that is named for him.

Linguistic research of a different kind forms the basis of *Deutsche Pflanzennamen* (1870). The goal of the work was to introduce German names for all plants grown in the German-language area.

An achievement of a much higher order is represented by Grassmann's work on the Sanskrit language. In 1860 he began an intensive study of the hymns of the *Rig-Veda*. His complete glossary of the *Rig-Veda* was modeled on the Biblical concordances, and the entry for each word indicates the grammatical form in which it appears. Although criticized on points of detail, the six-part *Wörterbuch zum Rigveda* (1873–75) was generally praised by specialists. His translation of the hymns appeared in two parts as *Rig-Veda. Übersetzt und mit kritischen Anmerkungen versehen* (1876–77). Unlike his mathematical works,

Grassmann's linguistic research was immediately well received by scholars.

In 1877 he prepared another edition of the *Ausdehnungslehre* of 1844 for publication; it appeared posthumously in 1878.

GRATIOLET, LOUIS PIERRE (*b. Ste. Foy-la-Grande, Gironde, France, 1815; d. Paris, France, 1865*), anatomy, anthropology.

Trained in medicine, turned to the science of anatomy under influence of Henri de Blainville at the Muséum d'Histoire Naturelle in Paris, where he worked as laboratory assistant to Blainville and later taught and was placed in charge of anatomical studies. Taught at the Faculty of Science, Paris (1862–65). Excelled as descriptive anatomist of the vascular and nervous systems, with emphasis on the brain and cranium. Believed that human intelligence was a function of cerebral convolutions, and that the Caucasian race might be superior due to fact that the frontal sutures of the developing cranium in whites closed later than those of other races. Founding member of the Société d'Anthropologie of Paris.

GRAUNT, JOHN (*b. London, England, 1620; d. London, 1674*), statistics, demography.

Although he had no formal mathematical training, his book, *Natural and Political Observations Mentioned in a Following Index, and Made Upon the Bills of Mortality* (1662), was the foundation of both statistics and demography. Received encouragement and assistance in the undertaking from William Petty. Listed kinds of knowledge to be gained from analyzing vital statistics, discussed the various kinds of defects in his data, and set forth statistical regularities evident from inspecting the data. Deduced various characteristics of populations, and introduced the use of statistical sampling.

GRAVE, DMITRY ALEKSANDROVICH (*b. Kirillov, Novgorod province, Russia, 1863; d. Kiev, U.S.S.R., 1939*), mathematics.

Educated at St. Petersburg University (master's, 1889; doctorate, 1896). Taught at Kharkov (1899–1902) and Kiev (from 1902). Mathematical researches connected with Chebyshev's school and were especially influenced by Korkin. Contributed to three-body problem and map projection research. Created a prominent school in algebra and number theory, and wrote a comprehensive study on algebraic calculus.

'sGRAVESANDE, WILLEM JACOB (*b. 'sHertogenbosch, Netherlands, 1688; d. Leiden, Netherlands, 1742*), physics, mathematics, philosophy.

Educated at home by a tutor who encouraged his natural mathematical gifts, and at Leiden University (1704–07). While practicing law at the Hague, collaborated in founding of the *Journal littéraire de la Haye* (1713), Was the earliest influential exponent of Newtonian philosophy in continental Europe; his association with English Newtonian philosophers began while he was on diplomatic mission to England. Began teaching at Leiden in 1717; by 1734 he and Boerhaave were established as the twin luminaries of Leiden, attracting hundreds of foreign students each year. Modeled lectures on Newton's *Principia* and *Opticks*, with influence from Boerhaave, Keill, and

Desaguliers. His *Physices elementa mathematica, experimentis confirmata. Sive, introductio ad philosophiam Newtonianam* (1720, 1721) was the most influential book of its kind. Also published texts for teaching mathematics and philosophy (1727, 1736).

GRAY, ASA (*b. Sauquoit, N.Y., 1810; d. Cambridge, Mass., 1888*), botany.

Obtained a medical degree, but turned his hobby of botany into a career, becoming the leading botanical taxonomist in America in the nineteenth century. Taught at University of Michigan (1838–39) and Harvard University (1842–73), leaving Harvard a permanent center of botanical study in the Botanic Garden and the Gray Herbarium. Collaborated with John Torrey on *Flora of North America*, which accomplished the shift from Linnaean classification, still prevalent in America in the 1830's, to a natural system modeled after A. L. de Jussieu and A. P. de Candolle, but also established the practice of thoroughly basing the taxonomy of American plants on the type specimens. Also devoted much of their time to elaborating in reports the plants of collections sent in from various American expeditions. His *Manual of the Botany of the Northern United States* is still used. Correspondence with Charles Darwin led to agreement with his theory of origin of species by natural selection even before publication of *Origin of Species*. Gray became a leading voice in Darwin's defense, although Darwin rejected Gray's assertion that natural selection had not damaged the argument from design in nature.

GRAY, HENRY (*b. London[?], England, 1825/27; d. London, 1861*), anatomy, physiology.

Studied and spent his medical career at St. George's Hospital. Published important papers on development of the retina and of the ductless glands. His *Anatomy, Descriptive and Surgical* (1858) became an institution in its own right, due not only to its logical arrangement of material, but also to its illustrations and the introduction of remarks on surgical anatomy.

GRAY, STEPHEN (*b. Canterbury, England, 1666; d. London, England, 1736*), electricity.

Worked as a dyer; perhaps self-taught in science, but may have studied in London or perhaps in Greenwich under John Flamsteed, explaining his command of optics and astronomy. Early work included a water droplet microscope and accurate, quantitative observations of eclipses, sunspots, and the revolutions of Jupiter's satellites. In 1719 became a "gentleman pensioner" at Sutton's Hospital (London Charterhouse). Performed many electrical experiments which led to the discovery of conduction. In attempting to transmit electricity, substituting brass wire for silk, he stumbled upon the fundamental qualitative distinction between insulators and conductors. He and his associates then enjoyed a monopoly in the study of communicated electricity, identifying substances which might serve as supporters (insulators) or receivers, and mapping the course of transmitted electricity.

GREEN, GEORGE (*b. Nottingham, England, 1793; d. Sneinton, near Nottingham, 1841*), mathematics, natural philosophy.

Self-taught in mathematics, eventually receiving B.A. from Caius College, Cambridge (1837). Among his works, the most important, *An Essay on the Application of Mathematical Analysis to the Theories of Electricity and Magnetism* (1828), developed the general mathematical theory of potential. Through William Thomson and Maxwell, this theory would lead to mathematical theories of electricity underlying twentieth-century industry. Green coined the term "potential" to denote results obtained by adding masses of all the particles of a system, each divided by its distance from a given point. The formula connecting surface and volume integrals, now known as Green's theorem, was introduced, as was "Green's function," the concept now extensively used in the solution of partial differential equations.

GREEN, JACOB (*b. Philadelphia, Pa., 1790; d. Philadelphia, 1841*), chemistry, biology, botany, dissemination of knowledge.

Received B.A. (1807) from University of Pennsylvania; studied medicine, law, and theology. Taught chemistry, experimental philosophy, and natural history at Princeton (1818–22) and chemistry at Jefferson Medical College (1825–41), having been a founder of the latter (1825). Published works in several fields: chemistry, astronomy, botany, electricity.

GREENOUGH, GEORGE BELLAS (*b. London, England, 1778; d. Naples, Italy, 1855*), geology.

Studied at Cambridge and Göttingen. A founder and first president of the Geological Society of London. Prepared geological maps of England, Wales, and India; in 1819 published *A Critical Examination of the First Principles of Geology; in a Series of Essays*.

GREENWOOD, ISAAC (*b. Boston, Mass., 1702; d. South Carolina, 1745*), natural philosophy, education.

After graduation from Harvard College, installed in 1727 as first Hollis professor of mathematics and natural and experimental philosophy. His contribution to science in America lay in strengthening and modernizing the science program at Harvard College, and in inspiring many students, including John Winthrop.

GREGORY, DAVID (*b. Aberdeen, Scotland, 1659; d. Maidenhead, Berkshire, England, 1708*), mathematics, astronomy, optics.

Received M.A. from Edinburgh University (1683); taught at Edinburgh (1683–91) and Oxford (from 1691). Sought in his lectures on elementary optics, astronomy, and mechanics to impart to his students basic insights into the "new" science of Descartes, John Wallis, and Newton. Published some 400 manuscripts and memoranda on mathematical, physical, and astronomical topics; no definitive assessment of his scientific achievement is possible until detailed examination of these is made. His true role in development of seventeenth-century science is not that of original innovator, but that of custodian of certain precious papers and verbal communications passed to him by his uncle (James Gregory, 1638–75) and, as privileged information, by Newton.

GREGORY, DUNCAN FARQUHARSON (*b. Edinburgh, Scotland, 1813; d. Edinburgh, 1844*), mathematics.

Studied at Geneva and Edinburgh; received M.A. from Trinity College, Cambridge (1841), where he remained as lecturer and tutor and later fellow. A founder and first editor of the *Cambridge Mathematical Journal* (1838). Major contribution to mathematics was his theory of algebra: in papers on differential and difference equations, he used a method that came to be known as the calculus of operations. He did not live long enough to create a large-scale abstract algebra to illustrate his view.

GREGORY, FREDERICK GUGENHEIM (*b. London, England, 1893; d. London, 1961*), plant physiology.

Graduated from Royal College of Science (1915). His scientific career was spent in association with the Imperial College of Science and Technology, a constituent college of the University of London. His work extended over an enormous range of topics. A few of his chief contributions were: 1) development of new methods of growth analysis and introduction of the term "net assimilation rate" to denote average photosynthetic efficiency of leaves; 2) vernalization of "winter" rye to a "spring" rye; 3) determination of physiological causes underlying crop growth; 4) invention of the resistance porometer and diffusion porometer; 5) increase in the knowledge of factors affecting cotton production.

GREGORY (more correctly **GREGORIE**), **JAMES** (*b. Drumoak, near Aberdeen, Scotland, 1638; d. Edinburgh, Scotland, 1675*), mathematics, optics, astronomy.

Gregory received his early education from his mother. He was later sent to Aberdeen, first to grammar school and later to Marischal College. After graduating there, he devoted himself to studies in mathematical optics and astronomy.

In 1662 he traveled to London, there publishing *Optica promota* (1663). To improve his scientific knowledge, Gregory went to Italy, studying geometry, mechanics, and astronomy under Evangelista Torricelli's pupil Stefano degli Angeli at Padua (1664–67) and publishing *Vera circuli et hyperbolae quadratura* (1667) and *Geometriae pars universalis* (1668). He returned to London and was elected to the Royal Society. Soon after, he made Huygens' attack upon the originality and validity of his *Vera quadratura* and also the publication of Nicolaus Mercator's *Logarithmotechnia* an opportunity for publishing in riposte certain newly composed *Exercitationes geometricae* of his own. In late 1668 he was nominated to the new chair of mathematics at St. Andrews in Scotland, and in 1674 accepted the newly endowed professorship of mathematics at Edinburgh, but died within a year after the appointment.

GREGORY, OLINTHUS GILBERT (*b. Yaxley, England, 1774; d. Woolwich, England, 1841*), applied mathematics, science education.

One of the self-taught or privately tutored mathematicians who swelled the ranks of British mathematics during the eighteenth and early nineteenth centuries. Taught at Royal Military Academy at Woolwich (1803–38). His *A Treatise of Mechanics* (1806) was one of the most complete works on pure and applied mechanics that had appeared in English, an example of what would now be described as "engineering mechanics." A founder of London University.

GREGORY, WILLIAM (*b. Edinburgh, Scotland, 1803; d. Edinburgh, 1858*), chemistry, biology.

Graduated from Edinburgh (1828). Worked as assistant to several chemists on the Continent, most notably Liebig at Giessen. Taught successively at Anderson College, Glasgow; a Dublin medical school; King's College, Aberdeen (1839–44); and Edinburgh (1844–58). Translated into English many works of Liebig on organic, agricultural, and physiological chemistry. Wrote important works on animal magnetism and on diatoms.

GREN, FRIEDRICH ALBRECHT CARL (*b. Bernburg, Germany, 1760; d. Halle, Germany, 1798*), chemistry, physics.

Educated (M.D., 1786; Ph.D., 1787) and taught at Halle University (1783–98). Made his mark as author of texts, journal editor, and theorist in chemistry and physics. Wrote textbooks on chemistry and pharmacology. Inspired by former teacher and patron Lorenz von Crell, founded the *Journal der Physik* (1790), now called the *Annalen der Physik*. As one of Germany's phlogistonists, was involved in bitter debate with German proponents of Lavoisier's antiphlogistic theory. When Gren and his allies were discredited, his eventual acceptance of the compromise phlogiston theory of Leonhardi and Richter helped prepare the way for the ultimate acceptance of Lavoisier's theory. Also helped prepare the way for penetration of Kant's "dynamic system" into German chemistry and physics.

GRESSLY, AMANZ (*b. Bärschwyl, Switzerland, 1814; d. Bern, Switzerland, 1865*), geology, stratigraphy, paleontology.

Became interested in geology while studying medicine at Strasbourg. During the period of subdivision of major units of the geological column, the theoretical framework of geology required the abandonment of simplistic Wernerian doctrines of simultaneous worldwide depositions of lithologically similar formations—the "onionskin" view of stratigraphy. Gressly made a major contribution to this development by his identification and definition of the concept of facies or "aspects de terrain," in "Observations géologiques sur le Jura Soleurois" (1838). This and his 25,000-specimen fossil collection brought him to the attention of Louis Agassiz, who engaged him as assistant at Neuchâtel. After Agassiz left for America, Gressly worked in engineering geology for the construction of alpine railroads. His work of 1838 establishes him as a pioneer in, if not the founder of, paleogeography.

GREW, NEHEMIAH (*b. Mancetter, Warwickshire, England, 1641; d. London [?], England, 1712*), plant morphology, plant anatomy.

Received B.A. at Cambridge (1661) and M.D. at Leiden. Returned to England and practiced medicine as a means of livelihood at Coventry and later in London. Scientific distinction rests on his outstanding contribution to plant anatomy. *The Anatomy of Plants* (1682) made a tremendous advance in knowledge, partly because Grew started with naked-eye observations and then used the microscope. Primary aim was to discover physiological functions of various tissues. Also made important contributions to plant morphology.

GRIESS, JOHANN PETER (*b. Kirchhosbach, Germany, 1829; d. Bournemouth, England, 1888*), chemistry.

Studied at the Polytechnic in Kassel, at Jena, and at Marburg under A. W. H. Kolbe. Worked as a chemist for the brewers Allsopp and Sons, after return to England (1861–88). Main contribution to chemistry stemmed from discovery of formation of a new type of organic nitrogen compound by the action of nitrous acid on certain amines. Named the compound diazodinitrophenol, the first use of the term "diazo."

GRIFFITH, RICHARD JOHN (*b. Dublin, Ireland, 1784; d. Dublin, 1878*), geology.

Studied chemistry and mineralogy under William Nicholson in London, and chemistry and natural history under Thomas Hope and Robert Jameson in Edinburgh. After his return to Ireland, he succeeded Richard Kirwan as inspector general of the royal mines in Ireland, and was appointed mining engineer to the Royal Dublin Society, later commissioner for general valuation of lands. Greatest contribution was the first geological map of Ireland, a noteworthy feature being his division of Carboniferous Limestone into five different groups. This led him to amass a large collection of fossils from the formation, which he published and followed with a similar work on Silurian fossils of Ireland.

GRIFFITH, WILLIAM (*b. Ham Common, Surrey, England, 1810; d. Malacca, India, 1845*), botany.

Studied at University of London under John Lindley, in Paris under Charles Mirbel, and at Sir Hans Sloane's garden in Chelsea. Served as assistant surgeon for East India Company from 1832 until his death. Traveled extensively in India and neighboring countries, collecting plants; his goal was to write a flora of India including ecology, physiology, morphology, and anatomy of the native plants. After his death at age 35, many of Griffith's observations were confirmed by Wilhelm Hofmeister, although his conclusions differed.

GRIGNARD, FRANÇOIS AUGUSTE VICTOR (*b. Cherbourg, France, 1871; d. Lyons, France, 1935*), chemistry.

After completing studies in mathematics at Lyons, he switched to chemistry and received the doctor of physical sciences degree (1901), with his thesis on organomagnesium compounds and their applications in synthesis. Developed the reaction that became one of the most fruitful methods of synthesis in organic chemistry. He treated magnesium turnings in anhydrous ether with methyl iodide at room temperature, preparing what came to be known as the Grignard reagent, which could be used for reaction with a ketone or an aldehyde without first being isolated. Awarded the Nobel Prize for chemistry for this discovery (1912). Taught at Besançon (1905), Nancy (1909–13), and Lyons (1906–08 and 1919–35). In army service (1914–19) worked on toluene production and war gases.

GRIJNS, GERRIT (*b. Leerdam, Netherlands, 1865; d. Utrecht, Netherlands, 1944*), physiology.

Received M.D. from University of Utrecht (1901); studied at Leipzig under Carl Ludwig. Joined Christiaan Eijkman at Batavia, Java, at his small laboratory for pathological anatomy and bacteriology, later becoming director

(1912). Pursued research on cause of beriberi; advanced the idea that a deficiency of "protective substances" was the causative factor and that the absence in food of not only proteins, carbohydrates, fats, and minerals, but also of other substances, could result in disease. This idea of "partial hunger" became the starting point and the basis of the modern theory of vitamins. In 1917 returned to the Netherlands, and in 1921 was appointed professor of animal physiology at State Agricultural University, Wageningen, retiring in 1935.

GRIMALDI, FRANCESCO MARIA (*b. Bologna, Italy, 1618; d. Bologna, 1663*), astronomy, optics.

In 1632 entered Society of Jesus; studied at Novellara, Parma, Ferrara, and Bologna. Taught at Bologna; received doctorate in 1647. Astronomical work done with G. B. Riccioli at Bologna; made important contributions to Riccioli's *Almagestum novum,* namely free fall experiments and devising, building, and operating new observational instruments. Made a particularly accurate selenograph of the moon, probably with a micrometer eyepiece. His primary contribution to positive science was the discovery of optical diffraction. In his experiments, he used bright sunlight introduced into a completely darkened room via a hole about 1/60 inch across. The cone of light thus produced was projected to a white screen at an angle so as to form an elliptical image of the sun on the screen. In his comprehensive treatise on light, he presents opposing views on the substantial nature of light and is concerned to show color to be nothing more than a modification of light. His experiments showed him that a new mode of transmission of light had been discovered and that this mode contradicts the notion of an exclusively rectilinear passage of light. His work had an influence on the work of Hooke and Newton.

GRINNELL, JOSEPH (*b. Indian agency forty miles from Fort Sill [now Oklahoma], 1877; d. Berkeley, Calif., 1939*), zoology.

Received B.A. from Throop Polytechnic Institute (now California Institute of Technology) (1897), and M.A. and Ph.D. from Stanford (1901, 1913). Director of Museum of Vertebrate Zoology at University of California (1908–39); taught at Berkeley after 1913. Contributed extensively to knowledge of distribution and ecology of Californian vertebrates.

GRISEBACH, AUGUST HEINRICH RUDOLF (*b. Hannover, Germany, 1814; d. Göttingen, Germany, 1879*), botany, taxonomy.

Studied at Göttingen and Berlin. Taught at Göttingen (from 1841). Extensive travels in Balkan peninsula, northwestern Asia Minor, the western Alps, Norway, southern France and the Pyrenees, and the Carpathian Mountains led to publications establishing his reputation as a botanical taxonomist and phytogeographer. Coined the modern term "geobotany." His main work, *Die Vegetation der Erde nach ihrer klimatischen Anordnung* (1872), gave a lively picture of the earth's plants emphasizing the effect of climate on the composition and distribution of the flora.

GRISOGONO, FEDERICO, also known as **Federicus De Chrysogonis** (*b. Zadar, Dalmatia, Yugoslavia, 1472; d. Zadar, 1538*), cosmography, astrology.

Received doctorate from Padua (1506 or 1507), then taught astrology and mathematics there for a short time. Returned to Zadar, practicing medicine and making astronomical observations. In medical publications, an aggressive advocate of astrology. Chief contribution to science concerns the theory of tides resulting from combined action of sun and moon. Constructed a mathematical model which predicted high tide quite accurately.

GRODDECK, ALBRECHT VON (*b. Danzig, Germany [now Gdansk, Poland], 1837; d. Clausthal, Germany, 1887*), geology, mineralogy.

Worked in mining industry before studying at Berlin, Breslau, and the mining school at Clausthal; employed at the latter in 1864, eventually becoming director (1867). Presented doctoral thesis to Göttingen in 1867. In 1871 became director of the School of Mines. Cooperated in detailed mapping of the Harz Mountains. In studying the link between lithology and ore geology, made a major step in a direction that was almost entirely lost for 80 years and which has been rediscovered only recently: observational classification of ore deposits, taking into account facts of congruence between the host rock and the deposits.

GROSSETESTE, ROBERT (*b. Suffolk, England, ca. 1168; d. Buckden, Buckinghamshire, England, 1253*), natural philosophy, optics, calendar reform.

Educated at Oxford and possibly Paris. Probably taught at Oxford before appointment as chancellor. Became bishop of Lincoln in 1235. As bishop and ecclesiastical statesman, was governed by three principles: belief in the supreme importance of the cure of souls; belief that the papacy, under God, was the center and source of spiritual life and energy; and belief in the superiority of church over state because salvation of souls was more vital. As a university scholar and teacher, he took a leading part in introducing Greek and Arabic philosophical and scientific writings into university teaching. His commentaries on Aristotle's *Posterior Analytics* and *Physics* were some of the first and most influential of the medieval commentaries on this fundamental work. His important treatises on astronomical subjects expounded elements of both Aristotelian and Ptolemaic theoretical astronomy. His plan for reforming the calendar was threefold: accurate measure of the length of the solar year; calculate the relationship between this and the mean lunar month; and use these results for an accurate reckoning of Easter. He also wrote important treatises on sound, comets, heat, and optics (including lenses and the rainbow, with special attention to refraction, reflection, and color). Roger Bacon took up his work on optics and the calendar. Albertus Magnus first made serious use of his commentary on the *Posterior Analytics,* as did John Duns Scotus of that on the *Physics.*

GROSSMANN, ERNST A. F. W. (*b. Rothenburg, near Bremen, Germany, 1863; d. Munich, Germany, 1933*), astronomy.

Received doctorate at Göttingen (1891). Assistant at Göttingen observatory (1891–96), at Moritz Kuffner's observatory in Vienna (1896–98), at Leipzig observatory (1898–1902), and at Kiel observatory (1902–05). In 1905 became an observer at Munich, retiring in 1928. An important worker with meridian instruments: all of his work is devoted to questions concerning fundamental astrometric measurements.

GROSSMANN, MARCEL (*b. Budapest, Hungary, 1878; d. Zurich, Switzerland, 1936*), mathematics.

Received doctorate from Zurich (1912). Taught geometry in Frauenfeld and Basel; appointed professor of descriptive geometry at the Eidgenössische Technische Hochschule (Zurich) in 1907. Classmate of Einstein. When Einstein sought to formulate mathematically his ideas on general relativity theory, he turned to Grossmann for assistance. They set forth their fundamental discoveries in joint works.

GROTE, AUGUSTUS RADCLIFFE (*b. Aigburth, near Liverpool, England, 1841; d. Hildesheim, Germany, 1903*), entomology.

Authority on taxonomy of Lepidoptera, especially noctuid moths. From about 1860 to 1880 held various positions at Buffalo (N.Y.) Society of Natural Sciences. Greatest contribution was accurate description of vast number of species. Published over 600 papers. Sold valuable collection of Lepidoptera to British Museum in 1884, taking up residence in Bremen and later Hildesheim, where he became honorary curator of Roemer-Museum.

GROTH, PAUL HEINRICH VON (*b. Magdeburg, Germany, 1843; d. Munich, Germany, 1927*), mineralogy, crystallography.

Studied at the Freiberg Mining Academy and Dresden Polytechnical School; received doctorate from Berlin (1868). Taught at University of Berlin and at the mining academy in Berlin (1870–72), at Strasbourg (1872–83), and at Munich (1883–1924). First mineralogical work (1866) dealt with titanite discovered in the Plauenscher Grund, near Dresden, later named grothite by J. D. Dana. A silicate probably related to harstigite was named grothine by F. Zambonini in 1913. His most important contribution was his explanation of connections between chemical composition and crystal structure. His views on morphotropy and isomorphism and on chemical crystallography in general have become firmly embodied in chemical literature. Remarkable advances in knowledge of crystal structure as result of development of X-ray analysis are in large measure due to Groth's long and enthusiastic advocacy of the point system theory of crystal structure. Founded the *Zeitschrift für Kristallographie und Mineralogie* (1877).

GROTTHUSS, THEODOR (CHRISTIAN JOHANN DIETRICH) VON (*b. Leipzig, Germany, 1785; d. Geddutz, near Jelgava, Courland, Russia [now Lithuanian S.S.R.], 1822*), chemistry, physics.

Educated at home, completing his studies in Leipzig, Paris, Naples, Rome, and the École Polytechnique in Paris. After his return from France, conducted scientific experiments and constructed new theories at his mother's estate in Russia. Published more than seventy articles and notes. Discovered experimentally the basic laws of photochemistry, produced original theories on the nature of phosphorescence and color, and attempted to develop a unified electromolecular conception of vari-

ous chemical and physical phenomena (which anticipated certain elements of the modern kinetic-molecular theory).

GROVE, WILLIAM ROBERT (*b. Swansea, Wales, 1811; d. London, England, 1896*), electrochemistry, physics.

Educated privately and at Brasenose College, Oxford (B.A., 1832; M.A., 1835). Practiced law, pursued scientific interests simultaneously. Taught experimental philosophy at the London Institution (1841–46). Soon gained a reputation in the comparatively new but rapidly growing science of electrochemistry, particularly with development of the Grove cell, an improved form of voltaic cell with a positive electrode of platinum, later replaced by carbon by Bunsen. Not to be confused with his "gas battery," the earliest fuel cell, with electrodes of platinum immersed in hydrogen and oxygen respectively and an electrolyte of acidulated water. His book, *On the Correlation of Physical Forces* (1846), was an early statement of the principle of the conservation of energy. Knighted 1872.

GRUBB, HOWARD (*b. Dublin, Ireland, 1844; d. Monkstown, Ireland, 1931*), optical engineering.

Studied civil engineering at Trinity College, Dublin; left studies to assist his father (Thomas Grubb, 1800–78) at his factory for manufacture of machine tools and telescopes, taking control of the factory in 1868. Soon established a reputation as a maker of large telescopes of improved design. Constructed seven identical photographic telescopes used in the *Carte du Ciel,* an international photographic survey of the entire heavens. Patented a novel form of optical gunsight and perfected the submarine periscope. Knighted in 1887.

GRUBB, THOMAS (*b. 1800; d. Dublin, Ireland, 1878*), optical engineer.

Self-taught mechanic with a small private observatory and factory for manufacture of machine tools and reflecting telescopes. Greatest achievement was construction of a 48-inch equatorial cassegrainian reflector for Melbourne, Australia. Assisted and succeeded at the factory by his son, Howard (1844–1931).

GRUBENMANN, JOHANN ULRICH (*b. Trogen, Appenzell, Switzerland, 1850; d. Zurich, Switzerland, 1924*), mineralogy, petrography.

Studied at the Swiss Federal Institute of Technology; received Ph.D. from Zurich (1886). Taught at cantonal school of Frauenfeld (1874–88) and at the Mineralogical and Petrographical Institute of the Institute of Technology and the University of Zurich (1888–1920). Founded *Schweizerische mineralogische und petrographische Mitteilungen* (1921), which he edited until his death. Carried out petrographic fieldwork in the volcanic areas of Hegau, Germany, and of Italy, and in the Alps. Published classic treatises on crystalline schists of the eastern Alps (1903, 1904–07). Made important contributions to rock classification and nomenclature, as well as to mineralogy. Founded the Swiss Geotechnical Commission to locate natural raw materials in Switzerland.

GRUBER, MAX VON (*b. Vienna, Austria, 1853; d. Berchtesgaden, Germany, 1927*), hygiene.

Studied at the First Chemical Institute of the University of Vienna, and in Munich and Leipzig. Taught at Vienna (1882–84 and 1887–1902) and at the Institute for Hygiene at the University of Graz, Austria (1884–1887). Director of Institute for Hygiene in Munich (1902–23). While in Vienna, discovered agglutination which gained him international fame. Found that blood serum of animals inoculated with typhoid or cholera bacteria some time before agglutinated these bacteria. The reverse problem of diagnosing typhoid fever by showing evidence of specific agglutinins in the serum of patients was correctly recognized. The serological diagnosis method today is called the Gruber-Widal reaction.

GRUBY, DAVID (*b. Kis-Kér, Hungary [now Bačko Dobro Polje, Yugoslavia], 1810; d. Paris, France, 1898*), microbiology, medical mycology, parasitology.

Graduated from Vienna (1839), where his dissertation included some of his early microscopic observations on pathology of body fluids—demonstrated that every one of the body fluids contained living elements (leukocytes). Settled in Paris to practice medicine (1840); also gave courses in microscopic anatomy and pathology. In 1841 began announcing discoveries of various microscopic fungi that produce skin diseases. Among others he discovered the *Microsporum* that causes a form of tinea (ringworm) in man—also called microsporia or Gruby's disease. In 1843 discovered and named *Trypanosoma* in the blood of the frog. During his life, he was known mainly as an eccentric physician famous for extravagant cures prescribed for his distinguished patients.

GUA DE MALVES, JEAN PAUL DE (*b. near Carcassonne, France, ca. 1712; d. Paris, France, 1786*), mathematics, mineralogy, economics.

Little is known of his life; he gradually acquired a thorough grounding in science. His first publication, a work on analytic geometry aimed at developing a theory of algebraic plane curves of any degree based essentially on algebra, contributed to the rise of the theory of curves in the eighteenth century and partially inspired subsequent works of Euler, Cramer, Dionis du Séjour, and Goudin. Adjoint geometer of Royal Academy of Sciences, and later pensioner in natural history and mineralogy. Taught at the Collège Royal (Collège de France) from 1742 to 1748.

GUCCIA, GIOVANNI BATTISTA (*b. Palermo, Italy, 1855; d. Palermo, 1914*), mathematics.

Studied at Palermo and at Rome, where he was one of Luigi Cremona's best students. Taught at Palermo (1889–1914). His works concern primarily Cremona's plane transformations, classification of linear systems of plane curves, singularities of curves and of algebraic surfaces, and certain geometric loci. His chief merit lies in founding the Circolo Matematico di Palermo (1884) and editing its publications.

GUDDEN, JOHANN BERNHARD ALOYS VON (*b. Cleves, Germany, 1824; d. Lake Starnberg, near Schloss Berg, Germany, 1886*), psychiatry, neuroanatomy.

Studied medicine in Bonn, Halle, and Berlin. Worked at Siegburg asylum (1849–50), Illenau hospital (1851–55), Werneck asylum (1855–68), and mental hospitals in Burghölzli, near Zurich (1869–72) and Munich (from 1872). While in Zurich and Munich, also taught psychiatry at the universities. Contributed significantly to liberating mental patients from treatment by physical force, granting them an unprecedented measure of personal freedom. Major scientific work was in fields of care of the mentally ill, craniology, and cerebral anatomy. Developed the "Gudden method" in cerebral anatomy: by systematically destroying, on one side only, parts of the nervous system and brain in a newborn animal, he was able to induce atrophy of the conducting paths and centers, thus determining the functions of nerve fibers and nuclei.

GUDERMANN, CHRISTOPH (*b. Vienenburg, near Hildesheim, Germany, 1798; d. Münster, Germany, 1852*), mathematics.

Studied in Göttingen. Taught at the Theological and Philosophical Academy in Münster (1832–52). Wrote books on spherical geometry (*Grundriss der analytischen Sphärik*, 1830) and on theory of special functions (*Theorie der Potenzial- oder cyklisch-hyperbolischen Funktionen*, 1833; *Theorie der Modular-Functionen und der Modular-Integrale*, 1844). Introduced a notation for elliptical functions—*sn*, *cn*, and *dn*. His most famous student, Karl Weierstrass, using Gudermann's idea of the development of functions into series and products, formed the principal, mighty, and accurate tool of the theory of functions.

GUENTHER, ADAM WILHELM SIEGMUND (*b. Nuremberg, Germany, 1848; d. Munich, Germany, 1923*), mathematics, geography, meteorology, history of science.

Studied at Erlangen, Heidelberg, Leipzig, Berlin, and Göttingen; received doctorate from Erlangen (1872). Taught at Weissenburg, Bavaria, and Erlangen (1872–74); Munich Polytechnicum (1874–76); the Gymnasium in Ansbach (1876–86); and at the Munich Technische Hochschule (1886–1920). Wrote numerous articles and books on pure mathematics and its history, physics, geophysics, meteorology, geography, and astronomy.

GUERICKE (GERICKE), OTTO VON (*b. Magdeburg, Germany, 1602; d. Hamburg, Germany, 1686*), engineering, physics.

Studied at Leipzig, Helmstedt, Jena, and Leiden. Diplomacy and politics consumed the major part of his life, particularly in Magdeburg; devoted his leisure time to scientific experimentation. As a result of experiments to prove the existence of a vacuum, he invented the air pump—discovering the pumping capacity and the elasticity of air. His work stimulated Huygens and Boyle to repeat and extend his experiments and work on an improved air pump. To support his notion that the heavenly bodies interacted with each other across empty space through magnetic force, he cast a sphere composed of a variety of minerals with a large proportion of sulfur. By rubbing the sphere he produced static electricity; but since he did not recognize these electrical effects as special phenomena, but as demonstrations of the *virtues* of a celestial body, he cannot properly be credited with the invention of the first electrical machine. Also concerned himself with the question of the boundedness of space and number of worlds therein, reasoning that both are unbounded.

GUERTLER, WILLIAM MINOT (*b. Hannover, Germany, 1880; d. Hannover, 1959*), metallography, metallurgy.

Studied at the Technische Hochschule in Hannover, University of Munich, and received his doctorate from Göttingen (1904). Held various teaching and administrative positions: Göttingen (1904–06); Technische Hochschule, Berlin (1906–08, 1909–29); M.I.T. (1908–09, 1911, and as a guest in retirement); Institute for Applied Metallurgy, Berlin (1930–45); Technische Hochschule, Dresden (1936–45); and Technical University in Istanbul (guest in retirement). His lifework concerned pure and applied metallurgy; he considered both theoretical and technological aspects and applied his results to the metal industry. Established many new metallurgical concepts, including segregation and peritectonics. Wrote more than 300 scientific papers and books, was awarded some 100 patents for his methods and devices. Founded journals and societies in the field.

GUETTARD, JEAN-ÉTIENNE (*b. Étampes, Seine-et-Oise, France, 1715; d. Paris, France, 1786*), geology, natural history, botany.

Educated in Étampes, Montargis, and Paris. Worked as assistant to Réaumur in Paris. *Médecin botaniste* to Louis, duc d'Orléans, and his son, Louis-Philippe, with a laboratory at his disposal; devoted himself entirely to scientific research, making many long field trips, corresponding widely, and publishing numerous articles. Discovered the volcanic nature of Auvergne (1751). He was commissioned along with Lavoisier to prepare a geological survey of France. Although unfinished, it was published later by Antoine Monnet as the *Atlas et Description minéralogiques de la France.* His maps featured chemical symbols and the location of rock formations and mineral deposits.

GUIBERT, NICOLAS (*b. St. Nicolas-de-Port, Lorraine, ca. 1547; d. Vaucouleurs, France, ca. 1620*), chemistry.

Received medical degree from University of Perugia; traveled in Italy, France, Germany, and Spain, becoming well known as an alchemist. Practiced medicine in Casteldurante, Italy; later worked as an alchemist for the archbishop of Augsburg. Growing frustration with alchemical pursuits led to vehement criticism of the profession, in *Alchymia ratione et experientia ita demum viriliter impugnata et expugnata* (1603). Branded writings of Ibn-Sīnā, Albertus Magnus, and Thomas Aquinas as spurious, and those of Arnald of Villanova, Roger Bacon, Agrippa, and Paracelsus as quackery and heresy. Controversy with Libavius led to *De interitu alchymiae* (1614), in which he attacked Libavius' position.

GUIDI, GUIDO (also known as **Vidus Vidius**) (*b. Florence, Italy, 1508; d. Pisa, Italy, 1569*), anatomy, surgery.

Practiced medicine in Rome and Florence. In Paris, named royal physician and first professor of medicine at the Collège Royal; in the latter position inaugurated a method of vivisection. From 1548 taught at University of Pisa. He carried out important anatomical investigations, recorded in *Anatomia* (ca. 1560), which has not yet been studied. His name is still attached to the *canalis vidianus* of the sphenoid bone and to the nerve that traverses this canal. Described a new childhood disease (chicken pox) and invented an original method for tracheotomy.

GUIGNARD, JEAN-LOUIS-LÉON (*b. Mont-sous-Vaudrey [Jura], France, 1852; d. Paris, France, 1928*), botany.

Received advanced qualification in pharmacy from the Paris School of Pharmacy and doctorate in natural sciences from the Faculty of Sciences (1882). His outstanding theses on the embryo sac in angiosperms and investigation of the embryogeny in leguminous plants established him as a botanist of considerable ability. Taught at Faculty of Sciences in Lyons (1883–86) and at Paris School of Pharmacy (1887–1927). Most important were contributions to embryology, cytology, fertilization, morphology and development of the seed, and study of reproductive organs in plants. Also did research on sites of specific plant principles, organs of secretion, and bacteriology.

GUILANDINUS. *See* **Wieland, Melchior.**

GUILLAUME, CHARLES ÉDOUARD (*b. Fleurier, Switzerland, 1861; d. Sèvres, France, 1938*), metallurgy, physics.

Studied at the Zurich Polytechnikum. Strongly influenced by Arago's *Éloges académiques.* Worked at the International Bureau of Weights and Measures at Sèvres, near Paris, throughout his career, becoming its director. Participated in preparation of the national meters, marking the origin of modern metrology. Investigation of metal alloys led to discovery of invar, an alloy less expansible than the constituent metals, which immediately found numerous applications, particularly in clockmaking. He also helped solve the problem of compensation in ordinary watches through the discovery of elinvar, an alloy whose elasticity does not vary with temperature. These successes won him the 1920 Nobel Prize in physics.

GUILLET, LÉON ALEXANDRE (*b. Saint Nazaire, France, 1873; d. Paris, France, 1946*), metallurgy.

Received engineering degree at the École Centrale des Arts et Manufactures (1897) and a doctorate in physical sciences from the Faculté des Sciences of Paris (1902). Taught at the Conservatoire National des Arts et Métiers (1906–11) and the École Centrale (from 1911). As director of the laboratory of a large automobile factory, he transformed it into the first department of scientific research in an industrial plant (1905). His scientific work was related almost entirely to the theory of alloys: research on special steels, bronzes, and brasses. Many of his disciples became well-known engineers and scientists.

GUILLIERMOND, MARIE ANTOINE ALEXANDRE (*b. Lyons, France, 1876; d. Lyons, 1945*), botany.

Received doctorate at Lyons (1902). His teaching career was brilliant at Lyons, Paris (1913–35), and the Sorbonne (1935–42). His first works dealt with lower organisms: blue-green algae, bacteria, and especially yeasts. His studies of yeasts form the basis of our scientific knowledge, especially in the field of sexuality. He published *Les levures* (1911) and tables of yeasts in the *Tabulae biologicae.* His second area of work dealt with the morphological constituents of the cytoplasm. He obtained valuable results using only the ultramicroscope, before the electron microscope existed.

302

GUINTER, JOANNES (*b. Andernach, Germany, ca. 1505; d. Strasbourg, France, 1574*), medicine.

Studied at Leipzig and Liège; received M.D. at Paris (1532). Taught anatomy at the Paris Faculty of Medicine (1534–38). In conjunction with his course he published a dissection manual, *Institutiones anatomicae* (1536). A major Greek scholar of his day, he translated the larger part of Galen's writings and those of Paul of Aegina and Alexander of Tralles. His later publications reflected his interest as a practicing physician.

GULDBERG, CATO MAXIMILIAN (*b. Christiania [now Oslo], Norway, 1836; d. Christiania, 1902*), chemistry, physics.

Graduated from the University of Christiania (1859). He taught at the Royal Military College (1863–1902) and at the University of Christiania (from 1869). The names of Guldberg and Waage are linked for their joint discovery of the law of mass action. The combined efforts of the theorist Guldberg and the empiricist Waage led to the first general mathematical and exact formulation of the role of the amounts of reactants in chemical equilibrium systems. Guldberg also made important contributions on general equations of state for gases, liquids, and solids from a kinetic molecular approach; he did important research on the thermodynamics of solution and of dissociation, and discovered and correctly explained cryohydrates.

GULDIN, PAUL (*b. St. Gall, Switzerland, 1577; d. Graz, Austria, 1643*), mathematics.

Studied in Rome and taught mathematics at the Jesuit colleges in Rome and Graz and at the University of Vienna. His main work was *Centrobaryca seu de centro gravitatis trium specierum quantitatis continuae* (1635–41). In the first volume he determined the centers of gravity of plane rectilinear and curvilinear figures and of solids in the Archimedean manner. Volume II contains what is known as Guldin's theorem: "If any plane figure revolve about an external axis in its plane, the volume of the solid so generated is equal to the product of the area of the figure and the distance traveled by the center of gravity of the figure." In Volume III he determined the surface and volume of a cone, cylinder, sphere, and other solids of revolution and their mutual proportions. Volume IV criticized Kepler and Cavalieri for their methods of using indivisibles.

GULLAND, JOHN MASSON (*b. Edinburgh, Scotland, 1898; d. Goswick, England, 1947*), organic chemistry, biochemistry.

Graduated from Edinburgh University (1921). At St. Andrews and Manchester he and Robert Robinson established the structures of an important group of alkaloids including morphine. From 1924 he was at Oxford with W. H. Perkin, Jr., and worked on strychnine and brucine. He is remembered mainly for his work on the chemistry of nucleic acids at the Lister Institute of Preventive Medicine, London (1931–36), and as professor of chemistry at University College, Nottingham (1936–47). He was one of the first to use methods other than those of classical chemistry to study the structure of nucleic acids.

GULLSTRAND, ALLVAR (*b. Landskrona, Sweden, 1862; d. Uppsala, Sweden, 1930*), ophthalmology, geometrical optics.

Studied in Uppsala, Vienna, and Stockholm, receiving his doctorate in 1890. At the University of Uppsala he taught ophthalmology (1894–1913) and did research on physiological and physical optics. He received the 1911 Nobel Prize in physiology or medicine for his investigations of the dioptrics of the eye. His greatest achievements lie in the field of ophthalmological optics, the study of the human eye as an optical system. He invented a slit lamp which, in combination with a microscope, allowed him to locate a foreign body in the eye. In geometrical optics he developed the theory of the fourth-order aberration of a general optical ray, independent of the axis of a rotational symmetry system, and made contributions to the knowledge of umbilic points. He solved difficult mathematical problems simply by developing the necessary quantities in a series around the coordinates of the principal ray.

GUNDISSALINUS, DOMINICUS, also known as **Domingo Gundisalvo** or **Gonsález** (*fl. Toledo, Spain, second half of the twelfth century*), science translation, philosophy of science.

Although archdeacon of Segovia, his intellectual activity centered at Toledo, where a flourishing school of translators introduced a considerable amount of Arabic and Judaic materials to the Latin West. He translated works of Ibn Sīnā, al-Ghazzālī, Ibn Gabirol, al-Fārābī, al-Kindī, and Isaac Israeli. He wrote five philosophical works which drew heavily on his translations as well as on Latin sources. He was the first to provide the Latin West with an introduction to Arabic-Judaic Neoplatonism and the first to blend this tradition with the Latin Christian Neoplatonism of Boethius and Augustine.

GUNTER, EDMUND (*b. Hertfordshire, England, 1581; d. London, England, 1626*), navigation, mathematics.

Graduated from Christ Church, Oxford (B.A., 1603; M.A., 1605). Entered holy orders and received B.D. in 1615. Taught astronomy at Gresham College, London (1619–26). A practical mathematician, he devised instruments which simplified calculations in astronomy, navigation, and surveying. His *Canon triangulorum* (1620) was the first table of common logarithms of sines and tangents. In *De sectore et radio* (1623) he gave an account of his sector, which was used by the British navy for two centuries and was a precursor of the slide rule. Gunter's chain, used in surveying, is sixty-six feet long and divided into 100 equal links, thus allowing decimal measurement of acreage.

GÜNTHER, JOHANN. *See* **Guinter, Joannes.**

GURVICH, ALEKSANDR GAVRILOVICH (*b. Poltava, Russia, 1874; d. Moscow, U.S.S.R., 1954*), biology.

Graduated from the Faculty of Medicine of the University of Munich (1897). Taught in St. Petersburg and at the Universities of Simferopol (Crimea) and Moscow. Head of experimental biology at the Institute of Experimental Medicine in Leningrad (1930–42) and at the All-Union Institute of Experimental Medicine (1942–48). His early researches on morphogenesis allowed him to establish that the arrangement of morphological structures is governed by the character of the vector field. This became known as the theory of the biological field. His study of the causes of cell division led to his discovery of the resolving factor of mitosis, and paved the way for further developments in molecular biology.

GUTBIER, FELIX ALEXANDER (*b. Leipzig, Germany, 1876; d. Jena, Germany, 1926*), chemistry.

Received a doctorate at Erlangen under Otto Fischer (1899). Held various academic and administrative positions at Erlangen, the Technische Hochschule in Stuttgart, and Jena. His publications treat many branches of inorganic chemistry. Beginning with the colloids of tellurium, he went on to the description of the metallic colloids silver, gold, platinum and the platinum metals, and of other colloidal elements. He obtained a wealth of results in the chemistry of coordination complexes. He worked out quantitative determinations and methods of separation for tellurium, palladium, and selenium. He also succeeded in the difficult field of atomic weight determination. He invented the high-speed dialyzer.

GUTENBERG, BENO (*b. Darmstadt, Germany, 1889; d. Pasadena, Calif., 1960*), seismology.

Studied seismology under Emil Wiechert at Göttingen (Ph.D., 1911). Assistant at International Seismological Association in Strasbourg (1911–18); taught at University of Frankfurt-am-Main (1918–30) and California Institute of Technology (1930–58). In seismology he considered most of the presently known sources for microseismic disturbances. He computed the travel times of waves that would be affected by a low-velocity core of the earth, searched seismograms for them, demonstrated the existence of the core and measured its depth to an accuracy that still stands. With Charles F. Richter, he derived improved travel-time curves for earthquakes. He derived improved methods of epicenter and depth determinations, extended Richter's magnitude scale to deep-focus shocks, and, with Richter, determined the quantitative relations between magnitude, energy, intensity, and acceleration. His most outstanding works are "On Seismic Waves" (1934–39), *Internal Constitution of the Earth* (1939), and *Seismicity of the Earth* (1941).

GUY DE CHAULIAC. *See* **Chauliac, Guy de.**

GUYE, CHARLES-EUGÈNE (*b. St. Christophe, Switzerland, 1866; d. Geneva, Switzerland, 1942*), physics, electromagnetism, molecular physics.

Received doctorate at Geneva (1889). Taught at Zurich's Polytechnique (1894–1900) and at Geneva (1900–30). He gained recognition for his precise measurements of variation of the mass of electrons as a function of their velocity, and as director of physical laboratories at Geneva. Bolometry, induction coefficients, and analysis of electrical measuring instruments were his specialties. He designed highly accurate instruments for such work. He carried out a series of increasingly elaborate experiments with charged particles moving through electromagnetic fields. As a result, he defended the Lorentzian theory of the electron and Einstein's special theory of relativity.

GUYER, MICHAEL FREDERIC (*b. Plattsburg, Mo., 1874; d. New Braunfels, Tex., 1959*), zoology.

Received Ph.D. at Chicago (1900); taught at Cincinnati (1900–11) and Wisconsin (1911–45). He carried on research on spermatogenesis of pigeons, guinea fowl, chickens, and hybrids between the latter two. Among his best-known works are *Animal Micrology* (1906); *Being Well Born* (1916), which aroused widespread interest in human heredity and its significance as a predisposing factor to crime, disease, and mental deficiency; and *Animal Biology* (1931), a leading zoology textbook. In cytology he was one of the first to determine the chromosome number in human spermatocytes.

GUYONNEAU DE PAMBOUR, F. M. *See* **Pambour, F. M. Guyonneau de.**

GUYOT, ARNOLD HENRI (*b. Boudevilliers, Switzerland, 1807; d. Princeton, N.J., 1884*), geography, glacial geology.

Studied at Neuchâtel, Karlsruhe, and Berlin, receiving doctorate in 1835. At Agassiz's suggestion he spent six weeks in the Alps making a series of fundamental observations on the moraines, the differential flow of glaciers, and the banded structure of the ice. He also did a major study of the distribution of erratic boulders in Switzerland. His results were not published as promised by Agassiz, so he did not receive proper credit. He taught at Neuchâtel (1839–48), Lowell Technological Institute in Boston (1848–54), and Princeton (from 1854). His chief work, *Earth and Man* (1849), represents a far-reaching synthesis in which he visualized a divine law of progress common to Genesis, the evolution of the earth, and the history of humanity. In his honor the term "guyot" is applied to a seamount, generally deeper than 200 meters, whose top is a relatively smooth platform.

GUYTON DE MORVEAU, LOUIS BERNARD (*b. Dijon, France, 1737; d. Paris, France, 1816*), chemistry, aeronautics.

Guyton was entirely self-taught in science, studying initially Baumé and Macquer, and spending most of his scientific career at the Dijon Academy. In *Digressions académiques* (1772) he continued Chardenon's work by proving that every metal invariably gains weight on calcination; his proof was one of the factors that led Lavoisier to investigate combustion and calcination. His lectures in chemistry at Dijon were published as *Élémens de chymie* (1777–78). He became a leading reformer of chemical nomenclature, contributing fourteen articles to the *Encyclopédie méthodique* (1786). He collaborated with Lavoisier, Berthollet, and Fourcroy on *Méthode de nomenclature chimique* (1787). In metallurgical research, he discovered that cast iron, wrought iron, and steel differed only in carbon content. His manufacture of saltpeter at Dijon led to a new analytical method of calculating how much potash was needed to form the maximum quantity of saltpeter free from chloride—one of the earliest applications of volumetric analysis.

In the new field of aeronautics, Guyton tested various gases for balloon flights, eventually using hydrogen on his flights, publishing his research on balloon construction and gas production in *Description de l'aérostate* (1784). He moved to Paris in 1791, where he aided the military during the war with his scientific applications, and taught at the École Polytechnique (1794–1811). He did important research on the disinfection of air (*Traité des moyens de désinfecter l'air*, 1801).

GWYNNE-VAUGHAN, DAVID THOMAS (*b. Llandovery, Wales, 1871; d. Reading, England, 1915*), botany.

Graduated from Christ's College, Cambridge (1893). Worked at the Jodrell Laboratory, Kew, and at Bower's laboratory in Glasgow. Taught at Birkbeck College, London (1907–09), Queen's University of Belfast (1909–14), and University College (1914–15). The following are the results of his research: "The Arrangement of the Vascular Bundles in Certain Nymphaeaceae" (1896), "On a New Case of Polystely in Dicotyledons" (1896), "Observations on the Anatomy of Solenostelic Ferns" (1901–03), and "On the Fossil Osmundaceae" (1907–14).

GYLLENHAAL, LEONHARD (*b. Ribbingsberg, Sweden, 1752; d. Höberg, near Skara, Sweden, 1840*), entomology.

Gyllenhaal was an amateur scientist who became one of Sweden's foremost authorities on Coleoptera. His *Insecta Suecica descripta* (1808–27) is concerned entirely with Coleoptera—conceived on the highest level and executed in the most minute detail. His extensive collection of Coleoptera is now at Uppsala.

HAAK, THEODORE (*b. Neuhausen, near Worms, Germany, 1605; d. London, England, 1690*), learned correspondence, translation.

Studied at Oxford and Cambridge; became an important conveyor of knowledge and information between England and the Continent. As a translator, he undertook the immense task of the *Dutch Bible and Annotations* (1657). His correspondence with Mersenne and John Winthrop stated aspirations that were shared by Samuel Hartlib's Comenian group and by the members of the early Royal Society: natural philosophy is the crucial prerequisite for the successful achievement of Comenian pansophy. He was chiefly active in the promotion and maintenance of correspondence with the learned world abroad, especially in Germany, and acted as intermediary between Hooke and Leibniz.

HAAR, ALFRÉD (*b. Budapest, Hungary, 1885; d. Szeged, Hungary, 1933*), mathematics.

Received Ph.D. (1909) at Göttingen. Taught at Göttingen, the Technical University of Zurich, Klausenburg University, and at Szeged University, where with F. Riesz he founded *Acta scientiarum mathematicarum* (1920). His research in analysis led him to the character theory of commutative groups as a precursor of Pontryagin on duality. His most important contribution to variational calculus (1917–19) features an analogous principle, Haar's lemma, an extension of Paul du Bois-Reymond's to double integrals. His name is most firmly attached to Haar's measure on groups: in 1932 he showed that every locally compact group possesses an invariant measure which assigns positive numbers to all open sets. This theorem is now one of the cornerstones of those areas of mathematics where algebra and topology meet.

HAAS, ARTHUR ERICH (*b. Brünn, Moravia [now Brno, Czechoslovakia], 1884; d. Chicago, Ill., 1941*), physics, history of physics.

Studied at Göttingen and Vienna (doctorate, 1906); taught at Vienna, Leipzig, and the University of Notre Dame. He became the first to apply a quantum formula to the clarification of atomic structure. Haas's quantum rule $E_{pot} = h\nu$ agrees, for the ground state, with the condition later stated by Bohr; thus Haas obtained the correct "Bohr" radius of the hydrogen atom. Influenced by Mach's and Ostwald's interest in the history of science, his numerous books on the subject were widely disseminated and translated into many languages.

HAAS, WANDER JOHANNES DE (*b. Lisse, Netherlands, 1878; d. Bilthoven, Netherlands, 1960*), physics.

Received doctorate (1912) and taught (1924–48) at Leiden University; with W. H. Keesom, he directed the Kamerlingh Onnes Laboratory of Experimental Physics. In Berlin in 1915 he performed an experiment suggested by Einstein, known as the Einstein-de Haas effect: the sudden magnetization of a suspended iron cylinder in a vertical solenoid causes a momentary torque in the cylinder. Other lines of research led to the so-called Van Alphen-de Haas effect on the anomalous behavior of the resistance of a metal crystal in a magnetic field.

HAAST, JOHANN FRANZ JULIUS VON (*b. Bonn, Germany, 1822; d. Christchurch, New Zealand, 1887*), geology.

Studied geology and mineralogy at Bonn. Traveled extensively throughout New Zealand with Ferdinand von Hochstetter's expedition, publishing results of his topographic and geologic survey. As geologist for Canterbury province, he founded the Philosophical Institute of Canterbury (1862), the Canterbury Museum (1870), the Canterbury Collegiate Union (later University of Canterbury), and the Imperial Institute. He was later director of the museum and professor at the university.

ḤABASH AL-ḤĀSIB, AḤMAD IBN ʿABDALLĀH AL-MARWAZĪ (*b. Marw, Turkestan [now Mary, Turkmen S.S.R.]; d. 864–874*), trigonometry, astronomy.

Worked as an astronomer at Baghdad (825–835). The following works are ascribed to him: (1) reworking of the *Sindhind;* (2) the *Mumtaḥan Zīj,* the best known of his works, which relies on Ptolemy and is based on his own observations; (3) the *Shāh Zīj,* the shortest of his *ziyajāt;* (4) the *Damascene Zīj;* (5) the *Maʾ mūnī Zīj* (or *Arabic Zīj*) —this and the *Damascene Zīj* are based on the Hijra calendar rather than on the Yazdigird or Seleucid eras; (6) on the *Rukhāmāt* and Measurements; (7) on the Celestial Spheres; (8) on Astrolabes; (9) on the Oblique and Perpendicular Planes; (10) on the Distances of the Stars.

His important trigonometric contributions included defining the sine and versed sine and compiling a table of tangents. For the solution of problems in spherical astronomy, transformations of coordinates, time measurements, and many other problems, Ḥabash gives standard astronomical tables of functions. His other astronomical work involved theories of the sun, moon, and planets; latitude of the moon and planets; parallax theory; and visibility theory.

HABER, FRITZ (*b. Breslau, Germany [now Wrocław, Poland], 1868; d. Basel, Switzerland, 1934*), chemistry.

Studied at Berlin and Heidelberg; received Ph.D. at the Charlottenburg Technische Hochschule (1891). Assisted Ludwig Knorr at Jena, and taught at the Karlsruhe Technische Hochschule (1896–1912). Director of Kaiser Wilhelm Institute for Physical Chemistry and Electrochemistry at Dahlem (1912–33). His outstanding achievement was the combination of nitrogen and hydrogen to form ammonia. It was through the work of Bosch and others that the process came to be the first successful high-pressure industrial chemical reaction. During World War I he developed the use of chlorine gas as a war weapon and served as chief of the Chemical Warfare Service. He was awarded the Nobel Prize in chemistry in 1919. Under his direction, the Kaiser Wilhelm Institute became a great scientific research center, producing more than 700 publications and many outstanding physical chemists. He served Germany well in his relations with foreigners—his laboratories at Karlsruhe and Dahlem always had foreign students. When the Nazis came to power, he resigned rather than dismiss all of his Jewish workers.

HABERLANDT, GOTTLIEB (*b. Ungarisch-Altenburg, Hungary, 1854; d. Berlin, Germany, 1945*), botany.
Received Ph.D. at Vienna (1876); influenced greatly by works of Sachs and Schwendener. Taught at Vienna, Graz, and at Berlin (1910–23), where he established the Institute for Plant Physiology. His most influential book was *Physiologische Pflanzenanatomie* (1884), which considered plant anatomy from a physiological point of view. Many of his basic ideas have been incorporated into modern biology. In *Eine botanische Tropenreise* (1893) he describes his trip to Java and Ceylon. He wrote a number of other books and numerous papers. He hypothesized the statolith function of certain starch grains, thus exerting a lasting influence on plant physiology.

HACHETTE, JEAN NICOLAS PIERRE (*b. Mézières, Ardennes, France, 1769; d. Paris, France, 1834*), geometry, theory of machines, physics.
The son of a bookseller, Hachette studied at the University of Rheims (1785–87). In 1792 he was professor of hydrography at Collioure and Port Vendres. In 1793 he became professor of mathematics at the École Royale de Génie of Mézières. A fervent revolutionary, Hachette carried out various technological assignments (military applications of balloons, manufacture of weapons, and so on) for the Committee of Safety in 1794. He also took an active part in the creation of the École Polytechnique in 1794. He taught descriptive geometry there until 1816, when the Restoration government forced him out.
Collaborated with Gaspard Monge in writing an exposition of three-dimensional analytic geometry, dealing especially with changes of coordinates and the theory of second-degree surfaces. In pure and descriptive geometry, Hachette developed effective procedures for studying diverse properties of space curves and surfaces by the methods of synthetic geometry joined to perspective and projective geometry. His results heralded the development of projective geometry and modern geometry in the nineteenth century.

HADAMARD, JACQUES (*b. Versailles, France, 1865; d. Paris, France, 1963*), mathematics.

Hadamard received his *docteur ès sciences* in 1892 and taught in numerous institutions, including the École Polytechnique from 1912 to 1937. His interest in pedagogy led to his *Leçons de géométrie élémentaire* (1898, 1901), which are still studied. In 1896 Hadamard solved the ancient and famous problem concerning the distribution of prime numbers. He demonstrated that the function of $\pi(x)$ designating the number of prime numbers less than x is asymptotically equal to $x/\log x$. This is certainly the most important result ever obtained in number theory. In all his works, Hadamard emphasized the importance of "the problem correctly posed." He especially influenced hydrodynamics, mechanics, probability, and even logic.

HADFIELD, ROBERT ABBOTT (*b. Attercliffe, Sheffield, England, 1858; d. Kingston, Surrey, England, 1940*), metallurgy.
After studying at Collegiate School, Sheffield, Hadfield set up a laboratory in his father's steel castings plant. In 1882 he began a study of iron alloys. He developed valuable new steel products, including silicon steel with exceptionally low magnetic hysteresis. After 1888 he headed his father's company and influenced the systematic improvement of steel and steel products. He was created a baronet in 1917.

HADLEY, JOHN (*b. Hertfordshire, England, 1682; d. 1744*), optical instrumentation.
In 1719 Hadley developed the form of reflecting telescope introduced by Newton in 1668. He also produced a reflecting octant, which was the precursor of the modern nautical sextant.

HAECKEL, ERNST HEINRICH PHILIPP AUGUST (*b. Potsdam, Germany, 1834; d. Jena, Germany, 1919*), zoology.
Haeckel earned his medical degree at Berlin in 1857 and taught comparative anatomy and zoology at Jena. After 1865 he headed the Zoological Institute at Jena. He was profoundly influenced by the publication of Darwin's *On the Origin of Species*, whose theories are reflected in all Haeckel's work, including *Generelle Morphologie* (1866), one of the earliest Darwinian treatises. His definition of "ecology" and "chorology" are the generally accepted ones. He led numerous scientific expeditions and catalogued about 4,000 new species of lower marine animals. He published *Systematische Phylogenie* (1894–96).
Haeckel took the side of Lamarck in his belief in the "inheritance of acquired characteristics," which was opposed by the "Neo-Darwinism" of August Weismann. He failed to grasp the importance of Mendel's findings, and he was late in appreciating the importance of *Homo neanderthalensis*.
Haeckel's more popular works—in lectures, essays, and books—had a far greater influence than his scientific ones. His *Die Welträthsel* (1899) states his belief in the "truth of the monistic philosophy." It achieved great success in numerous translations. Haeckel's advocacy of Darwin's ideas contributed to the breakthrough in evolutionary thinking. His scientific importance consists principally in his suggestions that stimulated further work. His lasting contribution lies not in the solutions he proposed but rather in the questions he asked.

HAFFKINE, WALDEMAR MORDECAI WOLFE (*b. Odessa, Russia, 1860; d. Lausanne, Switzerland, 1930*), bacteriology.

Haffkine attended the Gymnasium in Berdyansk and the university of Odessa, a graduating doctor of science in 1884. He was then offered a teaching position at the university on the condition that he convert to the Russian Orthodox Church, which he refused to do. Instead he accepted an appointment as assistant in the Odessa Museum of Zoology, which he held until 1888. While there he became a member of the Society of Naturalists of Odessa. He left Odessa to teach physiology for a year under Moritz Schiff at the University of Geneva. In 1889 Metchnikoff, who was working at the Pasteur Institute, offered him the only position vacant there—that of librarian. Haffkine accepted and in 1890 became assistant to the director of the institute, Emile Roux.

Haffkine took up cholera research during the 1888 epidemic. By early July 1892 he was able to report that his vaccine was safe for human use. Haffkine went to Calcutta in March 1893 and immediately set to work, as cholera struck one village after another reducing the rate of death from cholera by 70 percent.

In 1895 Haffkine contracted malaria and left India for England to try to recover his health. He returned to Calcutta in March 1896; six months later he was reassigned to Bombay, where plague was epidemic. He improvised a laboratory in a corridor of Grant Medical College and began experiments with his antiplague vaccine on laboratory animals. By December, Haffkine was convinced of the efficacy of the vaccine on animals; on 10 January 1897 a doctor agreed to inoculate him in secret and the principal of the college agreed to be a witness. Haffkine developed a high fever and pain at the site of the injection; nevertheless, he attended a meeting of the Indian Medical Service.

In 1902 plague was epidemic in the Punjab and an all-out inoculation campaign was planned. At the end of October, nineteen people, of the tens of thousands inoculated, contracted tetanus and died. All had been inoculated from the same bottle of vaccine; no unusual results were traced to the five other bottles used the same day. The British medical officials publicly accused Haffkine and his laboratory of having sent contaminated vaccine to the Punjab and Haffkine was suspended without pay before proper investigations were even begun. Haffkine was exonerated and began negotiations that took him back to the work in India that he realized was unfinished. The Institut de France awarded him the Prix Briant, its highest honor, in 1909, and the Tata Institue of Science in Bangalore elected him to its Court of Visitors. In 1929 he created the Haffkine Foundation, which still exists, for fostering religious, scientific, and vocational education in Eastern European yeshivas. In 1915 the Plague Research Institute that he founded in Bombay was renamed in his honor and still bears that name.

HAGUE, ARNOLD (*b. Boston, Mass., 1840; d. Washington, D.C., 1917*), geology.

Graduated (Ph.B.) from the Sheffield Scientific School of Yale. His professors included James D. Dana, George J. Brush, and Samuel W. Johnson, and among his fellow students were J. Willard Gibbs, Ellsworth Daggett, Clarence King, and O.C. Marsh.

After graduation Hague went to Germany where he studied with R. W. Bunsen. He then attended the Bergakademie at Freiberg, Saxony. There he met S. F. Emmons and came under the personal guidance of Bernhardt von Cotta.

Hague returned to Boston in 1866 and shortly thereafter visited King who invited him to join the proposed goelogical survey across the western cordilleras. Hague, Emmons, and King accomplished much for geology in their geological exploration of the fortieth parallel (1867–72). Hague became government geologist for Guatemala in 1877, and in the following year went to northern China to study various mines for the Chinese government.

In 1879 the U.S. Geological Survey was established by Congress, and King was made its first director. He was appointed government geologist with Joseph P. Iddings and, later, Charels D. Walcott and W. H. Weed were made assistants. From 1883 to 1889 Hague directed the survey of Yellowstone National Park and vicinity, returning again in 1893 with T. A. Jaggar, Jr., as an assistant.

In collaboration with King and Emmons, Hague made a geological reconnaissance of a 100-mile-wide belt extending from the eastern California border to the Great Plains of Wyoming and Colorado, embracing the line of the first transcontinental railroad. This was the first of the extensive surveys which took note of the petrography of the extrusive rocks. Hague suggested that the name Laramie be used for a great series of sedimentary beds covering hundreds of square miles in the Rocky Mountains and Great Plains. The Laramie formation, which marks the end of the Mesozoic era, gave rise to one of the most prolonged controversies in the Paleontological dating of rocks in the history of American geology. Hague also explored Mount Hood, Oregon, collecting volcanic rocks and studying the glacial phenomena. In addition he mapped the famous silver-lead district of Eureka, Nevada. He was a member of the National Academy of Sciences (1885) and served as its home secretary from 1901–13. He also served as president of the Geological Society of America (1910) and vice-president of the International Geological Congress on three occasions (1900, 1910, 1913).

HAHN, OTTO (*b. Frankfurt am Main, Germany, 1879; d. Göttingen, Germany, 1968*), radiochemistry.

Hahn received his doctorate in organic chemistry from Marburg University in 1901 and became an assistant there to Theodor Zincke. In 1904 he went to England, where he obtained a place in Sir William Ramsay's laboratory at University College, London. While there he discovered by chance a new radioelement: radiothorium. In order to attain greater mastery over radioactivity, he worked under Rutherford briefly at McGill University in Montreal, where he discovered radioactinium. In 1906 he took up a position in Emil Fischer's chemical institute at the University of Berlin. In 1907 he proved his belief in a long-lived radioelement between thorium and radiothorium; he separated it and named it mesothorium. He also began a fruitful thirty-year collaboration with the physicist Lise Meitner. After 1912 he was part of the Kaiser Wilhelm Gesellschaft.

Radiochemistry was transformed into nuclear chemistry in the 1930's, and Hahn was one of its leading scientists. He succeeded in splitting the uranium nucleus in 1938, a process named "fission" by Meitner. Hahn was little concerned with the energy released by fission and played no part in the German atomic bomb project. Instead, he devoted himself to the study of fission fragments. He was arrested by the Allied troops in 1945 and removed to England, where he learned that he had been awarded the 1944 Nobel Prize in chemistry. After the war, he headed the Kaiser Wilhelm Gesellschaft, now renamed the Max Planck Gesellschaft.

HAHNEMANN, CHRISTIAN FRIEDRICH SAMUEL (*b. Meissen, Germany, 1755; d. Paris, France, 1843*), medicine, chemistry.

Hahnemann received his medical degree from the University of Erlangen in 1779. In 1796 he published his first paper setting forth the view that later formed the basis of homeopathy. These ideas were more fully expressed in *Organon der rationellen Heilkunde* (1810) and *Materia medica pura* (1811). He later became a highly successful practitioner of homeopathic medicine, eventually settling in Paris. He is considered the founder of homeopathy, and his followers increased throughout the nineteenth century:

HAIDINGER, WILHELM KARL (*b. Vienna, Austria, 1795; d. Dornbach, near Vienna, 1871*), mineralogy, geology.

In 1812 Haidinger became assistant to Friedrich Mohs at Landesmuseum Joanneum. In 1823 he moved to Edinburgh to work for Thomas Allen, a banker interested in mineralogy. In 1825 he translated Mohs's textbook into English. He did important studies on pseudomorphs and in 1848 he designed an instrument, known as Haidinger's dichroscope, that measured the absorption of light in crystals. A charter member of the Vienna Academy of Sciences, Haidinger sponsored the first geological survey of Austria.

HAKLUYT, RICHARD (*b. London, England, ca. 1552; d. London, 1616*), geography, history.

Hakluyt was the leading advocate and chronicler of English overseas expansion in the reigns of Elizabeth I and James I. A graduate of Christ Church, Oxford, and a clergyman, Hakluyt became a student of the rapidly developing subject of geography. He was an advocate of English colonization in America. His major contribution to knowledge and literature lies in his three great collections: *Divers Voyages Touching the Discoverie of America* (1582); *The Principall Navigations, Voiages and Discoveries of the English Nation* (1589); and an enlarged three-volume edition of the latter book (1598–1600).

HALDANE, JOHN BURDON SANDERSON (*b. Oxford, England, 1892; d. Bhubaneswar, Orissa, India, 1964*), physiology, biochemistry, genetics.

The son of John Scott Haldane, he was educated at Oxford and studied biochemistry under Frederick Hopkins at Cambridge. In 1922 he formulated Haldane's Law, covering the crossing of animal species to produce an offspring of which one sex is absent or sterile. He did important work on the mathematics of natural selection, set forth in his classic *The Causes of Evolution* (1932). After 1933 Haldane occupied the chair of genetics and then of

biometry at University College, London. Here he gave increasing time to human genetics. He also became a member of the Communist party and contributed numerous articles on popular science to the *Daily Worker*. In 1957 he emigrated to India, where he set up a genetics and biometry laboratory. The uniqueness of Haldane's contribution to science lay in his ability to bring about the "cross fertilization of ideas" from among the various scientific disciplines.

HALDANE, JOHN SCOTT (*b. Edinburgh, Scotland, 1860; d. Oxford, England, 1936*), physiology.

In respiratory physiology, Haldane was the prime mover of modern times. The younger brother of Richard Burdon Haldane, he attended the University of Edinburgh, where he received a medical degree in 1884. Shortly thereafter, he began doing research work under his uncle, John Burdon-Sanderson, professor of physiology at Oxford. Oxford was to be his base for the rest of his life. As a result of his inquiries into coal mine disasters, he produced a classic paper on the lethal effects of carbon monoxide. He devised, in principle, the Haldane gas analysis apparatus, and with Joseph Barcroft developed a method for determining blood gas content from small amounts of blood. Later he unraveled the basic enigmas surrounding heatstroke, caisson disease (bends), and the physical effects of high altitude. His *Respiration* (1922) was for many years the standard textbook in respiratory physiology.

HALDANE, RICHARD BURDON (*b. Edinburgh, Scotland, 1856; d. Cloan, Perthshire, Scotland, 1928*), philosophy.

Haldane studied philosophy at the University of Edinburgh and became a lawyer. He entered the House of Commons as a Liberal in 1885 and later served in several Liberal governments. He was, variously, lord chancellor and secretary of war. In 1924 he became lord chancellor in the first Labour government. In philosophy, Haldane was a follower of Hegel, whose views he developed in *The Pathway to Reality* (1903). He sketches the mathematical context of the various theories of relativity and explores the metaphysical connotations of relativity in *The Reign of Relativity* (1921).

HALE, GEORGE ELLERY (*b. Chicago, Ill., 1868; d. Pasadena, Calif., 1938*), astrophysics.

Shortly after graduation from the Massachusetts Institute of Technology, Hale invented (*ca.* 1892) the spectroheliograph, an instrument that photographs solar prominences and other solar phenomena. In 1892 Hale was appointed associate professor of astrophysics at the new University of Chicago, and in 1897 he established the Yerkes Observatory. Later, he established the Mount Wilson and Palomar observatories. Each of the three was in its time the greatest observatory in the world. Hale was the designer and builder of giant telescopes for these observatories, culminating in the 100-inch reflecting telescope, which solved problems that had previously seemed insoluble. He was one of the founders of the American Astronomical Society, and in 1895 he founded the *Astrophysical Journal*, which is still the leading journal in the field. A life-long internationalist, Hale was the leader in the founding of the International Research

Council. Hale was chiefly responsible for the present-day cultural and scientific importance of Pasadena, California. He transformed the small Throop Polytechnic Institute into the California Institute of Technology and was responsible for bringing the Henry E. Huntington Library and Art Gallery to the city. In 1938, ten years after his death, a 200-inch telescope he had designed was set up on Palomar Mountain and named in his honor. In 1969 the Mount Wilson and Palomar observatories were renamed the Hale Observatories. Among Hale's many writings are *The Study of Stellar Evolution* . . . (1908), *Ten Years' Work of a Mountain Observatory* (1915), *The Depths of the Universe* (1924), *Beyond the Milky Way* (1926), and *Magnetic Observations of Sunspots, 1917–1924* (2 volumes, 1938).

HALE, WILLIAM (*b. Colchester, England, 1797; d. London, England, 1870*), rocketry.

Hale was largely self-educated. His first studies concerned hydrodynamics. He patented (1827) a method of propelling vessels by the principle of the Archimedean screw: water was sucked in and expelled, thereby driving the vessel forward by a crude form of jet propulsion. He was widely honored for this invention. In 1844 he patented a rotating rocket. This "rotary" or "stickless" rocket, which applied Newton's third law of motion, greatly advanced the science of rocketry. Among Hale's works are *Treatise on the Comparative Merits of a Rifle, Gun and Rotary Rocket* (1863).

HALES, STEPHEN (*b. Bekesbourne, Kent, England, 1677; d. Teddington, Middlesex, England, 1761*), physiology, public health.

Hales entered Benet College (now Corpus Christi), Cambridge, in 1696. In 1703 he became a fellow of his college and was awarded an M.A. He was ordained in 1709 and became "perpetual curate" or minister at Teddington, a village near Hampton Court. He held this position for the rest of his life, and most of his scientific experiments were carried out in his laboratory at Teddington. Hales's years at Cambridge coincided with the great awakening of interest in science there—Isaac Newton left Cambridge the year that Hales arrived there. Hales was a great admirer of Newton and a close student of his work. John Ray, Richard Bentley, Roger Cotes, and William Whiston were other Cambridge scientists of Hales's years there.

One of Hales's closest colleagues at Cambridge was William Stukeley, in whose laboratory he and Hales performed chemical experiments and dissected frogs and other small animals. It was about this time (1706) that Hales carried out his first blood pressure experiments on dogs. After he assumed his duties at Teddington, however, Hales's scientific experiments lapsed, partly because he was "discouraged by the disagreeableness of anatomical Dissections."

In 1717/18 Hales was elected to the Royal Society, and soon thereafter he began the plant experiments that made him the acknowledged founder of the science of plant physiology and the leading English scientist of his day. His experiments concerning "fixed air"—and the apparatus he devised, the pneumatic trough—laid the foundations of British pneumatic chemistry for the next century.

In 1719 Hales began his experiments to discover the movement of sap in plants, recognizing its analogy to blood pressure in animals. In 1724/25 he submitted his book *Vegetable Staticks* to the Royal Society, where it was read at successive meetings. Hales next turned to completing and publishing his experiments on animal circulation. This was published in 1733 as *Haemastaticks* (published with the Third Edition of *Vegetable Staticks* under the overall title *Statical Essays*). Hales's experiments had convinced him that the force of blood pressure was not sufficient to account for muscular motion. This he attributed to "some more vigorous and active Energy, whose force is regulated by the Nerves." Hales was therefore the first physiologist to suggest, with some evidence, the role of electricity in neuromuscular phenomena.

Hales's experiments with sap movement may have suggested to him the role that transpiration—or, as he called it, perspiration—might play in plant life. He also became aware of the importance of air. He wrote that air is "absolutely necessary for the support of the life and growth of Animals and Vegetables." His chapter "Analysis of Air" was to have momentous consequences for the later development of chemistry. Hales's many experiments produced a wide variety of "airs," in fact, gases. His most famous apparatus, the pneumatic trough, was devised for these experiments. With his trough, Hales was able to collect air from a number of sources and to differentiate them. He also discovered the properties of "elastic" air and "vitiated" air. Experimenting on himself, he found he could rebreathe his own expired air for only a minute. But by fitting the bladder into which he breathed with flannel diaphragms soaked with salt of tartar, he discovered he could rebreathe his air for as long as eight and a half minutes; the salt, in fact, had absorbed much of the carbon dioxide of his expired air.

With the publication of his *Haemastaticks*, Hales's career in pure science came to an end. From 1733 to the end of his life, he devoted himself to applying his scientific knowledge and technical skills to alleviating human problems, both medical and social. He campaigned against the excessive use of alcohol and is credited with helping pass the Gin Act of 1736. He attempted to alleviate the painful afflictions of kidney and bladder stones. He suggested ways of keeping water sweet during sea voyages and explored the obstinate problem of distilling fresh water from sea water. Hales's experiments with air and respiration led to the invention that more than any other contributed to his contemporary fame: the ventilators he contrived to remove fetid air from enclosed spaces. Hales's ventilators were installed in His Majesty's ships, in merchant ships, in slave ships, and in hospitals and prisons. They seem to have markedly reduced mortality rates, and Hales deserves his reputation as a pioneer in the field of public health.

HALL, ASAPH (*b. Goshen, Conn., 1829; d. Goshen, 1907*), astronomy.

Hall studied briefly under Franz Brünnow, director of the University of Michigan Observatory. Determined to become an astronomer despite his poverty, Hall took a low-paying job at the Harvard College Observatory. This led in 1862 to a job as assistant astronomer at the U.S. Naval Observatory. A year later he was given the position of professor of mathematics there. He led various sighting expeditions for the observatory to Siberia, Sicily, Colorado, and Texas (between 1869 and 1882), and the success of these expeditions assured his career as an astronomer. In 1877 he made his great discovery: he identified the two satellites of Mars, which he named Deimos and Phobos. Although primarily known for those discoveries, Hall's contributions to astronomy were far more extended. He became known as the caretaker of the satellites, and in 1884 he showed that the position of the elliptical orbit of Saturn's satellite Hyperion was retrograding by about twenty degrees per year. He was also an assiduous observer of double stars. After retiring from the Naval Observatory (1891), he taught celestial mechanics at Harvard (1898–1903).

HALL, CHARLES MARTIN (*b. Thompson, Ohio, 1863; d. Daytona, Fla., 1914*), commercial chemistry.

Hall graduated from Oberlin College, where he became interested in the problem of inventing a cheap method of producing aluminum from bauxite ore. By 1886 he had perfected the electrolytic method. (In France Paul T. Héroult had developed a similar method concurrently, so the process is known as the Hall-Héroult process.). Hall was one of the founders of the Aluminum Company of America.

HALL, EDWIN HERBERT (*b. Great Falls [now North Gorham], Me., 1855; d. Cambridge, Mass., 1938*), physics.

Hall graduated from Bowdoin in 1875 and entered Johns Hopkins graduate school to study physics under Henry Rowland. In 1879, as a consequence of his dissertation research, he discovered the "Hall effect." He found that a current through a gold conductor in a magnetic field produced an electrical potential perpendicular to both the current and the field. Hall's discovery was recognized as being of prime importance and sparked widespread interest in the area. Hall spent his academic career at Harvard and was particularly noted for his pedagogical aids to the teaching of physics in secondary schools.

HALL, GRANVILLE STANLEY (*b. Ashfield, Mass., 1846; d. Worcester, Mass., 1924*), psychology, education.

Hall attended Williams College (B.A., 1867; M.A., 1870). He also studied at Bonn, Berlin, Heidelberg and Leipzig. After teaching English, modern languages, and philosophy at Antioch and Harvard, Hall completed his Ph.D. at Harvard in physiology. In 1881 he began teaching psychology and pedagogy at Johns Hopkins, where he established the first formal laboratory in psychology in the United States. In 1888 Hall became president of Clark University, but continued his psychological studies, particularly the mental development of children and adolescents. This in turn led to pioneering work in educational methods, particularly as applied to teaching techniques. Hall was a pioneer in the application of psychology to education and saw the profession advance from a scattered handful to a multitude.

HALL, SIR JAMES (*b. Dunglass, East Lothian, Scotland, 1761; d. Edinburgh, Scotland, 1832*), geology, chemistry.

Hall attended Cambridge and the University of Edinburgh. In 1783 he moved to Europe, where he became interested in the great scientists of the period. He became

a convert of the new chemical ideas of Antoine Lavoisier, with whom he became acquainted. In 1786 he returned to Scotland and lived there the rest of his life, taking part in the scientific activities of his day. Hall is remembered chiefly for his geological experiments to prove the theories contained in James Hutton's *Theory of the Earth.* In one important experiment, Hall conceived the idea that igneous rocks, if they had cooled slowly, as seemed probable under natural conditions, would form crystalline rocks rather than a glass. In 1797 he carried out a series of experiments that were sufficiently convincing to scientists of his day.

Between 1798 and 1805 Hall carried out more than 500 experiments, in a classic case of proceeding by trial and error. In most cases, he was forced to design and construct his own apparatus. It was many years before Hall's experiments were repeated successfully, and his results aroused great interest in Europe. He made many other geological experiments and field studies, and is today regarded as one of the founders of experimental geology.

HALL, JAMES, JR. (*b. Hingham, Mass., 1811; d. Bethlehem, N.H., 1898*), paleontology, geology.

Hall was educated in the progressive environment of the newly created Rensselaer Technical Institute at Troy, New York, then under the directorship of Amos Eaton. He received a B.S. in 1832 and an M.A. in 1833. In 1837 Hall assisted Eaton in a geological survey of New York state, and in 1843 he was appointed state paleontologist. Out of this position grew Hall's monumental *Paleontology of New York*, a lifetime work that eventually comprised thirteen volumes. As a collector, Hall was unsurpassed, and part of his collection formed an important part of the collection of the American Museum of Natural History. Hall's long career was marked by controversy and disputes with other scientists. Nevertheless, at his death he was recognized as the foremost invertebrate paleontologist of his day.

HALL, MARSHALL (*b. Basford, near Nottingham, England, 1790; d. Brighton, England, 1857*), physiology, clinical medicine.

Hall received his medical degree from Edinburgh University Medical School in 1812. He practiced medicine at Nottingham from 1816 to 1826. In 1817 he published *On Diagnosis,* then a new topic. After 1826 Hall practiced in London, where he maintained a large practice and did his experimental work. Hall wrote nineteen books and over 150 papers. His importance lies in his studies on the physiology of reflex action, particularly the role of the independent spinal cord system. Hall is also remembered for a method of resuscitating the drowned, known as the Marshall Hall method. In it the subject is placed in the prone position and pressed upon the back, causing an active expiration. Hall was an active campaigner for the abolition of slavery in America and for the improvement of sewerage systems.

HALLER, (VICTOR) ALBRECHT VON (*b. Bern, Switzerland, 1708; d. Bern, 1777*), anatomy, physiology, botany, bibliography.

Haller studied medicine at Tübingen and at Leiden. At age eighteen he received his medical degree. In 1727–28 he studied mathematics at Bern and began the botanical collection that was to form the basis for his massive work on Swiss flora.

In 1736 Haller became professor of anatomy, surgery, and medicine at the new University of Göttingen, where he remained until 1753. Thereafter, he lived mostly in Bern, combining his scientific and literary work with an active public life. His poetry, especially "Die Alpen" of 1732, brought him youthful fame. In his old age, Haller turned to fiction and wrote three philosophical romances: *Usong* (1771), *Alfred* (1773), and *Fabius und Cato* (1774). He also compiled a *Bibliotheca medica* that comprised 50,000 titles (even though it was never completed).

In anatomy Haller did important early work on the cell tissue, which he named *tela cellulosa.* He regarded it as the basis for the tendons, cartilage, ligaments, and bones—as well as the soft tissues and organs—thereby permitting arguments for a general theory of tissues. Haller also did important work on the heart, in which he examined both structure and activity exhaustively. He attributed cardiac activity to muscle irritability. He went on to designate as irritable all the parts of the human or animal body that have external contact. What Haller understood as irritability is identical with the contractibility of muscle fibers. Haller's experiments and conclusions, with all their limitations, can be taken as the basis for modern neurophysiology. His studies of the structure of the blood vessels are similarly pioneering; and he was able to supply the first accurate picture of the structure and function of the diaphragm.

Among his botanical works is the two volume *Bibliotheca botanica* (1771–72). His extensive herbarium is preserved in the Muséum National d'Histoire Naturelle in Paris.

HALLEY, EDMOND (*b. London, England, 1656* [*?*]*; d. Greenwich, England, 1743*), astronomy, geophysics.

Halley showed an early interest in astronomy and took with him to Queen's College, Oxford, a valuable collection of astronomical instruments purchased for him by his father. Upon receiving his M.A. from Oxford, he visited Johannes Hevelius at Danzig. Halley contributed editorial aid to Newton when he was writing *Principia* and paid for its publication. He became an expert on the fortification of seaports and was sent (1702–03) on diplomatic missions to Europe for that purpose by Queen Anne. He published archaeological papers and designed an improved diving bell and helmet. He was an active member of the Royal Society and edited (1685–93) its *Philosophical Transactions.* He was in active and continuous correspondence with most of the leading scientists of his day. He obtained the Savilian chair of geometry at Oxford in 1704. In 1720 he was named astronomer royal and thereafter devoted most of his time to astronomy. Under Halley the Greenwich Observatory became the site of some of the most important astronomical work of the early eighteenth century.

Halley's best-known scientific achievement was a scheme for computing the motion of comets and establishing their periodicity in elliptical orbits. He correctly predicted the return of a bright comet in December 1758, which was fifteen years after his death. The comet appeared a few days later than he had predicted, but it was in the part of the sky he had predicted. The comet's

return on schedule electrified the world, and it was named Halley's Comet in his honor. (It appears every 75 or 76 years, the last time being in 1910.) Halley's cometary views were published in 1705 as *A Synopsis of the Astronomy of Comets.* Halley also made important contributions to astronomy in calculating the distance of the sun, in positional and navigational astronomy, and in general stellar astronomy. His most notable achievement in stellar astronomy was his discovery of stellar motion.

In mathematics he prepared definitive translations of works by Apollonius, Serenus, and Menelaus of Alexandria, in addition to publishing papers on pure mathematics, ranging from higher geometry to computation of logarithms and trigonometric functions. He applied mathematics to calculation of trajectories in gunnery and the computation of focal length of thick lenses. Halley was also a pioneer in social statistics and the founder of scientific geophysics. His most significant geophysical contribution was his theory of terrestrial magnetism (1683, 1692). He was the first to adopt isogonic lines ("Halleyan lines") to connect points of equal magnetic variation as a means of determining longitude at sea.

HALLIER, ERNST HANS (*b. Hamburg, Germany, 1831; d. Dachau, Germany, 1904*), botany, parasitology.

Hallier studied botany and philosophy at the universities of Berlin, Jena, and Göttingen and received his doctorate from Jena in 1858. According to Hallier, fungi were the causative agents of numerous infectious diseases, including cholera, typhoid, measles, smallpox, syphilis, and gonorrhea. Hallier did not succeed in sufficiently isolating those microorganisms, and his work is only of historical interest today. His sole merit is in having been one of the first to maintain that infectious diseases are due to pathogenic microorganisms.

HALLWACHS, WILHELM LUDWIG FRANZ (*b. Darmstadt, Germany, 1859; d. Dresden, Germany, 1922*), physics.

Hallwachs studied at the universities of Berlin and Strasbourg and received his doctorate from the latter in 1883. In 1888 he investigated photoelectric activity and identified the process, known as the photoelectric effect, or the Hallwachs effect, that forms the basis for the photoelectric cell. He became the leading expert in this field, and he summarized his findings in 1914 in the treatise "Die Lichtelektrizität."

HALM, JACOB KARL ERNST (*b. Bingen, Germany, 1866; d. Stellenbosch, Union* [*now Republic*] *of South Africa, 1944*), astronomy.

After studying at the universities of Giessen, Berlin, and Kiel, Halm became the chief assistant at the Royal Observatory in Capetown. There he conducted extensive research on stellar statistics and did intensive work to create good standard sequences to be used for photographic photometry in the southern sky.

HALPHEN, GEORGES-HENRI (*b. Rouen, France, 1844; d. Versailles* [*?*]*, France, 1889*), mathematics.

Halphen entered the École Polytechnique, Paris, in 1862 and was awarded a doctorate in mathematics in 1878. His mathematical reputation rests primarily on his work in analytical geometry. He made a complete classification of all algebraic space curves up to the twentieth degree, the solution to a very difficult problem. His last work was a monumental treatise on elliptical functions. The amount and quality of Halphen's work is impressive, and his eminence in his field is unquestioned.

HALSTED, GEORGE BRUCE (*b. Newark, N.J., 1853; d. New York, N.Y., 1922*), mathematics, education.

Halsted received his B.A. from Princeton in 1875 and his M.A. in 1878. He also attended the Columbia School of Mines and received his Ph.D. from Johns Hopkins in 1879. He taught at numerous universities, most notably the University of Texas (1894–1903), where he held the chair of pure and applied mathematics. Halsted established himself as an internationally known scholar, teacher, and promoter and popularizer of mathematics. He was noted for his translations of and commentaries on historical mathematical works.

HALSTED, WILLIAM STEWART (*b. New York, N.Y., 1852; d. Baltimore, Md., 1922*), surgery.

After graduation from Yale, Halsted entered the College of Physicians and Surgeons (now part of Columbia University) in 1874. He later taught there, but in 1884 he became addicted to cocaine hydrochlorate while experimenting with it as a surgical anesthetic. After overcoming his addiction, he went to Johns Hopkins, where he became surgeon in chief and professor of surgery. He is credited with developing a method of local anesthesia by means of cocaine injections. He was widely regarded as an innovative teacher of medicine, and his system of residency training was widely adopted.

HAMBERG, AXEL (*b. Stockholm, Sweden, 1863; d. Djursholm, Sweden, 1933*), geography, geology.

Hamberg received his doctorate from the University of Stockholm in 1901 and became professor of physical geography and historical geology there. In 1907 he moved to the University of Uppsala, where he remained until he retired in 1928. Hamberg had wide training in chemistry, physics, geology, and geography and was soon attracted to hydrology and glaciology. He conducted several meticulously planned expeditions to examine arctic conditions. Many aspects of modern glaciology can be traced back to his research.

AL-HAMDĀNĪ, ABŪ MUHAMMAD AL-HASAN IBN AHMAD IBN YAʿQŪB, also known as **Ibn al-Hāʾik, Ibn Dhi 'l-Dumayna,** or **Ibn Abī 'l-Dumayna** (*b. Ṣanʿāʾ, Yemen, 893 [?]; d. after 951[?]*), geography, natural science.

Al-Hamdānī is chiefly remembered for two works, *al-Iklīl* ("The Crown") and *Ṣifat Jazīrat al-ʿArab* ("Description of the Arabian peninsula"). The former, which has survived only in parts, is a historical work recounting the history and genealogies of the South Arabian tribes, one of which was the author's own tribe. *Ṣifat Jazīrat al-ʿArab*, a geographical work, is based primarily on the author's own observations, but occasionally he used information from other geographers. The work also includes observations on fruits and vegetables, precious stones and metals, and linguistic matters. The work shows the influence of Greek and Persian learning on Arabian culture.

HAMID IBN KHIDR AL-KHUJANDI. See **al-Khujandi.**

HAMILTON, WILLIAM (*b. Glasgow, Scotland, 1788; d. Edinburgh, Scotland, 1856*), philosophy, logic.

Hamilton received his education at the University of Edinburgh and Balliol College, Oxford. He returned to Edinburgh to practice law, but after a series of important philosophical papers published in the *Edinburgh Review*, in 1836 he was named to the chair of logic and metaphysics at the University of Edinburgh. He remained there until his death. Hamilton was the first of the series of British logicians (which included George Boole, Augustus De Morgan, and John Venn) who radically transformed logic and created the algebra of logic and mathematical logic. Hamilton and De Morgan carried on a long and acrimonious argument over the relative merits of their innovations in logic. Most logicians agree that De Morgan had the best of the argument, but Hamilton's contribution to modern logic is considerable.

HAMILTON, WILLIAM (*b. Scotland, 1730; d. London, England, 1803*), archaeology, geology.

Hamilton is best known for his diplomatic career and also for his wife Emma's notorious affair with Horatio Nelson. Hamilton's scientific reputation rests on his hobbies—the study of volcanism and the collection of antiquities. While serving as envoy to the court of Naples, he made an intensive study of Vesuvius, collecting lavas, ashes, and minerals produced by volcanism. He later extended his studies to include earthquakes. Hamilton's collection of antiquities, especially Greek vases, was famous. Part of it was sold to the British Museum.

HAMILTON, WILLIAM ROWAN (*b. Dublin, Ireland, 1805; d. Dunsink Observatory [near Dublin], 1865*), mathematics, optics, mechanics.

Hamilton was raised and educated from the age of three by his uncle James Hamilton, curate of Trim. William's enthusiasm for mathematics caught fire in 1822, and he began studying furiously. He took the entrance examination for Trinity College in 1823 and came out first in a field of 100 candidates.

In 1827 Hamilton was appointed astronomer royal at Dunsink Observatory and Andrews professor of astronomy at Trinity College. As a practical astronomer Hamilton was a failure, but life at the observatory gave him time for his mathematical and literary pursuits. Hamilton's major contributions were in the algebra of quaternions, optics, and dynamics.

In the "Theory of Systems of Rays" (1827) Hamilton continued the work of his paper "On Caustics" (1824), but he applied the analysis explicitly to geometrical optics and introduced the characteristic function. Only the first of three parts planned for the essay was actually published, but Hamilton continued his analysis in three published supplements between 1830 and 1832. In the "Theory of Systems of Rays," Hamilton considered the rays of light emanating from a point source and being reflected by a curved mirror.

The long third supplement of 1832 was Hamilton's most general treatment of the characteristic function in optics and was essentially a separate treatise. He applied his characteristic function to the study of Fresnel's wave surface and discovered that for the case of biaxial crystals there exist four conoidal cusps on the wave surface. From this discovery he predicted that a single ray incident in the correct direction on a biaxial crystal should be refracted into a cone in the crystal and emerge as a hollow cylinder. He also predicted that if light were focused into a cone incident on the crystal, it would pass through the crystal as a single ray and emerge as a hollow cone.

Hamilton's theoretical prediction of conical refraction and Humphrey Lloyd's verification caused a sensation. Unfortunately it also involved Hamilton in an unpleasant controversy over priority with his colleague James Mac-Cullagh, who had come very close to the discovery in 1830.

Shortly after completion of his third supplement Hamilton undertook to apply his characteristic function to mechanics as well as to light. The analogy was obvious from his first use of the principle of least action. He applied his theory first to celestial mechanics in a paper entitled "On a General Method of Expressing the Paths of Light and of the Planets by the Coefficients of a Characteristic Function" (1833). He subsequently bolstered this rather general account with a more detailed study of the problem of three bodies using the characteristic function. The latter treatise was not published, however, and Hamilton's first general statement of the characteristic function applied to dynamics was his famous paper "On a General Method in Dynamics" (1834), which was followed the next year by a second essay on the same subject.

The major part of the first essay was devoted to methods of approximating the characteristic function in order to apply it to the perturbations of planets and comets.

In the second essay, Hamilton deduced from the principal function the now familiar canonical equations of motion and showed that the same function was equal to the time integral of the Lagrangian between fixed points. The statement that the variation of this integral must be equal to zero is now referred to as Hamilton's principle.

A solution to Hamilton's principal function was very difficult to obtain in most actual cases, and it was K.G.J. Jacobi who found a much more useful form of the same equation. Since the canonical transformation depends on a single function, Jacobi was able to drop the second of Hamilton's two equations, and the problem was reduced to the solution of the single partial differential equation which is usually referred to as the Hamilton-Jacobi equation.

Hamilton extended his general method in dynamics to create a "calculus of principal relation," which permitted the solution of certain total differential equations by the calculus of variations. Another important contribution was the hodograph, the curve defined by the velocity vectors of a point in orbital motion taken as drawn from the origin rather than from the moving point. Hamilton also attempted to apply his dynamics to the propagation of light in a crystalline medium.

All of Hamilton's work in optics and dynamics depended on a single central idea, that of the characteristic function. It was the first of his two great "discoveries." The second was the quaternions, which he discovered in 1843 and to which he devoted most of his efforts during the remaining twenty-two years of his life.

Hamilton raised two questions: (1) Is there any other algebraic representation of complex numbers that will reveal all valid operations on them? (2) Is it possible to find a hypercomplex number that is related to three-dimensional space just as a regular complex number is related to two-dimensional space? If such a hypercomplex number could be found, it would be a "natural" algebraic representation of space, as opposed to the artificial and somewhat arbitrary representation by coordinates.

In 1833 Hamilton read a paper on algebraic couples to the Royal Irish Academy in which he presented his answer to the first question. His algebraic couples consisted of all ordered pairs of real numbers, for which Hamilton defined rules of addition and multiplication. He then demonstrated that these couples constituted a commutative associative division algebra, and that they satisfied the rules for operations with complex numbers. On June 1, 1835 Hamilton presented a second paper on number couples entitled *Preliminary and Elementary Essay on Algebra as the Science of Pure Time,* in which he identified the number couples with steps in time. He combined this paper with his earlier paper of 1833, added some *General Introductory Remarks,* and published them in the *Proceedings of the Royal Irish Academy* of 1837.

Hamilton had less success in answering the second question, whether it would be possible to write three-dimensional complex numbers, or, as he called them, "triplets." Addition of triplets was obvious, but he could find no operation that would follow the rules of multiplication. In searching for the elusive triplets, Hamilton sought some way of making his triplets satisfy the law of the moduli, since any algebra obeying this law is a division algebra. By analogy to complex numbers, Hamilton wrote the triplet as $x + iy + jz$ with $i^2 = j^2 = -1$ and took as its modulus $x^2 + y^2 + z^2$. The product of two such moduli can be expressed as the sum of squares; but it is the sum of four squares not the sum of three squares, as would be the case if it were the modulus of a triplet.

The fact that he obtained the sum of four squares for the modulus of the product must have indicated to Hamilton that possibly ordered sets of four numbers, or "quaternions," might work where the triplets failed. Thus, he tested hypercomplex numbers of the form $(a + ib + jc + kd)$ to see if they satisfied the law of the moduli. They worked, but only by sacrificing the commutative law. Hamilton's great insight came in realizing that he could sacrifice commutativity and still have a meaningful and consistent algebra. The laws for multiplication of quaternions then followed immediately

$$ij = k = -ji,$$
$$jk = i = -kj,$$
$$ki = j = -ik,$$
$$i^2 = j^2 = k^2 = ijk = -1.$$

Hamilton was convinced that in the quaternions he had found a natural algebra of three-dimensional space. The quaternion seemed to him to be more fundamental than any coordinate representation of space, because operations with quaternions were independent of any given coordinate system. The scalar part of the quaternion caused difficulty in any geometrical representation, and Hamilton tried without notable success to interpret it as an extraspatial unit. The geometrical significance of the quaternion became clearer when Hamilton and A. Cayley independently showed that the quaternion operator rotated a vector about a given axis.

Hamilton's books on quaternions were too long and too difficult to attract much of an audience. The first readable book on quaternions was P. G. Tait's *Elementary Treatise on Quaternions* (1867). Tait was Hamilton's most prominent disciple, and during the 1890's entered into a heated controversy with Gibbs and Heaviside over the relative advantages of quaternions and vectors.

The quaternions were not the only contribution that Hamilton made to mathematics. In 1837 he corrected Abel's proof of the impossibility of solving the general quintic equation and defended the proof against G. B. Jerrard, who claimed to have found such a solution. He also became interested in the study of polyhedra and developed in 1856 what he called the "Icosian Calculus," a study of the properties of the icosahedron and the dodecahedron.

HAMPSON, WILLIAM (*b. Bebington, Cheshire, England, ca. 1854; d. London, England, 1926*), chemical engineering.

Hampson received his M.A. from Trinity College, Oxford, in 1881. In 1895 he patented a machine for making liquid air using the "cascade" system. His invention was taken up by what later became the British Oxygen Company, with which Hampson became connected. Hampson's work on inert gases led directly to the discovery of neon.

HAMY, MAURICE THÉODORE ADOLPHE (*b. Boulogne-sur-Mer, France, 1861; d. Paris, France, 1936*), celestial mechanics, astronomy, optics.

Hamy received his science *licence* at Paris in 1884. He then went to the Paris Observatory, where in time (1904) he became chief astronomer. A mathematician and physicist, Hamy did research in various areas of astronomy. Those of most interest today concern the study of stellar and planetary diameters through interferometry.

HANKEL, HERMANN (*b. Halle, Germany, 1839; d. Schramberg, near Tübingen, Germany, 1873*), mathematics, history of mathematics.

Hankel was the son of Wilhelm Gottlieb Hankel and was educated at Leipzig, Göttingen, and Berlin universities. After receiving his doctorate from Leipzig (1862), he taught there and later at Erlangen. Hankel's contributions to mathematics were concentrated in three areas: the study of complex and higher complex numbers, the theory of functions, and the history of mathematics.

HANKEL, WILHELM GOTTLIEB (*b. Ermsleben, Harz, Germany, 1814; d. Leipzig, Germany, 1899*), physics, chemistry.

Hankel belongs among the older nineteenth century physicists who typically represented the classical scientist. He was educated at the University of Halle, where he also taught. As an experimenter, Hankel investigated primarily piezoelectric and thermoelectric phenomena in crystals and was a pioneer in that special field. He was the father of Hermann Hankel.

HANN, JULIUS FERDINAND VON (*b. Mühlkreis, near Linz, Austria, 1839; d. Vienna, Austria, 1921*), meteorology, climatology.

Hann received his Ph.D. in physical geography from the University of Vienna in 1868 and taught meteorology, climatology, and oceanography there. In 1877 he was named professor of physics. Hann was one of the most prominent meteorologists of his day. His importance rested less on the creation of new theoretical concepts than on his efforts to coordinate empirical and theoretical results into a coherent structure. He attracted scientists of the highest ability to Vienna, including Max Margules, J.M. Perntner, Wilhelm Trabert, F.M. Exner, and A. Merz. He was a driving force in the establishment of mountain observatories, where he studied upper-air data from many different aspects. He produced the first comprehensive climatologies of both the tropics and the polar regions. He was knighted in 1910.

HANSEN, EMIL CHRISTIAN (*b. Ribe, Denmark, 1842; d. Hornbaek, Denmark, 1909*), botany, physiology.

Hansen became intensely interested in botany and financed his education by writing novels. He never achieved his M.Sc., but in 1876 he received a gold medal from Copenhagen University for an essay on fungi. In 1879 he became superintendent of the laboratories of the Carlsberg breweries, a position he held until his death. In 1883 he successfully developed a cultivated yeast that revolutionized beer-making around the world. (Hansen refused to patent his method, and it was freely adopted by other brewers.) He left a large fortune to a foundation to bear his name, the income of which was to be used for prizes for biological papers.

HANSEN, GERHARD HENRIK ARMAUER (*b. Bergen, Norway, 1841; d. Florø, Norway, 1912*), bacteriology.

In 1866 Hansen received his medical degree from the University of Christiania (now Oslo), and in 1868 he began serving in the leprosy hospital in Bergen. In 1873 Hansen discovered the rod-shaped bodies *Mycobacterium leprae*, also called Hansen's bacillus. He believed the bacillus to be the causative agent of leprosy. (Scientists of the period regarded that affliction as hereditary.) Therefore, he became the first investigator to suggest that a chronic disease might be caused by microorganisms. He was leprosy medical officer of Norway from 1875 until his death, and he was chiefly responsible for the dramatic decline of that disease there.

HANSEN, PETER ANDREAS (*b. Tondern, Schleswig, Germany, 1795; d. Seeberg, Germany, 1874*), astronomy.

Hansen, a leading German theoretical astronomer of the mid-nineteenth century, began his career as a clockmaker. In 1820 he became a volunteer assistant to Heinrich Christian Schumacher, a leading Danish astronomer. He accompanied Schumacher on expeditions, and after 1823 he assisted in the editing of *Astronomische Nachrichten* and was a frequent contributor. In 1825 he became director of the private observatory of the duke of Mecklenburg, near Gotha. He remained there the rest of his life. Hansen's contributions to astronomy were diversified, but he was above all a theoretician, concerned with the motion of the moon and planets in terms of Newtonian celestial mechanics. In 1857, under British sponsorship, he published extensive tables of lunar motions; they proved to be extraordinarily accurate and were a significant contribution to the science of astronomy. Today

Hansen is regarded as the greatest master of celestial mechanics since Laplace.

HANSEN, WILLIAM WEBSTER (*b. Fresno, Calif., 1909; d. Palo Alto, Calif., 1949*), physics, microwave electronics.

Hansen entered Stanford University at the age of sixteen, studied electrical engineering and physics, and received his doctorate (1933) in X-ray excitation. While teaching at Stanford, Hansen turned his attention to the problem of accelerating electrons for experiments in X-ray physics. From 1937 to 1940 Hansen helped elaborate the theory and practices of the new field he had founded, microwave electronics. He pioneered novel configurations, measurement techniques, and solutions of radiation problems generally. During World War II Hansen's group moved to the Sperry Gyroscope Company's laboratory in Garden City, New York. There he worked on the klystron and other electronic devices, including Doppler radar and blind landing systems for aircraft. Hansen returned to Stanford in 1945, but weakened by hard work during the war, he died in his fortieth year.

HANSKY, ALEKSEY PAVLOVICH (*b. Odessa, Russia, 1870; d. the Crimea, Russia, 1908*), astronomy.

Hansky graduated from Novorossisk University (now Odessa University) in 1894. In 1896 he went to Pulkovo Observatory in St. Petersburg, where he began his research on the form of the solar corona in relation to the phases of solar activity. He drowned in 1908, cutting short a promising career. In addition to his solar research, he studied gravimetry, measuring gravitational force atop Mont Blanc and in the depths of a coal mine, conducted research on the zodiacal light, and made observations of Jupiter and the meteors. At Pulkovo, Hansky had striking success in photographing sunspots and details of solar granulation.

HANSTEEN, CHRISTOPHER (*b. Christiania [now Oslo], Norway, 1784; d. Christiania, 1873*), physics, astronomy.

In 1802 Hansteen began studying law but dropped it in 1806 and devoted the rest of his life to astronomy and physics, particularly geomagnetism. After 1814 he was at the University of Christiania. In 1815 he established the first astronomical laboratory in Norway. In 1819 he published a magnetic atlas, to which he added over the years. His most important contribution to astronomy was a method for time measurements with simple instruments by observing a star in the vertical plane of the polestar.

HANTZSCH, ARTHUR RUDOLF (*b. Dresden, Germany, 1857; d. Dresden, 1935*), chemistry.

Hantzsch attended the Dresden Polytechnic (now Technische Hochschule) and received his doctorate from the University of Würzburg. Hantzsch's investigations broadened the conception of acids, showing that their properties depended on reaction with a solvent. His earliest work was in organic synthesis, and he synthesized thiazole in 1887. In 1890 Hantzsch and his student Alfred Werner launched the stereochemistry of nitrogen compounds. He extended his theory to nitrogen-nitrogen double bonds in 1894. After 1899 he developed a general theory of pseudo acids and bases as neutral compounds that can undergo reversible isomeric change into acids and bases respectively.

HARCOURT, A.G. VERNON (*b. London, England, 1834; d. Hyde, Isle of Wight, 1919*), chemistry.

Harcourt was a student assistant of Benjamin Brodie at Balliol College, Oxford, and later held a chemistry professorship at Christ Church College. In 1872 he was appointed to the board that prescribed tests and purity standards for London gas; as a member he introduced the pentane lamp for brightness measurement. In the realm of pure chemistry, Harcourt in 1866, aided by his mathematician colleague William Esson discovered independently of Guldberg and Waage, the law of mass action in its simplest form: "The velocity of chemical change is directly proportional to the quantity of substance undergoing change."

HARDEN, ARTHUR (*b. Manchester, England, 1865; d. Bourne End, Buckinghamshire, England, 1940*), biochemistry.

Harden graduated from the University of Manchester in 1885 with first-class honors in chemistry. He received his doctorate from the University of Erlangen in 1888 and returned to teach at Manchester. In 1897 he became head of the chemistry department of what is now the Lister Institute. Most of Harden's studies were related to alcoholic fermentation and the enzyme action involved. He shared the 1929 Nobel Prize for chemistry with Hans von Euler-Chelpin, and was knighted in 1936.

HARDING, CARL LUDWIG (*b. Lauenburg, Germany, 1765; d. Göttingen, Germany, 1834*), astronomy.

Harding studied theology—along with mathematics and physics—at Göttingen. While working on a stellar chart at a private observatory at Lilienthal, Harding discovered (1804) the third asteriod and named it Juno Georgia. He was transferred to the new Göttingen observatory, where he observed planets, comets, and variable stars. He also discovered three comets: 1813 II, 1824 II, and 1832 II.

HARDY, CLAUDE (*b. Le Mans, France, ca. 1598; d. Paris, France, 1678*), mathematics.

An acquaintance of Descartes, Hardy concerned himself with a favorite seventeenth-century mathematical problem: the effort to duplicate the cube. Hardy owed his greatest fame, however, to his knowledge of Arabic and in particular to his edition of Euclid's *Data* (1625).

HARDY, GODFREY HAROLD (*b. Cranleigh, England, 1877; d. Cambridge, England, 1947*), mathematics.

Hardy attended Trinity College, Cambridge, and in 1900 was elected a fellow. Between 1900 and 1911 he published many papers on the convergence of series and integrals and allied topics. In 1908 he published *A Course of Pure Mathematics*, the first rigorous English exposition of number, function, limit, and so on, for the undergraduate; it transformed university teaching of mathematics.

In 1910 Hardy established a partnership with J.E. Littlewood that was to last thirty-five years. Jointly they wrote nearly a hundred papers, covering such topics as

Diophantine approximation, additive and multiplicative theory of numbers and the Riemann zeta function, inequalities, series and integrals in general, and trigonometric series. In 1913 Hardy discovered the Indian mathematician Srinivasa Ramanujan and brought him to England. Together, they arrived at spectacular solutions of problems about the partition of numbers. Hardy is generally recognized as the leading English pure mathematician of his day.

HARDY, WILLIAM BATE (*b. Erdington, England, 1864; d. Cambridge, England, 1934*), biology, colloid chemistry.

Hardy entered Gonville and Caius College, Cambridge, in 1884, and he was associated with it throughout his life. Hardy began as a histologist, but in 1899 he published an important paper questioning the validity of the fixing and staining techniques used to reveal the details of cell structure. It marked his transition from a biologist to a colloidal chemist. Later he studied the colloidal properties of proteins.

HARE, ROBERT (*b. Philadelphia, Pa., 1781; d. Philadelphia, 1858*), chemistry.

Hare helped manage the family brewery at Philadelphia until he was thirty-seven. From 1818 to 1847 he was professor of chemistry at the University of Pennsylvania, then the nation's largest university. He made his major contribution at the age of twenty, when he hit upon the idea of burning a mixture of hydrogen and oxygen as a means of producing high temperatures. He devised an ingenious gasholder and blowtorch that formed the basis of the Drummond light and limelight.

HARIDATTA I (*fl. India, 683*), astronomy.

Haridatta wrote the *Grahacāranibandha,* the principal text of the *parahita* system of astronomy, which prevailed in Kerala until the fifteenth century.

HARIDATTA II (*fl. India, 1638*), astronomy.

Haridatta composed the *Jagadbhūṣaṇa,* which consists of tables for computing planetary positions and solar and lunar positions.

HARIOT, THOMAS. *See* **Harriot, Thomas.**

HARKER, ALFRED (*b. Kingston-upon-Hull, England, 1859; d. Cambridge, England, 1939*), petrology.

Harker attended St. John's College, Cambridge, and spent his entire scientific career there. Very early in his career, he was recognized as the leading British petrologist. Harker's original research related mostly to igneous rocks of the British Isles. Much of his work is still authoritative.

HARKINS, WILLIAM DRAPER (*b. Titusville, Pa., 1873; d. Chicago, Ill., 1951*), physical chemistry.

Harkins received his Ph.D. from Stanford University in 1907. After 1912 he was at the University of Chicago. Early in his career, he was recognized as an expert in smelter pollution. At Chicago he began work on the structure and the reactions of atomic nuclei, then a novel field. Harkins's eighty papers on nuclear reactions and isotopes include several important contributions to theory and experiment, and for some years were the only significant American contributions in this field. Throughout his career, Harkins showed exceptional foresight in choosing important fields of research.

HARKNESS, WILLIAM (*b. Ecclefechan, Scotland, 1837; d. Jersey City, N.J., 1903*), astronomy.

Graduated from the University of Rochester (M.A., 1861) and the New York Homeopathic Medical College (1862). Joined the U.S. Naval Observatory in 1862 and was associated with it until his retirement in 1899. He was much involved in the design of the present Naval Observatory building and its equipment. He was civilian director of the observatory from 1892. In 1879 he published a theory of the focal curve of achromatic telescopes.

HARLAN, RICHARD (*b. Philadelphia, Pa., 1796; d. New Orleans, La., 1843*), comparative anatomy.

In 1818 Harlan received his M.D. from the University of Pennsylvania. In 1821 he wrote a paper on the generation of animal heat and he was the first American to devote a major part of his time to vertebrate paleontology. In 1825 he published *Fauna Americana,* the first systematic presentation of the zoology of North America. Despite his errors due to insufficient data and his haste, Harlan contributed significantly to taxonomic knowledge.

HARPER, ROBERT ALMER (*b. Le Claire, Iowa, 1862; d. Phenix, Va., 1946*), botany.

Harper was educated at Oberlin, Johns Hopkins (Ph.D., 1896), and Bonn. Taught at Wisconsin (1898–1911) and Columbia (1911–30). His most important research was on the cytology of fungi. His work at the New York Botanical Garden was a substantial contribution to plant pathology; he installed equipment to combat insect pests and fungus diseases.

HARPER, ROLAND McMILLAN (*b. Farmington, Me., 1878; d. Tuscaloosa, Ala., 1966*), botany, geography, demography.

Harper graduated from the University of Georgia, and received his Ph.D. from Columbia University in 1905. He joined the Geological Survey of Georgia as botanist and geographer, serving chiefly there and in the Florida Geological Survey for the next sixty-one years. Harper published over 500 titles on the natural resources of the Southeast. These were especially valuable because the vegetation was represented by photographs.

HARPESTRAENG, HENRIK (*d. Roskilde, Denmark, 1244*), medicine, pharmacy.

Harpestraeng, also known as Henricus Dacus, was the author of several medical treatises. He was canon of the cathedral at Roskilde at the time of his death. He is also believed to have been the physician to King Eric Plovpenning. His Latin texts include *De Simplicibus medicinis laxativis,* on herbs and drugs and their medicinal use; *Liber herbarum,* a herbal for medical use; and the *Remedium contra sacrum ignem,* now lost, a therapeutical treatise on St. Anthony's fire. His later works were in Danish. Harpestraeng showed no great originality; his importance was his establishment of European medicine in Scandinavia. His Danish works are also of linguistic interest.

HARRIOT (or **HARIOT**), **THOMAS** (*b. Oxford, England, ca. 1560; d. London, England, 1621*), mathematics, astronomy, physics.

Harriot finished his Oxford studies in 1580 and went into the service of Sir Walter Raleigh, who needed a cartographer and an expert on the theory of oceanic navigation for his colonizing venture in Virginia. Harriot went to Virginia in 1585, where he investigated the life, language, and customs of the Indians (including learning how to "drink" tobacco smoke). He also surveyed the coast, islands, and rivers. His account of this trip was published in 1588 as *A Briefe and True Report of the New Found Land of Virginia*. He later went into the service of the ninth earl of Northumberland and was imprisoned briefly with the earl after the Gunpowder Plot of 1605.

From 1610 to 1613 Harriot undertook prolonged telescopic observations of Jupiter's satellites and of sunspots. Harriot was an accomplished mathematician who enriched algebra with a comprehensive theory of equations. His convenient notation system simplified algebra and the other branches of mathematics. His *Artis analyticae praxis* was published posthumously in 1631. It contains an interesting attempt at a uniform treatment of algebraic equations.

Harriot also studied optics and prismatic colors, making important contributions in both fields. He is believed to have conducted chemical experiments as well. Harriot's papers disappeared sometime after 1649, and his contributions to science and mathematics were difficult to gauge. In 1784 some were rediscovered, and as a result of comprehensive and penetrating studies of them in recent years, his name is becoming increasingly important.

HARRIS, JOHN (*b. Shropshire [?], England, ca. 1666; d. Norton Court, Kent, England, 1719*), natural philosophy, dissemination of knowledge.

Harris received his B.A. from Trinity College, Oxford, in 1686 and his M.A. from Hart Hall, Oxford, in 1689. He took orders and held a variety of ecclesiastical posts during his lifetime. He showed a lifelong interest in natural philosophy, and he defended the consonance of scientific knowledge and orthodox religion against the Hobbists and the atheists. His most famous work was the *Lexicon technicum* (1704), which was the first general scientific encyclopedia. In it Harris called upon the specialized knowledge of the greatest scientific authorities of his day, including Isaac Newton, John Ray, Edmond Halley, Robert Boyle, and John Collins.

HARRISON, JOHN (*b. Foulby, Yorkshire, England, 1693; d. London, England, 1776*), horology.

Harrison and his brother James designed many scientific instruments, including a cumbersome marine clock designed to find longitude at sea. In 1737 the device was tested on a voyage to Lisbon and was found to be successful. The Board of Longitude, which had offered a £20,-000 prize for such a clock, raised various previously unstipulated obstacles to the payment of the money. Eventually, King George III had to intervene on behalf of Harrison, and in 1773 the award was made. Although soon superseded by simpler mechanisms, the use of timekeepers to find longitude stemmed directly from Harrison's invention.

HARRISON, ROSS GRANVILLE (*b. Germantown, Pa., 1870; d. New Haven, Conn., 1959*), biology.

Harrison received his Ph.D. in zoology from Johns Hopkins University in 1894. In 1899 he received an M.D. from Bonn University but never practiced. After teaching at Bryn Mawr College and Johns Hopkins, he became professor of comparative anatomy at Yale University (1907), where he remained the rest of his life.

Harrison was one of the pioneers of experimental embryology, and his single most important contribution was the hanging drop method of tissue culture. A number of investigators had been attempting for a decade or more to grow tissues or cells in isolation *in vitro* or *in vivo*. Harrison's experiments, published in 1907, were by far the most successful, and established tissue and cell culture as a technique adaptable to the solution of a wide variety of problems in biology and medicine. The observation of the activities of cells in culture is still one of the most important pursuits of developmental biologists. Harrison also contributed to biology by developing a method of embryonic grafting. He and his students experimented widely, principally in amphibian embryos. Experimental embryology, which Harrison was so crucial in establishing as a science, was an important bridge between the old morphology of the nineteenth century and the new molecular biology of the twentieth.

HART, EDWIN BRET (*b. Sandusky, Ohio, 1874; d. Madison, Wis., 1953*), biochemistry, nutrition.

Hart received his B.S. from the University of Michigan in 1897. He then studied protein chemistry with Albrecht Kossel at the universities of Marburg and Heidelberg. From 1906 to his retirement in 1944, he headed the agricultural chemical department at the University of Wisconsin. Hart's department, often in collaboration with other departments at Wisconsin, was unique in its success in establishing basic scientific principles while pursuing practical objectives. His department was in the forefront of nutritional research when the role of organic and mineral trace nutrients was only beginning to be understood. At one time or another, Hart worked on most of the vitamins and minerals of nutritional significance. He also worked on such varied subjects as copper anemia, the irradiation of milk to enhance vitamin D content, and cheese curing.

HARTIG, THEODOR (*b. Dillenburg, Germany, 1805; d. Brunswick, Germany, 1880*), plant physiology, forestry, entomology.

Hartig studied forestry at the University of Berlin from 1824 to 1827. In 1838 he became professor of forestry at the Collegium Carolinum in Brunswick, where he remained until he retired in 1878 as *Oberforstrat*. In 1837 he established his reputation as an entomologist with the work *Adlerflügler Deutschlands*. Thereafter, he devoted more and more time to plant physiology. In *Neue Theorie der Befruchtung der Pflanzen* (1842), he considered the theory of plant fertilization. He also wrote extensively on the practical questions of forestry.

HARTING, PIETER (*b. Rotterdam, Netherlands, 1812; d. Amersfoort, Netherlands, 1885*), microscopy, zoology.

Harting received his medical degree from Utrecht University in 1835. He practiced medicine and taught pharmacology at Utrecht, but did his most important work there in research in microscopy. In 1848 he began publishing his multivolume treatise *Het Mikroskoop,* the first full historical treatment of the subject. He developed a new system for measuring the enlarging properties of microscopes uniformly, introducing a new factor, μ. Harting was one of the earliest supporters of Darwin. He occupied the chair in zoology at Utrecht and wrote a textbook on the subject.

HARTLEY, DAVID (*b. Armley, Yorkshire, England, ca. 1705; d. Bath, England, 1757*), psychology.

Hartley studied classics, mathematics, and divinity at Jesus College, Cambridge, from which he received an M.A. in 1729. He went into medicine and practiced at Newark, later settling at Bath. In 1749 he published *Observations on Man, His Frame, His Duty, and His Expectations;* in it he expanded on the "association of ideas" principle of John Locke. In the century following publication of *Observations,* the work came to be seen as the fountainhead of some of the most important ideas in biological, psychological, and social thought. It was the first work in English to use the term "psychology"; and his unification of sensation, motion, association, and vibrations in a coherent mechanistic theory of experience and behavior provided the grounds for modern theories in biology, neurophysiology, human and comparative psychology, neurology, psychiatry, psychoanalysis, and social and political theory.

HARTLIB, SAMUEL (*b. Elbing, Prussia [now Elblag, Poland]; d. London, England, 1662*), science education, reform, publishing, promotion.

Hartlib studied at Cambridge from about 1621 to 1626 and settled permanently in England in 1628. He was a tireless promoter of useful inventions and was involved in a wide variety of public issues, including Protestantism and educational reform. He edited many books and published some sixty-five of his own. His best-known work was *A Description of the Famous Kingdome of Macaria* (1641), a utopian romance.

HARTMANN, CARL FRIEDRICH ALEXANDER (*b. Zorge, Harz, Germany, 1796; d. Leipzig, Germany, 1863*), mineralogy, mining, metallurgy.

In 1818 he began attending the University of Berlin, where he studied mineralogy under Christian Weiss, and in 1826 he received a doctorate in jurisprudence from the University of Heidelberg. During this period, Hartmann's first major work on mining science was published, and in 1829 he was named commissioner of mines in Brunswick. He continued to publish important works. Hartmann did no independent research. Nevertheless, his contribution to the literature of mining and metallurgy was great: by setting down on paper anything that could further technical knowledge, he contributed to the dissemination of the latest information.

HARTMANN, GEORG (*b. Eggolsheim, near Forchheim, Germany, 1489; d. Nuremberg, Germany, 1564*), instrument making, mathematics.

In Italy in 1518, Hartmann began designing sundials, and discovered the magnetic dip. Settling in Nuremberg in 1518, he designed and produced timepieces, as-

trolabes, globes, quadrants, armillary spheres, a star altimeter, and the caliber gauge. Among his works were *Joh. Pisani Perspectiva communis* (1542) and an astrological work, *Directorium* (1554).

HARTMANN, JOHANNES (*b. Amberg, Oberpfalz, Germany, 1568; d. Kassel, Germany, 1631*), iatrochemistry, medicine, mathematics.

Hartmann studied at the universities of Jena and Wittenberg before receiving a master's degree from Marburg in 1591. In 1592 he became professor of mathematics there. He also studied medicine at Marburg and received his medical doctorate in 1606 and became court physician to Landgrave Moritz. Thereafter, he combined his interest in mathematics, astronomy, and alchemy with medicine. In 1609 he introduced pharmaceutical and medical chemistry into the medical curriculum by becoming professor of those subjects at Marburg. This new field, newly emerging from alchemy, was soon split between the Galenists and the iatrochemists. Hartmann sought to mediate between the two factions. His principal work was *Praxis chymiatrica.*

HARTMANN, JOHANNES FRANZ (*b. Erfurt, Germany, 1865; d. Göttingen, Germany, 1936*), astronomy.

Hartmann studied astronomy at Tübingen, Berlin, and Leipzig. He received his Ph.D. from Leipzig in 1891 and was with its observatory until 1896 when he moved to the Potsdam observatory. There he was chiefly active in the fields of instrumentation and spectrography. He also designed a spectrograph and a spectrocomparator for the observatory; both employed original techniques. In 1904 he discovered the stationary calcium lines in the spectrum of δ Orionis; he thus proved the existence of interstellar matter for the first time. In 1909 Hartmann went to the University of Göttingen. In 1921 he became director of the La Plata Observatory in Argentina. He remained there until he retired in 1935.

HARTREE, DOUGLAS RAYNER (*b. Cambridge, England, 1897; d. Cambridge, 1958*), applied mathematics, theoretical physics.

Hartree received a Ph.D. from Cambridge University in 1926. He taught theoretical mathematics and theoretical physics for many years at the University of Manchester and later at Cambridge. Hartree's chief contribution to science was his development of powerful methods of numerical mathematical analysis, which made it possible to apply successfully the so-called self-consistent field method to the calculation of atomic wave functions of polyelectronic atoms. He also applied his methods to problems of ballistics, atmospheric physics, hydrodynamics, and to the control of chemical engineering processes.

HARTSOEKER (or **HARTSOECKER**), **NICOLAAS** (*b. Gouda, Netherlands, 1656; d. Utrecht, Netherlands, 1725*), physics, technology.

Hartsoeker may have attended the University of Leiden briefly but is believed to have been largely self-educated. He became a noted lensmaker in Passy, outside Paris, where he also made microscopes and telescopes. In 1704 he became professor of mathematics at the University of Dusseldorf. He was in correspondence with the noted scientists of his day, debating the conclusions of Leibniz,

Newton, and Jakob I Bernoulli. Among his many books are *Essai de dioptrique* (1694) and *Suite de conjectures physiques* (1708).

HARTWIG, (CARL) ERNST (ALBRECHT) (*b. Frankfurt am Main, Germany, 1851; d. Bamberg, Germany, 1923*), astronomy.

After studying at several German universities, Hartwig received his Ph.D. from Strasbourg in 1880. Soon afterward he was sent on an inspection tour of modern observatories throughout Europe and went on a sighting expedition to Argentina. In 1886 he became director of the observatory at Bamberg and spent the rest of his life there. Hartwig's work was devoted to two main branches of research: the measurement of stars and planets and the observation of variable stars. He performed a most valuable series of measurements of the diameters of planets and the physical libration of the moon. In 1885 he independently discovered S Andromedae, the first known extragalactic supernova.

HARVEY, WILLIAM (*b. Folkestone, Kent, England, 1578; d. London or Roehampton, Surrey, England, 1657*), physiology, anatomy, embryology, medicine.

Studied at Gonville and Caius College, Cambridge, and received doctorate in medicine at Padua (1602). Practiced medicine in London; in 1609 was appointed physician to St. Bartholomew's Hospital. Lectured on surgery for the Royal College of Physicians (1615–56). Served as a royal physician (1618–47); Charles I provided him with deer from the royal parks for some of his investigations.

Harvey used Aristotle's physiological doctrines in preference to the prevailing ideas of Galen: one of the most convincing elements of Galenic physiology was the centrifugal flow of venous blood from the liver to all parts of the body. By 1616 Harvey had accepted the newer view of the heart and arteries as sanguineous organs, with the transmission of blood to the arteries as one of the most important functions of the heart. In early experiments leading eventually to his discovery of circulation of the blood, he was strongly influenced by Colombo's description of active and passive phases in the heart's movement. Harvey sought to establish that the heartbeat consists of only one active movement, beginning with the auricles and proceeding to the apex of the ventricles, and that the heart's essential action is to contract and expel materials rather than to dilate and attract them. He maintained that the pulse of the arteries is simply the result of the impulsion of blood by the heart and is not an active movement. His ultimate success resulted largely from the study of the hearts of dying animals, in which the heartbeat is considerably slowed down; he also studied the simpler hearts of cold-blooded animals and observed excised beating hearts, both whole and in section.

His discovery of circulation was announced in *Exercitatio anatomica de motu cordis et sanguinis in animalibus* (1628). In the first half he presents his conclusions about the movements of the heart and arteries, bolstered by vivisectional, anatomical, pathological, and embryological observations. He describes how he first took up the study of the movement of the heart; presents his conclusions about the ventricles, arteries, and auricles; defends the pulmonary circuit of the blood; and relates how he

went beyond this early work to the discovery of circulation. From this account it seems clear that he first conceived of the centripetal flow of venous blood as a necessary consequence of his conclusions about the heartbeat, rather than as the result of a direct investigation of the veins. He realized that over a relatively short period of time the heart transmits from the veins to the arteries even more than the whole mass of the blood; the rate of transmission is in fact so large that if it took place in only one direction, the veins would soon be drained and the arteries filled to bursting. Only if blood somehow returns from the arteries to the veins at the periphery could these absurdities be avoided. He then began to consider whether the blood might have a kind of circular motion, and the second half of *De motu cordis* presents evidence to confirm the circular movement. He strengthened the original quantitative argument by showing that the heart must expel at least some blood to the arteries at each beat, and by making a rough calculation of the resulting rate of transmission. He demonstrated by the use of ligatures that there is a passage of blood from the arteries to the veins at the periphery, and gave a more direct demonstration of centripetal venous flow, based on the existence of the venous valves. Since antiquity ideas about physiology and pathology of most parts of the body had been based on assumptions about the functions of the heart and blood vessels, and by fundamentally changing the latter, Harvey pointed the way to a reform of all of physiology and medicine. Most of the reaction to the publication was favorable, but his ideas also found some major opponents. In 1649 he published *Exercitationes duae de circulatione sanguinis,* replying to Jean Riolan and other critics. Subsequent developments in physiology have led to great changes in thinking about the functions of the circulation, but have abundantly confirmed the importance of Harvey's discovery as the cornerstone of modern physiology and medicine.

In addition to the nutritive and pneumatic systems, which he amalgamated into one circulatory system, Harvey was also interested in the third great system of classical physiology: the organs concerned with locomotion and sensation. His "De motu locali animalium" was primarily concerned with applying the general principles of Aristotle's treatises on animal movement to a detailed study of muscles, nerves, and other organs involved in locomotion. Only the rough draft has survived, and shows that he had begun to develop some important insights into the physiology of sensation and locomotion. In his *Exercitationes de generatione animalium* (1651) he discussed some related themes that had a direct and significant influence on the development of the concept of tissue irritability.

By 1616 Harvey had already begun his lifelong study of generation. In *De generatione* he reported a wealth of observations on all aspects of reproduction in a wide variety of animal species, focusing primarily on domestic fowl and deer as representatives of the ovipara and vivipara, respectively. His description of the day-to-day development of the chick embryo was notably more accurate than earlier ones, while his direct study of viviparous generation by dissecting the uteri of deer at various stages during mating and pregnancy was quite without precedent. These observations formed the basis of a critical evaluation of earlier theories of generation, especially those of Aristotle, Galen, and Fabrici; and, finding all of the latter deficient, Harvey went on to formulate the first fundamentally new theory of generation since antiquity. Subsequent investigation has undermined much of Harvey's theory of generation, but his views nevertheless represented a major advance over those of his predecessors.

HARVEY, WILLIAM HENRY (*b. Limerick, Ireland, 1811; d. Torquay, England, 1866*), botany.

While colonial treasurer of Cape Town, Harvey produced *The Genera of South African Plants* (1838). In 1844 he became keeper of the herbarium of Trinity College, Dublin, where he produced *Phycologia Britannica* (three volumes, 1846–51). Later he toured the eastern United States and published (1852–58) an account of the marine algae of North America.

AL-ḤASAN IBN MUḤAMMAD AL-WAZZĀN. *See* **Leo the African.**

AL-ḤASAN IBN MŪSĀ IBN SHĀKIR. *See* **Banū Mūsā.**

HASENÖHRL, FRIEDRICH (*b. Vienna, Austria, 1874; d. near Vielgereuth, South Tirol, Austria, 1915*), physics.

Hasenöhrl received his Ph.D. from Vienna University in 1897. In 1905 he went to Vienna Technical University, where he taught until he was killed in World War I. He is best known for his series of papers on electromagnetic radiation. He also attacked the problems in statistical mechanics and considered their relation to the foundations of quantum theory.

HASSENFRATZ, JEAN-HENRI (*b. Montmartre [now in Paris], France, 1755; d. Paris, 1827*), chemistry.

In 1782 Hassenfratz joined the Service des Mines and was sent to central Europe to study steel manufacturing and the exploitation of mines. He worked in Lavoisier's laboratory and taught physics at the École des Mines from 1786 to 1788. He was a militant and active democrat during the Revolution. Later in his career he taught at the École des Mines again and at the École Polytechnique. The four volumes of his *Sidérotechnie* (1812) constitute his most important publication.

HASSLER, FERDINAND RUDOLPH (*b. Aarau, Switzerland, 1770; d. Philadelphia, Pa., 1843*), geodesy.

Hassler immigrated to the United States in 1805, bringing with him a set of metric weights and measures and an interest in the determination of the figure of the earth. Reflecting French influences, he was largely responsible for the transfer of European scientific skills and high professional standards to the young United States. He taught at Union College and West Point and served in the Coast Survey (now Coast and Geodetic Survey) and was superintendent of the Office of Weights and Measures (now National Bureau of Standards).

HATCHETT, CHARLES (*b. London, England, 1765; d. London, 1847*), chemistry.

A skilled mineral analyst, Hatchett was the effective discoverer of the element niobium (columbium) in 1801. He also did important analysis of shell, bone, and dental enamel.

HATSCHEK, BERTHOLD (*b. Kirwein, Moravia, Austria, 1854; d. Vienna, Austria, 1941*), zoology.

Hatschek received his doctorate from the University of Leipzig in 1876. After teaching at several institutions, he was head (1896–1925) of the Zoological Institute of the University of Vienna. He studied the growth and metamorphosis of larva of annelids and formulated important theories concerning the systematic placing of animals.

HAUG, GUSTAVE EMILE (*b. Drusenheim, Alsace, France, 1861; d. Paris, France, 1927*), stratigraphy, structural geology, paleontology.

Haug received a doctorate in natural history from the University of Strasbourg in 1884. After 1887 he was at the Sorbonne. Between 1907 and 1911 he published *Traité de géologie*, which rapidly became one of the indispensable reference volumes of the profession. It combined profound erudition with sweeping synthetic view of all fields of geology. He also produced important works on the fundamental aspects of paleontology, stratigraphy, and tectonics.

HAUKSBEE, FRANCIS (*b. Colchester [?], England, ca. 1666; d. London, England, 1713*), experimental physics, scientific instrumentation.

Hauksbee's experiments in electricity, especially luminescence, are regarded as the beginning of sustained study in that field; they opened the way for such diverse scientists as Stephen Gray, Charles de Cisternay Dufay, and Benjamin Franklin. Newton and Laplace also reflect the influence of Hauksbee's experiments.

Little is known of Hauksbee's early life or his scientific training. He burst upon the scientific world with a series of sensational demonstrations before the Royal Society, the first taking place in 1703. These were under the sponsorship of Isaac Newton, who was the newly elected president of the society. Hauksbee's experiments, which concerned electroluminosity, static electricity, and capillarity, were eventually published in his *Physico-Mechanical Experiments on Various Subjects* (1709). It was widely read throughout the eighteenth century.

In the first, and most dramatic, of Hauksbee's Royal Society demonstrations, he created "a Shower of Fire" by rushing mercury into the evacuated receiver of his new model air pump. He went on later to investigate other ways to produce light by the friction of glass. He also did impressive experiments that resulted in demonstrations of interparticulate attraction. In this field, in particular, Newton showed interest. The 1706 edition of his *Optics* shows the considerable influence that Hauksbee's experiments had on Newton's theory of matter.

HAUKSBEE, FRANCIS (*b. London, England, 1688; d. London, 1763*), experimental physics, scientific instrumentation.

The nephew of the elder Francis Hauksbee, he assisted his uncle in his famous experiments and did independent experimentation largely derived from those of his uncle. He was also a competent maker of scientific instruments; a reflecting telescope of his had a certain success.

HAUSDORFF, FELIX (*b. Breslau, Germany [now Wrocław, Poland], 1868; d. Bonn, Germany, 1942*), mathematics.

Hausdorff graduated from the University of Leipzig in 1891. His early main interests were philosophy and literature, and he wrote poetry, philosophical essays, and even a successful farce. After 1902, when he began teaching at Leipzig, he devoted more time to mathematics. From 1913 to 1935 he taught at Bonn. Set theory and topology were his main fields. His major work, *Grundzüge der Mengenlehre,* was published in 1913. It contained the beginnings of the theories of topological and metric spaces, which are now included in all textbooks. Thus, Hausdorff can rightly be considered the founder of general topology and of the special theory of metric spaces. As a Jew, Hausdorff was forced into retirement in 1935 and his later work was published only outside Germany. He committed suicide in 1942.

HAUTEFEUILLE, PAUL GABRIEL (*b. Étampes, Seine-et-Oise, France, 1836; d. Paris, France, 1902*), chemistry.

In 1865 Hautefeuille received a doctorate in the physical sciences from the École Normale Supérieure. In 1885 he was named to the chair of mineralogy at the Sorbonne. His best-known studies were his reproductions of numerous crystallized minerals by utilizing mineral catalysts and varied temperature conditions.

HAÜY, RENÉ-JUST (*b. St.-Just-en-Chaussée, Oise, France, 1743; d., Paris, France, 1822*), crystallography, mineralogy.

Haüy was educated at the Collège de Navarre in Paris and was ordained a priest in 1770. He became interested in mineralogy and in 1784 he published *Essai d'une théorie sur la structure des cristaux,* which laid the foundation of the mathematical, or geometric, theory of crystal structure. He was to devote the rest of his life to the elaboration of his crystal theory and its application to mineralogical classification. In 1801 he published his major work, *Traité de minéralogie,* the first volume of which presented his crystal theory. It is an irony of history that Haüy's geometrical definition of mineral species has acquired importance in twentieth-century mineralogy through acquiring the opposite sense, that of substitution of "vicarious" isomorphic constituents.

HAVERS, CLOPTON (*b. Stambourne, Essex, England, ca. 1655; d. Willinggale, Essex, England, 1702*), osteology.

In 1689 and 1690 Havers, a physician, read five discourses to the Royal Society that provided the first full description of the microscopic structure of the bone lamellae and canals, with a discussion of bone physiology. They formed the substance of his book *Osteologia nova, or Some New Observations of the Bones* (1691).

HAWORTH, ADRIAN HARDY (*b. Hull, England, 1768; d. Chelsea, London, England, 1833*), botany, entomology.

Haworth wrote over sixty works, primarily concerned with Lepidoptera and with succulent plants. His *Lepidoptera Britannica* (1803–28) was the first comprehensive study of British butterflies and moths and the standard work for fifty years.

HAWORTH, WALTER NORMAN (*b. Chorley, England, 1883; d. Birmingham, England, 1950*), organic chemistry.

Haworth graduated from the University of Manchester in 1906 and later received a doctorate from the University of Göttingen. Haworth devoted most of his time to the study of carbohydrates, and in 1929 he published *The*

Constitution of Sugars. He identified vitamin C and coined the name "ascorbic acid." In 1933 he succeeded in synthesizing vitamin C, the first for any vitamin. He won (along with Paul Karrer) the Nobel Prize for chemistry in 1937 for his work on carbohydrates and for his synthesis of vitamin C.

IBN ḤAWQAL, ABŪ'L-QĀSIM MUḤAMMAD (*b. Nisibis, Upper Mesopotamia [now Nusaybin, Turkey]; fl. second half of the tenth century*), geography.

A merchant and perhaps a Fāṭimid missionary, Ibn Ḥawqal traveled through most of the Muslim world, going as far west as Spain. He wrote an important geography, *Kitāb al-masālik wa'l-mamālik* ("Book of Routes and Kingdoms").

HAYDEN, FERDINAND VANDIVEER (*b. Westfield, Mass., 1829; d. Philadelphia, Pa., 1887*), geology.

Hayden graduated from Oberlin College in 1850 and received his M.D. from Albany Medical College in New York in 1853. In 1865 he became professor of geology at the University of Pennsylvania, and from 1867 to 1879 he headed the U.S. Geological and Geographical Survey of the Territories. His greatest contribution during this period was his stratigraphic work on the American West. His topographers drew contour maps for which quantitative accurate cross sections and long-distance extrapolations of formulations could be made. Hayden was successful in having Yellowstone Park set aside for the people.

HAYFORD, JOHN FILLMORE (*b. Rouses Point, N.Y., 1868; d. Evanston, Ill., 1925*), geodesy.

Hayford graduated as a civil engineer from Cornell University in 1889 and joined the U.S. Coast and Geodetic Survey. Hayford is an important member of a little-studied scientific tradition: determining the figure of the earth. In his great work, *The Figure of the Earth and Isostasy From Measurements in the United States* (1909), he inaugurated the modern procedure in this field. It is also the first work to take isostasy into consideration in arriving at the figure of the earth.

IBN AL-HAYTHAM, ABŪ ʿALĪ AL-ḤASAN IBN AL-ḤASAN, called **al-Baṣrī** (of Baṣra, Iraq), **al-Miṣrī** (of Egypt); also known as **Alhazen** (*b. 965; d. Cairo, ca. 1040*), optics, astronomy, mathematics.

About Ibn al-Haytham's life we have several, not always consistent, reports, most of which come from the thirteenth century. His autobiography, written at the end of 417 A.H./A.D. 1027, when the author was sixty-three lunar years old, and clearly modeled after Galen's *De libris propriis,* lists his works up to that date but speaks only in general terms about his intellectual development.

Among the subjects on which Ibn al-Haytham wrote are logic, ethics, politics, poetry, music and theology; but neither his writings on these subjects nor the summaries he made of Aristotle and Galen have survived. His extant works belong to the fields in which he was reputed to have made his most important contributions: optics, astronomy, and mathematics.

Ibn al-Haytham's theory of light and vision is neither identical with nor directly descendant from any one of the theories known to have previously existed in antiquity or in Islam. His writings on optics included a treatise written "in accordance with the method of Ptolemy," whose *Optics* was available to him in an Arabic translation lacking the first book and the end of the fifth and last book, and a summary of Euclid and Ptolemy in which he "supplemented the matters of the first Book, missing from Ptolemy's work." The two works are now lost. His major work, the *Optics* or *Kitāb al-Manāzir,* in seven books, is not a philosophical dissertation on the nature of light but an experimental and mathematical investigation of its properties, particularly insofar as these relate to vision.

The main part of Ibn al-Haytham's general theory of light and vision is contained in book I of the *Optics.* In book II he expounded an elaborate theory of cognition, with visual perception as the basis. Book III deals with binocular vision and with the errors of vision and of recognition. Reflection is the subject of book IV, and here Ibn al-Haytham gave experimental proof of the specular reflection of accidental as well as essential light, a complete formulation of the laws of reflection, and a description of the construction and use of a copper instrument for measuring reflections from plane, spherical, cylindrical, and conical mirrors, whether convex or concave. He gave much attention to the problem of finding the incident ray, given the reflected ray to a given position of the eye. This is characteristic of the whole of the *Optics*—an eye is always given with respect to which the problems are to be formulated. The investigation of reflection—with special reference to the location of images—is continued in book V where the well-known "problem of Alhazen" is discussed, while book VI deals with the errors of vision due to reflection. Book VII is devoted to the theory of refraction.

The extant writings of Ibn al-Haytham include a number of optical works other than the *Optics: The Light of the Moon; The Halo and the Rainbow; On Spherical Burning Mirrors; On Paraboloidal Burning Mirrors; The Formation of Shadows; The Light of the Stars; Discourse on Light; The Burning Sphere; The Shape of the Eclipse.*

No fewer than twenty of Ibn al-Haytham's extant works are devoted to astronomical questions. Many of these works are short tracts that deal with minor or limited, although by no means trivial, theoretical or practical problems (sundials, determination of the direction of prayer, parallax, and height of stars), and none of them seems to have achieved results comparable to the great astronomers.

As a writer on astronomy Ibn al-Haytham has been mainly known as the author of a treatise *On the Configuration of the World.* The treatise was widely known in the Islamic world, and it is his only astronomical work to have been transmitted to the West in the Middle Ages.

The longest of the astronomical works of Ibn al-Haytham that have come down to us is a commentary on the *Almagest.* In this work he sought to explain basic matters relating to the construction of Ptolemy's own tables, and he meant his commentary to be read in conjunction with the *Almagest,* whose terminology and order of topics it followed.

Ibn al-Haytham's fame as a mathematician has rested on his treatment of the problem known since the seventeenth century as "Alhazen's problem." In book V of his *Optics,* he set out to solve the problem for all cases of spherical, cylindrical, and conical surfaces, convex and concave. Although he was not successful in every particular, his performance showed him to be in full command of the higher mathematics of the Greeks.

Apart from the mathematical sections of the *Optics,* some twenty of the writings of Ibn al-Haytham which deal exclusively with mathematical topics have come down to us. Most of these writings are short and they vary considerably in importance.

HEATH, THOMAS LITTLE (*b. Barnetby le Wold, Lincoln, England, 1861; d. Ashtead, Surrey, 1940*), mathematics, antiquity.

After attending the grammar school at Caistor, Heath went to Clifton and thence, with a foundation scholarship, to Trinity College, Cambridge, where he became a fellow in 1885 and an honorary fellow in 1920. The University of Oxford conferred an honorary degree on him; the Royal Society elected him a fellow (1912); and he served on the council of the society. He was a fellow of the British Academy and president of the Mathematical Association from 1922 to 1923.

Heath was one of the leading authorities on mathematics in antiquity. His *History of Greek Mathematics* is usually regarded as his most famous contribution. In *The Thirteen Books of Euclid's Elements* he made available those books of the *Elements* that had hitherto been considered unintelligible; in particular his treatment of book X is a masterpiece.

HEAVISIDE, OLIVER (*b. Camden Town, London, England, 1850; d. Paignton, Devonshire, England, 1925*), physics, electrical engineering.

Despite the lack of a formal education—he was almost entirely self-taught—Heaviside became expert in mathematical physics and played an important role in the development of the electromagnetic theory of James Clerk Maxwell and in its practical application. He proved to be right in an extended controversy over the effect of inductance in long-distance cables. He predicted the existence of a reflecting ionizing region surrounding the earth; at first called the Kennelly-Heaviside layer, it is now known as the ionosphere.

HECATAEUS OF MILETUS (*fl. late sixth century and early fifth century* B.C.), geography.

Hecataeus is important as one of the earliest Greek prose writers and especially as the author of the earliest geographical work, the *Periegesis,* only fragments of which have survived. It was originally in two volumes, entitled "Europe" and "Asia." The latter included Africa. Apparently it described briefly the main features, region by region, of the largely coastal areas of the Mediterranean world then known to the Greeks.

HECHT, DANIEL FRIEDRICH (*b. Sosa, near Eibenstock, Germany, 1777; d. Freiberg, Germany, 1833*), mathematics, mechanics.

Hecht graduated from the Freiberg Bergakademie, became a mine manager, and taught mathematics. In 1816 he joined the Bergakademie, becoming a full professor of mathematics in 1826. He later devoted his teaching activity to mechanics and mining activity, especially to mechanical engineering. This was reflected in his book, *Erste Gründe der mechanischen Wissenschaften* (1819).

HECKE, ERICH (*b. Buk, Posen, Germany [now Poznan, Poland], 1887; d. Copenhagen, Denmark, 1947*), mathematics.

Hecke studied at the universities of Breslau, Berlin, and Göttingen, receiving his Ph.D. from Göttingen in 1910. He taught there and at Basel before going to the University of Hamburg in 1919, where he remained until his death. Most of Hecke's work dealt with analytic number theory.

HEDIN, SVEN ANDERS (*b. Stockholm, Sweden, 1865; d. Stockholm, 1952*), geography.

Hedin received his B.S. from Uppsala University in 1888 and his Ph.D. from Halle in 1892. He then began advanced studies at Berlin under Ferdinand von Richthofen, specializing in the geology and geography of Asia, through which he made numerous expeditions. He combined the qualities of a great explorer, a great writer, and a trail blazer preparing the way for trained specialized scientists. He was the last of the classical explorers of the nineteenth century, but his solid academic training made him one of the most active representatives of the modern trend in regional geographic research. Among his many works (by their English titles) are *Through Asia* (two volumes, 1898), *Central Asia and Tibet* (two volumes, 1903), *Southern Tibet* (eleven volumes, 1916–1922), and *My Life as an Explorer* (1925).

HEDWIG, JOHANN (*b. Kronstadt [now Braşov], Transylvania [now Rumania], 1730; d. Leipzig, Germany, 1799*), botany.

Hedwig received his M.D. from the University of Leipzig in 1759. Although he became a busy and successful physician, he gave much time to the study of plants, specializing in mosses and liverworts. In 1782 he published *Fundamentum historiae naturalis muscorum frondosorum*, which attracted wide international attention. His best known and probably most significant contribution was the better understanding of the life history—especially the sexual reproduction—of the lower plants resulting from his observations on mosses.

HEER, OSWALD (*b. Niederutzwyl, St. Gallen, Switzerland, 1809; d. Zurich, Switzerland, 1883*), paleontology, botany.

After attending the University of Halle, Heer taught at the University of Zurich, and in 1852 he became full professor of botany and entomology. For almost fifty years he engaged in the teaching of taxonomic botany, pharmaceutical and economic botany, paleobotany, and entomology (particularly beetles and fossil insects). As early as 1835 he published the first monograph on plant geography of the Swiss Alps; it became the classic foundation for all his subsequent works. At the end of his life he returned to the same subject, publishing *Über die nivale Flora der Schweiz* (1883). In between, he achieved world fame for his paleobotanical investigations, especially of Tertiary flora. The chief works in this area were *Flora tertiaria Helvetiae* (1855–59), *Flora fossilis Helvetiae* (1876), and *Flora fossilis arctica* (1868–83).

HEFNER-ALTENECK, FRIEDRICH FRANZ VON (*b. Aschaffenburg, Germany, 1845; d. Berlin, Germany, 1904*), engineering.

Hefner-Alteneck spent most of his professional life on the technical staff of an electrical apparatus manufacturer in Berlin. He invented (1872) the drum armature principle for dynamos, which is still in use. He invented numerous other mechanisms that enormously accelerated the early growth of the electrical industry.

HEIDENHAIN, MARTIN (*b. Breslau, Germany [now Wrocław, Poland], 1864; d. Tübingen, Germany, 1949*), microscopic anatomy, microtechnique.

The son of Rudolf Heidenhain, Martin Heidenhain was educated at the universities of Breslau and Würzburg. In 1890 he received his Ph.D. from Freiburg im Breisgau. In 1899 he began his life-long association with the University of Tübingen, where he taught microscopy, embryology, and anatomy. In 1891 he discovered the still widely used iron-hematoxylin staining method that bears his name. Subsequently he invented the mercuric chloride method of tissue fixation and pioneered the use of aniline dyes for the staining of tissue. Heidenhain's magnum opus is the two-volume cytology text *Plasma und Zelle* (1907–11).

HEIDENHAIN, RUDOLF PETER HEINRICH (*b. Marienwerder, East Prussia [now Kwidzyn, Poland], 1834; d. Breslau, Germany [now Wrocław, Poland], 1897*), physiology, histology.

After attending several German universities, Heidenhain received (1854) his M.D. at Berlin with a dissertation containing important work on heart activity. Two years later he published *Physiologische Studien*, and in 1859 he assumed the chair of physiology at the University of Breslau. He continued his work on muscles and nerves, and in 1867 he began systematic studies of the physiology of glands and of secretion and absorption processes. They remained his chief field of interest. He showed that secretion of saliva is largely independent of the blood flow and studied the effects of stimulation of nerves. Heidenhain also studied secretion in the pancreas, the liver, and the intestinal glands. (One of his students was I.P. Pavlov, who later improved some of Heidenhain's experiments.) Heidenhain's reliance on experiment as a sure guide in the search for truth, his technical skill, and his wide-ranging work greatly influenced his contemporaries.

HEIM, ALBERT (*b. Zurich, Switzerland, 1849; d. Zurich, 1937*), geology.

Heim graduated from the Zurich Institute of Technology in 1869 with a dissertation on glaciers. In 1878 he published the two-volume *Mechanismus der Gebirgsbildung* (shortened title) and between 1916 and 1922 his monumental *Geologie der Schweiz*. Heim's talent lay in his power to describe accurately the most complex geological structures and to illustrate them with brilliant drawings, cross sections, and models.

HEIM, ALBERT ARNOLD (*b. Zurich, Switzerland, 1882; d. Zurich, 1965*), geology, geography.

The son of Albert Heim (1849–1937), Albert Arnold Heim studied geology with his father and received his Ph.D. from the University of Zurich in 1905. He taught at Zurich, at Sun Yat Sen University in Canton, China, and in Buenos Aires and Teheran. Heim's initial fame as a geologist came from his studies of the Swiss Alps. His constant expeditionary activity, primarily in the Alps, resulted in over 300 scientific works, which included full accounts of the flora and fauna of the region visited. He also wrote on birds, insects, and bats and developed his own musical notation system to record their sounds.

HEINE, HEINRICH EDUARD (*b. Berlin, Germany, 1821; d. Halle, Germany, 1881*), mathematics.

Heine received his Ph.D. in mathematics from Berlin University in 1842. After 1848 he settled at Halle University. He published about fifty mathematical works, including his *Handbuch der Kugelfunctionen* (1861). Its second edition (1878–81) was long the standard text on spherical functions, for which subject (along with Lamé functions and Bessel functions) Heine is best known. His name is attached to the Heine-Borel covering theorem, although there is controversy as to his contribution to the theorem.

HEISTER, LORENZ (*b. Frankfurt am Main, Germany, 1683; d. Bornum, near Königslutter, Germany, 1758*), anatomy, surgery, medicine.

After studying at various German universities, Heister went to Amsterdam, at the time one of the few places where anatomy could be studied by practical dissection. He received his M.D. from the University of Harderwijk in 1708. Heister made many minor anatomical discoveries, but his main significance was as a teacher and author. At the universities of Altdorf and Helmstedt, where he taught, he trained a large number of surgeons and physicians. His books on anatomy, surgery, and medicine dominated the field for several generations. His works, translated into Japanese, introduced Western methods to Japanese medicine.

HEKTOEN, LUDVIG (*b. Westby, Wis.; 1863; d. Chicago, Ill., 1951*), pathology, microbiology.

After attending Luther College (Decorah, Iowa) and the University of Wisconsin, Hektoen received his M.D. from the College of Physicians and Surgeons in Chicago in 1888. By 1901, when he became head of the pathology department at the University of Chicago, he was recognized as one of the foremost physicians in the Midwest. In 1902 he was appointed director of the newly founded John McCormick Institute of Infectious Diseases (now the Hektoen Institute for Medical Research); there he did important work on scarlet fever and measles. He was one of the pioneers in the rapidly developing field of immunology. Modern techniques of blood transfusion also owe much to his pioneering efforts.

HELL (or HÖLL), MAXIMILIAN (*b. Schemnitz [now Banská Štiavnica, Slovakia [now Czechoslovakia], 1720; d. Vienna, Austria, 1792*), astronomy.

A Jesuit priest, Hell studied philosophy (which then comprised astronomy, mathematics, and physics) at the University of Vienna; he received his Ph.D. in 1752. In 1755 the Hapsburgs established a new astronomical observatory outside Vienna and Hell was named director. In 1769 he observed the transit of Venus from a specially constructed observatory in Lapland. He was later accused of having falsified his data on this observation. The controversy raged on and was not finally resolved until 1883, when Simon Newcomb fully redeemed Hell's reputation by a careful evaluation of his manuscripts.

HELLINGER, ERNST (*b. Striegau, Germany, 1883; d. Chicago, Ill., 1950*), mathematics.

Hellinger taught at the University of Frankfurt am Main from 1914 until 1936, when, as a Jew, he was forced to retire. He was placed in a concentration camp in 1938 but was allowed to emigrate. He settled in the United States, where he taught at Northwestern University. His monumental work on integral equations and equations with infinitely many unknowns (first published in 1927) has attained the status of a classic document.

HELLOT, JEAN (*b. Paris, France, 1685; d. Paris, 1766*), industrial chemistry.

Hellot was appointed inspector general of dyeing in 1740, and his major contributions were to the chemistry and technical aspects of dyeing and to mining and assaying. His *L'art de la teinture des laines* (1750) contained a careful discussion of dyeing techniques and was a standard work for the remainder of the century.

HELLRIEGEL, HERMANN (*b. Mausitz, near Pegau, Saxony, Germany, 1831; d. Bernburg, near Halle, Germany, 1895*), agricultural chemistry.

As director of agricultural research for the dukedom of Anhalt-Bernburg, Hellriegel conducted experiments on the conditions required for the raising of sugar beets. He discovered that certain legumes assimilate nitrogen from the air and convert it into a utilizable bound form in the sandy soil in which beets are grown, thereby greatly adding to the nutrients of the soil. The discovery of this symbiotic cooperation of intermediate crops was of considerable importance.

HELMERSEN, GRIGORY PETROVICH (*b. Duckershof, Latvia, 1803; d. St. Petersburg, Russia, 1885*), geology.

Most of Helmersen's career was spent at the Mining Institute of St. Petersburg and from 1865 to 1872 he was its director. Helmersen played a major role in the development of geological mapping in Russia. He was a prominent coal geologist and was familiar with coal deposits in Russia and Poland. He also compiled (1846) a map of the goldfields in eastern Siberia.

HELMERT, FRIEDRICH ROBERT (*b. Freiberg, Saxony, Germany, 1843; d. Potsdam, Germany, 1917*), geodesy, astronomy.

Helmert studied at the Polytechnische Schule in Dresden and the University of Leipzig, from which he received his Ph.D. in 1867. After 1870 he taught geodesy at the University of Aachen. While there he wrote his masterpiece, *Die mathematischen und physikalischen Theorien der höheren Geodäsie* (1880–84). After 1886 he was connected with the University of Berlin. Helmert was always concerned with improvement in the gravitational formula and in the reduction of determinations of gravity. In 1909 he calculated the value of the flattening of the earth as $1:298.3 \pm 0.7$. He also investigated the state of equilibrium of the masses of the earth's crust, the depth of the isostatic surface, and the accuracy of the dimensions of Hayford's ellipsoidal earth.

HELMHOLTZ, HERMANN VON (*b. Potsdam, Germany, 1821; d. Berlin, Germany, 1894*), energetics, physiological acoustics, physiological optics, epistemology, hydrodynamics, electrodynamics.

At the Potsdam Gymnasium Helmholtz' interests turned very early to physics, but his father did not have the money to send him to the university, and he persuaded his son to turn to medicine, for which there existed the prospect of state financial aid. In 1837 Helmholtz obtained a government stipend for five years' study at the Königlich Medizinisch-chirurgische Friedrich-Wilhelms-Institut in Berlin. In return he committed himself to eight years' service as an army surgeon. He passed his *Abitur* with distinction and left for Berlin in September 1838.

While at the Friedrich Wilhelm Institute, Helmholtz took courses at the University of Berlin. During the winter of 1841 he began research for his dissertation under Johannes Müller and later moved into the circle of Müller's students. Chief among these were Ernst Brücke and Emil du Bois-Reymond. Confident and sophisticated, du Bois-Reymond seems to have taken the younger Helmholtz as his protégé and Brücke quickly won Helmholtz to their program for the advancement of physiology. With Karl Ludwig the three made up the "1847 school" of physiology. Their program reacted sharply against German physiology of previous decades. Philosophically they rejected any explanation of life processes which appealed to nonphysical vital properties or forces. Methodologically they aimed at founding physiology upon the techniques of physics and chemistry. All of Helmholtz' minor papers published between 1843 and 1847, most of which treated problems of animal heat and muscle contraction, clearly reflect the mechanistic tenets of the school.

Helmholtz received the M.D. degree in November 1842. After completing the state medical examinations he was appointed surgeon to the regiment at Potsdam. He maintained his Berlin connections, though, and in 1845 du Bois-Reymond brought the shy young doctor into the newly founded Physikalische Gesellschaft. On 23 July 1847 Helmholtz read to the society his epic memoir "Über die Erhaltung der Kraft," in which he set forth the mathematical principles of the conservation of energy.

In 1848 Brücke resigned his chair of physiology at Königsberg to accept a post at Vienna. When du Bois-Reymond refused the vacant post, Helmholtz was released from his military duty and appointed associate professor of physiology at Königsberg; there he measured the velocity of the nerve impulse, published his first papers on physiological optics and acoustics, and won a European reputation with his invention of the ophthalmoscope in 1851. In 1855, with the help of Alexander von Humboldt, Helmholtz obtained a transfer to the vacant chair of anatomy and physiology at Bonn.

At Bonn, Helmholtz continued his research into sensory physiology, publishing in 1856 volume I of his massive *Handbuch der physiologischen Optik.* His work took a wholly new turn with his seminal paper on the hydrodynamics of vortex motion (1858). He was never satisfied at Bonn. Anatomy was an unfamiliar subject, and there were whispered reports to the minister of education that his anatomy lectures were incompetent. Helmholtz angrily dismissed these reports as the grumblings of medical traditionalists who opposed his mechanistic-physiologi-

cal approach. At the same time he was becoming the most famous young scientist in Germany. In 1857 the Baden government offered him a chair at Heidelberg, then at the peak of its fame as a scientific center; the promise of a new physiology institute convinced him to accept in 1858.

The following thirteen years at Heidelberg were among the most productive of Helmholtz' career. He carried on his research in sensory physiology, publishing in 1862 his influential *Die Lehre von den Tonempfindungen als physiologische Grundlage für die Theorie der Musik.* His treatises on physics included "Über Luftschwingungen in Röhren mit offenen Enden" (1859) and his analysis of the motion of violin strings. By 1860 he had begun research for volume III of his *Handbuch der physiologischen Optik* in which visual judgments of depth and magnitude were to be treated. The study led him directly into the nativist-empiricist controversy and inaugurated a decade of intense concern with epistemological issues. He developed the empiricist position latent in his earlier work. He began that development in volume III of the *Handbuch* (1867), which was an extended defense of the empirical theory of visual perception. In 1868 and 1869 Helmholtz carried that position still further in his work on the foundations of geometry. He summarized his epistemology in the famous popular lecture of 1878, "Die Thatsachen in der Wahrnehmung."

By 1866 Helmholtz had completed his great treatises on sensory physiology and was contemplating abandoning physiology for physics. The scope of physiology had already become too great for any individual to encompass, he wrote in 1868, and while a flourishing school of physiology existed in Germany, German physics was stagnating for lack of well-trained young recruits. When Gustav Magnus' death in 1870 left vacant the prestigious chair of physics at Berlin, Helmholtz and G. R. Kirchhoff, his colleague at Heidelberg, became the primary candidates for the post. The Berlin philosophical faculty preferred Kirchhoff, whom they regarded as the superior teacher. When he refused the post, the nomination went to Helmholtz. Helmholtz' price was high: 4,000 taler yearly plus the construction of a new physics institute to be under his full control. Prussia readily agreed to his terms. He accepted the Berlin post early in 1871.

Helmholtz inaugurated his new position with a series of papers critically assessing the various competing theories of electrodynamic action. This work first brought Maxwell's field theory to the attention of Continental physicists and inspired the later research of Helmholtz' pupil Heinrich Hertz, who entered the Berlin institute in 1878. After 1876 Helmholtz contributed papers on the galvanic cell, the thermodynamics of chemical processes, and meteorology. He devoted the last decade before his death in 1894 to an unsuccessful attempt at founding not only mechanics but all of physics on a single universal principle, that of least action.

By 1885 Helmholtz had become the patriarch of German science and the state's foremost adviser on scientific affairs. This position was recognized in 1887, when he assumed the presidency of the newly founded Physikalisch-technische Reichsanstalt for research in the exact sciences and precision technology. Helmholtz' friend, the industrialist Werner von Siemens, had donated 500,000 marks to the project, and he himself had been among its foremost advocates. Under his administration the Reichsanstalt stressed purely scientific research.

HELMONT, JOHANNES (JOAN) BAPTISTA VAN
(*b. Brussels, Belgium, 1579; d. Brussels, 1644*), chemistry, natural philosophy, medicine, mysticism.

A Flemish aristocrat, Helmont received his M.D. in 1599 and continued his studies in Switzerland, France, and England. He is chiefly remembered as the first person to identify gas as a separate class of substance (from liquid and solid) and as the first person to use the term "gas" in the modern scientific way. He also discovered carbon dioxide. He did important work on the role of acids in digestion and his theories on the character of diseases represented an important step forward from the traditional view of disease an an upset of humoral balance.

Despite the scientific soundness of many of Helmont's theories and experiments, he was also deeply involved in the alchemy and mysticism then widespread in learned circles in Europe. He was a follower of Paracelsus and at one time even defended the efficacy of a pseudo-Paracelsian ointment applied not to the wound but to the weapon and acting by sympathy over long distances. In 1674, he was briefly placed under ecclesiastical custody for his "monstrous superstitions," and his work was condemned. Two years before his death, however, church proceedings against him were dropped and he received the imprimatur for his treatise on fever.

HENCKEL, JOHANN FRIEDRICH
(*b. Merseburg, Germany, 1678; d. Freiberg, Saxony, Germany, 1744*), chemistry, mineralogy.

Henckel received his M.D. from the University of Halle and established a practice at Freiberg. He soon became proficient in using heat and fire for the chemical analysis of mineral substances. He made his reputation in the 1720's with three major books: *Flora saturnizans* (1722), an inquiry into the relations and similarities between plants and animals; *Pyritologia* (1725), an encyclopedic study of the pyrites; and *De mediorum chymicorum* (1727), an investigation of medical reactions. In 1732 he became councilor of mines and established a large laboratory for metallurgical chemistry; it later achieved great renown.

HENDERSON, LAWRENCE JOSEPH
(*b. Lynn, Mass., 1878; d. Boston, Mass., 1942*), biochemistry, physiology.

Henderson attended Harvard College, received his M.D. from Harvard in 1902, and spent virtually the rest of his life there. His studies on the complex buffer system of the organism and on acidosis contributed greatly to the understanding of these subjects. He began his study of blood in 1919, and his description of it as a physicochemical system was summarized in his classic book *Blood: A Study in General Physiology* (1928). Henderson also wrote on sociology and philosophy, notably *Pareto's General Sociology: A Physiologist's Interpretation* (1935).

HENDERSON, THOMAS
(*b. Dundee, Scotland, 1798; d. Edinburgh, Scotland, 1844*), astronomy.

Despite the lack of a formal education in astronomy and very poor eyesight, Henderson was able to make his mark, especially by developing new methods of computation. Most of his early astronomical work was done in his spare time, but after 1834 he was astronomer royal of Scotland, professor of practical astronomy at the University of Edinburgh, and director of the Calton Hill observatory.

HENDERSON, YANDELL
(*b. Louisville, Ky., 1873; d. La Jolla, Calif., 1944*), physiology.

Henderson was educated at Yale University, from which he received a Ph. D. in 1898, and spent the rest of his career there. His physiological researches were devoted almost exclusively to respiration and circulation. He introduced the technique of administering a mixture of carbon dioxide and oxygen, instead of only oxygen, as a method of resuscitation, which proved very successful and saved countless lives. He supervised the construction of gas masks during World War I.

HENFREY, ARTHUR
(*b. Aberdeen, Scotland, 1819; d. London, England, 1859*), botany.

Trained as a physician, Henfrey never practiced. Instead he turned to botany. Eventually he held the chair in botany at King's College, London (1854). He was an advocate of the emerging Continental emphasis on physiological anatomy and comparative morphology. He was influential as an editor, translator, and author of textbooks and manuals in communicating these new theories to British naturalists. Among his works is *Elementary Course in Botany: Structural, Physiological and Systematic* (1857), for a time probably the leading British textbook on botany.

HENKING, HERMANN
(*b. Jerxheim, Germany, 1858; d. Berlin, Germany, 1942*), zoology.

Henking was educated at the University of Göttingen and taught there until he joined the German Fisheries Association in 1892. In the course of his studies on arachnids, he made the first observation of sex chromosomes, although he did not so identify them. Most of his work dealt with scientific fisheries research, and he developed statistical procedures for the German fishing industry. He also made pioneering studies on the migration of fish.

HENLE, FRIEDRICH GUSTAV JACOB
(*b. Fürth, near Nuremberg, Germany, 1809; d. Göttingen, Germany, 1885*), anatomy, pathology.

Henle helped prepare the way for cytology through his studies on epithelia; created the first histology based on extensive microscopical investigations; and, through his theory of miasma and contagion, was among the precursors of modern microbiology. He was educated at the universities of Heidelberg and Bonn; he received his Ph. D. from the latter in 1831 and his M.D. in 1832. He became assistant to Johannes Müller, his great mentor. He was arrested (1835) for belonging to a radical students' movement, sentenced to seven years in prison, but soon released and allowed to resume his academic career. After teaching at Zurich and Heidelberg, he settled (1852) at Göttingen, where he spent thirty-three years. Important works of their time were Henle's *Handbuch der rationellen Pathologie* (2 vols., 1846–53) and *Handbuch der systematischen Anatomie des Menschen* (3 vols., 1855–71). Henle's name is best known today for the loop-shaped portion of the nephron named for him.

HENRI. *See* **Henry.**

HENRICHSEN, SOPHUS (*b. Kragerø, Norway, 1845; d. Oslo, Norway, 1928*), physics.

Henrichsen's main scientific achievements were measurements of the dependence of certain physical quantities on temperature. His first scientific work was an experimental determination of the relation between temperature and electric conductivity in a sulfuric acid solution. He wrote several textbooks and coedited a popular scientific journal.

HENRION, DENIS or **DIDIER** (*b. ca. 1580; d. Paris [?], France, ca. 1632*), mathematics.

Henrion is chiefly remembered for his translation of Euclid's works into French (from Latin texts). His *Traité des logarithmes* (1626), although not original, was the second work on the subject published in France.

HENRY BATE OF MALINES (*b. Malines, Belgium, 1246; d. ca. 1310*), astronomy.

Bate studied at Paris under Albertus Magnus, receiving his M.A. before 1274 and perhaps a master of theology before 1301. His works include translations of astrological treatises by Abraham ibn Ezra, original astronomical and astrological writings, and a philosophical encyclopedia. The last, his most important work, is known as *Speculum divinorum et quorumdam naturalium* (ca. 1305). It is in twenty-three parts and follows the curriculum of the Faculty of Arts in Paris.

HENRY OF DENMARK. *See* **Harpestraeng, Henrik.**

HENRY OF HESSE (*b. Hainbuch, Germany, 1325; d. Vienna, Austria, 1397*), physics, astronomy.

Henry of Hesse received his doctorate in theology at Paris in 1376. He was forced to leave France during the Great Schism, eventually settling in Vienna. He wrote his first astronomical treatise on the comet of 1368 and in 1373 he wrote *Tractatus contra astrologos coniunctionistas de eventibus futurorum,* in which he asserted that the foundations of astrology are based on false astronomical data.

HENRY OF MONDEVILLE (*b. Mondeville, near Caen, or Emondeville, Manche, France, ca. 1260[?]; d. Paris, France, ca. 1320*), surgery, medicine.

Henry of Mondeville is regarded as a key link between Italian and French surgery (he had studied in both countries). He was surgeon in the services of Philip the Fair, Charles of Valois, and Louis X. He taught anatomy and surgery. His reputation today is derived from his unfinished treatise on surgery, which was not published until the nineteenth century. Although his book contains some modern precepts, such as keeping surgical instruments clean, they seem to have had little influence in his own day.

HENRY, JOSEPH (*b. Albany, N.Y., 1797; d. Washington, D.C., 1878*), physics.

Born to a poor family, Henry struggled to attend Albany Academy; after graduating in 1822 he taught there and did private tutoring. His reputation grew and in 1832 he accepted a chair at the College of New Jersey (now Princeton University). In 1846 he became head of the newly formed Smithsonian Institution. He guided it through its early years and was chiefly responsible for setting it on a course of supporting important scientific research.

While still at Albany, Henry began his important work in electricity and magnetism. He greatly improved the electromagnet and in 1832 he independently discovered self-induction. Henry and his British contemporary, Michael Faraday, cooperated with each other and exchanged experimental data. Henry's contributions to the field of electromagnetism are considered second only to Faraday's.

HENRY, PAUL PIERRE, and **HENRY, PROSPER MATHIEU** (*Paul Pierre Henry, b. Nancy, France, 1848; d. Montrouge, near Paris, France, 1905. Prosper Mathieu Henry, b. Nancy, 1849; d. Pralognan, Savoy, France, 1903*), astronomy, optics.

The Henry brothers were united in their careers and their work cannot be separated. Beginning in 1868, they set up a small optical workshop in their home and constructed a thirty-centimeter mirror and its mounting. In 1871 they were invited to join the equatorial telescope section of the Paris observatory, where they continued their work on a map of the stars in the ecliptic zone. Between 1872 and 1878 they discovered fourteen minor planets. They built a photographic telescope that changed the course of astronomy. The Henry instrument was adopted in 1887 as the prototype for the international project of the Carte du Ciel. Seventeen of their instruments were built and placed at various latitudes around the world.

HENRY, THOMAS (*b. Wrexham, Wales, 1734; d. Manchester, England, 1816*), chemistry.

A practicing apothecary, Henry became active in Manchester scientific circles, and translated (1776) Lavoisier's *Opuscules.* Henry's most profitable venture was the manufacture and sale of calcined magnesia for medicinal purposes.

HENRY, WILLIAM (*b. Manchester, England, 1774; d. Manchester, 1836*), chemistry.

The son of Thomas Henry, he left Edinburgh University after one year to superintend the family manufacturing business. Eventually, however (in 1807) he received his M.D. from Edinburgh. In 1801 he published *Elements,* which in numerous editions became the most popular and successful chemistry text in English for more than thirty years. He was long associated with John Dalton in the study of various gases, and his was a significant contribution to the progress of the gas industry. He is sometimes confused with his son William Charles Henry, who is best known for his biography of Dalton.

HENSEL, KURT (*b. Königsberg, Germany [now Kaliningrad, U.S.S.R.], 1861; d. Marburg, Germany, 1941*), mathematics.

Hensel studied mathematics at the universities of Bonn and Berlin. At Berlin, under the guidance of Leopold Kronecker, he took his Ph.D. in 1884. He spent years editing Kronecker's papers. His scientific work was based on Kronecker's arithmetical theory of algebraic number fields. He developed this fully in *Theorie der algebraischen*

Funktionen (1902), *Theorie der algebraischen Zahlen* (1908), and *Zahlentheorie* (1913). From 1901 until retirement in 1930 he was at the University of Marburg.

HENSEN, (CHRISTIAN ANDREAS) VICTOR (*b. Schleswig, Germany, 1835; d. Kiel, Germany, 1924*), physiology, marine biology.

Hensen studied at various German universities and received (1858) his medical degree from the University of Kiel. He was associated with Kiel for most of his career. In physiology, he preferred the histophysiological method and, using it, settled essential questions regarding the basic conditions of hearing and sight. In marine biology—originally a hobby—he investigated the fauna of the oceans, especially plankton (a term he coined). He led large plankton expeditions and may be regarded as the originator of quantitative marine research.

HENSLOW, JOHN STEVENS (*b. Rochester, Kent, England, 1796; d. Hitcham, Suffolk, England, 1861*), botany.

At Cambridge, from which he received his M.A. in 1821, Henslow studied mathematics, chemistry, and mineralogy; he was professor of minerology (1822) and then of botany (1825). He was also an ordained minister. His main scientific interests were plant geography, morphology, and physiology. Charles Darwin was one of his students, and it was Henslow who recommended Darwin as naturalist for the voyage of H.M.S. *Beagle*. Henslow received and took care of all the specimens sent back by Darwin.

HERACLIDES PONTICUS (*b. Heraclea Pontica [now Ereğli, Turkey], ca. 390 B.C.; d. Heraclea Pontica, after 339 B.C.*), astronomy.

Heraclides was a student at Plato's Academy (before 360 B.C.) and also attended Aristotle's lectures. His many books were greatly admired in antiquity, but not a single one has survived. Mostly, they contained the kind of prescientific speculation common to early Greek philosophy. Today he is famous chiefly for an astronomical theory holding that the orbits of Venus and Mercury have the sun as their center, while the sun itself moves around the earth. (Evidence for this attribution to him is incomplete, however). He is the earliest known philosopher to have held that the earth is central and stationary and turns on its axis once a day. It is this assertion alone that gives him a definite place in the history of astronomy.

HERACLITUS OF EPHESUS (*fl. ca. 500 B.C.*), moral philosophy, natural philosophy.

Heraclitus, whose works have survived only in fragments, is the first Greek philosopher to emerge as a personality. He is most famous for his physical doctrine that "all things are in flux and nothing is stable," and that "it is not possible to step twice into the same river." Both Plato and Aristotle discussed his cosmology, but it is not clear how developed his cosmological system was.

HERAPATH, JOHN (*b. Bristol, England, 1790; d. Lewisham, England, 1868*), theoretical physics, journalism.

Herapath was largely self-educated and for most of his life earned his living in journalism. He became (1836) editor of *Railway Magazine and Annals of Science* (later *Herapath's Railway and Commercial Journal*), and it was in this journal that he published his scientific papers. He is best known as the first to work out extensive calculations and applications of the kinetic theory of gases. In 1832 he published the first known calculation of the speed of a molecule from the kinetic theory of gases, although Joule is ordinarily credited with this accomplishment.

HERAPATH, WILLIAM BIRD (*b. Bristol, England, 1820; d. Bristol, 1868*), medicine, chemistry.

A cousin of John Herapath, William Bird Herapath was awarded an M.B. in 1844 from London University and in 1851 became an M.D. He published many articles in medical, chemical, and scientific journals. His most successful feat was producing small but usable crystals of iodosulfate of quinine (now called herapathite after him), which he patented for optical use. He also devised new methods for detecting arsenic and other substances and developed new methods for pathological investigations. He was interested in domestic sanitation and worked for a close alliance between chemistry and medical research.

HERBART, JOHANN FRIEDRICH (*b. Oldenburg, Germany, 1776; d. Göttingen, Germany, 1841*), philosophy, psychology, pedagogy.

Herbart was strongly influenced by the Enlightenment thought of his period, particularly Kant's ethics and Fichte's metaphysics. In 1808 he took over Kant's chair at Königsberg, where he established the first pedagogical institute with an experimental school. According to Herbart, the structure and operation of human perception are conditioned by the changing complex of ultimate entities of reality, which he called the "reals" (*Realen*); they were modeled after Leibniz' monads. He believed that mental processes can be described with the exactness of mathematical laws. In pedagogy, he saw the goal of education as the uniting of five ideas: inner freedom (harmony of moral insight and will), perfection (health of body and soul), benevolence (toward the will of others), justice (balancing of interests, respect for the rights of others), and equity (suitability of reward and punishment).

HERBERT, WILLIAM (*b. Highclere, Hampshire, England, 1778; d. London, England, 1847*), natural history.

An English aristocrat, Herbert attended Eton and Oxford and served (1806–07, 1811–12) in the House of Commons. Plant life held the greatest scientific attraction for Herbert. His classification of the Amaryllidaceae, published in 1837, established his reputation as a botanist. He aimed at a "natural" classification and was generally more advanced in his views than most botanists of his day. He was among the earliest in Britain to study hybridization on a large scale. He considered it a factor in evolution, and Darwin made numerous mentions of Herbert's findings.

HERBRAND, JACQUES (*b. Paris, France, 1908; d. La Bérarde, Isère, France, 1931*), mathematics, logic.

Herbrand gave early signs of mathematical gifts. He received his doctorate in 1929 at the École Normale Supérieure and then studied under John von Neumann, Emil Artin, and Emmy Noether. He was killed in a fall in the Alps at the age of twenty-three. Herbrand's contributions fall into two categories: mathematical logic and modern algebra. The Herbrand theorem, as it is now known, is the most fundamental result in quantification theory and establishes a bridge between quantification theory and sentential logic. In modern algebra Herbrand's contributions are in class-field theory. He wrote ten papers in this field, simplifying previous proofs, generalizing theorems, and discovering important new results.

HÉRELLE, FÉLIX D' (*b. Montreal, Canada, 1873; d. Paris, France, 1949*), microbiology.

A French-Canadian, d'Hérelle was educated in Paris and Leiden. He taught microbiology in the medical school in Guatemala City. In 1915 he identified the phenomenon of bacteriophagy. (An English scientist, Frederick Twort, had observed the phenomenon slightly earlier but did not continue his investigations.) In 1921 d'Hérelle published *Le bactériophage, son rôle dans l'immunité,* for which he received wide acclaim. In the following decades, he traveled to many parts of the world, organizing programs to study the bacteriophage as it applies to various human and animal infectious diseases.

HÉRIGONE, PIERRE (*d. Paris [?], France, ca. 1643*), mathematics.

Hérigone was apparently a Basque who spent most of his life teaching mathematics in Paris; little else is known of him. His only important work is *Cursus mathematicus* (1634–42), a six-volume compendium of elementary and intermediate mathematics that shows an extensive knowledge and understanding of contemporary mathematics. Although he introduced in it a complete system of mathematical and logical notation, it seems to have been ignored by his contemporaries.

HERING, KARL EWALD KONSTANTIN (*b. Alt-Gersdorf, Germany, 1834; d. Leipzig, Germany, 1918*), physiology, psychology.

Hering studied medicine at the University of Leipzig. He practiced medicine, taught physiology, and published (1861–64) a five-part study on visual space perception. He challenged the great master in that field, Hermann von Helmholtz, proposing alternative views that emphasized the physiological rather than the physical aspects of sensation. With Josef Breuer he discovered reflex reactions originating in the lungs and mediated by the fibers of the vagus nerve. As the main representative of the phenomenological tradition, Hering exerted a great influence on the evolution of modern psychology, particularly Gestalt theory. In general, Hering's theories did not prove correct in the new era of nerve and sensory physiology that began in the 1920's.

HERMANN (HERMANNUS) THE LAME (also known as **Hermannus Contractus** or **Hermann of Reichenau**) (*b. Altshausen, Germany, 1013; d. Altshausen, 1054*), astronomy, mathematics.

Hermannus is one of the key figures in the transmission of Arabic astronomical techniques and instruments to the Latin West before the period of translation. He is one of the earliest Latin authors responsible for the introduction or reintroduction into the West from the Islamic world (undoubtedly Spain) of three astronomical instruments: the astrolabe, the chilinder (a portable sundial),

and the quadrant with cursor. Since the thirteenth century a *De mensura astrolabii* has been ascribed to him. The first section of a second work, often called in its entirety *De utilitatibus astrolabii,* was attributed to Gerbert as early as the twelfth century. The second section of the *De utilitatibus,* containing a description of the chilinder and the quadrant, is generally considered to be by Hermannus.

In mathematics Hermannus composed a treatise teaching multiplication and division with the abacus (*Qualiter multiplicationes fiant in abbaco*); the work uses Roman numerals only. He also wrote the earliest treatise on rithmomachia (*De conflictu rithmimachie*), a very complex game based on Pythagorean number theory derived from Boethius.

Hermannus composed an excellent world chronicle dating from the birth of Christ which was continued by Berthold and was used by later German historians. He was also the author of a work on music (*Opuscula musica*) and wrote poems and hymns.

HERMANN, CARL HEINRICH (*b. Lehe, near Bremerhaven, Germany, 1898; d. Marburg, Germany, 1961*), solid-state physics, crystallography.

Hermann studied mathematics and physics at Göttingen; he obtained his Ph.D. in 1923 under Max Born. From 1925 to 1937 he taught at Stuttgart, during which time he published *Strukturberichte* (1931–37) and *Internationale Tabellen zur Bestimmung von Kristallstrukturen* (2 vols., 1935). Hermann's work on modern crystallography and solid-state theory helped to guide their development along sound mathematical lines. His structure theory calls for the investigation of all possible spatially periodic arrangements of matter that differ in their internal symmetry. Any of the 230 "space groups" thus determined can serve as the repeat scheme for the arrangement of atoms in a crystal. A Quaker, Hermann was forced out of his teaching position by the Nazis but continued his work in the X-ray laboratories of I.G. Farbenindustrie. He was in prison during the latter half of World War II. He ended his teaching career after the war at the University of Marburg.

HERMANN, JAKOB (*b. Basel, Switzerland, 1678; d. Basel, 1733*), mathematics.

Hermann devoted much of his time to mathematics while studying theology at the University of Basel (under the guidance of Jacob I Bernoulli). At an early age, he was able to join the small group of the most important mathematicians. In 1707, assisted by Leibniz, he became professor of mathematics at Padua. (He later also taught at Bologna.) While in Italy, Hermann finished his principal scientific work, the *Phoronomia* (1716). This textbook advanced mechanics in the modern sense and was considered an important work, very favorably reviewed by Leibniz himself. From 1724 to 1731 he was at the Academy in St. Petersburg.

HERMANNUS CONTRACTUS. *See* **Hermann the Lame.**

HERMBSTAEDT, SIGISMUND FRIEDRICH (*b. Erfurt, Germany, 1760; d. Berlin, Germany, 1833*), chemistry, technology.

An apothecary by profession (with a doctorate in chemistry), Hermbstaedt became Prussian court apothecary in Berlin in 1790. In 1791 he was given the title of professor and wrote a three-volume textbook and translated (1792) Lavoisier's *Traité élémentaire de chimie.* His reputation in the field of technology was of the highest and when the University of Berlin opened in 1810, he became professor of technological chemistry. His *Grundriss der Technologie* (1814) was widely consulted by merchants, factory owners, and officials—both Prussian and foreign. After the Napoleonic Wars, he headed the organization charged with the task of rebuilding the Prussian economy.

HERMES TRISMEGISTUS, *philosophy, astrology, magic, alchemy.*

The ancient Greeks identified their god Hermes with the Egyptian Thoth and gave him the epithet Trismegistus, or "Thrice-Greatest," for he had given them their vaunted arts and sciences. A vast literature in Greek was ascribed to Hermes Trismegistus; the cited number of works ranges from 20,000 (Seleucus) to 36,525 (Manetho).

The so-called *Corpus Hermeticum,* a collection of religious and philosophical works, is best known and has received considerable attention from scholars and those interested in the occult. Most of its seventeen or eighteen works were probably written in the second century.

Besides the works of the *Corpus,* a work entitled *Asclepius* exists in a Latin translation. The work, a dialogue between Asclepius and Hermes Trismegistus, is of interest for its purported description of the ancient Egyptian religion.

A strong Hermetic tradition persisted in the Middle Ages and Hermes Trismegistus was usually associated with alchemy and magical talismans. Medieval chemistry was often called the "hermetic science."

The magical and philosophical literature attributed to Hermes Trismegistus received widespread currency in the Renaissance. Traditional Hermetism was erroneously considered to be of ancient Egyptian origin and thus much older than the esteemed Greek philosophers who had been influenced by Egyptian beliefs.

Both philosophical and magical Hermetism declined rapidly in the seventeenth century after Isaac Casaubon showed in 1614 that the Hermetic writings were of the post-Christian era. Hermetism continued thereafter only among the Rosicrucians and other secret societies and occult groups.

HERMITE, CHARLES (*b. Dieuze, Lorraine, France, 1822; d. Paris, France, 1901*), mathematics.

Hermite was educated at the École Polytechnique in Paris, receiving his *baccalauréat* and *licence* in 1847. By that time, despite his youth, he had already achieved some renown for his work in general function theory as well as on elliptic and hyperelliptic functions. He rose quickly at the École Polytechnique, finally becoming professor in 1869. His textbooks in analysis became classics, famous even outside France. Throughout his lifetime and for years afterward, Hermite was an inspiring figure in mathematics. In today's mathematics, he is remembered chiefly for Hermitean forms (a complex generalization of quadratic forms) and for Hermitean polynomials. An interpolation procedure is also named after him. More important, however, were the discoveries that laid the groundwork for breakthroughs by other mathematicians.

HERNÁNDEZ, FRANCISCO (*b. Montalban, near Toledo, Spain, 1517; d. Toledo, 1587*), natural history.

Hernández was physician to Philip II, on whose orders he went to Mexico, where, from 1570 to 1577, he studied the flora and fauna. His efforts resulted in sixteen books, which formed the foundation for later works on Mexican natural history.

HERO OF ALEXANDRIA (*fl. Alexandria, Egypt,* A.D. *62*), mathematics, physics, pneumatics, mechanics.

Virtually nothing, aside from his surviving works, is known of Hero (or Heron) of Alexandria. The construction of his most famous work, *Pneumatics,* indicates that he taught mathematics, physics, pneumatics, and mechanics, probably at the University of Alexandria. *Pneumatics* can best be regarded as a collection of notes for a textbook. The work treats the occurrence of a vacuum in nature and the pressure of air and water. He discusses siphons, a fire pump, and a water organ. He also describes in great detail numerous playthings and apparatuses for parlor magic. Some of the toys described were powered by hot air or steam. The theoretical sections of *Pneumatics* contain some theory that is right, some that is wrong; but it was the best theoretical explanation to be had at the time.

Another work, the *Mechanics,* is a textbook for architects, engineers, builders, and contractors, divided into three books. Book 1 deals with the theoretical and practical knowledge necessary for the builder: the theory of the wheel, the theory of motion, the theory of balance, and how to construct both plane and solid figures in a given figure. Book 2 contains the theory of the five simple "powers": the winch, the lever, the pulley, the wedge, and the screw. It also discusses gravity and the distribution of weight on supports. Book 3 describes various devices: sledges, wine presses, cranes, and so forth.

Hero's reputation as a mathematician rests primarily on his *Metrica,* a work discovered in manuscript in 1896. Traditionally, he was regarded as a mere "technician," ignorant or neglectful of the theoretical sophistication of his predecessors. In the light of recent scholarship, however, he now appears as a well-educated and often ingenious applied mathematician, as well as a vital link in a continuous tradition of practical mathematics from the Babylonians, through the Arabs, to Renaissance Europe.

HERODOTUS OF HALICARNASSUS (*b. Halicarnassus, Caria, Asia Minor, fifth century* B.C.; *d. Thurii, near the site of Sybaris, southern Italy, 430–420* B.C.), history.

Although Herodotus was primarily concerned with narrating and explaining the course of events (i.e., history), especially the conflicts between Greeks and Asiatics, his work contains much information on subjects that would now be classified as geography, ethnography, and anthropology. He had some value as a researcher. He knew the value of autopsy and of direct firsthand information. He frequently gives alternative versions of an incident, sometimes reciting both of them with a healthy skepticism. On the other hand, he tells us little that is useful about contemporary science or technology.

HERON. *See* **Hero of Alexandria.**

HEROPHILUS (*b. Chalcedon, Bithynia, last third of the fourth century* B.C.), anatomy, physiology.

Little is known of the life of Herophilus and all of his writings have perished. He taught and practiced medicine at Alexandria, then probably the only Greek city in which dissection of the human body could be practiced. Herophilus acquired great prestige and students flocked to his school in Alexandria (which survived after his death). It was in anatomy that Herophilus made his greatest contributions, conducting important anatomical investigations of the brain, eye, nervous and vascular systems, and the genital organs; he discovered the nerves and demonstrated their origin in the brain, and was first to isolate the lacteals. He also wrote on obstetrics and gynecology, and held an elaborate quantitative theory of the pulse. Several medical terms, some still in use, were coined by him. In addition to anatomy, he wrote a treatise on dietetics, and recommended gymnastics as a means of preserving health. His true importance lies in the fact that he, together with Erasistratus, laid the foundations for the scientific study of anatomy and physiology.

HÉROULT, PAUL LOUIS TOUSSAINT (*b. Thury-Harcourt, Normandy, France, 1863; d. Cannes, France, 1914*), metallurgy.

Héroult studied at the École des Mines at Paris under Henry Le Chatelier, who communicated to him his great interest in aluminum. In 1886, when he was only twenty-three, Héroult registered his patent for a process for manufacturing aluminum—the process still in use today. Later he invented a highly successful furnace for producing steel.

HERRERA, ALFONSO LUÍS (*b. Mexico City, Mexico, 1868; d. Mexico City, 1942*), biology.

Trained in pharmacy, Herrera became (1889) professor of botany and zoology at the Normal School. In 1904 he published a textbook, *Nociones de biología,* and he also published for the National Museum catalogs of its collections of fauna. In 1915 he organized and headed (until he retired in 1930) the Direction of Biological Studies, the country's largest center for biological research. Herrera specialized in problems of biological adaptation to high altitudes, publishing the results of his experiments in *La vie sur les hauts plateaux* (1899).

HERRICK, CHARLES JUDSON ·and **HERRICK, CLARENCE LUTHER** (*Charles Judson Herrick, b. Minneapolis, Minn., 1868; d. Grand Rapids, Mich., 1960. Clarence Luther Herrick, b. Minneapolis, 1858; d. Socorro, N.M., 1904*), comparative neurology, psychobiology.

Clarence Luther Herrick received his B.A. in 1880 from the University of Minnesota. In 1885 he became professor of geology and natural history at Denison University. In 1888 he went to the University of Cincinnati, where he founded the *Journal of Comparative Neurology.* Charles Judson Herrick studied under his older brother at Cincinnati, receiving his B.S. in 1891. In 1893 he became a graduate student under his brother again, this time at Denison, to which Clarence Luther Herrick had returned the prior year as professor of biology. Clarence was forced to resign for medical reasons (pulmonary tuberculosis) and moved to New Mexico. He spent the rest of his life there, becoming (1897) the second president of

the University of New Mexico. While still at Denison, he had launched the new science of psychobiology, aided by his brother and, later, George Ellett Coghill. The three men encouraged comparative anatomists, physiologists, and psychiatrists to coordinate their attack upon the mind-body problem.

Charles Judson Herrick assumed most of his brother's duties at Denison when the latter moved to New Mexico. He received his Ph.D. from Columbia University in 1900. Under him, the journal, later renamed the *Journal of Comparative Neurology and Psychology,* became one of the outstanding biological journals in America. Charles became (1907) professor of neurology at the University of Chicago. He remained there until he retired in 1934. His major work, *The Evolution of Human Nature,* was published in 1956.

HERSCHEL, a family of distinguished scientists of German origin, established in England in 1757. Its most notable members, on whom separate articles follow, were William Herschel (1738–1822), his sister Caroline Lucretia Herschel (1750–1848), and his only son, John Frederick William Herschel (1792–1871). The central position that the Herschel family held in British astronomy extended over a century. They were connected by marriage to the Maclean and Waterfield families.

HERSCHEL, CAROLINE LUCRETIA (*b. Hannover, Germany, 1750; d. Hannover, 1848*), astronomy.

Caroline Herschel followed her brother, William Herschel, from Hannover to England in 1772. At first a professional singer, she gradually became immersed in astronomy along with her brother. In 1782 she turned full time to the study of astronomy, assisting her brother and on her own, sweeping the skies for nebulae. She discovered three new nebulae in 1783, and between 1786 and 1797 she discovered eight comets. Her work was recognized by a royal pension and in 1798 her revision of Flamsteed's catalog of stars was published by the Royal Society. She was also a major influence on her nephew John Frederick William Herschel.

HERSCHEL, JOHN FREDERICK WILLIAM (*b. Slough, Buckinghamshire, England, 1792; d. Hawkhurst, Kent, England, 1871*), astronomy, physics, chemistry.

The only son of William Herschel, John Herschel was educated at Eton and St. John's College, Cambridge University, where he achieved an impressive reputation as a mathematician. He and George Peacock translated Lacroix's *Traité du calcul différentiel et du calcul intégral* (1816). He was also accomplished in chemistry, but after some vacillation took up astronomy out of "filial devotion" to his father, whose own powers were waning. His aunt, Caroline Herschel, also exerted a strong influence on his choice of astronomy as a career. His affluence allowed him the luxury of extensive travel. On his journeys, he made many physical and meteorological experiments and he met with most of the leading astronomers of his day.

John Herschel's choice of research topics was characteristically diverse: physical and geometrical optics, polarization and birefringence of crystals, spectrum analysis, and the interference of light and sound waves. In 1819 he discovered that sodium thiosulfate dissolved silver salts, a fact that later was of great importance in the newly discovered process of photography. He published numerous scientific papers and contributed important articles to the encyclopedias of the day.

In 1834, he established an observatory and laboratory at Cape Town, from where he did extensive astronomical, oceanographical, and meteorological experiments. Using new processes and equipment, he cataloged the southern skies, counting stars, and comparing their brightness by the use of his invention called an astrometer. He left South Africa in 1838 and was created a baronet. In his later years, Herschel did important work on the new process of photography. (He coined the terms "positive image" and "negative image.") Because his interests in photography were mainly scientific, he has not received the credit due him in the practical development of photography. John Herschel had twelve children, several of whom carried on the family's scientific traditions.

HERSCHEL, WILLIAM (*b. Hannover, Germany, 1738; d. Observatory House, Slough, Buckinghamshire, England, 1822*), astronomy.

Friedrich Wilhelm (William) Herschel, a professional musician, emigrated to England from Hannover in 1757. He supported himself by copying music, teaching, performing (on the oboe and the organ), conducting, and composing. In 1773, with the aid of his sister Caroline Herschel, he began manufacturing reflecting telescopes. He also began a systematic review of the heavens. In 1781 he made a sensational discovery: Uranus, a primary planet of the solar system. As a result, he became world famous and was named astronomer royal, which gave him a royal pension. He was now able to devote himself solely to astronomy. In 1789 he completed a monster telescope (40 feet) that, despite its cumbersomeness, was one of the wonders of the world. It immediately revealed a sixth satellite of Saturn. (He later discovered the seventh.) In 1783 Herschel embarked on a twenty-year program for sweeping the skies for nebulae and eventually raised the total of those known to 2,500 (from little more than 100). In his attempt to determine the distance of stars by studying double stars, or binary stars, he discovered that double stars are gravitationally connected (even though his hypothesis regarding the relative brightness of the double stars proved wrong). In the course of his experiments, he identified about 800 double stars.

Herschel's most important single achievement consisted in his development of far-reaching theories of "the construction of the heavens." His powerful telescopes showed him that the nebulae are in fact clusters of stars. He concluded that the universe began with stars scattered throughout infinite space. Under the action of the forces of attraction, in time the stars condensed toward regions where they eventually formed tightly packed clusters. Herschel considered that the groups of nebulae he discovered represented the fragments of larger associations of stars, and he took a similar view of the star clusters of the Milky Way. In 1811 and 1814 he published a theory of the development of a star cluster: an "extensive diffused nebulosity" gradually condenses into stars, which in turn cluster together even more tightly.

Although Herschel's studies of the sun, moon, planets, and comets are less significant than his investigations of the sidereal universe, they nevertheless represent solid achievements. He confirmed the existence of infrared

heat rays and he showed that heat obeys laws of reflection and refraction analogous to those of light. He was knighted in 1816.

HERTWIG, KARL WILHELM THEODOR RICHARD VON (*b. Friedberg, Hessen, Germany, 1850; d. Schlederlohe, Germany, 1937*), biology.

Richard Hertwig and his brother, Oscar Hertwig, studied under Ernst Haeckel at Jena from 1868 to 1871. The brothers remained at Jena, and in 1872 Richard Hertwig became lecturer of zoology, and professor in 1878. Shortly after that he went to Königsberg, and later to Bonn. In 1885 he went to Munich, where he remained until he retired in 1925. He contributed to many fields of biology: he was a protozoologist, an embryologist, and a cytologist. In the 1870's he and his brother published works on the nervous system, the sense organs, and the musculature of various coelenterates. During the next decade the two brothers did important work in embryology, especially artificial hybridization. Richard Hertwig's *Textbook of Zoology* was highly influential.

HERTWIG, WILHELM AUGUST OSCAR (*b. Friedberg, Hessen, Germany, 1849; d. Berlin, Germany, 1922*), zoology.

Oscar Hertwig and his brother, Richard Hertwig, studied under Ernst Haeckel at Jena from 1868 to 1871. They remained at the university, Oscar Hertwig becoming professor of anatomy in 1881. From 1888 until 1921 he held the first chair of cytology and embryology and directed the new Anatomical-Biological Institute. He did important work in embryology. In 1875 he established the fact that fertilization occurs by the union of the nuclei of the male and female sex cells. He also established that the transfer of hereditary material is part of the same nuclear process. His most important research was on the egg of the sea urchin. He often experimented and wrote papers in collaboration with his brother. Oscar Hertwig's textbooks were highly successful, especially *Lehrbuch der Entwicklungsgeschichte des Menschen und der Wirbeltiere* (2 vols., 1886–88) and *Die Zelle und die Gewebe* (2 vols., 1893–98; retitled *Allgemeine Biologie*, 2nd ed., 1906). His demonstration of nuclear continuity and conjugation—his greatest contribution to science—is contained in his *Habilitationsschrift* (1875).

HERTZ, HEINRICH RUDOLF (*b. Hamburg, Germany, 1857; d. Bonn, Germany, 1894*), physics.

Hertz entered the Johanneum Gymnasium when he was fifteen. After his *Abitur* in 1875 he went to Frankfurt to prepare for a career in engineering. After a short time at the Dresden Polytechnic in 1876, he put in his year of military service 1876–77. He then moved to Munich in 1877 with the intention of studying further at the Technische Hochschule there. He matriculated in 1877 at the University of Munich instead of at the Technische Hochschule—relieved at having decided on an academic and scientific career.

After a year in Munich, Hertz went to Berlin where he met Hermann von Helmholtz, who was to have a profound influence on him throughout his career. He responded eagerly to the intensive research environment in Berlin and in German physics in general. He wrote a doctoral dissertation on electromagnetic induction in rotating conductors, a purely theoretical work that took him only three months to complete.

In 1880 he began as a salaried assistant to Helmholtz in the practical work of the Berlin Physical Institute, a position he held for three years. In 1883 he moved to Kiel, where he discovered that he was a successful lecturer and teacher.

Hertz spent four years at Karlsruhe, from 1885 to 1889. In 1886 he began the experimental studies that were to make him world-famous. In the rich Karlsruhe physical cabinet he came across induction coils that enabled him to tackle the problem on Maxwell's theory that Helmholtz had set several years earlier for the 1879 Berlin Academy prize. By the end of 1888 he had gone beyond the terms of Helmholtz' problem and had confirmed the existence of finitely propagated electric waves in air. All the time he was in close touch with Helmholtz, sending him his papers to communicate to the Berlin Academy for quick publication before sending them later to *Annalen der Physik*. In December 1888 the Prussian *Kultusministerium* offered Hertz the physics professorship at the University of Bonn which he accepted. He moved to Bonn in 1889. The main advantage of the Bonn position over that at Karlsruhe was that it required less teaching and left Hertz more time for research. In Bonn he continued the theoretical study of Maxwell's theory that he had begun in Karlsruhe; this research led to two classic papers on the subject, published in *Annalen der Physik* in 1890. In the spring of 1891 he began the research that would occupy him almost exclusively until his death: a purely theoretical study of the principles of mechanics inspired by Helmholtz' new work on the principle of least action. The one distraction from his mechanical study was the request at the end of 1891 by J. A. Barth, the publisher of *Annalen der Physik*, that he collect his papers on electric waves for publication in book form, which he did, and dedicated the collection to Helmholtz.

Hertz's chief contribution to physics was in bringing about a decision regarding the proper principles for representing electrodynamics. His experimental researches in Karlsruhe settled once and for all the long conflict in nineteenth-century physics over the merits of action at a distance versus contiguous action. After Hertz it was eccentric to continue to advocate action at a distance in electrodynamics—or for that matter in any other part of physics.

He perceived early on that Helmholtz had more to offer him than did any other German physicist. His relation to Helmholtz was a disciple. His dependence on him lay in his recognition of Helmholtz' sure grasp of the central, soluble problems of physics. In his brief career Hertz revealed himself not so much as an innovator of concepts, but as one having an uncommonly critical and lucid intelligence in addressing the conceptual problems of physics that others, Helmholtz above all, had marked out.

HERTZSPRUNG, EJNAR (*b. Frederiksberg, Denmark, 1873; d. Roskilde, Denmark, 1967*), astronomy.

Hertzsprung graduated in chemistry from the Polytechnical Institute in Copenhagen in 1898 and spent the next few years as a chemist in St. Petersburg. In 1901 he studied photochemistry under Wilhelm Ostwald in Leipzig; thereafter he devoted himself to astronomy. He taught and directed observatories at several German universities. After 1919, until he retired in 1944, he was at the University of Leiden.

When Hertzsprung began as an astronomer, the use of photography in astronomy was in its infancy. His knowledge of chemistry and photochemistry aided him in devising new methods of photography. In two classic papers (1905,1907) he demonstrated a new method for measuring luminosity. His method, under the title "spectroscopic parallaxes," has become one of the most powerful means for determining stellar distances, galactic structure, and distances to other galactic systems.. In 1905 he discovered high-luminosity, or giant, stars. He and the American astronomer H.N. Russell, working independently, devised what is now known as the Hertzsprung-Russell diagram. It divides stars into two categories: main sequence and high luminosity. Its graph shows the luminosity of a star to be a function of its temperature. During the 1920's he concentrated on variable stars. He took 1,792 plates of the skies and made about 50,000 estimates of brightness of variable stars. By following his own principles of unceasing observation and hard work, he placed himself among the great astronomers of all time.

HESS, GERMAIN HENRI (*b. Geneva, Switzerland, 1802; d. St. Petersburg, Russia [now Leningrad, U.S.S.R.], 1850*), chemistry.

Hess was taken to Russia at age three and lived there all his life. He took a medical degree from the University of Dorpat (now Tartu, Estonia) in 1825 and established a practice at Irkutsk. During the 1830's he established himself as an academician and taught at several educational institutions in St. Petersburg. He was noted chiefly for his thermochemical investigations, which laid the groundwork for later research in chemical thermodynamics. His work was later continued by Thomsen and Berthelot. He was very influential in the development of chemistry in Russia, particularly through his textbook *Osnovania chistoy khimii* (1831).

HESS, VICTOR FRANZ (FRANCIS) (*b. Schloss Waldstein, Styria, Austria, 1883; d. Mount Vernon, N.Y., 1964*), physics.

Hess received the Ph.D. from the University of Graz in 1906 and did advanced work there with Franz Exner and Egon von Schweidler. Later he joined Exner in Vienna, where ionization in the atmosphere was to become a principal area of study for him. In 1911 he began a series of ten balloon ascensions (reaching a height of 5,350 meters), which proved that radiation at 5,000 meters is several times greater than at sea level and that it was not the result of the direct rays of the sun. Thus he concluded that the rays entered the atmosphere from above and were of cosmic origin. The discovery of cosmic rays won him the Nobel Prize in physics in 1936 (shared with C. D. Anderson). From 1920 to 1938 he was mostly at the University of Graz. After fleeing the Nazis in 1938, he settled in New York City, where he taught at Fordham University.

HESSE, LUDWIG OTTO (*b. Königsberg, Germany [now Kaliningrad, U.S.S.R.], 1811; d. Munich, Germany, 1874*), mathematics.

Hesse studied mathematics and the natural sciences at the University of Königsberg, where he continued to teach after graduation in 1840. Hesse's mathematical works are important for the development of the theory of algebraic functions and the theory of variants. His work was closely related to that of C.G.J. Jacobi, under whom Hesse studied at Königsberg. Hesse's textbooks were especially influential; his collected works appeared in 1897 under the title *Gesammelte Werke*.

HESSEL, JOHANN FRIEDRICH CHRISTIAN (*b. Nuremberg, Germany, 1796; d. Marburg, Germany, 1872*), mineralogy, crystallography.

Hessel's most important scientific contribution was his mathematical derivation, from consideration of the symmetry elements of crystals, of the fact that there can be only thirty-two crystal classes and only two-, three-, four-, and sixfold axes of symmetry can occur. Hessel spent his entire career at the University of Marburg and published more than forty scientific books and papers. Although he enunciated his crystal theory in 1830, it drew no attention until 1891, long after his death.

HEURAET, HENDRIK VAN (*b. Haarlem, Netherlands, 1633; d. 1660 [?]*), mathematics.

Van Heuraet studied medicine and mathematics at the University of Leiden. There, in collaboration with Christian Huygens, Frans van Schooten, and Jan Hudde, he devised methods for tangent determinations and quadratures of algebraic curves. Van Heuraet's own general method of rectification of curves drew attention because it broke the spell of Aristotle's dictum that curved lines could not in principle be compared with straight ones.

HEURNE, JAN VAN (or **Johannes Heurnius**) (*b. Utrecht, Netherlands, 1543; d. Leiden, Netherlands, 1601*), medicine.

Van Heurne studied medicine at Louvain and graduated (1571) from Padua, then the most famous center of medical education in Europe. At Padua, van Heurne had been exposed to the new practice of the teaching of medical students at the bedside. Later, in 1591, while teaching medicine at the University of Leiden, he proposed introducing the practice there. His proposal was turned down, and it was not until forty-five years later (when his son Otto van Heurne had succeeded to his chair) that bedside teaching was finally introduced at Leiden. It was still the first introduction of the practice into northern Europe.

HEVELIUS, JOHANNES (*b. Danzig [now Gdańsk], Poland, 1611; d. Danzig, 1687*), astronomy, instrument making.

Hevelius studied mathematics and astronomy under Peter Krüger and jurisprudence at the University of Leiden. After 1639 he conducted systematic astronomical observations. He built his own observatory (one of the world's best at the time), constructed his own instruments, and began collecting the data for his catalog of 1,564 stars. He maintained a correspondence with all the leading astronomers of his day, including Halley, Hooke, Kepler, and Scheiner. He was assisted in his work by his wife Elisabetha Koopman, who edited his unpublished works after his death. His *Selenographia*

(1647) was noted for its lunar maps. Many of the names given by Hevelius to the physical features of the moon are still used today.

HEVESY, GYÖRGY (*b. Budapest, Hungary, 1885; d. Freiburg im Breisgau, Germany, 1966*), radiochemistry, physical chemistry, analytical chemistry, biochemistry.

Hevesy was educated at the universities of Budapest, Berlin, and Freiburg and spent some important years at Rutherford's laboratory in Manchester, England, acquainting himself with radioactive phenomena. While there, he began (1913) his experiments in using isotopes as tracers in studying chemical processes. (In 1943 he was to receive the Nobel Prize in physics for these efforts.) After 1913 Hevesy contributed much to the definitive clarification of the question of isotopes. After having unambiguously established their chemical identity, he demonstrated the identity of their electrochemical properties. He also discovered (along with Dirk Coster) element 72 (hafnium) in the periodic table.

HEWSON, WILLIAM (*b. Hexham, Northumberland, England, 1739; d. London, England, 1774*), hematology.

A physician educated in London and Edinburgh, Hewson was a partner at William Hunter's anatomy school in London. In 1767 he published the first practical account of paracentesis of the thorax in cases of emphysema. In 1768–69 he published accounts of his explorations of the lymphatic system of the lower vertebrates. He did important early microscopical research on blood, ascertaining the role of fibrinogen and giving the first valid account of coagulation. He was also the first to describe clearly the three parts of the blood.

HEYN, EMIL (*b. Annaberg, Germany, 1867; d. Berlin, Germany, 1922*), technology, metallography.

A protégé of Adolf Martens, Heyn continued the microscopic investigations of metals and alloys begun by Martens, applying them to practical problems. In 1904 he became deputy director of the Königliche Material-prüfungsamt at Berlin-Dahlern. There he produced a great number of papers on interesting defects, on the constitution of steels, on problems of nonferrous metals, and on inner stresses. After 1911 Heyn played a major role in the reorganization of technological education in German colleges.

HEYNITZ (HEINITZ), FRIEDRICH ANTON VON (*b. Dröschkau, near Torgau, Germany, 1725; d. Berlin, Germany, 1802*), mining.

From 1763 to 1774 Heynitz was director of the Saxon mining industry, during which time he took over and reorganized the Saxon salt works. He resigned after a dispute with the elector and headed, for a year and a half, certain Spanish mines. In 1777 Frederick the Great named him a Prussian state minister and inspector general of mines. In that position, he greatly expanded the Prussian mining industry, constructing turnpikes, canals, and railways. His social programs for the miners—relief funds, housing, and health insurance—were forward-looking.

HEYROVSKÝ, JAROSLAV (*b. Prague, Czechoslovakia, 1890; d. Prague, 1967*), electrochemistry.

Heyrovský was educated at Charles-Ferdinand (now Prague) University and University College, London. In 1918 he received his Ph.D. with a thesis on the electro-affinity of aluminum. His work on the electrochemical properties of aluminum brought him a D.Sc. from the University of London in 1921. He rose quickly in the physical chemistry department of Charles University. He remained there through the 1930's and was allowed to keep his chair during the German occupation of Czechoslovakia during World War II.

Heyrovský was awarded the Nobel Prize for chemistry in 1959 for his discovery of polarography. In 1921 his inclinations toward electrochemistry and his recent experience in the field transformed the study of electrocapillarity into polarography. He reported his findings in Czech in 1922 and a year later in English. The term "polarography" was not coined until 1925, when a co-worker, Masuzo Shikato, published a description of an instrument they called a Polarograph. It automatically registered the current-voltage curves, or polarograms, on a cylinder covered with photographic paper. The polarographic investigations animated by Heyrovský gave a new impetus to the study of electrode processes. Nevertheless, the scientific world was slow to take notice of the importance of polarography. The major breakthrough occurred in 1933. Since then interest in polarography has deepened and widened because of its extensive uses not only in electrochemical and other research but also in industrial and hospital laboratories. It has been called one of the "top five" analytical methods of contemporary chemical analysis. In 1929 Heyrovský was the cofounder of the journal *Collection of Czechoslovak Chemical Communications.* The early volumes contained many of the significant contributions to polarography by Heyrovský and his school. The journal is still flourishing and is now published in German and Russian as well as Czech.

HEYTESBURY, WILLIAM (*fl. Oxford, England, ca. 1335*), logic, kinematics.

Heytesbury was one of several scholars at Merton College, Oxford, during the second quarter of the fourteenth century whose writings formed the basis of the late medieval tradition of *calculationes,* the discussion of various modes of quantitative variation of qualities, motions, and powers in space and time. The influence of the Mertonian scholars (about whom little is known) spread to the Continent later in the fourteenth century and to the Italian universities in the fifteenth century and again at Paris and the Spanish universities in the early sixteenth century. Thereafter, it lost impetus with the shift of interests consequent upon the humanist movement.

Heytesbury's two best-known works are *Sophismata* and *Regule solvendi sophismata,* both written probably about 1335. The works provide rules for the resolution of different classes of logical fallacies and deal intensively with thirty-two particular sophisms. An important last chapter of the *Regule* deals with the quantitative description of motion or change in the three Aristotelian categories of place, quantity, and quality. The principal aim is to establish the proper velocity in the given category. In the case of augmentation, Heytesbury adopts a measure involving the exponential function. It exhibits an almost exclusive concern of the Mertonian *calculatores* with quantitative description of hypothetical cases. Galileo is known to

have been familiar with the writings of Heytesbury and the other Mertonians, but their influence on his own science of motion is questionable.

HIÄRNE, URBAN (*b. Skworitz, Ingria, Sweden, 1641; d. Stockholm, Sweden, 1724*), medicine, chemistry, mineralogy.

Hiärne studied medicine at the University of Uppsala and in England and France. In 1674 he established what became a considerable practice in Stockholm. His interests increasingly turned to chemistry and about 1678 he and several interested colleagues established a chemical research laboratory, which later became a national institution. The main purpose of the laboratory was the examination of minerals and ores. Extensive pharmaceutical research was also included. Hiärne's contribution to applied chemistry included work on improved methods for producing alum and vitriols, on impregnating agents to safeguard trees against rot, and on rust preventatives. He is best known for his work on formic acid, which he produced throughout the distillation of ant specimens.

IBN HIBINTĀ (*fl. Iraq, ca. 950*), astrology.

Ibn Hibintā lived at the time of the first two Buwayhid rulers of Baghdad. The only work by which he is known is his vast collection of astrological and astronomical lore. Its importance lies in the many quotations it contains from earlier authorities, including Ptolemy, Dorotheus of Sidon, al-Khwārizmī, and Kanaka.

HICETAS OF SYRACUSE (*fl. fifth century,* B.C.), astronomy.

So little is known about Hicetas of Syracuse that even his existence as a historical person has been disputed. The ancients connected him with Philolaus, the Pythagorean of the late fifth century B.C. Diogenes Laertius states that Philolaus "was the first to say that the earth moves in a circle, but some assert that Hicetas the Syracusan was the first." Other sources cite him as an adherent of the Heraclidean theory of the axial rotation of the earth.

HIGGINS, BRYAN (*b. Collooney, County Sligo, Ireland, 1737 or 1741; d. Walford, Staffordshire, England, 1818*), chemistry.

Higgins received his M.D. from the University of Leiden and in 1774 opened a "school of practical chemistry" in London. An extant syllabus refers to the course given there as one of philosophical, pharmaceutical, and technical chemistry. Higgins moved in London's beau monde and among his auditors were Samuel Johnson, Benjamin Franklin, Edward Gibbon, and Joseph Priestley. In 1793 he founded the society of Philosophical Experiments and Conversations, which met in his laboratory. Besides lecturing, experimenting, consulting, and advising across a broad range of chemical topics, Higgins also manufactured and sold reagents and chemicals. His many publications interweave detailed discussions of problems in technical chemistry with speculative theoretical views. His *Philosophical Essay Concerning Light* (1776) saw short-range-force explanations of the interactions of light, heat, and matter as central to any coherent natural philosophy. From 1796 to 1801 he advised the Jamaican government on the making of sugar and rum, for which he was handsomely paid. After returning to England, he virtually retired from scientific activity.

HIGGINS, WILLIAM (*b. Collooney, County Sligo, Ireland, 1762 or 1763; d. Dublin, Ireland, 1825*), chemistry.

William Higgins was the nephew of Bryan Higgins, with whom he lived in London from boyhood. From his uncle he developed a strong taste for, and considerable expertise in, experimental chemistry. He attended Oxford from 1786 to 1788 but left without a degree. In 1792 he became a chemist with the Irish Corporation of Apothecaries in Dublin. Later he became professor of chemistry for the Royal Dublin Society. He did important work for the Irish linen and hemp industries, especially in new methods of bleaching. In 1789 and 1791 Higgins published two editions of his most important work, the *Comparative View of Phlogistic and Anti-Phlogistic Theories,* which favored antiphlogistic chemisty. The work contains a brilliant and highly individualistic exploitation of dominant Newtonian assumptions about the forces of chemical affinity. It also contains among its unstated assumptions ideas on combining proportions that were later to be made explicit in chemical atomic theory. Humphry Davy, a colleague of Higgins, later vigorously promoted Higgins as the discoverer of the chemical atomic theory against the claims of John Dalton. Although most scientists today give the credit to Dalton, Higgins still has his champions and the debate has never died down.

HIGHMORE, NATHANIEL (*b. Fordingbridge, England, 1613; d. Sherborne, Dorset, England, 1685*), anatomy, medicine.

Highmore received an M.A. from Trinity College, Oxford, in 1638 and then studied medicine, receiving his M.D. in 1643. He was a colleague of William Harvey, with whom he did joint experiments in embryology. He settled at Sherborne, where he practiced for forty years, while still interesting himself in scientific research. His most important work, *Corporis humani disquisitio anatomica* (1651), contains the first description of the antrum of Highmore (maxillary sinus) and of the *corpus Highmori* (mediastinal testis). It was the first anatomical textbook to accept Harvey's theory of the circulation of the blood. Although Highmore's physiology reflects the still medieval thinking of the time, the book was the standard textbook for some years and brought the author immediate renown.

HIKETAS. *See* **Hicetas.**

HILBERT, DAVID (*b. Königsberg, Germany* [*now Kaliningrad, R.S.F.S.R.*], *1862; d. Göttingen, Germany, 1943*), mathematics.

From 1870 Hilbert attended the Friedrichskolleg in Königsberg; his last year of high school was spent at the Wilhelms-Gymnasium. He studied at the University of Königsberg from 1880 to 1884, except for his second semester, when he went to Heidelberg. After his doctoral examination in 1884 and receipt of his Ph.D. in 1885, he traveled to Leipzig and Paris. In June 1886 he qualified as Privatdozent at Königsberg University. In 1892 Hilbert was appointed professor extraordinary to replace Adolf Hurwitz at Königsberg. In 1893 he was appointed ordinary professor, succeeding F. Lindemann. He was appointed to a chair at Göttingen University in

1895, remaining there until his official retirement in 1930.

At Königsberg under the influence of F. Lindemann, Hilbert became interested in the theory of invariants, his first area of research. The mathematician whose work most profoundly influenced Hilbert was the number theoretician Leopold Kronecker.

Hilbert's scientific activity can be roughly divided into six periods, according to the years of publication of the results: up to 1893 (at Königsberg), algebraic forms; 1894–99, algebraic number theory; 1899–1903, foundations of geometry; 1904–09, analysis (Dirichlet's principle, calculus of variations, integral equations, Waring's problem); 1912–14, theoretical physics; after 1918, foundations of mathematics.

Hilbert perplexed his contemporaries by a revolutionary approach to the theory of invariants. His approach was a direct, nonalgorithmic method, foreshadowing and perparing what would be called abstract algebra in the twentieth century.

From the theory of invariants Hilbert turned to algebraic number theory. At the 1893 meeting at Munich the Deutsche Mathematiker-Vereinigung, which Hilbert had presented with new proofs of the splitting of the prime ideal, charged Hilbert and Minkowski with preparing a report on number theory within two years. Minkowski soon withdrew, although he did read the proofs of what would be known as *Der Zahlbericht,* dated by Hilbert 10 April 1897. The *Zahlbericht* is infinitely more than a report; it is one of the classics, a masterpiece of mathematical literature. For half a century it was the bible of all who learned algebraic number theory. In it Hilbert collected all relevant knowledge on algebraic number theory, reorganized it under striking new unifying viewpoints, reshaped formulations and proofs, and laid the ground work for the still growing edifice of class field theory.

He then turned to foundations of geometry, but the impact of his work in foundations of geometry cannot be compared with that of his work in the theory of invariants, in algebraic number theory, and in analysis. There is hardly one result of his *Grundlagen der Geometrie* which would not have been discovered in the course of time if Hilbert had not written this book. But what matters is that one man alone wrote this book, and that it is a fine book. *Grundlagen der Geometrie,* published in 1899, reached its ninth edition in 1962.

In 1904 Hilbert perplexed the mathematical world by salvaging the Dirichlet principle, which had been brought into discredit by Weierstrass' criticism. He proved the Dirichlet principle by brute force, as straightforwardly as he had solved the finiteness problem of the theory of invariants.

Hilbert also enriched the classical theory of variations, but his most important contribution to analysis is integral equations, dealt with in a series of papers from 1904–10.

Today the least studied and the most obsolete among Hilbert's papers are probably those on integral equations. Their value is now purely historical, as the most important landmark ever set out in mathematics: the linear space method in analysis, with its geometrical language and its numerous applications, quite a few of which go back to Hilbert himself. From Hilbert's analytic period also came the interesting and often overlooked proof of Waring's hypothesis.

From about 1909 Hilbert showed an ever increasing interest in physics. It is generally acknowledged that his achievements in this field lack the profundity and the inventiveness of his mathematical work proper. The same is true of his highly praised work in the foundations of mathematics.

One desire of Hilbert's first axiomatic period was still unfulfilled: after the relative consistency of geometry he wanted to prove the consistency of mathematics itself— or, as he put it, the consistency of number theory.

He conceived the idea of formalism: to reduce mathematics to a finite game with an infinite but finitely defined treasure of formulas. The mathematical world did not have to decide whether formalism was relevant. In 1931 Kurt Gödel proved that Hilbert's approach was not feasible.

HILDEBRANDT, GEORG FRIEDRICH (*b. Hannover, Germany, 1764; d. Erlangen, Germany, 1816*), chemistry.

Hildebrandt studied pharmacy at the University of Göttingen, received his M.D. in 1783, and taught medicine and later chemistry at the University of Erlangen. He possessed a profound knowledge of anatomy, physiology, chemistry, physics, and pharmacy. He was an early advocate of Lavoisier's oxidation theory. His 1794 book *Anfangsgründe der Chemie* reflected a preference for the antiphlogiston theory. He published papers on such varied topics as mercury compounds, the nature of quicklime, mineral waters, ammonia, and the analytical separation of iron from alum. He also wrote textbooks on pharmacology (1787) and anatomy (1789–92).

HILDEGARD OF BINGEN (*b. Bermersheim, Germany, 1098; d. Rupertsberg, near Bingen, Germany, 1179*), cosmology.

Also called Hildegardis de Pinguia and often St. Hildegard, Hildegard was a writer on nature and medicine (probably also a practicing physician), a visionary, and a transmitter and original transformer of Oriental, Judeo-Christian, and Greek cosmological and allegorical ideas. A nun, she founded her own convent in 1147. Encouraged by Pope Eugene III and Bernard of Clairvaux, she became the spiritual center to which popes, kings, and ecclesiastical and secular dignitaries turned. Her influence was felt as far as Greece and Palestine, and in 1163 her convent was placed under the protection of Frederick Barbarossa, the Holy Roman emperor. Her mystical, visionary, and spiritual works include *Liber Scivias* (1141–51), *Liber vitae meritorum* (1158–63), and *Liber divinorum operum* (1163–70). Her naturalistic and medical works include *Liber simplicis medicinae* (*ca.* 1150–60), on plants, trees, animals, stones, metals, and elements; and *Liber compositae medicinae*, on the nature of diseases and their causes, notably the forces of the elements. The phlegm figures as the main cause of disease, reflecting her fundamental Galenic humoralism. Many of her medical sources were probably folk medicine and popular tradition. The curative virtue of precious stones plays a prominent part. Hildegard admitted that knowledge can come from *magia*, including information from evil spirits. She remains original in both her natural and mystical work, and her influence lasted far into the Renaissance.

HILDITCH, THOMAS PERCY (*b. London, England, 1886; d. Birkenhead, England, 1965*), chemistry.

Hilditch received the D. Sc. from the University of London in 1911. From 1911 to 1925 he was a research chem-ist for a soap and chemical manufacturer. From 1925 to his retirement in 1951 he was professor of industrial chemistry at the University of Liverpool. Hilditch was mainly responsible for the advances in knowledge of the chemical constitution of natural oils from 1925 to 1950. Prior to then, the chemistry of fats was a neglected field. He and his students published more than 300 papers, dealing mainly with the component acids and glycerides of natural fats. His major work was *The Chemical Constitution of Natural Fats* (1940).

HILL, GEORGE WILLIAM (*b. New York, N.Y., 1838; d. West Nyack, N.Y., 1914*), mathematical astronomy.

Hill studied under Theodore Strong at Rutgers College, from which he graduated in 1859. In 1861 he joined the staff of the *American Ephemeris and Nautical Almanac*, an astronomical journal. He contributed articles to it for half a century. His work on the theories of Jupiter and Saturn represented one of the most important contributions to nineteenth-century mathematical astronomy. His 1878 paper "Researches in the Lunar Theory" initiated a new approach to the study of three mutually attracting bodies, and the article became fundamental in the development of celestial mechanics. From 1898 to 1901 he taught celestial mechanics at Columbia University.

HILL, JOHN (*b. Peterborough [?], England, 1707 [?]; d. London, England, 1775*), botany.

An apothecary, Hill developed an interest in plants and wrote voluminously on botany. Some of his works were popular handbooks for gardeners, or like the *Useful Family Herbal*, guides to the use of herbs as medicaments. Others, like his twenty-six-volume compendium *Vegetable System* (1759–75), are works in taxonomic and descriptive botany. He also wrote on mineralogy and zoology.

HILL, LESTER SANDERS (*b. New York, N.Y., 1890; d. Bronxville, N.Y., 1961*), mathematics.

A graduate of Columbia University (B.A., 1911; M.A., 1913) and Yale University (Ph.D., 1926), Hill spent most of his career at Hunter College, New York City. He is best known for his mathematical approaches to cryptography and cryptoanalysis. He did important secret code systems for the government during World War II. Most of his research in developing a modular algebraic cipher-code system is still classified information and has never been published.

HIND, JOHN RUSSELL (*b. Nottingham, England, 1823; d. Twickenham, England, 1895*), astronomy.

Hind was educated privately and showed an early affinity for astronomy. After a short stint (1840–44) at the Royal Observatory, Greenwich, he became supervisor of George Bishop's private observatory at Regent's Park, London. Hind discovered ten asteroids (including Iris and Flora), two comets, a variable nebula in Taurus, and several variable stars. He was also the long-time editor of the *Nautical Almanac*.

HINDENBURG, CARL FRIEDRICH (*b. Dresden, Germany, 1741; d. Leipzig, Germany, 1808*), mathematics.

Hindenburg was educated at the University of Leipzig and from 1786 until his death was professor of physics there. He was the founder of the "combinatorial school" of mathematics, his first paper on the subject being published in 1778. He and his school developed a complicated system of symbols for fundamental combinatorial concepts, such as permutations, variations, and combinations; but its cumbersomeness soon made it outmoded. The school's influence was limited to Germany, and no leading contemporary mathematician was a member.

HINSHELWOOD, CYRIL NORMAN (*b. London, England, 1897; d. London, 1967*), chemistry.

Hinshelwood was educated at Oxford University and spent most of his career there. He is noted for his extensive and comprehensive contributions to the development of chemical kinetics, on both the experimental and theoretical levels. He was knighted in 1948 and in 1956 was awarded (along with N.N. Semenov) the Nobel Prize in chemistry.

HIPPARCHUS (*b. Nicaea, Bithynia [now Iznik, Turkey], first quarter of second century* B.C.*; d. Rhodes [?], after 127* B.C.), astronomy, mathematics, geography.

The only certain biographical datum concerning Hipparchus is his birthplace, Nicaea, in northwestern Asia Minor. His scientific activity is dated by a number of his astronomical observations quoted in Ptolemy's *Almagest*. The earliest observation indubitably made by Hipparchus himself is of the autumnal equinox of 26/27 September 147 B.C. The latest is of a lunar position on 7 July 127 B.C. Ptolemy reports a series of observations of autumnal and vernal equinoxes taken from Hipparchus, ranging from 162 to 128 B.C., but it is not clear whether the earliest in the series had been made by Hipparchus himself or were taken from others; Ptolemy says only that "they seemed to Hipparchus to have been accurately observed." We can say, then, that Hipparchus' activity extended over the third quarter of the second century B.C. and may have begun somewhat earlier.

It is probable that Hipparchus spent the whole of his later career at Rhodes: observations by him ranging from 141 to 127 B.C. are specifically attributed to Rhodes by Ptolemy. In Ptolemy's *Phases of the Fixed Stars*, however, it is stated that the observations taken from Hipparchus in that book were made in Bithynia (presumably Nicaea). We may infer that Hipparchus began his scientific career in Bithynia and moved to Rhodes some time before 141 B.C. He is most famous for his discovery of the "precession of the equinoxes," the slow motion of the solstitial and equinoctial points from east to west through the fixed stars.

Hipparchus is a unique figure in the history of astronomy in that, while there is a general agreement that his work was of profound importance, we are singularly ill-informed about it. Of his numerous works only one (the commentary on Aratus) survives, and that a comparatively slight one (although valuable in the absence of the others). We derive most of our knowledge of Hipparchus' achievements in astronomy from the *Almagest;* and although Ptolemy obviously had studied Hipparchus' writings thoroughly and had a deep respect for his work, his main concern was not to transmit it to posterity but to use it and, where possible, improve upon it in constructing his own astronomical system.

Both in antiquity and in modern times Hipparchus has been highly praised and misunderstood. Since Delambre modern scholarship has tended to treat Hipparchus as if

he had written a primitive *Almagest,* and to extract his "doctrine" by discarding from the extant *Almagest* what are thought to be Ptolemy's additions. This unhistorical method has obscured Hipparchus' real achievement. Greek astronomy before him had conceived the idea of explaining the motions of the heavenly bodies by geometrical models, and had developed models that represented the motions well qualitatively. What Hipparchus did was to transform astronomy into a quantitative science. His main contributions were to develop mathematical methods enabling one to use the geometrical models for practical prediction, and to assign numerical parameters to the models. For the latter, his use of observations and of constants derived from Babylonian astronomy was crucial (without them his lunar theory would not have been possible). His own observations were also important (he and Ptolemy are the only astronomers in antiquity known to have observed systematically). Particularly remarkable is his open-mindedness, his willingness to abandon traditional views, to examine critically, and to test by observation his own theories as well as those of others. Remarkable too, in antiquity, was his attitude toward astronomy as an evolving science that would require observations over a much longer period before it could be securely established. Related to this were his attempts to assemble observational material for the use of posterity.

It seems that Hipparchus never gave an account of astronomical theory, or even part of it, starting from first principles (Ptolemy often inferred Hipparchus' opinion on a topic from incidental remarks). Hipparchus did not, then, construct an astronomical system: he only made such a system possible and worked out some parts of it.

In Western tradition the influence of Hipparchus was channeled solely through the *Almagest.* But there is much evidence that Indian astronomy of the *Siddhāntas* preserves elements of Hipparchus' theories and methods.

HIPPIAS OF ELIS (*b. Elis, Greece; fl. 400* B.C.), philosophy, mathematics.

Hippias was a contemporary of Plato and is mentioned in Plato's dialogues, including the *Hippias Major,* the *Hippias Minor,* and the *Protagoras.* He was a Sophist and thus came under Plato's scorn. In these dialogues, Hippias is represented as a naïve and humorless boaster who cannot stand up to the remorseless logic of Socrates. The real Hippias could not have been the ridiculous figure that Plato made him to be, for he was frequently sent on diplomatic missions to other states. He wrote and lectured over a wide range of disciplines: rhetoric, politics, poetry, music, painting, sculpture, and astronomy, as well as the philosophy and mathematics on which his fame chiefly rests. None of his voluminous works has survived. His *Synagoge* is regarded by some as the earliest work in both Greek philosophy and Greek literature, and it is believed by some to have been Aristotle's source for his knowledge of the theories of Thales. Hippias' teaching has to be reconstructed from the scattered references to him in Greek and Latin authors. One important discovery is attributed to him: the transcendental curve known as the quadratrix (although the term "quadratrix" was probably coined later).

HIPPOCRATES OF CHIOS (*b. Chios; fl. Athens, second half of the fifth century* B.C.), mathematics, astronomy.

The name by which Hippocrates the mathematician is distinguished from the contemporary physician of Cos implies that he was born on the Greek island of Chios; but he spent his most productive years in Athens and helped to make it, until the foundation of Alexandria, the leading center of Greek mathematical research. There are indications that he stood in the Pythagorean tradition supported by what is known of his astronomical theories, which have affinities with those of Pythagoras and his followers.

When Hippocrates arrived in Athens, three special problems—the duplication of the cube, the squaring of the circle, and the trisection of an angle—were already engaging the attention of mathematicians, and he addressed himself at least to the first two. In the course of studying the duplication of the cube, he used the method of reduction or analysis. He was the first to compose an *Elements of Geometry* in the manner of Euclid's famous work. In astronomy he propounded theories to account for comets and the galaxy.

HIPPOCRATES OF COS *(b. Cos, 460 B.C.; d. Larissa, ca. 370 B.C.),* medicine.

Little is known about the life of Hippocrates, although it may be stated with a fair degree of certainty that he was a physician, taught at Cos, traveled widely in Greece, and enjoyed exceptional fame in his lifetime. He contributed to a significant body of medical writings, but it is difficult to determine precisely which works of the corpus are actually his, which are by his contemporaries at Cos, and which belong to the school of Cnidus. The *Collection* consists of about sixty medical works, the great majority of which date from the last decades of the fifth century B.C. and from the first half of the fourth; they were probably brought together in Alexandria.

Since it is not practicable to determine the nature and degree of Hippocrates' originality as a scientist, given the limitations of our attribution, the essential step is to define the contribution of the school of Cos and its relation to the school of Cnidus. The doctrine of humors is found in the teachings of both schools. The Coan writings imply the four humors specified in *Nature of Man*—phlegm, blood, yellow bile, and black bile. The Cnidian humors are those set forth in *Diseases* IV, namely water, blood, phlegm, and bile. Ambient factors and diet are fundamental to the medical teachings at Cos; the treatise *Airs, Waters, Places* is devoted to the role of such factors as air, location, climate, and season. Cnidian writings also allude to these factors, although no Cnidian treatises present a systematic exposition of them. The importance of diet is stated in the Coan *Regimen in Acute Diseases; Nature of Man; Prognostic;* and *Fractures, Joints;* as well as in the para-Cnidian *Regimen.* Prognosis consisted of stating the past and present state of the disease and predicting its course after making an examination of the current symptoms but before questioning the patient. Both schools showed a further concern for the psychology of the patient and the effect of the psyche on the organism. They were united in their repudiation of medicine based directly on philosophical principles, and rejected any sort of magico-religious medicine. A frequent generalization is that the medicine of Cos was more sensitive to the patient, while that of Cnidus was more greatly concerned with the disease (Coan: *Regimen in Acute Diseases;* Cnidian:

Diseases II). The rivalry between the schools seems to have been the result of divergences in detail which must be grossly magnified to achieve any significance. Still, it is necessary to consider these small differences in an attempt to identify the originality of the school of Cos and of Hippocrates.

We must now determine the level and the value of Hippocratic medicine. The followers of Hippocrates wished to promote a strictly scientific medicine, advocating a rigorous rational technique. Practitioners were advised that examining the body requires sight, hearing, smell, touch, taste, and reason *(Epidemics* VI; *In the Surgery; Precepts).* This rational approach to observation and synthesis allowed them to recognize their errors and to be aware of the methodological value of admitting and analyzing them *(Joints; Diseases* III). The same rationality led them to a firm principle of causality—that each disease has a nature of its own, and none arises without its natural cause *(Airs, Waters, Places; The Art).* They accepted as self-evident the unity of the animal kingdom, man being one species among others *(Joints; The Sacred Disease).* In the field of deontology the school of Cos set forth principles that are still valid, and the *Oath* known to all physicians makes this explicit.

It is also necessary to consider the reservations which must be held concerning Hippocratic medicine. The therapeutic use of excrement reveals the archaic mentality that prizes all living beings and their products. The preference for right over left is also archaic, and appeared in conjunction with the idea that women are inferior *(Aphorisms; Epidemics).* What are certainly archaic ideas were further manifested in imitative errors *(Regimen).* Concrete examples of situations where deduction may have supplanted observation appear in *Nature of Man* and *Nature of the Child,* where observation is short-circuited by a priori thinking, and the Hippocratic author sees what he wishes to see.

A departure in practice from the declared Hippocratic intention of observation is its emphasis on qualities: the most serious illnesses affect the strongest part of the body; drinking mixed waters is dangerous; the location of a city plays an important role in health. Here, too, what might appear to be the result of systematic observation, in truth represents a deduction from a preliminary postulate.

The Hippocratic physicians explained most diseases by fluxes of humors. The mechanical functions of the organs form a physics of the receptacle which, together with the qualities of the humors in motion, define the entire physiology and internal pathology of the schools of both Cos and Cnidus. It is important to note the role of analogy in this medical thought. The functioning of the organism is conceived of in terms familiar from elementary mechanics, from such devices as the pump, the cupping glass, and communicating vessels. This tendency is most consciously expressed in *Generation-Nature of the Child-Diseases* IV, but it exists everywhere.

The most striking aspect of the dietetics *(Regimen in Acute Diseases)* is the horror of change. The author dramatizes the least departure from the diet. The physician was limited in the therapeutic possibilities available to him, in the face of common and often fatal diseases, and needed to make the most of what little he had. As for the pharmacopoeia, the two schools were in close agreement. In this area there is a want of specificity: long lists of recipes prescribe a host of substances for a single malady and, conversely, a single substance is recommended for a host of ills. Particular value was placed on products made from living matter or of human products. The area of fractures or luxations (dislocations) was virtually the only area of medicine in which the techniques of the time were adequate to produce very satisfactory results.

In summary, we might say that Hippocratic medicine was rational, but that its reason was not the scientific reason of today. Even as prescientific medicine, however, the medicine of the Hippocratics represented a knowledge infinitely more valuable than the magic which it supplanted. The proof of their success may be found in that for two millennia no better work was accomplished, and often worse was done.

HIRAYAMA, KIYOTSUGU (*b. Miyagi prefecture, Japan, 1874; d. Tokyo, Japan, 1943*), celestial mechanics.

Hirayama studied at the University of Tokyo, Yale University, and the U.S. Naval Observatory. He then taught at Tokyo and was on the staff of the Tokyo Astronomical Observatory. Hirayama developed an important hypothesis on the movements of asteroids and satellites, based on the theory that those bodies from the same origin would have similar eccentricity, mean motion, and inclination. He successfully identified several asteroid families. His other achievements are in latitudinal change, variable-star theory, and the history of Oriental astronomy.

HIRN, GUSTAVE ADOLFE (*b. Logelbach, near Colmar, Alsace, France, 1815; d. Colmar [then Germany], 1890*), thermodynamics.

Hirn was privately educated in chemistry and physics. He and his brother, the inventor Charles Ferdinand Hirn, became technical directors of a textile mill using an 1824 Boulton & Watt steam engine. Hirn, as a result, became one of the first to investigate the internal phenomena of the steam engine. His *Exposition analytique et expérimentale de la théorie mécanique de la chaleur* (1862) was among the first systematic treatises on thermodynamics. He was also interested in astronomy, climatology, and meteorology.

HIRSZFELD, LUDWIG (*b. Warsaw, Poland, 1884; d. Wrocław, Poland, 1954*), serology, bacteriology.

Hirszfeld completed his doctoral dissertation "Uber Blutagglutination" at the University of Berlin, thus establishing his specialty. At the Heidelberg Institute for Experimental Cancer Research, he formed a close working relationship with E. von Dungern. While there, Hirszfeld discovered the heritability of blood groups and established serological paternity exclusion. He and von Dungern were responsible for naming the blood groups A, B, AB, and O. Hirszfeld was the first to foresee the serological conflict between mother and child, confirmed by the discovery of the Rh factor. In 1911 Hirszfeld went to the Hygiene Institute of the University of Zurich, where he did work on anaphylaxis and anaphylatoxin. During World War I he discovered the bacillus now known as *Salmonella hirszfeldi*. After the war, he went to the University of Warsaw and the State Hygiene Institute. During World War II he was forced to resign his offices and was

moved to the Warsaw ghetto. Later he was forced to hide out with the underground. After the war, he helped found the University of Lublin and became director of the Institute for Medical Microbiology at Wrocław.

HIS, WILHELM (*b. Basel, Switzerland, 1831; d. Leipzig, Germany, 1904*), anatomy, histology, embryology.

His studied medicine at various universities, including Berlin, where his teachers were Johannes Müller and Robert Remak. He taught at the universities of Basel (1857–72) and Leipzig (from 1872). His's accomplishments lay in research and in the teaching of anatomy, histology, and embryology. His investigations dealt with the lymph vessels and lymph glands and with the thymus. In 1865 he published *Die Häute und Höhlen des Körpers,* his first important embryological work. His's work in embryology displayed new methodology. In 1866 he constructed the first microtome, and he also built an embryograph, which permitted him to make exact drawings of the microscopic sections. He encouraged the introduction of photography in anatomy, and he introduced standardized charts in embryology. He was responsible, in 1895, for identifying the remains of Johann Sebastian Bach.

HISINGER, WILHELM (*b. Skinnskatteberg, Västmanland, Sweden, 1766; d. Skinnskatteberg, 1852*), chemistry, mineralogy, geology, paleontology.

Hisinger, a wealthy landowner and proprietor of an iron foundry, worked privately as a scientist. In 1803, he discovered the element cerium and investigated (1806) the effect of electric current on salt solutions, thus preparing the way for the electrochemical theories of Davy and Berzelius. Those studies were published in *Afhandlingar i Fysik, Kemi och Mineralogi* (1806–18). He also wrote works on mineralogy and on animal and plant fossils from Swedish deposits. He gave his extensive geological, mineralogical, and paleontological collections to the Swedish natural history museum.

HITCHCOCK, ALBERT SPEAR (*b. Owosso, Mich., 1865; d. at sea, crossing the North Atlantic, 1935*), botany.

Hitchcock, educated at the University of Iowa, became the leading agrostologist in the United States and was acknowledged around the world. He botanized virtually all over the world, assembling at the National Herbarium, Washington, D.C., one of the world's most comprehensive grass collections. His most important work was *Manual of the Grasses of the United States* (1935).

HITCHCOCK, EDWARD (*b. Deerfield, Mass., 1793; d. Amherst, Mass., 1864*), geology.

Hitchcock, the son of a hatter, worked his way through Deerfield Academy, where he showed an affinity for science, especially astronomy. He audited classes at Yale to prepare himself for science-teaching and in 1825 was named professor of chemistry and natural history at Amherst College. In 1844 he became president of Amherst and continued to teach. He wrote extensively on the relation of science to religion (from 1821 to 1825 he had served as a Congregationalist minister), on the geomorphology of the Connecticut River Valley, on fossil tracks found in that area, and on the metamorphosis of sediments.

HITTORF, JOHANN WILHELM (*b. Bonn, Germany, 1824; d. Münster, Westphalia, Germany, 1914*), chemistry, physics.

Hittorf is remembered chiefly for his experimental work in the transport of charge by ions in electrolytic solutions and the study of electrical conduction through gases. His work was a continuation of that of Faraday and Daniell. Hittorf was educated at the University of Berlin and taught at the universities of Bonn and Münster.

HITZIG, (JULIUS) EDUARD (*b. Berlin, Germany, 1838; d. Luisenheim zu St. Blasien, Germany, 1907*), neurophysiology, psychiatry.

After initially studying law, Hitzig turned to medicine and studied at the universities of Berlin and Würzburg. After an important paper on the function of the cerebral cortex, he was named (1875) professor at the University of Zurich and director of the Berghölzli mental asylum there. Later he became associated with the University of Halle, from which he retired in 1903. His contributions to medicine were to the physiology of the cerebral cortex and to clinical psychiatry. Believing that the brain was the instrument of the mind, he attempted to place the treatment of psychiatric patients on a more scientific basis and to bring attention to the inadequate care then available.

HJORT, JOHAN (*b. Christiania [now Oslo], Norway, 1869; d. Oslo, 1948*), marine biology.

Hjort was educated at the universities of Oslo and Munich and at the Zoological Station at Naples. He founded and headed, from 1900 to 1916, the Norwegian governmental fisheries. In 1914 he published a substantial contribution to marine knowledge, his paper "Fluctuations in the Great Fisheries of Northern Europe." From 1921 to 1939, when he retired, he was professor of marine biology at Oslo. His consuming interests included the sigmoid curve, yeasts, the "optimum catch," and whales. In the field of marine ecology, he is probably best known for the classic volume, co-authored with Sir John Murray, *The Depths of the Ocean* (1913).

HOAGLAND, DENNIS ROBERT (*b. Golden, Colo., 1884; d. Oakland, Calif., 1949*), plant physiology.

Hoagland graduated from Stanford University in 1907 with a degree in chemistry. He taught animal nutrition at the University of California at Berkeley for two years and in 1910 joined the Food and Drug Administration of the U.S. Department of Agriculture. In 1914 he went back to Berkeley, where he taught agricultural chemistry until he retired in 1949. Hoagland is best known for his research in processes of salt absorption by plants, in plant and soil interrelations, and in the utilization of various elements in soil solutions. Our current understanding of the field of plant nutrition owes much to his significant contribution, particularly his experiments after he discovered that plants could be grown in water containing salts. His views on plant nutrition were summarized in *Lectures on the Inorganic Nutrition of Plants* (1948).

HOBBES, THOMAS (*b. Malmesbury, England, 1588; d. Hardwick, Derbyshire, England, 1679*), political philosophy, moral philosophy, geometry, optics.

Hobbes was born into an impoverished family in Wiltshire. His uncle recognized signs of precocity in him and underwrote the cost of his education. When he was seven, he was sent to school at the house of Richard Latimer, where he was given a solid grounding in Latin and Greek. At age fourteen he matriculated at Magdalen Hall (later called Hertford College), Oxford.

In 1608 Hobbes was recommended by the principal of his college to be tutor to the son of William Cavendish, Baron Hardwicke, who later became the second earl of Devonshire. Thus he was introduced to a cultured, aristocratic world where he was able to mingle with his master's guests. He came to know many of the intellectuals of his day and had at his disposal an excellent library.

To a second branch of the Cavendish family residing at Welbeck Abbey, Hobbes owed the awakening of his interest in natural science. Sir Charles Cavendish was a skilled mathematician; and his more famous brother William, duke of Newcastle, was a scientific amateur who maintained a private laboratory. Both men accepted Hobbes as a friend; and Newcastle, who had a passion for horses as well as a curiosity about optics and geometry, persuaded Hobbes to combine these interests in a curious treatise entitled "Considerations Touching the Facility or Difficulty of the Motions of a Horse on Straight Lines, or Circular."

In 1610 Hobbes set out on a grand tour of the Continent with his pupil. On this first tour, he perfected his knowledge of foreign tongues and resolved, on his return, to become a scholar. In the library at Chatsworth he immersed himself in classical studies and in 1628–29 published a brilliant translation of Thucydides' *Peloponnesian War*.

For a brief period before the Thucydides was published, Hobbes served as secretary to Francis Bacon and assisted him in the Latin translation of several of his (Bacon's) *Essaies*.

In June of 1628 Hobbes's master and friend, the second earl of Devonshire, died. Hobbes accepted a new appointment as tutor and cicerone to the son of Sir Gervase Clinton of Nottinghamshire, with whom he embarked, in 1629, on a second tour of Europe.

By November of 1630 Hobbes was recalled to the Cavendish family to serve as tutor in Latin and rhetoric to the next earl of Devonshire. With this young man, Hobbes, now in his forties, made his third grand tour of the Continent, the one which had the most important consequences for the development of his interest in natural science. That interest had not previously been dormant, since as Hobbes himself tells us, he had formulated a theory of light and sound as early as 1630. On the third journey Hobbes made personal contact with scientific minds. He met Galileo, Marin Mersenne, Gassendi, Roberval, and read Descartes.

His deepest scientific interest was in optics. A large part of the short tract of 1630 on sensation and appetite was devoted to optics. His views were expressed in three manuscript treatises, one in English and two in Latin. The first of the Latin treatises, "Tractatus opticus," was communicated to Mersenne, who published it as book VII of the "Optics" in his *Universae geometriae* (Paris, 1644). Mersenne had also published an optical treatise by Walter Warner which Hobbes had given him in Paris, and in 1641 he had published the *Objectiones ad Cartesii Meditationes,* the third "objection" of which was by Hobbes.

When he was forty-nine he thought it was time to put his ideas in order and he formulated the outline of a large philosophical system, to be composed of three parts—body, man, and citizenship—and to be described in that order, since for Hobbes body or matter is the ultimate constituent of all things, including human society. Hobbes's early scientific manuscripts may be considered as preparation for *De corpore,* his formal account of the first principles of science, which he intended to put first in his system but which the pressure of events forced him to lay aside and not publish until 1655.

In 1640 while Parliament and king were locked in political combat, Hobbes considered it prudent for his safety to return to France. In Paris Hobbes renewed his scientific contacts and almost immediately corresponded with Descartes about questions raised by the latter's *Méditations* and *Dioptriques.*

In the spring of 1640, while still in England, he wrote a short treatise on politics which circulated widely in manuscript and was published in 1650 in two parts under the titles *Humane Nature* and *De corpore politico, or the Elements of Law.* In Paris he wrote *De cive,* published in 1642. But *De cive* was written in Latin; and although it was separately translated into French by Samuel Sorbiere and du Verdus, two of Hobbes's friends, it remained inaccessible to the general English reader. Hobbes therefore set to work on an English treatise, *Leviathan,* published in 1651. The outlook of *Leviathan* is nominalist, materialist, and anticlerical, and fully one-third of the book examines the implications of Hobbes's political philosophy in a Christian society. Not unexpectedly, Hobbes's views in *Leviathan,* taken altogether, raised a storm of opposition. He was embroiled in controversy for the rest of his life.

On the recommendation of Newcastle, Hobbes was appointed tutor in mathematics to the prince of Wales, the future Charles II. Because of fears expressed by clergymen that the prince would be contaminated with atheism, Hobbes was obliged to promise that he would teach mathematics only, and not politics or religion. When *Leviathan* was published, no one of the English court in France liked it. Charles ordered Hobbes to leave the English colony in France, and in 1652 the philosopher returned to England, but the shock inflicted by *Leviathan* on clerical and lay opinion produced a rising tide of hostile criticism, some of it intelligent and philosophical, but much of it in the form of abuse.

Part of Hobbes's difficulties can be traced to controversy between himself and John Bramhall, bishop of Derry (Londonderry) and later archbishop of Armagh. The two had met in 1645 at Paris, where they debated the subject of free will. Bramhall committed his ideas to paper; Hobbes wrote a rejoinder. Both agreed to publish what they had written, but Hobbes's side of the question was put into print without his permission in a little treatise called *Of Liberty and Necessity* (1654). Bramhall, outraged by what he considered to be Hobbes's discourtesy in ignoring his side, published in 1655 all that had passed between them. Thus was launched a controversy which continued until Hobbes had the last word with the posthumous publication of *An Answer to a Book by Dr Bramhall Called The Catching of the Leviathan* (1682).

Hobbes was not molested personally during this last period of his life because he enjoyed the protection of Charles II. Nevertheless, the king refused to license a history in English by Hobbes of the Long Parliament, published posthumously as *Behemoth,* and the crown prohibited Hobbes from publishing any other works in English on the subject of politics or religion. Not included in this ban was the Latin translation of *Leviathan,* made by Henry Stubbe and first published at Amsterdam in 1668 and at London in 1678.

A second controversy, even more absorbing of Hobbes's energy than his debate with Bramhall, was his dispute with John Wallis on questions of geometry. The issue between the two men was whether Hobbes had succeeded as he claimed, both in squaring the circle and in duplicating the cube. Neither Hobbes nor Wallis doubted the possibility of quadrature, a proof of its impossibility not having been discovered until the nineteenth century. Nevertheless, Wallis was able to show that Hobbes's claim of success was unfounded.

Hobbes, in his sixties when he began his dispute with Wallis, was out of touch with the generation of rising young scientists and mathematicians. In 1661 he wrote a brief but barbed attack on Robert Boyle's experiments on the vacuum pump, to which Boyle replied calmly, though forcefully, in *Examen of Mr. Hobbes, His Dialogus* (1662) and *Dissertation on Vacuum Against Mr. Hobbes* (1674). Not surprisingly, Hobbes was excluded from membership in the Royal Society, a fact which he resented, although he publicly declared that he was lucky to be out of it.

In his eighties Hobbes published translations of the *Iliad* and the *Odyssey.* And when he was ninety he published *Decameron physiologicum,* a set of dialogues on physical principles containing also a last salvo fired off against Wallis.

HOBSON, ERNEST WILLIAM (*b. Derby, England, 1856; d. Cambridge, England, 1933*), mathematics.

Hobson had a brilliant career as a student at Christ's College, Cambridge, and spent the rest of his life teaching and doing research there. In 1891 he published *A Treatise on Trigonometry,* an early textbook on mathematical analysis. In 1907 he published his *Theory of a Real Variable,* which introduced to English readers the vital Borel-Lebesgue concepts of measure and integration.

HODGKINSON, EATON (*b. Anderton, near Great Budworth, Cheshire, England, 1789; d. Manchester, England, 1861*), applied mathematics, structural mechanics.

Hodgkinson, whose widowed mother operated a pawn brokerage in Manchester, was almost completely self-taught in mathematics. He began publishing papers about 1824, mostly on the stresses and tensions in metals. His further publications covered a wide variety of problems in structural mechanics, and in 1847 he became one of the commissioners appointed to study the application of iron to railway structures. In 1847 he also became professor of mechanical principles of engineering at University College, London.

HODIERNA, GIOVANNI. *See* **Odierna, Giovanni.**

HOEK, MARTINUS (*b. The Hague, Netherlands, 1834; d. Utrecht, Netherlands, 1873*), astronomy.

Hoek is known chiefly for his discovery that several comets move in the same orbit ("comet groups") and for his investigations of optical phenomena in moving bodies. He studied astronomy at the University of Leiden and in 1857 became extraordinary professor of astronomy at the University of Utrecht.

HOËNÉ-WROŃSKI (or HOEHNE), JÓZEF MARIA (*b. Wolsztyn, Poland, 1776; d. Neuilly, near Paris, France, 1853*), philosophy, mathematics.

Beginning in 1797 he studied philosophy at several German universities. In 1800 he settled in Marseilles, where he became a French citizen and addressed himself to scientific research. About 1810 he adopted the surname Wroński and most of his writings are signed Hoëné-Wroński, without a first name. His first published work, *Philosophie critique découverte par Kant* (1803), was the first exhaustive presentation of Kant's teachings in French. Hoëné-Wroński's own philosophical system was based on the sudden revelation of the "Absolute," a concept never made precise. He attempted to apply his philosophy to mathematics in his various works. In them rigorous mathematical proof retreats before arguments of the absolute philosophy. His universal solution of algebraic equations, published in 1812, proved to be faulty, although his solutions applied in particular cases. Despite the irrelevancies of his work—and the marked evidences of the author's psychopathological tendencies in them—close investigations shows him to have been a highly gifted mathematician whose contribution, unfortunately, was overshadowed by the imperatives of his all-embracing absolute philosophy.

HOEVEN, JAN VAN DER (*b. Rotterdam, Netherlands, 1801; d. Leiden, Netherlands, 1868*), comparative anatomy, natural history, anthropology.

Van der Hoeven received the Ph.D. in 1822 from the University of Leiden, and in 1824 he received the M.D. After 1826 he was professor of zoology at Leiden. His textbook, *Handboek der Dierkunde* (1828–33), unlike most textbooks of the time, starts with the lower animals and progresses to the vertebrates in order to illustrate the increasing complexity. All his works display an underlying religious viewpoint. Accordingly, he rejected any idea of evolution.

HOFF, KARL ERNST ADOLF VON (*b. Gotha, Germany, 1771; d. Gotha, 1837*), geology, geography.

Hoff was educated at the universities of Jena and Göttingen and entered the diplomatic service of the duchy of Gotha. He represented Gotha at numerous European diplomatic conclaves, while at the same time establishing his reputation in scientific research, notably in geology and geography. In 1801 Hoff began publishing his works, which earned him the friendship of Humboldt, Buch, and Goethe. He was one of the earliest proponents of the *Aktualismus*, or the actualist theory of the alterations of the earth's crust (as opposed to the catastrophist theory).

HOFFMANN, FRIEDRICH (*b. Halle, Germany, 1660; d. Halle, 1742*), medicine, chemistry.

Hoffmann was a leading medical systematist of the first half of the eighteenth century. He systematized coherently the Galenic, iatromechanical, and iatrochemical aspects of the phenomena of health and disease. He focused attention on the nervous system in physiology and pathogenesis, which contributed to the gradual shift in medical approach from the study of the humors and vascular hydrodynamics.

Hoffmann was the son of a well-known phsycician in Halle (also named Friedrich Hoffman) and studied at the University of Jena. In 1693 he became the first professor of medicine at the new University of Halle and was charged with the organization of its medical school. He thus began a long and distinguished career as physician and teacher; he was from time to time pressed into service as private physician to various German rulers. His most important work is *Medicinae rationalis systematicae* (1718–20). His formulations of a series of general principles for understanding the human organism, along with those of other eighteenth-century systematists, led to the more precise investigations that laid the theoretical foundations of modern medicine.

HOFMANN, AUGUST WILHELM VON (*b. Giessen, Germany, 1818; d. Berlin, Germany, 1892*), organic chemistry.

Hofmann studied law and languages at Giessen; he gradually shifted to chemistry under the influence of Liebig. He obtained his doctorate in 1841 and taught at the University of Bonn. In 1845, under the sponsorship of Prince Albert, he went to England, where he became director of the Royal College of Chemistry, London. He stayed there until 1865, when he was given the chemistry chair at the University of Berlin. He was ennobled on his seventieth birthday.

Hofmann's influence on British and German chemistry was profound. He was responsible for continuing the method of science teaching by laboratory instruction that had been established and popularized by Liebig at Giessen and for transporting it to England and Berlin. He created his own school of chemists who were interested primarily in experimental organic chemistry and its industrial applications. Much of his experimentation had to do with coal tar and its derivatives. In 1843 he established that many substances obtainable from coal tar naphtha and its derivatives were all of a single nitrogenous base, aniline. His discoveries—and those of his school—laid the foundation for the coal tar products industries. He also did important work on the chemistry of dyes.

HOFMEISTER, WILHELM FRIEDRICH BENEDIKT (*b. Leipzig, Germany, 1824; d. Lindenau, near Leipzig, 1877*), botany.

Hofmeister, almost completely self-taught in botany, began his serious botanical studies in 1841, after entering his father's music publishing business. (His father was himself an avid amateur botanist, having constructed a large herbarium for his own use.) His early papers dealt with cell division, and they met with such success that in 1851 the University of Rostock awarded him (at age twenty-six) an honorary doctorate. Later that year he published the work he is best remembered for and the work that was to change the direction of nineteenth-century botany: *Vergleichende Untersuchungen*. Concentrating on conifers, the work described the alternation of generations and described correctly the fertilization process. The details of structure and life history are described and copiously illustrated, and each plant is placed in the hierarchy of complexity. The amount of new information in it was immense, and with this single publication the core of botany passed from its Middle Ages to the modern period. In 1863 Hofmeister was given the chair of botany at Heidelberg, and in 1872 he assumed the chair at the University of Tübingen, both almost unheard of accomplishments for a self-taught scholar.

HOHENHEIM, THEOPHRASTUS BOMBASTUS VON. *See* **Paracelsus, Theophrastus.**

HOLBACH, PAUL HENRI THIRY, BARON D' (*b. Edesheim, Palatinate, Germany, 1723; d. Paris, France, 1789*), philosophy of science.

D'Holbach completed his studies at the University of Leiden and settled in Paris in 1749, where he became a French citizen. In 1753 he inherited his title and a considerable fortune. He was a major contributor to the *Encyclopédie* and became the leader of an important coterie of thinkers, writers, scientists, and artists. In 1770 he published his masterpiece, the *Système de la nature, on des lois du monde physique et du monde moral.* It was a methodical and intransigent affirmation of materialism and atheism. His scientific articles for the *Encyclopédie* (some 400 signed ones and at least as many that remained unsigned) showed d'Holbach to be mainly a skillful propagator and popularizer of technical and scientific information. He also wrote articles on psychology, the history of religion, and on what now would be called anthropology and ethnology. He translated numerous German scientific works into French.

HOLBORN, LUDWIG CHRISTIAN FRIEDRICH (*b. Göttingen, Germany, 1860; d. Berlin, Germany, 1926*), physics.

After attending the Realschule in Göttingen, he studied natural sciences at the university in that city from 1879 to 1884 and earned a teaching diploma in mathematics and physics. From 1884 to 1889 he was an assistant to E. Schering at the geomagnetic observatory in Göttingen. In 1887 he received his doctorate for a dissertation on the daily mean values of magnetic declination and horizontal intensity, an investigation in which he carried out measurements of terrestrial magnetism. In 1903 he constructed a torsion magnetometer with F. W. G. Kohlrausch.

In 1890 Holborn changed his field of research and worked under Helmholtz, and later Kohlrausch, at the newly founded (1889) Physikalisch-Technische Reichsanstalt in Berlin; he became an actual member of the organization in 1898. Holborn became director of the thermodynamic laboratories in 1914 and representative of the president of the Reichsanstalt in 1918.

In his work on gas temperatures, Holborn determined, along with W. Wien and A. L. Day, the accuracy of measurements made with thermoelements and investigated the various fixed points, including that for oxygen. In 1901 he and F. Kurlbaum built an optical or incandescent-filament pyrometer having an adjustable brightness setting. In addition, Holborn compared the temperature scales and gave crucial support to the introduction by law, in 1924, of the thermodynamic scale in Germany. He examined the thermocaloric properties of gases and of water vapor, as well as the compressibility of gases. Holborn also plotted the isothermal lines for monoatomic gases at temperatures greater than 100°C., without, however, offering a theoretical interpretation.

HOLBROOK, JOHN EDWARDS (*b. Beaufort, S.C., 1794; d. Norfolk, Mass., 1871*), herpetology, ichthyology.

Holbrook received the B.A. from Brown University in 1815 and the M.D. from the University of Pennsylvania in 1818. After continuing his studies at Boston, London, Edinburgh, and Paris, he settled in Charleston, South Carolina, in 1822 and established a practice. In 1824 he was one of the founders of the Medical College of South Carolina and served as its professor of anatomy until about 1854. During the Civil War, he served in the Confederate Army and was chief medical examiner for the state of South Carolina.

Despite his eminence as a physician, Holbrook is chiefly remembered as a herpetologist. In 1840 he published *North American Herpetology,* at the time the most accurate and comprehensive work on American reptiles. His thorough scholarship made his work a contribution of lasting value. Many reptiles, discovered and catalogued by him, still carry the genus name *Holbrookia* or the species name *holbrookii.* He later turned his attention to the study of fishes and published *Ichthyology of South Carolina* (1855).

HOLDEN, EDWARD SINGLETON (*b. St. Louis, Mo., 1846; d. West Point, N.Y., 1914*), astronomy.

Holden designed the Lick Observatory in California and was its first director. He was president of the University of California from 1886 to 1888. Holden graduated from Washington University, St. Louis, in 1866 and from the U.S. Military Academy, West Point, in 1870. After teaching at West Point, he was with the U.S. Naval Observatory and the Washburn Observatory at the University of Wisconsin. During the 1870's he helped plan the observatory that the Californian philanthropist James Lick wanted to be the world's greatest. Holden's plan became the basis for the observatory's construction and upon its completion he became the first director, a position he held until 1897. From 1901 until his death he was librarian at the U.S. Military Academy, West Point.

HÖLDER, OTTO LUDWIG (*b. Stuttgart, Germany, 1859; d. Leipzig, Germany, 1937*), mathematics.

Hölder studied mathematics with Weierstrass at the University of Berlin. There he developed the continuity condition for volume density that bears his name. It appeared in his dissertation (*Beiträge zur Potentialstheorie*), which he presented at Tübingen in 1882. The Hölder continuity is sufficient for the existence of all second derivatives of the potential and for the validity of the Poisson differential equation. Next he investigated analytic functions and summation procedures by arithmetic means as evidenced in his *Habilitationsschrift,* submitted in 1884 at Göttingen. After teaching at Tübingen and Königsberg, he went to Leipzig in 1899, where his interest turned to geometrical questions; his inaugural lecture there was *Anschauungen und Denken in der Geometrie* (1900). Later he turned to the logico-philosophical foundations of mathematics. These studies resulted in *Die mathematische Methode* (1924).

HOLMBOE, BERNT MICHAEL (*b. Vang, Norway, 1795; d. Christiania [now Oslo], Norway, 1850*), mathematics.

Holmboe's greatest contribution to mathematics was the discovery and nurturing (at the University of Christiania, where he taught) of the genius of Niels Henrik Abel. After Abel's death, Holmboe edited his works. He also published a number of elementary school texts and a more advanced calculus text influenced by Abel's research.

HOLMES, ARTHUR (*b. Hebburn on Tyne, England, 1890; d. London, England, 1965*), geology, geophysics, petrology.

Holmes was educated at Imperial College, London, where he afterward taught. He was a major contributor in three main lines of research: geochronology, the genesis of igneous rocks, and physical geology. He later worked for an oil company in Burma and taught at the universities of Durham and Edinburgh. He made a great impact through his pioneer work on radiometric methods of rock dating, his controversial views on the origins of deep-seated rocks, and his brilliant synthesis of the contributions of geophysics and geomorphology to the understanding of the history of the earth. Among his works is *Principles of Physical Geology* (1944).

HOLMGREN, FRITHIOF (*b. West Ny, Sweden, 1831; d. Uppsala, Sweden, 1897*), physiology.

Holmgren studied medicine at the University of Uppsala (1850–60) and then physiology at Vienna, Leipzig, Berlin, and Paris. In 1864 he returned to Uppsala and became the first professor of physiology in Sweden. He discovered (about 1864) the retina's electrical response to light, today's electroretinogram. In the 1870s, he did important work on color-blindness, and the tests he devised were adopted all over the world and were credited with preventing countless industrial accidents. His book on color-blindness was widely translated.

HOMBERG, WILHELM or **GUILLAUME** (*b. Batavia, Java [now Jakarta, Indonesia], 1652; d. Paris, France, 1715*), chemistry.

Homberg was educated at Jena and Leipzig and became a practicing lawyer in Magdeburg in 1674. His interest turned to scientific subjects—botany, astronomy, experimental physics—and he took up the study of medicine, receiving his degree from Wittenberg. He settled in Paris under the protection of Philippe II, duke of Orléans.

Homberg is credited with introducing the new scientific chemistry into France. In his "Essais de chimie" (1702–10), he discussed the general concept of principles or elements. Probably most important was his work on the strength of acids and the quantity of acid required to neutralize a given quantity of alkali.

HOME, EVERARD (*b. Hull, England, 1756; d. London, England, 1832*), surgery, comparative anatomy.

Home was a surgical student of John Hunter, who was his brother-in-law. After Hunter's sudden death in 1793, Home replaced him as surgeon at St. George's Hospital, London. He taught comparative anatomy and in 1822 became the first president of the Royal College of Surgeons. He was a brilliant and resourceful surgeon and an excellent teacher. His career was tainted by the scandal arising from his burning of John Hunter's papers and the later discovery that he had published some of Hunter's ideas as his own. He was sergeant surgeon to George III and was close to the prince regent. He was created a baronet in 1813.

HONDA, KOTARO (*b. Aichi prefecture, Japan, 1870; d. Tokyo, Japan, 1954*), physics.

Honda was educated at Tokyo Imperial University and at Göttingen and Berlin. In 1911 he became a professor at Tohoku Imperial University. He was its president from 1931 to 1940. From 1949 to 1953 he was president of Tokyo Science University.

Honda's fame is based on his study of magnetic substances as well as of the metallurgy of iron and steel. After investigating (1926–35) the magnetization of single crystals of iron, nickel, and cobalt, he discovered anisotropic magnetism.

HÖNIGSCHMID, OTTO (*b. Hořovice, Bohemia [now Czechoslovakia], 1878; d. Munich, Germany, 1945*), chemistry.

Hönigschmid studied chemistry under Guido Goldschmiedt at the German University in Prague. In 1909 he went to Harvard University, where he studied atomic weights under T.W. Richards; while there he made his first achievements as an atomic scientist. In the years following, he taught at the German Technical University in Prague and, after 1918, at the University of Munich. It was there that he established his famous atomic weight laboratory, his primary interest for the rest of his life. He perfected preparative and analytic methods, and with a large circle of students and colleagues, he successfully determined the atomic weight of some fifty elements. Among these were the first weight estimates for hafnium and rhenium.

HOOKE, ROBERT (*b. Freshwater, Isle of Wight, England, 1635; d. London, England, 1702*), physics.

Hooke showed himself to be a child prodigy at Westminster School and entered Christ Church, Oxford, in 1653. His facility for mechanics was quickly recognized by the scientific community there, among whom were Thomas Willis and Robert Boyle; Hooke was for a time assistant to each of these men. He was assistant to Boyle when Boyle's law was devised; Hooke's contribution to it is unclear.

Upon the restoration of Charles II, the informal scientific circle at Oxford formed the nucleus of the new Royal Society, and in 1662 Hooke was made its curator of experiments. For the next fifteen years, he poured out a continuous stream of brilliant ideas and experiments. In 1664 he took up residence at Gresham College, where, in one capacity or another, he was to remain the rest of his life.

In 1665 Hooke published *Micrographia*, one of the scientific masterpieces of the seventeenth century. Among other things, it contained the first descriptions and drawings of units he called cells—a term he coined. In *Lectiones Cutlerianae* (1679), a collection of six brief works, he enunciated Hooke's law, the law of elasticity stating that the stress is proportional to the strain. He also contributed a revolutionary insight that reformulated the approach to circular motion in general and to celestial dynamics in particular. In a celebrated correspondence with Isaac Newton, Hooke stated his conviction that gravity decreases in power in proportion to the square of the distance—a theory that stimulated Newton toward the inverse square relation—and put him on the track to universal gravitation.

Hooke was an important geologist; his theories of the origin of fossils were a foreshadowing of the nineteenth century. He is also regarded as the first catastrophist. He was also an accomplished architect. After the Great Fire, he was named surveyor to Sir Christopher Wren in the elaborate plan to rebuild London.

Perhaps Hooke's most important contribution to science, however, lay in the field of instrumentation. He added something to every important instrument developed in the seventeenth century. He invented the air pump in its enduring form. He advanced horology and microscopy. He developed the crosshair sight for the telescope, the iris diaphragm, and a screw adjustment from which the setting could be read directly. He has been called the founder of scientific meteorology. He invented the wheel barometer, on which the pivoted needle registers the pressure. He suggested the freezing temperature of water as the zero point on the thermometer and devised an instrument to calibrate thermometers. His weather clock recorded barometric pressure, temperature, rainfall, humidity, and wind velocity on a rotating drum. The universal joint was also his invention.

HOOKER, JOSEPH DALTON (*b. Halesworth, England, 1817; d. Sunningdale, England, 1911*), botany.

Hooker was the son of Sir William Jackson Hooker. He received the M.D. from Glasgow University in 1839. From 1839 to 1843 he was assistant surgeon and naturalist aboard H.M.S. *Erebus* and *Terror* on an expedition to determine the position of the south magnetic pole. Hooker's botanical findings on that expedition were published (between 1844 and 1860) in a great work known as *The Botany of the Antarctic Voyage of H.M. Discovery Ships 'Erebus' and 'Terror.'* It established Hooker as one of the world's leading botanists.

From 1847 to 1850 he was in Sikkim and Nepal doing botanical exploration and topographical surveying. He also made detailed meteorological and geological observations. Afterward he botanized in other parts of India, resulting in his monumental work, *Flora of British India* (1872–97). It remains the classic work on the subject. Hooker was mainly responsible for the introduction of the rhododendron (a native of Sikkim) into England.

Hooker's father was director of the Royal Botanic Gardens at Kew, London, and in 1855 he became assistant director there. In 1865 his father died and he succeeded as director. He continued his father's work in making Kew an international center for botanical research. He also continued his botanizing expeditions, traveling to the Middle East, Morocco, and western North America. He was a champion of Charles Darwin, and his later works emphasized Darwinian evolutionist theory. He was knighted in 1877.

HOOKER, WILLIAM JACKSON (*b. Norwich, England, 1785; d. Kew, England, 1865*), botany.

In 1804, when he was nineteen, Hooker discovered a new moss (*Buxbaumia aphylla*) and his career as a botanist was set. His patron (who later became his father-in-law), Dawson Turner, commissioned Hooker to illustrate his *Historia fucorum*, a thirteen-year task. In 1809 Hooker went to Iceland, becoming the first scientist to botanize there. In 1816 he published *British Jungermanniae*, a work that established hepaticology as an independent entity and made Hooker's reputation as a botanist. He also wrote four books on mosses during this period.

In 1820, despite his lack of formal education, Hooker became regius professor of botany at the University of Glasgow. In 1821 he published *Flora scotica*. He also greatly improved Glasgow's botanic garden. (It grew from 8,000 species to 20,000, making it the equal of any garden in Europe.) Hooker was knighted in 1836 and in 1841 became the first director of the newly established Royal Botanic Garden at Kew. He set about turning it into a garden of international renown, bringing to it specimens from every corner of the British Empire. He attacked the problem of malaria in India by sending to Peru for the *Cinchona* plant, a cheap source of quinine. He acclimated *Cinchona* at Kew and then successfully established it in India. In 1855 his son Joseph became his assistant at Kew. Ten years later, upon his death, he was succeeded by his son. After his death, the nation bought his herbarium library of 4,000 volumes and his enormous botanical collection of dried speciments.

HOPE, THOMAS CHARLES (*b. Edinburgh, Scotland, 1766; d. Edinburgh, 1844*), chemistry.

Hope entered the University of Edinburgh at thirteen, studied botany, and received the M.D. in 1787. He taught chemistry and medicine at the University of Glasgow until 1795, when he returned to Edinburgh. There he eventually succeeded Joseph Black as professor of chemistry. Hope is remembered for his contributions to the discovery of strontium and his demonstration that water reaches its maximum density just above its freezing point.

HOPF, HEINZ (*b. Breslau, Germany [now Wrocław, Poland], 1894; d. Zollikon, Switzerland, 1971*), mathematics.

Hopf received the Ph.D. in topological research from the University of Berlin in 1925. After an academic year (1927–28) at Princeton University, he was appointed (1931) a full professor at the Eidgenössische Technische Hochschule in Zurich. The greater part of Hopf's work was algebraic topology; no topologist of that period inspired so great a variety of important ideas. Hopf's work during the 1930's constituted the beginnings of the research into homotopy of spheres that developed after World War II.

HOPKINS, FREDERICK GOWLAND (*b. Eastbourne, Sussex, England, 1861; d. Cambridge, England, 1947*), biochemistry.

Hopkins is regarded as the father of British biochemistry and was a major contributor to biochemical thought and experimental biochemistry throughout the world. Hopkins's first career was as an analyst; working for the Home Office as an expert medical jurist, he helped solve a number of celebrated murder cases. At age twenty-seven, a small inheritance allowed him to enter the medical school at Guy's Hospital. After qualifying in chemistry, he continued to work at Guy's. In 1898, when he was thirty-seven, he finally was able to enroll at Cambridge. Michael Foster, who was professor of physiology there, encouraged Hopkins to undertake the development and teaching of what was then known as chemical physiology. So rigorous was his program that he suffered a breakdown in 1910. While he was recuperating, Trinity College, Cambridge, named him a fellow and elected him to a praelectorship in biochemistry, an honor that he credited with helping him to recover. Thus Hopkins was almost fifty before he entered into a full-time career in biochemistry.

In 1912 he published his most famous paper, "Feeding Experiments Illustrating the Importance of Accessory Food Factors in Normal Dietaries." It was this paper that firmly and finally established the existence of vitamins. In 1914 Hopkins became the first professor of biochemistry at Cambridge, and his new department became the mecca of biochemists the world over. Later he was chiefly responsible for the introduction of biochemistry into the curriculum of all British universities.

During World War I, Hopkins began his experiments with margarine, a project that eventually (1926–27) resulted in the first "vitaminized" margarines, that is, products into which vitamins A and D were added, thereby making margarine the nutritional equal of butter. He also devised an accurate and superior method for determining the presence of uric acid in urine. Hopkins was knighted in 1925, won the Nobel Prize in physiology or medicine (along with Eijkmann) in 1929, and became president of the Royal Society in 1931.

HOPKINS, WILLIAM (*b. Kingston-on-Soar, Derbyshire, England, 1793; d. Cambridge, England, 1866*), geology, mathematics.

In 1822 Hopkins entered St. Peter's College (Peterhouse), Cambridge, where his talent for mathematics was recognized. After receiving the B.A. in 1827 he tutored mathematics. After 1833 he was primarily interested in the application of mathematics to proving geological theories. His interest in pure mathematics was evidenced in the two-volume *Elements of Trigonometry* (1833–47). His theoretical investigations into the constitutions of the interior of the earth were supported later in the works of Poisson, Ampère, George H. Darwin, and Lord Kelvin.

HOPKINSON, JOHN (*b. Manchester, England, 1849; d. Evalona, Switzerland, 1898*), electricity, physics.

Hopkinson was educated at London University and Trinity College, Cambridge. He taught electrical engineering at King's College, London University, and directed the Siemens laboratory there. His investigation in the application of electricity and magnetism to motors and dynamos resulted in more than sixty books and papers.

HOPPE-SEYLER, (ERNST) FELIX (IMMANUEL) (*b. Freiburg im Breisgau, Germany, 1825; d. Lake Constance, Germany, 1895*), physiological chemistry.

In 1851 Hoppe-Seyler received the M.D. from the University of Berlin, and after a year of clinical training in Prague established a practice in Berlin. In 1861 he went to the University of Tübingen as professor of applied chemistry. After 1872 he was professor of physiological

chemistry at the University of Strasbourg. His most important work was done (while he was at Tübingen) on a substance he called hemoglobin. He also did important work on lecithin and cholesterol. At Strasbourg he concentrated on problems relating to the nature of intracellular oxidation processes. He was influential in the establishment of physiological chemistry as a distinct discipline.

HORBACZEWSKI, JAN (*b. Zarubince, near Ternopol, Austria-Hungary [now R.S.F.S.R], 1854; d. Prague, Czechoslovakia, 1942*), biochemistry.

Horbaczewski taught at the University of Prague and during World War I he was for a short time (1917–18) minister of health in a multinational government of the Austro-Hungarian monarchy. (He was of Lithuanian descent.) Today he is chiefly remembered as the first to synthesize (1882) uric acid. Later he produced the first direct experimental proof that uric acid was not a constituent of protein but was part of the cell nucleus metabolism.

HORN, GEORGE HENRY (*b. Philadelphia, Pa., 1840; d. Beesley's Point, N.J., 1897*), coleopterology.

After earning the M.D. at the University of Pennsylvania in 1861, Horn practiced obstetrics in Philadelphia for many years. He developed an interest in zoology, specifically the Coleoptera, on which he published (from 1860 to 1896) more than 200 works. During his life he described a total of 1,583 species and varieties of Coleoptera. His works still retain much of their usefulness.

HORN D'ARTURO, GUIDO (*b. Trieste, 1879; d. Bologna, Italy, 1967*), astronomy.

Horn D'Arturo graduated from the University of Vienna in 1902. After working at various Italian observatories, in 1920 he was named director of the Bologna Observatory, which he completely renovated. He also held the astronomy chair at Bologna. In 1938 he was removed from both posts because he was a Jew. He was reinstated after World War II and retired in 1954. He was active in positional astronomy, cosmography, and optical astronomy. In the last, he demonstrated how the density of photographic stellar tracks may be measured by using the diffraction of light.

HORNE (HORNIUS), JOHANNES VAN (*b. Amsterdam, Netherlands, ca. 1621; d. Leiden, Netherlands, 1670*), anatomy.

He entered the University of Leiden at age fifteen and later studied medicine at Utrecht and Padua. In 1651 he became professor of anatomy at Leiden and gave anatomical demonstrations. He was the first to describe (1652) the *ductus chyliferus* (thoracicus) in man. He also wrote an important introduction to anatomy (1660).

HORNER, LEONARD (*b. Edinburgh, Scotland, 1785; d. London, England, 1864*), geology.

Horner attended Edinburgh University and after moving to London became active in the Geological Society and the Royal Society. After 1827 he was connected with University College, London, and supervised the formation of its revolutionary scientific curriculum. Horne's work in promoting science-based education at all levels was more important than his original geological work, although the latter was far from negligible. He was an early supporter of Charles Darwin.

HORNER, WILLIAM GEORGE (*b. Bristol, England, 1786; d. Bath, England, 1837*), mathematics.

Horner was educated at Kingswood School, Bristol, where he later became headmaster. Horner's only significant contribution to mathematics lay in the method of solving algebraic equations that still bears his name. First published in 1819, its use spread quickly throughout England; it occupied a prominent place in English and American textbooks through the early twentieth century. Its use declined with the development of computer methods.

HORNSBY, THOMAS (*b. Oxford, England, 1733; d. Oxford, 1810*), astronomy.

Hornsby is best remembered for his part in the foundation of the Radcliffe Observatory at Oxford. He made an accurate evaluation of the solar parallax. Hornsby earned the M.A. from Corpus Christi College, Oxford, in 1757 and later became professor of astronomy at Oxford. He successfully promoted the building of the Radcliffe Observatory, which was completed in 1778. Employing equipment of the master instrument maker, John Bird, it was unequalled in its day.

HORREBOW, CHRISTIAN (*b. Copenhagen, Denmark, 1718; d. Copenhagen, 1776*), astronomy.

He obtained the M.S. from the University of Copenhagen in 1738 and became the assistant of his father, Peder Nielsen Horrebow, at the Round Tower Observatory. Gradually he and his brother Peder took over and continued their father's work. Eventually (1764) Christian obtained the chair in astronomy at Copenhagen. His systematic observations of sunspots came to play a role in the later investigation of the period of sunspot activity.

HORREBOW, PEDER NIELSEN (*b. Løgstør, Denmark, 1679; d. Copenhagen, Denmark, 1764*), astronomy.

The son of a fisherman, Horrebow worked his way through Copenhagen University. He became assistant to Ole Römer and in 1714 became professor of astronomy and director of the observatory, a position he held for fifty years, assisted in his later years by his two sons. In 1728 a fire destroyed Römer's papers, and Horrebow set about the task of reconstructing Römer's scientific experiments for posterity. His book on Römer, *Basis astronomiae* (1734–35), is a classic. In *Atrium astronomiae* (1732) Horrebow advanced what later came to be called the Horrebow-Talcott method for determining geographical latitude.

HORROCKS, JEREMIAH (*b. Lancashire, England, 1618; d. Toxteth Park, England, 1641*), astronomy.

Horrocks attended Emmanuel College, Cambridge, but left in 1635 without taking a degree. His astronomy was largely self-taught. In his short career he studied all aspects of astronomy. He redetermined the astronomical constants of several planets, improved the theory of lunar motion, considered the scale of the solar system, began a study of the tides, and theorized on the motions of the planets. Much of his work was in collaboration with William Crabtree. He was an ardent disciple of Tycho and Kepler. In 1639 he predicted and observed the transit of Venus, the first astronomer to do so. This event is described in *Venus in sole visa,* published posthumously in 1662. Much of his manuscript has not survived.

HORSFORD, EBEN NORTON (*b. Moscow [now Livonia], N.Y., 1818; d. Cambridge, Mass., 1893*), chemistry.

Horsford studied at Rensselaer Institute under Amos Eaton. From 1844 to 1846 he studied chemistry under Liebig at Giessen, Germany, and was instrumental in the transfer of chemical skills and knowledge from Europe to America. In 1847 he became Rumford professor at Harvard. With the founding of the Lawrence Scientific School, he transferred there and established the first laboratory in America for analytical chemistry. Primarily interested in nutrition, he developed a phosphatic baking powder. He became rich from the Rumford Chemical Company, which he helped found to market it. He abandoned his academic career, but was one of the patrons of the newly founded Wellesley College.

HORSLEY, VICTOR ALEXANDER HADEN (*b. Kensington, London, England, 1857; d. Amara, near Baghdad, Mesopotamia [now Iraq], 1916*), neurosurgery, pathology, social reform.

A graduate (1880) of University College Hospital Medical School, Horsley taught pathology at University College, London, and carried on a private surgical practice. His many contributions to medicine fall in three general areas: experimental work, surgical innovation, and political and social reform. His experimental work was mainly concerned with thyroid physiology and pathology and on cerebral cortical function. He was a pioneer brain surgeon, making experimental lesions in the deep parts of the brain. He did a breakthrough removal of a spinal tumor, and his operation for trigeminal neuralgia was another important advance. In social reform, he was active in the temperance, women's suffrage, and anti-smoking movements. He was knighted in 1902.

HORSTMANN, AUGUST FRIEDRICH (*b. Mannheim, Germany, 1842; d. Heidelberg, Germany, 1929*), physical chemistry.

Horstmann stimulated the application of thermodynamics to chemical reactions when he showed that the Clausius-Clapeyron equation adequately explained the heats of dissociation of ammonium chloride upon sublimation. He studied at Zurich, Bonn, and at Heidelberg, where he received his doctorate in 1865 and where he taught the rest of his life.

HORTENSIUS, MARTINUS, also known as **Ortensius,** or **Van den Hove, Maarten** (*b. Delft, Netherlands, 1605; d. Leiden, Netherlands, 1639*), astronomy.

Hortensius' chief contributions were in the diffusion of Copernican astronomy and in his measurements of the angular size of the sun. He studied at Leiden, Ghent, and probably in Italy. In 1635 he became professor of astronomy at the Amsterdam Atheneum and in 1639 at the Leiden university. He collaborated with Philip van Lansberge and carried on correspondence with Descartes, Mersenne, Gassendi, Huygens, and Galileo.

HOSACK, DAVID (*b. New York, N.Y., 1769; d. New York, 1835*), botany, medicine.

After studying at Columbia College and the College of New Jersey (now Princeton University), Hosack received his medical education at the University of Pennsylvania (M.D., 1791). After several years in Great Britain, where he became interested in botany, he became professor of botany at Columbia in 1795 and later professor of materia medica. He founded the Elgin Botanic Garden in 1801. In medicine, he was a strong believer in the contagion theory of yellow fever. He also maintained a large private practice. (He was attending physician at the Hamilton-Burr duel.) He was instrumental in the founding (1820) of Bellevue Hospital.

HOSEMANN. *See* **Osiander, Andreas.**

HOÜEL, GUILLAUME-JULES (*b. Thaon, Calvados, France, 1823; d. Périers, near Caen, France, 1886*), mathematics, astronomy.

Hoüel received his doctorate from the Sorbonne in 1855 for research in celestial mechanics. He held the chair of pure mathematics at Bordeaux from 1859 until his death. His reputation rests primarily on the quality and quantity of his activities in mathematical exposition. In his *Théorie élémentaire des quantités complexes* (1874), he introduced to France the work of the leading foreign mathematicians. He also wrote a major four-volume text in analysis, *Cours de calcul infinitésimal* (1878–81).

HOUGH, GEORGE WASHINGTON (*b. Tribes Hill, N.Y., 1836; d. Evanston, Ill., 1909*), astronomy, meteorology.

Hough's main contributions to astronomy were his discovery of 627 double stars and his floating island theory of the great red spot on the planet Jupiter. He devised many instruments with astrological and meteorological applications. He received the M.A. from Union College, Schenectady, in 1856, later studied at Harvard and in 1862 became director of the Dudley Observatory in Albany. In 1879 he became head of the Dearborn Observatory in Chicago, where he began his systematic observations of Jupiter and his search for new double stars.

HOUGHTON, DOUGLASS (*b. Troy, N.Y., 1809; d. Eagle River, Mich., 1845*), medicine, geology.

A physician, Houghton delivered scientific lectures in Detroit, then a bustling frontier city. He served twice as mayor of Detroit, and in 1837 he became the first state geologist and professor of geology, mineralogy, and chemistry at the newly founded University of Michigan. Until his death by drowning at age thirty-six, he conducted important geological and geographical surveys of the frontier.

HOUSSAY, BERNARDO ALBERTO (*b. Buenos Aires, Argentina, 1887; d. Buenos Aires, 1971*), physiology, pharmacology, medicine.

Houssay was one of the leading South American scientists of the twentieth century. For more than twenty-five years, his Institute of Physiology at the University of Buenos Aires was the scientific beacon for all of South America. He was educated in medicine at the University of Buenos Aires; his doctoral dissertation (1911) con-

cerned the physiological activities of pituitary extracts. This area and his studies of the effects of insulin led to a recognition of the role played by the anterior lobe of the hypophysis in carbohydrate metabolism. For this work he won the 1947 Nobel Prize in physiology or medicine (shared with G.T. and C.F. Cori). He also studied the pancreatic secretion of insulin, the hormonal control of fat metabolism, and the factors regulating arterial blood pressure.

HOWARD, LELAND OSSIAN (*b. Rockford, Ill., 1857; d. Bronxville, N.Y., 1950*), applied entomology.

After graduation from Cornell University, Howard became (1878) assistant to Charles Valentine Riley, chief of the Division of Insects in the United States Department of Agriculture. Howard succeeded Riley in 1894 and retained the post until 1924. Howard was intimately involved in studies of such economically important insects as the boll weevil, gypsy moth, San José scale, and the mosquito. Of the last, he described twenty-two new species. He published more than one thousand papers.

HOWE, JAMES LEWIS (*b. Newburyport, Mass., 1859; d. Lexington, Va., 1955*), chemistry.

After receiving the B.A. from Amherst College in 1880, Howe received the M.A. and Ph.D. in 1882 from the University of Göttingen. From 1894 to 1938 he headed the chemistry department at Washington and Lee University. Howe was regarded as the outstanding American expert on the platinum metals in general and the undisputed world authority on the chemistry of ruthenium. His magnum opus was *Bibliography of the Platinum Metals* (1947–56).

HÖWELCKE, JOHANN. *See* **Hevelius, Johannes.**

HOWELL, WILLIAM HENRY (*b. Baltimore, Md., 1860; d. Baltimore, 1945*), physiology.

Howell was educated at Johns Hopkins University, where he received the Ph.D. in 1884. His dissertation, "The Origin of the Fibrin Formed in the Coagulation of Blood," was the forerunner of the later research in which he made his greatest contribution. In 1893 Howell became the first professor of physiology at Johns Hopkins, where he was to remain all his career. Howell's early contributions dealt with the circulatory system, nerve tissue, and the components of the blood. He was one of the founders of the American Physiological Society, and in the early years of the twentieth century was regarded as America's outstanding physiologist. In 1910 he isolated thrombin; in 1918 he discovered the anticoagulant heparin; and in his last years he proved the theory that blood platelets are formed in the lungs.

HRDLIČKA, ALEŠ (*b. Humpolec, Bohemia [now Czechoslovakia], 1869; d. Washington, D.C., 1943*), physical anthropology.

Hrdlička's parents immigrated to New York City while he was a youth. In 1894 he completed training at the New York Homeopathic College. In 1896 he went to Paris to study anthropology with L.P. Manouvrier. After 1903 he was connected with the Smithsonian Institution and was its curator from 1910 to 1943. He led numerous field investigations and became an expert on Eskimos and Indians of North and Central America. In *The Question of Ancient Man in America* (1937) he formulated the theory that America had been peopled from Asia via the Bering Strait—a theory generally accepted today.

HUBBLE, EDWIN POWELL (*b. Marshfield, Mo., 1889; d. San Marino, Calif., 1953*), observational astronomy, cosmology.

Hubble studied mathematics and astronomy at the University of Chicago, and in 1910 he went to Queen's College, Oxford, as a Rhodes scholar. In 1912 he received the B.A. in jurisprudence from Oxford. He was admitted to the bar in Kentucky and practiced law briefly before going to the Yerkes Observatory at the University of Chicago. In 1917 he was awarded the Ph.D. After serving in World War I, he joined G.E. Hale at the Mount Wilson Observatory, Pasadena, California. In 1925 he was the first to introduce a significant classification system for galaxies. It is the basis for the system still used.

Hubble was a founder of modern extragalactic astronomy and the first to provide observational evidence for the expansion of the universe. This he formulated in what is known as Hubble's law. It states that the distances between galaxies are constantly increasing and that, therefore, the universe is expanding. He formulated the law in 1929 and based it on his analysis of the light received from the distant galaxies. The colors emitted from the stars in these galaxies move toward the red end of the spectrum (the red shift) as the galaxies move away from our own galaxy, the Milky Way. It was this discovery that made his name known far beyond the ranks of professional astronomers.

HUBER, JOHANN JACOB (*b. Basel, Switzerland, 1707; d. Kassel, Germany, 1778*), anatomy, botany.

Huber's main contributions to science were his anatomical studies. In his *De medulla spinali* (1741), he gave the first detailed and accurate description of the spinal cord. He received his medical degree from the University of Basel in 1733 and taught at Göttingen and Kassel.

HUBER, MAKSYMILIAN TYTUS (*b. Krościenko, Poland, 1872; d. Cracow, Poland, 1950*), mechanics, theory of elasticity.

Huber's main areas of scientific contribution were the theory of orthotropic (orthogonally anisotropic) plates and strength theories. He studied at the Lvov Institute of Technology and the University of Berlin. He later taught at Lvov and at the Warsaw Institute of Technology. He was active in the Polish underground during World War II and after the war taught at Gdańsk and Cracow.

HUBRECHT, AMBROSIUS ARNOLD WILLEM (*b. Rotterdam, Netherlands, 1853; d. Utrecht, Netherlands, 1915*), zoology, comparative embryology.

Hubrecht received his doctorate in 1874 from Utrecht University, where he studied zoology under Harting and Donders. From 1875 to 1882 he was curator of fishes at the natural history museum at Leiden. During that period he also spent six months (in 1878) in Naples studying nemerteans. In 1882 he became professor of zoology and comparative anatomy at Utrecht. He held that chair until 1910, when he became extraordinary professor of em-

bryology, a chair especially created for him. From about 1888 Hubrecht studied the early embryology and placentology of mammals. In particular, he cleared up many obscure points in the development of the fetal membranes and the placenta. He was a convinced Darwinian. In his 1889 paper on mammalian embryology, concerning the hedgehog (*Erinaceus*), he coined the term "trophoblast" for the outer cell layer of the early mammalian embryo, a term still used.

HUDDE, JAN (*b. Amsterdam, Netherlands, 1628; d. Amsterdam, 1704*), mathematics.

Hudde studied law at the University of Leiden around 1648, at which time he became interested in mathematics under the tutelage of Frans van Schooten. Hudde's contributions to mathematics apparently were all made between 1654 and 1663; after that he seems to have devoted himself to the civic government of Amsterdam. In Hudde's small quantity of extant mathematical works (Leibniz noted that Hudde had many unpublished mathematical writings, which are now lost) two main problems are confronted: the improvement of Descartes's algebraic methods with the intention of solving equations of higher degree by means of an algorithm; and the problem of extreme values (maxima and minima) and tangents to algebraic curves. In the latter, Hudde accomplished the algorithmizing of Fermat's method, with which he had become acquainted through Schooten. Hudde was also interested in physics and astronomy, and in 1665 he worked with Spinoza on the construction of telescopic lenses.

HUDSON, CLAUDE SILBERT (*b. Atlanta, Ga., 1881; d. Washington, D.C., 1952*), chemistry.

Hudson received the B.S. (1901) and Ph.D. (1907) in physics from Princeton University. He also studied physical chemistry at the universities of Berlin and Göttingen. His career was spent almost entirely in government laboratories in Washington, D.C., where he trained many followers in the chemistry of the sugars.

HUDSON, WILLIAM (*b. Kendal, Westmorland, England, 1733; d. London, England, 1793*), botany.

Hudson was apprenticed to an apothecary in London after a grammar school education. In 1757 and 1758 he was sublibrarian of the British Museum, while studying at the Sloane herbarium. In 1762 he published *Flora Anglica*, which quickly became the standard English flora and won over most English naturalists to the Linnean sexual system, which it employed. From 1765 to 1771 Hudson was director of the Apothecaries' Garden, although he retained his apothecary practice throughout his life.

HUFNAGEL, LEON (*b. Warsaw, Poland, 1893; d. Berlin, Germany, 1933*), astronomy.

Hufnagel studied at the University of Warsaw and the University of Vienna, from which he received the Ph.D. in 1919. From 1919 to 1926 he was at the Free University in Warsaw and from 1926 to 1928 at the Lund Observatory in Sweden. He then went to America (Mt. Wilson, Lick, and Harvard observatories) and Germany. In his most important papers, Hufnagel considered the velocity distributions of faint stars and the influence on such distributions of accidental errors in proper motions.

HUGGINS, WILLIAM (*b. London, England, 1824; d. Tulse Hill, London, 1910*), astrophysics.

Huggins was mostly educated by private tutors and in 1842 he took over his father's mercery business. Despite his lack of university education, he was well grounded in the sciences and his spare time was devoted to the microscope and telescope. In 1854 he sold his mercery business and devoted himself wholly to science. He moved to Tulse Hill (then still in the country), where he set up a private observatory and carried out his astronomical research. His wife, Margaret Lindsay Murray, took an active part in his research and coauthored some of his publications. He and W. A. Miller designed a spectroscope and he began his spectroscopic observations of stars. His findings were published in 1863–64 by the Royal Society. His general conclusion was that the brightest stars, at least, resemble the sun in structure. In 1864 he made a still more sensational discovery: He proved that some nebulae are clusters of stars while others are uniformly gaseous. Two years later (1866), he made the first spectroscopic observations of a nova. Huggins was knighted in 1897. In 1899 he and his wife published the *Atlas of Representative Stellar Spectra*.

HUGH OF ST. VICTOR (*d. Paris, France, 1141*), scientific classification, geometry.

Hugh came to Paris at an early age and joined the canons regular of the abbey of St. Victor. He lectured on theology in the famous school attached to this monastery, and was its greatest representative. He wrote a very large number of exegetical, philosophical, and theological works which exercised a profound influence on the scholasticism of the twelfth and thirteenth centuries. The most famous of them is the *De sacramentis christianae fidei*.

Preoccupied with giving a scientific basis to the teaching of theology, Hugh wrote an introductory treatise to the sacred sciences, the *Didascalicon* or *De studio legendi*, composed before 1125. Book II of this work contains a division of philosophy which is a classification of the sciences, inspired by that of Boethius.

The division of the sciences in the *Didascalicon* was resumed a short time later in a dialogue entitled *Epitome Dindimi in philosophiam*. The interest that he had shown for mathematics reappeared in *Practica geometriae*. Composed at about the same time as the *Didascalicon*, this treatise, which shows the influence of Macrobius and especially of Gerbert d'Aurillac, testifies to the state of geometry in the West before the great diffusion of Arabic science.

HUGONIOT, PIERRE HENRI (*b. Allenjoie, Doubs, France, 1851; d. Nantes, France, 1887*), mechanics, ballistics.

In 1868 he entered the École Polytechnique in Paris. After completing the two-year general course, he chose military engineering as his speciality and graduated in 1872 with an appointment to the naval artillery. He held a teaching post at the École d'Artillerie de la Marine in Lorient. In 1884, on the basis of his scientific work, Hugoniot was made *répétiteur auxiliaire* of mechanics at the École Polytechnique and, a year later, *répétiteur*.

Hugoniot's first research, done with H. Sébert, concerned the effect of powder gases on the bore of a weapon (1882) and was based on the analysis of experimental materials. In 1884 he collaborated with Félix

Hélie in preparing a revised and substantially enlarged edition of Hélie's *Traité de balistique expérimentale*, first published in 1865.

His theory was published in an extensive two-part memoir (pt. 1, 1887; pt. 2, 1889); its basic conclusions had been announced in a series of articles published in the *Comptes rendus* (1885–86) of the Paris Academy.

Hugoniot's earliest work on the mechanics of gases was written with Sébert in 1884. In 1885 Hugoniot developed, on a sufficiently general physical basis, the theory of discontinuous flows. It was the first theory to apply the law of conservation of energy in an obvious manner. The correspondence that he found between the pressure and the density of gas before and after discontinuity (the pressure jump)—which was called "Hugoniot's adiabatic curve"—is one of the bases of modern shock-wave theory.

HULL, ALBERT WALLACE (*b. Southington, Conn., 1880; d. Schenectady, N.Y., 1966*), electron physics.

Hull studied Greek at Yale and after graduation taught French and German at Albany Academy for one year. Recognizing an enthusiasm for physics, he returned to Yale for graduate work, obtained the doctorate in 1909, and taught for five years at Worcester Polytechnic Institute in Massachusetts.

Hull joined the famed General Electric Research Laboratory at Schenectady, New York, in 1914; his first work was on electron tubes, X-ray crystallography, and (during World War I) piezoelectricity. The work for which he is best known was done after the war, when he published the classic paper on the effect of a uniform magnetic field on the motion of electrons between coaxial cylinders. His other electron tube work in the 1920's concerned noise measurements in diodes and triodes.

In the 1930's Hull's interests broadened to metallurgy and glass science.

HUMBERT, MARIE-GEORGES (*b. Paris, France, 1859; d. Paris, 1921*), mathematics.

Humbert received his doctorate in mathematics in 1885 from the École Polytechnique in Paris and became professor of analysis there in 1895. Previous to 1885 he had worked as a mining engineer and taught at the École Polytechnique and the École des Mines. He was elected to the Academy in 1901 and after 1904 he taught higher mathematics at the Collège de France. A brilliant representative of the French school of mathematics, Humbert distinguished himself primarily through his works in fields pioneered by Poincaré and Hermite. He completed the work of Hermite by pursuing the applications to number theory throughout his life. The progressive alliance of geometry, analysis, and arithmetic in Humbert's works is a splendid example of how a broad mathematical education can assist discovery. All his memoirs and articles were collected in *Oeuvres de Georges Humbert* (2 vols., 1929–36).

HUMBERT, PIERRE (*b. Paris, France, 1891; d. Montpellier, France, 1953*), mathematics, history of science.

The son of Georges Humbert, Pierre entered the École Polytechnique in Paris in 1910 and from 1913 to 1914 attended the University of Edinburgh, where he studied under Edmund Whittaker. He received his doctorate in

1918 and taught at the University of Montpellier, where he remained throughout his career. In the field of mathematics, Humbert directed his efforts chiefly toward the development of symbolic calculus. He also undertook scholarly research in the history of science, specializing in the study of seventeenth-century astronomy.

HUMBOLDT, FRIEDRICH WILHELM HEINRICH ALEXANDER VON (*b. Berlin, Germany, 1769; d. Berlin, 1859*), natural science.

From 1787 to 1792 Humboldt studied at various German schools, including the universities of Frankfurt an der Oder and Göttingen, the academy of commerce in Hamburg, and the academy of mining in Freiberg. He acquired a broad background in technology, economics, geology, mining science, and botany. In 1792 he entered the Prussian mining service, where he invented several mining safety devices and founded, with his own money, a "free mining school" for miners.

In 1795 Humboldt made an extensive expedition through the Swiss, French, and Italian Alps; there he learned about altitude effects on climate and plants and became interested in geomagnetism. Thus he began his lifelong interest in natural interrelationships. Although he is indisputably one of the founders of geography as a science, he had as a major goal a comprehensive view of nature to which the earth sciences would contribute significantly.

Becoming financially independent in 1796, Humboldt resigned from the civil service and began preparations for the "great journey beyond Europe." At Jena in 1797 he conducted experiments on galvanism and chemical effects on animals and plants. He learned techniques for making geodesic and geophysical measurements, and especially for taking astronomical bearings. He also renewed his contacts with Goethe and Schiller. In 1798 he and the French botanist Aimé Bonpland went to Spain where Humboldt busied himself with geodetic measurements and botanic field studies. In 1799 he received permission to make a research tour of the Spanish colonies, and on 16 July 1799 he and Bonpland landed in what is now Venezuela. For the next five years, the two journeyed through what is now Venezuela, Cuba, Colombia, Peru, Ecuador, and Mexico. They recorded, sketched, described, measured, and compared what they observed. They also collected some 60,000 plant specimens, 6,300 of which were unknown in Europe. Humboldt made maps and amassed exhaustive data in countless fields—magnetism, meteorology, climatology, geology, mineralogy, oceanography, zoology, and ethnography. He navigated the Orinoco and Magdalena rivers and proved the connection between the Orinoco and the Amazon.

In 1804, on his way back to Europe, Humboldt visited the United States, where he conferred with President Jefferson and was elected a member of the American Philosophical Society. He returned to Paris, where he was enthusiastically received in scientific circles. His American travel journals were published in twenty-three volumes under the general title *Voyages aux régions équinoxiales du Nouveau Continent...* (1805–1834). This classic work gave a major impetus to the study of the Americas. Humboldt studied the discovery and history of America; its economics and politics; its human productivity and property relationships; and its physical attributes in all dimensions.

Humboldt, having bankrupted himself, returned to Berlin and the civil service in 1827. In 1829, however, he set out on a trip to Siberia as a guest of the Russian government. He again made systematic investigations in wide areas of interest. He returned to Berlin in late 1829 and thereafter lived alternately there and in Paris. In his last decades, he devoted himself primarily to his writings, and produced, among others, his monumental *Kosmos* (5 vols, 1845–62), a popular scientific work in the best sense of the term. He also interested himself in a wide range of humane and social causes. He was a strong opponent of slavery and spoke out against anti-Semitism and racism.

HUME, DAVID (*b. Edinburgh, Scotland, 1711; d. Edinburgh, 1776*), philosophy, economy, political theory, history.

Hume matriculated at the University of Edinburgh at age twelve but left three years later without a degree. He studied law, but at age eighteen he reported that he made a great discovery that "opened up a new scene of thought," and he determined to devote himself wholly to working out his new ideas. However, he did enter the business world until 1734, when he took up residence at La Flèche, France, where he developed an intimate acquaintance with French philosophy. While there he completed his *Treatise of Human Nature,* although it was not completely published until 1740, by which time he had returned to Britain. The unenthusiastic reception of the work was a severe disappointment to Hume, who had expected it to create a sensation. His later philosophical works include *Essays Moral and Political* (1741–42), *Philosophical Essays Concerning Human Understanding* (1748), *Enquiry Concerning the Principles of Morals* (1751), *Dialogues on Natural Religion* (written *ca.* 1751, but published posthumously in 1779), and *Four Dissertations* (1757). Although Hume today is famous for his skeptical philosophy, in his own day it was his six-volume *History of Great Britain* (1754–62) that made his reputation; it was enormously successful and was the standard work on the subject for several decades.

Hume's analysis of reasoning begins from the presumption that what we are directly acquainted with are "perceptions in our mind," as distinct from independently existing physical objects. He divides these perceptions into two classes, impressions and ideas. Impressions are direct sense perceptions, and ideas are the "faint images of impressions." They are what men have before their mind when they think, as distinct from when they feel. Thus all ideas are derived from sense experience; and such metaphysical concepts as "substance" and "essence" are meaningless or mere word play. He denied the possibility that any ultimate scientific verification of the truth of impressions and ideas is possible. Instead, both science and common sense take it for granted that there are independently existing objects necessarily linked one with another. But man's belief in an orderly systematic world is justified only by virtue of the fact that similar perceptions recur in particular ordered sequences (e.g., we can predict the sun will rise tomorrow morning only because it has risen on every other morning in the past). Hume's skepticism, which went beyond that of Locke and Berkeley, had a profound effect on subsequent metaphysics and logic.

HUME-ROTHERY, WILLIAM (*b. Worcester Park, Surrey, England, 1899; d. Iffley, Oxfordshire, England, 1968*), metallurgy, chemistry.

Hume-Rothery's plan to enter the military was cut short when meningitis left him totally deaf. He subsequently entered Magdalen College, Oxford, graduating in 1922. He then studied metallurgy at the Royal School of Mines at London University and received the Ph.D. in 1926. He taught and did research at Oxford, and in 1957, under pressure from the metallurgical profession, the School of Metallurgy was established there with Hume-Rothery as the first professor. His scientific contributions are related to the principles underlying the crystal structures of alloy phases. His influence on metallurgical education was worldwide. His book *The Structures of Metals and Alloys* (1936) was particularly important.

ḤUNAYN IBN ISḤĀQ AL-ʿIBĀDĪ, ABŪ ZAYD, known in the Latin West as **Johannitius** (*b. near Ḥīra, Iraq, 808; d. Baghdad, Iraq, 873*), medicine, philosophy, theology, translation of Greek scientific works.

Ḥunayn, a physician, philosopher, and theologian, was the most famous ninth-century translator of works from Greek antiquity into Arabic and Syriac. While still young, Ḥunayn learned Arabic and Syriac, perfecting his knowledge of the former at Baṣra. He went to Baghdad to study medicine but because of difficulties with his teacher, left Baghdad for several years, during which time he made a profound study of Greek. When he returned, the teacher who had sent him away recognized his abilities, was reconciled with Ḥunayn, and accepted him as a disciple.

Ḥunayn possessed the best knowledge of Greek of anyone of his time and translated the works of Plato and Aristotle and their commentators. Even more important were his translations of the major portion of the works of the three founders of Greek medicine, whose ideas were also central to the development of Arab medicine: Hippocrates, Galen, and Dioscorides. Ḥunayn's scientific activity consisted mainly of producing translations or revisions of earlier translations, but also included a number of original works.

HUNDT (HUND, CANIS), MAGNUS (*b. Magdeburg, Germany, 1449; d. Meissen, Germany, 1519*), anatomy, medicine.

Magnus Hundt, known as the Elder, received the B.A. from Leipzig University in 1483, a baccalaureate in medicine in 1499, and a licentiate in theology in 1504. Thereafter he was a professor at Leipzig for many years. His best-known work, *Antropologia de hominis dignitate, natura et proprietatibus de elementis* (1501), is one of the three or four earliest printed books to include anatomical illustrations. (At one time it was looked upon as the oldest but that is no longer believed to be the case.) It contains five full-page wood cuts, two of the head. There are also illustrations of the hand, thorax, abdomen, stomach, intestines, and cranium.

HUNT, JAMES (*b. Swanage, England, 1833; d. Hastings, England, 1869*), anthropology.

Hunt continued the work of his father, Thomas Hunt, who had developed a method of treating stammering. James may have attended Cambridge University, al-though there are no records of his having done so. He is said to have treated 1,700 cases of stammering, and in 1854 he published *A Treatise on the Cure of Stammering*. In 1863 he was one of the founders of the Anthropological Society of London and the *Anthropological Review*. His racial theories, especially that the Negro is a separate species, were highly controversial.

HUNT, THOMAS STERRY (*b. Norwich, Conn., 1826; d. New York, N.Y., 1892*), chemistry, geology.

Hunt's desultory education was augmented by the scientific training he received under both Benjamin Silliman and his son. From 1846 to 1872 he was mineralogist and chemist to the Geological Survey of Canada, during which period he also taught at the University of Laval, Quebec, and at McGill University. From 1872 to 1878 he was professor of geology at the Massachusetts Institute of Technology. As a chemist, Hunt rejected atomism for a continuum physics in which all chemical changes were explained by interpenetration or solution. In geology, his primary interest was in Paleozoic rocks, the history of which, he argued, could be deduced by extrapolating from the existing mineral species that they contained, the supposed prehistoric chemical conditions necessary for their origin.

HUNTER, JOHN (*b. Long Calderwood, near East Kilbride, Lanarkshire, Scotland, 1728; d. London, England, 1793*), surgery, anatomy.

In 1748 Hunter began studying anatomy under the supervision of his brother William in London. He spent eleven years working with William in Covent Garden, during which time he made detailed studies of the lymphatic vessels and of bone. His interest in the organ of hearing was concentrated on various types of fish. In 1768 he was admitted to the Company of Surgeons (later the Royal College of Surgeons) and was appointed to a post at St. George's Hospital. Thereafter his time was divided among his practice, his dissections and experiments on live animals, and teaching. He was also active in the scientific societies. In 1776 he was appointed surgeon-extraordinary to King George III. His museum of 14,000 specimens was purchased after his death by the Company of Surgeons.

HUNTER, WILLIAM (*b. Long Calderwood, near East Kilbride, Lanarkshire, Scotland, 1718; d. London, England, 1783*), anatomy.

Hunter was sent at age thirteen to the University of Glasgow, where he spent four years studying Greek, logic, and natural philosophy. In 1739 he began a year of studying medicine at the University of Edinburgh. He then continued his studies in London. In 1746 he began a series of highly successful lectures on anatomy, including dissection. He continued those lectures after he was admitted to the Company of Surgeons (later the Royal College of Surgeons) in 1747. In 1748 he was joined in his teaching and experimentation by his brother John. He later received the M.D. (1750) from the University of Glasgow and transferred his membership from the Company of Surgeons to the College of Physicians. He received many honors and was personal physician to Queen Charlotte during her first pregnancy. His anatomy school continued after his death, and his museum and library went to the University of Glasgow, where they were housed in a special building.

HUNTINGTON, EDWARD VERMILYE (b. Clinton, N.Y., 1874; d. Cambridge, Mass., 1952), mathematics.

Huntington received the B.A. and M.A. from Harvard University in 1895 and 1897 and the Ph.D. from the University of Strasbourg in 1901. He spent his professional life at Harvard, where from 1919 to his retirement in 1941 he was professor of mechanics. His major scientific work was in the logical foundations of mathematics. He constructed sets of axioms for many branches of mathematics, one of which was Euclidean geometry, and developed techniques for proving their independence and completeness. His book *The Continuum* (1917) was for many years the standard introduction to the theory of sets of points and transfinite numbers.

HURWITZ, ADOLF (b. Hildesheim, Germany, 1859; d. Zurich, Switzerland, 1919), mathematics.

Hurwitz attended the Munich Technical University, Berlin University, and Leipzig University, from which he received the Ph.D. in 1880 with a thesis on modular functions. After teaching at the universities of Göttingen and Königsberg, he settled at the Zurich Polytechnical University, where he remained the rest of his life. Much of his work was done under the influence of Felix Klein, whose student he was. Klein's new view of modular functions was fully exploited by Hurwitz. In algebraic number theory, Hurwitz devised new proofs from the fundamental theorem on ideas. And it is in this area that Hurwitz's name will be remembered. In 1898 he proved that the classical examples exhausted the algebras over the reals with a quadratic norm. Hurwitz's theorem has become of fundamental importance; many new proofs have been given, and it has been extended several times.

HUSCHKE, EMIL (b. Weimar, Germany, 1797; d. Jena, Germany, 1858), anatomy, embryology, physiology.

Huschke began studying at the University of Jena in 1813, then the center of *Naturphilosophie*. He received the Ph.D. and continued to teach there for the rest of his career. He was greatly influenced by Lorenz Oken, a leading promoter of *Naturphilosophie*. In fact, Huschke can be considered one of the links between that school and the biology of the second half of the nineteenth century. On the one hand, he transmitted his philosophical ideas—mainly through his pupil and son-in-law Ernst Haeckel—to the following generation of biologists. On the other hand, he was one of the German scientists of his era who introduced an exact methodology into the life sciences. His central interest was the question of the origin and development of a particular organ or function. He was especially interested in the origin and transformation of the visceral skeleton during embryogenesis. He paid special attention to the development of the sense organs. The incisorlike folds in the ear are named for him; other eponyms are Huschke's foramen, valve, cartilage, canal, and ligament.

HUSSEY, WILLIAM JOSEPH (b. Mendon, Ohio, 1862; d. London, England, 1926), astronomy.

Hussey graduated from the University of Michigan in civil engineering in 1889. His interest turned to astron-

omy. From 1896 to 1905 he was at the Lick Observatory at Stanford University. He then became professor of astronomy at the University of Michigan and director of the Detroit observatory, where he remained until his death. Hussey's scientific reputation in research rests largely on his extensive discovery and measurement of double stars. He also established a reputation as an outstanding observatory director and advised in the operation of a number of observatories, including La Plata (Argentina), Blomfontein (South Africa), and, in the United States, Mount Wilson and Mount Palomar.

HUTCHINSON, JOHN (b. Ryton, near Newcastle-upon-Tyne, England, 1811; d. Fiji, Sandwich Islands, 1861), physiology.

John Hutchinson carried out fundamental research on respiratory function in health and disease. He attended London University College (now University College, London) and was admitted to the Royal College of Surgeons in 1836. From 1852 to 1861, he was in Australia, collecting gold bearing rocks. In 1861, on his return trip to England, he died on Fiji. Hutchinson studied the mechanical aspects of respiratory function, in particular the action of the intercostal muscles. He invented the spirometer in order to measure accurately the amount of air taken into the lungs with a single deep inspiration. His machine was the forerunner of all modern methods of estimating pulmonary function.

HUTTON, CHARLES (b. Newcastle-upon-Tyne, England; 1737; d. London, England, 1823), mathematics.

The son of a colliery worker, Hutton was largely self-educated. After establishing himself as a schoolmaster at Newcastle, he wrote a tract on the equilibrium of bridges (1772), an elementary textbook on arithmetic (1764), and a treatise on mensuration (1767). In 1773 he became professor of mathematics at the Royal Military Academy at Woolwich, where he remained for thirty-four years. He wrote many papers and his mathematical contributions, if unoriginal, were useful and practical. The *Mathematical and Philosophical Dictionary* (1795) is the best known of his works. It has served as a valuable source for historians of mathematics.

HUTTON, JAMES (b. Edinburgh, Scotland, 1726; d. Edinburgh, 1797), geology, agriculture, physical sciences, philosophy.

Studied at Edinburgh and Paris, and received his M.D. at Leiden (1749). He decided against practicing medicine and took up farming (1750–68). While traveling in England, Holland, Belgium, and northern France to study agriculture, he acquired the habit of examining rock outcrops, stimulating his interest in geology. After 1768 he settled in Edinburgh, devoting his time to experimental chemistry and making further field excursions in England, Wales, Scotland, and the Isle of Man. After 1788 he prepared his lesser known works on chemistry, physics, and philosophy.

His most important contribution to science was his theory of the earth. In essence it was simple, yet it was of such fundamental importance that Hutton has been called the founder of modern geology. It was first published in condensed form in a thirty-page pamphlet entitled *Abstract of a Dissertation . . . Concerning the System of the*

Earth, Its Duration, and Stability (1785). He ignored the biblical account of creation as a source of scientific information, stating that the facts of the history of the earth were to be found in "natural history." His method employed a careful examination of the rocks of the earth's crust, and a study of the natural processes that operated on the earth's surface. He concluded that rocks in general (sedimentary rocks) are composed of the products of the sea (fossils) and of other materials similar to those found on the seashore (the products of erosion). Hence they could not have formed part of the original crust of the earth, but were formed by a "second cause" and had originally been deposited at the bottom of the ocean. He deduced that two further processes had been necessary to convert the land into a permanent body resistant to the operations of water: the consolidation of the loose incoherent matter at the sea bottom, and the elevation of the consolidated matter. Consolidation was achieved through fusion of the sediments by the great heat he believed to exist beneath the lower regions of the earth's crust; he concluded that this extreme heat must be capable of "producing an expansive force, sufficient for elevating the land from the bottom of the ocean to the place it now occupies." He next claimed that his theory could be extended to all parts of the world, a justifiable generalization since similar rocks occur in other countries. In discussing the length of time the earth had existed as a habitable world, he rejected the possibility of estimating geological time by measuring the rate at which erosion is wearing down the land, and concluded that "it had required an indefinite space of time to have produced the land which now appears."

From 1785 onward Hutton continued to collect new information to support his theory, which he published later in *Theory of the Earth: With Proofs and Illustrations; in Four Parts* (2 vols., 1795). The most important advance in geological science embodied in his theory was his demonstration that sedimentation is cyclical, a principle now accepted as axiomatic. He showed that the cyclic process of degradation through erosion, consolidation of sediments on the sea bottom, and elevation of new land surfaces must have been repeated an indeterminate number of times in the past, and he assumed it would continue indefinitely. His theory formulated for the first time the general principle that some fifty years later came to be known as uniformitarianism.

Hutton also made important contributions in the field of igneous geology. From his detailed study of numerous outcrops of igneous rocks he distinguished two types, lavas and intrusions, and established for the first time the existence of the intrusive igneous rocks. He concluded that all igneous rocks originated in the "mineral region," a subcrustal zone of undefined depth in which heat of sufficient intensity to melt rocks prevailed. He also established the igneous origin of granite (1788). The school of geologists who accepted his ideas about the origin of igneous rocks came to be known as "plutonists," a name first used by Kirwan.

It was not until after 1830 that Hutton's theory of the earth began to gain general acceptance, largely because of Playfair's *Illustrations of the Huttonian Theory of the Earth* (1802) and Lyell's *Principles of Geology* (1830); this was due to the natural conservatism of many geologists, reluctance to abandon belief in the biblical account of crea-

tion, the widespread influence of geologists of the Wernerian school, and the rise of catastrophism.

His continuing interest in farming resulted in a manuscript, "Principles of Agriculture," prepared shortly before his death. Most noteworthy is a section on animal husbandry, where he outlined a theory of evolution. Raising the question of how so many varieties in every species are procured, and using the dog as a model, he suggested that originally the "species" had existed in only one form, and there was inherent in the constitution of the animal "a general law or rule of seminal variation" which would bring about constant changes in the animal, to a greater or lesser extent, "by the influence of external causes." For example, "where dogs are to live by the swiftness of their feet and the sharpness of their sight, the form best adapted to that end will be the most certain of remaining."

In 1792 he published *Dissertations on . . . Natural Philosophy*. Part 1, on meteorology, contains his theory on the origin of rain as a mixture of air currents of different temperatures, saturated or nearly saturated with moisture. In part 2, on phlogiston, he accepts the major advances made by Lavoisier, but takes the view that the concept of phlogiston was too hastily rejected. He held that heat, light, and electricity were all modifications of what he called "solar substance." Part 3 contains his theory of matter. Briefly summarized, this theory suggests that to describe a body as made of small particles does not explain its nature, because if we suppose these particles to possess magnitude, we do no more than say large bodies are made of smaller bodies. Therefore the elements of a body must be something unextended. To these elements he gave the name "matter," reserving the name "body" to combinations of matter subject to powers or forces acting in various directions. He continued his discussion of phlogiston in *Philosophy of Light, Heat, and Fire* (1794), raising the question whether there might be a species of light capable of producing heat in bodies without affecting the sense of sight. A few years later, Herschel confirmed Hutton's suggestion.

From his studies of the physical sciences came his three-volume treatise on metaphysics and moral philosophy, *An Investigation of the Principles of Knowledge* (1794). He acknowledged the existence of a God defined as "the superintending mind . . . a Being with perfect knowledge and absolute wisdom." He considered nature as subordinate to God, for God is infinite and unchangeable, but nature limited and changing. The term "nature" properly meant the whole of that action from which, in necessarily inferring design, we learn the existence of a superintending being.

HUXLEY, THOMAS HENRY (*b. Ealing, Middlesex, England, 1825; d. Hodeslea, Eastbourne, Sussex, England, 1895*), zoology, evolution, paleontology, ethnology.

For his general education Huxley was largely self-taught. He studied medicine at Charing Cross Hospital. His first scientific paper was on his discovery of a layer of cells (Huxley's layer) directly within Henle's layer in the root sheath of hair. He passed the M.B. examination at London University in 1845 and soon afterward that for membership in the Royal College of Surgeons. He joined the Royal Navy and was assigned to the *Rattlesnake* as ship's surgeon on a surveying voyage to the Torres

Straits off Australia (1846–50). The natural history investigations he undertook on the voyage set the course of his career toward zoology rather than medicine. Between 1850 and 1854 in London he published about twenty papers on materials from the *Rattlesnake*. Most important are four memoirs on invertebrates: an 1849 paper on the Medusae; two 1851 papers on tunicates ("Observations on the Anatomy and Physiology of Salpa and Pyrosoma" and "Remarks Upon Appendicularia and Doliolum, Two Genera of Tunicates"); and "On the Morphology of the Cephalous Mollusca . . ." (1853). For the Medusae, Ascidians, and Cephalous Mollusca he sought and found a typical structure (archetype) of which each genus and species is a modification.

In 1854 he became lecturer in natural history at the Government School of Mines and soon afterward naturalist with the Geological Survey; although preferring a post in physiology, he held the appointments for over thirty years. He organized and taught at the Museum of Practical Geology (from 1855), and taught at the School of Mines and the Royal Institution. His interests shifted rapidly to vertebrates, and he became deeply involved in paleontology and geology. In the late 1850's he began a detailed study of the embryology of vertebrates. In "On the Theory of the Vertebrate Skull" (1858) he made an important methodological contribution to morphology by insisting that comparisons of adult structures are insufficient for the demonstration of homologies, and that only by studying embryological development can we say that various structures are homologous. He revived studies by K. E. von Baer and M. H. Rathke showing the inadequacies of the vertebral theory of the skull originated by Goethe, elaborated by Oken, and developed to its fullest by Owen. Huxley's conclusions helped to prepare the way for later disputes between him and Owen.

Huxley is known today primarily as the protagonist of evolution in the controversies immediately following the publication of *On the Origin of Species* late in 1859. Darwin sent Huxley one of three prepublication copies, and Huxley was quick to praise the *Origin* publicly—in a review for the London *Times;* in an article for the *Westminster Review;* and in a discourse at the Royal Institution ("On Species and Races, and their Origin") which set a model for many later defenses of the *Origin.* His success in an encounter with Samuel Wilberforce, bishop of Oxford, established Huxley as principal spokesman for Darwin and gave convincing evidence that the evolutionists were not going to be cowed by the Church. His dispute with Owen was more prolonged (1857–63), and involved scientific details concerning the classification of Mammalia. Owen constructed a taxonomy based on certain characteristics of the mammalian brain, the most famous of these being a small internal ridge known as the *hippocampus minor,* which became well known to the public and gave its name to this controversy. Owen asserted that man was zoologically distinct from all other mammals. Huxley gave a direct and unqualified contradiction in "On the Zoological Relations of Man With the Lower Animals" (1861), demonstrating clearly that the differences between man and the apes were smaller than those between the apes and the lower primates. Therefore, man had to be considered zoologically a member of the primates. He did not accept Darwin's hypothesis uncritically, however, and did not consider that the problem was finally settled nor that

natural selection was by any means proven as the mechanism. For him it remained a hypothesis because of the lack of experimental proof.

Huxley did important work on all the major groups of vertebrates; of particular interest was the first comprehensive, comparative study of a single avian organ system (1867). His study set a model for much later avian taxonomic work.

His early paleontological work on Devonian fishes led him into a revision of much of the material and a memoir on their classification which remained a standard work for several decades. He made other important studies of the classification of reptiles, birds, fishes, and amphibians. His series of ancestral forms of horses was the first extensive series to give proof that the kinds of modifications demanded by Darwin's hypothesis had taken place and that the ancestral stages were more generalized than their more recent representatives.

In addition to his extensive scientific output, Huxley was an active teacher from 1854 until near the end of his life. His lectures and laboratory classes were highly innovative, with students doing the dissecting and observing to verify the facts in the text and lectures. He put a strong emphasis on clear and distinct ideas, very much in the Cartesian tradition. He emphasized an active skepticism, from which he believed freedom of thought would necessarily flow. In this context he coined the term "agnosticism," which to him embodied no belief nor implied any. He regarded the Bible highly, both as one of the great works of English literature and as a defense of freedom and liberty. In this context he first became involved in Biblical controversy, on the subject of the authority of Genesis. Huxley applied agnosticism, as a method, to this and other Biblical problems, including the divine inspiration of the New Testament Gospels and various revelations and miracles.

He was the grandfather of Julian, Aldous, and Andrew Fielding Huxley.

HUYGENS, CHRISTIAAN (also **Huyghens, Christian**) (*b. The Hague, Netherlands, 1629; d. The Hague, 1695*), physics, mathematics, astronomy, optics.

Huygens came from a family with strong educational and cultural traditions. Christiaan and his brother Constantijn were educated at home up to the age of sixteen by their father and private teachers.

From 1645 until 1647 Christiaan studied law and mathematics at the University of Leiden, the latter with Frans van Schooten. During this period his father called Mersenne's attention to his son's study on falling bodies, and this opened up a direct correspondence between Christiaan and Mersenne. From 1647 until 1649 Christiaan studied law at the newly founded Collegium Arausiacum (College of Orange) at Breda, of which his father was a curator and where Pell taught mathematics.

Huygens at first concentrated on mathematics: determinations of quadratures and cubatures, and algebraic problems inspired by Pappus' works. In 1651 the *Theoremata de quadratura hyperboles, ellipsis et circuli* appeared, including a refutation of Gregory of St. Vincent's quadrature of the circle. The *De circuli magnitudine inventa* followed in 1654. In the subsequent years Huygens studied the rectification of the parabola, the area of surfaces of revolution of parabolas, and tangents and quadratures of various curves such as the cissoid, the cycloid (in connection with a problem publicly posed by Pascal in 1658), and the logarithmica. In 1657 he published a treatise on probability problems, the *Tractatus de ratiociniis in aleae ludo.*

A manuscript on hydrostatics had already been completed in 1650, and in 1652 Huygens formulated the rules of elastic collision and began his studies of geometrical optics. In 1655 he applied himself to lens grinding. He and his brother built microscopes and telescopes, and in the winter of 1655–56 he discovered the satellite of Saturn and recognized its ring, as reported in his *De Saturni lunâ observatio nova* and *Systema Saturnium,* respectively.

In 1656 Huygens invented the pendulum clock. This is described in 1658 in the *Horologium* (not to be confused with the later *Horologium oscillatorium*) and formed the occasion for the discovery of the tautochronism of the cycloid (1659), and for the studies on the theory of evolutes and on the center of oscillation. Huygens' study of centrifugal force also dates from 1659. In these years he corresponded with increasing intensity with many scholars. Studies on the application of the pendulum clock for the determination of longitudes at sea occupied much of his time from 1660 onward.

As a prominent member of the Académie Royale des Sciences (1666–81), Huygens received an ample stipend and lived in an apartment in the Bibliothèque Royale. In the Academy, he encouraged a Baconian program for the study of nature. He participated actively in astronomical observations and in experiments with the air pump. He expounded his theory of the cause of gravity in 1669, and in 1678 he wrote the *Traité de la lumière,* which announced the wave, or more accurately, the pulse theory of light developed in 1676–77. In the years 1668–69 he investigated, theoretically and experimentally, the motion of bodies in resisting media. In 1673 he cooperated with Papin in building a *moteur à explosion,* and from that year onward he was also in regular contact with Leibniz. Huygens began his studies of harmonic oscillation in 1673 and designed clocks regulated by a spring instead of a pendulum, about which a controversy with Hooke ensued. In 1677 he did microscopical research.

Huygens left Paris in 1681 and decided to stay in Holland. He continued his optical studies, constructed a number of clocks, which were tested on several long sea voyages, and wrote his *Cosmotheoros.* Discussions with Fatio de Duillier, correspondence with Leibniz, and the interest created by the latter's differential and integral calculus drew Huygens' attention back to mathematics in his last years.

HYATT, ALPHEUS (*b. Washington, D.C., 1838; d. Cambridge, Mass., 1902*), invertebrate paleontology, zoology.

Hyatt graduated from the Lawrence Scientific School of Harvard University in 1862. He then taught at the Massachusetts Institute of Technology and at Boston University, where he was professor of biology from 1877 until his death. An influential evolutionist, Hyatt was not a Darwinian. Instead he was co-founder (with E.D. Cope) of the neo-Lamarckian theory. He and Cope believed that most new characters of organisms arose from the mechanical activities of the animals themselves and that this is why structure is so well adapted to function. Hyatt's most imaginative and original contribution to evolutionary thought was his "old age" theory that species, like

individuals, have a natural cycle of youth, maturity, and old age leading to extinction. This theory was fairly popular until the 1930's, when the "modern synthesis" of evolutionary theory was formulated.

HYLACOMYLUS. *See* **Waldseemüller, Martin.**

HYLLERAAS, EGIL ANDERSEN (*b. Engerdal, Norway, 1898; d. Oslo, Norway, 1965*), physics.

Hylleraas graduated from the University of Christiania (now Oslo) in 1924, where he studied mathematics and physics. From 1926 to 1928 he studied at Göttingen under Max Born. In 1937 he became professor of theoretical physics at Oslo, a chair he held until his death. After World War II, he also taught in the United States, at Princeton and the University of Wisconsin. In 1926, at Born's suggestion, he attacked the problem of the ionization energy of the ground state of the helium atom. To manage his very extensive calculations, he used an electric Mercedes-Euklid calculating machine, probably the first time that machine calculation played an important part in physics. In 1930 he demonstrated the theoretical stability of the negative hydrogen ion. Hylleraas always considered the helium atom and the negative hydrogen ion his special domains and never really relinquished his hegemony over them. His ability was mathematical and his belief in the efficacy of a numerical and computational approach to physics, often combined with the use of calculating machines, anticipated what is perhaps the main structure of modern science.

HYPATIA (*b. Alexandria, Egypt, ca. 370; d. Alexandria, 415*), mathematics, philosophy.

Although documentation of Hypatia's activities is lacking, it is known that she lectured on mathematics and on the Neoplatonic doctrines of Plotinus and that about A.D. 400 she became head of the Neoplatonic school in Alexandria. It is believed that she assisted Theon of Alexandria in writing his eleven-part treatise on Ptolemy's *Almagest* and possibly in the revised and improved version of Euclid's *Elements.* She was murdered by a fanatic mob objecting to her friendship with Orestes, the Roman prefect of Alexandria. She has been the subject of much romantic drama and fiction.

HYPSICLES OF ALEXANDRIA (*fl. Alexandria, first half of second century* B.C.), mathematics, astronomy.

Hypsicles is attested by the more definitive manuscripts to be the author of book XIV of Euclid's *Elements,* which is concerned with the inscription of regular solids in a sphere. Arabic tradition suggests that he also had something to do with book XV (exactly what is unclear). One other work by Hypsicles survives, the *Anaphorikos,* or *On the Ascension of Stars,* which is notable for being the first work in which the ecliptic is divided into 360 parts or degrees. In this work, he also considers the problems of the longest and shortest days in relation to the various signs of the zodiac.

HYRTL, JOSEPH (*b. Kismarton, Hungary [now Eisenstadt, Austria], 1810; d. Perchtoldsdorf, Austria, 1894*), anatomy.

In 1835 Hyrtl earned his doctorate in Vienna, where he studied under Joseph Berres. In 1837 he became professor of anatomy at Prague, and he returned to Vienna in

1845, where he succeeded to Berres's chair. Hyrtl was one of the anatomists responsible for making anatomy in the middle and latter parts of the nineteenth century the most important of the basic sciences on which medicine drew. His scientific reputation stemmed especially from his *Lehrbuch der Anatomie des Menschen mit Rücksicht auf physiologische Begründung und praktische Anwendung* (1846). He also won a worldwide reputation as a technical anatomist and was regarded as the most scintillating anatomy teacher of his time.

IAMBLICHUS (*b. Chalcis, Syria, ca.* A.D. *250; d. ca.* A.D. *330*), philosophy.

Helped systematize Neoplatonism; wrote biography of Pythagoras and encyclopaedic work of traditional Pythagorean claims; commentaries on Aristotle are unoriginal; his work on Egyptian magic stimulated Renaissance interest in hieroglyphics.

IBÁÑEZ E IBÁÑEZ DE IBERO, CARLOS (*b. Barcelona, Spain, 1825; d. Nice, France, 1891*), geodesy.

Educated at Academy of Army Engineers where he later taught. Concerned mainly with precision in measurement and scientific organization. Improved probable error in geodesic bases; won Poncelet Prize of the Academy of Sciences of Paris (1889) for precision of his remeasurement of the arc of meridian. Helped found (and served in) many scientific institutions, including International Geodesic Association (1866) and International Office of Weights and Measures (1875).

IBN. *See next element of name.*

IBRĀHĪM IBN SINĀN IBN THĀBIT IBN QURRA (*b. Baghdad [?], 908; d. Baghdad, 946*), mathematics, astronomy.

Born into a family of scholars (father was Sinān ibn Thābit, grandfather was Thābit ibn Qurra). Left a notable body of work on geometry, apparent motions of sun, solar hours, and the astrolabe; two most important contributions were discussions of quadrature of the parabola and of relations between analysis and synthesis. His grandfather had already solved the parabola problem, but Ibn Sinān gave an even more economical demonstration which did not depend upon reduction to the absurd; instead, he used the proposition that proportionality of areas is invariant under affine transformation. One of the foremost Arab mathematicians in mathematical philosophy; attempted to revive Apollonius' methods of analysis and synthesis.

IBRĀHĪM IBN YA⁽QŪB AL-ISRĀ⁾AĪLĪ AL-TUR-ṬUSHI (*b. Tortosa, Spain; fl. second half tenth century*), geography.

Ibrāhīm ibn Ya⁽qūb was a Spanish Jewish merchant and diplomat who traveled throughout Europe (*ca.* 965). His travel accounts (only fragments remain) are among the best of the period (especially on Slavic areas) and were quoted by later Arab geographers. Careful observer of commerce, agriculture, local customs, health conditions, etc.

IDDINGS, JOSEPH PAXSON (*b. Baltimore, Md., 1857; d. Brinklow, Md., 1920*), petrology.

Graduated Yale University (1877); studied at Heidelberg (1879–80) under K. H. F. Rosenbusch. Taught at Yale and Columbia University's School of Mines (where influenced by Clarence King) before joining U. S. Geological Survey (1880–92); taught at University of Chicago until 1908, when he retired to private study. One of the foremost petrographers of his time; one of first to study thin rock sections with microscope; his studies of igneous rocks of Yellowstone Park emphasized physicochemical factors, influencing the course of petrology; with C. W. Cross, L. V. Pirsson, and G. H. Williams, Iddings helped revise classification of rocks in terms of quantitative chemical composition (referred to, after authors, as C.I.P.W. system).

IDELSON, NAUM ILICH (*b. St. Petersburg, Russia, 1885; d. near Riga, Latvian S.S.R., 1951*), astronomy, history of astronomy.

Graduated in law and mathematics, St. Petersburg University (1909). Joined P. F. Lesgaft Scientific Institute (1918); headed project of State Computing Institute for computing astronomical yearbook; headed astronomical section of Leningrad Astronomical Institute (1923); directed Petrograd section of Pulkovo Observatory (1920). Taught at Leningrad University (from 1933); held chair in mechanics at Leningrad Institute of Precision Mechanics and Optics (1930–37). Idelson's works on the theory of ephemerides, potential theory, and theory of the shape of the earth gained wide recognition; his important writings on history of astronomy not yet translated.

AL-IDRĪSĪ, ABŪ ⁽ABD ALLĀH MUḤAMMAD IBN MUḤAMMAD IBN ⁽ABD ALLĀH IBN IDRĪS, AL-SHARĪF AL-IDRĪSĪ (*b. Ceuta, Morocco, 1100; d. Ceuta, 1166*), geography, cartography.

After education in Córdoba, al-Idrīsī traveled widely, settling with court of Roger II, Norman king of Sicily; lived in Palermo until Roger's death (1138–54), when he returned to Ceuta. Under Roger's patronage, collaborated with Christian scholars to construct a large silver map of the world; only sectional maps (reproduced from silver map) and accompanying descriptions are extant today; text is rich in information and maps are somewhat distorted (not drawn mathematically) and unoriginal (rely heavily on Ptolemy); best example of Arab-Norman scientific collaboration in geography of Middle Ages; popular in Europe as textbook for several centuries.

IKHWĀN AL-ṢAFĀ⁾ Secret association (also known as Brothers of Purity) founded at Basra *ca.* 983; also a group of epistles by the same name (referred to as *Encyclopedia of the Brothers of Purity*).

A compendium of all sciences known in tenth century and first complete exposition of the Ismaili philosophical system; represents new syncretism, combining an earlier Hellenistic syncretism emphasizing Platonism and Neoplatonism with Hindu, Persian, and Christian elements, all of which are integrated with Shiite Islamic doctrines. According to Ismaili doctrine, there is hierarchy of all beings and human souls, which God sustains through the intermediary of the imams—divinely appointed successors of Muḥammad in the line of ⁽Alī—who alone are entitled to rule the Muslim community (much of the epistles is propaganda for such doctrines); the epistles may have been written by Jaᶜfar al-Ṣādiq and developed by his successors, the secret imams, as well as four propagandists; while some passages may have been written earlier than 909, the *Ikhwān* probably did not receive definitive form until after conquest of Egypt (969).

IMAMURA, AKITUNE (*b. Kagoshima, Japan, 1870; d. Tokyo, Japan, 1948*), seismology.
Graduated in physics from Tokyo Imperial University (1894; D.Sc., 1905; professor, 1923), where he established department of seismology (1924). Interested in scientific and human aspects of seismology: helped develop seismograph; among first to relate ground tilting and earthquakes; studied foreshocks and aftershocks; drew maps of expected earthquake intensities; campaigned to educate public on earthquake precautions; worked to improve safety of buildings.

INFELD, LEOPOLD (*b. Cracow, Poland, 1898; d. Warsaw, Poland, 1968*), theoretical physics.
Studied physics at Jagiellonian University in Cracow; met Einstein in Berlin (1920) while working on doctoral dissertation on general relativity. Taught at University of Lvov (1929–33) where he studied spinor analysis; Rockefeller Foundation Fellow in Cambridge, England (1933–34), where with Max Born developed Born-Infeld theory of non-linear electrodynamics. Fellow at Institute for Advanced Study in Princeton (1936–38), where he worked with Einstein on motion of heavy bodies according to general relativity; at University of Ontario (1938–50) worked on factorization method of solving differential equations. Professor at University of Warsaw (1950–68), where he greatly advanced theoretical physics in Poland.

INGEN-HOUSZ, JAN (*b. Breda, Netherlands, 1730; d. Bowood Park, near Calne, Wiltshire, England, 1799*), medicine, plant physiology, physics.
Educated at University of Louvain (M.D., 1753); studied medicine at Leiden (1755) under H. D. Gaubius, anatomy under B. S. Albinus, physics under van Musschenbroek. Traveled to Edinburgh and London, meeting many scientists, including Priestley and Franklin. At Foundling Hospital in London (1766), he utilized newly revived practice of inoculation against smallpox, in which live smallpox was introduced under the patient's skin; assisted Thomas Dimsdale in inoculating 700 persons during smallpox epidemic (1768); wrote pamphlets defending Dimsdale's inoculation techniques. Sent by George III to Austrian court in Vienna (1768), where he successfully inoculated the royal family; appointed court physician with lifelong income by Empress Maria Theresa (provided freedom to travel and do research rest of life); with Vienna as base, traveled to France, Holland, and England (admitted to Royal Society 1771); alarmed by violence in Paris (1789), moved permanently to England. Best known for discovery of photosynthesis (reported in 1779 book); stimulated by Priestley's discovery (1771) that plants can "restore" air made unfit for respiration, Ingen-Housz determined that only green parts can do this, only when illuminated by sunlight, and that the active part of the sun's radiation is in visible light, not heat radiation; also determined that all parts of plants, like animals, respire and produce fixed air (CO_2), and

that respiration continues day and night; further studies convinced him that plants and animals mutually support each other, the animals consuming dephlogisticated air (oxygen) and producing fixed air, the plants doing the reverse; also stated that carbon dioxide in air, and not decayed plant and animal matter in soil, is the origin of carbon in plants (1796). In studies of algae, he discovered swarm spores and suggested use of cover glass for liquid microscopic preparations; discovered Brownian motion (1827) and showed that lifeless particles display the motion as well as microorganisms. First to use oxygen therapy; experimented with explosive gases; first to burn steel wire in pure oxygen. Earliest scientific interest was in electricity: first to use disks in electrostatic generators; in Bakerian Lecture to Royal Society (1778) used Franklin's theory of positive and negative electricity to explain Volta's electrophore. Discovered paramagnetism of platinum.

INGRASSIA, GIOVANNI FILIPPO (*b. Regalbuto, Sicily, ca. 1510; d. Palermo, Sicily, 1580*), medicine.
Studied medicine at Palermo and University of Padua (M.D., 1537). Taught at University of Naples; called to Palermo as *protomedicus* (1556), where he was concerned with hygiene, epidemiology, and administration of Sicilian medicine; established one of the first sanitary codes and council of public health; a founder of study of legal medicine. Best known for anatomical studies based on work of Vesalius; wrote commentary on Galen's work on osteology (published posthumously, 1603).

INNES, ROBERT THORBURN AYTON (*b. Edinburgh, Scotland, 1861; d. Surbiton, England, 1933*), astronomy.
Self-taught after age twelve, Innes was elected fellow of Royal Astronomical Society at age seventeen. Became secretary at Cape Observatory, South Africa, where he compiled a catalog of southern double stars. Appointed director of the Transvaal Observatory in Johannesburg (1903). First to place double-star research in the southern hemisphere on a sound footing, discovering 1,628 new doubles. Other work includes pioneering use of the blink microscope and first definite proof of variability of earth's rotation.

INŌ, TADATAKA (*b. Ozekimura, Yamabegun, Kazusanokuni, Japan, 1745; d. Kameshimachō, Hacchōbori, Tokyo, Japan, 1818*), astronomy, surveying, cartography.
Inō's scientific studies did not begin until age fifty, when he retired from the brewery business and went to study astronomy in Tokyo. In order to find length of a meridian, he undertook a geodetic survey, producing a rough map of northeastern Japan. In 1804 he undertook a more accurate survey of the western seacoast; calculated length of meridian which agreed within several tenths of a degree with figure in Lalande's *Astronomie;* determined longitude by measuring distances on the earth's surface, reducing accuracy of maps. Energetic observer but devised no new theories; unfamiliar with Western astronomy. However, Inō's map of Japan was far superior to previous maps; its influence limited by government's suppression of publication; copy smuggled out by German natural historian P. F. von Siebold in 1826 (Japanese astronomer T. Kageyasu, who gave map to

Siebold, arrested and died in prison); Siebold revised map and published it (1840); revision reimported to Japan. H.M.S. *Acteon* asked shogunate permission to survey coastline (1861); due to xenophobia, the government instead gave a copy of Inō's map which the British found fairly accurate; Japanese maps produced during 1870's and 1880's all based on Inō's map.

IOFFE, ABRAM FEDOROVICH (*b. Romna, Poltava gubernia, Russia, 1880; d. Leningrad, U.S.S.R., 1960*), physics, technology.

Graduated from St. Petersburg Technical Institute in technical engineering (1902); studied physics at Röntgen's Physical Institute, University of Munich (Ph.D., 1905). Taught at St. Petersburg Polytechnical Institute, Institute of Mines, and St. Petersburg University; received doctorate in physics (1915). Organized Faculty of Physics and Mechanics at Polytechnical Institute (1919); helped found Physical and Technological X-ray Institute (director for twenty-five years). Fields of interest included X rays, electronic phenomena, atomic nuclei, dielectric crystals, and semiconductors. Discovered internal photoeffect in halite crystals subjected to X rays.

IPATIEV, VLADIMIR NIKOLAEVICH (*b. Moscow, Russia, 1867; d. Chicago, Ill., 1952*), chemistry.

Graduated from Artillery Academy, St. Petersburg (1892); became professor there (1899). First to synthesize isoprene (1896); introduced high pressures into heterogeneous catalysis (1904); introduced autoclave into chemical practice, using it for first synthesis of methane; first to use multicomponent catalysts (1912); author of catalysis theory assigning basic role to metallic oxides; developed use of oxides in petrochemical industry; first to polymerize ethylene in reduction (1913). In 1930 became director of Catalytic High Pressure Laboratory (now bearing his name) at Northwestern University.

IBN ʿIRĀQ. *See* **Manṣūr ibn ʿIrāq.**

IRINYI, JÁNOS (*b. Nagyléta, Hungary, 1817; d. Vértes, Hungary, 1895*), chemistry.

Studied chemistry at Vienna Polytechnikum. Contributed to development of friction (safety) match; suggested substitution of lead oxide for potassium chlorate, obtaining an explosionless match (1835).

ISAAC ISRAELI (*b. Egypt, fl. ninth-tenth century*), medicine, philosophy.

Court physician in Ifriqiya (now Tunisia); his medical works on fevers and urine were highly regarded. Wrote on Neoplatonic philosophy; his *Book of Definitions and Descriptions* translated into Latin by Gerard of Cremona and widely used by Schoolmen.

ISAAC JUDAEUS. *See* **Isaac Israeli.**

ISAACS, CHARLES EDWARD (*b. Bedford, N.Y., 1811; d. Brooklyn, N.Y., 1860*), medicine.

First American to study experimental kidney physiology; settled controversy concerning connection of Malpighian bodies with uriniferous tubules; demonstrated that Malpighian bodies separated dyes from blood, ex-

creting them into the urine; demonstrated presence of nucleated cells on surface of Malpighian tuft. Studied at College of Physicians and Surgeons of New York and at University of Maryland (M.D., 1833). Taught medicine in New York City; established successful practice. Presented papers on the kidney to New York Academy of Medicine (1856, 1857), attracting worldwide attention. Helped found New York Pathological Society (served as president).

ISHĀQ IBN ḤUNAYN, ABŪ YAʿQŪB (*b. Baghdad, 910 or 911*), medicine, scientific translation.

Trained under father's supervision in Greek sciences and translation (knew Greek, Syriac, Arabic). Both Isḥāq and his father (Ḥunayn ibn Isḥāq) were court physicians to caliphs; associated with translation movement in Baghdad which flourished even after decline of the academy founded by Caliph al-Maʾmūn for scientific translation. Few original works; *History of Physicians* based on work by John Philoponus. Most notable contributions are translations from Greek and Syriac. Translated Galen and other medical works with his father; translated philosophical works of Galen, Aristotle, and Plato, including commentaries and epitomes. Of special consequence are mathematical translations: Euclid's *Elements, Optics,* and *Data;* Ptolemy's *Almagest;* Archimedes' *On the Sphere and the Cylinder,* and others. The *Elements, Optics,* and *Almagest* were revised and improved by the mathematician Thābit ibn Qurra.

ISHIWARA, JUN (*b. Tokyo, Japan, 1881; d. Chiba prefecture, Japan, 1947*), physics.

Graduated in theoretical physics, University of Tokyo (1906); studied in Munich, Berlin, Zurich (1912–14), influenced by Sommerfeld and Einstein; taught at Tohoku Imperial University. Fields of study included electron theory of metal, special and general theories of relativity, and quantum theory. Edited Japanese translation of Einstein and wrote popular works on physics.

ISIDORE OF SEVILLE (*b. Spain [?], ca. 560; d. Seville, Spain, 636*), dissemination of knowledge.

Educated by his brother, whom he succeeded as bishop of Seville and Catholic primate of Spain (599). Isidore's scientific writings, intended as textbooks, are contained in a glossary, two works on cosmology, and a great encyclopedic dictionary, the *Etymologiae.* His work is entirely derivative, though of great influence in Middle Ages and Renaissance; good source for lexicography and preserves much scientific lore from the late Roman period.

ISIDORUS OF MILETUS (*b. Miletus; fl. Constantinople, sixth century*), architecture, mathematics.

Associated with Anthemius of Tralles in construction of church of Hagia Sophia at Constantinople. May have headed a school of mathematics; edited Eutocius' commentaries on Archimedes' *On the Sphere and the Cylinder* and *Measurement of the Circle.*

ISSEL, ARTURO (*b. Genoa, Italy, 1842; d. Genoa, 1922*), geology.

Graduated University of Pisa (1863); taught at Genoa (1866–1917). A geologist, Issel also did work in geography, seismology, petrography, paleethnology, paleontology, and malacology. Made two trips to Red Sea (1865, 1870); in *Malacologia del Mar Rosso* (1869) described eighty-five new species of mollusks found there; geological observations published 1899. Geological work mainly concerned with recent events in Mediterranean basin; established "Tyrrhenian" geological stage of Pleistocene marine series; wrote on oscillations of ground (1883). Studied natural history of Liguria region, especially prehistoric man.

IVANOV, ILYA IVANOVICH (*b. Shigry, Kursk guberniya, Russia, 1870; d. Alma-Ata, Kazakh S.S.R., 1932*), biology.

Studied biology at University of Moscow and University of Kharkov; studied at Pasteur Institute, Paris (1897–98). Main interests were in reproductive biology, interspecies hybridization, and artificial insemination of domestic animals; began research on these topics in 1898 at laboratories of Academy of Sciences; concluded that the sole necessary condition for impregnation is meeting and union of spermatozoon and egg (semen and sex act not required); also found that spermatozoa could retain motility and ability to cause conception for a period of time outside the organism if favorable conditions maintained; developed methods for artificial insemination by spermatozoa in both natural and artificial media; established full viability of offspring; promoted hybridization of livestock with wild animals; founded world's first center for artificial insemination of horses (1901).

IVANOV, PIOTR PAVLOVICH (*b. St. Petersburg [now Leningrad], Russia, 1878; d. Kostroma, U.S.S.R., 1942*), embryology.

Graduated from St. Petersburg University (1901; M.S. and began teaching, 1912; appointed head of embryological laboratory, 1922); headed departments of zoology and biology at Psychoneurological Institute (1924–42). Developed theory of the larval body of segmented animals, in which only segments whose structure is characteristic for larval stage regenerate after fore end amputated.

IVANOVSKY, DMITRI IOSIFOVICH (*b. Gdov, Russia, 1864; d. U.S.S.R., 1920*), botany, microbiology.

Graduated from St. Petersburg University (1888; M.S. and began teaching, 1895); taught at Technological Institute (1896–1901); named extraordinary professor at University of Warsaw (1901). D.Sc. at Kiev (1903). Published investigation of mosaic disease in tobacco (1892), the first study containing factual proof of the existence of viruses, which he believed were living parasitic microorganisms; discovered crystals in diseased plants which he associated with mosaic disease; abandoned study of viruses after defending doctoral dissertation ("Mosaic Disease in Tobacco"); moved to Warsaw (1908) where he studied photosynthesis in relation to pigments of green leaves; theorized that yellow pigments protect chlorophyll from destructive action of blue-violet rays.

IVES, HERBERT EUGENE (*b. Philadelphia, Pa., 1882; d. New York, N.Y., 1953*), physics.

Worked for his father, Frederic Eugene Ives, on color photography apparatus (1898–1901); graduated University of Pennsylvania (B.S. 1905); Ph.D. from Johns Hop-

kins (1908). Before World War I concerned with colorimetry and photometry; after the war with Bell Telephone Laboratories until 1947, where he studied photoelectric effect and television; beginning in 1927 made successful television transmissions; with G.R. Stilwell, detected transverse Doppler effect predicted by Einstein (1938, 1941). Received more than 100 patents.

IVORY, JAMES (*b. Dundee, Scotland, 1765; d. London, England, 1842*), mathematics.

Educated at universities of St. Andrews (M.A. 1783) and Edinburgh (1785–86); Taught mathematics at Dundee and at Royal Military College at Great Marlow until ill health forced early retirement (1819); remainder of his life devoted to mathematics. Main interest was in application of mathematics to physical problems; not an original thinker but one of the first in England to understand and comment on the work of Laplace.

JĀBIR IBN AFLAḤ AL-ISHBĪLĪ, ABŪ MUḤAMMAD (*fl. Seville, first half of the twelfth century*), astronomy, mathematics.

Known in West as Geber, Jābir's most important work was a reworking of Ptolemy's *Almagest*, titled *Iṣlāḥ al-Majistī* ("Correction of the *Almagest*"); principal difference is replacement of Menelaus' theorem by theorems on right spherical triangles; also, does not present theorems in the form of numerical examples as Ptolemy did; changes similar to those made by Abu'l Wafāʾ and may have had a common source; Jābir severely criticized Ptolemy, especially on placing of Venus and Mercury below the sun (Jābir placed them above); as trigonometer important only because his work was translated into Latin (Abu'l Wafāʾ was not) by Gerard of Cremona; most important influence upon Regiomontanus' *De triangulis* (published 1533), which systematized trigonometry for Latin West.

JĀBIR IBN ḤAYYĀN (*fl. late eighth and early ninth centuries*), alchemy.

Supposed author of very extensive corpus of alchemical and other scientific writings in Arabic, but by no means author of all writings which bear his name. P. Kraus has concluded that *Corpus Jābirianum* is the work of a school; that it presupposes translations from Greek by Ḥunayn ibn Isḥāq; that it contains Ismaʿili propaganda of the epistles of the Brethren of Purity; that the works were not written until the tenth century; and that Jābir was a student or favorite of the Shiite imam named Jaʿfar ibn Muḥammad al-Ṣādiq. M. Berthelot has proven that Latin alchemical writings appearing under the name of Geber were not written by Jābir. Most books of the corpus still unedited; alchemy dominates writings but all sciences and some non-sciences represented; writings contain many quotations from ancient authors, especially from the Greek alchemical corpus. Jābir unites his scientific system with religious doctrine through his allegorical interpretation of Koranic concept of balance (*mīzān*); *mīzān* is the basic principle of Jābir's scientific monism, in opposition to Manichaean dualism, in which the qualities of all natural objects are determined by the numerical balance or mixture of substances from the three kingdoms (animal, mineral, and vegetable); this theory led him to believe in artificial production of natural objects and the homunculus; numerology and astrology play prominent roles in Jabir's system. Medicine plays a major role in his alchemical sciences; remarkable medical knowledge is displayed in the *Poison Book*. Jābir is among the pioneers of the completion of "spirits," that is, of the volatile substances sulfur, mercury, and arsenic, through a fourth one, sal ammoniac, which was unknown to Greeks. Aquainted with the best works of Greek science (Aristotle, Alexander of Aphrodisias, Galen, Archimedes, and pseudo-Plutarch).

JACCARD, AUGUSTE (*b. Culliairy, Neuchâtel, Switzerland, 1833; d. Le Locle, Neuchâtel, Switzerland, 1895*), geology, paleontology.

Assisted in family watchmaking business until 1875, and operated his own business until 1885. Little formal education, but learned geology and paleontology from local physician and from Desor, professor at Academy of Neuchâtel; succeeded Desor as professor of geology (1873–95). Writings concerned mostly with Swiss Jura; worked on geological mapping; collaborated on geological map of Switzerland (1861); studied hydrology, hydrogeology, and occurence of bitumen, petroleum, and asphalt in Switzerland; among the first to declare petroleum to be of organic origin.

JACKSON, CHARLES THOMAS (*b. Plymouth, Mass., 1805; d. Somerville, Mass., 1880*), medicine, chemistry, mineralogy, geology.

Graduated from Harvard Medical School (1829); studied medicine at the University of Paris (1829) and attended geology lectures by Élie de Beaumont. Established first instructional laboratory in analytical chemistry in America (Boston, 1836). First state geologist of Maine (1837), Rhode Island (1839), and New Hampshire (1839); appointed U.S. geologist in Lake Superior region (1847), but was soon discharged. A descriptive geologist, he was interested in mineralogy to the exclusion of stratigraphy; probably first to observe tellurium and silenium in America. Made disputed claims to discovery of guncotton, telegraph, and use of ether as an anesthetic. Died insane.

JACKSON, JOHN HUGHLINGS (*b. Providence Green, Green Hammerton, Yorkshire, England, 1835; d. London, England, 1911*), clinical neurology, neurophysiology.

Apprenticed to a doctor at age fifteen, he completed education at St. Bartholomew's Hospital Medical School, London (1855–56); house surgeon at York Hospital (1856–59); returned to London and took M.D. at University of St. Andrews (1860) and spent rest of his life as physician at various hospitals and in private practice; elected Fellow of Royal College of Physicians of London (1868) and Fellow of Royal Society (1878); first president of Neurological Society (1885). Jackson's writings (1861–1909) are rich and voluminous but were never systematized; by applying data of abnormal functioning to normal action of the nervous system, he profoundly influenced development of clinical neurology, neurophysiology, and psychology in the nineteenth and twentieth centuries; acclaimed as greatest British scientific clinician of nineteenth century, though he performed no experiments. Early life influenced by four men: Thomas Laycock, Jonathan Hutchinson, Charles Brown-Séquard, and Herbert Spencer; early papers dealt mainly with ophthalmological problems; Jackson was one of first to relate ocular and cerebral disease; first to place site of origin of epileptic phenomena in cerebral cortex instead of medulla oblongata, as previously thought; deduced that localized epilepsy (now known as "Jacksonian epilepsy") is limited to a certain area of one cerebral hemisphere; suggested nutritional disturbance of brain cells as cause of epilepsy; contended that function is localized to areas of cerebral cortex; studied physiological basis of speech; believed that the cerebellum controlled continuous (tonic) movements and cerebrum controlled changing (clonic) movements; envisaged functional localization in cerebellum, only recently demonstrated. Jackson's most basic neurological concept is evolution and dissolution of the nervous system (Croonian lectures, 1884).

JACOB BEN MĀCHIR IBN TIBBON. *See* **Ibn Tibbon.**

JACOBI, CARL GUSTAV JACOB (*b. Postdam, Germany, 1804; d. Berlin, Germany, 1851*), mathematics.

After being educated by his mother's brother, Jacobi entered the Gymnasium at Potsdam in 1816. Graduated from the Gymnasium in 1821. In the fall of 1824 Jacobi passed his preliminary examination for *Oberlehrer* and was offered a position at the prestigious Joachimsthalsche Gymnasium in Berlin. At the age of twenty he began a university career as *Privatdozent* at the University of Berlin. There being no prospect for a promotion at Berlin in the near future, it was suggested that Jacobi transfer to the University of Königsberg, where a salaried position might be available sooner. When he arrived there in May 1826, the physicists Franz Neumann and Heinrich Dove were just starting their academic careers, and Friedrich Bessel, then in his early forties, occupied the chair of astronomy. Joining these colleagues, Jacobi soon became interested in applied problems. In 1827 he was appointed associate professor. Appointment as full professor followed in 1832. Jacobi created a sensation among the mathematics world with his investigations into the theory of elliptic functions, carried out in competition with Abel. Most of Jacobi's fundamental research articles in the theory of elliptic functions, mathematical analysis, number theory, geometry, and mechanics were published in Crelle's *Journal für die reine und angewandte Mathematik*. With an average of three articles per volume, Jacobi was one of its most active contributors and quickly helped to establish its international fame.

The outburst of Jacobi's creativity at the very beginning of his career caused him to seek contacts with some of the foremost mathematicians of his time. He summarized his first two years' research, a good deal of which had been obtained in competition with Abel, in his masterpiece *Fundamenta nova theoriae functionum ellipticarum* (1829). His previous publications in *Astronomische Nachrichten* and in Crelle's *Journal* were here systematically collected, greatly augmented, and supplemented by proofs—he had previously omitted these, thereby arousing the criticism of Legendre, Gauss and others.

The *Fundamenta nova* deals in the first part with the transformation, and in the second with the representation, of elliptic functions. The second part is devoted to the evolution of elliptic functions into infinite products and series of various kinds.

In his ten hours a week of lecturing in the winter of 1835–36 Jacobi for the first time founded the theory on the theta function, proving the famous theorem about the sum of products of four theta functions and defining the kinds of elliptic functions as quotients of theta functions. He continued this work in his lectures of 1839–40, the second part of which is published in volume I of his *Gesammelte Werke*. Volume II contains a historical summary, "Zur Geschichte der elliptischen und Abel'schen Transcendenten," composed by Jacobi probably in 1847, which documents his view of his favorite subject toward the end of his life.

In number theory, the theory of residues, the division of the circle into *n* equal parts, the theory of quadratic forms, the representation of integers as sums of squares or cubes, and related problems were studied by Jacobi. In 1839 Jacobi's *Canon arithmeticus* on primitive roots was published; for each prime and power of a prime less than 1,000 it gives two companion tables showing the numbers with given indexes and the index of each given number.

Most of Jacobi's work is characterized by linkage of different mathematical disciplines. He introduced elliptic functions not only into number theory but also into the theory of integration, which in turn is connected with the theory of differential equations where, among other things, the principle of the last multiplier is due to Jacobi. Most of his investigations on first-order partial differential equations and analytical mechanics were published posthumously (in 1866, by Clebsch) as *Vorlesungen über Dynamik*.

Among Jacobi's work in mathematical physics is research on the attraction of ellipsoids and a surprising discovery in the theory of configurations of rotating liquid masses.

The theory of determinants, which begins with Leibniz, was presented systematically by Jacobi early in 1841. He introduced the "Jacobian" or functional determinant; a second paper—also published in Crelle's *Journal*—is devoted entirely to its theory, including relations to inverse functions and the transformation of multiple integrals.

In the 1840's Jacobi became involved in the planning of an edition of Euler's works. He drew up a very detailed plan of distributing the immense number of publications among the volumes of the projected edition. Unfortunately, the project could be realized only on a much reduced scale. It was not until 1911 that the first volume of *Leonhardi Euleri opera omnia*—still in progress —appeared.

JACOBI, MORITZ HERMANN VON (*b. Potsdam, Germany, 1801; d. St. Petersburg, Russia, 1874*), physics.

Studied architecture at Göttingen; taught civil engineering at University of Dorpat; moved to St. Petersburg (1837), where he joined Imperial Academy of Sciences (1839) and did research on electricity and its applications; published interesting studies but had little impact. His most interesting work was a study of power of the electromagnet as a function of various parameters (1838); built one of the first practical electric motors (1834); constructed an electromagnetic telegraph similar to Morse's first receiver (1839); discovered process of "galvanoplasty" (electrotyping) in 1838.

JACOBS, WALTER ABRAHAM (*b. Brooklyn, N.Y., 1883; d. Los Angeles, Calif., 1967*), organic chemistry.

Took B.S. and M.S. at Columbia University; studied under Emil Fischer in Berlin (Ph.D., 1907); fellow in chemistry at Rockefeller Institute for Medical Research until retirement. Early research on nucleic acids; with Michael Heidelberger developed Tryparsamide which was highly effective in treating African sleeping sickness; turned to structural investigations of pharmacologically significant natural products from plants (1922); last twenty-five years of career spent studying alkaloids.

JACQUET, PIERRE ARMAND (*b. St. Mande, France, 1906; d. at sea, off coast of Spain, 1967*), chemical engineering.

Diploma from École Nationale Supérieure de Chimie (1926); discovered electrolytic polishing (1929) and by 1940 had established methods for polishing most ordinary metals; made important micrographs and contributed to various metallurgical problems; with E. Mencarelli developed a method of rendering metallography nondestructive.

JACQUIN, NIKOLAUS JOSEF (*b. Leiden, Netherlands, 1727; d. Vienna, Austria, 1817*), botany, chemistry.

Studied medicine in Paris and at University of Vienna; sent by Francis I to West Indies and South America to augment imperial natural history collections (1754–59); appointed to chair of chemistry and botany in Medical Faculty, University of Vienna (1768–96); member of Royal Society, Academy of Sciences in Paris. Significance in chemistry is his acceptance of Joseph Black's explanation of burning lime by escape of special air, contrary to prevailing phlogiston theory; proved that I. C. Meyer's criticisms of Black were wrong; wrote influential chemistry text. As a botanist, was the most important younger contemporary of Linnaeus; first German writer to extensively use binomial nomenclature; described many new species.

JAEGER, FRANS MAURITS (*b. The Hague, Netherlands, 1877; d. Haren, near Groningen, Netherlands, 1945*), crystallography, physical chemistry.

Graduated from University of Leiden (1900); studied at University of Berlin (1900–02); Ph.D. at Leiden (1903); taught physical chemistry at University of Groningen (1908–44). Most important work was study of molten salts and silicates at very high temperatures; with help from A. L. Day of Carnegie Institution he opened a laboratory for this purpose at Groningen (1912); wrote on crystals and history of chemistry.

JAEGER, GEORG FRIEDRICH (*b. Stuttgart, Germany, 1785; d. Stuttgart, 1866*), paleontology, medicine.

M.D. at Tübingen (1808); studied osteology and fossil skeletons under G. Cuvier at Paris; established medical practice in Stuttgart, where he was also inspector of royal natural history cabinet (1817–56); taught at Stuttgart Obergymnasium (1822–42). Principal contributions in paleontology; also wrote on abnormal growth and anatomy of man and animals, effects of poisons on plants, parasitism, mammalian systematics and distribution, geology, and anthropology.

JAEKEL, OTTO (*b. Neusalz an derOder, Germany* [*now Nowa Sól, Poland*], *1863; d. Peking, China, 1929*), paleontology.

Ph.D. in paleontology at Munich (1886); chair of paleontology at University of Greifswald (Pomerania), 1906–28; appointment at Sun Yat-sen University, Canton, China (1928). Primary research in paleontology, especially echinoderms and vertebrates; founded Paleontological Society (1912).

JAʿFAR AL-BALKHĪ. *See* **Abū Maʿshar.**

JAGANNĀTHA (*fl. India, ca. 1720–1740*), astronomy, mathematics.

Under patronage of Jayasiṃha II, translated Euclid's *Elements* (before 1727) and Ptolemy's *Syntaxis Mathēmatikē* (1732) from Arabic into Sanskrit.

JAGGAR, THOMAS AUGUSTUS, JR. (*b. Philadelphia, Pa., 1871; d. Honolulu, Hawaii, 1953*), geology, volcanology.

Ph.D. from Harvard University (1897); postgraduate study at universities of Munich and Heidelberg (1894–95). With U.S. Geological Survey (1898–1901); provided first estimate for geological survey of Hawaii. Taught Harvard (1901–06); headed geology department Massachusetts Institute of Technology (1906–11). Founded Hawaii Volcano Observatory in 1911 (director until 1940); this work was summarized in "Origin and Development of Craters" (1947). Most of Jaggar's work was qualitative; he made significant contributions on development of volcanoes and role of groundwater in explosive eruptions.

AL-JĀḤIẒ, ABŪ ʿUTHMĀN ʿAMR IBN BAḤR (*b. Basra, Iraq, ca. 776; d. Basra, 868/869*), natural history.

Taught by philologists and men of letters al-Aṣmaʿī, Abū ʿUbayda, and Abū Zayd; he was tutor to children of Caliph al-Mutawakkil; earned much money from 200 writings on politics, religion, and science (less than thirty extant). Most important scientific work on animals (*Kitāb al-Ḥayawān*), is a literary work for entertainment; summarizes Arab and Greek knowledge of larger mammals, important birds, and insects. He cites his own studies and makes his own judgments; a zoology book of this scope never appeared again in Islamic world.

JAHN, HANS MAX (*b. Küstrin, Germany* [*now Kostrzyn, on the Oder, Poland*], *1853; d. Berlin, Germany, 1906*), physical chemistry.

Ph.D., University of Berlin (1875), where he later taught electrochemistry. Most important publications were on decomposition of simple organic compounds by means of zinc dust.

JAMES OF VENICE, also known as **IACOBUS VENETICUS GRECUS** (*d. after 1147*), philosophy, law, Aristotelian translations.

Probably most important of the scholars who provided knowledge of Aristotle for the Latin Middle Ages; first to translate *Physics, De anima, Metaphysics, Parva naturalia,* and *Posterior Analytics.* He translated and wrote influential commentary on *Sophistici elenchi.* Some of James's translations became recognized "authentic" texts for over three centuries.

JAMES, WILLIAM (*b. New York, N.Y., 1842; d. Chocorua, N.H., 1910*), psychology, philosophy.

Son of Henry James, Sr. and brother of novelist Henry James. Studied chemistry and biology at Harvard (1861–64) where he attended Agassiz's lectures; joined Agassiz's Amazon expedition (1865); M.D. from Harvard (1869) though he never practiced medicine; beginning in 1873 he taught anatomy, physiology, and philosophy at Harvard. *Principles of Psychology* published 1890 was one of the first attempts to treat psychology as natural science. He believed the mind was subject to both Darwinian evolutionary principles and to acts of will; proposed a physiological base for emotions. Major work of descriptive psychology was *The Varieties of Religious Experience* (1902); he used a pluralistic approach to illustrate the pragmatic value of religion. James's theory of "pragmatism," first asserted by Charles Peirce, was developed in *Pragmatism: A New Name for Some Old Ways of Thinking* (1907); highly influential in United States. Last complete work, *A Pluralist Universe* (1909), asserted the multiplicity of standards of truth and rationality.

JAMESON, ROBERT (*b. Leith, Scotland, 1774; d. Edinburgh, Scotland, 1854*), geology, natural history.

Studied geology and mineralogy under John Walker at Edinburgh University; traveled about British Isles studying local natural history (1794–99); observations recorded in two works (1798, 1800). An advocate of A. G. Werner's theories, Jameson studied under Werner at the Bergakademie in Freiberg (1800–02). Succeeded Walker in Regius chair of natural history at Edinburgh (1804–54). Published three-volume *System of Mineralogy* (1804–08); third volume contains first detailed English account of Werner's geognostic theories and strata classification; Jameson was the leader of Scottish Wernerians (Neptunists); helped found Wernerian Natural History Society in 1808 (president until death). Co-founder of *Edinburgh Philosophical Journal* (1819; editor 1824–54); edited and annotated works by Cuvier, Buch, and others; increased Edinburgh University museum collections; by 1852 its natural history holdings were second in Great Britain only to British Museum. Made no considerable direct contributions to geology, but observations still of interest and his teaching inspired many naturalists and instructed far more students in Wernerian doctrine than did Werner himself.

JAMSHĪD IBN MAḤMŪD AL-KĀSHĪ. *See* **al-Kāshī.**

JANISZEWSKI, ZYGMUNT (*b. Warsaw, Poland, 1888; d. Lvov, Poland* [*now U.S.S.R.*], *1920*), mathematics.

Studied mathematics at Zurich, Munich, Göttingen, and Paris (Ph.D., Sorbonne, 1911); Hilbert, H. Minkowski, Zermelo, Goursat, Hadamard, Lebesgue, Picard, and Poincaré were among his teachers. Taught mathematics at Société des Cours des Sciences (1911–13); obtained *agrégation* in mathematics from University of Lvov, where he taught until World War I; after the war taught at University of Warsaw (1918–20). Early research (1910–12) on concepts of arc, curve, and surface; sketched first construction of a curve without arcs (1912); three topological theorems are associated with his name. With S. Mazurkiewicz and W. Sierpiński, founded the contemporary Polish school of mathematics and its journal, *Fundamenta mathematicae,* devoted to set theory and allied fields.

JANSEN, ZACHARIAS (*b. The Hague, Netherlands, 1588; d. Amsterdam, Netherlands, ca. 1631*), optics.

A Middleburg optician and counterfeiter of Spanish coins. Invention of the telescope wrongly attributed to him by Pierre Borel (*De vero telescopii inventore*, 1655–56) on basis of a false claim by Jansen's son, Johannes Sachariassen, who told Middleburg authorities that his father invented the telescope in 1590.

JANSSEN, PIERRE JULES CÉSAR (*b. Paris, France, 1824; d. Meudon, France, 1907*), physical astronomy, spectroscopy, photography.

Graduated University of Paris (*licence ès sciences*, 1852; doctorate of science, 1860); for doctorate studied absorption of radiant heat in mediums of the eye. Stimulated by Kirchhoff's discovery (1859) of terrestrial elements in the sun, Janssen devoted his career to physical astronomy. With a home-made observatory and spectroscope, established that certain dark bands in solar spectrum are of terrestrial origin, and named them "telluric rays" (1862–63); determined that the intensity of telluric rays is lessened at high elevations where atmosphere is less dense (1864) and increased by high humidity; stated that telluric rays could reveal chemical composition of planetary atmospheres, and in 1867 announced presence of water vapor in atmosphere of Mars. Studied spectra of solar prominences during total eclipse in India (1868), where he developed a method of observing lines of prominences without eclipses; during observations in Himalayas created the first spectrohelioscope (1868). Appointed professor of physics at École Spéciale d'Architecture; first director of French government's Meudon observatory for physical astronomy (1876–1907). His most famous project at Meudon was an atlas of solar photographs made between 1876 and 1903. At Mont Blanc (1888 and 1890) determined that dark rays of oxygen are entirely telluric; erected observatory at Mont Blanc (1891–93). Pioneered in use of balloons for celestial observations; used balloon to measure intensity of Leonid meteor shower (1898). Worked on improvement of solar photography; developed photographic revolver for observing transit of Venus (1874), which used revolving disks to photograph successive positions of the planet. Elected to Academy of Sciences (1873) and Bureau of Longitudes (1875).

JARS, ANTOINE GABRIEL (*b. Lyons, France, 1732; d. Clermont-Ferrand, Auvergne, France, 1769*), mining engineering, metallurgy.

Son of copper mine owner; studied chemistry at College of Lyons; entered École des Ponts-et-Chaussées at Paris about 1754; sent by French government to study mines in Europe and Great Britain in effort to modernize industrial practices; gave first demonstration in France of melting iron with coke (1769); probably first professional French metallurgist.

AL-JAWHARĪ, AL-ʿABBĀS IBN SAʿĪD (*fl. Baghdad, ca. 830*), mathematics, astronomy.

One of the astronomers for the ʿAbbāsid Caliph al-Maʾmūn; worked in astrology, observing, instrument construction, and geometry. Three works attributed to al-Jawharī (two on Euclid's *Elements* and a book of astronomical tables) are not extant. Naṣīr al-Dīn al-Ṭūsī ascribes to al-Jawarī an "Emendation of the Elements"

and quotes his attempt to prove Euclid's parallels postulate, the earliest extant proof of the Euclidean postulate written in Arabic. The proof takes its starting point from Simplicius but fails to establish the intended general case; also extant are "additions" to book V of the *Elements*.

JAYASIMHA (*b. Amber, Rajasthan, India, 1686; d. Jaipur, Rajasthan, 1743*), astronomy.

Maharaja of Amber (though subordinate to Mogul emperor) who revived Brahman culture and attempted to restore Indian astronomy by introducing Islamic and European scientific works and instruments; had Islamic astronomical works translated into Sanskrit by Jagannātha and Nayanasukhopādhyāya (1727–32); had astronomical tables prepared (dedicated to Mogul emperor in 1728); constructed five observatories (Delhi, Jaipur, Ujjain, Benares, and Mathurā); had instruments constructed of metal and stone; Jayasimha himself wrote Sanskrit work describing astrolabe. His reform of astronomy failed, the observatories were abandoned, and European advances were ignored by Indian scientists until 1835.

AL-JAYYĀNĪ, ABŪ ʿABD ALLĀH MUHAMMAD IBN MUʿĀDH (*b. Cordoba [?], Spain, ca. 989/990; d. after 1079*), mathematics, astronomy.

"Jayyānī" means from Jaén, the capital of the Andalusian province of same name. Wrote "On the Total Solar Eclipse" and "On the Dawn," the latter translated by Gerard of Cremona into Latin and of wide interest in the Latin Middle Ages and Renaissance. Gerard also translated al-Jayyānī's *Tabulae Jahen* which is based on the tables of al-Khwārizmī converted to longitude of Jaén; in it, al-Jayyānī rejects previous astrological theories. His treatise *On Ratio* is a defense of Euclid's fifth book, definition 5 (doctrine of proportions), whose abstract form was dissatisfying to Arab mathematicians; al-Jayyānī was the most successful of the Arabs who tried to explain the Greek technique of equimultiples in terms of more basic concepts and methods; his approach shows understanding comparable to that of Isaac Barrow.

AL-JAZARĪ^c, BADĪ^cAL-ZAMĀN, ABU-L-ʿIZZ ISMĀʿĪL IBN AL-RAZZĀZ (*fl. Diyār Bakr, 1206*), machinery, techniques of construction.

In the service of the family of Nāṣir al-Dīn, the Artuqid king of Diyār Bakr in Mesopotamia; wrote "Book of Knowledge of Mechanical Devices", grouped into six parts: water clocks and candle clocks; vessels and figures for drinking; pitchers and basins for phlebotomy and ritual washing; fountains that change shape and machines for the perpetual flute; machines for raising water; and miscellaneous instruments. Al-Jazarī^c was not primarily an inventor but an engineer who perfected earlier, mainly Islamic, machines; most important machine is a double-cylinder slot-rod pump driven by paddle wheel; more important were individual components and constructional techniques, such as conical valves, casting of brass and copper, static balancing of large pulley wheels, use of wooden templates, use of paper models in design, calibration of orifices, lamination of timber to minimize warping, use of true suction pipes, tipping buckets, and segmental gears; many of al-Jazarī^c's components and techniques reappeared in Europe, apparently as reinventions, centuries later.

JEAN. *See* **John.**

JEANS, JAMES HOPWOOD (*b. Ormskirk, Lancashire, England, 1877; d. Dorking, Surrey, England, 1946*), physics, astronomy.

Entered Trinity College, Cambridge, 1896 (M.A., 1903); professor of applied mathematics Princeton University (1905–09); fellow of Royal Society (1907); Stokes lecturer in applied mathematics at Cambridge (1910–12), after which Jeans devoted his life to research and writing; president of Royal Astronomical Society (1925–27); won Royal Medal of Royal Society (1919); knighted in 1928; from 1928 ceased research and popularized science. His scientific life had four parts: The first period devoted to molecular physics (1903–14) studied foundations of kinetic molecular theory; published *The Dynamical Theory of Gases* (1904), which became a standard textbook; corrected error in Rayleigh's law concerning blackbody radiation (1905; became known as Rayleigh-Jeans law); *Mathematical Theory of Electricity and Magnetism* (1908) was widely used; *Report on Radiation and the Quantum Theory* (1914) helped spread acceptance of quantum theory. The second phase of his career concerned rotating liquid masses; work summarized in *Problems of Cosmogony and Stellar Dynamics* (1919); concluded that rotation of a contracting mass could not form a planetary system; favored tidal theory in which planets formed by close passage of two stars. In the third phase of his career he continued astrophysical work (1919–28); applied kinetic theory arguments to stars in clusters or galaxies; criticized A.S. Eddington's theory of internal constitution of stars; ideas summarized in *Astronomy and Cosmogony* (1928), much of which has not held up with time. The fourth phase of his career began with radio lectures in 1928 (published as *The Universe Around Us*, 1929); the Rede lecture in 1930 led to the immensely popular *The Mysterious Universe*.

JEAURAT, EDME-SÉBASTIEN (*b. Paris, France, 1724; d. Paris, 1803*), astronomy.

Studied mathematics under Lieutaud; professor at École Militaire in Paris; early work on perfecting planetary tables; went to live at royal observatory (1770); edited twelve volumes of the *Connaissance des temps;* member of Paris Adacemy of Sciences (1763); director (1792).

JEFFERSON, THOMAS (*b. Goochland [now Albemarle] County, Va., 1743; d. Albemarle County, 1826*), agriculture, botany, cartography, diplomacy, ethnology, meteorology, paleontology, surveying, technology.

Entered school of philosophy, College of William and Mary (1760); studied mathematics and sciences with Reverend William Small; read for the law in Williamsburg (1762–67), where he practiced law (1767–69); elected House of Burgesses (1769–75); appointed county surveyor of Albemarle County (1773); served in Continental Congress (1775) and House of Delegates (1776–79); helped draft Declaration of Independence (1776); governor of Virginia (1779–81); retired to Monticello estate (1781–83). Wrote *Notes on the State of Virginia* (first printed in France, 1784–85), which describes the geography, climate, flora and fauna, topography, and other aspects of the region; refutes Buffon's conclusions concerning American animals and aborigines. Elected Continental

Congress (1783–85); minister to France (1785–89), where he observed the state of sciences and technology; designed an improved moldboard, based on the French plow, which was widely used in America; introduced dry rice, olive trees, and Merino sheep to America. Appointed secretary of state (1790); involved with survey of national capital; instrumental in developing patent office; elected American Philosophical Society (1780; president 1797–1815); read papers on fossilized bones of sloth and his moldboard (1797, 1798); vice-president of United States (1797–1801); president (1801–09); launched Lewis and Clark expedition (1803) and Zebulon Pike's expedition down the Mississippi River, leading to formation of U.S. Geological Survey (1879); recommended founding of United States Coast Survey; retired to Monticello where he founded the University of Virginia (chartered 1819).

JEFFREY, EDWARD CHARLES (*b. St. Catherines, Ontario, 1866; d. Cambridge, Mass., 1952*), botany.

Graduated University of Toronto (B.A., 1888; fellow in biology, 1889–92); taught botany at Toronto (1892–1902); papers on comparative morphology (1899–1905) established reputation; Ph.D. in botany at Harvard (1899); taught vegetable histology Harvard (1902–06); professor of plant morphology at Harvard (1907–33); vigorous defender of theory of evolution.

JEFFREYS, JOHN GWYN (*b. Swansea, Wales, 1809; d. London, England, 1885*), marine zoology.

Retired from legal profession to devote life to study of European Mollusca; published five-volume treatise, *British Conchology* (1862–69), still a standard reference work today. Directed scientific work on cruises of Admiralty survey ship *Porcupine* (1869, 1870); by dredging to depth of 2,435 fathoms, disproved Edward Forbes's hypothesis of an azoic zone below 300 fathoms and the current belief in a universal minimum temperature of seawater at low depths. Helped found Marine Biological Association of the United Kingdom. Jeffreys' unrivalled collection of British mollusks was sold to Smithsonian Institution.

JEFFRIES, ZAY (*b. Willow Lake, S.D., 1888; d. Pittsfield, Mass., 1965*), industrial metallurgy.

Graduated in mechanical engineering South Dakota School of Mines and Technology (1910); Ph.D. at Harvard (1918); consultant for Aluminum Company of America and General Electric Company; did research on measurement of grain size of metals, grain growth, and with Robert S. Archer developed slip-interference theory of hardening.

JENKIN, HENRY CHARLES FLEEMING (*b. near Dungeness, Kent, England, 1833; d. Edinburgh, Scotland, 1885*), engineering.

Fleeming (pronounced "Fleming") Jenkin received the M.A. from University of Genoa (1851); worked in design and manufacture of submarine cables; worked in British Association for Advancement of Science to establish the ohm as the absolute unit of resistance; made first absolute measurement of capacitance (1867). His objections to theory of evolution influenced Darwin (1867). Fellow of Royal Society (1865).

JENKINSON, JOHN WILFRED (*b. London, England, 1871; d. Gallipoli, Turkey, 1915*), comparative embryology, experimental embryology.

Studied zoology under W. F. R. Weldon, University College, London; further research with embryologist A. A. W. Hubrecht in Utrecht; D.Sc. at Oxford (1905); university lecturer in comparative and experimental embryology (1906); research fellow, Exeter College (1909); killed at Gallipoli in World War I; wrote texts on experimental embryology (1909) and vertebrate embryology (1913); studied mammalian placenta; interested in vitalism.

JENNER, EDWARD (*b. Berkeley, Gloucestershire, England, 1749; d. Berkeley, 1823*), natural history, immunology, medicine.

Apprenticed to a surgeon (1761–70); studied anatomy and surgery under John Hunter in London (1770–73); returned to Berkeley and practiced medicine (1773–1823). Frequently asked to give smallpox inoculations, a dangerous practise; began to use improved method of Robert Sutton, but found that patients who had had cowpox were immune; learned that only one kind of cowpox conferred immunity and only when the matter was taken from cowpox pustules before it was too old (1780); mistakenly thought true cowpox was identical with disease of horses and transmitted to cattle by milkmen; made first successful vaccination on eight-year old boy (1796); published *An Inquiry Into the Causes and Effects of the Variolae Vaccinae* (1798), in which Jenner described twenty-three cases in which cowpox conferred lasting immunity to smallpox; introduced the term "virus" to describe matter producing cowpox; after publication of the book, the practice of vaccination spread very quickly and Jenner's life was devoted to providing vaccine, explaining details of his procedure, and defending the practice against critics; founder of immunology and first pioneer of modern science of virology.

JENNINGS, HERBERT SPENCER (*b. Tonica, Ill., 1868; d. Santa Monica, Calif., 1947*), zoology.

Graduated from University of Michigan (B.S., 1893); graduate study at Harvard (M.A., 1895; Ph.D., 1896); further study with Max Verworn at Jena (1896–97) and at Naples zoological station (1897); taught experimental zoology Johns Hopkins University (1906–38), where he was named director of the zoological laboratory (1910); after retirement (1938) was research associate University of California, Los Angeles. Studies focused on two types microorganisms, Rotifera and Protozoa; early work on Rotifera is descriptive and systematic; later work concerning physiology and adaptation, is summarized in *Behavior of the Lower Organisms* (1906), a classic of zoology and comparative psychology; his final work made important contributions to genetics; studied constancy and variability of protozoan lines of inheritance (1908–16); after 1916 wrote popular works on genetics and philosophical implications of experimental biology (*The Biological Basis of Human Nature*, 1930; *The Universe and Life*, 1933).

JENSEN, CARL OLUF (*b. Frederiksberg, Copenhagen, Denmark, 1864; d. Middelfart, Denmark, 1934*), veterinary medicine.

Studied bacteriology at Koch's institute in Berlin (1887); taught at Royal Veterinary and Agricultural College (1889–1934); made contributions in pathology, serology, and surgery (first veterinarian to use X-ray investigations in surgery); investigated relation between human and animal tuberculosis (1902–1908). Beginning 1901, experimented with cancer transplantation; developed standardized method for preparation of thyroid hormone for medical use (1920). Appointed *Veterinaerfysicus*, highest veterinary office in Denmark (1922).

JENSEN, JOHAN LUDVIG WILLIAM VALDEMAR (*b. Nakskov, Denmark, 1859; d. Copenhagen, Denmark, 1925*), mathematics.

Essentially self-taught; never held academic position; employed by Copenhagen Telephone Company (1881–1924); developed Jensen's theorem (1899); did important study of convex functions and inequalities between mean values (1906).

JEPSON, WILLIS LINN (*b. Little Oak Ranch, Vacaville, Calif., 1867; d. Berkeley, Calif., 1946*), botany.

Known as "high priest of California Flora"; graduated from University of California at Berkeley (B.A., 1889; Ph.D., 1899). He wrote nearly sixty field books; his *Manual of the Flowering Plants of California* (1925) was the leading book in its field. His best taxonomic work is in *A Flora of California;* he founded the California Botanical Society (1913).

JERRARD, GEORGE BIRCH (*b. Cornwall, England, 1804; d. Long Stratton, Norfolk, England, 1863*), mathematics.

Graduated from Trinity College (1827); best known for important theorem in theory of equations given in *Mathematical Researches* (1832–35).

JEVONS, WILLIAM STANLEY (*b. Liverpool, England, 1835; d. Hastings, England, 1882*), logic, economics, philosophy of science.

While an undergraduate at University College, London, he took a job as assayer at the Australian mint, Sydney (1853–58); returned to England and earned master's degree, University College (1863). Taught "logic and mental and moral philosophy" and political economy at Owens College, Manchester (1863–76); taught at University College (1876–80); retired to write (1880) but drowned two years later. Best known as economist; wrote *The Coal Question* (1865); developed theory that trade cycles are correlated to sunspot activity; defined value as function of utility, leading to use of calculus by economists. Helped spread Boolean symbolic logic, to which he made improvements; developed a logical calculus based on the substitution of similars; devised a logic machine (the "logical piano") which was exhibited at Royal Society (1870). Jevons' *Elementary Lessons in Logic* (1870) was a popular textbook; ideas on logic were summarized in *The Principles of Science* (1874), his most celebrated book and a landmark in nineteenth-century philosophy of science. Perhaps the first writer to insist that absolute precision is beyond human reach; a subjectivist, Jevons believed the theory of probability is essential to logical method. He was a naïve disciple of probabilist theories of Laplace and Augustus De Morgan.

JEWETT, FRANK BALDWIN (*b. Pasadena, Calif., 1879; d. Summit, N.J., 1949*), telecommunications.

Ph.D. University of Chicago (1902), where he worked with Albert Michelson; with American Telephone and Telegraph Company (1904–25; in charge of research 1912–25), where worked on telephone link between New York and San Francisco; with Bell Telephone Laboratories (1925–44; first president), which Jewett helped establish as a leading center of industrial research in communications.

JOACHIM, GEORG. *See* **Rheticus.**

JOACHIMSTHAL, FERDINAND (*b. Goldberg, Germany [now Złotoryja, Poland], 1818; d. Breslau, Germany [now Wrocław, Poland] 1861*), mathematics.

Studied under best mathematicians of the day (Kummer, Dirichlet, Steiner, Jacobi, Bessel, and O. Rosenberger); studied in Berlin (1836–37) and Königsberg (1838–39); Ph.D. at Halle (1840); taught at University of Berlin (1845–53), where his lectures attracted many students; taught at Halle (1853–55) and Breslau (1855–61); primarily concerned with analytic applications in geometry; interested in theory of surfaces; known today for Joachimsthal surfaces, the Joachimsthal theorem, and a theorem on the ellipse; persuaded by Jacobi to write an *Analytische Geometrie der Ebene* as supplement to *Geometrie des Raumes* (published posthumously, 1863).

JOBLOT, LOUIS (*b. Bar-le-Duc, Meuse, France, 1645; d. Paris, France, 1723*), microscopy, physics.

Probably educated at Collège Gilles de Trèves; taught mathematics at École Nationale des Beaux-Arts (1680–1721); began research in microscopy about the time Huygens and Hartsoeker demonstrated microscopes in Paris (1678); publication of *Descriptions et usages de plusieurs nouveaux microscopes* (1718) established Joblot as first French microscopist and contains the earliest treatise on Protozoa; performed experiments with Infusoria disproving the doctrine of spontaneous generation; designed first *porte loupe* microscope; constructed first artificial magnet (1701); developed his own theory of magnetism contrary to Descartes'.

JOHANNES. *See also* **John.**

JOHANNES LAURATIUS DE FUNDIS (*fl. Bologna, 1428–1473*), astronomy, astrology.

Lecturer in astrology at University of Bologna; wrote several texts and treatises which L. Thorndike has determined to be unoriginal; his *Nova theorica planetarum* reveals how planetary theory was taught around the middle of the fifteenth century.

JOHANNES LEO. *See* **Leo the African.**

JOHANNSEN, ALBERT (*b. Belle Plaine, Iowa, 1871; d. Winter Park, Fla., 1962*), petrology, petrography.

Educated at universities of Illinois (B.S., 1894), Utah (B.A., 1898), and Johns Hopkins (Ph.D., 1903); with U.S. Geological Survey (1903–25); taught University of Chicago (1910–37); major work was *Descriptive Petrography of the Igneous Rocks* (1931–38), still a standard reference today, which introduced a now outmoded quantitative mineralogical classification of igneous rocks.

JOHANNSEN, WILHELM LUDVIG (*b. Copenhagen, Denmark, 1857; d. Copenhagen, 1927*), biology.

Apprenticed to pharmacist (1872); worked in Danish and German pharmacies; became assistant in chemistry at Carlsberg laboratory (1881), where he worked under Johan Kjeldal; research centered on plant metabolic processes; discovered method of breaking dormancy of winter buds (1887); taught botany and plant physiology at Copenhagen Agricultural College (1892–1905); taught plant physiology University of Copenhagen (beginning 1905). Strongly influenced genetics (1900–15); main concern was heredity of normal characters which vary quantitatively; in *Elemente der exakten Erblichkeitslehre* ("The Elements of Heredity," 1909), the first and most influential textbook of genetics in Europe, Johannsen introduced the concepts of "gene," "genotype," and "phenotype"; introduced concept of "pure line" in a paper on the work of Francis Galton (1903), proving existence of two kinds of variability—heritable and nonheritable—eliminating need for theory of inheritance of acquired characteristics. Wrote a book condemning mysticism in biology (1914) and a work on history of ideas on heredity (1923).

JOHN BURIDAN. *See* **Buridan, Jean.**

JOHN DANKO OF SAXONY. *See* **John of Saxony.**

JOHN DE' DONDI. *See* **Dondi, Giovanni.**

JOHN OF DUMBLETON (*b. England; d. ca. 1349*), natural philosophy.

May have been fellow of Merton College, Oxford, between 1338 and 1348; in 1340 was named as one of original fellows of Queen's College. Dumbleton's huge *Summa logicae et philosophiae naturalis* provides an invaluable source for current Oxford opinions; used a more mathematical approach to standard problems, such as the Ockhamist definition of motion; accepted Bradwardine's "law of motion," and gave an interesting proof of the "Merton mean speed theorem."

JOHN DUNS SCOTUS. *See* **Duns Scotus, John.**

JOHN OF GMUNDEN (*b. Gmunden am Traunsee, Austria, ca. 1380–1384; d. Vienna, Austria, 1442*), astronomy, mathematics, theology.

Graduated from the University of Vienna (B.A., 1402; M.A., 1406). His career can be divided into four periods. In the first (1406–16), lectures were on nonmathematical subjects, including theology; received appointment to Collegium Ducale (1409). In the second (1416–25), lectures were on mathematics and astronomy, leading to first professorship in these fields at University of Vienna; writing on mathematics was unoriginal and only one, an arithmetic book with sexagesimal fractions, was printed. The third period (1425–31) began when he retired from Collegium Ducale and became canon of a chapter of St. Stephen; devoted himself to writings on astronomical tables, calendars, and instruments. Through John of Gmunden's writings and teaching, Vienna became a center of astronomical research in Europe; he made few observations and disapproved of astrology; especially concerned with preparation of calendars, bringing out four editions covering the years from 1415–1514 (fourth edition printed on Gutenberg's press, 1448); works on astronomical instruments explain the operation and construction of an astrolabe, quadrant, albion, equatorium, torquetum, and cylindrical sundial. In the fourth period (1431–42) John received an ecclesiastical post in Laa an der Thaya. John's work reflects the Scholastic goal of teaching science from existing books and not advancing it; influential in both his teaching and writings; greatly influenced Peurbach and Regiomontanus, both of whom knew him personally (though were not students of his) and studied his writings, and whose achievements later overshadowed those of John's.

JOHN OF HALIFAX. *See* **Sacrobosco, Johannes de.**

JOHN OF HOLYWOOD. *See* **Sacrobosco, Johannes de.**

JOHN OF LIGNÈRES, or **Johannes de Lineriis** (*fl. France, first half of fourteenth century*), astronomy, mathematics.

Lived in Paris from about 1320 to 1335; published astronomical and mathematical works which diffused the Alfonsine tables throughout the Latin West; work includes tables and canons of tables, a theory of planets, and treatises on instruments. The canons known as *Canones super tabulas magnas* (*ca.* 1320) provide information on planetary motions in an unexceptional form; the accompanying tables of equations are completely original. Another set of canons with corresponding tables (1322) is in three parts: daily movement of sun, movements of the planets, and determination of eclipses; John of Saxony wrote commentary on first part (*ca.* 1335); the planetary tables preserve the general structure of the Castilian tables, though reduced to the meridian of Paris. Also wrote canons beginning *Quia ad inveniendum loca planetarum . . .* (*ca.* 1322–27) which deal with Alfonsine tables; John of Lignères himself may have contributed to converting Alfonsine Tables to sexagesimal form in Paris in 1320's; also compiled an almanac (1321). John's theory of planets is presented in *Spera concentrica vel circulus concentricus dicitur . . .* (*ca.* 1335) and gives justification of the compound motion of the eighth sphere; he also included treatises on three instruments: the saphea (an astrolabe with a peculiar system of stereographic projection), the equatorium (described in two treatises), and the directorium (a device similar to the astrolabe used in astrology); also wrote on an "armillary instrument" which probably derived from the new quadrant; treatises on instruments are not dated but probably written about 1320. Continued work on sexagesimal numeration in astronomical tables in *Algorismus minutiarum,* which was widely read.

JOHN MARLIANI. *See* **Marliani, Giovanni.**

JOHN OF MURS (*fl. France, first half of the fourteenth century*), mathematics, astronomy, music.

Active in science 1317–1345; wrote most works in Paris, at Sorbonne, where he was already master of arts in 1321; clerk to Philippe III d'Évreux, king of Navarre, (between 1338 and 1342); in 1344 he was canon of Mézières-en-Brenne; date of death unknown; wrote on music, mathematics, and astronomy. Musical works show originality, take a mathematical approach, and

were widely diffused until the end of the Middle Ages. Mathematical works are his most developed; earliest mathematical work is *Tabula tabularum* (1321) which uses sexagesimal notation; wrote a short treatise on trigonometry; *De arte mensurandi* (*ca.* 1344) utilizes William of Moerbeke's translations of Archimedes; most famous mathematical work is *Quadripartitum numerorum* (1343), whose arithmetic derives from al-Khwārizmī, algebra from Leonardo Fibonacci, and whose final book (four in all) on practical applications discusses music and mechanics.

In astronomy, John of Murs was a partisan of the Toulouse tables in 1317, but learned of the Alfonsine tables between 1317 and 1321, and along with John of Lignères helped introduce them into medieval science; *Expositio tabularum Alfonsi regis Castelle* (1321) is a technical study of certain values given by the Alfonsine tables; he did not compose canons of the tables in their definitive version until 1339. "Prima tabula docet differentiam unius ere . . ." attempted to perfect and simplify tables and calculating procedures for determining planetary positions on a given date; his tables of 1321, bearing the canons "Si vera loca planetarum per presentes tabulas invenire . . . ," represent one of the most original productions of medieval astronomy, and are based on generalization to all planets of calculating procedures for solar and lunar conjunctions and oppositions; developed new tables to further simplify calculation of solar and lunar conjunctions and oppositions; in *Patefit* he continues simplification of tables and includes an improved calendar; in 1337 work, "De regulis computistarum quia cognite sunt a multis . . . ," strongly urges reform of the ecclesiastical calendar; with Firmin de Belleval in 1345 he presented a memoir ("Sanctissimo in Christo patri ac domina . . .") to Pope Clement VI in Avignon suggesting two methods of calendar reform, neither of which was adopted; later corresponded with Clement VI on astrological matters.

JOHN OF PALERMO (*fl. Palermo, Sicily, 1221–1240*), translation of scientific works.

Worked at court of Emperor Frederick II; only known work is Latin translation of an Arabic tract (author unknown) on the hyperbola.

JOHN PECKHAM. *See* **Pecham, John.**

JOHN PHILOPONUS (*b. Caesarea* [*?*], *late fifth century; d. Alexandria, second half of sixth century*), philosophy, theology.

One of last the holders of the chair of philosophy in Alexandria; his philosophical background was Neoplatonic, but he was a member of a Monophysite sect; gives dates of two of his books: commentary on Aristotle's *Physica* (517) and book against Proclus (529); main significance is as first thinker to seriously attack Aristotle's physics and cosmology. Philoponus' philosophy of nature was the first to combine scientific cosmology and monotheism; rejected Aristotle's doctrines of eternity of universe, dichotomy of heaven and earth, and indestructible character of celestial bodies (composed of the fifth element, ether); believed different appearance of stars indicates different constitutions and hence they are not indestructible; anticipated Descartes' assertion that all bodies have extension; held that the world, once created by God, continues to exist automatically by natural law.

Objected to parts of Aristotle's dynamics; criticized analysis of falling bodies; raised doubts about natural motion of light and heavy bodies; rejected theory of forced motion, specifically the necessity for continuous contact between mover and the moved object; instead, concluded that "impetus" was imparted to objects, anticipating modern concepts of momentum and kinetic energy; believed that light is emitted from luminous object to our eyes and is a "force" similar to the "impetus" imparted to moving objects. Gave ingenious solution to problem of how one physical property of a substance may remain unaltered while another is visibly changing; interpreted uniform and circular motion of celestial bodies as inertial motion; utilized concept of "fitness" to amplify Aristotle's requirements for physical action and to defend Plato's doctrine of soul as mover of the body. Philoponus' Neoplatonic background was evident in discussion of resonance; gave ingenious physical illustration to explain perturbation of system by external forces; rejected existence of the infinite not only as actual entity, as Aristotle did, but also excluded potentially infinite; used the argument against the infinite to show the impossibility of eternity of universe; used the concept of infinite cardinal numbers (anticipating modern mathematics) in another argument against eternity of the world, later used by Islamic philosophers.

JOHN OF SACROBOSCO. *See* **Sacrobosco, Johannes de.**

JOHN OF SAXONY (*fl. France, first half of the fourteenth century*), astronomy.

Probably from Germany; active in science in Paris between 1327 and 1335; considered himself a student of John of Lignères. Published canons on Alfonsine tables (1327): "Tempus est mensura motus ut vult Aristoteles . . ."; in early 1320's probably worked with John of Lignères and John of Murs on putting Alfonsine tables in sexagesimal form. John of Saxony's 1327 canons apply to these modified tables, enjoyed considerable success, and were included in the first printed edition of the Alfonsine tables (1483). Also helped spread knowledge of the Alfonsine tables by working out examples in the *Exempla super tabulas et canones primi mobilis* of John of Lignères ("Quia plures astrologorum diversos libros . . .," *ca.* 1335); compiled ephemeris for 1336–80 for meridian of Paris with short canon to allow young people to determine planetary positions without making tedious calculations from tables. Wrote commentary on astrological treatise of al-Qabisi (Alcabitius) known as *Liber isagogicus* (written 1331, printed 1485); possibly wrote a computus and commentary in 1297.

JOHN SCOTTUS ERIUGENA. *See* **Eriugena, Johannes Scottus.**

JOHN OF SICILY (*fl. France, second half of the thirteenth century*), astronomy.

Part of Paris scientific community at end of thirteenth century; only extant work is commentary on "Quoniam cujusque actionis quantitatem . . . ," Gerard of Cremona's translation of canons of tables of al-Zarqal (*ca.* 1291); discusses solar and lunar calendars, the *primum mobile,* and planetary motions; comments on mo-

tion of "accession and recession" advocated by al-Zarqal, preferring instead Ptolemy's simple movement of precession.

JOHN SIMONIS OF SELANDIA (*fl. France, fifteenth century*), astronomy.

Of Danish or Dutch origin; *doctor artium;* wrote *Speculum planetarum* in Vienne (1417), his only known work. A well-known treatise, it was copied by Regiomontanus and Arnald of Brussels describes construction and use of new type equatorium (no specimen of actual instrument is known).

JOHNSON, DOUGLAS WILSON (*b. Parkersburg, W.Va., 1878; d. Sebring, Fla., 1944*), geomorphology.

Studied at the University of New Mexico, assisting Clarence Luther Herrick in geological fieldwork; Ph.D., Columbia University (1903); taught at Massachusetts Institute of Technology while studying physical geography at Harvard under W. M. Davis; became disciple of Davis, using Davis's "analytical method of presentation" in his work, *The Origin of the Carolina Bays* (1942). Taught geology at Harvard (1907–11), where he produced many Ph.D.'s; received grant (1911) to study eastern shoreline of United States; after moving to Columbia University (1912) published *Shore Processes and Shoreline Development* (1919), *The New England-Acadian Shoreline* (1925), and *Origin of Submarine Canyons* (1939). Made many contributions to "military geography" (served in intelligence division U. S. Army in World War I). Johnson's work in geomorphology was his most important; after Davis's death (1934) he was America's most influential geomorphologist; major and most lasting work is *Stream Sculpture on the Atlantic Slope* (1931), one of the masterpieces of denudation chronology. President of both Geological Society of America and Association of American Geographers.

JOHNSON, MANUEL JOHN (*b. Macao, China, 1805; d. Oxford, England, 1859*), astronomy.

While lieutenant in British East India Company on the island of St. Helena, operated observatory provided by East India Company, and compiled *Catalogue of 606 Principal Fixed Stars of the Southern Hemisphere* (1835); returned to England, graduated Magdalen College, Oxford (B.A., 1839; M.A., 1842); became Radcliffe observer, Radcliffe Observatory, Oxford (1839); compiled *Radcliffe Catalogue of 6317 Stars, Chiefly Circumpolar* (1860).

JOHNSON, THOMAS (*b. Selby* [?], *Yorkshire, England, ca. 1600, d. Basing, Hampshire, England, 1644*), botany.

Apprenticed to London apothecary (1620); made free brother Society of Apothecaries (1628); established apothecary's shop in London by 1633; acquainted with John Goodyear and John Parkinson, who with Johnson himself were ablest British botanists of first half of the seventeenth century. Johnson's *Iter plantarum* (1629) is first local flora of Britain. He revised John Gerard's *Herball* (1597), correcting many mistakes and adding first history of botany in English (1633). In his two-part work, *Mercurius botanicus* (1634, 1641), he intended to catalogue all 900 known British plants. His translation of works of French surgeon Ambroise Paré (1634) profoundly influenced British surgery.

JOHNSON, WILLARD DRAKE (*b. Brooklyn, N.Y., 1859; d. Washington, D.C., 1917*), geomorphology.

Graduated Yale University, joining U.S. Geological Survey (1879–1913); performed numerous topographical surveys throughout United States; best scholarly work was "The Profile of Maturity in Alpine Glacial Erosion" (1904); transfer to U.S. Forest Service (1913) was unsuccessful; remainder of life plagued with poor mental and physical health; did much to improve mapmaking procedures; patented Johnson tripod head (1887).

JOHNSON, WILLIAM (*b. ca. 1610; d. London, England, 1665*), chemistry.

Chemical operator to Royal College of Physicians (1648–65), preparing chemical medicines as samples and for sale; granted freedom of Society of Apothecaries (1654); published *Lexicon chemicum* (1652), gleaned from other sources; defended chemical Galenism in *Some Brief Animadversions* (1665).

JOHNSON, WILLIAM ERNEST (*b. Cambridge, England, 1858; d. Northampton, England, 1931*), logic.

Educated at King's College, Cambridge; held various Cambridge positions (1883–1902); appointed Sidgwick lecturer in moral science (1902–31); published three-volume *Logic* (1921–24); primary contributions in foundations of logic and of probability theory.

JOLIOT, FRÉDÉRIC (*b. Paris, France, 1900; d. Paris, 1958*), nuclear physics.

Admitted to École Supérieure de Physique et de Chimie Industrielle, Paris (1920), where he received an engineering degree; influenced by physicist Paul Langevin, director of studies. After military service, became personal assistant to Mme. Curie at Institut du Radium of University of Paris (1925); research on electrochemical properties of polonium was subject of doctoral thesis (defended in 1930). Married Mme. Curie's daughter, Irène, an assistant at Radium Institute (1926), with whom he collaborated on research, beginning 1931. Continued research under scholarship arranged by Jean Perrin from Caisse Nationale des Sciences to study ionizing radiations emitted by radioactive substances, designed improved Wilson cloud chamber with which he and Irène discovered artificial radioactivity (1934); their experiments showed that Bothe-Becker radiation ejects nuclei from hydrogen and helium (1932); discovered that positive electrons are emitted from light elements bombarded by α particles (1933); discovered that artificial radioactivity could be induced in aluminum by exposure to α rays, which transmute aluminum atoms into radioactive isotopes of phosphorus (1934); they were awarded Nobel Prize for this work (1935). Joliot became professor Collège de France (1937); with H. von Halban and L. Kowarski was first to prove that fission of uranium atoms (discovered by O. Hahn) induced by one neutron produces an emission of several neutrons and could possibly create nuclear chain reaction (1939). Research interrupted by World War II; after war became head of new atomic energy commission (1945); supervised France's first atomic pile (1948) and building of nuclear research center; activities in Communist party lead to dismissal from atomic energy commission (1950); after Irène Joliot-Curie died (1956), succeeded her as head of Radium Institute.

JOLIOT-CURIE, IRÈNE (*b. Paris, France, 1897; d. Paris, 1956*), radioactivity, nuclear physics.

Famous mainly from discoveries made with husband, Frédéric Joliot, particularly artificial radioactivity, for which they shared Nobel Prize in chemistry (1935). Daughter of scientists Pierre Curie and Marie Sklodowska Curie, who discovered radium; educated at teaching co-operative by Marie Curie and colleagues (Paul Langevin, Jean Perrin); B.A. at Collège Sévigné (1914); during World War I was an army nurse, assisting her mother with radiography apparatus; became assistant at the Radium Institute (1918), of which mother was director; took examinations for *licence* in physics and mathematics at Sorbonne (1920). First important research was on fluctuations in range of α rays, which was basis for doctoral thesis (1925); married Frédéric Joliot (1926) and began collaboration (1931) leading to Nobel Prize. Best individual work was before World War II after elected professor at Sorbonne (1937): studied bombardment of uranium with neutrons with P. P. Savic, leading to Otto Hahn's discovery that the neutron can induce bipartition (fission) of a uranium atom into two atoms of comparable mass. Named director of Radium Institute (1946) and helped create new laboratories; died of leukemia like her mother, a consequence of exposure to X and γ radiations.

JOLLY, PHILIPP JOHANN GUSTAV VON (*b. Mannheim, Germany, 1809; d. Munich, Germany, 1884*), physics.

Studied universities of Vienna and Heidelberg (Ph.D., 1834); taught mathematics and physics at Heidelberg (1839–54), where he was often consulted by J. R. von Mayer; Taught at the University of Munich (1854–84); well-known for improved measuring devices. Demonstrated variability of oxygen content of air (1879).

JOLY, JOHN (*b. Holywood, King's County [now Offaly], Ireland, 1857; d. Dublin, Ireland, 1933*), geology, experimental physics, chemistry, mineralogy.

Graduated Trinity College, Dublin (B.A. 1882); taught geology Trinity College (1897–1933). Invented steam calorimeter, which he used to determine specific heats of minerals and, for first time, specific heats of gases at constant volume; devised new method of producing color photographs (1895); estimated age of earth (1899), supporting those scientists unwilling to accept much lower estimates of Lord Kelvin. After the discovery of radioactivity wrote *Radioactivity and Geology* (1909) and *The Surface History of the Earth* (1925).

JONES, HAROLD SPENCER. *See* **Spencer Jones, Harold.**

JONES, HARRY CLARY (*b. New London, Md., 1865; d. Baltimore, Md., 1916*), physical chemistry.

Graduated Johns Hopkins University, (B.A., 1889; Ph.D., 1892); additional study in Europe with Ostwald, Arrhenius, and van't Hoff; taught physical chemistry Johns Hopkins (1894–1916). Later research concerned attempt to develop theory of solutions similar to Mendeleev's; most successful book was *Elements of Physical Chemistry* (1902).

JONES, WILLIAM (*b. Llanfihangel Tw'r Beird, Anglesey, Wales, 1675; d. London, England, 1749*), mathematics.

Mathematics tutor to great London families. In 1702 he published *A New Compendium of the Whole Art of Navigation*. His *Synopsis palmariorum matheseos* (1706) attracted attention of Halley and Newton, the latter maintaining close touch with Jones and allowing Jones to print several of his works; works of Newton as well as others are contained in Jones's collection of manuscripts and correspondence.

JONQUIÈRES, ERNEST JEAN PHILIPPE FAUQUE DE (*b. Carpentras, France, 1820; d. Mousans-Sartoux, near Grasse, France, 1901*), mathematics.

Entered École Navale at Brest (1835); thirty-six years in French navy; became vice-admiral (1879); main interest geometry; won two-thirds Grand Prix of Paris Academy (1862) for work in theory of fourth-order plane curves.

JONSTON, JOHN (*b. Sambter, Poland, 1603; d. Liegnitz, Poland, 1675*), natural history, medicine.

Attended many European universities; M.D. degrees in 1632 at Cambridge and Leiden; briefly taught medicine at Frankfurt; practiced medicine at Leiden; books are mere compilations but helped spread interest in natural history; best medical writing is *Idea Universae Medicinae Practicae* (1644).

JORDAN, (CLAUDE THOMAS) ALEXIS (*b. Lyons, France, 1814; d. Lyons, 1897*), botany.

Member of distinguished family; cousin of mathematician Camille Jordan; member Linnaean Society of Lyons; assisted director of Lyons Botanical Garden, where he worked on French floras; made frequent botanical journeys (1836–46) assembling important private herbarium. Argued that Linnaean system of classification was too schematic; began cultural experimentation in his own gardens; asserted invariability of true species, which Jordan distinguished not by difference in one characteristic but by series of small but stable details. His ideas were rejected by both conservative botanists and Darwinists, though certain experiments were confirmed; Jordan's concept of fixity is now outdated but survives in conclusions that acquired characteristics are not transmissible and that species is a blending of separate but closely related homogeneous types. In 1916 J. P. Lotsy introduced term "Jordanon" to distinguish Jordan's sense of species from Linnaeus's.

JORDAN, CAMILLE (*b. Lyons, France, 1838; d. Paris, France, 1921*), mathematics.

Born into well-to-do family; cousin of botanist Alexis Jordan; entered École Polytechnique (1855); engineer until 1885; taught at École Polytechnique and Collège de France (1873–1912); elected to Academy of Sciences (1881). A "universal" mathematician who wrote on many branches of mathematics; his *Cours d'analyse* set standards for analysis in late nineteenth century; made important contribution to topology in proof on decomposition of plane into two regions by simple closed curve; at age thirty became master of group theory; Jordan first to systematically develop theory of finite groups and its applications in directions opened by Galois; studied solvable finite groups; work on permutation groups collected in *Traité des substitutions* (1870), the bible of group theory

for thirty years; most profound algebraic work is "finiteness theorems," which Jordan proved during twelve years after publication of the *Traité;* students included F. Klein and S. Lie.

JORDAN, DAVID STARR (*b. Gainesville, N.Y., 1851; d. Stanford, Calif., 1931*), ichthyology, education.

Graduated Cornell University (M.S., 1872); taught at Butler University (1875–79); became professor at Indiana University (1879), and later president (1885–91); became first president of Leland Stanford Junior University, and later chancellor (1913). Inspired to enter ichthyology by Louis Agassiz (1873); with his first paper on fishes (1874) he dominated ichthyology, then in its infancy in United States; made extensive expeditions throughout world; named 1,085 genera and more than 2,500 species of fishes, as well as writing synopses of the classification. An early Darwinian, he derived Jordan's law: species most closely related to another is found just beyond a barrier to distribution; concluded that extreme specialization along given line of development is followed by progressive degeneration; published thirteen editions *Manual of Vertebrates* (1876–1929).

JORDAN, EDWIN OAKES (*b. Thomaston, Me., 1866; d. Lewiston, Me., 1936*), bacteriology.

Graduated Massachusetts Institute of Technology (1888); graduate study in zoology at Clark University under C. O. Whitman (Ph.D., 1892); taught bacteriology at University of Chicago forty-one years; joint editor, beginning 1904, of *Journal of Infectious Diseases* of John McCormick Institute for Infectious Diseases; editor of *Journal of Preventive Medicine* (1926–33); authority on waterborne diseases; wrote *Textbook of General Bacteriology* (1908); also wrote authoritative *Food Poisoning* (1917) and *Epidemic Influenza* (1927).

JORDANUS DE NEMORE (*fl. ca. 1220*), mechanics, mathematics.

Most important mechanician, and one of most significant mathematicians, of the Middle Ages; meaning of "de Nemore" unknown, though could signify "of Nemus" (an unknown place), or corruption of "de numero" from Jordanus' arithmetic works. Mechanics was his principal legacy, especially "science of weights" (statics); although twelve treatises are ascribed to Jordanus, only one is definitely his work, *Elementa Jordani super demonstrationem ponderum;* in this treatise he introduces component forces into statics with concept of "positional gravity" (the heaviness or force of a weight) which, although erroneous when applied to arcal constrained paths, led to brilliant results when applied to rectilinear constrained paths; introduced infinitesimal considerations into statics with principle of virtual displacement; gave important proof of law of lever by principle of work. *De ratione ponderis* is most significant medieval statical treatise; uses positional gravity and principle of work to formulate first proof of conditions of equilibrium of unequal weights on planes inclined at different angles; also used principle of work in first proof of bent lever, anticipating concept of static moment. Jordanus' approach to statics was innovative blend of current Aristotelian dynamics and abstract mathematical physics of Archimedes. Extensive commentary literature developed on Jordanus' work, much of which was printed in sixteenth century and influenced leading mechanicians, including Galileo.

Jordanus' role in mathematics not is yet evaluated; his *Liber Philotegni de triangulis* is medieval Latin geometry at highest level; *De numeris datis,* an algebraic treatise, was praised by Regiomontanus, and may have anticipated Viète in application of analysis to algebraic problems; *Arithmetica,* most widely known of his mathematical works, became a standard source of theoretical arithmetic in the Middle Ages; minor arithmetic treatises include *Demonstratio Jordani de algorismo,* which deals with Arabic number system, and an algorithm of fractions, called *Liber* or *Demonstratio de minutiis.*

JØRGENSEN, SOPHUS MADS (*b. Slagelse, Denmark, 1837; d. Copenhagen, Denmark, 1914*), chemistry.

Graduated University of Copenhagen in chemistry (M.S., 1863; Ph.D., 1869); taught at Copenhagen (1871–1908). Main studies in coordination compounds (1878–1906), which Jørgensen interpreted in own version of C. W. Blomstrand's chain theory; "Blomstrand-Jorgensen theory" was accepted for fifteen years before successfully challenged by Alfred Werner's radically new coordination theory.

JOULE, JAMES PRESCOTT (*b. Salford, near Manchester, England, 1818; d. Sale, England, 1889*), physics.

Member of a wealthy family; privately educated; never engaged in any profession; experiments performed in his own laboratory at his own expense. In his early creative period he developed the general law of energy conservation and established the dynamical nature of heat (1837–47); thirty years of skillful, but less important experiments (1847–78) followed. Began research on electromagnets under influence of William Sturgeon (1837); abandoned study of electromagnetic machines when he realized their efficiency was lower than that of existing steam engines, and turned to thermal effects of voltaic electricity (1841–43); derived quantitative law of heat production by a voltaic current (proportional to resistance and to square of intensity of current); by measuring heat produced by operating a dynamo enclosed in a container filled with water, obtained the first determination of coefficient of equivalence (1843); further experiments measured heat produced by various mechanical processes, e.g., friction of rotating paddle wheels in water (1847); his results stimulated William Thomson to form his own theory of thermodynamics; last contribution was precise determination of the equivalent (1878).

JUAN Y SANTACILLA, JORGE (*b. Novelda, Alicante, Spain, 1713; d. Madrid, Spain, 1773*), geodesy.

Educated in sciences while midshipman at Cádiz; one of Spanish representatives in Hispano-French commission which measured one degree of arc of a meridian near equator (1736–45); results confirmed Newton's theory of shape of earth (spheroid flattened at poles), which had been challenged by Cassini; founded astronomical observatory of Cádiz.

JUDAY, CHANCEY (*b. Millersburg, Ind., 1871; d. Madison, Wis., 1944*), limnology.

Graduated University of Indiana (B.A., 1896; M.A., 1897), where he studied with Carl Eigenmann; geologist

with Wisconsin Geological and Natural History Survey (1899–1930); taught at universities of California, Colorado, and Wisconsin; wrote numerous papers on Wisconsin lakes.

JUEL, SOPHUS CHRISTIAN (*b. Randers, Denmark, 1855; d. Copenhagen, Denmark, 1935*), mathematics.

Graduated University of Copenhagen (Ph.D., 1885); taught at Polytechnic Institute in Copenhagen (from 1894); editor of *Matematisk Tidsskrift* (1889–1915); made substantial contributions to projective geometry and to theory of curves and surfaces.

JUKES, JOSEPH BEETE (*b. Summerhill, near Birmingham, England, 1811; d. Dublin, Ireland, 1869*), geology, geomorphology.

Studied geology at Cambridge under Sedgwick (graduated 1836); worked for Geological Survey of Great Britain (1846–69); best known for study of river action in Ireland (1862), forcing Lyell and Darwin to modify their adherence to marine erosion theory.

JULIUS, WILLEM HENRI (*b. Zutphen, Netherlands, 1860; d. Utrecht, Netherlands, 1925*), solar physics.

Studied at University of Utrecht; taught physics University of Amsterdam (from 1890) and University of Utrecht (from 1896); studied various solar phenomena.

IBN JULJUL, SULAYMĀN IBN ḤASAN (*b. Córdoba, Spain, 944; d. ca. 994*), medicine, pharmacology.

Studied medicine with group of Hellenists in Córdoba; personal physician of Caliph Hishām II; "Generations of Physicians and Wise Men" is oldest and most complete extant summary in Arabic—excepting Isḥāq ibn Ḥunayn's work—on history of medicine; uses both Eastern and Western sources and contains fifty-seven biographies.

JUNCKER, JOHANN (*b. Londorf, Germany, 1679; d. Halle, Germany, 1759*), chemistry, medicine.

Received M.D. degree at Erfurt (1717); appointed to chair of medicine Royal Pedagogical Institute and Orphanage at Halle (1729), where he was influenced by colleagues Georg Stahl and Friedrich Hoffmann. Juncker's medical treatises developed and promoted Stahl's vitalism and censure of iatrochemical tradition; most important chemical text was *Conspectus chemiae theoretico-practicae* (1730), a systematic exposition of work of Becher and Stahl.

JUNG, CARL GUSTAV (*b. Kesswil, Switzerland, 1875; d. Küsnacht, Switzerland, 1961*), analytical psychology.

Graduated from the University of Basel in medicine; doctoral thesis, on parapsychological phenomena experienced by Jung in séances, delivered at faculty of medicine of University of Zurich (published 1902); after séance work and reading Krafft-Ebing, decided to become psychiatrist; with aid of Eugen Bleuler at Burghölzli Asylum performed association tests, developing a theory of complexes which used the repression theory of Freud, with whom he formed a close relationship (1907). Lectured at University of Zurich (1905–09); edited *Jahrbuch für psychoanalytische und psychopathologische Forschungen,* main psychoanalytic journal; first president International

Psychoanalytical Association; wrote *Wandlungen und Symbole der Libido* (1912), which applied psychoanalytic theory to myths and was criticized by psychoanalysts. Jung's attempt to resolve conflict by a theory of psychological types was unsuccessful; severed connections with psychoanalysis and formed his own school of analytical psychology (1914); developed concept of substratum of historical structures in the psyche in *The Psychology of Consciousness* (1913); personal dreams and visions of period 1914–17 became the basis of Jung's structural theory of conscious and unconscious systems; developed energy concept to account for dynamic relations of elements of psyche; methods were empirical and comparative; published paper stating that World War I was not the end of European psychological problems and that Germany would again threaten the world (1918); his ideas attracted attention of scholars world-wide, including Richard Wilhelm, Carl Kerényi, and Wolfgang Pauli. After World War II studied alchemy, gnosticism, Christianity, and developed theory of synchronicity (meaningfulness of random occurrences); named professor at Eidgenössische Technische Hochschule (1935); and at University of Basel (1943); a pioneer, with Freud and Adler, in early stages of dynamic psychology. His influence was also felt in religion, art, history, economics, and philosophy of science.

JUNGIUS, JOACHIM (*b. Lübeck, 1587; d. Hamburg, Germany, 1657*), natural science, mathematics, logic.

Studied at University of Rostock (1906–08); graduated University of Giessen (M.A., 1608), where he taught mathematics until 1614; M.D. at Padua (1619); practiced medicine various places, taught medicine University of Helmstedt, and taught mathematics at Rostock (1624–28), before being appointed professor of natural science Akademisches Gymnasium at Hamburg, which he held until death; wrote prolifically but published little; most of his manuscripts lost in fire. He applied mathematics in two ways: solved problems (one of first to use exponents to represent powers, made astronomical observations and calculations); and used mathematics as model for general theory of science and scientific method, as outlined in "Protonoeticae philosophiae sciagraphia" (1654). Made morphological studies in botany which were used by John Ray and communicated to the Royal Society (1663). Developed corpuscular theory of chemistry in two *Disputationes* (1642) and in *Doxoscopiae physicae minores* (1662).

JUSSIEU, ADRIEN HENRI LAURENT DE (*b. Paris, France, 1797; d. Paris, 1853*), botany.

Last in long line of botanists; son of Antoine-Laurent de Jussieu; thesis on Euphorbiaceae (1824); succeeded father as professor of botany at Muséum National d'Histoire Naturelle (1826). His *Botanique. Cours élémentaire d'histoire naturelle* went through twelve editions (1842–84).

JUSSIEU, ANTOINE DE (*b. Lyons, France, 1686; d. Paris, France, 1758*), botany, paleontology.

First in botanical dynasty including younger brothers Bernard and Joseph and nephew Antoine-Laurent; studied medicine, botany at Montpellier (M.D., 1707) under Pierre Magnol, first French botanist to attempt natural classification of plants; professor of botany Jardin du Roi (1710–58); made modest contributions to natural science; first to give scientific description of coffee plant (1715); main activities were development of Jardin du Roi and training of pupils; forerunner of *philosophes*, pioneer in colonial agriculture, and originator of botanical hypotheses ahead of their time.

JUSSIEU, ANTOINE-LAURENT DE (*b. Lyons, France, 1748; d. Paris, France, 1836*), botany.

Nephew of Antoine, Bernard, and Joseph de Jussieu; graduated University of Paris (doctorate, 1770), soon after becoming deputy to L. G. Le Monnier, professor of botany Jardin du Roi; his epoch-making *Genera plantarum* (1789) arranged genera in a natural system based on correlation of many characteristics; this system was accepted within a few decades by leading botanists, especially Robert Brown and A. P. de Candolle; became professor of botany (1793) and later director (1800) of Muséum National d'Histoire Naturelle (the reorganized Jardin du Roi).

JUSSIEU, BERNARD DE (*b. Lyons, France, 1699; d. Paris, France, 1777*), botany.

M.D. at Montpellier and another at Paris (1726); taught field courses and supervised gardens at Jardin du Roi (from 1722); greatest gift was teaching; though published little, influence was unequaled; most famous for arrangement of botanical garden of Trianon according to natural system of classification, as set forth in the *General plantarum* (1789) by his uncle Antoine-Laurent de Jussieu.

JUSSIEU, JOSEPH DE (*b. Lyons, France, 1704; d. Paris, France, 1779*), natural history.

Like brothers Antoine and Bernard, pursued career in medicine and interest in botany; accepted position as physician and naturalist on expedition to Peru to measure arc of meridian (1735–43); unable to return to France because of lack of money and ill health; spent next twenty-five years traveling about South America studying flora and fauna and practicing medicine; returned to France (1771); most papers left in Lima and later destroyed.

JUSTI, JOHANN HEINRICH GOTTLOB VON (*b. Brücken, Thuringia, Germany, 1720; d. Küstrin, Germany, 1771*), political economy, mining.

Studied law at University of Wittenberg; also studied in Jena and Leipzig (concluded in 1747); professor of cameralistics at Theresian Academy in Vienna (1751–54); held a number of civil service positions concerning finances and mining in Austria, Denmark, and Germany; main contributions in political science.

KABLUKOV, IVAN ALEXSEVICH (*b. Selo Prussi, Moskovskaya Guberniya, Russia, 1857; d. Tashkent, U.S.S.R., 1942*), chemistry.

Graduated from School of Physics, Mathematics, and Sciences of University of Moscow, where he studied under V. V. Markovnikov; taught at University of Moscow (beginning 1885); helped develop Russian physical chemistry; discovered effect of anomalous conductivity; helped develop theory of ionic hydration; formulated laws on reaction capacity of organic compounds.

KAEMPFER, ENGELBERT (*b. Lemgo, Germany, 1651; d. Lemgo, 1716*), geography, botany.

Studied at universities of Thorn (1674–76), Cracow (1676–80), and Königsberg (1680–81); secretary to ambassador sent by King Charles XI of Sweden to shah of Persia (1683); during journey through Persia studied language, geography, and flora; joined Dutch East India Company as physician and traveled to India, Java, and Nagasaki, where he studied Japanese history, geography, customs, and flora. Returned to Holland (1693), taking M.D. at University of Leiden; became court physician to Friedrich Adolf, count of Lippe (1694–1716). Only one book published on Kaempfer's journeys during lifetime, *Amoenitatum exoticarum* (1712); after his death, the manuscript on Japan was bought by Sir Hans Sloane, who had it translated and published as *History of Japan* (1727), which for more than a century was a chief source of Western knowledge of Japan.

KAESTNER, ABRAHAM GOTTHELF (*b. Leipzig, Germany, 1719; d. Göttingen, Germany, 1800*), mathematics.

Graduated University of Leipzig (1739), where he taught until 1756; professor of mathematics and physics University of Göttingen (1756–1800); made no important discoveries but was influential through teaching and writing; most popular work *Mathematische Anfangsgründe* (1757–1800); promoted interest in foundations of parallel theory.

KAGAN, BENJAMIN FEDOROVICH (*b. Shavli, Kovno [Kaunas] district [now Siauliai, Lithuanian S.S.R.], 1869; d. Moscow, U.S.S.R., 1953*), mathematics.

Received master's degree University of St. Petersburg (1895); taught at Novorossysky University (beginning 1897); and at Moscow University (from 1922); studied various problems in geometry; at Moscow created large scientific school in geometry; edited Lobachevsky's complete works (1946–51).

KAHLENBERG, LOUIS ALBRECHT (*b. Two Rivers, Wis., 1870; d. Sarasota, Fla., 1941*), chemistry.

Graduated University of Wisconsin (B.S., 1892; M.S., 1893); studied at University of Leipzig in Ostwald's laboratory (Ph.D., 1895); taught at University of Wisconsin until 1940, directing studies of twenty doctoral candidates; rigid opponent of Arrhenius' theory of ionization; formed pharmaceutical company with son Herman.

KAISER, FREDERIK (*b. Amsterdam, Netherlands, 1808; d. Leiden, Netherlands, 1872*), astronomy.

Graduated University of Leiden (1831), where he was awarded a doctoral degree *honoris causa* (1835) for most accurate prediction of Halley's comet's return (1835); best known for reorganization of Leiden observatory (became director 1837; new observatory inaugurated 1861–62), and for his work on fundamental coordinates of stars (published in *Annalen der Sternwarte in Leiden*).

KALBE, ULRICH RÜLEIN VON. See **Rülein, Ulrich.**

KALM, PEHR (*b. Ångermanland, Sweden, 1716; d. Turku, Finland, 1779*), natural history.

Studied at University of Åbo (1735); completed studies under Linnaeus at University of Uppsala; became professor University of Åbo (1747); made botanical expedition to North America and Canada (1748–51); made friends with Benjamin Franklin, John Bartram, and Cadwallader Colden; published material from diary of this trip in three volumes during lifetime; informative source on eighteenth-century American colonial life; Kalm was cited for ninety botanical species, sixty of them new, in *Species plantarum* of Linnaeus.

KALUZA, THEODOR FRANZ EDUARD (*b. Ratibor, Germany [now Raciborz, Poland], 1885; d. Göttingen, Germany, 1954*), mathematical physics.

Earned Ph.D. University of Königsberg, where he also taught (1909–29); taught at University of Kiel (1929–35) and at University of Göttingen (1935–54); attempted to explain electromagnetic effects by postulating five-dimensional manifold, as Einstein had explained gravitational effects in terms of four-dimensional Riemannian manifold (Einstein encouraged Kaluza's work); worked on models of atomic nucleus; wrote on epistemological aspects of relativity.

KAMĀL AL-DĪN ABU'L ḤASAN MUḤAMMAD IBN AL-ḤASAN AL-FĀRISĪ (*d. Tabriz [?], Iran, 1320*), optics, mathematics.

Disciple of Quṭb al-Dīn al-Shīrāzī, mathematician, astronomer, and commentator on Ibn Sīnā; though he wrote on mathematics, his essential contribution was in optics; at suggestion of al-Shīrāzī, wrote commentary on "Book of Optics" of Ibn al-Haytham, but chose to extend commentary to many other works on optics of al-Haytham; more of a revision than a commentary in the medieval sense, for Kamāl al-Dīn refutes, extends, and in some cases replaces al-Haytham's theories with his own ideas, e.g. his theory of the rainbow. Kamāl al-Dīn's work on the rainbow can be considered an extension of reforms initiated by al-Haytham, who introduced mathematical and experimental norms into problems where light and vision are united; while al-Haytham advocated direct experimental study of optical effects to verify geometrical hypotheses, this was impractical for complex phenomena like rainbows; Kamāl al-Dīn's innovation was abandoning direct study and substituting study of a more manageable analogue or model; on basis of Ibn Sīnā's conception of rainbow as reflection of light from water droplets in sky, Kamāl al-Dīn developed analogy between drop of water and glass sphere filled with water; used glass sphere in experimental procedure (independently rediscovered by Descartes) to verify geometrical hypotheses.

KAMALĀKARA (*b. Benares, India, ca. 1610*), astronomy.

A scion of family of astronomers; leading rival of Munīśvara Viśvarūpa among Benares astronomers; combined Indian astronomy with Aristotelian physics and Ptolemaic astronomy as presented by Islamic scientists; wrote commentary (in family tradition) on works of Gaṇeśa; most important work is *Siddhāntatattvaviveka* (1658).

KAMERLINGH ONNES, HEIKE (*b. Groningen, Netherlands, 1853; d. Leiden, Netherlands, 1926*), physics.

Graduated from University of Groningen (Ph.D., 1879); studied with Bunsen and Kirchhoff at Heidelberg (1871–1873); taught at Polytechnic School at Delft

(1880–82), during which time he was in close contact with van der Waals in Amsterdam; appointed professor of experimental physics (first in Netherlands) at Leiden (1882–1924). Main research goal was to give experimental support to van der Waals's corpuscular theory of gases at low temperatures; liquefied hydrogen (1906) and helium (1908) for first time; also studied resistance of metals at low temperatures, discovering superconductivity (1911); for research on properties of matter at low temperatures, Kamerlingh Onnes won Nobel Prize (1913).

KANAKA (*b. India; fl. Baghdad* [*?*], *ca. 775–820*), astronomy.

Indian astrologer who practiced his art in Baghdad during reign of al-Rashīd (late eighth–early ninth centuries), but whose works in Arabic fall within Abbasid traditions of astrology (derived from Greek and Iranian sources) and at least in existing fragments display no specifically Indian traits.

KANE, ROBERT JOHN (*b. Dublin, Ireland, 1809; d. Dublin, 1890*), chemistry.

Graduated Trinity College, Dublin (B.A., 1835); published *Elements of Practical Pharmacy,* founded *Dublin Journal of Medical and Chemical Science;* taught natural philosophy at the Royal Dublin Society (1834–47); studied three months at Liebig's laboratory at Giessen (1836); editor of *Philosophical Magazine* (1840–90); wrote *Elements of Chemistry* (1840–41); appointed director Museum of Economic Geology in Dublin (1845); became president Queen's College, Cork (1845); knighted (1846); fellow of Royal Society (1849).

KANT, IMMANUEL (*b. Königsberg, Germany* [*now Kaliningrad, R.S.F.S.R.*] *1724; d. Königsberg, 1804*), philosophy of science.

Kant received his doctorate in philosophy at Königsberg in 1755, lectured there as *Privatdozent* for fifteen years, and held the chair of logic and metaphysics from 1770 until 1797. He is considered to be one of the greatest philosophers produced by Western civilization, but he was also much interested in science and especially in the philosophy of science. He was not an experimental scientist and did not contribute to the body of scientific knowledge, but was much concerned with the foundations of science. This is to say that he was not interested in gleaning facts and data but that he speculated concerning the grand scheme in which the facts gleaned by others are arrayed. The two main influences on Kant in his speculations were Leibniz and Newton, and especially the opposition between the two regarding the nature of space and time. For Kant space and time are based epistemologically on the nature of the mind rather than ontologically on the nature of things, either as a relation among monads (Leibniz) or as a thing (Newton's absolute space). He held in the *Critique of Pure Reason* (1781) that both are passive forms of sensuous intuition by means of which a manifold of sensa are presented to the understanding, which has the active function of synthesizing this manifold. Space is the form of all appearances of the external senses, just as time is the form of all appearances of the internal sense. As such, space and time are nothing but properties of the human mind. Everything in our knowledge belonging to spatial intuition contains nothing but relations: locations in an intuition (extension), change of location (motion), and the laws of moving forces according to which change of location is determined. The representations of the external senses are set in time, which contains nothing but relations of succession, coexistence, and duration.

Material objects are the things which are located in an intuition and which change location by moving. As in the case of space and time, so here Kant's mature theory of matter as put forth in the "Dynamics" of the *Metaphysical Foundations of Natural Science* (1786) developed as an opposition to the atomic view held by Newton and the monadist view held by Leibniz. But he was more like Leibniz and less like Newton in that for matter he put the emphasis on force rather than on atomic particles of impenetrable mass. For him motive forces were the fundamental attributes of matter. Only two kinds of moving forces are possible: repulsive and attractive. If two bodies (regarded as mathematical points) are being considered, then any motion which the one body can impress on the other must be imparted in the straight line joining the two points. They either recede from one another or approach one another; there are no other possibilities. Since forces are what cause bodies to move, the only kinds of forces are therefore repulsive and attractive. When one body tries to enter the space occupied by another body, the latter resists the intrusion and the former is moved in the opposite direction. The repulsive (or expansive) force exerted here is also called elastic. All matter is originally elastic, infinitely compressible but impenetrable—one body cannot compress another to the extent that the first occupies all the space of the second. He called such elasticity "relative impenetrability" and contrasted it with the absolute impenetrability posited by atomism. Unless there were another force acting in an opposite direction to repulsion, that is, acting for approach, matter would disperse itself to infinity. By means of universal attraction all matter acts directly on all other matter and so acts at all distances. This force is usually called gravitation, and the endeavor of a body to move in the direction of the greater gravitation is called its weight. If matter possessed only gravitational force, it would all coalesce in a point. The very possibility of matter as an entity filling space in a determinate degree depends on a balance between repulsion and attraction. Kant appealed to these forces to account for the specific varieties of matter. Attraction depends on the mass of the matter in a given space and is constant. Repulsion depends on the degree to which the given space is filled; this degree can vary widely. For example, the attraction of a given quantity of air in a given volume depends on its mass and is constant, while its elasticity is directly proportional to its temperature and varies accordingly. This means that repulsion can, with regard to one and the same attractive force, be originally different in degree in different matters. Consequently, a spectrum of different kinds of matter each having the same mass (and therefore having the same attraction) can vary widely in repulsion—running, for instance, from the density of osmium to the rarity of the ether. Hence matter is a continuous quantity involving a proportion between the two fundamental forces of attraction and repulsion.

Heretofore motion has been mentioned several times, but it has not been examined up till now in any detail. In contrast to Newton, Kant claimed in the "Phenomenology" of the *Metaphysical Foundations of Natural Science* that all motion is relative. He established this by considering three principal cases. For rectilinear motion, change of place may be attributed either to the matter (that is, space at rest and matter moving with respect to it) or to the space (that is, matter at rest and space moving with respect to it). In the case of rotatory motion (for example, the earth turning on its axis), the change of place must be attributed to the matter. In the case of colliding bodies, both the matter and the (relative) space must necessarily be represented as moved at the same time. Motion is relative in all three cases by reference to absolute space: in the first case by reference to absolute space *outside of* the body, in the second to absolute space *inside of* the body, and in the third to absolute space *between* two bodies.

All the occurrences in the inanimate world can be explained in terms of the motion of matter in space and enduring through time, but for living things Kant thought that such efficient causes are not enough—they must be explained in terms of an end and hence require final causes in addition to efficient ones. A machine has only motive power, while an organized being possesses inherent formative power, which is imparted to rare materials devoid of form. But he insisted that final causes are merely regulative concepts which human beings use for the comprehension of biological organisms, which are dealt with by means of an analogy with artifacts (it is as though a tree or any other living thing organized itself in a way not unlike that in which an artisan forms his product). Finality is read into the facts, and teleological principles are nothing but heuristic maxims whose justification resides in their fruitfulness for providing systematic comprehension of living organisms, as he carefully points out in the *Critique of Teleological Judgment* (1790). For example, the processes of digestion are not understood by any appeal to the principle that such processes enable the organism to live and thrive; rather, such processes are understood by accounting for the passage of chemical substances through membranes, but why such membranes permit the passage only of certain chemical substances and no others may not be able to be accounted for on the basis of mechanical causes alone.

He worked out his theory of efficient causation in the Second Analogy of Experience on the "Transcendental Analytic" of the *Critique of Pure Reason* largely in opposition to Hume's position on the subject. Hume held that the idea of necessary connection between cause and effect arises when we develop a habit of association from a repeated subjective succession of perceptions (fire always burns). Kant questioned this. For example, one walks into a warm room and sees a glowing stove. As far as the *subjective order* of the perceptions is concerned, one first feels warm and only later sees the stove concealed behind a screen in the corner. But one says that the stove causes the room to be warm and not that the warm room causes the stove to glow. In order to have knowledge one must put the perceptions in an *objective order,* that is, one must connect them in their objective time relations. There is no necessity in the subjective order of perceptions, but there certainly is in one's synthetic reorganization of that order. Kant claimed that the objective reordering of the subjective succession of sense awareness

(which is based on sense perception and imagination) is actually a synthetic reorganization of the a posteriori order of perception. This synthetic reorganization is an a priori act of the human understanding. In other words, the causal ordering of cognitions is an act of the intellect that is brought to experience (or, even better, that makes experience) and is not an ordering derived from experience (as Hume claimed). Time, space, matter, force, motion, cause—the major portions of Kant's philosophy of nature—have now been examined in terms of these most fundamental concepts of natural science.

Kant's emphasis on causality in conformity with law and on mathematical rigor in conformity with experience contributed important elements to the philosophical depth and seriousness that animated the German scientific movement from the middle of the nineteenth century onwards and that distinguished it from the scientific traditions of other cultures. In particular, Helmholtz and Schwann were greatly influenced by Kant; and they in turn influenced the first great generation of German science that includes Miller, Schleiden, Mayer, du Bois-Reymond, and Virchow. In the twentieth century Kant's thought has not had the direct influence on experimental scientists that it had on Helmholtz and Schwann, but in the philosophy of science Ernst Cassirer gave a Kantian interpretation of the metaphysical and epistemological foundations of relativity theory, and C. F. von Weizsäcker gave a Kantian interpretation of quantum theory.

KAPTEYN, JACOBUS CORNELIUS (*b. Barneveld, Netherlands, 1851; d. Amsterdam, Netherlands, 1922*), astronomy.

Received Ph.D. University of Utrecht; observer at Leiden observatory (1875–78); professor of astronomy and theoretical mechanics University of Groningen (1878–1921). Major contributions were in stellar astronomy, particularly space distribution and motions of stars, in which Kapteyn's work was the first major step after works of William and John Herschel; influenced astronomy not only by his analyses but by establishing continuing observational projects. First major achievement was compilation, with David Gill, of *Cape Photographic Durchmusterung* (published 1896–1900), a catalogue of stars in the southern hemisphere. To process photographic plates made by Gill at Cape Town observatory, Kapteyn started an "astronomical laboratory" which soon became world famous. Regarding structure of the stellar system, he tried to solve two unknowns: space density of stars as function of distance from sun, and distribution of stars according to brightness per unit volume; final solutions published by Kapteyn and van Rhijn in *Contributions from the Mount Wilson Solar Observatory* (1920). Some results of lasting value, though some superseded because they failed to account for interstellar absorption. In studies using proper motion to determine stellar distances, he discovered stellar motions are not random, as previously supposed, but that stars move in two "star streams" (announced in 1904). Devised international plan for determining stellar magnitudes, proper motion, parallax, spectral type, and radial velocity (1906); work on Kapteyn's "plan of selected areas" continues today. Presented dynamical theory of stellar system in "First Attempt at a Theory of the Arrangement and Motion of the Sidereal System" (1922); attempted to explain density distribution and motions in terms of gravitational forces, assuming system in equilibrium and spheroidal (spheroidal system has not been upheld). Made essential contributions in other fields: improved upon measurement of parallaxes and stellar magnitudes; improved system of declinations. Introduced many standard concepts in astronomy, such as absolute magnitude and color index.

AL-KARAJĪ (or AL-KARKHĪ), ABŪ BAKR IBN MU-ḤAMMAD IBN AL ḤUSAYN (or AL-ḤASAN) (*fl. Baghdad, end of tenth century/beginning of eleventh*), mathematics.

His work is important in the history of mathematics because it presents the only theory of algebraic calculus among Arabs; he established a new beginning of algebra by means of systematic application of operations of arithmetic to the interval, made possible by familiarity with algebra of al-Khwārizmī and reading of arithmetical work of Diophantus; new approach extended by al-Karajī's successors, notably al-Samawʾal; may have influenced Leonardo Fibonacci and Levi ben Gerson. His *al-Fakhrī* presented the first account of algebra of polynomials; attempted to apply arithmetical operations to irrational terms and expressions. For al-Karajī, the aim of algebra is to show how unknown quantities are determined by known quantities through the transformation of the given equations. Two preoccupations evident in solutions: to find methods of ever greater generality and to increase number of cases in which conditions of solution should be examined.

KÁRMÁN, THEODORE VON (*b. Budapest, Hungary, 1881; d. Aachen, Germany, 1963*), aerodynamics.

Graduated from Technical University of Budapest, where he taught three years; studied three years under Ludwig Prandtl, the "father of aerodynamics," at Göttingen, where he taught three years. Collaborated with Max Born in an attempt to explain temperature dependence of specific heat; also discovered Kármán vortices. Taught at Technische Hochschule in Aachen until 1929, where he worked on aviation, especially after working on planes during World War I; developed new law of turbulence. Became director Guggenheim Aeronautical Laboratory at California Institute of Technology in Pasadena (1929); put teaching of aeronautical engineering on scientific basis and trained many graduate students; helped develop Caltech's Jet Propulsion Laboratory. Kármán and students laid foundations for aerodynamic design leading to supersonic flight; proposed organization of NATO-related Advisory Group for Aeronautical Research and Development, which led to founding of international aerodynamics school later known as Von Kármán Center.

KARPINSKI, LOUIS CHARLES (*b. Rochester, N.Y., 1878; d. Winter Haven, Fla., 1956*), history of mathematics, cartography.

Received A.B. Cornell University (1901); received doctorate of natural philosophy from Kaiser Wilhelm American College of University of Strasbourg (1903); taught mathematics University of Michigan (1904–48); became interested history of science (1909); with David E. Smith wrote the still authoritative *The Hindu-Arabic Numerals* (1911); photographed and collected historic maps and atlases; elected president History of Science Society (1943).

KARPINSKY, ALEXANDR PETROVICH (*b. Bogoslovsk [now Karpinsk], Russia, 1847; d. Moscow, U.S.S.R., 1936*), geology.

Graduated Mining Corps (later Mining Institute) in St. Petersburg (1866; defended dissertation, 1869); taught at Mining Institute (1868–96); president Soviet Academy of Sciences (1917–36). First works were in petrography, especially on Urals; one of first to use microscope for research on metamorphic rock; also interested in methods of petrographic research; opposed classification of rock by chemical composition alone, considering mineralogical composition more important. Near end of century, geological-paleontological interests prevailed; in three works (1887, 1893, 1894), generalized material on Russian geology accumulated by end of nineteenth century; Karpinsky's description of the development of the Russian platform was later confirmed by Soviet geologists. He made important contributions to tectonics (1887, 1894); believed tectonic movements all due to contraction of earth's crust (contraction hypothesis); in second edition of his works (1919), Karpinsky expanded tectonic and paleogeographical conclusions with additional data; tectonic works important not only as synthesis but as methodology for research on the platform. Made major contributions to paleontology concerning ammonoids (for which he received Cuvier Prize of French Academy), fossil sharks of Edestidae family, and study of Devonian algae, the charophytes. Was a Darwinist. Works in stratigraphy related to other research; classification of sedimentary formations accepted at Second International Geological Congress (1881). Geological research always had practical cast; many works devoted to study of deposits and theoretical questions of ore formation, influencing development of Russian industry.

KARRER, PAUL (*b. Moscow, Russia, 1889; d. Zurich, Switzerland, 1971*), chemistry.

Entered University of Zurich (1908), studying chemistry with Alfred Werner; went to Frankfurt to work with Ehrlich (1912); taught at University of Zurich (1918–71). Versatile organic chemist; his *Lehrbuch der organischen Chemie* (1928) went through fourteen editions. During 1920's began lifelong study of natural products, especially plant pigments and vitamins; shared Nobel Prize for chemistry for his "researches into the constitution of the carotenoids, flavonoids, and vitamins A and B" (1937).

KARSTEN, KARL JOHANN BERNHARD (*b. Bützow, Germany, 1782; d. Berlin, Germany, 1853*), metallurgy, mining.

Studied sciences and law at University of Rostock (1799–1800); did editing work in Berlin while continuing studies (from 1801), eventually obtaining doctoral degree. Served in Prussian government as mining administrator (1804–50); as privy councilor (appointed 1821), administered entire metallurgical and salt-mining industry in Prussia for thirty years. With publication of *System der Metallurgie* (1831), Karsten achieved fame as a founder of scientific metallurgy.

378

AL-KĀSHĪ (or AL-KĀSHĀNĪ), GHIYĀTH AL-DĪN JAMSHĪD MASᶜŪD (*b. Kāshān, Iran; d. Samarkand [now in Uzbek, U.S.S.R.], 1429*), astronomy, mathematics.

Although a physician, his main interest was in mathematics and astronomy; after a long period of penury and wandering, he finally obtained a secure position at Samarkand under Sultan Ulugh Beg, himself a great scientist. Al-Kāshī occupied the most prominent place on the scientific staff of *madrasa*—school of theology and science founded by Ulugh Beg in 1417–20; until the assassination of Ulugh Beg in 1449, Samarkand was the most important scientific center in the East; al-Kāshī helped organize the observatory and was close collaborator on Ulugh Beg's *Zīj.* Best-known work is *Miftāḥ al-ḥisāb* ("The Key of Arithmetic," 1427), an encyclopedia of elementary mathematics which served as a manual for hundreds of years; describes method of extracting roots of integers and gives first methodical treatment of decimal fractions (possibly influenced propagation of decimal fractions in Europe). Greatest mathematical achievements are *Risāla al-muḥīṭiyya* ("The Treatise on the Circumference," 1424) and *Risᵊla al-watar waʾl-jaib* ("The Treatise on the Chord and Sine"); in the former work, he determines value of 2π to sixteen decimal places. In latter work, he calculates value of sine of 1° to ten correct sexagesimal places. His method of numerical solution of the trisection equation is one of the best achievements in medieval algebra.

Only three astronomical works of al-Kāshī have been studied: his *Khāqānī Zīj* was revision of *Īlkhānī Zīj* of Naṣīr al-Dīn al-Ṭūsī; his *Risāla dar sharḥ-i ālāt-i raṣd* ("Treatise on the Explanation of Observational Instruments") describes construction of eight astronomical instruments; in *Nuzha al-hadāiq* al-Kāshī describes two instruments he had invented, a planetary equatorium and a device for performing a linear interpolation.

KATER, HENRY (*b. Bristol, England, 1777; d. London, England, 1835*), geodesy.

After serving in British army as surveyor, briefly educated at Royal Military College at Sandhurst; prominent in Royal Engineers. Most significant contributions were improvements in geodetic instruments, refinements of geodetic measurements, and standardization of weights and measures; devised reversible pendulum ("Kater's Pendulum").

IBN KAṬĪR AL-FARGHĀNĪ. *See* **al-Farghānī.**

KAUFMANN, NIKLAUS. *See* **Mercator, Nicolaus.**

KAUFMANN, WALTER (or **Walther**) (*b. Elberfeld [Wuppertal], Germany, 1871; d. Freiburg, Germany, 1947*), physics.

Studied at Berlin and Munich (Ph.D. Munich, 1894); became associate professor at Bonn (1903); professor and director of Physics Institute of Königsberg (1908–35). Major work was attempt to measure and characterize "apparent" (electromagnetic) mass of electrons; determined that apparent mass was about three times larger than real mass (1901); produced evidence that mass of electrons was entirely electromagnetic and varies with velocity (1902), thus contradicting Newtonian principle that mass was invariant with velocity. While at Bonn per-

formed experiments indicating Lorentz-Einstein theory of contraction of electrons was in error and supporting Bucherer's and Abraham's theories (1906); significance of Kaufmann's measurements challenged by Max Planck (1906) and Einstein (1907); Bucherer published more accurate data supporting Lorentz-Einstein viewpoint (1908).

KAVRAYSKY, VLADIMIR VLADIMIROVICH (*b. Zherebyatnikovo, Simbirsk province [now Ulyanovsk oblast], Russia, 1884; d. Leningrad, U.S.S.R., 1954*), astronomy, geodesy, cartography.

Studied mathematics at University of Moscow (1903–05); graduated Kharkov University (1916); long career in naval service (1916–49); astronomer at observatory of Main Hydrographical Administration (1918–26); astronomer at Pulkovo observatory (1926–30); member Leningrad Institute of Geodesy and Cartography (1930–38). All of Kavraysky's works were devoted to problems of navigation; improved known methods of solving practical problems of astronomy, geodesy, and mathematical cartography.

KAY, GEORGE FREDERICK (*b. Virginia, Ontario, 1873; d. Iowa City, Iowa, 1943*), geology.

Degrees at University of Toronto (B.A., 1900; M.S., 1901) and University of Chicago (Ph.D., 1914) under Joseph Iddings; professor of geology, University of Iowa (1907–43). With J. S. Diller mapped nickel, copper, and gold deposits in Oregon (before 1910); studied Pleistocene geology of Iowa.

KAYSER, HEINRICH JOHANNES GUSTAV (*b. Bingen, Germany, 1853; d. Bonn, Germany, 1940*), physics.

Studied in Strasbourg, Munich, and Berlin with Kundt, Helmholtz, and Kirchhoff (1873–79; Ph.D., 1879); with Heinrich Hertz became assistant to Helmholtz at Berlin Physical Institute (1878–85); taught physics at Hannover Technical University (1885–94); succeeded Hertz as professor of physics, University of Bonn (1894). With Carl Runge at Hannover made important investigations in spectroscopy; determined exact frequencies of many spectral lines and showed that many elements have regular spectral structure; this work (and that of Rydberg) was indispensable to Rutherford and Bohr's atomic theory twenty-five years later. Wrote eight-volume *Handbuch der Spektroskopie* (1900–32); also studied spectra of comets and stars.

KECKERMANN, BARTHOLOMEW (*b. Danzig [now Gdansk], Poland, 1571/73; d. Danzig, 1609*), astronomy, mathematics, methodology.

Studied at Wittenberg, Leipzig, and Heidelberg (M.A. at Heidelberg, 1595; doctor of divinity, 1602); professor of philosophy at Danzig Gymnasium (1602–09). At Danzig he attempted reform of curriculum according to views of Petrus Ramus and Jacopo Zabarella (a progressive Aristotelian). In *Praecognita* he gave the first theoretical discussions of systems (the set of precepts characterizing each science); Keckermann's systematic method was reflected in *Systema physicum* (1610), which discussed physics, astronomy, and natural philosophy in Aristotelian terms, and contains serious errors and gaps. *Systema compendiosum totius mathematices* (1617) consists of lectures on geometry, optics, astronomy, and geography.

KEELER, JAMES EDWARD (*b. La Salle, Ill., 1857; d. San Francisco, Calif., 1900*), astronomy.

Graduated Johns Hopkins University (B.A., 1881); became assistant to Samuel P. Langley, director of Allegheny Observatory (1881); studied at Heidelberg under G. H. Quincke and at Berlin under Helmholtz (1883); became astronomer at new Lick Observatory (1888), where he measured wavelengths of bright lines in nebular spectra (1890). Appointed successor to Langley as director of Allegheny Observatory (1891); designed spectrograph and with it proved James Clerk Maxwell's prediction that rings of Saturn are meteoritic in nature (1895). Became director of Lick Observatory (1898); with thirty-six-inch Crossley reflecting telescope took photographs that established the abundance of spirals among the nebulae (later identified as exterior galaxies).

KEESOM, WILLEM HENDRIK (*b. Texel, Netherlands, 1876; d. Oegstgeest, Netherlands, 1956*), physics.

Studied physics under J. D. van der Waals at Amsterdam University (Ph.D., 1904); became close collaborator of Kamerlingh Onnes at University of Leiden, assisting him in liquefaction of helium (1908); appointed to chair in experimental physics at Leiden (1923). As director of Kamerlingh Onnes laboratory, continued tradition of low-temperature research, especially on helium.

KEILIN, DAVID (*b. Moscow, Russia, 1887; d. Cambridge, England, 1963*), biochemistry, parasitology.

Studied at University of Liège and University of Paris (Ph.D., 1917); influenced by Maurice Caullery, the distinguished parasitologist; became research assistant at Quick laboratory, University of Cambridge (1915), which became part of Molteno Institute (1921); became professor of biology and director of Molteno Institute (1931–52). In parasitology, Keilin became known for work on the life cycle of parasitic and free-living Diptera; editor of *Parasitology* (1934–63). Began studies in biochemistry with discovery of cytochrome (1924), an intracellular respiratory pigment. Also studied comparative biochemistry of hemoglobin and problem of anabiosis. Exerted profound influence on development of science at Cambridge.

KEILL, JAMES (*b. Edinburgh, Scotland, 1673; d. Northampton, England, 1719*), physiology, anatomy.

Younger brother of John Keill, the distinguished Newtonian mathematician; studied at Edinburgh, Paris, and Leiden; M.D. degree from Aberdeen was probably bought (1699); subsequent life combined research with practice in Northampton. Keill's anatomical texts provided sound basic knowledge to generations of students; his physiology showed iatromechanical bias and utilized Newtonian-inspired theories of attraction developed by his brother, and was a rational attempt at quantification.

KEILL, JOHN (*b. Edinburgh, Scotland, 1671; d. Oxford, England, 1721*), physics, mathematics.

Received M.A. at University of Edinburgh, where he studied under David Gregory, first to teach on basis of Newtonian philosophy; became Savilian professor of as-

tronomy at Oxford (1712–21). Keill was an important disciple of Newton's who propagated his philosophy and influenced its development; his *An Examination of Dr. Burnet's Theory of the Earth* (1698) offers Newtonian views as antidote to "world-making" of Cartesian philosophy; Newton's acceptance of Keill's criticism was incorporated in 1706 in the famous 31st Query of the *Opticks*. Keill's *Introductio ad veram physicam . . .* (1701) was the first series of experimental lectures on Newtonian natural philosophy ever given and influenced later publications; Keill's charge that Leibniz plagiarized from Newton's invention of calculus brought hostile attacks from the Continent.

KEIR, JAMES (*b. Edinburgh, Scotland, 1735; d. West Bromwich, England, 1820*), chemistry.

Studied medicine at University of Edinburgh, where he befriended Erasmus Darwin, who later brought Keir into the Lunar Society of Birmingham. Managed glass factory at Stourbridge (1771–78) and co-founder of Tipton Chemical Works (1780), which manufactured alkalies; prepared chemical dictionary; developed the first commercially successful process for making synthetic alkali.

KEITH, ARTHUR (*b. Persley, Aberdeen, Scotland, 1866; d. Downe, Kent, England, 1955*), anatomy, anthropology.

Graduated University of Aberdeen (M.D., 1894); became fellow of Royal College of Surgeons of England (1894); worked under Wilhelm His at Leipzig (1895); head of London Hospital anatomy department (1899–1908); wrote and edited books on anatomy. Became conservator at Royal College of Surgeons Museum (1908), where interests turned to anthropology; published numerous books on early man, and several popular works; became master of research institute at Downe, founded by Royal College of Surgeons at Keith's urging, where he continued anthropological studies (1933–55).

KEKULE VON STRADONITZ (KEKULÉ), (FRIEDRICH) AUGUST (*b. Darmstadt, Germany, 1829; d. Bonn, Germany, 1896*), chemistry.

Began chemistry studies at University of Giessen (1849), where he assisted in Liebig's laboratory; studied in Paris (1851) where he became familiar with Gerhardt's unitary theory of chemistry; Ph.D. Giessen (1852); as assistant at St. Bartholomew's Hospital in London (1853–55) befriended A. W. Williamson, who influenced Kekulé's theories and instigated his study of reaction of phosphorus pentasulfide on acetic acid, Kekulé's first mature work (1854). Taught organic chemistry at University of Heidelberg (1856–1858); worked out theory of tetravalence of carbon and carbon's ability to link in chains and form polyvalent radicals (1857–58), thus laying foundation of structural chemistry. Taught at University of Ghent (1858–67), where Adolf von Baeyer became his research assistant; organized first International Congress of Chemists (1860). He was concerned with chemical structure of organic acids, and in a new laboratory built for him, Kekulé studied unsaturated dibasic acids, publishing theory of unsaturates in 1862. The solution for ring structure of benzene came in a vision of a snake biting its tail (1863). Much of subsequent work devoted to experimental confirmation of benzene theory, not publicly announced until 1865; also studied azo and diazo derivatives of aromatic substances (beginning

1865). Kekulé's discovery that sulfonic derivatives of benzene fuse with potash to create phenols became important in industrial production of phenols. Appointed professor and director of new chemical institute at University of Bonn (1867); resumed study of sulfonic derivatives of phenol and nitrophenol, extended investigations of aromatic compounds, and revived attempt to find experimental evidence for benzene theory; in attempting to prove superiority of benzene theory over theories of A. Claus, H. Wichelhaus, and A. Ladenburg, Kekulé created the complementary "oscillation theory" (1872); with Franchimont synthesized triphenylmethane, which proved crucial to development of synthetic dyes and resulted in rapid growth of German aniline dye industry (1872); Kekulé's further experiments on benzene theory confirmed the superiority of his formula. Many of Kekulé's results were described in fascicles of his *Lehrbuch der organischen Chemie* (1859–87).

KELLNER, DAVID (*b. Gotha, Germany, mid-seventeenth century; d.* [?]), medicine, chemistry.

Studied medicine in Helmstedt (M.D., 1670); wrote two surgical dissertations and a reference work on bone injuries, *Schenkeldiener* (1690); practiced medicine in Nordhausen; most scientific writings in metallurgical chemistry, which Kellner wished to free from fantasies of alchemists; wrote comedy excoriating alchemy (1700).

KELLOGG, ALBERT (*b. New Hartford, Conn., 1813, d. Alameda, Calif., 1887*), botany.

M.D. at Transylvania College, Lexington, Kentucky; moved to San Francisco (1849), where he helped found California Academy of Sciences (1853); first resident botanist of California; his *Forest Trees of California* (1882) was state's first dendrological report.

KELLOGG, VERNON LYMAN (*b. Emporia, Kan., 1867; d. Hartford, Conn., 1937*), entomology, zoology.

Graduated University of Kansas (B.A., 1889; M.A., 1892); taught entomology at Stanford University (1894–1920); work on silkworms (1908) was pioneer study in genetics; did extensive studies of *Mallophaga;* wrote numerous books on evolution; became permanent secretary National Research Council (1920).

KELSER, RAYMOND ALEXANDER (*b. Washington, D.C., 1892; d. Philadelphia, Pa., 1952*), veterinary medicine, microbiology.

D.V.M. degree George Washington University (1914); joined Veterinary Corps of U.S. Army (1918–46); improved test for detecting botulinus toxin; Ph.D., American University (1923); while serving in Philippines (1925–28) developed vaccine for cattle plague; determined mechanism of transmission of virus of equine encephalomyelitis (1928–33); professor of bacteriology at University of Pennsylvania (1946–52).

KELVIN. *See* **Thomson, William.**

KENDALL, EDWARD CALVIN (*b. South Norwalk, Conn., 1886; d. Princeton, N.J., 1972*), endocrinology, biochemistry.

Graduated Columbia University (B.S., 1908; M.S., 1908; Ph.D., 1910); did research and taught physiological chemistry at new laboratories of Mayo Clinic, Rochester, Minnesota (1914–51); first to isolate crystalline thyroxine (1914), though C.R. Harington in England was the first to work out the structure (1926); began search for hormones of adrenal cortex (1930); with Philip S. Hench discovered that cortisone alleviated effects of rheumatoid arthritis (1949), for which they and T. Reichstein were awarded Nobel Prize in physiology or medicine (1950); became research professor Princeton University (1951–72), where he continued work on adrenal extracts.

KENNEDY, ALEXANDER BLACKIE WILLIAM (*b. Stepney, London, England, 1847; d. London, 1928*), kinematics of mechanisms, testing of materials and machines.

Served as apprentice, draftsman, and consultant in construction and design of marine steam engines. As a young man he made significant contributions to kinematics of mechanisms and to laboratory testing of machines as part of engineering training; professor of engineering at University College, London (1874–89); from 1889 was consulting electrical engineer on electrical power systems.

KENNELLY, ARTHUR EDWIN (*b. Colaba, near Bombay, India, 1861; d. Boston, Mass., 1939*), electrical engineering.

Primarily self-educated in engineering; immigrated to United States (1887) and became assistant to Thomas Edison; professor of engineering at Harvard University (1902–30); also taught at Massachusetts Institute of Technology (1913–24); made contributions in theory and practice of electrical engineering, evolution of electrical units and standards, and in study of ionosphere (once called the Kennelly-Heaviside layer).

KEPLER, JOHANNES (*b. Weil der Stadt, Germany, 1571; d. Regensburg, Germany, 1630*), astronomy, physics.

Although Kepler is remembered today chiefly for his three laws of planetary motion, these were but three elements in his much broader search for cosmic harmonies and a celestial physics. An enthusiatic Copernican, Kepler found an astronomy whose clumsy geocentric or heliostatic planetary mechanisms typically erred by several degrees and he left it with a unified and physically motivated heliocentric system nearly 100 times more accurate.

Kepler was the son of Heinrich, a mercenary soldier who abandoned his family in 1588, and of Katharina Guldenmann. Kepler first attended school in Leonberg, where his family moved in 1576. At 13 he entered a regional preparatory school. In 1587 he matriculated at the University of Tübingen, but he did not take up actual residence there until 1589. In 1591 Kepler received his master's degree and thereupon entered the theological course. Halfway through his last year, however, he was sent to teach in the high school at Graz in southern Austria.

In April, 1594, Kepler became a teacher and provincial mathematician. Soon after his arrival, Kepler's fertile imagination hit upon what he believed to be the secret key to the universe. He was already a devoted Copernican, having learned of the heliocentric cosmology from the cautious Michael Maestlin at Tübingen. Kepler began to wonder "why it was this way and not another—the number, the dimensions, and the motions of the orbs.'' The outlines of a solution struck him during a class lecture. His invention consisted of nesting the five Platonic solids (octahedron, icosahedron, dodecahedron, tetrahedron, and cube) between the successive spheres of Mercury, Venus, Earth, Mars, Jupiter, and Saturn. Astonishingly, Kepler's scheme predicts the planetary distances, except for Jupiter, within 5 percent accuracy.

Kepler published these conceptions in his *Mysterium cosmographicum* (1596). Quixotic as Kepler's polyhedrons may appear today, we must remember their revolutionary context: his book was the first unabashedly heliocentric treatise since that of Copernicus. Kepler sent copies of his book to various scholars, including Galileo and Tycho Brahe. Although the principal idea of the *Mysterium cosmographicum* was erroneous, Kepler established himself in the front rank of astronomers as the first, and until Descartes the only, scientist to demand physical explanations for celestial phenomena. Seldom in history has so wrong a book been so seminal in directing the future course of science.

In 1600 he set out to visit Tycho Brahe, who had just taken up residence outside Prague. Kepler quickly perceived the quality of Tycho's observations, and by the spring of 1601, using a circular orbit with an arbitrarily placed equant, had calculated the longitudes of Mars far more accurately than any of his predecessors. Kepler continued to chafe under the secretive jealously with which Tycho guarded his observations, when, suddenly, the Danish astronomer fell ill and died (in October 1601). Altogether Kepler had worked with Tycho only ten months. Emperor Rudolph appointed Kepler to Tycho's post of imperial mathematician, but at a greatly reduced salary that was often in arrears.

Following Tycho's death, Kepler continued to work on his orbit for Mars, but he soon realized that his scheme failed to predict the latitudes correctly. Kepler sought a unified, physically acceptable model that worked accurately for both the planetary longitudes and latitudes, but the best compromise left errors of about 8'. Believing that Tycho's observations were better than this, Kepler set out on a new trail, reviving his earlier speculations about a planetary driving force, analogous to magnetism, that emanated from the sun. In this process he discovered that the radius vector from the sun to the planet swept out equal areas in equal times. Today this is called his second law, although nowhere in his great book on Mars is it clearly stated.

Shortly thereafter Kepler discovered that the orbit of Mars was not circular, although the exact shape was difficult to establish. Finally, in 1605, he realized that an ellipse would satisfy the observations, and at last he found a geometrical way to reconcile the ellipse with his magnetic hypothesis, thus arriving at what we now call his first law, that planetary orbits are ellipses with the sun at one focus. The publication of his work proceeded slowly, and not until 1609 was the *Astronomia nova* distributed.

Simultaneously with his analysis of Mars, Kepler undertook other researches. A brilliant nova appeared in 1604; Kepler's extensive collection of observations and opinions appeared in 1606 in a long work, *De stella nova.* During the same period Kepler laid the foundations of geometrical optics in his *Astronomiae pars optica* published in 1604.

In April 1610 Kepler received a copy of Galileo's *Sidereus nuncius* together with a request for an opinion on the startling new telescopic discoveries. Kepler promptly published his *Dissertatio cum Nuncio sidereo.* Galileo later wrote, "I thank you because you were the first one, and practically the only one, to have complete faith in my assertions."

Kepler's earlier work on optics allowed him to work out the theory of the telescope, completing his *Dioptrice* (1611) within a few months after receiving Galileo's book. In August 1610 Kepler finally had an opportunity to borrow a telescope. He observed Jupiter for nearly two weeks, publishing the results in *Narratio de Jovis satellitibus* (1611). Other short works from Kepler's Prague period include *Phaenomenon singulare* (1609) in which he incorrectly reported a presumed transit of Mercury in 1607, *Tertius interveniens* (1610) an astrological work in which Kepler argued in German that "the stars do not compel, but they impress upon the soul a special character," and *Strena* (1611) in which he pondered why snowflakes are hexagonal.

By 1611 Kepler was at the peak of his career, when his world suddenly collapsed. The strife of the Thirty Years' War swept into Prague, and Emperor Rudolph was forced to abdicate. His children were stricken with smallpox, and his wife died. Yet not until Rudolph's death early in 1612 was Kepler free to leave Prague for a fourteen-year sojourn in Linz.

That Kepler, engulfed in a sea of personal troubles, published no astronomical works from 1612 through 1616 is not surprising. Yet the *Stereometria doliorum vinariorum* (1615) and its popular German version, the *Messekunst Archimedis* (1616), are regarded as significant contributions in the prehistory of the calculus.

After completing his *Ephemerides* for 1617, he revived his comparatively dormant cosmological studies, which soon appeared in his *Harmonice mundi* (1619). Kepler's favorite book, the *Harmonice* appears as a great cosmic vision, woven out of science, poetry, philosophy, theology, and mysticism. Kepler developed his theory of harmony in four areas: geometry, music, astrology, and astronomy. In the *Mysterium cosmographicum* the young Kepler had been satisfied with the rather approximate planetary spacings predicted by his nested polyhedrons and spheres; now, he could no longer dismiss its error. In the astronomical book V of the *Harmonice* he asked: By what secondary principles did God adjust the original archetypal model based on the regular solids? He found the supposed reason in the silent harmonies corresponding to the velocities of the planets at their perihelia and aphelia. In the course of his investigation he hit upon the relation now called his third or harmonic law: The ratio that exists between the periodic times of any two planets is precisely the ratio of the 3/2 power of their mean distances.

At about the same time, Kepler also wrote out his longest and most influential work, the *Epitome astronomiae Copernicanae.* The first of the three books finally appeared in 1617. By that time his seventy-year-old mother had been charged with witchcraft, and the astronomer felt obliged to go to Wurttemberg to aid in her legal defense. The second installment appeared in 1620. The final section was completed in 1621, just as his mother won acquittal in the witchcraft trial. In the *Epitome* Kepler sought to establish a "celestial physics" in which causes were assigned to "every size, motion, and proportion in the heavens." Within the book he gave an accurate statement of his law of areas, an interesting (but quite false) derivation of his harmonic law, and an introduction to what is now called Kepler's equation for the solution of motion in an elliptical orbit constrained by the law of areas.

In his own eyes Kepler was a cosmologist; to his imperial employers he was a mathematician charged with completing Tycho's planetary tables. This task hung over him as a burden as well as a challenge, but ultimately his *Tabulae Rudolphinae* (1627) provided the chief vehicle for the recognition of his astronomical accomplishments. Soon after Kepler saw Napier's newly-invented logarithms, he grasped their potentialities. He created his own tables by a new geometrical procedure. These were published in the *Chilias logarithmorum* (1624), and the Rudolphine Tables became the first scientific work to employ this new computational device. His tables provided an astonishing improvement over earlier methods; for example, the predictions for Mars previously erred up to 5°, but Kepler's tables kept within $\pm 10'$ of the actual position.

In 1628 Kepler entered the employment of the imperial commander-in-chief, Albrecht von Wallenstein, a general eager to have close access to an astrologer. Thus Kepler moved to Sagan, where he finally began to print a pioneering science fiction tale: *Somnium seu astronomia lunari*. In the fantasy framework of a voyage to the moon, Kepler produced an ingenious polemic for the Copernican system.

In Sagan Kepler waited in vain for his back salary, and finally he set out for the electoral congress at Regensburg to consult about a new residence. A few days after reaching Regensburg, he became ill with an acute fever and died. His son-in-law, Jacob Bartsch, defended the penniless family, but failed to collect the 12,694 guldens still owed by the state treasury.

Kepler's scientific thought was characterized by his profound sense of order and harmony, which was intimately linked with his theological view of God the Creator. He wrote prolifically, but his intensely personal cosmology was not very appealing to the rationalists of the generations that followed. A much greater audience awaited a more gifted polemicist, Galileo, who became the persuasive purveyor of the new astronomy. Yet for the professionals, Kepler's improved planetary positions were a forceful testimony to the efficacy of the Copernican system, and when Newton's *Principia* was introduced to the Royal Society, it was described as "a mathematical demonstration of the Copernican hypothesis as proposed by Kepler."

KERÉKJÁRTÓ, BÉLA (*b. Budapest, Hungary, 1898; d. Gyöngyos, Hungary, 1946*), mathematics.

Ph.D. at Budapest University (1920); taught at Szeged University (1922–38); appointed professor at Budapest University (1938). Kerékjártó's monograph on topology (1923) was one of first on subject, but exerted little influence because most material was hardly intelligible and apparently wrong; his later studies were generally correct and continued the work of Brouwer and Hilbert on mappings of surfaces and topological groups acting upon surfaces.

KERR, JOHN (*b. Ardrossan, Ayrshire, Scotland, 1824; d. Glasgow, Scotland, 1907*), physics.

Graduated University of Glasgow (M.A., 1849), where he studied under William Thomson; taught mathematics at the Free Church Normal Training College for Teachers in Glasgow (1857–1901). Discovered birefringence in glass in intense electric field (1875); also discovered Kerr effect: the elliptical polarization of a beam of plane polarized light when reflected from the pole of an electromagnet (1876).

KERR, JOHN GRAHAM (*b. Arkley, Hertfordshire, England, 1869; d. Barley, Hertfordshire, England, 1957*), zoology.

Studied at Edinburgh University; joined an expedition of the Argentine navy to survey Pilcomayo River (1889–91), which he described in *A Naturalist in the Gran Chaco* (1950); after graduating from Christ's College, Cambridge, led expedition to Paraguay (1896–97); taught zoology at the University of Glasgow (1902–35); continued research on dipnoan anatomy and embryology; one of the last of famous zoologists of the nineteenth century.

KEŚAVA (*fl. Nandod, Gujarat, India, 1496*), astronomy.

First of line of astronomers at Nandigrāma (Nandod) that includes his sons Ananta, Rāma, and Gaṇeśa and his grandson Nṛsiṃha; in addition to works on astronomy and astrology, Keśava also wrote on Hindu law; his *Jātakapaddhati* is a short treatise on horoscopy which has been immensely popular in India.

KETTERING, CHARLES FRANKLIN (*b. Loudonville, Ohio, 1876; d. Loudonville, 1958*), engineering, invention.

Graduated from Ohio State University (1904) in electrical engineering; founded Dayton Engineering Laboratories Company (Delco) with Edward A. Deeds (1909), which became subsidiary of General Motors. Developed the electric starter for automobiles, first installed on the Cadillac car (1912); discovered that cause of engine knock was imperfect combustion of fuel and with Thomas Midgley, Jr. and T. A. Boyd found the remedy in the addition of tetraethyl lead; ethyl gasoline was first marketed in 1922; Kettering became head of General Motors Research Corporation (1919); helped improve the diesel engine during 1930's.

KEULEN, LUDOLPH VAN. *See* **Ceulen, Ludolph van.**

KEYNES, JOHN MAYNARD (*b. Cambridge, England, 1883; d. Firle, Sussex, England, 1946*), economics, mathematics.

Graduated Kings College, Cambridge (1905) in mathematics; studied an additional year at Cambridge (1905–06); worked in India Office of British Treasury (1906–08). In 1911 completed *Treatise on Probability* (published 1921), which attempted to provide firm mathematical basis for probability theory; though *Treatise* was innovative in expressing probability in terms of modern-type symbolism, two of its doctrines are not accepted today. With the British Treasury (1915–19); he resigned because he regarded German reparations payments unfair; wrote *The Economic Consequences of the Peace* (1919), which brought him much fame. Returned to Kings College,

Cambridge; studied German reparations, monetary theory, and advocated public works to cure unemployment; published *The General Theory of Employment, Interest and Money* (1936), which contains Keynes' final synthesis. Keynes was the first economist to provide systematic "macrostatics," which analyzes economy as a whole; after serious illness (1937) invited into British Treasury on honorary basis (1940); helped found International Monetary Fund; joint editor *Economic Journal* (1912–45).

KEYS, JOHN. *See* **Caius, John.**

KEYSERLING, ALEXANDR ANDREEVICH (*b. Kabillen farm, Courland, Latvia, 1815; d. Raikül estate, Estonia, 1891*), geology, paleontology, botany.

Studied geology at Berlin University (Ph.D., 1842); being financially secure, settled on an estate in Estonia and continued scientific research; made a number of expeditions in Carpathians, Alps, European Russia, and the Urals; geological papers contain elements of facies analysis, which was quite new at that time; also interested in botany; espoused evolutionary views (1853) which were praised by Darwin in *The Origin of Species* (1859).

IBN KHALDŪN (*b. Tunis, 1332; d. Cairo, 1406*), history, sociology.

Completed education at court of Abū 'Inān in Fez (1354–57) where he was imprisoned because of Tunisian connections (1357–58); in Granada (1362–65); returned to northwest Africa (1365) but turbulent politics forced Ibn Khaldūn to take refuge in a small village in Algerian hinterland (1375–78); here he completed the introduction to his world history (became known as independent work, *Muqaddima*); returned to Tunis but politics forced him to flee to Egypt (1382) where he remained rest of his life. Appointed to academic positions and judgeship by ruler Barqūq (1382–99). *Muqaddima* was the first large-scale attempt to analyze group relationships that govern political and social organization on the basis of environmental and psychological factors. He gives an acceptable account of medieval science and scholarship.

AL-KHALĪLĪ, SHAMS AL-DĪN ABŪ 'ABDALLĀH MUHAMMAD IBN MUHAMMAD (*fl. Damascus, Syria, ca. 1365*), astronomy, mathematics.

Astronomer associated with Umayyad Mosque in Damascus; a *muwaqqit,* or astronomer concerned with timekeeping by sun and stars and regulating times of Muslim prayer; colleague of Ibn al-Shātir, also a *muwaqqit.* His major work—a culmination of medieval Islamic achievement in spherical astronomy—was a set of tables for astronomical timekeeping; some of these tables were used in Damascus until the nineteenth century and used in Cairo and Istanbul for several centuries; Al-Khalīlī's computational ability is best revealed by a table for determining *qibla,* the direction of Mecca, one of the most complicated problems of medieval Islamic trigonometry; he wrote at least one treatise on the use of the quadrant with trigonometric grid.

KHARASCH, MORRIS SELIG (*b. Kremenets, Ukraine, Russia* [*formerly Krzemieniec, Poland*], *1895; d. Chicago, Ill., 1957*), organic chemistry.

Graduated University of Chicago (B.S., 1917; Ph.D., 1919); taught chemistry at the University of Chicago (1928–57); best known for studies on addition of hydrogen bromide to unsaturated organic compounds.

AL-KHAYYĀMĪ (or **KHAYYĀM**), **GHIYĀTH AL-DĪN ABU'L-FATH 'UMAR IBN IBRĀHĪM AL-NĪSĀBŪRĪ** (or **AL-NAYSĀBŪRĪ**), also known as **Omar Khayyam** (*b. Nīshāpūr, Khurasan* [*now Iran*], *1048* [*?*]; *d. Nīshāpūr, 1131* [*?*]), mathematics, astronomy, philosophy.

Probably educated at Nīshāpūr; possibly became tutor; about 1070 obtained support of chief justice of Samarkand, Abū Tāhir, under whose patronage he wrote a great algebraical treatise on cubic equations, *Risāla fi'l-barāhīn 'alā masā'il al-jabr wa'l-muqābala* ("Treatise on Demonstration of Problems of Algebra and Almuqabala"). Invited to Isfahan by Seljuk sultan, Jalāl al-Dīn Malik-shāh, and his vizier, Nizām al-Mulk, to supervise astronomical observatory there (spent eighteen years in Isfahan); under al-Khayyāmī's guidance, astronomers at Isfahan (the best of the time) compiled *Zīj Malik-shāhī* ("Malik-shāh Astronomical Tables"); presented plan for calendar reform (*ca.* 1079); served as court astrologer, though he did not believe in judicial astrology; finished commentaries on Euclid's theory of parallel lines and theory of ratios (1077), which with *Risāla* is his most important scientific contribution; wrote on philosophical subjects (*ca.* 1080). Al-Khayyāmī fell into disfavor after Malik-shāh died and vizier Nizām al-Mulk murdered; financial support withdrawn from observatory; left Isfahan after 1118 to live in Merv (now Mary, Turkmen S.S.R.), the new Seljuk capital, where he probably wrote "Balance of Wisdoms" and "On Right Qustas"; the former work gives an algebraic solution to problem of determining quantities of gold and silver in given alloy by means of specific weights. Al-Khayyāmī's treatise "Problems of arithmetic," though not extant, probably used the Chinese method of reckoning in the decimal positional system by means of ten numbers for extracting cube roots. Wrote work on music, "Discussion on Genera Contained in a Fourth," which took up problem of dividing a fourth into three intervals corresponding to diatonic, chromatic, and enharmonic tonalities. Books II and III of commentaries on Euclid are concerned with theoretical foundations of arithmetic as manifested in study of theory of ratios; developed theory of ratios equivalent to Euclid's; book III is concerned with compound ratios, geometry, theory of music, and trigonometry. Regarding algebra, al-Khayyāmī's construction of geometrical theory of cubic equations is the most successful one accomplished by a Muslim scholar; first to state that a cubic equation cannot be generally solved by reduction to quadratic equations but can be solved by application of conic sections. He was the first to demonstrate that cubic equation might have two roots; gave one of first definitions of algebra. Devoted his first book of commentaries on Euclid to reworking theory of parallels and establishing it on a basis different from Euclid's fifth postulate. Wrote five philosophical and religious treatises. More than 1,000 quatrains, written in Persian, are now published under al-Khayyāmī's name, though the authenticity of many is uncertain.

AL-KHĀZIN, ABŪ JAʿFAR MUḤAMMAD IBN AL-ḤASAN AL-KHURĀSĀNĪ (*d. 961/971*), astronomy, mathematics.

A Sabaean of Persian origin; probably with court of Buwayhid ruler Rukn al-Dawla (932–976) of Rayy; best known work was *Zīj al-ṣafāʾiḥ* ("Tables of the Disks [of the astrolabe]"); wrote other works on astronomy and mathematics, most of which are not extant.

AL-KHĀZINĪ, ABUʾL-FATḤ ʿABD AL-RAḤMĀN [sometimes **Abū Manṣūr ʿAbd al-Raḥmān** or **ʿAbd al-Raḥmān Manṣūr**] (*fl. Merv, an Iranian city in Khurāsān [now Mary, Turkmen S.S.R.], ca. 1115–ca. 1130*), astronomy, mechanics, scientific instruments.

A slave-boy of Byzantine origin, al-Khāzinī was owned by Abuʾl-Ḥusayn ʿAlī ibn Muḥammad al-Khāzin al-Marwazī, who was treasurer of the court at Merv and who seems to have been sometime chancellor there. His master gave the young man the best possible education in mathematical and philosophical disciplines. Al-Khāzinī "became perfect" in the geometrical sciences and pursued a career as a mathematical practitioner under the patronage of the Seljuk court. His work seems to have been done at Merv, a capital of Khurāsān and a brilliant center of literary and scientific activity renowned for its libraries. The known works of al-Khāzinī, seemingly all extant, are the following: *al-Zīj al-Sanjarī* ("The Astronomical Tables for Sanjar"), also in a summary *(wajīz)* by the author; *Risāla fiʾl-ālāt* ("Treatise on [Astronomical] Instruments"), which actually may not be the work mentioned by the biobibliographers; and *Kitāb mīzān al-ḥikma* ("Book of the Balance of Wisdom"), a wide-ranging work that deals primarily with the science of weights and the art of constructing balances. To the manuscripts listed should be added 1) Sipahsālār Mosque [madrasa] Library (Teheran) 681–682 (cataloged as "Zīj-i Sanjarī" but containing a collection of al-Khāzinī's works including *Risāla fiʾl-ālāt* but not the complete *zīj*), and 2) the manuscript used for the Cairo edition of *Kitāb mīzān al-ḥikma.*

It is hard to assess the importance of al-Khāzinī. His hydrostatic balance can leave no doubt that as a maker of scientific instruments he is among the greatest of any time. As a student of statics and hydrostatics, even in their most practical aspects, he is heavily dependent upon earlier workers and borrows especially from al-Bīrūnī and al-Asfizārī; but his competence is not to be denied, and *Kitāb mīzān al-ḥikma* is of outstanding importance to the historian of mechanics, whatever its claims to originality or comprehensiveness may prove to be. In astronomy, as in mechanics, al-Khāzinī's direct predecessors are ʿUmar al-Khayyāmī and al-Asfizārī. His *zīj* takes its place in the Eastern Islamic astronomical tradition after those of al-Bīrūnī and ʿUmar al-Khayyāmī and is succeeded by those produced by the labors of the Marāgha Observatory (Naṣīr al-Dīn al-Ṭūsī and Quṭb al-Dīn al-Shīrāzī) and the Samarkand observatory (al-Kāshī [*d. ca.* 1430] and Ulugh Beg [the sultan; *d.* 1449]). Al-Khāzinī is one of twenty-odd Islamic astronomers known to have performed original observations. His *zīj* is rated very highly.

In mechanics no works are known that follow in the tradition of *Kitāb mīzān al-ḥikma;* treatments of balances or the science of weights become mere manuals for craftsmen who make simple scales or steelyards, or for merchants or inspectors who use them or check them. That branch of learning ceases to be a part of the scientific tradition.

Although al-Khāzinī's publications were well known in the Islamic world, and particularly in the Iranian part of it, they do not seem to have been used elsewhere save in Byzantium.

KHINCHIN, ALEKSANDR YAKOVLEVICH (*b. Kondrovo, Kaluzhskaya guberniya, Russia, 1894; d. Moscow, U.S.S.R., 1959*), mathematics.

Studied at Moscow University (1911–16); became professor of mathematics Moscow University (1927); with A. N. Kolmogorov, Khinchin was one of founders of Moscow school of probability theory.

AL-KHUJANDĪ, ABŪ MAḤMŪD ḤĀMID IBN AL-KHIDR (*d. 1000*), mathematics, astronomy.

For a time lived under patronage of Buwayhid ruler Fakhr al-Dawla (976–997); may have discovered sine theorem relative to spherical triangles; proved (imperfectly) that the sum of two cubic numbers cannot be a cubic number; geometry text and work on obliquity of ecliptic have been ascribed to al-Khujandī. Under patronage of Fakhr, al-Dawla he constructed a large instrument called *al-suds al-Fakhrī* ("sixth of a circle") for measurement of obliquity of ecliptic. Al-Khujandī and Ulugh Beg represent extreme examples of Islamic tendency to increase precision of astronomical instruments by increasing size; using his own observations he compiled his *Zīj al-Fakhrī* (not extant).

KHUNRATH (or **KUNRATH** or **KUHNRAT[H]** or **CUNRADIUS** or **CONRATHUS), CONRAD** (*b. Leipzig, Germany; d. not later than 1614*), medicine, preparation of medicines, chemistry.

Main work is *Medulla Destillatoria et Medica* (Schleswig, 1594), a masterpiece of clear, practical prescriptions. Khunrath was a follower of Paracelsus, whom he knew personally; also influenced by metallurgical knowledge of Georg Agricola and Conrad Gesner.

KHUNRATH (or **KUNRATH**), **HEINRICH** (*b. Leipzig, Germany, ca. 1560 [?]; d. Dresden [Leipzig?], Germany, 1605*), theosophy, alchemy, medicine.

Received M.D., University of Basel (1588); practiced medicine. An adept in alchemy dominated by Paracelsian belief in divine science of medicine as privilege of the initiated; combined theosophical experience and experience from natural observations in attempt to develop *physicochemica,* a chemical art grounded on general principles; Khunrath's *Amphitheatrum* was condemned by the Sorbonne for its mixture of Christianity and magic (1625).

IBN KHURRADĀDHBIH (or **IBN KHURDĀDHBIH), ABUʾ L-QĀSIM ʿUBAYD ALLĀH ʿABD ALLĀH** (*b. ca. 820; d. ca. 912*), geography, history, music.

Chief of posts and information in al-Jibāl (Media); wrote on history, genealogy, geography, music, and wines and cookery; main contribution was geographical compendium (846–847), an indispensable source of knowledge for later geographers and travelers.

AL-KHUWĀRIZMĪ, ABŪ ʿABD ALLĀH MUHAM-MAD IBN AHMAD IBN YŪSUF (*fl. in Khuwarizm ca. 975*), transmission of science.

Author of *Mafātih al-ʿulūm* ("Keys of the Sciences"), composed after 977; intended as manual for perfect secretary, this work contains all knowledge possessed by a cultured person living at that time in eastern Persia.

AL-KHWĀRIZMĪ, ABŪ JAʿFAR MUHAMMAD IBN MŪSĀ (*b. before 800; d. after 847*), mathematics, astronomy, geography.

While his ancestors were probably from Khwārizm, al-Khwārizmī was probably from Qutrubbullī, a district near Baghdad; under Caliph al-Maʾmūn (reigned 813–833) he became a member of the "House of Wisdom," an academy of scientists at Baghdad patronized by al-Maʾmūn. The *Algebra,* dedicated to al-Maʾmūn, is a work of elementary mathematics and may have been the first book on algebra written in Arabic; scholars dispute the extent of material derived from Greek, Hindu, and Hebrew sources. Another mathematical work, composed sometime after the *Algebra,* is an elementary arithmetical treatise using Hindu (or, as they are misnamed, "Arabic") numerals; it was the first work to systematically expound decimal place-value system (also from India). Also dedicated to al-Maʾmūn was *Zīj al-sindhind,* the first Arabic astronomical work to survive in entirety, the form of the tables being influenced by Ptolemy's tables. The geography, *Kitāb ṣūrat al-ard* ("Book of the Form of the Earth"), written soon after 816–817, consists almost entirely of lists of longitudes and latitudes of cities and localities; probably based on al-Maʾmūn's world map (on which al-Khwārizmī himself had probably worked), which in turn was based on Ptolemy's *Geography;* more accurate than Ptolemy's work in some respects, especially for Islamic areas. Only other surviving work is short treatise on Jewish calendar (823–824). Also wrote two works on astrolabe. Al-Khwārizmī's scientific achievements are mediocre but uncommonly influential, for they provided an introduction to Greek and Hindu science; a part of *Algebra* was twice translated into Latin in the twelfth century and was the chief influence on medieval European algebra; his treatise on Hindu numerals had the greatest impact in the West after a Latin translation appeared in the twelfth century; al-Khwārizmī's name became synonomous with any work on the "new arithmetic" (hence the modern term "algorithm"). *Zīj* was not so influential, but was the first such work to reach the West, in Latin translation by Adelard of Bath in twelfth century. Al-Khwārizmī's astronomical tables reached a wider audience in West after they were incorporated, along with other Arabic tables, into *Toledan Tables,* translated into Latin by Gerard of Cremona in the late twelfth century and were very popular for at least 100 years; his *Geography* remained unknown in Europe until the late nineteenth century.

KIDD, JOHN (*b. London, England, 1775; d. Oxford, England, 1851*), chemistry, anatomy.

Graduated Christ Church, Oxford (B.A., 1797; M.A., 1800); received medical degrees at Oxford (M.B., 1801; M.D., 1804). Taught chemistry at Oxford (from 1801), and later mineralogy and geology (William Buckland was a student of his); also taught anatomy (from 1816) and

medicine (from 1822) at Oxford. Wrote pamphlet on role of science in education, texts on geology and mineralogy, and several works on natural theology; contributed to *Bridgewater Treatises.*

KIELMEYER, CARL FRIEDRICH (*b. Bebenhausen, Württemberg, Germany, 1765; d. Stuttgart, Germany, 1844*), comparative physiology, anatomy, chemistry.

Entered Karlsschule near Stuttgart (1774), where Georges Cuvier and Friedrich von Schiller were his classmates; after completing philosophical course, studied medicine (certified in 1786 but never practiced); additional study at Göttingen with J.F.Blumenbach, J. F. Gmelin, and G. C. Lichtenberg; taught chemistry and later botany at University of Tübingen (1796–1816); director of Württemberg state art and scientific collections and of the state library, all at Stuttgart (1816–39). Published very little but greatly influenced friends and students, especially Cuvier. Although influenced by *Naturphilosophie,* Kielmeyer's regard for Kant and adherence to concrete evidence precluded excesses of radical idealism; sought to develop all-inclusive system of nature based on concept of developmental force, which accounts for all changes in organisms, chemical transformation, and physical change in general; outlook was spiritualistic, anti-mechanistic, and probably Christian; perhaps the preeminent teacher of physiology in Germany.

KIMURA, HISASHI (*b. Kanazawa, Japan, 1870; d. Setagaya-ku, Tokyo, Japan, 1943*), astronomy.

Graduated in astronomy from Tokyo University (1892); after graduate study there became director of Mizusawa Latitude Observatory (1899–1936); devoted life to observation of latitude variation.

AL-KINDĪ, ABŪ YŪSUF YAʿQŪB IBN ISHĀQ AL-SABBĀH (*b. ca. 801; d. Baghdad, ca. 866*), philosophy, science.

Ancient biobibliographers, as well as writers report many legends concerning the life of al-Kindī, but little certain, or even fairly reliable, information has come down to us. Even the years of his birth and death are not definitely known. It has been established, however, that al-Kindī was descended from a noble branch of the Kinda tribe of Yemen and that he began his education in Kūfa, Iraq, completing it in Baghdad—both centers of intellectual activity. It was in Baghdad that al-Kindī came to the attention of Caliph al-Maʾmūn, who took him into his court and named him to the "Academy" of Baghdad—Dār al-Hikma—with the task of improving the often defective translations made from the Greek. Al-Maʾmūn's successor, al-Muʿtasim, chose al-Kindī as tutor to his son Ahmad, on whose behalf al-Kindī wrote several philosophical essays.

The "first Arab philosopher," as he was commonly called by the bibliographers, al-Kindī participated in the expansion and dissemination of what might be called the contemporary encyclopedia of knowledge. In addition, he played an important role in the elaboration and definitive formulation of Arabic philosophical and, in some cases, scientific terminology.

Some fifteen philosophical works by al-Kindī have been preserved. Given the present state of knowledge it is difficult, if not impossible, to offer anything approaching a complete, systematic exposition of al-Kindī's scientific work. Encyclopedic in scope, it comprises writings on arithmetic, geometry, astronomy, music, medicine, pharmacology, and other fields.

Except for a few short treatises, al-Kindī's scientific writings have not fared as well as his more abundant philosophical works. Moreover, the difficulty of presenting his ideas applies to his scientific as well as to his philosophical concepts, for he followed an ancient tradition of basing his philosophical reflection on scientific investigation.

Nevertheless, two abiding concerns may be detected in the corpus of al-Kindī's scientific writings. The first is that of the commentator, the transmitter of Hellenic scientific works, whose goal is to prepare his readers for the study of philosophy. The other is the completion and, if possible, the augmentation of the body of inherited scientific knowledge.

KING, CLARENCE RIVERS (*b. Newport, R.I., 1842; d. Phoenix, Ariz., 1901*), geology.

Studied chemistry at Yale's Sheffield Scientific School (bachelor of philosophy degree, 1862), where he learned geology from James Dwight Dana; audited Louis Agassiz's lectures on glaciers (1863); directed U.S. Geological Exploration of Fortieth Parallel, where Union Pacific and Central Pacific railroad ran; first director U.S. Geological Survey (1879–81); worked as mining geologist (1882–93) until he suffered a nervous breakdown. Proposed neocatastrophist theory (1877); his assertion that Darwin's theory of evolution was only true for geologically quiet times helped diastrophism and neo-Lamarckianism gain a hearing.

KINNERSLEY, EBENEZER (*b. Gloucester, England, 1711; d. Pennepack, Pa., 1778*), electricity.

Ordained as Baptist minister, but never received a pulpit because of polemics against church. Wrote tracts on electricity which Benjamin Franklin published. With Franklin's help he toured the colonies (1749–53) giving public lectures on electricity and became professor of English at Philadelphia Academy (1753–72); helped Franklin clarify several points of electrical theory; best-known contribution is electrical air thermometer.

KIPPING, FREDERICK STANLEY (*b. Manchester, England, 1863; d. Criccieth, England, 1949*), chemistry.

Graduated in chemistry at Owens College in Manchester; graduate study at University of Munich (Ph.D., 1887), where he worked in A. von Baeyer's laboratory under W. H. Perkin, Jr.; taught chemistry at University College in Nottingham (1897–1936); coauthor with Perkin of popular textbook *Organic Chemistry* (1894). Kipping's studies led to synthesis of silicone polymers, which became important industrial products during World War II.

KIRCH. A family of scientists who flourished in Germany in the seventeenth and eighteenth centuries.

Four of its members were astronomers: **Kirch, Gottfried** (*b. Guben, Germany, 1639; d. Berlin, Germany, 1710*); his wife, **Maria Margarethe Winkelmann** (*b. Panitsch near Leipzig, Germany, 1670; d. Berlin, 1720*); his son, **Christfried** (*b. Guben, 1694; d. Berlin, 1740*); his daughter, **Christine** (*b. ca. 1696; d. Berlin, 1782*); astronomy.

Gottfried Kirch was apprenticed to Hevelius at Danzig; made his living by computing and publishing calendars and ephemerides; his calendars were very popular; the ephemerides, based on Rudolphine Tables, were known throughout Europe. Kirch was one of the earliest astronomers to search the skies systematically with a telescope; discovered several comets; studied variable stars. Appointed first astronomer at the observatory founded by Frederick I of Prussia (1700–10), but the building was not completed until after Kirch's death. He continued observations at home and at the private observatory of Baron von Krosigk.

Maria Margarethe worked with her husband making observations and doing calculations for calendars; after his death she continued to publish on her own; discovered the comet of 1702; made astrological prognostications; worked in Krosigk's observatory (1712–14); joined son Christfried when he was appointed astronomer at Berlin observatory (1716).

Christfried Kirch studied astronomy in Leipzig, Königsberg, and Danzig, where he restored Hevelius' old observatory; astronomer of Berlin observatory (1716–40).

Christine Kirch assisted her brother Christfried with observations and calculations.

KIRCHER, ATHANASIUS (*b. Geisa at the Ulster, Germany, 1602 [or 1601]; d. Rome, Italy, 1680*), polymathy, dissemination of knowledge.

Studied wide variety of subjects at Paderborn (until 1622), Cologne, Koblenz (1623), and Mainz (ordained Jesuit priest, 1628); taught philosophy and mathematics at University of Würzburg (1628–31); lectured at Avignon on astronomy, hieroglyphics, and surveying (1631–33); professor of mathematics at College of Rome (1638–46); rest of life spent in independent study in Rome. Wrote forty-four books and 2,000 extant letters and manuscripts covering most fields of humanities and sciences. Kircher's works were popular but not original, though he made some scientific contributions; in *Ars magnesia* (1631) he described a device for measuring magnetic power with a balance (published four other books on magnetism combining scientific and fantastic theories). In *Ars magna lucis et umbrae* (1646) he argued that light behaves like magnetism; supplied astronomers G. B. Riccioli, G. D. Cassini, and Hevelius with valuable information. *Mundus subterraneus* (1665) discusses hydrologic cycle and subterranean regions of fire. His mathematical work was both mystical and practical. Recorded the first description of a speaking trumpet (1650).

KIRCHHOF, KONSTANTIN SIGIZMUNDOVICH (GOTTLIEB SIGISMUND CONSTANTIN) (*b. Teterow, Mecklenburg-Schwerin [now D.D.R.], 1764; d. St. Petersburg, Russia, 1833*), chemistry.

Moved to Russia (1792), where he was journeyman apothecary; became pharmacist (1805–09) at St. Petersburg Chief Prescriptional Pharmacy, where he began chemical studies; helped develop method for refining vegetable oil and co-founded oil purifying plant in St. Petersburg; discovered catalytic enzyme hydrolysis of starch in 1811 (first controlled catalytic reaction), which laid foundation for scientific study of brewing and distilling.

KIRCHHOFF, GUSTAV ROBERT (*b. Königsberg, Germany, 1824; d. Berlin, Germany, 1887*), physics.

Graduated from University of Königsberg (1847), where he studied under Franz Neumann; taught at Breslau (1850–54) and became friends with Bunsen, who later arranged for Kirchhoff to join him at the University of Heidelberg (1854–75); accepted the chair of theoretical physics at Berlin (1875–86) after ill health hindered his experimental work. First scientific work, under Neumann, was formulation of laws of distribution of tension and current intensity in networks of linear conductors (1845–46); achieved correct mathematical unification of electrostatics and theory of voltaic currents (1849); developed general theory of motion of electricity in conductors (1857). Although he realized that currents move at the velocity of light in an ideal conductor, he failed to see the unity of optical and electromagnetic waves; discovered a fundamental law of electromagnetic radiation: for all material bodies, the ratio of absorptive and emissive power for such radiation is a universal function of wavelength and temperature (1859). Kirchhoff's law was the key to the whole thermodynamics of radiation, and in Planck's hands became the key to quantum physics. Kirchhoff made this discovery while investigating spectra of chemical elements with Bunsen, thus founding the method of spectral analysis (1860). Introduced concept of a "black body," which absorbs completely every radiation incident on it (1862).

KIRKALDY, DAVID (*b. Dundee, Scotland, 1820; d. London, England, 1897*), metallurgy, mechanical engineering.

Testing consultant and manufacturer of testing machinery; wrote *Results of an Experimental Enquiry* (1862). Main contribution was establishing testing of materials as essential factor in civil engineering construction.

KIRKMAN, THOMAS PENYNGTON (*b. Bolton, England, 1806; d. Croft, near Warrington, England, 1895*), mathematics.

Graduated with arts degree from Dublin University (1833; M.A., 1850); ordained into Anglican Church; educated self in mathematics; elected into Royal Society (1857); main contributions were in combinatorics, especially his Fifteen Schoolgirls Problem.

KIRKWOOD, DANIEL (*b. Harford County, Md., 1814; d. Riverside, Calif., 1895*), astronomy.

Entered York County Academy (1834) where he studied and later taught mathematics; after a time in high school administration (1843–51), taught mathematics at Delaware College (1851–56), where he was also college president (1854–56); taught mathematics at Indiana University (1856–86). Kirkwood's research and writings mainly concerned the solar system, especially lesser members—asteroids, comets, meteors, and meteoritic bodies; most important astronomical discovery was of "gaps" in distribution of mean distances of asteroids from sun (1857; formal publication not until 1866); anticipated asteroid "families," listing thirty-two groups with similar orbits (1892). Began to question Laplace's nebular hypothesis (from 1869), and advanced his own modifications (1880–85); gave first convincing demonstration of association between meteors and comets (1861); first to consider (1866–67) possible relationship

of comets and asteroids and of shower meteors and stony meteorites.

KIRKWOOD, JOHN GAMBLE (*b. Gotebo, Okla., 1907; d. New Haven, Conn., 1959*), theoretical chemistry.

Graduated University of Chicago (B.S., 1926); did graduate work at Massachusetts Institute of Technology, followed by postdoctoral study in U.S. and abroad; assumed academic positions at Cornell University (1934), University of Chicago (1937), California Institute of Technology (1947), and Yale University (1951). Kirkwood's scientific contributions were in the theory of chemical physics.

KIRWAN, RICHARD (*b. Cloughballymore, County Galway, Ireland, 1733 [?]; d. Dublin, Ireland, 1812*), chemistry, mineralogy, geology, meteorology.

Studied at University of Poitiers (1750–54); inherited family estates and returned to Ireland; studied law and practiced in Ireland (1766–68); moved to London (1777–87), where he did most of his work in chemistry; returned to Ireland (1787–1812). In three-part paper (1781–83), sought to measure degrees of attraction between substances by determining weights of bases and metals that neutralized or dissolved in a given weight of acid; these measurements of affinity were equivalents and contributed to formulation of law of reciprocal proportions advanced by Richter. Best-known work is *Essay on Phlogiston* (1787), in which he defended phlogiston theory against Lavoisier; Kirwan abandoned phlogiston theory in 1791 because he failed to show conclusively the formation of fixed air (carbon dioxide) from phlogiston and oxygen. In paper of 1793, attacked James Hutton's geomorphological theory, leading Hutton to expand his ideas in *Theory of the Earth* (1795).

KITAIBEL, PÁL (or **PAUL**) (*b. Nagymarton, Hungary [now Mattersdorf, Austria], 1757; d. Pest, Hungary, 1817*), botany, chemistry, mineralogy.

Although qualified as physician (1785) after study at the University of Pest, he never practiced medicine; became assistant and later professor of botany at Institute for Chemistry and Botany at University of Pest; classified many unknown plants; published flora of Hungary (1799–1812); independently discovered tellurium (1798), though already discovered by Franz Müller (1784).

KITASATO, SHIBASABURO (*b. Oguni, Kumamoto, Japan, 1852; d. Nakanojo, Gumma, Japan, 1931*), bacteriology.

Received medical degree University of Tokyo (1883); became research assistant at Public Health Bureau; was sent to Germany to study at Robert Koch's laboratory (1886–91). Published paper on deriving first pure culture of the bacillus that causes tetanus (1889); paper written with Behring opened field of serology and gave first evidence that immune serum can serve in curing an infectious disease (1890); identified causative bacterium of 1894 outbreak of bubonic plague in Hong Kong as *Pasteurella pestis*. On return to Japan (1892) became director of Institute for Infectious Diseases; resigned in 1914 to found Kitasato Institute; first president Japanese Medical Association (1923); one of the foremost Japanese bacteriologists.

KJELDAHL, JOHANN GUSTAV CHRISTOFFER (*b. Jagerpris, Denmark, 1849; d. Tisvildeleje, Denmark, 1900*), analytical chemistry.

Studied chemistry at Technological Institute in Copenhagen; passed state examination in applied science (1873). Appointed director of Carlsberg Laboratory (1876); best known for "Kjeldahl method" for estimation of nitrogen in organic substances (1883); Kjeldahl's method was extremely important for agriculture, medicine, and drug manufacturing, and is still used today in its original form.

KLAPROTH, MARTIN HEINRICH (*b. Wernigerode, Germany, 1743; d. Berlin, Germany, 1817*), chemistry.

Became apprentice in apothecary shop (1759); after becoming journeyman (1764), moved to Hannover (1766), where he began reading chemistry; settled in Berlin (1771), where he started own apothecary shop (1780). From 1782 worked his way up through Prussian medical bureaucracy; also taught at Berlin's Medical-Surgical College (1782–1810), Mining School (1784–1817), and University of Berlin (1810–17). Appointed as Berlin Academy's representative for chemistry (1800), and worked in academy's laboratory (1803–17). Leading analytical chemist in Europe from late 1780's until early 1800's; discovered or co-discovered numerous elements (zirconium, 1789; uranium, 1789; titanium, 1792; etc.). A significant contribution was insistence on importance of "small" losses and gains in weight in analytical work; helped facilitate German acceptance of Lavoisier's antiphlogistic theory.

KLEBS, GEORG ALBRECHT (*b. Neidenburg, Germany, 1857; d. Heidelberg, Germany, 1918*), botany.

Studied at University of Königsberg; became assistant to leading plant physiologists: J. Sachs at Würzburg and W. Pfeffer at Tübingen; taught at Tübingen (1883), Basel (1887), Halle (1898), and Heidelberg (1907). Most lasting contribution was creating method for, and hence founding, developmental physiology. His books were published in 1896 and 1903; specifically, he was first to make logically consistent division of influences affecting development into external conditions, internal conditions, and specific structure.

KLEIN, CHRISTIAN FELIX (*b. Düsseldorf, Germany, 1849; d. Göttingen, Germany, 1925*), mathematics.

Studied mathematics and physics at University of Bonn (Ph.D., 1868); further studies at Göttingen, Berlin, and Paris (1869); taught at Göttingen (1871–72), Erlangen (1872–75), Technische Hochschule in Munich (1875–80), University of Leipzig (1880–86), and University of Göttingen (1886–1925). One of the leading mathematicians of his age; made contributions to almost all branches of mathematics; helped make Göttingen chief center of exact sciences in Germany. Assisted J. Plücker in physics lectures at Bonn while still a student; completed Plücker's book on line geometry after he died. With S. Lie, Klein discovered the fundamental properties of the asymptotic lines of the famous Kummer surface (1870). Most important achievements in geometry were the projective foundation of the non-Euclidean geometries and creation of the "Erlanger Programm"; in two works entitled *Über die sogenannte nicht-euklidische Geometrie*

(1871, 1873) he established that hyperbolic, elliptic, and Euclidean geometries can be constructed purely projectively; "Erlanger Programm" (1872) established that every geometry known so far is based on a certain group, and the task of any geometry is to set up invariants of this group. Klein considered his work in function theory, which developed Riemann's ideas, to be his best. He provided an account of his conception of Riemann surface in *Riemanns Theorie der algebraischen Funktionen und ihre Integrale* (1882); established the Riemann surface as an indispensable component of function theory; derived a complete theory of the general algebraic equation of the fifth degree from a consideration of the icosahedron; also studied elliptic modular functions, algebraic function fields, and automorphic functions (simultaneously developed by Poincaré). Sought to apply mathematics to physics and engineering and to encourage use of mathematics by engineers; wrote textbook on theory of gyroscope with A. Sommerfeld (1897–1910); founded Göttingen Institute for Aeronautical and Hydrodynamical Research.

KLEIN, HERMANN JOSEPH (*b. Cologne, Germany, 1844; d. Cologne, 1914*), astronomy, meteorology.

After an early career as bookdealer in Cologne, entered University of Giessen (Ph.D., 1874); based on own observations, advocated lunar vulcanism (later confirmed); became director of meteorological and astronomical observatory at Lindenthal, near Cologne (1880–1914); one of the foremost popularizers of meteorology and astronomy of his day.

KLEIN, JACOB THEODOR (*b. Königsberg, East Prussia, 1685; d. Danzig [now Gdansk, Poland], 1759*), zoology.

Studied law at University of Königsberg; served as court secretary in Danzig (from 1714); Klein's *Naturalis dispositio Echinodermatum* (1734) was one of earliest monographic treatments of sea urchins.

KLEINENBERG, NICOLAUS (NICOLAI) (*b. Liepaja, Russia, 1842; d. Naples, Italy, 1897*), biology.

Studied medicine at University of Dorpat (1860–67), where he attended lectures of M. J. Schleiden; studied with Ernst Hallier at Jena (1868), where he was influenced by Ernst Haeckel, Anton Dohrn, and Ernst Abbe; assisted Haeckel at Zoological Institute (1869–70); received doctorate (1871). Helped Dohrn establish first marine biological station in Naples (1873–75); taught zoology and comparative anatomy at University of Messina (1879–95); taught same subjects at Palermo (from 1895). Kleinenberg's zoological work was not extensive; his dissertation contains first detailed investigation of development of freshwater polyp (1871); favored physiological over phylogenetic approach to embryological processes.

KLEIST, EWALD GEORG VON (*b. probably Prussian Pomerania, ca. 1700; d. Köslin [?], Pomerania [now Koszalin, Poland], 1748*), physics.

A member of Prussian administrative squirearchy; he began experiments which culminated in the invention of a condenser (1745–46), though it was P. van Musschenbroek's experiment with the Leyden jar (or Kleist vial) that was most influential in changing the theory of electricity.

KLINGENSTIERNA, SAMUEL (*b. near Linköping, Sweden, 1698; d. Stockholm, Sweden, 1765*), physics.

After studying at University of Uppsala, began study tour of Marburg, Basel, Paris, and London (1727); taught at Uppsala (1728–54); became member of Swedish court (1754–64); most important contributions were in geometrical optics; proved that, contrary to Newton, achromatic refraction is possible (1754), a discovery which John Dollond used, but did not acknowledge, in constructing the first achromatic lenses (1758). Klingenstierna presented general theory of achromatic and aplanatic lens systems in a classic paper (1760).

KLÜGEL, GEORG SIMON (*b. Hamburg, Germany, 1739; d. Halle, Germany, 1812*), mathematics, physics.

Studied mathematics University of Göttingen (1760–65); held chair of mathematics and physics at University of Halle; most important contribution was in trigonometry; Klügel's *Analytische Trigonometrie* (1770) unified trigonometric formulas and introduced concept of trigonometric function.

KLUYVER, ALBERT JAN (*b. Breda, Netherlands, 1888; d. Delft, Netherlands, 1956*), microbiology, biochemistry.

Received chemical engineering degree from Technical University of Delft (1910); did graduate work on biochemical sugar determinations; appointed to the chair of general and applied microbiology at Technical University of Delft (1922–56). Greatly influenced chemical study of microorganisms; most important contribution was statement of principle of hydrogen transfer (oxidation) as fundamental feature of all metabolic processes; also studied microbial morphology with electron microscope during World War II. His interest in commercial applications led to collaboration with Netherlands Yeast and Alcohol Manufacturing Company; co-founded Biophysical Research Group Delft-Utrecht.

KNESER, ADOLF (*b. Grüssow, Germany, 1862; d. Breslau, Germany [now Wrocław, Poland], 1930*), mathematics.

Graduated University of Berlin (Ph.D, 1884); taught at University of Breslau (1905–30); one of most distinguished German mathematicians *circa* 1900; two main contributions in analysis: linear differential equations and the Sturm-Liouville problem (from 1896), and the calculus of variations (from 1897).

KNIGHT, THOMAS ANDREW (*b. near Ludlow, Herefordshire, England, 1759; d. London, England, 1838*), botany, horticulture.

Graduated Balliol College, Oxford (before 1791); was independently wealthy. His scientific work recorded in correspondence with Sir Joseph Banks was read by Banks to the Royal Society. Knight's research was intended to improve produce from his farm; most important contribution was application of scientific principles and techniques to the practical needs of grower or breeder. Most famous work was on geotropisms (1806); performed experiments with seedlings attached to a rotating wheel to eliminate influence of earth's gravitation, concluding that geotropism has a strictly mechanical explanation.

KNIPOVICH, NIKOLAI MIKHAILOVICH (*b. Suomenlinna, Finland, 1862; d. Leningrad, U.S.S.R., 1939*), marine biology, marine hydrology.

Graduated from Physics and Mathematics Faculty of St. Petersburg University (1886); headed a number of research expeditions to Russian seas from late 1880's to early 1930's; a pioneer in study of marine fishes and their close connection to hydrological conditions.

KNOPP, KONRAD (*b. Berlin, Germany, 1882; d. Annecy, France, 1957*), mathematics.

Graduated University of Berlin (1907); taught at Berlin (1911–15), Königsberg University (1915–26), and Tübingen University (1926–50); a specialist in generalized limits, he wrote popular books on complex functions.

KNORR, GEORG WOLFGANG (*b. Nuremberg, Germany, 1705; d. Nuremberg, 1761*), engraving, paleontology.

A protogeologist intermediate between collectors of natural history cabinets and those who first made use of fossils for identification and mapping of stratigraphic succession; an engraver of detailed and accurate scientific copper plates; his best work is *Sammlung . . .* ("Collection of Natural Wonders and Antiquities of the Earth's Crust"), 1755.

KNOTT, CARGILL GILSTON (*b. Penicuik, Scotland, 1856; d. Edinburgh, Scotland, 1922*), natural philosophy, seismology.

Graduated Edinburgh University; taught physics at Imperial University of Japan (1883–91), where he helped inaugurate the modern era in earthquake study by applying seismology to determine internal mechanical properties of the earth; organized first comprehensive magnetic survey of Japan.

KNOX, ROBERT (*b. Edinburgh, Scotland, 1793; d. Hackney, London, England, 1862*), anatomy.

Received medical degree, specializing in anatomy, from University of Edinburgh; became hospital assistant with British forces in Europe and South Africa; after returning to Edinburgh went to Paris to study with G. Cuvier and G. Saint-Hilaire (1821–22). In Edinburgh again he published a study on the eye asserting it was muscle, not ligament (1823); founded museum of comparative anatomy with backing of Royal College of Surgeons; took over John Barclay's extramural school of anatomy (1825); extremely popular teacher who also gave public lectures. While Knox attempted to gain Parliamentary sanction to dissect unclaimed bodies of paupers, in the meantime he bought cadavers regardless of source; scandal erupted when one supplier of bodies was found to be obtaining them through murder (1828). Though Knox was cleared of wrong-doing, his reputation was tarnished and he ceased his research on human anatomy; affair prompted Parliament to pass anatomy act permitting use of unclaimed bodies of paupers for study (1832). Another unrelated scandal resulted in withdrawal of accreditation for Knox's lectures by Edinburgh College of Surgeons (1847); managed to be appointed pathological anatomist to London Cancer Hospital (1856–62).

KNUDSEN, MARTIN HANS CHRISTIAN (*b. Hansmark, Denmark, 1871; d. Copenhagen, Denmark, 1949*), physics, hydrography.

Graduated University of Copenhagen (M.S., 1896); taught at University of Copenhagen (1901–41); scientific work concerned properties of gases at low pressure; he confirmed Maxwell's law of distribution of velocity; developed laws of molecular diffusion; discovered absolute manometer (now called Knudsen manometer); also studied properties of seawater.

KNUTH, PAUL ERICH OTTO WILHELM (*b. Greifswald, Germany, 1854; d. Kiel, Germany, 1900*), botany.

Graduated University of Greifswald (Ph.D., 1876); taught at Oberrealschule (1881–1900); studied at botanical garden in Buitenzorg, Java (1898–99); best known for work on fertilization of flowers; his *Handbuch der Blütenbiologie* (1898–99) remains the definitive work on flower pollination.

KÖBEL (or **KOBEL** or **KOBILIN** or **KIBLIN** or **CABALLINUS), JACOB** (*b. Heidelberg, Germany, ca. 1460; d. Oppenheim, Germany, 1533*), mathematics, law, publishing, municipal administration.

Graduated University of Heidelberg (B.A., 1481); while active in book trade also studied law, receiving bachelor's degree (1491); studied mathematics at Cracow, where he was reported to be fellow student of Copernicus. In Oppenheim *circa* 1494, where in addition to being town clerk, official surveyor, and manager of a municipal wine tavern, Köbel also wrote extensively and was printer and publisher. He published ninety-six works between 1499 and 1532, some his own and some by others. Importance lies in his dissemination of mathematical knowledge, especially of new Hindu ("Arabic") numerals and methods, among broad segments of the population (wrote in German); wrote three arithmetic books (1514, 1515, 1525), a work on the astrolabe (1532), and books of law, imperial history, and poetry.

KOCH, HEINRICH HERMANN ROBERT (*b. Clausthal, Oberharz, Germany, 1843; d. Baden-Baden, Germany, 1910*), bacteriology, hygiene, tropical medicine.

Many of the basic principles and techniques of modern bacteriology were adapted or devised by Koch, who therefore is often regarded as the chief founder of that science. His isolation of the causal agents of anthrax, tuberculosis, and cholera brought him worldwide acclaim as well as leadership of the German school of bacteriology. Directly or indirectly he influenced authorities in many countries to introduce·public health legislation based on knowledge of the microbic origin of various infections, and he stimulated more enlightened popular attitudes toward hygienic and immunologic measures for controlling such diseases.

Koch studied natural sciences at Göttingen University beginning in 1862. After studying botany, physics, and mathematics for two semesters, he transferred to medicine because of a disinclination for professional teaching and the realization that natural science interests were compatible with a medical career. Upon graduation from Göttingen in January 1866, he visited Berlin to attend the Charité clinics and Rudolf Virchow's course in pathology.

In 1868 Koch established a small-town practice in the province of Posen and later migrated eastward settling in Rakwitz, where his practice flourished. This was interrupted by the Franco-Prussian War and Koch volunteered for service as a field hospital physician. He gained invaluable experience, but early in 1871, responding to a petition from Rakwitz citizens, he left the army and resumed practice. Shortly afterward he passed the quali-

fying examinations for district medical officer and was advised to apply for a vacant position at Wollstein, where he was appointed in 1872.

Koch became involved in the current controversies about the etiology of infection and he extended the scale of his investigations, which he conducted in a small section of his house he had converted to a laboratory.

At thirty years of age Koch turned his attention to anthrax. His classic report on the etiology of anthrax, proving that the disease was caused by a specific bacterium, was published in 1876. In 1877 he published another paper in which he described techniques for dry-fixing thin films of bacterial culture on glass slides, for staining them with aniline dyes, and for recording their structure by microphotography.

Koch's reputation and ambitions soon outgrew his environment, and obligations to patients conflicted with his keeping abreast of specialized literature and with conducting laboratory researches that demanded more apparatus and experimental animals than the household could accommodate. In 1880 he was appointed government adviser with the Imperial Department of Health in Berlin, and his home was henceforth in the capital city.

Upon returning to Berlin, Koch extended his earlier work on bacteriological methods. He stressed the importance of avoiding contamination through use of strictly sterile techniques and advocated nutrient gelatin as a solid medium that allowed individual colonies to be selected, thus ensuring pure cultures. He also specified that newly isolated pathogens should be investigated for transferability to animals, portals of entry and localizations in the host, natural habitats, and susceptibility to harmful agents. This work, illustrated with microphotography, long remained the basic instructional manual for bacteriological laboratories.

Koch also launched experiments on tuberculosis, convinced of its chronic infectious nature. In a lecture entitled "Ueber Tuberculose," he identified the tuberculosis bacilli. Within three weeks Koch's paper appeared in the *Berliner klinische Wochenschrift* as "Die Aetiologie der Tuberculose."

Koch's tuberculosis researches were interrupted by the 1883 Hygiene Exhibition in Berlin, which he helped to organize, but a more challenging diversion was an outbreak of cholera in the Nile delta that summer. Koch traveled there and his research rapidly led him to the identification of the cholera bacillus.

In 1890, at the tenth International Medical Congress in Berlin, Koch ended his address on bacteriological research by announcing that after testing many chemicals, he had discovered a substance capable of preventing the growth of tubercle bacilli both *in vitro* and *in vivo*. In January 1891 Koch published the long-awaited formula in "Fortsetzung der Mittheilungen über ein Heilmittel gegen Tuberkulose"; but the report proved anticlimactic. Widespread doubts arose about the remedy. Still undaunted, Koch endeavored to improve tuberculin's safety and efficacy and to determine its optimal dosage. In "Ueber neue Tuberkulinpräparate" (1897), describing three new forms of tuberculin, Koch asserted that nothing better of this kind could be produced. Eventually the specific diagnostic value of the hypersensitive response of tuberculous patients and cattle to tuberculin injections helped to restore the prestige lost through excessive confidence in the agent's curative powers.

Koch always had a thirst for foreign travel. He studied bubonic plague in upper India, rinderpest in German East Africa (where instead he found two protozoan diseases—surra, a trypanosomiasis affecting horses, and Texas cattle fever, identified as a piroplasmosis by Theobald Smith). He began to study malaria and blackwater fever—soon attributing the latter to quinine intoxication—and detected an endemic plague focus at Kisiba on Lake Victoria.

Returning to Berlin in May 1898, after eighteen months' absence, Koch delivered an address entitled "Aertzliche Beobachtungen in den Tropen." He described four types of malaria, favored the mosquito-borne theory, compared immunity in malaria and Texas fever, and asserted that he had pioneered new routes and set new goals in malaria research. The various accomplishments were recounted in *Reise-Bericht über Rinderpest, Bubonenpest in Indien und Afrika . . .* (1898).

Shortly thereafter Koch proposed another visit to Italy, followed by an extensive tropical expedition. That autumn, working in the Lombardy plains, the Campagna di Roma, and other Italian malarial districts, he confirmed Ronald Ross's discovery of the avian malaria parasite's life cycle.

Koch returned to Berlin in 1900, having spent only nine months there in four years. Early in 1903 he departed for Bulawayo, Southern Rhodesia, where he had been invited to investigate "Rhodesian redwater," another cattle epizootic, a tick-borne piroplasmosis resembling Texas fever.

Koch returned to Berlin in 1904 to retire from state service, and although the battle against tuberculosis remained his prime concern, he spent most of the next three years in equatorial Africa. Early in 1905 he arrived at Dar-es-Salaam. On this expedition he investigated the life cycles of the piroplasmas of Coast and Texas fevers, and of sleeping sickness trypanosomes in *Glossina* (tsetse flies). He also showed African relapsing fever to be a spirochetosis transmitted by *Ornithodoros moubata*, a tick infesting caravan routes and native huts. Three months later, in Stockholm, he received the 1905 Nobel Prize for physiology or medicine for his work on tuberculosis.

The remainder of Koch's life was devoted to tuberculosis control, and he worked daily at the Institute until his death.

KOCH, HELGE VON (*b. Stockholm, Sweden, 1870; d. Stockholm* [*?*], *1924*), mathematics.

Known principally for work in theory of infinitely many linear equations and study of matrices derived from such infinite systems; also did work in differential equations and in theory of numbers; his work was a first step on the long road to functional analysis.

KOCHIN, NIKOLAI YEVGRAFOVICH (*b. St. Petersburg, Russia* [*now Leningrad, U.S.S.R.*], *1901; d. Moscow, U.S.S.R.,* *1944*), physics, mathematics.

Graduated from Petrograd University (1923), where he taught mechanics and mathematics (1924–34); taught at Moscow University (1934–44); worked in Mathematics Institute of Soviet Academy of Sciences (1932–39); head of mechanics section of Mechanics Institute of the Academy (1939–44). Made contributions in meteorology, gas

dynamics, hydrodynamics, aerodynamics, mathematics, and theoretical mechanics.

KOELLIKER, RUDOLF ALBERT VON (*b. Zurich, Switzerland, 1817; d. Würzburg, Germany, 1905*), comparative anatomy, histology, embryology, physiology.

Entered University of Zurich (1836), where his teachers included O. Heer and L. Oken; studied for a semester in Bonn (1839) followed by three semesters in Berlin, where he was influenced by J. Müller, F. G. J. Henle, and R. Remak; awarded Ph.D. at Zurich for determining cellular nature of spermatazoa of invertebrates (1841); awarded M.D. from Heidelberg (1842). Assisted Henle at Zurich (1840–43); taught physiology and comparative anatomy at Zurich (1843–47); recognized cellular nature of muscle fibers (1846); taught at University of Würzburg (1847–97). Published *Mikroskopische Anatomie* (1850–54), which presented study of tissue in terms of cell theory; Koelliker's classification of tissues, presented in *Handbuch der Gewebelehre des Menschen* (1852), became accepted throughout Europe. Also employed cell theory in interpreting development of the embryo; demonstrated that same types of developmental processes occur in both invertebrates and vertebrates; viewed the egg as single cell. Suggested that the nucleus transmitted inherited characteristics (1841) and foreshadowed De Vries's theory of mutations; helped substantiate doctrine of the neuron as basic unit of nervous system (*circa* 1884); continued research after retirement from teaching (1897). Founder and co-editor of *Zeitschrift für wissenschaftliche Zoologie* (1848). His students included Haeckel and Gegenbaur; during his tenure, Würzburg became an important center for medical education, and he helped establish histology and cytology as independent branches of science.

KOELREUTER, JOSEPH GOTTLIEB (*b. Sulz, Germany, 1733; d. Karlsruhe, Germany, 1806*), botany.

Graduated University of Tübingen (1755); became keeper of natural history collections of Imperial Academy of Sciences in St. Petersburg (1755–61); returned to Germany (1761), where he was appointed professor of natural history and director of gardens in Karlsruhe (1761–86). Initiated scientific study of plant hybridization; although Koelreuter's world view belonged to seventeenth century (emphasizing harmony and purposiveness of nature, and alchemical notions), his experimentation was not surpassed until Mendel. Helped support preformationist view of fertilization as mixing of liquids; performed experiments with tobacco hybrids supporting theory of plant sexuality. He believed sterility of "natural" plant hybrids was purposive mechanism for maintaining harmony of nature; rejected counterevidence of fertile hybrids developed in botanical gardens by distinguishing between natural and artificial worlds. Drew an analogy between pollen and sulfur of the alchemist, and between female seed and mercury of alchemist; succeeded in "transmuting" *Nicotiana rustica* into *N. paniculata* (1763). These experiments supported theory of bisexual heredity and weakened preformation theory.

KOENIG (KÖNIG), JOHANN SAMUEL (*b. Büdingen, Germany, 1712; d. Zuilenstein, near Amerongen, Netherlands, 1757*), mathematics, physics.

Studied mathematics in Basel (1730–35) under Johann I Bernoulli, Daniel Bernoulli, and Jakob Hermann; studied under Leibniz' disciple, Christian von Wolff, in Marburg (1735–37); practiced law in Bern while unsuccessfully pursuing chair at Lausanne (1737–38); in Paris (1739) instructed Voltaire's friend, marquise du Chatelet; returned to Bern (1740), where he was exiled for liberal political views (1744). Became professor at University of Franeker in Netherlands, and moved to The Hague (1749) as privy councillor and librarian. Best known for his essay on principle of least action (1751), which triggered the famous scientific dispute with Maupertuis, Euler, Frederick II, and Voltaire.

KOENIG, JULIUS (*b. Györ, Hungary, 1849; d. Budapest, Hungary, 1914*), mathematics.
Studied at Vienna and Heidelberg (Ph.D., 1870), where he was influenced by Helmholtz; taught at Budapest's technical university; in later years was civil servant in Ministry of Education. His most important work (1903) develops Kronecker's theory of polynomial ideals.

KOENIG, KARL RUDOLPH (*b. Königsberg, East Prussia [now Kaliningrad, R.S.F.S.R.], 1832; d. Paris, France, 1901*), acoustics.
Graduated from University of Königsberg (Ph.D., 1851), where he studied with Helmholtz; became apprentice to violin maker in Paris (1851). He began his own business producing equipment used for acoustical research; also conducted important research, collected in *Quelques expériences d'acoustique* (1882).

KOENIGS, GABRIEL (*b. Toulouse, France, 1858; d. Paris, France, 1931*), differential geometry, kinematics, applied mechanics.
Graduated École Normale Supérieure in Paris (Ph.D., 1882); taught mathematics at École Normale (1886–95); taught physical and experimental mechanics at Sorbonne (from 1895); a disciple of Darboux, Koenigs did work in infinitesimal geometry, kinematics, and applied thermodynamics.

KOFOID, CHARLES ATWOOD (*b. Granville, Ill., 1865; d. Berkeley, Calif., 1947*), zoology.
Studied at Oberlin (B.S., 1890) and Harvard (Ph.D., 1894); director of Biological Station at University of Illinois (1895–1901); taught zoology at University of California at Berkeley (1901–36); his research centered on plankton and pelagic life of Pacific ocean. He helped found Scripps Institution of Oceanography at La Jolla, California.

KÖHLER, AUGUST KARL JOHANN VALENTIN (*b. Darmstadt, Germany, 1866; d. Jena, Germany, 1948*), microscopy.
Studied at universities of Heidelberg and Giessen (passed state exam for teachers in 1888); became assistant at Institute of Comparative Anatomy of University of Giessen (1891–1900); joined Carl Zeiss firm in Jena (1900–48). Though he did research in zoology, his main interest was in improving microphotography; helped develop the ultraviolet microscope (1904), which did not become popular until thirty years later.

KOHLRAUSCH, FRIEDRICH WILHELM GEORG (*b. Rinteln, Germany, 1840; d. Marburg, Germany, 1910*), chemistry, physics.
Educated at universities of Marburg, Erlangen, and Göttingen (Ph.D., Göttingen, 1863), where he studied under W. Weber; taught at Göttingen (1866–70), the Polytechnikum at Zurich (1870–71), Darmstadt (1871–75), and University of Würzburg (1875–88); director of physical laboratory at Strasbourg (1888–94); director of Physikalisch Technische Reichsanstalt at Charlottenburg (from 1894). He is best known for research on electrical conductivity of solutions, which led to Arrhenius' electrolytic dissociation theory of solution structure.

KOHLRAUSCH, RUDOLPH HERRMANN ARNDT (*b. Göttingen, Germany, 1809; d. Erlangen, Germany, 1858*), physics.
Father of physicist F. W. Kohlrausch; taught at several gymnasiums before appointments at University of Marburg (1853–58) and University of Erlangen (1857–58). Best known for showing, with W. Weber, that ratio of absolute electrostatic unit of charge to absolute electromagnetic unit of charge equals speed of light.

KOLBE, ADOLF WILHELM HERMANN (*b. Eliehausen near Göttingen, Germany, 1818; d. Leipzig, Germany, 1884*), chemistry.
Entered University of Göttingen (1838), where he studied under Wöhler; while a student he met Berzelius, whose theories greatly influenced Kolbe; finished dissertation at Marburg, where he was assistant to Bunsen and learned Bunsen's methods of gas analysis; assisted L. Playfair at School of Mines in London (1845–47), where he met E. Frankland, with whom he conducted joint studies. Edited *Handwörterbuch der Chemie* (1847–51); taught at Marburg (1851–65); taught at Leipzig (from 1865), where he built largest and best equipped chemical laboratory of its day (completed in 1868). Edited *Journal für praktische Chemie* (from 1870), in which Kolbe violently criticized contemporaries such as Kekulé, van t'Hoff, and Le Bel. A brilliant experimenter, whose work in organic chemistry resulted in discovery of many important compounds and reactions. He developed his own method of representing structure of compounds which involved incorrect ideas, e.g., he refused to abandon equivalent weights for atomic weights until 1869, and refused to abandon Berzelius' concept of radicals. Kolbe's criticisms of type theory prepared way for acceptance of Kekulé's structural theory, which was similar to Kolbe's but simpler; in later years he developed a method for large-scale synthesis of salicylic acid.

KOLOSOV, GURY VASILIEVICH (*b. Ust, Novgorod guberniya, Russia, 1867; d. Leningrad, U.S.S.R., 1936*), theoretical physics, mechanics, mathematics.
Graduated in physics and mathematics from St. Petersburg (now Leningrad) University (1889), where he passed master's examination (1893) and taught theoretical mechanics (1913–36); research concerned mechanics of solid bodies and theory of elasticity.

KOLTZOFF, NIKOLAI KONSTANTINOVICH (*b. Moscow, Russia, 1872; d. Leningrad, U.S.S.R., 1940*), zoology, cytology, genetics.

Graduated in natural sciences from Moscow University (1894); after three years additional study at Moscow, studied abroad in laboratories of Flemming at Kiel and of O. Bütschli in Heidelberg, and at several biological stations (1897–99, 1902–4); awarded master's degree (1901), but refused to defend doctoral dissertation (1906) for political reasons. Taught at Moscow University (1903–11); left university as political protest and taught at Shanyavsky People's University; returned to Moscow University (1918–30), where he headed Institute of Experimental Biology (1917–39), the first Russian biological institute. Koltzoff's career concerned three areas of interest; after initial work in comparative anatomy, he studied experimental cytology, in which he advanced the principle of skeletal structure in the cell (the Koltzoff principle), and he experimented with spermatozoan and other cell structures; his second area of research was physicochemical and colloidal biology; third area was genetics, in which he made prophetic theoretical contributions.

KOMENSKY, JAN AMOS. *See* **Comenius, John Amos.**

KONDAKOV, IVAN LAVRENTIEVICH (*b. Vilyuisk, Yakutia, Russia* [*now Yakut A.S.S.R.*], *1857; d. Elva, Estonia, 1931*), chemistry.

Graduated St. Petersburg University (1884); worked at Warsaw University (1886–95); taught at University of Yurev (Tartu) (1895–1918); main contribution was discovery of methods of polymerization of diisopropenyl, providing basis of industrial production of synthetic "methyl rubber," accomplished in Germany (1915).

KÖNIG, ARTHUR (*b. Krefeld, Germany, 1856; d. Berlin, Germany, 1901*), physics.

Graduated from the University of Berlin (Ph.D., 1882), where he was assistant to Helmholtz; became professor and head of physics division of physiological institute of University of Berlin (1889). He devoted studies to physiological optics; an excellent experimenter, who defended the Young-Helmholtz theory of color perception and studied color blindness. He was active in editing periodicals.

KÖNIG, EMANUEL (*b. Basel, Switzerland, 1658; d. Basel, 1731*), natural history, medicine.

Graduated from University of Basel (M.D., 1682), where he taught Greek (from 1695), physics (from 1703) and medicine (from 1711). His main importance was as popularizer of natural history and medicine; wrote *Regnum animale* (1682), *Regnum minerale* (1686), and *Regnum vegetabile* (1688); his books are well reasoned and well researched, though credulous of superstitions.

KÖNIGSBERGER, LEO (*b. Posen, Germany* [*now Poznań, Poland*], *1837; d. Heidelberg, Germany, 1921*), mathematics.

Graduated from University of Berlin (1860), influenced by Weierstrass; taught at University of Heidelberg (1869–75; 1884–1914); made contributions to analysis and analytical mechanics; best-known works are biography of his close friend, Helmholtz (1902), and a biographical *Festschrift* for C.G.J. Jacobi (1904).

KONINCK, LAURENT-GUILLAUME DE (*b. Louvain, Belgium, 1809: d. Liège, Belgium, 1887*), chemistry, paleontology.

Graduated University of Louvain with doctorate in medicine, pharmacy, and natural sciences (1831); practiced medicine for only a short time; visited German chemical laboratories (1834–35); taught chemistry at University of Liège (1836–76), although his principal activity was in paleontology; chief work concerned fauna of Carboniferous limestone; he remained convinced of fixity of species which led him to exaggerate number of species; work is valuable for precise descriptions and for the number of fossil forms it helped make known.

KONKOLY THEGE, MIKLÓS VON (*b. Budapest, Hungary, 1842; d. Budapest, 1916*), astronomy, geophysics.

Graduated from University of Berlin (Ph.D. in astronomy, 1862); established observatory at his estate at Ógyalla (1869), donating it to Hungarian government in 1898; directed Hungarian Meteorological Service (from 1890).

KONOVALOV, DMITRY PETROVICH (*b. Ivanovka, Ekaterinoslav guberniya* [*now Dnepropetrovsk oblast*], *Russia, 1856; d. Leningrad, U.S.S.R., 1929*), chemistry.

Graduated from Institute of Mines, St. Petersburg University (1878), where he taught from 1886; studied under Mendeleev at St. Petersburg (from 1890); director of St. Petersburg Institute of Mines (from 1904); director of government's Department of Mines (from 1907). His research was mainly in theory of solutions, kinetics, and catalysis; he formulated Konovalov's laws concerning vapor pressure of solutions (1884), which made possible industrial distillation of solutions; the Ostwald-Konovalov formula expresses the fundamental law of autocatalysis (developed independently by Ostwald in 1888 and Konovalov in 1885).

KOPP, HERMANN (*b. Hanau, Electoral Hesse, 1817; d. Heidelberg, Germany, 1892*), chemistry.

Kopp's interest in chemistry was stimulated by L. Gmelin at University of Heidelberg (entered in 1836); received Ph.D. at Marburg (1838); taught at Giessen (1839–63), where he worked with Liebig; taught crystallography and history of chemistry at Heidelberg (1863–90). His chief interest was in the connection between physical properties and chemical nature of substances; his work involved tedious purifications and laborious calculation, but Kopp enjoyed this type of study, despite his poor health. He studied specific gravity, specific heat, boiling points, and other physical constants; involved in disputes with H. G. F. Schröder, whose work paralleled Kopp's. With Liebig, he continued publication of *Jahresbericht über die Fortschritte der Chemie* after death of Berzelius, its founder. He edited *Justus Liebigs Annalen der Chemie;* his best-known works were on history of chemistry; he wrote four-volume *Geschichte der Chemie* (1843–47), the first complete, accurate, and readable history of chemistry. *Die Entwicklung der Chemie in der neueren Zeit* (1873) discussed recent chemical developments. He was involved in polemical disputes with Berthelot, a French historian of chemistry.

KOROLEV, SERGEY PAVLOVICH (*b. Zhitomir, Russia, 1907; d. Moscow, U.S.S.R., 1966*), mechanics, rocket and space technology.

Graduated from Faculty of Aeromechanics of Bauman Higher Technical School in Moscow (1929), defending his thesis on the SK-4 airplane, which he had built himself. Korolev's interest turned to rocket and space technology, and he joined Institute for Jet Research after its creation (1933); his building of long-distance rockets resulted in launching of first artificial earth satellite (1957); he directed Soviet launches of probes to Venus (1961–65) and Mars (1962).

KORTEWEG, DIEDERIK JOHANNES (*b. 's Hertogenbosch, Netherlands, 1848; d. Amsterdam, Netherlands, 1941*), mathematics.

Graduated from University of Amsterdam (Ph.D., 1878), where he taught mathematics (1881–1918) and helped raise mathematics in Netherlands to modern level; his main scientific work was in applied mathematics; edited *Oeuvres* of C. Huygens (1911–27).

KOSSEL, KARL MARTIN LEONHARD ALBRECHT (*b. Rostock, Germany, 1853; d. Heidelberg, Germany, 1927*), nucleoprotein chemistry.

Received M.D. from University of Strasbourg (before 1877), where he was influenced by Germany's foremost physiological chemist, F. Hoppe-Seyler. Became director of chemical division of Berlin physiological institute (1883–93); received chair of physiology and directorship of physiological institute in Marburg (1893–1901). Received chair of physiology at Heidelberg (1901–24) and directed new institute for study of proteins (1924–27). Received Nobel Prize in physiology or medicine (1910). Began to study nucleins (nucleoproteins) in 1879; with his students, he discovered adenine, thymine, cytosine, and uracil (1885–1901), which he demonstrated were breakdown products of nucleic acids and can be used to distinguish between true nucleins and paranucleins. He established that the function of nuclein is formation of fresh tissue; isolated histone (1884). Developed a scheme of protein synthesis in attempt to unite chemical description with physiological function.

KOSSEL, WALTHER (LUDWIG JULIUS PASCHEN HEINRICH) (*b. Berlin, Germany, 1888; d. Kassel, Germany, 1956*), physics.

Son of Albrecht Kossel (1853–1927). Studied physics under Philipp Lenard at University of Heidelberg (Ph.D., 1911); further study at University of Munich and Technische Hochschule, where Laue, Friedrich, and Knipping had shown that X rays could be diffracted by crystals (1912). His first important contribution to physics was extension of Bohr's theory to mechanism of X-ray emission; also contributed to theories of valence and bonding. He asserted that the number of electrons in outer ring determines chemical properties of an atom, and that the chemical bond was due largely to electrostatic forces (1916). Taught theoretical physics and was director of Institute for Theoretical Physics at University of Kiel (1921–32); taught experimental physics and was director of Institute for Experimental Physics at Technische Hochschule in Danzig (now Gdańsk, Poland) (1932–45). At Danzig discovered interference effects (the so-called Kossel effect) produced by characteristic Roentgen rays excited in a single crystal (1935); he also contributed to theory of electron diffraction. Left Danzig because of

Russian occupation (1945). From 1947, he taught experimental physics and directed Experimental Physics Institute at University of Tübingen.

KOSTANECKI, STANISŁAW (*b. Myszakow, Poznań province, Poland, 1860; d. Würzburg, Germany, 1910*), chemistry.

Entered Faculty of Philosophy of University of Berlin (1883), where he became Liebermann's assistant and jointly published papers establishing Liebermann-Kostanecki rule, which states that the only technically satisfactory dyestuffs are those hydroxyanthraquinone ones with two hydroxyl groups attached. Received doctorate University of Basel (1890); taught organic and theoretical chemistry at University of Bern (1890–1910). Did research mainly in structural problems of vegetable dyestuffs.

KOSTINSKY, SERGEY KONSTANTINOVICH (*b. Moscow, Russia, 1867; d. Pulkovo, near Leningrad, U.S.S.R., 1936*), astronomy.

Graduated from Faculty of Physics and Mathematics of Moscow University (1890); began work at Pulkovo observatory (1890), where he became senior astronomer (1902); taught at Petrograd-Leningrad University (from 1919). His main research was in astrophotography (from 1898). He discovered effect of mutual repulsion of very close stellar images on negatives (Kostinsky effect). He used photographs to measure proper motions and parallaxes of stars; at Pulkovo, he established school of specialists in photographic astrometry.

KOTELNIKOV, ALEKSANDR PETROVICH (*b. Kazan, Russia, 1865; d. Moscow, U.S.S.R., 1944*), mechanics, mathematics.

Graduated from Kazan University (1884), where he began teaching (1893) and obtained doctorate in both pure and applied mathematics (1899). Taught at Kiev (1899–1904), Kazan (1904–14), Kiev Polytechnical Institute (1914–24), and Bauman Technical College in Moscow (1924–44). Developed generalization of vector calculus to non-Euclidean spaces; edited the works of Zhukovsky and Lobachevsky.

KOTŌ, BUNJIRO (*b. Tsuwano, Iwami [now Shimane prefecture], Japan, 1856; d. Tokyo, Japan, 1935*), geology, seismology.

Graduated from Tokyo Imperial University (1879), where he was first student to specialize in geology; further study at University of Munich and University of Leipzig (Ph.D., 1884), where he was taught by Credner and Zirkel; he taught at Tokyo University (1885–1921). His early research was in metamorphic rocks of Japan, but after great Nobi earthquake (1891), he studied volcanoes, earthquakes, and geotectonics.

KOVALEVSKY, ALEKSANDR ONUFRIEVICH (*b. Daugavpils district, Vitebsk region, Russia [now Latvian S.S.R.], 1840; d. St. Petersburg, Russia, 1901*), embryology.

Graduated in natural sciences St. Petersburg University (M.A., 1865; Ph.D., 1866); further study at Heidelberg (1860) and Tübingen (1861–62, 1863–64); taught at Kazan University (1868–69), University of St. Vladimir in Kiev (1869–73), Novorossisk University in Odessa (1873–

90), and St. Petersburg University (1891–94). The leading Russian embryologist of late nineteenth century and a Darwinist, he established that many organisms develop from a bilaminar sac (gastrula) produced by invagination.

KOVALEVSKY, SONYA (or **Kovalevskaya, Sofya Vasilyevna**) (*b. Moscow, Russia, 1850; d. Stockholm, Sweden, 1891*), mathematics.

The greatest woman mathematician prior to twentieth century, she took part in the movement to emancipate women in Russia—one technique of which was arranging a marriage of convenience in order to study at a foreign university. Married Vladimir Kovalevsky, young paleontologist whose brother, Aleksandr, was a renowned zoologist; they went to Heidelberg (1869), where Vladimir studied geology and Sonya took courses with Kirchhoff, Helmholtz, Koenigsberger, and du Bois-Reymond. Sonya went to Berlin while Vladimir went to Jena to obtain doctorate (1871). Since women were not admitted to university lectures, Weierstrass tutored Sonya privately for four years; by 1874 she had written three papers on partial differential equations, Abelian integrals, and Saturn's rings, which qualified her for her doctorate *in absentia* from the University of Göttingen. Because she was unable to obtain an academic position anywhere in Europe, she returned to Russia, where she was reunited with her husband and had her first and only child (1878). When Vladimir was unable to get a lectureship at Moscow University, he and Sonya worked at odd jobs. An involvement with shady speculations for an unscrupulous company led to Vladimir's disgrace and suicide (1883). Through a disciple of Weierstrass, Gösta Mittag-Leffler, Sonya was appointed to life professorship in mathematics at the University of Stockholm (1889); her memoir, *On the Rotation of a Solid Body About a Fixed Point* (1888), won the Prix Bordin of the French Academy of Sciences; she was elected to the Russian Academy of Sciences (1889); two years later died of influenza complicated by pneumonia. Best-known in mathematics for Cauchy-Kovalevsky theorem, basic to the theory of partial differential equations. Also attempted a simultaneous career in literature; her novels include *The University Lecturer*, *The Nihilist*, *The Woman Nihilist*, and *A Story of the Riviera;* collaborated with Mittag-Leffler's sister, A. C. Leffler-Edgren, who wrote a biography of Sonya, in writing a drama, *The Struggle for Happiness*, which was favorably received when produced in Moscow.

KOVALEVSKY, VLADIMIR ONUFRIEVICH (*b. Dünaberg, Vitebsk region, Russia [now Daugavpils, Latvian S.S.R.], 1842; d. Moscow, Russia, 1883*), paleontology.

Graduated from School of Jurisprudence (1861); married Sonya (Sofya) Korvin-Krukovsky in 1869 (see article above). Studied natural sciences in European universities and museums (1869–74); passed doctoral examinations in Jena (1872); awarded master's degree (1875); associate professor at Moscow University (1880–83). A Darwinist, Kovalevsky's paleontological research dealt with evolution of teeth and skull of mammals as related to change of plant food composition.

KOVALSKY, MARIAN ALBERTOVICH (VOYTEK-HOVICH) (*b. Dobrzhin, Russia [now Dobrzyn nad Wisła, Poland], 1821; d. Kazan, Russia, 1884*), astronomy.

Graduated in mathematics from St. Petersburg University (1841; M.S., 1847); participated in Russian Geographical Society expedition to Urals to determine astronomical coordinates. Taught astronomy at Kazan University (1850–84); defended doctoral dissertation on theory of motion of Neptune (1852); director of Kazan Observatory (from 1855). Made contributions to celestial mechanics, astronomy, and stellar astronomy; developed first practical method of discovering rotation of the Galaxy from proper motion of stars (1860; rotation not confirmed until 1927 by J. H. Oort).

KOWALEWSKY. *See* **Kovalevsky.**

KOYRÉ, ALEXANDRE (*b. Taganrog, Russia, 1892; d. Paris, France, 1964*), history of science, of philosophy, and of ideas.

Koyré's work was threefold: he exercised a formative influence upon the entire generation of historians of science, especially in the U.S.; he initiated a revival of Hegelian studies in 1930's; he made important contributions to the history of Russian thought. A philosophical idealist who believed the object of philosophical reasoning is reality; also a Platonist, as seen in his *Discovering Plato* (1945). His secondary education was at Tiflis and Rostov-on-Don; studied at Göttingen (1908–11) under Husserl (phenomenology) and Hilbert (mathematics); studied at Sorbonne in Paris under Bergson and L. Brunschvicg (1911–14). After fighting in French and Russian armies, he returned to Paris, where a theological work on Descartes (1922) earned Koyré the diploma of the École Pratique and a teaching position there, which he maintained the rest of his life; a theological work on St. Anselm (1923) earned him a doctorate from the Sorbonne. His early theological works concerned the ontological arguments of Descartes and Anselm for the existence of God; only later in *Entretiens sur Descartes* (1944) did Koyré discuss Descartes' role in the history of science. Though Koyré came to devote his life to history of science, he remained in the section for the "sciences réligieuses" at the École Pratique since there was no provision for the history of science in the Parisian academic structure. Another theological work by Koyré, *La Philosophie de Jacob Boehme* (1929), remains the most considerable and reliable study of Boehme; soon after it appeared, Koyré began teaching at Montpellier (1930–31); he resumed teaching at the École Pratique (1932), where he prepared a translation and interpretation of book I of Copernicus' *De revolutionibus* (1934), his first contribution to the history of science proper. Taught on a visiting basis at the University of Cairo (1934; 1936–37; 1937–38), where he composed his masterpiece, *Études galiléennes* (1940); returned to Paris just as the city surrendered (1940), so he returned to Cairo and offered his services to De Gaulle, who asked him to go to U.S. to promote Gaullist views. In New York he helped found the École Libre des Hautes Études and taught at the New School for Social Research throughout the war. The *Études galiléennes* became very popular in the U.S.; the theme is the emergence of classical physics from the effort to formulate the law of falling bodies and the law of inertia. Attributing the law of inertia to Descartes was one of the most original and surprising of Koyré's findings in the *Études;* in Koyré's view, the concept of inertia resulted in a more decisive mutation in man's sense of himself in the world than any intellectual event since the beginnings of civilization. After the war, he continued teaching in Paris in addition to Harvard, Yale, Johns Hopkins, Chicago, and the University of Wisconsin; from 1955 until 1962 he spent half the year at the Institute for Advanced Study in Princeton and half the year at the École Pratique in Paris. The last book Koyré left in finished form was *La révolution astronomique* (1961), which dealt with Kepler, Copernicus, and Borelli. His essay on Newtonian synthesis in *Newtonian Studies* (published in 1965 after his death) is one of his best writings; he collaborated with I. Bernard Cohen and A. Whitman on a variorum edition of Newton's *Principia* (1972); *From the Closed World to the Infinite Universe* (1957) explored metaphysical and theological implications of the transition to "world-feelings" epitomized in the title; central theme is alienation of consciousness from nature by its own creation of science.

KRAFT, JENS (*b. Fredrikstad, Norway, 1720; d. Sorø, Denmark, 1765*), mathematics, physics, anthropology, philosophy.

Received master's degree University of Copenhagen (1742); studied philosophy with C. Wolff in Germany, and mathematics and physics in France; first professor of mathematics and philosophy in reestablished academy for nobility at Sorø (1747–65). Though he wrote on many subjects, his best-known work is textbook on theoretical and technical mechanics (1763–64); also wrote ethnological book regarded as pioneering work in social anthropology (1760). A Newtonian, Kraft helped diminish influence of Cartesianism in Denmark.

KRAMERS, HENDRIK ANTHONY (*b. Rotterdam, Netherlands, 1894; d. Oegstgeest, Netherlands, 1952*), theoretical physics.

Studied theoretical physics with P. Ehrenfest at Leiden (obtained equivalent of master's degree in 1916); at Copenhagen became close collaborator of Niels Bohr (1916–26); taught physics at Utrecht (1926–34), and succeeded Ehrenfest at Leiden (1934–52). At Copenhagen worked on further development of quantum theory of atom; his paper on helium atom (1923) was important in demonstrating inadequacy of the provisional quantum theory. Coauthor of famous paper by Bohr, Kramers, and J.C. Slater (1924), which suggested conservation of energy might not hold in elementary processes (not substantiated); in this paper and one with Heisenberg (1924), they developed theory of dispersion. Later work may be divided into four groups: papers dealing with mathematical formalism of quantum mechanics; papers on paramagnetism, magneto-optical rotation, and ferromagnetism, some of which were done with J. Becquerel; contributions, with J. Kistemaker, to kinetic theory of gases; and papers on relativistic formalisms in particle theory and on theory of radiation. Kramers' work covers almost entire field of theoretical physics and shows outstanding mathematical skill and careful analysis of physical principles.

KRAMP, CHRÉTIEN or **CHRISTIAN** (*b. Strasbourg, France, 1760, d. Strasbourg, 1826*), physics, astronomy, mathematics.

Studied medicine and practiced in Rhineland cities; professor of mathematics and dean of Faculty of Science of Strasbourg (from around 1809); published works on aerostatics (1783), crystallography and double refraction (1793), medicine (1786, 1794, 1812), astronomy (*Analyse des réfractions astronomiques et terrestres*, 1798), and mathematics (*Éléments d'arithmétique universelle*, 1808); a disciple of K.F. Hindenburg, Kramp was a representative of the combinatorial school, which played an important role in German mathematics.

KRASHENINNIKOV, STEPAN PETROVICH (*b. Moscow, Russia, 1711; d. St. Petersburg, Russia [now Leningrad, U.S.S.R.], 1755*), geography, ethnography, botany, history.

Studied at University of St. Petersburg Academy of Sciences (1732–33) before joining Academy's expedition to Kamchatka (1733–43); appointed professor of natural history and botany at Academy (1750); worked mainly on material gathered on expedition.

KRASNOV, ANDREY NIKOLAEVICH (*b. St. Petersburg, Russia, 1862; d. Tbilisi, Russia, 1915*), geography, geobotany.

Graduated in natural sciences at St. Petersburg University (1885; M.S., 1889; Ph.D., 1894); taught geography at Kharkov University (1889–1912); his research was mainly on steppe and tropical and subtropical plants; wrote first original Russian university textbooks in geography.

KRASOVSKY, THEODOSY NICOLAEVICH (*b. Galich, Kostroma guberniya, Russia, 1878; d. Moscow, U.S.S.R., 1948*), earth sciences, mathematics.

Graduated Moscow Geodetic Institute (1900), where he taught (from 1902); additional study at Moscow University and Pulkovo observatory (1900–03); contributed to study of geometry of the figure of the earth.

KRAUS, CHARLES AUGUST (*b. Knightsville, Ind., 1875; d. East Providence, R.I., 1967*), chemistry.

Graduated in engineering from University of Kansas (B.A., 1898); after year as research fellow at Johns Hopkins University, taught physics at University of California (1901–04); Ph.D. in chemistry at Massachusetts Institute of Technology (1908), where he taught and did research (1908–14); taught chemistry and was head of chemical laboratory at Clark University (1914–23); professor of chemistry and director of chemical research at Brown University (1924–46). With E.C. Franklin wrote eight papers on ammonia solution (1898–1905); published over twenty-five papers on metal-organic systems; with C. Callis designed economical quantity synthesis of tetraethyl lead, which reduced engine knock when added to gasoline (1922).

KRAUSE, ERNST LUDWIG, also known as **Carus Sterne** (*b. Zielenzig, Germany [now Sulęcin, Poland], 1839; d. Eberswalde, Germany, 1903*), scientific popularization.

After training to be apothecary, studied science at University of Berlin (beginning 1857); after receiving doctorate at University of Rostock (1874), he lived in Berlin. Wrote popular works against spiritualism and in support of Darwin's theory of evolution; Krause's *Werden und Vergehen* (1876) was well-received; it introduced many readers to theory of evolution and explained its effect on anthropomorphic concept of God; edited *Kosmos* (1877–

83). His essay on Erasmus Darwin is indispensable for studying history of theory of evolution.

KRAYENHOFF, CORNELIS RUDOLPHUS THEODORUS (*b. Nijmegen, Netherlands, 1758; d. Nijmegen, 1840*), geodesy, engineering.

Received two degrees, in science (1780) and in medicine (1784) from Harderwijk; after ten years of medical practice in Amsterdam, was persuaded to take up military career. Became minister of war under King Louis Bonaparte, but was relieved in a year and studied arts of war, especially fortification. Krayenhoff's defense works were admired by Napoleon, who summoned him to Paris to join commission on fortifications. Under King William I, worked on fortifications and hydraulic engineering. Pensioned in 1830, he devoted full time to physics and astronomy. After 1798, he worked on map of Netherlands in order to divide it into *départements* and *arrondissements*, following French example. In *Précis historique* (1815) he recounts how he made extensive system of triangles, and demonstrates use of "the rule of sines in a polygon" in geodesy for the first time.

KROGH, SCHACK AUGUST STEENBERG (*b. Grenå, Jutland, Denmark, 1874; d. Copenhagen, Denmark, 1949*), zoology, physiology.

Graduated from University of Copenhagen (M.Sc., 1899), where he studied physiology under C. Bohr; after graduation became assistant to Bohr. More interested in physical than in chemical problems in biology; his first internationally known work was a paper demonstrating that free nitrogen takes no part in respiratory exchanges; though he at first adhered to secretion theory of pulmonary gas exchange, he later concluded that diffusion was responsible (1910). Left Bohr's laboratory for professorship of zoophysiology at University of Copenhagen (1908–46), where he was later given a laboratory (1910). Developed many instruments for studying blood flow and respiration: rocker spirometer, electromagnetic bicycle ergometer, and gas analysis apparatus. For his demonstration that the capillaries of muscles were partially closed during rest and mostly open during work, Krogh was awarded the Nobel Prize in physiology or medicine (1920). With co-workers from all over the world, he showed that capillary movements were influenced by nerves and hormones; published a monograph on anatomy and physiology of capillaries (1922). The Rockefeller Foundation provided funds for new laboratories for Krogh, named Rockefeller Institute (opened in 1928 in Juliane Mariesvej), where Krogh continued studies on heavy muscle work. He never lost interest in zoophysiology, demonstrating the importance of diffusion for insect respiration; also studied metabolism of sea animals and flight of insects and birds.

KRONECKER, HUGO (*b. Liegnitz, Germany [now Legnica, Poland], 1839; d. Bad Nauheim, Germany, 1914*), physiology.

Brother of mathematician L. Kronecker. Received doctorate from University of Berlin (1863), where he studied physiology under du Bois-Reymond; also studied at Pisa and Heidelberg, where he assisted H. von Helmholtz and W. Wundt in studies on muscles. Registered as a medical practitioner (1865); received clinical training at Berlin

under W. Kühne; in Leipzig assisted C. Ludwig at Physiologische Anstalt (1868–75), and was lecturer (1875–77). In charge of "special physiological department" of Institute of Physiology at Berlin (1878–84); professor of physiology at Bern (1884–1914). Kronecker's main studies concerned muscles, the heart and circulation, mechanism of deglutition, and mountain sickness; discovered use of saline solution as blood substitute (1884).

KRONECKER, LEOPOLD (*b. Liegnitz, Germany [now Legnica, Poland], 1823; d. Berlin, Germany, 1891*), mathematics.

Brother of physiologist H. Kronecker. Encouraged to do mathematics by E. E. Kummer at Liegnitz Gymnasium; received doctorate from University of Berlin (1845), where he attended lectures by Dirichlet and Steiner; also studied at Bonn and Breslau; Kronecker was greatly influenced by Dirichlet and especially by Kummer, and remained close friends with both. Called away from Berlin on family business, he returned to Berlin as a financially independent private scholar, the same year that Kummer succeeded Dirichlet at the University of Berlin (1855); as a member of the Berlin Academy (1861), Kronecker was entitled to give lectures at the University of Berlin (1862–83); principal topics were theory of algebraic equations, theory of numbers, theory of determinants, and theory of simple and multiple integrals. While he did not attract many students, he was very influential in the affairs of the Academy, particularly in recruiting eminent mathematicians for membership; succeeded C. W. Borchardt as editor of *Journal für die reine und angewandte Mathematik* (1880). Succeeded Kummer in the chair of mathematics at Berlin (1883–91), and was named codirector of mathematics seminar with Weierstrass. He eventually broke with Weierstrass because of personal and scholarly differences: Kronecker objected to Weierstrass' methods of analysis, believing that "God Himself made the whole numbers—everything else is the work of men." He believed all arithmetic could be based upon whole numbers only, while Weierstrass granted irrational numbers equal validity; the conflict was ended only by Kronecker's death (1891). His greatest mathematical achievements lie in efforts to unify arithmetic, algebra, and analysis, and particularly in his work on elliptical functions; Kronecker stressed the use of the algorithm for calculation, rather than as a concept; though his mathematics lacked a systematic theoretical basis, Kronecker was preeminent in uniting the separate mathematical disciplines.

KRÖNIG, AUGUST KARL (*b. Schildesche, Westphalia, Germany, 1822; d. Berlin, Germany, 1879*), physics.

Graduated University of Berlin (Ph.D., 1845); taught at Berlin Königliche Realschule and edited several journals. Though commonly recognized as originator of kinetic theory of gases (1859), Krönig may have inadvertently utilized the conclusions of a paper by Waterston, an abstract of which he had reviewed while editor of *Die Fortschritte der Physik* (1855–59); not a significant figure in the Berlin scientific community.

KROPOTKIN, PETR ALEKSEEVICH (*b. Moscow, Russia, 1842; d. Dmitrov, Moscow oblast, U.S.S.R., 1921*), geography.

After education at School of Pages in St. Petersburg (1857–62), Kropotkin enlisted in the Amur Cossack army in order to study Siberia; served as adjutant to General Kukel; took part in military missions for geographical investigations to the Transbaikal region and to the basins of Vitim and Olekma rivers, and published observations (1865, 1873). Published a paper on orography of eastern Siberia (1875); left army to study mathematics at St. Petersburg University (1867). After a visit to Finland and Sweden to study glacial phenomena on behalf of Russian Geographic Society, he presented a paper to the Society refuting the view that huge boulders had been transported to European fields by ice floes (1874). His major contribution was thus in corroborating the theory of ancient continental glaciation. In 1874 he was arrested for espousing anarchism, and was imprisoned at St. Petersburg (1874–76); escaped to Edinburgh (1876), and lived in Switzerland and France, where he was arrested and imprisoned for disseminating anarchist propaganda (1883–86); after release lived in London. While visiting the United States in 1897, Kropotkin agreed to write his memoirs for *Atlantic Monthly;* the work appeared in English (1899) and was translated into Russian (1902) as a separate book entitled *Memoirs of a Revolutionist;* it received wide circulation in western countries and was frequently reprinted in the Soviet Union (7th ed., Moscow, 1966); after the February Revolution (1917), he returned to Russia.

KR̥ṢṆA (*fl. 1653 at Taṭāka, Mahārāṣṭra, India*), astronomy.

Wrote the *Karaṇakaustubha* at the command of the bhūpati Śiva (*ca.* 1653); the *Karaṇakaustubha* is based on the *Grahalāghava* of Gaṇeśa and is an astronomical work.

KRUBER, ALEKSANDR ALEKSANDROVICH (*b. Voskresensk [now Istra], Moscow guberniya, Russia, 1871; d. Moscow, U.S.S.R., 1941*), geography.

Graduated from Moscow University (1896), where he subsequently taught geography (1897–1927) and received master of geography degree (1915); director of Moscow University Scientific Research Institute of Geography (1923–27); one of the founders of scientific study of karstic phenomena in Russia.

KRYLOV, ALEKSEI NIKOLAEVICH (*b. Visyaga, Simbirskoy province [now Ulyanovskaya oblast], Russia, 1863; d. Leningrad, U.S.S.R., 1945*), mathematics, mechanics, engineering.

Graduated from Maritime Academy (1890), where he taught theoretical and engineering sciences for almost fifty years. Krylov's work covered wide spectrum of naval science: theories of buoyancy, stability, rolling and pitching, vibration, and performance, and compass theories. Director of Physics and Mathematics Institute of Soviet Academy of Sciences (1927–32); author of numerous works in history of science, including Russian translation of Newton's *Principia* (1915).

KRYLOV, NIKOLAI MITROFANOVICH (*b. St. Petersburg, Russia, 1879; d. Moscow, U.S.S.R., 1955*), mathematics.

Graduated from St. Petersburg Institute of Mines (1902), where he later taught (1912–17); also taught at

Crimea University (1917–22); appointed chairman of mathematical physics department Academy of Sciences of Ukrainian S.S.R. (1922); Krylov's works were mainly in theory of interpolation, of approximate integration of differential equations, and of nonlinear mechanics.

KUENEN, JOHANNES PETRUS (*b. Leiden, Netherlands, 1866; d. Leiden, 1922*), physics.

Graduated from University of Leiden (Ph.D., 1892) where he was appointed assistant to H. Kamerlingh Onnes (1889); also studied in London with Sir William Ramsay and at University of Dundee, where he taught physics (1895–1906); taught physics at Leiden (1906–22); known chiefly for his work on phase equilibria; discovered phenomenon of retrograde condensation.

KÜHN, ALFRED (*b. Baden-Baden, Germany, 1885; d. Tübingen, Germany, 1968*), zoology.

Graduated from University of Freiburg im Breisgau (Ph.D., 1908), where he studied with A. Weismann and later taught (from 1910). After World War I, taught zoology at University of Göttingen (1920–37); director of Kaiser Wilhelm Institute for Biology in Berlin-Dahlem (1937–58), which was later moved to Tübingen and renamed the Max Planck Institute for Biology (1951). His main studies concerned genetics and early development; helped develop concept that genes achieve their effects by means of specific enzymes.

KUHN, RICHARD (*b. Vienna-Döbling, Austria, 1900; d. Heidelberg, Germany, 1967*), chemistry.

Graduated from University of Munich (Ph.D., 1922), where he studied under Willstätter; director of new Chemistry Institute of Kaiser Wilhelm Institute for Medical Research at Heidelberg (1929–67); became director of entire Kaiser Wilhelm Institute for Medical Research (1937); helped transform Kaiser Wilhelm Society for Scientific Research into Max Planck Society for the Advancement of Science (1946–48). Preoccupied with problems in optical stereochemistry for most of his life; his studies on carotenoids and vitamins won Kuhn the Nobel Prize in chemistry (1939).

KUHN, WERNER (*b. Maur, near Zurich, Switzerland, 1899; d. Basel, Switzerland, 1963*), physical chemistry.

Graduated in chemical engineering at Eidgenössische Technische Hochschule in Zurich (Ph.D., 1924); also studied at Institute for Theoretical Physics of the University of Copenhagen; taught at Physico-Chemical Institute of the University of Basel (from 1939); chief fields of research were macromolecules and optical activity.

KÜHNE, WILHELM FRIEDRICH (*b. Hamburg, Germany, 1837; d. Heidelberg, Germany, 1900*), physiology, physiological chemistry.

Graduated from University of Göttingen (Ph.D., 1856), where he studied under Wöhler, Henle, and Rudolph Wagner; worked in Berlin with E. du Bois-Reymond on myodynamics and with Hoppe-Seyler. Did additional study in Paris and in Vienna with Ernst Brücke and Carl Ludwig. Succeeded Hoppe-Seyler as assistant in the chemical department of Rudolf Virchow's institute of pathology in Berlin (1861), and later succeeded Helmholtz in the chair of physiology at Heidelberg (1871–99).

Kühne substantially advanced research in physiology of metabolism and digestion, physiology of muscle and nerves, physiology of protozoa, and physiological optics. He demonstrated usefulness of cytophysiological investigations for solving problems of general physiology; author of *Lehrbuch der physiologischen Chemie* (1868). He was the first to perceive migrating pigments in the living retina (1877–78).

KUMMER, ERNST EDUARD (*b. Sorau, Germany [now Zary, Poland], 1810; d. Berlin, Germany, 1893*), mathematics.

Graduated from University of Halle (Ph.D., 1831); taught at Gymnasium in Liegnitz [now Legnica, Poland] (1832–42); students included L. Kronecker and F. Joachimsthal; corresponded with Jacobi and Dirichlet, and with their help was appointed professor at University of Breslau, now Wrocław, Poland (1842–55). When Dirichlet left Berlin to succeed Gauss at Göttingen, Kummer succeeded Dirichlet (1855–83) and arranged for Joachimsthal to be his successor at Breslau; with Weierstrass he established Germany's first seminar in pure mathematics (1861). Kummer's lectures drew large numbers of students and his doctoral students included famous mathematicians: P. du Bois-Reymond, P. Gordan, H.A. Schwarz, G. Cantor, and A. Schoenflies. Kummer's work falls into three periods: during function-theory period at Leignitz he developed hypergeometric series; during arithmetical period in Breslau he formulated a theory of ideal prime factors (1845–47); and during geometric period in Berlin he used an algebraic approach to the theory of ray systems. Gauss and Dirichlet exerted the most lasting influence on Kummer, who in turn had the strongest influence on Kronecker. A conservative in both politics and mathematics: advocated constitutional monarchy during revolutionary events in 1848; believed mathematics should be pursued without regard to applications.

KUNCKEL, (VON LOEWENSTERN), JOHANN (*b. Hutten, Schleswig-Holstein, Germany, ca. 1630; d. Stockholm, Sweden [or nearby], ca. 1703*), chemistry.

Learned chemistry from his father and practical chemistry from pharmacists and glassworkers; chemist and gentleman of the bedchamber to Johann Georg II, elector of Saxony, for about ten years (from 1667). Head of chemical laboratory at Berlin under Frederick William, elector of Brandenburg (1679–88); minister of mines under King Charles XI of Sweden (from 1688) in Stockholm. Best-known work outside Germany was *Chymische Anmerckungen* (1677). He claimed to have discovered phosphorus (1678), though probably first learned that it could be made from urine from H. Brand. R. Boyle was first to publish a method of preparation. Also wrote on glassmaking (1679). Kunckel's views are a mixture of alchemy and rational natural philosophy.

KUNDT, AUGUST ADOLPH (*b. Schwerin, Germany, 1839; d. Israelsdorf, near Lübeck, Germany, 1894*), physics.

Graduated from University of Berlin (Ph.D., 1864), where he studied under G. Magnus; succeeded Helmholtz in chair of physics at Berlin (1888); worked primarily in optics, acoustics, and gas theory; famous for method of determining speed of sound in gases. A leading experimental physicist of the nineteenth century.

KUNKEL VON LÖWENSTERN. *See* **Kunckel (von Loewenstern), Johann.**

KUNTH, CARL SIGISMUND (*b. Leipzig, Germany, 1788; d. Berlin, Germany, 1850*), botany.

Studied botany under Willdenow at University of Berlin; through his uncle he became acquainted with Alexander von Humboldt, who invited Kunth to stay with him in Paris and publish botanical sections of Humboldt and Bonpland's *Voyage aux régions équinoxiales du Nouveau Continent*, which he worked on from 1813 to 1829; in dealing with the 3,600 new species brought home by Humboldt and Bonpland, he contributed significantly to the development of the natural system of classification; became professor at the University of Berlin and head of Berlin botanical garden (1829).

KUNTZE, CARL ERNST OTTO (*b. Leipzig, Germany, 1843; d. San Remo, Italy, 1907*), botany.

Essentially a self-taught scientist. After he established a successful factory for manufacturing volatile oils and essences at Leipzig (1868), he retired from business and devoted his life to travel and botany (1873); Kuntze described his journey around the world (1874–76) in *Reise um die Erde* (1881); received doctorate in botany from University of Freiburg im Breisgau (1878). Published botanical results of a journey around the world in *Revisio generum plantarum* (1891), in which he attacked defects in Alphonse de Candolle's nomenclature as approved by International Botanical Congress in Paris (1867). He wanted to change names of 25,000–30,000 plants, causing chaos in botanical establishment; issues raised by Kuntze's reforms were not finally resolved until Fifth International Congress of Botany at Cambridge (1930); although few of his changes were adopted, Kuntze had forced botanists to straighten out nomenclature problems; also wrote on history of botany.

KURCHATOV, IGOR VASILIEVICH (*b. Sim, Ufimskaya guberniya [now Ufimskaya oblast], Russia, 1903; d. Moscow, U.S.S.R., 1960*), physics.

Graduated from University of the Crimea (1923); entered Leningrad Physical-Technical Institute (1927), where he conducted experiments on dielectrics and ferroelectricity. In the early thirties, he became head of nuclear physics department, where he supervised construction of what was then the largest cyclotron in Europe. During World War II, he headed research on atomic energy and atomic weapons; supervised building of new laboratory in Moscow (later named the I. V. Kurchatov Institute of Atomic Energy). With co-workers developed first atomic reactor in Europe (late 1946), the first Soviet atomic bombs (1949), and conducted first hydrogen bomb test (12 August 1953).

KURLBAUM, FERDINAND (*b. Burg, near Magdeburg, Germany, 1857; d. Berlin, Germany, 1927*), physics, especially optics.

Studied under H. Kayser in Helmholtz's laboratory in Berlin (completed dissertation in 1887); worked under O. Lummer at Physikalisch-Technische Reichsanstalt in Berlin (1891–1904), where he also taught (from 1899). With Lummer published famous work on hollow-space radiation (1898); with H. Rubens made long-wave measurements that contradicted Wien's law of radiation. Soon after Rubens communicated their results to Planck (7 October 1900), Planck discovered his own law of radiation (mid-October) and quantum theory had begun. Kurlbaum finished his career as professor at Technical College of Berlin-Charlottenburg (from 1904).

KURNAKOV, NIKOLAI SEMYONOVICH (*b. Nolinsk, Vyatka guberniya, Russia, 1860; d. Moscow, U.S.S.R., 1941*), chemistry.

Graduated from St. Petersburg Institute of Mines (1882) where he later taught (from 1893); professor of chemistry at St. Petersburg Polytechnic Institute (1902–30); Kurnakov's main accomplishment was the creation of physicochemical analysis based on the study of equilibrium systems by measuring their characteristics in relation to changes in composition and by constructing phase diagrams.

KÜRSCHÁK, JÓZSEF (*b. Buda, Hungary, 1864; d. Budapest, Hungary, 1933*), mathematics.

Graduated from Technical University in Budapest (Ph.D., 1890) where he taught (1891–1933). His main achievement was founding the theory of valuations (1912), which was later developed into an important arithmetical theory of fields. Among Kürschák's pupils were mathematicians and physicists of first rank, including John von Neumann.

KUSHYĀR IBN LABBĀN IBN BĀSHAHRĪ, ABU' L-ḤASAN, AL-JĪLĪ (*fl. ca. 1000*), astronomy, trigonometry, arithmetic.

Lived in Baghdad; only three of Kushyār's works have received scholarly attention, two *zījes* (astronomical tables) and an arithmetic, "Elements of Hindu Reckoning." He probably did not make astronomical observations of his own; he helped develop the study of trigonometric functions started by Abu'l-Wafāʾ and al-Battānī; his "Elements" introduced Hindu methods into astronomical calculations, which were formerly done by finger reckoning and sexagesimal calculation.

KÜTZING, FRIEDRICH TRAUGOTT (*b. Ritteburg, near Artern, Saxony, Germany, 1807; d. Nordhausen, Germany, 1893*), botany.

Served as apprentice and later assistant to apothecaries in numerous German towns, during which he also studied chemistry and botany; studied at University of Halle (1832–33); discovered that walls of diatoms are silicified (1834); taught chemistry and natural history in Nordhausen (1835–83); received Ph.D. from University of Marburg (1837). Best known for work on algae; his *Tabulae phycologiae* (1845–71) is still the best reference on the habit of many species of algae. His *Die kieselschaligen Bacillarien oder Diatomeen* (1844) received worldwide recognition and contained illustrations of 700 species engraved by Kützing himself.

KYLIN, JOHANN HARALD (*b. Ornunga, Älvsborg, Sweden, 1879; d. Lund, Sweden, 1949*), botany.

Graduated from University of Uppsala (Ph.D., 1907) where he was docent (1907–20); professor of botany at University of Lund (1920–44). His main studies concern the morphology, biochemistry, and physiology of algae, particularly of the west coast of Sweden. Kylin's greatest contributions to phycology were morphological and systematic studies of the class Florideophycidae, which includes most of the red algae (from 1914); his last great work, *Die Gattungen der Rhodophyceen* (1956) is the standard reference on red algae.

LA BROSSE, GUY DE (*b. Paris, France, ca. 1586; d. Paris, 1641*), botany, medicine, chemistry.

Founder and first director of Royal Botanical Garden in Paris; studied chemistry in Paris; physician to Henry II de Bourbon, Prince de Condé (by 1619); physician in ordinary to Louis XIII (1626). Hoped to secure establishment of a botanical garden, not merely for study of medicinal herbs, but where chemistry would be taught as a handmaiden to medicine; first approached Louis XIII through J. Hérouard, chief physician of king (1616); a royal edict (1626) authorized the garden's establishment and appointed La Brosse as director. To assure support and financing for the project, Guy published pamphlets defending his plan and criticizing the Paris medical faculty, which distrusted the medical chemistry he advocated; most of these pamphlets are reprinted in his major book, *De la nature, vertu et utilité des plantes* (1628). Finally a house and grounds were purchased (1633); by 1636 there were 1,800 species and varieties under cultivation; formal opening occurred in 1640, a year before Guy's death. His earliest book was on plague, the *Traicté de la peste* (1623), which demonstrates affinity with Paracelsian doctors in its emphasis on external factors rather than traditional theory of internal imbalances of fluids. His major concern was medical botany; *De la nature des plantes* is not just a defense of the garden project but a theoretical work about plants in general, discussing generation, growth, and nutrition of plants, the influence of stars, and whether plants have souls; anticipating Stephen Hales by a century, La Brosse argued for the nutritive role of air in plants, although on inadequate evidence.

LACAILLE, NICOLAS-LOUIS DE (*b. Rumigny, near Rheims, France, 1713; d. Paris, France, 1762*), astronomy, geodesy.

An immensely industrious observational astronomer whose expedition to the Cape of Good Hope made him "the father of southern astronomy." Completed course of philosophy at Collège de Lisieux in Paris (1731); while studying theology at Collège de Navarre, he became interested in mathematical astronomy; rather than apply for bachelor of theology degree, spent money on science books; sometime during his education he received title of abbé, though never practiced as clergyman. Worked at observatory in Paris under J. Cassini (1737–41); led measurement of degrees of latitude and resolved controversy between Newtonians and Cartesians over shape of the earth in favor of Newton, who asserted earth an oblate spheroid (1741); taught mathematics at Collège Mazarin (1741–46); worked at observatory made available for him at Collège de Lisieux (1746–50), where he used transit instruments, little known in France at that time. With endorsement of Academy of Sciences and government support, he moved to the Cape of Good Hope to observe southern stars (1751–53); in a small observatory he made observations of parallax of sun and moon, mapped nearly 10,000 stars, and completed the naming of southern constellations (fourteen), which as an astronomer of the Enlightenment he named not after classical mythology but after modern tools of arts and sciences. He also measured the meridian, though his results mistakenly supported the Cartesian assertion that the earth is a prolate spheroid; before returning to France, he established positions of two French islands in Indian Ocean. Lavish praise greeted Lacaille on his return to Paris, including a pension from the Academy. He published *Astronomiae fundamenta* (1757); a complete catalog of Lacaille's southern stars did not appear until 1847.

LACAZE-DUTHIERS, FÉLIX-JOSEPH HENRI DE (*b. Château de Stiguederne, Lot-et-Garonne, Montpezat, France, 1821; d. Las-Fons, Dordogne, France, 1901*), zoology.

Received M.D. at Paris (1851); doctor of sciences at Faculty of Sciences (1853), where he studied with H. Milne-Edwards; taught zoology at Lille (1854–64); professor at Muséum d'Histoire Naturelle (1865–69) and at Faculty of Sciences (from 1869). Did research on marine mollusks and zoophytes; wrote *Histoire naturelle du corail* (1864); insisted, contrary to Claude Bernard, that zoology can be an experimental science; founded *Archives de zoologie expérimentale et générale* (1872).

LACÉPÈDE, BERNARD-GERMAIN-ÉTIENNE DE LA VILLE-SUR-ILLON, COMTE DE (*b. Agen, France, 1756; d. Épinay-sur-Seine, France, 1825*), zoology.

Privately educated; commissioned colonel of a German regiment (which he never saw) (1777); invited by Buffon to work on continuation of *Histoire naturelle;* published *Histoire naturelle des quadrupèdes ovipares* (1788), and *Histoire naturelle des serpents* (1789) which appeared after Buffon's death; completed Buffon's plan by publishing works on fishes (1798–1803) and on cetaceans (1804). Held political positions during Revolution; chosen by Directory as member of new Institut de France (1795). After completion of *Histoire naturelle* (1804), Lacépède turned to public affairs; after Napoleon's fall he retired to Épinay where he worked on moral and historical writings.

LA CONDAMINE, CHARLES-MARIE DE (*b. Paris, France, 1701; d. Paris, 1774*), mathematics, natural history.

Educated at Collège Louis-le-Grand in Paris; fought in war with Spain; wrote memoir on mathematical observations made on a trip to the Levant (1732); chosen by the Academy to participate in the mission known as *Académiciens du Pérou*, whose purpose was to verify Newton's hypothesis on flattening of the globe in polar regions (1735). While Maupertuis, Clairaut, and Le Monnier went to Lapland to measure a meridian arc, Godin, Bouguer, and La Condamine measured the meridian near the equator in Peru; the mission was marked by lack of funds (La Condamine contributed some of his own money) and internal dissension. After work was completed (1743) La Condamine returned to Paris (1745) via dangerous Amazon route, collecting natural history specimens which he gave to Buffon; results of the expedition confirmed the correctness of Newton's theory. Bouguer and La Condamine were unable to agree on joint publication of their works; though La Condamine was a less gifted scientist

than Bouguer and Godin, he often received more credit. Helped popularize inoculation for smallpox.

LACROIX, ALFRED (*b. Mâcon, France, 1863; d. Paris, France, 1948*), mineralogy, petrology, geology.

Received diploma in pharmacy (1887); also took mineralogy courses at Muséum d'Histoire Naturelle and assisted F. Fouqué until obtaining doctorate (1889); married Fouqué's daughter (1889); took chair of mineralogy at museum (1893–1936). Helped transform mineralogy from purely descriptive to interpretive science; published a major study on Madagascar (1922–23); made important observations of volcanoes. Was named *secrétaire perpetuel* of Académie des Sciences (1914–48); wrote series of biographies of French scientists.

LACROIX, SYLVESTRE FRANÇOIS (*b. Paris, France, 1765; d. Paris, 1843*), mathematics.

Studied mathematics at Collège des Quatre Nations in Paris; attended free courses given by G. Monge (1780), who became his patron and obtained a position for him at École des Gardes de la Marine at Rochefort (from 1782); taught at Lycée and École Militaire in Paris (until 1788); taught at École Royale d'Artillerie in Besançon; became *chef de bureau* of Commission Exécutive de l'Instruction Publique (1794); taught at École Centrale des Quatre Nations, also succeeding to Lagrange's chair at École Polytechnique (until 1809); taught transcendental mathematics at Lycée Bonaparte (1805–15); professor of calculus and dean of Faculté des Sciences of Paris (until 1821); held chair of mathematics at Collège de France (1812–28). Best-known work was *Traité du calcul différentiel et du calcul intégral* (1797–98), a successful synthesis of works of Euler, Lagrange, Laplace, Monge, Legendre, Poisson, Gauss, and Cauchy. His mathematical work was not original. Was first to propose the term "analytic geometry." Also wrote on history of mathematics.

LADENBURG, ALBERT (*b. Mannheim, Germany, 1842; d. Breslau, Germany [now Wrocław, Poland], 1911*), chemistry.

Studied chemistry at Heidelberg where inspired by Bunsen and Kirchhoff (Ph.D., 1863); worked under Kekulé at Ghent (1865) and under Wurtz in Paris (1866); invited by Friedel to work at École des Mines (1866–68); taught history of chemistry at Heidelberg (published lectures 1869); taught at University of Kiel (1872–89) and at Breslau (from 1889). Chief contributions were elucidation of structure of alkaloids and their synthesis; also pioneered studies of organic compounds of silicon and tin and advanced theories on the structure of aromatic compounds.

LADENBURG, RUDOLF WALTHER (*b. Kiel, Germany, 1882; d. Princeton, N.J., 1952*), physics.

Son of chemist Albert Ladenburg; graduated University of Munich (Ph.D., 1906); taught at University of Breslau (1906–24); at invitation of Haber, became head of physics division at Kaiser Wilhelm Institute in Berlin (1924–31); professor of physics at Princeton University (1931–50). Most original work was in elucidation of anomalous dispersion in gases (before 1931); Ladenburg's successful formula for anomalous dispersion, which ignored Bohr orbital frequencies in favor of line frequencies, was of critical importance to development of the new quantum theory in 1920's; also known for introduction in United States of optical interferometry as a quantitative tool to map density distribution in high-speed flows (after World War II). Worked to aid displaced colleagues during 1930's and 1940's.

LAENNEC, THÉOPHILE-RENÉ-HYACINTHE (*b. Quimper, France, 1781; d. Kerbouarnec, Brittany, France, 1826*), medicine.

Learned medicine from uncle, a physician in Nantes; worked as surgeon in Nantes during French Revolution; entered École Pratique in Paris (1801) where he studied dissection and published papers on anatomy with Bichat (1802–03); poor health forced several stays in Brittany. Published *De l'auscultation médiate* (1819), which greatly advanced knowledge of chest diseases; after many disappointments, finally obtained chair of medicine at Collège de France in Paris (1822).

LA FAILLE, (JEAN) CHARLES DE (*b. Antwerp, Belgium, 1597; d. Barcelona, Spain, 1652*), mathematics.

Entered Jesuit order (1613); became disciple of Gregory of St. Vincent, known for work on quadrature of circle, at Antwerp; taught at Imperial College in Madrid (1629–44); appointed by Philip IV as preceptor to his son Don Juan of Austria (1644–52); best known for *Theoremata de centro gravitatis partium circuli et ellipsis* (Antwerp, 1632), in which the center of gravity of a sector of a circle was determined for first time.

LAGNY, THOMAS FANTET DE (*b. Lyons, France, 1660; d. Paris, France, 1734*), mathematics, computation.

Probably studied with Jesuits in Lyons and at Faculty of Law in Toulouse; collaborated with L'Hospital on several publications (1690–91); professor of hydrography at Rochefort (1697–1716); *pensionnaire* of Académie Royale des Sciences (1719–33); Lagny's work was outmoded: while the idea of function was gaining dominance, he continued computations with aid of numerical tables.

LAGRANGE, JOSEPH LOUIS (*b. Turin, Italy, 1736; d. Paris, France, 1813*), mechanics, celestial mechanics, astronomy, mathematics.

Lagrange's life can be divided into three periods. The first comprises the years spent in his native Turin (1736–66). The second is that of his work at the Berlin Academy, between 1766 and 1787. The third is in Paris, from 1787 until his death in 1813.

The first two periods were the most fruitful in terms of scientific activity, which began as early as 1754 with the discovery of the calculus of variations and continued with the application of the latter to mechanics in 1756. He also worked in celestial mechanics in this first period, stimulated by the competitions held by the Paris Academy of Sciences in 1764 and 1766.

The Berlin period was productive in mechanics as well as in differential and integral calculus. Yet during that time Lagrange distinguished himself primarily in the numerical and algebraic solution of equations, and even more in the theory of numbers. His years in Paris were dedicated to didactic writings and to the composition of the great treatises summarizing his mathematical conceptions. These treatises, while closing the age of eigh-

teenth-century mathematics, prepared and in certain respects opened that of the nineteenth century.

Lagrange's father destined him for the law, but having begun the study of physics under the direction of Beccaria and of geometry under Filippo Antonio Revelli, he quickly became aware of his talents and henceforth devoted himself to the exact sciences. In 1757 some young Turin scientists, among them Lagrange, Count Saluzzo, and the physician Giovanni Cigna, founded a scientific society that was the origin of the Royal Academy of Sciences of Turin. One of the main goals of this society was the publication of a miscellany in French and Latin, *Miscellanea Taurinensia ou Mélanges de Turin*, to which Lagrange contributed fundamentally; the first three volumes contained almost all the works he published while in Turin.

Lagrange's activity in celestial mechanics was often centered around competitions proposed by the various scientific societies but it was not solely confined to these competitions. In Turin his work had often taken an independent direction and in 1782 he wrote to d'Alembert and Laplace that he was working on the theory of the secular variations of the aphelia and of the eccentricities of all the planets. This research led to the *Théorie des variations séculaires des éléments des planètes* and the memoir "Sur les variations séculaires des mouvements moyens des planètes," the latter published in 1785.

His work in Berlin far surpassed this classical aspect of celestial mechanics. Soon after his arrival he presented "Mémoire sur le passage de Vénus du 3 Juin 1769," a work that disconcerted the professional astronomers and contained the first somewhat extended example of an elementary astronomical problem solved by the method of three rectangular coordinates. He later returned sporadically to questions of pure astronomy.

In October 1773 he composed *Nouvelle solution du problème du mouvement de rotation d'un corps de figure quelconque qui n'est animé par aucune force accélératrice*. A by-product of this study of dynamics was his famous *Solutions analytiques de quelques problèmes sur les pyramides triangulaires*. Here he expressed the surface, the volume, and the radii of circumscribed, inscribed, and escribed spheres and located the center of gravity of every triangular pyramid as a function of the lengths of the six edges.

Lagrange began works inspired by Euler as soon as he arrived in Berlin. First he presented in the *Mémoires* of the Berlin Academy for 1767 (published in 1769) "Sur la solution des problèmes indéterminés du second degré," in which he copiously cited his predecessor at the Academy and utilized the "Euler criterion." In 1768 he sent "Solution d'un problème d'arithmétique" to the *Mélanges de Turin* for inclusion in volume 4. Through a series of unfortunate circumstances this second memoir was not published until October 1773. In it Lagrange alluded to the preceding memoir, and through a judicious and skillful use of the algorithm of continued fractions he demonstrated that Fermat's equation $x^2 - ay^2 = 1$ can be solved in all cases where $x, y,$ and a are positive integers, a not being a perfect square and y being different from zero. This is the first known solution of this celebrated problem. The last part of this memoir was developed in "Nouvelle méthode pour résoudre des problèmes indéterminés en nombres entiers," presented in the Berlin *Mémoires* for 1768 but not completed until February 1769 and published in 1770. In the Berlin *Mémoires* for 1770 (published 1772) he presented "Démonstration d'un théorème d'arithmétique." On the basis of Euler's unsuccessful but nevertheless fruitful attempts, he set forth the first demonstration that every natural integer is the sum of at most four perfect squares.

A fundamental memoir on the arithmetic theory of quadratic forms, modestly entitled "Recherches d'arithmétique," appeared in two parts, the first in May 1775 in the Berlin *Mémoires* for 1773 and the second in June 1777, in the same periodical's volume for 1775. In 1777 Lagrange read another paper before the Academy: "Sur quelques problèmes de l'analyse de Diophante." His known arithmetical works end at this point, while he was still in Berlin. "Essai d'analyse numérique sur la transformation des fractions," published at Paris in the *Journal de l'École polytechnique* (1797–98), shows that he did not lose interest in problems of this type, but the main portion of his work in this area is concentrated in the first ten years of his stay in Berlin (1767–77). During these ten years he also tackled algebraic analysis—or, more precisely, the solution of both numerical and literal equations.

Two important memoirs appeared in 1769 and 1770, respectively: "Sur la résolution des équations numériques" and "Addition au mémoire sur la résolution des équations numériques." In them Lagrange utilized the algorithm of continued fractions, and in the "Addition" he showed that the quadratic irrationals are the only ones that can be expressed as periodic continued fractions. The two memoirs later formed the framework of the *Traité de la résolution des équations numériques de tous les degrés*, the first edition of which dates from 1798. The culmination of his research in the theory of equations was a memoir read in 1771: "Réflexions sur la résolution algébrique des équations."

Lagrange's works in infinitesimal analysis are for the most part later than those concerned with number theory and algebra and were composed at intervals from about 1768 to 1787. More in agreement with prevailing tastes, they assured him a European reputation during his lifetime.

The considerable place that mechanics, and more particularly celestial mechanics, occupied in Lagrange's works resulted in contributions that were scattered among numerous memoirs and he thought it proper to present his ideas in a single comprehensive work, a *Traité de mécanique analytique*, which appeared at the beginning of 1788; in it he proposed to reduce the theory of mechanics and the art of solving problems in that field to general formulas, the mere development of which would yield all the equations necessary for the solution of every problem. The *Traité* united and presented from a single point of view the various principles of mechanics, demonstrated their connection and mutual dependence, and made it possible to judge their validity and scope. It is divided into two parts, statics and dynamics, each of which treats solid bodies and fluids separately. There are no diagrams. The methods presented require only analytic operations, subordinated to a regular and uniform development. Each of the four sections begins with a historical account which is a model of the kind.

Lagrange decided, however, that the work should have a second edition incorporating certain advances. In the *Mémoires de l'Institut* he had earlier published some essays

that represented a last, brilliant contribution to the development of celestial mechanics, and he included some of this theory in the first volume of the revised *Traité* (1811).

LAGUERRE, EDMOND NICOLAS (*b. Bar-le-Duc, France, 1834; d. Bar-le-Duc, 1886*), mathematics.

Studied at École Polytechnique in Paris; left school for army (1854–64); taught at École Polytechnique (1864–86); also taught at Collège de France (1883–86). Although more than half of Laguerre's published works were in geometry, his major influence was in analysis. He discovered the set of differential equations known as Laguerre equations and their polynomial solutions (Laguerre's polynomials); as brilliant as he was, he worked only on details and never drew them together into a single theory.

LA HIRE, GABRIEL-PHILIPPE (or **PHILIPPE II**) **DE** (*b. Paris, France, 1677; d. Paris, 1719*), astronomy, geodesy, architecture.

Son of Philippe de La Hire; educated at Paris Observatory, where he lived after 1682; succeeded father as *pensionnaire* of Academy of Sciences (1718); involved in dispute with J. Le Fèvre (1701); produced work as varied as his father's, though more limited in extent.

LA HIRE, PHILIPPE DE (*b. Paris, France, 1640; d. Paris, 1718*), astronomy, mathematics, geodesy, physics.

Educated among artists and technicians; throughout life pursued parallel study of art, science, and technology, under the influence of Desargues. Studied geometry and art during a stay in Venice for health reasons (1660–64). Published several treatises on conic sections (1673, 1679, 1685) which helped make known Desargues's projective ideas; very conservative in acceptance of infinitesimal calculus. Also studied astronomy, physics, and applied mathematics; was *astronome pensionnaire* to Academy of Sciences (1678–1718); published astronomical tables (1687, 1702); took part in geodesic and surveying projects; at Collège Royale (from 1682) lectured on many mathematical applications; professor at Académie Royale d'Architecture (1687–1717). La Hire's *Traité de mécanique* (1695) marks significant step toward a modern manual of practical mechanics for engineers of several disciplines. Was also interested in descriptive zoology, respiration, and physiological optics.

LALANDE, JOSEPH-JÉRÔME LEFRANÇAIS DE (*b. Bourg-en-Bresse, France, 1732; d. Paris, France, 1807*), astronomy.

Extremely well known during his lifetime because of vast writings and love for limelight; mainly a practical astronomer, maker of tables, and writer of astronomical textbooks, his most important contribution. Educated by Jesuits at Collège de Lyon; attended lectures of J. Delisle in Paris and assisted him in astronomical observations; also attended lectures of P. Le Monnier, who permitted Lalande to take his place in measurement of lunar parallax in Berlin in conjunction with Abbé N. de La Caille's measurements at Cape of Good Hope (1751); publication of his observations led to election to Paris Academy (1753; became *pensionnaire*, 1772). Lost friendship with Le Monnier in controversy over best way to correct for flattening of earth in calculating lunar parallax; aligned with Clairaut against d'Alembert and Le Monnier in controversy over solution to three-body problem and prediction of return of Halley's comet (1759). Editor of *Connaissance des temps* (1760–76; 1794–1807); succeeded Delisle as professor of astronomy at Collège Royale (1760).

His most important textbook was *Traité d'astronomie* (1764); also wrote on practical arts and travel. Lalande took a major organizational role in observation of the transit of Venus (1769); his discussion of possibility of collision of a comet with earth provoked panic among Parisian public (1773). Helped organize many institutions of the *ancien régime*, such as the famous Lodge of Nine Sisters of the Masonic order (1777), composed of elite leaders of arts and sciences, including Voltaire; political views were cautiously royalist; desire for fame and reputation as freethinker led him into conflict with Napoleon, who insisted Lalande be censured.

LALLA (*fl. India, eighth century*), astronomy.

One of leading Indian astronomers of eighth century; wrote *Śiṣyadhīvṛddhidatantra,* an astronomical text which is most extensive extant exposition of views of the Āryapakṣa school; also surviving is *Jyotiṣaratnakośa,* an influential work on catarchic astrology.

LALOUVÈRE, ANTOINE DE (*b. Rieux, Haute-Garonne, France, 1600; d. Toulouse, France, 1664*), mathematics.

Entered Jesuit order (1620) at Toulouse, where he was later professor of humanities, rhetoric, Hebrew, theology, and mathematics; chief book is *Quadratura circuli* (1651). Best known for dispute with Pascal (1658), who falsely accused Lalouvère of plagiarizing in contest on cycloid problems (1658).

LAMARCK, JEAN BAPTISTE PIERRE ANTOINE DE MONET DE (*b. Bazentin-le-Petit, Picardy, France, 1744; d. Paris, France, 1829*), botany, invertebrate zoology and paleontology, evolution.

Lamarck left the Jesuit school in Amiens to fight with French army in Seven Years' War; after the war he spent five years (1763–68) at various French forts where he began botanizing; he left the army (1768) and later studied medicine in Paris for four years. His personal life was marked by tragedy and poverty: three of his wives died; Lamarck himself went blind (1818); one son was deaf, another insane.

Lamarck's scientific recognition in botany came from his *Flore française* (1779), whose dichotomous keys were much easier to use in identifying plants than Linnaeus' artificial system or the natural system; his other major work in botany was the first three and a half volumes of *Dictionnaire de botanique* (1783–95). In "Discours preliminaire" of the *Flore,* he showed philosophical concern for nature as a whole, its processes, and interrelations; in the same work he demonstrated an awareness of the influence of environment on vegetable development though he still believed in fixity of species. His belief in the idea of progress is most evident in "Discours préliminaire" in *Dictionnaire de Botanique.* After 1800, when he began advocating his theory of evolution, he wrote only one work on botany, *Introduction à la botanique* (1803), which stressed that a natural order of classification from simplest class to most complex class reflected the order by which nature had produced these groups in time.

With Buffon's help, he was elected to the Académie des Sciences as adjoint botanist (1779; pensioner, 1790). His most significant affiliation was with the Jardin du Roi, where he held various botanical positions (from 1788); he was professor of zoology after it was transformed during the Revolution into the Muséum National d'Histoire Naturelle (1793).

Lamarck began studying chemistry in the 1770's when the four-element theory (earth, air, water, and fire) was current; he continued to believe in four elements throughout his life despite the chemical revolution. Although his chemical views were ignored, they play a prominent role in *Recherches sur l'organisation des corps vivans* (1802), the first full exposition of his evolutionary theories; his chemical ideas provided a materialistic definition of life and its maintenance, appearance, and gradual development, fire was key element in all these processes.

In the field of meteorology he tried to explain all meteorological change as result of one general cause, the moon, and believed that laws of climate would help understand changes in organisms. He published *Annuaire météorologique* (1800–10), which was ridiculed by Napoleon (1810), bringing an end to Lamarck's meteorological work.

In the area of invertebrate zoology and paleontology he came to be regarded as expert in conchology. The pressing question of the late 1790's was to explain differences and similarities between living and fossil forms; Lamarck was unable to accept extinction or migration as possible causes and chose an evolutionary explanation in late 1799 or early 1800. His most important paleontological work was *Mémoires sur les fossiles des environs de Paris* (1802–06).

Lamarck's perception of slowly changing environment and resulting changes in organisms may have led to his theory of evolution that the main geological force was water acting under influence of the moon according to uniformitarian principles over millions of years; *Hydrogéologie* published in 1802. He never used the term "evolution" but spoke of a path or order which nature followed in producing all living organisms. He first presented in a course on invertebrates at the museum (1800) and published it in *Système des animaux sans vertèbres* (1801). He asserted that nature formed the simplest animals and plants by spontaneous generation, though he did not explain how, and suggested that changes in environment led to new habits and gradual modifications in organs or parts. He still viewed structural organization in terms of "degradations" from most complex to simplest, as the natural classification scheme was then organized. His ideas were developed further in *Recherches sur l'organisation des corps vivans* (1802), where he realized the need to reverse his classification scheme to reflect the order of production in nature and time. He began to talk of a natural tendency in organic realms toward increasing complexity. His chemistry was used to explain how evolution works: spontaneous generation of life occurred from the action of heat, sunlight, and electricity on matter; from this point on, the natural tendency of organic movement toward increasing complexity took over through interaction of contained fluids in an organism and subtle fluids in the environment; changes that occurred through the use of parts were preserved through inheritance. He also made a preliminary attempt to provide a materialistic explanation for the functioning of the nervous system. His best-known work on evolution is *Philosophie zoologique* (1809), which presents more details of his two-factor theory. His next best-known work is the "Introduction" to the seven-volume *Histoire naturelle des animaux sans vertèbres* (1815–22), where he summarizes the four laws of evolution. While he gave a few examples to support his theories, Lamarck was never systematic; he felt that the theories were so obvious they did not need extensive proof. The reasons for his changing his mind on the fixity of species range from his own work to the influence of other scientists.

Lamarck left few followers; his ideas were generally ignored. Cuvier's eulogy for the Academy condemned Lamarck's theories but they were revived mainly by Darwin's enemies (neo-Lamarckians) to suit their own purposes. With wide acceptance of Darwinism, much of Lamarckism has died out; he nevertheless made significant contributions in botany, invertebrate zoology, and paleontology, and developed one of the first complete theories of evolution.

LAMB, HORACE (*b. Stockport, England, 1849; d. Manchester, England, 1934*), applied mathematics, geophysics.

Educated in mathematics at Queen's College, Cambridge; taught mathematics Owen's College, Manchester (1885–1920). One of world's greatest applied mathematicians; best known for work in fluid mechanics embodied in *Hydrodynamics* (1895; first publ. in 1879 as *A Treatise on the Motion of Fluids*). His contributions to geophysics include fundamental papers on theoretical seismology; also studied the theory of tides and terrestrial magnetism.

LAMBERT, JOHANN HEINRICH (*b. Mulhouse, Alsace, 1728; d. Berlin, Germany, 1777*), mathematics, physics, astronomy, philosophy.

Lambert grew up in impoverished circumstances and acquired almost all his training and scholarship by self-instruction. In 1748 he became tutor at Chur, in the home of the Reichsgraf Peter von Salis, who had been ambassador to the English court. He remained tutor for ten years and was able to study intensively in the family library and pursue his own critical reflections.

Seeking a permanent scientific position, Lambert at first hoped for a chair at the University of Göttingen. When this hope came to nothing, he went to Zurich, where he made astronomical observations with Gessner, was elected a member of the city's Physical Society, and published *Die freye Perspektive*. At Augsburg in 1759 he met the famous instrument maker George Friedrich Brander. (Their twelve-year correspondence is available in *Lamberts deutscher gelehrter Briefwechsel*, vol. III.) Lambert also found a publisher for his *Photometria* and his *Cosmologische Briefe*.

Lambert produced more than 150 works for publication. Of his philosophical writings only his principal works, *Neues Organon* and *Anlage zur Architectonic*, as well as three papers published in *Nova acta eruditorum*, appeared during his lifetime. Although the composition of the main books and papers was done during the period of his appointment to the Berlin Academy in the winter of 1764–65, Lambert was occupied with philosophical questions at least as early as 1752, as his *Monatsbuch* testifies.

During the last ten years of his life his interest centered on problems in mathematics and physics.

The two main aspects of Lambert's philosophy, the analytic and the constructive, were both strongly shaped by mathematical notions; hence logic played an important part in his philosophical writing. Following Leibniz' ideas, Lambert early tried to create an *ars characteristica combinatoria*, or a logical or conceptual calculus. He investigated the conditions to which scientific knowledge must be subjected if it is to enjoy the same degree of exactness and evidence as mathematical knowledge. This interest was expressed in two smaller treatises, *Criterium veritatis* and *Über die Methode, die Metaphysik, Theologie und Moral richtiger zu beweisen.*

In *Neues Organon, oder Gedanken über die Erforschung und Bezeichnung des Wahren und dessen Unterscheidung vom Irrthum und Schein* he further develops the idea that proofs in metaphysics can be given with the same evidence as mathematical ones.

In his second large philosophical work, *Anlage zur Architectonic, oder Theorie des Einfachen und des Ersten in der philosophischen und mathematischen Erkenntnis*, Lambert proposed a far-reaching reform of metaphysics, stemming from discontent with the Wolffian system. Modeled on mathematical procedures, the body of general sciences so constructed was to be true both logically and metaphysically.

Lambert's work in physics and astronomy must be seen in relation to his general philosophical outlook and his attempts to introduce mathematical exactness and certitude into the sciences. His interest in the paths of comets was stimulated by the appearance of a comet in 1744. While studying the properties of such paths, he discovered interesting geometrical theorems, one of which carries his name. It was later proven analytically by Olbers, Laplace, and Lagrange. In 1770 Lambert suggested an easy method of determining whether the distance between the earth and the sun is greater than the distance from the earth to a given comet.

Lambert's efforts to improve communication and collaboration in astronomy were noteworthy. He promoted the publication of astronomical journals and founded the *Berliner astronomisches Jahrbuch oder Ephemeriden.*

Of special interest among Lambert's astronomical writings—apart from applications of his physical doctrines—are his famous *Cosmologische Briefe über die Einrichtung des Weltbaues.*

Lambert's numerous contributions to physics center on photometry, hygrometry, and pyrometry. In his famous *Photometria sive de mensura et gradibus luminis, colorum et umbrae*, Lambert laid the foundation for this branch of physics independently of Bouguer, whose writings on the subject were unknown to him. Lambert carried out his experiments with few and primitive instruments, but his conclusions resulted in laws that bear his name. The exponential decrease of the light in a beam passing through an absorbing medium of uniform transparency is often named Lambert's law of absorption, although Bouguer discovered it earlier. Lambert's cosine law states that the brightness of a diffusely radiating plane surface is proportional to the cosine of the angle formed by the line of sight and the normal to the surface. Such a diffusely radiating surface does therefore appear equally bright when observed at different angles, since the apparent size of the surface is also proportional to the cosine of the said angle.

Lambert's *Hygrometrie* was first published in two parts in French as articles entitled *Essai d'hygrometrie*. A result of his meteorological studies, this work is mostly concerned with the reliable measurement of the humidity of the atmosphere.

The *Pyrometrie oder vom Maasse des Feuers und der Wärme* was Lambert's last book, completed only a few months before his death; his first publication also had dealt with the question of measuring heat.

In mathematics Lambert's largest publication was the *Beyträge zum Gebrauch der Mathematik und deren Anwendung*. This is not at all a systematic work but rather a collection of papers and notes on a variety of many topics in pure and applied mathematics.

One of Lambert's most famous results is the proof of the irrationality of pi and *e*. It was based on continued fractions, and two such fractions still bear his name. Of importance also is Lambert's series in which the coefficient 2 occurs only when the exponent is a prime number.

Lambert's second book, *Die freye Perspektive, oder Anweisung, jeden perspektivischen Aufriss von freyen Stücken und ohne Grundriss zu verfertigen*, was intended for the artist wishing to give perspective drawing without first having to construct a ground plan. It is nevertheless a masterpiece in descriptive geometry, containing a wealth of geometrical discoveries.

Lambert contributed significantly to the theory of map construction. For the first time the mathematical conditions for map projections (to preserve angles and area) were stated.

One of Lambert's most important contributions to geometry was his posthumously published *Theorie der Parallel-Linien*.

LAMÉ, GABRIEL (*b. Tours, France, 1795; d. Paris, France, 1870*), mathematics.

Graduated from École Polytechnique (1817) and École des Mines (1820); accompanied Clapeyron to Russia (1820–32), where he taught at and directed the School of Highways and Transportation in St. Petersburg; held chair of physics at École Polytechnique (1832–44); appointed chief engineer of mines (1836); taught mathematical physics and probability at University of Paris (1844–62). His greatest contribution to mathematics was the introduction of curvilinear coordinates and their use in pure and applied mathematics; also contributed to number theory, thermodynamics, and applied mechanics; was considered an excellent engineer.

LAMÉTHERIE, JEAN-CLAUDE DE (*b. La Clayette [Mâconnais], France, 1743; d. Paris, France, 1817*), scientific editing and journalism, mineralogy, geology, biology, chemistry, natural philosophy.

While in the seminary at age sixteen, was influenced by Madame du Châtelet's *Institutions de physique;* abandoned the seminary, obtained a medical degree, and practiced medicine in La Clayette (1770–80); published *Principes de la philosophie naturelle* (1778); abandoned medicine to become chief editor (1785–1817) of *Observations sur la physique* (renamed *Journal de physique* in 1794). As editor he sought to bring attention to his favorite ideas and to reduce the influence of scientists like Lavoisier, whom he

regarded as a dictatorial force; blocked publication of the work of his enemies; helped draw attention to work of foreign scientists. He espoused a number of losing causes, such as the four-element scheme in chemistry and the phlogistonist theory of combustion and calcination. His only teaching position was at Collège de France (from 1801). His greatest influence was in mineralogy; his expanded edition of Bergman's *Sciagraphia regni mineralis* contributed to the acceptance of chemical composition as an important criterion in distinguishing minerals.

LA METTRIE, JULIEN OFFRAY DE (*b. Saint-Malo, France, 1709; d. Berlin, Germany, 1751*), medicine, physiology, psychology, philosophy of science.

Studied medicine at University of Paris (1728–33); obtained his degree at Rheims; did further study at Leiden, where he was greatly influenced by H. Boerhaave. After a short medical practice he became an army doctor (1743–46), during which time his *Histoire naturelle de l'âme* (1745) created scandal with its materialistic theory of the "soul" and was condemned by the Paris Parlement. He wrote satires on the medical profession (1746–50) which made him many enemies and forced him to flee to Holland (1747); in Holland he published his most notorious book, *L'homme machine* (1748), whose atheism and materialism outraged the Dutch as well. He found refuge with Frederick II of Prussia, whose personal physician he became; here he wrote *Discours sur le bonheur* (1748), which denied that vice and virtue have meaning. His main service to medicine was spreading Boerhaave's iatromechanistic philosophy through French translations and commentaries published in late 1730's. *L'homme machine* is a synthesis of iatromechanistic tradition and Cartesian automatist biology; he gave a strictly mechanistic interpretation of living things, explaining all mental faculties as products of the nervous system; believed man and his psychic activities should be explored with quantitative, mechanical principles. *Système d'Epicure* (1750) is among the earliest statements in the modern era of the evolution of ideas. La Mettrie's influence on the history of science was in promoting the mechanistic school of biology, and in advocating the science of psychology based on physiological method.

LAMONT, JOHANN VON (*b. Braemar, Scotland, 1805; d. Bogenhausen, near Munich, Germany, 1879*), astronomy, physics.

Educated at St. Jacob Scottish Foundation in Regensburg; sent to astronomical observatory at Bogenhausen (1827), where he became assistant (1828) and director (from 1833). Continued the work of previous director, Soldner, with the meridian circle; his zone catalog was one of the most important of its kind in the nineteenth century. Became interested in meteorology; founded *Annalen für Meteorologie und Erdmagnetismus* (1842–44). His most enduring achievements were in terrestrial magnetism: made numerous observations and improved measuring instruments; discovered that variations in earth's magnetism occur in periods of about ten years. Assumed chair of astronomy at University of Munich (1852), where his popular lectures attracted large audiences.

LAMOUROUX, JEAN VINCENT FÉLIX (*b. Agen, France, 1776; d. Caen, France, 1825*), natural history.

Earned M.D. in Paris (1809); professor of natural history at Caen (from 1809); attracted to study of marine algae by Bory de Saint-Vincent. In 1813 he separated for first time, though imperfectly, the brown, red, and green algae, eliminating much confusion; this inspired C. A. Agardh, who with Lamouroux is considered a founder of modern phycology.

LAMY, BERNARD (*b. Le Mans, France, 1640; d. Rouen, France, 1715*), mathematics, mechanics.

A priest educated in Oratorian pedagogy; his principal work in this field, *Entretiens sur les sciences* (1683), was admired by Rousseau; his staunch Cartesianism caused him to be exiled (1676); principal scientific works written in seminary in Grenoble, but not original; although he stated the rule of the parallelogram of forces at the same time as Varignon (1687), he did not see all its implications.

LAMY, GUILLAUME (*b. Coutances, France; d. Paris, France* [*?*]), philosophy, medicine.

Received doctorate from Faculty of Medicine at Paris (1672); earlier he had published philosophical work, *De principiis rerum* (1669), critiquing Peripatetic, Cartesian, and Epicurean thought. Among first to contradict advocates of transfusion (1667); his best-known medical work was *Discours anatomiques* (1675), which asserts man is not physically superior to animals. In a 1677 work he criticized mechanical explanations of the senses, passions and voluntary motion. *Dissertation sur l'antimoine* (1682) favored medical use of antimony, renewing "antimony war" of fifteen years before. Popular with public, Lamy had fervent disciples and impassioned enemies.

LANCHESTER, FREDERICK WILLIAM (*b. Lewisham, England, 1868; d. Birmingham, England, 1946*), engineer.

General manager and chief engineer of Lanchester Motor Company, a motor car manufacturer (founded 1899). His vortex theory of lift (1894) was ignored by learned societies. He published *Aerial Flight* (1907–08) which had considerable influence; a leader in history of aeronautical sciences.

LANCISI, GIOVANNI MARIA (*b. Rome, Italy, 1654; d. Rome, 1720*), medicine.

Obtained medical degree at the Sapienza (1672), where he taught anatomy (1684–97). Became pontifical doctor (1688); at papal request studied epidemic deaths in Rome, publishing two studies on cardiac pathology (1707, 1728). Did important research on malaria, which he believed was spread by mosquitoes; helped bring treatment of malaria by cinchona bark into common practice; published Eustachi's anatomical tables at his own expense.

LANCRET, MICHEL ANGE (*b. Paris, France, 1774; d. Paris, 1807*), differential geometry, topography, architecture.

Studied at École Polytechnique (1794–97); as engineer of bridges and highways, participated in Egyptian expedition (1798–1801); edited *Description de l'Égypte* (1809–18). Lancret's mathematical work places him among most direct disciples of Monge in infinitesimal geometry.

LANDAU, EDMUND (*b. Berlin, Germany, 1877; d. Berlin, 1938*), mathematics.

Studied mathematics at University of Berlin with G. Frobenius (Ph.D., 1899), where he also taught (1901–9); succeeded H. Minkowski at University of Göttingen (1909). He was active until stopped by National Socialist regime. Main field was analytic number theory and, specifically, distribution of prime numbers. Landau's *Handbuch der Lehre von der Verteilung der Primzahlen* (1909) gave first systematic presentation of analytic number theory; greatly influenced development of number theory in his time.

LANDAU, LEV DAVIDOVICH (*b. Baku, Russia, 1908; d. Moscow, U.S.S.R., 1968*), theoretical physics.

Graduated in physics from Leningrad University (1927); graduate study at Leningrad Institute of Physics and Technology (1927–29); toured Europe (1929–31), where he met Bohr, Pauli, Ehrenfest, and Heisenberg; awarded doctoral degree without defending dissertation at Kharkov University (1934), where he taught (1935–37). Director of theoretical physics of Institute of Physical Problems of U.S.S.R. Academy of Sciences in Moscow (1937–68). Studied wide range of topics in theoretical physics, influencing a number of students; awarded Nobel Prize in physics (1962).

LANDEN, JOHN (*b. Peakirk, near Peterborough, England, 1719; d. Milton, near Peterborough, 1790*), mathematics.

A surveyor who served as a land agent (1762–88). In his leisure, he wrote on dynamics and on summation of series; best known for work on elliptic arcs (*Philosophical Transactions*, 1775).

LANDOLT, HANS HEINRICH (*b. Zurich, Switzerland, 1831; d. Berlin, Germany, 1910*), chemistry.

Obtained doctorate at Breslau; after further study at Heidelberg, taught at Bonn (1857–69), Aachen (1869–80), Agricultural Institute in Berlin (1880–91), and Second Chemical Laboratory, Berlin (1891–1904). A physical chemist, Landolt's main work was on molecular refractivity of organic compounds.

LANDRIANI, MARSILIO (*b. Milan, Italy, ca. 1751; d. Vienna, Austria, not later than 1816*), scientific instrumentation.

After teaching physics in Milan and advising government on science and technological development, he moved to Vienna (1794–1816). Landriani's name is often linked to Volta's inventions, especially eudiometer, which he named.

LANDSBERG, GEORG (*b. Breslau, Germany, [now Wrocław, Poland], 1865; d. Kiel, Germany, 1912*), mathematics.

Graduated University of Breslau (Ph.D., 1890); taught at Heidelberg (1893–1904), Breslau (1904–06), and Kiel (1906–12). His most important contribution was development of theory of algebraic functions of one variable.

LANDSBERG, GRIGORY SAMUILOVICH (*b. Vologda, Russia, 1890; d. Moscow, U.S.S.R., 1957*), physics.

Graduated Moscow University (1913); worked at Institute of Physics and Biophysics (from 1920); in studying

Rayleigh scattering in crystals with L. I. Mandelshtam, he discovered combination scattering (1927). C. V. Raman announced discovery of analogous effect (now known as the Raman effect) in liquids several weeks before Landsberg and Mandelshtam, and received 1930 Nobel Prize in physics; Landsberg continued research on combination scattering and methods and devices for spectral analysis at Lebedev Physical Institute of U.S.S.R. Academy of Sciences (from 1932).

LANDSTEINER, KARL (*b. Vienna, Austria, or Baden [near Vienna], Austria, 1868; d. New York, N.Y., 1943*), medicine, serology, immunology.

Has been called father of immunology. Graduated from University of Vienna (M.D., 1891), where he studied chemistry with Ludwig; continued chemical studies with E. Fischer at Würzburg, in Munich, and with Hantzsch in Zurich (1892–94). Assisted M. Gruber (1896–97) and Weichselbaum (1897–1908) at University of Vienna; prosector at Royal-Imperial Wilhelminen Hospital in Vienna (1908–19); prosector at RK Hospital, The Hague (1919–22). Accepted a position at the Rockefeller Institute in New York (1922); awarded Nobel Prize in physiology or medicine (1930). Landsteiner's discovery of human blood groups (1900) made possible safe transfusion of blood, operations on the heart, lungs, and circulatory system, and complete blood exchanges; his work on the individuality of blood made serological genetics possible. Postulated viral cause for poliomyelitis and devised a serum diagnostic test for it (1909–12). With A. Wiener and P. Levine, he discovered rhesus (Rh) factor in human blood (1940).

LANE, JONATHAN HOMER (*b. Genesee, N.Y., 1819; d. Washington, D.C., 1880*), physics.

Graduated from Yale (1846). Employed by the U.S. Coast Survey, Washington, D.C. (1847). Conferred with Joseph Henry about experiments to determine speed of propagation of solar light and heat (1848); with Henry's help, appointed an examiner in U.S. Patent Office. From 1857–66, concerned with attempt to develop a low-temperature apparatus, using the expansion of gases for cooling. Joined Office of Weights and Measures (1869); the same year, read "On the Theoretical Temperature of the Sun" before the National Academy of Sciences; paper included careful calculations of mass and heat relationships in the sun. Work on star structure contributed to the developing evidence of stellar evolution.

LANE FOX, AUGUSTUS HENRY. *See* **Pitt-Rivers, Augustus Henry Lane Fox.**

LANG, ARNOLD (*b. Oftringen, Switzerland, 1855; d. Zurich, Switzerland, 1914*), zoology.

Took doctorate at Jena (1876). Appointed full professor at the University of Zurich (1889). Influenced by Karl Vogt and Ernst Haeckel. Translated Lamarck's *Philosophie zoologique* into German; wrote the popular *Lehrbuch der vergleichenden Anatomie der wirbellosen Tiere* (1888–94) on the anatomy of invertebrates.

LANG, KARL NIKOLAUS (*b. Lucerne, Switzerland, 1670; d. Lucerne, 1741*), paleontology.

Gave original descriptions of many of the fossils of Switzerland. Maintained that marine fossils originated from tiny, seminal seeds of living marine animals.

LANG, WILLIAM HENRY (*b. Withyham, Groombridge, Sussex, England, 1874; d. Storth, Westmorland, England, 1960*), botany.

Attended University of Glasgow (B.Sc., 1894; M.B., C.M., 1895); junior assistant in botany under Frederick Bower; worked under D. H. Scott at the Jodrell Laboratory at Kew; D.Sc. from Glasgow (1900). Interest in alternation of generations led him to study apospory in *Anthoceros laevis* and the prothallia in Lycopodiales and Ophioglossales; for specimens he visited Ceylon and Malaya (1899). Published paper on a theory of alternation of generations based on ontogeny (1909). With Robert Kidstone, wrote five classic papers (1917–21) on the silicified plants (probably Lower Devonian) of the Rhynie chert; a new order, Psilophytales, was created for these ancient vascular plants.

LANGE, CARL GEORG (*b. Vordingborg, Denmark, 1834; d. Copenhagen, Denmark, 1900*), medicine, psychology.

M.D. from Copenhagen University (1859); internship in Copenhagen (1859–67). Studied in Florence with Moritz Schiff. Was first to describe acute bulbar paralysis (1866); paper on spinal meningitis (1872) anticipated later neuron doctrine. Lectured at Copenhagen University from 1869. Published *Om Sindsbevaegelser* (1885), which argued that excitement is the result of vasomotor manifestations not of mental entities (the James-Lange theory), *Periodiske depressionstilstande* (1886), and *Bidrag til nydelsernes fysiologi* (1899) on pleasurable sensations in emotions.

LANGERHANS, PAUL (*b. Berlin, Germany, 1847; d. Funchal, Madeira, 1888*), anatomy, pathology.

Studied at the University of Jena (1865–66) and at Berlin (M.D., 1869). Working under Virchow and Cohnheim, studied the Malpighian layer of the epidermis, describing oblong bodies with processes branching into this layer, later called Langerhans' cells; his inaugural dissertation (1869) related his discovery of characteristic cell islands in the pancreas (Islets of Langerhans); also, with F. A. Hoffman, did pioneer investigation of the macrophage system. Contracted tuberculosis (1874); moved to Madeira where he practiced medicine.

LANGEVIN, PAUL (*b. Paris, France, 1872; d. Paris, 1946*), physics.

Was the leading practitioner and expositor of modern mathematical physics in France. Placed first in entrance exam for the École Normale Supérieure (1893), having already done laboratory work supervised by Pierre Curie. Worked in Cambridge at the Cavendish Laboratory under J. J. Thomson on ionization of X rays (1897). Doctoral dissertation at the Sorbonne on ionized gases (1902). Taught at the Collège de France from 1902. First theoretical papers (1904, 1905) dealt with the concept of electromagnetic mass, its rate of increase with velocity, and the related contraction hypothesis which suggested the impossibility of determining the earth's motion through the ether; his thoughts were developing on lines close to Einstein's. Most important paper (1905) gave a quantitative account of paramagnetism and diamagnetism, demonstrating the possibility of using the electron hypothesis to give precise meaning to the molecular models of Ampère and Weber. Produced a still-standard treatment of Brownian motion (1908). In World War I he developed a submarine detector using amplified ultrasonic waves. Arrested by the Wehrmacht (1940); fled to Switzerland. His body now lies in the Pantheon.

LANGLEY, JOHN NEWPORT (*b. Newbury, England, 1852; d. Cambridge, England, 1925*), physiology, histology.

Professor of physiology at Cambridge from 1903; renowned for his studies of glandular secretion and of the autonomic, or involuntary, nervous system. As a student at Cambridge, was inspired by Michael Foster to read for the natural sciences. (Graduated B.A., 1875; M.A., 1878; Sc.D., 1896.) In investigations of glandular secretion (1875–90), he radically disagreed with findings of Rudolf Heidenhain. His work on the involuntary nervous system arose from the discovery (announced jointly with William Lee Dickinson, 1889) that nicotine could selectively interrupt nerve impulses at the sympathetic ganglia; this offered a technique for distinguishing which nerve fibers ended in the nerve cells of a ganglion and which merely ran through. Mapped out much of the involuntary system in detail. Suggested (1906) that every cell connected with an efferent fiber contains a substance responsible for the chief function of the cell, as well as other "receptive substances," a concept which stimulated many subsequent studies.

LANGLEY, SAMUEL PIERPONT (*b. Roxbury [now part of Boston], Mass., 1834; d. Aiken, S.C., 1906*), astrophysics.

From an old and prominent New England family. Appointed director of the Allegheny Observatory and professor of physics and astronomy at Western University of Pennsylvania (now University of Pittsburgh) in 1867. Founded the Smithsonian Astrophysical Observatory (1890). Did research in aerodynamics; successfully flew machine-powered airplane models, but his man-carrying plane failed (1906). Developed a new instrument (1879–81), the bolometer, to measure energy of radiation as a function of wavelength; used it to study the solar constant (integrating energy versus wavelength curves) and the selective absorption of the earth's and sun's atmospheres. At Mount Whitney (1881), discovered significant solar radiation beyond a wavelength of one micron (thought to be the limit).

LANGLOIS, CLAUDE (*b. France, ca. 1700; d. France, ca. 1756*), instrumentation.

The most highly regarded maker of scientific instruments in France. Commissioned to build for the Paris observatory a wall quadrant of six-foot radius. Made an improved pantograph for the Académie des Sciences; chosen by the Académie as official instrument maker of the French astronomers (*ca.* 1740).

LANGMUIR, IRVING (*b. Brooklyn, N.Y., 1881; d. Falmouth, Mass., 1957*), chemistry, physics.

Studied at the Columbia University School of Mines (graduated 1903) and the University of Göttingen, where he worked under Walther Nernst; doctoral dissertation (1906) on the dissociation of gases by glowing platinum wire. Employed in the General Electric Company's research laboratory in Schenectady, New York (1909–50). Awarded Nobel Prize in chemistry (1932). Discovered that filling a lamp with inert gases increases its lifetime and efficiency. Invented the atomic-hydrogen welding torch. Independently derived for electrons the relationship shown by C. D. Child for ions; this Child-Langmuir space-charge equation (current between electrodes is proportional to voltage raised to the 3/2 power) underlies the design of many electron tubes. Major work was in surface chemistry: his new theory of adsorption stated that every molecule that strikes a surface remains for a time, so that a monolayer is formed; he characterized the catalytic effect of an adsorbing surface by considering the chemical reaction as occurring in the film, a valuable explanatory concept. Studied electric discharges in gases; coined the term "plasma" for the complex, inherently unstable medium of a space-charge-free ionized gas. A great outdoorsman, in retirement Langmuir (with V. J. Schaefer) studied atmospherics and developed a method of "seeding" clouds with solid carbon dioxide particles. Mount Langmuir in Alaska is named after him.

LANGREN, MICHAEL FLORENT VAN (*b. Mechlin or Antwerp, Belgium, ca. 1600; d. Brussels, Belgium, 1675*), engineering, cartography, selenography.

Used lunar observations in an attempt to determine longitude at sea. Created maps of the moon. Wrote on the structure of the port of Ostend and on the fortification of Brussels.

LANKESTER, EDWIN RAY (*b. London, England, 1847; d. London, 1929*), zoology, natural history.

Graduated from Oxford University. Taught at University College, London, and at Oxford (from 1891). A friend and supporter of Darwin. Systematized the field of embryology.

LANSBERGE, PHILIP VAN (*b. Ghent, Belgium, 1561; d. Middelburg, Netherlands, 1632*), geometry, astronomy.

Was a Protestant minister. Wrote text on trigonometry, *Triangulorum geometriae libri IV* (1591). Taught Copernican theory of the earth's motion.

LAPICQUE, LOUIS (*b. Épinal, France, 1866; d. Paris, France, 1952*), physiology, anthropology.

Studied at the Paris Medical School; professor at the Muséum d'Histoire Naturelle and the Sorbonne (1919–36). Investigated the circulation of iron in vertebrates; studied the peoples of the Indian Ocean, also the relation between brain and body weight in man and animals. Essential work was on the time factor in nervous processes; proposed fruitful theory that transmission of excitation between two nerve cells was optimal when cells had the same chronaxie (a measure of functional rapidity).

LAPLACE, PIERRE-SIMON, MARQUIS DE (*b. Beaumont-en-Auge, Normandy, France, 1749; d. Paris, France, 1827*), celestial mechanics, probability, applied mathematics, physics.

Laplace was among the most influential scientists in all history. His career was important for his technical contributions to exact science, for the philosophical point of view he developed in the presentation of his work, and for the part he took in forming the modern scientific disciplines. The main institutions in which he participated were the Académie Royale des Sciences (until its suppression in the Revolution, and then its replacement), the scientific division of the Institut de France, together with two other Republican foundations, the École Polytechnique and the Bureau des Longitudes. His scientific life passed through four stages, the first two in the context of the old regime and the latter two in that of the French Revolution, the Napoleonic regime, and the Restoration.

In the first stage, 1768–78, Laplace was composing memoirs on problems of the integral calculus, mathematical astronomy, cosmology, theory of games of chance, and causality. During this formative period, he established his style, reputation, philosophical position, certain mathematical techniques, and a program of research in two areas, probability and celestial mechanics, in which he worked mathematically for the rest of his life.

In the second stage, 1778–89, he reached in both areas many of the major results for which he is famous and which he later incorporated into the great treatises *Mécanique céleste* (1799–1825) and *Théorie analytique des probabilités* (1812). They were informed in large part by the mathematical techniques that he introduced and developed, then or earlier, most notably generating functions, the transform since called by his name, the expansion also named for him in the theory of determinants, the variation of constants to achieve approximate solutions in the integration of astronomical expressions, and the generalized gravitational function that, through the intermediary of Poisson, later became the potential function of nineteenth-century electricity and magnetism. It was also during this period that Laplace entered on the third area of his mature interests, physics, in his collaboration with Lavoisier on the theory of heat, and that he became, partly in consequence of this association, one of the inner circle of influential members of the scientific community. In the 1780's he began serving on commissions important to the government and affecting the lives of others.

In the third stage, 1789–1805, the Revolutionary period and especially that of the Directory brought him to his zenith. The early 1790's saw the completion of the great series of memoirs on planetary astronomy and involved him centrally in the preparation of the metric system. More important, in the decade from 1795 to 1805 his influence was paramount for the exact sciences in the newly founded Institut de France; and his was a powerful position in the counsels of the École Polytechnique, which was training the first generation of mathematical physicists. The educational mission attributed to all science in that period of intense civic consciousness changed the mode of scientific publication from academic memoir to general treatise. The first four volumes of *Méchanique céleste* (Laplace himself coined the term), generalizing the laws of mechanics for their application to the motions and figures of the heavenly bodies, appeared from 1799 through 1805. The last parts of the fourth volume and the fifth volume, really a separate work that appeared in installments from 1823 to 1825, contain important material (on physics) not already included in the sequence of Laplace's original memoirs published previously by the old Academy.

Laplace accompanied both *Mécanique céleste* and *Théorie analytique des probabilités* by verbal paraphrases addressed to the intelligent public in the French tradition of *haute vulgarisation*. The *Exposition du système du monde* preceded the *Mécanique céleste* and appeared in 1796. The *Essai philosophique sur les probabilités*, published in 1814 as an introduction to the second edition of *Théorie analytique* and printed separately earlier in the same year, originated in a course of lectures at the École Normale in 1795.

The work of the fourth stage, occupying the period from 1805 until 1827, exhibits elements of culmination and of decline. It was then that the mature—perhaps the aging—Laplace, in company with Berthollet, formed a school, surrounding himself with disciples in the informal Société d'Arcueil. But the science that he set out to shape was not astronomy. The center of their interest, following Volume IV of *Mécanique céleste,* was in physics—capillary action, the theory of heat, corpuscular optics, and the speed of sound. The Laplacian school of physics has had a bad scholarly press since its identity was established, excessively so perhaps. But whatever else may be said about it, there can be no doubt about the encouragement that it gave to the mathematization of the science.

Beginning in 1810, Laplace turned his attention to probability again, moving back by way of error theory into the subject as a whole. Mathematically speaking, the *Théorie analytique des probabilités* (1812) may be said to belong to the previous phase of drawing together and generalizing the researches on special topics of his younger years. There were important novelties in the application, however, notably in the treatment of least squares, in the extension of probability in later editions to analysis of the credibility of witnesses and the procedures of judicial panels and electoral bodies, and in the increasing sophistication of the statistical treatment of geodesic and meteorological data.

LAPPARENT, ALBERT-AUGUSTE COCHON DE (*b. Bourges, France, 1839; d. Paris, France, 1908*), geology.

Graduated first in class from the École des Mines (1864). Supervised surveying for six maps of the Paris Basin. On committee to study feasibility of tunnel under English Channel (concluded it was possible). Taught at the newly-founded Catholic University (later the Catholic Institute) from 1876. Wrote *Traité de géologie* (1882).

LAPWORTH, ARTHUR (*b. Galashiels, Scotland, 1872; d. Manchester, England, 1941*), chemistry.

Studied at Birmingham; worked in London under H. E. Armstrong (on naphthalene chemistry) and with F. S. Kipping (studies on camphor). Taught at the University of Manchester from 1909. For work on reaction mechanisms, he is regarded as one of the founders of modern "physical-organic chemistry." Son of Charles Lapworth.

LAPWORTH, CHARLES (*b. Faringdon, Berkshire, England, 1842; d. Birmingham, England, 1920*), geology.

Became schoolmaster in Scotland (1864); as an amateur, developed a genius for geology. Did major research in Southern Uplands and Highlands of Scotland; findings impressed him with importance of tangential stress in earth's crust. Proposed (1879) classification of Lower Paleozoic rocks into Cambrian, Ordovician (a new system), and Silurian. Appointed (1881) to chair of geology at Mason College (now University of Birmingham).

LA RAMÉE, PIERRE DE. *See* **Ramus, Peter.**

LARGHI, BERNARDINO (*b. Vercelli, Italy, 1812; d. Vercelli, 1877*), surgery.

Graduated in surgery, University of Turin (1833); in medicine, University of Genoa (1836). Practiced in Vercelli. Known chiefly for performance of subperiosteal resection.

LA RIVE, ARTHUR-AUGUSTE DE (*b. Geneva [then French], 1801; d. Marseilles, France, 1873*), physics.

Studied law at the Académie de Genève, where his father, Charles Gaspard de La Rive, was a professor. Through father's influence, appointed professor of physics at the Academy (1823). Was a leader of the Swiss scientific community, but his own work, chiefly on the chemical pile, was of no lasting significance.

LA RIVE, CHARLES-GASPARD DE (*b. Geneva, 1770; d. Geneva, Swiss Confederation, 1834*), physics, chemistry, medicine.

Of a noble family, prominent in Geneva's Protestant patriciate. Studied law at the Académie de Genève; emigrated to Edinburgh during the Revolution, where he received his doctorate (1797). Returned to Geneva (1799); became an honorary professor at the Academy; influential in reforms to free the Academy of ecclesiastical control and strengthen the science faculty. Was a defender of Ampère.

LARMOR, JOSEPH (*b. Magheragall, County Antrim, Ireland, 1857; d. Holywood, County Down, Ireland, 1942*), theoretical physics.

Studied at Queen's University, Belfast, and Cambridge (fellow, 1880). Taught at Cambridge (1885–1932). Knighted (1909); member of Parliament from Cambridge University (1911–22). Major work concerned electron theory and the related problem of the effect of the motion of matter through the ether. In *Aether and Matter* (1900), his electron theory is constructed from a rotationally elastic ether, derived from the concepts of James MacCullagh. Larmor worked in the tradition of classical mathematical physics; was generally critical of quantum theory and the relativity theories.

LA ROCHE, ESTIENNE DE (*b. Lyons, France; fl. Lyons, ca. 1520*), arithmetic.

Known as Villefranche, he was a pupil of Nicolas Chuquet. His famous *Larismetique* (1520) was later discovered to be mostly a copy of Chuquet's ms. "Triparty" (1484), with the most striking features omitted.

LARSEN, ESPER SIGNIUS, JR. (*b. Astoria, Ore., 1879; d. Washington, D.C., 1961*), geology.

Was the foremost descriptive and theoretical petrologist in the U.S. Studied under A. C. Lawson at the University of California (B.S., 1906). Served with the U.S. Geological Survey (1909–23, 1949–58); professor at Harvard University (1923–49). Major work in field of optical crystallography; with H. Berman wrote *The Microscopic Determination of the Nonopaque Minerals* (1934). Developed a hollow prism for measuring directly the index of refraction of immersion liquids, and a method for determining the age of igneous rocks.

LARTET, ÉDOUARD AMANT ISIDORE HIPPOLYTE (*b. St.-Guiraud, Gers, France, 1801; d. Seissan, Gers, 1871*), paleontology, prehistory.

Although trained in law, Lartet devoted his life to his estate in Gers and to natural history. Discovered (1834) the rich fossil deposit of Sansan; showed the contemporaneity of man and extinct animal species in excavations at Massat and Aurignac (1860); with Henry Christy, explored grottoes of La Madeleine, Le Moustier, and Les Eyzies, rich in prehistoric art. Author, *Reliquiae acquitanicae* (1865–75).

LARTET, LOUIS (*b. Castelnau-Magnoac, Hautes-Pyrénées, France, 1840; d. Seissan, Gers, France, 1899*), geology, prehistory.

Was the son of Édouard Lartet. Noted for his study of the Cro-Magnon deposit.

LASHLEY, KARL SPENCER (*b. Davis, W. Va., 1890; d. Poitiers, France, 1958*), psychology, neurophysiology.

One of the world's foremost physiological psychologists. Received Ph.D. from Johns Hopkins (1914); was research professor of neuropsychology at Harvard University (1935–55) and director of the Yerkes Laboratories of Primate Biology (from 1942). Author, *Brain Mechanisms and Intelligence* (1964).

LASSAR-COHN. *See* **Cohn, Lassar.**

LASSELL, WILLIAM (*b. Bolton, Lancashire, England, 1799; d. Maidenhead, Berkshire, England, 1880*), astronomy.

Originally a brewer. Began to construct reflecting telescopes (*ca.* 1820); made improvements in their design. Discovered the satellites Triton (1846) and Hyperion (1848, seen simultaneously by W. C. Bond), and 600 nebulae.

LĀṬADEVA (*fl. India, ca.* A.D. *505*), astronomy.

Perhaps originally from Lāṭadeśa in Gujarat, was a pupil of Āryabhaṭa I. Said by Varāhamihira to have commented on the *Romakasiddhānta* and the *Pauliśasiddhānta;* evidently also revised the *Sūryasiddhānta.*

LATIMER, WENDELL MITCHELL (*b. Garnett, Kan., 1893; d. Oakland, Calif., 1955*), chemistry.

Studied and taught at the University of Kansas; took Ph.D. at Berkeley (1919); became full professor there (1931). With W. H. Rodebush, expressed first clear recognition of the hydrogen bond as distinct from ordinary dipoles (1920); wrote *The Oxidation States of the Elements and Their Potentials in Aqueous Solutions* (1938, 1952).

LATREILLE, PIERRE-ANDRÉ (*b. Brive-la-Gaillarde, France, 1762; d. Paris, France, 1833*), entomology, zoology.

The natural son of baron d'Espagnac; ordained a priest (1786); career interrupted by the Revolution. Pursued natural history to bolster frail health. Worked under Lamarck at the Muséum d'Histoire Naturelle (from 1805), taking over his course (1820), but did not accept his evolutionary views. Classified insects, arachnids, and crustaceans according to "natural method" (combining approaches of Linnaeus and Fabricius). Was one of the foremost entomologists of his day; wrote *Genera crustaceorum et insectorum* (1806–09).

LAU, HANS EMIL (*b. Odense, Denmark, 1879; d. Usserød, Denmark, 1918*), astronomy.

Received master's degree at University of Copenhagen (1906). Working from his own small observatory, made important contributions on a wide range of phenomena; did pioneer work on photographic observations.

LAUE, MAX VON (*b. Pfaffendorf, near Koblenz, Germany, 1879; d. Berlin, Germany, 1960*), theoretical physics.

Studied at the universities of Strasbourg, Göttingen, and Berlin; influenced by Woldemar Voigt, Otto Lummer, and especially Max Planck, his lifelong friend. Interested in optical problems; doctoral dissertation (1903, under Planck) on theory of interference in plane parallel plates. An early adherent of the special theory of relativity, Laue provided a proof (1907) based on Fizeau's formula for the velocity of light in moving water. Became *Privatdozent* at the Institute for Theoretical Physics, directed by Arnold Sommerfeld, University of Munich. Suggested sending X rays through crystals (1912), a procedure that both confirmed the wave nature of X rays and revealed the atomic structure of the crystal. For this work, creating the field of X-ray structural analysis, received Nobel Prize in physics (1914). As a professor at the University of Berlin, courageously opposed the Nazis.

LAURENS, ANDRÉ DU (LAURENTIUS) (*b. Tarascon, near Arles, France, 1558; d. Paris, France, 1609*), anatomy, medicine.

Took M.D. degrees at Avignon (1578) and Montpellier (1583); studied under Louis Duret in Paris; appointed to chair of medicine at Montpellier (1583). Served as a royal physician (from 1596, under Henry IV). Became chancellor at Montpellier (1603). Author, *Historia anatomica* (1600), a widely used textbook, which supported Galen's views.

LAURENT, AUGUSTE (or **AUGUSTIN**) (*b. St.-Maurice, Haute-Marne, France, 1807; d. Paris, France, 1853*), chemistry.

Studied at the École des Mines in Paris (graduated 1830). Worked under J. B. Dumas at the École Centrale des Arts et Manufactures (1830–31) and under Alexandre Brongniart, Dumas's father-in-law, at the royal porcelain works at Sèvres (1832–34). His main doctoral thesis for the Sorbonne (1837) developed the principal ideas of his theory of fundamental and derived radicals in organic chemistry. Appointed (1838) to chair of chemistry at Bordeaux. With C. F. Gerhardt, edited the journal, *Comptes-rendus mensuels des travaux chimiques* (from 1845). Became assayer at the Paris Mint (1848). Was a central figure in the emergence of organic chemistry as a mature science. Original theories formulated 1835–37; modified after 1842. Did exhaustive studies of naphthalene and action of bromine on camphor. Extending work of Dumas, generalized that all organic compounds could be understood as derivatives of hydrocarbons. Influenced by Haüy's work in crystallography, theorized that the basic hydrocarbons corresponded to the fundamental crystalline structure; basic hydrocarbons were thus called fundamental radicals, their substitution and addition products, derived

radicals. Suggested a pyramidal model for structure of organic substances, with carbon atoms at the angles; as long as the central structure of carbon atoms was unaffected in reactions, the resulting compounds belonged to the same family; if any one of the carbon atoms were to be destroyed, a wholly different type of product would be formed. Laurent wrote two books: *Précis de cristallographie* ... (Paris, 1847) and *Méthode de chimie* (Paris, 1854).

LAURENT, MATTHIEU PAUL HERMANN (*b. Echternach, Luxembourg, 1841; d. Paris, France, 1908*), mathematics, higher education.

Laurent's father, Auguste, was a noted chemist. Laurent took his doctorate at the University of Nancy (1865); taught at the École Polytechnique and (from 1889) at the École Agronomique; served as actuary for Compagnie d'Assurance de l'Union. Was most important for his teaching activities. Wrote *Traité des séries* (1862); *Traité des résidus* (1865); and *Traité d'analyse* (1885–91) on the differential and integral calculus.

LAURENT, PIERRE ALPHONSE (*b. Paris, France, 1813; d. Paris, 1854*), mathematics, optics.

Trained as an engineer (École Polytechnique, École d'Application at Metz), worked chiefly on the study leading to the enlargement of the port of Le Havre. Wrote memoirs in pure mathematics and optics, including an extension of a theorem of A. L. Cauchy, reported by Cauchy to the Académie des Sciences (1843). Rejected use of single material points in determining equations of motion of light; used instead a system combining the spheroids and a system of material points. Developed a theorem for study of the equilibrium of temperatures in a body and the phenomenon of elasticity.

LAUSSEDAT, AIMÉ (*b. Moulins, France, 1819; d. Paris, France, 1907*), photogrammetry.

Studied at the École Polytechnique; taught at this school and the Conservatoire des Arts et Métiers. Did pioneer work in the use of aerial photography to prepare topographic maps.

LAVANHA, JOÃO BAPTISTA (*b. Portugal, ca. 1550; d. Madrid, Spain, 1624*), cosmography, mathematics.

Became professor of mathematics at Madrid (1583); also served as chief engineer and chief cosmographer; maintained chair in Lisbon for teaching navigational mathematics. Author, *Regimento nautico* (1595).

LAVERAN, CHARLES LOUIS ALPHONSE (*b. Paris, France, 1845; d. Paris, 1922*), medicine, biology, parasitology.

Studied medicine in Strasbourg. With the Army in Algeria (1878–83), discovered the living agent of malaria (1880). Awarded Nobel Prize (1907) for work on pathogenic protozoans. At Pasteur Institute (from 1896).

LAVOISIER, ANTOINE-LAURENT (*b. Paris, France, 1743; d. Paris, 1794*), chemistry, physiology, geology, economics, social reform.

A versatile scientist and public servant, Lavoisier was first of all a chemist of genius; he discovered the role of oxygen in chemical reactions and was the architect of a revolutionary reform of chemistry. He died on the guillotine in his fifty-first year, a martyr of the Reign of Terror.

Lavoisier was the son of a lawyer; following the death of his mother (1748), he was raised by an aunt. He attended the remarkable Collège des Quatres Nations (usually called the Collège Mazarin); studied under the astronomer Lacaille; received his baccalaureate in law (1763). Soon he turned from law to science, working with the geologist Jean-Étienne Guettard; took courses in chemistry from G. F. Rouelle at the Jardin du Roi; with Guettard, worked on a geologic and mineralogic atlas of France. Formulated a theory of stratification (1766) postulating that the *terre nouvelle* (the strata believed to have been deposited when the sea covered the continent of Europe) was formed in a succession of epochs by a cyclically advancing and retreating sea. First chemical investigation was a study of gypsum (1764) intended to be the beginning of a systematic analysis of mineral substances; his method was to study reactions in solution; his approach was characterized by careful quantitative investigation. Did paper for the Academy of Sciences (1764) on improving the street lighting of Paris; was awarded a gold medal but not elected to the Academy as he had hoped. Read to the Academy (1768) a paper on hydrometry, describing his design of an instrument of the constant-immersion type, and a paper on the analysis of water from different sources; considered water the chief agent in shaping the earth. Was now elected to the Academy.

Entered the Ferme Générale (1768), a private consortium for the collection of certain taxes; married the daughter of one of his colleagues there (1771); his bride a girl of fourteen, trained herself to be her husband's collaborator; they had no children. Was appointed a commissioner of the Royal Gunpowder Administration (1775); took up residence in the Paris Arsenal; equipped a fine laboratory there.

In connection with a plan to bring to Paris the waters of the Yvette river, Lavoisier studied the problem of transmutation: whether water, on distillation, could in part be transmuted to earth; many, including Van Helmont and Boyle, believed in this transmutation; in a famous experiment (1768), Lavoisier repeatedly distilled water in a pelican (a glass vessel), obtaining eventually particles of solid matter; the weight of these particles equalled weight lost from the pelican; the "earth" (silica) was from the glass. Speculation on the nature of the elements led Lavoisier to the first steps of his "revolution in chemistry": the overthrow of the dominant phlogiston theory, the recognition that the atmosphere is composed of different gases, the demonstration that oxygen gas is the agent active in combustion and calcination. (Phlogiston was a hypothetical element, assumed to be the cause of combustion and to be given off in combustion.) Lavoisier had been impressed by Stephen Hales's finding that air could exist "fixed" in a wide variety of substances; and a book by L. B. Guyton de Morveau (1772) on the characteristic weight gains of different metals when calcined suggested to Lavoisier that the fixation of air might be what accounted for these gains. In 1775, Lavoisier discovered that the air produced by the reduction of red mercury calx was not Hales's "fixed air": Instead of extinguishing a candle's flame, it caused the flame to burn brighter; it was "more pure than the air in which we live." Priestley, who in a visit to Paris (1774) had described his own work with mercury calx to Lavoisier, believed that

Lavoisier had simply followed his lead; however, Lavoisier and others in France had begun work with mercury calx before Priestley's visit. Now (1775) Priestley published his conclusion that this new air was "dephlogisticated air": because it supported combustion better than common air, it must be a better receptacle for phlogiston, therefore it must have less phlogiston already in it. Extending Priestley's work, Lavoisier discovered that the residual air left after prolonged calcination of mercury (nitrogen) did not support combustion by itself, but did so when mixed with "dephlogisticated air" (five parts to one); he also found that the latter supported respiration much longer than common air; he further concluded (somewhat rashly) from a series of experiments on the nature of acids that this "eminently respirable air" might be the "acidifiable principle," combining with substances to create acids; therefore he named it *principe oxigine* ("oxygen principle"), i.e., "begetter of acids."

Working with Jean Bucquet (1777), he experimented with the "inflammable air" (hydrogen) produced by the action of weak acids on iron or copper; continuing these experiments with Laplace, he designed an apparatus for burning "inflammable air" together with oxygen; meanwhile it was reported that Cavendish had already obtained pure water by this means; after making his own experiment, Lavoisier announced (1783) that water was not a simple substance, an element, but rather a compound of the two gases. From a series of experiments with Laplace on vaporization and heat production, he concluded that gases owe their aeriform, elastic state to their combination with the "matter of fire," and so the heat and light given off during combustion must come from the fire matter released by the "vital air" (oxygen gas); he published his definitive attack on the old theory of combustion in "Réflexions sur le phlogistique" (1786); this attack and a general exposition of his methods and conclusions formed the subject of his classic book, *Traité élémentaire de chimie* (1789). In the meantime, Lavoisier was also considering the question of respiration; he suggested (1777) that oxygen might be exchanged in the lungs for carbon dioxide or converted to carbon dioxide; the latter event might account for the production of animal heat; finding that experimental animals gave off less carbon dioxide than the intake of oxygen had led him to expect, Lavoisier argued (1785) that either some of the oxygen unites with the blood or combines with hydrogen to form water; collaborative experiments done with Armand Seguin (1789–91) persuaded him that both occur; he also found that the quantity of oxygen consumed increases with the temperature and is greater during digestion and exercise; he concluded that combustion occurs in the tubules of the lungs.

Upon the death of his father (1775), Lavoisier inherited a title associated with an honorific office his father had purchased; shortly thereafter he bought an estate near Blois where he carried out agricultural experiments. Politically liberal and probably a Freemason, he took an active part in the events leading to the Revolution; he was elected to the Commune of Paris, became a Director of the Discount Bank, and brought out (1791) a statistical study of the agricultural resources of the nation; at the Academy he was active in working to establish the metric system. Nevertheless, he was attacked by Marat and other radicals. In 1793, all members of the Ferme Générale were arrested, including Lavoisier and his father-in-law. All were tried by the Revolutionary Tribunal on the morning of May 8, 1794, and executed that same afternoon. After Lavoisier's death, Lagrange remarked, "It took them only an instant to cut off that head, and a hundred years may not produce another like it."

LAVRENTIEV, BORIS INNOKENTIEVICH (*b. Kazan, Russia, 1892; d. Moscow, U.S.S.R., 1944*), histology.

Graduated in medicine from Kazan University (1914), and was prosector in histology there (1921–25) after serving as an army doctor. From 1927 he worked primarily in Moscow, hoding professorships at various institutes. Did experimental studies of the histophysiology of the autonomic nervous system; investigated degeneration and regeneration of severed nerves; supported concept of the tropic effect of the nervous system, and theory of its neuronal structure; demonstrated existence and functions of interneuron bonds (synapses) both in sections and intravitally in isolated heart of the frog; established relative independence of synapses from the neurons they connect.

LAWES, JOHN BENNET (*b. Rothamsted, Hertfordshire, England, 1814; d. Rothamsted, 1900*); and **GILBERT, JOSEPH HENRY** (*b. Hull, England, 1817; d. Harpenden, England, 1901*), agricultural chemistry.

Lawes inherited estate at Rothamsted (1834); devised method of treating ground bones to make a "superphosphate," universally effective as fertilizer; acquired factory at Deptford Creek for its manufacture. Gilbert studied chemistry at Glasgow University, University College, London, and under Liebig at Giessen. Engaged (1834) by Lawes to assist in agricultural experiments; together they built Rothamsted into a world-famous institution. Disproved Liebig's view that nitrogen was unnecessary in action of manures. Evolved "chessboard system" of random plots.

LAWRENCE, ERNEST ORLANDO (*b. Canton, S.D., 1901; d. Palo Alto, Calif., 1958*), physics.

Studied at the University of South Dakota (graduated, 1922), the University of Minnesota (M.A. under W. F. G. Swann), the University of Chicago, and Yale University (Ph.D., 1925). Left teaching post at Yale to join the physics department at the University of California at Berkeley, which under his leadership and that of his colleagues, including J. R. Oppenheimer, became a world-renowned research center. With N. E. Edlefsen and M. S. Livingston, Lawrence developed a circular accelerator (later called the cyclotron), which, being capable of producing energy of millions of electron volts, ushered in the era of high-energy physics. Received Nobel Prize, 1939. Helped to devise method of obtaining fissionable materials used in the atomic bomb. His support (with Edward Teller) of the development of the hydrogen bomb led to a dramatic conflict with Oppenheimer.

LAWRENCE, WILLIAM (*b. Cirencester, Gloucestershire, England, 1783; d. London, England, 1867*), anatomy, physiology, surgery.

A distinguished surgeon with St. Bartholomew's Hospital, London (1824–65); became sergeant-surgeon to Queen Victoria (1858); awarded baronetcy (1867). Apprenticed with Dr. John Abernathy at St. Bartholomew's; appointed his demonstrator in anatomy (1799); diploma from Royal College of Surgeons (1805). Surgeon for the London Infirmary for Curing Diseases of the Eye (later the London Ophthalmic Infirmary, 1814–26). Author, *Treatise on the Diseases of the Eye* (1833) and the controversial *Lectures on Physiology* (1819), proposing that all mental activity is a function of the brain, not the soul.

LAWSON, ANDREW COWPER (*b. Anstruther, Scotland, 1861; d. San Leandro, Calif., 1952*), geology.

Studied at the University of Toronto (bachelor's degree, 1883; master's, 1885) and Johns Hopkins University (doctorate, 1888). At the University of California at Berkeley (1890–1950); chairman of Department of Geology for 20 years. Published papers on isostasy (1920–50), on the region northwest of Lake Superior, and on the western coastal area; supervised official state report on California earthquake of 1906; helped to found the Seismological Society of America.

LAX, GASPAR (*b. Sariñena, Aragon, Spain, 1487; d. Zaragoza, Spain, 1560*), mathematics, logic, natural philosophy.

Studied the arts and theology in Zaragoza; taught in Paris and Zaragoza. Was a nominalist, "the Prince of the Parisian *sophistae*"; wrote *Arithmetica speculativa* and *Proportiones* (both 1515).

LAZAREV, MIKHAIL PETROVICH (*b. Vladimir, Russia, 1788; d. Vienna, Austria, 1851*), navigation, oceanography.

Trained at the Naval Academy in St. Petersburg; made three voyages around the world, one with Bellinsgauzen's expedition to the Antarctic.

LAZAREV, PETR PETROVICH (*b. Moscow, Russia, 1878; d. Alma-Ata, U.S.S.R., 1942*), physics, biophysics, geophysics.

Trained as a medical doctor in Moscow; studied physics and mathematics on his own; doctoral thesis (1912, Moscow University) was a fundamental investigation in prequantum photochemistry. Studied the biophysics of the sense organs; developed ion theory of nerve excitation. Supported the October Revolution; established prospecting surveys, which (1919) revealed enormous national reserves of iron ore.

LEA, ISAAC (*b. Wilmington, Del., 1792; d. Philadelphia, Pa., 1886*), malacology.

A businessman and publisher, Lea was also a dedicated naturalist, noted for his collection of minerals, rocks, and fossils (begun with his lifelong friend Lardner Vanuxem) and for his exhaustive work on freshwater mollusks. Author, *Contributions to Geology* (1833) and *Synopsis of the Family of Naïades* (1836).

LEAKEY, LOUIS SEYMOUR BAZETT (*b. Kabete, Kenya, 1903; d. London, England, 1972*), archaeology, human paleontology, anthropology.

The son of a missionary, Leakey was raised in a Kikuyu village. Attended Cambridge University (Ph.D. in African prehistory). Did archaeological and paleontological research in East Africa from 1924. With wife, Mary, and sons began large-scale work at the Olduvai Gorge (1959), which yielded major finds: skull of *Australopithecus boisei;* first remains of *Homo habilis;* skull of *Homo erectus.*

LEAVITT, HENRIETTA SWAN (*b. Lancaster, Mass., 1868; d. Cambridge, Mass., 1921*), astronomy.

Received A.B., Radcliffe College (1892); became chief, photographic photometry department, Harvard College Observatory. Discovered 2,400 variable stars and the period-luminosity relationship of the Cepheid variable stars.

LEBEDEV, PETR NIKOLAEVICH (*b. Moscow, Russia, 1866; d. Moscow, 1912*), physics.

Studied at Strasbourg University and Moscow University (Ph.D., 1900). A leader among Russian physicists; noted for ingenious experimental work on the ponderomotive action of waves on resonators and on the pressure of light.

LEBEDEV, SERGEI VASILIEVICH (*b. Lublin, Poland, 1874; d. Leningrad, U.S.S.R., 1934*), chemistry.

Attended University of St. Petersburg (Ph.D., 1913); taught at Military Medical Academy (from 1917). Led group that synthesized rubber (1927), polymerizing divinyl in presence of sodium.

LEBEDINSKY, VYACHESLAV VASILIEVICH (*b. St. Petersburg, Russia [now Leningrad, U.S.S.R.], 1888; d. Moscow, U.S.S.R., 1956*), chemistry.

A student of Chugaev; graduated from St. Petersburg University (1913). Noted for studies of complex compounds of rhodium.

LE BEL, JOSEPH ACHILLE (*b. Pechelbronn, Bas-Rhin, France, 1847; d. Paris, France, 1930*), chemistry.

Educated at the École Polytechnique; active in managing petroleum workings at Pechelbronn. At laboratory of C.-A. Wurtz, developed (independently of van't Hoff) the theory of the relation of stereochemical structure to optical activity in organic compounds (1874).

LEBESGUE, HENRI LÉON (*b. Beauvais, France, 1875; d. Paris, France, 1941*), mathematics.

Studied at the École Normale Supérieure and the Sorbonne (Ph.D., 1902). Extending Camille Jordan's and Émile Borel's work on the Riemann integral, Lebesgue formulated the theory of integration that bears his name and that became the foundation for subsequent work in integration theory; with his generalization of Riemann's integral was able to solve many of the difficulties associated with Riemann's theory of integration.

LE BLANC, MAX JULIUS LOUIS (*b. Barten, East Prussia [now Poland], 1865; d. Leipzig, Germany, 1943*), chemistry.

Educated at the universities of Tübingen, Munich, and Berlin. Helped to develop the technical institute at Karlsruhe and the physical chemical institute at Leipzig. Studied electrochemical polarization; introduced the hydrogen electrode (1893).

LEBLANC, NICOLAS (*b. Ivoy-le-Pré, France, 1742; d. Paris, France, 1806*), chemistry.

Attended École de Chirurgie, Paris; entered service of the duc d'Orléans. Discovered the Leblanc process for the artificial preparation of soda (1789).

LE BOUYER DE FONTENELLE, BERNARD. *See* **Fontenelle, Bernard Le Bouyer de.**

LE CAT, CLAUDE-NICOLAS (*b. Blérancourt, Picardy, France, 1700; d. Rouen, France, 1768*), surgery, anatomy, physiology, biomechanics.

Received M.D. (1733) and master's degree in surgery from University of Rheims. Specialized in operating for vesicular stones. Established school for anatomy and surgery in Rouen (1736). An early adherent of a mechanistic approach to physiology.

LE CHÂTELIER, HENRY LOUIS (*b. Paris, France, 1850; d. Miribel-les-Échelles, Isère, France, 1936*), chemistry, metallurgy.

From a prominent family of scientists and technologists. Attended the École Polytechnique and the École des Mines, where he also taught (1877–1919); held additional professorships at the Collège de France and the Sorbonne; appointed inspector general of mines (1907). Studied the setting of plaster of Paris and of cements composed of calcium silicates; doctoral thesis on the latter (1887). With Ernest Mallard appointed to investigate causes of mine accidents (1882). Study of reactions in blast furnaces led to formulation of the Le Châtelier principle: "Every change in one of the factors of an equilibrium occasions a rearrangement of the system in such a direction that the factor in question experiences a change in the sense opposite to the original change" (as stated in his summary article, *Annales des Mines,* 1888). Did experimental research on metallic alloys and on the chemistry and metallurgy of iron and steel. In *Le Taylorisme* (1928), advocated the application of the ideas of the industrial engineer F. W. Taylor.

LECLERC. *See* **Buffon, Georges-Louis Leclerc, Comte de.**

L'ÉCLUSE (CLUSIUS), CHARLES DE (*b. Arras, France, 1526; d. Leiden, Netherlands, 1609*), botany.

Known to botanists as Clusius. Trained as a lawyer at Louvain; interest in botany awakened (1551) in Provence while gathering plants. Held chair of botany of the University of Leiden (1593–1609). Author, *Rariorum plantarum historia* (1601) and *Exoticorum libri decem* (1605)

LECONTE, JOHN (*b. near Savannah, Ga., 1818; d. Berkeley, Calif., 1891*), physics, natural history.

Attended College of Physicians and Surgeons of New York (M.D., 1841). Wrote on a wide range of scientific subjects. With younger brother, Joseph, moved to the newly-founded University of California (1869), held chair of physics; was president (1876–81). Promoted use of statistics in medical research. Discovered the sensitive flame (1858).

LECONTE, JOSEPH (*b. near Savannah, Ga., 1823; d. Yosemite Valley, Calif., 1901*), natural history, physiology, geology.

The younger brother of John LeConte. Attended the College of Physicians and Surgeons of New York (M.D., 1845). Studied under Louis Agassiz at Harvard. Went with brother to the new University of California (1869), became its first president. Wrote on diverse scientific subjects.

LECOQ DE BOISBAUDRAN. *See* **Boisbaudran, Paul Émile Lecoq de.**

LECORNU, LÉON FRANÇOIS ALFRED (*b. Caen, France, 1854; d. St.-Aubin-sur-Mer, Calvados, France, 1940*), mechanics, mechanical engineering.

Trained at the École Supérieure des Mines; served in the Corps des Mines; doctorate in science from the Sorbonne (1880). Applied classical methods to engineering problems, such as the determination of the conditions of rupture of air balloons.

LE DANTEC, FÉLIX (*b. Plougastel-Daoulas, France, 1869; d. Paris, France, 1917*), biology.

Trained under Pasteur; became full professor at the Sorbonne (1908). Sought to reconstruct biology in accordance with the precise language of chemistry.

LE DOUBLE, ANATOLE FÉLIX (*b. Rocroi, France, 1848; d. Tours, France, 1913*), anatomy.

Took medical degree at University of Paris (1873); became a surgeon in Tours; appointed professor of anatomy at the Hospice Général in Tours (1885). Wrote on anomalies of the human body.

LEEUWENHOEK, ANTONI VAN (*b. Delft, Netherlands, 1632; d. Delft, 1723*), natural sciences, microscopy.

Né Thoniszoon, he took surname ("Lion's Corner") from a corner house owned by his father, near the Lion's Gate in Delft. Became a prominent civil servant (from 1660). Built his first microscope (1671), a minute lens, ground by hand from a globule of glass, clamped between two metal plates, with specimen holder affixed; went on to grind about 550 lenses; the best that has survived has a magnifying power of 270 and a resolving power of 1.4μ. Believed inorganic and organic nature are similar and that all living creatures are similar in form and function. In 1674, recognized that microorganisms are alive; communicated observations on these "little animals" to the Royal Society (1676), causing a sensation. Subsequently described bacteria, protozoa, rotifers, and ciliate reproduction. From study of spermatozoa, postulated that these penetrate the egg, but (against the followers of Harvey) denied a generative role to the egg (identified life with motility), also denied Aristotelian theory of spontaneous generation. Investigated the transport of nutrients in plants and animals; believed that the blood transports food particles but not air. With Malpighi and Grew, was a founder of the study of plant anatomy.

LE FEBVRE, NICAISE (*b. Sedan, France, ca. 1610; d. London, England, 1669*), pharmacy, chemistry.

Became an apprentice in father's pharmacy (1625); received M.D. and Ph.D. degrees from the Calvinist academy of Sedan. Taught pharmacy in Paris; appointed demonstrator in chemistry at the Jardin du Roi (1652);

became royal professor of chemistry and apothecary to Charles II in London (1660). Wrote *Traicté de la chymie* (1660).

LE FÈVRE (or **LE FÈBVRE), JEAN** (*b. Lisieux, France, ca. 1652; d. Paris, France, 1706*), astronomy.

Assisted Picard in Paris; did calculations for the *Connaissances des temps*.

LEGALLOIS, JULIEN JEAN CÉSAR (*b. Cherrueix, near Dol, France, 1770; d. Paris, France, 1814*), physiology.

The son of a Breton farmer. Medical studies interrupted by the Revolution; graduated (1801) from the École de Santé, Paris. Was the first great French physiologist to base his conclusions on animal experiments. Localized the respiratory center in the medulla; anticipated understanding of internal secretions; argued the importance of arterial blood to maintaining or reviving life in the tissues (bleeding was still the therapy of choice); demonstrated metameric organization of spinal cord. Served as physician to the poor of the twelfth district of Paris.

LEGENDRE, ADRIEN-MARIE (*b. Paris, France, 1752; d. Paris, 1833*), mathematics.

Educated at the Collège des Quatres-Nations (called the Collège Mazarin) (thesis, 1770); taught mathematics at the École Militaire in Paris (1775–80); elected to the Academy (1783). The Revolution wiped out his "small fortune" and disrupted his career at the Academy, but, a tireless worker, he succeeded in various projects and appointments; replaced Lagrange at the Bureau des Longitudes upon the latter's death (1813). Favorite areas of research were celestial mechanics, number theory, and the theory of elliptic functions. In a paper on the planets (1784) the famous "Legendre polynomials" first appeared. A year later, he published an account of the law of reciprocity of quadratic residues and the theorem: "Every arithmetical progression whose first term and ratio are relatively prime contains an infinite number of prime numbers." His theorem on spherical triangles appeared in 1787 along with his method of indeterminate corrections. In an important paper (1787) stimulated by Monge's studies of minimal surfaces, the Legendre transformation was stated. Given the partial differential equation

$$R \frac{\partial^2 z}{\partial x^2} + S \frac{\partial^2 z}{\partial x \, \partial y} + T \frac{\partial^2 z}{\partial y^2} = 0.$$

Set $\partial z/\partial x = p$ and $\partial z/\partial y = q$. Suppose R, S, T are functions of p and q only. Legendre is concerned with the plane tangent to the surface being sought: $z = f(x, y)$. The equation of this plane being $pX + qY - Z - v = 0$, he shows that v satisfies the equation

$$R \frac{\partial^2 v}{\partial q^2} - S \frac{\partial^2 v}{\partial p \, \partial q} + T \frac{\partial^2 v}{\partial p^2} = 0.$$

Later, writing on elliptic functions (1826), he used an analogous procedure to demonstrate "the manner of expressing every integral as an arc length of a curve." In a book on the comets (1806), in a supplement, he gave the first statement and first published application of the method of least squares (used by Gauss since 1795). Legendre is a precursor of analytic number theory. His *Essai sur la théorie des nombres* appeared in three editions (1798, 1808, 1830). In it he included improved demonstrations of the reciprocity of quadratic residuals (based on work by Gauss and Jacobi); in a supplement (1825) on Fermat's theorem, he showed the impossibility of finding an integral solution of the equation $x^n + y^n + z^n = 0$; his law of the distribution of prime numbers, which he said he had found by induction, took the form: If y is the number of prime numbers less than x, then $y = \dfrac{x}{\log x - 1.08366}$. Legendre is also the founder of the theory of elliptic functions. He expanded his early work (1786) on integration by elliptic arcs and on the comparison of these arcs in *Exercices de calcul intégral* (1811) and *Traité des fonctions elliptiques* (1825–28). In 1786, he gave a new demonstration of Landen's theorem and proved that every given ellipse is part of an infinite sequence of ellipses, related in such a way that by the rectification of two arbitrarily chosen ellipses the rectification of all the others is possible; with this theorem it was possible to reduce the rectification of a given ellipse to that of two others differing arbitrarily little from a circle. In 1826, discussing elliptic functions, he presented a symbolic calculus, inspired by Lagrange, linking the expansion of a function by Taylor's formula with the calculation of its finite differences of various orders. Legendre's very successful *Éléments de géométrie* (1794) contains (apart from two beautiful theorems) little but paralogisms, for he was governed by a blind belief in absolute Euclidean space.

LE GENTIL DE LA GALAISIÈRE, GUILLAUME-JOSEPH-HYACINTHE-JEAN-BAPTISTE (*b. Coutances, France, 1725; d. Paris, France, 1792*), astronomy.

Attended Delisle's lectures at the Collège Royal in Paris; trained in the observatory. Spent eleven years in the East, studying Brahman astronomy and making his own observations; wrote *Voyage dans les mers d'Inde . . .* (1779–81).

LÉGER, URBAIN-LOUIS-EUGÈNE (*b. Loches, France, 1866; d. Grenoble, France, 1948*), zoology, protistology, hydrobiology.

Took doctorates in zoology (Poitiers, 1892) and medicine (Montpellier, 1895). Taught these subjects at Grenoble (from 1898). About 300 publications; in protistology, wrote on parasitic species; also studied fresh water fish and their environment.

LEHMANN, JOHANN GOTTLOB (*b. Langenhennersdorf, near Pirna, Germany, 1719; d. St. Petersburg, Russia [now Leningrad, U.S.S.R.], 1767*), medicine, chemistry, metallurgy, mineralogy, geology.

Studied medicine at the universities of Leipzig and Wittenberg (M.D., 1741). In Dresden, developed interest in mining and metallurgy; did noted work in this field. In 1756, moved to Berlin and published *Versuch einer Geschichte von Flötz-Gebürgen,* a fundamental work in geology; described and compared sequences of strata; developed the laws governing the formation of mountains. Became professor of chemistry at the University of St. Petersburg, Russia (1761).

LEHMANN, OTTO (*b. Konstanz, Germany, 1855; d. Karlsruhe, Germany, 1922*), crystallography, physics.

Received doctorate from the University of Strasbourg (1876); succeeded Heinrich Hertz as professor of physics at the Technische Hochschule at Karlsruhe (1889). Discovered (1889) liquid crystals: substances which behave mechanically as liquids but display many of the optical properties of crystalline solids.

LEIBENSON, LEONID S. *See* **Leybenzon, Leonid S.**

LEIBNIZ, GOTTFRIED WILHELM (*b. Leipzig, Germany, 1646; d. Hannover, Germany, 1716*), mathematics, philosophy, metaphysics.

The position of Leibniz at the beginning of modern science is analogous to that of Aristotle at the beginning of ancient science. He was a man with an encyclopedic multiplicity of interests, who made numerous original contributions and verged on even more discoveries.

Leibniz's father was professor of moral philosophy at the University of Leipzig, and Leibniz received most of his formal training there; he also studied Euclidean geometry under Erhard Weigel at Jena; he received his doctorate in law at Altdorf (1666). Leibniz spent most of his life in government service. He worked in Mainz for the elector Johann Philipp von Schönborn, developing a program for legal reform of the Holy Roman Empire and designing a calculating machine (a model was built in 1672). In Hannover, he served Johann Friedrich, the duke of Brunswick-Lüneburg (from 1676) and his brother who succeeded him (1680), Ernst August; his particular patrons were the latter's wife, Sophia, and daughter, Sophia Charlotte; throughout much of his life he worked on a history of the House of Brunswick. At the end of his life, he was imperial privy councillor in Vienna for Peter the Great of Russia (1712–14). Leibniz died (1716) quite neglected by the noblemen he had served; but this service had enabled him to travel and to maintain a vast network of acquaintances and advisers. Among his most important associations were his friendship with Huygens (from 1672) and his meeting with Spinoza (1676).

Leibniz's lifelong quest was to establish a unified system of knowledge; his search for the ultimate ground of mechanism led him to metaphysics. In physics, Leibniz (against Newton) regarded motion as relative: the real difference between a moving body and a body at rest cannot consist of a change of position; and, as the principle of inertial motion precludes an external impulse for a body moving with constant speed, the cause of motion must be an inherent force. He saw the correct measure of force as the central problem of dynamics; he believed that this internal force, or *vis viva,* is preserved in all interactions; he discovered the principle of the conservation of momentum.

In general science, he sought to create a universal language of all knowledge and a method that would permit "truths of reason in any field whatever to be attained, to some degree at least, through a calculus, as in arithmetic or algebra." He proposed (1666) a calculus of concepts, in which, in marked contrast to the traditional theories of concepts and judgments, he discussed the possibility of transforming rules of inference into schematic deductive rules and using a mechanical procedure for decision making.

Leibniz stands at the very beginning of formal logic, for he succeeded in casting the older syllogistics into the form of a logical calculus, which he intended to lend the same certainty to deductions concerning concepts as that possessed by algebraic deduction; this calculus (introduced about 1686) was made up of symbols for predicates, an operational sign, four relational signs, and the logical particles in vernacular form; the rules covered the principles of implication and logical equivalence and a substitution formula. He held that in every true proposition of the subject-predicate form, the concept of the predicate is contained originally in the concept of the subject; when the predicate concept simply repeats the subject concept or is implicit in it, the proposition is necessary; contingent propositions cannot be reduced practically to identical propositions, although God, through an infinite number of steps could do so; but we can know contingent truths *a priori*.

In his metaphysics, Leibniz taught that the ultimate constituents of physical bodies are real unities (i.e., indivisibles), not mathematical points (which are mere nothings) but points of unextended substance, whose essence is an intensive quality of the nature of force or mind; these ultimate constituents he called monads. On an analogy between individual concepts and the individual monads, Leibniz held that each monad represents or mirrors the whole universe just as each concept includes the infinite conjunction of predicates appertaining to that individual. The inner activity and essence of monads is perception; since no real interaction would be possible for such purely intensive unities, he introduced the concept of a preestablished harmony to explain the orderliness of events, that is, the mutual compatibility of the internal activities of the monads.

Leibniz was essentially self-taught in mathematics, although his discovery of the integral and differential calculus (independently of Newton) is his most famous achievement. He began with study of the arithmetic triangle (1666), and was further stimulated by discussions with Huygens and by the work of Mercator, Barrow, and Pascal. Studying infinitesimals, he mastered (1673) the characteristic triangle and found by means of a transmutation, i.e., the integral transformation

$$\frac{1}{2}\int_0^x [y(\bar{x}) - x \frac{dy}{dx}(\bar{x})] \cdot d\bar{x},$$

for the determination of a segment of a plane curve, a method developed on a purely geometrical basis by means of which he could uniformly derive all the previously stated theorems on quadrature. His most important results were the arithmetical quadrature of the circle, including the tangent series, and the quadrature of a cycloidal segment. In 1675, investigating Cavalieri's methods of quadrature, he made his greatest discovery: the symbolic characterization of limiting processes by means of the calculus. He sought to clarify the conditions under which an algebraic function can be integrated algebraically; he also established that not every differential equation can be solved exclusively through the use of quadratures and was immediately cognizant of the vast importance of symbolism and technical terminology.

In a draft of a letter, he gave an example of the method of series expansion through gradual integration (later named for Cauchy and Picard). In 1682, he hinted at the derivation of the law of refraction by means of the extreme value method; in the 1690's, he worked on several problems in dynamics, including the determination of the isochrona paracentrica and of the brachistochrone. The breadth of his mathematical achievement and intuition, especially as revealed in his correspondence, was extraordinary; his remarks on the solvability of higher equations, for example, actually anticipate Galois's theory. The dispute between Leibniz and Newton over the priority of their discoveries eventually became an embarrassment to both parties; the finding of the Royal Society (1712) that Leibniz had borrowed improperly from Newton's work is now recognized as unfair, a product of the nationalism that inflamed the controversy.

LEIDY, JOSEPH (*b. Philadelphia, Pa., 1823; d. Philadelphia, 1891*), biology.

Received M.D. from the University of Pennsylvania (1844). Noticing tiny specks in pork, discovered that *Trichinella spiralis* infests flesh of pigs. Appointed professor of anatomy, University of Pennsylvania (1853). Began studies of intestinal flora and fauna (1848); suggested all life has evolved from simple circumstances. His discovery that the larval eye of Cirripedia persists into the adult stage noted by Darwin. Author, "The Extinct Mammalian Fauna of Dakota and Nebraska" (1869) and *Fresh-Water Rhizopods of North America* (1879).

LEMAIRE, JACQUES (*fl. Paris, France, 1720–40*), and **PIERRE** (*fl. Paris, 1733–60*), instrument making.

Jacques Lemaire invented the front-view reflecting telescope. His workshop was maintained by his son, Pierre, the outstanding French compass maker.

LEMERY, LOUIS (*b. Paris, France, 1677; d. Paris, 1743*), chemistry, anatomy, medicine.

The son of Nicolas Lemery; graduated M.D. from Faculty of Medicine of Paris (1698); practiced at the Hôtel Dieu (from 1710); held chair of chemistry at the Jardin du Roi (from 1730). Wrote on organic analysis of plants (1719–21); held that monsters were product of accidental factors influencing embryo in the womb; wrote on nutritional value of edibles.

LEMERY, NICOLAS (*b. Rouen, France, 1645; d. Paris, France, 1715*), chemistry, pharmacy.

Apprenticed as an apothecary with uncle in Rouen. In Paris, became associated with the household of Louis, prince of Condé; established successful apothecary business (1674); career interrupted by persecution of Protestants; converted to Catholicism after revocation of Edict of Nantes (1685). Wrote the very popular *Cours de chymie* (1675); also *Pharmacopée universelle* (1697) and *Traité des drogues simples* (1698). His use of mechanical modes of explanation was an advance over the Paracelsian-Helmontian tradition, but Lemery did not develop a fully Cartesian or atomistic system; explained chemical reactions in terms of particle shape and movement. Questioned probity of use of fire as means of vegetable analysis, which provoked much discussion in the Academy of Sciences. Wrote a major work on antimony (1707).

LEMOINE, ÉMILE MICHEL HYACINTHE (*b. Quimper, France, 1840; d. Paris, France, 1912*), mathematics.

Was an influential amateur musician and mathematician. Considered, with John Casey, a founder of the newer geometry of the triangle; wrote "Sur quelques propriétés d'un point remarquable [the symmedian point] du triangle" (1873).

LE MONNIER, LOUIS-GUILLAUME (*b. Paris, France, 1717; d. Montreuil, France, 1799*), botany, physics.

Was the younger brother of Pierre-Charles Le Monnier, the astronomer. Investigated flow-times of liquids, conduction of electricity, and lightning. Practiced medicine at the Hospital of Saint-Germain-en-Laye, with the Hanoverian army (1756), and at courts of Louis XV and XVI. Had charge of the botanical garden at Trianon.

LE MONNIER, PIERRE-CHARLES (*b. Paris, France, 1715; d. Herils, Calvados, France, 1799*), astronomy.

Was the older brother of Louis-Guillaume Le Monnier, the botanist. Accompanied Clairaut and Maupertuis on voyage to Lapland (1736) to measure a degree of an arc of meridian. Was a favorite of Louis XV before whom he made observations of the transits of Mercury (1753) and Venus (1761). Studied lunar motion. Wrote *Institutions astronomiques* (1746).

LENARD, PHILIPP (*b. Pressburg, Austria-Hungary [now Bratislava, Czechoslovakia], 1862; d. Messelhausen, Germany, 1947*), physics.

Took doctorate in physics at Heidelberg (1886). Began research in phosphorescence. Became assistant to Hertz at Bonn, continuing Hertz's work when he died; racial views led him to detect effects in Hertz's work of his Jewish inheritance. In connection with cathode ray experiments, built a tube with a "Lenard window" to direct rays away from the discharge space for further study; also claimed to have been the first to discover electrons; developed a model of the atom that anticipated Rutherford's; received Nobel Prize for these results (1905). As professor and director of laboratory at Kiel (1898–1907), did important work on photoelectric effect; at Heidelberg also became professor and director of the physics and radiology laboratory (1907). Was an early, fanatic supporter of Hitler; led the assault on Einstein.

LENIN (ULYANOV), VLADIMIR ILYICH (*b. Simbirsk, Russia [now Ulyanovsk, U.S.S.R.], 1870; d. Gorki, U.S.S.R., 1924*), politics, statesmanship, philosophy.

Leader of the Bolshevik Revolution (1917); founder of the Soviet state. Studied law at St. Petersburg; informally began study of Marxism and natural science. In *Materialism and Empiriocriticism* (1909), he defended dialectical materialism against the positivism of Ernst Mach and Richard Avenarius; in "On the Significance of Militant Materialism" (1922) and other writings, advocated union between scientists and Marxists.

LENNARD-JONES, JOHN EDWARD (*b. Leigh, Lancashire, England, 1894; d. Stoke-on-Trent, England, 1954*), theoretical physics, theoretical chemistry.

Attended Manchester and Cambridge universities (Ph.D., 1924); taught at the universities of Bristol (1925–32) and Cambridge (from 1932). Formulated the Lennard-Jones potential energy function for interatomic forces (1931):

$$V(r) = -\frac{A}{r^6} + \frac{B}{r^{12}},$$

where *r* is the distance between the centers of two atoms (negative values correspond to an attractive force, positive ones to a repulsive force).

LENZ, EMIL KHRISTIANOVICH (Heinrich Friedrich Emil) (*b. Dorpat, Russia [now Tartu, Estonian S.S.R.], 1804; d. Rome, Italy, 1865*), physics, geophysics.

Entered Dorpat University (1820). Sailed with Admiral I. F. Krusenstern on a voyage around the world (1823–26); made observations on the salinity of oceans. Taught at several schools, including the University of St. Petersburg (1836–65). Investigated electromagnetism (1831–58); formulated Lenz's law (1833) relating phenomena of induction to those of the ponderomotive interaction of currents and magnets: the induced current is in such a direction as to oppose the motion of the magnet or coil that produced the induction.

LEO (*fl. Athens, first half of fourth century* B.C.), mathematics.

Evidently of the Platonic school. Is the first Greek mathematician specifically said to have worked on *diorismos* (the conditions of the possibility of solutions of problems).

LEO THE AFRICAN, also known as **al-Ḥasan ibn Muḥammad al-Wazzān al-Zayyāti al-Gharnāṭi** (*b. Granada, Spain, ca. 1485; d. Tunis, Tunisia, after 1554*), geography.

A Moroccan ambassador and geographer. Captured by Italian pirates (1518); given as a slave to Pope Leo X, whose name he took upon baptism; returned to Tunis (1519) and reconverted to Islam. Author of the important *Della descrittione dell' Africa*.

LEO THE MATHEMATICIAN, also known as **Leo the Philosopher** (*b. Constantinople [?], ca. 790; d. Constantinople [?], after 869*), mathematics, astronomy.

Taught in Constantinople; archbishop of Thessalonica (840–43); head of the "Philosophical School" founded by Caesar Bardas (*d.* 866) in Constantinople (from 855). Important mainly for role in transmission of Greek scientific literature and in the restoration of Byzantine learning.

LEO SUAVIUS. *See* **Gohory, Jacques.**

LEODAMAS OF THASOS (*b. Thasos, Greece; fl. Athens, ca. 380* B.C.), mathematics.

Evidently a figure of importance. Plato is said to have communicated the method of analysis to him, but the interpretation of this is not clear.

LEONARDO DA PISA. *See* **Fibonacci, Leonardo.**

LEONARDO DA VINCI (*b. Vinci, near Empolia, Italy, 1452; d. Amboise, France, 1519*), anatomy, technology, mechanics, mathematics, geology.

Was the illegitimate son of Piero da Vinci, a Florentine notary, and a peasant girl named Caterina. Apprenticed by his father to Andrea del Verrocchio (*ca.* 1467), with whom he studied painting, sculpture, and mechanics. Entered the employ of Ludovico Sforza, duke of Milan (1482–99); during these years in Milan, his interest in mechanics (including problems of flight), in the physics of light, in mathematics, and in the physiology of vision grew rapidly; his artistic output peaked with the great equestrian statue of Francesco Sforza and the fresco "The Last Supper"; he collaborated with the mathematician Luca Pacioli on his *Divina proportione,* drawing the figures for the first book.

After the French captured the duke of Milan, Leonardo left for Venice; eventually returned to Florence (1500–06); employed by Cesare Borgia as chief inspector of fortifications and military engineer in the Romagna; thereafter was responsible for an unsuccessful attempt to divert the Arno near Pisa. In these years he began the portrait "Mona Lisa" and the ill-fated fresco "Battle of Anghiari"; did systematic research in anatomy; increasingly was occupied with mathematics and mechanics; began to couple study of the problem of human flight with research on bird flight and meteorology; did studies on the movement of water, later compiled into *Treatise on the Movement and Measurement of Water.* Returned to Milan (1506); enjoyed the patronage of the French governor, Charles d'Amboise; produced brilliant anatomical drawings; had now come to feel that mathematics held the key to the "powers" of nature; sought the geometrical "rules" for those powers through visual experience, experiment, and reason. After the French were expelled from Milan (1513), moved to Rome; in 1516 travelled with the French king, Francis I, to Amboise; died there of a stroke. The great part of his written work and notebooks has been lost; in addition to the *Treatise on . . . Water,* a *Treatise on Painting* was compiled after his death.

At a time when theology was queen of the sciences, Leonardo believed that there is a logic in nature, detectable by the senses and comprehensible to the mind; for him, science was basically visual: patterns of natural phenomena can conform with patterns of form created in the mind; natural causes, effects, and laws can be expressed visually in a geometry that includes the movement of things as well as their resting forms. He thus linked geometry with physics, and denied the term "science" to any investigation not capable of "mathematical" demonstration. Via geometry, he believed, human experience can interpret nature. In the geometry of vision, he worked with a concept of the spread of light from a source analogous to the transverse wave-spread set up by dropping a stone into still water: the light wave varies in power with the force of percussion and inversely with its distance in the form of an infinite number of pyramids (like perspective), diminishing as they approach the eye: the pupil forms the base of another cone or pyramid of light rays; the image is carried neurologically to the "imprensiva" of the brain, where it joins impressions made by "percussions" from the nerves that serve the other senses, all of which are activated by similar percussive mechanisms and follow similar pyramidal laws. He also applied the pyramidal form to the propagation of the four "powers" of nature: movement, force, weight, and percussion. His investigations were characterized by careful measurement and the use of models (e.g., a glass cast of an aorta with valves) and markers (e.g., floats in water); he advocated repetition of experiments and rejection of "rules" not confirmed by experiment; he himself had to reject the Aristotelian rule that "if a power moves a mobile object with a certain speed, it will move half this object twice as swiftly."

Leonardo gave special attention to the eye, optic nerves, cranial nerves, spinal cord, and peripheral nervous system; he injected the cerebral ventricles with wax, finding their approximate shape, size, and situation; constructed a glass model of the eye and lens, into which he inserted his own head with his eye in the position of the optic nerve; concluded that the optic nerve was the sensitive visual receptor organ; here his experimental brilliance deceived him. Against Aristotle and Galen, noted (on pithing a frog) that the spinal cord seems to be the foundation of movement and life. Approach to sensation and movement was primarily mechanical; he regarded the bones as levers and their attached muscles as the lines of force acting upon them. Made the first known representation of the appendix; hypothesized that it took up superfluous wind. Studying the heart, recognized the atria as contracting chambers which propel blood into the ventricles (this opposed Galenic physiology); experiments indicated that the aortic valve cusps close in vertical, not horizontal, apposition; deduced the relation of systole to the pulse and apex beat; missed the concept of circulation. In botany, saw the sap as analogous to blood; believed sunlight was necessary to give "spirit and life"; perceived upward and downward movement of sap; realized that the ring formation in trees indicates age and which years were wet or dry.

Technology was the most important of Leonardo's interests; his vocation for the technical arts flowered in Milan; thereafter his concern shifted from practice to theory. He took note of all interesting mechanical devices he saw or heard about, and suggested numerous improvements and innovations. Limitations of mechanical engineering of the time stemmed from inadequacies of construction (producing excessive friction and wear) and from insufficient understanding of the possibilities of mechanical systems; Leonardo was the first to try systematically to overcome these shortcomings; was the first to recognize that each machine was a composition of certain universal mechanisms (in this he anticipated Leupold). His contemporaries believed that the work done by a given prime mover could be increased indefinitely; Leonardo rejected this idea (*ca.* 1492); his argument against perpetual motion machines is the same as that put forward later by Huygens and Parent; his recognition that machines do not perform work but only modify its application was later clearly formulated by Galileo. Leonardo formulated the basic concepts of what are known today as work and power; his variables for these include force, time, distance, and weight; he concluded, "It is impossible to increase the power of instruments used for weight-lifting, if the quantity of force and motion is given." He had an intuitive grasp of the principle of conservation of energy.

Leonardo was aware that the main impediment of all mechanical motions is friction, and devised ingenious experimental equipment, which included friction banks identical to those used by Coulomb 300 years later. To reduce rolling friction, suggested the use of bearing blocks with split, adjustable bushings of antifriction metal; was also the first to suggest true ball and roller bearings; designed thrust bearings with conical pivots turning on cones, rollers, or balls. Worked persistently to produce gearings to overcome frictional resistance; some of his gears are unmistakably cycloidal; among his new gear forms was a globoidal gear, including a worm gear shaped to match the curve of the toothed wheel it drives (rediscovered by Henry Hindley *ca.* 1740). Drew hundreds of crank and rod combinations; belt techniques included tightening devices; described both hinged link chains and continuous chain drives with sprocket wheels. Concern with efficient use of prime movers related to interest in flying machine based on muscle power (from 1487); designed descending platforms to use weight of men or animals to raise a weight. Re water power, concluded that the weight of the percussion is proportional to height, and therefore to gravitational acceleration; in maturity returned to horizontal designs for waterwheels; sketched forerunners of the reaction turbine and Pelton wheel; drew completely encased waterwheels. Re steam as power, came close to correct estimation of volume of steam evolved through the evaporation of a given quantity of water; suggested a steam cannon; described the first impulse turbine moved by a jet of steam. A thermal engine he proposed consisted of cylinder, piston, and valve. Studied behavior and resistance of materials; described various machine tools; made very original plans for canal-building machines; invented a technique of relief etching that was later reinvented by William Blake; studied gliders; made projects for distillation apparatus; anticipated the operations of modern plastic technology in instructions for making decorative objects of imitation agate, jasper, etc. Described several projects using important concept of transmission of power to various operating machines, including a complete oil factory with a single power source.

Leonardo was increasingly concerned with mechanics from 1508. In statics, his major sources were *Elementa de ponderibus* by Jordanus de Nemore, *Liber de ratione ponderis,* also attributed to Jordanus, and Archimedes' *On the Equilibrium of Planes.* His most original work was the discovery and use of a basic concept in analyzing string tensions: "The ratio of the tension in a cord segment to the weight supported by the cord is equal to the inverse ratio of the potential lever arms through which the tension and weight act, where the fulcrum of the potential bent lever is in the point of support of the other segment of the cord." (The potential arm is the horizontal distance to the vertical through the center of motion in the case of bent levers.) He also went beyond Archimedes in the determination of centers of gravity in solids; discovered that the center of gravity in a tetrahedron lies at the intersection of the segments joining the midpoint of each edge with the midpoint of the opposite edge and that each of these segments is bisected by the center of gravity. In hydrostatics he noted that a quantity of water will never lift another quantity of water to a level higher than its own; appears to have discovered, in observations of fluid motion, the principles of continuity and of equal circulation.

In dynamics and kinematics, he never quite reached the concepts of mass and inertia, as opposed to weight; he used the "halfway" concept of impetus ("All moved bodies continue to move as long as the impression of the force of their motors remains in them"). Although he disproved the Aristotelian relationship between force, weight, and velocity, he did not reach the concept of acceleration resulting from the action of force on a moving body; he did anticipate Newton's third law by stating that "An object offers as much resistance to the air as the air does to the object," adding that water acts in the same way as air; gravity he defined as the force of weight which is exerted "along a central line which with straightness is imagined from the thing to the center of the world"; concluded that velocity is proportional to the time of fall, but incorrectly that the distance of fall is also proportional directly to the time, not to its square; saw weight as an accidental power produced by a displaced element "desiring" to return to its natural place in its own element; force was caused by violent movement stored within bodies; percussion was an end of movement created in an indivisible period of time. He virtually invented the study of percussion as a branch of mechanics, groping for adequate laws of impact; concluded that in a rebound, the angle of incidence is equal to that of rebound.

Leonardo's admiration for mathematics was unbounded and he was particularly proud of his "discoveries" in this field, although many were erroneous; he was not, strictly, a mathematician. Euclid's *Elements* was his main source, and proportions and proportionality his chief interest; he investigated curvilinear angles, the squaring of curvilinear surfaces, and how to transform a parallelepiped into a cube; proposed to vary "to infinity" one or more surfaces while maintaining the same quantity. It was his profound intuition that the infinite forms in nature must be infinite variations of a fundamental "equation"; this view identified form as function and integrated into the concept of function the medieval notion of substance.

Leonardo described the configuration of the earth's crust as the result of actual processes, principally fluvial, operating over immense periods of time, a system of geology which Duhem described as "perhaps his most complete and lasting invention." He believed that similar laws operate in the microcosm, that is, the human body, as in the macrocosm, and that the body is composed of elements similar to those present in the earth. He saw the land of the world as emerging from its surrounding element of water by a process of growth, a concept that is summarized in the background of his "Mona Lisa." The Windsor drawings of the Alps above the Po are the ultimate expression of his visual apprehension of topography; he estimated that 200,000 years were required for the Po to lay down its plain (he had clearly abandoned the Judeo-Christian time scale). In his system, the highest peaks of the Alps and Appenines were former islands in an ancient sea; mountains are continually eroded by winds and rains; every valley is carved by its river; alluvial deposition continually extends the area of land at the expense of the sea; mountains made lighter by erosion rise slowly to maintain the earth's center of gravity at the center of the universe, bringing up petrified marine strata with their accompanying flora and fauna. His views were derived from meticulous observation, especially in the course of building canals, moats, and roadways. Bringing his sense of fantasy to the subject as well, he showed in the foreground of the "Virgin of the Rocks" alternately horizontal and vertical strata, with caves widening into tunnels so that the roofs form natural bridges, some of them falling in; such hollowing out from underneath and falling in of the back is the mechanism used by Nicholas Steno (1669) to account for the inclination of strata. Duhem has argued cogently that Leonardo's ideas were transmitted through Cardano and Palissy to the modern world. There may also be a connection with the influential *Telliamed* of Benoit de Maillet (1749). G. B. Venturi's studies of the geologic material in Leonardo's notebooks was published in 1797 (when catastrophic views of earth history were dominant); in later editions of his *Principles of Geology* (1830), Charles Lyell notes that his attention was drawn to the passages in Venturi by H. Hallam. Leonardo considered his geologic investigations to be a vital aspect of his science, writing, "The understanding of times past and of the site of the world is the ornament and the food of the human mind."

LEONHARD, KARL CÄSAR VON (*b. Rumpenheim bei Hanau, Germany, 1779; d. Heidelberg, Germany, 1862*), mineralogy, geology.

Attended the University of Göttingen (1798). Pursued science as an avocation while employed in various civil service positions. In *Handbuch einer allgemeinen topographischen Mineralogie* (1805–10) took Werner's position on neptunism; turned to volcanism in *Zur Naturgeschichte der Vulkane* (1818). Founded the journal *Taschenbuch für die gesammte Mineralogie* (1807). Appointed professor of mineralogy at Heidelberg (1818). Other writings include *Charakteristik der Felsarten* (1823) and *Die Basaltgebilde* (1832).

LEONHARDI, JOHANN GOTTFRIED (*b. Leipzig, Saxony, 1746; d. Dresden, Saxony, 1823*), chemistry, medicine, pharmacy.

Received baccalaureate in medicine from the University of Leipzig (1771); taught there and at the University of Wittenberg (from 1782). Chief accomplishment was *Chymisches Wörterbuch* . . . (1781–83), a new, much expanded, and richly annotated edition in translation of P.-J. Macquer's *Dictionnaire de chimie*.

LEONICENO, NICOLÒ (*b. Vicenza, Italy, 1428; d. Ferrara, Italy, 1524*), medicine, philology.

One of the leading Greek scholars of his age. Took doctorate at Padua (*ca.* 1453); taught at the University of Ferrara (from 1464). Under his leadership Ferrara became the center for the revival of Galenic medicine. Was a pioneer in the effort to recover and edit works of Greek physicians and to prepare faithful Latin translations. Wrote the first scholarly treatise on syphilis, which showed the disease had occurred in the remote past.

LE PAIGE, CONSTANTIN (*b. Liège, Belgium, 1852; d. Liège, 1929*), mathematics.

After graduating from the University of Liège (1875), stayed on to teach there (until retirement, 1922). Investigated the geometry of algebraic curves and surfaces, and the theory of invariants and involutions; best-known achievement was the construction of a cubic surface given by nineteen points.

LEPEKHIN, IVAN IVANOVICH (*b. St. Petersburg, Russia [now Leningrad, U.S.S.R.], 1740; d. St. Petersburg, 1802*), geography, natural history.

Attended the universities at St. Petersburg and Strasbourg (M.D., 1766). Elected to the Academy of Sciences in St. Petersburg (1768); led expedition organized by the Academy (1768), traveling from Moscow to Tyumen, and then to the area around the White Sea. Was head of the Botanical Garden of the Academy (1774–1802) and of the Gymnasium (1777–94). Wrote *Diaries of a Journey Through Various Provinces of the Russian State* (1771–1805). Believed that changes in the earth's surface were the result of the slow influence of water and underground fire.

LE POIVRE, JACQUES-FRANÇOIS (*fl. France, early eighteenth century*), mathematics.

A minor figure in the early history of projective geometry, known only for his *Traité des sections du cylindre et du cône* (1704).

LERCH, MATHIAS (*b. Milínov, near Sušice, Bohemia, 1860; d. Sušice, Czechoslovakia, 1922*), mathematics.

Studied in Prague and Berlin; teaching appointments included full professorships at the University of Fribourg (1896–1906) and at the Czech technical institute in Brno. Described and applied important new methodological principles: the principle of the introduction of an auxiliary parameter for meromorphic functions and the principle of most rapid convergence. Developed the Lerch theory on the generally unique solution ϕ of the equation $J(a) = \int_0^\infty \exp(-ax) \phi(x) dx$—which is fundamental in modern operator calculus; and the Lerch formula for the derivative of the Kummerian trigonometric development of log $\Gamma(v)$.

LEREBOULLET, DOMINIQUE-AUGUSTE (*b. Épinal, France, 1804; d. Strasbourg, France, 1865*), zoology, embryology.

Studied at the University of Strasbourg (M.D., 1832; licentiate in natural science, 1837; Ph.D., 1838); taught at Strasbourg (from 1838). Noted for research in comparative embryology (from 1849); having learned to fertilize fish eggs artificially, was able to study fish development from the earliest stages. Was a follower of Cuvier.

LE ROY, CHARLES (*b. Paris, France, 1726; d. Paris, 1779*), physics, meteorology, medicine.

Of a distinguished family of scientists and scholars; was the brother of Jean-Baptiste LeRoy. Studied and taught medicine at Montpellier. Published theory of evaporation (1751): vapors are to air as salts are to water. The theory was important for its emphasis on analogy and for turning attention from arcane mechanical explanations to a clear, testable hypothesis.

LE ROY, ÉDOUARD (*b. Paris, France, 1870; d. Paris, 1954*), mathematics, philosophy.

Although trained as a mathematician (École Normale Supérieure, D. Sc., 1898), was inspired by Bergson to turn to philosophy; taught at the Collège de France (1914–41). Developed views similar to those of his friend Teilhard de Chardin: an inventive psychic factor exists at the basis of life and is still vital in man; scientific facts are not just received passively by the mind but are to some extent created by it.

LE ROY, JEAN-BAPTISTE (*b. Paris, France, 1720; d. Paris, 1800*), physics, scientific instrumentation.

Of a distinguished family of scientists and scholars; was the brother of Charles Le Roy. Active in the Paris Academy of Sciences (from 1751). Defended Benjamin Franklin's concept of a single electric stream; contributed articles on scientific instruments to the *Encylopédie*.

LESAGE, GEORGE-LOUIS (*b. Geneva, Switzerland, 1724; d. Geneva, 1803*), physics.

A teacher of mathematics. Noted for his ingenious attempt to explain gravitational phenomena mechanistically by hypothesizing the existence of tiny, atom-like particles not subject to gravity, which could push two masses toward each other; the theory was essentially untestable.

LESLEY, J. PETER (*b. Philadelphia, Pa., 1819; d. Milton, Mass., 1903*), geology.

Served briefly as a Presbyterian minister. Worked under Henry Darwin Rogers in the first state survey of Pennsylvania; became director of the second survey (1873). Writings include *A Manual of Coal and Its Topography* (1856) and *The Iron Manufacturers' Guide* (1859).

LESLIE, JOHN (*b. Largo, Scotland, 1766; d. Coates, Fife, Scotland, 1832*), natural philosophy.

Studied at the University of St. Andrews and at Edinburgh; taught mathematics and natural philosophy at the University of Edinburgh (from 1805); knighted for scientific work (1832). Author, *An Experimental Inquiry Into the Nature and Propagation of Heat* (1790–1804), which established several fundamental laws of heat radiation; held a corpuscular theory of heat. Discovered (1800) the wet- and dry-bulb hygrometer and the theory of its operation.

LEŚNIEWSKI, STANISŁAW (*b. Serpukhov, Russia, 1886; d. Warsaw, Poland, 1939*), philosophy of mathematics.

Received Ph.D. in philosophy at Lvov (1912); taught at the University of Warsaw (from 1919). Influenced by Łukasiewicz; focused on mathematical logic; analyzing Russell's antinomy of the class of all those classes which are not members of themselves; constructed an original, elegant system of logic and of the foundations of mathematics.

LESQUEREUX, LEO (*b. Fleurier, Neuchâtel, Switzerland, 1806; d. Columbus, Ohio, 1889*), botany, paleontology.

Was encouraged by Agassiz to immigrate. Specialized in fossil plants and bryology. Wrote *Coal Flora of Pennsylvania* (1879–84).

LESSON, RENÉ-PRIMEVÈRE (*b. Cabane-Carée, Rochefort, France, 1794; d. Rochefort, 1849*), natural history, scientific exploration.

A naval pharmacist and prominent naturalist-voyager. Wrote extensively about the voyage of the *Coquille* (1822–25), commanded by L. I. Duperrey.

LESUEUR, CHARLES-ALEXANDRE (*b. Le Havre, France, 1778; d. Le Havre, 1846*), natural history.

A naval officer, his talent in sketching led him to natural history. Traveled on the expedition to Tasmania and Australia under Nicolas Baudin (1800–04); helped to write the official report. Lived in the U.S. (1816–37) in Philadelphia and New Harmony, Indiana; explored the Mississippi Valley and studied the fishes of North America.

LE TENNEUR, JACQUES-ALEXANDRE (*b. Paris, France; d. after 1652*), physics, mathematics.

A friend of Mersenne and correspondent of Gassendi; described as a patrician of Paris on title page of his book *De Motu naturaliter accelerato* (1649). In this work Le Tenneur showed himself to be the only mathematical physicist of his time to understand precisely Galileo's rejection of the proportionality of speeds in free fall to the distance traversed. Probably also wrote the more conservative *Traité des quantitez incommensurables*.

LE TONNELIER DE BRETEUIL. *See* **Châtelet, Gabrielle-Émilie Le Tonnelier de Breteuil, Marquise du.**

LEUCIPPUS (*fl. Greece, fifth century* B.C.), philosophy.

The first of the Greek atomists; probably founded the school of Abdera; was succeeded by his pupil Democritus. Originally probably came from Miletus in Ionia.

LEUCKART, KARL GEORG FRIEDRICH RUDOLF (*b. Helmstedt, Germany, 1822; d. Leipzig, Germany, 1898*), zoology, parasitology.

Studied medicine at the University of Göttingen (M.D., 1845); became assistant to Rudolf Wagner (1845). Taught at Göttingen (1847–50), Giessen (1850–69), and Leipzig (from 1869). His unfinished *Die menschlichen Parasiten und die von ihnen herrührenden Krankheiten* is a classic of parasitology based on extensive original research. Correctly predicted course of development of roundworm and tapeworm (confirmed 1916). Discovered *Trichina* (1860), simultaneously with Zenker. His study of marine invertebrates (1848) led to the establishment of the phylum Coelenterata.

LEURECHON, JEAN (*b. Bar-le-Duc, France, ca. 1591; d. Pont-à-Mousson, France, 1670*), mathematics.

A Jesuit teacher, remembered for his collection of mathematical recreations.

LEURET, FRANÇOIS (*b. Nancy, France, 1797; d. Nancy, 1851*), psychiatry, public health, comparative anatomy.

Studied at Charenton (M.D., 1826). Chief psychiatrist at Bicêtre (from 1839). Opposed phrenology and the identification of morbid brain anatomy with mental illness; defended "moral" (psychological) therapy; also used punitive methods such as cold showers.

LEVADITI, CONSTANTIN (*b. Galați, Romania, 1874; d. Paris, France, 1953*), medicine, bacteriology.

Received the M.D. at Paris (1902). At the Pasteur Institute (from 1900). Did major work on the tubercle bacillus; antitetanus vaccine; streptococcus; syphilis; lethargic encephalitis; the etiology of poliomyelitis; sulfamides; antibiotics; discovered what are today called interference phenomena.

LEVAILLANT (LE VAILLANT), FRANÇOIS (*b. Paramaribo, Netherlands Guiana [now Surinam], 1753; d. La Noue, near Sézanne, France, 1824*), natural history.

Traveled in Africa (1781, 1783). Writings, including *Voyages de F. Le Vaillant dans l'intérieur de l'Afrique* (1790) and *Histoire naturelle des oiseaux d'Afrique* (1796–1812), popularized the exotic fauna of Africa and of the tropics.

LEVENE, PHOEBUS AARON THEODOR (*b. Sagor, Russia, 1869; d. New York, N.Y., 1940*), biochemistry.

Emigrated to New York (1891) but returned that year to finish studies for his M.D. at the Imperial Medical Academy in St. Petersburg. Was in charge of biochemical studies at the Rockefeller Institute for Medical Research (1905–39). Carried out extensive research on conjugated proteins; was particularly noted for pioneering work on nucleoproteins and nucleic acids.

LE VERRIER, URBAIN JEAN JOSEPH (*b. Saint-Lô, France, 1811; d. Paris, France, 1877*), astronomy, celestial mechanics, meteorology.

Studied and taught at the École Polytechnique. Derived (1839–40) precise limits for the eccentricities and inclinations of the seven planets, given the masses accepted at that time; from perturbations of Uranus hypothesized the existence of an unknown planet; J. G. Galle, using Le Verrier's information re position, found the planet, Neptune (1846). Le Verrier showed (1859) that Mercury moves as if an unknown agent produced an advance of its perihelion of about 38 seconds per century; Karl Schwarzschild demonstrated (1916) that an advance of 43 seconds per century is predicted by Einstein's general relativity theory. Le Verrier was also one of the founders of modern meteorology, initiating a service using telegraphic communication to warn sailors of approaching storms.

LEVI BEN GERSON (*b. Bagnols, Gard, France, 1288; d. 1344*), mathematics, astronomy, physics, philosophy, religious commentary.

Was also called RaLBaG, Gersonides, Gersoni, Leo de Bannolis or Balneolis, Leo Judaeus or Hebraeus. Wrote five works on mathematics and *Milhamot Adonai* ("The Wars of the Lord"), which includes a treatise on astronomy (1328, revised 1340); this treatise, in Latin translation, was influential until the 18th century. Levi here described the Jacob's staff, used for measuring angles; it consists of a graduated rod and a plate that moves along the rod perpendicular to it. Levi rejected Ptolemy's planetary system as not conforming with his own observations, which he made using the Jacob's staff and the camera obscura; he postulated 48 spheres, some concentric with the earth, and movement transmitted from the innermost sphere by an intermediate nonresistant fluid. In his measurements of distances he enlarged the Ptolemaic universe.

LEVI, GIUSEPPE (*b. Trieste, Austria-Hungary, 1872; d. Turin, Italy, 1965*), human anatomy, histology, embryology.

Studied at Florence (M.D., 1895). Taught at Turin (1919–38); dismissed under fascist racial laws; taught at the University of Liège (1938–41); returned to Italy (1945). Did a major study on the structure of the nucleus of nerve cells; made other important investigations of nerves and cells; concluded size of the neurons is proportional to the size of the body (Levi's law); was a pioneer in cultivating tissues *in vitro*.

LEVI-CIVITA, TULLIO (*b. Padua, Italy, 1873; d. Rome, Italy, 1941*), mathematical physics.

Graduated (1894) from the University of Padua; taught there (1897–1918) and at Rome. Wrote "Sulle trasformazioni delle equazioni dinamiche" (1896), characterized by the use of absolute differential calculus. Introduced (1917) the concept of parallelism in curved space that now bears his name.

LEVINSON-LESSING, FRANZ YULEVICH (*b. St. Petersburg, Russia, 1861; d. Leningrad, U.S.S.R., 1939*), geology, petrography.

Graduated from St. Petersburg University (1883). Taught at the University of Yurev (1893–1902); was at the Polytechnical Institute in Leningrad (1902–30). Created petrography as an independent field; proposed (1898) the first rational chemical classification of rocks; wrote "The Problem of the Genesis of Magmatic Rock and the Means of Solving It" (1934).

LÉVY, MAURICE (*b. Ribeauvillé, France, 1838; d. Paris, France, 1910*), mathematics, engineering.

Had a distinguished career as a practicing engineer, teacher, and researcher. Author, *La statique graphique et ses applications aux constructions* (1874).

LÉVY, SERVE-DIEU ABAILARD (called **ARMAND**) (*b. Paris, France, 1795; d. le Pecq, near Saint-Germain, France, 1841*), mineralogy.

Catalogued (1820–27) the collection of minerals sold by Henry Heuland to Charles Hampden Turner; discovered important new mineral species; devised a system of notation (the Haüy-Lévy notation), which is still used today.

LEWIS, GILBERT NEWTON (*b. West Newton, Mass., 1875; d. Berkeley, Calif., 1946*), physical chemistry.

Studied at Harvard (B.S., 1896; Ph.D., 1899), with W. Nernst at Göttingen, and with W. Ostwald at Leipzig. Taught at Harvard (1901–04); spent a year at the Bureau of Weights and Measures in Manila; attracted by A. A. Noyes to the Massachusetts Institute of Technology (1905). Early interests were in thermodynamics, blackbody radiation, and valence theory; realized that only free energy and entropy could provide an exact chemical thermodynamics; developed concept of the "cubic atom," built up of a concentric series of cubes with electrons at the corners; was an early supporter of Einstein. Became dean and chairman of the College of Chemistry of the University of California at Berkeley (1912); with modernized curriculum and methods, built an outstanding department. With Merle Randall did intense research on free-energy data, culminating in their book, *Thermodynamics and the Free Energy of Chemical Substances* (1923); with William Bray, proposed (1913) a new, nonpolar chemical bond, not involving electron transfer; published (1916) the very fruitful suggestion that the chemical bond was a pair of electrons shared or held jointly by two atoms. Made intensive studies (1933–34) of deuterium, some in collaboration with E. O. Lawrence. After a nonproductive period, began (1938) important investigations in photochemistry. Re compounds, such as the triphenylcarbonium salts, that exist in different colors, Lewis suggested that these forms were of two "electromeric" types, differing only in the distribution of electrons in the molecule; after making studies of phosphorescence, he proposed (1943) that the two electromeric states were the singlet and triplet states of quantum theory.

LEWIS, THOMAS (*b. Cardiff, Wales, 1881; d. Rickmansworth, England, 1945*), physiology, cardiology, clinical science.

Took his M.D. (1907) at University College Hospital, London, his medical home for the rest of his life. At the suggestion of James Mackenzie, began study of irregular heart action; demonstrated (1909) the role of atrial fibrillation; during World War I, developed idea of judging the state of the heart from exercise tolerance; emphasized importance of research with living persons. His many books include *The Mechanism of the Heart Beat* (1911), *The Blood Vessels of the Human Skin and Their Responses* (1927), and *Pain* (1942).

LEWIS, TIMOTHY RICHARDS (*b. Llanboidy, Carmarthenshire, Wales, 1841; d. Southampton, England, 1886*), tropical medicine.

The second son of William Lewis. Studied at Aberdeen (M.B., 1867); affiliated with the Army Medical School at Netley. Studying cholera, published first authentic account of amoebas from the human intestine (1870); did major work on blood parasites of man and animals, including microfilariae, spirochetes, and trypanosomes (subsequently named *Trypanosoma lewisi*).

LEWIS, WILLIAM (*b. Richmond, Surrey, England, 1708; d. Kingston, Surrey, England, 1781*), chemistry, pharmacy, chemical technology.

Studied at Oxford and Cambridge (M.B., 1731); major interest was applied chemistry, especially pharmacy. Author, *The New Dispensatory* (1753), based on Quincy's *Complete English Dispensatory*, and *Commercium philosophico-technicum*, relating chemical knowledge to industrial problems.

LEXELL, ANDERS JOHAN (*b. Åbo, Sweden [now Turku, Finland], 1740; d. St. Petersburg, Russia, 1784*), mathematics, astronomy.

Worked at the St. Petersburg Academy of Sciences (from 1768). Demonstrated that the moving body discovered by W. Herschel (1781) was a new planet (Uranus); predicted existence of Neptune. In mathematics, did innovative work in analysis and geometry.

LEYBENZON, LEONID SAMUILOVICH (*b. Kharkov, Russia, 1879; d. Moscow, U.S.S.R., 1951*), mechanical engineering, geophysics.

Took his doctorate at Yurev University (1917); taught at Moscow University (from 1922). Major achievements were in the science and technology of petroleum and in elasticity theory and the resistance of materials.

LEYDIG, FRANZ VON (*b. Rothenburg-ob-der-Tauber, Germany, 1821; d. Rothenburg-ob-der-Tauber, 1908*), comparative anatomy.

Received M.D. at Würzburg; taught at Würzburg, Tübingen (1857–75), and Bonn. Author, *Lehrbuch der Histologie des Menschen und der Tiere* (1857). Discovered mucous cell of epidermis of fish (later named for him), interstitial cells that occur in the seminiferous tubules of the testes and secrete testosterone, and the gland of Leydig, thought to secrete a stimulant to movement of spermatozoa.

L'HÉRITIER DE BRUTELLE, CHARLES LOUIS (*b. Paris, France, 1746; d. Paris, 1800*), botany.

Appointed superintendent of the waters and forests of the Paris region (1772). Author of the sumptuous *Stirpes novae* (1785–1805).

L'HOSPITAL (L'HÔPITAL), GUILLAUME-FRAN-ÇOIS-ANTOINE DE (Marquis de Sainte-Mesme, Comte d'Entremont) (*b. Paris, France, 1661; d. Paris, 1704*), mathematics.

His name is remembered now for the rule for finding the limiting value of a fraction whose numerator and denominator tend to zero; famous in his time for *Analyse des infiniment petits . . .* (1696), first textbook of the differential calculus.

L'HUILLIER (or LHUILIER), SIMON-ANTOINE-JEAN (*b. Geneva, Switzerland, 1750; d. Geneva, 1840*), mathematics.

Studied at the Calvin Academy. Was tutor in Poland (1777–88) to the son of Prince Adam Czartoryski; wrote mathematics texts for use in Polish schools; did a prizewinning memoir for the Berlin Academy (1786) on mathematical infinity. Held chair of mathematics at the Geneva Academy (1795–1823); with Pierre Prevost, wrote four major papers (1796, 1797) on probabilities of causes.

LHWYD, EDWARD (*b. Cardiganshire, Wales, 1660; d. Oxford, England, 1709*), paleontology, botany, philology.

Studied at Jesus College, Oxford. Became keeper of the Ashmolean Museum (1691). Collected plants around the hill mass of Snowdon. As an appendix to his catalogue (1699) of shells in the Ashmolean, published a letter to John Ray hypothesizing that marine fossils were formed by the "seed" of marine animals, taken up in mist and distributed over land by rain. Wrote first comparative study (1707) of the Celtic languages.

LI CHIH, also called **LI YEH** (*b. Ta-hsing [now Peking], China, 1192; d. Hopeh province, China, 1279*), mathematics.

Li Chih (literary name, Jen-ch'ing; appellation, Ching-chai) was one of the greatest mathematicians of his time and of his race. His father, Li Yü, served as an attaché under a Jurchen officer called by the Chinese name Hu Sha-hu. Li Yü later sent his family back to his home in Luan-ch'eng, Hopeh province. Li Chih went alone to the Yüan-shih district in the same province for his education.

In 1230 Li Chih went to Loyang to take the civil service examination; after he passed, he was appointed registrar in the district of Kao-ling, Shensi province. Before he reported for duty, however, he was made governor of Chün-chou (now Yü-hsien), Honan province. In 1232 the Mongols captured the city of Chün-chou, and Li Chih was forced to seek refuge in Shansi province. The kingdom of the Jurchen fell into the hands of the Mongols in 1234.

From that time on, Li Chih devoted himself to serious study, frequently living in poverty. It was during this period that he wrote his most important mathematical work, the *Ts'e-yüan hai-ching* ("Sea Mirror of the Circle Measurements").

About 1251 Li Chih, finding himself in an improved financial position, returned to the Yüan-shih district of Hopeh province and settled near Feng-lung, a mountain in that district. Although he continued to lead the life of a scholarly recluse, he counted Chang Te-hui and Yuan Yü among his friends; the three of them became popularly known as "the Three Friends of [Feng-]Lung Mountain." In 1257 Kublai Khan sent for Li Chih and asked him about the government of the state, the selection and deployment of scholars for civil service, and the reasons for earthquakes. Li Chih completed another mathematical text, the *I-ku yen-tuan* ("New Steps in Computation") in 1259. Kublai Khan ascended the throne in 1260 and the following year offered Li Chih a government post, which was politely declined with the plea of ill health and old age. In 1264 the Mongolian emperor set up the Han-lin Academy for the purpose of writing the official histories of the kingdoms of Liao and Jurchen, and the following year Li Chih was obliged to join it. After a few months he submitted his resignation, again pleading infirmity and old age. He returned to his home near Feng-lung, and many pupils came to study under him.

Li Chih changed his name to Li Yeh at some point in his life because he wished to avoid having the same name as the third T'ang emperor, whose dynastic title was T'ang Kao-tsung (650–683). This circumstance has given rise to some confusion as to whether Li Yeh was a misprint for Li Chih.

Besides the *Ts'e-yüan hai-ching* and the *I-ku yen-tuan*, Li Chih wrote several other works, including the *Fan shuo*, the *Ching-chai ku-chin chu*, the *Wen chi*, and the *Pi-shu ts'ung-hsiao*. Before his death Li Chih told his son, Li K'e-hsiu, to burn all his books except the *Ts'e-yüan hai-ching*, because he felt that it alone would be of use to future generations. We do not know to what extent his wishes were carried out; but the *I-ku yen-tuan* survived the fire, and the *Ching-chai ku-chin chu* has also come down to us. His other works are now lost, although some passages from the *Fan shuo* are quoted in the *Ching-chai ku-chin chu*. Only the *Ts'e-yüan hai-ching* and the *I-ku yen-tuan* have mathematical or scientific interest.

The *Ts'e-yüan hai-ching* was studied by many eighteenth- and nineteenth-century Chinese mathematicians, such as K'ung Kuang-shen (1752–86) and Li Shan-Ian (1811–82).

The *I-ku yen-tuan* was completed in 1259 and was published in 1282. It has been regarded as a later version of a previous mathematical text, the *I-ku-chi*, which is no longer extant. The *I-ku yen-tuan* is incorporated in both the *Chih-pu-tsu-chai ts'ung-shu* and the *Pai-fu-t'ang suan-hsüeh ts'ung-shu* collections.

Li Chih introduced an algebraic process called the *t'ien yüan shu* ("method of the celestial elements" or "coefficient array method") for setting up equations to any degree. The *t'ien yüan shu* occupied a very important position in the history of mathematics in both China and Japan. From the early fourteenth century until algebra was brought to China from the West by the Jesuits, no one in China seemed to understand this method.

LI SHIH-CHEN (*tzu* Tung-pi, *hao* P'in-hu) (*b. Wa-hsiao-pa, near Chichow [now Hupeh province], China, 1518; d. 1593*), pharmacology.

Of a family of medical practitioners and pharmacologists, his skill as a physician won him renown. His greatest work is the *Pen-ts'ao kang mu* ("Systematic Pharmacopoeia," published posthumously, 1596), it is the culmination of the pharmacognostic tradition, correcting the previously standard Sung dynasty series of pharmacognostic treatises. The *Pen-ts'ao kang mu* is more than a pharmacopoeia, for its wide-ranging discussions form a comprehensive treatise on mineralogy, metallurgy, botany, and zoology. Li rearranged the Sung dynasty taxonomy of T'ang Shen-wei, using instead a hierarchy of being from the inorganic world to man; he also classified substances according to diseases cured, with careful notes on the physiological functions of each drug with respect to the disease. The first Japanese edition of this work appeared in 1637; a copy of the Chinese original was sent to Europe at the end of the 17th century; Darwin cited the book in his *Variation of Animals and Plants Under Domestication*.

LI YEH. *See* **Li Chih.**

LIBAVIUS (or **LIBAU**), **ANDREAS** (*b. Halle, Saxony, ca. 1560; d. Coburg, 1616*), chemistry, medicine, logic.

Studied at the universities of Jena (Ph.D. and poet laureate, 1581) and Basel (M.D., 1588); taught at Jena; was municipal physician and inspector of schools in Rothenburg (1592–1607); was rector (from 1607) of the Gymnasium founded by Duke John Casimir of Coburg. Wasted the greater part of his life on fruitless medical, philosophical, and theological polemics. Is valued for extraordinarily voluminous alchemical works, especially *Alchymia* (1606; enlarged edition of *Alchemia*, 1597). Was a first-rate chemist and a founder of chemical analysis.

LICEAGA, EDUARDO (*b. Guanajuato, Mexico, 1839; d. Mexico City, Mexico, 1920*), medicine, public health.

Studied at the School of Medicine in Mexico City (M.D., 1866) and taught there (1868–1911). As chairman of the Council of Public Health, led successful campaigns against plague, yellow fever, and malaria.

LICHTENBERG, GEORG CHRISTOPH (*b. Oberramstadt, near Darmstadt, Germany, 1742; d. Göttingen, Germany, 1799*), physics.

Studied and taught at the University of Göttingen, where he was enormously popular. Was the leading German expert not only in physics but also in geodesy, geophysics, meteorology, astronomy, chemistry, statistics, and geometry. Questioned the validity of Euclid's postulates; suggested that the undulatory and corpuscular theories of light might both be right; emphasized interconnectedness of things. Discovered basic process of xerographic copying. In psychology, developed concepts of subconscious mechanisms and motivations. In superb satiric and aphoristic writings, took the role of "heretic" and "antifaust."

LIE, MARIUS SOPHUS (*b. Nordfjordeide, Norway, 1842; d. Christiania [now Oslo], Norway, 1899*), mathematics.

Sophus Lie first attended school in Moss (Kristianiafjord), then, from 1857 to 1859, Nissen's Private Latin

School in Christiania. He studied at Christiania University from 1859 to 1865, mainly mathematics and sciences. After his examination in 1865, he gave private lessons, became slightly interested in astronomy, and tried to learn mechanics; but he could not decide what to do. The situation changed when, in 1868, he hit upon Poncelet's and Plücker's writings. Later, he called himself a student of Plücker's, although he had never met him. Plücker's momentous idea to create new geometries by choosing figures other than points—in fact straight lines—as elements of space pervaded all of Lie's work.

Lie's first published paper brought him a scholarship for study abroad. He spent the winter of 1869–70 in Berlin, where he met Felix Klein, whose interest in geometry also had been influenced by Plücker's work. This acquaintance developed into a friendship that, although seriously troubled in later years, proved crucial for the scientific progress of both men.

Lie and Klein spent the summer of 1870 in Paris, where they became acquainted with Darboux and Camille Jordan. Here Lie, influenced by the ideas of the French "anallagmatic" school, discovered his famous contact transformation, which maps straight lines into spheres and principal tangent curves into curvature lines. He also became familiar with Monge's theory of differential equations.

In 1871 Lie was awarded a scholarship to Christiania University. He also taught at Nissen's Private Latin School. In July 1872 he received his Ph.D. During this period he developed the integration theory of partial differential equations now found in many textbooks, although rarely under his name. Lie's results were found at the same time by Adolph Mayer, with whom he conducted a lively correspondence.

In 1872 a chair in mathematics was created for him at Christiania University. In 1873 Lie turned from the invariants of contact transformations to the principles of the theory of transformation groups. Together with Sylow he assumed the editorship of Niels Abel's works.

His main interest turned to transformation groups, his most celebrated creation, although in 1876 he returned to differential geometry. In the same year he joined G. O. Sars and Worm Müller in founding the *Archiv för mathematik og naturvidenskab*. In 1882 the work of Halphen and Laguerre on differential invariants led Lie to resume his investigations on transformation groups.

Lie was quite isolated in Christiania. He had no students interested in his research. Abroad, except for Klein, Mayer, and somewhat later Picard, nobody paid attention to his work. In 1884 Klein and Mayer induced F. Engel, who had just received his Ph.D., to visit Lie in order to learn about transformation groups and to help him write a comprehensive book on the subject. Engel stayed nine months with Lie. Thanks to his activity the work was accomplished, its three parts being published between 1888 and 1893, whereas Lie's other great projects were never completed. F. Hausdorff, whom Lie had chosen to assist him in preparing a work on contact transformations and partial differential equations, got interested in quite different subjects.

This happened after 1886 when Lie had succeeded Klein at Leipzig, where, indeed, he found students, among whom was G. Scheffers. With him Lie published textbooks on transformation groups and on differential

equations, and a fragmentary geometry of contact transformations. In the last years of his life he turned to foundations of geometry, which at that time meant the Helmholtz space problem.

LIEBER, THOMAS. *See* **Erastus, Thomas.**

LIEBERKÜHN, JOHANNES NATHANAEL (*b. Berlin, Germany, 1711; d. Berlin, 1756*), anatomy.

Studied at the academy at Jena and at Leiden (M.D., 1739). Was first to describe the glands (Lieberkühnian glands) attached to intestinal villi; explored circulatory vessels with specially-devised microscopes; credited with invention of a type of solar microscope.

LIEBERMANN, CARL THEODORE (*b. Berlin, Germany, 1842; d. Berlin, 1914*), chemistry.

Studied at the university in Berlin and at Heidelberg (1861) with Bunsen. Worked in Baeyer's laboratory and became his assistant; taught at the Gewerbeakademie in Berlin (from 1873). Specialized in aromatic organic chemistry.

LIEBIG, JUSTUS VON (*b. Darmstadt, Germany, 1803; d. Munich, Germany, 1873*), chemistry.

Liebig taught at the University of Giessen (1825–51) and the University of Munich (from 1851).

Began chemical work as a child in a small family laboratory. Studied with W. G. Kastner at Bonn and at Erlangen (Ph.D., 1822); found Kastner unskilled in analysis. A grant from Grand Duke Louis I of Hesse enabled Liebig to study in Paris; his work on fulminates attracted the attention of Humboldt, who arranged for him to work with Gay-Lussac, where he learned rigorous, quantitative, experimental chemistry. Appointed professor at Giessen; with colleagues, set up a laboratory for teaching and experimental work; in a new approach, guided students sytematically from elementary operations to independent research.

Established lifelong association with Wöhler when Wöhler published an analysis of silver cyanate, giving same composition that Liebig and Gay-Lussac had found for silver fulminate; Liebig confirmed this surprising result; drew from it the important new idea that two compounds with different properties could have the same elementary composition, differing only in the manner in which the elements are joined; collaborated with Wöhler (1829) in study of the relationship between cyanic acid and a similar acid discovered by G. Serullas; Liebig found that the two had the same percentage composition; Wöhler inferred that the two were isomers (according to Berzelius' recent definition); called them cyanic and cyanuric acid.

Liebig next turned to the study of uric acid, which led him from inorganic to organic chemistry; improved techniques of analysis of organic acids by using a method he and Gay-Lussac had devised for burning compounds in a vacuum and by measuring the hydrogen in a separate analysis. Studying alkaloids, he made a crucial technical innovation: a device in which combustion gases passed through a tube containing calcium chloride, which absorbed the water vapor, and then entered a triangular tube with five bulbs; here a caustic potash solution absorbed the carbonic acid. He could then simply measure the increase in weight of the tube (for non-nitrogenous compounds—he could not find such a satisfactory solution for measurement of nitrogen). This process eliminated much of the tedium and extraordinary skill formerly demanded, and his laboratory began turning out hundreds of analyses daily; his combustion apparatus became a symbol of the new era of organic chemistry.

Liebig now turned to the question of how the atoms of organic compounds are ordered in the molecules. Initially he rejected suggestion by Dumas and P. Boullay that some groups of atoms function as units, but soon began to apply similar reasoning; in 1832, with Wöhler, extended experiments of P. Robiquet and A. Boutron-Charlard with oil of bitter almonds; was able to show that the conversion of this oil to benzoic acid can be represented as replacement of two atoms of hydrogen by one of oxygen; produced a series of related compounds; deduced that a "benzoyl radical," $C^{14}H^{10}O^2$, persisted unchanged through all these reactions. Particular attention was being given at that time to the analysis of alcohol, ethers, and related compounds. Liebig discovered chloral (1831) by decomposing alcohol with chlorine gas, and another product which Dumas later renamed chloroform. Liebig partially supported Berzelius' view that ether and alcohol were oxides of different radicals, as opposed to the theory of Dumas and Boullay, who postulated an etherin radical that acts as a base analogous to ammonia; Liebig, however, believed that the radical, which he named ethyl (C^4H^{10}), was common to both alcohol and ether, alcohol being the hydrate of ether. Working in the same line, discovered acetal (1833) and aldehyde; by 1839 he had devised a new system in which neither etherin nor ethyl were used as fundamental radicals; instead ether and related compounds were represented as based on an acetyl radical (Ac=C_4H_6); this approach was compatible both with his own view of ether as an organic oxide and with Dumas's view that the compounds of ether resemble those of ammonia.

In the 1830's Lavoisier's oxygen theory of acids was no longer intact; acids were considered to be either oxacids or hydracids. Liebig, however, considered the division unnatural; in "Über die Constitution der organischen Säuren" (1838) he gave detailed arguments for considering all acids as hydrogen acids and for believing that some organic acids neutralize more than one base; this brought him into opposition with his revered friend Berzelius. In 1836–37, working with Wöhler, he precipitated from an emulsion of almonds a substance they named "emulsin," with an action similar to yeast; this helped to generalize the concept of specific fermenting actions. Also with Wöhler published a description (1838) of numerous decomposition products of uric acid.

In 1840, tired of the disputes involving his findings, Liebig turned to new subjects; began systematically to study the relation of organic chemistry to agriculture and physiology; published *Die organische Chemie in ihre Anwendung auf Agricultur und Physiologie* (1840; translation, *Organic Chemistry in Its Applications to Agriculture and Physiology,* 1840). Concluded that plants derive carbon from the atmosphere and nitrogen from ammonia dissolved in rainwater; plants need alkalies and alkaline earths to neutralize their essential acids, therefore cultivation of the same crop year after year gradually diminishes the fertility of the soil; recommended rotation of crops and use of a

fertilizer, composed of bases such as lime, potash, and magnesias, as well as phosphoric acid (because it is present in all plants); thought some ammonia might be helpful as a supplement. Had difficulty defending his views not only because of error regarding nitrogen, but also because in his fertilizer formula he fused potash with calcium carbonate to prevent its being washed away; it was several years before he realized that the salts should be in a soluble form.

In 1842, published *Die Thierchemie oder die organische Chemie in ihre Anwendung auf Physiologie und Pathologie* (translation, *Animal Chemistry or Organic Chemistry in Its Applications to Physiology and Pathology,* 1842); extending a concept of Lavoisier's, he maintained that animal heat is produced solely by the oxidation to carbon dioxide and water of the carbon and hydrogen of the nutrient compounds; perceived that the respiratory oxidations were net reactions, encompassing the cumulative results of all the transformations nutrients may undergo in the body; also examined the mutual proportionalities between the internal nutritive metamorphoses in an animal, its respiratory exchanges, intake of food, excretions, and production of heat or work. Liebig's work in physiology, like his work in scientific agriculture, provided an impetus for future investigations which outlasted the refutation of some of his specific theories.

LIESGANIG, JOSEPH XAVER (*b. Graz, Austria, 1719; d. Lemberg, Galicia [now Lvov, U.S.S.R.], 1799*), astronomy, geodesy.

Entered the Society of Jesus (1734); studied and taught at the Jesuit College in Vienna; also taught at the University of Vienna. Was appointed prefect of the Jesuit astronomical observatory (1756); with Joseph Ramspoeck, constructed a zenith sector that indicated tangents; determined the latitude of Vienna; made many other geodesic calculations.

LIEUTAUD, JOSEPH (*b. Aix-en-Provence, France, 1703; d. Versailles, France, 1780*), anatomy, medicine.

Received M.D. at Aix. In Paris, was appointed a royal physician (1755); eventually retired to pursue his own research. Oriented toward practical medicine learned at the bedside and in the autopsy room; undertook to determine correlation between symptoms during life and lesions found after death; inoculated patients against smallpox. Author, *Essais anatomiques* (1742), *Précis de la médecine pratique* (1759), and *Précis de la matière médicale* (1766), recommending use of simple medicines with well-known effects. His name is associated with Lieutaud's sinus, Lieutaud's uvula, and Lieutaud's body.

LIGNIER, ÉLIE ANTOINE OCTAVE (*b. Pougy, Aube, France, 1855; d. Paris, France, 1916*), botany.

Took doctorate in natural sciences at the University of Paris (1887); taught in the Faculty of Sciences at Caen. Noted for theories on evolution and proposed classifications.

LILLIE, FRANK RATTRAY (*b. Toronto, Canada, 1870; d. Chicago, Ill., 1947*), embryology, zoology.

Studied at the University of Toronto; worked as a fellow with C. O. Whitman at the Marine Biological Laboratory at Woods Hole, Massachusetts; accompanied Whitman to the University of Chicago (doctorate in zoology, 1894). Taught at the University of Michigan, at Vassar, and at Chicago (from 1900). Played a vital role in the development of the Marine Biological Laboratory; served as director (1910–26) and as president of the corporation and board of trustees (1925–42). Was active in founding the Woods Hole Oceanographic Institution (1930). His early work (1892–1909) dealt primarily with mechanisms of cleavage and with early development of eggs of invertebrates, especially the freshwater mussel *Unio* and the marine annelid *Chaetopterus;* emphasized how special features of cleavage in each species are adapted to future needs; focused attention on the necessity of studying the ultramicroscopic organization of the egg. Wrote a classic text on chick embryology (1908). Studied fertilization in the annelid *Nereis* and the sea urchins *Arbacia* and *Strongylocentrotus* (1910–21); hypothesized the existence of specific combining groups in sperm and in eggs; developed a "fertilizin theory" of the role of union (linkage) of such combining groups. Explained the development of the freemartin (1917) in terms of the influence of male hormone from the male twin upon the development of the female; this led to the concept of a comparable role for fetal sex hormones in all vertebrates.

LINACRE, THOMAS (*b. Canterbury, England, ca. 1460; d. London, England, 1524*), medicine.

Studied at Oxford; continued studies in Greek and in medicine in Italy; graduated M.D. from Padua (1496); did further work with Nicolò Leoniceno. Returned to Oxford; privately tutored Thomas More in Greek; became a physician to Henry VIII (1509); took holy orders to increase income. Translated Galen's works into Latin; helped to found the College of Physicians of London.

LIND, JAMES (*b. Edinburgh, Scotland, 1716; d. Gosport, Hampshire, England, 1794*), medicine.

Was apprenticed to a physician (1731); entered the British navy as a surgeon's mate (1739); promoted to surgeon (1747); after leaving the navy, obtained M.D. from the University of Edinburgh (1748). In 1747, on H.M.S. *Salisbury,* Lind carried out classic experiments which showed that citrus fruit is a cure for scurvy. Published *A Treatise of the Scurvy* (1753), which led to his appointment as chief physician at the Royal Naval Hospital; his scurvy cure, however, was not officially adopted by the Navy until after his death.

LINDBLAD, BERTIL (*b. Örebro, Sweden, 1895; d. Stockholm, Sweden, 1965*), astronomy.

Received doctorate from Uppsala University (1920) with thesis on radiative transfer in the solar atmosphere; did research at the Lick and Mount Wilson observatories (1920–22); returned to Uppsala; was appointed director of the Stockholm observatory (1927); was in charge of building the new observatory in Saltsjöbaden. Early work was on problem of determining absolute magnitudes of stars; later turned to stellar dynamics; advanced concept of the galactic system rotating around a distant center.

LINDE, CARL VON (*b. Berndorf, Germany, 1842; d. Munich, Germany, 1934*), engineering, cryogenics.

Attended the Eidgenössische Polytechnikum in Zurich (1861–64). Established first engineering laboratory in

Germany (1875) at the Munich Polytechnische Schule. Research on heat theory led to the development of the first successful compressed ammonia refrigerator. Succeeded in liquefying air (1895); among other inventions, developed a device for obtaining pure oxygen by means of rectification (1902).

LINDELÖF, ERNST LEONHARD (*b. Helsingfors, Sweden [now Helsinki, Finland], 1870; d. Helsinki, 1946*), mathematics.

Educated at Helsinki, Paris, and Göttingen. Taught at the University of Helsinki (1895–1938). In the theory of differential equations, investigated the existence of solutions ("Sur l'intégration de l'équation différentielle de Kummer," 1890); also wrote *Le calcul des résidus . . .* (1905).

LINDEMANN, CARL LOUIS FERDINAND (*b. Hannover, Germany, 1852; d. Munich, Germany, 1939*), mathematics.

Received doctorate from Erlangen (1873). Was a leading educator; taught at several universities, ending at Munich (from 1893); supervised doctoral work of David Hilbert. Did paper (1882) on the transcendence of pi, which definitively settled the problem of the quadrature of the circle.

LINDEMANN, FREDERICK ALEXANDER, later **Lord Cherwell** (*b. Baden-Baden, Germany, 1886; d. Oxford, England, 1957*), physics.

Studied in Scotland and Germany; took Ph.D. with Nernst (1910); with him, formulated the Nernst-Lindemann theory of specific heats; at the same time, derived the (Lindemann) formula relating the melting point of a crystal to the amplitude of vibration of its atoms. Became head of the Clarendon Laboratory at Oxford (1919). His wide interest in physics is reflected in the Lindemann electrometer, Lindemann glass for transmitting X rays, and the Dobson-Lindemann theory of the upper atmosphere. Was an important advisor to Churchill on air defense and other scientific and economic problems.

LINDENAU, BERNHARD AUGUST VON (*b. Altenburg, Germany, 1779; d. Altenburg, 1854*), astronomy.

Studied at Leipzig. Worked at the Gotha observatory (from 1801; director, 1808–18). Produced tables of planets for calculation of ephemerides of Mercury, Venus, and Mars.

LINDGREN, WALDEMAR (*b. Kalmar, Sweden, 1860; d. Brookline, Mass., 1939*), geology.

Studied at the Royal Mining Academy in Freiberg, Saxony; emigrated to the U.S. (1883); worked at the U.S. Geological Survey (1884–1912) and at the Massachusetts Institute of Technology (1912–33). Was a leader in the science of ore deposition and use of the petrographic microscope.

LINDLEY, JOHN (*b. Catton, near Norwich, England, 1799; d. Turnham Green, Middlesex, England, 1865*), botany, horticulture.

The son of a nurseryman. Active in the Horticultural Society of London (from 1820); taught at the University of London (from 1828); prepared report that led to the founding of the Royal Gardens at Kew. Among his many works are *The Theory of Horticulture* (1840) and *Genera and Species of Orchidaceous Plants* (1830–40). Orchids were his speciality.

LINK, HEINRICH FRIEDRICH (*b. Hildesheim, Germany, 1767; d. Berlin, Germany, 1851*), zoology, botany, chemistry, geology, physics.

Received the M.D. from the University of Göttingen (1789). Published in all the fields listed above as well as in the philosophy of science. Taught at Rostock, Breslau, and Berlin.

LINNAEUS (or **VON LINNÉ**), **CARL** (*b. Södra Råshult, Småland, Sweden, 1707; d. Uppsala, Sweden, 1778*), botany, zoology, geology, medicine.

The son of a country parson who greatly loved flowers, Linnaeus in his youth set himself the task of establishing new systems for describing and ordering animals, plants, and minerals. He studied at the universities in Lund, Uppsala, and in Harderwijk, Holland, where he obtained his M.D. In Holland (1735–38) worked as superintendent of George Clifford's botanical garden near Haarlem; published *Systema naturae* (1735), presenting his new system of taxonomy. Returned to Sweden; was appointed a physician to the admiralty (1739); helped to found the Swedish Academy of Science; became a professor of medicine at the University of Uppsala (1741); renovated the university's botanical garden, where he lived for the rest of his life; was elevated to the nobility (1762). Published his most influential work, *Philosophia botanica*, in 1751 (an expansion of *Fundamenta botanica*, 1736); in *Species plantarum* (1753) he described about 8,000 plant species; his definitive 10th edition of *Systema naturae* appeared 1758–59. Linnaeus brought an urgently needed simplicity to the classification of plants; as early as 1730, he had worked out a sexual system, grouping plants in classes, according to the number and order of stamens, and then into orders, mostly according to the number of pistils; although he realized that this was an artificial structure, he did not fully work out a more "natural" system; was the first to work with species as a clearly defined concept; introduced binomial nomenclature based on genus and species; concluded that for every natural plant order, only one species had been created originally. In *Oeconomia naturae* (1749) and *Politia naturae* (1760) he developed concepts of the balance and competition in nature among the insects, animals, and plants. Was less influential in classification of the animal and mineral kingdoms, but did group man with the apes, and was the first to recognize whales as mammals; his insect orders are still recognized.

LIOUVILLE, JOSEPH (*b. St.-Omer, Pas-de-Calais, France, 1809; d. Paris, France, 1882*), mathematics.

Graduated from the École des Ponts et Chaussées (1830). Taught at the École Polytechnique and the Collège de France; received doctorate (1836); taught at the Sorbonne (1857–74). Founded (1836) the important *Journal des mathématiques pures et appliquées* (soon called *Journal de Liouville*), which he directed until 1874; published the influential papers of Galois (1846). Liouville investigated the determination of the nature of roots of algebraic equations higher than the fourth degree.

Demonstrated (1840) the impossibility, in general, of reducing the solution of differential equations either to a finite sequence of algebraic operations and indefinite integrations or—independently of Cauchy—to a particular aspect of the method of successive approximations (1837–38). With Sturm, published memoirs on the equation of vibrating strings; concepts related to the beginning of the theory of linear integral equations. In number theory, published notes in the *Journal des mathématiques* (1858–65) stating without demonstration a set of theorems that constitute the foundation of "analytic" number theory.

LIPPMANN, GABRIEL JONAS (*b. Hollerich, Luxembourg, 1845; d. at sea, 1921*), physics, instrumental astronomy.

Of a French family, attended the École Normale Supérieure and the Sorbonne (Ph.D., 1875); taught at the Sorbonne (from 1883). Developed the capillary electrometer, sensitive to changes in potential of 1/1,000 of a volt. Invented the coelostat, which enables photography of a region of the sky without apparent movement (an improvement on the siderostat). Devised a method for measurement of the difference in longitude between two observatories by means of radio waves and photography, and a method for measuring the difference between the periods of two pendulums using high-speed flash photography. Was awarded the Nobel Prize (1908) "for his method, based on the interference phenomenon, for reproducing colours photographically."

LIPSCHITZ, RUDOLF OTTO SIGISMUND (*b. near Königsberg, Germany [now Kaliningrad, R.S.F.S.R.], 1832; d. Bonn, Germany, 1903*), mathematics.

Studied at Königsberg and at Berlin under Dirichlet (doctorate, 1853); taught at Berlin, Breslau, and Bonn. In basic analysis he is remembered for the Lipschitz condition, important for proofs of existence and uniqueness and for approximation theory and constructive function theory. In algebraic number theory he obtained a hypercomplex system that is today termed a Lipschitz algebra. Did important investigations of n-dimensional differential forms, extending the work of Riemann; was one of the first to employ cogradient differentiation; showed that the vanishing of a certain expression (a fourth-degree curvature quantity) is a necessary and sufficient condition for a Riemannian manifold to be Euclidean; was especially successful in his study of the properties of Riemannian submanifolds V_m of dimension m in a Riemannian manifold V_m of dimension n.

LISBOA, JOÃO DE (*b. Portugal; d. Indian Ocean, before 1526*), navigation.

Was a pilot; voyaged to Brazil, northern Africa, and the Indies. In *Tratado da agulha de marear* (1514), describes his attempt to determine magnetic declination.

LISSAJOUS, JULES ANTOINE (*b. Versailles, France, 1822; d. Plombières, France, 1880*), physics.

Received his doctorate from the Sorbonne (1850). Developed an optical method for studying vibration by reflecting light; produced a characteristic kind of curve, the "Lissajous figure," by successively reflecting a light beam from mirrors on two tuning forks that are vibrating about mutually perpendicular axes.

LISTER, JOSEPH (*b. Upton, Essex, England, 1827; d. Walmer, Deal, Kent, England, 1912*), surgery.

Lister's practice and teaching of antiseptic techniques transformed surgery into an enlightened art governed by scientific disciplines. He led the way in reducing the appalling mortality rates resulting from traumatic and post-operative sepsis to the point that surgery could be undertaken with confidence of a successful outcome.

As a boy, Lister was introduced to microscopy and natural history by his father, Joseph Jackson Lister. He attended University College, London (M.B. and fellowship of the Royal College of Surgeons, 1852). Became assistant to James Syme at the University of Edinburgh (1853); married Syme's eldest daughter, Agnes (1855); began work in the post of assistant surgeon at the Royal Infirmary (1855). In investigations of inflammation, he related it to "adhesiveness" of the blood corpuscles; this led to study of coagulation; his reports on these subjects resulted in his election to the Royal Society of London (1860). Became regius professor of surgery at the University of Glasgow (1860); explored the greater opportunities afforded in surgery by use of anesthesia (he favored chloroform); invented several ingenious devices, e.g., slender-bladed sinus forceps, and innovative procedures, e.g., radical mastectomy for breast cancer and wiring of fractured patellae. But although his patients fared better than those in other wards, the risk of infection was severe. Lister began to consider suppuration to be a form of decomposition and to doubt Liebig's dictum that the cause was a form of combustion resulting from contact with oxygen; began to experiment with potassium sulfite administered orally, and with applications of carbolic acid. Thomas Anderson, a professor of chemistry at Glasgow, drew Lister's attention to the work of Pasteur (1865), which provided him with the key to the control of hospital diseases. Using carbolic acid, he had good results treating compound fractures and indolent abscesses; this he reported in *The Lancet* (1867); then began to apply the antiseptic principle to surgical wounds, with excellent effects. His accomplishments were for many years received with hostility or apathy by many of his peers in England; however, he became renowned abroad, and was also supported by his students and assistants. In several studies, confirmed and extended Pasteur's theories. While serving as professor of clinical surgery at the University of Edinburgh (1869–77), began to work in surgery with a carbolic spray, which he later rejected in favor of antiseptic dressings; using a rubber drainage tube (invented in France by P. M. E. Chaussaignac), he treated Queen Victoria for an axillary abscess. Became professor of surgery at King's College, London (1877–92); gradually overcame the resistance to the use of his methods. Helped to found and was first chairman of the British Institute of Preventive Medicine (1891). Was raised to the peerage (1897).

LISTER, JOSEPH JACKSON (*b. London, England, 1786; d. West Ham, Essex, England, 1869*), optics.

The father of Joseph Lister. Of a Quaker family, Lister joined his father's wine firm at age 14, but was already interested in optics. In 1830, he read a paper to the Royal

Society reporting that an achromatic combination of a negative flint-glass lens with a positive crown-glass lens has two aplanatic focal points; with this knowledge he was able to use two sets of achromatic lens combinations to remove fuzziness of image caused by chromatic and spherical aberrations and to nullify coma. This design was an essential step in changing the microscope from a toy to a vital scientific instrument.

LISTER, MARTIN (*christened Radclive, Buckinghamshire, England, 1639; d. Epsom, England, 1712*), zoology, geology.

Attended St. John's College, Cambridge (B.A., 1658; M.A., 1662); studied medicine at Montpellier (1663–66), but did not graduate; received M.D. from Oxford (1684) largely because of his donations to Ashmolean Museum. Did pioneer studies in invertebrate zoology, especially on mollusks, spiders, and several parasites. Believed fossils had a geological origin.

LITKE, FYODOR PETROVICH (*b. St. Petersburg, Russia, 1797; d. St. Petersburg, 1882*), earth sciences, geography.

Became a sailor in the Baltic fleet (1812). Best known for his command of the sloop *Senyavin* on a round-the-world voyage (1826–29) to survey the little-known islands of the central Pacific and the coast of the Bering Sea.

LIU HUI (*fl. China, ca.* A.D. *250*), mathematics.

All that is known of the life of Liu Hui is that he flourished in the kingdom of Wei towards the end of the Three Kingdoms Period (A.D. 221–265). His commentary on the *Chiu-chang suan-shu* ("Nine Chapters on the Mathematical Art") has exerted a profound influence on Chinese mathematics for well over 1,000 years. The *Chiu-chang suan-shu,* which may already have been in existence in the third century B.C., was intended as a practical handbook for engineers, architects, officials, and tradesmen. Chapter I, on land surveying, gives the rules for finding the areas of various figures and for calculations with fractions; of special interest is that Liu Hui gave 3.14 as the value of pi, which he obtained by taking the ratio of the perimeter of a regular polygon of 96 sides to the diameter of a circle enclosing this polygon. In Chapter IV, the use of the least common multiple in fractions is shown, and the extraction of square roots and cube roots is demonstrated. Chapter VII presents the method of "excess and deficiency" for solving problems of the type $ax + b = 0$ in a roundabout way, which in Europe came to be known as the rule of false position. Chapter VIII, concerned with simultaneous linear equations, in one problem presents five unknowns but only four equations, thus heralding the indeterminate equation. Some scholars believe that in Chapter IX, on applications of the Pythagorean theorem, essentially the same method is used to solve numerical equations of the second and higher degrees as that developed by Horner (1819). Liu Hui also wrote *Hai-tao suan-ching* ("Sea Island Mathematical Manual," so called because the first problem deals with an island), as an appendix to the *Chiu-chang suan-shu.* In the preface to this brief work (only nine problems in all), Liu Hui describes the classical Chinese method of determining the distance from the sun to the earth by means of double triangulation; he goes on to show how the same method can be applied to more immediately practical questions, such as finding the depth of a valley.

LIVINGSTON, BURTON EDWARD (*b. Grand Rapids, Mich., 1875; d. Baltimore, Md., 1948*), plant physiology, physiological ecology.

Studied at the University of Michigan (B.S., 1898) and the University of Chicago (Ph.D., 1901). Taught at Johns Hopkins (1909–40). Interests centered mainly on the water relations of plants. Wrote *The Role of Diffusion and Osmotic Pressure in Plants (1903)*. Invented the porous cup atmometer, an instrument for measuring the evaporating capacity of air, and the auto-irrigator to control soil moisture in potted plants.

LLOYD, HUMPHREY (*b. Dublin, Ireland, 1800; d. Dublin, 1881*), physics.

Graduated from Trinity College, Dublin (1819); became a professor and provost there. In 1832, W. R. Hamilton asked Lloyd to investigate "conical refraction" within a crystal; Lloyd's findings gave new support to the wave theory of light. In 1834, he found that Fresnel's interference pattern could be produced with a single reflecting surface; in studying this phenomenon was able to establish Fresnel's prediction that the intensity of light reflected at a 90° incidence is equal to that of direct light; also that a half-wavelength phase acceleration takes place upon reflection by a higher-density medium. Also studied the earth's magnetic field.

LLOYD, JOHN URI (*b. West Bloomfield, N.Y., 1849; d. Van Nuys, Calif., 1936*), pharmacy, chemistry.

Was educated mostly at home; apprenticed to a pharmacist at age fourteen; with his two brothers, gained control of the pharmaceutical firm of H. M. Merrell of Cincinnati, which became known as Lloyd Brothers; taught chemistry at the Cincinnati College of Pharmacy (1883–87) and at the Eclectic Medical Institute (1878–1907). His commitment to eclecticism, which stressed the use of botanical drugs, led him to concentrate his scientific studies on plants. He developed and patented several useful techniques, including Lloyd's reagent—hydrous aluminum silicate—which adsorbed alkaloids from solutions. He was a pioneer in the application of physical chemistry to pharmaceutical techniques. Was also a novelist.

LLWYD, EDWARD. *See* **Lhwyd, Edward.**

LOBACHEVSKY, NIKOLAI IVANOVICH (*b. Nizhni Novgorod* [*now Gorki*], *Russia, 1792; d. Kazan, Russia, 1856*), mathematics.

Lobachevsky entered Kazan University in 1807 and received the master's degree in physics and mathematics in 1812. His subsequent career in the university (from 1814) included both teaching and administrative duties; he was made professor ordinarius in 1822, and served as librarian of the university (1825–35), rector (1827–46), and assistant trustee for the Kazan educational district (1846–55). He was raised to the hereditary nobility in 1837.

Although he wrote on such topics as mechanics, astronomy, probability theory, analysis, and algebra, the chief thrust of Lobachevsky's scientific endeavor was geometrical; his later work was devoted exclusively to his new non-Euclidean geometry, which was first set out in a paper of 1826 and first published in 1829–30. In his early lectures, Lobachevsky himself attempted to prove the fifth postulate; his own geometry is derived from his later insight that a geometry in which all of Euclid's axioms except the fifth postulate hold true is not in itself contradictory. He called such a system "imaginary geometry," proceeding from an analogy with imaginary numbers. If imaginary numbers are the most general numbers for which the laws of arithmetic of real numbers prove justifiable, then imaginary geometry is the most general geometrical system. It was Lobachevsky's merit to refute the uniqueness of Euclid's geometry, and to consider it as a special case of a more general system.

In Lobachevskian geometry, given a line a and a point A not on it, one can draw through A more than one coplanar line not intersecting a. It follows that one can draw infinitely many such lines which, taken together, constitute an angle of which the vertex is A. The two lines bordering that angle are called parallels to a, and the lines contained between them are called ultraparallels, or diverging lines; all other lines through A intersect a. For all triangles in the Lobachevskian plane the sum of the angles is less than two right angles. Lobachevsky also constructed a space geometry. He discovered that the formulas of trigonometry in the space he defined can be derived from formulas of spherical trigonometry if the sides a, b, c of triangles are regarded as purely imaginary numbers (or if the radius r of the sphere is considered as purely imaginary); in this he saw evidence of the noncontradictory nature of his geometry.

In "Voobrazhaemaya geometriya" ("Imaginary Geometry") (1835) he built up the new geometry analytically, proceeding from its inherent trigonometrical formulas and considering the derivation of these formulas from spherical trigonometry to guarantee its internal consistency. In a later work he developed the idea of a geometry independent of the fifth postulate. His last two books, *Geometrische Untersuchungen* (1840) and *Pangéométrie* (1855–56), represent summaries of his previous work; the former dealt with the elements of the new geometry, while the latter applied differential and integral calculus to it.

Lobachevsky's work was little heralded in his lifetime; such men as Ostrogradsky and Cayley failed to understand it. Gauss spoke to Lobachevsky flatteringly of *Geometrische Untersuchungen* and supported his election to the Göttingen Gesellschaft der Wissenschaften (1842), but never publicly commented on his discovery. The new geometry achieved recognition through translations by Houël (1866) and A. V. Letnikov (1868), and was studied and extended by Beltrami, Weierstrass, Klein, Poincaré, and Riemann. The presence of specifically Lobachevskian geometry is felt in modern physics in the isomorphism of the group of motions of Lobachevskian space and the Lorentz group. Within the framework of the general theory of relativity, the problem of the geometry of the real world, to which Lobachevsky had devoted much attention, was solved; the geometry is that of variable curvature, which is on the average much closer to Lobachevsky's than to Euclid's.

L'OBEL (or **LOBEL**), **MATHIAS DE** (*b. Lille, France, 1538; d. Highgate, near London, England, 1616*), botany.

Studied at the University of Montpellier. With Pierre Pena wrote *Stirpium adversaria nova* (1570 or 1571), one of the milestones of modern botany.

LOCKE, JOHN (*b. Wrington, Somersetshire, England, 1632; d. Oates, Essex, England, 1704*), philosophy.

Locke was the most important British philosopher of the Age of Reason; in his work two streams of thought merged: the semiskeptical rationalism of Descartes and the *ad hoc* scientific experimentation of Bacon and the Royal Society. He was the son of a lawyer; attended Westminster School and Christ Church, Oxford. Met (1666) Anthony Ashley Cooper, later the first earl of Shaftesbury, who became his patron. His most important work, which won him immediate fame, was *An Essay Concerning Human Understanding* (1689–90). In the *Essay*, he rejected the opinion that people are born with certain innate ideas; maintained that all ideas are derived from experience. Argued that the object of perception is not a thing itself but rather an idea derived in part from things and in part from our own minds; in perception there are three elements: the observer, the idea, and the object that the idea represents. Distinguished between primary qualities (impenetrability, extension, figure, mobility, number), which he thought belonged to material bodies themselves, and secondary qualities (color, taste, sound), which depend on the observer's mind.

LOCKYER, JOSEPH NORMAN (*b. Rugby, England, 1836; d. Salcombe Regis, England, 1920*), astrophysics.

Entered the English War Office (1857), but success as an amateur astronomer led to his appointment as director of the Solar Physics Observatory at South Kensington; when it was transferred to Cambridge University (1911), he retired and established his own observatory in Salcombe Regis, now attached to the University of Exeter. In 1868 Lockyer, almost simultaneously with Jules Janssen, observed the solar prominences (at a time when there was not a total solar eclipse); he was using a spectroscope attached to a refracting telescope. Later suggested that there existed in the sun an unknown element, which he named helium. Further spectroscopic studies led him to formulate several speculative theories, which have not survived the test of time, but which include some striking ideas; e.g., he believed that a sufficiently strong stimulus would break up atoms into subatoms having their own characteristic spectra; but the observation that prompted this hypothesis was faulty. Perhaps the most lasting of Lockyer's achievements was his creation of the great scientific journal *Nature* (1869), which he edited for fifty years.

LODGE, OLIVER JOSEPH (*b. Penkhull, Staffordshire, England, 1851; d. Lake, near Salisbury, England, 1940*), physics.

Received the D.Sc. from University College, London (1877); taught at University College, Liverpool (1881–1900); was principal of the University of Birmingham (1900–19). In an ingenious experiment (1893) he disproved the notion that the ether in the vicinity of moving matter moves along with it (contradicting the conclusion drawn from the Michelson-Morley experiment of 1887);

thus Lodge set the stage for abandonment of the ether theory. Also did major work on electromagnetic radiation, and participated in the beginnings of radiotelegraphy.

LOEB, JACQUES (*b. Mayen, Rhine Province, Prussia, 1859; d. Hamilton, Bermuda, 1924*), physiology, biology.

Brother of Leo Loeb. Studied at Strasbourg (M.D., 1884); taught at Würzburg, where he was influenced by Julius von Sachs's work on plant tropisms. Emigrated to the U.S., where he held several teaching posts, ending at the Rockefeller Institute (from 1910). Was an ardent mechanist, seeking to demonstrate tropisms in animals and to explain biological processes in terms of physicochemical agencies; achieved artificial parthenogenesis of sea urchin eggs. Was widely known for his materialism and socialism. Wrote the popular *The Mechanistic Conception of Life* (1912).

LOEB, LEO (*b. Mayen, Germany, 1869; d. St. Louis, Mo., 1959*), medicine, pathology.

The younger brother of Jacques Loeb. Received his M.D. (1897) from the University of Zurich; emigrated to the U.S. Was professor of pathology at Washington University in St. Louis (from 1915). Noted for studies of transplanted tissue; helped to inaugurate experimental approach to the study of cancer in the U.S.

LOEFFLER (LÖFFLER), FRIEDRICH AUGUST JOHANNES (*b. Frankfurt an der Oder, Germany, 1852; d. Berlin, Germany, 1915*), microbiology, medicine.

Received his M.D. from the Friedrich Wilhelm Institut for military doctors in Berlin. Among numerous appointments, was a professor at the University of Greifswald (1888–1913). Became an assistant to Robert Koch in Berlin (1880). Elucidated the characteristics of the diphtheria bacillus and its growth in pure culture (1884), extending the work of Edwin Klebs; suggested that this bacillus produced a toxin responsible for some of the effects of the disease; found that healthy people may be carriers of the disease. Also identified the infectious agent of glanders and the cause of swine erysipelas and of swine plague; with Paul Frosch, showed that one of the newly-discovered filterable viruses could cause disease, specifically, aphthous fever (foot-and-mouth disease).

LOEWI, OTTO (*b. Frankfurt am Main, Germany, 1873; d. New York, N.Y., 1961*), pharmacology, physiology.

Shared with Henry Dale the Nobel Prize for physiology or medicine (1936) for work relating to the chemical transmission of nerve impulses. As a student, was more interested in art and philosophy than science. Received his M.D. from the University of Strasbourg (1896), where he was impressed by Bernhard Naunyn's clinical lectures and by reading W. H. Gaskell's Croonian lecture (1883) on the isolated heart of the frog. Visited England (1902–03), meeting the leading English physiologists. Became professor at the University of Graz (1909–38); was arrested by the Gestapo; allowed to leave only after turning over his savings. In the U.S.A. (from 1940) as research professor of pharmacology at the College of Medicine, New York. His most famous experiment (1921) was done with two isolated frog hearts attached to Straub canulas filled with Ringer solution; when the vagus nerve of one

434

heart was stimulated and the solution transferred to the other, the beat slowed; a similar, opposite reaction could be provoked following stimulation of the accelerator nerve; later Loewi identified the vagus-transmitting substance as acetylcholine (with E. Navratil, 1926) and the accelerant as adrenaline (epinephrine—1936).

LOEWINSON-LESSING. *See* **Levinson-Lessing, Franz Yulevich.**

LOEWNER, CHARLES (KARL) (*b. Lany, Bohemia* [*now Czechoslovakia*], *1893; d. Stanford, Calif., 1968*), mathematics.

Attended the University of Prague (Ph.D., 1917). Taught at universities of Prague, Berlin (1922–28), Cologne (1928–30), and at Charles University (1930–39). Emigrated to the U.S. when the Nazis occupied Czechoslovakia; last teaching appointment was at Stanford University (1951–63). Noted for application of Lie theory concepts and methods to semigroups, and applying semigroups to unexpected mathematical situations; made the first significant contribution (1923) to the Bieberbach hypothesis: proved *schlicht* function in the case $n = 3$.

LOEWY, ALFRED (*b. Rawitsch, Germany* [*now Rawicz, Poznan, Poland*], *1873; d. Freiburg im Breisgau, Germany. 1935*), mathematics.

Studied at Munich (Ph.D., 1894); taught at Freiburg. Noted for work on linear groups, on the algebraic theory of linear and algebraic differential equations, and on actuarial mathematics.

LOGAN, JAMES (*b. Lurgan, Ireland, 1674; d. Germantown, Pa., 1751*), dissemination of knowledge.

Was the son of a Scotch Quaker school teacher who emigrated to England in 1690. Became William Penn's secretary (1699); thereafter administered Penn's affairs. Served as mayor of Philadelphia (1722–23), Chief Justice of the Supreme Court of Pennsylvania (1731–39), and acting governor of the colony (1736–37). Did original work in botany and optics. Gave scientific help and advice to Thomas Godfrey, John Bartram, Benjamin Franklin, and Cadwallader Colden. Disseminated the work of numerous European scientists in the colonies, including that of Newton, Halley, Linnaeus, and Huygens.

LOGAN, WILLIAM EDMOND (*b. Montreal, Canada, 1798; d. Llechryd, Wales, 1875*), geology.

Attended Edinburgh University. A businessman, Logan began geological study in connection with the management of a copper-smelting and coal-mining venture in Wales; from 1838, devoted himself solely to geology. Was director (1842–69) of the Geological Survey of Canada, producing the still valuable "Report on the Geology of Canada" (1863).

LOHEST, MARIE JOSEPH MAXIMIN (called **MAX**) (*b. Liège, Belgium, 1857; d. Liège, 1926*), geology, mineralogy, paleontology.

Studied and taught at the School of Mines in Liège. Investigated Paleozoic fishes. Stratigraphy and tectonics were major interests; was an ardent partisan of actualism. Participated in discovery (1886) of a characteristic Neanderthal fossil man in the terrace of Spy cavern.

LÖHNEYSS (or **LÖHNEIS** or **LÖHNEYSSEN**), **GEORG ENGELHARDT VON** (*b. Witzlasreuth, Germany, 1552; d. Remlingen, near Wolfenbüttel, Germany, 1625* [*?*]), mining, metallurgy.

Of a noble family, held various administrative positions relating to the mines of Germany. His greatly admired *Bericht vom Bergwerck* (1617) is filled with shameless plagiarism from works of Agricola and Ercker.

LOHSE, WILHELM OSWALD (*b. Leipzig, Germany, 1845; d. Potsdam, Germany, 1915*), astronomy.

Received the Ph.D. from the University of Leipzig (1865). Collaborated with Vogel for more than 30 years, succeeding him as director of the astrophysical observatory at Potsdam.

LOKHTIN, VLADIMIR MIKHAYLOVICH (*b. St. Petersburg, Russia, 1849; d. Petrograd, Russia, 1919*), hydrotechnology, hydrology.

Graduated from the St. Petersburg Institute of Communications Engineers (1875). Held various research and administrative posts in the civil service. Was one of the founders of the hydrology of rivers. Author, *O mekhanizme rechnogo rusla* ("On the Mechanism of a Riverbed," 1895).

LOMONOSOV, MIKHAIL VASILIEVICH (*b. Mishaninskaya, Archangelsk province, Russia, 1711; d. St. Petersburg, Russia, 1765*), chemistry, physics, metallurgy, optics.

Poet, polymath, and scientist of wide accomplishment. Studied at the University of St. Petersburg and at Marburg with Christian Wolff. As adjunct of the St. Petersburg Academy of Sciences, he developed original theories in physics provoking such controversy that he was imprisoned (1743) for eight months; but when Euler lavishly praised his works, Lomonosov was appointed professor of chemistry, and opened the first scientific chemical laboratory in Russia (1748). In practical areas, studied mining, navigation, atmospheric electricity, and built a mosaic workshop (1756). In theoretical physics, developed an atomic theory (a materialistic monadology) in which the particles of matter were endowed with motion; the system was based on the most general concept of the law of conservation of matter and motion. He argued against phlogiston; explained heat and cold in terms of changes in the velocity of motion of material particles; and predicted a deviation from Boyle's law in air subjected to very great pressure.

LONDON, FRITZ (*b. Breslau, Germany* [*now Wrocław, Poland*], *1900; d. Durham, N.C., 1954*), physics, theoretical chemistry.

Fritz and Heinz London were the only children of prosperous German-Jewish parents; their father was a professor of mathematics. London received his Ph.D. from the University of Munich (1921) with a dissertation on the theory of knowledge, based on the methods of Russell, Whitehead, and Peano. From 1925 he worked with Sommerfeld, P. P. Ewald, and Schrödinger, successively. Nazi persecution forced him and his brother to emigrate (1933); London came to the U.S. (via Oxford and Paris), and taught at Duke University (from 1939).

435

In 1927, in a classic study of the hydrogen molecule, London and W. Heitler set themselves the problem of determining the energy of a quantum-mechanical system having two electrons in motion about two charged nuclei; this requires precise knowledge of the probability function for the distribution of electrons. Toward a solution, they applied two ideas: 1) a method devised by Lord Rayleigh for estimating the energy of vibration in a complex system; and 2) a concept put forward by Heisenberg, that since in quantum mechanics the two electrons are indistinguishable, they may be supposed to change places without altering the system; therefore a better approximation to the wave function will be

$$\psi_{AB}(1, 2) = \psi_A(1) \, \psi_B(2) \pm \psi_A(2) \, \psi_B(1). \qquad (1)$$

rather than the standard

$$\psi_{AB}(1, 2) = \psi_A(1) \, \psi_B(2). \qquad (2)$$

From these bases, and using (1) with the positive sign, London and Heitler were able to obtain an expression of the total energy of the molecule, which compared well with experimental values. The solution was later corrected in detail and simplified by others; but the idea of treating complex molecules as resonating between a number of simple structures has been amazingly fruitful.

In 1937, while studying the benzene ring, London began to form notions about long-range order that became central to his important work on superconductivity. In 1935, he and his brother had proposed an equation relating the current in a superconductor to the magnetic field; this work was done in response to the discovery by W. Meissner and R. Ochsenfeld that a superconductor not only shields internal points from changes in the external magnetic field, it actually tends to expel the field present in its interior before cooling. Gradually London came to see a deeper meaning in his and his brother's equation; he discovered that it is equivalent to

$$\text{curl } \mathbf{p}_s = 0. \qquad (3)$$

where $\mathbf{p}_s$ is the average momentum of the superconducting electrons. In the special case of an ideal solid superconductor, the solution of (3) is $\mathbf{p}_s = 0$, while for a wire of constant cross section fed at its ends by a current, the wave functions of the electrons extend uniformly throughout the material. This led London to a radical new concept. In quantum mechanical systems, unlike the situation in classical mechanics, at absolute zero there is still a residual kinetic energy because the positions and momenta of the particles are subject to Heisenberg's uncertainty relation; hence, London conjectured, there might in some circumstances be an advantage in energy for particles to condense with respect to momentum rather than position; this would account for the uniformity of $\mathbf{p}_s$ throughout the wire; the current would constitute a macroscopic quantum state, describable by a single wave function; a corollary is that the magnetic flux through a superconducting ring should be quantized, since there must be an integral number of waves around the ring (flux quantization was later demonstrated). Lon-

don did not complete work on the question of what mechanism accounts for the cooperative behavior of superconducting electrons; however, an answer was reached later, the crucial idea being suggested by L. N. Cooper: Pairs of electrons moving in opposite directions with opposite spins become briefly paired through interaction with the ionic lattice of the metal.

On a related problem, London made an important (at the time controversial) suggestion. To account for certain abnormal properties of the superfluid liquid helium II, he revived a speculation by Einstein that at a low temperature a quantum gas would have more particles than the number of particle states available, and would undergo a kind of condensation, with the surplus molecules concentrated in the lowest possible quantum state. The idea had been abandoned, but London theorized that it was valid, could apply to liquids as well, and would account for the peculiar behavior of liquid helium II. Eventually, he was shown to be right.

LONDON, HEINZ (*b. Bonn, Germany, 1907; d. Oxford, England, 1970*), physics.

The younger brother of Fritz London. Did graduate work at Breslau under F. E. Simon (Ph.D., 1934); followed Simon to Oxford, and worked with him on the British atomic bomb project; worked at Harwell (from 1946). In his thesis on superconductors he suggested that alternating-current high-frequency losses (which he had not yet been able to demonstrate) probably occur because there exist two groups of electrons, one subject to losses, the other not; direct currents, then, flow only in the superconducting electrons, while alternating currents couple inductively to both groups in parallel, and so cause dissipation; he wrote an acceleration equation for the superconducting electrons, $\Lambda \mathbf{J} = \mathbf{E}$, where $\mathbf{E}$ is the internal field, $\mathbf{J}$ the current, and Λ a constant (the London order parameter) equal to m/ne^2, where m and e are the mass and charge of the electrons and n their number density. London continued investigating superconductors in the work done with his brother relating current to magnetism (described in the article above). In 1939 he was finally able to show the high-frequency losses; discovered the "anomalous skin effect" in normal metals; he also investigated superconductivity of thin metallic films.

In work on helium, he devised an experiment that helped to establish the two-fluid model of helium II (a model suggested by L. Tisza, extending concepts of Fritz London): Helium II is considered as a mixture of two fluids, superfluid and normal, analogous to the two-fluid model of superconductivity. London also was able to prove from thermodynamic arguments that the superfluid component does not carry entropy. Proposed (1946) an experiment to test Lev Landau's conclusion that the superfluid is subject to the condition curl $\mathbf{v}_s = 0$, making it incapable of rotation. The experiment involved using a rotating container containing helium I, and cooling it until well below the lambda point; if Landau were correct, the container would have to start to rotate more rapidly to preserve the total angular momentum; the experiment was finally done successfully (1965), confirming Landau's theory. London's later work encompassed methods for the production of carbon 13 as a stable tracer element for medical research, and the development of the He^3-He^4 dilution refrigerator.

LONGOMONTANUS. *See* **Severin, Christian.**

LONICERUS (LONITZER), ADAM (*b. Marburg, Germany, 1528; d. Frankfurt, Germany, 1586*), botany.

Received his M.D. from Marburg (1554); also taught there. His herbals remained influential for more than 200 years.

LONITZER, ADAM. *See* **Lonicerus, Adam.**

LONSDALE, DAME KATHLEEN YARDLEY (*b. Newbridge, Ireland, 1903; d. London, England, 1971*), crystallography, chemistry, physics.

Attended Bedford College for Women (B.Sc., 1922); worked in X-ray crystallography at University College, London, and then at the Royal Institution in London; was the first woman to be admitted as a Fellow of the Royal Society (1945). Demonstrated that the benzene ring is hexagonal and planar (findings published, 1929); in study of the magnetic anisotrophy of crystals she established the reality of the concept of molecular orbitals. Principal editor of the International Tables for X-Ray Crystallography (from 1952).

LONSDALE, WILLIAM (*b. Bath, England, 1794; d. Bristol, England, 1871*), geology.

Was an army officer (1812–15). Became curator and librarian at the Geological Society of London (1829–42). His analysis of the age of the older strata of Devonshire helped to establish the validity of correlating strata by means of fossils.

LOOMIS, ELIAS (*b. Willington, Conn., 1811; d. New Haven, Conn., 1889*), meteorology, mathematics, astronomy.

Graduated from Yale (1830); taught at Western Reserve College, the University of the City of New York (1844–60), and Yale (from 1860); wrote many textbooks; published the first "synoptic" weather map (1846). Rediscovered (with D. Olmsted, 1835) Halley's comet and computed its orbit.

LORENTZ, HENDRIK ANTOON (*b. Arnhem, Netherlands, 1853; d. Haarlem, Netherlands, 1928*), theoretical physics.

Studied at the University of Leiden (Ph.D., 1875); was appointed to the new chair of theoretical physics at Leiden (1877). Most productive period dates from 1892, when he began work on his influential electron theory. Shared the Nobel Prize in physics with Pieter Zeeman (1902). Moved to Haarlem (1912); served as a curator in Teyler's Stichting, a museum in which, for the first time, he had his own laboratory. Was the regular president of the Solvay Congresses for physics (1911–27); he was venerated by Einstein and others of the younger generation of physicists for his knowledge, intellectual daring, and helpful, nonmanipulative leadership.

His doctoral thesis (1875) on electromagnetic optics was inspired by a paper by Helmholtz on Maxwell (1870); it included an electromagnetic derivation of Fresnel's amplitudes for light reflected at a dielectric interface, and closed with a prophetic vision of the unifying potential for physics in the combination of Maxwell's electromagnetic theory of light with the molecular theory of matter.

Lorentz here took a first step toward distinguishing the electromagnetic field from matter; interpreted the ether as the only proper dielectric. In a sequel paper (1878) on the optical theory of matter he assumed that the ether everywhere (except possibly in the immediate vicinity of material molecules) has the same properties that it has in a vacuum. Re the dispersion of light in a material body, theorized that incident light waves in the ether cause the electric particles in the body to vibrate and to send out secondary waves that interfere with the incident ones, thus making the propagation of light through the body depend on frequency; predicted a relation between the density of a body and its index of refraction (the Lorentz-Lorenz formula, developed independently by L. V. Lorenz in 1869).

In formulating his electron theory, Lorentz applied a particulate concept of electricity, a stationary ether, and an explicit separation of the roles of ether and matter. Also (1891) accepted the theory of contiguous action in electromagnetic processes (following Hertz). Assumed that electrons are contained in all molecules of ordinary matter and have either a positive or negative charge; the electrons create the electromagnetic field, the seat of which is the ether, and the field in turn acts ponderomotively on ordinary matter through the electrons in material molecules. He postulated the following formula (the Lorentz force) for the electric force of the ether on ponderable matter: $\mathbf{E} = 4\pi c^2 \mathbf{d} + \mathbf{v} \times \mathbf{H}$ (where $\mathbf{d}$ is the dielectric displacement, c the velocity of light, $\mathbf{v}$ the velocity of the electric charge, and $\mathbf{H}$ the magnetic force).

Given the concept of a stationary ether, it was necessary to account for the absence of any detectable ether "wind" associated with the earth's motion (the absence of wind effects having been demonstrated most significantly by the Michelson-Morley experiment, 1887). Lorentz first introduced transformations for the field magnitudes, spatial coordinates, and a "local time," and showed that in first-order approximation the equations describing an electric system in a moving frame were identical with those for the corresponding system in a frame at rest in the ether; to account for second-order experiments (such as Michelson-Morley) he referred to the contraction hypothesis (proposed independently by Fitzgerald), stating that the arms of an interferometer contract by a factor of $\sqrt{1 - v^2/c^2}$ in the direction of the earth's motion through the ether. He introduced the idea that the second-order transformations imply that the mass of an electron varies with velocity, and that the mass is different for motions parallel and perpendicular to the direction of translation through the ether.

In his famous 1904 paper ("Electromagnetic Phenomena in a System Moving With Any Velocity Smaller Than That of Light"), Lorentz refined his transformations to hold for all orders of smallness for the case of electromagnetic systems without charges; thus, no experiment on such systems could reveal the translation of the apparatus through the ether. He foresaw a physical universe consisting solely of ether and charged particles, or possibly of ether alone. In 1908, he was one of the first to speak out in favor of Planck's quantum theory and to emphasize the antithesis between quantum hypotheses and those of the electron theory. Lorentz never, however, embraced Einstein's reinterpretation of the equations of his electron theory (1905); he held to the belief that the ether is a reality and that absolute space and time are meaningful concepts.

LORENZ, HANS (*b. Wilsdruff, Germany, 1865; d. Sistrans, near Innsbruck, Austria, 1940*), mechanics, mechanical engineering.

Studied at the Dresden Polytechnical Institute and the University of Munich (Ph.D., 1894). Held the chair of mechanics at the Technische Hochschule of Danzig (from 1904). A versatile engineer, noted especially for work on refrigeration. Founded *Zeitschrift für die gesamte Kälteindustrie*.

LORENZ, LUDWIG VALENTIN (*b. Elsinore, Denmark, 1829; d. Copenhagen, Denmark, 1891*), physics.

Studied civil engineering at the Technical University of Denmark in Copenhagen. Supported himself by teaching and in last years through grants from the Carlsberg Foundation. Was a brilliant and original physicist, although little known in his lifetime. Did major work in optics, developing (1867) an electromagnetic theory of light independently of Maxwell, and also in heat and electricity conductivities of metals. Made first determination of the number of molecules in a given volume of air (1890). Developed a complete theory of currents in telephone cables. Stated that Lorenz law: the ratio between the conductivities of heat and electricity is proportional to the absolute temperature (with same constant of proportionality for all metals).

LORENZ, RICHARD (*b. Vienna, Austria, 1863; d. Frankfurt am Main, Germany, 1929*), physical chemistry.

Received his doctorate at Jena; was an assistant to Nernst at Göttingen (1892–96); taught at Frankfurt (from 1910). Specialized in the electrochemistry of substances in the fused state; demonstrated that Faraday's law is completely valid for fused salts.

LORENZONI, GIUSEPPE (*b. Rolle di Cisón, Treviso, Italy, 1843; d. Padua, Italy, 1914*), astronomy, astrophysics, geodesy.

Studied and taught at the University of Padua, and was director of its observatory (from 1878). Did important work in astrophysics, classical astronomy, and geodesy; established Padua as gravimetric reference point.

LORIA, GINO (*b. Mantua, Italy, 1862; d. Genoa, Italy, 1954*), mathematics, history of mathematics.

Studied at Turin; taught at Genoa (from 1886). Noted for studies of new applications of algebraic concepts in geometry and for work in the history of mathematics.

LORRY, ANNE CHARLES (*b. Crosnes, France, 1726; d. Bourbonne-les-Bains, France, 1783*), medicine.

Received his M.D. in Paris (1748). Patients included the Richelieus, Voltaire, and (briefly) Louis XV. Remembered now for writings on dermatology and on mental depression.

LOSCHMIDT, JOHANN JOSEPH (*b. Putschirn, near Carlsbad, Bohemia [now Karlovy Vary, Czechoslovakia], 1821; d. Vienna, Austria, 1895*), physics, chemistry.

Of a peasant family; educated in parochial school, in Prague, and at the University of Vienna. In private indus-

try, rediscovered a process for converting sodium nitrate to potassium nitrate (used in making gunpowder); nevertheless, went bankrupt (1854). Became a science teacher in Vienna; was allowed to do research at the university's Institute of Physics. Published at his own expense *Chemische Studien* (1861); for benzene he envisioned a ring-shaped chain formula of carbon atoms. In *Zur Constitution des Aethers* (1862), extending Herbart's metaphysics, he attempted to formulate a mathematical theory for luminiferous ether; conceived of an energy sphere surrounding each atom. Made the first accurate estimations of the size of air molecules; Loschmidt's figure (also called Avogadro's constant) states that one mole of gas contains $6.03 \cdot 10^{23}$ molecules. Appointed professor at the University of Vienna (1868). In connection with a dispute with Ludwig Boltzmann (one of his pupils), he was the first to apply the second law of thermodynamics to the theory of solutions and chemical compounds.

LOSSEN, KARL AUGUST (*b. Kreuznach, Germany, 1841; d. Berlin, Germany, 1893*), geology, petrology.

Studied at the University of Halle (graduated, 1866); worked at the Geological Survey of Prussia; taught at the University of Berlin (from 1870). Main work was the mapping and description of the Harz Mountains; also did essential work in microscopical petrology.

LOTKA, ALFRED JAMES (*b. Lemberg, Austria [now Lvov, Ukrainian S.S.R.], 1880; d. Red Bank, N.J., 1949*), demography, statistics.

Of American parents; received an international education; worked for the Metropolitan Life Insurance Company of New York (from 1924). Author of *Elements of Physical Biology* (1925), treating the whole biological world in a mathematico-physical way.

LOTSY, JAN PAULUS (*b. Dordrecht, Netherlands, 1867; d. Voorburg, Netherlands, 1931*), botany.

Studied at the Wageningen Agricultural College and at Göttingen. Initiated the founding of the Association Internationale de Botanistes; erected experimental gardens in Haarlem and Velp. Was convinced that species originated and evolved by hybridization. Founded the journal *Genetica* (1919).

LOTZE, HERMANN RUDOLPH (*b. Bautzen, Germany, 1817; d. Berlin, Germany, 1881*), theoretical biology, metaphysics.

Studied philosophy and medicine at the University of Leipzig (Ph.D. and M.D., 1838); taught at Leipzig and at Göttingen, where he succeeded Herbart. Among his voluminous writings, *Mikrokosmus* (1856–64) is the most comprehensive. Rejected vitalism; viewed the organism as a combination of mechanical processes, but saw all nature as directed toward spiritual goals and activated by the immanence of an infinite being.

LOVE, AUGUSTUS EDWARD HOUGH (*b. Weston-super-Mare, England, 1863; d. Oxford, England, 1940*), applied mathematics, geophysics.

Attended St. John's College, Cambridge; taught at Oxford (from 1899). Wrote classic *Treatise on the Mathematical Theory of Elasticity* (1892–93). Noted for analysis of surface seismic waves (Love waves).

LOVEJOY, ARTHUR ONCKEN (*b. Berlin, Germany, 1873; d. Baltimore, Md., 1962*), epistemology, history of ideas.

Studied under William James at Harvard; taught at Johns Hopkins (1910–38). Wrote *Revolt Against Dualism* (1930), expressing a temporalistic epistemological dualism, and, in the history of ideas, *The Great Chain of Being* (1936).

LOVELL, JOHN HARVEY (*b. Waldoboro, Me., 1860; d. Waldoboro, 1939*), botany, entomology.

Attended Amherst (graduated 1882); was independently wealthy. Investigated colors of flowers and color preferences of insects; studied wild bees.

LOVÉN, SVEN (*b. Stockholm, Sweden, 1809; d. near Stockholm, 1895*), marine biology.

Attended the University of Lund (M.A., 1829) and studied in Berlin (1830); worked at the Museum of Natural History in Stockholm (1841–92). Studied plankton, mollusks, and fossil shells.

LOVITS (LOWITZ), JOHANN TOBIAS (in Russian, **Tovy Yegorovich**) (*b. Göttingen, Germany, 1757; d. St. Petersburg, Russia, 1804*), chemistry.

Was orphaned in Russia (1768) when his father was killed by a Cossack revolutionary. Studied at St. Petersburg and Göttingen; became court apothecary in St. Petersburg (1787). Did original work in several areas, especially in studies of adsorptive qualities of charcoal and studies of the crystallization of substances from solutions. Introduced the concepts of supercooling and supersaturation; explained the role of seeding in crystal growth. Isolated strontium and chrome, and was the first to isolate a number of organic substances in the pure state.

LOWELL, PERCIVAL (*b. Boston, Mass., 1855; d. Flagstaff, Ariz., 1916*), astronomy.

Of a distinguished New England family; graduated from Harvard (1876); traveled in Japan and Korea. Built an observatory in Flagstaff (1894); became famous for thesis that Mars is the abode of intelligent life, expounded in *Mars and Its Canals* (1906) and *Mars as the Abode of Life* (1908); also wrote *The Evolution of Worlds* (1909). Predicted the existence of a trans-Neptunian planet; when found (1930) it was named Pluto, with its symbol depicting also the initials of Percival Lowell.

LOWER, RICHARD (*b. Tremeer, Cornwall, England, 1631; d. London, England, 1691*), medicine, physiology.

Of an old, affluent family. Perhaps the best seventeenth-century English physiologist after Harvey. Studied at Christ Church, Oxford (B.A., 1653; M.A., 1655; B.M. and doctor of physic, 1665), chiefly under Thomas Willis; moved with Willis to London (1666); admitted to the Royal Society (1667), where he performed important experiments with Hooke on respiration. Concluded a series of experiments on transfusion of medicinal liquids and blood with a successful demonstration of human transfusion (1667). In his *Tractatus de corde* (1669) Lower rejected ideas, derived from Willis, which he had formerly propounded, namely that an energetic effervescence of blood in the heart accounts for the blood's mo-

tion and for the difference in color between arterial and venous blood; citing particularly his work with Hooke, he showed that contact with air causes the change in color, and he stressed the role of cardiac systole in moving the blood.

LOWITZ, J. T. *See* **Lovits, Johann Tobias.**

LUBBOCK, SIR JOHN (LORD AVEBURY) (*b. London, England, 1834; d. Kingsgate Castle, Kent, England, 1913*), entomology, anthropology, botany.

A banker and amateur scientist (as was his father, J. W. Lubbock). Became a protégé of Darwin (1842), and then his lifelong friend and advocate. Discovered the first fossil remains of musk-ox in England (1855), evidence of an ice age. In *Pre-Historic Times* (1865) and *The Origin of Civilisation* (1871) he identified prehistoric cultures as evolutionary precursors of modern civilization; coined the terms *Neolithic* and *Paleolithic.* Did ingenious experiments with ants and on insect vision and color sense, reported in *Ants, Bees, and Wasps* (1882) and *On the Senses, Instincts, and Intelligence of Animals* (1888). Was a Liberal member of Parliament; was made a peer in 1900.

LUBBOCK, JOHN WILLIAM (*b. London, England, 1803; d. High Elms, near Farnborough, England, 1865*), astronomy.

Inherited (1840) a mercantile bank and baronetcy. As an amateur scientist, did major work on probability and the theory of tides. Was the father of John Lubbock.

LUBBOCK, RICHARD (*b. Norwich, England, 1759 [?]; d. Norwich, 1808*), chemistry.

Studied at the University of Edinburgh; practiced medicine at Norwich. Noted for his M.D. dissertation (1784) rejecting the phlogiston theory.

LUCAS, FRANÇOIS-ÉDOUARD-ANATOLE (*b. Amiens, France, 1842; d. Paris, France, 1891*), mathematics.

In Paris, taught at the Lycée Saint-Louis and the Lycée Charlemagne. Noted for contributions to number theory and writings on recreational mathematics; devised the modern method, essentially, of testing the primality of Mersenne's numbers.

LUCAS, KEITH (*b. Greenwich, England, 1879; d. over Salisbury Plain, near Aldershot, England, 1916*), physiology.

Studied at Trinity College, Cambridge (B.A., 1901; M.A., 1905; D.Sc., 1911), and taught there; was a director of the Cambridge Scientific Instrument Company (1906–14). Enlisted during World War I; did aeronautical research and designed improved instrumentation; died in a plane crash. Investigated the properties of nerve and muscle, especially the nature of waves of excitation; made innovations in design of physiological instruments, particularly the capillary electrometer. Established (1905, 1909) that the "all or none" law of cardiac muscle also applies to ordinary skeletal muscle (each muscle fiber, when stimulated, contracts maximally or not at all). With E. D. Adrian, developed the theory of summation (summation results in any excitable tissue when successive stimuli coincide with a temporary postrecovery phase, following the refractory period, of supernormal excitability).

LUCIANI, LUIGI (*b. Ascoli Piceno, Italy, 1840; d. Rome, Italy, 1919*), physiology.

Graduated in medicine from the University of Bologna (1868); studied under Carl Ludwig in Leipzig (1872–73); last of several teaching appointments was in Rome (1893–1917). Most important work was on the physiology of the cerebellum.

LUCRETIUS (*b. Italy, ca. 95 B.C.; d. ca. 55 B.C.*), natural philosophy.

Probably of a Roman aristocratic family. Wrote the great poem *De rerum natura*, propounding an Epicurean atomism: Everything is made up of ungenerated, indestructible atoms; all of nature can be explained by mechanical causes.

LUDENDORFF, F. W. HANS (*b. Thunow, Germany, 1873; d. Potsdam, Germany, 1941*), astronomy.

The younger brother of General Erich Ludendorff (whose political views he did not share). Studied at Berlin (Ph.D., 1897). Affiliated with the observatory at Potsdam (from 1898, as director from 1921–39). Worked mainly in spectrography.

LUDWIG, CARL FRIEDRICH WILHELM (*b. Witzenhausen, Germany, 1816; d. Leipzig, Germany, 1895*), physiology.

A great experimenter and teacher, one of the creators of modern physiology; sought to explain vital phenomena through laws of physics and chemistry. Received his M.D. at the University of Marburg (1840); taught at Marburg, at Zurich, and at the Josephinum in Vienna. At Leipzig (from 1865), planned and directed the influential physiological institute. Did outstanding work on the structure of the kidneys and on cardiac activity. Invented the kymograph (later modified by Marey and Chauveau), the mercurial blood pump, and the stream gauge. Did fundamental research on diffusion of liquid through a membrane in renal and salivary secretion. Author, *Lehrbuch der Physiologie* (1852–56).

LUEROTH (or **LÜROTH**), **JAKOB** (*b. Mannheim, Germany, 1844; d. Munich, Germany, 1910*), mathematics.

Graduated from the University of Giessen (Ph.D., 1866); last teaching appointment was at the University of Freiburg (1883–1910). Made contributions in analytical geometry, linear geometry, and theory of invariants. He is remembered eponymously for the "Lueroth quartic" (a covariant of a given ternary form of fourth degree), the "Lueroth theorem" (whereby each uni-rational curve is rational), and the "Clebsch-Lueroth method."

LUGEON, MAURICE (*b. Poissy, France, 1870; d. Lausanne, Switzerland, 1953*), geology.

Pursued studies in science while working in a bank; accompanied Eugène Renevier in mapping the mountains of Savoy; received doctorate from the University of Lausanne (1895), and began teaching there. In his most important paper (1901), described the macrostructure of the whole Alpine chain and the interrelationships of a vast series of recumbent folds and thrust sheets; his radical view was based on tectonic theories that have since been applied to all parts of the world; Lugeon himself extended them to the Carpathians (1903). One of his students was Émile Argand.

LUGININ, VLADIMIR FEDOROVICH (*b. Moscow, Russia, 1834; d. Paris, France, 1911*), chemistry.

A former artillery officer and member of revolutionary circles, turned to science exclusively (1867). Published articles with Berthelot; established first thermochemical laboratory in Russia, at Moscow University.

ŁUKASIEWICZ, JAN (*b. Lvov, Austrian Galicia [now Ukrainian S.S.R.], 1878; d. Dublin, Ireland, 1956*), mathematical logic.

Earned doctorate at Lvov (1902). Taught at the universities of Lvov and Warsaw and at the Royal Irish Academy, Dublin (from 1946). With Leśniewski, founded the Warsaw school of logic. Did brilliant work on many-valued logics.

LULL, RAMON (*b. Ciutat de Mallorques [now Palma de Mallorca], ca. 1232; d. Cuitat de Mallorques, 1316*), polymathy.

Invented an "art of finding truth" which inspired Leibniz's dream of a universal algebra four centuries later. Of a noble family, was converted to a religious life (*ca.* 1263), with a special mission to convert Muslims, toward which his Art was directed. Wrote at least 292 works in Catalan, Arabic, and Latin, including the encyclopedia *Arbor scientiae* (1295–96); among his sources were cabalistic and Neoplatonic writings and the cosmology of John Scotus Eriugena. Sought systematically to relate everything to God, examining how Creation was structured by the active manifestation of the divine attributes, or Dignities; developed letter codes for the Dignities, for principles of relation, and for subjects, as well as combinatory systems for these elements, sometimes using semimechanical techniques; thus, the Art anticipated modern symbolic logic and computer science. Lull's ideas influenced Nicholas of Cusa and Giordano Bruno.

LUMMER, OTTO RICHARD (*b. Gera, Germany, 1860; d. Breslau, Germany [now Wrocław, Poland], 1925*), optics.

Became Helmholtz's assistant (1884); taught at the University of Berlin and at Breslau (from 1904). Developed the basic concept and mechanism of the Lummer-Gehrcke interference spectroscope; did important work on blackbody radiation with Pringsheim. In 1889 he constructed, with Brodhun, an exact photometer, the Lummer-Brodhun cube.

LUNA, EMERICO (*b. Palermo, Italy, 1882; d. Palermo, 1963*), anatomy.

Studied and taught at the University of Palermo; founded the Italian Anatomical Society. Investigated the cerebellum; was one of the first to suture the heart successfully and to introduce the teaching of radiological anatomy.

LUNGE, GEORG (*b. Breslau, Prussia [now Wrocław, Poland], 1839; d. Zurich, Switzerland, 1923*), chemistry.

Took his doctorate at Breslau (1859); was in private industry in Silesia and in England; taught at the Eidgenössische Polytechnikum Schule in Zurich (from 1875). A leader in the chemical raw-materials industry. Invented Lunge's plate towers for the acid industry.

LUSITANUS, AMATUS (RODRIGUES, JOÃO) (*b. Castelo Branco, Portugal, 1511; d. Salonika, Greece [then Turkish], 1568*), medicine, botany.

Studied medicine at Salamanca. Practiced in Antwerp, Italy, and Greece. Author of seven collections of case histories, *Curationem medicinalium centuria* (1551–61).

LUSK, GRAHAM (*b. Bridgeport, Conn., 1866; d. New York, N.Y., 1932*), physiology, nutrition.

Studied at Columbia University School of Mines and in Munich (Ph.D., 1891); taught at Yale, New York University, and Cornell Medical College (from 1909). Investigated metabolic processes, using the calorimeter. His important research on diabetes demonstrated a constant ratio between dextrose and nitrogen excreted in the urine and that carbohydrates are not normally produced in the metabolism of fats.

LUSTIG, ALESSANDRO (*b. Trieste, Austria [now Italy], 1857; d. Marina di Pietrasanta, Lucca, Italy, 1937*), pathology, bacteriology.

Studied at Vienna (M.D., 1882); taught at Florence (1890–1932). Investigated cholera; did pioneer work in the study of antigens and the production of antibodies. Successfully extracted from *Bacterium pestis* a substance having the chemical characteristics of nucleoproteids; from this he was able to immunize animals and obtain immune sera, and subsequently to successfully treat plague victims in Bombay (1897–98).

LUTHER, C. ROBERT (*b. Schweidnitz, Germany [now Swidnica, Poland], 1822; d. Düsseldorf, Germany, 1900*), astronomy.

Studied at Berlin under Encke; became director of the observatory at Bilk, outside Düsseldorf. Did extensive, original work on the planetoids, discovering twenty-four.

LUZIN, NIKOLAI NIKOLAIEVICH (*b. Tomsk, Russia, 1883; d. Moscow, U.S.S.R., 1950*), mathematics.

Studied at Moscow, Göttingen, and Paris (Ph.D., Moscow University, 1915). Taught at Moscow University, and became the central figure in the Moscow school of function theory (1914–24). Most creative work was related to the theory of functions of a real variable in its two branches, metric and descriptive.

LYAPUNOV, ALEKSANDR MIKHAILOVICH (*b. Yaroslavl, Russia, 1857; d. Odessa, U.S.S.R., 1918*), mathematics, mechanics.

Studied at St. Petersburg University; was greatly influenced by P. L. Chebyshev; received doctorate (1892) with a brilliant dissertation on the stability of motion. Taught at Kharkov (1893–1901); affiliated with the St. Petersburg Academy of Sciences (from 1901); following the death of his wife from tuberculosis, Lyapunov committed suicide. His work focused on 1) the stability of equilibrium and motion of a mechanical system having a finite number of degrees of freedom (such as the solar system); 2) the stability of figures of equilibrium of a uniformly rotating liquid; 3) the stability of figures of equilibrium of a rotating liquid. With respect to the first subject, his work is fundamental to the qualitative theory of ordinary differential equations; his findings coincided with Poincaré's, but his approach was purely analytic. Lyapunov's investigations into mathematical physics (1886–1902) created the basis of a number of classic methods for solving boundary-value problems. In the theory of probability, he substantially generalized La-

place's limit theorem in application to sums of random independent values.

LYELL, CHARLES (*b. Kinnordy, Kirriemuir, Angus, Scotland, 1797; d. London, England, 1875*), geology, evolutionary biology.

Lyell's father was a lawyer, a wealthy landowner, and an amateur botanist. As a boy, Lyell studied insects; at Oxford he was introduced to mineralogy and geology by William Buckland. Travels in Scotland and the Alps reinforced his interest in geology, a subject which he established as a science.

Lyell studied law at Lincoln's Inn, London, and was called to the bar (1822); but chronic eye pain required him to take time off from reading and the law, time which he used for geological expeditions. With Constant Prévost he examined the geology of the Paris basin (1823), and was led by him to see that the formations could be explained naturally, without resort to catastrophes. Lyell expanded this view in an article in the *Quarterly Review* (September, 1826); he theorized that geological causes now active, such as earthquakes and volcanic action, could account for geological change, including raising sedimentary strata from the bottom of the sea to their present places in hills and mountains.

In further travels in France and Italy, Lyell gathered more evidence of the similarity of conditions in the geologic past and present. Experts on local fossils led him to try to distinguish among Tertiary formations according to the proportion of living species among their fossils; he thought that at Vesuvius and Etna he would find younger strata and a larger proportion of fossils of still-living species. In Sicily, however, he was astonished to note many fossils of living species in very old strata; he realized that the shell species of the Mediterranean are an ancient fauna that have changed very little over time, and that therefore modern conditions must indeed be analogous to those of the past. Furthermore, he was now certain that the Tertiary formations he had seen in the Paris basin, in Italy, and in Sicily were not parallel and contemporary but rather represented different and successive periods of time, the whole Tertiary representing a much greater period than he had dreamed. In Paris, meetings with Jules Desnoyers and Paul Deshayes (1829) led to the idea of arranging Tertiary formations in a chronological series according to differences in their characteristic groupings of fossil shell species.

In Volume I of *Principles of Geology* (1830), Lyell argued for the uniformity of the order of nature in the past and present. In Volume II (1832), he maintained that the life of a species is dependent upon physical conditions, including relationships with other species; geological processes, which change habitats, and competition with other species gradually lead to the extinction of some species and the increase of others. Lyell rejected Lamarck's theory, but he did not attempt to explain the emergence of new species. In Volume III (1833), he answered various criticisms, and introduced the classification of Tertiary formations into four epochs: Eocene, Miocene, and older and newer Pliocene. Lyell continued to revise and update the *Principles* throughout his life.

He was appointed professor at King's College, London (1831); he married in 1832. In 1836 he became friends with Darwin, who had taken the *Principles* with him on the voyage of the *Beagle*. Darwin went on to defend Lyell's uniformity theory in a paper on the geology of South America (1838); that same year, Lyell published *Elements of Geology*, a descriptive work, which he also revised many times. In 1858, Lyell and Joseph Hooker presented to the Linnean Society papers by Darwin and A. R. Wallace on natural selection; their ideas and his own observations on Madeira and the Canary Islands had led Lyell to accept tentatively the transmutation of species. In *The Geological Evidences of the Antiquity of Man* (1862), he presented all the evidence and arguments suggesting that man evolved gradually from lower species, but did not commit himself to this conclusion, which apparently was alien to his sentiments. Darwin was disappointed; but in 1864 Lyell publicly announced that he now did accept Darwin's theory of the modification of species by natural selection.

Lyell was by now universally recognized as one of the great men of his era. He came to America three times to give the Lowell lectures (1841, 1845, 1852); he was knighted (1848) and made a baronet (1864). After 1869, his health began to fail and he gradually became blind; he continued to work, however, until the sudden death of his beloved wife in 1873. He did not recover from the blow, and died himself less than two years later.

LYMAN, BENJAMIN SMITH (*b. Northampton, Mass., 1835; d. Philadelphia, Pa., 1920*), geology.

Was introduced to geology by his uncle, J. P. Lesley. Educated at Harvard, School of Mines at Paris, and Freiberg Mining Academy. Devised method of representing subsurface structure by structural contour lines (*ca.* 1866); did major surveys in Japan.

LYMAN, CHESTER SMITH (*b. Manchester, Conn., 1814; d. New Haven, Conn., 1890*), astronomy, geology.

A graduate of Yale; combined a career as a minister with his interest in science; taught astronomy at Yale (from 1859). Credited as the first to obtain reliable evidence for an atmosphere surrounding Venus.

LYMAN, THEODORE (*b. Boston, Mass., 1874; d. Brookline, Mass., 1954*), physics.

Studied at Harvard (Ph.D., 1900), and briefly at Cavendish Laboratory and Göttingen. Spent entire career at Harvard. Investigated the ultraviolet spectrum, extending its known extreme region. Discovered (1914) the fundamental series of hydrogen.

LYONET, PIERRE (*b. Maastricht, Netherlands, 1706; d. The Hague, Netherlands, 1789*), entomology.

Gave up a Calvinist pastorate to study law (graduated from Leiden, 1831); was also an official codebreaker; believed that nature was a cipher that could be clarified by tracing every detail of its perfect design. Author of *Traité anatomique . . .* (1760) on the goat worm caterpillar and *Recherches . . .* on insects in the vicinity of The Hague.

LYOT, BERNARD (*b. Paris, France, 1897; d. Cairo, Egypt, 1952*), astronomy, optics.

Graduated from École Supérieure d'Électricité (1917). Spent his career at the observatory at Meudon. Studied the polarization of light reflected from the surfaces of the planets; invented the coronograph for observing the sun's corona (1930), and the photoelectric polarimeter.

MAANEN, ADRIAAN VAN (*b. Sneek, Netherlands, 1884; d. Pasadena, Calif., 1946*), astronomy.

From a long line of aristocrats; graduated from the University of Utrecht (Sc.D., 1911); on staff at the Mount Wilson Observatory (from 1912). Made accurate studies of the parallaxes of more than 500 stars and discovered the second known white dwarf (now "van Maanen's star"); obtained influential but inaccurate results on the proper motion of spirals and on the magnetic field of the sun.

MACALLUM, ARCHIBALD BYRON (*b. Belmont, Ontario, Canada, 1858; d. London, Ontario, 1934*), biochemistry, physiology.

Studied at the University of Toronto and Johns Hopkins (Ph.D., 1888); taught at Toronto and McGill University. Remembered for theory that there is a significant relationship between the inorganic composition of vertebrate blood plasma and that of the ancient oceans.

MACAULAY, FRANCIS SOWERBY (*b. Witney, England, 1862; d. Cambridge, England, 1937*), mathematics.

Graduated from St. John's College, Cambridge. A brilliant teacher at St. Paul's School, London (1885–1911); among his pupils were G. N. Watson and J. E. Littlewood. Did major work in algebraic geometry and on the theory of algebraic polynomials and of modular systems.

MACBRIDE, DAVID (*b. Ballymoney, Antrim, Ireland, 1726; d. Dublin, Ireland, 1778*), medicine, chemistry.

Was a successful doctor in Dublin. In *Experimental Essays* (1764) he attempted to apply some of Stephen Hales's ideas on air to medicine. Advocated an infusion of malt to prevent scurvy.

MacBRIDE, ERNEST WILLIAM (*b. Belfast, Ireland, 1866; d. Alton, Hampshire, England, 1940*), embryology.

Graduated from Cambridge (1891); became the first professor of zoology at McGill University. From 1909 to 1934, taught at Imperial College of Science and Technology. Author, *Textbook of Embryology*, Volume I, *Invertebrata* (1914).

McCLUNG, CLARENCE ERWIN (*b. Clayton, Calif., 1870; d. Philadelphia, Pa., 1946*), cytology, zoology.

Studied at the University of Kansas (Ph.D., 1902) and briefly under E. B. Wilson at Columbia University and W. M. Wheeler at the University of Chicago, both of whom were interested in chromosomes. Taught at Kansas until 1912, when he moved to the University of Pennsylvania. Best known for his papers of 1901 and 1902, which suggested that the accessory, or X, chromosome could be a sex determiner. His work, and subsequently that of E. B. Wilson and Nettie M. Stevens, substantiated the concept of the individuality of the chromosome: each chromosome does not bear a full complement of hereditary information but rather the information for one specific set of characteristics.

McCOLL, HUGH (*b. 1837; d. Boulogne-sur-Mer, France, 1909*), mathematical logic.

Did comparative analysis of the logical calculus of propositions and classes which helped to clarify the subject in the hundred-year period between Boole and Whitehead.

McCOLLUM, ELMER VERNER (*b. near Fort Scott, Kan., 1879; d. Baltimore, Md., 1967*), organic chemistry, nutrition.

Studied at the University of Kansas and at Yale (Ph.D., 1906). Employed (1907) by the Wisconsin Agricultural Experiment Station to do chemical analyses on the food and excreta of dairy cattle; instead, established first white rat colony in the U.S. for the same purpose. Discovered vitamins that he at first called "fat-soluble A" and "water-soluble B." Moved (1917) to Johns Hopkins, where he helped in the elucidation of the substance now called vitamin D.

MacCULLAGH, JAMES (*b. near Strabane, County Tyrone, Ireland, 1809; d. Dublin, Ireland, 1847*), physics.

Studied and taught at Trinity College, Dublin. Clarified Fresnel's wave optics in "On the Laws of Crystalline Reflexion and Refraction" (1837); similar conclusions were simultaneously reached by F. E. Neumann. In another major paper on optics (1839), sought to deduce the phenomena from dynamical principles.

MACCULLOCH, JOHN (*b. Guernsey, Channel Islands, 1773; d. Poltair, Cornwall, England, 1835*), geology, chemistry.

Studied medicine at Edinburgh University (M.D., 1793); employed by the Army's Board of Ordnance (until 1826) and then by the Treasury; began career as a chemist but shifted to geology. Author, *A Description of the Western Isles of Scotland* (1819). In 1835, the year of his marriage and his death (in a carriage accident), he completed the first large-scale geological map of Scotland (published, 1836).

MACELLAMA. *See* **Māshāʾallāh.**

MACH, ERNST (*b. Chirlitz-Turas, Moravia [now Chrlice-Tuřany, Czechoslovakia], 1838; d. Vaterstetten, near Haar, Germany, 1916*), physics, physiology, psychology.

Mach was the oldest child of well-educated, idealistic parents, who lived on a farm near Vienna; he did not go to school (except for one year) until he was fourteen; his father was his main teacher, and taught observation as well as academic subjects. Mach attended the University of Vienna (Ph.D., 1860), and taught there until 1864. His first work represented a fairly traditional approach to physics (e.g., experiments to support Doppler's controversial law), and he appeared to accept the prevailing atomic-molecular theory of matter and the kinetic theory of gases. But before moving to the University of Graz (1864), his interest began to shift to the physiology and psychology of sensation and the new discipline of psychophysics. At Graz, he discovered what are now called Mach bands, observed when a spatial distribution of light results in a sharp change of illumination at some point (these were essentially rediscovered in the 1950's). In 1867, he married and became professor of experimental physics at Charles University in Prague; he did his most important work there. In 1887 he published, with P. Salcher, his celebrated paper on supersonics, showing that the angle α, which the shock wave surrounding the

envelope of an advancing gas cone makes with the direction of its motion, is related to the velocity of sound v and the velocity of the projectile ω as $\sin \alpha = v/\omega$ when $\omega > v$. (The ratio ω/v is now termed the "Mach number.") In 1895, Mach became a professor of philosophy at the University of Vienna. In 1897 he suffered a stroke, but recovered and continued to be active until the time of his death.

Mach was best known for his work in the history and philosophy of science. His major writing in this area was *Die Mechanik* (1883), an historical study of the development of the principles of statics and dynamics; the purpose of the study was to consider how we inherit scientific concepts and theories and to examine certain epistemological problems in the philosophy of science. His general objective was to rid science of concepts that have no parallel in our experience. He believed that what we perceive are sensations; the so-called objects of experience (things, bodies, matter, etc.) are thought symbols for combinations of sensations. Science has its origins in the need of an organism to organize the overwhelmingly complex experience of sensations in the most economical way for a behavioral response that favors self-preservation. These views led Mach to reject theories based on the existence of entities, such as atoms, that cannot be defined in terms of elements of sensation. According to what is sometimes called "Mach's criterion," a theory should employ only those propositions from which statements about observable phenomena can be deduced; "proofs" must be tied to experience. This position is related to the skepticism of eighteenth-century empiricism and subjective idealism, and also caused Mach to be identified with the positivists, most famously by Lenin (1909). Mach was convinced that understanding science demands understanding the psychology and physiology of the scientist; sensations can be investigated equally from the point of view of physics, psychology, or physiology; phenomena are a complex of interrelated sensations, embracing both what is sensed and the senser, such that the distinction between them disappears.

Mach's approach influenced younger scientists, including Einstein, who in the development of his gravitational theory was motivated by a desire to accommodate "the Mach principle": a generalization of Mach's claim that the inertia of an isolated body can have no meaning. Mach's claim arose in his discussion of Newton in *Die Mechanik*, a discussion that challenged Newton's views on absolute space, time, and motion. Mach suggested redefining inertia in terms of the body's relationship to all observable matter in the universe at large; the inertia of a system would be thus reduced to a functional relationship between the system and the rest of the universe. In the end, Einstein was not completely successful in giving mathematical expression to the Mach principle, and he rejected the restriction to finite space-time boundary conditions that it implied. Nevertheless, in various interpretations, the principle is still debated.

MACHEBOEUF, MICHEL (*b. Châtel-Guyon, France, 1900; d. Paris, France, 1953*), biochemistry.

Affiliated with the Pasteur Institute, the University of Bordeaux, and the Sorbonne. Discovered the protidolipidic "cenapse" of the blood plasma. Worked on immunochemistry of the tubercle bacillus, and was the first to investigate ultra high pressures on bacteria, bacterial spores, and viruses.

McINTOSH, WILLIAM CARMICHAEL (*b. St. Andrews, Scotland, 1838; d. St. Andrews, 1931*), marine zoology.

Received M.D. from Edinburgh (1860); superintendent at the Perthshire Asylum at Murthly (1863–82); taught natural history at St. Andrews (1882–1918). Wrote *Monograph of the British Marine Annelids* (4 vols., 1873–1923); established the first marine laboratory in Great Britain, the Gatty Laboratory at St. Andrews.

MACLAURIN, COLIN (*b. Kilmodan, Scotland, 1698; d. Edinburgh, Scotland, 1746*), mathematics.

A precocious student at the University of Glasgow (M.A., 1715); appointed professor of mathematics at Aberdeen while still in his teens. Visited London (1719); met Newton and became his staunchest advocate. In *Geometrica Organica* (1720, published with Newton's imprimatur), a discussion of conics and of the higher plane curves, Maclaurin gave proofs of many important theorems; some had been used by Newton (without proof), others Maclaurin had discovered himself. In 1725, with Newton's help, he was appointed professor at Edinburgh. In *Treatise of Fluxions* (1742) he tried to provide a geometrical framework for Newton's doctrine of fluxions; solved a great number of problems in geometry, statics, and theory of attractions (including the attraction of an ellipsoid on an internal point); and gave for the first time the correct theory for distinguishing between maximum and minimum values of a function.

MACLEAN, JOHN (*b. Glasgow, Scotland, 1771; d. Princeton, N.J., 1814*), chemistry.

Raised with his cousin Charles Macintosh (inventor of the waterproof cloth); went to the University of Glasgow at age thirteen. In Paris, was won over to Lavoisier's views. Came to the U.S. (1795) and was first professor of chemistry at Princeton. His *Two Lectures on Combustion* (1797) was important in the overthrow of the phlogiston theory.

MACLEAR, THOMAS (*b. Newton Stewart, Tyrone, Ireland, 1794; d. Mowbray, near Cape Town, South Africa, 1879*), astronomy.

A practicing physician and amateur astronomer; appointed Her Majesty's astronomer at the Cape of Good Hope (1833).

MACLEOD, JOHN JAMES RICKARD (*b. Cluny, near Dunkeld, Perthshire, Scotland, 1876; d. Aberdeen, Scotland, 1935*), physiology.

Studied medicine at Aberdeen (M.B., Ch.B., 1898); taught at London Hospital Medical College, Western Reserve University, Cleveland, and at the University of Toronto. Specialized in carbohydrate metabolism; was in charge of the laboratory at Toronto where insulin was discovered (1921). With F. G. Banting, was awarded Nobel Prize (1923) for insulin discovery.

MACLURE, WILLIAM (*b. Ayr, Scotland, 1763; d. St. Angelo, Mexico, 1840*), geology.

A wealthy businessman and an influential and imaginative amateur geologist; his speculation on the origins of primitive rock, for example, comes close to the present-day concept of granitization. Best known for *Observations on the Geology of the United States* (1817).

MacMAHON, PERCY ALEXANDER (*b. Malta, 1854; d. Bognor Regis, England, 1929*), mathematics.

An Army officer, civil servant, and master of classical algebra. Did major work on invariants; wrote an outstanding treatise on combinatorial analysis (1915–16).

MACMILLAN, WILLIAM DUNCAN (*b. La Crosse, Wis., 1871; d. St. Paul, Minn., 1948*), astronomy, mathematics.

Educated at Chicago (Ph.D., 1908), where he spent most of his working life. Interested in cosmogony; proposed a steady-state theory. Author, *Theoretical Mechanics* (1927–36). Contributed to potential theory, theory of automorphic functions, and theory of differential equations.

MACQUER, PIERRE JOSEPH (*b. Paris, France, 1718; d. Paris, 1784*), chemistry.

Graduated from the Paris Faculty of Medicine (1742); practiced briefly; studied chemistry under G. F. Rouelle. Discovered the previously unknown salt potassium arsenate and a new method of dyeing with Prussian blue. Wrote the conservative but influential texts *Élémens de chymie théorique* (1749) and *Élémens de chymie pratique* (1751). Taught at the Paris Faculty of Medicine (1752–73) and at the Jardin du Roi (1770–83). His principal book, *Dictionnaire de chymie* (1766), was a great success, although also conservative.

MACROBIUS, AMBROSIUS THEODOSIUS (*b. North Africa [?], fl. early fifth century* A.D.), Neoplatonic commentary.

In the smaller of his two extant works, *Commentary on the Dream of Scipio*, Macrobius created the most satisfactory and widely read Latin compendium on Neoplatonism that existed during the Middle Ages. His lengthy excursuses on Pythagorean number lore, cosmography, world geography, and the harmony of the spheres established him as one of the leading popularizers of science in the Latin West.

MÄDLER, JOHANN HEINRICH (*b. Berlin, Germany, 1794; d. Hannover, Germany, 1874*), astronomy.

Mädler, a seminary teacher in Berlin, became astronomer in a private observatory and after 1836 at the Berlin observatory. From 1840 to 1865 he was observer at Dorpat, a professor of astronomy, and the author of numerous works. They include *Populäre Astronomie* (1841), which was widely read, and *Geschichte der Himmelskunde* (1873). Both works contained valuable historical data.

MAESTLIN, MICHAEL. *See* **Mästlin, Michael.**

MAGALHÃES. *See* **Magellan.**

MAGALOTTI, LORENZO (*b. Rome, Italy, 1637; d. Florence, Italy, 1712*), dissemination of science.

Studied at Pisa with Viviani; traveled as a diplomat for the Medicis. Magalotti was secretary of the Florentine

Accademia del Cimento and reported on its activities in the *Saggi di naturali esperienze fatte nell' Accademia del Cimento* (1667). It attracted widespread interest and Magalotti acquired considerable fame. His descriptions of experiments in physics are written in colorful, almost dramatic, language. He was also interested in linguistics.

MAGATI, CESARE (*b. Scandiano, Modena, Italy, 1579; d. Bologna, Italy, 1647*), surgery.

Magati obtained a doctorate in philosophy and medicine at Bologna in 1597. He was one of the forerunners of modern surgery, being among the first to prescribe a rational treatment of wounds. His major work was *De rara medicatione vulnerum* (1616), in which he advocated that wounds be lightly dressed and the dressings left in place for five to six days, thereby permitting nature to do its work in the best way.

MAGELLAN, JEAN-HYACINTHE (Magalhães, João Jacinto de) (*b. Aveiro, Portugal, 1722; d. Islington, England, 1790*), chemistry, physics, scientific instrumentation.

An Augustinian monk, Magellan became a recognized master of astronomy. In about 1755 he left his order and, after traveling about Europe, settled in England and eventually converted to Protestantism. Not an original scientist himself, Magellan is known chiefly for disseminating new scientific information. He wrote more about scientific instruments than about any other subject. He also translated into English several works on mineralogy.

MAGENDIE, FRANÇOIS (*b. Bordeaux, France, 1783; d. Sannois, Seine-et-Oise, France, 1855*), physiology, medicine.

After an apprenticeship to a surgeon, Magendie entered the Hôpital Saint-Louis in 1803 as a medical student. While still a student, he gave lectures on anatomy and physiology at the École de Médecine, and received his degree in 1808. In 1811 he became anatomy demonstrator at the Faculté de Médecine, but in 1813 he resigned and established his private course in physiology. Those courses, featuring experiments on living animals, aroused the curiosity of the medical world and attracted students from all over Europe. These foreign physiologists carried the seeds of the new experimental physiology to neighboring schools where it developed rapidly. During that period, Magendie wrote *Précis élémentaire de physiologie* (2 vols, 1816–17); quickly translated into other languages, it exerted a very profound influence on physiologists and biologists.

Magendie made discoveries in almost all fields of physiology, including the workings of the stomach, liver, nervous system, and cerebrospinal fluid. His name is associated with the Bell-Magendie law (the anterior spinal roots are motor, the posterior are sensory). After 1830 Magendie was connected with the Collège de France, where his interest turned to the study of cholera and yellow fever. After 1838 he concentrated on the nervous system and on nutrition.

MAGGI, BARTOLOMEO (*b. Bologna, Italy, 1477; d. 1552*), surgery.

Maggi was professor of surgery at the University of Bologna and the private physician of Pope Julius II. He was among the first to teach a rational method of treating

gunshot wounds, thus earning a place in medical history. His theories were published posthumously in 1552 in *De vulnerum bombardorum et sclopetorum, globulis illatorum, et de eorum symptomatum curatione, tractatus.*

MAGINI, GIOVANNI ANTONIO (*b. Padua, Italy, 1555; d. Bologna, Italy, 1617*), mathematics, astronomy, geography, cartography.

Magini graduated in philosophy from the University of Bologna in 1579, and after 1588 taught mathematics and astronomy there. In astronomy, he was a conservative who rejected Copernican theory and he was the enemy of his contemporary Galileo. In 1609 he brought out extremely accurate trigonometric tables. Today, however, he is chiefly remembered as a geographer and cartographer. He did a commentary on Ptolemaic geography and produced an ambitious atlas of Italy, with maps of each region and exact nomenclature.

MAGIOTTI, RAFFAELLO (*b. Montevarchi, Italy, 1597; d. Rome, Italy, 1656*), physics, hydrostatics, hydrodynamics.

Maggiotti was a student of Galileo in Florence. He entered the priesthood and became well known as a scholar in mathematics, law, medicine, theology, and letters. After 1636 he held a position in the Vatican library. Magiotti encouraged experiments on siphons and the vacuum. In hydrodynamics, he aided Torricelli in formulating his theory of flow (1643). In his book *Renitenza dell' Acqua alla Compressione* (1648), he announced the near incompressibility of water at a constant temperature.

MAGNENUS, JOHANN CHRYSOSTOM (*b. Luxeuil–les–bains, France, ca. 1590; d. 1679* [?]), natural philosophy, medicine.

Magnenus received an M.D. from the University of Dôle and established himself in Italy, where he taught medicine and philosophy at the University of Pavia. His importance derives from his attempt to reinstate the Democritean theory of atomism as a respectable part of seventeenth-century natural philosophy. His major work was *Democritus reviviscens* (1646).

MAGNI, VALERIANO (*b. Milan, Italy, 1586; d. Salzburg, Austria, 1661*), physics.

A member of the Capuchin order, Magni gained a reputation in Prague, Linz, and Vienna as a preacher and teacher. In 1613 he became professor of philosophy at Vienna. He became a power within the Catholic Church, but his zealous opposition to the Jesuits led to his arrest for heresy in 1655. He was released, however, and never tried. In philosophy, Magni was an anti-Aristotelian and an admirer of Galileo and Descartes. In physics, he demonstrated the existence of a vacuum, although at the time he was accused of plagiarizing the experiments of others.

MAGNITSKY, LEONTY FILIPPOVICH (*b. Ostashkov, Russia, 1669; d. Moscow, Russia, 1739*), mathematics.

In 1702 Peter the Great brought Magnitsky to the newly formed Navigation School in Moscow. He taught there the rest of his life and was its director after 1715. His *Arithmetic* (1703) was the first guide to mathematics published in Russia and was the basic textbook for the next fifty years; as such, it had an enormous influence on Russian mathematics.

MAGNOL, PIERRE (*b. Montpellier, France, 1638; d. Montpellier, 1715*), botany.

Magnol received an M.D. in 1659 and began a serious study of plants. His reputation as a botanist spread rapidly, and he was soon in correspondence with all the great botanists of Europe. In 1676 he published *Botanicum Monspeliense*, which described 1,354 species. An innovator in classification, Magnol was the first to use the term "family" in the sense of a natural group.

MAGNUS, HEINRICH GUSTAV (*b. Berlin, Germany, 1802; d. Berlin, 1870*), physics, chemistry.

Magnus entered the University of Berlin in 1822 and published his first paper (on pyrophoric iron) in 1825. After receiving his doctorate in 1827, he studied under Berzelius in Stockholm, thereby beginning a lifelong friendship and professional association. Magnus' research interests were varied; among the most important are his contributions to the theory of heat, thermal expansion of gases, boiling of liquids, vapor formation, electrolysis (Magnus' rule), induced and thermoelectric currents, optics, hydrodynamics, magnetism, and mechanics. He uncovered much valuable physical and chemical information—notably the Magnus effect.

MAGNUS, OLAUS. *See* **Olaus Magnus.**

MAGNUS, RUDOLF (*b. Brunswick, Germany, 1873; d. Pontresina, Switzerland, 1927*), neurophysiology, pharmacology.

Magnus received an M.D. from Heidelberg in 1898 and began his career in pharmacology. He remained at Heidelberg until 1908, when he became professor at the University of Utrecht. He also worked closely with British research laboratories. The major corpus of his work deals with the reflex control of postures. His *Die Körperstellung* (1924) is a classic work on reflex physiology, and present concepts of the body's equilibratory system are principally an outgrowth of Magnus' work.

MAGNUS, VALERIANUS. *See* **Magni, Valeriano.**

MAHĀDEVA (*fl. western India, 1316*), astronomy.

Mahādeva wrote a lengthy set of astronomical tables (called the *Mahādevi*). They were extremely popular; more than 100 manuscripts of them have been identified.

AL-MĀHĀNĪ, ABŪ ʿABD ALLĀH MUḤAMMAD IBN ʿĪSĀ (*b. Mahān, Kerman, Persia; fl. Baghdad, ca. 860; d. ca. 880*), mathematics, astronomy.

Using an astrolabe, al-Māhānī calculated three lunar eclipses within a half hour's accuracy. His main contributions, however, were in mathematics. He was the first to attempt an algebraic solution of the Archimedean problem of dividing a sphere by a plane. He wrote commentaries on Euclid, which were influential among the Arabic mathematicians.

MAHĀVĪRA (*fl. Mysore, India, ninth century*), mathematics.

Little is known of Mahāvīra, except that he was a Jain. His only work was a major treatise on mathematics, *Gaṇitasārasaṅgraha*.

MAHENDRA SŪRI (*fl. western India, 1370*), astronomy.

A Jain, Mahendra Sūri wrote the first Sanskrit treatise on the astrolabe, the *Yantrarāja* (1370).

MAḤMŪD IBN MASʿŪD AL-SHĪRĀZĪ. *See* **Quṭb al-Dīn al-Shīrāzī.**

MAIER, MICHAEL (*b. Rensburg, Holstein, Germany, ca. 1568; d. Magdeburg, Germany, 1662*), alchemy.

Maier studied at several universities before receiving an M.D. at the University of Basel. Maier traveled widely, receiving the patronage of numerous rulers and nobles; among these was Emperor Rudolf II, who named him count palatine. He was an ardent alchemist, a follower of Paracelsus and neo-Hermetic ideas. He was a defender of the Rosicrucians and an implacable enemy of the Roman Catholic Church. His works were highly prized by the alchemists, especially *Symbola aureae mensae* (1617), *Fama fraternitatis* (1616), and *Viatorum . . . de montibus planetarium* (1618).

MAIGE, ALBERT (*b. Auxonne, France, 1872; d. Lille, France, 1943*), botany.

Maige taught botany at Algiers (1900–10), Poitiers (1911–19), and Lille (1920–43). In *Flore forestière de l'Algérie* (1914), he dealt with phytogeography, silviculture, and the natural history of the woody plants of Algeria. The work also included a key to identifying specimens. Later he studied the potato blight and "yellow spot," a disease of the cork oak. He also conducted research in cytophysiology.

MAIGNAN, EMANUEL (*b. Toulouse, France, 1601 [?]; d. Toulouse, 1676*), physics.

A member of the order of Minims, Maignan taught at their convent in Rome (1636–50). Originally an Aristotelian (and honored in his day as a philosopher), he turned to mathematics and physics. His experiments toward creating a void space in nature were valuable to later experimenters of the vacuum, such as Torricelli. His *Cursus philosophicus* (1653) contains a full account of these experiments. He also did work on optics, and his *Perspectiva horaria* (1648) is an exhaustive treatise on the sundial.

MAILLET, BENOÎT DE (*b. St. Mihiel, France, 1656; d. Marseilles, France, 1738*), geology, oceanography, cosmogony.

Born into a noble family, Maillet received a classical education and made a career in the diplomatic service. His major work was (in its English title) *Telliamed: Or Discourses Between an Indian Philosopher and a French Missionary on the Diminution of the Sea* (1748). An important historical and sociological work, it presents an ultraneptunian theory of the earth, based largely on Maillet's observations during extensive travels throughout Egypt and other Mediterranean countries. His unorthodox and highly materialistic system did not admit God as an omnificent ruler, postulating instead an eternal universe undergoing natural changes at random. Everything was explained by the action of a retreating sea, a concept that was of major importance to eighteenth-century geology.

MAIMONIDES, RABBI MOSES BEN MAIMON, also known by the acronym **RaMBaM** (*b. Córdoba, Spain,*

1135 or 1138; d. Cairo [or Fuṣṭāṭ], Egypt, 1204), medicine, codification of the Jewish law, philosophy.

Maimonides was the foremost representative of the school known as Jewish Aristotelianism, and one of the towering figures in the history of Jewish philosophy and theology. His family fled Córdoba while he was a youth (after its invasion by the Almohads). He eventually (1166) settled in Cairo, where he became court physician and head of the Jewish community. He spent the rest of his life there.

Maimonides' work covers a wide range. His *Mishnah Torah* (written in Hebrew; all his other works were in Arabic) is a codification of the Talmudic law; *Maqāla fī ṣināʿat al-manṭiq* is a treatise on logic; and *The Guide of the Perplexed* deals unsystematically with physics and metaphysics and is a popular guide to the lay person. He also wrote numerous medical treatises.

Maimonides' emphasis on the limitation of human science is perhaps his most significant contribution to general philosophical thought. He accepted Aristotle's physics insofar as it is concerned with the sublunar world; in this connection, he apparently preferred a mechanistic explanation. He believed that man is unable to give a satisfactory scientific account of the world of the spheres, and he rejected both Aristotle and the Muslim philosophers and astronomers. Many later scholars were profoundly influenced by Maimonides. They include Spinoza, Leibniz, Solomon Maimon, Thomas Aquinas, and Jean Bodin.

MAIOR (or **MAIORIS**), **JOHN** (frequently cited as **Jean Mair**) (*b. Gleghornie, near Haddington, Scotland, 1469; d. St. Andrews, Scotland, 1550*), logic, mathematics, natural philosophy, history.

Maior was educated at Cambridge and the University of Paris; he received a doctorate in theology in 1506. He taught philosophy and theology variously at the universities of Glasgow, St. Andrews, and Paris. His importance in the physical sciences derives from his applications of logic and mathematics to the problems of natural philosophy. He was the conduit through which the Mertonians (Bradwardine, Heytesbury, Swineshead, *et al.*) exerted an influence on European scientists (e.g., the young Galileo). Among Maior's works are *Historiae Majoris Britanniae, tam Angliae quam Scotiae* (1521) and *Propositum de infinito* (1506).

MAIR, SIMON. *See* **Mayr, Simon.**

MAIRAN, JEAN JACQUES D'ORTOUS DE (*b. Béziers, France, 1678; d. Paris, France, 1771*), physics.

Mairan studied the classics at Toulouse and physics and mathematics at Paris. He was concerned with a wide variety of subjects, including heat, light, sound, motion, the shape of the earth, and the aurora. Although he remained basically a Cartesian, he incorporated some Newtonian ideas in his theories.

MAIRE, RENÉ-CHARLES-JOSEPH-ERNEST (*b. Lons-le-Saunier, France, 1878; d. Algiers, Algeria, 1949*), botany.

Maire studied at the Faculties of Science and Medicine at Nancy and by age twenty he had published about twenty papers. He was chiefly interested in the phanerogams and the fungi. His doctoral dissertation on the Basidiomycetes is still a basic work. Much of his field work

was done in North Africa, where he was chairman of botany at the French University of North Africa from 1911.

IBN MĀJID, SHIHĀB AL-DĪN AḤMAD IBN MĀJID (*fl. Najd, Saudi Arabia, fifteenth century* A.D.), navigation.

Of the Arab navigators of the Middle Ages, none surpassed Ibn Mājid in the intimate knowledge of both the Red Sea and the Indian Ocean. He was well versed in the works of both Muslim and Greek geographers, astronomers, and navigators and he himself wrote thirty-eight works, twenty-five of which are extant. His *Kitāb al-Fawāʾid* (1490) was the most valuable to navigators; it is a synthesis of the nautical sciences of the Middle Ages. Ibn Mājid did not actually invent the marine compass (an accomplishment once attributed to him) but he did make important improvements on it.

MAJORANA, ETTORE (*b. Catania, Sicily, 1906; d. at sea, near Naples, 1938*), physics.

Majorana studied physics under Fermi at the University of Rome, receiving his doctorate in 1929. After studying at Leipzig, Copenhagen, and the Istituto di Fisica at Rome, he was named professor of physics at the University of Naples in 1937. Long plagued by bad health, he committed suicide the following year. He wrote a total of nine papers. Six were on problems of atomic and molecular physics, and three on nuclear physics or the properties of elementary particles.

AL-MAJRĪṬĪ, ABUʾL-QĀSIM MASLAMA IBN AḤ-MAD AL-FARAḌĪ (*b. Madrid, Spain, second half of the tenth century; d. Córdoba, Spain, ca. 1007*), astronomy.

Little is know of al-Majrīṭī's life; he was probably educated by the hellenizing scholars of Córdoba, and he was engaged in making astronomical observations in about A.D. 979. He revised the astronomical tables of al-Khwārizmī. His disciples spread his influence throughout Muslim Spain, and some of their works are attributed to al-Majrīṭī himself. Among his works that are considered genuine are the *Commercial Arithmetic* and *Treatise on the Astrolabe.*

AL-MAJŪSĪ, ABUʾL-ḤASAN ʿALĪ IBN ʿABBĀS (latinized as **Haly Abbas**) (*b. al-Ahwāz-Khūzistān, near Shiraz, Persia, first quarter of the tenth century; d. Shiraz,* A.D. *994*), medicine, pharmacology, natural science.

His only work, *Kāmil al-Ṣināʿah al-Ṭibbiyyah*, consists of twenty treatises on the theory and practice of medicine. Its detailed coverage of medical matters won it a high prestige in Islam. It was translated into Latin and enjoyed wide acceptance in East and West for five centuries.

MAKARANDA (*fl. Benares, India, 1478*), astronomy.

Makaranda wrote an extremely influential set of tables, entitled *Makaranda*. These tables are calendaric, planetary, and for eclipses. There are almost 100 manuscripts of them still extant.

MAKAROV, STEPAN OSIPOVICH (*b. Nikolayev, Russia, 1849; d. aboard the battleship Petropavlovsk, Port Arthur, Russia, 1904*), oceanography.

Makarov graduated from naval school in 1865, entered the navy, and commanded a steamer during the Russo-Turkish War. He conceived the idea of opening up navigation in the northern waters with the aid of icebreakers and supervised the construction of the icebreaker *Ermak* (1899–1901). In his main oceanographic work, *Vityaz i Tikhy okean* ("The *Vityaz* and the Pacific Ocean," 1894), he explained the hydrological observations carried out on a round-the-world voyage. In it Makarov compiled the first water temperature tables for the North Pacific Ocean.

MAKSIMOV, NIKOLAY ALEKSANDROVICH (*b. St. Petersburg [now Leningrad], Russia, 1880; d. Moscow, U.S.S.R., 1952*), plant physiology.

Maksimov studied physics and mathematics at St. Petersburg University (graduated 1902; master's, 1913); after working in Java and Tiflis he returned to Leningrad in 1921 and worked in the main botanical gardens of the U.S.S.R.; he later worked in Saratov (1933–39) and at the Timiryazev Agricultural Academy in Moscow (1943–51). He was one of the most important pioneers in the study of the ecological physiology of plants. His basic research was connected with the study of frost resistance and drought resistance.

MAKSUTOV, DMITRY DMITRIEVICH (*b. Odessa, Russia, 1896; d. Pulkovo [near Leningrad], U.S.S.R., 1964*), optics, astronomy.

Maksutov was a child prodigy in astronomy. He was elected to the Russian Astronomical Society at age fifteen, and while in the cadet corps in Odessa, he directed the astronomical observatory and conducted classes in cosmography. He was variously connected with the Leningrad Optical Institute and the Pulkovo Observatory; among the instruments he prepared were the 381-mm. Schmidt telescope for the Engelhardt observatory, the 820-mm. Pulkovo refractor, and—interested in replacing glass for the reflector with metal—a number of silvered mirrors, the largest of which was a 720-mm. parabolic mirror of high optical efficiency.

MALEBRANCHE, NICOLAS (*b. Paris, France, 1638; d. Paris, 1715*), philosophy, science.

Malebranche received an M.A. from the University of Paris in 1656. He studied theology at the Sorbonne, and in 1664 he was ordained a priest. The stimulus for his intellectual development came from Descartes; he assimilated the whole of the Cartesian heritage and attempted to elaborate, on theological foundations, an original, rationalist-oriented speculative system.

Malebranche's major work, begun in 1668, was *De la recherche de la vérité*. It ran to several volumes and was revised constantly. Like Descartes, Malebranche rejected sensible qualities and held that things are to be judged solely by the ideas that represent them to us according to their intelligible essence. God was seen as the sole efficient cause and natural causes as only "occasional" causes—hence occasionalism, as Malebranche's system is called. Among his other works are *Conversations chrétiennes* (1677) and *Traité de la nature et de la grâce* (1680). The latter was aimed at refuting Jansenist ideas concerning grace and predestination. It ran afoul of Rome, however, and was placed on the Index in 1690.

Malebranche's influence in mathematics was chiefly through his collaboration with younger mathematicians. Himself busy with his philosophical writings, he hoped to lead these mathematicians toward a mathematical synthesis of Cartesianism that would match his own philosophical synthesis. His first protégé was Jean Prestet, who published *Élémens de mathématiques* in 1675. It aroused the interest of the mathematical world, including Leibniz. Prestet died in 1691, and Malebranche turned to the Marquis de L'Hospital to continue the search for a new mathematics; by 1696, however, the latter had asserted his independence, and a work of his published that year showed little influence of Malebranche. In 1698 Malebranche turned to Charles-René Reyneau, who in 1708 produced *Analyse démontrée*. It was the first textbook of the new mathematics and justified Malebranche's long search.

At the age of sixty, Malebranche turned seriously to the study of science. He improved on Mariotte's collision theory, studied luminous phenomena, and provided an account of universal gravitation, of planetary motion, and of gravity. He worked to fashion a suitable basis for the union of the rational and the experimental and thereby made a genuine contribution to the autonomy of science. His activity was always inspired by his Christian philosophy, however, and the final separation of science from philosophy and theology would be completed by later scientists.

MALESHERBES, CHRÉTIEN-GUILLAUME DE LAMOIGNON DE (*b. Paris, France, 1721; d. Paris, 1794*), agronomy, botany.

Malesherbes was a member of the nobility and a magistrate by profession. He was one of the most enlightened officials of the *ancien régime*, and in 1792 he considered it his duty to undertake the defense of Louis XVI. Subsequently accused of "acts of treason," he was tried by the Revolutionary Tribunal and guillotined.

Malesherbes studied botany with Bernard de Jussieu and chemistry with G.-F. Rouelle, and maintained a lifelong interest in natural history. He was concerned with the improvement of herds of livestock, the cultivation of wastes, and the naturalization in France of "exotic" plants and trees. He maintained a wide correspondence with botanists, and his correspondents included Benjamin Franklin and Thomas Jefferson. He arranged to have shipments of North American seeds and seedlings sent to France for possible naturalization. Although he considered himself an amateur whose role it was to encourage the work of professional scientists, those scientists disagreed and looked upon him as their colleague.

MALFATTI, GIAN FRANCESCO (*b. Ala, Trento, Italy, 1731; d. Ferrara, Italy, 1807*), mathematics.

Malfatti was educated at Bologna, then founded a school of mathematics in Ferrara. In 1771 he was appointed professor of mathematics at the new University of Ferrara. He became famous for a paper published in 1770 in which he constructed what became known as the Malfatti resolvent. In 1802 he gave the first, brilliant solution of the problem that bears his name, which was the restatement of a problem that had long perplexed mathematicians: "Describe in a triangle three circumferences that are mutually tangent, each of which touches two sides of the triangle."

IBN MALKĀ. *See* **Abu'l-Barakāt.**

MALL, FRANKLIN PAINE (*b. Belle Plaine, Iowa, 1862; d. Baltimore, Md., 1917*), anatomy, embryology, physiology.

Mall received an M.D. from the University of Michigan in 1883 and continued his studies at Heidelberg and Leipzig, where he was a student of His. In 1893 he settled at Johns Hopkins University at its new school of medicine. His reputation is based chiefly on his accomplishments in embryological research, and he made valuable studies of the development of the intestinal canal, the body cavities, and the abdominal walls. With Franz Keibel he edited the *Handbook of Human Embryology* (2 vols., 1910–12), which was written by American and German experts. It has not yet been superseded.

Mall was an influential medical educationist, being the chief proponent of the so-called concentration system. Under that system, medical students concentrated on only one or two subjects at a time. The system, begun at Johns Hopkins, was generally adopted by American medical schools. He was also a proponent of full-time professors of medicine as opposed to private practitioners who only devoted a portion of their time to teaching.

MALLARD, (FRANÇOIS) ERNEST (*b. Châteauneuf-sur-Cher, France, 1833; d. Paris, France, 1894*), mineralogy, mining engineering.

Mallard graduated in 1853 from the École des Mines. He worked as a geologist for the Corps des Mines and taught mineralogy at the École des Mineurs at Saint-Étienne and in 1872 filled the chair of mineralogy at the École des Mines. In 1879 he published *Traité de cristallographie géométrique et physique,* an important work, which his colleagues described as being responsible for elevating crystallography to the rank of a rational science.

MALLET, ROBERT (*b. Dublin, Ireland, 1810; d. London, England, 1881*), technology, seismology.

Mallet received a B.A. from Trinity College, Dublin, in 1830. He joined his father's copper and brass foundry and built it into one of the most important engineering works in Ireland. He himself became an inventive designer-engineer and versatile researcher. His multifarious engineering projects included ordnance, hoisting and moving apparatuses, printing plants, bridges, ventilators and heaters, lighthouses, and coal mines. In research, Mallet did work on corrosion, the science of materials, and, especially, on earthquakes. He coined the word "seismology," and made an experimental seismograph with features of which Palmieri made use. In 1846 he produced *On the Dynamics of Earthquakes.*

MALOUIN, PAUL-JACQUES (*b. Caen, France, 1701; d. Versailles, France, 1778*), medicine, chemistry.

Malouin studied first law and then medicine in Paris. He established a successful practice and from 1767 to 1775 was professor of medicine at the Collège Royal. He also maintained an interest in chemistry and contributed to Diderot's *Encyclopédie.* In a practical vein, he developed a more efficient method of grinding wheat and mixing flour.

MALPIGHI, MARCELLO (*b. Crevalcore, Bologna, Italy, baptized 1628; d. Rome, Italy, 1694*), medicine, microscopic and comparative anatomy, embryology.

Malpighi received an M.D. and Ph.D. from Bologna in 1653. Most of his career was spent at Bologna, but he also taught at Pisa and Messina. In 1691 he went to Rome as personal physician to Pope Innocent XII. In his major work, *De pulmonibus observationes anatomicae* (1661), Malpighi demonstrated his mastery of microscopic technique. He observed the movement of the blood through the capillaries, and described the structure of the lungs. In *De lingua* (1665) he described the structure of the various layers of the tongue, and in *De cerebro* (1665) and *De cerebro cortice* (1666) he constructed a mechanism to encompass the entire neural course from the cortex of the brain to the nerve endings.

In the field of embryology, Malpighi studied the three stages of the silkworm and brought a fine structural content to embryology and used the morphology of lower forms of life to clarify more highly developed ones. His embryological writings include *De formatione pulli in ovo* (1673) and *De bombyce* (1669).

MALTHUS, THOMAS ROBERT (*b. near Guildford, Surrey, England, 1766; d. near Bath, England, 1834*), political economy.

Malthus graduated from Jesus College, Cambridge, in 1788 with a degree in mathematics. He was ordained and given a curacy in Surrey. From 1803 until his death he held a sinecure in Lincolnshire. In 1805 he also became professor of history and political economy at the college newly formed at Hertford (later moved to Haileybury) by the East India Company. Together these positions gave him the security and income that allowed him to devote himself to writing and lecturing.

Malthus is famous for his pessimistic theory that population, when unchecked, increases in a geometric ratio while food production increases only in arithmetical ratio, the result being eventual famine. This theory was propounded in *Essay on the Principle of Population* (1798; rev. ed., 1803). His work had an enormous influence in the social sciences, but in the history of science it is important chiefly because of its influence on Charles Darwin. Malthus' essay was a crucial contribution to Darwin's thinking about natural selection. In the *Origin of Species* he wrote that the struggle for existence "is the doctrine of Malthus applied with manifold force to the whole animal and vegetable kingdoms." Today, modern methods of food production have rendered some of Malthus' pessimism inapplicable in the more developed nations, but his theory still applies in much of the Third World.

MALTSEV (or **Malcev**), **ANATOLY IVANOVICH** (*b. Misheronsky, near Moscow, Russia, 1909; d. Novosibirsk, U.S.S.R., 1967*), mathematics.

Maltsev received an M.S. in 1937 and a D.S. in 1941 from the University of Moscow and became professor of mathematics there in 1944. He also taught at various other Soviet institutions of higher learning. Maltsev's most important work was in algebra and mathematical logic. In algebra, he concentrated on the theory of Lie groups. In the last ten years of his life he obtained important results in the synthesis of algebra and mathematical logic, as is evidenced in his posthumous work *Algebraicheskie sistemy* ("Algebraic Systems," 1970).

MALUS, ÉTIENNE LOUIS (*b. Paris, France, 1775; d. Paris, 1812*), optics.

After studying (1794–96) at the École Polytechnique, Malus served in Napoleon's army in Egypt and Syria in the engineering corps. Upon his return to France, he became immersed in scientific circles. His first paper, "Traité d'optique," was published in 1807. In it he considered the phenomenon of double refraction and posited what became known as the Malus theorem. Although he died at an early age, he greatly influenced the science of optics in the early nineteenth century.

MANARDO, GIOVANNI (*b. Ferrara, Italy, 1462; d. Ferrara, 1536*), medicine, botany.

Manardo received his doctorate in arts and medicine from the University of Ferrara in 1482. He spent most of his life at Ferrara, eventually becoming professor of medicine and personal physician to the duke of Ferrara. He also traveled and taught widely in Europe and was for a while royal physician to two rulers of Hungary (Ladislaus Jagellon and Louis II). Manardo brought to his science new methods of interpretation, analysis, and classification; he divided diseases into groups, according to their natures and cures. He established syphilis as a specific venereal disease, and he made a distinction between cataracts and glaucoma. His major work was *Epistolae medicinales* (20 books, 1521–40).

MANASSE(H). *See* **Māshāʾallāh.**

MANDELSHTAM, LEONID ISAAKOVICH (*b. Mogilev, Russia, 1879; d. Moscow, U.S.S.R., 1944*), physics.

Mandelshtam studied at Novorossysk University in Odessa and at Strasbourg University, from which he received a Ph.D. in 1902. He taught at various Russian institutions and eventually (1925) settled at Moscow State University. There he began his long collaboration with G.S. Landsberg. Together they discovered combination scattering (1928), which consists of a regular variation in the frequency of light scattering in crystals. With Papaleksi, he invented the radio-interference method of precise measurement (radiogeodesy). His scientific research centered fundamentally on optics and radio physics.

MANFREDI, EUSTACHIO (*b. Bologna, Italy, 1674; d. Bologna, 1739*), astronomy, hydraulics.

Educated by the Jesuits, Manfredi took a law degree in 1692 but never practiced. He was also a well-known poet. He studied mathematics and hydraulics under Domenico Guglielmini and was self-taught in astronomy. In Bologna, he founded (1690) what later became the Academy of Sciences and also taught mathematics. In 1711 he was named astronomer of the Institute of Sciences. His work was concerned with ephemerides, and observations and descriptions of solar and lunar eclipses, comets, transits of Mercury, and an aurora borealis.

MANGIN, LOUIS ALEXANDRE (*b. Paris, France, 1852; d. Grignon, France, 1937*), botany.

Mangin may be considered one of the founders of phytopathology. He published studies on mycorrhiza of fruit trees, on wheat foot-rot, and on vine diseases. From 1906 to 1932 he was professor of cryptogamy at the Muséum National d'Histoire Naturelle in Paris, and was its director after 1920. He pioneered in the use of color reactives for microscopic investigation.

MANILIUS, MARCUS (*fl. Rome, beginning of the first century* A.D.), astrology.

Manilius is known to us only through an incomplete Latin poem on astrology, *Astronomicôn libri V*. It is important chiefly because of its antiquity; it is our oldest connected treatise on astrology.

MANNHEIM, VICTOR MAYER AMÉDÉE (*b. Paris, France, 1831; d. Paris, 1906*), geometry.

Mannheim was educated and taught at the École Polytechnique. He worked in many branches of geometry, with his primary interest in projective geometry. He also made significant contributions to the theory of surfaces.

MANSION, PAUL (*b. Marchin, near Huy, Belgium, 1844; d. Ghent, Belgium, 1919*), mathematics, history and philosophy of science.

Mansion was educated at the University of Ghent and taught there. He was a founder (1874) of *Nouvelle correspondance mathématique,* which later became *Mathesis* (1881).

MANSON, PATRICK (*b. Old Meldrum, Aberdeen, Scotland, 1844; d. London, England, 1922*), tropical medicine.

Manson received an M.D. from Aberdeen Medical School in 1866. He became a medical officer on Formosa and later on the China mainland, at Amoy. He did important work on elephantiasis and established *Filaria sanguinis hominis* (F.S.H.) as the cause. He also determined the role of the mosquito in "nursing" F.S.H. and spreading disease. In 1890 Manson set up practice in London and carried out prolonged observations on malaria and posited the role of the mosquito in transmitting that disease (1894). He worked closely with Ronald Ross, who carried out the crucial experiments in India. He was the principal founder of the London School of Tropical Medicine. His major work was *Tropical Diseases. A Manual of the Diseases of Warm Climates* (1898), which is still a classic textbook.

MANṢŪR IBN ʿALĪ IBN ʿIRĀQ, ABŪ NAṢR (*fl. Khwarizm [now Kara-Kalpakskaya, A.S.S.R.]; d. Ghazna [?] [now Ghazni, Afghanistan], ca. 1036*), mathematics, astronomy.

Abū Naṣr's fame is due in large part to his collaboration with al-Bīrūnī; it began some time before the year 1000, at which time al-Bīrūnī described Abū Naṣr as "my master." The tendency of al-Bīrūnī to credit the older man with all their joint work makes it impossible today to sort out all those works actually written by Abū Naṣr. Their collaboration included a method for determining the position, ortive amplitude, and maximum declination of the sun. In trigonometry, Abū Naṣr was one of three mathematicians (the others being Abu'l Wafāʾ and Abū Maḥmūd al-Khujandī) to whom the discovery of the sine law was attributed. Of the twenty-two works that are known to be by Abū Naṣr, seventeen are extant.

MANTEGAZZA, PAOLO (*b. Monza, Italy, 1831; d. San Terenzo di Lerici, Italy, 1910*), medicine, anthropology.

Mantegazza attended the universities of Pisa and Pavia, receiving an M.D. from the latter in 1853. In 1860 he assumed the chair of general pathology at Pavia. In 1870 he became the first professor of anthropology in Italy at the University of Florence, where he founded an important museum of anthropology. In medicine, he did research on the physiology of reproduction, opotherapy, and endocrinology. He speculated on the feasibility of artificial insemination, and showed for the first time that bacteria reproduce by spores. In addition to his scientific writings he was a great popularizer, and he wrote important works on hygiene and sex education. He was also a novelist.

MANTELL, GIDEON ALGERNON (*b. Lewes, Sussex, England, 1790; d. London, England, 1852*), geology.

Educated as a surgeon, Mantell's prime interest was always geology. He assembled an important collection of fossils, which eventually was bought by the British Museum. His most important work was *The Fossils of the South Downs* (1822). He is best known for his discovery of the first dinosaur ever to be described properly.

AL-MAQDISĪ (or **Muqaddasī**), **SHAMS AL-DĪN ABŪ ʿABDALLĀH MUḤAMMAD IBN AḤMAD IBN ABĪ BAKR AL-BANNĀʾ AL-SHĀMĪ AL-MAQDISĪ AL-BASHSHĀRĪ** (*b. Bayt al-Maqdis [Jerusalem], ca. A.D. 946; d. ca. the end of the tenth century*), geography, cartography.

Al-Maqdisī's great geographical work, *Kitāb aḥsan al-taqāsim fī maʿrifat al-aqālim*, completed in 985, described the Islamic world. (He saw no reason to visit or describe the countries of the infidel.) He divided the Islamic world into fourteen regions and drew a highly stylized map of each. His book indicates that he was also knowledgeable in Islamic jurisprudence and displayed a highly ornamental literary style. He used the local dialect of each region in describing it and occasionally made use of rhymed prose.

MARALDI, GIACOMO FILIPPO (MARALDI I) (*b. Perinaldo, Imperia, Italy, 1665; d. Paris, France, 1729*); **MARALDI, GIOVANNI DOMENICO (MARALDI II)** (*b. Perinaldo, Imperia, Italy, 1709; d. Perinaldo, 1788*), astronomy, geodesy.

Maraldi I was the nephew of Cassini I, one of the founders of the Paris observatory. In 1687, after an education in the classics and mathematics, Maraldi I went to work with his uncle in Paris, where he started production on a new catalog of the fixed stars, a lifelong project. In 1701 he went to Rome for two years, making various astronomical observations—including one on the zodiacal light. Although Maraldi's personal work was only of the second rank, his thirty years at the Paris observatory contributed significantly to the realization of important astronomical and geodesic projects.

In 1726 Maraldi brought his nephew Giovanni Domenico (Maraldi II) to Paris. Maraldi II had studied at San Remo and Pisa. He carried out regular astronomical and meteorological observations and collaborated with Cassini II and Cassini III. His primary activity was concerned with positional astronomy, but he also participated in various geodesic operations.

MARCGRAF, GEORG. *See* **Markgraf, Georg.**

MARCHAND, RICHARD FELIX (*b. Berlin, Germany, 1813; d. Halle, Germany, 1850*), chemistry.

Marchand studied medicine and chemistry at the University of Halle, from which he graduated in 1837. After 1843 he taught there. He died of cholera at thirty-six. In his short career, he accomplished an impressive amount of experimental work encompassing biochemistry, organic chemistry, determinations of atomic weights, and ethyl sulfuric acid.

MARCHANT, JEAN (*b. 1650; d. Paris, France, 1738*); **MARCHANT, NICOLAS** (*d. Paris, 1678*), botany.

Jean Marchant was the son and successor of Nicolas Marchant. Both men devoted much of their effort to the preparation of *Histoire des plantes*, a huge project never completed or published. Nicolas Marchant held a degree in medicine from the University of Padua and was apothecary to the duc d'Orléans, who maintained a botanic garden. He collaborated in editing *Mémoires pour servir à l'histoire des plantes* (1676). He was a founder of the Académie Royale des Sciences and was its only botanist member for many years. In 1674 he became director of the Jardin du Roi.

Jean Marchant succeeded his father at the Jardin du Roi in 1678 and as a member of the academy. He assembled a great collection of foreign specimens sent to him from abroad. Much of his work, along with the *Histoire des plantes*, remains unpublished.

MARCHI, VITTORIO (*b. Novellara, Reggio nell' Emilia, Italy, 1851; d. Iesi, Ancona, Italy, 1908*), pathology.

Marchi received a degree in chemistry and pharmacy from the University of Modena in 1873 and a further degree in medicine and surgery in 1882. In 1883 he went to Golgi's general pathology laboratory at the University of Pavia, where he did research on the fine structure of the corpus striatum and optic thalamus. He developed a system of staining fat globules ("Marchi's globules") in the nerve fiber. His most important work was his experiments on the descending degeneration that results from extirpation of the cerebellum. The tractus tectospinalis is known as "Marchi's tract."

MARCHIAFAVA, ETTORE (*b. Rome, Italy, 1847; d. Rome, 1935*), pathology, anatomy.

Marchiafava graduated from the University of Rome in 1869 and studied briefly under Koch in Berlin, who was investigating tuberculosis. In 1872 he went to the University of Rome and remained there throughout his career. He early developed an interest in bacteriology and parasitology. From 1880 to 1891 he made the study that resulted in his discovery that malarial infection is transmitted through the blood. In 1884, with A. Celli, he identified meningococcus as the etiological agent of meningitis. His name is also remembered for the Marchiafava-Bignami syndrome (in alcoholism), the Marchiafava postpneumonic triad (in meningitis), and the Marchiafava-Micheli syndrome (in jaundice).

MARCHLEWSKI, LEON PAWEŁ TEODOR (*b. Włocławek, Poland, 1869; d. Cracow, Poland, 1946*), chemistry.

In 1892 Marchlewski received a doctorate from the University of Zurich, where he was assistant to Georg Lunge. He went to England, where he worked under

Edward Schunck at Kersal, near Manchester, studying plant pigments. Schunck and Marchlewski published papers on natural glucosides, including arbutin, phlorizin, and datiscin. In 1900 he returned to Poland, where he taught at Jagiellonian University and took up the study of chlorophyll. His last important achievement was the discovery of phylloerythrin.

MARCI OF KRONLAND, JOHANNES MARCUS (*b. Lanškroun, Bohemia [now Czechoslovakia], 1595; d. Prague, Bohemia [now Czechoslovakia], 1667*), physics, mathematics, medicine.

Marci received an M.D. from the University of Prague in 1625, then began to lecture at the Prague Faculty of Medicine. He was a renowned physician—the personal attendant to two emperors, Ferdinand III and Leopold I. He was professor of medicine at Prague University from 1620 to 1660. He was knighted in 1654.

Marci's book *De proportione motus* (1639) contained his theory of the collision of bodies and other problems of mechanics. *Thaumantias liber de arcu coelesti* (1648) dealt with optical experiments designed to explain the rainbow. He also wrote a work describing epilepsy as a nervous disease (1678). His medical and scientific works became involved with philosophical as well as theoretical problems. His philosophy represents a Catholic mysticism incoherently fused with Aristotelian and Platonic ideas.

MARCONI, GUGLIELMO (*b. Bologna, Italy, 1874; d. Rome, Italy, 1937*), engineering, physics.

Marconi's private education included special instruction in physics. In 1894 he became interested in Hertz's apparatus for the transmission of electromagnetic waves, finding that increased transmission distance could be obtained with larger antennas. By 1895, a distance of 1.5 miles had been achieved and the idea of "wireless telegraphy" was conceived. By 1900—now in London—Marconi increased the distance to 150 miles and was preparing for transatlantic transmission. This was accomplished in 1901 and, at twenty-seven, Marconi became world famous. From 1902 he devoted himself to managing his companies, the Marconi Wireless Telegraph Co. and later the Radio Corporation of America. He was awarded (with K.F. Braun) the Nobel Prize in physics in 1909.

MARCOU, JULES (*b. Salins, France, 1824; d. Cambridge, Mass., 1898*), geology, paleontology, topography.

Marcou studied at the Collège Saint-Louis in Paris but ill health forced his return to his native Jura. The natural history of that region had much to do with determining the course of his work, and in 1845 he published a highly original analysis of Jurassic fossils. He was named professor of mineralogy at the Sorbonne (1846), where he placed himself under the guidance of Louis Agassiz. His outstanding contributions were in stratigraphical geology and geological mapping. After 1864 he joined Agassiz at Harvard and thereafter considered Cambridge, Massachusetts, as home. His biography of Agassiz (2 vols., 1895) was a particular success.

Marcou's American studies were surrounded by controversy. Disdainful of American geologists, his theories in general were in opposition to theirs. His geological map of the United States, published in 1892, met with especially harsh criticism. At the heart of the controversy was Marcou's identifying large portions of the United States as belonging to the Jurassic and Triassic periods. Subsequent investigations demonstrated that he was at least partially correct.

MARCUS, JOHANNES. *See* **Marci of Kronland.**

MAREY, ÉTIENNE-JULES (*b. Beaune, France, 1830; d. Paris, France, 1904*), physiology.

Marey studied medicine at the Faculty of Medicine at Paris. His early work was on the circulation of the blood; he established the first private laboratory in Paris for the study of experimental physiology. In 1868 he went to the Collège de France, assuming the chair of "natural history of organized bodies." Marey's central significance for the development of physiology in France lies in his adoption and advocacy of two fundamental techniques in experimental physiology: graphical recording and cinematography. His most impressive accomplishment was the study of human locomotion, which he compared with the flight of birds and insects and the leg motions of trotting horses.

MARGERIE, EMMANUEL MARIE PIERRE MARTIN JACQUIN DE (*b. Paris, France, 1862; d. Paris, 1953*), geology, physical geography.

Margerie was privately educated. Independently wealthy, he was director (1918–33) of the geological service for Alsace and Lorraine. He published 265 scientific works, primarily in regional geology, tectonics, physical geography, and geographic and geological cartography. Many of these served to bring to the attention of French scientists the work of foreign geologists and geographers; as such, they were and continue to be of outstanding importance for the study of geology. His great reputation among scientists stemmed from his six-volume translation of Suess's *Das Antlitz der Erde* (1897–1918). His last major work was *Études américaines. Géologie et géographie* (1952).

MARGGRAF, ANDREAS SIGISMUND (*b. Berlin, Prussia, 1709; d. Berlin, 1782*), chemistry.

The son of the royal apothecary of Berlin, Marggraf was apprenticed to the leading apothecaries and chemists of the day. He quickly achieved the reputation of a masterful experimental chemist due to the extraordinary range of his interests and the painstaking nature of his procedures. His interest in chemistry for its own sake, refinement of analytical tools, and use of the balance anticipated the chemical revolution. His most significant contribution was the extraction and crystallization of sugar from plants commonly grown in Europe (1747). He also did important work on phosphorus, alumina, and magnesia.

MARGULES, MAX (*b. Brody, Galicia [now Ukrainian S.S.R.], 1856; d. Perchtoldsdorf, near Vienna, Austria, 1920*), meteorology, physics.

Margules was one of the most important meteorologists of the early twentieth century. He provided the first thorough, theoretical analyses of atmospheric energy processes and deeply influenced the evolution of present concepts of such processes. His work dealt with such widely varied subjects as the oscillation periods of the earth's atmosphere, the kinetic energy displayed in storms, and cold and warm air masses and sudden variations in barometric pressure during storms. He was educated at the universities of Vienna and Berlin. In 1877 he joined the staff of Zentralanstalt für Meteorologie in Vienna, and spent most of his time there until he gave up meteorology in 1906. After that time he concentrated on physical chemistry, apparently embittered at the lack of recognition received for his work as a meteorologist. Something of a recluse, he literally starved to death during the austerities of postwar Vienna.

MARIANO, JACOPO. *See* **Taccola, Mariano di Jacomo.**

MARIE, PIERRE (*b. Paris, France, 1853; d. Normandy, France, 1940*), neurology.

Marie studied law before entering medical school. He began his work in neurology under J.-M. Charcot, quickly becoming his chief assistant. In 1907 he joined the Faculty of Medicine, and in 1918 he was named to the chair of clinical neurology at the Salpêtrière. He devoted most of his time to the study and treatment of neurological traumas of the wounded. A brilliant technician, Marie wrote numerous books and articles and established an influential school of neurology. He was the first to define muscular atrophy type Charcot-Marie (1886); pulmonary hypertrophic osteoarthropathy (1890); cerebellar heredoataxia (1893); cleidocranial dysostosis (1897); and rhizomelic spondylosis (1898). He provided the first description and study of acromegaly, a fundamental contribution to the nascent field of endocrinology.

MARIGNAC, JEAN CHARLES GALISSARD DE (*b. Geneva, Switzerland, 1817; d. Geneva, 1894*), inorganic chemistry, physical chemistry.

Marignac studied at the École Polytechnique and the École des Mines in Paris. In 1841 he assumed the chair of chemistry at the Académie de Genève (later the University of Geneva), and in 1845 he also became professor of mineralogy. He won a worldwide renown for his analytical accuracy. In inorganic chemistry he accurately determined the atomic weights of nearly thirty elements and helped to unravel the tortuous chemistry of niobium and tantalum, the silicates, the tungstates, and the rare earths. He is generally regarded as the discoverer of ytterbium and gadolinium.

MARINUS (*b. Neapolis [the Biblical Shechem, now Nablus], Palestine; fl. second half of the fifth century* A.D.*; d. Athens [?]*), philosophy.

Marinus studied at Plato's Academy while Proclus headed it and later headed it himself. His *Life of Proclus* is looked upon as an important source for information on the late Neoplatonists. Marinus exerted an influence on Arabic philosophers, especially al-Fārābī and Ibn Sīnā.

MARION, ANTOINE FORTUNÉ (*b. Aix-en-Provence, France, 1846; d. Marseilles, France, 1900*), zoology, geology, botany, plant paleontology.

Marion attended the *lycée* in Aix, and in 1862 was named an assistant in natural history at the Faculté des Sciences at Marseilles, where he eventually received a doctorate. He taught at the *lycée* in Marseilles and in 1876 was given the newly created chair of geology at the Faculté des Sciences, and in 1880 he became director of the Museum of Natural History at Marseilles.

Beginning in 1858, Marion maintained a long collaboration with the Marquis Gaston de Saporta; together they wrote a number of works on botany and paleontology. The most noteworthy being *L'évolution du règne végétal* (3 vols., 1881–85). Marion received considerable recognition for his struggle against phylloxera, which constituted a threat to French vineyards. His extremely important zoological work dealt with marine invertebrates. Always looking for practical applications, he advocated the establishment of "maritime fields" where marine animals would be raised for food.

MARIOTTE, EDME (*d. Paris, France, 1684*), experimental physics, mechanics, hydraulics, optics, plant physiology, meteorology, surveying, methodology.

Honored as the man who introduced experimental physics into France, Mariotte played a central role in the work of the Paris Academy of Sciences from shortly after its formation in 1666 until his death. He became, in fact, so identified with the Academy that no trace remains of his life outside of it or before joining it. Lack of biographical information makes it impossible to determine what drew him to the study of science and when or where he learned what he knew when named to the Academy.

Mariotte's works have two basic characteristics: they treat subjects discussed at length in the Academy, and they rest in large part on fundamental results achieved by others. His own strength lay in his talent for recognizing the importance of those results, for confirming them by new and careful experiments, and for drawing out their implications. His career was an Academy career, which embodied the pattern of research envisaged by the founders of the institution. Although named as *physicien*, he soon shared in the work of the *mathématiciens* as well.

In 1668 Mariotte published his first work, *Nouvelle découverte touchant la veüe*, which immediately embroiled him in a controversy that lasted until his death, although no one denied the discovery itself. Curious about what happened to light rays striking the base of the optic nerve, Mariotte devised a simple experiment: placing two small white spots on a dark background, one in the center and the other two feet to the right and slightly below the center line, he covered his left eye and focused his right eye on the center spot. When he backed away about nine feet, he found that the second spot disappeared completely, leaving a single spot on a completely dark surface; the slightest motion of his eye or head brought the second spot back into view. By experiments with black spots on a white background and with the spots reversed for the left eye, he determined that the spot disappeared when the light from it directly struck the base of the optic nerve, which therefore constituted a blind spot or, as he called it, defect of vision in the eye.

As early as 1670 Mariotte had announced his intention to compose a major work on the impact of bodies. Completed and read to the Academy in 1671, it was published in 1673 as *Traité de la percussion ou choc des corps*. The first comprehensive treatment of the laws of inelastic and elastic impact and of their application to various physical problems, it long served as the standard work on the subject and went through three editions in Mariotte's lifetime.

For all its apparent diversity, Mariotte's research reflects a continuing concern with the motion of bodies in a resisting medium. The subject forms the core of his letter to Huygens in 1668 and of part II of the *Traité de la percussion* in 1673. Moreover, it was the subject of a full Academy investigation in 1669. A report in 1676 on the reflection and refraction of cannon balls striking water, and one in 1677 on the resistance of air to projectile motion, pursued the issue further. It was, however, only in 1678 that Mariotte broached the topic that would unite this research in a common theme: natural springs, artificial fountains, and the flow of water through pipes. His long report formed the basis for his *Traité du mouvement des eaux et des autres corps fluides*, published posthumously by La Hire in 1686. Mariotte was still working on the treatise at his death; his last two reports to the Academy dealt with the dispersion of water fired from a cannon and with the origin of the winds.

As an active member of the Academy for over twenty-five years, Mariotte exerted influence over scientific colleagues both within and without that institution. His closest associate seems to have been La Hire, but during his tenure he carried out joint investigations with most of the other members, including Huygens. His work was known to the Royal Society and was cited by Newton in the *Principia.* Mariotte conducted an extensive correspondence (as yet unpublished) with Leibniz, for whom he was a source of information about the work of the Academy in the early and mid-1670's and who in turn cooperated with Mariotte's meteorological survey. Huygens' accusation of plagiarism in 1690 seems to have done little to dim the reputation Mariotte had earned during his career.

MARIUS, SIMON. *See* **Mayr, Simon.**

MARKGRAF (or **Marcgraf), GEORG** (*b. Liebstadt, Meissen, Germany, 1610; d. Luanda, Angola, 1644*), astronomy, botany, zoology.

Markgraf was privately educated and was already proficient in mathematics, the natural sciences, and medicine when he entered the University of Leiden in 1636. In 1638 he joined a military and scientific expedition (under Count Maurice of Nassau) to Brazil, where he made maps and assembled botanical and zoological collections. Maurice founded the town of Mauritzstad (now part of Recife) and installed nearby an observatory for Markgraf on the island of Antonio Vaz. There Markgraf made important observations, including those of the planet Mercury and the solar eclipse of 1640.

MARKHAM, CLEMENTS ROBERT (*b. Stillingfleet, Yorkshire, England, 1830; d. London, England, 1916*), geography.

Markham became a cadet in the Royal Navy in 1844 and left the service in 1851. Most of his education took place during that period. After a year in Peru (1852–53) studying Inca ruins, he joined the India Office. In 1860 he planned and executed the project for the acclimatization of the Peruvian cinchona (the source of quinine) in India, an enterprise of immense social and economic importance. While in India he wrote extensively on geography, economic botany, and technology. Markham left the India Office in 1877 and devoted himself to geographical research, exploration, and education. He was especially interested in promoting exploration of the polar regions. Instrumental in planning the exploration of Antarctica, he played an active role in preparations for R.F. Scott's *Discovery* voyage (1901–04) and the fatal expedition of 1910–12. He helped found a school of geography at Oxford and wrote and edited numerous works of geography and exploration.

MARKOV, ANDREI ANDREEVICH (*b. Ryazan, Russia, 1856; d. Petrograd [now Leningrad], U.S.S.R., 1922*), mathematics.

In 1874 Markov entered the mathematics department of St. Petersburg University and enrolled in a seminar for superior students, led by A. N. Korkin and E. I. Zolotarev. He also attended lectures by the head of the St. Petersburg mathematical school, P. L. Chebyshev, and afterward became a consistent follower of his ideas.

In 1878 he graduated from the university with a gold medal for his thesis, "On the Integration of Differential Equations by Means of Continued Fractions," and remained at the university to prepare for a professorship. In 1880 he defended his master's thesis, "On the Binary Quadratic Forms With Positive Determinant," and began teaching in the university as a docent. In 1884 he defended his doctoral dissertation, devoted to continued fractions and the problem of moments.

For twenty-five years Markov combined research with intensive teaching at St. Petersburg University. In 1886 he was named extraordinary professor and in 1893, full professor. In this period he studied many questions: number theory, continued fractions, functions least deviating from zero, approximate quadrature formulas, integration in elementary functions, the problem of moments, probability theory, and differential equations. His lectures were distinguished by an irreproachable strictness of argument, and he developed in his students that mathematical cast of mind that takes nothing for granted. He included in his courses many recent results of investigations, while often omitting traditional questions. The lectures were difficult, and only serious students could understand them. He was also a faculty adviser for a student mathematical circle. Nominated by Chebyshev, Markov was elected in 1886 an adjunct of the St. Petersburg Academy of Sciences; in 1890 he became an extraordinary academician and in 1896 an ordinary academician. In 1905, after twenty-five years of teaching, Markov retired to make room for younger mathematicians. He was named professor emeritus, but still taught the probability course at the university, by his right as an academician. At this time his scientific interests concentrated on probability theory and in particular on the chains later named for him.

MARKOVNIKOV, VLADIMIR VASILEVICH (*b. Knyaginino, Nizhegorodskaya [now Gorki Region], Russia, 1837 or 1838; d. Moscow, Russia, 1904*), chemistry.

Markovnikov graduated from Kazan University in 1860 and became assistant to Butlerov, his mentor there. After further study in Germany, he returned to Kazan in 1867 and succeeded Butlerov as professor of chemistry. From 1871 to 1873 he was at the University of Odessa; thereafter he was at Moscow University, where he established a new chemical laboratory and trained a whole generation of chemists. He devoted almost twenty-five years to the study of the hydrocarbons of Caucasian petroleum and to the chemistry of alicyclic hydrocarbons. He also studied the history of chemistry.

MARLIANI, GIOVANNI (*b. Milan, Italy, early fifteenth century; d. Milan, 1483*), physics, mechanics, medicine.

Marliani's early life is obscure, but he probably studied at Pavia University. By 1440 he was a physician and taught natural philosophy, medicine, "astrologia," and mathematics variously at the universities of Pavia and Milan. He also held the profitable position of physician to the Sforzas. He was a gifted mathematician and wrote on heat and kinetics. He was highly regarded by the humanists of his day, even though his physics had a decidedly Aristotelian, Scholastic cast. His important works include *Tractatus de reactione* (1448) and *Disputatio cum Joanne de Arculis* (1461).

MARSH, OTHNIEL CHARLES (*b. Lockport, N.Y., 1831; d. New Haven, Conn., 1899*), vertebrate paleontology.

Marsh studied at Yale and taught paleontology there from 1866 until his death. From 1882 to 1892 he was also the first vertebrate paleontologist of the U.S. Geological Survey. He acquired a vast collection of fossils for the Peabody Museum at Yale, a gift of his uncle, George Peabody. Marsh's classifications and descriptions of extinct vertebrates—especially dinosaurs, the early horse, and horned mammals—were major contributions to knowledge of evolution.

MARSILI (or **Marsigli**), **LUIGI FERDINANDO** (*b. Bologna, Italy, 1658; d. Bologna, 1730*), natural history.

Marsili achieved high rank in the imperial army and accumulated a vast knowledge of history, politics, geography, and the natural sciences. He traveled widely in Europe and made several sea voyages; in all of his travels he made good use of his keen observations as a student of natural history. His writings covered a wide range: military affairs; the structure of mountains and the natural condition of the sea, lakes, and rivers; and especially oceanography. In 1725 he published the first treatise on oceanography, *Histoire physique de la mer.*

MARSILIUS OF INGHEN (or **Inguem** or **de Novimagio**) (*b. near Nijmegen, Netherlands; d. Heidelberg, Germany, 1396*), natural philosophy.

Marsilius received an M.A. from the University of Paris in 1362 and remained there for twenty years. The university became a battleground of the Great Schism and Marsilius removed himself to the recently founded University of Heidelberg, where he remained until his death.

Marsilius was a disciple of Jean Buridan, the master of the new physics of the fifteenth and sixteenth centuries and the precursor of Galileo and Leonardo. These new physicists formulated the concept of impetus, which they applied to the theory of gravity, acceleration, and the motion of projectiles. Marsilius himself occupied a moderate and traditionalist position among these men, and he never accepted the really novel implications for dynamics inherent in the doctrine of impetus. He avoided

mechanical interpretations of the physical world, holding in particular that the motions of the heavens are spiritual, eternal, and incorruptible. The initial source of this perfect motion is the First Mover, or God. Marsilius regarded the world as a plenum and accepted the Aristotelian theory of the *horror vacui.*

MARTENS, ADOLF (*b. Backendorf bei Hagenow, Mecklenburg-Schwerin, Germany, 1850; d. Berlin, Germany, 1914*), materials testing, metallography.

Martens studied mechanical engineering from 1868 to 1871 at the Königliche Gewerbeakademie in Berlin (later the Technische Hochschule of Berlin-Charlottenburg). He then joined the Prussian State Railway, where he was involved in the building of railway bridges. He also began his research on metallurgy, specializing in iron. In 1884 he was appointed director of the Mechanisch-Technische Versuchsanstalt, which in 1903 became the Königliche Materialprufungsamt of Berlin-Dahlem; its brilliant design and organization were essentially Martens' work. His major published work was *Handbuch der Materialienkunde* (1899).

MARTÍ FRANQUÉS (or **Martí d'Ardenya**), **ANTONIO DE** (*b. Altafulla, Tarragona, Spain, 1750; d. Tarragona, 1832*), biology, geology, meteorology, chemistry.

Martí Franqués attended the University of Cervera briefly but was mostly self-educated. He took an early interest in developing the cotton-spinning, weaving, and chinaware industries of Tarragona. He did analyses of air pressure and air temperature, invented a forerunner of the burette, and determined that the oxygen content of air is from 21 to 22 percent. He did experiments in plant reproduction and supported Linnaeus.

MARTIANUS CAPELLA (*b. Carthage; fl. Carthage, ca. A.D. 365–440*), transmission of knowledge.

Martianus was the author of *De nuptiis philologiae et Mercurii,* the most popular textbook in the Latin West in the early Middle Ages. A compendium of the liberal arts, it became the foundation of the medieval curriculum of the trivium (books III–V) and quadrivium (books VI–IX). Martianus' quadrivium books provide the best means of reconstructing the ancient Roman mathematical disciplines, and book VIII, *De astronomia,* is the best extant ancient Latin treatise on astronomy. Book IX is important for its Latin definitions of musical terms; Martianus, next to Boethius, is the most important ancient Latin authority on music.

MARTIN, BENJAMIN (*b. Worplesdon, Surrey, England, 1704 [?]; d. London, England, 1782*), experimental philosophy, scientific instrumentation.

Martin was probably self-educated in science. He became a teacher, and in 1735 published *The Philosophical Grammar,* a highly successful account of experimental philosophy. In 1756 he opened a scientific instrument shop in London and also conducted demonstration-lectures there. His shop soon became well known for its extensive stock and for the extensive catalogs and pamphlets he published on a wide variety of scientific subjects. Instruments bearing Martin's name are to be found today in many museums. He was responsible for various improvements, especially on the microscope.

MARTIN, HENRY NEWELL (*b. Newry, County Down, Ireland, 1848; d. Burley-in-Wharfedale, Yorkshire, England, 1896*), physiology.

Martin studied medicine at University College, London, and became interested there in the physiology research of Michael Foster. He followed Foster to Cambridge, where he became the assistant to T.H. Huxley. By the time he received a D.Sc. in physiology in 1875 (the first ever granted at Cambridge), he was recognized as one of England's most promising physiologists. On Huxley's recommendation he was named professor at the newly formed Johns Hopkins University in Baltimore. From his strategic position there, Martin was to exert a significant influence on the evolution of scientific education in the United States, especially in the development of physiology as an independent discipline. He died at age forty-eight and published only fifteen papers, notably a report on his experiments on a mammalian heart.

MARTIN, RUDOLF (*b. Zurich, Switzerland, 1864; d. Munich, Germany, 1925*), anthropology.

Martin studied law, philosophy, and zoology at Baden State University in Freiburg and at Leipzig. At Freiburg he came under the influence of the neo-Darwinist zoologist Weismann. His preoccupation with Kant's ideas on anthropology probably led to his choice of anthropology as a career. In 1897 he began work at Zurich's Institute of Anatomy and was a professor there from 1899 until ill health forced his retirement in 1911. He lived in France until 1914, when he returned to Germany. Martin is recognized as one of Germany's leading anthropologists. His classic work, *Die Inlandstämme der malaiischen Halbinsel* (1905), dealt with primitive Malaysian tribes, which he observed on his 1897 expedition. His textbook *Lehrbuch der Anthropologie in systematischer Darstellung* (1914) was highly successful and helped establish anthropology as an independent science.

MARTÍNEZ, CRISÓSTOMO (*b. Valencia, Spain, 1638; d. Flanders, 1694*), anatomy.

Martínez was associated with a circle of anatomists at the University of Valencia until 1687, when a royal grant allowed him to study in Paris. His genius at anatomical drawings is most evident in his microscopic studies of the human bone. In his essay "Generalidades acerca de los huesos" he attempted to explain ossification from the embryo to the adult bone.

MARTINI, FRANCESCO DI GIORGIO, also known as **Francesco di Siena** (*b. Siena, Italy, 1439; d. Siena, 1501*), architecture, sculpture, painting, technology.

Francesco was trained as a painter, and in 1477 entered the service of the duke of Urbino. He was architect and decorator of the duke's new palace. Later he became the duke's military engineer, designing his fortresses and engines of war and artillery. His fame spread, and he did work for various Italian rulers, including the Sforzas, for whom he designed the dome for the Milan Cathedral. He also collaborated with Leonardo da Vinci. Francesco's reputation lay in his work as painter, sculptor, and architect until his authorship of technological treatises was discovered. His importance to the history of technology lies in these works, among whose subjects are civil and military engineering, surveying, hydraulic engineering, war machinery, millwork, cranes and lifting devices, and devices for raising water.

MARTINOVICS, IGNÁC (*b. Pest, Hungary, 1755; d. Buda, Hungary, 1795*), chemistry.

Martinovics traveled widely as an army chaplain, becoming familiar with the great scientists of Europe and being exposed to the progressive ideas of the French Enlightenment. In 1783 he became professor of physics at the University of Lemberg (Lvov). His *Praelectiones physicae experimentalis*, which still adhered to the phlogiston theory, was published in 1787. He was beheaded after being caught in a conspiracy to proclaim Hungary a republic.

MARTIUS, KARL FRIEDRICH PHILIPP VON (*b. Erlangen, Germany, 1794; d. Munich, Germany, 1868*), botany, ethnology.

Martius received an M.D. from Erlangen University in 1814. In 1817 he published *Flora cryptogamica Erlangensis,* which resulted from his position as assistant conservator of the botanic garden. From 1817 to 1820 he was part of a specimen-collecting expedition to Brazil. The success of this expedition assured Martius' career, which included royal support and the botany chair at the University of Munich.

MARTONNE, EMMANUEL-LOUIS-EUGÈNE DE (*b. Chabris, France, 1873; d. Sceaux, France, 1955*), geography, geomorphology, hydrography.

After studying at the École Normale Supérieure, Martonne taught geography at the University of Rennes. In 1909 he became head of the geography department in the Faculty of Letters at the Sorbonne, a post he held for thirty-five years. From that position he became the recognized leader of the French school of geography, which he helped develop into an autonomous science. In his personal research he showed a lasting interest in hydrography, especially in drainage and runoff areas and their relation to aridity.

MARUM, MARTIN (MARTINUS) VAN (*b. Delft, Netherlands, 1750; d. Haarlem, Netherlands, 1837*), natural philosophy, medicine, botany.

Van Marum received a Ph.D. and an M.D. from Groningen University in 1773. He established a practice in Haarlem and began the study of electricity. In 1783 he was made director of Teyler's Museum, which became famous for its electrical apparatuses, for which van Marum was responsible. His experiments on a large electrical machine were greatly admired and were repeated all over Europe. Franklin and Volta were among his admirers, and van Marum coined the term "Voltaic pile." He and van Troostwijk discovered carbon monoxide, and he did important experiments to decompose and synthesize water. After 1795 he devoted himself to paleontology and geology.

AL-MARWAZĪ. *See* Ḥabash al-Ḥāsib.

MARX, KARL (*b. Trier, Prussian Rhineland, 1818; d. London, England, 1883*), economics, history, philosophy, political science, sociology, history and sociology of science and technology.

Marx was educated (1830–35) at the Friedrich-Wilhelm Gymnasium in Trier, formerly a Jesuit school. During 1835–41, he studied at the universities of Bonn and Berlin, reading law at his father's request but turning to philosophy and history. After initial resistance, he studied Hegel thoroughly, in part through the lectures of Eduard Gans but more deeply with an intellectual club of somewhat older philosophers, among them Bruno Bauer and, later, Arnold Ruge. Hoping for an academic career, he submitted a dissertation entitled "The Difference Between the Democritean and Epicurean Philosophies of Nature" to the University of Jena in 1841 and was awarded the doctorate. Central to that dissertation was Marx's praise for Epicurus' addition of spontaneity—the famous "swerve"—to the determinism of the Democritean atomic dynamics, and for the Epicurean recognition of an animate level of human will along with the inanimate mechanisms of natural necessity.

Immersed for some time in the history of philosophy, Marx followed Hegel's cultural setting of philosophical thought in an inherently rational and explicable sequence that is the historical as well as the systematic maturation of awareness and self-awareness of the human spirit. Marx joined with the Young Hegelians in seeing basic challenge and change to be central for Hegel, with progress the recurring theme of the increasing self-awareness of human consciousness, in the larger society as much as in the philosophical mind.

If only on ideological grounds, Marx was unable to begin an academic career. His friend Bauer was dismissed from his teaching post at Bonn because of his secular critique of the Christian Gospels, and Marx, seeing his academic hopes disappearing, turned to journalism. He joined the staff of a liberal newspaper in Cologne, the *Rheinische Zeitung;* became editor by October 1842; and resigned early in 1843, just before the paper was closed by the Prussian censor. He met Friedrich Engels briefly in Cologne, and by their second meeting in Paris in 1844, a friendship had flourished that was to last until Marx's death.

Marx went to Paris in October 1843, already committed to a life that would combine scientific work with political activity. He joined the radical German colony in Paris, and collaborated in a short-lived publication, Arnold Ruge's radical *Deutsch-französischer Jahrbücher.* From those years come his incisive and profound notebooks, published a century later (the influential *Economic and Philosophic Manuscripts of 1844*), and his first writings with Engels.

Deported from France in 1845, Marx lived in Brussels until the revolutionary year of 1848, when he returned briefly to Paris at the invitation of the provisional government; he then went to Cologne to organize the *Neue Rheinische Zeitung.* Within six months he had been charged with incitement to rebellion and tried in court. Although acquitted in February 1849, Marx was expelled once more. He stayed briefly in Paris, was again ordered from France, and in July 1849 settled himself and his family permanently in London. Engels came to London in November of that year; and in 1850 he settled in Manchester to work in his father's textile firm, thereby providing Marx's principal financial support. Aside from some ten years writing political commentary, mainly for the *New York Tribune* (1852–62), Marx had no regular income.

His political activities were manifold, from his first contacts with working-class people in the early 1840's to his repeated organizational efforts: the German Communist League in Brussels (1847); various workers' and democratic associations in subsequent years; the *Manifesto of the Communist Party,* written with Engels and published in 1848; the International Working Men's Association of 1864, with its several congresses and its national sections (ultimately dissolved in 1876, after a struggle with Bakunin); the uniting of the various German workers' parties in 1875; continuing relations with the Chartists and with other British labor organizations; efforts to assist refugees after the fall of the Paris Commune in 1871; and, throughout his life, a voluminous correspondence with European and American socialists and sympathetic thinkers and activists.

He saw the first volume of his chief work, *Das Kapital,* published in 1867; the second volume (1885) and the third (1894) were edited from Marx's notes and drafts by Engels; further portions (1905–10) were edited by Karl Kautsky. The important preparatory outlines and studies for *Kapital,* the *Grundrisse* of 1857–58, were first published at Moscow in 1939–41, but became widely available only with the Berlin edition of 1953. Aside from these, Marx's works comprise more than a dozen monographs and treatises, and hundreds of shorter articles. Since 1957 the collected *Marx-Engels Werke* have appeared in forty volumes.

The principal contribution of Karl Marx to the understanding of the sciences was his emphasis on their social character. Although he admired the great advances in knowledge that the sciences have provided, especially since the Renaissance—that is, he acknowledged the cognitive successes of the sciences—Marx nevertheless comprehended them as social phenomena. For Marx, man and nature have a history together; man encounters nature in his own species' history, each encounter within a specific concrete stage of that history. Without doubt, for Marx, nature had its own history; but that was not so much his own view as one he thought increasingly demonstrated by the natural sciences themselves. For him this was evident from developments in geology, astronomy, and, above all, evolutionary biology.

MASCAGNI, PAOLO (*b. Pomarance, Volterra, Italy, 1755; d. Florence, Italy, 1815*), anatomy.

Mascagni graduated from the University of Siena in 1775 and four years later was named professor there. In 1784 he published *Vasorum lymphaticorum historia,* illustrated with numerous plates. It paved the way for progress in anatomy, physiology, and clinical medicine, for 50 percent of the lymphatic vessels now known were discovered by Mascagni. His renown was such that the Tuscan government created at the University of Florence a special chair of anatomy, physiology, chemistry, and the teaching of art anatomy for him. There he began an ambitious project of preparing life-size anatomical models of the human body. He died before its completion.

MASCART, ÉLEUTHÈRE ÉLIE NICOLAS (*b. Quarouble, France, 1837; d. Paris, France, 1908*), physics.

Mascart received a doctorate from the École Normale Supérieure in Paris in 1864. He taught in secondary schools and published *Éléments de mécanique* (1866). In

1868 he went to the Collège de France, where he held the chair in physics from 1872 until his death. His scientific career was marked by a steady stream of first-rate experimental and theoretical work in optics, electricity, magnetism, and meteorology. His major works include *Traité d'optique* (3 vols., 1889–93), *Traité d'électricité statique* (2 vols., 1876), and *Leçons sur l'électricité et le magnétisme*, written with J. Joubert (2 vols., 1882–86). The last became a standard textbook for both engineers and physicists.

MASCHERONI, LORENZO (*b. Castagneta, near Bergamo, Italy, 1750; d. Paris, France, 1800*), mathematics.

Mascheroni was ordained a priest at seventeen and taught physics and mathematics in the seminary at Bergamo. In 1786 he became professor of algebra and geometry at the University of Pavia. He is best known for his *Geometria del compasso* (1797), in which he shows that all plane construction problems that can be solved by ruler and compass can be solved by compass alone. In his *Adnotationes ad calculum integrale Euleri* (1790) he calculated Euler's constant, sometimes called the Euler-Mascheroni constant, to thirty-two decimal places.

MASERES, FRANCIS (*b. London, England, 1731; d. Reigate, Surrey, England, 1824*), mathematics.

Maseres attended Clare College, Cambridge, was called to the bar, and served as attorney general of Quebec. Back in England, he went to the Exchequer, where he served until age ninety-three. He wrote on political matters, especially the problems of the American colonies, and on mathematics. On the latter, his work was marked by his rejection of significant parts of the new discoveries, particularly in algebra. He strove to bring mathematics to a wide public, and he reprinted at his own expense works of distinguished mathematicians.

MĀSHĀ'ALLĀH (*fl. Baghdad, 762–ca. 815*), astrology.

Māshā'allāh, a Jew, was one of the early ^{c}Abbāsid astrologers who introduced the Sassanian version of that science to the Arabs. He flourished during the reign of al-Manṣūr, and he participated in the decision to found Baghdad in 762. He wrote on virtually every aspect of astrology, and his works are of especial interest to historians of astronomy.

MASKELYNE, NEVIL (*b. London, England, 1732; d. Greenwich, England, 1811*), astronomy.

Maskelyne graduated from Trinity College, Cambridge, in 1754 and was ordained in 1755. He accepted a curacy near London, but spent much of his time assisting the astronomer royal, James Bradley. He was sent on several observing missions by Bradley. In 1765 he succeeded Bradley as astronomer royal. During his tenure he was responsible for supervising the publication of the annual *Nautical Almanac*, which is Maskelyne's greatest monument to astronomy.

MASON, CHARLES (*b. Wherr, Gloucestershire, England, baptized 1728; d. Philadelphia, Pa., 1786*), astronomy, geodesy.

Mason was on the staff of the Royal Observatory, when in 1763 he and Jeremiah Dixon were named to go to the North American colonies to resolve the common boundaries of Pennsylvania, Maryland, Delaware, and Virginia. The results of this expedition, or more precisely, the east-west demarcation, became known as the Mason-Dixon Line, the traditional separation of North from South. Mason worked on the annual editions of the *Nautical Almanac* for many years. He immigrated to Pennsylvania in 1786 but fell ill on shipboard and died shortly after landing.

MASSA, NICCOLO (*b. Venice, Italy, 1485; d. Venice, 1569*), medicine.

Massa received an M.D. from Padua and practiced in Venice. In 1536 he published *Liber introductorius anatomiae*, which remained the best textbook of anatomy for a generation. It is based partly on the work of earlier writers and partly on Massa's own dissections. Despite its shrewd observations and considerable new findings, the text does not reflect to any large degree the most up-to-date anatomical research of the time.

MASSON, ANTOINE-PHILIBERT (*b. Auxonne, France, 1806; d. Paris, France, 1860*), physics.

Masson received a B.S. from the École Normale Supérieure in Paris. In 1834 he observed independently the self-induction of a voltaic circuit. He also constructed some of the earliest induction coils. In 1836 he successfully defended his doctoral thesis elaborating Ampère's work in electrodynamics.

MAST, SAMUEL OTTMAR (*b. Ann Arbor, Mich., 1871; d. Baltimore, Md., 1947*), botany.

Mast received a B.S. from the University of Michigan in 1899 and a Ph.D. in zoology in 1906 from Harvard. After teaching at Hope and Goucher colleges, he went to Johns Hopkins in 1911. He published *Light and the Behavior of Organisms* in 1911. It and much of his later research was on the reaction of lower organisms to stimuli, especially light. Also classic is his study of the colorless flagellate *Chilomonas paramecium* (1933).

MÄSTLIN, MICHAEL (*b. Göppingen, Germany, 1550; d. Tübingen, Germany, 1631*), astronomy.

Mästlin, the first person to explain earthshine in print and the teacher who converted Kepler to Copernican astronomy, received a B.A. (1569) and an M.A. (1571) from Tübingen University. In 1573 his essay on the nova of 1572 so impressed Tycho Brahe that he reprinted it in his *Progymnasmata*. Mästlin taught briefly at Tübingen, and in 1580 he became professor of mathematics at Heidelberg. In 1584 he returned to Tübingen. His *Epitome of Astronomy* (1582) was a highly popular introductory textbook. In his classroom Kepler heard Mästlin expound the Copernican astronomy over the Ptolemaic. At one time, legend held that Mästlin was responsible for the Copernican views of Galileo, but that legend is without factual basis. Mästlin was often involved in religious controversy. He computed Jesus' birth more than four years before the conventional date, and he denounced the Gregorian Calendar as a Roman Catholic plot. In 1590 Pope Sixtus V placed all his works on the Index.

AL-MAS^{c}ŪDĪ, ABU'L-ḤASAN ^{c}ALĪ IBN AL-ḤUSAYN IBN ^{c}ALĪ (*b. Baghdad; d. al-Fusṭāṭ [old Cairo], Egypt, 956 or 957*), geography, history.

Al-Mas^cūdī left Baghdad about 915 and spent the rest of his life traveling throughout the Middle East, India, and East Africa. He was a prolific writer on a great variety of subjects: history, geography, jurisprudence, theology, genealogy, and the art of government. He made important contributions to Arab historiography, believing as he did that a historian ought to consult the primary sources available and not depend on secondary sources. His history of Iran was a good example of his principles at work. He looked upon geography as a necessary prerequisite of history. He gave especial importance to the animal and plant life of a particular region. His geographical system was based more on the "secular" Greek model than on the Islamic geographers, who made Mecca the center of the world and made their geographical ideas conform to the Koran. He was deeply interested in Greek philosophy and was one of the most original thinkers of medieval Islam.

MATHER, WILLIAM WILLIAMS (*b. Brooklyn, Conn., 1804; d. Columbus, Ohio, 1859*), geology.

Mather graduated from West Point Military Academy in 1828 and taught chemistry, mineralogy, and geology in the service. His *Elements of Geology for the Use of Schools* (1833) went through five editions. In 1836 he resigned from the army and became a geologist for the New York survey. His most important work is embodied in his massive final report for that survey. Later he taught at Ohio University and Marietta College. An expert on coal geology, he had large interests in the development of Ohio coal lands, and served as mineral consultant for railroads.

MATHEWS, GEORGE BALLARD (*b. London, England, 1861; d. Liverpool, England, 1922*), mathematics.

Mathews was educated at University College, London, and St. John's, Cambridge. He taught at University College of North Wales at Bangor, and at Cambridge. His main interest was in the classical theory of numbers. He also produced books on Bessel functions and projective geometry.

MATHIEU, ÉMILE LÉONARD (*b. Metz, France, 1835; d. Nancy, France, 1890*), mathematics, mathematical physics.

Mathieu received a D.Sc. from the École Polytechnique in Paris in 1859 with a thesis on transitive functions. In 1869 he was appointed to the chair of mathematics at Besançon, and in 1874 he moved permanently to Nancy. His main efforts were devoted to the continuation of the great tradition of French mathematical physics, and he extended in sophistication the formation and solution of partial differential equations for a wide range of physical problems. Most of his papers in these fields were collected in his *Traité de physique mathématique* (7 vols., 1874–90).

MATHURĀNĀTHA ŚARMAN (*fl. Bengal, India, 1609*), astronomy.

Mathurānātha composed the *Ravisiddhāntamañjarī* in 1609. It is an astronomical text accompanied by extensive tables, based on the parameters of the *Saurapakṣa*.

MATRUCHOT, LOUIS (*b. Verrey-sous-Salmasse, near Dijon, France, 1863; d. Paris, France, 1921*), mycology.

Matruchot graduated from the École Normale Supérieure in 1888, became a science librarian there, and in 1901 began teaching mycology and botany at the Sorbonne. He applied Pasteur's techniques to the study of the effects of various culture media upon the polymorphism and reproduction of fungi. His research on fungi pathogenic to humans and animals opened a whole new field of medical investigation.

MATTEUCCI, CARLO (*b. Forlì, Italy, 1811; d. Leghorn, Italy, 1868*), physiology, physics.

Matteucci graduated from the University of Bologna in 1828 with a degree in physics. He studied further at the Sorbonne, and in 1840 he was appointed professor of physics at the University of Pisa. In the meantime, he began carrying out electrophysical investigations, and in 1842 at Pisa he made his most famous discovery, the induced twitch. His most important work was on the neural mechanisms of the electric discharge of torpedoes, on the resting potential of the frog's muscle, and especially on the action currents, which he discovered. When Italy was united, Matteucci became a senator for life, and in 1862, as minister of education, reorganized the Scuola Normale Superiore in Pisa to become Italy's first institute for advanced studies.

MATTHIESSEN, AUGUSTUS (*b. London, England, 1831; d. London, 1870*), chemistry

Matthiessen received a Ph.D. in agricultural chemistry from the University of Giessen in 1853. From 1853 to 1857 he worked in Bunsen's laboratory at the University of Heidelberg. In 1857 he returned to London, where he soon set up his own laboratory, studying particularly the chemistry of narcotine and related opium alkaloids. He also pursued research on the electrical, physical, and chemical properties of metals and their alloys. He lectured at the medical schools of the University of London.

MATTIOLI, PIETRO ANDREA GREGORIO (*b. Siena, Italy, 1501; d. Trento, Italy, 1577*), medicine, botany.

Mattioli received an M.D. from the University of Padua in 1523. After living in Siena, Perugia, and Trento, he settled in Gorizia, where his interest in medical and natural history increased, particularly in phytology. In 1544 he published *Di Pedacio Dioscoride anazarbeo libri cinque*, which made him famous. He was called to Prague to serve at the courts of Ferdinand I and Maximilian II. He wrote on a wide range of medical and botanical subjects, including an examination of the origins and treatment of syphilis.

MATUYAMA (MATSUYAMA), MOTONORI (*b. Uyeda [now Usa], Japan, 1884; d. Yamaguchi, Japan, 1958*), physics, geophysics, geology.

Matuyama graduated from Hiroshima Normal College (now the University of Hiroshima) in 1907 and did graduate work at the Imperial University in Kyoto. With Toshi Shida he began work on what became one of his chief fields of research, the determination of gravity by pendulum. Except for a period (1919–21) studying under T.C. Chamberlin at the University of Chicago, his whole career was spent at the Imperial University. He did important gravity surveys in the Japan Trench and the area surrounding it. He also studied the distribution of coral reefs in the South Seas, the remnant magnetization of rocks, and seismology.

MAUGUIN, CHARLES VICTOR (*b. Provins, France, 1878; d. Paris, France, 1958*), crystallography, mineralogy.

Mauguin received a doctorate from the École Normale Supérieure in Paris in 1910. He became Frédéric Wallerant's assistant at the Sorbonne, studying liquid crystals. He taught at Bordeaux and Nancy before settling at the Sorbonne in 1919. All of his researches were concerned essentially with the diffraction of X rays by crystals. He published the atomic structure of cinnabar, calomel, and graphite, and determined the chemical composition of a great number of micas.

MAUNDER, EDWARD WALTER (*b. London, England, 1851; d. London, 1928*), astronomy.

Maunder took the first British Civil Service Commission examination ever given for the post of photographic and spectroscopic assistant at the Royal Observatory. He worked at Greenwich for forty years, mostly measuring sunspots. His wife, Annie S.D. Russell, a Cambridge-educated astronomer, worked closely with him. They also collaborated on papers, articles, and books.

MAUPAS, FRANÇOIS ÉMILE (*b. Vaudry, Calvados, France, 1842; d. Algiers, Algeria, 1916*), zoology, biology.

Maupas studied at the École des Chartes and spent his vacations working in the laboratories of the Muséum d'Histoire Naturelle and the Sorbonne. In 1870 he became archivist in Algiers and then curator of the Bibliothèque Nationale. His scientific work was devoted entirely to sexuality and reproduction among the protozoans, rotifers, nematodes, and oligochaetes. He also published geological and botanical observations and translated important German scientific works.

MAUPERTUIS, PIERRE LOUIS MOREAU DE (*b. St.-Malo, France, 1698; d. Basel, Switzerland, 1759*), mathematics, biology, physics.

Maupertuis was privately educated in mathematics and was elected to the Academy of Sciences at age twenty-five. After a trip to London in 1728, he became the foremost French proponent of the Newtonian movement. In 1735 he headed an expedition to Lapland that proved Newton's theory of the flattening of the earth toward the poles. In 1745 he accepted the invitation of Frederick the Great to move to Berlin and rehabilitate the academy of sciences there. He was successful in attracting eminent scientists to Berlin—La Mettrie, Mérian, Meckel, and even Voltaire—but his brusque manner involved him in numerous arguments and personal vendettas against fellow scientists. His estrangement from his old friend Voltaire (who satirized him unmercifully) was especially painful to him and marred his last days. His "Discours sur les différentes figures des astres" (1732) contained his Newtonian theories. *Système de la nature* (1751) was a theoretical speculation on the nature of biparental heredity. It also contained an attempt to reconcile Newton and Leibniz. In his philosophical writings, Maupertuis anticipated the utilitarianism of Bentham and Beccaria.

MAURER, JULIUS MAXIMILIAN (*b. Freiburg im Breisgau, Germany, 1857; d. Zurich, Switzerland, 1938*), meteorology, astronomy.

Maurer received his doctorate in 1882 from the University of Zurich. He spent his entire career at the Schweizerische Meteorologische Zentralanstalt in Zurich. He worked mainly on radiation problems, and he wrote papers on total solar radiation and on nighttime heat loss by radiation.

MAURO, FRA (*d. Murano, near Venice, Italy, 1459 [?]*), geography.

Fra Mauro, author of the last of the great medieval world maps, was a Camaldolese monk and probably head of the Camaldolese cartographic workshop near Venice. His work is a milestone in the history of geography and cartography for the wealth of its information. It contains the first mention of "Zimpagu," or Japan, on a European map.

MAUROLICO, FRANCESCO (*b. Messina, Italy, 1494; d. near Messina, 1575*), mathematics, astronomy, optics.

Maurolico was a priest and a Benedictine who lived his whole life in Sicily. His patrons included Charles V's viceroy and the Ventimiglias, the leading noble family of Sicily. He held high positions: head of the mint, architect in charge of the fortifications of Messina, and official historian. His history of Sicily was published in 1562. From 1569 he was professor of mathematics at the University of Messina. His main mathematical writings are gathered in the *Opuscula mathematica* (1575), a collection of eight treatises. It includes, in particular, a treatment of polygonal numbers. He wrote extensively on the ancient mathematicians. He also did important work in optics, especially *Photismi de lumine et umbra ad perspectivam et radiorum incidentiam facientes* (possibly 1575; certainly 1611), which has been called the most important work on optics of the Renaissance. Maurolico also wrote on meteorology, music, mechanics, and magnetism.

MAURY, ANTONIA CAETANA DE PAIVA PEREIRA (*b. Cold Spring-on-Hudson, N.Y., 1866; d. Dobbs Ferry, N.Y., 1952*), astronomy.

Maury graduated from Vassar in 1887 and went to work at the Harvard Observatory, where she did creative and perceptive work, particularly on spectroscopic binaries; she herself discovered the second such star, Beta Aurigae. She spent many years investigating the complex spectrum of the binary Beta Lyrae, and did an elaborate classification of 681 bright stars of the northern skies.

MAURY, MATTHEW FONTAINE (*b. near Fredericksburg, Va., 1806; d. Lexington, Va., 1873*), physical geography, meteorology, oceanography.

Maury followed a career in the U.S. Navy until 1861, when he joined the Confederate Navy. After the war, he was in the service of Emperor Maximilian of Mexico, and from 1868 to his death he was professor of physics at Virginia Military Institute.

Maury was head of the U.S. Naval Observatory from 1844 to 1861, but his poor qualifications as an astronomer held back the work of one of the world's great observatories. His major interest was navigation. The *Wind and Current Charts* he published regularly were an important tool of maritime commerce. He was also a pioneer in the use of submarine telegraphy; the first bathymetrical chart was prepared by him. His best-known work was *Physical Geography of the Sea* (1855). It was received enthusiastically in general and religious publications, critically in scientific journals. His tendency to couch his theories in the pious language of natural theology damaged them in the eyes of scientists. Although his cherished theories never won acceptance, he was widely honored for his technical achievements and for the stimulus those achievements gave to other scientists. He was one of the founders of the American Association for the Advancement of Science.

MAWSON, SIR DOUGLAS (*b. Bradford, Yorkshire, England, 1882; d. Adelaide, Australia, 1958*), geology.

Mawson received a B.S. in 1904 and a D.Sc. in 1909 from the University of Adelaide. He was on the faculty there from 1905 until his retirement in 1952. He became its first professor of geology in 1920. Mawson was foremost an explorer-geologist. He made expeditions to the New Hebrides and especially to Antarctica, where he ascended Mt. Erebus and mapped the position of the South Magnetic Pole. His exploits in the Australian Antarctic Expedition (1911–14) are recorded in *The Home of the Blizzard* (1915).

MAXIMOW. *See* **Maksimov.**

MAXWELL, JAMES CLERK (*b. Edinburgh, Scotland, 1831; d. Cambridge, England, 1879*), physics.

From 1841 Maxwell attended Edinburgh Academy, where he met his lifelong friend and biographer, the Platonic scholar Lewis Campbell, and P. G. Tait. He entered Edinburgh University in 1847 and came under the influence of James David Forbes and Sir William Hamilton. In 1850 he went up to Cambridge (Peterhouse one term, then Trinity), where he studied under the great private tutor William Hopkins and was also influenced by G. G. Stokes and William Whewell. He graduated in 1854 and became a fellow of Trinity in 1855. Maxwell held professorships at Marischal College, Aberdeen, and King's College, London, from 1856 to 1865, when he retired from regular academic life to write his celebrated *Treatise on Electricity and Magnetism.* In 1871 he was appointed first professor of experimental physics at Cambridge and planned and developed the Cavendish Laboratory.

Maxwell wrote four books and about one hundred papers. He was joint scientific editor with T. H. Huxley of the famous ninth edition of the *Encyclopaedia Britannica,* to which he contributed many articles. His grasp of both the history and the philosophy of science was exceptional, as may be seen from the interesting philosophical asides in his original papers and from his general writings. His *Unpublished Electrical Researches of the Hon. Henry Cavendish* (1879) is a classic of scientific editing, with a unique series of notes on investigations suggested by Cavendish's work.

In addition to the revolutionary investigations in electromagnetism and the kinetic theory of gases that earned him a lasting place in the history of science, Maxwell made substantial contributions in several other fields. His first paper, on a new method of constructing a perfect oval, was published when he was fourteen; other early work was on geometrical optics, including discovery of the "fish-eye" lens (1853), and on photoelasticity (1850) using a pair of polarizing prisms given him by William Nicol. Maxwell began experiments on color mixing in 1849 in Forbes's laboratory, and went on to create the science of quantitative colorimetry. He proved that all

colors may be matched by mixtures of three spectral stimuli, provided subtraction as well as addition of stimuli is allowed; he revived Thomas Young's three-receptor theory of color, vision and demonstrated that color blindness is due to the ineffectiveness of one or more receptors; and he projected the first trichromatic color photograph (1861).

Much of Maxwell's time between 1855 and 1859 was spent in mathematical studies of the motions and stability of the rings of Saturn. He first took up the theory of the solid ring where Laplace had left it, and performed calculations proving that the hypothesis of a solid ring was untenable; he then applied his analysis to nonrigid, semirigid, and other gaseous and liquid rings, and concluded that the only stable structure was concentric circles of small satellites, each moving at a speed appropriate to its distance from Saturn. Such rings attract one another, and Maxwell presented a lengthy investigation of mutual perturbations; he estimated the rate of loss of energy and deduced that the whole system of rings would slowly spread out, as the observations indicated.

The determining influences on Maxwell's study of electricity were Faraday and William Thomson. Faraday's discoveries sprang from the search for correlations of forces and formed, in Maxwell's words, "the nucleus of everything electric since 1830." Among Thomson's contributions was the first exact mathematical description of lines of electric force (1845); later Thomson and Maxwell between them established a general similitude among static vector fields subject to the conditions of continuity and incompressibility, proving that identical equations describe (1) streamlines of frictionless incompressible fluids through porous media, (2) lines of flow of heat, (3) current electricity, and (4) lines of force in magnetostatics and electrostatics.

Maxwell's electrical researches began in 1854; they fall into two broad cycles, with 1868 roughly the dividing point: the first a period of five major papers on the foundations of electromagnetic theory, the second a period of extension with the *Treatise on Electricity and Magnetism,* the *Elementary Treatise on Electricity,* and a dozen shorter papers on special problems.

In the first paper, "On Faraday's Line of Force" (1855–56), after a discussion of the use of analogy, he extended Thomson's treatment of the analogy between lines of force and streamlines in an incompressible fluid by considering the resistive medium through which the fluid moves. Applying the analogy to magnetism, he distinguished two vectors, magnetic induction and magnetic force (**B** and **H**); in electricity the parallel quantities were current density and electromotive intensity (**I** and **E**). He then made an important mathematical distinction between two classes of vector functions: "quantities" (later "fluxes") vs. "intensities" (later "forces"). In Part 2 of this paper he developed a new formal theory of electromagnetic processes, obtaining a complete set of equations between the four vectors **E, I, B, H** and going on to derive a new vector function (**A**, the electrotonic function); the new function provided equations to represent ordinary magnetic action, electromagnetic induction, and the forces between closed currents, and was later identified as a generalization of Neumann's electrodynamic potential. The next paper, "On Physical Lines of Force" (1861–62), began as an attempt to devise a medium occupying space which would account for the stresses associated by Faraday with lines of magnetic force, and ended with the stunning discovery that vibrations of the medium have properties, identical with light: "we can scarcely avoid the inference that *light consists in the transverse undulations of the same medium which is the cause of electric and magnetic phenomena.*" His third paper, written for the electrical standards committee of the British Association, gave the first exposition of the dual system of electrical units commonly but incorrectly known as the Gaussian system by setting forth definitions of electric and magnetic quantities related to measures M, L, T of mass, length, and time; for every quantity the ratio of the two absolute definitions, based on electric and magnetic forces, proved to be some power of a constant c whose value was very nearly the velocity of light.

Maxwell's fourth paper, "A Dynamical Theory of the Electromagnetic Field" (1865), provided a new theoretical framework based on electrical experiments and a few general dynamical principles, from which the propagation of electromagnetic waves through space followed without any special assumptions about molecular vortices or the forces between electric particles; in working out the theory he replaced the vortex hypothesis with a new macroscopic analogy between inductive circuits and coupled dynamical systems. Helmholtz and Thomson had applied energy principles to deduce the law of induction from Ampère's force law; Maxwell inverted and generalized their argument to calculate forces from the induction formulas. Thus his first analytic treatment of the electrotonic function was metamorphosed into a complete dynamical theory of the field. In his fifth major paper (1868) he simplified the equations for the electromagnetic field, writing them in an integral form, without the function **A**, based on four postulates derived from electrical experiments.

In the *Treatise on Electricity and Magnetism* (2 vols., 1873) Maxwell extended the dynamical formalism by a more thoroughgoing application of Lagrange's equations than he had attempted in 1865; the use he made of Lagrangian techniques was new to the point of being almost a new approach to physical theory. In his analysis of cross-terms linking electrical and mechanical phenomena he identified three possible electromechanical effects, later detected by Barnett (1908), Einstein and de Haas (1916), and Tolman and Stewart (1916). Maxwell's eight equations describing the electromagnetic field embody the principle that electromagnetic processes are transmitted by the separate and independent action of each charge (or magnetized body) on the surrounding space rather than by direct action at a distance. Formulas for the forces between moving charged bodies may indeed be derived from his equations, but the action is not along the line joining them and can be reconciled with dynamical principles only by taking into account the exchange of momentum with the field.

Maxwell gave three distinct proofs of the existence of electromagnetic waves in 1865, 1868, and 1873. The disturbance has dual form, consisting in waves of magnetic force and electric displacement with motions perpendicular to the propagation vector and to each other; an alternative view given in the *Treatise* is to represent it as a transverse wave of the function **A**. In either version the theory yields strictly transverse motion, automatically eliminating the longitudinal waves which had embar-

rassed previous theories of light. Further contributions of the *Treatise* include establishing that light exerts a radiation pressure (confirmed experimentally by Lebedev in 1900); initiation of research on connections between electrical and optical properties of bodies; application of Tait's quaternion formulas to the field equations, paving the way for Heaviside's and Bibbs's developments of vector analysis; application of reciprocal theorems to electrostatics; a general treatment of Green's functions; topological methods in field and network theory; the beautiful polar representation of spherical harmonic functions; and important contributions to experimental technique, such as the well-known "Maxwell bridge" circuit for determining the magnitude of an inductance.

Maxwell was led to his second major field of accomplishment, the kinetic theory of gases, by his study of Saturn's rings, which raised the problem of determining the motions of large numbers of colliding bodies; by papers of Clausius (1857, 1858) with ideas of probability and free path; and by early reading on statistics. The first five propositions of his "Illustrations of the Dynamical Theory of Gases" (1860) led to a statistical formula for the distribution of velocities in a gas at uniform pressure, and marked the beginning of a new epoch in physics with the extraordinary novelty of Maxwell's idea of describing actual physical processes by a statistical function.

In a second paper he offered a new derivation of the distribution law tied directly to molecular encounters; he then applied the distribution function to evaluate coefficients of viscosity, diffusion, and heat conduction, as well as other properties of gases not studied by Clausius. He interpreted viscosity as the transfer of momentum between successive layers of molecules moving, like Saturn's rings, with different transverse velocities, and found that viscosity is independent of pressure; he gave as the physical explanation for this that although the number of molecules increases with pressure, the average distance over which each one carries momentum decreases with pressure. He calculated the numerical value for the free path as 5.6×10^{-6} cm. for air at atmospheric pressure and room temperature. The calculations for diffusion and heat conduction proceeded along similar lines by determining the number of molecules and quantity of energy transferred in the gas. On considering the distribution of energy among different modes of motion of the molecules, he deduced that equal volumes of gas at fixed temperature and pressure contain the same number of molecules.

The measurements of gaseous viscosity at different pressures and temperatures made by Maxwell and his wife in 1865 were their most useful contribution to experimental physics. The "Dynamical Theory of Gases," which followed (1867), was Maxwell's greatest single paper; in it he developed a new theory treating gas molecules as point centers of force subject to an inverse nth-power repulsion, and replacing the characteristic mean free path by a characteristic time, the "modulus of time of relaxation" of stresses in the gas. Processes short compared with relaxation time are elastic; processes of longer duration are viscous. This theory of stress relaxation formed the starting point of the science of rheology and affected indirectly every branch of physics.

In further studies of gas theory Maxwell went on to perfect his transfer equation for molecular encounters; to determine the scattering integrals and calculate physical properties of gases; to find an expression for the thermal conductivity of a gas in terms of its viscosity, density, and specific heat (the ratio of these quantities, the "Prandtl number," is one of several dimensionless ratios used in applying similarity principles to the solution of problems in fluid dynamics); to give a revised theory of diffusion for the hard-sphere gas, from which he developed estimates of the size of molecules (1873); and to give a new theory of capillarity, based on considerations about intermolecular forces, which stimulated new research on surface phenomena (1876).

In his last two years Maxwell produced two powerful papers on molecular physics. The main conclusion of "On Boltzmann's Theorem on the Average Distribution of Energy in a System of Material Points" was that the validity of the distribution and equipartition laws in a system of material particles is not restricted to binary encounters; an important result of a more technical kind was an exact calculation of the microcanonical density of the gas. Together with Boltzmann's articles this paper marks the emergence of statistical mechanics as an independent science. "On Stresses in Rarefied Gases Arising From Inequalities of Temperature" gave a theory for the radiometer effect and thermal transpiration, and created the science of rarefied gas dynamics.

Maxwell's textbook *Theory of Heat* was published in 1870 and went through several editions with extensive revisions. Chiefly an exposition of standard results, it did contain one far-reaching innovation, the "Maxwell relations" between the thermodynamical variables—pressure, volume, entropy, and temperature—and their partial derivatives. In conceptual spirit they resemble Maxwell's field equations in electricity, by which they were obviously suggested; they are an ordered collection of relationships between fundamental quantities from which practically useful formulas follow. One more important personage in the *Theory of Heat* was Maxwell's "sorting demon" (so named by Thomson), a member of a class of "very small BUT lively beings incapable of doing work but able to open and shut valves which move without friction and inertia" and thereby defeat the second law of thermodynamics. The demon points to the statistical character of the law.

MAYER, ALFRED MARSHALL (*b. Baltimore, Md., 1836; d. Hoboken, N.J., 1897*), physics.

Mayer was a self-educated analytical chemist who published his first paper at age nineteen; at age twenty he was named assistant professor of physics and chemistry at the University of Maryland. He taught in various universities until 1871, when he organized the department of physics at the newly founded Stevens Institute of Technology. He remained there until his death. He invented the method of floating tiny magnets in a magnetic field, a method much used at the time as a key to discovering and illustrating atomic structure. His major work was in acoustics: Mayer's Law gives a quantitative relation between pitch and the duration of residual auditory sensation.

MAYER, CHRISTIAN (*b. Meserisch, Moravia [now Mederizenhi, Czechoslovakia], 1719; d. Heidelberg, Germany, 1783*), astronomy.

Mayer, a Jesuit, was professor of mathematics and physics at Heidelberg University from 1752. In 1762 the elector palatine named him court astronomer and built him an observatory at Schwetzingen. He observed the transits of Venus across the sun in 1761 and 1769. In 1776 he turned to a branch of astronomy not previously investigated: the observation of double stars. The controversy engendered by his conclusions gave an important impetus to this new branch of astronomy.

MAYER, CHRISTIAN GUSTAV ADOLPH (*b. Leipzig, Germany, 1839; d. Gries bei Bozen, Austria [now Bolzano, Italy], 1908*), mathematics,

Mayer studied mathematics and physics at several German universities before receiving his doctorate from Heidelberg in 1861. He spent his entire career there. His mathematical researches dealt essentially with the theory of differential equations, the calculus of variations, and theoretical mechanics.

MAYER, JOHANN TOBIAS (*b. Marbach, near Stuttgart, Germany, 1723; d. Göttingen, Germany, 1762*), cartography, astronomy.

Mayer was reared in an orphanage and showed an early talent for architectural drawing. In 1739 he produced a book of plans and drawings of military fortifications. Self-taught in mathematics, at age eighteen he published a book devoted to the solution of geometrical problems. In 1746 he began five-years' work with the Homann Cartographic Bureau in Nuremberg, where he improved the state of cartography. The maps he drew were both geographical and astronomical. By 1750 he had achieved a reputation as a cartographer and practical astronomer and was named professor at the Georg-August Academy in Göttingen. He chiefly taught applied mathematics and did research. His chief scientific concerns were the investigation of astronomical refraction and lunar theory. He drew up new lunar and solar tables of high accuracy, and he undertook an investigation of the celestial positions of the moon at conjunction and opposition. In 1765 the British Parliament authorized a payment of £3,000 to his widow as one of the prizes offered to "any Person or Persons as shall Discover the Longitude at Sea"; the lunar theory that brought him that prize was contained in *Theoriae lunae juxta systema Newtonianum*.

MAYER, JULIUS ROBERT (*b. Heilbronn, Württemberg [now Baden-Württemberg], Germany, 1814; d. Heilbronn, 1878*), physics, physiology.

Robert Mayer was one of the early formulators of the principle of the conservation of energy. He received an M.D. from the University of Tübingen in 1838. He became a ship's physician on a Dutch merchant ship on a voyage to the East Indies. While in Java, certain physiological observations convinced him that motion and heat were incontrovertible manifestations of a single, indestructible force in nature and that this force was quantitatively conserved in any conversion. He elaborated on this insight in papers published in the 1840's after he had settled into a successful practice in his native Heilbronn. The events of the Revolution of 1848 depressed him and he suffered recurrent fits of insanity in the 1850's. His health improved after 1860, and he gradually achieved international recognition.

Mayer's most original and comprehensive paper is *Die organische Bewegung in ihrem Zusammenhang mit dem Stoffwechsel* (1845). In it he set out the physical basis of his theory, extending the ideal of force conservation to magnetic, electrical, and chemical forces. He described the basic force conversions of the organic world. Plants convert the sun's heat and light into latent chemical force; animals consume this chemical force as food; the animals then convert that force to body heat and mechanical muscle force in their life processes. In 1848 he published *Dynamik des Himmels.* In it he showed that tidal friction deflects the major axis of the earth, and that the moon's gravitation exercises a constant retarding couple on the earth's rotation.

MAYER-EYMAR, KARL (*b. Marseilles, France, 1826; d. Zurich, Switzerland, 1907*), paleontology, stratigraphy.

Mayer-Eymar studied medicine, natural history, and geology at the University of Zurich, graduating about 1851. From 1858 he was at the geology institute of the Zurich Polytechnische Hochschule, where he was successively assistant, curator, and professor. His main interest was the biostratigraphy and paleontology of mollusks. He published voluminous lists and descriptions. His stratigraphical works were of great importance and have been of some influence until the present day.

MAYO, HERBERT (*b. London, England, 1796; d. Bad Weilbach, Germany, 1852*), neurology.

Mayo received an M.D. from Leiden in 1818. He practiced surgery and taught anatomy in London from 1819 to 1843. He founded the Middlesex Hospital Medical School in 1836 and wrote many successful textbooks. Mayo announced his discoveries of the physiology of the nerves in his *Anatomical and Physiological Commentaries* (part one, 1822; part two, 1823). He classified nerves as being either sentient or voluntary and wrote that "An influence may be propagated from the sentient nerves of a part to their correspondent nerves of motion through the intervention of that part alone of the nervous system to which they are mutually attached," an early description of reflex action.

MAYOW, JOHN (*b. Bray, near Looe, England, 1641; d. London, England, 1679*), physiology, chemistry.

Mayow received a bachelor of law degree from Oxford in 1670 and entered medical practice at Bath and, probably, London. He is best known for his studies on the interrelated problems of atmospheric composition, aerial nitre, combustion, and respiration. He has been regarded by some as the unappreciated precursor of Lavoisier, especially in describing the role of oxygen in respiration and combustion. His first book, *Tractatus duo* (1668), contains a tract on respiration and one on rickets. It was the former that gave the work its importance. In it, Mayow described "nitrous air," a substance necessary for respiration. The nitrous particles react with the "sulphureous" parts of the blood, causing a gentle and necessary fermentation in the pulmonary vessels, heart, and arteries. It is essential to the beating of the heart, which results from an "explosion" that occurs microscopically within its fibers. In a later work, *Tractatus quinque* (1674), Mayow described a substance he called nitro-aerial spirit that is responsible for sustaining combustion and producing

fermentation. Lavoisier was aware of Mayow's experiments and theories, giving rise to the controversy over his exact contributions to the development of the modern science of chemistry.

MAYR (MARIUS), SIMON (*b. Gunzenhausen, Germany, 1573; d. Ansbach, Germany, 1624*), astronomy.

Mayr studied at Heilbronn from 1589 to 1601. He studied medicine and began serious astronomical observation. In 1607 he was convicted of plagiarizing Galileo. Today he is remembered mostly for being the first to mention in print the nebula in Andromeda, to publish tables of the mean periodic motions of the four satellites of Jupiter then known, and for bestowing on them the names by which they are still known.

AL-MĀZINĪ. *See* **Abū Ḥāmid al-Gharnāṭī.**

MAZURKIEWICZ, STEFAN (*b. Warsaw, Poland, 1888; d. Grodzisk, Mazowiecki, near Warsaw, 1945*), mathematics.

Mazurkiewicz studied mathematics at the universities of Cracow, Lvov, Munich, and Göttingen. He received a Ph.D. from Lvov in 1913, and in 1915 he was named professor of mathematics at the University of Warsaw, a position he held until his death. Mazurkiewicz, along with Zygmunt Janiszewski and Wacław Sierpiński, was a founder of the contemporary Polish mathematical school and of its journal *Fundamenta mathematicae,* which is concerned chiefly with set theory and related fields, including topology and foundations of mathematics. A particular interest of Mazurkiewicz was the theory of probability. The manuscript for his book on that subject was destroyed in 1944 during the German burning of Warsaw. Mazurkiewicz, gravely ill, rewrote part of it, but died before he could complete the task. The work was published eleven years after his death.

MÉCHAIN, PIERRE-FRANÇOIS-ANDRÉ (*b. Laon, Aisne, France, 1744; d. Castellón de la Plana, Spain, 1804*), geodesy, astronomy.

Méchain was a mathematical prodigy who was brought to the attention of Lalande, who in 1772 procured for him a position as hydrographer at the naval map archives in Versailles. He became an expert mapmaker and became active as an astronomical observer. In 1781 he discovered two comets and calculated their orbits. From 1788 to 1794 he edited *Connaissance des temps,* the French national almanac. In 1790 the National Assembly named Méchain and Delambre to the task of establishing a decimal system of measurement. The unit was to be the meter, which was intended to be one ten-millionth part of the distance from the equator to the terrestrial pole. It was to be based on an extended survey from Dunkerque to Barcelona. Méchain was given the difficult task of surveying the stretch over the Pyrenees. The project was beset with all manner of problems: the French Revolution, mechanical accidents, war between Spain and France, and Méchain's own poor health. The task was completed in 1798 and Méchain was honored by being named director of the Paris Observatory. In 1803, however, still dissatisfied, he returned to Spain to make corrections in his survey. He died there of yellow fever exacerbated by exhaustion and poor diet.

MECHNIKOV, ILYA. *See* **Metchnikoff, Elie.**

MECKEL, JOHANN FRIEDRICH (*b. Halle, Germany, 1781; d. Halle, 1833*), anatomy, embryology, comparative anatomy.

Meckel studied at the universities of Halle and Göttingen, receiving his doctorate from the former in 1802. In 1808 he became professor of normal and pathological anatomy, surgery, and obstetrics at Halle, remaining there until his death. He was one of the greatest anatomists of his time. His painstaking observations in comparative and pathological anatomy furnished a wealth of new knowledge. Meckel's teratology was the first comprehensive description of birth defects. He discovered the diverticulum—which now carries his name—in the distal small bowel.

MEDICUS, FRIEDRICH CASIMIR (Medikus, Friedrich Kasimir) (*b. Grumbach, Rhineland, Germany, 1736; d. Mannheim, Germany, 1808*), botany.

Medicus studied medicine at Tübingen, Strasbourg, and Heidelberg, and served as a garrison doctor in the Palatine army. In 1766 he abandoned medicine for botany and became director of the Mannheim botanic garden. He became a leading opponent of Linnaeus—prolific, bitter, witty, and sarcastic. In addition, his works contain many firsthand botanical observations that are of both historical and nomenclatural importance.

MEDINA, PEDRO DE (*b. Seville [?], Spain, 1493; d. Seville, 1576*), cosmography, navigation.

Medina was a cleric and may have graduated from the University of Seville. He was the librarian to the duke of Medina-Sidonia, and in 1538 King Charles I gave him a warrant to draw charts and prepare pilot books for navigation to the Indies. He also made astrolabes, quadrants, mariner's compasses, forestaffs, and other navigational instruments. His book *El arte de navegar* (1545) is one of the prime works of Spain's golden maritime age.

MEEK, FIELDING BRADFORD (*b. Madison, Ind., 1817; d. Washington, D.C., 1876*), paleontology, geology.

Meek was self-educated in natural history and supported himself as a portrait painter. From 1852 to 1858 he assisted James Hall, who was New York State paleontologist. In 1857 he first recognized the occurrence of Permian fossils in the United States, and he felt, probably justifiably, that Hall took credit for this and other of his discoveries. In 1858 he became the first full-time paleontologist with the Smithsonian Institution. There he described Paleozoic fossils of Illinois and supervised the survey of the Territories.

MEGGERS, WILLIAM FREDERICK (*b. Clintonville, Wis., 1888; d. Washington, D.C., 1966*), physics.

Meggers received a doctorate from Johns Hopkins in 1917 and began his career in spectroscopy at the U.S. Bureau of Standards. He remained there until 1958. His achievements, which provide a lasting contribution to our knowledge of atomic structure, consisted of observing, measuring, and interpreting optical spectra. He was long associated with international efforts toward establishing standard wavelengths of light.

MEINESZ, F. A. VENING. *See* **Vening Meinesz, Felix A.**

MEINZER, OSCAR EDWARD (*b. near Davis, Ill., 1876; d. Washington, D.C., 1948*), ground-water hydrology.

Meinzer graduated from Beloit College in 1901, attended the University of Chicago (1906–07), and received a Ph.D. in 1922. He began his career with the U.S. Geological Survey in 1906 and was chief of its ground-water division from 1913 until he retired in 1946. He became the main architect in the development of the modern science of ground-water hydrology. He trained a large number of scientists and engineers who became recognized international authorities. In developing the science, he established new methods for determining the quality and quantity of available ground water. He was the author or co-author of more than 100 reports and papers, among them *Outline of Ground-Water Hydrology* (1923) and *The Occurrence of Ground Water in the United States* (1923).

MEISSNER, GEORG (*b. Hannover, Germany, 1829; d. Göttingen, Germany, 1905*), anatomy, physiology.

While a student at the University of Göttingen (from which he received his doctorate in 1853), Meissner came under the influence of Rudolph Wagner, who was professor of physiology, comparative anatomy, and zoology. After further study in Berlin and Munich and teaching at Basel and Freiburg im Breisgau, he returned to Göttingen in 1860. There he became the first occupant of the separate chair of physiology. He held the chair until 1901, when he retired. Before 1857 his work dealt chiefly with problems of microscopy, especially as related to the skin (Meissner's tactile cells). In 1857 he described the submucosal nerve plexus of the intestinal wall (Meissner's plexus). After 1858 he wrote largely on physiological-chemical problems.

MEITNER, LISE (*b. Vienna, Austria, 1878; d. Cambridge, England, 1968*), physics.

Meitner was the second woman to receive (1905) a doctorate in science from the University of Vienna. In Berlin she began her long association with Otto Hahn, and together they set to work measuring radiation. In 1917 they discovered the element protactinium. In 1918 she was appointed head of the physics department of the Kaiser-Wilhelm Institut and continued her work toward clarifying the relationship between beta and gamma rays. She was also on the faculty of the University of Berlin.

In 1938 Meitner fled Hitler's Germany and settled in Stockholm. There she made her most famous contribution: she bombarded the uranium nucleus with slow neutrons. The result of the fission was the release of great amounts of energy. It was a result that contributed to the development of the nuclear-fission bomb, although Meitner herself refused to work on the project.

MELA, POMPONIUS. *See* **Pomponius Mela.**

MELLANBY, EDWARD (*b. West Hartlepool, Durham, England, 1884; d. Mill Hill, near London, England, 1955*), biochemistry, physiology, biomedical research and administration.

Mellanby received a B.A. from Emmanuel College, Cambridge, in 1905. He studied medicine at St. Thomas' Hospital, London, from which he received an M.A. (1910), an M.B. (1910), and an M.D. (1915). He taught physiology at King's (later Queen Elizabeth) College for Women, London (1913–20); and from 1920 to 1933 was professor of pharmacology at the University of Sheffield. From 1933 to 1949 he was secretary (chief executive) of the Medical Research Council, the most important post in medical research in Great Britain. He was knighted in 1937.

Mellanby did pioneer work on dietary deficiency diseases. In particular, he discovered (1918–21) that it was the absence of vitamin D, which he isolated, that caused rickets. Since vitamin D was readily available in such animal fats as cod-liver oil, butter, and suet, within a decade no case of rickets could be found in London's clinics. His later research included work on the effects of vitamin A deficiency.

MELLO, FRANCISCO DE (*b. Lisbon, Portugal, 1490; d. Évora, Portugal, 1536*), mathematics.

A protégé of King Manuel I, Mello studied theology and mathematics in Paris and returned to be tutor to the king's children. He enjoyed considerable prestige as a scientist, but many of his works were destroyed in the fire that followed the great Lisbon earthquake of 1755. Among his extant works are a commentary on Euclid and a work on geometry based on Jābir ibn Aflaḥ.

MELLONI, MACEDONIO (*b. Parma, Italy, 1798; d. Portici, Italy, 1854*), physics.

Melloni was professor of physics at the University of Parma from 1824 and 1831. He was a political exile from 1831 to 1839; he returned to Italy to become director of a physics conservatory in Naples and director of the meteorological observatory on Vesuvius. Melloni was mostly concerned with the properties of radiant heat, or calorific radiation as it was then called, and how it differed from light. His detailed investigations into the behavior of heat were important to later generations.

MELTZER, SAMUEL JAMES (*b. Ponevyezh, Russia [now Panevezhis, Lithuanian S.S.R.], 1851; d. New York, N.Y., 1920*), physiology, pharmacology.

Meltzer received an M.D. from the University of Berlin in 1882 and soon settled in New York City in medical practice. In 1904 he joined the recently created Rockefeller Institute for Medical Research; he headed the department of physiology there until he retired in 1919. His early work was on the reflex act of swallowing, and he did later work on artificial respiration. He did an important study on the pharmacological effect of magnesium salts. Perhaps his most important contribution was as a liaison between practitioners and scientific investigators.

MELVILL, THOMAS (*b. Glasgow [?], Scotland, 1726; d. Geneva, Switzerland, 1753*), astronomy, physics.

Melvill studied divinity at the University of Glasgow, where he acquired a taste for experimental philosophy. He noted the yellow spectrum of sodium, and considered a means of testing a relation between the velocity of light and its color, developing an observation of Bradley re-

garding color aberration. He died at twenty-seven, depriving physics of a gifted and ingenious experimenter.

MENABREA, LUIGI FEDERICO (*b. Chambéry, Savoy, 1809; d. St. Cassin [near Chambéry], France, 1896*), structural and military engineering, mathematics.

Menabrea is known to scientists as one of the most important men in the development of energy methods in the theory of elasticity and structures. He was also a distinguished general and statesman. He studied engineering and mathematics at the University of Turin. He entered the army corps of engineers but soon resigned to become professor of mechanics and construction at the University of Turin and at the Military Academy there. The king of Sardinia entrusted him with various diplomatic missions, while at the same time he rose in rank in the Sardinian army and commanded important military campaigns. In 1860 he was appointed senator and was given the title of count. He held several portfolios in the government, culminating with premier and foreign minister from 1867 to 1869. He opposed Garibaldi and the temporal power of the pope. He was later ambassador to London. He was created marquis of Valdora in 1875 and retired from public life in 1892. In science, Menabrea's place has been overshadowed by the greater fame of Castigliano, even though Menabrea's methods form the essential foundation for Castigliano's accomplishments. During the period 1857–58 and later in 1868, Menabrea enunciated his "principle of elasticity," calling it also "principle of least work," stating that when an elastic system attains equilibrium under external forces, the work done by the tensions and compressions in ther internal members of the system is a minimum. His methods placed these concepts for the first time very clearly before the engineering profession.

MENAECHMUS (*fl. Athens and Cyzicus, middle of fourth century, B.C.*), mathematics.

Menaechmus may have headed the mathematical school at Cyzicus and may have been mathematical tutor to Alexander the Great, possibly introduced to that position by Aristotle. He is known to have written a commentary on Plato's *Republic*, and he must have written at least one work describing his discovery of the conic sections, but none of his works has survived. Modern knowledge of him and his work is all derived from secondary sources, much of it from the Neoplatonic philosopher Plotus.

Plotus attributes to Menaechmus the discovery of the conic sections. He appears to have been aware of all three types and saw them as sections of a cone—that is, not as plane curves that he later identified with sections of a cone. He also knew the properties of the asymptotes of a hyperbola. There are no signs of any knowledge of the conic sections before Menaechmus, but with him it suddenly blossomed forth in full flower.

MENDEL, JOHANN GREGOR (*b. Heinzendorf, Austria [now Hynčice, Czechoslovakia], 1822; d. Brno, Austria [now Czechoslovakia], 1884*), genetics, meteorology.

In 1840 Mendel enrolled at the University of Olmütz (Olomouc). His physics professor, F. Franz, recommended his admission to the Augustinian monastery in Brno, and Mendel entered the monastery in 1843 with the name Gregor.

During his theological studies (1844–48) Mendel also attended courses at the Philosophical Institute in agriculture, pomology, and viticulture given by F. Diebl, who in his textbook of plant production had described artificial pollination as the main method of plant improvement. In these lectures Mendel also learned of the methods of sheep breeding introduced by F. Geisslern.

Mendel was then sent to the University of Vienna. He attended lectures on experimental physics by Doppler and on the construction and use of physical apparatus by Andreas von Ettinghausen. Mendel also thoroughly studied Gaertner's *Versuche und Beobachtungen über die Bastardzeugung im Pflanzenreich* (Stuttgart, 1849), in which nearly 10,000 separate experiments with 700 plant species yielding hybrids were described. During his studies Mendel published his first two short communications (1853, 1854), on damage to plant cultures by some insects.

In 1868 Mendel was elected abbot of the monastery, which involved many official duties. He also became a member of the Central Board of the Agricultural Society and was entrusted with distribution of subsidies for promoting farming. He took an active part in the organization of the first statistical service for agriculture. Later he also reported on scientific literature and cooperated with the editorial board of the society's journal, *Mittheilungen der K. K. Mährisch-schlesischen Gesellschaft zur Beförderung des Ackerbaues, der Natur- und Landeskunde.*

Mendel began his meteorological studies in 1856 and was soon recognized as the only authority on this subject in Moravia. In his first meteorological paper (1863) he summarized graphically the results of observations at Brno, using the statistical principle to compare the data for a given year with average conditions of the previous fifteen years. Between 1863 and 1869, the paper was followed by five similar communications concerned with the whole of Moravia. Later Mendel published three meteorological reports describing exceptional storm phenomena. He also devoted much time to the observation of sunspots, assuming that they had some relation to the weather. In 1877, with his support, weather forecasts for farmers in Moravia were issued, the first in central Europe.

Mendel's principal work in plant hybridization was the outcome of ten years of tedious experiments. His approach was the common one of reducing the problem to an elementary level and formulating a hypothesis that could be proved or disproved by experiments.

Between 1856 and 1863 Mendel cultivated and tested at least 28,000 plants, carefully analyzing seven pairs of seed and plant characteristics. This was his main experimental program. His original idea was that heredity is particulate, contrary to the model of "blending inheritance" generally accepted at that time. In the pea plants hereditary particles to be investigated are in pairs. Mendel called them "elements" and attributed them to the respective parents. From one parent plant comes an element determining, for instance, round seed shape; from the other parent, an element governing the development of the angular shape. In the first generation all hybrids are alike, exhibiting one of the parental characteristics (round seed shape) in unchanged form. Mendel called such a characteristic "dominant"; the other (angular shape), which remains latent and appears in the next generation, he called "recessive." The "elements" deter-

mining each paired character pass in the germ cells of the hybrids, without influencing each other, so that one of each pair of "elements" passes in every pollen (sperm) and in every egg (ovule) cell. In fertilization, the element marked by Mendel *A,* denoting dominant round seed shape, and the element *a,* denoting the recessive angular shape, meet at random, the resulting combination of "elements" being

$$\tfrac{1}{4} \, AA \; + \; \tfrac{1}{4} \, Aa \; + \; \tfrac{1}{4} \, aA \; + \; \tfrac{1}{4} \, aa.$$

In hybrid progeny both parental forms appear again; and Mendel's explanation of this segregation of parental traits was called, after 1900, Mendel's law (or principle) of segregation.

In his simplest experiments with crossing pea plants that differed in only one trait pair, Mendel cultivated nearly 14,000 plants and explained the progeny of the hybrid in terms of the series $A + 2 Aa + a$. At the same time he conformed to the view of K. F. von Gaertner and J. G. Koelreuter that hybrids have a tendency to revert to the parental forms. Mendel then called his explanation of hybrid progeny "the law of development thus found," which he tested further in a case "when several different traits are united in the hybrid through fertilization." Hereditary elements belonging to different pairs of traits, for example A and a for the round and angular seed shapes and B and b for the yellow and green seed colors, recombine the individual series $A + 2 Aa + a$ and $B + 2 Bb + b$, resulting in terms of a combination series

$$\begin{aligned} AB + Ab + aB + ab + 2\,ABb + 2\,aBb \\ + 2\,AaB + 2\,Aab + AaBb. \end{aligned}$$

In his paper Mendel also illustrated a recombination of three trait pairs, showing every expected combination of characteristics and relevant elements in actual counts of offspring. He also observed that 128 constant associations of seven alternative and mutually exclusive characteristics were actually obtained—that being the expansion of 2^7, and the maximum number theoretically possible. His conclusion was that the "behavior of each of different traits in a hybrid association is independent of all other differences in the two parental plants," which principle was later called Mendel's law of independent assortment.

The generalization of Mendel's explanation was that "if n denotes the number of characteristic differences in two parental plants, then 3^n is the number of terms in the combination series, 4^n the number of individuals that belong to the series, and 2^n the number of combinations that remain constant."

Mendel's introduction of simple symbols that permitted comparing the experimental results definitively with the theory was very important. Altogether new was his use of large populations of experimental plants, which allowed him to express his experimental results in numbers and subject them to mathematical treatment. By the statistical analysis of large numbers Mendel succeeded in extracting "laws" from seemingly random phenomena.

The main results of Mendel's experiments and their interpretation, which constituted his whole theory, were reported in "Versuche über Pflanzenhybriden" (1866). This memoir was his magnum opus, one of the most important papers in the history of biology, and the foundation of genetic studies.

After 1866, however, he published only a single short paper on *Hieracium* hybrids (1869). But the great efforts he devoted to this goal are evident from his letters written from 1866 to 1873 to Naegeli.

After 1871 Mendel conducted hybridization experiments on bees, hoping to prove his theory in the animal kingdom. He kept about fifty bee varieties, which he attempted to cross in order to obtain "a new synthetic race." He was not successful, however, because of the complex problem of the controlled mating of queen bees. In these experiments he also proved the hybrid effect on fertility of bees.

Mendel received no recognition of his scientific work and even Naegeli missed its essential feature and did not grasp the historical significance of his theory. Mendel was not understood in his time. Only in the following decades did the discoveries of the material basis of what was later called Mendelian—behavior of the nucleus in cell division, constancy in each species of the number of chromosomes, the longitudinal splitting of chromosomes, the reduction division during the maturation of germ cells, and the restitution of the number of chromosomes in fertilization—prepare the way for understanding the cytological basis of Mendelian inheritance and for its general acceptance.

The absence of response and recognition was one of the reasons that Mendel stopped publishing the results of his later experiments and observations. He did, nonetheless, take satisfaction and pleasure in the application of his theory in the breeding of new varieties of fruit trees and in propagating the idea of hybridization among local gardeners and horticulturists.

MENDEL, LAFAYETTE BENEDICT (*b. Delhi, N.Y., 1872; d. New Haven, Conn., 1935*), physiological chemistry.

Mendel graduated from Yale in 1891, and received a Ph.D. from the Sheffield Scientific School at Yale in 1893. He studied at Breslau and Freiburg, and in 1897 returned to Sheffield. He spent the rest of his career at Yale. In addition to his scientific work, Mendel was renowned as a teacher. He is remembered chiefly as coauthor, with Thomas B. Osborne, of more than one hundred papers on nutrition. His experiments on laboratory rats created the first convincing proof that certain amino acids are essential components of the diet and cannot be synthesized by the animal organism. He also identified vitamin A in butter (McCollum at Wisconsin independently discovered it at about the same time and published his results first and is, therefore, usually credited with the discovery); his experiments led directly to the discovery of vitamin B. Largely through his own efforts, nutrition was transformed during his lifetime from empiricism to a clearly recognized branch of biochemistry. His contributions to the modern meat and poultry industries (with their attention to animal nutritional needs) is almost incalculable.

MENDELEEV, DMITRY IVANOVICH (*b. Tobolsk, Siberia [now Tyumen Oblast, R.S.F.S.R.], Russia, 1834; d. St. Petersburg [now Leningrad], Russia, 1907*), chemistry.

Mendeleev entered the Tobolsk Gymnasium when he was seven, and graduated from it in 1849. In 1850 he enrolled in the Main Pedagogical Institute from which he graduated in 1855 with a brilliant record, but his hot temper led him into a quarrel with an important official of the Ministry of Education, and his first teaching assignment was therefore to the Simferopol Gymnasium, which was closed because of the Crimean War.

After two months in the Crimea, where he was unable to work, Mendeleev went to Odessa as a teacher in the lyceum, and there took up the continuation of his early scientific work. He had already begun to investigate the relationships between the crystal forms and chemical composition of substances. On graduating from the Institute, he had written a dissertation entitled "Isomorphism in Connection With Other Relations of Form to Composition."

In September 1856 Mendeleev defended a master's thesis at the University of St. Petersburg, expressing his adherence to the chemical ideas of Gerhardt. Among other topics, he made known his agreement with unitary and type theories and his opposition to Berzelius' electrolytic theory of the formation of chemical compounds. Mendeleev adhered to Gerhardt's ideas all his life, and in consequence later years found him resisting Arrhenius' electrolytic theory, rejecting the concept of the ion as an electrically charged molecular fragment, and refusing to recognize the reality of the electron. He was opposed in general to linking chemistry with electricity and preferred associating it with physics as the science of mass. His predilection found its most brilliant vindication in the correlation he achieved between the chemical properties and the atomic weights of elements. Nor was he a chemical mechanist in the methodological sense then fashionable in certain quarters. Chemistry in his view was an independent science, albeit a physical one.

In October 1856 Mendeleev defended a thesis *pro venia legendi* to obtain the status of privatdocent in the university. His subject was the structure of silicon compounds. In January 1857 he began to give lectures in chemistry and to conduct research at the university's laboratories. In 1859–60 Mendeleev worked at the University of Heidelberg, where he first collaborated with Bunsen, and then established his own laboratory. He studied capillary phenomena and the deviations of gases and vapors from the laws of perfect gases. In 1860, he discovered the phenomenon of critical temperature—the temperature at which a gas or vapor may be liquefied by the application of pressure alone—which he called the "absolute temperature of boiling." He was thereby led to consider once again the relationship between the physical and chemical properties of particles and their mass.

In 1861 Mendeleev published "Attempt at a Theory of Limits of Organic Compounds," in which he stated that the percentage of such elements as oxygen, hydrogen, and nitrogen could not exceed a certain maximum value when combined with carbon—a theory that brought him into direct opposition to the structural theories of organic chemistry. On this theory he based his text *Organicheskaya khimia,* which was published in the same year.

From 1864 to 1866 Mendeleev was professor of chemistry at the St. Petersburg Technological Institute and a docent on the staff of the university. In addition, he traveled abroad on scientific assignments for three or four months of each year, wrote books, edited translations, and participated in the compilation of a technical encyclopedia, for which he wrote articles on the production of chemicals and technical chemistry, including the production of alcohol and alcoholometry. In 1865 he defended a thesis for the doctorate in chemistry, "On the Compounds of Alcohol With Water." In it he first developed the characteristic view that solutions are chemical compounds and that dissolving one substance in another is not to be distinguished from other forms of chemical combination. In this thesis, he also adhered to the principles of chemical atomism. Mendeleev was also active in the growth of Russian chemical organizations during the 1860's.

A turning point in his career occurred in October 1867, when he was appointed to the chair of chemistry at the University of St. Petersburg. He found nothing which he could recommend as a text, so he set out to write his own. He derived his basic plan for his book from Gerhardt's theory of types, whereby elements were grouped by valence in relation to hydrogen.

Mendeleev's work toward the *Osnovy khimii* thus led him to the periodic law, which he formulated in March 1869: "Elements placed according to the value of their atomic weights present a clear periodicity of properties." The necessity to establish correct atomic weights was what first led Mendeleev to investigate the connections among the elements; from this investigation he proceeded inductively to the periodic law, upon which he was then able to construct a system of elements.

At first Mendeleev could subsume under the periodic law only isomorphism and atomic weight; in each of these early papers, too, he presented only the quantitative argument for the analytical expression of the law in the form of the increase of atomic weights. The first paper in particular contained many ambiguities and imprecisions. Having been occupied with studies leading up to the law for fifteen years—since 1854—Mendeleev then formulated it in a single day. He spent the next three years in further perfecting it, and continued to be concerned with its finer points until 1907.

Mendeleev himself summarized the studies that had brought him to the periodic law in a later edition of *Osnovy khimii,* in which he commented on "four aspects of matter," representing the measurable properties of elements and their compounds: "(a) isomorphism, or the similarity of crystal forms and their ability to form isomorphic mixtures; (b) the relation of specific volumes of similar compounds or elements; (c) the composition of their compound salts; and (d) the relations of the atomic weights of elements."

The *Osnovy khimii* was finished in February 1871. Among the important ideas that the work embodied was Mendeleev's notion of the complexity of the chemical elements and their formation from "ultimates." In March 1871, two years after his discovery of the law, Mendeleev first named it "periodic." That summer he published in *Justus Leibigs Annalen der Chemie* his article "Die periodische Gesetzmässigkeit der chemischen Elemente," which he later characterized as "the best summary of my views and ideas on the periodicity of the elements and the original after which so much was written later about this system."

The majority of scientists did not accept Mendeleev's discovery for some time; the first textbook on organic chemistry to be based on the law was published in St. Petersburg by Richter only in 1874. The discovery of gallium was incorporated into the third edition of *Osnovy khimii* in 1877. The fourth edition, of 1881–82, mentioned the discovery of scandium—the ekaboron predicted by Mendeleev—by Nilson, in 1879. Winkler discovered germanium in 1886; its properties matched precisely those of Mendeleev's ekasilicon, and the discovery of germanium figured in the fifth edition of Mendeleev's book in 1889.

After 1884, Mendeleev concerned himself with the expansion of liquids and in particular with the specific weights of aqueous solutions of various substances. He thus arrived at a chemical theory of solutions, which he opposed to the theory of electrolytic dissociation of dilute aqueous solutions set forth by Arrhenius. Mendeleev stated his theory both in his "Research on Aqueous Solutions According to Their Specific Weight" of 1887 and in the fifth edition of *Osnovy khimii.*

From the late 1870's Mendeleev was also concerned with the production of petroleum. In 1876 he visited the United States; in the resultant book, "Petroleum Production in the North American State of Pennsylvania and in the Caucasus," he advanced a theory of the inorganic origin of petroleum. In 1880–81, Mendeleev wrote a series of reports of the results of his Caucasian journeys, and thus became engaged in a dispute with Nobel over the proper location of petroleum refineries. In 1883, with "On a Question of Petroleum," he entered into a discussion with Markovnikov; he also wrote a series of works on the refining of both Baku and American oil.

From 1892 on, Mendeleev was concerned in the regulation of the system of weights and measures in Russia. In 1893 he was named director of the newly created Central Board of Weights and Measures, a post that he held until his death. In the 1890's Mendeleev was also actively involved in problems of shipbuilding and the development of shipping routes. He participated in the design of the icebreaker *Ermak* (launched in 1899) and wrote on the progress of research in the northern Arctic Ocean (1901).

From 1892 Mendeleev took an active part in the preparation of the great Brockhaus encyclopedia, which provided another vehicle for the dissemination of his ideas in western Europe. He introduced a section on chemistry and the production of chemicals and wrote the articles on matter, the periodic regularity of the chemical elements, and technology, among a number of other topics.

MENEGHETTI, EGIDIO (b. *Verona, Italy, 1892; d. Padua, Italy, 1961*), experimental pharmacology.

Meneghetti graduated from the University of Padua in 1916. He taught there except between 1926 and 1932, when he taught at Camerino and Palermo. He was named professor of pharmacology at Padua in 1932, and in 1951 founded the Centro di Studio per la Chemoterapia there. He worked in the sometimes overlapping fields of colloids and toxicology. He wrote more than a hundred scientific works, including reports on the toxicology of arsenic, erythrocytes, antimony, sulfur, and the histiocytic system. His *Elementi di Farmacologia* (1934) went through many editions and revisions.

MENELAUS OF ALEXANDRIA (*fl. Alexandria and Rome*, A.D. *100*), geometry, trigonometry, astronomy.

Nothing is known of the life of Menelaus, although Ptolemy records that he was making astronomical observations in Rome in A.D. 98. His major contribution to the rising science of trigonometry was contained in his *Sphaerica*. It is this work that entitles him to be regarded as the founder of spherical trigonometry and the first to have disengaged trigonometry from spherics and astronomy. He also wrote a work on chords in the circle, an elements of geometry, a book on the triangle, a work on hydrostatics, a treatise on the signs of the zodiac, and a series of astronomical observations that may have amounted to a catalog of the fixed stars. His works have not survived in Greek, but are known to us through Arabic translations.

MENGHINI, VINCENZO ANTONIO (*b. Budrio, Italy, 1704; d. Bologna, Italy, 1759*), medicine, chemistry.

Meneghini graduated from the University of Bologna in philosophy and medicine in 1726. He taught theoretical and practical medicine there for most of his life. He identified the red corpuscles as the chief site of iron within the organism.

MENGOLI, PIETRO (*b. Bologna, Italy, 1625; d. Bologna, 1686*), mathematics.

Mengoli took a degree in philosophy in 1650 at the University of Bologna and went on to further degrees in philosophy and civil and canon law. He was ordained a priest, taught at the university, and served a parish in Bologna until his death. His mathematical works, widely distributed in the seventeenth century, are significant because of the transitional position of his mathematics, midway between Cavalieri's method of indivisibles and Newton's fluxions and Leibniz' differentials. In his major writings, he took up Cataldi's work on infinite algorithms (1650), and set out a logical arrangement of the concepts of limit and definite integral (1659).

MENSHUTKIN, NIKOLAY ALEKSANDROVICH (*b. St. Petersburg, Russia, 1842; d. St. Petersburg, 1907*), chemistry.

Menshutskin received a B.S. (1862), an M.S. (1866), and a Ph.D. (1869) from St. Petersburg University. He was professor there until 1902, when he went to the Petersburg Polytechnic Institute. His work was chiefly in chemical kinetics. He developed a kinetic method of determining the isomers of alcohols which was used to determine the structure of newly synthesized alcohols. He published (1871) a highly successful textbook on analytic chemistry, a detailed course of organic chemistry (1883–84), and the first original work on the history of chemistry in the Russian language.

MENURET DE CHAMBAUD, JEAN JACQUES (*b. Montélimar, France, 1733; d. Paris, France, 1815*), physiology, medicine.

Menuret received his medical degree from Montpellier and went to Paris, where he established a medical practice and contributed articles to the Diderot-d'Alembert *Encyclopédie*. His central preoccupation was the art of medicine. He claimed to regard practice as being far more important than theory. For this reason, the prospective physician required more the clinical experience won through apprenticeship or in the hospital and less a rigorous introduction to the sciences ancillary to medicine.

MÉRAY, HUGUES CHARLES ROBERT (*b. Chalon-sur-Saône, France, 1835; d. Dijon, France, 1911*), mathematics.

Méray was educated at the École Normale Supérieure and became a *lycée* teacher. In 1867 he became a professor at the University of Dijon, where he spent the remainder of his career. He is remembered for having anticipated (in 1869) Cantor's theory of irrational numbers, one of the main steps in the arithmetization of analysis.

MERCATI, MICHELE (*b. San Miniato, Italy, 1541; d. Rome, Italy, 1593*), medicine, natural sciences.

Mercati studied at the University of Pisa under Cesalpino. Pope Pius V named him director of the Vatican botanical garden, a position he continued to hold under Gregory XIII and Sixtus V. The grand duke of Tuscany elevated him to the aristocracy. As a naturalist, his greatest interest lay in collecting minerals and fossils; that collection later formed the basis of the work that made him famous: *Metallotheca*, published posthumously in 1717. He was one of the founders of paleontology; he understood the origin of stone implements in a day when they were generally considered the product of lightning.

MERCATOR, GERARDUS (or **Gerhard Kremer**) (*b. Rupelmonde, Flanders, 1512; d. Duisburg, Germany, 1594*), geography.

Mercator's family name was Kremer, but he latinized it on entering the University of Louvain in 1530. He studied philosophy and theology and became concerned with mathematics and astronomy. He was a man of many talents and also a great artist whose contributions to calligraphy and engraving influenced several generations of artisans. His lasting fame rests on his contributions to mapmaking; he was undoubtedly the most influential of cartographers. His maps cover a variety of subjects. At Duisburg, where he was cosmographer to the duke of Cleves, he published the first modern maps of Europe and Britain, and in 1569 he published his famous world map. It was created on a new projection that still bears his name. His son, Rumold, published a collection of his maps in 1595 under the title "Atlas—or Cosmographic Meditations on the Structure of the World." It was the first time the word "atlas" was used to designate a collection of maps.

MERCATOR, NICOLAUS (Kauffman, Niklaus) (*b. Eutin [?], Schleswig-Holstein, Denmark [now Germany], ca. 1619; d. Paris, France, 1687*), mathematics, astronomy.

Mercator graduated from the University of Rostock in 1642 and was appointed to the Faculty of Philosophy. He also taught at Copenhagen University, where he produced several short textbooks on elementary and spherical astronomy. His tract on calendar improvement (1653) caught Cromwell's eye in England, and Mercator moved to London, where he continued to reside for thirty years. He supported himself as a mathematical tutor, and he is remembered above all as a mathematician. His best-known work was *Logarithmotechnia* (1668). However, his

Hypothesis astronomica nova (1664) was also important. His enunciation of Kepler's hypothesis (that planets travel in elliptical orbits round the sun, with the sun at one focus) was instrumental in propagating that theory. Newton is known to have used Mercator's works to fill in his rather shaky knowledge of planetary and lunar theory.

MERICA, PAUL DYER (*b. Warsaw, Ind., 1889; d. Tarrytown, N.Y., 1957*), metallurgy.

Merica received a B.A. from the University of Wisconsin in 1908 and a Ph.D. from the University of Berlin in 1914. He taught at Wisconsin and in Hangchow, China. From 1914 to 1919 he was a physical metallurgist for the U.S. Bureau of Standards. There he collaborated on developing a new alloy, Duralumin, which made use of precipitation hardening—the first new hardening process since classical times. After 1919 Merica was with the International Nickel Company, where he continued his research.

MERRETT, CHRISTOPHER (*b. Winchcomb, England, 1614; d. London, England, 1695*), natural history, glassmaking.

Merrett received an M.B. from Oxford in 1636 and an M.D. in 1643. He practiced in London. He translated a pioneer work in glassmaking, Antonio Neri's *L'arte vetraria* (1612), adding considerable original material applicable to Britain. His *Pinax rerum naturalium Britannicarum* (1666) was notable because the section on mammals and birds was the first attempt to construct a British fauna.

MERRIAM, CLINTON HART (*b. New York, N.Y., 1855; d. Berkeley, Calif., 1942*), biology.

Merriam studied at Yale University and received an M.D. from the College of Physicians and Surgeons (now part of Columbia University) in 1879. He practiced medicine for six years, and then became an ornithologist at the U.S. Department of Agriculture for what later became the Bureau of Biological Survey. Although most widely known for his definition of life zones of faunal distribution, he also did significant groundwork in mammalian studies. He was also active in early conservation efforts.

MERRIAM, JOHN CAMPBELL (*b. Hopkinton, Iowa, 1869; d. Oakland, Calif., 1945*), paleontology.

Merriam received a B.S. from Lenox College, Iowa, studied at the University of California at Berkeley, and received a Ph.D. in vertebrate paleontology from Munich in 1893. Taught at University of California (1894–1920); president of Carnegie Institution of Washington (1920–38). He published papers on Tertiary echinoids and Triassic Ichthyosauria. He did studies of the John Day Basin in Oregon and the Rancho La Brea tar pits in California.

MERRILL, ELMER DREW (*b. East Auburn, Me., 1876; d. Forest Hills, Mass., 1956*), botany.

Merrill graduated from what is now the University of Maine in 1898 and remained as an assistant in the natural sciences. From 1902 to 1923 he was with the Philippine Bureau of Agriculture. He established an important herbarium, taught at the University of the Philippines, and in 1919 became director of the Bureau of Science. From 1924 to 1930 he was at the University of California at Berkeley. From 1930 to 1935 he was professor of botany at Columbia University and director of the New York Botanical Garden. After that he was professor at Harvard University, director of the Arnold Arboretum, and administrator of botanical collections. Merrill was acknowledged the "American Linnaeus." He amassed a million plant specimens of tropical floras, and he designed a comprehensive field label for plant vouchers. His *Plant Life of the Pacific World* (1945) was the distillation of his years in the tropics. He designed the "Merrill case" for housing plant specimens.

MERRILL, GEORGE PERKINS (*b. Auburn, Me., 1854; d. Auburn, 1929*), geology, meteoritics.

Merrill received a B.Sc. from what is now the University of Maine in 1879. He joined the Smithsonian in 1881, where he was put in charge of petrology and physical geology at the U.S. National Museum. From 1897 he was head of its geology department. From 1893 to 1915 he was also professor of geology and mineralogy at Columbian College (now George Washington University). He assembled the great geological collection of the Smithsonian and was a world-recognized expert on rock weathering. His most successful works were *Stones for Building and Decoration* (1891) and especially *A Treatise on Rocks, Rock Weathering, and Soils* (1897). He also did notable work on identifying meteorites and craters.

MERSENNE, MARIN (*b. Oizé, Maine, France, 1588; d. Paris, France, 1648*), natural philosophy, acoustics, music, mechanics, optics, scientific communication.

Mersenne studied theology at the Sorbonne and in 1611 joined the Order of Minims. He spent virtually the rest of his life in their convent in Paris. In his earliest works, he defended the Christian orthodoxy against such ancient and Renaissance doctrines scepticism, atheism, alchemy, magic, deism, atomism, and a whole range of Hermetic, Cabalist, and "natural" doctrines of occult powers and harmonies. After about 1625 he devoted himself to scientific and mathematical matters. His *Harmonie universelle* (1636–37) was devoted to his theory of music, harmonics, and acoustics, and the pendulum. His posthumously published *L'optique et la catoptrique* (1651) discussed current hypotheses on the nature of light.

Mersenne's chief importance, however, lay in his role as the propagator of the new science of the seventeenth century. His regular visitors or correspondents came to include Peiresc, Gassendi, Descartes, the Roman musicologist Giovanni Battista Doni, Roberval, Beeckman, J.B. van Helmont, Fermat, Hobbes, and the Pascals. Although he defended in varying degrees Copernicus, Francis Bacon, and Galileo, in general he continued to support orthodox theology. For example, he condemned Giordano Bruno for having made "underhanded attacks on the Christian religion." On the other hand, his insistence on the careful specification of experimental procedures, repetitions of experiments, and the publication of the numerical results of actual measurements all marked a notable step in the organization of experimental science in the seventeenth century.

MÉRY, JEAN (*b. Vatan, France, 1645; d. Paris, France, 1722*), anatomy, surgery, pathology.

Méry studied surgery at the Hôtel-Dieu and served there as surgeon for most of his life; he was chief surgeon from 1700. Méry's researches were mostly comparative-anatomical and pathological. He made a number of valuable contributions to the anatomy of a wide range of animals. He described the urethral glands named after Cowper before Cowper described them, and he preceded Winslow in a designation of the eustachian valve.

MESHCHERSKY, IVAN VSEVOLODOVICH (*b. Arkhangelsk, Russia, 1859; d. Leningrad, U.S.S.R., 1935*), mechanics, mathematics.

Meshchersky graduated from St. Petersburg University in 1882, took a master's degree in mathematics there in 1889, and in 1897 received a doctorate. He taught there and at the St. Petersburg Polytechnic Institute. He was an innovative pedagogue and published a scientific–methodological guide to the teaching of mathematics and mechanics; his own course in theoretical mechanics became famous; and his textbook on theoretical mechanics went through twenty-four editions and was a standard work: His purely scientific work was devoted to the motion of bodies of variable mass. His pioneering studies formed the basis for much of the rocket technology and dynamics that was developed rapidly following World War II.

MESMER, FRANZ ANTON (*b. Iznang, Germany, 1734; d. Meersburg, Germany, 1815*), medicine, origins of hypnosis.

Mesmer attended the Jesuit University of Dillingen (Bavaria), the University of Ingolstadt, and the University of Vienna (M.D., 1766). He established a highly successful practice in Vienna and began building up a repertory of techniques and cures. He applied magnets to the bodies of patients, for example. But he is remembered as the man who introduced hypnotism, or mesmerism, as a therapeutic device. Mesmerism became a *cause célèbre;* scores of mesmerists entered the field, producing at least 200 books and pamphlets, many of which were sensationalist in nature and made excessive claims for the procedure. Mesmer himself never systematized his ideas, and confined his writings on the subject to two pamphlets. A royal commission issued a highly critical report in 1784, and Mesmer virtually retired from practice and the movement declined. Hypnotism, shorn of its occultism and vitalist influences, reemerged as a medical practice late in the nineteenth century.

MESNIL, FÉLIX (*b. Ormonville-la-Petite, Manche, France, 1868; d. Paris, France, 1938*), zoology, general biology, tropical medicine.

Mesnil received a doctorate in 1895 from the École Normale Supérieure in Paris. After spending several months at universities in central Europe, he entered the Institut Pasteur, where he remained throughout his career. His work was varied, much of it oriented toward general biology; important papers dealt with systematic, ecological, and etiological zoology. His investigations of the French coasts resulted in the description of many new genera and species of annelids, crustaceans, enteropneusts, turbellarians, Orthonectida, and protozoans. His major book, written with A. Laveran, was *Trypanosomes et trypanosomiases* (1904).

MESSAHALA. *See* **Māshāʾāllāh.**

MESSIER, CHARLES (*b. Badonviller, Lorraine, France, 1730; d. Paris, France, 1817*), astronomy.

Messier, with no astronomical education, became a clerk to Joseph-Nicolas Delisle in 1751, moving in 1755 to the observatory in the Hôtel de Cluny. In 1759 Delisle set Messier to searching for the reappearance of Halley's comet. Messier found it, but observers in Saxony reported it first and claimed the credit. In 1760 Delisle retired, and for the next fifteen years Messier claimed a virtual monopoly on comet discoveries. He also observed nebulae, eclipses, occultations, sunspots, the new planet Uranus, and the transits of Mercury and Venus. His catalog of nebulae and star clusters, first published in 1771, remains his most enduring contribution to astronomy.

MESYATSEV, IVAN ILLARIONOVICH (*b. 1885; d. Moscow, U.S.S.R., 1940*), earth science, oceanography.

Mesyatsev graduated from Moscow University in 1912 and remained there a professor of zoology throughout his career. His scientific interests were centered on marine ichthyology and its importance to the fishing industry. He was especially active in exploring the Barents Sea and served on and headed numerous government commissions related to fishing.

METCHNIKOFF, ELIE (*b. Ivanovka, Kharkov Province, Russia, 1845; d. Paris, France, 1916*), embryology, comparative anatomy, pathology, bacteriology, immunology.

Metchnikoff studied at the university in Kharkov, with Rudolf Leuckart at Giessen, at Göttingen and Munich, and at St. Petersburg, where he received his doctorate. He taught at the new University of Odessa off and on, until 1888, when he moved to Paris to enter the Pasteur Institute. He remained there the rest of his life. In 1882, while in Messina, he made his greatest discovery, the role of phagocytes in the defense of the animal body. (He also coined the term "phagocyte.") His theory of phagocytosis was vigorously opposed, and Metchnikoff and his followers were forced to devise new experiments and new arguments to ward off attacks on his brainchild. He also did important work on immunology and on the problem of fever and the mechanisms of infection. His book *L'immunité dans les maladies infectieuses* (1901), was a resounding success, and in 1908 he shared the Nobel Prize with Paul Ehrlich for their researches illuminating the understanding of immunity.

METIUS, ADRIAEN (*b. Alkmaar, Netherlands, 1571; d. Franeker, Frisia [now Netherlands], 1635*), mathematics, instrument making; **[METIUS], ADRIAEN ANTHONISZ** (*b. Alkmaar [?], Netherlands, ca. 1543; d. Alkmaar [?], 1620*), *military engineering, cartography;* **METIUS, JACOB** (*b. Alkmaar, Netherlands; d. Alkmaar, 1628*), mathematics, instrument making.

Adriaen Anthonisz, the father, was cartographer and military engineer for the States of Holland and burgomaster of Alkmaar. He gave the value of 335/113 for what we now denote by pi, stating that it differs from the true value by less than 1/100,000. He built fortifications, drew charts of cities and military works, and wrote on sundials and astronomical problems.

His second son, Adriaen, studied at the University of Franeker in Frisia and at the University of Leiden. He worked under Tycho Brahe at his observatory on Hven, taught at Rostock and Jena, assisted his father in the Netherlands, and in 1598 became professor at Franeker, a position he held until his death. He taught mathematics, surveying, navigation, military engineering, and astronomy. He was a popular and efficient teacher, who followed Tycho Brahe's theory of the solar system. His books included *Doctrina spherica* (1598) and *Geometria practica* (1625).

His brother Jacob became an instrument maker in Alkmaar, specializing in lens grinding. He was intensely shy about his inventions and destroyed them before his death. According to Descartes and Jacob's brother Adriaen, his "perspicilla" was actually the first telescope.

METON (*fl. Athens, second half of fifth century* B.C.), astronomy.

Meton, about whom little is known, was famous in antiquity for his introduction of a nineteen-year lunisolar calendaric cycle, in modern times often called the Metonic cycle. Although some scholars have asserted that he aimed to reform the Athenian civil calendar, the evidence is that his purpose was to provide a fixed calendrical scheme for recording astronomical data. His calendar (with corrections) was so used as late as Hipparchus (128 B.C.). He is also credited with being the first Greek of whom we can say with certainty that he undertook serious astronomomical observations. His solstice observations (even if inaccurate by one day) are the earliest Ptolemy thought worthy of attention. He is also assumed to have observed equinoxes. His observatory was on the hill of the Pnyx in Athens, but we do not know what his instruments were.

METTENIUS, GEORG HEINRICH (*b. Frankfurt am Main, Germany, 1823; d. Leipzig, Germany, 1866*), botany.

Mettenius received a doctorate at Heidelberg in 1845. After further studies at various universities, he became professor of botany and director of the botanic garden at Leipzig (1852). He made an intensive study of ferns and had become one of the leading pteridologists of his day when he died suddenly of cholera at age forty-two.

METZGER, HÉLÈNE (*b. Chatou, near Paris, France, 1889; d. on the way to Auschwitz, Poland, 1944*), chemistry, history of science, philosophy.

Hélène Bruhl studied mineralogy with Frédéric Wallerant at the Sorbonne, receiving her diploma in 1912. In 1913 she married Paul Metzger, a professor of history and geography at Lyons, who died the next year in World War I. She received her doctorate in 1918, with her dissertation on the history of crystallography. She gave a synthetic view of the history of chemistry in *La chimie* (1930).

Drawn to philosophical reflection and preoccupied with epistemological problems, she devoted her last two decades to the philosophy of science and the history of science. A disciple of Émile Meyerson and Lucien Lévy-Bruhl (her uncle), she was not satisfied with a strictly positivist position. For her, religious, metaphysical, and scientific ideas formed a unified whole in a given historical period and must be studied together. It is a view widely accepted today. Her views are contained in *La*

science, l'appel de la religion et la volonté humaine (published posthumously, 1954). She was arrested by German troops occupying France in 1944 and died on her way to a concentration camp.

MEUSNIER DE LA PLACE, JEAN-BAPTISTE-MARIE-CHARLES, (*b. Tours, France, 1754; d. Mainz, Germany, 1793*), mathematics, physics, engineering.

Meusnier was privately tutored until he entered the military academy at Mézières, from which he graduated in 1775 and entered the Engineering Corps. His mathematics teacher was Gaspard Monge, under whom Meusnier did his only published mathematical work, on the theory of surfaces. It was "Mémoire sur la courbure des surfaces," (read in 1776, published in 1785) and it contained Meusnier's theorem on the curvature, at a point of a surface, of plane sections with a common tangent. It is now a standard theorem in differential geometry. From 1779 to 1788 he was a military engineer improving the harborworks of Cherbourg. The first balloon ascensions in 1783 caused him to study the theory of this new field, aerostation. He and Lavoisier collaborated on the synthesis and analysis of water. Its success was a heavy blow to the phlogiston theory.

MEYEN, FRANZ JULIUS FERDINAND (*b. Tilsit, Prussia [now Sovetsk, U.S.S.R.], 1804; d. Berlin, Germany, 1840*), botany.

Meyen received an M.D. in 1826 from the Friedrich Wilhelms Institut, where military physicians were trained. He also studied botany and zoology at the University of Berlin. In 1830 he became ship's doctor on a royal cargo ship, with the assignment of collecting natural history specimens and making scientific observations. In 1834 he became a professor at the University of Berlin and continued his study of phytotomy and plant physiology. His importance for botany lies in his intensive and wide-ranging study of microscopic anatomy in connection with physiology. His most important works were *Phytotomie* (1830) and *Neues System der Pflanzen-Physiologie* (3 vols, 1837–39).

MEYER, CHRISTIAN ERICH HERMANN VON (*b. Frankfurt, Germany, 1801; d. Frankfurt, 1869*), paleontology.

Meyer studied finance and natural science, especially geology and mineralogy, at several German universities, He became a respected paleontologist, publishing numerous works in rapid succession, although finance remained his career. In 1837 he entered the financial administration of the Bundestag of the German Confederation, becoming its director of finances in 1863. His main scientific area of interest was the fossil vertebrates, and his chief work was *Fauna der Vorwelt* (4 vols., 1845). He considered all types of vertebrates and was one of the most distinguished scientists in the field; his descriptions were characterized by great accuracy and clarity of expression.

MEYER, JOHANN FRIEDRICH (*b. Osnabrück, Hannover [now German Federal Republic], 1705; d. Osnabrück, 1765*), chemistry.

Meyer was apprenticed to an apothecary and worked as a journeyman, studying mining and metallurgy, before inheriting his grandmother's apothecary shop (1737). Today, he is best known for being wrong: He argued that causticity in alkalies arose from a substance, *acidum pingue*, that entered the mild alkalies from the fire. His theory was accepted by a number of chemists, but with the explication over the next fifteen years of the role of oxygen in combustion and acidification, Meyer's claim as a builder of eighteenth-century chemistry received a blow from which it has never recovered.

MEYER, JULIUS LOTHAR (*b. Varel, Oldenburg, Germany, 1830; d. Tübingen, Germany, 1895*), chemistry.

Meyer received an M.D. from Würzburg in 1854 and went to Heidelberg to study physiological chemistry under Bunsen. In 1856 he went to Königsberg to attend Franz Neumann's lectures on mathematical physics. In 1859 the University of Breslau awarded him the Ph.D. for his study of the effect of carbon monoxide on the blood. He taught at Breslau, where he published *Die modernen Theorien der Chemie und ihre Bedeutung für die chemische Statik* (1864). In 1866 he was called to the School of Forestry at Neustadt-Eberswalde, in 1868 to the Karlsruhe Polytechnic Institute, and in 1876 to Tübingen, where he taught until his death.

Meyer is known for his work on the periodic table, which he developed independently of Mendeleev. Mendeleev's 1869 paper on the periodic table of the elements led Meyer to publish his findings the next year. In 1882 he and Mendeleev jointly received the Davy Medal of the Royal Society for the creation of the table. He went on to plead with chemists to systematize inorganic chemistry on the basis of the periodic table, in order to approach the organization of subject matter achieved in organic chemistry.

MEYER, KURT HEINRICH (*b. Dorpat, Russia, 1883; d. Menton, France, 1952*), organic chemistry.

Meyer studied chemistry at the universities of Marburg, Freiburg, and Leipzig. After receiving the doctorate in 1907, he traveled for a year and then settled in Munich, where the school of organic chemistry was led by Adolf von Baeyer. There he carried out the studies on keto-enol tautomerism that first made his reputation. In 1917 he worked with Haber on chemical warfare.

After the war Meyer isolated the pure enol form of ethyl acetoacetate by "aseptic distillation," working with H. Hopff. In 1921 he left academic life to become director of the headquarters laboratories of the firm of Badische Anilin- und Sodafabrik (BASF) at Ludwigshafen. His own interests became increasingly centered on the chemistry of natural high polymers. In 1932 he left the country to take the chair of inorganic and organic chemistry at the University of Geneva.

MEYER, VICTOR (*b. Berlin, Germany, 1848; d. Heidelberg, Germany, 1897*), chemistry.

Meyer received the Ph.D., *summa cum laude,* at the age of eighteen from the University of Heidelberg. He remained there one year as Bunsen's assistant and then became Baeyer's assistant at Berlin. From 1872 to 1885 he was professor at Zurich. He then went to Göttingen and finally back to Heidelberg, where he became Bunsen's successor. He remained there until his death.

Meyer explored the area of nitro compounds so thoroughly that at the time of his death, almost all that was known about them was due to Meyer and his students. His name is most closely associated with his vapor density method, which he perfected in 1878. In it, the vapor of a weighed substance displaced an equal volume of air, which in turn was measured by means of a burette. This method is still more commonly used than any other, and Meyer's apparatus is found in most chemical laboratories. The vapor density studies led to a further series of pyrochemical researches. He studied vapors at temperatures up to 3000°C. In 1885 he published *Pyrochemische Untersuchungen,* which dealt with those researches. In 1883 he discovered and named thiophene. His comprehensive treatise on organic chemistry, *Lehrbuch der organischen Chemie* (2 vols, 1893–1903), written with Paul Jacobson and uncompleted at the time of his death, remains the best extended treatment of the subject.

MEYER, WILHELM FRANZ (*b. Magdeburg, Germany, 1856; d. Königsberg, Germany [now Kaliningrad, U.S.S.R.], 1934*), mathematics.

Meyer studied in Leipzig and Munich, where he received his doctorate in 1878. He taught at Tübingen, at the Bergakademie of Claustha-Zellerfeld, and from 1897 until retirement at the University of Königsberg. Meyer was a many-sided mathematician whose list of writings includes 136 titles. His principal field of interest was geometry, especially algebraic geometry and the related projective invariant theory, of which he was one of the leading experts.

MEYERHOF, OTTO (*b. Hannover, Germany, 1884; d. Philadelphia, Pa., 1951*), biochemistry.

Meyerhof received an M.D. from the University of Heidelberg in 1909. His interest turned to cellular physiology, and he pursued that field at the University of Kiel (1913–24), the Kaiser Wilhelm Institute for Biology in Berlin-Dahlem (1924–29), and the Kaiser Wilhelm Institute for Medical Research at Heidelberg (1929–38). He fled the Nazis in 1938, eventually settling at the School of Medicine at the University of Pennsylvania. Meyerhof's work on the chemical processes in the muscle laid the basis for the elucidation of the chemical pathway in the intracellular breakdown of glucose to provide energy for biological processes. Meyerhof and A.V. Hill shared the 1922 Nobel Prize in physiology or medicine. His influence on the development of biochemistry was profound. He published some 400 scientific articles; his books include *Chimie de la contraction musculaire* (1933).

MEYERSON, ÉMILE (*b. Lyublin, Russia [now Lublin, Poland], 1859; d. Paris, France, 1933*), history and philosophy of science.

Meyerson was educated in Germany at the universities of Göttingen, Heidelberg, and Berlin and at the Còllege de France. In 1898 he became head of the Jewish Colonization Association, and thereafter retained an attachment to Zionism. He became a French citizen and maintained an influential philosophical salon in Paris. His first and most famous work was *Identité et réalité* (1908). It is basically a demonstration of the key role of causality in the physical sciences. He held scientific thought to be a continuation of common sense and saw science as a progressive rationalization of reality. His other important works were *De l'explication dans les sciences* (1921), *La déduction relativiste* (1925), and *Du cheminement de la pensée* (1931).

MICHAEL PSELLUS. *See* **Psellus, Michael.**

MICHAEL SCOT (*b. before 1200; d. ca. 1235*), astrology, popularization of science, translation of scientific and philosophical works from the Arabic.

Nothing is known of Michael's background; despite the epithet "Scot," there is no indication that he was Scottish, or, as the term sometimes meant, Irish. He was in Toledo in about 1217, where he probably learned Arabic and, perhaps, Hebrew. By 1224 he was a priest and was given benefices in Britain. Pope Honorius III named him archbishop of Cashel, Ireland, a position he declined. There are also indications that he studied or taught at Bologna and Paris.

Today Michael Scot is chiefly remembered as an astrologer and magician. Contemporary scientists—e.g., Albertus Magnus and Roger Bacon—were scathing in their assessments of his scientific knowledge and honesty. Bacon did, however, credit him for having introduced some Aristotle and Ibn Rushd to the West. His translations, particularly of Arabic commentaries on Aristotle, were widely used by the early Scholastic philosophers. He was astrologer to the Emperor Frederick II, and his most famous books probably grew out of that position. *Liber introductorius* and *Liber particularis* deal primarily with astronomy, partly mixed with and partly distinguishable from astrology; general geography and meteorology; the tides; and such other matters as advice on food, on curing mental states with the help of enchantresses, music, the calendar, important numbers (especially seven), and some theology. *Physionomia* deals with human anatomy and physiology but not in the accepted scientific manner. *Ars alchemie* deals directly with alchemy.

MICHAEL, ARTHUR (*b. Buffalo, N.Y., 1853; d. Orlando, Fla., 1942*), chemistry.

Michael studied chemistry under Hofmann at Berlin (1871, 1875–78), under Bunsen at Heidelberg (1872–74), and under Wurtz at Paris (1879). He was professor of chemistry at Tufts College (1881–89, 1894–1907) and Harvard University (1912–36). He was a severe critic of mechanical interpretations of chemical phenomena, and he introduced thermodynamic conceptions into organic chemical theory.

MICHAUX, ANDRÉ (*b. Satory, near Versailles, France, 1746; d. Madagascar [now Malagasy Republic], 1802*), botany.

Michaux studied under the leading French botanists of his day and botanized with Lamarck and André Thouin. He was sent to North America, particularly to investigate potential sources of ship timbers. That trip—and subsequent ones—led to his compiling the first flora for eastern America (1803). He introduced many American plants into French horticulture and disseminated the camellia, silk tree, and tea olive in the Carolinas. Among his works is *Histoire des chênes de l'Amérique* (1801).

MICHELI, PIER ANTONIO (*b. Florence, Italy, 1679; d. Florence, 1737*), botany.

Micheli, the son of a laborer, was completely self-educated in plant life. He eventually obtained the patronage of the Medici, whose generosity permitted him to devote his full time to botany. The results of his collecting expeditions throughout southern and central Europe are contained in *Nova plantarum genera* (1729). In it he considered 1,900 species, 1,400 of which were new. His classifications are considered cautious and perspicacious.

MICHELINI, FAMIANO (*b. Rome, Italy, 1604; d. Florence, Italy, 1665*), hydraulics, medicine.

Michelini was a member of the Piarists, a teaching order, and he was sent (1629) to Florence to teach. His mathematical gifts came to the attention of Galileo and Benedetto Castelli. He taught mathematics at the Florentine court and in 1648 became professor at Pisa. He was much interested in medicine although he was not a doctor. He is generally credited with paving the way for Redi's experiments and Borelli's theories. Among other things, he recommended the use in many illnesses of orange and lemon juice, and advised people to control their weight. He was also regarded as an expert on hydraulics. Although his works on running water and riverbeds contain errors, they also contain many good suggestions.

MICHELL, JOHN (*b. Nottinghamshire [?], England, 1724 [?]; d. Thornhill, near Leeds, England, 1793*), astronomy.

Michell earned a permanent place in the history of stellar astronomy for two signal accomplishments: he was the first to make a realistic estimate of the distance of the stars, and he discovered the existence of physical double stars. He graduated from Queen's College, Cambridge, with an M.A. (1752) and a B.D. (1761). From 1762 to 1764 he was geology professor at Cambridge. After 1767 he was rector of a church at Thornhill. He was a man of wide interests; in addition to astronomy. They included music and the study of the causes of earthquakes.

MICHEL-LÉVY, AUGUSTE (*b. Paris, France, 1844; d. Paris, 1911*), geology, mineralogy.

Michel-Lévy attended the École Polytechnique and the École des Mines, from which he graduated in 1867. He entered the service of the Carte Géologique, where he remained throughout his career. In 1907 he became its inspector general. Michel-Lévy collaborated with Ferdinand Fouqué in introducing into France the study of rocks by microscopical petrography. They co-authored *Minéralogie micrographique* (2 vols., 1879) and *Synthèse des minéraux et des roches* (1882), which incorporated their work in synthesizing igneous rocks artificially. Alone, Michel-Lévy did work on the feldspars and devoted twenty years to field work in the Massif Central, the Morvan Massif, and the western Alps.

MICHELSON, ALBERT ABRAHAM (*b. Strelno, Prussia [now Poland], 1852; d. Pasadena, Calif., 1931*), physics, optics, metrology.

Michelson, whose family immigrated to America when he was four, graduated from the Naval Academy at Annapolis in 1873. From 1880 to 1882 he studied in Europe with Helmholtz, Quincke, Cornu, Mascart, and Lippmann. He taught at the academy and several universities before going in 1893 to the new University of Chicago to head its physics department. From 1920 he did research at Mt. Wilson observatory and at the California Institute of Technology.

In 1907 Michelson became the first American citizen to win a Nobel Prize in one of the sciences "for his precision optical instruments and the spectroscopic and metrological investigations conducted therewith." He had measured the speed of light in 1878 as his first venture into scientific research. He invented the interferometer to aid him in his measurements. He and Edward W. Morley conducted ether-drift experiments with the interferometer in 1887; their null results led indirectly to Einstein's relativity theory. In 1892–93 he measured the Paris meter bar, finding it was equal to 1,553,163.5 wavelengths of the red cadmium line. So elegant were the success and precision of this project that Michelson became internationally famous. His books are *Light Waves and Their Uses* (1903) and *Studies in Optics* (1927).

MICHURIN, IVAN VLADIMIROVICH (*b. Dolgoye, Ryazan gubernia, Russia, 1855; d. Kozlov [now Michurinsk], U.S.S.R., 1935*), plant breeding, genetics.

Michurin was the owner of a small private experimental nursery at the time of the Russian Revolution. It became a state institution, and Michurin achieved great fame and power, becoming known as the "Russian Burbank." He was put in charge of an institute directing fruit breeding for almost the entire country. His real fame came after his death in 1935, when "Michurinism" became the official name for the genetics doctrine of Lysenko. Even after Lysenko lost political support in 1965, official sanction continued to bestow on Michurin the status of a breeder of genius whose unusual methods can be explained by genetics. Because of this official sanction, his genuine contributions to horticulture are difficult to determine. He believed in "vegetative blending"—grafting different species onto one another to predispose them for cross-pollination. He resented efforts to subject his methods and beliefs to rigorous tests. He placed high value on practical intuition as a guide to the breeder.

MIDDENDORF, ALEKSANDR FEDOROVICH (*b. St. Petersburg, Russia, 1815; d. Khellenurme [now Estonian S.S.R.], 1894*), biogeography.

Middendorf received an M.D. from Dorpat University in 1837, and he studied zoology, botany, and geognosy in various universities. He taught zoology at Kiev University and then undertook a two-year scientific expedition to northern and eastern Siberia. The result was his masterpiece, *Reise in den aussersten Norden und Osten Sibiriens während der Jahre 1843 und 1844* (4 vols, 1848–75), which dealt with the climatology, geognosy, botany, zoology, and ethnography of the region.

MIDGLEY, THOMAS, JR. (*b. Beaver Falls, Pa., 1889; d. Worthington, Ohio, 1944*), chemistry.

Midgley graduated from Cornell University in 1911 with a degree in mechanical engineering, but devoted himself thereafter to industrial chemistry. From 1916 he worked with Charles F. Kettering on the problem of gaseous detonation, or knock, in the internal combustion engine. Eventually (1921) he discovered the substance tetraethyl lead, which reduced knock and aided fuel econ-

omy. He then became general manager of the Ethyl Gasoline Corporation. Later, for General Motors, he discovered the refrigerant dichlorodifluoromethane.

MIE, GUSTAV (*b. Rostock, Germany, 1868; d. Freiburg im Breisgau, German Federal Republic, 1957*), physics.

Mie received a doctorate from the University of Heidelberg in 1891, where he had studied mathematics and the physical sciences. In 1897 he became *Privatdozent* at the Physics Institute of the Technische Hochschule in Karlsruhe and from 1902 to 1917 he was at the University of Greifswald. He was at the University of Halle until 1924 and thereafter at the University of Freiburg im Breisgau. Mie's research into light diffraction led to the discovery (known as the Mie effect) of the asymmetry in the intensity distribution and the precise determination of the optical constants of suspended particles. It had increasing importance in the investigation of interstellar matter. He also did important work on the electromagnetic field, and his theory of matter had a great influence on later physicists.

MIELI, ALDO (*b. Leghorn, Italy, 1879; d. Florida, Argentina, 1950*), chemistry, history of science.

Mieli graduated in chemistry from the University of Pisa and was Paterno's assistant in chemistry at the University of Rome from 1905 to 1912. Thereafter, he devoted himself to the history of science, one of the first scholars to consider this study an autonomous discipline. He edited numerous bibliographies, journals, and series of books on the history of science. Political considerations caused him to flee to France in 1928 and again to Argentina in 1939. There he continued to edit *Archeion*, the journal he had begun to edit in 1921, when it was known as *Archivio di storia della scienza*. He also taught at the Universidad Nacional del Litoral in Santa Fé. At his death, he had completed only part of his monumental *Panorama general de historia de la ciencia*, which was finished by others and eventually published in twelve volumes.

MIERS, HENRY ALEXANDER (*b. Rio de Janeiro, Brazil, 1858; d. London, England, 1942*), mineralogy.

Miers graduated from Oxford in 1881 with a degree in mathematics. He became an assistant to Lazarus Fletcher at the British Museum, where he was largely concerned with descriptions of crystal forms. His invention of an inverted goniometer permitted him to measure crystal faces while they were growing. In 1886 he began teaching crystallography at what later became part of Imperial College, and in 1895 he became professor of mineralogy at Oxford. In 1902 his highly successful textbook on mineralogy was published. After 1908 he was at the universities of London and (after 1915) Manchester. He was chiefly interested in crystal growth and was a renowned teacher.

MIESCHER, JOHANN FRIEDRICH II (*b. Basel, Switzerland, 1844; d. Davos, Switzerland, 1895*), physiology, physiological chemistry.

Miescher was educated at the University of Basel, where his father (who had the same name) was professor of pathological anatomy. After further study at Tübingen and Leipzig he returned to Basel, where in 1871 he became professor of physiology. He discovered nucleins, a new class of compounds rich in organic phosphorus and forming the major constituent of cell nuclei. He also established a clear chemical distinction between the nucleus and cytoplasm.

MIKLUKHO-MAKLAY, MIKHAIL NIKOLAEVICH (*b. Rozhdestvensky, Novgorod gubernia, Russia, 1857; d. Leningrad, U.S.S.R., 1927*), geology.

Miklukho (the suffix Maklay was added to the name later) graduated from the St. Petersburg Mining Institute in 1886 and then studied at Strasbourg University. Upon his return to Russia, he worked for the Mining Institute and did geological investigations for the Imperial Russian Mineralogical Society in various parts of Russia. Between 1886 and 1897 he compiled an index to geological literature, *Russkaya geologicheskaya biblioteka.*

MILHAUD, GASTON (*b. Nîmes, France, 1858; d. Paris, France, 1918*), mathematics, philosophy of science.

Milhaud graduated from the École Normale Supérieure in 1881 and taught mathematics at Le Havre for ten years. In 1891 he became professor of mathematics at Montpellier. In 1894, at Paris, he defended his Ph.D. thesis, on the conditions and limits of logical certainty. This remarkable work was decisive for his career, and he quickly became a respected authority in a new field. After 1909 he occupied a specially created chair at the Sorbonne in the history of philosophy as it related to science.

MILL, JOHN STUART (*b. London, England, 1806; d. Avignon, France, 1873*), philosophy, economics.

Mill was educated at home by his father James Mill, the leading exponent of utilitarianism. At age twenty-four he began his most important work in pure philosophy, *System of Logic,* which was published thirteen years later in 1843. In 1848 he published *Principles of Political Economy.* These and his other works made him the most influential British philosopher of the nineteenth century. His central endeavor as a philosopher was to provide science with a better claim to truth than that afforded by the skeptical philosophers of the seventeenth and eighteenth centuries. He believed that all knowledge is derived from sensory observation and denied the existence of innate, rational knowledge. He sought to vindicate the importance of knowledge derived inductively and claimed that even mathematics, in a way, is inductive. In political philosophy, he was a partisan of democratic government and an eloquent champion of freedom of the individual. In ethics, he generally followed the utilitarian precepts of James Mill and Jeremy Bentham.

MILLER, DAYTON CLARENCE (*b. Strongsville, Ohio, 1866; d. Cleveland, Ohio, 1941*), physics.

Miller attended Baldwin-Wallace College, and in 1890 he received a D.Sc. from Princeton University. His entire career was spent at the Case School of Applied Science (now Case Western Reserve University) in Cleveland, where he became professor of physics. He was an expert on architectural acoustics, consulting on the design of, among others, Severance Hall in Cleveland. His efforts to refute Einstein's theory of relativity were less successful.

MILLER, GEORGE ABRAM (*b. Lynnville, Pa., 1863; d. Urbana, Ill., 1951*), mathematics.

Miller graduated from Muhlenberg College in 1887 and received an M.A. from there in 1890. In 1892 he received a doctorate from Cumberland University. He taught in various institutions and in 1893 he came under the influence of Frank Nelson Cole at the University of Michigan. Thereafter, group theory engaged his talents for the rest of his life. After studying in Europe, he taught at Cornell and Stanford before settling at the University of Illinois in 1906. He remained there the rest of his life. Miller's studies in the theory of finite groups resulted in more than 800 papers, many of which made direct scientific contributions to that theory.

MILLER, HUGH (*b. Cromarty, Scotland, 1802; d. Portobello, Scotland, 1856*), geology.

By profession Miller was consecutively a stonemason, accountant, and religious editor. He was self-educated in geology. His *Scenes and Legends of the North of Scotland* (1835) contained a chapter on geology and brought him recognition. He was editor of *The Witness,* a newspaper of the "nonintrusion" faction of the Church of Scotland controversy. His articles for that journal, combining geology and religion, were assembled for his first scientific book, *The Old Red Sandstone* (1841). He believed that the fossil record confirmed in broad outline the cosmic drama depicted symbolically in the Bible. *Foot-Prints of the Creator* (1847) continued his opposition to evolutionary theory. Miller's scientific work was of limited scope, and his importance lies in his use of outstanding literary abilities to broaden the taste for science, especially geology.

MILLER, PHILIP (*b. Bromley, Greenwich, or Deptford, London, England, 1691; d. Chelsea, London, 1771*), botany, horticulture.

Miller, the most important horticultural writer of the eighteenth century, was curator of the Chelsea Physic Garden from 1722 to 1770. The son of a gardener, he set himself up in business as a florist and nurseryman. When Sir Hans Sloane transferred his private physic garden to the Society of Apothecaries, Miller became its curator and established it as the world's preeminent horticultural institution. He was editor of eight editions of the monumental *Gardeners Dictionary.*

MILLER, WILLIAM ALLEN (*b. Ipswich, England, 1817; d. Liverpool, England, 1870*), chemistry, spectroscopy, astronomy.

After being apprenticed in surgery and medicine in London, Miller took his M.B. and M.D. in 1841–42 from King's College, London. He became professor of chemistry there in 1845. His textbooks on organic and inorganic chemistry went through many editions. Miller was an early researcher into the spectra of flames and was possibly the first to publish drawings of flame and absorption spectra. He also drew the spectra of calcium, copper, barium chlorides, boric acid, and strontium nitrate. He and William Huggins, paying especial attention to the spectra of the moon, Jupiter, and Mars, concluded that all stars have much chemically in common with the sun.

MILLER, WILLIAM HALLOWES (*b. Llandovery, Carmarthenshire, Wales, 1801; d. Cambridge, England, 1880*), crystallography, mineralogy.

Miller received a B.A. in mathematics from St. John's College, Cambridge, in 1826. He remained there throughout his career. He wrote two highly successful textbooks, *The Elements of Hydrostatics and Hydrodynamics* (1831) and *An Elementary Treatise on the Differential Calculus* (1833). After 1832 he was professor of mineralogy and his main contribution to crystallography is contained in *A Treatise on Crystallography* (1839). In it, he presented his own system of indexing. The algebraic advantages of these "Millerian indices" were immediately apparent, but their full significance was not recognized until the twentieth century.

MILLER, WILLIAM LASH (*b. Galt, Canada, 1866; d. Toronto, Canada, 1940*), chemistry.

Miller received a B.A in natural philosophy at the University of Toronto in 1887. He then studied at Berlin, Göttingen, and Munich, from which he received a Ph.D. in 1890. He received a second Ph.D. from Leipzig in 1892, where he studied under Ostwald. He became familiar with the thermodynamic approach of Josiah Willard Gibbs. Most of his academic life, spent at the University of Toronto, was devoted to translating Gibbs's theories into laboratory terms, especially extending the theories to polycomponent systems.

MILLIKAN, ROBERT ANDREWS (*b. Morrison, Ill., 1868; d. Pasadena, Calif., 1953*), physics.

Millikan graduated from Oberlin College in 1891 and received an M.A. from there in 1893. He studied under M. I. Pupin at Columbia University and received a Ph.D. in 1895. After advanced study in Europe, he joined the faculty of the University of Chicago in 1896. Except for government and military service in World War I, he remained there until 1921, when he went to the California Institute of Technology. He was largely responsible for turning it into one of the most distinguished scientific centers in the world. He spent the rest of his career there.

In 1909 Millikan measured the charge of the electron, a feat for which he won the 1923 Nobel Prize in physics. He also did important work on the photoelectric effect, confirming the validity of Einstein's equation in every detail. During the 1920's he did research in the "hot spark" spectra; by 1924 he and I. S. Bowen had identified some 1,000 new lines of the ultraviolet spectra of the lighter elements. He also began an increasingly intensive program of research into the penetrating radiation for which he coined the term "cosmic rays." During his long career, he published close to 300 scientific papers. His books included the textbook *First Course in Physics* (1906), *The Electron* (1917), and *Time, Matter, and Values* (1932).

MILLINGTON, THOMAS (*b. Newbury, Berkshire, England, 1628; d. London, England, 1704*), medicine.

Millington received a B.A from Trinity College, Cambridge, in 1649. He moved to Oxford, where he received an M.A. in 1651 and a B.D. and M.D. in 1659. He became professor of natural philosophy at Oxford in 1675; although he retained the chair until his death, he seems to have resided mainly in London. He was physician to William and Mary and to Queen Anne, and was knighted in 1680. His claim upon the attention of posterity is threefold: as a physician, as a man of wide-ranging intellectual achievements, and as the reputed discoverer of sexuality in plants.

MILLON, AUGUSTE-NICOLAS-EUGÈNE (*b. Châlons-sur-Marne, France, 1812; d. St.-Seine-l'Abbaye, France, 1867*), chemistry, agronomy, pharmacy.

Millon received his medical training at the Val-de-Grâce military teaching hospital in Paris and served as an army surgeon. He received an M.D. in 1836 from the Paris Faculty of Medicine, but his interest in chemistry prompted him to take up military pharmacy. His entire career was spent in the army. Particularly noteworthy were his studies (1837–47) of the nitrides of bromine, iodine, and cyanogen; of oxides of chlorine and iodine; of reactions of nitric acid on metals and of mercury salts with ammonia; and of the nature of catalytic reactions.

MILLS, WILLIAM HOBSON (*b. London, England, 1873; d. Cambridge, England, 1959*), organic chemistry.

Mills graduated from Jesus College, Cambridge, in 1896–97. After further study at Tübingen, he taught at Northern Polytechnic Institute in London until 1912, when he returned to Cambridge. He remained there the rest of his life. The major part of his scientific work was devoted to stereochemistry and the cyanine dyes.

MILNE, EDWARD ARTHUR (*b. Hull, England, 1896; d. Dublin, Ireland, 1950*), astrophysics, cosmology.

Milne was one of the foremost pioneers of theoretical astrophysics and modern cosmology. He entered Trinity College, Cambridge, in 1916, and while an undergraduate he did important war service in research concerned with ballistics and sound ranging and involving problems related to the atmosphere of the earth. He remained at Cambridge until 1924, when he went to the University of Manchester. In 1929 he became professor of mathematics at Oxford, a position he held until his death. He was again actively involved in war service during World War II.

Milne's scientific work falls into three distinct phases: from 1920 to 1929 his researches centered on problems of radiative equilibrium and the theory of stellar atmospheres; from 1929 to 1932 he was mainly concerned with the theory of stellar structure; after 1932 he concentrated on relativity and cosmology. His books include *Relativity, Gravitation and World-Structure* (1935) and a valuable textbook, *Vectorial Mechanics* (1948).

MILNE, JOHN (*b. Liverpool, England, 1850; d. Shide, Isle of Wight, England, 1913*), seismology.

Milne was educated at King's College, London, and at the Royal School of Mines. His early years were spent as a mining engineer in many parts of the world, and he assembled numerous geological notes and a large collection of skeletons of the great auk from Funk Island. From 1875 to 1895 he was professor of mining and geology at the Imperial College of Engineering in Tokyo; there he studied earthquakes and volcanoes, for which he became world famous. He was a founder of the Seismological Society of Japan, the first in the world, and his researches touched on nearly all aspects of seismology. He helped develop that science as a full-scale branch of geophysics. With his colleagues Ewing and Gray he developed a seismograph (1892) for recording horizontal components of ground motion; reliable, compact, and simple, it could be installed on a worldwide basis. Milne compiled important earthquake catalogs, including one covering the seismic history of Japan from 295 B.C.

MILNE-EDWARDS, HENRI (*b. Bruges, Belgium, 1800; d. Paris, France, 1885*), zoology.

A naturalized French citizen, Milne-Edwards studied medicine in Paris, acquiring a solid background in zoology. In 1832 he became professor of hygiene and natural history at the École Centrale des Arts et Manufactures, where he undertook a vast program of research on the invertebrates. In 1841 he became professor of entomology at the Museum of Natural History and later also professor of the Faculty of Sciences. He first concentrated on the study of crustaceans, which resulted in his classic *Histoire naturelle des crustacés* (3 vols., 1834–40). His voluminous writings on animal organization set forth the law of division of labor within higher organisms: tissue in lower animals can adapt to different functions; in higher zoological orders, tissue specialization is found.

MINDING, ERNST FERDINAND ADOLF (or **Ferdinand Gotlibovich**) (*b. Kalisz, Poland, 1806; d. Dorpat, Russia [now Tartu, Estonian S.S.R.], 1885*), mathematics.

Minding graduated from the University of Berlin in 1827 and received a Ph.D. from Halle in 1829. He taught at Berlin until 1843; he then went to the University of Dorpat and remained there until 1883. His most important discoveries were in the differential geometry of surfaces, continuing the researches of Gauss; especially remarkable were his studies on the bending or the applicability of surfaces.

MINEUR, HENRI (*b. Lille, France, 1899; d. Paris, France, 1954*), astronomy, astrophysics, mathematics.

Mineur graduated from the École Normale Supérieure in 1921 and received a doctorate in 1924 for his work on functional equations. In 1925 he went to the Paris observatory as an astronomer. He made important contributions to stellar astronomy, celestial mechanics, analytic mechanics, statistics, and numerical calculus. He corrected the coordinates of the galactic center; he also showed that an important correction had to be made in the zero of the period-luminosity relation of the Cepheids, which led to a doubling of the scale of distances in the universe. He was the founder of the Institut d'Astrophysique in 1936.

MINKOWSKI, HERMANN (*b. Alexotas, Russia [now Lithuanian S.S.R.], 1864; d. Göttingen, Germany, 1909*), mathematics.

Minkowski was educated at the universities of Berlin and Königsberg, from which he received his doctorate in in 1885. He taught at Bonn, Königsberg, and Zurich before going to Göttingen (1902), where he taught until his death. Minkowski was the co-winner of the French Grand Prix des Sciences Mathématiques at age eighteen for his work on the theory of quadratic forms in *n* variables. It was a subject he returned to throughout his career. His most original achievement was his "geometry of numbers," which led him to the geometrical properties of convex sets in *n*-dimensional space. In mathematical physics, he was the first to conceive of a four-dimensional "space-time" which became the frame of all later developments of relativity theory and led Einstein to his bolder conception of generalized relativity.

MINNAERT, MARCEL GILLES JOZEF (*b. Bruges, Belgium, 1893; d. Utrecht, Netherlands, 1970*), astronomy.

Minnaert, one of the pioneers of solar research in the first half of the twentieth century, was professor at the University of Utrecht and director of its observatory from 1937 to 1963. He received his doctorate in biology from the University of Ghent in 1914, studied physics at Leiden, and taught at Ghent until 1918, at which time he settled at Utrecht. He transformed the Utrecht observatory into an astronomical institute devoted mainly to the investigation of solar and stellar spectra. He also studied comets and gaseous nebulae and was involved in lunar photometry. His *Photometric Atlas of the Solar Spectrum* (1940, written with Houtgast and Mulders) is still a standard reference.

MINOT, CHARLES SEDGWICK (*b. Roxbury, Mass., 1852; d. Milton, Mass., 1914*), anatomy, embryology.

Minot graduated from the Massachusetts Institute of Technology in 1872 and did graduate work at Leipzig and Harvard, receiving a doctorate from the latter in 1878; he remained at Harvard throughout his career. In 1886 he invented the automatic rotary microtome, still in worldwide use in sectioning vertebrate embryos. In 1892 he published *Human Embryology*, a masterly summation of the subject.

MINOT, GEORGE RICHARDS (*b. Boston, Mass., 1885; d. Brookline, Mass., 1950*), medicine.

Minot received a B.A. from Harvard College in 1908 and his M.D. from the Harvard Medical School in 1912. He was a professor of medicine throughout his career. His outstanding contribution to medical science was the discovery in 1926, with William P. Murphy, of the successful treatment of pernicious anemia by liver feeding, for which they won the 1934 Nobel Prize in physiology or medicine (shared with George H. Whipple).

MIQUEL, FRIEDRICH ANTON WILHELM (*b. Neuenhaus, Germany, 1811; d. Utrecht, Netherlands, 1871*), botany.

Miquel was trained as a physician at the University of Groningen. He specialized in botany and his career was spent as botanist at various Dutch universities and botanic gardens. His work dealt mainly with the floras of the former Netherlands East Indies, Surinam, and Japan. He played an important background role in the development of the East Indian quinine industry.

MIRBEL, CHARLES FRANÇOIS BRISSEAU DE (*b. Paris, France, 1776; d. Paris, 1854*), botany.

Mirbel's education was brought to an end by the French revolution. Later he did work in military history and topography, but he was forced into exile in the Pyrenees in 1796. While there he did research into the geological configuration of the Pyrenees. In 1798 he returned to Paris and a post in the Museum of Natural History. He was in the service of Napoleon and Louis Bonaparte, king of Holland, and after 1808 was professor of botany at the Faculty of Sciences in Paris. He was also appointed (1829) administrator of the Jardin des Plantes. Mirbel wrote a series of articles on the structure of plants and on the seed and embryo, thereby inaugurating the study of microscopical plant anatomy in France. He laid the groundwork for embryogenic classifications that are still in use today. His *Éléments de botanique* (1815) revealed his talents as a draftsman and contributed to the acceptance of his ideas.

MISES, RICHARD VON (*b. Lemberg, Austria [now Lvov, U.S.S.R.], 1883; d. Boston, Mass., 1953*), mathematics, mechanics, probability.

Von Mises earned his doctorate at Vienna in 1907 and taught at universities in Europe and Turkey. From 1939 he was in the United States and from 1944 was professor of aerodynamics and applied mathematics at Harvard. In 1913 he gave what is probably the first university course on the mechanics of powered flight. During World War I he designed a military plane for the Austrian air arm. He was also interested in probability and statistics, and in 1919 he published a famous paper that spliced the probability theory of John Venn and that of a random sequence of events. In 1928 he published *Probability, Statistics, and Truth.*

MITCHELL, ELISHA (*b. Washington, Conn., 1793; d. on Mount Mitchell, N.C., 1857*), natural history.

Mitchell graduated from Yale University in 1813 and in 1817 became professor of mathematics and natural history at the University of North Carolina. He later taught chemistry, geology, and mineralogy there. In 1842 he published the first geologic map of North Carolina. He wrote on meteorology, and was a pioneer in applied soil science and in conservation. He drowned while remeasuring the altitude of the mountain, first measured by him in 1839, that was later named in his honor. His *Elements of Geology* (1842) was a successful textbook.

MITCHELL, MARIA (*b. Nantucket, Mass., 1818; d. Lynn, Mass., 1889*), astronomy.

Mitchell, the first woman astronomer in America, was taught by her father, an amateur astronomer. She was librarian in Nantucket and it was there that she conducted her astronomical observations. She became world famous in 1847 by discovering a new telescopic comet. From 1849 to 1868 she was employed by the U.S. Nautical Almanac office to compute the ephemerides of the planet Venus. After 1865 she also taught astronomy at Vassar.

MITCHELL, SILAS WEIR (*b. Philadelphia, Pa., 1829; d. Philadelphia, 1914*), medicine, neurology.

Mitchell received an M.D. from Jefferson Medical College in 1850 and joined his father in practice in Philadelphia. He became widely recognized as the outstanding American neurologist and was especially interested in hysteria. He popularized the "rest cure" for the treatment of nervous disease. He wrote widely on numerous subjects, including gunshot wounds, neuralgia, the physiology of the cerebellum, and the pharmacology of bromides, lithium, and chloral hydrate. He was also renowned as a novelist, short story writer, and poet.

MITSCHERLICH, EILHARD (*b. Neuende, Oldenburg, Germany, 1794; d. Berlin, Germany, 1863*), chemistry, mineralogy.

After studying at the universities of Heidelberg and Paris, Mitscherlich studied medicine at Göttingen. His interest turned to chemistry, particularly crystallography.

He worked in Berzelius' laboratory in Stockholm from 1820 to 1822, when he went to the University of Berlin. Early in his career (about 1820) he discovered the principle of isomorphism, a crucial development in nineteenth-century chemistry. He continued to refine his work on isomorphism throughout his career. In 1834 he obtained benzene by the dry distillation of the calcium salt of benzoic acid and went on to conduct experiments on various benzene derivatives. He maintained an interest in geology and mineralogy and produced artificial minerals. His process for extracting cellulose from wood (Mitcherlich process) formed the basis for the German cellulose industry. His textbook *Lehrbuch der Chemie* (1829) went through numerous editions and was highly praised by his contemporaries.

MITTAG-LEFFLER, MAGNUS GUSTAF (GÖSTA) (*b. Stockholm, Sweden, 1846; d. Stockholm, 1927*), mathematics.

Mittag-Leffler was a mathematical prodigy as a child, and he received a doctorate from the University of Uppsala in 1872. In 1877 he became professor of mathematics at the University of Helsinki, and in 1881 he went to the newly established Högskola, which later became the University of Stockholm. His most important work was done on the theory of elliptic functions and showed the influence of Weierstrass. In the area now known as the theory of summability, certain infinite matrices are now known as Mittag-Leffler matrices. He founded, and for many years was chief editor of, the highly influential *Acta mathematica.*

MITTASCH, ALWIN (*b. Grossdehsa, Germany, 1869; d. Heidelberg, Germany, 1953*), physical chemistry.

Mittasch was a leading authority on contact catalysis. As head of catalytic research for the Badische Anilin- und Soda-Fabrik (BASF), he guided important chemical research. A protégé of Ostwald, he did his doctoral dissertation on catalysis; it led directly to his career. He was at BASF from 1904 to 1934, when he retired.

MIVART, ST. GEORGE JACKSON (*b. London, England, 1827; d. London, 1900*), biology, natural history.

Mivart was admitted to the bar in 1851, but his primary interests were in natural history. He achieved a modest reputation in comparative anatomy and knew many of the naturalists of his day, including Owen and Huxley. A Roman Catholic convert, he attempted to reconcile evolutionism with his religion. He only succeeded in alienating both sides: Huxley and the Darwinians broke with him, and he was excommunicated from the church. Among his works are *On the Genesis of Species* (1871), *Man and Apes* (1873), and *Contemporary Evolution* (1873–76).

MÖBIUS, AUGUST FERDINAND (*b. Schulpforta, near Naumburg, Germany, 1790; d. Leipzig, Germany, 1868*), mathematics, astronomy.

Möbius studied at Leipzig, Göttingen, and Halle. He earned his doctorate from Leipzig in 1814, where he became professor of astronomy and observer at the observatory and was responsible for its refurbishing in 1821. Although he was employed as an astronomer, his main contributions were in mathematics. His greatest work, published in 1827, was *Der barycentrische Calcul: Ein neues Hülfsmittel zur analytischen Behandlung der Geometrie*, a mathematical classic. It was also the source of much of his later work. Möbius is now most frequently remembered for his discovery of the one-sided surface called the Möbius strip.

MÖBIUS, KARL AUGUST (*b. Eilenburg, Germany, 1825; d. Berlin, Germany, 1908*), zoology.

Möbius studied natural history at the University of Berlin and then taught at a Hamburg grammar school. In 1855 he went to the Hamburg Museum of Natural History and was a cofounder of the Hamburg zoo and aquarium. Later he taught at Kiel, conducted expeditions to the tropics, and was director of the natural history museum in Berlin. He introduced the ecological concept of "life community" ("Biocönose"). The major portion of his work was devoted to marine biology, including the formation of pearls and the biology and anatomy of the whale.

MOCIÑO, JOSÉ MARIANO (*b. Temascaltepec, Mexico, 1757; d. Barcelona, Spain, 1820*), botany.

After medical training at the University of Mexico, Mociño became committed to botany. From 1790 to 1804 he was part of the Royal Botanical Expedition to New Spain (Mexico), which traveled as far afield as California. He spent many years preparing *Plantae novae Hispaniae* (1887–91) and *Flora Mexicana* (1891–97), which comprise the findings of the expedition and which were published long after his death.

MOENCH, CONRAD (*b. Kassel, Germany, 1744; d. Marburg, Germany, 1805*), botany.

Moench, a pharmacist by profession, became in 1781 professor of botany at the Collegium Medicum Carolinianum at Kessel, which in 1785 became part of the Philipps-Universität at Marburg. He founded the Marburg botanic garden and instituted a new method of teaching botany. A follower of C.F. Medicus, he was a bitter opponent of Linnaeus and published in 1794 one of the leading anti-Linnaean works, *Methodus plantas horti botanici.* . . . Some of the generic names coined in it are still the accepted ones.

MOERBEKE, WILLIAM OF, also known as **Guillelmus de Moerbeka** (*b. Moerbeke, Belgium* [?]*, ca. 1220–35; d. before 1286*), philosophy, geometry, biology.

Moerbeke, a Dominican, was one of the most productive and eminent translators from Greek into Latin of early philosophical and scientific works. Legend has it that Aquinas encouraged Moerbeke to translate Aristotle; it is known that Aquinas used Moerbeke's translations. In addition to Aristotle, he translated works of Plato, Archimedes, Proclus, Alexander of Aphrodisias, Themistius, Ammonius, Philoponus, Simplicius, Hero of Alexandria, Ptolemy, Galen, and Pseudo-Hippocrates. It would be difficult to overestimate the importance of Moerbeke's work: he introduced into the Western Latin world works that had practically been lost. The consequent extensive study of these works in universities and ecclesiastical and monastic schools of the later Middle Ages was initally made possible by Moerbeke. Only one original work by Moerbeke is preserved, *Geomantia* ("Divination From Earth").

MOFFETT (MOUFET, MUFFET), THOMAS (*b. London, England, 1553; d. Bulbridge, Wiltshire, England, 1604*), medicine, entomology.

Moffett graduated from Cambridge in 1573 and read medicine in Basel, where he received an M.D. in 1578. He established a practice in England and was a Member of Parliament from 1597 to his death. He is remembered today chiefly for two works, both published posthumously. *Theatrum insectorum* (1634) is a systematic treatise dealing with the habits, habitat, breeding, and economic importance of insects. *Health's Improvement* (1655), designed for the layman, is concerned mainly with food and diet, but includes descriptions of animals and fishes used for food, and observations on wild birds. (It includes the first printed list of British birds.) He was also one of the first to recognize migration in birds.

MOHL, HUGO VON (*b. Stuttgart, Germany, 1805; d. Tübingen, Germany, 1872*), biology.

Mohl received a doctorate from Tübingen in 1828. In 1832 he was appointed professor of physiology at Bern and in 1835 professor of botany at Tübingen, where he remained until his death. In 1846 Mohl wrote a manual on microscopy. He remains famous for his works on the microscopic anatomy of plants and for his contributions to knowledge of the plant cell. The history of biology credits him with the invention of the term "protoplasm."

MOHN, HENRIK (*b. Bergen, Norway, 1835; d. Christiania [now Oslo], Norway, 1916*), meteorology, oceanography.

Mohn received his master's degree in mineralogy from the University of Christiania in 1858. From 1866 to 1913 he occupied the first chair of meteorology there. He was also director of the Norwegian Meteorological Institute, which grew under his guidance to 450 stations throughout Norway. With G. O. Sars, Mohn planned and participated in the three Norwegian North Atlantic expeditions (1876–78).

MOHOROVIČIĆ, ANDRIJA (*b. Volosko, Istria, Croatia, 1857; d. Zagreb, Yugoslavia, 1936*), meteorology, seismology.

A graduate of the University of Prague, Mohorovičić taught meteorology and oceanography at the Royal Nautical School in Bakar (Buccari), and in 1897 he received his doctorate from the University of Zagreb. He remained there teaching, and directing the observatory, which under his guidance became the Royal Regional Center for Meteorology and Geodynamics. When he retired in 1921 it was reorganized as the Geophysical Institute. Mohorovičić's fame rests on the results of his investigations of the destructive earthquake of 1909, which occured near Zagreb. His study contained important new discoveries about the features of earthquakes, including the boundary now known as the Mohorovičić discontinuity, the boundary separating the earth's crust from the mantle, which he had discovered by seismological means. His son Stjepan also became a distinguished seismologist.

MOHR, CARL FRIEDRICH (*b. Koblenz, then France [now Germany], 1806; d. Bonn, Germany, 1879*), analytical chemistry, physical chemistry, agricultural chemistry, geology.

Mohr took over his father's pharmacy business after studying at the universities of Bonn, Heidelberg, and Berlin. His most lasting contribution was in titration. His *Lehrbuch der chemisch-analytischen Titriermethode* (1855) was the first successful compendium in this new field of analytical chemistry; it went through eight editions and was widely translated. Mohr invented many new titration procedures and improved others. Many apparatuses and methods bear his name: the Mohr test for iron and chloride determination, the Mohr pinchcock burrette, the Mohr balance for determining specific gravity, and Mohr's salt.

MOHR, CHRISTIAN OTTO (*b. Wesselburen, Holstein, 1835; d. Dresden, Germany, 1918*), civil engineering.

After studying engineering at the Polytechnic Institute of Hannover, Mohr became an engineer for the state railroads of Hannover and Oldenburg and was involved in building some notable bridges. He published original research papers and taught at Stuttgart and Dresden. He was regarded as a remarkable teacher. He was concerned with the problem of stress, and in an 1882 paper he made his most widely known contribution—what became known as "Mohr's stress circle." His theory of failure, based on the concept of the stress circle, has been widely accepted in engineering practice.

MOHR, GEORG (*b. Copenhagen, Denmark, 1640; d. Kieslingswalde, near Görlitz, Germany, 1697*), mathematics.

Mohr studied mathematics in Holland, England, and France. He remained aloof from official positions until 1695, when Tschirnhausen lured him to Kieslingswalde to participate in his mathematical projects. Although he is believed to have written three books, only *Euclides danicus* (1672) is known today. That work was rediscovered in 1928. In it Mohr dealt with a problem made famous 125 years later by Mascheroni, namely, that of making constructions with only a compass.

MOHS, FRIEDRICH (*b. Gernrode, Anhalt-Bernburg, Germany, 1773; d. Agordo, Tirol, Italy, 1839*), mineralogy, geology.

Mohs studied at the universities of Halle and Freiberg and participated in numerous mineralogical and geological expeditions. In 1811 he became curator of the mineral collection of the newly established Johanneum in Graz, and in 1812 became professor of mineralogy there. In the same year, he revealed his new classificatory system, in which he first proposed his hardness scale for minerals. He continued perfecting his system, giving particular attention to the possible arrangement of minerals in crystal systems based on external symmetry. After about 1820, his system was generally employed by mineralogists. In 1822 and 1824 he published his two-volume *Grund-Riss der Mineralogie*. Later he taught at Freiberg and Vienna, and ended his career as imperial counselor of the exchequer in charge of mining and monetary affairs.

MOISEEV, NIKOLAY DMITRIEVICH (*b. Perm, Russia, 1902; d. Moscow, U.S.S.R., 1955*), celestial mechanics, astronomy, mathematics.

Moiseev graduated from Moscow University in 1923, having specialized in astronomy, and did his graduate work at the State Astrophysics Institute. From 1929 to

1947 he taught mathematics at the N.E. Zhukovsky Military Air Academy. He also taught at the University of Moscow and at the P.K. Sternberg Astronomical Institute (formerly the State Astrophysics Institute). The recognized leader of the Moscow school of celestial mechanics, Moiseev published more than 120 works.

MOISSAN, FERDINAND - FRÉDÉRIC - HENRI (*b. Paris, France, 1852; d. Paris, 1907*), chemistry.

Moissan studied at the University of Paris, the École Supérieure de Pharmacie, and the Faculté des Sciences, from which he received his doctorate in 1880. He then began his remarkable research on the compounds of fluorine. Academic recognition came quickly, and in 1886 he became professor of toxicology at the École Supérieure de Pharmacie. In 1899 he became professor of inorganic chemistry there, and in 1900 was given the same chair at the Faculté des Sciences. He was regarded as an effective teacher and attracted increasing numbers of students. In 1906 he was awarded the Nobel Prize for chemistry.

MOIVRE, ABRAHAM DE (*b. Vitry-le-François, France, 1667; d. London, England, 1754*), probability.

De Moivre, a Protestant, emigrated to England after the Edict of Nantes in 1685. He read Newton's *Principia* and mastered the work quickly. Despite his wide acquaintanceship in British scientific circles, he found little patronage and was forced to eke out a living as tutor, author, and expert on practical applications of probability in gambling and annuities. His masterpiece is *The Doctrine of Chances* (1718), one of the earliest systematic treatises on probability. The most memorable of his discoveries is his approximation to the binomial probability distribution, which, as the normal or Gaussian distribution, became the most fruitful single instrument of discovery used in probability theory and statistics for the next two centuries.

MOLDENHAWER, JOHANN JACOB PAUL (*b. Hamburg, Germany, 1766; d. Kiel, Germany, 1827*), plant anatomy.

Moldenhawer was one of the principal founders of plant anatomy. His chief work, *Beiträge zur Anatomie der Pflanzen* (1812), reflects substantially the extensive knowledge of the period. A theology student at Keil and Copenhagen, Moldenhawer turned his interest to science during the 1780's. His first botanical work, on Peripatetic botany based on ancient sources, was published in 1791. In 1792 he was named professor of botany and fruit-tree culture at the University of Kiel. The *Beiträge*, representing his lifework, is notable for its critical insights and methodical observations. It contains important findings concerning plant anatomy.

MOLESCHOTT, JACOB (*b. 's Hertogenbosch, Netherlands, 1822; d. Rome, Italy, 1893*), medicine, physiology.

Moleschott received an M.D. from Heidelberg in 1845, established a practice at Utrecht, and taught physiology at Heidelberg, Zurich, Turin, and the "Sapienza" in Rome. His special interests were in the metabolism of plants and animals, and in the effect of light on it in nutrition. His most important work, *Kreislauf des Lebens* (1852), concerned the structure and function of the brain.

MOLIÈRES, JOSEPH PRIVAT DE. *See* **Privat de Molières, Joseph.**

MOLIN, FEDOR EDUARDOVICH (*b. Riga, Russia, 1861; d. Tomsk, U.S.S.R., 1941*), mathematics.

Molin graduated from Dorpat University (now Tartu University) in 1883. He did graduate work at Leipzig University and received his master's degree from Dorpat in 1885 and his doctorate in 1892. His academic career was spent at Tomsk Technological Institute and Tomsk University. Molin's mathematical interests were focused on the theory of algebras and the theory of representation of groups.

MOLINA, JUAN IGNACIO (*b. Guaraculen, Talca, Chile, 1740; d. Bologna, Italy, 1829*), natural history.

A Jesuit, Molina was expelled from Chile in 1768 when all Jesuits were banished from Spanish dominions. Settling in Italy, he became professor of natural sciences at the Institute of Bologna in 1774. His classic account of the natural history of Chile was published in 1776.

MOLL, FRIEDRICH RUDOLF HEINRICH CARL (*b. Culm, Germany, 1882; d. Berlin, Germany, 1951*), naval engineering, wood technology.

In 1909 Moll received a doctorate in engineering from the Technische Hochschule in Berlin-Charlottenburg. He was chiefly concerned with the preservation of wood. From 1911 he privately built wood-treatment works in a number of countries, and his operations acquired an international reputation. Especially notable was his kyanizing process for impregnating telephone poles with mercuric chloride. He also worked on techniques for protection against shipworms.

MOLL, GERARD (*b. Amsterdam, Netherlands, 1785; d. Amsterdam, 1838*), astronomy, physics.

Moll received a Ph.D. from the University of Amsterdam in 1809. His academic career was at the University of Utrecht, where he was professor of physics and director of the observatory. His contributions ranged from observing the transit of Mercury on 5 May 1832 to determining the speed of sound. The latter was accomplished by measuring the interval between the light flash and sound of a fired cannon.

MÖLLER, DIDRIK MAGNUS AXEL (*b. Sjörup, Sweden, 1830; d. Lund, Sweden, 1896*), astronomy.

Moller was educated at the University of Lund and spent his entire career there, where he also founded the observatory. His main contribution to astronomy concerned the motion of Faye's comet, discovered in 1843, and that of the asteroid Pandora.

MOLLIARD, MARIN (*b. Châtillon-Colligny, Loiret, France, 1866; d. Paris, France, 1944*), plant physiology.

Molliard graduated from the École Normale Supérieure and was connected with the Faculty of Sciences of the Sorbonne for fifty years. A Lamarckian, he occupied the first chair of plant physiology in France. He devoted all his writings to the influence of the environment on plants. He was the leading authority on plant physiology in France, and virtually two generations of plant physiologists were his students. His most important work is *Nutrition de la plante* (4 vols., 1923).

MOLLIER, RICHARD (*b. Trieste, 1863; d. Dresden, Germany, 1935*), thermodynamics.

Mollier studied at the universities of Graz and Munich before transferring to the Technische Hochschule in Munich, from which he graduated in 1888. He received his doctorate from Munich in 1895. He spent virtually his entire academic career at the Technische Hochschule of Dresden, as professor of the theory of machines and director of the machine laboratory. A pure theoretician, he centered his interest on the properties of thermodynamic media and their effective presentation in the form of charts and diagrams. He introduced the concept of *enthalpy*, which had been defined earlier by Gibbs as "heat function for constant pressure," and also published (1897) an important study of heat transfer.

MOLLWEIDE, KARL BRANDAN (*b. Wolfenbüttel, Germany, 1774; d. Leipzig, Germany, 1825*), astronomy, mathematics.

Mollweide graduated from the University of Halle. From 1811 he was at Leipzig University, as professor of astronomy and mathematics. Certain trigonometric formulas and a conformal map projection are named for him. He is also remembered for a dispute with Goethe over the Newtonian theory of colors.

MOLYNEUX, SAMUEL (*b. Chester, England, 1689; d. Kew, England, 1728*), astronomy, optics.

Molyneux, the son of William Molyneux, received a B.A in 1708 and an M.A. in 1710 from Trinity College, Dublin. He settled at Kew House, London, where he devoted himself to the study of astronomy and optics, much of it done in collaboration with James Bradley. Also active in public life, he sat in both the English and Irish parliaments and was Lord of the Admiralty.

MOLYNEUX, WILLIAM (*b. Dublin, Ireland, 1656; d. Dublin, 1698*), astronomy, physics.

Molyneux received a B.A. from Trinity College, Dublin, in 1675. He studied for the law, but his main interest was in natural philosophy. In 1683 he founded the Dublin Philosophical Society, the Irish equivalent of the Royal Society. He moved to England in 1689, where he wrote his best-known scientific work, the *Dioptrica nova* (1692). It was a popular treatise on optical knowledge to which was appended Halley's famous theorem for finding the foci of lenses. He is perhaps best known for the Molyneux problem: Would a blind man, suddenly granted his vision, be able to distinguish by sight alone between a sphere and a cube that he had touched when sightless? Both Molyneux and Locke, as well as Berkeley, decided in the negative. He was an advocate of Irish autonomy and wrote a famous book arguing that cause, *The Case of Ireland's Being Bound by Acts of Parliament in England Stated* (1698).

MONARDES, NICOLÁS BAUTISTA (*b. Seville, Spain, ca. 1493; d. Seville, 1588*), medicine, natural history.

Monardes graduated from the University of Alcalá de Henares and received an M.D. from Seville in 1547. He was involved in the importation of drugs from the Americas and carried on a successful practice in Seville. He was the best-known and most widely-read Spanish physician in the sixteenth century, and through his books the

American materia medica began to be known. His careful description of drugs and the tests he carried out on animals to ascertain their medicinal properties caused him to be considered one of the founders of pharmacognosy and experimental pharmacology.

MOND, LUDWIG (*b. Kassel, Germany, 1839; d. London, England, 1909*), industrial chemistry.

Mond is remembered for three contributions to the chemical industry: the establishment of the ammonia soda process in England; the development of an efficient power gas plant; and the discovery of nickel carbonyl. Mond studied under Kolbe at Marburg and under Bunsen at Heidelberg. In 1867 he settled in England, where he set up several chemical corporations which developed his breakthroughs in chemical processes.

MONDEVILLE. *See* **Henry of Mondeville.**

MONDINO DE' LUZZI (also **Liucci** or **Liuzzi**) (*b. Bologna, Italy, ca. 1275; d. Bologna, 1326*), anatomy.

Mondino received an M.D. from the University of Bologna in 1300 and joined the faculty of the college of medicine and philosophy there. Mondino's chief work, *Anatomia Mundini,* completed in 1316, dominated anatomy for over two hundred years. It was the first medieval anatomy text that was based on the dissection of the human cadaver.

MONGE, GASPARD (*b. Beaune, France, 1746; d. Paris, France, 1818*), geometry, calculus, chemistry, theory of machines.

Monge revived the study of certain branches of geometry, and his work was the starting point for the remarkable flowering of that subject during the nineteenth century. Beyond that, his investigations extended to other fields of mathematical analysis, in particular to the theory of partial differential equations, and to problems of physics, chemistry, and technology. A celebrated professor and peerless *chef d'école,* Monge assumed important administrative and political responsibilities during the Revolution and the Empire. He was thus one of the most original mathematicians of his age, while his civic activities represented the main concerns of the Revolution more fully than did those of any other among contemporary French scientists of comparable stature.

Monge was a brilliant student at the Oratorian *collège* in Beaune. From 1762 to 1764 he completed his education at the Collège de la Trinité in Lyons, where he was placed in charge of a course in physics. After returning to Beaune in the summer of 1764, he sketched a plan of his native city. The high quality of his work attracted the attention of an officer at the École Royale du Génie at Mézières, and this event determined the course of his career.

He became *répétiteur* to the professor of mathematics, Charles Bossut. In January 1769 Monge succeeded the latter, even though he did not hold the rank of professor. The following year he succeeded the Abbé Nollet as instructor of experimental physics at the school. In this double assignment, devoted partially to practical ends, Monge showed himself to be an able mathematician and physicist, a talented draftsman, a skilled experimenter, and a first-class teacher.

Parallel to this brilliant professional career, Monge very early commenced his personal work. His youthful investigations (1766–72) were quite varied but exhibit several characteristics that marked his entire output: an acute sense of geometric reality; an interest in practical problems; great analytical ability; and the simultaneous examination of several aspects of a single problem: analytic, geometric, and practical.

During the period 1777–80 Monge was interested primarily in physics and chemistry and arranged for a well-equipped chemistry laboratory to be set up at the École du Génie. Moreover, having for some time been responsible for supervising the operation of a forge belonging to his wife, he had become interested in metallurgy.

His election to the Academy of Sciences as *adjoint géomètre* in June 1780 altered Monge's life, obliging him to stay in Paris on a regular basis. In Paris he participated in the Academy's projects and presented memoirs on physics, chemistry, and mathematics. A list of the subjects of his communications to the Academy attests to their variety: the composition of nitrous acid, the generation of curved surfaces, finite difference equations, and partial differential equations (1785); double refraction and the structure of Iceland spar, the composition of iron, steel, and cast iron, and the action of electric sparks on carbon dioxide gas (1786); capillary phenomena (1787); and the causes of certain meteorological phenomena; and a study in physiological optics (1789).

When the Revolution began in 1789, Monge was among the most widely known of French scientists. A very active member of the Academy of Sciences, he had established a reputation in mathematics, physics, and chemistry. As an examiner of naval cadets he directed a branch of France's military schools, which were then virtually the only institutions offering a scientific education of any merit. This position also placed him in contact, in each port he visited, with bureaucracy that was soon to come under his administration. It also enabled him to visit iron mines, foundries, and factories, and thus to become an expert on metallurgical and technological questions. Furthermore, the important reform of teaching in the naval schools that he had effected in 1786 prepared him for the efforts to renew scientific and technical education that he undertook during the Revolution.

In 1794 he became responsible for establishing an École Centrale des Travaux Publics (later École Polytechnique). Appointed instructor of descriptive geometry in 1794, Monge supervised the operation of the training school of the future *chefs de brigade,* or foremen, taught descriptive geometry in "revolutionary courses" designed to complete the training of the future students, and was one of the most active members of the governing council. After a two-month delay caused by political difficulties, the school—soon to be called the École Polytechnique—began to function normally in June 1795. Even though his duties as senator took him away on several occasions from his courses at the École Polytechnique, he maintained his intense concern for the school. He kept careful watch over the progress of the students, followed their research, and paid close attention to the curriculum and the teaching.

Most of Monge's publications in this period were written for the students of the École Polytechnique. The wide success of his *Géométrie descriptive* (1799) was responsible

484

for the rapid spread of this new branch of geometry both in France and abroad. It was reprinted several times.

In 1798 Monge took part in the preparations for Napoleon's Egyptian expedition and joined it reluctantly at first. During the three and a half years he was gone from France, he observed mirages and studied viticulture and metallurgy. On his return he was on the commission to supervise the publication of material collected by the expedition.

Monge's scientific work encompasses mathematics (various branches of geometry and mathematical analysis), physics, mechanics, and the theory of machines. His mathematical work constitutes a coherent ensemble in which analytic developments were closely joined with material drawn from pure, descriptive, analytic, and infinitesimal geometry, even though his investigations in physics, mechanics, and the theory of machines were also intimately linked.

Throughout his career infinitesimal geometry remained Monge's favorite subject. Here his investigations were directed toward two main topics: families of surfaces defined by their mode of generation, which he examined in connection with the corresponding partial differential equations, and the direct study of the properties of surfaces and space curves. In his study of partial differential equations, he introduced such basic notions as characteristic curve, integral curve, characteristic developable trajectory of characteristics, and characteristic cone. He contributed exceptionally fruitful methods for approaching the theory of these equations.

Although the details regarding Monge's contributions to physics are poorly known, because he never published a major work in this field, his reputation among his contemporaries was solid. His main contributions concerned caloric theory, acoustics (theory of tones), electrostatics, and optics (theory of mirages).

His most important research in chemistry dealt with the composition of water. As early as 1781 he effected the combination of oxygen and hydrogen in the eudiometer, and in 1783 he achieved the synthesis of water—at the same time as Lavoisier and independently of him. Although Monge's apparatus was much simpler, the results of his measurements were more precise. On the other hand, his initial conclusions remained tied to the phlogiston theory, whereas Lavoisier's conclusions signaled the triumph of his new chemistry and the overthrow of the traditional conception of the elementary nature of water. Monge soon adhered to the new doctrine. In February 1785 he took part in the great experiment on the synthesis and analysis of water; he was subsequently an ardent propagandist for the new chemistry and actively participated in its development.

In the experimental realm, in 1784 Monge achieved, in collaboration with Clouet, the first liquefaction of a gas, sulfurous anhydride (sulfur dioxide). Finally, between 1786 and 1788 Monge investigated with Berthollet and Vandermonde the principles of metallurgy and the composition of irons, cast metals, and steels.

MONIZ, EGAS. *See* **Egas Moniz, A. A. F.**

MONNET, ANTOINE-GRIMOALD (*b. Champeix, Puy-de-Dôme, France, 1734; d. Paris, France, 1817*), chemistry, mineralogy.

Monnet was France's first (from 1776) *inspecteur général des mines et minières du royaume.* He was responsible for suggesting improvements in the French mining industry, and his writings reflected contemporary theories in mining and metallurgy. His adherence to the phlogiston theory eventually isolated him from the scientific community.

MONRO, ALEXANDER (Primus) (*b. London, England, 1697; d. Edinburgh, Scotland, 1767*), anatomy.

After three years at Edinburgh University, Monro was apprenticed to his father, a military surgeon, in 1713. He later studied in London, Paris, and Leiden. In 1720, at age twenty-two, he became the first professor of anatomy at the University of Edinburgh. In 1726 he published his major work *The Anatomy of the Humane Bones.* The work was in use for more than one hundred years. Although not a great innovator, Monro was a supreme teacher and demonstrator. His reputation attracted students from all over Europe, and he raised the reputation of the Edinburgh Medical School to the highest level.

MONRO, ALEXANDER (Secundus) (*b. Edinburgh, Scotland, 1733; d. Edinburgh, 1817*), anatomy.

Monro began attending his father's anatomy classes at the University of Edinburgh when he was eleven years old. At age twelve he matriculated there, and in 1750 began studying medicine with the best physicians of the era. In 1754 he was named joint occupant of his father's anatomy chair, and in 1755 he received his M.D. He studied on the Continent, but after 1758 his father's illness forced him to take over the anatomy lectures at Edinburgh. He was an even more successful teacher than his father had been. In 1798 his elder son, Alexander, thereafter known as Monro Tertius, was named joint professor of anatomy with him. Secundus retired in 1808, at age seventy-five.

Monro Secundus' *Observations on the Structure and Functions of the Nervous System* (1783) described the foramen connecting the lateral and third ventricles of the brain, thereafter known as the "foramen of Monro." He was also involved in a long dispute with William Hunter over who had priority in discovering that the lymphatics were absorbents and distinct from the circulatory system. His book on the structure and physiology of fishes, published in 1785, was an important early work on comparative anatomy.

MONTANARI, GEMINIANO (*b. Modena, Italy, 1633; d. Padua, Italy, 1687*), astronomy, geophysics, biology, ballistics.

Montanari studied law at Florence and received degrees in both church and civil law from Salzburg. He established a law practice in Vienna and developed an interest in mathematics and natural sciences, and especially in the works of Galileo. For reasons unclear, he was forced to return to Italy, where he was in the service of several Italian rulers. In 1664 he was given the chair of mathematics at Bologna, a position he held for fourteen years. He then became professor of astronomy and meteorology at Padua. He organized and directed the mint of the Republic of Venice and advised Venice in the control of its rivers, lagoon, and on its fortification. His talents were diverse: It has been said that he was an astronomer in Modena, a physicist in Bologna, and an engineer in Venice. His most important contributions were in astronomy, particularly in his observations of the star Algol, which contributed to one of the earliest and most important chapters in the history of astrophysics, the study of the variable stars. He was passionately opposed to astrology and was largely responsible for the banning it from the universities.

MONTE, GUIDOBALDO, MARCHESE DEL (*b. Pesaro, Italy, 1545; d. Montebaroccio, 1607*), mechanics, mathematics, astronomy.

Guidobaldo, who studied at the University of Padua, was a prominent figure in the renaissance of the mathematical sciences. His first book, *Liber mechanicorum* (1577), was regarded by his contemporaries as the greatest work on statics since the Greeks. Its most fruitful section dealt with pulleys, reducing them to the lever. Guidobaldo was a longtime friend and patron of Galileo. He also wrote works on astronomy and perspective.

MONTELIUS, GUSTAV OSCAR (*b. Stockholm, Sweden, 1843; d. Stockholm, 1921*), archaeology.

Montelius joined the Swedish Archaeological Service at age twenty and worked at the Swedish National Museum for fifty years, retiring as its director and state antiquary. He was strongly influenced by the great Scandinavian archaeologists Thomsen, Worsaae, and Nilsson, the creators of the scientific method of archaeology. He adopted the three-age system (Stone, Bronze, and Iron) and expanded it into a four-age system comprising the Paleolithic, Neolithic, Bronze, and Iron. He established a historical chronology of prehistoric Europe, and his *The Orient and Europe* (1894) is a classic statement of the theory of megalithic origins in the eastern Mediterranean.

MONTESQUIEU, CHARLES-LOUIS DE SECONDAT, BARON DE LA BRÈDE ET DE (*b. La Brède, near Bordeaux, France, 1689; d. Paris, France, 1755*), philosophy, political theory.

Montesquieu was born into a noble family and studied the law at Bordeaux. His most significant work was in the social and political sciences, of which he has been considered a founder. He is noted for his *Lettres persanes* (1721) and his most important work, *L'esprit des lois* (1748). He was also interested in the natural sciences, and he was long occupied in compiling a physical history of the earth. He also wrote on insects, parasitic plants, and the anatomy of the frog. His major contribution, however, lay in his attempt to establish a science of social and political facts based on the conviction that a rational order exists in seemingly diverse phenomena, a conviction shared by most scientists of the age. Montesquieu's originality consists in his having applied this approach to human societies and institutions.

MONTGÉRY, JACQUES-PHILIPPE MÉRIGON DE (*b. Paris, France, 1781; d. Paris, 1839*), military technology.

Montgéry's career was spent in the French navy, in which he rose to the rank of captain in 1828. As a member of the Conseil des Travaux de la Marine, he undertook extensive scientific and military studies. He was a strong advocate of steamships, ironclads, mines, torpedoes, and rockets. His *Traité des fusées de guerre* (1825) was the first

documented history of rocketry and became the standard work on the subject.

MONTGOLFIER, ÉTIENNE JACQUES DE (*b. Vidalon-les-Annonay, France, 1745; d. Serrières, France, 1799*); **MONTGOLFIER, MICHEL JOSEPH DE** (*b. Vidalon-les-Annonay, 1740; d. Balaruc-les-Bains, France, 1810*), technology, aeronautics.

The Montgolfier brothers, both adept at mathematics and technology, became interested in the problem of flight, and in 1782 they lifted a balloon filled with hydrogen. In 1783 the first human flight was made in one of their hot-air balloons, known as "Montgolfières." They also did experiments with parachutes, but after 1784 did no further work on aeronautics. Joseph de Montgolfier subsequently invented a widely adopted hydraulic ram—a simple device for raising water.

MONTGOMERY, EDMUND DUNCAN (*b. Edinburgh, Scotland, 1835; d. Hempstead, Tex., 1911*), cell biology, philosophy.

Montgomery studied medicine at various German universities, although there is doubt whether he received the M.D. While a student he met the sculptor Elisabet Ney, whom he later married. He practiced medicine in London, Madeira, Italy, and Munich. In order to escape social pressures resulting from their nonconformist behavior, they moved to the United States, settling on a Texas plantation in 1873. They remained there the rest of their lives, and Montgomery became a United States citizen in 1886. Montgomery performed intensive microscopical investigations of protozoans and multicellular organisms in his private laboratory and published articles in European and American scientific and philosophic journals. *The Vitality and Organization of Protoplasm* (1904) put forth his theory that the vital properties of life resided in the protoplasm of living organisms. He was a careful observer with original thoughts, but his isolation from the scientific community adversely affected his work.

MONTGOMERY, THOMAS HARRISON, JR. (*b. New York, N.Y., 1873; d. Philadelphia, Pa., 1912*), zoology.

Montgomery attended the University of Pennsylvania and received a Ph.D. at Berlin in 1894. Most of his career was spent teaching zoology at the University of Pennsylvania. Within the span of his brief life (thirty-nine years) he became one of the leaders in American zoology and was a major figure in cytology. He published more than eighty papers, twenty-five of which were on cytology. He experimented mainly on Hemiptera-Heteroptera, or true bugs, and his conclusions contain the essentials of the chromosomal basis of biparental inheritance. Later theories of inheritance were to a large extent based on his theories.

MONTMOR, HENRI LOUIS HABERT DE (*b. Paris [?], France, ca. 1600; d. Paris, 1679*), scientific patronage.

A member of a rich and politically influential family, Montmor sponsored or encouraged the leading scientists of his day, including Descartes and Gassendi. The scientific salon that grew up around his Paris household came to be called the Académie Montmor and is generally regarded as a forerunner to the Académie Royale des

Sciences. Among its members were Chapelain, Sorbière, Clerselier, Rohault, Pierre Huet, Roberval, and Huygens. Montmor was regarded as a fine scholar but very few of his writings have survived. He collected and edited the posthumous edition (1658) of Gassendi's works.

MONTMORT, PIERRE RÉMOND DE (*b. Paris, France, 1678; d. Paris, 1719*), probability.

Montmort abandoned his law studies to travel to England and Germany, where he toured extensively. He returned to France in 1699 to study under Malebranche. His book on probability, *Essay d'analyse sur les jeux de hazard* (1708), made his reputation as a scientist and led to a fruitful collaboration with Nikolaus I. Bernoulli. The greatest value of his book lay perhaps not in its solutions but in its systematic setting out of the problems about games, which are shown to have mathematical properties worthy of further scientific consideration.

MONTUCLA, JEAN ÉTIENNE (*b. Lyons, France, 1725; d. Versailles, France, 1799*), mathematics, history of mathematics.

Montucla received a thorough education in mathematics and ancient languages at Jesuit *collège* at Lyons and studied law at Toulouse. He then studied mathematics in Paris, and in 1758 he published his masterpiece, *Histoire des mathématiques*. The work included sections on mechanics, astronomy, optics, and music—all then considered branches of mathematics. It was by far the most comprehensive and accurate work on the subject up to that time.

MOORE, ELIAKIM HASTINGS (*b. Marietta, Ohio, 1862; d. Chicago, Ill., 1932*), mathematics.

Moore received a B.A. from Yale University in 1883 and a Ph.D. in 1885. He studied in Germany for a year and was at Northwestern University academy and Yale before going in 1892 to the new University of Chicago, where he headed the mathematics department. His work in the area of integral equations and general analysis set a trend for precision in American mathematical literature at a time when vagueness and uncertainty were common.

MOORE, JOSEPH HAINES (*b. Wilmington, Ohio, 1878; d. Oakland, Calif., 1949*), astronomy.

Moore graduated from Wilmington College in 1897 and received a Ph.D. from Johns Hopkins University in 1903. He immediately went to the Lick Observatory, where he remained until he retired as director in 1945. He then taught at the University of California at Berkeley. His principal scientific work was concerned with astronomical spectroscopy, in particular with the measurements of radial velocities of stars. He took part in five eclipse expeditions, obtaining important spectroscopic information on the structure and composition of the solar corona.

MOORE, WILLIAM (*fl. ca. 1806–23*), rocketry.

Moore's origin and education are unknown. From 1806 to 1823 he taught mathematics at the Royal Military Academy at Woolwich, England. His theories on rockets, appearing in 1810 and 1811, were the world's first mathematical treatises on rocket dynamics. He correctly demonstrated that Newton's third law of motion explained the principle of rocket motion.

MORAT, JEAN-PIERRE (*b. St.-Sorlin, Saône-et-Loire, France, 1846; d. La Roche-Vineuse, near St.-Sorlin, 1920*), physiology.

Morat received his medical degree from the Faculty of Medicine in Paris in 1873 and taught at Lyons and Lille. He contributed to physiological knowledge primarily by his studies of what is now called the autonomic nervous system; in particular, he and Albert Dastre showed in 1880 that stimulation of the cervical portion of the sympathetic nerve led to vasodilation in the gums and hard palate of the dog. His subsequent research emphasized the general significance of vasodilator nerves in the regulation of organic function.

MORAY (or MURREY or MURRAY), SIR ROBERT (*b. Scotland, 1608 [?]; d. London, England, 1673*), chemistry, metallurgy, mineralogy, natural history.

A soldier, statesman, and diplomat, Moray served (1660–73) as the first president of the Royal Society and contributed significantly to its survival and growth during the early years. He was knighted by Charles I in 1643, and his close friendship with Charles II aided in obtaining a charter for the Royal Society. His varied scientific interests included fishing, lumbering, mining, ship-building, windmills, watermills, magnetism, mineralogy, chronometry, and chemistry.

MORE, HENRY (*b. Grantham, Lincolnshire, England, 1614; d. Cambridge, England, 1687*), philosophy, theology.

More received a B.A. from Christ's College, Cambridge, in 1636 and an M.A. in 1639. He took orders and became a fellow at the college, a position he held, refusing preferment, all his life. He became a doctor of divinity in 1660. In the history of philosophy, More is counted among the leading Cambridge Platonists. His Platonism was rather vague and eclectic, and his theology emphasized moral goodness over asceticism. His main scientific contribution lay in introducing generations of students to Descartes in his writings. Newton was one of his students.

MORGAGNI, GIOVANNI BATTISTA (*b. Forlì, Italy, 1682; d. Padua, Italy, 1771*), medicine, anatomy, pathological anatomy.

Morgagni took a degree in philosophy and medicine from Bologna in 1701. He remained in Bologna, working in hospitals and, from 1704, headed the Accademia degli Inquieti. His *Adversaria anatomica prima*, published in 1706, earned him international fame. His discoveries represented new contributions to the mechanical interpretation of the structure of the organism, It was a subject that continued to hold his interest throughout his long career. His major work, published in 1761, was *De sedibus et causis morborum per anatomen indagatis*. Its thesis is the notion that the organism can be considered as a mechanical complex. Life therefore represents the sum of the harmonious operation of organic machines, subject to deterioration and breakdowns. These breakdowns give rise to functional impairments that produce disharmony proportional to their location and nature. Morgagni may be considered to be the founder of pathological anatomy.

MORGAN, CONWY LLOYD (*b. London, England, 1852; d. Hastings, England, 1936*), comparative psychology, philosophy.

Lloyd Morgan was a pioneer of animal psychology and an outstanding contributor to the evolutionary understanding of animal behavior. He was educated at the School of Mines at the Royal College of Science in London. He worked under T. H. Huxley, who influenced him profoundly. After teaching in South Africa (1878–83), he held the chair of geology and zoology at University College, Bristol, for the rest of his career. He was one of the first psychologists to recognize the need for an experimental as well as an observational approach to learning, and he resorted to rigorously controlled experiments. His "law of parsimony," also known as "Lloyd Morgan's canon" states that "in no case is an animal activity to be interpreted as the outcome of the exercise of a higher psychical faculty, if it can be fairly interpreted as an outcome of the exercise of one which stands lower in the psychological scale." His literary output was prodigious; among his works are *Animal Life and Intelligence* (1890–91) and *Animal Behavior* (1900).

MORGAN, HERBERT ROLLO (*b. Medford, Minn., 1875; d. Washington, D.C., 1957*), astronomy.

Morgan studied at the University of Virginia (B.A., 1899; Ph.D., 1901). Long with the U.S. Naval Observatory, he carried out a series of fundamental observations of the sun, moon, planets, and selected stars with the nine-inch transit circle. His "Catalog of 5,268 Standard Stars, 1950.0 Based on the Normal System N30," published in 1952, is probably the most accurate source of positions and proper motions available today.

MORGAN, THOMAS HUNT (*b. Lexington, Ky., 1866; d. Pasadena, Calif., 1945*), embryology, genetics.

Morgan entered the preparatory department of the State College of Kentucky in 1880 and, after two years, the college itself (now the University of Kentucky). In 1886 he received a B.S., *summa cum laude*, in zoology.

The summer before he entered graduate school (1886), Morgan went to the Boston Society of Natural History's marine biological station at Annisquam, Massachusetts. This was his first experience in working with marine organisms, an interest he was to continue throughout his life, primarily in association with the Marine Biological Laboratory, Woods Hole, Massachusetts.

In 1890 he completed his doctoral work on sea spiders and received his Ph.D. at Johns Hopkins. He stayed on for a postdoctoral year, and in the fall of 1891 he went to Bryn Mawr College, where he remained until 1904, when E. B. Wilson offered him the chair of experimental zoology at Columbia. In 1928 he resigned to found the division of biological sciences at California Institute of Technology. He remained at Cal Tech and was active in scientific and administrative work until his death.

Morgan's research methods were largely experimental. Between 1895 and 1902 he focused on experimental embryology; between 1903 and 1910, on evolution and on heredity and cytology in relation to sex determination; between 1910 and 1925, on problems of heredity in *Drosophila;* and from 1925 to 1945, on embryology and its relations to heredity and evolution.

Although known best for his studies in heredity with the small vinegar fly *Drosophila melanogaster* (often called fruit fly), Morgan contributed significantly to descriptive and experimental embryology, cytology, and, to a lesser extent, evolutionary theory. In recognition of his work in establishing the chromosome theory of heredity (the idea that genes are located in a linear array on chromosomes), Morgan was awarded the Nobel Prize in medicine or physiology for 1933.

The major early findings of the *Drosophila* research group were summarized in an epoch-making book, *The Mechanism of Mendelian Heredity,* published in 1915. They presented evidence to suggest that genes were linearly arranged on chromosomes and that it was possible to regard the Mendelian laws as based on observable events taking place in cells. Most important, however, they demonstrated that heredity could be treated quantitatively and rigorously. For almost the first time since the advent of experimental embryology in the 1880's, a previously descriptive area of biology had proved itself accessible to quantitative and experimental methods.

In 1916 Morgan published his second major work on evolution, *A Critique of the Theory of Evolution* (revised in 1925 as *Evolution and Genetics*), showing clearly his altered views about Darwinian selection. Although he had previously regarded de Vries's mutation theory as an alternative to natural selection, Mendelism now provided a mechanism for understanding the Darwinian theory itself. Mendelian variations (called also "mutations" by Morgan) were not as large or as drastic as those postulated by de Vries. Yet they were more distinct and discontinuous than the slight individual variations which Darwin had emphasized. Most important, they could be shown to be inherited in a definite pattern and were therefore subject to the effects of selection. The Mendelian theory filled the gap which Darwin had left open so long before.

Morgan found it more difficult to make explicit the relationships which he instinctively knew existed between the new science of heredity and the old problems of development (such as cell differentiation or regeneration). In 1934 Morgan attempted to make these connections in a book titled *Embryology and Genetics.*

Morgan's influence was central to the transformation of biology in general, and heredity and embryology in particular, from descriptive and highly speculative sciences arising from a morphological tradition, into ones based on quantitative and analytical methods. Beginning with embryology, and later moving into heredity, he brought first the experimental, and then the quantitative and analytical, approach to biological problems. Morgan's work on the chromosome theory of heredity alone would have earned him an important place in the history of modern biology.

MORICHINI, DOMENICO LINO (*b. Civitantino, Aquila, Italy, 1773; d. Rome, Italy, 1836*), medicine, chemistry.

In 1792 Morichini graduated from the University of Rome with a degree in medicine and philosophy. He practiced medicine, held several public health positions, and taught at the University of Rome. He is remembered for finding elemental flourine in fossil elephant and human teeth.

MORIN, JEAN-BAPTISTE (*b. Villefranche, Beaujolais, France, 1583; d. Paris, France, 1656*), medicine, astronomy, astrology.

Originally a medical doctor, Morin was professor of mathematics at the Collège Royal (now Collège de France) from 1630 until his death. He was interested in hermetic literature, astrology, mining, optics, and philosophy. He attacked Descartes and Galileo and presented himself as the champion of the immobility of the earth.

MORISON, ROBERT (*b. Dundee, Scotland, 1620; d. London, England, 1683*), botany.

Morison received an M.A. from Aberdeen University in 1638 and taught there until 1644, when his position as a Royalist in the Civil War forced him to flee to France. He studied medicine there and received an M.D. from Angers in 1648. His interest turned to botany, and in 1660 the restored Charles II brought him back to England as royal physician and botanist. In 1669 he became professor of botany at Oxford. There he developed a taxonomic system based on fruit and seed characteristics. He is regarded as one of the founders of the science of modern taxonomy. Among his works are *Praeludia botanica* (1669) and *Plantarum Historiae . . .* (incomplete at his death).

MORLAND, SAMUEL (*b. Sulhamstead Bannister, Berkshire, England, 1625; d. Hammersmith, Middlesex [now London], England, 1695*), mathematics, technology.

Morland entered Magdalene College, Cambridge, in 1644, became a fellow there, and continued his mathematics studies until 1653. He held important posts in Cromwell's foreign service but switched sides and worked as an agent to restore Charles II. In 1660, after the Restoration, Charles II knighted him, and he became a courtier. In 1681 he was named the king's "Master of Mechanicks." Morland's most important work was in the field of hydrostatics. He invented an ingenious apparatus for raising water by using gunpowder to expel air from a cistern, thereby creating a vacuum into which water rose. His manuscript version of *Élévation des eaux* (1685) describes one of the first uses of steam power to raise water.

MORLEY, EDWARD WILLIAMS (*b. Newark, N.J., 1838; d. West Hartford, Conn., 1923*), chemistry, physics.

Morley received the B.A. from Williams College in 1860 and continued his studies there along with his theological studies at Andover Theological Seminary. Ordained in the Congregational ministry, he became a minister in Twinsburg, Ohio, and taught at what is now Case Western Reserve University. He held the chair of chemistry and natural history until he retired in 1901. He also taught (1873–88) at the Cleveland Medical School.

Morley undertook to analyze the oxygen content of the atmosphere and designed a painstaking program to determine the atomic weight of oxygen relative to hydrogen taken as unity. The final period of his career was characterized by extensive collaborative studies with A.A. Michelson and others. His famous ether-drift experiments with Michelson reflect a fascination with the sensitivity of the interferometer and measuring techniques based on the wavelengths of light.

MORO, ANTONIO-LAZZARO (*b. San Vito del Friuli, Italy, 1687; d. San Vito del Friuli, 1764*), geology.

Despite an irregular education, Moro distinguished himself in mathematics, music, languages, literature,

natural sciences, and ecclesiastical studies. He took orders and served in various ecclesiastical posts, including professor of philosophy and rhetoric at the seminary at Feltre. In 1740 he published his best-known work, *Dei crostacei e degli altri corpi marini che si trovano sui monti*, a study of fossiliferous deposits. In it he gives a stratigraphic compilation of various fossilized marine flora and fauna, and in important respects it anticipates nineteenth-century geology. He rejected the neptunist view of the origin of rocks and mountain formations. His work provoked vehement reactions among European scientists, polarizing them into neptunists and plutonists.

MOROZOV, GEORGY FEDOROVICH (*b. St. Petersburg, Russia, 1867; d. Simferopol, U.S.S.R., 1920*), biogeography, ecology.

Morozov graduated from the Pavlovsk military academy in 1886 and went into the army. In 1889 he entered the St. Petersburg Forestry Institute. After graduation in 1894 he became a forester, and after 1896 he studied forestry in Germany and Switzerland for two years. Back in Russia, he became director of the Kammeno-Steppe experimental forestry preserve. An 1899 paper on "Soil Science and Forestry" attracted wide attention, and in 1901 he was named professor of forestry at St. Petersburg University. He was a follower of Dokuchaev, who had founded soil science in Russia, and Morozov's work laid the theoretical bases for rational forest management; especially important was his theory of the forest as a single complex organism.

MORSE, EDWARD SYLVESTER (*b. Portland, Me., 1838; d. Salem, Mass., 1925*), zoology.

Morse was a special student of Louis Agassiz at Harvard, where he had an assistantship from 1859 to 1862. During his career, he was associated with the Essex Institute, Bowdoin College, Tokyo University, and, especially, the Peabody Academy of Science (later Peabody Museum) of Salem, Massachusetts. His specialty was mollusks, primarily brachiopods, which were then considered mollusks. (Morse proved them to be more closely affiliated with worms.)

MORSE, JEDIDIAH (*b. Woodstock, Conn., 1761; d. New Haven, Conn., 1826*), geography.

Morse graduated from Yale College in 1783 and remained in New Haven, studying theology and conducting a school for young girls. From 1789 until 1819 he was a minister of the First Parish Church in Charlestown, Massachusetts, where he was a leading defender of orthodox Calvinism against the growing liberal Unitarianism. He was a founder of the Andover Theological Seminary, a bastion of conservative theology.

In 1784 Morse wrote the school text, *Geography Made Easy*, the first geography published in the United States. In 1789 he published his revised and extended version, *American Geography; or A View of the Present Situation of the United States of America*. It was an immediate success and was widely reprinted in Europe. He was quickly established as the "American Geographer," and as such he commanded the field for the next twenty-five years. His work, which went through about twenty editions, contained much historical and political material, in addition to geology and topography. He was the father of the inventor Samuel Finley Breese Morse.

MORTILLET, LOUIS-LAURENT GABRIEL DE (*b. Meylan, Isère, France, 1821; d. St.-Germain-en-Laye, France, 1898*), archaeology, anthropology.

Mortillet was educated in Jesuit seminaries in Chambéry and Paris. A revolutionary freethinker, he took part in the revolution of 1848 and was forced to leave France in 1849. While in Switzerland and Savoy, he engaged in scientific and archaeological work, particularly zoology and geology. Back in France in 1864, he held a number of important academic positions and became one of the founders of the new discipline of prehistory. In his *Musée préhistorique* (1881, written with his son Adrien), Mortillet subdivided the four-age system (Paleolithic, Neolithic, Bronze, and Iron) into periods and the periods into epochs. His fourteen epochs system predominated until the 1920's and was an important stepping-stone in the development of prehistory and anthropology. He was one of the first to recognize the importance of the Altamira cave paintings after they were discovered in 1879.

MORTON, JOHN (*b. England, 1671; d. Great Oxendon, England, 1726*), natural history.

Morton, a clergyman, wrote *The Natural History of Northamptonshire* (1712), which describes the topography, general geography, natural history, and prehistory of the county. Morton assumed the biblical Deluge to be responsible for the presence of fossils and the geological features. His botanical section is notable for his attempt to arrange the local flora systematically.

MORTON, SAMUEL GEORGE (*b. Philadelphia, Pa., 1799; d. Philadelphia, 1851*), anthropology.

Morton graduated from the University of Pennsylvania Medical School and received a second M.D. from Edinburgh in 1823. Long interested in scientific study, he wrote a description of the fossil remains collected by Lewis and Clark: *Synopsis of the Organic Remains of the Cretaceous Group of the United States* (1834). It marks him as a founder of invertebrate paleontology in the United States. His *Crania Americana* (1839), a comparative study of the human cranium, was a landmark in anthropology. It contained his theory of the origin of the world's races.

MOSANDER, CARL GUSTAF (*b. Kalmar, Sweden, 1797; d. Ångsholm, Sweden, 1858*), chemistry, mineralogy.

Apprenticed as a pharmacist as a teenager, Mosander receive his M.D. as an army surgeon in 1825. In 1832 he succeeded Berzelius as professor of chemistry and pharmacy at the Caroline Institute, a post he held until his death. His research was on minerals containing rare earth elements. He isolated and named lanthana, and mosandrite was named for him by A. Erdmann.

MOSELEY, HENRY GWYN JEFFREYS (*b. Weymouth, Dorsetshire, England, 1887; d. Gelibolu, Gallipoli Peninsula, Turkey, 1915*), physics.

A member of a distinguished scientific family, Moseley attended Trinity College, Oxford, on a science scholarship, and after graduation obtained (1910) a post in the Physics department at the University of Manchester. A

protegé of Rutherford, he specialized in the X-ray spectra of elements. His collaboration with C. G. Darwin resulted in an important paper, "The Reflexion of X Rays" (1913). He also wrote "The High-Frequency Spectra of the Elements" (1914).

MOSS, WILLIAM LORENZO (*b. Athens, Ga., 1876; d. Athens, 1957*), medicine, pathology.

Moss received a B.S. from the University of Georgia in 1902 and an M.D. from Johns Hopkins in 1905. He spent his career teaching and doing research at Johns Hopkins, Yale, Harvard, the New York State Institute for the Study of Malignant Diseases, and the University of Georgia School of Medicine. His most renowned contribution to medicine was a classification system, based on the content of the serum, of the four blood groups, which he designated by the roman numerals I through IV. His system has been replaced by the Landsteiner classification (A, B, O, and AB).

MOSSO, ANGELO (*b. Turin, Italy, 1846; d. Turin, 1910*), physiology, archaeology.

Mosso received an M.D. from the University of Turin in 1870. He did further work at Florence and Leipzig. Returning to Turin, he became (1875) professor of pharmacology and (1879) professor of physiology. Under him, Turin became an extremely active center for research in experimental physiology and biology. He pursued two main lines of research, the analysis of motor functions and the relationship between physiological and psychic phenomena. He perfected the plethysmograph, which measured slow changes in the volume of the blood vessels. Bad health forced him to give up his physiological studies in 1904, and his last years were devoted to archaeology. He acquired as great fame in archaeology as he had in physiology, conducting studies in the Roman Forum, Crete, and Southern Italy.

MOSSOTTI, OTTAVIANO FABRIZIO (*b. Novara, Italy, 1791; d. Pisa, Italy, 1863*), physics.

Mossotti attended the University of Milan, worked at the Milan observatory, and was professor of physics at the University of Buenos Aires. He taught at the Ionian University at Corfu, and in 1841 he became professor of mathematics, theoretical astronomy, and geodesy at the University of Pisa, where he remained until his death. Mossotti's outlook and methods—derived from Laplace, Poisson, and Ampère—were based on the belief that the proper way to explain all physical phenomena was by means of forces acting centrally at a distance between various fluids. Mossotti's success in accounting for dielectric behavior may be considered together with the impact of Faraday's work to illustrate the conceptual flux that characterized the study of electricity and magnetism from 1840 to 1870. He made an extensive analysis of the internal conditions in a dielectric subject to electrical action, obtaining expressions for the force in a small element of the dielectric resulting from the distribution of the molecules therein. This result is the Clausius-Mossotti relation in its original form. Mossotti's work was not very influential theoretically; it used none of Faraday's newer ideas on the distribution of force in space. However, it was an important formal development, even though Faraday's theories eventually won out.

MOTTRAM, JAMES CECIL (*b. Slody, Norfolk, England, 1879; d. London, England, 1945*), medicine, natural history.

Mottram qualified as a doctor in 1903 at University College Hospital, London. His professional life was mainly devoted to the study of cancer: at Middlesex Hospital School (1908–19), the Radium Institute (1919–37), and Mount Vernon Hospital (1937–45). His work was in three phases: (1) the effects of X rays and radium on the cells of normal and malignant tissues; (2) carcinogenesis; and (3) the methods of treating cancer. His work on X rays pointed both to the treatment of tumors by exposure to radium and to the potential damage to persons working with X rays and radium. His most important discovery (1913) was that plant and animal cells are more vulnerable to damage by beta and gamma radiation when they are in the process of division than in the resting stage. He also wrote an important work on the coloration of animals, *Controlled Natural Selection and Value Marking* (1914).

MOUCHEZ, ERNEST BARTHÉLÉMY (*b. Madrid, Spain, 1821; d. Wissous, Seine-et-Oise, France, 1892*), cartography, astronomy.

Mouchez prepared for a career in the navy at the École Navale. During his naval career, he made important hydrographical studies along the coasts of Korea, China, South America, and Algeria. He also explored several rivers and islands. In 1874 he observed the transit of Venus for the Académie des Sciences, and in 1878 became director of the Paris observatory.

MOULTON, FOREST RAY (*b. Osceola County, Mich., 1872; d. Wilmette, Ill., 1952*), astronomy, mathematics.

Moulton received a B.A. in 1894 from Albion College and a Ph.D. in astronomy from the University of Chicago in 1899. He remained at Chicago until he retired in 1926. He collaborated with Thomas Crowder Chamberlin in investigating the origin of the earth. Their study of the eruptive nature of the sun, photographed during a solar eclipse in 1900, resulted in the Moulton-Chamberlin hypothesis of 1904, also known as the planetesimal hypothesis. The theory proposed that nebula flaring away from the sun quickly cooled and solidified, creating small chunks of matter, the planetesimals. He also did pioneering work in ballistics and in educational broadcasting.

MOUTARD, THÉODORE FLORENTIN (*b. Soultz, Haut-Rhin, France, 1827; d. Paris, France, 1901*), geometry, engineering.

Moutard attended the École Polytechnique (1844–46), graduated from the École des Mines in 1849, and entered the engineering corps. From 1875 he was professor of mechanics at the École des Mines. His mathematical work was primarily in the theory of algebraic surfaces.

MOUTON, GABRIEL (*b. Lyons, France, 1618; d. Lyons, 1694*), mathematics, astronomy.

Mouton spent his entire life in Lyons, where he was a clergyman. He also acquired a certain renown as mathematician and astronomer. The book that made him famous, *Observationes diametrorum solis et lunae apparentium* (1670), was concerned with the project of a universal standard of measurement based on the pendulum. Leibniz arrived at the same general ideas by using a different method but acknowledged the similarity of their theories. Mouton constructed a remarkably precise astronomical pendulum.

MUHYI 'L-DĪN AL-MAGHRIBĪ (Muḥyi 'l-Milla wa 'l-Dīn Yaḥyā ibn Muḥammad ibn Abi 'l-Shukr al-Maghribī al-Andalusī) (*fl. Syria, and later Marāgha, ca. 1260–65*), trigonometry, astronomy, astrology.

Al-Maghribī was a Hispano-Muslim mathematician and astronomer about whom little is known. He was born in the Islamic West and was active in Syria and in Marāgha, where he joined the astronomers directed by Naṣīr al-Dīn al-Ṭūsī. His writings on trigonometry contain original developments. For example, two proofs are given of the sine theory for right-angled spherical triangles, and one of them is different from those given by Naṣīr al-Dīn al-Ṭūsī; this theorem is generalized for other triangles. Al-Maghribī also worked in several other branches of trigonometry.

MUIR, MATTHEW MONCRIEFF PATTISON (*b. Glasgow, Scotland, 1848; d. Epsom, England, 1931*), chemistry.

Muir was educated at the universities of Glasgow and Tübingen, and from 1877 taught chemistry at Gonville and Caius College, Cambridge. His laboratory investigations chiefly related to compounds of bismuth, and he wrote a number of chemistry textbooks. In the 1880's, he turned to philosophical and historical studies of chemistry, and in this field made his greatest contributions, particularly in his biographical work on famous chemists.

MULDER, GERARDUS JOHANNES (*b. Utrecht, Netherlands, 1802; d. Bennekom, Netherlands, 1880*), chemistry.

Mulder received an M.D. from the University of Utrecht in 1825 and established practices in Amsterdam and Rotterdam, where he also taught botany, chemistry, mathematics, and pharmacy to medical and apothecary students. From 1840 to 1868 he was professor of chemistry at the University of Utrecht. The works of Faraday and Berzelius exerted a great influence on him, and his scientific works were written in the spirit of their theories. His analysis of proteins (1838) received widespread attention.

MÜLLER, FRANZ (FERENC), BARON DE REICHENSTEIN (*b. Nagyszeben, Transylvania [now Sibiu, Rumania], 1740; d. Vienna, Austria, 1825*), chemistry.

Müller studied law in Vienna and mining and metallurgy at Selmecbánya (Schemnitz, in Hungary). In 1768 he entered the service of the state saltworks in Transylvania. Later he was director of state mines in southern Hungary and the Tirol. After 1802 he headed the council that had jurisdiction over all minting and mining in Austria and Hungary. He discovered the chemical element tellurium, a variety of tourmaline, and the variety of opal known as Müller glass. Upon retirement in 1818 he was raised to the peerage.

MÜLLER, FRITZ (JOHANN FRIEDRICH THEODOR) (*b. Windischholzhausen, Thuringia, Germany, 1822; d. Blumenau, Brazil, 1897*), natural history.

Müller received a Ph.D. from the University of Berlin in 1844. He completed his medical studies at the Univer-

491

sity of Greifswald in 1849 but was not allowed certification because of his free-thinking religious views. In 1852 he went to Brazil, where his important scientific work was done. He is regarded as one of the greatest and most original naturalists of the nineteenth century. His book *Für Darwin* (1864) was a fundamental contribution to evolutionary biology at a critical moment during its infancy; and his name has been immortalized in scientific literature with the term "Müllerian mimicry," in which two or more distasteful but unrelated species resemble one another. Müller explained that predators must learn through warning characteristics which species are palatable, and that in this process some of the prey population must be sacrificed. If there are two or more similar, unpalatable species, then predators will be educated faster by the warning characteristics, the similar species will be better protected, fewer deaths will result, and the losses will be absorbed by a larger group. He maintained a correspondence with Charles Darwin, who sponsored the English translation of Müller's book, published in 1869 as *Facts and Arguments for Darwin*.

MÜLLER, GEORG ELIAS (*b. Grimma, Germany, 1850; d. Göttingen, Germany, 1934*), psychology.

After attending the universities of Leipzig and Berlin, Müller received a Ph.D. from the University of Göttingen in 1873, where he had studied philosophy and psychology under Lotze. Except for a year as professor of philosophy at Czernowitz, his entire academic career was spent at Göttingen. His psychological research laboratory there was highly regarded. His contributions in psychophysics comprised articles on method and the muscle basis of weight judgments, and a definitive handbook of psychophysics. He extended Ebbinghaus's work on the learning and memory of nonsense syllables, and he and Schumann invented the memory drum for more accurate presentations. In work on vision, his study of color sensation led to his lengthy *Über die Farbenempfindungen: Psychophysische Untersuchungen* (1930). His position at the beginnings of phenomenology and Festalt psychology was extremely important.

MÜLLER, GUSTAV (*b. Schweidnitz, Germany [now Świdnica, Poland], 1851; d. Potsdam, Germany, 1925*), astronomy, astrophysics.

Müller studied mathematics and natural science at Leipzig (1870–72) and astronomy at Berlin and at Potsdam, where he received his doctorate in 1877. He became an observer at Potsdam in 1882, chief observer in 1888, and professor in 1891. His most important photometric project was the *Potsdamer Durchmusterung*, in which he used an astrometer he had constructed himself to ascertain the luminosities of more than 14,000 stars in the Northern skies. Its preparation lasted from 1886 to 1907, and it is still an indispensable standard work, He participated in many great scientific expeditions, ranging from the United States to Russia.

MULLER, HERMANN JOSEPH (*b. New York, N.Y., 1890; d. Indianapolis, Ind., 1967*), genetics, evolution, eugenics.

Muller received a B.A. from Columbia College in 1910, an M.A. in 1912, and a Ph.D. in 1916. His teaching posts were widespread: Rice Institute, Columbia, the Univer-

sity of Texas, the Brain Research Institute in Berlin, the Soviet Academy of Sciences in Leningrad and Moscow, Edinburgh University, Amherst College, and Indiana University. Muller induced genetic mutations by exposing *Drosophila* to X rays. In 1927 he reported his findings in "Artificial Transmutation of the Gene." It won him an international reputation that culminated in the 1946 Nobel Prize in physiology or medicine. Muller worked at the Soviet Academy of Sciences from 1933 to 1937, chiefly concerned with radiation genetics, cytogenetics, and gene structure. He opposed the theories of Lysenko, which eventually made his work in the Soviet Union unfeasible. His later years were spent conducting his campaign against medical, military, and industrial abuse of radiation.

MÜLLER, JOHANN. *See* **Regiomontanus.**

MÜLLER, JOHANN (HEINRICH JACOB) (*b. Kassel, Germany, 1809; d. Freiburg im Breisgau, Germany, 1875*), physics.

Müller attended the universities of Bonn and Giessen. In 1833 he received a Ph.D. from Giessen with a thesis on the optics of crystals. He remained at Giessen until 1844, when he was named professor of physics and technology at the University of Freiburg. Early in his career, Müller developed a systematic concept of physics, which was partially determined by his didactic talent. His synopses of topics related to physics were contained in his textbook, *Lehrbuch der Physik und Meteorologie*. Its first edition was published in 1842, and Müller regularly revised and enlarged it. It remained well known and in use until the 1930's. His studies of Fraunhofer lines led him to measure with L. Babot (1855), the first Fraunhofer lines beyond the violet end of the spectrum.

MÜLLER, JOHANNES PETER (*b. Coblenz, Germany, 1801; d. Berlin, Germany, 1858*), physiology, anatomy, zoology.

Müller received an M.D. from the University of Bonn in 1822 and continued his studies at the University of Berlin. There he came under the influence of Carl Rudolphi, Germany's preeminent anatomist. Returning to Bonn, he taught physiology, anatomy, and general pathology; and in 1826, at age twenty-five, he became extraordinary professor. In 1830 he was named full professor. He taught at Berlin for the rest of his life. After Rudolphi's death, Müller assumed his chair in anatomy and physiology. After publication of his major work, *Handbuch der Physiologie des Menschen* in 1840, his interests turned to comparative anatomy and zoology, especially the study of marine animals. Müller suffered from depression during several periods of his life, and his death in 1858 was suspected of being by his own hand.

Müller introduced a new era of biological research in Germany and pioneered the use of experimental methods in medicine. He overcame the inclination to natural-philosophical speculation widespread in German universities during his youth and inculcated respect for careful observation and physiological experimentation. Anatomy and physiology, pathological anatomy and histology, embryology and zoology—in all these fields he made numerous fundamental discoveries. Among them were new findings on human and animal vision, including perceptive analyses of human vision; the discovery of the anatomy of the embryonic duct (now known as "Müller's duct"); his confirmation of the Bell-Magendie law by a simple, classic operation on a frog; and his demonstrations of the sensory and motor activities of the cranial nerves.

MÜLLER, OTTO FREDERIK (*b. Copenhagen, Denmark, 1730; d. Copenhagen, 1784*), botany, zoology.

Müller studied theology and law at the University of Copenhagen. From 1756, for nearly twenty years, he was tutor to a noble Danish family and traveled throughout Europe with them. In 1773 he married a wealthy widow, thereby enabling him to devote his last years to the study of science. Early in his career as tutor, Müller became interested in the local flora and fauna. In 1764 he published *Fauna insectorum Fridrichsdalina*, which described 858 "insects" found at his patrons' estate Frederiksdal, in northern Zealand. *Flora Fridrichsdalina* (1766) described 1,100 species and was intended to represent most of the Danish flora. But Müller's main work in systematics consisted of studying animal groups that were very little known before he identified them: the Hydrachnida, the Tardigrada, the Entomostraca, and the Infusoria. His study of the Infusoria, published in 1786, was for many years accepted as the best study of the group. His placement is still accepted by most authors. Müller also wrote *Zoologiae Danicae prodromus* (1776), the first manual on the fauna of Norway and Denmark and for many years the most comprehensive.

MÜLLER, PAUL (*b. Olten, Solothurn, Switzerland, 1899; d. Basel, Switzerland, 1965*), chemistry.

Müller received his doctorate in chemistry from the University of Basel in 1925. He became a research chemist in the dye factory of J.R. Geigy A.G., where he remained all his career, eventually specializing in pest-control research. In 1939 he developed a new insecticide, 4,4'-dichloro-diphenyl-trichloro-ethane, which he called DDT and for which he secured the Swiss patents. He was awarded the Nobel Prize in physiology or medicine in 1948.

MÜLLER-BRESLAU, HEINRICH (FRANZ BERN-HARD) (*b. Breslau, Germany [now Wrocław, Poland], 1851; d. Berlin, Germany, 1925*), theory of structures.

Müller (he styled himself Müller-Breslau after the 1870's) served with the Prussian army engineers and later became a civil engineer. Although he studied engineering and mathematics at the Gewerbeakademie and the University of Berlin, he never took a degree. He specialized in the design of iron structures, chiefly bridges. His first major book was *Theorie und Berechnung der eisernen Bogenbrücken* (1880). He taught bridge design at the Polytechnic Institute of Hannover from 1883 to 1888. In 1888 he was appointed to the chair of structural engineering at the Berlin-Charlottenburg Institute of Technology, where he remained the rest of his life. Müller-Breslau has been termed the founder of modern structural engineering in Germany. He designed bridges, the new cathedral in Berlin, and participated in the construction of the Zeppelin airships.

MUNCKE, GEORG WILHELM (*b. Hillingsfeld, near Hameln, Germany, 1772; d. Grosskmehlen, Germany, 1847*), physics.

In 1810 Muncke became professor of physics at the University of Marburg, and from 1817 to his death was at the University of Heidelberg. Muncke's chief importance lies in his critical opposition toward much of the scientific speculation of his time, in particular in his opposition to Kant's dynamical theory of matter. His major works were *System der atomistischen Physik* (1809) and *Handbuch der Naturlehre* (1829–30).

MUNIER-CHALMAS, ERNEST CHARLES PHILIPPE AUGUSTE (*b. Tournus, France, 1843; d. Saint-Simon, near Aix-les-Bains, France, 1903*), paleontology, stratigraphy.

After successfully teaching himself geology, Munier-Chalmas became assistant in the Sorbonne's geology department in 1863. In 1882 he began teaching at the École Normale, and in 1891 he succeeded Edmond Hébert, his closest collaborator, to the chair of geology at the Sorbonne. His doctoral thesis was never published. He and Hébert collaborated on paleontological investigations, and he was also concerned with the stratigraphy of the Cenozoic of the Paris Basin.

MUNĪŚVARA VIŚVARŪPA (*b. Benares, India, 1603*), astronomy, mathematics.

Munīśvara was born into a noted family of astronomers who had settled in Benares. His greatest work, the *Siddhāntasārvabhauma* (1646) demonstrates some knowledge of Islamic astronomy and generally embraced the Saurapakṣa position. He seems to have enjoyed the patronage of Shāh Jahān.

MUÑJĀLA (*fl. India, 932*), astronomy.

Munjala was the author of a *Bṛhanmānasa*, only fragments of which survive, and the *Laghumānasa*, which is extant. The latter is an eclectic work, borrowing from different schools, with some original insights into lunar theory.

MÜNSTER, SEBASTIAN (*b. Nieder-Ingelheim, Germany, 1489; d. Basel, Switzerland, 1552*), geography.

Münster studied at Heidelberg and entered the Minorite order at age sixteen. He became an important Hebrew scholar and was elected to the chair of Hebrew at Basel in 1527. In 1529 he became a Protestant and married. In 1540 he published a Latin translation of Ptolemy's *Geography*, and in 1544 published his most important work, *Cosmographei*, a "description of the whole world and everything in it." It ran to 660 pages and set a new standard in the field; especially valuable are the sections dealing with Germany and Central Europe.

MURALT, JOHANNES VON (*b. Zurich, Switzerland, 1645; d. Zurich, 1733*), surgery, medicine, anatomy.

After extensive foreign studies, Muralt received an M.D. from the University of Basel in 1671. Early in his career he encountered opposition for his public dissection of animals, but later the Zurich authorities allowed him to dissect the bodies of executed criminals and of hospital patients who had died of rare diseases. Muralt was a skillful surgeon who developed new procedures.

MURCHISON, RODERICK IMPEY (*b. Tarradale, Ross and Cromarty, Scotland, 1792; d. London, England, 1871*), geology.

Murchison enjoyed a private income; his interest was turned toward science through his acquaintance with Humphry Davy. His geological studies brought him worldwide fame and recognition. Stratigraphy was his chief area of interest. He became convinced of the superiority of fossils over lithology as criteria of geological age. He discovered (and named) in 1835 the Silurian, a major system of strata that marked a major period in the history of the earth. By the time his report, *The Silurian System,* was published in 1839, its validity had already been recognized. Two expeditions to Russia (1840, 1841) established still further the validity of his findings. His *Geology of Russia* (1845) resulted from those expeditions. Always intolerant to criticism, he became increasingly involved in bitter disputes, particularly with Henry de la Beche and his former collaborator, Adam Sedgwick. He was totally opposed to Darwin's evolutionary theory, and equally opposed to Louis Agassiz's glacial theory. During his later years, he was well known as a geographer and was a patron of David Livingstone's expeditions. The Murchison Falls of the Nile are named for him. He was knighted in 1846 and created a baronet in 1866.

MURPHY, JAMES BUMGARDNER (*b. Morganton, N.C., 1884; d. Bar Harbor, Me., 1950*), biology.

Murphy received a B.S. from the University of North Carolina in 1905 and an M.D. in 1909 from Johns Hopkins University. From 1910 until retirement in 1950, he pursued and directed research on cancer and related physiological problems at the Rockefeller Institute in New York City. The results of studies under his guidance included, by 1935, the discovery that certain tumors in mice could be transplanted, that specific chemical substances produced malignancies after repeated exposure to them, that certain cancers occurred more frequently when ancestors had expressed the same disease, and that chicken tumors were transplantable. His personal achievements included perfection of the techique of virus culture in fertilized eggs.

MURRAY, GEORGE ROBERT MILNE (*b. Arbroath, Scotland, 1858; d. Stonehaven, Scotland, 1911*), botany.

Murray was educated at Arbroath and Strasbourg. In 1876 he began his lifelong career in the botany department of the British Museum; he was put in charge of the cryptogamic collections. Before he was twenty-one he was invited to write the fungi article for the *Encyclopaedia Britannica*. His work on the reproduction of diatoms by asexual spore formation was published in 1897. He was involved in numerous botanizing expeditions, generally under the auspices of the British Museum.

MURRAY, JOHN (*b. Cobourg, Ontario, Canada, 1841; d. Kirkliston, Scotland, 1914*), oceanography, marine geology.

Murray studied medicine and physics at the University of Edinburgh, but never took a degree. In 1872 he became an assistant to C. Wyville Thomson, the scientific director of the circumnavigation voyage of H.M.S. *Challenger.* During his three-and-one-half years aboard, Mur-

ray took over the newest of the *Challenger's* scientific quests: investigating the deposits on the sea bottom. In 1877 he began assisting Thomson in preparing the massive report of the expedition. Thomson died in 1882 and Murray took over the project. The result was a monumental fifty-volume report, published between 1880 and 1895. It included his own masterly *Summary* (1895) and the two-volume *Deep-Sea Deposits* (1891, written with Alphonse Renard) and established his preeminence as an oceanographer. His study of coral reefs led him to oppose Darwin's theory on the subject but his views have not held up. He amassed a fortune by developing phosphate mining on Christmas Island and left most of it to subsidize oceanographic research.

MŪSĀ IBN MUḤAMMAD IBN MAḤMŪD AL-RŪMĪ QĀḌĪZĀDE. *See* **Qāḍī Zāda al-Rūmī.**

MŪSĀ IBN SHĀKIR, SONS OF. *See* **Banū Mūsā.**

MUSHET, DAVID (*b. Dalkeith, Scotland, 1772; d. Monmouth, Wales, 1847*), metallurgy.

Mushet was the son of an iron founder, and he began his experiments in 1793 as an employee of the Clyde ironworks, near Glasgow. After 1800 he was associated in various ironwork partnerships, all the while writing and publishing scientific papers on the iron and steel industry. Mushet was granted five patents for metallurgy processes. In the 1870's there was considerable controversy over the technical value of those processes. His son, Robert Forester Mushet, whose contributions to the iron and steel industry were more spectacular, was an aggressive defender of his father's contributions.

MUSHKETOV, IVAN VASILIEVICH (*b. Alekseevskaya, Voronezh, Russia, 1850; d. St. Petersburg, Russia, 1902*), geology, geography.

Mushketov graduated from the St. Petersburg Mining Institute in 1872, where he studied mineralogy and petrography. He spent many years doing research in Turkestan and central Asia, the results of which were published in *Turkestan* (2 vols., 1886–1906). He taught geology and physical geography at the Mining Institute. His work was especially influential in the study of the geology of central Asia, tectonics, seismology, and glaciology. His major publication was *Fizicheskaya geologia* (2 vols., 1888–91).

MUSSCHENBROEK, PETRUS VAN (*b. Leiden, Netherlands, 1692; d. Leiden, 1761*), physics.

Musschenbroek belonged to a well-known family of brass founders and instrument makers. He received an M.D. from the University of Leiden in 1715 and a Ph.D. in 1719. He taught at Duisburg and from 1723 to 1740 he occupied the chair of natural philosophy and mathematics at Utrecht. From 1740 until his death he taught at Leiden. He maintained the reputation that Leiden had acquired under Boerhave and 'sGravesande, and students interested in experimentation came from all parts of Europe. Musschenbroek was primarily a lecturer and author, and his fame was achieved through the wide dissemination of his lecture notes, collected in ever larger volumes. He devised many experiments, and developed what came to be known as the Leyden jar. In his experiments he often used apparatus made by his brother Jan, who was carrying on the family tradition as an instrument maker.

MUTIS Y BOSSIO, JOSÉ CELESTINO BRUNO (*b. Cadiz, Spain, 1732; d. Sante Fe de Bogotá, Nueva Granada [now Bogotá, Colombia], 1808*), botany, astronomy.

Mutis received a degree in medicine at Seville in 1755 and continued his education at Madrid (1757–60). In 1760 he went to America, where he successfully opposed smallpox inoculation, helped found the Sociedad de Amigos del País (1802), and initiated the study of the exact sciences. In 1803 he founded the astronomical observatory at Bogotá. His major contribution was *La Flora de la real expedición botánica del Nuevo Reino de Granada,* publication of which began in 1954.

MYDORGE, CLAUDE (*b. Paris, France, 1585; d. Paris, 1647*), mathematics, physics.

Mydorge belonged to one of France's richest and most illustrious families. He pursued a legal career. He met Descartes in about 1625 and became one his most faithful friends, defending him against his detractors. Although an amateur, Mydorge was held in high repute by his contemporaries. His work in geometry was directed to the study of conic sections. In 1631 he published a two-volume work on the subject, which was enlarged to four volumes in 1639 and later reprinted under the title *De sectionibus conicis.* It contains hundreds of problems published for the first time, as well as a multitude of ingenious and original methods that later geometers frequently used, usually without giving credit to Mydorge.

MYLON, CLAUDE (*b. Paris, France, ca. 1618; d. Paris, ca. 1660*), mathematics.

The son of a counselor to Louis XIII, Mylon was admitted to the bar. He became concerned with mathematics and came into contact with such mathematicians as Schooten, Huygens, Mersenne, Debeaune, and Roberval. His place in the history of science derives from the service he provided in facilitating communication among such learned men. His own attempts at mathematical achievement were largely unsuccessful.

NAEGELI, CARL WILHELM VON (*b. Kilchberg, near Zurich, Switzerland, 1817; d. Munich, Germany, 1891*), botany, microscopy.

Naegeli studied medicine at the University of Zurich and botany at the University of Geneva, from which he received a Ph.D. in 1840. After short periods working at Jena, Zurich, and Freiburg, he accepted the chair of botany at the University of Munich (1857), where he remained the rest of his life. He is regarded as one of the nineteenth century's foremost botanists and influential theoreticians. In 1858 he arrived at his micellar theory of cell ultrastructure, according to which such amorphous substances as starch and cellulose consist of building blocks—which he later termed "micelles"—packed in crystalline array. This theory stimulated studies of ultrastructure and initiated a tradition of the study of botanical ultrastructure in Germany and Switzerland. His final statements on heredity, growth, and ultrastructure are in *Mechanisch-physiologische Theorie der Abstammungslehre* (1884).

IBN AL-NAFĪS, ʿALĀʾ AL-DĪN ABU ʾL-ḤASAN ʿALĪ IBN ABI ʾL-ḤAZM AL-QURASHĪ (or AL-QARASHĪ) (*b. al-Qurashiyya, near Damascus, thirteenth century; d. Cairo, 1288*), medicine.

Ibn al-Nafīs studied medicine at Damascus and eventually became chief of physicians under the Mamluk ruler al-Ẓāhir Baybars al-Bunduqdārī (reigned 1260–77). He also lectured on jurisprudence. He wrote a voluminous book on the art of medicine (*Kitāb al-Shāmil*) when in his thirties, which contains an interesting section on surgical technique and details of the duties of the surgeon to his patients. In an earlier work, *Sharh Tashrīh al-Qānūn,* he gave the earliest known account of the pulmonary blood circulation. The date of his discovery of the lesser circulation has been fixed at no later than 1242, three centuries before those published by Servetus (1553) and Colombo (1559).

NAGAOKA, HANTARO (*b. Nagasaki, Japan, 1865; d. Tokyo, Japan, 1950*), physics.

After receiving a Ph.D. from the University of Tokyo, Nagaoka studied in Berlin, Munich, and Vienna from 1893 to 1896. From 1901 to 1925, as professor at the University of Tokyo, he was primarily responsible for promoting the advancement of physics in Japan. He is known for his Saturnian atomic model, published in 1904.

NĀGEŚA (*fl. Gujarat, India, ca. 1630*), astronomy.

Nāgeśa's principal astronomical work is an unpublished *Grahaprabodha,* which gives instructions for computing the true longitudes of the sun, moon, and planets. His son Śiva was also an astronomer.

AL-NAIRĪZĪ. *See* **al-Nayrizi.**

NAIRNE, EDWARD (*b. Sandwich [?], England, 1726; d. London, England, 1806*), mathematics, optics, physics.

Nairne achieved an international reputation as one of the foremost makers of mathematical, optical, and philosophical instruments of the eighteenth century. These included electrical machines, microscopes, telescopes, vacuum pumps, measuring equipment, and artificial magnets. He was a longtime acquaintance of Benjamin Franklin.

NAJĪB AL-DĪN. *See* **al-Samarqandī, Najib al-Din.**

NAMETKIN, SERGEY SEMENOVICH (*b. Kazan, Russia, 1876; d. Moscow, U.S.S.R., 1950*), chemistry.

Nametkin was educated (1896–1902) at the University of Moscow and from 1938 to 1950 was head of the organic chemistry department there, after teaching at the Second Moscow University. From 1927 to 1950 he was also professor at the Moscow Mining Academy. His scientific work concentrated on the nitration of saturated hydrocarbons, the chemistry of terpenes (in which he discovered the Nametkin rearrangement), stereochemistry, the chemistry and technology of petroleum, and the synthesis of growth stimulators and perfumes.

NANSEN, FRIDTJOF (*b. Store-Fröen, near Oslo, Norway, 1861; d. Oslo, 1930*), zoology, oceanography.

While a student at the University of Christiania (now Oslo) in 1882, Nansen took part in an Arctic expedition of the sealer *Viking,* and his subsequent career as an Arctic explorer was set by that voyage. In 1888 he received a Ph.D. from Oslo for a thesis on nerve fibers, and set off on an expedition to Greenland which confirmed that Greenland is completely covered with ice and produced meticulous meteorological observations that have remained basic to an understanding of the influence of weather conditions in northern Europe and the United States. In 1893 a vessel, the *Fram* ("Forward"), was specially built to his specifications to withstand the pressure of ice; it spent almost three years in the Arctic, at times frozen in the ice for long periods. Nansen and F. H. Johansen left the ship at 85°55′N. lat. and went on towards the pole, reaching 86°14′N before having to turn back (1895). The publication of the results of that expedition provided an important stimulus to physical oceanography. Nansen made extensive studies of ice drift, oceanic thermometry, and salinity, and devised useful apparatus. With the outbreak of World War I he turned to humanitarian work. He was Norway's first delegate to the League of Nations, a post he held to his death. In 1921 he was named commissioner for refugees for the League. He received the 1922 Nobel Peace Prize.

NAPIER, JOHN (*b. Edinburgh, Scotland, 1550; d. Edinburgh, 1617*), mathematics.

A Scottish aristocrat and landowner, Napier studied briefly at St. Andrews University and probably abroad. Although he is remembered today as the inventor of logarithms, his early reputation was made in theology. His book *A Plaine Discovery of the Whole Revelation of Saint John* (1593) took the Protestant position; it went through several editions and was widely translated. Napier is believed to have become interested in mathematics early in his life; he seems to have begun work on logarithms about 1590. That work culminated in his two important treatises, *Descriptio* (1614) and *Constructio* (1619). Very little is known of the preliminary work that led him to invent the logarithm tables, and one observer, Lord Moulton, called it a "bolt from the blue"; Joost Bürgi, a Swiss mathematician, independently prepared a set of tables at about the same time. Napier's writings also made a valuable contribution to the development and systematization of spherical trigonometry, and publicized and facilitated the adoption of decimal notation. His *Rabdologiae* (1617) contains several elementary calculating devices, including the popular engraved rods ("Napier's bones") that functioned as a mechanical multiplication table.

NĀRĀYAṆA (*fl. India, 1356*), mathematics.

Nārāyaṇa was one of the most renowned Indian mathematicians of the medieval period. His major work was *Gaṇitakaumudī* (1356); it consists of rules and examples of arithmetic and geometry.

AL-NASAWĪ, ABU 'L-ḤASAN, ʿALĪ IBN AḤMAD (*fl. Baghdad, 1029–44*), arithmetic, geometry.

Al-Nasawī probably was born at Nasā, in Khurasan. His major work was *al-Muqniʿ fī 'l-Ḥisāb al-Hindī,* written at the behest of Sharaf al-Mulūk, the vizier of Jalāl al-Dawla, the ruler of Baghdad. Al-Nasawī is generally remembered as a forerunner in the use of the decimal concept, but his priority has recently been questioned.

NAṢĪR AL-DĪN AL-ṬŪSĪ. *See* **al-Ṭūsī, Muḥammad ibn Muḥammad ibn al-Ḥasan.**

NASMYTH, JAMES (*b. Edinburgh, Scotland, 1808; d. London, England, 1890*), engineering, astronomy.

Nasmyth was educated privately and not well, but he acquired some knowledge of chemistry, mathematics, and natural philosophy. He was skilled in model engineering and established a highly successful business in Manchester. The steam hammer (1839) was his most successful invention. He also designed a milling machine, a planing machine, and a steam pile driver. He helped William Lassell build a very fine Newtonian reflector, and he published astronomical observations of some interest, including the book *The Moon Considered as a Planet, a World, and a Satellite* (1874, written with James Carpenter).

NATALIS, STEPHANUS. *See* **Noël, Étienne.**

NATANSON, WŁADYSŁAW (*b. Warsaw, Poland, 1864; d. Cracow, Poland, 1937*), physics.

Natanson, who came from a distinguished literary and scientific family, studied at the University of St. Petersburg, the Cavendish Laboratory in England, the University of Dorpat, and the Jagiellonian University in Cracow; his entire career was spent at the Jagiellonian University. He pioneered in the thermodynamics of irreversible processes, publishing two important papers on the subject in 1896 and 1897. He later worked on the hydrodynamics of viscous liquids and on optics.

NATHORST, ALFRED GABRIEL (*b. Väderbrunn, Södermanland, Sweden, 1850; d. Stockholm, Sweden, 1921*), paleobotany, geology, exploration.

Nathorst studied at Malmö, Lund, and Uppsala before receiving his doctorate in 1874 from the University of Lund. He was on the staff of the Geological Survey of Sweden until 1884, when he went to the Swedish Museum of Natural History; there he was professor and director of the Department of Archegoniates and Fossil Plants until he resigned in 1917. He published a series of works on the vegetational history of Sweden in postglacial times, but his international reputation is based on his monographs on the Tertiary floras of Japan (1882, 1888) and on the Paleozoic and Mesozoic floras of the Arctic (1894–1920).

NAUDIN, CHARLES (*b. Autun, France, 1815; d. Villa Thuret, near Antibes, France, 1899*), horticulture, experimental botany.

Naudin received a baccalaureate from Montpellier in 1837 and a doctorate at Paris in 1842. A severe nervous disorder, resulting in deafness and constant pain, precluded a regular academic career. Instead he supervised botanic gardens and carried out research at Collioure (1869–78) and then at Antibes. His primary interests focused on acclimatization and economic botany; his most celebrated work was done on problems of plant hybridization. He regarded hybridization, rather than natural selection or environmental action, as the primary agency of evolutionary change.

NAUMANN, ALEXANDER (*b. Eudorf, near Alsfeld, Prussia, 1837; d. Giessen, Germany, 1922*), chemistry.

Naumann studied at the University of Giessen; from 1862 he taught at Giessen, first at the Gymnasium and then (from 1864) at the university as well; he retired in 1913. His research contributed significantly to preparing the way for later important discoveries in chemical thermodynamics. His most important books are *Grundriss der Thermochemie* (1869) and *Lehr- und Handbuch der Thermochemie* (1882).

NAUMANN, KARL FRIEDRICH (*b. Dresden, Germany, 1797; d. Dresden, 1873*), mineralogy, geology.

Naumann studied at the mining academy at Freiberg and at the universities of Leipzig and Jena, where he received his doctorate in 1819. His academic career was spent at Jena, Leipzig, and Freiberg. He discovered tetartohedrism in the isometric, tetragonal, and hexagonal crystal systems. He was the first to observe hemimorphism. His *Lehrbuch der Geognosie* (1850–54) was the most authoritative work on petrography in the mid-nineteenth century and served as a standard textbook for decades.

NAVASHIN, SERGEY GAVRILOVICH (*b. Tsarevshin, Saratov guberniya, Russia, 1857; d. Detskoye Selo [now Pushkin], U.S.S.R., 1930*), biology, plant cytology, plant embryology.

Studied at St. Petersburg Academy of Medicine and Surgery and at University of Moscow. Taught at Moscow and at Petrov Academy, then became Borodin's assistant at University of St. Petersburg (1888; master's degree, 1894); later taught at universities of Kiev (from 1894) and Tbilisi (from 1915); director of K. A. Timiryazev Institute of Plant Physiology, Moscow (1923–29). Did research on morphology and taxonomy of mosses and parasitic fungi; discovered chalazogamy in birches (1895) and other trees (1899). In 1898 he discovered double fertilization in angiosperms, thus leading to the discovery that the endosperms of angiosperms and gymnosperms are not homologous. Later work contributed to the comparative karyological trend in cytology.

NAVIER, CLAUDE-LOUIS-MARIE-HENRI (*b. Dijon, France, 1785; d. Paris, France, 1836*), engineering, mechanics.

Studied at École Polytechnique and École des Ponts et Chaussées (graduated 1806), and later taught at both schools. In the process of editing the engineering works of his granduncle, Emiland Gauthey, and the *Science des ingénieurs* of Bélidor, Navier became a theoretician who wrote textbooks for practicing engineers. During the period 1807–20 he made mathematical analysis a fundamental tool of the civil engineer and codified the nascent concept of mechanical work for the science of machines. In considering the performance of iron as a structural material he used the traditional engineering approach to study the forces resisting compression and extension, and the analytical approach to study forces resisting bending. In revising Bélidor's *Architecture hydraulique* Navier sought a quantitative criterion for the study of machines and was led to the concept of quantity of action (the action of a force over a distance), which Coriolis shortly afterward transformed into that of mechanical work. After 1820 Navier worked in theoretical science and in practical engineering, designing a con-

troversial suspension bridge over the Seine; he developed mathematical expressions for the motion of solid and liquid bodies based on the view that bodies are made up of particles which are close to each other and which act on each other by means of two opposing forces—one of attraction and one of repulsion—which, when in a state of equilibrium, cancel each other out. When equilibrium is disturbed in a solid, a restoring force acts which is proportional to the change in distance between the particles; in a liquid, this force becomes proportional to the difference in speed of the particles.

AL-NAYRĪZĪ, ABU'L-ᶜABBĀS AL-FADL IBN ḤĀTIM (*fl. Baghdad, ca. 897; d. ca. 922*), geometry, astronomy.

Wrote astronomical handbooks and works on meteorology, on instruments for determining the distances of objects, on Euclid's parallel postulate, on the construction and use of the spherical astrolabe (the most complete treatment of the subject in Arabic), and on the direction of the *qibla*. Also wrote commentaries on Ptolemy's *Almagest* and *Tetrabiblos*, and a commentary on Euclid's *Elements*, the latter being the work for which he is best known. His commentary was based on an Arabic translation of Euclid, and quotes extensively from commentaries by Hero and Simplicius; Simplicius' *Commentary*, almost entirely reproduced by al-Nayrīzī, played a significant part in arousing the interest of Islamic mathematicians in methodological problems and also quotes verbatim the influential proof by "Aghānīs" (probably Agapius) of the parallel postulate.

NEANDER, MICHAEL (*b. Joachimsthal, Bohemia, 1529; d. Jena, Germany, 1581*), mathematics, medicine.

Studied at Wittenberg (baccalaureate, 1549; master's, 1550); taught at Jena (from 1551; M.D., 1558; professor of medicine, 1560). Wrote textbooks for students at faculty of arts; considered writings of the ancients, especially Galen, to be absolutely authoritative. In his *Methodorum in omni genere artium . . .* (1556) he distinguished the analytic and synthetic methods and introduced proof by contradiction as a third independent possibility. His *Elementa sphaericae doctrinae* (1561) endorsed Melanchthon's rejection of the Copernican view of the universe.

NECKER, LOUIS-ALBERT, known as **NECKER DE SAUSSURE** (*b. Geneva, Switzerland, 1786; d. Portree, Skye, Scotland, 1861*), geology, mineralogy, zoology.

Studied at Academy of Geneva and at University of Edinburgh; appointed professor of mineralogy and geology at Geneva Academy (1810) and remained there for over two decades, combining teaching with geological field work. Emphasized the dependence of mineralogists and geologists upon real characteristics of actual objects, as opposed to abstractions; objected to chemical composition, which he considered abstract, as a criterion for mineral classification. Made the first geological map of the whole of Scotland (1808). Resisted theoretical schemes, but became convinced of the igneous origin of granite; investigated origins of mineral deposits and concluded that metalliferous veins are formed by sublimation from igneous intrusions. Published notable studies of birds and of meteorological optics.

NEEDHAM, JOHN TURBERVILLE (*b. London, England, 1713; d. Brussels, Belgium, 1781*), biology, microscopy.

Ordained a priest in 1738. Settled in Brussels in 1768 as director of what was to become the Royal Academy of Belgium. His scientific interests were motivated largely by a desire to defend religion; he became renowned as an empirical scientist, and found himself at the focal point of the controversy over generation. In 1748 Needham and Buffon examined fluids extracted from the reproductive organs of animals and infusions of plant and animal tissue, and observed globules that Buffon interpreted as genetic factors; in his famous experiment with boiled mutton gravy (1748) Needham thought he actually did see new organisms taking shape out of disorganized material. His theory of generation placed him in the vitalist camp through its reliance on principles peculiar to living things and its assignment of self-patterning powers to matter; for him, the embryo was not preformed but predetermined. Needham's claim to have observed spontaneous generation was disproved in 1765, when Spallanzani showed that the mutton gravy had been incompletely sterilized.

NEES VON ESENBECK, CHRISTIAN GOTTFRIED (DANIEL) (*b. Reichenberg Castle, near Erbach, Hesse, 1776; d. Breslau, Silesia [now Wrocław, Poland], 1858*), botany.

While studying at University of Jena (1796–99) Nees was drawn into the Weimar circle and became a personal friend of Goethe. Received doctorate from Giessen (1800) and for a time practiced medicine. His botanical career began in 1818 as professor of botany first at Erlangen and then at Bonn. Moved to Breslau (1830), where he reorganized the botanical garden and played an active role in civic affairs; he became a radical democrat, founded (in Berlin) the German Workers' Brotherhood (1848), and was banished from Berlin for life "because of dangerous socialistic tendencies." He was dismissed from his professorship in 1852 for well-camouflaged political reasons. His botanical activity was largely taxonomic: he became a world expert on widely diverse groups, and did intensive work on liverworts (*Naturgeschichte der europäischen Lebermoose* [1833–38]) on a completely new level of detail. In zoology he made major contributions to the taxonomy of ichneumon flies. His greatest contribution to science, however, was his rejuvenation of the Academia Caesarea Leopoldina-Carolina Naturae Curiosorum, of which he was elected president in 1818: the academy had lost its viability in Erlangen, and Nees arranged to bring it with him when he moved to Bonn, with guaranteed financial support from the Prussian government. He remained its president, and personally edited forty-seven volumes of its *Nova acta*, sparing no expense to insure the high quality of the publications. He also acted as a transmitter of outstanding foreign publications, most notably through his five-volume edition of Robert Brown's botanical works (1825–34).

NEF, JOHN ULRIC (*b. Herisau, Switzerland, 1862; d. Carmel, Calif., 1915*), chemistry.

Graduated from Harvard (1884), then studied under Adolf von Baeyer at Munich (Ph.D., 1886); held academic positions at Purdue (1887–89), Clark (1889–92), and Chicago (1892–1915) universities. A great experimentalist and pioneer in theoretical organic chemistry, whose theoretical work clearly contains the germs of the present concepts of free radicals, transition states, and polymerization. Topics studied included the apparently bivalent carbon compounds and their dissociation, and the action of alkali and alkaline oxidizing agents on the sugars. He was instrumental in establishing postdoctoral fellowship study in the United States.

NEGRI, ADELCHI (*b. Perugia, Italy, 1876; d. Pavia, Italy, 1912*), pathology.

Studied medicine and surgery at Pavia University (graduated 1900); became Golgi's assistant, and in 1909 became first official teacher of bacteriology at Pavia. Conducted research in histology, hematology, cytology, protozoology, and hygiene. His fundamental contribution was discovery (1903) of the rabies corpuscles, now known as Negri bodies: he found that certain cells of the nervous system of animals with rabies, especially the pyramidal cells of the horn of Ammon, contain bodies consisting of single or multiple eosinophile, spherical, ovoid, or pyriform endocytoplasmic (never endonuclear) formations with a well-defined outline, varying in size from two to more than twenty microns and containing minute basophil granules of 0.2–0.5 micron diameter. The significance of the bodies has not been clarified, but their specificity and importance for diagnosis are universally recognized.

NEHRING, ALFRED (*b. Gandersheim, Germany, 1845; d. Berlin, Germany, 1904*), paleontology, zoology.

Studied natural sciences at universities of Göttingen and Halle (doctorate, Halle, 1867). Professor of zoology, Agricultural College in Berlin (from 1881). His research covered Recent, post-glacial, and Pleistocene vertebrates, particularly domestic animals; their domestication; their history; their relations in the wild; and the zoology of untamed game animals. His publications on Pleistocene mammals are of major importance; *Über Tundren und Steppen der Jetzt- und Vorzeit* (1890), filled with numerous and exact data, is among the most important foundations of the paleoecology and paleobiogeography of the later Pleistocene in central and western Europe.

NEISSER, ALBERT LUDWIG SIGESMUND (*b. Schweidnitz, Germany [now Swidnica, Poland], 1855; d. Breslau, Germany [now Wrocław, Poland], 1916*), dermatology.

Medical training and career were at Breslau (M.D. 1877; lecturer, 1880; professor, 1907). Discovered micrococcus of gonorrhea (1879), named gonococcus by Ehrlich. The same year, he found bacilli in secretion smears from leprosy patients; publication of his findings in 1880 brought a priority claim from G. H. A. Hansen, who had seen the bacilli as early as 1873. While Hansen first discovered the bacillus, Neisser was the first to identify it as the etiological agent of the disease; he continued to study the etiology, diagnosis, and prophylaxis of leprosy for much of his career. He also devoted intensive study to syphilis: his observations in Java yielded valuable data concerning reinfection and superinfection. He encouraged Wassermann to study seroreaction in syphilis in 1906; with him and with Carl Bruck, he developed the serological test now named for Wassermann. He tested the therapeutic use of arsenic preparations, and contributed to Ehrlich's introduction of Salvarsan (1910). Active in the field of public health, he was a founder of the Deutschen Gesellschaft sur Bekämpfung der Geschlechtskrankheiten.

NEKRASOV, ALEKSANDR IVANOVICH (b. Moscow, Russia, 1883; d. Moscow, 1957), mechanics, mathematics.

Graduated from Faculty of Physics and Mathematics, Moscow University (1906), and taught there from 1912; from 1917 he also taught and conducted research at the Higher Technical School, Central Aerohydrodynamics Institute, Sergo Orjonikidze Aviation Institute, and the Institute of Mechanics of the Academy of Sciences of the U.S.S.R. A brilliant representative of the precise mathematical trend in hydromechanics and aeromechanics, he published basic works on the theory of waves, theory of whirlpools, theory of jet streams, and gas dynamics. He also enriched mathematics with the first fruitful investigations of nonlinear integral equations with symmetrical nuclei.

NEMESIUS (fl. Emesa [now Homs], Syria, A.D. 390–400), medicine.

Bishop of Emesa. Author of On the Nature of Man, the major contribution of which was to establish the idea (proposed earlier by Posidonius) that the mental faculties were localized in the ventricles of the brain, a belief that was generally accepted and retained as late as the sixteenth century. According to Nemesius' doctrine, all sensory perceptions were received in the anterior (now called lateral) ventricles; the middle (now called third) ventricle was the region of the faculty of intellect; memory was located in the cerebellum (according to later interpretations, in the fourth ventricle).

NEMORE, JORDANUS DE. See Jordanus de Nemore.

NENCKI, MARCELI (b. Boczki, near Kielce, Russia [now Poland], 1847; d. St. Petersburg, Russia, 1901), biochemistry.

Studies at University of Berlin (M.D., 1870) included two years of work in Baeyer's laboratory. Did research on oxidation of aromatic compounds in the body and on chemistry of uric acid and similar compounds. Taught at University of Bern, then organized new institute of experimental medicine in St. Petersburg (1890). Partly in collaboration with Pavlov, Nencki showed that urea is formed chiefly in the liver; he stated that it did not preexist in the protein molecule, but was synthesized from amino groups of amino acids and from carbon dioxide. Studied degradation products of hemoglobin, comparing results with Marchlewski, who was studying chlorophyll: both finally obtained the same substance, hemopyrrole, leading to Nencki's hypothesis on the chemical relationship between the animal and plant kingdoms.

NERI, ANTONIO (b. Florence, Italy, 1576; d. Pisa or Florence, ca. 1614), chemical technology.

A priest who led a wandering life and is remembered only for L'arte vetraria (1612), a small book in which many of the closely guarded secrets of glassmaking were printed for the first time. Topics discussed, although with not much detail and no illustrations, included the coloring of glass with metallic oxides, making lead glass of high refractive index, and making enamel glass by the addition of tin oxide. The book served as a nucleus for the observations of later writers.

NERNST, HERMANN WALTHER (b. Briesen, West Prussia [now Wąbrzeżno, Poland], 1864; d. Zibelle manorial estate, near Bad Muskau, Oberlausitz [now German Democratic Republic], 1941), chemistry, physics.

Although Nernst's worldwide reputation resulted from a broad range of fundamental contributions to the new developments in physical chemistry, especially in electrolytic solution theory, his crowning achievement was in chemical thermodynamics. For this work he received the Nobel Prize for chemistry in 1920. The Nernst heat theorem of 1906, or the third law of thermodynamics, as he preferred to call it, was at first recognized chiefly as a practical means for computing chemical equilibria. The feasibility of directly calculating the entropy constants for gases from quantum theoretical formulations led to a new recognition of Nernst's work prior to World War I. During the 1920's quantum statistical considerations initiated a controversy—even serious reservations in some quarters—over the general validity of Nernst's theorem for solids. By the late 1920's, when Nernst no longer was actively engaged in thermodynamic investigations, several special formulations of the heat theorem, and notably that of Francis Simon, led to the acceptance of Nernst's fundamental idea, in its refined form, as a general law of thermodynamics.

In 1883 Nernst graduated first in his class from the Gymnasium in Graudenz [now Grudziadz, Poland], where his studies had focused on the classics, literature, and the natural sciences. From 1883 to 1887 he studied physics at the universities of Zurich, Berlin, Graz, and Würzburg. In 1887 he became Ostwald's assistant at the University of Leipzig. In Leipzig theoretical and experimental chemistry were pursued conjointly. The emphasis fell on the electrolytic theory of ionization; the colligative properties of gases and liquids; and thermodynamics, or "energetics" in the Ostwald sense. Besides Arrhenius, van't Hoff, and Nernst, others who belonged to Ostwald's circle included Tammann (Nernst's successor at Göttingen), Le Blanc (Ostwald's successor at Leipzig), James Walker, Wilhelm Meyerhofer, Ernst Otto Beckmann, and Julius Wagner—all pioneers in the establishment and exploration of physical chemistry as an academic discipline.

In the context of this group of Ioner, as they were called, Nernst soon became totally absorbed with the problems of physical chemistry. On the whole, his early investigations fit the pattern of chemistry laid out by Ostwald and the Ioner. Until he was about forty years of age, his efforts were directed predominantly toward the refinement of methods to explore principles already current among chemists. Within a year he had published his derivation of the law of diffusion for electrolytes in the simple case when only two kinds of ions are present. Thus for the first time (1888) he was able to calculate the diffusion coefficient for infinitely dilute solutions and to show the relationship between ionic mobility, diffusion coefficient, and electromotive force in concentration cells. This in turn was based upon the idea that, for two solutions of differing concentrations separated by a semipermeable partition, the driving force responsible for the diffusion is given by the difference in osmotic pressures on opposite sides of the partition. The fundamental relationship between electromotive force and ionic concentration was developed more fully in his Leipzig *Habilitationsschrift* of 1889, *Die elektromotorische Wirksamkeit der Ionen.* The classical Nernst treatment of ionic diffusion (in terms of mobility and transport number) was based on Arrhenius' theory of electrolytic dissociation and was expressed in terms of the electromotive force of concentration cells and galvanic elements. Nernst had assumed that a metal immersed in an electrolyte acts like a reservoir of ions having properties characteristic of electrolytic solvation pressure. Thus he was able to calculate maximum electric work (electromotive forces) from fundamental principles such as the relation to the gas constant. This work gave Nernst, then in his mid-twenties, an international reputation in electrochemistry.

Nernst's distribution law, which relates the equilibrium concentrations of a solute distributed between immiscible liquid phases, appeared in two papers in 1890 and 1891. The case that Nernst studied theoretically and experimentally was the distribution of benzoic acid between water and benzene. His work called attention to the fact that a simple distribution law can be expected to be valid only if, on dissolving, the solute undergoes no changes such as dissociation—that is, only when the concentrations (or activities) of the same molecular species in each phase are considered. The Nernst distribution equation represents an important type of phase equilibrium, and was put to practical use in extraction process calculations and in analyzing the distribution of substances in different parts of a living organism.

After a semester at Heidelberg, Nernst returned to Leipzig and in 1891 accepted a post as associate professor in physics at the University of Göttingen. During the early Göttingen period of his career, his conception of the goals and significant advances in theoretical chemistry was fashioned and published in his *Theoretische Chemie vom Standpunkte der Avogadroschen Regel und der Thermodynamik* (1893), the preeminent textbook of physical chemistry in Germany until 1926. As Nernst conceived it, the most important guide to presenting the theoretical treatment of chemical processes was first, to recognize the central importance of Avogadro's hypothesis, which he referred to as "an almost inexhaustible 'horn of plenty' for the molecular theory," and second, to accentuate the law of energy that governs all natural processes.

In 1894 Nernst was offered a chair in physical chemistry and a new Institut für Physikalische Chemie und Elektrochemie in Göttingen—the only such post in Germany, apart from Ostwald's in Leipzig. Although Nernst sometimes disagreed with Ostwald on matters of interpretation, he retained a lifelong appreciation of this old master who had turned him in the direction of chemical pursuits. In 1895 Nernst and Schoenflies published their *Einführung in die mathematische Behandlung der Naturwissenschaften,* dedicated to Ostwald; by 1931 it had passed through eleven editions.

From 1891 to 1904 at Göttingen, Nernst managed to assemble an international group of scholars to cooperate in the intensive and comprehensive investigation of experimental and theoretical physicochemical problems. In 1905 he was called to the University of Berlin, upon the retirement of Landolt. On 23 December of the same year

Nernst was back in Göttingen to present to the Academy his now-classic forty-page "heat theorem" paper, "Ueber die Berechnung chemischer Gleichgewichte aus thermischen Messungen." It is apparent that the work and deliberations that led to the heat theorem and its sequel, the enunciation of the third law of thermodynamics, had been carried out mostly in Göttingen. Undoubtedly that is the reason that led Nernst to present his ideas on this fundamental topic in Göttingen. The paper was published in 1906 in the *Nachrichten von der Gesellschaft der Wissenschaften zu Göttingen.*

For over a decade after the 1906 paper appeared, virtually the entire facilities and personnel of the physical chemistry institute of the University of Berlin were organized into a huge work program to experimentally test Nernst's *Wärme-Theorem.* The immediate consequence of Nernst's new idea was that radically different thermochemical techniques were put into practice to elucidate chemical equilibrium. These involved the determination at very low temperatures (in fact as close to zero as possible) of the specific heats and thermal coefficients of specific heats for the constituents of the chemical reactions under investigation. In a series of seven papers (1910–1914) Nernst and his co-workers (F. Koref, F. A. Lindemann, and F. Schwers) presented impressive experimental evidence to support Nernst's theorem based on the electrical measurement of electrically induced temperature changes. The rigorous test of the validity of the theorem was soon seen to be an enormously challenging experimental undertaking. To approach this objective the Nernst group constructed ingenious electrical and thermal devices, developed a vacuum calorimeter, and built a small hydrogen liquefier (1911) to achieve temperatures low enough to be able to extrapolate safely to absolute zero. Nernst tackled all these problems imaginatively and successfully, and step by step came increasingly to believe that his hypothesis should be elevated to the rank of a bona fide law of thermodynamics.

In 1912 Nernst stated his heat theorem in terms of the theoretically decisive principle of the unattainability of absolute zero. According to this principle, it is impossible to build a caloric machine that will allow a substance to be cooled to absolute zero; and from this negative assertion Nernst concluded that the thermal coefficients of all the physical properties of solid bodies would vanish in the approach to absolute zero.

With the outbreak of World War I, Nernst's academic pursuits virtually came to a halt as he was drawn into military administration, chemical gas warfare, and service as automobile chauffeur for the German army on the move from Belgium to France. As is evident from the preface to his 1918 monograph, *Die theoretischen und experimentellen Grundlagen des neuen Wärmesatzes,* he was able to immerse himself further in the new theoretical physics, namely, quantum mechanics, and to reflect on its meaning and implications for his beloved and not yet controversial *Wärmesatz.* In this volume he presented in a most comprehensive way his mature ideas on chemical thermodynamics.

Until his retirement in 1934 Nernst was again actively involved with the pursuit of physical chemistry at Berlin, but he now took up a number of new topics. With the accumulation of experimental data in the 1920's, his heat theorem, which had enjoyed the successes of early quantum theory, encountered serious difficulties as experimental anomalies with condensed systems appeared that could not be squared with the general theorem. Nernst took relatively little part in the discussion of these problems. He felt that his theorem should apply in a straightforward way to all systems using a thermodynamic mode of reasoning and without appealing to statistical considerations. He was convinced that further experimental and theoretical research would confirm his theorem as a general law. His participation in the extensions, criticisms, and reformulations of his heat theorem was rather that of a spectator; it was his students who were involved in new contributions. Nernst was totally absorbed in other scientific matters. Thus while low-temperature investigations continued to command the attention of experimentalists and theoreticians alike, he explored new leads in photochemistry, chemical kinetics, and chemical astrophysics.

When he returned to his physical chemistry institute in Berlin, he was to become entrenched once again in more decisively chemical topics than third-law investigations. Until his retirement in 1934, Nernst continued to devote his efforts to physical chemistry and to serve as director of the physical laboratory.

Nernst also played the conspicuous role of organizer for the first Solvay Conference of 1911. He was the effective promoter in the creation of a post for Einstein at the Berlin Academy of Sciences. He was the prime mover for the establishment of the Kaiser Wilhelm Institut. He was a founder of the Deutsche Elektrochemische Gesellschaft (later called Deutsche Bunsengesellschaft) and for several years edited its *Zeitschrift für Elektrochemie*. With J. A. W. Borchers, beginning in 1895, Nernst edited the *Jahrbuch für Elektrochemie*.

NETTESHEIM. *See* **Agrippa, Heinrich Cornelius.**

NETTO, EUGEN (*b. Halle, Germany, 1848; d. Giessen, Germany, 1919*), mathematics.
Studied under Kronecker, Kummer, and Weierstrass at University of Berlin (graduated 1870); taught at universities of Strasbourg (1879–82), Berlin (1882–88), and Giessen (1888–1913). His textbook *Substitutionentheorie und ihre Anwendung auf die Algebra* (1882) is a milestone in the development of abstract group theory, uniting the theory of permutation groups and that of implicit group-theoretical thinking in number theory.

NEUBERG, JOSEPH (JEAN BAPTISTE) (*b. Luxembourg City, Luxembourg, 1840; d. Liège, Belgium, 1926*), geometry.
Studied at University of Ghent; professor at University of Liège (1884–1910). One of the founders of the modern geometry of the triangle. With Catalán and Mansion, published *Nouvelle correspondance mathématique* (1874–80); subsequently collaborated with Mansion in publishing *Mathesis*.

NEUMANN, CARL GOTTFRIED (*b. Königsberg, Prussia [now Kaliningrad, R.S.F.S.R.], 1832; d. Leipzig, Germany, 1925*), mathematics, theoretical physics.
Son of Franz Ernst Neumann. Attended University of Königsberg (doctorate, 1855); taught at Halle (1858), Basel (1863), Tübingen (1865), and University of Leipzig (1868–1911). Did notable research in potential theory:

developed method of the arithmetical mean for solution of boundary value problems; coined the term "logarithmic potential"; the second boundary value problem of potential theory still bears his name. Founded and edited *Mathematische Annalen.*

NEUMANN, CASPAR (*b. Züllichau, Germany [now Sulechów, Poland], 1683; d. Berlin, Germany, 1737*), chemistry.
Apprenticed to a pharmacist. Served as court apothecary and traveled widely; studied with Boerhaave (1712), experimented with C. J. and E. F. Geoffroy, gave courses in London (1713–16), Paris (*ca.* 1717–18), and at Berlin Medical-Surgical College (from 1724). In his travels he conveyed knowledge of German techniques and theories to chemists in London and Paris; through his writings he contributed significantly to the establishment of Stahlian chemistry both in Germany and abroad. Neumann distinguished clearly between pure and applied chemistry and insisted that the chemical approach to nature was vastly superior to the mechanical philosophy.

NEUMANN, FRANZ ERNST (*b. Joachimsthal, Germany [now Jáchymov, Czechoslovakia], 1798; d. Königsberg, Germany [now Kaliningrad, R.S.F.S.R.], 1895*), mineralogy, physics, mathematics.
Studied at University of Jena and under Christian S. Weiss at Berlin (doctorate, 1825); appointed curator of minerals at Berlin (1823). Taught at University of Königsberg (from 1826), where he inaugurated the German *mathematisch-physikalische* seminar to supplement his lectures and to introduce his students to research methodology (1833). Early publications (1823–30) concerned crystallography: he introduced the method of spherical projection and extended Weiss's work on the law of zones. Under the influence of Bessel, Dove, and Jacobi he turned to mathematical physics. He investigated the specific heats of minerals and extended the Dulong-Petit law to include compounds having similar chemical constitutions; he arrived at what has been termed Neumann's law, that the molecular heat of a compound is equal to the sum of the atomic heats of its constituents (1831). His work in optics contributed to the establishment of the dynamical theory of light; his mathematical formulation of the laws of induction of electric currents (1845, 1848) made him a founder of the electrodynamic school in Germany. He also aided in developing the theory of spherical harmonics. He made known many of his discoveries in heat, optics, electrodynamics, and capillarity during his lectures, thinking that priority of discovery extended to lectures as well as to publications; thus he made numerous contributions to the theory of heat without receiving credit.

NEUMAYR, MELCHIOR (*b. Munich, Germany, 1845; d. Vienna, Austria, 1890*), paleontology, geology.
Studied law in Munich but soon turned to paleontology and geology (doctorate, 1867); joined Imperial Austrian Geological Survey (1868) in Vienna; subsequently taught at University of Heidelberg (1872) and at Vienna (from 1873). Made fundamental contributions to knowledge of the geological structure of Greece and the Aegean Islands (1874–76); compiled first geological history of the eastern Mediterranean (1882). His studies of Upper Tertiary freshwater mollusks and their gradual morphologi-

cal transformation led to the first concise demonstration of the Darwinian theory of variation and evolution of species in invertebrate fossils (1875). His writings raised paleontology—previously considered simply a study of index fossils—to the level of a basic biological science.

NEUYMIN, GRIGORY NIKOLAEVICH (*b. Tiflis, Georgia [now Tbilisi, Georgian S.S.R.], 1886; d. Leningrad, U.S.S.R., 1946*), astronomy.

Graduated from St. Petersburg University (1910); worked at Pulkovo Observatory (1908–12; 1922–25; director, 1944–46) and at its southern section, Simeiz Observatory (1912–22; director, 1925–41). Neuymin developed a broad program at Simeiz for the systematic search and photographic observation of comets and asteroids; he himself discovered comet Neuymin II and five others, sixty-three numbered asteroids, and thirteen variable stars. He developed a special method of calculating the planetary perturbations of cometary orbits and a method for photographic discovery of short-period variable stars, and compiled a catalog of galaxies for attachment to his catalog of faint stars.

NEWALL, HUGH FRANK (*b. Gateshead, England, 1857; d. Cambridge, England, 1944*), astrophysics.

Read mathematics as an undergraduate at Cambridge and subsequently worked under J. J. Thomson in the Cavendish Laboratory; when his father donated a twenty-five-inch refracting telescope to Cambridge, Newall turned to astronomy in order to put the telescope into service. His interest focused increasingly on the sun; he studied flash and coronal spectra, polarization of the corona, sunspot spectra, and solar rotation. Appointed professor of astrophysics in 1909.

NEWBERRY, JOHN STRONG (*b. Windsor, Conn., 1822; d. New Haven, Conn., 1892*), paleontology, geology.

Studied at Western Reserve College (graduated 1846), Cleveland Medical School (M.D., 1848), and at Jardin des Plantes, Paris (1849–50); practiced medicine from 1851 to 1855. Served as physician-naturalist for several important army exploring expeditions in the West (1855–59); doctor and executive with U. S. Sanitary Commission (1861–65); professor of geology at Columbia University School of Mines (from 1866); paleobotanist for the Hayden and Powell Surveys; director of Ohio State Geological Survey (1869–74). As a field scientist, he contributed to nearly every branch of geology; his particular interest was in paleobotany, especially that of American coal beds. He argued for a Cretaceous age for the Western lignites (1859). Best known for his accurate description of the Grand Canyon as erosion on a large scale (1861).

NEWCOMB, SIMON (*b. Wallace, Nova Scotia, Canada, 1835; d. Washington, D.C., 1909*), astronomy.

The most honored American scientist of his lifetime. Apprenticed at sixteen to a doctor who turned out to be a quack, Newcomb ran away after two years and made his way to Maryland, where he taught school and studied mathematics by reading Newton's *Principia*. In 1856 he met Joseph Henry, who helped him obtain employment at the Nautical Almanac Office (then located in Cambridge, Mass.). While in Cambridge (1857–61) he showed that the orbits of several asteroids did not inter-

sect and that therefore they were not the fragments of a former larger planet, and he also studied at Lawrence Scientific School, Harvard, graduating in 1858. In 1861 he joined the Naval Observatory, where he revolutionized the observational methods; in 1877 he was appointed superintendent of the Nautical Almanac Office, which by then had been transferred to Washington; he proceeded to reform the entire theoretical and computational basis of the *American Ephemeris;* he was also one of the first lecturers at the Johns Hopkins University (professor from 1884). Newcomb did important work on lunar, solar, and planetary theory. His discovery of the departure of the moon from its predicted position led to investigations on the variations in rate of rotation of the earth; the planetary theories and astronomical constants that he derived are either still in official use or have been superseded only recently. His study of the transits of Mercury confirmed Leverrier's conclusion that the perihelion of Mercury is subject to an anomalous advance; his value for the mass of Jupiter has not been significantly improved; he showed that the fourteen-month period found by Chandler in the variation of latitude is due to some lack of rigidity of the earth. His many writings include popular works on astronomy and several books on economics; his influence on professional astronomers and laymen is still widely felt today.

NEWCOMEN, THOMAS (*b. Dartmouth, England; christened 1663; d. London, England, 1729*), steam technology.

An ironmonger in partnership with John Calley, who assisted him in developing the steam engine. The Newcomen engine (1712), product of years of trials, combined familiar elements—piston and cylinder, pumps, levers, valves, and pressure from the condensation of steam—with the important innovation, discovered accidentally, of the injection of cold water directly into the cylinder. Since the engine was designed to drive a pump to remove water from mines, it was covered by Thomas Savery's broad patent, and Newcomen was required to build his engines under license from Savery. James Watt significantly increased the efficiency of the engine through his invention of the separate condenser (1765), which avoided the necessity of alternately heating and cooling the cylinder.

NEWLANDS, JOHN ALEXANDER REINA (*b. London, England, 1837; d. London, 1898*), chemistry.

Studied under A. W. Hofmann at Royal College of Chemistry. Worked as assistant chemist to Royal Agricultural Society (until 1864), as an independent analytical chemist (1864–68), as chief chemist in a sugar refinery (1868–86), and as an analyst in partnership with his brother (from 1886). He was one of the precursors of Mendeleev in the formulation of the concept of periodicity in the properties of the chemical elements. In his writings on the numerical relationships existing between the atomic weights of similar elements he considered the triads and predicted (1864) the existence of germanium between silicon and tin. In tabulating the elements he formulated the Law of Octaves (1865), that "the eighth element starting from a given one is a kind of repetition of the first"; the manipulation of the elements to fit them into his rigid framework weakened his case, and his paper was widely criticized. After the publication of Mendeleev's table (1869), Newlands continued to seek numerical relationships among atomic weights, while attempting to establish his priority.

NEWPORT, GEORGE (*b. Canterbury, England, 1803; d. London, England, 1854*), entomology, natural history.

While an apprentice wheelwright he taught himself entomology through the facilities of the Canterbury Philosophical and Literary Institution; from 1825 to 1828 he was employed by the institution as lecturer and exhibitor. He then studied surgery as an apprentice and at the University of London (licensed, 1835); he was one of the original fellows of the Royal College of Surgeons of England. Did important studies on the turnip fly, on insect structure, and on the embryology and physiology of the Insecta. His most outstanding contribution to biology was his discovery that during fertilization in higher animals impregnation of the ovum by the spermatozoon is by penetration and not just by contact as previously thought (observed in the frog, 1851).

NEWTON, EDWIN TULLEY (*b. Islington, London, England, 1840; d. Canonbury, London, 1930*), paleontology.

Studied at Royal School of Mines; from 1865, worked at Geological Survey Museum. In early research, he invented a new method for making microsections of coal. Studied wide range of fossils, but was noted especially for vertebrate paleontology; wrote important monographs on the brain of the pterodactyl and on Permotriassic reptiles. Discovered dicynodonts and pareiasaurs for the first time in Europe.

NEWTON, HUBERT ANSON (*b. Sherburne, N.Y., 1830; d. New Haven, Conn., 1896*), astronomy, mathematics.

Graduated from Yale (1850) and taught mathematics there (from 1853; professor, 1855). His interest began to shift to astronomy and meteorology, and he wrote on the orbits and velocities of meteors (1860–62). He analyzed observations (which he had helped to make) of the Leonid shower of 1861, and published (1864) the important finding that the shower had occurred thirteen times since A.D. 902, in a cycle of 33.25 years; J. C. Adams calculated the planetary perturbations of several hypothetical orbits, and proved the Leonids to be in an elliptical orbit with a period of 33.25 years; the Leonids were positively identified with a comet on their reappearance in 1866. Newton's later pioneering studies included the effect of large planetary perturbations on the distribution of cometary orbits; he accumulated statistical data indicating that long-period comets could be captured by Jupiter, shortening their periods. He was also active in teaching and educational reform; a founder of the American Metrological Society, promoting the metric system; an original member of the National Academy of Sciences; and an associate editor of the *American Journal of Science*.

NEWTON, ISAAC (*b. Woolsthorpe, Lincolnshire, England, 1642; d. London, England, 1727*), mathematics, dynamics, celestial mechanics, astronomy, optics, natural philosophy.

Of a family of yeomen, Newton was born prematurely and was a frail child. His father had died before his birth; within three years his mother remarried, leaving her son in the care of his maternal grandmother. Such difficult early years no doubt influenced Newton's mature personality, for he was often harsh and suspicious toward others. In his youth, he was interested in mechanical contrivances; with the encouragement of an uncle and the master of the school in nearby Grantham that Newton attended, he was spared a career as a farmer, and admitted to Trinity College, Cambridge (1661; B.A., 1665). During eighteen months (from June 1665), when the University was closed because of plague, Newton spent much of his time in Lincolnshire; in this period he laid the foundations of his work in mathematics, optics, and celestial mechanics. The episode of the falling apple, which "occasioned" the concept of gravitation, must have occurred at or near his home; but contrary to common belief, he probably did make at least one visit back to Cambridge during these months.

Newton became a fellow of Trinity (1667); was created M.A. (1668); was appointed Lucasian professor (1669) at age twenty-six, succeeding Isaac Barrow; and became a fellow of the Royal Society (1672). He was productive throughout most of his life, but next to the famous return to Lincolnshire, his most fruitful work was done in 1685–86, when he composed his great *Principia* (*Philosophiae naturalis principia mathematica*, 1687). He was active in defending the university's rights in a dispute with James II, and was elected (1689) by the university constituency to serve as member of the Convention Parliament. In 1693, he suffered a severe depression and possibly a sort of mental breakdown. In 1696, his friend and former pupil Charles Montague arranged for Newton's appointment as warden of the mint; following his second election as M.P. (1701), Newton resigned from Trinity College. He was made President of the Royal Society (1703) and was knighted (1705). His last years were marred by an acrimonious dispute with the astronomer Flamsteed and by the famous quarrel with Leibniz concerning the invention of the infinitesimal calculus, in which Newton accused Leibniz of plagiarism and generally behaved with gratuitous vindictiveness.

In his maturity and old age, Newton was also keenly interested in alchemy, mysticism, and theology. This has occasioned considerable speculation, on issues ranging from Newton's health to his possible association with an hermetic tradition and the relationship of his alleged hermeticism to his scientific work. While Newton's nonscientific, mystical concerns should not be dismissed as irrelevant aberrations produced by senility or a mental disorder, his early manuscripts, in which he recorded his purely scientific discoveries and innovations, are free from any tinges of alchemy or hermeticism.

Newton made contributions to algebra and number theory, classical and analytic geometry, the classification of curves, methods of computation and approximation, and even probability; but he was most influential by his creation of the calculus and his theory of infinite series (most notably the general binomial expansion). He was himself most influenced by Descartes's *Géométrie* and Wallis' *Arithmetica infinitorum;* the latter led directly to his discovery (1665) of the general binomial theorem, or expansion of $(a + b)^n$. Later (1676), in two letters transmitted to Leibniz, Newton explained that fractions "are reduced to infinite series by division; and radical quantities by extraction of roots . . ."; he discussed his development of his method; and he made the important statement that in dealing with infinite series all operations are carried out "in the symbols just as they are commonly carried out in decimal numbers." The key step in his breakthrough was changing Wallis' fixed upper boundary to a free variable x. Wallis had obtained the quadrature of certain curves by a technique of indivisibles yielding $\int_0^1 (1 - x^2)^n dx$ for certain positive integral values of n (0, 1, 2, 3); attempting to find the quadrature of a circle of unit radius, he had sought to evaluate the integral of $\int_0^1 (1 - x^2)^{1/2} dx$ by interpolation; he showed that

$$\frac{4}{\pi} = \frac{1}{\int_0^1 (1 - x^2)^{1/2} dx} = \frac{3 \cdot 3 \cdot 5 \cdot 5 \cdot 7 \cdot 7 \cdots}{2 \cdot 4 \cdot 4 \cdot 6 \cdot 6 \cdot 8 \cdots} .$$

Newton then was stimulated to go considerably further, freeing the upper bound and deriving the infinite series expressing the area of a quadrant of a circle of radius x:

$$x - \frac{1/2\, x^3}{3} - \frac{1/8\, x^5}{5} - \frac{1/16\, x^7}{7} - \frac{5/128\, x^9}{9} - \cdots .$$

Thus he was led to recognize that the terms, identified by their powers of x, displayed the binomial coefficients; the factors 1/2, 1/8, 1/16, 5/128, ... stand out plainly as $\binom{q}{1}, \binom{q}{2}, \binom{q}{3}, \binom{q}{4}, \ldots$, in the special case $q = \frac{1}{2}$ in the generalization

$$\int_0^1 (1 - x^2)^q dx = X - \binom{q}{1} \cdot \frac{1}{3} X^3 + \binom{q}{2} \cdot \frac{1}{5} X^5$$
$$- \binom{q}{3} \cdot \frac{1}{7} X^7 + \frac{q}{5} \cdot \frac{1}{9} X^9 + \ldots ,$$

where

$$\binom{q}{n} = \frac{q\,(q-1) \ldots (q-n+1)}{n!} .$$

Newton (*ca.* 1665) found the power series (i.e., the sequence of coefficients) for

$$\sin^{-1} x = x + \frac{1}{6} x^3 + \frac{3}{40} x^5 + \ldots$$

and, most important of all, the logarithmic series; he also computed the area of the hyperbola with this method of infinite series. He devised a general differentiation procedure, using the "little zero," o, an indefinitely small, ultimately vanishing element of a variable. From the derivative of an algebraic function $f(x)$ conceived as

$$\lim_{o \to \text{zero}} \frac{1}{o} [f(x+o) - f(x)]$$

he developed general rules of differentiation. He next developed a new theoretical basis for his calculus, reject-

ing the element represented by o in favor of "fluxions" of variables (instantaneous "speeds" of flow); and he invented a true partial-derivative symbolism.

In 1669, alarmed by Nicolaus Mercator's close approach to his own accomplishments, Newton began to write up his mathematical researches. His first tract, *De analysi per aequationes infinitas,* was not printed but was later read in manuscript by Leibniz (1676); scholars now tend to agree that Leibniz was interested only in the series expansion and not the fluxional method. The main parts of *De analysi* were incorporated into *Methodus fluxionum et serierum infinitarum* (1670); in the preface to the English version of this work, John Colson wrote that the chief principle of the method of fluxions is that "Mathematical Quantity, particularly Extension, may be conceived as generated by continued local Motion." Subsequently, in *Tractatus de quadratura curvarum* (1704), Newton explained that lines are generated "not by the Apposition of Parts, but by the continued Motion of Points," areas are generated by the motion of lines, solids by the motion of surfaces, etc.; and he connected fluxions with infinite series: "These Fluxions are as the Terms of an infinite converging series" (he was aware of the importance of convergence as a necessary condition for expansion in an infinite series). In *Methodus fluxionum,* Newton solved the differentiation of any algebraic function $f(x)$; the integration of such a function by the inverse process; and, more generally, the "inverse method of tangents," or the solution of a first-order differential equation; the "little zero" now stands for an "infinitely" small interval (as opposed to the former "indefinitely" small interval).

Newton preferred geometric methods to purely analytical ones; he is one of the originators of polar coordinates, and did pioneering work in the theory of projections (which he called "shadows"). He halted most of his mathematical activity after being appointed warden of the mint; but he did solve in that year (1696) the famous problem set by Johann [I] Bernoulli: find the curve of swiftest descent. Newton replied briefly that the "brachistochrone" is a cycloid.

Newton's election to the Royal Society followed upon exhibition there of a reflecting telescope he had invented; he then (1672) wrote the society an account of the discovery that had led him to his invention. In 1666, he had passed white light through a tiny hole in a shutter and through a triangular glass prism; the multi-colored image was oblong rather than circular as required by the laws of refraction. This led him to his renowned "experimentum crucis" in which he used a second prism to pick up a narrow beam of light of a single color from the first prism; he found that the second prism did not produce any further dispersion of the "homogeneal" light (i.e., light of about the same color). He therefore concluded that "Light it self is a *Heterogeneous mixture of differently refrangible Rays";* he asserted an exact correspondence between color and "degree of Refrangibility," and also that colors are original and connate properties of light rays; and he concluded that it could no longer be a subject of dispute "whether Light be a Body." It seems likely, however, that Newton's assertion of a corpuscular theory of light and his other conclusions were not strictly the product of these experiments, but were drawn earlier from profound speculation and insight, and demonstrated by these experiments.

Newton's report precipitated a four-year debate with Hooke and the further elaboration of Newton's ideas. He suggested that light is something capable of causing "vibrations in the aether," assuming an etherial medium much rarer than air and strongly elastic; he even supposed that gravitational attraction might "be caused by the continual condensation of some other such like aethereal spirit." Building on experiments of Hooke's, Newton discovered the "rings" produced by light passing through a thin wedge or layer of air between two pieces of glass.

In his *Opticks* (1704), Newton described considerable investigation of interference effects (as they are now called). He concluded that the smallest possible subdivisions of matter must be transparent, and their dimensions optically determinable; in relation to refraction, he developed his concept of "fits," stating that a ray of light passing through a refracting surface "is put into a certain transient Constitution or State, which in the progress of the Ray returns at equal Intervals, and disposes the Ray at every return to be easily transmitted through the next refracting Surface, and between the returns to be easily reflected by it." The fits of easy refraction and easy reflection could be described as a numerical sequence: if reflection occurs at distances 0, 2, 4, 6, . . ., from some central point, then refraction (or transmission) must occur at 1, 3, 5, 7, . . .; Newton thus integrated the periodicity of light into his theoretical work, although he did not attempt to explain it.

Some of the most import ideas in the *Opticks* are contained in the queries at the end, especially in those appended to the second English edition (1717–18). Here Newton suggested that bodies act on light at a distance to bend the rays; heat is said to consist in having the parts of a body put into a vibrating motion; vibrations are also suggested as the cause of sight, "being propagated along the solid Fibres of the optick Nerves into the Brain"; radiant heat may be transmitted by vibrations in the ether; rays of light are possibly composed of "very small Bodies emitted from shining Substances," and light rays could be put into fits of easy reflection and transmission if these small bodies, by their power of attraction or some other force, stirred up "Vibrations in what they act upon." In his later work Newton held that the ether must be very rare; its resistance is said to be inconsiderable; and he had apparently, at least at one point, doubted its existence. With regard to the exact nature of the ether, Newton noted (Query 28, 1717) that "the main Business of natural Philosophy is to argue from Phaenomena without feigning Hypotheses." With regard to the nature of light, he preferred the corpuscular theory, but, challenged by Hooke, he associated ether waves with these corpuscles; unlike either Hooke or Huygens (who is usually held to be the founder of the wave theory), Newton postulated periodicity as a fundamental property of waves of (or associated with) light, and he suggested that a particular wavelength characterizes the light producing each color.

When Newton as an undergraduate began to consider the principles of motion, the main influences on his thought were Descartes and Galileo. By 1664, his notes show a quantitative approach to inelastic collision; before long he had corrected Descartes's law of conservation, noted rules for elastic collision, declared a principle of inertia, asserted a relation between "force" and change

of motion, and evidently had learned the law of centrifugal force (almost a decade before Huygens). His famous contemplation of the fall of an apple led him to postulate that since the moon is sixty times as far away from the center of the earth as the apple, by an inverse-square relation it would have an acceleration of free fall $1/(60)^2 = 1/3600$ that of the apple. This "moon test" proved the inverse-square law of force which Newton said he "deduced" from combining Kepler's third law ("of the periodical times of the Planets being in a sesquialterate proportion of their distances from the Centers of the Orbs") with the law of central (centrifugal) force.

After 1679, following an exchange with Hooke, Newton came to see the significance of Kepler's area law, which he had apparently just encountered:

> I found now that whatsoever was the law of the forces which kept the Planets in their Orbs, the areas described by a Radius drawn from them to the Sun would be proportional to the times in which they were described. And . . . that their Orbs would be such Ellipses as Kepler had described [when] the forces which kept them in their Orbs about the Sun were as the squares of their . . . distances from the Sun reciprocally.

Newton's solution is based on his method of limits, and on the use of infinitesimals. He considered the motion along an ellipse from one point to another during an indefinitely small interval of time, and evaluated the deflection from the tangent during that interval, assuming the deflection to be proportional to the inverse square of the distance from a focus; as one of the two points approaches the other, the area law supplies the essential condition in the limit. Thus, the true significance of Kepler's first two laws of planetary motion was revealed: that the area condition was equivalent to the action of a central force, and that the ocurrence of the ellipse under this condition demonstrates that the force is as the inverse square of the distance. Newton further showed the law of areas to be only another aspect of the law of inertia; he also proved that a homogeneous sphere will gravitate as if all its mass were concentrated at its geometric center.

In 1684, Halley asked Newton about the path a planet would follow under the action of an inverse-square force; Newton replied that it would be an ellipse; he could not find his calculations, but promised to do them over. Thus, he began work on *De motu corporum*, which led immediately to the creation of the *Principia*. This supreme work is often described as a synthesis of Kepler's planetary hypotheses and Galileo's laws of falling bodies; but Newton introduced important modifications to both men's theories. Thus, he proved that Kepler's laws must be modified by the mutual attraction of each of any pair of bodies, and by the perturbation of a moving body by any and all neighboring bodies; and he also showed that the rate of free fall of bodies is not constant, but varies with latitude and with distance from the center of the earth. One of the most original aspects of the book is its novel mathematical character, the calculus being used throughout. In Book I, Newton first stated various definitions; he distinguished mass from weight, defined centripetal force, and (in a celebrated scholium) opted for concepts of absolute space and absolute time. He then gave three axioms, or "Laws of Motion." The first is the law of inertia. The second states a proportionality between change in motion (momentum) and "the motive force impressed"; the latter phrase is ambiguous: it may be interpreted as referring either to impulse or to continuous force, but Newton considered these to be infinitesimally equivalent. The third law is that for every action there is an equal and opposite reaction. Newton then went on to treat mathematically motion under the action of impressed forces in free spaces (i.e., spaces devoid of resistance). Book II, which was not part of the original plan, is something of a digression; it deals with the motion of bodies in resisting mediums, and contains the first clear recognition that mass determines both weight and inertia. In Book III, the findings of Book I are applied to solving astronomical and physical problems; it is here that the law of universal gravitation is given.

Thus, the *Principia* demonstrated that one and the same law of force, gravitation, operates both in the centrally-directed acceleration of planetary bodies and of satellites and in the linear downward acceleration of freely falling bodies; and it is this force that also controls the motion of comets and the phenomena of tides. In the well-known general scholium added at the end of Book III, Newton made the often misinterpreted statement, "Hypotheses non fingo," which here clearly means that he will not hypothesize concerning the cause of gravitation, not that he would never make hypotheses. He concluded with observations about God, for he believed that the ultimate cause of natural phenomena could not be mechanical, and in general that the study of natural philosophy would provide evidence for the existence of God the Creator.

NICERON, JEAN-FRANÇOIS (*b. Paris, France, 1613; d. Aix-en-Provence, France, 1646*), geometrical optics.

Studied under Mersenne at Collège de Nevers in Paris and then entered the Order of Minims; appointed professor of mathematics at Trinità dei Monti, in Rome (1639), and thereafter traveled frequently for his order. His journeys enabled him to communicate to Italian scientists the results of French investigations and to disseminate Italian work in Paris. His *Perspective curieuse* (1638) concentrated primarily on the practical applications of perspective, catoptrics, and dioptrics, and on the illusory effects of optics then traditionally associated with natural magic; it presented techniques of anamorphosis, and also contains perhaps the first published reference to Descartes's derivation of the law of refraction.

NICHOLAS CHUQUET. *See* **Chuquet, Nicolas.**

NICHOLAS OF CUSA. *See* **Cusa, Nicholas.**

NICHOLAS OF DAMASCUS. *See* **Nicolaus of Damascus.**

NICHOLAS ORESME. *See* **Oresme, Nicole.**

NICHOLAS, JOHN SPANGLER (*b. Allegheny, Pa., 1895; d. New Haven, Conn., 1963*), biology.

Educated at Pennsylvania (now Gettysburg) College (B.S., 1916; M.S., 1917) and at Yale (Ph.D., 1921); taught at University of Pittsburgh (1921–26) and at Yale (1926–

63). Conducted original and pioneering investigations in embryology: his vital staining experiments on amphibian eggs showed that extensive movements take place in the endoderm before gastrulation; he made an important contribution to the study of teleost development by improvising a method for removing the horny covering of the egg; he was the first to carry out an intensive program of study of mammalian eggs. By transplanting single blastomeres into the uteri of foster mothers he was the first to demonstrate the flexible nature of mammalian development and to prove that the important embryological principles of induction and progressive differentiation are applicable to higher as well as to lower vertebrates.

NICHOLS, ERNEST FOX (*b. Leavenworth, Kan., 1869; d. Washington, D.C., 1924*), physics.

Graduated from Kansas State College of Agriculture (1888); studied at Cornell University (1888–92, D.Sc. 1897) and with Warburg at Berlin (1894–96). Worked at Colgate (1892–98), Dartmouth (1898–1903; president, 1909–16), Columbia (1903–09), Yale (1916–20), M.I.T. (president, 1920), and as director of research at National Electric Light Association (Cleveland, Ohio, 1921–24). Coeditor of *Physical Review* (1913–16). His scientific reputation rested on his development and use of the Nichols radiometer, constructed with the help of Ernst Pringsheim in Berlin; his radiometer was far more sensitive than any other then in existence and superior for measurements in the infrared range. With it he successfully explored the reflection and transmission of infrared rays, measured the relative heats of stars, and quantitatively confirmed the existence of the pressure of light predicted by Maxwell's laws.

NICHOLSON, JOHN WILLIAM (*b. Darlington, England, 1881; d. Oxford, England, 1955*), mathematical physics, astrophysics.

Studied at University of Manchester and at Trinity College, Cambridge. Taught at Cavendish Laboratory, Cambridge; Queen's University, Belfast; King's College, London (professor, 1912); and Balliol College, Oxford (1921–30). Created an original atomic theory of coronal and nebular spectra (1911–12): he assumed that the spectral lines of unknown origin were produced by elements that were primary in an evolutionary sense to terrestrial elements, and viewed an atom of such an element as a single, planetary ring of electrons rotating about a small, massive, positively charged nucleus. Associating the frequencies of the unidentified spectral lines with those of the transverse modes of oscillation of the electrons about their equilibrium path, he accounted for most coronal and nebular lines with impressive numerical accuracy, even predicting a new nebular line that was soon observed. The spectral capability of Nicholson's theory led Bohr to explore the spectral implications of his own very different quantum theory.

NICHOLSON, SETH BARNES (*b. Springfield, Ill., 1891; d. Los Angeles, Calif., 1963*), observational astronomy.

Studied at Drake University (B.S., 1912) and at Berkeley (Ph.D., 1915); joined staff of Mt. Wilson Observatory (1915). Discovered four faint moons of Jupiter (IX, 1914; X and XI, 1938; XII, 1951). Made long-term, detailed observations of the surface features and spectrum of the sun. Measured surface temperatures of stars, planets, and the eclipsed moon.

NICHOLSON, WILLIAM (*b. London, England, 1753; d. London, 1815*), chemistry, technology.

Spent time in service of East India Company (1769–76) and in Amsterdam before settling in London (*ca.* 1780); subsequently taught mathematics and served as a patent agent and a water engineer. Nicholson's scientific interests were expressed in his translations of works of Fourcroy, Kirwan, Chaptal, and others; in his *Dictionary of Chemistry* (1795) and other books; in his various inventions, which were technically excellent and commercially unrewarding; and, most of all, in his decision to found a monthly journal of scientific news and commentary (1797). The success of the *Journal of Natural Philosophy, Chemistry and the Arts* invited emulation, and in 1813 it merged into Alexander Tilloch's *Philosophical Magazine* (founded 1798). The *Journal*'s reliable news of scientific discoveries, technical processes, instruments, books, translations, and meetings met an evident demand; its greatest coup was in July 1800, when it gave the first report of its proprietor's sensational electrolysis of water, in collaboration with Anthony Carlisle.

NICOL, WILLIAM (*b. 1768; d. Edinburgh, Scotland, 1851*), optics, petrology, paleontology.

Lectured in natural philosophy at University of Edinburgh. Achieved fame as inventor of the first polarizer, the Nicol prism: he split a parallelepiped of calcite spar along its shorter diagonal and cemented the halves together with Canada balsam (whose index of refraction is intermediate to the two indices of the crystal). The balsam allows the extraordinary ray to pass almost undeviated through the prism while it reflects the ordinary beam, and the two beams can thus be used independently. Also important, but slower of recognition, were his technique for preparing transparent slivers of crystals and rocks for viewing directly through a microscope, revealing their innermost structure, and his application of the technique to fossil woods.

NICOLAI, FRIEDRICH BERNHARD GOTTFRIED (*b. Brunswick, Germany, 1793; d. Mannheim, Germany, 1846*), astronomy.

Studied mathematics under Gauss at Göttingen; worked at observatories of Seeberg (from 1813) and Mannheim (director from 1815). Made important preliminary calculations of lunar occultations, and pointed out the distorting influence of the profile of the moon. Did influential work on the determination of differences of longitude from lunar observations. Improved the value of the mass of Jupiter.

NICOLAUS OF DAMASCUS (*b. Damascus, 64* B.C.), botany.

A prestigious commentator on Aristotelian philosophy whose life was spent in the service of Herod the Great. Author of a two-volume *De plantis* that was so Peripatetic in style and structure as to have been believed to be the work of Aristotle himself. The original Greek text has been lost; it was translated successively into Syriac, Arabic, Latin, and Greek, and became the most important single source for later medieval botany.

NICOLLE, CHARLES JULES HENRI (*b. Rouen, France, 1866; d. Tunis, Tunisia, 1936*), medicine, bacteriology.

Studied medicine at Rouen and Paris; wrote doctoral dissertation under Émile Roux at Institut Pasteur (M.D., 1893). Worked and taught in Rouen before going to Tunis (1902) as director of the Pasteur Institute, which he transformed into a prestigious institution equipped for large-scale manufacture of vaccines as well as for scientific research. It became a training ground for bacteriologists and specialists in tropical medicine. Awarded Nobel Prize (1928) for his experimental proof of the role of lice in the transmission of exanthematous typhus. Elucidated etiology of many Mediterranean diseases. Originated the concept of unapparent infection. Lectured at Collège de France (1932–35), frequently on philosophical topics.

NICOMACHUS OF GERASA (*fl. ca.* A.D. *100*), mathematics, harmonics.

Author of several works, of which two are extant. The *Introduction to Arithmetic*, in two books, discusses the philosophical importance of mathematics, number per se, relative number, plane and solid numbers, and proportions; it was influential until the sixteenth century and gave its author the undeserved reputation of being a great mathematician. His *Manual of Harmonics* exhibits characteristics of both the Aristoxenian and the Pythagorean schools of music.

NICOMEDES (*fl. ca. 250* B.C. [?]), mathematics.

Nicomedes became famous for discovering the curve known as conchoid, cochlioid, or cochloid, whose advantages are that it is very easy to construct and that it can be used to solve a variety of problems, including duplication of the cube and trisection of an angle. As far as is known, all applications of the conchoid made in antiquity were developed by Nicomedes himself; interest in it revived in the late sixteenth century, and new applications and properties were discovered by such mathematicians as Viète, Descartes, Fermat, Roberval, Huygens, and Newton.

NICOT, JEAN (*b. Nîmes, France, ca. 1530; d. Paris, France, 1604*), philology, botany.

Studied letters at Nîmes and at Paris. While on a diplomatic mission to Portugal (1560) he sent to France seeds and leaves of tobacco, pointing out the therapeutic value of the plant (whose cultivation later spread from France). In his French-Latin dictionary, *Thresor de la langue francoyse* (1606), he called tobacco "the nicotian plant"; his name was preserved in the Linnaean designation *Nicotiana tabacum*.

NIEBUHR, CARSTEN (*b. Altendorf, Holstein, 1733; d. Meldorf, Holstein, 1815*), cartography, exploration.

Studied mathematics and astronomy at University of Göttingen. Hired as cartographer for a Danish expedition to Arabia (1761–67); made very exact determinations of longitude and latitude in the eastern Mediterranean and made maps of the Middle East that were the best available for a long time. On his return trip he made exact copies of cuneiform inscriptions at Persepolis that were used by later interpreters of the cuneiform alphabet.

NIELSEN, NIELS (*b. Ørslev, Denmark, 1865; d. Copenhagen, Denmark, 1931*), mathematics.

Studied at University of Copenhagen (doctorate, 1895), where he later taught (from 1905). His principal achievements were his many textbooks dealing with various classes of special functions, particularly cylindrical functions (1904) and the gamma function (1906). Later work was on number theory and on the history of mathematics.

NIEPCE, JOSEPH (later **NICÉPHORE**) (*b. Chalon-sur-Saône, France, 1765; d. St. Loup de Varenne, France, 1833*), photography.

After brief careers as a professor, a soldier, and a civil administrator, Niepce took up technological research with his brother Claude. Together they developed the "pyréolophore" (1807), an internal combustion engine fueled by lycopodium powder which was sufficiently powerful to move a boat, but which never became practical; their other inventions were less successful. By 1813 Niepce had taken up lithography, and from this he was led to the invention of photography; a letter to Claude of May 1816 refers to a photographic apparatus that produced a negative image, using paper impregnated with silver chloride fixed with nitric acid; by 1821 he was producing images on both glass and metal. In 1822 he recorded the first fixed positive image. Financial difficulties led him to sign an agreement of cooperation with Daguerre in 1829, but little is known of the development of this association.

NIESTEN, JEAN LOUIS NICOLAS (*b. Visé, Liège, Belgium, 1844; d. Laeken, Brussels, Belgium, 1920*), astronomy.

Served as captain of artillery and wrote two textbooks on military science. Resigned from the service (1877) and became assistant astronomer at Brussels observatory (*chef de service*, 1884). A systematic observer, particularly interested in planetary astronomy; wrote many articles on physical aspects of the planets. One of the founders of *Ciel et terre* (1880).

NIEUWENTIJT, BERNARD (*b. Westgraftdijk, North Holland, 1654; d. Purmerend, North Holland, 1718*), mathematics, philosophy.

Studied medicine at Leiden and Utrecht (M.D., 1676) and went into practice. Engaged in a controversy with Leibniz and his school on the foundations of calculus (1695–1700); his *Analysis infinitorum* (1695) was the first comprehensive book on the subject. Became famous for the publication (1714) of a lengthy teleological work, one of the first to review the whole of natural sciences to show in detail how marvelously things fitted in the world, and for a second major work (1720) opposing rationalism and presenting an empirical methodology of science. Nieuwentijt distinguished himself from the British empiricists by his closeness to mathematics and exact sciences.

NIEUWLAND, JULIUS ARTHUR (*b. Hansbeke, Belgium, 1878; d. Washington, D.C., 1936*), organic chemistry.

Graduated from Notre Dame University (1899); studied for the priesthood (ordained, 1903); studied botany and chemistry at Catholic University (Ph.D., 1904); taught botany and then chemistry at Notre Dame. Founded *American Midland Naturalist* (1909). Studied reactions of acetylene; his discovery of the reaction between acetylene and arsenic trichloride (which he did not pursue) led to the development of the poison gas and vesicant lewisite in World War I. Collaborated with Du Pont chemists in polymerization of acetylene and development of Chloroprene, which in turn could be polymerized to the first really successful synthetic rubber, "Duprene" or neoprene.

NIFO, AGOSTINO (*b. Sessa Aurunca, Italy, ca. 1469–70; d. Sessa Aurunca, 1538*), medicine, natural philosophy, psychology.

Studied at University of Padua, taught there and at universities of Naples, Salerno, Rome, and Pisa; created count palatine by Leo X (1520), with the right to use the Medici name and to grant degrees in his own name. Wrote commentaries on almost all the works of Aristotle, usually providing his own translation; in some cases he wrote a second, revised commentary. Although he initially held to the doctrine of Averroës on the unity of the intellect, he later rejected this as the true interpretation of Aristotle (in *De intellectu*, 1503) and came to prefer the Greek commentators. He attempted to reconcile Aristotle with the impetus theory by making impetus the principal mover, and later added the interesting refinement that a *vis impressa* is communicated not only to the projectile but also to the medium; he developed Averroës' doctrine of natural minima by further refining the notion of qualitative minima, and by using the theory of minima to explain physical structure and chemical reactions.

NIGGLI, PAUL (*b. Zofingen, Switzerland, 1888; d. Zurich, Switzerland, 1953*), crystallography, mineralogy, petrology, geology, chemistry.

Studied in Zurich at the Eidgenössische Technische Hochschule (M.S., 1911) and at the university (Ph.D., 1912), and later taught at both institutions (from 1920); visited the Geophysical Laboratory of the Carnegie Institution (1913) and worked with N. L. Bowen. Edited *Zeitschrift für Kristallographie,* and strove to maintain a unified system of crystallographic terminology. Niggli published over sixty papers on crystal structures and summarized the field in *Lehrbuch der Mineralogie und Kristallchemie* (2 vols., 1941–44), the first volume of which contains the foundation of a statistical morphological science. In his last years he showed that even the wave-mechanical approach to crystal physics required the assistance of morphological concepts. In attacking the gigantic task of petrographic classification and geochemical interpretation he modified the CIPW-norm procedures, creating "molecular values," which were soon used throughout the world and were known as Niggli values; they greatly facilitated the calculation of the possible mineralogical composition of a rock. He went on to develop the principle of magmatic crystallization and the influence of the volatile fraction; the principle of gravitative crystallization differentiation in magmas; the principle of petrographic-geochemical provinces; and the importance of calculation and comparison of the normative and the modal composition of rocks. He also applied his molecular values and norm calculations to metamorphic and sedimentary rocks to show that extreme transformist or relatively migrationist interpretations were oversimplifications.

Other areas that attracted his attention included applied petrology, snow petrology, clastic sediments, and ore deposits. Throughout his career he emphasized the importance of physical chemistry; his influence is still felt in virtually all fields of applied and pure crystallography, mineralogy, and petrology.

NIKITIN, SERGEY NIKOLAEVICH (b. *Moscow, Russia, 1851; d. St. Petersburg, Russia, 1909*), geology.

Studied at Moscow University (graduated, 1871; master's, 1878). One of the organizers of the Moscow Natural History Courses for Women; senior geologist with Russian Geological Survey (from 1882). Concerned with the stratigraphy of the Russian platform: investigated coal deposits, named the Tatar layer; divided Jurassic deposits, according to the ammonites, into seven paleontological zones; established a phylogenetic series of Kelloveyskikh and Oxford ammonites. Studied Quaternary deposits. Laid the foundation for systematic hydrogeological and hydrological research in Russia.

NĪLAKAṆṬHA (b. *Tṛ-k-kaṇṭiyūr* [*Kuṇḍapura*], *Kerala, ca. 1444; d. after 1501*), astronomy.

A follower of Parameśvara's *dṛggaṇita* system of astronomy. Author of at least eight works, including the *Āryabhaṭīyabhāṣya*—an extensive and important commentary on the *Āryabhaṭīya* of Āryabhaṭa I—and two works on eclipses.

NILSSON-EHLE, HERMAN (b. *Skurup, Sweden, 1873; d. Lund, Sweden, 1949*), genetics, plant breeding.

Studied at University of Lund (candidate's degree, 1894; licentiate, 1901; Ph.D., 1909) and taught there (chair of physiological botany, 1915; chair of genetics, 1917); assistant at Swedish Seed Association (from 1900), and later its director (1925–39). First to demonstrate that economically important properties in cultivated plants are inherited according to Mendel's laws and may be recombined in a specific way; recommended (1906) artificial crosses as the best method of obtaining a recombination of various desirable properties. Demonstrated (1908–11) that quantitative characters are inherited in the same Mendelian way as qualitative characters, but are conditioned by a relatively high number of polymeric genes. Advocated mutation research. As professor emeritus, he became actively interested in forestry and horticulture.

NISSL, FRANZ (b. *Frankenthal, Germany, 1860; d. Munich, Germany, 1919*), psychiatry, neuropathology.

Studied medicine at Munich and became Gudden's assistant (1884–86); worked at psychiatric hospital in Frankfurt (1886–95); taught at University of Heidelberg (1895–1918). Known for the discovery of a granular basophilic substance, now called Nissl's bodies, that is found in the nerve cell body and the dendrites. He also coined the term *nervöses grau*, or gray nerve network, a misleading concept of a diffuse interconnection of all nerve processes; and made a detailed study of dementia paralytica whose results are still valid, paying special attention to the behavior of microglia.

NOBEL, ALFRED BERNHARD (b. *Stockholm, Sweden, 1833; d. San Remo, Italy, 1896*), chemistry.

Son of an industrialist and inventor, Nobel was tutored privately and improved his knowledge of chemistry on a two-year study trip to Germany, France, Italy, and North America (1850–52). He then worked in his father's firm, and in 1863 developed his first important invention, the Nobel patent detonator for liquid nitroglycerin; in 1867 he patented dynamite, an easily handled, solid, and ductile explosive that consisted of nitroglycerin absorbed by kieselguhr, a very porous diatomite. Further research with explosives produced blasting gelatin (1875), a colloidal solution of nitrocellulose in nitroglycerin; Ballistite (1887), a nearly smokeless blasting powder; and progressive smokeless powder (1896). His later work covered electrochemistry, optics, biology, and physiology; he was granted no fewer than 355 patents in different countries, and became a multimillionaire through his patents and through his skill as an industrialist. Nobel left his total fortune to a foundation that would award prizes "to those who, during the preceding year, shall have conferred the greatest benefit on mankind."

NOBERT, FRIEDRICH ADOLPH (b. *Barth, Pomerania* [*now German Democratic Republic*], *1806; d. Barth, 1881*), clockmaking, optical instruments.

Became a clockmaker after a scanty education; encouraged by Encke, he constructed a telescope and made astronomical measurements. Studied at the Technical Institute at Charlottenburg in Berlin (1833–34), learned dividing methods and made a circle-dividing engine. Appointed *Universitätsmechaniker* at Greifswald (1835). Invented a technique for using the dividing engine to rule parallel lines on glass for microscope micrometers; extended his technique to produce a resolution plate for the microscope. His first test plate (1845) consisted of ten bands of ruled lines, the first and tenth bands being ruled to a spacing of 2.25 and 0.56 microns respectively; his seventh test plate (1873) contained a band ruled to a spacing of 0.11 micron, well below the resolution limit of the optical microscope. Nobert also supplied diffraction gratings to Ångström and others, and made compound microscopes and objective lenses.

NOBILI, LEOPOLDO (b. *Trassilico, Italy, 1784; d. Florence, Italy, 1835*), physics.

After an early career as an artillery captain, Nobili became a professor of physics at Florence and conducted research on electricity. Developed theory that an electric current is a flow of heat or caloric, and that the currents produced with wet conductors do not result from direct chemical action but are created by the heat generated in the chemical action. Opposed the Voltaic theory of the decomposition of water, reasoning that when the ends of a copper-zinc strip were submerged in water, a true electrical current or caloric flow was immediately engendered between the submerged ends; the current, while attempting to increase in length because of the self-repulsion of its parts, exerted a powerful force at the terminals and this force wrenched the water particles apart. He thus concluded that the generation of current by Voltaic means was not due to the release of statical electricity by electrochemical decomposition, but rather, the release was itself the result of the presence of an electric current; this conclusion was essential to the ultimate acceptance of Maxwellian electrodynamics.

NODDACK, WALTER (*b. Berlin, Germany, 1893; d. Bamberg, West Germany, 1960*), chemistry.

Studied at University of Berlin (doctorate, 1920); worked in Berlin (1920–35), Freiburg (1935–41), Strasbourg (1941–45), and Bamberg (1945–60). With Ida Tacke (later his wife) Noddack discovered (1925) element seventy-five of the periodic table, called rhenium, by X-ray spectroscopy in columbite that had been systematically enriched; they also claimed to have discovered element forty-three, masurium, but this discovery was disproved. Noddack believed that every element was present in every mineral but could not be detected unless it surpassed a threshold concentration, and he calculated this concentration for various elements. His studies in photochemistry included photographic sensitizing and visual pigments.

NOËL, ÉTIENNE (*b. Bassigny, Haute-Marne, France, 1581; d. La Flèche, France, 1659*), physics.

A Jesuit who taught in several colleges, principally at La Flèche (where he taught the young Descartes, with whom he later corresponded). Held to Aristotelian physics, but was receptive to new ideas, particularly those of Descartes. In correspondence and in *Le plein du vide* (1648) Noël disputed Pascal's theory of the vacuum in Torricelli's barometer.

NOETHER, AMALIE EMMY (*b. Erlangen, Germany, 1882; d. Bryn Mawr, Pa., 1935*), mathematics.

Daughter of Max Noether. Studied mathematics at universities of Erlangen (1900–02) and Göttingen (1903–04) as a nonmatriculated auditor; permitted to matriculate at Erlangen in 1904 (Ph.D., 1907). Taught in various capacities at Göttingen (1915–33), Moscow (1928–29), and Frankfurt (summer of 1930); dismissed from Göttingen by the Nazis and came to the United States, where she lectured and did research at Bryn Mawr and at the Institute for Advanced Study. While teaching under Hilbert she provided an elegant pure mathematical formulation for several concepts of the general theory of relativity. Her most important contributions were in the area of abstract algebra; from 1920 to 1926 she developed the theory of ideals, relating group and ring structures to the ideals, showing the importance of the ascending chain condition, formulating the concept of primary ideals (a generalization of Dedekind's prime ideals), and using polynomial ideals to rigorize, generalize, and give pure mathematical form to the concepts and methods of algebraic geometry as developed by her father and the Italian school of geometers. She also studied noncommutative rings in linear algebras, contributed notably to the theory of representations (1927–29), and probed profoundly into the structure of noncommutative algebras by means of her concept of the *verschränktes* (cross) product (1932–34).

NOETHER, MAX (*b. Mannheim, Germany, 1844; d. Erlangen, Germany, 1921*), mathematics.

Taught himself university-level mathematics, and then earned a doctorate (1868) at Heidelberg University. Affiliated with Heidelberg (1870–75) and with Erlangen (1875–1919). One of the guiding spirits of nineteenth-century algebraic geometry. Following Cremona, Noether studied the invariant properties of an algebraic variety subjected to birational transformations; obtained a number of important theorems for quadratic transformations. In 1873 he proved what came to be his most famous theorem: Given two algebraic curves $\Phi(x,y) = 0$, $\Psi(x,y) = 0$, which intersect in a finite number of isolated points, then the equation of an algebraic curve which passes through all those points of intersection can be expressed in the form $A\Phi + B\Psi = 0$ (where A and B are polynomials in x and y) if and only if certain conditions (today called "Noetherian conditions") are satisfied. If the intersections are nonsingular points of both curves, the desired form can readily be achieved.

NOGUCHI, (SEISAKU) HIDEYO (*b. Sanjogata, Okinashima-mura, Fukushima, Honshu, Japan, 1876; d. Accra, Gold Coast, 1928*), microbiology.

Largely self-taught in medicine; briefly attended a proprietary medical school in Tokyo (practitioner's diploma, 1897). While working at Kitasato Institute he met Simon Flexner, and followed him to the University of Pennsylvania (1900); research assistant at Carnegie Institution with one-year fellowship at the Statens Seruminstitut, Copenhagen (1903–04); worked at Rockefeller Institute from 1904. Early researches were on snake venoms and antivenins. With Flexner, was first in America to confirm Schaudinn's discovery of *Spirochaeta pallida* (1905); became preoccupied with problems of syphilis, worked on serodiagnostic methods and discovered *Sp. pallida* in the brain of paretics. Working with the Rockefeller Foundation yellow fever commission in Ecuador (1918), Noguchi isolated an organism that he named *Leptospira icteroides* and that he considered to be the causal agent of yellow fever; his theory was finally discredited in 1927. He elucidated the puzzling relationship between Oroya fever (Carrión's disease) and verruga peruana by isolating *Bartonella bacilliformis* (previously uncultivated) from sufferers of both diseases, thus establishing the etiologic unity of the two diseases. He died of yellow fever while investigating the new viral theory of its causation.

NOLLET, JEAN-ANTOINE (*b. Pimprez, near Noyon, France, 1700; d. Paris, France, 1770*), physics.

From a peasant family, Nollet initially planned an ecclesiastical career; however, while studying in Paris (M.Th., 1724; diaconate, *ca.* 1728) he became attracted to science and technology, and withdrew from the clerical world with the title "abbé." Active with Société des Arts from 1728; assisted Dufay and Réaumur with wide-ranging experiments in early 1730's, learning laboratory technique and a useful, moderate Cartesian approach to physical theory. In order to finance his own physics apparatus he built and sold duplicate instruments; from 1735 he lectured publicly, and his *cours de physique* was perhaps the most popular exhibition of its kind ever given (described in *Leçons de physique*, 6 vols., 1743–48). Entered the Academy as "adjunct mechanician" (1739); held the first chair of physics at the University of Paris; appointed preceptor to the royal family. Proposed a theory (1745) of the simultaneous effluence and affluence of electricity: electricity consists in the action of a particular matter in motion; the matters of electricity and light are fundamentally the same, and thus one can infer from the appearance of a brush discharge that the electrical matter leaves a charged body in divergent conical jets; environing objects and even the air return an "affluence" to the body, the two currents nearly or exactly balancing so that a body can never be emptied of its electrical matter; and all "attractions" and "repulsions" arise from the direct impact of the electrical matter in motion ("mechanical explanations are the only ones capable of advancing experimental physics"). Nollet immediately became the chief of the European electricians, but by 1752 he was under attack by Franklinists led by Buffon; he replied in *Lettres sur l'électricité* (1753 and two later vols.), capitalizing on Franklin's occasional obscurities and imprecisions, and his arguments stimulated the evolution of classical electrostatics. Another achievement was the discovery and clear explanation of osmotic pressure (1748).

NORDENSKIÖLD, (NILS) ADOLF ERIK (*b. Helsinki, Finland, 1832; d. Dalbyö, Sweden, 1901*), geography, geology, mineralogy, history of cartography.

Educated at University of Helsinki; moved to Sweden (1858) and became chief of the mineralogy division of the National Museum. Made numerous Arctic expeditions, culminating in the voyage of the *Vega* (1878–79) which penetrated the seas north of Asia to reach the Pacific, thus achieving the long-sought northeastern passage to the Orient and earning Nordenskiöld a barony. Was responsible for making scientific work an integral part of Arctic exploration; the five-volume report of the *Vega* voyage marked the beginning of serious polar studies. Did important work in history of science; his *Facsimile-atlas to the Early History of Cartography* (1889) and *Periplus—An Essay on the Early History of Charts and Sailing Directions* (1897) laid the foundations of the history of cartography.

NORDENSKIÖLD, NILS ERIK (*b. Frugård, Nyland [now Uusimaa], Finland, 1872; d. Stockholm, Sweden, 1933*), zoology, history of biology.

Studied at University of Helsinki; did graduate work at Padua and Leipzig. Taught at Helsinki (1899–1917) and at Stockholm (from 1926). Studied the systematics, anatomy, histology, and spermatogenesis of the Acarina. Most important contribution was in history of biology: his series of lectures at the University of Helsinki (1916–17), published in Swedish in three volumes as *Biologiens historia* (1921–24), was soon translated into German and English and received great international acclaim.

NORMAN, ROBERT (*fl. England, late sixteenth century*), navigation, magnetism.

Served as a sailor and later sold navigational instruments. In *The Newe Attractive* (1581), one of the few writings on magnetism favorably referred to by William Gilbert, Norman discussed his discovery of the dip of the magnetic needle from the horizontal, gave its value at London as 71°50′, and expressed an interest in finding its value at other points of the earth's surface. Also published *The Safegarde of Saylers* (1590), a book of sailing directions translated from Dutch.

NORTON, JOHN PITKIN (*b. Albany, N.Y., 1822; d. Farmington, Conn., 1852*), agriculture, agricultural chemistry.

Attended lectures at Yale, worked in the laboratory of Benjamin Silliman, Jr., attended lectures in Boston (1842–43), and spent two years learning agricultural chemistry in Scotland (1844–46). With the Sillimans (father and son) Norton promoted the study of applied chemistry at Yale (leading to the creation of Sheffield Scientific School); he was named professor of agricultural chemistry, probably the first in the U.S., and awarded an honorary M.A. (1846—his only degree). Analyzed plant proteins and the chemical constitution of oats, emphasized soil analysis, led the scientific farming movement in the U.S. Wrote an excellent textbook, *Elements of Scientific Agriculture* (1850).

NORWOOD, RICHARD (*b. Stevenage, Hertfordshire, England, 1590; d. Bermuda, 1665*), mathematics, surveying, navigation.

Taught himself mathematics while serving as a seaman. Mapped Bermuda (1614–17; map published in 1622). In London (1617–38) he taught mathematics and wrote a number of books on mathematics and navigation, including *Trigonometrie, or, The Doctrine of Triangles* (1631), intended as a navigational aid to seamen, and *The Seaman's Practice* (1637), which was especially concerned with the length of a degree and improvements in the log line (his value for the degree, measured along the meridian between London and York, was 367,167 English feet, a surprisingly good measurement; on the basis of this, he reknotted the log line, putting a knot every fifty feet). Norwood was the first to use consistently the trigonometric abbreviations s for sine, t for tangent, sc for sine complement, tc for tangent complement, and sec for secant.

NOSTRADAMUS, MICHAEL (latinized form of **Nostredame, Michel de**) (*b. Saint-Rémy, France, 1503; d. Salon, France, 1566*), medicine, astrology.

Having studied liberal arts at Avignon, Nostradamus endeavored to study medicine at Montpellier but was hindered first by an outbreak of plague, which he worked to combat for four years, and then by a jealous and hostile faculty; he left Montpellier in 1532, spending some years in travel and some in Agen with Scaliger's circle before settling in Salon (1547). While still practicing some medicine, he concentrated on producing his *Prophecies*, deliberately vague forebodings in verse form for which he claimed divine inspiration. The first edition (1555: three centuries, or groups of 100 quatrains, plus part of a fourth) brought him instant success; he was invited to cast royal horoscopes, and went on to write a total of ten centuries. His work attracted harsh criticism from some contemporaries, and continues to draw supporters and adversaries.

NOVARA, DOMENICO MARIA (*b. Ferrara, Italy, 1454; d. Bologna, Italy, 1504*), astronomy.

Professor of astronomy at Bologna University (1483–1504) where Copernicus was one of his pupils. Determined date of conjunction of Jupiter and Saturn in 1484 that was thought by many to have caused the outbreak of syphilis in southern Europe. Attributed difference in latitudes between Ptolemy's time and his own to a gradual shift of the terrestrial north pole toward the zenith in a cycle of 395,000 years; this thesis was quoted in Magini's planetary tables and then repeated by William Gilbert, Snel, Gassendi, and Riccioli.

NOVY, FREDERICK GEORGE (*b. Chicago, Ill., 1864; d. Ann Arbor, Mich., 1957*), microbiology.

Studied and worked at University of Michigan (B.S., 1886; M.S., 1887; D.Sc., 1890; M.D., 1891; professor and chairman of bacteriology, 1902–35; dean of medical school, 1933–35). Learned bacteriological techniques in Koch's laboratory (Berlin, 1888) and became one of the pioneers of bacteriology in the U.S. Early work, with Victor Vaughan, dealt with the toxic products of pathogenic bacteria, which they held to play a major role in infectious diseases. Made extensive studies on trypanosomes and spirochetes, as well as on microbial respiration and anaphylaxis; developed the Novy jar for anaerobic culture; discovered and isolated *Clostridium novyi* (1894), a gas gangrene bacillus; was apparently the first to cultivate a pathogenic protozoan in an artificial culture medium. Novy's approach to science formed part of the character of Max Gottlieb in Sinclair Lewis' *Arrowsmith*.

NOYES, ARTHUR AMOS (*b. Newburyport, Mass., 1866; d. Pasadena, Calif., 1936*), chemistry.

Studied at M.I.T. (B.S., 1886; M.S., 1887) and Leipzig (Ph.D., 1890). Taught analytical, organic, and physical chemistry at M.I.T. and wrote widely-used textbooks; directed Research Laboratory of Physical Chemistry (1903–19); acting president, 1907–09. Moved to California Institute of Technology in 1919, and with G. E. Hale worked to develop it into a great center of education and research; his estate was left to C.I.T. for the support of chemical research. Founded *Review of American Chemical Research* (1895), which became *Chemical Abstracts* (1907); chairman of National Research Council during World War I. One of his important contributions, carried out with many collaborators, was the thorough study of the chemical properties of the rarer elements and the development of a complete system of chemical analysis including these elements (*A System of Qualitative Analysis for the Rare Elements* [1927], with W. C. Bray). Was one of the first chemists to surmise that large deviations from unity of the activity coefficients of ions might be ascribed to the interaction of the electric charges of the ions.

NOYES, WILLIAM ALBERT (*b. Independence, Iowa, 1857; d. Urbana, Ill., 1941*), chemistry.

Earned degrees from Grinnell College (A.B. and B.S., 1879; A.M., 1882) and from Johns Hopkins (Ph.D., 1882). Worked at University of Minnesota (1882), University of Tennessee (1883–86), and Rose Polytechnic Institute, Terre Haute, Indiana (1886–1903); chief chemist at National Bureau of Standards (1903–07); director of chemical laboratories at University of Illinois (1907–26). Editor of *Journal of the American Chemical Society* (1902–17) and first editor of *Chemical Abstracts* (1907–10), *Chemical Reviews* (1924–26), and *American Chemical Society Scientific Monographs* (1919–41). Studied structure of camphor and its derivatives. While at National Bureau of Standards, working on atomic weights, he obtained a value of 1.-00787:16 for the critical hydrogen:oxygen weight ratio, which still stands as one of the most precise chemical determinations ever made.

NUMEROV, BORIS VASILIEVICH (*b. Novgorod, Russia, 1891; d. 1943*), astronomy, gravimetry.

Graduated from St. Petersburg University (1913) and remained in the department of astronomy (professor from 1924); supernumerary astronomer at Pulkovo Observatory, 1913–15. In 1919 he organized the Computation Bureau (now the Institute of Theoretical Astronomy of the Soviet Academy of Sciences), the aim of which was to compile an astronomical yearbook, and directed it from 1920 through 1936. Headed (1930–34) the Astronomical Committee created to plan and organize astronomical institutions in the Soviet Union and to coordinate their work, and traveled to foreign observatories. Notable in Soviet astronomy for having organized the construction and manufacture of gravimetric and astronomical instruments and equipment. Numerov's new program and method (1916) of analyzing zenith telescope observations was used in determining variations in latitude and was later adopted at Pulkovo; he developed a theory of universal and photographic transit instruments; he developed useful tables and charts for computing geographical and Gauss-Kruger rectangular coordinates; his new method of computing planetary perturbation was widely used in compiling the annual reference book that he founded, *Efemeridi malykh planet* ("Ephemerides of Asteroids"); he gave a theoretical basis to the analysis of star catalogs by means of observational data on asteroids, and proposed an original plan for international cooperation in determining the constants that characterize star catalogs. He also introduced into practice the pendulum gravimeter and the variograph for studying the upper layers of the earth's crust in geological prospecting, and planned the general gravimetrical survey of the Soviet Union.

NUÑEZ SALACIENSE, PEDRO (*b. Alcácer do Sol, Portugal, 1502; d. Coimbra, Portugal, 1578*), mathematics, cosmography.

After independent studies at the University of Salamanca, Nuñez went to Lisbon and studied mathematics and astrology while earning a bachelor's degree in medicine (*ca.* 1525; licentiate, 1532); held professorships at Lisbon (1529–37) and at Coimbra (1537–62); was appointed royal cosmographer (1529) and chief royal cosmographer (1547–78); served as adviser for the projected reform of weights and measures (1572–74). Considered the greatest of Portuguese mathematicians, Nuñez was a first-rate geographer, physicist, cosmologist, geometer, and algebraist who published works in both Portuguese (*Tratado da sphera,* 1537) and Latin on such topics as solar and lunar motions, the transformation of astronomical coordinates, spherical trigonometry, the duration of twilight, the geometrical errors of Oronce Fine, and Aristotle's mechanical problem of propulsion by oars. He contributed to instrument design with his invention of the nonius, an attachment for the astrolabe consisting of forty-four concentric circles ranging in number of divisions from 46 (on the smallest circle) to 89 (on the largest); the nonius permitted measurement of fractions of a degree and was a forerunner of the vernier. In navigation he made the significant discovery that the rhumb line (the course of a ship while sailing on a single bearing) was not equivalent to the great circle (the shortest distance between any two terrestrial points); his conception and drawing of rhumb lines (1534–37) exerted great influence on the making of charts for navigation.

NUSSELT, ERNST KRAFT WILHELM (*b. Nuremberg, Germany, 1882; d. Munich, Germany, 1957*), heat transfer, thermodynamics.

Studied mechanical engineering at Technischen Hochschulen of Munich and Charlottenburg (Berlin); received doctorate from Munich (1907). Held various teaching and industrial positions until 1925, when he was named to the chair in theoretical mechanics at the Technische Hochschule in Munich (retired 1952). Nusselt was the first significant contributor to the subject of analytical convective heat transfer. In "The Basic Law of Heat Transfer" (1915) he set up the dimensionless functional equations for both natural and forced convection, thus making it possible for experimentalists to generalize limited data; in "The Film Condensation of Steam" (1916) he provided a simple description of the film condensation of any liquid by linearizing the temperature profile and ignoring inertia in the liquid. He later provided an important description of the similarity between heat and mass transfer (1930), and published a book on technical thermodynamics (2 vols.; 1934, 1944).

NUTTALL, THOMAS (*b. Long Preston, near Settle, Yorkshire, England, 1786; d. Nut Grove Hall, near St. Helens, Lancashire, England, 1859*), botany, ornithology, natural history.

A printer by training, Nuttall sailed for Philadelphia in 1808 and became a friend of and plant collector for Benjamin Smith Barton. He taught himself the principles of botany and made important collections from the Missouri River region (1810–11); he reported on this trip in *The Genera of North American Plants, and a Catalogue of the Species, to the Year 1817* (1818), which was the first comprehensive study of American flora and established his reputation as a botanist. From 1822 to 1834 he was curator of the botanic garden at Cambridge and lecturer in natural history at Harvard; his textbook *An Introduction to Systematic and Physiological Botany* (1827; 2nd ed., enl., 1830) partially anticipated Schleiden's cell theory in its descriptions of the cellular composition of plants. His last major collecting trip took him across the continent to Oregon (1834–36) and to Hawaii; he included some of his data on western plants in his contribution to Torrey and Gray's *Flora of North America* and in his three-volume appendix for a new edition of Michaux's *North American Sylva* (1842–49). His achievements outside botany included a report on the geology and fossils of the Mississippi Valley (1820) in which he suggested a similarity between the geological formations of America and Europe, and *A Manual of the Ornithology of the United States and Canada* (1832–34). He returned to England in 1842, and his last years were not scientifically productive.

NYLANDER, FREDRIK (*b. Uleåborg [now Oulu], Russia [now Finland], 1820; d. Contrexéville, Vosges, France, 1880*), botany, medicine.

Studied botany and medicine at University of Helsinki (master's, 1840; doctorate in botany, 1844; M.D., 1853) and lectured on botany (1843–53); later career (from 1853) was in the health service of Uleåborg (municipal physician from 1865). Was the first to study the flora of Finland critically, making many expeditions and publishing important papers; pioneered in the botanical exploration of the then almost unknown Kola Peninsula.

NYLANDER, WILLIAM (*b. Uleåborg [now Oulu], Russia [now Finland], 1822; d. Paris, France, 1899*), botany.

Brother of Fredrik Nylander. Received M.D. from University of Helsinki (1847) but never practiced. Early papers were on entomology, particularly the identification of Finnish ants and bees. From 1848 he studied and published much about lichens, acquiring the reputation of being able to identify lichens from any part of the world and amassing the world's largest and richest private lichen herbarium; in 1857 he became the first professor of botany at the University of Helsinki, but he resigned in 1863 and emigrated to France. At the pinnacle of his career in 1868, he fell rapidly from favor through his vitriolic rejection of the new symbiotic theory of lichen composition and became a paranoid recluse.

OBRUCHEV, VLADIMIR AFANASIEVICH (*b. Klepenino, Rzhev district, Tver [now Kalinin] guberniya, Russia, 1863; d. Moscow, U.S.S.R., 1956*), geology, geography.

Graduated from St. Petersburg Mining Institute (1886). Held numerous positions and made expeditions throughout Russia, earning a worldwide reputation as an explorer and geologist. His study of the action of the wind as a geological agent in the Transcaspian depression (1886–88) inspired a lifelong interest in wind processes, particularly in the production of loess; he discovered convincing evidence that the Transcaspian sands were of triple origin—marine, continental, and fluviatile—and suggested practical measures for combating migrating sands. In 1888 he went to eastern Siberia as staff geologist of the Irkutsk Administration of Mines, to study geological structure and the distribution of useful minerals, especially gold; the geology of Siberia subsequently remained his main scientific topic. He concluded that the depression of Lake Baikal had originated by recent faulting; he also developed an original theory of the origin of gold deposits from thin quartz veins and from pyrite dispersed through certain layers of bedrock. From 1892 to 1895 Obruchev traveled through Mongolia and China as a member of the central Asian expedition, extending Richthofen's research deep into central Asia to the north, northwest, and west; his two-volume diary of the expedition (1900–01) remains the only source material on certain areas of central Asia. Later important studies were of Transbaikalia (1895–98), during which he developed a concept of the prime role of faulting in the formation of the surface and geological structure of Siberia, and of the Altay mountain system (*Altayskie etyudy*, 1915). In 1921 he was appointed to the chair of applied geology at Moscow Mining Academy; he later headed the Geological Institute and Committee for the Study of Permafrost of the Soviet Academy of Sciences; in 1939 he became editor of the geological series of *Izvestiya Akademii nauk SSSR*. He retained a lifelong interest in the geography of Siberia, especially in the former glaciation of the northern region and in the formation of the topography; his delineation and characterizations of ten geomorphological regions have retained their importance.

OCAGNE, PHILBERT MAURICE D' (*b. Paris, France, 1862; d. Le Havre, France, 1938*), mathematics, applied mathematics, history of mathematics.

Studied at École Polytechnique; taught there (*répétiteur;* professor, 1912) and at École des Ponts et Chaussées. Active as both researcher and teacher, publishing extensively; his name remains linked especially with graphical calculation procedures and with the systematization he gave to that field under the name of nomography (*Traité de nomographie,* 1899). Also published many articles on history of science, some of which were collected.

OCHSENIUS, CARL (*b. Kassel, Germany, 1830; d. Marburg, Germany, 1906*), geology, sedimentology.

Studied mining engineering and geology at Polytechnische Schule in Kassel. Spent twenty years in Chile (1851–71), serving in various positions and investigating coal, salt, guano, and sulfur deposits. Best known for *Die Bildung der Steinsalzlager und ihrer Mutterlaugensalze* (1877), in which he presented his "bar theory" of the origin of salt deposits (evaporites precipitate in lagoons separated by bars from the ocean proper).

OCKENFUSS, LORENZ. *See* **Oken, Lorenz.**

OCKHAM, WILLIAM OF (*b. Ockham, near London, England, ca. 1285; d. Munich, Germany, 1349*), philosophy, theology, political theory.

Traditionally regarded as the initiator of the movement called nominalism, which dominated the universities of northern Europe in the fourteenth and fifteenth centuries and played a significant role in shaping modern thought, Ockham ranks, with Thomas Aquinas and Duns Scotus, as one of the three most influential Scholastic philosophers.

He is assumed to have become a Franciscan friar at an early age; he entered Oxford around 1310 and became a *baccalaureus formatus,* or *inceptor,* in 1319, but never received his doctorate due to the controversial nature of his teachings. He was summoned to Avignon in 1324 to face charges of heresy; while there he supported Michael of Cesena against the pope on the question of evangelical poverty, a position that necessitated his flight (1328) to Munich and the protection of the German emperor, Louis of Bavaria. His flight caused his excommunication.

Ockham's works fall into three main groups: philosophical, including commentaries on Porphyry and Aristotle, an incomplete *Philosophia naturalis,* and a *Summa logicae* that gave full expression to his philosophy of language and logical doctrines; theological, including a set of questions on the *Sentences* of Peter Lombard, and two works of both logical and theological interest *(De praedestinatione . . .* and *De sacramento altaris);* and political, many polemical but some containing important discussions of moral, legal, and political concepts and issues pertinent to the controversies over the powers of pope and emperor, of church and state. His contributions to philosophy of language, metaphysics, and theory of knowledge were the direct result of his effort, as a theologian, to meet the twofold commitment to faith and reason. This commitment was expressed repeatedly in two maxims: the first is that God can bring about anything whose accomplishment does not involve a contradiction; the second, known as Ockham's Razor because of his frequent use of it, is the methodological principle of economy in explanation, frequently expressed in the formula "What can be accounted for by fewer assumptions is explained in vain by more." The two maxims determine a view of the universe as radically contingent in its being, a theory of knowledge that is thoroughly empiricist, and a rejection of all realist doctrines of common natures and necessary relations in things—all of which constitute what is called Ockham's nominalism.

ODDI, RUGGERO (*b. Perugia, Italy, 1864; d. Tunis, Tunisia, 1913*), medicine.

Studied medicine at Perugia (1883–87), Bologna (1887–88), and Florence (graduated 1889). Worked at Physiology Institute in Florence, did research at University of Strasbourg, directed Physiology Institute at University of Genoa (1894–1900), and worked as a physician in the Belgian Congo. Known for his discovery, while still a student (Perugia, 1886–87), of the sphincter of the choledochus; also perfected a device to measure the tone of the sphincter.

ODIERNA (or **Hodierna**), **GIOANBATISTA** (*b. Ragusa, Sicily, 1597; d. Palma di Montechiaro, Sicily, 1660*), astronomy, meteorology, natural history.

A self-taught scholar who taught school in Ragusa and later studied theology at Palermo, he served the barons of Montechiaro as a cleric and as court mathematician. Was given a telescope by Galileo; observed the comets of 1618–19, attempted to determine periods of revolution of the four satellites of Jupiter, observed Saturn. An early experimentalist, studying the passage of light through prisms and offering a vague explanation of the rainbow and of the spectrum (1647, 1652). In natural history his explanation of the structure and function of the poison fangs of vipers anticipated the work of Redi; in his studies on the eyes of flies and other insects he used a microscope and a camera obscura.

ODINGTON. *See* **Walter of Odington.**

ODLING, WILLIAM (*b. Southwark, London, England, 1829; d. Oxford, England, 1921*), chemistry.

One of England's leading theoretical chemists during the vital period 1850–70. Gave his first public lecture (on chemical affinity, 1844) before entering Guy's Hospital; became one of the hospital's first students to take the London University M.D. (1851). Taught at Guy's (1856–62), St. Bartholomew's Hospital (1863–70), the Royal Institution (1867–72), and Oxford (Waynflete professor, 1872–1912). Translated Laurent's *Méthode de chimie* (1854–55) and became a formidable spokesman for the type theory and for two-volume formulas; he was uncommitted to atomism per se, however, and preferred to regard formulas as heuristic devices. In a paper of 1853 he extended Williamson's use of the multiple water type and showed how all salts, however complex, could be reduced to "the types of one or more atoms of water"; he introduced the useful notation of superscript vertical lines to indicate the equivalence, or "replaceable value," of the element or group within the type formula compared with hydrogen (he recognized, and allowed for, elements with variable equivalence), and introduced "mixed types." His work had an influence on Kekulé, among others. He also published several prescient schemes (1857–65) of the relationships between chemical elements, stressing the physical and chemical analogies between elements and their compounds rather than atomic weights. He supported revision of atomic weights. He wrote several textbooks, including *A Course of Practical Chemistry, Arranged for the Use of Medical Students* which was read by Mendeleev in its Russian translation (1867).

OENOPIDES OF CHIOS (*b. Chios; fl. fifth century* B.C.), astronomy, mathematics.

None of his works has survived, nor are the titles of any known. He was reported by Theon of Smyrna to have discovered the obliquity of the zodiac, and it was probably he who settled on the value of 24°, which was accepted in Greece until refined by Eratosthenes. Theon also attributed to Oenopides the discovery of the period of the Great Year (the least number of solar years that coincided with an exact number of lunations); his value was reported by Aelian as fifty-nine years, and by Censorinus as 21,557 days. In geometry, according to Eudemus, he first stated the problems of dropping a perpendicular from a given point to a given line, and of constructing a rectilinear angle, equal to a given angle, at a given point on a given straight line. It may have been he who introduced the limitation of the use of instruments in all plane constructions to the ruler and compasses.

OERSTED, HANS CHRISTIAN (*b. Rudkøbing, Langeland, Denmark, 1777; d. Copenhagen, Denmark, 1851*), physics.

Oersted gained a working knowledge of chemistry while still a schoolboy by assisting in his father's pharmacy; he graduated in pharmacy from the University of Copenhagen (1797) and received his doctorate in 1799. He was profoundly influenced by Kantianism, stating its importance for natural philosophy in his dissertation. His study travels (1801–04) in pursuit of information on galvanism took him to Berlin, Göttingen, Weimar, and Paris, and introduced him to *Naturphilosophie* and to the chemical theories of Johann Ritter and J. J. Winterl; his uncritical defense of Ritter and Winterl in Paris destroyed, for a time, his scientific credibility and delayed his academic career. He was appointed extraordinary professor at Copenhagen (1806); in 1824 he founded the Society for the Promotion of Natural Science, and in 1829 became director of the Polytechnic Institute in Copenhagen. He was a superb teacher and, almost single-handed, raised the level of Danish science to that of the major countries of Europe; he was also an ardent popularizer of science.

Having found that experiment failed to support the physical systems of Winterl and Ritter, Oersted created his own system, based on forces (Kant's *Grundkräfte*); his *Recherches sur l'identité des forces chimiques et électriques* (1813 translation of the 1812 German work) sought to explain combustion and the neutralization of acids and bases through attraction and repulsion, and included a discussion of the convertibility of other forces. He predicted the existence of the electromagnetic effect, deducing the particular conditions for the conversion of electricity into magnetism from the nature of electricity (for him, it was a conflict of the positive and negative aspects of magnetism, which conflict spread out in wave fashion in space and was converted to heat, light, and, he thought, magnetism by increasing confinement in narrow-gauge wire). He was wrong, of course, on the conditions, and didn't

make the actual discovery until 1820, when he tried a new technique during a lecture demonstration and found that a current-carrying wire is surrounded by a circular magnetic field, thus opening a new epoch in the history of physics. His second major area of research involved the compressibility of gases and fluids, perhaps with the aim of testing the atomic hypothesis; his last researches were on diamagnetism.

OHM, GEORG SIMON (*b. Erlangen, Bavaria, 1789; d. Munich, Bavaria, 1854*), physics.

Ohm's father gave his sons a solid education in mathematics, physics, chemistry, and the philosophies of Kant and Fichte. After attending the Erlangen Gymnasium, Ohm studied at the University of Erlangen, receiving his Ph.D. in 1811. He subsequently taught mathematics as a *Privatdozent,* his only university affiliation until near the end of his life. Lack of money and the poor prospects for advancement at Erlangen forced Ohm to seek other employment from the Bavarian government; but the best he could obtain was a post as a teacher of mathematics and physics at the *Realschule* in Bamberg, where he worked with great dissatisfaction from 1813 until the school's dissolution in 1816. From 1816 until his release from Bavarian employ in 1817, he taught mathematics at the Bamberg *Oberprimärschule.*

Ohm took the position of *Oberlehrer* of mathematics and physics at the recently reformed Jesuit Gymnasium at Cologne in 1817. Here he studied the French classics—at first Lagrange, Legendre, Laplace, Biot, and Poisson, later Fourier and Fresnel—and, especially after Oersted's discovery of electromagnetism in 1820, did experimental work in electricity and magnetism. It was not until early in 1825, however, that he undertook research with an eye toward eventual publication. In 1826 Ohm was granted a year's leave of absence to go to Berlin to continue this work. When his leave ended in 1827, he had not yet attained his fervently sought goal of a university appointment.

Not wishing to return to Cologne, Ohm accepted a temporary job teaching mathematics at the Allgemeine Kriegsschule in Berlin. Continuing to find all higher academic doors closed to him in Prussia, Ohm hoped to have better luck in Bavaria; but although his ample qualifications were duly recognized, he could elicit no better offer (1833) than the professorship of physics at the Polytechnische Schule in Nuremberg.

Finally Ohm began to receive belated official recognition of the importance of his earlier work: he became a corresponding member of the Berlin (1839) and Turin (1841) academies, and on 30 November 1841 he received the Royal Society's Copley Medal. He became a full member of the Bavarian Academy in 1845 and was called to Munich in 1849 to be curator of the Academy's physical cabinet, with the obligation to lecture at the University of Munich as a full professor. He did not receive the chair of physics until 1852, less than two years before his death.

Ohm's first work was an elementary geometry text, *Grundlinien zu einer zweckmässigen Behandlung der Geometrie als höheren Bildungsmittels an vorbereitenden Lehranstalten* (Erlangen, 1817), which embodied his ideas on the role of mathematics in education.

His first scientific paper was "Vorläufige Anzeige des Gesetzes, nach welchem Metalle die Contaktelektricität leiten" (1825). In it he sought a functional relationship between the decrease in the electromagnetic force exerted by a current-carrying wire and the length of the wire. One of the striking features of this and Ohm's other early papers was their direct foundation on experiment. Indeed, several could be taken as models of inductive derivation of mathematical laws from empirical data. In his mature work of 1827, however, Ohm, under the influence of Fourier, adopted a highly abstract theoretical mode of presentation that obscured the theory's close relationship with experiment.

It is not obvious why Ohm chose to measure the loss in force and not the force itself. It should be noted, however, that he nowhere spoke of measuring the current; rather, he wanted to find out by what amount the electromagnetic force exerted by a given conductor was weakened when another, longer conductor was placed in the same circuit.

In February and April 1826, Ohm published two important papers that dealt separately with the two major aspects of his ultimately unified theory of galvanic electricity. The first, "Bestimmung des Gesetzes, nach welchem Metalle die Contaktelektricität leiten, nebst einem Entwurfe zu einer Theorie des Voltaischen Apparates und des Schweiggerschen Multiplicators," announced a comprehensive law for electric current that brought order into the hitherto confused collection of phenomena pertaining to the closed circuit, including the solution to the problem of conductibility as he and others had conceived of it. The second paper, "Versuch einer Theorie der durch galvanische Kräfte hervorgebrachten elektroskopischen Erscheinungen," broke new ground in associating an electric tension with both open and closed galvanic circuits.

Ohm's experimental procedure in the first of these papers was analogous to that which he had used earlier but was modified in several significant ways at Poggendorff's suggestion.

The second paper announced the beginnings of a comprehensive theory of galvanic electricity based, he said, on the fact that the contact of heterogeneous bodies produced and maintained a constant electric tension (Spannung). He deferred the systematic exposition of this theory to a later work, however, and limited himself to stating without derivation the two equations that constituted its heart: $X = kw(a/l)$ and $u - c = \pm (x/l)a$, where X is the strength of the electric current in a conductor of length l, cross section w, and conductibility (Leitungsvermögen) k produced by a difference in electric tension a at its end points; where u is the electroscopic force at a variable point x of the conductor; and where c is a constant independent of x. By means of the first equation one can, with respect to overall conducting power (or resistance), reduce the actual length of a wire of whatever cross section and conductibility to the equivalent length of one wire chosen arbitrarily as a standard. Letting l now be this equivalent length—called the reduced length (reducirte Länge) of the conductor—Ohm wrote his first law in the simpler form $X = a/l$, the expression which has become known as Ohm's law.

The fully developed presentation of his theory of electricity appeared in Ohm's great work, Die galvanische Kette, mathematisch bearbeitet (1827).

OKEN (or **Okenfuss**), **LORENZ** (b. Bohlsbach bei Offenburg, Baden, Germany, 1779; d. Zurich, Switzerland, 1851), natural science, philosophy, scientific congresses.

Studied at universities of Freiburg, Würzburg, and Göttingen. After graduating from Freiburg (1804), he held various teaching posts at Göttingen, Jena, Munich, and Erlangen before settling at the University of Zurich (1832–51). A prolific, controversial writer and proponent of Naturphilosophie, who took an active interest in all branches of natural history and of human knowledge in general. He made important contributions to comparative anatomy, but of more interest to the historian is his formulation of a number of fundamental concepts. In Die Zeugung (1805) he discussed the elementary units of living organisms, the "infusoria" or "primal animals (Urthiere)": every organism, both animal and vegetable, is a fusion of primal beings, each element having lost its individuality in favor of a higher unity; the infusoria originated in a primal slime formed along the boundary of the seas and the earth; the genesis of the organism is merely the accumulation of an infinite number of infusoria. These formulations prefigure some of the fundamental concepts of nineteenth-century natural science. Oken published his own journal, Isis (1817–47), which by the variety of its contents (largely written by Oken himself) offers a remarkable picture of the development of natural history. He founded the Gesellschaft Deutscher Naturforscher und Aerzte (1822) and has been called the father of scientific meetings.

OLAUS MAGNUS (b. Linköping, Sweden, 1490; d. Rome, Italy, 1557), geography, ethnology.

A Swedish cleric with a degree from the University of Rostock, Olaus traveled extensively in Scandinavia as deputy to the papal seller of indulgences; the notes made on his travels were later incorporated in his two pioneering works on Scandinavian geography: Carta marina (1539), based partly on older maps, executed in woodcut with vivid illustrations; and Historia de gentibus septentrionalibus (1555), large parts of which were copied from older European literature, dealing with climate, physical geography, agriculture and mining, wild animals, and the Swedish people in their daily occupations.

OLBERS, HEINRICH WILHELM MATTHIAS (b. Arbergen, near Bremen, Germany, 1758; d. Bremen, 1840), medicine, astronomy.

While studying medicine at Göttingen (M.D., 1780), Olbers continued his self-education in astronomy. His lifelong concern with comets dates from January 1779, when he calculated the orbit of Bode's comet. After a study trip to Vienna (1781) he settled in Bremen with a medical practice specializing in ophthalmology; it was mainly through his efforts that inoculation was introduced in the city. In 1820 he retired from active medical practice to devote the rest of his life to astronomy; his private library became one of the best in Europe, and was bought for Pulkovo Observatory. His achievements in astronomy included discovery of comets and calculation of their orbits (his new method of calculation of parabolic orbits, reported in Über die leichteste und bequemste Methode, die Bahn eines Kometen aus einigen Beobachtungen zu berechnen [1797], made his reputation); discovery of the asteroids Pallas (1802) and Vesta (1807); and his explanation of the paradox of the dark night sky (Olbers' paradox) by the assumption that space is not absolutely transparent (1823). He was proudest of having led F. W. Bessel to become a professional astronomer.

OLDENBURG, HENRY (*b. Bremen, Germany, ca. 1618; d. London, England, 1677*), scientific administration.

Little is known of Oldenburg's early life and career. He studied at the Gymnasium Illustre of Bremen (M.Th., 1639) and at the University of Utrecht; he most likely traveled abroad as a tutor before going to England on a diplomatic mission to Cromwell (1653). Once in England, he developed an acquaintance with many of the leading thinkers, especially with Robert Boyle (several of whose books he translated into Latin). In the first royal charter granted to the Royal Society (1662) he was named one of its two secretaries; in the ensuing fifteen years of service he founded a complete system of records, created an international correspondence among scientists, and founded (1665) the *Philosophical Transactions,* the first purely scientific journal containing both formal contributions and short notes about work in progress, as well as book reviews, which became the principal vehicle of interchange between English and Continental science.

OLDHAM, RICHARD DIXON (*b. Dublin, Ireland, 1858; d. Llandrindod Wells, Wales, 1936*), geology, seismology.

Son of Thomas Oldham. Studied at Royal School of Mines. Joined Geological Survey of India (1879–1903): became superintendent, wrote some forty of its publications, and devoted much energy to completing the unfinished work of his father. Became famous for his report on the great Assam earthquake of 12 June 1897, far surpassing in quality all previous reports; its most far-reaching result was the first clear identification on seismograms of the onsets of the primary *(P),* secondary *(S),* and tertiary (surface) waves, previously predicted mathematically. He also supplied the first clear evidence (1906) that the earth has a central core, through analysis of records of large earthquakes.

OLDHAM, THOMAS (*b. Dublin, Ireland, 1816; d. Rugby, England, 1878*), geology.

Received a B.A. from Trinity College, Dublin (1836), and studied engineering at Edinburgh. Taught at Trinity College (from 1844) and was Irish director of the Geological Surveys (from 1846) before going to India (1850) as surveyor to the East India Company. He immediately named himself "Superintendent of the Geological Survey of India" and began to recruit other geologists, thereby creating the Survey; under his guidance a remarkable amount of work was carried out, particularly the survey of Indian coalfields. He initiated the scientific study of earthquakes in India and published a catalog of earthquakes. Edward Forbes gave the name *Oldhamia* to what is now thought to be a trace fossil, discovered by Oldham in Cambrian rocks (1849).

OLIVER, GEORGE (*b. Middleton-in-Teesdale, Durham, England, 1841; d. Farnham, Surrey, England, 1915*), physiology.

Studied medicine at University College, London (M.B., 1865; M.D., 1873); practiced medicine in Harrogate

(1876–1908) and spent winters in London. Contributed to the development of more scientific methods of diagnosis and therapy, notably through introduction of urinary testing papers and of his hemacytometer, hemoglobinometer, arteriometer, and sphygmomanometer. With Edward A. Schäfer (later Sharpey-Schafer) he elucidated the cardiovascular effects of the administration of extracts of the adrenal medulla and of the pituitary, the first detailed study of the effect of the active principle of a ductless gland (1893–95).

OLSZEWSKI, KAROL STANISŁAW (*b. Broniszow, Poland, 1846; d. Cracow, Poland, 1915*), chemistry, physics.

Studied natural science at Cracow and at Heidelberg (doctorate, 1872); taught at Cracow (professor from 1891). Pioneer in the field of low-temperature phenomena. With Z. von Wroblewski he liquefied air, oxygen, nitrogen, and carbon monoxide (1883); they were able to liquefy hydrogen only in its dynamic state. He determined the inversion temperatures of oxygen and nitrogen and, in 1902, of hydrogen; he also liquefied argon and fluorine. He improved Dewar's methods of liquefaction and adapted them to practical laboratory work.

OLUFSEN, CHRISTIAN FRIIS ROTTBØLL (*b. Copenhagen, Denmark, 1802; d. Copenhagen, 1855*), astronomy.

Studied at University of Copenhagen and with Bessel at Königsberg; worked at University of Copenhagen observatory (professor and director from 1832; doctorate, 1840). With P. A. Hansen, produced new fundamental solar tables (1853). Investigated systematic errors in observations made with the Greenwich mural quadrant (1831). Took over the right ascension l^h for the *Akademische Sternkarten* of the Berlin Academy.

OLYMPIODORUS (*b. Thebes, Egypt, ca. 360–385; d. after 425*), history, alchemy.

Known primarily for a work preserved only in fragments—*Materials for History*—continuing the work of Eunapius and covering the period 407–25. May have written "The Philosopher Olympiodorus to Pelasius . . . on the Divine and Sacred Art," presenting a poor explanation of alchemy and comparing the views of alchemists and philosophers on the origin of matter.

OMALIUS D'HALLOY, JEAN BAPTISTE JULIEN D' (*b. Liège, Belgium, 1783; d. Brussels, Belgium, 1875*), geology.

D'Omalius was educated in the family tradition of law and public service, but became attracted to science in Paris and studied seriously from 1803; he attended lectures of Lacépède, Fourcroy, and Cuvier, and made geological observations throughout France. His scientific reputation was established by "Essai sur la géologie du nord de la France," in which he began, on the Continent, stratigraphic subdivision of the major Wernerian classes by superposition and paleontological criteria, and opposed Wernerian geology by arguing that the inclination of strata is not due to deposition and that, in the same basin, inclined strata are older than horizontal strata. From 1809 to 1813 he worked for the Bureau of Statistics, preparing a geological map of the Empire (1823); he then served in a succession of public offices, before returning to geology (1830). In his textbook *Éléments de géologie* (1831) he argued against uniformitarianism and insisted that the deepest structures had been formed by heat agencies no longer intensely active; he defended the theory of organic evolution, believing that species change in response to changes in environment.

OMAR KHAYYAM. *See* **al-Khayyāmī.**

OMORI, FUSAKICHI (*b. Fukui, Japan, 1868; d. Tokyo, Japan, 1923*), seismology.

Graduated in physics from Imperial University, Tokyo (1890); lectured there from 1893, and became professor of seismology (1897) after study in Italy and Germany. One of the world's great early seismologists. Encouraged by John Milne to make the first precise studies of earthquake aftershocks; developed a formula (1894) for rate of falloff of aftershocks following major earthquakes. Designed instruments, including a horizontal-pendulum seismograph and the tiltmeter. Carried out pioneering work on earthquake zoning.

ONNES, HEIKE KAMERLINGH. *See* **Kamerlingh Onnes, Heike.**

OPPEL, ALBERT (*b. Hohenheim, Württemberg, Germany, 1831; d. Munich, Germany, 1865*), paleontology, biostratigraphy.

Studied under Quenstedt at Tübingen (doctorate, 1853); toured Jurassic exposures and met leading European geologists. Worked at Bavarian State Paleontological Collection, Munich (from 1858), and taught at the university (from 1861). In *Die Juraformation Englands, Frankreichs und des südwestlichen Deutschlands* (1856–58) he divided the Jurassic into thirty-three zones, each characterized by typical animal species, mostly ammonites; although based on Linnaeus' immutability of species and Cuvier's catastrophism, his concept of the zone remains an indispensable resource of modern biostratigraphy. In his last work he distinguished the Tithonian stage of the Jurassic (1865).

OPPENHEIM, SAMUEL (*b. Braunsberg, Moravia* [*now Brušperk, Czechoslovakia*], *1857; d. Vienna, Austria, 1928*), astronomy.

Received teaching diploma (1880) and Ph.D. from University of Vienna. Taught intermittently at secondary schools and worked in observatories; from 1911, full professor at University of Vienna. In theoretical astronomy he published valuable contributions to the three-body and *n*-body problem and to the theory of gravitation; studied motions of stars and stellar statistics; calculated orbits of numerous comets and asteroids. Astronomical editor of *Encyklopädie der Mathematischen Wissenschaften* (from 1917).

OPPENHEIMER, J. ROBERT (*b. New York, N.Y., 1904; d. Princeton, N.J., 1967*), theoretical physics.

Oppenheimer achieved great distinction through his personal research, as a teacher, as director of Los Alamos, and as the elder statesman of postwar physics. He went from the Ethical Culture School in New York to Harvard, where he graduated *summa cum laude* after three years (1925); he then went to Europe and established himself as a theoretical physicist. His first two papers (1926), written in Cambridge, England, with help from R. H. Fowler and Paul Dirac, were on the quantum mechanics of molecular band spectra and of the hydrogen atom, and show him already in full command of the new methods. He went next to Göttingen (1926) and received his Ph.D. (1927) under Max Born; together they developed the Born-Oppenheimer method for handling the electronic, vibrational, and rotational degrees of freedom of molecules, now one of the classical parts of quantum theory. He remained in Europe until 1929, learning from both Ehrenfest and Pauli. From 1929 to 1942 he divided his time between Berkeley and the California Institute of Technology, as an outstanding teacher of theoretical physics and as a productive researcher; his achievements in this period include prediction (1930) of a positive electron (Anderson's positron) and development (1937, with J. F. Carlson) of an elegant method for investigating electron-photon showers in cosmic rays.

During World War II he directed research on the atomic bomb, first as head of a theoretical group at Berkeley and then as director of the army's "Manhattan District," brought together, at his suggestion, at Los Alamos. He was one of a panel of four scientists (the others being Compton, Fermi, and Lawrence) who supported the decision to use the bomb on Japan. After the war he took part in the drafting of the "Acheson-Lilienthal Report," proposing international control of atomic energy; from 1946 to 1952 he served as advisor to the Atomic Energy Commission. In 1947 he became director of the Institute for Advanced Study in Princeton; he expanded its population by bringing in many young scientists, mostly as short-term members. Under his influence the physics group became one of the centers at which the current problems of modern physics were most clearly understood; he was at his best in guiding the intense debate and discussion and in helping people to understand each other ("What we do not know we try to explain to each other"), and did not resume personal research on any substantial scale. In December 1953, in the height of the McCarthy era, Oppenheimer's loyalty was questioned and his security clearance was withdrawn; he requested hearings, and the Personnel Security Board found him to be "a loyal citizen" but censured him for opposing the hydrogen-bomb program. The Atomic Energy Commission did not censure him, but confirmed withdrawal of his clearance. He continued as director of the Institute and with his writing and lecturing; in 1963 he was given the A.E.C.'s Enrico Fermi Award.

OPPOLZER, THEODOR RITTER VON (*b. Prague, Bohemia* [*now Czechoslovakia*], *1841; d. Vienna, Austria, 1886*), astronomy, geodesy.

Studied astronomy and medicine in Vienna (M.D., 1865) and built a private observatory. Taught at University of Vienna (from 1866; professor, 1875); director of Austrian geodetic survey (from 1873). Published more than 300 papers, mostly on determination and improvement of the orbits of comets and asteroids; developed new formulas, computed ephemerides. His *Lehrbuch zur Bahnbestimmung der Cometen und Planeten* (2 vols., 1870–80) comprises all the materials then necessary for understanding and determining both preliminary and definitive orbits. Organized—partly at his own expense—the "Canon der Finsternisse," containing the relevant data of every lunar and solar eclipse, with minor exceptions, from 1207 B.C. to A.D. 2163.

ORBELI, LEON ABGAROVICH (*b. Tsakhkadzor, Russia, 1882; d. Leningrad, U.S.S.R., 1958*), physiology.

Graduated from Medical Military Academy, St. Petersburg (1904); worked with Pavlov, as well as with Hering in Germany, Langley and Barcroft in England, and at the Stazione Zoologica, Naples. Spent scientific career in the leading Russian physiological centers; was departmental chairman at Military Medical Academy (1925–50) and at First Leningrad Medical Institute (1920–30); directed I. P. Pavlov Institute of Physiology; organized I. M. Sechenov Institute of Evolutionary Physiology (1956). Wrote more than 200 works on a varied range of problems in physiology and theoretical medicine, including neurophysiology and environmental physiology. Created the theory of the adaptive-trophic role of the sympathetic nervous system (the Orbeli-Ginedinsky phenomenon, 1923). Responsible for the development of evolutionary physiology.

ORBIGNY, ALCIDE CHARLES VICTOR DESSALINES D' (*b. Couëron, Loire-Atlantique, France, 1802; d. Pierrefitte-sur-Seine, near Saint-Denis, France, 1857*), paleontology.

Studied zoology in Paris under Cordier. From 1826 to 1834 he explored the entire continent of South America on a commission for the Muséum d'Histoire Naturelle; his report (10 vols., 1834–47)—covering zoology, geography, geology, paleontology, ethnography, and anthropology—constituted the most detailed description of a continent ever made. His paleontological theories aroused criticism that hindered his career; he finally obtained a professorship (created for him in 1853) at the Muséum d'Histoire Naturelle. He published many works and contributed to others. In *Tableau méthodique de la classe des Céphalopodes* (1826) he reclassified the microscopic forms of living and fossil cephalopods under the name Foraminifera. One of the founders of modern biostratigraphy through his *Prodrome de paléontologie stratigraphique universelle* (1850–52), in which he divided the sediments and their invertebrate fossil contents into twenty-seven "stages" named for localities or regions; his theory of successive destructions and creations is no longer useful, but the concept of the stage is still valid.

ORESME, NICOLE (*b. France, ca. 1320; d. Lisieux, France, 1382*), mathematics, natural philosophy.

Nothing is known of Nicole Oresme's early academic career. Apparently he took his arts training at the University of Paris in the 1340's and studied with Jean Buridan. After teaching arts and pursuing his theological training, he took his theological mastership in 1355 or 1356; he became grand master of the College of Navarre in 1356, was appointed canon at Rouen in 1362. A few months later he was appointed canon at Sainte-Chapelle, Paris; a year later (1364) he was appointed dean of the cathedral of Rouen. It is presumed that from 1364 to 1380 Oresme divided his time between Paris and Rouen, probably residing regularly in Rouen until 1369 and in Paris thereafter. From about 1369 he was busy translating certain Aristotelian Latin texts into French and writing commentaries on them, at the behest of King Charles V. In 1377 he was appointed bishop of Lisieux; he moved there in 1380.

The writings of Oresme show him at once as a subtle Schoolman disputing the fashionable problems of the day, a vigorous opponent of astrology, a dynamic preacher and theologian, an adviser of princes, a scientific popularizer, and a skillful translator of Latin into French. In his *Questiones de celo* he stressed the essential differences between the mechanics governing terrestrial motion and that involved in celestial motions. In two passages of his last work, *Livre du ciel et du monde d'Aristote*, he suggests (1) the possibility that God implanted in the heavens at the time of their creation special forces and resistances by which the heavens move continually like a mechanical clock, but without violence, the forces and resistances differing from those on earth; and (2) that "it is not impossible that the heavens are moved by a power or corporeal quality in it, without violence and without work, because the resistance in the heavens does not incline them to any other movement nor to rest but only [effects] that they are not moved more quickly."

One of these passages in which the clock metaphor is cited leads into one of Oresme's most intriguing ideas—the probable irrationality of the movements of the celestial bodies. The idea itself was not original with Oresme, but the mathematical argument by which he attempted to develop it in his treatise *Proportiones proportionum ("The Ratios of Ratios")* was certainly novel. His point of departure in this tract is Thomas Bradwardine's fundamental exponential relationship, suggested in 1328 to represent the relationships between forces, resistances, and velocities in motions:

$$\frac{F_2}{R_2} = \left(\frac{F_1}{R_1} \right)^{\frac{V_2}{V_1}}.$$

Oresme went on to give an extraordinary elaboration of the whole problem of relating ratios exponentially. It is essentially a treatment of fractional exponents conceived as "ratios of ratios," in which he made a new and apparently original distinction between irrational ratios of which the fractional exponents are rational, for example, $\left(\frac{2}{1} \right)^{1/2}$, and those of which the exponents are themselves irrational, apparently of the form $\left(\frac{2}{1} \right)^{\sqrt{1/2}}$. In making this distinction he introduced new significations for the terms *pars, partes, commensurabilis*, and *incommensurabilis*. He also composed an independent tract, the *Algorism of Ratios*, in which he elucidated in an original way the rules for manipulating ratios.

Oresme's consideration of a very old cosmological problem, the possible existence of a plurality of worlds, was also novel. Like the great majority of his contemporaries, he ultimately rejected such a plurality in favor of a single Aristotelian cosmos, but before doing so he stressed the possibility that God by His omnipotence could so create such a plurality.

In examining his views on terrestrial physics, we should note first that Oresme accepted the conclusion that the earth could move in a small motion of translation which would be brought about by the fact that the center of gravity of the earth is constantly being altered by climatic and geologic changes and strives always for the center of the world. His discussion is of interest mainly because of its application of the doctrine of center of gravity to large bodies. Still another question of the motion of the earth fascinated Oresme, that is, its possible rotation, which he discussed in some detail in at least three different works. His treatment in the *Du ciel* is well known, but many of its essential arguments for the possibility of the diurnal rotation of the earth already appear in his *Questiones de celo* and his *Questiones de spera*.

In discussing the motion of individual objects on the surface of the earth, Oresme seems to suggest (against the prevailing opinion) that the speed of the fall of bodies is directly proportional to the time of fall, rather than to the distance of fall, implying as he does that the acceleration of falling bodies is of the type in which equal increments of velocity are acquired in equal periods of time. He did not, however, apply the Merton rule of the measure of uniform acceleration of velocity by its mean speed, discovered at Oxford in the 1330's, to the problem of free fall, as did Galileo almost three hundred years later. Oresme knew the Merton theorem, to be sure, and in fact gave the first geometric proof of it in another work, but as applied to uniform acceleration in the abstract rather than directly to the natural acceleration of falling bodies. In his treatment of falling bodies, despite his different interpretation of *impetus,* he did follow Buridan in explaining the acceleration of falling bodies by continually accumulating impetus. Furthermore, he presented (as Plutarch had done in a more primitive form) an *imaginatio*—the device of a hypothetical, but often impossible, case to illustrate a theory—of a body that falls through a channel in the earth until it reaches the center. Its impetus then carries it beyond the center until the acquired impetus is destroyed, whence it falls once more to the center, thus oscillating about the center.

Oresme's work of unusual scope and inventiveness was the *Tractatus de configurationibus qualitatum et motuum,* composed in the 1350's while he was at the College of Navarre. This work applies two-dimensional figures to hypothetical uniform and nonuniform distributions of the intensity of qualities in a subject and to equally hypothetical uniform and nonuniform velocities in time. While many of the laws and doctrines contained in the *De configurationibus* had already been anticipated in his *Questions on the Physics* and *Questiones super geometriam Euclidis,* in this work he takes the opportunity to refine or elaborate on many complex ideas contained in his earlier work.

ORIBASIUS (*fl. Pergamum, fourth century*), medicine.

An iatrosophist who studied medicine in Alexandria; he became physician in ordinary to Emperor Julian the Apostate and also held political office. Important for his role in preserving earlier, more important medical authors in such works as *Iatrikai synagogai* (or *Collectiones medicae*). His writings inspired other authors, found a large audience in the Latin West, and were drawn on freely by the Arabs.

ORLOV, ALEKSANDR YAKOVLEVICH (*b. Smolensk, Russia, 1880; d. Kiev, Ukrainian S.S.R., 1954*), astronomy, gravimetry, seismology.

Studied at St. Petersburg University (graduated 1902; master's, 1910) and at the Sorbonne, Lund, and Göttin-

gen. Taught at universities of Yurev (1908–11), Novorossysk (1912), Odessa (doctorate, 1915; professor, 1915–17), and Kiev (rector, 1919), and at P. K. Sternberg Astronomical Institute, Moscow (professor, 1934–38). Worked at observatories of Yurev (1905–06 and 1908–11; director of seismic station from 1909), Pulkovo (1906–08), Odessa (director from 1912), and the Ukrainian Academy of Sciences (director, 1944–50). Organized the seismic station in Tomsk (1911) and the gravimetric observatory in Poltava (1924; director, 1924–34, 1938–51). President of commission on latitude of the Astronomical Council of the Soviet Academy of Sciences (1939–52). Did important work on motion of the poles and variations in latitude: developed a graphic method of selecting pairs of stars for determining latitudes from observations by the method of equal zenith angles (1909); introduced a new definition of "mean latitude"; discovered slow nonpolar variations of latitude and devised a method for excluding them; developed a new method of determining polar coordinates from latitude observations at an isolated station; discovered the annual secular motion of the pole to be $0.004''$ per year, along a meridian of 69° W. Also studied tidal deformations of the earth, solar rotation, eclipses, brightness curves of variable stars, radial velocity curves of spectroscopic binaries, and comets, as well as seismology, geodesy, and geophysics.

ORLOV, SERGEY VLADIMIROVICH (*b. Moscow, Russia, 1880; d. Moscow, 1958*), astronomy, astrophysics.

Studied at Moscow University (graduated 1904; doctorate, 1935). Taught at First Gymnasium in Moscow (1906–20), Perm University (1920–22), and Moscow University (professor from 1926); acting director of State Astrophysical Institute (1923–31); vice-director (1931–35) and director (1943–52) of P. K. Sternberg Astronomical Institute. President of Commission on Comets and Meteors of the Astronomical Council of the USSR Academy of Sciences (1935–57). Published more than seventy studies on the astronomy of comets, including the mechanical theory of comet forms and spectroscopic studies. Developed a classification of the forms of comet heads; improved calculation of the repulsive accelerations of the action of the sun on the particles of comets' tails; established the integral, or absolute stellar, magnitudes of many comets and noted that a comet's brightness depends on the phase of solar activity; determined the gas composition of straight-tail comets; was first to identify nickel in cometary spectra. Hypothesized that comets form as a result of accidental collisions between two asteroids.

ORNSTEIN, LEONARD SALOMON (*b. Nijmegen, Netherlands, 1880; d. Utrecht, Netherlands, 1941*), physics.

Received doctorate (1908) under Lorentz at Leiden. Lectured at University of Groningen (1909–14); succeeded Debye in chair of theoretical physics at Utrecht (1914); became acting director (1920) and director (1925) of Utrecht physical institute. He applied statistical mechanics to molecular theory; with Zernicke (1914–17) he studied the formation of molecular "swarms" and added an important correction to the Einstein-Smoluchowski theory of opalescence of a fluid at its critical point. At Utrecht his work shifted from theory to experiment; he charted an ambitious, coordinated program for systematic investigation of techniques of radiation intensity measurement, and his group's publications on the sum rules of spectral lines provided important data for the development of quantum mechanics.

ORTA, GARCIA D' (or **da Orta**) (*b. Castelo de Vide, Portugal, ca. 1500; d. Goa, India, ca. 1568*), botany, pharmacology, tropical medicine, anthropology.

Studied at the universities of Salamanca and Alcalá de Henares; qualified in medicine (1526) and moved to Lisbon, where he taught at the university (1530–34). Traveled extensively along the western coast of India and Ceylon (1534–38) before settling permanently in Goa as vice-regal physician. His *Coloquios dos simples e drogas he cousas medicinais da India* (1563) included information on the materia medica (with Indian, Greek, and Arabic synonymy), local food plants, diseases, and sociology of India, and provided Western scholars with their introduction to tropical medicine. L'Écluse published an epitome of d'Orta's book as *Aromatum et simplicium . . . historia* (1567), and Italian and French translations were also published. D'Orta was one of the first European scholars to express admiration for the civilization of China.

ORTEGA, JUAN DE (*b. Palencia, Spain, ca. 1480; d. ca. 1568*), mathematics.

Member of the Order of Preachers; taught arithmetic and geometry in Spain and Italy. His *Tractado subtilisimo d'aritmética y de geometria* (1512), on commercial arithmetic and practical rules of geometry, became famous throughout Europe and was the first book on commercial arithmetic to be published in French (Lyons, 1515); it contains surprisingly close approximations to the numerical values of square roots.

ORTELIUS (or **Oertel**), **ABRAHAM** (*b. Antwerp, Brabant [now Belgium], 1527; d. Antwerp, 1598*), cartography, geography.

Supported himself by buying, coloring, and selling maps until encouraged by Mercator (1559–60) to draw his own maps; he soon became one of the principal cartographers of his time. He published maps of the world (1564), Egypt (1565), Asia (1567), and Spain (1570) before undertaking a comprehensive atlas of the world. *Theatrum orbis terrarum* (1570) was an immediate success and went through a long series of revised editions and translations; its original 70 maps had increased to 161 by the 1601 edition. A useful feature for historians was Ortelius' list of 87 map makers (183 by 1601) as authorities for his own work. In later life he spent much time on classical studies, including numismatics and geography.

ORTON, JAMES (*b. Seneca Falls, N.Y., 1830; d. Lake Titicaca, Bolivia, 1877*), natural history, exploration.

Studied at Williams College (B.A., 1855) and Andover Theological Seminary. Directed three expeditions in the Andes (1867, 1873, 1876), collecting for specialists and making observations; his *Andes and Amazon* (1870) was dedicated to Darwin. Introduced natural history instruction at Vassar College (1869). Wrote an influential text, *Comparative Zoology, Structural and Systematic* (1876), expounding Agassiz's functional approach.

OSBORN, HENRY FAIRFIELD (*b. Fairfield, Conn., 1857; d. Garrison, N.Y., 1935*), vertebrate paleontology.

Graduated from Princeton (1877) and did postgraduate work under Huxley and Balfour in London. Taught at Princeton (1881–91) before being called to Columbia University to found a department of biology and to the American Museum of Natural History to found a department of mammalian paleontology; remained at Columbia until 1910 and was first dean of graduate faculty; remained at the museum until his death, serving as president for twenty-five years and bringing it to world eminence. Published extensively on paleontology and on evolution theory.

OSBORNE, THOMAS BURR (*b. New Haven, Conn., 1859; d. New Haven, 1929*), protein chemistry.

Studied at Yale (graduated 1881; Ph.D., 1885). Joined staff of Connecticut Agricultural Experiment Station (1886) as an analytical chemist; developed the Osborne beaker method for the mechanical analysis of soils. In 1889 he began investigating the proteins of plant seeds, using methods of isolation that showed an instinctive appreciation of the physicochemical properties of proteins well ahead of contemporary theory. He stated in 1894 that the crystalline globulins extracted from different seeds were identical, having essentially the same content of carbon, hydrogen, nitrogen, and sulfur; later intensive studies of amino acid composition (1906–16), partly in collaboration with H. Gideon Wells (1911–16), demonstrated the specificity of vegetable proteins with respect to source. His studies with Lafayette Mendel on the nutritive properties of seed proteins (1909–28) revealed that tryptophan and lysine are essential in the diet, and that growth could be quantitatively controlled in rats by the supply of lysine; they also did important work on the natural distribution of vitamin A (having announced its existence in a paper submitted just three weeks after E. V. McCollum's paper on the same discovery), and on the effects of different diets. In 1919 he and Alfred J. Wakeman prepared the first vitamin-rich concentrate from an extract of brewer's yeast.

OSGOOD, WILLIAM FOGG (*b. Boston, Mass., 1864; d. Belmont, Mass., 1943*), mathematics.

Studied at Harvard (A.B., 1886; A.M., 1887), where he was influenced by B. O. Peirce; at Göttingen under Klein (1887–89); and at Erlangen (Ph.D., 1890). Taught at Harvard (1890–1933), and at National University of Peking for two years. An outstanding mathematics teacher and expert on the theory of functions. His *Lehrbuch der Funktionentheorie* (1907) became the standard treatise.

OSIANDER, ANDREAS (*b. Gunzenhausen, Bavaria, Germany, 1498; d. Königsberg, Germany [now Kaliningrad, U.S.S.R.], 1552*), theology, astronomical and mathematical publishing.

Taught at Nuremberg, was ordained a priest (1520), and became an outspoken Lutheran; appointed professor of theology at Königsberg (1549). His doctrinal views were bitterly opposed by the more orthodox Lutherans in the "Osiander Controversy," which continued after his death. Replaced Rheticus as editor of Copernicus' *De revolutionibus* and surreptitiously added an unsigned preface composed by himself and expounding his anti-Copernican fictionalism. Also edited Cardano's *Artis magnae*.

OSMOND, FLORIS (*b. Paris, France, 1849; d. St. Leu, Seine-et-Oise, France, 1912*), metallography.

Studied metallurgy at École Centrale des Arts et Manufactures; worked in industry before returning to Paris (1884) to conduct private research. Early studies on the heating and cooling of steel led to his theory that allotropic modifications of iron cause all the phenomena observed in the hardening of steel. Developed a method of polish attack for metallographic samples. Identified and named sorbite, austenite, and troostite.

OSTROGRADSKY, MIKHAIL VASILIEVICH (*b. Pashennaya [now in Poltava oblast], Russia, 1801; d. Poltava [now Ukrainian S.S.R.], 1862*), mathematics, mechanics.

Studied at Kharkov University and passed examinations for the candidate's degree (1820), but was denied his diploma on politico-religious grounds; he continued his studies in Paris (1822–27), achieving important work in mathematical physics and integral calculus and earning the friendship and respect of the senior French mathematicians. In 1828 he arrived in St. Petersburg; the same year he was elected a junior academician of the Academy of Sciences, and by 1832 was a full academician. His work at the Academy restored to it the brilliance in mathematics that it had won in the eighteenth century but had lost in the first quarter of the nineteenth. In addition to manifold activity at the Academy he did much to improve mathematical instruction in Russia through his textbooks, through his teaching at various institutes and colleges, and as chief inspector (from 1847) for the teaching of the mathematical sciences in military schools.

Ostrogradsky may be considered the founder of the Russian school of theoretical mechanics. His scientific work closely bordered upon the developments originating in the École Polytechnique in applied mathematics and in directly related areas of analysis. Topics to which he made significant contributions include the theories of heat and elasticity, the method of separating variables, boundary-value problems, the theory of multiple integrals, the theory of ordinary differential equations, the theory of algebraic functions and their integrals, probability theory, algebra, the principle of virtual displacements, and percussion theory. His most important investigations in mechanics dealt with generalizations of its basic principles and methods, especially the development of variational principles. Ostrogradsky's theorem (also called Gauss's theorem, Green's theorem, or Riemann's theorem) for the reduction of certain volume integrals to surface integrals, in modern terms, states that the volume integral of the divergence of a vector field A taken over any volume v is equal to the surface integral of A taken over the closed surface s surrounding the volume v. In applied science, his ballistics papers of 1839–41 stimulated the creation of the Russian school of ballistics in the second half of the nineteenth century.

OSTWALD, CARL WILHELM WOLFGANG (*b. Riga, Latvia, Russia, 1883; d. Dresden, Germany, 1943*), colloid chemistry, zoology.

Second child of Friedrich Wilhelm Ostwald. Studied at Leipzig, and taught there (from 1907) after two years in

Berkeley, California, as research assistant to Jacques Loeb; professor of colloid chemistry (from 1915) and director of the colloid chemistry division of the physical-chemical institute at Leipzig (from 1923). Editor of *Zeitschrift für Chemie und Industrie der Kolloide* (from 1907) and of *Kolloidchemische Beihefte* (from 1909). One of the founders of colloid chemistry. He defined colloids as disperse systems that are generally polyphasic and that possess particles 1–100 millimicrons in size. He discovered the rule of color dispersion in the optics of colloidal systems, explained colloids' irregular flow behavior, textural viscosity, and textural turbulence, and developed a method of foam analysis.

OSTWALD, FRIEDRICH WILHELM (*b. Riga, Latvia, Russia, 1853; d. Leipzig, Germany, 1932*), physical chemistry, color science.

Together with van't Hoff and Arrhenius, Ostwald established physical chemistry as a recognized and independent professional discipline and was its most important spokesman and organizer. His early reputation was based upon investigations into the fundamental principles governing chemical equilibrium and reactivity. A skillful experimentalist, he continued to give chemical affinity a central position in his research on electrolytic dissociation, electrical conductivity, mass action, catalysis, and reaction velocity. Ostwald received the Nobel Prize in chemistry in 1909 for his work in physical chemistry, and especially in recognition of his studies on catalysis. He was also one of the leading twentieth-century researchers in color science, and enriched chromatics through his quantitative theory of colors and his subjective chromatic system. Ostwald was at the same time an inspiring teacher who restored the significance of general chemistry and induced a generation of chemists in Europe and the Americas to adopt a receptive attitude toward theoretical and physical chemistry in their teaching and research.

In 1872 Ostwald enrolled at the University of Dorpat (now Tartu), where he studied chemistry under Carl Schmidt and Johann Lemberg and physics under Arthur von Oettingen; in 1878 he earned the doctorate in chemistry. In 1881 he was appointed professor of chemistry at the Riga Polytechnic Institute, where he quickly proved to be an outstanding teacher and began two important undertakings that made him widely known. First, in 1885–87 he wrote the ambitious *Lehrbuch der allgemeinen Chemie* (called "der grosse Ostwald" in order to distinguish it from "der kleine Ostwald" of 1889, *Grundriss der allgemeinen Chemie*). The work was a substantial contribution to the establishment of physical chemistry as a separate branch of the discipline and was published in a partial second edition between 1897 and 1902. Second, with van't Hoff, Ostwald began to publish *Zeitschrift für physikalische Chemie*, which became the mouthpiece of the Leipzig school of physical chemistry. This journal quickly established its importance and became the organizational link uniting physical chemists of various countries.

Ostwald expanded his activity as a teacher and researcher in 1887, when he accepted an appointment at Leipzig to the only chair of physical chemistry then existing in Germany. In 1898 he celebrated the official dedication of the new physical chemistry institute of the University of Leipzig, which became a training center for generations of physical chemists. Ostwald, however, remained there for barely a decade. As early as 1894 he had wished to be free of teaching and official duties; he retired to Grossbothen in 1906, after having been appointed as the first German exchange professor to Harvard University (academic year 1905–06).

Ostwald's achievements as a young chemist lay primarily in chemical affinity studies that, along with both general and inorganic chemistry, had been relatively neglected. In his *Volumchemische Studien über Affinität* (master's thesis, 1877) he determined the volume changes that take place during the neutralization of acids by bases in dilute solution. In his *Volumchemische und optisch-chemische Studien* (doctoral dissertation, 1878), he enlarged his investigations to include the determination of the coefficients of refraction of a large group of acid-base and other double decomposition reactions; he obtained values for chemical reactivity that confirmed those obtained by the specific-volume method, but felt that the optical method was less trustworthy. In addition, his chemical affinity studies were extended to incorporate the analysis of both homogeneous and heterogeneous reactions as a function of temperature. In this way Ostwald was able to attach specific numerical values to the term "affinity," which had long been referred to in the literature in a qualitative and often arbitrary way.

In his first teaching post (at Riga) Ostwald pursued the studies on chemical reaction kinetics with resolution. His *Studien zur chemischen Dynamik* (1881) treated the reaction velocity for the acid-catalyzed saponification of acetamides and the hydrolysis of esters. In 1885 he initiated a comprehensive program to redetermine, using Arrhenius' electrolytic conductivity method, the affinities of the acids he had studied earlier by other physical methods. He concluded that electrolytic conductivity measurements were far more elegant and less tedious than his own specific volume method. His experiments showed that for strong monobasic acids in aqueous solution, the molecular conductivity gradually increases with dilution and asymptotically approaches a maximum value at infinite dilution. Ostwald's dilution law (*Verdünnungsgesetz*), in its essentially modern form, was theoretically derived in 1888 and was supported with impressive experimental evidence the following year.

In 1891 Ostwald formulated a theory of acid-base indicators in which he used the principle of ionic equilibrium to account for the ratio of un-ionized weak acid (of one color) to ionized weak acid (of another color). Subsequent investigations, stimulated by Ostwald's contributions, revealed, as Hantzsch and his pupils showed in 1906, that the organic indicators were pseudo acids and pseudo bases—that is, nonelectrolytes susceptible to the formation of metallic derivatives by changing into acidic and basic isomers. The new views did not substantially alter the quantitative formulation of Ostwald's theory. The entire field encompassed by the theory of chemical reaction based on electrolytic dissociation, including indicator theory, was expounded in great detail in Ostwald's *Die wissenschaftlichen Grundlagen der analytischen Chemie* (1894), a work that revolutionized the teaching of analytical chemistry.

Important experimental work on catalytic processes was carried out in Ostwald's institute. This work is conveniently summarized in his paper "Über Katalyse" (1901). The most important aspects of the experimental contributions on this subject by Ostwald and his co-workers are the ones that treat the process of crystallization from super-saturated solution—for both homogeneous and heterogeneous reactions—and the effect of enzymes. The work on supersaturation and supercooling showed that a system moving from a less stable to a more stable state goes by stages to the one lying closest at hand, and not necessarily to the most stable of all possible states. This is known as Ostwald's law of stages.

After his retirement, Ostwald worked with great determination on the development of color science. Starting from color standardization, which around 1912 was a question of topical interest, he systematically investigated colors, developed a quantitative color theory, and produced color samples and coloring substances in his laboratory. From color standardization he turned to color harmony. Because he chose his color scales in accord with the characteristics of human perception—that is, they were logarithmically graded—he was able to construct harmonies, as in music. He enthusiastically set forth his views in *Harmonie der Farben* (1918), *Die Farbe* (1921–26), and *Harmonie der Formen* (1922).

During the last thirty years of his life, Ostwald spoke and wrote in a grandiloquent style in support of humanistic, educational, and cultural causes. In 1909 he published *Grosse Männer* and classified persons of genius into two broad types according to mental temperament: classicists and romanticists. He believed that mutual understanding among scholars was indispensable from a humanistic standpoint. In his *Forderung des Tages* (1910), dedicated to Arrhenius, he integrated his views on energetics with scientific methodology and systematics, psychology, scientific genius, general cultural problems, public instruction in the sciences, and the introduction of an international language (while at Harvard he had studied Esperanto, and later he created his own artificial language, Ido). He had a mania for reform movements. His *Der energetische Imperativ* (1912) was a rousing, prophetic declaration of the urgency for man to adopt internationalism, pacifism, and a systematic plan for the preservation of natural energy resources. In a similar vein, *Die Philosophie der Werte* (1913) was given over largely to a discussion of the second law of thermodynamics, its history, applications, and prognostic comments.

Ostwald strongly advocated the study of the history of science and frequently used historical materials in both his scientific and his more philosophical writings. His most important single work devoted to the history of science was *Elektrochemie. Ihre Geschichte und ihre Lehre* (1896), a book of more than 1,100 pages that exhibits Ostwald's complete command of the scientific literature on electrochemistry and allied areas. The monumental enterprise known as Ostwalds Klassiker der Exakten Wissenschaften began in 1889 with Helmholtz' 1847 work "Ueber die Erhaltung der Kraft"; 243 volumes had been published by 1938, and 256 volumes by 1977.

OTT, ISAAC (*b. Northampton County, Pa., 1847; d. Easton, Pa., 1916*), physiology.

Received B.A. and M.A. from Layafette College, and M.D. from University of Pennsylvania (1869); did postgraduate study at Leipzig, Würzburg, and Berlin. Held appointments in physiology at University of Pennsylvania

(1873–78), in biology at Johns Hopkins (1879–94), and in physiology at the Medico-Chirurgical College of Philadelphia (from 1894). Developed valuable methods in neurophysiology and discovered the heat-regulating center of the brain (1887); discovered the path and decussation of the sudorific, sphincter-inhibitory, and thermoinhibitory fibers in the spinal cord and the innervation of the sphincters; studied the physiological action of drugs.

OUDEMANS, CORNEILLE ANTOINE JEAN ABRAM (*b. Amsterdam, Netherlands, 1825; d. Arnhem, Netherlands, 1906*), medicine, botany, mycology.

M.D. from Leiden (1847); lecturer at clinical school of Rotterdam (1848–59); professor at the Athenaeum of Amsterdam (1859–96) and its first *rector magnificus* (from 1877). National expert on fungi of the Netherlands; his *Révision des champignons* (1892–97) and *Catalogue raisonné* (1904) are still standard works. In *Enumeratio systematica fungorum* (5 vols., 1919–24) he described all the known European parasitic fungi.

OUGHTRED, WILLIAM (*b. Eton, Buckinghamshire, England, 1575; d. Albury, near Guildford, Surrey, England, 1660*), mathematics.

Entered King's College, Cambridge, at fifteen (fellow, 1595; B.A., 1596; M.A., 1600); ordained in 1603 and served as a parish priest, pursuing mathematics in his spare time. His treatise on arithmetic and algebra (*Clavis mathematicae*, 1631) earned him wide recognition; it employed many symbols, of which those for multiplication and proportion are still used. In *Trigonometria* (1657), which included seven-place tables of logarithms and of sines, tangents, and secants, he used the abbreviations *s, t, se, sco, tco,* and *seco*. He invented the slide rule (as early as 1621) and claimed, along with his pupil Delamain, invention of the circular slide rule.

OUTHIER, RÉGINALD (*b. La Marre-Jousserans, near Poligny, France, 1694; d. Bayeux, France, 1774*), astronomy, cartography.

One of the many provincial amateur scientists who provided the Paris academicians with observations; correspondent of Jacques Cassini and later of Cassini de Thury. Invented (1727) a celestial globe showing the path of the sun and motions of the moon. Surveyed with Cassini (1733); participated in Academy's expedition to Lapland (1736–37), drew maps, and published a journal of the voyage (1744). Drew a highly accurate map of the Pleiades (1752). Reported to the Academy on eclipses, a transit of Venus (1761), and local weather.

OVERTON, CHARLES ERNEST (*b. Stretton, Cheshire, England, 1865; d. Lund, Sweden, 1933*), cell physiology, pharmacology.

Studied at University of Zurich (Ph.D., 1889); taught at Zurich (1890–1901), Würzburg (1901–07), and Lund (1907–30). Did pioneering work in plant cytology (1890–93), showing that the haploid chromosome number is characteristic of the whole gametophyte. Studied permeability of cells, found plant and animal cells to be similar; found a striking parallel between permeating powers of different substances and their relative fat solubility and formulated (1899) Overton's lipoid (or lipide) theory of plasma permeability, that the invisible plasma membranes are "impregnated" with fatlike substances; discussed (1896) active transport. Studied the relation between muscle irritability and passage of sodium ions. Observed high lipide solubility of narcotic agents.

OWEN, DAVID DALE (*b. New Lanark, Scotland, 1807; d. New Harmony, Ind., 1860*), geology.

Son of utopian Robert Owen. Studied chemistry under Andrew Ure in Glasgow; came to New Harmony in 1828, returned to London to study chemistry (1831–33), and studied medicine in Cincinnati (graduated 1837). State geologist of Indiana (1837); appointed to survey mineral lands of the Dubuque lead district (1839) and the Chippewa land district (1847); state geologist of Kentucky (1854), Arkansas (1857), and Indiana (1859). A superb field geologist and talented artist whose survey reports contain meticulous and accurate descriptions, reasonable analysis of origin, and wide correlation with American and foreign strata. Introduced European Paleozoic terminology to America. Wrote on paleontology, stratigraphy, mineralogy, structure, and economic geology. In Kentucky, he related certain diseases to soil and mineral types. First American to use the term "Carboniferous" in the present restricted sense.

OWEN, GEORGE (*b. Henllys, Pembrokeshire, Wales, 1552; d. 1613*), geology.

Eminent as a local historian and topographer. His "Description of Pembrokeshire" (1603) included an account of the occurrence of the (Carboniferous) limestone and coal measures of South Wales, tracing the course of the limestone across country, which was the first attempt to "map" a British geological formation, if only verbally.

OWEN, RICHARD (*b. Lancaster, England, 1804; d. Richmond Park, London, England, 1892*), comparative anatomy, vertebrate paleontology, geology.

Introduced to anatomy as an apprentice surgeon; studied in Edinburgh (1824–25) and at St. Bartholomew's Hospital, London; qualified for the Royal College of Surgeons (1826) and set up practice. Appointed assistant to William Clift to catalogue the Hunterian Collection; Hunterian professor (1836); and conservator of the Museum of the Royal College of Surgeons (succeeding Clift). As superintendent of natural history at the British Museum (1856–84) he planned the new Natural History Museum in South Kensington. After retirement he was made K.C.B.

Owen was a superb Cuvierian comparative anatomist who wrote quantities of detailed monographs and papers, making known many new organisms (both recent and fossil), helping to delineate several natural groups, and laying the bases for much later work by many investigators. Among other achievements he described the parasite that causes trichinosis (1835), elucidated the reproduction and taxonomic place of monotremes and marsupials, described Darwin's fossils from South America in the first volume of *The Zoology of the Voyage of H.M.S. "Beagle"* (1840), made a major study of teeth (*Odontography,* 1840–45), wrote a series of papers on flightless birds, and prepared an exhaustive *History of British Fossil Reptiles* (4 vols., 1849–84). Primates in general and anthropoid apes in particular were of early and lasting interest to Owen, especially in their relation to man. He separated man from the anthropoid apes into a separate subclass of Mammalia, the Archencephala, primarily on the basis of several supposed differences in the gross structure of their brains.

He is principally remembered as Huxley's antagonist in the debates over Darwinism (1860). He did not dispute the fact of evolution, but felt that Darwin's mechanism, natural selection, had not been demonstrated as adequate; he thought "an innate tendency to deviate from parental type" the most probable secondary cause of speciation (*On the Anatomy and Physiology of the Vertebrates,* 1866–68).

OZANAM, JACQUES (*b. Bouligneux, Bresse, France, 1640; d. Paris, France, 1717 [?]*), mathematics.

Ozanam was educated for the clergy but pursued mathematics, which he taught in Lyons and Paris. Wrote popular treatises and reference works on "useful and practical mathematics," and an extremely popular work on mathematical recreations (1694) which drew heavily on Bachet de Méziriac, Mydorge, Leurechon, and Daniel Schwenter and was later augmented and revised by Montucla.

OZERSKY, ALEKSANDR DMITRIEVICH (*b. Chernigov guberniya, Russia, 1813; d. St. Petersburg, Russia, 1880*), mining engineering, geology.

Graduated from Mining Cadet Corps and then taught there (1833–57); head of Altay mines (1857–64) and civilian governor of Tomsk; worked in Mining Department, St. Petersburg (from 1864). In his early work in chemical analysis he established the composition of a number of Russian minerals. In Transbaikalia he found that ore deposits do not depend upon the enclosing strata but are directly associated with intrusive igneous rocks, and he determined a pattern according to which all the deposits of Transbaikalia could be grouped into several isolated stretches. He was the first to compile a detailed sequence of Silurian strata of the Baltic provinces. A plutonist, he also admitted the possibility of alternating ascending and descending movements, suggesting that they be called oscillation movements. His translation (1845) of Murchison's *The Geology of Russia* included much new information.

PACCHIONI, ANTONIO (*b. Reggio nell' Emilia, Italy, 1665; d. Rome, Italy, 1726*), medicine.

Studied in his native town (M.D., 1688); practiced in Rome (1689–93), Tivoli (1693–99), and again in Rome. In anatomy, he was guided by Malpighi and collaborated with Lancisi, with whom he wrote the explanatory text to Eustachi's *Tabulae anatomicae* (1714). Explored the structure and functions of the dura mater; his *Dissertatio epistolaris de glandulis conglobatis durae meningis humanae* (1705) contains his description of the arachnoidal, or so-called Pacchioni, granulations.

PACINI, FILIPPO (*b. Pistoia, Italy, 1812; d. Florence, Italy, 1883*), anatomy, histology.

Graduated in surgery (1839) and in medicine (1840) from the University of Pisa; taught in Pisa and at the Lyceum in Florence (from 1847; professor and director of anatomical museum, 1849). Discovered the Pacini corpuscles (named by Koelliker, 1844) in 1831; although Abraham Vater had observed them in 1741, Pacini was

first to describe their distribution in the body, their microscopic structure, and their nerve connections. Also discovered the cholera vibria ("Osservazioni microscopiche e deduzioni patologiche sul cholera asiatico," 1854), which was rediscovered by Koch in 1884. Advocated the teaching of microscopic anatomy and published studies of the human retina and of the structure of bone, among others. Wrote on practical anatomy; developed (1870) a method of artificial respiration.

PACINOTTI, ANTONIO (*b. Pisa, Italy, 1841; d. Pisa, 1912*), electrophysics.

Graduated from University of Pisa (1861), where his father was a professor of mathematics and physics; taught at Florence, Bologna, and Cagliari before returning to the University of Pisa. Noted for the invention (reported in 1864) of a new form of armature that became a key element in the evolution from the magnetoelectric generator to the commercial self-excited dynamo during the next decade; the Pacinotti armature consisted of an iron ring with projecting teeth interspersed with coils which formed a closed series circuit with connections to a commutator (Gramme developed a similar design, apparently independently, by 1869).

PACIOLI, LUCA (*b. Sansepolcro, Italy, ca. 1445; d. Sansepolcro, 1517*), mathematics, bookkeeping.

Pacioli may have studied under Piero della Francesca, whose works Vasari accused him of plagiarizing. As a Franciscan friar and a teacher of mathematics, he lived in many of the cities of Italy and taught in court, university, and ecclesiastic settings. While at the court of Ludovico Sforza, duke of Milan, he met Leonardo da Vinci; in 1499 they journeyed together to Florence, where they shared quarters. Leonardo consulted Pacioli on mathematics, and drew the figures of solid bodies for the first part of *Divina proportione*. Pacioli made no original contribution to mathematics, but his encyclopedic *Summa de arithmetica . . .* (1494), written in Italian, enabled his countrymen to contribute to the advancement of algebra in the sixteenth century; "De computis et scripturis," contained in the *Summa*, was the first printed work setting out the "method of Venice," that is, double-entry bookkeeping. *Divina proportione* (1509), also in Italian, comprised a book on the golden section or divine proportion (the ratio obtained by dividing a line in extreme and mean ratio); a treatise on architecture, based on Vitruvius; and an Italian translation of Piero della Francesca's *De corporibus regularibus*. Also in 1509 Pacioli published his Latin translation of Euclid's *Elements*, based on Campanus (and vindicating him) but containing his own emendations and annotations. His extensive collection of mathematical recreational problems, "De viribus quantitatis," was not published.

PACKARD, ALPHEUS SPRING, JR. (*b. Brunswick, Me., 1839; d. Providence, R.I., 1905*), entomology.

Graduated from Bowdoin College (1861); earned M.D. from Maine Medical School (1864) while simultaneously studying under Louis Agassiz at Lawrence Scientific School. From 1864 to 1877 he moved frequently, writing, editing, and holding short appointments at various institutions and agencies; he was subsequently appointed professor of zoology and geology at Brown University.

Widely interested in zoology and geology, but his most enduring work was on invertebrate taxonomy, particularly of insects (*Monograph of the Bombycine Moths of North America* [3 vols., 1895–1914]). The first serious American student of insect embryology and one of the first to introduce the concept of comparative embryology. His *Cave Fauna of North America* (1888) was a pioneer masterpiece, combining taxonomy, anatomy, and evolution. Packard was a founder of the neo-Lamarckian movement.

PADOA, ALESSANDRO (*b. Venice, Italy, 1868; d. Genoa, Italy, 1937*), mathematical logic, mathematics.

Attended engineering school in Padua and graduated from University of Turin (1895); taught in secondary schools and lectured in universities. An effective popularizer of the Peano school of mathematical logic. The first to devise a method for proving that a primitive term of a theory cannot be defined within the system by the remaining primitive terms (1900).

PAGANO, GIUSEPPE (*b. Palermo, Sicily, 1872; d. Palermo, 1959*), physiology.

Received medical degree from University of Palermo (1895); honorary professor emeritus of human physiology at Palermo (1950), after an intermittent academic career. Discovered (1895) the physiological toxicity of blood for certain cellular elements. His systematic experimental exploration of the sensitivity of the heart and blood vessels (from 1897) revealed the existence of the carotid reflexes; he asserted that many of the phenomena previously attributed to direct stimulation of the encephalomedullary centers were of indirect origin, produced through the excitation of sensitive surfaces. His results were confirmed by L. Siciliano in 1900, but were slow to find acceptance.

PAINLEVÉ, PAUL (*b. Paris, France, 1863; d. Paris, 1933*), mathematics.

Graduated from École Normale Supérieure (1886); doctorate, 1887. Taught at Lille (1887–92), and then in various faculties in Paris (from 1892). Turned to politics (1910), created the Service des Inventions pour les Besoins de la Défense Nationale (1914), served as minister of war (1917). In mathematics, he introduced biuniform transformations of algebraic curves and surfaces; studied singular points of algebraic differential equations, defining new transcendentals and determining every equation of the second order and first degree whose critical points are fixed; and applied his results to analytical mechanics.

PAINTER, THEOPHILUS SHICKEL (*b. Salem, Va., 1889; d. Fort Stockton, Tex., 1969*), genetics, cytogenetics.

B.A., Roanoke College (1908); Ph.D., Yale (1913); postgraduate studies under Boveri at Würzburg. Taught at Yale (1914–16) and at University of Texas (from 1916; professor, 1922; acting president, 1944–46; president, 1946–52). Best known for introducing the use of the giant salivary gland chromosomes of fruit fly larvae into cytogenetic studies, demonstrating (1933) that Mendelian genes could be identified with specific bands on the chromosomes. Pioneered in structural analysis of human chromosomes and suggested ways of relating chromosomal aberrations to disease; it was his count of

the human karyotype that established the erroneous total of 48 (rather than 46), long believed to be correct.

PALEY, WILLIAM (*b. Peterborough, England, 1743; d. Lincoln, England, 1805*), natural theology.

A graduate (B.A., 1763; D.D., 1795) and fellow (1766) of Christ's College, Cambridge; Paley's career was more ecclesiastic than academic. He earned fame as a writer of textbooks (*Principles of Moral and Political Philosophy* [1782]; *Evidences of Christianity; Natural Theology* [1802]), which were used at Cambridge for several decades after his death and which brought him advancement in the church. *Natural Theology* is perhaps most significant for Paley's efforts to reconcile liberal orthodox Christianity with divine providence. His underlying belief was that the world is essentially a happy place. Nature was God and God was good; the proof of the goodness of God and Nature could be found in day-to-day experiences and in the efficiency of design and happiness of all creatures. His work helped to create the atmosphere so hostile to Charles Darwin in the 1850's and 1860's.

PALISA, JOHANN (*b. Troppau, Austrian Silesia [now Czechoslovakia], 1848; d. Vienna, Austria, 1925*), astronomy.

Studied at University of Vienna. Director of naval observatory at Pola (1871–83), where he invented the chronodeik, a small instrument for determining time by measuring equal heights of stars east and west of the meridian, and discovered 28 asteroids. Continued observation of asteroids at new observatory in Vienna (1883–1924), discovering 120 more and collaborating with Max Wolf (who was at Heidelberg) to determine many orbits. Published catalogs of 4,696 stars and, with Wolf, 210 sheets of photographic charts of the sky.

PALISSY, BERNARD (*b. La Capelle Biron, France, ca. 1510; d. Paris, France, ca. 1590*), natural history, hydrology.

Initially an artisan of stained glass, Palissy experimented for sixteen years to perfect a technique for making a "rustic" enameled earthenware that brought him fame and a modest fortune. He moved to Paris with a commission to decorate the new Tuileries palace; his public lectures on natural history (from 1575) attracted the most learned men in Paris. His two major books, *Recepte véritable* (1563) and *Discours admirables* (1580), dealt with a wide variety of topics. The views on hydrology and paleontology in the *Discours* are of particular interest: he was one of the few men of his century to have a correct notion of the origins of rivers and streams; he recognized the relation between fossils and living species and, in some cases, extinct ones, and was one of the first to hold a reasonably correct view of petrification. His classification of salts was nearly correct, and he suggested the concept of superposition for the development of sedimentary rocks.

PALLADIN, VLADIMIR IVANOVICH (*b. Moscow, Russia, 1859; d. Petrograd [now Leningrad], U.S.S.R., 1922*), biochemistry, plant physiology.

Graduated from Moscow University (1883; M.A., 1886); received doctorate (1889) from University of Warsaw. Taught at universities of Kharkov (1889) and St. Petersburg (1901); from 1914 he worked at the Academy of Sciences. Earned an international reputation with work on plant respiration: stated that oxidation-reduction processes, representing a chain of strictly coordinated enzyme reactions, are the basis of respiration; clarified the enzymatic details of the anaerobic and aerobic phases of respiration; discovered (1912) respiratory pigments as intermediaries between oxidases and carbohydrates, and found that they activate the hydrogen in carbohydrates, rather than oxygen in the air, with the aid of the enzyme reductase (dehydrogenase).

PALLAS, PYOTR SIMON (*b. Berlin, Germany, 1741; d. Berlin, 1811*), natural science, geography.

Received M.D. after studies at the Medical-Surgical Academy of Berlin and the universities of Halle, Göttingen, and Leiden. From 1767 he worked at the St. Petersburg Academy of Sciences; he participated in the "Academic expeditions" of 1768–74 and published *Reise durch verschiedenen Provinzen des russischen Reichs . . .* (1771–76), containing large quantities of empirical data. He studied the southern provinces of Russia (1793–94, pub. 1799–1801) and moved to the Crimea in 1795. His main goal was publication of *Zoographia Rosso-Asiatica . . .* (1811–31). He sought to advance from merely describing nature to finding the causal interrelationships and hidden regularities of natural phenomena. His research in comparative anatomy provided the foundations for animal taxonomy. He described hundreds of species of animals and plants; expressed interesting ideas on their relationships to the environment; and noted the boundaries and areas of their distribution, which led to the development of the science of biogeography. In geology, his was the first general hypothesis of the formation of mountains: the granite skeleton of the earth emerged as marine islands; volcanic processes caused the raising of mountains and the receding of the seas. His work was influential in the development of evolutionary ideas of nature.

PALMER, EDWARD (*b. Hockwold cum Wilton, England, 1831; d. Washington, D.C., 1911*), natural history.

Came to the U.S. in 1849; after serving as hospital steward on a naval expedition to Paraguay (1853–55) he attended the Homeopathic College in Cleveland, Ohio (1856–57), and then worked as a physician and surgeon at army posts and an Indian agency. From 1869 he devoted himself exclusively to collecting in Mexico and the western U.S., with intermittent governmental and private support; from 1878 he sold subscriptions to his sets of exsiccatae. His botanical specimens were often from areas seldom or never before visited by experienced collectors, and provided a basis for modern taxonomic and phytogeographic studies. His observations of Indian customs and collections of artifacts are among the more important sources of information on the ethnology and archaeology of western Indian tribes.

PAMBOUR, FRANÇOIS MARIE GUYONNEAU DE (*b. Noyon, France, 1795*), civil engineering.

Studied at École Polytechnique and entered the military. Published many papers, and two successful books: *Théorie de la machine à vapeur* (1837) and *Traité théorique et pratique des machines locomotives* (1835). He improved the theory of the steam engine by discarding Boyle's law in the calculation of work obtained, assuming that the steam

remained saturated and that its temperature varied, and using an empirical formula that involved two experimentally determined constants.

PANDER, CHRISTIAN HEINRICH (*b. Riga, Latvia, Russia, 1794; d. St. Petersburg, Russia, 1865*), embryology, anatomy, paleontology.

Studied at University of Dorpat (1812–14) under Burdach, at Berlin and Göttingen, and at Würzburg (M.D., 1817) under Döllinger. In his dissertation research on embryology (1817) he discovered the trilaminar structure of the chick blastoderm (a term he coined); his work inspired Baer's research, but he himself never pursued the subject further. His later work in St. Petersburg (Academy of Sciences, 1821–26; Zoological Academy, 1826–27; Mining Institute, from 1842) was on comparative osteology, geology, and paleontology. He developed a Lamarckian theory of animal evolution which was endorsed by Goethe and was known to Darwin through secondary sources.

PANETH, FRIEDRICH ADOLF (*b. Vienna, Austria, 1887; d. Mainz, Germany, 1958*), radiochemistry, inorganic chemistry.

Son of Joseph Paneth (discoverer of Paneth's granular cells). Studied at universities of Munich, Glasgow, and Vienna (Ph.D., 1910). Held positions at Vienna Institute for Radium Research (1912–18), Hamburg University (1919–22), University of Berlin (1922–29), University of Königsberg (1929–33), Imperial College of Science and Technology, London (1933–38), University of London (1938–39), University of Durham (1939–53), and Max Planck Institute for Chemistry, Mainz (from 1953). Contributed significantly to the development of radioactive tracer techniques, synthesized and characterized new metal hydrides, and experimentally verified the existence of free radicals in the thermal decomposition of organic compounds. Developed sensitive methods for determining trace amounts of helium and used them to date rocks and meteorites, to measure the rate of diffusion through glass, and to determine the composition of the stratosphere as a function of altitude up to 45 miles.

PANNEKOEK, ANTONIE (*b. Vaassen, Netherlands, 1873; d. Wageningen, Netherlands, 1960*), astronomy.

An amateur astronomer since his youth, Pannekoek studied astronomy at Leiden and worked for a time at the observatory there, became a teacher of Marxist theory in Germany and the Netherlands, and was named professor (1925) at the municipal university of Amsterdam where he founded a modest but very active astronomical institute. He made detailed drawings, and later extrafocal photographs, of the northern and southern Milky Way, studying our galaxy as a function of galactic longitude as well as latitude; discovered the typical groups of early stars that were later called associations; was first to apply "detailed analysis" to stellar atmospheres; and published (1928, with Minnaert) the first quantitative analysis of the solar flash spectrum. He also wrote on the history of astronomy and the evolution of man.

PAPANICOLAOU, GEORGE NICHOLAS (*b. Kími, Greece, 1883; d. Miami, Fla., 1962*), anatomy, cytology.

527

Received M.D. from University of Athens (1904) and studied biology at Jena, Freiburg, and Munich (Ph.D., 1910). Worked in pathology at New York Hospital (1913–61) and in anatomy at Cornell Medical College (1914–61); director of Miami Cancer Institute (now Papanicolaou Cancer Research Institute) from November 1961 until his death. Developed the Papanicolaou smear, or "Pap test," for the cytologic diagnosis of cancer, especially cancer of the uterus, as an extension of his technique for studying the estrous cycle in laboratory animals via cytologic cycles in vaginal discharge. He first reported the test in 1928, but it gained clinical acceptance only after publication of *Diagnosis of Uterine Cancer by the Vaginal Smear* (1943, with Herbert Traut).

PAPIN, DENIS (*b. Blois, France, 1647; d. London* [?], *England, ca. 1712*), technology.

M.D., University of Angers (1669). Lived intermittently in Paris (1669–75, 1680), where he performed experiments under Huygens' direction (*Nouvelles expériences du vuide,* 1674); in London (1675–80, 1684–87), where he worked with Robert Boyle and at the Royal Society; in Venice (1681–84); in Marburg (1687–95); and at the court of the landgrave of Hesse, in Kassel (1695–1707). His technical achievements included an air pump; the "steam digester," a pressure cooker for which he invented a safety valve that was to be of use in the development of steam power; and a single-cylinder steam pump (1690), in which water was both boiled and condensed in a tube beneath the piston, atmospheric pressure forcing the piston down again.

PAPPUS OF ALEXANDRIA (*b. Alexandria, fl.* A.D. *300–350*), mathematics, astronomy, geography.

In the silver age of Greek mathematics Pappus stands out as an accomplished and versatile geometer. His treatise known as the *Synagoge* or *Collection* is a chief, and sometimes the only, source for our knowledge of his predecessors' achievements.

The *Collection* is in eight books, perhaps originally in twelve, of which the first and part of the second are missing. That Pappus was an Alexandrian is affirmed by the titles of his surviving books and also by an entry in the *Suda Lexicon.* The dedication of the seventh and eighth books to his son Hermodorus provides the sole detail known of his family life. Only one of Pappus' other works has survived in Greek, and that in fragmentary form—his commentary on Ptolemy's *Syntaxis* (the *Almagest*). A commentary on book X of Euclid's *Elements,* which exists in Arabic, is generally thought to be a translation of the commentary that Pappus is known to have written, but some doubts may be allowed. A geographical work, *Description of the World,* has survived in an early Armenian translation.

PARACELSUS, THEOPHRASTUS PHILIPPUS AUREOLUS BOMBASTUS VON HOHENHEIM (*b. Einsiedeln, Switzerland, ca. 1493; d. Salzburg, Austria, 1541*), chemistry, medicine, natural philosophy, cosmology, theology, occultism, iatrochemistry.

"Paracelsus," a nickname dating from about 1529, may denote "surpassing Celsus"; it might also represent a latinization of "Hohenheim," or even refer to his authorship of "para [doxical]" works that overturned tradition.

Paracelsus received his early education—particularly in mining, mineralogy, botany, and natural philosophy—from his father who practiced medicine from 1502–34. He was later taught by several bishops and apparently by Johannes Trithemius, abbot of Sponheim and a famous exponent of the occult, who was also in contact with Heinrich Cornelius Agrippa von Nettesheim. Paracelsus did practical work in the Fugger mines of Hutenberg, near Villach, and in those of Siegfried Fueger at Swaz. It is possible that he took a lower medical degree at Ferrara, as may be borne out by his subsequent service as a military surgeon.

Paracelsus led an unsettled life, traveling to various cities and towns of central Europe in search of medical work. When he was able to secure positions (such as municipal physician and professor of medicine at Basel, 1527–28) he soon lost them, due to his outspoken nonconformity. He was an angry man, committed to the reformation of religion and society. His wholesale condemnation of traditional science and medicine found its parallel in his rough behavior and in his unwillingness to make concessions to custom and authority. His works might at times have appeared to be the ravings of a megalomaniac, enjoining the whole learned world to follow him in new paths. His ideas—those of a naturalist physician, spiritualist and symbolist thinker, and passionate fighter against perceived evil—are reflected in the contradictory interpretations that posterity has placed upon his work.

Only a few of Paracelsus' works were published during his lifetime. Among these were some astrological-mantic forecasts; his critical appraisal of the treatment of syphilis by guaiacum (*Vom Holtz Guaiaco gründlicher heylung* [Nuremberg, 1529]); a related treatise on the "impostures" committed therein (*Von der Französischen kranckheit Drey Bücher* [Nuremberg, 1530]); a booklet on Bad Pfäfers; and the *Grosse Wundartzney* (Augsburg, 1536). Most of his writings came to light in the decades following his death, and their publication reached a peak in about 1570 with the *Archidoxis,* a handbook of Paracelsian chemistry that went through many editions.

Among Paracelsus' practical achievements was his conservative management of wounds and chronic ulcers, and his recognition of the superiority of chemicals taken internally over the traditional, mostly herbal, internal medicines. His description of miners' diseases was the first to identify silicosis and tuberculosis as occupational hazards. He was also the first to recognize the congenital form of syphilis, and to distinguish it from postpartum infection. He studied visceral—notably osseous and nervous—syphilis in its protean manifestations, and differentiated it from hydrargyrosis, the morbid syndrome caused by toxic doses of mercury. (He did, however, regard syphilis as a specific modification of other diseases, rather than as a separate entity.) He also gave the first purely medical account of dancing mania and chorea, proposing a natural explanation in place of previous supernatural theories, and described the symptoms of hysteria, including hysterical blindness. Paracelsus further drew the connection between cretinism and goiter, which he identified as being endemic and related to the mineral content of drinking water. He recognized the significance of acid in mineral waters as a powerful aid to gastric digestion.

Chief among Paracelsus' contributions to medical theory was his new concept of disease. He demolished the ancients' notion of disease as an upset of humoral balance—either an excess *(hyperballonta)* or an insufficiency *(elleiponta)*—or as a displacement or putrefaction of humors, and emphasized instead the external cause of a disease, its selection of a particular locus, and its consequent seat. This new idea of disease led him to new modes of therapy. For Galenic remedies derived from plants, he substituted specifics, often applied on homeopathic principles. Here his notion of "signatures" came into play, in the selection of herbs that in color and shape resembled the affected organ. His search for such specifics led him to attempt to isolate the *quinta essentia* of each substance; his method was thus to separate drugs into their component parts, rather than to compound them as the ancients had done.

In nontherapeutic chemistry Paracelsus described new products arising from the combination of metals, devised a method of concentrating alcohol by freezing out its watery component, and found a new way to prepare aquafortis. He was the first to attempt to construct a chemical system. In the *Archidoxis* he grouped chemicals according to their susceptibility to similar chemical processes, although it has been stated (and disputed) that many of the chemicals that he believed to be discrete entities were in fact identical distillates containing nitric or hydrochloric acid.

Paracelsus' general natural philosophy is spiritualist. The important forces in nature are the invisible "spirits," such as the *quintae essentiae;* these are the life substances of objects, and the *magus* may know how to extract them, particularly from herbs and chemicals. Earth, air, and fire also occur in the Paracelsian world, not in the ancient sense of elements, but rather in the Platonic and cabalistic sense of mothers; they are the wombs that give birth to groups of objects, each specific to its source. The three Paracelsian principles—salt, sulfur, and mercury—are neither elements nor matter, but rather principles within matter that condition the state in which matter can occur. Salt, responsible for the solid state, is of particular importance in medicine: it represents a state of fixation, of coagulation and sedimentation, and appears in the pathological form of tartar.

Paracelsus made a distinct contribution to medicine and chemistry in his nomenclature for substances that were already known—for example, he substituted the word "alcohol" (which had previously meant any subtle substance in dispersion) for "spirit of wine" and "synovia" for the "gluten" contained within the joints.

In sum, Paracelsus was a great doctor and an able chemist. His views encompassed both astrological superstitions and quite conspicuously modern descriptions of diseases, together with shrewd appraisals of their nature and causes. He remained ignorant of a number of important surgical methods that were practiced widely by his contemporaries and, although repudiating astrological beliefs in many instances, he nonetheless incorporated them into his own work and added multifarious mantic lore of his own.

PARAMEŚVARA (*b. Ālattūr, Kerala, India, ca. 1380; d. ca. 1460*), astronomy.

Author of commentaries on standard astronomical texts; of revisions of eclipse-computation techniques, based on his own observations (which extended from 1393 to 1432); and of *Dṛgganita* (1431), a set of new parameters of planetary motions modifying those of the *parahita* system of Āryabhaṭa I.

PARDIES, IGNACE GASTON (*b. Pau, France, 1636; d. Paris, France, 1673*), physics.

Educated by the Jesuits; ordained in 1663, admitted to the order in 1665; taught at Bordeaux (1656–60, 1668–70), La Rochelle (1666–68), and the Collège Clermont, Paris (1670–73). Was continually obliged by his superiors to compromise his true views on philosophy and science, to the point that they cannot be established with certainty. In *Discours du mouvement local* (1670), *Élémens de géométrie* (1671), and *La statique ou la science des forces mouvantes* (1673) he strove for the most economical axioms obtained through rational reflection on empirical data. His thoughtful correspondence aided the pioneers of physics, such as Newton and Huygens, to clarify difficult points of their theories.

PARÉ, AMBROISE (*b. Laval, Mayenne, France, 1510 [?]; d. Paris, France, 1590*), surgery.

Apprentice to a provincial barber-surgeon, then house surgical student at Hôtel-Dieu, Paris. Served as military surgeon (from *ca.* 1536), as *chirurgien ordinaire* to Henry II, and as *premier chirurgien* to Charles IX and to Henry III. Revolutionized the treatment of gunshot wounds by substituting a "digestive" dressing for cautery (*La méthode de traicter les playes . . .*, 1545). Advocated ligature of blood vessels during amputations and devised a hemostat for this purpose; revived the ancient technique of podalic version for difficult obstetric deliveries. His many publications, written in the vernacular and also translated into both Latin and modern languages, circulated throughout Europe and had a lasting influence.

PARENAGO, PAVEL PETROVICH (*b. Ekaterinodar [now Krasnodar], Russia, 1906; d. Moscow, U.S.S.R., 1960*), astronomy.

Studied and worked at University of Moscow (graduated, 1929; doctorate, 1935; professor of astronomy, 1938; head of department of stellar astronomy, 1940). Studied variable stars, discovered statistical relationships of their physical and kinematic properties to their spatial distribution, and used them to study galactic structure. Developed a method of taking into account the absorption of light in galactic space by particles of interstellar dust; published a new, evolutionary meaning for the concept of subsystems of various objects in the galaxy and obtained fundamental quantitative properties of these subsystems; developed a new theory of galactic potential, and the theory of the galactic orbit of stars and the sun.

PARENT, ANTOINE (*b. Paris, France, 1666; d. Paris, 1716*), physics.

Studied law and then mathematics, attending the lectures of La Hire and Sauveur; from 1699, an *élève* at the Académie des Sciences. Wrote anti-Cartesian, utilitarian works on astronomy, cartography, chemistry, biology, sensationalist psychology and epistemology, music, mathematics, and mechanics (particularly strength of materials and the effects of friction on motion). His most comprehensive publication, *Essais et recherches de mathématiques et de physique* (3 vols., 1713), included a detailed critique of Descartes's *Principia philosophiae.* In describing the conditions of stress on a loaded beam, Parent first recognized the existence of a shear stress (1713).

PARKHURST, JOHN ADELBERT (*b. Dixon, Ill., 1861; d. Williams Bay, Wis., 1925*), astronomy.

Attended Wheaton College (1878–81); graduated from Rose Polytechnic Institute (B.S., 1886; M.S., 1897). Initially a businessman and amateur astronomer, he went to Yerkes Observatory in 1898 as a volunteer and was employed there from 1900 (associate professor, 1919). His specialty was stellar photometry, both visual and photographic; "Yerkes Actinometry" (1912) contains his determination of the visual and photographic magnitudes, color indexes, and spectral classes of all stars brighter than 7.5 between $+73°$ north declination and the celestial north pole.

PARKINSON, JAMES (*b. Hoxton Square, London, England, 1755; d. London, 1824*), medicine, paleontology.

After a period of political crusading, he began (1799) a series of popular medical works aimed toward improvement of the general health and well-being of the population; he also wrote treatises of interest to the profession: a work on gout (1805), perhaps the earliest English description of a perforated and gangrenous appendix with peritonitis (1812), and *An Essay on the Shaking Palsy* (1817). In the essay he gave the classic clinical description of the illness now known as Parkinson's disease: "Involuntary tremulous motion, with lessened muscular power, in parts not in action and even when supported; with a propensity to bend the trunk forwards, and to pass from a walking to a running pace: the senses and intellect being uninjured." A side interest in geology and paleontology led to his *Chemical Pocket-Book* (1799); *Organic Remains of a Former World* (3 vols., 1804–11), with many plates that were later republished by Mantell; and *Outlines of Oryctology* (1822). He theorized that coal and peat originated from plants by "bituminous fermentation"; he opposed evolution theory, favoring the idea of successive creations. A founder (1807) of the Geological Society of London.

PARKINSON, SYDNEY (*b. Edinburgh, Scotland, ca. 1745; d. at sea, 1771*), natural history drawing.

An extremely gifted and versatile draftsman and colorist, who worked with Joseph Banks from 1767 and accompanied him on the *Endeavour* (1768–71); during the voyage he made nearly 1,000 drawings of plants, about 300 of animals, and some 200 topographical and ethnographical drawings. He also recorded Polynesian and other vocabularies, and listed eighty-one Tahitian plants with their economic uses.

PARMENIDES OF ELEA (*b. ca. 515* B.C.*; d. after 450* B.C.), natural philosophy.

The thought of Parmenides, which he expressed in a poem, has come to us through citations by Simplicius and through the comments of Plato, Aristotle, Theophrastus, and the doxographers. He attempted to apply the exigencies of logical proofs to thought and its object, and concluded that logic did not permit the existence of non-being, and that that which is (being) must be ungenerated, imperishable, homogeneous, changeless, immovable, complete, and unique; thus mortals' opinions about the phenomenal world, and the change therein, are meaningless, since they refer to something that has no existence whatever.

PARMENTIER, ANTOINE-AUGUSTIN (*b. Montdidier, France, 1737; d. Paris, France, 1813*), chemistry, nutrition, agriculture, public health, pharmacy.

A military pharmacist who had attended the lectures of Nollet, Bernard de Jussieu, and G.-F. Rouelle, Parmentier was deeply interested in food chemistry and nutrition; his earliest study (1771) was on the chemical and nutritive constituents of the potato, which he promoted as a food crop. He worked on formulating cheap and nutritious soups for the poor; studied the technology of bread-making and helped to found (1780) the first government-sponsored school of baking in France; analyzed wheat and flour (1776), chestnuts (1780), milk (1790 and 1799), and chocolate (1786 and 1803); and studied the preservation and adulteration of food and grain. In public health, he was concerned with water quality, cesspools, and exhumations, and worked to provide free smallpox vaccinations to the poor. Author of *Économie rurale et domestique* (6 vols., 1788–93); contributor to *Cours complet d'agriculture* and to *Nouveau dictionnaire d'histoire naturelle.* A founding member of the Société d' Encouragement pour l'Industrie Nationale.

PARNAS, JAKUB KAROL (*b. Tarnopol, Poland [now Ukrainian S.S.R.], 1884; d. Moscow, U.S.S.R., 1949*), biochemistry.

Studied at universities of Berlin, Strasbourg, Zurich, and Munich (Ph.D., 1907). Taught chemistry at Strasbourg (1913) and physiological chemistry at Warsaw (1916–19) and Lvov (1920–41); head of the Biological and Medical Chemistry Institute of the Soviet Academy of Medical Sciences, Moscow (from 1943). Did influential work on muscle metabolism: discovered the phosphorolysis of glycogen, and, by establishing reaction sequences linking the metabolism of carbohydrates with that of phosphorus, initiated the method of studying life processes now characteristic of molecular biology. Was one of the first to apply P^{32} to biochemical investigations (1937): by studying the metabolism of muscles in vitro he established the enzymatic pathway sometimes known as the Embden, Meyerhof, and Parnas (EMP) scheme.

PARSEVAL DES CHÊNES, MARC-ANTOINE (*b. Rosières-aux-Salines, France, 1755; d. Paris, France, 1836*), mathematics.

Little is known of Parseval's life or work. The second of his five memoirs presented to the Académie des Sciences contains the famous Parseval theorem on the summation of infinite series (1799); in later memoirs he applied his theorem to the solution of differential equations suggested by Lagrange and d'Alembert. It was taken up by Lacroix in 1800 and shortly thereafter by Prony and Poisson.

PARSONS, WILLIAM, third Earl of Rosse (*b. York, England, 1800; d. Monkstown, Ireland, 1867*), astronomy.

Attended Trinity College, Dublin (1818–19), and graduated from Magdalen College, Oxford (1822). While active as an administrator and public servant, Parsons (styled Lord Oxmantown until the death of his father, 1841) made important contributions to astronomical instrumentation, particularly the design and construction of large telescopes. He succeeded in casting a six-foot metal reflector which he incorporated into the "Leviathan of Parsonstown," a telescope with a focal length of fifty-four feet; with this telescope he was able to make detailed studies of nebulae, and he was the first to detect the spiral nature of some nebulae. He also took some of the earliest lunar photographs.

PARTINGTON, JAMES RIDDICK (*b. Bolton, Lancashire, England, 1886; d. Weaverham, Cheshire, England, 1965*), chemistry, dissemination of knowledge.

Remembered primarily for his outstanding last work, *A History of Chemistry* (4 vols., 1961–70), Partington studied chemistry at the University of Manchester, did research under Nernst in Berlin, was knighted for work on the purification of water and the oxidation of nitrogen for the Ministry of Munitions during World War I, and continued research on the specific heats of gases as professor of chemistry at Queen Mary College, London University (1919–51). He also wrote numerous chemical textbooks.

PASCAL, BLAISE (*b. Clermont-Ferrand, Puy-de-Dôme, France, 1623; d. Paris, France, 1662*), mathematics, mechanical computation, physics, epistemology.

The young Pascal began his scientific studies about 1635 with the reading of Euclid's *Elements*. In 1639, not yet sixteen, he began to participate in the activities of Mersenne's academy. In that year Girard Desargues had just published his *Brouillon project d'une atteinte aux événemens des rencontres du cone avec un plan*. Grasping the significance of Desargues's new conception of conics, Pascal adopted the basic ideas of the *Brouillon project*. As early as June 1639 he made his first great discovery, that of a property equivalent to the theorem now known as Pascal's "mystic hexagram"; according to it, the three points of intersection of the pairs of opposite sides of a hexagon inscribed in a conic are collinear.

In 1640 he wrote *Essay pour les coniques*, a pamphlet, of which only a few copies were published. A plan for further research, illustrated with statements of several typical propositions that he had already discovered, the *Essay* constituted the outline of a great treatise on conics that he had just conceived and begun to prepare. In 1648 Pascal obtained a purely geometric definitive general solution to the celebrated problem of Pappus. In 1654 he indicated that he had nearly completed the treatise which was never published. It seems that only Leibniz saw it in manuscript, and the most precise details known about the work were provided by him. Although the few elements of Pascal's treatise preserved by Leibniz do not provide a complete picture of its contents, they are sufficient to show the richness and clarity of Pascal's conceptions once he had become fully aware of the power of projective methods.

Anxious to assist his father (Étienne Pascal), whose duties entailed a great deal of accounting, Pascal next sought to mechanize the two elementary operations of arithmetic, addition and subtraction. Toward the end of 1642 he began a project of designing a machine that would reduce these operations to the simple movements of gears. After having constructed, in his words, "more than fifty models, all different," he finally produced the definitive model in 1645. He himself organized the manufacture and sale of the machine. This activity is the context of Pascal's second publication.

In October 1646, in Rouen, Pascal and his father assisted Pierre Petit in repeating Torricelli's experiment on the barometric vacuum. At the end of November 1646 Petit described the event in a letter to Pierre Chanut. Meanwhile, Pascal, seeking to arrive at firm conclusions, had repeated the experiment in various forms, asserting that the results contradicted the doctrine of the *horror vacui*. In early 1647 he conducted a series of further experiments with water and wine, using tubes of different shapes, some as long as twelve meters, affixed to the masts of ships; these experiments became known in Paris in the spring of 1647. Gassendi wrote the first commentary on them, and Mersenne and Roberval undertook their own experiments. The first printed account of the entire group of Pascal's experiments was *Discours sur le vide* by P. Guiffart, of Rouen, written in April 1647 and published in August of that year. Pascal also wrote a thirty-two-page pamphlet published in October 1647 as *Expériences nouvelles touchant le vide*. In this "abridgment" of a larger work that he planned to write, Pascal admitted that his initial inspiration derived from the Italian barometric experiment and stated that his primary goal was to combat the idea of the impossibility of the vacuum. From his experiments he had deduced the existence of an apparent vacuum, but he asserted that the existence of an absolute vacuum was still an unconfirmed hypothesis.

Pascal also conceived one of the variants of the famous experiment of the vacuum within the vacuum, designed to verify the hypothesis of the column of air. He seems, however, to have expected a still better confirmation of the hypothesis from a program of simultaneous barometric observations at different altitudes (at Clermont-Ferrand and at the summit of Puy de Dôme), the execution of which he entrusted to his brother-in-law, Périer. One of these observations, now known as the "Puy de Dôme experiment," was carried out on 19 September 1648. Pascal immediately published a detailed, twenty-page account of it, *Récit de la grande expérience de l'équilibre des liqueurs . . . .*

At the beginning of 1649 Périer, following Pascal's instructions, began an uninterrupted series of barometric observations designed to ascertain the possible relationship between the height of a column of mercury at a given location and the state of the atmosphere. The *expérience continuelle*, which was a forerunner of the use of the barometer as an instrument in weather forecasting, lasted until March 1651 and was supplemented by parallel observations made at Paris and Stockholm. Pascal continued working on a major treatise on the vacuum; but only a few fragments, dating from 1651, have survived.

Pascal soon put aside his great treatise on the vacuum in order to write a shorter but more synthetic work. Divided into two closely related parts, this work is devoted to the laws of hydrostatics and to the demonstration and description of the various effects of the weight of air. It was completed about the beginning of 1654 and marked the end of his active research in physics. It was published posthumously by Périer, along with several appendices, in 1663 as *Traités de l'équilibre des liqueurs et de la pesanteur de la masse de l'air* . . . . The fruit of several years of observations, experiments, and reflection, it is a remarkable synthesis of new knowledge and theories elaborated since the work of Stevin and Galileo.

In 1654 Pascal not only did the last refining of his treatises on geometry and physics but also conducted his principal studies on arithmetic, combinatorial analysis, and the calculus of probability. This work can be seen in his correspondence with Fermat and his *Traité du triangle arithmétique.*

Unsatisfied by his worldly life and intense scientific activity, Pascal was drawn to religious concerns. He abandoned his scientific work in order to devote himself to meditation and religious activity and to assist the Jansenists in their battle against many enemies, particularly the Jesuits. Working anonymously, between 13 January 1656 and 24 March 1657 he composed the eighteen *Lettres provinciales* with the assistance of his friends from Port-Royal, Antoine Arnauld and Pierre Nicole. A masterpiece of polemic, this eminent contribution to the debate then agitating Christian doctrine was first published as a collection in 1657 under the pseudonym Louis de Montalte. This unfinished project was the source of several posthumously published writings, the most important being the *Pensées,* published in 1670. The object of numerous commentaries and penetrating critical studies, this basic work fully displays Pascal's outstanding philosophical and literary talents.

Around 1657, at the request of Arnauld, Pascal prepared a work entitled *Éléments de géométrie,* of which there remain only a few passages concerning methodology: the brief "Introduction à la géométrie," preserved among Leibniz's papers [18]; and two fragments, "De l'esprit géométrique" and "De l'art de persuader." During 1658 and the first months of 1659 Pascal devoted most of his time to perfecting the "theory of indivisibles," a forerunner of the methods of integral calculus. This new theory enabled him to study problems involving infinitesimals: calculations of areas and volumes, determinations of centers of gravity, and rectifications of curves.

At the beginning of 1658 Pascal believed that he had perfected the calculus of indivisibles by refining his method and broadening its field of application. Persuaded that in this manner he had discovered the solution to several infinitesimal problems relating to the cycloid or *roulette,* he decided to challenge other mathematicians to solve these problems. In an unsigned circular distributed in June 1658, he stated the conditions of the contest and set its closing date at 1 October. In further unsigned circulars and pamphlets, issued between July 1658 and January 1659, he modified or specified certain of the conditions and announced the results. He also responded to the criticism of some participants and sought to demonstrate the importance and the originality of his own solutions. Most of the leading mathematicians of the time followed the contest with interest. At the end of the contest Pascal published his own solutions to some of the original problems and to certain problems that had been added in the meantime. In December 1658 and January 1659 he brought out, under the pseudonym A. Dettonville, four letters setting forth the principles of his method and its applications to various problems concerning the cycloid, as well as to such questions as the quadrature of surfaces, cubature of volumes, determination of centers of gravity, and rectification of curved lines. In February 1659 these four pamphlets were collected in *Lettres de A. Dettonville contenant quelques-unes de ses inventions de géométrie* . . . . Pascal's outstanding work in this field marked an important stage in the transition from the calculus of indivisibles to integral calculus.

PASCAL, ÉTIENNE (*b. Clermont-Ferrand, France, 1588; d. Paris, France, 1651*), mathematics.

Father of Blaise Pascal. A public official, Pascal settled in Paris (1631–38) and devoted himself to his son's education while gaining a reputation as a talented mathematician and musician. Frequented "Mersenne's academy" and was in contact with Roberval, Desargues, and Mydorge. Introduced "Pascal's limaçon" (named by Roberval), the conchoid of a circle with respect to one of its points, to be applied to the trisection of an angle. Participated with his son and P. Petit (1646) in the first repetition in France of Torricelli's experiment.

PASCH, MORITZ (*b. Breslau, Germany [now Wrocław, Poland], 1843; d. Bad Homburg, Germany, 1930*), mathematics.

Studied mathematics under Heinrich Schroeter at Breslau and under Weierstrass and Kronecker at Berlin; professor (from 1875) and administrator at University of Giessen. The axiomatic method as it is understood today was initiated by Pasch in his *Vorlesungen über neuere Geometrie* (1882). It consists in isolating from a given study certain notions that are left undefined and certain theorems that are accepted without proof, and deriving all other notions and theorems from these using logical arguments; the initial notions and theorems should be founded on observations. "Pasch's axiom" states that in a plane, if a line meets one side of a triangle, then it meets another.

PASCHEN, LOUIS CARL HEINRICH FRIEDRICH (*b. Schwerin, Mecklenburg, 1865; d. Potsdam, Germany, 1947*), experimental physics.

Paschen, one of the greatest experimental spectroscopists of his time, came from a family of German officers with scientific ability. He obtained his doctorate (1888) under August Kundt at Strasbourg, with research that established "Paschen's law": that the sparking voltage depends only on the product of the gas pressure and the distance between the electrodes—one of the first and most important of the numerous scaling laws in this field. He investigated electrolytic potentials as Hittorf's assistant in Münster (1888–91), and then went to Hannover where he assisted Heinrich Kayser; he remained at Hannover as lecturer in physics and photography until 1901, when he became professor of physics at Tübingen. His last post was the presidency of the Physikalisch-Technische Reichsanstalt in Berlin (1924, succeeding Nernst), from which he was ousted by Stark in 1933; he was also president of the Deutsche Physikalische Gesellschaft (1925–27), and lectured at the University of Berlin.

His ten years in Hannover were largely spent in bolometric studies, in an effort to clarify Kirchhoff's function; corrected Rubens' measurements of the dispersion of fluorite, determined the infrared absorption by carbon dioxide and water vapor (his results remained in 1913 the strongest evidence for Bjerrum's quantum theory of molecular absorption), and demonstrated that heat alone could bring gases to radiate. By 1894 he had evidence that $\lambda_{max} \cdot T =$ constant, "or: the frequency of the main thermal vibrations of the molecular parts of an absolutely black body is proportional to the absolute temperature" By 1896 he had found $I = c_1 \lambda^{-\alpha} \exp(-c_2 / \lambda T)$ with $\alpha = 5.5$, for an iron oxide surface; Wien immediately published his derivation of the same law, with $\alpha = 5$, and by 1898 Paschen supported this value.

Paschen's remarkable work on spectral series began in Hannover, where he and Runge achieved instant fame for their elucidation of the helium lines (1895), and resumed in Tübingen. He discovered the "Paschen series" of hydrogen lines (1908) by looking at the frequencies suggested by Ritz on the basis of his new combination principle. With his students he used the Zeeman effect, which Thomas Preston had shown (1899) to be characteristic within series, to identify series lines; the large number of apparent exceptions to Preston's rule led Paschen and Ernst Back to discovery of the "Paschen-Back effect": that in sufficiently strong magnetic fields all the splitting patterns transform themselves into the "normal" pattern of a single line rather than showing the superposition of splittings of the components of a group. In 1916 he published his important data on the fine structure of the helium lines predicted by Sommerfeld's relativistic extension of Bohr's theory. During Paschen's last six years there (1918–24) Tübingen was the major center of atomic spectroscopy in Germany. Paschen's own outstanding successes were the ordering of the neon spectrum—almost 1,000 lines—into spectral series; the evocation of the missing combinations between complex spectral terms by magnetic fields of appropriate strength; and the first analysis of the spectra of an atom in its doubly ionized, as well as its neutral, and singly ionized states. In all his work Paschen accepted, as few other experimentalists did, the priorities and guidance of atomic theorists.

PASTEUR, LOUIS (*b. Dole, Jura, France, 1822; d. Château Villeneuve-1'Étang, near Paris, France, 1895*), crystallography, chemistry, microbiology, immunology.

Pasteur's work was characterized by clear thinking, extraordinary experimental skill, and extreme tenacity of purpose. He was ambitious and opportunistic, which in part accounts for his concern with pursuing the practical consequences of his findings. By taking this direction, he greatly benefitted both science and humanity. But he later expressed regret at abandoning his youthful research. His early, relatively little-known investigations into the relationship between optical activity, crystalline structure, and chemical composition in organic compounds were profound and original; they opened the way to a consideration of the disposition of atoms in space; his memoirs here constitute founding documents of stereochemistry; if he had continued in his attempt to resolve the relationship between asymmetry and life, he might indeed have become the Newton or Galileo of biology.

Of a *petit bourgeois* family (his father was a tanner), Pasteur as a young boy was distinguished only by artistic talent; but at the Collège d'Arbois his enthusiasm for

studies was eventually aroused. Despite setbacks, he entered the École Normale Supérieure in Paris (1843) as a science student; he remained there as a *préparateur* in chemistry while studying for his doctorate (1847).

Pasteur's interest in optical activity, asymmetry, and crystal structure had emerged by 1847; it was intensified by his association with Auguste Laurent, with whom he worked (1846–47). In particular, Pasteur studied tartaric acid and paratartaric, or racemic, acid. J.-B. Biot and Eilhard Mitscherlich had already established that aqueous solutions of tartaric acid and its derivatives rotate the plane of polarized light to the right, whereas the paratartrates are optically inactive; Mitscherlich had claimed that in the case of the sodium-ammonium double salts the tartrates and paratartrates were completely identical, even in crystalline form and atomic arrangement, but not with respect to optical activity. Inspired by his teacher G. Delafosse, a specialist in hemihedrism, Pasteur became convinced that the molecular asymmetry of optically active liquids should find expression in an asymmetry, or hemihedrism, in their crystalline form; he then did succeed in finding hemihedral facets in all the tartrates. Surprisingly, in the case of sodium ammonium paratartrate, where he had predicted symmetry, he also found hemihedral facets; investigating further, he discovered that the substance included right-handed and left-handed crystals, i. e., crystals which incline in opposite directions. Pasteur separated the crystals by hand and then tested them in solution; each polarized light in a direction opposite to the other, but when the solutions were mixed together there was no optical activity. He concluded that the components were mirror images of each other and that their separate, opposite optical activities compensated for, or canceled, each other. This was confirmed by Biot and Pasteur himself, and led to Pasteur's appointment (1848) to the Faculty of Sciences in Strasbourg.

Thereafter, Pasteur and others turned up various exceptions to the principles he believed he had established, and he qualified his claims to some extent; e.g., he increasingly emphasized optical activity as the index of molecular asymmetry, relegating crystalline form to a secondary position. In 1860 he suggested, with regard to atomic arrangements and molecular asymmetry, that atoms of, say, a right-handed compound might be "arranged in the form of a right-handed spiral" or be "at the corners of an irregular tetrahedron"; it was left to others to link this concept with Kekulé's theory of the tetrahedral carbon atom, but from this linkage emerged the concept of the asymmetrical carbon atom, which underlies all subsequent developments in stereochemistry.

By 1852, Pasteur had become firmly committed to the idea that optical activity was somehow intimately connected with life and could not be produced artificially by ordinary chemical procedures. These preconceptions guided his continuing investigations in this area, including his prize-winning work on methods of obtaining racemic acid and his discovery of two new methods (one chemical, one biological) of separating racemic acid into its left- and right-handed components. His own unexpected production of racemic acid from a tartrate (1853) forced him to retreat from the view that such was impossible; but he continued to insist that the artificial production of racemic substances was not comparable to the production of a single optically-active substance unaccompanied by its inverse form; this he perceived as a barrier between organic and inorganic phenomena. He began to devise unusual experiments to try to reveal certain effects of "asymmetrical forces" in the cosmos, for he believed that these forces (including sunlight) must somehow generate asymmetry (and thus life) in matter; he admitted later that he must have been a "little mad" in this quest, but he never abandoned the hope that life might someday be created or profoundly modified in the laboratory under the influence of such asymmetric forces; moreover, subsequent research has supported his conviction that optical activity and life are somehow intimately associated, and that the production of a single optically-active substance without its mirror image maybe indeed be essentially nature's prerogative.

Pasteur was apparently led to the study of fermentation by two factors. In 1854, he became professor of chemistry and dean of the Faculty of Sciences at Lille, where there was strong interest in relating science to local industry. Second, he was interested in amyl alcohol (one of the optically-active products of fermentation), which he discovered was an exception to his "law of hemihedral correlation" (1856). His tendency to associate asymmetry with life may have inspired him to assume that fermentation depends on living organisms; this position was not new, but it had recently been overwhelmed by Liebig and Berzelius, who held that the process is chemical. By 1857, having completed a study of lactic fermentation, Pasteur had concluded definitely that microorganisms feed on the fermenting medium; he also believed that a specific organism is responsible for each fermentation. He demonstrated and elaborated this view in further studies on alcoholic fermentation, on butyric fermentation, on acetic fermentation and vinegar (*Études sur le vinaigre,* 1868), and on wine (*Études sur le vin,* 1866); he developed a method of cultivating microorganisms in a medium free of organic nitrogen; and he suggested that fermentation is merely "nutrition without the consumption of free oxygen gas," and that putrefaction is an analogous process involving both anaerobes, who live on nitrogenous materials in the absence of air, and aerobes, who transform the products of the initial putrefaction into water, ammonia, and carbonic acid. Thus, "life takes part in the work of death," and death is essential to life, for it is this process which makes carbon, nitrogen, and oxygen available as nutrients. He found (as had others) that heating wine can preserve it, and his name now became generally known abroad, as the procedure was termed "pasteurization."

From the beginning, his work on fermentation involved him in the controversial issue of spontaneous generation, and having moved to Paris (1857) as administrator and director of scientific studies at the École Normale, he was literally in the center of things. Following the publication of Félix Pouchet's *Hétérogénie ou Traité de la génération spontanée* (1859), the Académie des Sciences instituted a prize for the best experimental work on the subject. Pasteur eagerly opposed Pouchet's claims for spontaneous generation, in part because such claims were associated with materialism, radical politics, and attacks on religion (Pasteur was strictly conservative in his political and philosophical views). With ingenious experiments and impressive arrogance he overwhelmed the opposition, at least temporarily. Developing work done

by Theodor Schwann and others, he aspirated atmospheric air through guncotton, thus collecting any solid bodies from the air; he then introduced a small wad of this guncotton directly (i.e., without the opportunity for further contamination) into a flask containing only boiled, sugared yeast water and calcined air; in less than thirty-six hours the liquid swarmed with familiar microorganisms. In another famous experiment, using "swan-necked" flasks, contact with the atmosphere could be controlled by manipulating the unsealed necks of the flasks; thus Pasteur was able to test the distribution of atmospheric microorganisms in different locations and altitudes. Pasteur won the Academy's prize with his classic paper "Mémoire sur les corpuscules organisés qui existent dans l'atmosphère" (1861); the Academy ruled definitively in his favor in 1864.

In the 1860's, Pasteur was involved in exhausting work; in addition to his duties at the École Normale, he participated actively in the affairs of the Academy (to which he'd been elected in 1862); he was also teaching at the École des Beaux-Arts (1863–67); he continued his own personal research; and from 1865 to 1870, at the request of his friend Dumas, he spent several months each year investigating a blight afflicting silkworms that was devastating France's silk industry. It took painstaking study to discover that the cause of the blight was not one disease (as had been supposed) but two: a parasitic disease (*pébrine*) and a disorder (*flacherie*) caused by a susceptibility to certain intestinal bacteria which, under special circumstances, become pathogenic in silkworms. Pasteur explained his findings in *Études sur la maladie des vers à soie* (1870).

By now overwork and personal losses had taken a toll on Pasteur: his father had died in 1865; a year later a young daughter died; a student protest led to his dismissal (1867) from the administration of the École Normale; and in 1868 he suffered a debilitating stroke. Although newly appointed as director of the laboratory of physiological chemistry at the École Normale (1867–88) and as professor of chemistry at the Sorbonne (1867–74), Pasteur withdrew to the country during the Franco-Prussian War and the Commune. Throughout the decade of the 1870's he also faced some sharp challenges to his theories on fermentation and spontaneous generation. Liebig published a wide-ranging critique (1871) that was taken up after his death (1873) by several French chemists. Pasteur's position on the negative role of oxygen was particularly vulnerable, and he responded by admitting (*Études sur la bière,* 1876) that a small quantity of oxygen was essential in fermentation; he avoided the issue raised by his own finding that an aerobic organism is involved in acetic fermentation simply by denying that this process is true fermentation. In retrospect it is clear that Liebig and Pasteur were actually close to a possible agreement, for the former was prepared to admit that living yeast cells might secrete a soluble chemical ferment, and Pasteur maintained that this would not be inconsistent with his own position. With regard to spontaneous generation, Pasteur came out strongly against the possibility of the transformation of one microbial species into another (admitting that he had been in error in believing in the past that he had observed such a transmutation); he also engaged in a celebrated debate with the English naturalist H. C. Bastian, who claimed to be able to produce microorganisms spontaneously in neutral or alkaline urine (the organisms involved proved merely to be highly heat resistant).

Pasteur shared the quite common belief that fermentation and disease were analogous, and he had always been aware of the potential medical implications of his research; in advocating the germ theory of disease, he championed a position that already had its advocates, but which was weak compared to the traditional view that disease is an interior, spontaneous process. It might seem that his investigation of silk worms was good evidence for the germ theory, but evidence of microbial participation in certain insect diseases had long existed without transforming the traditional view. More influential was the dramatic success of Lister's use of Pasteur's ideas in antiseptic surgery; also, C. J. Davaine and Robert Koch had made good headway in studying the possible role of a bacillus in the etiology of anthrax, the disease with which Pasteur made his own entry into medicine. Pasteur's first objective was to counter a claim (1877) by Paul Bert that anthrax was caused by a "virus," i.e., a soluble poison or other inanimate agent; this Pasteur accomplished, first by diluting a drop of anthrax blood to the point of virtual disappearance and then demonstrating that it still retained its original virulence, and second by showing that filtered liquid from an anthrax culture was not virulent. He next confirmed Koch's suggestion that anthrax was transmitted through food, and discovered that anthrax spores are brought from animal graves to the surface of the earth by earthworms. He went on to implicate microbes in other diseases: septicemia, furuncles, osteomyelitis, and puerperal fever (in the last case infuriating physicians by his insistence that they themselves transmitted the disease).

In 1879, while studying fowl cholera, Pasteur discovered (really by accident) a method of reducing the virulence of the microbes in a culture, namely by leaving it alone for several months; almost equally adventitiously, he found that chickens inoculated with the mild form of the culture became immune to the effects of the highly virulent form. Preventive vaccination for the so-called viral diseases was not new (Jenner's smallpox vaccination was well established); but this was the first time that immunization had been observed in a microbial disease, the first clear link between microbial diseases and those believed to be caused by a non-living virus. Soon thereafter, Pasteur and his associates developed two types of anthrax vaccine; the second, highly practical for storing and transporting, was tested (1881) in a internationally-reported field trial at Pouilly-le-Fort; the results constituted a triumph for Pasteur.

In developing the anthrax vaccine, Pasteur had exploited the fact that attenuated viruses (or microbes) gradually could be returned to their original virulence by successive cultures in appropriate animals (to immunize, he used a series of inoculations of progressively stronger cultures); now, in studies on the "saliva microbe" (a pneumococcus) and "horse typhoid," he found that successive passages through one species could reduce the virulence of a microbe toward another species; he applied this principle in his next important success, the discovery (1882) of the vaccine against swine erysipelas, largely accomplished by his young assistant Louis Thuillier, who died a year later in Egypt of cholera.

Pasteur had by now already embarked on his search for a vaccine against rabies, a search that may have been in part inspired by a childhood trauma in which a rabid wolf had bitten several persons in the area near his home. It should be mentioned that in this venture, as in all his later work, Pasteur was greatly helped by generous government support and the aid of talented assistants; since his entry into medicine, these included J. Joubert, E. Duclaux, C. E. Chamberland, Thuillier, A. Loir, and (especially with regard to rabies) Émile Roux. The significance of the conquest of rabies lay not only in the horror of the disease; it was also the first disease of humans Pasteur had addressed and the first true virus disease, which meant (although Pasteur did not know it) that cultivation *in vitro* was perhaps impossible (it has not yet been done) —but he decided early on to work only with living organisms as the culture medium. Despite difficulties, success came fairly quickly; using the series method of inoculation, he succeeded first in immunizing dogs. In 1885 he decided somewhat impulsively to treat his first human patient, nine-year-old Joseph Meister; the survival of Meister and the next patient was properly hailed as a great accomplishment. By March 1886 he had treated 350 patients, of whom one had died; although the failure was not Pasteur's fault (the patient had not arrived for treatment until thirty-seven days after being attacked), he was the subject of sharp attacks for this and occasional subsequent failures that occurred for various reasons (in this century it was discovered that a dead vaccine is safer than Pasteur's live vaccine). Nevertheless, each year thousands of people came to him for rabies treatment, with a less than 1% mortality rate. Not only was rabies on the way to being conquered, but scientists were moving toward a conceptual grasp of the immunization process; Pasteur himself had abandoned his early belief that the microbes consumed some element in their host essential for their survival; he now suspected that they produced a substance toxic to themselves. Thus, he retained his flexibility of mind to the end of his life, and in his last years he was deeply gratified by the many honors accorded him, including election to the Académie Française (1881), the establishment of the Institut Pasteur (1888), and a moving jubilee celebration at the Sorbonne (1892).

PASTOR, JULIO REY. *See* **Rey Pastor, Julio.**

PATRIZI, FRANCESCO (also **Patrizzi** or **Patricio**; Latin form, **Franciscus Patricius**) (*b. Cherso, Istria, Italy, 1529; d. Rome, Italy, 1597*), mathematics, natural philosophy.

Studied at Ingolstadt, the University of Padua (1547–54), and Venice; held chairs of philosophy at Ferrara (1578–92) and at Rome (1592–97). Published works in many fields, blending Platonism and natural philosophy with a very strong anti-Aristotelian bent (particularly in *Discussiones peripateticae*, 1571). His importance rests primarily on his highly original views on the nature of space, as set out in *De rerum natura libri II priores, alter de spacio physico, alter de spacio mathematico* (1587) and in *Nova de universis philosophia* (1591): he argued that the physical existence of a void is possible and that space is a necessary precondition of all that exists in it, being "merely the simple capacity *(aptitudo)* for receiving bodies and nothing else." His distinction between "mathematical" and "physical" space points the way toward later philosophical and scientific theories.

PAUL OF AEGINA (*b. Aegina; fl. Alexandria*, A.D. *640*), medicine.

Author of *Epitome medicae libri septem,* a medical encyclopedia that transmitted the whole range of classical Greek medical thought to the Islamic world. Based primarily on Oribasius' Galenic encyclopedia, the work contains books on hygiene and regimen, fevers, bodily afflictions arranged topically, cutaneous complaints and intestinal worms, toxicology, surgery, and properties of medicines (in the Dioscoridean tradition). Paul was interested in the establishment of the proper regimen for every stage of human development; he maintained that man is in his best temperament when in a middle position between all extremes; he discussed dietary therapeutics, and classified sixty-two varieties of pulse; and he described manipulations of the fetus for proper presentation. The book on surgery contains one of the most detailed descriptions of ophthalmic surgery in antiquity, as well as techniques for tracheotomies, tonsilectomies, nasal polyps, abdominal paracentesis, catheterization, hemorrhoidectomies, lithotomies, and surgical removal of the fetus; it was used extensively by al-Zahrāwī, al-Rāzī, and Fabrici.

PAUL OF ALEXANDRIA (*fl. Alexandria, ca.* A.D. *378*), astrology.

Author of a popular elementary textbook of astrology, *Eisagogika,* whose sources included Ptolemy and Hermes Trismegistus. Two erroneous modern theories deserve mention: that the Indian astronomer Pauliśa was actually Paul of Alexandria, and that there is a dependence between a geographical list in Acts of the Apostles and the geography of Paul's text; both theories have been disproved by recent scholarship.

PAUL OF VENICE (*b. Udine, Italy, ca. 1370; d. Padua, Italy, 1429*), natural philosophy, logic.

A highly respected scholar and leader of the Hermits of St. Augustine. Studied at Oxford and (probably) Paris; taught at various times at Padua, Siena, Bologna, Paris, and Rome; served briefly as Venetian ambassador to the king of Poland (1413). Widely known as a prominent rationalist with Averroist tendencies, whose work in natural philosophy was widely read, he was more important in the field of logic. His four logical works, while not markedly original, probably constitute the most thorough and encyclopedic medieval exposition of terminist logic; his *Logica* was a required text at Venice, Padua, and Ferrara, and was still used in Jesuit schools late in the seventeenth century. In natural philosophy he often attempted unsuccessfully to reconcile Averroistic positions with the assertion of divine omnipotence. The geological theories in his *De compositione mundi* derived largely from the work of Ristoro.

PAULI, SIMON. *See* **Paulli, Simon.**

PAULI, WOLFGANG (*b. Vienna, Austria, 1900; d. Zurich, Switzerland, 1958*), physics.

Son of Wolfgang Pauli, a professor of chemistry; godson of Ernst Mach. After reading Einstein's relativity theory independently while in high school, Pauli studied under Sommerfeld in Munich; on Sommerfeld's recommendation he wrote on relativity theory for Klein's *Encyklopädie,* achieving a masterful, critical presentation of the mathematical foundations of the theory as well as its physical significance. He received his doctorate in 1922 and then assisted Max Born in Göttingen, Niels Bohr in Copenhagen, and Wilhelm Lenz in Hamburg before being appointed Debye's successor at the Eidgenössische Technische Hochschule (1928); during World War II he was active at the Institute for Advanced Study, Princeton, but he later returned to Zurich. He received the Nobel Prize in physics in 1945.

Pauli early studied the anomalous Zeeman effect, and proposed that it be understood as resulting from the properties of the valence electron, rather than from those of the atomic core, thus retaining Bohr's "permanence of the quantum numbers": each electron, even in a closed shell, could in principle be described by quantum numbers (to the already known n, l, and m he added a fourth, s, for spin). He went on to study the structure of the core, and announced his famous exclusion principle (1925): "There can never be two or more equivalent electrons in an atom, for which in a strong field the values of all the quantum numbers n, k_1, k_2 and m are the same. If an electron is present, for which these quantum numbers (in an external field) have definite values, then this state is 'occupied.' " The number of possible configurations of the various unclosed electron shells could now be ascertained. His later studies covered many areas of theoretical physics, including relativistic quantum electrodynamics, wave mechanics (1933), and discrete symmetries in field theory. One of his most significant discoveries came in 1930 at Zurich, when he explained the puzzling continuous spectrum of β decay by assuming the emission of a neutral particle (christened "neutrino" by Fermi) along with the electron.

Sensing the irrational source of apparently rational physical theory, and endeavoring to master the consequent inner conflicts, Pauli took up the ideas of Jung in order better to understand the meaning of scientific activity; together they published *Naturerklärung und Psyche* (1952).

PAULIŚA (*fl. India, fourth or fifth century*), astronomy.

Sometimes falsely identified with Paul of Alexandria. Author of a textbook largely based on Greek adaptations of Mesopotamian astronomy, the *Pauliśasiddhānta,* which was revised by Lāṭadeva (*fl.* 505) and is known to us only through the *Pañcasiddhāntikā* of Varāhamihira (*fl. ca.* 550).

PAULLI, SIMON (*b. Rostock, Mecklenburg, 1603; d. Copenhagen, Denmark, 1680*), botany, anatomy.

Received medical degree at Wittenberg (1630) after studies at Rostock, at Leiden, and under Jean Riolan at Paris. Professor at Rostock (1639–48) and then at Copenhagen; physician in ordinary to the Danish king. His notable contributions to the technical literature of anatomy and botany included *Quadripartitum botanicum de simplicium medicamentorum facultatibus . . .* (1640), in which plants are arranged according to the seasons; *Flora Danica* (1648), also seasonal, with 393 illustrations; descriptions of scurvy and venereal diseases (1660); and discussions of the use of tobacco and tea.

PAULY, AUGUST (*b. Munich, Germany, 1850; d. Munich, 1914*), zoology, entomology.

Assisted Siebold, under whom he had studied (doctorate, 1877), at University of Munich; became an expert in avian pathological anatomy, and lectured on forest entomology; appointed extraordinary professor of applied zoology (1896). His uniquely vitalistic neo-Lamarckian theory of evolution was presented in *Darwinismus und Lamarckismus. Entwurf einer psychophysischen Teleologie* (1905): evolution was the result of an "inner teleology," a capacity for change in response to a consciously apprehended need within the organism itself; adaptive changes were inherited but could be maintained only through use. He referred the underlying psychic circumstances not only to the brain but also to each organ and cell, in plants as well as in animals.

PAVLOV, ALEKSEI PETROVICH (*b. Moscow, Russia, 1854; d. Bad Tölz, Germany, 1929*), geology.

Studied at Moscow University (graduated 1878; master's, 1884; doctorate, 1886), where he became a professor (1886) after teaching in secondary schools, doing field research in the Volga region, and traveling to Paris, the Auvergne, and Vienna. His students at the university, the Moscow Archaeological Institute, and the Moscow Mining Academy formed the nucleus of the Moscow school of geologists; he was also concerned with the reform of secondary education. His scientific interests included stratigraphy, paleontology, tectonics, Quaternary geology, and practical geology. His comparative stratigraphic analysis revealed a great similarity between the Jurassic fauna of the Volga region and that of Europe. He established that there had been two Boreal periods in the Lower Cretaceous and that the sea which had flooded the lower Volga in the Albian stage had been connected to the sea of Western Europe. He distinguished two types of glacial deposits, talus and proluvium, and compared Russian and Western European Neogene and Quaternary deposits to establish threefold glaciation. He proposed (1900) a new genetic classification for fossil organisms, based upon phylogenetic properties, and discovered the phenomenon of phylogenetic acceleration. He found a new element in the structure of the Russian platform, the great gentle down-warpings that he called "synclines," which he interpreted as local uplifts and depressions in the earth's crust; he compared the topography of the moon and the earth (1908), and emphasized the importance of the study of lunar topography for understanding terrestrial processes. In practical geology, he treated the distribution of forces acting in massive landslides and suggested preventive measures; provided a classification of rocks for engineering purposes; and stressed the geological processes of soil formation. He published also on the history of science and on popular science.

PAVLOV, IVAN PETROVICH (*b. Ryazan, Russia, 1849; d. Leningrad, U.S.S.R., 1936*), physiology, psychology.

After graduating from St. Petersburg University (1875), Pavlov studied theoretical medicine at the Military Medical Academy, where he received his M.D. (1879) and Ph.D. (1883), and became *Privatdozent* in physiology (1883) and professor of pharmacology (1890). In 1884–86 he worked in the laboratories of Karl Ludwig in Leipzig and Rudolf Heidenhain in Breslau. An able administrator, he organized a number of major research centers, including the physiological section of the Institute of Experimental Medicine, the Institute of Physiology of the Soviet Academy of Sciences that now bears his name, and the biological station at Koltushy (now Pavlovo).

He enriched physiology and the natural sciences with a new methodology, derived from his view that the living organism must be studied under the conditions of its normal activity; he considered the main problem of experimental physiology to be the study of reciprocal influence and reciprocal action within the organism, and the relation of the organism to its environment. He conceived the method of long-term experiment.

Pavlov's research was in three main areas: physiology of the circulation of the blood (1874–88), physiology of digestion (1879–97), and physiology of the brain and of higher nervous activity (1902–36). He described the role of the nerve mechanism in the adaptive activity of the blood vessels, specifying the role of the vagus as a regulator of blood pressure; he showed that cardiac function is governed by four nerves which respectively inhibit, accelerate, weaken, and intensify it (1883); and he proposed that the influence of the intensifying nerve be understood as trophic (1888). He devised new techniques for surgical intervention on the entire digestive tract, allowing him to observe the normal activity of a particular digestive gland in a healthy animal. He showed a close connection between the properties of salivary secretion and the kind of food consumed (the Pavlovian curves of salivary secretion); he elucidated the role of enzymes in digestion and, with N. P. Shepovalnikov, discovered enterokinase in the intestinal secretion (1894); and he demonstrated specific irritability in various parts of the digestive tract.

He then turned to the physiology of behavior, drawing upon Darwin's theory of evolution and Sechenov's reflexology to create his own theory. He investigated the activity of the cortex and the cerebral hemispheres by studying the salivary glands, whose activity could be measured quantitatively; he saw the "psychic" stimulation of the salivary glands as a phenomenon analogous to the normal digestive reflex: he termed the latter an unconditioned reflex, and the activity of the salivary glands, stimulated by various environmental agents, a conditioned reflex (1903). He noted that the chief characteristics of conditioned reflexes are that they are developed throughout the life of an organism (and are therefore subject to change), and that they are provoked by stimuli that act as signals; they thus ensure the organism a completely individual adaptive activity. He localized conditioned-reflex activity in the cerebral cortex, and showed that with the formation of conditioned reflexes in the functional state of nerve centers, displacements occur in the form of increases in irritability; the neural cells must therefore undergo definite subtle structural and physicochemical changes. An important concomitant of this work was his creation of experimental neuroses by offering the subject contradictory stimuli; he attributed the neuroses to the disturbance of balance between the cortical processes of excitation and inhibition. With his co-workers, he established the existence of four basic types of behavior, classified according to the strength, mobility, and constancy of the basic nerve processes. At Koltushy, he explored the genetic study of behavior.

PAVÓN Y JIMÉNEZ, JOSÉ ANTONIO (*b. Casatejada, Cáceres, Spain, 1754; d. Madrid, Spain, 1840*), botany.

Pavón worked as a pharmacist but was apparently never licensed. The central event in his life was serving as junior partner to Hipólito Ruiz on the royal botanical expedition to Peru (1777–88); in the subsequent publications (all but one of which named Ruiz as senior author) they announced 141 new genera still recognized today and named over 500 species. Pavón took charge of the project after Ruiz's death (1816), but three-quarters of the expedition's findings remained unpublished. He helped to spread knowledge of Spanish-American plants by selling thousands of herbarium duplicates to foreign collectors, principally to Aylmer Bourke Lambert.

PAYEN, ANSELME (*b. Paris, France, 1795; d. Paris, 1871*), industrial chemistry, agricultural chemistry.

Son of a chemical manufacturer, he studied chemistry privately with Vauquelin and Chevreul; he later taught at the École Centrale des Arts et Manufactures (from 1829) and the Conservatoire des Arts et Métiers (from 1839). Published many papers, mostly on technological matters of local and temporary concern; he advocated animal charcoal as superior to wood charcoal for decolorizing purposes in the beet-sugar industry. He is remembered mainly for his work on carbohydrates, some of it done with Persoz; in 1833 they found that starch was hydrolyzed to sugar by a substance contained in malt, which they called diastase. He showed that starch from different plant species has the same chemical composition, and distinguished (1838) two components in woody tissue, one of which he named cellulose (the other was later called lignin).

PAYKULL, GUSTAF (*b. Stockholm, Sweden, 1757; d. Vallox-Säby, Sweden, 1826*), entomology.

A civil servant (royal chamberlain, 1796; master of the royal household, 1815), Paykull became a baron in 1818. He amassed the largest private collection of zoological specimens ever assembled in Scandinavia; it was donated to the state in 1819 and became the nucleus of the present National Museum of Natural History in Stockholm. In entomology he concentrated on beetles and accurately described a great many new species; his major publication was *Fauna Suecica* (3 vols., 1789–1800).

PEACOCK, GEORGE (*b. Denton, near Darlington, Durham, England, 1791; d. Ely, England, 1858*), mathematics.

Educated at Trinity College, Cambridge (B.A., 1813; M.A., 1816; D.D., 1839), where he taught until being appointed dean of Ely (he had been ordained in 1822); he was instrumental in reforming the teaching of mathematics at Cambridge, and remained active in university affairs after moving to Ely. With Babbage and John Herschel he published a translation of an elementary calculus text by Lacroix (1816). In *A Treatise on Algebra* (1830) he attempted to put the theory of negative and complex numbers on a firm and logical basis by dividing the field of algebra into arithmetical algebra and symbolic algebra, and extended the domain of the symbols in the latter by his principle of the permanence of equivalent

forms. Wrote a biography of Thomas Young and was one of the editors of his works.

PEALE, CHARLES WILLSON (*b. Queen Anne's County, Md., 1741; d. Philadelphia, Pa., 1827*), museum direction.

A skilled portraitist, Peale settled in Philadelphia in 1776, served as a militia officer in the Revolution and painted its officers and men, designed large patriotic displays, and established the first natural history museum in the U.S. (in his house, 1786; moved to American Philosophical Society, 1794; moved to State House [now Independence Hall], 1802; collections sold, 1848 and 1854). He viewed the museum as an educational tool and hoped it would become a national institution; his exhibits were arranged by a modified Linnaean system and were displayed as naturalistically and as informatively as possible. His sons Rubens and Rembrandt established similar institutions in Baltimore and New York.

PEALE, REMBRANDT (*b. near Richboro, Pa., 1778; d. Philadelphia, Pa., 1860*), natural history, technology.

Son of Charles Willson Peale (1741–1827). Studied art (and, informally, science) in London (1802–03) and France (1808–10); lived and painted for various periods in Baltimore, Philadelphia, New York, Italy, and England before finally settling in Philadelphia in 1834. Known for his portraits, many of which were of scientists. Interested in technology, he observed some of Fulton's early steam navigation experiments (1807, reported in 1848); experimented with gas lighting (Baltimore, 1816–20); was among the first Americans to experiment with lithography (1820's); and is credited with importing from France the encaustic method of painting, in which pigments are fixed in wax rather than in oils. With his father, he excavated mastodon skeletons from the peat bogs of Orange County, N.Y. (1801); he popularized their find by traveling with a skeleton to display in New York and London (1802), by publishing three descriptions of the creature (1802, 1803), and by displaying the skeleton at the museum he founded at Baltimore (1814–30).

PEALE, TITIAN RAMSAY (*b. Philadelphia, Pa., 1799; d. Philadelphia, 1885*), natural history.

Son of Charles Willson Peale. Participated in numerous natural history expeditions, collecting and drawing; contributed plates to T. Say's *American Entomology* (vol. I, 1824); drew all but one of the plates for C. L. Bonaparte's *American Ornithology* (1825), having collected many of the specimens. Issued a prospectus for *Lepidoptera Americana* (1833), a project that proved too expensive to publish. Participated in Wilkes's South Seas expedition (1838–42) and prepared *Mammalia and Ornithology* (1848; rewritten by John Cassin, 1858) for the expedition's report, although the best of his specimens were lost in a shipwreck. Later an examiner in the U.S. Patent Office (1849–72).

PÉAN DE SAINT-GILLES, LÉON (*b. Paris, France, 1832; d. Cannes, France, 1862*), analytical chemistry.

Independently wealthy and privately educated, he taught himself chemistry, acquired practical laboratory experience under Pelouze, and worked in his own laboratory. He extended the use of potassium permanganate as a titrimetric solution for the quantitative determination of nitrite and iodide, as well as of oxalic acid and other organic substances; his procedures are still used. With Berthelot he studied the esterification of alcohols with acids and found that "the amount of ester formed in each moment is proportional to the product of the reacting substances"; this was the crucial reaction referred to by Guldberg and Waage in their enunciation of the law of mass action (1864).

PEANO, GIUSEPPE (*b. Spinetta, near Cuneo, Italy, 1858; d. Turin, Italy, 1932*), mathematics, logic.

Graduated with high honors from the University of Turin (1880); assisted D'Ovidio (1880–81) and Genocchi (1881–89); extraordinary professor, 1890; ordinary professor, 1895–1932. Taught also at the military academy in Turin (1886–1901). Active in the Academy of Sciences of Turin; knight of the Order of the Crown of Italy and of the Order of Saint Maurizio and Saint Lazzaro. Peano considered his most important work to be that in analysis. His books *Angelo Genocchi, Calcolo differenziale e principii di calcolo integrale, publicato con aggiunte dal D.ʳ Giuseppe Peano* and *Lezione di analisi infinitesimale* (1893) were highly acclaimed in *Encyklopädie der mathematischen Wissenschaften;* he was the first to show (1886) that the first-order differential equation $y' = f(x,y)$ is solvable on the sole assumption that f is continuous. Much of his work in analysis, such as his clarification of the notion of area of a surface (1882), his work with Wronskians, Jacobians, and other special determinants, and with Taylor's formula, and his generalizations of quadrature formulas, was designed to clarify and to make rigorous the current definitions and theories; his most famous counterexample to commonly accepted notions in mathematics was the space-filling curve (1890).

Peano's lasting reputation is as a pioneer of symbolic logic and a promoter of the axiomatic method; in this area his influence was strongly felt by Bertrand Russell, and his "school" included Pieri and Burali-Forti. The first statement of his famous postulates for the natural numbers appeared in *Arithmetices principia, nova methodo exposita* (1889), which also included important innovations in logical notation. He founded *Rivista di matematica* (1891) and announced in it his *Formulario* project: to publish all known theorems and their proofs, using his logical notation (5th ed., 1908, contained some 4200 theorems). For him the purpose of mathematical logic was to "analyze the ideas and reasoning that especially figure in the mathematical sciences."

In geometry, he reduced the number of undefined terms to three (1894): point, segment, and motion; developed a "geometrical calculus"; and popularized the vectorial methods of H. Grassmann. He also contributed to actuarial mathematics, rational mechanics, pedagogy, and mathematical historiography. His promotion of an international language for science, Interlingua (a "Latin without grammar," 1903), eclipsed his role as professor of mathematics and led him to the algebra of grammar and to philology, culminating in publication of *Vocabulario commune ad latino-italiano-français-english-deutsch* (1915) with 14,000 entries.

PEARL, RAYMOND (*b. Farmington, N.H., 1879; d. Hershey, Pa., 1940*), biology, genetics.

Studied at Dartmouth (A.B., 1899), University of Michigan (Ph.D., 1902), University of Leipzig (1905), and

under Karl Pearson at University College, London (1905–06). Held academic positions at University of Pennsylvania (1906–07) and Johns Hopkins University (1918–40); also worked at Maine Agricultural Experiment Station (1907–18), and led the statistical division of U.S. Food Administration (1917–19), where he studied the relationship of food to population. A prodigious researcher and a voluminous and articulate writer who achieved renown as a pioneer in world population changes, birth and death rates, and longevity. Founded and edited *Quarterly Review of Biology* from 1926 and *Human Biology* from 1929.

PEARSON, GEORGE (*b. Rotherham, England, 1751; d. London, England, 1828*), chemistry.

One of the first chemists in Britain to accept the "antiphlogistic" theories of Lavoisier, Pearson studied chemistry and medicine at Edinburgh (M.D., 1773) and practiced medicine in Doncaster and London. In 1794 he published a translation of the chemical table from Lavoisier's *Méthode de nomenclature chimique;* the enlarged 2nd ed. (1799) included tables of chemical affinity and the symbols of Hassenfratz, Adet, Bergman, and Geoffroy. His chemical researches included discovery of calcium phosphide by heating phosphorus with quicklime (extending the work of Smithson Tennant).

PEARSON, KARL (*b. London, England, 1857; d. Coldharbour, Surrey, England, 1936*), applied mathematics, biometry, statistics.

Pearson was the founder of twentieth-century statistics. At Cambridge he studied mathematics under E. J. Routh, G. G. Stokes, J. C. Maxwell, Arthur Cayley, and William Burnside, and received his B.A. in 1879. He then went to Germany, where he studied physics under G. H. Quincke and metaphysics under Kuno Fischer, and where he also attended lectures of Emil du Bois-Reymond on Darwinism. He received an LL.B. from Cambridge University in 1881 and an M.A.. in 1882, but he never practiced. He taught applied mathematics and mechanics at University College, London (1884–1911), and became the first Galton professor of eugenics (1911–33). From 1891 to 1894 he also lectured in geometry at Gresham College, London. Pearson was well on the way to a respectable career as a teacher of applied mathematics and philosopher of science when two events changed the direction of his career: the publication of Galton's *Natural Inheritance* (1889), and the appointment of W. F. R. Weldon as professor of zoology at University College (1890). Weldon began to apply, extend, and improve Galton's methods of measuring variation and correlation, in pursuit of concrete evidence to support Darwin's "working hypothesis" of natural selection, and turned to Pearson for help. Pearson saw Galton's work as bringing psychology, anthropology, medicine and sociology in large parts into the field of mathematical treatment, and began to lay the foundations of the new science of statistics that he was to develop almost single-handed during the next decade and a half. The main purpose of his work was not development of statistical theory and techniques for their own sake but, rather, "development and application of statistical methods for the study of problems of heredity and evolution."

Among his numerous contributions to statistical theory and practice were his "method of moments," developed to provide a general method for determing the values of the parameteres of a frequency distribution of some particular form selected to describe a given set of observational or experimental data, and his system of diverse frequency curves (Pearson curves). His χ^2 test for goodness of fit is one of his greatest contributions; in its original and extended forms it has remained one of the most useful of all statistical tests.

Pearson's more than 648 publications included over 400 on the theory of statistics and its applications to biological, social, and other problems, and 37 on pure and applied mathematics and physical science. He was the principal editor of *Biometrika* from its founding to his death, and for many years he was the sole editor. Under his guidance it became the world's leading medium of publication of papers on, and mathematical tables relating to, statistical theory and practice. In 1925 he founded *Annals of Eugenics* and served as editor of the first five volumes (1925–33). The *Tables of the Incomplete Beta-Function* (1934), a compilation prepared under his direction over a period of several decades, remains a monument to him and his co-workers.

PEASE, FRANCIS GLADHELM (*b. Cambridge, Mass., 1881; d. Pasadena, Calif., 1938*), astronomy.

Graduated from Armour Institute of Technology, Chicago (B.S., 1901); worked at Yerkes Observatory with G. W. Ritchey, and then at Mount Wilson (from 1904) where he contributed significantly to the design of several large instruments (including the 200-inch telescope). Studied rotations and radial velocities of spiral nebulae. Associated with A. A. Michelson in the first determination of stellar diameters (1921), using interferometers for measurement of fringes as a function of mirror separation; assisted Michelson and Pearson in redetermining the velocity of light (1935) and in repeating the Michelson-Morley experiment.

PECHAM, JOHN (*b. Sussex, England, ca. 1230–35; d. Mortlake, Surrey, England, 1292*), optics, cosmology, mathematics.

Studied at Paris and Oxford; became a Franciscan, and studied theology in Paris (doctorate, 1269); taught theology in Paris, Oxford, and Italy; was elected archbishop of Canterbury, and maintained a zealous program of reform. Saw himself as an expositor of scientific matters in elementary terms, and was a leader in the defense of Augustinianism against Aristotelian and Thomist innovations. His success was greatest in the case of his *Perspectiva communis*, which is still extant in more than sixty manuscripts and went through twelve printed editions between 1482 and 1665. Central to his optical system was a theory of direct vision that endeavored to reconcile all the available authorities—Aristotle, Euclid, Augustine, al-Kindī, Ibn al-Haytham, Ibn Rushd, Grosseteste, and Bacon: the primary agent of sight is the ray coming to the eye from a point on the visible object; the ray falls perpendicularly on the cornea and penetrates without refraction to the sensitive ocular organ, the glacial humor; it is further propagated through the vitreous humor and optic nerve to the common nerve of both eyes, and eventually to the anterior part of the brain and the "place of interior judgment"; visual rays from the eye serve to moderate the luminous rays from the visible object and make them

"commensurate with the visual power." In this book and in the more rambling *Tractatus de perspectiva* Pecham treated the full range of elementary optical matters; his other scientific works are *Tractatus de numeris* (or *Arithmetica mystica*) and *Tractatus de sphera* (a rival to, rather than a commentary on, Sacrobosco's work). He also wrote three works on the soul, which contain material of considerable scientific import.

PECQUET, JEAN (*b. Dieppe, France, 1622; d. Paris, France, 1674*), anatomy.

Studied medicine in Paris (*ca.* 1646–51) and at Montpellier (doctorate, 1652); returned to Paris and had both worldly and scientific careers. His only important scientific accomplishment was discovery of the chyle reservoir (which he called *receptaculum chyli*): using a dog that was digesting, he showed that 1) if the heart has been resected, pressure on the mesenteric root causes the chyle to spurt into the superior vena cava; 2) the chyle is directed toward the subclavian veins by two paravertebral canals; 3) the origin of the ascending chyliferous ducts is in a prevertebral and subdiaphragmatic ampulla, the "sought-after sanctuary of the chyle"; 4) the posterior part of Aselli's "pancreas" is composed of lymphatic ganglia; and 5) no mesenteric chyliferous vessel goes to the liver, and the inferior vena cava, incised above the liver, reveals no trace of chyle. His discovery provoked sharp debate, particularly with Riolan.

PEIRCE, BENJAMIN (*b. Salem, Mass., 1809; d. Cambridge, Mass., 1880*), mathematics, astronomy.

Graduated from Harvard (1829; M.A., 1833), where he was a tutor (1831–33) and professor (1832–80). In mathematics, he amended N. Bowditch's translation of Laplace's *Mécanique céleste* (1829–39); proved (1832) that there is no odd perfect number with fewer than four prime factors; published popular elementary textbooks; discussed possible systems of multiple algebras in *Linear Associative Algebra* (republished posthumously, 1881, by his son C. S. Peirce); and set forth, in *A System of Analytic Mechanics* (1855), the principles and methods of that science as a branch of mathematical theory, developed from the idea of the "potential." In astronomy, he studied comets; worked on revision of planetary theory and was the first to compute the perturbing influence of other planets on Neptune; and worked on the mathematics of the rings of Saturn, deducing that they were fluid. From 1852 he worked with the U.S. Coast Survey on longitude determination, and developed (1852) "Peirce's criterion" for judgment of observational errors (since demonstrated invalid); head of the survey (1867–74) he superintended measurement of the arc of the thirty-ninth parallel in order to join the Atlantic and Pacific systems of triangulation. Influential in founding the Smithsonian Institution and the National Academy of Sciences.

PEIRCE, BENJAMIN OSGOOD, II (*b. Beverly, Mass., 1854; d. Cambridge, Mass., 1914*), mathematics, physics.

First research student of Trowbridge at Harvard (1872–76); also studied under Wiedemann in Leipzig (Ph.D., 1879) and worked in Helmholtz' laboratory in Berlin (1880). Taught at Harvard (instructor, 1881; professor, 1888); a founder of American Physical Society; an editor of *Physical Review*. One of first to study retinal sensitivity by means of the spectrum instead of revolving discs (1883); his major works are *Elements of the Theory of the Newtonian Potential Function* (1888), *A Short Table of Integrals* (1889), and *Mathematical and Physical Papers, 1903–1913* (1926).

PEIRCE, CHARLES SANDERS (*b. Cambridge, Mass., 1839; d. Milford, Pa., 1914*), logic, geodesy, mathematics, philosophy, history of science.

Son of Benjamin Peirce. Graduated from Harvard (1859; M.A., 1862; Sc.B., Lawrence Scientific School, 1863). Worked with U.S. Coast Survey (1861–91), where he did pioneering astronomical studies (1869–75) attempting to reform existing scales of magnitudes with the aid of instrumental photometry, published as *Photometric Researches* (1878). In 1872 he was put in charge of pendulum experiments; he traveled to Europe (1875–76) to learn new techniques and compare results, and there made a name as a research geodesist by his discovery of an error in European measurement due to the flexure of the pendulum stand. In 1879 he succeeded in determining the length of the meter from a wavelength of light. His quincuncial map projection (1876), the first application of elliptic functions and Jacobian elliptic integrals to conformal mapping for geographical purposes, grew out of his studies of gravity. He pursued mathematical problems while lecturing in logic at Johns Hopkins University (1879–84); influenced by his father's mathematics, Peirce was the first to recognize the quadrate linear associative algebras identical with matrices in which the units are letter pairs.

For Peirce, mathematical procedure resolves itself into four parts: (1) the creation of a model that embodies the condition of the premise; (2) mental modification of the diagram to obtain auxiliary information; (3) mental experimentation on the diagram to bring out a new relation between parts not mentioned in its construction; and (4) repetition of the experiment. The concern of the mathematician is to reach the conclusion, whereas the logician desires to understand the process. Mathematics is a study of what is or is not logically possible, with no concern for what actually exists, while philosophy discovers what it can from everyday experience. Logical truth has the same source as mathematical truth, which is derived from the observation of diagrams. He greatly enlarged Boolean algebra by introducing a new kind of abstraction, the dyadic relation called "inclusion." The logic of relatives developed by Peirce treats of "systems" in which objects are brought together by any kind of relation, while ordinary logic deals with "classes" of objects brought together by the relation of similarity. His contribution to the foundations of lattice theory is widely recognized.

Peirce's Scotistic realism led to his famous pragmatic axiom, first stated in 1877 and later brought to the world's attention by William James: "Consider what effects, that might conceivably have practical bearings, we conceive the object of our conception to have. Then, our conception of these effects is the whole of our conception of the object." The maxim underlies Peirce's epistemology. He held that chance, law, and continuity are basic to the explanation of the universe; chance accounts for the origin of fruitful ideas, which associate with allied ideas in a mind prepared for them. He considered this law of association to be the one law of intellectual development.

His concern with the "economy of research" underlay his application of the pragmatic maxim and became an important objective in his approach to problems in political economy.

PEIRESC, NICOLAS CLAUDE FABRI DE (*b. Belgentier, Var, France, 1580; d. Aix-en-Provence, France, 1637*), astronomy, scientific patronage.

Widely traveled and well educated, with a law degree from Montpellier, Peiresc lived primarily in Aix but spent the years 1616–23 in Paris. He held various legislative positions and in 1618 was granted an abbacy; his main interest, however, was the pursuit of science as he understood it. He felt that cooperation and free communication are the basis on which sound knowledge—that is, science—and therefore human wisdom can advance; to this end he maintained a large correspondence and was a patron and amateur of science, the arts, and erudition. His outlook was that of a collector rather than of a systematist; his gardens at Belgentier were in their day the third largest in France. Interested in collecting animals, he introduced the Angora cat to Europe; he also studied fossils and crystals, and sponsored anatomical dissections in his own house. His chief personal contributions were in astronomy, largely in collaboration with Gassendi (who lived with him from 1634 and wrote an influential biography of him). He was first in France to see the four satellites of Jupiter (1610, with Joseph Gaultier), and first to see the nebula in the sword of Orion (1611; announced by Huygens, 1658). His interest in recording the positions and times of observation of Jupiter's satellites (1610–12), and later the timing of lunar eclipses (1628), led to longitude calculations and culminated in the training and equipping of a network of priests, merchants, and embassy personnel who in 1635 observed the lunar eclipse of 28 August and provided data permitting determination of the length of the Mediterranean with a good deal of accuracy.

PEKELHARING, CORNELIS ADRIANUS (*b. Zaandam, Holland, 1848; d. Utrecht, Holland, 1922*), physiological chemistry, medicine.

Studied and practiced medicine at Leiden (licensed, 1872; M.D., 1877); worked at veterinary school in Utrecht (1878–81) and at University of Utrecht (1881–1918). His research topics included protein digestion, bacteriology (anthrax), the role of leukocytes in inflammation and phagocytosis, and the role of calcium in blood clotting. With C. Winkler and Eijkman he studied beriberi in the Dutch East Indies (1886–87); his interest subsequently turned to nutrition, and in 1905 he reported his conclusion that milk contains an unknown substance which is essential to the diet. Instrumental in founding the Netherlands Institute of Nutrition.

PELETIER, JACQUES (*b. Le Mans, France, 1517; d. Paris, France, 1582*), mathematics, medicine.

After schooling in philosophy and law he trained himself in Greek, mathematics, and medicine; from 1547 he lived as a vagabond, working alternately as a teacher and as a surgeon. He promoted the use of French in literature and science, publishing scientific poetry (*L'amour des amours*, 1555), the first vernacular textbook on theoretical and practical arithmetic (*L'arithmétique*, 1549), and *L'al-*

gèbre (1554), which discussed German and Italian techniques. Was the first mathematician to see relations between coefficients and roots of equations. His geometrical ideas were disputed by Clavius and Buteo.

PELL, JOHN (*b. Southwick, Sussex, England, 1611; d. London, England, 1685*), mathematics.

A graduate of Trinity College, Cambridge (B.A., 1629; M.A., 1630), and a member of the Comenian group in London (from 1638); professor at Amsterdam (1643) and Breda (1646); Commonwealth agent in Zurich (1654–58); held ecclesiastical posts in Restoration England, and died in poverty. Author of *Idea of Mathematics* (1638) and *Controversiae de vera circuli mensura* (1647), which were well received. Has been credited with innovations in algebra, particularly the symbol for division, setting out equations in three columns, and the Pell equation: $x^2 = 1 + Ay^2$.

PELLETIER, BERTRAND (*b. Bayonne, France, 1761; d. Paris, France, 1797*), chemistry.

Studied pharmacy; became d'Arcet's assistant at the Collège de France (1782); was appointed manager of Rouelle pharmacy (1783), and later bought it (still called Pharmacie Pelletier). Received M.D. from Rheims (1790). A skillful chemist, concerned more with experiment than with theory, he made few original contributions. He made valuable reports on industrial processes to the Bureau de Consultation des Arts et Métiers, the Commission Temporaire des Arts, and the Institut de France, and was an editor of *Annales de chimie;* his own research included the first preparation of many metal phosphides, and development of a process for recovering copper from bell metal by oxidation with manganese dioxide.

PELLETIER, PIERRE-JOSEPH (*b. Paris, France, 1788; d. Paris, 1842*), chemistry, pharmacy.

Son of Bertrand Pelletier. Studied and taught at the École de Pharmacie (graduated, 1810; *docteur ès sciences,* 1812; assistant professor, 1815; professor, 1825; assistant director, 1832); also directed the family pharmacy and a chemical plant at Clichy. His early studies were mainly on analysis of gum resins and coloring matter in plants, culminating in the isolation of emetine from ipecac root (1817, with Magendie). His collaborators included Dumas, Philippe Walter, and H. Sainte-Claire Deville, but his most famous work was with Caventou, principally their study and naming of chlorophyll (1817) and their discovery of a number of plant alkaloids: strychnine (1818), brucine (1819), veratrine (1819), quinine (1820), and caffeine (1821).

PELOUZE, THÉOPHILE-JULES (*b. Valognes, Manche, France, 1807; d. Paris, France, 1867*), chemistry.

A pharmacist, Pelouze became student and assistant to Gay-Lussac and quickly established himself as an outstanding analytical and experimental chemist; he published at least 90 papers, alone or with other eminent chemists. His discoveries included ethyl cyanide (1834), oenanthic ester and the corresponding acid (with Liebig, 1836), nitrocellulose (1838), and the formula for potassium dinitrosulfite (1835); he studied curare with Claude Bernard (1850), and American petroleum with Cahours (1862–64). Professor at the École Polytechnique (1831–

46) and at the Collège de France (1831–50); assayer at Paris mint; founded the most important private laboratory school of chemistry in France.

PELTIER, JEAN CHARLES ATHANASE (*b. Ham, France, 1785; d. Paris, France, 1845*), physics.

Initially a clockmaker, he retired in 1815 and pursued science; he was led to the study of electricity by Magendie's vivisection demonstrations. In 1830 he showed that chemical effects can be obtained from a dry pile with plates of sufficiently large surface area. He later constructed a thermoelectric thermoscope to measure temperature distribution along a series of thermocouple circuits, and discovered that a cooling effect can take place at one junction and excessive heating at the other; the importance of this "Peltier effect" was not fully recognized until after the thermodynamic work of William Thomson twenty years later.

PEMBERTON, HENRY (*b. London, England, 1694; d. London, 1771*), physics, mathematics, physiology, medicine.

Earned a medical degree under Boerhaave at Leiden (1719) with an important thesis on accommodation of the eye to objects at different distances by changes in shape of the crystalline lens; did not practice medicine extensively, but taught physics at Gresham College for several years (from 1728). Brought himself to the attention of Newton, and served as editor of the third edition of the *Principia* (1726). Also wrote a nonmathematical popularization of Newtonianism, *A View of Sir Isaac Newton's Philosophy* (1728); translated the *Principia* into English, but was beaten into print by Andrew Motte; and reedited and translated *The Dispensatory of the Royal College of Physicians* (1746).

PENCK, ALBRECHT (*b. Reuditz [near Leipzig], Germany, 1858; d. Prague, Czechoslovakia, 1945*), geomorphology, geology, paleoclimatology, hydrology, cartography.

Penck's fruitful work in geology began while he was a student at Leipzig, where his teachers included Kolbe, Credner, and Zirkel; in 1877 he assisted Credner in a geological survey of Saxony. In 1879 he postulated at least three main glacial phases, interspersed with two interglacial periods during which rivers had laid down normal, bedded deposits. The following year he worked under Zittel at Munich; he summarized his local fieldwork in *Die Vergletscherung der deutschen Alpen . . .*, which soon became a standard reference and was his *Habilitationsschrift* as *Privatdozent* in geography at the University of Munich (1883). In 1885 he won the chair of physical geography at Vienna; from 1906 to 1926 he held the chair of geography at Berlin and directed the Geographisches Institut. The outbreak of World War I caused his attention to turn to socio-political themes; his inaugural discourse (1917) as rector of the university was a study of frontiers: the best frontiers coincided with the living space *(Lebensraum)* indispensable to the life and security of a state. He played a considerable role in the revival of German nationalism after the war. Throughout his career he traveled widely. After retiring from Berlin he continued to write, primarily on Quaternary chronology, cartography, and population problems. He also wrote several competent biographies.

In Quaternary geology his studies of Alpine valleys with Eduard Brückner culminated in *Die Alpen im Eiszeitalter* (3 vols., 1901–09), which gave indisputable sedimentation evidence for at least four main ice advances (named Günz, Mindel, Riss, and Würm) and provided a nomenclature and a time scale for European Pleistocene studies for nearly half a century. His major contributions in geomorphology were to the general classification of landforms, to knowledge of individual landform types, and to the significance of climatic change in landform analysis. His *Morphologie der Erdoberfläche* (2 vols., 1894) was the first unified text of geomorphology. He emphasized form or shape in relation to genetic processes rather than to functional processes, and differentiated six fundamental forms (plain, escarpment, valley, mount, cup-shaped hollow, and cavern), differentiated by their slopes, that can arise from either erosion, accumulation, or dislocation. He contributed to the knowledge of glacial landform types, stressing the importance of the over-deepening of glacial valleys and the significance of glacial through valleys. He was one of the first to insist (1905) that "we see on the earth's surface not only the features of the present climate but also those of a past climate." His detailed accounts of the Danube (1891) and Oder (1899) rivers were among the earliest scientific analyses of the water budget and the flow regime of Central European rivers. In cartography, he advocated (1891) the production of Prussian maps on the scale of 1:100,000 for general purposes and of a standard series of global maps on a scale of 1:1,000,000; the latter idea was eventually realized in the IMW maps.

PENCK, WALTHER (*b. Vienna, Austria, 1888; d. Stuttgart, Germany, 1923*), geology.

Son of Albrecht Penck. Studied at University of Berlin, traveled with his father (1908–09), graduated from University of Heidelberg, and continued his studies in Vienna. In 1912–14, as geologist to the Dirección General de Minas in Buenos Aires, he mapped some 4,500 square miles and made a reconnaissance across the Andes; his observations led him, like his father, to posit temporal patterns of uplift much more varied than the pattern of rapid uplift followed by long quiescence that was accepted by W. M. Davis. Penck believed that most tectonic movements began and ended slowly; much of his geomorphic work was an attempt to provide physiographic support for the general pattern of uplift that he had previously inferred from stratigraphical evidence. After serving in the German army, he was appointed (1915) professor of mineralogy and geology at Constantinople; his last post was as unsalaried professor at Leipzig, where he developed an influential theory of landform interpretation through analysis of the ratios between endogenetic (diastrophic) and exogenetic (erosional) processes. He divided diastrophic movements into two major types, *Grossfalt* (great fold) and regional arching; where the two types of crustal movements occur together, as in the Alps, he thought that a more complex deformation was produced in which the regional doming, often outlasting the *Grossfalt*, was responsible for the general relief. Penck published little on these views; his book *Die morphologische Analyse* (1924), only part of a contemplated larger work, was assembled and edited by his father and was fragmentary, hurriedly written, and often unclear. It

is unfortunate that, for more than twenty years, the only English interpretation of his ideas was a highly critical article (1932) by his major opponent, W. M. Davis, who grossly misrepresented him.

PENNANT, THOMAS (*b. Downing, near Holywell, Flintshire, Wales, 1726; d. Downing, 1798*), natural history.

An eminent gentleman-naturalist who had studied at Queen's College, Oxford (no degree), and was active in politics, Pennant contributed to organizing, popularizing, and promoting the study of natural history. His writings include *British Zoology* (4 vols., 1768–70) and *Arctic Zoology* (2 vols., 1784–85), both standard texts. It was at his suggestion that Gilbert White began writing the letters that became *The Natural History and Antiquities of Selborne*.

PENNY, FREDERICK (*b. London, England, 1816; d. Glasgow, Scotland, 1869*), analytical chemistry, toxicology.

Apprenticed (1833–38) to a pharmacist and analytical chemist; attended lectures of Brande and Faraday at the Royal Institution. From 1839 he held the poorly paid chair of chemistry at Anderson's College, Glasgow, earning extra money in legal and commercial consultancy; in 1843 he visited Liebig at Giessen and was awarded the Ph.D. there on the basis of his published work (all of which was related to practical problems). Noteworthy for his polished reappraisal (1839) of the equivalent weights (oxygen = 8) of chlorine, nitrogen, potassium, sodium, and silver; this work was highly praised by, and later influential on, J. S. Stas.

PENSA, ANTONIO (*b. Milan, Italy, 1874; d. Pavia, Italy, 1970*), anatomy, histology, embryology.

Graduated in medicine and surgery at Pavia University (1898) and lectured there (1900–15); professor of human anatomy at Sassari (1915–20), Parma (1921–29; also rector of the university), and Pavia (1930–48); from 1950, director of Pavia's Center for the Study of Neuroanatomy. Made important contributions to human and comparative morphology, histology, and microscopic anatomy; animal and plant cytology; and embryology. His extensive research on the nervous system added to knowledge of its structure, especially to interpretation of the concepts inherent in Golgi's doctrine of the diffused network and in that of the neuron according to Ramón y Cajal.

PERCY, JOHN (*b. Nottingham, England, 1817; d. London, England, 1889*), metallurgy.

Studied medicine in Paris and Edinburgh (M.D., 1838) and obtained a hospital post in Birmingham, where his interest in chemistry was reawakened by the local metal industries. Through research and teaching (at Royal School of Mines, 1851–79) he exerted a profound influence on the progress of British metallurgy, transforming it from a repertoire of practices into a scientific discipline. His comprehensive (but unfinished) *Treatise on Metallurgy* (4 vols., 1864–80) included his survey of the national resources of iron ore.

PEREIRA (or **Pererius**), **BENEDICTUS** (*b. Ruzafa [near Valencia], Spain, 1535; d. Rome, Italy, 1610*), physics, mechanics, astrology.

A Jesuit who taught in Rome, Pereira wrote an important Aristotelian commentary on natural philosophy, *De communibus omnium rerum naturalium* (or *Physicorum . . . libri;* 1562), which was widely read and was used as a philosophy textbook in Jesuit schools. He followed the Italian tradition in rejecting Parisian dynamics. The *De communibus* was quoted frequently in the Renaissance debate on the nature of mathematics. His popular *Adversus fallaces et superstitiosas artes* (1591) was an outright attack on the occult arts.

PEREIRA, DUARTE PACHECO (*b. Santarém* [?], *Portugal, ca. 1460; d. Lisbon* [?], *Portugal, 1533*), navigation.

A sailor and pilot whose expeditions are incompletely documented, he became a national hero for his successful defense of the weak king of Cochin against the powerful King Samorim of Calicut. His *Esmeraldo de situ orbis*, begun in Lisbon in 1505, is known only from incomplete copies; it may be considered a routier, or collection of sailing directions, with an introduction on contemporary seamanship, which departs from the style of the medieval routiers.

PÉRÈS, JOSEPH JEAN CAMILLE (*b. Clermont-Ferrand, France, 1890; d. Paris, France, 1962*), mathematics, mechanics.

Agrégé in mathematics at the École Normale Supérieure (1911); earned a doctorate (1915) under the supervision of Volterra. Professor of mechanics at Marseilles (1921–32), where he founded an institute of fluid mechanics. Called to the Sorbonne in 1932; dean of Paris Faculty of Sciences (1954–61) and active in major research organizations. His results on integral equations extended those of Volterra, notably regarding composition products of permutable functions with a given function, and, later, the composition of functions of arbitrary order; these findings are now considered classical, as is his theory of symbolic calculus. His influential work in fluid mechanics was aimed at various applications, especially in aeronautics. In two other fields he obtained results now bearing his name: Levi-Civita parallelism (1919), and impact with friction (1924; one of the last great successes of rational mechanics).

PÉREZ DE VARGAS, BERNARDO (*b. Madrid, Spain, ca. 1500–33*), astronomy, biology, metallurgy.

Son of a distinguished family, but few biographical data are known. Author of the first extensive book on metallurgy in Spanish, *De re metalica* (licensed, 1564; published in 1568), composed of nine books and largely copied from Biringuccio's *Pirotechnia* (1540). Also wrote *Sumario de cosas notables* (1560) and *Repertorio perpetuo o fábrica del universo* (1563).

PERKIN, WILLIAM HENRY (*b. London, England, 1838; d. Sudbury, England, 1907*), organic chemistry.

Enrolled in Royal College of Science at fifteen and studied under A. W. von Hofmann. In 1856, while trying to synthesize quinine by treating an aniline salt with bichromate of potash in his home laboratory, he isolated mauve, or aniline purple, the first dye-stuff to be produced commercially from coal-tar. With his father's support he built a factory, devised new techniques and apparatus, and patented his process; Perkin's mauve was an instant success in dyehouses and gave impetus to a new coal-tar dyestuffs industry. In 1868–69 he developed new methods of manufacturing alizarin, and by 1871 his company was producing 220 tons a year. Other discoveries included "Perkin's synthesis" of coumarin, stemming from studies of the action of acetic anhydride on aromatic aldehydes, which led in turn to the synthesis of cinnamic acid from benzaldehyde—a discovery that made possible the first synthesis of indigo by Baeyer and Caro. In 1874 he sold his factory and turned full time to research in pure chemistry; from 1881 he studied the relationship between magnetic rotatory polarization and organic molecular structure, thereby developing an important tool. He was knighted in 1906.

PERKIN, WILLIAM HENRY, JR. (*b. Sudbury, Middlesex, England, 1860; d. Oxford, England, 1929*), organic chemistry.

Eldest son of William Henry Perkin. Studied at Royal College of Chemistry, under Wislicenus at Würzburg (1880–82), and under Baeyer at Munich (1882–86). Taught at Heriot-Watt College in Edinburgh (1887–92), Owens College in Manchester (1892–1912), and Oxford (Waynflete professor, from 1912). As a young man he made the first derivatives of cyclopropane and cyclobutane; his later work was concerned almost entirely with elucidation of the structures of natural products by degradation and synthesis.

PÉRON, FRANÇOIS (*b. Cérilly, France, 1775; d. Cérilly, 1810*), zoology, natural history.

Studied theology (1791–92), fought in Alsace, and studied at École de Médecine, Paris. Sailed with an expedition (1800–04) to New Holland (Australia) as a zoologist, and subsequently wrote various zoological and oceanographical memoirs, some jointly with Lesueur.

PÉROT, JEAN-BAPTISTE GASPARD GUSTAV ALFRED (*b. Metz, France, 1863; d. Paris, France, 1925*), physics.

Studied at the École Polytechnique; earned *docteur ès sciences* (1888) after working under Blondlot at Nancy. He then joined the University of Marseilles, where he studied dielectric properties and electromagnetic waves and became an expert on industrial electricity. With Charles Fabry he developed a new method of optical interferometry (1894–1901); they used their "Fabry-Pérot interferometer" to determine the mass of a cubic centimeter of water and to analyze the solar spectrum. In 1901 he went to the Conservatoire des Arts et Métiers as laboratory director; from 1908 he did research at Meudon Observatory and taught at the École Polytechnique.

PERRAULT, CLAUDE (*b. Paris, France, 1613; d. Paris, 1688*), zoology, medicine, plant and animal physiology, architecture, mechanical engineering.

Brother of fairy-tale writer Charles Perrault and hydrologist Pierre Perrault. Studied at Collège de Beauvais and then trained as a physician; presented his thesis at Paris in 1639 and practiced medicine quietly until invited to be a founding member of the Académie des Sciences (1666). He became a leader of the Academy's anatomists and has been credited with many of their anonymously published dissection descriptions. He claimed to have conceived independently a theory of the circulation of sap in plants (1667, not strictly a circulatory theory) and an embryonic preformation theory (1668). In 1680 he began publishing an all-embracing natural philosophy which shows clear Cartesian influence; in his longest essay, he explained sound as an agitation of the air which affects only the ear. From 1667 he was also active as an architect, working principally on plans for the Louvre and for the observatory of the Academy; this led in turn to mechanical inventions to overcome friction in machines, as well as other inventions.

PERRAULT, PIERRE (*b. France, 1611; d. France, 1680*), natural history.

Elder brother of Claude Perrault. A lawyer and government administrator who was dismissed as tax collector for borrowing on revenues (1664), Perrault is now known to be the author of *De l'origine des fontaines* (published anonymously, 1674). This work, with its proof, by measurement and calculation, that only one-sixth of the annual rainfall was necessary to sustain the flow of the Seine, marks him as a pioneer in experimental hydrology; his findings were later confirmed by Mariotte.

PERRIER, EDMOND (*b. Tulle, France, 1844; d. Paris, France, 1921*), zoology.

Studied under Lacaze-Duthiers at École Normale Supérieure (*licence ès sciences*, 1866; *agrégation*, 1867). Worked primarily at Muséum d'Histoire Naturelle (*aidenaturaliste*, 1867–72; *doctorat ès sciences naturelles*, 1869; professor-administrator, 1876–1900; director from 1900). His major work was devoted to the anatomy, physiology, and taxonomy of invertebrates, particularly oligochaetes and echinoderms. In *Les colonies animales* (1881) he attempted a theory of the evolutionary formation of groups of organisms. One of the principal evolutionists in France, he was largely responsible for the revival of Lamarckism. In "Tachygenèse" (1902) he sought to explain apparent difficulties of the biogenetic law by the phenomenon of embryogenic acceleration and by the occurrence of embryonic adaptations that modify the subsequent development of the organism.

PERRIER, GEORGES (*b. Montpellier, France, 1872; d. Paris, France, 1946*), geodesy.

Graduated from the École Polytechnique (1894) as an artillery officer. Played a major role in preparing and executing a scientific mission (1901–06) sent to Peru and Ecuador to measure an arc of meridian; on his return he was placed in charge of evaluating and processing all the measurements and of publishing the results. From 1919 until his death he was secretary-general of the Association Internationale de Géodésie, where he suggested and encouraged many undertakings, improved existing publications, and created new ones.

PERRIN, JEAN BAPTISTE (*b. Lille, France, 1870; d. New York, N.Y., 1942*), physical chemistry.

While still a student at the École Normale Supérieure (doctorate, 1897), where he was strongly influenced by Marcel Brillouin, Perrin proved that cathode rays are negatively charged by collecting them in a "Faraday cup" (1895). Developing a course in physical chemistry at the Sorbonne, his interest shifted to ion transport and thence

to Brownian motion. In 1908 he showed that the number of colloidally suspended particles undergoing Brownian motion decreases exponentially with increasing height and that this variation follows from kinetic theory; in auxiliary experiments he proved that Stokes's law was valid for particles as small as 0.1 micron. This work brought him recognition: from 1910 to 1940 he held a chair created for him at the Sorbonne, and in 1926 he won the Nobel Prize for physics. His most fundamental conclusion—that he had proved the existence of atoms—was soon universally accepted and was popularized in his book *Les atomes* (1913). In 1940 his antifascism made it necessary for him to emigrate from France to the U.S., where he helped establish the French University of New York.

PERRINE, CHARLES DILLON (*b. Steubenville, Ohio, 1867; d. Villa General Mitre, Argentina, 1951*), astronomy.

Initially a businessman, he joined the staff of Lick Observatory in 1893 and soon became widely known for his discovery, observation, and calculation of orbits of comets and for his determination of solar parallax from observations of the asteroid Eros. In 1904 and 1905 he discovered the sixth and seventh satellites of Jupiter; he then did important research on nebulae and star clusters. From 1909 until 1936, when forced to retire for political reasons, he directed the Argentine National Observatory at Cordoba.

PERRONCITO, EDOARDO (*b. Viale d'Asti, Italy, 1847; d. Pavia, Italy, 1936*), parasitology, bacteriology.

Studied veterinary medicine at University of Turin and held a professorship there (from 1873); in 1875 the first chair of parasitology in Italy was created for him at Turin. Did research on many aspects of the infective pathology and parasitology of animals (and of some plants). Among his important studies were those on Echinococcus, cysticercosis, and other parasitic infections in animals that are easily transmitted to man by infected food; on bovine tuberculosis, which he showed to be identical to human tuberculosis; and on miners' anemia, which he found to be caused by *Anchylostoma duodenale* and for which he developed a medicine based on the oil of the male fern.

PERRONET, JEAN-RODOLPHE (*b. Suresnes, France, 1708; d. Paris, France, 1794*), civil engineering.

First director of the Bureau Central des Dessignateurs of the Corps des Ponts et Chaussées (1747), which became the École des Ponts et Chaussées; also inspector general (from 1750) and then head (from 1763) of the Corps des Ponts et Chaussées, and inspector general of France's saltworks (1757–86). A noted designer of bridges (including Pont de Neuilly and Pont de la Concorde), he developed the classical stone arch bridge to its ultimate perfection.

PERROTIN, HENRI JOSEPH ANASTASE (*b. St. Loup, Tarn-et-Garonne, France, 1845; d. Nice, France, 1904*), astronomy.

Studied with F. Tisserand at the Faculté des Sciences of Toulouse, and worked with him at Toulouse observatory. Made astrometric and astrophysical observations and discovered six asteroids before turning to celestial mechanics. His doctoral dissertation (1879) established the first precise theory of the asteroid Vesta. From 1879 he directed the Nice observatory; his slotted-wheel determination of the speed of light as 299,880 kilometers per second (1902) was considered the best estimate for more than thirty years.

PERSEUS (*fl. third century* B.C. [*?*]), mathematics.

Perseus is known to us only from two passages in Proclus. In the first, his name is associated with "spiric" curves; in the second, Proclus says that Perseus wrote an epigram upon his discovery, "Three lines upon five sections finding, Perseus made offering to the gods therefor." In another place Proclus says that a spiric surface is generated by the revolution of a circle standing upright and turning about a fixed point that is not its center; wherefore there are three kinds of spiric surface according as the fixed point is on, inside, or outside the circumference. The spiric surface is thus the modern "tore"; the exact interpretation of Perseus' epigram, however, remains unclear.

PERSONNE, JACQUES (*b. Saulieu, Côte-d'Or, France, 1816; d. Paris, France, 1880*), chemistry, pharmacy.

A graduate of the Paris School of Pharmacy, he taught there while serving as chief pharmacist at three Paris hospitals: Midi (1849–57), Pitié (1857–78), and Charité (1878–80). At the same time he carried on unremitting research, most notably a chemical and botanical study of lupulin (1854); the first experimental evidence of the superiority of red phosphorus to regular phosphorus in the production of hydrobromic and hydriodic acids and their esters (1861); development of standards of identity and purity for chloral hydrate; and discovery and study of chloral alcoholate (1869–70). He earned his *docteur ès sciences physiques* in 1877.

PERSOON, CHRISTIAAN HENDRIK (*b. Cape of Good Hope, South Africa, 1761; d. Paris, France, 1836*), botany, mycology.

Studied theology at Halle (1783–86), medicine at Leiden (1786), and medicine and natural sciences at Göttingen (1787–1802); never completed his studies, but was awarded an honorary Ph.D. (1799); moved to Paris in 1802. He is known in particular for his mycological publications, culminating in *Synopsis fungorum* (1801; an incomplete, greatly revised version was titled *Mycologia europaea* [1822–26]), considered the basis of modern mycology. His *Synopsis plantarum* (1805–07) sought to describe briefly all the phanerogams then known.

PERSOZ, JEAN-FRANÇOIS (*b. Cortaillod, Neuchâtel, Switzerland, 1805; d. Paris, France, 1868*), chemistry.

Earned *docteur ès sciences physiques* from Paris Faculty of Sciences (1833) after studies with Thenard at Collège de France. Worked in Strasbourg (1833–50), then returned to Paris as *suppléant* to Dumas; taught at the École Normale Supérieure and the Conservatoire des Arts et Métiers. Wrote many papers on analytical chemistry and chemical technology, a large work on textile printing (1846), and an influential book on the chemistry of molecular combinations, *Introduction à l'étude de la chimie moléculaire* (1839). With Payen (1833), he reported the isolation of diastase from malt extract and the conversion of starch into sugar by diastase; with Biot (1833) he stud-

ied the production of dextrorotatory substances by hydrolysis of sugar or starch with mineral acids.

PETER ABANO. *See* **Abano, Pietro d'.**

PETER ABELARD. *See* **Abailard, Pierre.**

PETER OF AILLY. *See* **Ailly, Pierre d'.**

PETER BONUS. *See* **Petrus Bonus.**

PETER OF DACIA. *See* **Peter Philomena of Dacia.**

PETER PEREGRINUS, also known as **Pierre de Maricourt** (*fl. ca. 1269*), magnetism.

Virtually nothing is known of him; he may have earned the honorific title "Peregrinus" by participating in the siege of Lucera, perhaps in the capacity of engineer. He is known as author of an influential treatise on the magnet, *Epistola Petri Peregrini de Maricourt ad Sygerum de Foucaucourt, Militem, De Magnete* (1269). He is conjectured to have written a treatise on the construction of an astrolabe; he is also conjectured to be the "Magister Petrus" lavishly praised by Roger Bacon in *Opus tertium*. It seems evident that he was greatly, and perhaps primarily, interested in the construction of instruments and devices.

The *Epistola* ranks as one of the most impressive scientific treatises of the Middle Ages; it is the earliest extant treatise devoted exclusively to magnetism, and was drawn upon by William Gilbert in *De magnete* (1600). Its first part, in ten chapters, describes the properties and effects of the lodestone, while the second, in three chapters, is devoted to the construction of three instruments utilizing the special properties and powers of the magnet. In discussing the spherical magnet (called a *terrella* by William Gilbert but perhaps first shaped and used by Peregrinus) it gives the first extant account of magnetic polarity and methods for determining the poles of a magnet, and in distinguishing north and south poles it presents a qualitative description of the fundamental law of magnetic polarity. To explain attraction and repulsion between the poles of magnets, Peregrinus resorted to the agent-patient relationship so popular in medieval natural philosophy; he believed that the poles receive their virtue from the celestial poles, a theory deriving from his knowledge that Polaris, the pole star, does not rest at the celestial north pole but revolves around it (a fact virtually unknown to astronomers or seamen). Interested in practical applications of magnetism, he suggested a device using magnetic power as a source of perpetual motion; he also described two compasses, one wet and one dry, which, in their use of divisions and of movable sights enabling azimuthal readings to be taken, represent a considerable improvement over previous instruments.

PETER PHILOMENA OF DACIA, also known as **Petrus Dacus, Petrus Danus, Peter Nightingale** (*fl. 1290–1300*), mathematics, astronomy.

Peter's career is incompletely documented. He is known to have been canon of Roskilde, to have taught at the University of Bologna (1291–92), to have been in Paris 1292–93, and to have returned to Roskilde by 1303; he has incorrectly been considered a Dominican. His mathematical works included a commentary on Sacrobosco's arithmetic, with some original contributions. In astronomy, represented by numerous writings, he is especially noteworthy for his work on computing instruments (he was the first to invent a computer that calculated longitudes for all the planets with a single instrument) and for his astronomical tables. His calendar, computed in Paris as a substitute for the much-used calendar of Robert Grosseteste, which had run out, remained in constant use for 150 years; it had the peculiar feature (stemming, perhaps, from Scandinavian astronomy) that for each day of the year it listed both the declination of the sun and the length of the day.

PETERS, CARL F. W. (*b. Pulkovo, Russia, 1844; d. Königsberg, Germany [now Kaliningrad, R.S.F.S.R.], 1894*), astronomy, geodesy.

Son of Christian A. F. Peters, he became his father's assistant at Altona observatory after studies at Kiel, Berlin, Munich, and Göttingen (Ph.D., 1868); in this post he made determinations of the length of the seconds pendulum and worked with Bessel's pendulum apparatus. In 1883 he became director of the chronometer *Observatorium* of the imperial navy, due to his extremely careful investigations of the rate of chronometers (he found them to be influenced by humidity and magnetism as well as by temperature). In 1888 he was made professor at the University of Königsberg and director of its observatory.

PETERS, CHRISTIAN AUGUST FRIEDRICH (*b. Hamburg, Germany, 1806; d. Kiel, Germany, 1880*), astronomy.

Received Ph.D. from University of Königsberg; worked at Hamburg observatory (1834–38), Pulkovo observatory (1839–48), University of Königsberg (1849–54), Altona observatory (from 1854), and University of Kiel (from 1874). Both a student and a successor of Bessel, Peters sought to ascertain the base of spherical astronomy. His investigations concerning nutation, the proper motion of Sirius, and parallaxes of the fixed stars are his main achievements. From 1855 till his death he was editor of *Astronomische Nachrichten.* Father of Carl F. W. Peters.

PETERS, CHRISTIAN HEINRICH FRIEDRICH (*b. Coldenbüttel, Schleswig, Denmark [now Schleswig-Holstein, Germany], 1813; d. Clinton, N.Y., 1890*), astronomy.

Studied under Encke at Berlin (Ph.D., 1836) and under Gauss at Göttingen. Surveyed in Sicily (1838–48); immigrated to U.S. (1854) after five years in Constantinople. Employed by Coast Survey in Cambridge and in Albany; from 1858, professor of astronomy and director of Litchfield Observatory at Hamilton College in Clinton. His primary scientific interest was observational positional astronomy: charted proper motions and internal developments of sunspots; attempted to chart, without photography, all stars down to (and even below) the fourteenth magnitude within 30° of the ecliptic, coincidentally discovering 48 asteroids. Collated the star catalogs in Continental manuscripts of Ptolemy's *Almagest.*

PETERSEN, JULIUS (*b. Sorø, Denmark, 1839; d. Copenhagen, Denmark, 1910*), mathematics.

Studied at College of Technology in Copenhagen and later taught there (1871–87); graduated from University of Copenhagen (1866; doctorate, 1871), and was a pro-

fessor there (1887–1909). His textbooks exerted a very strong influence on Danish mathematical education (particularly *Methods and Theories for the Solution of Problems of Geometrical Constructions,* 1866) and several were translated into other languages. An important contribution was his theory of regular graphs (1891), inspired by a problem in the theory of invariants.

PETERSON, KARL MIKHAILOVICH (*b. Riga, Russia [now Latvian S.S.R.], 1828; d. Moscow, Russia, 1881*), mathematics.

Received the degree of bachelor of mathematics from the University of Dorpat (1853) for a remarkable thesis (not published in his lifetime) on the theory of surfaces; its first part established certain new properties of curves on surfaces, and its second continued Gauss's and Minding's works on the bending of surfaces. From 1865 he taught at the German Peter and Paul School in Moscow; he also took an active part in the organization of the Moscow Mathematical Society and in its work. His later works elaborated new methods in the differential geometry of surfaces. He was awarded an honorary doctorate (1879) for studies on the theory of characteristics of partial differential equations.

PETIT, ALEXIS THÉRÈSE (*b. Vesoul, France, 1791; d. Paris, France, 1820*), physics.

Graduated from the École Polytechnique in 1809 and was immediately taken onto the staff; in 1815 he succeeded to Hassenfratz's chair of physics. His most important research was in collaboration with Pierre Dulong (q.v.): their classic experimental investigation (1815–18) established the gas thermometer as the only reliable standard and put the approximate nature of Newton's law of cooling beyond all doubt. In 1819 they accidentally discovered their law of atomic heats ("the atoms of all elementary substances have exactly the same capacity for heat"), the exactness of which was in doubt from the start. Petit had a great talent for mathematics, as evidenced by his doctoral thesis (1811) on the theory of capillary action and by a paper on the theory of machines (1818).

PETIT, PIERRE (*b. Montluçon, France, 1594 or 1598; d. Lagny-sur-Marne, France, 1677*), physics, astronomy.

A governmental official who also pursued science, Petit was a member of Mersenne's Academia Parisiensis and a leader of the Académie Montmor. His private collection of telescopes and instruments was among the best in Paris; his inventions included a perfected filar micrometer later used by Cassini I. His *Dissertation sur la nature des comètes* (1665) was highly praised, as were his studies on magnetic declination. In 1646 he collaborated with Blaise Pascal in repeating Torricelli's barometric vacuum experiment. His correspondence with Oldenburg facilitated the exchange of ideas between England and France.

PETOSIRIS, PSEUDO- (*fl. Egypt, second and first centuries* B.C.), astrology.

During antiquity several texts relating to divination and astrology circulated under the names Petosiris and Nechepso (Nechepso was a king in the twenty-sixth Egyptian dynasty, *ca.* 600 B.C., and the most famous Petosiris was high priest of Thoth, *ca.* 300 B.C. [?], but whether the author of the works circulating under their names had these two individuals in mind is uncertain). The fragments of these works fall into four main groups: (1) those using astral omens as developed by the Egyptians in the Achemenid and Ptolemaic periods from Mesopotamian prototypes to give general indications, and including the earliest evidence known to us of a theory of astral influence; (2) those derived from a revelation-text in which Nechepso the king, guided by Petosiris, sees a vision that grants him a knowledge of horoscopic truth; (3) a treatise on astrological medical botany and another on decanic medicine; and (4) treatises on numerology. These influential works illuminate the invention of a new science of astrology based on Greek astronomy and physics in conjunction with Hellenistic mysticism and Egypto-Babylonian divination from astral omens.

PETRIE, (WILLIAM MATTHEW) FLINDERS (*b. Charlton, Kent, England, 1853; d. Jerusalem, Palestine [now Israel], 1942*), Egyptology, archaeology.

Prevented by delicate health from attending school or university, he was taught by his parents and developed a keen interest in antiquities and surveying. His first book (1877) was *Inductive Metrology*. In 1883 he published *The Pyramids and Temples of Gizeh* after two years' surveying. He subsequently worked with the Egyptian Exploration Fund (later Society) 1883–93, 1896–1906, and founded and directed the British School of Archaeology in Egypt (1905–26), before turning his attention to Palestine. He was professor of Egyptology at the University of London (1892–1933) and was knighted in 1923. His later publications included *Diospolis Parva* (1901), in which he systematically arranged the predynastic Egyptian material for the first time and invented the technique of sequence-dating; and *Methods and Aims in Archaeology* (1904), in which he further described the technique. His revolutionary techniques and remarkable finds (including the early royal tombs at Abydos; the Tell el-Amarna correspondence and the numerous relics at Tell el-Amarna itself; the discoveries of Mycenaean and Pre-Mycenaean pottery at Ghurob and Kahun; and discovery of the predynastic cultures of Egypt, particulary at Nakada, Ballas, and Diospolis Parva) made the last quarter of the nineteenth century the ''heroic age'' of Egyptian archaeology.

PETROV, NIKOLAY PAVLOVICH (*b. Trubchevsk, Orlovskaya Oblast, Russia, 1836; d. Tuapse, U.S.S.R., 1920*), mechanics, engineering.

Studied under Vyshnegradsky and Ostrogradsky at Nikolaevskaya Engineering Academy (graduated 1858), and taught there and at St. Petersburg Technological Institute. Active in the technical study and governmental administration of transportation, particularly railroads, he was the first to arrive at equations for the motion of wheels in the presence and absence of braking, as well as an equation for the motion of the center of gravity of a train during braking (1878); he then found the true maximum speed for any possible braking system. His most important work was in the hydrodynamic theory of lubricants; computing the equations of motion of a viscous liquid, integrating them, and using Newton's formula for the force of resistance of a viscous liquid with one layer in motion relative to another layer (which he had confirmed experimentally), he discovered the law of friction that bears his name.

PETROV, VASILY VLADIMIROVICH (*b. Oboyan, Russia, 1761; d. St. Petersburg, Russia, 1834*), physics, chemistry.

From 1795 Petrov taught at the Medical-Surgical Academy in St. Petersburg, where he created a first-class *cabinet de physique* and did basic research in physical chemistry, electrostatics, and galvanism. He actively promoted Lavoisier's theory of combustion; in applying it to the study of various forms of phosphorescence he showed that luminescence of rotten wood can occur only in the presence of oxygen, and by demonstrating that the phosphorescence of minerals does not depend on the presence of oxygen he distinguished photoluminescence from chemiluminescence. In publications of 1803 and 1804 he described studies with a battery of 2,100 copper-zinc elements. He also made meteorological observations and conducted a study of the relation of velocity of vaporization of ice and snow to atmospheric pressure, temperature, and wind force.

PETROVSKY, IVAN GEORGIEVICH (*b. Sevsk, Orlov guberniya, Russia, 1901; d. Moscow, U.S.S.R., 1973*), mathematics.

A graduate of Moscow University (1927), he combined a career there (professor from 1933; doctorate, 1935; rector, 1951–73) with activity at various scientific and teaching institutions. Editor-in-chief of *Matematicheskii sbornik* for many years. He achieved important results in the theory of partial differential equations (1937–38), where he was first to distinguish elliptical, hyperbolic, and parabolic systems; topology of algebraic curves and surfaces; and probability theory (1934), including the method of upper and lower sums, which became the basic analytical method of research in this field.

PETRUS. *See also* **Peter.**

PETRUS BONUS, also known as **Bonus Lombardus** or **Buono Lombardo of Ferrara** (*fl. ca. 1323–30*), alchemy.

Author of *The Precious New Pearl*, a scholastic exposition of the arguments, with the names of appropriate authorities, for and against the validity of the alchemical art; it is significant for the light that it sheds on current practices, theories, and authorities in alchemy and in other areas of natural science in the early fourteenth century. Petrus Bonus held that the substance and material cause of the philosophers' stone was quicksilver alone, and that divine assistance was necessary for success in alchemy.

PETTENKOFER, MAX JOSEF VON (*b. Lichtenheim [near Neuberg], Germany, 1818; d. Munich, Germany, 1901*), chemistry, hygiene, epidemiology.

Pettenkofer studied intermittently at the University of Munich, was an apprentice in the court pharmacy, qualified as pharmacist and physician in 1843, studied medical chemistry at Würzburg (1843–44) and Giessen (1844, under Liebig), wrote romantic poems glorifying chemistry and its adepts (*Chemische Sonette*), and worked at the Royal Mint (1845–47) before receiving an appointment to teach medical chemistry at Munich (1847; professor from 1852). From 1850 he also directed the royal pharmacy. His early achievements in chemistry include improvement of Marsh's test for arsenic, development of the Pettenkofer color reaction for bile (Würzburg, 1844), discovery of creatinine in human urine

(Giessen, 1844), an anticipation of the periodic law of the elements (1850), and numerous inventive solutions of practical problems.

His lasting fame, however, is as founder of experimental hygiene. His studies in this field originated in the king's inquiry as to the drying effects and possible health hazards of the new hot-air heating in the palace, which led him to an awareness of environmental influences on health. He developed new methods and apparatus for the quantitative study of air quality and air exchange in occupied rooms. With Carl Voit, he established many basic nutritional facts using an airtight metallic respiratory apparatus, and his fame grew. In 1865 he was made professor of hygiene; in 1879 the first Institute of Hygiene was opened under his direction; in 1883 he was one of the founders and editors of the *Archiv für Hygiene,* and was granted hereditary nobility. His special interest in the hygienic importance of air focused on its relationship to clothing and particularly to soil. In studying outbreaks of cholera—the grimmest challenge to hygiene in the nineteenth century—he became convinced that its cause lay in the combination of a specific germ with particular soil conditions (moisture, porosity, and pollution) that fostered the germ's dissemination, and that the germ alone could not produce the disease. His views brought him into conflict with Koch and his followers after 1883. Nevertheless, his efforts toward the improvement of the water supply, drainage, and sewerage of Munich brought him wide acclaim and greatly reduced the incidence of cholera and typhoid in that city. Indirectly, by elevating hygiene to an accepted discipline in medical training, he stimulated a new social outlook that encouraged the physician to provide not only relief from disease, but counsel and leadership toward healthful living.

PETTERSSON, HANS (*b. Kälhuvudet, Marstrand, Bohuslän, Sweden, 1888; d. Göteborg, Sweden, 1966*), oceanography.

Son of an outstanding oceanographer, Pettersson studied at Stockholm, Uppsala, and under Sir William Ramsay. In 1913 he joined the staff of the Svenska Hydrografiska-Biologiska Kommissionen; from 1914 he taught at Göteborgs Högskola; he was largely responsible for persuading businessmen to finance the Oceanografiska Institutet in 1939, and directed it until 1956. His research interests included differences of flow in stratified water, waves on internal boundary surfaces, radioactivity in seawater and sediments, penetration of light into the sea, changes of sea level caused by meteorological factors, and the effect of oceans on climate. He is best known for his round-the-world, Swedish deep-sea expedition in the *Albatross* (1946–48).

PETTY, WILLIAM (*b. Romsey, Hampshire, England, 1623; d. London, England, 1687*), economics, demography, geography.

Studied medicine in Utrecht, Leiden, and Amsterdam (1643–44), and anatomy with Hobbes in Paris (1645); by 1649 he was at Oxford, where John Wilkins and others met to study experimental philosophy in his lodgings. In 1650 he earned the doctorate of physic from Oxford, and soon received appointments at Brasenose College, Oxford, and then at Gresham College, London. He went to Ireland in 1652 as physician-general to Cromwell's army. He then supervised the Down Survey of forfeited lands

(1655–56); as a supplement to the survey he undertook the complete mapping of Ireland: a general map and thirty-five county and barony maps were printed around 1685—the most detailed maps ever published for a whole country. By 1659 he had returned to London, and in 1662 was a charter member of the Royal Society.

A thoroughgoing Baconian, Petty emphasized the collection of information and the practical application of scientific principles and knowledge. His most enduring achievement was in "political arithmetic": he was the first economic theorist to make a significant attempt to base economic policy upon statistical data, the first to emphasize the value of labor as a part of national wealth, and provided an important analysis of rents. His *Treatise of Taxes and Contributions* (1662) is perhaps his best work; *Verbum sapienti* (written *ca.* 1665, publ. 1691) is more quantitative and contains the first estimate of national incomes and the first discussion of the velocity of money. Among his other writings, seven contemporaries credited him with authorship of John Graunt's *Natural and Political Observations . . . Upon the Bills of Mortality* (1662).

PEURBACH (or **PEUERBACH**), **GEORG** (*b. Peuerbach, Austria, 1423; d. Vienna, Austria, 1461*), astronomy, mathematics.

A student at the University of Vienna (bachelor's, 1448; master's, 1453), where he later taught; for part of the period 1448–53 he traveled in Germany, France, and Italy, lectured in Padua and Ferrara, and perhaps met Nicholas Cusa—having already acquired an international reputation. In the 1450's he also became court astrologer to King Ladislaus V of Hungary, and then to Emperor Frederick III.

Peurbach's first valuable work in astronomy appears to have been the *Theoricae novae planetarum* (1454), an elementary but thorough textbook that went through many editions and was the subject of numerous commentaries; it contains very careful and detailed descriptions of solid sphere representations of Ptolemaic planetary models, derived perhaps from Ibn al-Haytham, that remained the canonical physical description of the structure of the heavens until Tycho disproved the existence of solid spheres. Its many definitions helped to establish the technical terminology of astronomy through the early seventeenth century. His most impressive work was *Tabulae eclipsium* (*ca.* 1459), an expansion and rearrangement of the Alphonsine Tables designed to save the calculator much tedious labor; it was still used (although critically) by Tycho near the end of the sixteenth century.

Peurbach is credited by Regiomontanus, his student and collaborator, with authorship of the first six books of *Epitoma Almagesti Ptolemaei;* the work, written at the request of Cardinal Bessarion, was completed by Regiomontanus after Peurbach's death. It was the most important and most advanced Renaissance textbook on astronomy, giving astronomers an understanding of Ptolemy that they had not previously been able to achieve. It served as the fundamental treatise on Ptolemaic astronomy until the time of Kepler and Galileo, and remains the best exposition of the subject next to the *Almagest* itself. The precise extent of Peurbach's contribution is unclear, however, for books I through VI follow closely the so-called *Almagesti minoris libri VI* (an unfinished textbook, apparently of the late thirteenth century).

In addition to his many astronomical works, Peurbach wrote on the computation of sines and chords *(Tractatus super propositiones Ptolemaei de sinubus et chordis)*, compiled a table of sines at intervals of 0;10°, and wrote a popular elementary textbook on practical computation *(Algorismus* or *Elementa arithmetices* or *Introductorium in arithmeticam).*

PEYER, JOHANN CONRAD (*b. Schaffhausen, Switzerland, 1653; d. Schaffhausen, 1712*), physiology.

Studied medicine in Basel, at Paris with Duverney, and at Montpellier with Vieussens. With his teacher Johann Jakob Wepfer and with Johann Conrad Brunner he formed the "Schaffhausen trio," whose important contributions to the new methodology of medical research were the explanation of symptoms by connecting them with the lesion in the body, considered as the site of the disease, and experimentation on animals *(anatomia animata)* to study either the functioning of organs or the effects of medicines on the organism. In 1682 Peyer described the lymphatic nodules and masses located in the walls of the ileum that now bear his name (he supposed them to be glands excreting the digestive juices). In 1681 he succeeded in making the hearts of dead animals—and even of hanged criminals—beat by blowing air into the veins or by utilizing other stimuli, achieving an artificial cardiac activity lasting several hours.

PEYSSONNEL, JEAN ANDRÉ (*b. Marseilles, France, 1694; d. Guadeloupe, 1759*), botany, zoology.

Received a medical degree from the University of Aix and began practice in Marseilles, but pursued marine natural history. Sent by the king to the Barbary Coast, he reported his finding that corals are not plants, but animals (1726)—a finding that was disputed by other naturalists until 1740. Also in 1726, he published *Mémoire sur les courans de la Méditerranée,* the first work written on the subject. In 1727 he went to Guadeloupe as "royal botanist to the American islands," and spent the rest of his life there.

PEZARD, ALBERT (*b. Neuflize, Ardennes, France, 1875; d. Paris, France, 1927*), endocrinology.

Studied at the École Normale of Charleville and of St.-Cloud; received master's from University of Paris; taught at two Paris *collèges,* and worked at the Station Physiologique du Collège de France. In his experimental studies of birds he established the true secondary sexual characters in the male bird and showed their strict dependence upon an endocrine secretion; he also deduced from the effects of total castration of females that the ovary normally secretes a substance that inhibits the evolution of plumage and of spurs—the first demonstration of the inhibitory action of an endocrine secretion. His pioneer work on the experimental production of sexual inversion and hermaphroditism showed that a threshold amount of the specific hormone must be secreted in order to elicit a given secondary sexual character, thus introducing into endocrinology the "all or none law." With Fernand Caridroit and Knud Sand he concluded that hormones do not interfere with the fundamental genotypic complex, but act as regulators of dominances.

PEZENAS, ESPRIT (*b. Avignon, France, 1692; d. Avignon, 1776*), hydrography, astronomy, physics.

A Jesuit, he taught in Lyons and in Aix before being named professor of hydrography at the École Royale d'Hydrographie at Marseilles (1728–49); he next directed the Observatoire Ste.-Croix in Marseilles, retiring to Avignon when the Jesuit order was suppressed in 1763. Author of notable treatises on piloting, gauging of barrels and ships, and nautical astronomy. He played a major role in the diffusion in France of English science through his translations of works by Maclaurin, Desaguliers, Henry Baker, John Harrison, and Robert Smith, among others.

PFAFF, JOHANN FRIEDRICH (*b. Stuttgart, Germany, 1765; d. Halle, Germany, 1825*), mathematics.

After legal studies he turned to science, studying mathematics with Kaestner and physics with Lichtenberg at Göttingen, astronomy with Bode at Berlin, and traveled extensively. He was professor of mathematics at Helmstedt (1788–1810), where Gauss was one of his students and lived in his house (1798), and then at Halle (from 1810; from 1812, he also directed the observatory). His early work was strongly marked by Euler's influence. In *Versuch einer neuen Summationsmethode . . .* (1788) he uncritically employed divergent series in his treatment of Fourier expansions; he edited Euler's posthumous writings (1792), and published an introductory treatise on analysis written in the spirit of Euler: *Disquisitiones analyticae maxime ad calculum integralem et doctrinam serierum pertinentes* (1797). His most important achievement, the theory of Pfaffian forms, was presented in an article of 1815, but its importance was not appreciated until Jacobi wrote on it in 1827. It constituted the starting point of a basic theory of integration of partial differential equations which, through the work of Jacobi, Lie, and others, has developed into the modern Cartan calculus of extreme differential forms.

PFEFFER, WILHELM FRIEDRICH PHILIPP (*b. Grebenstein, near Kassel, Germany, 1845; d. Leipzig, Germany, 1920*), botany, chemistry.

Pfeffer was apprenticed to his father, an apothecary with broad scientific interests, and was introduced by him to nature study; an uncle took him on excursions into the Alps, and he became one of the earliest climbers of the Matterhorn. He earned a doctorate in chemistry and botany from the University of Göttingen (1865) after barely four semesters; he then studied pharmacy at Marburg and worked as an apothecary before turning to academic botany. After studies with Pringsheim at Berlin and with Sachs at Würzburg he received appointments at Marburg (1871), Bonn (1873), Basel (1877), Tübingen (1878), and Leipzig (1887); from 1895 he was also coeditor of *Jahrbuch für wissenschaftliche Botanik.* His early researches were on germination of *Selaginella,* on the effects of external stimuli on plant growth, on protein metabolism in plants, and on plant irritability. His classic investigations of osmosis (reported in *Osmotische Untersuchungen,* 1877) were undertaken in an effort to explain irritability phenomena. He devised his *Pfeffer-Zelle* ("pepper pots")—unglazed, porous porcelain cells within which he precipitated membranes of copper ferrocyanide—in order to make direct measurements of various solutions at different concentrations and temperatures; his results showed osmotic pressure to be proportionate to concentration and to temperature. He also made the first direct measurements of osmotic pressures in plants, which were to provide van't Hoff with the values for his calculations. His comprehensive *Pflanzenphysiologie* (1881) became a well-known reference work. He was ingenious at devising apparatus for acute measurements and was an innovative experimenter; using aniline dyes, he pioneered the method of vital staining. He followed specific phenomena in his search for ultimate causes.

PFEIFFER, PAUL (*b. Elberfeld [now Wuppertal], Germany, 1875; d. Bonn, Germany, 1951*), chemistry.

Pfeiffer studied under Kekulé and Anschütz at Bonn, under Werner at Zurich (doctorate, 1898), under Ostwald at Leipzig, and under Hantzsch at Würzburg. After teaching at Zurich, Rostock, and Karlsruhe, he succeeded to Kekulé's chair at Bonn (1922–47). His work covered both inorganic and organic chemistry, as well as the territory between them; his main interest was in coordination compounds, particularly those of chromium. He was the first to apply Werner's coordination theory to crystals, and pioneered in the field of halochromism (the formation of colored substances from colorless organic bases by the addition of acids or solvents).

PFLÜGER, EDUARD FRIEDRICH WILHELM (*b. Hanau, Germany, 1829; d. Bonn, Germany, 1910*), physiology.

Studied medicine briefly at Heidelberg and Marburg; received M.D. from Giessen (1851) and from Berlin (1855, under Johannes Müller). Working on electrotonus (under the supervision of du Bois-Reymond) he determined the basic laws of the changes in sensitivity in a section of nerve subjected to a direct current which, due to polarization, spreads "extra-polarly"; Pflüger's law of convulsion—that sensitivity changes are dependent on the polarity, direction, and strength of the current—forms the basis for the diagnostic and therapeutic applications of electricity in medicine. In 1859 he succeeded Helmholtz in the chair of physiology at Bonn. Later topics of study included embryonal development of the ovary (1861–63; "Pflüger's tubes" are tubular sacs, containing closely packed vesicles, which form the ovary); nerve endings in salivary glands (1866); metabolism of nutritive substances; and gas exchange in blood and in cells. In the last field he showed that the energy requirement of the cell determines the magnitude of oxygen consumption, the blood respiring comparatively little; he developed the concept of "respiratory quotient," and showed that respiratory action is stimulated by a surplus of carbon dioxide and a lack of oxygen; and he performed the famous "table-salt frog" experiment: a frog in which the blood was replaced by a physiological salt solution displayed no significant decrease in gas exchange. From 1868 he edited the influential *Archiv für die gesamte Physiologie des Menschen und der Tiere;* he was the most feared critic of his time.

PHILINUS OF COS (*b. Cos; fl. ca. 250 B.C.*), medicine.

A student of Herophilus, Philinus severed relations with his teacher and thus helped to establish the empirical school of medicine (which had close contacts with the philosophy of skepticism). An etiological nihilist, he denied the utility of reading the pulse.

PHILIP, ALEXANDER PHILIPS WILSON (*b. Shieldhall, Scotland, 1770; d. Boulogne, France, 1851 [?]*), medicine, physiology.

Was christened Alexander Philips Wilson, but in 1811 changed his name to A. P. W. Philip. Studied medicine at Edinburgh (M.D., 1792) and London; practiced in Edinburgh, Winchester, and Worcester before going to London (1820), where he soon became a leading physician. Was a critical and accurate observer of disease and wrote successful treatises on many medical topics, including indigestion and fevers, but is more important for his work in physiology. In *An Experimental Enquiry Into the Laws of the Vital Functions* (1817) he reported that digestion ceased with section of the vagus, that gastric secretion could be decreased by damage or removal of parts of the brain or spinal cord, and that movement of the gut could be independent of brain control. Equally significant were his demonstrations that cardiac acceleration and inhibition were produced by stimulation of the nervous system, and that the heart and blood vessels could be affected by drugs that acted on the nervous system.

PHILLIPS, JOHN (*b. Marden, Wiltshire, England, 1800; d. Oxford, England, 1874*), geology, paleontology.

Nephew of geologist William Smith, whom he assisted from 1815. In 1824 he was engaged by the museum at York, and in 1831 played a leading part in organizing at York the general meeting of British scientists that became the British Association for the Advancement of Science; he was executive officer of the Association until 1859, and was a major contributor to its success. Professor of geology at King's College, London (1834–40); joined Geological Survey (1840); taught at Trinity College, Dublin (1844–45), and at Oxford (from 1853), where he was keeper of the new University Museum. A practical field geologist, he was skilled in the making of geological maps. In volumes on the geology of Yorkshire he introduced the term "Yoredale series" (1836). His descriptions and illustrations of the stratigraphy and characteristic fossils of particular formations facilitated progress in stratigraphical classification and correlation. He introduced the term "Mesozoic" to include the "New Red" (Triassic), "Oolitic" (Jurassic), and Cretaceous periods (1841). From 1852 he studied the moon's surface for the British Association (using photography, from 1853).

PHILLIPS, THEODORE EVELYN REECE (*b. Kibworth, Leicestershire, England, 1868; d. Headley, Surrey, England, 1942*), astronomy.

An amateur astronomer, he graduated from St. Edmund Hall, Oxford (B.A., 1891), was ordained (1891), and held a series of clerical appointments. In 1896 he began systematic observation of the planets; his work on Jupiter included tables with deduced rotation periods for different latitudes (1897–98) and the recording of more than 30,000 spot transits. President of British Astronomical Association (1914–16) and Royal Astronomical Society (1927–29).

PHILLIPS, WILLIAM (*b. London, England, 1775; d. London, 1828*), geology.

A printer and bookseller with a strong interest in natural science; one of the founders of the London Geological

Society (1807). Author of numerous papers, mainly on mineralogy; two popular textbooks of mineralogy (1815, 1816); and a digest of English geology (1818). The latter text was enlarged in collaboration with Conybeare and became *Outlines of the Geology of England and Wales, With an Introductory Compendium of the General Principles of That Science, and Comparative Views of the Structure of Foreign Countries* (1822); the stratigraphical framework popularized in it became of worldwide significance.

PHILO OF BYZANTIUM *(fl. ca. 250 B.C.)*, physics, mechanics, pneumatics.

Mentioned in antiquity by Vitruvius, Hero, and Eutocius. Author of *Mechanics*, a textbook whose contents have been reconstructed as: 1) Introduction; 2) On the lever; 3) On the building of seaports; 4) On catapults; 5) On pneumatics; 6) On automatic theaters; 7) On the building of fortresses; 8) On besieging and defending towns; 9) On stratagems. Of these, book 4 *(Belopoeica)*, book 5 *(Pneumatica)*, book 7 *(Paraskeuastica)*, and book 8 *(Poliorcetica)* are extant. Book 4 contains a method of doubling the cube that was cited by Eutocius; it is quite similar to Hero's method.

PHILOLAUS OF CROTONA *(fl. second half of fifth century B.C.)*, philosophy, astronomy, medicine.

A Pythagorean who settled in Tarentum after the democratic rebellion and is said to have taught Archytas. The actual nature and extent of his writings is uncertain; his existence is established by Plato's *Phaedo*. His medical doctrines were quoted by Menon. Ancient tradition credited him with a comprehensive Pythagorean treatise that was bought and publicized by Plato. His importance lies in his astronomical system as made known to us by Aëtius, Achilles Tatius, and Aristotle: the center of the universe is occupied not by the earth but by a central fire (not the sun), around which the earth moves at considerable speed (the earth always turns the same side to the central fire and we live on the opposite side); a "counter-earth" exists on the opposite side of the fire but at a lesser distance; the other heavenly bodies also revolve around the fire (in the order moon, sun, Mercury, Venus, Mars, Jupiter, Saturn); outermost is the fiery sphere of the fixed stars; the sun serves to focus the light of the fire (according to Aëtius) or of the stars (according to Achilles) toward the earth. Philolaus' suggestion that the earth is not at rest encouraged the inventors of the heliocentric system.

PHILOPONUS. See John Philoponus.

PIANESE, GIUSEPPE *(b. Civitanova del Sannio, Campobasso, Italy, 1864; d. Naples, Italy, 1933)*, pathological anatomy and histology.

Graduated in medicine and surgery from Naples (1887) and spent most of his career there (professor of pathological histology, 1906; head of Anatomical-Pathological Institute, 1917). His name was particularly linked to infective splenic anemia of infancy, which he first recognized as caused by a species of *Leishmania*. Did experimental splenectomy of guinea pigs (1903) and noted manifold effects on bodily development, resistance to infections, various organic reactions, and the morphological constitution of hematopoietic organs. Other impor-

tant work included minute cytological analysis of malignant tumors, confirming the morbidity of the tumor cells.

PIAZZI, GIUSEPPE *(b. Ponte in Valtellina, Italy [now Switzerland], 1746; d. Naples, Italy, 1826)*, astronomy.

Joined Theatine Order as a young man; earned a doctorate in philosophy and mathematics in Rome. From 1780 he held the chair of higher mathematics at Palermo, and established the observatory there (1790) with instruments he had ordered in England; from 1817 he was also in charge of establishing the Naples observatory. At Palermo he made precise determinations of the coordinates of the fixed stars, and in 1803 published a prize-winning catalog of the median positions of 6,748 stars; his catalog of 1813 contained the mean positions of 7,646 stars. In the course of his regular observations he discovered a new comet or planet on 1 January 1801, and recorded its motion until it came too near the sun to be observable; Gauss calculated its reappearance and F. X. von Zach found it as predicted, thus proving it to be a planet. In 1802 Piazzi named it Ceres for the patron goddess of Sicily.

PICARD, CHARLES ÉMILE *(b. Paris, France, 1856; d. Paris, 1941)*, mathematics.

With Poincaré, he was the most distinguished French mathematician of his generation. He entered the École Normale Supérieure in 1874, and passed the *agrégation* in 1877, having already made several important discoveries and having received the *docteur ès sciences* degree. From 1881 he lectured at the Sorbonne and at the École Normale Supérieure; from 1885 he was a chaired professor at the Sorbonne. He also taught at the École Centrale des Arts et Manufactures (1894–1937), and was permanent secretary of the Académie des Sciences (1917–41). Noted especially for work in mathematical analysis and algebraic geometry; his *Traité d'analyse* (3 vols., 1891–96) immediately became a classic. In 1879 he discovered the first Picard theorem: Let $f(z)$ be an entire function. If there exist two values of A for which the equation $f(z) = A$ does not have a finite root, then $f(z)$ is a constant. Picard's second theorem (1880), extending a result of Weierstrass', states: Let $f(z)$ be a function, analytic everywhere except at a, where it has an essential isolated singularity; the equation $f(z) = A$ has in general an infinity of roots in any neighborhood of a. Although the equation can fail for certain exceptional values of the constant A, there cannot be more than two such values. This result led to a classification of regular analytic functions. Worked also in theoretical physics, applying analysis to theories of elasticity, heat, and electricity; wrote on the history and philosophy of science; and participated in publication of works of Hermite and Halphen.

PICARD, JEAN *(b. La Flèche, France, 1620; d. Paris, France, 1682)*, astronomy, geodesy.

Seems to have taken religious orders, and may have become a prior. Assisted Gassendi for a time (from 1645) and is reputed to have succeeded him at the Collège Royal, but this has not been substantiated. A founder of the Académie Royale des Sciences (1666) and in charge of its project to remeasure an arc of meridian (1668–70); using Snell's method of skeleton triangulation, but greatly improving the observational techniques by use of instruments fitted with telescopes, quadrants, and sectors for angular measurements, he attained a precision thirty to forty times greater than that achieved previously. His result of 57,060 toises for the terrestrial degree, published in *Mesure de la terre* (1671), enabled Newton in 1684 to confirm the accuracy of his principle of gravitation. His other achievements include perfection of the movable-wire micrometer (with Auzout), and determination of the coordinates of Brahe's castle, Uraniborg (with Ole Römer, 1671–72), during which he noted an annual displacement of the polestar. In 1673 he moved into the Paris observatory and collaborated with Cassini, Römer, and P. de La Hire on astronomical and geodetic programs. He was one of the first to observe the fixed stars in full daylight; he also pointed out the phenomenon of "barometric glow."

PICCARD, AUGUSTE (*b. Basel, Switzerland, 1884; d. Lausanne, Switzerland, 1962*), physics.

Doctorate in mechanical engineering from Federal Institute of Technology, Zurich; taught in Zurich and Brussels. Attracted world attention in 1931 by ascending with Paul Kipfer, in a free balloon, to 51,775 feet; this was a new altitude record and marked the first use of a pressurized cabin for manned flight. In 1932, with Max Cosyns, he attained 53,153 feet. From 1937 he worked on developing his "bathyscaphe" to penetrate the depths of the sea; in 1953 his second model carried him and his son Jacques to a depth of 10,168 feet, trebling Beebe's record. A third model, the *Trieste,* was sold to the U.S. Navy; Jacques Piccard and Lt. Don Walsh, USN, descended in it to 35,800 feet in the Marianas Trench (1960).

PICCOLOMINI, ARCANGELO (*b. Ferrara, Italy, 1525; d. Rome, Italy, 1586*), medicine, anatomy, physiology.

Received doctorate in philosophy and medicine at Ferrara; taught philosophy at University of Bordeaux. Went to Rome, and became papal physician (from 1559); taught medicine and anatomy at the Sapienza (from 1575). His lectures were published as *Anatomicae praelectiones* (1586), in which morphological description is generally subordinate to the discussion of highly abstract questions of psychology and physiology; his thought reveals Neoplatonic, Aristotelian, and Galenic influences, but his physiological scheme had many characteristic features of its own. He upheld the supreme hegemony of the brain and refuted the pulmonary circulation.

PICKERING, EDWARD CHARLES (*b. Boston, Mass., 1846; d. Cambridge, Mass., 1919*), astronomy.

Graduated from Lawrence Scientific School at Harvard (1865), and taught there (1865–67); he then went to M.I.T. (1867–77), where he revolutionized the teaching of physics and established the first instructional physics laboratory in America (his *Elements of Physical Manipulation* [2 vols., 1873–76] was the first American laboratory manual of physics). From 1877 he directed the Harvard College Observatory, which he developed into the major distributing house of astronomical news and where he did pioneering work in astrophysics. In visual photometry, he developed the meridian photometer, in which the image of a star crossing the meridian is brought alongside the image of Polaris (Pickering's arbitrary standard)

by suitable arrangement of mirrors and prisms, and made more than 1.5 million readings, culminating with publication of the *Revised Harvard Photometry* (1908) listing magnitudes of more than 45,000 stars. He led a team including W. P. Fleming, A. J. Cannon, and A. C. Maury in producing the *Henry Draper Catalogue* (1918–24), in which nearly a quarter of a million stellar spectra were measured by Cannon and placed into one of twelve main spectral classes. In 1903 he issued a *Photographic Map of the Entire Sky,* the first such map ever published, picturing stars down to the twelfth magnitude on fifty-five plates. His habit of routinely photographing as large a portion of the visible sky as possible on every clear night resulted in the unique Harvard Photographic Library, providing a history, on some 300,000 glass plates, of all stars down to the eleventh magnitude. He was instrumental in founding the American Association of Variable Star Observers.

PICKERING, WILLIAM HENRY (*b. Boston, Mass., 1858; d. Mandeville, Jamaica, 1938*), astronomy.

Brother of E. C. Pickering. Graduated from M.I.T. (1879); taught there, and at Harvard observatory (from 1887). In 1891 he set up Harvard's Boyden Station at Arequipa, Peru; led expeditions to Jamaica (*ca.* 1900), and from 1911 was in charge of a permanent Harvard observing station there (it became his private observatory on his retirement, 1924). Pioneered in dry-plate celestial photography; took early pictures of Mars (1888) and long-unexcelled lunar photographs (1900). Discovered Phoebe on photographic plates and demonstrated its retrograde orbit. Also made extensive visual observations of planets and their satellites. From 1907 he paid considerable attention to predicting the location of trans-Neptunian planets.

PICTET, MARC-AUGUSTE (*b. Geneva, Switzerland, 1752; d. Geneva, 1825*), physics.

Turned to science after qualifying in law (1774); influenced by H. B. de Saussure, who had him appointed to chair of philosophy at Academy of Geneva (1786). Always prominent in public life, and also in scientific circles of Paris; joint founder and editor of *Journal de Genève* (1787–91) and of *Bibliothèque britannique* (1796; renamed *Bibliothèque universelle,* 1815). Did research in geology, geodesy, astronomy, and meteorology, as well as physics. Published *Essai sur le feu* (1790), which was widely read but unremarkable; it described experiments on heat and hygrometry and discussed theories of heat, favoring the idea of a fluid caloric. His lectures of 1790 gave the first public support in Geneva to Lavoisier's views.

PICTET, RAOUL-PIERRE (*b. Geneva, Switzerland, 1846; d. Paris, France, 1929*), low-temperature physics.

Studied physics and chemistry in Geneva and Paris (1868–70); returned to Geneva and began experimentation in cryogenics. Developed a compression refrigeration system using sulfur dioxide as coolant; he later patented *liquide Pictet* (sulfur dioxide plus carbon dioxide) and claimed it to be exempt from the second law of thermodynamics. In 1877, almost simultaneously with Cailletet, he liquefied oxygen, the first liquefaction of an atmospheric gas; he used the "cascade process," with sulfur dioxide in the first cycle, carbon dioxide in the second, and oxygen in the last. Held chair of industrial physics at University of Geneva (1879–86) before establishing an industrial research laboratory in Berlin.

PIERCE, GEORGE WASHINGTON (*b. Webberville, Tex., 1872; d. Franklin, N.H., 1956*), applied physics.

Graduated from University of Texas (1893); earned Ph.D. at Harvard (1900), where he spent his entire career (first director of Cruft Laboratory, 1914; professor from 1917). Wrote basic papers of great lucidity on resonant circuits and crystal detectors used in early radiotelegraphy, extended the use of semiconductor crystals to electroacoustics, and showed how mercury-vapor discharge tubes could be used for current control and sound recording. In collaboration with Kennelly, discovered the concept of motional impedance. Offered the first postgraduate course anywhere on underwater sound signaling. Best remembered for work on piezoelectricity, leading to development of quartz-crystal "Peirce oscillator"; and on magnetostriction, leading to generators of underwater sound. Later studied sound generation by bats and insects.

PIERI, MARIO (*b. Lucca, Italy, 1860; d. Sant' Andrea di Còmpito [Lucca], Italy, 1913*), projective geometry, foundations of geometry.

Studied at University of Bologna (1880–81) and at the Scuola Normale Superiore of Pisa (graduated 1884). Taught in Pisa, at military academy and University of Turin (1888–1900), at University of Catania (1900–08), and at Parma. Worked primarily in projective geometry until turning to foundations of mathematics in 1895; influenced by von Staudt, Peano, and Burali-Forti. In 1898 he used two undefined terms, projective point and the join of two projective points, to construct projective geometry as a logical-deductive system based on nineteen sequentially independent axioms. In 1899 he reduced the undefined terms for ordinary geometry to two: point and motion, the latter understood as the transformation of one point into another. Wrote also on foundations of arithmetic.

PIERO DELLA FRANCESCA. *See* **Francesca, Piero della.**

PIERRE. *See* **Peter.**

PIETTE, LOUIS-ÉDOUARD-STANISLAS (*b. Aubigny, Ardennes, France, 1827; d. 1906*), archaeology, paleontology.

While trained as a lawyer and active as a magistrate, he made major contributions to Paleolithic archaeology by his own discoveries, his championship of Paleolithic art, his special study and valuable collection of portable art (now at St.-Germain-en-Laye), and his ideas on classification. He discovered Gourdan, Lortet, Mas-d'Azil, and Brassempouy, and excavated prehistoric barrows at Avezac-Prat, Bartres, Osun, and La Halliade, near Lourdes.

PIGOTT, EDWARD (*b. 1753; d. Bath, England, 1825*), and **PIGOTT, NATHANIEL** (*b. Whitton, Middlesex, England; d. 1804*), astronomy.

Nathaniel Pigott, a surveyor, landed proprietor, and amateur astronomer, spent much of his life on the Conti-

nent, settling for a while at Caen before returning to England in 1771. He made a series of meteorological and longitudinal measurements in the Low Countries (1770–78) and observed a solar eclipse (1765), a transit of Venus (1769), and a transit of Mercury (1786); he was assisted by his son Edward, some of whose achievements have been ascribed to Nathaniel. Edward Pigott discovered a nebula in Coma Berenices and three comets, determined proper motions of several stars, and wrote important papers on the method of observing stars with a transit instrument. In 1783 he struck up a friendship with John Goodricke; his attention was subsequently directed to variable stars, and in 1784 he noted that η Aquilae is periodically variable, the first of several such discoveries.

PILATRE DE ROZIER, JEAN FRANÇOIS (*b. Metz, France, 1754; d. Wimille, near Boulogne, France, 1785*), education, aeronautics.

Studied pharmacy in Metz and sciences in Paris, but did little research of merit. Under the patronage of the Comte de Provence, brother of Louis XVI, he founded the Musée (1781), a private institution for higher education; after his death it was reorganized and called the Lycée (changed to Lycée Républicain in 1792 and to Athénée de Paris in 1802), and played an important part in the scientific and cultural life of Paris until the 1840's. In 1783 he made the first human balloon flight, traveling nearly six miles at about 3,000 feet; with Proust (23 June 1784) he reached a height of about 11,000 feet. He died attempting to cross the English Channel in an experimental balloon of his own design.

PINCHERLE, SALVATORE (*b. Trieste, Austria [now Italy], 1853; d. Bologna, Italy, 1936*), mathematics.

Studied under Betti and Dini at University of Pisa (graduated 1874) and under Weierstrass in Berlin (1877–78). Taught at universities of Palermo (1880) and Bologna (1880–1928). Founder and first president of Italian Mathematical Union (1922). One of the principal founders of functional analysis; studied in depth the Laplace transformation, iteration problems, and series of generalized factors. Author of several textbooks.

PINCUS, GREGORY GOODWIN (*b. Woodbine, N.J., 1903; d. Boston, Mass., 1967*), endocrinology.

Received B.S. at Cornell (1924), M.S. and Sc.D. at Harvard (1927); studied at Cambridge University and Kaiser Wilhelm Institute (1929–30); taught at Harvard (1931–38), Clark (1938–44), Tufts (1945–51), and Boston University (from 1951). With Hudson Hoagland he established the Worcester Foundation for Experimental Biology (1944). Made significant contributions to knowledge of the effects, metabolism, and biosynthesis of steroid hormones. With M. C. Chang (1951) he found that several progestational compounds administered orally could prevent pregnancy; with J. Rock and C. R. Garcia he immediately extended these studies to humans and perfected the oral contraceptive pill.

PINEL, PHILIPPE (*b. Jonquières, near Castres, France, 1745; d. Paris, France, 1826*), medicine.

Studied theology (1767–70), mathematics, and medicine at Toulouse (M.D., 1773); studied further at Montpellier (1774–78), where he began to formulate and to practice the principles that he later recommended to his students: "Take written notes at the sickbed and record the entire course of a severe illness." From 1778 he was in Paris; he frequented the *salon* of Mme Helvétius, became editor of *Gazette de santé* (1784), was appointed doctor to the Hospice de Bicêtre (1793), was chief physician of the Hospice de la Salpêtrière (from 1795), and was professor of medical pathology at the École de Santé (from 1795). Founding member of Académie de Médecine (1820). One of the founders of psychiatry, he effectively transformed the prison for the insane into a hospital. His classification of mental diseases retained the old divisions but made finer distinctions; he considered emotional disorders the primary factor in precipitating intellectual dysfunctions, and also took into account heredity, morbid predisposition, and individual sensitivity. His therapeutics ("traitement moral") represented the first attempt at individual psychotherapy and was marked by gentleness and understanding; his findings were synthesized in a paper of 1799 and in *Traité medico-philosophique de l'aliénation mentale* (1801). Was also noteworthy for work in internal medicine; his *Nosographie philosophique* (1798) contained an authoritative division of diseases into five classes: fevers, phlegmasias, hemorrhages, neuroses, and diseases caused by organic lesions, each class being further subdivided. He believed every disease to be "an indivisible whole from its commencement to its conclusion, a regular ensemble of characteristic symptoms."

PINGRÉ, ALEXANDRE-GUI (*b. Paris, France, 1711; d. Paris, 1796*), astronomy.

Entered the order of Ste. Geneviève de Senlis (1727); professor of theology at University of Ste. Geneviève (1735–45). Astronomer to academy of sciences in Rouen (1749–53); recalled to Paris by his order in 1753, where he worked with P. C. Le Monnier on *État du ciel à l'usage de la marine* and gained a reputation as an astronomer and a computer. Later became astronomer-geographer to the navy, and chancellor of his old university (1769). Observed transit of Mercury (1753); on commission to examine Picard's meridian measurement (1755); active in organizing observations of transits of Venus. Observed transit of 1761 from Rodriguez Island in Indian Ocean, made longitude determinations, calculated solar parallax at 10.6″; observed 1769 transit in Haiti, announced solar parallax of 8.8″ (1772). Author of important *Cométographie ou traité historique et théorique des comètes* (2 vols., 1783–84) and of *Annales célestes du dix-septième siècle* (ed. by Bigourdan, 1901). Expanded Lacaille's *L'art de vérifier les dates* (1770); translated and edited *Astronomica* of Marcus Manilius and *Phaenomena* of Aratus of Soli.

PIRES, TOMÉ (*b. Portugal, ca. 1470; d. China, ca. 1540*), pharmacology.

Apothecary in Portugal, Cochin (1511–13), and Malacca (1513); ambassador on first Portuguese voyage to China (1516). Only known work is *Suma oriental*, a masterpiece on the geography, ethnography, and commerce of the Orient at the beginning of the sixteenth century.

PIRĪ RAIS (or **Re'is**), **MUḤYĪ AL-DĪN** (*b. Gelibolu* [*Gallipoli*], *Turkey, 1470; d. Egypt, 1554*), geography, cartography.

Served in Turkish navy and under the corsair Khair al-Din Barbarossa; conquered Alexandria (1517); appointed admiral of the South Seas (1526) and of the Red and Arabian seas. Known for two maps and a book. His map of 1513 shows the Iberian Peninsula, the western bulge of North Africa, the Atlantic Ocean, and the coast and islands of America, with colored pictures and marginal notes about countries, peoples, animals, and plants; it is a portolano chart based on twenty other maps, including one that had belonged to Columbus, and on personal experience. The map of 1528 includes the newly discovered regions of North and Central America. *Kitab-ī Bahriye* ("On Navigation," 1521) is basically a naval guidebook; its main portion is devoted to the Mediterranean coast and islands, but it also includes all that was known about the discovery of America at the time.

PIROGOV, NIKOLAY IVANOVICH (*b. Moscow, Russia, 1810; d. Vishnya, Ukraine, Russia, 1881*), surgery, anatomy.

Graduated in medicine at Moscow (1828); studied surgery and anatomy at Dorpat University (doctorate, 1832); professor of surgery at Dorpat (1836–41); head of surgery at St. Petersburg Medical-Surgical Academy, founded its clinic, taught pathological anatomy, and found its museum of anatomical pathology. Pioneered in anesthesiology: first to use ether under battle conditions (1847); first to administer anesthetic rectally; first to give ether intravenously; first in Russia to use chloroform. Founder of topographical anatomy and discoverer of new methods of anatomical research; by dissecting frozen cadavers and removing organs from them he produced a work (1851–59) comprising four volumes of drawings and explanatory text. During the Crimean War he developed the basic principles of field surgery and was the first to use plaster casts. Pavlov credited him with placing surgery on a scientific basis.

PISANO, LEONARDO. *See* **Fibonacci, Leonardo.**

PISO, WILLEM (*b. Leiden, Netherlands, ca. 1611; d. Amsterdam, Netherlands, 1678*), medicine, pharmacy.

Began medical studies at University of Leiden at age twelve; received M.D. at Caen (1633) and established a practice in Amsterdam. His fame as a pioneer of tropical medicine rests on his work as physician of the Dutch settlement in Brazil (1636–44); he was the first to point out that the health of Europeans in the tropics is best preserved by adopting the way in which the natives live. His findings were recorded in the first four books of *Historia naturalis Brasiliae* (1648), the other eight books being the work of Georg Markgraf, and in a later edition, *De Indiae utriusque re naturali et medica* (1658), whose authorship is less clearly delineated. First to distinguish yaws from venereal disease; stated that defective nutrition was the cause of hemeralopia; fully discussed tropical intestinal disorders, particularly dysentery (for which he recommended ipecacuanha, thus bringing this drug to the attention of the Western medical world). His description of the chigoe, its effects, and its treatment has never been surpassed.

PITCAIRN, ARCHIBALD (*b. Edinburgh, Scotland, 1652; d. Edinburgh, 1713*), medicine, physiology.

Studied at the University of Edinburgh (M.A., 1671), Paris, and Reims (M.D., 1680); became one of the first three medical professors at Edinburgh (1685). As a close friend of the mathematician David Gregory, he assisted in Gregory's correspondence with Newton; visited Newton (1692). Launched his "mathematical physick" while lecturing at Leiden (1692–93); relying heavily on the work of Lorenzo Bellini, constructed a hydraulic theory to explain all symptoms of illness, with a mathematical certainty, as the result of different impairments of the circulation of the blood; controversial at first, his ideas became widely accepted as part of the Newtonian philosophy.

PITISCUS, BARTHOLOMEO (b. Grünberg, Silesia [now Zielona Góra, Poland], 1561; d. Heidelberg, Germany, 1613), mathematics.

Court chaplain at Breslau and later for Elector Frederick IV of the Palatinate, but his many theological works are overshadowed by those in mathematics. Coined the term "trigonometry," first printed in his Trigonometria (1595), a systematic textbook containing all six of the trigonometric functions.

PITOT, HENRI (b. Aramon, Languedoc, France, 1695; d. Aramon, 1771), hydraulics.

Starting as Réaumur's assistant, was associated for some twenty years with the Académie des Sciences in Paris; worked as a civil engineer (from 1740). Invented the "Pitot tube" for measuring local velocity in liquids.

PITT-RIVERS, AUGUSTUS HENRY LANE FOX (b. Yorkshire, England, 1827; d. Rushmore, England, 1900), archaeology, anthropology.

A lieutenant-general in the British army, his meticulous work on prehistoric sites in Dorset (Excavations in Cranborn Chase, 1887–98) helped to establish modern field techniques in archaeology. Was one of the first to arrange artifacts by type in evolutionary sequences; with Flinders Petrie, worked to turn archaeology from the study of objects of art to the study of all objects.

PLANA, GIOVANNI (b. Voghera, Italy, 1781; d. Turin, Italy, 1864), mathematics, astronomy.

A student of Lagrange at the École Polytechnique in Paris; professor of astronomy and director of the observatory at Turin. Made contributions in mathematical analysis (Eulerian integrals, elliptical functions) and geodesy (the extension of an arc of latitude from Austria to France). Author, Théorie du mouvement de la lune (1832).

PLANCK, MAX KARL ERNST LUDWIG (b. Kiel, Germany, 1858; d. Göttingen, Germany, 1947), theoretical physics, philosophy of physics.

Planck studied at the Universities of Munich and Berlin. Independently, he studied Clausius' Mechanische Wärmetheorie in detail and later remarked that this private study was what had finally drawn him into physics. These investigations also led him to the preparation of his doctoral dissertation on the second law of thermodynamics, for which he was awarded the Ph.D. degree at the University of Munich in 1879.

In 1880 he was given the venia legendi at the University of Munich for his paper Gleichgewichtszustände isotroper Körper in verschiedenen Temperaturen, in which he extended the mechanical theory of heat, using the entropy concept, to treat elastic forces acting on bodies at different temperatures. His habilitation lecture in the same year was "Über die Prinzipien der mechanischen Gastheorie," in accord with the lectures given by his colleagues at Munich.

An appointment as professor extraordinarius at the University of Kiel in 1885 gave Planck greater scientific independence. In his publications during this period, he still concentrated, as he had done in Munich, on applications of his ideas to physical chemistry. After completing his prize essay on Das Princip der Erhaltung der Energie (1887), which included a ninety-one page historical introduction, he turned again to the "second principle" and in three papers tried to generalize it to cover the theory of dilute solutions and thermoelectricity. These studies later culminated in his monograph Grundriss der allgemeinen Thermochemie (1893), which had a thirty-one page historical introduction, and in his Vorlesungen über Thermodynamik (1897), which was effective for more than thirty years as an exceptionally clear, systematic, and skillful presentation of thermodynamics.

In 1888 Planck was appointed successor to Kirchhoff as assistant professor at the University of Berlin and director of the Institute for Theoretical Physics (founded for him).

The bulk of Planck's systematic work may be divided into thermodynamics, radiation theory, relativity, and philosophy of science. The first culminated in his Vorlesungen über Thermodynamik. By 1895 he was fully occupied with irreversible processes, especially in electrodynamics. He connected his early studies on thermodynamic irreversibility with Maxwell's electromagnetic theory of light, in the form given it by Helmholtz, Heaviside, and Hertz. He combined Clausius' phenomenological method with Kirchhoff's theorem that light and heat radiation in thermal equilibrium are independent of the nature of the substance. This combination, along with the statistical methods of calculation, was what would lead him in 1900 to the energy elements of the new radiation law. His third major interest, relativity, arose in the winter of 1905–06 from the publications of Lorentz and Einstein, but not without knowledge of the work of Poincaré. It is characteristic of Planck that, in 1907, he connected the "principle of relativity" with his quantum of action h.

Planck had always been inclined toward generalization, and encouraged by finding himself in the spotlight of publicity, he attacked even more general questions in some twenty published lectures devoted to developing and explaining his scientific views. This pursuit of general ideas going back to the 1890's started with his lecture "Einheit des physikalischen Weltbildes" given at Leiden in 1908, and continued in following years with numerous reflections on the relations of science to philosophy, religion, and human nature.

Planck received the high distinction of the 1918 Nobel Prize in physics and he witnessed the founding of the Max Planck Gesellschaft zur Förderung der Wissenschaften, successor to the Kaiser Wilhelm Gesellschaft founded in 1911. (He had been its president from 1930–37.)

PLANUDES, MAXIMUS (b. Nicomedia, Bithynia, ca. 1255; d. Constantinople, 1305), polymathy.

A monk and leading scholar in Byzantium. His *Calculation According to the Indians, Which Is Called Great* is notable for using Indian numerals in their eastern Arabic form.

PLASKETT, JOHN STANLEY (*b. Hickson, Ontario, 1865; d. Esquimalt, British Columbia, 1941*), astronomy.

Spent his early years as a mechanic; graduated from the University of Toronto (1899). Worked at the Dominion Observatory in Ottawa (1903–17); director of the Dominion Astrophysical Observatory in Victoria, British Columbia (1917–35). A leader in instrument design; studied binary stars and discovered Plaskett's twins.

PLATE, LUDWIG HERMANN (*b. Bremen, Germany, 1862; d. Jena, Germany, 1937*), zoology.

Studied at Bonn, Munich, and Jena (Ph.D., 1885). Succeeded Haeckel, his former teacher, as professor of zoology and director of the Phyletische Museum at Jena (1909). An influential neo-Darwinist and painstaking in his studies, Plate nevertheless larded his lectures with anti-Semitic, pro-Fascist opinions. Founder and coeditor for biology of the *Archiv für Rassen- und Gesellschafts- biologie* (1904).

PLATEAU, JOSEPH ANTOINE FERDINAND (*b. Brussels, Belgium, 1801; d. Ghent, Belgium, 1883*), physics, visual perception.

Studied law and science at the University of Liège (Sc.D., 1829). Taught at the Institut Gaggia in Brussels (1830–34) and at the State University of Ghent (1835–72). A pioneer in physiological psychology; investigated the perception of color, the phenomenon of irradiation, and invented an early stroboscope. Went blind (1843), apparently from staring at the sun in one of his experiments; turned to work on molecular forces and thin films. Lack of rigor in his work on thin films led other mathematicians to formulate the "problem of Plateau" (to show that across any Jordan space curve there may be stretched a minimal surface). Was an ingenious experimenter but his theoretical explanations are not generally accepted.

PLATER, FÉLIX. *See* **Platter, Félix.**

PLATO (*b. Athens [?], 427 B.C.; d. Athens, 348/347 B.C.*), theory of knowledge; advocacy, in theory and practice, of education based on mathematics; organization of research.

Plato's enthusiasm for mathematics, astronomy, and musical theory appears everywhere in his writings, and he also displays a far from superficial knowledge of the medicine and physiology of his day. In ancient times competent judges held that he had promoted the advance of mathematics, especially geometry, in his lifetime. Theodore of Cyrene and Archytas of Tarentum were his friends, and Eudoxus of Cnidus, Theaetetus, and Menaechmus his colleagues or pupils. His critics assert that his theory of knowledge rules out any empirical science and that, owing to his idealism, he had a radically false idea of the procedure and value of the mathematics that he admired. Even so, it can be said that the Academy, founded by him at Athens at a date not exactly known (380 B.C.[?]), became a center where specialists—not all of them sympathizers with his philosophy and epistemol-

ogy—could meet and profit by discussion with him and with one another.

The first dialogues and the *Apology* must have been written during the years 399–388 B.C. He felt it his duty to defend the memory of Socrates, especially since controversy about his aims had been revived by hostile publications. As the chance of political action remained remote, he gradually developed the idea of a training of the young not in rhetoric but in mathematics—and in Socratic interrogation only after the mathematical foundation had been laid. Part of his diagnosis of the ills of Athens was that young men had bewildered themselves and others by engaging too soon in philosophical controversy; these ideas probably found little sympathy among the Megarians. About 390 he resolved to visit the West, where Archytas of Tarentum survived as a maintainer of the Pythagorean system of education and was also active in research.

Plato's views at the time of departure on his journey to the West are well seen in the *Gorgias,* his first major constructive effort as a moralist.

Plato returned to Athens, after two years' absence, in 388 B.C. Nothing definite is recorded about his personal life during the ensuing twenty-two years. But the Academy was founded, or gradually grew up, during this time, and he composed further dialogues in Socratic style. The *Meno* and *Euthyphro, Euthydemus, Phaedo, Symposium,* and *Republic* must all be assigned to these years. In them he puts forward the distinctive account of knowledge which has taken shape in his mind; explains his purpose and method in education and shows the continuity of his aims with those of Socrates; and differentiates himself, where necessary, from the Italian Pythagoreans. It is natural to place the *Republic* at the end of this series, and to regard it as either a prospectus for a proposed school or as a statement to the Athenian public of what was already being carried out among them.

Aristotle gives a clear analysis of the factors which produced Plato's doctrine of Forms. Plato was acquainted from youth with an Athenian named Cratylus, who declared with Heraclitus that there is no stable substance, or hold for human knowledge, in the sense world. Plato did not deny this then or later but, wishing to take over and continue the Socratic search for universals, in the sphere of morals, which do remain permanent, he necessarily separated the universals from sensible particulars. It was he who termed them Ideas and Forms. In his view particulars (that is, things and states of things, actions and qualities) derive reality from Forms by "participation"; and when we name or speak of these particulars, we in effect name Forms.

In the dialogues Plato often starts from a contrast between knowledge and opinion. To live in a state of opinion is to accept assertions, either of fact or of principle, on authority or from mere habit. The opinion may be true and right; but since it is held without a rational ground, it may be driven from the mind by emotion and is less proof against forgetfulness than knowledge is. The holder of it may also be deceived in an unfamiliar instance. Based as it is on habit, an opinion cannot easily be transmitted to another; or, if the transmission takes place, this is not teaching. In terms of the theory of Forms, the holder of knowledge knows the Forms and can relate particular instances to them (although Plato did not successfully explain how this occurs), whereas the contented holder of opinions moves about among half-real particulars.

In middle life, then, Plato had advanced from his Socratic beginnings toward beliefs, held with assurance, from which many practical consequences flowed. The chief elements were the knowledge-opinion contrast; the belief in a realm of immutable Forms, with which human minds can make intermittent contact and which on such occasions the minds recognize as "their own" or as akin to them; given this, the soul, or its intellectual part, is seen to be likewise eternal; and the belief that the Forms, each of which infuses reality into corresponding particulars, in turn derive their existence, intelligibility, and truth from one supreme Form, the Good.

The advance from the plurality of Forms to their source is in consequence regarded as the ultimate stage in human study, *megiston mathēma;* it is a step which will be taken by only a few, but for the welfare of mankind it is important that a few should take it. Within the dialogue it is described but cannot be accomplished. There are hints of a methodical derivation of the other Forms from the Good; but for the present the image, whereby the Good is shown to have the same relation to other objects of intellection as the sun has to other visible things, takes its place. In reading the *Republic* and later dialogues, one must therefore reckon with the possibility that in the school Plato amplified or corrected the exposition which he chose to commit to writing.

The Athenians thought it suitable that young men should exercise themselves in argument on abstract themes before turning to serious business, and were prepared to tolerate "philosophy" on these terms. But Plato, as has been said, speaks out against this practice and holds that it has brought philosophy into discredit. Indeed, according to him, the order of procedure should be reversed. Argument, or its theory, is the hardest branch of philosophy and should come later. Men and women to whom legislation and administration are ultimately to be entrusted should undergo discipline in the sciences (including reflection on their interrelation) before they embark, say, at the age of thirty, on dialectical treatment of matters which have to be grasped by the intellect without the help of images. Such a discipline will single out those who have capacity for dialectic. To them will fall the task of making good laws, if these are not found in existence, and of interpreting and applying them if they are. For this purpose knowledge must be reinforced by experience. Lawless government is the common fault of despotism and democracy.

Plato holds that ignorance of mathematical truths which are in no way recondite, for example, the wrong belief that all magnitudes are commensurable, is a disgrace to human nature. It is not, however, this that is emphasized in his educational plan in the *Republic.* He explains that it is characteristic of mathematical studies that they gently disengage the intellect from sensible appearances and turn it toward reality; no other discipline does this. They induce a state of mind (which Plato terms *dianoia,* discursive thought) clearer than "opinion" and naïve trust in the senses but dimmer than knowledge and reason. In geometry, for instance, the learner is enabled or compelled, with the aid of figures, to fix his attention on intelligible objects. Also, mathematicians "lay down as

hypotheses the odd and even, various figures, and the three kinds of angles and the like" but leave them unexamined and go on to prove that the problem that gave rise to their investigation has been solved. In this respect mathematical procedure tends to divert the mind from reality and can provide only conditional truth. But such studies, pursued steadily and without continual talk of their practical use, are a good preparation for methodical treatment of such relations among Forms as cannot be visibly depicted.

Arithmetic and plane geometry will be the basis of an education which is to end in knowledge; the geometry of three-dimensional figures must also be studied. When, in the dialogue, Glaucon observes that this hardly yet exists as a science, Socrates says that there are two reasons for this: first, no state at present honors the study and encourages men to devote themselves to it; and second, a director is needed in order to coordinate the research. Such a man will be hard to find; and at present even if he existed the researchers are too self-confident to defer to him. Even without these conditions, and even when the researchers do not succeed in explaining what they are striving to achieve, the intrinsic charm of the study of three-dimensional figures is carrying it forward. This is one of the passages in which speakers in Plato's dialogues refer prophetically, but in veiled terms, to circumstances at the time of writing. It is somewhat enigmatic for us. The intention is perhaps to compliment Theaetetus, who had discovered constructions for inscribing in a sphere the regular octahedron and icosahedron. Either he or Plato himself is cast for the role of a director, and there is a plea for public support of the Academy so that research can continue.

There is a similar personal reference in the treatment of the sciences of astronomy and musical theory. Socrates dissociates himself from the Pythagoreans while approving of their statement that the two sciences are closely akin. Their theory of harmony is restricted to a numerical account of audible concords; and the aim of their astronomy is to discover the proportion between month, year, and the period of revolution of the planets. Instead of this, heard harmonies should be studied as a special case of the harmonies between numbers; and the proportion between month, year, and so forth (which is doubtless not unvarying) as an application of some wider theory dealing with the spatial relations of any given number of bodies of any shape, moving at any regular speeds at any distances. The visible universe will be to the "true astronomer" what a beautifully contrived diagram might be to the geometer, that is, an aid to the science, not the object of contemplation. Here Plato is indicating that he has not simply established on Athenian soil a replica of the Pythagorean schools. Attachment to the sense world must be loosened and the sciences taught with emphasis on their affinity to one another; for it is the power of synopsis, the perception of common features, that is to be strengthened. Those few who excel in this are to be set apart and trained to pursue another method which treats hypotheses as provisional until they have been linked to the unconditionally real and so established.

If we consider Plato's relation to Theaetetus and Eudoxus and also bring in the evidence of Aristotle, his personal role in the Academy begins to appear. He probably committed all the specialist instruction to them. He took note of their research and sometimes criticized their methods, speaking as a person with authority; he guided the juniors in that reflection about first principles and about the interrelation of sciences that in *Republic* VII is designated as suitable for them; and he confided to some an ethicomathematical philosophy in which two ultimate principles, from which Form-Numbers were derived, were found by analysis. The Academy was not a place in which *all* science was studied for its own sake but one in which selected sciences were taught and their foundations examined as a mental discipline, the aim being practical wisdom and legislative skill, which in Plato's opinion are inseparable from contemplative philosophy. It was an area to the northeast of the city which had been laid out as a park, including a public gymnasium. According to Lysias, the Spartans encamped there during the troubled year 403 B.C. Plato may have commenced teaching in the gymnasium itself; but he soon purchased an adjoining garden and erected buildings there, and from this moment he may be said to have instituted a school. Hitherto he could not exclude chance listeners. The buildings may have included lodgings for students or visitors, and Plato himself presumably lived in the neighborhood. Common meals had been a feature of Pythagorean life, and this precedent was followed. Legal recognition was secured by making the Academy a religious fraternity devoted to the Muses. The story that the words "Let no man unversed in geometry enter" were inscribed over the door cannot be traced back further than John Philoponus (sixth century). In the first century B.C., "academic" teaching was being given in the gymnasium of Ptolemy near the agora of Athens.

PLATO OF TIVOLI (*fl. Barcelona, first half of twelfth century*), mathematics, astronomy, astrology, medicine [?].

One of the first Iberian scientists to provide the Latin West with the work of Greek authors as transmitted or elaborated in Arabic and Hebrew; the first to edit Ptolemy in Latin; helped to translate from Hebrew a geometry text by Savasorda that introduced the solution of quadratic equations to the West.

PLATTER, FÉLIX (*b. Basel, Switzerland, 1536; d. Basel, 1614*), botany, medicine, psychiatry.

Studied at Montpellier; received M.D. from Basel (1557). A disciple of Vesalius; best known for works on human pathology, especially *De corporis humani structura* (1583).

PLATTNER, KARL FRIEDRICH (*b. Klein-Waltersdorf bei Freiberg, Germany, 1800; d. Freiberg, 1858*), metallurgy.

Studied at Königliche Bergakademie, Freiberg (1817–20), worked in industry, and held chair of metallurgy at Freiberg from 1840. Perfected the quantitative use of the blowpipe and wrote a work on smelting (1856).

PLAYFAIR, JOHN (*b. Benvie, near Dundee, Scotland, 1748; d. Edinburgh, Scotland, 1819*), mathematics, physics, geology.

Studied at St. Andrews and at Edinburgh; professor at the University of Edinburgh from 1785. Devoted his professional career to physics and mathematics; his *Elements of Geometry* (1795) contains "Playfair's axiom" for parallel lines (that two intersecting straight lines cannot be both

parallel to the same straight line). However, his fame rests on his work in geology, in which, five years after the death of his friend James Hutton, he presented Hutton's revolutionary concept of the geological cycle (*Illustrations of the Huttonian Theory of the Earth*, 1802).

PLAYFAIR, LYON (*b. Chunar, India, 1818; d. London, England, 1898*), chemistry.

One of the first government scientists in Britain. Studied medicine at Glasgow's Andersonian Institution and at Edinburgh; assisted Thomas Graham in London; collaborated with Joule and Bunsen; discovered nitroprussides. Member of Parliament (1868–83); knighted (1883) and created Baron Playfair (1892).

PLENČIČ (or **PLENCIZ**), **MARCUS ANTONIUS** (*b. Solkan, Austria [now Yugoslavia], 1705; d. Vienna, Austria, 1786*), medicine.

Studied at Vienna and Padua, where Morgagni was among his teachers. Following Leeuwenhoek's discovery of animacules, published a comprehensive germ theory of contagion in *Opera medico-physica* (1762), a century before Pasteur and Koch.

PLINY (GAIUS PLINIUS SECUNDUS) (*b. Como, Italy, ca. A.D. 23; d. near Pompeii, Italy, A.D. 79*), natural history.

Military commander, civil administrator, historian, man of affairs, and author of the encyclopedic *Natural History* (completed *ca.* A.D. 77). This great work treated (in 37 books) the universe, the earth, and terrestrial phenomena; geography; man; other animals; botany; materia medica from botanical sources and from animal sources; and metals and stones. Though not always reliable in quoting or using his sources, Pliny was a remarkable purveyor of the knowledge of the past. He died while trying to rescue people living across the bay from Pompeii during the eruption of Vesuvius that destroyed that city.

PLOT, ROBERT (*b. Borden, Kent, England, 1640; d. Borden, 1696*), natural history, archaeology, chemistry.

Studied at Oxford (LL.D., 1671); secretary of the Royal Society (1682–84, 1692); first keeper of the Ashmolean Museum (appointed 1683); professor of chemistry at Oxford. An omnivorous gatherer of specimens and observations in the Baconian tradition. Author of *Natural History of Oxfordshire* (1677) and *Natural History of Staffordshire* (1686).

PLOTINUS (*b. ca. A.D. 204; d. southern Italy, A.D. 270*), philosophy.

Had a Greek education; studied philosophy in Alexandria; taught in Rome (from *ca.* 243). The foremost Neoplatonist, his works were published posthumously in six books, the *Enneads*.

PLUCHE, NOËL-ANTOINE (*b. Reims, France, 1688; d. La Varenne-Saint-Maur, near Paris, 1761*), scientific popularization.

A seminary teacher, ordained in 1712, Pluche had to give up his post (1717) after being identified with the Jansenists; became a private tutor and a writer, producing the immensely popular *Le spectacle de la nature* (8 vols.,

1732–50). Here and in his other books, Pluche was strongly influenced by the natural theology of John Ray and other English writers.

PLÜCKER, JULIUS (*b. Elberfeld, Germany, 1801; d. Bonn, Germany, 1868*), mathematics, physics.

Studied in Bonn, Heidelberg, Berlin, and Paris, receiving his doctorate *in absentia* from the University of Marburg (1824). Spent almost his entire career at the University of Bonn. Plücker dedicated many years to physics, investigating the magnetic properties of gases and crystals, electrical discharges in evacuated gases, and the spectra of gaseous substances; but he was essentially a geometer, noted for the elegance of his algebraic operations. He created the field of line geometry, the subject of many researches until the twentieth century; introduced the notions (still used) of complexes, congruences, and ruled surfaces for subsets of lines of three, two, or one dimension; and initiated the study of quadratic complexes. His *Analytisch-geometrische Entwicklungen* (1828–31) gave a detailed explanation of the principle of reciprocity (now called duality); *Theorie der algebraischen Kurven* (1839) contained his proofs of the formulas now known as "Plücker's equations"; *Neue Geometrie des Raumes . . .* (1868), on line geometry, was completed after Plücker's death by his assistant, Felix Klein.

PLUMIER, CHARLES (*b. Marseilles, France, 1646; d. El Puerto de Santa María, near Cádiz, Spain, 1704*), natural history, botany.

Sent as botanist to the Caribbean three times (1689, 1693, 1695) by Louis XIV; noted for his excellent drawings and descriptions in *Nova plantarum americanarum genera* (1703) and other works.

PLUMMER, ANDREW (*b. Scotland, ca. 1698; d. Edinburgh, Scotland, 1756*), medicine.

Studied at Leiden (M.D., 1722). Taught medical chemistry at the University of Edinburgh (from 1726), introducing to Britain the modern approach of Boerhaave, one of his teachers at Leiden. Invented "Plummer's pills" for treating venereal diseases and other complaints.

PLUMMER, HENRY CROZIER (*b. Oxford, England, 1875; d. Oxford, 1946*), astronomy.

Graduated Oxford (1901); astronomer royal of Ireland (1912–21). Best known for *Dynamical Astronomy* (1918), a still-valued text.

POGGENDORFF, JOHANN CHRISTIAN (*b. Hamburg, Germany, 1796; d. Berlin, Germany, 1877*), physics, biography, bibliography.

Studied at the University of Berlin and spent his entire teaching career there. Invented a galvanoscope (multiplier), independently of Schweigger; it was used by Gauss in measuring magnetism. Edited *Annalen der Physik und Chemie* (1824–76); produced (1863) an indispensable biographical-bibliographical reference work in the history of the exact sciences that is now called simply "Poggendorff."

POGGIALE, ANTOINE-BAUDOIN (or **Baudouin**) (*b. Valle di Mezzana, Corsica, 1808; d. Bellevue, Seine-et-Oise, France, 1879*), chemistry, public health, pharmacy.

Received M.D. from the Faculty of Medicine in Paris (1833); became top-ranking pharmacist in the French army (1858). Was an outstanding analytical chemist; did studies of bread (1853), of blood, and of drinking water and mineral water.

POINCARÉ, JULES HENRI (*b. Nancy, France, 1854; d. Paris, France, 1912*), mathematics, mathematical physics, celestial mechanics.

Poincaré is the most important figure in the theory of differential equations and the mathematician who after Newton did the most remarkable work in celestial mechanics. In 1873 he entered the École Polytechnique at the top of his class; his professor at Nancy is said to have referred to him as a "monster of mathematics." After graduation he followed courses in engineering at the École des Mines and worked briefly as an engineer while writing his thesis for the doctorate in mathematics which he obtained in 1879. Shortly afterward he started teaching at the University of Caen, and in 1881 he became a professor at the University of Paris, where he taught until his untimely death in 1912. At the early age of thirty-three he was elected to the Académie des Sciences and in 1908 to the Académie Française. He was also the recipient of innumerable prizes and honors both in France and abroad.

Before he was thirty years of age, Poincaré became world famous with his epochmaking discovery of the "automorphic functions" of one complex variable (or, as he called them, the "fuchsian" and "kleinean" functions) and the general theory of automorphic functions of one complex variable is one of the few branches of mathematics where he left little for his successors to do.

But the theory of automorphic functions is only one of his many contributions to the theory of analytic functions, each of which was the starting point of extensive theories. In a short paper of 1883 he was the first to investigate the links between the genus of an entire function (defined by properties of its Weierstrass decomposition in primary factors) and the coefficients of its Taylor development or the rate of growth of the absolute value of the function; together with the Picard theorem, this was to lead, through the results of Hadamard and E. Borel, to the vast theory of entire and meromorphic functions that is not yet exhausted after eighty years.

Automorphic functions had provided the first examples of analytic functions having singular points that formed a perfect non-dense set, as well as functions having curves of singular points. Poincaré gave another general method to form functions of this type by means of series $\sum_n \dfrac{A_n}{z - b_n}$ of rational functions, leading to the theory of monogenic functions later developed by E. Borel and A. Denjoy.

It was also a result from the theory of automorphic functions, namely the parametrization theorem of algebraic curves, that in 1883 led Poincaré to the general "uniformization theorem," which is equivalent to the existence of a conformal mapping of an arbitrary simply connected noncompact Riemann surface on the plane or on an open disc. This time he saw that the problem was a generalization of Dirichlet's problem, and Poincaré was the first to introduce the idea of "exhausting" the Riemann surface by an increasing sequence of compact regions and of obtaining the conformal mapping by a limiting process. Here again it was difficult at that time to build a completely satisfactory proof, and Poincaré himself and Koebe had to return to the question in 1907 before it could be considered as settled.

Poincaré was even more an initiator in the theory of analytic functions of several complex variables—which was practically nonexistent before him. His first result was the theorem that a meromorphic function F of two complex variables is a quotient of two entire functions, which in 1883 he proved by a very ingenious use of the Dirichlet principle applied to the function $\log |F|$; in a later paper (1898) he deepened the study of such "pluriharmonic" functions for any number of complex variables and used it in the theory of Abelian functions. Still later (1907), after the publication of F. M. Hartogs' theorems, he pointed out the completely new problems to which led the extension of the concept of "conformal mapping" for functions of two complex variables. These were the germs of the imposing "analytic geometry" (or theory of analytic manifolds and analytic spaces) which we know today.

Finally, Poincaré was the first to give a satisfactory generalization of the concept of "residue" for multiple integrals of functions of several complex variables, after earlier attempts by other mathematicians had brought to light serious difficulties in this problem.

As soon as he came into contact with the work of Riemann and Weierstrass on Abelian functions and algebraic geometry, Poincaré was very much attracted by those fields. His papers on these subjects occupy in his complete works as much space as those on automorphic functions, their dates ranging from 1881 to 1911. One of the main ideas in these papers is that of "reduction" of Abelian functions. Generalizing particular cases studied by Jacobi, Weierstrass, and Picard, Poincaré proved the general "complete reducibility" theorem.

The most remarkable contribution of Poincaré to algebraic geometry is in his papers of 1910–11 on algebraic curves contained in an algebraic surface $F(x, y, z) = 0$.

Poincaré was a student of Hermite, and some of his early work deals with Hermite's method of "continuous reduction" in the arithmetic theory of forms, and in particular the finiteness theorem for the classes of such forms (with nonvanishing discriminant) that had just been proved by C. Jordan. These papers bring some complements and precisions to the results of Hermite and Jordan, without introducing any new idea. In connection with them Poincaré gave the first general definition of the genus of a form with integral coefficients, generalizing those of Gauss and Eisenstein; Minkowski had arrived independently at that definition at the same time.

Poincaré's last paper on number theory (1901) was most influential and was the first paper on what we now call "algebraic geometry over the field of rationals" (or a field of algebraic numbers). The subject matter of the paper is the Diophantine problem of finding the points with rational coordinates on a curve $f(x,y) = 0$, where the coefficients of f are rational numbers. Poincaré never studied algebra for its own sake, but only when he needed algebraic results in problems of arithmetic or analysis. He returned to noncommutative algebra in a 1903 paper on algebraic integrals of linear differential equations. His method led him to introduce the group algebra of the group of the equation (which then is finite), and to split it (according to H. Maschke's theorem, which apparently he did not know but proved by referring to a theorem of Frobenius) into simple algebras over $\mathbf{C}$ (that is, matrix algebras). He then introduced for the first time the concepts of left and right ideals in an algebra, and proved that any left ideal in a matrix algebra is a direct sum of minimal left ideals (a result usually credited to Wedderburn or Artin).

Poincaré was one of the few mathematicians of his time who understood and admired the work of Lie and his continuators on "continuous groups," and in particular the only mathematician who in the early 1900's realized the depth and scope of E. Cartan's papers. In 1899 Poincaré became interested in a new way to prove Lie's third fundamental theorem and in what is now called the Campbell-Hausdorff formula; in his work Poincaré substantially defined for the first time what we now call the "enveloping algebra" of a Lie algebra (over the complex field) and gave a description of a "natural" basis of that algebra deduced from a given basis of the Lie algebra; this theorem (rediscovered much later by G. Birkhoff and E. Witt, and now called the "Poincaré-Birkhoff-Witt theorem") has become fundamental in the modern theory of Lie algebras.

The theory of differential equations and its applications to dynamics was clearly at the center of Poincaré's mathematical thought; from his first (1878) to his last (1912) paper, he attacked the theory from all possible angles and very seldom let a year pass without publishing a paper on the subject. The whole theory of automorphic functions was from the start guided by the idea of integrating linear differential equations with algebraic coefficients. Poincaré simultaneously investigated the local problem of a linear differential equation in the neighborhood of an "irregular" singular point, showing for the first time how asymptotic developments could be obtained for the integrals. A little later (1884) he took up the question, also started by I. L. Fuchs, of the determination of all differential equations of the first order (in the complex domain) algebraic in y and y' and having fixed singular points; his researches were to be extended by Picard for equations of the second order, and to lead to the spectacular results of Painlevé and his school at the beginning of the twentieth century.

The most extraordinary production of Poincaré, also dating from his prodigious period of creativity (1880–83) (reminding us of Gauss's *Tagebuch* of 1797–1801), is the qualitative theory of differential equations. It is one of the few examples of a mathematical theory that sprang apparently from nowhere and that almost immediately reached perfection in the hands of its creator. Everything was new in the first two of the four big papers that Poincaré published on the subject between 1880 and 1886.

After 1885 most of his papers on differential equations were concerned with celestial mechanics, and more particularly the three-body problem. It seems that his interest in the subject was first aroused by his teaching at the Sorbonne; then, in 1885, King Oscar II of Sweden set up a competition among mathematicians of all countries on the n-body problem. Poincaré contributed a long paper, which was awarded first prize, and which ranks with his papers on the qualitative theory of differential equations as one of his masterpieces. Its central theme is the study of the periodic solutions of the three-body problem when the masses of two of the bodies are very small in relation to the mass of the third (which is what happens in the solar system). In 1878 G. W. Hill had given an example of such solutions; in 1883 Poincaré proved—by a beautiful application of the Kronecker index—the existence of a whole continuum of such solutions. Then in his prize memoir he gave another proof for the "restricted" three-body problem, when one of the small masses is neglected, and the other μ is introduced as a parameter in the Hamiltonian of the system. He published close to a hundred papers concerning various aspects of the theory of the solar system, in which he suggested innumerable improvements and new techniques. Most of his results were developed in his famous three-volume *Les méthodes nouvelles de la mécanique céleste* and later in his *Leçons de mécanique céleste.*

Another famous paper of Poincaré in celestial mechanics is the one he wrote in 1885 on the shape of a rotating fluid mass submitted only to the forces of gravitation.

Poincaré became an expert in practically all parts of theoretical physics, and published more than seventy papers and books on the most varied subjects, with a predilection for the theories of light and of electromagnetic waves. On two occasions he played an important part in the development of the new ideas and discoveries that revolutionized physics at the end of the nineteenth century. His remark on the possible connection between X rays and the phenomena of phosphorescence was the starting point of H. Becquerel's experiments which led him to the discovery of radioactivity. On the other hand, Poincaré was active in the discussions concerning Lorentz' theory of the electron from 1899 on; Poincaré was the first to observe that the Lorentz transformations form a group, isomorphic to the group leaving invariant the quadratic form $x^2 + y^2 + z^2 - t^2$; and many physicists consider that Poincaré shares with Lorentz and Einstein the credit for the invention of the special theory of relativity.

This persistent interest in physical problems was bound to lead Poincaré into the mathematical problems raised by the partial differential equations of mathematical physics, most of which were still in a very rudimentary state around 1880. It is typical that in all the papers he wrote on this subject, he never lost sight of the possible physical meanings (often drawn from very different physical theories) of the methods he used and the results he obtained. This is particularly apparent in the first big paper (1890) that he wrote on the Dirichlet problem. The main leitmotiv of Poincaré's mathematical work is clearly the idea of "continuity": whenever he attacks a problem in analysis, we almost immediately see him investigating what happens when the conditions of the problem are allowed to vary continuously. He was therefore bound to encounter at every turn what we now call topological problems. He himself said in 1901, "Every problem I had attacked led me to *Analysis situs,*" particularly the researches on differential equations and on the periods of multiple integrals. Starting in 1894 he inaugurated in a remarkable series of six papers—written during a period of ten years—the modern methods of algebraic topology. Until then the only significant step had been the generalizations of the concept of "order of connection" of a surface, defined independently by Riemann and Betti,

and which Poincaré called "Betti numbers" (they are the numbers $1 + h_j$, where the h_j are the present-day "Betti numbers"); but practically nothing had been done beyond this definition. The machinery of what we now call simplicial homology is entirely a creation of Poincaré: concepts of triangulation of a manifold, of a simplicial complex, of barycentric subdivision, and of the dual complex, of the matrix of incidence coefficients of a complex, and the computation of Betti numbers from that matrix. With the help of these tools, Poincaré discovered the generalization of the Euler theorem for polyhedra (now known as the Euler-Poincaré formula) and the famous duality theorem for the homology of a manifold; a little later he introduced the concept of torsion. Furthermore, in his first paper he had defined the fundamental group of a manifold (or first homotopy group) and shown its relations to the first Betti number. In the last paper of the series he was able to give an example of two manifolds having the same homology but different fundamental groups. In the first paper he had also linked the Betti numbers to the periods of integrals of differential forms (with which he was familiar through his work on multiple integrals and on invariant integrals), and stated the theorem which G. de Rham first proved in 1931. It has been rightly said that until the discovery of the higher homotopy groups in 1933, the development of algebraic topology was entirely based on Poincaré's ideas and techniques.

In addition, he also showed how to apply these new tools to some of the problems for which he had invented them.

POINSOT, LOUIS (*b. Paris, France, 1777; d. Paris, 1859*), mathematics, mechanics.

Studied at École Polytechnique (1794–97), where he later taught (1809–12) and served as admissions examiner (1816–26), and at École des Ponts et Chaussées (1797–1800). Was named to Bureau des Longitudes (1843) and held political positions. Poinsot was a fervent disciple of Monge and a leader of the revival of geometry in France. Author, *Éléments de statique* (1803), in which he introduced the concept of the couple.

POISEUILLE, JEAN LÉONARD MARIE (*b. Paris, France, 1797; d. Paris, 1869*), physiology, physics.

Studied at the École Polytechnique in Paris. Invented a hemodynamometer, which he used in research for his doctorate (1828) on blood pressure. Discovered (1840) what is now called the Hagen-Poiseuille law governing the movement of liquids in capillary tubes.

POISSON, SIMEON-DENIS (*b. Pithiviers, Loiret, France, 1781; d. Paris, France, 1840*), mathematical physics.

Having failed in his attempt to learn surgery, Poisson was guided toward other professions by his father. At the École Centrale of Fontainebleau he made such great progress in mathematics that he was encouraged to prepare for the competitive entrance examination at the École Polytechnique. He was admitted first in his class in 1798, and his success in his studies attracted the attention of both Lagrange and Laplace.

Poisson possessed undoubted ability in mathematical analysis and displayed this gift in 1799–1800 in a paper on the theory of equations and on Bezout's theorem. At a time when it was difficult to recruit suitably qualified teaching personnel, this asset was sufficient to gain him nomination as *répétiteur* at Polytechnique immediately after his graduation in 1800. He was named professor in 1802 and four years later replaced Fourier as titular professor. In 1808 he was appointed astronomer at the Bureau des Longitudes and, in 1809, professor of mechanics at the Faculty of Sciences.

The early stages of Poisson's research can be studied in the *Journal de 'l École polytechnique* and in the second series of the *Bulletin de la Société philomatique de Paris.* They indicate that he was particularly drawn to the integration of differential and of partial differential equations, and to their possible application in the study of the oscillations of a pendulum in a resisting medium and in the theory of sound. This initial selection was decisive for his career, since it continued to guide all his subsequent research which included probability, definite integrals, and electromagnetic theory.

Much of his work, especially that on the Fourier series, set the stage for the following generation of mathematicians. Poisson had the habit of saying: "Life is good for only two things: to study mathematics and to teach it." Poisson himself was not impeded by the obstacles encountered in scientific publishing, at their worst around 1810. He submitted three major papers to the Academy, all of which received flattering reports from committees that included Laplace: "Sur les inégalités des moyens mouvements des planètes" (20 June 1808), "Sur le mouvement de rotation de la terre" (20 March 1809), and "Sur la variation des constantes arbitraires dans les questions de mécanique" (15 October 1809). Poisson's career was thus off to a most promising start, and his election to the Academy came just at the moment when Biot was scheduled to report on his fourth major memoir, "Sur la distribution de l'électricité à la surface des corps conducteurs" (9 March 1812). This report was never delivered, since Poisson himself had become one of the judges. During this period he composed two other works, a new edition of Clairaut's *Théorie de la figure de la terre* (1808) and the two-volume *Traité de mécanique* (1811), a textbook.

In the first memoir Poisson simply pursued problems raised and mathematically formulated by Laplace and Lagrange regarding the perturbations of planetary motions with respect to Kepler's solution of the problem of motion for two bodies. Even here, however, he improved the demonstration of the stability of the major axes of the orbits and of the mean motions. In finding approximate solutions by means of various series expansions, he also showed that determination of the possibility of secular inequalities required the inclusion of higher-order terms in the calculation. Finally, he simplified the mathematical treatment of these difficult equations by perceptive suggestions regarding the notation and disposition of the terms representing the perturbing function.

In his efforts to extend the use of mathematics in the treatment of physical problems, he studied many subjects. In some cases he limited himself to brief outlines, one of which, that concerning the potential in the interior of attracting masses (1813), later gave rise to important results in electrostatistics. He was more ambitious in the memoirs on electricity and magnetism and on the theory of elastic surfaces. The second of these, read to the Academy on 1 August 1814, represented his attempt to block

the progress of Sophie Germain, who he knew was competing—under the guidance of Legendre—for the prize in physics.

Poisson worked closely with Laplace, under whose influence he investigated a number of topics. One of these was the speed of sound in gases. In other studies Poisson considered the propagation of heat, elastic vibration theory, and what was later called potential. He took up ideas that Laplace had proposed and at the same time conducted a vast amount of his own research.

The physics of heat, which was attracting a growing number of researchers during this period, consists of phenomena other than those that, like radiation, suggest the adoption of a hypothesis concerning events occurring on an infinitesimal, molecular scale. Poisson made worthwhile contributions to the understanding of these other areas, largely through his insistent amassing of theoretical and experimental data.

In "Sur la chaleur des gaz et des vapeurs," published in August 1823 in *Annales de chimie et de physique,* Poisson developed ideas published four months before by Laplace in Book XII of *Mécanique céleste.*

It cannot be denied that Poisson showed real tact in "subjecting" physical phenomena to mathematical calculation. It is in this context that Poisson's contribution to the mathematical treatment of attractive force must be mentioned. His interest in this subject dates from his analysis in 1812–13 of James Ivory's work; and here again Laplace was the source for his examination of the integral V of the inverse of the distance function, which function was first called potential by George Green. Late in 1813 Poisson pointed out that in addition to the equation for the attraction exerted by a mass on an external point, namely

$$\Delta V = \frac{\partial^2 V}{\partial x^2} + \frac{\partial^2 V}{\partial y^2} + \frac{\partial^2 V}{\partial z^2} = 0,$$

the equation $\Delta V = -4\pi\rho$ must also be considered, where ρ is the density around the point $x, y, z,$ when this point is inside the attracting mass. The demonstration provoked several objections, and Poisson attempted to prove it, notably in two memoirs of 1824 published in the *Mémoires de l'Académie des sciences.* In 1826 he stated the triple equation,

$$\Delta V = 0, \quad = -2\pi\rho, \quad = -4\pi\rho,$$

depending on whether the point x, y, z is internal to, on the surface of, or external to the attracting mass.

"Mathematicians have long known of the first of these cases," he added. "An investigation several years ago led me to the third. To it I now add the second, thus completing this equation. Its importance in a great number of questions is well known."

The last period of Poisson's life was dominated by his feeling of being the chosen leader of French science—at a time when he already felt called upon to guide the future of the French university system. Since it was during this last period that he decided to publish books, this sense of a twofold mission determined the form that they took; and these works are therefore treatises, concerned primarily with pedagogical matters. Although ably written and including clear historical accounts of the topics treated, they did little to advance contemporary research.

Toward the end of his life, Poisson turned his attention to other subjects, producing two works of considerable repute. The first, *Recherches sur la probabilité des jugements en matière criminelle et en matière civile* (1837), is significant for the author's participation in an important contemporary debate. The legitimacy of the application of the calculus to areas relating to the moral order, that is to say within the broad area of what is now called the humanistic sciences, was bitterly disputed beginning in 1820 in politically conservative circles as well as by Saint-Simonians and by such philosophers as Auguste Comte. Poisson was bold enough to take pen in hand to defend the universality of the probabilistic thesis and to demonstrate the conformability to the order of nature of the regularities that the calculus of probability, without recourse to hidden causes, reveals when things are subjected to a great number of observations. It is to Poisson that we owe the term "law of large numbers." He improved Laplace's work by relating it explicitly to Jacob Bernoulli's fundamental theorem and by showing that the invariance in the prior probabilities of mutually exclusive events is not a necessary condition for calculating the approximate probabilities. It is also from Poisson that we derive the study of a problem that Laplace had passed over, the case of great asymmetry between opposite events, such that the prior probability of either event is very small. The formula for evaluation that he proposed for this case, which is to be substituted for Laplace's general formula, was not recognized or used until the end of the nineteenth century.

The second work in this category, *Recherches sur le mouvement des projectiles dans l'air* (1839), was far better known in its day. It is the first work to deal with the subject by taking into account the rotation of the earth and the complementary acceleration resulting from the motion of the system of reference.

The very multiplicity of Poisson's undertakings might be considered a reason for his failure to enjoy the good fortune of which Cournot spoke. He constantly exploited the ideas of other scientists, often in an unscrupulous manner. Still, he was frequently the first to show their full significance, and he did much to disseminate them.

POIVRE, PIERRE (*b. Lyons, France, 1719; d. La Freta, near Lyons, 1786*), botany.

Introduced clove and nutmeg plants to Île-de-France (Mauritius) in an effort to circumvent Dutch control of the spice trade.

POLENI, GIOVANNI (*b. Venice, Italy, 1683; d. Padua, Italy, 1761*), mathematics, physics, ancient history, archaeology.

Trained as a judge. Taught astronomy, physics, and mathematics at the University of Padua, corresponded with Euler, Maupertuis, the Bernoullis, and Cassini III.

POLI, GIUSEPPE SAVERIO (*b. Molfetta, Italy, 1746; d. Naples, Italy, 1825*), physics, natural sciences.

Studied at Padua under Morgagni and Caldani, professor of experimental physics at the University of Naples. Expert in many fields; founded botanical garden of Naples, regarded as the founder of the study of mollusks.

POLINIÈRE, PIERRE (*b. Coulonces, near Vire, Normandy, France, 1671; d. Coulonces, 1734*), physics, experimental natural philosophy.

Educated at Caen and Paris. A precursor of Nollet; gave public demonstrations of experimental natural philosophy at the University of Paris (from *ca.* 1700); investigated electroluminescence; was an early advocate of Newton's theory of color.

POLLENDER, ALOYS (*b. Barmen, Germany, 1800; d. Barmen, 1879*), medicine.

Attended the University of Bonn (M.D., 1824); went into medical practice; a bachelor until age 70, he then married a woman 42 years younger. In 1849, when anthrax broke out near his home, he examined the blood of the infected cows microscopically; with the aid of an iodine staining solution (the first use of a staining method), he found many fine "rodlike corpuscles," which he thought must be a form of plant life. He did not publish his results until 1855 and his claim to priority was contested: "granulated threads" had already been observed (1842) by a veterinarian, C. J. Fuchs. But Pollender was the first to recognize the bacilli as plant organisms and to discuss whether they could be the cause of anthrax.

POMPONAZZI, PIETRO (*b. Mantua, Italy, 1462; d. Bologna, Italy, 1525*), natural philosophy.

A philosopher in the Aristotelian tradition; taught at the universities of Padua (where he had also studied), Ferrara, and Bologna. Argued in *De immortalitate* (1516), *Apologia* (1518), and *Defensorium* (1519) that the soul perishes with the body. Although he tried to prevent a conflict with religious doctrine by separating philosophy from faith, Pomponazzi's views sparked a considerable debate, and he was nearly tried for heresy. He became more circumspect, and his *De incantationibus* and *De fato*, both written about 1520, were only published posthumously. In the first he developed naturalistic explanations for miracles; in the second, he tried to reconcile the doctrines of predestination and free will.

POMPONIUS MELA (*fl.* A.D. *44*), geography.

Author of *De chorographia*, a compendious, largely derivative work, giving a general descriptive survey of the world as known *ca.* A.D. 43; it is the first extant geographical work in Latin.

PONCELET, JEAN VICTOR (*b. Metz, France, 1788; d. Paris, France, 1867*), geometry, theory of machines, industrial mechanics.

Studied at the École Polytechnique in Paris; entered corps of military engineers (1810); graduated from the École d'Application of Metz (1812); began original mathematical work while a prisoner of war in Russia (1812–14). Held various military and teaching posts, retiring as commandant of the École Polytechnique; was chairman of the division of industrial machines and tools at the Universal Expositions of London (1851) and Paris (1855); his report (1857) on the London Exposition is a major study of nineteenth-century advances in this field. In geometry, his most important work is *Traité des propriétés projectives des figures* (1822). As the first book devoted wholly to projective geometry, it played a decisive role in the early development of this new discipline.

Poncelet here systematically introduced elements at infinity and imaginary elements; he made extensive use of central projections and profitably used other types of transformations; his distinction between projective and metric properties prefigured the modern concept of structure. In applied mechanics, he was occupied with hydraulic engines (his undershot water wheel with curved paddles won a prize from the Académie des Sciences in 1825), regulators and dynamometers, and fortification techniques.

PONS, JEAN-LOUIS (*b. Peyre, Dauphiné, France, 1761; d. Florence, Italy, 1831*), astronomy.

Learned astronomy as the concierge of the Marseilles observatory; became the most successful finder of comets in history, discovering thirty-seven from 1801 to 1827.

PONTEDERA, GIULIO (*b. Vicenza, Italy, 1688; d. Lonigo, Italy, 1757*), botany.

Graduated from the University of Padua (1715), where he taught and was prefect of the botanical garden (from 1719). In *Anthologia sive de floris natura* (1720) he tried to demonstrate the nonsexuality of plants.

POOR, CHARLES LANE (*b. Hackensack, N.J., 1866; d. New York, N.Y., 1951*), astronomy.

Educated at City College of New York (B.S., 1886; M.S., 1890) and Johns Hopkins University (Ph.D., 1892); taught at Johns Hopkins (1892–99) and Columbia University (1903–44). Known for his excellent work on comets and his polemical stand against relativity theory.

POPE, WILLIAM JACKSON (*b. London, England, 1870; d. Cambridge, England, 1939*), organic chemistry.

Studied at the City and Guilds of London Institute under H. E. Armstrong, a believer in the heuristic teaching method, who forbade his students to take examinations; thus Pope left school without a degree (1891). Worked at the Institute of the Goldsmiths' Company in New Cross and, in Manchester, taught at the Municipal School of Technology and at the university (1901–08); elected professor of chemistry at the University of Cambridge (1908), a post he held until his death; was knighted for technological work during World War I; presided at the chemical conferences of the Solvay Foundation in Brussels (1922–36). Pope's many accomplishments included the production of sobrerol (with H. E. Armstrong); the study of camphor and the production of new halogenocamphors (with F. S. Kipping); the crystallization of sodium chlorate from aqueous solution (with Kipping); the optical resolution of "tetrahydropapaverine" (with S. J. Peachey), and the study of asymmetric nitrogen compounds (with J. Read). Pope and W. Barlow attempted to correlate chemical constitution and crystal structure (1906–10); though their valency-volume theory has been discarded, they revealed many factors that helped in the evolution of modern crystallography. Pope also worked on the synthesis of 1-methylcyclohexylidene-4-acetic acid (with W. H. Perkin, Jr.) and of chloroiodomethane sulfonic acid (with J. Read). During World War I he worked on photographic sensitizers (with W. H. Mills) and on the manufacture of mustard gas (with C. S. Gibson). Later, his research with F. G. Mann on complex metallic compounds led to the first systematic use of terti-

ary phosphines and arsines, thus opening an important field of coordination chemistry.

POPOV, ALEKSANDR NIKIFORIVICH (*b. Vitebsk region [oblast], Russia, 1840 [?]; d. Warsaw, Russia [now Poland], 1881*), chemistry.

Studied and taught at Kazan University (1861–69); then moved to Warsaw University. Best known for his rule (1869) relating to the oxidation of ketones.

POPOV, ALEKSANDR STEPANOVICH (*b. Turinsk mining village [now Krasnoturinsk, Sverdlovsk oblast], Russia, 1859; d. St. Petersburg, Russia, 1906*), physics, technology.

Graduated from St. Petersburg University (1882). Taught at the Torpedo School at Kronstadt (1888–1900) and at St. Petersburg Institute of Electrical Engineering (1901–05). Independently of Marconi, and at almost the same time, built an apparatus for detecting electromagnetic signals from an oscillator eighty meters away; gave the world's first public demonstration of such a receiver (1895).

PORETSKY, PLATON SERGEEVICH (*b. Elisavetgrad [now Kirovograd], Russia, 1846; d. Joved, Grodno district, Chernigov guberniya, Russia, 1907*), mathematics, astronomy.

Russia's first eminent scholar in mathematical logic. Graduated from Kharkov University; worked there as an astronomer, earning his Ph.D. in 1886; taught at Kazan University (1886–89). Elaborated Boolean algebra in papers published 1880–1908.

PORRO, IGNAZIO (*b. Pinerolo, Italy, 1801; d. Milan, Italy, 1875*), topography, optics, geodesy.

While a member of the Piedmontese Corps of Engineers, invented several instruments, which revolutionized topographical practice. These included the telemeter (1835); a telescopic objective giving several views at different scales (1848); and the cleps (1875), an improved tachymeter.

PORTA, GIAMBATTISTA DELLA (*b. Vico Equense, Italy, 1535; d. Naples, Italy, 1615*), natural philosophy, mathematics.

Of a noble family; probably self-educated; a lay brother of the Jesuits by 1585. Porta dealt in both magic and science. His *Magiae naturalis libri xx* (1589) combines an insatiable desire for the marvelous with a serious attempt to describe and define natural magic and to make use of mathematical and experimental techniques; book XVII, on refraction, is the basis of the attribution of priority to Porta in inventing the telescope. Porta founded an academy in Naples for the study of the secrets of nature; this may have been the cause of his being examined by the Inquisition; his works were banned (1592–98). He became a member of the Accademia dei Lincei in Rome (1610).

PORTA, LUIGI (*b. Pavia, Italy, 1800; d. Pavia, 1875*), surgery.

Studied at University of Pavia (M.D., 1826) and with A. Scarpa in Vienna. Professor of clinical surgery at Pavia from 1832. Did research on the pathological changes caused to arteries by ligation and torsion, thereby contributing to the foundations of modern vascular surgery. Investigated how collateral circulation was established after obliteration of parts of arteries. Also worked in anesthesiology, thyroid pathology, urology, and traumatology.

PORTAL, ANTOINE (*b. Gaillac, France, 1742; d. Paris, France, 1832*), medicine.

Studied at Montpellier (1762–65); moved to Paris; appointed anatomy teacher to the dauphin (the future Louis XVI) in 1766. A greatly respected physician, he held posts of high honor throughout his life; noted for diagnosis of abdominal disorders; used methods bordering on charlatanism. Author, *Histoire de l'anatomie et de la chirurgie* (1770–73), a still-valuable reference.

PORTEVIN, ALBERT MARCEL GERMAIN RENÉ (*b. Paris, France, 1880; d. Abano Terme, Italy, 1962*), metallurgy.

Studied engineering at the École Centrale des Arts et Manufactures; named professor there (1925); appointed editor-in-chief of the *Revue de métallurgie* (1907). Noted especially for studies of chrome steels.

PORTIER, PAUL (*b. Bar-sur-Seine, France, 1866; d. Bourg-la-Reine, France, 1962*), biology, physiology.

Spent his entire career at the University of Paris; was director of the Institut Océanographique. With Charles Richet, discovered (1901) the phenomenon of negative immunization, which they called "anaphylaxis," thereby opening the field of allergy studies. He was the first to show that the spout of a blowing marine animal is visible because of the condensation of water vapor.

POŠEPNÝ, FRANZ (*b. Starkenbach, Bohemia, 1836; d. Döbling, near Vienna, Austria, 1895*), geology.

Studied and taught at the School of Mines in Příbram, Bohemia. Noted for a work on the genesis of ore deposits (1895) in which he held that ore deposits are characteristically confined to decomposed rocks. Although it was well received, particularly in the U.S., it was misguided in its theoretical aspect.

POSIDONIUS (*b. Apameia, Syria, ca. 135* B.C.; *d. ca. 51* B.C.), philosophy, science, history.

Of Greek parentage; studied at Athens; became head of the Stoic school at Rhodes (between 100 and 95 B.C.); traveled as ambassador from Rhodes to Rome (87–86); was a friend of Pompey and Cicero. Posidonius' works are known to us only as used or mentioned by other authors. He described a spherical universe, a spherical revolving heaven, and a minute, spherical motionless earth, all alive and forming the being of God. Made a portable orrery, with good estimates of sizes and distances; but in *On Ocean* gave a very low figure for the meridian circumference of the earth (which influenced Columbus). His *Histories* deal with the period from about 146–63 B.C.

POST, EMIL LEON (*b. Augustów, Poland, 1897; d. northern New York, 1954*), mathematics, logic.

Came to the U.S. at age seven; studied at the College of the City of New York and at Columbia University (Ph.D., 1920); taught at the former (from 1935). In his doctoral thesis (1920) proved the consistency as well as

the completeness of Russell and Whitehead's propositional calculus. He worked with multi-valued propositional systems; anticipated the results of Gödel; discovered (independently) the concept of a recursive function.

POTANIN, GRIGORY NIKOLAEVICH (*b. Semiyarsky, Russia, 1835; d. Tomsk, U.S.S.R., 1920*), geography, biogeography, ethnography.

As a member of the Russian Geographical Society, made five major expeditions through Inner Asia (1876–99). His writings gave the first extensive information on the geography and geology of Mongolia. Discovered many plants and published on the flora and fauna of Inner Asia.

POTT, JOHANN HEINRICH (*b. Halberstadt, Saxony, 1692; d. Berlin, Prussia, 1777*), technical chemistry.

Studied under F. Hoffmann and G. E. Stahl at University of Halle. Professor of theoretical chemistry at the Collegium Medico-Chirurgicum in Berlin. Did a vast, systematic examination of mineral substances in an attempt (ordered by the king of Prussia) to duplicate Meissen porcelain.

POUCHET, FÉLIX-ARCHIMÈDE (*b. Rouen, France, 1800; d. Rouen, 1872*), biology, natural history.

A physician, teacher, and director of Museum d'Histoire Naturelle in Rouen, Pouchet was an excellent popularizer of science and did some important original work; but he is remembered for his opposition to Pasteur.

POUILLET, CLAUDE-SERVAIS-MATHIAS (*b. Cusance, Doubs, France, 1790; d. Paris, France, 1868*), physics.

An eminent teacher, textbook writer, and administrator; with the Faculty of Sciences in Paris (1826–52). His own research included work on expansion and compressibility of gases; verified Ohm's law of resistance (1827).

POURFOUR DU PETIT, FRANÇOIS (*b. Paris, France, 1664; d. Paris, 1741*), physiology, surgery.

Studied medicine in Paris, at the Charité hospital, and at Montpellier (M.D., 1690). A physician-surgeon in the armies of Louis XIV; practiced opthalmic medicine in Paris. Is most famous for his investigations of brain damage and paralysis and of the origin of the sympathetic nerve.

POURTALÈS, LOUIS FRANÇOIS DE (*b. Neuchâtel, Switzerland, 1823 or 1824; d. Beverly Farms, near Salem, Mass., 1880*), oceanography.

A favorite student of Louis Agassiz in Neuchâtel; came with him to the U.S. (1847); served with the U.S. Coast Survey (1848–73); "keeper" of Agassiz's Museum of Comparative Zoology at Harvard. Was a pioneer in marine biology and submarine geology; studied the coast from Cape Cod to Florida; extended the technology of dredging to depths as great as 850 fathoms. Author, *Deep Sea Corals* (1871).

POWALKY, KARL RUDOLPH (*b. Neudietendorf, near Gotha, Germany, 1817; d. Washington, D.C., 1881*), astronomy.

Trained at the Hamburg observatory (1842–47); received doctorate at age forty-seven from the University of

Kiel; held various posts in Germany and the U.S. Studied comets, the planets, and especially the minor planets.

POWELL, BADEN (*b. Stamford Hill, England, 1796; d. London, England, 1860*), physics.

Studied mathematics at Oriel College, Oxford (1814–17); was ordained in 1820; appointed professor of geometry at Oxford (1827). Investigated radiant heat and light; was involved in prolonged religious controversy for his support of Lyell and other modern scientists. One of his sons was Robert Baden-Powell, founder of the scouting movement.

POWELL, CECIL FRANK (*b. Tonbridge, Kent, England, 1903; d. near Bellano, Lake Como, Italy, 1969*), physics.

Studied at Sidney Sussex College and the Cavendish Laboratory, Cambridge; did Ph.D. (1927) under C. T. R. Wilson; spent teaching career at Bristol University; awarded Nobel Prize for physics (1950). In the late 1930's began to investigate the use of photographic emulsions to record the tracks of fast-moving electrically-charged particles, thus opening the way for the study of elementary particle physics as it is known today; discovered (1947) the pi-meson, or pion. Worked for international, socially-responsible collaboration among scientists.

POWELL, JOHN WESLEY (*b. Mount Morris, N.Y., 1834; d. Haven, Me., 1902*), geology, ethnology.

Although largely self-educated, Powell was one of the most influential scientists in the U.S. Became a national hero for his exploration of the unknown canyons of the Green and Colorado rivers (1869). Was placed in charge of the government survey of the Rocky Mountain region (1870); his reports and those of his colleagues did much to formulate the basic principles of structural geology. Worked passionately for government reform to preserve the land of the West from destruction; his views not appreciated until the Dust Bowl years of the 1930's. Directed the Bureau of Ethnology at the Smithsonian Institution, leading in the systematic study of Indian tribes; headed the U.S. Geological Survey (1881–94).

POWER, FREDERICK BELDING (*b. Hudson, N.Y., 1853; d. Washington, D.C., 1927*), pharmacy, chemistry.

Educated at the Philadelphia College of Pharmacy and the University of Strasbourg (doctorate, 1880); specialized in phytochemistry. Among many appointments, was the first director of the distinguished department of pharmacy at the University of Wisconsin (1883–92).

POWER, HENRY (*b. Halifax, Yorkshire, England, 1623; d. New Hall, Yorkshire, England, 1668*), microscopy.

Studied at Cambridge (M.D., 1655); wrote the first book in English on microscopy (1664), *Experimental Philosophy, in Three Books.*

POYNTING, JOHN HENRY (*b. Monton, near Manchester, England, 1852; d. Birmingham, England, 1914*), physics.

Did his graduate work at Cambridge; taught at Mason College, Birmingham (from 1880). Best known for the derivation (1884) of the expression for the flow of energy in an electromagnetic field (Poynting flux).

PRANDTL, LUDWIG (*b. Freising, Germany, 1875; d. Göttingen, Germany, 1953*), fluid mechanics.

The founder of the boundary layer theory and originator of the German school of aerodynamics; taught at Göttingen for most of his career. Received his doctorate at the Technische Hochschule in Munich (1900) under August Föppl; did significant work in the mechanics of solids. In trying to improve an industrial suction device, discovered the boundary layer in fluids of small viscosity (1904); made lasting contributions to the theory of supersonic flow; helped to develop the first German wind tunnel (1909); with Theodore von Kármán, did major research on airfoil theory, drag, and turbulent flow (summary paper published 1933).

PRATT, FREDERICK HAVEN (*b. Worcester, Mass., 1873; d. Wellesley Hills, Mass., 1958*), physiology.

Graduated from Harvard (A.B., 1896; A.M., 1898; M.D., 1906). During a long teaching career, spent mostly at Boston University (1921–42), Pratt studied heart and muscle physiology, especially muscle fiber contraction.

PRATT, JOHN HENRY (*b. London, England, 1809; d. Ghazipur, India, 1871*), mathematics.

Graduated from Gonville and Caius College, Cambridge (1833), and received M.A. (1836) from Christ's and Sidney Sussex colleges. A chaplain and archdeacon (from 1850) in Calcutta. Author of a book on the shape of the earth (1836; expanded edition, 1860).

PRAXAGORAS OF COS (*b. Cos, ca. 340 B.C.*), anatomy, physiology.

Of a medical family, wrote some half-dozen books on science and medicine, none of which has survived. Is credited with distinguishing between veins and arteries and with the theory that the pneuma moves through the latter and blood through the former.

PREGL, FRITZ (*b. Laibach, Austria [now Ljubljana, Yugoslavia], 1869; d. Graz, Austria, 1930*), analytical chemistry.

Studied medicine at the University of Graz and spent almost entire career there. He received training in physiological and physical chemistry at Tübingen, Leipzig, and Berlin. Developed modern methods of organic microanalysis. Awarded Nobel Prize in chemistry (1923).

PRESL, KAREL BORIWOJ (*b. Prague, Czechoslovakia, 1794; d. Prague, 1852*), botany.

Custodian at the National Museum in Prague (1822–36) and then professor of natural history and technology at Charles University, where he had also studied medicine (M.D., 1818). Noted for works on ferns.

PRESTWICH, JOSEPH (*b. Clapham, London, England, 1812; d. Shoreham, Kent, England, 1896*), geology.

A wine merchant and one of England's foremost geologists. Most important investigations were into the older Tertiary formations in southeastern England and (from 1859) into the Quaternary deposits of England and France containing the traces of early man. Knighted, 1896.

PRÉVOST, ISAAC-BÉNÉDICT (*b. Geneva, Switzerland, 1755; d. Montauban, France, 1819*), natural philosophy, mathematics, physics, chemistry.

A cousin of Pierre Prevost and tutor in the home of the Delmas family of Montauban. His discovery of a fungus parasite as the cause of the smut of wheat (1807) was a major step in the understanding of contagious disease.

PREVOST, JEAN-LOUIS (*b. Geneva, Switzerland, 1790; d. Geneva, 1850*), physiology, embryology, medicine.

One of the first biochemists. Studied in Paris and Edinburgh (M.D., 1818); in Geneva founded, for the care of the poor, the first outpatient hospital in Europe. Was a pioneer in embryology and hematology; did major work on spermatozoa, the digestive tract, and the circulation of the blood; was the first to use a "galvanic current" in experiments on muscle contraction.

PRÉVOST, LOUIS-CONSTANT (*b. Paris, France, 1787; d. Paris, 1856*), geology.

Taught geology at the Paris Athénée and the Sorbonne. Was a founder of the Société Géologique de France (1830). Collaborated with Lyell in comparing Tertiary and "Secondary" strata on both sides of the English channel. His work with strata emphasized the importance of interpretations based on analogy with present conditions. He held unorthodox views on sedimentation and vulcanism, opposed the paroxysmal dynamics of Cuvier and Élie de Beaumont, and questioned the validity of d'Orbigny's use of fossils simply as indices of geological age.

PREVOST, PIERRE (*b. Geneva, Switzerland, 1751; d. Geneva, 1839*), philosophy, physics.

A lawyer, classics scholar, politician, and scientist; professor at Geneva (1793–1823). His theory of exchanges (1791) stated that all bodies are constantly radiating heat and that an equilibrium of heat between two bodies consists in an equality of exchange.

PREYER, THIERRY WILLIAM (*b. Moss Side, near Manchester, England, 1841; d. Wiesbaden, Germany, 1897*), physiology.

Received doctorate in science at Heidelberg (1862) and his medical degree from Bonn (1866); taught at Jena (1867–88). One of the founders of modern developmental psychology. Author, *Die Seele des Kindes* (1882) on child development.

PRICHARD, JAMES COWLES (*b. Ross, Herefordshire, England, 1786 d. London, England, 1848*), anthropology.

Studied medicine at Edinburgh and practiced in Bristol (from 1811). Expanded his doctoral thesis (1808) into *Researches Into the Physical History of Mankind,* a monumental work that went into many editions. Argued originally that animal and plant varieties arise from changes in the ovum or germ of the parents, but later retreated from this position; also argued for a single origin for mankind.

PRIESTLEY, JOHN GILLIES (*b. Cottingley Hall, Bingley, Yorkshire, England, 1879; d. Oxford, England, 1941*), physiology, medicine.

Taught physiology at Oxford following medical service in World War I. With J. S. Haldane produced a classic paper on the regulation of lung ventilation (1905).

PRIESTLEY, JOSEPH (*b. Birstal Fieldhead, Yorkshire, England, 1733; d. Northumberland, Pa., 1804*), chemistry, electricity, natural philosophy, theology.

Educated for the dissenting ministry and employed most of his adult life as a teacher or preacher, Priestley wrote books, pamphlets, and articles on theology, history, education, metaphysics, language, aesthetics, and politics, as well as on scientific subjects. In his own day he was as well known for his religious and political views as for his science, although he is chiefly remembered as the discoverer of oxygen.

Completing his studies, Priestley went to preach, first at Needham Market, Suffolk, and then at Nantwich, Cheshire. At Nantwich he opened a school that proved so successful that he was invited to become tutor of languages and belles lettres at the recently founded dissenting academy at Warrington, to which he moved in 1761. While at Warrington he published *The Rudiments of English Grammar* (1761) and *A Course of Lectures on the Theory of Language* (1762). He also prepared *A Course of Lectures on Oratory and Criticism,* published several years later (1777).

Priestley's general philosophy of education was described in an *Essay on a Course of Liberal Education for Civil and Active Life* (1765) and *Miscellaneous Observations Relating to Education* (1778), and his teaching in history and law was outlined in *Lectures on History and General Policy,* prepared at Warrington but not published until 1788. The *Essay on the First Principles of Government* (1768), from which Jeremy Bentham declared that he had derived his Utilitarian formula: "The greatest happiness of the greatest number," was, therefore, but one of many protoutilitarian works written by Priestley.

While at Warrington, Priestley was ordained and obtained an LL.D. from the University of Edinburgh (1764). There he also began his scientific career, with the writing of his *History of Electricity* for which he enlisted the support of Benjamin Franklin, John Canton, Richard Price, and William Watson, whom he met in London late in 1765.

Priestley resigned his teaching position to become minister of Mill-Hill Chapel, a major Presbyterian congregation in Leeds. The *History of Electricity* (1767) and the *History of Optics* (1772) were published while he was at Leeds, and he there began his most famous scientific researches, those into the nature and properties of gases.

In 1773 William Petty, Earl of Shelburne and later Marquis of Lansdowne, prevailed on Priestley to enter his service. Priestley became Shelburne's resident intellectual, although officially he served as librarian and adviser to the household tutor. During this period Priestley did most of his scientific work, preparing five of the six major volumes of experiments on gases. He also wrote his major philosophical works, including the only books that come close to relating explicitly his theological and scientific philosophies, the *Disquisitions Relating to Matter and Spirit* (1777) and the *Doctrine of Philosophical Necessity, Illustrated* (1777).

Priestley settled with his family in Birmingham and became preacher at New Meeting House, one of the most liberal congregations in England, and was soon associated with the Lunar Society, an informal collection of provincial intellectuals, scientists, and industrialists. The Lunar Society—comprised during Priestley's years of Matthew Boulton, Erasmus Darwin, Richard Lovell Edgeworth, Samuel Galton, Jr., Robert Augustus Johnson, James Keir, Jonathan Stokes, James Watt, Josiah Wedgwood, and William Withering—combined widely ranging curiosity about nature with pragmatic concerns that would most appeal to Priestley. The members supported his researches intellectually and financially. He began there his opposition to the new chemical system of Lavoisier and devoted much of his experimentation to the application of scientific phenomena to practical pursuits.

Priestley's major preoccupations, however, were increasingly theological. He became the chief propagandist and protagonist for Unitarian beliefs in England, but increasing signs of political persecution, including economic sanctions against his sons, prompted him to emigrate to the United States in 1794.

Priestley's scientific work was begun as a logical extension of his interests in education. *The History and Present State of Electricity, With Original Experiments* was conceived as a methodized account of previous discoveries and an assessment of contemporary electrical studies, to encourage further work on the subject.

Priestley's experiments relate primarily to conductivities of different substances, although he also examined other modes of the motion of the electrical fluid. He discovered the conductivities of charcoal and of metallic salts, ranged the metals in a table of comparative conductivities, first noted the distinctive marks left by spark discharges on metallic surfaces—now known as "Priestley's rings"—and examined the phenomena of "electric wind" and sideflash. His most remarkable electrical discovery came as an interpretation of an experiment by Franklin. From the observation that pith balls lowered within an electrified metallic cup were not influenced by electricity, Priestley deduced, on Newtonian grounds, the inverse-square form of the force law between electrical charges.

In 1772 Priestley published his *History and Present State of Discoveries Relating to Vision, Light, and Colours* (usually referred to as the *History of Optics*). Although the *History of Optics* contains much useful information, it was considerably less successful than the *History of Electricity*. Yet it remained the only English work on the subject for a hundred and fifty years and the only one in any language for over fifty.

From the publication of the *History of Optics*, Priestley continued into his major metaphysical writings. His *Examination of Dr. Reid's Inquiry Into the Human Mind . . .* (1774) criticized the Scottish philosophy of common sense for its multiplication of entities (in this case independent instincts or affections of the mind) in contradiction to Newton's "Rules of Reasoning" and to the reductionist principles of Hartley, whose work, minus the mechanistic physiology, Priestley edited as *Hartley's Theory of the Human Mind . . .* in 1775. His edition of Hartley emphasized the deterministic and associationist aspects of Hartley's psychology and led him to the *Disquisitions Relating to Matter and Spirit* (1777).

Priestley's concentration on pneumatic studies began comparatively late in his career (at the age of thirty-seven). This interest lasted for the remainder of his life; and during those thirty-odd years, and chiefly in the first ten of them, he was to establish himself as one of the world's foremost pneumatic chemists. His discoveries of new gases and new processes were to make the chemistry of his day seem untenable; but Priestley never developed a new system to encompass his discoveries, and he refused to adopt the system developed by Lavoisier, which did so.

His first "chemical" publication was a pamphlet: *Directions for Impregnating Water With Fixed Air, in Order to Communicate to it the Peculiar Spirit and Virtue of Pyrmont Water, . . .* (1772). His experiments were carried on at such a prolific rate, that following the paper of 1772, it was decided that he should publish his accounts of them in book form. The first volume of *Experiments and Observations on Different Kinds of Air* appeared in 1774, the second in 1775, and the third in 1777. In 1779 Priestley began a new series, *Experiments and Observations Relating to Various Branches of Natural Philosophy*, continued with a second volume in 1781 and a third in 1786. (These six volumes are generally cited as forming a single series; in 1790 they were combined and edited in three volumes as *Experiments and Observations on Different Kinds of Air, and Other Branches of Natural Philosophy.*) These works were supplemented by an occasional paper in the *Philosophical Transactions* (including the "Account of Further Observations on Air" [1775], in which he announced his discovery of "dephlogisticated air," later to be defined as oxygen), and an extensive correspondence with other scientists in Britain and on the Continent.

During this period—in addition to his discovery of oxygen—Priestley described the isolation and identification of ammonia, sulfur dioxide, nitrous oxide and nitrogen dioxide, and silicon tetrafluoride. He discussed the properties of mineral acids; further extended the knowledge of photosynthesis; defined the role of the blood in respiration; and noted, unknowingly, the differential diffusion of gases through porous containers. More than any other person, he established the experimental techniques of pneumatic chemistry. For over a decade Priestley dominated the scientific scene in Britain and attracted the attention of scientists throughout Europe. In 1784 he was elected one of the eight foreign associates of the Royal Academy of Sciences in Paris, and he was similarly honored by nearly a score of memberships in other scientific societies from Boston and Philadelphia to Stockholm and St. Petersburgh. His reign came to an end with the development of Lavoisier's new chemistry.

In his *Heads of Lectures on a Course of Experimental Philosophy, Particularly Including Chemistry* (1794), Priestley declared that changes in the properties of bodies may result from the addition of substances, from a change in the texture of the substance itself, or from the addition of something not a substance. It was the first of these methods of interpretation that had introduced the imponderable fluids of electricity, heat, and phlogiston and it was in this mode of explanation that Lavoisier's chemistry achieved its revolution, through its emphasis on mass as a parameter and on gravimetrics as a technique for defining the elements that entered into chemical composition. Priestley's training and instincts led him to prefer the second method of explanation as he twice declared—in the *Experiments on the Generation of Air From Water* (1793) and again in "Miscellaneous Observations Relating to the Doctrine of Air," in *New York Medical Repository* (1802), when he emphasized that the principle and mode of arrangement of elements in substances was the object of his investigations.

PRINGLE, JOHN (*b. Roxburgh, Scotland, 1707; d. London, England, 1782*), medicine.

A distinguished Army physician and scientist. Author, *Diseases of the Army* (1752).

PRINGSHEIM, ALFRED (*b. Ohlau, Silesia, Germany, 1850; d. Zurich, Switzerland, 1941*), mathematics.

Studied at Berlin and Heidelberg (Ph.D., 1872); taught at Munich (1877–1922). The most consequent follower of Weierstrass; his field was pre-Lebesgue real functions and complex functions. His best-known discovery concerns power series with positive coefficients: they have a singularity in the intersection of the positive axis and the circle of convergence.

PRINGSHEIM, ERNST (*b. Breslau, Germany [now Wroclaw, Poland], 1859; d. Breslau, 1917*), physics.

Received his Ph.D. at Berlin under Helmholtz (1882); taught at Berlin and at Breslau. With his close collaborator, Otto Lummer, conducted major studies of radiation; verified Stefan's and Boltzmann's law for the temperature dependence of total radiated energy (1900).

PRINGSHEIM, NATHANAEL (*b. Wziesko, Silesia, 1823; d. Berlin, Germany, 1894*), botany, plant physiology.

Took his Ph.D. at Berlin (1848); independently wealthy, spent most of his career in private research. He helped revolutionize the science of botany by shifting attention from collection and taxonomy to the dynamics of cell development and life history. His chief contribution was to identify (1855–58) in the lower cryptogams, and especially in the algae, those basic reproductive modes (notably sexual union and the alternation of generations) that Hofmeister and others had already established for the higher cryptogams. Later in his career he developed the remarkable theory that chlorophyll plays no direct role in photosynthesis; this was based, however, upon the important observation that highly concentrated light destroys chlorophyll. Founded (1857) and edited the *Jahrbücher für wissenschaftliche Botanik;* was also the chief founder of the German Botanical Society (1882) and president until his death.

PRITCHARD, CHARLES (*b. Alberbury, Shropshire, England, 1808; d. Oxford, England, 1893*), astronomy, astrophysics.

Graduated from Cambridge (1830); founded and ran the Clapham Grammar School in London; practiced amateur astronomy. At age sixty-two, appointed professor of astronomy at Oxford; thereafter, played important role in demonstrating that accurate measurements of position can be obtained from photographic plates.

PRIVALOV, IVAN IVANOVICH (*b. Nizhniy Lomov, Penza guberniya [now oblast], Russia, 1891; d. Moscow, U.S.S.R., 1941*), mathematics.

Spent almost his entire career at the University of Moscow. Wrote principally on the boundary properties of analytic functions.

PRIVAT DE MOLIÈRES, JOSEPH (*b. Tarascon, Bouches-du-Rhône, France, 1677; d. Paris, France, 1742*), physics.

An intimate of Malebranche, and one of the major supporters of Cartesian physics versus the Newtonian science.

PROCHÁSKA, GEORGIUS (JIŘÍ) (*b. Blížkovice, Moravia, 1749; d. Vienna, Austria, 1820*), anatomy, physiology.

Studied at Olomouc and Vienna; taught at Prague (1778–91) and Vienna (1791–1819). Did his early research on movement of blood through the blood vessels. A 1781 treatise on the generation and origin of monsters set out his views on embryology, opposing preformation. His principal work, *Commentatio de functionibus systematis nervosi* (1784), analyzed the function of the nervous system, carefully differentiating between facts and theories.

PROCLUS (*b. Byzantium, 410 [?]; d. Athens, 485*), philosophy, mathematics, astronomy.

The last great representative of Neoplatonism; studied at the Platonic Academy in Athens, taught there, and became its head. Among his few extant writings is *Commentary on the First Book of Euclid's Elements,* the earliest contribution to the philosophy of mathematics; his other works included an elaborate exposition of the Ptolemaic system and commentaries on Plato's dialogues.

PROCTOR, RICHARD ANTHONY (*b. London, England, 1837; d. New York, N.Y., 1888*), astronomy.

Proctor began adult life as an indifferent student, strictly amateur astronomer, and obscure science writer. Became a hugely successful popularizer and did original work relating to Venus, Mars, and to the Galaxy. In 1870, charting directions and proper motions of *ca.* 1600 stars, he found the phenomenon he called "star drift."

PROFATIUS TIBBON. *See* **Ibn Tibbon, Jacob ben Machir.**

PRONY, GASPARD-FRANÇOIS-CLAIR-MARIE RICHE DE (*b. Chamelet, France, 1755; d. Asnières, France, 1839*), engineering.

France's leading engineer and engineering educator (from 1800). Graduated from the École des Ponts et Chaussées (1780); became its director in 1798. Was highly-placed in the civil service of several successive governments. Wrote a number of textbooks using Lagrangian analysis and graphic geometrical representations. Work in Italy led to his treatises on earth thrust (1802) and on the measure of the flow of liquids through orifices (1802) and in pipes and canals (1804). Developed the Prony brake in 1821, while testing steam engines.

PROUST, JOSEPH LOUIS (*b. Angers, France, 1754; d. Angers, 1826*), chemistry.

The son of an apothecary; went to Paris (*ca.* 1774); studied chemistry with H.-M. Rouelle; from 1778–1806, held several teaching posts in Spain; in 1820, took over his brother's pharmacy in Angers. Proust's outstanding accomplishment was his formulation of the law of definite proportions, published rather suddenly in a paper on iron oxides (1794). Its fundamental tenet is that combining substances can combine in only a small number of proportions; specifically, Proust maintained (in this paper and later ones) that most metals form two and only two oxides at fixed proportions and only one sulfide. Although his law is logically related to Daltonian chemical atomism, Proust did not develop in detail any such theoretical underpinnings; there are, however, in his writings, occasional echoes of chemical affinity theory and, rarely, formulations of chemical combination in something like molecular terms. Proust's view involved him in a prominent controversy with Berthollet, who found intermediate oxides and sulfides; there is no evidence of any direct influence on Dalton. It was apparently left to Berzelius (1811) to give Proust his due by establishing the connection between Proust's and Dalton's ideas and by awarding proper credit to Proust for the law of definite proportions.

PROUT, WILLIAM (*b. Horton, Gloucestershire, England, 1785; d. London, England, 1850*), chemistry, biochemistry.

Studied at Edinburgh (M.D., 1811); practiced as a physician in London; noted for his elaborate and accurate organic analyses. Did important work on the urine and on digestion; demonstrated (1824) that the gastric juices contain hydrochloric acid; classified foodstuffs into water, carbohydrates, fats, and proteins. Calculated (1815) that the atomic weights of all elements are integral when the weight of hydrogen is taken as unity; added (1816) that hydrogen might be the primary matter from which all other "elements" were formed; these hypotheses were greatly fruitful in stimulating interest in atomic theory. Later (1834) Prout published a corpuscular philosophy that led him to conclusions similar to those of Avogadro (1811).

PROWAZEK (PROVÁZEK), STANISLAUS VON LANOV (*b. Jindřichův Hradec, Bohemia, 1875; d. Cottbus, Germany, 1915*), microbiology, parasitology.

Studied at Prague and Vienna (Ph.D., 1899); became director of the Institut für Schiffs- und Tropenkrankheiten in Hamburg (1906). Investigated microbial diseases; in the course of his work, died of typhus.

PRUDDEN, THEOPHIL MITCHELL (*b. Middlebury, Conn., 1849; d. New York, N.Y., 1924*), pathology, bacteriology, public health, archaeology.

A founder of pathology as a field of research and teaching in the U.S. Studied at Yale (M.D., 1875), at Heidelberg, and under Koch (1885) in Berlin. Worked under Francis Delafield in his laboratory for pathology and histology in New York; became its director (1882); also taught at Yale (1880–86) and Columbia universities (1892–1909). With Delafield, wrote a landmark text of pathology (1885).

PRUNER BEY, FRANZ IGNACE (*b. Pfreimd, Germany, 1808; d. Pisa, Italy, 1882*), medicine, anthropology.

Studied at University of Munich (M.D., 1830). Travelled and practiced medicine in the Near East, especially Egypt where he became the personal physician to Abbas Pasha (1849), with the title "Bey." Studied and wrote on the Arab peoples and culture.

PRYANISHNIKOV, DMITRY NIKOLAEVICH (*b. Kyakhta, Transbaikalia, Siberia, 1865; d. Moscow, U.S.S.R., 1948*), agricultural chemistry.

Studied and taught at Moscow University (doctorate, 1900); affiliated with the Petrovskaya Agricultural Academy from 1895. Worked to improve agricultural education in Russia; specialized in the study of plant nutrition.

PRZHEVALSKY, NIKOLAY MIKHAYLOVICH (*b. Kimbarovo, Smolensk guberniya, Russia, 1839; d. Karakol [now Przhevalsk], Russia, 1888*), geography, natural science.

One of the great Russian explorer-researchers; made five major expeditions (1866–85) for the Russian Geographical Society to the Ussuri region, to Mongolia and northern China, to Lob Nor, and to Tibet (two journeys). Was a disciple of Humboldt, and considered his main task to be the study of nature. Six volumes on the zoology, botany, and meteorology of central Asia appeared (1888–1912), based on the accounts of his travels.

PSELLUS, MICHAEL (baptized **CONSTANTINE**) (*b. near Constantinople, 1018; d. Constantinople [?], 1078*), philosophy.

Despite an active political career, full of successes and setbacks, Psellus, a Neoplatonist, was instrumental in reviving an interest in philosophy and science in Byzantium. Among his vast writings are valuable compendia of excerpts from various sources on the sciences and theology, dating from the third through fifth centuries.

PTOLEMY (or **Claudius Ptolemaeus**) (*b. ca.* A.D. *100; d. ca.* A.D. *170*), mathematical sciences, especially astronomy.

Our meager knowledge of Ptolemy's life is based mostly on deductions from his surviving works, supplemented by some dubious information from authors of late antiquity and Byzantine times. The best evidence for his dates is the series of his observations reported in his major astronomical work, the *Almagest,* a manual covering the whole of mathematical astronomy as the ancients conceived it. Ptolemy assumes in the reader nothing beyond a knowledge of Euclidean geometry and an understanding of common astronomical terms; starting from first principles, he guides him through the prerequisite cosmological and mathematical apparatus to an exposition of the theory of the motion of those heavenly bodies which the ancients knew (sun, moon, Mercury, Venus, Mars, Jupiter, Saturn, and the fixed stars, the latter being considered to lie on a single sphere concentric with the earth) and of various phenomena associated with them, such as eclipses. For each body in turn Ptolemy describes the type of phenomena that have to be accounted for, proposes an appropriate geometric model, derives the numerical parameters from selected observations, and finally constructs tables enabling one to determine the motion or phenomenon in question for a given date.

Later Ptolemy published a "popular" résumé of the results of the *Almagest* under the title *Planetary Hypotheses,* in two books. Only the first part of book I survives in Greek, but the whole work is available in Arabic translation, and it goes beyond the *Almagest* in several respects.

A work in two books named *Phases of the Fixed Stars* dealt in detail with a topic not fully elaborated in the *Almagest,* the heliacal risings and settings of bright stars.

Much greater scientific interest attaches to two small works applying mathematics to astronomical problems. The first is the *Analemma* surviving, apart from a few palimpsest fragments, only in William of Moerbeke's Latin translation from the Greek. It is an explanation of a method for finding angles used in the construction of sundials, involving projection onto the plane of the meridian and swinging other planes into that plane. The actual determination of the angles is achieved not by trigonometry (although Ptolemy shows how that is theoretically possible) but by an ingenious graphical technique which in modern terms would be classified as nomographic. Although the basic idea was not new the sophisticated development is probably Ptolemy's. The other treatise is the *Planisphaerium*. This treatise survives only in Arabic translation; a revision of this translation was made by the Spanish Islamic astronomer Maslama al-Majrītī (*d.* 1007/1008) and was in turn translated into Latin by Hermann of Carinthia in 1143. It treats the problem of mapping circles on the celestial sphere onto a plane. Ptolemy projects them from the south celestial pole onto the plane of the equator. This projection is the mathematical basis of the plane astrolabe, the most popular of medieval astronomical instruments. Since the work explains how to use the mapping to calculate rising times, one of the main uses of the astrolabe, it is highly likely that the instrument itself goes back to Ptolemy (independent evidence suggests that it goes back to Hipparchus). These two treatises are an important demonstration that Greek mathematics consisted of more than "classical" geometry.

To modern eyes it may seem strange that the same man who wrote a textbook of astronomy on strictly scientific principles should also compose a textbook of astrology. Ptolemy, however, regards the *Tetrabiblos* as the natural complement to the *Almagest*: as the latter enables one to predict the positions of the heavenly bodies, so the former expounds the theory of their influences on terrestrial things.

The *Geography*, in eight books, is an attempt to map the known world. The bulk of it consists of lists of places with longitude and latitude, accompanied by very brief descriptions of the chief topographical features of the larger land areas. It was undoubtedly accompanied in Ptolemy's own publication by maps like those found in several of the manuscripts. But knowing how easily maps are corrupted in copying, Ptolemy takes pains to ensure that the reader will be able to reconstruct the maps on the basis of the text alone.

The *Optics*, in five books, is lost in Greek. An Arabic translation was made from a manuscript lacking book I and the end of book V; from this translation, which is also lost, Eugenius of Sicily produced the extant Latin translation in the twelfth century. Despite the incompleteness and frequent obscurity of the text, the outlines of Ptolemy's optical theory are clear enough. The establishment of theory by experiment, frequently by constructing special apparatus, is the most striking feature of the work. Whether the subject matter is largely derived or original, the *Optics* is an impressive example of the development of a mathematical science with due regard to the physical data, and is worthy of the author of the *Almagest*.

A work on music theory *Harmonica*, in three books, deals with the mathematical intervals (on a stretched string) between notes and their classification according to various traditional Greek systems. It seeks a middle ground between the two schools of the Pythagoreans and the followers of Aristoxenus, of whom the former, according to Ptolemy, stressed mathematical theory at the expense of the ear's evidence, while the latter did the reverse. Again we see Ptolemy's anxiety to erect a theory

that is mathematically satisfactory but also takes due account of the phenomena. According to the commentary of Porphyry (late third century), the *Harmonica* is mostly derivative, especially from the work of one Didymus (first century). We have no means of checking this statement.

In estimating Ptolemy's stature and achievement as a scientist, it is unfortunately still necessary to react against the general tendency of nineteenth-century scholarship to denigrate him as a mere compiler of the scientific work of his predecessors. This extreme view, exemplified in the writings of Delambre, is no longer held by anyone competent but still persists in handbooks. With a candor unusual in ancient authors Ptolemy freely acknowledges what parts of his theory he owes to Hipparchus. It is certain that a great part of the theory in the *Almagest* is his personal contribution, and it is unlikely that the situation was radically different in all his other scientific work. On the other hand, his was not an original genius: his method was to take existing theory and to modify and extend it so as to get good agreement with observed facts. In this method, however, Ptolemy was no different from the vast majority of scientists of all periods; and he in no way deserves the reputation of a hack. His work is remarkable for its blend of knowledge, ingenuity, judgment, and clarity. The authority that it achieved in several fields is not surprising.

PUISEUX, VICTOR (*b. Argenteuil, Val-d'Oise, France, 1820; d. Frontenay, Jura, France, 1883*), mathematics, mechanics, celestial mechanics.

Studied (doctorate, 1841) and taught at the École Normale Supérieure in Paris; succeeded Cauchy in the chair of mathematical astronomy at the Faculty of Sciences (1857–82), was a pioneer alpinist. Expert in several areas of physics and mathematics, his most original work (1850–51) involved developing, correcting, and completing major aspects of the theory of functions of a complex variable that had been elaborated by Cauchy: z defined by $f(u,z)=0$.

PULFRICH, CARL (*b. Strässchen [near Burscheid], Solingen, Germany, 1858; d. Baltic Sea, near Timmendorferstrand, Germany, 1927*), physics.

Studied at the University of Bonn (Ph.D., 1882); assisted Clauius and Hertz (1883–90); employed under Ernst Abbe at the Zeiss works in Jena. A disciple of Abbe; expert in photometry and refractometry; considered the father of stereo-photogrammetry.

PUMPELLY, RAPHAEL (*b. Owego, N.Y., 1837; d. Newport, R.I., 1923*), geology, geography, enthnology.

Studied geology at the Freiberg Bergakademie; influenced by Breithaupt and von Cotta; developed technique of drawing hypotheses from the two vantage points of sequential and multiple analysis. Traveled in the Far East in the 1860's; in the U.S. investigated copper-bearing rocks; wrote on the origin of Chinese loess. Headed several official geological surveys. Went to Central Asia (1903, 1904), studying the pattern of human settlements and migrations following the glacial period.

PUNNETT, REGINALD CRUNDALL (*b. Tonbridge, England, 1875; d. Bilbrook, Somerset, England, 1967*), morphology, genetics.

Spent most of his career at Cambridge and (after 1930) in private research. First studied the morphology of nemertines. In collaboration with Bateson (1904–10), confirmed several basic discoveries of classical Mendelian genetics; founded and edited the *Journal of Genetics* (1911); continued this research, working primarily with poultry. Wrote *Mendelism* (1905) and *Heredity in Poultry* (1923).

PUPIN, MICHAEL IDVORSKY (*b. Idvor, Banat [now Yugoslavia], 1858; d. New York, N.Y., 1935*), applied physics.

Immigrated to the U.S. alone at age fifteen; studied at Columbia University, at Cambridge, and at Berlin (doctorate, 1889); taught at Columbia (from 1889). Most important contribution was to the technology of telephone lines. His autobiography (1924) won the Pulitzer Prize.

PURKYNĚ (PURKINJE), JAN EVANGELISTA (*b. Libochovice, Bohemia [now Czechoslovakia], 1787; d. Prague, Bohemia, 1869*), physiology, histology, embryology, education.

A very resourceful and versatile scientist. Was educated by the Piarists and took holy orders; abandoned an ecclesiastical career (1807); did private tutoring to support his studies in Prague; was influenced by his teacher Bernard Bolzano. Taught at Prague and at Breslau (1823–50), overcoming initial hostility caused by his liberal, nonconformist views. Investigated subjective sensory phenomena (1818–25), especially visual sensations (including the "Purkyně phenomenon," or "Purkyně shift"); postulated that to each subjective sensation there corresponds a physiological process in the relevant sensory organ, and was thus led to many important discoveries (including the physiological inability of peripheral parts of the retina to distinguish colors); tried to determine the physical properties of the sensory organs; anticipated Helmholtz's design of the ophthalmoscope. His 1823 Breslau dissertation contained his renowned classification of fingerprints. Studied vertigo (1820–27) and the role of the cerebellum in muscular reactions to rotation, the early development of the avian egg (discovered the germinal vesicle, or "Purkyně's vesicle"), the effects of drugs (notably digitalis and belladona), and plant structures. Acquiring a new microscope (1832) by S. Plössl, began a patient, systematic study of structure as the material basis of life phenomena; made major discoveries in the digestive tract, nervous system (including Purkyně's cells in the cerebellum), and in the heart (Purkyně fibers); was the first to describe cells as ubiquitous formations in the central nervous system of vertebrates and in their ganglia; with Gabriel Valentin, discovered ciliary motion in higher animals. Opened a modest independent physiological institute in Breslau (1839), the first of its kind. Returned to Prague (1850) as professor of physiology; devoted most of his final years to organizing and expanding science education.

PURSH, FREDERICK (Friedrich Traugott Pursch) (*b. Grossenhain, Saxony [now German Democratic Republic], 1774; d. Montreal, Canada, 1820*), botany.

Held a variety of posts in Dresden, the U.S., England, and Canada. His *Flora Americae Septentrionalis* (1814) was the first work to describe plants of the Pacific Coast.

PUTNAM, FREDERIC WARD (*b. Salem, Mass., 1839; d. Cambridge, Mass., 1915*), archaeology, anthropology.

Studied at Harvard under Louis Agassiz. Became curator of the Peabody Museum of American Archaeology and Ethnology at Harvard (1874) and also Peabody professor (1887); chief of the ethnology and archaeology department of the World's Columbian Exposition in Chicago (1893); his chief assistant was Franz Boas, whom he employed again upon becoming curator of the American Museum of Natural History (1894).

PYTHAGORAS OF SAMOS (*b. Samos, ca. 560 B.C.; d. Metapontum, ca. 480 B.C.*), mathematics, theory of music, astronomy.

Most of the sources concerning Pythagoras' life, activities, and doctrines date from the third and fourth centuries A.D., while the few more nearly contemporary (fourth and fifth centuries B.C.) records of him are often contradictory, due in large part to the split that developed among his followers soon after his death.

A few decades after Pythagoras' death, two groups evolved into sharp factions and began a controversy over which of them was most truly Pythagorean. One group based their claim on their literal adherence to Pythagoras' own words the other seems to have developed Pythagoras' ideas to such an extent that they were no longer in complete agreement with their originals. The matter was further complicated because, according to ancient tradition, Pythagoras chose to reveal his teachings clearly and completely to only his most advanced disciples. The later Pythagorean tradition thus includes a number of strange prescriptions and doctrines interpreted with absolute literalness; the more rationalistic group (led at one time by Aristoxenus, who was also a disciple of Plato and Aristotle) preferred a symbolic and allegorical interpretation.

This obscurity concerning Pythagoras' intent has led historians of science into differences of opinion as to whether Pythagoras could really be considered a scientist or even an initiator of scientific ideas. It is further debatable whether those ancient authors who made real contributions to mathematics, astronomy, and the theory of music can be considered to have been true Pythagoreans, or even to have been influenced by authentically Pythagorean ideas. Nonetheless, apart from the theory of metempsychosis (which is mentioned by his contemporaries), ancient tradition assigns one doctrine to Pythagoras and the early Pythagoreans that can hardly have failed to influence the development of mathematics. This is the broad generalization, based on rather restricted observation (a procedure common in early Greek science), that all things are numbers.

Pythagoras' number theory was based on three observations. The first of these was the mathematical relationships of musical harmonies—that is, that when the ratio of lengths of sound-producing instruments (such as strings or flutes) is extended to other instruments in which one-dimensional relations are involved, the same musical harmonies result. Secondly, the Pythagoreans noted that any triangle formed of three sticks in the ratio 3:4:5 is always a right triangle, whatever the length of its segments. Their third important observation derived from the fixed numerical relations of the movements of heavenly bodies. It was thereby apparent to them that since the same musical harmonies and geometric shapes can be produced in different media and sizes by the same combination of numbers, the numbers themselves must express the harmonies and shapes and even the things having those harmonies and shapes. It could thus be said that these things—or, as they were later called, the essences of these things—actually were numbers. The groups of numbers that embodied the essence of a thing, and by which it might be reproduced, were called a term that later came to mean "ratio."

The theory of "means" is also undoubtedly Pythagorean and probably of considerable antiquity.

Although the contributions made by Pythagoras and his early successors to arithmetic and number theory can be determined with some accuracy, their contributions to geometry remain problematic. The so-called Pythagorean theorem had been known in Babylonia at the time of Hammurabi, and it is possible that Pythagoras had learned it there. It is not known whether the theorem was proved during Pythagoras' lifetime, or shortly thereafter. The pentagram, which played an important role in Pythagorean circles in the early fifth century B.C., was also known in Babylonia, and may have been imported from there. This figure, a regular pentagon with its sides extended to intersect in the form of a five-pointed star, has the interesting property that its sides and diagonals intersect everywhere according to the golden section; the Pythagoreans used it as a symbol by which they recognized each other.

Of the mathematical discoveries attributed by ancient tradition to the Pythagoreans, the most important remains that of incommensurability. According to Plato's *Theaetetus*, this discovery cannot have been made later than the third quarter of the fifth century B.C., and although there has been some scholarly debate concerning the accuracy of this assertion, there is no reason to believe that it is not accurate. It is certain that the Pythagorean doctrine that all things are numbers would have been a strong incentive for the investigation of the hidden numbers that constitute the essences of the isosceles right-angled triangle or of the regular pentagon; if, as the Pythagoreans knew, it was always possible to construct a right triangle given sides in the ratio 3:4:5, then it should by analogy be possible to determine the numbers by which a right-angled isosceles triangle could be constructed.

Pythagoras (or, according to another tradition, Hippasus) is also credited with knowing how to construct three of the five regular solids, specifically the pyramid, the cube, and the dodecahedron.

The notion that all things are numbers is also fundamental to Pythagorean music theory. Early Pythagorean music theory would seem to have initially been of the same speculative sort as early Pythagorean mathematical theory. It was based upon observations drawn from the lyre and the flute, the most widely used instruments; from these observations it was concluded that the most beautiful musical harmonies corresponded to the most beautiful (because simplest) ratios or combinations of numbers, namely the octave (2:1), the fifth (3:2), and the fourth (4:3).

In addition to its specifically Pythagorean elements, Pythagorean astronomy would seem to have comprised both Babylonian observations and theories (presumably brought back by Pythagoras from his travels) and certain theories developed by Anaximander of Miletus, whose disciple Pythagoras is said to have been. Their knowledge of the periodicity of the movements of the stars undoubtedly strengthened the Pythagoreans in their belief that all things are numbers. They attempted to develop astronomical theory by combining it with this general principle, among others (including the principle of beauty that had figured in their axiomatic foundations of the theory of music). Their concern with musical intervals led them to try to determine the sequence of the planets in relation to the position of the earth. According to their theory, probably the earliest of its kind, the order of the planets, in regard to their increasing distance from the earth, was the moon, Mercury, Venus, the sun, Mars, Jupiter, and Saturn—a sequence that was later refined by placing Mercury and Venus above the sun, since no solar transits of these bodies had been observed.

Further theories by which the distances and periods of revolution of the heavenly bodies are correlated with musical intervals are greatly various, if not actually contradictory. Indeed, a number of them make very little sense in the context of musical theory. It is almost impossible to tell what the original astronomical-musical theory on which these variants are based actually was, although it was almost certainly of considerable antiquity. It may be assumed, however, that in any original theory the celestial spheres were likened to the seven strings of a lyre, and were thought to produce a celestial harmony called the music of the spheres. Ordinary mortals could not hear this music (Aristotle suggested that this was because they had been exposed to it continuously since the moment of their birth), but later Pythagoreans said that it was audible to Pythagoras himself.

Another mystical notion, this one adopted from the Babylonians, was that of the great year. This concept, which was used by the Pythagoreans and probably by Pythagoras, held that since the periods of revolution of all heavenly bodies were in integral ratio, a least common multiple must exist, so that exactly the same constellation of all stars must recur after some definite period of time (the "great year" itself). It thereupon followed that all things that have occurred will recur in precisely the same way.

Pythagorean ideas of beauty required that the stars move in the simplest curves. This principle thus demanded that all celestial bodies move in circles, the circle being the most beautiful curve, a notion that held the utmost importance for the development of ancient astronomy. There may have been—even before Plato asked the non-Pythagorean mathematician Eudoxus to create a model showing the circular movements of all celestial bodies—a Pythagorean theory that explained the movements of Mercury and Venus as epicycles around the sun, and thus represented the first step toward a heliocentric system.

PYTHEAS OF MASSALIA (*fl. Massalia [now Marseilles, France], 330* B.C.), geography.

One of the greatest explorers of antiquity. Traveled in Britain, the North Sea, and the Frisian Islands; discovered Thule (usually said to be Iceland). The recorded history of Britain begins with him.

AL-QABAJĀQĪ. *See* **Baylak al-Qibjāqī.**

AL-QABĪṢĪ, ABŪ AL-ṢAQR ʿABD AL-ʿAZĪZ IBN ʿUTHMĀN IBN ʿALĪ (*fl. ca. 950, Aleppo, Syria*), astrology.

An authority on Ptolemy's *Almagest.* Wrote a vastly popular "Introduction to Astrology," now valued only for its quotations from ancient sources.

QĀḌĪ ZĀDA AL-RŪMĪ (more properly **Salah al-Dīn Mūsā Pasha**) (*b. Bursa, Turkey, ca. 1364; d. Samarkand, Uzbekistan, ca. 1436*), mathematics, astronomy.

Studied in Bursa with the theologian and encyclopedist Mullā Shams al-Dīn Muḥammad al-Fanārī. In Samarkand, was named director of the new university and professor of mathematics and astronomy (1421) by Ulugh Beg; became director of the observatory (1429). Was the great-grandfather of the Turkish mathematician Mīram Chelebi.

AL-QALAṢĀDĪ (or **AL-QALṢĀDĪ**), **ABU'L-ḤASAN ʿALĪ IBN MUḤAMMAD IBN ʿALĪ** (*b. Basṭa [now Baza], Spain, 1412; d. Béja, Tunisia, 1486*), arithmetic, algebra.

The last known Spanish-Muslim mathematician. Wrote a commentary on Ibn al-Yāsmīnī's poem on algebraic rules. His own text on arithmetic, in simplified and shortened versions, was widely used in North African schools.

AL-QARASHĪ. *See* **Ibn al-Nafīs.**

AL-QAZWĪNĪ, ZAKARIYĀ IBN MUḤAMMAD IBN MAḤMŪD, ABŪ YAḤYĀ (*b. Qazwīn [now Kasvin], Persia, ca. 1203; d. 1283*), cosmography, geography.

Of a family of Arab jurists; was in Damascus by 1233, where he was influenced by the mystic Ibn al-ʿArabī (*d.* 1240); served as a judge in Wāsiṭ and Ḥilla (Iraq). Wrote two works: one on cosmography, which marks him as the greatest Muslim cosmographer of medieval times, and a geographical dictionary in two versions (1262, 1275). In the Ṣūfī tradition, al-Qazwīnī saw all of creation as a manifestation of the divine wisdom and intelligence; he had a vast if uncritical knowledge of science, and quoted liberally from written and oral sources.

QUATREFAGES DE BRÉAU, JEAN-LOUIS-ARMAND DE (*b. Valleraugues, France, 1810; d. Paris, France, 1892*), medicine, zoology, anthropology.

Studied in Strasbourg; had a medical practice in Toulouse. In Paris (from 1840), was greatly influenced by his teacher and friend Milne-Edwards; undertook extensive zoological studies, especially of marine invertebrates; set forth a theory of degeneration of organisms, in which he hypothesized the disappearance of the circulatory system in certain creatures (e.g., the gastropod marine mollusks). Obtained the chair of the natural history of man at the Muséum d'Histoire Naturelle (1855); believed in the antiquity of man but opposed Darwinian theory.

QUENSTEDT, FRIEDRICH (*b. Eisleben, Germany, 1809; d. Tübingen, Germany, 1889*), paleontology, mineralogy, geology.

Studied at Berlin, and taught at Tübingen from 1837. In crystallography, extended the work of Christian Weiss, and in geology that of Leopold von Buch; most signifi-

cant work concerned the paleontology and stratigraphy of the Juraissic series of Swabia.

QUERCETANUS, JOSEPHUS. *See* **Duchesne, Joseph.**

QUETELET, LAMBERT-ADOLPHE-JACQUES (*b. Ghent, Belgium, 1796; d. Brussels, Belgium, 1874*), statistics.

Studied at the University of Ghent (doctorate, 1819); taught at the Athénée of Brussels; appointed astronomer at the Brussels Royal Observatory (1828). Specialized in social statistics; with the publication of his *Sur l'homme et le développement de ses facultés, essai d'une physique sociale* (1835), he became famous throughout Europe. He hoped to create a social physics; although he did not apply sophisticated mathematics, he did give science new aims and new tools.

IBN AL-QUFF, AMĪN AL-DAWLAH ABŪ AL-FARAJ IBN MUWAFFAQ AL-DĪN YAʿQŪB IBN ISḤĀQ AL-MASĪḤĪ AL-KARAKĪ (*b. Karak, Jordan, 1233; d. Damascus, Syria, 1286*), medicine, physiology, natural sciences, philosophy.

A great physician-surgeon with the Mamluk army, the best-known medical educator in Syria, and a prolific author. Wrote the largest Arabic text devoted to surgery of the medieval period, *Kitāb al-ʿUmdah;* described the importance of the capillaries (nearly four centuries before Malpighi); explained the function of the cardiac valves. His *Jāmiʿ al-Gharaḍ* contains original ideas on embryology, health preservation, and other topics.

AL-QŪHĪ (or **AL-KŪHĪ**), **ABŪ SAHL WAYJAN IBN RUSTAM** (*fl. Baghdad, ca. 970–1000*), mathematics, astronomy.

Of Persian origin. Built (988) and directed an observatory for Sharaf al-Dawla. In geometry he solved problems that would have led to equations of higher than the second degree; analyzing the equation $x^3 + a = cx^2$, he concluded that it had a (positive) root if $a \leq 4c^3/27$; was the first to describe the so-called conic compass.

QUINCKE, GEORG HERMANN (*b. Frankfurt-an-der-Oder, Germany, 1834; d. Heidelberg, Germany, 1924*), physics.

Educated at Berlin (doctorate, 1858) and Königsberg; taught at Berlin (1865–72) and Würzburg (1872–75); succeeded Kirchhoff at Heidelberg (1875). Was mainly concerned with the determination and collection of data on the properties and constants of materials.

QUOY, JEAN-RENÉ-CONSTANT (*b. Maillé, Vendée, France, 1790; d. St.-Jean-de-Liversay, France, 1869*), zoology.

Of a family of surgeons (even one grandmother was a surgeon); became a naval surgeon and rose to the highest office in the Naval Health Service. Served as zoologist on the world voyage of the *Uranie* (1817–20) and on the voyage of the *Astrolabe* (1826–29) to Australia, New Zealand, and New Guinea.

IBN QURRA. *See* **Thābit ibn Qurra.**

QUSṬĀ IBN LŪQĀ AL-BAʿLABAKKĪ (*fl. Baghdad and Armenia, 860–900*), medicine, translation of scientific literature.

A Christian of Greek origin; was a doctor in Baalbek; served Caliph al-Mustaʿīn in Baghdad and the ruler Sanhārīb in Armenia. Wrote on medicine, mathematics, astronomy, music, and philosophy; was especially valued for his translations of Greek scientific works.

IBN QUTAYBA, ABŪ MUḤAMMAD ʿABDALLĀH IBN MUSLIM AL-DĪNAWARĪ AL-JABALĪ (*b. Baghdad or Kufa, Iraq, 828; d. Baghdad, 884 or 889*), transmission of knowledge.

Served as judge in Dīnawar (northern Persia); taught in Baghdad; was primarily a philologist and lexicographer. His *Kitāb al-anwāʾ* is a compilation of popular lore concerning astronomy, meteorology, and related phenomena.

QUṬB AL-DĪN AL-SHĪRĀZĪ (*b. Shīrāz, Persia, 1236; d. Tabrīz, Persia, 1311*), optics, astronomy, geography, medicine, philosophy.

At age fourteen, assumed his late father's duties as physician and ophthalmologist at the Muẓaffarī hospital in Shīrāz; left after ten years to pursue further studies; became associated (*ca.* 1262) with the teacher Naṣīr al-Dīn al-Ṭūsī at Marāgha, with whom he studied the astronomy and philosophy of Ibn Sīnā; was also a disciple of the famous Ṣūfī Ṣadr al-Dīn al-Qunyawī in Konya; then became a judge in Sivas and Molatya; moved to Tabrīz where he attracted the attention of the ruler of Persia, who sent him to Egypt as an ambassador; after returning to Tabrīz, became renowned for his vast knowledge; was also an expert chess player and lutist. As a philosopher and theologian, Quṭb al-Dīn contributed to the revival of the thought of Ibn Sīnā; his *Durrat al-tāj* . . . is the outstanding Persian encyclopedia of Peripatetic philosophy. He also wrote on geometry, astronomy, and geography; his *Nihāyat al-idrāk* . . . , a masterpiece of astronomy, contains sections on optics, and the first correct explanation of the rainbow; he emphasized the relation between the sun and the planets in a manner which prepared the way for Copernicus. In medicine, his major work was his commentary on the *Canon* of Ibn Sīnā. In *Sharḥ Ḥikmat al-ishrāq* he developed a physics of light, in which light is considered as the source of all motion.

RABELAIS, FRANÇOIS (*b. "La Devinière," near Chinon, France, 1494 [?]; d. Meudon, France, 1553 [?]*), medicine.

In addition to his careers as cleric, politician, diplomat, Humanist scholar, and writer, Rabelais was also a physician (M.D., Montpellier, 1537). He wrote books on Hippocrates and Galen; taught and practiced medicine (1530–39); and conducted a public dissection of a human corpse (1537).

RABL, CARI (*b. Wels, Oberösterreich, Austria, 1853; d. Leipzig, Germany, 1917*), anatomy, embryology, cytology.

Inspired by Haeckel, studied medicine at Vienna (M.D., 1882) and zoology at Jena with Haeckel. Taught at Ferdinand University in Prague (1885–1904) and at Leipzig (from 1904). His outstanding contribution was the first clear expression of the concept of the continuity of the chromosomes throughout cellular division (1885).

RADEMACHER, HANS (*b. Wandsbeck, Schleswig-Holstein, Germany, 1892; d. Haverford, Pa., 1969*), mathematics.

Studied at Göttingen (doctorate, 1916), and held several teaching posts in Germany, before coming to the U.S. (1933); taught at Swarthmore College and the University of Pennsylvania. His chief field of interest was analytic number theory.

RÁDL, EMANUEL (*b. Pyšely, Bohemia [now Czechoslovakia], 1873; d. Prague, Czechoslovakia, 1942*), philosophy, history of biological sciences.

Spent almost his entire career at the University of Prague; was a friend and follower of T. G. Masaryk; proposed a nonformalized western Christianity as a unifying philosophy. In the history of science, wrote *Geschichte der biologischen Theorien* (1905–09).

RADÓ, TIBOR (*b. Budapest, Hungary, 1895; d. New Smyrna Beach, Fla., 1965*), mathematics.

Held several teaching posts in Hungary and the U.S., retiring as research professor at Ohio State University. Contributed to the creation of a modern theory of surface area measure.

RADON, JOHANN (*b. Tetschen, Bohemia [now Decin, Czechoslovakia], 1887; d. Vienna, Austria, 1956*), mathematics.

Received his doctorate from Vienna (1910) and eventually returned there as full professor (1947). His major field was the calculus of variations.

RAFFLES, THOMAS STAMFORD BINGLEY (*b. at sea off Port Morant, Jamaica, 1781; d. London, England, 1826*), natural history.

A high official of the East India Company in Malaya, Java, and Singapore; was also an important explorer and collector. Author, *History of Java* (1817).

RAFINESQUE, CONSTANTINE SAMUEL (*b. Galata, near Constantinople, 1783; d. Philadelphia, Pa., 1840*), natural history, archaeology.

Neglected by his peers (partly because of his own failings), but nevertheless an original scientist. Traveled widely in Europe and the U.S.; made important botanical explorations west of the Alleghenies; anticipated Darwin in his view of the ordering of plants; was the first to suggest (1822) that the Mayan ideographs are partly syllabic.

RĀGHAVĀNANDA ŚARMAN (*fl. Bengal, India, 1591–99*), astronomy.

A Bengālī Brāhmaṇa; wrote a series of astrological and astronomical works; was a follower of the Saurapakṣa.

RAMAN, CHANDRASEKHARA VENKATA (*b. Tiruchirapalli [Trichinopoly], India, 1888; d. Bangalore, India, 1970*), physics, physiology of vision.

Of a family of scholars; received his B.A. at age sixteen from the University of Madras and his M.A. three years later. Ill health forced him to abandon further study and to enter the civil service, but he continued to do research, particularly on vibrations and sound and on the theory of musical instruments; appointed professor of physics at Calcutta (1917). Showed how the scattering of light causes the color of the sea (1922). Published a definitive article on musical instruments and their sounds (1927). With associates, discovered a new type of secondary radiation of incident light, with several lines shifted toward longer wavelengths, the shift indicating a characteristic absorption of energy by the scattering molecule; this Raman effect can be explained by the quantum theory, and had been predicted by A. Smekal (1923); R. W. Wood called it "one of the most convincing proofs of the quantum theory of light." Raman was knighted (1929) and awarded the Nobel Prize (1930). He served with the Indian Institute of Science in Bangalore (1933–48) and as head of the Raman Research Institute (from 1948). Continuing his work in optics, he also studied the structure of crystals, optical effects in gems and minerals, and colors and their perception.

RAMANUJAN, SRINIVASA AAIYANGAR (*b. Erode, Tanjore district, Madras province, India, 1887; d. Chetput, near Madras, India, 1920*), mathematics.

A failed student, occasional clerk, and self-educated genius in mathematics; was helped by several friends; invited to England by G. H. Hardy; admitted to Trinity College, Cambridge (1914). The most lasting aspect of his work is probably his investigation of the partition of numbers into summands. Elected fellow of the Royal Society (1918).

RAMES, JEAN BAPTISTE (*b. Aurillac, France, 1832; d. Aurillac, 1894*), botany, geology.

A pharmacist. Studied fossil remains in the Toulouse region. Did outstanding investigations of the volcanoes of the Cantal.

RAMMELSBERG, KARL (or **CARL**) **FRIEDRICH** (*b. Berlin, Germany, 1813; d. Gross-Lichterfelde, near Berlin, 1899*), chemistry.

Spent entire career at the University of Berlin. Most important works were his comprehensive compilations on mineral chemistry and on chemical crystallography.

RAMON, GASTON (*b. Bellechaume, France, 1886; d. Paris, France, 1963*), immunology.

Trained as veterinarian; affiliated with the Pasteur Institute (1911–49); head of the Bureau of Epizootic Diseases in Paris (1949–58). Did vital work on vaccines.

RAMÓN Y CAJAL, SANTIAGO (*b. Petilla de Aragón, Spain, 1852; d. Madrid, Spain, 1934*), neuroanatomy, neurohistology.

Studied at Zaragoza (M.D., 1873); taught at Valencia, Barcelona, and Madrid (1892–1922). Shared the Nobel Prize for physiology or medicine with Golgi (1906). Using Golgi's potassium dichromate-silver nitrate technique, showed that axons always end independently of other axons; thus he established what was later called the neuron doctrine against the more popular belief that there was a network of axon terminals. Also did fundamental work on the cortex, on neurofibrils, and on traumatic degeneration and regeneration of nervous structures. His book on the nervous system (1904) is a classic.

RAMOND DE CARBONNIÈRES, LOUIS FRANÇOIS ÉLISABETH (*b. Strasbourg, France, 1755; d. Paris, France, 1827*), geology, botany.

Combined careers in politics and natural history; secretary to Cardinal Louis de Rohan; professor of natural history at Tarbes; appointed prefect of Puy-de-Dôme by Napoleon (1806). Studied the Alps and especially the Pyrenees, where he made the revolutionary discovery of abundant fossils in calcareous sediments at high altitudes.

RAMSAUER, CARL WILHELM (*b. Osternburg, Oldenburg, Germany, 1879; d. Berlin, Germany, 1955*), physics.

Received his doctorate from the University of Kiel (1902); held several posts, retiring (1953) as director of the physics institute of the Berlin Technische Hochschule. Discovered (1920) the Ramsauer effect in which the penetrability of gas atoms by electrons of decreasing velocity is at a certain point unexpectedly increased; this could not be explained until the development of wave mechanics.

RAMSAY, ANDREW CROMBIE (*b. Glasgow, Scotland, 1814; d. Beaumaris, Wales, 1891*), geology.

A failed businessman and self-taught geologist; affiliated with the Geological Survey of Great Britain (from 1841); knighted in 1881. His main contributions were his theories concerning general denudation, the development of river systems, and glaciation.

RAMSAY, WILLIAM (*b. Glasgow, Scotland, 1852; d. Hazlemere, Buckinghamshire, England, 1916*), physical chemistry.

For his discovery of the family of inert gases, awarded the 1904 Nobel Prize in chemistry. Studied organic chemistry under Fittig at Tübingen, earning the Ph.D. at age nineteen. Taught at Glasgow, at University College, Bristol (1880–87), and at University College, London (1887–1912). At Glasgow investigated pyridine and its derivative alkaloids; was one of the first to suggest a plausible explanation for Brownian motion. Next (1880–94) he studied the critical states of liquids and gases. Following Lord Rayleigh's announcement (1892) reconsidering the discrepancy between atmospheric and chemical nitrogen, he speculated that there might be a heavy gas in the former; discovered argon (1894) and with Rayleigh determined that it is monatomic with an atomic weight of about 40. Discovered helium (1895); with M. W. Travers went on to study the properties of helium and to discover and study krypton, neon, and xenon. With F. Soddy, investigated the new gas, "emanation," linked to thorium and radium; jointly suggested (1902) that the excess of atmospheric and terrestrial helium might be connected with radioactivity. From 1903, Ramsay was increasingly interested in research on radioactivity.

RAMSDEN, JESSE (*b. Halifax, England, 1735; d. Brighton, England, 1800*), instrument design.

The most skillful instrument maker of the 18th century. Opened his own shop in London (1762). Greatest achievement was his dividing engine of 1775, in which the error was reduced to less than one-half second of arc.

RAMSEY, FRANK PLUMPTON (*b. Cambridge, England, 1903; d. Cambridge, 1930*), mathematical logic.

Spent his brief life at Cambridge, where his father was president of Magdalene College. Criticized the Whitehead-Russell axiom of reducibility; following Wittgenstein, he reinterpreted the concept of propositional functions, thus obviating the need for this axiom.

RAMUS, PETER, also known as **Pierre de La Ramée** (*b. Cuts, Vermandois, France, 1515; d. Paris, France, 1572*), logic and method, pedagogy, physics.

Studied and taught at the University of Paris; was principal there of the Collège de Presles (from 1545). An extremely popular and influential teacher, Ramus was also highly controversial for his attacks on contemporary Aristotelianism and his conversion to Calvinism (1561); despite explicit royal protection, he was murdered in the St. Bartholomew's Day Massacre. Ramus extended the pedagogical ideas of Rudolf Agricola, calling for a revival in the curriculum of mathematics, astronomy, and physics, with the emphasis on their application to practical problems; was not certain of the proper role of algebra but did suggest a link between algebra and Greek geometrical analysis; urged a return to the observational astronomy of the Babylonians and Egyptians. With his dual concern for mathematics and problem-solving, Ramus helped to formulate the quest for operational knowledge of nature that marks the Scientific Revolution.

RAṄGANĀTHA (son of Ballāla) (*fl. 1603 at Benares, India*), astronomy.

Of a learned Brāhmaṇa family. Wrote a commentary (1603) on the *Sūryasiddhānta*.

RANKINE, ALEXANDER OLIVER (*b. Guildford, England, 1881; d. Hampton, Middlesex, England, 1956*), physics, geophysics.

A university teacher; chief physicist with the Anglo-Iranian Oil Company (1937–47). Invented the "Rankine viscosimeter" for measuring the viscosity of a gas.

RANKINE, WILLIAM JOHN MACQUORN (*b. Edinburgh, Scotland, 1820; d. Glasgow, Scotland, 1872*), engineering, physical science.

A practicing civil engineer; invented what is now called Rankine's method for laying out circular curves on railways (1841); began to publish papers in physical science in 1849. Rejecting Fresnel's luminiferous ether, he proposed "the hypothesis of molecular vortices," in which the atoms composing matter were made up of circulating streams of elastic matter around small nuclei; the nuclei formed the luminiferous medium. Extended this hypothesis most successfully to the theory of heat. Developed a general theory of energy, distinguishing (1853) between "actual" and "potential" energy; founded "the science of energetics," in which energy and its transformations, rather than force and motion, were regarded as basic. Rankine taught at Glasgow (from 1855) and published a very successful set of engineering textbooks.

RANVIER, LOUIS-ANTOINE (*b. Lyons, France, 1835; d. Vendranges, Loire, France, 1922*), histology.

The foremost French histologist of the period 1850–1900. Received his M.D. in Paris (1865); affiliated with the Collège de France (1867–1900). Best known for his researches on the peripheral nervous system; discovered (1871) the annular constrictions of medullated nerves (the nodes of Ranvier). Author, *Traité technique d'histologie* (1875–82).

RANYARD, ARTHUR COWPER (*b. Swanscombe, Kent, England, 1845; d. London, England, 1894*), astrophysics.

A lawyer, mathematician, photographer, and astronomer; lived in London; specialized in the observation of solar eclipses and published a memoir (1879) collecting all nineteenth-century eclipse observations.

RAOULT, FRANÇOIS MARIE (*b. Fournes, France, 1830; d. Grenoble, France, 1901*), chemistry.

Supported himself by teaching while earning his B.A. and B.S. degrees (College of St. Dié, Reims) and his doctorate (University of Paris, 1863); taught at the University of Grenoble (from 1867). Best known for his experimental examination of the freezing point and vapor pressure of various solutions and of water as affected by different salts.

RASPAIL, FRANÇOIS-VINCENT (*b. Carpentras, France, 1794; d. Arcueil, near Paris, 1878*), biology, medicine.

Of a poor family; prepared for the priesthood but instead became active in politics; was a prominent figure in the Revolutions of 1830 and 1848; endured numerous political trials, long prison terms, and exile; was exceedingly popular with the public and quite unpopular with the established scientists of his day. Self-educated in science, his definitions and descriptions of the cell are remarkable and helped to prepare the way for the rise of cell theory; he was one of the founders of cytochemistry and cellular pathology. Discovered the histochemical reactions specific to protides and glucides. Applied the iodine-starch color reaction to the cell. Determined the agent of scabies. Established his own pharmacopoeia; set up dispensaries in which he gave free consultations; published an annual health manual to spread medical knowledge.

RASPE, RUDOLF ERICH (*b. Hannover, Germany, 1737; d. Muckross, Ireland, 1794*), literature, geology.

While a clerk at the Royal Library of Hannover, was inspired by the great Lisbon earthquake (1755) and his "discovery" of Hooke's nearly forgotten treatise on earthquakes (published 1705) to write *Specimen Historiae Naturalis Globi Terraquei . . .* (1763); this very successful book was never followed by the comprehensive work on the earth which it promised, but Raspe did go on to publish important writings by Leibniz and an influential account of the origin of basalt in the Kassel region (suggested by Desmarest's discussion of basalt in Auvergne). Then his luck turned for the worse. He put forth hasty, erroneous geological theories; was arrested for theft from a collection of which he was curator; escaped and began a new life in Great Britain, working in publishing, mining, and mineralogy; died while prospecting in Ireland. His most famous book, *Baron Münchausen's Narrative . . .* (1786) was published anonymously and brought him little profit.

RATEAU, AUGUSTE CAMILLE EDMOND (*b. Royan, Charente-Maritime France, 1863; d. Paris, France, 1930*), fluid mechanics, turbomachinery.

A civil engineer, teacher, and designer and manufacturer of turbine engines; invented the pressure-stage impulse turbine; was probably the first to apply the turbosupercharger to aircraft engines (1916–17).

RATHKE, MARTIN HEINRICH (*b. Danzig, Prussia [now Gdańsk, Poland], 1793; d. Königsberg, Prussia [now Kaliningrad, U.S.S.R.], 1860*), embryology, anatomy.

Received his M.D. at Berlin (1818); with the faculty at Königsberg from 1835. One of the founders of modern embryology; discovered the gill slits and gill arches in embryo birds and mammals. Rathke's pocket—a small pit on the dorsal side of the oral cavity that marks the point of invagination of the hypophysis—is named for him.

RATZEL, FRIEDRICH (*b. Karlsruhe, Germany, 1844; d. Ammerland, Germany, 1904*), geography, ethnography.

Studied zoology at Heidelberg and Jena; influenced by Darwin, Haeckel, and by Moritz Wagner's ideas on the migration of species; visited North America (1874–75); taught geography at Leipzig from 1886. Studied the diffusion of cultures; attempted to formulate a "scientific political geography." Was the founder of modern human geography but is remembered for the political misuse and distortion of his concept of *Lebensraum.*

RAULIN, JULES (*b. Mézières, France, 1836; d. Lyons, France, 1896*), plant physiology.

While assistant director of Pasteur's laboratory, did a major study of the mineral nutrition of yeast (1870). Taught chemistry at the University of Lyons from 1876.

RAUWOLF, LEONHARD (*b. Augsburg, Bavaria, 1535; d. Waitzen [now Vac], Hungary, 1596*), botany.

Studied at the universities of Wittenberg, Montpellier, and Valence, where he received the M.D. degree; lived in Augsburg and Linz; died fighting the Turks. In 1573–76, visited the Near East (Tripoli, Aleppo, Bir, Baghdad, Jerusalem); was the first modern botanist to collect and describe the flora of these regions; published a fine book on his travels (1582).

RAY, JOHN (*b. Black Notley, Essex, England, 1627; d. Black Notley, 1705*), natural history.

Ray's career as student and then fellow of Trinity College, Cambridge (B.A., 1648; M.A., 1651), ended when he refused to take the oath required by the Act of Uniformity (1662); he was supported by his friend and collaborator, Francis Willughby, until the latter's death (1672). At Cambridge, Ray was deeply influenced by the Platonists and came to see the study of nature as the means to reveal the workings of God; he was the chief author of an anonymous catalog of plants of the Cambridge region (1660) and a general catalog of British plants (1670). With Willughby, he began to compose a comprehensive *systema naturae* (Ray being responsible for the botany). Published a full revision of his catalog of British plants, *Synopsis stirpium Britannicarum* (1690), and his magnum opus, *Historia Plantarum* (1686–1704), intended to be comprehensive for Europe; also undertook to complete Willughby's work, with books on birds, fish, quadrupeds and snakes, and finally insects (published posthumously). In these and related works, Ray made major contributions to scientific knowledge and method, but none of these books compared in influence and significance with his theologically oriented books, *Three Physico-Theological Discourses* (1693) and *The Wisdom of God* (1691). The former attempted to formulate scientific theories reconcilable with the Scriptural doctrines of the Deluge and Creation; the latter, which was extremely popular, was a general survey of nature in which Ray, with great virtuosity, expressed his conviction that nature is the manifestation of Divinity.

RAY, PRAFULLA CHANDRA (*b. Raruli, Khulna, India [now Bangladesh], 1861; d. Calcutta, India, 1944*), chemistry.

Studied at Edinburgh (D.Sc., 1887); taught and did research at the Presidency College (1889–1916) and the University College of Science and Technology (from 1916), both in Calcutta; founded the Bengal Chemical & Pharmaceutical Works, Ltd., and other industries. Author, *The History of Hindu Chemistry* (1902–08).

RAYET, GEORGES ANTOINE PONS (*b. Bordeaux, France, 1839; d. Floirac, near Bordeaux, 1906*), astronomy.

At the Paris observatory, collaborated with Charles Wolf in the discovery of what is now called the Wolf-Rayet stage in the life of a nova (1866) and the discovery of "Wolf-Rayet" stars (1867). Taught at Bordeaux from 1876; also director of the Floirac observatory from 1879.

RAYLEIGH, LORD. **See Strutt, John William.**

RAYMOND OF MARSEILLES (*fl. France, ca. 1141*), astronomy.

Author of three works: a treatise on the astrolabe, a text on the courses of the planets, and a treatise on astrology.

RAYMOND, PERCY EDWARD (*b. New Canaan, Conn., 1879; d. Cambridge, Mass., 1952*), paleontology, geology.

Graduated from Yale (Ph.D., 1904). Taught at Harvard from 1912; described many new Paleozoic fossils; his lifelong specialty was trilobites, on which he wrote a classic book (1920).

AL-RĀZĪ, ABŪ BAKR MUḤAMMAD IBN ZAKA-RIYYĀ, known in the Latin West as **Rhazes** (*b. Rayy, Persia [now Iran], ca. 854; d. Rayy, 925 or 935*), medicine, alchemy, philosophy.

Directed a hospital in Rayy and later one in Baghdad. Taught that all men have a sufficient share of reason to reach correct views on both practical and theoretical issues; men do not need religious leaders to guide them; in fact religion is harmful, engendering hatred and war. Was sceptical of authority in all areas. In medicine, wrote *Doubts Concerning Galen;* wrote on alchemy, apparently believing that no reported phenomena should be dismissed out of hand. Consistent with his view of human reason, argued against the Aristotelians and in favor of absolute space and time, which he maintained were known as immediate a priori certainties. Developed an atomism somewhat similar to Democritus'; believed in the temporal creation of the world and five preeternal principles: creator, soul, matter, time, and space. Held that in our world evil predominates over good. Al-Rāzī had wide clinical experience, and many of his medical works were translated into Latin; he was, however, sharply criticized by his contemporaries because of his philosophical and religious opinions.

RAZMADZE, ANDREI MIKHAILOVICH (*b. Chkhenisi, Russia [now Samtredia district, Georgian S.S.R.], 1889; d. Tbilisi, U.S.S.R., 1929*), mathematics.

One of the most prominent Georgian scientists and educators; a founder of Tbilisi University (1918) and professor there for most of his life. Specialized in the calculus of variations, particularly in discontinuous, or, as he called them, "angular," solutions.

RÉAUMUR

RÉAUMUR, RENÉ-ANTOINE FERCHAULT DE (*b. La Rochelle, France, 1683; d. near St.-Julien-du-Terroux, France, 1757*), mathematics, technology, natural history, biology, experimental physics.

Réaumur was most likely educated by either the Oratorians or the Jesuits at La Rochelle, and was then probably sent to study with the Jesuits at Poitiers. In 1703 he went to live in Paris where he became acquainted with the great mathematician Pierre Varignon, who became his friend, teacher, and guide, and in 1708 nominated Réaumur to be his "student geometer" at the Academy of Sciences.

Réaumur's first three communications to the Academy, on geometrical subjects, were presented in 1708 and 1709, and demonstrate a degree of mathematical sophistication.

In 1709, however, he changed the course of his career by reading a paper on the growth of animal shells. From then on, his work would be characterized by its extraordinary richness and diversity, but never again would he devote himself to the pure mathematical research that had so fascinated him in his youth.

Shortly after the formation of the Paris Academy of Sciences, Louis XIV's finance minister, Colbert, charged it with the task of collecting a description of all the arts, industries, and professions. The work was intended to be a sort of industrial encyclopedia presenting the secret processes of industrial technology so that they might be better examined and improved. Réaumur was one of the earliest and most enthusiastic supporters of this technocratic function of the Academy, and perhaps it was for this reason that he was given charge of writing the vast industrial encyclopedia that Colbert had projected.

His most significant and original contribution to industrial technology was unquestionably his investigation of the iron and steel industry, the results of which he presented in a series of memoirs read before the Academy in 1720, 1721, and 1722. He also studied and worked in the tinplate industry, and from 1717 he undertook a lengthy and intensive investigation of the porcelain industry. He was perhaps best known for the thermometer scale that he invented and that bears his name.

Réaumur was among the greatest naturalists of his age. His greatest work in natural history was his *Mémoires pour servir à l'histoire des insectes*, published in six volumes between 1734 and 1742. He had originally intended to publish ten volumes on insects; but after the six published during his lifetime, nothing remained of the project but fragments in manuscript, some of which were not published until the twentieth century.

Réaumur's biological and genetical notions were dominated by the ideas of the preformationists, although he never accepted all the ideas of preformationism, for he was too aware of the difficulties some aspects of the theory entrained. He also made a significant contribution to physiology in his brilliantly conceived experimental investigation of the process of digestion in birds.

RECK, HANS (*b. Würzburg, Germany, 1886; d. Lourenço Marques, Mozambique, 1937*), geology, paleontology.

Conducted major expeditions in Africa; made the first systematic excavations in the Olduvai Gorge (1913–14), returning with Louis Leakey in 1931–32. Did many vol-

REECH

canologic studies, particularly on the Santorini island group in the Aegean.

RECLUS, ÉLISÉE (*b. Sainte-Foy-la-Grande, France, 1830; d. Thourout, Belgium, 1905*), geography.

A well-traveled and largely self-taught geographer; particularly admired Carl Ritter and Humboldt; their influence is apparent in his vast writings, including *La terre* (2 vols., 1868–69) and *Nouvelle géographie universelle* (19 vols., 1876–94).

RECORDE, ROBERT (*b. Tenby, Pembrokeshire, Wales, ca. 1510; d. London, England, 1558*), mathematics.

Educated at Cambridge (M.D., 1545). Early in his career as a civil servant, while comptroller of the Bristol mint (1549), Recorde provoked the enmity of Sir William Herbert (later third earl of Pembroke); this eventually led to Recorde's death, apparently in King's Bench prison. Recorde was one of the outstanding scholars of his generation, the founder of the English school of mathematical writers, and a most skillful teacher. He wrote a series of mathematical textbooks characterized by lucidity and a refreshingly critical attitude toward established authority; the most popular was *The Ground of Artes* (1543).

REDFIELD, WILLIAM C. (*b. Middletown, Conn., 1789; d. New York, N.Y., 1857*), meteorology, paleontology.

A saddle and harness maker, shopkeeper, and (from 1822) in the business of river and rail transportation. From an initial observation of the hurricane of 3 September 1821, he developed the theory that storm winds blow counterclockwise around a moving center. Was also the first American specialist in fossil fish.

REDI, FRANCESCO (*b. Arezzo, Italy, 1626; d. Pisa, Italy, 1697 or 1698*), entomology, parasitology, toxicology.

Head physician and superintendent of the pharmacy and foundry at the Medici court. Author of a beautifully researched study of snake venom (1664); of *Esperienze intorno alla generazione degli insetti* (1668), a masterpiece disproving the doctrine of spontaneous generation of insects in decaying substances; and of a major treatise on parasites (1684).

REDOUTÉ, PIERRE-JOSEPH (*b. St.-Hubert, Belgium, 1759; d. Paris, France, 1840*), botanical illustration.

One of the world's great botanical artists; trained by the botanist C. L. L'Héritier de Brutelle and by Gerardus van Spaendonck, professor of flower painting at the Jardin du Roi.

REDTENBACHER, FERDINAND JAKOB (*b. Steyr, Austria, 1809; d. Karlsruhe, Germany, 1863*), mechanics, engineering.

Graduated from Polytechnikum of Vienna. Through his teaching and textbooks gave the German *Technische Hochschule* its characteristic structure and blend of theory and practice. Taught at the Polytechnische Schule of Karlsruhe; was its director from 1857.

REECH, FERDINAND (*b. Lampertsloch, Alsace, France, 1805; d. Lorient, France, 1884*), marine engineering.

Studied at École Polytechnique. Affiliated with the École du Génie (as director, from 1831). Remembered for the first formulation of the hydraulic-model law of gravitational similitude, the necessary proportionality between the velocity of a ship and the square root of its length.

REED, WALTER (*b. Belroi, near Gloucester, Va., 1851; d. Washington, D.C., 1902*), medicine.

Entered the University of Virginia at age fifteen; received the M.D. degree (1869) and took a second M.D. (1870) at Bellevue Hospital medical school in New York. Held several appointments in New York City before receiving a commission as assistant surgeon in the Army Medical Corps (1874). Until 1893, worked at bases in the West, except for a period studying pathology at Johns Hopkins. In 1893, was appointed curator of the Army Medical Museum in Washington, D.C., and professor at the new Army Medical College. Headed the Typhoid Board in the Spanish-American War and the Yellow Fever Board (1900–01) that freed Havana of this age-old plague.

REGENER, ERICH RUDOLPH ALEXANDER (*b. Schleussenau, near Bromberg, Germany [now Bydgoszcz, Poland], 1881; d. Stuttgart, Germany, 1955*), physics.

Taught at Berlin and at the Technische Hochschule in Stuttgart, from which he was dismissed (1937) because his wife was Jewish (she then emigrated with their two children); ran a research station for stratospheric physics built for him by the Kaiser-Wilhelm-Gesellschaft; after the war was again affiliated with the Stuttgart school. In 1909, determined the elementary electric charge through the use of α radiation. In 1933, linked unusually strong cosmic radiation with an eruption on the solar surface.

REGIOMONTANUS, JOHANNES (*b. Königsberg, Franconia, Germany, 1436; d. Rome, Italy, 1476*), astronomy, mathematics.

The greatest astronomer of the fifteenth century. Enrolled in the University of Vienna at age thirteen; upon joining the faculty (1457) became close friends with Peuerbach; both were influenced by Cardinal Bessarion (a native of Trebizond) to study Greek authors; after Peuerbach's death Regiomontanus completed the translation Peuerbach had begun of Ptolemy's *Mathematical Syntaxis*, complete with revisions and critical reflections. *Ca.* 1461–65, Regiomontanus accompanied Bessarion to Rome, Padua, and Venice; during *ca.* 1467–71, he was in Buda, Hungary, where he worked with the royal astronomer, Martin Bylica; in Nuremberg (1471–75) he became the first publisher of astronomical and mathematical literature; he died in Rome (1476), probably a victim of the plague but, according to rumor, murdered by the sons of a scholar he had criticized. Besides his outstanding work on Ptolemy, Regiomontanus wrote the monumental *On All Classes of Triangles; Tables of Directions* (computed with Bylica) and *Table of the First Movable* [*Sphere*], both relating to the apparent daily rotation of the heavens; and the *Ephemerides* (used by Columbus in Jamaica). It is possible that Regiomontanus anticipated Copernicus by accepting the concept of a moving earth.

REGNAULT, HENRI VICTOR (*b. Aix-la-Chapelle, France [now Aachen, Germany], 1810; d. Paris, France, 1878*), physics, chemistry.

Studied at the École Polytechnique; taught there and at the Collège de France; was director of the porcelain factory at Sèvres from 1854. Studied the action of chlorine on ethers; discovered vinyl chloride, dichloroethylene, trichloroethylene, and carbon tetrachloride. From 1842, researched the thermal properties of gases.

REICHENBACH, GEORG FRIEDRICH VON (*b. Durlach [now part of Karlsruhe], Germany, 1771; d. Munich, Germany, 1826*), instrument making, mechanical engineering.

A leader in the industrialization of Germany. Trained as an army engineer; founded firms famous for surveying and astronomical instruments; his civil engineering projects included large power machinery.

REICHENBACH, HANS (*b. Hamburg, Germany, 1891; d. Los Angeles, Calif., 1953*), philosophy of science.

Took his doctorate in philosophy at the University of Erlangen; with Einstein's support, appointed professor at the University of Berlin (1926); with Rudolf Carnap, founded (1930) and edited the journal *Erkenntnis;* dismissed following the election of Hitler to power; taught at the University of Istanbul (1933–38) and the University of California at Los Angeles (from 1938), among his students was Carl Hempel. Held that physical theories must contain conventional elements, however, their truth is not a matter of convention but rather of empirical confirmation; extended and reformulated the work of the logical positivists, particularly to justify theories predicting probabilities; defined causality in terms of inductive inference, and denied that it applies to the subatomic realm of quantum theory.

REICHENBACH, KARL (or **CARL) LUDWIG** (*b. Stuttgart, Germany, 1788; d. Leipzig, Germany, 1869*), chemistry, speculative science.

A successful industrialist and chemist, but (from *ca.* 1844) increasingly obsessed with trying to prove the existence of paranormal sensitivities to stimuli and of a universal force called "Od."

REICHERT, KARL BOGISLAUS (*b. Rastenburg, East Prussia [now Kętrzyn, Poland], 1811; d. Berlin, Germany, 1883*), embryology, histology.

Graduated from the University of Berlin (1836); returned there as professor of anatomy (1858). Remembered especially for his introduction of cell theory into embryology and for his opposition, late in life, to new ideas.

REID, HARRY FIELDING (*b. Baltimore, Md., 1859; d. Baltimore, 1944*), geophysics.

A great grandnephew of George Washington and the first geophysicist in the U.S. Studied and taught at Johns Hopkins. Made a masterful exposition of the "elastic rebound theory" of earthquakes, accounting for breakage along faults.

REIDEMEISTER, KURT WERNER FRIEDRICH (*b. Brunswick, Germany, 1893; d. Göttingen, Germany, 1971*), mathematics.

Had a distinguished teaching career, concluding at Göttingen (from 1955). Researched the foundations of geometry and topology on a purely combinatorial and group-theoretical basis; also, wrote on the historical origins of mathematical and rational thought.

REIL, JOHANN CHRISTIAN (*b. Rhaude, Germany, 1759; d. Halle, Germany, 1813*), medicine, physiology.

Studied and taught at the University of Halle, serving as director of its clinical institution and as municipal physician; invited (1810) by Humboldt to participate in the reorganization of the medical school of the University of Berlin; died from typhus contracted trying to help the wounded in the Napoleonic wars. Was a shrewd clinician and an outstanding educator; did important neuroanatomical research; regarded pyschiatric patients as victims of cerebral malfunctions and advocated humane treatment by a psychological method. After 1904, was increasingly influenced by Schelling's speculative philosophy.

REINHOLD, ERASMUS (*b. Saalfeld, Germany, 1511; d. Saalfeld, 1553*), astronomy.

After Copernicus, the leading mathematical astronomer of his era; spent his entire career at the University of Wittenberg. Early appreciated Copernicus and revised his tables for easier use; but was silent about the heliocentric view, apparently regarding it as simply a mathematical hypothesis of secondary interest.

RE'IS, PIRĪ. *See* **Piri Rais.**

REMAK, ROBERT (*b. Posen, Germany [now Poznan, Poland], 1815; d. Kissingen, Germany, 1865*), histology, embryology, neurology.

Took his M.D. (1838) at the University of Berlin; became (1847) the first Jew ever to teach there. Among many achievements in neurology, did a major study of medullary nerve fibers; discovered the marrowless nerve fibers in the sympathetic nervous system and correctly confirmed that they originate in the ganglion cells. Began the study of chicken embryos, particularly the "germinal layer" (endoderm); published an outstanding work on pathological anatomy (1845); returned to the study of the germinal layer, publishing (1850–55) *Untersuchungen über die Entwicklung der Wirbelthiere*, a text which established the position of histology among the sciences; asserted (1852) that the cleavage of the frog egg is due to a continuous process of division that begins with the nucleus.

REMSEN, IRA (*b. New York, N.Y., 1846; d. Carmel, Calif., 1927*), chemistry, education.

Taught chemistry at Johns Hopkins from 1876; was president there (1901–13); introduced teaching methods he had learned in Germany under Fittig. Remsen specialized in the benzene ring and related groups.

RENARD, ALPHONSE FRANÇOIS (*b. Renaix [now Ronse], Belgium, 1842; d. Brussels, Belgium, 1903*), geology, mineralogy.

Ordained as a priest (1877); was already renowned in the sciences as a chemist, petrographer, and field geologist; resigned from the priesthood (1884); taught at Ghent from 1888. With Sir John Murray, wrote the monumental *Deep-Sea Deposits* (1891).

RENAULT, BERNARD (*b. Autun, France, 1836; d. Paris, France, 1904*), paleobotany.

A protégé of Adolphe Brongniart; assistant naturalist at the Muséum d'Histoire Naturelle in Paris from 1876; specialized in the anatomy of Carboniferous and Permian plants.

RENAUT, JOSEPH-LOUIS (*b. La Haye-Descartes, Indre-et-Loire, France, 1844; d. Lyons, France, 1917*), medicine, histology.

Studied at Tours and at Paris. A brilliant young intern in Paris at the time of the Franco-Prussian war; appointed (1877) to the chair of anatomy and histology at the new Medical Faculty of Lyons. Author, *Traité d'histologie pratique* (1889–99).

RENEVIER, EUGÈNE (*b. Lausanne, Switzerland, 1831; d. Lausanne, 1906*), geology.

Studied at Stuttgart, Geneva, and Paris. Taught at Lausanne from 1859; did valuable work on the High Calcareous Alps and Prealps; was a founder (1882) and first president of the Société Géologique Suisse; led the movement for international standardization of geological nomenclature, classification, and graphics.

RENNELL, JAMES (*b. Upcott, near Chudleigh, Devon, England, 1742; d. London, England, 1830*), geography.

A former naval officer and surveyor for the East India Company, he specialized (from 1777) in the geography of Asia and North Africa; wrote an account of the Ganges (1781) and a book on Atlantic Ocean currents (1832).

REPSOLD, ADOLF (*b. Hamburg, Germany, 1806; d. Hamburg, 1871*); **REPSOLD, JOHANN ADOLF** (*b. Hamburg, Germany, 1838; d. Hamburg, 1919*); **REPSOLD, JOHANN GEORG** (*b. Wremen, near Bremerhaven, Germany, 1770; d. Hamburg, 1830*), instrument making.

The Repsold family produced three generations of outstanding designers and builders of astronomical instruments. Johann Georg Repsold established the original shop in Hamburg by 1800; an officer of the city fire department, he was killed on duty (1830); he was succeeded in his instrument business by his sons Adolf and Georg, and eventually by Adolf's sons Johann Adolf and Oskar.

RESPIGHI, LORENZO (*b. Cortemaggiore, near Piacenza, Italy, 1824; d. Rome, Italy, 1889*), astronomy.

As director of the Campidoglio observatory in Rome, was noted for his studies of solar phenomena, especially the spectra of sun spots. Also wrote on differential calculus.

RETZIUS, ANDERS ADOLF (*b. Stockholm, Sweden, 1796; d. Stockholm, 1860*), anatomy, histology, anthropology.

A pioneer in Scandinavia in the biological sciences; strongly opposed the speculative *Naturphilosophie* prevalent in Germany; sponsored by Berzelius, was appointed professor (1824) and also inspector (1830) at the Karolinska Institutet in Stockholm. Also professor of veterinary science at Stockholm Veterinary Institution (1823–40). Discovered the interrenal organ of elasmobranch fishes; did major work on *Amphioxus*, the only link between vertebrates and invertebrates; made microscopic studies of the structure of teeth; made numerous discoveries in gross anatomy. By systematizing the measurement and classification of human skulls, Retzius initiated the science of physical anthropology.

RETZIUS, MAGNUS GUSTAF (*b. Stockholm, Sweden, 1842; d. Stockholm, 1919*), anatomy, histology, anthropology.

The son of Anders Adolf Retzius; followed his father in teaching at the Karolinska Institutet; resigned (1890) to pursue pure research. Published more than 300 papers, lavishly illustrated, in numerous fields; specialized in neuroanatomy and neurophysiology.

REULEAUX, FRANZ (*b. Eschweier, Germany, 1829; d. Berlin, Germany, 1905*), mechanical engineering.

A prolific writer, his most influential work was the first volume of his *Theoretische Kinematik . . .* (1875), published while he was teaching at the Gewerbe Institut in Berlin; this book founded modern kinematics. Although Reuleaux's thought was marred by a disregard for dynamic phenomena, his system of classifying mechanisms proved definitive. He was also a major spokesman for modern technology.

REUSS, AUGUST EMANUEL (*b. Bilin, Bohemia [now Bílina, Czechoslovakia], 1811; d. Vienna, Austria, 1873*), paleontology, stratigraphy.

Educated largely by his father, F. A. Reuss; gave up his medical practice to teach mineralogy at Prague and then Vienna. Was an expert in paleontology and stratigraphy; most interested in Foraminifera of the Cretaceous period.

REUSS, FRANZ AMBROSIUS (*b. Prague, Czechoslovakia, 1761; d. Bilin, Bohemia [now Bílina, Czechoslovakia], 1830*), mineralogy, geology.

An important physician and civic official in Bilin; became a specialist in the geology and chemistry of mineral springs; trained his son August Emanuel in geology and mineralogy. Author, *Lehrbuch der Mineralogie* (1801–06), promoting Werner's neptunist theories.

REY, ABEL (*b. Châlon-sur-Saône, France, 1873; d. Paris, France, 1940*), philosophy.

Studied at the Sorbonne; returned there (1919) as professor of the history and philosophy of science. Also taught at Dijon and Paris. Wrote *Le retour éternel et la philosophie de la physique* (1922) and the four volumes on the Greeks (1930–48) in the series "Évolution de l'Humanité."

REY, JEAN (*b. Le Bugue, France, ca. 1582; d. ca. 1645*), chemistry.

Took his M.D. at Montpellier (1609). Wrote *Essays de Jean Rey . . .* (1630), anticipating Lavoisier's recognition (1772) that calcination involves combination with air.

REY PASTOR, JULIO (*b. Logroño, Spain, 1888; d. Buenos Aires, Argentina, 1962*), mathematics.

Had a distinguished teaching career in Spain and Argentina. His works include *Fundamentos de la geometría proyectiva superior* (1916), on the synthetic geometry of

space in *n* dimensions, and the now-classic *Elementos de análisis algebraico* (1917).

REYE, THEODOR (*b. Ritzebüttel, near Cuxhaven, Germany, 1838; d. Würzburg, Germany, 1919*), mathematics.

Took his doctorate at Göttingen (1861); taught at Zürich, Strasbourg, and Würzburg. Founded what was later called point-series geometry.

REYNA, FRANCISCO DE LA (*b. Spain [?], ca. 1520*), physiology.

A veterinarian of Zamora. A controversial passage on the anatomy and physiology of the horse, in his *Libro de Albeyteria* (1546), in part anticipates Harvey's concept of blood circulation.

REYNEAU, CHARLES RENÉ (*b. Brissac, Maine-et-Loire, France, 1656; d. Paris, France, 1728*), mathematics.

Priest and mathematics professor. Chosen by Malebranche to write the textbook (1708) introducing the new mathematics, *Analyse démontrée.*

REYNOLDS, OSBORNE (*b. Belfast, Ireland, 1842; d. Somerset, England, 1912*), engineering, physics.

A Cambridge graduate, civil engineer, and (from 1868) professor at Owens College, Manchester. Did important work on streamline and turbulent flow in pipes; on film lubrication; on the mean specific heat of water (in terms of work) between the freezing and boiling points; on group-velocity; and on several other subjects. Developed a model of the universe as completely filled with rigid granules.

RHAZES. *See al-Rāzī.*

RHEITA, ANTON MARIA SCHYRLAEUS DE (Antonín Maria Šírek z Vrajtu) (*b. Bohemia, 1597; d. Ravenna, Italy, 1660*), astronomy.

A Capuchin priest, his scientific reputation rests on *Oculus Enoch et Eliae . . .* (Antwerp, 1645). Here he described a telescopic eyepiece, of his own invention, that left the image reverted; he coined the terms "ocular" and "objective"; and he included the first map of the moon with its southernmost part at the top, as in an inverting telescope.

RHETICUS, GEORGE JOACHIM (*b. Feldkirch, Austria, 1514; d. Kassa, Hungary [now Košice, Czechoslovakia], 1574*), mathematics, astronomy.

Unable by law to use his own surname (his father had been beheaded for sorcery), Rheticus chose a name to indicate that he came from the ancient Roman province of Rhaetia. Was a student and teacher at Wittenberg (M.A., 1536). Met Copernicus (1539), who permitted him to write a *Narratio prima (First Report,* 1540) on *De revolutionibus*; in 1542, Rheticus arranged for the printing of *De revolutionibus* itself in Nuremberg. Rheticus became a professor at Leipzig (1542) but his tenure was disrupted by misfortune and scandal; he next studied medicine in Prague (1551–52); finally settled in Cracow, where he practiced medicine and became a famous astrologer. In mathematics, he is noted for his innovative and monumental trigonometric tables, including *Canon of the Doctrine of Triangles* (1551), the first table to give all six trigonometric functions, and *Opus Palatinum de triangulis* (1596), completed by his student L. V. Otho.

RIBAUCOUR, ALBERT (*b. Lille, France, 1845; d. Philippeville* [*now Skikda*], *Algeria, 1893*), mathematics, engineering.

An exceptionally talented engineer; worked in Algeria from 1886. Pursued mathematics primarily in his spare time; specialized in differential geometry, particularly the study of minimal surfaces, in which he achieved a wealth of results.

RIBEIRO SANTOS, CARLOS (*b. Lisbon, Portugal, 1813; d. Lisbon, 1882*), engineering.

Of a poor family; became an army officer, politician, and Portugal's first major geologist; a leader and adviser in numerous national science and engineering projects.

RICCATI, JACOPO FRANCESCO (*b. Venice, Italy, 1676; d. Treviso, Italy, 1754*), mathematics.

Of a noble family; internationally famous for his private research in mathematics; was an expert in hydraulics; in studies of central forces, enthusiastically advocated Newton's ideas. In his work with differential equations, achieved notable results in lowering the order of equations and in the separation of variables.

RICCATI, VINCENZO (*b. Castelfranco, near Treviso, Italy, 1707; d. Treviso, 1775*), mathematics.

The second son of J. F. Riccati; joined the Jesuit order (1726). Was skilled in hydraulic engineering; carried out government flood control projects; studied the integration of differential equations, including some derived from geometrical problems. Introduced the use of hyperbolic functions to obtain the roots of certain types of algebraic equations, particularly cubic equations; together with his collaborator, Girolamo Saladini, carried out extensive investigation of hyperbolic functions, anticipating Lambert; their *Institutiones analyticae* (1765–67) is the first extensive treatise on integral calculus, predating that of Euler.

RICCI, MATTEO (*b. Macerata, Italy, 1552; d. Peking, China, 1610*), dissemination of knowledge.

A Jesuit and founder of the first modern Catholic missions in China. Remembered for his Chinese-language works in the sciences, especially his Chinese version (1607) of Euclid's *Elements*, and for his map of the world (1584).

RICCI, MICHELANGELO (*b. Rome, Italy, 1619; d. Rome, 1682*), mathematics.

An internationally-known member of the school of Galileo; influenced by Torricelli; exceptionally competent in algebra; his only surviving work is the booklet *Geometrica exercitatio* (1666), usually called *De maximis et minimis*. Ricci, although not ordained, was made a cardinal in 1681.

RICCI, OSTILIO (*b. Fermo, Italy, 1540; d. Florence* [?], *Italy, 1603*), mathematics, engineering.

A teacher and military engineer. Tutored Galileo in mathematics (1583) and perspective (*ca.* 1585); recommended him for posts at the universities of Bologna and Pisa.

RICCI-CURBASTRO, GREGORIO (*b. Lugo, Italy, 1853; d. Bologna, Italy, 1925*), mathematics.

Took his doctorate at the Scuola Normale Superiore at Pisa; taught at the University of Padua from 1880. Best known for the invention of the absolute differential calculus (1884–94), modifying the differential calculus in such a way that the formulas and results retain the same form whatever the system of variables used; he came to this invention through the study of Riemann, Lipschitz, and, most immediately, Christoffel's idea of covariant derivation. Published (1896) a paper on intrinsic geometry, examining the congruences of lines on an arbitrary Riemannian variety, and applying the absolute calculus; found the contract tensor ("Ricci's tensor") that plays a fundamental role in the general theory of relativity; with his student Levi-Civita, wrote two papers (1900, 1911) on the absolute calculus and its applications; still, the innovation was little appreciated until Einstein found that it enabled him to write his gravitational equations, and further investigations by Levi-Civita and others confirmed its validity.

RICCIOLI, GIAMBATTISTA (*b. Ferrara, Italy, 1598; d. Bologna, Italy, 1671*), astronomy, geography.

A Jesuit and an ardent opponent of Galileo and the Copernican system (while nevertheless acknowledging its mathematical superiority); devised ingenious experiments to disprove Galileo's conclusions that instead ratified them; perfected the pendulum for the measurement of time; made important astronomical and geographical measurements and observations.

RICCÒ, ANNIBALE (*b. Modena, Italy, 1844; d. Rome, Italy, 1919*), geophysics, astrophysics.

As an assistant at the Palermo observatory and for forty years at the Catania observatory, which he founded (1885), Riccò studied solar prominences and sunspots and their influence on terrestrial phenomena.

RICHARD SWINESHEAD.   *See* **Swineshead, Richard.**

RICHARD OF WALLINGFORD (*b. Wallingford, Berkshire, England, ca. 1292; d. St. Albans, Hertfordshire, England, 1336*), mathematics, astronomy, horology.

Priest, Oxford graduate (B.Th., 1327), and abbot of St. Albans (1327–36). Author of *Quadripartitum*, the first comprehensive European (non-Islamic) treatise on trigonometry of the medieval period, and *Tractatus albionis*, on his instrument, the "Albion" ("all by one"), for astronomical calculations. Designed an extraordinary astronomical clock for St. Albans.

RICHARD, JULES ANTOINE (*b. Blet, Cher, France, 1862; d. Châteauroux, Indre, France, 1956*), mathematics.

Received his doctorate at Paris (1901); became a lycée teacher. Noted for his work in the philosophy of science, especially mathematics; in set theory, he proposed (1905) "Richard's paradox or antinomy."

RICHARD, LOUIS PAUL ÉMILE (*b. Rennes, France, 1795; d. Paris, France, 1849*), mathematics.

A brilliant teacher; at the Collège Louis-le-Grand from 1822; prepared students, including E. Galois, for the mathematics entrance exam for the École Polytechnique.

RICHARDS, FRANCIS JOHN (*b. Burton-upon-Trent, England, 1901; d. Wye, Kent, England, 1965*), plant physiology.

Educated at the University of Birmingham; worked under F. G. Gregory in London; from 1958, directed projects for the Agricultural Research Council in Rothamsted and Wye. Noted for his research on the mineral nutrition of cereal crops.

RICHARDS, THEODORE WILLIAM (*b. Germantown, Pa., 1868; d. Cambridge, Mass., 1928*), chemistry.

Educated at home until entering college; graduated from Harvard at age 18 and received doctorate two years later; taught there for the rest of his life. Best known for his determinations of the atomic weights of 25 elements, for which he became the first U.S. chemist to receive the Nobel Prize (1914).

RICHARDSON, BENJAMIN WARD (*b. Somerby, Leicestershire, England, 1828; d. London, England, 1896*), medicine, pharmacology.

An eminent physician (M.A., M.D., St. Andrews, 1854) and active reformer in temperance, public hygiene, and sanitation. Tried to determine the physiological effects of specific radicals in compounds.

RICHARDSON, OWEN WILLANS (*b. Dewsbury, Yorkshire, England, 1879; d. Alton, Hampshire, England, 1959*), physics, electronics, thermionics.

A scholarship student at Trinity College, Cambridge University; studied at the Cavendish Laboratory under J. J. Thomson, and remained there after graduation; published (1901) two papers on radiation from heated metallic filaments; in one, announced a law (now named for him) regarding the emission behavior of electric "corpuscles" per unit time from heated platinum surfaces in a vacuum. Continued research on thermionics (he coined the term in 1909) at Princeton (1906–13); proved that the electric current in tungsten is carried by electrons; returned to the University of London as an authority on metallic conduction, electrons, and heat; worked on telecommunications during World War I; was awarded the 1928 Nobel Prize in physics for his work in thermionics, especially the discovery of his law. Wrote *The Electron Theory of Matter* (1914), *The Emission of Electricity from Hot Bodies* (1916), and *Molecular Hydrogen and Its Spectrum* (1934).

RICHE DE PRONY, GASPARD-FRANÇOIS-CLAIR-MARIE. *See* **Prony, Gaspard-François-Clair-Marie Riche de.**

RICHER, JEAN (*b. 1630; d. Paris, France, 1696*), astronomy, physics.

On Cayenne Island (1672–73), at the direction of the Académie Royale des Sciences, made astronomical observations (especially of perigean Mars) simultaneously with others being made in Paris; as a result, he enabled the calculation of the distance from the earth to the sun; he also found that the seconds pendulum is shorter in Cayenne than in Paris; this prompted Newton to basic deductions concerning the shape of the earth.

RICHER DE BELLEVAL, PIERRE. *See* **Belleval, Pierre Richer de.**

RICHET, CHARLES ROBERT (*b. Paris, France, 1850; d. Paris, 1935*), physiology, psychology.

As an intern in Paris, turned from medicine to physiology; served (1876) as an assistant to the surgeon Aristide Verneuil, who led him to study pain perception and digestion; published (1878) a comprehensive memoir on the properties of gastric juice. After becoming *professeur agrégé* at the Faculty of Medicine (1878), undertook a major investigation of muscle contraction; from 1883, studied animal heat, especially the role of the central nervous system in controlling temperature. After 1880, was increasingly concerned with the biological effects of microorganisms; influenced by Pasteur, began to look for toxins secreted by microbes and for chemical substances that would oppose these toxins in immune animals; with Jules Héricourt, discovered that transfusions from dogs inoculated with a type of staphylococcus bacterium conferred immunity on rabbits from infection by this bacterium; attempted to treat tuberculosis on this principle but with little success. In 1900, with Paul Portier, on the yacht of Prince Albert of Monaco, extracted toxin from the Portuguese man-of-war; discovered that inoculation with this toxin caused *increasing* sensitivity to the effects of the toxin; named this phenomenon "anaphylaxis." In 1907, Richet began to construct a general theory of anaphylaxis; published a comprehensive monograph (1911); was awarded a Nobel Prize (1913) for his contributions to this field.

RICHMANN, GEORG WILHELM (*b. Pernau, Estonia [now Pärnu, U.S.S.R.], 1711; d. St. Petersburg, Russia [now Leningrad, U.S.S.R.], 1753*), physics.

Studied at Halle, Jena, and St. Petersburg. Taught at the St. Petersburg Academy of Sciences. Devoted himself to the measurement of physical phenomena, especially heat phenomena and electricity; performed perhaps the earliest experiments (1745) to determine the capacity of conductors; killed by a bolt of lightning while trying to read an indicator on an insulated pole.

RICHTER, JEREMIAS BENJAMIN (*b. Hirschberg, Germany [now Jelenia Gora, Poland], 1762; d. Berlin, Germany, 1807*), chemistry.

Took his doctorate at the University of Königsberg (1789); spent his life as a working chemist, without gaining his due recognition. Convinced that all chemical processes are based upon mathematical laws, dedicated himself to "stoichiometry," i.e., "the science of measuring the mass ratios in which chemical elements stand to one another." Developed the law of neutrality (1791): Neutralization should occur in all chemical decompositions by double affinity, to the extent that the compounds used in the decomposition are themselves neutral. Concluded from this that compounds have a certain fixed ratio of mass so that the compositions of resulting products can be calculated mathematically. Experiments led him to the view that the amount of oxygen in any base is the same as that needed to saturate a constant given amount of acid, and that when one metal precipitates another from a neutral salt, the quantities of both metals that will dissolve in the same amount of acid will also unite with identical quantities of oxygen to form oxides. Studied alkaline earths and acids with the notion that the combining proportions in a compound form arithmetical or geometrical series; concluded that the equivalent weights of bases follow the former series and that acids follow the latter. Richter's findings and theories were published in his *Anfangsgründe der Stöchyometrie . . .* (1792–94) and *Ueber die neuern Gegenstande der Chemie* (1791–1802).

RICHTHOFEN, FERDINAND VON (*b. Karlsruhe, Silesia* [*now Poland*], *1833; d. Berlin, Germany, 1905*), geology, geography.

Graduated in geology from the University of Berlin; among his major expeditions were trips to the Alps (1857), the U.S. (1862–68), and China (1868–72); taught at the universities of Bonn, Leipzig, and Berlin. His chief contributions were to Alpine stratigraphy, the geology and geography of China, and geographical methodology. His books include the monumental *China . . .* (1877–1912).

RICHTMYER, FLOYD KARKER (*b. Cobleskill, N.Y., 1881; d. Ithaca, N.Y., 1939*), physics.

Spent his entire student and teaching career at Cornell University; specialized in X-ray spectra. Author of the celebrated text *Introduction to Modern Physics* (1928).

RICKETTS, HOWARD TAYLOR (*b. Findley, Ohio, 1871; d. Mexico City, Mexico, 1910*), pathology.

Pioneered research on what we now call the rickettsial diseases. While a professor of pathology at the University of Chicago, began (1906) intensive study of Rocky Mountain spotted fever; died while investigating typhoid fever.

RIDGWAY, ROBERT (*b. Mt. Carmel, Ill., 1850; d. Olney, Ill., 1929*), ornithology.

Appointed zoologist of the U.S. Geological Survey (1867); then, curator of birds at the U.S. National Museum. Works include *Manual of North American Birds* (1887–1919).

IBN RIDWĀN, ABŪ'L-ḤASAN ʿALĪ IBN ʿALĪ IBN JAʿAFAR AL-MIṢRĪ (*b. El Gīzah, Egypt,* A.D. *998; d. Cairo, Egypt,* A.D. *1061 or 1069*), medicine.

Chief of all physicians of Egypt, probably appointed by caliph al-Mustanṣir. His medical writings include treatises on various diseases and treatments and commentaries on, and summaries of, Hippocrates and Galen (masters to whom he was strictly faithful).

RIECKE, EDUARD (*b. Stuttgart, Germany, 1845; d. Göttingen, Germany, 1915*), physics.

From 1870, when he began his graduate studies, spent his academic life at the University of Göttingen. Following the lead of Helmholtz, sought to to establish granular theories of electricity and crystal structure; did influential research on conduction in metals and a granular theory of the properties of metals. Author of *Lehrbuch der Physik* (1896); editor of *Physikalische Zeitschrift* (from 1899).

RIEMANN, GEORG FRIEDRICH BERNHARD (*b. Breselenz, near Dannenberg, Germany, 1826; d. Selasca, Italy, 1866*), mathematics, mathematical physics.

From 1846 to 1851 Riemann studied at the universities of Berlin and Göttingen. In 1851 he submitted his thesis on complex function theory and Riemann surfaces, to earn the Ph.D. at Göttingen.

Riemann then prepared for his *Habilitation* as a *Privatdozent,* which took him two and a half years. At the end of 1853 he submitted his *Habilitationsschrift* on Fourier series, with a list of three possible subjects for his *Habilitationsvortrag.* Against Riemann's expectation Gauss chose the third: "Über die Hypothesen, welche der Geometrie zu Grunde liegen." Both papers were posthumously published in 1867.

Riemann's first course as a *Privatdozent* was on partial differential equations with applications to physics. His courses in 1855–56, in which he expounded his theory of Abelian functions, were attended by C.A. Bjerknes, Dedekind, and Ernst Schering; the theory itself, one of the most notable masterworks of mathematics, was published in 1857. Meanwhile he had published a paper on hypergeometric series.

When Gauss died early in 1855, his chair went to Dirichlet. After Dirichlet's death in 1859, Riemann became a full professor.

What Riemann's work lacks in quantity is more than compensated for by its superb quality. One important factor in the dissemination of Riemann's results, if not his ideas, was C. Neumann's *Vorlesungen über Riemann's Theorie . . .* , which helped one work with concepts such as Riemann surfaces, crosscuts, degree of connection, and integration around rather abstract domains.

Riemann also taught courses in mathematical physics. A few have been published: *Partielle Differentialgleichungen und deren Anwendung auf physikalische Fragen* and *Schwere, Electricität und Magnetismus.* Continuing work of Dirichlet, in 1861 Riemann studied the motion of a liquid mass under its own gravity, within a varying ellipsoidal surface. His most important contribution to mathematical physics was his 1860 paper on sound waves.

A few other contributions, all posthumous, by Riemann to real calculus should be mentioned: his first manuscript, of 1847, in which he defined derivatives of nonintegral order by extending a Cauchy formula for multiple integration; his famous *Habilitationsschrift* on Fourier series of 1851, which contains not only a criterion for a function to be represented by its Fourier series but also the definition of the Riemann integral, the first integral definition that applied to very general discontinuous functions; and a paper on minimal surfaces—that is, of minimal area if compared with others in the same frame. Riemann noticed that the spherical mapping of such a surface by parallel unit normals was conformal.

His *Habilitationsvortrag,* "Über die Hypothesen, welche der Geometrie zu Grunde liegen" made a strong impact upon philosophy of space. Riemann, philosophically influenced by J. F. Herbart rather than by Kant, held that the a priori of space, if there was any, was topological rather than metric. The topological substratum of space is the *n*-dimensional manifold—Riemann probably was the first to define it. The metric structure must be ascertained by experience. Although there are other possibilities, Riemann decided in favor of the simplest: to describe the metric such that the square of the arc element is a positive definite quadratic form in the local differentials:

$$ds^2 = \Sigma \, g_{ij} \, dx^i \, dx^j.$$

The structure thus obtained is now called a Riemann space. It possesses shortest lines, now called geodesics, which resemble ordinary straight lines. In fact, at first approximation in a geodesic coordinate system such a metric is flat Euclidean, in the same way that a curved surface up to higher-order terms looks like its tangent plane. Beings living on the surface may discover the curvature of their world and compute it at any point as a consequence of observed deviations from Pythagoras' theorem. Likewise, one can define curvatures of n-dimensional Riemann spaces by noting the higher-order deviations that the ds^2 shows from a Euclidean space.

Riemann's lecture contains nearly no formulas. A few technical details are found in an earlier mentioned paper. The reception of Riemann's ideas was slow. Riemann spaces became an important source of tensor calculus. Covariant and contravariant differentiation were added in G. Ricci's absolute differential calculus (from 1877). T. Levi-Civita and J. A. Schouten (1917) based it on infinitesimal parallelism. H. Weyl and E. Cartan reviewed and generalized the entire theory.

In the nineteenth century Riemann spaces were at best accepted as an abstract mathematical theory. As a philosophy of space they had no effect. In the twentieth century some of Riemann's works became known as great classics of mathematics.

RIES (or **RISZ, RIESZ, RIS,** or **RIESE**), **ADAM** (*b. Staffelstein, upper Franconia, Germany, 1492; d. Annaberg-Buchholz, Germany, 1559*), mathematics, mining.

Taught mathematics in Erfurt and in Annaberg, where he also held important positions in the ducal mining administration. Wrote an excellent *Coss* (algebra text) at Erfurt (never printed); the most comprehensive of his very successful arithmetic texts is *Rechenung nach der lenge, auff den Linihen vnd Feder* (1550).

RIESZ, FRIGYES (FRÉDÉRIC) (*b. Györ, Hungary, 1880; d. Budapest, Hungary, 1956*), mathematics.

Took his doctorate at Budapest; taught at the University of Kolozsvár (which was moved to Szeged, 1920) and at Budapest (from 1946). Concentrated on abstract and general theories connected with mathematical analysis, especially functional analysis; remembered for the Riesz-Fischer theorem (1907, also discovered by Emil Fischer) and the Riesz representation theorem; created the topic of subharmonic functions.

RIGHI, AUGUSTO (*b. Bologna, Italy, 1850; d. Bologna, 1920*), physics.

Studied at Bologna, graduating from the School of Engineering (1872); returned (1889) as professor at the university's Institute of Physics. Is remembered for studies on electric oscillations, which contributed to wireless telegraphy, but did much other work of great importance.

RIMA, TOMMASO (*b. Mosogno, Ticino, Switzerland, 1775; d. Venice, Italy, 1843*), medicine.

A military surgeon; discovered the blood reflux in varicose veins of the leg; devised the surgical procedure for their treatment.

RINGER, SYDNEY (*b. Norwich, England, 1835; d. Lastingham, Yorkshire, England, 1910*), medicine, physiology.

For his entire professional career was associated with University College Hospital, London; was an outstanding bedside teacher. His *Handbook of Therapeutics* (1869) reflects his lifelong interest in pharmacology. Did basic work on the actions of inorganic salts on living tissues; developed "Ringer's solution" for the perfusion of isolated organs.

RINMAN, SVEN (*b. Uppsala, Sweden, 1720; d. Ekskilstuna, Sweden, 1792*), metallurgy.

Of a family famous for its contributions to mining and metallurgy; did substantial work (both theoretical and practical) on the improvement of iron and steel production.

RÍO, ANDRÉS MANUEL DEL (*b. Madrid, Spain, 1764; d. Mexico City, Mexico, 1849*), mineralogy, geology.

Internationally educated; spent most of his professional life at the Colegio de Minería in Mexico City; introduced modern methods to Mexico's mining industry. Discovered vanadium (1801), which he called panchromium or erythronium.

RÍO-HORTEGA, PÍO DEL (*b. Portillo, Valladolid province, Spain, 1882; d. Buenos Aires, Argentina, 1945*), neurohistology.

Took his M.D. at the University of Valladolid; worked in Madrid at the laboratory of Nicolás Achúcarro and at the National Institute of Cancer; moved to Argentina (1940). Specialized in the study of the interstitial cells of the nervous system and tumors of the central nervous system.

RIOLAN, JEAN, JR. (*b. Paris, France, 1580; d. Paris, 1675*), anatomy.

Took his M.D. in 1604; affiliated for all of his professional life with the University of Paris and the Collège Royal; principal physician to Marie de Médicis (1633–42). Restored Paris to eminence in anatomy; but fiercely defended conservative, Galenic medicine, notably against Harvey's concept of blood circulation.

RISNER, FRIEDRICH (*b. Herzfeld, Hesse, Germany; d. Herzfeld, ca. 1580*), mathematics, optics.

The protégé and colleague of Peter Ramus; their collaboration resulted in the immensely influential edition (1572) of the optical works of Ibn al-Haytham and Witelo.

RISTORO (or **RESTORO**) **D'AREZZO** (*b. Arezzo, Italy, ca. 1210–20 [?]; d. after 1282*), natural history.

Wrote *Composizione del mondo* (1282), the oldest surviving scientific text in Italian; it described every known celestial and terrestrial phenomenon, in a compilation from ancient authors enlivened by critical comments and personal observations.

RITCHEY, GEORGE WILLIS (*b. Tupper's Plains, Ohio, 1864; d. Azusa, Calif., 1945*), astronomy.

Sponsored by George Ellery Hale, was named chief optician at the Yerkes Observatory (1896) and head of instrument construction at Mt. Wilson (1906). Taught at University of Chicago (1901–06); directed astrophotagraphy at National Observatory in Paris (1920's); research director at U.S. Naval Observatory (1931–36). Ritchey fashioned some of the largest instruments of his era; used them in meticulous and important observations.

RITT, JOSEPH FELS (*b. New York, N.Y., 1893; d. New York, 1951*), mathematics.

Took his Ph.D. at Columbia University (1917). Noted for investigations of the algebraic aspects of the theory of differential equations.

RITTENHOUSE, DAVID (*b. Paper Mill Run, near Germantown, Pa., 1732; d. Philadelphia, Pa., 1796*), technology, astronomy, natural philosophy.

An outstanding maker of clocks and mathematical instruments. Was active in the American Revolution; served as treasurer of Pennsylvania (1777–89) and first director of the U.S. Mint (1792–95); succeeded Franklin as president of the American Philosophical Society. Did original work in astronomy, mathematics, and physics.

RITTER, JOHANN WILHELM (*b. Samitz, near Haynow [now Chojnów, Poland], Silesia, 1776; d. Munich, Germany, 1810*), chemistry, physics, physiology.

At the University of Jena, encouraged by Alexander von Humboldt, began galvanism studies; did research mainly in electrochemistry and electrophysiology (1797–1804); appointed to the court of Gotha (1801); lectured at Jena (1803–04); moved to Munich (1804) as a full member of the Bavarian Academy of Sciences. His many unique discoveries were little known or appreciated, partly because of an interest in the occult that influenced his later work.

RITZ, WALTER (*b. Sion, Switzerland, 1878; d. Göttingen, Germany, 1909*), theoretical physics.

At the Eidgenössische Technische Hochschule in Zurich, was (with Einstein) a mathematics student; transferred (1901) to Göttingen, where he studied under Voigt. His dissertation (1902), on a theory of spectral series, yielded novel series laws and anticipated the energy of a Rutherford-Bohr atom; he conceived atoms to be elastic continua, and postulated that line spectra originate in the proper vibrations of two-dimensional structures (indeed, in the transverse normal modes of a plane square plate). His frail health failed (1904); he was forced to retire, but, in the last year and a half of his life, published eighteen papers on theoretical spectroscopy, the foundations of electrodynamics, and a method for the numerical solution of boundary-value problems.

Ritz took on the problem set by the Paris Academy of Sciences (1904) as a contest, "to perfect in some important respect the problem in analysis relating to the equilibrium of an elastic plate in a rigid frame"; his ingenious solution was applicable not only for the case of static equilibrium but also for standing waves. In 1907, returning to the topic of line spectra, he abandoned his elastic-body model as the basis for explaining their causal mechanism; developed instead a magnetic-field model; on the question of how the interconnections between the series formulas ought to be extended and generalized, he proposed a "combination principle," according to which the subtractive (or additive) "combination" of any two terms from any two series, or even from one and the same series, gives the frequency of an actually existing spectral

line. In electrodynamics, he set forth a positivist program to replace not only the ether but also the electromagnetic potentials, the fields derived from them, and the equations governing them, by "elementary actions" between spatially separated charged particles; "the waves of the ether," he said, "will be replaced by a distribution of the emanation of luminous energy, periodic in time and space."

RIVA-ROCCI, SCIPIONE (*b. Almese, Piedmont, Italy, 1863; d. Rapallo, Liguria, Italy, 1937*), medicine.

A physician, surgeon, and teacher; invented (1896) the mercury sphygmomanometer for measuring blood pressure.

RIVETT, ALBERT CHERBURY DAVID (*b. Port Esperance, Tasmania, Australia, 1885; d. Sydney, Australia, 1961*), chemistry, scientific administration.

Left the chair of chemistry of the University of Melbourne (1927) to become the chief executive officer and later chairman (1945–49) of the Council for Scientific and Industrial Research; in shaping the national science policy, he emphasized original and fundamental research.

RIVIÈRE DE PRÉCOURT, ÉMILE-VALÈRE (*b. Paris, France, 1835; d. Paris, 1922*), anthropology.

Explored the caves of Baoussé-Roussé in Italy, uncovering several skeletons, which he correctly concluded were Cro-Magnon. Discovered (1887) the cave art of the grotto of La Mouche in the Dordogne.

RIVINUS, AUGUSTUS QUIRINUS. *See* **Bachmann, Augustus Quirinus.**

ROBERT OF LINCOLN. *See* **Grosseteste, Robert.**

ROBERTS, ISAAC (*b. Groes, North Wales, 1829; d. Crowborough, Sussex, England, 1904*), astronomy.

A businessman and amateur astronomer; famous for his dramatic photographs of stars, star clusters, and nebulae.

ROBERTS-AUSTEN, WILLIAM CHANDLER (*b. Kennington, Surrey, England, 1843; d. London, England, 1902*), metallurgy.

Studied at the Royal School of Mines, returning there as professor of metallurgy (1880); affiliated with the royal mint from 1869, serving as "chemist and assayer of the mint" from 1882 until his death. In his fundamental study of the constitution of alloys, introduced new physico-chemical theories and new experimental techniques.

ROBERVAL, GILLES PERSONNE (or **PERSONIER**) **DE** (*b. near Senlis, France, 1602; d. Paris, France, 1675*), mathematics, mechanics, physics.

Of a simple farm family; arrived in Paris (1628) and joined the scientists of the Mersenne circle; taught at the Collège Royale from 1634. Was one of the leading proponents of the geometry of infinitesimals, which he claimed to have taken directly from the work of Archimedes (not from Cavalieri); came closer to the integral calculus than did Cavalieri; completed the definite integration of the rational power *ca.* 1636; achieved the integration of the sine; reported to be the first to square the surface of the oblique cone; introduced the "compagne" ($x = r\theta, y = r - r\cos\theta$) of the original cycloidal curve and appears to have succeeded in the quadrature of the latter and in the cubature of the solid that it generates in turning around its base; knew how to extend these results to the general case:

$$x = a\,\theta - b\sin\theta, y = a - b\cos\theta.$$

For his method of the "composition of movements," may be called the founder of kinematic geometry; applied this procedure to the construction of tangents, to comparison of the lengths of curves, and to determining extrema. Dreamed of a vast physical theory based uniquely on the composition of motions; inspired by Kepler, based his astronomy on the existence of universal attraction. Tended to reject speculation in favor of a positivist approach. On the problem of the vacuum he did ingenious experiments, which supported the work of his friend Pascal.

ROBIN, CHARLES-PHILLIPE (*b. Jasseron, Ain, France, 1821; d. Jasseron, 1885*), biology, histology.

Studied and taught at the Faculty of Medicine in Paris. Made significant contributions to biology, especially histology. Was a dedicated positivist, the leading proponent of the Société de Biologie. Urged the study of the anatomical element as an independent subject; believed that life depended ultimately on "a particular molecular state," and therefore that microscopic investigation should be followed by chemical analysis; but rejected the progress made by Virchow, Pasteur, and others.

ROBINET, JEAN-BAPTISTE RENÉ (*b. Rennes, France, 1735; d. Rennes, 1820*), literature, philosophy, natural history.

A writer and metaphysician, remembered in science primarily for his treatise *De la nature* (4 vols., 1761–66), in which several important contemporary themes are prominent: the unity of nature, the chain of beings, universal dynamism and sensibility, and vitalism.

ROBINS, BENJAMIN (*b. Bath, England, 1707; d. Fort St. David, India, 1751*), mathematics, military engineering.

An ardent defender of Newton. Best known as the inventor of the ballistic pendulum, described in his *New Principles of Gunnery* (1742).

ROBIQUET, PIERRE-JEAN (*b. Rennes, France, 1780; d. Paris, France, 1840*), chemistry, pharmacy.

Taught in Paris at the École Polytechnique and the École de Pharmacie (from 1811). Was a leader in the search for "proximate principles"; among his discoveries were caffeine (1821) and codeine (1832); with Antoine Boutron-Charlard, did work on bitter almonds that was later elucidated by Wöhler and Liebig.

ROBISON, JOHN (*b. Boghall, Stirlingshire, Scotland, 1739; d. Edinburgh, Scotland, 1805*), physics, applied mechanics.

Attended the University of Glasgow (M.A., 1756); worked under Admiral Knowles in Russia to improve the Russian navy; taught at Glasgow (1766–70) and Edinburgh (from 1774). Best known for the remarkable sci-

ence articles he contributed to the third edition of the *Encyclopaedia Britannica*, the most influential being those on applied structural mechanics.

ROCHE, ÉDOUARD ALBERT (*b. Montpellier, France, 1820; d. Montpellier, 1883*), celestial mechanics, geophysics.

Spent almost his entire adult life at the University of Montpellier. Made basic and lasting contributions to the study of the internal structure and form of the free surface of celestial bodies; did a critical analysis of Laplace's cosmogonic hypothesis; proposed the first "earth model" with a solid nucleus.

RODRIGUES, JOÃO. *See* **Lusitanus, Amatus.**

ROEBUCK, JOHN (*b. Sheffield, England, 1718; d. Borrowstounness, Scotland, 1794*), technology.

Founded the Carron ironworks (1759), the basis of the Scottish iron industry.

ROEMER. *See also* **Römer.**

ROEMER, FERDINAND (*b. Hildesheim, Germany, 1818; d. Breslau, Germany [now Wrocław, Poland], 1891*), geology, paleontology.

Taught at the universities of Bonn (1847–55) and Breslau (from 1855). Wrote on the geology of the Rhenish mountains, Texas, and Silesia; also on Cretaceous and Paleozoic fossils and Pleistocene mammals. Was the brother of F. A. and Hermann Roemer, both also geologists.

ROEMER, FRIEDRICH ADOLPH (*b. Hildesheim, Germany, 1809; d. Clausthal, Germany, 1869*), stratigraphy, paleontology.

The older brother of Ferdinand Roemer; served as judicial official; taught at Mining School in Clausthal (from 1843). Wrote on the fossils and stratigraphy of the northwestern German Jurassic and Cretaceous and of the northwestern Harz Paleozoic.

ROENTGEN, WILHELM. *See* **Röntgen, Wilhelm Conrad.**

ROESEL VON ROSENHOF, AUGUST JOHANN (*b. Arnstadt, Germany, 1705; d. Nuremberg, Germany, 1759*), natural science, science illustration.

Of a noble family; trained as a painter; an enthusiastic student of insects and later of amphibians and reptiles. Author of *Der monatlich-herausgegebenen Insecten-Belustigung* (4 vols., 1746–61) and *Historia naturalis ranarum* (1753–58).

ROGER OF HEREFORD (*fl. England, ca. 1170–80*), astronomy, astrology.

Wrote several works on astronomy and on astrology, was instrumental in bringing Arabic scientific materials to the Latin West.

ROGERS, HENRY DARWIN (*b. Philadelphia, Pa., 1808; d. Shawlands, near Glasgow, Scotland, 1866*), and
ROGERS, WILLIAM BARTON (*b. Philadelphia, Pa., 1804; d. Boston, Mass., 1882*), geology.

Did extraordinary work on the stratigraphy and structure of the Appalachians; were active in organization of the Association of American Geologists (1840) and in its transformation into the A.A.A.S. (1848). William Rogers became the first president of the Massachusetts Institute of Technology (1862) after both brothers had vigorously advocated its founding; Henry was appointed professor of natural history at Glasgow University (1857).

ROHAULT, JACQUES (*b. Amiens, France, 1620; d. Paris, France, 1675*), natural philosophy, scientific methodology.

The leading advocate and teacher of Descartes's natural philosophy among the first generation of Cartesians; famous for the weekly lectures he gave in his house in Paris (from *ca.* 1655). In both his lectures and writings he sought to join Cartesian explanatory principles to experimental practice and to give a probabilistic interpretation of specific explanations. His masterwork, the *Traité de physique* (1671), was the leading textbook of its time on natural philosophy.

ROHN, KARL (*b. Schwanheim, Hesse, Germany, 1855; d. Leipzig, Germany, 1920*), mathematics.

Spent most of his teaching career at Leipzig. Specialized in forms of algebraic curves and surfaces up to degree 4, linear and quadratic congruences, and complexes of lines in P_3.

ROLANDO, LUIGI (*b. Turin, Italy, 1773; d. Turin, 1831*), medicine, anatomy, physiology, zoology.

Studied medicine at Turin; taught at Sassari University, in Sardinia, and at Turin. Most important studies were of the anatomy, physiology, and embryology of the brain; the "Rolandic fissure" is named for him.

ROLFINCK, GUERNER (*b. Hamburg, Germany, 1599; d. Jena, Germany, 1673*), medicine, chemistry, botany.

Taught at the University of Jena (from 1629); was six times rector; built the first anatomical theater at Jena; gave lectures involving human dissection; established the botanical garden (1631) and the chemical laboratory (1638). Opposed alchemy and "superstition."

ROLLE, MICHEL (*b. Ambert, Basse-Auvergne, France, 1652; d. Paris, France, 1719*), mathematics.

A scribe and reckoner; became famous for solving a problem posed (1682) by Ozanam; was sponsored by Colbert and the minister Louvois. His *Traité d'algèbre* (1690), on the algebra of equations, is remembered for its method of "cascades" for separating the roots of an algebraic equation. Rolle briefly but vigorously opposed infinitesimal analysis (1699–1706).

ROLLESTON, GEORGE (*b. Maltby, Yorkshire, England, 1829; d. Oxford, England, 1881*), anatomy, zoology, anthropology.

Spent most of his career at Oxford; was Linacre professor of anatomy and physiology (from 1860). Supported T. H. Huxley against Richard Owen in their debate on human and simian brains; influenced by Huxley, introduced the still-dominant "type" system of zoological instruction, in which a few representative organs are selected for dissection.

ROLLET, JOSEPH-PIERRE-MARTIN (*b. Lagnieu, Ain, France, 1824; d. Lyons, France, 1894*), venereology.

Was chief of surgery (1855–64) at the Antiquaille Hospital, which specialized in treatment of venereal disease. Did outstanding research on syphilis.

ROMANES, GEORGE JOHN (*b. Kingston, Ontario, 1848; d. Oxford, England, 1894*), physiology, comparative psychology, evolution.

Of wealthy family; educated at home; studied physiology under Michael Foster at Cambridge. Met Darwin (1874); became his close friend and influential supporter. Did important work with E. A. Schäfer on the nerve system of the medusa (this influenced Charles Sherrington's development of the synapse concept); drew a significant analogy between the rhythmic motion of the medusa and heartbeat. Published three books on animal intelligence, introducing a relatively critical approach to the study of animal behavior. With Herbert Spencer, argued that natural selection is not the sole factor at work in evolution; proposed (1886) a role for isolation, specifically mutual infertility between two or more portions of a species population prior to morphological or other distinctions.

ROMÉ DE L'ISLE (or DELISLE), JEAN-BAPTISTE LOUIS (*b. Gray, France, 1736; d. Paris, France, 1790*), crystallography, mineralogy.

Turned from a military career to science, studying chemistry under B. G. Sage, who became his sponsor and supporter. Began to investigate mineralogy (1767) while cataloguing a private collection of curiosities; published *Essai de cristallographie* (1772), identifying 110 crystal forms. In his major work, *Cristallographie* (1783), drawing on discoveries and techniques developed by his assistant, Arnould Carangeot, he formulated the law of constancy of interfacial angles as the criterion for identifying a species of crystal; he maintained that secondary crystal forms can be derived geometrically from primary ones by means of truncation of solid angles or edges, and that the form of the integrant molecules of a crystal must be identical with its primitive form and must exist in fixed proportions. Romé's other major works were a book on the external characteristics of minerals (1784) and *Métrologie* (1789), comparing ancient and modern weights and measures.

ROMER, EUGENIUSZ MIKOŁAJ (*b. Lvov, Poland [now U.S.S.R.], 1871; d. Cracow, Poland, 1954*), geography, cartography.

Took his doctorate at Lvov; returned there (1911) as professor of geography; from 1945, taught at Jagiellonian University in Cracow. Active in cartography, producing many atlases, maps, and globes and founding institutes of geography (1919) and cartography (1921) and the *Polish Cartographic Review* (1923); also made significant contributions to climatology and geomorphology.

RÖMER. *See also* **Roemer.**

RÖMER, OLE CHRISTENSEN (or ROEMER, OLAUS) (*b. Aarhus, Denmark, 1644; d. Copenhagen, Denmark, 1710*), astronomy.

Studied at the University of Copenhagen under the brothers Thomas and Erasmus Bartholin; with the latter and Jean Picard, made observations of the first satellite of Jupiter (1671) from the observatory at Hven; accompanied Picard to Paris and, from the Royal Observatory, continued to study Jupiter's satellites; was able to show (1676) that the cause of the differences in the periodic times of eclipses of the satellite Io was the finite speed of light; thus Römer disproved the prevalent concept that light propagates itself instantaneously; he also arrived at a good approximation of its speed. Returned to Denmark (1681) to become professor of mathematics at Copenhagen and astronomer royal; incidentally invented an advanced thermometer that greatly influenced Fahrenheit. Held numerous civil positions, including mayor of Copenhagen, prefect of police, senator, and head of the state council of the realm.

RONDELET, GUILLAUME (*b. Montpellier, France, 1507; d. Réalmont, Tarn, France, 1566*), ichthyology, medicine, anatomy.

Received his M.D. from Montpellier University (1537), eventually becoming the chancellor there (1556); was a friend of Rabelais, personal physician to François Cardinal Tournon, and an internationally popular lecturer in anatomy. Wrote *Libri de piscibus marinis* (1554–55), a compendium on all aquatic animals, marine and freshwater, covering over 300 species.

RÖNTGEN (ROENTGEN), WILHELM CONRAD (*b. Lennep im Bergischen [now part of Remscheid], Rhine Province, Germany, 1845; d. Munich, Germany, 1923*), physics.

Rebellious and unstudious as a youth, Röntgen won by examination admission to the Polytechnic at Zurich (Ph.D., 1869); became assistant to his physics teacher, August Kundt, and traveled with him; gradually earned academic recognition, becoming (1894) rector of the University of Würzburg; accepted (1900) the chair of physics and directorship of the Physical Institute at Munich. Did important work on the rotation of the plane of polarization of light in gases, on crystals and pyroelectrical and piezoelectrical phenomena, and on the compressibility of liquids and solids; his fame, however, rests on two discoveries outside his normal field of research. In 1888, he discovered the magnetic effects (predicted by Maxwell) produced in a dielectric when moved between two electrically charged condenser plates; this finding and Röntgen's analysis of it led to the theories of Lorentz and to modern theories of electricity. In 1895, while researching cathode rays, Röntgen discovered X rays; for this, he became known worldwide, and was awarded (1901) the first Nobel Prize for physics.

ROOD, OGDEN NICHOLAS (*b. Danbury, Conn., 1831; d. New York, N.Y., 1902*), physics.

Professor of physics at Columbia University (from 1863). Invented technique of flicker photometry for comparing brightness of colors; wrote *Modern Chromatics* (1879).

ROOKE, LAWRENCE (*b. Deptford [now part of London], England, 1622; d. London, 1662*), astronomy, natural philosophy.

Esteemed for his learning, experiments, and observations in physics and astronomy. Moved from Oxford to Gresham College, London (1652); with Christopher Wren, initiated weekly meetings that led to the founding of the Royal Society.

ROOMEN, ADRIAAN VAN (*b. Louvain, Belgium [?], 1561; d. Mainz, Germany, 1615*), mathematics, medicine.

A much-traveled and honored teacher of medicine and mathematics; an important part of his work dealt with trigonometry and the calculation of chords in a circle. Among his treatises are *Ideae mathematicae pars prima* (1593), *Speculum astronomicum* (1606), and *Canon triangulorum sphaericorum* (1609); the latter two contain the first systematic use of a trigonometric notation.

ROOZEBOOM, HENDRIK WILLEM BAKHUIS (*b. Alkmaar, Netherlands, 1854; d. Amsterdam, Netherlands, 1907*), physical chemistry.

Took his doctorate at Leiden (1884); became professor of general chemistry at Amsterdam (1896). Important for his fruitful application of J. W. Gibbs's phase rule to the study of heterogeneous equilibriums.

ROSA, DANIELE (*b. Susa, near Turin, Italy, 1857; d. Novi Ligure, Italy, 1944*), zoology.

Taught zoology and comparative anatomy at various universities in Sardinia and Italy. Held that extinction of species results from a steady decrease in variability.

ROSANES, JAKOB (*b. Brody, Austria-Hungary [now Ukrainian S.S.R.], 1842; d. Breslau, Germany [now Wrocław, Poland], 1922*), mathematics.

Took his Ph.D. at Breslau (1865), and remained there for the rest of his career. Specialized in algebraic geometry and invariant theory.

ROSCOE, HENRY ENFIELD (*b. London, England, 1833; d. Leatherhead, Surrey, England, 1915*), chemistry.

The founder of the Manchester school of chemistry. Studied at University College (B.A., 1853) and the Birbeck Laboratory in London and at Heidelberg under Bunsen (Ph.D., 1853); selected (1857) for the chair of chemistry at Owens College in Manchester. Helped to turn this faltering college into a leading center for science education; used Continental teaching methods; stressed the practical, economic value of science; was extremely active in local civic affairs and in the general science community.

ROSE, GUSTAV (*b. Berlin, Germany, 1798; d. Berlin, 1873*), mineralogy, crystallography.

Of a family of scientists (his older brother Heinrich was a chemist); spent almost his entire career at the University of Berlin. Discovered about fifteen new minerals; his goniometric measurements contributed to the development of the concept of isomorphism.

ROSE, HEINRICH (*b. Berlin, Germany, 1795; d. Berlin, 1864*), chemistry.

Of a family of scientists (his brother Gustav became a mineralogist); influenced by Berthollet and Berzelius; took his doctorate at Kiel; taught at Berlin (from 1822). Noted for his analyses of inorganic substances and minerals, and for study of the influence of temperature and concentration on chemical decomposition. Discovered niobium. Author of the great textbook *Handbook of Analytical Chemistry* (1829).

ROSENBERG, HANS OSWALD (*b. Berlin, Germany, 1879; d. Istanbul, Turkey, 1940*), astronomy, astrophysics.

Taught in Germany, the U.S., and Turkey. Specialized in photometric and spectrophotometric studies of stars; made improvements in instrument design.

ROSENBERGER, JOHANN KARL FERDINAND (*b. Lobeda, Germany, 1845; d. Oberstdorf, Germany, 1899*), history of physics.

Studied at Jena (Ph.D., 1870); taught at the Musterschule in Frankfurt am Main. His history of physics (1882–90) focused on the emergence of the modern scientific method; his book on Newton (1895) examined the function of authority in the scientific community.

ROSENBERGER, OTTO AUGUST (*b. Tukums, Latvia, 1800; d. Halle, Germany, 1890*), astronomy.

A protégé of F. W. Bessel's; taught at Königsberg and Halle. Noted for observations of stars and comets.

ROSENBLUETH, ARTURO (*b. Ciudad Guerrero, Mexico, 1900; d. Mexico City, Mexico, 1970*), neurophysiology.

Received his M.D. at Paris; taught at Harvard; became (1944) director of research at the Institute of Cardiology in Mexico City; founded (1961) the National Polytechnical Institute of Mexico. With Walter B. Cannon, did research on the sympathetic nervous system that decisively confirmed the theory of "chemical mediation"; with Norbert Wiener, did functional analysis of the nervous system that led Wiener to edify the new science of cybernetics.

ROSENBUSCH, HARRY (KARL HEINRICH FERDINAND) (*b. Einbeck, Germany, 1836; d. Heidelberg, Germany, 1914*), geology.

Professor of mineralogy at Heidelberg (1878–1908). Helped to establish petrography as a true geological science; stressed the genetic and mineralogical (as opposed to chemical) classification of rocks. Wrote a two-volume text that became the standard work on igneous rocks.

ROSENHAIN, JOHANN GEORG (*b. Königsberg, Prussia, 1816; d. Königsberg, 1887*), mathematics.

Is remembered for his prize-winning essay (1851) extending Jacobi's findings in the theory of elliptic functions.

ROSENHAIN, WALTER (*b. Berlin, Germany, 1875; d. Kingston Hill, Surrey, England, 1934*), metallurgy.

Did graduate work at Cambridge under J. A. Ewing and at Melbourne, Australia (D.Sc., 1909). At Cambridge, using the micrographic technique of Henry Sorby, discovered slip lines in deformed metal strips that enabled him to confirm that metals consist of crystalline grains. Affiliated with the National Physical Laboratory, Teddington (1906–31). Helped to create the new science of physical metallurgy.

ROSENHEIM, ARTHUR (*b. New York, N.Y., 1865; d. Berlin, Germany, 1942*), chemistry.

Took his Ph.D. at Berlin (1888) and remained there for most of his teaching career until forced to retire (1933) by the Nazis. Noted for his extremely careful analyses; although he primarily extended and corrected the work

of others, his findings were so excellently researched that they have needed only minor updating.

ROSENHOF, AUGUST JOHANN ROESEL VON. *See* **Roesel von Rosenhof, August Johann.**

ROSS, FRANK ELMORE (*b. San Francisco, Calif., 1874; d. Altadena, Calif., 1960*), astronomy.

One of the most versatile astronomers of his time. Received his Ph.D. at the University of California at Berkeley (1901); was director of the International Latitude Observatory at Gaithersburg, Maryland (1905–15); physicist at the Eastman Kodak Company (1915–24); on the staff of the Yerkes Observatory and professor at the University of Chicago (1924–39). Noted for his many valuable observations and his instrument (especially lens) designs.

ROSS, JAMES CLARK (*b. London, England, 1800; d. Aylesbury, England, 1862*), polar navigation, geomagnetism.

A naval officer and explorer, expert in magnetic observations; discovered the north magnetic pole (1831), and Victoria Land and Mount Erebus in Antarctica (1841).

ROSS, RONALD (*b. Almora, Nepal, 1857; d. Putney, London, England, 1932*), medicine.

Studied medicine at St. Bartholomew's Hospital, London, but was more interested in mathematics and the arts (became a successful writer). While in the Indian Medical Service, grew concerned with medical problems; on furlough in England (1894), was inspired by Patrick Manson to study malaria, which Manson thought might be transmitted by mosquitoes. Working in India with human patients and then with caged birds (1897), Ross was able to identify the vector mosquito *(Anopheles)* and to demonstrate the parasite life cycle. There were disputes over priority, but these were largely stilled when Ross was awarded the Nobel Prize (1902).

ROSSBY, CARL-GUSTAV ARVID (*b. Stockholm, Sweden, 1898; d. Stockholm, 1957*), meteorology, oceanography.

Trained under V. F. Bjerknes in Bergen, Norway; came to the U.S. (1926); helped to create modern American meteorology. Was particularly influential in positions at the Massachusetts Institute of Technology (1928–39) and at the University of Chicago (1941–50); returned to Sweden (1950). His original contributions include work on atmospheric turbulence and the theory of atmospheric pressure; studies of the general circulation of the atmosphere; investigation of the circumpolar system of "Rossby waves"; and improved prediction methods.

ROSSE, WILLIAM. *See* **Parsons, William, third Earl of Rosse.**

ROSSETTI, FRANCESCO (*b. Trento, Italy, 1833; d. Padua, Italy, 1885*), physics.

Taught at Venice and Padua. Noted for investigations of electrical piles and electrical generators and of solar temperature.

ROSTAN, LÉON LOUIS (*b. St.-Maximin, Var, France, 1790; d. Paris, France, 1866*), medicine.

An immensely popular teacher of clinical medicine at La Salpêtrière and the Hôtel-Dieu, both in Paris; sought always to explain clinical symptoms by specific organic lesions.

ROTH, JUSTUS LUDWIG ADOLPH (*b. Hamburg, Germany, 1818; d. Berlin, Germany, 1892*), geology, petrology.

Taught at the University of Berlin (from 1867). His masterwork was his advanced textbook on general and chemical geology, *Allgemeine und chemische Geologie* (1879–93).

ROTHMANN, CHRISTOPH (*b. Bernburg, Anhalt, Germany; d. Bernburg, 1599–1608*), astronomy.

Mathematicus to William IV of Hesse, his importance lies mainly in his correspondence with Tycho Brahe (published, 1596).

ROUELLE, GUILLAUME-FRANÇOIS (*b. Mathieu, Calvados, France, 1703; d. Passy, Seine, France, 1770*), chemistry, geology.

Universally considered an extraordinary teacher, Rouelle lectured in chemistry at the Jardin du Roi in Paris (1742–46) and at his own laboratory (from 1746); he also taught geology, and in both fields introduced original, advanced concepts. Among his students were Lavoisier, Desmarest, and Diderot.

ROUELLE, HILAIRE-MARIN (*b. Mathieu, Calvados, France, 1718; d. Paris, France, 1779*), chemistry.

Assisted his older brother Guillaume-François in most of his activities; carried on their work after his brother's death.

ROUELLE, JEAN (*b. probably Douzy [Ardennes], France, ca. 1751; d. unknown*), chemistry, natural history.

Nephew of the Rouelle brothers. Taught science in the U.S. (1788–98).

ROUGET, CHARLES MARIE BENJAMIN (*b. Gisors, France, 1824; d. Paris, France, 1904*), physiology, histology.

Trained at the Collège Sainte-Barbe and the teaching hospitals of Paris; taught at Montpellier and at the Muséum d'Histoire Naturelle in Paris. Is remembered particularly for research on animal reproductive organs and functions, the eye and vision, capillary contractility, and nerve endings; extending the work of Claude Bernard, speculated that diabetes mellitus is caused by an internal nutritive disorder.

ROUILLIER, KARL FRANTSOVICH (*b. Nizhny-Novgorod [now Gorky], Russia, 1814; d. Moscow, Russia, 1858*), biology, paleontology, geology.

A leader in the development of evolutionary concepts. Studied at the Moscow Medical and Surgical Academy; became a military physician; then held the chair of zoology at Moscow University. Wrote classical studies of the Jurassic, Carboniferous, and Quaternary deposits of the Moscow basin (1840–48). Taught that the evolution of animal forms is gradual and influenced by the organism's relation to the environment (including other organisms). Rouillier was intolerably harassed by authorities, including the minister of education.

ROUTH, EDWARD JOHN (*b. Quebec, Canada, 1831; d. Cambridge, England, 1907*), mechanics.

Had a brilliant undergraduate career (he bested J. C. Maxwell in Cambridge's mathematical tripos, 1854); became the most famous of the Cambridge "coaches" (teachers who prepare students for their public examinations). Wrote a series of treatises that became the standard texts of classical applied mathematics; noted also for his theorem of the "modified Lagrangian function."

ROUX, PIERRE PAUL ÉMILE (*b. Confolens, Charente, France, 1853; d. Paris, France, 1933*), baceriology.

A founder of medical baceriology. Worked under Pasteur and at the Institut Pasteur (as director after 1904). Known especially for research on rabies and diptheria.

ROUX, WILHELM (*b. Jena, Germany, 1850; d. Halle, Germany, 1924*), embryology, anatomy.

A leader in the creation of modern experimental embryology; the founder of *Entwicklungsmechanik* (developmental mechanics, with an emphasis on experimentalism and a broadly mechanistic interpretation); a ferocious propagandist for his own accomplishments. Had a distinguished teaching career at Breslau, Innsbruck, and finally at Halle, where he was director of the anatomical institute (1895–1921). Roux did his doctoral dissertation (1878) at Jena, under Schwalbe; in making an analogy between hydrodynamics and hemodynamics, Roux began his search for a causal relation between form and function. In a highly speculative treatise (1881), he suggested that the evolutionary struggle for existence takes place at the cellular and molecular level. In orthopedic studies (1883–85), introduced the concept of "functional adaptation" in the development of form. His most important investigations (1883–88) were of early cleavage patterns of frog eggs; stimulated by an experiment of Eduard Pflüger's, Roux moved from a descriptive to experimental approach; began injury experiments (piercing blastomeres with needles); he was now explicitly seeking to isolate causal factors in early development; focusing on the interaction between nucleus and cytoplasm, he came to conceive of the course of development as moments of independent and dependent variation. In his celebrated "half-embryo" paper (1888), he believed that he had shown that the nucleus of each blastomere is capable of directing a specific independent line of differentiation; he also concluded (in part from this research) that the nucleus is composed of hereditary particles.

ROVERETO, GAETANO (*b. Mele, near Voltri, Genoa, Italy, 1870; d. Genoa, 1952*), geology.

Of an aristocratic family; a self-taught geologist and specialist in geomorphology; professor at the University of Genoa (from 1922). Best known for studies of Liguria.

ROWE, ALLAN WINTER (*b. Gloucester, Mass., 1879; d. Boston, Mass., 1934*), physiological chemistry.

Took his doctorate in chemistry at Göttingen; affiliated with the Boston University School of Medicine (from 1906) and the Robert Dawson Evans Memorial for Clinical Research and Preventive Medicine (from 1910). Specialized in endocrine disorders; with T. W. Richards, studied the thermochemistry of electrolytes.

ROWLAND, HENRY AUGUSTUS (*b. Honesdale, Pa., 1848; d. Baltimore, Md., 1901*), physics.

Studied civil engineering at Rensselaer Polytechnic Institute; accepted the chair in physics at Johns Hopkins University (1875), where he developed the best physics laboratory in the U.S. Known especially for the invention and ruling of the concave spectral grating.

ROWNING, JOHN (*b. Ashby, Lincolnshire, England, 1701 [?]; d. London, England, 1771*), mathematics, natural philosophy.

A graduate of Magdalene College, Cambridge; rector of Anderby, Lincolnshire (from 1738). Wrote *A Compendious System of Natural Philosophy* (1735), one of the most popular texts of its era.

ROZHDESTVENSKY, DMITRY SERGEEVICH (*b. St. Petersburg, Russia, 1876; d. Leningrad, U.S.S.R., 1940*), physics.

Studied at St. Petersburg University; became the founder and director (1918–32) of the State Optical Institute. His research centered on anomalous dispersion near the lines of absorption in atomic spectra, theory of atomic spectra, and theory of the microscope.

RUBENS, HEINRICH (Henri Leopold) (*b. Wiesbaden, Germany, 1865; d. Berlin, Germany, 1922*), physics.

Studied under August Kundt at the University of Berlin (Ph.D., 1889); returned there (1906) as professor of experimental physics and director of the Königliches Physikalisches Institut. His lifework was the investigation of the far-infrared region; with E. F. Nichols, discovered *Reststrahlen* (residual rays); with Henri Du Bois and Ernst Hagen, confirmed the validity of the electromagnetic theory as applied to the infrared.

RUBNER, MAX (*b. Munich, Germany, 1854; d. Berlin, Germany, 1932*), physiology, hygiene.

Studied medicine at Munich; taught hygiene at Marburg; succeeded Robert Koch (1891) at Berlin. His most original work involved the clarification of the specific dynamic effect of foodstuffs, and the establishment of the validity of the principle of the conservation of energy in living organisms.

RUDBECK, OLOF (*b. Västerås, Sweden, 1630; d. Uppsala, Sweden, 1702*), medicine, anatomy, botany.

The son of the bishop of Västerås, an important ecclesiastic. Studied medicine at Uppsala and the University of Leiden. Discovered the lymphatic system prior to and independently of Thomas Bartholin. Taught at Uppsala (from 1655); active in the reform of the university, establishing with his own money the fine botanical garden, and building an anatomical theater. Published (1679–1702) his *Atland eller Manhem*, arguing that Sweden was Plato's lost Atlantis. Employing a large staff, began work on an illustrated book on all known plants; only two parts were published when the great fire of 1702 destroyed almost all the work that had been prepared; Rudbeck died soon thereafter. His son, Olaf, became Linnaeus' patron.

RÜDENBERG, REINHOLD (*b. Hannover, Germany, 1883; d. Boston, Mass., 1961*), electrical engineering.

Taught in Germany and in the U.S. at Harvard University (1939–52); created the first 60-MVA turbine generator (1916). Wrote on heavy-current and light-current engineering.

RUDIO, FERDINAND (*b. Wiesbaden, Germany, 1856; d. Zurich, Switzerland, 1929*), mathematics, history of science.

A mathematician, teacher of mathematics at the Zurich Polytechnic (from 1881), and author in the history of mathematics; edited the collected works of Euler.

RUDOLFF (or **RUDOLF**), **CHRISTOFF** (*b. Jauer, Silesia [now Jawor, Poland]; fl. 1525–30; d. Vienna, Austria*), mathematics.

Studied algebra under Grammateus at the University of Vienna; wrote an algebrà text, or *Coss* (1525), and an arithmetic book (1526), supplemented by a book of examples (1530). His *Coss* is the first comprehensive algebra text in German, remarkable for its advanced concepts and for improvements in symbolism.

RUDOLPHI, KARL ASMUND (*b. Stockholm, Sweden, 1771; d. Berlin, Germany, 1832*), anatomy, physiology, helminthology.

Studied and taught at Greifswald; appointed (1810) to the chair of anatomy and physiology at Berlin. With H. F. Link, studied the cellular tissue of plants; did pioneering work in helminthology and comparative histology (studies of intestinal villi in vertebrates). His textbook on physiology opposed the romantic, speculative approach then prevailing in Germany.

RUEDEMANN, RUDOLF (*b. Georgenthal, Germany, 1864; d. Albany, N.Y., 1956*), paleontology, geology.

Took his doctorate at the University of Jena (1887); taught at Strasbourg; immigrated to the U.S. (1892); affiliated with the New York State Museum (from 1899); became state paleontologist (1925). Investigated the paleontology and geology of the principal valleys of New York; was the foremost graptolite expert in the U.S.

RUEL, JEAN, also known as **RUELLIUS** (*b. Soissons, France, 1474; d. Paris, France, 1537*), medicine, botany.

Physician to Francis I; later entered holy orders and obtained a canonry at Notre-Dame. His works include *De natura stirpium* (1536), a compilation, but a notable early attempt to popularize botany.

RUFFER, MARC ARMAND (*b. Lyons, France, 1859; d. eastern Mediterranean, ca. 1917*), paleopathology.

Internationally educated; director of the British Institute of Preventive Medicine; professor of bacteriology at the Cairo Medical School; knighted (1916); killed at sea in a torpedo attack. Working with mummies, revolutionized techniques for the microscopic examination of ancient human tissues; made numerous important discoveries in paleopathology.

RUFFINI, ANGELO (*b. Pretare, near Arquata del Tronto, Italy, 1864; d. Baragazza, near Castiglione dei Pepoli, Italy, 1929*), histology embryology.

Studied medicine at Bologna; taught histology at Siena and at Bologna. Did important research on proprioceptive sensibility and amphibian embryology.

RUFFINI, PAOLO (*b. Valentano, Italy, 1765; d. Modena, Italy, 1822*), mathematics, medicine, philosophy.

Exceptionally versatile, Ruffini was both a professor of mathematics (at Modena) and an active practicing physician. His most important work was the discovery of what is now known as the Abel-Ruffini theorem: a general algebraic equation of higher than the fourth degree cannot be solved by means of radical-rational operations. In this, Ruffini contributed to the transition from classical to abstract algebra. His philosophical writings reflect his religious faith.

RUFFO, GIORDANO (*b. Gerace [?], Calabria, Italy; fl. Italy, ca. 1250*), veterinary medicine.

Of a noble family; became farrier at the court of the emperor Frederick II; was blinded (1256) by Frederick's illegitimate son Manfred; apparently died in captivity. Author of the influential *De medicina equorum* (completed between 1250–54), based on his expert knowledge of horses and veterinary medicine; the book distinguishes between veins and arteries.

RUFINUS (*fl. Italy, second half of the thirteenth century*), botany, medicine.

An Italian monk and priest; author of *De virtutibus herbarum* (finished after 1287), containing many excellent passages of descriptive botany.

RUFUS OF EPHESUS (*fl. late first century* B.C. *to mid-first century* A.D. *[?]*), medicine.

A Greek physician, native to Ephesus; lived for a long time in Egypt, mainly Alexandria. Notable for the breadth of his knowledge, his rich clinical observations, and his care in drawing conclusions. Wrote on melancholy, amnesia, kidney and bladder ailments, sexual function, joint diseases, and many other subjects.

RÜHMKORFF, HEINRICH DANIEL (*b. Hannover, Germany, 1803; d. Paris, France, 1877*), technology.

Founded (1855) a shop in Paris, known to physicists worldwide, especially for the quality of its electrical apparatus. Designed an induction coil capable of producing sparks a foot or more in length.

RUINI, CARLO (*b. Bologna, Italy, ca. 1530; d. Bologna, 1598*), anatomy, veterinary surgery.

A Bolognese aristocrat, senator, and lawyer, remembered chiefly for his comprehensive *Anatomia del cavallo, infermità et suoi rimedii* (1598), a pioneering study in (equine) anatomy.

RUIZ, HIPÓLITO (*b. Belorado, Burgos province, Spain, 1754; d. Madrid, Spain, 1816*), botany.

Was first botanist of a French-Spanish expedition to Peru (1778–85); wrote on the plants of Peru, including cinchona.

RULAND, MARTIN (*b. Lauingen, Germany, 1569; d. Prague, Bohemia, 1611*), medicine, iatrochemistry.

Physician to Emperor Rudolf II; favored Paracelsian reforms and the use of chemically-prepared medicines.

RÜLEIN, ULRICH (usually called **ULRICH RÜLEIN VON CALW**) (*b. Calw [?], Germany, 1465/69; d. Germany, 1523*), geology, mining, medicine.

A leading figure of the German Renaissance. Earned his master's and doctor's degrees in 1490, at Leipzig, and his M.D. (1496 or 1497), probably also at Leipzig. Designed the (silver) mining cities of Annaberg and Marienberg; for more than twenty years (from 1497), was municipal physician, a mining expert and surveyor, and a leading politician in Freiberg. Wrote *Ein nützlich Bergbüchlein* (*ca.* 1500), a landmark in the development of the science of mining, incorporating the personal experiences of miners with ores and ore deposits.

RUMFORD. *See* **Thompson, Benjamin.**

AL-RŪMĪ. *See* **Qāḍi Zāda al-Rūmī.**

RUMOVSKY, STEPAN YAKOLEVICH (*b. Stary Pogost, near Vladimir, Russia, 1734; d. St. Petersburg, Russia, 1812*), astronomy, mathematics, geodesy.

A skilled mathematician and astronomer; studied and taught at the university of the St. Petersburg Academy of Sciences; also trained with Euler and A. N. Grischow. Made very precise geodesic determinations; helped to found the university at Kazan.

RUNGE, CARL DAVID TOLMÉ (*b. Bremen, Germany, 1856; d. Göttingen, Germany, 1927*), mathematics, physics.

Of a merchant family; studied at Munich and at Berlin (doctorate, 1880) under Weierstrass. Did his *Habilitationsschrift* (1883) under Leopold Kronecker; obtained a general procedure for the numerical solution of algebraic equations in which the roots were expressed as infinite series of rational functions of the coefficients, and the traditional procedures for numerical solutions of Newton, Bernoulli, and Gräffe were derived as special cases from a single function-theoretic theorem. Appointed to the Technische Hochschule at Hannover (1886); married one of the daughters, Aimée, of Emil du Bois-Reymond (1887). Began to work in "applied mathematics," a shift that was regarded as nearly treasonous. With Heinrich Kayser, did basic research on spectral lines; but Runge was not as successful here as Rydberg, whose formulas were more fruitful. With Friedrich Paschen, did outstanding work on the spectral series of helium and on magnetic splitting; Runge found not only that the splitting was characteristic of a series, and quantitatively as well as qualitatively identical for analogous series in the spectra of different elements, but also that all the splittings were rational fractions of the "normal" splitting given by the Lorentz theory of the Zeeman effect; this last result, "Runge's rule," met with great applause but eventually proved to be largely misleading. Runge went to Göttingen (1904) as the first (and last) full professor of "applied mathematics," which he conceived as treating the theory and practice of numerical and graphical computation.

RUNGE, FRIEDLIEB FERDINAND (*b. Billwärder, near Hamburg, Germany, 1794; d. Oranienburg, Germany, 1867*), chemistry.

As a chemist at the factory in Oranienburg owned by the Royal Maritime Society, did important research on synthetic dyes; was a pioneer in the use of paper chromatography.

RUSCELLI, GIROLAMO (or **Alexis of Piedmont** [?]) (*b. Viterbo, Italy; d. Venice, Italy, ca. 1565*), medicine, technological chemistry.

Author of *Secreti nuovi* (1567); possibly also, as he claimed, author of the vastly popular *Secreti* (mid-1550's), attributed to "Alessio Piemontese," a collection of empirically discovered recipes, including formulas for medicines, cosmetics, and for the chemical technology of pigments and dyes, metallurgy, and jewelry.

RUSH, BENJAMIN (*b. Byberry, Pa., 1746; d. Philadelphia, Pa., 1813*), chemistry, medicine, psychiatry.

Educated at the Presbyterian College of New Jersey (later Princeton) and at the University of Edinburgh, where he studied chemistry under Joseph Black and obtained his M.D. Appointed professor of chemistry (1769) at the College of Philadelphia (now the University of Pennsylvania Medical College); became professor of medicine (1789). Holding a theory of medicine based on the responsiveness of the arterial system, Rush overenthusiastically applied bleeding and other depleting remedies to his patients; in neither chemistry nor medicine did he appreciate the value of the experimental method. Nevertheless, he was an inspiring teacher, who evinced the best qualities of the Enlightenment; he believed that science should serve the needs of society; he was an active reformer, a signer of the Declaration of Independence, and an opponent of slavery and capital punishment. Placed in charge of the insane at the Philadelphia Hospital (1787), he taught that body and mind are "intimately united"; in *Medical Inquiries and Observations Upon Diseases of the Mind* (1812) he observed that not only intellect but also behavior and emotions can be disturbed, and his attempts to understand these phenomena represent his most creative contribution to psychiatric thought.

IBN RUSHD, ABU'L-WALĪD MUḤAMMAD IBN AḤMAD IBN MUḤAMMAD, also known as **Averroës** (*b. Cordoba, Spain, 1126; d. Marrakech, Morocco, 1198*), astronomy, philosophy, medicine.

Ibn Rushd, who was called the Commentator in the Latin Middle Ages, came from an important family of jurists and received a very good Muslim education. He studied medicine under Abū Jaʿfar Hārūn al-Tajālī, a noted figure in Seville who was versed in the works of Aristotle and the ancient physicians. Thoroughly familiar with the principles and various branches of medical science, he was an excellent practitioner, and his cures were frequently successful. It is likely therefore that Abū Jaʿfar played an important role in the life of his student, teaching him not only medicine but also Aristotelian philosophy.

The biographers make no mention of Ibn Rushd's philosophical studies. Ibn Abī Uṣaibiʿa confirms that it was under Abū Jaʿfar that Ibn Rushd became interested in the philosophical sciences, and Ibn al-Abbār notes simply that he "inclined towards the sciences of the Ancients." These meager data are sufficient to substantiate the idea that he approached philosophical problems with a scientific outlook, though without forgetting his early instruction in legal reasoning. To an important degree, therefore, it was his scientific and legal training that gave Ibn Rushd's thinking its particular cast.

He was also interested in astronomy and acquainted with the history of its theories. Capable of explaining what Aristotle said about the systems of Eudoxus and Callippus, he was just as well informed about the work of Ptolemy, and, through the latter, he had some knowledge of the ideas of the ancients who preceded Hipparchus. He also knew the writings of the Arab astronomers. Ibn Rushd aligned himself with those astronomers who advocated a return to Aristotle, but in order to sort out his own ideas, he took into account the whole of the history of the subject that separates him from the Greek philosopher. In fact, the abundance and the weakness of the contending theories left him very perplexed. Although he treated the scientific aspects of these problems as an expert, he hesitated to offer definitive solutions.

Ibn Rushd was almost certainly influenced by the "moderns," but he did not follow them blindly. He remarked that if one considers the plurality of the planetary motions, one can distinguish three kinds: (1) those accessible to the naked eye; (2) those that can be detected only with the use of observational instruments—which sometimes take place over periods exceeding the lifetime of an individual and sometimes over shorter periods; and finally, (3) those whose existence is established only by reasoning.

He found the system of eccentrics and epicycles, adopted and developed by Ptolemy, completely unacceptable. From the time of Plato the task of astronomy had been to save the phenomena by providing a rational account of the irregular apparent motions of the planets. The burden of Ibn Rushd's criticism of this type of explanation is that it is mathematical and not physical.

The philosophical writings of Ibn Rushd are divided into two groups, the commentaries on the works of Aristotle, and the personal writings, which are entitled *Faṣl al-Maqāl, Kitāb al-Kashf,* and *Tahāfut al-Tahāfut.*

As a commentator on Aristotle, Ibn Rushd attempted to restore the Stagirite's own thought, and to supplant the Neoplatonic interpretations of al-Fārābī and Ibn Sīnā. Ibn Rushd regarded Aristotelianism as the truth, inasmuch as truth is accessible to the human mind.

Although Ibn Rushd had a more complete knowledge of the *corpus Aristotelicum* and analyzed it more carefully and more accurately than did his predecessors al-Fārābī and Ibn Sīnā, he continued to view Aristotle essentially as the master of logic, and it was the logical rigor of the demonstrations in the Stagirite's philosophical and scientific writings that produced the greatest impression on him.

Ibn Rushd made an important qualification in his evaluation of Aristotle, however; he cautioned that while the Greek philosopher possessed the totality of the truth available to man, he did not possess the Truth itself.

The obscurity of many Aristotelian texts permitted wide latitude in their interpretation. The Commentator (as Ibn Rushd was called in the Latin West) naturally did not always give the correct explanation, especially since he often had to work with defective and even incomprehensible translations. In any case, it is clear that he always interpreted the texts in such a way as to accomplish two things: emphasis on the opposition between Aristotle and Plato, and criticism and correction of the positions advanced by Ibn Sīnā. Ibn Rushd rejected the view of metaphysics as the universal science that gives to all the other sciences their goals and principles, as well as the corollary to this view, that all human knowledge can, in principle at least, be deduced from metaphysics. At the same time, he opposed a cosmology that claimed to deduce, by the process of emanation, the celestial world of the Intelligences and of the spheres from the existence of the First Principle *(al-Awwal)* or Necessary Being. Nor did he accept the idea that the last of the Intelligences, that of the sphere of the moon (also called the Active Intellect), is the *dator formarum (wāhib al-suwar),* which gives form to the material beings of the sublunary world. In short, he rejected the Avicennian world view that explained the universe as having started from above and as having then proceeded downward, moving from the superior to the inferior. In Ibn Rushd's eyes this was Platonism.

His theory of the intellect is important both in itself and for its influence on the Latin Middle Ages. In order to understand it properly, one must constantly bear in mind that Ibn Rushd's main goal was to explain intellection without appealing to such separate intelligible entities as the Platonic Ideas.

In his personal writings he sets forth his positions on the religious problems of his time, notably on the agreement between reason and faith and on the interpretation and speculative use that can be made of the verses of the Koran.

Methodological questions form the subject of his *Decisive Treatise and Exposition of the Convergence of the Religious Law and Philosophy.* He also wrote *Kitāb al-Kashf,* the full title of which may be rendered as *Exposition of the Methods of Demonstration Relative to the Religious Dogmas and to the Definition of the Equivocal Meanings and Innovations Encountered in the Process of Interpretation and which Alter the Truth and Lead to Error.* In this work he examined the theories of the major theological sects, particularly the demonstrations of the existence of God, of His unicity, and of His attributes, and conceptions about the origin of the universe and the infinite chain of causation, as well as about predestination and human freedom.

After the *Kashf,* which prepared the way for it, the *Tahāfut al-Tahāfut* may be considered the most complete exposition of Ibn Rushd's personal thought. It takes the form of a critique of the *Tahāfut al-Falāsifa,* in which the theologian al-Ghazāli refutes Ibn Sīnā in the name of religious dogma, using arguments that Ibn Rushd attacks because they are not demonstrative. While he considers al-Ghazāli's refutation worthless, he nevertheless thinks that Ibn Sīnā's ideas should be combated, and marshals a number of demonstrative proofs against the major themes of Avicennian thought. In the process, Ibn Rushd presents virtually an entire philosophical treatise. On the whole, he sought to replace Arab Neoplatonism with what he thought were Aristotle's real views, at the same time taking into account the demands of religious faith.

Ibn Rushd's major work in medicine, *al-Kulliyyāt* ("Generalities"), was written between 1153 and 1169. Its subject matter leans heavily on Galen, and occasionally Hippocrates' name is mentioned.

RUSSELL, BERTRAND ARTHUR WILLIAM (*b. Trelleck, Monmouthshire, England, 1872; d. Plas Penrhyn, near Penrhyndeudraeth, Wales, 1970*), mathematical logic.

Like many Victorian children of the upper class, Russell was educated at home by a succession of tutors, so that when he entered Trinity College, Cambridge, as a scholar in 1890, he had had no experience of communal life in an educational establishment save for a few months in a "cramming" school in London.

A great stimulus to Russell's development was his election in 1892 to the Apostles. This was a small, informal society, founded about 1820, that regarded itself—not without some justification—as composed of the intellectual cream of the university; its main object was the completely unfettered discussion of any subject whatsoever.

One mode of encouragement for intellectual life at Trinity was the establishment of prize fellowships, awarded for original dissertations; such a fellowship lasted for six years and involved no special duties, the object being to give a young man an unhindered opportunity for intellectual development. Russell was elected in 1895, on the strength of a dissertation on the foundations of geometry, published in 1897. During the later part of his tenure and after it lapsed, he was not in residence; but in 1910 the college appointed him to a special lectureship in logic and the philosophy of mathematics.

During World War I pacifism excited emotions much more bitter than was the case in World War II. Russell's strongly held views made him unpopular in high places; and when in 1916 he published a leaflet protesting the harsh treatment of a conscientious objector, he was prosecuted on a charge of making statements likely to prejudice recruiting for and discipline in the armed services, and fined £100. The Council, the governing body of Trinity, then dismissed him from his lectureship, and Russell broke all connection with the college by removing his name from the books. In 1918 another article of his was judged seditious, and he was sentenced to imprisonment for six months. The sentence was carried out with sufficient leniency to enable him to write his very useful *Introduction to Mathematical Philosophy* in Brixton Prison.

Many members of Trinity felt that the Council's action in dismissing Russell in 1916 was excessively harsh. After the war the breach was healed: in 1925 the college invited Russell to give the Tarner lectures, later published under the title *The Analysis of Matter;* and from 1944 until his death he was again a fellow of the college.

A long list of books bears witness to Russell's endeavor to encourage human beings to think clearly, to understand the new scientific discoveries and to realize some of their implications, and to abhor injustice, violence, and war. *The Impact of Science on Society, History of Western Philosophy, Common Sense and Nuclear Warfare, Marriage and Morals, Freedom and Organisation,* and *Prospects of Industrial Civilisation,* to name only a few, show how earnestly he sought to promote his ideals.

Russell's fellowship thesis was revised for publication in 1897 as *An Essay on the Foundations of Geometry.* Its basic theme was an examination of the status assigned to geometry by Kant in his doctrine of synthetic a priori judgments. To Russell, non-Euclidean spaces were possible, in the philosophical sense that they are not condemned by any a priori argument as to the necessity of space for experience. However, in the light of modern views on the nature of a geometry, these investigations must be regarded as meaningless or at least as devoted to the wrong kind of question. What remains of interest in the *Foundations of Geometry* is the surgical skill with which Russell can dissect a corpus of thought, and his command of an easy yet precise English style.

Following the publication of the *Foundations of Geometry,* Russell settled down to the composition of a comprehensive treatise on the principles of mathematics, to expound his belief that pure mathematics deals entirely with concepts that can be discussed on a basis of a small number of fundamental logical concepts, deducing all its propositions by means of a small number of fundamental logical principles.

Volume I of *Principles of Mathematics* was not published until 1903. The second edition (1937) is perhaps more valuable for the study of the development of Russell's ideas, for it both reprints the first edition and contains a new introduction in which Russell gives his own opinion on those points on which his views had changed since 1903; but in spite of Hilbert and Brouwer, he is still firm in his belief that mathematics and logic are identical.

The second volume of the *Principles,* to be written in cooperation with Whitehead, never appeared because it was replaced by the later *Principia Mathematica.* It was to have been a completely symbolic account of the assimilation of mathematics to logic, of which a descriptive version appears in volume I. The main sections of volume I treat indefinables of mathematics (including a description of Peano's symbolic logic), number, quantity, order, infinity and continuity, space, and matter and motion.

In the three volumes of *Principia Mathematica* (1910–13) Whitehead and Russell took up the task, attempted in Russell's uncompleted *Principles,* of constructing the whole body of mathematical doctrine by logical deduction from the basis of a small number of primitive ideas and a small number of primitive principles of logical inference, using a symbolism derived from that of Peano but considerably extended and systematized. The second edition (1925–27) was mainly a reprint of the first, with small errors corrected; but it's worth to the student is considerably increased by the addition of a new introduction, of some thirty-four pages, in which the authors give an account of modifications and improvements rendered possible by work on the logical bases of mathematics following the appearance of the first edition.

The publication of the *Principia* gave a marked impulse to the study of mathematical logic. The deft handling of a complicated but precise symbolism encouraged workers to use this powerful technique and thus avoid the ambiguities lurking in the earlier employment of ordinary language. The awkwardness and inadequacy of the theory of types and the axiom of reducibility led not only to further investigations of the Whitehead-Russell doctrine but also to an increased interest in rival theories, particularly Hilbert's formalism and Brouwer's intuitionism. Perhaps because none of these three competitors can be regarded as finally satisfactory, research on the foundations of mathematics has produced new results and opened up new problems the very existence of which could hardly have been foreseen in the early years of this century. Whitehead and Russell may have failed in their valiant attempt to place mathematics once and for all on an unassailable logical basis, but their failure may have contributed more to the development of mathematical logic than complete success would have done.

The *Introduction to Mathematical Philosophy* (1919), written while Russell was serving a sentence in Brixton Prison, is a genuine introduction but certainly is not "philosophy without tears"; it may perhaps best be described as *une oeuvre de haute vulgarisation.* The aim is to expound work done in this field, particularly by Whitehead and Russell, without using the complex symbolism of *Principia Mathematica.* Russell's mastery of clear and precise English stood him in good stead for such a task, and many young students in the decade 1920–30 were first drawn to mathematical logic by a study of this efficient and readable volume.

The last six chapters of the *Introduction* are concerned with the theory of deduction and the general logical bases of mathematics, including an analysis of the use and nature of classes and the need, in Russell's theory, for a doctrine of types.

Among the essays collected in *Mysticism and Logic* (1921) are some that deal, in popular style, with Russell's views on mathematics and its logical foundations.

Russell's gifts as a popularizer of knowledge are shown in a number of his other books, such as *The Analysis of Matter* and *The ABC of Relativity,* in which problems arising from contemporary physics are discussed.

A few of Russell's many honors were fellowship of the Royal Society in 1908, the Order of Merit in 1949, and the Nobel Prize for literature in 1950.

RUSSELL, EDWARD JOHN (*b. Frampton-on-Severn, Gloucestershire, England, 1872; d. Goring-on-Thames, Oxfordshire, England, 1965*), agricultural chemistry, agronomy.

Studied at University College of Wales at Aberystwyth, Owens College (B.Sc., 1896); received D.Sc. from London University (1901). Taught at Wye Agricultural College (1901–07) and joined Rothamsted Experimental Station, Hertfordshire (1901; director, 1912–43). His courses at Wye formed the basis of his highly significant *Soil Conditions and Plant Growth* (1912). At Rothamsted he pioneered in soil microbiology, discovering that partial sterilization would increase soil productiveness. His trips abroad extended his influence on agricultural science and provided source material for *World Population and World Food Supplies* (1954). Knighted, 1922.

RUSSELL, HENRY CHAMBERLAINE (*b. West Maitland, New South Wales, Australia, 1836; d. Sydney, Australia, 1907*), astronomy, meteorology.

Received B.A. (1858) at Sydney University; became assistant at the Sydney observatory in 1859, and government astronomer in 1870, retiring in 1905. His most widely known contributions to astronomy were photographic; first to photograph the nebula η Argus. His day-to-day astronomical and meteorological recording is still of value, and he played an important part in the establishment of scientific and technical education in Australia.

RUSSELL, HENRY NORRIS (*b. Oyster Bay, N.Y., 1877; d. Princeton, N.J., 1957*), astrophysics, spectroscopy.

Received doctorate (1900) and taught (1905–47) at Princeton. Held research appointments at Mt. Wilson Observatory (1921–47) and at Lick and Harvard observatories after 1947. Member of numerous scientific societies and received many medals. Concerned himself with most of the major problems of astrophysics. Presented

(1912) the earliest systematic analysis of the variation of light received from eclipsing binary stars; with Shapley he extended the results to those with limb-darkened components. On the basis of his parallax studies, Russell developed a theory of stellar evolution that stimulated other astrophysicists, especially Eddington, and was the original context of the Hertzsprung-Russell diagram (graphs plotting absolute magnitudes of stars against their spectral types). His quantitative investigations of the absorption-line spectrum of the sun resulted in a reliable determination of the abundance of various chemical elements in the solar atmosphere, and provided clear evidence of the predominance of hydrogen in the sun and, by inference, in most stars. In calculating the relative populations of excited states of atoms in different stars, he and Walter Adams discovered that in cooler stars the dependence on excitation potential was not what was expected (the Adams-Russell effect), leading them to believe that the atmospheres of cool stars were not in thermodynamic equilibrium. He carried out, with various co-workers, extensive analyses of the spectra of a number of elements, most notably calcium, titanium, and iron. In this work he developed empirical rules for the relative strengths of lines of a given multiplet, and with F. A. Saunders devised the theory of L-S coupling to explain spectra produced by atoms with more than one valence electron. His approach to the theory of stellar structure led to the Vogt-Russell theorem, that on very general grounds the properties of a star can be expected to be completely determined by its mass and chemical composition.

RUTHERFORD, DANIEL (*b. Edinburgh, Scotland, 1749; d. Edinburgh, 1819*), chemistry.

Received M.D. and taught at Edinburgh. His place in the history of chemistry depends solely on his discovery of nitrogen (*Dissertatio inauguralis de aere fixo dicto, aut mephitico*, 1772). There is little doubt about his priority of publication, but priority of discovery seems attributable to Cavendish, Priestley, or Scheele.

RUTHERFORD, ERNEST (*b. between the settlements of Brightwater and Spring Grove, near Nelson, New Zealand, 1871; d. Cambridge, England, 1937*), physics, chemistry.

Rutherford received a scholarship to Nelson College, a nearby secondary school and a second scholarship took him in 1889 to Canterbury College, Christchurch. For his postgraduate work he obtained the M.A. in 1893, with double first-class honors in mathematics and mathematical physics and in physical science.

He was encouraged to stay at Canterbury for another year, during which he began research on the magnetization of iron by high-frequency discharges, work that earned him the B.Sc. in 1894.

In this first research Rutherford examined the magnetization of iron by a rapidly alternating electric current, such as the oscillatory discharge of a Leyden jar, and showed it to occur even with frequencies of over 10^8 cycles per second. This discovery enabled him to devise a detector of wireless signals before Marconi began his experiments, and during the next year or two Rutherford endeavored to increase the range and sensitivity of his device.

In 1895 he was awarded a scholarship, the terms of which required attendance at another institution, and Ru-

therford chose Cambridge University's Cavendish Laboratory, of which the director, J.J. Thomson, was the leading authority on electromagnetic phenomena. The university had just altered its rules to admit graduates of other schools, thereby enabling Rutherford to become the laboratory's first research student. He brought with him to England his wireless wave detector and soon was able to receive signals from sources up to half a mile away. This work so impressed a number of Cambridge dons, J. J. Thomson included, that Rutherford quickly made a name for himself. Upon the discovery of X rays, Thomson asked Rutherford in early 1896 to join him in studying the effect of this radiation upon the discharge of electricity in gases.

Out of this collaboration came a joint paper famous for its statement of a theory of ionization. The idea—that the X rays created an equal number of positive and negative carriers of electricity, or "ions," in the gas molecules—presumably was Thomson's, while much of the experimentation that placed this formerly descriptive subject on a quantitative basis was Rutherford's. The latter continued this work through 1897, measuring ionic velocities, rates of recombination, absorption of energy by gases, and the electrification of different gases while Thomson independently determined the existence of the particle later called the electron. Rutherford logically next examined the discharge of electricity by ultraviolet light, then conducted a similar study of the effects of uranium radiation. Again his inclination to pursue the most recent—and significant—problems led to a more detailed study of radioactivity. This was his field of endeavor for the next forty years.

Rutherford's interest in the field of radioactivity began by examining the Becquerel rays from uranium. Indeed, until about 1904 the emissions received far more attention than the emitters. Passage of the radiation through foils revealed one type that was easily absorbed and another with greater penetrating ability: these Rutherford named alpha and beta, "for simplicity."

Accepting the professorship of physics at McGill University in Montreal in 1898, Rutherford's first inclination was to examine thorium substances, since the activity of this element had been noticed only half a year earlier. When a colleague obtained erratic ionization measurements, Rutherford succeeded in tracing the irregularity to a gaseous radioactive product escaping from the thorium; and because he was uncertain of the nature of this product, in 1900 he gave it the deliberately vague name "emanation."

The number of known radioelements was increasing. Rutherford added several more to the list, the next being thorium active deposit, which in time was resolved into thorium A, B, C, and so on. The active deposit, or excited activity, which was laid down on surfaces touched by the decaying emanation, was found by Rutherford because of the apparent breakdown of good insulators and was described in *Philosophical Magazine* just one month after his announcement of the emanation. A curious feature he immediately noticed was that, unlike uranium, thorium, and radium, such materials as thorium emanation, radium emanation, their active deposits, and polonium lost their activities over periods of time. Moreover, the rate of this decrease was unique for each radioelement and thus an ideal identifying label. This meant that an exponential curve could be plotted for the half-life of each radioelement with a discernible decay period, and theory could thereby be compared with experiment.

By this time Rutherford had recognized the need for skilled chemical assistance in this radioactivity investigations and had secured the services of a young chemistry demonstrator at McGill, Frederick Soddy. Together they removed most of the activity from a thorium compound, calling the active matter thorium X; but found that the X product lost its activity and that the thorium recovered its original level in a few weeks. Had Becquerel's similar finding for uranium not been immediately at hand, they might have searched for errors in their work. In early 1902, however, they began to plot the activities as a function of time, seeing evidence of a fundamental relationship in the equality of the time for thorium X to decay to half value and thorium to double in activity.

This work led directly to Rutherford's greatest achievement at McGill, for with Soddy he advanced the still-accepted explanation of radioactivity. Their iconoclastic theory, variously called transformation, transmutation, and disintegration, first appeared in 1902 and was refined in the following year.

Although alchemy had long been exorcised from scientific chemistry, they declared that "radioactivity is at once an atomic phenomenon and the accompaniment of a chemical change in which new kinds of matter are produced." The radioactive atoms decay, they argued, each decay signifying the transmutation of a parent into a daughter element, and each type of atom undergoing its transformation in a characteristic period. This insight set the course for their next several years of research, for the task was then to order all the known radioelements into decay series and to search for additional members of these families.

The theory explained the experimental decay and rise curves as a measure of a radioelement's quantity and half-life. At equilibrium the same number of atoms of a parent transform as the number of atoms of its daughter and its granddaughter, and so on until a stable end product is obtained. But when a chemical process separates members of a series, the parent must regain its former activity as it produces additional daughters while its own numbers are maintained constant, unless it is the very first member of the family—whose numbers can only decrease. The daughter side of a chemical separation, however, is destined only to decay, for there is no means of replenishing its stock of transformed atoms.

Soddy left Montreal in 1903 for London, where he and Ramsay proved spectroscopically that helium is produced during transformations from radium emanation. Such work was highly important, for there were numerous radioelements of which the chemical identity and place in the decay series were uncertain.

Helium, while not a radioelement, was of particular interest because of Rutherford's certainty that, as a positive ion, it was identical with the alpha particle. And the alpha particle, being of ponderable mass, he saw as the key in the change from an element of one atomic weight to an element of another. It fascinated Rutherford also because he could appreciate the enormous speed and energy with which it is ejected from a decaying atom. In 1903 he was able to deflect it in electric and magnetic fields, thereby showing its positive charge, but his

charge-to-mass ratio measurement lacked the precision required to distinguish between a helium atom with two charges and a hydrogen atom with one charge. The proof of the particle's identity awaited Rutherford's transfer to Manchester, although he determined many useful facts about the alpha particle, such as the number emitted per second from one gram of radium, a constant that is the basis for several other important quantities, including the half-life of radium, and in 1906 made another assault upon the e/m ratio.

Halfway between Soddy's departure in 1903 and Otto Hahn's arrival at McGill in 1905, Rutherford found another chemist of comparable skill upon whom he could rely. This was Bertram Boltwood (working at Yale), who had proved circumstantially that uranium and radium are related, thus linking two previously separate decay series, and who in 1907 discovered ionium, the immediate parent of radium, which went far in proving the uranium-radium connection directly.

Boltwood showed the universal occurrence of lead with uranium minerals; considered this the series' final product; and, using Rutherford's value for radium's half-life and their figure for the amount of radium in a gram of uranium, was able to calculate the rate of formation for lead. The ages of some of his rock samples were over a billion years, furnishing for the first time quantitative proof of the antiquity of the earth.

Rutherford's time was also consumed in writing *Radio-Activity*, the first textbook on the subject and recognized as a classic at its publication in 1904.

His nine years at McGill were filled with great work and he received the Nobel Prize for chemistry in 1908.

When Arthur Schuster offered to resign from his chair at the University of Manchester on the condition that Rutherford succeed him, the post and the laboratory were sufficiently attractive for Rutherford to make a move in 1907. Most of his initial investigations at Manchester were extensive studies of radium emanation.

Never one to limit the scope of his investigations—he preferred to advance across radioactivity in a wide path—Rutherford pursued "his" alpha particles. In 1908 he and Geiger were able to fire alpha particles into an evacuated tube containing a central, charged wire and to record single events. Ionization by collision, a process studied by Rutherford's former colleague at Cambridge, J. S. E. Townsend, caused a magnification of the single particle's charge sufficient to give the electrometer a measurable "kick." By this means they were able to count, for the first time accurately and directly, the number of alpha particles emitted per second from a gram of radium.

This experiment enabled Rutherford and Geiger to confirm that every alpha particle causes a faint but discrete flash when it strikes a luminescent zinc sulfide screen, and thus led directly to the widespread method of scintillation counting. It was also the origin of the electrical and electronic methods of particle counting in which Geiger later pioneered. But at this time the scintillation technique, now proved reliable, was more convenient. This counting work also led Rutherford and Geiger to the most accurate value of the fundamental electric charge e before Millikan performed his oildrop experiment. They measured the total charge from a radium source and divided it by the number of alphas counted to obtain the charge per particle. Since this figure was about twice the previous values of *e,* they concluded that the alpha was indeed helium with a double charge.

As in Montreal, Rutherford found chemical help in Manchester of the highest quality. Boltwood spent a year with him, during which time they redetermined more accurately the rate of production of helium by radium. By combining these results with those from the counting experiments, they obtained Avogadro's number more directly than ever before.

Rutherford's greatest discovery at Manchester—in fact, of his career—was of the nuclear structure of the atom.

By the end of 1910, he had begun tying several factors into a new atomic model and theory of scattering. The alpha projectile, he said, changed course in a single encounter with a target atom. But for this to occur, the forces of electrical repulsion (or attraction—it made no difference for the mathematics) had to be concentrated in a region of 10^{-13} centimeters, whereas the atom was known to measure 10^{-8} centimeters. This meant that the atom consisted largely of empty space, with a very tiny and very dense charged nucleus at the center and opposite charges somehow placed in the surrounding void. Rutherford next calculated the probability of such single scattering at a given angle and found his predictions confirmed experimentally by Geiger and Ernest Marsden.

More was yet to come from Rutherford's school concerning the nucleus. Marsden had noticed scintillations on a screen placed far beyond the range of alpha particles when these particles were allowed to bombard hydrogen. Rutherford repeated the experiment and showed that the scintillations were caused by hydrogen nuclei or protons. This was easily understood, but when he substituted nitrogen for the hydrogen, he saw the same proton flashes. The explanation he gave in 1919 stands beside the transformation theory of radioactivity and the nuclear atom as one of his most important discoveries. This, he said, was a case of artificial disintegration of an element. Unstable, or radioactive, atoms disintegrated spontaneously; but here a stable nucleus was disrupted by the alpha particle, and a proton was one of the pieces broken off.

This line of work was to be the major theme for the remainder of Rutherford's career, which he spent at Cambridge from 1919. In that year Thomson was appointed master of Trinity College and decided to resign as director of the Cavendish Laboratory. The postwar period saw great activity in the game of professorial "musical chairs," but to no one's surprise Rutherford was elected as Thomson's successor. With him came James Chadwick, a former research student at Manchester who had spent the war years interned in Germany; he was to become Rutherford's closest collaborator. During the 1920's they determined that a number of light elements could be disintegrated by bombardment with swift alpha particles; as a corollary, they measured the distance of closest approach between projectile and target to ascertain both the size of the nucleus and that the inverse-square force law applied at this small distance.

Not long after the discovery of heavy water in the United States, Rutherford obtained a small quantity of it and in 1934, with Marcus Oliphant and Paul Harteck, bombarded deuterium with deuterons. This reaction was notable for the first achievement of what is now called fusion, as well as for the production of tritium.

RUTHERFURD, LEWIS MORRIS (*b. New York, N.Y., 1816; d. Tranquility, N.J., 1892*), astrophysics.

Studied at Williams College and set up an observatory on the family estate, working on astronomical photography and spectroscopy and sometimes making his own instruments. Produced fine lunar photographs as well as images of Jupiter, Saturn, the sun, and stars of the fifth magnitude. Made spectroscopic studies of the sun, moon, Jupiter, Mars, and sixteen fixed stars. In 1864 he displayed a never-published photograph of the solar spectrum 15 centimeters wide and 78.7 centimeters between lines H and F, and produced diffraction gratings superior to the best then made. He helped Columbia University found its department of geodesy and practical astronomy, donating the equipment of his observatory.

RÜTIMEYER, KARL LUDWIG (*b. Biglen, Bern Canton, Switzerland, 1825; d. Basel, Switzerland, 1895*), vertebrate paleozoology, geography.

Received doctorate in medicine at Bern (1850), where his interests in natural history and geology were stimulated by Studer. He had a distinguished teaching and research career at Basel (1855–93), making significant contributions to the natural history and evolutionary paleontology of ungulate mammals, especially the artiodactyls. His comparative odontography of ungulates (1863) was perhaps the first serious attempt after Darwin's *Origin* to interpret fossil mammals as parts of evolutionary lineages by showing the gradual change in dentitions. His work advanced the study of mammalian evolution and biogeography.

RUYSCH, FREDERIK (*b. The Hague, Netherlands, 1638; d. Amsterdam, Netherlands, 1731*), botany, obstetrics, anatomy, medicine.

Studied medicine at Leiden (M.D., 1664) while managing a chemist's shop in The Hague. Served as praelector of anatomy for the surgeon's guild in Amsterdam (1666–1731), city obstetrician (1672–1712), and doctor of the court of justice (from 1679), and taught botany at the Athenaeum Illustre (from 1685). Conducted serious anatomical studies in addition to his teaching and public dissections, and developed his own method of preserving bodies and organs. In 1743 it was revealed that Ruysch used a mixture of talc, white wax, and cinnabar for injecting vessels, whereas his embalming fluid (liquor balsamicus) consisted of alcohol (prepared from wine or corn) to which some black pepper was added. His collection of 935 preserved items became a major attraction for foreign visitors.

RYDBERG, JOHANNES (JANNE) ROBERT (*b. Halmstad, Sweden, 1854; d. Lund, Sweden, 1919*), mathematics, physics.

Received doctorate (1879) and taught (1880–1919) at the University of Lund. His involvement with spectra had its origin in his interest in the periodic system of the elements. He held that the effective force between atoms must be a periodic function of their atomic weights and that study of the periodic motions of atoms, which presumably gave rise to the spectral lines and were dependent on the effective force, might lead to a better knowledge of the mechanics, nature, and structure of atoms and molecules. His major spectral work was "Recherches sur la constitution des spectres d'émission des éléments chimiques" (1890). He developed the Rydberg formula, similar to that of Balmer, for expressing the wave numbers of the lines in a spectral series. The universal constant in the formula became known as Rydberg's constant. His formula allowed him to note some important relationships: the difference between the common limit of the diffuse and sharp series and the limit of the corresponding principal series gave the wave number of the common first-member term of the sharp and principal series (Rydberg-Schuster law). In 1897 he suggested that certain characteristics of the elements could be more simply organized by using an atomic number instead of atomic weights. The physical reality that underlay Rydberg's atomic-number proposal was later interpreted as the positive charge on the atomic nucleus expressed in elementary units of charge.

SABATIER, ARMAND (*b. Ganges, Hérault, France, 1834; d. Montpellier, Hérault, France, 1910*), comparative anatomy, philosophy.

Received doctorate and taught at University of Montpellier. His *Études sur le coeur et la circulation centrale dans la série des vertébrés. Anatomie, physiologie comparée, philosophie naturelle* (1873) established his reputation as an anatomist. From his research he established the general laws that govern the functional evolution of the heart from fishes to mammals. He founded the Station Zoologique de Sète (1879), one of the earliest marine laboratories.

SABATIER, PAUL (*b. Carcassonne, France, 1854; d. Toulouse, France, 1941*), chemistry.

Received doctorate at the Collège de France (1880). Taught at Toulouse from 1881. Was instrumental in founding three schools of applied science at Toulouse—chemistry, electrical engineering, and agriculture. For his work on hydrogenating organic compounds in the presence of finely disintegrated metals, he received the 1912 Nobel Prize. He demonstrated the general applicability of his method to the hydrogenation of nonsaturated and aromatic carbides, ketones, aldehydes, phenols, nitriles, and nitrate derivatives. His *La catalyse en chimie organique* (1913) set forth his theory of catalytic mechanism, later termed "chemisorption."

SABIN, FLORENCE RENA (*b. Central City, Colo., 1871; d. Denver, Colo., 1953*), anatomy, immunology.

Received B.S. at Smith College (1893) and M.D. at Johns Hopkins Medical School (1900) under the strong influence of Franklin P. Mall. First woman faculty member at Johns Hopkins (1902–25). *An Atlas of the Medulla and Midbrain* (1901), a three-dimensional model of the mid- and lower brain, quickly became a popular text. In work on the origin of the lymphatics, she showed that they arose from the veins directly, by a series of small endothelial buds. In 1925 she established a laboratory at the Rockefeller Institute in New York devoted to the cellular aspects of the immune response. After retiring to Denver (1938), she worked for the passage of new health laws in Colorado.

SABINE, EDWARD (*b. Dublin, Ireland, 1788; d. Richmond, Surrey, England, 1883*), geophysics.

Graduated from the Royal Military Academy, Woolwich. Accompanied John Ross on expedition seeking Northwest Passage (1818) and was with William Edward Parry on his 1819–20 Arctic expedition. Sent by Royal Society on pendulum expedition in 1821–22 around the Atlantic to determine the true figure of the earth. His work was of a Humboldtian nature—the gathering and analysis of geophysical data on a large, even global, scale. In the 1830's Sabine, Humphrey Lloyd, James Clark Ross, and others completed the magnetic survey of the British Isles; Sabine repeated it in 1858–61. He was distinguished by his successful promotion and administration of a world-wide effort to gather terrestrial magnetism observations, designated the "magnetic crusade." He had a key role in the British dispatching an expedition to the southern hemisphere and establishing a network of magnetic and meteorological observatories. He was active in the management of the Kew observatory, which became a leading center of geophysics. His publication of known intensity observations in the world (1837) enabled Gauss to do requisite calculations for the *Allgemeine Theorie*. In 1851 Sabine discovered the relation between Schwabe's sunspot cycle and the periodicity of magnetic storms, and announced his important finding that the daily magnetic variation consists of two superimposed variations, one deriving from within and the other from outside the earth.

SABINE, PAUL EARLS (*b. Albion, Ill., 1879; d. Colorado Springs, Colo., 1958*), acoustics.

Received baccalaureate (1903), master's (1911) and doctorate (1915) at Harvard. Taught at Worcester Academy (1903–10) and Case School of Applied Science in Cleveland (1916–18). Director of acoustical research at the Wallace Clement Sabine Laboratory of Acoustics (Riverbank Laboratory) in Geneva, Illinois (1919–47). The bulk of his work followed directly from that of his cousin, Wallace (1868–1919). The Riverbank Laboratory had been built for Wallace's use in determining the sound-absorptive properties of architectural materials as well as the sound absorption and transmission characteristics of architectural elements and types of construction. Sabine was also active as an acoustical consultant to architects, notably in the design of Radio City Music Hall and Fels Planetarium, and in remodeling the U.S. Capitol Building.

SABINE, WALLACE CLEMENT WARE (*b. Richwood, Ohio, 1868; d. Cambridge, Mass., 1919*), physics.

Received A.B. at Ohio State University (1886) and M.A. at Harvard (1888); taught at Harvard (1890–1917). Turned architectural acoustics from a qualitative, rule-of-thumb practice into a quantitative engineering science. He managed, with the ingenious use of graphs, to derive an acoustical law of general applicability. He showed that the product of the reverberation time and the summed absorptive power of the walls, furnishings, and materials of appointment equaled a constant; and that this constant was directly proportional to the volume of the room. The formula enabled him to predict the acoustical properties of an auditorium in advance of construction. In his honor, the unit of sound-absorbing power is called the sabin.

SACCHERI, (GIOVANNI) GIROLAMO (*b. San Remo, Italy, 1667; d. Milan, Italy, 1733*), mathematics.

Received Jesuit education; ordained at Como (1694); taught at Turin, Jesuit College of Pavia, and the University of Pavia (1699–1733). His two most important works were *Logica demonstrativa* (1697) and *Euclides ab omni naevo vindicatus* (1733). *Logica* is divided into four parts corresponding to Aristotle's *Analytica priora, Analytica posteriora, Topica,* and *De sophisticis Elenchis,* and treats questions relating to the compatibility of definitions. He was one of the first to draw explicit attention to the question of consistency and compatibility of axioms. In the *Euclides* Saccheri applied his type of *reductio ad absurdum* to Euclid's parallel axiom. He took as true Euclid's first twenty-six propositions and then assumed that the fifth postulate was false. Among the consequences of this hypothesis he sought a proposition to test the postulate itself. He found it in what is now called the quadrilateral of Saccheri. He was a precursor of the discoverers of non-Euclidean geometry.

SACCO, LUIGI (*b. Varese, Lombardy, Italy, 1769; d. Milan, Italy, 1836*), medicine.

Obtained degree in medicine and surgery at University of Pavia (1792). Practiced medicine in Milan. Following Jenner's publication of his work on cowpox inoculation, Sacco found a spontaneous cowpox stock in the neighborhood of Varese and began inoculating people in many regions of Italy. In 1809 he published *Trattato di vaccinazione,* presenting the important conclusions from his ample statistics. His stock was also sent to Vienna, Baghdad, and the East Indies.

SACHS, JULIUS VON (*b. Breslau, Silesia [now Wrocław, Poland], Germany, 1832; d. Würzburg, Germany, 1897*), botany, plant physiology.

Received Ph.D. at Prague (1856), where he was personal assistant to the physiologist Purkyně and was strongly influenced by Zimmermann. He was the first to teach plant physiology at a Germany university (Prague, 1857–59); also taught at agricultural colleges in Tharandt and Poppelsdorf, at Freiburg im Breisgau, and at Würzburg (1868–97). The field of plant physiology became developed only through his work, which extended to nearly all branches of the subject. He discovered the transformation of oil into starch in *Ricinus* seeds; investigated the culture of plants in pure nutrient solution; discovered the corrosive action of roots on marble slabs; studied the influence of temperature on life processes; and discovered the law of "cardinal points," according to which each vital process has a minimum, an optimum, and a maximum temperature that are mutually related. He demonstrated that starch in the chloroplasts is the first visible product of assimilation and that carbon dioxide assimilation (photosynthesis) actually occurs in chloroplasts. His studies of growth and its mechanisms in roots and shoots led to the discovery of the "great period of growth." He also devoted attention to plant tropisms and to the transport of nutrients and water. He invented or substantially improved many devices that were long prominent in botany laboratories, and was responsible for innovations in experimental technique. His books were long the definitive works in plant physiology, giving results both of his own research and of that of many contemporaries, such as Hofmeister and Naegeli.

SACROBOSCO, JOHANNES DE (or **John of Holywood**) (*b. Holywood, Yorkshire, England, end of twelfth century; d. Paris, France, 1256 [1244?]*), astronomy.

Very little is known of his life; it is commonly held that he was educated at Oxford. Entered orders and became canon regular at monastery of Holywood in Nithsdale. About 1220 went to Paris, where he eventually became an outstanding mathematician and astronomer at the university. His chief extant works are elementary textbooks on mathematics and astronomy. His fame rests on his *De sphaera* (*ca.* 1220), a small work based on Ptolemy and his Arabic commentators. It was quite generally adopted as the fundamental astronomy text, and from the middle of the thirteenth century it was taught in all the schools of Europe, still being used as late as the seventeenth century. It often appeared with commentaries by the most distinguished scholars of the time. His *De computo ecclesiastico* deals with the division of time—marked out by the movements of the sun and moon and their interrelationship—into days and years. *De algorismo* discusses the art of calculating with nonnegative integers, and examines numeration, addition, subtraction, mediation, duplication, multiplication, division, progression, and extraction of both the square and cube roots of numbers.

AL-ṢADAFĪ. *See* **Ibn Yūnus, Abu'l-Ḥasan ꜥAlī ibn ꜥAbd al-Raḥmān ibn Aḥmad ibn Yūnus al-Ṣadafī.**

SAGE, BALTHAZAR-GEORGES (*b. Paris, France, 1740; d. Paris, 1824*), metallurgy, assaying, chemistry.

Studied at the Collège des Quatre Nations and attended public lectures by Nollet and Rouelle. At the family pharmacy he gave public lectures in chemistry and assaying, also beginning his extensive mineral collection. His publications and teaching showed his dubious qualifications as a chemist—he continued to believe in the reality of phlogiston, and opposed Lavoisier's new chemistry. The creation of the Paris École des Mines is his major claim to distinction. He served as director and professor of mineralogy for at least seven years, but in his teaching there was no trace of the classification made possible by recent advances in chemistry and by the new crystallography of Haüy. He made a few minor chemical discoveries.

SAGNAC, GEORGES M. M. (*b. Périgueux, France, 1869; d. Meudon, France, 1928*), physics.

Studied at the École Normale Supérieure and at University of Paris (doctorate, 1900); taught at Lille (1900–11) and at Paris (from 1911). He worked mainly on the radiation produced by X rays and the optics of interference. He is remembered today mainly for his design of a rotating interferometer and for the experimental results it provided. In the theoretical analysis of optics of moving systems his approach was classical, and he interpreted the results of his optical experiments as contradicting Einstein's theory of relativity.

SAHA, MEGHNAD (*b. Scoratali, Dacca district, India [now Bangladesh], 1894; d. New Delhi, India, 1956*), theoretical physics.

Studied at Calcutta Presidency College (M.A., 1915; D.Sc, 1918); taught at the University College of Science (1916–19), University of Allahabad (1923–38), and University of Calcutta (from 1938). His work on thermal ionization was the starting point of modern astrophysics. By boldly applying thermodynamics and quantum theory to stellar matter and by drawing an analogy between chemical dissociation and atomic ionization, he derived a formula by which the degree of ionization in a very hot gas could be expressed in terms of its temperature and electron pressure (1920). At Calcutta he created an institute of nuclear physics. In 1935 he founded the journal *Science and Culture.*

IBN AL-ṢAʾIGH. *See* **Ibn Bājja, Abū Bakr Muḥammad ibn Yaḥyā ibn al-Ṣāʾigh.**

SAINTE-MESME, MARQUIS DE. *See* **L'Hospital (L'Hôpital), Guillaume-François-Antoine de.**

SAINT-HILAIRE, AUGUSTIN FRANÇOIS CÉSAR PROUVENÇAL (usually known as **Auguste de**) (*b. Orléans, France, 1779; d. La Turpinière, near Sennely, Loiret, France, 1853*), natural history.

Surveyed the flora and fauna of Brazil for six years, returning to Paris with 24,000 plants, 2,000 birds, 16,000 insects, 135 quadrupeds, and many reptiles, fishes, and minerals to classify. He published *Flora Brasiliae meridionalis* (1825–33) and other works on his travels, including several diaries.

ST. JOHN, CHARLES EDWARD (*b. Allen, Mich., 1857; d. Pasadena, Calif., 1935*), astronomy.

Received B.S. from Michigan Agricultural College (1887) and Ph.D. at Harvard (1896). Taught at Oberlin College (1897–1908), spending summers at the Yerkes Observatory with George Ellery Hale; and joined the Mount Wilson Observatory (1908–30). His research was mainly in solar physics. His principal contribution was his *Revision of Rowland's Preliminary Table of Solar Spectrum Wavelengths, With an Extension to the Present Limit of the Infra-Red,* with Moore, Ware, Adams, and Babcock (1928). He paid particular attention to the problem of measuring the relativistic deflection of the lines in the solar spectrum.

SAINT-VENANT, ADHÉMAR JEAN CLAUDE BARRÉ DE (*b. Villiers-en-Bière, Seine-et-Marne, France, 1797; d. St.-Ouen, Loir-et-Cher, France, 1886*), mechanics, geometry.

Graduated from the École Polytechnique; joined the Service des Poudres et Salpêtres, transferring to the Service des Ponts et Chaussées (1823–43). Spent rest of life teaching and doing research. His investigations deal chiefly with the mechanics of solid bodies, elasticity, hydrostatics, and hydrodynamics, frequently with immediate applications to road- and bridge-building, control of streams, and agriculture. He set forth a vector calculus displaying certain analogies with the conceptions of Grassmann. His lectures on this vector calculus at the Institut Agronomique were published as *Principes de mécanique fondés sur la cinématique* (1851).

ST. VICTOR, HUGH OF. *See* **Hugh of St. Victor.**

SAINT VINCENT, GREGORIUS (*b. Bruges, Belgium, 1584; d. Ghent, Belgium, 1667*), mathematics, astronomy.

Studied at various Jesuit colleges; was ordained in 1613 at Louvain. Taught at several schools, including Antwerp, Louvain, and Ghent. Elaborated the theory of conic sections on the basis of Commandino's editions of Archimedes, Apollonius, and Pappus. Developed a fruitful method of infinitesimals and was recognized as one of the great pioneers in infinitesimal analysis. His major work, *Opus geometricum quadraturae circuli et sectionum coni* (1647), included introductory theorems on the circle and on triangles as well as geometrically clothed algebraic transformations; sums of geometric series; books on the circle, ellipse, parabola, and hyperbola; and Gregorius' remarkable quadrature method—a summation procedure related to the method of indivisibles developed by Cavalieri. Another section is devoted to the quadrature of the circle.

SAKHAROV, VLADIMIR VLADIMIROVICH (*b. Simbirsk [now Ulyanovsk], Russia, 1902; d. Moscow, U.S.S.R., 1969*), genetics.

Graduated from the Second Moscow State University (1926). Combined teaching and research at the Institute of Experimental Biology (1929–48), Moscow Pharmaceutical Institute (1950–56), Laboratory of Radiation Genetics of the Institute of Biophysics (1956–65), Laboratory of Polyploids of the Institute of General Genetics (1966–67), Institute of Biology of Development (1967–69), and the Timiryazev Institute of Plant Physiology. His research was basically in experimental chemical mutagenesis, polyploids, radiation genetics, and human genetics. He discovered the role of factors inherent in the mutational process (aging of sperm, hibernation, inbreeding, and hybridization). He did a comparative study of sensitivity of diploid and autotetraploid forms to the action of radiation and chemical mutagenesis (for example, on buckwheat and meadow brown butterflies), discovering the physiological protection of polyploids against the influence of mutagenesis.

SAKS, STANISŁAW (*b. Warsaw, Poland, 1897; d. Warsaw, 1942*), mathematics.

Received doctorate from the Polish University of Warsaw (1921). A member of the Polish school of mathematics that flourished between the two world wars, he taught at Warsaw Technical University (1921–39) and the University of Warsaw (1926–39). Most of his research involved the theory of real functions and the properties of Denjoy-Perron integrals. He wrote two important books: *Théorie de l'intégrale* (1933), which systematically developed the theory of integration and differentiation from the standpoint of countably additive set functions; and *Funkcje analityczne* (1938), which has become a standard reference work on complex analysis.

SALA, ANGELO (Angelus) (*b. Vicenza, Italy [?], 1576; d. Bützow, Germany, 1637*), pharmaceutics, chemistry, medicine.

Little is known of his education. He practiced medicine in a number of cities, settling in The Hague in 1612, where he also taught chemistry to medical students from various countries. From 1617 to 1620 he was physician to the Count of Oldenburg, and later to the rulers of Mecklenburg. His chemical ideas proved to be historically influential. He performed the earliest known experiment in which a synthesis was confirmed by analysis. Closely connected with his conception of the constitution of vitriol out of constituent parts is his notion that the possibility of *reductio* is proof that no genuine transmutation has occurred.

SALERNITAN ANATOMISTS (*fl. eleventh to thirteenth centuries, Salerno, Italy*), anatomy.

The contribution made by the school of anatomists at Salerno followed the arid millennium in the history of anatomy that began after the death of Galen (A.D. 199/200). The situation changed radically with the arrival at Salerno of Constantine the African (*d.* 1087), translator of numerous works from the Arabic. By the mid-eleventh century Salerno was rapidly approaching its zenith as the undisputed center of medical teaching in the Western world. An annual public demonstration of porcine anatomy became a traditional occurrence, with publication of four dissections in particular having great influence. The first, *Anatomia porci*, attributed to a Master Copho (*fl. ca.* 1080–1115), served as a working tool in book form from 1502 to 1655. The second pig dissection, the *Demonstratio anatomica*, has been attributed to Master Bartholomaeus (*fl.* first half of twelfth century); the third, *Anatomia mauri*, to Master Maurus (*d.* 1214); and the fourth to Urso of Calabria, whose Scholastic method and terminology excluded any practical approach to the subject.

SALISBURY, ROLLIN DANIEL (*b. Spring Prairie, Wis., 1858; d. Chicago, Ill., 1922*), geology, physical geography.

Received bachelor's degree at Beloit College (1881). Taught at Beloit (1884–91), Wisconsin (1891–92), and Chicago (1892–1922). Best known for collaboration with T. C. Chamberlin on geological textbooks that profoundly influenced the growth of the earth sciences during the first third of the twentieth century. His field studies, especially in Wisconsin, New Jersey, and Greenland, contributed notably to the then new science of glaciology.

SALLO, DENYS DE (*b. Paris, France, 1626; d. Paris, 1669*), scientific journalism.

Details of Sallo's life are scarce; he was educated at the Collège des Grassins and studied law. In 1664 he began preparing the first scholarly periodical, *Journal des sçavans;* it was an international record of new books, a readable and critical account of current writings, with reports of current scientific and technological developments. Jean Gallois took over its publication in 1666.

SALMON, GEORGE (*b. Cork, Ireland, 1819; d. Dublin, Ireland, 1904*), mathematics.

Graduated from Trinity College, Dublin (1838), and taught there from 1841, becoming head of the divinity school in 1866 and provost in 1888. His chief fame rests on his series of mathematics textbooks that appeared between 1848 and 1862 on conic sections, higher plane curves, modern higher algebra, and the geometry of three dimensions. He played an important part in the applications of the theory of invariants and covariants of algebraic forms to the geometry of curves and surfaces. He exchanged voluminous mathematical correspondence with Cayley and Sylvester.

SALOMONSEN, CARL JULIUS (*b. Copenhagen, Denmark, 1847; d. Copenhagen, 1924*), medicine, bacteriology.

Received M.D. (1871) at Copenhagen. His thesis, "Studier over Blodets Forraadnelse," became the fundamental starting point for the study of bacteriology in Denmark and gave effective support to the school of Ferdinand Cohn, who maintained that the bacteria were distinct species. He practiced medicine and traveled extensively, meeting many influential scientists, and taught at Copenhagen (from 1883). Was responsible for creation of the State Serum Institute (1902), directing it until 1909. Was a cofounder (1907) of the Danish Museum for the History of Medicine. In 1885 he published his important textbook, *Ledetraad i Bakteriologisk Teknik.* In his various bacteriological researches, he studied the relationship between bacteria and pyemic processes; demonstrated the specificity of tuberculosis (1878, with Cohnheim); investigated immunity, diphtheria, and anthrax; reformed vaccination procedures in Denmark; and showed the physiological effects of radium on amoebas and trypanosomes. He also worked for the improvement of education.

SALVIANI, IPPOLITO (*b. Citta di Castello*[*?*]*, Italy, 1514; d. 1572*), medicine, natural history.

Little known of his life; served as papal physician. Published one successful medical book, *De crisibus ad Galeni censuram* (1556); better known for his monumental work on natural science, *De piscibus tomi duo* (1554?). The latter describes, in two folio volumes, the fishes of the Mediterranean and is accompanied by beautiful copper engravings by various contemporary artists.

AL-SAMARQANDĪ, NAJĪB AL-DĪN ABŪ ḤAMID MUḤAMMAD IBN ᶜALĪ IBN ᶜUMAR (*d. Herat, Afghanistan, 1222*), medicine, materia medica.

Little known of his life; practiced medicine. Most important medical work is *al-Asbāb wa'l-ᶜalāmāt* ("Etiology and Symptoms [of Diseases]"). In his works he displayed originality in not considering the theory of humors of decisive importance in therapeutics.

AL-SAMARQANDĪ, SHAMS AL-DĪN MUḤAMMAD IBN ASHRAF AL-ḤUSAYNĪ (*b. Samarkand, Uzbekistan, Russia, fl. 1276*), mathematics, logic, astronomy.

A noted logician, best known to mathematicians for his *Kitāb Ashkāl al-taᵓsīs* ("Book on the Fundamental Theorems"). Became famous for his book on dialectics, *Risāla fī ādāb al-baḥth* ("Tract on the Methods of Enquiry").

AL-SAMAWᵓAL, IBN YAḤYĀ AL-MAGHRIBĪ (*b. Baghdad, Iraq; d. Marāgha, Iran* [*?*]*, ca. 1180*), mathematics, medicine.

Studied medicine with Abu'l-Barakāt; taught himself mathematics. His only extant medical work is *Nuzhat al-aṣḥāb* ("The Companions' Promenade in the Garden of Love"), a treatise on sexology and a collection of erotic stories. He describes diseases and sexual deficiencies, states of virile debility, and diseases of the uterus and their treatment. His fame as a mathematician stems from his book on algebra, *Al-bāhir* ("The Dazzling"). In it he brought together the algebraic rules formulated by, in particular, al-Karajī. The first part provides an account of operations on polynomials in one unknown with rational coefficients; he was the first Arab algebraist to undertake the study of relative numbers. The second part deals with second-degree equations, indeterminate analysis, and summations. The third is chiefly concerned with the classification of irrationals found in Book X of Euclid's *Elements.* The fourth presents the application of algebraic principles to a number of problems.

SAMOYLOV, ALEKSANDR FILIPPOVICH (*b. Odessa, Ukraine, Russia, 1867; d. Kazan, U.S.S.R., 1930*), physiology, electrophysiology, electrocardiography.

Studied at Novorossysk University; received M.D. at Dorpat (1891). From 1892 to 1903 worked in laboratories of Pavlov, Sechenov, Ludimar Hermann, Nagel, and von Kries. Taught at Kazan (from 1903) and Moscow (from 1924). Conducted more than 120 original experimental and theoretical investigations in electrophysiology, physiology of sense organs, clinical physiology, and history of science. Made improvements in methods of string galvanometry. With Einthoven, laid the foundations for clinical and theoretical electrocardiography.

SAMPSON, RALPH ALLEN (*b. Skull, County Cork, Ireland, 1866; d. Bath, England, 1939*), astronomy.

Graduated from St. John's College, Cambridge (1888); studied astronomical spectroscopy with Newall. Taught at University of Durham (1893–1910); astronomer royal for Scotland and professor at Edinburgh (from 1910). In "A Discussion of the Eclipses of Jupiter's Satellites 1878–1903" (1909) he developed a new theory for the motions of the four satellites, and in 1910 he published *Tables of the Four Great Satellites of Jupiter.* His tables have since formed the basis for computing the phenomena for the national ephemerides.

SANARELLI, GIUSEPPE (*b. Monte San Savino, Italy, 1864; d. Rome, Italy, 1940*), hygiene.

Obtained degree in medicine and surgery at University of Siena (1889). Taught at Siena, Bologna, and Rome; set up institute of experimental hygiene at University of Montevideo. Did important research on pathogenesis of typhoid fever and cholera; study of choleraic algidity led to his discovery (1916) of the hemorrhagic allergy, or "Sanarelli's phenomenon." Was first to propose concept of hereditary immunity to tuberculosis. Isolated *Bacterium icteroides,* earliest discovered (1897) human exit-paratyphoid. Pioneered in field of nasal vaccination (1924).

SANCHEZ (or **SANCHES**), **FRANCISCO** (*b. diocese of Braga, Portugal, ca. 1550; d. Toulouse, France, 1623*), philosophy, medicine.

Received doctorate in medicine at Montpellier (1574). Taught philosophy (from 1585) and medicine (from 1612) at Toulouse; director of Hospital of Saint Jacques. He was a shrewd clinical observer in the Hippocratic tradition; his anatomical works show the influence of Colombo, Vesalius, and Falloppio. His major philosophical work, *Quod nihil scitur* (1576), attacked the Aristotelian concept of science for being too abstract and the syllogistic method of doing science as self-fulfilling. In 1577 he extended his skeptical critique to astrology, in a long versified comment on the hysterical reactions to the comet of that year.

SANCTORIUS. *See* **Santorio, Santorio.**

SANDERSON, EZRA DWIGHT (*b. Clio, Mich., 1878; d. Ithaca, N.Y., 1944*), entomology, rural sociology.

Received B.S. at Michigan Agriculture College (1897) and Cornell (1898), and Ph.D. in sociology at Chicago (1921). Between 1899 and 1915 held various academic and entomological positions in Delaware, Texas, New Hampshire, and West Virginia. His fundamental and pioneering entomological researches appeared in the *Journal of Economic Entomology,* which he helped establish, and are considered landmarks in the development of insect ecology. From 1918 to 1943 he headed the Rural Social Organization at Cornell, attracting many graduate students to the cause of rural sociology and providing guidelines for ameliorating the plight of many rural communities.

SANDERSON, JOHN S. B. *See* **Burdon-Sanderson, John Scott.**

SANIO, KARL GUSTAV (*b. Lyck, East Prussia [now Elk, Poland], 1832; d. Lyck, 1891*), botany.

Studied at Berlin and Königsberg (Ph.D., 1858). Conducted botanical research in Lyck after 1858. His work mainly concerned ferns, the Characae, the moss genus *Drepanocladus (Harpidium),* and, most importantly, the anatomy of wood. He gave a classic explanation of the structure and development of cork, explained the formation of annual rings, and established the first table for identifying woods on the basis of anatomical features (1863).

SANTORINI, GIOVANNI DOMENICO (*b. Venice, Italy, 1681; d. Venice, 1737*), medicine, anatomy.

Studied at Bologna, Padua, and Pisa; doctorate, 1701. Outstanding anatomist of his time, carefully dissecting and delineating many difficult gross features of the human body. His name has been given to some of these structures, such as the arytenoid cartilages, the risorius muscle, and the *plexus pudendalis venosus.*

SANTORIO, SANTORIO, also known as **Sanctorius** (*b. Justinopolis, Venetian Republic [now Koper, Yugoslavia], 1561; d. Venice, Italy, 1636*), medicine, physiology, invention of measuring instruments.

Obtained doctor's degree at the Archilyceum of Padua (1582). After twelve years in Croatia, he established a medical practice in Venice (1599). His first book, *Methodi vitandorum errorum omnium qui in arte medica contingunt* (1602), was a comprehensive study on how to avoid making errors in healing. From 1611 to 1624 he taught at Padua. As professor of theoretical medicine, he published most of his own views in the restricted form of scholarly commentaries on Galen, Hippocrates, and Ibn Sīnā. His creed was that one must believe first in one's own senses and experience, then in reasoning, and only then in the authority of the ancients. His most famous work is *De statica medicina* (1614), a short work on the variation in weight experienced by the human body as a result of ingestion and excretion. His great achievement was the introduction of quantitative experimentation into biological science. With the aid of a chair scale, he systematically observed daily variations in the weight of his body and showed that a large part of excretion takes place invisibly through the skin and lungs (*perspiratio in-*

sensibilis). He invented instruments to measure ambient humidity and temperature; he was the first to add a scale to the thermoscope, transforming it into a thermometer. Among his other measuring instruments and medical devices were a hygrometer, a pendulum for measuring pulse rate, a trocar, a special syringe for extracting bladder stones, and a bathing bed. After returning to Venice (1624) he published his commentaries on Ibn Sīnā's *Canon (Commentaria in primam fen primi libri Canonis Avicennae,* 1625), which revealed the principles of construction of various instruments. Undoubtedly inspired by the ideas of Galileo, Santorio opened the way to a mathematical and experimental analysis of physiological and pathological phenomena.

SAPORTA, LOUIS CHARLES JOSEPH GASTON DE (*b. St. Zacharie, France, 1823; d. St. Zacharie, 1896*), paleobotany.

Saporta's interest in botany was encouraged by Adolphe Brongniart, and he devoted his initial research to the Tertiary flora of France. His subsequent publications on Mesozoic flora brought his services into demand, and he traveled to Belgium, Portugal, Greece, and the United States. In other major publications he gave a synoptic view of the stages through which vegetation on earth had passed. In his work he attempted both to give a precise description of a species and to relate it to historical developments; he was particularly concerned with elucidating climatic conditions of an era.

SARPI, PAOLO (*b. Venice, Italy, 1552; d. Venice, 1623*), natural philosophy, theology.

A member of the Servite Order, Sarpi received the degree of doctor of theology at Padua (1578). Served as procurator general in Rome, and state theologian and adviser to the Venetian Senate. Chiefly remembered now for his highly biased *Istoria del Concilio Tridentino* (1619), Sarpi was well versed in works of all the Scholastic philosophers. His *Arte di ben pensare,* in which he distinguishes between sensation and reflection and examines the relationship of the senses to cognition, anticipated Locke's *Essay Concerning Human Understanding.* Although Sarpi was highly praised for his mathematical and speculative abilities by his contemporaries, all that remains by which one can judge his originality are some letters and notebooks. The notebooks consist of more than 600 chronologically annotated entries touching upon every aspect of contemporary science, from the corpuscular nature of light to an enumeration of the properties of conic sections. Of particular interest are his ideas on optical relativity, his negation of the concept of absolute rest, correct interpretation of the function of the venous valves, and discovery of circulation of the blood—for which Harvey later provided experimental proof.

SARS, MICHAEL (*b. Bergen, Norway, 1805; d. Christiania [Oslo], Norway, 1869*), marine biology.

Studied theology and received candidate's degree in 1828. From 1828 to 1854 served as teacher, vicar, and later rector of seashore communities, often traveling by boat and devoting much of his time to zoological studies. Taught zoology at University of Christiania (1854–69). Natural history study trips to Holland, France, Germany, Prague, Denmark, Sweden, the Mediterranean and the Adriatic increased his knowledge and brought him in contact with the leading zoologists of Europe. One of the fathers of marine zoology, from 1830 to 1860 he made what is perhaps the greatest single contribution to the elucidation of the life cycles of marine invertebrates. His findings on the alternation of generations in coelenterates were among the most important evidence for Steenstrup's classical work. Sars's numerous discoveries of deep-sea organisms by dredging were a sensation in his day because it had been universally assumed that the depths of the ocean where light did not penetrate were without life. His exciting results led to the conception and organization of the *Challenger* and other deep-sea expeditions.

SARTON, GEORGE ALFRED LÉON (*b. Ghent, Belgium, 1884; d. Cambridge, Mass., 1956*), history of science.

Graduated from University of Ghent (D.Sc., 1911). Sarton was the first deliberate architect of the history of science as an independent and organized discipline. The transition from his dawning conviction of the importance of a passionate history of the physical sciences to the systematic work of equipping a new discipline with tools and standards, and more especially the transition to paid employment in an as-yet-nonexistent profession, was to prove slow and complex. While still in Ghent (1912), he founded *Isis,* his *"Revue consacrée à l'histoire de la science,"* recruiting a distinguished editorial board of scientists, historians, sociologists, and historians of philosophy. The journal provided Sarton with the first institutional tool he needed. To Sarton himself the creation of the history of science as a discipline was only preliminary and minor compared with achieving the "new humanism," the holistic and all-embracing synthesis which would be based on a just appreciation of science in history.

The German invasion of Belgium in 1914 forced him to abandon his library and notes and flee to London and then the United States. In the U.S., due to the strong influence of Robert S. Woodward and L. J. Henderson, he began a lifelong association with the Carnegie Institution and an unpaid appointment at Harvard. Secure in the great Widener Library at Harvard, with his salary guaranteed by Carnegie, and with his notes retrieved from Belgium, he began his most ambitious and significant work. The first volume of *Introduction to the History of Science* appeared in 1927, the final volume in 1948, but its chronological survey reached only as far as A.D. 1400; it deals with the emergence and growth of positive knowledge by means of contemporaneous surveys across all disciplines, races, and cultures, and by systematic division into half-century time units. Critical bibliography was another essential basis of the work—hence the deliberate cross-linking of information with that contained in *Isis* (and its later occasional fellow-journal *Osiris*). Among his other many publications were two volumes of the projected eight-volume *History of Science,* from antiquity to the present: *Ancient Science Through the Golden Age of Greece* (1952) and *Hellenistic Science and Culture in the Last Three Centuries B.C.* (1959). Sarton came to epitomize the history of science to both European and American audiences and automatically served as the central reference point for the ideal type of historian of science as researcher, scholar, and teacher. He opened the way for Koyré to have a major impact on the first generation of

American "professional" historians of science. His presence at Harvard was crucial to the later creation of a department that is now one of the world's major centers of the history of science.

SARYCHEV, GAVRIIL ANDREEVICH (*b. St. Petersburg, Russia, 1763; d. St. Petersburg, 1831*), hydrography.

Entered Naval Cadet Corps in Kronstadt (1775), commissioned in 1781; became hydrographer-general (1808) and admiral (1829). With Joseph Billings participated in extensive surveying expedition to northeastern Siberia, the Aleutian Islands, and the shores of North America (1785–93). Beginning in 1802 spent many years surveying the Baltic Sea. Among his publications is his great achievement, "Atlas of the Northern Part of the Eastern Ocean" (1826).

ŚATĀNANDA (*fl. India, 1099*), astronomy.

Wrote the *Bhāsvatī* in 1099 on the basis of Varāhamihira's summary of Lāṭadeva's recension of the *Sūryasiddhānta*. The *Bhāsvatī* was instrumental in spreading this version of the *Sūryasiddhānta* throughout northern and, especially, eastern India, as can be seen from the existence of numerous manuscripts, commentaries, and editions.

SATŌ NOBUHIRO (*b. Ugo [now Akita] prefecture, Japan, 1769; d. Edo [now Tokyo], Japan, 1850*); **SATŌ NOBUKAGE** (*b. Nishimonai, 1674; d. Nishimonai, 1732*); **SATŌ NOBUSUE** (*b. 1724; d. 1784*), mining, agriculture, economics.

The Satō family served the feudal lords of Ugo as physicians. Their concern with agricultural subjects led Satō Nobusue and his father, Satō Nobukage, to study agricultural administration and natural science. They wrote works on agricultural management and mining. Their accomplishments can be understood only in the context of the secrecy in which science and technology were held in feudal Japan. Knowledge was jealously guarded and mostly passed on orally from father to son. Satō Nobusue's son, Satō Nobuhiro, studied science in Edo and published the knowledge accumulated by the Satō family. His best-known work concerns mining, describing a method for predicting the presence of ores, methods for refining ores, and management of mines, with particular emphasis on the well-being of miners. In another work he presented a system for the management of the whole civil state. He was a popularizer of western thought and wrote the first Japanese works on western science and history.

SAURIN, JOSEPH (*b. Courthézon, Vaucluse, France, 1659; d. Paris, France, 1737*), mathematics, mechanics, cosmology.

Turned from the ministry to mathematics, which he studied and then taught. Mathematics editor for the *Journal des sçavans* (1702); member of Academy of Sciences (1707). Made no original contributions to mathematics. Rather, firmly committed to the new infinitesimal calculus, he explored the limits and possibilities of its methods and defended it against criticism based on lack of understanding. His study of multivalued curves became the basis for correcting Guisnée's and Crousaz's misunderstanding of the nature of extreme values and of their

expression in the new calculus. He defended Huygens' theory of the pendulum against Parent and Liouville.

SAUSSURE, HORACE BÉNÉDICT DE (*b. near Geneva [Conches], 1740; d. Geneva, 1799*), geology, meteorology, botany, education.

Graduated from University of Geneva (1759); taught at Academy of Geneva (1762–86). His passion for mountains led to extensive alpine investigations that he described in his *Voyages dans les Alpes, précédés d'un essai sur l'histoire naturelle des environs de Genève* (4 vols., 1779–96). He abstracted and grouped the results of his journeys into three sections, of which one concerned his work in the area of Mont Blanc, another his trips through the Mont Cenis pass to the Italian and French Rivieras and his return through Provence, and the last his numerous expeditions to the area of the Gries, the St. Gotthard, and the Italian lakes. The success of his expedition on Mont Blanc won him an international reputation. With his son, Nicolas-Théodore, he made meteorological, geological, and topological observations on Mont Blanc, the Col du Géant, and on Monte Rosa. In his theory of the earth he came close to an accurate understanding of the structure of the Alps. His dedicated work was of great importance in the development of geology since, among other things, it provided James Hutton with fundamental documentation. In addition, he devised a number of useful instruments and performed some experiments on the fusion of granites and porphyries that entitled him to be considered the first experimental petrologist.

SAUSSURE, NICOLAS-THÉODORE DE (*b. Geneva, Switzerland, 1767; d. Geneva, 1845*), chemistry, plant physiology.

Son of Horace-Bénédict de Saussure. Assisted his father in making meteorological and barometric observations on expeditions to Mont Blanc, the Col du Géant, and Monte Rosa. Became passionately interested in chemistry and plant physiology, and accumulated original observations, particularly on the mineral nutrition of plants. Published three remarkable articles on carbonic acid and its formation in plant tissues (1797) and an important study of the role of soil in the development of plants, which brought him recognition of his fellow scientists. His *Recherches chimiques sur la végétation* (1804) laid the foundations of phytochemistry. He examined the chief active components of plants, their synthesis, and their decomposition. He specified the relationships between vegetation and the environment, doing pioneering work in the fields of pedology and ecology. He published a series of important articles (from 1808) devoted to a rigorous analysis of biochemical reactions occurring in the plant cell. He was a founding member of the Société Helvétique des Sciences Naturelles (1815).

SAUVAGEAU, CAMILLE-FRANÇOIS (*b. Angers, Maine-et-Loire, France, 1861; d. Vitrac [near Sarlat], Dordogne, France, 1936*), botany.

Received doctorate at Montpellier (1891). Taught at Lyons, Dijon, and at the Faculty of Sciences of Bordeaux (1901–32). The bulk of his research was devoted to marine algae, almost exclusively the study of Phaeophyceae (brown algae). He did important work on Ectocarpaceae, Myrionemaceae, and Cutleriaceae. His "Remarques sur les Sphacelariacées" (1900–14), a series of papers totaling more than six hundred pages, is a model systematic and ecological study. He discovered alternation of generations in the Laminariaceae. He greatly elucidated the extremely complex cycles of brown algae, and his discoveries form the basis of all our present knowledge concerning Phaeophyceae—its classification and the evolution of its reproductive cycles.

SAUVEUR, ALBERT (*b. Louvain, Belgium, 1863; d. Cambridge, Mass., 1939*), metallurgy, metallography.

Studied at the École de Mines in Liège (1881–86) and graduated from M.I.T. (1889). In 1891 he set up a laboratory at the Illinois Steel Company and became the first in the United States to study effectively the microscopy of steel. He showed how grain-size was affected by mechanical and thermal treatment, and how, in turn, the properties of steel depend on grain-size. He founded and edited the journal *Metallographist* (1898–1906); published in the most active period of metallographic discovery, the journal is a prime source for metallurgical history. Taught at Harvard (1899–1939).

SAUVEUR, JOSEPH (*b. La Flèche, France, 1653; d. Paris, France, 1716*), physics.

Studied at the Jesuit school of La Flèche and in Paris. Was an influential teacher of practical mathematics at the Collège Royal (from 1686). Worked on early problems in the physics of sound, especially beats, harmonics, and the determination of absolute frequency. He began his work in acoustics by developing a method of classifying temperaments of the musical scale. His first work on the physics of vibration concerned the determination of absolute frequency; he was the first to use beats to determine frequency difference. He later derived the frequency of a string theoretically. Through Sauveur and the Paris Academy ideas about harmonics became well known in the early eighteenth century. His terminology, including "harmonics" and "node," was adopted and is still current.

SAVART, FÉLIX (*b. Mézières, France, 1791; d. Paris, France, 1841*), physics.

Received medical degree at University of Strasbourg (1816), but his interest in physics led to a position teaching acoustics at the Collège de France (1828). He made experimental studies of many phenomena involving vibration. With Biot he showed that the magnetic field produced by the current in a long, straight wire is inversely proportional to the distance from the wire. He gave the first explanation of the function of certain parts of the violin, and generalized this work to analyze the vibrations of coupled systems. His results were relevant for the contemporary analyses of vibration and elasticity made by Poisson, Cauchy, and Lamé.

SAVASORDA. *See* **Abraham bar Ḥiyya ha-Nasi.**

SAVIGNY, MARIE-JULES-CÉSAR LELORGNE DE (*b. Provins, Brie, France, 1777; d. Versailles, France, 1851*), biology.

Studied at the local Collège des Oratoriens and in Paris at the École de Santé and the Muséum d'Histoire Naturelle. Cuvier urged him to join Napoleon's expedition to Egypt as zoologist: he would study invertebrates while Geoffroy Saint-Hilaire studied vertebrates. They remained in Egypt from 1798 until 1802; Savigny spent the rest of his life in Paris and Versailles. His *Mémoires sur les animaux sans vertèbres* (1816) became a model for the morphological zoology that flourished in the nineteenth century. By example rather than precept, he demonstrated the value of comparative morphology, showing unsuspected homologies among invertebrates. Geoffroy Saint-Hilaire did the same with the bones of reptiles and fish, and Savigny's work encouraged him to search for homologies between vertebrates and arthropods.

SAXTON, JOSEPH (*b. Huntingdon, Pa., 1799; d. Washington, D.C., 1873*), scientific instrumentation.

Apprenticed to a local watchmaker, Saxton acquired a taste for precision craftsmanship. In Philadelphia (1818) his earliest major achievements included a clock with a unique temperature-compensating pendulum and an oil-less escapement, a device for shaping clock gear teeth, and a "reflecting pyrometer and comparator" for checking the precision of pendulums. In London (1829) he built many of the permanent exhibits for the newly constructed Adelaide Gallery and various precision instruments for Wheatstone and other scientists. Returned to Philadelphia in 1837 to take charge of the precision assay balance he had built for the Philadelphia Mint. He pioneered in daguerreotype photography and engraved a diffraction grating that enabled J. W. Draper to make the first photograph of the diffraction spectrum. From 1844 to 1873 directed the U.S. Coast Survey Office of Weights and Measures.

SAY, THOMAS (*b. Philadelphia, Pa., 1787; d. New Harmony, Ind., 1834*), entomology, conchology.

Say was one of the generation of self-taught naturalists. A charter member of the Academy of Natural Sciences of Philadelphia (1812), he lived in the Academy building, tended the small museum, and studied his own collections. In 1818 he began a series of zoological expeditions to the Sea Islands of Georgia, Spanish Florida, and the Missouri and Mississippi Rivers. He settled in New Harmony, Indiana, in 1825, and was among the victims of this unsuccessful idealistic community. His two major works, *American Conchology* (6 vols., 1830–34) and *American Entomology; or Descriptions of the Insects of North America* (3 vols., 1817–28), are classics in their fields. He described many important economic insects, which bear his name.

SCALIGER (BORDONIUS), JULIUS CAESAR (*b. Padua, Italy, 1484; d. Agen, France, 1558*), natural philosophy, medicine, botany.

The details of Scaliger's life before 1524 are in dispute, but there is evidence that he received his doctorate in arts in 1519 at Padua. He arrived in Agen in southern France in 1524, becoming a well-known and respected physician. Of a disputatious nature, Scaliger first established his fame by a savage literary attack on the satire of Erasmus against the Ciceronian stylists. Later he wrote the more lasting *Poetics*, a re-working of Aristotelian aesthetics in order to form an important early statement of neo-classicism. The creative approach to classical thought is manifest in his writings on botany. He sought to advance botany and simples by his admirable editions of three ancient treatises: the *De plantis* of pseudo-Aristotle (Nico-

609

laus of Damascus) and the two works of Theophrastus on plants. All three works benefit from the editor's knowledge of actual specimens. In medicine Scaliger considered himself an empirical Averroist, who relied upon observation and experience rather than system. This led to a great hostility between him and Rabelais, who preferred systematic "ancient" medicine. His *Exotericarum exercitationum* (1557) is a spirited critique of Cardano's *De subtilitate libri XXI*. Following its target, the work ranges over the whole of natural philosophy.

SCARPA, ANTONIO (*b. Motta di Livenza, near Treviso, Italy, 1752; d. Pavia, Italy, 1832*), anatomy, neurology.

Graduated from Padua (1770); taught at Modena (1772–83) and at Pavia (1783–1803). Director of medical school at Pavia (1815–18). He was responsible for construction of anatomical amphitheaters at Modena and Pavia. He was an eminent anatomist, a skilled surgeon, and one of the powerful teachers at Pavia during its period of greatest renown. His greatest works were in descriptive anatomy. He began with comparative investigation of the ear. In *Anatomicae disquisitiones de auditu . . .* (1789, 1794) he described his discoveries of the membrane labyrinth and its endolymph, the vestibule, the membrane semicircular canals with their ampullae and the utricle, and the vestibular nerve and its ganglion (named for him). His *De organo olfactus praecipuo . . .* (1785) presented the first illustration of the human olfactory nerves, bulbs, and tracts, the sphenopalatine ganglion, and the interior nasal nerves. These classic works were part of a broad plan of research on the nervous system, the premise of which had been set forth in Scarpa's *De nervorum gangliis et plexubus* (1779), the first accurate analysis of these nerve structures. His great neurological work, *Tabulae . . . neurologicae* (1794), contains seven life-size plates illustrating the human glossopharyngeal, vagus, and hypoglossal nerves. Of particular interest are the two plates on the cardiac nerves. He decisively first demonstrated cardiac innervation.

SCHAEBERLE, JOHN MARTIN (*b. Württemberg, Germany, 1853; d. Ann Arbor, Mich., 1924*), practical astronomy.

Graduated from University of Michigan (1876); worked at the university observatory (1876–88) and at the Lick Observatory (1888–97). Devised new astronomical instruments, particularly for photography. Discovered two comets (1880–81) and the thirteenth-magnitude companion of Procyon (1896). Took excellent large-scale photographs of four eclipses and developed a mechanical theory of the solar corona.

SCHAFER. *See* **Sharpey-Schäfer, Edward Albert.**

SCHARDT, HANS (*b. Basel, Switzerland, 1858; d. Zurich, Switzerland, 1931*), geology.

Studied at Lausanne (graduated 1883) and Geneva (D.Sc., 1884). Taught at Lausanne (1891–97), Neuchâtel (1897–1911), and Zurich (1911–28). His research encompassed tectonics, hydrology, stratigraphy, and engineering geology. His most important work, however, lay in his discovery of the older, rootless exotic complexes of the Alps, which, floating on younger series, led him to the hypothesis concerning the great alpine mass displace-

ments that became known as the nappe theory. The theory was not fully accepted for a number of years; in the meantime, Argand drew upon Schardt's studies of Jurassic folding, thrusting, and strike-slip faults for his own theory of cover folds. Schardt explored the Simplon area and advised on the construction of the Simplon tunnel.

SCHAUDINN, FRITZ RICHARD (*b. Röseningken, Germany, 1871; d. Hamburg, Germany, 1906*), zoology, medicine.

Received doctorate at Berlin (1894). Made successful expeditions to study Arctic fauna. Worked at the Zoological Institute of the University of Berlin; director of zoological station in Rovinj (now Rovinj, Yugoslavia) on the Dalmatian coast (1901–04). In studies on malaria he observed the entrance of the sporozoite into the red blood cell; he clearly revealed the amoebic nature of tropical dysentery. Directed the newly established Institute for Protozoology at the Imperial Ministry of Health in Berlin (1904–06). Confirmed that the larvae of the hookworm enters the body through the skin of the feet or legs. The culmination of his investigations was the discovery of the microorganism responsible for venereal syphilis, first named *Spirochaeta pallida*, later *Treponema pallidum* or Schaudinn's bacillus.

SCHEELE, CARL WILHELM (*b. Stralsund, Swedish Pomerania, 1742; d. Köping, Sweden, 1786*), pharmacy, chemistry.

Scheele received excellent training at the pharmacy of Martin Bauch in Göteborg (1757–65) and spent the next ten years as a journeyman in pharmacy laboratories in Malmö (1765–68), Stockholm (1768–70), and Uppsala (1770–75). In 1775 he settled at his own pharmacy in Köping. In 1777 he took his long-postponed pharmacy examination and swore the pharmacist's oath. His most important work was done in his ten years as journeyman: *Scheele's Brown Book*, extremely difficult to decipher, includes his laboratory notes, drafts of papers and letters, and part of his vast correspondence. More thorough study is needed of this collection to clarify all of his contributions to the edifice of chemistry. His correspondence with Retzius, Gahn, Bergman, and Lavoisier is a great source of information on his discoveries.

His refusal to accept phlogiston as an element of combustibility led not only to the formulation of his theories of combustion and calcination, but also to the discovery of oxygen. From his research came the isolation of tartaric acid and the discovery of hydrofluoric acid, chlorine, and "Scheele's green" (copper hydrogen arsenite). In a letter to Lavoisier (1774) he freely disclosed his discovery of oxygen—the earliest known description of the detailed method of producing oxygen, together with complete information on its chemical nature and physiological properties. His study of air and fire was summarized in *Chemische Abhandlung von der Luft und dem Feuer* (1777). He proved that air liberated from aerial acid (carbon dioxide) and water vapor consists of two gases: fire air (oxygen), which can support combustion, and vitiated, foul air (nitrogen), which cannot. He gave the first correct description of the properties of hydrogen sulfide, was the first to record a synthesis of the gas through the heating of sulfur in hydrogen, and gave the first description of hydrogen polysulfides. In a letter to Bergman (1780) he discussed his thorough study of tungsten (*lapis ponderosus,* now called scheelite, CaWO$_4$).

His contributions to organic chemistry were even more imposing, since he had no precedent. He had obtained excellent results in inorganic chemistry by oxidation, and the same methods in organic chemistry led to the discovery of many new acids. When this work is added to his researches in protein and fats, it is clear that his influence in organic chemistry was fundamental. He found that his acid of sorrel and acid of sugar were identical (oxalic acid). In 1776 he separated from both kidney stones and urine the acid of calculus (uric acid). In 1765 he discovered prussic acid. The capstones of Scheele's gigantic chemical edifice were his discovery of glycerol and of the art of preserving vinegar by heating the vessel containing it in a kettle with boiling water—pasteurization a century before Pasteur.

SCHEFFERS, GEORG (*b. Altendorf, near Holzminden, Germany, 1866; d. Berlin, Germany, 1945*), mathematics.

Received doctorate at Leipzig (1890) under strong influence of Sophus Lie. Taught at Leipzig (1890–96), the Technische Hochschule in Darmstadt (1896–1907), and the Technische Hochschule in Charlottenburg (1907–35). His main field of study was geometry, particularly the differential geometry of intuitive space. His reputation was based largely on his books on geometry, which went through several editions.

SCHEGK, JAKOB (in Latin, **Jacobus Schegkius** or **Scheggius**; also sometimes called **Jakob Degen**) (*b. Schorndorf, Germany, 1511; d. Tübingen, Germany, 1587*), medicine, natural philosophy, methodology of science.

Received baccalaureate (1528), master's (1530), and doctorate (1539) at Tübingen and taught there (1532–77). One of the most prominent sixteenth-century spokesmen for German Scholasticism, Schegk published more than thirty works on philosophy, theology, and medicine, including numerous commentaries and treatises on Aristotle's works.

SCHEINER, CHRISTOPH (*b. Wald, near Mindelheim, Swabia, Germany, 1573; d. Neisse, Silesia [now Nysa, Poland], 1650*), astronomy.

Scheiner joined the Jesuit Order in 1595, was ordained in 1617, and held various academic and administrative positions throughout his life. He invented the pantograph, an instrument for copying plans on any scale (*Pantographice, seu ars delineandi,* 1631). With a telescope he constructed, he was one of the first to observe sunspots, but believed they were small planets circling the sun. Having observed the lower conjunction of Venus with the sun, he concluded that Venus and Mercury revolve around the sun. He organized public debates on current issues in astronomy, upheld the traditional view that the earth is at rest at the center of the universe, and discussed the theory behind sundials and explained their construction. In experiments on the physiology of the eye, he showed that the retina is the seat of vision. His refutation of the Copernican system was published posthumously in 1651.

SCHEINER, JULIUS (*b. Cologne, Germany, 1858; d. Potsdam, Germany, 1913*), astrophysics, astronomy.

Received doctorate at Bonn (1882), working in the observatory until 1887, when he moved to the Royal Astrophysical Observatory at Potsdam for the rest of his life. Taught at Berlin (from 1894). At Potsdam collaborated with Hermann Vogel in applying Vogel's new instrument, the spectrograph, inaugurating the era of accurate measurement of stellar radial velocities. Supervised publication of six large volumes of the international astrographic chart (1899–1912). Later collaborated with J. Wilsing; among other things they determined the temperatures of more than 100 stars.

SCHELLING, FREDERICK WILHELM JOSEPH (later **von Schelling**) (*b. Leonberg, Württemberg, Germany, 1775; d. Bad Ragaz, Switzerland, 1854*), philosophy.

Received master's degree in philosophy (1792) and in theology (1795) at Tübingen, where he was strongly influenced by the works of Kant and Fichte. Taught at Jena (1798–1803), Würzburg (1803–06), Munich (1806–20, 1827–41), Erlangen (1820–27), and Berlin (1841–46). His philosophy can be presented in a strictly chronological order: philosophy of nature and transcendental philosophy, philosophy of identity, and philosophy of religion. In his *Naturphilosophie* he dealt with all the important physical, chemical, and biological phenomena and processes that occupied the scientists of his day: ether, light, weight, heat, air, gravitation, the atom, matter, combustion, electricity, magnetism, and evolution. To Kant's mechanistic theory of the formation of the cosmos, Schelling opposed an organic theory according to which the universe came into being through the expansion and contraction of the primary matter. His philosophy of nature was well received by poets, writers, and scientists of the Romantic school, but contemporary scientists and philosophers who favored mechanistic explanations were repelled by Schelling's notions. In his transcendental philosophy, which is partly a reworking and partly a major revision of Fichte's *Wissenschaftslehre,* he treated the problem of nature from the point of view of consciousness. With the philosophy of nature, it completed the theoretical part of his doctrines. He took up questions concerning the freedom of the will, the moral law and natural law, and the philosophy of history. He asserted that the summit of subjective activity is attained, not in morality, as Kant and Fichte held, but in the free creative act of the artist. With the philosophy of identity, he went one step farther: real and ideal, and nature and mind are seen to be identical when conceived with sufficient understanding. His thinking on the philosophy of religion was stimulated by the ideas of Jacob Boehme. Overcoming the impasse of Romanticism, he arrived at a new realism—that of struggling man, the fundamental concept of existentialism. A direct line can be drawn from this formulation to the work of Kierkegaard, the founder of this new philosophy and for a time Schelling's student at Berlin. His collected works were edited by one of his sons as *Sämtichle Werke* (14 vols., 1856–61).

SCHEUCHZER, JOHANN JAKOB (*b. Zurich, Switzerland, 1672; d. Zurich, 1733*), medicine, natural history, mathematics, geology, geophysics.

Received doctorate at Utrecht (1694). Taught at the Carolinum in Zurich (1716–33). His numerous Alpine excursions led to a voluminous correspondence with many European scholars and to his greatest work in natural history and geophysics, *Helvetiae stoicheiographia* (1716–18). He is considered the moving force in the establishment of paleontology in Switzerland, the founder of paleobotany, and the founder of European paleontology.

SCHIAPARELLI, GIOVANNI VIRGINIO (*b. Savigliano, Cuneo province, Italy, 1835; d. Milan, Italy, 1910*), astronomy.

Received civil engineering degree at Turin (1854); studied astronomy at Turin and at observatories of Berlin and Pulkovo. Was appointed astronomer at the Brera Observatory in Milan (1860), becoming director in 1862. Discovered the asteroid Hesperia. His accurate study of the shape and position of the tails of comets led him to new theories on the repulsive action exerted by the sun. In 1871 he published a complete elaboration of his theory that "meteor showers are the product of the dissolution of the comets and consists of very minute particles that they . . . have abandoned along their orbit because of the disintegrating force that the sun and the planets exert on the very fine matter of which they are composed." His hypothesis has been confirmed in many cases. In studying the planet Mars (1877–90), he was the first to classify the features as "seas" and "continents"; the term "canal" had been used by Secchi in his observations of 1859. Schiaparelli observed that certain canals seemed to be splitting into two parts, and his last aerographic map depicts most of the canals as split. He also observed Saturn and the few dark spots visible on Mercury in the form of shadowy bands. He concluded that Mercury revolves about the sun in the same manner that the moon does around the earth—with the same side always turned to the sun. He collaborated with Nallino on the translation into Latin of al-Battānī's *Opus astronomicum*. His three volumes on the history of ancient astronomy provide data and information of inestimable value.

SCHICKARD, WILHELM (*b. Herrenberg, Germany, 1592; d. Tübingen, Germany, 1635*), astronomy, mathematics, natural philosophy.

Studied at Tübingen (B.A., 1609; M.A., 1611), teaching there from 1619. A polymath who knew several Near Eastern languages, Schickard wrote treatises on Semitic studies, mathematics, astronomy, optics, meteorology, and cartography. He invented and built a working model of the first modern mechanical calculator and proposed to Kepler the development of a mechanical means of calculating ephemerides.

SCHIFF, HUGO JOSEF (*b. Frankfurt, Germany, 1834; d. Florence, Italy, 1915*), chemistry.

Brother of the distinguished physiologist Moritz Schiff. Received doctorate at Göttingen (1857). Taught at Bern, the Museo di Storia Naturale in Florence (1863–76), Turin (1876–79), and the Istituto di Studi Superiori in Florence (1879–1915), modeling his teaching methods on those of Berzelius and Wöhler. In 1871, with Cannizzaro and Selmi, founded the journal *Gazzetta chimica italiana*. In 1864 he discovered the condensation products of aldehydes and amines, later known as "Schiff bases." In 1866 he devised the nitrometer that bears his name, an improved version of the Dumas method for the determination of nitrogen.

SCHIFF, MORITZ (*b. Frankfurt, Germany, 1823; d. Geneva, Switzerland, 1896*), zoology, physiology.

Studied at the Senckenberg Institute, Heidelberg, Berlin, and Göttingen (medical degree, 1844). Practiced medicine and conducted physiological experiments before beginning academic career. Taught at Bern, Florence, and Geneva. Schiff was one of the eminent biologists who pioneered the experimental method in the new science of physiology. Following in the steps of his teacher Magendie, he approached the subject matter from a biological point of view instead of carrying out reductionist physicochemical studies like those of du Bois-Reymond and Helmholtz. His often controversial vivisections uncovered details in spinal cord physiology, clarified the role of the autonomic nervous system, and revealed the importance of certain internal secretions.

SCHIMPER, ANDREAS FRANZ WILHELM (*b. Strasbourg, France, 1856; d. Basel, Switzerland, 1901*), botany.

Son of the botanist Wilhelm Philipp Schimper. Received doctorate at Strasbourg (1878). His many botanical expeditions throughout his life included Florida, the West Indies, South America, and Indonesia. He worked with de Bary at Strasbourg, Sachs at Würzburg, and Strasburger at Bonn (1882–98). Taught at Bonn (1883–98) and Basel (from 1898). Wrote very important medico-pharmaceutical books. His study of the growth of starch grains induced him to abandon Naegeli's intussusception theory. In July 1898 he joined the important German marine expedition on board the *Valdivia*, during which he studied the oceanic plankton flora and the vegetation of the Canary Islands, Kerguelen, the Seychelles, Cameroon, the Congo and eastern Africa, Sumatra, and the Cape of Good Hope.

SCHIMPER, KARL FRIEDRICH (*b. Mannheim, Germany, 1803; d. Schwetzingen, near Heidelberg, Germany, 1867*), botany, geology, zoology, meteorology.

Studied at Heidelberg and at Munich (doctorate, 1829). Remained in Munich until 1841, returned to Mannheim, and settled in Schwetzingen in 1849. Lacking a permanent position and a regular income, he was constantly in financial difficulties. In botany his principal concern was to formulate a theory of phyllotaxy. He collaborated on *Flora Manhemiensis* and *Flora Friburgensis*. His study of prehistoric animals led to his proposal of the existence of a succession of different faunas and floras, in a schema similar to a genealogical tree, contradicting Cuvier's catastrophist theory. Much of his account was similar to the theory of evolution, but he completely rejected Darwin's theory of natural selection. In geology he studied traces of Pleistocene glaciers in the northern Alpine foothills; his ideas anticipated the contraction theory proposed by Suess in 1875. In 1843 he presented a paper on prehistoric climatic conditions, postulating an Ice Age preceded by warmer weather.

SCHIMPER, WILHELM PHILIPP (GUILLAUME PHILIPPE) (*b. Dossenheim, Alsace, France, 1808; d. Strasbourg, France [then part of Germany], 1880*), botany.

Graduated from Strasbourg (degree in natural sciences, 1845; doctorate, 1848). Worked at the Strasbourg Natural History Museum in various capacities from 1835, eventually becoming its director. Also taught at Strasbourg. His most famous work, *Bryologia Europaea* (6 vols., 1836–55), set a new standard in the description and delineation of mosses. His study of the structure and development of the sphagna is particularly valuable, and he made important contributions to paleobotany.

SCHJELLERUP, HANS CARL FREDERIK CHRISTIAN (*b. Odense, Denmark, 1827; d. Copenhagen, Denmark, 1887*), astronomy.

Studied at the Polytechnic School of Copenhagen and received doctorate at Jena (1857). Senior astronomer at the Copenhagen observatory (1851–87). His catalog of 10,000 positions of faint stars in declinations between $-15°$ and $+15°$ (1864), outstanding at the time for its completeness and accuracy, was used as recently as 1952 for determining the constant of precession. He also compiled two catalogs of colored stars (1866, 1874) and wrote a French translation of an Arabic astronomical manuscript by al-Ṣūfī.

SCHLÄFLI, LUDWIG (*b. Grasswil, Bern, Switzerland, 1814; d. Bern, Switzerland, 1895*), mathematics.

Studied at Bern; taught mathematics and science in Thun for ten years before joining Steiner, Jacobi, Dirichlet, and Borchardt on a trip to Rome (1843). He studied higher mathematics with these leading mathematicians of the day, and obtained a position at Bern (1848). He was concerned with two major problems, one in elimination theory and the other in *n*-dimensional geometry. The first is discussed in "Ueber die Resultante eines Systems mehrerer algebraischer Gleichungen. Ein Beitrag zur Theorie der Elimination," which led to an extensive correspondence with Cayley. The second work, "Theorie der vielfachen Kontinuität," consisted of the detailed theory of regular bodies in Euclidean space R_n of n dimensions and the associated problems of the regular subdivision of the higher-dimensional spheres. He based his investigation of regular polytopes on his discovery that such objects can be characterized by certain symbols now known as Schläfli symbols. The second section of the paper contains the theory of Schläfli functions and a detailed treatment of the decomposition of an arbitrary spherical simplex into right-angled simplexes. The third section contains both applications of theorems of Binet, Monge, Chasles, and Dupin to quadratic continua in R_n and Schläfli's own discoveries. In function theory he wrote an outstanding work on elliptic modular functions (1870) that gave rise to the designation "Schläfli modular equation."

SCHLEIDEN, JACOB MATHIAS (*b. Hamburg, Germany, 1804; d. Frankfurt am Main, Germany, 1881*), botany, natural science, scientific popularization.

After abandoning his law practice, Schleiden studied natural science at Göttingen, Berlin (with Humboldt, Brown, Müller, and Schwann), and Jena (doctorate, 1839). He taught briefly at Jena and Dorpat, then became a *Privatgelehrter* and thereafter moved frequently from one city to another. His liberality and combative nature constantly involved him in debates and harsh polemics

with the most eminent scientists and thinkers of the age, among whom were Amici, Fechner, Liebig, Mohl, Nees von Esenbeck, and Schelling. His "Beiträge zur Phytogenesis" (1838) fixed his name in the history of biology. He starts from Robert Brown's discovery of the cell nucleus, which Schleiden called the cytoblast, and then indicates its role in the formation of cells. According to Schleiden, as soon as the cytoblast reaches its final size, a fine, transparent vesicle forms around it: this is the new cell. The cell then crystallizes within a formative liquid. This clearly announced the advent of plant cytology. Despite increasing evidence of nuclear activity during division, and despite Virchow's definitive aphorism, "omnis cellula a cellula," the notion of the formative blastema long survived. Schleiden contributed greatly to the introduction of the microscope in biological research. He based his description of cytogenesis on an examination of the pollen tube. His botany textbook, *Grundzüge der wissenschaftlichen Botanik* (1842) was a frontal attack against the ideas of nature philosophy and introduced new pedagogical standards that were to dominate the teaching of botany for years.

SCHLESINGER, FRANK (*b. New York, N.Y., 1871; d. Lyme, Conn., 1943*), astronomy.

Graduated from City College of New York (1890), and received Ph.D. from Columbia University (1898). His dissertation, based on measurements of star positions on plates photographed many years before by Lewis Rutherfurd, was a forerunner in his distinguished career in astrometry. After two years at Yerkes Observatory (1903–05) he became director of the Allegheny Observatory in Pittsburgh, and later, director of the Yale University Observatory (1920–41). His work included improvement of instrumentation for parallax work, spectroscopic studies of eclipsing and spectroscopic binary stars, and preparation of "zone catalogues" to provide accurate positions and proper motions of many thousands of stars to the ninth and fainter magnitudes.

SCHLICK, (FRIEDRICH ALBERT) MORITZ (*b. Berlin, Germany, 1882; d. Vienna, Austria, 1936*), theory of knowledge, philosophy of science.

Studied at Heidelberg, Lausanne, and Berlin (doctorate, 1904); abandoned science for a philosophical career, teaching at Rostock, Kiel, and Vienna (from 1922). Became the center of the Vienna Circle, a group of thinkers with predominantly scientific and mathematical backgrounds who were devoted to the cultivation and development of a scientific philosophy, as opposed to the then prevailing metaphysical orientation of Continental, and especially German, philosophy. His main reputation rests on his work in theory of knowledge and philosophy of science. His first work in this area was a brief expository, interpretive book on Einstein's theory of relativity, *Raum und Zeit in der gegenwärtigen Physik* (1917), stressing the profound philosophical implication of Einstein's work. *Allgemeine Erkenntnislehre* (1918), his major work, examines a very wide range of problems and concepts relating to scientific knowledge. His broad conception of science by no means excluded systematic knowledge relating to questions of life and values. In his works *Lebensweisheit, Natur und Kultur,* and *Fragen der Ethik* he explores the pleasure-happiness value of the senses, the instincts, and of personal and social relations and institutions.

SCHLIEMANN, HEINRICH (*b. Neu Buckow, Mecklenburg-Schwerin, Germany, 1822; d. Naples, Italy, 1890*), archaeology.

In 1858 Schliemann retired from a successful business career to devote his time and great fortune to the study of prehistoric archaeology, and especially to finding the remains of Homer's Troy. He studied ancient and modern Greece, traveled extensively in Europe, Egypt, Syria, and Greece, and studied archaeology in Paris. He began to dig at Hissarlik in Asia Minor in 1871—the first such operation conducted upon a tell and the first large-scale dissection of a dryland settlement unguided by the remains of great monuments. His discovery of seven occupation levels at Troy gave considerable impetus to the application of the principles of stratigraphy to archaeology. He designated the levels by Roman numerals, the deepest being Troy I. He identified Troy II as Homeric Troy and in 1873 found "Priam's treasure," a magnificent cache of gold objects that he hastily smuggled out of Turkey. Wilhelm Dörpfeld later identified Troy VI as the Homeric city. At Mycenae he dug for the tombs of Clytemnestra and Agamemnon and found the now-famous shaft graves, the contents of which far surpassed "Priam's treasure" in richness. At Orchomenus he excavated the treasury of Minyas, and at Tiryns he uncovered the royal palace. Results of his excavations were published quickly: *Trojanische Altertümer* (1874), *Mycenae* (1877), *Ilios* (1881), and *Orchomenos* (1881). What Schliemann had in fact discovered, in both Greece and western Anatolia, was the great pre-Hellenic civilization of the eastern Mediterranean, and this marks his chief contribution to prehistoric archaeology.

SCHLOTHEIM, ERNST FRIEDRICH, BARON VON (*b. Almenhausen, Thuringia, Germany, 1765; d. Gotha, Germany, 1832*), geology, paleontology.

Studied under Blumenbach at Göttingen and under Werner at Freiberg. Entered Gotha civil service in 1792, rising to minister and lord high marshal by 1828. Served as superintendent of the ducal art, natural history, coin, and book collections in Gotha. He published observations of the countryside, reporting on the stratigraphy of the calcareous tufa at Gräfentonna. His later investigations were concerned primarily with paleontology. He was the first to insist that the species of the fossils must be determined in order to distinguish the various formations. He called for the establishment of a nomenclature in paleontology analogous to that provided by Linnaeus for existing organisms.

SCHLUMBERGER, CHARLES (*b. Mulhouse, France, 1825; d. Paris, France, 1905*), micropaleontology.

Studied at the École Polytechnique. While in the navy corps of engineers he made many field trips and collected fossils, leading to his career as a micropaleontologist specializing in Foraminifera. Became guest scientist at the laboratory of paleontology of the Muséum d'Histoire Naturelle and later at the École des Mines. With E. Munier-Chalmas, he discovered the dimorphism in Miliolidae, later continuing his research alone on other groups of Foraminifera.

SCHMERLING, PHILIPPE-CHARLES (*b. Delft, Netherlands, 1791; d. Liège, Belgium, 1836*), paleontology.

Received M.D. at Liège (1825). While practicing medicine, he noticed a poor quarry worker's children playing with some unusual bones unearthed at the nearby quarry. Stimulated by this find, the first known excavation of fossil bones in Belgium, Schmerling traveled extensively in the region and within less than four years located more than forty similar sites. He collected the remains of some sixty animal species. Those that made him famous were human bones in an indisputably fossil state. The most famous human remains, found in the Engis cave, were later shown to be Neanderthal (the first such example ever found) and Cro-Magnon man. He was the first to demonstrate the existence of fossil man by means of irrefutable stratigraphic arguments. His 1836 memoir on paleopathology was one of the first of its kind, recognizing the importance of this discipline.

SCHMIDEL (or **Schmiedel**), **CASIMIR CHRISTOPH** (*b. Bayreuth, Germany, 1718; d. Ansbach, Germany, 1792*), medicine, natural history.

Received M.D. at Jena (1742), learning natural history on his own. Taught at the Friedrichs-Akademie and at Erlangen and practiced medicine. He is best known for his studies of the morphology of the cryptogams and for his editing of Konrad Gesner's posthumous botanical publications. He also wrote many essays on general medicine and anatomy.

SCHMIDT, BERNHARD VOLDEMAR (*b. Naissaar, Estonia [now Estonian S.S.R.], 1879; d. Hamburg, Germany, 1935*), optics.

Studied in Göteborg, Sweden, and in Mittweida, Saxony, where he set up his own small observatory. He constructed and improved astronomical instruments, his most famous being a reflector without coma. Photographs could then be taken which yielded undistorted star images over a large field.

SCHMIDT, CARL AUGUST VON (*b. Diefenbach, Württemberg, Germany, 1840; d. Stuttgart, Germany, 1929*), geophysics, astrophysics.

Obtained doctorate at Tübingen (1863), also studying in Paris and Stuttgart. Taught at the Realgymnasium in Stuttgart (1868–1904) and worked for the Württemberg office of statistics, the central weather bureau in Stuttgart, and the earthquake research center in Strasbourg. In 1892 established an earthquake observatory in Hohenheim. One of his notable works (most of which dealt with geophysics and astrophysics) demonstrated that seismic waves do not spread rectilinearly from the focus of an earthquake but in curved paths (1888). He also established the law, named for him, concerning the turning point in the apparent propagation velocity of seismic waves. He contributed to meteorology through work on the application of thermodynamics and the kinetic theory of gases to the study of the atmosphere (1889) and introduced the concept of barometric tendency into weather forecasting.

SCHMIDT, ERHARD (*b. Dorpat, Germany [now Tartu, E.S.S.R.], 1876; d. Berlin, Germany, 1959*), mathematics.

Studied at Dorpat, Berlin, and Göttingen (doctorate, 1905). After short periods teaching at Bonn, Zurich, Erlangen, and Breslau, in 1917 he went to the University of Berlin for the rest of his life. Was first director of the Research Institute for Mathematics of the German Academy of Sciences (1946–58) and a founder of *Mathematische Nachrichten* (1948). His most significant contributions were in integral equations and in the founding of Hilbert space theory. Specifically, he simplified and extended Hilbert's results in the theory of integral equations; and he formalized Hilbert's distinct ideas on integral equations into the single concept of a Hilbert space, in the process introducing many geometrical terms. In addition he made contributions in the fields of partial differential equations and geometry. Although his methods were classical rather than abstractionist, nevertheless he must be considered a founder of modern functional analysis. His paper on integral equation included the well-known Gram-Schmidt process for the construction of a set of orthonormal functions from given set of linearly independent functions. In an extension of the symmetric to the unsymmetric case, Schmidt broadened Hilbert's result in the Hilbert-Schmidt theorem.

SCHMIDT, ERNST JOHANNES (*b. Copenhagen, Denmark, 1877; d. Copenhagen, 1933*), marine biology.
Studied at University of Copenhagen (M.Sc., 1898; Ph.D., 1903). Attached to Botanical Institute of the University (1899–1909), and from 1910 directed the Carlsberg Physiological Laboratory in Copenhagen. As a member of the Danish Commission for the Investigation of the Sea, he went on several marine biological expeditions in the North Atlantic, and his fame rests chiefly on his research there. In studying the life cycle of eels, he succeeded in locating the breeding grounds in the Sargasso Sea.

SCHMIDT, GERHARD CARL NATHANIEL (*b. London, England, 1865; d. Münster, Germany, 1949*), physical chemistry.
Studied at Tübingen, Berlin, Strasbourg, Greifswald, and Basel (Ph.D., 1891). Taught at Erlangen, Königsberg, and Münster. Most famous for his discovery of the radioactivity of thorium (1898). (Marie Curie soon made the same discovery independently.)

SCHMIDT, JOHANN FRIEDRICH JULIUS (*b. Eutin, Germany, 1825; d. Athens, Greece, 1884*), astronomy, geophysics.
Studied astronomy and worked at observatories in Hamburg, Bilk (near Düsseldorf), Bonn, Olmütz, and Athens. He is known chiefly for his selenographic observations.

SCHMIEDEL. *See* **Schmidel, Casimir Christoph.**

SCHNEIDER, FRIEDRICH ANTON (*b. Zeitz, Germany, 1831; d. Breslau, Germany [now Wrocław, Poland], 1890*), zoology, comparative anatomy, cytology.
Studied at Bonn and Berlin (doctorate, 1854). Made field trips to Norway and Italy studying marine biology. Taught at Giessen (1869–81) and Breslau (1881–90). His zoological interests were in morphology and systematization. After years of studying the roundworms and flat-

worms, he reported in "Untersuchungen über Plathelminthen" (1873) his various laboratory observations of the life history of the Platyhelminthes. The paper contains the first description of the process of cell division and the visible changes during its successive stages—a detailed account of Schneider's microscopic investigations, with drawings of the nucleus and the chromosomal strands as he had seen them in the flatworm *Mesostomum ehrenbergii.*

SCHNEIDERHÖHN, HANS (*b. Mainz, Germany, 1887; d. Sölden, near Freiburg im Breisgau, Germany, 1962*), geology.
Studied geology and mineralogy at Freiburg, Munich, and Giessen. While mineralogist for the Tsumeb mine in South-West Africa, he discovered "Rosa Erz," now known as germanite. Also examined many deposits in Europe, North America, and Turkey, becoming one of the classical authors on ore microscopy. Taught at Giessen (1919–24), Aachen (1924–26), and Freiburg im Breisgau (1926–55).

SCHOENFLIES, ARTHUR MORITZ (*b. Landsberg an der Warthe, Germany [now Gorzów, Poland], 1853; d. Frankfurt am Main, Germany, 1928*), mathematics, crystallography.
Received Ph.D. at Berlin (1877); taught at Göttingen (1884–99), Königsberg (1899–1911), and Frankfurt (1911–22). His investigations on Euclidean motion groups and regular space division culminated in his magnum opus, *Kristallsysteme und Kristallstruktur* (1891), containing the 230 crystallographic groups. He also published important articles on topology, set theory, kinematics, and projective geometry.

SCHÖNBEIN, CHRISTIAN FRIEDRICH (*b. Metzingen, Swabia [now West Germany], 1799; d. Sauersberg, near Baden-Baden, Germany, 1868*), physical chemistry.
Schönbein acquired a profound knowledge of theoretical and applied chemistry through his work in chemical and pharmaceutical factories and through private study. He taught at Basel (1835–68). The influence of *Naturphilosophie* is evident in all his work, especially in his speculative views that lack a sufficient experimental basis. He published more than 350 works, mostly qualitative, covering a wide range of research—but especially ozone, autoxidation, induced reactions, guncotton, electrochemistry, and passive iron. He discovered ozone in 1839, was the first to produce guncotton (1846), and from it collodion. His general ideas on chemistry, and particularly on catalysis, are discussed in *Beiträge zur physikalischen Chemie* (1844). His dynamical ideas are also emphasized. He was opposed to the atomic theory.

SCHÖNER, JOHANNES (*b. Karlstadt, Germany, 1477; d. Nuremberg, Germany, 1547*), astronomy, geography.
Studied at University of Erfurt; served as a Roman Catholic priest until 1525. Taught at the Melanchthon Gymnasium (1526–46). Published his astronomical works on his own printing press. Made his own globes: his earliest terrestrial globe was the first to name the recently discovered continental mass "America." He wrote valuable editions of many previously unpublished works by Regiomontanus.

SCHÖNFELD, EDUARD (*b. Hildburghausen, Germany, 1828; d. Bonn, Germany, 1891*), astronomy.

Studied at Kassel, Marburg, and Bonn (doctorate, 1854). Directed observatories at Mannheim (1859–75) and Bonn (from 1875). Collaborated with Argelander on the *Bonner Durchmusterung,* a catalog of all stars down to the ninth magnitude. He also observed nebulae, variable stars, and comets.

SCHÖNHERR, CARL JOHAN (*b. Stockholm, Sweden, 1772; d. Sparresäter, near Skara, Sweden, 1848*), entomology.

Schönherr was completely self-taught. Wrote important works on beetles: his exemplary descriptions of weevils and the analyses of synonyms and explanations of nomenclature have remained of lasting value. He amassed a great entomological book collection as well as an insect collection of about 37,700 specimens.

SCHONLAND, BASIL FERDINAND JAMIESON (*b. Grahamstown, South Africa, 1896; d. Winchester, England, 1972*), atmospheric electricity, scientific administration.

Graduated from Gonville and Caius College, Cambridge (1920), and registered for the Ph.D. at Cavendish Laboratory. Taught at universities of Cape Town (1922–36) and Witwatersrand (1937–54). In *Atmospheric Electricity* (1932) and *The Flight of Thunderbolts* (1950) he described the apparatus he designed to photograph lightning discharges, and confirmed Charles Wilson's theory that positive ions are carried to the top rather than to the bottom of a thundercloud. Knighted in 1960.

SCHÖNLEIN, JOHANN LUCAS (*b. Bamberg, Germany, 1793; d. Bamberg, 1864*), medicine.

Studied at universities of Landshut and Würzburg (graduated, 1816). Taught and eventually became director of the medical clinic at the Julius Hospital in Würzburg (1819–32). At the clinic percussion and auscultation were first routinely used in Germany as diagnostic aids. Blood, urine, and various secretions were examined under the microscope and chemical reagents were utilized; autopsies provided still further information. His methods and teaching gave a new direction to German medicine. Later became professor of medicine at Zurich (1833–39) and at Berlin (1840–59). His brief paper on favus, which recognized for the first time a fungus parasite as the cause of a disease in man, contributed importantly to the understanding of contagious disease.

SCHOOLCRAFT, HENRY ROWE (*b. Albany County, now Guilderland, N.Y., 1793; d. Washington, D.C., 1864*), ethnology.

Studied at Union College and Middlebury College, Vermont. His six-thousand-mile tour of the Mississippi valley, the Ozark Mountains, and the lead district, published in 1819 as *A View of the Lead Mines of Missouri,* led to his assignment to further expeditions. His major scientific accomplishment resulted from his appointment as Indian agent in 1822 at Sault Ste. Marie, Michigan Territory. For over ten years he edited the six-volume *Historical and Statistical Information Respecting the History, Condition and Prospects of the Indian Tribes of the United States,* an unassorted, lavishly illustrated compendium of material gathered by other agents and by himself. His reports on

mineral occurrences were among the earliest such descriptions in the United States.

SCHOOTEN, FRANS VAN (*b. Leiden, Netherlands, ca. 1615; d. Leiden, 1660*), mathematics.

Studied at and later taught at the University of Leiden. Prepared a collected edition of the mathematical writings of Viète (1646), changing the notation in several places to simplify the mathematical statements and to make the material more accessible. A voluminous correspondence developed between him and his student Christiaan Huygens. From Schooten's Latin edition of Descartes's *Géométrie* (1649) contemporary mathematicians lacking proficiency in French first learned Cartesian mathematics. His first independent work was a study of the kinematic generation of conic sections (1646). He made an original contribution to mathematics with his *Exercitationes mathematicae* (1657). Worth noting, in particular, is the restatement of Hudde's method for the step-by-step building-up of equations for angular section and the determination of the girth of the folium of Descartes; and also the determination of Heronian triangles of equal perimeter and equal area (Roberval's problem) according to Descartes's method.

SCHOPFER, WILLIAM-HENRI (*b. Yverdon, Switzerland, 1900; d. Geneva, Switzerland, 1962*), biology, microbiology, biochemistry.

Received two *licences* in natural sciences (1923, 1925) and doctorate (1928) from Geneva. Taught at Geneva (1929–33) and Bern (1933–62). He published 299 scientific works, directed twenty-two doctoral dissertations, and was actively involved with several scientific societies and journals. In his remarkable work on the sexuality of mushrooms (1927) he treated a completely new problem, the comparative biochemistry of sexual reproduction. Henceforth all of his and most of his students' works were devoted to the study of the role of organic factors controlling the growth of microorganisms. He opened the immense area of research on microbial vitamins, in which plant and animal biochemists and physiologists met. His experiments on the mold *Phycomyces blakesleeanus* became classics, and in 1931 he made a series of studies that were decisive for the new science of vitaminology. His results were included in the collaborative work, *Plants and Vitamins* (1943).

SCHORLEMMER, CARL (*b. Darmstadt, Germany, 1834; d. Manchester, England, 1892*), organic chemistry, history of chemistry.

Studied at Darmstadt, Giessen, and Manchester. Taught at Owens College, Manchester, becoming England's first professor of organic chemistry. His important contributions to the development of modern organic chemistry included investigations of the compounds "methyl" and "ethyl hydride." In other studies, he presented the history of chemistry from a sociological point of view and discovered important relations between chemistry, economics, and philosophy.

SCHOTT, CHARLES ANTHONY (*b. Mannheim, Germany, 1826; d. Washington, D.C., 1901*), geophysics.

Graduated from the Technische Hochschule in Karlsruhe; immigrated to the United States (1848) and joined the U.S. Coast Survey (1848–1901). His division was responsible for processing the data gathered by Survey parties. On him depended the precision and theoretical adequacy of the Survey's work; this involved not only study of instruments, observational techniques, and data, but also appraisals of proposed innovations, including theoretical changes. He also made studies of the influence of the aurora, relations of sunspots and magnetic storms, and climatology.

SCHOTT, GASPAR (*b. Königshofen, near Würzburg, Germany, 1608; d. Würzburg, 1666*), mathematics, physics, technology.

In 1627 Schott entered the Society of Jesus and was sent to Würzburg, studying under Athanasius Kircher; completed studies at Palermo, teaching there and at Würzburg. His main contribution was essentially that of an editor who prepared the researches of others for the press without adding much of consequence. He did much to popularize the achievements of contemporary physicists—notably Guericke, Boyle, and Torricelli. His chief works are *Magia universalis* (1657–59), *Physica curiosa* (1662), and *Technica curiosa* (1664).

SCHOTT, OTTO FRIEDRICH (*b. Witten, Germany, 1851; d. Jena, Germany, 1935*), glass chemistry, glass manufacture.

Studied at Aachen, Würzburg, Leipzig, and Jena (doctorate, 1875). A leading pioneer in glass chemistry, Schott created new types of glass of outstanding quality for use in optics, in the laboratory, and in industry. The Jena glassworks of Schott and Associates (founded in 1884) soon achieved world fame for its glass. Collaborated closely with Ernst Abbe at the glassworks and in testing optical properties of new types of glass.

SCHOTTKY, FRIEDRICH HERMANN (*b. Breslau, Germany [now Wrocław, Poland], 1851; d. Berlin, Germany, 1935*), mathematics.

Studied at Breslau and at Berlin (Ph.D., 1875); taught at Berlin, Zurich, and Marburg. He made important contributions to the conformal mapping of multiply connected plane domains and to the realm of Picard's theorem (Schottky's theorem). The greater part of his work concerned elliptic, Abelian, and theta functions.

SCHOUTE, PIETER HENDRIK (*b. Wormerveer, Netherlands, 1846; d. Groningen, Netherlands, 1923*), mathematics.

Received Ph.D. at Leiden (1870); taught at high schools in Nijmegen and The Hague, and at the University of Groningen. Investigated quadrics, algebraic curves, complexes, and congruences; the geometry in Euclidean spaces of more than three dimensions; and regular polytopes (generalizations of regular polyhedrons).

SCHOUTEN, JAN ARNOLDUS (*b. Nieuweramstel [now part of Amsterdam], Netherlands, 1883; d. Epe, Netherlands, 1971*), tensor analysis.

Received doctorate at Leiden (1914); taught at Delft and Amsterdam, and was a founder, teacher, and later director of the Mathematical Center at Amsterdam. His scientific contributions virtually all relate to tensor analysis and its applications to differential geometry, Lie groups, relativity, unified field theory, and Pfaffian systems of differential equations. Was one of the founders of the "Ricci calculus."

SCHOUW, JOAKIM FREDERIK (*b. Copenhagen, Denmark, 1789; d. Copenhagen, 1852*), plant geography, climatology.

Received Ph.D. (1816) and taught (1820–53) at Copenhagen University. Made botanical expeditions to Norway, Italy, and Sicily. Was greatly interested in popularizing science and improving the teaching of natural history. He became well known through his editorship of *Dansk Ugeskrift*, in which many of his popular-science lectures were printed.

SCHREIBERS, KARL (or **CARL**) **FRANZ ANTON VON** (*b. Pressburg, Hungary [now Bratislava, Czechoslovakia], 1775; d. Vienna, Austria, 1852*), zoology.

Studied natural science and medicine at Vienna (M.D., 1798); practiced medicine briefly, then taught at Vienna (from 1800), becoming director of the zoological and mineralogical museums (1806). Improved and enlarged the museum collections, partly through expeditions, notably to Brazil (1817–22). Active mainly in zoology, his most lasting works are his large monographs on the fauna of Austria and his investigations of the salamander *Proteus anguinus*.

SCHRÖDER, FRIEDRICH WILHELM KARL ERNST (*b. Mannheim, Germany, 1841; d. Karlsruhe, Germany, 1902*), mathematics.

Studied at Heidelberg (doctorate, 1862) and Königsberg. After teaching in Karlsruhe, Zurich, Pforzheim, Baden-Baden, and Darmstadt, he accepted a post at the Technische Hochschule in Karlsruhe, becoming director in 1890. His works deal almost exclusively with the foundations of mathematics, notably with combinatorial analysis; the theory of functions of a real variable; and mathematical logic. Particularly noteworthy was his early support of Cantor's ideas on set theory, which he was one of the first to accept. His ideas furnished the fundamental notion of mathematical logic: the partition of objects into classes.

SCHRÖDINGER, ERWIN (*b. Vienna, Austria, 1887; d. Alpbach, Austria, 1961*), theoretical physics.

Schrödinger studied at the University of Vienna and received his doctorate under Hasenöhrl (1910). The following year he became assistant to Exner at the university's Second Physics Institute, where he remained until the outbreak of World War I. After the war he worked again at the Second Physics Institute in Vienna.

After short stays in Jena and Breslau, he was offered the chair formerly held by Einstein and Max von Laue at Zurich. While at Zurich, Schrödinger worked chiefly on problems related to the statistical theory of heat. He wrote papers on gas and reaction kinetics, oscillation problems, and the thermodynamics of lattice vibrations and their contribution to internal energy; in other works he elucidated aspects of mathematical statistics. In an article on the theory of specific heats and in a monograph on statistical thermodynamics he gave a comprehensive account of the latter subject.

Although he published several contributions to the old quantum theory, he did not pursue that topic systematically. His first papers on relativity pointed to a second major field of interest. In addition to these works, and his early papers on relativity, he made a detailed study, through both measurement and computation, of the metric of color space and the theory of color vision. The main results of his efforts were an article in J. H. J. Müller and C. S. M. Pouillet's *Lehrbuch der Physik* and the acceptance by physiologists of his interpretation of the relationship between the frequency of red-green color blindness and that of the blue-yellow type.

In 1925 he became very interested in the theory of the Broglie waves and shortly before December of that year completed a paper on the topic, "Zur Einsteinschen Gastheorie." Seeking to apply the new ideas to the problem of atomic structure, he "took seriously the de Broglie-Einstein wave theory of moving particles, according to which the particles are nothing more than a kind of 'wave crest' on a background of waves."

The intensity of Schrödinger's work on the problem increased as he saw that he was on the track of a "new atomic theory." On 27 December 1925 he wrote to Wilhelm Wien, editor of the *Annalen der Physik* in Munich that he was very optimistic: "I believe that I can give a vibrating system . . . that yields the hydrogen frequency *levels* as its eigenfrequencies." The frequencies of the emitted light rays are then obtained, as he observed, by establishing the differences of the two eigenfrequencies respectively.

Schrödinger originally developed a relativistic theory. It must be emphasized, therefore, that he worked out the relativistic version only at the end of 1925. The equation now known as the "Klein-Gordon equation" does yield the correct nonrelativistic Balmer term, but it gives an incorrect description of the fine structure. He was deeply disappointed by this failure and must have thought at first that his whole method was basically wrong. Today it is known that the reason for the failure lay not in his bold initial approach but in the application of the theory of relativity, which, however, has itself been abundantly confirmed. The relativistic Schrödinger equation is obviously correct, but it describes particles without spin, whereas a description of electrons requires the Dirac equation. At the time, however, only the first steps had been taken toward an understanding of electron spin.

After a brief interruption Schrödinger took up his method again, but this time he treated the electron nonrelativistically. It soon became apparent that he had arrived at a theory that correctly represented the behavior of the electron to a very good approximation. The result was the emergence of wave mechanics in January 1926. He published the results of his research in a series of four papers in the *Annalen der Physik* bearing the overall title "Quantisierung als Eigenwertproblem." The first installment contains the first appearance in the literature of his famous wave equation, written out for the hydrogen atom. The solution of this equation follows, as Schrödinger put it, from the "well-known" method of the separation of variables. The radial dependency gives rise to the differential equation

$$\frac{d^2\chi}{dr^2} + \frac{2}{r}\frac{d\chi}{dr} + \left(\frac{2mE}{K^2} + \frac{2me^2}{K^2 r} - \frac{n(n+1)}{r^2} \right) \chi = 0.$$

In fulfilling the boundary conditions one obtains solutions only for certain values of the energy parameters, the stationary values. This seemed to Schrödinger to be the "salient point," but in Bohr's original theory—as its creator stressed from the beginning—it was one of the two fundamental postulates that had remained unexplained.

In his second paper Schrödinger gave a sort of "derivation" of his *undulatorischer Mechanik* in which he drew on the almost century-old work of William Rowan Hamilton. In Hamilton's work Schrödinger found an analogy between mechanics and geometrical optics. And, since geometrical optics "is only a gross approximation for light," he conjectured that the same cause was responsible for the failure of classical mechanics "in the case of very small orbital dimensions and very strong orbital curvature." Both would be only approximations for small wavelengths. Therefore, he said:

> Perhaps this failure is a complete analogy to the failure of geometrical optics, that is, the optics with infinitely small wavelengths; [a failure] that occurs, as is known, as soon as the "obstacles" or "openings" are no longer large relative to the real, finite wavelength. Perhaps our classical mechanics is the *complete* analogue of geometrical optics and, as such, false. . . . Therefore, we have to seek an "undulatory mechanics"—and the way to it that lies closest at hand is the wave-theoretical elaboration of Hamilton's model.

Consequently, Schrödinger introduced into his development of wave mechanics conceptions that differed completely from those underlying the quantum mechanics formulated by the Göttingen school. He himself stated: "It is hardly necessary to emphasize how much more agreeable it would be to represent a quantum transition as the passage of energy from one vibrational form into another, rather than to represent it as the jumping of electrons." In many passages Schrödinger (like Heisenberg) expressed his views in an almost polemical tone: "I . . . feel intimidated, not to say repelled, by what seem to me the very difficult methods [of matrix mechanics] and by the lack of clarity."

Despite his distaste for matrix mechanics, Schrödinger was "convinced of [its] inner connection" with wave mechanics. Hermann Weyl, to whom he had presented his purely mathematical problem, was unable to "provide the connecting link." Thereupon Schrödinger temporarily put aside his conjectures on the matter; but by the beginning of March 1926, much earlier than he had thought possible, he was able to show the formal, mathematical identity of the two theories.

The starting point for this analysis was the following observation:

> Given the extraordinary disparity, it is . . . odd that these two new quantum theories agree with each other even where they deviate from the old quantum theory. I note above all the peculiar "half-integrality" in the case of the oscillator and the rotator. This is truly remarkable, for the starting point, conception, method, and . . . entire mathematical apparatus appear to be fundamentally different for each theory.

He proceeded to show the complete mathematical equivalence of the two theories. The matrices can be constructed from Schrödinger's eigenfunctions, and vice versa.

With the demonstration of the mathematical identity of wave mechanics and matrix mechanics, physicists at last came into possession of the "new quantum theory" that had been sought for so long. In working with it they could use either of two mathematical tools: matrix computation or the method of setting up and solving a partial differential equation. Schrödinger's wave equation proved to be easier to handle and thus his methods were more widely adopted for the mathematical treatment of the new theory. He contributed substantially to the elaboration of that treatment in his next two papers, especially through the development of his perturbation theory.

In 1927 Schrödinger succeeded Max Planck in the chair of theoretical physics at the University of Berlin. At the same time he became a member of the Prussian Academy of Sciences. But in 1933, deeply outraged at the new regime and its dismissal of outstandingly qualified scientists, he moved to Oxford. In the same year he was awarded the Nobel Prize in physics, jointly with P.A.M. Dirac.

As early as May 1938 Eamon de Valera, who had once been professor of mathematics at the University of Dublin, attempted to find a way of bringing Schrödinger to Ireland. At the beginning of September 1939, Schrödinger, as a German émigré, suddenly found himself an enemy alien; but de Valera came to his assistance. Through the Irish high commissioner in Great Britain, he arranged for a letter of safe conduct to be issued for Schrödinger, who on 5 October 1939 passed through England on his way from Ghent to Dublin with a transit visa valid for twenty-four hours. Schrödinger spent the next seventeen years in the Irish capital, where he was able to work in his new position undisturbed by external events. He devoted an especially fervent effort, as did Einstein in his later years, to expanding the latter's theory of gravitation into a "unified field theory," the metric determination of which was to be established from a consideration of all the known forces between particles.

Soon after the end of the war, Austria tried to convince him to return home, but he did not return definitively until 1956, when he was given his own chair at the University of Vienna.

SCHROEDER VAN DER KOLK, JACOBUS LUDOVICUS CONRADUS (b. Leeuwarden, Netherlands, 1797; d. Utrecht, Netherlands, 1862), medicine.

Received M.D. at Groningen (1820); established medical practice in Amsterdam (1826) and taught at Utrecht (1827–62). Made important contributions in anatomy and physiology. In studying brain disorders he examined closely the structure of the central nervous system; his most important discovery was the connection between the nervous fibers of the anterior roots of the medulla oblongata and the large branched cells of the anterior gray horns of the spinal cord. He was deeply influenced by vitalism in both his physiology and clinical psychiatric concepts. He always strove for better care for the insane and prompted legislation for general reform in the care of the mad.

SCHROETER, HEINRICH EDUARD (b. Königsberg, Germany [now Kaliningrad, R.S.F.S.R.], 1829; d. Breslau, Germany [now Wrocław, Poland], 1892), mathematics.

Studied at Königsberg (doctorate, 1854) and at Berlin under Jakob Steiner; taught at Breslau (1855–92). Steiner's influence on Schroeter led him to devote almost all his research to synthetic geometry. His extensive book of 1880 on the theory of second-order surfaces and third-order space curves continues Steiner's work. Schroeter's name has been given to the generation of a third-degree plane curve and to two generations of a third-degree surface.

SCHRÖTER, JOHANN HIERONYMUS (b. Erfurt, Germany, 1745; d. Erfurt, 1816), astronomy.

Studied law at Göttingen but also attended lectures in mathematics, physics, and astronomy. The observatory he built and equipped at Lilienthal was a center of astronomical research for thirty years, becoming world-famous for the excellence of its instruments. First to observe the surface of the moon and the planets systematically over a long period; discovered and named the lunar rills. He had important influence on Harding, Bessel, and J. F. J. Schmidt.

SCHRÖTTER, ANTON VON (b. Olmütz, Austria [now Olomouc, Czechoslovakia], 1802; d. Vienna, Austria, 1875), chemistry.

Studied at Vienna; taught at the Technische Hochschule of Graz (1827–43), where he set up an impressive laboratory, and at the Technische Hochschule in Vienna (from 1843). Chief director of the mint (1868–74). Best known for his conclusive demonstration that red phosphorus (believed to be an oxide of white phosphorus) is truly an allotropic form of the element. His suggestion of using amorphous phosphorus led to the development of the safety match.

SCHUBERT, HERMANN CÄSAR HANNIBAL (b. Potsdam, Germany, 1848; d. Hamburg, Germany, 1911), mathematics.

Studied at Berlin and Halle (doctorate, 1870); taught in secondary schools in Hildesheim and Hamburg. His most important work was in enumerative geometry, which is concerned with all those problems and theorems of algebraic geometry that involve a finite number of solutions. One of his achievements was to combine "the principle of the conservation of the number" with the Chasles correspondence principle, thus establishing the foundation of a calculus. In Kalkül der abzählenden Geometrie (1879) the formulation of his fundamental problem included appropriate elementary sets that have since been known as Schubert sets.

SCHUCHERT, CHARLES (b. Cincinnati, Ohio, 1858; d. New Haven, Conn., 1942), paleontology.

Schuchert began his career as an untrained amateur collector of fossils and completed it as perhaps the most influential synthesizer of historical geology in North America. For much of the nineteenth century, the "Cincinnati school" of enthusiastic amateurs was a vital part of the American study of paleontology. After a successful career with various geological surveys and as curator at the U.S. National Museum, Schuchert began a second career teaching at Yale (1904). His most important publications were *Synopsis of American Fossil Brachiopoda* (1897), *A Text-Book of Geology* (1915), "Paleogeography of North America" (1910), and *Historical Geology of North America* (vol. I, 1935). A direct outgrowth of his teaching efforts was the summarization of numerous stratigraphic details on maps to give a better picture of the changing distribution of land and seas during 600 million years.

SCHULTZE, MAX JOHANN SIGISMUND (*b. Freiburg im Breisgau, Germany, 1825; d. Bonn, Germany, 1874*), anatomy, microscopy.

Graduated from University of Greifswald (M.D., 1849); taught at Greifswald (1850–54), Halle (1854–59), and Bonn (from 1859). Schultze played a leading role in the movement to reform the cell theory as originally set forth by Schleiden and Schwann. Above all, he disputed their emphasis on the cell wall and directed attention instead to the living substance (protoplasm) found within all cells, whether plant or animal. His next most important work was on the sense organs, particularly the retina, elucidating the physiological role of the rods and cones. He also did valuable descriptive and taxonomic work, especially on rhizopods and sponges. He founded in 1865 and edited until his death the *Archiv für mikroskopische Anatomie und Entwicklungsmechanik.*

SCHULZE, FRANZ FERDINAND (*b. Naumburg, Germany, 1815; d. Rostock, Germany, 1873*), chemistry, microbiology.

Schulze's career was centered principally around teaching agricultural chemistry at Eldena and chemistry and pharmacy at Rostock. The core of much of his work was his expertise in analytical chemistry; he made a number of useful modifications to existing analytical techniques and equipment, such as in gas analysis and in the use of the blowpipe in the production of laboratory glassware. In studies of well water, he contributed significantly to the controversy over spontaneous generation.

SCHUMACHER, HEINRICH CHRISTIAN (*b. Bad Bramstedt, Holstein, Germany, 1780; d. Altona, Germany, 1850*), astronomy, geodesy.

After earning a law degree Schumacher obtained a salaried position at Göttingen (1807) and studied astronomy under Gauss, who became a lifelong friend. He also studied mathematics in Hamburg and made observations at its observatory. Directed observatory at Mannheim (1813–15), taught at Copenhagen (1815–17), worked at the Altona observatory for many years, and directed geodetic surveys. His founding of *Astronomische Nachrichten* (1823), a journal to which astronomers of all nations could contribute, is perhaps his greatest contribution to astronomy.

SCHUMANN, VICTOR (*b. Markranstödt, near Leipzig, Germany, 1841; d. Leipzig, 1913*), photography.

After training as an engineer, Schumann was co-founder of an engineering works in Leipzig (1865) and served as its technical director. He took up photography as a hobby while it was still in its infancy. He developed methods leading to shorter exposure times and to markedly improved tint contrasts. His development of

photographic plates capable of registering ultraviolet light made him a pioneer of spectroscopy and of atomic physics.

SCHUNCK, HENRY EDWARD (*b. Manchester, England, 1820; d. Kersal, near Manchester, 1903*), organic chemistry.

Studied under Rose and Magnus at Berlin and with Liebig at Giessen before entering his father's printing works in 1842. Later was able to detach himself from management duties and devote himself to research, mainly to chemistry of the natural coloring matters. Made important contributions to the study of the polyhydroxy anthraquinones, and was among the first to use absorption spectroscopy as a tool for the identification of colored compounds. Although he never held an academic post, he was the leading figure in the scientific life of Manchester for fifty years, and his laboratory and extensive library were bequeathed to the University.

SCHUR, ISSAI (*b. Mogilev, Russia, 1875; d. Tel Aviv, Palestine [now Israel], 1941*), mathematics.

Attended and spent most of his scientific career at Berlin. Also taught at Bonn (1911–16). His principal field was the representation theory of groups; certain of the functions appearing in his dissertation on the subject have been named "S-functions" in his honor. In 1905 he reestablished the theory of group characters—the keystone of representation theory. The most important tool involved is "Schur's lemma." In 1906 he considered the fundamental problems that appear when an algebraic number field is taken as the domain; a number appearing in this connection is now called the Schur index.

SCHUSTER, ARTHUR (*b. Frankfurt, Germany, 1851; d. Yeldall, near Twyford, Berkshire, England, 1934*), physics, applied mathematics.

Studied at Owens College, Manchester, and at Heidelberg (Ph.D., 1873). Taught at Owens College (1881–1907). In 1897 Schuster independently discovered and published the relationship known as the Rydberg-Schuster law, which relates the convergence frequencies of different spectral series of the same substance. He made important investigations of the spectra produced by the discharge of electricity through gases in otherwise evacuated tubes. Among his many other interests, his work on terrestrial magnetism deserves special notice: in 1889 he showed that daily magnetic variations are of two kinds, internal and atmospheric. He was knighted in 1920.

SCHWABE, SAMUEL HEINRICH (*b. Dessau, Germany, 1789; d. Dessau, 1875*), astronomy.

Schwabe studied at Berlin and worked as an apothecary from 1812 until 1829, when he sold the business to devote his time to science. In 1827 he rediscovered the eccentricity of Saturn's rings. In 1843 he made his first definite statement regarding the periodicity of sunspots, giving statistics for 1826–43. His carefully compiled results demonstrated the existence of periodicity, although he wrongly estimated the period to be about ten years. His discovery remained unnoticed until Humboldt drew attention to it in 1851.

SCHWANN, THEODOR AMBROSE HUBERT (*b. Neuss, Germany, 1810; d. Cologne, Germany, 1882*), physiology.

Schwann obtained his bachelor's degree in 1831 at Bonn, studied in Würzburg, and received the M.D. in 1834 at Berlin, where he became one of Johannes Müller's assistants. Schwann's contributions to Müller's *Handbuch der Physiologie* inaugurated the quantitative period of physiology. He envisaged experiments in which it would be possible to subject the physiological properties of an organ or tissue to physical measurement; one such experiment used the "muscular balance" and in a sense established the first tension-length diagram for muscle contraction. Dissociating itself from the teaching of Müller and resolutely abandoning the notion of vital force for the study of molecular mechanisms, the school stemming from Schwann's experiment was distinguished particularly by the work of his successors at Berlin, du Bois-Reymond and Helmholtz. Parallel with his experiments on muscle, Schwann pursued the researches that led to his discovery of pepsin. In 1836 his experiments with fermentation led to the conclusion that alcoholic fermentation is the work of a live organism.

In 1839, in his *Mikroskopische Untersuchungen*, Schwann formulated his cell theory, which insists on the common cellular origin of every living thing. By "cell" Schwann meant "a layer around a nucleus" that could differentiate itself. He also thought (incorrectly) that cells form around a nucleus within a "blastema," an amorphous substance that can be intracellular or extracellular. Schwann's cell theory can be regarded as marking the origin in biology of the school of mechanistic materialism that Brücke, du Bois-Reymond, Helmholtz, and Carl Ludwig made famous. According to Schwann, the theory that led from the chemical molecule to the organism by way of the universal stage of the cell, was inspired by an intellectual, mechanistic reaction to Müller's vitalism. Erroneous as it appears now in certain of its aspects, this theory led him to the inestimably significant discovery of the development of organisms through cellular differentiation. His short and brilliant scientific career extended from 1834 to 1839, after which he became professor, inventor, and theologian. He taught at Louvain (1839–48) and Liège (1848–79). While at Louvain he developed a method of utilizing the biliary fistula for the study of the role of bile in digestion, and concluded that a lack of bile secretion in the digestive tract is incompatible with survival.

SCHWARZ, HERMANN AMANDUS (*b. Hermsdorf, Silesia [now Sobiecin, Poland], 1843; d. Berlin, Germany, 1921*), mathematics.

Received doctorate at Berlin (1864); taught at Halle, the Eidgenössische Technische Hochschule in Zurich, Göttingen, and Berlin. The influence of Weierstrass at Berlin led Schwarz to place his geometric ability in the service of analysis, and this synthesis was the basis of his contribution to mathematics. His work most important to the history of mathematics was the "rescue" of some of Riemann's achievements. The question centered on the "main theorem" of conformal mapping. Schwarz first solved the mapping problem explicitly for various simple geometric figures and then in general for polygons. His solutions included "Schwarz's lemma." In his most important work, a *Festschrift* for Weierstrass, Schwarz set himself the task of completely answering the question of whether a given minimal surface really yields a minimal area. He employed the inequality for integrals that is today known as "Schwarz's inequality."

SCHWARZSCHILD, KARL (*b. Frankfurt am Main, Germany, 1873; d. Potsdam, Germany, 1916*), astronomy.

Schwarzschild's precocious mastery of celestial mechanics resulted in two papers on double star orbits, written when he was barely sixteen. Studied at Strasbourg and at Munich (Ph.D., 1896). The main thrust of his work at the Kuffner observatory near Vienna (1896–99) was stellar photometry, substituting a photographic plate for the human eye at the telescope. His practical and theoretical work culminated in his "Aktinometrie" (1910), so called because light producing a photochemical effect was then referred to as "actinic." It contains the earliest catalog of photographic magnitudes. According to the photochemical law, the image of a given star should be identical with that produced for a star half as bright when exposed for twice the time; Schwarzschild was the first to quantify the particular "failure of reciprocity" that occurs with faint stars. He modified the law by raising the exposure time to the power p (Schwarzschild's exponent), with p less than unity but a constant for any given combination of emulsion and development process (Schwarzschild's law). While serving as *Privatdozent* at Munich (1899–1901) he developed theories on the curvature of space and on the tails of comets.

From 1901 to 1909 he taught at Göttingen and was director of its observatory. The observatory soon became a center for young intellectuals of all disciplines. He devised a special plateholder—his "Schraffierkassette"—to improve his photographic images of stars. *Aktinometrie, Teil B* (1912) contains for each star its fully corrected photographic magnitude and an indication of its surface temperature in the form of its color index. To the tradition of geodetic measurements at Göttingen he contributed in 1903 a suspended zenith camera of his own design. In 1905 he photographed the total solar eclipse in Algeria; he took sixteen photographs of the solar spectrum in thirty seconds. In 1906 he published a theoretical work on the transfer of energy at and near the surface of the sun. He developed a theory of radiative exchange and equilibrium that was quantitative, and therefore susceptible to experimental verification. His first approximation to a solution of the integral equations involved is usually referred to as the Schuster-Schwarzschild model for a gray atmosphere, although the two men arrived at it independently. Other work done by Schwarzschild at Göttingen includes papers on electrodynamics, geometrical optics, stellar statistics, and publication of his popular lectures on cosmology.

In 1909 he became director of the Astrophysical Observatory in Potsdam, where his interests turned more toward spectroscopy. He designed a spectrographic objective, which was built by Zeiss. While serving in the war (1914–16) he wrote two papers on general relativity. The first, dealing with the gravitational field of a point mass in empty space, was the first exact solution of Einstein's field equations. The well-known "Schwarzschild radius" appears in the second of these papers, which treated the gravitational field of a fluid sphere with constant density throughout. Should a star, undergoing gravitational collapse, shrink down inside this radius, it becomes a "black hole" that emits no radiation and can be detected only by its gravitational effects.

SCHWEIGGER, JOHANN SALOMO CHRISTOPH (*b. Erlangen, Bavaria, 1779; d. Halle, Prussia, 1857*), physics, chemistry.

Received Ph.D. at Erlangen (1800); his main academic career was at Halle (1819–57). Best known as founder of the *Journal für Chemie und Physik,* of which he edited fifty-four volumes (1811–28). He published several papers in which he questioned the validity of Volta's contact theory of electricity (1806, 1808), and shared with Poggendorff the honor of constructing the first simple galvanometer (1810).

SCHWEIKART, FERDINAND KARL (*b. Erbach, Germany, 1780; d. Königsberg, Germany [now Kaliningrad, R.S.F.S.R.], 1859*), mathematics.

Received doctorates in law (Jena, 1798) and philosophy (Königsberg); taught at Giessen, Kharkov, Marburg, and Königsberg. He holds an important place in the prehistory of non-Euclidean geometry. In his only publication in mathematics (1807) he considered the problem of parallel lines, and later arrived at the beginnings of a hyperbolic geometry, which he called astral geometry.

SCHWENDENER, SIMON (*b. Buchs, St. Gallen, Switzerland, 1829; d. Berlin, Germany, 1919*), plant anatomy.

Studied at Zurich (Ph.D., 1856) under the strong influence of Candolle and Naegeli. While at Munich (1857–67) he collaborated with Naegeli on *Das Mikroskop* (2 vols., 1865–67), demonstrating a number of details of plant anatomy and setting out principles that Abbe used in his optical work. At Basel (1867–77) he continued his previous work on lichens, and first stated (1869) that lichens are a composite of algae and fungi. He moved to Tübingen in 1877 and to Berlin in 1878. He demonstrated that the principles of mechanics govern the structure of the stems of plants and that leaf arrangement is the result of displacement by contact between leaf primordia. The latter remains an important theory of phyllotaxy.

SCILLA, AGOSTINO (*b. Messina, Sicily, 1629; d. Rome, Italy, 1700*), geology.

One of best painters of the seventeenth-century Sicilian school. In science he is particularly remembered for *La vana speculazione disingannata dal senso* (1670), today considered one of the classics of geology. He described with admirable clarity and critical sense his observations on the fossiliferous sedimentary terrains of both shores of the Strait of Messina. At a time when most scientists still thought fossils were born within rocks, Scilla considered them to be animal remains imprisoned in rocks that are now hard but were originally muddy or sandy soil.

SCLATER, PHILIP LUTLEY (*b. Tangier Park, Hampshire, England, 1829; d. Odiham, Hampshire, England, 1913*), ornithology.

Sclater took his B.A. at Oxford (1849). His most engrossing duties were with the Zoological Society of London, as Council member (from 1857) and secretary (1860–1903). Took a prominent part in founding *Ibis,* the journal of the British Ornithologists' Union (1858), becoming its first editor. In his paper "On the General Geographic Distribution of the Members of the Class Aves" (1858) he classified the zoogeographical regions of the world on the basis of their bird life. Among his almost 1,400 publications were four volumes of the monumental *Catalogue of the Birds in the British Museum* (1886–91).

SCOT. *See* **Michael Scot.**

SCOTT, DUKINFIELD HENRY (*b. London, England, 1854; d. Basingstoke, England, 1934*), botany, paleobotany.

Attended Christ Church, Oxford (B.A., 1876), and Würzburg (doctor of philosophy, 1882). Returned to England and taught at University College and the Royal College of Science, doing experiments in the Jodrell Laboratory in Kew Gardens. Collaborated with W. C. Williamson of Manchester on several memoirs on the anatomy of fossil species. Wrote two admirable textbooks which together make up *An Introduction to Structural Botany:* pt. I, *Flowering Plants;* pt. II, *Flowerless Plants* (1896). His lectures at University College, London were published as *Studies in Fossil Botany,* which became and has remained a classic. One of those who laid the foundations of scientific botany and paleobotany, he also wrote *The Evolution of Plants* (1911) and *Extinct Plants and Problems of Evolution* (1922).

SCOTT, WILLIAM BERRYMAN (*b. Cincinnati, Ohio, 1858; d. Princeton, N.J., 1947*), vertebrate paleontology, geology.

Studied at the College of New Jersey (now Princeton), in England, and in Germany (doctorate, Heidelberg). Taught at Princeton for 67 years. His research was almost entirely devoted to fossil mammals. Edited and wrote in part *Reports of the Princeton University Expeditions to Patagonia* (1905–12). Wrote several large volumes on the Oligocene mammals of the beds of the White River, South Dakota (1936–41); a standard geology textbook; and *History of Land Mammals in the Western Hemisphere* (1913).

SCOTUS, JOHN DUNS. *See* **Duns Scotus, John.**

SCROPE, GEORGE JULIUS POULETT (*b. London, England, 1797; d. Fairlawn [near Cobham], Surrey, England, 1876*), geology.

Scrope was educated at Harrow; Pembroke College, Oxford (1815–16); and St. John's College, Cambridge (1816–21). He was a member of Parliament from 1833 to 1868. On the basis of his geological fieldwork in France, Italy, Sicily, and the Lipari Islands, studying Vesuvius, Mount Etna, and Stromboli, he wrote two books. *Considerations on Volcanos* (1825) has been called "the earliest systematic treatise on vulcanology." His partial restatement of the ideas of Hutton, Playfair, and Hall, together with his theory of a cooling earth, provided the basis for a catastrophist opposition to the uniformitarianism of Lyell. His second book, *Memoir on the Geology of Central France* (1827), was more uniformitarian in approach and influenced the development of Lyell's views. Therefore, Scrope can, paradoxically, be regarded as a parent of both uniformitarianism and its catastrophist opposition in Great Britain; he never committed himself to either side. He assisted Lyell in completing the first volume of his *Principles of Geology* (1830), which had as a principal objective the extermination of theological influence on geology. In two articles (1856, 1859) he helped to refute the theory of "craters of elevation" of Humboldt, Buch, and Élie de Beaumont.

SCUDDER, SAMUEL HUBBARD (*b. Boston, Mass., 1837; d. Cambridge, Mass., 1911*), systematic entomology.

Attended Williams College (1853–57) and studied with Agassiz at Harvard (1857–64). Held various positions in Cambridge and Boston; worked as paleontologist in the U.S. Geological Survey (1886–92). Noteworthy works include *Catalogue of Scientific Serials of All Countries . . . 1633–1876* (1879); *Nomenclator zoologicus* (1882–84); and *Butterflies of the Eastern United States and Canada* (1888–89). One of the most learned and productive American systematic entomologists of his day, his main contributions were in the study of Orthoptera.

SEARES, FREDERICK HANLEY (*b. near Cassopolis, Mich., 1873; d. Honolulu, Hawaii, 1964*), astronomy.

Studied at University of California in Berkeley (B.S., 1895), at the Sorbonne, and at Berlin. After eight years at Laws Observatory he began a thirty-six-year career at the Mount Wilson Observatory. His principal contribution lay in the field of photographic photometry: he standardized the stellar magnitude system and extended it to include stars fainter than the eighteenth magnitude. He developed an exposure ratio method for direct determination of the color index of stars.

SECCHI, (PIETRO) ANGELO (*b. Reggio nell'Emilia, Italy, 1818; d. Rome, Italy, 1878*), astronomy, astrophysics.

Secchi entered the Jesuit order in Rome, studied at the Collegio Romano, and became the director of its observatory (1849). He determined to build a new observatory with better equipment and to reshape the course of research performed there, placing a new emphasis on astrophysics. He began his study of the sun by measuring its radiation during the eclipse of 1851; he made several daguerreotypes that are among the earliest applications of photography to the study of celestial bodies. He made important spectroscopic studies of sunspots, chromospheric eruptions, solar prominences, and eclipses; studied the physical constitution of comets; and established the similarity of falling stars, asteroids, and aerolites. He determined the physical characteristics of Saturn, including its polar flattening and the eccentricity of its ring; introduced the term "canals" for those observed on Mars; measured and made a detailed drawing of the crater of Copernicus on the moon; and concluded from spectroscopic studies of Jupiter and Saturn that their atmospheres contained elements different from terrestrial ones. His spectroscopic research on luminous stars began in 1863. He examined at least 4,000 stars and was able to divide them into five types, with the high-temperature white stars at one end of the scale and the low-temperature red stars at the other. This classification still bears his name; it was soon adopted almost universally. He also classified nebulae according to his spectroscopic examination, into planetary, elliptical, and irregular forms.

SECHENOV, IVAN MIKHAYLOVICH (*b. Teply Stan [now Sechenovo], Simbirsk guberniya [now Arzamas oblast], Russia, 1829; d. Moscow, Russia, 1905*), physiology, physical chemistry, psychology.

After graduating from Moscow University (1856), Sechenov studied and worked in Germany in the laboratories of Johannes Müller, E. du Bois-Reymond, Helmholtz, and Ludwig; and in the Paris laboratory of Claude Bernard. Taught at the St. Petersburg Medico-Surgical Academy (1860–70), where he founded the first Russian school of physiology; and at Novorossysk University (1871–76), St. Petersburg (1876–88), and Moscow (1891–1901). In 1862 he reported on "central inhibition," the repressive effects of thalamic nerve centers on spinal reflexes, thus inaugurating research on inhibition phenomena in the central nervous system. He then suggested the theory of cerebral behavior mechanisms, according to which all conscious and unconscious acts are reflexes in terms of their structure. This theory provided the basis for the development of neurophysiology and objective psychology in Russia, including the investigations of Pavlov and Bekhterev. He also established the existence of periodic spontaneous fluctuations of bioelectric potentials in the brain; and, maintaining that the reality of sensation is rooted in the reality of the motor act, developed a new approach to the functions of the sensory organs.

SEDERHOLM, JOHANNES JAKOB (*b. Helsinki, Finland, 1863; d. Helsinki, 1934*), geology, petrology.

Studied at Helsinki (B.A., 1885); Stockholm, under the strong influence of Brøgger; and Heidelberg (doctorate, 1892). At Heidelberg he wrote important papers on the eruptive rocks of southern Finland and on the rapakivi granites. Became director of the Geological Commission (1892–1933), the first geological survey of Finland with geological mapping; he not only created a modern research institution for basic and economic geology, but also established new standards for the study of the world's crystalline basements, the Precambrian continental shields. He improved methods by mapping crucially important areas or outcrops on a finer scale and publishing them on separate sheets. His eagerness to find conglomerates was rewarded by his important discovery of such formations in the sedimentary series of Lake Näsijärvi, near Tampere, in 1899. This was a triumph for uniformitarian principles, and the area became a classic site often visited by foreign geologists.

A new level of research was intercalated between the petrographic level, based mainly on microscopic study and large-scale mapping. He created a new apparatus of descriptive and interpretive terms: migmatites, "agmatites," "nebulites," ptygmatic veins, and palingenetic and anatectic granites. He published a series of maps of the basement of Finland, perfected after progressive mapping, in the *Atlas of Finland,* on whose editorial staff he served (1899–1925). In "The Average Composition of the Earth's Crust in Finland" (1925), another study of old crystalline basements, he attempted to characterize the average geochemical composition of deeply eroded crustal areas. He classified granite into four families, which also were groups of different relative age that occupy special places in the evolution of the crustal sector. He studied special textures: orbicular, spotted, and nodular granites and the rapakivi (1928). He produced a hitherto unsuspected picture of crustal evolution in a historical perspective.

SEDGWICK, ADAM (*b. Dent, Yorkshire, England, 1785; d. Cambridge, England, 1873*), geology.

Graduated from Trinity College, Cambridge (1808), became a fellow in 1810, and was ordained in 1817. Taught geology at Cambridge from 1818. His lectures had tremendous influence on successive generations of Cambridge students, and hence on the shaping of English educated opinion on geology. His geological collection expanded into one of the finest geological museums in the world. His most important geological work, which led to the foundation of the Cambrian system, seems to have been motivated by a desire to penetrate the fossil record back to its farthest limits, and to demonstrate that life had indeed had a beginning in time. The wide relevance of his conclusions lay in his interpretation of strata as the products of long-continued processes, and in his emphasis on the strata as conformable "connecting links" from the Coal Measures below to the Jurassic above.

Sedgwick's joint works with Murchison were "A Sketch of the Structure of the Eastern Alps . . ." (1832), "On the Physical Structure of Devonshire, and on the Subdivisions and Geological Relations of Its Older Stratified Deposits, &c." (1840), and "On the Distribution and Classification of the Older or Palaeozoic Deposits of the North of Germany and Belgium, and Their Comparisons With Formations of the Same Age in the British Isles" (1842). Their studies of strata in North Wales (Sedgwick's "Cambrian"), the Welsh Borderland (Murchison's "Silurian"), and Devonshire (which they termed "Devonian") had important implications for the understanding of the earliest part of the fossil record. Their conflict over Murchison's Lower Silurian strata, which Sedgwick called Upper Cambrian, was settled much later, when the discovery of earlier faunas in Wales rehabilitated the term Cambrian for what had been Sedgwick's Lower Cambrian; and an "Ordovician" system was proposed for the disputed strata (that is, Sedgwick's "Upper Cambrian" and Murchison's "Lower Silurian") between the newly restricted Cambrian and Silurian systems. Sedgwick gave Charles Darwin his first training as a field geologist; he later rejected his pupil's evolutionary theory, feeling that no purely natural mechanism could ever account for the origin of new organic species. His influential *Discourse on the Studies of the University* (1833) linked a reassertion of the place of geology within the tradition of natural theology with a trenchant criticism of utilitarian moral philosophy.

SEDOV, GEORGY YAKOVLEVICH (*b. Krivaya Kosa, on the Sea of Azov, Russia, 1877; d. during an expedition to the North Pole, 1914*), hydrography, polar exploration.

In 1901 Sedov was assigned to the Main Hydrographical Administration of the Naval Ministry in St. Petersburg. In 1909 he explored the mouth of the Kolyma River, directing meteorological and hydrological observations and gathering ethnographical and geological material and making astronomical observations. On his fatal expedition to the North Pole he and the other members made meteorological and magnetic observations, investi-

gated and mapped Novaya Zemlya, gave geological descriptions of Hooker Island and Franz Josef Land, made observations on the condition of the ice, and determined astronomical points.

SEE, THOMAS JEFFERSON JACKSON (*b. near Montgomery City, Mo., 1866; d. Oakland, Calif., 1962*), astronomy.

Graduated from University of Missouri (1889); doctorate from Berlin (1892). Directed observatory at Mare Island, California (1903–30). Studied evolution of the stars, earth, and the solar system. First to do an experimental study of craters formed by high-velocity projectiles. Formulated the wave theory of gravitation and suggested the red shift of galaxies was due to interaction of light and gravity waves. His numerous publications were considered unorthodox, but many of his ideas are in striking agreement with current theories.

SEEBECK, THOMAS (*b. Tallinn, Estonia, 1770; d. Berlin, Germany, 1831*), electricity, magnetism, optics.

Studied at Berlin and Göttingen (M.D., 1802). Decided to devote himself to research in the natural sciences rather than practice medicine. In Jena he investigated the heating and chemical effects of the different colors of the solar spectrum, and studied polarization in stressed glass. In Berlin he repeated the discovery made independently by Arago and Davy, that an electric current can induce magnetism in iron and steel, and that a steel needle is strongly magnetized when drawn around a conductor. His most significant discovery was that of thermoelectricity—or thermomagnetism, as he called it—in 1822.

SEELIGER, HUGO VON (*b. Biala, near Bielitz, Austrian Silesia [now Bielsko Biala, Poland], 1849; d. Munich, Germany, 1924*), astronomy.

Studied at Heidelberg and Leipzig (doctorate, 1871). Worked at observatories at Leipzig, Bonn, Gotha (director from 1881), and Munich (director from 1882). Main interest was theoretical astronomy: made important contribution to study of stellar statistics. First to develop the fundamental equations of the relations between various statistical functions of the stars. His important papers on the illumination of cosmic objects deal especially with Saturn and the zodiacal light. His research on the law of gravitation provided a strong impetus to astronomical cosmology.

SEGNER, JÁNOS-ANDRÁS (JOHANN ANDREAS VON) (*b. Pressburg, Hungary [now Bratislava, Czechoslovakia], 1704; d. Halle, Germany, 1777*), mathematics, physics.

Received M.D. at Jena (1730), where he also studied physics and mathematics. Taught at Jena (1732–35), Göttingen (1735–55), and Halle (1755–77). He invented one of the first reaction hydraulic turbines, named for him, consisting of a wheel rotating under the action of water streaming from parallel and oppositely directed tubes. Segner's wheel is now used for horticultural irrigation. He constructed and perfected other scientific devices, studied the theory of tubes, and wrote on various problems of physics and mathematics. Carried on mutually fruitful correspondence with Euler.

SEGRE, CORRADO (*b. Saluzzo, Italy, 1863; d. Turin, Italy, 1924*), mathematics.

Received doctorate (1883) and taught (1883–1924) at Turin. All of his work was linked by a common concern with the problem of space. He wrote articles on the geometric properties that are invariant under linear transformations of space, and a series of works on the properties of algebraic curves and ruled surfaces subjected to birational transformations. In studying the role of imaginary elements in geometry, he laid the basis of a new theory of hyperalgebraic entities by representing complex points of S_n by means of the ∞^{2n} real points of one of the varieties V_{2n} (Segre variety). Darboux's *Leçons sur la théorie générale des surfaces* inspired him to investigate infinitesimal geometry. He introduced a new system of lines, analogous to those studied by Darboux, traced on the surface; they were named Segre lines, and their differential equation was established by Fubini. Segre wrote a classic article on hyperspaces for the *Encyklopädie der mathematischen Wissenschaften.*

SÉGUIN, ARMAND (*b. Paris, France, 1767; d. Paris, 1835*), chemistry, chemical technology, physiology.

Little is known of his education; by the mid-1780's he had become part of Lavoisier's circle, and was his assistant from 1789 until the latter's death in 1794. Séguin's papers on respiration, animal heat, and caloric are all derivative from Lavoisier's work and ideas. As director of a tanning works at Sèvres, an enterprise based on processes of his own devising, he shortened the time for tanning hides from more than a year to a few weeks. He collaborated with Fourcroy and Vauquelin in experiments on the synthesis of water.

SEGUIN, MARC, also known as **Seguin Aîné** (*b. Annonay, France, 1786; d. Annonay, 1875*), engineering, physics.

Studied in Paris, where his interest in science and engineering was stimulated and decisively shaped by his granduncle Joseph Montgolfier. In 1825, at Tournon on the Rhone, he and his brothers erected the first successful suspension bridge in France to use cables of iron wire. They organized the company that built France's first modern railroad, a line between Saint-Étienne and Lyons completed in 1832. In 1827 Seguin invented the multitubular, or fire tube, boiler. His most important publication was *De l'influence des chemins de fer* (1839), a handbook for the design and construction of railroads, in which he rejected the caloric theory, stating that, "It appears more natural to me to suppose that a certain quantity of heat disappears in the very act of the production of force or mechanical power, and conversely; and that the two phenomena are linked together by conditions that assign to them invariable relationships." This assumption was the basis for his later claim to priority over Joule and Mayer for the statement of the convertibility and conservation of heat and work.

SEIDEL, PHILIPP LUDWIG VON (*b. Zweibrücken, Germany, 1821; d. Munich, Germany, 1896*), astronomy, mathematics.

Studied at Berlin, Königsberg, and Munich (doctorate, 1846). Taught at Munich. His photometric measurements of fixed stars and planets were the first true measurements of this kind. The precise evaluation of his observations by methods of probability theory, considering atmospheric extinction, are worthy of special mention. In his mathematical investigations he filled important gaps left by his teacher, Dirichlet—for instance, introducing the concept of nonuniform convergence.

SEKI, TAKAKAZU (*b. Huzioka* [?], *Japan, 1642* [?]; *d. Edo* [*now Tokyo*], *Japan, 1708*), mathematics.

Knowledge of Seki's life is meager and indirect. Worked as chief of the Bureau of Supply in Edo (now Tokyo). Of particular influence on Seki's mathematics was Chu Shih-chieh's *Suan-hsüeh ch'i-mêng,* a collection of problems solved by the Chinese method *t'ien-yuan shu,* which makes it possible to solve a problem by transforming it into an algebraic equation with one variable. In his *Hatubi sanpō* (1674) Seki solved fifteen problems unsolvable by Chu Shih-chieh's method. Seki introduced Chinese ideographs and wrote them to the right of a vertical; this notation (*bōsyohō*) was the basis of his *endan zyutu* ("*endan* method"), which enabled him to represent known and unknown quantities by Chinese ideographs, and led him to form equations with literal coefficients of any degree and with several variables. The method was later renamed *tenzan zyutu.* Some of his theorems were collected and published posthumously by his disciples as *Katuyō sanpō* (1709).

Seki first treated general theories of algebraic equations. The notion of a discriminant of an algebraic equation was introduced by him. The method that he named *syōsahō* for determining coefficients gave a solution similar to the method of finite difference. Another method, *daseki zyutu,* was used to find values of $s_p = 1^p + 2^p + \ldots + n^p$ for $p = 1,2,3,\ldots$. *Enri* ("principle of the circle") consists of rectification of the circumference of a circle, rectification of a circular arc, and cubature of a sphere. He also created a method of approximation called *reiyaku zyutu,* by which he theoretically obtained 355/113 as an approximate value of π, a value found much earlier in China.

SELWYN, ALFRED RICHARD CECIL (*b. Kilmington, Somerset, England, 1824; d. Vancouver, British Columbia, 1902*), geology.

Educated in England and Switzerland. Did outstanding geological mapping for the Geological Survey of Great Britain (1845–52) and the Geological Survey of Victoria, Australia (1852–69). Served as director of the Geological Survey of Canada (1869–94). He investigated gold fields and made surveys of possible railroad routes, broadening his knowledge of Canadian geology and the hardships of fieldwork in Canada. He increased the survey staff to over thirty; set up sections for chemistry, mineralogy, paleontology, natural history, topographic mapping, and administration; expanded the library into one of the great scientific libraries in North America; and initiated new sections for mines, borings, water supply, and statistics of mineral production. His term was, however, marked by much internal dissension, possibly because of his authoritarian attitude, and agitation by malcontents both inside and outside the survey.

SEMMELWEIS, IGNAZ PHILIPP (*b. Buda, Hungary, 1818; d. Vienna, Austria, 1865*), medicine.

Received education at University of Pest and University of Vienna (doctorate, 1844). At the First Obstetrical Clinic of the Vienna General Hospital, he made his discoveries concerning the etiology and prevention of puerperal (childbed) fever. Suspecting a connection between cadaveric contamination and puerperal fever, he made a detailed study of mortality statistics and concluded that he and his students carried infecting particles on their hands from the autopsy room to the patients they examined during labor. He instituted the use of a solution of chlorinated lime for washing hands between autopsy work and examination of patients. In barely one month the mortality from puerperal fever in his clinic declined from 12.24 percent to 2.38 percent. He gradually widened his prophylaxis to include all instruments coming in contact with patients in labor. An initial lack of proper publicity among Viennese and foreign visiting physicians led to misunderstandings and an incomplete assessment of the intended procedure, and it failed to gain widespread support. Semmelweis finally left Vienna and returned to Pest, implementing his new prophylaxis at St. Rochus Hospital and at the University of Pest's hospital. He finally published his momentous discovery in book form in 1861. His increasing bitterness and frustration at the lack of acceptance of his method at last broke his spirit, and he died in an asylum.

SEMON, RICHARD WOLFGANG (*b. Berlin, Germany, 1859; d. Munich, Germany, 1918*), zoology, anatomy.

Studied at Heidelberg and at Jena (Ph.D., 1883; medical degree, 1886). Taught at Jena (1887–97), thereafter working as a private scholar in Munich. Made comparative anatomical and embryological studies of echinoderms, snails, fish, and birds. In Australia (1891–93) he was concerned mainly with the habitats, sexual reproduction, and development of the lungfish *Ceratodus forsteri*, as well as the monotremata. Out of his attempt to bring together into a unified concept "all those phenomena in the organic world that involve reproduction of any kind" emerged his hypothesis of "the mneme [cell memory] as the enduring principle in changes occurring in organic life."

SEMPER, CARL GOTTFRIED (*b. Altona, Germany, 1832; d. Würzburg, Germany, 1893*), zoology, ecology.

Graduated from Würzburg (1856); traveled to the Palau Islands and to the Philippines (1858–65); taught at Würzburg (1866–93). His magnificent zoological and ethnographic collections laid a permanent foundation for future research in the Philippines. His ten-quarto-volume *Reisen im Archipel der Philippinen* (1868–1905) is an important source book, particularly for the Philippine mollusks. His best-known work is *Die natürlichen Existenzbedingungen der Thiere* (1880), the first textbook on animal ecology, in which he discusses the influence of the physical and biotic environment on the structure, distribution, and habits of organisms.

SEMYONOV-TYAN-SHANSKY, PETR PETROVICH (*b. near Urusov, Ryazan guberniya, Russia, 1827; d. St. Petersburg, Russia, 1914*), geography, statistics.

Graduated from St. Petersburg University (1848; master's degree, 1851). In preparing for an expedition

to Tien Shan, he studied at Berlin, traveled through the mountainous regions of western Europe and Switzerland, studied volcanic phenomena, and made seventeen ascents of Vesuvius. In 1855 he returned to Russia, and published (1856) the first volume of his translation of Ritter's *Die Erdkunde von Asien*, devoted to Mongolia, Manchuria, and northern China. He introduced the terms "upland," "plateau," "hollow," and "foothills," and corrected some of the geographical theories of Ritter and Humboldt. In 1856 he reached Tien Shan, and in 1857 crossed the northern chain of the Terskey Ala-Tau range. His route enabled him to trace the overall configuration of the country and to discover the actual structure of the interior of Asia. The vast collection of geological and botanical specimens that he amassed included insects, mollusks, and ethnographical material.

After his return to Russia in 1857 he became active as a scientific encyclopedist. His thirty-year study of Russian economics and statistics was reflected in the five-volume *Geografichesko-statistichesky slovar* ("Geographical-Statistical Dictionary," 1863–85). As head of the Central Statistical Committee from 1864 he introduced the geographical method into the study of landed property, sowing area, and yields. As president of the Section of Physical Geography of the Russian Geographical Society he organized many expeditions to central Asia, the results of which substantially altered existing ideas. In 1888 he visited central Asia again, passing through Ashkhabad and Bukhara to Samarkand and Tashkent. His descriptions of the natural history and economy of the area are still of scientific value.

SENAC, JEAN-BAPTISTE (*b. near Lombez, Gascony, France, ca. 1693; d. Paris, France, 1770*), anatomy, physiology, medicine, chemistry (?).

Little is known of Senac's life; possibly received M.D. at Montpellier or Reims. In 1724 he published anonymously *L'anatomie d'Heister*, a detailed account of human anatomy and physiology. Between 1724 and 1729 he wrote several anatomical memoirs, principally on the respiratory organs. After twenty years of research on the structure, action, and diseases of the heart he published his most important work, *Traité de la structure du coeur . . .* (1749), making new observations on both healthy and diseased hearts. Several other works on anatomy, physiology, medicine, and chemistry have been attributed to him.

SÉNARMONT, HENRI HUREAU DE (*b. Broué, Eure-et-Loire, France, 1808; d. Paris, France, 1862*), crystallography, mineralogy.

Studied at the École Polytechnique, worked as a mining engineer, and taught at the École des Mines and the École Polytechnique. His importance is based on his demonstration of the directional dependency of the physical properties of crystals and on his experiments on the synthesis of minerals under conditions corresponding to those in nature. In studies between 1840 and 1851 he introduced a thin layer of mica for measuring phase differences, discussed perpendicular incidence on calcite, made important contributions to isomorphism, provided a method for measuring the binormal angle in convergently polarized light, provided a thorough account of all of the phenomena related to parallel and convergent polarized light beams, developed the formulas for conic sections in optically uniaxial crystals and in certain optically biaxial crystals, demonstrated that thermal conductivity is dependent on crystal symmetry, established the directional dependence of surface conductivity in crystals, and was the first to describe the production of artificial pleochroism in strontium nitrate pentahydrate. Altogether he succeeded in synthesizing twenty-nine vein minerals from the alkali sulfides and carbonates commonly found in thermal springs with metallic salts. In 1851 he confirmed the dimorphism of Sb_2O_3, and Dana gave the name senarmontite to its isometric form.

SENDIVOGIUS (SĘDZIMIR or SĘDZIWÓJ), MICHAEL (*b. Skorsko or Łukawica, Poland, 1566; d. Cravar, Silesia, 1636*), alchemy.

Attended the universities of Leipzig and Vienna; served as a royal courier in Prague and in Poland. On his many official missions he met prominent political figures and scientists, including several alchemists. His treatise *De lapide philosophorum* (1604), in which he claimed to be the "true possessor" of the "mystery of the philosophical stone," is of great value for the history of science. Besides recipes for the philosophers' stone, it contains interesting notes concerning the components of air. He believed that the air contained a hidden life-giving and fire-supporting agent, the "invisible niter" or "philosophical saltpeter"—the first idea of the existence of oxygen. He also established many smithies and iron and brass foundries in Krzepice, and lead foundries in Silesia.

SENEBIER, JEAN (*b. Geneva, Switzerland, 1742; d. Geneva, 1809*), physiology.

After holding several ecclesiastical positions, Senebier became librarian for the Republic of Geneva. His French translations introduced Spallanzani's works to French readers. Senebier's *Action de la lumière sur la végétation* was a study of photosynthesis that established his reputation as a physiologist (1779). His other important contribution was the three-volume *Essai sur l'art d'observer et de faire des expériences* (1802), which sums up the fundamental theses of the experimental method.

SENECA, LUCIUS ANNAEUS (*b. Córdoba, Spain, ca. 4 B.C.–A.D. 1; d. near Rome, A.D. 65*), physical science.

Seneca was educated at Rome and became a leading orator, writer, and philosopher. For eight years he was an influential advisor to the emperor Nero. His tragedies and ethical works are his best-known writings, but also extant is one of his scientific books, *Naturales quaestiones* (*ca. A.D. 62*). The surviving part deals with meteorological phenomena, rivers, earthquakes, meteors, and comets. It is the main source for the history of Greek meteorology after Aristotle, since it draws heavily on Greek sources and mentions the theories of many individuals whose works are lost, Posidonius in particular. A typically Roman scientific writing, it contributes no original ideas, but stresses the need for further careful investigation of natural phenomena.

SENNERT, DANIEL (*b. Breslau, Germany [now Wrocław, Poland], 1572; d. Wittenberg, Germany, 1637*), medicine, chemistry.

Sennert attended the universities of Leipzig, Jena, Frankfurt an der Oder, and Wittenberg (master's, 1598; doctor of medicine, 1601). Served as physician in Wittenberg and professor at the university (1602–37). His many medical works attempt to reconcile the theories of Aristotle, Galen, Paracelsus, and the supporters of the traditional atomic hypotheses. Strongly rooted in the ancient tradition, he retained the Peripatetic notion of form even where he conceived from a corpuscular point of view the constituents joined together under the form. In the theory proper of change in natural processes—which includes what we call "chemistry"—Sennert followed to some extent the views of Jean Fernel, Ibn Sīnā, and Ibn Rushd.

SERENUS (*b. Antinoupolis, Egypt, fl. fourth century A.D. [?]*), mathematics.

Serenus was the author of two treatises on conic sections, which have survived, and a commentary on the *Conics* of Apollonius, which has not. *On the Section of a Cylinder* counters the prevalent belief that the curve formed by the oblique section of a cylinder differs from the curve formed by the oblique section of a cone known as the ellipse. *On the Section of a Cone* deals mainly with the areas of triangular sections of right or scalene cones made by planes passing through the vertex.

SERGENT, EDMOND (*b. Philippeville [now Skikda], Algeria, 1876; d. Andilly-en-Bassigny, France, 1969*), epidemiology, immunology.

Sergent studied at Algiers and under Roux at the Institut Pasteur in Paris. From 1912 until 1963 he was director of the Institut Pasteur at Algiers. With his brother Étienne, both in the laboratory and in the field, he tirelessly studied the factors involved in the spread of malaria: the protozoan (pathogenic agent), the *Anopheles* (vector), and man (reservoir of the parasite).

SERRES, ANTOINE ÉTIENNE REYNAUD AUGUSTIN (*b. Clairac, France, 1786; d. Paris, France, 1868*), comparative anatomy, embryology.

Serres received his medical degree in Paris in 1810, worked at the Hôtel Dieu (1808–22) and at the Hôspital de la Pitié (from 1822), and taught comparative anatomy at the Jardin des Plantes (from 1839). He did research into the development of the bones and teeth in normal and abnormal fetuses and studied the comparative anatomy of a number of vertebrate organs. He was clearly influenced by the work of Cuvier, although his theoretical position was closer to Geoffroy Saint-Hilaire, who regarded Serres as his collaborator. Serres believed that there was only one underlying animal type and that in the course of their development, the organs of the higher animals repeated the form of the equivalent organs in lower organisms. Meckel claimed that the higher animals pass through development stages analogous to the adult forms of lower animals (sometimes called the Serres-Meckel Law). Haeckel's biogenetic law—each animal in its development recapitulates its evolutionary history—has much in common with the Serres-Meckel law.

SERRES, OLIVIER DE (or DES) (*b. Villeneuve-de-Berg, Ardèche, France, 1539; d. Villeneuve-de-Berg, 1619*), agronomy.

Serres spent most of his life on the family estate, Pradel, where he worked towards its improvement and published his main work, *Théâtre d'agriculture* (1600). His aim was to present a complete survey of all aspects of agriculture, starting with advice on the proper way to run a household and proceeding, by way of discussions of various types of soil, to describe all the domesticated animals and plants known to him and to give useful hints on their cultivation. He was an enthusiastic advocate of irrigation, careful drainage, and conservation of water. He gave one of the first detailed accounts of the life cycle of the silkworm, devised a method of manufacturing coarse cloth from mulberry trees, introduced hops to France, and encouraged the cultivation of maize and potatoes.

SERRES DE MESPLÈS, MARCEL PIERRE TOUSSAINT DE (*b. Montpellier, France, 1780; d. Montpellier, 1862*), zoology, geology.

Serres studied in Paris, investigated technology in Austria and Bavaria which might be of value to France, and taught at Montpellier. His 300 writings encompass the natural and physical sciences, technology, jurisprudence, social and economic statistics, and travel accounts. The most detailed and original of his studies on Orthoptera concerned the organs of vision. He was apparently the first, in 1817, to consider dating fossil bones by their fluorine concentration. He sought to reconcile science and the Bible in *Cosmogonie de Moïse comparée aux faits géologiques* (1838–59).

SERRET, JOSEPH ALFRED (*b. Paris, France, 1819; d. Versailles, France, 1885*), mathematics.

Graduated from the École Polytechnique (1840); taught at the Collège de France and the Sorbonne. Worked at Bureau des Longitudes. He greatly advanced differential calculus (1840–65), and the fundamental formulas in the theory of space curves bear his name and that of Frenet.

SERTOLI, ENRICO (*b. Sondrio, Italy, 1842; d. Sondrio, 1910*), physiology, histology.

Graduated from Pavia (1865); taught at the Advanced Royal School of Veterinary Medicine in Milan (from 1870), founding the Laboratory of Experimental Physiology. An outstanding exponent of microscopic anatomy, he identified and described the branched cells in the seminiferous tubules of the human testicle, still known as Sertoli cells. He also did research on blood proteins and on the persistent excitability and extreme sensitivity to thermal stimuli of the smooth muscles.

SERTÜRNER, FRIEDRICH WILHELM ADAM FERDINAND (*b. Neuhaus, near Paderborn, Germany, 1783; d. Hameln, Germany, 1841*), pharmacology.

Sertürner was trained as an apothecary and took over the town pharmacy of Hameln in 1820. He laid the foundations for alkaloid chemistry by his isolation of morphine from opium, calling the newly discovered "sleep-inducing factor" a "vegetable alkali," the first representative of a new class of plant matter. His tendency toward speculation explains why his two further important discoveries were ignored. He developed a theory on the formation of ether from alcohol and sulfuric acid and established the formulas for three different "sulphovinic

acids" (ethyl sulfuric acids). He was the first to discover a toxic, self-reproducing living agent as the real cause of cholera.

SERULLAS, GEORGES-SIMON (*b. Poncin, Ain, France, 1774; d. Paris, France, 1832*), chemistry, pharmacy.

While serving as a military pharmacist during a campaign in the Alps, Serullas learned botany, physics, and chemistry. He later taught pharmacy at the military hospital in Metz and at the Val de Grâce, and chemistry at the Jardin des Plantes. His research involved sugar and sugar substitutes and studies of iodine and bromine and their compounds. He discovered iodoform (1823), cyanuric chloride (1828), and cyanamide and cyanuric acid (1827).

SERVETUS, MICHAEL (*b. Villanueva de Sixena [?], Spain, 1511 [?]; d. Geneva, Switzerland, 1553*), biology, philosophy.

Servetus spent his early years in Spain, Toulouse, and Basel, before convincing a printer in Strasbourg to print his first work, *De trinitatis erroribus* (1531). Servetus denied the doctrine of the Trinity and brought on himself the condemnation of both Catholics and Protestants. Forced to leave Strasbourg and later Basel, he moved to France, assuming the name of Michel de Villeneuve. He left Paris for Lyons, becoming a corrector and editor for the famous publishers, the brothers Trechsel. He prepared corrected editions of Ptolemy's *Geography* (1535, 1541) and developed an interest in medicine. His first medical work, *In Leonardum Fuchsium apologia* (1536), expounded his belief in the healing powers of certain herbs. Its continuation, the *Syruporum universa ratio* (1537), centered on the use of syrups for curative purposes and contained a significant passage on the use of "correct" foods as aids in digestion. Meanwhile, Servetus had returned to Paris to study medicine. After his book on astrology was confiscated, he returned to practice medicine in Lyons. His magnum opus, the *Christianismi restitutio* (1553), was a theological treatise containing his imperishable contribution to science as the first man in the West to discover the lesser circulation of the blood. His assertion that blood passes through the lungs for oxygenation and his further statement that the "vital spirit is then transfused from the left ventricle of the heart into the arteries of the whole body" showed that he had arrived at the threshold of the complete circulation. The publication of this work and his earlier letters to Calvin revealed the true identity of Michel de Villeneuve. He was imprisoned, escaped into hiding, but was captured in Geneva and burned at the stake.

SERVOIS, FRANÇOIS-JOSEPH (*b. Mont-de-Laval, Doubs, France, 1767; d. Mont-de-Laval, 1847*), mathematics.

As a teacher of mathematics in military schools, Servois closely followed developments in mathematics. His first publication, on pure and applied geometry, *Solutions peu connues de différents problèmes de géométrie pratique . . .* (1805), Poncelet considered "a truly original work, notable for presenting the first applications of the theory of transversals to the geometry of the ruler or surveyor's staff." His formalist conception of algebra made him one of the chief precursors of the English school of symbolic algebra. In his "Essai sur un nouveau mode d'exposition des principes du calcul différentiel" (1814) he sought to provide differential calculus with a rigorous foundation, developing the first elements of what became the calculus of operations. He introduced the fundamental notions of "commutative property" and "distributive property."

SESSÉ Y LACASTA, MARTÍN DE (*b. Baraguas, Aragón, Spain, 1751* [?]; *d. Madrid, Spain, 1808*), botany.

Sessé studied medicine, practiced in Madrid, and served as army doctor in Spain and Cuba. In 1787 was named director of the Royal Botanical Expedition to New Spain and director of the Royal Botanical Garden in Mexico City. He took part in long field excursions to western Mexico, to the Atlantic slope of Mexico, and to Cuba and Puerto Rico. In 1803 he returned to Spain with the expedition's collection of over 10,000 botanical specimens. Two posthumous works are attributed jointly to Sessé and Mociño. *Plantae Novae Hispaniae* (1887–91) is a complete flora, including the species of flowering plants studied by the Botanical Expedition. *Flora Mexicana* (1891–97) contains many notes on individual plant-species from many parts of Spanish America.

SETCHELL, WILLIAM ALBERT (*b. Norwich, Conn., 1864; d. Berkeley, Calif., 1943*), botany, geography.

Graduated from Yale and Harvard; taught at University of California at Berkeley. Setchell was the acknowledged authority on marine algae of the northern Pacific, and on the role of crustaceous algae in coral reef formation. He also advanced knowledge of the role of temperature in delimiting plant distributions, and initiated studies on the genus *Nicotiana*.

SEVERGIN, VASILY MIKHAYLOVICH (*b. St. Petersburg, Russia, 1765; d. St. Petersburg, 1826*), mineralogy, chemistry, technology.

Studied at the St. Petersburg Academy of Sciences and at Göttingen; taught at St. Petersburg (from 1789). Among his many works was an enlarged and supplemented Russian translation of Kirwan's *Elements of Mineralogy* (1791), classifying and describing minerals on the basis of their chemical composition. His "Foundations of Mineralogy" (1798) was the first textbook in Russian on the subject. The first volume of "An Attempt at the Mineralogical Description of the Territory of the Russian State" (1809) is a physical-geographical survey and describes structures and lithology as well as the hydrographic network; the second volume deals with the geographical distribution of minerals. He also published a translation of the book on minerals of Pliny's *Natural History*.

SEVERI, FRANCESCO (*b. Arezzo, Italy, 1879; d. Rome, Italy, 1961*), mathematics.

Severi's interest in algebraic geometry was stimulated by studying with Segre at the University of Turin and while assisting Enriques at Bologna and Bertini at Pisa. He perfected the theory of birational invariants of algebraic surfaces and created an analogous theory for algebraic varieties of arbitrary dimension. His work on algebraic geometry can be divided into five sections: (1) enumerative and projective geometry, intersections, and questions on the foundations of algebraic geometry; (2) series and systems of equivalence; (3) geometry on algebraic surfaces; (4) geometry on algebraic varieties; and (5) Abelian and quasi-Abelian varieties.

SEVERIN, CHRISTIAN, also known as **Longomontanus** (*b. Longberg, Jutland, Denmark, 1562; d. Copenhagen, Denmark, 1647*), astronomy.

Severin worked with Tycho Brahe from 1588 until Tycho left Denmark (1597). After receiving his M.A. at the University of Rostock, he taught at the University of Copenhagen (1607–47). As Tycho's sole disciple, he assumed the responsibility for completing his program for the restoration of astronomy. He selected and integrated Tycho's observational data into accounts of the motions of the planets and presented the results of the entire program in his voluminous *Astronomia danica* (1622).

SEVERINO, MARCO AURELIO (*b. Tarsia, Calabria, Italy, 1580; d. Naples, Italy, 1656*), biomedical sciences.

Received medical degree at Salerno (1606); while studying medicine at Naples, he learned from Campanella the rudiments of Telesio's philosophical system, which formed the basis of the critical anti-Aristotelianism that marked Severino's later work. He practiced medicine in Naples and taught at the university (from 1615), becoming a famous surgeon and teacher, and corresponding with many important physicians and scientists of his time. His *Zootomia Democritea* (1645) has been called "the earliest comprehensive treatise on comparative anatomy." Severino studied the anatomy of man, animals, and plants to uncover a clearer knowledge of divine creation. The *Antiperipatias* (1655, 1659) illustrates his critical attitude toward the Aristotelians, arguing against the Peripatetic view that fish do not breathe air.

SEVERINUS, PETRUS (or **PEDER SØRENSON**) (*b. Ribe, Jutland, Denmark, ca. 1542; d. Copenhagen, Denmark, 1602*), chemistry, medicine.

Severinus received his Master of Arts at Copenhagen and his M.D. in France, also studying at other European universities. Returning home, he served as a physician to the court for thirty years. His major work, *Idea medicinae philosophicae* (1571), purported to contain the "entire doctrine of Paracelsus, Hippocrates, and Galen" and was immediately accepted as one of the most authoritative documents of the Paracelsian school. It was a defense of the Paracelsian doctrines in opposition to the traditional medicine and the "mathematical" approach of Galen. He fully accepted Paracelsus' endorsement of the macrocosm-microcosm universe, accepted the doctrine of signatures, and firmly condemned the humoral pathology of the ancients. His views on the primacy of the heart and the blood—as well as his espousal of epigenesis—show an Aristotelian influence and also mark him as a significant precursor of Harvey.

SEVERTSOV, ALEKSEY NIKOLAEVICH (*b. Moscow, Russia, 1866; d. Moscow, 1936*), comparative anatomy, evolutionary morphology.

Severtsov graduated from Moscow University (master's, 1895; doctorate, 1898). He did scientific and administrative work at Dorpat (1898–1902), Kiev (1902–11), and Moscow (1911–30). In 1930 he founded at Moscow University what was to become the A. N. Severtsov Institute of Evolutionary Morphology and Animal

Ecology. Severtsov chose comparative anatomy as his specialty, recognizing the necessity of extending morphology and evolutionary theory. His classic research on metameres of the vertebrate head (1895) revealed the evolution of the head. He attempted to restate the evolution of the lower vertebrates in three articles (1916, 1917, 1925). Opposing a dogmatic interpretation of Darwin's theory, he favored a bold posing of new problems and the introduction of new ideas. The result of his work was the strict theory of the morphological regularities of evolution, the nucleus of which was the theory of phyloembryogeny and the morphobiological theory of evolution. His study of the relationship of ontogeny and phylogeny on the level of the whole organism, of separate organs, and of tissues showed the universality of the theory of phyloembryogeny. First formulated on the basis of the study of vertebrates, this theory was later recognized in the morphology of vertebrates, the morphology of plants, histology, physiology, and anthropology.

SEWARD, ALBERT CHARLES (*b. Lancaster, England, 1863; d. London, England, 1941*), paleobotany.

Seward received his degree in geology and botany at Cambridge, taught at St. John's College, Cambridge (1890–1936), and was master of Downing College (1915–36). He worked on the whole range of fossil plants, but about half his papers dealt with the Mesozoic. His great revision of the English Weald flora (1895) brought him fame; collections of fossil plants from all over the world poured into his laboratory. His synthetic papers dealt with the history of floras, especially with past climates as deduced from fossil plants and with the ways in which changing climates altered the geographical distribution of vegetation.

SEXTUS EMPIRICUS (*fl. ca.* A.D. *200*), medicine, skeptical philosophy.

Presumably Sextus was a practicing physician of the Empirical school, which claimed to understand and treat diseases without postulating theoretical causes like "humors" or "spirits." His historical importance is in the field of philosophy. His surviving works include *Pyrrhonian Hypotyposes*, in three books, of which the first outlines the skeptical position and the second and third criticize other philosophical schools, subject by subject. These criticisms are expanded in the rest of his work, usually grouped under the single title *Adversus mathematicos*, or *Against the Professors*. His criticisms of the Stoic school constitute the fullest source of information on Stoic logic and have been used extensively in the recent reconstruction of the logical theory of the Stoics.

SEZAWA, KATSUTADA (*b. Yamaguchi, Japan, 1895; d. Tokyo, Japan, 1944*), applied mathematics, theoretical seismology.

Sezawa graduated from and taught at the Imperial University of Tokyo, and was associated with the Earthquake Research Institute of the university (from 1925). Through his mathematical analysis of seismic surface waves he derived useful estimates of layering in the earth's crust. He produced a body of theory important to such seismological problems as seiches in lakes and tsunami (seismic sea waves) generated by large earthquakes, and the mechanism of earthquake generation. He

studied vibrations excited in buildings and bridges by strong earthquakes, and contributed to the theory of designing structures to withstand earthquakes.

SHAKERLEY, JEREMY (*b. Halifax, Yorkshire, England, 1626; d. India, ca. 1655*), astronomy.

Shakerley was self-educated, having acquired his knowledge from the works of Kepler and Boulliau. He was the first mathematician to recognize the significance of the work of Jeremiah Horrocks, using material from Horrocks' surviving papers in his attack on Vincent Wing's faulty lunar theory (*Anatomy of "Urania Practica,"* 1649), in his *Tabulae Britannicae* (1653), and in his almanac for 1651 (*Synopsis compendiana*), in which he correctly predicted the 1651 transit of Mercury. After emigrating to India, he observed the predicted Mercury transit. He was the second man ever to witness a Mercury transit, probably the first Englishman to undertake systematic astronomical observations in India, and one of the earliest to interest himself in the astronomy of the Brahmins.

SHALER, NATHANIEL SOUTHGATE (*b. Newport, Ky., 1841; d. Cambridge, Mass., 1906*), geology.

Shaler received his S.B. degree (1862) and taught at the Lawrence Scientific School of Harvard University. He also worked intermittently for the U.S. Coast Survey, the Kentucky Geological Survey, and the U.S. Geological Survey and attained recognition through his popularization of geology. In reports on inundated lands of the eastern United States and their reclamation value, Shaler stated that an interesting reclamation alternative to irrigation of arid western lands would be the drainage of swamps and marshes. His *Aspects of the Earth* (1889) was intended to show the necessity for human understanding of the environment. *Nature and Man in America* (1891) was an important work on the environmental interpretation of history.

SHANKS, WILLIAM (*b. Corsenside, Northumberland, England, 1812; d. Houghton-le-Spring, Durham, England, 1882*), mathematics.

Shanks's contributions to mathematics lie entirely in the field of computation. He kept a boarding school in Houghton-le-Spring, and carried out his laborious and generally reliable calculations, most of which concerned the constant π, the ratio of the circumference of a circle to its diameter. His most accurate calculation gave the value of π to 530 places.

SHAPLEY, HARLOW (*b. Nashville, Mo., 1885; d. Boulder, Colo., 1972*), astronomy.

Shapley received his B.A. (1910) and M.A. (1911) from the University of Missouri, and his doctorate from Princeton (1913). From 1914 to 1921 he worked at the Mount Wilson Observatory. The globular star clusters that became the focal point of his work are extremely remote and highly concentrated stellar systems, arranged in a spherical form and consisting of tens of thousands of stars. He enlarged on Bailey's and Leavitt's work by discovering many new Cepheid variables in globular clusters and by devising a method of measuring distances to these clusters. He established a radically altered conception of the size of the Milky Way system, indicating that the equatorial diameter of the system was about 300,000 light-years, with a center some 60,000 light-years distant. He outlined his findings on the large dimensions of the Galaxy in the now famous debate with Heber D. Curtis on the scale of the universe before the National Academy of Sciences in Washington in 1920. He published over 100 papers during his seven years at Mount Wilson.

From 1921 until 1952 he was director of the Harvard Observatory, where he created an extraordinarily stimulating environment which drew astronomers from all over the world. With Annie Jump Cannon and Lindblad, he began extensive researches into the distribution and distances of stars of various spectral types. Since the Harvard Observatory maintained a station in the southern hemisphere, Shapley established a virtual monopoly on the study of the Magellanic Clouds, the objects in the southern hemisphere in which the period-luminosity relation for Cepheids had first been established. His principal work on galaxies took the form of vast surveys that recorded tens of thousands of these objects in both hemispheres. An early result of these surveys was the "Shapley-Ames Catalogue" of 1,249 galaxies, including 1,025 brighter than the thirteenth magnitude. His major discovery of the 1930's, a consequence of the galaxy surveys, was the identification of the first two dwarf systems, in the southern constellations Sculptor and Fornax, both now firmly established as members of our local family of galaxies. One of his proudest achievements during the late 1940's was his role in the formation of the United Nations Educational, Scientific, and Cultural Organization (UNESCO).

AL-SHARĪF AL-IDRĪSĪ. *See* **Al-Idrīsī, Abū ʿAbd Allāh Muḥammad ibn Muḥammad ibn ʿAbd Allāh ibn Idrīs, al-Sharīf al-Idrīsī.**

SHARONOV, VSEVOLOD VASILIEVICH (*b. St. Petersburg, Russia, 1901; d. Leningrad, U.S.S.R., 1964*), astronomy, geophysics.

Sharonov studied at Petrograd University, Leningrad Astronomical Institute, and the University of Leningrad (doctorate, 1940). At Leningrad he also taught, organized a photometric laboratory, and directed its astrophysics laboratory and astronomical observatory. Having studied the photometric wedge as the most convenient instrument for astronomical and geophysical observations, Sharonov developed original instruments for aerophotometry. He applied the absolute methods of photometry and colorimetry to study the lunar surface, the solar corona, and the planets.

SHARPEY, WILLIAM (*b. Arbroath, Scotland, 1802; d. London, England, 1880*), anatomy, physiology.

Sharpey received his M.D. at the University of Edinburgh. He taught anatomy extramurally in Edinburgh (1831–36), and held the chair of anatomy and physiology at University College, London (1836–74). Many considered him the real founder of the British school of physiology. He was a great and inspiring teacher who did all he could to further the development of physiology. His students included Joseph Lister, Michael Foster, and E. A. Schäfer, who added Sharpey's name to his own. Among Sharpey's few publications is a description in Quain's *Elements of Anatomy* of what are still referred to as Sharpey's bone fibers.

SHARPEY-SCHÄFER, EDWARD ALBERT (*b. London, England, 1850; d. North Berwick, Scotland, 1935*), histology, physiology.

Schäfer was educated at University College, London, under William Sharpey, whose name he later added to his own. He taught there from 1874 to 1899 and at Edinburgh from 1899 to 1933. He was knighted in 1913. His catholicity of interest was impressive. He edited and contributed six chapters on topics as diverse as the biochemistry of blood, the ductless glands, the neuron, and cerebral localization to the *Textbook of Physiology*. His *Essentials of Histology* (1885) was one of the most widely used books on the subject in English. In an important paper on nerve cells he found that each nerve fiber was distinct from and nowhere structurally continuous with any other. He collaborated with Victor Horsley in an important series of experiments on cerebral localization. His papers with George Oliver on the effects of suprarenal and of pituitary extracts are landmarks in the history of physiology. He suggested that the islets of Langerhans of the pancreas might act collectively as an organ of internal secretion by means of which the pancreas produced its effect on the blood sugar level. He suggested the name "insuline" for the still hypothetical substance and also introduced the terms "autocoid" and "chalone" into endocrinology. His name became familiar through his method of artificial respiration, particularly in cases of drowning —now superseded by mouth-to-mouth resuscitation. In 1908 he founded the *Quarterly Journal of Experimental Physiology*.

SHARROCK, ROBERT (*b. Adstock, England, 1630; d. Bishop's Waltham, England, 1684*), botany.

Sharrock was educated at Winchester College and New College, Oxford, and held several ecclesiastical positions. He took a scientific interest in the cultivation of plants. His *History of the Propagation and Improvement of Vegetables by the Concurrence of Art and Nature* (1660) shows his experimental approach to botany as well as a profound knowledge of methods of propagating plants by seeds, vegetative reproduction, budding, and grafting, and of the improvement of soil by cultivation and by leguminous crops.

IBN AL-SHĀṬIR, ʿALĀʾ AL-DĪN ABU'L-ḤASAN ʿALĪ IBN IBRĀHĪM (*b. Damascus, Syria, ca. 1305; d. Damascus, ca. 1375*), astronomy.

Ibn al-Shāṭir studied astronomy in Cairo and Alexandria. He was perhaps the most distinguished Muslim astronomer of the fourteenth century. His most significant contribution to astronomy was his planetary theory, the essence of which is the apparent removal of the eccentric deferent and equant of the Ptolemaic models, with secondary epicycles used instead. The ultimate object was to produce a planetary theory composed of uniform motions in circular orbits rather than to improve the bases of practical astronomy. With the reservation that they are geocentric, his models are the same as those of Copernicus. His planetary theory was investigated for the first time in the 1950's, and the discovery that his models were mathematically identical to those of Copernicus raised the very interesting question of a possible transmission of his planetary theory to Europe.

Ibn al-Shāṭir also compiled prayer tables, that is, a set of tables displaying the values of certain spherical astronomical functions relating to the times of prayer; designed and constructed a magnificent horizontal sundial; wrote on the ordinary planispheric astrolabe and designed an astrolabe that he called "the universal instrument"; and wrote on the almucantar and sine quadrants. He also designed two modifications of the sine quadrant.

SHATUNOVSKY, SAMUIL OSIPOVICH (*b. Znamenka, Melitopol district, Tavricheskaya guberniya, Russia, 1859; d. Odessa, U.S.S.R., 1929*), mathematics.

Shatunovsky received his master's degree in 1905 and taught at Novorossysky (Odessa) University and at the Women's School for Higher Education. His principal works concern the foundations of mathematics. Independently of Hilbert he elaborated an axiomatic theory of the measurement of areas of rectilinear figures. He developed a theory for measuring the volumes of polyhedrons and an axiomatic general theory of scalar quantities. In elementary mathematics he stated a general principle for solving trigonometrical problems and a classification of problems connected with this principle.

SHAW, PETER (*b. Lichfield, Staffordshire, England, 1694; d. London, England, 1764*), chemistry.

Little is known of Shaw's early life or education. He learned classics, medicine, and chemistry, and made his living by translating, writing, and editing books on the latter two subjects and by practicing medicine. His edition of Boyle's works and his translations of Boerhaave and Stahl were popular and influential. The most important of his own early writings was *A New Practice of Physic* (1726), based on the teachings of Sydenham and Boerhaave.

SHAW, WILLIAM NAPIER (*b. Birmingham, England, 1854; d. London, England, 1945*), meteorology, physics.

Shaw studied at King Edward's School in Birmingham and Emmanuel College, Cambridge (graduated, 1876). He worked and taught at the Cavendish Laboratory (1879–1900) and became director of the Meteorological Office (1905–20), which he transformed through the introduction of a trained scientific staff and the consequent emphasis on studies of the physics of the atmosphere. His most important publications were *The Life History of Surface Air-Currents* (1906), which pointed the way toward air-mass analysis and the concept of fronts; and his four-volume *Manual of Meteorology* (1926–31), a unique account of the historical roots and the physical and mathematical basis of the subject. He was knighted in 1915.

SHAYN, GRIGORY ABRAMOVICH (*b. Odessa, Russia, 1892; d. Abramtsevo, near Moscow, U.S.S.R., 1956*), astrophysics.

After receiving his master's degree at Perm (1920), to which Yurev (Dorpat) University had been evacuated, Shayn taught briefly and then worked at the Simeiz section of the Pulkovo observatory. He participated in building a large modern astrophysical observatory in the mountains of the central Crimea. In 1945 he was named director of the Crimean Astrophysical Observatory of the Soviet Academy of Sciences. He did important research on the evolution of double stars and the rotation of stars; discovered several dozen spectroscopic binaries; con-

ducted important research on isotopes in the atmospheres of stars; developed a special method of photography based on the fact that gas nebulae radiate all their energy in certain bright emission lines; discovered more than 150 new emission nebulae; and published several catalogs of diffuse nebulae. He formulated the important cosmogonic statement of the common formation of the association of hot stars and nebulae.

SHEN KUA (*b. 1031, registered at Ch'ien-t'ang [now Hangchow, Chekiang province], China; d. Ching-k'ou, Jun prefecture [now Chinkiang, Kiangsu province], China, 1095*), polymathy, astronomy.

Of a gentry family, Shen spent his life in minor provincial posts, with several years in the capital judiciary (then the only conventional road to advancement for educated people). Shortly after he was assigned to the court he became a confidant of the emperor and played a brilliant part in resolving the crises of the time, contributing to nearly every field of New Policies activity, both civil and military; but within slightly over a decade his career in the capital was ended by impeachment. He received his first appointment in 1054, and began notable work in land reclamation. In 1063 he was posted to Yangchow and was recommended for a court appointment. In 1072 he received an additional appointment as director of the Astronomical Bureau, and in collaboration with his remarkable commoner protégé Wei P'u he undertook a major calendar reform and planned an ambitious series of daily observations to extend over five years, using renovated and redesigned instruments (political opposition prevented the carrying-out of the project, however). After several years spent traveling as troubleshooter and negotiator, he returned to China—with biological specimens and maps of the territories he had passed through—to become a Han-lin academician, to be given charge of a large-scale water control survey in the Yangtze region, and then to become head of the Finance Commission; while in the latter position he produced penetrating writings on political economy. His fortunes rose and fell as varying factions controlled the emperor's favor; by 1082 his career was over. After six years in fixed probationary residence, forbidden to engage in official matters, he retired in 1088 to a garden estate (*Meng ch'i,* or Dream Brook).

Shen's writings, of which only a few are extant even in part, include commentaries on Confucian classics, two atlases, reports on his diplomatic missions, literary works, and monographs on rituals, music, mathematical harmonics, administration, mathematical astronomy, astronomical instruments, defensive tactics and fortification, painting, tea, medicine, and poetry. "Brush Talks From Dream Brook" (*Meng ch'i pi t'an*) and its sequels, written in Shen's last years, is one of the most remarkable documents of early science and technology; it is a collection of about six hundred recollections and observations, ranging from one or two sentences to about a page of modern print, loosely grouped under topics, a large fraction being devoted to fate, divination, and portents. It has become a major source for early technology, both of Shen's time and of ancient times. Archaeology was beginning to emerge as a distinct branch of investigation in the eleventh century, and Shen utilized its findings to enrich the present through understanding what the practical arts had been capable of. Examples of his effort to understand lost processes are his reconstruction of ancient crossbow markmanship, and his discussion of the proportion system of the Timberwork Canon, used in the modular construction of public buildings. The most famous example of Shen's descriptions of contemporary technology is his account of the invention of movable-type printing—using ceramic type imbedded in a layer of resin, wax, and paper ash in an iron form—by the artisan Pi Sheng (*fl.* 1041–48). Scientific topics treated in "Brush Talks" include astronomy, cosmology, mathematics, and medicine.

The major contributions of Shen to astronomy were his attempts to visualize motions spatially, his arc-sagitta methods that for the first time moved algebraic techniques toward trigonometry, and his insistence on daily observational records as a basis for his calendar reform. The most noteworthy of his cosmological hypotheses attempted to account for variations in the apparent planetary motions (of little interest to traditional astronomers) with a model in which the planet traced out a figure like a willow leaf attached at one side to the periphery of a circle. His ideas played a considerable part in the highest achievement of traditional Chinese mathematical astronomy, the Season-Granting (*Shou shih*) system of Kuo Shou-ching (1280). Shen also recorded a calendric scheme that was most remarkable for his time and place (and was therefore poorly received): he proposed abandoning the traditional lunisolar calendar for a purely solar one, based on the twelve divisions of the tropical year, with alternate months of thirty and thirty-one days (using pairs of short months as necessary to approach the average of 30.43697 days).

Shen used mathematics in the formulation of policy arguments more consistently than most of his colleagues, as well as applying it to astronomical uses. His originality in abstract mathematics is particularly evident in two problems treated in "Brush Talks": in the first, in computing the frustum of a solid rectangular pyramid, Shen worked out the volume of the same figure if composed of stacked articles with interstices; this may have been a step in the direction of geometric exhaustion methods, and is the earliest known case in China of a problem involving higher series. The second problem of interest deals with the number of possible situations on a *go* board, and is the only known discussion of permutations in traditional Chinese mathematics.

By Shen's time medicine had accumulated a classical tradition; not only was each new treatise consciously built upon its predecessors, but a major goal of new work was restoring an understanding that medical scholars believed was deepest in the oldest writings. Shen's most characteristic contribution was undoubtedly his emphasis on his own experience; he not only omitted from his writings any prescription the efficacy of which he had not witnessed, but appended to most a description of the circumstances in which it had succeeded. Perhaps his most famous writing on general medical matters is one in which he refuted (by reasoning, not dissection) the common belief that there are three passages in the throat.

Shen studied magnetic needles and recognized the existence of magnetic declination. He has been credited as the first to use a compass in mapmaking; he recorded bearings between points using a twenty-four-point compass rose that he substituted for the old eight compass points. In his study of the earth he developed a theory of the shaping role of erosion; he reported finds of petrified plants and animals, and conjectured prehistoric changes in climate to account for petrified bamboo roots found in an area too dry to grow bamboo. He noted the blackness of soot from petroleum and began an industry to manufacture solid cakes of carbon ink, to replace the ink made by burning pine resin. A poem of his is among the earliest records of the economic importance of coal, then beginning to replace charcoal as a fuel. He saw the fiscal function of the state as the provision of wealth from nature; he encouraged extractive industries and manufactures, and mobilization of the popular strength for land reclamation, in order to increase national wealth.

SHERARD, WILLIAM (*b. Bushby, Leicestershire, England, 1659; d. London, England, 1728*), botany.

Sherard received his bachelor's degree (1683) and doctorate (1694) in common law from St. John's College, Oxford. During tours of the Continent and while serving as consul at Smyrna he collected botanical specimens; he left his herbarium of 12,000 to 14,000 specimens to Oxford. Although an excellent and knowledgeable botanist, he wrote and published little; he corresponded with nearly every major botanist of his day, and was especially generous with gifts of specimens, seeds, and living plants. Sherard's assistance is acknowledged by Bobart in his *Historia oxoniensis* and by Ray in his *Historia plantarum.*

SHERRINGTON, CHARLES SCOTT (*b. London, England, 1857; d. Eastbourne, England, 1952*), neurophysiology.

Sherrington graduated from Caius College, Cambridge, and did graduate study and research in Europe under Goltz, Virchow, and Koch, gaining a superb grounding in physiology, morphology, histology, and pathology. He taught at Liverpool (1895–1912) and Oxford (1913–35). Sherrington's classic investigations dealt primarily with reflex motor behavior in vertebrates, detailing the nature of muscle management at the spinal level. The data, terms, and concepts that he introduced have become a fundamental part of the neurosciences. His early study of the knee jerk reflex (1891, 1892) showed him a major gap in neuroanatomical knowledge—the distribution of the sensory and motor fibers of the spinal cord. His three major contributions to neuroanatomy were mapping motor pathways (1892), establishing the existence of sensory nerves in muscles (1894), and tracing the cutaneous distribution of the posterior spinal roots (1894, 1898). In his research on the reflex functions of the spinal cord he used the classic spinal animal and the decerebrate animal; he named decerebrate rigidity and established it as a phenomenon in its own right (1898). His analysis of the reciprocal innervation of antagonistic muscles led to his classic definition of reciprocal innervation as that form of coordination in which "inhibito-motor spinal reflexes occur quite habitually and concurrently with many of the excito-motor" (1897). In the same year he introduced the term and concept of synapse in Michael Foster's *Textbook of Physiology:* "So far as our knowledge goes we are led to think that the tip of a twig of the [axon's] arborescence is not continuous with but merely in contact with the substance of the dendrite or cell body on which it impinges. Such a connection of one nerve-cell with another might be called a synapsis."

The Integrative Action of the Nervous System (1906) provides a succinct statement of the meaning and scope of his concept of integrative action: (1) the nervous system is one, if not the only, major integrating agent in complex multicellular organisms; (2) the reflex is the unit reaction in nervous integration; (3) there are two grades of reflex coordination—that effected by the simple reflex and that effected by the simultaneous and successive combination of reflexes.

Three fundamental publications of his tenure at Oxford were his papers on the stretch reflex (1924), central excitatory and inhibitory states (1925), and the motor unit (1930). His research with Liddell on the stretch reflex, the basic reflex used in standing, led to the definition of the nature of autogenetic excitation and inhibition and to our present understanding of muscle tones, attitude, and posture. His concept of on central excitatory and inhibitory states has been confirmed, expanded, and reformulated in terms of postsynaptic excitatory and inhibitory potentials by Sir John Eccles and others, using such techniques as intracellular recordings from motoneurons. The concept of the motor unit can be seen as a more sophisticated, experimentally based development of his principle of the common path. The motor unit, in simple terms, is a spinal motoneuron (or motor cell in the ventral horn of the spinal cord) which, by the branching of its axon, controls and coordinates the actions of more than 100 muscle fibers. Sherrington received the Nobel Prize in 1932 specifically for his isolation and functional analysis of the motor unit.

SHIBUKAWA, HARUMI (*b. Kyoto, Japan, 1639; d. Edo [now Tokyo], Japan, 1715*), astronomy.

Harumi's distinguished service in calendar reform led to his appointment in 1685 as official astronomer. The Chinese lunisolar Hsuan-ming calendar, adopted in Japan in 862, had not been reformed for more than eight hundred years, and the discrepancy in the length of a solar year had increased so that by Harumi's time there was a two-day delay in the winter solstice. Harumi pointed out faults in the Hsuan-ming calendar and began conducting astronomical observations, probably the first systematic observations made in Japan. In 1683 he proposed a calendar revision to the emperor—the first calendar devised by a Japanese independent of the Chinese calendars. His revision (the Jokyo calendar) was implemented in 1684. Harumi was a leader of those Japanese astronomers who initiated the acknowledgment of Western superiority and the modernization of Japan.

SHILOV, NIKOLAY ALEKSANDROVICH (*b. Moscow, Russia, 1872; d. Gagry, U.S.S.R., 1930*), chemistry.

Graduated from Moscow University (master's degree, 1905); taught at Moscow Commercial Institute (from 1911). His research demonstrated the central role of intermediary products in the kinetics of conjugate oxidation reactions. The terminology he developed became generally accepted in chemical literature: chemical induction, induction factor, actor, inductor, and acceptor. During World War I he established a laboratory at the front where he studied gas adsorption, introducing Zelinsky's charcoal filter gas mask. In investigating hydrolytic adsorption he gave the first explanation of the principle of the action of ion exchangers.

SHIRAKATSÍ, ANANIA (also known as **Ananias of Shirak**) (*b. Shirakavan [now Ani], Armenia, ca. 620; d. shortly after 685*), mathematics, geography, philosophy, astronomy.

Shirakatsí is a representative of the progressive Armenian scholars of the seventh century. He studied at Trebizond under the Greek scientist Tychicus, later returning to Shirak and opening a school. His advanced philosophical and cosmological views led to his persecution by both lay and church authorities. He believed in the spherical form of the earth, that "the Milky Way is a mass of thickly clustered and weakly shining stars," and that the moon reflects the light of the sun. He gave a correct explanation for solar and lunar eclipses and developed precise tables of the lunar cycle. His textbook of arithmetic is one of the oldest known Armenian textbooks.

AL-SHĪRĀZĪ. *See* **Quṭb al-Dīn al-Shīrāzī.**

SHIZUKI, TADAO (*b. Nagasaki, Japan, 1760; d. Nagasaki, 1806*), natural philosophy.

At a time when Japanese knowledge of western science was very limited, Tadao translated the only sources for Copernicanism and Newtonianism, which were books brought in by the Dutch. His translation of Keill's *Introductio ad veram physicam* and the *Introductio ad veram astronomiam* led to Tadao's becoming the first Newtonian in the East, and he had to invent Japanese vocabulary to embrace the concepts of corpuscle, vacuum, gravity, and force. The concept of atomism was also unknown in the Orient, and Tadao attempted to adopt the neo-Confucian idea of *ch'i* as a corresponding notion. He also applied Western principles of attractive force and the traditional idea of Yin-Yang to the explanation of the phenomenal world. In his own major work, *Rekisho shinso* ("New Treatise on Calendrical Phenomena"), he commented systematically on Newtonian dynamics—although he was concerned primarily with their metaphysical basis.

SHMALHAUZEN, IVAN IVANOVICH (*b. Kiev, Russia, 1884; d. Moscow, U.S.S.R., 1963*), biology.

Shmalhauzen graduated from Kiev University (1909) and Moscow University (master's, 1914; doctorate, 1916). He taught at Yuriev (Tartu) University, Kiev, and Moscow, and directed the Biological Institute at the Ukrainian Academy of Sciences and the A. N. Severtsov Institute of Evolutionary Morphology. He began as a comparative anatomist and later expanded to the study of individual development and directed research in experimental embryology. In specialized monographs he examined the course and regularities of the evolutionary process. In 1938 he suggested that methods of cybernetics might be applied to the study of ontogenetic and phylogenetic development. He also wrote textbooks on comparative anatomy and on Darwinism.

SHNIRELMAN, LEV GENRIKHOVICH (*b. Gomel, Russia, 1905; d. Moscow, U.S.S.R., 1938*), mathematics.

Shnirelman graduated from and taught at Moscow University. With Lyusternik he made important contributions to the qualitative (topological) methods of the calculus of variations. In 1930 he introduced an original and profound idea into number theory which allowed him to prove that any natural number is the sum of a certain finite number k of prime numbers. He also stated several arithmetical propositions.

SHOKALSKY, YULY MIKHAYLOVICH (*b. St. Petersburg, Russia, 1856; d. Leningrad, U.S.S.R., 1940*), oceanography, geography.

Shokalsky was educated at the Naval College in St. Petersburg and at the Naval Academy; he taught at the Naval College, Naval Academy, and Leningrad University. From 1900 to 1915 he developed a large-scale project for oceanographic research and participated in the preparations for the expedition of the icebreakers *Taymyr* and *Vaygach* to the Arctic Ocean. He made major contributions to cartography, geomorphology, terrestrial hydrology, glaciology, and geodesy, with over 1,300 publications. In *Okeanografia* (1917), his most important work, he postulated the mutual dependence of all marine phenomena. He planned and determined the methodology of a comprehensive oceanographic expedition to the Black Sea (1923–35); fifty-three voyages were made, and over 1,600 hydrological samples and approximately 2,000 soil and biological samples were taken.

SHORT, JAMES (*b. Edinburgh, Scotland, 1710; d. Stoke Newington, Essex, England, 1768*), optics.

Short studied at the University of Edinburgh, and received his M.A. from the University of St. Andrews in 1753. In his workshop in London, he gained an international reputation for his reflecting telescopes. He started making mirrors for reflecting telescopes, first of glass, then of speculum metal. The perfecting of these metal mirrors was his lifework, and he made a total of 1,370 reflecting telescopes.

SHTOKMAN, VLADIMIR BORISOVICH (*b. Moscow, Russia, 1909; d. Moscow, 1968*), earth science, oceanography.

Shtokman studied at Moscow and began his work at the Institute of Oceanography, leading an oceanographic expedition to the Barents Sea. He later worked for the All-Union Scientific Research Institute of Ocean Fisheries and Oceanography at Baku and in Moscow. By applying probability theory and random functions to the study of ocean turbulence, he was a pioneer in introducing new statistical ideas and methods of studying this phenomenon into the U.S.S.R. He also developed direct techniques of measuring turbulent pulsation and current velocity at a series of points. From 1943 until 1968 he worked at the laboratory which grew into the Institute of Oceanography of the Soviet Academy of Sciences. He was the first to show clearly the important role in the dynamics of ocean currents of the transverse irregularities of tangential stress exerted by wind on water.

SHUJĀᶜ IBN ASLAM, AL-MIṢRI. *See* **Abū Kāmil Shujāᶜ ibn Aslam ibn Muḥammad ibn Shujāᶜ.**

SHULL, AARON FRANKLIN (*b. Miami County, Ohio, 1881; d. Ann Arbor, Mich., 1961*), genetics, evolution.

Shull received his A.B. at Michigan (1908) and his Ph.D. at Columbia (1911). He taught at Michigan (1911–

51), where he was a stimulating lecturer and a prolific writer of monographs and textbooks that introduced countless students to modern, experimental biology and to rigorous concepts in general biology, heredity, and evolution, at a time when most biology courses were organized along phylogenetic and "type specimen" lines. The focus of his research was the relationship between heredity and environment in determining the phenotype of an organism. His three main works were *Principles of Animal Biology* (1934), *Evolution* (1936), and *Heredity* (1938).

SIDGWICK, NEVIL VINCENT (*b. Oxford, England, 1873; d. Oxford, 1952*), chemistry.

Sidgwick studied at Christ Church, Oxford, and at Leipzig and Tübingen. In 1900 he was elected a fellow of Lincoln College, Oxford, where he spent the rest of his working life. His important publications began with *Organic Chemistry of Nitrogen* (1910), his first essay in applying the ideas and quantitative methods of physical chemistry to the facts and systematics of descriptive chemistry. His major accomplishment was establishing that there can be a definite bond between a group containing a fairly acidic hydrogen atom and an oxygen-rich group. He was inspired by Ernest Rutherford to try to explain chemical behavior in terms of atomic structure: *Electronic Theory of Valency* (1927) was intended as an exposition of principles to be followed by a second volume applying them systematically. The second volume did not appear until 1950, as *Chemical Elements and Their Compounds.* After meeting L. Pauling, one of Sidgwick's main preoccupations was to expound the concept of resonance in molecules to British chemists. In 1933 he published *Some Physical Properties of the Covalent Link in Chemistry,* which dealt mainly with the new experimental methods for investigating structure, such as heats of formation, lengths, and electric dipole moments of bonds.

SIEBOLD, CARL THEODOR ERNST VON (*b. Würzburg, Germany, 1804; d. Munich, Germany, 1885*), medicine, zoology.

Siebold studied at Göttingen and Berlin (M.D., 1828); practiced medicine in Heilsberg, Königsberg, and Danzig; and taught at the Friedrich Alexander University in Erlangen, the University of Freiburg, Breslau, and the Ludwig Maximilian University in Munich. His investigations on the phenomena of generation in jellyfish, intestinal worms, and insects foreshadowed Steenstrup's fundamental work on the alternation of generations. In 1848 Siebold and Koelliker created the *Zeitschrift für wissenschaftliche Zoologie,* a new journal of botany and zoology. Siebold's *Lehrbuch der vergleichenden Anatomie der wirbellosen Thiere* (1848) was one of the most important systematic reforms since the work of Cuvier; in it Siebold divided the Radiata into groups and characterized the Protozoa as single-celled organisms. At Breslau Siebold discovered the parthenogenesis of the honeybee. In 1863 he published a monograph on the fishes of Central Europe, illustrated with sixty-four woodcuts and two colorplates.

SIEDENTOPF, HENRY FRIEDRICH WILHELM (*b. Bremen, Germany, 1872; d. Jena, Germany, 1940*), physics.

Studied at Leipzig and Göttingen (doctorate, 1896). Worked at the Zeiss optical works in Jena (1899–1938) and taught at the University of Jena (from 1918). Developed the "slit ultramicroscope," which he perfected in collaboration with Zsigmondy (1902–03). Siedentopf also created the cardioid ultramicroscope and made important advances in microphotography and microcinematography.

SIEDLECKI, MICHAŁ (*b. Cracow, Poland, 1873; d. Sachsenhausen, Germany, 1940*), zoology, cytology.

Received M.D. at Jagiellonian Cracow University (1895). His outstanding contributions were in protozoology. Published a joint paper with Schaudinn on the life histories of *Coccidium schnedieri* and *Adelea ovata* (1897), the first to describe correctly the life cycle of Coccidia. He also was the first to describe the sexual cycle of *Klossia octospina* (1898) and the first to publish the complete life cycle of a gregarine living in *Lithobius forficatus.* Taught at Cracow (1900–18); rector at University of Vilna (1919–21).

SIEMENS, CHARLES WILLIAM (CARL WILHELM) (*b. Lenthe, near Hannover, Germany, 1823; d. London, England, 1883*), engineering.

After receiving a sound German technical education, Siemens went to England and promoted inventions of his brother Werner (founder of the Germany company of Siemens and Halske), later becoming a partner in his subsidiary British company. He developed a highly successful meter for measuring water consumption and invented the regenerative gas furnace with application to open-hearth steelmaking and other industrial processes. In 1874 he designed the cable ship *Faraday* and assisted in laying the first of several transatlantic cables that it completed.

SIEMENS, ERNST WERNER VON (*b. Lenthe, near Hannover, Germany, 1816; d. Berlin-Charlottenburg, Germany, 1892*), electrical science, technology.

Studied at the Prussian artillery and engineering school in Berlin; while a military officer, used his free time to apply science to practical inventions. First successful invention was an improved process for gold- and silverplating. After improving upon the indicator telegraph of Wheatstone, he developed an entire telegraph system; in 1847, together with Halske, he founded the Telegraphenbauanstalt von Siemens & Halske to manufacture and construct telegraph systems, eventually expanding to London, St. Petersburg, and Vienna. Helped design the first special cable-laying ship, the *Faraday,* and organized and constructed the Indo-European telegraph from London to Calcutta (1870). His most outstanding contribution was his discovery of the dynamo principle and its practical applications to streetcars and mine locomotives, in electrolysis, and in central generating stations.

SIERPIŃSKI, WACŁAW (*b. Warsaw, Poland, 1882; d. Warsaw, 1969*), mathematics.

Received degree from University of Warsaw (1904); taught at the University of Lvov and at Warsaw. Published some six hundred papers on set theory and a hundred on number theory. Most important on set theory are *Hypothèse du continu* (1934) and *Cardinal and Ordinal Numbers* (1958); chief work on number theory was *Elementary*

Theory of Numbers (1964). His papers contained new and important theorems (some of which bear his name), geometrical constructions (Sierpiński curves), concepts, and original and improved proofs of earlier theorems. With Janiszewski and Mazurkiewicz (1920) created a Polish school of mathematics centered on foundations, set theory, and applications.

SIGAUD DE LAFOND, JOSEPH-AIGNAN (*b. Bourges, France, 1730; d. Bourges, 1810*); experimental physics. chemistry, medicine.

Studied with the Jesuits in Bourges and in Paris at Saint-Côme; was strongly influenced by the public lectures of the Abbé Nollet. Taught at the Collège Louis-le-Grand, Saint-Côme, and Bourges. Also practiced medicine in Paris. A prolific writer in experimental physics, chemistry, medicine, and theology; most of his publications were written for the enlightened layman rather than the professional researcher. His positive contributions were in the area of experimental technique. He is sometimes attributed with the invention of the glass insulator and the circular glass plate in electrical machines. Collaborated with Macquer in investigating the aeriform fluids of "airs," newly discovered by Priestley. Achieved a certain notoriety in medicine for performing section of the pubic symphysis rather than cesarean section in certain cases.

SIGER OF BRABANT (*b. Brabant, ca. 1240; d. Orvieto, Italy, 1281/84*), philosophy.

Became master of arts at University of Paris between 1260 and 1265; taught at the Faculty of Arts, was summoned by the inquisitor of France for his heterodox propositions, but fled and took refuge at the papal court. Siger's historical role was fundamental because of the reactions he provoked in university circles and on such men as Bonaventure, Thomas Aquinas, Albert the Great, and John Peckham. He was concerned primarily with metaphysics and psychology, and secondarily with logic and natural philosophy; several questions on ethics also have been discovered. His contributions to science can be found in his writings on psychology and natural philosophy, in which areas connections can be made between philosophy and science.

SIGORGNE, PIERRE (*b. Rembercourt-aux-Pots, France, 1719; d. Mâcon, France, 1809*), physics, science popularization.

Received theological degrees at the Sorbonne and assumed chair of philosophy at the Collège Duplessis (Paris) in 1740. His *Institutions léibnitiennes* (1767) was an accurate but critical account of Leibniz's cosmological theories. His main importance lies in his vigorous and effective popularization of Newtonian ideas. His lectures at the Collège Duplessis provided a detailed and sophisticated treatment of recent physical theories, notably the Newtonian concept of universal gravitation. His main works were *Institutions newtoniennes, ou introduction à la philosophie de Newton* (1747), and *Examen et refutation des leçons de physique expliquées par M. de Molières* (1741). His most successful effort to apply the concept of universal gravitation is his explanation of capillary phenomena by the laws of attraction.

636

SIGÜENZA Y GÓNGORA, CARLOS DE (*b. Mexico City, 1645; d. Mexico City, 1700*), mathematics, astronomy, natural history.

Studied at the Jesuit Colegio de Tepozotlán, the Colegio del Espíritu Santo at Puebla, and the University of Mexico, teaching astrology and mathematics at Mexico (from 1672). Among his works were *Manifiesto filosófico contra los cometas* (1681), written to calm fears aroused by a comet, and *Libra astronómica y philosóphica* (1690), of great significance for its sound mathematical background, anti-Aristotelian outlook, and familiarity with modern authors: Copernicus, Galileo, Descartes, Kepler, and Tycho Brahe. As royal cosmographer, he made valuable observations and drew good maps.

AL-SIJZĪ, ABŪ SAʿĪD AHMAD IBN MUHAMMAD IBN ʿABD AL-JALĪL (*b. Sijistān, Persia, ca. 945; d. ca. 1020*), geometry, astronomy, astrology.

Evidence indicates al-Sijzī was an older contemporary of al-Biruni (973–ca. 1050); in 969–970 he assisted at the observations of the meridian transits in Shīrāz conducted by al-Ṣūfī. His main scientific activity was in astrology: he summarized three works by Abī Maʿshar and wrote *Kitāb Zarādusht suwar darajāt al-falak* ("The Book of Zoroaster on the Pictures of the Degrees of the Zodiac") and *Zāʾirjāt*, a book on horoscopes. His mathematical papers are more significant and he is better known as a geometer: he wrote original treatises on spheres and conic sections, the construction of a conic compass, and the trisection of an angle by intersecting a circle with an equilateral hyperbola.

SILLIMAN, BENJAMIN (*b. North Stratford [now Trumbull], Conn., 1779; d. New Haven, Conn., 1864*), chemistry, mineralogy, geology.

Graduated from Yale College in 1796, continued his scientific studies in Philadelphia, England, Holland, and Edinburgh, and took the newly established professorship of chemistry and natural history at Yale. He made Yale the leading center in the U.S. for training in chemistry, geology, and mineralogy; helped found the medical school (1813), and laid the groundwork for the Graduate School and the Sheffield Scientific School. In 1818 he launched the *American Journal of Science,* which quickly became the leading American scientific journal. His popular lectures did much to generate interest in science throughout the country. As consulting chemist and geologist, he inspected mining properties in several eastern states.

His best-known original investigations were his description and chemical analysis of the Weston meteor of 14 December 1807 and his experiments with the oxyhydrogen blowpipe and the deflagrator. His scientific work is commemorated in the name of the mineral sillimanite. Father of Benjamin Silliman, Jr., chemist and geologist.

SILLIMAN, BENJAMIN, JR. (*b. New Haven, Conn., 1816; d. New Haven, 1885*), chemistry, geology.

Son of Benjamin Silliman (1779–1864), under whom he studied at Yale College (M.A., 1840). Assisted his father on the internationally known *American Journal of Science and Arts,* continuing in various editorial capacities for 47 years. He had a long and effective career as teacher at Yale, helping to establish the Department of Philosophy and the Arts. He was the author of two important textbooks: *First Principles of Chemistry* (1847) and *First Principles of Physics or Natural Philosophy* (1859). One of the many reports he wrote for private clients launched the world's petroleum industry (1855): he set forth his methods and results in a chemical analysis of rock oil and recommended uses of the several products discovered. He used fractional distillation to break down the components; he identified kerosene, paraffin, lubricants, and an illuminating gas of high quality. Another important publication was *American Contributions to Chemistry,* a biographical dictionary of American chemists including bibliographies of their work (1874). On trips to undeveloped lands in the West he identified both potential oil-yielding sites and gold and silver mines. His controversial claims of oil in southern California were justified in the late 1870's when improved methods and machinery yielded rich oil strikes.

SIMON BREDON. *See* **Bredon, Simon.**

SIMON DE PHARES (*b. Meung-sur-Loire [?], France, ca. 1450; d. Paris, France, after 1499*), astrology.

Simon studied in Orléans, Paris, Oxford, and Montpelier, and traveled in Egypt, Italy, and Switzerland. In 1488 he settled in Lyons and established an astrological office. His success brought accusations of sorcery, and he moved to Paris. The work he wrote justifying his activities, *Recueil des plus célèbres astrologues et quelques hommes doctes,* is a panegyric of astrologers who had honored their profession by the success of their predictions, and he should therefore be considered the first historiographer of astronomy. The *Recueil* is a series of accounts, arranged in theoretically chronological order, devoted to famous astrologers and their works.

SIMON, FRANZ EUGEN (FRANCIS) (*b. Berlin, Germany, 1893; d. Oxford, England, 1956*), physics.

Received Ph.D. at Berlin (1921), remaining to teach and to found his school of low-temperature physics. In 1931 he moved to the Technical University of Breslau and in 1933 to the Clarendon Laboratory, Oxford. His dissertation had concerned the measurement of specific heats at low temperatures, a line of research that was closely connected with Nernst's heat theorem, now generally known as the third law of thermodynamics. The subject remained the basis of Simon's scientific interest throughout his life. At Oxford he built up a new research school in low-temperature physics. Much of his work was taken up with developing the method of cooling by adiabatic demagnetization and with investigating the properties of matter at temperatures below 1°K. A few months before his death he achieved his final goal of cooling nuclear spins by adiabatic demagnetization.

His other large body of outstanding work was directed toward the proof and elucidation of the third law of thermodynamics, which requires that, as absolute zero is approached, any system must tend to a state of zero entropy. His work on high pressure was an investigation of the melting curves of solidified gases, especially that of helium. It was Simon's great achievement to develop small-scale apparatus of novel and ingenious design that permitted many laboratories to liquefy helium.

SIMPLICIUS (*b. Cilicia, ca. 500; d. after 533*), philosophy.

Received education in Alexandria at the school of Ammonius Hermiae and in Athens at the school of Damascius, both of whom had a great influence on his philosophy. One of the most famous representatives of Neoplatonism in the sixth century, Simplicius endeavored to harmonize and reconcile Plato and Aristotle by reducing the differences between them to a question of vocabulary, point of view, or even misunderstanding of some Platonic theories by Aristotle. His extensive commentaries on Aristotle contain much valuable information on previous Greek philosophy, including the pre-Socratics. His earliest preserved work seems to be his commentary on Epictetus' *Enchiridion.* His commentaries on Aristotle's work included *In de Caelo, In Physicorum, In de Anima,* and *In Categorias.* Only fragments have been preserved of the commentary on the *Premises* of the first book of the *Elementa Euclidis.* His most influential works, on the *Categoriae* and on the *De Caelo,* were translated into Latin by William of Moerbeke (1266, 1271).

SIMPSON, THOMAS (*b. Market Bosworth, Leicestershire, England, 1710; d. Market Bosworth, 1761*), mathematics.

Simpson was primarily self-taught; his first mathematical contributions to the well-known *Ladies' Diary* (1736) showed that he was already versed on the subject of fluxions. His first book, *A New Treatise of Fluxions* (1737), led to his career as mathematics teacher, editor, and textbook writer. He was appointed second mathematical master at the Royal Military Academy, Woolwich, in 1743. His three best-seller textbooks were *Algebra* (1745–1826), *Geometry* (1747–1821), and *Trigonometry* (1748–99). From 1754 he edited the *Ladies' Diary.* His other important publications were *The Laws of Chance* and *Essays on Several Subjects* (1740), *Annuities and Reversions* (1742), *Mathematical Dissertations* (1743), and *Doctrine and Applications of Fluxions* (1750). He is now best remembered for Simpson's rule for determining the area under a curve.

SIMSON, ROBERT (*b. West Kilbride, Ayrshire, Scotland, 1687; d. Glasgow, Scotland, 1768*), geometry.

Studied at Glasgow, spent a year at the mathematical school at Christ's Hospital, London, and returned to Glasgow as professor of mathematics (1711) to set up a proper course in mathematics. His lifework was devoted to the restoration of "lost" works of the Greek geometers and to the preparation of definitive editions of those works that had survived: Euclid's porisms, the *loci plani* of Apollonius, and Euclid's *Elements* and *Data.* His four posthumously published books are *De porismatibus tractatus, De sectione determinata, De logarithmis liber,* and *De limitibus quantitatum et rationum, fragmentum.*

IBN SĪNĀ, ABŪ ῾ALĪ AL-ḤUSAYN IBN ῾ABDAL-LĀH, also known as **Avicenna** (*b. Afshana, near Bukhara, central Asia [now Uzbek S.S.R.], 980; d. Hamadān, Persia [now Iran], 1037*), philosophy, science, medicine.

Displaying an extraordinary precocity, Ibn Sīnā rapidly mastered contemporary knowledge of the various sciences and, at the age of sixteen, began to practice medicine. While continuing to pursue science he was active in the political life of his time: after serving as jurist at Korkanj, teacher of science at Gorgan, and administra-

tor at Rayy and at Hamadān, he was named vizier of Shams al-Dawla. His bibliography comprises nearly 270 titles in a number of widely divergent fields.

Ibn Sīnā's major philosophical work, *Al-Shifā᾽* ("The Cure" [of ignorance]), is an immense encyclopedia in four parts: logic, corresponding very closely to Aristotle's Organon; physics; mathematics (geometry, arithmetic, music, and astronomy); and metaphysics. His philosophy largely derived from Aristotelianism, heavily laden with elements of Neoplatonism stemming mainly from Plotinus and Proclus. He sought to integrate all aspects of science and religion in a grand metaphysical vision founded on a theory of necessary emanation (from a God in whom essence and existence are identical) and progressive descent.

In physics, the study of natural bodies and of movement, he refuted at length the atomistic conception of body and of reality in general, advocating instead continuity and hylomorphism. Matter, which cannot exist without form, is homogeneous and can receive all possible forms. Movement is an act and a primary perfection; it exists in a time between pure potentiality and pure act, and is found in quantity, quality, place, and position. All motion in a body exists only through a cause (either external or internal) distinct from the body itself. The universe is full because a vacuum does not exist. The outer sphere, that of the fixed stars, envelops all that exists; the stars and their spheres move on the inside of this sphere with an eternal circular motion. The center of the earth is the center of the universe. Bodies enveloped by other bodies have places; every natural body has its own natural place. Composite bodies are formed by different combinations of the four simple bodies, each of which contains two qualitative powers: fire (hot and dry), water (hot and wet), earth (cold and wet), and air (cold and dry). This scheme is sufficient to explain the formation of the corruptible bodies in the sublunar world: minerals, stones, and metals; plants; animals; and man.

Ibn Sīnā elaborated a broad theory of science as wisdom, and classified the spectrum of sciences known in his time under two broad headings—practical or speculative—and numerous subdivisions. His writings on psychology, the science of the soul, enjoyed great success in the Latin Middle Ages. He refuted the claims of the astrologers; he also denied the validity of alchemy, after study of its foundations and personal experimentation.

Al-Qānūn, Ibn Sīnā's medical encyclopedia, was very well received; it was translated into Latin by Gerard of Cremona in 1473 and was a textbook at the universities of Montpellier and Louvain until 1650. It borrowed extensively from al-Rāzī's *al-Ḥāwī,* which it eclipsed in popularity. Its five books were on medical theory (elements, temperaments, humors, and forces; etiology; hygiene; and therapeutics); materia medica; "head-to-toe diseases" of specific organs, with anatomical accounts of compound organs; diseases not specific to certain organs; and compound drugs.

SINĀN IBN THĀBIT IBN QURRA, ABŪ SA῾ĪD (*b. ca. 880; d. Baghdad, 943*), medicine, astronomy, mathematics.

Son of Thābit ibn Qurra al-Ḥarrānī (836-901) and father of Ibrāhīm ibn Sinān ibn Thābit (908-946). Sinān belonged to the sect of the Sabians originating in Ḥarrān;

one of the most famous physicians of his time, he worked mainly in Baghdad. None of his work is extant. Ibn al-Qiftī lists two mathematical treatises by Sinān: one connected with Archimedes' *On Triangles;* and a correction, with additions, of Aqātun's *On Elements of Geometry.* In astronomy, the content of the *Kitāb al-Anwāʾ* is somewhat known through excerpts by al-Bīrūnī: Sinān discusses the meteorological qualities of the individual days by comparing weather in the past, and relates an Egyptian theory and one by Hipparchus, on where to fix the beginnings of the seasons. Another astronomical treatise is on the assignment of the planets to the days of the week.

SITTER, WILLEM DE (*b. Sneek, Netherlands, 1872; d. Leiden, Netherlands, 1934*), astronomy.

De Sitter received his doctorate from the University of Groningen (1901), taught at Leiden (from 1908), and was director of the Leiden observatory (from 1919). His main contributions lie in the fields of celestial mechanics (particularly his research into the intricate problem of the dynamics of the satellites of Jupiter), the rotation of the earth, the determination of the fundamental astronomical constants, and the theory of relativity applied to cosmology. In one of his papers on "Einstein's Theory of Gravitation and Its Astronomical Consequences" (1917), he introduced what soon became known as the "De Sitter universe" as an alternative to the "Einstein universe." De Sitter showed that in addition to Einstein's representation of a static universe, a second model was possible with systematic motions—particularly the "expanding universe"—provided the density of matter could be considered negligible. Subsequent work led to solutions satisfying more accurately both theory and observations, from which modern cosmology has emerged.

ŠKODA, JOSEF (*b. Pilsen, Bohemia [now Czechoslovakia], 1805; d. Vienna, Austria, 1881*), internal medicine.

Graduated from the Faculty of Medicine at Vienna, practiced medicine, and became professor of internal diseases at Vienna (1846). His most important research was on the fundamentals of percussion and auscultation. Basing his investigations on physical acoustics, he simplified and unified the terminology, developing a physical classification of percussion sound in four categories: from full to empty, from clear to muffled, from tympanous to nontympanous, from high to deep. In the theory of auscultation he first distinguished reverberations (heart sounds) from cardiac murmurs; he established the principles of the clinical physiology of heart diseases. His critical approach to therapy led him to replace obsolete, inefficient methods with rational new methods; his principles formed the basis of diagnoses and a simpler and more humane therapy.

SKOLEM, ALBERT THORALF (*b. Sandsvaer, Norway, 1887; d. Oslo, Norway, 1963*), mathematics.

Studied in Göttingen and received his doctorate at Oslo (1926), teaching at the latter (1938–50). His main field was foundations of mathematics; also worked on algebra, number theory, set theory, algebraic topology, group theory, lattice theory, and Dirichlet series. Developed a *p*-adic method in connection with his work on Diophantine equations. In 1920 stated the Skolem-

Löwenheim theorem: If a finite or denumerably infinite sentential set is formulable in the ordinary predicate calculus, then it is satisfiable in a denumerable field of individuals. He freed set theory from Cantor's definitions. In 1923 he presented the Skolem-Noether theorem on the characterization of the automorphism of simple algebras.

SKRAUP, ZDENKO HANS (*b. Prague, Czechoslovakia, 1850; d. Vienna, Austria, 1910*), chemistry.

Skraup was educated at the German Technische Hochschule in Prague. He taught at the Technische Hochschule in Graz, the University of Graz, and at Vienna. His synthesis of quinoline resulted in the development of heterocyclid chemistry of the quinoline series and became a general method for the preparation of quinolines.

SKRYABIN, KONSTANTIN IVANOVICH (*b. St. Petersburg, Russia [now Leningrad, U.S.S.R.], 1878; d. Moscow, U.S.S.R., 1972*), helminthology, public health.

Studied at Dorpat Veterinary Institute and at Dorpat University; held various veterinary, academic, and administrative posts in Russia. Organized three important helminthological research institutes in Moscow. Headed the Laboratory of Helminthology of the U.S.S.R. Academy of Sciences (1942–72). His more than 700 varied works included geography of helminths, helminthiasis, and the development of principles and radical methods for eliminating helminths in man and animals. The more than 340 expeditions he organized played a major role in disseminating knowledge of helminths. He described more than 200 new species and 100 new genera of helminths. His methods of prophylaxis led to the total liquidation of a number of helminthiases in certain areas of the Soviet Union. His special interest in the trematode and the diseases it causes resulted in "Trematodes of Animals and Man."

SLIPHER, EARL C. (*b. Mulberry, Ind., 1883; d. Flagstaff, Ariz., 1964*), planetary astronomy.

Received B.S. at Indiana University; worked at the Lowell Observatory at Flagstaff, Arizona, from 1905 until his death. A pioneer in planetary photography; the quality of his photographs has seldom been surpassed. His special interest was the study of Mars, and culminated in *Mars, the Photographic Story* (1962). His photographs of Mars, Jupiter, Saturn, and Venus are unique. He was one of the first to recognize that multiple-image printing could improve the quality of information extracted from a series of photographs.

SLIPHER, VESTO MELVIN (*b. Mulberry, Ind., 1875; d. Flagstaff, Ariz., 1969*), astronomy.

Received B.A. (1901), M.A. (1903), and Ph.D. (1909) at Indiana University. Worked at Lowell Observatory at Flagstaff, Arizona, from 1901, serving as director from 1926 till 1952. His main contributions were to spectroscopy and can be divided into three areas: planetary atmospheres and rotations, diffuse nebulae and the interstellar medium, and rotations and radial velocities of spiral nebulae. He measured the rotation periods of Venus, Mars, Jupiter, Saturn, and Uranus. His research on interstellar space was extremely important, for he demonstrated the existence of both dust and gas. His most significant research dealt with spiral nebulae. For over ten years he was the only observer investigating the velocities of extragalactic nebulae. Hubble's velocity-distance relationship was made possible by Slipher's velocity measurements. Slipher's work prepared the way for investigations of the motions of galaxies and for cosmological theories based on an expanding universe. He also measured rotations of spiral nebulae.

SLOANE, SIR HANS (*b. Killyleagh, County Down, Northern Ireland, 1660; d. Chelsea, London, England, 1753*), medicine, natural history.

Studied in London, Paris, and Montpellier; graduated Doctor of Physick from the university in the town of Orange in Provence (1683). Made important contributions to medicine and to natural history. Accompanying an expedition to Jamaica as a physician gave him firsthand experience of the flora and fauna of a little-known island and enabled him to search for new drugs. The description of the voyage and the observations on the inhabitants, diseases, plants, animals, and meteorology of the West Indies make his book on the natural history of Jamaica indispensable even today. He practiced medicine in London and was elected president of the Royal College of Physicians. A main event of his presidency was the publication of the fourth *London Pharmacopoeia,* which reflected his efforts to rationalize medical prescriptions, get rid of disgusting ingredients, discard superstition, and include a catalog of medicinal herbs with clear definitions of their properties and the methods by which they could be identified. He was consulted on precautions to be taken against the threat of the plague of Marseilles and played an important part in establishing the practice of inoculation for smallpox in England. He served as president of the Royal Society from 1727 until 1741. Throughout his life he amassed collections. His herbarium fills 337 folio volumes. In addition to botanical specimens from France and the West Indies, he added other collections of plants, animals, insects, fossils, minerals, precious stones, and ethnographical specimens. His library of over 50,000 books and 3,500 bound volumes of manuscripts became part of the new British Museum.

SLUSE, RENÉ-FRANÇOIS DE (*b. Visé, Principality of Liège [now Belgium], 1622; d. Liège, 1685*), mathematics.

Obtained doctorate in law at University of Rome; held many high ecclesiastical positions in Liège; followed his scientific interests through extensive correspondence with leading mathematicians: Pascal, Huygens, Oldenburg, Wallis, and Ricci. He solved a number of problems related to the cycloid, discussed solutions of third- and fourth-degree equations, and discovered a general method for the construction of tangents to algebraic curves. His major work was *Mesolabum seu duae mediae proportionales inter extremas datas per circulum et ellipsim vel hyperbolam infinitis modis exhibitae* (1659, 1668).

SLUTSKY, EVGENY EVGENIEVICH (*b. Novoe, Yaroslavskaya guberniya, Russia, 1880; d. Moscow, U.S.S.R., 1948*), mathematics, statistics.

Graduated from Kiev University (1911); taught in Kiev and Moscow and worked in Moscow government statistical offices. A pioneer of the theory of random functions,

he generalized or introduced stochastic concepts of limits, derivative, and integral, and obtained the conditions of measurability of functions. He discovered that multiple moving averages obtained from a series of independent random variables generate series close to periodic ones. An important group of his papers is devoted to the classical theory of correlations of related series for a limited number of trials. He contributed to economics what is now known as the fundamental equation of value theory.

SLYKE, DONALD DEXTER VAN. *See* **Van Slyke, Donald Dexter.**

SMEATON, JOHN (*b. Austhorpe, England, 1724; d. Austhorpe, 1792*), civil engineering, applied mechanics.

One of the foremost British civil engineers of eighteenth century; distinguished himself through experimental research on applied hydraulics. Best-known achievement was the rebuilding of the Eddystone lighthouse (1756–59). Established himself as a consultant in fields of structural engineering and river and harbor works, adopting the term "civil engineer" to distinguish civilian consultants from military engineers; was responsible for many engineering projects, including bridges, steam engine facilities, power stations run by wind or water, mill structures and machinery, and river and harbor improvements. His research on waterwheels showed that overshot wheels are twice as efficient as undershot wheels. In the field of natural philosophy, his support of the *vis viva* school of thought played a prominent role in the recurrent controversy over the measure of "force."

SMEKAL, ADOLF GUSTAV STEPHAN (*b. Vienna, Austria, 1895; d. Graz, Austria, 1959*), physics.

Received doctorate at University of Graz (1917), continuing studies at Berlin; taught at the Technische Hochschule in Vienna (1919–28), Halle (1928–45), and Graz (from 1949). Published works on the foundations of quantum statistics, abstracted publications on quantum theory for the *Physikalische Berichte,* and did research on the quantum, the Bohr theory, and the problem of X-ray spectra. His name is better known through the effect predicted by him in 1923 and discovered experimentally by Raman in 1928: the alteration of the frequency of light upon being scattered by an atomic-molecular system—a decrease, or increase, by an amount equal to the frequency of the light that would be absorbed or emitted in transitions between the stationary states of that system. He later advanced his conception of the irregularities in the structure of real crystals arising as a "frozen Brownian molecular motion," and became a world authority on brittleness and the technology of pulverization.

SMITH, EDGAR FAHS (*b. York, Pa., 1854; d. Philadelphia, Pa., 1928*), chemistry.

Received Ph.D. at Göttingen (1876); taught at Muhlenberg College, Wittenberg College, and University of Pennsylvania. In electrochemistry he developed the rotating anode; he used electrolytic and chemical methods to determine more precisely the atomic weights of eighteen elements; other research was on complex inorganic acids. He was also a prominent historian of chemistry in the U.S.

SMITH, EDWARD (*b. Heanor, Derbyshire, England, 1818* [?]; *d. London, England, 1874*), physiology, nutrition, public health.

Obtained his M.B. (1841) and M.D. (1843) at the Royal Birmingham Medical School, which soon became Queen's College (London B.A. and LL.B., 1848). Practiced medicine in Birmingham and London, worked at Charing Cross Medical School, Brompton Hospital for Consumption, and for the Poor Law Board. Smith made great innovations in the quantitative study of respiration and metabolism, and in the nutrition of populations. He was the first to devise quantitative methods suitable for studies on the human being during exercise. His monumental data on inspiratory volume, respiratory and pulse rates, and carbon dioxide production at rest and at various levels of exercise served as the basis for much of the work on muscular exercise in the latter part of the nineteenth century. A social reformer at heart, his research led to improved conditions in prisons and among the poor.

SMITH, ERWIN FRINK (*b. Gilbert's Mills, N.Y., 1854; d. Washington, D.C., 1927*), plant pathology, bacteriology.

Received B.Sc. (1886) and doctorate (1889) from University of Michigan. Served in the U.S. Dept. of Agriculture from 1899 and later was director of the plant pathology laboratory of the Bureau of Plant Industry. His researches made him the most distinguished of the early American plant pathologists. His work fully established that bacteria cause plant disease—a view vigorously contested by his European counterparts. His most important works are *Bacteria in Relation to Plant Diseases* (1905–14) and *An Introduction to Bacterial Diseases of Plants* (1920).

SMITH, GRAFTON ELLIOT. See **Elliot Smith, Grafton.**

SMITH, HENRY JOHN STEPHEN (*b. Dublin, Ireland, 1826; d. Oxford, England, 1883*), mathematics.

Graduated from (1849) and taught at Balliol College, Oxford, devoting considerable effort to educational administration and reform. His best work was on number theory: he presented important papers on systems of linear indeterminate equations and congruences, and established a general theory of n-ary quadratics permitting the derivation of theorems on expressing any positive integer as the sum of five and seven squares. He extended many of Gauss's theorems for real quadratic forms to complex quadratic forms; his work in elliptic functions was especially elegant.

SMITH, HOMER WILLIAM (*b. Denver, Colo., 1895; d. New York, N.Y., 1962*), physiology, evolutionary biology.

Received A.B. from University of Denver (1917) and D.Sc. from Johns Hopkins (1921). Taught at the University of Virginia School of Medicine (1925–28) and at the New York University College of Medicine (1928–61), where his laboratory became an international center of renal physiology. He brought his comparative studies of renal physiology in various animals to bear on his most important research, the functions of the mammalian (and especially human) kidney. He played a major part in the development of contemporary understanding of the kidney. His main works were *The Physiology of the Kidney*

(1937), *The Kidney: Structure and Function in Health and Disease* (1951), and *Principles of Renal Physiology* (1956).

SMITH, JAMES EDWARD (*b. Norwich, England, 1759; d. Norwich, 1828*), botany.

Smith studied at Edinburgh, London, and Leiden (M.D., 1786); his life was shaped and influenced by his purchase of Linnaeus' library, manuscripts, herbarium, and specimens. He studied the material, some of which he rearranged and relabeled, and translated several of Linnaeus' works, although he was aware of the need for change and latterly acknowledged the importance of Jussieu's system. He was a founder and first president (1788–1828) of the Linnean Society. He lectured at the Royal Institution and at Cambridge, tutored the queen and princesses in botany, and was knighted in 1814. Most of his personal research was in taxonomy, and he wrote several books popularizing botany and accurately and comprehensively describing the flora of Great Britain and other countries.

SMITH, PHILIP EDWARD (*b. DeSmet, S.D., 1884; d. Florence, Mass., 1970*), anatomy, endocrinology.

Smith received his B.S. at Pomona College (1908) and his M.S. (1910) and Ph.D. (1912) at Cornell. He taught at the University of California, Berkeley (1912–26), and Columbia (1927–54), and worked as a research associate at Stanford from 1956 until his final retirement in 1963. He became internationally known for his classic experiments on the pituitary gland, first working with amphibians, then rats and rhesus monkeys. He developed a surgical approach through the neck to the base of the skull, where he drilled a small hole that exposed the hypophysis directly without any contact being made with the brain. The results of removal by this route resulted in a number of symptoms, which were completely reversible by daily implants of the anterior lobe of the hypophysis from donor animals into the operated animal. He showed that uncomplicated hypophysectomy in mammals resulted in cessation of growth; loss of weight; atrophy of the reproductive system, the thyroid gland, and the cortex of the adrenal gland; and a number of other symptoms. Two classics among his many publications are "The Pigmentary, Growth and Endocrine Disturbances Induced in the Anuran Tadpole by the Early Ablation of the Pars Buccalis of the Hypophysis" (1920) and "Hypophysectomy and a Replacement Therapy in the Rat" (1930).

SMITH, ROBERT (*b. Lea, near Gainsborough, England, 1689; d. Cambridge, England, 1768*), physics.

Educated at Trinity College, Cambridge (B.A., 1711; M.A., 1715; LL.D., 1723; D.D., 1739), where he also taught (1716–60). In 1738 he published *A Compleat System of Opticks in Four Books, viz. A Popular, a Mathematical, a Mechanical, and a Philosophical Treatise,* the most influential optical textbook of the eighteenth century. It helped to establish the conviction that light is particulate. He developed a comprehensive set of geometric propositions applicable to lenses and mirrors and derived a particular case of the relationship now known as the Smith-Helmholtz formula or the theorem of Lagrange. Using a relationship between the magnification and location of object and image for one lens, he showed that the same relationship was invariant within a system of any combination of lenses. The principal objective of his *Harmonics, or the Philosophy of Musical Sounds* (1749) was to describe his system of tempering a musical scale by making "all the consonances . . . as equally harmonious as possible."

SMITH, ROBERT ANGUS (*b. Glasgow, Scotland, 1817; d. Colwyn Bay, North Wales, 1884*), chemistry.

Smith received his Ph.D. (1841) at Giessen, where he worked in Liebig's laboratory. In 1843 he became assistant at the Royal Manchester Institution, commencing his long, distinguished career as a sanitary chemist. His pioneering studies on atmospheric and water pollution are collected in *Air and Rain* (1872), and his papers on disinfection in *Disinfectants and Disinfection* (1869). A pioneer also in the chemistry of disinfection, he patented a successful disinfectant powder which was largely carbolic acid.

SMITH, SIDNEY IRVING (*b. Norway, Me., 1843; d. New Haven, Conn., 1926*), zoology.

Graduated from the Sheffield Scientific School at Yale (1867) and taught in the zoology department (1867–1906). Participated in many zoological expeditions in New England, Lake Superior, and Canada. The value of his work was the large volume of careful identification and description, with accurate drawings, and some observations of behavior, of many species of aquatic Crustacea, hitherto little studied. His early papers on the North American lobster are models.

SMITH, THEOBALD (*b. Albany, N.Y., 1859; d. New York, N.Y., 1934*), microbiology, comparative pathology.

The most distinguished early American microbiologist and probably the leading comparative pathologist in the world. His greatest accomplishment was the elucidation of the causal agent and mode of transmission of Texas cattle fever, and the first conclusive proof that an infectious disease could be arthropod-borne. He graduated from Cornell (Ph.B., 1881; M.D., 1883) and worked for the Bureau of Animal Industry of the U.S. Department of Agriculture (1884–95), where his research resulted in *Hog Cholera: Its History, Nature and Treatment* (1889); *Special Report on the Cause and Prevention of Swine Plague* (1891); and *Investigations Into the Nature, Causation, and Prevention of Texas or Southern Cattle Fever* (1893). His research on the bacteriology of water supplies culminated in the *Standard Methods of Water Analysis* (1905) of the American Public Health Association.

From 1886 until 1895 he taught at the present George Washington University, and in 1895 became director of an antitoxin laboratory for the Massachusetts State Board of Health and professor of zoology at Harvard. Within six months he produced potent diphtheria antitoxin. His preliminary observations on two varieties of mammalian tubercle bacilli led to his classic report, "A Comparative Study of Bovine Tubercle Bacilli and of Human Bacilli From Sputum" (1898). He was the first scientist in North America to adopt Ehrlich's standardized antitoxic unit. In studying the antigenic properties of toxin-antitoxin mixtures, he foresaw their application to the active immunization of humans. His observation of the sudden death of guinea pigs following second injections of anti-toxin led to the designation of this serum-hypersensitivity as the "Theobald Smith phenomenon." As early as 1896 Smith

conjectured that malaria was mosquito-borne. His convictions about the importance of comparative pathology were permeated increasingly by the concept of host-parasite interrelationships.

He resigned from the State Board of Health (1914) and from Harvard (1915) to head the new department of animal pathology at Princeton. His publications number almost 300 titles, and his contributions to the conquest of disease are thought comparable to those of Pasteur and Koch.

SMITH, WILLIAM (*b. Churchill, Oxfordshire, England, 1769; d. Northampton, England, 1839*), geology.

Often called the "founder of stratigraphical geology," Smith received early training as a surveyor, and received most of his geological knowledge while surveying, becoming familiar with strata through which mine tunnels and canals passed. His various surveying tasks offered him prospects of traveling and seeing more of England's geology. He made early lists of strata and the fossils characteristic of each.

Unlike certain naturalists, Smith did not concern himself with the extinction of species or the living analogues of fossils. His knowledge of biology was minimal and he regarded fossils solely as a means of identifying a particular stratum. He did not recognize any age difference in these beds. Hence his approach was quite different from that of those naturalists who had concluded that rocks containing fossils of which there were no known living representatives must be older than those containing fossils part or all of which resembled creatures living in modern oceans. Smith did, however, recognize before 1800 that fossils worn by attrition found in alluvial beds indicated that the beds were deposited later than those containing unworn fossils. His major achievements were (1) the recognition of a regular succession in the strata of England, first confirmed in the southwest and then established across most of the country; (2) the discovery that many individual beds have a characteristic fossil content that can be used to distinguish them from other beds that are lithologically similar; and (3) the utilization of these two discoveries in the preparation of a large-scale geological map of the whole country.

His great work, *Delineation of the Strata of England and Wales, With Part of Scotland* (1815), was a major cartographic and scientific achievement. It represented about 65,000 square miles, was the first large-scale geological map of any country, and was based on the scientific principles discovered by Smith himself. Moreover, the coloring was designed to indicate not only the surface area of any one geological formation, but, by using a deeper shade along the base of a formation, an attempt was also made to show how the beds were superimposed; thus a structural factor was introduced.

SMITH, WILSON (*b. Great Harwood, Lancashire, England, 1897; d. Newbury, Berkshire, England, 1965*), microbiology.

Received diploma in bacteriology at Manchester University; in 1927 began studying viruses at the National Institute for Medical Research in London. He elucidated the mechanisms of protection that immunized animals acquire against viral infections. His most important contribution was the isolation of the influenza virus, and he became one of the leading virologists in the United Kingdom. He taught bacteriology at Sheffield University (1939–46) and at University College Hospital Medical School (1946–60), and continued his research at the Microbiological Research Establishment, Porton, after his retirement in 1960.

SMITHELLS, ARTHUR (*b. Bury, Lancashire, England, 1860; d. Highgate, London, England, 1939*), chemistry.

Studied at Glasgow; Owens College, Manchester; University of London (B.Sc., 1881); Munich; and Heidelberg. Taught at University of Leeds (1885–1923) and directed the Salters' Institute of Industrial Chemistry (1923–37). He was an articulate spokesman for chemistry, chemical education, and the larger cultural dimensions of chemistry; his research contributed to the understanding of combustion and the structure of flames.

SMITHSON, JAMES LOUIS MACIE (*b. Paris, France, 1765; d. Genoa, Italy, 1829*), chemistry.

Smithson received his master of arts at Pembroke College, Oxford (1786), became a fellow of the Royal Society (1787), and was a charter member of the Royal Institution. In his most important work, "A Chemical Analysis of Some Calamines" (1802), he analyzed zinc ores from various European deposits and showed them to be primarily zinc carbonate (later named smithsonite). He is remembered chiefly because he left money for founding the Smithsonian Institution in Washington, D.C.: "an Establishment for the increase & diffusion of knowledge among men."

SMITS, ANDREAS (*b. Woerden, Netherlands, 1870; d. Doorn, Netherlands, 1948*), physical chemistry.

Studied at Utrecht and at Giessen (Ph.D., 1896). Worked at Municipal Gasworks in Amsterdam, and taught at Amsterdam (1901–06, 1907–40) and Delft (1906–07). His major research was in phase theory, especially in three-component systems with critical endpoints where two phases are identical; and in so-called pseudobinary systems. Many of his investigations are summarized in *Die Theorie der Allotropie* (1921) and *Die Theorie der Komplexität und der Allotropie* (1938).

SMOLUCHOWSKI, MARIAN (*b. Vorderbrühl, near Vienna, Austria, 1872; d. Cracow, Poland, 1917*), physics.

Received doctorate at Vienna (1895); also studied in Paris, Glasgow (LL.D., 1901), and Berlin. Taught at the University of Lvov (1899–1913) and at the Jagiellonian University in Cracow (1913–17). His work on rarefied gases ("Über Wärmeleitung in verdünnten Gasen," 1898) was of special importance, for by publishing it Smoluchowski joined the dispute on the validity of atomic conceptions. These, represented in physics mainly by the kinetic theory of gases developed by Boltzmann, were far from accepted at the end of the nineteenth century; and their recognition was partly due to Smoluchowski. From about 1900 he worked on Brownian movement ("An Outline of the Kinetic Theory of Brownian Movement," 1906). In other research he laid the foundations of the theory of fluctuations, calculated the times of return for macro states, linked the theory to measurable parameters, and proved the actual existence of fluctuations. He discovered that blueness of the sky

was caused by fluctuations in the density of the air. He also obtained important results in the physics of colloids.

SMYTH, CHARLES PIAZZI (*b. Naples, Italy, 1819; d. Clova, near Ripon, Scotland, 1900*), astronomy, meteorology.

Smyth served as assistant to Maclear at the royal observatory, Cape of Good Hope (1835–45), and in 1845 was appointed director of the Edinburgh observatory, a position that included the titles astronomer royal for Scotland and professor of practical astronomy at the University of Edinburgh. In 1856 he led an expedition to the Peak of Tenerife, making astronomical observations ". . . Above the Clouds." On another expedition (1865) he measured the orientation, sizes, and angles of the Great Pyramid at Giza, and correlated the results with astronomical phenomena. He also charted the spectra of the sun, aurora, zodiacal light, the atmosphere under different meteorological conditions, and—in the laboratory—of various luminous gases.

SNEL (Snellius or **Snel van Royen), WILLEBRORD** (*b. Leiden, Netherlands, 1580; d. Leiden, 1626*), mathematics, optics, astronomy.

Studied at Leiden (M.A., 1608), Würzburg, Prague, Altdorf, Tübingen, and Paris; succeeded his father as professor at Leiden (1613). His early work translating mathematical texts was followed by geodetic work. In 1615 he became deeply involved in the determination of the length of the meridian, selecting for this purpose the method of triangulation, which he developed to such an extent that he may rightfully be called the father of triangulation. His other works included descriptions of comets, calculation of π, studies of navigation, and books on plane and spherical trigonometry. His best-known discovery, the law of refraction of light rays, which was named after him, was formulated probably in or after 1621, and was the result of many years of experimentation and of study of books by Kepler and Risner; it was first published by Descartes (1637).

SNOW, JOHN (*b. York, England, 1813; d. London, England, 1858*), medicine, anesthesiology, epidemiology.

Graduated from University of London (M.B., 1843; M.D., 1844); practiced medicine in London. After ether was introduced as an anesthetic in 1846, Snow invented an apparatus for its administration, based on physiological principles. He became the premier anesthetist of the country, publishing his masterly book *On Ether* in 1847. When chloroform was introduced into anesthesia (1847), Snow quickly appreciated its advantages and disadvantages, and constructed new pieces for its administration. His other important contribution was his theory and proof of the transmission of cholera by water infected with fecal matter. The vibrio of cholera was not to be described by Koch until 1884; Snow's reasoned argument was that cholera was propagated by a specific living, water-borne, self-reproducing cell or germ.

SODDY, FREDERICK (*b. Eastbourne, England, 1877; d. Brighton, England, 1956*), radiochemistry, science and society.

Graduated from Merton College, Oxford (1898); taught at McGill University (1900–03), Glasgow (1904–

14), Aberdeen (1914–19), and Oxford (1919–36). Soddy developed with Lord Rutherford (1901–03) the disintegration theory of radioactivity, confirmed with Sir William Ramsay (1903) the production of helium from radium, advanced in 1910 the concept of isotope (named in 1913), proposed in 1911 the alpha-ray rule leading to the full displacement law of 1913, and was the 1921 Nobel laureate in chemistry, principally for his investigations into the origin and nature of isotopes.

SOEMMERRING, SAMUEL THOMAS (*b. Torun, Poland, 1755; d. Frankfurt, Germany, 1830*), comparative anatomy, human anatomy, anthropology, physiology.

Received M.D. at Göttingen (1778); taught and did research at the Collegium Carolinum in Kassel (1779–84), the University of Mainz (1784–97), and the Bavarian Academy of Sciences in Munich (1805–20); practiced medicine in Frankfurt (1797–1805, 1820–30). His dissertation on the base of the brain and the origin of the cranial nerves provided such solid grounds for the order of the twelve cranial nerves that it is still taught. His writings made him the most famous German anatomist of the early nineteenth century. Among his varied researches he concluded that Negroes and Europeans belong to the same species; gave the pituitary gland its current name (hypophysis); published a handbook of human anatomy, *Vom Baue des menschlichen Körpers* (5 vols., 1791–96); discovered that arterial trunks always lie on the bent side of the joints and that the small part of the trigeminal nerve always lies against the third branch; and discovered the fovea centralis in the macula lutea, stimulating his interest in the anatomy of the sense organs.

SOHNCKE, LEONHARD (*b. Halle, Germany, 1842; d. Munich, Germany, 1897*), crystallography, physics, meteorology.

Studied at Halle and at Königsberg (doctorate, 1866); taught at Königsberg, the Technische Hochschule in Karlsruhe (1871–83), Jena (1883–86), and the Technische Hochschule in Munich (1886–97). His main contribution was in the field of crystallography; in studying the internal symmetry of crystals, he extended the lattice theory of Bravais to arrive at sixty-five of the 230 possible space groups. He introduced two new symmetry elements: the screw axis and the glide plane. He published his results in *Die Entwicklung einer Theorie der Krystallstruktur* (1879). While at Karlsruhe he also directed the network of meteorological stations in the province of Baden. In order to popularize meteorology he published *Über Stürme und Sturmwarnungen* (1875).

SOKHOTSKY, YULIAN-KARL VASILIEVICH (*b. Warsaw, Poland, 1842; d. Leningrad, U.S.S.R., 1927*), mathematics.

Sokhotsky was educated at St. Petersburg University (bachelor of mathematics, 1866; master's degree, 1868; doctorate, 1873). Taught at St. Petersburg (1868–1923) and at the Institute of Civil Engineers (from 1875). He belonged to the Chebyshev school of mathematics. Elaborating the foundations of the theory of residues, he discovered and demonstrated one of the principal theorems of the theory of analytical functions. According to this theorem, a single-valued analytical function assumes in every vicinity of its essential singular point all complex values.

SOKOLOV, DMITRY IVANOVICH (*b. St. Petersburg, Russia [now Leningrad, U.S.S.R.], 1788; d. St. Petersburg, 1852*), geology.

Graduated from the Mining Cadet Corps (1805), which later became the Institute of the Corps of Mining Engineers; he remained associated with this institution throughout his life. Taught at St. Petersburg University for more than twenty years (from 1822). Early training as an experimental chemist enabled him to approach classification of minerals in a new way. He attached primary importance to chemical composition and classified minerals according to their cations; he outlined their natural groupings long before Mendeleev's periodic system. In his petrographic descriptions he attempted to give rocks not only a chemical and mineralogical description but also an account of their genesis. He attached decisive importance to processes occurring deep within the earth. His distinction of metalliferous zones and belts of varying composition laid the foundation of modern concepts of metallogenetic provinces. At his suggestion, the first geological maps of European Russia were made, using a summarized stratigraphic table compiled by Sokolov. His three-volume textbook *Kurs geognosii* (1839) contains a detailed description of all the geological systems then known.

SOLANDER, DANIEL CARL (*b. Piteå, Sweden, 1733; d. London, England, 1782*), natural history.

Solander studied at the University of Uppsala, where he helped Linnaeus classify and index natural history collections; in 1756 published *Caroli Linnaei Elementa botanica,* an epitome of Linnaeus' general botany. Chosen by Linnaeus to help popularize the Linnaean system in England, he soon established himself as a link between Linnaeus and English naturalists and received a post at the newly established British Museum (1763). On Captain James Cook's *Endeavour* expedition (1768–71), he and Joseph Banks collected plant and animal specimens and conducted observations of the natural history and inhabitants. Solander Island (off the southern coast of South Island, New Zealand) and Cape Solander (the south side of Botany Bay, New South Wales, Australia) were named during the voyage, and Solander devised the Solander case, a book-shaped box that is still used, to guard the manuscript records of the voyage. In 1872 he made a four-month journey to the western coast of Britain, Iceland, and the Orkneys.

SOLDANI, AMBROGIO (or **Baldo Maria**) (*b. Pratovecchio, Arezzo, Italy, 1736; d. Florence, Italy, 1808*), geology.

A monk of the Camaldolese Congregation, Soldani taught mathematics at the University of Siena (from 1781) and was also an ardent naturalist. In deposits of the Pliocene Tuscan sea, especially near Siena and Volterra, he identified three layers: abyssal, formed by material of marine origin; littoral, formed by material of terrestrial origin; and intermediate, formed by both marine and terrestrial material. His studies distinguished him as a leader in establishing the interrelation of zoology and paleontology, and as a founder of micropaleontology.

SOLDNER, JOHANN GEORG VON (*b. Georgenhof, near Feuchtwangen, Germany, 1776; d. Bogenhausen, Munich, Germany, 1833*), geodesy, astronomy.

Self-taught astronomer; became known first through his contributions to Bode's *Astronomisches Jahrbuch.* While working for the Bavarian Land Survey, he developed his famous method for calculation of a triangle network. In 1815 he became director of the Bogenhausen observatory, responsible for supervising the construction and equipping of the new observatory.

SOLEIL,   JEAN-BAPTISTE-FRANÇOIS (*b.   Paris, France, 1798; d. Paris, 1878*), optical instruments.

Soleil was intimately associated with the work of Fresnel (1823–27). He directed the construction of the annular lenses and the mechanism to rotate them that Fresnel had designed for use in lighthouses, and constructed most of the apparatus used by Fresnel in his optical research based on the experimental demonstration of the wave theory by Thomas Young. Among the instruments he invented was the diffraction bench.

SOLLAS, WILLIAM JOHNSON (*b. Birmingham, England, 1849; d. Oxford, England, 1936*), geology, paleontology, anthropology.

Studied at the Royal School of Mines, London, and at St. John's College, Cambridge. Taught at Bristol (1880–83), Trinity College, Dublin (1883–97), and Oxford (1897–1936). A versatile investigator and experimentalist, he made significant contributions to many branches of the geological sciences and to biological research. He wrote an early work on fossil and modern sponges, carried out petrological and mineralogical investigations of the granites of Ireland, and devised improved methods for studying crystals and fossils. In 1911 he published *Ancient Hunters and Their Modern Representatives.*

SOLVAY, ERNEST (*b. Rebecq-Rognon, near Brussels, Belgium, 1838; d. Brussels, 1922*), industrial chemistry.

Solvay worked in his father's salt-making business and then at his uncle's gasworks in Brussels. In 1861 he noted the ease with which ammonia, salt solution, and carbon dioxide react to form sodium bicarbonate, which can be converted easily to the soda ash of commerce. He established a factory for soda production, patenting every stage of the process. His key contribution was the invention of a carbonating tower in which ammoniacal brine could be mixed thoroughly with carbon dioxide. He founded the Solvay International Institutes of Chemistry, of Physics, and of Sociology, which held periodical international conferences.

SOMERVILLE, MARY FAIRFAX GREIG (*b. Jedburgh, Roxburghshire, Scotland, 1780; d. Naples, Italy, 1872*), scientific and mathematical exposition, experimentation on the effects of solar radiation.

One of the foremost women of science of the nineteenth century, she had a profound and beneficial effect in advancing the cause of science and of women's education and emancipation. She taught herself mathematics, physics, and astronomy at a time when it was feared that the strain of abstract thought would injure tender female frames. Her second husband, a cosmopolitan army doctor, staunchly supported her aspirations, and wherever they traveled they came into contact with the prominent scientists of the day. Her first paper, in which she designed and carried out experiments on the magnetizing

effects of sunlight, had a vitalizing effect on investigations of the alleged phenomenon. Her other well-known publications were *The Mechanism of the Heavens* (1831), a translation of Laplace's *Mécanique céleste; On the Connexion of the Physical Sciences* (1834) and *Physical Geography* (1848), both of which strongly endorsed the new geology of Lyell, Murchison, and Buckland; and *On Molecular and Microscopic Science* (1869), dealing with the constitution of matter and the structure of microscopic plants.

SOMMERFELD, ARNOLD (JOHANNES WILHELM) (*b. Königsberg, Prussia [now Kaliningrad, U.S.S.R.], 1868; d. Munich, Germany, 1951*), theoretical physics.

Received doctorate at University of Königsberg (1891); his dissertation developed the methods that were to underlie his most important scientific work in the following decade—the application of the theory of functions of a complex variable to boundary-value problems, especially diffraction phenomena. He taught at Göttingen (1895–97), the Bergakademie in Clausthal (1897–1900), the Technische Hochschule of Aachen (1900–1906), and at Munich (from 1906). At Clausthal he applied his extraordinary ingenuity in boundary-value problems to the propagation of electromagnetic waves along wires of finite diameter (obtaining the first rigorous solution) and to the diffraction of X rays by a wedge-shaped slit. He collaborated with Felix Klein on *Theorie des Kreisels* (1897–1910). At Aachen he collaborated with Föppl, Schlick, and von Borries. Of fundamental importance were his investigations of the hydrodynamics of viscous fluids, aiming at an explanation of the onset of turbulence and a theory of the lubrication of machines. His series of papers on the general dynamics of electrons (1904–05) made him one of the most advanced theoretical physicists.

In 1907 he defended Einstein's relativity theory—thus placing himself among the earliest converts. One of his most striking applications of the theory was the prediction of a forward shift and narrowing of the direction in which an electron decelerated from relativistic velocities emits the greatest amount of energy (distribution of *Bremsstrahlung*). After the appearance of Niels Bohr's first paper on the constitution of atoms and molecules (1913), Sommerfeld worked on applying Bohr's model to the Zeeman effect (the splitting of spectral lines emitted in a magnetic field). By 1916 he found the definitive formulation of his quantization rules yielding a quantum theory of the normal Zeeman effect. This extraordinary extension, enrichment, and precision of Bohr's theory contributed decisively to its rapid and widespread acceptance. Sommerfeld's *Atombau und Spektrallinien* (1919) immediately became the bible of atomic physics. He also pioneered a new style of theoretical spectroscopy, wrote one of the first textbooks of wave mechanics (1929), and turned out an enormous number of doctorates in theoretical physics.

SOMMERING. *See* **Soemmerring, Samuel Thomas.**

SOMMERVILLE, DUNCAN MCLAREN YOUNG (*b. Beawar, Rajasthan, India, 1879; d. Wellington, New Zealand, 1934*), mathematics.

Sommerville was educated in Scotland at the Perth Academy and the University of St. Andrews. Taught at St.

Andrews (1902–14) and at Victoria University College, Wellington, New Zealand (from 1915). Evidence of his outstanding teaching ability is reflected in his four textbooks; among them are *The Elements of Non-Euclidean Geometry* (1914) and *An Introduction to the Geometry of n Dimensions* (1929), whose titles indicate his two major research specialties and whose contents develop geometric concepts that he created. His *Bibliography of Non-Euclidean Geometry* (1911) is also a bibliography of *n*-dimensional geometry.

SOMOV, OSIP IVANOVICH (*b. Otrada, Moscow gubernia [now Moscow oblast], Russia, 1815; d. St. Petersburg, Russia [now Leningrad, U.S.S.R.], 1876*), mathematics, mechanics.

Received master's degree at Moscow and doctorate at St. Petersburg. Taught at Moscow Commercial College (1839–41) and at St. Petersburg (1841–66). Originator of the geometrical trend in theoretical mechanics in Russia during second half of nineteenth century. Was first in Russia to deal with the solution of kinematic problems.

SONIN, NIKOLAY YAKOVLEVICH (*b. Tula, Russia, 1849; d. Petrograd [now Leningrad], Russia, 1915*), mathematics.

Studied at Moscow University and at Warsaw University (master's, 1871; doctorate, 1874). Taught at Warsaw (1872–93) and at the University for Women in St. Petersburg (1894–99), and held high educational administrative positions. Made a substantial contribution to the theory of special functions; especially important were his discoveries in the theory of cylindrical functions.

SONNERAT, PIERRE (*b. Lyons, France, 1748; d. Paris, France, 1814*), natural history.

Sonnerat rose from clerk in the overseas service of the Ministry of Naval Affairs to commissioner of the colonies, ending his career as commandant of the French settlement at Yanam, India. His fame rests on his determination to adhere, despite lack of sympathy from his superiors, to the enlightened policy of collecting essential scientific information on the overseas territories he administered. His two successful publications were *Voyage à la Nouvelle Guinée* (1776) and *Voyage aux Indes orientales et à la Chine* (1782). He sent botanical specimens to Adanson, A.-L. de Jussieu, Linnaeus the younger, and Lamarck; collections of reptiles from India and of tropical fishes were sent to Lacépède; and his notes and drawings were used by Cuvier. His elegant drawings of exotic birds are fundamental for the study of ornithology. His name is commemorated in the genus *Sonneratia* (mollusk) and in six or eight species of mangrove swamp plants of the eastern tropics. His understanding of contrasting cultures and civilizations made him a forerunner of modern social anthropologists.

SORANUS OF EPHESUS (*fl. Rome, second century* A.D.), medicine.

One of the major Greek physicians in the Roman Empire at the beginning of the second century; a member of the methodist sect; an important physician of the Ephesian school. The extent of his work demonstrates that, with Galen, he was the greatest medical author of late antiquity. That almost all his works were lost, whereas

Galen's were widely preserved, is a result of the fact that Galen and his theory of crasis dominated medical thought during the following 1,500 years and deprived the atomistic and cellular-pathological approach of any chance of acceptance. Although a master of the "method," Soranus looked beyond the limits of his school, and his work would have been impossible without the preliminary studies of the Herophileans. His major extant work, *Gynaecia,* comprised four books: the necessary qualities and the work of a midwife; obstetrics; women's diseases; and women's diseases that can be treated surgically and pharmaceutically. His magnum opus, on acute and chronic diseases, is lost, as are other works on midwifery, sperm and the genesis of creatures, causes of diseases, treatment of fevers, medical resources, surgery, ophthalmology, hygiene, and psychology. However, in addition to the works of translators and physicians of the Western Empire, of etymologists, lexicographers, and theologians, important chapters of Soranus' works appeared in the compilations of Byzantine medical science.

SORBY, HENRY CLIFTON (*b. Woodbourne, near Sheffield, England, 1826; d. Sheffield, 1908*), microscopy, geology, biology, metallurgy.

Sorby attended no university; he did full-time independent research in a laboratory in his own house. His most influential work was on the application of the microscope to geology and metallurgy (1849–64). He developed the basic techniques of petrography, using the polarizing microscope to study the structure of thin rock sections. He began with sedimentary rocks, returning to the subject shortly before his death and publishing a paper (1908) summarizing his whole approach. His new methods were taken up by Zirkel, who established petrography as a broad and systematic science. Turning to metals (1863–64), Sorby studied the structure of meteorites and proceeded to the local steel, identifying three separate crystalline compounds that differed in their reaction to nitric acid. His paper (1864) showing photomicrographs of steel was the true foundation of metallography, although no one followed this start.

His other major interest was spectrum analysis. Quickly developing the necessary combination of microscope and spectroscope, he first examined minerals in rock sections, then studied the coloring matter in animal and plant tissues. Carotene was one of his discoveries. He later became increasingly concerned with public policy in support of science, and advocated separation of research and teaching. Beginning in 1880 he worked to promote the formation of Firth College in Sheffield, and served as its president from 1882 to 1897. In 1878 he equipped his thirty-five-ton yawl as a floating laboratory, studying marine biology and geology. His only lasting contribution in this field was his technique for differentially staining biological tissues and mounting soft-bodied animals as permanent lantern slides for demonstration and study.

SØRENSEN, SØREN PETER LAURITZ (*b. Havrebjerg, Slagelse, Denmark, 1868; d. Copenhagen, Denmark, 1939*), chemistry.

Received doctorate at University of Copenhagen (1899); was director of the chemical department of the Carlsberg Laboratory in Copenhagen (1901–38). His investigations can be divided into four classes: synthesis of amino acids, analytical studies, work on hydrogen ion concentration, and studies on proteins.

SOSIGENES (*fl. Rome, middle of first century* B.C.), astronomy.

Sosigenes was one of the scientists who helped Julius Caesar with his reform of the calendar. Caesar's adoption of the $365\frac{1}{4}$ - day solar year may have been one result of Sosigenes' advice, and the statesman's seasonal calendar another.

SOTO, DOMINGO DE (*b. Segovia, Spain, ca. 1494; d. Salamanca, Spain, 1560*), logic, natural philosophy.

Soto was educated at the University of Alcalá (baccalaureate, 1516), the University of Paris (master's degree), and the College of San Ildefonso (licentiate in theology). He taught at San Ildefonso (1520–24), entered the Dominican order, and taught at San Esteban in Salamanca (1525–32) and the University of Salamanca (1532–60). His commentary and questions on the *Physics* of Aristotle (1545) were particularly important, since he was the first to apply the expression "uniformly difform" to the motion of falling bodies, thereby indicating that they accelerate uniformly and thus adumbrating Galileo's law of falling bodies. His best-known work, *De iure et iustitia* (1553–54), developed concepts of natural law and a "translation theory" of the origin of political authority.

SOULAVIE, JEAN-LOUIS GIRAUD (*b. Largentière, Ardèche, France, 1752; d. Paris, France, 1813*), geology.

Ordained in 1776, Soulavie was one of the many philosophical *abbés* and pamphleteers active before the Revolution. A self-taught amateur scientist, he explored the volcanic regions of Vivarais and Velay. His major geological publication was the eight-volume *Histoire naturelle de la France méridionale* (1780–84). The first seven volumes deal with "minerals," and the eighth with the plant kingdom. He used the principle of superposition not only to determine the relative ages of strata, but he also attempted to correlate age with fossil remains.

SOULEYET, LOUIS-FRANÇOIS-AUGUSTE (*b. Besse, Var, France, 1811; d. Martinique, 1852*), zoology.

One of several health officers in the French navy who won renown for zoological work connected with a voyage of circumnavigation. He did research on the *Bonite* voyage (1836–37), collecting new species, especially microscopic mollusks, in South America, Hawaii, the Philippines, and various parts of the Indian and Chinese seas. The results of his anatomical and physiological investigations of pteropod and gastropod mollusks are contained in the second volume of the zoology of the *Bonite* voyage and in various memoirs. From 1844 he was involved in a controversy with Armand de Quatrefages on the subject of "phlebenterism."

SOUTH, JAMES (*b. Southwark, London, England, 1785; d. Campden Hill, Kensington, London, 1867*), astronomy.

South gave up his medical practice in 1816 to devote himself to astronomy, establishing several observatories in the environs of London and Paris, where he worked with some of the finest telescopes available. With John Herschel, he reobserved the double stars charted originally by William Herschel, mainly for the purpose of detecting position changes. He published two catalogs of double stars. His great disappointments in, and severe criticisms of, contemporary scientific institutions often overwhelmed his actual scientific accomplishments. He was knighted in 1831.

SOWERBY, JAMES (*b. London, England, 1757; d. London, 1822*), natural history, geology.

Sowerby was trained as an artist and studied at the Royal Academy of Arts. Among the works he illustrated were James Edward Smith's *English Botany; or Coloured Figures of British Plants, With Their Essential Characters, Synonyms, and Places of Growth* (1790–1814); *British Mineralogy; Exotic Mineralogy; Mineral Conchology of Great Britain;* and William Smith's *Strata Identified by Organized Fossils.* He maintained a vast correspondence with naturalists in Britain and abroad.

SPALLANZANI, LAZZARO (*b. Scandiano, Italy, 1729; d. Pavia, Italy, 1799*), natural history, experimental biology, physiology.

Spallanzani received his doctorate at the University of Bologna in 1753 or 1754, took minor orders, and was ordained a priest. Apart from casual religious commitments, and despite an insatiable enthusiasm for travel, his career was wholly academic. He taught at the College (later University) of Reggio Emilia (1755–63), at the university and College of Nobles in Modena (1763–69), and at Pavia (1769–99). At Pavia he took charge of the public Museum of Natural History, building its collections to become among the most magnificent in Italy.

Among the many dedicated natural philosophers of the eighteenth century, Spallanzani stands preeminent for applying bold and imaginative experimental methods to an extraordinary range of hypotheses and phenomena. His main scientific interests were biological, and he acquired a mastery of microscopy; but he probed also into problems of physics, chemistry, geology, and meteorology, and pioneered in volcanology. Acute powers of observation and a broadly trained and logical mind helped him to clarify mysteries as diverse as stone skipping on water; the resuscitation of Rotifera and the regeneration of decapitated snail heads; the migrations of swallows and eels and the flight of bats; the electric discharge of the torpedo fish; and the genesis of thunderclouds or a waterspout. His ingenious and painstaking researches illuminated the physiology of blood circulation and of digestion in man and animals, and also of reproduction and respiration in animals and plants. The relentless thoroughness of his work on the animalcules of infusions discredited the doctrine of spontaneous generation and pointed the way to preservation of foodstuffs by heat. He made numerous excursions to various parts of Italy, along the shores of the Mediterranean, and even to Turkey to collect natural history specimens.

His early work on the animalcules of infusions (*Saggio di osservationi microscopiche . . .*, 1765) was finalized in *Opuscoli di fisica animale e vegetabile . . .* (1776), which also confirmed and extended Leeuwenhoek's observations on spermatozoa. Volume one of his *Dissertazioni di fisica animale e vegetabile* (1780) discussed his experiments involving "gastric juice"—a term introduced by him; volume two, on the generation of certain animals and plants, had

had its prelude in *Prodromo di un opera da imprimersi sopra le riproduzioni animali* (1768). He adduced abundant evidence that actual contact between eggs and seminal fluid is essential to fertilization, and recorded the first artificial insemination of a viviparous animal. He detailed his experiments involving more than 700 decapitated snails in *Resultati di esperienze sopra la riproduzione della testa nelle lumache terrestri* (1782, 1784). A fascinating account of his journeys, *Viaggi alle due Sicilie e in alcune parti dell'Appennino*, appeared in 1792.

SPEMANN, HANS (*b. Stuttgart, Germany, 1869; d. Freiburg im Breisgau, Germany, 1941*), embryology.

Spemann studied at Heidelberg, received his doctorate at Würzburg, taught at Würzburg (1894–1908), Rostock (1908–14), and Freiburg im Breisgau (1919–38), and directed the Kaiser Wilhelm Institute of Biology in Berlin-Dahlem (1915–18). His contact with Gustaf Wolff at Heidelberg led to his lifelong interest in embryology. To study the development of the lens of the amphibian eye, he invented a number of refined instruments for carrying out complicated surgical operations on eggs and embryos only a millimeter or two in diameter. In this way he became almost solely responsible for founding the techniques of microsurgery, one of his greatest contributions to biology. In experiments with newts' eggs, he discovered that a process he called "determination" takes place after the early stages of development, after which the developmental fate of the parts is fixed. He devised experimental procedures that revealed a causal sequence of events leading up to the determination of the main organ that appears in early stages of development: the central nervous system. He discovered the first known example of a causal mechanism that makes it possible to control precisely the direction in which a part of the embryo will develop; by surgical manipulation of its neighboring cells, it can be determined whether this embryonic part will develop into nerves or into skin. He also discovered that the character of the induced organ depends much more on its own intrinsic (presumably genetic) constitution than on that of the inducer. He was awarded the Nobel Prize for physiology or medicine in 1935.

SPENCER, HERBERT (*b. Derby, England, 1820; d. Brighton, England, 1903*), philosophy, biology, psychology, sociology.

Spencer was virtually self-taught, learning his science from reading, attending lectures, and, later, associating with working scientists. He is important for his synthesis of so much of the accepted science of his day in the integrating framework of evolution. His view of evolution was quite distinct from Darwin's: to show how progress or development in all areas of the universe—the solar system, the totality of organic species, the maturation of each organism, the psychic development and socialization of the individual, the evolution of society and culture—consists of one fundamental, determinate motion from an incoherent homogeneity to a complex and interdependent heterogeneity. In an early essay, "A Theory of Population" (1852), Spencer applied Malthusian principles to animal populations, deduced a struggle for survival, and coined the phrase "survival of the fittest." His *First Principles* (1862), with its doctrine of an ultimate unknowable force, sought to reconcile science and religion and to lay the metaphysical underpinnings of all

evolution. *The Principles of Biology* (1864–67) analyzes the principles by which higher forms emerge from a gradual process of adaptation to the environment. He insisted on the inheritance of acquired characteristics as a major mechanism of evolution. *The Principles of Psychology* (1855) marked the transition of psychology from a heavily epistemological phase to one in which it was closely dependent on physiology.

SPENCER, LEONARD JAMES (*b. Worcester, England, 1870); d. London, England, 1959*), mineralogy.

Spencer studied at the Royal College of Science for Ireland, Dublin; Sidney Sussex College, Cambridge; and in Munich. In 1894 he began his lifelong career at the British Museum and with the Mineralogical Society of Great Britain and Ireland. In descriptive mineralogy, he established relationships between three lead antimony sulfides, gave a model description of enargite, and named eight new minerals. Made the British Museum mineral collection the best-documented and best-indexed in the world. Started publication of *Mineralogical Abstracts* by the Mineralogical Society, editing twelve volumes (1920–55) and contributing two-thirds of the text himself. Wrote *The World's Minerals* (1911) and *A Key to Precious Stones* (1936).

SPENCER JONES, HAROLD (*b. Kensington, London, England, 1890; d. Greenwich, England, 1960*), astronomy.

After attending Jesus College, Cambridge, Spencer Jones spent his astronomical career as assistant at the Greenwich Royal Observatory (1913–23), H.M. Astronomer at the Cape of Good Hope (1923–33), and astronomer royal (1933–55). He was knighted in 1943. His scientific interests were connected mainly with the tasks of the observatories: primarily the problems of positional and fundamental astronomy. His outstanding personal contributions were a study of the speed of rotation of the earth, and one of the solar parallax.

SPERRY, ELMER AMBROSE (*b. Cortland County, N.Y., 1860; d. Brooklyn, N.Y., 1930*), technology, engineering.

A self-taught inventor and engineer, Sperry founded his own company in Chicago to market his generator and arc light (1882). In Chicago, Cleveland, and Brooklyn, he was successful as an independent inventor concentrating successively upon the electric streetcar, mining machinery, the automobile, and industrial chemistry. The U.S. Navy adopted his improved gyrocompass, used his gyrostabilizer, and tested his airplane stabilizer. Before World War I he founded the Sperry Gyroscope Company. An analysis of his 350 patents reveals his consistent focus on automatic controls. The Sperry automatic ship pilot and the Sperry automatic airplane pilot enhanced his reputation as a pioneer in automatic controls.

SPEUSIPPUS (*b. Athens, ca. 408 B.C.; d. Athens, 339 B.C.*), philosophy.

A member of the Academy in Athens, Speusippus became its head after Plato's death. Only scattered fragments of his works have survived, a large portion being from his work, "Similar Things," dealing with zoological classifications. The importance of such classifications can be inferred from his assumption that every being is fully determined by the totality of its logical relations to all other beings. This seems to correspond to the doctrine that the concatenation of the levels of existence is constituted by logical relations (analogies).

SPHUJIDHVAJA (*fl. western India*, A.D. *269*), astronomy, astrology.

Sphujidhvaja's *Yavanajātaka* (written 269 A.D.) was a versification of a prose translation into Sanskrit of a Greek astrological textbook. It became the foundation of genethlialogy and interrogational astrology in India, adapting the foreign Greco-Egyptian material for an Indian context.

SPIEGEL, ADRIAAN VAN DEN (also **Spieghel, Spigelius, Spiegelius, Adriano Spigeli**) (*b. Brussels, Belgium, 1578; d. Padua, Italy, 1625*), botany, anatomy, medicine.

Studied at universities of Louvain and Leiden, and later at Padua under Fabrici and Casserio; succeeded Casserio at Padua as professor of anatomy and surgery (1616). During his lifetime only two works were published: *Isagoge in rem herbariam libri duo* (1606), on the tapeworm; and a work on malaria. The work that established his renown as an anatomist, *De humani corporis fabrica,* was edited and published by Bucretius (1627).

SPIEGELIUS. *See* **Spiegel, Adriaan van den.**

SPIX, JOHANN BAPTIST VON (*b. Höchstadt an der Aisch, Germany, 1781; d. Munich, Germany, 1826*), zoology.

Received M.D. at Würzburg; in 1811 became an *Adjunkt* and later full member and curator of the zoological collections at the Munich Academy. From 1817 to 1820 he and K. F. P. Martius accomplished one of the most important scientific expeditions of the nineteenth century—exploring the Amazon in South America. Their collections included specimens of eighty-five species of mammals, 350 species of birds, nearly 2,700 species of insects, and fifty-seven living animals, providing material for a vast number of works by other scientists.

SPOERER, GUSTAV FRIEDRICH WILHELM (*b. Berlin, Germany, 1822; d. Giessen, Germany, 1895*), astronomy.

Graduated from Berlin University (1843), worked at the Berlin observatory, taught in secondary schools, and became an observer at the new Potsdam observatory (1874). His main accomplishments were his very careful observations of the sun. He determined the elements of the solar rotation and improved the law for the decrease of the rotation of the sun from the equator to the poles. His statistics contain much material on proper motions and on the evolution and distribution of sunspots during a sunspot period.

SPORUS OF NICAEA (*fl. second half of third century*), mathematics.

Our knowledge of Sporus stems only from such secondary sources as the works of Pappus and various commentators. He concerned himself intensively with two mathematical problems: that of squaring the circle and that of doubling the cube. He contributed chiefly through his constructive criticism of existing solutions.

SPRAT, THOMAS (*b. Beaminster, Dorset, England, 1635; d. Bromley, Kent, England, 1713*), history of science.

Received B.A. (1654) and M.A. (1657) at Wadham College, Oxford, and was ordained in 1660. His loyalties being pliable, he held many ecclesiastical offices under different rulers of England. His fame rests entirely on his *History of the Royal Society* (1667), although questions have been raised from the seventeenth century to the present day concerning its historical reliability. The *History* was designed as a public relations piece, to explain the nature, organization, work, and aims of the Royal Society to the public, thus showing that the promotion of its affairs was a national, even a patriotic, enterprise. Part one presents a survey of ancient, medieval, and Renaissance philosophy and its influence on the Society. Part two contains the history proper: prehistory and first meetings; methods of inquiry and manner of discourse; reputation and correspondence abroad; and fourteen examples of Society papers. Part three is an apology for the Society that tries to meet all conceivable objections to its enterprise—it poses no threat to learning, education, or the universities, and is a great ally of religion.

SPRENGEL, CHRISTIAN KONRAD (*b. Brandenburg, Germany, 1750; d. Berlin, Germany, 1816*), botany.

Sprengel was educated at Halle University, taught at the Friedrichs-Hospital School and the military academy in Berlin (1774–1780), and served as rector and taught at the Great Lutheran Town School at Spandau (1780–95). In 1787 he began observing the pollination of *Geranium* flowers. These relationships of flower structure, insect visitors, and pollination mechanisms culminated in the publication of his great work, *Das entdeckte Geheimniss der Natur im Bau und in der Befruchtung der Blumen* (1793). His discovery of dichogamy led him to one of his major conclusions: "Nature appears not to have intended that any flower should be fertilized by its own pollen." This doctrine, together with the even more important view of the close integration of floral structures with insect visitation, was the first attempt to explain the origin of organic forms from definite relations to the environment. The insect-plant mutualism so elegantly and minutely described profoundly influenced Darwin and provided him with evidence for his theory of evolution.

SPRENGEL, KURT POLYCARP JOACHIM (*b. Boldekow, Germany, 1766; d. Halle, Germany, 1833*), botany, medicine.

Sprengel graduated from (1787) and taught at (from 1789) the University of Halle, also maintaining a lucrative private medical practice for several years. One of the most prestigious professors in Germany, he taught pathology, legal medicine, semeiology, medical history, and botany. His most important publication was a medical history, *Versuch einer pragmatischen Geschichte der Arzneikunde* (1792–99). He also made numerous translations, edited five journals, and was a vigorous critic of the emerging speculative currents in German medicine. He strongly promoted the microscopic examination of plants and studied their structure.

SPRING, WALTHÈRE VICTOR (*b. Liège, Belgium, 1848; d. Tilff, Belgium, 1911*), chemistry, physics.

Spring received a diploma in mining engineering from the University of Liège (1872), studied under Kekulé at Bonn, and returned to teach at Liège (1875–1911). In early research, he produced a valuable series of papers on the oxyacids of sulfur and on the polythionates, in which he synthesized new compounds and found new chemical reactions. His most important work, however, was in physical chemistry: he investigated the effects of pressure on phase equilibria, on chemical equilibria, on the chemical reactions of solids, and on the ability or inability of one metal to diffuse into another; studied the actual color of natural and chemically pure waters; and supplied ideas and emphasis that contributed significantly to the development of the ultramicroscope.

SPRUCE, RICHARD (*b. Ganthorpe, near Malton, England, 1817; d. Coneysthorpe, Castle Howard, near Malton, 1893*), botany.

In 1844 Spruce left his role of schoolmaster to make botany his career. He made botanical expeditions to the Pyrenees, where he discovered bryophytes previously unrecorded in the region; to South America, studying the rich vegetation of the Amazon valley and dispatching to England specimens of more than 7,000 species; and to Andean Ecuador, collecting cinchona plants suitable for cultivation in India. His "Palmae Amazonicae" (1869) and "Hepaticae Amazonicae et Andinae" (1884) gave results of his expeditions.

SPRUNG, ADOLF FRIEDRICH WICHARD (*b. Kleinow, near Perleberg, Germany, 1848; d. Potsdam, Germany, 1909*), meteorology.

Received doctorate at Leipzig (1876); worked at the naval observatory in Hamburg (1876–86), directed the instrument division of the Prussian Meteorological Institute in Berlin (1886–92), and became director of the meteorological-magnetic observatory in Potsdam (1892–1909). He became the first to apply the theorems of mathematical physics to the interpretation of meteorological processes, thereby laying the foundations for the theory of the dynamics of the atmosphere, with which meteorology became an exact science. His *Lehrbuch der Meteorologie* (1885) was the first complete work on dynamic meteorology. He also enriched the field with his remarkable new designs of meteorological instruments.

SPURZHEIM, JOHANN CHRISTOPH (*b. Longuich, near Trier, Germany, 1776; d. Boston, Mass., 1832*), psychology, psychiatry, neuroscience.

Studied at the universities of Trèves (now Trier), Vienna (M.D., 1813), and Paris. Worked at Vienna with Franz Joseph Gall on neuroanatomical research, collaborating with him on the founding of phrenology. After breaking with Gall in 1813, Spurzheim formalized his views in *The Physiognomical System of Drs. Gall and Spurzheim: Founded on an Anatomical and Physiological Examination of the Nervous System in General, and of the Brain in Particular; and Indicating the Dispositions and Manifestations of the Mind* (1815). As a result of his conviction of phrenology's truthfulness, he inspired inquiries that in some cases led to the establishment of phrenology's inherent incorrectness.

ŚRĪDHARA (*fl. India, ninth century*), mathematics.

Śrīdhara wrote two works on arithmetic, and one work, now lost, on algebra. The *Pāṭīgaṇita* covers metrological definitions; basic mathematical operations; finding squares and square roots and cubes and cube roots; frac-

tions; proportions; and solutions for problems involving mixtures, series, plane figures, volumes, shadows, and zero. His *Triśatikā* summarizes much of the material in the above work, including parts no longer available to us.

ŚRĪPATI (*fl. Rohiṇīkhaṇḍa, Mahārāṣṭra, India, 1039-56*), astronomy, astrology, mathematics.

Śrīpati is one of the most renowned authorities on astrology in India, although his works on astronomy and mathematics are not negligible. His works include: *Dhīkoṭidakaraṇa* (1039), on solar and lunar eclipses; *Dhruvamānasa* (1056), on calculating planetary longitudes, gnomon problems, eclipses, horns of the moon, and planetary transits; *Siddhāntaśekhara*, a major work on astronomy; *Gaṇitatilaka*, a mathematical treatise; *Jyotiṣaratnamālā*, the most influential work in Sanskrit on *muhūrta* or catarchic astrology; and *Jātakapaddhati* or *Śrīpatipaddhati*, one of the fundamental textbooks for later Indian genethlialogy.

STÄCKEL, PAUL GUSTAV (*b. Berlin, Germany, 1862; d. Heidelberg, Germany, 1919*), mathematics, history of science.

Graduated from Berlin (1885); wrote *Habilitationsschrift* at Halle (1891); held chairs at various German universities, teaching finally at Heidelberg. Specialized in analytical mechanics, related questions in geometry, and properties of analytical functions. In the history of mathematics, he was especially noted for his role in instituting the publication of Euler's *Opera omnia*.

STAHL, GEORG ERNST (*b. Ansbach, Germany, ca. 1660; d. Berlin, Germany, 1734*), medicine, chemistry.

Stahl studied medicine at Jena and received his degree in 1684. He then devoted himself to scientific work and lectured in chemistry at the university, attaining considerable reputation. In 1687 he became court physician at Weimar, and in 1694 joined the medical faculty of the new University of Halle. In 1715 he went to Berlin to be court physician, remaining there until his death. Stahl has aroused much controversy. As a physician he was outstanding; he held the highest academic positions, enjoyed a very active practice, and through his writings became vastly influential. As a philosopher he supported the viewpoint known as vitalism and wove that concept into the fabric of his medical system. As a chemist he elaborated and maintained the doctrine of phlogiston, which, until outgrown later in the eighteenth century, provided a reasoned explanation for many chemical phenomena. But his teachings, particularly his stand on vitalism, in large part ran counter to the trend of the times; his chemical theories were overthrown; his vitalist doctrine, in the form that he elaborated it, could not stand up against the onrushing tide of research and experimentation; while his system of medical practice faded away before numerous competitors. Yet, even though he seemed to be discredited, Stahl influenced the whole of eighteenth-century medicine.

His prolix writing contains certain recurrent themes that serve as a foundation for his more specific discussions. Foremost among his basic concepts is the irreducible difference between the living and the nonliving. Mind and matter are distinct and ultimate. While both living and nonliving are composed of matter, only living creatures have an *anima.* A second major principle involves the concept of goal or purpose. Behavior is not blind or mechanical. Living creatures can be understood only if we pay attention to their striving toward particular ends or purposes. The directive agent is the *anima.* A third principle concerns the place of mechanism in the scheme of things. All nonliving creatures are entirely mechanical. Living creatures, up to a point, also are mechanical; but the mechanism involved represents only the instrument of the directing agent or *anima.* The *anima,* in brief, is an intelligent agent that wills certain ends and therefore must have organs suitable for achieving them. The human body is the organ of the rational *anima* and is formed for its needs. Medicine has to do with the whole living organism, presided over by the *anima,* rather than with specific actions of specific parts, which are only instruments.

In chemistry as in biology, Stahl strongly disavowed the mechanical viewpoint. He relied heavily on the doctrines of Becher, who believed in three elementary principles—air, water, and earth. Air, however, did not enter into combinations, so that water and earth formed the material bases of objects. "Earth," however, comprehended three different types: the first, having to do with substantiality, rendered bodies solid and vitrifiable; the second provided color, odor, and combustibility; the third supplied weight, ductility, and volatility. Stahl adopted these views from Becher and used the name "phlogiston" to designate the second earth—the principle of combustibility. The experimental bases for phlogiston rested principally on the behavior of minerals and metals. When a metal was heated intensely, the phlogiston was released. For minerals the expulsion or reception of phlogiston was a reversible process, but this was not the case in the animal or vegetable kingdoms. Plants were particularly rich in phlogiston; but once it was driven out, the original compound could not be reestablished. Phlogiston was an element or substance and not an abstract quality or property. The Stahlian chemistry held a theory of recycling—the phlogiston in the air passed into plants and thence could pass into animal bodies through the ingestion of plant material.

STALLO, JOHANN BERNHARD (*b. Sierhausen, Oldenburg, Germany, 1823; d. Florence, Italy, 1900*), philosophy of science.

After immigrating to the United States in 1839, Stallo taught at St. Xavier College in Cincinnati (1841–44) and at St. John's College (now Fordham University), New York City (1844–48), studied and practiced law (1847–83), and served as American ambassador in Florence (1884–89). The development of his thought can be characterized as a gradual transition from post-Kantian idealism in his youth to his own version of positivistically oriented phenomenalism in his mature years. One idea was common to all phases of his thought: that things are not "insular existences" but complexes of relations. In 1848 he published *The General Principles of the Philosophy of Nature, With an Outline of Its Recent Developments Among the Germans; Embracing the Philosophical Systems of Schelling and Hegel and Oken's System of Nature,* indicating his exclusive commitment to *Naturphilosophie* and documenting the early stage of his philosophical development. His critical essay on materialism, *Naturphilosophische Untersuchungen.*

Der Materialismus (1855), represents an intermediate stage between his early Hegelianism and his mature work in the philosophy and epistemology of science. The main purpose of his *Concepts and Theories of Modern Physics* (1881) was an epistemological criticism of the corpuscular-kinetic theory of nature. As one of the prophets of twentieth-century physics, he correctly recognized the inadequacy of the classical corpuscular-kinetic models on the microphysical scale and questioned the absolutistic assumptions of Newton. He had especially great influence on philosophers of science, rather than on scientists.

STAMPIOEN, JAN JANSZ, DE JONGE (*b. Rotterdam, Netherlands, 1610; d. The Hague, Netherlands [?], after 1689*), mathematics.

Stampioen began his career in 1632 with *Kort byvoeghsel der sphaerische triangulen,* a fully algebraic treatment of spherical trigonometry appended to his edition of Frans van Schooten's *Tabula sinuum.* From 1633 to 1645 he was a mathematics teacher and tutor in Rotterdam and The Hague, and had a printing shop where he published his *Algebra ofte nieuwe stelregel* (*Algebra, or the New Method*), 1639. His new method of solving cubic equations led to disputes with Descartes and Waessenaer and to a series of polemic pamphlets.

STANNIUS, HERMANN FRIEDRICH (*b. Hamburg, Germany, 1808; d. Sachsenburg, Germany, 1883*), comparative anatomy, physiology.

Studied at Berlin and Breslau (doctorate, 1831). Worked at the Friedrichstädter-Krankenhaus (1831–37) and taught at Rostock (1837–62). His various studies in comparative anatomy and physiology included notable works on entomology, general pathology, and an outstanding monograph which was the second volume of *Lehrbuch der vergleichenden Anatomie der Wirbeltiere* (1846). In a noted work (1852), he ligatured a frog heart and established the location of the stimulus-building center with the *sinus venosus* ("Stannius' experiment").

STANTON, THOMAS ERNEST (*b. Atherstone, Warwickshire, England, 1865; d. Pevensey Bay, Sussex, England, 1931*), engineering.

Studied at Owens College, Manchester, and University College, Liverpool (D.Sc., 1898); in addition to the above, he taught at University College, Bristol, and became superintendent of the engineering department at the National Physical Laboratory (1901–30). His work was mainly in hydrodynamics (*Friction,* 1923), strength of materials, heat transmission, lubrication, and aerodynamics. Knighted in 1928.

STARK, JOHANNES (*b. Schickenhof, Upper Palatinate, Germany, 1874; d. Traunstein, Upper Bavaria, Germany, 1957*), experimental physics.

Received doctorate at Munich (1897); taught at Munich, Göttingen, Hannover, Aachen, Greifswald, and Würzburg. His main interest was electrical conduction in gases; in 1904 he founded *Jahrbuch der Radioaktivität und Elektronik* to publish studies in the newly developing field of particle physics. He discovered the Doppler effect in canal rays (1905) and attempted to make the optical Doppler effect a proof of Einstein's theory of special relativity, and later, with the quantum hypothesis as well. The latter led to a vigorous dispute with Arnold Sommerfeld on quantum theory. In 1914 he published his discovery of the effect (Stark effect) produced on spectrum lines by subjecting the source of light to an intense electric field. Received 1919 Nobel Prize for physics. After the Nazi seizure of power, Stark, as a partisan of Hitler, led the fight against modern theoretical physics, retiring shortly before the outbreak of the war.

STARKEY, GEORGE (*b. Bermuda, 1628; d. London, England, 1665*), medicine, alchemy.

Received master's degree at Harvard College (1646) and practiced medicine in Boston and London. He engaged in a wide range of experiments, including the production of alchemical metals and the preparation of chemical medicines. His most important works were *The Marrow of Alchemy* (1654–55), *Natures Explication and Helmont's Vindication* (1657), *Pyrotechny Asserted and Illustrated* (1658), and *Introitus apertus* (1667).

STARLING, ERNEST HENRY (*b. London, England, 1866; d. Kingston, Jamaica, 1927*), physiology, education.

Received education at King's College School and Guy's Hospital Medical School (M.B., London, 1889), and spent influential periods in Heidelberg in Kühne's laboratory and with Heidenhain at Breslau. Collaborated with William Maddock Bayliss at University College on hormonal function. Their 1902 paper established the existence and role of secretin, a product of the duodenum; and in 1905 Starling coined the word "hormone" to designate the body's "chemical messengers" produced by the endocrine glands. On the basis of his studies of lymph production, capillary permeability, and the physiological effects of osmotic forces, he began the synthesis of the "Starling equilibrium," referring to the balance between intravascular pressure and osmotic forces at the capillary level. His most significant work was on the heart itself. The "Starling sequence," embracing both central circulatory function and fluid exchange at the capillary level, remains the unifying theme of contemporary circulatory theory. He was also a responsible and pragmatic activist in education.

STAS, JEAN-SERVAIS (*b. Louvain, Belgium, 1813; d. Brussels, Belgium, 1891*), chemistry.

Received M.D. at University of Louvain (1835); did chemical research on apple tree roots, isolating a crystalline glucoside, phlorizin. In Paris he collaborated with Dumas, splitting phlorizin into phloretin and glucose. Taught at the Military School in Brussels (1840–68), working on atomic weights. In several papers he discredited Prout's hypothesis that atomic weights are whole-number multiples of the atomic weight of hydrogen. In toxicology he developed a method for detecting alkaloids in cases of poisoning.

STASZIC, STANISŁAW WAWRZYNIEC (*b. Piła, Poland, 1755; d. Warsaw, Poland, 1826*), geology, organization of educational and scientific institutions.

Studied at universities of Leipzig and Göttingen and at the Collège Royal de France. Served as a tutor in Poland and Vienna, obtained a doctorate in canon and civil law from the Academy of Zamość (1782), and in 1797 began

geologic investigations in Silesia, Saxony, and the Tatra Mountains. In 1807 he published "On the Statistics of Poland," and from 1807 he concentrated on the organization of educational institutions and on the development of the mining industry in the duchy of Warsaw. He became a high-ranking official in the kingdom of Poland (1815), and initiated a systematic development of the mining and metallurgical industries; he established the directorate of mining and founded the first mining academy in Poland. His investigations of the structure of geological formations were compiled in 1815 as "On the Geology of the Carpathians and of Other Mountain Ranges and Plains of Poland."

STAUDINGER, HERMANN (*b. Worms, Germany, 1881; d. Freiburg im Breisgau, Germany, 1965*), organic and macromolecular chemistry.

Staudinger studied in Darmstadt, Munich, Halle, and at Strasbourg, where he discovered the highly reactive ketenes; he taught at the Technische Hochschule in Karlsruhe (1907–12), Eidgenössische Technische Hochschule of Zurich (1912–26), and Freiburg im Breisgau (1926–50). Staudinger's main studies were in macromolecular chemistry, for which he received the Nobel Prize in chemistry (1953). In Karlsruhe Staudinger achieved a new synthesis of isoprene (the basis of synthetic rubber); in Zurich and Freiburg im Breisgau he began studies of polymers; he first expressed preference for long-chain conception of polymers over the aggregate hypothesis in 1920, and spent much of his life trying to confirm it; his formulation of the Staudinger law relating specific viscosity and molecular weight was made in the attempt to strengthen his viscosimetric data for long-chain molecules. Staudinger's pioneer work in macromolecular chemistry (*Makromolekulare Chemie und Biologie*, 1947) was a major foundation for molecular biology. Helped found the journal, *Makromolekulare Chemie* (1947).

STAUDT, KARL GEORG CHRISTIAN VON (*b. Rothenburg-ob-der-Tauber, Germany, 1798; d. Erlangen, Germany, 1867*), mathematics.

Staudt attended the University of Gottingen (1818–22), where he was introduced to astronomy by Gauss; his calculations of a comet's orbit in 1821 were praised by Gauss, and on the basis of this work he received the doctorate from the University of Erlangen (1822), though he never again studied astronomy. Staudt taught mathematics most of his life at the University of Erlangen (1835–67). His fame as an innovator stems from his work in projective geometry, the subject of his *Geometrie der lage* (1847), his principal publication; Staudt was the first to adopt a fully rigorous approach in projective geometry, free from all metrical considerations; he made an essential contribution to synthetic geometry through his elegantly formulated introduction of the complex projective spaces of one, two, and three dimensions. Staudt is also known for the Staudt-Clausen theorem in the theory of Bernoulli numbers (1840).

STEACIE, EDGAR WILLIAM RICHARD (*b. Westmount, Quebec, Canada, 1900; d. Ottawa, Ontario, Canada, 1962*), physical chemistry.

Steacie received the Ph.D. from McGill University, with further study in Frankfurt, Leipzig, and King's College,

London; he taught at McGill (1937–39), then moved to the National Research Council of Canada (president from 1952 to 1962); his principal work was *Atomic and Free Radical Reactions* (1946).

STEAD, JOHN EDWARD (*b. Howden-on-Tyne, Northumberland, England, 1851; d. Redcar, Yorkshire, England, 1923*), metallurgy, analytical chemistry.

After apprenticeship to the chemical analyst of Newcastle-upon-Tyne, Stead became his partner (1876) and remained an analyst the rest of his life; he studied eutectics in steels, the crystalline structure of metals, and the effects of phosphorus on steel; elected fellow of Royal Society (1903).

STEBBING, THOMAS ROSCOE REDE (*b. London, England, 1835; d. Tunbridge Wells, England, 1926*), zoology.

Stebbing was educated at King's College, London (B.A., 1855), and Worcester College, Oxford (B.A., 1857; M.A., 1859), where he held several teaching and administrative positions until resigning in 1868. Stebbing became interested in natural history and devoted most of his life to the study of amphipod Crustacea and to writing both scholarly and popular works. An early convert to Darwinism, many of Stebbing's essays were written in support of it.

STEENSTRUP, (JOHANNES) JAPETUS SMITH (*b. Vang, Denmark, 1813; d. Copenhagen, Denmark, 1897*), zoology.

Though he took no university degree, Steenstrup taught for six years at the Sorö Academy, where two publications (1842) on bogs and metagenesis earned him an appointment as professor of zoology at the University of Copenhagen (1846–85); for nearly fifty years he initiated and guided Danish research in natural history.

STEFAN, JOSEF (*b. St. Peter, near Klagenfurt, Austria, 1835; d. Vienna, Austria, 1893*), physics.

Stefan studied at the University of Vienna (beginning 1853), where he worked with Carl Ludwig and later became a full professor of mathematics and physics (1863); three years later he was appointed director of the Institute for Experimental Physics; he was a brilliant experimenter and a well-liked teacher. Stefan's most important work deals with heat radiation (1879); he refined Newton's law so that it agreed with measurements in all temperature ranges; the law is now known as the Stefan-Boltzmann law, for Boltzmann established its theoretical basis (1884). Other important work by Stefan concerns heat conduction in gases; and in the theory of mutual magnetic effects of two electric currents, he showed, in opposition to Ampére and Grassman, that clear results can be achieved only by means of the Faraday-Maxwell theory of continuous action.

STEIN, JOHAN WILLEM JAKOB ANTOON, S.J. (*b. Grave, Netherlands, 1871; d. Rome, Italy, 1951*), astronomy.

Stein entered the Society of Jesus in 1889 and studied physics and astronomy at the University of Leiden (1894–1901) under Lorentz; he directed the Vatican observatory (1930–51); his major publication (with J. G. Hagen, 1924) concerned variable stars.

STEINER, JAKOB (*b. Utzensdorf, Bern, Switzerland, 1796; d. Bern, Switzerland, 1863*), mathematics.

The son of a small farmer and tradesman, Steiner did not learn to write until he was fourteen; he left home in 1814 to attend J. H. Pestalozzi's school at Yverdon, where he was both student and teacher; inspired by Pestalozzi's revolutionary ideas on education, Steiner advocated independent reflection by students, a practice responsible for his great success as a teacher; he gave private instruction in Heidelberg (1818–21) and taught briefly at the Werder Gymnasium before being dismissed in 1822 (a fiery temperament, liberal political views, and crude behavior and speech alienated many people); after studying at the University of Berlin (1822–24), Steiner served as assistant and then senior master at the technical school in Berlin (1825–34), where he also experienced difficulties; in 1834 he was appointed extraordinary professor at the University of Berlin, a post he held until his death.

His work was guided by one goal: to discover the organic unity of all the objects of mathematics, an aim realized especially in his fundamental research on synthetic geometry; many of his theorems are founded on the stereographic projection of the plane onto the sphere. At Berlin, he became friendly with Abel, Crelle, and Jacobi, and together they introduced a fresh, new current into mathematics; Steiner contributed many articles to the journal founded by Crelle, *Journal für die reine und angewandte Mathematik*, in whose first volume he published the first systematic development of the theory of the power of a point with respect to a circle and of the points of similitude of circles (1826); also in this work Steiner proved his famous theorem on series of circles. Most of the articles published in Crelle's *Journal* and Gergonne's *Annales de mathématiques* were problems to be solved or theorems to be proved, providing a stimulating influence on geometric research that was strengthened by his first book, *Systematische Entwicklung* (1832), on projective geometry; the eighty-five "Problems and Theorems" appended in a supplement proved stimulating to a generation of geometers; his second book appeared a year later (1833) and enjoyed great success.

Other research interests included conic sections and surfaces, new methods of determining second-order curves, the theory of second-degree surfaces, center-of-gravity problems, and the principle of symmetrization which he developed (1840–41). In a short paper of fundamental importance (1848), Steiner first defined and examined the various polar curves of a point with respect to a given curve, and introduced the "Steiner curves." His work was continued by L. Cremona and R. Sturm, among many others.

STEINHEIL, KARL AUGUST (*b. Rappoltsweiler [now Ribeauvillé], Alsace, 1801; d. Munich, Germany, 1870*), physics, astronomy.

Steinheil received the Ph.D. from Königsberg (1825) under Bessel's supervision; taught mathematics and physics at Munich University (1832–49), organized telegraph communications in Austria (1849–52), and worked as a government technical consultant; a keen-witted discoverer and inventor, especially in optics and telegraphy, he exerted great influence on scientific life at Munich.

653

STEINITZ, ERNST (*b. Laurahütte, Silesia, Germany [now Huta Laura, Poland], 1871; d. Kiel, Germany, 1928*), mathematics.

Steinitz received the Ph.D. from Breslau (1894); he taught at Technical College in Breslau (1910–20) and University of Kiel (1920–28); in his most important publication, "Algebraische Theorie der Körper" (1910), he gave an abstract and general definition of the concept of a "field."

STEINMETZ, CHARLES PROTEUS (*b. Breslau, Germany [now Wrocław, Poland], 1865; d. Schenectady, N.Y., 1923*), engineering.

Steinmetz studied at the University of Breslau, where he became an ardent socialist; shortly before completing the Ph.D. in mathematics he was forced to flee to Zurich (1887), where he studied mechanical engineering. Immigrating to the U.S. in 1889, Steinmetz was employed as draftsman for a company later purchased by General Electric, which made him a consulting engineer (1895–1923). At General Electric he was responsible for 195 patents for electrical inventions; he repeatedly demonstrated the profitability of applying sophisticated mathematical methods to practical problems. Many legends accumulated around the idiosyncratic Steinmetz, who was physically small and crippled from birth.

STEJNEGER, LEONHARD HESS (*b. Bergen, Norway, 1851; d. Washington, D.C., 1943*), ornithology, herpetology.

Stejneger graduated in law (1875) at the University of Kristiania (Oslo) though he had long been interested in birds. Arriving in the U.S. (1881), he was hired at the Smithsonian Institution, where he became acting curator, and later curator, of reptiles and amphibians (1889–1911), and curator of the department of biology (1911–43). He made extensive collections for the Smithsonian, and with T. Barbour published the highly useful *Check-list of North American Amphibians and Reptiles* (1917). His "Poisonous Snakes of North America" is a classic in herpetology.

STEKLOV, VLADIMIR ANDREEVICH (*b. Nizhni Novgorod [now Gorky], Russia, 1864; d. Gaspra, Crimea, U.S.S.R., 1926*), mathematics, mechanics.

Steklov was educated at the University of Kharkov (Ph.D., 1902), where he taught mechanics and applied mathematics (1891–1906); appointed to the chair of mathematics at St. Petersburg University (1906), he was noted for profound lectures and acute criticism of the tsarist order; A.A. Friedmann was among his pupils. From 1916 Steklov devoted most of his time to the Academy of Sciences; he suggested the founding of the Institute of Physics and Mathematics (1921) and served as its director until his death. Steklov's early works were devoted mostly to mechanics; his principal field, however, was mathematical physics and corresponding problems of analysis. In his later years he wrote on the theory of quadratures, Chebyshev's polynomials, a monograph on mathematical physics, a popular book on the importance of mathematics, and biographies of Galileo and Newton.

STELLER, GEORG WILHELM (*b. Windsheim, Germany, 1709; d. Tyumen, Siberia, Russia, 1746*), geography, biology.

Steller entered the medical faculty of the University of Halle (1731), though apparently he never passed a medical examination; he was accepted as physician in the Russian army (1734), where he assisted a botanist. Steller was a pioneer in the study of natural history and geography of Kamchatka and Alaska, both of which he visited as research member of the second Bering expedition. He was the first natural historian to land on the coast of Alaska (1741).

STELLUTI, FRANCESCO (*b. Fabriano, Italy, 1577; d. Fabriano, 1652*), microscopy, scientific organization.

Stelluti studied law at Rome, where he was influenced by F. Cesi and J. Eck, and with them helped found the Accademia dei Lincei (1603). Harassment of the Lincei forced him to leave for Fabriano; he then went to Parma, returning to Rome with Eck in 1608 or 1609. Stelluti was elected procurator, or business manager, of the Academy (1612), and as such he supervised the publication and distribution of works by Galileo, Cesi, and other Academy members; Stelluti himself produced synoptic tables of G. della Porta's *De humana physiognomia* (1637).

STENSEN, NIELS, also known as **Nicolaus Steno** (*b. Copenhagen, Denmark, 1638; d. Schwerin, Germany, 1686*), anatomy, geology, mineralogy.

Stensen studied medicine at the University of Copenhagen (beginning 1656), where he was influenced by S. Paulli and T. Bartholin. The customary study journey took him to Amsterdam and the University of Leiden, from which he received the M.D. in 1664; he traveled to Montpellier (1665), Pisa (1666), and Tuscany (1666–68), where he stayed at the court of Grand Duke Ferdinand II in Florence; although from a Lutheran family, Stensen converted to Catholicism (1667). After a stay in Denmark (1668–70), he returned to Florence and explored several grottoes for the Accademia del Cimento; called to Denmark to be royal anatomist, Stensen again returned to Florence, where he was consecrated a priest (1675), renounced his scientific research, and tutored the crown prince; in Rome (1677) he was appointed apostolic vicar of northern missions and made titular bishop of Titiopolis; after serving as assistant bishop of Münster (1680–83), he spent the last years of his life in apostolic activity in Hamburg and Schwerin.

Stenson's scientific work can be divided into four periods. The first period was devoted to the glandular and lymphatic system; in Amsterdam he discovered in 1660 the duct of the parotid gland (Stensen's duct), although his teacher Blasius claimed priority; in Leiden he continued his studies and worked with J. van Horne, F. Sylvius, and Jan Swammerdam; the controversy with Blasius led Stensen to further study of the glands, publishing *Observationes anatomicae* (1662) and *Apologiae prodromus* (1663); he considered every fluid in the body a glandular secretion, or "lymph," as he called them, for he was not yet able to distinguish between them chemically and physiologically; he determined the purpose of the lachrymal fluid and discovered the nasal glands; many of these results were summarized in *De musculis et glandulis* (1664), which also marks the beginning of his second period of research on muscles. Stensen challenged the traditional overestimation of the heart, arguing that the heart is merely a muscle and that it is neither the seat of joy nor the source of blood or of the *spiritus vitales;* the controversy over his views led him to publish *Elementorum myologiae specimen* (1666/67), which dealt with muscle contraction and swelling; Stensen's refutation of Descarte's view of the heart as a hearth of fire made him skeptical of the whole geometrical philosophy. The third period (1665–67) involved brain anatomy, embryology, and comparative anatomy; in his *Discours . . . sur l'anatomie du cerveau* (1669), Stensen opposed Descartes's mechanical theory of the brain and refuted his anatomical errors; from 1667 to 1669 he contributed two concepts about the ovum and the ovary, oviduct, and uterus (published in 1675). The fourth and greatest period of Stensen's research began in Florence (1666) when he made anatomical studies of a shark, leading him to studies of fossil shark's teeth and to paleontological, geological, and mineralogical discoveries; his great work, the *Prodomus* (1669) outlines the principles of modern geology.

STEPANOV, VYACHESLAV VASSILIEVICH (*b. Smolensk, Russia, 1889; d. Moscow, U.S.S.R., 1950*), mathematics.

Stepanov studied physics and mathematics at Moscow University, with additional study at Göttingen under Hilbert and E. Landau; a lecturer at Moscow University (from 1915), he later directed the Research Institute of Mathematics and Mechanics there (1939–50). Influenced by Egorov and Luzin, he wrote on the theory of functions of a real variable (1923, 1925); his most widely known works treated the theory of almost periodic functions; he also studied the qualitative theory of differential equations.

STEPHAN, ÉDOUARD JEAN MARIE (*b. Ste.-Pezenne, Deux Sevres, France, 1837; d. Marseilles, France, 1923*), astronomy.

After graduating from the École Normale Supérieure (1862), Stephan was invited by Le Verrier to the Paris observatory; after defending his doctoral thesis (1865), he was named director of the Marseilles branch of the Paris observatory (1866); he was also professor of astronomy at the University of Marseilles (1879–1907). His main studies were of nebulae, of which he discovered about 350; he was the first to study stellar diameters.

STEPHANUS (or **STEPHEN**) **OF ALEXANDRIA** (*fl. first half of seventh century* A.D.), philosophy, mathematics, astronomy, alchemy.

Stephanus was a public lecturer in Constantinople at the court of Emperor Heraclius; primarily a mathematician, he taught and wrote on many subjects, including astronomy; a Greek treatise on alchemy attributed to Stephanus, *De chrysopoeia,* is uncritical and shows no experimental work.

STEPHANUS, CAROLUS. *See* **Estienne (Stephanus), Charles.**

STEPHEN OF ANTIOCH (*fl. first half of the twelfth century*), translation.

Stephen, according to one source, was a Pisan who went to Syria (possibly with the First Crusade), learned Arabic, and translated the *Kitāb al-mālikī* of Haly Abbas in 1127; his translation is inferior to Constantine the African's. He may be identical to Stephanus Philosophus, who wrote several works on astronomy based on Arabic and Greek sources.

STEPLING, JOSEPH (*b. Regensburg, Germany, 1716; d. Prague, Bohemia [now Czechoslovakia], 1778*), astronomy, physics, mathematics.

Admitted to the Jesuit order in 1733, Stepling took a course of philosophy at Brno (1735–38), studied mathematics, physics, and astronomy in Prague (1741–43), studied theology there (1743–47), and in 1745 took holy orders. He was appointed to the chair of mathematics at the University of Prague, where he set up a laboratory of experimental physics, built an observatory, was named director of the faculty of philosophy by Empress Maria Theresia (1753), and founded a scientific study group.

STERN, OTTO (*b. Sohrau, Upper Silesia, Germany [now Zory, Poland], 1888; d. Berkeley, Calif., 1969*), physics.

Stern studied at the universities of Freiburg im Breisgau, Munich, and Breslau, from which he received the Ph.D. in physical chemistry (1912); he attended lectures by A. Sommerfeld, O. Lummer, and E. Pringsheim; the books of Boltzmann, Clausius, and Nernst influenced him to study thermodynamics and molecular theory.

Stern's scientific work can be divided into two periods: theoretical (1912–19) and experimental (1919–45). In the first period, he was influenced by Einstein in Prague and Zurich (1912–13), by Ehrenfest and Laue in Zurich, and by Max Born in Frankfurt after the war. Stern served in the German army from 1914 to 1918; during this period he studied problems in statistical thermodynamics. Assigned to Nernst's laboratory at the University of Berlin in the last years of the war, Stern met J. Franck and M. Volmer, who probably influenced his shift from theoretical to experimental work. At the Institute for Theoretical Physics in Frankfurt (1918–21), he continued theoretical work, publishing a paper with Max Born on surface energy of solids; thereafter, he sought experimental confirmation for molecular theory, developing a successful method of measuring molecular velocities in a gas with the molecular beam (1919), and beginning the second period of his research. With W. Gerlach, Stern used the molecular-beam method to prove the reality of space quantization (1920–21), establishing Stern's reputation.

He taught at the University of Rostock (1921–23) and the University of Hamburg, where he directed the Institute for Physical Chemistry (1923–33) and provided experimental confirmation of de Broglie's assertion of the wave nature of particles. His measurements of magnetic moments of protons and electrons helped win him the Nobel Prize in physics in 1943. Stern, who was of Jewish origin, resigned his post with the advent of the Nazi regime in 1933, and moved to the Carnegie Institute of Technology as research professor in physics, though the momentum of the Hamburg laboratory was never regained; he retired in 1946.

STERNBERG, KASPAR MARIA VON (*b. Prague, Bohemia [now in Czechoslovakia], 1761; d. Březina castle, Radnice, 1838*), botany, geology, paleontology.

After studying theology in Rome, Sternberg pursued an ecclesiastical career in Regensburg and Freisingen; in

1808 he inherited the family estate at Radnice and thereafter devoted himself to botanical studies, especially Carboniferous phytopaleontology. His chief work (1820–33) described 200 fossil species of plants; he and A.-T. Brongniart were the two leading paleobotanists in the world by the end of his life. He was one of the chief founders of the Bohemian National Museum, Prague (1818–21), he also had close dealings with Goethe.

STERNBERG, PAVEL KARLOVICH (*b. Orel, Russia, 1865; d. Moscow, U.S.S.R., 1920*), astronomy, gravimetry.

Educated at Moscow University (M.S. 1903, Ph.D. 1913), Sternberg began as an assistant at the university observatory (1888) and became director in 1916; in 1914 he was elected extraordinary professor of astronomy and geodesy. From 1905 Sternberg was an active Social Democrat (Bolshevik), and in October 1917 he led the revolutionary forces of the Zamoskvoretsky district of Moscow; as a military commissar he toured the Eastern Front where he became ill and died. He was a distinguished researcher and innovator in gravimetry, the variations of latitude in relation to the motion of the earth's poles, and photographic astrometry.

STEVENS, EDWARD (*b. St. Croix, Virgin Islands, ca. 1755; d. St. Croix, 1834*), medicine, physiology.

Stevens graduated from King's College, now Columbia College (A.B., 1774) and received his M.D. at the University of Edinburgh (1777); in his dissertation research he was the first to isolate human gastric juice. After practicing medicine in St. Croix (1783–93), he moved to Philadelphia, where he became involved in a controversy over methods of treating the yellow fever epidemic there. After teaching at King's College (1795–99), he was United States consul-general to Santo Domingo (1799–1800), and returned to St. Croix around 1804.

STEVIN, SIMON (*b. Bruges, Netherlands [now Belgium], 1548; d. The Hague, Netherlands, ca. 1620*), mathematics, engineering.

Little is known of Stevin's early life; he entered the university at Leiden in 1583, and from 1604 was quartermaster-general of the States of the Netherlands; at the same time he tutored Maurice of Nassau, prince of Orange. He organized a school of engineers at Leiden and served as administrator of Maurice's domains. Stevin's published works include books on mathematics, mechanics, astronomy, navigation, military science, engineering, music theory, civics, dialectics, bookkeeping, geography, and house building; almost all were written in the vernacular and are characterized by versatility, the combining of theory and practice, and clarity of argument. Stevin's *De Thiende* (1585) introduced decimal fractions for general purposes; his *L'arithmétique* (1585) is a general treatment of the arithmetic and algebra of his time. *De Deursichtighe* is a mathematical treatment of perspective; *De Beghinselen der Weeghconst* (1586) is his chief work in mechanics, chiefly statics, and contains Stevin's famous discovery of the law of the inclined plane, which he demonstrated with the *clootcrans*, or wreath of spheres. Beneath his diagram of the *clootcrans* Stevin inscribed "Wonder en is gheen wonder"—"What appears a wonder is not a wonder," a rallying cry for the new science; the device also appears as the colophon of this *Dictionary*.

Stevin's next work on mechanics, *De Beghinselen des Waterwichts*, is the first systematic treatise on hydrostatics since Archimedes, and gives a simple explanation for the Archimedean principle of displacement; his chief book on astronomy, *De Hemelloop* (1608) is one of the first presentations supporting the Copernican system. Stevin wrote several works related to navigation, including a theory of the tides, a method of determining longitude by magnetic deviation, and a method of steering a ship along a loxodrome. A considerable body of Stevin's other work is related to his military duties and interests, such as the art of fortification (*De Sterctenbouwing*) and a description of field encampment during Maurice's campaigns (*De Legermeting);* his engineering works discuss sluices, locks and wind-driven drainage mills. Stevin's *Van de Spiegeling der Singconst* applied new methods to the theory of musical tuning; his *Het Burgherlick Leven* is a handbook to guide the citizen through periods of civil disorder. In the last years of his life Stevin returned to mathematics, collecting his mathematical works into two folio volumes of his *Wisconstighe Ghedachtenissen* (1605–08).

STEWART, BALFOUR (*b. Edinburgh, Scotland, 1828; d. Drogheda, Ireland, 1887*), physics, meteorology, terrestrial magnetism.

Stewart was educated at the universities of St. Andrews and Edinburgh; after a ten-year career in business, he sought a career in science, first as an assistant at the Kew observatory and then as assistant to J.D. Forbes at Edinburgh; there he made original contributions to the study of radiant heat (infrared radiation), extending a theory of Prevost's (1858) and pre-dating Kirchhoff's similar but more influential conclusions by two years; Stewart directed the Kew Observatory (1859–70) where he did important work on geomagnetism; he was appointed professor of natural philosophy at Owens College, Manchester (1870), where J. J. Thomson was one of his students. Stewart's textbooks and popularizations were widely read (Ernest Rutherford, at age ten, owned one of them); his popular book, *The Unseen Universe,* written with P.G. Tait, was intended to reconcile science and religion.

STEWART, GEORGE NEIL (*b. London, Ontario, 1860; d. Cleveland, Ohio, 1930*), physiology.

Stewart was educated at the University of Edinburgh (D.Sc., 1887; M.D., 1891), where he was an assistant to P.G. Tait (1879); he also studied with du Bois-Reymond at Berlin (1886–87). After a year at Harvard as instructor in physiology (1893), Stewart taught physiology and histology at Western Reserve University School of Medicine, in Cleveland, with the exception of four years at the University of Chicago (1903–07). Stewart's main contribution was transmitting modern methods of teaching and research in physiology to American medical education.

STEWART, MATTHEW (*b. Rothesay, Isle of Bute, Scotland, 1717; d. Catrine, Ayrshire, Scotland, 1785*), geometry, astronomy, natural philosophy.

Stewart entered the University of Glasgow (1734), where he was greatly influenced by the mathematician R. Simson; he also studied with C. Maclaurin at the University of Edinburgh; in 1747 he was elected to the chair of mathematics at Edinburgh, largely on the reputation of his celebrated book, *General Theorems* (1746). Stewart's interests then turned to astronomy and natural philosophy; he used geometric methods to calculate the distance of the earth from the sun (1763), but was shown to be greatly in error by J. Dawson (1768).

STIELTJES, THOMAS JAN (*b. Zwolle, Netherlands, 1856; d. Toulouse, France, 1894*), mathematics.

Stieltjes received his principal schooling at the École Polytechnique in Delft; he served at the observatory in Leiden for six years (1877–83); after several years at the University of Groningen, he went to live in Paris, where he received his doctorate of science in 1886; he then taught at the University of Toulouse until his death eight years later. Best known today for Stieltjes integral—a generalization of the ordinary Riemann integral with wide applications in physics—Stieltjes's published work encompasses almost all of analysis of his time; he made contributions to the theory of ordinary and partial differential equations, studied gamma functions and elliptical functions, and worked in interpolation theory. He is the father of the analytic theory of continued fractions, and his integral was developed as a tool for its study. His integral first appears in his last memoir, "Recherches sur les fractions continues" (1894–95); a mathematical milestone, this paper is the first general treatment of continued fractions as part of complex analytic function theory.

STIFEL (STYFEL, STYFFEL, STIEFFELL, STIFELIUS, or STIEFFEL), MICHAEL (*b. Esslingen, Germany, ca. 1487; d. Jena, Germany, 1567*), mathematics, theology.

Stifel was ordained priest at Esslingen (1511); an early follower of Luther, after 1520 he was preoccupied with mystical numbers in the Bible; because of his religious views, he was forced to flee to Kronberg (1522) and then to Wittenberg, where Luther lodged him in his own house and helped him become pastor at Annaberg (1528). Arrested for prophesying the end of the world (1533), Stifel received another parish at Holzdorf with the help of Luther and Melanchthon (1535). He now devoted himself to mathematics, taking his master's degree from the University of Wittenberg and giving private instruction. He also wrote his best works at Holzdorf: *Arithmetica integra* (1544), which added original contributions to a summary of current arithmetic and algebra; *Deutsche arithmetica* (1545), which sought to make algebra more accessible to German readers by eliminating foreign words; and *Welsche Practick* (1546). Next in Haberstroh, near Königsberg, where he was forced to flee by the Schmalkaldic War (1547), Stifel lectured on theology and mathematics at the University of Königsberg and brought out a new edition of C. Rudolff's *Coss*, to which he added material of his own. Involved in theological controversy, especially with A. Osiander, he returned to Saxony (1554), where in Jena he lectured on arithmetic and geometry at the university, and was pastor at Brück until about 1559.

A principal concern of Stifel's books was establishing generally valid laws; he was the first to present a general method for solving equations; he introduced into western mathematics a general method for computing roots using binomial coefficients. Stifel also surpassed his predecessors in the division of general polynomials and extraction of their roots, as well as in computing with irrational numbers; his *Arithmetica integra* contributed to the preliminary stages of logarithmic computation. Stifel was also a pioneer in the development of algebraic symbolism; although his work at Holzdorf is most admired today, Stifel declared that he valued his "word calculus" (number mysticism) above all the computations he had ever made; he was the greatest German algebraist of the sixteenth century.

STILES, CHARLES WARDELL (*b. Spring Valley, N.Y., 1867; d. Baltimore, Md., 1941*), zoology, public health.

After studies in Paris, Göttingen, and Berlin, Stiles concentrated in zoology at the University of Leipzig (Ph.D., 1890), where he studied with R. Leuckart. Returning to the U.S., he became principal zoologist at the Bureau of Animal Industry of the Department of Agriculture in Washington (1891); he was chief of the division of zoology at the Hygienic Laboratory of the United States Public Health Service (1902–32). Stiles's greatest contribution to health was his work on hookworms; he discovered a new variety in 1902 and lead a campaign against it.

STILLE, WILHELM HANS (*b. Hannover, Germany, 1876; d. Hannover, 1966*), tectonic geology.

Stille graduated from the University of Göttingen (1899), where he studied geology and later taught (1913–32); he also taught at the University of Berlin (1932–50). Stille was a leader in German geology, an outstanding investigator and collator of the history of global tectonic events, and a highly admired teacher.

STIMPSON, WILLIAM (*b. Roxbury, Mass., 1832; d. Ilchester, Md., 1872*), marine zoology.

After graduating from high school Stimpson became a special student in L. Agassiz's laboratory at Harvard College (1850) and also became curator of mollusks at the Boston Society of Natural History. He was chosen as naturalist for the United States North Pacific Exploring and Surveying Expedition (1853–56), after which he was in charge of the invertebrate section of the Smithsonian Institution (1856–65); he directed the Chicago Academy of Sciences (1865–72); Stimpson is remembered as the first naturalist to dredge systematically along the Atlantic coast and for the description of 948 new species of marine invertebrates.

STINE, CHARLES MILTON ALTLAND (*b. Norwich, Conn., 1882; d. Wilmington, Del., 1954*), organic chemistry.

Stine studied at Gettysburg College (M.S., 1905) and Johns Hopkins University (Ph.D., 1907). He began a lifelong association with the Du Pont Company in 1907, becoming chemical director in 1924 and retiring as vice-president in 1945. Stines was responsible for establishing, by 1927, a program of fundamental research that made Du Pont an industrial pioneer in American science; under his direction Du Pont produced neoprene, nylon, and whole new families of fibers, films, plastics, paints, elastomers, and other applications of polymer chemistry.

STIRLING, JAMES (*b. Garden, Stirlingshire, Scotland, 1692; d. Edinburgh, Scotland, 1770*), mathematics.

Stirling studied at Balliol College, Oxford (1711–16); because of his Jacobite sympathies he refused to take the oaths needed to continue his scholarship and did not graduate. His first book, *Lineae tertii ordinis Neutonianae* (1717), won him a considerable reputation, the support of Newton, and a post in Venice; in the book Stirling proved Newton's enumeration of seventy-two species of cubic curves and added four more. By 1724 he had moved to London, where Newton helped secure his fellowship in the Royal Society (1726), and he became a partner of the Little Tower Street Academy, one of the most successful schools in London. His main work, *Methodus differentialis* (1730), was written during this period, and discusses summation and interpolation. After 1735, when Stirling became a successful administrator for the Scottish Mining Company in the lead mines at Leadhills, Lanarkshire, he continued his mathematical correspondence but did little significant work.

STOCK, ALFRED (*b. Danzig, West Prussia [now Gdansk, Poland], 1876; d. Aken, Germany, 1946*), chemistry.

After graduating from the University of Berlin (Ph.D., 1899), Stock spent a year in Paris as an assistant to Moissan; he returned to Berlin to do research (1900–09) before moving to Breslau to direct the new Inorganic Chemistry Institute (1909–16). At the Kaiser Wilhelm Institute in Berlin (1916–26), Stock was concerned with problems related to the war and to the restoration of German chemistry afterward. After learning that his deteriorating health was caused by mercury poisoning (1924), he began a program of research into the analysis and pathology of mercury that continued to the end of his active life. He directed the Chemical Institute at Karlsruhe until his retirement (1926–36). Stock pioneered in the development of the chemistry of the boron and silicon hydrides, developed the chemical high-vacuum technique, held numerous high positions in chemical organizations and educational institutes, and made important contributions to chemical education and nomenclature; some of his work had important technological applications.

STOCK, CHESTER (*b. San Fransicso, Calif., 1892; d. Pasadena, Calif., 1950*), paleontology.

Stock graduated from the University of California, Berkeley (Ph.D., 1917), where his interest in prehistoric animals was stimulated by J. C. Merriam's lectures; he also taught there (1921–26) before moving to the California Institute of Technology, where he became chairman of its Division of Earth Sciences (1947); he also served on the staff of the Los Angeles County Museum. Stock's early studies were on Pleistocene vertebrates, especially ground sloths, on which he published a major monograph (1925); most of his publications consist of meticulous descriptions of fossil material.

STODOLA, AUREL BOLESLAV (*b. Liptovský Mikuláš, Hungary [now Czechoslovakia], 1859; d. Zurich, Switzerland, 1942*), mechanical engineering.

Stodola graduated from the Eidgenössische Technische Hochschule (1880) as a mechanical engineer; after designing steam engines for a company in Prague (1886–92), he returned to the Eidgenössische Technische Hochschule of Zurich to occupy the chair for thermal machinery (1892–1929). Stodola was the leading authority on the steam turbine; his first publications dealt with the

theory of automatic control, but at the turn of the century his attention shifted to the steam turbine, the focus of his most important work, *Die Dampfturbinen und die Aussichten der Wärmekraftmaschinen* (1903), which used entropy charts to analyze heat engines. Stodola also did pioneer work in the flow of steam through Laval nozzles, as well as in pure mechanics.

STOKES, GEORGE GABRIEL (*b. Skreen, County Sligo, Ireland, 1819; d. Cambridge, England, 1903*), physics, mathematics.

Stokes graduated from Pembroke College, Cambridge (1841), where he read mathematics with W. Hopkins, an outstanding private tutor. After a fellowship at Pembroke, Stokes became the Lucasian professor at Cambridge (1849–1903), restoring the chair to the eminence it had when held by Newton. Stokes also taught at the Government School of Mines in London in the 1850's to augment his income. He was an active member of the Cambridge Philosophical Society (president from 1859 to 1861); he was secretary (1854–85) and president (1885–90) of the Royal Society of London; he was also president of the Victoria Institute of London (1886–1903), a society founded in 1865 to examine the relationship between Christianity and contemporary thought, especially science. He was knighted in 1889.

Stokes's theoretical and experimental investigations covered the entire realm of natural philosophy; he systematically explored areas of hydrodynamics, the elasticity of solids, and the behavior of waves in elastic solids including the diffraction of light. He also investigated problems in light, gravity, sound, heat, meteorology, solar physics, and chemistry. Stokes's analysis of the internal friction of fluids appeared in 1845, though some of the work had already appeared in the French literature of mathematical physics, a common situation in Cambridge; Stokes became well known in England through a report on recent developments in hydrodynamics (1846); in one of his most important papers on hydrodynamics (1850), he applied his theory of internal friction of fluids to the behavior of pendulums. He became the foremost British authority on the principles of geodesy.

Stokes's earliest investigations in the wave theory of light, which he accepted, were on the nature of the ether (from 1845); in a major paper on the dynamical theory of diffraction (1849), he treated the ether as a sensibly incompressible elastic medium. His paper on fluorescence (1852), which won him the Rumford Medal of the Royal Society, showed how it could be used to study the ultraviolet segment of the spectrum (this work typifies Stokes's exploitation of light to study other aspects of nature). His final major mathematical study on light was on the dynamical theory of double refraction (1862). In the early years of his career, Stokes was a pivotal figure in furthering the dissemination of French mathematical physics at Cambridge; and he was an important formative influence on many Cambridge men, including Maxwell. His output of papers dropped rapidly as he took on increasing administrative duties in the 1850's. Although he never published a treatise on optics, his Burnett lectures on light at the University of Aberdeen (1883–85) were published in a single volume; the Gifford lectures on natural theology at Edinburgh (1891, 1893) were also published; a devoutly religious man, Stokes was deeply interested in the relationship of science to religion.

STOLETOV, ALEKSANDR GRIGORIEVICH (*b. Vladimir, Russia, 1839; d. Moscow, Russia, 1896*), physics.

After graduating from Moscow University, Stoletov continued his studies in Germany, where he attended the lectures of Helmholtz, Kirchhoff, and Wilhelm Weber, and worked in H. G. Magnus' laboratory. He returned to Moscow University in 1865, where he taught physics and obtained his master's degree (1869) and doctoral degree (1872); he helped establish a physics institute there in 1887. In his most distinguished work, "Actinoelectric Investigations" (1889), Stoletov experimentally established the basic laws of the external photoelectric effect and certain fundamental regularities of electrical discharge in rarefied gases.

STOLZ, OTTO (*b. Hall [now Solbad Hall in Tirol], Austria, 1842; d. Innsbruck, Austria, 1905*), mathematics.

Stolz received the Ph.D. at the University of Vienna (1864); he attended courses given by Weierstrass, Kummer, and Kronecker at Berlin, and by Clebsch and Klein at Göttingen (1869–71); he taught at the University of Innsbruck (1872–1905). His earliest papers were on analytic or algebraic geometry, including spherical trigonometry, though his later research was on real analysis.

STONEY, GEORGE JOHNSTONE (*b. Oakley Park, Kingstown [now Dún Laoghaire], County Dublin, Ireland, 1826; d. London, England, 1911*), mathematical physics.

Stoney graduated from Trinity College, Dublin (1848); after teaching natural philosophy at Queen's College, Galway, for five years, he spent the rest of his working life as secretary to Queen's University in Dublin (1857–93). He is best known for coining the term "electron" (1891); he also put forward important ideas on atomic structure based on spectrum analysis.

STØRMER, FREDRIK CARL MÜLERTZ (*b. Skien, Norway, 1874; d. Oslo, Norway, 1957*), mathematics, geophysics.

Størmer graduated from the University of Oslo (Ph.D., 1903), where he taught pure mathematics (1903–44). Though his first papers were on number theory, much of his life was devoted to studies of polar aurora, which he studied both experimentally and through mathematical analysis. His last book, *The Polar Aurora* (1955), is his final summary and an up-to-date and authoritative study; he was also an excellent popularizer.

STRABO (*b. Amasia, Asia Minor, 64/63 B.C.; d. Amasia, ca. A.D. 25*), history, geography.

A Greek by language and education, Strabo studied under the rhetorician Aristodemus at Nysa in Caria, and may also have known the Stoic polymath Posidonius. About 44 B.C. he went to Rome to study with the geographer Tyrannion and the philosopher Xenarchus, and became a convert to Stoicism; he spent five years (25–20 B.C.) in Alexandria, where he may have studied in the great library. Although it is known Strabo composed a number of historical works, only one, the *Geographica*, is extant; part of the *Geographica* was published about 7 B.C., while a finished work in seventeen books appeared later,

perhaps after his death. Although he traveled widely, his *Geographica* was based less upon his personal observations than on his reading, including Eratosthenes, Eudoxus, Hipparchus, Posidonius, Polybius, Artemidorus, and Apollodorus of Athens. His presentation is mathematical, chorographical, topographical, physical, political, and historical, although his scientific skills were limited and he tended to underestimate science; nevertheless, he produced an excellent account of parts of western Europe, Asia Minor, Egypt, and Gaul. Strabo followed Eratosthenes in showing the known world as a single ocean-girt landmass on the northern half of a motionless sphere within a revolving spherical universe. Although Strabo was fond of digressions and was sometimes argumentative and obsessive, the *Geographica* is nonetheless highly valuable in its exposition of the development of geography; it marked the first attempt to assemble all available geographical knowledge into a single treatise; it is unlike any other surviving work of ancient geography.

STRACHEY, JOHN (*b. Sutton Court, Chew Magna, Somerset, England, 1671; d. Greenwich, England, 1743*), geology.

After studying law at Middle Temple, London, Strachey resided mainly at Sutton Court, though the latter part of his life was spent in Edinburgh. It was probably his interest in the coal mines near Sutton Court that led him to study geology, for he published two geological papers and a pamphlet on occurences of coal. His 1725 paper contained the first clear demonstration by a British author of an angular unconformity, the importance of which was not realized until much later. His work is of value as an early attempt to establish a stratigraphical succession.

STRASBURGER, EDUARD ADOLF (*b. Warsaw, Poland, 1844; d. Poppelsdorf, Germany, 1912*), botany, plant cytology.

After studying at the Sorbonne (1862–64) and at the University of Bonn, Strasburger went to Jena (Ph.D., 1866), studied with N. Pringsheim and E. Haeckel, the latter influencing him to become an evolutionist and to apply phylogenetic interpretations to the structure and developmental history of plants. He soon succeeded Pringsheim and was made director of the botanical gardens; he accompanied Haeckel on a scientific trip to Egypt and the Red Sea (1873). After twelve years in Jena he taught at the University of Bonn, where he spent the rest of his career; his laboratory at the Botanical Institute of the University of Bonn became the leading center for the study of plant cytology. Strasburger clarified the phenomena of cell division and the role of the nucleus and chromosomes in heredity; his cytological observations at Jena are recorded in the three editions of his *Zellbildung und Zelltheilung* (1875, 1876, 1880). He noted stages in plant cell division that were parallel to those observed by his colleagues in the more easily observable division of animal cells, leading him to postulate the common descent of vegetable and animal cells, as Haeckel had maintained. He originated a number of terms, including "phototaxis," "chloroplast," "cytoplasm," "nucleoplasm," "haploid," and "diploid." In 1884 he independently concluded, as did Hertwig, A. Weismann, and A. von Koelliker at about the same time, that the nucleus was responsible for heredity; he believed that the cell nucleus was essential in fertilization and that in a way it governed the cytoplasm and controlled metabolism and growth. He investigated both sexual and asexual reproduction in plants, as well as the anatomy, life history, and aspects of physiology of plants. He helped train students from all over the world, including D. H. Campbell and C. J. Chamberlain from America; he became co-editor with W. Pfeffer of the *Jahrbucher für wissenschaftliche Botanik* (1894).

STRATO OF LAMPSACUS (*b. Lampsacus, Mysia; d. Athens, 271/268* B.C.), natural philosophy.

The dominant influence on Strato's thought was Aristotle's school at Athens, where he spent considerable time studying under Theophrastus; for a time he was tutor to the future Ptolemy II Philadelphus, who ruled Egypt from 283 to 246 B.C.. On Theophrastus' death *ca.* 287, Strato succeeded him as head of the Lyceum. Since Strato's works are not extant, knowledge of them is derived from later sources of two types: 1) short passages where Strato is quoted or referred to by name (the most important are in a commentary on Aristotle's *Physics* by Simplicius); and 2) writings in which Strato is not named but which are derived from his work (the most important are the introduction to the *Pneumatica* of Hero of Alexandria and an extract from a book *On Sounds* wrongly attributed to Aristotle).

Strato wrote on logic, ethics, cosmology, psychology, physiology, zoology, and inventions, but his interest was centered on physics, broadly defined. While some historians have represented Strato as an eclectic trying to combine the systems of Aristotle with Democritus, in reality his thought was a development of Aristotle's views along lines marked out by Theophrastus. Strato stripped the Aristotelian world picture of its transcendental elements, refusing to acknowledge the reality of anything not subject to natural laws of the sub-lunary world. He differed from the Stoics in denying that nature is conscious and provident, and from the atomists in positing a regulating principle to which all worldly processes are subordinated. He also differed from the atomists in that atoms and void were the starting point of atomist physics, while particles and interstices were the end point of Strato's (e.g., Strato's particles were mere divisions of matter resulting from the primary qualities of hot, cold, moist, and dry; to the atomists, the atoms were basic and the qualities were epiphenomena of their shapes and sizes). While Strato's system in many ways continued those of Aristotle and Theophrastus, it showed real originality in combining philosophical and scientific reasoning to produce a unified explanation of the world in which theories were shaped by observed facts, and the facts themselves interpreted in the light of simple and consistent theories. He was the first to use experiments systematically to establish a fundamental cosmological doctrine; nevertheless his influence was limited; the centrifugal tendency among the sciences could not be arrested, and philosophical cosmology came to be dominated by religious considerations.

STRATTON, FREDERICK JOHN MARRION (*b. Birmingham, England, 1881; d. Cambridge, England, 1960*), astronomy.

Stratton was educated at Gonville and Caius College, Cambridge, where he was elected a fellow (1904) and after the First World War became a tutor; he became assistant director (1913) and later director (1928) of the Solar Physics Observatory at Cambridge; he educated many bright young men in astronomy.

STREETE, THOMAS (*b. Cork, Ireland [?], 1622; d. Westminster, London, England, 1689*), astronomy.

Streete spent most of his life in London as a clerk in the Excise Office under E. Ashmole; he frequented Gresham College and knew many leading astronomers. His most important work, *Astronomia Carolina* (1661), was one of the most popular expositions on astronomy in the second half of the seventeenth century, and served as a textbook for Newton, Flamsteed, and Halley. It was an important vehicle for dissemination of Kepler's astronomical ideas.

STREETER, GEORGE LINIUS (*b. Jamestown, N.Y., 1873; d. Gloversville, N.Y., 1948*), embryology.

Streeter took his M.D. at the College of Physicians and Surgeons of Columbia University (1899). In 1902 he studied at Frankfurt and at Leipzig with W. His, who influenced him to devote himself to embryology, particularly to the development of the human nervous system. His main appointment was in the newly organized department of embryology of the Carnegie Institution, located at Johns Hopkins Medical School in Baltimore, directed by F. P. Mall. When Mall died, Streeter succeeded him as director (1917–40). Streeter's studies of the early embryology of the pig and the rhesus monkey (1927–41) are among the most accurate descriptions of early mammalian development ever published; he helped turn attention to genetic factors in pathological aspects of human prenatal development.

STRÖMBERG, GUSTAF BENJAMIN (*b. Göteborg, Sweden, 1882; d. Pasadena, Calif., 1962*), astronomy.

Strömberg obtained his Ph.D. from the University of Lund (1916); he spent most of his working life at the Mount Wilson observatory (1916–46), where he was astronomer. His main contributions were statistical analyses of stellar motions; he provided an early confirmation of Shapley's theory, and also supplied data used by Lindblad and Oort in developing the presently accepted picture of galactic rotation.

STRÖMGREN, SVANTE ELIS (*b. Hälsingborg, Sweden, 1870; d. Copenhagen, Denmark, 1947*), astronomy.

Strömgren received his Ph.D. at the University of Lund (1898); his main appointment was as professor of astronomy at Copenhagen University and director of the observatory (1907–40). His research belongs to the tradition of classical celestial mechanics; his dissertation derived the definitive orbit of Comet 1890 II and was crucial for work on the cosmogony of comets. Strömgren was active in international astronomical collaboration.

STRUSS (or STRUTHIUS), JÓZEF (*b. Poznan, Poland, 1510; d. Poznan, 1568*), medicine.

Struss took his diploma in the seven liberal arts at Cracow (1531) and his medical degree at Padua (1535), where Vesalius was his fellow pupil and later his teacher. After teaching medicine at Padua and Cracow, and service to the governor of Greater Poland, Struss established a successful practice in Poznan (1545) and became personal physicain to King Sigismund Augustus. His main work is *Sphygmicae artis* (1555), perhaps the first work in the history of medicine that suggested the pulse as a reliable source of clinical data and of diagnostic and prognostic information.

STRUTT, JOHN WILLIAM, THIRD BARON RAYLEIGH (*b. Langford Grove, near Maldon, Essex, England, 1842; d. Terling Place, Witham, Essex, England, 1919*), experimental and theoretical physics.

At Cambridge Strutt became a pupil of E.J. Routh and was inspired by the lectures of Sir George Stokes; he graduated there in 1865 and became a fellow of Trinity College, Cambridge (1866). After a trip to the United States, he began experimenting in a laboratory he set up at the family seat in Terling Place (1868), where he would do much of his scientific work. A trip up the Nile was the genesis of his monumental work, *The Theory of Sound* (1877–78). After succeeding to the title and taking up residence at Terling (1873), Rayleigh began serious experiments; he had already established himself as a leading authority on sound by his paper on the theory of resonance. In a paper of 1871 he had explained the blue color of the sky; he then began experimental studies of optical instruments, and was first to publish formally a clear definition of resolving power of an optical device.

In 1879, after Maxwell died, Rayleigh succeeded him, somewhat reluctantly, in the Cavendish chair of experimental physics at Cambridge; there he succeeded in putting laboratory instruction in elementary physics on a firm basis, ultimately influencing higher educational institutions throughout the country. He also led a program to redetermine three electrical standards: the ohm, the ampere, and the volt (completed 1884). In 1884 he resigned his professorship and retired to his laboratory at Terling, though he did continue to give some lectures at the Royal Institution in London (1887–1905).

During the middle and late 1880's, Rayleigh published results of experimental and theoretical work on radiation both optical and acoustical, electromagnetism, general mechanical theorems, vibrations of elastic media, capillarity, thermodynamics, the filtration of waves in periodic structures; he also became interested in the complete radiation law which governs the distribution of energy in the spectrum of blackbody radiation (what is now known as the Rayleigh-Jeans law was first enunciated by Rayleigh in 1900). He also made his most famous (though not most important) discovery: the isolation of argon, which he announced with Sir W. Ramsay (1895), and which won him the Nobel Prize in physics (1904). An 1899 paper of his led to the establishment of the field of molecular acoustics.

Although Rayleigh kept up with the development of quantum and relativity theories, revolutionary ideas were distasteful to him, and he could never support them with much enthusiasm. Rayleigh devoted considerable attention to professional scientific societies and governmental applied science; he was a leader in the movement culminating in establishing the National Physical Laboratory at Teddington. Rayleigh was one of the greatest ornaments of British science in the last half of the nineteenth century and the first two decades of the twentieth; he

conducted research continuously from 1865 until his death; he may justly be considered the last great polymath of physical science. Though not profound or boldly imaginative, he did advance enormously the applicability of practically every branch of classical physics.

STRUTT, ROBERT [ROBIN] JOHN, FOURTH BARON RAYLEIGH (*b. Terling Place, Witham, Essex, England, 1875; d. Terling, 1947*), physics.

The son of renowned physicist J. W. Strutt, third Baron Rayleigh, Strutt studied at Trinity College, Cambridge; he was professor of physics at Imperial College, London, until becoming Baron Rayleigh in 1919. Though his early research was on radioactivity, he is best known for his work on atmospheric optics. Strutt and Alfred Fowler confirmed in 1916 the presence of ozone in the atmosphere. Because of his pioneering quantitative research on atmospheric airglow, the unit of sky brightness is called the rayleigh.

STRUVE, FRIEDRICH GEORG WILHELM (or **Vasily Yakovlevich**) (*b. Altona, Germany, 1793; d. Pulkovo, Russia, 1864*), astronomy, geodesy.

Struve was sent by his parents to live with his brother in Dorpat, Russia, to avoid conscription; he graduated from the University of Dorpat (1810) with a degree in philology, but continued his studies in astronomy, mathematics, and geodesy, earning his doctorate in 1813 and beginning a twenty-five year career as a teacher. He also gave widely popular public lectures. Struve did significant research in observation of double stars; determination of stellar parallaxes and distribution of stars in space; observation of planets, the moon, comets, and auroras; meridian measurements; statistical techniques; and the design and refinement of astronomical and geodetic instruments. In 1834, he was appointed director of the new observatory at Pulkovo, near St. Petersburg, which was completed in 1839 and soon achieved worldwide fame.

Struve published a number of catalogs of double stars, the latest and most complete being *Stellarum fixarum imprimis duplicium et multiplicium positiones mediae* (1852); he was one of the first to make reliable determination of stellar parallaxes, making it possible to calculate the actual values of stellar distances; he also conducted investigations on stellar distribution to determine whether there is a statistical dependence between the brightness of stars and their distances. He confirmed earlier suggestions that the interstellar medium is incompletely transparent and determined the value of the obscuration effect in outer space (1846). He was also active in a number of geodetic studies throughout his career. He discovered rational methods for the determination of latitude, time, and azimuth that allowed him to eliminate many systematic errors.

STRUVE, GEORG OTTO HERMANN (*b. Pulkovo, Russia, 1886; d. Berlin, Germany, 1933*), astronomy.

Struve was the son of Karl Hermann Struve, the astronomer; he studied at the universities of Heidelberg and Berlin (Ph.D., 1910). After serving as astronomer at the Wilhelmshaven naval observatory (1913–19), Struve was observer at the Berlin-Babelsberg observatory (from 1919), where he also was professor (1929–33). He published a number of works on Saturn.

STRUVE, GUSTAV WILHELM LUDWIG (or **Ludwig Ottovich**) (*b. Pulkovo, Russia, 1858; d. Simferopol, Russia, 1920*), astronomy, geodesy.

Struve, the son of astronomer Otto Wilhelm Struve, graduated from the University of Dorpat (1880; Ph.D., 1887), where he served as observational astronomer until 1894. At Dorpat Struve's chief interest was the positions and motions of stars; at Kharkov (1894–1919), he was professor and director of the university observatory, and participated in geodetic projects; in 1919 he moved to the Crimea, where he was professor at the Tauris University at Simferopol.

STRUVE, KARL HERMANN (or **Hermann Ottovich**) (*b. Pulkovo, Russia, 1854; d. Neubabelsberg, near Potsdam, Germany, 1920*), astronomy.

Struve, the son of astronomer Otto Wilhelm Struve, graduated from the University of Dorpat (1877; Ph.D., 1882) and began work at the Pulkovo Observatory, where he later became senior astronomer (1890–95). He was director of the observatory at the University of Königsberg (1895–1904), director of the Berlin-Babelsberg Observatory (1904–13), and director of the Neubabelsberg Observatory (1913–20). His most important work (1898) concerns Saturn.

STRUVE, OTTO (*b. Kharkov, Russia, 1897; d. Berkeley, Calif., 1963*), astronomy.

Struve was the son of astronomer Gustav Wilhelm Ludwig Struve; after serving in the Russian army during World War I, he was soon recalled when civil war broke out; in 1920 he was evacuated from the Crimea to Turkey. Unable to find work or housing in Constantinople, Struve wrote to his astronomer uncle Georg Hermann Otto Struve in Berlin; though his uncle had died, his widow wrote to his colleagues of their nephew's plight, and E. B. Frost, director of the Yerkes Observatory in Williams Bay, Wisconsin, invited him to come to the U.S. as assistant observer in stellar spectroscopy. Struve arrived at Yerkes in November, 1921, where he began work and continued his studies at the University of Chicago, which administered Yerkes (Ph.D. 1923).

Struve quickly rose to prominence at Yerkes, and soon became director (1932–47); he also served as professor of astrophysics at the University of Chicago (1932–47). Struve was instrumental in founding the McDonald Observatory in Texas; he was director of the new observatory (until 1947), which was dedicated in 1939 and featured an eighty-two-inch telescope, then the second-largest in the world. From 1950 to 1959 he was chairman of the department of astronomy at the University of California at Berkeley, and director of its Leuschner Observatory. He returned to Yerkes briefly before becoming director of the new National Radio Astronomical Observatory at Green Bank, West Virginia. His health forced him to resign in 1962, though he soon accepted a joint professorship at the Institute of Advanced Study, Princeton, and the California Institute of Technology.

Although much of Struve's career was devoted to administration, he nevertheless found time to conduct his own investigations; his chief interests lay in spectroscopic investigations of binary and variable stars and researches into stellar atmospheres, stellar rotation, the gaseous constituents of cosmic matter, and stellar evolution. His work was strongly influenced by Henry Norris Russell, particularly by Russell's "Some Problems of Sidereal Astronomy" (1919). One of his most important contributions was his discovery of the presence of areas of ionized hydrogen in interstellar space, a discovery crucial to modern radio astronomy (1938). In 1928, with G. A. Shayn, Struve confirmed the axial rotation of single stars that had been suggested as early as the time of Galileo. Though his hypothesis of stellar formation in his *Stellar Evolution* (1950) was not widely accepted, much of his research was greeted enthusiastically. Struve was also concerned with popularization and with communication among astronomers; he edited the *Astrophysical Journal* (1932–47) and wrote many articles for *Sky and Telescope.*

STRUVE, OTTO WILHELM (or **Otton Vasilievich**) (*b. Dorpat, Russia [now Tartu, Estonian S.S.R.], 1819; d. Karlsruhe, Germany, 1905*), astronomy, geodesy.

The son of F. G. W. Struve, Struve graduated from the University of Dorpat (1839); he spent fifty years at the Pulkovo Observatory, becoming director in 1862. Struve collaborated with his father on a number of projects and shared his broad astronomical and geodetic interests; he discovered and described several hundred double stars, and for almost forty years investigated the motion of binary and multiple stars. In the 1850's he determined a value for the constant of precession that was used throughout the world until S. Newcomb derived a more accurate one in 1895; he participated in a number of astronomical, geodetic, and geographic expeditions; under his guidance an astrophysical laboratory was established at Pulkovo.

STUART, ALEXANDER (*b. Aberdeen [?], Scotland, 1673; d. London [?], England, 1742*), physiology.

After receiving his M.A. from Marischal College, Aberdeen (1691), Stuart earned the M.D. at Leiden (1711); in 1728 he was designated physician to the queen and elevated to a fellowship in the College of Physicians; in 1738 he became the first Croonian lecturer in muscle physiology at the Royal Society. Stuart's main concern, both in his *Dissertatio de structura et motu musculari* (1738) and in his Croonian lectures, was to demonstrate that a strict hydraulic iatromechanism was the best theory to account for muscular motion (contemporary British writers attributed muscular action to wavelike movement of animal spirits and the jiggling of elastic nerve fibers). His theory may have been derived from Boerhaave's analogous ideas in his *Institutiones medicinae.* Though not original with him, Stuart's decapitated "spinal frog" experiment became fixed in the imagination of later eighteenth-century physiologists, helping to clarify the articulation of reflex theory.

STUDER, BERNHARD (*b. Büren, Switzerland, 1794; d. Bern, Switzerland, 1887*), geology.

After taking a degree in theology, Studer studied mathematics and science at Bern and then Göttingen (1816–18); he became professor of geology and mineralogy at the University of Bern shortly after its founding (1834–73). Studer's scientific writings are devoted to the geology of Switzerland, particularly to the Swiss Alps; with A. Escher von der Linth, he published the first geological map of Switzerland (1853) with an accompanying text, *Geologie der Schweiz* (1851–53), which contains the first comprehensive description of the structure of the Swiss Alps. With Escher, he was one of the founders of modern Alpine geology in Switzerland.

STUDY, EDUARD (*b. Coburg, Germany, 1862; d. Bonn, Germany, 1930*), mathematics.

Study received the doctorate from the University of Munich (1884); he also studied mathematics and science at Jena, Strasbourg and Leipzig. After brief stays at Marburg, Johns Hopkins University, Göttingen, and Greifswald, he succeeded Lipschitz at Bonn (1904–27). Study was largely self-taught in mathematics, and his writings reflect a highly individual way of thinking; he worked in many areas of geometry but did not accept the geometric axiomatics of Pasch and Hilbert; he published a number of works on invariant theory, but most of them provoked little response even at the time of publication. In his long work, *Geometrie der Dynamen* (1903), he made a particularly thorough examination of Euclidean kinematics.

STURGEON, WILLIAM (*b. Whittington, Lancashire, England, 1783; d. Prestwick, Manchester, England, 1850*), physics.

After apprenticeship to a shoemaker and service in the army, Sturgeon became a bootmaker in Woolwich (1820). Having developed mechanical skills useful for making scientific apparatus, he lectured on science to schools and other groups, including the East India Company Royal Military College of Addiscombe; he was superintendent of the Royal Victoria Gallery of Practical Sciences (1840–44). Sturgeon's major achievements concerned electromagnetism; in addition to his refinements to the design of the electromagnet, he designed apparatus for displaying electromagnetic phenomena, exemplifying the small but important group of instrumentmakers and lecturers who sought means of exhibiting electrical science in graphic and exciting ways. He founded *Annals of Electricity* (1836), which lasted until 1843.

STURM, CHARLES-FRANÇOIS (*b. Geneva, Switzerland, 1803; d. Paris, France, 1855*), mathematics, physics.

At the Geneva Academy Sturm attended the mathematics lectures of S. L'Huillier and the physics lectures of Marc-Auguste Pictet and P. Prevost; among Sturm's fellow students was Daniel Colladon, his best friend and collaborator. In 1823 Sturm moved to the château of Coppet near Geneva to tutor the son of Mme. de Staël; also living at the chateau was Duke Victor de Broglie, who introduced Sturm to scientific circles in Paris. Sturm then gave up teaching for research (1824) and with Colladon undertook a study of the compression of liquids, which had been set by the Paris Academy as the subject of the grand prize in mathematics and physics. At the Sorbonne and at the Collège de France, they attended lectures of Ampère and Gay-Lussac in physics and of Cauchy and Lacroix in mathematics; they also visited Fourier and Arago. Sturm and Colladon submitted their memoir to the Academy but no paper won the prize; they repeated their experiments and their new memoir won the grand prize for 1827. Meanwhile, Sturm and Colladon had been appointed assistants to Ampère; henceforth their careers diverged.

Through Ampère's influence, Sturm was appointed chief editor for mathematics of the *Bulletin des sciences et de l'industrie* (1829); also in that year he presented to the Academy "Mémoire sur la résolution des équations numériques," containing the famous theorem known by his name. Arago was able to have Sturm named professor of mathematics at the Collège Rollin; he was elected to the Académie des Sciences following the death of Ampère; in 1838 he was named répétiteur of analysis in Liouville's course at the École Polytechnique, where he became professor of analysis and mechanics in 1840; he also assumed the chair of mechanics at the Faculty of Sciences. Around 1851 his health deteriorated and he suffered a nervous breakdown. In addition to Sturm's contributions to plane geometry, differential equations, and infinitesimal geometry, he also published many articles on mechanics and analytical mechanics; his *Cours de mécanique* (1861) and *Cours d'analyse* (1857–59) remained classics for half a century. Sturm's combining of mathematics with physics in his work makes him appear a very modern scientist.

STURM, FRIEDRICH OTTO RUDOLF (*b. Breslau, Germany [now Wrocław, Poland], 1841; d. Breslau, 1919*), mathematics.

Sturm received his doctorate at the University of Breslau (1863); he taught at Munster (1878–92) and Breslau (1892–1919); his principal interest was in pure synthetic geometry; almost all his articles are collected in *Die Lehre von den geometrischen Verwandtschaften* (1908, 1909); he also authored several textbooks.

STURTEVANT, ALFRED HENRY (*b. Jacksonville, Ill., 1891; d. Pasadena, Calif., 1970*), genetics.

Sturtevant entered Columbia University in 1908, where he studied under T. H. Morgan; Morgan, impressed by an article Sturtevant wrote on the inheritance of coat colors in horses, encouraged him to publish it (which he did in 1910), and gave him a desk in his laboratory. After completing his doctorate under Morgan (1914), Sturtevant remained at Columbia as a research investigator for the Carnegie Institution of Washington; he worked there, along with two other students, C. B. Bridges and H. J. Muller, until 1928, when he became professor of genetics in the new division of biology that Morgan established at the California Institute of Technology; he remained at Caltech until his death.

In addition to his principal publications on the genetics and taxonomy of *Drosophila*, Sturtevant contributed papers on the genetics of horses, fowl, mice, moths, snails, iris, and especially the evening primroses. He was also a leading authority on the taxonomy of several groups of Diptera; he was much interested in the social insects and published papers on ant behavior; his discoveries of the principle of gene mapping, of the first reparable gene defect, of the principle underlying fate mapping, of the phenomena of unequal crossing-over, and of position effect were perhaps his greatest scientific achievements.

Sturtevant's work on gene mapping, which he began as an undergraduate, has enabled geneticists to map the chromosomes of a wide variety of higher organisms, including man; his discovery of the first reparable gene defect in 1920 was the basis of much of modern biochemical genetics; his discovery of the principle underlying a kind of embryological-genetic mapping process now known as fate mapping, has became a powerful tool of developmental and behavioral genetics; the process of unequal crossing-over demonstrated by Sturtevant (1924) has come to be regarded as possibly one of the main forces of evolution; and Sturtevant's determination that the position of a gene in the chromosome can affect its function was the first demonstration that primary genic interactions occur at the site of the genes rather than in the nucleus or cytoplasm. His last major work was *A History of Genetics* (1965).

SUBBOTIN, MIKHAIL FEDOROVICH   (*b. Ostrolenka [now Ostroleka], Lomzhinsk province, Russia [now Poland], 1893; d. Leningrad, U.S.S.R., 1966*), astronomy, mathematics.

Subbotin graduated from Warsaw University (1914) and obtained his master's degree at Rostov-on-Don (1917); he directed the Tashkent division of the State Astrophysical Institute (1922–30) before moving to Leningrad University, where he held several teaching and administrative positions (from 1930); he became director of the Leningrad Astronomical Institute in 1942. While Subbotin's first scientific work was devoted to the theory of functions and probability theory, he later worked entirely on celestial mechanics and theoretical astronomy and related areas of mathematics; he also wrote on the history of astronomy.

SUCHTEN (or **Zuchta**), **ALEXANDER**   (*b. Tczew [?], Poland, ca. 1520; d. Bavaria, 1590 [?]*), chemistry, medicine.

After studying at Elblag (1535–39), Suchten studied at Louvain, Rome, Ferrara, Bologna, and at Padua, where he received the doctorate; he was a court physician in Königsberg, the Rhineland, and Poland. His two treatises, *De tribus facultatibus* and *Decem et octo propositiones* (1564), created a storm of protest by stating that doctors of medicine with degrees from Bologna, Padua, Ferrara, Paris, Louvain, and Wittenberg were frauds, and endorsing the views of Paracelsus; probably as a consequence, Suchten was dismissed by his patron, Sigismund II Augustus. After short stays in Königsberg and Strasbourg, where he published *Liber unus de secretis antimonii* (1570), he settled somewhere in Bavaria. Suchten was a distinguished Paracelsian who attacked deceit and charlatanism in medicine; he was perhaps the first scholar to write on the history of chemistry.

SUDHOFF, KARL FRIEDRICH JAKOB   (*b. Frankfurt am Main, Germany, 1853; d. Salzwedel, Germany, 1938*), history of medicine.

Sudhoff studied medicine at the universities of Erlangen, Tübingen, and Berlin, taking the M.D. in 1875; he practiced medicine in Bergen and Hochdahl (1878–1905), during which time he studied the history of medicine and published his two-volume *Bibliographia Paracelsica* (1894–99). He was instrumental in founding the German Society for the History of Medicine and Science (1901). From 1905 to 1925 he held the chair in the history of medicine at the University of Leipzig, where he developed the first German department for the history of medicine (it served as a model for other such departments in Europe and elsewhere). He edited a number of important periodicals and founded the *Archiv für Geschichte der Medizin und der Naturwissenschaften* (1907), later called *Sudhoffs Archiv*. His own research was in ancient, medieval, and Renaissance medicine and in epidemiology; his chief contribution to science was espousing a strict historical method based upon objective and thorough study of original sources,

SUESS, EDUARD   (*b. London, England, 1831; d. Marz, Burgenland, Austria, 1914*), geology.

An autodidact, Suess received no formal training in paleontology or geology, though he did study briefly at Prague and the Technical University in Vienna; in Vienna he was active in the Society of the Friends of Science, where he met W. Haidinger; Suess was imprisoned (1850) for his political activities (he had participated in the revolutionary demonstrations of 1848), but was released through the efforts of Haidinger; he then devoted himself to geology at the Geological Survey, of which Haidinger was director, and became an assistant at the Imperial Mineralogical Collection (1852), where he classified brachiopods. With Haidinger's recommendation, and despite his lack of the doctorate, Suess was appointed extraordinary professor of paleontology at the University of Vienna (1856), where he spent the rest of his career.

In addition to his scientific work, Suess promoted educational improvements, organized public works projects (dredging the Danube Canal and building an aqueduct for Vienna), and wrote books on gold and silver (1877, 1892). Suess began his scientific career as a paleontologist; graptolites, brachiopods, ammonites, and the mammals of the Tertiary period especially attracted his attention. Emphasizing the unity of the living world, he created the concept of the biosphere; his studies gradually shifted from stratigraphy to tectonics, of which he must be considered a creator. Commissioned to write a treatise on the geology of the Austrian Empire, the result was *Die Entstehung der Alpen* (1875), which gives an overall view of the genesis and structure of mountain chains. Suess's masterpiece was *Das Antlitz der Erde* (1883–1909), whose notions, principles, and ways of reasoning have entered so profoundly into the thinking of geologists that many are unaware of their origin and consider them archetypes.

AL-ṢŪFĪ, ABU'L-ḤUSAYN ʿABD AL-RAḤMĀN IBN ʿUMAR AL-RĀZĪ   (*b. Rayy, Persia, 903; d. 986*), astronomy.

Little is known of al-Ṣūfī's life except that he was closely associated with members of the Buwayhid dynasty in Iran and Baghdad. He is best known for his observations and descriptions of the fixed stars, as presented in his "Book on the Constellations of the Fixed Stars"; this work gives the first critical revision of Ptolemy's star catalog and became a classic of Islamic astronomy for many centuries; it was also known to medieval Western science, where al-Ṣūfī was known as Azophi. The scientific significance of this work lies in the valuable records of real star observations and in the exact astronomical identification of several hundred old Arabic star names. Al-Ṣūfī also wrote "Book on the Use of the Astrolabe," "Introduction to the Science of Astrology," and a "Book on the Use of the Celestial Globe."

SUMNER, FRANCIS BERTODY (*b. Pomfret, Conn., 1874; d. La Jolla, Calif., 1945*), biology.

Sumner took his B.S. at the University of Minnesota (1894) and the Ph.D. at Columbia University (1901), where he was attracted to zoology by B. Dean, E. B. Wilson, and H. F. Osborn. He taught natural history at the College of the City of New York for seven years and spent most of his summers at Woods Hole, Massachusetts, where he took up a summer appointment as director of the laboratory of the U. S. Bureau of Fisheries at Woods Hole (1903). In 1913 he moved to the Scripps Institution for Biological Research in La Jolla, California, where he engaged in research on population studies of the deer mouse and on the pigments of fishes.

SUMNER, JAMES BATCHELLER (*b. Canton, Mass., 1887; d. Buffalo, N.Y., 1955*), biochemistry.

Sumner graduated from Harvard College in chemistry (1910) and later returned to earn the Ph.D. (1914). He began teaching biochemistry at the Ithaca division of the Cornell University Medical College (1914), where he later became director of a new laboratory of enzyme chemistry (1947). Convinced that enzymes are proteins, Sumner decided in 1917 to isolate an enzyme, succeeding nine years later in obtaining a crystalline globulin with high urease activity; however, it was only after 1930 that the merit of his work was recognized. In 1946 he was awarded one-half the Nobel Prize in chemistry (the other half was shared by J. H. Northrop and W. M. Stanley).

SUNDMAN, KARL FRITHIOF (*b. Kaskö, Finland, 1873; d. Helsinki, Finland, 1949*), astronomy.

After studying at the University of Helsinki and the Pulkovo Observatory, Sundman taught at Helsinki (1902–41) and was director of the Helsinki observatory (1918–41). In the field of celestial mechanics he made two important contributions: first, he extended Laplace's propositions concerning the convergence of the series in unperturbed elliptic motion to the perturbation problem; second, he developed a general solution to the three-body problem.

SURINGAR, WILLEM FREDERIK REINIER (*b. Leeuwarden, Netherlands, 1832; d. Leiden, Netherlands, 1898*), botany.

Suringar received his doctorate from the University of Leiden in botany (1857) and was immediately appointed extraordinary professor of botany, remaining there until his death. As *conservator herbarii* of the Netherlands Botanical Society (1857) and director of the national herbarium (1868), he was a leading plant taxonomist of the Netherlands; his flora of the Netherlands (1870) was the leading work until the turn of the century.

SUTER, HEINRICH (*b. Hedingen, Zurich canton, Switzerland, 1848; d. Dornach, Switzerland, 1922*), mathematics, Oriental studies.

Suter received his doctorate from the University of Zurich (1871), though he also studied at Berlin; his dissertation emphasized the significance of mathematics for cultural history. Most of his career was spent teaching mathematics and physics at the cantonal school of Zurich (1886–1918), where he learned Arabic and became the outstanding expert of his time on Muslim mathematics.

SUTHERLAND, WILLIAM (*b. Dumbarton, Scotland, 1859; d. Melbourne, Australia, 1911*), theoretical physical chemistry, molecular physics.

Sutherland studied at the University of Melbourne (B.A. 1879, M.A. 1883) and University College, London (B.Sc. 1881); although he remained indirectly attached to the University of Melbourne, he held no regular appointment. From 1885 he published several major scientific articles per year, mostly in the *Philosophical Magazine;* he investigated such topics as the viscosity of gases and liquids, molecular attraction, valency, ionization, ionic velocities, and atomic sizes; his later research dealt with the electronic theory of matter.

SUTTON, WALTER STANBOROUGH (*b. Utica, N.Y., 1877; d. Kansas City, Kan., 1916*), biology, medicine.

Sutton graduated from the University of Kansas at Lawrence (B.A. 1900, M.A. 1901), where he worked in cytology under C. E. McClung; he did graduate work at Columbia University under E. B. Wilson, and though he never completed a Ph.D. thesis, during the years 1901–03 he formulated the theory of the chromosomal basis of Mendelism, his most noteworthy discovery; these results were recounted in "The Chromosomes in Heredity" (1903), a major landmark in biologic literature. After two years as foreman in the oil fields of Kansas (1903–05), Sutton returned to the College of Physicians and Surgeons of Columbia University and received the M.D. (1907); from 1909 until his premature death from a ruptured appendix, he practiced surgery in Kansas City, Kansas, and in Kansas City, Missouri.

SVEDBERG, THE (THEODOR) (*b. Fleräng, Valbo, near Gävle, Seeden, 1884; d. Örebro, Sweden, 1971*), physical chemistry.

Svedberg graduated from the University of Uppsala (Ph.D. 1907), with which he remained associated the rest of his life; he was appointed the first Swedish chair of physical chemistry (1912) and was head of the new Gustaf Werner Institute of Nuclear Chemistry (1949–67). He received the 1926 Nobel Prize in chemistry for his work on disperse systems, and he helped create the first research council in Sweden, the Research Council for Technology (1942).

Svedberg's research was focused on the new field of colloid chemistry for almost two decades; his studies (1906) provided an experimental confirmation of Einstein's and of Smoluchowski's theories on Brownian movement. He also had a lifelong interest in radioactive processes; his discovery, with D. Strömholm, that thorium X crystallized with lead and barium salts, but not with others, indicated to them the existence of isotopes before that conception was introduced into chemistry by Soddy. From 1913 to 1923 Svedberg continued his studies of the physicochemical properties of colloidal solutions; with J. B. Nichols he constructed the first optical centrifuge in which the settling of the particles could be followed photographically during the run (1923); he and Rinde proposed the name "ultracentrifuge" for the improved instrument developed in 1924. Svedberg's interest then focused on using his ultracentrifuge to study other colloidal systems, such as proteins; with the aid of a new high-speed oil-turbine centrifuge, he concluded that certain rules existed for the molecular weights of the proteins (1929), asserting that in most cases the soluble proteins had molecules with a well-defined uniform size; while these ideas were skeptically received by many scientists at first, they were confirmed by other studies in the early 1930's. In the late 1930's and early 1940's, however, it became evident that the multiple law did not have the generality that Svedberg had expected; nevertheless this hypothesis was very important to the development of protein chemistry. He remained intensively engaged in the development of his ultracentrifuge, extending his interest in macromolecules of biological origin to include the polysaccharides.

During World War II he was charged with developing Swedish production of synthetic rubber. Svedberg's interest in radiation chemistry was revived in the late 1930's, and in 1946 he convinced Gustaf Werner, a wealthy industrialist, to give funds for a cyclotron; with additional funds from the Swedish government, Svedberg supervised construction of a 185 MEV synchrocyclotron, which began operation in 1951 at the new Gustaf Werner Institute of Nuclear Chemistry; the institute soon became the center in Sweden for research in the area between high-energy physics, chemistry, and biology.

SVEDELIUS, NILS EBERHARD (*b. Stockholm, Sweden, 1873; d. Uppsala, Sweden, 1960*), phycology.

Svedelius received the doctorate from the University of Uppsala (1901), where he taught botany until 1938; although he had a lifelong interest in the algae of the Baltic, his most important contributions were in the elucidation of the various life cycles in the red algae and their evolutionary value.

SVERDRUP, HARALD ULRIK (*b. Sogndal, Norway, 1888; d. Oslo, Norway, 1957*), geophysics.

Sverdrup studied at the University of Norway, where he worked with V. Bjerknes, the leading authority on atmospheric circulation, whom he followed to the University of Leipzig in 1913; at Leipzig Sverdrup completed his doctoral dissertation (published in 1917). He served as chief scientist on several expeditions to the North Pole (1918, 1922), after which he succeeded Bjerknes as professor of geophysics at the University of Bergen in Norway (1926–31). After being a researcher at the Christian Michelsens Institute (1931–35), Sverdrup became director of the Scripps Institute of Oceanography (1935–48); at Scripps he studied the boundary layer between the atmosphere and the sea and wrote *The Oceans* (1942), a monumental handbook that remains an important introduction. As director of the Norwegian Polar Institute in Oslo (from 1948), he organized several expeditions; in 1949 he became professor of geophysics at the University of Oslo.

SWAINSON, WILLIAM (*b. Newington Butts, London, England, 1789; d. Wellington, New Zealand, 1855*), zoology.

Swainson spent the early part of his life with the army commissariat, for which he traveled widely, making extensive zoological collections on his own time; after 1823 he engaged in scientific writing for a living, publishing on vertebrates, mollusks, and insects. He emigrated to New Zealand in 1840; his claim to remembrance rests on his zoological work and his fine zoological illustrations; however, his adherence to the "quinary system" of W. S. Macleay distorted some of his work.

SWAMMERDAM, JAN (*b. Amsterdam, Netherlands, 1637; d. Amsterdam, 1680*), biology.

Swammerdam received the M.D. from the University of Leiden (1667), though he probably never practiced medicine; from 1664 to 1665 he was a guest of M. Thévenot in Paris and an active member of Thévenot's scientific academy, an informal club that met to watch experiments and dispute over Cartesian ideas. In Amsterdam again (1665), he joined a group of physicians called the Private College of Amsterdam, which included G. Blaes (Blasius), and met irregularly until 1672. Swammerdam devoted his life to scientific investigation, but he was interrupted by illness, by his father's insistence that he earn a living, and by periods of depression and religious anxiety. He was a friend of the mystical prophetess Antoinette Bourignon, whom he visited in Schleswig-Holstein (1675–76); he apparently rejected science—at least temporarily—about this time, for his friend N. Stensen (Steno) reported that he had destroyed the manuscript to his study of silkworm anatomy and urged his friends to pray for him in his search for God.

Swammerdam's biological researches fall into two distinct categories which both sought mechanistic types of explanation: studies of insects and medical work (most of his work was of the latter type); his medical thesis offers a perfectly Cartesian mechanical explanation of the motion of the lungs and the function of breathing, supplemented by the iatrochemistry of Sylvius. Through demonstrations with frogs performed as eary as 1663, though not published until 1738, Swammerdam provided classic proof that muscles do not increase in volume upon contraction. In working with van Horne in Leiden (1666–67), he claimed to have discovered that mammals have ovaries like those of egg-laying animals, but the Royal Society assigned priority to Steno. Though Swammerdam pursued a lifelong inquiry into the nature of lower animals, all he managed to publish was the *Historia insectorum generalis*, Part I (1669), and a monograph on the mayfly, which, in the period of his religious crisis, became the occasion for an extended hymn to the Creator; the rest of his entomological works were published posthumously as provided for in his will (Boerhave published the *Biblia naturae* in 1737–38).

Swammerdam's thesis about insects was new, significant, and rejected three Aristotelian arguments that placed the insects far below the higher animals: spontaneous generation, the lack of internal anatomy, and development by metamorphosis; the *Historia* sought to eliminate the supposed difference between the epigenetic development of higher animals and the metamorphic origin of lower animals, asserting that those changes that seem metamorphic are really no different from the obviously gradual ones, except that they go on invisibly, under the skin. In 1669 Swammerdam demonstrated the presence of rudimentary wings and limbs under the skin of a caterpillar. He asserted that the pupa is the basis of all insect development (the egg being itself a type of pupa), proposing four modes of insect development. After 1669 he attacked the other two arguments; with his exceptional skills at microdissection he destroyed the idea that insects consisted internally of humors (his dissections formed a good portion of the study of all invertebrate anatomy before Cuvier). Swammerdam opposed both spontaneous generation and metamorphosis on the grounds that they led to atheism by allowing chance and accident to rule instead of law and regularity; the basic law of living things was that they came from parents of the same kind by means of eggs. That Swammerdam is called the founder of preformation theory is ironic because he consciously avoided conjecture; still, his work did contribute to the development of the idea of preexistence and even emboîtement. Although some biographers describe Swammerdam as a mystic, his work is certainly not mystical, for his was a mechanistic world, instituted by God and operating like clockwork.

SWANN, WILLIAM FRANCIS GRAY (*b. Ironbridge, Shropshire, England, 1884; d. Swarthmore, Pa., 1962*), experimental physics, theoretical physics.

Swann received the D.Sc. degree from the University of London (1910); after working at the Carnegie Institution of Washington on terrestrial magnetism, he taught physics at the universities of Minnesota, Chicago, and Yale; he was director of the Bartol Research Foundation of the Franklin Institute (1927–59), located at Swarthmore College. He made the Foundation into one of the world's great centers in cosmic ray studies; his chief contributions lay in experimental and theoretical studies of cosmic radiation, theoretical research in electromagnetic theory and relativity, and work in philosophy of physics, which appeared in the highly successful book *The Architecture of the Universe* (1934).

SWARTS, FRÉDÉRIC JEAN EDMOND (*b. Ixelles, Belgium, 1866; d. Ghent, Belgium, 1940*), chemistry.

Swarts obtained doctorates in chemistry (1889) and medicine (1891) from the University of Ghent, where he spent his entire career; he made the first extensive investigations of organic-fluorine compounds, for which he developed a double decomposition process using inorganic fluorides, known as the Swarts reaction (1892); this process led to the development of commercial fluorochemicals.

SWARTZ, OLOF (*b. Norrköping, Sweden, 1760; d. Stockholm, Sweden, 1818*), botany.

Swartz received his doctorate from Uppsala University (1781), where he studied with Linnaeus the younger; his studies made on a botanical tour of the West Indies were summed up in his *Flora Indiae Occidentalis I–III* (1797–1806), in which he described nearly 900 species, most of them new. After 1791 he held several appointments in the service of the Royal Swedish Academy of Sciences. Swartz is also known for his taxonomic studies of specific plant groups, including orchids, mosses, and sepecially ferns.

SWEDENBORG, EMANUEL (*b. Stockholm, Sweden, 1688; d. London, England, 1772*), technology, geology, cosmogony, physiology, theology.

After studying at the University of Uppsala, Swedenborg stayed in England (1710–13), where he read Newton and met Flamsteed, Halley, and J. Woodward. Beginning in 1716, he served for many years with the Swedish Board of Mines as a metallurgist; being wealthy, he also published at his own expense Sweden's first, short-lived (1716–18) scientific journal, *Daedalus hyperboreus*. Interested in many fields, Swedenborg was least successful as an astronomer and at his best in geology and paleontology; in 1719 he published proof that Scandinavia had once been covered by an ocean. In his grandiose *Principia rerum naturalium* (1734) he developed a modified Cartesian cosmogony in which physical reality developed from the mathematical point; though his ideas heralded the later planetary theories of Buffon, Kant, and Laplace, there is no evidence of a direct influence. As he developed his materialistic explanation of the universe to its furthest point, concluding that the human soul also derived from the movements of small particles, his interest shifted to the body-soul problem; he now sought to explain everything in terms of psyche, considering even the body as a manifestation of divine origin. After wrestling with the problem of devising a logical-mathematical universal language in the early 1740's, Swedenborg experienced a religious crisis, culminating in a vision of God while in London (1745); his dreams and visions are recounted in *Drömboken* (1859); at the age of fifty-seven, he abandoned his scientific investigations to become a visionary, prophet, and founder of a new universal religion represented by the Swedenborgian New Church. His theory of the spiritual world is developed in the eight volumes of *Arcana coelestia* (1749–56); Swedenborg's theology is characterized by rigorous logic and is obviously rooted in his previous concern with the physical sciences.

SWIETEN, GERARD VAN (*b. Leiden, Netherlands, 1700; d. Schönbrunn Palace, Vienna, Austria, 1772*), medicine.

Van Swieten studied at Louvain before moving to the University of Leiden (M.D., 1725), where he attended the lectures of Boerhaave; he established a medical practice in Leiden and continued to attend Boerhaave's lectures. Unable to succeed Boerhaave at the university because he was Catholic, van Swieten left Leiden to take charge of physicians at the court of the empress of Austria, Maria Theresa (1745); while there he also reorganized the medical faculty at the University of Vienna, which became world-famous at the turn of the century. His contributions to medicine include his *Commentaria* (5 vols., 1742–72), which increased the dissemination of Boerhaave's ideas; his modification of the traditional treatment of venereal disease with mercurials; and overcoming the aversion of Viennese physicians to inoculation against smallpox, introduced to Austria by J. Ingen-Housz in 1768.

SWINDEN, JAN HENDRIK VAN (*b. The Hague, Netherlands, 1746; d. Amsterdam, Netherlands, 1823*), electricity, magnetism, meteorology, metrology.

Van Swinden received his doctorate from Leiden University (1766), where he was greatly influenced by Newton's *Principia* (he subsequently took every opportunity to popularize Newtonian philosophy); he held the chair of philosophy, logic, and metaphysics at Franeker University (1767–85), after which he taught philosophy, natural philosophy, mathematics, and astronomy at the University of Amsterdam. His best-known work in magnetism was *Mémoires sur l'analogie de l'électricité et du magnétisme* (1784), in which he included a comparison of Mesmer's animal magnetism with electricity; he was best

667

known outside the Netherlands for his accurate meteorological observations.

SWINESHEAD (Swyneshed, Suicet, etc.), RICHARD (*fl. ca. 1340–55*), natural philosophy.

The name Richard Swineshead is best known as that of the author of the *Liber calculationem* (*ca.* 1340–50), famous for its extensive use of mathematics within physics; there were, however, at least two or three men named Swineshead, whose identities have become confused. They were probably: 1) John Swineshead (*d.* 1372). fellow of Merton College, Oxford (from *ca.* 1343), who pursued a career in law and left no extant works. 2) Roger Swineshead (*d. ca.* 1365), also at Oxford, author of the logical works *De insolubilibus* and *De obligationibus* and the physical work *De motibus naturalibus*; he was possibly a Benedictine monk and theologian. 3) The Richard Swineshead mentioned above, associated with Merton College, and possibly also the author of two extant *opuscula*, *De motu* and *De motu locali*, and of at least a partial *De caelo* commentary. This article will cover the extant physical works attributed to any Swineshead.

De motibus naturalibus was written at Oxford (*ca.* 1335), probably by Roger Swineshead; it contains not only logicomathematical natural philosophy but also large sections of traditional natural philosophy, and is thus, in a way, transitional between thirteenth-century cosmological and fourteenth-century logicomathematical natural philosophy. The treatment of motion reflects an Aristotelian or medical base; the author considers first the effects of motion (rather than its cause), and begins with the effects of alteration (rather than of local motion); the basic notions of the measurement of motion come from the category of quality, with the emphasis on mean degrees, as in medical theory. The author rejects the Aristotelian position that velocity is proportional to force and inversely proportional to resistance; he states that resistance is not required for natural motion; he concludes, in modern terms, that velocity is proportional to the difference between the force and resistance. In measuring a quality he postulates so-called uniform degrees; the "uniformly difform degree" is a divisible part of a latitude (range) of quality, each degree containing a linearly increasing series of degrees above some minimum and below some maximum; by contrast, the "uniform degree" is not a component part of a latitude, but rather is equally intense throughout. Roger Swineshead tried to find means of dealing with nonuniform distributions of qualities, but succeeded only in establishing criteria for uniform and uniformly varying distributions; it is very likely that the work of Richard Swineshead was motivated by the failures of Roger.

Liber calculationem by Richard Swineshead (often called "the Calculator") provides techniques for calculating the values of physical variables and their changes, or for solving problems or sophisms; the author's approach is to generate results almost exhaustively from various positions, or propositions, and to analyze such results; he shows little interest in the contexts in which one might expect the situations represented by these results to occur, nor does he investigate whether they can occur; his purpose appears to have been to provide techniques which would enable the reader to handle problems of all sorts, whether physical, logical, medical, theological, or

whatever. The *Liber calculationem* begins with four treatises dealing with the qualitative degrees of simple and mixed subjects insofar as the degrees of the subjects depend on the degrees in their various parts; the discussion is of course related to the Aristotelian theory that each terrestrial element (earth, air, fire, or water) is qualified in some degree by a combination of two of the four elemental qualities (hotness, coldness, wetness, dryness). In treatises V and VI the author introduces density and rarity, which are mathematically more complex than qualitative intensity because two variables, amount of matter and quality, are involved in even the simplest cases; treatises VII and VIII consider whether reaction is possible and how powers and resistances are to be measured. Swineshead and the other Oxford calculators of this period did not accept Oresme's concept of quantity of quality but rather favored quantifications in terms of intensities alone. Swineshead held the so-called addition of part to part theory of qualitative change; he supported (with some uneasiness) the position that the measure of intensity of a whole corresponds to the mean degree of the qualified subject (i.e., the whole); reasoning that in a difform subject with uniform halves, a quality extended through a half "denominates the whole only half as much as it denominates the half," he generalized this rule, opening the possibility of considering "stair-step" distributions. In measuring intensity, he worked with, in our terms, convergent and divergent infinite series, but it would be anachronistic to credit him with thinking in terms of anything tending toward zero or to set down the general term of a series; he was more interested in apparent paradoxes regarding infinite and finite intensity. In dealing with the problem of reaction, or how two qualified bodies act on each other, Swineshead was faced with a most difficult problem, thanks especially to the Aristotelian emphasis on alteration rather than local motion; he had to consider the additivity, or summability, of the relevant forces and resistances, and appears to concede that great problems ensue if one attempts to treat subjects as the sums of their parts in any simple fashion.

Treatises IX and X treat difficulty of action and maxima and minima; here Swineshead clears away certain Aristotelian objections to Bradwardine's function. In treatise XI there appears the most mathematically sophisticated passage of the book, a consideration of the problem of whether in free fall, assuming a void, a heavy body (in this case a rod) will ever reach the center of the universe in the sense that the center of the body will eventually coincide with the center of the universe. In one proof, the author employs a discontinuous step function; in another, he comes more directly to grip with his variables as exhibiting a continuous function. Treatises XII and XIII are on light; and treatise XIV presents a very full discussion of local motion. The author accepts Bradwardine's view that (in modern terms) arithmetic changes in velocities correspond to geometric changes in the relevant force-resistance ratios. The medieval tradition of compounding proportions was at the base of Bradwardine's logarithmic-type function; Swineshead makes this explicit in his initial rules, which, together with Bradwardine's function, are the key to his conclusions: the first fundamental rule is that "whenever a force increases with respect to a constant resistance, then it will acquire as much proportionally relative to that resistance as it will itself be rendered greater"—i.e., if a force F_1 acting on a constant resistance R increases to F_2, then the proportion $F_2 : F_1$ equals the increase of $F_2 : R$ over $F_1 : R$. Swineshead always compares at least *pairs* of $F : F$ or $R : R$ proportions, and velocity increments (even negative increments) are thus always added. His most signal success is his connection of variations in resistance over time with variations in resistance over space; this he accomplished by "translating" spatial increments of resistance into temporal ones, thus circumventing a troublesome double dependency (for in the medieval view a variation in the resistance of a medium would determine the velocity of a body in motion in it, while at the same time the velocity would determine where in the medium the mobile would be and hence the resistance it would encounter). The final treatises (XV and XVI) continue study of the problems raised in treatise XIV.

Richard Swineshead's *In librum de caelo* is a fragment, apparently of a commentary on *De caelo*; the first part of the fragment deals with Aristotle's proofs that an infinite body cannot move locally, and the second with the relation of substances to their qualities, in connection with the possibility of action and passion between infinite bodies. *De motu* is not explicitly ascribed to Swineshead but is so similar to *De motu locali,* which is so ascribed, that there is little doubt of the authorship; both these works represent a stage in the author's thought leading to the *Liber calculationem.*

SYDENHAM, THOMAS (*b., or at least baptized, Wynford Eagle, Dorset, England, 1624; d. London, England, 1689*), medicine.

Soon after entering Magdalen Hall, Oxford (1642), Sydenham left to serve in the army of the Parliament during the civil war; he later returned to the university, where he may have been made master of arts; his war service and family connections with Cromwell's cause led to his being made bachelor of medicine (1648) and to his election as fellow of All Souls College (1648–55). Soon after his marriage (1655), he began to practice medicine in Westminster, where he remained for the rest of his life; he obtained his license to practice from the Royal College of Physicians of London in 1663; he was admitted member of Pembroke College, Cambridge, in 1676, and received an M.D. at that time. His associates included R. Boyle and John Locke, who may have been Sydenham's collaborator or, more likely, his student. Sydenham's philosophy was that of a skeptical physician, emphasizing the importance of observing, and depreciating book knowledge and university education; his notebook of clinical observations from 1669 to 1674 resulted in his magnum opus, *Observationes medicae circa morborum acutorum historiam et curationem* (1676). His effort to tie treatment deductively to the observable phenomena, and his concern for epidemic variations, gave an impetus to the more careful bedside observation of disease. Sydenham's fame came from his contributions to therapy: his moderate treatment of smallpox, his use of cinchona, and his invention of liquid laudanum; he became known as the "English Hippocrates."

SYLOW, PETER LUDVIG MEJDELL (*b. Christiania [now Oslo], Norway, 1832; d. Christiania, 1918*), mathematics.

After studying at Christiania University, Sylow won a scholarship to travel abroad to Berlin and Paris (1861); he was not able to obtain a chair at Christiania University until 1898, with the help of S. Lie, with whom he had collaborated on a new edition of N. H. Abel's works (1873–81); he is best known for certain theorems in group theory.

SYLVESTER II, POPE. *See* **Gerbert,** also known as **Gerbert d'Aurillac.**

SYLVESTER, JAMES JOSEPH (*b. London, England, 1814; d. London, 1897*), mathematics.

Sylvester was educated at the University of London (later University College); the Royal Institution in Liverpool; St. John's College, Cambridge; and Trinity College, Dublin (B.A. and M.A., 1841). He taught at University College, London (1838–41); University of Virginia (1841–43); Royal Military Academy, Woolwich (1855–70); Johns Hopkins (1876–83); and Oxford (1883–94). His greatest achievements were in algebra. With Cayley he helped to develop the theory of determinants and their application to nonalgebraic subjects. He was instrumental in helping to turn the attention of algebraists from such studies as the theory of equations—in which he nevertheless did important work—to the theory of forms, invariants, and linear associative algebras generally.

A number of his early writings concern the reality of the roots of numerical equations, Newton's rule for the number of imaginary roots, and Sturm's theorem. In connection with Newton's rule, the method of Sturm's proof was applied to a quite different problem. Sylvester supposed x to vary continuously, and investigated the increase and decrease in the changes of sign. Newton's first statement of his incomplete rule for enumerating imaginary roots dates from 1665–66. Although valid, the rule was not justified before Sylvester's proofs of the complete rule.

Another problem of great importance concerned the nature of the roots of a quintic equation.

He also showed interest in the theory of numbers when he published a beautiful theorem on a product formed from numbers less than and prime to a given number (1838). He made numerous later contributions to the theory of numbers, especially in the partition of numbers, his most novel contribution being his use of a graphical method. This graphical representation greatly simplified and showed the way to proofs of many new results in the theory of partitions. Sylvester's and Cayley's discussions on the algebra of forms led to their theory of annihilators, which was closely linked to that of generating functions for the tabulation of the partitions of numbers.

Sylvester played an important part in the creation of the theory of canonical forms. What may be his most widely known theorem states that a general binary form of odd order $(2n-1)$ is a sum of $n(2n-1)$-th powers of linear forms. Early in his study of the effects of linear transformations on real quadratic forms, Sylvester discovered (and named) the law of inertia of quadratic forms. Another memorable result in the theory of linear transformations and matrices is Sylvester's law of nullity. For Sylvester the "nullity" of a matrix was the difference between its order and rank, wherefore he wrote his law of nullity. He published no lengthy volume of mathematics, although his books on versification and its mathematical principles are numerous.

SYLVIUS, FRANCISCUS DELE BOË (*b. Hanau, Germany, 1614; d. Leiden, Netherlands, 1672*), medicine.

Sylvius studied medicine at Leiden (1633–35) before taking his degree at Basel (1637); he gave private lectures on anatomy in Leiden (1638–41), where he was one of the first to defend Harvey's new theory of the circulation of the blood and to demonstrate it on dogs. In Amsterdam (1641), Sylvius established a lucrative practice, leaving to become professor of medicine at Leiden in 1658; his enthusiasm inspired the anatomical and physiological work of J. Swammerdam, N. Steno, and R. de Graaf. Sylvius' accomplishments were in anatomy and medical chemistry; he was the first to describe the tubercles in phthisis, among other things, and was the most brilliant representative of the iatrochemical school of Paracelsus and J. B. van Helmont. Though his speculative and exaggerated theories may have caused much harm in the medical practice of his students, he was a promoter of scientific medical research.

SYLVIUS, JACOBUS. *See* **Dubois, Jacques.**

SYMMER, ROBERT (*b. Galloway, Scotland* [*?*], *ca. 1707; d. London, England, 1763*), electricity.

After taking the M.A. at the University of Edinburgh (1735), where he studied natural philosophy, Symmer eventually became head clerk of the office of the Treasurer of the Chamber (until 1757). In his leisure time he experimented with electricity from 1758; he concluded that the contrary electricities of Franklin derived from two distinct, opposed, positive principles, perhaps in the form of two fluids. His experiments, though not his theories, were repeated and improved by Nollet and Cigna, leading the latter to develop the electrophore, a device as important as the Leyden jar for the development of electrical theory; before the end of the eighteenth century his dualist theory had captured the Continent, although English electricians remained with the singlist theories.

SYNESIUS OF CYRENE (*b. Cyrene, ca. 370; d. ca. 414*), astronomy, physics.

Synesius was a gifted pupil of Hypatia; a landed proprietor, he became bishop of Ptolemais in 410. He is well known for his essays, letters, and hymns, but his scientific achievements are also noteworthy; he invented a "perfected" astrolabe, or planisphere.

SZEBELLÉDY, LÁSZLÓ (*b. Rétság, Hungary, 1901; d. Budapest, Hungary, 1944*), analytical chemistry.

After earning a degree in pharmacy at the University of Budapest (1923), Szebellédy became assistant to L. Winkler at the Inorganic Chemistry Institute of the University of Budapest (1925), where he also taught analytical chemistry (from 1934); he studied catalytic ultramicroreactions and, with Z. Somogyi, invented the coulometric titration method (1938), which is widely used in analytical chemistry.

SZILARD, LEO (*b. Budapest, Hungary, 1898; d. La Jolla, Calif., 1964*), physics, biology.

After serving in World War I, Szilard obtained the doctorate in physics at the University of Berlin (1922); his

dissertation, under the direction of Max von Laue, led to his famous paper establishing the connection between entropy and information and foreshadowing modern cybernetic theory (1929). In Berlin, as a researcher at the Kaiser Wilhelm Institute and then as *Privatdozent* at the university, he began to patent his long series of pioneering discoveries, including an electromagnetic pump for liquid refrigerants now used in nuclear reactors, which he developed with Einstein. In England, after fleeing Germany in 1933, he conceived the idea of achieving a nuclear chain reaction, leading to the establishment of the Szilard-Chalmers reaction and the discovery of the γ-ray induced emission of neutrons from beryllium. In the United States (from 1938) at Columbia University, he undertook experiments to demonstrate the release of neutrons in the fission process; with Fermi he organized research there that led to the first controlled nuclear chain reaction on 2 December 1942, at Chicago. More than any other individual, Szilard was responsible for establishing the Manhattan Project; it was he who arranged for the letter from Einstein to President Roosevelt that brought it about, and he also worked in a futile effort to convince President Truman to use the first atomic bomb in a non-lethal demonstration to the Japanese. After the war Szilard turned to biology. Throughout his life he had a strong social consciousness; he helped found the Academic Assistance Council for refugee scientists, and was a leader in the successful effort by Manhattan Project alumni for a bill establishing civilian control over peaceful development of nuclear energy.

SZILY, PÁL (*b. Budapest, Hungary, 1878; d. Mosonmagyaróvár, Hungary, 1945*), chemistry.

After obtaining his medical degree at the University of Budapest, Szily became an assistant at the Institute of Physiology there, where he carried out his fundamental research on the colorimetric determination of hydrogen ion concentration (1903); his invention of artificial buffer solutions was extended by S. P. L. Sørensen, who introduced the concept of pH in 1909. After Szily became director of the Budapest Jewish Hospital (1909), his research was purely medical.

AL-ṬABARĪ, ABU'L-ḤASAN AḤMAD IBN MU-ḤAMMAD (*b. Ṭabaristān, Persia, first quarter of the tenth century; d. Ṭabaristān, fourth quarter of the tenth century*), philosophy, natural science, medicine.

Al-Ṭabarī studied under the physician Abū Māhir Mū sā ibn Sayyār; he became court physician to the Buwayhid king Rukn al-Dawla (reigned 932–976), during a period of great cultural and scientific productivity in Persia and Iraq under the Abbasid caliphate. He won wide recognition for his only known work, *al-Muᶜālajāt al-Buqrāṭiyya*, which consists of ten treatises on Hippocratic medical treatment; he was the first practitioner to describe and recommend effective treatment for scabies.

AL-ṬABARĪ, ABU'L-ḤASAN ᶜALĪ IBN SAHL RAB-BĀN (*b. Marw, Persia, ca. 808; d. Baghdad, ca. 861*), medicine, natural science, theology, government.

Ṭabarī was educated by his father, a learned and highly placed government official; after they moved to Ṭabaristān, ᶜAlī became known as al-Ṭabarī; from 840 he served under three Abassid caliphs. His two best-known books are *Firdaws al-ḥikma* ("Paradise of Wisdom," 850), a medical encyclopedia based on Greek, Syriac, and Indian medical compendiums and the first of its kind in Arabic with such scope and comprehensiveness; and *Al-Dīn wā 'l-dawla* ("On Religion and Government," 855).

TABOR, JOHN (*b. Faccombe, Hampshire, England, 1667*), medicine.

Tabor graduated B.A. at Merton College, Oxford (1687), and received his medical degree there in 1694. An adherent of the English iatromathematical school that developed under the aegis of Newtonianism during the early eighteenth century, he attempted to incorporate medical animism into a mathematical framework in his *Exercitationes medicae* (1724), drawing heavily on the work of Borelli; his work attempted to reconcile reductionist and vitalist traditions in physiological theory, but had little influence.

TACCHINI, PIETRO (*b. Modena, Italy, 1838; d. Spilamberto, Modena province, Italy, 1905*), astronomy, meteorology.

After obtaining his engineering degree at the *archiginnasio* of Modena, Tacchini studied astronomy at the observatory of Padua; he became deputy director of the Modena observatory (1859), adjunct astronomer at the Palermo observatory (1863), and director of the observatory at the Collegio Romano and director of the Central Meteorological Office (1879). His main research was on solar physics using the spectroscope; he directed many astronomical expeditions, and helped found the Society of Italian Spectroscopists (1871).

TACCOLA, MARIANO DI JACOMO (*b. Siena, Italy, 1381; d. Siena, 1453/1458*), mechanics.

A sculptor in his early life, by 1427 Taccola became interested in mechanical technology; he was appointed a *nobile familiare* (1432) to the future emperor Sigismund, and accompanied him to fight the Turks; returning to Siena by 1435, Taccola worked on finishing his "De machinis libre decem" (1449). With Brunelleschi and G. Fontana, he was a founder of the Italian school of Renaissance engineers; though his work was not greatly original, he did invent the chain transmission system and the compound crank with connecting rod; the latter converted rotary motion to reciprocal motion, a crucial concept for postmedieval Western technology.

TACHENIUS, OTTO (*b. Herford, Westphalia; d. probably Venice, Italy*), medical chemistry, pharmaceutical chemistry.

Apprenticed to an apothecary, from whose service he was dismissed for theft, he then acquired an M.D. from Padua (1652) and settled in Venice, where he sold a "viperine salt" (*sal viperinum*) as a sovereign remedy; his work was greatly criticized by J. Zwelfer, among others, to whom Tachenius replied in *Hippocrates chemicus* (1666), a defense of the viperine salt. In his *Clavis* (1668) he espoused a version of the Helmontian theory of acid and alkali as the governing principles of human physiology.

TACQUET, ANDREAS (*b. Antwerp, Belgium, 1612; d. Antwerp, 1660*), mathematics.

Entering the Jesuit order in 1629, Tacquet studied logic, physics, mathematics, and theology in Louvain; he took his vows in 1646 and subsequently taught mathematics in the *collèges* of Louvain (1649–55) and Antwerp (1645–49, 1655–60). His most important mathematical work, *Cylindricorum et annularium* (1651), contained original theorems on cylinders and rings and, most importantly, adopted an essentially Archimedean method; his most popular work was *Elementa geometriae* (1654). Tacquet's importance was mainly pedagogical.

IBN ṬĀHIR. *See* **Al-Baghdādī, Abū Manṣūr ʿAbd al-Qāhir ibn Ṭāhir ibn Muḥammad ibn ʿAbdallah, al-Tamīmī, al-Shāfiʿī.**

TAIT, PETER GUTHRIE (*b. Dalkeith, Scotland, 1831; d. Edinburgh, Scotland, 1901*), physics, mathematics.

After graduating from Peterhouse, Cambridge (1852), Tait was professor of mathematics at Queen's College, Belfast (1854–60), and professor of natural philosophy at Edinburgh (1860–1901). He performed much experimental work in thermodynamics; with J. Dewar he experimented with the Crookes radiometer and gave the first satisfactory explanation of it (1875); a series of papers on the kinetic theory of gases (1886–92) contained, according to Kelvin, the first proof of the Waterston-Maxwell equipartition theorem. Tait was engaged in several controversies; his *Sketch of the History of Thermodynamics* (1868) was a highly prejudiced and pro-British account. He strongly promoted the use of quaternions, as opposed to Gibb's and Heaviside's vector methods.

TALBOT, WILLIAM HENRY FOX (*b. Melbury House, Dorsetshire, England, 1800; d. Lacock Abbey, Wiltshire, England, 1877*), photochemistry, mathematics.

Talbot graduated from Trinity College, Cambridge (1821); after traveling on the Continent as a gentleman scholar, he established himself at the family estate in the late 1820's and successfully ran for Parliament (1833–34). Heavily influenced by Romanticism, he began a life-long series of translations from ancient languages and of historical and philological studies in 1830. After graduating from Cambridge Talbot did mathematical work, but he became increasingly interested in chemistry and optics, and adopted a unified, dynamic view of physical phenomena; in pursuing the problem of light-matter interaction, he suggested in 1835 a connection between spectral lines and chemical composition. His love of nature and artistic interests led to his development, with N. Henneman, of the first negative-positive process in photography (1835), though Daguerre's process (announced in 1839 by Arago at the Académie des Sciences) proved vastly superior; in the middle 1840's he published two of the earliest books illustrated with photographs.

TAMM, IGOR EVGENIEVICH (*b. Vladivostok, Russia, 1895; d. Moscow, U.S.S.R., 1971*), physics.

Graduated from Moscow University (1918), where he became head of the department of theoretical physics (1924–41); after he was named director of the theoretical section of the P. N. Lebedev Physical Institute of the Academy of Sciences of the U.S.S.R. (1934), his activity was concentrated there. Tamm's first scientific research was on electrodynamics of anisotropic media, crystal optics in the theory of relativity, quantum theory of paramagnetism, and nonrelativistic quantum mechanics; from 1934 he devoted his research to the atomic nucleus and cosmic rays, while also publishing works with S. A. Altshuler on the magnetic moment of the neutron. In 1937–39 Tamm and I. M. Frank developed the theory of radiation of the electron, which moves through a medium with a velocity exceeding the velocity of light in that medium; this theory led to an understanding of the nature of the radiation discovered by S. I. Vavilov and P. A. Cherenkov, resulting in a Nobel Prize for Tamm (with Frank and Cherenkov) in 1958. During World War II he carried out practical investigations, formulating the Tamm-Dankov method of calculating the interaction of molecules (1945). Of very great importance was the theory of gas discharge in a powerful magnetic field developed in 1950 by Tamm and A. D. Sakharov; it was the basis of all subsequent Soviet research on guided thermonuclear reactions and led to important results. In his last years he searched for ways to remove fundamental difficulties in the theory of elementary particles.

TAMMANN, GUSTAV HEINRICH JOHANN APOLLON (*b. Yamburg [now Kingisepp, R.S.F.S.R.], St. Petersburg gubernia, Russia, 1861; d. Göttingen, Germany, 1938*), physical chemistry.

Tamman belonged to the generation of scientists who created physical chemistry; he was a founder of metallography, and he pioneered the study of solid-state chemical reactions. He began to study chemistry at Dorpat (1879), where he assisted C. Schmidt (1883) and specialized in plant physiology; after defending his master's essay (1885), he worked in Helmholtz's institute at Charlottenburg and with Ostwald at Leipzig, where he became friends with Arrhenius and Nernst. In Dorpat again he taught (1890–1903) and succeeded Schmidt as institute director (1892); when a chair of inorganic chemistry (the second in Germany) and a new institute were established at Göttingen (1903), Tammann was chosen to head the institute; when Nernst went to Berlin, he succeeded to the latter's professorship at Göttingen (1907), thus becoming director of the Institute of Physical Chemistry; he retired in 1930.

Tammann's more than five hundred scientific writings cover a very broad range of subjects. In 1907 he published the results of many experiments on solvents and his theory of internal pressure in homogeneous systems (which has been generally confirmed). In two monographs (1903, 1922) he put forth his theory of heterogeneous equilibria, which was later shown by P. W. Bridgman to be of little practical significance, yet led him to postulate a twofold division of matter into an isotropic phase and an anisotropic phase; his studies of the transition from the isotropic to the anisotropic phase culminated in his *Aggregatzustände* (1922). By 1903 he had perfected the indispensable method of "thermic analysis," which he used to explore the intermetallic compounds; his research in mixed crystals culminated in his frequently cited publication (1919) on the resistance limits of binary systems as a function of the mixing proportion, in which he set forth the so-called $n/8$ law and his theory of "superlattices."

Tammann's extended series of works on metal physics, begun in 1910, have greatly influenced techniques of metal-working; having derived the malleability of metals in the solid state from crystallographic slipping, he saw crystalline rearrangement as the cause of the alterations in the mechanical properties of metals during cold-working, especially the hardening. He summarized his experiments on the phenomenon of allotropy or polymorphism in his *Kristallisieren und Schmelzen* (1903); in 1915 he solved the problem of the flow of glacial ice by showing it to be the result of crystalline slipping. He began to study reactions of solid bodies with other solids and with gaseous substances in 1911; in determining the temperature (later named for him) at which mixtures of crystalline powders sinter, he laid the foundation of solid-state chemistry; his investigation of the tarnish that forms on metallic surfaces was of the greatest importance for the theory of oxidation. Tammann's theoretical work did not always attract the interest of his contemporaries, and since later research has often taken paths that have diverged from those he followed, many problems that he isolated remain unsolved; by having trained more than one hundred doctoral candidates and assistants, he helped to determine the conceptions and methods of an entire generation of chemical physicists and metallurgists.

TANFILEV, GAVRIIL IVANOVICH (*b. Tallinn, Russia, 1857; d. Odessa, U.S.S.R., 1928*), geography, phytogeography, soil science.

Tanfilev graduated from St. Petersburg University (1883) and taught at the universities of St. Petersburg (1895–1903) and Novorossysk (1904–28). His classic work "Main Features of the Vegetation of Russia" (1897) took an historical approach to the formation of vegetation zones in post-Tertiary time; a major five-volume work concerned the physical geography of Russia (1916–31).

TANNERY, JULES (*b. Mantes-sur-Seine, France, 1848; d. Paris, France, 1910*), mathematics.

Tannery was the younger brother of the engineer and historian of science Paul Tannery, who gave him a taste for philosophy and Greek antiquity. He was educated at the École Normale where he defended a thesis in 1874; two years later he became editor of the *Bulletin des sciences mathématiques*, on which he collaborated with Darboux, Hoüel, and Picard until his death; he was assistant director of scientific studies at the École Normale (1884–1910). His *Introduction a la théorie des fonctions d'une variable* (1886) was a great influence on younger generations of mathematicians; his vast culture, nobility of character, and innate sense of a rationally grounded morality are reflected in his *Pensées*, a collection of his thoughts on friendship, the arts, and beauty.

TANNERY, PAUL (*b. Mantes-la-Jolie, Yvelines, France, 1843; d. Pantin, Seine-St. Denis, France, 1904*), history of science, history of mathematics.

An engineer and administrator by profession, Tannery could devote only his leisure hours to scholarship, yet became one of the most influential figures in the rapidly developing study of the history of science at the beginning of the twentieth century. The older brother of Jules Tannery, Paul graduated from the École Polytechnique (1863); as an apprentice engineer he read Comte's *Cours de philosophie positive,* which profoundly influenced his approach to the history of science. In Bordeaux, while supervising construction at the state tobacco factory, he began his historical studies, eventually publishing hundreds of memoirs, articles, notes, and reviews in about fifteen periodicals while pursuing a brilliant career in the state tobacco administration; he subsequently worked at factories in Le Havre (1877–83), Paris (1883–86), Tonneins (Lot-et-Garonne) (1886–88), Bordeaux (1888–90), Paris (1890–93), and Pantin, near Paris (1893–1904). While in Pantin he taught at the Collège de France for several years and would have succeeded to the chair of history of science there, following the death of P. Laffitte (1903), but was unfairly passed over for a less qualified positivist philosopher; the "scandal of 1903" did great damage to the development of the history of science in France.

Tannery's historical works occupy five of the seventeen volumes of the *Mémoires scientifiques* (1912–50), which was compiled by his wife Marie with the aid of several historians of science and includes almost all his works; his principal area of interest was the history of mathematics. In the very productive Paris period (1883–86), he began his two major editorial projects, the two volumes of Diophantus' *Opera omnia* (1893, 1895) and the three volumes of the *Oeuvres de Fermat,* with C. Henry (1891–96). With C. Adam he was co-editor of a new critical edition of the works and correspondence of Descartes (1897–1904); known as the "Adam-Tannery" Descartes, it was a major contribution to the history of ideas, and sparked a renewal of interest in Cartesian philosophy. With C. de Waard, Marie Tannery began work on the edition of the *Correspondance du P. Marin Mersenne* that her husband had hoped to undertake. The most notable characteristic of Tannery's work is an unwavering concern for rigor and precision; he viewed his detailed studies, a large number of which still retain their value, as only a step toward broader syntheses; more important is the fruitful influence of his work on historians of science in the twentieth century.

TARDE, JEAN (*b. La Roque-Gageac, France, 1561 or 1562; d. Sarlat, France, 1636*), astronomy, geography.

After receiving a doctorate in law from the University of Cahors, Tarde continued his studies at the Sorbonne and was ordained a priest; in addition to an explanation of a surveying quadrant equipped with a compass needle (1621), he published a work (*Borbonia sidera,* 1620) based on his conversations with Galileo, whom he visited in Florence (November 1614); he concluded that the newly discovered sunspots, which he discussed with Galileo, were planets.

TARGIONI TOZZETTI, GIOVANNI (*b. Florence, Italy, 1712; d. Florence, 1783*), natural history.

Targioni Tozzetti received his degree in medicine at Pisa (1734); for the rest of his life he practiced medicine in Florence, where, among other things, he promoted prophylactic inoculation against smallpox. He studied with the botanist P. A. Micheli for six years (1731–37) and became director of Florence's botanical garden (1737). In his study of the relations between normal hydrography and landform, he outlined the morphological evolution of certain landscapes for the first time; his *Prodromo*

(1754) outlines a plan for a full description, never completed, of Tuscany. He was one of the precursors of modern human geography and one of the most active Italian naturalists of the eighteenth century.

IBN ṬĀRIQ. *See* **Yaᶜqūb ibn Ṭāriq.**

TARTAGLIA (also **Tartalea** or **Tartaia**), **NICCOLÒ** (*b. Brescia, Italy, 1499 or 1500; d. Venice, Italy, 1557*), mathematics, mechanics, topography, military science.

Niccolò acquired the nickname Tartaglia because of a speech impediment; from a poor family, he was essentially self-educated. In Verona (from *ca.* 1516), he rose to head of a school in the Palazzo Mazzanti; he was "professor of mathematics" in Venice (1534–57), where he died poor and alone. Tartaglia's most important contribution to mathematics was his rediscovery of the solution of third-degree equations (1535), which was published against his will by G. Cardano (1545); this led to an exchange of polemic pamphlets known as the *Cartelli* (1547–48) and a personal debate in Milan (1548) between Tartaglia and L. Ferrari. Of special importance to geometry was Tartaglia's Italian translation, with commentary, of Euclid's *Elements* (1543), the first printed translation of the work into any modern language; he also produced an edition (1543) of William of Moerbeke's Latin version of some of Archimedes' works, and published an Italian translation, with commentary, of part of one of Archimedes' writings (1551). His contributions to the art of warfare and other nonmathematical areas is demonstrated in the *Quesiti* (1546); he was a pioneer in the theory of projectile motion, concluding through an erroneous argument that the trajectory is a curved line everywhere, and that the maximum range is obtained with a firing elevation of 45°. One historian has asserted that Tartaglia was responsible for "the major advances in practical geometry of the first half of the sixteenth century"; among his pupils was G. B. Benedetti.

TASHIRO, SHIRO (in Japanese sources called **Tashiro Shirosuke**) (*b. Kagoshima prefecture, Japan, 1883; d. Cincinnati, Ohio, 1963*), biochemistry.

After immigrating to the U.S. in 1901, Tashiro graduated B.S. from the University of Chicago (1909; Ph.D., 1912), where he taught physiological chemistry (1913–19); he was appointed to the University of Cincinnati College of Medicine as associate professor of biochemistry (1919), where he remained until 1952, except for several years in Japan, where he received the M.D. from Kyoto University (1923). He invented, with H. N. McCoy, the biometer, the first method of analyzing minute quantities of carbon dioxide.

TAUBER, ALFRED (*b. Pressburg, Slovakia [now Bratislava, Czechoslovakia], 1866; d. Theresienstadt, Germany [now Terezin, Czechoslovakia], 1942 [?]*), mathematics.

Tauber obtained his doctorate from the University of Vienna (1888), where he qualified as a *Privatdozent* (1891); he taught there and (from 1899) at the Technical University until 1938, and also headed the mathematics department of the Phönix insurance company of Vienna (1892–1908). His most important work was on function theory and potential theory; his most important memoir was "Ein Satz aus der Theorie der unendlichen Reihen" (1897).

TAURINUS, FRANZ ADOLPH (*b. Bad König, Odenwald, Germany, 1794; d. Cologne, Germany, 1874*), mathematics.

After studying law at Heidelberg, Giessen, and Göttingen, Taurinus lived in Cologne as a man of independent means, pursuing science at his leisure. His mathematical investigations are presented in *Die Theorie der Parallellinien* (1825) and *Geometriae prima elementa* (1826); his work was stimulated by his uncle F. K. Schweikart, who also worked on the problem of parallel lines.

TAYLOR, BROOK (*b. Edmonton, Middlesex, England, 1685; d. London, England, 1731*), mathematics.

Taylor studied at St. John's College, Cambridge (LL.D. 1714), where John Keill was among his teachers; he served as secretary of the Royal Society (1714–18) but resigned because of ill health; after several trips to France for health and social reasons, he began corresponding with P. R. de Montmort. Taylor's most mathematically productive years were 1714–19, when he published his two mathematical books, *Methodus incrementorum directa et inversa* (1715) and *Linear Perspective* (1715). He is best known for the theorem or process for expanding functions into infinite series that commonly bears his name; the method of "Taylor's series," though the subject of a priority dispute, was developed independently by Taylor, who was the first to state it explicitly and in a general form; his first statement of this theorem was in a letter of 26 July 1712 to J. Machin, in which he remarked that this discovery grew out of a conversation in Child's Coffeehouse about the use of "Sir Isaac Newton's series" to solve Kepler's problem, and "Dr. Halley's method of extracting roots" of polynomial equations. His book on linear perspective served as a basis for work by Lambert and for the development of photogrammetry. In his later years, Taylor turned to religious and philosophical writings; his third book, *Contemplatio philosophica*, was published posthumously in 1793.

TAYLOR, CHARLES VINCENT (*b. near Whitesville, Mo., 1885; d. Stanford, Calif., 1946*), biology.

After obtaining his B.A. at Mount Morris College, Illinois, Taylor took the Ph.D. at the University of California in Berkeley (1917), where he worked with C. Kofoid; during the years he taught there (1920–23), he spent some of his summers at the Marine Biological Station at Woods Hole, Massachusetts, where he did microsurgical experiments on the function of motor organelles and of the micronucleus in *Euplotes;* his papers on these topics (1920, 1924) are classics. A member of Stanford University's biology department (from 1925), he later became dean of the School of Biological Sciences (1934); the series of papers that he and his collaborators published (1930–46) on the encystment and excystment of the ciliate *Colpoda duodenaria* has not been superseded or surpassed.

TAYLOR, FRANK BURSLEY (*b. Fort Wayne, Ind., 1860; d. Fort Wayne, 1938*), geology.

Taylor entered Harvard in 1882 and took courses in geology and astronomy until ill health forced him to drop out (1886); for the next several years he was accompanied by a physician on travels through the Great Lakes region, studying its postglacial geological history. He was an assistant in the glacial division of the U.S. Geological Survey (1900–16) under the direction of T. C. Chamberlin and then of Frank Leverett, with assignments in New England and in the Great Lakes area; he was supported by his father's estate for his remaining life. Taylor's work on glacial history, in which he postulated a pattern of glacial retreat and partial readvance, culminated in *The Pleistocene of Indiana and Michigan and the History of the Great Lakes* (1915), which he wrote with Leverett. He also elaborated a theory of the origin of the planetary system (1898) based on the notion that the moon had once been a comet; this same work also contained his first articulation of a theory of continental drift caused by tidal forces resulting from the earth's capture of the moon; his ideas differed from those of A. Wegener, whose theory of continental drift was published in 1912; not only did Taylor require astronomical events to explain earth movements, but he rejected Wegener's use of isostatic adjustment as a mechanism for crustal movements; thus Taylor's theory did not fully anticipate the features of plate tectonics.

TAYLOR, FREDERICK WINSLOW (*b. Germantown [part of Philadelphia], Pa., 1856; d. Philadelphia, 1915*), engineering.

At a steel company in Philadelphia, Taylor rose from laborer to chief engineer in six years; he obtained the M.E. degree by correspondence from Stevens Institute of Technology (1883). With J. M. White he discovered the process, named for them, for the heat treatment of tool steel (1898); also known as "high-speed steel," it doubled the speed of metal-cutting machinery. His best-known achievement was his development of "scientific management," which used time-and-motion studies to calculate the optimum time for any task; it had a profound influence on modern management thought.

TEALL, JETHRO JUSTINIAN HARRIS (*b. Northleach, England, 1849; d. Dulwich, England, 1924*), petrography, geology.

Teall graduated from St. John's College, Cambridge (M.A., 1876), where he attended A. Sedgwick's geology course and was elected to a fellowship (1875–79); from 1872 to 1888 he lectured at various institutions, did research at Cambridge, and published his definitive work, *British Petrography* (1888). In 1888 he joined the Geological Survey of Great Britain (director, 1901–12).

TEICHMANN, LUDWIK KAROL (*b. Lublin, Poland, 1823; d. Cracow, Poland, 1895*), anatomy.

Teichmann studied medicine at Heidelberg and worked under F. G. J. Henle, before following Henle to Göttingen and taking his M.D. (1855). He is best known for the first (1853), and for ten years the only, test for the presence of blood in stains, which was widely used in forensic medicine. Most of his career was spent at Cracow, where he taught anatomy (1861–94); his main scientific interest was in the lymphatic vessels and their origin.

TEILHARD DE CHARDIN, PIERRE (*b. near Orcines, Puy-de-Dôme, France, 1881; d. New York, N.Y., 1955*), paleontology, geology.

After entering the Jesuit order (1898) and studying at Aix-en-Provence and the Isle of Jersey, Teilhard taught science at a Jesuit school in Cairo (1905–08), where his interest in geology began; at the Jesuit house at Hastings, England (1908–12), he studied paleontology as well as theology; ordained a priest, he returned to Paris (1912) and studied with M. Boule at the Museum of Natural History and at the Sorbonne. In 1926 he departed for China in virtual exile after being forbidden to continue teaching geology at the Catholic Institute in Paris, where opposition arose to his evolutionary interpretations of theology. In China Teilhard wrote *Le milieu divin,* in which man is seen as the culmination of the evolutionary impulse; his ideas were strongly influenced by Bergson's *L'évolution créatrice,* by the Bergsonian philosopher E. Le Roy, and by the geologist V. I. Vernadsky. Continuing work on Quaternary and Tertiary mammals, he became scientific advisor (1929) and then acting director (1934) of the Chinese Geological Survey, and demonstrated the earliness of the human cranium of *Sinanthropus,* discovered by Pei Wen-chung (1929); from 1931 to 1938 he produced a series of essays contributing to his synthesis of Asian geology and paleontology. After the war Teilhard returned to Paris, where he vainly tried to publish *Le phénomène humain* (finally printed in 1955); the rest of his life was in a second "exile" in New York (1951–55), where he held a research appointment at the Wenner-Grenn Foundation for Anthropological Research.

The Teilhardian thesis is not a scientific theory but a philosophical world view based on evolutionary themes and expressed in mystical, often poetic, terms; he asserted that the historical development of the cosmos was marked by an increasing degree of complexity in organization and by a corresponding increase in degree of consciousness. Although he is typically interpreted as a neo-Lamarckian exponent of orthogenesis, toward the end of his life his views drew closer to the neo-Darwinian synthesis; his evolutionism helped popularize the theory of evolution among previously hostile groups. Teilhard's teleological interpretation of evolution has been well received by European Marxists, especially in the Soviet Union.

TELESIO, BERNARDINO (*b. Cosenza, Italy, 1509; d. Cosenza, 1588*), natural philosophy.

Telesio was one of the group of sixteenth-century Italian speculators known to scholars as "nature philosophers"; having learned Latin and Greek from his uncle, he went to Padua where he became profoundly dissatisfied with the Aristotelian doctrines presented there. Leaving Padua, he worked on his own system at a Benedictine monastery; he began to write while staying at Naples. While he is considered an arch anti-Aristotelian, his style of thinking is very much like that of Aristotle. His major work was *De rerum natura iuxta propria principia* (1565), but despite its Lucretian title, Telesio was not an atomist; in this work he deployed certain Aristotelian concepts so as to achieve a new system of physical explanation, rejecting metaphysical entities that had no explanatory role in physics. Though he was not an empiricist per se he did base his doctrine on sense, and explained the world in terms of heat, cold, and *materia;* he also anticipated the absolute space and time of Newtonian physics.

TENNANT, SMITHSON (*b. Selby, Yorkshire, England, 1761; d. Boulogne, France, 1815*), chemistry.

Tennant attended Joseph Black's lectures at Edinburgh as a medical student (1781) before moving to Christ's College, Cambridge (M.B., 1788; M.D., 1796); he was appointed professor of chemistry at Cambridge in 1813. His most important work was the discovery of two new elements—iridium and osmium—in platinum ore (1804); he and W. Wollaston became partners in a platinum boiler business.

TENNENT, DAVID HILT (*b. Janesville, Wis., 1873; d. Bryn Mawr, Pa., 1941*), biology.

Tennent received the B.S. (1900) from Olivet College in Michigan and the Ph.D. (1904) from Johns Hopkins University, where he studied under W. K. Brooks; he taught at Bryn Mawr (1904–38). The major part of his work was in marine biology, and consisted principally of experiments on marine eggs. His most important investigations dealt with echinoderm hybridization; he confirmed Boveri and Driesch's conclusions that maternal factors control the earliest phases of echinoderm development while paternal factors are expressed in later development.

TEN RHYNE, WILLEM (*b. Deventer, Netherlands, 1647; d. Batavia, Netherlands Indies [now Djakarta, Indonesia], 1700*), medicine, botany.

After receiving his medical degree at the University of Leiden (1668), where he studied with Sylvius and became an adherent of his iatrochemical school, ten Rhyne traveled to the Cape of Good Hope, Batavia, Japan, and Sumatra as physician to the Dutch East India Company. Governor of the leper colony in Batavia (1677–79), he published a classic work on leprosy in 1687; he also wrote on tea culture, tropical flora, acupuncture, and gout.

TERMIER, PIERRE (*b. Lyons, France, 1859; d. Grenoble, France, 1930*), metamorphic petrology, structural geology, geotectonics.

Termier's grandiose synthesis of the geological structure of the Alps (1903) made him the founder of modern tectonics and geodynamics. He studied in Paris at the École Sainte-Geneviève (1876–78), the École Polytechnique (1878–80), and the École des Mines, where he attended the mineralogy course of E. Mallard. While professor of physics and electricity and later of mineralogy and geology at the École des Mines in Saint-Étienne (1885–94), he began a fruitful cooperation with Marcel-Alexandre Bertrand; Termier's report of 1891 of their explorations of the Haute Vanoise was an epoch-making contribution to Alpine geology. In 1894 he succeeded Mallard as professor of mineralogy and petrology at the École des Mines in Paris; he also was elected director of the Service de la Carte Géologique de la France (1911), and in 1914 was elected inspector general of mines. Termier's field research was directed toward the metamorphic rather than structural history of the areas he studied, and by 1903 he had rejected the widely accepted theory of dynamic metamorphism. His contributions to regional tectonics effected revolutionary changes in the perception of global dynamics; he emerged as the new leader of the French structuralists, who adhered to the concepts of E. Suess. Although he did not accept A. Wegener's notion of continental drift, he insisted that considerable lateral motion of Alpine crustal blocks had occurred; his classic perception of the structure of the Alps underwent much modification, but its basic implication of large-scale plate motion was reaffirmed by E. Argand and others.

TESLA, NIKOLA (*b. Smiljan, Croatia [now Yugoslavia], 1856; d. New York, N.Y., 1943*), physics, electrical engineering.

Tesla studied at the Joanneum, the polytechnical college of Graz, Austria, and at the University of Prague (1879), but left the latter without a degree when his father died; in Budapest, working for a telephone company, he thought of the principle of the rotating magnetic field, the basis of all polyphase induction motors. As an engineer with the Continental Edison Company in Strasbourg he built a crude prototype (1883) of his alternating current motor; in New York (1884), trying to promote his motor, he was employed by Edison for a year before forming his own laboratory. With the backing of G. Westinghouse, Tesla's polyphase system of alternating-current dynamos, transformers, and motors triumphed in the "battle of the currents" against Edison's direct-current system; it made possible the first large-scale harnessing of Niagara Falls and provided the basis for the whole modern electric power industry. He also invented the Tesla coil, an air-core transformer, and in 1893—two years before Marconi's first experiments—Tesla predicted wireless communication. Working in Colorado (1899–1900) he proved the earth to be a conductor and produced giant flashes of artificial lightning 135 feet long. Tesla seldom bothered to patent his inventions and died an impoverished, eccentric recluse.

TESTUT, JEAN LÉO (*b. Saint-Avit Sénieur, Dordogne, France, 1849; d. Cauderán, near Bordeaux, France, 1925*), anatomy, anthropology.

Testut received his M.D. at Paris (1877); he was professor of anatomy at Lyons (1886–1919). His most important work, *Traité d'anatomie humaine* (3 vols., 1889–92), was used throughout the world.

THĀBIT IBN QURRA, AL-ṢĀBIʾ AL-ḤARRĀNĪ (*b. Ḥarrān, Mesopotamia [now Turkey], 836; d. Baghdad, 901*), mathematics, astronomy, mechanics, medicine, philosophy.

Thābit ibn Qurra belonged to the Sabian (Mandaean) sect, descended from the Babylonian star worshippers; his native language was Syriac, but he also knew Greek and Arabic and most of his scientific works were written in the latter. In his youth he was a money changer in Ḥarrān, but was invited to Baghdad by Muḥammad ibn Mūsā ibn Shākir, one of three sons of Mūsā ibn Shākir, who was impressed by his knowledge of languages; there, under the guidance of the brothers, he became a great scholar in mathematics and astronomy. He was also a distinguished physician and leader of a Sabian community in Iraq; during his last years he was in the retinue of the Abbasid Caliph al-Muʿtaḍid (892–902). His son Sinān and his grandsons Ibrāhīm and Thābit were well-known scholars.

Thābit's mathematical writings played an important role in preparing the way for such important discoveries

as the extension of the concept of number to (positive) real numbers, the integral calculus, theorems in spherical trigonometry, analytic geometry, and non-Euclidean geometry. Working in almost all areas of mathematics, he translated many ancient works from the Greek, particularly those of Archimedes, and wrote commentaries on Euclid's *Elements* and Ptolemy's *Almagest*. Thābit wrote many astronomical works and was one of the first reformers of the Ptolemaic system; he wrote two works on the sundial, and others on the uneven apparent motion of the sun, the apparent motion of the moon, and the visibility of the new moon; in another work he explained precession with an "eighth celestial sphere" (that of the fixed stars), and the "trepidation" of the equinoxes with a ninth sphere. In the natural sciences, Thābit wrote two treatises on weights that are devoted to mechanics, and treatises on the saltiness of seawater, the formation of mountains, and on the striking of fire from stones; he also wrote two works on music.

He was one of the best-known physicians of the medieval East and wrote many works on Galen and medicinal treatises, which are almost completely unstudied, including general guides to medicine, works on the circulation of the blood, on embryology, on the cure of various illnesses, and on medicines; he also wrote on the anatomy of birds and on veterinary medicine, and commented on *De plantis* (ascribed to Aristotle). A philosophical treatise by Thābit is comprised of answers to questions posed by a student; another work criticizes the views of Plato and Aristotle on the motionlessness of essence. He also wrote on logic, psychology, ethics, the classification of sciences, the grammar of the Syriac language, politics, and the symbolism of Plato's *Republic*, and is said to have produced many works in Syriac on religion and the customs of the Sabians.

THADDAEUS FLORENTINUS. *See* **Alderotti, Taddeo.**

THALES (*b. Miletus, Ionia, 625 B.C. [?]; d. 547 B.C. [?]*), natural philosophy.

Thales is considered by Aristotle to be the founder of Ionian natural philosophy. Even in antiquity there was considerable doubt concerning Thales' written works; some authorities declare that he left no book behind; others credit him with a work on navigation, but this is doubtful. Much evidence of practical activities associated with Thales has survived, testifying to his versatility as statesman, tycoon, engineer, mathematician, and astronomer; in the century after his death he became an epitome of practical ingenuity. He achieved his fame as a scientist for having predicted an eclipse of the sun, which occurred on 28 May 585 B.C. While it has been believed that Thales used the so-called "Babylonian saros," a cycle of 223 lunar months, to perform this feat, Neugebauer has demonstrated that the "saros" was an invention of the English astronomer E. Halley in a weak moment; while it could be assumed that Thales simply made an extremely lucky guess, a more likely explanation is that he happened to be the *savant* around at the time and it was assumed he *must* have been able to predict it (as Anaxagoras was said to have predicted the fall of a huge meteorite in 468–467 B.C.). Claims by the Greeks that they derived their mathematics from Egypt through

Thales are unlikely. Our knowledge of Thales' cosmology is virtually dependent on two passages in Aristotle, who says that Thales considered water to be the material constituent of things, and on Seneca, who adds that Thales used the idea of the earth as floating on water to explain earthquakes. Although he was influenced by mythological precedents, his use of a simple, natural explanation for earthquakes, instead of the supernatural agencies invoked by Homer and Hesiod, makes him the first philosopher; the search for natural explanations and a unifying hypothesis paved the way for science.

THAN, KÁROLY (*b. Óbecse, Hungary [now Bečej, Yugoslavia], 1834; d. Budapest, Hungary, 1908*), chemistry.

After taking the doctorate in pharmacy at the University of Vienna (1858), Than studied with Bunsen in Heidelberg and with Wurtz in Paris; from 1860 he was professor of chemistry at the University of Budapest. His research embraced many fields of chemistry; he discovered carbonyl sulfide (1867) and defined the concept of the molecular volume of a gas (1887).

THAXTER, ROLAND (*b. Newtonville [part of Newton], Mass., 1858; d. Cambridge, Mass., 1932*), cryptogamic botany.

After graduating from Harvard (A.B., 1882; A.M. and Ph.D., 1888) in natural history, Thaxter taught cryptogamic botany there (from 1891). His chief research was on the entomogenous fungi; his work has had a profound and lasting influence on the development of mycology and of cryptogamic botany generally.

THAYER, WILLIAM SYDNEY (*b. Milton, Mass., 1864; d. Washington, D.C., 1932*), medicine.

Thayer received his B.A. from Harvard University (1885) and his M.D. from Harvard Medical School (1889); after continuing his studies in the principal pathological laboratories of Berlin and Vienna, he became resident physician at Johns Hopkins Hospital (1890), where he spent his entire medical career except for wartime service; he rose to professor of clinical medicine (1905) and professor of medicine and physician-in-chief (1919). He studied a number of diseases and the blood cell's response to them, and published two important works on malarial fevers (1895, 1897); he also wrote a number of important papers on cardiology. Thayer was known as a clinician's clinician and was widely sought out for difficult diagnoses; he influenced many students.

THEAETETUS (*b. Athens, ca. 417 B.C.; d. Athens, 369 B.C.*), mathematics.

Theaetetus studied under Theodorus of Cyrene and at the Academy with Plato; at some time he taught in Heraclea, and he may have been the teacher of Heraclides Ponticus; Plato regarded Theaetetus with a respect and admiration second only to that he felt for Socrates, and he made him a principal character in the *Theaetetus* and the *Sophist*. The former dialogue is the chief source of knowledge of Theaetetus' life, and mentions that Theaetetus died while fighting in the Athenian army against Corinth. Although no writing of his has survived, Theaetetus had a major influence in the development of Greek mathematics; he made important contributions in three fields. First, he laid the foundation of the elaborate clas-

sification of irrationals, which is found in a commentary on Euclid's tenth book of the *Elements;* and in particular he discovered, and presumably named, the medial, binomial, and apotome. While one scholar has asserted that the entire tenth book of the *Elements* is the work of Theaetetus, it is likely that only part of it is due to him. Secondly, Theaetetus was probably the first to give a theoretical construction for all the five regular solids and to show how to inscribe them in a sphere; such a theoretical construction is found in Euclid, *Elements* XIII, and Theaetetus must be regarded as the main source of the book. Theaetetus' third contribution was his probable development of a general theory of proportion—applicable to incommensurable and to commensurable magnitudes—before the theory was developed by Eudoxus and set out in book V of Euclid's *Elements*. Although in Plato's dialogue named after him, Theaetetus was given the rare Greek compliment of being "a thorough gentleman," it was the beauty of his mind rather than of his body that impressed his compatriots, for, like Socrates, he had a snub nose and protruding eyes.

THEGE, MIKLÓS VON KONKOLY. *See* **Konkoly Thege, Miklós von.**

THEMISTIUS (*b. Paphlagonia, A.D. 317 [?]; d. Constantinople, ca. 388*), philosophy, politics.

Themistius attended his father's philosophy lectures, probably at Constantinople, and began teaching philosophy in 345, influencing many students. His chief interest was in ethics and, like his father, he adhered mainly to Aristotle without neglecting Plato; his paraphrases of, and commentaries on, Aristotle's texts were frequently used and quoted by medieval Arabic philosophers; he also wrote some philosophical treatises, but made no effort to be original; he began a long political career as a senator (355), and thirty-one of his speeches are completely preserved. Some of his ideas are still vital, including his doctrine of toleration and universal philanthropy.

THENARD, LOUIS JACQUES (*b. La Louptière [now Louptière-Thenard], Aube, France, 1777; d. Paris, France, 1857*), chemistry.

With the intention of becoming a pharmacist, Thenard went to Paris to study; he attended the public courses of Vauquelin and Fourcroy and was taken into the Vauquelin household as a bottle washer and scullery boy. Vauquelin eventually allowed him to deputize for him in his lecture course and Thenard succeeded to his chair at the Collège de France in 1804. With the founding of the faculties of sciences (1808), he was appointed professor of chemistry at the Paris Faculty; he was elected to the chemistry section of the First Class of the Institute (1810). From 1845 to 1852 he was chancellor of the University of France—the highest post in the French educational system. Thenard's early work in plant and animal chemistry was influenced by Vauquelin and Fourcroy; he obtained a new acid in 1801 which he called sebacic acid, but his most important organic work was on the esters, then called "ethers"; his quantitative study of "acetic ether" (ethyl acetate) is a model for its time; in his early study of nickel (1802), he announced the discovery of a new, higher oxide of nickel; nevertheless, his study of cobalt compounds (1804), in which he described a new blue pigment which became known as "Thenard's Blue," brought him greater fame. Much of his research was concerned with the combining proportions of elements in certain compounds, particularly metal oxides; he soon acquired a reputation as an analyst and collaborated on several important studies with Biot. A considerable amount of research was done with Gay-Lussac in 1808–1811; in 1808 they announced they had prepared potassium by purely chemical means and, later that year, announced the isolation of a new element, boron. They also made pioneering contributions to photochemistry and did important work on the combustion analysis of vegetable and animal substances (1810). Other work by Thenard includes a memoir (1803) on alcoholic fermentation which was the basis for much of Leibig's work; Thenard's greatest single discovery was that of hydrogen peroxide, which he announced in 1818 (his complete work on hydrogen peroxide was summarized in an 1820 article); he also collaborated with Dulong in making significant contributions to knowledge of surface catalysis. Thenard authored an important chemistry textbook, *Traité de chimie élémentaire,* which went through six editions from 1813 to 1836; this book helped restore France to its traditional role as supplier of chemistry textbooks to the rest of the world.

THEODORIC BORGOGNONI OF LUCCA. *See* **Borgognoni of Lucca, Theodoric.**

THEODORIC OF FREIBERG. *See* **Dietrich von Freiberg.**

THEODORUS OF CYRENE (*b. Cyrene, North Africa, ca. 465* B.C.; *d. Cyrene* [?], *after 399* B.C.), mathematics.

Theodorus was the mathematical tutor of Plato and Theaetetus and is known for his contribution to the early development of the theory of irrational quantities. Iamblichus includes him in his catalog of Pythagoreans; he is made a character by Plato in the *Theaetetus,* the *Sophist,* and the *Politicus.* According to the *Theaetetus* he had been a disciple of Protagoras but had turned at an early age from abstract speculation to geometry; in the dialogue, Theaetetus relates how Theodorus demonstrated to him that the square roots of 3, 5, and so on up to 17 (excluding 9 and 16, it being understood) are incommensurable with the unit. Thus it appears that Theodorus was the first to demonstrate the irrationality of these numbers; the reason why he started at $\sqrt{3}$ is that the irrationality of $\sqrt{2}$ was already known to the earlier Pythagoreans; this discovery led Theodorus and others to look for further examples of irrationality, and made necessary a recasting of Greek mathematical theory. As to why Theodorus stopped with $\sqrt{17}$, where he evidently ran into difficulties, one suggestion by H. G. Zeuthen is that Theodorus used the process of finding the greatest common measure of two magnitudes as set out in Euclid's *Elements,* X.2, and actually made a test of incommensurability by Euclid, a process which is periodic and will never end for $\sqrt{17}$. However, Wilbur Richard Knorr has more recently asserted that Theodorus stopped with $\sqrt{17}$ because his proofs were based on a method using "Pythagorean triples" of numbers that may be set out as the sides of a right triangle, which encounters difficulties with $\sqrt{17}$.

THEODOSIUS OF BITHYNIA (*b. Bithynia, second half of the second century* B.C.), mathematics, astronomy.

Theodosius was the author of *Sphaerics,* a textbook on the geometry of the sphere, and minor astronomical and astrological works; he was probably a younger contemporary of Hipparchus, also a Bithynian, and he may have survived into the first century B.C.. Much of Theodosius' *Sphaerics* is probably derived from some pre-Euclidean textbook, of which some have conjectured that Eudoxus was the author. Two other surviving works attributed to Theodosius are *On Habitations,* which treats the phenomena caused by the rotation of the earth, and *On Days and Nights,* which studies the arc of the ecliptic traversed by the sun each day. These three works were included in the collection Pappus called "The Little Astronomy" and were translated into Arabic in the ninth century; Vitruvius claims Theodosius invented a sundial suitable for any region but nothing is known about it.

THEON OF ALEXANDRIA (*fl. Alexandria, second half of fourth century*), mathematics, astronomy.

According to one ancient source, Theon lived under the emperor Theodosius I (reigned 379–395); he was certainly a pagan, as was his daughter Hypatia, a famous mathematician in her own right who, as a Neoplatonic philosopher, was torn to pieces by a mob of fanatic Christians at Alexandria in 415. He also was said to be a member of the "Museum" at Alexandria, an institution for advanced learning established about 300 B.C., but which by Theon's time had declined (Theon is the last attested member). Whether he was connected with the Museum or not, he was actively engaged in higher education, and all of his extant works, being either commentaries on or editions of classics of mathematics and astronomy, were intended for the use of students. Theon's most extensive work is his commentary on Ptolemy's *Almagest,* which is merely exegetic and never critical. He also published two commentaries on the *Handy Tables* of Ptolemy, claiming to be the first to do so. All other extant works by Theon are editions of previous authors or, rather, a reworking of the original in a form more suitable for students; the most notable one is his edition of Euclid's *Elements,* which was so influential that it consigned the original text to near oblivion; though it did not improve on the original, it may have been easier for his students to use. Theon also produced editions of Euclid's *Data* and *Optics,* and he may have produced a version of Euclid's *Catoptrics.* Among lost works attributed to Theon is a "Treatise on the Small Astrolabe," evidently meaning the planispheric astrolabe as opposed to the "armillary sphere"; no work on the astrolabe predating the sixth century survives, but it is most unlikely that Theon invented the astrolabe, which may well predate Ptolemy. Theon was a competent mathematician, but completely unoriginal, typifying the scholastic of later antiquity who was content to expound classics in his field without attempting to go beyond them; for a man of such mediocrity, however, Theon was uncommonly influential, especially with his version of Euclid's *Elements.* His edition of the *Handy Tables* passed to Islamic astronomers and thence (via al-Battānī's work and the Toledan Tables) to Latin Europe in the twelfth century; the work on the astrolabe was probably the main, if not the sole, source of transmission of the theory of that instrument to Islamic astronomy, whence it came to medieval Europe.

THEON OF SMYRNA (*fl. early second century* A.D.), mathematics, astronomy.

Theon is known chiefly for his handbook, usually called *Expositio rerum mathematicarum ad legendum Platonem utilium;* it is valuable for its wide range of citation from earlier sources; it shows little originality and is mainly a handbook for philosophy students, written to illustrate how arithmetic, geometry, stereometry, music, and astronomy are interrelated. The arithmetic section treats the types of numbers in the Pythagorean manner, and the music section sometimes descends into number mysticism. The astronomical section, which depends much on Adrastus, is of great merit, particularly the brief fragment from Eudemus on pre-Socratic astronomy; other works by Theon are lost, including a commentary on Plato's *Republic.*

THEOPHILUS (Theophilus Presbyter, also called **Rugerus)** (*fl. Helmarshausen, Germany* [*?*], *early twelfth century*), metallurgy, chemistry.

Theophilus is the pseudonymous author of *De diversis artibus,* an instructive treatise on practical arts for the adornment of the church, perhaps written in 1122–23 in answer to Bernard of Clairvaux's animadversions on ecclesiastical luxury. Theophilus wrote it with the Benedictine monk Roger, who was active as a goldsmith in Helmarshausen around 1100; the three parts of the work discuss the art of the painter, the art of the worker in glass, and the art of the metalworker. The latter two sections constitute the earliest firsthand accounts of many pyrotechnological processes that later bore fruit in chemical science and engineering, as well as in the entire modern materials industry. There is little quantitative measurement and no philosophical speculation on the nature of materials, but Theophilus reflects the practical bent of prescientific technology. He did not invent or discover any of the processes he records, some of which had existed for centuries without being written down.

THEOPHRASTUS (*b. Eresus, Lesbos, ca. 371* B.C.; *d. Athens, ca. 287* B.C.), botany, mineralogy, philosophy.

Theophrastus was associated with Aristotle for more than two decades and succeeded him (322) as head of the Peripatetic school at the Lyceum; during his tenure of thirty-five years he had two thousand students, among them the physician Erasistratus; so well was he regarded by the Athenians that an attempt to prosecute him for impiety failed. The Hellenistic lists of Theophrastus' writings contain over two hundred titles covering science, philosophy, history, law, literature, music, poetics, and politics; there survive only two longer works on botany, a few short treatises on science, an essay on metaphysics, the *Characters,* and fragmentary excerpts and paraphrases in the works of later writers; he has generally been considered a botanist who was heavily dependent on Aristotle, but these are unwarranted assumptions based on meager and unbalanced evidence. The general trend of Theophrastus' thought is seen in the *Metaphysics,* in which he does not deviate from Aristotle's assumptions, but points out difficulties in their application; while offering no new answers, he suggests an approach using

different kinds of knowledge and different methods appropriate to different types of objects. In *De igne* he takes issue with Aristotle's theory of four qualitatively distinguished simple bodies, demonstrating that the fire of our experience is different from elemental fire and that the various phenomena associated with it do not have a single explanation. Theophrastus' *De lapidibus,* a systematic discussion of stones and mineral earths, is the first methodical study of mineralogy and the only one before Agricola's in the sixteenth century that considers mineral substances for themselves rather than for their curative or magical properties; his reliance on reports of others lead him to include fantastic reports, such as stones formed by the urine of the lynx. His works on botany correspond to Aristotle's works on animals; *Historia plantarum* is concerned with description, classification, and analysis, and *De causis plantarum* with etiology; although he follows Aristotle in his typological procedure and physiological theory, he adopts a different perspective in which he concentrates on the plants themselves and avoids systematization beyond his immediate subject; as in the *Metaphysics,* he insists on a method appropriate to plants because of their differences from other objects; by assembling his data impartially, classifying and discussing them within an elastic system, and withholding judgement (even regarding nonsensical tales) when it was not secured by facts, Theophrastus created what he called an appropriate method and laid the groundwork for modern botany. Theophrastus was also influential as a historian and critic of science, and wrote a general history known as the *Physicorum opiniones,* a compilation of Aristotle's accounts of earlier theories, supplemented by quotations, biographical data, and other information. It provided many of the details of pre-Aristotelian theories later compiled in the summaries of the doxographers.

THEUDIUS OF MAGNESIA (*fl. fourth century* B.C.), mathematics.

An early member of the Academy, Theudius is known only from a passage in Proclus' commentary on Euclid's *Elements.* He was a contemporary of Aristotle, and some of the propositions in elementary geometry that are quoted by Aristotle were probably taken from Theudius' *Elements.*

THÉVENOT, MELCHISÉDECH (*b. Paris, France, ca. 1620; d. Issy* [*now Issy-les-Moulineaux*], *France, 1692*), scientific correspondence and translation, natural philosophy.

Thévenot was one of the important correspondents linking Paris to the rest of the European scientific world; he influenced the organization and founding of the French Academy of Sciences and was an intimate of C. Huygens, H. Oldenburg, A. Auzout, and other personages. Not much is known about his personal life; after his formal education he traveled about Europe; he knew a number of foreign languages and was a bibliophile and man of letters. From about 1658 Thévenot attended the philosophical discussions at the house of H. L. H. de Montmor in Paris known as the "Montmor Academy"; partly because of squabbles among the participants, which included Auzout, P. Petit, I. Boulliau, B. F. de Bessy, J. Rohault, and G. Desargues, Thévenot held additional meetings at his country house at Issy after about 1662, where he supported Frenicle de Bessy and N.

Stensen. After the demise of the Montmor Academy (1664), Thévenot became involved in a plan for a new utilitarian academy of scientists; the Academy of Sciences was formed in 1666, but was influenced more by C. Perrault's design for a less practical and more philosophical academy than by Thévenot's. Thévenot did not become a member until 1685, perhaps because he was an amateur. His only notable direct contribution to science was a bubble level (1681), later improved by R. Hooke and Huygens; he was also known for his celebrated translation and publication of voyages of discovery, *Relations de divers voyages . . .* (1663–72).

THIELE, F. K. JOHANNES (*b. Ratibor, Upper Silesia, Germany [now Raciborz, Poland], 1865; d. Strasbourg, Germany [now France], 1918*), chemistry.

Thiele obtained his doctorate at the University of Halle (1890); he taught at Munich (1893–1902) and at Strasbourg (from 1902), and in 1910 he became editor of *Justus Liebig's Annalen der Chemie.* His most important research dealt with conjugated unsaturated organic molecules, which stimulated extensive research and was a direct precursor of electronic theories of organic reaction mechanisms. Thiele's extensive research on nitrogen chemistry led to the discovery of numerous new compounds and new synthetic processes.

THIELE, THORVALD NICOLAI (*b. Copenhagen, Denmark, 1838; d. Copenhagen, 1910*), astronomy, mathematics, actuarial mathematics.

Thiele took his doctorate at the University of Copenhagen (1866), where he was professor of astronomy and director of the university laboratory (1875–1906). He developed a new method of orbit determination, now known as the Thiele-Innes method, and was a pioneer in the numerical search for solutions to the three-body problem, developing the Thiele (or Thiele-Burrau) transformation for this purpose. He also managed a life insurance company for nearly forty years.

THIERRY OF CHARTRES, also known as **Magister Theodoricus Carnotensis** (*b. Brittany, France, last quarter of the eleventh century; d. ca. 1155*), philosophy, theology.

Thierry is believed to have taught at the cathedral school of Chartres as early as 1121; he also taught in Paris during the 1130's. Although his fame was based on his courses on the trivium (grammar, logic, rhetoric), he is believed to have taught mathematics successfully, and is considered to have introduced the use of the *rota* or zero into European mathematics. Today Thierry is best known for his short commentary on the introductory chapters of Genesis, the *Tractatus de sex dierum operibus,* part of which explains the unfolding of the universe on the basis of physical laws.

THIRY, PAUL HENRI. *See* **Holbach, Paul Henri Thiry, Baron d'.**

THISELTON-DYER, WILLIAM TURNER (*b. Westminster, England, 1843; d. Witcombe, Gloucestershire, England, 1928*), botany.

After Thiselton-Dyer took his B.A. at Christ Church, Oxford (1865), where he read mathematics under H.J.S. Smith and chemistry under B. C. Brodie, he studied natu-ral history there under G. Rolleston. He obtained his B.S. from the University of London (1870), and then taught botany at the Royal Horticultural Society at South Kensington (1872–76), where he acted as botanical demonstrator in T. H. Huxley's famous and influential course in biology for government school teachers. There he helped extend to botanical circles Huxley's emphasis on evolutionary principles and pioneering efforts in laboratory teaching. As assistant director (1875–85) and then director (1885–1905) of the Royal Botanic Gardens at Kew, he engineered and oversaw the immense expansion of economic botany throughout the British Empire; although he made no important contribution to scientific knowledge, he played a central role in the botanical life of late Victorian England; as director of the Jodrell Laboratory at Kew (from 1876), he supervised the work of the new school of British botany, including F. O. Bower and D. H. Scott.

THÖLDE, JOHANN. *See* **Valentine, Basil.**

THOLLON, LOUIS (*b. Ambronay, Ain, France, 1829; d. Nice, France, 1887*), solar physics.

Thollon's scientific career began at the Nice observatory (1878), where he designed a high dispersion light spectroscope. In 1879 he carried out a classic experiment in which he demonstrated the Doppler-Fizeau effect in a concrete manner; he published in 1890 the last and most important chart of the solar spectrum based on data from a spectroscope (spectrographic data was used henceforth).

THOMAS OF CANTIMPRÉ, also known as **Thomas Brabantinus (Brabançon)** (*b. Leeuw-Saint Pierre, Brabant, Belgium, ca. 1186–1210; d. Louvain, between 1276 and 1294*), theology, natural history, encyclopedism.

Thomas entered the Dominican Order in Louvain (1232) and was educated in the schools of Liège, Cologne, and Paris (Collège St. Jacques). While primarily a theologian who composed biographies of ecclesiastics and saints, he also wrote on natural and pseudo science; his major work on natural phenomena, *De naturis rerum,* completed between 1228 and 1244, was avowedly intended to provide materials for use in sermons and arguments to bolster faith, yet reveals a lively interest in the real and natural world. Its twenty books deal with man, animals, the vegetable kingdom, bodies of water, meteorology, astronomy, and astrology. This work reveals many current beliefs about natural phenomena, including astrology and the occult and an undue reliance on the credibility of his authorities; it also helped disseminate knowledge of significant technological developments such as the mariner's compass.

THOMAS, HUGH HAMSHAW (*b. Wrexham, Denbighshire, Wales, 1885; d. Cambridge, England, 1962*), paleobotany.

Thomas graduated from Downing College, Cambridge (1908), where he was influenced by the botanist A. C. Seward; afterwards, he continued his research in Cambridge with E. A. N. Arber. He was curator of the Botany School Museum (1909–23) and was elected a fellow of Downing College (1914). His scientific work was important because of the comprehensiveness of his collecting and fieldwork, his techniques of interpretation, and his detailed work on the systematics of fossil plant groups.

THOMAS, SIDNEY GILCHRIST (b. London, England, 1850; d. Paris, France, 1885), metallurgy.

When his father died, Thomas was forced to abandon his plans to study medicine and became a clerk at the Thames police court in Stepney (1868–79). While a clerk, he pursued his interests in metallurgy and applied chemistry in courses at the Royal School of Mines and the Birkbeck Literary and Scientific Institution (now Birkbeck College). With the help of his cousin, P. C. Gilchrist, he developed the basic process for dephosphorizing pig iron in the making of wrought iron and steel (their first commercial success was in 1879). As a result of his work, vast deposits of phosphoric iron ores that were previously unsuitable could be converted into steel by either the Bessemer or open-hearth methods. By the early twentieth century most steel was being made by the basic, or Thomas-Gilchrist, process.

THOMAZ, ALVARO (also known as **Alvaro Tómas** or **Alvarus Thomas**) (b. Lisbon, second half of the fifteenth century; place and date of death unknown), physics, mathematics.

Thomaz is mentioned in the archives of the University of Paris as a master of arts at that college in 1513; his principal work is "Book on the Three [Kinds of] Movement, With Ratios Added . . ." (Paris, 1509), a guide to the thought of R. Swineshead. It helped make available the teachings of fourteenth-century English calculators and Parisian terminists to a wide audience of European scholars in the sixteenth century, and revived Parisian interest in the Mertonian approach to mathematical physics.

THOMPSON, BENJAMIN (COUNT RUMFORD) (b. Woburn, Mass., 1753; d. Auteuil, France, 1814), physics.

An active Tory in the early part of the American Revolution, Thompson fled to London, where he became undersecretary of state for the colonies. After a brief career in the British army, he retired as colonel at age thirty-one. At the Bavarian court, he rose to head of the Bavarian army, and was made a count by the Bavarian duke (1793). After 1800 he settled briefly in Paris, where he made an unsuccessful marriage to the widow of A. Lavoisier, after which he retired to Auteuil, near Paris, to write and work on science and technology; he established the Royal Institution of Great Britain in London as a museum of technology primarily for the education of artisans and the poor. Throughout his life, Thompson studied the force of gunpowder, and it was his investigations of cannon that led him to accept the vibratory theory of heat, which he actively championed. He carried out many experiments to demonstrate the falseness of the caloric (fluid) theory of heat, the most famous being his demonstration of the heat generated by boring cannon with a dull drill. As military commander in Bavaria, Thompson showed a genius for technological improvement, and many of his innovations are still used. He made improvements in the heat insulating properties of clothes and experimented with many cheap foods for mass feeding, introducing the potato into Central Europe. He designed a kitchen range and championed the use of the pressure cooker. In his studies of the efficiency of illumination, he invented the shadow photometer that bears his name and designed the so-called Rumford oil lamp; he also introduced the concept of a standard candle, which became the international unit of luminosity until the twentieth century. He studied air currents in open fireplaces in the attempt to eliminate smoky fireplaces, and introduced the smoke shelf, the throat, and the damper used in modern chimneys; he demonstrated at the same time as did J. Leslie that mat surfaces radiate heat better than shiny ones.

THOMPSON, D'ARCY WENTWORTH (b. Edinburgh, Scotland, 1860; d. St. Andrews, Scotland, 1948), natural history, classics, mathematics, oceanography.

Thompson was educated at the University of Edinburgh (1877–80), where he studied anatomy under W. Turner and chemistry under A. C. Brown, and at Trinity College, Cambridge (1880–83), where he read zoology under F. M. Balfour and physiology under M. Foster. He taught at University College, Dundee (1884–1917) and at St. Andrews (from 1917). His most important contribution is *On Growth and Form* (1917), which made a revolutionary departure from contemporary zoology by treating morphological problems by mathematics, and influenced research in embryology, taxonomy, paleontology, and ecology. Thompson was equally a scholar, scientist, naturalist, classicist, mathematician, and philosopher.

THOMPSON, JOHN VAUGHAN (b. Berwick-upon-Tweed, England [?], 1779; d. Sydney, New South Wales, Australia, 1847), natural history.

After studying medicine and surgery in northern England, Thompson became a British army surgeon (1799), eventually rising to be deputy inspector general of hospitals (1830). He was posted as medical officer to the convict settlements in New South Wales (1835–44); in his army service he traveled to Gibraltar, Guiana, the West Indies, France, the Netherlands, and the Mascarene Islands. He was stationed at Cork in Ireland (1816–35), where he undertook much of his research on marine invertebrates. Thompson's biological writings fall into three categories. His earliest writings are on botany and he also wrote general works on zoology, but his most important work was on marine invertebrates. He successfully exploited the plankton or tow net, which he was one of the first persons to use (1816), in making observations of living animals. One of his principal contributions, reported in the first memoir of his *Zoological Researches* (1828–34), was the discovery that certain planktonic forms of crustacean undergo metamorphoses until recognizable as the young of the European edible crab; an acrimonious conflict resulted with the zoological establishment in London until his findings were confirmed. His second important achievement in marine biology was his discovery that cirripeds are Crustacea, described in the fourth memoir of *Zoological Researches;* his third major achievement in marine biology was the recognition of the class of animals he named Polyzoa (now named Bryozoa).

THOMPSON, SILVANUS PHILLIPS (b. York, England, 1851; d. London, England, 1916), applied physics, electrical engineering, history of science and technology.

After sitting for the external B.A. at the University of London (1869), Thompson continued his scientific studies and earned the B.Sc. (1875) and D.Sc. (1878); while still a graduate student he narrowly missed demonstrating Maxwell's theory of electromagnetic propagation, which Hertz accomplished in 1887–1888. He taught physics at University College, Bristol (1876–85) before he became principal of Finsbury Technical College in London (1885–1916); he was a popular and prolific lecturer and author of textbooks on electricity that made him famous; his biographies of Gilbert, Faraday, and Kelvin are considered excellent of their sort.

THOMSEN, CHRISTIAN JÜRGENSEN (*b. Copenhagen, Denmark, 1788; d. Copenhagen, 1865*), archaeology.

Privately educated, Thomsen ran the family shipping business until his mother died in 1840. He began a second career in museum administration in 1816 as secretary of the Danish Commission for the Preservation of Antiquities and director of their museum. His use (1820) of a new chronology for prehistoric artifacts—dividing them into the Stone, Iron, and Bronze Ages—became widely accepted. He established the first ethnographical museum (1841), organizing its exhibits in terms of his "principle of progressive culture"; in 1849 he became director of a complex of museums of art, archaeology, and history in Copenhagen. Thomsen was one of the first to use museums as a tool for popular education, and was one of the first to open his collections to the public free of charge.

THOMSEN, HANS PETER JÖRGEN JULIUS (*b. Copenhagen, Denmark, 1826; d. Copenhagen, 1909*), chemistry.

Thomsen obtained his M.Sc. degree in applied natural sciences at Polytekniske Laereanstalt (1846), where he was assistant in the chemical laboratory (1847–53) and instructor in agricultural chemistry (1850–56); he took a study tour to France and Germany in 1853–54). He taught chemistry at the University of Copenhagen (1864–1901), while also teaching at the Polytekniske Laereanstalt. Thomsen's first chemical work was elaboration of a method for the fabrication of soda from cryolite, on which he obtained a monopoly and opened several factories (from 1859). His main studies were in thermochemistry, and are collected in his *Thermochemische Untersuchungen* (1882–86). His fundamental thought was that the evolution of heat accompanying a chemical reaction is an exact expression of the chemical affinity of the reaction, a theory also advanced a short time later by Berthelot, who disputed Thomsen's priority. Thomsen later publicly admitted that his theory was only an approximation, while Berthelot upheld it for many years, despite the facts.

THOMSON, SIR CHARLES WYVILLE (*b. Bonsyde, Linlithgow, Scotland, 1830; d. Bonsyde, 1882*), natural history, oceanography.

Thomson studied medicine at the University of Edinburgh for three years before he was forced to give up because of ill health; even so, he became a lecturer in botany at the University of Aberdeen (1851–53), professor of natural history at Queen's College, Cork (1853–54), professor at Queen's College, Belfast (1854–68), professor of botany at the Royal College of Science, Dublin (1868–70), and regius professor of natural history at the University of Edinburgh (from 1870). His interest in whether life existed at great depths in the sea led him to

participate in several deep-sea dredging voyages. His cruises on the H. M. S. *Lightning* (1868) and H. M. S. *Porcupine* (1869) led to his disputing the accepted theory of a constant submarine temperature of 4° C and cast doubts upon Forbes's azoic theory. His studies culminated with the voyage of H. M. S. *Challenger* (1872–76), which discovered marine life at depths near three thousand fathoms; the *Challenger Reports*, for which he established the format, were published after his death (1880–95).

THOMSON, ELIHU (*b. Manchester, England, 1853; d. Swampscott, Mass., 1937*), electrical engineering.

Thomson taught at the high school in Philadelphia from which he had graduated, and collaborated in experiments with E. J. Houston; together they he started the Thomson-Houston Co., a predecessor of the General Electric Co., with which Thomson remained associated throughout his career. Thomson's inventions made possible significant improvements in alternating-current motors and transformers; he invented electric resistance welding, and received more than seven hundred patents. He was acting president of the Massachusetts Institute of Technology from 1921 to 1923.

THOMSON, JOSEPH JOHN (*b. Cheetham Hill, near Manchester, England, 1856; d. Cambridge, England, 1940*), physics.

After receiving an engineering degree at Owens College, where he studied under O. Reynolds, H. Roscoe, and B. Stewart, Thomson went to Trinity College, Cambridge, where he spent the rest of his life; coached by E. J. Routh, he emerged second from the mathematical tripos (1880), and was awarded a fellowship at Trinity in 1881.

Thomson followed Maxwell's practice of developing theories with two approaches: by using mechanical models or analogies, and the phenomenological approach of deducing basic equations from the most general dynamical relationships. Thomson's use of models is seen in his *Treatise* (1883), which won the Adams Prize of 1882, on the interaction of two closed vortices in a perfect incompressible fluid; he extended this work to include a study of Kelvin's theory of the vortex atom, in which the atoms of a gas are likened to smoke rings in air, and unsuccessfully attempted to apply it to the problem of chemical constitution; his work was guided by the experiments of A. M. Mayer as interpreted by Kelvin. A second line in Thomson's early researches followed Maxwell's phenomenological procedure; he developed the idea that the potential energy of a given system might be replaced by the kinetic energy of imaginary masses connected to it in an appropriate way. This work is described in *Applications of Dynamics* (1888), in which he developed the important notion that electricity flows in much the same way in metals as in electrolytes. The third of Thomson's early research lines was the mathematical development of Maxwell's electrodynamics; his results (1881) included the discovery of the so-called electromagnetic mass, or extra inertia, and the calculation (in error by a factor of two) of what is now known as the Lorentz force; these results sparked the rapid harvest of Maxwellian fruits by Fitzgerald, Heaviside, Lamb, Poynting, and Thomson himself.

In 1884 Thomson succeeded Lord Rayleigh as Cavendish Professor of Experimental Physics, and began studying the discharge of electricity in gases; guided by his theory of the vortex atom, he introduced the important idea that the gas discharge proceeds in analogy to electrolysis, by the disruption of chemical bonds. In the early 1890's, Thomson's attention was turned to cathode rays, which became a source of controversy between English physicists, who believed them to be streams of charged particles, and German physicists, who considered them an "aether disturbance"; about the same time, Roentgen discovered X rays, which Thomson and his assistants proceeded to exploit as a more convenient means for producing gaseous ions than disruptive discharge; the result was the famous *Conduction of Electricity Through Gases* (1903). Influenced by P. Lenard's work on Hertz's discovery that rays could be passed through metal foil impermeable to particles of gas-theoretical dimensions, Thomson began to think that the cathode rays consisted of bodies smaller than atoms; he then used Schuster's technique of magnetic bending to calculate the ratio of electric charge to mass of the "corpuscles," from which he inferred that they have very small size and mass and are constituents of all chemical atoms. In other words, Thomson had discovered what was later called the electron (1897); at least two other physicists, E. Wiechert and W. Kaufmann, possessed almost all the relevant data but failed to realize its significance; Thomson proceeded to erroneously assert that atoms were composed entirely of electrons; he later succeeded in measuring the charge of the electron but his value turned out to be 30 percent too high. Zeeman's discovery (1897) that the corpuscle was also contained in *normal* atoms and was responsible for their line spectra helped add weight to Thomson's discovery.

Thomson next turned to the problem of what causes the electrons of an atom to arrange themselves in the periodic manner implied by the table of the elements; he attempted to represent positive electrification by a diffuse sphere of constant charge density through which electrons move subject solely to electrostatic forces, though this theory was disproved by Rutherford; he discovered that the order of magnitude of the number of electrons in an atom was much less than previously thought, indicating that the chief part of the atomic mass must belong to the positive charge. His last important experimental work was devoted to determining the nature of positive electricity; in the course of this work he became the first to isolate isotopes of stable elements (1921), in which he was assisted by E. Everett and F. Aston, who later perfected the mass spectrometer, which brought him the Nobel Prize.

Thomson was an excellent teacher and lecturer; he became Professor of Natural Philosophy at the Royal Institution in 1905 (in addition to his Cambridge post). For the benefit of advanced students at the Cavendish he established the Cavendish Physical Society (1893), a seminar in which recent work was criticized; he was not himself a good experimentalist, being clumsy with his hands, but he had a genius for designing apparatus and diagnosing its ills. He resigned his Cavendish chair in 1919 in favor of Rutherford before his lack of sympathy with Bohr's new physics could do any damage. He received the Nobel Prize in 1906.

THOMSON, THOMAS (*b. Crieff, Scotland, 1773; d. Kilmun, Scotland, 1852*), chemistry.

Thomson studied at the University of St. Andrews before going to the University of Edinburgh (M.D., 1799), where he was inspired to devote his life to chemistry by Joseph Black's lectures. While a private lecturer on chemistry in Edinburgh (1800–11), he published his bestselling *A System of Chemistry* (1802), the first systematic treatise of a nonelementary kind to break the French monopoly of such works; it went through six editions in eighteen years. He edited his own journal, *Annals of Philosophy* (1813–20), and taught chemistry at the University of Glasgow (1817–52). Thomson was an ambitious self-made chemist who was distinguished more for unflagging industry than for brilliant originality. From 1807 he was John Dalton's warmest advocate, and in January 1808 he was the first to submit an experimental illustration of the law of multiple proportions; much of his journal was devoted to Dalton's chemical atomic theory and to W. Prout's hypothesis that the atomic weights of elements were whole-numbered multiples of that of hydrogen. His experiments on Dalton's and Prout's theories, reported in *An Attempt to Establish the First Principles of Chemistry by Experiment* (1825), were severely criticized. He was a pioneer in emphasizing the laboratory teaching of practical chemistry; at Glasgow in 1818 he established the first school of practical chemistry in a British university.

THOMSON, SIR WILLIAM (Baron Kelvin of Largs) (*b. Belfast, Ireland, 1824; d. Netherhall, near Largs, Ayrshire, Scotland, 1907*), physics.

William and his brother James were educated at home by their father who was a professor of engineering and mathematics. In 1834 both boys matriculated at Glasgow. Having been stimulated to read Fourier's *Théorie analytique de la chaleur* and Laplace's *Mécanique céleste*, by William Meickleham, his teacher at Glasgow, Thomson's earliest interests centered on questions drawn from both these treatises.

Between 1841 and 1845 he attended Cambridge. Soon after his graduation he journeyed to Paris to work in Regnault's laboratory. On arriving there he was warmly received by Liouville and introduced to many of the leading scientists of his day. Thomson's extensive contact with Liouville led him to think more deeply about electrical theory. Liouville had heard of Faraday's work in electrostatics, or at least of the aspects in which Faraday claimed to have found that electrical induction occurs in "curved lines." The conception seemed to conflict with the action-at-a-distance approach, and Liouville asked Thomson to write a paper clarifying the differences between Faraday on the one hand and Coulomb and Poisson on the other. This request prompted Thomson to bring together ideas he had been turning over in his mind during the previous three years.

In 1842, and again early in 1845, Thomson attempted to envision the physical characteristics of the electrical fluid, and reached disquieting conclusions. He found that if electricity is thought of as a fluid the parts of which exert only inverse-square forces upon one another, then the electrical layer at the surface of a conductor can have no physical thickness at all. That result implied that electricity must be a set of point centers of force. At the time he completely rejected that notion. Later, in 1860, he attributed it to Bošković. But this rejection made it increasingly difficult for him to conceive of Poisson's fluid as a real physical entity at all. Thus, Liouville's request for a discussion of the issue between Faraday's approach and that of action-at-a-distance led Thomson to attempt a restatement of both theories in terms free from physical hypotheses (as he termed hypotheses concerning unobservable entities). In making that effort, Thomson found himself to be constructing an entire methodology for scientific explanation.

After his 1845 sojourn in Paris, Thomson returned to Scotland, where he succeeded to the professorship in natural philosophy at Glasgow, a post that he held for the rest of his life. Neither in Scotland nor in England was there then a university research laboratory or any other in which students could work. Thomson, having had access to Regnault's laboratory, was interested in establishing similar opportunities for students, and he obtained a small sum from the university for that purpose. It made possible the first teaching laboratory in Britain. He was also greatly interested in developing highly accurate measuring instruments, and the facilities of his new laboratory in Glasgow made that possible also.

Thomson's studies in France not only led him to a new approach to electrical theory and to an interest in experimental work and instrumentation; he was also introduced to Sadi Carnot's theory of the motive power of heat, as developed analytically by Clapeyron in 1834. Thomson was deeply impressed by the power of Carnot's theory (although he had read only Clapeyron's explication of it at this date), and especially by the rationalization it afforded for the production of mechanical effect by thermal processes. In an 1848 paper Thomson employed Carnot's theory for the first time in an attempt to establish an "absolute" thermometric scale. The old scale was a merely "arbitrary series of numbered points of reference sufficiently close for the requirements of practical thermometry." By an absolute scale Thomson meant one based on some completely general natural law. That law he took from Carnot—a given amount of heat passing between two given temperatures can produce at most a certain amount of work. In the old scale, based on the air thermometer, the amount of work done by a standard quantity of heat in falling through one degree varied at different points of the scale, as Clapeyron had shown. An absolute scale would be one in which the "value of a degree" would be independent of temperature. Thomson constructed this measure using the results of Regnault, Steele, and others. (The modern Kelvin scale was defined later, following the elucidation of the concept of the conservation of energy.)

Thomson at first rejected ideas that heat could be converted into mechanical energy. Steam remains saturated during its expansion after its escape at high pressure through an orifice (an expansion rapid enough to be essentially adiabatic). Its condition is evident in that it does not scald, as it would had it become partially liquefied. By mid-1850 Thomson saw this phenomenon as conclusive evidence in favor of Joule's contention that heat can be generated from something else: Thomson thought he knew the source of this extra heat. "There is no possible way," he wrote to Joule, "in which the heat can be acquired except by the friction of the steam as it rushes

through the orifice. Hence I think I am justified in saying that your discovery alone can reconcile Mr. Rankine's discovery with known facts." It was at this time also that Thomson first learned of Clausius' work of the previous April; although he had not read it by October, he commented that Clausius' methods "differ from those of Carnot only in the adoption of your [Joule's] axiom instead of Carnot's. . . ." Within five months Thomson himself had assimilated in full the "dynamical theory of heat" and had so modified Carnot's theory as to be in accord with it—an act accomplished independently, without any detailed knowledge of Clausius' work.

Thomson's central concern during these months was the discovery of a principle from which the essential elements of Carnot's theory could be derived while dispensing with the fundamental axiom concerning the conservation of heat *qua* heat. This was not a simple task; without the fundamental axiom, it is extremely difficult to produce a measure of the effect resulting from purely thermal action. The beginning of a solution lay in the new meaning given to the concept of "latent heat" by the dynamical theory, where it is thought of as the work done against the internal, molecular forces of a body. They then store it in the resulting molecular configuration. This notion relieved Thomson of his earlier concern that a body can be returned to its initial state only if the entire amount of heat that has entered it leaves in the same form. He now understood that heat can be converted into a "new" form—"attraction through space" in Joule's terminology—and yet be entirely removed from the transferring engine because the "latent heat" of the engine, its forced molecular configuration, can be directly converted through the performance of work into something of the same kind, namely, the "attraction through space" of external bodies. The problem, therefore, became the discovery of a principle that could be taken as the expression of the essential contents of Carnot's theory once conversion had been admitted. In other words, now that heat could be envisioned as both *vis viva* and molecular configuration, the problem ceased to concern the way in which purely thermal actions could be measured, for thermal actions were reducible to mechanical processes.

Despite Thomson's deep theoretical concerns, he was always strongly interested in physical instrumentation. He felt that existing instruments were inadequate for precisely determining important physical constants. Instrumentation became even more important as electrical phenomena began to be employed in Britain's increasingly complex industrial economy, and Thomson was involved in the design and implementation of many new devices.

His interest and reputation brought him to the attention of a consortium of British industrialists who, in the mid-1850's, proposed to lay a submarine telegraph cable between Ireland and Newfoundland. Telegraphy by then was a well-developed and extremely profitable business, and the idea of laying such a cable was not new. The undertaking provides perhaps the first instance of a complex interaction between large-scale industrial enterprise and theoretical electricity. Thomson was brought in early in the project as a member of the board of directors, and he played a central role.

The directors had entrusted the technical details of the project to an industrial electrician, E. O. W. Whitehouse;

and the many difficulties that plagued it from the outset resulted from Whitehouse's insistence on employing his own system of electrical signaling, despite theoretical objections from Thomson. Thomson had developed a very sensitive apparatus, the mirror-galvanometer, to detect the minuscule currents transmitted through miles of cable, but Whitehouse refused to use it. The Whitehouse-Thomson controversy stemmed primarily from Whitehouse's jealousy of Thomson's reputation. Thomson had asserted that the length of cable would, by a process of statical charging of its insulation, substantially reduce the rate at which signals could be sent unless small voltages were used, so small that only his galvanometer could detect the currents.

The first attempt to lay the cable, in 1857, ended when it snapped and was lost. The second attempt, a year later, was successful, but the large voltages required by the Whitehouse method reduced the ability of the cable to transmit signals rapidly, just as Thomson had predicted. Whitehouse privately recognized the inadequacy of his own instruments and surreptitiously substituted Thomson's galvanometer while claiming success for his own methods. This deception was soon discovered, and the ensuing controversy between Whitehouse, the board of directors, and Thomson combined theoretical science, professional vanity, and financial ignominy. A third cable was laid in 1865, and, with the use of Thomson's instruments, it proved capable of rapid, sustained transmission. Thomson's role as the man who saved a substantial investment made him a hero to the British financial community and to the Victorian public in general; indeed, he was knighted for it. It also was the foundation for a large personal fortune.

Thomson also became involved in a geochronology controversy with the contention that geological theory had to conform to the well-established theories of physics. By 1862 he had provided detailed support for his argument that the sun has cooled considerably and that it is an incandescent liquid mass receiving no heat from without. On that basis, Thomson further calculated, given his estimate of the solar specific heat and the present rate of radiation, that the sun probably has "not illuminated the earth for 100,000,000, and almost [certainly for not more than] 500,000,000 years."

His deduction of a maximum limit for the age of the sun was in direct conflict with those geological Uniformitarians who assumed that geological time cannot be given absolute limitations. Thomson soon presented a second paper supporting his earlier belief that the earth also must have been much hotter in the past. He showed that Fourier's laws of the transfer of heat require that, given the present rate of decrease of the heat of the earth with depth, the earth must have solidified from its primordial molten state not less than 20,000,000 and not more than 400,000,000 years ago. These limits were rigorous deductions from Fourier's laws applied to the case of a molten sphere cooling through emission of radiant heat. They include a probable estimate of the magnitude of the effect due to the formation of the earth's crust; and they hold good provided that the earth has no sources of energy beyond its own central heat.

Thomson's original intention in writing the 1862 papers had been to attack Lyell and the extreme Uniformitarian approach to geology.

The two central concerns of his life were the application of the ideas of mechanics to physics and the development of sensitive measuring devices. By the time of his death, Thomson, then Baron Kelvin of Largs, while perhaps behind the times in his adherence to dynamical modes of thought, was generally looked upon as the founder of British physics.

THORPE, JOCELYN FIELD (*b. London, England, 1872; d. London, 1940*), chemistry.

Thorpe received his doctorate in chemistry at the University of Heidelberg (1895); after joining the research group of W. H. Perkin, Jr., at the University of Manchester, he served in the chair of organic chemistry at the Imperial College of Science and Technology in London (until 1938); his most valuable contribution was his study of the formation and reactions of imino compounds.

THORPE, THOMAS EDWARD (*b. Barnes Green, Harpurhey, near Manchester, England, 1845; d. Salcombe, England, 1925*), chemistry, history of science.

Thorpe graduated from Owens College, Manchester (1867), where he studied chemistry under H. E. Roscoe; he worked with Bunsen at the University of Heidelberg, where he received his doctorate, and studied with Kekulé at Bonn. He taught at what became the Imperial College of Science and Technology in London (1885–94) and was director of government laboratories (1894–1909). An important figure in inorganic chemical research, he is best known for his numerous textbooks and histories of chemistry.

THOUIN, ANDRÉ (*b. Paris, France, 1747; d. Paris, 1824*), botany.

Thouin spent his entire life at the Jardin des Plantes in Paris; at age seventeen he succeeded his father as head gardener. A student of B. de Jussieu and Buffon, he assisted the latter in reorganizing the Jardin des Plantes; in collaboration with A. P. de Candolle in 1806, he studied the influence of light on a number of plants; he was an early proponent of the teaching of agriculture and horticulture.

THUE, AXEL (*b. Tönsberg, Norway, 1863; d. Oslo, Norway, 1922*), mathematics.

Thue received his doctorate from Oslo University, where he taught applied mathematics (1903–22); he also studied with Sophus Lie at Leipzig (1890–91); his famous article of 1909 contained an important theorem in number theory.

THUNBERG, CARL PETER (*b. Jönköping, Sweden, 1743; d. Tunaberg, near Uppsala, Sweden, 1828*), botany.

Thunberg obtained his M.D. at Uppsala University (1770), but his main interest was in botany, and Linnaeus soon considered him a protégé. He was invited to follow a Dutch merchant ship to Japan, which was closed to all European nations except Holland; en route to Japan he stopped to learn Dutch in Cape Colony, South Africa (1772–75), where he also made extensive botanical collections. He became the first Western scientist to investigate Japan botanically through the aid of Japanese interpreters employed by the traders (1776); returning to Sweden, he became professor of botany at Uppsala University (1784–1828); his findings in Japan were published in *Flora japonica* (1784), while the the material from Cape Colony is described in *Flora capensis* (1807–23).

THUNBERG, THORSTEN LUDVIG (*b. Torsåker, Sweden, 1873; d. Lund, Sweden, 1952*), physiology.

Thunberg studied medicine at the University of Uppsala (1891–1900) and obtained the M.D. degree with a dissertation on epidermal sensory perception; he held the chair in physiology at Lund (1905–38). While his first work was in sensory physiology, from 1903 Thunberg made his most important contributions in his studies of biological metabolism. From 1910 he integrated the studies of H. Wieland with his own and finally determined that the oxidative degradation of food is accomplished by a chain of consecutive splittings of hydrogen atoms carried out by a series of dehydrogenases, each with a specific purpose. He also invented a microrespirometer, which he used in 1905 to show that nerve tissue respires.

THURET, GUSTAVE ADOLPHE (*b. Paris, France, 1817; d. Nice, France, 1875*), botany.

Thuret studied law in Paris and began a diplomatic career before devoting himself to botanical research; a very wealthy man, he remained an amateur and never sought a university post; he became a corresponding member of the Académie des Sciences in 1857. He was assisted in his studies of marine algae by E. Bornet; together they elucidated the extremely varied reproductive modes of the different groups of algae. After leaving Paris for Cherbourg (1852), Thuret demonstrated the role of the spermatozoids of *Fucus* in fertilization (1854), thus clarifying the formerly mysterious fertilization process; he described his discoveries in two books, both of which were completed after his death by Bornet: *Notes algologiques* (1876–80) and *Études phycologiques* (1878). After 1856 he continued his research at Cap d'Antibes. The outstanding characteristic of Thuret's research was his concern for fully observing live algae in their natural environment, an unusual practice at that time.

THURNAM, JOHN (*b. Lingcroft, near York, England, 1810; d. Devizes, England, 1873*), psychiatric medicine, anthropology.

Thurnam studied medicine and received his first qualification in 1834; he was medical superintendent at the Retreat asylum at York (1839–49), and thereafter at the Wiltshire County Asylum, Devizes. In medicine his most important work was *Observations and Essays on the Statistics of Insanity* (1845), which played an important role in the application of statistics to psychiatry; in anthropology, he co-edited *Crania Britannica* (1865).

THURNEYSSER, LEONHARD (or **Thurnyser, Lienhart**) (*b. Basel, Switzerland, 1531; d. Cologne, Germany, 1596*), alchemy.

Thurneysser became a goldsmith, like his father, and studied with a Dr. Huber, a physician and alchemist; he was forced to flee Basel when he was discovered to be selling gold-covered lead as pure gold (1548). Eventually he entered the service of Archduke Ferdinand in the Tyrol (1560–70), where he published several alchemical tracts; he then became court physician to Johann Georg, elector of Brandenburg, and established a laboratory and printing house in Berlin. His chief alchemical works, *Megaln chymia* and *Melisath*, were published in 1583 and contained many quotations from Paracelsus invented by Thurneysse himself; his works were severely criticized by other physicians, and Thurneysser would certainly seem to be a charlatan, though a rich one. He conducted a school of alchemy of sorts, which numbered the distinguished apothecary M. Aschenbrenner among its students.

THURSTON, ROBERT HENRY (*b. Providence, R.I., 1839; d. Ithaca, N.Y., 1903*), engineering education, steam engineering, testing of materials.

Thurston graduated from Brown University (1859) with a major in science and minor in civil engineering; after serving as an engineer in the navy during the Civil War, he taught natural and experimental philosophy at the U. S. Naval Academy in Annapolis for six years; he then became head of the school of mechanical engineering at Stevens Institute of Technology in Hoboken, New Jersey (1871–85). At Cornell University he became director of the Sibley College of Mechanical Engineering (1885); he was the first president of the American Society of Mechanical Engineers, which he helped found (1880). He was a prolific writer of textbooks, reference works, and technical and popular articles, and exerted wide and lasting influence on the American engineering profession.

THYMARIDAS (*fl. Paros, first half [?] of fourth century* B.C.), mathematics.

An early Pythagorean, Thymaridas was a number theorist from the Aegean island of Paros; his chief contribution to number theory was his "bloom," a rule which leads to the solution of a certain set of n simultaneous simple equations connecting n unknowns.

IBN TIBBON, JACOB BEN MACHIR (*b. Marseilles, France [?], ca. 1236; d. Montpellier, 1305*), astronomy, science translation.

Jacob was from a family of translators, including Moses Ben Samuel ibn Tibbon, that moved from Granada in 1150; their translations helped make Arabic learning and Greek scientific traditions available to medieval European scholars. Jacob studied medicine and spent most of his life in Lunel and Montpellier; he translated from Arabic into Hebrew works by Autolycus of Petane, Euclid, Menelaus of Alexandria, Qusṭā ibn Lūqā, Ibn al-Ṣaffār, al-Zarqālī, al-Ghazālī, Jābir ibn Aflaḥ, and Ibn Rushd. His own works, which deal with astronomy, were cited by Copernicus, Reinhold, Clavius, and Kepler; they include the *Almanac* (1301) and "Quadrant of Israel" (written between 1288 and 1293), which describes a new astronomical instrument known as the *quadrans novus*, a type of simplified astrolabe.

IBN TIBBON, MOSES BEN SAMUEL (*b. Marseilles, France; fl. Montpellier, France, 1240–1283*), medicine, philosophy, translation.

Moses ben Samuel was related to Jacob ben Machir ibn Tibbon and spent most of his life in Montpellier; he is most significant as a translator from Arabic into Hebrew of Ibn Rushd, Themistius, al-Baṭalyūsī, Maimonides, Euclid, Geminus, Theodosius of Bithynia, Jābir ibn Aflaḥ,

Muhammad al-Ḥaṣṣār, al-Biṭrūjī, Ibn Sīnā, Ibn al-Jazzār, Ḥunayn ibn Isḥāq, al-Rāzī, and al-Fārābī.

TIEDEMANN, FRIEDRICH (*b. Kassel, Germany, 1781; d. Munich, Germany, 1861*), anatomy, physiology.

Tiedemann received his M.D. degree from Marburg (1804), where he remained to attend F. J. Gall's courses; he also studied with F. von Schelling at Würzburg and with G. Cuvier in Paris; he was professor of comparative anatomy and morphology at the Landshut Medical Faculty (1807–16) and professor of anatomy, comparative anatomy, physiology, and zoology at the University of Heidelberg (1816–49); from 1822 he devoted all his time to physiology. Tiedemann's first work at Landshut was an unfinished textbook on zoology (1808–1814), the most comprehensive compendium of zoological data since Cuvier's own *Léçons d'anatomie comparée;* he also did important work in morphology and embryology at this time, particularly his study of brain development (1816). At Heidelberg he was influenced by the chemist L. Gmelin, with whom he collaborated on physiological studies; in 1820 they published their researches on the passage of substances from the stomach or intestines to the blood, on the function of the spleen, and on the hypothetical hidden urinary ducts, which they showed could not exist. Stimulated by a prize offered by the Paris Académie des Sciences, they expanded their work on digestion, showing that it is a complicated series of processes involving a number of organs and, for some substances, resulting in chemical transformation; awarded only half the prize, they declined their share and published their results in *Die Verdauung nach Versuchen* (1826); advances in the study of digestion beyond this work became possible only with advances in chemistry. Tiedemann also published one of the earliest works of physical anthropology (1836), which showed that no substantial differences could be found between the brains of the races of men.

VAN TIEGHEM, PHILIPPE (*b. Bailleul, Nord, France, 1839; d. Paris, France, 1914*), botany.

Van Tieghem received his doctorate in the physical sciences from the École Normale Supérieure, where his dissertation was supervised by Pasteur; he became *maître de conférences* in botany there in 1864, and received a doctorate in the natural sciences in 1867. Appointed professor-administrator at the Muséum d'Histoire Naturelle in 1879, he also taught at the École Centrale des Arts et Manufactures (1873–1886), the École Normale Supérieure des Jeunes Filles at Sèvres (1885–1912), and at the Institut Agronomique (1898–1914). His research covered five fields of botany: cryptogamy, fermentation, anatomy and biology of phanerogams, the application of anatomy to classification, and plant physiology; his publications are characterized by approaching function in relation to structure and development; students still find his *Traité de botanique* useful.

TIEMANN, JOHANN CARL WILHELM FERDINAND (*b. Rübeland, Germany, 1848; d. Meran, Austria [now Merano, Italy], 1899*), chemistry.

Tiemann studied chemistry under A. W. von Hofmann at the University of Berlin where, after serving in the Franco-Prussian War, he spent the rest of his career. He edited the *Berichte der Deutschen chemischen Gesellschaft*

(1882–97); he discovered the commercial method of preparing vanillin from eugenol (1891); with his students he published many papers on hydroxyaldehydes and related compounds.

TIETZ, J. D. *See* **Titius, Johann Daniel.**

AL-TĪFĀSHĪ, SHIHĀB AL-DĪN ABU' L-ᶜABBĀS AḤMAD IBN YŪSUF (*b. Tīfāsh, 1184; d. Cairo, 1253/1254*), mineralogy, physiology.

Al-Tīfāshī was educated in Tīfāsh, Cairo, and Damascus, after which he returned to Tīfāsh and obtained a judgeship; he later settled in Cairo. He wrote "Blossoms of Thoughts on Precious Stones," a book on sense perception of which only an extract is preserved, and three books on sexual relations.

TIKHOV, GAVRIIL ADRIANOVICH (*b. Smolevichi, near Minsk, Russia, 1875; d. Alma-Ata, Kazakhstan S.S.R., 1960*), astrophysics, astrobotany.

Tikhov graduated from Moscow University (1897); he studied in Paris at the Sorbonne (1898–1900) and worked in J. Janssen's astrophysics observatory in Meudon; he began working at the Pulkovo observatory in 1906 and received the degree of master of astronomy and geodesy in 1913. He lectured on astrophysics at the University of Leningrad (1919–31) and directed the astrophysics laboratory of the P. F. Lesgaft Scientific Institute (1919–41). In his colorimetric studies of Algol variable stars he detected what is now known as the Tikhov-Nordmann effect; he developed the "longitudinal spectrograph" and his photographic studies of Mars led to the new fields of astrobotany and astrobiology; he invented an instrument for registering astral scintillation (1912) which he used to determine the angular diameter of stars.

TILAS, DANIEL (*b. Gammelbo, Västmanland, Sweden, 1712; d. Stockholm, Sweden, 1772*), geology, mining.

Tilas studied at the University of Uppsala (1723–26, 1728–32); he became assistant at the Office of Mines which controlled the Swedish mining industry (1732); he developed an ambitious project to map all of Sweden geologically, though he only produced an unpublished geological map of two provinces of Finland and of a large number of mines. His views on the origin of fossils and erratic boulders seem rather modern; he was one of the first geologists to work with oil (1740) and to describe its economic exploitation.

TILDEN, SIR WILLIAM AUGUSTUS (*b. London, England, 1842; d. London, 1926*), chemistry.

Apprenticed to a pharmacist in 1857, Tilden eventually graduated from London University (B.Sc., 1868; D.Sc., 1871); he taught at Clifton College (1872–80), Mason College (1880–1894), and at what became the Imperial College in London (from 1894). From his first work in 1877 with the nitroso derivatives, he continued to study terpenes throughout his career.

TILLET, MATHIEU (*b. Bordeaux, France, 1714; d. Paris, France, 1791*), agronomy, chemistry.

Little is known about Tillet's early life; in 1758 he entered the Paris Académie des Sciences, where he worked his way up from botanist, assayer, and chemist to the position of director (1779). His chemical papers are concerned with assaying and refining metals for the mint and contributed to the creation of accurate chemical standards; he is best remembered for his investigations of diseases of wheat known as smuts and bunts.

TILLO, ALEKSEY ANDREEVICH (*b. Kiev, Russia, 1839; d. St. Petersburg, Russia [now Leningrad, U.S.S.R.], 1900*), geography, cartography, geodesy.

Tillo's education and career were with the military; he completed the theoretical course of the geodesy section of the General Staff Academy (1864); and then worked two years at the Pulkovo observatory under Otto Struve; his research, which was associated mainly with the Russian Geographical Society, was in geodesy; his chief works concerned the hypsometry and orography of Russia; he published an important hypsometrical map of European Russia (1889).

TILLOCH, ALEXANDER (*b. Glasgow, Scotland, 1759; d. Islington, London, England, 1825*), natural philosophy, science journalsim.

After graduating from the University of Glasgow (1771), Tilloch developed a number of inventions related to printing, including the rediscovery of stereotyping (1781). In London he bought a newspaper, the *Star* (1787), which he edited until 1821; he also founded the monthly *Philosophical Magazine* (1798); in competing with Thomas Thomson's *Annals of Philosophy,* it became of major importance in disseminating original scientific news (from 1810).

TILLY, JOSEPH-MARIE DE (*b. Ypres, Belgium, 1837; d. Schaerbeek, Belgium, 1906*), geometry.

Tilly, one of the most profound Belgian mathematicians, had a military career and education; he was commandant and director of studies at the École Militaire for ten years before being dismissed for ostensibly overemphasizing scientific education. He was the first to study non-Euclidean mechanics; in his *Essai de géométrie analytique générale* (1892), the synthesis and crowning achievement of his work, he established that geometry is the mathematical physics of distances.

IBN AL-TILMĪDH, AMĪN AL-DAWLA ABU'L-ḤASAN HIBAT ALLĀH IBN ṢAĪD (*b. Baghdad, ca. 1073; d. Baghdad, 1165*), medicine, pharmacy, logic, education, literature.

After completing his medical education, Ibn al-Tilmīdh practiced in Persia for several years; after returning to Baghdad he served under several caliphs, especially al-Muqtafī (1136–60), who appointed him court physician and chief of the important ʿAḍudī hospital. He had the largest private medical school in Baghdad in his time and attracted many students; he wrote fourteen books, including pharmaceutical formularies and medical commentaries, some of which were cited by later Arab physicians for more than a century after his death.

TIMIRYAZEV, KLIMENT ARKADIEVICH (*b. St. Petersburg, Russia [now Leningrad, U.S.S.R.], 1843; d. Moscow, U.S.S.R., 1920*), plant physiology.

Timiryazev attended St. Petersburg University and received the Candidate of Sciences degree (1865); he also studied under Mendeleev in Simbirsk province, and worked with Helmholtz, G. Kirchhoff, Bunsen, and Hofmeister in Germany (1868–70); in France, he worked with Berthelot, J. B. Boussingault, and C. Bernard. On returning to Russia he earned his master's degree (1871) and his doctorate (1875); he became professor of anatomy and plant physiology at the University of Moscow (1877), but was prevented from teaching in 1898 because of troubles with the government; he supported the October Revolution, and his position was restored in 1917. Timiryazev's basic research was in plant physiology, particularly photosynthesis; his work is summarized in "The Cosmical Function of the Green Plant" (1903); the theoretical basis he provided for the energetics of photosynthesis is still valid.

TINSEAU D'AMONDANS, CHARLES DE (*b. Besançon, France, 1748; d. Montpellier, France, 1822*), mathematics.

Tinseau graduated as a military engineer from the École Royale du Génie at Mézières (1771), where his interest in mathematics was awakened by G. Monge. Tinseau was Monge's first disciple, and although he published only three memoirs, they are of great interest as additions to Monge's earliest works. Until 1791 he was an officer in the engineering corps, after which he lived in various émigré communities until 1816, conducting a propaganda campaign against the Revolution and later against the Empire.

TISELIUS, ARNE WILHELM KAURIN (*b. Stockholm, Sweden, 1902; d. Stockholm, 1971*), physical biochemistry.

Tiselius studied at the University of Uppsala under The Svedberg, the leading physical chemist in Sweden; he received the M.A. in chemistry, physics, and mathematics in 1924, and the doctorate in 1930; his dissertation was on electrophoresis. He became a docent in chemistry at Uppsala and later held the chair in biochemistry (1938–68). Tiselius was awarded the 1948 Nobel Prize in chemistry "for his work on electrophoresis and adsorption analysis and especially for his discovery of the complex nature of the proteins in blood serum." He entered Svedberg's laboratory as research assistant in 1925, and his first paper was written with Svedberg (1926) on a new method for determining the mobility of proteins. While Svedberg worked on his ultracentrifuges, Tiselius continued the study of electrophoresis; while at Princeton University on a Rockefeller Foundation fellowship (1934–35), he began a total reconstruction of his electrophoresis apparatus. With his new instrument he detected three electrophoretically different components in serum globulin, which he named α, β, and γ globulin, each of which consisted of many individual proteins. He then worked on adsorption methods and, with S. Claesson, introduced interferometric methods to measure the concentration of eluate (1942). In the following decade he and his co-workers worked on improving his method of displacement analysis (1943); he also made decisive contributions to chromatography. His contributions to the development of new methods for analysis and separation of biological systems mark an era in the study of macromolecules and have contributed to the enormous development in biochemistry since the end of the 1930's.

TISSERAND, FRANÇOIS FÉLIX (*b. Nuits-St.-Georges, Côte-d'Or, France, 1845; d. Paris, France, 1896*), celestial mechanics, astronomy.

After graduating from the École Normale Supérieure (1866), Tisserand began working under Le Verrier at the Paris observatory; he received the doctorate in 1868. He directed the Toulouse observatory and was professor of astronomy at that city's university (1873–78) before leaving to teach at the Paris Faculty of Sciences (1878–92); he became director of the Paris observatory in 1892. He did important work on the three-body problem (1885) and established the relationship known as "Tisserand's criterion" (1889). The criterion is applied to the two orbits of an asteroid or comet before and after it passes close to a planet. It is widely used to establish the identity, or lack of identity, of two objects observed at different times and following distinct orbits. His greatest work is his *Traité de mécanique céleste* (1889–96), an up-to-date version of Laplace's *Mécanique céleste*.

TITCHMARSH, EDWARD CHARLES (*b. Newbury, England, 1899; d. Oxford, England, 1963*), mathematics.

Titchmarsh received his mathematical training at Oxford, but did not take a doctorate; he was Savilian professor of geometry at Oxford (1931–63). He made significant contributions in various branches of analysis; his text *The Theory of Functions* (1932) was his best-known book.

TITIUS (TIETZ), JOHANN DANIEL (*b. Konitz, Germany [now Chojnice, Poland], 1729; d. Wittenberg, Germany, 1796*), astronomy, physics, biology.

Titius received the master's degree from the University of Leipzig (1752); he began teaching at the University of Wittenberg in 1756, where he remained the rest of his life; in addition to teaching mathematics and physics, he also lectured on philosophy, natural theology, and natural law. His chief scientific activity was in physics, particularly thermometry, and biology, in which he published classifications of plants, animals, and minerals based on the Linnaean system. He is famous chiefly for the Titius-Bode law governing the distances between the planets and the sun (1766), confirmed by Bode in 1772. He edited six series of periodicals which popularized new scientific results.

TODHUNTER, ISAAC (*b. Rye, Sussex, England, 1820; d. Cambridge, England, 1884*), mathematics.

Todhunter received the B.A. (1842) and the M.A. (1844) from University College, London, where he was a student of the mathematician A. De Morgan; he obtained another B.A. at St. John's College, Cambridge (1848), where he held a fellowship (1849–64). He was not an original mathematician, but his mathematical textbooks were extremely popular and influential; his reputation rests on his publications on the history of mathematics.

TOEPLITZ, OTTO (*b. Breslau, Germany [now Wrocław, Poland], 1881; d. Jerusalem, 1940*), mathematics.

Toeplitz studied at the University of Breslau (Ph.D., 1905); he taught at the University of Kiel (1913–28) and at the University of Bonn (1928–33), from which he was dismissed by the National Socialist regime. He moved to Jerusalem in 1938. His chief interest was the theory of infinite linear, bilinear, and quadratic forms, and of the associated infinite matrices, as a framework for concrete problems of analysis.

TOLMAN, RICHARD CHACE (*b. West Newton, Mass., 1881; d. Pasadena, Calif., 1948*), physical chemistry, mathematical physics.

Tolman received a B.S. degree in chemical engineering from the Massachusetts Institute of Technology (1903); he returned there after studying at the Technische Hochschule at Charlottenburg, Germany, to join A. A. Noyes's Research Laboratory of Physical Chemistry and earn his Ph.D. (1910). He was director of the Fixed Nitrogen Research Laboratory (1920–22) and with Noyes's help became professor of physical chemistry and mathematical physics at the California Institute of Technology (1922). The main thrust of his work in statistical mechanics, relativistic thermodynamics, and cosmology was mathematical and theoretical. He published important papers concerning chemical kinetics in gaseous systems; with G. N. Lewis, he published the first American exposition of the special theory of relativity (1909).

TORRE, MARCANTONIO DELLA (*b. Verona, Italy, 1481; d. Riva, Italy, 1511*), medicine, anatomy.

Torre received the doctorate in philosophy (1497) and in medicine (1501) at the University of Padua; he subsequently taught medicine there until 1510, when he transferred to the University of Pavia, where he soon died of plague. He is supposed to have collaborated with Leonardo da Vinci on a treatise on anatomy; while they were probably friends, the collaboration of Torre, a Galenist, and Leonardo, who was unfettered by scholasticism, is unlikely.

TORRES QUEVEDO, LEONARDO (*b. Santa Cruz de Iguña, Santander, Spain, 1852; d. Madrid, Spain, 1936*), engineering.

Torres Quevedo studied civil engineering (1870–76) and produced inventions which made him famous; the Centro de Ensayos de Aeronáutica was created for him by royal decree (1904), as was the Laboratorio de Mecánica Aplicada (1907, 1911). He developed several calculating devices, including a chess-playing robot (1912) and an electromechanical calculating machine (1920); he also invented the Telekino, a remote control device employing Hertzian waves (patented in 1902).

TORREY, JOHN (*b. New York, N.Y., 1796; d. New York, N.Y., 1873*), botany.

Torrey became interested in botany when he befriended the scientist Amos Eaton, who was in a prison administered by Torrey's father. His degree was in medicine (1818) and his teaching was in chemistry and mineralogy; in the 1820's he taught at West Point and the College of Physicians and Surgeons in New York; he taught at Princeton (1830–54) during the summer terms. He became assayer of the United States Mint in New York (1851) and from 1860 lived on the campus of Columbia College, where he taught chemistry. Torrey initiated the practice of gathering in one work all that was known of American flora (1824) and he led American botanists in the adoption of the natural system of classification developed by A.-L. de Jussieu and A. P. de Candolle. With his protégé Asa Gray, whose career he helped advance, he published several fascicles of *Flora of North America* (1836–43); he also published *Flora of the State of New York* (1843) and wrote many reports on specimens brought back by explorers from the western United States. His extensive herbarium became the basis of the New York City Botanical Garden.

TORRICELLI, EVANGELISTA (*b. Faenza, Italy, 1608; d. Florence, Italy, 1647*), mathematics, physics.

Torricelli attended the Jesuit school at Faenza and the school in Rome run by Benedetto Castelli. He assisted Galileo during the last three months before the latter's death, and succeeded him as mathematician and philosopher to the Grand Duke Ferdinando II of Tuscany. He remained in Florence until his death. His only work to be published during his lifetime was *Opera geometrica* (1644), which diffused Cavalieri's new geometry of indivisibles. In the first section, *De sphaera et solidis sphaeralibus libri duo*, Torricelli extended Cavalieri's theory by using curved indivisibles. He gave a brilliant application of the principle to solid figures by proving a new theorem: in modern terms Torricelli's process is described by saying that an integral in Cartesian coordinates is replaced by an integral in cylindrical coordinates. In applying the geometry of indivisibles to the determination of the center of gravity of figures, he developed the "universal theorem," still considered the most general possible even today, which allows determination of the center of gravity of any figure through the relation between two integrals. He also directed his attention to rectification of arcs of a curve. In addition to these contributions to the integral calculus, he discovered many relationships of differential calculus. He determined the point still known as Torricelli's point on the plane of a triangle for which the sum of the distances from the vertices is minimum.

In the second section of his *Opera, De motu gravium,* he continued the study of the parabolic motion of projectiles begun by Galileo. He seeks to demonstrate Galileo's principle regarding equal velocities of free fall of weights along inclined planes of equal height. He bases his demonstration on another principle, now called Torricelli's principle, according to which a rigid system of a number of bodies can move spontaneously on the earth's surface only if its center of gravity descends. Among the many theorems of external ballistics, he shows that the parabolas corresponding to a given initial speed and to different inclinations are all tangents to the same parabola (known as the safety parabola or Torricelli's parabola, the first example of an envelope curve of a family of curves). His experiments on the movement of water led Ernst Mach to proclaim Torricelli the founder of hydrodynamics. His aim was to determine the efflux velocity of a jet of liquid spurting from a small orifice in the bottom of a receptacle. He deduced the theorem that bears his name: The velocity of the jet at the point of efflux is equal to that which a single drop of the liquid would have if it could fall freely in a vacuum from the level of the top of the liquid at the orifice of efflux.

Torricelli is often credited with having converted Galileo's primitive air thermoscope to a liquid thermometer. There is good evidence of his technical ability in working telescope lenses. The success of his lenses was due to accurate machining of the surfaces, selecting good-quality glass, and not fastening the lenses "with pitch, or in any way with fire."

Torricelli's name is linked above all to the barometric experiment named after him. He filled a simple glass tube about one meter long to the rim with mercury, closed it with one finger and overturned it, and immersed the open end in mercury in a bowl. The mercury sank in the tube until it was balanced by the atmospheric pressure. According to Torricelli, the force that supports the mercury column is not internal to the tube but external, produced by the atmosphere that weighs on the mercury in the bowl. Torricelli's experiment gave rise to flourishing experimental and theoretical activity, changing the appearance of physics just as the telescope changed that of astronomy.

TOSCANELLI DAL POZZO, PAOLO (*b. Florence, Italy, 1397; d. Florence, 1482*), astronomy, geography, medicine.

Toscanelli began his studies in medicine, mathematics, and astronomy at the University of Florence but later transferred to the University of Padua, where he became friends with Nicolas of Cusa. On returning to Florence he practiced judicial astrology; he designed a gnomon, an important astronomical instrument incorporated in the cupola of the basilica of Santa Maria del Fiore, built by Brunelleschi. His observations of comets were very accurately mapped; he apparently sent to Christopher Columbus a copy of a map he made of the Atlantic Ocean, which demonstrated a shorter western route to the Orient.

TOULMIN, GEORGE HOGGART (*b. Southwark, Surrey, England, 1754; d. Wolverhampton, England, 1817*), geology.

Toulmin studied medicine at Edinburgh University (M.D., 1779); he probably practiced medicine the rest of his life. His only geological work, *The Antiquity and Duration of the World* (1780), is chiefly remarkable for having anticipated in a general way some of the conclusions in James Hutton's *Theory of the Earth* (1788). While Hutton based his work on extensive field studies, Toulmin cites no such evidence at all; the work was almost completely ignored by contemporary geologists.

TOURNEFORT, JOSEPH PITTON DE (*b. Aix-en-Provence, France, 1656; d. Paris, France, 1708*), botany, medicine.

Tournefort's early education was from the Jesuits; from 1677 to 1683 he divided his time between herborizing and courses in chemistry, medicine, and botany (taught by Magnol) at the University of Montpellier. He became substitute for G. Fagon, professor at the Jardin du Roi (1683), which involved teaching and collecting; he entered the Académie des Sciences in 1691. His major publications were *Élémens de botanique* (1694) and an account of his voyage to the Levant (1717). Tournefort was one of Europe's most noted botanists whose teaching and publications exerted enormous influence until the end of the eighteenth century, despite the fact that he knew nothing of plant sexuality, refused to employ the microscope, and divided the plant into almost independent parts. His main contribution was the concept of genus in the modern sense which was elaborated by Linnaeus, B. de Jussieu, and Adanson; above all, Tournefort carefully distinguished the act of describing from that of naming; Tournefort's genera—he accepted 725—have largely been retained. A physician with a considerable practice, he played a decisive role in emancipating botany from medicine.

TOWNELEY, RICHARD (*b. Towneley Hall, near Burnley, Lancashire, England, 1629; d. York, England, 1707*), natural philosophy.

Towneley was from a wealthy family and could devote most of his energies to science. With H. Power he collaborated on experiments (1660–61) that led to a recognition of the air pressure-volume relationship, later known as Boyle's law. His most significant achievement was an improved micrometer, which he applied to astronomical uses; from 1670 he and J. Flamsteed collaborated on astronomical observations.

TOWNSEND, JOHN SEALY EDWARD (*b. Galway, Ireland, 1868; d. Oxford, England, 1957*), physics.

Townsend graduated from Trinity College, Dublin (1890), and became a research student at the Cavendish Laboratory under J. J. Thomson. In 1897 he made a direct determination of the absolute unit of charge and his result compared favorably with R. A. Millikan's value (1911). He was elected as Wykeham professor of physics at Oxford (1900), by which time he had published a preliminary report of his unique collision theory of ionization; the collision principle was the basis of the 1908 particle detector of E. Rutherford and H. Geiger. In 1924 he reported a new physical effect in which monatomic gases seemed particularly transparent to low energy electrons; this Ramsauer-Townsend effect later became important in understanding the wave nature of the electron.

TOWNSEND, JOSEPH (*b. London, England, 1739; d. Pewsey, Wiltshire, England, 1816*), medicine, geology, economics.

Townsend graduated from Clare Hall, Cambridge University (B.A., 1762; M.A., 1765); he studied medicine in Edinburgh (1762–63), attending classes of W. Cullen and R. Whytt. He was ordained a Calvinistic Methodist minister in 1765 and traveled through England for a number of years evangelizing; his popular travel account, *Journey Through Spain* (1791), emphasized the economic importance of population; he wrote two very popular manuals for physicians (1781, 1795). A friend of William Smith, he published one of the first accounts of Smith's method of correlating strata by the kinds of fossils in them in *The Character of Moses . . .* (1813–1815).

TOZZI, DON BRUNO (*b. Florence, Italy, 1656; d. Vallombrosa, Italy, 1743*), botany.

Tozzi became a monk in the order of Vallombrosa (1676), eventually becoming abbot of the order; he was an able teacher (P. A. Micheli was a student and friend) and an authority on the Italian flora, his *Catalogus plantarum etruriae et insularum adjacentium* included 200 of his own plant illustrations.

TRADESCANT, JOHN (*b. Suffolk [?], England, ca. 1570; d. South Lambeth, Surrey, England, 1638*), natural history.

A gardener for Robert Cecil, earl of Salisbury (beginning 1604), Tradescant began a long series of collecting trips in 1610; in 1618 he made the first botanical visit to Russia and in 1620 he joined an expedition against the Barbary corsairs in order to make natural history collections. After 1628 he set up a garden and museum in South Lambeth, a pioneer enterprise, which was visited by Charles I, for whom he became gardener; doubtless the most famous exhibit was the stuffed dodo; his *Catalogus* (1634) lists 750 garden plants grown at South Lambeth.

TRADESCANT, JOHN (*b. Meopham, Kent, England, 1608; d. South Lambeth, Surrey, England, 1662*), natural history.

Traveler, collector, and gardener, Tradescant carried on the activities of his father of the same name; though the circumstances are confused, E. Ashmole seems to have obtained a signed bequest of the South Lambeth museum from Tradescant during a drinking party (1659); in 1674 Ashmole removed the Tradescant collections to his house and three years later delivered his and Tradescant's "rarities" to Oxford, where they were displayed in what became known as the Ashmolean Museum.

TRAGUS, HIERONYMUS. *See* **Bock, Jerome.**

TRAUBE, MORITZ (*b. Ratibor, Silesia [now Racibórz, Poland], 1826; d. Berlin, Germany, 1894*), physiological chemistry.

Traube began his scientific education in Berlin but soon transferred to Giessen, where he studied under Liebig (Ph.D., 1847); he abandoned his studies in 1849 when he was obliged to take over the family business; he subsequently led a double existence as a businessman and a researcher, working in private laboratories; he encountered prejudice because he held no academic post. Traube's experiments in physiological chemistry proved of great importance in general chemistry; he discovered oxygen-carrying ferments, or enzymes as they are now called (1858), semipermeable membranes (1867), and artificial models of the cell (1875); his discovery of semipermeable membranes provided the basis for Pfeffer's measurement of osmotic pressure and for van't Hoff's theoretical interpretation of osmosis.

TRAVERS, MORRIS WILLIAM (*b. Kensington, London, England, 1872; d. Stroud, Gloucestershire, England, 1961*), physical chemistry, cryogenics, industrial chemistry.

Travers graduated from University College, London (B.Sc., 1893; D.Sc., 1898), where he worked with W. Ramsay (who discovered argon and helium) and began teaching (1898). Travers and Ramsay together discovered three more inert gases: krypton, neon, and xenon (1898); in his cryogenic research Travers made probably the first accurate temperature measurements of liquefied gases; he directed the Indian Institute of Science in Bangalore (1906–14) and established a research group at University College, Bristol, where he was made honorary professor of chemistry (1927); he completed a biography of Ramsay in 1955.

TREBRA, FRIEDRICH WILHELM HEINRICH VON (*b. Allstedt, Weimar, Germany, 1740; d. Freiberg, Germany, 1819*), mining.

Trebra studied law, philosophy, mathematics, and natural science at the University of Jena before enrolling in the mining academy at Freiberg, Saxony (1766); a year later he became assessor for the Bureau of Mines at Freiberg, soon afterward becoming inspector of mines at Marienberg, Saxony (1767), where he introduced many technical improvements into silver mining; he eventually became head of the Saxon mining industry (1801–19).

TRELEASE, WILLIAM (*b. Mount Vernon, N.Y., 1857; d. Urbana, Ill., 1945*), botany.

Trelease graduated from Cornell University (B.S., 1880) and Harvard University (Sc.D., 1884), where he studied under Asa Gray; he then became head of the new Missouri Botanical Garden in St. Louis and then he headed the department of botany at the University of Illinois (1913–26); he was an internationally known botanist, teacher, and administrator.

TREMBLEY, ABRAHAM (*b. Geneva [now Switzerland], 1710; d. Petit Sacconex, near Geneva, 1784*), zoology.

Trembley was educated at the Academy of Geneva, and in 1733 found employment as a tutor in Holland; while tutoring near The Hague in the early 1740's he carried out the researches on the hydra that made him famous. He was generously rewarded for his tutoring of the young duke of Richmond so that he never again needed to work for a living (1756); he devoted himself to the instruction of his children and to writing books on education, politics, religion, and moral philosophy. In 1740 he discovered that hydra would multiply by artificial division; he devoted much time to a detailed study of the budding process, regeneration, and artificial production of monsters, and made the first permanent graft of animal tissues (with hydra) in 1742; his work on hydra is summarized in his *Mémoires* (1744). He was also the first to describe multiplication and colony formation in Protozoa and multiplication by budding in Oligochaeta and Polyzoa; he was also the first to witness cell division of a uninucleate cell. It is often said that he was the father of experimental zoology.

TREUB, MELCHIOR (*b. Voorschoten, Holland, 1851; d. St. Raphael, France, 1910*), botany.

Treub graduated from the University of Leiden (Ph.D., 1873), where he remained for seven years as docent and assistant in the botanical institute under his former tutor, W. F. R. Suringar. From 1880 he directed the botanical gardens at Buitenzorg (now Bogor), West Java; Treub successfully publicized the work of the gardens and convinced both the government and the colonial planters of the value of applied scientific research; he thus was able to revitalize the institution by adding new laboratories, a chain of experimental stations, a zoological museum, and a new library; these became the nucleus for the Java General Agriculture Experiment Station. The most significant botanical studies published during Treub's tenure include *Flore de Buitenzorg* and the *Icones Bogoriensis;* he also found time to do research of his own and write a history of the Buitenzorg botanic garden (1886).

TREVIRANUS, GOTTFRIED REINHOLD (*b. Bremen, Germany, 1776; d. Bremen, 1837*), zootomy, physiology.

Treviranus studied medicine and mathematics at the University of Göttingen (M.D., 1796); from 1797 he was professor of mathematics and medicine at the Bremen lyceum. His magnum opus, *Biologie* (1802–22), which sought to summarize all basic knowledge of his time about the structure and function of living matter, greatly influenced his contemporaries; his ideas appeared in more condensed form in *Erscheinungen und Gesetze* (1831–32), a classic in theoretical biology. He introduced the idea of biology as a distinct discipline into Germany and was one of the first to express the idea that the cell is the structural unit of living matter. As an adherent of *Naturphilosophie* all his studies focused on finding what universal laws underlie nature; he anticipated Lamarck in stating that changes in the environment could induce corresponding changes in organic structures (1802). He also did work on the anatomy and physiology of sense organs.

TREVIRANUS, LUDOLPH CHRISTIAN (*b. Bremen, Germany, 1779; d. Bonn, Germany, 1864*), plant anatomy, plant physiology.

Treviranus studied medicine at the University of Jena (M.D., 1801), where he was a student of F. W. Schelling. Like his brother, the biologist Gottfried R. Treviranus, he became an adherent of *Naturphilosophie* and denied any difference between organic and inorganic forces. He held the chair in botany at the University of Rostock, after which he taught at Breslau (1816–30) and Bonn (from 1830). His major work is *Physiologie der Gewächse* (1835–38), a study of the relation between structure and function in plants which is of interest for its historical introductions to the subjects; of more physiological importance are his observations on the influence of chemical substances on plants, on the movement of particles in the cell, and the movement of sap in trees; with his brother Gottfried he published a work on anatomy and physiology (1816–21) and founded *Zeitschrift für Physiologie* (1824).

TREVISANUS. *See* **Bernard of Trevisan.**

TRIANA, JOSÉ GERÓNIMO (or **JERÓNIMO**) (*b. Zipaquirá, Colombia, 1826; d. Paris, France, 1890*), botany.

Triana began the study of botany at Bogotá as the private pupil of F. J. Matis, the last survivor of the Mutis botanical expedition; he was appointed associate botanist by the government on a commission for preparing a geographical map of Colombia (1850), in the course of which he amassed a large herbarium and much data on economic and medical botany; he visited Europe on behalf of the government to publicize Colombian plants of economic value (1856–58); with J. Planchon of Montpellier he collaborated on *Prodromus florae Novogranatensis* (1862–67).

TRILIA, BERNARD OF. *See* **Bernard of Le Treille.**

TRISMEGISTUS. *See* **Hermes Trismegistus.**

TROJA, MICHELE (*b. Andria, Apulia, Italy, 1747; d. Naples, Italy, 1827*), medicine.

Troja studied medicine at Naples and in 1774 won a scholarship to study in Paris; he was appointed to the chair of ophthalmology at the University of Naples (1779); he is known for his studies on the nutrition and regeneration of bones in which he considerably improved the techniques of study.

TROMMSDORFF, JOHANN BARTHOLOMÄUS (*b. Erfurt, Germany, 1770; d. Erfurt, 1837*), chemistry, pharmacy.

Trommsdorff completed his apprenticeship to a chemist in Weimar in 1787 and took over the family apothecary shop; he held a chair in chemistry at Erfurt University, but his work as a pharmacist was more important; he wrote popular texts, established the leading periodical *Journal der Pharmacie* (1794–1834), and taught over 300 students in his "Chemical-physical-pharmaceutical Boarding School" (1795–1828); he thus played a major role in training the founding generation of the German drug industry.

TROOST, GERARD (*b. 'sHertogenbosch, Netherlands, 1776; d. Nashville, Tenn., 1850*), geology, mineralogy, paleontology, natural history.

Troost received his master of pharmacy degree from the Athenaeum in Amsterdam and his M.D. from the University of Leiden, but he never practiced medicine and was a pharmacist only briefly. He studied mineralogy and crystallography in Paris (1807) and collected specimens for two years on behalf of King Louis Bonaparte; Louis Bonaparte abdicated and Troost decided to remain in the United States; he was a founder of the Academy of Natural Sciences of Philadelphia and was its first president (1812); he became professor of geology and mineralogy at the University of Nashville (1828–50) and state geologist of Tennessee (1831–39), and prepared the first geologic map of the state. His private natural history museum was one of the finest west of the Appalachians; his important study of fossil crinoids was not published until 1909.

TROOST, LOUIS JOSEPH (*b. Paris, France, 1825; d. Paris, 1911*), chemistry.

Troost received his doctorate (1857) in Paris and was appointed to the chair of chemistry at the Sorbonne (1874); most of his research was on isomerism, allotropy, and dissociation; he worked in Deville's thermochemical laboratory (from 1857) and collaborated with Hautefeuille (from 1868).

TROOSTWIJK, ADRIAAN PAETS VAN (*b. Utrecht, Netherlands, 1752; d. Nieuwersluis, Netherlands, 1837*), chemistry.

Although van Troostwijk worked in Amsterdam as a merchant most of his life (1770–1816), he became an important Dutch chemist who published thirty-five works on his experiments in chemistry and electricity between 1778 and 1818. Nothing is known of his education except that he was greatly influenced by M. van Marum, director of Teyler's Museum in Haarlem. A phlogistonist until 1788, he was a founder of the Batavian Club, better known as the Society of Dutch Chemists (1791), which was instrumental in securing recognition in the Netherlands for Lavoisier's discoveries.

TROPFKE, JOHANNES (*b. Berlin, Germany, 1866; d. Berlin, 1939*), history of mathematics.

Tropfke took the state examination at the University of Berlin in mathematics, physics, philosophy, botany, zoology, Latin, and Greek (1889), but his dissertation was on the theory of functions; he was director of the

Kirschner Oberrealschule (1912–32); the second edition of his *Geschichte der Elementarmathematik in systematischer Darstellung* (1921–24) encouraged teachers to devote greater attention to historical development in mathematical education.

TROUGHTON, EDWARD (*b. Corney, Cumberland, England, 1753; d. London, England, 1836*), mathematics, optics, physics.

Troughton was apprenticed to his elder brother, an instrument maker (1770), after which they became partners (1779); he became one of the most competent mathematical instrument makers of his time; his most notable achievement was the improvement of the method of dividing a circle (1809); his instruments can be found in museums around the world.

TROUTON, FREDERICK THOMAS (*b. Dublin, Ireland, 1863; d. Downe, Kent, England, 1922*), physics.

Trouton received degrees in engineering and physical science at Trinity College, Dublin, where he remained as assistant to G. F. Fitzgerald, who greatly influenced him; he was Quain professor of physics, University College, London, from 1902 until he was partially paralyzed by an illness (1912); he carried out a number of studies in applied research, but he is remembered for his attempts to determine the relative velocity of the earth and ether (i.e. the ether wind); his experiments with H. R. Noble (1903) and with A. O. Rankine (1908) obtained null results.

TROUVELOT, ÉTIENNE LÉOPOLD (*b. Guyencourt, Aisne, France, 1827; d. Meudon, France, 1895*), natural history, astronomy.

Trouvelot came to America in 1857 and worked with the fifteen-inch refractor at Harvard Observatory (1872–74); in 1869 he imported to Massachusetts the European gypsy moth for experimentation; unfortunately some escaped and proliferated alarmingly, defoliating many trees in the northeastern United States; he returned to France (1882) and joined the staff of the new Meudon observatory; his drawings were considered the most accurate pictures of celestial objects available until the perfection of dry-plate photography.

TROWBRIDGE, JOHN (*b. Boston, Mass., 1843; d. Cambridge, Mass., 1923*), physics.

Trowbridge graduated from the Lawrence Scientific School of Harvard University (1865), where he taught physics (1870–1910); he was a pioneer in establishing serious scientific research in late nineteenth-century America; he was responsible for construction of the Jefferson Physical Laboratory at Harvard (1884), which he directed (1888–1910); his main line of research was in electrical phenomena; his most important book is *What is Electricity?* (1897); he was associate editor of the *American Journal of Science* (1880–1920).

TRULLI, GIOVANNI (*b. Veroli, Frosinone province, Italy, 1598; d. Rome, Italy, 1661*), medicine.

Trulli was trained in France in surgery, particularly lithotomy; he was surgeon to Cardinal Francesco Barberini in Rome (1636–44) and probably played a role in the contacts between Barberini and William Harvey

(1636); he was a strong supporter of the doctrine of circulation of the blood; his written consultation sent to Galileo in 1638 is the most important medical document on Galileo's blindness.

TRUMPLER, ROBERT JULIUS (*b. Zurich, Switzerland, 1886; d. Oakland, Calif., 1956*), astronomy.

Trumpler received his Ph.D. from the University of Göttingen (1910); most of his career was spent at the Lick Observatory (1919–51) and in teaching astronomy at the University of California, Berkeley (1938–51); his most significant work was on galactic star clusters.

TSCHERMAK, GUSTAV (*b. Littau [now Litove], near Olomouc, Czechoslovakia, 1836; d. Vienna, Austria, 1927*), petrography, mineralogy.

Tschermak studied chemistry and mineralogy at the University of Vienna, passing his teacher's examinations in 1860; he received the doctorate from the University of Tübingen later that year. He began his teaching career in 1861 at the University of Vienna, where he also held curatorial positions at the imperial mineral collection (1862–77); his petrographical researches and his later work on meteorites brought him an international reputation; his most significant contribution is his work on feldspar, recounted in his *Die Feldspatgruppe* (1864). He established that the great variety of chemical composition of the rock-forming silicates may be explained by the isomorphic mixture of simple compounds, from which changes in physical properties emerge naturally and in obedience to a law.

TSCHERMAK VON SEYSENEGG, ERICH (*b. Vienna, Austria, 1871; d. Vienna, 1962*), botany, genetics.

Tschermak was the son of Gustav Tschermak; he received the agricultural diploma (1895) and the Ph.D. (1896) from the University of Halle; from 1900 he taught at the Hochschule für Bodenkultur. Mendel's laws of heredity were rediscovered independently and simultaneously by Tschermak, H. de Vries, and C. Correns (1900). Tschermak's greatest service was his exclusive, immediate recognition of their importance and his application of these laws in his own breeding experiments; his discovery and elucidation of a cryptomeric heredity among the gillyflowers is a classic work in theoretical genetics, and his investigations of intergeneric hybridization led to basic discoveries about hybridization.

TSCHIRNHAUS, EHRENFRIED WALTHER (*b. Kieslingswalde, near Görlitz, Germany, 1651; d. Dresden, Germany, 1708*), mathematics, physics, philosophy.

Tschirnhaus studied philosophy, mathematics, and medicine at the University of Leiden (1668–72), where he was influenced by Sylvius and by Descartes's ideas. He moved to Paris (1675), where he tutored one of Colbert's sons and exchanged ideas with Leibniz and Huygens, though he never grasped the significance of Leibniz's infinitesimal symbolism; he was unwilling to accept suggestions from other mathematicians, although he would later adopt them as his own inventions and publish them as such. This tactic led to bitter controversies, particularly with Leibniz over the possibility of algebraic quadratures of algebraic curves (1682–84). His *Medicina corporis et mentis* (1686–87) was of considerable philosoph-

ical importance and was influential in the early stages of the Enlightenment.

TSERASKY (or CERASKY), VITOLD KARLOVICH (*b. Slutsk, Minsk guberniya, Russia, 1849; d. Meshcherskoe, near Podolsk, Moscow oblast, U.S.S.R., 1925*), astronomy.

Tserasky entered Moscow University in 1867 and after graduating worked at the observatory; becoming director, in 1890. He obtained his doctorate in 1887 and began teaching astronomy at Moscow University in 1882. From 1877 he conducted pioneering work in stellar photometry; from the astrophotographic studies he organized, his wife, Lidia Petrovna Shelekhova, discovered more than 200 variable stars; he made the first experimental determination of the lower limit of the temperature of the sun (1895).

TSIOLKOVSKY, KONSTANTIN EDUARDOVICH (*b. Izhevsk, Ryazan guberniya, Russia, 1857; d. Kaluga, U.S.S.R., 1935*), mechanics, aeronautics, astronautics.

At the age of nine Tsiolkovsky became almost completely deaf, yet in Moscow he was able to pass the teaching examination (1879) without attending lectures. He began teaching arithmetic and geometry in the Borovsk district school (1880) and moved to teach at Kaluga (1892). In the mid-1880's he began research in aerostatics, publishing plans for a metal dirigible (1892), an airplane (1894), and a spaceship (1903); his ideas did not find acceptance until after the October Revolution, when he became a member of the Academy (1918) and received a personal pension (1921). During the 1920's he elaborated his theory of multistage rockets and began working out his theory of the flight of jet engines, and his works on rocket engineering and space flight began to win international recognition.

TSU CH'UNG-CHIH (*b. Fan-yang prefecture [modern Hopeh province], China, ca. A.D. 429; d. China, ca. A.D. 500*), mathematics.

Tsu Ch'ung-chih was in the service of the emperor Hsiao-wu (r. 454–464) of the Liu Sung dynasty in Nanhsü (in modern Kiangsu province) and then in Chienk'ang (modern Nanking); he also did work in mathematics and astronomy; when the emperor died (464), he left the imperial service to devote himself entirely to science; he is known for calculating a more accurate value of π and for his attempt to reform the calendar; his proposed system was based on a cycle of 4,836 lunations in 391 years instead of the old system of 235 lunations in nineteen years, but was never implemented.

TSVET (or TSWETT), MIKHAIL SEMENOVICH (*b. Asti, Italy, 1872; d. Voronezh, Russia, 1919*), plant physiology, plant biochemistry.

Tsvet received the B.S. (1893) and the Ph.D. (1896) from the University of Geneva; in 1896 he moved to Russia and continued his studies at the Academy of Sciences and the St. Petersburg Biological Laboratory. Because foreign scientific degrees were not legally recognized in Russia, he obtained a master's degree in botany at Kazan University (1901) and a doctorate in botany (1910) at Warsaw Technical University. He taught botany and microbiology at the latter (1908–16) and was briefly at Yuryev (now Tartu) University (1917–18) before his health broke. Tsvet's main interest was in applying chemical methods to the study of cytophysiology; he discovered that there are two types of chlorophyll (now known as chlorophyll *a* and chlorophyll *b*) in leaves (1900). He also developed a physical method using adsorption, which he called chromatography, for isolating and separating plant pigments (summarized in his 1910 doctoral dissertation); with his new method he obtained pure forms of the chlorophylls and discovered chlorophyll *c* in brown and diatomic algae, also finding new forms of xanthophyll; acceptance of Tsvet's chromatographic method was very limited. The wide use of chromatography began in the 1930's, when R. Kuhn, L. Zechmeister, and P. Karrer simultaneously used it to study the chemistry of carotene and vitamin A.

IBN ṬUFAYL, ABŪ BAKR MUḤAMMAD (Abubacer) (*b. Guadix, Spain, before 1110; d. Marrakesh, Morocco, 1185*), medicine, philosophy.

Ibn Ṭufayl was a Spanish Muslim who received a broad education in Islam and the sciences; he was a physician at Granada, Ceuta, and Tangier, and was court physician to the Almohad sultan of Morocco and Andalusia (1163–82); he is best known for his book, "The Living, Son of the Wakeful," which presents Neoplatonic philosophy in the form of a myth, and which probably influenced Defoe's *Robinson Crusoe*.

TULASNE, LOUIS-RENÉ (*b. Azay-le-Rideau, France, 1815; d. Hyères, France, 1885*), mycology.

Tulasne studied law in Poitiers but on inheriting a large sum of money he joined his brother Charles in Paris, and they decided to devote themselves to botany, Christian religion, and charitable activities; he attended the lectures of Brongniart and A. de Jussieu, and collaborated with A. de Sainte-Hilaire; his principal work was on cryptogams, and his *Fungi hypogaei* (1851) remains one of the foundations of modern study; his major publication was *Selecta fungorum carpologia* (1857–65).

TULP, NICHOLAAS (*b. Amsterdam, Netherlands, 1593; d. The Hague, Netherlands, 1674*), medicine, anatomy.

Tulp received his M.D. degree from the University of Leiden (1614) and established a practice in Amsterdam; he was appointed *praelector* of anatomy (1628–52) and was charged with teaching all the surgeons in the city; his main work, *Observationum medicarum libri tres* (1641), contains descriptions of 228 cases; he gave the first description of beriberi and the chimpanzee, and suggested, and probably wrote, the first pharmacopoeia of the Netherlands (1636); he is best known from the painting by Rembrandt commissioned by the Surgeon's Guild in 1632, "Anatomy Lesson of Dr. Tulp."

TUNSTALL, CUTHBERT (*b. Hackforth, Yorkshire, England, 1474; d. London, England, 1559*), theology, diplomacy, mathematics.

Tunstall became doctor of both canon and civil laws at Padua (*ca.* 1505); he was appointed bishop of London (1522) and later bishop of Durham (1530); his arithmetic, *De arte supputandi* (1522), was a compilation of available works which was greatly admired on the Continent but was not popular in England; he was a close friend of Sir Thomas More and Erasmus.

TUPOLEV, ANDREY NIKOLAEVICH (*b. Pustomazovo, Tver [now Kalinin] guberniya, Russia, 1888; d. Moscow, U.S.S.R., 1972*), mechanics, aeronautical engineering.

Tupolev graduated from Moscow Technical School (1918), where he was influenced by N. E. Zhukovsky; he was assistant director of the Central Aerohydrodynamics Institute in Moscow (1918–35) and designed planes for the military during World War II; he built the first Russian jet passenger airplane (1955) and tested the first supersonic passenger airplane (1968).

TÜRCK, LUDWIG (*b. Vienna, Austria, 1810; d. Vienna, 1868*), medicine, laryngology, neurology.

Türck qualified as a physician at the medical school in Vienna (1836) and studied in Paris (1844); he then headed the neurological clinic at the General Hospital in Vienna until he was appointed physician in chief at the new and largest hospital in Vienna (1857); besides his neurological investigations, he is known for the independent construction and clinical application of the laryngoscope (1855). The mammalian temporo-pontine tract is named the "bundle of Türck" in his honor.

TURGOT, ANNE-ROBERT-JACQUES (*b. Paris, France, 1727; d. Paris, 1781*), economics, philosophy.

After studying for the priesthood at the Séminaire St.-Sulpice and the Sorbonne, Turgot decided (1751) to enter public service; he became intendant of Limoges (1761–74), where his reforms gained him national prominence; he then became controller general of finance in the first government formed by Louis XVI (1774–76), attempting many bold reforms. His interests were encyclopedic and extended far beyond his modern image as an economist; he studied Newtonian physics with Abbé Sigorgne and chemistry with G.-F. Rouelle, and wrote on physics, chemistry, and geology. The only scientific work he published in his lifetime was the article "Expansibilité" in the Diderot *Encyclopédie* (1756), which influenced Lavoisier. More significant was Turgot's role as a patron and a public official who regularly sought the advice of scientific experts, for he was convinced that applied science was a key to progress; he was the patron of the Society of Agriculture of Limoges, a co-founder with F. Vicq d'Azyr of what later became the Société Royale de Médecine (1776), and arranged the botanical and agricultural mission of Dombey to South America (1775). With Condorcet, his friend and closest consultant, he developed a project for a uniform system of weights and measures (1775), which was discontinued when Turgot fell from power. He appointed Condorcet, Bossut, and d'Alembert to a committee to investigate new canal projects (1775), also soon discontinued; a more lasting innovation was his creation of the Régie des Poudres to reform the manufacture of gunpowder (1775), appointing Lavoisier one of the *régisseurs;* his philosophy, if not all of his reforms, had a long-lasting influence.

TURGOT, ÉTIENNE-FRANÇOIS (*b. Paris, France, 1721; d. Château of Bons, Calvados, France, 1788*), botany, agronomy.

An older brother of A.-R.-J. Turgot, he served briefly as governor of Guiana (1764–65), after which he devoted himself to agricultural experiments and study.

TURING, ALAN MATHISON (*b. London, England, 1912; d. Wilmslow, England, 1954*), mathematics, mathematical logic, computer technology.

Turing graduated from King's College, Cambridge, where he was elected a fellow (1935). While working at Princeton University he published an important paper, "On Computable Numbers, With an Application to the *Entscheidungsproblem*" (1937); in it he analyzed the processes that can be carried out in computing a number to arrive at a concept of a theoretical "universal" computing machine (the "Turing machine"), capable of operating upon any sequence of zeros and ones; he also proved that Hilbert's *Entscheidungsproblem* is not solvable by these means. He worked on the automatic computing engine (ACE) at the National Physical Laboratory (1945–48) and then on the University of Manchester's automatic digital machine (MADAM) beginning in 1950; his studies of machine intelligence were presented in "Computing Machinery and Intelligence" (1950).

TURNER, EDWARD (*b. Kingston, Jamaica, 1796; d. Hampstead, London, England, 1837*), analytical chemistry.

Turner studied medicine at the University of Edinburgh (1816–19), chemistry and physics in Paris under Gay-Lussac, P.-J. Pelletier, and Robiquet (1820), and chemistry and mineral analysis at Göttingen (1821–23); he was appointed professor of chemistry and lecturer in geology at the new University of London, now University College, London (1827). He wrote one of the best nineteenth-century textbooks on chemistry, *Elements of Chemistry* (1827). At first he was a naïve disciple of Thomas Thomson, who adhered to Prout's hypothesis that atomic weights were integral multiples of the atomic weight of hydrogen; Turner later demonstrated that Thomson's atomic weights for chlorine, nitrogen, sulfur, lead, and mercury were wrong, confirming instead those of Berzelius, and concluding that integral atomic weights were only approximations.

TURNER, HERBERT HALL (*b. Leeds, England, 1861; d. Stockholm, Sweden, 1930*), astronomy, seismology.

Turner graduated from Cambridge University (1882), was chief assistant at the Royal Observatory, Greenwich (1884–93), and was Savilian professor of astronomy at Oxford (1893–1930); he is best known for organizing international scientific projects, including a number of eclipse expeditions and the publication of the quarterly *International Seismological Summary*, which he edited from 1918 to 1927.

TURNER, PETER (*b. London, England, 1586; d. London, 1652*), mathematics.

The grandson of William Turner (1508–68), Peter Turner graduated from Oxford (B.A., 1605; M.A., 1612), and became a fellow of Merton College (1607); he was the second Gresham professor of geometry (1620–30) and second Savilian professor of geometry (1630–48); he was one of the first scholars to enlist for King Charles in 1641, and was ejected from his professorship and his Merton fellowship by the Parliamentary Visitors (1648); he left no mathematical writings.

TURNER, WILLIAM (*b. Morpeth, Northumberland, England, 1508; d. London, England, 1568*), natural history, medicine.

Turner graduated from Pembroke Hall, Cambridge (B.A., 1529/30; M.A., 1533), where he became a fellow (1530–37). An ardent religious reformer, he periodically was forced by the threat of persecution to leave the country; in his first period of exile (1540–46), he obtained an M.D. at either Ferrara or Bologna. He was made dean of Wells cathedral (1551) before leaving for a second period of exile (1553–58), during which he was a medical practitioner in Weissenburg; after his second return to England he was restored to the deanery of Wells. His major botanical work is his *New Herball* (1551–68); one estimate is that Turner's pioneering flora provided the first descriptions of 238 species of native plants; his descriptions were unorthodox in being written in the vernacular and by including many firsthand observations; the work was not well known to later botanists with the exception of J. Bauhin and John Ray.

TURNER, WILLIAM (*b. Lancaster, England, 1832; d. Edinburgh, Scotland, 1916*), anatomy, academic administration.

After an apprenticeship with a medical practitioner and a stint at St. Bartholomew's Hospital, London, Turner qualified with the membership of the Royal College of Surgeons of England (1853); he was made senior demonstrator in anatomy at the University of Edinburgh (1854), and succeeded to the chair in anatomy (1867), resigning only to become principal of the university (1903–16). He was president of a number of scientific and medical societies, founded the *Journal of Anatomy and Physiology* (1867) and the Anatomical Society of Great Britain and Ireland (1887), and made important contributions to the Medical Act of 1886, which still largely governs medical education in Britain. He placed British anthropology on a new footing; he corresponded with Darwin, and many of his observations were included in the *Descent of Man*.

TURNER, WILLIAM ERNEST STEPHEN (*b. Wednesbury, Staffordshire, England, 1881; d. Sheffield, England, 1963*), glass technology.

Turner graduated from Birmingham University (B.S., 1902; M.S., 1904); his entire career was spent at Sheffield University, where he helped establish a Department of Glass Technology during World War I, which held unchallenged world leadership in glass research for a generation. He founded the Society of Glass Technology (1916) and edited its *Journal* (1917–59).

TURPIN, PIERRE JEAN FRANÇOIS (*b. Vire, France, 1775; d. Paris, France, 1840*), botany.

Turpin studied drawing at the École des Beaux-Arts in Vire and learned botany from A. Poiteau, a gardener at the Paris Muséum d'Histoire Naturelle, while stationed in Haiti in the French army; he returned to France in 1802 and became a botanical artist whose fame was equal to that of Redouté. He collaborated on a number of the most important botanical publications of the early nineteenth century, including Humboldt's *Plantae aequinoctiales* and several works with Poiteau; he defended the idea of organ types in a number of works and participated in the elaboration of cell theory.

TURQUET DE MAYERNE, THEODORE (*b. Mayerne, near Geneva, Switzerland, 1573; d. London, England, 1655*), medicine, chemistry.

Turquet studied at the University of Heidelberg and at Montpellier, where he received the M.D. degree (1597); he became a successful royal physician to Henry IV in Paris, where he worked under J. Ribit; both Ribit and Turquet supported the use of chemical therapeutics in medicine and they were probably instrumental in establishing J. Beguin's chemistry courses in Paris. Turquet was censured by the Paris Medical Faculty for his publication (1603) defending Paracelsian remedies, but as a royal physician was able to continue in practice. After the assassination of Henry IV, he moved to England (1611), where he was incorporated M.D. at the University of Oxford (1606), and became first physician to James I and later to Charles I; at the outbreak of the English Civil War he retired to Chelsea. Although not a prominent scientific figure, he aided the introduction of chemical therapeutics in medicine.

AL-ṬŪSĪ, MUḤAMMAD IBN MUḤAMMAD IBN AL-ḤASAN, usually known as **NAṢĪR AL-DĪN** (*b. Ṭūs, Persia, 1201; d. Kadhimain, near Baghdad, 1274*), astronomy, mathematics, mineralogy, logic, philosophy, ethics, theology.

Al-Ṭūsī is one of the best-known and most influential figures in Islamic intellectual history. He studied the religious sciences and elements of the "intellectual" sciences with his father and studied logic, natural philosophy with his uncle; he completed his studies in Nīshāpūr, where he gained a reputation as an outstanding scholar. Al-Ṭūsī found protection from advancing the Mongols in the forts of the Ismāʿīlī ruler, Naṣīr al-Dīn Muḥtashim, sometime before 1232; this allowed him to write some of his important ethical, logical, philosophical, and mathematical works, including his most famous work, the *Nasirean Ethics*. When Hūlāgū ended the rule of the Ismāʿīlīs (1256), al-Ṭūsī was retained in his service and allowed to construct a major observatory at Marāgha (begun 1259). Most of the 150 known treatises and letters by al-Ṭūsī were written in Arabic; his breadth of knowledge and influence is comparable to that of Ibn Sīnā, though the latter was the better physician and al-Ṭūsī the better mathematician. Of his five works on logic, his "Foundations of Inference" is the most important. In mathematics he composed a series of recensions upon the works of Autolycus, Aristarchus, Euclid, Apollonius, Archimedes, Hypsicles, Theodosius, Menelaus, and Ptolemy; his most important original works on arithmetic, geometry, and trigonometry include "The Comprehensive Work on Computation with Board and Dust," "The Satisfying Treatise," and a work known as the *Book of the Principle of Transversal*, which influenced Regiomontanus. The best-known of his astronomical works are "The Īlkhānī Tables" (1271) and "Treasury of Astronomy"; he also wrote "The Book of Precious Materials" and works on astrology. Probably al-Ṭūsī's most outstanding contribution to mathematics was in trigonometry; in *Book of the Principle of Transversal* he was the first to develop trigonometry without using Menelaus' theorem or astronomy; he also described clearly for the first time the theorem of sines, a landmark in the history of mathematics; in astronomy, his "Treasury of Astronomy" is perhaps the most

thorough criticism of Ptolemaic astronomy in medieval times and presents the only new mathematical model of planetary motion to appear in medieval astronomy; it most likely influenced Copernicus through Byzantine intermediaries and, with the work of al-Ṭūsī's followers, contains all the novelty of Copernicus' astronomy except the heliocentric hypothesis; al-Ṭūsī is best-known as an astronomer and his observatory constitutes a major scientific institution in the history of science. His "Book of Precious Materials" is second in importance only to al-Bīrūnī's work on that subject. Al-Ṭūsī was one of the foremost philosophers of Islam, reviving the Peripatetic teachings of Ibn Sīnā after they had been eclipsed for two centuries by *Kalām;* he marks the first stage in the gradual synthesis of the Peripatetic and Illuminationist schools. His *Nasirean Ethics* has been the most popular ethical work among the Muslims of India and Persia for centuries; his "Catharsis" is the foundation of systematic theology for the Twelve Imām Shīʿites. Al-Ṭūsī was probably more responsible for the revival of the Islamic sciences than any other individual.

AL-ṬŪSĪ, SHARAF AL-DĪN AL-MUẒAFFAR IBN MUḤAMMAD IBN AL-MUẒAFFAR (*b. Ṭūs [?], Iran; d. Iran, ca. 1213/1214*), astronomy, mathematics.

Al-Ṭūsī taught at Damascus about 1165; after teaching in Aleppo for about three years, he was apparently in Mosul in the years preceding 1175; he returned to Iran, where he died at an advanced age. He is known for his linear astrolabe (al-Ṭūsī's staff), a simple wooden rod with graduated markings but without sights, which he described in several treatises; although inexpensive to construct, it was less accurate than the ordinary astrolabe, less decorative and of little interest to collectors, and not a single linear astrolabe has survived. His greatest achievement is recorded in *Kitāb fi'l-jabr wa'l-muqābala,* a reworking of a mathematical treatise of al-Ṭūsī's by an unknown author; it deals with the numerical solutions of twenty-five equations up to the third degree.

TUTTON, ALFRED EDWIN HOWARD (*b. Stockport, Cheshire, England, 1864; d. Dallington, Sussex, England, 1938*), crystallography.

Tutton graduated from the Royal College of Science in London (1886); he was inspector of technical schools (1895–1924) and served successively in the Oxford, London, and Plymouth districts; he published about fifty papers between 1890 and 1929 on the precise goniometric and optical study of isomorphous salts; his data added substantially to the understanding of isomorphism.

TWENHOFEL, WILLIAM HENRY (*b. Covington, Ky., 1875; d. Atlanta, Ga., 1957*), geology.

Twenhofel earned the baccalaureate (1904) from National Normal University at Lebanon, Kansas, and earned three degrees in geology at Yale University (B.A., 1908; M.A., 1910; Ph.D., 1912), where he was influenced by C. Schuchert and J. Barrell; he joined the University of Wisconsin (1916), where he taught for thirty years. His demonstration of the transitional nature of the Ordovician-Silurian boundary in northeastern North America brought him international recognition as an authority on Ordovician and Silurian stratigraphy and paleontology;

more than anyone else in his time, he led and promoted the study of sedimentation as a branch of geology.

TWORT, FREDERICK WILLIAM (*b. Camberley, London, England, 1877; d. Camberley, 1950*), microbiology.

Twort attended St. Thomas' Hospital Medical School in London, where he qualified (1900) as member of the Royal College of Surgeons and licentiate of the Royal College of Physicians. He entered the field of microbiology as assistant to W. Bulloch at the London Hospital (1902–09); he was superintendent of the Brown Animal Sanatory Institution in London (1909–44) and was appointed professor of bacteriology in the University of London (1919). His work centered on his thesis that pathogenic bacteria have evolved from wild ancestors; he was first to discover (1915) the lytic phenomena caused by what F. d'Hérelle named bacteriophage in 1917.

TYNDALL, JOHN (*b. Leighlinbridge, County Carlow, Ireland, 1820; d. Hindhead, Surrey, England, 1893*), natural philosophy, microbiology, popularization of science.

A draftsman and civil engineer in the Irish Ordnance Survey, Tyndall was transferred to the English survey at Preston, Lancashire (1842), where he was dismissed for his protests against repressive policies. After working as a surveyor and engineer (1844–45), he taught mathematics and drawing at Queenwood College, Hampshire (1847–48); he left (1848) with his fellow teacher, the chemist E. Frankland, to study at the University of Marburg, where he completed a mathematical dissertation for the doctorate and collaborated with K. H. Knoblauch on studies of diamagnetism. Jobless in England for two years, like his friend T. H. Huxley, he was obliged, like Huxley, to write, lecture, and examine in order to survive; he became professor of natural philosophy at the Royal Institution (1853) and later succeeded Faraday as superintendent and as adviser to Trinity House and the Board of Trade (1867–85). Tyndall's research can be described in two phases: the first (1853–74) was a steady progression within physics, while the second, between 1874 and the early 1880's, saw the amplification of his work in other domains; he is remembered chiefly for his efforts to verify the high absorptive and radiative power of aqueous vapor, to measure the absorption and transmission of heat by different gases and liquids, to explain the selective influence of the atmosphere on different sounds, and to establish the principle of "discontinuous heating" ("Tyndallization") as a sterilizing technique. Tyndall occupied a unique place in the popular exposition of science; he gave over fifty Friday discourses, over 300 afternoon lectures, and twelve Christmas courses for young people at the Royal Institution; in 1859 he joined Huxley in writing a regular column for the *Saturday Review,* he acted as scientific adviser to *The Reader* (1863–67), and he helped inaugurate the journal *Nature* (1869); his republished essays and lectures were very popular; the American edition of *Fragments of Science* (1871), for instance, was sold out on the day of publication, and *Forms of Water* (1872) went through twelve English editions by 1897; his lectures in America (1872–73) were published in *Six Lectures on Light* (1873). Tyndall was involved in many public disputes, particularly after his provocative presidential address to the British Association (1874), in which he placed science against religious authority.

TYRRELL, JOSEPH BURR (*b. Weston, Ontario, Canada, 1858; d. Toronto, Canada, 1957*), geology, exploration, mining.

Tyrrell graduated from the University of Toronto and began his career as a field assistant with the Geological Survey of Canada; he participated in the exploration of many remote areas of Canada, and discovered the first remains of giant carnivorous dinosaurs found in Canada. He is remembered for his recognition that three major Pleistocene ice sheets had covered northern and eastern Canada. After a visit to the Yukon during the Klondike gold rush (1898), Tyrrell left the Geological Survey and returned to the Yukon as a consultant; his greatest achievement was the discovery of the Kirkland Lake gold deposit, which he predicted from structural reasoning.

TYSON, EDWARD (*b. Bristol, England, ca. 1650; d. London, England, 1708*), comparative anatomy, medicine.

Tyson graduated from Magdalen Hall, Oxford (B.A., 1670; M.A., 1673; bachelor of medicine, 1677), where he was influenced by Plot; while maintaining an active medical practice in London (1677–1708), he lectured on anatomy at Surgeons Hall (1684–99), was physician to Bethlehem and Bridewell Hospitals (beginning 1684), and conducted research in comparative anatomy. He was elected a fellow of the Royal College of Physicians (1683) and received a doctorate in physics from Cambridge; his first major contribution in comparative anatomy, *Phocaena, or the Anatomy of a Porpess . . .* (1680), was a description of a dolphin and did much to set the style and direction for comparative-anatomical work in the late seventeenth century. His best-known work is *Orang-Outang, Sive Homo Sylvestris: or, the Anatomy of a Pygmie Compared With That of a Monkey, an Ape, and a Man* (1699); it concludes that the "Orang-Outang" (actually a chimpanzee) occupied a rung immediately below man in the Great Chain of Being; the identification of such graduational links was one of his objectives for comparative anatomy.

UBALDO, GUIDO. *See* **Monte, Guidobaldo, Marchese del.**

UEXKÜLL, JAKOB JOHANN VON (*b. Keblas, Estonia [now Estonian S. S. R.], 1864; d. Capri, Italy, 1944*), biology.

Uexküll studied zoology at the University of Dorpat (now Tartu), where he was influenced by the writings of K. E. von Baer and J. Müller; he worked on muscle physiology with Kühne at Heidelberg (1888) and with Marey in Paris; he was director of the Institut für Umweltforschung at the University of Hamburg (1925–36), where he was also an honorary professor (1925–44). He is known for his *Umweltlehre,* which has stimulated research in ethology by K. Lorenz and others; the theory assumes that within its own subjective "self-world," a living being perceives only that which its sense organs convey to it and deals only with those factors that its locomotive organs can affect; his concept of a functional circle anticipates the notion of a control loop in cybernetics.

UKHTOMSKY, ALEXEI ALEXEIVICH (*b. Rhurik, Russia, 1875; d. Leningrad, U.S.S.R., 1942*), physiology.

Ukhtomsky studied at the Moscow Theological Academy at Zagorsk, where he became a member of the Old

Believers, a dissenting group in the Russian Orthodox Church; his interests changed, however, and he entered the University of St. Petersburg (1902) and specialized in animal physiology. While working as a demonstrator after graduating, he stumbled on the phenomenon that led to his theory of a dominant focus of cortical excitation operating to exclude and inhibit other concurrent functions, which became the subject of his master's thesis (1912) and guided his later work. He became a docent at St. Petersburg (1912) and later succeeded to the chair of physiology (1922).

ULLOA Y DE LA TORRE GIRAL, ANTONIO DE (*b. Seville, Spain, 1716; d. Isla de Léon, Cádiz, Spain, 1795*), natural history.

A mariner by profession, Ulloa and J. Juan y Santicilla accompanied the expedition sent to America by the Paris Academy of Sciences to measure an arc of meridian (1736–45); with Juan he published *Relación histórica del viaje a la América meridional* (1748), which includes the first scientific description of the platinum found in Colombia (1736). He served as the first Spanish governor of Louisiana (1766–68) and published other works on the natural history of the Americas.

ULRICH OF STRASBOURG (or **ULRICUS DE ARGENTINA** or **ULRICH ENGELBERTI**) (*b. early thirteenth century; d. Paris, ca. 1278*), natural philosophy.

A student of Albertus Magnus at Cologne (1248–54), Ulrich became his devoted disciple; he lectured at Strasbourg for many years. His chief work is *Summa de summo bono* ("A Summary Concerning the Supreme Good"); the portions on astronomy are largely derived from Albertus Magnus and indicate the latter's all-pervading influence on scientific matters on the Continent.

ULRICH, EDWARD OSCAR (*b. Cincinnati, Ohio, 1857; d. Washington, D.C., 1944*), stratigraphy, paleontology.

Ulrich's formal education was limited to intermittent terms at two Ohio colleges during the 1870's; his career was typical of those nineteenth-century paleontologists who, beginning as self-taught amateur collectors, reached professional status through independent publication, then commissions for state or territorial geologic surveys, and finally, a permanent position with the federal survey, a large museum, or a major university. Ulrich's first permanent position was with the U. S. Geological Survey (1901), at which time his research shifted from paleontology to stratigraphy; he was appointed associate in paleontology at the U. S. National Museum (1914), and occupied that position after his retirement from the U. S. Geological Survey (1932). He was an eminent authority on American lower Paleozoic stratigraphy during the first three decades of the twentieth century, and dominated the discipline; Ulrich believed stratigraphic syntheses to be his most lasting contributions; perhaps his most important influence during his years on the U. S. Geological Survey was the controversial aspect of his research and his disputative nature, which caused contemporaries to re-examine critically their own investigations.

ULSTAD, PHILIPP (*fl. early sixteenth century*), medicine, alchemy.

Ulstad was a Nuremberg patrician who taught medicine at the Academy in Fribourg, Switzerland; his *Coelum philosophorum . . .* (1525) was an extremely popular standard authority on the preparation and use of distillates for nearly a century; it contributed to the rise of the iatrochemistry of Paracelsus and his followers by demonstrating that drugs and other medicinals depend for their efficacy upon pure spirits or essences that can be extracted by the methods of chemistry; he influenced K. Gesner and A. Libavius.

ULUGH BEG (*b. Sulṭāniyya, Central Asia, 1394; d. near Samarkand, Central Asia [now Uzbek S.S.R.], 1449*), astronomy.

Ulugh Beg was raised at the court of his grandfather, Tamerlane, and from 1409 was ruler of Maverannakhr, the chief city of which was Samarkand. In 1420 he founded a *madrasa*, or institution of higher learning, in which astronomy was the most important subject; besides Ulugh Beg, the lecturers included Qāḍī Zāda and al-Kāshī; He soon erected a three-story observatory (1424), whose main instrument was a "Fakhrī sextant," used in determining the basic constants of astronomy related to the sun; the radius of the Fakhrī sextant was 40.04 meters, which made it the largest astronomical instrument in the world of that type. An important result of Ulugh Beg's school was the astronomical tables called the *Zīj* of Ulugh Beg or the *Zīj-i Gurgānī;* originally written in the Tadzhik language, this work consists of a theoretical section and the results of the observatory observations; the latter include tables of calendar calculations, of trigonometry, and of the planets, as well as a star catalog; the ruins of the observatory, which was destroyed in the sixteenth century, were located in 1908, and the tomb of Ulugh Beg was discovered in 1941.

ULYANOV, VLADIMIR ILYICH. *See* **Lenin (Ulyanov), Vladimir Ilyich.**

ʿUMAR AL-KHAYYĀMĪ. *See* **ʿAl-Khayyāmī** (or **Khayyām**), **Ghiyāth al-Dīn Abu'l-Fatḥ ʿUmar ibn Ibrāhīm al-Nīsābūrī** (or **al-Naysābūrī**), also known as **Omar Khayyam.**

ʿUMAR IBN AL-FARRUKHĀN AL-ṬABARĪ (*fl. Baghdad, Iraq, 762–812*), astrology, astronomy.

ʿUmar was one of those Persian scholars who made the early Abbasid court a center for the translation of Pahlavi scientific texts into Arabic; he was one of a group of astrologers, including Māshāʾallāh and al-Fazārī, whom al-Manṣūr asked to select an auspicious time for the foundation of Baghdad. Among his extant works are a paraphrase of Ptolemy's *Tetrabiblos* (812) and a paraphrase of the astrological work of Dorotheus of Sidon.

AL-UMAWĪ, ABŪ ʿABDALLĀH YAʿĪSH IBN IBRĀHĪM IBN YŪSUF IBN SIMĀK AL-ANDALUSĪ (*fl. Damascus, fourteenth century*), arithmetic.

Al-Umawī was a Spanish Arab who lived in Damascus, where he taught arithmetic; his *Marāsim al-intisāb fī ʿilm al-ḥisāb* represents a trend of Arabic arithmetic in which, as early as the tenth century, the Indian "dust board" calculations had begun to be modified to suit paper and ink, and arithmetic was enriched by concepts from traditional finger reckoning and the Pythagorean theory of numbers; the trend seems to have started in Damascus and probably had greater influence in the West than in the East; the work is especially interesting in connection with the early history of number theory.

UNANUE, JOSÉ HIPÓLITO (*b. Arica, Peru [now Chile], 1755; d. Lima, Peru, 1833*), natural history.

Unanue, the outstanding figure of the Peruvian enlightenment, received his medical degree in 1784 and by 1789 was professor of anatomy at the University of San Marcos; his major work, *Observaciones sobre el clima de Lima* (1806), purported to correlate climate with disease in Lima and had tremendous local influence, despite its archaic cast, and denial of the relevance of chemistry to medical practice; he planned and directed the new medical school, the College of San Fernando (opened in 1811).

UNGER, FRANZ (*b. Der Gute Amthof, near Leutschach, Austria, 1800; d. Graz, Austria, 1870*), botany.

Unger studied at the universities of Vienna and Prague, qualifying to practice medicine in 1827; he was professor of botany at Graz (1835–49) and professor of plant anatomy and physiology at the University of Vienna (1849–66). His fame rested chiefly on the *Grundzüge der Botanik* (1843), which he wrote with S. Endlicher; in advocating cell multiplication by cell division it made him Schleiden's first opponent on the question of the origin of cells; his popular articles on evolution were collected in *Botanische Briefe* (1852), and provoked a violent personal attack from the Catholic press. Unger's work may have played a crucial role in equipping Gregor Mendel, a student of his at Vienna, for the cytological interpretation of his breeding experiments.

UNZER, JOHANN AUGUST (*b. Halle, Germany, 1727; d. Altona, Germany, 1799*), physiology, medicine.

Unzer studied medicine at Halle under J. Juncker, a disciple of Stahl, and under Stahl's opponent, F. Hoffman (M.D., 1748); he practiced medicine and conducted research in Hamburg and then in Altona. He gradually abandoned his Stahlian animism for a more anatomical and physiological approach, directed mainly to the role of the nervous system in animal functions; his major work is *Erste Gründe* (later translated into English as *The Principles of Physiology of the Proper Animal Nature of the Animal Organism*) (1771). Although his original contribution to physiology is slight, his essentially correct presentation of the mechanical and material aspects of nerve functions became the basis of a considerable body of work on the nervous system in the nineteenth century.

AL-UQLĪDĪSĪ, ABU'L-ḤASAN AḤMAD IBN IBRĀHĪM (*fl. Damascus, 952–953*), arithmetic.

Al-Uqlīdīsī is known only from a unique copy of his work entitled *Kitāb al-fuṣūl fi'l-ḥisāb al-hindī*, written at Damascus in 952–953 and copied in 1157; it is the most important of some one hundred extant Arabic arithmetic texts; it is the earliest known text that contains a direct treatment of decimal fractions, and it is the first text to tell us clearly that Indian arithmetic depended on the dust abacus; al-Uqlīdīsī suggests a modification of the Indian arithmetical operations whereby the abacus can be dispensed with, and paper and ink can be used instead; this modification presents a first step in a long chain of attempts that resulted in discarding the abacus completely, first in western Islam and, many centuries later, in the eastern part.

URBAIN, GEORGES (*b. Paris, France, 1872; d. Paris, 1938*), chemistry, mineralogy.

Urbain graduated from École de Physique et de Chimie (1894), where he was influenced by Pierre Curie; he received the doctorate from the University of Paris (1899); he became a professor at the Sorbonne (1906) and was appointed director of the Institut de Chimie de Paris (1928); his name is linked with his important studies of the rare earths (1895–1912), especially with his separation of ytterbium into ytterbium and lutetium and his determination of their atomic weights; after 1912 he studied theoretical complex chemistry; he extended A. Werner's coordination theory and proposed his own theory of homeomerism in the hope of unifying organic and inorganic chemistry.

URE, ANDREW (*b. Glasgow, Scotland, 1778; d. London, England, 1857*), chemistry.

Ure graduated M.D. at the University of Glasgow (1801) and became professor of natural philosophy at the Andersonian Institution (now the University of Strathclyde), Glasgow (1804), where his evening lectures in chemistry and mechanics for artisans were extremely popular. He made no significant contributions to science yet was an indefatigable writer and encyclopedist, and his major work, the *Philosophy of Manufactures . . .* (1835), while containing ridiculous passages, contains the first clear recognition that what came to be called the industrial revolution was a novel and irreversible alteration in the human condition. His *System of Geology* (1829) was an outdated attempt to reconcile contemporary geology with the Mosaic account of the Creation, and was heavily criticized by A. Sedgwick. After disputes with the managers of the Institution, he resigned (1830) and moved to London, where he became probably the first consulting chemist in Great Britain.

URYSON, PAVEL SAMUILOVICH (*b. Odessa, Russia, 1898; d. Batz, France, 1924*), mathematics.

Uryson graduated from the University of Moscow (1919), where he was appointed assistant professor in mathematics (1921); he drowned off the coast of Brittany at the age of twenty-six while on vacation; although his scientific activity lasted only five years, he greatly influenced the development of topology, particularly regarding topological space and the theory of dimensionality, and laid the foundations of the Soviet school of topology.

VAGNER (or **WAGNER**), **EGOR EGOROVICH** (*b. Kazan, Russia, 1849; d. Warsaw, Poland, 1903*), chemistry.

Vagner graduated from the University of Kazan (1874) and became professor at the Novo-Aleksandr Agricultural Institute (1882) and at the University of Warsaw (1886); he was one of the founders of the chemistry of terpenes; his Vagner oxidation method (developed 1882–88) made it possible in the nineteenth century to study the structure of complex unsaturated organic compounds, and is still important.

VAILATI, GIOVANNI (*b. Crema, Italy, 1863; d. Rome, Italy, 1909*), logic, philosophy of science, history of science.

Vailati graduated from the University of Turin in engineering (1884) and in mathematics (1888); he was G. Peano's assistant at the University of Turin (1892–95) and from 1899 held appointments in various secondary schools; he was best known to his contemporaries as the leading Italian exponent of pragmatism, but his essays in the history and methodology of science will perhaps be his most lasting contribution.

VAILLANT, LÉON-LOUIS (*b. Paris, France, 1834; d. Paris, 1914*), ichthyology, herpetology.

Vaillant obtained both the M.D. (1861) and the Ph.D. (1865) in Paris; he became assistant and then full professor at the Muséum National d'Histoire Naturelle in Paris, and occupied the chair of herpetology and ichthyology there (1875–1910); he published almost two hundred papers, each but a few pages long, and each containing a new detail that was significant in determining the precise classification of some little-known species; he also helped publish the results of expeditions that he had either participated in or had watched closely.

VAILLANT, SÉBASTIEN (*b. Vigny, Val d'Oise, France, 1669; d. Paris, France, 1722*), botany.

Vaillant studied medicine at the hospital in Pontoise and began to practice surgery at Évreux (1688) and then in Paris (1692); he became secretary to G. Fagon, who later became superintendent of the Jardin du Roi, where Vaillant was put in charge of the garden and became demonstrator of plants; his inaugural lecture there irrefutably established the existence of plant sexuality for the first time in France (1717); his *Botanicon parisiense* was published posthumously by Boerhaave.

VALDEN, PAVEL IVANOVICH. *See* **Walden, Paul.**

VALENCIENNES, ACHILLE (*b. Paris, France, 1794; d. Paris, 1865*), zoology.

After his education at the Collège de Rouen was cut off by the death of his father, who had worked at the Muséum d'Histoire Naturelle in Paris, Valenciennes became a *préparateur* (1812) and eventually an *aide-naturaliste* at the Muséum; he held the chair of annelids, mollusks, and zoophytes at the Muséum (from 1832). His major scientific achievement was his collaboration with Cuvier on eight volumes of the *Histoire naturelle des poissons* (1828–32); Valenciennes published an additional fourteen volumes (1832–49) after Cuvier's death.

VALENTIN, GABRIEL GUSTAV (*b. Breslau, Prussia [now Wrocław, Poland], 1810; d. Bern, Switzerland, 1883*), embryology, general and comparative anatomy, physiology.

Valentin received his medical degree from the University of Breslau (1832), where he was Purkyně's most important student; he was appointed to the chair of physiology and zootomy at the University of Bern (1836), becoming the first Jewish professor at a German-language university; he was also director of the Bern Anatomical Institute (1853–63). Although his initial research centered on the formation of plant and animal tissue (he concluded their development is not comparable), he also was interested in the processes of intracellular movement in plants, and in his studies of animals he was particularly concerned with embryology. He also pursued the microscopic examination of the structure of nerve tissue, becaming involved in controversies with J. Müller, R. Remak, and others. His two-volume work, *Lehrbuch der Physiologie des Menschen* (1844), is novel for its attempts to treat problems mathematically; this and his other textbook, *Grundriss der Physiologie des Menschen* (1846), were replaced after a decade of popularity by C. Ludwig's *Physiologie des Menschen* (1852–56). He published important research on the structure of the eye (1842), the hibernation of the marmot (1857–88), and on his polarization and spectroscopic studies; the latter are recorded in "Histologische und physiologische Studien" (1862–82). He also made seven studies on the effects of curare and other arrow poisons on muscles and nerves (1868–73); he was the first Jew to be granted citizenship by the city of Bern.

VALENTINE, BASIL (or **Basilius Valentinus**), chemistry, alchemy, iatrochemistry.

Supposedly Basil Valentine was a German Benedictine monk born at Mainz in 1394, who was elected prior of the monastery of St. Peter's in Erfurt in 1414; however, there is no contemporary evidence for any of the facts relating to his life. His *Zwölff Schlüssel* (1602), was a traditional book of alchemical symbolism that was to become one of the most frequently reprinted chemical-alchemical treatises of the seventeenth and eighteenth centuries; another work attributed to him, *Triumph Wagen Antimonii* (1604), contains a wealth of information on antimony and medical antimonial compounds. Although Valentine was a typical Paracelsian who emphasized the macrocosm-microcosm universe, his writings were used against Paracelsus by seventeenth century chemists who attempted to destroy his reputation by claiming he plagiarized Valentine's works.

VALERIANUS, MAGNUS. *See* **Magni, Valeriano.**

VALERIO (or **VALERI**), **LUCA** (*b. Naples, Italy, 1552; d. Rome, Italy, 1618*), mathematics.

Valerio was educated in Rome at the Collegio Romano, where Clavius was one of his teachers; he taught rhetoric and Greek at the Collegio Greco and, from 1600 until his death, mathematics at the Sapienza in Rome; a correspondent of Galileo, he was a member of the Accademia dei Lincei (1612–16), but was expelled for unknown reasons and spent his last two years in disgrace; he wrote *De centro gravitatis* (1604) and *Quadratura parabolae* (1606).

VALLÉE-POUSSIN, CHARLES-JEAN-GUSTAVE-NICOLAS DE LA (*b. Louvain, Belgium, 1866; d. Louvain, 1962*), mathematics.

Vallée-Poussin graduated from the Jesuit College at Mons and was elected to the chair of mathematics at the University of Louvain (1892), where he remained all his life; he was the outstanding Belgian mathematician of his generation; although the proof of the prime number theorem (1896) was his highest achievement, his main impact on mathematical thought was his *Cours d'analyse* (1903–06), which went through many editions.

VALLISNIERI (or VALLISNERI), ANTONIO (*b. Trassilico, Garfagnana district, Lucca province, Italy, 1661; d. Padua, Italy, 1730*), biology, medicine.

Vallisnieri received a bachelor's degree in Aristotelian philosophy (1682) from a Roman Catholic college in Reggio nell'Emilia; he studied under Malpighi at the University of Bologna and took his doctorate at Reggio (1684), and completed his medical training at Venice and Parma (1687–88); he held the chair of practical medicine (1700–10) and the first chair of theoretical medicine (1710–30) at the University of Padua. His first important scientific contribution was a complement to Redi's demonstration (1668) of the fallacy of the hypothesis of spontaneous generation; he developed to a considerable extent the theory of the "chain of beings" and was thus a precursor of the "ladder" established by C. Bonnet (1779). In a published letter (1715), he supported Cogrossi's hypothesis (1714) that a contagious disease such as cattle plague is due to microscopic parasites; he rejected Scholastic knowledge as well as occultist interpretations of natural phenomena, trusting solely in direct observation and in experiments.

VALMONT DE BOMARE, JACQUES-CHRISTOPHE (*b. Rouen, France, 1731; d. Paris, France, 1807*), mineralogy, natural history.

Valmont studied pharmacy and chemistry at Rouen; in Paris (1751) he obtained a commission from the government as a traveling naturalist, allowing him to make visits to most of Europe during the next twelve years; he introduced a highly successful public course in natural history at the Jardin des Plantes (1756–88). He became head of the cabinet of physics and natural history of the Prince de Condé at Chantilly (1769) and was professor of natural history at the École centrale in the Rue Saint-Antoine (1796–1806). His most important work was his *Dictionnaire raisonné universel d'histoire naturelle* (1764), which was highly successful in encouraging the popular study of natural history and served as a model for all similar works; he did not produce original scientific work, but was one of the most influential popularizers of natural history in France during the Enlightenment.

VALSALVA, ANTON MARIA (*b. Imola, Italy, 1666; d. Bologna, Italy, 1723*), anatomy.

Valsalva received the doctorate in medicine and philosophy (1687) at the University of Bologna, where he was the favorite pupil of Malpighi; he was lecturer and demonstrator in anatomy there from 1705 to 1723. His most famous work is *De aure humana tractatus* (1704), which treats the anatomy and physiology of the ear; he was an extremely skilled anatomist and pathologist, a fine physician, and an excellent surgeon for a quarter-century in the Bolognese hospitals; he considered madness to be a disease and was among the first to call for, and in part to implement, humanitarian treatment of the insane.

VALTURIO, ROBERTO (*b. Rimini, Italy, 1405; d. Rimini, 1475*), military technology, diffusion of knowledge.

Valturio served as apostolic secretary to Pope Eugene IV and in 1446 or 1447 became private secretary to the ruler of Rimini, Sigismondo Pandolfo Malatesta; at Sigismondo's request, Valturio wrote a treatise on the art of war known as *De re militari* (completed between 1455 and 1460); the first printed edition (1472) was a masterpiece of typography and woodcut, and passages of it were copied by Leonardo da Vinci; it gives only cursory coverage to the more recent military technology based on gunpowder.

VALVERDE, JUAN DE (*b. Amusco, Palencia, Spain, ca. 1520; d. Rome [?], Italy, ca. 1588*), medicine, anatomy.

Valverde studied at Valladolid University before going to Padua for anatomical training for several years under Vesalius and Colombo until 1543; he became assistant to Colombo when the latter went to Pisa (1544), and apparently accompanied Colombo to Rome (1548), where he became physician to Cardinal Álvarez de Toledo; his most famous work was the *Historia de la composición del cuerpo humano* (1556), which made many corrections and additions to Vesalius' *Fabrica* and came to be preferred to the latter.

VAN DE GRAAFF, ROBERT JEMISON (*b. Tuscaloosa, Ala., 1901; d. Boston, Mass., 1967*), physics.

Van de Graaff studied engineering at the University of Alabama (B.S., 1922; M.S., 1923), and physics at the Sorbonne and at Oxford, where he earned the Ph.D. (1928); as a National Research Fellow at Princeton (1929), he constructed the first working model of his belt-charged electro-static high-voltage generator. He came to the Massachusetts Institute of Technology as a research fellow (1931) and became associate professor of physics (1934–60); he worked on developing particle accelerators and in the late 1950's invented the insulating-core transformer; he also worked on accelerating heavy ions utilizing the tandem principle.

VANDERMONDE, ALEXANDRE-THÉOPHILE, also known as Alexis, Abnit, and Charles-Auguste Vandermonde (*b. Paris, France, 1735; d. Paris, 1796*), mathematics.

Although engaged in a musical career, Vandermonde developed an interest in mathematics through an acquaintance with A. Fontaine; he was elected to the Académie des Sciences (1771), to which he presented four mathematical papers (his total mathematical output) in 1771–72, two of which were of substantial importance; he is best known for the determinant that is named after him.

VAN DER WAALS, JOHANNES DIDERIK. *See* Waals, Johannes Diderik van der.

VAN HISE, CHARLES RICHARD (*b. Fulton, Wis., 1857; d. Milwaukee, Wis., 1918*), geology.

Van Hise taught geology at the University of Wisconsin (1879–1903), where he became president (1903); he also served in various positions with the U. S. Geological Survey (1883–1918); he was a pioneer in the use of the petrographic microscope for analyzing crystalline rocks and in the application of quantitative methods to the study of geologic phenomena; he established general principles—

still valid a half century later—for deciphering Pre-Cambrian rocks and understanding metamorphism.

VANINI, GIULIO CESARE (*b. Taurisano, Lecce, Italy, ca. 1585; d. Toulouse, France, 1619*), philosophy.

Vanini, a Carmelite friar, received a doctorate in both canon and civil law (1606); after a short-lived renunciation of the Catholic church (1612–13) in England, he moved to Paris and studied medicine; his *Amphitheatrum aeternae providentiae . . .* appeared in 1615 and his other surviving work, which dealt with the secrets of nature, was published in 1616; while in Toulouse practicing medicine, he was condemned to martyrdom and, after having his tongue cut off, burned at the stake.

VAN SLYKE, DONALD DEXTER (*b. Pike, N.Y., 1883; d. Garden City, N.Y., 1971*), biochemistry.

Van Slyke graduated in chemistry at the University of Michigan (B.S., 1905; Ph.D., 1907), where he worked under M. Gomberg; he was a research chemist in the biochemical laboratory of P. A. Levene at the Rockefeller Institute for Medical Research (1907–14), where he became chief chemist of the hospital (1914–49); from 1949 he was at the Brookhaven National Laboratory; his research concerned acid-base, gas, fluid, and electrolyte equilibriums in body fluids and the relation of these equilibriums to disease states; his joint effort with J. Peters, *Quantitative Clinical Chemistry* (1931–32), was a classic in its field.

VAN'T HOFF, JACOBUS HENRICUS (*b. Rotterdam, Netherlands, 1852; d. Steglitz [now Berlin], Germany, 1911*), physical chemistry.

Van't Hoff studied mathematics at the University of Leiden (1871–72) before going to work with Kekulé at Bonn (1872–73); after passing the doctoral examination in chemistry at the University of Utrecht (1873), he went to Paris for further study under Wurtz; in 1874 he returned to the Netherlands and published his theory of the asymmetric carbon atom, a work that inspired the development of stereochemistry; he obtained his Ph.D. at Utrecht (1874) and was successively professor of chemistry, mineralogy, and geology and head of the department of chemistry at the University of Amsterdam (1878–96). After 1877 he began his studies in chemical thermodynamics and affinity, and in 1884 stated his principle of mobile equilibrium; from 1885 to 1890 he published his studies on osmotic pressure and explored the analogy between dilute solutions and gases. He moved to Berlin (1896), where he lectured only once a week and devoted himself to research; he became the first Nobel laureate in chemistry (1901) for his work on osmotic pressure in solutions and on the laws of chemical dynamics. Van't Hoff's revolutionary theory of the asymmetric carbon atom was presented in extended form in *La chimie dans l'espace* (1875); his use of the concept of the tetrahedral carbon atom to explain the optical isomerism of a number of organic compounds was arrived at independently by Le Bel about the same time. In physical chemistry, he published *Études de dynamique chimique* (1884), which dealt not only with reaction rates but also with the theory of equilibrium and the theory of affinity based on free energy; his principle of mobile equilibrium was generalized by Le Châtelier (1884) and is known as the van't Hoff-Le

Châtelier principle. In his work on osmotic pressure he proved that the laws of thermodynamics are valid for dilute solutions as well as for gases, and his pressure law gave general validity to the electrolytic theory of Arrhenius; he also studied solid solutions and double salts. Van't Hoff made fundamental contributions to the unification of chemical kinetics, thermodynamics, and physical measurements; he was instrumental in founding physical chemistry as an independent discipline.

VANUXEM, LARDNER (*b. Philadelphia, Pa., 1792; Bristol, Pa., 1848*), geology.

After studying three years at the École des Mines in Paris with the mineralogists A. Brongniart and R.-J. Haüy, Vanuxem became professor of chemistry and mineralogy at South Carolina College (1819–26); he was one of the principal geologists on the geologic survey of New York state (beginning 1836), and his major scientific contribution was a report on the geology of the third geologic district of New York (1842).

VARĀHAMIHIRA (*fl. near Ujjain, India, sixth century*), astronomy, astrology.

Varāhamihira was the best-known and most respected astrologer of India; his numerous, though not original, writings covered all of the traditional fields of astrology and astronomy in India; his work is important as a source for studying three astronomical traditions in India: the Mesopotamian-influenced *vedāṅga*-astronomy; the Indian versions of Greco-Babylonian solar, lunar, and planetary theory; and the Indian versions of Hellenistic astronomy.

VARENIUS, BERNHARDUS (Bernhard Varen) (*b. Hitzacker, in the district of Hannover, Germany, 1622; d. Amsterdam, Holland, 1650*), physical geography.

Varenius studied at the universities at Königsberg (1643–45) and Leiden (1645–49), taking his medical degree at Leiden (1649) and settling in Amsterdam to practice medicine; the recent discoveries by Dutch navigators and his friendship with W. Blaeu and other geographers led him to concentrate on geography rather than medicine; his best-known work is his *Geographia generalis* (1650), which became the standard geographic text for more than a century; Newton revised parts of it for an English edition (1672).

VARIGNON, PIERRE (*b. Caen, France, 1654; d. Paris, France, 1722*), mathematics, mechanics.

Varignon's early life is not well known, but he probably studied at the Jesuit college in Caen; he earned his M.A. degree (1682) and became a priest (1683); he went to Paris (1686), where he was appointed to the new chair of mathematics at the Collège Mazarin (1688–1722). His pedagogical activity was his chief contribution to the progress of science and was the source of his fame; it is due to Lagrange that his name gained recognition in the teaching of mechanics in nineteenth-century France, and until rather recently his name was linked with a theorem on the composition of forces that is now identified with the properties of the vector product. His works include *Projet d'une nouvelle méchanique* (1687), *Nouvelles conjectures sur la pesanteur* (1690), and several posthumous works assembled by his disciples, including *Nouvelle mécanique*

(1725), *Éclaircissemens sur l'analyse des infiniment petits* (1725), and *Élémens de mathématiques* (1731), which was based on his courses at the Collège Mazarin.

VAROLIO, COSTANZO (*b. Bologna, Italy, 1543; d. Rome, Italy, 1575*), medicine.

Varolio studied medicine at the University of Bologna, where he received the medical degree (1567) and held the extraordinary chair of surgery (1569–72); in Rome after 1572, he may have joined the medical faculty of the Sapienza, the papal university, or entered the papal medical service; he wrote two books, *De nervis opticis* (1573) and the *Anatomiae sive de resolutione corporis humani libri IIII* (1591); he developed a new technique for dissecting the brain, which he used in contributing to knowledge of the course and terminations of the cranial nerves.

VARRO, MARCUS TERENTIUS (*b. Reate, Italy, 116 B.C.; d. Rome, 27 B.C.*), encyclopedism, polymathy, biology.

Varro devoted most of his life to public service (86 B.C.–46 B.C.), eventually reaching the rank of praetor; after escaping the death sentence from Antony (43 B.C.), he devoted himself to scholarship; he was the most prolific of all Roman authors; his most lasting scientific legacy was his *Disciplinarum libri IX* (not extant), which introduced the Greek encyclopedic tradition into Roman thought; this work also popularized the seven liberal arts, which became the basis for medieval education.

VASSALE, GIULIO (*b. Lerici, Italy, 1862; d. Modena, Italy, 1913*), endocrinology.

Vassale graduated from the University of Turin (1887), and taught at the University of Modena (1894–1913); though he began his studies in histology, most of his career (1890–1910) was spent in experimental research on internal secretions, principally those of the thyroid, parathyroid, and adrenal glands; he was one of the outstanding endocrinologists of his generation.

VASTARINI-CRESI, GIOVANNI (*b. Taranto, Italy, 1870; d. Naples, Italy, 1924*), anatomy, histology.

Vastarini-Cresi taught at the Naples Anatomical Institute and became director in 1919; he made excellent contributions to histological technique, especially with the method of glycogen-staining in tissues that bears his name.

VAṬEŚVARA (*b. 880 at Ānandapura [modern Wadnagar], Gujarat, India*), astronomy.

Vaṭeśvara wrote a *Vaṭeśvarasiddhānta* (904), which is extremely important for understanding the developments that took place in Indian astronomy between Brahmagupta (born 598) and Bhāskara II (born 1115).

VAUBAN, SÉBASTIEN LE PRESTRE DE (*b. St.-Léger-de-Fougeret [now St.-Léger-Vauban], near Avallon, Burgundy, France, 1633; d. Paris, France, 1707*), military engineering.

France's greatest military engineer and a dedicated public servant of Louis XIV, Vauban scarcely deserves to be called a scientist; he was a practical man of little culture and sparse scientific training who was skilled in the application of simple arithmetic and geometry and the elementary principles of surveying and civil engineering

to fortification and siegecraft. He directed some fifty sieges and fortified or radically strengthened nearly a hundred towns; his most famous success was the siege of Namur (1692), defended by the great Dutch engineer, Cohorn, and immortalized by Uncle Toby in L. Sterne's *Tristram Shandy.* He introduced the system of parallel trenches for approaching a fortress under cover at the siege of Maastricht, and first used the ricochet fire of mortars at the siege of Philippsburg; his major works were the citadel of Lille, Maubeuge, and Neuf-Brisach, considered his masterpiece; he urged improvements in artillery such as the use of iron cannon instead of bronze, the use of bayonets instead of pikes, and the use of the flintlock musket; he never published anything about his methods. Best known are Vauban's economic views; he had antimercantilist sentiments and strongly urged the reform of the system of taxation in his *Projet de capitation* (1695) and his anonymous *Dîme royale* (1707). Although made an honorary member of the Royal Academy of Sciences, it was less for any scientific achievements than for his long, devoted services to France; he was awarded the highest distinction his sovereign could bestow, the Ordre du Saint Esprit (1705).

VAUCHER, JEAN PIERRE ÉTIENNE (*b. Geneva, Switzerland, 1763; d. Geneva, 1841*), botany.

Ordained in 1787, Vaucher worked as a parish priest (1797–1822) while pursuing botany as a hobby; a close friend of A. P. de Candolle, he was honorary professor of botany at the University of Geneva (1798–1807) before transferring to the chair of ecclesiastical history (1807–1839); his most important work was his observation and interpretation of conjugation and spore formation in algae, particularly in *Ectosperma,* later renamed *Vaucheria* by de Candolle.

VAUQUELIN, NICOLAS LOUIS (*b. St. André d'Hébertot, Normandy, France, 1763; d. St. André d'Hébertot, 1829*), chemistry.

After serving as assistant to several pharmacists, Vauquelin became Fourcroy's laboratory and lecture assistant; he was professor of chemistry at what is now the École Polytechnique (1794–97), professor of chemistry at the Collège de France (1801–04), professor of applied chemistry at the Muséum d'Histoire Naturelle (from 1804), and professor of chemistry at the Faculté de Médecine (1811–22); he became master of pharmacy in 1795 and obtained his doctorate in medicine by 1811; he discovered two new elements, chromium and beryllia (1798).

VAVILOV, NIKOLAY IVANOVICH (*b. Moscow, Russia, 1887; d. Saratov, U.S.S.R., 1943*), botany, agronomy, genetics, phytogeography.

Vavilov was the brother of Sergey Vavilov, a well-known physicist; he graduated from the Moscow Agricultural Institute (1911), where he continued studies under D. N. Pryanishnikov in the department of special agriculture. He studied under R. C. Punnett at Cambridge and under W. Bateson in London (1913) before returning to Russia and acquiring his master's degree. He was simultaneously appointed professor of genetics, selection, and special agriculture at the Voronezh Agricultural Institute and professor of agronomy and selection at Saratov University (1917); he became director of the department of applied botany at Petrograd (1920) and, with Lenin's support, reorganized the department into the All-Union Institute of Plant Breeding (VIR). From 1923 he was also director of the State Institute of Experimental Agronomy at Leningrad, which he reorganized as the All-Union Lenin Academy of Agricultural Sciences (VASKhNIL), with the VIR at its core (1929), serving as its first president until 1935; during this period he earned a reputation as "the most widely traveled biologist of our day"; he became head of the genetics section of the Commission for the Exploitation of Productive Forces, transforming it into the Soviet Academy's Laboratory of Genetics, which became in 1933 its Institute of Genetics, which he directed until 1940. There he attracted a first-rate group of researchers, including H. J. Muller, and established the leading center of theoretical genetics research in the Soviet Union; he published more than 350 scientific books and articles. Vavilov's earliest scientific work concerned the genetic basis of plant immunity, which he treated from an evolutionary approach; he first presented his "law of homologous series in hereditary variation" in 1920. He showed that many variants found in a given species also are found in closely related species, and he thought he had found a law in the range of variability within plant species; he believed that just as the periodic table had served as the basis for predicting the existence of undiscovered elements, his "homologous series" tables could be used to predict the existence of undiscovered plant forms. He saw his law as evidence that the variability of species manifests an overall regularity; in response to criticisms of his theory, he published a revised version (1935). Vavilov's work on the origin of cultivated plants was largely responsible for his worldwide reputation; he used a "differential systematic geographical method," which relied heavily on genetic and cytological analysis. By 1935 he believed that he and his coworkers had located the center of origin of more than 600 species of cultivated plants. He sought to characterize selection as an independent scientific discipline in the mid-1930's, hoping to transform Soviet agriculture within a couple of decades. About 1921 Vavilov came to the attention of Lenin, and for the next fifteen years he enjoyed the strong support of the government, serving as one of the few non-Communist members of the Central Executive Committee (1926–35). Beginning in 1931 he began to attract criticism for failing to produce desired agricultural results, particularly from T. D. Lysenko, whom he had helped to bring to prominence. Lysenko's criticisms in 1935 led to Vavilov losing his post on the Central Executive Committee and as president of VAS-KhNIL (1935), and Lysenko assumed the latter post in 1938. In 1939 Vavilov became much more critical of Lysenko and was arrested the following year; he was sentenced to death (1941), and though the sentence was commuted to ten years' imprisonment he died in prison. After Stalin's death he was posthumously rehabilitated by the Soviet Supreme Court. In the West and the Soviet Union, he has come to be regarded as one of the outstanding geneticists of the twentieth century, a symbol of the best aspects of Soviet science, and a martyr for scientific truth.

VAVILOV, SERGEY IVANOVICH (*b. Moscow, Russia, 1891; d. Moscow, 1951*), physics.

Vavilov was the youngest brother of the botanist N. I. Vavilov; he studied at Moscow University with Lebedev and Lazarev (1909–11), following them to Shanyansky City University (1911); he became professor and head of the department of general physics at Moscow University (1929) and scientific director of the State Optical Institute, now named after him (1932); a major discovery made under Vavilov's supervision was the Vavilov-Cherenkov effect, a special kind of luminescence, for which Cherenkov, I. Y. Tamm, and I. M. Frank were awarded the Nobel Prize (1958).

VEBLEN, OSWALD (*b. Decorah, Iowa, 1880; d. Brooklin, Me., 1960*), mathematics.

Veblen earned two B.A. degrees (Iowa, 1898; Harvard, 1900) and received the Ph.D. from the University of Chicago (1903), where he studied under E. H. Moore; he taught at Princeton University (1905–32) and at the Institute for Advanced Study (1932–50); his exposition of the axiomatic method in *Projective Geometry* (1910–18) had extensive influence; his greatest contribution is probably his *Analysis Situs* (1922), which for nearly a decade was the only systematic treatment in book form of the pioneering ideas of Poincaré.

VEJDOVSKÝ, FRANTIŠEK (*b. Kouřim, Bohemia [now Czechoslovakia], 1849; d. Prague, Czechoslovakia, 1939*), zoology.

Vejdovský graduated from Charles University in Prague (Ph.D., 1876), where he taught zoology (1884–1920); he also taught at the Technical University of Prague (1877–1907); his most important work consisted of his embryological and cytological studies, conducted mainly on *Rhynchelmis limosella* (Annelida).

VEKSLER, VLADIMIR IOSIFOVICH (*b. Zhitomir, Russia, 1907; d. Moscow, U.S.S.R., 1966*), physics, engineering.

Veksler graduated from the Moscow Energetics Institute; he became director of the electrophysics laboratory of the Academy of Sciences (1954) and headed the high-energy laboratory of the Joint Institute for Nuclear Research (from 1956); he is best known for establishing the principle of phase stability of accelerated particles (1944); he supervised the construction of the largest Soviet accelerators.

VELLOZO, JOSÉ MARIANO DA CONCEIÇÃO (*b. San José, Minas Gerais, Brazil, 1742; d. Rio de Janeiro, Brazil, 1811*), botany.

A member of the Franciscan order, Vellozo completed his study of the flora of Rio de Janeiro province in 1790, though it was not published until 1825; the *Flora fluminensis* is regarded as the greatest creation of Enlightenment science in Brazil; in Lisbon from 1790 he directed a printshop and wrote a number of works of scientific and economic popularization, and a work on the economic botany of Brazil (1798–1806).

VENEL, GABRIEL FRANÇOIS (*b. Tourbes, near Pézenas, France, 1723; d. Montpellier, France, 1775*), chemistry, medicine.

Venel received the M.D. from the University of Montpellier (1742); his interests turned to chemistry while attending G.-F. Rouelle's chemistry lectures in Paris (1746); he secured the patronage of Louis, duc d'Orléans, who put him in charge of his laboratory at the Palais Royal; he later became professor at the University of Montpellier (1759); he wrote more than 700 articles on chemistry and materia medica in volumes three to seventeen (1753–65) of Diderot's *Encyclopédie;* he also studied the composition of vegetable matter and analyzed mineral waters; he came very close in 1750 to discovering that carbon dioxide was responsible for the effervescence in mineral waters, characterized in 1754 by J. Black, who called it fixed air.

VENETZ, IGNATZ (*b. Visperterminen, Valais, Switzerland, 1788; d. Saxon-les-Bains, Valais, Switzerland, 1859*), civil engineering, glaciology.

After studying science and mathematics, Venetz entered the Service des Ponts et Chausées, becoming chief engineer for the district; he is best known for his 1821 paper on advances and retreats of glaciers, which contributed to J. Charpentier's discovery of the Ice Age.

VENING MEINESZ, FELIX ANDRIES (*b. Scheveningen, Netherlands, 1887; d. Amersfoort, Netherlands, 1966*), geodesy, geophysics.

Vening Meinesz obtained a civil engineering degree at the Technical University of Delft (1910); he soon joined the gravimetric survey of the Netherlands sponsored by the government, and devoted his life to geodesy and geophysics. He developed a new method for making gravity measurements with pendulums on unstable peaty subsoils, and by 1921 had made measurements at fifty-one stations across the Netherlands; he then began to work on measuring gravity at sea, as recounted in his *Theory and Practice of Pendulum Observations at Sea* (1929–41). The first voyage to measure gravity at sea, from the Netherlands to Java (1923), yielded thirty successful observations made from submarines and led Vening Meinesz to construct an entirely new instrument, which was tested in 1925 with satisfactory results; many other gravity expeditions followed until World War II, and further refinements on the pendulum equipment were made with the aid of B. C. Browne. For over thirty years Vening Meinesz's apparatus provided the only means for measuring gravity at sea; it was superseded in the late 1950's by the spring gravimeter. In regard to geodesy, his observations helped establish that the equator must be represented by a circle rather than an ellipse. His model of the earth with an elastic crust on a viscous substratum led to his preference for interpretation in terms of regional isostasy, an approach which encounters great drawbacks, however. The most striking feature of the earth's gravity field was discovered by Vening Meinesz during his earlier cruises; the "Vening Meinesz negative gravity anomaly belts of island arcs," as they were called, with their bold, steeply descending lows of gravity, are not reduced to zero by any of the common suppositions. His explanation of the gravity anomalies by means of the buckling hypothesis brought strong reactions from geologists but eventually was favorably received, particularly after P. H. Kuenen's model experiments. Like other geoscientists, Vening Meinesz rejected Wegener's theory of continental drift, claiming that the continents were firmly fixed and the interior of the earth was the site of convection currents. He believed in the importance of interdisciplinary and international cooperation, and served as president of the Association Géodésique Internationale (1933–55) and of the International Union of Geodesy and Geophysics (1948–51).

VENN, JOHN (*b. Hull, England, 1834; d. Cambridge, England, England, 1923*), probability, logic.

Venn studied at Gonville and Caius College, Cambridge, where he took his degree in mathematics (1857); he held a fellowship there the rest of his life; he received the Cambridge Sc.D. in 1883; his *Logic of Chance* (1866) and *Symbolic Logic* (1881) were highly esteemed textbooks in the late nineteenth and early twentieth centuries; he is chiefly remembered for his systematic explanation and development of the method of geometrical representation of syllogistic logic; although Leibniz was the first to use logical diagrams, they are now generally called Venn diagrams.

VERANTIUS, FAUSTUS (also known as **FAUSTO VRANČIĆ** or **VERANZIO**) (*b. Šibenik, Dalmatia, 1551; d. Venice, Italy, 1617*), engineering.

Verantius studied philosophy and law at Padua (1568–70); although he was principally a man of letters and most of his career was spent as a diplomat, administrator, and bishop, he studied mechanics and mathematics in his leisure time; in 1616 he published a treatise on logic and, most important, a folio volume entitled *Machinae novae;* although some of his "machines" are not wholly original, many of them are explained in print for the first time, such as the parachute.

VERDET, MARCEL ÉMILE (*b. Nîmes, France, 1824; d. Nîmes, 1866*), physics.

Verdet studied at the École Normale Supérieure and received his doctorate from the Sorbonne (1848); he was one of the outstanding physics teachers of mid-nineteenth-century France, holding professorships at the École Normale Supérieure, the École Polytechnique, and the Faculté des Sciences in Paris; he introduced the new thermodynamics into the French scientific world, and conducted important experiments on the effects of a magnetic field on plane-polarized light.

VER EECKE, PAUL (*b. Menin, Belgium, 1867; d. Berchem, Belgium, 1959*), mathematics.

After graduating as a mining engineer from the University of Liège (1891), Ver Eecke worked at the Administration du Travail (1894–1932); his translations of Greek mathematical works into French, footnoted with proofs in modern notation, provided historians of science with a fairly accurate reflection of thought in antiquity and the scientific significance of the works.

VERHULST, PIERRE-FRANÇOIS (*b. Brussels, Belgium, 1804; d. Brussels, 1849*), statistics, sociology, probability theory, mathematics.

Verhulst, who studied and collaborated with Quetelet, was a professor at the Université Libre of Brussels and later at the Ècole Royale Militaire; his research on the law of population growth makes him a precursor of modern students of the subject.

VERNADSKY, VLADÍMIR IVANOVICH (*b. St. Petersburg, Russia, 1863; d. Moscow, U.S.S.R., 1945*), mineralogy, geochemistry, biogeochemistry.

Vernadsky graduated from St. Petersburg University (1885), where Mendeleev's lectures stimulated his interest in science; he traveled abroad (1888–1890), working under Groth at Munich and under Le Châtelier and Fouqué at the Collège de France. He became a *Privatdozent* at Moscow University (1890); after receiving his master's (1891) and doctorate (1897) degrees, he was appointed professor at Moscow University (1898); he left the university in protest against the Ministry of National Education (1911), and moved to St. Petersburg (1911–17); he moved to the Ukraine (1917–21) and after a time in Paris and Prague returned to Leningrad (1926), and continued his scientific work with the Academy of Sciences of the U.S.S.R. Vernadsky's research was concerned with crystallography and, primarily, mineralogy; he also studied geochemistry, radiogeology, and biogeochemistry. His great contribution to mineralogy was his research on silicates and aluminosilicate minerals; he opened a new evolutionary direction in mineralogy with his "Experiment in Descriptive Mineralogy" (1908–22) and "History of Minerals of the Earth's Crust" (1923–36). His geochemical research was generalized in *La géochimie* (1924), which includes much material on geospheres (the earth's layers). He was one of the first to recognize radioactivity as a powerful source of energy; in his work on the chemical composition of plants and animals he is considered the founder of the theory of the biosphere and of biogeochemistry.

VERNEUIL, PHILIPPE ÉDOUARD POULLETIER DE (*b. Paris, France, 1805; d. Paris, 1873*), geology, paleontology.

Verneuil began his career in law; he studied the geological lessons of E. de Beaumont and then in 1835, being of independent means, devoted himself to science; he conducted his research in five areas in Europe and America, including summer tours of Russia (1840, 1841) with the English geologist R. Murchison and the Russian naturalist A. Keyserling; they published their results in *Geology of Russia* . . . (1845); his major theoretical contribution to stratigraphy was his hypothesis that the Paleozoic deposits of the United States and Spain are parallel to those of Europe (1846–47)

VERNIER, PIERRE (*b. Ornans, France, 1584; d. Ornans, 1638*), military engineering, scientific instrumentation.

Vernier worked as a military engineer for the Spanish Hapsburgs; his reading of the works of Nuñez Salaciense, Clavius, and Tycho Brahe, combined with his experience in helping his father survey, led him to seek a new way to read off angles on surveying instruments; his use of a mobile concentric scale solved the difficulty of engraving many different concentric scales; he published his new invention (1631) but the vernier remained on the whole unknown until the early eighteenth century, perhaps because the extra precision it made possible was negated by the imprecision of open sights and methods of marking scales.

VERONESE, GIUSEPPE (*b. Chioggia, Italy, 1854; d. Padua, Italy, 1917*), mathematics.

Veronese studied at the Zurich Polytechnic and graduated from the University of Rome (1877); after further study at Leipzig (1880–81), he became professor of geometry at the University of Padua (1881–1917); he may be considered the main founder of the projective geometry of hyperspaces with *n* dimensions; he is also remembered for "Veronese's surface," a two-dimensional surface of a five-dimensional space, and for being one of the first to study non-Archimedean geometry; his pupils included G. Castelnuovo and T. Levi-Civita.

VERRILL, ADDISON EMERY (*b. Greenwood, Me., 1839; d. Santa Barbara, Calif., 1926*), zoology.

Of an old New England family; studied under Agassiz at Harvard. Held the chair of zoology at Yale (1864–1907); in charge of scientific investigations of the U.S. Commission of Fish and Fisheries. Made an outstanding contribution to the classification and natural history of corals; did basic taxonomic work on echinoderms, especially starfishes and brittle stars.

VERULAM, BARON. *See* **Bacon, Francis.**

VERWORN, MAX (*b. Berlin, Germany, 1863; d. Bonn, Germany, 1921*), physiology.

Studied at Berlin (Ph.D., 1887) and at Jena (M.D., 1889); taught at Jena, at Göttingen (1901–10), and at Bonn (from 1910). Investigated basic phenomena of life, such as irritability and paralysis; worked with unicellular organisms or the cells of higher organisms; was a major advocate of cellular physiology.

VESALIUS, ANDREAS (*b. Brussels, Belgium, 1514; d. Zákinthos, Greece, 1564*), medicine.

Vesalius was educated at the universities of Louvain (bachelor of medicine, 1537), Paris, and Padua (doctor of medicine, 1537). At Paris he studied under Guinter of Andernach and Jacobus Sylvius; since they were both supporters of the Galenic tradition, Vesalius remained under the influence of Galenic concepts of anatomy, although he acquired skill in the technique of dissection. After receiving his degree he continued his anatomical studies at Padua and lectured on surgery and anatomy until 1543, when he was appointed physician to the imperial household of Charles V. With the latter's abdication in 1555, Vesalius took service with his son Philip II of Spain as physician to the Netherlanders at the Spanish court and, from time to time, to the king himself. He remained in Spain from 1559 until the year of his death.

From his lecturing at Padua on Galen and from his own dissecting of cadavers, Vesalius began to realize that there were contradictions between Galen's texts and his own observations in the human body. His supply of dissection material became much greater when the Paduan criminal court made the bodies of executed criminals available to him. As a result, he became increasingly convinced that Galen's description of human anatomy was basically an account of the anatomy of animals in general and was often erroneous insofar as the human body was concerned. He boldly declared that human anatomy could be learned only from the dissection and observation of the human body. In his last year at Padua he published his great book, *De humani corporis fabrica*, and its *Epitome* (1543). In 1546 he published a long letter partly concerned with the discovery and therapeutic use of the chinaroot in the treatment of syphilis and partly to justify his anatomically heretical activities against the attack of the Galenic anatomists of Paris (*Epistola rationem modumque propinandi radicis chynae decocti pertractans*). During his service with the imperial army he was able to apply his unrivaled anatomical knowledge to surgery. His most notable contribution was the introduction of surgically induced drainage of empyema. As his experience became greater he realized the need for a new edition of the *Fabrica* (published in 1555).

Several motives underlay the composition and publication of the *Fabrica*. According to Vesalius medicine was properly composed of three parts: drugs, diet, and "the use of the hands," the last referring to surgical practice and its necessary preliminary, a knowledge of human anatomy. He hoped to persuade the medical world to appreciate anatomy as fundamental to all other aspects of medicine, and hoped that a genuine knowledge of human anatomy would be achieved by others, in contrast to the more restricted traditional outlook and the uncritical acceptance of Galenic anatomy. He felt it was desirable that human dissection be accompanied by a parallel dissection of the bodies of other animals in order to show the differences in structure and hence the source of Galen's errors. Because of Vesalius, Padua became the first great center of comparative as well as of human anatomical studies, a dual interest that continued to develop under his successors Falloppio, Fabrici, and Casserio.

His greatest contribution to the elucidation of anatomy is to be found in the illustrations to the *Fabrica*, most notably the three celebrated skeletal figures in book I, and the series of "muscle men" in book II. He endeavored in books I and II to identify and give the fullest possible description of every bone and muscle, respectively, and their functions; the first two books represent the major Vesalian achievement in terms of accuracy of description and present the most telling blows against Galenic anatomy. Books III through VII describe the vascular system; the nervous system; the abdominal organs, human generation and the organs of reproduction; the organs of the thorax; and the brain. In the *Fabrica* Vesalius made many contributions to the body of anatomical knowledge, by description of structures hitherto unknown, by detailed descriptions of structures known only in the most elementary terms, and by the correction of erroneous descriptions.

VESLING, JOHANN (*b. Minden, Germany, 1598; d. Padua, Italy, 1649*), anatomy, botany.

A student of medicine at Venice and Leiden, he served ably as professor of anatomy and surgery at Padua (from 1633). He wrote a very successful anatomy text, *Syntagma anatomicum* (1641), which contained a description of the chyle vessels and asserted that four is the normal number of pulmonary veins emptying into the left auricle. In 1638 he gave up lecturing on surgery and turned to botany. During a visit to Egypt (1628–33) he had made observations that resulted in *De plantis aegyptiis . . .* (1638). He also renovated the botanical gardens of Padua.

VESSIOT, ERNEST (*b. Marseilles, France, 1865; d. La Bauche, Savoie, France, 1952*), mathematics.

Studied at the École Normale Supérieure, and after teaching at Lille, Toulouse, Lyons, and Paris, returned there as director (retired, 1935). His research dealt with the application of the notion of continuous groups to the study of differential equations.

VICQ D'AZYR, FÉLIX (*b. Valognes, Manche, France, 1748; d. Paris, France, 1794*), anatomy, epidemiology, medical education.

Studied at Caen and Paris (M.D., 1774); elected to the Académie des Sciences (1774) and the Académie Française (1788); appointed physician to Marie Antoinette (1788). Specialized in comparative anatomy; studied the fibers in the white matter of the brain and the cerebral cortex. Served as professor of veterinary medicine at Alfort, and was particularly successful in the fight against epizootic diseases. Did pioneer work in public health and the improvement of medical education.

VIDIUS, VIDUS. *See* **Guidi, Guido.**

VIÈTE, FRANÇOIS (*b. Fontenay-le-Comte, Poitou [now Vendée], France, 1540; d. Paris, France, 1603*), mathematics.

Studied law at the University of Poitiers; bachelors degree, 1560. All of Viète's mathematical investigations are closely connected with his cosmological and astronomical work. The *Canon mathematicus, seu ad triangula cum appendicibus,* publication of which began in 1571, was intended to form the preparatory, trigonometric part of the "Harmonicon coeleste," five volumes which were never published, but which are available in manuscript. The *Canon* is composed of four parts, only the first two of which were published in 1579: "Canon mathematicus," which contains a table of trigonometric lines with some additional tables, and "Universalium inspectionum ad Canonem mathematicum liber singularis," which gives the computational methods used in the construction of the canon and explains the computation of plane and spherical triangles with the aid of the general trigonometric relations existing among the determinant components of such triangles. These relations were brought together in tables that allow the relevant proportion obtaining among three known and one unknown component of the triangle to be read off directly. The two other parts, devoted to astronomy, were not published.

The most important of Viète's many works on algebra was *In artem analyticem isagoge*, the earliest work on symbolic algebra (Tours, 1591). It also introduced the use of letters both for known quantities, which were denoted by the consonants B, C, D, and so on, and for unknown quantities, which were denoted by the vowels. Furthermore, in using A to denote the unknown quantity x, Viète sometimes employed A quadratus, A cubus . . . to represent x^2, x^3. . . . This innovation, considered one of the most significant advances in the history of mathematics, prepared the way for the development of symbolic algebra.

In 1593 Viete published *Zeteticorum libri quinque*, which is composed of five books, the first of which contains ten problems that seek to determine quantities of which the sum, difference, or ratio is known. The problems of the second book give the sum or difference of the squares or cubes of the unknown quantities, their product, and the ratio of this product to the sum or the difference of their squares. In the third book the unknown quantities are proportional, and one is required to find them if the sum or the difference of the extremes or means is given. This book contains the application of these problems to right triangles. The fourth book gives the solutions of second- and third-degree indeterminate problems. The fifth book contains problems of the same kind, but generally concerning three numbers.

By 1593 his tract *De aequationum recognitione* had already been completed, long before its publication by Alexander Anderson (1615). The tract begins with the following postulate: A straight line can be drawn from any point across any two lines (or a circle and a straight line) in such a way that the intercept between these two lines (or the line and the circle) will be equal to a given distance, any possible intercept having been predefined. The twenty-five propositions that follow can be divided into four groups:

1. Propositions 1–7 contain the solution of the problem of the mesographicum—to find two mean proportionals between two given straight line segments—and its solution immediately yields the solution of the problem of doubling the cube.

2. Propositions 8–18 contain the solution of the problem of the trisection of an angle and the corresponding cubic equation. The trigonometric solution of the cubic equation occurs twice: in propositions 16 and 17.

3. Propositions 19–24 contain the solution of the problem of finding the side of the regular heptagon that is to be inscribed in a given circle.

4. Proposition 25 explains the importance of the applied method: the construction of two mean proportionals, the trisection of an angle, and all problems that cannot be solved only by means of the ruler and compass but that lead to cubic and biquadratic equations, can be solved with the aid of the ancient *neusis* procedure.

In 1592 Viète began a lively dispute with J. J. Scaliger when the latter published a purported solution of the quadrature of the circle, the trisection of an angle, and the construction of two mean proportionals between two given line segments by means of the ruler and compass only. In that year Viète gave public lectures at Tours and proved that Scaliger's assertions were incorrect, without mentioning the name of the author. For this reason he decided in 1593 to publish book VIII of his *Variorum de rebus mathematicis responsorum Liber VIII, cuius praecipua capita sunt: De duplicatione cubi et quadratione circuli, quae claudit πρόχειρον seu ad usum mathematici canonis methodica.*

Since Scaliger could not defend himself against Viète's criticism, he left France for the Netherlands, where soon after his arrival in 1594 he published his *Cyclometrica elementa,* followed some months later by his *Mesolabium.* Viète responded with *Munimen adversus cyclometrica nova* (1594) and *Pseudomesolabium* (1595).

Viète's mathematical reputation was already considerable when the ambassador from the Netherlands remarked to Henry IV that France did not possess any geometricians capable of solving a problem propounded in 1593 by Adrian Romanus to all mathematicians and that required the solution of a forty-fifth-degree equation. The king thereupon summoned Viète and informed him of the challenge. Viète saw that the equation was satisfied by the chord of a circle (of unit radius) that subtends an angle $2\pi/45$ at the center. In a few minutes he gave the

king one solution of the problem written in pencil and, the next day, twenty-two more. He did not find forty-five solutions because the remaining ones involve negative sines, which were unintelligible to him.

Viète published his answer, *Ad problema, quod omnibus mathematicis totius orbis construendum proposuit Adrianus Romanus, responsum,* in 1595.

At the end of his work he proposed to Romanus, referring to Apollonius' *Tangencies,* the problem to draw a circle that touches three given circles.

In 1600 Viète presented a solution that had all the rigor desirable in his *Apollonius Gallus, seu exsuscitata Apollonii Pergaei Περὶ ἐξαφῶν geometria ad V.C.A. Romanum,* in which he gave a Euclidean solution using the center of similitude of two circles. Romanus was so impressed that he traveled to Fontenay to meet Viète, beginning an acquaintanceship that soon became warm friendship.

In the 1591 edition of the *Isagoge,* Viète had already given the outline of the *De numerosa potestatum purarum, atque adfectarum ad exegesin resolutione tractatus.* The "numerical resolution of powers" referred to in the title means solving equations that have numerical solutions, such as

$$x^2 = 2916 \text{ or } x^2 + 7x = 60750.$$

Viète also had a role in the improvements of the Julian calendar. He valued the studies involved in a reform of the calendar; and toward the end of his life he allowed himself to be carried away by them and to engage in unjustified polemics against Clavius, the result of which was the publication with Mettayer of *Libellorum supplicum in regia magistri relatio kalendarii vere Gregoriani ad ecclesiasticos doctores exhibita pontifici maximo Clementi VIII anno Christo 1600 iubilaeo* (1600). He gave the work to Cardinal Cinzio Aldobrandini, who transmitted it to Clavius. Since Clavius rejected the proposed corrections, Viète and Pierre Mettayer, the son of Jean, published a libel against Clavius that was as vehement as it was unjust: *Francisci Vietae adversus Christophorum Clavium expostulatio* (1602).

Francisci Vietae fontenaensis de aequationum recognitione et emendatione tractatus duo was published in 1615, under the editorship of Viète's Scottish friend Alexander Anderson. The treatise "De emendatione" contains the subject matter of the work as announced in the *Isagoge* under the title "Ad logisticen speciosam notae posteriores" and sets forth a series of formulas *(notae)* concerning transformations of equations. In particular it presents general methods for solving third- and fourth-degree equations.

In 1615 Anderson published Viète's treatise on angle sections. *Ad angularium sectionum analyticem theoremata καυολικώτερα a Francisco Vieta fontenaensis primum excogitata at absque ulla demonstratione ad nos transmissa, jam tandem demonstrationibus confirmata.* This treatise deals, in part, with general formulas of chords, sines, cosines, and tangents of multiple arcs in terms of the trigonometric lines of the simple arcs.

VIEUSSENS, RAYMOND (*b. Vigan, Lot, France, ca. 1635; d. Montpellier, France, 1715*), anatomy, medicine.

Studied medicine at Montpellier; upon obtaining doctorate (1670), was named physician at the Hôtel Dieu

St.-Éloi in Montpellier, where he remained for the rest of his life; among his many important patients was the duchess of Montpensier, the Grande Mademoiselle. Did important research on the nervous system; wrote *Nevrographia universalis* (1684). Made pioneer cardiological observations, which were little appreciated in his lifetime.

VIGANI, JOHN FRANCIS   (*b. Verona, Italy, ca. 1650; d. Newark-on-Trent, England, 1713*), chemistry, pharmacy.

Practiced chemistry at Cambridge from about 1682; became the first professor of chemistry at the university (1702). Author, *Medulla chemiae* (1682).

VIGO, GIOVANNI DA   (*b. Rapallo, Italy, 1450; d. 1525*), medicine.

Surgeon at the papal court of Julius II (Giuliano della Rovere) from 1503 to 1513. Specialized in trephination; was one of the first to advocate the use of mercury ointment in treating syphilis and distinguished between the primary and secondary stages of the disease. Wrote *Practica in arte chirurgica copiosa* (1514) and *Practica in arte chirurgica compendiosa* (1517).

VIJAYANANDA (or **VIJAYANANDIN**) (*fl. Benares, India, 966*), astronomy.

The son of a Brāhmaṇa of Benares who followed the Saurapakṣa; wrote a *Karaṇatilaka*.

VILLALPANDO, JUAN BAUTISTA (*b. Córdoba, Spain, 1552; d. Rome, Italy, 1608*), architecture, mathematics, mechanics.

A Jesuit, in Rome from 1592; author of an influential commentary on the book of Ezekiel. In his discussion of Solomon's temple, Villalpando demonstrated how it was constructed according to Vitruvius' principles of harmony and proportion; his treatment of "the center of gravity and the line of direction" is very advanced, the source of his ideas here being a matter of considerable conjecture.

VILLANOVA.   *See* **Arnald of Villanova.**

VILLARD DE HONNECOURT   (*b. Honnecourt, Picardy, France, ca. 1190*), architecture.

Author of the important *Bauhüttenbuch* (*ca.* 1225–35), in which the 207 drawings provide models for every type of worker in a builders' guild, and the long commentaries often express unusually personal value judgments.

VILLARD, PAUL (*b. Lyons, France, 1860; d. Bayonne, France, 1934*), physics.

Studied at the École Normale Supérieure (*agrégé,* 1884); returned to do research there. His main work involved the experimental study of cathode rays, X rays, radioactivity, and the aurora. Was the first to observe γ rays (1900).

VILLARI, EMILIO (*b. Naples, Italy, 1836; d. Naples, 1904*), physics.

Studied at the University of Pisa; taught there, at Bologna, and in Naples. Attempted to explain, from an action-at-a-distance standpoint, the peculiar effects of alternating currents on their conductors.

VILLEFRANCHE.   *See* **La Roche, Estienne de.**

VILMORIN, PIERRE LOUIS FRANÇOIS LEVEQUE DE (*b. Paris, France, 1816; d. Paris, 1860*), botany.

Succeeded his father (1843) as the head of the distinguished Paris seed firm Vilmorin-Andrieux et Cie; set up an experimental breeding farm at Verrières-le-Buisson. Bred a new variety of sugar beet with a high sugar content; bred plants of *Lupinus hirsutus* to study hereditary forces.

VINCENT OF BEAUVAIS (*b. Beauvais, France, ca. 1190; d. Beauvais, ca. 1264*), natural science.

A Dominican; probably studied in Paris; at the priory in Beauvais (from *ca.* 1233). His *Speculum maius* ("great mirror"), an encyclopedia of nature, history, and the learned arts financed by Louis IX, appeared in three versions (*ca.* 1244–55); although essentially a compilation of excerpts, it is the best encyclopedia from the Middle Ages.

VINCI, LEONARDO DA.   *See* **Leonardo da Vinci.**

VINOGRADSKY, SERGEY NIKOLAEVICH (*b. Kiev, Russia, 1856; d. Brie-Comte-Robert, France, 1953*), microbiology.

Graduated from St. Petersburg University (1881; M.A., 1884); affiliated with the Institute of Experimental Medicine at St. Petersburg (1891–1912); directed agricultural research in the Ukraine; became director (1922) of agricultural microbiology at the Pasteur Institute. His most important studies concerned the morphological variability of microbes, the discovery of microbes' capacity for chemosynthesis, and the creation and development of the bases for ecological and soil microbiology.

VIOLLE, JULES LOUIS GABRIEL (*b. Langres, France, 1841; d. Fixin, France, 1923*), physics.

Studied at the École Normale Supérieure; had a distinguished teaching career, concluding with his appointment (1892) as professor of physics at the Conservatoire des Arts et des Métiers. His major studies involved measurement of the solar constant and solar temperature and research on heat radiation and high temperatures.

VIRCHOW, RUDOLF CARL (*b. Schivelbein, Pomerania, Germany, 1821; d. Berlin, Germany, 1902*), medicine, pathology, public health, anthropology.

The most prominent German physician of his century, he played a crucial role in the ascendancy of German medicine after 1840. Received a military fellowship to study medicine at the Friedrich-Wilhelms Institut in Berlin (1839); awarded his M.D. by the University of Berlin (1843); became affiliated with the Charité Hospital in Berlin. In two influential speeches (1845) he emerged as a spokesman for a new vision of medical progress; rejected transcendental concerns; saw life as the sum of physical and chemical actions and as essentially the expression of cell activity. Became politically radicalized by his experiences among the destitute Polish minority of Upper Silesia during the typhus epidemic of 1848; participated in the uprisings (1848) in Berlin. At the University of Würzburg (1849–56), he developed his concept of "cellular pathology," reducing pathological processes to alterations at the cellular level; among his students were Edwin Klebs and Ernst Haeckel. Returned (1856) to Berlin University and the Charité Hospital; appointed (1859) to the Berlin City Council; active in pressing reforms, especially in public health. In his later years he became rigidly dogmatic; however, his skepticism concerning bacteriology was based in part on his belief that there is no one cause of disease and that sociological factors play a significant role. From 1870, was involved in anthropological studies and archaeological excavations.

VIREY, JULIEN-JOSEPH (*b. Hortes, Haute-Marne, France, 1775; d. Paris, France, 1846*), natural history, philosophy of nature.

Trained as a pharmacist and physician; wrote prolifically in many fields; vitalism and teleology were basic components of his natural philosophy. His M.D. thesis (Paris, 1814) was on daily-recurring physiological cycles; in *Hygiène philosophique* (1828), he explored the influence of social institutions and events on health.

VIRTANEN, ARTTURI ILMARI (*b. Helsinki, Finland, 1895; d. Helsinki, 1973*), biochemistry.

Studied at the University of Helsinki (M.S., 1916; doctorate, 1919); among other posts, served as director of the Biochemical Research Institute at Helsinki (from 1931). While director of laboratories for the Finnish Cooperative Dairies Association (1921–31), he made his famous discovery of the AIV method of fodder storage (the name deriving from his initials), for which he was awarded the Nobel Prize for chemistry in 1945.

VITALI, GIUSEPPE (*b. Ravenna, Italy, 1875; d. Bologna, Italy, 1932*), mathematics.

Studied at the Scuola Normale Superiore at Pisa; assistant to Ulisse Dini (1899–1901). Although Vitali worked most of his life in isolation, his results in the theory of functions of a real variable have established him as one of the great predecessors of Lebesgue.

VITELLIO (or **VITELO**). *See* **Witelo.**

VITRUVIUS POLLIO (*b. Italy, early first century* B.C.; *d. ca. 25* B.C.), architecture, architectural history.

Vitruvius, who may have been of northern Italian origin, worked in some capacity for Julius Caesar and then as military engineer for Octavianus (later the Emperor Augustus), to whom he dedicated his writings. *De architectura*, his only known work, comprises ten books, each with a separate preface. Book I, after a long introductory section defining the nature of architecture and the personality and ideal training of the architect, discusses town planning in very broad terms. Book II covers building materials and methods. Books III and IV are devoted to religious architecture and to a detailed discussion of the classical orders, and book V to other forms of public architecture, with special emphasis on the theater. Book VI deals with domestic architecture, and book VII with such practical matters as types of flooring, stuccowork, painting, and colors. Book VIII turns to the sources and transport of water, by conduit or aqueduct. After a long excursus on astronomy, book IX describes various forms of clocks and dials; book X covers mechanics, with partic-

ular reference to water engines, a hodometer, artillery, and military engineering.

What influence *De architectura* had on contemporary Roman architecture seems to have been in practical, rather than theoretical, matters. Vitruvius defined perfection in quantitative terms, and contrived to reduce temple planning to a series of strict numerical rules; there is nothing in the monuments to suggest that his precise forms were ever used, and his conservative tastes were not popular. Manuscripts of the work continued to be copied, however; it was "rediscovered" in 1414, and became an authority for Quattrocento architectural doctrine despite its many obscurities. Leone Battista Alberti's *De re aedificatoria* cited Vitruvius frequently and borrowed from him even more frequently.

The aspects of *De architectura* of most interest to modern historians include 1) the discussion of contemporary astronomy, which contains a possible reference to the theory that Mercury and Venus revolve about the sun, some fairly accurate figures for the sidereal periods of the outer planets, and a possible example of the notion that the absolute speed of all planets is the same; 2) an exposition of gnomonics, the science of sundials, with the first discussion of the analemma (a graphic method of determining the hour lines and day curves in a plane sundial with vertical gnomon, used as a basis for much of later mathematical dialing); and 3) a discussion of the anaphoric water clock, which employed a dial rotating once daily on which the constellations were represented by stereographic projection, and in front of which was fixed a "spider" of wires forming the civil hour curves, also constructed by stereographic projection (the earliest unambiguous evidence for the use of stereographic projection, the basic principle of the astrolabe).

VIVES, JUAN LUIS (*b. Valencia, Spain, 1492; d. Bruges, Netherlands* [*now Belgium*], *1540*), philosophy, psychology.

One of the greatest humanists of his day; studied in Paris; lived in the Netherlands and in England (1523–28). Developed an empirical psychology, including a theory of association of ideas.

VIVIANI, VINCENZO (*b. Florence, Italy, 1622; d. Florence, 1703*), mathematics.

Associated with the Medici court; collaborated with Galileo; edited works of ancient mathematicians, including Apollonius and Euclid, translated a work by Archimedes, and collected and arranged Torricelli's works. Proposed a famous problem, "the Florentine enigma," involving the determination of the area of a curved surface.

VIZE, VLADIMIR YULEVICH (*b. Tsarskoe Selo* [*now Pushkin*], *Russia, 1886; d. Leningrad, U.S.S.R., 1954*), Arctic geography.

Studied at Halle and Göttingen. Was a member of Sedov's expedition to the North Pole (1912–14); from the 1920's to the mid-1930's, directed many Soviet Arctic expeditions. Established polar stations and developed methods for ice forecasting.

VLACQ (**VLACK, VLACCUS**), **ADRIAAN** (*b. Gouda, Netherlands, 1600; d. The Hague, Netherlands, ca. 1666*), mathematics, publishing.

Famous for the publication (often in collaboration with Ezechiel De Decker) of logarithmic tables computed by himself and others.

VOEYKOV, ALEKSANDR IVANOVICH (*b. Moscow, Russia, 1842; d. Petrograd, Russia [now Leningrad, U.S.S.R.], 1916*), geography, climatology.

Studied at Heidelberg and Berlin and took his doctorate at Göttingen (1865); travelled worldwide, studying climate especially; taught at St. Petersburg University (from 1884). His basic work is *Klimaty zemnogo shara, v osobennosti Rossii* ("Climates of the Earth, Particularly Russia," 1884). Emphasized investigation of atmospheric circulation and solar radiation; also studied rivers and snow cover.

VOGEL, HERMANN CARL (*b. Leipzig, Germany, 1841; d. Potsdam, Germany, 1907*), astrophysics.

Studied at Leipzig; assisted Karl Bruhns in the university observatory; greatly influenced by J. K. F. Zöllner. Became director (1870) of the private observatory of F. G. von Bülow at Bothkamp, near Kiel; worked intensively on spectroscopic analysis of the stars. Next, worked at the new Potsdam Astrophysical Observatory (from 1879; as director, from 1882); began research in spectrophotometry; specialized in the spectroscopy of the fixed stars. Used photography in the determination of the radial components of stellar velocities from Doppler shifts in stellar spectra; thus demonstrated the value of both photographic techniques and Doppler's theory to astrophysics. His use of spectrography led to a sensational success (1889): the discovery of the first spectroscopic double stars (Algol and Spica).

VOGT, CARL (*b. Giessen, Germany, 1817; d. Geneva, Switzerland, 1895*), medicine, natural science.

Studied at Giessen (under Liebig) and Berne (M.D., 1839). Spent most of his adult life in Geneva, where he was a prominent educator and politician. Was a staunch supporter of scientific materialism; espoused Darwin's ideas; was one of the first anthropologists. Wrote widely in the sciences; specialized in marine biological research.

VOGT, JOHAN HERMANN LIE (*b. Tvedestrand, Norway, 1858; d. Trondheim, Norway, 1932*), geology.

The son of a physician; on his mother's side, the nephew of Sophus Lie; graduated (1880) as a mining engineer-geologist from the University of Christiania (Oslo); taught there (1886–1912) and at the Technical University of Norway at Trondheim (1912–29). Was a pioneer in ore geology and in the physical chemistry of silicates as a basis for igneous rock petrology; often called the father of modern physicochemical petrology.

VOGT, THOROLF (*b. Vang, Hedmark, Norway, 1888; d. Trondheim, Norway, 1958*), geology.

The son of J. H. L. Vogt, whom he succeeded as professor of mineralogy and geology at the Technical University of Norway at Trondheim. Noted for papers on the sulfide-rich Sulitjelma area, on metamorphism and the mineral facies of the Pentti Eskola, and on the geochemistry and geobotany of Røros.

VOIGT, JOHANN CARL WILHELM (*b. Allstedt, Germany, 1752; d. Ilmenau, Germany, 1821*), geology, mining.

Studied at Jena (1773–75) and the Freiberg mining academy (1776–79) under A. G. Werner; became a mining official. Was the leading German volcanist; thus, opposed Werner's neptunism. Was the first to draw attention to contact metamorphism.

VOIGT, WOLDEMAR (*b. Leipzig, Germany, 1850; d. Göttingen, Germany, 1919*), physics.

Studied at Leipzig and Königsberg; deeply influenced by Franz Neumann; taught at Königsberg and at Göttingen (from 1883). His chief interests were the understanding of crystals and the Zeeman effect and the electron theory; in a paper on the Doppler effect (1887) he established a set of transformations later known as the Lorentz transformations. Was an expert on music, especially Bach.

VOIT, CARL VON (*b. Amberg, Bavaria, 1831; d. Munich, Germany, 1908*), physiology.

Spent most of his adult life in Munich, where he trained in medicine (1848–54) and taught at the university (from 1859); he became the leading investigator of metabolism. As a former student of Liebig's, Voit originally adhered to Liebig's theories concerning the roles of nitrogenous and non-nitrogenous nutrients. With Theodor Bischoff, Voit carried out investigations of urea formation in dogs under various dietary conditions and in relation to different levels of muscle activity. With his former teacher Pettenkofer, Voit began (1861) the first combined feeding-respiration experiments; did the first comparative studies of the metabolism of healthy and ill humans (1865–66). By 1867, Voit's findings had led him to break with Liebig's views on both the source of muscle motion and the process of fat formation; although Voit's conclusions faced stiff opposition, his experimental findings were widely respected, and his laboratory became the center of activity in his field; among his numerous influential students was his successor, Otto Frank.

VOLKMANN, PAUL OSKAR EDUARD (*b. Bladiau, near Heiligenheil, Germany, 1856; d. Königsberg, Germany [now Kaliningrad, R.S.F.S.R.], 1938*), physics, epistemology, history of science.

Spent his entire professional life at the University of Königsberg. Studied the surface tension of water and aqueous solutions in capillary tubes and between flat plates; also wrote on axiomatics, epistemology, and figures in the history of science.

VOLNEY, CONSTANTIN-FRANÇOIS CHASSE-BOEUF, COMTE DE (*b. Craon, France, 1757; d. Paris, France, 1820*), geography, linguistics, sociology.

A disciple of the Idéalogues. Author of *Voyage en Égypte et en Syrie . . .* (1787), a pioneer work in physical and human geography; *Tableau du climat et du sol des États-Unis d'Amérique* (1803); and the deistic *Les ruines, ou méditations sur les révolutions des empires* (1791). Also taught history, was active in politics, and, in linguistics, pursued the development of a universal alphabet.

VOLTA, ALESSANDRO GIUSEPPE ANTONIO ANASTASIO (*b. Como, duchy of Milan, Italy, 1745; d. Como, 1827*), physics.

Volta's uncle took charge of his education, which began in 1757 at the local Jesuit college, until another uncle, the Dominican, who shared his order's opinion of Jesuits, put an end to the affair. Volta continued his education at the Seminario Benzi, where Lucretius' *De rerum natura* made a powerful impression upon him. His uncles wished to make him an attorney, a profession well represented on his mother's side of the family. Volta preferred to obey what he called his genius, which directed him, at the age of eighteen, to the study of electricity.

Volta enjoyed an active correspondence with Beccaria which lasted until 1769, when he published a Latin dissertation, *De vi attractiva,* which boldly reinterpreted Franklin's theory and Beccaria's latest experiments in terms of the unique attractive principle.

Volta's fundamental concept is that there exists for each body a state of saturation in which the integrated attractions of its particles for electric fluid are precisely satisfied. This integrated attraction may be altered by any process, mechanical or chemical, that displaces the particles relative to one another; friction, pressure, and, perhaps, evaporation electrify bodies by destroying the existing pattern of saturated forces and redistributing the electrical fluid.

To concoct his electrophore, the most intriguing electrical device since the Leyden jar, Volta combined the insight that resin retained its electricity longer than glass with the fact, emphasized by Cigna and Beccaria, that a metal plate and a charged insulator properly maneuvered can produce many flashes without enervating the electric. Beccaria inspired the combination. In 1772 he published a lengthy, difficult, updated version of *Elettricismo artificiale,* which emphasized more strongly than before his odd view that the contrary electricities destroy one another in the union of a charged insulator with a momentarily grounded conductor, only to reappear, "revindicated," in subsequent separations. Beccaria also criticized the hypothesis of the unique attractive force, without deigning to mention Volta, who in return conceived that, if he could greatly increase the duration of the effects ascribed to vindicating electricity, the implausible theory of alternate destructions and incomplete recuperations would fall to the ground. After many trials Volta found that an insulator made of three parts turpentine, two parts resin, and one part wax answered perfectly; and in June 1775 he informed Priestley of the invention of an *elettroforo perpetuo,* which "electrified but once, briefly and moderately, never loses its electricity, and although repeatedly touched, obstinately preserves the strength of its signs."

The device consisted of a metal dish containing a dielectric cake, and a light wooden shield covered with tin foil rounded to remove all corners and joined to an insulating handle. The cake is first charged, say negatively, by rubbing. The shield is then set upon it, and momentarily grounded, thereby charging positively by induction. The shield may then be removed and its charge given to, say, the hook of a Leyden jar; then replaced, touched, and again brought to the hook; and so on until the condenser is moderately charged. Any number of jars and electrophores may be electrified without regenerating the original; and if it should decline, it can be reinvigorated by lightly rubbing its cake with the coating of a Leyden jar that the shield had charged through the hook. Volta set

great store by this last property, which did seem to vouchsafe eternal life to the electrophore and to justify the term *elettricità vindice indeficiente,* with which he proposed to celebrate his victory over Beccaria.

The electrophore killed off not only vindicating electricity but also the last vestiges of the old doctrine of literal atmospheres. Accordingly, as contemporaries recognized, the electrophore caused electricians to take seriously the neglected approach of Aepinus.

The mid-1770's marked the beginning of Volta's career. In October 1774 he took his first academic job, principal or regent of the state Gymnasium in Como, then recently taken over from the Jesuits. Next came the electrophore and, at Volta's request, the professorship of experimental physics at the Gymnasium, which he garnered in 1775 without the usual examination. A sally into pneumatics brought the discovery of methane (1776) and a greater reputation, which helped him in 1777 to obtain state support for a trip to the chief centers of learning in Switzerland and Alsace.

As Volta's professional opportunity and acquaintance increased, his style of physics altered, at least in its public form. There is reason to believe that Volta read Cavendish's famous memoir of 1771, which most contemporary electricians ignored or misunderstood, and that he derived from it—and perhaps also from the works of Aepinus and even of Barletti, who first acquainted him with Aepinus—the clue for the transformation of his otiose notion, "natural saturation," into a serviceable substitute for the concept of potential.

Volta's thought is that the capacity C of a conductor and the tension T of its charge Q alter with its distance from other conductors. He had freed himself of the ideas that "anything real" passed between bodies interacting electrically beyond sparking range, and that the surplus electrical fluid of a positively charged body resided in the air about it. Volta embodied the quantities capacity and tension, and the implicit relation that he had established between them ($Q = CT$), in a new instrument, a "condensator" for rendering sensible atmospheric electricity otherwise too weak for detection.

He explained that owing to its great capacity the electrophore soaks up the electricity of the probe as often as it becomes charged, while the separated shield, being of small capacity, can reveal the weak collected electricity. He emphasized that the quantity of charge on a conductor increases as the product of its tension and its capacity, the former being the quantity measured by electrometers. Others soon incorporated this insight into ingenious multipliers of weak charges, such as the well-known "doubler" invented by William Nicholson.

Volta's interest in meteorology centered on atmospheric electricity, the study of which began in 1752 with the apparent confirmation of Franklin's hypothesis about the electrical character of lightning.

He accepted the Franklinist presumption that the instruments of atmospheric electricity measured the surplus (or deficiency) of electrical fluid in the lower atmosphere; and he had suggested in *De vi attractiva* that the fluid enters (or leaves) the air during evaporation. One of the first tasks he assigned his condensator was the detection of the supposititious electrification during change of state. He was then (1782) in France, and undertook the experiments in collaboration with Lavoisier and Laplace.

At first they failed, as they should have, there being no such effect; but shortly before Volta left Paris for London they succeeded, or believed they had, and made much of their success. According to Volta, everything depended on a change in electrical capacity suffered by water droplets in going from the liquid to the vapor state. They had probably detected electricity generated by the friction of bubbles against the evaporating pan. The subject was to remain confused for over a century.

Volta's work on gases shows the same genius for instrumentation and measurement, and the same failure or reluctance to establish general principles, that characterize his work on electrostatics. His first pneumatic studies concerned "inflammable air from marshes" (chiefly methane), which he discovered in November 1776 in Lago Maggiore. It was not a chance find. Inflammable air from metals (hydrogen released from acids) had been known since its isolation by Cavendish in 1766, and Franklin's description of a natural source of inflammable air had just been published by Priestley in a book quickly known in Italy. In the autumn of 1776 Volta's friend P. Carlo Giuseppe Campi had found a natural source near Pavia; and Volta himself, intrigued by the "ever more remarkable and interesting subject of the different kinds of air," had scoured the countryside for telltale bubbles. The testing of his new gas—new in source, flame color, and combustibility—led him into the faddish field of eudiometry.

Ever interested in large, reproducible effects, Volta had shifted his attention to hydrogen upon discovering that, when mixed with common air and sparked, Cavendish's inflammable air ignited more readily and burnt more fiercely than his own, whence Volta's famous "inflammable air pistol," filled with hydrogen and air or oxygen, and fired by a portable electrophore. To perfect this artillery (which could fire a lead ball with force enough to dent wood at fifteen feet) he looked for the mixture that destroyed the greatest quantity of gas. He thereby came to the problem of the eudiometer, but from a new side, and with a new eudiometric fluid, hydrogen, which could be obtained purer than the standard nitric oxide, and acted much more vigorously.

Volta's eudiometer set up one of the most important discoveries of the eighteenth century, the composition of water, detected by Lavoisier, among others, by sparking oxygen and hydrogen over mercury (1783).

Volta's later pneumatic studies centered on the action of heat on gases and vapors. His general conception of heat followed the fluid theories of Crawford and Kirwan, with one characteristic exception: whereas his sources ascribed the phenomenon of latent heat to a chemical combination responsible for change of state, he made the change primary, and the latent heat the result of a consequent jump in specific heat capacity.

Volta was more successful in measuring the dilation of air as a function of heat, or rather of temperature indicated on a mercury thermometer, but the journal to which he confided these results had little circulation outside Italy. His priority was ignored in favor of Gay-Lussac. In any case, the proposition, "the coefficient of expansion of air is constant," was restored to Volta by unanimous vote of the international congress of physicists meeting at Como in 1927 in observance of the centennial of his death.

In 1791 Galvani, professor of anatomy at the University of Bologna, published his now famous study of the electrical excitation of disembodied frog legs. He explained the jerking of a leg upon completing a circuit through the crural nerve and the leg muscle as the direct result of the discharge of a "nerveoelectrical fluid" previously accumulated in the muscle, which he supposed to act like a Leyden jar.

When Volta learned of Galvani's experiments he dismissed them as "unbelievable" and "miraculous." He had a low opinion of physicians, whom he found to be generally "ignorant of the known laws of electricity"; and he recognized "animal electricity" only in electrical fish, to which, however, he ascribed only the power of manipulating common electrical fluid. Moreover, even as late as 28 March 1792, just after he had first tried the experiments, "with little hope of success," under the urging of his colleagues in pathology and anatomy, his immediate research plans included only meteorology and the dilation of gases. But by 1 April the experiments had succeeded, and Volta had begun the brilliantly planned and executed experiments that step by step brought him to the invention of the pile.

Volta represented his discovery as an "artificial electric organ," an apparatus "fundamentally the same" as the natural electrical equipment of the torpedo. A medium-size pile, with forty or fifty pairs, gave anyone who touched its extremities about the same sensation he could enjoy grasping an electric fish.

It appears that Volta possessed most of the ingredients of the pile by 1796, including even an anticipation of the outstanding key discovery, the constructive combination of the generating pairs.

Napoleon patronized Volta, and predicted that the pile presaged a new era in science. Its chemical power, employed in electrolyzing alkali salts, soon revealed the existence of sodium and potassium, a discovery for which Davy won the medal established by Napoleon. Studies of the properties of the current led to the laws of Oersted, Ohm, and Faraday, and to the beginnings of electrotechnology. In all of this Volta played no part. He was not much interested in the chemical effects of the pile, which he considered to be secondary phenomena.

VOLTAIRE, FRANÇOIS MARIE AROUET DE (*b. Paris, France, 1694; d. Paris, 1778*), literature.

Voltaire's importance for the history of science lies in his popularization of Newton in *Éléments de la philosophie de Newton* (1738) and in his collaboration with his companion Mme. du Châtelet on her translation of the *Principia* into French. Voltaire's appreciation of English men of science developed in a visit to their country (1726–29); he never had an expert's understanding of Newton, but he emphasized those aspects of Newtonian science which he believed to be the most valuable in his great crusade against dogma and illusion.

VOLTERRA, VITO (*b. Ancona, Italy, 1860; d. Rome, Italy, 1940*), mathematics, natural philosophy.

Of a family of bankers and bibliophiles; as a child, he displayed a precocious talent in mathematics; while still a student published the first paper with examples of derivable functions the derivatives of which are not reconcilable with Riemann's point of view. After receiving his doctorate from the University of Pisa (1882), he became assistant to his former teacher Betti; he had a distinguished teaching career at Pisa, Turin, and Rome (from 1900). He was politically active, especially against Fascism. Volterra made important contributions in higher analysis, celestial mechanics, the mathematical theory of elasticity, and mathematical biometrics.

VOLTZ, PHILIPPE LOUIS (*b. Strasbourg, France, 1785; d. Paris, France, 1840*), geology.

Studied at École Polytechnique and École des Mines. Was chief engineer of the Strasbourg mineralogical district (1814–36); moved to Paris, (1836) as inspector-general of mines. Specialized in stratigraphic paleontology, published on fossil mollusks; introduced the notion of facies into geology (1828).

VON NEUMANN, JOHANN (or **JOHN**) (*b. Budapest, Hungary, 1903; d. Washington, D.C., 1957*), mathematics, mathematical physics.

Due to his unusual mathematical abilities, von Neumann was tutored in mathematics under the guidance of university professors, and by the age of nineteen he was already recognized as a professional mathematician and had published his first paper. He was *Privatdozent* at Berlin (1927–29) and Hamburg (1929–30); went to Princeton University for three years; and in 1933 joined the newly opened Institute for Advanced Study. During World War II he participated in various scientific projects related to the war effort, in particular the construction of the atomic bomb at Los Alamos. In 1954 he became a member of the Atomic Energy Commission. Von Neumann was equally at home in pure and applied mathematics and throughout his career maintained a steady production in both directions. His genius lay in analysis and combinatorics; as an analyst he belongs to the tradition of Hilbert, Weyl, and F. Riesz, in which analysis, while being as "hard" as any classical theory, is based on extensive foundations of linear algebra and general topology.

His work in pure mathematics was accomplished between 1925 and 1940. He made several valuable contributions to logic and set theory, measure theory, and Lie groups. The most dominant theme in his work is the spectral theory of operators in Hilbert space. For twenty years he was the undisputed master in this area, which contains what is now considered his most profound and most original creation, the theory of rings of operators. He extended the concepts of noncommutative algebra to algebras consisting of (bounded) operators in a given separable Hilbert space, to which he gave the vague name "rings of operators" and which are now known as "von Neumann algebras." After elucidating the relatively easy study of commutative algebras, von Neumann embarked in 1936, with the partial collaboration of F. J. Murray, on the general study of the noncommutative case. The six major papers in which they developed that theory between 1936 and 1940 rank among the masterpieces of analysis in the twentieth century.

His most famous work in theoretical physics is his axiomatization of quantum mechanics. When he began work in that field in 1927, the methods used by its founders were hard to formulate in precise mathematical terms. Von Neumann showed that mathematical rigor could be restored by taking as basic axioms the assumptions that the states of a physical system were points of a Hilbert space and that the measurable quantities were Hermitian (generally unbounded) operators densely defined in that space. This formalism has survived subsequent developments of quantum mechanics and is still the basis of nonrelativistic quantum theory. This and other work was developed and expanded in *Mathematische Grundlagen der Quantenmechanik* (1932).

Von Neumann's uncommon grasp of applied mathematics was nowhere more apparent than in his work on computers. Dissatisfied with the computing machines available immediately after the war, he examined from its foundations the optimal method that such machines should follow, and he introduced new procedures in their logical organization, the "codes" by which a fixed system of wiring could solve a great variety of problems. He supervised the construction of a computer at the Institute for Advanced Study, and must be considered one of the founders of a flourishing new mathematical discipline. His role as founder is even more obvious for the theory of games. He developed a quantitative mathematical model for games of chance by introducing the general concept of "strategy" and by constructing a model that made this concept amenable to mathematical analysis (1926). He applied his work to economics in his *Theory of Games and Economic Behavior* (1944, with O. Morgenstern).

VORONIN, MIKHAIL STEPANOVICH (*b. St. Petersburg, Russia [now Leningrad, U.S.S.R.], 1838; d. St. Petersburg, 1903*), mycology.

Studied at St. Petersburg University and with de Bary in Freiburg. Independently wealthy, he conducted most of his research at home, specializing in mycology. Discovered and studied the causal organisms of clubroot, sunflower rust, the mold on apples, and ergotism.

VORONOY, GEORGY FEDOSEEVICH (*b. Zhuravka, Poltava gubernia, Russia, 1868; d. Warsaw, Poland, 1908*), mathematics.

Studied at the University of St. Petersburg (doctorate, 1897); taught at University of Warsaw (from 1894). Did important work in number theory.

VRIES, HUGO DE (*b. Haarlem, Netherlands, 1848; d. Lunteren, Netherlands, 1935*), plant physiology, genetics, evolution.

De Vries studied at Leiden and Heidelberg; he was strongly influenced by reading Sachs's *Lehrbuch der Botanik* and Darwin's *Origin of Species*, and spent his summers doing experimental work in Sachs's laboratory at Würzburg. The reports of his experimental work there are found in Sachs's journal, *Arbeiten des botanischen Instituts in Würzburg.* Darwin greatly admired de Vries' work on the mechanism of the movements of climbing plants (1872) and praised it in his *Climbing Plants,* which started a correspondence between Darwin and de Vries. To qualify as a *Privatdozent* at Halle, de Vries defended a dissertation based on his work on the stretching of cells (1877). In later 1877 he became lecturer in plant physiology at the newly constituted University of Amsterdam, eventually succeeding Oudemans as senior professor of botany (1896–1918). Until about 1890 he conducted research on osmosis in plant cells—the famous experiments on plasmolysis. He found that if a plant cell is immersed in successively stronger salt solutions, the cell initially contracts; subsequently the protoplast starts contracting and frees itself from the cell wall until it becomes a globular body within the cell. He called this process "plasmolysis." He formulated a growth theory, stating that growth in plants is caused primarily by extension of the cell walls by turgor (cell fluid). Using plant cells as indicators, he formulated the law of isotonic coefficients. Using this law, he was able to determine the proportional contribution to the total osmotic pressure in the cell for each component of the cell fluid. His work on the isotonic coefficients of solutions led van't Hoff to his formula for the osmotic pressure of solutions, and van't Hoff's law in turn enabled de Vries to determine the total osmotic pressure in plant cells.

About 1890 de Vries abruptly switched to the study of heredity and variation. In his first work in this new field of interest, *Intracellulare Pangenesis* (1889), he presented his own theory. He considered the hereditary characteristics of living organisms as units that manifest themselves independently of each other and that can, therefore, be studied separately. Each independent characteristic is associated with a material bearer, which he called a "pangene." The pangene is a morphological structure, made up of numerous molecules, that can take nourishment, grow, and divide to yield two new pangenes. After cell division, each daughter cell receives one set of pangenes from the mother cell. A pangene can be either active or latent. Some characteristics may be represented by more than one pangene. Where conflicting characteristics are possible—for example, red or white flowers—the characteristic represented by the largest number of pangenes is dominant. In each reproductive cell at least one of the representative pangenes, either active or latent, is present. The pangene theory is remarkably close to the theory formulated later by geneticists; the name "gene," given to the hereditary unit by Johannsen, was derived from de Vries's pangene.

Deciding that experimental work in heredity should be performed with closely allied races or varieties, de Vries in 1896 demonstrated to his advanced students the segregation laws, now known as Mendel's laws, in *Papaver somniferum* var. *Mephisto* and var. *Danebrog*. After this rediscovery of Mendel's laws, de Vries concentrated on the phenomenon of mutation, which he believed explained the origin of new species and therefore gave necessary support to the theory of evolution. From 1886 till the end of his life he carried out extensive experiments with *Oenothera lamarckiana* (evening primrose); he called the new forms that appeared suddenly and unexpectedly "single variations," and later "mutations." He distinguished mutations that supply a useful characteristic ("progressive") and those that supply a useless or even harmful characteristic ("retrogressive"), and distinguished two kinds of crosses: bisexual and unisexual. His work on variability and mutation was reported in *Die Mutationstheorie . . .* (1901–03). The fact that his mutants were superseded does not mean that his work on the phenomenon of mutation was valueless. Many true mutations have been discovered in the animal and plant kingdoms and mutation is still the cornerstone of the theory of evolution. Next to the *Drosophila* experiments, the work with *Oenothera* has contributed most to the chromosome theory of heredity.

VULF, YURI VIKTOROVICH. *See* **Wulff, Georg.**

VVEDENSKY, NIKOLAY EVGENIEVICH (*b. Kochkovo, Vologodskaya gubernia, Russia, 1852; d. Kochkovo, 1922*), physiology.

Spent most of his adult life at St. Petersburg University (master's degree, 1884; professor, from 1895). Studied the regularities in the reaction of living tissue to various irritants; in his theory of parabiosis (1901), he generalized his ideas on the processes of excitation and inhibition, showing their identity.

VYSHNEGRADSKY, IVAN ALEKSEEVICH (*b. Vyshni Volochek, Tver gubernia [now Kalinin oblast], Russia, 1831; d. St. Petersburg, Russia, 1895*), mechanics, engineering.

Studied at St. Petersburg University (master's degree, 1854); an outstanding theoretician, civil engineer, and educator, he taught at the Mikhaylovsky Artillery Academy and the St. Petersburg Technological Institute and was minister of finance (1888–92). His most significant scientific contributions were in the theory of automatic regulation; his stability condition for a regulating system (1877) is known as the Vyshnegradsky criterion.

VYSOTSKY, GEORGY NIKOLAEVICH (*b. Nikitovka, Chernigov gubernia, Russia, 1865: d. Kharkov, U.S.S.R., 1940*), soil science, forestry.

Studied at Petrovsky Agricultural Academy. Directed numerous forestry projects. Established the scientific foundations of steppe forestry.

WAAGE, PETER (*b. Hitterø island [now Hidra], near Flekkefjord, Norway, 1833; d. Christiania [now Oslo], Norway, 1900*), chemistry, mineralogy.

Of a family of seamen; studied at the University of Christiania and under Bunsen at Heidelberg. In 1862, in collaboration with his brother-in-law C. M. Guldberg, he began studies of chemical affinity that led to their discovery of the law of mass action (1864). Taught at Christiania University (from 1861); did important work in nutrition and public health.

WAALS, JOHANNES DIDERIK VAN DER (*b. Leiden, Netherlands, 1837; d. Amsterdam, Netherlands, 1923*), physics.

While a headmaster at The Hague, did a dissertation for the University of Leiden (1873) that established his reputation. Using rather simple mathematics, he gave a molecular explanation for phenomena observed in vapors and liquids, especially the existence of a critical temperature below which a gas can be condensed to a two-phase system of vapor and liquid; this was one of the first descriptions of a collective molecular effect. Some years later he developed the law of corresponding states, which fits the experimental data somewhat better and was a useful guide in work on the liquefaction of the "permanent" gases. He taught at the University of Amsterdam until his retirement (1907); in 1910 he was awarded the Nobel Prize for physics.

WACKENRODER, HEINRICH WILHELM FERDINAND (*b. Burgdorf, near Hannover, Germany, 1798; d. Jena, Germany, 1854*), pharmacy.

An exceptionally successful pharmacist and professor of pharmacy at the University of Jena. Established pharmacy as an independent science. He discovered corydaline in the bulbs of *Corydalis tuberosa*, carotene in carrots, and solanine in potato sprouts. His name is commemorated by "Wackenroder's solution," a solution of polythionic acids.

IBN WĀFID, ABŪ AL-MUṬARRIF ʿABD AL-RAḤ-MAN, also known as **Abenguefit, Abenguéfith, Albenguéfith, Abel Nufit** (*fl. Toledo, Spain, ca. 1008–75*), pharmacology.

Built a botanical garden for King al-Maʾmūn of Toledo. Among his books is *Kitāb al-adwiya al-mufrada* ("Book of the Simple Medicines"), basically a synthesis of Dioscorides and Galen.

WAGNER, RUDOLPH (*b. Bayreuth, Germany, 1805; d. Göttingen, Germany, 1864*), comparative anatomy, physiology, anthropology.

Graduated M.D. from Würzburg (1826); taught at Erlangen (1829–40) and (from 1840) at Göttingen. His most important work concerned mammalian ova and sperm. Demonstrated that red blood corpuscles have no nuclei (1833).

WAGNER VON JAUREGG (or **WAGNER-JAUREGG**), **JULIUS** (*b. Wels, Austria, 1857; d. Vienna, Austria, 1940*), psychiatry.

Attended the University of Vienna medical school; by chance, took a post at the university psychiatric clinic. Taught at Graz (1889–93); returned to Vienna as full professor and director of the Psychiatric and Neurological Clinic. His studies of thyroid function, cretinism, and goiter led to the widespread use of iodized salt. He helped to develop the only effective treatment of general paresis prior to antibiotic therapy, malaria fever-therapy; in 1927 he received the Nobel Prize for his part in this achievement.

WAHLENBERG, GÖRAN (Georg) (*b. Skarphyttan, Sweden, 1780; d. Uppsala, Sweden, 1851*), botany.

Spent almost his entire life at Uppsala University (M.D., 1806). Travelled (1799–1814) to Gotland, in the Baltic Sea, Lapland, the Alps, and the Carpathians; this enabled his considerable contribution to phytogeography made in his introductions to his floras and in his geographical writings. Was an expert on the stratification of vegetation on mountains; emphasized the influence of climate on the differentiation of vegetation.

IBN WAḤSHIYYA, ABŪ BAKR AḤMAD IBN ʿALĪ IBN AL-MUKHTĀR (*b. Qussīn, near Janbalā, Iraq, ca. 860; d. Baghdad, ca. 935*), agronomy, toxicology, sorcery.

Practiced astrology and magical healing in Baghdad. Is best known for a book on agriculture and one on poisons and their antidotes, both supposedly translations from ancient Aramaic texts.

WALCH, JOHANN ERNST IMMANUEL (*b. Jena, Germany, 1725; d. Jena, 1778*), theology, philology, paleontology.

Studied, taught at, and was twice rector of the University of Jena. Admired in his day as a theologian and philologist; now remembered for transforming the muddled study of fossils into a science; created the first comprehensive paleontology ordered according to the zoological system.

WALCOTT, CHARLES DOOLITTLE (*b. New York Mills, N.Y., 1850; d. Washington, D.C., 1927*), paleontology.

A leading specialist in Cambrian rocks and fossils; discovered (1909) the Middle Cambrian Burgess shale deposit, rich in rare fossils. Was director of the U.S. Geological Survey (1894–1907); appointed secretary of the Smithsonian Institution (1907); founded the National Advisory Committee for Aeronautics; helped to found the Carnegie Institution of Washington; president of the National Academy of Sciences (1917–23).

WALD, ABRAHAM (*b. Cluj, Rumania, 1902; d. India, 1950*), mathematics, statistics, economics.

Of a Jewish family, almost all of whom were killed under Hitler; was educated at the universities of Cluj and Vienna; found employment with the economist Oskar Morgenstern; lived in the U.S. (from 1938); died in a plane crash. Founded and still dominates the fields of sequential analysis and the theory of decision functions. Did important work on the identification of economic relations and in geometry.

WALD, FRANTIŠEK (*b. Brandýsek, near Slaný, Czechoslovakia, 1861; d. Vítkovice [now part of Ostrava], Czechoslovakia, 1930*), chemistry.

Worked as a chemist at a leading ironworks at Kladno; taught at the Czech Technical University in Prague (from 1908). Noted for critiques of the conceptual foundations of chemistry.

WALDEN, PAUL (also known as **PAVEL IVANOVICH VALDEN**) (*b. Rosenbeck parish, Wenden district [now Latvian S.S.R.], Russia, 1863; d. Gammertingen, Germany, 1957*), chemistry.

Of a family of farmers; studied under F. W. Ostwald at the Riga Polytechnical School, where his first scientific work led to the discovery (1887) of the Ostwald-Walden empirical rule, enabling the determination of the basicity of polyatomic acids and bases according to molar electroconductivity; earned two doctorate degrees (1891, 1899); had a distinguished teaching career in St. Petersburg, Riga, and in Rostock, Germany (after 1919); was one of the founders of physical organic chemistry. His stereochemical research led him to the discovery in 1896 of "Walden's inversion"; did fundamental work in the electrochemistry of nonaqueous solutions.

WALDEYER-HARTZ, WILHELM VON (*b. Hehlen, Germany, 1836; d. Berlin, Germany, 1921*), anatomy.

Studied at Göttingen, Greiswald, and Berlin. A brilliant anatomy teacher; his academic posts included the chair of pathology at Breslau (1868–72), chair of anatomy at Strasbourg (1872–83), and, finally, director of the anatomy department at Berlin. He coined the terms "neuron" and "chromosome."

WALDSEEMÜLLER, MARTIN (*b. Radolfzell, Germany, 1470; d. St.-Dié, France, 1518 [?]*), geography.

Canon of St.-Dié; associated with the court of Duke René II of Lorraine; expert in cartography. Christened the New World "America" since he believed it was discovered by Amerigo Vespucci; his edition of Ptolemy's *Geographia* (1513), with new maps, is the first modern atlas.

WALKER, ALEXANDER (*b. Leith, Scotland, 1779; d. Leith, 1852*), physiology.

A versatile scientist and popularizer. Was the first to suggest that the roots of the spinal nerves differ in function (although he reversed their functions). His *Beauty in Women* (1836) remains a striking and scholarly work.

WALKER, JOHN (*b. Edinburgh, Scotland, 1731; d. Edinburgh, 1803*), botany, geology.

Studied at Edinburgh University; as a minister at Glencorse, met Henry Home, Lord Kames, who sponsored his geological investigations; appointed to the chair of natural history at Edinburgh (1779). Made many original contributions to geology and botany; developed teaching methods in geology that are still used today.

WALLACE, ALFRED RUSSEL (*b. Usk, Monmouthshire, Wales, 1823; d. Broadstone, Dorset, England, 1913*), natural history.

Wallace received no formal education past grammar school, teaching himself by reading the works of Humboldt, Malthus, Darwin, Chambers, Lyell, and Swainson, and making amateurish explorations in Charnwood Forest in Leicester with Henry Walter Bates. In 1848 Wallace and Bates left on an expedition to South America, where they eventually covered a sizeable portion of the Amazon basin. In 1850 they separated, with Wallace going to the Rio Negro and Uaupés rivers. His explorations were recounted in *A Narrative of Travels on the Amazon and Rio Negro* (1853). A major reason for the expedition had been to collect information on the variation and evolution of species. Wallace was converted to the belief that species arise through natural laws, rather than by divine fiat, but most of his splendid collections were lost at sea, and he hesitated to declare his views publicly.

After his rescue, and arrival in England (1852), he decided to embark on another lengthy expedition, this time to the Malay Archipelago (now Indonesia and Malaysia). During that period of extensive exploration (1854–62), Wallace formulated the principle of natural selection and made many other fundamental discoveries in biology, geology, geography, ethnography, and other natural sciences. His *The Malay Archipelago* (1869) went through countless editions and was translated into many foreign languages. The boundaries of the range of his explorations were the Aru Islands to the east; Malacca, Malaya, to the west; the northern tip of Celebes to the north; and as far south as southern Timor. He gathered precise scientific data on groups of animals in order to work out their geographical distribution and consequently to throw light on their origins through evolutionary processes. He concluded: "Every species has come into existence coincident both in space and time with a preexisting closely allied species," definitely announcing that he was an evolutionist. Wallace's paper "On the Tendency of Varieties to Depart Indefinitely From the Original Type" (1858) expounded his discovery of the principle of natural selection, the now famous mechanism of evolu-

tion, and was the final stimulus for Darwin to publish his *Origin*. Wallace's numerous publications included *Contributions to the Theory of Natural Selection* (1870), *Geographical Distribution of Animals* (1876), *Island Life* (1880), and *Darwinism* (1889). From the 1860's onward one of the forceful arguments used by Wallace to support evolution was mimicry, since it had been explained in terms of natural selection. He extended the work of Bates and Müller.

While Wallace was one of the founders of modern evolutionary biology, his views on man underwent significant alteration during the 1860's after his return from the Malay Archipelago, due mainly to his conversion to Spiritualism and his decision that natural selection could not adequately explain all aspects of man's development. He believed neither natural selection nor evolution could explain the origin of man's intellect. In exactly the reverse direction of a common trend since the eighteenth century, Wallace *added* deity to his mechanistic, self-regulating universe ("The Limits of Natural Selection as Applied to Man," 1867).

Another important result of his expedition to the Malay Archipelago was in geographical distribution. In 1860 Wallace published an elaborate discussion of the zoological geography of the archipelago, and in 1863 announced explicitly what became known as Wallace's Line, the zoogeographical line that extended between Bali and Lombok in the south and farther north between Borneo and Celebes, and continuing eastward around the Philippines. His investigations made it quite clear that zoogeography should be based on a wide range of geographical and geological facts interpreted by evolutionary doctrines. In his monumental two-volume *The Geographical Distribution of Animals* (1876) he established evolutionary zoogeography on its modern foundation.

WALLACE, WILLIAM (*b. Dysart, Scotland, 1768; d. Edinburgh, Scotland, 1843*), mathematics.

Self-taught in mathematics; professor of mathematics at Edinburgh (1819–38). Did original work in geometry.

WALLACH, OTTO (*b. Königsberg, Prussia [now Kaliningrad, R.S.F.S.R.], 1847; d. Göttingen, Germany, 1931*), chemistry.

Studied at Göttingen (doctorate, 1869); taught at Bonn for most of the period 1870–89; returned to Göttingen as director of the Chemical Institute (1889–1915). Made the fundamental discoveries in the field of terpene chemistry. Awarded the Nobel Prize in chemistry in 1910.

WALLER, AUGUSTUS VOLNEY (*b. Faversham, England, 1816; d. Geneva, Switzerland, 1870*), neurology.

Studied at Paris (M.D., 1840); in private practice in England (1841–51); thereafter engaged mainly in private research. Pioneered the method of secondary, or Wallerian, degeneration for studying the nervous system; using the simple technique of cutting the nerves in a frog's tongue (1849), reached findings that indicated the connection between nerve cell bodies and processes.

WALLERIUS, JOHAN GOTTSCHALK (*b. Stora Mellösa, Nerke, Sweden, 1709; d. Uppsala, Sweden, 1785*), chemistry, mineralogy.

An outstanding teacher of chemistry at the University of Uppsala (1741–67). His *Mineralogia eller Mineralriket*

(1747), which emphasized the essential chemical properties of minerals, opened a new epoch in mineralogy. Was called the father of agricultural chemistry; wrote *Agriculturae fundamenta chemica, Åkerbrukets kemiska grunder* (1761).

WALLICH, GEORGE CHARLES (*b. Calcutta, India, 1815; d. Marylebone, London, England, 1899)*, zoology.

Specialized in the study of deep-sea life, especially Protozoa; came to this interest when, as naturalist on the H.M.S. *Bulldog* (1860), he brought up living starfish from 1,260 fathoms, at which depth life was thought to be impossible.

WALLINGFORD. *See* **Richard of Wallingford.**

WALLIS, JOHN (*b. Ashford, Kent, England, 1616; d. Oxford, England, 1703)*, mathematics.

Wallis, son of a minister, attended the famous school of Martin Holbeach, Felsted, Essix; entered Emanuel College, Cambridge (B.A., 1637; M.A., 1640); and was ordained by the bishop of Winchester. For some years he earned his living as a private chaplain and minister in London; acted as secretary to the Assembly of the Divines at Westminster (from 1644); held a fellowship at Queens' College, Cambridge; was appointed Savilian professor of geometry at Oxford (1649), a position he held until his death; and was made Doctor of Divinity there (1654). After the restoration, he was confirmed in his offices for having signed the remonstrance against the execution of King Charles I, and was appointed royal chaplain to Charles II. Was a founder of the Royal Society. In addition to mathematics, his achievements included work in the decipherment of code letters for the government; logic; teaching deaf mutes to speak and the related grammatical and phonetical writings; and editions of mathematical and musical manuscripts of ancient Greek authors.

Wallis' interest in mathematics was first aroused (1647–48) when he chanced upon a copy of Wm. Oughtred's *Clavis mathematicae.* He rediscovered Cardano's solution of the cubic equation (not given by Oughtred) and composed a *Treatise of Angular Sections* (1648; pub. 1685); also gave an explanation of Descartes's treatment of the fourth-degree equation: to write the equation as a product of two quadratic factors. (Though this could be derived from Harriot's *Artis analyticae praxis* [pub. 1631], Wallis claimed not to have known the book.) His *Mathesis universalis seu opus arithmeticum* (1657) was a treatment of notation, including historical survey, stressed the great advantage of a suggested and unified symbolism, but reflects the rather weak state of mathematical learning in the universities of the time.

In the treatise *De sectionibus conicis* (1655) Wallis dealt with a classical subject in a new way. He considered the conic sections merely as plane curves, once he had obtained them by sections of a cone, and subjected them to the analytical treatment introduced by Descartes rather than to the traditional synthetic approach. In addition, he employed infinitesimals in the sense of Cavalieri and Toricelli. He also first introduced the sign for infinity.

His fame as a mathematician, however, is grounded on *Arithmetica infinitorium* (1656). It resulted from his study of Torricelli's *Opera geometrica* (1644). By an ingenius sequence of interpolations, he produced his famous result:

$$\frac{4}{\pi} = \frac{3}{2} \cdot \frac{3}{4} \cdot \frac{5}{4} \cdot \frac{5}{6} \cdot \frac{7}{6} \cdots$$

Wallis' main interest lay not with the demonstration, but with the investigation. Actually searching for the value of

$$\int_0^1 (1-x^2)^{\frac{1}{2}} \, dx = \frac{\pi}{4} ,$$

he considered the generalized integral

$$I(k,n) = \int_0^1 (1-x^{1/k})^n \, dx.$$

Its reciprocal $1:I(k,n)$ he tabulated first for integral values of k and n (receiving the symmetric array of the binomical coefficients or figurated numbers), then for the fractions $k = \frac{1}{2}, \frac{3}{2}, \frac{5}{2}, \ldots$; for, with $k = n = 1/2$, this should yield $1:I\left(\frac{1}{2},\frac{1}{2}\right) = \frac{4}{\pi}$, for which he wrote the symbol $\square$.

Then each second value of the row and column which met at $\square$ was a certain (fractional) multiple of $\square$. Assuming that all rows and columns in his table would continually increase, Wallis was able to derive two sequences of upper and lower bounds for $\square$, respectively. When these sequences are continued indefinitely, they yield his famous infinite product. William Brouncker soon transformed it into a regular continued fraction, which Wallis included in his book.

Wallis' method of interpolation—he himself gave it this name, which has become a *terminus technicus*—is based on the assumption of continuity, and, incidentally, seems closely related to the procedure he had to apply when he deciphered coded letters. To preserve this continuity and thereby the underlying mathematical law in his table, Wallis went to the utmost limit. He admitted fractional multiples of the type $A \cdot \frac{0}{1} \cdot \frac{2}{3} \cdot \frac{4}{5} \cdot \frac{6}{7} \cdots$, claiming that

A here should be infinite so that the value of the product was a finite number. One must emphasize the kind of "functional thinking" revealed here—not on the basis of geometric curves but of sequences of numerical expressions, that is, tabulated functions.

Wallis' last great mathematical book was *Treatise of Algebra, Both Historical and Practical* (1685). It was to combine a full exposition of algebra with its history, a feat never previously attempted. Of the hundred chapters, the first fourteen trace the history of the subject up to the time of Vite, with emphasis on the development of notation; chapters 15–63 are based almost entirely on Oughtred's *Clavis mathematicae,* Harriot's *Artis analyticae praxis* and *An Introduction to Algebra* (1668), and Thomas Brancker's translation of J. H. Rahn's *Teutsche Algebra* (1659); chapters 64–72 concern the application of algebra to geometry and geometrical interpretations of algebraic facts; and the final 28 chapters are devoted to a discussion of the methods of exhaustion and of indivisibles.

For over half a century Wallis helped shape the course of mathematics in England and was instrumental in raising it to the eminence it enjoyed on the Continent.

WALTER BURLEY. *See* **Burley, Walter.**

WALTER OF EVESHAM. *See* **Walter of Odington.**

WALTER OF ODINGTON (*fl. England, 1280* [*?*]*–1330* [*?*]), alchemy, music.

Was probably born at Odington in Oxfordshire; apparently became a monk at the Benedictine abbey at Evesham; was possibly at Merton College, Oxford, early in the fourteenth century. Works include a famous book on medieval music and the alchemical study *Icocedron,* in which he attempted to quantify qualitative intensities.

WALTER, PHILIPPE (*b. Cracow, Poland, 1810; d. Paris, France, 1847*), chemistry.

Received doctorate at Cracow. As a political refugee from Poland, joined the group around Dumas in Paris; taught at the École Centrale des Arts et Manufactures. Obtained (1842) the first indication that carbon could be replaced in organic compounds by other elements.

WALTON, IZAAK (*b. Stafford, England, 1593; d. Winchester, England, 1683*), literature, zoology.

A prosperous tradesman and writer. His biographies and *The Compleat Angler* (1653) are valuable in the history of science not only for their strictly scientific observations but also for an understanding of the close interaction in this era between religion and natural philosophy.

WANG HSI-SHAN (*b. 1628, registered at Wu-chiang, Soochow prefecture, China; d. 1682*), astronomy.

The son of an obscure gentry family; self-taught in mathematics and astronomy; after the Manchu conquest of his district (1645), Wang first attempted suicide, then renounced worldly ambition and dedicated himself to learning; his career was short, hampered by isolation and illness. Wang's achievements in astronomy were made at a time when the Jesuits, almost the sole source of knowledge of Western astronomy, had successfully denied Chinese scientists information on the theories of Copernicus, Galileo, and Kepler. Wang, Mei Wen-ting, and Hsueh Feng-tso were the first Chinese scholars to react to the exact sciences, and they effected a scientific revolution. Wang, working from what he knew of the system of Tycho Brahe, made considerable adaptations and improvements in it. His *Hsiao-an hsin fa* ("New Method," completed 1663) provided for the first time methods for predicting planetary occultations and solar transits. His *Wu hsing hsing tu chieh* ("On the Angular Motions of the Five Planets," completed 1673) displays a familiarity with modern trigonometry, and contains the original suggestion that planetary anomalies be explained by a force radiating from the outermost moving sphere and attracting each planet to an extent maximal at apogee; this is the first explicit assumption of forces to explain celestial motion in Chinese astronomy.

WANGERIN, ALBERT (*b. Greiffenberg, Pomerania, Germany, 1844; d. Halle, Germany, 1933*), mathematics.

Took his Ph.D. at Königsberg (1866); influenced by Franz Neumann, became expert in potential theory, spherical functions, and related fields. Was a very productive teacher (at Berlin and Halle), writer, and editor.

WANKLYN, JAMES ALFRED (*b. Ashton-under-Lyne, Lancashire, England, 1834; d. New Malden, Surrey [now part of London], England, 1906*), chemistry.

Studied at Owens College, Manchester; Heidelberg; and Edinburgh. Taught at London Institution, later establishing a private analytical laboratory and consultancy. Gained European reputation for research on organic synthesis, vapor densities, and qualitative analysis, but was ignored and despised by British academic chemists. Remembered for his stormy controversy with his former teacher and sponsor, Edward Frankland, over water analysis: Frankland's method was more accurate but too complex for use by public health analysts; Wanklyn's underestimated nitrogen content, but was more practical.

WARBURG, EMIL GABRIEL (*b. Altona, near Hamburg, Germany, 1846; d. Grunau, near Bayreuth, Germany, 1931*), physics.

Inspired by Kirchhoff to study physics; took his doctorate at the University of Berlin (1867). With August Kundt, at the Kaiser Wilhelm University at Strasbourg, made two famous studies on the kinetic theory of gases. At the University of Freiburg im Breisgau (1876–95), discovered and interpreted hysteresis in the cyclical magnetization of ferromagnetic materials; began studies of electrical conductivity in solids, liquids, and gases. As director of the prestigious Berlin physics institute (1895–1905), had a brilliant success as a teacher; continued studies of gas discharges; undertook others on spark discharges and point discharges and the resulting ozone formation. As president of the Physikalische Reichsanstalt (1905–22), strengthened this organization markedly; began investigations in photochemistry.

WARBURG, OTTO HEINRICH (*b. Freiburg im Breisgau, Baden, Germany, 1883; d. Berlin-Dahlem, Germany, 1970*), biochemistry.

The son of E. G. Warburg; studied chemistry under Emil Fischer at the University of Berlin where he obtained his doctorate; matured late, doing most of his important work after service in World War I; affiliated with the Kaiser Wilhelm Institute for Biology in Dahlem (from 1913); awarded the 1931 Nobel Prize in physiology or medicine for his discovery (1924) of iron oxygenase (*Atmungsferment*). The number and magnitude of his discoveries rank Warburg as the most accomplished biochemist of all time; he was a pioneer in methodology, who believed in the use of simple but new variations in experimental conditions; thus, he discovered the fermentation of tumor cells by increasing twentyfold the concentration of bicarbonate in the medium; discovered the energy cycle and one-quantum reaction of photosynthesis when the light-dark time intervals measured in manometry were shortened from five minutes to one minute; discovered iron oxygenase by raising the pressure of carbon monoxide from 5 to 95 percent or more. Worked more or less continuously for the last fifty years of his life on aspects of photosynthesis, demonstrating that this process can be made to take place with almost perfect thermodynamic efficiency; three cycles of illumination and of dark reaction (marked by a greatly increased rate of respiration) were shown to yield a net requirement of three quanta for the overall photosynthetic reaction.

He discovered in cancer cells greatly increased glucose fermentation accompanied by injured respiration; termed this the prime cause of cancer (i.e., the cause "found in every case of the disease"); in a controversial lecture (1966) recommended dietary additions of large amounts of the active groups of various respiratory enzymes (especially iron and certain of the B vitamins) for both prevention and treatment of cancer.

WARD, SETH (*b. Aspenden, Hertfordshire, England, 1617; d. Knightsbridge [now in London], England, 1689*), astronomy.

Mathematician, minister, and bishop; formulated an alternative to Kepler's law of areas that was widely used in planetary computations. With John Wilkins, wrote *Vindiciae academiarum* (1654).

WARGENTIN, PEHR WILHELM (*b. Sunne, Jämtland, Sweden, 1717; d. Stockholm, Sweden, 1783*), astronomy, demography.

Studied at Uppsala under Celsius (M.A., 1743); taught at Uppsala until 1749; investigated Jupiter's moons. Moved to Stockholm as secretary of the Royal Swedish Academy of Sciences, which he served with great energy; in connection with an Academy project, became one of the first modern experts in population statistics.

WARING, EDWARD (*b. Shrewsbury, England, ca. 1736; d. Plealey, near Shrewsbury, 1798*), mathematics.

Educated at Magdalene College, Cambridge (B.A., 1757; M.A., 1760); became Lucasian professor of mathematics. Works include *Miscellanea analytica . . .* (1762) on number theory.

WARMING, JOHANNES EUGENIUS BÜLOW (*b. Mandø, Denmark, 1841; d. Copenhagen, Denmark, 1924*), botany.

As secretary to the zoologist P. W. Lund in Brazil (1863–66) gathered a large botanical collection, the basis of his *Lagoa Santa, et bidrag til den biologiske plantegeografi* (1892). Became an ardent Lamarckian in the 1870's. Was professor of botany at Copenhagen (1886–1911). His *Plantes-amfund* (1895) laid the foundation of ecological plant geography.

WASHBURN, EDWARD WIGHT (*b. Beatrice, Neb., 1881; d. Washington, D.C., 1934*), physical chemistry.

Trained at the Massachusetts Institute of Technology (B.S., 1905; Ph.D., 1908). Held major posts at the University of Illinois, the National Bureau of Standards, the National Research Council, and others. Studied buffer solutions, indicators, the hydration of ions, ceramic engineering; obtained rubber in crystal form.

WASHINGTON, HENRY STEPHENS (*b. Newark, N.J., 1867; d. Washington, D.C., 1934*), geology.

A descendant of George Washington; studied at Yale and at Leipzig (Ph.D., 1893). Worked at the geophysical laboratory of the Carnegie Institution in Washington (from 1912). His enlarged edition (1917) of *Chemical Analyses of Igneous Rocks* was of fundamental importance in establishing standards of analysis.

WASSERMANN, AUGUST PAUL VON (*b. Bamberg, Germany, 1866; d. Berlin, Germany, 1925*), immunology, serology, bacteriology, cancer therapy.

Took his M.D. at Strasbourg (1888); worked under Robert Koch in Berlin (1891–1901); held several research and teaching posts, becoming director of the Institute for Experimental Therapy at the Kaiser Wilhelm Society for the Advancement of Science in Berlin (1913). Among many important studies, he did research on toxin-antitoxin bonds, which supported Ehrlich's side-chain theory; pointed out that a superior reagent exists in precipitins; pointed to the possibilities of differentiating albumen by a serologic procedure and of differentiating human and animal blood by specific antibodies for erythrocytes. After 1900, was increasingly occupied with problems relating to complement; began syphilis studies (1906); using the principle of the fixation of the complement, developed diagnostic procedures for syphilis; unexpectedly, found positive reactions in normal organs of infected persons. In his last years, investigated cancer therapy and tuberculosis.

WATERSTON, JOHN JAMES (*b. Edinburgh, Scotland, 1811; d. near Edinburgh, 1883*), physics, physical chemistry, astronomy.

Worked as a civil engineer in London and as a naval instructor (1839–57) with the East India Company in Bombay. Known in his lifetime chiefly for his investigations of solar radiation, done after his return to Edinburgh from India; his other valuable work on astronomy, physical chemistry, and molecular physics was largely unknown. Submitted (1845) to the Royal Society of London, a highly original and fundamental paper on the kinetic theory of gases; it was harshly rejected by Baden Powell and Sir J. W. Lubbock; the Society refused to return the ms. (the only copy) to the author, filing it in the archives. Only posthumously was it discovered by Lord Rayleigh and finally published.

WATERTON, CHARLES (*b. Walton Hall, Yorkshire, England, 1782; d. Walton Hall, 1865*), natural history.

Lord of Walton Hall; a militant Roman Catholic (which led to his official neglect); a courageous, ardent explorer and naturalist. Educated at Stonyhurst College. Wrote *Wanderings in South America* (1825); created a marvelous collection of specimens, using a new taxidermic technique of his invention; did early experiments with curare; set up, at Walton Hall, the world's first bird sanctuary.

WATSON, GEORGE NEVILLE (*b. Westward Ho!, Devon, England, 1886; d. Leamington Spa, England, 1965*), mathematics.

Studied at Trinity College, Cambridge; professor of mathematics at Birmingham (1918–51). Made wide-ranging contributions to complex variable theory; from 1929 to 1939, worked mainly from the notebooks of Srinivasa Ramanujan. Author, *A Course of Modern Analysis* (2nd ed., with E. T. Whittaker, 1915); *Treatise on the Theory of Bessel Functions* (1922).

WATSON, HEWETT COTTRELL (*b. Park Hill, Firbeck, Yorkshire, England, 1804; d. Thames Ditton, Surrey, England, 1881*), phytogeography, evolution, phrenology.

Studied at Edinburgh. Spent most of his life in private research; abandoned an early interest in phrenology in 1840. Began to publish in botany by 1832; accepted transformation of species by 1834; undertook phytogeographical studies from this viewpoint which were drawn upon by Darwin; accepted Darwin's theory enthusiastically. Helped to make British flora the best known in the world.

WATSON, RICHARD (*b. Heversham, Westmorland, England, 1737; d. Windermere, Westmorland, England, 1816*), chemistry.

Spent most of his career at Trinity College, Cambridge; became bishop of Llandaff (1782). Investigated phenomena of solution; wrote *Chemical Essays,* including a famous account of phlogiston theory.

WATSON, SERENO (*b. East Windsor Hill, Conn., 1826; d. Cambridge, Mass., 1892*), botany.

Studied at Yale. His career in botany began (1867) when he joined Clarence King's exploration of the fortieth parallel as a volunteer; became curator of the Gray Herbarium at Harvard (1874). Noted especially for *Botany,* vol. V of the fortieth parallel survey (1871), on the Great Basin region; and for *Botany of California* (1876–80).

WATSON, WILLIAM (*b. London, England, 1715; d. London, 1787*), physics, botany, medicine.

Apprenticed as an apothecary (1731–38); set up his own business. Active in the Royal Society, especially in communicating advances made abroad in botany and studies of electricity; did electrical investigations of his own; developed a crude electrical mechanics; became an adherent of Franklin's theory. Began a career in medicine (1759); was affiliated with the Foundling Hospital; knighted (1786).

WATT, JAMES (*b. Greenock, Scotland, 1736; d. Heathfield, England, 1819*), engineering, chemistry.

Son of a shipwright and nautical instrument maker; was appointed instrument maker to the University of Glasgow (1757); knew John Robison (who directed his attention to the steam engine) and Joseph Black. Invented the separate condenser for the Newcomen engine (1765); introduced many other inventions related to the steam engine in the next twenty-five years; in business with John Roebuck and later (1774–1800) with Mathew Boulton in Birmingham. In chemistry, he was the first to state that water is a compound. Also made contributions to commercial textile bleaching. His career marks the entrance by engineers into the world of research.

WAYJAN IBN RUSTAM. *See* **Al-Qūhi** (or **Al-Kūhī**), **Abū Sahl Wayjan ibn Rustam.**

AL-WAZZĀN AL-ZAYYĀTĪ AL-GHARNĀṬĪ, AL-ḤASAN IBN MUḤAMMAD. *See* **Leo the African.**

WEBER, ERNST HEINRICH (*b. Wittenberg, Germany, 1795; d. Leipzig, Germany, 1878*), anatomy, physiology, psychophysics.

The oldest of three brothers closely linked in scientific activity; important especially for their application of the exact methods of mathematical physics to physiology. Received his M.D. at Wittenberg (1815); taught at Leipzig, retiring from the chair of anatomy in 1871. Began with research in anatomy, discovering several important structures; proved definitively that digestive juices are specific products of glands. With his brother Wilhelm, wrote *Wellenlehre, auf Experimente gegründet* (1825) on

standing and travelling waves, focusing especially on flow in elastic tubes; was the first to apply hydrodynamics to the circulation of the blood; with his brother Eduard, discovered (1845) the effects of stimulation of the vagus nerve on heart action, the first instance known of nerve action inhibiting an autonomic activity. From about 1826, did classic studies of sensory physiology, introducing quantitative methods and the concept of threshold.

WEBER, HEINRICH (*b. Heidelberg, Germany, 1842; d. Strasbourg, Germany [now France], 1913*), mathematics.

Took his Ph.D. at Heidelberg (1863); had a distinguished career at several universities; Hermann Minkowski and David Hilbert were among his students. Worked mainly on analysis and its application to mathematical physics and number theory, with outstanding results.

WEBER, MAX WILHELM CARL (*b. Bonn, Germany, 1852; d. Eerbeek, Netherlands, 1937*), zoology.

Received the Ph.D. at Bonn (1877); spent most of his career at the University of Amsterdam. With his wife, Anna van Bosse, who aided in his research, studied whales in the North Atlantic and made expeditions to the Dutch East Indies, investigating aquatic fauna primarily. Author, *Die Säugetiere* (1904), on the anatomy and systematics of mammals.

WEBER, WILHELM EDUARD (*b. Wittenberg, Germany, 1804; d. Göttingen, Germany, 1891*), physics.

His early scientific work was inspired by his family's friend E. F. Chladni, the acoustician; with his older brother, Ernst Heinrich Weber, did the studies of waves reported in their *Wellenlehre, auf Experimente gegründet* (1825); at the University of Halle did his dissertation (1826) under J. S. C. Schweigger on the theory of reed organ pipes. His work on acoustics attracted the attention of Gauss, who arranged a professorship at Göttingen (1831–37); here he collaborated with Gauss in major studies of magnetism; with his younger brother Eduard wrote *Mechanik der menschlichen Gehwerkzeuge* (1836) on the physiology and physics of human locomotion. With six other professors, protested the revocation of Hannover's liberal constitution; was forced to leave Göttingen; joined his brothers at Leipzig. Here he began a series of works, published as *Elektrodynamische Maassbestimmungen* (1846–78); the first contained his famous law of electrical force, expressing the force between moving charges, and based on assumptions of central forces and of currents as consisting of equal and opposite flows of unlike charges; this law was eventually displaced by Maxwell's field theory. Returned to Göttingen (1849) where he remained until his retirement. With Rudolph Kohlrausch, determined (1856) the ratio between the electrodynamic and electrostatic units of charge. Devoted his later years to electrodynamics and the electrical structure of matter; his atomistic conception of electric charge, developed in collaboration with J. K. F. Zöllner, and his vision of the role of such charges in determining the electrical, magnetic, and thermal properties of matter made a lasting impression on physical theory; his successor at Göttingen, Eduard Riecke began the development of the electron theory of metals from Weber's ideas, a concept carried to completion in classical physics by Paul Drude and H. A. Lorentz.

WEBSTER, JOHN (*b. Thornton, Craven, England, 1610; d. Clitheroe, England, 1682*), chemistry, medicine, education.

A Puritan minister, surgeon, and chemist in the Paracelsian tradition. In *Academiarum examen* (1654) he attacked English universities for their emphasis on Aristotle and Galen. Also wrote on metals and on witchcraft (suggesting that "supernatural" effects would be found to have natural causes).

WEBSTER, THOMAS (*b. Orkney Islands, Scotland, 1773; d. London, England, 1844*), geology.

Gave up a career in architecture for geology; worked at the Geological Society and as the first professor of geology at University College, London. Studied the stratigraphy of the uppermost Jurassic, the Cretaceous, and the Tertiary rocks of southern England.

WEDDERBURN, JOSEPH HENRY MACLAGAN (*b. Forfar, Scotland, 1882; d. Princeton, N.J., 1948*), mathematics.

Studied at Edinburgh (M.A., 1903); spent most of his life at Princeton University. Proved that semisimple algebras are a direct sum of simple algebras, and that a simple algebra consists of all matrices of a given degree with elements taken from a division algebra; concerning skew fields, he showed that every field with a finite number of elements is commutative and therefore a Galois field.

WEDEL, GEORG WOLFGANG (*b. Golssen, Germany, 1645; d. Jena, Germany, 1721*), medicine, chemistry.

Took his M.D. at Jena (1669); became an influential professor there. Stood midway between medieval and modern views, defending astrology and alchemy and championing iatrochemistry.

WEDGWOOD, JOSIAH (*b. Burslem, England, 1730; d. Etruria, England, 1795*), ceramic technology, chemistry.

A great progressive British industrialist; entered the pottery business at age nine; founded his own firm in 1758. His lifelong interest in chemistry marks a new affiliation between technology and science.

WEGENER, ALFRED LOTHAR (*b. Berlin, Germany, 1880; d. Greenland, 1930*), meteorology, geophysics.

Studied at Heidelberg and Innsbruck; presented a thesis in astronomy at Berlin (1905); turned to meteorology and geology. Led or participated in four expeditions to Greenland, where he disappeared on his fiftieth birthday, and was not seen again; taught at Marburg (1908–12) and Graz (from 1924). Remembered for his theory of continental displacement, or drift, developed most fully in *Die Entstehung der Kontinente und Ozeane* (1915); interest in this theory faded after 1928, but was revived with the discovery of new evidence in the 1950's.

WEHNELT, ARTHUR RUDOLPH BERTHOLD (*b. Rio de Janeiro, Brazil, 1871; d. Berlin, Germany, 1944*), physics.

Studied at Berlin and at Erlangen (doctorate, 1898); returned to Berlin as full professor (1906); appointed director of its Physics Institute (1926). Became well known for discoveries concerning discharge in rarefied gases; developed the Wehnelt cylinder, as it is now known; was involved in the development of the radio tube, Röntgen tubes, and the oscilloscope.

WEICHSELBAUM, ANTON (*b. Schiltern, Austria, 1845; d. Vienna, Austria, 1920*), pathology.

Received M.D. at Military Hospital in Vienna (1869); practiced medicine and taught anatomy. Director of Pathological-anatomical Institute of the University of Vienna (1893–1916). Among first to recognize importance of bacteriology for pathological anatomy. Discovered meningococcus and the diplococcus which bears his name. Made important contributions to the study of miliary tuberculosis, diabetes mellitus, and in the new science of serology.

WEIERSTRASS, KARL THEODOR WILHELM (*b. Ostenfelde, Westphalia, Germany, 1815; d. Berlin, Germany, 1897*), mathematics.

Weierstrass entered the Catholic Gymnasium in Paderborn in 1829. In 1834 he entered the University of Bonn, but soon came to shun lectures and to restrict himself to studying mathematics on his own, beginning with the *Mécanique céleste* of Laplace. He also read Jacobi's *Fundamenta nova theoriae functionum ellipticarum* (1829). The work proved difficult for him based, as it was, on prior knowledge of Legendre's *Traité des fonctions elliptiques*, published shortly beforehand. A transcript of Christof Gudermann's lecture on modular functions rendered the theory of elliptic variables understandable to him and inspired him to initiate his own research.

After having passed the oral examinations in 1841, Weierstrass taught for a one-year probationary period at the Gymnasium in Münster, before transferring to the Catholic secondary school in Deutsch-Krone, West Prussia (1842–48), and then to the Catholic Gymnasium in Braunsberg, East Prussia (1848–55). In addition to mathematics and physics, he taught German, botany, geography, history, gymnastics, and even calligraphy.

His first publications on Abelian functions, which appeared in the Braunsberg school prospectus (1848–49), went unnoticed; but the following work, "Zur Theorie der Abelschen Functionen" (1854) elicited enormous interest and marked a decisive turning point in his life. In this memoir he demonstrated the solution to the problem of inversion of the hyperelliptic integrals, which he accomplished by representing Abelian functions as the quotients of constantly converging power series.

In 1854 the University of Königsberg awarded Weierstrass an honorary doctorate.

In the famous "Theorie der Abelschen Functionen" (1856), which contains an excerpt from the previously mentioned examination work, Weierstrass proved what previously he had only hinted. According to Hilbert, he had realized one of the greatest achievements of analysis —the solution of the Jacobian inversion problem for hyperelliptic integrals.

In 1856 Weierstrass accepted an appointment as professor at the Industry Institute in Berlin, a forerunner of the Technische Hochschule, and in the same year he became a member of the Berlin Academy. In 1864 he assumed a chair at the University of Berlin.

Over the years Weierstrass developed a great lecture cycle in which he erected the entire structure of his mathematics, using as building blocks only that which he himself had proven. In 1887, having already edited the works of Steiner and Jacobi, he decided to publish his own mathematical lifework, assured of the help of the younger mathematicians of his school.

In 1870, at the age of fifty-five, Weierstrass met the twenty-year-old Russian Sonya Kovalevsky, who had come to Berlin from Heidelberg, where she had taken her first semester under Leo Koenigsberger. Unable to secure her admission to the university, Weierstrass taught her privately; and his role in both her scientific and personal affairs far transcended the usual teacher-student relationship. In her he found a "refreshingly enthusiastic participant" in all his thoughts, and much that he had suspected or fumbled for became clear in his conversations with her. Through his intercession she received the doctorate *in absentia* at Göttingen in 1874.

What Weierstrass considered to be his main scientific task is now held to be less important than his accomplishments in the foundation of his theory. The special functions which he investigated, and the theory of which he lucidly elaborated or transformed, now elicit less interest than his criticism, rigor, generally valid concepts, and the procedures and propositions of the theory of functions. Weierstrass' name remains linked to his preliminary proposition, approximation propositions, double series proposition, proposition of products, and fundamental proposition—as well as the Casorati-Weierstrass proposition.

WEIGEL, CHRISTIAN EHRENFRIED (*b. Stralsund, Germany, 1748; d. Greifswald, Germany, 1831*), chemistry.

Supervisor of the botanical garden at Greifswald (from 1772) and professor of chemistry and pharmacy in the medical faculty. His *Grundriss der reinen und angewandten Chemie* (1777) was one of the first German chemistry texts directed to readers of all classes.

WEIGEL, VALENTIN (*b. Naundorf [near Dresden], Saxony, Germany, 1533; d. Zschopau, Saxony, Germany, 1588*), mysticism, philosophy of nature.

Educated at Leipzig and Wittenberg; became pastor of Zschopau (1567). Wrote (from 1570) a number of works, circulated in manuscript, challenging Lutheran orthodoxy; these, when finally printed (1609–18), became extremely influential. Weigel combined a mystical spiritualism with Paracelsian naturalism.

WEIGERT, CARL (*b. Munsterberg, Silesia [now Poland], 1845; d. Frankfurt am Main, Germany, 1904*), pathology, histology, neurology.

Studied at the universities of Breslau and Berlin (M.D., 1866); taught pathology at Leipzig, where his gentle modesty ruled against his advancement; became director of the pathological-anatomical institute of the Senckenberg Foundation in Frankfurt, where he remained until his death. Researching smallpox eruptions, he developed techniques that enabled him to demonstrate (1871) bacteria in tissue section; did important experiments on the staining of fibrin and elastic fibers; most important, he presented (1884) a method of staining medullary sheaths that enabled the creation of a reliable anatomy of the central nervous system.

WEINBERG, WILHELM (*b. Stuttgart, Germany, 1862; d. Tübingen, Germany, 1937*), human genetics, medical statistics.

A general practitioner and obsterician in Stuttgart for forty-two years. Published numerous original statistical studies; discovered what is now called the Hardy-Weinberg law; was a founder of population genetics; made first morbidity tables.

WEINGARTEN, JULIUS (*b. Berlin, Germany, 1836; d. Freiburg im Breisgau, Germany, 1910*), mathematics.

Received his Ph.D. from the University of Halle (1864); held various teaching posts in Berlin; was honorary professor at Freiburg im Breisgau (1902–08). Did important work in the theory of surfaces. He introduced those surfaces for which there exists a definite functional relationship between their principal curvatures (now called W-surfaces).

WEISBACH, JULIUS LUDWIG (*b. Mittelschmiedeberg, near Annaberg, Germany, 1806; d. Freiberg, Germany, 1871*), hydraulics.

Studied at Göttingen and Vienna; taught at the Freiberg Gymansium and at the Bergakademie. Contributed to the field of hydraulics and to mine surveying methods, introducing the theodolite. Published *Experimental-Hydraulik* (1855) and *Lehrbuch der Ingenieur- und Maschinenmechanik* (1845–1901).

WEISMANN, AUGUST FRIEDRICH LEOPOLD (*b. Frankfurt am Main, Germany, 1834; d. Freiburg im Breisgau, 1914*), zoology.

Took his M.D. at Göttingen (1856); entered practice in Frankfurt; studied briefly under Leuckart, who turned his attention to developmental studies of insects; habilitated at Freiburg University (1863); remained there for the rest of his life. Besides Leuckart and Henle (at Göttingen), the strongest influence on Weismann's thought was Darwin; Weismann became a leader among Neo-Darwinists, arguing for the sufficiency of natural selection and against the possibility of inheritance of acquired characteristics. He put forward and coherently defended a theory of the continuity of germ plasm, the substance of heredity, to explain heredity and development. He supported his theory with evidence from his studies of Diptera and 'small crustaceans, studies of the origins of sexual cells through generations of Hydromedusae (reported in *Die Entstehung der Sexualzellen bei den Hydromedusen*, 1883), and studies of mitosis (following indications from Wilhelm Roux) and meiosis. In 1884, several scientists including Weismann independently came to attribute the main role in heredity to the nucleus; Weismann located the germ plasm within the nucleus (1885); his theories regarding meiosis were extremely shrewd; he identified the "ids," linearly arranged on the "nuclear loops" (chromosomes), as the bearers of ancestral plasms. He presented his germ-plasm theory fully in *Das Keimplasma. Eine Theorie der Vererbung* (1892).

WEISS, CHRISTIAN SAMUEL (*b. Leipzig, Germany, 1780; d. Eger, Hungary, 1856*), crystallography.

Awarded the doctorate at Leipzig (1800) and admitted to the faculty; from 1810, occupied the chair of mineralogy at the University of Berlin; among his many gifted students was Franz Neumann. Regarded the directional aspect of crystals, in an abstract way, as the expression of processes of growth; developed the idea of crystallographic axes, which were at once a direction of growth and basis of classification; provided the first recognition of hemihedrism; Weiss's zone law (as simplified by Neumann) remains a powerful tool in crystallographic calculation.

WEISS, EDMUND (*b. Freiwaldau, Austrian Silesia [now Jesenik, Czechoslovakia], 1837; d. Vienna, Austria, 1917*), astronomy.

Studied and taught at the University of Vienna; succeeded Littrow as director of the observatory (1878). Specialized in determining the orbits of comets, minor planets, and meteor showers.

WEISS, PIERRE (*b. Mulhouse, France, 1865; d. Lyons, France, 1940*), magnetism.

Studied at the Zurich Polytechnikum and the École Normale Supérieure in Paris (doctorate, 1896). Taught at the Zurich Polytechnikum (1902–18) and directed the physics laboratory; in World War I, in Paris, helped to develop the "Cotton-Weiss" acoustical method for locating enemy gun emplacements; at the University of Strasbourg (1919–36) created and directed the physics institute. His phenomenological theory of ferromagnetism (extending the work of Paul Langevin) is founded on the hypothesis of a molecular field proportional to the magnetization and acting on the orientation of each atomic moment like a magnetic field of very high intensity; with this theory, he was able to account for the known characteristic properties of ferromagnetic bodies (notably the abrupt disappearance of ferromagnetism above a temperature known as the Curie point) and to discover the properties of spontaneous magnetization and magnetocaloric phenomena; modern quantum theories of ferromagnetism have substantiated Weiss's molecular field hypothesis as a first approximation.

WEIZMANN, CHAIM (*b. Motol, White Russia, 1874; d. Rehovot, Israel, 1952*), organic chemistry.

During his rise to leadership in the world Zionist movement, Weizmann also followed a career in chemistry; had considerable success developing dyes; his investigations of fermentation opened the microbiological road to the production of industrial chemicals. His scientific activities ended when he became president of Israel in 1948.

WELCH, WILLIAM HENRY (*b. Norfolk, Conn., 1850; d. Baltimore, Md., 1934*), pathology, public health, medical education.

Studied at Yale and the College of Physicians and Surgeons in New York (M.D., 1875). As an intern at Bellevue Hospital was led by Francis Delafield to pathology, an interest intensified by further study in Europe. Moved to the new Johns Hopkins medical school (1885) as professor of pathology; played a key role in the development of the school. Was a leader in alerting the medical profession to the practical applications of the germ theory of disease and in effecting public health reforms; was one of the most influential spokesmen for American medicine.

WELDON, WALTER FRANK RAPHAEL (*b. London, England, 1860; d. Oxford, England, 1906*), biometrics.

One of the founders of biometrics. Studied and taught at St. John's College, Cambridge; became professor (1890) at University College, London. Having decided that statistical studies of variations would help to solve the problems of Darwinism, did two classic papers (1890–92) on the shrimp *Crangon vulgaris*, using biometric techniques; from 1891, collaborated with Karl Pearson in promoting the statistical approach. Weldon's study of differential death rates in crabs (1894) provoked a storm of controversy for its conclusion that natural selection can operate on small variations, as opposed to large, discontinuous variations; two separate schools of genetics developed in England, divided by this issue; Weldon, who became Linacre professor at Oxford (1900), defended his position with an intensity that apparently led to his death.

WELLS, HARRY GIDEON (*b. Fair Haven [now New Haven], Conn., 1875; d. Chicago, Ill., 1943*), pathology.

Joined the department of pathology at the University of Chicago (1901); became its head (1932). Was the nation's chief authority on chemical aspects of pathology and immunology; wrote *Chemical Pathology* (1907).

WELLS, WILLIAM CHARLES (*b. Charleston, S.C., 1757; d. London, England, 1817*), meteorology, physiology, medicine, natural philosophy.

Received the M.D. from the University of Edinburgh (1780); physician at St. Thomas' Hospital in London (from 1795). Did numerous studies in physiology; his most important contribution to meteorology was "Essay on Dew" (1814), correctly describing the process of dew formation; Charles Darwin considered him a pioneer in the concept of evolution on the basis of a paper on human skin color and climate.

WENDELIN (VENDELINUS), GOTTFRIED (*b. Herck-la-Ville [or Herk], Belgium, 1580; d. Ghent, Belgium, 1667*), astronomy, natural science, humanism.

Priest, scholar, and scientist; courageously upheld the Copernican theory; made original observations concerning pendulum motion.

WENT, FRIEDRICH AUGUST FERDINAND CHRISTIAN (*b. Amsterdam, Netherlands, 1863; d. Wassenaar, near The Hague, Netherlands, 1935*), botany.

Studied at University of Amsterdam. As professor of botany and director of the botanical laboratory and gardens at the University of Utrecht (1896–1934), was the founder of the "Utrecht school," renowned for research in plant physiology and tropisms. Specialized in tropical agriculture.

WEPFER, JOHANN-JAKOB (*b. Schaffhausen, Switzerland, 1620; d. Schaffhausen, 1695*), medicine, physiology, toxicology.

Received M.D. at Basel (1647). As municipal physician of Schaffhausen, was famed for his skill; attracted many students. In pathology, used autopsies to great advantage; specialized in the brain; was the first to report that apoplexy involved hemorrhage from blood vessels. Was a pioneer in toxicology; did classic studies of the poison and water hemlocks; wrote on occupational diseases; was the first to warn workers concerning mercury poisoning.

WERNER, ABRAHAM GOTTLOB (*b. Wehrau, Upper Lusatia* [*now Osiecznica, Poland*], *1749; d. Dresden, Germany, 1817*), geology, mineralogy.

From a well-to-do family; his father was inspector of the Duke of Solm's ironworks. Studied at the Bergakademie Freiberg and the University of Leipzig (did not obtain a degree). While still a student, wrote *Von den äusserlichen Kennzeichen der Fossilien* (1774), a classification of external characteristics of minerals, designed to aid the worker in the field; it was an immediate success, for it offered an unprecedented number of characteristics with definitions. Throughout his life, Werner continued to study minerals and in particular their classification; his fullest exposition of his ideas on this subject appeared in "Werner's oryctognostische Classifikationslehre" (1816).

The success of his first book led to Werner's appointment (1775) as teacher of mining and curator of the mineral collection at the Bergakademie; he remained here for the rest of his life, and made the school world famous; among his students were Leopold von Buch, Alexander von Humboldt, Jean d'Aubuisson de Voisins, Robert Jameson, and Friedrich Mohs. Werner's celebrity arose especially from his work in geology, for he was the father of historical geology, the first to develop a complete, universally applicable geological system. His system was based on the principle of geological succession; its fundamental postulates were that the earth was once enveloped by an ocean and that all the important rocks that make up the earth's crust are either precipitates or sediments of that ocean; thus, the system was neptunist, as opposed to volcanist, but Werner personally did not link it to the biblical story of creation; his religious views were deistic. Werner's theories are exemplified in his "Kurze Klassifikation . . ." (1786), which helped to establish petrography as an independent study; and it was here that Werner first asserted that all basalt is of aqueous origin, thus precipitating the great basalt controversy that pitted neptunists against volcanists. In *Neue Theorie von der Entstehung der Gänge* (1791), Werner treated vein formation and ore deposits, making this field an integral part of historical geology, although his actual theories were later discarded.

WERNER, ALFRED (*b. Mulhouse, France, 1866; d. Zurich, Switzerland, 1919*), chemistry.

Being from Alsace, Werner was politically and culturally tied to France, while having great respect for German science and publishing mostly in German. From 1878 to 1885 he attended the École Professionelle, a technical school where he studied chemistry; he also built a laboratory in the barn behind his house, and wrote his first scientific paper. During 1885–86 he did compulsory military duty at Karlsruhe, and audited courses in organic chemistry at the Technische Hochschule. He then entered the Zurich Polytechnikum; after receiving a degree in technical chemistry (1889) he served as unsalaried assistant in Georg Lunge's laboratory while carrying out research under Arthur Hantzsch for which he received the doctorate in 1890.

Werner's three most important theoretical papers were produced during 1890–93. His doctoral dissertation, "Über räumliche Anordnung der Atome in stickstoff-haltigen Molekülen," was his first publication and remains his most popular and important work in organic chemistry. By extending the Le Bel and van't Hoff concept of the tetrahedral carbon atom to the nitrogen atom, Werner and Hantzsch for the first time placed the stereochemistry of nitrogen on a firm theoretical basis. In his *Habilitationsschrift*, "Beiträge zur Theorie der Affinität und Valenz," Werner attempted to replace Kekulé's concept of rigidly directed valences with his own more flexible approach, in which he viewed affinity as a variously divisible, attractive force emanating from the center of an atom and acting equally in all directions; using this concept he was able to derive the accepted van't Hoff configurational formulas.

During the winter of 1891–92 Werner worked with Berthelot at the Collège de France. In 1892 he returned to Zurich as *Privatdozent* at the Polytechnikum; in 1893 he became associate professor at the University of Zurich, and remained there (professor, 1895) until retiring a month before his death. His university appointment was largely due to the almost overnight fame he received from the publication of his most important paper, "Beitrag zur Konstitution anorganischer Verbindungen" (1893), in which he had proposed the basic postulates of his epochal and controversial coordination theory. In 1913 he became the first Swiss to be awarded the Nobel Prize in chemistry.

The solution to the problem of Kekulé's "molecular compounds" came to Werner like a flash of lightning at two in the morning; by five that afternoon he had finished the paper giving his coordination theory of inorganic compounds. He postulated two types of valence—primary or ionizable (*Hauptvalenz*) and secondary or nonionizable (*Nebenvalenz*)—and theorized that every metal in a particular oxidation state (primary valence) has a definite coordination number—that is, a fixed number of secondary valences that must be satisfied. Whereas primary valences can be satisfied only by anions, secondary valences can be satisfied also by neutral molecules such as ammonia, water, organic amines, sulfides, and phosphines; the secondary valences are directed in space around the central metal ion and the aggregate forms a "complex," which should exist as a discrete unit in solution. Werner was then able to predict series of unknown compounds, the eventual discovery of which confirmed his theory; he also recognized and named many types of inorganic isomerism: coordination, polymerization, ionization, hydrate, salt, coordination position, and valence isomerism; and he postulated explanations for polynuclear complexes, hydrated metal ions, hydrolysis, and acids and bases.

WERNER, JOHANN(ES) (*b. Nuremberg, Germany, 1468; d. Nuremberg, 1522*), astronomy, mathematics, geography.

Studied at the University of Ingolstadt and in Rome, where he was ordained; served as a priest in Nuremberg (from 1508). In astronomy was a skilled instrument maker; less talented in theoretical work. In mathematics, he is noted for a treatise on the theory of conic sections and an outstanding work in spherical trigonometry (written 1505–13) which surpassed Regiomontanus' books on triangles. Werner's writings in geography gained him widespread recognition; his commentary on Ptolemy's *Geography* gives a method for determining simultaneously the latitude and longitude of a place; in the same work he discussed the trade winds. In cartography, Werner outlined the principles of stereographic projection; he also developed three codiform map projections that resemble one another; the second gives an equal-area projection of the sphere. He did pioneer work in meteorology, attempting to put it on a scientific basis and to provide rational guidelines for weather forecasting.

WERNICKE, CARL (*b. Tarnowitz, Upper Silesia, Germany [now Tarnowskie Gory, Poland], 1848; d. Dörrberg im Geratal, Germany, 1905*), neuropsychiatry, neuroanatomy.

One of the disciples of Wilhelm Griesinger, who identified diseases of the mind with diseases of the brain. Wernicke specialized in aphasia; helped to establish the notion of right and left cerebral dominance; discovered "Wernicke's encephalopathy." Taught at the University of Breslau (1885–1904).

WERTHEIM, ERNST (*b. Graz, Austria, 1864; d. Vienna, Austria, 1920*), gynecology.

Received M.D. from Graz (1888). While still an assistant in gynecology and obstetrics, did major research on gonorrhea in females; later, developed a radical operation for cervical cancer that became the standard practice; also improved the treatment of uterine prolapse. Worked in Vienna at Elisabeth Hospital (1897–1910) and then as director of the First University Women's Clinic.

WESSEL, CASPAR (*b. Vestby, near Dröbak, Norway, 1745; d. Copenhagen, Denmark, 1818*), surveying, mathematics.

An official surveyor in Denmark. Wrote a remarkable paper (1798) that establishes his priority in publication of the geometric representation of complex numbers; his exposition (not appreciated at the time) is in some ways superior to and more modern than Robert Argand's independent work (1806).

WEYL, HERMANN (*b. Elmshorn, near Hamburg, Germany, 1885; d. Zurich, Switzerland, 1955*), mathematics, mathematical physics.

Studied at Göttingen; taught at the University of Zurich (1913–30); returned to Göttingen, succeeding his teacher Hilbert; with the advent of the Nazis, left Germany for the Institute for Advanced Study at Princeton (1933–51). Like Hilbert, Weyl believed in the value of deep analysis of concepts rather than blind computation; went beyond Hilbert's interests, becoming one of the most universal mathematicians of his generation; also contributed to mathematical physics, the subject of his two most famous books: *Raum, Zeit und Materie* (1918), on relativity theory, and *Gruppentheorie und Quantenmechanik* (1928). His *Habilitationsschrift* (1910), a major work in spectral theory, treated singular boundary conditions for second-order linear differential equations. He inaugurated another important chapter of spectral theory (1911) with his work on the asymptotic study of the eigenvalues of a self-adjoint compact operator U in Hilbert space H, giving special attention to applications to the theory of elasticity. His most famous paper (1916), on equidistribution modulo 1, is based on a completely new and amazingly simple method. In geometry, his *Die Riemannschen Fläche* (1913) is a classic in the theory of differential and complex manifolds; in 1915, he turned his attention to the

theory of infinitesimal and finite deformations of convex surfaces. In mathematical physics, he fell short of the "unitary theory" he hoped to attain, but laid the foundation for E. Cartan's general theory of connections. His masterpiece was his investigation of the theory of linear representations of Lie groups (1925–27); his papers on this subject are among the most influential ones in twentieth-century mathematics.

WHARTON, GEORGE (*b. Strickland, near Kendal, Westmorland, England, 1617; d. London, England, 1681*), astronomy.

From 1641, brought out almanacs full of astrological predictions favoring the Royalist cause; sentenced to death (1650); survived to be created a baronet (1677).

WHARTON, THOMAS (*b. Winston-on-Tees, Durham, England, 1614; d. London, England, 1673*), anatomy, endocrinology.

Graduated M.D. at Oxford (1647); had a London practice. His *Adenographia* (1656) gave the first thorough account of the glands of the human body. Discovered the duct of the submaxillary salivary gland and the jelly of the umbilical cord, both named for him; named and provided the first adequate account of the thyroid.

WHATELY, RICHARD (*b. London, England, 1787; d. Dublin, Ireland, 1863*), logic.

Studied at Oriel College, Oxford (B.A., 1808); returned (1825) as principal of St. Alban Hall; appointed archbishop of Dublin (1831). His *The Elements of Logic* (1826), a persuasive defense of the value of traditional formal deductive logic, stimulated the great progress made in this field in England in the nineteenth century.

WHEATSTONE, CHARLES (*b. Gloucester, England, 1802; d. Paris, France, 1875*), physics.

Of a family of musical instrument makers and dealers; had no formal scientific training. In acoustics, investigated the mechanical transmission of sound, visible demonstrations of vibrations, and properties of the vibrating air column; his results led to his appointment as professor of experimental physics at King's College, London (1834); became a fellow of the Royal Society (1836); knighted (1868). In electricity he devised the rotating-mirror technique to measure the velocity of an electrical discharge through a wire, invented the rheostat, and popularized the Wheatstone bridge (invented by Samuel Christie). Worked on electric telegraph systems from the early 1830's. In optics, he invented the stereoscope and the polar clock.

WHEELER, WILLIAM MORTON (*b. Milwaukee, Wis., 1865; d. Cambridge, Mass., 1937*), entomology.

The posts he held included curator of invertebrate zoology at the American Museum of Natural History in New York City (1903–08) and professor of entomology at the Bussey Institution of Harvard University, from which he retired in 1934. Was the foremost expert on ants and the social behavior of insects.

WHEWELL, WILLIAM (*b. Lancaster, England, 1794; d. Cambridge, England, 1866*), history and philosophy of science, physical astronomy, education.

The son of a master carpenter; in 1812, began a life-long career at Trinity College, Cambridge (M.A., 1819; D.D., 1844); ordained priest in the Church of England (1826); master of Trinity (from 1841). Was active in the reform of science education, especially in introducing the mathematical methods of French analysts; did basic studies of crystals and of tides; was one of the central figures in Victorian science. His ambitious *History of the Inductive Sciences* (3 vols., 1837) and *The Philosophy of the Inductive Sciences* . . . (2 vols., 1840) were masterpieces of the period.

WHISTON, WILLIAM (*b. Norton, Leicester, England, 1667; d. Lyndon, Rutland, England, 1752*), mathematics, cosmogony.

Newton's assistant in mathematics at Cambridge; succeeded him as Lucasian professor (1701); deprived of his chair (1710) for his Arian, anti-Trinitarian views. Among his many works is *A New Theory of the Earth* (1696), suggesting that a comet guided by God was responsible for the Flood; all cosmogonies based on the impact of celestial bodies owe something to Whiston's inventions.

WHITE, CHARLES (*b. Manchester, England, 1728; d. Sale, Cheshire, England, 1813*), obstetrics, surgery.

The most eminent surgeon in the north of England; made extensive contributions to surgery; was a pioneer in aseptic midwifery. Studied medicine in Manchester, London, and Edinburgh; helped to found the Manchester Infirmary (1752), Lying-in Charity Hospital (1790), and the Manchester Literary and Philosophical Society (1781). Published (1799) a treatise on evolution (unknown to Darwin), based on the study of skulls; concluded that acquired characteristics could not become hereditary.

WHITE, CHARLES DAVID (*b. near Palmyra, N.Y., 1862; d. Washington, D.C., 1935*), geology.

Served with the U.S. Geological Survey (from 1886). Became the foremost authority on carbonaceous deposits; developed the valuable carbon-ratio theory (1915).

WHITE, GILBERT (*b. Selborne, Hampshire, England, 1720; d. Selborne, 1793*), zoology, botany, horticulture.

A graduate of Oriel College, Oxford (M.A., 1746); pursued a modest church career. His daily notes and letters on his observations of natural phenomena in the region around his home were edited and published as *The Natural History and Antiquities of Selborne* (1789); it has become a classic of English literature and natural history.

WHITE, ISRAEL CHARLES (*b. Monongalia County, Va. [now W.Va.], 1848; d. Baltimore, Md., 1927*), geology.

Studied at West Virginia University (A.M., 1875) and University of Arkansas (Ph.D., 1880). As state geologist, headed the West Virginia Geological and Economic Survey (from 1897); was an authority on coal. Noted for the practical application of the anticlinal theory of oil and natural gas accumulation.

WHITE, THOMAS (*b. Runwell, Essex, England, 1593; d. London, England, 1676*), natural philosophy, theology.

A well-traveled priest and scholar; his works were condemned by the papacy for ideas similar to Jansenism. His scientific writings are amplifications of Aristotle's con-

cepts. The movement "Blackloism" maintained his theological positions for several decades after his death.

WHITEHEAD, ALFRED NORTH (*b. Ramsgate, Kent, England, 1861; d. Cambridge, Mass., 1947*), mathematics, mathematical logic, theoretical physics, philosophy.

Whitehead's career began at Trinity College, Cambridge, which he entered (1880) as a student and left (1910) as senior lecturer in mathematics. His writings in this period deal with mathematics and mathematical logic; they culminate in the monumental *Principia Mathematica* (3 vols., 1910–13), in which he collaborated with Bertrand Russell to demonstrate that logic is the basis for all mathematics; this work includes a brilliant exposition of sentential logic, but the fundamental premise was later refuted (1931) by Gödel's theorem.

From 1910 to 1924, Whitehead lived in London; he held posts at University College and the Imperial College of Science and Technology; in this period he was chiefly concerned with formulating a philosophy of science; in this connection, he considered basic issues in theoretical physics, primarily in *An Enquiry Concerning the Principles of Natural Knowledge* (1919), *The Concept of Nature* (1920), and *The Principle of Relativity* (1922). He challenged Einstein's special and general theories with "an alternative rendering of the theory of relativity"; hypothesized that space-time must possess a uniform structure everywhere and at all times; proposed a simple although now little-known gravitational theory, for which J. L. Synge has provided modern mathematical notation; it has been shown that the predictions of Whitehead's theory and Einstein's general theory are equivalent with respect to the four tests of relativity.

Whitehead's interests became increasingly philosophical in his final years, spent as professor of philosophy at Harvard University (from 1924); his outstanding work of this period is *Process and Reality* . . . (1929). Underlying all of his philosophical writings is his belief that we should reject the distinction between nature as it really is and our experiences of it; such experiences are nature itself. He examined how space and time are rooted in experience; in his middle writings, he identified noninstantaneous events as the basic elements of perceived nature, and stressed the intrinsically relational constitution of these events; space and time are derivative from the fundamental process by which the events are interrelated. In his later thought, Whitehead abandoned his view of nature as continuous, and instead saw it as "incurably atomic."

WHITEHEAD, JOHN HENRY CONSTANTINE (*b. Madras, India, 1904; d. Princeton, N.J., 1960*), mathematics.

His father was Bishop of Madras; his mother studied mathematics at Oxford; his uncle was A. N. Whitehead. J. H. C. Whitehead studied at Oxford and at Princeton University (Ph.D., 1932); taught at Oxford, where he built up an important school of topology. Is best remembered for developing the theory of homotopy equivalence by the strictly combinatorial method of allowed transformations.

WHITEHURST, JOHN (*b. Congleton, Cheshire, England, 1713; d. London, England, 1788*), geology.

A celebrated clockmaker and a geological pioneer. Established the succession of the Carboniferous strata; formulated the general proposition of a worldwide orderly superposition of strata.

WHITFIELD, ROBERT PARR (*b. Willowvale, near New Hartford, N.Y., 1828; d. Troy, N.Y., 1910*), invertebrate paleontology, stratigraphy.

A craftsman and self-taught naturalist; assisted James Hall in various projects (1856–76); became the first curator of the newly organized American Museum of Natural History (1877), with initial charge of geology. Was a superb illustrator; did studies of an array of fossil invertebrates, faunas, and their stratigraphic relations.

WHITMAN, CHARLES OTIS (*b. North Woodstock, Me., 1842; d. Chicago, Ill., 1910*), zoology.

Studied at Bowdoin College (B.A., 1868). While teaching at English High School in Boston, came under the influence of Louis Agassiz; took up marine biology; studied microscopy and embryology abroad; received his Ph.D. (1878). Among many important posts, taught zoology at the Imperial University in Tokyo (1879–81); helped in the founding of several new journals and institutions, including the Marine Biological Laboratory at Woods Hole, Massachusetts, where he was the first director (1893–1908). Did detailed research on the heredity and behavior of pigeons.

WHITNEY, JOSIAH DWIGHT (*b. Northampton, Mass., 1819; d. Lake Sunapee, N. H., 1896*), geology.

Studied at Yale College and in Europe; worked on five state geological surveys; appointed director of the California state survey (1860), where Clarence King was among the men he trained; became professor at Harvard (1865). His *The Metallic Wealth of the United States* (1854) is a milestone in the literature of ore deposits. Mount Whitney is named in his honor.

WHITTAKER, EDMUND TAYLOR (*b. Birkdale, Lancashire, England, 1873; d. Edinburgh, Scotland, 1956*), mathematics, physics, philosophy.

Studied at Trinity College, Cambridge; became astronomer royal for Ireland (1906) and professor of mathematics at the University of Edinburgh (1912–46). Published (1902) the most general solution of Laplace's equation in three dimensions, which is analytic about the origin, and the corresponding solution of the wave equation; from 1921, wrote ten papers on relativity theory. His textbooks have become classics.

WHYTLAW-GRAY, ROBERT (*b. London, England, 1877; d. Welwyn Garden City, Hertfordshire, England, 1958*), physical chemistry.

Studied at Glasgow; University College, London; and Bonn (Ph.D., 1906). Taught at University College, at Eton, and at Leeds. Did research for the War Office. Designed and utilized precision techniques for weighing aerosols and gases, notably radon.

WHYTT, ROBERT (*b. Edinburgh, Scotland, 1714; d. Edinburgh, 1766*), medicine, neurophysiology.

Studied at St. Andrews, at Edinburgh, and abroad; received M.D. degrees from Rheims (1736) and St. Andrews (1737). Investigating Joanna Stephens' remedy for urinary bladder stones, did research on the therapeutic value of limewater and soap, which led Joseph Black to begin the experiments resulting in the discovery of "fixed air" (carbon dioxide). Whytt became professor at Edinburgh (1747); specializing in animal experiments, he was the foremost neurologist of his day. He was the first to demonstrate reflex action in the spinal cord and to localize a reflex (Whytt's reflex); he investigated the peristaltic action of peripheral blood vessels and understood its function; he contended that all muscle action is governed by nervous control. Wrote *The Vital and Other Involuntary Motions of Animals* (1751), *Physiological Essays* (1755), *Observations on . . . Nervous, Hypochondriac or Hysteric Disorders* (1764), and *Observations on the Dropsy in the Brain* (1768), the first clear description of tuberculous meningitis in children.

WICKERSHEIMER, ERNEST (*b. Bar-le-Duc, France, 1880; d. Strasbourg, France, 1965*), history of medicine.

Received doctorate at Paris (1905). Administrator (1920–50) of the Bibliothèque Nationale et Universitaire (as it has been known since 1926). Wrote on French medicine in the Middle Ages and in the Renaissance.

WIDMAN (or **WEIDEMAN** or **WIDEMAN**), **JOHANNES** (*b. Eger, Bohemia* [*now Czechoslovakia*], *ca. 1462; d. Leipzig, Germany, after 1498*), mathematics.

Studied and taught at Leipzig; gave the first algebra lecture in Germany (1486). Wrote one of the first printed arithmetic books in German (1489).

WIDMANNSTÄTTEN (or **WIDMANSTETTER**), **ALOYS JOSEPH BECK EDLER VON** (*b. Graz, Austria, 1754; d. Vienna, Austria, 1849*), mineralogy.

Became a director of Emperor Francis I's private technology collection in Vienna (1807). Discovered the first "Widmannstätten figures" (1808) in an iron meteorite from Zagreb.

WIECHERT, EMIL (*b. Tilsit, Germany, 1861; d. Göttingen, Germany, 1928*), geophysics.

Graduated from Königsberg (1889), lectured there, and did research on the atomic structure of electricity and matter. Founded at the University of Göttingen a famous school of geophysics; from 1897 to 1914, Weichert and his students (including B. Gutenberg and L. Geiger) produced far-reaching results concerning the interior of the earth. Invented the inverted-pendulum seismograph.

WIED, MAXIMILIAN ZU (*b. Neuwied, Germany, 1782; d. Neuwied, 1867*), natural history, ethnology.

A minor German prince. After a military career, he studied natural history. Remembered for two excellent books based on his travels in Brazil (1815–17) and North America (1832–34); his ethnographical observations, particularly of the native tribes of Brazil and the Indians of the upper Missouri, are outstanding.

WIEDEMANN, GUSTAV HEINRICH (*b. Berlin, Germany, 1826; d. Leipzig, Germany, 1899*), physics, physical chemistry.

Studied under H. G. Magnus at Berlin (doctorate, 1847); taught at Berlin and Basel and at the Polytechnische Schule in Brunswick and Karlsruhe; appointed (1871) to Germany's first chair of physical chemistry, at

Leipzig; from 1877, edited *Annalen der Physik und Chemie*. With Rudolph Franz, discovered (1853) the law named for them stating that at a constant, not very low temperature, the electrical conductivity of metals is approximately proportional to their thermal conductivity; also did important work on endosmosis and magnetism. Wrote *Die Lehre vom Galvanismus* (1861–63).

WIEDERSHEIM, ROBERT (*b. Nürtingen, Baden-Württemberg, Germany, 1848; d. Lindau im Bodensee, Germany, 1923*), comparative anatomy, embryology.

Studied at Tübingen, Würzburg, and Freiburg; taught at Würzburg and Freiburg. Author of the world-famous *Vergleichende Anatomie der Wirbeltiere* on the comparison of vertebrates, and their embryologic and phylogenetic development.

WIEGLEB, JOHANN CHRISTIAN (*b. Langensalza, Germany, 1732; d. Langensalza, 1800*), pharmacy, chemistry.

Built his own pharmacy, with a model laboratory, in Langensalza (1759); in chemistry, was skilled in analytic procedures. Founded a school for pharmacists (1779); among its students were J. F. A. Göttling, Klaproth, Hermbstädt, and the botanist Willdenow. Wrote a book highly critical of alchemy (1777), but adhered to Stahl's phlogiston theory.

WIELAND, HEINRICH OTTO (*b. Pforzheim, Germany, 1877; d. Starnberg, Germany, 1957*), organic chemistry.

Received his Ph.D. at Munich (1901); remained there until 1917; did research on chemical warfare during World War I; then taught at the Technische Hochschule in Munich and at the University of Freiburg; became director of the Baeyer Laboratory at the University of Munich (1925). Best known for his investigation of the structure of bile acids, begun in 1912, done partly in concert with his friend A. O. R. Windaus; received the 1927 Nobel Prize in chemistry for this work; in 1932, revised his proposed structure for cholic acid, arriving at the presently accepted structure at the same time as, but independently of, the British chemists O. Rosenheim and H. King.

WIELAND (or GUILANDINUS), MELCHIOR (*b. Königsberg, Germany [now Kaliningrad, R.S.F.S.R.], ca. 1520; d. Padua, Italy, 1589*), botany.

Studied at Königsberg and Rome; traveled in Asia and the Mediterranean. Was a vastly knowledgeable and inventive director of the Padua botanical garden (from 1561).

WIELEITNER, HEINRICH (*b. Wasserburg am Inn, Germany, 1874; d. Munich, Germany, 1931*), mathematics, history of mathematics.

Served as *Oberstudiendirektor* at the Neue Realgymnasium in Munich (from 1926); also taught at the University. Wrote on geometry and on the history of mathematics.

WIEN, WILHELM CARL WERNER OTTO FRITZ FRANZ (*b. Gaffken, near Fischhausen, East Prussia [now Primorsk, R.S.F.S.R.], 1864; d. Munich, Germany, 1928*), physics, philosophy of science.

Studied under Helmholtz at the University of Berlin (doctorate, 1886); became his assistant at the Physikalisch-Technische Reichsanstalt (1890–96). Subsequently, Wien's positions included professorships at Würzburg (1900–20) and at Munich. On the basis of his discovery of several characteristics of the still unknown Kirchhoff energy distribution function, Wien achieved his energy distribution law (1896):

$$\phi_\lambda = C \, \lambda^{-5} \exp \left(\frac{c}{\lambda\theta} \right),$$

where ϕ_λ is the energy at a given small interval of the abscissa and θ is the temperature. Wien then focused on Röntgen and cathode radiation; the investigation of vacuum radiation of this kind occupied him for the rest of his life, and yielded important results. In 1911, he was awarded the Nobel Prize in physics "for his discoveries concerning the laws of the radiation of heat."

WIENER, LUDWIG CHRISTIAN (*b. Darmstadt, Germany, 1826; d. Karlsruhe, Germany, 1896*), mathematics, physics, philosophy.

Received Ph.D. at Giessen (1850). Taught at the Technische Hochschule in Karlsruhe (1852–96). Specialized in descriptive geometry and the construction of mathematical models; in physics, studied molecular phenomena and atmospheric radiation; developed an atomistic cosmology.

WIENER, NORBERT (*b. Columbia, Mo., 1894; d. Stockholm, Sweden, 1964*), mathematics.

Educated by his father; entered Harvard Graduate School at age fifteen; took his Ph.D. in philosophy and mathematics (1913); studied abroad with Bertrand Russell and others; joined (1919) the mathematics department of the Massachusetts Institute of Technology. Took up mathematics seriously only in 1918; began to work on integration in function spaces, which led to his greatest achievements, the first of which was differential space; not satisfied with a general integration theory, he looked for a physical embodiment to test the theory, which he found in Brownian motion (1921); conceived a measure in the space of one-dimensional paths that leads to the application of probability concepts in that space. Published (1923–25) papers that greatly influenced potential theory. The study of general stochastic processes and the mathematical needs of MIT's engineering department set him on the track of harmonic analysis, Fourier transforms, and Tauberian theorems; with J. D. Tamarkin, published a major paper (1930) on generalized harmonic analysis. With R. E. A. C. Paley, wrote *Fourier Transforms* (1934). Another cooperative achievement was the study of the Wiener-Hopf equation generalizing Eberhard Hopf's investigation on radiation equilibrium. From 1940, was led by technical problems (such as antiaircraft fire control and noise filtration in radar) to increasing interest in communication theory; linear prediction was investigated independently by A. N. Kolmogorov, but Wiener's approach dealt with prediction and filtering under one heading; he elaborated the fundamental concepts of his approach in a wartime report, belatedly published in 1949; this, although difficult to read, is a basic document in communication theory. With Y. W. Lee, investigated nonlinear filtering. Wiener's world-famous book *Cybernetics...* (1948), although badly organized and not his best work, popularized several important aspects of communication theory.

WIENER, OTTO (*b. Karlsruhe, Germany, 1862; d. Leipzig, Germany, 1927*), physics.

Received Ph.D. at Strasbourg (1887); taught at Giessen and Leipzig. A pioneer in the physics and techniques of thin plates; did his best work early in his career, achieving the experimental demonstration of standing light waves (1889).

WIESNER, JULIUS VON (*b. Tschechen, Moravia [now Czechoslovakia], 1838; d. Vienna, Austria, 1916*), plant anatomy, plant physiology.

Studied at Vienna and Jena (Ph.D., 1860); taught at Vienna and was director of the Institute of Plant Physiology (1873–1909). Writings include *Die Rohstoffe des Pflanzenreichs* (1873), on economically valuable plant materials, and *Der Lichtgenuss der Pflanzen* (1907), on plants and light.

WIGAND, ALBERT JULIUS WILHELM (*b. Treysa, Electoral Hesse, Germany, 1821; d. Marburg, Germany, 1886*), botany.

The last and most important member of Schleiden's school of botany. Was a professor at Marburg and director of the Botanical Garden and the pharmacognostic institute. Did research on teratology of plants and pioneered in microchemical staining techniques.

WILBRAND, JOHANN BERNHARD (*b. Clarholz, Germany, 1779; d. Giessen, Germany, 1846*), physiology.

After being released from serfdom (1803), studied medicine at Würzburg; became a professor at Giessen. Was a prominent and dogged adherent of Schelling's *Naturphilosophie*. Best-known work is *Physiologie des Menschen* (1815).

WILCKE, JOHAN CARL (*b. Wismar, Germany, 1732; d. Stockholm, Sweden, 1796*), physics.

The son of a German minister in Stockholm; received his doctorate in physics at Rostock (1757); worked (1755–57) with Franz Aepinus in Berlin on major experiments in electricity; with him, invented a large air condenser that gave a shock comparable to that from a well-charged bottle; this threatened the already moribund theory of electrical atmospheres. Returned to Sweden as a lecturer at the Royal Swedish Academy of Sciences, later becoming professor (1770) and secretary (1784–96). Continued electrical researches and began studies of heat, which led to his best-known work, the independent discovery of latent heat (1772); also investigated specific heat capacities. Studying magnetism, was responsible for several discoveries and inventions, including the creation of a systematic isoclinal chart and the demonstration of ways of magnetizing a soft iron needle.

WILCZYNSKI, ERNEST JULIUS (*b. Hamburg, Germany, 1876; d. Denver, Colo., 1932*), mathematics.

Extending the work of Halphen, created the subject of projective differential geometry. Taught at the University of Chicago (from 1910).

WILD, HEINRICH (*b. Uster, Zurich canton, Switzerland, 1833; d. Zurich, Switzerland, 1902*), meteorology.

Founded the magnetometeorological observatory at Pavlovsk, Russia (1876). Noted for improvements in meteorological instruments and techniques of observation.

WILEY, HARVEY WASHINGTON (*b. Kent, Ind., 1844; d. Washington, D.C., 1930*), chemistry.

Chief of the Division (later Bureau) of Chemistry of the U.S. Department of Agriculture (1883–1912). Was a leader in the campaign for the Food and Drug Act (1906), but then found enforcement frustrated by industrial interests. Thereafter, worked for *Good Housekeeping.*

WILHELM IV, LANDGRAVE OF HESSE (*b. Kassel, Germany, 1532; d. Kassel, 1592*), astronomy.

Refined techniques of astronomical observation; designed a precise astronomical clock (1560–61); began a much-needed new star catalogue; with his assistant Christoph Rothmann, made astonishingly accurate observations; introduced a new method for determining stellar positions.

WILHELMY, LUDWIG FERDINAND (*b. Stargard, Pomerania [now Poland], 1812; d. Berlin, Germany, 1864*), physics, chemistry.

Received his doctorate in chemistry at Heidelberg (1846). Was the first person to measure the velocity of a homogeneous chemical reaction (1850).

WILKINS, JOHN (*b. Northamptonshire, England, 1614; d. London, England, 1672*), theology, science, scientific and academic administration and organization.

After schooling at home, Wilkins began grammar school at the age of nine under the noted Greek and Latin scholar Edward Sylvester, and in May 1627 he matriculated at New Inn Hall, Oxford (later united with Balliol College). He soon transferred to Magdalen Hall, where his tutor was the Baptist divine John Tombes. He graduated B.A. in 1631, and gained the M.A. degree in 1634. At this time Wilkins was tutor in his college. A few years later he was ordained and became vicar of Fawsley. At this time he is reported to have become chaplain to William Fiennes, first viscount Saye and Seale, who was then a supporter of the Puritans and later sat in the Westminster Assembly. But in 1641 Wilkins dedicated his *Mercury* to George Lord Berkeley, signing himself "your lordship's servant and chaplain." His desire to move in high places was further gratified when he became chaplain to Charles Louis, the prince elector Palatine, the king's nephew. The elector lived in England during a good part of the 1640's, befriending the parliamentary party in the hope of securing the restitution of his lost possessions. During the early months of 1646, Wilkins was officially engaged as preacher at Gray's Inn; during these years he also preached at the Savoy.

On 13 April 1648, the Parliamentary Visitors made Wilkins warden of Wadham College. The holder of this office was required to take the degree of doctor of divinity, but on 5 March 1649, the Visitors gave him a year's dispensation.

Although published two years apart, the *Discovery* (1638) and the *Discourse* (1640) can be considered a single work. Addressed to the common reader, the primary aim was to make known and to defend the new world picture of Copernicus, Kepler, and Galileo by showing its agreement with reason and experience against subservience to Aristotelian doctrines and literal biblical interpretation.

Only a year later, in 1641, Wilkins published another book on a popular subject, entitled *Mercury, or the Secret and Swift Messenger, Showing How a Man May With Privacy and Speed Communicate His Thoughts to a Friend at Any Distance*. It mentions such old tricks as baking secret messages into loaves of bread, but Wilkins' chief interest was cryptography, of which he gives a wealth of examples, all ready for use. But he also deals with cryptology or secret communication by speaking, either by involving the sense in metaphors and allegories or by changing old words or inventing new ones, as is done by thieves, gypsies, and lovers; and with "semeology," that is communication by signs and gestures, as used for instance by deaf-mutes. Thus *Mercury* is not merely a practical guide in the use and decoding of ciphers, but a broadly based discussion of the means of communication, or what today would be called semiotics.

His *Mathematical Magick* (1648) is divided in two parts: "Archimedes or Mechanical Powers" and "Daedalus or Mechanical Motions."

The first part deals with the balance, lever, wheel, pulley, wedge, and screw in that order, all illustrated with line drawings and pictures. Then follow chapters that show how the combination of these devices may produce "infinite strength" so as to "pull up any oak by the roots with a hair, lift it up with a straw, or blow it up with one's breath," all illustrated with rather sensational pictures. The second part treats a miscellaneous collection of strange devices and possibilities, such as flying machines, moving and speaking statues, artificial spiders, the imitation of sounds made by birds and man, a land vehicle driven by sails, a submarine, Archimedes' screw, and perpetual motion.

In 1647, Parliament passed an ordinance which empowered a committee to look after "the better regulating and reformation of the University of Oxford, and the several colleges and halls in the same, and for the due correction of offences, abuses, and disorders, especially of late times committed there."

Within the next year the Parliamentary Visitors came to Oxford, ejected the old warden of Wadham College, and appointed Wilkins, who took charge on 13 April 1648. It proved a wise choice. At the young age of thirty-four, he must have impressed the authorities by his accomplishments in the university and in his varied public offices as well as by his forceful advocacy of new learning, his moderation in religious affairs, his energy, and his extensive connections. Under the guidance of a man who was not considered a bigot, the college admissions soon rose steeply, including a large number of country gentlemen and "cavaliers," a fact that may also have helped improve the finances. It is universally acknowledged that Wadham was a distinguished college during Wilkins' wardenship.

After the death of Oliver Cromwell, the Chancellor at Oxford, Wilkins had become a close adviser to Richard Cromwell, who appointed him master of Trinity College, Cambridge, "thinking he would be as serviceable in that, as he had been in the other university." He took possession in late summer, resigning from the wardenship of

Wadham on 3 September 1659. His tenure lasted barely a year.

Wilkins' departure from Cambridge was felt as a loss by many. With an uncertain future behind him, Wilkins now gravitated to London and the culmination of his career as the energetic center of the Royal Society.

In the midst of all his activities during the 1660's, Wilkins had also found time to prepare his greatest work, *An Essay Towards a Real Character and a Philosophical Language*, which with the official imprimatur of the Royal Society was presented to it on 7 May 1668.

The *Essay* is the largest and most complete work in a long tradition of speculation and effort to create an artificial language that would, in a contemporary phrase, "repair the ruins of Babel."

WILKS, SAMUEL STANLEY (*b. Little Elm, Tex., 1906; d. Princeton, N.J., 1964*), mathematical statistics.

Studied at the University of Texas (M.A., 1928), the University of Iowa (Ph.D., 1931), at Columbia University, and in England at University College, London, and Cambridge University; from 1933, was a member of the mathematics department at Princeton University. Made his greatest contributions to multivariate analysis; did penetrating studies of likelihood ratio tests for various hypotheses relating to multivariate normal distributions; made similar investigations relating to multinomial distributions and to independence in two-, three-, and higher-dimensional contingency tables; provided (1938) a compact proof of the basic theorem on the large-sample distribution of the likelihood ratio criterion for testing "composite" statistical hypotheses. In 1941, laid the foundations of the theory of statistical "tolerance limits"; also contributed to "nonparametric" methods of statistical inference. Was a founder of the Institute of Mathematical Statistics (1935); was active in government service; worked to improve mathematical education at all levels.

WILLDENOW, KARL LUDWIG (*b. Berlin, Germany, 1765; d. Berlin, 1812*), botany.

Received the M.D. at Halle (1789); took over his father's apothecary shop in Berlin. Introduced Alexander von Humboldt to botany; was named professor of natural history at the Berlin Medical-Surgical College (1798) and curator of the Berlin Botanical Garden (1801). His *Grundriss der Kräuterkunde* (1792), a greatly successful basic text, helped to lay the foundations of historical phytogeography.

WILLIAM OF AUVERGNE, also known as **Guilielmus Arvernus** or **Alvernus** (*b. Aurillac, Auvergne [now Cantal], France, ca. 1180–90; d. Paris, France, 1249*), philosophy, theology.

Bishop of Paris (from 1228); thus, sometimes called William of Paris; the first great scholastic philosopher. Author, *Magisterium divinale* (ca. 1231–36).

WILLIAM THE ENGLISHMAN (*fl. France, thirteenth century*), astronomy, astrology.

A physician who lived in Marseilles, known for four works (1220–31) on topics in astrology, astronomy, and natural history; his treatise on the saphea (similar to the astrolabe) represents the introduction of this instrument into the Latin West.

WILLIAM HEYTESBURY. *See* **Heytesbury, William.**

WILLIAM OF MOERBEKE. *See* **Moerbeke, William of.**

WILLIAM OF OCKHAM. *See* **Ockham, William of.**

WILLIAM OF SAINT-CLOUD (*fl. France, end of the thirteenth century*), astronomy.

Author of a treatise on the *Directorium* (a magnetic compass with a table for computing the duration of diurnal arcs); the *Calendrier de la reine,* a calendar dedicated to Queen Marie of Brabant, widow of Philip III; and an *Almanach* giving the daily planetary positions for twenty years (from 1292).

WILLIAM OF SHERWOOD, also **Shyreswood, Shirewode** (*b. ca. 1200–10, Nottinghamshire [?], England; d. ca. 1266–71*), logic.

Taught at Oxford; wrote approximately five treatises on logic; called by Roger Bacon "one of the famous wise men in Christendom."

WILLIAMS, HENRY SHALER (*b. Ithaca, N.Y., 1847; d. Havana, Cuba, 1918*), paleontology, stratigraphy.

Taught at Cornell and Yale universities. His *Geological Biology* (1895), little appreciated in his lifetime, is a minor classic; from the fossil record, Williams made excellent estimates of the durations of the great geological periods.

WILLIAMS, ROBERT RUNNELS (*b. Nellore, India, 1886; d. Summit, N.J., 1965*), chemistry, nutrition.

Studied at the University of Chicago (B.S., 1907; M.S., 1908). Remembered for his discovery and synthesis of the anti-beriberi factor (now called vitamin B_1) in rice polishings; from 1909, this was the major project of his career.

WILLIAMSON, ALEXANDER WILLIAM (*b. Wandsworth, London, England, 1824; d. Hindhead, Surrey, England, 1904*), organic chemistry.

The most influential chemist in Great Britain in the period 1850–70. Studied at Heidelberg and with Liebig at Giessen; had a private laboratory in Paris (1846–49), where he knew Laurent, Gerhardt, Wurtz, and Dumas; from 1849, taught at University College, London. Announced his elegant theory of etherization (1850). Stated that the relationship between alcohol and ether is not one of the loss or addition of water (as previously assumed), but rather of substitution, since ether contains two ethyl radicals but the same quantity of oxygen as alcohol; his research here laid the foundation for twentieth-century mechanistic studies; particularly important was his suggestion that analogies for the structures of both organic and inorganic substances should be based on the inorganic type, water, for this led to the final unification of organic and inorganic chemistry.

WILLIAMSON, WILLIAM CRAWFORD (*b. Scarborough, Yorkshire, England, 1816; d. Clapham Common, England, 1895*), botany, geology, natural history.

A physician and professor at Owens College in Manchester (from 1851). Among his wide-ranging contributions to natural history, he is best remembered for his series of studies of the fossil plants of the British coalfields (published 1871–93); these studies are part of the basis of our present knowledge of the earliest pteridophytes as well as of the early seed plants.

WILLIS, BAILEY (*b. Idlewild-on-Hudson, N.Y., 1857; d. Palo Alto, Calif., 1949*), geology.

Studied at Columbia University; worked for the Northern Pacific Railway (1880–82), the U.S. Geological Survey, and as professor and chairman of the geology department at Stanford University (from 1915). His major interests were Mount Rainier, the Appalachians, and earthquakes.

WILLIS, ROBERT (*b. London, England, 1800; d. Cambridge, England, 1875*), engineering, medieval archaeology.

Spent his entire career at Cambridge. Wrote *Principles of Mechanism* (1841), which anticipated and encouraged the subsequent development of kinematic analysis and synthesis of mechanisms. He introduced the term "kinematics" and helped change the study of machinery from a descriptive to an analytical science. Was an authority on medieval architecture; wrote an essay (1835) reputed to be the first work to call serious attention to the Gothic style.

WILLIS, THOMAS (*b. Great Bedwyn, Wiltshire, England, 1621; d. London, England, 1675*), anatomy, medicine.

Studied at Oxford University (B.A., 1639; M.A., 1642; B.Med., 1646) and taught there. The scientific club that met in his rooms was an early version of the Royal Society and included John Wilkins and Christopher Wren. In *De fermentatione* (completed by 1656), Willis suggested that a ferment of the blood in the heart is the basic process in generating heat and converting food into nutrient blood; he cast his explanations in atomistic and chemical terms. His *De febribus* (1659) is an important early contribution to English epidemiology in which he characterized epidemics of war-typhus, plague, measles, smallpox, and influenza, and gave the first clinical description of typhoid fever. *Cerebri anatome* (1664), drawings by Christopher Wren, is the foundation document of the anatomy of the central and autonomic nervous systems; Willis argued that voluntary functions are localized in the cerebrum, and that involuntary actions are performed especially by the "intercostal" and "vagal" nerves—respectively, the modern sympathetic and parasympathetic systems. He described the distribution of cranial nerves in detail and investigated cerebral blood flow. Moved to London (1667), where he set up a very successful private practice. Altered his theory of fermentation in *Tractatus de corde* (1669) to accommodate Richard Lower's finding that the heart is merely a muscle. In *De anima brutorum* (1672) he proposed that there is a corporeal soul in the nervous system that is subject to derangements that account for a wide range of disorders, from headache to delirium.

WILLISTON, SAMUEL WENDELL (*b. Roxbury, Mass., 1851; d. Chicago, Ill., 1918*), vertebrate paleontology, entomology, medicine.

While an assistant to O. C. Marsh of Yale, earned an M.D. (1880) and Ph.D. in entomology. Was active in public health and medical education; helped to found the medical school of the University of Kansas (where he had done undergraduate work); was its first dean (1898–1902). In geology and paleontology, taught at Kansas and (from 1902) at the University of Chicago; specialized in mosasaurs, plesiosaurs, and pterodactyls; did his most valuable work on labyrinthodont amphibians and early reptiles. Was known worldwide for his expertise on the Diptera of North America.

WILLSTÄTTER, RICHARD (*b. Karlsruhe, Germany, 1872; d. Locarno, Switzerland, 1942*), organic chemistry.

Studied under Adolf von Baeyer at the University of Munich, whom he succeeded (1916); after the rise of Hitler, emigrated to Switzerland (1939). Investigated cocaine and related tropine alkaloids. Best known for research on chlorophyll and the anthocyanins, for which he was awarded the Nobel Prize for chemistry (1915).

WILLUGHBY, FRANCIS (*b. Middleton, Warwickshire, England, 1635; d. Middleton, 1672*), natural history.

Graduated from Trinity College, Cambridge (1656). The lifelong friend, associate, and patron of John Ray. His observations were used by Ray; conversely, Ray completed Willughby's *Ornithologia* and *Historia piscium* (both published posthumously).

WILSING, JOHANNES (*b. Berlin, Germany, 1856; d. Potsdam, Germany, 1943*), astronomy.

Received doctorate from University of Berlin (1880); was affiliated with the Potsdam Astrophysical Observatory (1881–1921); made contributions to astrophysics and methodology. In calculating the diameters of stars, he used laws of radiation and the measured values of the surface temperature. His results were later confirmed by interferometry.

WILSON, ALEXANDER (*b. St. Andrews, Scotland, 1714; d. Edinburgh, Scotland, 1786*), astronomy.

A businessman and professor of practical astronomy (1760–84) at the University of Glasgow. Best known for his interpretation of sunspots, which influenced Herschel.

WILSON, ALEXANDER (*b. Paisley, Scotland, 1766; d. Philadelphia, Pa., 1813*), ornithology.

The founder of ornithology in America. Was the son of a smuggler; became a poet (his *Watty and Meg* was popular for generations); left Scotland in disgrace (1794) after being convicted of blackmail against a wealthy mill owner. As a schoolteacher in the United States, became interested in sketching and studying birds. At age forty, gave up teaching to research and produce his magnificent *The American Ornithology* (1808–13), in which he painted and described 264 species, adding forty-eight new species to those previously known to exist in the United States; having "sacrificed everything" in the creation of this masterpiece, Wilson died of dysentery at age forty seven; he had completed almost nine of the projected ten volumes.

WILSON, BENJAMIN (*b. Leeds, England, 1721; d. Bloomsbury, London, England, 1788*), electricity.

A successful artist, unsuccessful speculator on the Stock Exchange, and amateur physicist. In *Observations on a Series of Electrical Experiments* (1756) asserted the identity of electricity with the Newtonian aether. He engaged in an extraordinary public controversy with Franklin over the best shape for lightning rods.

WILSON, CHARLES THOMSON REES (*b. near Glencorse, Midlothian, Scotland, 1869; d. Carlops, Peeblesshire, Scotland, 1959*), atomic physics, meteorological physics.

Studied at Owens College, Manchester (B.Sc., 1887), and at Cambridge University, where he became friendly with Rutherford, Townsend, and McClelland; taught at Cambridge from 1900. With A. H. Compton, was awarded (1927) a Nobel Prize in physics for their work on the scattering of high-energy particles. Inspired by experiences on a vacation in the Highlands (1894), he began to study cloud formation; built (1895) the first apparatus (cloud chamber) to condense water vapor in dust-free air; used an X-ray tube to irradiate the expansion chamber (1896); designed an improved chamber (1910); used it to reveal the track of an alpha ray. His studies of atmospheric electricity led to the postulation of the existence of "cosmic radiation" (1911); as late as 1956, Wilson published an important paper on thundercloud formation.

WILSON, EDMUND BEECHER (*b. Geneva, Ill., 1856; d. New York, N. Y., 1939*), cytology, embryology, heredity.

Wilson studied at Antioch College in Ohio, the (old) University of Chicago, and Sheffield Scientific School at Yale (Ph.B., 1878). He received his Ph.D. from Johns Hopkins University in 1881. In 1882 he went abroad for further study at Cambridge, Leipzig and Naples.

On his return from Naples, Wilson taught for one year (1883–84) at Williams College. The following year he held a lectureship at the Massachusetts Institute of Technology, where he worked closely with his friend Sedgwick on a biology textbook they had begun planning several years earlier. In 1885 Wilson accepted an offer to head the biology department at Bryn Mawr College, where he remained until 1891, when he was appointed adjunct professor of zoology and chairman of the zoology department at Columbia. He remained at Columbia for the rest of his career, retiring as Da Costa professor of zoology in 1928.

Before assuming his official duties at Columbia, Wilson spent a year abroad, the first half with Theodor Boveri at Munich and the second half at Naples with the experimental embryologists Hans Driesch and Curt Herbst. During this and later years Wilson spent considerable time at marine stations and on collecting trips. His long association with the Marine Biological Laboratory, Woods Hole, Massachusetts (both as investigator and as trustee), and the Chesapeake Zoological Laboratory of Johns Hopkins were part and parcel of the importance he attached to studying living specimens, and especially marine forms as material for basic biological investigation.

Although Wilson always worked concurrently on a variety of problems, his career can be divided roughly into three periods, each of which was dominated by a particular set of interests: 1879–91, descriptive embryology and morphology (including studies of cell lineage); 1891–1903, experimental embryology (including the organization of the egg, the effects of various substances on differentiation, and artificial parthenogenesis); and 1903–38, heredity (including the relation of Mendelism to cytology, sex determination, and evolution). To Wilson these various topics converged in a single problem: How does the individual organism lie implicit in the fertilized (or even unfertilized) egg? He felt it was impossible fully to understand larger problems, such as those occurring on the tissue, organ, organismic, or population level, without a thorough knowledge of the cell—its structure, organization, and functions.

Although Wilson published two papers on the systematics of Pycnogonida (sea spiders) in 1879 and 1881, the result of work he had carried out for the Ph.B. at Yale, his earliest work of importance involved studies on the embryology and morphology of the coelenterate *Renilla.* This work was undertaken for his doctoral dissertation and consisted of comparing serial sections of embryos to determine the cellular changes occurring during development. It was published in the *Philosophical Transactions* in 1883.

His *General Biology,* published in 1886, was an attempt to treat the study of living organisms from a more analytical and integrated viewpoint than had been customary. To this end Wilson and Sedgwick treated life as a manifestation of chemical and physical laws: the properties of life were a result of the properties of its constituent atoms and molecules. They also included both plant and animal material in their discussion, and tried to show how all organic processes involved an interaction of the living system with its environment. *General Biology* provides one of the earliest examples of Wilson's broad perspective on biological problems, and as a textbook it was influential in bringing a new approach to the taxonomically and phylogenetically oriented introductory courses offered in most universities around the turn of the century.

After taking up his duties at Bryn Mawr in 1885, Wilson continued his studies on the cellular and morphological basis of early development with work on two annelids: *Lumbricus,* the earthworm, and *Nereis,* a marine polychaete.

Wilson's work on *Lumbricus* settled an existing controversy on the nature of mesoderm origin and showed, in conjunction with the subsequent work on *Nereis,* that spiral cleavage probably was characteristic of all annelids. The work on *Lumbricus* and *Nereis* also confirmed the study of cell lineage as an important embryological and morphological tool. It also established his reputation as a biologist of considerable observational skill and interpretive ability.

Wilson's first year as adjunct professor of zoology at Columbia was spent on leave in Europe (1891–92). During the first half he worked with Theodor Boveri at Munich, and during the second half at the zoological station in Naples. Particularly important during his stay in Munich were what Wilson learned about cytology and the strong personal relationship he developed with Boveri. At Naples, he was exposed to the new experimental embryology through the work of Hans Driesch and Curt Herbst, both of whom were testing Wilhelm Roux's mosaic theory of development, put forth in 1888. The questions of cell differentiation raised by the Roux-Driesch controversy greatly stimulated Wilson's imagination, and turned his attention away from the more morphologically oriented studies and toward more critical questions of experimental embryology.

Exposure to the problems and methods of the new school of experimental embryology (called by Roux's term, *Entwicklungsmechanik,* roughly translated as "developmental mechanics," or simply as "experimental embryology") raised in Wilson's mind the question of how differentiation *does* take place if it is not the result of a simple segregation of hereditary material among daughter cells. He reasoned that if differentiation were not a mosaic process, the key to both its regularity and its amazing flexibility somehow must reside in the organization of the egg cell, particularly the cytoplasm. Assuming, as Boveri and others had shown, that every daughter cell receives the same number and kind of chromosomes as the parent cell, he concluded that differentiation must be triggered by variations in the cytoplasm in which each nucleus lies. Thus, the egg cell's cytoplasm must be "preorganized" in such a way that regional localization of substances exists before cleavage begins. How the cytoplasm became structured in the first place was utter speculation, yet on the assumption of preorganization in the egg, Wilson could explain why some species seemed to show mosaic, and others nonmosaic, patterns of development. Those species appearing to have mosaic development simply showed cytoplasmic regionalization at a much earlier time in the embryo's life than those that seemed to be nonmosaic.

As a result of his work with Boveri, Wilson developed a strong interest in the cytological events surrounding cell division, particularly those involved in the maturation of the egg. On returning to the United States, he took up the study of chromosome movements, particularly spindle formation and the origin of the centrosomes (today called cell centrioles). In a lengthy study done with his pupil A. P. Mathews (1895), Wilson produced solid evidence against Hermann Fol's widely held theory of the "quadrille of the centers." (Fol maintained that the sperm and egg centrosomes fuse after fertilization, then divide, moving through the cytoplasm, like dancers changing partners in the eighteenth-century square dance quadrille, to form the two poles of the spindle apparatus.) Wilson showed that in echinoderms (especially the sea urchin) the poles were formed only by division of the sperm's centrosome. He went on to demonstrate in later papers that the centrosomes were formed within the cytoplasm, not within the nucleus, as had previously been thought. Close observation of the movements and doubling of centrosomes convinced Wilson that the replication of these bodies did not cause, and was not caused by, the replication of the chromosomes. The doubling of both sets of structures probably responded, he maintained, to some underlying rhythm in the cell's activity.

During his initial decade at Columbia, Wilson prepared the first edition of *The Cell in Development and Inheritance* (1896), the basis of which was a series of lectures he gave in 1892–93. *The Cell* was much more than a compilation of all the relevant information on various parts of the cell and various cell processes. It was not only a synthesis of a great deal of information (the bibliography in itself represents a prodigious effort) but also reflected Wilson's wide-ranging and balanced views of contemporary problems, and his special emphasis on the function of cytology in elucidating such topics as embryology, heredity, evolution, and general physiology.

The Cell went through three editions and numerous reprintings. It is estimated that this book has been the single most influential treatise on cytology during the twentieth century. Historically, one of the most important functions of *The Cell* was to pave the way for a more rapid acceptance of Mendelian theory, once it was reintroduced to the scientific community in 1900. By focusing attention on the cell nucleus, and particularly on the chromosomes as the seat of heredity, Wilson prepared many biologists—especially cytologists—to see the relationship between Mendel's laws and the events of maturation of the sperm and egg. Although two of the rediscoverers of Mendel's work—Carl Correns and Hugo de Vries—had offered a chromosomal interpretation of their own and Mendel's findings shortly after 1900, it was not based on much observational evidence.

In 1902 another former student of Wilson's, Clarence E. McClung, pointed out that the unpaired "accessory" chromosome (later called the X by Wilson), long known to exist in the males of some arthropods, might offer a clue to how sex was inherited. Wilson was intrigued by McClung's work and set out to study the occurrence and distribution of the accessory chromosome in a number of species, mostly insects. In 1905 Wilson and, independently, Nettie M. Stevens of Bryn Mawr published extensive cytological evidence suggesting a chromosomal basis for sex determination.[14] These works provided the missing link between cytology and heredity. Wilson and Stevens concluded that females normally have a chromosome complement of XX and males have one of XY. In oögenesis and spermatogenesis, the X and X (for oögenesis) and the X and Y (for spermatogenesis) separate, and end up, by meiotic division, in separate gametes. All eggs thus have a single X chromosome, while sperm can have either an X or a Y. When a Y-bearing sperm fertilizes an egg, the off-spring is a male (XY); when an X-bearing sperm fertilizes an egg, the offspring is a female (XX).

Wilson and Stevens recognized that a few groups of organisms have variations (or reversals) of this scheme—for instance, species that normally lack a Y or in which the females are XY and the males XX (the latter case is true for moths, butterflies, and birds). The 1905 papers by Wilson and Stevens not only cleared up a long-standing controversy on the nature of sex determination (for example, whether it was hereditarily or environmentally induced) but also were the first reports that any specific hereditary trait (or set of characteristics, such as those associated with sex) could be identified with one specific pair of chromosomes.

Wilson pursued studies on the chromosomes, particularly in relation to sex inheritance, over the next seven years (1905–12), producing a series of eight papers entitled "Studies on Chromosomes." In general these papers worked out the chromosomal theory of sex determination (essentially as it is understood today) in great detail, and supported its Mendelian nature. Among other things, Wilson showed that the Y chromosomes in different insect species are of widely different sizes in comparison with the X; in some species the X and Y are of virtually equal size, whereas in others the Y is very small, and in still others it is nonexistent. He also observed that in a species where the female is normally XX, some females have the combination XXY and some males have only a single X and no Y. Wilson interpreted these cases as having resulted from the failure of the X and the Y to separate during spermatogenesis in the organism's male parent. When the same phenomenon was observed in *Drosophila* by C. B. Bridges in 1913, he and Wilson jointly coined the term "nondisjunction" for the failure of two homologues to segregate during meiosis. These and other results led Wilson to postulate that the Y chromosome had degenerated over the course of evolutionary history. He felt it represented either inactive chromatin material or an excess that was duplicated elsewhere in the chromosome group. Wilson considered the X to be the active member of the sex chromosome pair, and therefore the causal agent of sex determination. Although we know today that the matter is not so simple, he was essentially correct in judging that the Y has little actual hereditary function, in relation to sex or anything else.

Wilson's studies on chromosomes provided the important cytological foundation upon which T. H. Morgan's later chromosome theory of inheritance was based. The keystone to the chromosome theory of inheritance was laid in the Columbia laboratory, where Morgan from the animal-breeding side, and Wilson from the cytological side, provided evidence that hereditary units exist as material entities located on chromosomes in the nucleus.

The years between 1902 and 1912 marked the zenith of Wilson's creative period. The eight studies on chromosomes were brilliant examples of his observational and analytical skill. In this work his broad-reaching mind incisively drew the connections between Mendelian theory and cytology, long before many other workers (including Morgan) were prepared to make the same bold leaps. The chromosomal concept of Mendelian heredity was a logical view for Wilson to maintain because it provided the link he had intuitively held for many years between the cell, heredity, and development. The main theme enunciated in *The Cell* (1896) was being realized in actuality by the parallel studies on chromosomes in Wilson's laboratory and on the process of heredity in Morgan's.

Wilson's studies after 1912 were variations of a single basic question: What cell constituents other than the chromosomes affect the hereditary process? There were really two aspects to this question. One was that of extrachromosomal inheritance: the replicative function of such organelles as chloroplasts or mitochondria, which by 1920 were known to be able to reproduce themselves without nuclear control. The other question was the effect of the cytoplasm on the expression of genetic potential in the nucleus.

The culminating work of Wilson's later years was the complete revision and expansion of *The Cell* into a third edition (1925). The revised edition, under the title *The Cell in Development and Heredity,* was awarded the Daniel Giraud Elliot Medal of the National Academy of Sciences (1928) and the gold medal of the Linnean Society of London (1928).

In all three editions of *The Cell* Wilson related the phenomena of heredity, cell structure and function, and development to organic evolution and adaptation. To him the central problem of evolution as posed by Darwin was how hereditary variations come about. In 1896 he recognized the importance of August Weismann's conception of the continuity of the germ plasm, and much of his future cytological work on chromosomes served to support the basic idea of a separation of germ and somatoplasm. Wilson's insight into this problem lay in his recognition that heredity was a cellular phenomenon —something that Darwin and his followers also had recognized. The Darwinian theory of pangenesis was, after all, only a cellular mechanism for how variations could occur. From his early studies of cells and his growing awareness that the nucleus was the locale of a cell's heredity, Wilson rejected the pangenesis theory. Because cell heredity was localized in the nucleus, specifically in the chromosomes, and because each set of chromosomes had continuity—that is, it transmitted its effects only vertically from one generation to the next—somatic variations could not be transmitted to the germ cells of the same organism.

WILSON, EDWIN BIDWELL (*b. Hartford, Conn., 1879; d. Brookline, Mass., 1964*), mathematics, physics.

Studied under Willard Gibbs at Yale (Ph.D., 1901), whose lectures on vector analysis he codified into a beautiful textbook (1901); also wrote on the foundations of geometry, on relativity, on aerodynamics, and on the applications of statistics to biology and astronomy; must be given priority in the discovery in statistics of what was later called the confidence interval. Was professor of vital statistics at the Harvard School of Public Health from 1922.

WILSON, JOHN (*b. Applethwaite, Westmorland, England, 1741; d. Kendal, Westmorland, England, 1793*), mathematics.

Studied mathematics at Cambridge; became a lawyer and judge. Remembered for Wilson's theorem: if p is prime number, then $1 + (p - 1)!$ is divisible by p. E. Waring published the theorem first (1770) and Lagrange, in 1773, gave its first proof in print.

WINCHELL FAMILY. Founded in America by Robert Winchell (d. 1669).

For four generations produced leaders in the broad organization of geology as a professional science in America.

WINCHELL, ALEXANDER (*b. Northeast, N.Y., 1824; d. Ann Arbor, Mich., 1891*), geology, education.

The older brother of Newton Horace Winchell; graduated from Wesleyan University (1847); taught at the University of Michigan (1853–73, 1879–91). Helped to organize geology as a science in America; was an effective popularizer; made important scientific observations in stratigraphy and paleontology.

WINCHELL, ALEXANDER NEWTON (*b. Minneapolis, Minn., 1874; d. New Haven, Conn., 1958*), mineralogy, petrology.

The youngest son of Newton Horace Winchell, with whom he began the project that became his magnum opus, the three-volume *Elements of Optical Mineralogy*. Also made contributions to petrology. Taught at the University of Wisconsin (1907–44).

WINCHELL, HORACE VAUGHN (*b. Galesburg, Mich., 1865; d. Los Angeles, Calif., 1923*), geology, mining engineering.

The oldest son of Newton Horace Winchell. Studied the Mesabi Range; worked in private industry and as a consultant; helped Anaconda Copper Mining Company in the development of the mine in Butte, Montana.

WINCHELL, NEWTON HORACE (*b. Northeast, N.Y., 1839; d. Minneapolis, Minn., 1914*), geology, archaeology.

Followed his older brother Alexander Winchell into geology; was state geologist of Minnesota (1872–1900); did original research on the geology of the United States; served in the Black Hills with Custer (1874); studied glaciation and early Indian sites. With his son Alexander Newton Winchell, wrote *Elements of Optical Mineralogy* (1909), which his son later expanded.

WINDAUS, ADOLF OTTO REINHOLD (*b. Berlin, Germany, 1876; d. Göttingen, Germany, 1959*), chemistry.

Studied under Emil Fischer at Berlin (B.S., 1897) and under Heinrich Kiliani at Freiburg im Breisgau (Ph.D., 1899); was professor of chemistry and director of the chemical laboratory at Göttingen (1915–44). Studied the structure of cholesterol and the "sterines" (steroids), partly in collaboration with his friend Heinrich Wieland; working with A. F. Hess in New York and A. Rosenheim in London, investigated the vitamin and provitamin involved in the cure of rickets, isolating what we now call vitamins D_1, D_2, and D_3. Received the Nobel Prize in 1928 for his work on the constitution of the sterols and their connection with other substances occurring in nature. Also discovered histamine and contributed to the synthesis of vitamin B_1.

WING, VINCENT (*b. North Luffenham. Rutland, England, 1619; d. North Luffenham, 1668*), astronomy.

A surveyor and astrologer, he produced the most popular almanacs of his time; accepted Keplerian astronomy by 1651.

WINKLER, CLEMENS (*b. Freiberg, Germany, 1838; d. Dresden, Germany, 1904*), chemistry.

Was educated at and became professor at the Freiberg School of Mines (1873–1902). Specialized in industrial gas analysis, developing the Winkler gas burette. Identified germanium.

WINKLER, LAJOS WILHELM (*b. Arad, Hungary [now Rumania], 1863; d. Budapest, Hungary, 1939*), chemistry.

Studied and taught at the University of Budapest. Specialized in analytical chemistry; created several new analytical methods; wrote *Die chemische Analyse* (1931–36).

WINLOCK, JOSEPH (*b. Shelby County, Ky., 1826; d. Cambridge, Mass., 1875*), astronomy, mathematics.

Graduated from and taught at Shelby College. Between 1857 and 1866 he taught mathematics at the U.S. Naval Academy, and was superintendent of the Nautical Almanac. Was professor of astronomy and director of the Harvard College Observatory (from 1866), where his primary concern was to develop and obtain better instruments.

WINSLØW, JACOB (or **JACQUES-BÉNIGNE**) (*b. Odense, Denmark, 1669; d. Paris, France, 1760*), anatomy.

Trained in Denmark under the barber-surgeon Johannes de Buchwald and Bartholin; studied in the Netherlands (1697–98) and in Paris under J.-G. Duverney, whom he eventually succeeded at the Jardin du Roi; was licensed to practice medicine (1704). Was regarded as the greatest anatomist of his day; Albrecht von Haller was among his students. Among his many treatises, he showed that a single muscle does not function alone as a flexor or supinator, but that muscles work in groups as synergists and always in relation to antagonists. Wrote the first treatise on descriptive anatomy (1732).

WINTHROP, JOHN (*b. Groton, Suffolk, England, 1606; d. Boston, Mass., 1676*), natural philosophy, medicine.

Educated at Trinity College, Dublin. Was the son of the governor of the Massachusetts Bay Colony; served as governor of Connecticut (from 1660). Was an enthusiastic amateur scientist and a founding member of the Royal Society of London. Searched for mineral resources; was a student of alchemy; dispensed herbal and chemical medicines.

WINTHROP, JOHN (*b. Boston, Mass., 1714; d. Cambridge, Mass., 1779*), astronomy, mathematics.

A friend and adviser of George Washington and a great-grand nephew of John Winthrop (*b.* 1606). Graduated from Harvard (1732). Became Hollis professor of mathematics and natural philosophy at Harvard College (1738), where he established the first experimental physics laboratory in America; did important work concerning the transits of Venus (1761, 1769)

WINTNER, AUREL (*b. Budapest, Hungary, 1903; d. Baltimore, Md., 1958*), mathematics.

Received the Ph.D. at Leipzig (1929); taught at Johns Hopkins (from 1930); editor of the *American Journal of Mathematics* (from 1944). Best known for *Analytical Foundations of Celestial Mechanics* (1941).

WISLICENUS, JOHANNES (*b. Klein-Eichstedt, near Querfurt, Germany, 1835; d. Leipzig, Germany, 1902*), chemistry.

Had a distinguished teaching career in Switzerland and Germany. With Adolf Fick, investigated the origin of muscle energy. Studied lactic and paralactic acids (1863–73); was the first to establish the structural identity of two different substances, and recommended three-dimensional formulas. Influenced van't Hoff; did an important paper on the stereoisomerism of unsaturated carbon compounds (1887).

WISTAR, CASPAR (*b. Philadelphia, Pa., 1761; d. Philadelphia, 1818*), anatomy.

A dedicated and admired physician, anatomy professor, and Abolitionist. Affiliated with the Pennsylvania Hospital (1793–1810); taught at the University of Pennsylvania (from 1792). The wisteria plant was named for him.

WITELO (Vitello) (*b. Poland, ca. 1230; d. ca. 1275*), optics, natural philosophy.

Was apparently born in Breslau (Wrocław); studied at the University of Paris in the early 1250's; studied canon law at Padua in the 1260's; became acquainted with William of Moerbeke in Viterbo (1268 or 1269); may have been an envoy from King Ottocar II of Bohemia to Gregory X (1274); possibly retired to the Premonstratensian abbey of Vicogne. His only extant works are *Tractatus de primaria causa penitentie et de natura demonum*, written in Padua, and *Perspectiva* (written after 1270), upon which his reputation rests. *Perspectiva* is an immense work, heavily influenced by Ibn al-Haytham's *Optics;* it falls generally into the Neoplatonic tradition; like Grosseteste and Bacon, Witelo considered optics the fundamental science of nature; the most substantial section of the book deals with catoptrics.

WITHAM, HENRY (*b. Minsteracres, Northumberland, England, 1779; d. Lartington Hall, Yorkshire, England, 1844*), geology, paleobotany.

Founded natural history societies in England. Wrote *Observations on Fossil Vegetables* (1831). In his investigations of *Pitus* fossil trees, he showed that gymnosperms were prevalent in Lower Carboniferous rocks.

WITHERING, WILLIAM (*b. Wellington, Shropshire, England, 1741; d. Birmingham, England, 1799*), medicine, botany, natural history.

Received M.D. at Edinburgh (1766). A practicing physician in Birmingham; member of the Lunar Society, which included Erasmus Darwin and Joseph Priestley. His *A Botanical Arrangement . . .*, on the plants of Great Britain, became a standard flora. He also published several chemical and mineralogical papers, a book on scarlet fever (1779), and *Account of the Foxglove . . .* (1785), a brilliant study of digitalis.

WITT, JAN DE (*b. Dordrecht, Netherlands, 1625; d. The Hague, Netherlands, 1672*), mathematics.

Studied at Leiden and Angers. Was in effect the prime minister of the Netherlands from 1653; with his brother Cornelis, was killed by a mob that favored the Orange faction. Witt's *Elementa curvarum linearum* (written before 1650, printed 1659–61) and John Wallis' *Tractatus de sectionibus conicis* (1655) are considered the first textbooks in analytic geometry; the two authors used different approaches. Witt first defined the conics geometrically in the plane and then showed that quadratic equations could be reduced to his normal forms. Witt was also among the first to apply the theory of probability to economic problems; in a treatise for the States of Holland (1671) he demonstrated mathematically that life annuities were being offered at too high a rate of interest relative to fixed annuities.

WITTGENSTEIN, LUDWIG (JOSEF JOHANN) (*b. Vienna, Austria, 1889; d. Cambridge, England, 1951*), philosophy.

One of the most original thinkers of the twentieth century. Was the son of a Viennese steel magnate and arts patron; studied under Bertrand Russell at Cambridge. Living in solitude in Norway, began (1913–14) to compose the *Tractatus Logico-Philosophicus* (1921); this influential work presented a theory of "logical atomism," postulating an isomorphism between the simplest elements of language and the possible states of affairs to which they ultimately refer. After working as a schoolteacher in several Austrian villages and as a gardener's assistant at a convent near Vienna, Wittgenstein returned to Cambridge to teach (1929); he worked in a medical school and medical laboratory during World War II. The masterpiece of his later thought, *Philosophical Investigations* (1953), rejects his former interest in the one and only "logical form" in favor of study of the natural history of language, the ways in which language is actually used; his aim was to show how philosophy has generated *insolubilia* and how such "philosophical sickness" can yield to rational treatment. In the *Tractatus*, he also made important technical contributions to the foundations of logic, probability theory, and the philosophy of science; he left voluminous manuscripts on the philosophy of mathematics still in the process of publication and evaluation.

WITTICH (or WITTICHIUS), PAUL (*b. Breslau, Silesia [now Wrocław, Poland], 1555 [?], d. Breslau, 1587*), mathematics.

Taught at Breslau (1582–84). Working with Tycho Brahe (1580), discovered—more precisely, rediscovered—the method of prostaphaeresis for simplifying trigonometric problems.

WOEPCKE, FRANZ (*b. Dessau, Germany, 1826; d. Paris, France, 1864*), mathematics, Oriental studies.

Graduated from Berlin (Ph.D., 1847). Spent most of his brief adult life in Paris studying the algebra of the Arabs, and Indian and Arab influence on Western mathematics; published some thirty texts. His own contributions deal mainly with curves and surfaces, equations of the nth degree, and function theory.

WÖHLER, AUGUST (*b. Soltau, Germany, 1819; d. Hannover, Germany, 1914*), engineering.

A railway engineer; named imperial railway director (1874). In 1855 he derived the formulas for calculating the sag of lattice girders, commonly called the equation of three moments. Gained broad recognition for his fatigue tests, which led him to universally valid results ("Wöhler's laws").

WÖHLER, FRIEDRICH (*b. Eschersheim, near Frankfurt-am-Main, Germany, 1800; d. Göttingen, Germany, 1882*), chemistry.

After taking his M.D. at Heidelberg (1823), studied for a year with Berzelius in Stockholm, becoming his lifelong friend and industrous translator. Became acquainted with Liebig (1825) in connection with finding that silver cyanate and silver fulminate both correspond to the empirical formula AgCNO; Liebig at first rejected this result, for it was generally assumed that two different compounds could not yield the same set of analytical percentages. Wöhler went on to discover a method for the extraction of aluminum (1827) and a method of preparing "artificial" urea, significant in that he had used inorganic materials to create a substance of animal origin. Liebig and Wöhler together did a half dozen famous studies, including one on what they ironically called allophanic ether ("unexpected" ether), produced when cyanic acid reacts with alcohol, and one on amygdalin, the first example of a glycoside; in their classic investigation of the oil of bitter almonds (1832), they established the existence of a body, the benzoyl radical, that remains constant from one compound to another. After 1840,

Wöhler was increasingly occupied with his duties as professor of chemistry at Göttingen (1836–82) and inspector general of the apothecaries of Hannover; he published a stream of interesting papers but none equal in importance to his early work.

WOLF, CHARLES JOSEPH ÉTIENNE (*b. Vorges, near Laon, Aisne, France, 1827; d. St.-Servan, Ille-et-Vilaine, France, 1918*), astronomy, history of science.

Received *agrégé* from the École Normale Supérieure (1851). Taught at Montpellier (1856–62) and at Paris (1875–1901). Among several achievements, he is remembered best for his discovery (1867) with Rayet of Wolf-Rayet stars, while they were both posted at the Paris Observatory.

WOLF, JOHANN RUDOLF (*b. Fällanden, near Zurich, Switzerland, 1816; d. Zurich, 1893*), astronomy, history of science.

Studied at universities of Zurich, Vienna, and Berlin. Taught astronomy in Bern and in Zurich. Noted for his studies of sunspot periods. Through his efforts, an observatory was constructed at Zurich.

WOLF, MAXIMILIAN FRANZ JOSEPH CORNELIUS (*b. Heidelberg, Germany, 1863; d. Heidelberg, 1932*), astronomy.

Studied and taught at the University of Heidelberg (Ph.D., 1888); working in his private observatory, became famous for his innovative photographic methods; promoted the construction of the Baden Observatory. Discovered hundreds of new asteroids; was an expert on the galactic nebulae; invented (with Pulfrich) the stereocomparator.

WOLFF, CASPAR FRIEDRICH (*b. Berlin, Germany, 1734; d. St. Petersburg, Russia [now Leningrad, U.S.S.R.], 1794*), biology.

Trained at the Medical-Surgical College in Berlin and at the University of Halle; was invited by Euler (1766) to join the St. Petersburg Academy of Sciences, and remained there for the rest of his life. Refuted the embryological theory of preformation with his studies of plant growth and chick embryos; discovered the embryonic kidneys (Wolffian bodies) and their ducts (Wolffian ducts). His research on the development of the intestine established the principles of formation of organs from foliate layers.

WOLFF, CHRISTIAN (*b. Breslau, Silesia [now Wrocław, Poland], 1679; d. Halle, Germany, 1754*), philosophy.

Studied at Jena and Leipzig (master's degree, 1702); taught at universities of Halle (1702–23) and Marburg. Essentially a popularizer, dependent on the ideas of Leibniz, but extremely influential, especially through his writings in German (rather than Latin). Wolff reinforced the German movement toward deism, determinism, and free thought, and set the major philosophical questions debated down to the time of Kant.

WOLLASTON, FRANCIS (*b. London, England, 1731; d. Chislehurst, Kent, England, 1815*), astronomy.

A liberal clergyman, father of William Hyde Wollaston, and amateur astronomer. Published practical aids for astronomers and navigators, including a star catalogue used by Herschel.

WOLLASTON, WILLIAM HYDE (*b. East Dereham, Norfolk, England, 1766; d. London, England, 1828*), chemistry, optics, physiology.

The son of Francis Wollaston, a vicar and fellow of the Royal Society, William entered Caius College, Cambridge (1782), as a medical student, graduated (1787), completed his studies in London, and first practiced in Huntingdon (1792). For reasons which are unclear, he abandoned medicine (1800) and formed a partnership with Smithson Tennant with whom he shared an interest in chemistry. Up to that time, platinum had resisted the efforts of chemists to produce it in a satisfactory malleable state. Tennant's experiments to that end led him to the discovery of osmium and iridium, new elements in the crude ore; but Wollaston went on (discovering along the way the new metals rhodium and palladium) to develop a process (1805) that was to yield malleable platinum: after producing a uniform powder of the platinum sponge and carefully removing its impurities, Wollaston compressed it in a powerful toggle press, dried it and forged it into a perfectly malleable state. His profit from the sale of platinum articles by 1826 had earned him some £ 15,000. His paper on the process (not read until 1828) won him the Royal Medal of the Royal Society.

In theoretical chemistry, Wollaston influenced the way in which the new atomic theory of Dalton was received. In 1808 he described his experiments on carbonates, sulfates, and oxalates which proved that the composition of these substances was regulated by the law of multiple proportions. In à paper on the structure of crystals (1812) he remarked that the existence of ultimate physical atoms was not established and that virtually spherical particles, consisting of mathematical points surrounded by forces of attraction and repulsion, would explain the structure of crystals equally well. This theory of unextended point centers of force was later accepted by Faraday in favor of the extended massy atoms of Dalton.

In 1813 Wollaston designed a logarithmic slide rule for the use of practical chemists, expressing the proportions in which the common chemical substances combined (referred to a standard oxygen unit of 10). This calculator, which he presented as being based on chemical facts and free from theoretical considerations, was in general use for over twenty years; Berzelius used it constantly.

In optics, Wollaston designed a dip sector, a modified sextant which was used by Ross and Parry on their arctic voyages (Wollaston Island in Baffin Bay is named for him). He developed (1802) an important method of determining refractive indices by total internal reflection. His observations on an impure spectrum led him to conclude that there were only four colors in the solar spectrum; he also discovered the dark lines there, later called Fraunhofer lines. He described (1803) his "periscopic spectacles," designed with meniscus lenses to allow clear vision in oblique directions; his camera lucida (1807), a quadrilateral glass prism, was widely used as an aid in drawing. He improved the camera obscura by introducing a meniscus lens and an aperture; it was employed as an early camera by Niepce and Daguerre. His well-known microscopic doublet was a combination of two planoconvex lenses used to reduce the aberration of the simple microscope.

His interest in physiology led him to characterize (1797) the principal constituents of urinary calculi; he identified (1812) a new and rare type of stone, which he called "cystic oxide" since it occurred in the bladder (later renamed "cystine"—the first amino acid to be discovered). He described for the first time (1809) the vibratory character of muscular action; investigated the physiology of the ear; and delivered the fullest explanation at the time (1824) of the nature of the problem of binocular vision.

Wollaston was associated with the attempts to bring uniformity to the system of weights and measures and recommended the introduction of the imperial gallon, accepted in 1824; was an active member of the Board of Longitude (1818–28), president of the Royal Society (1820), and foreign associate of the Académie des Sciences; and made notable donations for scientific research, including one thousand pounds to the Geological Society, which cast a die of his head for the "Wollaston Medal" (first given to William Smith, 1832), and has continued to be the annual prize of the Society.

WOLTMAN, REINHARD (*b. Axstedt, Germany, 1757; d. Hamburg, Germany, 1837*), hydraulics.

An expert in shore-erosion management; wrote two major books on hydraulics; invented the original "Woltman meter" for measuring the velocity of water currents (1790).

WOOD, HORATIO C. (*b. Philadelphia, Pa., 1841; d. Philadelphia, 1920*), pharmacology, therapeutics.

Received M.D. from University of Pennsylvania (1862), served in the Union Army, and entered private practice; held the chair of botany at the medical faculty of University of Pennsylvania (from 1866). Was a pioneer in experimental pharmacology and therapeutics; did extensive laboratory studies of the effects of drugs in animals. Wrote six medical books, including *Treatise on Therapeutics* . . . (1874); did prolific editorial work; and served as president of the U.S. Pharmacopeial Convention (1890–1910).

WOOD, ROBERT WILLIAMS (*b. Concord, Mass., 1868; d. Amityville, N.Y., 1955*), experimental physics.

Did undergraduate work at Harvard (B.A., 1891); did further study without obtaining a degree; taught at the University of Wisconsin (1897–1901) and at Johns Hopkins (from 1901). Was a brilliant experimenter; his spectroscopic studies were important in the development of atomic models, including Bohr's theory; investigated the optical properties of gases and vapors and the effect of magnetic and electric fields on spectrum lines. With A. L. Loomis researched high-frequency sound waves. Wrote *Physical Optics* (1905), *Supersonics, the Science of Inaudible Sounds* (1939), and the delightful *How to Tell the Birds From the Flowers* (1917).

WOODHOUSE, ROBERT (*b. Norwich, England, 1773; d. Cambridge, England, 1827*), mathematics.

Spent his entire career at Cambridge. His writings include *Principles of Analytical Calculation* (1803) and a text on trigonometry.

WOODWARD, JOHN (*b. Derbyshire, England, 1665; d. London, England, 1728*), geology, mineralogy, botany.

A physician and (from 1692) professor of physic at Gresham College, London. In experiments on plant nutrition (1691–92), achieved the first demonstration of transpiration; concluded that the food of plants is not water but mineral substances dissolved in the water. In *Essay Toward a Natural History of the Earth* (1695), argued persuasively that fossil organic remains in rocks derive from living plants or animals; focused attention on the worldwide similarity of geological strata. His 1729 catalogue of minerals and fossils was used for almost a century.

WOODWARD, ROBERT SIMPSON (*b. Rochester, Mich., 1849; d. Washington, D.C., 1924*), applied mathematics, geophysics.

Graduated from the University of Michigan (1872). Made several notable contributions while with the U.S. Geological Survey (1884–90), including studies of the cooling of homogeneous spheres and the diffusion of heat in rectangular masses; these led Woodward to criticize Kelvin's views on the earth's age. Taught at Columbia University (from 1893), and was president of the Carnegie Institution of Washington (1904–20).

WOOLLEY, CHARLES LEONARD (*b. Upper Clapton, London, England, 1880; d. London, 1960*), archaeology.

Graduated from New College, Oxford. Began his archaeological career as assistant to Sir Arthur Evans at the Ashmolean Museum. Directed excavations at Carchemish , Ur, Eridu, and al'Ubaid. His discovery of the great prehistoric cemetery at Ur inaugurated a brilliant revival of excavation in Mesopotamia. He wrote numerous successful books popularizing archaeology and ancient Mesopotamian history. Knighted in 1935.

WORM, OLE (or **OLAUS WORMIUS**) (*b. Aarhus, Jutland, Denmark, 1588; d. Copenhagen, Denmark, 1654*), natural history.

Received M.D. at Basel (1611). An eminent practicing physician, and professor at the University of Copenhagen; discovered the "Wormian bones" of the human skull. Was an expert on Danish antiquities, especially runes. His exotic natural history museum became a great popular attraction.

WORSAAE, JENS JACOB (*b. Vejle, Jutland, Denmark, 1821; d. Copenhagen, Denmark, 1885*), archaeology.

Became an assistant to C. J. Thomsen at age fifteen; succeeded him as director of the Museum of Northern Antiquities (now the National Museum) in 1865. In his excavation of prehistoric barrows, was able to classify them in Thomsen's three-age system (Stone Age, Bronze Age, Iron Age), a revolutionary achievement; his book on the antiquities of Denmark and England (1843) was extremely influential. Worsaae has been called the first full-time professional archaeologist. Taught archaeology at Copenhagen.

WOTTON, EDWARD (*b. Oxford, England, 1492; d. London, England, 1555*), medicine, natural history.

Studied at Magdalen College, Oxford, and Padua (M.D., 1526); became a distinguished London physician.

Wrote *De differentiis animalium* (1552), a zoological encyclopedia, essentially a learned but valuable compilation.

WOULFE, PETER (*b. Ireland [?], 1727 [?]; d. London, England, 1803*), chemistry.

His name is remembered for the familiar two-necked "Woulfe's bottle," which he seems to have used in distillation experiments (1767). He was a valued friend of Priestley; did many worthwhile chemical studies; achieved the first recorded preparation of picric acid.

WREN, CHRISTOPHER (*b. East Knoyle, Wiltshire, England, 1632; d. London, England, 1723*), mathematics, architecture.

One of the most accomplished men of his day in several branches of science and art. Was educated at Oxford, where he became closely associated with John Wilkins and the group that eventually became the Royal Society. Taught astronomy at Gresham College, London (1657–61), and at Oxford (1661–73); was an expert anatomist (did the drawings for Thomas Willis's *Cerebri anatome*); experimented with intravenous injections in living animals; was praised by Newton as a geometer (rectified the cycloid curve); gave a major report on the laws of impact to the Royal Society (1668); did pioneer investigations in meteorology and entomology. Is most famous as an architect; his buildings include St. Paul's Cathedral, London, the chapel of Pembroke College, Cambridge, and the Sheldonian Theatre at Oxford.

WRIGHT, ALMROTH EDWARD (*b. Middleton Tyas, Yorkshire, England, 1861; d. Farnham Common, Buckinghamshire, England, 1947*), pathology, bacteriology, immunology.

Earned a B.A. (1882) and a B.M. (1883) at Trinity College, Dublin; did further study and research abroad. As professor of pathology at the Army Medical School, Netley (1892–1902), did original work in blood coagulation and in bacteriology, discovering independently (1906) a vaccine against typhoid fever; was knighted for this achievement. At St. Mary's Hospital, London (1902–46), Wright developed a world-famous research center; Alexander Fleming was one of his workers. Wright originated vaccines against enteric tuberculosis and pneumonia, proved the worth of inoculations with dead microbes; studied opsonins. A notorious antifeminist, Wright was the model for Sir Colenso Ridgeon in Shaw's *The Doctor's Dilemma.*

WRIGHT, EDWARD (*b. Garveston, Norfolk, England, 1561; d. London, England, 1615*), mathematics, cartography.

A Cambridge-educated mathematician and navigator. An expedition to the Azores (1589) provided the inspiration for his book *Certaine Errors in Navigation* (1599). In it he presented the justification of the so-called Mercator map projection, a brilliant advance in cartography.

WRIGHT, FREDERICK EUGENE (*b. Marquette, Mich., 1877; d. Sagastaweka Island, near Garanoque, Ontario, Canada, 1953*), petrology.

Studied at Heidelberg (Ph.D., 1900); served as petrologist at the Carnegie Institution of Washington (1906–44). Contributed to the development of the petrographic microscope and its applications; did pioneer optical studies to determine the nature of materials on the surface of the moon.

WRIGHT, GEORGE FREDERICK (*b. Whitehall, N.Y., 1838; d. Oberlin, Ohio, 1921*), geology.

Educated at Oberlin College (B.A., 1859; M.A., 1862); became a Congregational minister and self-taught geologist; taught theology and geology at Oberlin College from 1881 to 1908; made extensive glacial investigations. Wrote on the glacial period and ancient man; argued for a relatively late end to the Ice Age and for the existence of man in North America during the Pleistocene.

WRIGHT, THOMAS (*b. Byers Green, near Durham, England, 1711; d. Byers Green, 1786*), astronomy.

A self-educated teacher of astronomy and navigation; was dedicated to reconciling the religious and scientific views of the universe. He assumed an identity between the moral and gravitational centers of the universe; proposed a disk-shaped model of the galaxy. Works include *Louthiana* (1748) and *An Original Theory or New Hypothesis of the Universe* (1750).

WRIGHT, WILBUR (*b. Millville, Ind., 1867; d. Dayton, Ohio, 1912*), and **WRIGHT, ORVILLE** (*b. Dayton, Ohio, 1871; d. Dayton, 1948*), aeronautics.

Sons of a bishop of the United Brethren Church; largely self-educated in science; set up the Wright Cycle Company (1892). Following the death of the pioneer aviator Otto Lilienthal (1896), they began to study flight; patented (1906) a fundamental system that achieved control about the airplane's three axes. After gliding trials at Kitty Hawk, North Carolina (1900, 1901), they designed a small wind tunnel to gather aerodynamic data; flew a powered airplane near the Kill Devil Hills, North Carolina, for 59 seconds (1903); after many rebuffs, gave successful demonstration flights in France and the United States (1909) that brought worldwide adulation. Wilbur Wright died of typhoid fever; after World War I, Orville devoted himself mainly to research.

WRIGHT, WILLIAM HAMMOND (*b. San Francisco, Calif., 1871; d. San Jose, Calif., 1959*), astronomy.

Worked for the Lick observatory from 1897 (as director, from 1935). Was a skillful designer of astronomical equipment, which he used to photograph the spectra of stars and nebulae; was the first to use six-color photography to study Mars.

WRÓBLEWSKI, ZYGMUNT FLORENTY VON (*b. Grodno, Lithuania, Russia, 1845; d. Cracow, Poland, 1888*), physics.

Famed mainly for his work on the liquefaction of gases done with K. S. Olszewski (1883).

WROŃSKI, JÓZEF MARIA. *See* **Hoëné-Wroński (or Hoehne), Józef Maria.**

WU, HSIEN (*b. Foochow, Fukien, China, 1893; d. Boston, Mass., 1959*), biochemistry, nutrition.

Studied at the Massachusetts Institute of Technology and at Harvard, where his doctoral dissertation (1919) reported techniques of blood analysis using small sam-

ples. Became China's foremost biochemist and nutrition scientist; renowned for the "Folin and Wu methods" of analysis. Returned to the United States, joining (1949) the Medical College of the University of Alabama.

WULFF, GEORG (**Yuri Viktorovich**) (*b. Nezhin, Russia [now Ukrainian S.S.R.], 1863; d. Moscow, U.S.S.R., 1925*), crystallography.

Had a distinguished teaching career in Poland and Russia; was professor at the University of Moscow (from 1918). Stimulated by Pierre Curie, he formulated (1916) the Curie-Wulff principle regarding the surface energies of crystals; also proposed the Wulff net method of stereographic projection of a sphere (1909); his goniometric research showed an essential deviation between ideal theory and the real crystal.

WUNDT, WILHELM (*b. Neckarau, Baden, Germany, 1832; d. Gross Bothen, Germany, 1920*), psychology.

Studied medicine at Heidelberg, becoming (1858) an assistant to Helmholtz; developed his lectures in "physiological psychology" into *Grundzüge der physiologischen Psychologie* (1873–74), which ran into many revised editions; appointed to professorships at Zurich (1874) and Leipzig (1875). Founded the first laboratory for experimental psychology; as a leader in establishing this discipline was enormously influential.

WURTZ, CHARLES-ADOLPHE (*b. Wolfisheim, near Strasbourg, France, 1817; d. Paris, France, 1884*), chemistry.

Took his doctorate in medicine at Strasbourg; studied under Liebig at Giessen; arrived in Paris in 1844 and joined Dumas at the Faculty of Medicine; succeeded him there in various posts. Was appointed (1874) to the chair of chemistry at the Sorbonne; was a brilliant teacher; in the 1870's attracted to his laboratory Le Bel, van't Hoff, and other giants of chemistry. Early championed the emerging concepts of atomicity and chemical types. In studies of the primary amines, he came to see that organic radicals could replace hydrogen without destroying the basic structure or type. Developed evidence supporting the theory that each molecule of hydrogen might comprise two equivalents or atoms of hydrogen, thus ratifying Avogadro's long-neglected molecular hypothesis. Wurtz's *La théorie atomique* (1879) included the idea of a characteristic combining power of the atoms; this when applied to the elements, precipitated the notion of valence.

WYMAN, JEFFRIES (*b. Chelmsford, Mass., 1814; d. Bethlehem, N.H., 1874*), anatomy, physiology.

Received his M.D. from Harvard Medical School (1837); returned (1847) to Harvard College as professor of anatomy and physiology; began a museum of anatomical specimens; became professor of American archaeology and ethnology (1866) and effectively the first director of the archaeological museum endowed by George Peabody. Noted for his work on the anatomy of gorillas, he supplied examples of natural selection used by Darwin. Among his students was William James.

XENOCRATES OF CHALCEDON (*b. Chalcedon, Bithynia [now Kadiköy, Turkey], ca. 396 B.C.; d. Athens, ca. 313 B.C.*), philosophy, mathematics.

A student of Plato and head of the Academy (from 339 B.C.). Produced a kind of codification of Plato's philosophy which was influential in the development of Neoplatonism.

XENOPHANES (*b. Colophon, Ionia, ca. 580–70* B.C.*; d. ca. 478* B.C.), theology, philosophy.

A poet and ardent advocate of the restoration of civil liberties to his native city; left Ionia after 545. Criticized anthropomorphic religion; proposed instead a single, omnipotent deity; maintained that man can have only probable knowledge of things; stimulated the emancipation of reason in theology and philosophy.

YAḤYĀ IBN ABĪ MANṢŪR (*d. near Aleppo, Syria, 832*), astronomy.

Of an important family of Persian scientists. He spent his life casting horoscopes and seeking methods to determine the positions of the stars with maximum precision. Under Caliph al-Maʾmūn, directed scholars at observatories in Baghdad and Damascus who were charged with the production of astronomical tables.

YAʿĪSH IBN IBRĀHĪM. *See* **Al-Umawī, Abū ʿAbdallāh Yaʿīsh ibn Ibrāhīm ibn Yūsuf ibn Simāk al-Andalusī.**

YANG HUI (*fl. China, ca. 1261–75*), mathematics.

Yang Hui was a great algebraist whose publications far surpassed those of his predecessors, yet all we know of his life is that he was a native of Ch'ien-t'ang (now Hangchow) and was probably a civil servant. The best known of his writings is *Hsiang-chieh chiu-chang suan-fa* ("Detailed Analysis of the Mathematical Rules in the Nine Chapters," 1261), a commentary on Liu Hui's classic *Chiu-chang suan-shu;* it gives detailed solutions to the problems, with occasional diagrams. This work contains the earliest illustration of the "Pascal triangle," showing the coefficients of the expansion of $(x + a)^n$ up to the sixth power; it also quotes a method of solving numerical equations higher than the second degree that is similar to that rediscovered independently by Ruffini and Horner for solving numerical equations of all orders by continuous approximation. His second work, *Jih-yung suan-fa* ("Mathematical Rules in Common Use," 1262), appears to be quite elementary.

The three works written in 1274–75 later came to be known under a single title, *Yang Hui suan-fa;* the collection was first printed in 1378. *Ch'eng-ch'u t'ung-pien pen-mo* ("Fundamental Mutual Changes in Multiplications and Divisions"; 3 vols., 1274) gives a detailed explanation of variations in the methods of multiplication, including the "additive" and "subtractive" methods; it shows how division can be conveniently replaced by multiplication by using the reciprocal of the divisor as the multiplier, and contains the first instance of division tables in Chinese mathematical texts. *T'ien-mou pi-lei ch'eng-ch'u chieh-fa* ("Practical Rules of Mathematics for Surveying"; 2 vols., 1275) is interesting mainly for its theory of equations; it contains the earliest explanations of the Chinese methods for solving quadratic equations, which may have been first derived geometrically by Yang Hui. The text shows that Yang Hui had a highly developed conception of decimal places, and preferred decimal fractions to common fractions. *Hsü-ku chai-ch'i suan-fa* ("Continuation of An-

cient Mathematical Methods for Elucidating the Strange Properties of Numbers," 1275) is the earliest Chinese text extant that gives magic squares higher than the third order and magic circles as well; it also deals with problems on indeterminate analysis, calendar computation, geometrical progressions, volumes and areas, and simultaneous linear equations of two and three unknowns.

IBN YAʿQŪB. *See* **Ibrāhīm ibn Yaʿqūb al-Isrāʾīlī al-Turṭushi.**

YAʿQŪB IBN ISḤĀQ. *See* **Al-Kindī, Abū Yūsuf Yaʿqūb ibn Isḥāq al-Ṣabbāḥ.**

YAʿQŪB IBN ṬĀRIQ (*fl. Baghdad, second half of the eighth century*), astronomy.

Was closely connected with (probably collaborated with) the Indian astronomer al-Fazārī in introducing the *Zīj al-Sindhind* to Islamic scientists.

YĀQŪT AL-ḤAMAWĪ AL-RŪMĪ, SHIHĀB AL-DĪN ABŪ ʿABDALLĀH YĀQŪT IBN ʿABD ALLĀH (*b. Rūm, Byzantine empire [now Turkey], 1179; d. Aleppo, Syria, 1229*), transmission of knowledge, geography.

Spent most of his life traveling in the Islamic world; earned his livelihood as a bookseller. As a biographer he was one of the outstanding scholars of medieval Islam (*Dictionary of the Learned Men*); equally concerned with geography, he wrote *Dictionary of the Lands,* an important historical and geographical reference work for scholars in the Islamic world as well as for Orientalists in the West.

YATIVṚṢABHA (*fl. India, sixth century*), cosmography, mathematics.

A Jain author; his *Tiloyapaṇṇattī,* a description of the universe, incorporates formulas representative of developments in Jain mathematics.

YAVANEŚVARA (*fl. western India, ca.* A.D. *150*), astrology, astronomy.

A Yavaneśvara was an official who acted on behalf of Greek merchants in western India (*ca.* the first four centuries A.D.). This Yavaneśvara translated a Greek astrology text into Sanskrit; it became a basic work in Indian horoscopy.

YERKES, ROBERT MEARNS (*b. Breadysville, Pa., 1876; d. New Haven, Conn., 1956*), comparative psychology.

Studied and taught psychology at Harvard (Ph.D., 1902); was largely in charge of U.S. Army psychological testing (1917–19); worked at the National Research Council (1919–24); affiliated with Yale (from 1924). By 1929, had founded an experimental station for the study of apes near Orange Park, Florida, which was the nucleus for the present Yerkes Regional Primate Research Center. With his wife wrote *The Great Apes: A Study of Anthropoid Life* (1929).

YERSIN, ALEXANDRE (*b. Aubonne, near Lausanne, Switzerland, 1863; d. Nha Trang, Annam, Vietnam, 1943*), medicine, bacteriology.

Joined the Institut Pasteur after Émile Roux saved his life with rabies serum; in Indochina, established a branch of the institute at Nha Trang and a study center in Hanoi. Developed independently an effective plague serum; also helped Indochina to control malaria.

YOUDEN, WILLIAM JOHN (*b. Townsville, Australia, 1900; d. Washington, D.C., 1971*), mathematical statistics.

Came to the United States in 1907; trained as a chemical engineer at the University of Rochester (B.S., 1921) and at Columbia (Ph.D., 1924); worked at the Boyce Thompson Institute for Plant Research at Yonkers, New York (1924–48), and at the National Bureau of Standards (1948–65). Took up statistical studies about 1928; began a "missionary" effort to acquaint research workers with statistical methods of value; created new experimental designs and statistical techniques, including "Youden squares" (an improvement on Latin square designs, broadly useful in biological and medical research), and "linked blocks" and "chain blocks" (for use in spectrographic chemical investigations).

YOUNG, CHARLES AUGUSTUS (*b. Hanover, N.H., 1834; d. Hanover, 1908*), astronomy.

His teaching posts included the Appleton professorship at Dartmouth (1866–77), a chair held by his father and grandfather before him. Specialized in solar research and spectroscopic studies; is credited with discovery of the "reversing layer" of the solar atmosphere (1870). Wrote several famous textbooks.

YOUNG, JOHN RICHARDSON (*b. Hagerstown, Md., 1782 [?]; d. Hagerstown, 1804*), physiology.

Remembered for his perspicacious M.D. thesis for the University of Pennsylvania on the digestive process (1803).

YOUNG, JOHN WESLEY (*b. Columbus, Ohio, 1879; d. Hanover, N.H., 1932*), mathematics, education.

His distinguished teaching career culminated at Dartmouth, where (from 1911) he modernized the mathematics department. Author of the excellent *Lectures on the Fundamental Concepts of Algebra and Geometry* (1911) and, with Oswald Veblen, volume I of *Projective Geometry* (1910). Instrumental in founding the Mathematical Association of America.

YOUNG, SYDNEY (*b. Farnworth, near Widnes, Lancashire, England, 1857; d. Bristol, England, 1937*), physical chemistry.

Studied at Owens College, Manchester; Strasbourg; and London University (D.Sc., 1883); taught at University College, Bristol (1882–1903). With William Ramsay, published an exhaustive series of researches concerning the vapor pressures of liquids; clarified crucial thermodynamic relationships for solids and liquids. Was also a pioneer in the separation and specification of pure organic compounds.

YOUNG, THOMAS (*b. Milverton, Somerset, England, 1773; d. London, England, 1829*), natural philosophy.

Young was raised as a member of the Society of Friends and was largely self-educated in languages and natural philosophy; later in life he formally became a member of the Church of England. He studied medicine at London, Edinburgh, Göttingen (M.D., 1796), and Emmanuel College, Cambridge (M.B., 1803; M.D., 1808). He practiced medicine in London, lectured on natural philosophy and the mechanical arts for the Royal Institution (1801–03), and in 1811 obtained a lifetime professional position as physician to St. George's Hospital. In the course of his very diverse writings Young made many "acute suggestions," as well as many ingenious "experimental illustrations" in physiological optics, the theory of light, mechanics, and Egyptian linguistics. In none of these fields, however, did he systematically develop his discoveries, hypotheses, or suggestions. Nor did he fully confront their implications. His failure to do this, despite the importance of some of his discoveries, partly accounts for his limited influence in science. He lived to see other men receive the credit and fame for completing what he had begun.

From 1791 to 1801 Young published most of his experiments and theories in physiological optics. He conjectured that the lens of the eye is composed of muscle fibers, and through his experiments refuted the opinions of Home, John Hunter, and Ramsden that accommodation of the eye to different distances was achieved by changes in the curvature of the cornea and the length of the eyeball. In 1801 he suggested that the retina responded to all colors in terms of variable amounts of three "principal colours"; Maxwell and Helmholtz later modified and extended his speculations into what has come to be called the Young-Helmholtz theory of color sensation.

Young's most sustained interest in natural philosophy was his attempt to gain acceptance for an undulatory theory of light. His failure was partly the result of hostile reviews and partly the result of the inherent limitations of his work. He never worked out a detailed mathematical theory; nor were his suggestions, except possibly for the principle of interference, influential on the man who did, Augustin Fresnel. Young's colleagues, however, quickly acknowledged the principle of interference as a major discovery. In 1802 Young made the first full announcement of this principle: ". . . whenever two portions of the same light arrive at the eye by different routes, either exactly or very nearly in the same direction, the light becomes most intense when the difference of the routes is any multiple of a certain length, and least intense in the intermediate state of the interfering portions; and this length is different for light of different colours."

Young described many of his mechanical discoveries and "suggestions" in his first book, *A Course of Lectures on Natural Philosophy and the Mechanical Arts* (1807), in which he juxtaposed lectures on motion, forces, and "passive strength" with ones on drawing, writing, modeling, and engraving; lectures on hydrostatics, hydraulics, and the friction of fluids with ones on hydraulic and pneumatic machines such as pumps, steam engines, and firearms; and lectures on astronomy, the physics of matter, electricity, and magnetism with ones on the study of meteors, vegetation, and animals. In his lecture "On Collision," he was probably the first person to suggest substituting the term "energy" for "living force" or *vis viva*. He defined a "modulus of elasticity" in his lecture "Passive Strength and Friction," which is almost impossibly obscure.

After Young ended his work on the theory of light he returned to his long-standing interest in languages. In

1813 he had started his attempts to decipher the Egyptian hieroglyphics, and by the following year he had translated the "enchorial" or demotic running script of the Rosetta Stone and had concluded that the enchorial was derived from the hieroglyphic. His final work was *Enchorial Egyptian Dictionary* (1830).

YOUNG, WILLIAM HENRY (*b. London, England, 1863; d. Lausanne, Switzerland, 1942*), mathematics.

Studied at Peterhouse, Cambridge; had a somewhat erratic academic career. Did fundamental work in the theory of real functions, the theory of Fourier series, and the basic differential calculus of functions of more than one variable; his textbook *The Fundamental Theorems of the Differential Calculus* (1910) has proved invaluable.

YULE, GEORGE UDNY (*b. Morham, near Haddington, Scotland, 1871; d. Cambridge, England, 1951*), statistics.

Taught statistics at University College, London, and at Cambridge (from 1912). His memoirs on correlation (1897, 1907) and association (1900) have proved to be fundamental; with Major M. Greenwood, laid the foundations of the theory of accident distributions. His first book, *An Introduction to the Theory of Statistics* (1911), was long the only comprehensive text on the subject; his paper on sunspots (1927) is a basic document in the study of oscillatory time series.

IBN YŪNUS, ABU'L-ḤASAN ᶜALĪ IBN ᶜABD AL-RAḤMĀN IBN AḤMAD IBN YŪNUS AL-ṢADAFĪ (*d. Fusṭāṭ, Egypt, 1009*), astronomy, mathematics.

One of the greatest astronomers of medieval Islam; also an astrologer and a widely acclaimed poet. His major work is *al-Zīj al-Ḥākimī al-kabīr,* a *zīj* being an astronomical handbook with tables; unlike other extant *zījes,* it begins with a list of observations made by Ibn Yūnus and by some of his predecessors. The observations described by Ibn Yūnus are of conjunctions of planets with each other and with Regulus, solar and lunar eclipses, and equinoxes; he also records measurements of the obliquity of the ecliptic and of the maximum lunar latitude; in spherical astronomy he reached a high level of sophistication; elegant solutions are presented for finding the meridian from three solar observations on the same day and for finding the time between two such solar observations. He appears also to be the author of tables of the sine and tangent functions for each minute of arc, tables of solar declination for each minute of solar longitude, and tables that display the equations of the sun and moon. He computed part of the corpus of spherical astronomical tables for timekeeping used in Cairo until the nineteenth century.

ZABARELLA, JACOPO (*b. Padua, Italy, 1533; d. Padua, 1589*), natural philosophy, scientific method.

Spent his adult life at the University of Padua; was a major figure in the Renaissance revival of Aristotelianism. Focused on biological rather than mathematical aspects of nature; was considered a leading authority on logic and scientific method. Works include *Opera logica* (1578) and *De rebus naturalibus* (1590).

ZACH, FRANZ XAVER VON (*b. Pest [now part of Budapest], Hungary, 1754; d. Paris, France, 1832*), astronomy.

Directed an observatory on the Seeberg near Gotha, built for him by Duke Ernst II of Saxe-Coburg. Had a gift for organizing ventures involving contributions from numerous observers.

ZACUTO (or ZACUT), ABRAHAM BAR SAMUEL BAR ABRAHAM (*b. Salamanca, Spain, ca. 1450; d. Portugal, ca. 1522*), astrology, astronomy.

A renowned astrologer in Salamanca; forced as a Jew to leave Spain; in Portugal (after 1492), helped king John II in developing the art of navigation. Wrote *Almanach perpetuum* (1496); computed tables of solar declination used by Vasco da Gama.

AL-ZAHRĀWĪ, ABU'L-QĀSIM KHALAF IBN ᶜABBĀS, also known as **Abulcasis** (*b. al-Zahrāʾ, near Córdoba, Spain, ca. 936; d. al-Zahrāʾ, ca. 1013*), medicine, pharmacology.

The most advanced surgeon of the Middle Ages until the thirteenth century, and a great educator and psychiatrist. Invented surgical instruments; was the first to recommend surgical removal of a broken patella and to practice lithotomy on women; ligatured arteries and discussed threads and catguts for suturing. Wrote a comprehensive medical encyclopedia, *al-Taṣrīf,* highly regarded in the West. Attempted to separate medical practice from alchemy, theology, and philosophy, advocating specialization in the health professions.

ZAKARIYĀ IBN MUḤAMMAD IBN MAḤMŪD. *See* **Al-Qazwīnī, Zakariyā ibn Muḥammad ibn Maḥmūd, Abū Yaḥyā.**

ZALUŽANSKÝ ZE ZALUŽAN, ADAM (*b. Mnichovo Hradištĕ, Bohemia [now Czechoslovakia], ca. 1558; d. Prague, Bohemia, 1613*), botany, medicine.

Was a teacher and administrator at Charles University; after 1594, was occupied with a medical practice in Prague. In his botanical treatise, *Methodi herbariae* (3 vols., 1592), he argued that botany should be an independent branch of science.

ZAMBECCARI, GIUSEPPE (*b. Castelfranco di Sotto, Italy, 1655; d. Pisa, Italy, 1728*), medicine.

A professor at Pisa. His most original work was done at Florence, where he experimented with removing organs from live animals in order to study the organs' functions.

ZAMBONINI, FERRUCCIO (*b. Rome, Italy, 1880; d. Naples, Italy, 1932*), chemistry, mineralogy.

The leading mineralogist in Italy of his period; among several teaching posts, held the chair of general chemistry at Naples (from 1923). Noted for studies of volcanic products, rare earths, isomorphism between ions of similar radii (Zambonini's rule), and optical properties of mixed crystals.

ZANOTTI, EUSTACHIO (*b. Bologna, Italy, 1709; d. Bologna, 1782*), astronomy, geometry.

Succeeded his godfather and teacher, Eustachio Manfredi, as director of the observatory at the University of Bologna (1739). Was a productive astronomer and an expert in hydraulics and geometry, and wrote an important work on perspective (1766).

ZARANKIEWICZ, KAZIMIERZ (*b. Czestochowa, Poland, 1902; d. London, England, 1959*), mathematics.

Took his Ph.D. at the University of Warsaw (1923); spent most of his teaching career at the Warsaw Polytechnic; was active in the International Astronautical Federation. His contributions in mathematics were in topology (mainly with regard to cut points and continua); in the theory of graphs; in the theory of complex functions (principally with regard to the kernel, *Kernfunktion,* and its applications); and in number theory (especially triangular numbers).

AL-ZARQĀLĪ (or **AZARQUIEL), ABŪ ISḤĀQ IBRĀHĪM IBN YAḤYĀ AL-NAQQĀSH** (*d. Córdoba, Spain, 1100*), astronomy.

An instrument maker and astronomer in Toledo and (after *ca.* 1078) in Córdoba. Constructed the water clocks of Toledo, predecessors of later planetary calendar devices; determined the longitude of Calbalazada (Regulus) in 1080 and the culmination of the planets (1081). His writings include the Toledan Tables, extraordinarily successful in the Latin world; a work based on twenty-five years of observations in which he discovered the proper motion of the solar apogee; a work on the trepidation theory, designed to explain the motion of the sphere of the fixed stars; and a work on the planets, in which he apparently anticipated Kepler by giving Mercury an "oval" orbit.

ZAVADOVSKY, MIKHAIL MIKHAYLOVICH (*b. Pokrovka, Kherson guberniya [now Kirovograd], Russia, 1891; d. Moscow, U.S.S.R., 1957*), biology.

Studied at Moscow University (M.S., 1918); associated with the First Moscow State University (1930–48). Specialized in experimental parasitology and research on the development of sex characteristics.

ZAVARZIN, ALEKSEY ALEKSEEVICH (*b. St. Petersburg, Russia [now Leningrad, U.S.S.R.], 1886; d. Leningrad, 1945*), histology, biology, embryology.

Studied at St. Petersburg; held numerous professorships in histology and embryology. Noted for works in which he developed the evolutionary trend in histology.

AL-ZAYYĀTĪ AL-GHARNĀṬĪ, AL-ḤASAN IBN MUḤAMMAD AL-WAZZĀN. *See* **Leo the African.**

ZEEMAN, PIETER (*b. Zonnemaire, Zeeland, Netherlands, 1865; d. Amsterdam, Netherlands, 1943*), physics.

Studied at the University of Leiden (doctorate, 1893), becoming H. A. Lorentz's assistant (1890). Interested in magnetic-optic phenomena, he interrupted his measurements of the Kerr effect (successfully completed a little later) to try to detect some change in the spectrum of a sodium flame burning in a magnetic field; initially failed, but repeated the experiment after a year (having learned that Faraday had tried the same approach). This time (1896) he observed a broadening of spectral lines, demonstrably caused by the magnetic field; further investigation showed that this Zeeman effect was beautifully comprehended by Lorentz's electromagnetic theory, which predicted related effects also discovered by Zeeman; for this work, both men shared the 1902 Nobel Prize for physics. From 1897 to 1935, Zeeman was at the University of Amsterdam, where a prolonged lack of appropriate equipment forced him to change the direction of his research; he studied the velocity of propagation of light in moving transparent media, ultimately confirming (1915–16) the Lorentz rather than the Fresnel expression. Established (1918) an equality of the inertial and gravitational mass for certain crystals and radioactive substances to within one part in twenty or thirty million; returned to studies of the Zeeman effect after 1923.

ZEILLER, RENÉ CHARLES (*b. Nancy, France, 1847; d. Paris, France, 1915*), paleobotany.

An eminent civil engineer (became president of the Conseil Général des Mines, 1911) and paleobotanist (taught at the École des Mines in Paris, from 1878); was especially interested in the Cycadofilicales.

ZEISE, WILLIAM CHRISTOPHER (*b. Slagelse, Denmark, 1789; d. Copenhagen, Denmark, 1847*), chemistry.

Taught chemistry at the University of Copenhagen (from 1822). Noted for his studies of organic sulfur compounds which led to the discovery of a new class of organic compounds (xanthates); played a role in the Dumas-Liebig dispute.

ZEJSZNER (or **Zeuschner), LUDWIK** (*b. Warsaw, Poland, 1805; d. Cracow, Poland, 1871*), geology.

The first Polish geologist in the modern sense. Took his doctorate at Heidelberg (1829); headed the mineralogy department at the University of Cracow (1830–33, 1848–57) and worked in the civil service. His first published treatise (1829) supported the magma origin of basalt; he specialized in field surveys of Poland, made thousands of barometric measurements, and studied the temperature of the springs in the Carpathian Mountains.

ZELINSKY, NIKOLAY DMITRIEVICH (*b. Tiraspol, Kherson province [now Moldavian S.S.R.], Russia, 1861; d. Moscow, U.S.S.R., 1953*), chemistry.

While working with Victor Meyer at Göttingen, accidentally synthesized mustard gas, becoming its first victim; later developed a universal gas mask. Taught at Moscow University from 1893 to 1953 (except 1911–17). Specialized in the chemistry of hydrocarbons and organic catalysis. Confirmed the organic theory of the origin of petroleum from plant and animal materials.

ZEMPLÉN, GÉZA (*b. Trencsén, Hungary [now Trenčín, Czechoslovakia], 1883; d. Budapest, Hungary, 1956*), organic chemistry.

Named professor at the Technical University of Budapest at age twenty-nine. Specialized in research on carbohydrates. Devised methods for establishing the structure of the disaccharides and for the production of oligosaccharides.

ZENODORUS (*b. Athens [?]; fl. early second century* B.C.), mathematics.

Was the author of a treatise on isoperimetric figures, now known only through other texts. Was apparently also an astronomer and posed a question to Diocles regarding what mirror surface would reflect the sun's rays to meet a point and cause burning.

ZENO OF CITIUM (*b. Citium, Cyprus, ca. 335* B.C.; *d. Athens, 263* B.C.), philosophy.

Of a Phoenician family; studied in Athens; set up his own school there (*ca.* 300 B.C.), called Stoic because he taught in the Stoa Poikile ("Painted Colonnade") the school survived until at least A.D. 260. The main emphasis of Stoic teaching was moral, and Stoicism had a wide acceptance in the Roman republic and the empire. In ethics, it identified goodness with virtue of the soul, and virtue with wisdom, especially the understanding of nature. It regarded the cosmos as a single material continuum, held together by a tendency of matter to contract upon its own center (a model that resembles a field theory); the interconnection of events in the continuum constitutes fate; the active elements in the cosmos he referred to collectively as "God". He taught that periodically the cosmos is consumed by the divine fiery *pneuma* and then formed again.

ZENO OF ELEA (*b. Elea, Lucania, ca. 490* B.C.; *d. Elea, ca. 425* B.C.), philosophy, mathematics.

A friend and disciple of Parmenides; according to legend, tortured and killed by a tyrant of Elea or Syracuse, against whom he had conspired. As reported by Diogenes Laërtius, Zeno developed a cosmology in which there existed several "worlds" composed of "warm" and "cold," "dry" and "wet," but no empty space. Zeno is best known, however, for his attempt to provide indirect evidence for Parmenides' view that only the (unchanging) One exists; to this end, Zeno presented some forty paradoxes designed to show that the assumption of plurality and motion leads to strange consequences; his paradoxes were all apparently based on analyses of the continuum. The most famous of his forty paradoxes asserts that in a race between Achilles and the tortoise, the former can never catch up with the latter; although Achilles may run a hundred times faster than the tortoise, by the time he has reached the tortoise's starting point, the tortoise will have traveled 1/100 of the original distance, and so on ad infinitum. In an alternate version, Achilles cannot even begin; the principle is similar to that which Zeno used in the paradox of the flying arrow that cannot move: At any given instant, the arrow occupies a space equal to its size; it cannot occupy a larger space or two spaces; and since there is nothing between one instant and the next, and the arrow cannot move in an instant, it cannot move at all. Mathematicians are still debating the correct solution.

ZENO OF SIDON (*b. Sidon, ca. 150* B.C.; *d. Athens, ca. 70* B.C.), philosophy, mathematics, logic.

Evidently a prolific writer and polymath. Made trenchant criticisms of Euclid's axiomatics. Against the Stoics, defended a version of Epicurean epistemology that anticipates J. S. Mill's theory of induction.

ZERMELO, ERNST FRIEDRICH FERDINAND (*b. Berlin, Germany, 1871; d. Freiburg im Breisgau, Germany, 1953*), mathematics.

Studied at Halle and Freiburg. Received his doctorate (1894) from Berlin with a dissertation on the calculus of variations; taught at Göttingen, Zurich, and Freiburg im Breisgau (from 1926, except 1935–46). In set theory, found his sensational proof of the well-ordering theorem (1904) after study of Cantor and conversations with Er-

hard Schmidt. Also (1908) set up an axiom system for Cantor's set theory that has proved of great importance in mathematics.

ZERNIKE, FRITS (*b. Amsterdam, Netherlands, 1888; d. Naarden, near Amsterdam, 1966*), physics.

An ingenious theoretician and technician; associated with the University of Groningen (1913–58). In the wave theory of light, introduced Zernike polynomials (the set of polynomials orthogonal on a circle); best-known for his method of phase contrast in wave theory, for which he received the Nobel Prize in physics (1953).

ZEUNER, GUSTAV ANTON (*b. Chemnitz, Germany [now Karl-Marx-Stadt, German Democratic Republic], 1828; d. Dresden, Germany, 1907*), mechanical engineering, thermodynamics.

Had a distinguished academic career, retiring (1890) as director of the Dresden Polytechnical Institute; Wilhelm Röntgen was among his students. Specialized in theoretical aspects of the steam engine; wrote a major text on thermodynamics (1860) which presented the first synthesis into a consistent system of the first and second laws of thermodynamics.

ZEUTHEN, HIERONYMUS GEORG (*b. Grimstrup, West Jutland, Denmark, 1839; d. Copenhagen, Denmark, 1920*), mathematics, history of mathematics.

Spent his entire academic career at the University of Copenhagen. Specialized in enumerative methods in geometry and the history of mathematics. Was editor of *Tidsskrift for Mathematik* (1871–1889).

ZHUKOVSKY, NIKOLAY EGOROVICH (*b. Orekhovo, Vladimir province, Russia, 1847; d. Moscow, U.S.S.R., 1921*), mechanics, mathematics.

Is called "the father of Russian aviation." Studied at the University of Moscow (doctorate, 1882); taught there and at the Moscow Technical School, where he taught special courses for pilots during World War I; became (1918) head of the N. E. Zhukovsky Academy of Military and Aeronautical Engineering (as it was called after 1922). Did important work in hydrodynamics in the 1880's; by 1890 was studying flight in heavier-than-air machines; the Zhukovsky-Chaplygin postulate (1910) enabled a solution to the problem of lift and the development of a profile for airplane wings.

ZININ, NIKOLAY NIKOLAEVICH (*b. Shusha, Transcaucasia [now Azerbaydzhan, S.S.R.], Russia, 1812; d. St. Petersburg, Russia, 1880*), chemistry.

Taught at the St. Petersburg Academy of Medicine and Surgery (1848–74). Investigated the aromatic compounds; He is known primarily for his research on the reduction of nitro compounds into amino derivatives by the action of ammonium sulfide. his research was later important in the creation of the aniline dye industry.

ZINSSER, HANS (*b. New York, N.Y., 1878; d. New York, 1940*), bacteriology, immunology.

Of a cultured German immigrant family; his writings include poetry, two engaging popular books, *Rats, Lice and History* (1935) and the autobiographical *As I Remember Him* (1940), as well as the successful technical works *Text-*

book of Bacteriology (1910) and Infection and Resistance (1914). Zinsser studied medicine at Columbia University (M.D., 1903), and taught at Columbia, Stanford, and (from 1923) at Harvard. Specialized in the study of typhus, especially Brill's disease (now Brill-Zinsser disease); also did important work on the nature of the antigen-antibody reaction, the etiology of rheumatic fever and on delayed hypersensitivity and allergy.

ZIRKEL, FERDINAND (b. Bonn, Germany, 1838; d. Bonn, 1912), geology, petrography, mineralogy.

Was professor at Lemberg (now Lvov), Kiel, and Leipzig (1870–1909). Is one of the founders of petrographic microscopy.

ZITTEL, KARL ALFRED VON (b. Bahlingen, Baden, Germany, 1839; d. Munich, Germany, 1904), paleontology, geology, history of geology.

The leading teacher of paleontology of his era; was associated with the University of Munich (from 1866). Wrote Handbuch der Palaeontologie (1876–93), a four-volume encyclopedia covering all forms of fossils; Grundzüge der Paläontologie (1895); and Geschichte der Geologie und Paläontologie (1899).

ZÖLLNER, JOHANN KARL FRIEDRICH (b. Berlin, Germany, 1834; d. Leipzig, Germany, 1882), astrophysics.

In connection with research for his Ph.D. (awarded at Basel, 1859), invented the astrophotometer; also designed the reversion spectroscope (1869) and the horizontal pendulum. Despite important contributions to the development of spectroscopy, to the theory of comets, and to other fields, Zöllner became increasingly isolated from the scientific community, in part because an obsession with Spiritualism.

ZOLOTAREV, EGOR IVANOVICH (b. St. Petersburg, Russia [now Leningrad, U.S.S.R.], 1847; d. St. Petersburg, 1878), mathematics.

Spent most of his brief adult life at the University of St. Petersburg. Produced fundamental works on mathematical analysis and number theory.

ZOSIMUS OF PANOPOLIS (b. Panopolis [now Akhmīm], Egypt; d. Alexandria, Egypt; fl. ca. A.D. 300), alchemy.

Apparently the earliest alchemist mentioned as an author in the Greek alchemical texts; his writings (not yet adequately studied) are imbued with mysticism.

ZSIGMONDY, RICHARD ADOLF (b. Vienna, Austria, 1865; d. Göttingen, Germany, 1929), colloidal chemistry.

A figure of paramount importance in his field. Took his Ph.D. at Munich (1890). In a period of private research (1900–07), invented the ultramicroscope and produced classic studies of gold sols, for which he was awarded the Nobel Prize (1925). Taught at Göttingen (from 1907).

ZUBOV, NIKOLAY NIKOLAEVICH (b. Izmail, Russia [now Ukrainian S.S.R.], 1885; d. Moscow, U.S.S.R., 1960), oceanography.

Trained as a naval officer and hydrographer; studied at the geophysics institute at Bergen, Norway. Took a leading role in many expeditions to the Soviet Union's northern seas. Specialized in research on the vertical mixing of sea water, ocean currents, and sea ice; emphasized the unity of the "air-ice-water" system. Created the world's first department of oceanology at the Hydrometeorological Center of the U.S.S.R. (1931). Taught oceanology at the University of Moscow (1949–60).

ZUBOV, VASILY PAVLOVICH (b. Aleksandrov, Ivanovo province [now Ivanovskaya oblast], Russia, 1899; d. Moscow, U.S.S.R., 1963), history of science.

Specialized in the history of physics, mathematics, and mechanics, especially of the Middle Ages and Renaissance. Associated (from 1945) with the U.S.S.R. Academy of Sciences.

ZUCCHI, NICCOLÒ (b. Parma, Italy, 1586; d. Rome, Italy, 1670), optics, astronomy.

A high-ranking Jesuit; met Kepler at the court of Emperor Ferdinand II. Is remembered for his invention of an early reflecting telescope with which he made observations of the spots on Mars.

IBN ZUHR, ABŪ MARWĀN ʿABD AL-MALIK IBN ABI'L-ʿALĀʾ (Latin, **ABHOMERON** or **AVENZOAR**) (b. Seville, Spain, ca. 1092; d. Seville, 1162), medicine.

Of a family of famous scholars and physicians; served in the courts of the Murābits (Almoravids) and their successors, the Muwaḥḥids. Was one of the best Muslim physicians in Spain; his writings remained influential in the West until the Renaissance.

ZWELFER, JOHANN (b. Rhenish Palatinate, 1618; d. Vienna, Austria [?], 1668), pharmacy, chemistry.

A pharmacist and physician. Received his M.D. at Padua and settled in Vienna. Famous for his abusive but well-founded commentary (1652) on the Pharmacopoeia Augustana, the standard official German pharmacopoeia.

Lists of Scientists By Field*

ASTRONOMY

Abetti
Abney
Abraham Bar Ḥiyya
Abū Ma'Shar
Abu'l-Wafā'
Acuta Pisārati
Adams, J. C.
Adams, W. S.
Adelard of Bath
Ailly
Airy
Aitken
Albertus Magnus
Albrecht
Alfonso El Sabio
Alzate y Ramírez
Anaximander
Andoyer
André
Angelus
Ångström
Anthelme
Antoniadi
Apian
Arago
Aratus of Soli
Argelander
Argoli
Aristarchus of Samos
Aristotle
Aristyllus
Arrest
Āryabhata I
Āryabhata II
Asada Gōryū
Autolycus of Pitane
Auwers, A. J. G. F. von
Auzout

Baade
Backlund
Bacon, R.
Bailey, S. I.
Bailly
Baily
Banachiewicz
Banū Mūsā
Barbier
Barnard
Barocius
Al-Battānī
Bayer
Beer
Benzenberg
Bergman
Bernard of Le Treille
Bernard of Verdun
Bernoulli, Jakob I

Bernoulli, Johann (Jean) III
Berti
Bessel
Bhāskara I
Bhāskara II
Bickerton
Biela
Bigourdan
Billy
Birmingham
Birt
Al-Bīrūnī
Al-Bitrūjī
Blazhko
Bochart de Saron
Bode
Boguslavsky
Bond, G. P.
Bond, W. C.
Borelli
Boškovic
Boss
Boulliau
Bour
Bouvard
Bowditch, N.
Bradley, J.
Brahe
Brahmadeva
Brahmagupta
Brandes
Bravais
Bredikhin
Bredon
Bremiker
Brendel
Brinkley
Brisbane
Brooks, W. R.
Brouwer, D.
Brown, E. W.
Bruhns
Brytte
Buot
Bürg
Bürgi
Burnham
Burrau
Busch

Calandrelli, G.
Calandrelli, I.
Caldas
Callandreau
Callippus
Campani
Campanus of Novara
Campbell, W. W.

Camus
Cannon, A. J.
Capra
Carrington
Cassini, G. D.
Cassini, J.
Cassini, J. D.
Cassini de Thury
Castelli
Cauchy
Cayley
Celcius
Challis
Chandler
Chappe d'Auteroche
Chaucer
Chazy
Chevallier, T.
Christie, W. H. M.
Christmann
Clairaut
Claude, F. A.
Clausen
Clavius
Cleomedes
Comas Solá
Common
Comrie
Comstock
Conon of Samos
Copernicus
Cosserat
Cotes
Cowell
Crabtree
Crommelin
Curtis
Curtiss
Cysat

Dalencé
D'Arcy
Darwin, G. H.
Dasabala
Dasypodius
Dawes
Delambre
De La Rue
Delaunay
Delisle, J. N.
Delporte
Dembowski
Deslandres
Dinakara
Dionis du Séjour
Dixon, J.
Dominicus de Clavasio
Donati

Dondi
Doppelmayer
Doppler
Dörffel
Dorno
Dorotheus of Sidon
Dositheus
Downing
Draper, H.
Dreyer
Dudith
Dugan
Duncan
Dunér
Dyson

Easton
Eckert
Eddington
Elkin
Ellis
Emanuelli
Embden, R.
Encke
Esclangon
Euclid
Euctemon
Eudoxus of Cnidus
Euler
Evershed
Ibn Ezra

Fabry, L.
Al-Farghānī
Faye
Al-Fazārī
Ferguson
Ferrel
Feuillée
Fine, O.
Fink
Firmicus Maternus
Flammarion
Flamsteed
Fleming, W. P.
Fontenelle
Foster, H.
Fouchy
Fowler, A.
Frenicle de Bessy
Freundlich, E. F.
Frisi
Frost
Fusoris
Fuss

*Initials, first names, or dates are given for those scientists with the same surname.

749

Gaillot
Galilei, G.
Galle
Gaṇeśa
Gascoigne
Gassendi
Gauss
Geminus
Gerard of Silteo
Gerasimovich
Giles of Lessines
Giles of Rome
Gill, D.
Glaisher, J. W. L.
Godin
Goodricke
Gould, B. A.
Graff
Gregory D.
Gregory J.
Grimaldi
Grisogono
Grossmann, E. A. F. W.

Ḥabash al-Ḥāsib
Hale, G. E.
Hall, A.
Halley
Halm
Hamy
Hansen, P. A.
Hansky
Hansteen
Harding
Haridatta I
Haridatta II
Harkness
Harriot
Hartmann, J. F.
Hartwig
Ibn al-Haytham
Hell
Helmert
Henderson, T.
Henry Bate of Malines
Henry of Hesse
Henry, P. M.
Henry, P. P.
Heraclides Ponticus
Hermann the Lame
Hermes Trismegistus
Herschel, C. L.
Herschel, J. F. W.
Herschel, W.
Hertzsprung
Hevelius
Ibn Hibintā
Hicetas of Syracuse
Hill, G. W.
Hind
Hipparchus of Rhodes
Hippocrates of Chios
Hirayama
Hoek
Holden
Horn d'Arturo
Hornsby
Horrebow, C.
Horrebow, P. N.
Horrocks
Hortensius
Hoüel
Hough
Hubble
Hufnagel

Humboldt
Huggins
Hussey
Huygens
Hypsicles of Alexandria

Ibrāhīm Ibn Sinān
Idelson
Innes
Inō

Jābir ibn Aflaḥ
Jagannātha
Janssen
Al-Jawharī
Jayasiṃha
Al-Jayyānī
Jeans
Jeaurat
Johannes Lauratius de Fundis
John of Gmunden
John of Lignères
John of Murs
John of Saxony
John of Sicily
John Simonis of Selandia
Johnson, M. J.

Kaiser
Kamalākara
Kanaka
Kapteyn
Al-Kāshī
Kavraysky
Keckermann
Keeler
Kepler
Keśava
Al-Khalīlī
Al-Khayyāmī
Al-Khāzin
Al-Khāzinī
Al-Khujandī
Al-Khwārizmī
Kimura
Kirch, G.
Kirch, M. M. W.
Kirch, Christfried
Kirch, Christine
Kirkwood, D.
Klein, H. J.
Konkoly Thege
Kostinsky
Kovalsky
Kramp
Kṛṣṇa
Kushyār

Lacaille
Lagrange
La Hire, G. P. de
La Hire, P. de
Lalande
Lalla
Lambert
Lamont

Langley
Lansberge
Laplace
Lassell
Lāṭadeva
Lau, H. E.
Lavanha
Leavitt
Le Fèvre
Le Gentil
Le Monnier, P. C.
Leo the Mathematician
Le Verrier
Levi ben Gerson
Lexell
Liesganig
Lindblad
Lindenau
Lippmann
Lockyer
Lohse
Loomis
Lorenzoni
Lowell
Ludendorff
Luther
Lyman, C. S.
Lyot

Maanen
Maclear
Macmillan
Mädler
Magini
Mahtādeva
Al-Māhānī
Mahendra Sūri
Al-Majrīṭī
Makaranda
Maksutov
Manfredi
Manilius
Manṣūr
Maraldi, G. F.
Maraldi, G. D.
Markgraf
Martianus Capella
Māshā'allāh
Maskelyne
Mason
Mästlin
Mathurānātha Sárman
Maunder
Maurer
Maurolico
Maury, A.
Mayer, C.
Mayer, J. T.
Mayr
Méchain
Melvill
Menelaus of Alexandria
Mercator
Messier
Meton
Michael Scot
Michell
Miller, W. A.
Milne, E. A.
Mineur
Minnaert
Mitchell, M.
Möbius, A. F.
Moiseev
Moll, G.

Möller
Mollweide
Molyneux, S.
Molyneux, W.
Montanari
Monte
Moore, J. H.
Morgan, H. R.
Morin
Mouchez
Moulton
Mouton
Muḥyi 'l-Dīn
Müller, G.
Munīśvara Viśvarūpa
Muñjāla
Mutis y Bossio

Nāgeśa
Nasmyth
Al-Nayrīzī
Neuymin
Newall
Newcomb
Newton, H. A.
Newton, I.
Nicholson, J. W.
Nicholson, S. B.
Nicolai
Niesten
Nīlakaṇṭha
Nostradamus
Novara
Numerov
Nuñez Salaciense

Odierna
Oenopedes of Chios
Olbers
Olufsen
Oppenheim
Oppolzer
Orlov, A. Y.
Orlov, S. V.
Outhier

Palisa
Pannekoek
Pappus of Alexander
Parameśvara
Parenago
Parkhurst
Parsons
Paul of Alexandria
Pauliśa
Pease
Peirce, B.
Peiresc
Pereira, B.
Pérez de Vargas
Perrine
Perrotin
Peter Philomena of Dacia
Peters, C. F. W.
Peters, C. A. F.
Peters, C. H. F.
Petit, J.
Petosiris
Peurbach

Pezenas
Phillips, T. E. R.
Philolaus of Crotona
Piazzi
Picard, J.
Pickering, E. C.
Pickering, W. H.
Pigott, E.
Pigott, N.
Pingré
Plana
Plaskett
Plato of Tivoli
Plummer, H. C.
Poincaré
Poleni
Pons
Poor
Poretsky
Powalky
Pritchard
Proclus
Proctor
Ptolemy
Puiseux
Pythagoras of Samos

Al-Qabīsī
Qāḍī Zāda
Al-Qūhī
Quṭb al-Dīn

Rāghavānanda Śarman
Ramus
Rañganātha
Ranyard
Rayet
Raymond of Marseilles
Regiomontanus
Reinhold
Respighi
Rheita
Rheticus
Ricci, Matteo
Riccioli
Riccò
Richard of Wallingford
Richer
Ritchey
Rittenhouse
Roberts
Roche

Roger of Hereford
Römer
Rooke
Rosenberg
Rosenberger, O. A.
Ross, F. E.
Rosse (Parsons)
Rothmann
Rumford (Thompson, B.)
Rumovsky
Ibn Rushd
Russell, H. N.
Russell, H. C.
Rutherfurd

Sacrobosco
St. John
Saint Vincent
Al-Samarqandī (fl. 1276)
Ṣampson
Satānanda
Schaeberle
Scheiner, C.
Scheiner, J.
Schiaparelli
Schickard
Schjellerup
Schlesinger
Schmidt, C. A. von
Schmidt, J. F. J.
Schöner
Schönfeld
Schröter
Schumacher
Schwabe
Schwarzschild
Seares
Secchi
See
Seeliger
Seidel
Severin
Shakerley
Shapley
Sharonov
Ibn al-Shāṭir
Shayn
Shen Kua
Shibukawa
Shirakatsí
Sigüenza y Góngora
Al-Sijzī
Simon de Phares
Ibn Sīnā
Sinān

Sitter
Slipher, E.
Slipher, V. M.
Smyth
Snel
Soldner
Somerville
Sosigenes
South
Spencer, J. H.
Sphujidhvaja
Ṣpoerer
Śrīpati
Stein
Steinheil
Stephan
Stephanus of Alexandria
Stepling
Sternberg, P. K.
Stewart, M.
Stratton
Streete
Strömberg
Strömgren
Struve, F. G. W.
Struve, G. O. H.
Struve, G. W. L.
Struve, K. H.
Struve, O.
Struve, O. W.
Subbotin
Al-Ṣūfī
Sundman
Synesius of Cyrene

Tacchini
Tarde
Thābit ibn Qurra
Theodosius of Bithynia
Theon of Alexandria
Theon of Smyrna
Thiele, T. N.
Thollon
Ibn Tibbon, J.
Tikhov
Tisserand
Titius
Toscanelli dal Pozzo
Trouvelot
Trumpler
Tserasky
Turner, H. H.
Al-Tūsī (Naṣir al-Dīn)
Al-Tūsī (Sharaf al-Dīn)

Ulugh Beg
'Umar ibn al-Farrukhān

Varāhamihira
Vaṭeśvara
Vijayananda
Vogel

Ibn Waḥshiyya
Wang Hsi-Shan
Ward
Wargentin
Waterston
Wendelin
Werner, J.
Wharton, G.
Whewell
Wilhelm IV
William of Saint-Cloud
William the Englishman
Wilsing
Wilson, Alexander (d. 1786)
Wing
Winlock
Winthrop, J. (d. 1676)
Winthrop, J. (d. 1779)
Wolf, C. J. E.
Wolf, J. R.
Wolf, M. F. J. C.
Wollaston, F.
Wright, T.
Wright, W. H.

Yaḥyā ibn Abī Manṣūr
Yaʿqūb ibn Ṭāriq
Yativṛsabha
Yavaneśvara
Young, C. A.
Ibn Yūnus

Zach
Zacuto
Zanotti
Al-Zarqālī
Zöllner

CHEMISTRY

Abel, J. J.
Accum
Achard
Adam of Bodenstein
Adams, R.
Adet
Agrippa
Albertus Magnus
Alder
Ampère
Anaxilaus of Larissa

Anderson, T.
Andrews
Anschütz
Arfvedson
Armstrong, E. F.
Armstrong, H. E.
Arrhenius
Aston
Atwater
Auwers, K. F. von
Avogadro

Babcock
Bach
Baekeland
Baeyer
Balandin
Balard
Bamberger
Bancroft
Barchusen
Barger
Barlow, W.
Barreswil

Baudrimont
Bauer, E.
Baumé
Baumhauer, E. H. von
Baumhauer, H. A.
Bayen
Ibn Al-Bayṭār
Béchamp
Becher
Beckmann, E. O.
Becquerel, A. C.
Beddoes

751

Beguin
Behrend
Beilstein
Beketov
Bellani
Benedict
Bérard, J. E.
Bergius
Bergman
Bergmann
Bernard of Trevesan
Bernthsen
Berthelot
Berthier
Berthollet
Bertrand, G.
Berzelius
Bischof
Bjerrum
Black, Joseph
Blagden
Blomstrand
Bodenstein
Boerhaave
Boisbaudran
Boltwood
Bonvicino
Borodin
Borrichius
Bosch
Bostock
Böttger
Bourdelin
Boussingault
Boyle
Braconnot
Brande
Brandt, G.
Brauner
Brodie, B. C. Jr.
Brønsted
Brown, A. C.
Brownrigg
Brunton
Buchanan
Buchner, E.
Bucholz
Bucquet
Bunsen
Butlerov
Buys Ballot

Cadet de Gassicourt, L. C.
Cadet de Gassicourt, C. L.
Cadet de Vaux
Cahours
Callinicos of Heliopolis
Cannizzaro
Caro
Carothers
Caventou
Centnerszwer
Cervantes
Chancel
Chapman, D. L.
Chaptal
Chardenon
Chardonnet
Charpy
Chenevix
Chernyaev
Chernov
Chevenard
Chevallier, J. B. A.

Chevreul
Chichibabin
Chittenden
Chugaev
Ciamician
Claisen
Clark T.
Clark, W. M.
Clarke, F. W.
Classen
Claus, A. C. L.
Claus, C. E.
Clément
Cleve
Clouet
Cohen, E. J.
Cohn, E. J.
Cohn, L.
Collet-Descotils
Collie
Cooke
Cooper
Copaux
Cordus, V.
Cori
Cornette
Cottrell
Couper
Courtois
Cramer
Crawford
Crell
Crollius
Cronstedt
Crookes
Crum
Cullen
Curtius
Cushny

Dale
Dalton, J.
Daniell
D'Arcet
Daubeny
Davison
Davy, H.
Davy, J.
Day
Debray
Debye
De La Rue
Delépine
Derosne
Desormes
Despagnet
Dessaignes
Deville
Dewar
Dickinson
Diels
Dioscorides
Dittmar
Dixon, H. B.
Döbereiner
Doelter
Domagk
Donnan
Dorn
Draper, J. W.
Duchesne
Duclaux
Duhamel du Monceau
Duhem
Dulong

Dumas
Dundonald

Eder
Ekeberg
Elhuyar, F. D'
Elhuyar, J. J. D'
Eller von Brockhausen
Elvehjem
Embden, G.
Ercker
Erdmann
Erlenmeyer
Esson
Eucken
Euler-Chelpin

Fankuchen
Faraday
Farkas
Favorsky
Favre
Fersman
Feulgen
Fischer E. H.
Fischer, H.
Fischer, H. O. L.
Fischer, N. W.
Fittig
Folin
Forchhammer
Fordos
Fourcroy
Fourneau
Fownes
Frankenheim
Frankland, E.
Frankland, P. F.
Franklin, R. E.
Freind
Frémy
Fresenius
Freundlich, H. M. F.
Friedel
Friend
Fritzsche
Fuchs, J. N. von
Funk
Fyodorov

Gabriel
Gadolin
Gahn
Galeazzi
Gaudin
Gaultier de Claubry
Gautier, A. E. J.
Gay-Lussac
Gehlen
Gelmo
Genth
Geoffroy, C. J.
Geoffroy, E. F.
Gerhardt
Geuther
Gibbs, O. W.
Giesel
Girtanner
Gladstone
Glaser, C.

Glauber
Gmelin, L.
Gobley
Gohory
Goldschmidt, V.
Goldschmidt, V. M.
Gomberg
Gore
Görgey
Graebe
Graham, T.
Green, J.
Gregory, W.
Gren
Griess
Grignard
Groth
Grotthuss
Grove
Guertler
Guibert
Guillaume
Guillet
Guldberg
Gulland
Gutbier
Guyton de Morveau

Haber
Hadfield
Hahn
Hahnemann
Haldane, John B. S.
Hall, C. M.
Hall, J.
Hampson
Hankel, W. G.
Hantzsch
Harcourt
Harden
Hardy
Hare
Harkins
Hartmann, C. F. A.
Hartmann, J.
Hassenfratz
Hatchett
Hautefeuille
Haüy
Haworth, W. N.
Hellot
Hellriegel
Helmont
Henckel
Henderson, L. J.
Henry, T.
Henry, W.
Herapath, W. B.
Hermann, C. H.
Hermbstaedt
Herschel, J. F. W.
Hess, G. H.
Hessel
Hevesy
Heyrovský
Hiärne
Higgins, B.
Higgins, W.
Hildebrandt
Hilditch
Hinshelwood
Hisinger
Hittorf
Hoffmann, F.

Hofmann, A. W. von
Homberg
Hönigschmid
Hope
Hopkins, F. G.
Hoppe-Seyler
Horbaczewski
Horsford
Horstmann
Houssay
Howe, J. L.
Hudson, C. S.
Hume-Rothery
Hunt, T. S.

Ipatiev
Irinyi

Jābir ibn Ḥayyān
Jackson, C. T.
Jacobs, W. A.
Jacquet
Jacquin
Jaeger, F. M.
Jahn
Jeffries
Johnson, W.
Joly
Jones, H. C.
Jørgensen
Juncker

Kablukov
Kahlenberg
Kane
Karrer
Karsten
Keilin
Keir
Kekule von Stradonitz
Kellner
Kendall
Kharasch
Khunrath, C.
Khunrath, H.
Kidd
Kielmeyer
Kipping
Kirchhof, K. S.
Kirkaldy
Kirkwood, J. G.
Kirwan
Kitaibel
Kjeldahl
Klaproth
Kluyver
Kohlrausch, F. W. G.
Kolbe
Kondakov
Koninck
Konovalov
Kopp
Kossel, K. M. L.
Kostanecki
Kraus
Kuhn, R.
Kuhn, W.
Kühne
Kunckel
Kurnakov

La Brosse
Ladenburg, A.
Lamétherie
Landolt
Langmuir
Lapworth
La Rive, C. G. de
Latimer
Laurent, A.
Lavoisier
Lawes, J. B.
Lawes, G. J. H.
Lebedev, S. V.
Lebedinsky
Le Bel
Le Blanc M. J. L.
Leblanc, N.
Le Châtelier
Le Febvre
Lehmann, J. G.
Lehmann, O.
Lemery, L.
Lemery, N
Lennard-Jones
Leonhardi
Levene
Lewis, G. N.
Lewis, W.
Libavius
Liebermann
Liebig
Link
Lloyd, J.U.
Lomonosov
London, F.
Lonsdale, K.
Lorenz, R.
Loschmidt
Lovits
Lubbock, R.
Luginin
Lunge

Macallum
Macbride, D.
McCollum
Macculloch
Macheboeuf
Maclean
Macquer
Magellan
Magnus H. G.
Maier
Malouin
Marchand
Marchlewski
Marggraf
Marignac
Markovnikov
Martí Franqués
Martinovics
Matthiessen
Mayow
Mellanby
Meltzer
Mendel, L. B.
Mendeleev
Meneghetti
Menghini
Menshutkin
Merica
Metzger
Meyer, J. F.
Meyer, J. L.
Meyer, K. H.

Meyer, V.
Meyerhof
Michael
Midgley
Mielli
Miescher
Miller, W. A.
Miller, W. L.
Millon
Mills
Mitscherlich
Mittasch
Mohr, C. F.
Moissan
Mond
Monge
Monnet
Moray
Morichini
Morley
Mosander
Muir
Mulder
Müller, Franz
Müller, P.
Mushet

Nametkin
Naumann, A.
Nef
Nencki
Neri
Nernst
Neumann, C.
Newlands
Nicholson, W.
Nieuwland
Niggli
Nobel
Noddack
Norton
Noyes, A. A.
Noyes, W. A.

Odling
Olszewski
Olympiodorus
Osborne
Osmond
Ostwald, C. W. W.
Ostwald, F. W.
Overton

Palladin
Paneth
Paracelsus
Parmentier
Parnas
Partington
Pasteur
Payen
Péan de Saint-Gilles
Pearson, G.
Pekelharing
Pelletier, B.
Pelletier, P. J.
Pelouze
Penny
Percy
Pérez de Vargas

Perkin, W. H.
Perkin, W. H. Jr.
Perrin
Personne
Persoz
Petrov, V. V.
Petrus Bonus
Pettenkofer
Pfeffer
Pfeiffer, P.
Plattner
Playfair, L.
Plot
Poggiale
Pope
Popov, A. N.
Pott
Power, F. B.
Pregl
Prévost, I. B.
Priestley, J.
Proust
Prout
Pryanishnikov

Rammelsberg
Ramsay, W.
Raoult
Ray, P. C.
Al-Rāzī
Regnault
Reichenbach, K. L.
Remsen
Rey, J.
Richards, T. W.
Richardson, B. W.
Richter
Rinman
Ritter
Rivett
Roberts-Austen
Robiquet
Roebuck
Rolfinck
Romé de l'Isle
Roozeboom
Roscoe
Rose, G.
Rose, H.
Rosenhain, W.
Rosenheim
Rouelle, G. F.
Rouelle, H.-M.
Rouelle, J.
Rowe
Ruland
Runge, F. F.
Ruscelli
Russell, E. J.
Rush
Rutherford, D.
Rutherford, E.

Sabatier, P.
Sage
Sala
Saussure, N. T. de
Scheele
Schiff, H. J.
Schmidt, G. C. N.
Schoenflies
Schönbein
Schopfer

Schorlemmer
Schott, O. F.
Schrötter
Schulze
Schunck
Schweigger
Sechenov
Séguin, A.
Sendivogius
Sennert
Sertürner
Serullas
Severgin
Severinus
Shaw, P.
Shilov
Sidgwick
Sigaud de Lafond
Silliman, B.
Silliman, B. Jr.
Skraup
Smith, Edgar F.
Smith, R. A.
Smithells
Smithson
Smits
Soddy
Solvay
Sørensen
Spring
Stahl
Starkey
Stas
Staudinger
Steacie
Stead
Stephanus of Alexandria
Stine
Stock, A.

Suchten
Sumner, J. B.
Sutherland
Svedberg
Swarts
Szebellédy
Szily

Tachenius
Talbot
Tammann
Tashiro
Tennant
Than
Thenard
Theophilus
Thiele, F. K. J.
Thomsen, H. P. J. J.
Thomson, T.
Thorpe, J. F.
Thorpe, T. E.
Thurneysser
Tiemann
Tilden
Tillet
Tiselius
Tolman
Traube
Travers
Trommsdorf
Troost, L. J.
Troostwijk
Tsvet
Turner, E.
Turquet de Mayerne
Tutton

Ulstad
Urbain
Ure

Vagner
Valentine
Van Slyke
Van't Hoff
Vauquelin
Venel
Vernadsky
Vigani
Virtanen

Waage
Wackenroder
Ibn Waḥshiyya
Wald, F.
Walden
Wallach
Wallerius
Walter of Odington
Walter
Wanklyn
Warburg, O. H.
Washburn
Waterston
Watson, R.
Watt
Webster, J.
Wedel
Wedgwood
Weigel, C. E.

Weizmann
Werner, A.
Whytlaw-Gray
Wiedemann
Wiegleb
Wieland, H. O.
Wiley
Wilhelmy
Williams, R. R.
Williamson, A. W.
Willstätter
Windaus
Winkler, C.
Winkler, L. W.
Wislicenus
Wöhler, F.
Wollaston, W. H.
Wood, H.
Woulfe
Wu
Wurtz

Young, S.

Al-Zahrāwī
Zambonini
Zeise
Zelinsky
Zemplén
Zinn
Zosimus of Panopolis
Zsigmondy
Zwelfer

EARTH SCIENCES

Abbe, C.
Abich
Abu'l Fidā'
Abū Ḥāmid al-Gharnāṭī
Acosta, J.
Adams, F. D.
Agassiz, A.
Agassiz, J. L. R.
Agricola
Albert I of Monaco
Alberti F. A. von
Albertus Magnus
Alzate y Ramírez
Ameghino
Anderson, E. M.
André
Andrusov
Anuchin
Anville
Apian
Arbos
Archiac
Arduino
Argand, E.
Aristotle
Arkell
Astbury
Aubuisson De Voisins
Azara

Babinet
Babington, W.
Baer
Baier
Bailey, E. B.
Bailey, L. W.
Bailey, S. I.
Baily, F.
Bakewell
Al-Bakrī
Barba
Barlow, W.
Barrande
Barrell
Barrois
Bassani
Bassler
Bather
Bauer
Baumhauer
Baylak Al-Qibjāqī
Becke
Becker
Béguyer De Chancourtois
Behaim
Belaiew
Bell, R.
Bellinsgauzen
Benzenberg
Berg
Bergman

Bering
Bernal
Berthier
Bertrand, M. A.
Bessel
Beudant
Beyrich
Billings
Birge
Al-Bīrūnī
Bischof
Bjerknes, V. F. K.
Black, James
Blaeu
Blanchard
Blomstrand
Bonaventura
Bonney
Boodt
Borelli
Born, I. E. von
Bosc
Bošković
Boucher
Boué
Bougainville
Bouguer
Boule
Boullanger
Bourguet

Bournon
Bowen
Bowie
Bowman, I.
Brandt, G.
Bravais
Breislak
Breithaupt
Brocard
Brocchi
Brochant de Villiers
Brøgger
Broili
Bromell
Brongniart, A.
Bronn
Brooks, A. H.
Broom
Bruce, J.
Brunhes
Bryan
Buache
Buch
Buchanan
Bucher
Buckland
Burnet
Bütschli
Buys Ballot

Cabeo
Caldas
Campanella
Cancrin
Carangeot
Carnall
Carpenter, H. C. H.
Cassini, G. D.
Cassini, J.
Cassini, J. D.
Cassini de Thury
Cayeux
Chamberlin
Chambers
Charcot, J. B.
Charpentier
Charpy
Chenevix
Chernov
Chernyshev
Chevenard
Childrey
Christol
Clarke, E. D.
Clarke, F. W.
Clarke, W. B.
Cleaveland
Cleve
Clift
Cloos
Clouet
Cocchi
Columbus
Conon of Samos
Conrad
Conybeare
Cook
Cordier
Coronelli
Cortés de Albacar
Cotta
Cotte
Credner
Croll
Cronstedt
Cross
Cushman
Cuvier, G.
Czekanowski
Czerski

Dainelli
Dalton, J.
Daly
Dana
Daniell
Danti
Darwin, C. R.
Daubeny
Daubenton
Daubrée
David
Davis
Dawson, J.
Dawson, J. W.
Day
Debenham
Dechen
DeGolyer
De La Beche
Delafosse
Delambre
Delisle, G.
Delisle, J.-N.
Deluc, J. A.

Deperet
Deryugin
Des Cloizeaux
Deshayes
Desmarest
Desor
Dicaearchus of Messina
Doelter
Dokuchaev
Dollo
Dolomieu
Dorno
Dove
Drygalski
Dudley
Dufrénoy
Duperrey
Du Toit
Dutton

Easton
Eaton
Ebel
Ehrenberg
Eichwald
Ekeberg
Ekman
Elhuyar, F. D'
Elhuyar, J. J. D'
Élie de Beaumont
Ellis
Emerson, B. K.
Emmons, E.
Emmons, S. F.
Ercker
Erman
Escher von der Linth
Escholt
Eskola
Espy
Evans, F. J. O.
Evans, L.

Falconer
Fankuchen
Farey
Faujas de Saint-Fond
Faye
Featherstonhaugh
Fenneman
Fenner
Ferrel
Fersman
Fichot
Fitton
Fitzroy
Fleming, J.
Flett
Foerste
Forbes, E.
Forbes, J. D.
Forchhammer
Forel
Forster, G. A.
Forster, J. R.
Foster, H.
Fouqué
Fraipont
Frankenheim
Franklin, B.
Freiesleben

Frenzel
Frere
Friedel
Fuchs, J. N. von
Füchsel
Fyodorov

Gabb
Gadolin
Gagnebin
Gahn
Gaimard
Gaudry
Geer, G. J. de
Geikie, A.
Geikie, J.
Gellibrand
Gemma Frisius
Genth
Germanus
Gessner
Gilbert, G. K.
Glaisher, J.
Glauber
Gmelin, J. G.
Godwin-Austen
Goethe
Goldschmidt, V.
Goldschmidt, V. M.
Golitsyn
Goodrich
Gosselet
Grabau
Gramont
Grand'eury
Granger
Greenough
Gressly
Griffith, R. J.
Groddeck
Groth
Grubenmann
Gua de Malves
Guenther
Guertler
Guettard
Guillaume
Guillet
Gunter
Gutenberg
Guyot

Haast
Hadfield
Hague
Haidinger
Hakluyt
Hall, J.
Hall, J. Jr.
Halley
Hamberg
Al-Hamdānī
Hamilton, W.
Hann
Harker
Harper, R. M.
Hartmann, C. F. A.
Hassler
Haug
Haüy
Ibn Hawqal
Hayden

Hayford
Hecataeus of Miletus
Hedin
Heer
Heim, A.
Heim, A. A.
Helmersen
Helmert
Henckel
Hermann, C. H.
Héroult
Hessel
Heyn
Heynitz
Hiärne
Hisinger
Hitchcock
Hoff
Holmes
Hopkins, W.
Horner, L.
Hough
Houghton
Humboldt
Hume-Rothery
Hunt, T. S.
Hutton, J.
Huxley, T. H.
Hyatt

Ibáñez e Ibáñez de Ibero
Ibrāhīm ibn Yaᶜqūb
Iddings
Al-Idrīsī
Imamura
Inō
Issel

Jaccard
Jackson, C. T.
Jaeger, F. M.
Jaeger, G. F.
Jaekel
Jaggar
Jameson
Jars
Jefferson
Jeffries
Johannsen, A.
Johnson, D. W.
Johnson, W. D.
Joly
Juan y Santacilla
Juday
Jukes
Jussieu, A. de
Justi

Kaempfer
Kalm
Karpinski
Karpinsky
Karsten
Kater
Kavraysky
Kay
Keyserling
Ibn Khurradādbih
Al-Khwārizmī

King
Kirkaldy
Kirwan
Kitaibel
Klein, H. J.
Knipovich
Knorr
Knott
Knudsen
Koninck
Konkoly Thege
Kotō
Kovalevsky, V. O.
Krasheninnikov
Krasnov
Krasovsky
Krayenhoff
Kropotkin
Kruber

Lacaille
Lacroix, A.
La Hire, G.P. de
La Hire, P. de
Lamarck
Lamb
Lamétherie
Lang, K. N.
Langren
Lapparent
Lapworth
Larsen
Lartet, E. A. I. H.
Lartet, L.
Laussedat
Lavanha
Lavoisier
Lawson
Lazarev, M.P.
Lazarev, P.P.
Leakey
Le Châtelier
Leconte, Joseph
Lehmann, J. G.
Lenz
Leo the African
Leonardo da Vinci
Leonhard
Lepekhin
Le Roy, C.
Lesley
Lesquereux
Lesson
Le Verrier
Levinson-Lessing
Lévy, S. D. A.
Leybenzon
Lhwyd
Liesganig
Lindgren
Link
Linnaeus
Lisboa
Lister, M.
Litke
Logan, W. E.
Lohest
Löhneyss
Lokhtin
Lomonosov
Lonsdale, W.
Loomis
Lorenzoni
Lossen
Love

Lugeon
Lyell
Lyman, B. S.
Lyman, C. S.

Macculloch
Maclure
Magini
Maillet
Ibn Mājid
Makarov
Mallard
Mallet
Mantell
Al-Maqdisī
Maraldi, G. D.
Maraldi, G. F.
Marcou
Margerie
Margules
Marion
Mariotte
Markham
Martí Franqués
Martonne
Mason
Al-Masʿūdī
Mather
Matuyama
Mauguin
Maurer
Mauro
Maury, M. F.
Mawson
Mayer, J. T.
Mayer-Eymar
Méchain
Medina
Meek
Meinzer
Mendel, J. G.
Mercator
Merica
Merriam, J. C.
Merrill
Mesyatsev
Metius, A. A.
Meyer, C. E. H. von
Michel-Lévy
Middendorf
Miers
Miklukho-Maklay
Miller, H.
Miller, W. H.
Milne, J.
Mitchell, E.
Mitscherlich
Mohn
Mohorovičić
Mohr, C. F.
Mohs
Molina
Monnet
Montanari
Montelius
Moray
Moro
Morozov
Morse, J.
Mortillet
Mosander
Mosso
Mouchez
Munier-Chalmas
Münster

Murchison
Murray, J.
Mushet
Mushketov

Nansen
Nathorst
Naumann, K. F.
Necker
Neumann, F. E.
Neumayr
Newberry
Nicol
Niebuhr
Niggli
Nikitin
Nordenskiöld, N. A. E.
Norman
Norwood
Numerov

Obruchev
Ochsenius
Odierna
Olaus Magnus
Oldham, R. D.
Oldham, T.
Omalius d'Halloy
Omori
Oppel
Oppolzer
Orbigny
Orlov, A. Y.
Ortelius
Orton
Osborn
Osmond
Outhier
Owen, D. D.
Owen, G.
Owen, R.
Ozersky

Palissy
Pallas
Pander
Pappus of Alexander
Parkinson, J.
Pavlov, A. A.
Peirce, C. S.
Penck, A.
Penck, W.
Percy
Pereira, D. P.
Pérez de Vargas
Perrier, G.
Peters, C. F. W.
Pettersson
Petty
Pezenas
Phillips, J.
Phillips, W.
Picard, J.
Piatte
Pirī Rais
Plattner
Playfair, J.
Poleni
Pomponius Mela

Porro
Porteviņ
Pošepny
Potanin
Pourtalès
Powell, J. W.
Prestwich
Prévost, L. C.
Przhevalsky
Pumpelly
Pythias of Massalia

Al-Qazwīnī
Quenstedt

Rames
Ramond de Carbonnières
Ramsay, A. C.
Rankine, A. O.
Raspe
Ratzel
Raymond
Reck
Reclus
Redfield
Reid
Renard
Renault
Renevier
Rennell
Reuss, A. E.
Reuss, F. A.
Ribeiro Santos
Ricci, Mateo
Riccioli
Riccò
Richthofen
Ries
Rinman
Río
Rittenhouse
Rivière de Précourt
Roberts-Austen
Roche
Roemer F.
Roemer, F. A.
Rogers, H. D.
Rogers, W. B.
Romé de l'Isle
Romer
Rose, G.
Rosenberger
Rosenbusch
Rosenhain, W.
Ross, J. C.
Rossby
Roth
Rouelle, G. F.
Rouillier
Rovereto
Ruedemann
Rülein
Rumovsky
Russell, H. C.
Rütimeyer

Sabine, E.
Sage
Salisbury

Saporta
Sarychev
Satō Nobuhiro
Satō Nobukage
Satō Nobusue
Saussure, H. B. de
Sauveur, A.
Schardt
Scheuchzer
Schimper, K. F.
Schlotheim
Schlumberger
Schmerling
Schmidt, C. A. von
Schmidt, J. F. S.
Schneiderhöhn
Schöner
Schott, C. A.
Schouw
Schuchert
Schumacher
Scilla
Scott, D. H.
Scott, W. B.
Scrope
Sederholm
Sedgwick
Sedov
Selwyn
Semyonov-Tyan-Shansky
Sénarmont
Serres de Mesplès
Setchell
Severgin
Seward
Sezawa
Shaler
Sharonov
Shaw, W. N.
Shirakatsí
Shokalsky
Shtokman
Silliman B.
Silliman, B. Jr.
Smith, William
Smyth
Sohncke
Sokolov

Soldani
Soldner
Sollas
Sorby
Soulavie
Sowerby
Spencer, L. J.
Sprung
Staszic
Stead
Steller
Stensen
Sternberg, K. M. von
Sternberg, P. K.
Stewart, B.
Stille
Stock, C.
Størmer
Strabo
Strachey
Struve F. G. W.
Struve, G. W. L.
Struve, O. W.
Studer
Suess
Sverdrup
Swedenborg
Swinden

Tachini
Tanfilev
Tarde
Taylor, F. B.
Teall
Teilhard de Chardin
Termier
Theophilus
Theophrastus
Thomas, H. H.
Thomas, S. G.
Thompson, D. W.
Thomson, C. W.
Al-Tīfāshī
Tilas
Tillo

Toscanelli dal Pozzo
Toulmin
Townsend, J.
Trebra
Troost, G.
Tschermak
Turner, H. H.
Al-Ṭūsī (Nasir al-Dīn)
Tutton
Twenhofel
Tyrrell

Ulrich, E. O.
Urbain

Valmont de Bomare
Van Hise
Vanuxem
Varenius
Venetz
Vening Meinesz
Vernadsky
Verneuil
Vize
Voeykov
Vogt, J. H. L.
Vogt, T.
Voigt, J. C. W.
Volney
Voltz
Vysotsky

Waage
Walch
Walcott
Waldseemüller
Walker, J.
Wallerius
Washington

Webster, T.
Wegener
Weiss, C. S.
Wells, W. C.
Wendelin
Werner, A. G.
Werner, J.
White, C. D.
White, I. C.
Whitehurst
Whitfield
Whitney
Widmannstätten
Wiechert
Wild
Williams, H. S.
Williamson, W. C.
Willis, B.
Williston
Winchell, A.
Winchell, A. N.
Winchell, H. V.
Winchell, N. H.
Witham
Woltmann
Woodward, J.
Woodward, R. S.
Wright, E.
Wright, F. E.
Wright, G. F.
Wulff

Yāqūt al-Ḥamawī al-Rūmī
Young, T.

Zach
Zambonini
Zeiller
Zejszner
Zirkel
Zittel
Zubov

LIFE SCIENCES

Abano
Abel, J. J.
Abel, O.
Abreu
Acharius
Achillini
Acosta, C.
Adam of Bodenstein
Adanson
Addison
Aëtius of Amida
Agardh, C. A.
Agardh, J. G.
Agassiz, A.
Agassiz, J. L. R.
Agathinus
Agrippa
Aiton, W.
Aiton, W. T.
Alberti, L. B.
Alberti, S.
Albertus Magnus

Albinus, B.
Albinus, B. S.
Albinus, C. B.
Albinus, F. B.
Alcmaeon of Crotona
Alderotti, Taddeo
Aldrovandi
Alexander of Myndos
Alexander of Tralles
Allen
Alpini
Alzate Y Ramírez
Ameghino
Amici
Ancel
Anguillara
Anuchin
Apáthy
Aranzio
Arber
Archiac
Archigenes

Aretaeus of Cappadocia
Argenville
Aristotle
Arkell
Arnald of Villanova
Aromatari
Arsonval
Artedi
Asclepiades
Aselli
Assalti
Astbury
Astruc
Athenaeus of Attalia
Atwater
Audouin
Audubon
Auenbrugger
Avery
Ibn al-ᶜAwwām
Azara

Babington, C. C.
Baccelli
Bachmann, A. Q.
Baer
Baier
Baglivi
Bailey, L. H.
Baillie
Baillou
Baird
Baker, J. G.
Balbiani
Balfour, F. M.
Balfour, I. B.
Balfour, J. H.
Banister
Banks
Banti
Banting
Bárány
Barbour
Barchusen

Barclay
Barcroft
Barrande
Barrois
Barry
Barthez
Bartholin, C.
Bartholin, T.
Bartolotti
Barton
Bartram, J.
Bartram, W.
Bassani
Bassi
Bassler
Bastian
Bataillon
Bates
Bateson
Bather
Baudrimont
Bauer, F. L.
Bauer, F. A.
Bauhin, G.
Bauhin, J.
Bayliss, L. E.
Bayliss, W. M.
Ibn al-Bayṭār
Beale
Beaumont
Beccari
Becquerel, P.
Beddoe
Beddoes
Beevor
Behring
Beijerinck
Bekhterev
Bell, C.
Bellardi
Belleval
Bellini
Belon
Beneden, E. van
Beneden, P. J. van
Benedetti, A.
Benedict
Benivieni
Bensley
Bentham
Bérard, J. F.
Berengario Da Carpi
Berg
Berger, H.
Berger, J. G.
Bergman
Bérigard
Beringer
Berkeley, M. J.
Bernal
Bernard, C.
Bernard, N.
Bernheim
Bernoulli, D.
Bernstein, J.
Bert
Berthold
Bertrand, C. E.
Bertrand, G.
Bessey
Bexon
Beyrich
Bezold
Bichat
Bidder
Bidloo
Bilharz
Billings

Billroth
Binet
Birge
Bischoff, G. W.
Bischoff, T. L. W.
Bizzozero
Black, D.
Black, James
Black, Joseph
Blackman
Blainville
Blair
Blanc
Blumenbach
Blyth
Boas
Bock
Bodenheimer
Boerhaave
Bogdanov
Bohn
Bolk
Bolos of Mendes
Bolotov
Bonaparte
Bonnet, C.
Bonnier
Bonomo
Bordet
Bordeu
Borel, P.
Borelli
Borgognoni of Lucca
Bory de Saint-Vincent
Bosc
Bose, J.
Bostock
Botallo
Bottazzi
Boucher
Bouin
Boule
Bourdelot
Bourguet
Boveri
Bowditch, H. P.
Bower
Bowman, W.
Brachet
Bradford
Bradley, R.
Brandt, J. F.
Braun, A. C. H.
Bravais
Bredon
Brefeld
Breschet
Bretonneau
Breuer
Breuil
Bridges
Bright
Brisson, M. J.
Britten
Britton
Broca
Brödel
Brodie, B. C.
Broili
Brongniart, A. T.
Bronn
Brooks, W. K.
Broom
Broussais
Broussonet
Brown A. C.
Brown, R.

Brown, T.
Brown-Séquard
Bruce, D.
Brücke
Brumpt
Brunfels
Brunschwig
Brunton
Bucholz
Buckland
Budd
Buffon
Buller
Bulloch
Bunge
Buonanni
Burdach
Burdenko
Burdon-Sanderson
Burger
Busk
Ibn Buṭlān
Bütschli

Cabanis
Cadet de Gassicourt, C. L.
Cadet de Vaux
Caius
Caldani
Caldas
Calkins
Calmette
Camerarius
Campbell, D. H.
Camper
Canano
Candolle, A. de
Candolle, A. P. de
Cannon, W. B.
Carangeot
Cardano
Carlisle
Carlson
Carpenter, W. B.
Carrel
Carroll
Carus, J. V.
Casal Julian
Casseri
Castaldi
Castle
Catesby
Cattell
Caullery
Cavanilles
Cels
Cervantes
Cesalpino
Cesi
Cestoni
Chabry
Chagas
Chamberlain
Chamberland
Chambers
Chamisso
Chaplin
Chapman, A. W.
Charcot, J. B.
Charcot, J. M.
Chardenon
Charleton
Chauliac
Chauveau
Cheyne

Chiarugi
Child
Childrey
Chittenden
Chodat
Christol
Claus, C. E.
Clements
Clerck
Clift
Coghill
Cogrossi
Cohn, E. J.
Cohn, F. J.
Coiter
Colden
Collinson
Collip
Colombo
Combes, R.
Commerson
Conklin
Conrad
Constantine the African
Cope
Cordus, E.
Cordus, V.
Cori
Cornette
Correns
Corti, A.
Corti, B.
Corvisart
Costantin
Cotugno
Coues
Councilman
Crawford
Creighton
Crollius
Croone
Cruikshank
Cruveilhier
Cruz
Cuénot
Cullen
Cushing
Cushman
Cushny
Cuvier, F.
Cuvier, G.
Czermak
Czerski

Dale
Daléchamps
Dalibard
Dall
Dalton, J. C.
Al-Damīrī
Danforth
Darlington
Darwin, C. R.
Darwin, E.
Darwin, F.
Daubenton
Davaine
Davenport
Davison
Davy, J.
Dawson, J.
Dean
De Bary
Déchellete
Delage

758

Delile
Denis
Deperet
Derham
Deryugin
Descartes
Descourtilz
Deshayes
Desor
Devaux
Digby
Dillenius
Diocles of Carystus
Dionis du Séjour
Dioscorides
Dixon, H. H.
Dobell
Dodart
Dodoens
Dogel
Dohrn
Dokuchaev
Döllinger
Dollo
Domagk
Dombey
Dominicus de Clavasio
Donaldson
Donders
Dondi
Dorn
Douglas, James
Draparnaud
Driesch
Dubini
Dubois
Dubois-Reymond, E. H.
Duboscq
Duchesne
Duclaux
Duggar
Du Hamel
Duhamel du Monceau
Dujardin
Duméril
Dunglison
Dutrochet
Duval
Duverney
Dyadkovsky

East
Eaton
Ebel
Eberth
Edwardes
Edwards
Egas Moniz
Ehrenberg
Ehret
Ehrlich
Eichler
Eichwald
Eigenmann
Eijkman
Einthoven
Eller von Brockhausen
Elliot Smith
Elvehjem
Embden
Emerson, R.
Engelmann, G.
Engelmann, T. W.
Engler
Ent

Erasistratus
Erastus
Erlanger
Erman
Errera
Escherich
Eschscholtz
Estienne
Euler-Chelpin
Eustachi
Evans, A. W.
Evans, W. H.
Evelyn
Ewing, J.

Fabre
Fabrici
Fabricius
Falconer
Falloppio
Farmer
Fechner
Fée
Fernald
Fernel
Ferrein
Ferrier
Feuillée
Feulgen
Fick
Fiessinger
Fink
Finlay
Finsen
Fischer, H. O. L.
Fisher, R. A.
Fitch
Flechsig
Fleming, A.
Fleming, J.
Flemming
Fletcher
Flexner
Florey
Flourens
Flower
Fludd
Foerste
Fol
Folin
Fontana
Forbes, A.
Forbes, E.
Forbes, S. A.
Forel
Forsskål
Foster, M.
Fourcroy
Fracastoro
Fraipont
Frankland, P. F.
Franklin, R. E.
Frazer
Frederick II of Hohenstaufen
Fredericq
Freind
Freud
Frey
Fries, E. M.
Fritsch
Fuchs, L.
Fuhlrott
Fulton
Funk

Gaertner, J.
Gaertner, K. F. von
Gaffky
Gagliardi
Gaimard
Gaines
Galeazzi
Galen
Gall
Galton
Galvani
Gamaleya
Garnett
Garnot
Garreau
Gaskell
Gasser
Gates
Gaudry
Gaultier de Claubry
Gay
Gayant
Geer, C. de
Gegenbaur
Geminus, T.
Geoffroy, C. J.
Geoffroy, E. F.
Geoffroy, E. L.
Geoffroy Saint-Hilaire, E.
Geoffroy Saint-Hilaire, I.
Gerard, J.
Gerbezius
Gesell
Gesner
Gessner
Ghini
Ghisi
Giard
Giles of Rome
Gill, T. N.
Girtanner
Glaser, C.
Glaser, J. H.
Glauber
Gleichen-Russworm
Glisson
Gmelin, J. G.
Goebel
Goedaert
Goeppert
Goethe
Goette
Gohory
Goldberger
Goldschmidt, R. B.
Golgi
Goltz
Goodrich
Goodsir
Gosselet
Gould, A. A.
Gould, J.
Graaf
Grabau
Gram
Grand'eury
Granger
Grassi
Gratiolet
Gray, A.
Gray, H.
Green, J.
Gregory, F. G.
Gregory, W.
Gressly
Grew
Griffith, W.
Grijns

Grinnell
Grisebach
Grote
Gruber
Gruby
Gudden
Guettard
Guidi
Guignard
Guilliermond
Guinter
Gulland
Gullstrand
Gurvich
Guyer
Gwynne-Vaughan
Gyllenhaal

Haberlandt
Haeckel
Haffkine
Hahnemann
Haldane, John B. S.
Haldane, John Scott
Hales
Hall, G. S.
Hall, J. Jr.
Hall, M.
Haller
Hallier
Halsted, W. S.
Al-Hamdānī
Hansen, E. C.
Hansen, G. H. A.
Harden
Hardy
Harlan
Harper, R. A.
Harper, R. M.
Harpestraeng
Harrison, R. G.
Hart
Hartig
Harting
Hartley
Hartmann, J.
Harvey, W.
Harvey, W. H.
Hatschek
Haug
Havers
Haworth, A. H.
Hedwig
Heer
Heidenhain, M.
Heidenhain, R. P. H.
Heister
Hektoen
Helmholtz
Helmont
Henderson, L. J.
Henderson, Y.
Henfrey
Henking
Henle
Henry of Mondeville
Hensen
Henslow
Herapath, W. B.
Herbart
Herbert
Hérelle
Hering
Hernández
Herophilus

LIST OF SCIENTISTS BY FIELD

Herrera
Herrick, C. J.
Herrick, C. L.
Hertwig, K. W. T. R. von
Hertwig, W. A. O.
Heurne
Hewson
Hiärne
Highmore
Hill, J.
Hippocrates of Cos
Hirszfeld
His
Hitchcock
Hitzig
Hjort
Hoagland
Hoeven
Hoffmann, F.
Hofmeister
Holbrook
Holmgren
Home
Hooker, J. D.
Hooker, W. J.
Hopkins, F. G.
Hoppe-Seyler
Horbaczewski
Horn
Horne
Horsley
Hosack
Houghton
Houssay
Howard
Howell
Hrdlička
Huber, J. J.
Hubrecht
Hudson, W.
Humboldt
Ḥunayn ibn Isḥāq
Hundt
Hunt, J.
Hunter, J.
Hunter, W.
Huschke
Hutchinson
Hutton, J.
Huxley, T. H.
Hyatt
Hyrtl

Ingen-Housz
Ingrassia
Isaac Israeli
Isaacs
Isḥāq ibn Ḥunayn
Ivanov, I. I.
Ivanov, P. P.
Ivanovsky

Jaccard
Jackson, C. T.
Jackson, J. H.
Jacquin
Jaeger, G. F.
Jaekel
Al-Jāḥiz
James, W.
Jameson
Jefferson

Jeffrey
Jeffreys
Jenkinson
Jenner
Jennings
Jensen, C. O.
Jepson
Joblot
Johannsen, W. L.
Johnson, T.
Jonston
Jordan, C. T. A.
Jordan, D. S.
Jordan, E. O.
Juday
Ibn Juljul
Juncker
Jung
Jungius
Jussieu, A. de
Jussieu, A. H. L. de
Jussieu, A. L. de
Jussieu, B. de
Jussieu, J. de

Kaempfer
Kalm
Keilin
Keill, James
Keith
Kellner
Kellogg, A.
Kellogg, V. L.
Kelser
Kendall
Kerr, J. G.
Keyserling
Khunrath, C.
Khunrath, H.
Kidd
Kielmeyer
Kitaibel
Kitasato
Klebs
Klein, J. T.
Kleinenberg
Kluyver
Knight
Knipovich
Knorr
Knox
Knuth
Koch, H. H. R.
Koelliker
Koelreuter
Kofoid
Köhler
Koltzoff
König, E.
Koninck
Kossel, K. M. L.
Kovalevsky, A. O.
Kovalevsky, V.
Kraft
Krasheninnikov
Krasnov
Krogh
Kronecker, H.
Kühn, A.
Kühne
Kunth
Kuntze
Kützing
Kylin

La Brosse
Lacaze-Duthiers
Lacépède
La Condamine
Laennec
Lamarck
Lamétherie
La Mettrie
Lamouroux
Lamy, G.
Lancisi
Landsteiner
Lang, A.
Lang, K. N.
Lang, W. V.
Lange
Langerhans
Langley
Lankester
Lapicque
Larghi
La Rive, C. G. de
Lartet, E. A. I. H.
Lartet, L.
Lashley
Latreille
Laurens
Laveran
Lavoisier
Lavrentiev
Lawrence, W.
Lazarev, P. P.
Lea
Leakey
Le Cat
L'Écluse
Leconte, John
Leconte, Joseph
Le Dantec
Le Double
Leeuwenhoek
Le Febvre
Legallois
Leger
Lehmann, J. G.
Leidy
Lemery, L.
Lemery, N.
Le Monnier, L. G.
Leonardo da Vinci
Leonhardi
Leoniceno
Lepekhin
Lereboullet
Le Roy, C.
Lesquereux
Lesson
Lesueur
Leuckart
Leuret
Levaditi
Levaillant
Levene
Levi
Lewis, Thomas
Lewis, Timothy R.
Lewis, W.
Leydig
L'Héritier de Brutelle
Lhwyd
Libavius
Liceaga
Lieberkühn
Liebig
Lieutaud
Lignier
Lillie
Linacre

Lind
Lindley
Link
Linnaeus
Li Shih-Chen
Lister, J.
Lister, M.
Livingston
Lloyd, J. U.
L'Obel
Loeb, J.
Loeb, L.
Loeffler
Loewi
Lohest
Lonicerus
Lorry
Lotsy
Lotze
Lovell
Lovén
Lower
Lubbock, J.
Lucas, K.
Luciani
Ludwig
Luna
Lusitanus
Lusk
Lustig
Lyell
Lyonet

Macallum
Macbride, D.
MacBride, E. W.
McClung
McCollum
Mach
Macheboeuf
McIntosh
Macleod
Magati
Magendie
Maggi
Magnenus
Magnol
Magnus, R.
Maimonides
Maire
Al-Majūsī
Maksimov
Malesherbes
Mall
Malouin
Malpighi
Manardo
Mangin
Manson
Mantegazza
Marchant, J.
Marchant, N.
Marchi
Marchia Fava
Marci of Kronland
Marcou
Marey
Marie
Marion
Mariotte
Markgraf
Marliani
Marsh
Marsili
Marsilius of Inghen

Martí Franqués
Martin, H. N.
Martin, R.
Martínez
Martius
Marum
Mascagni
Massa
Mast
Matruchot
Matteucci
Mattioli
Maupas
Maupertuis
Mayer, J. R.
Mayer-Eymar
Mayo
Mayow
Meckel
Medicus
Meek
Meissner
Mellanby
Meltzer
Mendel, J. G.
Mendel, L. B.
Meneghetti
Menghini
Menuret de Chambaud
Mercati
Merriam, C. H.
Merriam, J. C.
Merrill
Mersenne
Méry
Mesmer
Mesnil
Metchnikoff
Mettenius
Meyen
Meyer, C. E. H. von
Meyerhof
Michaux
Micheli
Michelini
Michurin
Middendorf
Miescher
Miller, P.
Millington
Millon
Milne-Edwards
Minot, C. S.
Minot, G. R.
Miquel
Mirbel
Mitchell, E.
Mitchell, S. W.
Mivart
Möbius, K. A.
Mociño
Moench
Moerbeke
Moffett
Mohl
Moldenhawer
Moleschott
Molina
Molliard
Monardes
Mondino de' Luzzi
Monro, A. (I)
Monro, A. (II)
Montanari
Montgomery, E. D.
Montgomery, T. H.
Morat
Moray

Morgagni
Morgan, C. L.
Morgan, T. H.
Morichini
Morin
Morison
Morozov
Morse, E. S.
Mortillet
Morton, J.
Morton, S. G.
Moss
Mosso
Mottram
Müller, Fritz
Müller, G. E.
Muller, H. J.
Müller, J. P.
Müller, O. F.
Munier-Chalmas
Muralt
Murphy
Murray, G. R. M.
Mutis y Bossio

Naegeli
Ibn al-Nafīs
Nansen
Nathorst
Naudin
Navashin
Neander
Necker
Needham
Nees von Esenbeck
Negri
Nehring
Neisser
Nemesius
Nencki
Neumayr
Newberry
Newport
Newton, E. T.
Nicholas
Nicol
Nicolaus of Dafnascus
Nicolle
Nicot
Nifo
Nilsson-Ehle
Nissl
Noguchi
Nordenskiöld, N. E.
Norton
Nostradamus
Novy
Nuttall
Nylander, F.
Nylander, W.

Oddi
Odierna
Oken
Olaus Magnus
Olbers
Oliver
Oppel
Orbeli
Orbigny
Oribasius,
Orta
Orton

Osborn
Ostwald, C. W. W.
Ott
Oudemans
Overton
Owen, R.

Pacchioni
Pacini
Packard
Pagano
Painter
Palissy
Palladin
Pallas
Palmer
Pander
Papanicolaou
Paré
Parkinson, J.
Parkinson, S.
Parmentier
Parnas
Pasteur
Paul of Aegina
Paulli
Pauly
Pavlov, I. P.
Pavón y Jiménez
Paykull
Peale, R.
Peale, T. R.
Pearl
Pearson, K.
Pecquet
Pekelharing
Peletier, J.
Pelletier, P. J.
Pembertom
Pennant
Pensa
Pérez de Vargas
Péron
Perrault, C.
Perrault, P.
Perrier, E.
Perroncito
Personne
Persoon
Petrie
Pettenkofer
Peyer
Peyssonnel
Pezard
Pfeffer
Pflüger
Philinus of Cos
Philip
Phillips J.
Philolaus of Crotona
Pianese
Piccolomini
Piette
Pincus
Pinel
Pires
Pirogov
Piso
Pitcairn
Pitt-Rivers
Plate
Plato of Tivoli
Platter
Plenčič

Pliny
Plot
Plumier
Plummer, A.
Poggiale
Poiseuille
Poivre
Poli
Pollender
Pontedera
Porta, G. della
Porta, L.
Portal
Portier
Potanin
Pouchet
Pourfour du Petit
Powell, J. W.
Power, F. B.
Power, H.
Pratt, F. H.
Praxagoras of Cos
Presl
Prevost, I. B.
Prevost, J. L.
Preyer
Prichard
Priestley, J. G.
Pringle
Pringsheim, N.
Procháska
Prout
Prowazek
Prudden
Pruner Bey
Pryanishnikov
Przhevalsky
Pumpelly
Punnett
Purkyně
Pursh
Putnam

Quatrefages de Bréau
Quenstedt
Ibn al-Quff
Quoy
Qusṭa ibn Lūqā
Quṭb al-Dīn

Rabelais
Rabl
Rádl
Raffles
Rafinesque
Raman
Rames
Ramon
Ramond de Carbonnières
Ramón y Cajal
Ranvier
Raspail
Rathke
Ratzel
Raulin
Rauwolf
Ray, J.
Raymond
Al-Rāzī
Réaumur
Reck
Redfield
Redi

761

Redouté
Reed
Reichert
Reil
Remak
Renault
Renaut
Renevier
Retzius, A. A.
Retzius, M. G.
Reuss, A. E.
Reyna
Richards, F. J.
Richardson, B. W.
Richet
Ricketts
Ridgway
Ibn Riḍwān
Rima
Ringer
Río-Hortega
Riolan
Ristoro
Rittenhouse
Ritter
Riva-Rocci
Rivière de Précourt
Robin
Robinet
Robiquet
Roemer, F.
Roemer, F. A.
Roesel von Rosenhof
Rolando
Rolfinck
Rolleston
Rollet
Romanes
Rondelet
Roomen
Rosa
Rosenblueth
Ross, R.
Rostan
Rouelle, J.
Rouget
Rouillier
Roux, P. P. E.
Roux, W.
Rowe
Rubner
Rudbeck
Rudolphi
Ruedemann
Ruel
Ruffer
Ruffini, A.
Ruffini, P.
Ruffo
Rufinus
Rufus of Ephesus
Ruini
Ruiz
Ruland
Rülein
Ruscelli
Rush
Ibn Rushd
Russell, E. J.
Rütimeyer
Ruysch

Sabatier, A.
Sabin
Sacco

Sachs
Saint-Hilaire
Sakharov
Sala
Salernitan Anatomists
Salomonsen
Salviani
Al-Samarqandi (d. 1222)
Al-Samaw'al
Samoylov
Sanarelli
Sanchez
Sanderson
Sanio
Santorini
Santorio
Saporta
Sars
Saussure, H. B. de
Saussure, N. T. de
Sauvageau
Savigny
Say
Scaliger
Scarpa
Schaudinn
Scheele
Schegk
Scheuchzer
Schiff, M.
Schimper, A. F. W.
Schimper, K. F.
Schimper, W. P.
Schleiden
Schlotheim
Schlumberger
Schmerling
Schmidel
Schmidt, E. J.
Schneider
Schönherr
Schönlein
Schoolcraft
Schopfer
Schouw
Schreibers
Schroeder van der Kolk
Schuchert
Schultze
Schulze
Schwann
Schwendener
Sclater
Scott, D. H.
Scott, W. B.
Scudder
Sechenov
Séguin, A.
Semmelweis
Semon
Semper
Senac
Senebier
Sennert
Sergent
Serres, A. E. R. A.
Serres, O. de
Serres de Mesplès
Sertoli
Sertürner
Serullas
Servetus
Sessé y Lacasta
Setchell
Severino
Severinus
Severtsov
Seward

Sharpey
Sharpey-Schäfer
Sharrock
Sherard
Sherrington
Shmalhauzen
Shull
Siebold
Siedlecki
Sigaud de Lafond
Sigüenza y Góngora
Ibn Sīnā
Sinān
Škoda
Skryabin
Sloane
Smith, Edward
Smith, Erwin F.
Smith, H. W.
Smith, J. E.
Smith, P. E.
Smith, S. I.
Smith, T.
Smith, Wilson
Snow
Soemmerring
Solander
Sollas
Sonnerat
Soranus of Ephesus
Sorby
Souleyet
Sowerby
Spallanzani
Spemann
Spencer, H.
Spiegel
Spix
Sprengel, C. K.
Sprengel, K. P. J.
Spruce
Spurzheim
Stahl
Stannius
Starkey
Starling
Stebbing
Steenstrup
Stejneger
Steller
Stelluti
Stensen
Sternberg, K. M. von
Stevens
Stewart, G. N.
Stiles
Stimpson
Stock, C.
Strasburger
Streeter
Struss
Stuart
Sturtevant
Suchten
Sudhoff
Sumner, F. B.
Sumner, J.
Suringar
Sutton
Svedelius
Swainson
Swammerdam
Swartz
Swedenborg
Swieten
Sydenham
Sylvius
Szilard

Al-Ṭabarī (11th cent.)
Al-Ṭabarī (9th cent.)
Tabor
Tachenius
Targioni Tozzetti
Tashiro
Taylor, C. V.
Teichmann
Teilhard de Chardin
Tennent
Ten Rhyne
Testut
Thābit ibn Qurra
Thaxter
Thayer
Theophrastus
Thiselton-Dyer
Thomas, H. H.
Thompson, D. W.
Thompson, J. V.
Thouin
Thunberg, T. L.
Thuret
Thurnam
Ibn Tibbon, M.
Tiedemann
Van Tieghem
Al-Tīfāshī
Tikhov
Tillet
Ibn al-Tilmīdh
Timiryazev
Tiselius
Titius
Torre, M. della
Torrey
Toscanelli dal Pozzo
Tournefort
Townsend, J.
Tozzi
Tradescant, J. I
Tradescant, J. II
Traube
Trelease
Trembley
Treub
Treviranus, G. R.
Treviranus, L. C.
Triana
Troja
Trommsdorf
Troost, G.
Trouvelot
Trulli
Tschermak von Seysenegg
Tsvet
Ibn Ṭufayl
Tulasne
Tulp
Türck
Turgo, E. F.
Turner, W. (d 1568)
Turner, W. (d. 1916)
Turpin
Turquet de Mayerne
Twort
Tyndall
Tyson

Ukhtomsky
Ulloa
Ulrich
Ulstad
Unanue
Unger

Unzer
Uexküll

Vaillant, L. L.
Vaillant, S.
Valenciennes
Valentin
Vallisnieri
Valmont de Bomare
Valsalva
Valverde
Van Slyke
Varolio
Varro
Vassale
Vastarini-Cresi
Vaucher
Vavilov, N. I.
Vejdovský
Vellozo
Venel
Verneuil
Verrill
Verworn
Vesalius
Vesling
Vicq d'Azyr
Vieussens
Vigani
Vigo
Vilmorin
Vinogradsky
Virchow
Virey

Virtanen
Vogt, C.
Voit, C. von
Voronin
Vries
Vvedensky

Wackenroder
Ibn Wāfid
Wagner
Wagner von Jauregg
Wahlenberg
Ibn Waḥshiyya
Walch
Walcott
Waldeyer-Hartz
Walker, A.
Walker, J.
Wallace, A. R.
Waller
Wallich
Walton
Wanklyn
Warburg, O. H.
Warming
Wassermann
Waterton
Watson, H. C.
Watson, S.
Watson, W.
Weber, E. H.
Weber, M. W. C.
Webster, J.
Wedel

Weichselbaum
Weigert
Weinberg
Weismann
Weizmann
Welch
Weldon
Wells, H. G.
Wells, W. C.
Went
Wepfer
Wernicke
Wertheim
Wharton, T.
Wheeler
White, C.
White, G.
Whitfield
Whitman
Whytt
Wickersheimer
Wied
Wiedersheim
Wiegleb
Wieland, M.
Wiesner
Wigand
Wilbrand
Willdenow
Williams, H. S.
Williams, R. R.
Williamson, N. C.
Willis, T.
Williston
Willughby
Wilson, Alexander (d. 1813)
Wilson, Edmund B.

Wilson, Edwin B.
Winsløw
Winthrop
Wistar
Witham
Withering
Wolff, C. F.
Wollaston, W. H.
Wood, H.
Woodward, J.
Worm
Wotton
Wright, A. E.
Wu
Wundt
Wyman

Yerkes
Yersin
Young, T.

Al-Zahrāwī
Zalužansky
Zambeccari
Zavadovsky
Zavarzin
Zeiller
Zinsser
Zittel
Ibn Zuhr
Zwelfer

MATHEMATICS

Abel, N. H.
Abraham Bar Hiyya
Abū Kāmil
Abul'-Wafā'
Adams, J. C.
Adelard of Bath
Adrain
Aepinus
Agnesi
Aguilon
Ahmad Ibn Yūsuf
Aida Yasuaki
Ajima Naonobu
Albert of Saxony
Alberti, L. B.
Albertus Magnus
Alembert
Alzate y Ramírez
Ampère
Amsler
Anatolius of Alexandria
Anderson, O. J. V.
Andoyer
Angeli
Anthemius of Tralles
Antiphon
Apollonius of Perga
Apell
Arbogast
Arbuthnot
Archimedes
Archytas of Tarentum
Argand, J. R.

Aristaeus
Aristarchus of Samos
Aristotle
Aristoxenus
Arnauld
Aronhold
Artin
Āryabhaṭa I
Āryabhaṭa II
Atwood
Autolycus of Pitane
Auzout
Azara

Babbage
Bachelier
Bachet de Méziriac
Bachmann, P. G. H.
Bacon, R.
Al-Baghdādī
Baire
Balbus
Balmer
Banach
Ibn Al-Bannā'
Banū Mūsā
Barbier
Barlow, P.
Barocius
Barrow

Bartholin, E.
Bateman
Al-Battānī
Bayes
Beaugrand
Bell, E. T.
Bellavitis
Beltrami
Benedetti, G. B.
Bernoulli, D.
Bernoulli, Jakob I
Bernoulli, Jakob II
Bernoulli, Johann I
Bernoulli, Johann II
Bernoulli, Johann III
Bernoulli, Nikolaus I
Bernoulli, Nikolaus II
Bernstein F.
Bernstein, S. N.
Bertini
Bertrand, J. L. F.
Berwick
Bessel
Betti
Bezout
Bhāskara II
Bianchi
Bienaymé
Billy
Birkhoff
Al-Bīrūnī
Bjerknes, C. A.
Blaschke

Blasius of Parma
Blichfeldt
Bliss
Bobillier
Bôcher
Boethius
Bohl
Bohr, H.
Bolyai, F.
Bolyai, J.
Bolza
Bolzano
Bombelli
Bonnet, P. O.
Boole
Borchardt
Borda
Borel, E.
Borelli
Bortkiewicz
Bortolotti
Boškovic
Bosse
Bossut
Bougainville
Boulliau
Bouquet
Bour
Bourbaki
Boussinesq
Boutroux
Bouvelles
Bradwardine

Braikenridge
Bramer
Brashman
Braunmühl
Bredon
Bret
Brianchon
Briggs
Brill
Brillouin
Bring
Brinkley
Brioschi
Briot
Brisson
Brocard
Bromwich
Brouncker
Brouwer, L. E. J.
Brożek
Bryson of Heraclea
Budan de Boislaurent
Bugaev
Bunyakovsky
Buot
Burali-Forti
Bürgi
Burnside
Burrau
Buteo

Cabeo
Calandrelli, I.
Callippus
Campanus of Novara
Camus
Cantor, G.
Cantor, M. B.
Caramuel y Lobkowitz
Carathéodory
Carcavi
Cardano
Carnot, L. N. M.
Cartan
Castel
Castelnuovo
Castillon
Cataldi
Cauchy
Cavalieri
Cayley
Čech
Cesàro
Ceulen
Ceva, G.
Ceva, T.
Chaplygin
Chasles
Chebotaryov
Chebyshev
Cheyne
Ch'in Chiu-Shao
Christmann
Christoffel
Chrystal
Chu Shih-Chieh
Chuquet
Ciruelo
Clairaut
Clarke, S.
Clausen
Clavius
Clebsch
Clifford
Codazzi

Cole
Collins
Commandino
Comte
Condorcet
Conon of Samos
Coolidge
Cosserat
Cotes
Cournot
Couturat
Craig
Cramer
Crelle
Cremona
Crousaz
Culmann
Cunha
Curtze
Cusa

Dandelin
Danti
Darboux
D'Arcy
Darwin, C. G.
Darwin, G. H.
Dasypodius
Davidov
Debeaune
Dechales
Dedekind
Dee
De Groot
Dehn
Delamain
Democritus
De Morgan
Deparcieux
Desargues
Descartes
Dickson
Dickstein
Digges, L.
Digges, T.
Dini
Dinostratus
Diocles
Dionis du Séjour
Dionysodorus
Diophantus of Alexandria
Dirichlet
Dodgson
Dominicus de Clavasio
Domninus of Larissa
Doppelmayr
Doppler
Dositheus
Douglas, Jesse
Drach
Du Bois-Reymond, P. D. G.
Dudith
Duhamel
Dupin
Dupré
Dürer
Dyck

Egorov
Eisenhart
Eisenstein
Engel

Enriques
Eratosthenes
Esclangon
Euclid
Eudoxus of Cnidus
Euler
Eutocius of Ascalon
Ibn Ezra

Fabri
Fagnano dei Toschi, G. F.
Fagnano dei Toschi, G. C.
Fano
Farrar
Fatou
Faulhaber
Feigl
Fejér
Fermat
Ferrari
Ferrel
Ferro
Feuerbach
Fibonacci
Fields
Fine, H. B.
Fine, O.
Fink
Fisher, R. A.
Fontaine
Fontenelle
Forsyth
Fourier
Fraenkel
Français, F. J.
Français, J. F.
Francesca
Frank, P.
Fredholm
Frege
Frenet
Frenicle de Bessy
Friedmann
Fries, J. F.
Frisi
Frobenius
Fubini
Fuchs, I. L.
Fueter
Fuss
Fyodorov

Galerkin
Galois
Galton
Gauss
Geiser
Gelfond
Gellibrand
Geminus
Gemma Frisius
Gentzen
Gerard of Brussels
Gerbert
Gergonne
Germain
Ghetaldi
Giorgi
Girard, A.
Glaisher, J. W. L.
Goldbach
Gompertz

Göpel
Gordan
Gossett
Goursat
Gräffe
Grandi
Grassman
Graunt
Grave
'sGravesande
Green, G.
Gregory, D.
Gregory, D. F.
Gregory, J.
Gregory, O. G.
Grossmann, M.
Gua de Malves
Guccia
Gudermann
Guenther
Guldin
Gunter

Haar
Ḥabash al-Ḥāsib
Hachette
Hadamard
Halley
Halphen
Halsted, G. B.
Hamilton, W.
Hamilton, W. R.
Hankel, H.
Hardy, C.
Hardy, G. H.
Harriot
Hartmann, G.
Hartmann, J.
Hartree
Hausdorff
Ibn al-Haytham
Heath
Hecht
Hecke
Heine
Hellinger
Henrion
Hensel
Heraclides Ponticus
Herbrand
Hérigone
Hermann the Lame
Hermann, J.
Hermite
Hero of Alexandria
Hesse
Heuraet
Heytesbury
Hilbert
Hill, G. W.
Hill, L. S.
Hindenburg
Hipparchus
Hippias of Elis
Hippocrates of Chios
Hobbes
Hobson
Hodgkinson
Hoëné-Wroński
Hölder
Holmboe
Hopf
Hopkins, W.
Horner, W. G.
Hoüel

Hudde
Hugh of St. Victor
Humbert, M. G.
Humbert, P.
Huntington
Hurwitz
Hutton, C.
Huygens
Hypatia
Hypsicles of Alexandria

Ibrāhīm ibn Sinān
Isidorus of Miletus
Ivory

Jābir ibn Aflah
Jacobi, C. G. J.
Jagannātha
Janiszewski
Al-Jawharī
Al-Jayyānī
Jensen, J. L. W. V.
Jerrard
Jevons
Joachimsthal
John of Gmunden
John of Lignères
John of Murs
Johnson, W. E.
Jones, W.
Jonquières
Jordan, C.
Jordanus de Nemore
Juel
Jungius

Kaestner
Kagan
Kaluza
Kamāl al-Dīn
Al-Karajī
Al-Kāshī
Keckermann
Keill, John
Kerékjártó
Keynes
Al-Khalīlī
Al-Khayyāmī
Al-Khāzin
Khinchin
Al-Khujandī
Al-Khwārizmī
Kirkman
Klein, C. F.
Klügel
Kneser
Knopp
Köbel
Koch, H. von
Kochin
Koenig, J.
Koenig, J. S.
Koenigs
Kolosov
Königsberger
Korteweg
Kotelnikov
Kovalevsky, S.
Kraft

Kramp
Krasovsky
Kronecker, L.
Krylov, A. N.
Krylov, N. M.
Kummer
Kürschák
Kushyār

La Condamine
Lacroix, S. F.
La Faille
Lagny
Lagrange
Laguerre
La Hire, P. de
Lalouvère
Lamb
Lambert
Lamé, G.
Lamy, B.
Lancret
Landau, E.
Landen
Landsberg, G.
Lansberge
Laplace
La Roche
Laurent, M. P. H.
Laurent, P. A.
Lavanha
Lax
Lebesgue
Legendre
Leibniz
Lemoine
Leo
Leo the Mathematician
Leodamas of Thasos
Leonardo da Vinci
Le Paige
Le Poivre
Lerch
Le Roy, E.
Lesniewski
Le Tenneur
Leurechon
Levi ben Gerson
Levi-Civita
Lévy, M.
Lexell
L'Hospital
L'Huillier
Li Chih
Lie
Lindelöf
Lindemann, C. L. F.
Liouville
Lipschitz
Liu Hui
Lobachevsky
Loewner
Loewy
Loomis
Loria
Lotka
Love
Lucas, F. E. A.
Lueroth
Łukasiewicz
Lull
Luzin
Lyapunov

Macaulay
McColl
Maclaurin
MacMahon
Macmillan
Magini
Magnitsky
Al-Māhānī
Mahāvīra
Maior
Malebranche
Malfatti
Maltsev
Mannheim
Mansion
Mansūr
Marci of Kronland
Markov
Martianus Capella
Mascheroni
Maseres
Matthews
Mathieu
Maupertuis
Maurolico
Mayer, C. G. A.
Mazurkiewicz
Mello
Menabrea
Menaechmus
Menelaus of Alexandria
Mengoli
Méray
Mercator
Mersenne
Meshchersky
Metius, A.
Metius, A. A.
Metius, J.
Meusnier de la Place
Meyer, W. V.
Milhaud
Miller, G. A.
Miller, W. H.
Minding
Mineur
Minkowski
Mises
Mittag-Leffler
Möbius, A. F.
Moerbeke
Mohr, G.
Moiseev
Moivre
Molin
Mollweide
Monge
Monte
Montmort
Montucla
Moore, E. H.
Morland
Moulton
Moutard
Mouton
Muhyi 'l-Dīn
Muniśvara Viśvarūpa
Mydorge
Mylon

Nairne
Napier
Nārāyana
Al-Nasawī
Al-Nayrīzī

Neander
Nekrasov
Netto
Neuberg
Neumann, C. G.
Neumann, F. E.
Newton, H. A.
Newton, I.
Nicholson, J. W.
Nicomachus of Gerasa
Nicomedes
Nielsen
Nieuwentijt
Noether, A. E.
Noether, M.
Norwood
Nuñez Salaciense

Ocagne
Oenopedes of Chios
Oresme
Ortega
Osgood
Ostrogradsky
Oughtred
Ozanam

Pacioli
Padoa
Painlevé
Pappus of Alexander
Parseval des Chênes
Pascal, B.
Pascal, E.
Pasch
Patrizi
Peacock
Peano
Pearson, K.
Pecham
Peirce, B.
Peirce, B. O. II
Peirce, C. S.
Peletier, J.
Pell
Pemberton
Pérès
Perseus
Peter Philomena of Dacia
Petersen
Peterson
Petrovsky
Peurbach
Pfaff
Picard, C. E.
Pieri
Pincherle
Pitiscus
Plana
Planudes
Plato of Tivoli
Playfair, J.
Plücker
Poincaré
Poisson
Poinsot
Poleni
Poncelet
Poretsky
Porta, G. della
Post
Pratt, J. H.

LIST OF SCIENTISTS BY FIELD

Prévost, I. B.
Pringsheim, A.
Privalov
Privat de Molières
Proclus
Ptolemy
Puiseux
Pythagoras of Samos

Qāḍī Zāda
Al-Qalaṣādī
Quetelet
Al-Qūhī

Rademacher
Radó
Radon
Ramanujan
Ramsden
Ramsey
Ramus
Razmadze
Réaumur
Recorde
Regiomantanus
Reichenbach, H.
Reidemeister
Reye
Reyneau
Rey Pastor
Rheticus
Ribaucour
Ricatti, J. F.
Ricatti, V.
Ricci, Matteu
Ricci, Michelangelo
Ricci, O.
Ricci-Curbastro, G.
Richard, J. A.
Richard, L. P. E.
Richard of Wallingford
Riemann
Ries
Riesz
Risner
Ritt
Roberval
Robins
Rohn
Rolle
Roomen
Rosanes
Rosenhain, J. G.
Rowning
Rudio
Rudolff
Ruffini, P.
Rumovsky
Runge, C. D. T.
Russell, B. A. W.
Rydberg

Saccheri
Sacrobosco
Saint-Venant
Saint-Vincent

Saks
Salmon
Al-Samarqandī (*fl.* 1276)
Al-Samaw'al
Saurin
Scheffers
Scheuchzer
Schickard
Schläfli
Schmidt, E.
Schoenflies
Schooten
Schott, G.
Schottky
Schoute
Schouten
Schröder
Schroeter
Schubert
Schur
Schuster
Schwarz
Schweikart
Segner
Segre
Seidel
Seki
Semyonov-Tyan-Shansky
Serenus
Serret
Servois
Severi
Sezawa
Shanks
Shatunovsky
Shen Kua
Shirakatsí
Shnirelman
Sierpiński
Sigüenza y Góngora
Al-Sijzī
Simpson
Simson
Sinān
Skolem
Sluse
Slutsky
Smith, H. J. S.
Snel
Sokhotsky
Somerville
Sommerville
Somov
Sonin
Şporus of Nicaea
Şrīdhara
Śrīpati
Stäckel
Stampioen
Staudt
Steiner
Steinitz
Steklov
Stepanov
Stephanus of Alexandria
Stepling
Stevin
Stewart, M.
Stieltjes
Stifel
Stirling
Stokes
Stolz
Stoney
Størmer

Study
Sturm, C.-F.
Sturm, F. O. R.
Subbotin
Suter
Swineshead
Sylow
Sylvester

Tacquet
Tait
Talbot
Tannery, J.
Tannery, P.
Tartaglia
Tauber
Taurinus
Taylor, B.
Thābit ibn Qurra
Theaetetus
Theodorus of Cyrene
Theodosius of Bithynia
Theon of Alexandria
Theon of Smyrna
Theudius of Magnesia
Thiele, T. N.
Thomaz
Thompson, D. W.
Thue
Thunberg, C. P.
Thymaridas
Tilly
Tinseau d'Amondans
Titchmarsh
Todhunter
Toeplitz
Tolman
Torricelli
Tropfke
Troughton
Tschirnhaus
Tsu Ch'ung-Chih
Tunstall
Turing
Turner, P.
Al-Tūsī (Naṣir al-Dīn)
Al-Tūsī (Sharaf al-Dīn)

Al-Umawī
Al-Uqlīdīsī
Uryson

Valerio
Vallée-Poussin
Vandermonde
Varignon
Veblen
Venn
Ver Eecke
Verhulst
Veronese
Vessiot
Viète
Villalpando

Vitali
Viviani
Vlacq
Volterra
Von Neumann
Voronov

Wald, A.
Wallace, W.
Wallis
Wangerin
Waring
Watson, G. N.
Weber, H.
Wedderburn
Weierstrass
Weingarten
Werner, J.
Wessel
Weyl
Whiston
Whitehead, A. N.
Whitehead, J. H. C.
Whittaker
Widman
Wieleitner
Wiener, L. C.
Wiener, N.
Wilczynski
Wilks
Wilson, Edwin B.
Wilson, J.
Winlock
Winthrop, J. (*d.* 1779)
Wintner
Witt
Wittich
Woepcke
Woodhouse
Woodward, R. S.
Wren
Wright, E.

Xenocrates of Chalcedon

Yang Hui
Yativṛṣabha
Youden
Young, J. W.
Young, W. H.
Yule
Ibn Yūnus

Zanotti
Zarankiewicz
Zenodorus
Zeno of Elea
Zeno of Sidon
Zermelo
Zeuthen
Zhukovsky
Zolotarev
Zucchi

HISTORY, PHILOSOPHY, DISSEMINATION of KNOWLEDGE

Abailard
Abano
Abu'l-Barakāt
Abu'l-Fidā
Adanson
Agrippa
Ailly
Alain de Lille
Albert of Saxony
Albertus Magnus
Alcuin of York
Alexander of Aphrodisias
Alfonso el Sabio
Alsted
Ames, W.
Ammonius
Anatolius of Alexandria
Anaxagoras
Anaximander
Anaximenes of Miletus
Andreae
Antiphon
Apelt
Aquinas
Arago
Archytas of Tarentum
Aristotle
Armstrong, H. E.
Ashmole
Atwater
Augustine of Hippo

Bachelard
Bacon, F.
Bacon, R.
Bain
Baird
Ibn Bājja
Baranzano
Bartholin, C.
Basso
Ibn Baṭṭūṭa
Bede
Bellarmine
Bergson
Bérigard
Berkeley, G.
Bernard of Chartres
Bernard of Le Treille
Bernard Silvestre
Al-Bīrūnī
Bisterfeld
Al-Biṭrūjī
Blasius of Parma
Boehme
Boethius
Bogdanov
Bolzano
Boncompagni
Borro
Bošković
Bossut
Bourdelot
Bourguet
Boutroux
Boyle
Bradwardine
Braunmühl
Bridgman
Bruno

Brunschvicg
Büchner, F. K. C. L.
Buonamici
Burgersdijk
Buridan
Burley

Cabanis
Calcidius
Campanella
Campbell, N. R.
Cardano
Carr
Carus, P.
Cassiodorus
Cassirer
Cattell
Celaya
Celsus
Cesalpino
Censorinus
Cesi
Charleton
Châtelet
Christmaan
Chrystal
Chwistek
Ciruelo
Clarke, S.
Clerselier
Cohen, M. R.
Collinson
Comenius
Comte
Condillac
Constantine the African
Coronel
Cournot
Couturat
Creighton
Crell
Crelle
Crescas
Crousaz
Cudworth
Cusa

Darwin, C. R.
Della Torre
Democritus
Derham
Descartes
Dicaearchus of Messina
Dickstein
Diderot
Dietrich von Freiberg
Digby
Dingler
Domninus of Larissa
Driesch
Du Hamel
Duhem
Dullaert of Ghent
Duns Scotus
Dyadkovsky

Eaton
Empedocles of Acragas
Engels
Enriques
Epicurus
Erastus
Eriugena
Eudemus of Rhodes

Fabri
Al-Fārābī
Flourens
Folkes
Fontenelle
Forster, G. A.
Forster, J. R.
Fracastoro
Francis of Marchia
Francis of Meyronnes
Franck, S.
Frank, P.
Franklin, B.
Frederick II Hohenstaufen
Fries, J. F.

Galen
Gallois
Garnett
Gassendi
Geminus
Gerard of Cremona
Giles of Lessines
Giles of Rome
Glanvill
Glisson
'sGravesande
Green, J.
Greenwood
Grosseteste
Gundissalinus

Haak
Haldane, R. B.
Hamilton, W.
Harris
Hartlib
Heath
Helmholtz
Helmont
Heraclides Ponticus
Heraclitus of Ephesus
Herbart
Hermes Trismegistus
Herodotus of Halicarnassus
Heytesbury
Hildegard of Bingen
Hipparchus of Rhodes
Hippias of Elis
Hobbes
Höené-Wroński
Holbach
Hugh of St. Victor
Humbert, P.
Humboldt

Hume
Ḥunayn ibn Isḥāq
Hutton, J.
Huxley, T. H.
Huygens
Hypatia

Iamblichus
ıkhwān al-Ṣafāʾ
Isaac Israeli
Ishaq ibn Hunayn
Isidore of Seville

James of Venice
James, W.
Jevons
John of Dumbleton
John of Gmunden
John of Palermo
John Philoponus
Johnson, W. E.
Jungius

Kant
Karpinski
Ibn Khaldūn
Al-Khayyāmī
Khunrath, H.
Al-Khwārizmī
Al-Kindī
Kircher
Köbel
Koyré
Kraft
Krause

La Condamine
Lamarck
Lambert
Lamétherie
La Mettrie
Lamy, G.
Lax
Leibniz
Lenin
Le Roy, E.
Lesniewski
Leucippus
Levi ben Gerson
Libavius
Linacre
Locke
Logan, J.
Lotze
Lovejoy
Lucretius
Łukasiewicz
Lull
Lyell

McColl
Mach
Macrobius
Magalotti
Magnenus
Maimonides
Maior
Malebranche
Malthus
Mansion
Marinus
Marsilius of Inghen
Martianus Capella
Martin, B.
Marum
Marx
Mersenne
Metzger
Meyerson
Michael Scot
Mieli
Milhaud
Mill
Moerbeke
Montesquieu
Montgomery, E. D.
Montmor
Montucla
More
Morgan, C. W.

Ibn al-Nafīs
Newton, I.
Nieuwentijt
Nifo

Ockham
Oken
Oldenburg
Olympiodorus
Oresme
Oribasius
Osiander

Padoa
Paley
Pappus of Alexandria
Paracelsus
Parmenides of Elea
Partington
Pascal, B.
Patrizi
Paul of Aegina
Paul of Venice

Peale, C. W.
Peano
Pecham
Peirce, C. S.
Peiresc
Petty
Philolaus of Crotona
Planck
Planudes
Plato
Plotinus
Pluche
Poggendorff
Polinière
Pomponazzi
Porta, G. della
Posidonius
Post
Prevost, P.
Priestley, J.
Proclus
Psellus
Purkyně
Pythogoras of Samos

Al-Qazwīnī
Ibn al-Quff
Qusṭā ibn Lūqā
Ibn Qutayba
Quṭb al-Dīn

Rádl
Ramus
Ray, P. C.
Al-Rāzī
Reichenbach, H.
Rey, A.
Rittenhouse
Robinet
Roger of Hereford
Rohault
Rosenberger, J. K. F.
Rowning
Rudio
Ruffini, P.
Ibn Rushd
Russell, B. A. W.

Sabatier, A.
Sacrobosco
Sallo
Al-Samarqandī (*fl.* 1276)
Sanchez
Sarpi

Sarton
Scaliger
Schegk
Schelling
Schleiden
Schlick
Schliemann
Seneca
Servetus
Sextus Empiricus
Shen Kua
Shizuki
Siger of Brabant
Sigorgne
Simplicius
Ibn Sīnā
Smithson
Solvay
Soto
Spencer, H.
Speusippus
Sprat
Stallo
Staszic
Stephen of Antioch
Strabo
Strato of Lampsacus
Sudhoff
Swedenborg
Swineshead

Al-Ṭabarī (11th cent.)
Al-Ṭabarī (9th cent.)
Tannery, P.
Teilhard de Chardin
Telesio
Thābit ibn Qurra
Thales
Themistius
Theophrastus
Thévenot
Thierry of Chartres
Thomas of Cantimpré
Thompson, D. W.
Thompson, S. P.
Thomsen, C. J.
Ibn Tibbon, J.
Ibn Tibbon, M.
Tilloch
Towneley
Ibn Ṭufayl
Tunstall
Turgot, A. R. J.
Al-Ṭūsī (Naṣir al-Dīn)
Tyndall

Ulrich of Strasbourg

Vailati
Vanini
Varro
Venn
Vincent of Beauvais
Vives
Vlacq
Volkmann
Volney
Voltaire

Wallace, A. R.
Weigel, V.
Wendelin
Whately
Whewell
Whiston
White, T.
Whitehead, A. N.
Whittaker
Wickersheimer
Wieleitner
Wien
Wiener, L. C.
Wilkins
William of Auvergne
William of Sherwood
Winthrop, J. (*d.* 1676)
Witelo
Wittgenstein
Wolf, J. R.
Wolff, Casper F.
Wolff, Christian
Wooley
Worsaae

Xenocrates of Chalcedon
Xenophanes

Yāqūt al-Ḥamawī al-Rūmī
Young, T.

Zabarella
Zeno of Citium
Zeno of Elea
Zeno of Sidon
Zittel

PHYSICS

Abbe, E.
Abraham
Abu'l-Barakāt
Achard
Adams, W. S.
Aepinus
Aguilon

Albert of Saxony
Alberti, L. B.
Albertus Magnus
Aldini
Alembert
Amagat
Ames, J. S.

Amici
Amontons
Ampère
Andronov
Angeli
Ångström
Apell

Appleton
Arago
Archimedes
Atchytas of Tarentum
Aristotle
Arkadiev
Arnold

Arrhenius
Arsonval
Artsimovich
Astbury
Aston
Atwood
Aubuisson de Voisins
Austin
Auzout
Avogadro

Babinet
Bache
Back
Bacon, R.
Baker, H.
Baldi
Baliani
Balmer
Barkhausen
Barkla
Barlow, P.
Barrow
Bartels
Bartholin, E.
Bartoli
Barus
Bateman
Bauer, E.
Bauer, L. A.
Beccaria
Becquerel, A. E.
Becquerel, A. C.
Becquerel, A. H.
Beeckman
Béghin
Bélidor
Bellani
Belopolsky
Benedetti, G. B.
Benedicks
Benoit
Benzenberg
Bergman
Bérigard
Bernoulli, D.
Bernoulli, Jakob I.
Bertholon
Berti
Bhabha
Białobrzeski
Biot
Bjerknes, C. A.
Bjerknes, V. F. K.
Bjerrum
Black, Joseph
Blagden
Blasius of Parma
Blondlot
Bohr, N. H. D.
Boltwood
Boltzmann
Borda
Borelli
Born
Borries
Bose, G. M.
Bose, J.
Bose, S.
Bošković
Bothe
Bouguer
Bour
Bourguet

Boussinesq
Boyle
Boys
Brace
Bragg, W. H.
Bragg, W. L.
Brandes
Braun, F.
Bravais
Brewster
Bridgman
Brillouin
Briot
Brisson, M. J.
Broglie
Bucherer
Buckingham
Buono
Buot
Burger
Buridan
Burley

Cabrera
Cagniard de la tour, C.
Cailletet
Callan
Callendar
Campbell, N. R.
Camus
Canton
Cardano
Carlisle
Carnot, N. L. S.
Cassegrain
Castel
Castelli
Catalán
Cauchy
Cavallo
Cavendish
Charles
Chladni
Christiansen
Christie, S. H.
Chrystal
Clairaut
Clausius
Clay
Coblentz
Cockcroft
Colden
Colding
Combes, C. P. M.
Compton, A. H.
Compton, K. T.
Coriolis
Cornu
Corti, B.
Cosserat
Coster
Coulomb
Courtivron
Crawford
Crookes
Cumming
Curie, M.
Curie, P.

Dalencé
Dalton, J.
Daniell

Darwin, C. G.
Davidov
Davisson
Debye
De Forest
De Groot
Delaunay
Deluc
Democritus
Deprez
Desaguliers
Descartes
Des Cloizeaux
Deslandres
Devaux
Dewar
Dickinson
Dietrich von Freiberg
Diocles
Diviš
Dollond
Dominis
Donnan
Doppelmayer
Doppler
Dove
Drebbel
Drude
Duane
Dubois-Reymond, E. H.
Du Buat
Dufay
Duhamel
Duhem
Dullaert of Ghent
Dulong
Du Moncel
Dunoyer de Segonzac
Duperrey
Dupré
Dutrochet

Eddington
Ehrenfest
Eichenwald
Einstein
Ellis
Elster
Emden, R.
Enskog
Eötvös
Erman
Esclangon
Eucken
Euclid
Euler
Evershed
Ewing, J. A.

Fabbroni
Fabry, C.
Fahrenheit
Fankuchen
Faraday
Farkas
Farrar
Feddersen
Fermi
Ferraris
Fessenden
Fitzgerald
Fizeau

Fleischer
Fleming, J. A.
Föppl
Forbes, J. D.
Foucault
Fourier
Fowler, A.
Fowler, R. H.
Franck, J.
Frank, P.
Frankenheim
Franklin, B.
Franklin, R. E.
Fraunhofer
Frenicle de Bessy
Frenkel
Fresnel
Friedel
Friedmann
Fries, J. F.
Frisi
Froude
Fyodorov

Galerkin
Galilei, G.
Galilei, V.
Galvani
Gamow
Gascoigne
Gassiot
Gauss
Gautier, P. F.
Gay-Lussac
Geiger
Geitel
Gerasimovich
Gibbs, J. W.
Gilbert, N.
Giles of Rome
Giorgi
Glazebrook
Goddard
Goethe
Goldschmidt, V.
Goldstein
Golitsyn
Gordon
Gore
Gouy
Graham, T.
Gramont
Grashof
'sGravesande
Gray, S.
Green, G.
Gregory, D.
Gregory, J.
Gren
Grimaldi
Grosseteste
Groth
Grotthuss
Grove
Guericke
Guillaume
Guldberg
Gullstrand
Guye
Guyton de Morveau

Haas A. E.
Haas, W. J. de

Hachette
Hahn
Hale, G. E.
Hall, E. H.
Halley
Hallwachs
Hamilton, W. R.
Hamy
Hankel, W. G.
Hansen, W. W.
Hansteen
Harkins
Harriot
Hartree
Hartsoeker
Hasenöhrl
Hauksbee, Francis (d. 1713)
Hauksbee, Francis (d. 1763)
Ibn al-Haytham
Heaviside
Helmholtz
Henrichsen
Henry of Hesse
Henry, J.
Henry, P. M.
Henry, P. P.
Herapath, J.
Hermann, C. H.
Hero of Alexandria
Herschel, J. F. W.
Hertz
Hess, V. F.
Hessel
Hevesy
Heytesburg
Heyrovsky
Hirn
Hittorf
Hobbes
Hodgkinson
Holborn
Honda
Hooke
Hopkinson
Horstmann
Huber, M. T.
Huggins
Hugoniot
Hull
Humboldt
Hume-Rothery
Hutton, J.
Huygens
Hyleraas

Infeld
Ingen-Housz
Ioffe
Ishiwara
Ives

Jacobi, M. H. von
Jaeger, F. M.
Jahn
Janssen
Jeans
Joblot
Joliot
Joliot-Curie
Jolly
Joly

Jones, H. C.
Jordanus de Nemore
Joule
Julius

Kaluza
Kamāl al-Dīn
Kamerlingh Onnes
Kármán
Kaufmann
Kayser
Keesom
Keill, John
Kelvin (W. Thomson)
Kennedy
Kennelly
Kepler
Kerr, J.
Al-Khāzinī
Kinnersley
Kirchhof, G. R.
Kleist
Klingenstierna
Klügel
Knudsen
Kochin
Koenig, J. S.
Koenig, K. R.
Koenigs
Kohlrausch, F. W. G.
Kohlrausch, R. H. A.
Kolosov
König, A.
Konkoly Thege
Korolev
Kossel, W. L. J. P. H.
Kotelnikov
Kraft
Kramers
Kramp
Krönig
Krylov, A. N.
Kuenen
Kuhn, W.
Kundt
Kurchatov
Kurlbaum

Ladenburg, R. W.
Lagrange
La Hire, P. de
Lamb
Lambert
Lamont
Lamy, B.
Landau L. D.
Landriani
Landsberg, G. S.
Lane
Langevin
Langley
Langmuir
Laplace
La Rive, A. A. de
La Rive, C. G. de
Larmor
Laue
Laurent, P. A.
Lawrence, E. O.
Lazarev, P. P.
Lebedev, P. N.
Le Cat

Le Châtelier
Leconte, John
Lecornu
Leeuwenhoek
Lehmann, O.
Leibniz
Le Monnier, L. G.
Lenard
Lennard-Jones
Lenz
Leonardo da Vinci
Le Roy, C.
Le Roy, J. B.
Lesage
Leslie
Le Tenneur
Le Verrier
Levi ben Gerson
Levi-Civita
Lewis, G. N.
Leybenzon
Lichtenberg
Linde
Lindemann, F. A. (Lord Cherwell)
Link
Lippmann
Lissajous
Lister, J. J.
Lloyd, H.
Lockyer
Lodge
Lomonosov
London, F.
London, H.
Lonsdale, K.
Lorentz, H. A.
Lorenz, H.
Lorenz, L. V.
Lorenz, R.
Lorenzoni
Loschmidt
Love
Lummer
Lyapunov
Lyman, T.
Lyot

MacCullagh
Mach
Magellan
Magiotti
Magnenus
Magni
Magnus, H. G.
Maignan
Mairan
Majorana
Maksutov
Malebranche
Mallet
Malus
Mandelshtam
Manfredi
Marci of Kronland
Marconi
Margules
Mariotte
Marliani
Marsilius of Inghen
Martianus Capella
Mascart
Masson
Mathieu
Matteucci

Matuyama
Mauguin
Maupertuis
Maurolico
Maxwell
Mayer, A. M.
Mayer, J. R.
Meggers
Meitner
Melloni
Melvill
Merica
Mersenne
Meshchersky
Meusnier de la Place
Michelini
Michelson
Mie
Miller, D. C.
Miller, W. H.
Miller, W. A.
Millikan
Milne, E. A.
Mineur
Mises
Mittasch
Mohr, C. F.
Moiseev
Moll, G.
Mollier
Molyneux, S.
Molyneux, W.
Monge
Montanari
Monte
Moore, W.
Morley
Moseley
Mossotti
Müller, G.
Müller, J. H. J.
Muncke
Musschenbroek
Mydorge

Nagaoka
Nairne
Natanson
Navier
Nekrasov
Nernst
Neumann, C. G.
Neumann, F. E.
Newall
Newton, I.
Niceron
Nichols
Nicholson, J. W.
Nicol
Niggli
Nobili
Noel
Nollet
Norman
Numerov
Nusselt

Oersted
Ohm
Olszewski
Oppenheimer
Orlov, S. V.

Ornstein
Osmond
Ostrogradsky
Ostwald, F. W.

Pacinotti
Paneth
Pardies
Parent
Pascal, B.
Paschen
Pasteur
Pauli
Pecham
Peirce, B. O. II
Peltier, J. C. A.
Pemberton
Pereira, B.
Pérès
Pérot
Perrin
Peter Peregrinus
Petit, A. T.
Petit, P.
Petrov, N. P.
Petrov, V. V.
Pezenas
Philo of Byzantium
Piccard
Pictet, M.-A.
Pictet, R. -P.
Pierce
Planck
Plateau
Playfair, J.
Plücker
Poggendorff
Poincaré
Poinsot
Poiseuille
Poisson
Poleni
Poli
Polinière
Poncelet
Popov, A. S.
Porro
Pouillet
Powell, B.
Powell, C. F.
Power, H.
Poynting
Prandtl
Prévost, I.-B.
Prevost, P.
Priestley, J.
Pringsheim, E.
Pritchard
Privat de Molières
Puiseux
Pulfrich
Pupin

Quincke

Raman
Ramsauer
Ramsay, W.

Ramsden
Ramus
Rankine, A. O.
Rankine, W. J. M.
Ranyard
Rateau
Rayleigh (Strutt)
Réaumur
Redtenbacher
Reech
Regener
Regnault
Reichenbach, G. F. von
Reid
Reuleaux
Reynolds
Ricci-Curbastro
Ricco
Richardson, O. W.
Richer
Richmann
Richtmyer
Riecke
Riemann
Righi
Risner
Ritter
Ritz
Roberval
Robison
Roche
Röntgen
Rood
Roozeboom
Rosenberg
Rosenberger, J. K. F.
Ross
Rossetti
Routh
Rowland
Rozhdestvensky
Rubens
Rüdenberg
Runge, C. D. T.
Russell, H. N.
Rutherford E.
Rutherfurd
Rydberg

Sabine, E.
Sabine, P. E.
Sabine, W. C. W.
Sagnac
Saha
Saint-Venant
Saurin
Sauveur, J.
Savart
Scheiner, J.
Schmidt, B. V.
Schmidt, C. H. von
Schmidt, G. C. N.
Schoenflies
Schönbein
Schonland
Schrödinger
Schuster
Schweigger
Secchi
Sechenov
Seebeck
Segner
Seguin, M.
Sénarmont

Seneca
Sharanov
Shaw, W. N.
Shayn
Short
Siedentopf
Sigaud de Lafond
Sigorgne
Simon
Smeaton
Smekal
Smith, R.
Smits
Smoluchowski
Snel
Soddy
Sohncke
Somerville
Sommerfeld
Somov
Spring
Stark
Steacie
Stefan
Steinheil
Steinmetz
Steklov
Stepling
Stern
Stewart, B.
Stokes
Stoletov
Stoney
Störmer
Strutt, J. W.
Strutt, R. J.
Sturgeon
Sturm, J. C. F.
Sutherland
Svedberg
Sverdrup
Swann
Swinden
Swineshead
Symmer
Synesius of Cyrene
Szilard

Taccola
Tait
Tamm
Tammann
Tartaglia
Tesla
Thābit ibn Qurra
Thollon
Thomaz
Thompson B.
Thompson, S. P.
Thomson, J. J.
Thomson, W.
Tikhov
Tiselius
Tisserand
Titius
Tolman
Torricelli
Towneley
Townsend, J. S. E.
Travers
Troughton
Trouton
Trowbridge
Tschirnhaus

Tsiolskovsky
Tupolev

Van de Graaff
Van't Hoff
Varignon
Vavilov, S. I.
Veksler
Verdet
Villalpando
Villard
Villari
Violle
Vogel
Voigt, W.
Volkmann
Volta
Von Neumann
Vyshnegradsky

Waals
Warburg, E. G.
Washburn
Waterston
Watson, W.
Watt
Weber, W. E.
Wehnelt
Wegener
Weiss, C. S.
Weiss, P.
Weyl
Wheatstone
Whitehead, A. N.
Whittaker
Whytlaw-Gray
Wiechert
Wiedemann
Wien
Wiener, L. C.
Wiener, O.
Wilcke
Wilhelmy
Wilson, B.
Wilson, C. T. R.
Wilson, Edwin B.
Witelo
Wollaston, W. H.
Wood, R. W.
Woodward, R. S.
Wren
Wróblewski
Wulff

Young, S.
Young, T.

Zeeman
Zernike
Zeuner
Zeuthen
Zhukovsky
Zöllner

TECHNOLOGY, ENGINEERING

Amsler
Armstrong, E. H.

Beckmann, J.
Bell, A. G.
Berti
Bertin
Bessemer
Betancourt y Molina
Bion
Bird
Blondel, A. E.
Blondel, N. F.
Biringuccio
Bourdon
Brashear
Breguet
Brinell
Brioschi
Brisson, B.
Brunelleschi

Campani
Carnot, L. N. M.
Castigliano
Chaplygin
Chardonnet
Clapeyron
Clark, A.
Clark, A. G.
Clark, G. B.
Clark, J. L.
Claude, G.
Congreve
Cottrell
Courtivron
Ctesibius

De La Rue
Deprez
Derosne
Diderot
Divini
Drebbel
Dufour
Duhamel du Monceau

Edison
Eichenwald
Eytelwein

Ferguson
Ferraris
Fessenden
Fleming, J. A.
Föppl
Fortin
Foucault

Fourneyron
Fraunhofer
Froude

Gambey
Gautier, P. F.
Gay-Lussac
Geissler
Giorgi
Girard, P. S.
Goddard
Godfrey
Graham, G.
Gramme
Grashof
Gregory, O. G.
Grubb, H.
Grubb, T.
Guericke

Hadley
Hale, W.
Hampson
Harrison, J.
Harting
Hartmann, G.
Hartsoeker
Hauksbee, F. (d. 1713)
Hauksbee, F. (d. 1763)
Hefner-Alteneck
Hellot
Hermbstaedt
Héroult
Hevelius
Heyn
Hodgkinson
Huygens

Ioffe

Jacquet
Jansen
Jars
Al-Jazarī
Jefferson
Jeffries
Jenkin
Jewett
Joblot

Kennedy
Kennelly
Kettering
Al-Khāzinī
Kirkaldy
Köhler
Korolev

Krayenhoff
Krylov, A. N.

Lanchester
Landriani
Langlois
Langren
Le Châtelier
Lecornu
Leeuwenhoek
Lemaire, J.
Lemaire, P.
Leonardo da Vinci
Le Roy, J. B.
Lévy, M.
Leybenzon
Linde
Lippmann
Lorenz, H.
Lunge

Magellan
Mallard
Mallet
Marconi
Martens
Martin, B.
Martini
Medina
Menabrea
Merett
Metius, A.
Metius, A. A.
Metius, J.
Meusnier de la Place
Mohr, C. O.
Moll, F. R. H. C.
Montgéry
Montgolfier, E. J. de
Montgolfier, M. J. de
Morland
Moutard
Müller-Breslau
Mushet

Nasmyth
Navier
Neri
Newcomen
Nicholson, W.
Niepce
Nobel
Nobert

Pambour
Papin
Percy
Perrault, C.
Perronet
Petrov, N. P.
Pilatre de Rozier

Pitot
Plattner
Poleni
Popov, A. S.
Portevin
Pouillet
Prony

Rankine, W. J. M.
Rateau
Réaumur
Redtenbacher
Reech
Repsold, A.
Repsold, J. A.
Repsold, J. G.
Reuleaux
Ribaucour
Ribeiro Santos
Ricci, O.
Rittenhouse
Robins
Roebuck
Rosenhain, W.
Rüdenberg
Rühmkorff

Santorio
Sauveur, A.
Saxton
Schott, G.
Schott, O. F.
Schumann
Seguin, M.
Siemens, C. W.
Siemens, E. W. von
Smeaton
Soleil
Solvay
Sperry
Stanton
Stead
Steinmetz
Stevin
Stodola
Swedenborg

Taylor, F. W.
Tesla
Thomas, H. H.
Thompson, S. P.
Thomson, E.
Thurston
Torres Quevedo
Towneley
Travers
Tupolev
Turner, W. E. S.

Valturio
Vauban

Venetz
Verantius
Vernier
Villard de Honnecourt
Vitruvius
Vyshnegradsky

Watt
Wedgwood
Weisbach
Willis, R.
Wöhler, A.
Woltman

Wright, O.
Wright, W.

Zucchi